You don't have to look any further for the complete service to South America

TRAILFINDERS ✈

THE TRAVEL EXPERTS

194 Kensington High Street, London W8 7RG
0171-938 3939

22-24 The Priory Queensway, Birmingham B4 6BS
0121-236 1234

48 Corn Street, Bristol BS1 1HQ
0117-929 9000

254-284 Sauchiehall Street, Glasgow G2 3EH
0141-353 2224

58 Deansgate, Manchester M3 2FF
0161-839 6969

4/5 Dawson Street, Dublin 2
01-677 7888

OPEN 7 DAYS A WEEK
MON - SAT 9am - 6pm • THURS 9am - 7pm • SUN 10am - 6pm (Dublin closed)

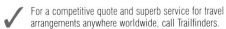

CONTACT US FOR INFORMATION ON SOUTH AMERICA
OR ANY OTHER WORLDWIDE DESTINATION

✓ For a competitive quote and superb service for travel arrangements anywhere worldwide, call Trailfinders.

✓ Trailfinders offers a complete tailormade service - including flights, tours, accommodation, immunisation, travel insurance, maps & books, information centre, foreign exchange and visa & passport service.

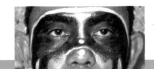

Tour Operators Licence No. V0989

ABTA A3921 IATA

ATOL 1458

All that Latin America has to offer.
All the more accessible with Iberia.

Nowhere offers such a wealth of contrasts, cultures and ancient civilisations as Latin America. And no one offers a better way to explore this spectacular continent than Iberia.

Half a century ago, as Spain has always provided the natural link between Europe and Latin America, Iberia became the first airline to connect the two lands. Today, the Iberia Group remains as progressive as ever, serving an extensive network of 25 destinations and providing unmatched frequencies on all key routes.

So if you don't want to miss all that Latin America has to offer, make sure you travel with the airline that leads the way.

To book, call Iberia Group Reservations on **0171-830 0011**
or contact your specialist travel agent.

Leading the way to Latin America

South American Handbook

Ben Box

Footprint Handbooks

*The whole Brazilian plain seemed to lie beneath us,
extending away and away until it ended in dim blue
mists upon the farthest sky-line ...
I was still drinking in this wonderful panorama when
the heavy hand of the Professor fell upon my shoulder.
"This way, my young friend," said he; "vestigia nulla
retrorsum. Never look rearwards, but always to our
glorious goal."*

Sir Arthur Conan Doyle

Footprint Handbooks

™

6 Riverside Court, Lower Bristol Road
Bath BA2 3DZ England
T 01225 469141 F 01225 469461
E mail handbooks@footprint.cix.co.uk

ISBN 1 900949 02 4 ISSN 0309-4529
CIP DATA: A catalogue record for this book is
available from the British Library

In North America, published by

PASSPORT BOOKS
NTC/Contemporary Publishing Company

4255 West Touhy Avenue, Lincolnwood
(Chicago), Illinois 60646-1975, USA
T 847 679 5500 F 847 679 24941
E mail NTCPUB2@AOL.COM

ISBN 0-8442-4783-9
Library of Congress Catalog Card
Number: on file
Passport Books and colophon are registered
trademarks of NTC Publishing group

©Footprint Handbooks Limited
74th Edition
September 1997

™ Footprint Handbooks and the Footprint mark
are a trademark of Footprint Handbooks Ltd

First published in 1924 by South American
Publications Ltd

Title page quotation taken from Sir Arthur
Conan Doyle, *The Lost World* (taken from
*Traveller's Literary Companion South and
Central America*)

Cover design by Newell and Sorrell;
photography by Jamie Marshall and Dave
Saunders

Production: Design by Mytton Williams;
Secretarial assistance Rhoda Williams;
Typesetting by Jo Morgan and Ann Griffiths;
Maps by Sebastian Ballard, Kevin Feeney and
Aldous George; Proofread by Rod Gray.

Printed and bound in Great Britain by
Clays Ltd., Bungay, Suffolk

Contents

4

4 Rounding up   1645

We try as hard as we can to make each Footprint Handbook as
up-to-date and accurate as possible but, of course, things always
change. Many people write to us with new information,
amendments or simply comments. Please do get in touch. In return
we will send you details of our special guidebook offer.

See page 1650 for more information

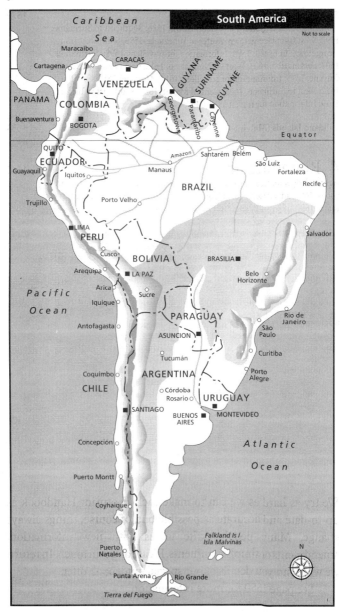

South America

Not to scale

Caribbean Sea

PANAMA

Maracaibo
Cartagena
CARACAS
VENEZUELA
COLOMBIA
Buenaventura
BOGOTA
GUYANA
SURINAME
GUYANE
Georgetown
Paramaribo
Cayenne

Equator

QUITO
ECUADOR
Guayaquil
Iquitos
Amazon
Santarém
Belém
Manaus
São Luiz
Fortaleza
Trujillo
Porto Velho
BRAZIL
Recife

LIMA
PERU
Cusco
BOLIVIA
BRASILIA
Salvador
Arequipa
LA PAZ
Belo
Horizonte
Arica
Sucre

Pacific
Ocean

Iquique
Antofagasta
PARAGUAY
Rio de
Janeiro
São
Paulo
ASUNCION
Tucumán
Curitiba
Coquimbo
ARGENTINA
Porto
Alegre
CHILE
Córdoba
Rosario
URUGUAY
SANTIAGO
BUENOS
AIRES
MONTEVIDEO

Concepción

Atlantic
Ocean

Puerto Montt

Coyhaique

Falkland Is /
Isla Malvinas

N

Puerto
Natales
Punta Arena
Río Grande

Tierra del Fuego

The Editor

Ben Box

A doctorate in medieval Spanish and Portugese studies provided very few job prospects for Ben Box, but a fascination for all things Latin. While studying for his degree, Ben travelled extensively in Spain and Portugal. He turned his attention to contemporary Iberian and Latin American affairs in 1980, beginning a career as a freelance writer at that time. He contributed regularly to national newspapers and learned tomes, and after increasing involvement with the *South American Handbook*, became its editor in 1989. Although he has travelled from the US/Mexico border to southern Chile (not all in one go) and in the Caribbean, Ben recognises that there are always more places to explore. He also edits jointly the *Mexico and Central American Handbook* and the *Caribbean Islands Handbook* with Sarah Cameron and is series editor of Footprint Handbook's South American series. To seek diversion from a household immersed in Latin America, he plays village cricket in summer and cycles the lanes of Suffolk.

Editorial team

Special thanks go to our regular subeditors Charlie Nurse (Argentina, Chile), Alan Murphy (Bolivia, Ecuador, Peru, Venezuela), Peter Pollard (Colombia), Rachel Rogers (Paraguay, Uruguay, The Guianas) and Steve Collins (Brazil).

Specialist contributors: Sarah Cameron for economics sections; Nigel Gallop for music and dance; Paul Davies of Journey Latin America for details of air transport; John Alton of Strand Cruise and Travel Centre for details of sea transport; John Lewis for information on business travel; Binka and Robin le Breton for motoring; Ashley Rawlings for motorcycling; Hallam Murray for cycling; Hilary Bradt for hiking and trekking; Richard Robinson for world wide radio information; Mark Eckstein of David Bellamy Associates for responsible tourism and Dr David Snashall for health.

Correspondents: We are most grateful to our correspondents in the region, who are thanked at the end of the relevant chapters.

Acknowledgements
Much additional help has been received during the preparation of this edition. All contributions have been tremendously helpful and are duly acknowledged on page 1645.

South America

WHY VISIT South America? For the uninitiated, South America may seem a daunting prospect, a tantalizing mixture of enticing images and ambiguous press reports. The pictures are clear to see: ancient cities in Peru; Spanish and Portuguese colonial splendours; the flora and fauna of a vast array of habitats; Indian markets; adventure sports; ranches where you can simply relax, watch nature, be a cowhand or help shear the sheep. Behind the brochures and holiday TV programmes, the reality is as magnificent as the images suggest. But it is not just the places themselves that captivate, it is their context: the contrasts of so many different elements, the variety of climates, the juxtapositions of traditional and modern (in architecture, agriculture, transport, music), rich and poor, timeless and transient. And then, of course, there is the good old gringo trail, like some exotic plant – lop off one branch here and another grows elsewhere – a well-trodden path off which pioneers each year uncover new treasures. Latin America has something for everyone, of all ages and most budgets.

It is undeniable that some aspects of South America have received a negative press. The stereotyped 'bandido' has become the drug-trafficker, the guerrilla, the urban criminal. However, no country in all of Latin America can be categorized as politically unstable, a health risk or very dangerous to visit. Elections are due in several countries in the next 12-18 months and the increase in political activity is based on democracy, not the prospect of coups and violence. Even those rare parts of the sub-continent which still host guerrilla movements may be travelled without peril if the essential precaution is taken of asking local advice in the parts of the country which are affected. As for crime, we now live in a world where crime is a fact of life and South America is no better or worse than many other places.

Ask tour operators specializing in adventurous holidays about new destinations for 1997 and the countries constantly mentioned are in Latin America (Peru, Chile, Mexico, Cuba, Costa Rica or Belize) or Asia (Cambodia, Laos and Vietnam). Seeing Mexico, Central America and South America as untapped markets, American Airlines and Continental recently introduced several new routes and anticipate adding more. Press reports from late 1996, early 1997 predict a boom in tourism to Latin America, within a worldwide trend whose potential for economic development is seen as enormous. Now is the time to go to Latin America, while the continent is still regarded as 'adventurous'. One final note of caution: South America is a big place. Do not be too ambitious with your itinerary, you can always go again.

Over the years, a unique relationship has built up between the *South American Handbook* and its readers. This has inspired an enormous post-bag without which it would be difficult to keep abreast of developments 'on the ground'. That's not to say that the Footprint editorial team is not in touch with South America. Our network of correspondents in the region also grows annually, three members of our team have made extensive trips in the past year and, as soon as this preface is finished, the editor will be flying to Brazil. We hope that this, our 74th annual edition, will inspire you to travel too and give you all the necessary materials for a successful trip.

Ben Box, The Editor

Responsible Tourism

Much has been written about the adverse impacts of tourism on the environment and local communities. It is usually assumed that this only applies to the more excessive end of the travel industry such as the Spanish Costas and Bali. However it now seems that travellers can have an impact at almost any density and this is especially true in areas "off the beaten track" where local people may not be used to western conventions and lifestyles, and natural environments may be very sensitive.

Of course, tourism can have a beneficial impact and this is something to which every traveller can contribute. Many National Parks are part funded by receipts from people who travel to see exotic plants and animals, the Galápagos (Ecuador) and Manu (Peru) National Parks are good examples of such sites. Similarly, travellers can promote patronage and protection of valuable archaeological sites and heritages through their interest and entrance fees.

However, where visitor pressure is high and/or poorly regulated, damage can occur. It is also unfortunately true that many of the most popular destinations are in ecologically sensitive areas easily disturbed by extra human pressures. This is particularly significant because the desire to visit sites and communities that are off the beaten track is a driving force for many travellers. Eventually the very features that tourists travel so far to see may become degraded and so we seek out new sites, discarding the old, and leaving someone else to deal with the plight of local communities and the damaged environment.

Fortunately, there are signs of a new awareness of the responsibilities that the travel industry and its clients need to endorse. For example, some tour operators fund local conservation projects and travellers are now more aware of the impact they may have on host cultures and environments. We can all contribute to the success of what is variously described as responsible, green or alternative tourism. All that is required is a little forethought and consideration.

It would be impossible to identify all the possible impacts that might need to be addressed by travellers, but it is worthwhile noting the major areas in which we can all take a more responsible attitude in the countries we visit. These include, changes to natural ecosystems (air, water, land, ecology and wildlife), cultural values (beliefs and behaviour) and the built environment (sites of antiquity and archaeological significance). At an individual level, travellers can reduce their impact if greater consideration is given to their activities. Canoe trips up the headwaters of obscure rivers make for great stories, but how do local communities cope with the sudden invasive interest in their lives? Will the availability of easy tourist money and gauche behaviour affect them for the worse, possibly diluting and trivialising the significance of culture and customs? Similarly, have the environmental implications of increased visitor pressure been considered? Where does the fresh fish that feeds the trip come from? Hand caught by line is fine, but is dynamite fishing really necessary, given the scale of damage and waste that results?

Some of these impacts are caused by factors beyond the direct control of travellers, such as the management and operation of a hotel chain. However, even here it is possible to voice concern about damaging activities and an increasing number of hotels and travel operators are taking "green concerns" seriously, even if it is only to protect their share of the market.

Environmental Legislation Legislation is increasingly being enacted to control damage to the environment, and in some cases this can have a bearing on travellers. The establishment of National Parks may involve rules and guidelines for visitors and these should always be followed. In addition there may be local or national laws controlling behaviour and use of natural resources (especially wildlife) that are being increasingly enforced. If in doubt, ask. Finally, international legislation, principally the Convention on International Trade in Endangered Species of Wild Fauna and Flora (CITES), may affect travellers.

CITES aims to control the trade in live specimens of endangered plants and animals and also "recognizable parts or derivatives" of protected species. Sale of Black Coral, Turtle shells, protected Orchids and other wildlife is strictly controlled by signatories of the convention. The full list of protected wildlife varies, so if you feel the need to purchase souvenirs and trinkets derived from wildlife, it would be prudent to check whether they are protected. Every country included in this Handbook is a signatory of CITES. In addition, most European countries, the USA and Canada are all signatories. Importation of CITES protected species into these countries can lead to heavy fines, confiscation of goods and even imprisonment. Information on the status of legislation and protective measures can be obtained from Traffic International, UK office T (01223) 277427, F (01223) 277237, e-mail traffic@wcmc.org.uk.

Green Travel Companies and Information The increasing awareness of the environmental impact of travel and tourism has led to a range of advice and information services as well as spawning specialist travel companies who claim to provide "responsible travel" for clients. This is an expanding field and the veracity of claims needs to be substantiated in some cases. The following organizations and publications can provide useful information for those with an interest in pursuing responsible travel opportunities.

Organizations Green Flag International Aims to work with travel industry and conservation bodies to improve environments at travel destinations and also to promote conservation programmes at resort destinations. Provides a travellers' guide for "green" tourism as well as advice on destinations, T (UK 01223) 890250. Tourism Concern Aims to promote a greater understanding of the impact of tourism on host communities and environments; Stapleton House, 277-281 Holloway Road, London N7 8HN, T UK (0171) 753-3330, F UK (0171) 753 3331, e-mail tourconcern@gn.apc.org). Centre for Responsible Tourism CRT coordinates a North American network and advises on N American sources of information on responsible tourism. CRT, PO Box 827, San Anselmo, California 94979, USA. Centre for the Advancement of Responsive Travel CART has a range of publications available as well as information on alternative holiday destinations. T (UK – 01732) 352757.

Section 2

Introduction and hints

GETTING THERE

AIR

All the main airlines plying to each country are given in the "Information for travellers" sections. Airlines will only allow a certain weight of luggage without a surcharge; this is normally 30 kg for first class and 20 kg for business and economy classes, but these limits are often not strictly enforced when it is known that the plane is not going to be full. On some flights from the UK special outbound concessions are offered (by Iberia, Air France, Avianca) of a 2-piece allowance up to 32 kg, but you may need to request this. Passengers seeking a larger baggage allowance can route via USA, but with certain exceptions, the fares are slightly higher using this route. On the other hand, weight limits for internal flights are often lower; best to enquire beforehand.

Prices and discounts

1 It is generally cheaper to fly from London rather than a point in Europe to Latin American destinations; fares vary from airline to airline, destination to destination and according to time of year. Check with an agency for the best deal for when you wish to travel.

2 Most airlines offer discounted fares of one sort or another on scheduled flights. These are not offered by the airlines direct to the public, but through agencies who specialize in this type of fare. In UK, these include Journey Latin America, 14-16 Devonshire Road, Chiswick, London, W4 2HD (T 0181-747 8315) and 28-30 Barton Arcade, 51-63 Deansgate, Manchester, M3 2BH (T 0161 832 1441); Trailfinders, 194 Kensington High Street, London, W8 7RG (T 0171-938 3939); South American Experience, 47 Causton Street, Pimlico, London, SW1P 4AT (T 0171-976 5511); Last Frontiers, Swan House, High Street, Long Crendon, Buckinghamshire, HP18 9AF (T 01844 208405); Passage to South America, Fovant Mews, 12 Noyna Road, London, SW17 7PH (T 0181 767 8989); STA Travel, Priory House, 6 Wrights Lane, London, W8 6TA (T 0171-361 6166); Encounter Overland, 267 Old Brompton Road, London, SW5 9JA (T 0171 370 6845); Hayes & Jarvis, 152 King Street, London, W6 0QU (T 0181 222 7844); Cox & Kings Travel, St James Court, 45 Buckingham Gate, London (T 0171-873 5001).

The very busy seasons are 7 Dec – 15 Jan and 10 July – 10 Sept. If you intend travelling during those times, book as far ahead as possible. Between Feb-May and Sept-Nov special offers may be available.

3 Other fares fall into three groups, and are all on scheduled services:

● **Excursion (return) fares** with restricted validity eg 5-90 days. Carriers are introducing flexibility into these tickets, permitting a change of dates on payment of a fee.

● **Yearly fares**: these may be bought on a one-way or return basis. Some airlines require a specified return date, changeable upon payment of a fee. To leave the return completely open is possible for an extra fee. You must, fix the route (some of the cheapest flexible fares now have 6 months validity).

● **Student (or Under 26) fares** Some airlines are flexible on the age limit, others strict. One way and returns available, or 'Open Jaws' (see below). Do not assume that student tickets are the cheapest; though they are often very flexible, they are usually more expensive than A or B above. On the other hand, there is a wider range of cheap one-way student fares originating in Latin America than can be bought outside the continent. **NB** If you foresee returning home at a busy time (eg Christmas-beginning of January, August), a booking is advisable on any type of open-return ticket.

4 For people intending to travel a linear route and return from a different point from that which they entered, there are 'Open Jaws' fares, which are available on student, yearly, or excursion fares.

5 Many of these fares require a change of plane at an intermediate point, and a stopover may be permitted, or even obligatory, depending on schedules. Simply because a flight stops at a given airport does not mean you can break your journey there – the airline must have traffic rights to pick up or set down passengers between points A and B before it will be permitted. This is where dealing with a specialized agency (like Journey Latin America!) will really pay dividends. There are dozens of agencies that offer the simple returns to Rio or Lima at roughly the same (discounted) fare. On multi-stop itineraries, the specialized agencies can often save clients hundreds of pounds.

6 Although it's a little more complicated, it's possible to sell tickets in London for travel originating in Latin America at substantially cheaper fares than those available locally. This is useful for the traveller who doesn't know where

he will end up, or who plans to travel for more than a year. Because of high local taxes (see paragraph 7) a one-way ticket from Latin America is more expensive than a one-way in the other direction, so it's always best to buy a return (but see **Student fares**, above). Taxes are calculated as a percentage of the full IATA fare; on a discounted fare the tax can therefore make up as much as 30-50% of the price.

7 Certain Latin American countries impose local tax on flights originating there. Among these are Ecuador, Peru, Bolivia, Uruguay and Mexico. This often applies if you happen to have bought a ticket, say, London-Rio-Santiago-Lima-Los Angeles and then on to Australia.

8 There are several cheap French charters to Colombia, Ecuador, Peru, Bolivia and the southern countries, but no-one in the UK sells them.

Travellers starting their journey in continental Europe should make local enquiries about charters and agencies offering the best deals.

9 If you buy discounted air tickets *always* check the reservation with the airline concerned to make sure the flight still exists. Also remember the IATA airlines' schedules change in March and October each year, so if you're going to be away a long time it's best to leave return flight coupons open (but see **NB** under **Student fares**, above).

In addition, check whether you are entitled to any refund or re-issued ticket if you lose, or have stolen, a discounted air ticket. Some airlines require the repurchase of a ticket before you can apply for a refund, which will not be given until after the validity of the original ticket has expired. The Iberia group and Air France, for example, operate this costly system. Travel insurance in some cases covers lost tickets.

10 Note that some South American carriers change departure times of short-haul or domestic flights at short notice and, in some instances, schedules shown in the computers of transatlantic carriers differ from those actually flown by smaller, local carriers. If you book, and

reconfirm, both your transatlantic and onward sectors through your transatlantic carrier you may find that your travel plans have been based on out of date information. The surest solution is to reconfirm your outward flight in an office of the onward carrier itself.

Air passes

AeroPerú operates Sudameripass, a 60-day return ticket which is one of the cheapest ways of flying around the continent. If starting a journey in Miami, Mexico City or Cancún, it costs US$1,099 for up to 6 coupons on AeroPerú's network; if starting in Buenos Aires or Los Angeles it costs US$1,299. Extra coupons can be bought for US$100 each. There are seasonal permutations. AeroPerú, AeroMéxico and Mexicana have the Mexi-AmeriPass, available until end-1997, which covers the whole of Latin America; the region is divided into 10 zones and a minimum of 3 flights must be purchased (domestic or international); fares start at US$50-70 for single domestic coupons, rising to US$400 for the longest legs (validity 3-90 days). Check with JLA for up-to-date details. Iberia and Aerolíneas Argentinas offer Latin American Circular Fares: available from the UK only, the fares are for circular routes (no back-tracking) in North, Central and South America. There are two zones, mid-Atlantic and South Atlantic, and a flat fare applies to each: mid-Atlantic £847 high season, £680 low; South Atlantic £968 high, £793 low. Two free stopovers are allowed, plus Caracas on mid-Atlantic routes, or Buenos Aires on South Atlantic routes. Additional stops are £35 each. Fares are valid for 3 months (extensions and business class available). Also worth noting here is the Mercosur Airpass which applies to Brazil, Argentina, Uruguay and Paraguay, using 9 local carriers, available to any passenger with a return ticket to a Mercosur country. It must be bought in conjunction with an international flight; minimum stay is 7 days, maximum 30, at least 2 countries must be visited. Maximum number of coupons is eight. Fares are calculated on a mileage basis and range from US$225 to US$870. Servivensa/Avensa of Venezuela have an airpass which covers these airlines internal and international network, minimum 3 flights, US$40 per leg.

Miami is a good place for connections between South and Central America and Europe. Non-US citizens should note that it is very difficult to check air tickets purchased outside the USA through an agent in Miami and that it is unlikely that you will be allowed by US Immigration to enter the USA without an onward ticket already in your possession. Continental Airlines' hub, Houston, is another good place for connections.

If you buy internal airline tickets in Latin American countries you may find cash refunds difficult to get if you change your plans: better to change your ticket for a different one. Overbooking by Latin American airlines is very common (largely due to repeated block bookings by travel agents, which everyone knows will not be used), so always reconfirm the next stage of your flight within 72 hrs of your intended departure. And it does no harm to reconfirm yet again in the last 24 hrs, just to show them you mean it, and turn up for the flight in good time (at least 2 hrs before departure). Also provide the airline with a contact phone number for the week prior to departure.

We advise people who travel the cheap way in Latin America to pay for all transport as they go along, and not in advance. This advice does not apply to people on a tight schedule: paying as you go along may save money, but it is likely to waste your time somewhat. The one exception to this general principle is in transatlantic flights; here money is saved by booking as far as possible in one operation. International air tickets are very expensive if purchased in Latin America. If buying airline tickets routed through the USA, check that US taxes are included in the price.

The national airlines of Argentina, Bolivia, Brazil, Chile, Colombia, Peru and Venezuela operate airpass schemes within those countries at a set price. See the respective country sections.

The Amerbuspass covers the whole of Latin America, from Mexico City to Ushuaia, and entitles the holder to 15-20% discounts on tickets with participating operators; bookable in all Latin American capitals, Europe, Asia, Africa, Oceania, it is valid for 9,999 miles, up to 180 days. Unlimited stopovers, travel with either a confirmed or open itinerary. Contact TISA Internacional, B Irigoyen 1370, Oficina 25/26, 1138 Buenos Aires, Argentina, T 307-1956/631-1108, F 300-5591, PO Box 40 Suc 1 (B), 1401 Buenos Aires.

TRAVEL TO THE USA

Although visa requirements for British air travellers with round-trip tickets to the USA have been relaxed, it is advisable to have a visa to allow entry by land, or on airlines from South and Central America which are not "participating carriers" on the Visa Waiver scheme. If you are thinking of travelling via the USA, or of visiting the USA after Latin America, you are strongly advised to get your visa from a US Consulate in your own country, not while travelling.

The US Department of Agriculture places restrictions on agricultural items brought to the United States from foreign countries as well as those brought to the mainland from Hawaii, Puerto Rico, and the US Virgin Islands. Prohibited items can harbour foreign animal and plant pests and diseases that could seriously damage America's crops, livestock, pets and the environment.

Because of this threat, travellers are required to list on the Customs' declaration form any meats, fruits, vegetables, plants, animals, and plant and animal products they are bringing into the country. The declaration must list all agricultural items carried in baggage, hand luggage and in vehicles coming across the border.

USDA inspectors will confiscate illegal items for destruction. Travellers who fail to declare items can be fined up to US$100 on the spot, and their exit from the airport will be delayed. Some items are permitted. Call 301-436-5908 for a copy of the helpful pamphlet, "Travelers Tips". The best advice is to check before purchasing an agricultural item and trying to bring it back to the United States.

SEA

Voyages on passenger-carrying cargo vessels between South America and Europe, the USA, or elsewhere, are listed here: the Grimaldi Line sails from Tilbury to Brazil (Vitória, Santos, Paranaguá, Rio) and Buenos Aires via Hamburg, Amsterdam and Antwerp, Le Havre, round trip about 51 days, US$3,040-5,400, also from Genoa to Paranaguá, Santos and Rio for US$1,100-1,400 (round trip or S-bound only, no N-bound only passages). Fyffes has regular sailings Portsmouth-Suriname, 6 passengers on a banana boat, 35-38 day round trip only, £1,980 pp.

A number of German container ships sail the year round to the E coast of South America: Felixstowe, Hamburg, Antwerp, Bilbao or Algeciras, Santos, Buenos Aires, Montevideo, Rio Grande do Sul, Itajaí, Santos, Rio de Janeiro, Rotterdam, Felixstowe (about 45 days, £3,100-3,500 pp round trip). There are also German sailings from Genoa or Livorno (Italy), or Spain to the E coast of South America. Projex Line's *EWL West Indies* sails Felixstowe, Paramaribo, Georgetown, Port of Spain, La Guaira, Puerto Cabello, Willemstad, Oranjestad, Cartagena, Santa Marta, Bremen, Rotterdam, Felixstowe, 44-day round trip, £2,600 pp. Flensburger Befrachtungskontor UC Hansen of Germany has a 50-day round trip on *Rickmers Brazil* and *Hapag Lloyd Amazonas*, Antwerp, Manaus, Itacoatiara, Belém, Rouen/Honfleur, Bremen, costing £3,500.

To W coast South America from Europe: CGM's *Magellan* (on charter to Furness Withy) sails from Felixstowe to Antwerp, Le Havre, Bilbao, Kingston (Jamaica), Cristóbal, Buenaventura, Guayaquil, Callao, Arica, Valparaíso, Callao, Paita, Guayaquil, Buenaventura, Bahía Málaga, Cristóbal, Kingston, Bilbao, Amsterdam, Hamburg,

Felixstowe, 69-day round trip, £4,590 pp. The *Tamayo* and *Andacollo* make an 80-day round trip Felixstowe, Bilbao, Cartagena, Guayaquil, Callao, Iquique, Valparaíso, Talcahuano, Antofagasta, Callao, Bilbao, Liverpool, £4,350 pp.

A cheaper option is Polish Ocean Line's services: E coast, Gdynia to Buenos Aires, Montevideo and Santos (2-2½ months); W coast, Hamburg, Antwerp, Guayaquil, Callao, Arica, Antofagasta, Valparaíso, Hamburg (2½-3 months), £2,700 pp double, £2,900 single; South and Central America, Gdynia, La Guaira, Puerto Cabello, Cartagena, Puerto Limón, Puerto Cortés, Santo Tomás de Castilla, New Orleans, Houston, Gdynia (2½-3 months), £2,650 pp double, £2,800 single.

From the USA, Ivaran Lines serve East Coast USA, Brazilian ports, Montevideo and Buenos Aires; the *Americana* container ship carries 80 passengers in luxury accommodation (New Orleans, Houston, Puerto Cabello, La Guaira, Rio, Santos, Buenos Aires, Montevideo, Rio Grande do Sul, Itajaí, Paranaguá, Santos, Salvador, Fortaleza, Bridgetown, San Juan, Veracruz, Tampico, New Orleans, £6,645-11,340 pp round trip, fares depend on season, one-way N or S possible). Ivaran also have the *San Antonio*, carrying 12 passengers on the route Port Elizabeth (New Jersey), Baltimore, Norfolk, Savannah, Miami, Puerto Cabello, La Guaira, Rio, Santos, Buenos Aires, Montevideo, Rio Grande do Sul, Itajaí, Santos, Rio (possibly Salvador and Fortaleza), Port Elizabeth; 44-day round trip £4,085-4,825 pp, one-way subject to availability. *Sven Ottmann*, 2-week round trip Fort Lauderdale, Oranjestad, Willemstad, Puerto Cabello, La Guaira, Fort Lauderdale £1,300 pp; Chilean Line's *Laja* and *Lircay*, New Orleans, Houston, Tampico, Cristóbal, Panama Canal, Guayaquil, Callao, Antofagasta, San Antonio, Arica, Callao, Buenaventura, Panama Canal, Cristóbal, New Orleans, 48-day round trip, US$4,800-5,280 pp.

Uniline has 6 tramp cargo vessels which sail around South America, either from Rio de Janeiro, or from Buenos Aires, calling at a large number of ports on

about 7-week trips on the E and W coast (fares and schedules from Strand Cruise and Travel Centre; see below).

Enquiries regarding passages should be made through agencies in your own country, or through John Alton of Strand Cruise and Travel Centre, Charing Cross Shopping Concourse, The Strand, London WC2N 4HZ, T 0171-836 6363, F 0171-497 0078. Strand Cruise and Travel are booking agents for all the above, except Fyffes, whose booking agent is Cargo Ship Voyages Ltd, Hemley, Woodbridge, Suffolk, IP12 4QF, T/F 01473-736065 (who can also advise on the other sailings). In Europe, contact Wagner Frachtschiffreisen, Stadlerstrasse 48, CH-8404, Winterthur, Switzerland, T (052) 242-1442, F 242-1487. In the USA, contact Freighter World Cruises, 180 South Lake Ave, Pasadena, CA 91101, T (818) 449-3106, or Travltips Cruise and Freighter Travel Association, 163-07 Depot Road, PO Box 188, Flushing, NY 11358, T (800) 872-8584. Do not try to get a passage on a non-passenger carrying cargo ship to South America from a European port; it is not possible.

Details on shipping cars are given in **Motoring**, below, and in the relevant country sections.

NB Some countries in Latin America officially require travellers who enter their territory to have an onward or return ticket. (Look under 'Information for travellers' sections for the countries you intend to visit.) In 1996-97 this regulation was rarely enforced by any country. (It does not apply to travellers with their own vehicles.) In lieu of an onward ticket out of the country you are entering, any ticket out of another Latin American country (or a ticket home) may suffice, or proof that you have sufficient funds to buy a ticket (a credit card will do).

ON ARRIVAL

APPEARANCE

There is a natural prejudice in all countries against travellers who ignore personal hygiene and have a generally dirty and unkempt appearance. Most Latin

Americans, if they can afford it, devote great care to their clothes and appearance; it is appreciated if visitors do likewise. How you dress is mostly how people will judge you. Buying clothing locally can help you to look less like a tourist. It may be advantageous to carry a letter from someone in an official position testifying to one's good character, on official-looking notepaper.

Men wearing earrings are liable to be ridiculed in more "macho" communities (eg parts of Argentina). A medium weight shawl with some wool content is recommended for women: it can double as pillow, light blanket, bathrobe or sunscreen as required. For men, a smart jacket can be very useful.

COURTESY

Remember that politeness – even a little ceremoniousness – is much appreciated. In this connection professional or business cards are useful. Men should always remove any headgear and say "con permiso" ("com licença" in Brazil) when entering offices, and be prepared to shake hands (this is much commoner in Latin America than in Europe or North America); always say "Buenos días" (until midday) or "Buenas tardes" ("Bom dia" or "Boa tarde" in Brazil) and wait for a reply before proceeding further. Always remember that the traveller from abroad has enjoyed greater advantages in life than most Latin American minor officials, and should be friendly and courteous in consequence. Never be impatient; do not criticize situations in public: the officials may know more English than you think and they can certainly interpret gestures and facial expressions. Be judicious about discussing politics with strangers. Politeness can be a liability, however, in some situations; most Latin Americans are disorderly queuers. In commercial transactions (buying a meal, goods in a shop, etc) politeness should be accompanied by firmness, and always ask the price first.

Politeness should also be extended to street traders; saying "No, gracias/Não, obrigado" with a smile is better than an arrogant dismissal. Whether you give money to beggars is a personal matter, but your decision should be influenced by whether a person is begging out of need or trying to cash in on the tourist trail. In the former case, local people giving may provide an indication. Giving money to children is a separate issue, upon which most agree: don't do it. There are occasions where giving food in a restaurant may be appropriate, but first inform yourself of local practice.

Moira Chubb, from New Zealand, suggests that if you are a guest and are offered food that arouses your suspicions, the only courteous way out is to feign an allergy or a stomach ailment. If worried about the purity of ice for drinks, ask for a beer.

CULTURE

Literature

This Handbook does not at present have space to contain sections on Latin American literature. Interested readers are recommended to see Jason Wilson, *Traveller's Literary Companion, South and Central America* (Brighton, UK: In Print, 1993), which has extracts from works by Latin American writers and by non-Latin Americans about the various countries and has very useful bibliographies.

Music and dance

The aim of the Music and Dance sections (specially written for us by Nigel Gallop) has been to give an overview of the traditional and popular music and dances of each country. Considerations of space and the desire to avoid a tedious inventory has meant that by no means every song style, dance or instrument has been noted. As to the performers mentioned, the choice has also been selective, giving preference to those who have achieved local fame over those who, for commercial or political reasons, have based themselves in Europe or North America and are probably already familiar to the overseas visitor. Space has not been devoted to the forest indians, who are nevertheless present in most of the countries covered and whose music and dancing tends to exist only in its isolated cosmos, rarely relating to, or connecting with, national or regional musical cultures. Also not discussed, at present, is the classical music of the region.

DOCUMENTS

Passports

Latin Americans, especially officials, are very document-minded. You should always carry your passport in a safe place about your person, or if not going far, leave it in the hotel safe. If staying in a country for several weeks, it is worth while registering at your Embassy or Consulate. Then, if your passport is stolen, the process of replacing it is simplified and speeded up. Keeping photocopies of essential documents, including your flight ticket, and some additional passport-sized photographs, is recommended.

It is your responsibility to ensure that your passport is stamped in and out when you cross frontiers. The absence of entry and exit stamps can cause serious difficulties: seek out the proper migration offices if the stamping process is not carried out as you cross. Also, do not lose your entry card; replacing one causes a lot of trouble, and possibly expense. Citizens of countries which oblige visitors to have a visa (eg France) can expect more delays and problems at border crossings.

If planning to study in Latin America for a long period, make every effort to get a student visa in advance.

Identity and Membership Cards

Membership cards of British, European and US motoring organizations can be useful for discounts off hotel charges, car rentals, maps, towing charges, etc. Student cards must carry a photograph if they are to be of any use in Latin America for discounts. Business people should carry a good supply of visiting cards, which are essential for good business relations in Latin America. Identity, membership or business cards in Spanish or Portuguese (or a translation) and an official letter of introduction in Spanish or Portuguese are also useful.

If you are in full-time education you will be entitled to an International Student Identity Card, which is distributed by student travel offices and travel agencies in 77 countries. The ISIC gives you special prices on all forms of transport (air, sea, rail etc), and access to a variety of other concessions and services. If you need to find the location of your nearest ISIC office contact: The ISIC Association, Box 9048, 1000 Copenhagen, Denmark T (+45) 33 93 93 03.

It is possible to get jobs in some countries of South America, *Jobs Abroad* will arrange work permits, visas and immigration, send 2 x 25p stamps for information to Worldwide House, Broad St, Port Ramsgate, Kent, CT11 8NQ.

KEEPING IN TOUCH

Mail

Postal services in most countries are not very efficient, and pilfering is frequent. All mail, especially packages, should be registered. Check before leaving home if your Embassy will hold mail, and for how long, in preference to the Poste Restante/General Delivery (*Lista de Correos*) department of a country's Post Office. (Cardholders can use American Express agencies.) If there seems to be no mail at the Lista under the initial letter of your surname, ask them to look under the initial of your forename or your middle name. Remember that there is no W in Spanish; look under V, or ask. For the smallest risk of misunderstanding, use title, initial and surname only. If having items sent to you by courier (eg DHL), do not use poste restante, but an address such as a hotel: a signature is required on receipt.

Phones

AT&T's "USA Direct", Sprint and MCI are all available for calls to the USA. It is much cheaper than operator-assisted calls. Details given under individual countries. Other countries have similar systems, eg UK, Canada; obtain details before leaving home.

Communicating by fax is a convenient way of sending messages home. Many places with public fax machines (post offices, telephone companies or shops) will receive messages as well as send. Fax machines are often switched off; you may have to phone to confirm receipt.

Insurance tips

Insurance companies have tightened up considerably over recent years and it is now almost impossible to claim successfully if you have not followed procedures closely. The problem is that these often involve dealing with the country's red tape which can lead to some inconvenience at best and to some quite long delays at worst. There is no substitute for suitable precautions against petty crime.

The level of insurance that you carry is often dictated by the sums of medical insurance which you carry. It is inevitably the highest if you go through the USA. Also don't forget to obtain sports extensions if you are going to go diving, rafting, climbing etc. Most policies do not cover very high levels of baggage/cash. Don't forget to check whether you can claim on your household insurance. They often have worldwide all risks extensions. Most policies exclude manual work whilst away although working in bars or restaurants is usually alright.

Here are our tips: they apply to most types of policies but always check the details of your own policy before you leave.

1. Take the policy with you (a photocopy will do but make sure it is a complete one).

2. Do not travel against medical advice. It will invalidate the medical insurance part of the cover.

3. There is a 24 hour medical emergency service helpline associated with your insurance. You need to contact them if you require in-patient hospital treatment or you need to return home early. The telephone number is printed on the policy. Make sure you note the time of the call, the person you were talking to and get a reference number. Even better get a receipt from the telephone company showing the number you called. Should you need to be airlifted home, this is always arranged through the insurance company's representative and the hospital authorities. Ironically this can lead to quite intense discussions which you will not be aware of: the local hospital is often quite keen to keep you!

4. If you have to cancel your trip for whatever reason, contact your travel agent, tour operator or airline without delay.

5. If your property is damage by an airline, report it immediately and always within 3 days and get a "property irregularity report" from them.

6. Claims for baggage left unattended are very rarely settled unless they were left in a securely locked hotel room, apartment etc; locked in the boot of a car and there is evidence of a forced entry; cash is carried on your person or is in a locked safe or security box.

7. All loss must be reported to the police and/or hotel authorities within 24 hours of discovery and a written report obtained.

8. If medical attention is received for injury or sickness, a medical certificate showing its nature must be obtained, although some companies waive this if only out-patient treatment is required. Keep all receipts in a safe place as they will be needed to substantiate the claim.

9. Check your policy carefully to see if there is a date before which claims must be submitted. This is often within 30 days of returning home. It is now usual for companies to want your policy document, proof that you actually travelled (airline ticket or travel agent's confirmation of booking), receipts and written reports (in the event of loss). **NB** photocopies are not accepted.

E-mail

E-mail is becoming more common and public access to the Internet is fairly widespread with cybercafés opening in both large and small towns. There is usually a charge per page sent or received, which compares favourably with fax charges.

World Band Radio

South America has more local and community radio stations than practically anywhere else in the world; a shortwave (world band) radio offers a practical means to brush up on the language, sample popular culture and absorb some of the richly varied regional music. International broadcasters such as the BBC World Service, the Voice of America, Boston (Mass)-based Monitor Radio International (operated by *Christian Science Monitor*) and the Quito-based Evangelical station, HCJB, keep the traveller abreast of news and events, in both English and Spanish.

Compact or miniature portables are recommended, with digital tuning and a full range of shortwave bands, as well as FM, long and medium wave. Detailed advice on radio models (£150 for a decent one) and wavelengths can be found in the annual publication, *Passport to World Band Radio* (Box 300, Penn's Park, PA 18943, USA). Details of local stations is listed in *World TV and Radio Handbook* (WTRH), PO Box 9027, 1006 AA Amsterdam, The Netherlands, US$19.95. Both of these, free wavelength guides and selected radio sets are available from the BBC World Service Bookshop, Bush House Arcade, Bush House, Strand, London WC2B 4PH, UK, T 0171-257 2576.

LANGUAGE

Without some knowledge of Spanish you can become very frustrated and feel helpless in many situations. English, or any other language, is absolutely useless off the beaten track. Some initial study, to get you up to a basic Spanish vocabulary of 500 words or so, and a pocket dictionary and phrase-book, are most strongly recommended: your pleasure will be doubled if you can talk to the locals. Not all the locals speak Spanish, of course; apart from Brazil's Portuguese, you will find that some Indians in the more remote highland parts of Bolivia and Peru, and lowland Indians in Amazonia, speak only their indigenous languages, though there will usually be at least one person in each village who can speak Spanish (or Portuguese).

The basic Spanish of Hispanic America is that of south-western Spain, with soft "c's" and "z's" pronounced as "s", and not as "th" as in the other parts of Spain. Castilian Spanish is readily understood, but is not appreciated when spoken by non-Spaniards; try and learn the basic Latin American pronunciation. There are several regional variations in pronunciation, particularly in the River Plate countries, which are noted in the Argentine section **Information for travellers**.

Differences in vocabulary also exist, both between peninsular Spanish and Latin American Spanish, and between the usages of the different countries.

If you are going to Brazil, you should learn some Portuguese. Spanish is not adequate: you may be understood but you will probably not be able to understand the answers. Language classes are available at low cost in a number of centres in South America, for instance Quito. See the text for details, under **Language Courses**.

The Linguaphone Language Centre, 124-126 Brompton Road, Knightsbridge, London SW3 1JD, T 0171 589 2422, F 0171 584 7052, offers the full range of Linguaphone self-study courses including Latin American Spanish. It also supplies many other courses and dictionairies by the world's leading publishers. (**NB** Readers of the South American Handbook qualify for a 10% discount off all Linguaphone branded products by referring to their advertisement.)

AmeriSpan, PO Box 40007, Philadelphia, PA 19106, T 800-879-6640, offers Spanish immersion programs, volunteer and internship positions throughout Latin America. Language programs are offered in Buenos Aires, Santiago, Cuenca, Quito, Cuzco, Huancayo, Montevideo, Caracas and Mérida as well as throughout Central America and its Dominican Republic. Contact AmeriSpan at above address or Web: http://www.amerispan.com for details. In Ecuador, they also offer a discount card for use in hotels, restaurants and shops.

MONEY

The three main ways of keeping in funds while travelling are with US dollars cash, US dollars travellers' cheques (TCs), or plastic.

Cash

Sterling and other currencies are not recommended. Though the risk of loss is greater, the chief benefit of US dollar notes is that better rates and lower commissions can usually be obtained for them. In many countries, US dollar notes are only accepted if they are in excellent, if not perfect condition (likewise, do not accept local currency notes in poor condition). Low-value US dollar bills should be carried for changing into local currency if arriving in a country when banks or *casas de cambio* are closed (US$5 or US$10 bills). They are very useful for shopping: shopkeepers and exchange shops (*casas de cambio*) tend to give better exchange rates than hotels or banks (but see below). The better hotels will normally change travellers' cheques for their guests (often at a rather poor rate), but if you are travelling on the cheap it is essential to keep in funds; watch weekends and public holidays carefully and never run out of local currency. Take plenty of local currency, in small denominations, when making trips into the interior.

Travellers' cheques

These are convenient but they attract thieves (though refunds can of course be arranged) and you will find that they are more difficult than dollar bills to change in small towns (denominations of US$50 and US$100 are preferable, though one does need a few of US$20). American Express, Visa or Thomas Cook US$ TCs are recommended, but less commission is often charged on Citibank or Bank of America TCs, if they are cashed at Latin American branches of those banks. These TCs are always accepted by banks, even though they may not be as well known outside banks as those of American Express, Visa or Thomas Cook. (It is also easier to obtain refunds for stolen TCs with the last three than with Citicorp cheques.) It is a good idea to take 2 kinds of cheque: if large numbers of one kind have recently been forged or stolen, making people suspicious, it is unlikely to have happened simultaneously with the other kind. Several banks charge a high fixed commission for changing TCs – sometimes as much as US$5-10 a cheque – because they don't really want to be bothered. Exchange houses (*casas de cambio*) are usually much better for this service. Some establishments may ask to see the customer's record of purchase before accepting.

Exchange Rates		
COUNTRY	**Unit of currency**	**Exchange rate/US$**
ARGENTINA	Peso	1.00
BOLIVIA	Boliviano	5.24
BRAZIL	Real	1.08
CHILE	Chilean peso	416.27
COLOMBIA	Colombian peso	1,102.48
ECUADOR	Sucre	3,987.00
GUYANA	Guyanese dollar	142.30
GUYANE	French franc	5.91
PARAGUAY	Guaraní	2,159.00
PERU	New sol	2.65
SURINAME	Suriname guilder	401.00
URUGUAY	Peso Uruguayo	9.52
VENEZUELA	Bolivar	488.45
Correct at 4 July 1997		

Plastic

It is straightfoward to obtain a cash advance against a credit card and, in the text, we give the names of banks that do this.

There are two international **ATM** (automatic telling machine) acceptance systems, Plus and Cirrus. Many issuers of debit and credit cards are linked to one, or both (eg Visa is Plus, Mastercard is Cirrus). Look for the relevant symbol on an ATM and draw cash using your PIN. Frequently, the rates of exchange on ATM withdrawals are the best available. Find out before you leave what ATM coverage there is in the countries you will visit and what international 'functionality' your card has. Check if your bank or credit card company imposes handling charges. Obviously you must ensure that the account to which your debit card refers contains sufficient funds. With a credit card, obtain a credit limit sufficient for your needs, or pay money in to put the account in credit. If travelling for a long time, consider a direct debit to clear your account regularly. Do not rely on one card, in case of loss. If you do lose a card, immediately contact the 24-hr helpline of the issuer in your home country (keep

this number in a safe place). (With thanks to Nigel Baker, Debit Card Manager, Natwest Bank plc, London.)

For purchases, credit cards of the Visa and Mastercard (Eurocard, Access), American Express (Amex), Carte Blanche and Diners Club can be used. Make sure you know the correct procedure if they are lost or stolen. Credit card transactions are normally at an officially recognized rate of exchange; they are often subject to tax. Many establishments in Latin America charge a fee of about 5% on credit card transactions; although forbidden by credit card company rules there is not a lot you can do about this, except get the charge itemized on the receipt and complain to the card company. For credit card security, insist that imprints are made in your presence and that any imprints incorrectly completed should be torn into tiny pieces. Also destroy the carbon papers after the form is completed (signatures can be copied from them).

NB In many countries, one can get at least US$500 in Amex travellers' cheques on the American Express card (US$1,000 on the gold card). One can also obtain cash at

American Express via personal cheques, eg Eurocheque. If you are having additional sums of money sent out during a tour of Latin America, try to have it sent to one of the countries where you can easily exchange dollar travellers' cheques for dollars cash; see under the individual countries below for the current situation.

Money can be transferred between banks. A recommended method is, before leaving, to find out which local bank is correspondent to your bank at home, then when you need funds, telex your own bank and ask them to telex the money to the local bank (confirming by fax). Give exact information to your bank of the routing number of the receiving bank. Cash in dollars, local currency depending on the country can be received within 48 banking hours.

Exchange

Most of the countries described in this book have freedom of exchange between US dollars and the local currency. A few have a parallel rate of exchange which is not always better than the official rate. Local conditions are described in the relevant chapters. Changing money on the street: if possible, do not do so alone. If unsure of the currency of the country you are about to enter, check rates with more than one changer at the border, or ask locals or departing travellers.

Whenever you leave a country, sell any local currency before leaving, because the further away you get, the less the value of a country's money. **NB** If departing by air, do not leave yourself too little money to pay the airport departure tax, which is never waived.

Americans should know that if they run out of funds they can usually expect no help from the US Embassy or Consul other than a referral to some welfare organization. Find out before you go precisely what services and assistance your embassy or consulate can provide if you find yourself in difficulties.

PHOTOGRAPHY

Always ask permission before photographing people. The price of film varies from country to country, being cheapest in Chile (in the Iquique and Punta Arenas Tax Free Zones), Bolivia (in markets of major cities and in all free zones – Zofri) and Paraguay (always check the expiry date). Pre-paid Kodak slide film cannot be developed in South America; it is also very hard to find. Kodachrome is almost impossible to buy. Some travellers (but not all) have advised against mailing exposed films home; either take them with you, or have them developed, but not printed, once you have checked the laboratory's quality. Note that postal authorities may use less sensitive equipment for X-ray screening than the airports do. Modern controlled X-ray machines are supposed to be safe for any speed of film, but it is worth trying to avoid X-ray as the doses are cumulative. Many airport officials will allow film to be passed outside X-ray arches; they may also hand-check a suitcase with a large quantity of film if asked politely.

Dan Buck and Anne Meadows write: A note on developing film in South America. Black and white is a problem. Often it is shoddily machine-processed and the negatives are ruined. Ask the store if you can see an example of their laboratory's work and if they hand-develop.

Jeremy Till and Sarah Wigglesworth suggest that exposed film can be protected in humid areas by putting it in a balloon and tying a knot. Similarly keeping your camera in a plastic bag may reduce the effects of humidity.

SAFETY
Drugs

Users of drugs, even of soft ones, without medical prescription should be particularly careful, as some countries impose heavy penalties – up to 10 years' imprisonment – for even the simple possession of such substances. In this connection, the planting of drugs on travellers, by traffickers or the police, is not unknown. If offered drugs on the street, make no response at all and keep walking. Note that people who roll their own cigarettes are often suspected of carrying drugs and subjected to intensive searches. Advisable to stick to commercial brands of cigarettes – but better still not to smoke at all.

Keeping safe

Generally speaking, most places in Latin America are no more dangerous than any major city in Europe or North America. In provincial towns, main places of interest, on day time buses and in ordinary restaurants the visitor should be quite safe. Nevertheless, in large cities (particularly in crowded places, eg bus stations, markets), crime exists, most of which is opportunistic. If you are aware of the dangers, act confidently and use your common sense you will lessen many of the risks. The following tips, all endorsed by travellers, are meant to forewarn, but not alarm, you. Keep all documents secure; hide your main cash supply in different places or under your clothes: extra pockets sewn inside shirts and trousers, pockets closed with a zip or safety pin, moneybelts (best worn below the waist rather than outside or at it or around the neck), neck or leg pouches, a thin chain for attaching a purse to your bag or under your clothes and elasticated support bandages for keeping money and cheques above the elbow or below the knee have been repeatedly recommended (the last by John Hatt in *The Tropical Traveller*). Keep cameras in bags (preferably with a chain or wire in the strap to defeat the slasher) or briefcases; take spare spectacles (eyeglasses); don't wear wrist-watches or jewellery. If you wear a shoulder-bag in a market, carry it in front of you. Backpacks are vulnerable to slashers: a good idea is to cover the pack with a sack (a plastic one will also keep out rain and dust) with maybe a layer of wire netting between, or make an inner frame of chicken wire. Use a pack which is lockable at its base.

Ignore mustard smearers and paint or shampoo sprayers, and strangers' remarks like "what's that on your shoulder?" or "have you seen that dirt on your shoe?" Furthermore, don't bend over to pick up money or other items in the street. These are all ruses intended to distract your attention and make you easy for an accomplice to steal from. If someone follows you when you're in the street, let him catch up with you and "give him the eye". While you should take local advice about being out at night, do not assume that daytime is safer than nighttime. If walking after dark, walk in the road, not on the pavement/sidewalk.

Be wary of "plainclothes policemen"; insist on seeing identification and on going to the police station by main roads. Do not hand over your identification (or money – which he should not need to see anyway) until you are at the station. On no account take them directly back to your lodgings. Be even more suspicious if he seeks confirmation of his status from a passer-by. If someone tries to bribe you, insist on a receipt. If attacked, remember your assailants may well be armed, and try not to resist.

It is best, if you can trust your hotel, to leave any valuables you don't need in safe-deposit there, when sightseeing locally. Always keep an inventory of what you have deposited. If you don't trust the hotel, lock everything in your pack and secure that in your room (some people take eyelet-screws for padlocking cupboards or drawers). If you lose valuables, always report to the police and note details of the report – for insurance purposes.

When you have all your luggage with you at a bus or railway station, be especially careful: don't get into arguments with any locals if you can help it, and lock all the items together with a chain or cable if you are waiting for some time. Take a taxi between airport/bus station/railway station and hotel, if you can possibly afford it. Keep your bags with you in the taxi and pay only when you and your luggage are safely out of the vehicle. Make sure the taxi has inner door handles, in case a quick exit is needed. Avoid night buses; never arrive at night; and watch your belongings whether they are stowed inside or outside the cabin (roof top luggage racks create extra problems, which are sometimes unavoidable – make sure your bag is waterproof). Major bus lines often issue a luggage ticket when bags are stored in the bus' hold. When getting on a bus, keep your ticket handy; someone sitting in your seat may be a distraction for an accomplice to rob you while you are sorting out the problem. Finally, never accept food, drink, sweets or cigarettes from unknown fellow-travellers on buses or trains. They may be drugged, and you would wake up hours later without your belongings. In this connection, never accept a bar drink from an opened bottle (unless you can see that that bottle is in general use): always have it uncapped in front of you.

For specific local problems, see under the individual countries in the text.

Rape This can happen anywhere in the world. If you are the victim of a sexual assault, you are advised in the first instance to contact a doctor (this can be your home doctor if you prefer). You will need tests to determine whether you have contracted any sexually-transmitted diseases; you may also need advice on post-coital contraception. You should also contact your embassy, where consular staff are very willing to help in cases of assault.

Police

Whereas in Europe and North America we are accustomed to law enforcement on a systematic basis, in general, enforcement in Latin America is achieved by periodic campaigns. The most typical is a round-up of criminals in the cities just before Christmas. In December, therefore, you may well be asked for identification at any time, and if you cannot produce it, you will be jailed. If a visitor is jailed his/her friends should provide food every day. This is especially important for people on a diet, such as diabetics. In the event of a vehicle accident in which anyone is injured, all drivers involved are automatically detained until blame has been established, and this does not usually take less than 2 weeks.

Never offer a bribe unless you are fully conversant with the customs of the country. (In Chile, for instance, it would land you in serious trouble if you tried to bribe a *carabinero*.) Wait until the official makes the suggestion, or offer money in some form which is apparently not bribery, eg "In our country we have a system of on-the-spot fines (*multas de inmediato*). Is there a similar system here?" Do not assume that an official who accepts a bribe is prepared to do anything else that is illegal. You bribe him to persuade him to do his job, or to persuade him not to do it, or to do it more quickly, or more slowly. You do not bribe him to do something which is against the law. The mere suggestion would make him very upset. If an official suggests that a bribe must be paid before you can proceed on your way, be patient (assuming you have the time) and he may relent.

SOUVENIRS

Remember that these can almost invariably be bought more cheaply away from the capital, though the choice may be less wide. Bargaining seems to be the general rule in most countries' street markets, but don't make a fool of yourself by bargaining over what, to you, is a small amount of money.

If British travellers have no space in their luggage, they might like to remember Tumi, the Latin American Craft Centre, who specialize in Mexican and Andean products and who produce cultural and educational videos for schools: at 23/2A Chalk Farm Road, London NW1 8AG (F 0171-485 4152), 8/9 New Bond Street Place, Bath BA1 1BH (T 01225 462367, F 01225 444870), 1/2 Little Clarendon St, Oxford OX1 2HJ (T/F 01865-512307), 82 Park St, Bristol BS1 5LA (T/F 0117 929 0391). Tumi (Music) Ltd specializes in different rhythms of Latin America. See *Arts and Crafts of South America*, by Lucy Davies and Mo Fini, published by Tumi (1994), for a fine introduction to the subject. There are similar shops in the USA.

TRAVELLING ALONE

Many points of security, dress and language have been covered already. First time exposure to countries where sections of the population live in extreme poverty or squalor and may even be starving can cause odd psychological reactions in visitors. So can the exceptional curiosity extended to visitors, especially women. Simply be prepared for this and try not to over-react. These additional hints have mainly been supplied by women, but most apply to any single traveller. When you set out, err on the side of caution until your instincts have adjusted to the customs of a new culture. If, as a single woman, you can befriend a local woman, you will learn much more about the country you are visiting. Unless actively avoiding foreigners like yourself, don't go too far from the beaten track; there is a very definite "gringo trail" which you can join, or follow, if seeking company. This can be helpful when looking for safe accommodation, especially if arriving after dark (which is best avoided). Remember that for a single woman a taxi at night can be as dangerous as wandering around on her own. At borders dress as smartly as possible. Travelling by train is a good way to meet locals, but buses are much easier for a person alone; on major routes your seat is often reserved and your luggage can usually be locked in the hold. It is easier for men to take the friendliness of locals at face value; women may be subject to much unwanted attention. To help minimize this, do not wear suggestive clothing and, advises Alex Rossi of Jawa Timur, Indonesia, do not flirt. By wearing a wedding ring, carrying a photograph of your "husband" and "children", and saying that your "husband" is close at hand, you may dissuade an aspiring suitor. If politeness fails, do not feel bad about showing offence and departing. When accepting a social invitation, make sure that someone knows the address and the time you left. Ask if you can bring a friend (even if you do not intend to do so). A good rule is always to act with confidence, as though you know where you are going, even if you do not. Someone who looks lost is more likely to attract unwanted attention. Do not disclose to strangers where you are staying. (Much of this information was supplied by Alex Rossi, and by Deirdre Mortell of Carrigaline, Co Cork).

WHAT TO TAKE

Everybody has his/her own list. In addition to items already suggested above, those most often mentioned include air cushions for slatted seats, inflatable travel pillow for neck support, strong shoes (and remember that footwear over 9½ English size, or 42 European size, is difficult to obtain in Latin America except Argentina and Brazil); a small first-aid kit and handbook, fully waterproof top clothing, waterproof treatment for leather footwear, wax earplugs (which are almost impossible to find outside large cities) and airline-type eye mask to help you sleep in noisy and poorly curtained hotel rooms, sandals (rubber-thong Japanese-type or other – can be worn in showers to avoid athlete's foot), a polyethylene sheet 2 x 1 metres to cover possibly infested beds and shelter your luggage, polyethylene bags of varying sizes (up to heavy duty rubbish bag size) with ties, a toilet bag you can tie round your waist, if you use an electric shaver, take a rechargeable type, a sheet sleeping-bag and pillow-case or separate pillow-case – in some countries they are not changed often in cheap hotels; a 1½-2m piece of 100% cotton can be used as a towel, a bedsheet, beach towel, makeshift curtain and wrap; a mosquito net (or a hammock with a fitted net), a straw hat which can be rolled or flattened and reconstituted after 15 mins soaking in water, a clothes line, a nailbrush (useful for scrubbing dirt off clothes as well as off oneself), a vacuum flask, a water bottle, a small dual-voltage immersion heater, a small dual-voltage (or battery-driven) electric fan, a light nylon waterproof shopping bag, a universal bath- and basin-plug of the flanged type that will fit any waste-pipe (or improvise one from a sheet of thick rubber), string, velcro, electrical insulating tape, large penknife preferably with tin and bottle openers, scissors and corkscrew – the famous Swiss Army range has been repeatedly recommended (for knife sharpening, go to a butcher's shop), alarm clock or watch, candle, torch (flashlight) – especially one that will clip on to a pocket or belt, pocket mirror, pocket calculator, an adaptor and flex to enable you to take power from an electric-light socket (the Edison screw type is the most commonly used), a padlock (combination lock is best) for the doors of the cheapest and most casual hotels (or for tent zip if camping), spare chain-lengths and padlock for securing luggage to bed or bus/train seat. Remember not to throw away spent batteries containing mercury or cadmium; take them home to be disposed of, or recycled properly.

Useful medicaments are given at the end of the "Health" section (page 48); to these might be added some lip salve with sun protection, and pre-moistened wipes (such as "Wet Ones"). Always carry toilet paper. Natural fabric sticking plasters, as well as being long-lasting, are much appreciated as gifts. Dental floss can be used for backpack repairs, in addition to its original purpose. **Never** carry firearms. Their possession could land you in serious trouble.

A note for **contact lens wearers**: most countries have a wide selection of products for the care of lenses, so you don't need to take kilos of lotions. Lens solution can be difficult to find in Peru and Bolivia and outside major cities. Ask for it in a chemist/pharmacy, rather than an optician's.

Be careful when asking directions. Women probably know more about the neighbourhood; men about more distant locations. Policemen are often helpful. However, many Latin Americans will give you the wrong answer rather than admit they do not know.

Lastly, a good principle is to take half the clothes, and twice the money, that you think you will need.

WHERE TO STAY

HOTELS

For about US$10, a cheap but not bad hotel room can be found in most countries, although in some of the Andean countries you may not have to pay that much. For those on a really tight budget, it is a good

Hotel prices

Our hotel price ranges, including taxes and service charges but without meals unless stated, are as follows:

L1	Over US$200	**L2**	US$151-200	**L3**	US$101-150
A1	US$81-100	**A2**	US$61-80	**A3**	US$46-60
B	US$31-45	**C**	US$21-30	**D**	US$12-20
E	US$7-11	**F**	US$4-6	**G**	Up to US$3

NB Prices are for double rooms, except in **F** and **G** ranges where the price is almost always per person.

Unless otherwise stated, all hotels in range **D** and above have private bath. Assume friendliness and cleanliness in all cases.

Other abbreviations used in the book (apart from pp = per person; a/c = air conditioned; rec = recommended; T = telephone; TCs = travellers' cheques; s/n = "sin número", no street number; p = piso – floor, in Spanish-speaking countries) should be self-explanatory.

idea to ask for a boarding house – *casa de huéspedes, hospedaje, pensión, casa familial* or *residencial*, according to country; they are normally to be found in abundance near bus and railway stations and markets. Good value hotels can also be found near truckers' stops/service stations; they are usually secure. There are often great seasonal variations in hotel prices in resorts. Note that in the text "with bath" usually means "with shower and toilet", not "with bath tub". Remember, cheaper hotels don't always supply soap, towels and toilet paper; in colder (higher) regions they may not supply enough blankets, so take your own or a sleeping bag. Useful tips: book even cheap hotels in advance by registered mail, if you receive no reply don't worry. In any class, hotel rooms facing the street may be noisy; always ask for the best, quietest room. To avoid price hikes for gringos, ask if there is a cheaper room.

Experiment in International Living Ltd, 287 Worcester Road, Malvern, Worcestershire, WR14 1AB, T 01684-562577, F 562212, or Ubierstrasse 30, 5300 Bonn 2, T 0228-95-7220, F 0228-35-8282, can arrange stays with families from 1 to 4 weeks in Chile, Ecuador and Brazil; EIL has offices in 38 countries. This has been recommended as an excellent way to meet people and learn the language.

NB The electric showers used in innumerable hotels should be checked for obvious flaws in the wiring; try not to touch the rose while it is producing hot water.

Cockroaches

These are ubiquitous and unpleasant, but not dangerous. Take some insecticide powder if staying in cheap hotels; Baygon (Bayer) has been recommended. Stuff toilet paper in any holes in walls that you may suspect of being parts of cockroach runs.

Toilets

Many hotels, restaurants and bars have inadequate water supplies. **Almost without exception used toilet paper should not be flushed down the pan, but placed in the receptacle provided**. This applies even in quite expensive hotels. Failing to observe this custom will block the pan or drain, a considerable health risk. It is quite common for people to stand on the toilet seat (facing the wall – easier to balance).

CAMPING

Organized campsites are referred to in the text immediately below hotel lists, under each town. If there is no organized site in town, a football pitch or gravel pit might serve. Obey the following rules for "wild" camping: (1) arrive in daylight and pitch your tent as it gets dark; (2) ask permission to camp from the parish priest, or the fire chief, or the police, or a farmer regarding his own property; (3) never ask a group of people – especially young people; (4) never camp on a beach (because of sandflies and thieves). If you can't get information from anyone, camp in a spot where you can't be seen from the nearest inhabited place, or road, and make sure no one saw you go there. In Argentina and Brazil, it is common to camp at gas/petrol stations. As Béatrice Völkle of Gampelen, Switzerland, adds, camping wild may be preferable to those organized sites which are treated as discotheques, with only the afternoon reserved for sleeping.

If taking a cooker, the most frequent recommendation is a multifuel stove (eg MSR International, Coleman Peak 1), which will burn unleaded petrol or, if that is not available, kerosene, *benzina blanca*, etc. Alcohol-burning stoves are simple, reliable, but slow and you have to carry a lot of fuel: for a methylated spirit-burning stove, the following fuels apply, *alcohol desnaturalizado*, *alcohol metílico*, *alcohol puro (de caña)* or *alcohol para quemar*. Ask for 95%, but 70% will suffice. In all countries fuel can usually be found in chemists/pharmacies. Gas cylinders and bottles are usually exchangeable, but if not can be recharged; specify whether you use butane or propane. Gas canisters are not always available. The Camping Clube do Brasil gives 50% discounts to holders of international campers' cards.

YOUTH HOSTELS

Organizations affiliated to the Youth Hostels movement exist in Argentina, Brazil, Colombia, Chile, Peru and Uruguay. There is an associate organization in Ecuador. Further information in the country sections and from the IYHA.

FOOD

In all countries except Brazil and Chile (where cold meats, cheese, eggs, fruit etc generally figure) breakfast usually means coffee or tea with rolls and butter, and anything more is charged extra. In Colombia and Ecuador breakfast usually means eggs, a roll, fruit juice and a mug of milk with coffee; say "breakfast without eggs" if you do not want that much. There is a paragraph on each nation's food under "Information for travellers". Vegetarians should be able to list all the foods they cannot eat; saying "Soy vegetariano/a" (I'm a vegetarian) or "no como carne" (I don't eat meat) is often not enough. Most restaurants serve a daily special meal, usually at lunchtime, which is cheap and good. Other than that you can expect to pay between US$10-15 on breakfast and dinner per day.

GETTING AROUND

NB See above for details of air transport including air passes.

Before you start, remember that distances are great and journeys by land are long: plan accordingly and do not try to do too much in the time available.

BUSES AND TRAINS

The continent has an extensive road system for motor traffic, with frequent bus services. The buses are often comfortable; the difficulties of Andean terrain affect the quality of vehicles. In mountainous country do not expect buses to get to their destination after long journeys anywhere near on time. Do not turn up for a bus at the last minute; if it is full it may depart early. Tall travellers are advised to take aisle rather than window seats on long journeys as this allows more leg room. When the journey takes more than 3 or 4 hrs, meal stops at country inns or bars, good and bad, are the rule. Usually, no announcement is made on the duration of a stop: follow the driver, if he eats, eat. See what the locals are eating – and buy likewise, or make sure you're stocked up well on food and drink at the start. For drinks, stick to bottled water or soft drinks or coffee (black). The food sold by vendors at bus stops may be all right: watch if locals are buying, though unpeeled fruit is of course reliable. (See above on **Security** in buses.)

Where they still run, trains are slower than buses. They tend to provide finer scenery and you can normally see much more wildlife than from the road – it is less disturbed by one or two trains a day than by the more frequent road traffic. Moreover, so many buses now show video films that you can't see the countryside because the curtains are drawn. Complaining to the conductor that you cannot see the beautiful landscape may persuade him to give you his seat at the front.

MOTORING
The machine

What kind of motoring you do will depend on what kind of car you set out with. Four-wheel drive is not necessary, but it does give you greater flexibility in mountain and jungle territory, although you may not get far in Amazonas, where roads are frequently impassable. In Patagonia, main roads are gravel rather than paved: perfectly passable without four-wheel drive, just rough and dusty. Consider fitting wire guards for headlamps, and for windscreens too, if you don't mind peering out through a grill like a caged chimpanzee. Wherever you travel you should expect from time to time to find roads that are badly maintained, damaged or closed during the wet season, and delays because of floods, landslides and huge potholes. Don't plan your schedules too tightly.

Diesel cars are much cheaper to run than petrol ones, and the fuel is easily available; in Venezuela you may have to look hard for it outside Caracas. Most towns can supply a mechanic of sorts, and probably parts for Bosch fuel injection equipment. Watch the mechanics like a hawk, since there's always a brisk market in spares, and some of yours may be highly desirable. That apart, they enjoy a challenge, and can fix most things, eventually.

For prolonged motoring over 3000 metres, you may need to fit high altitude jets on your carburettors. Some fuel injection engines need adjusting too, and ignition settings may have to be changed: check the manufacturer's recommendations. The electronic ignition and fuel metering systems on modern emission controlled cars are allergic to humidity, heat and dust, and cannot be repaired by bush mechanics. Standard European and Japanese cars run on fuel with a higher octane rating than is commonly available in North, South or Central America, and in Brazil petrol (gasolina) is in fact gasohol, with a 12% admixture of alcohol. A high compression fuel injection engine will not like this. Unleaded fuel is available in Chile, Colombia and Ecuador, and to an increasing extent in Argentina and coastal Peru. The most easily maintained petrol engined cars, then, are the types manufactured in Latin American countries, ie pre-emission control models such as the VW Kombi with carburettors and conventional (non-electronic) ignition, or the old type Toyota Landcruisers common in Central America. Older model American cars, especially Ford or GM pickups, are easily maintained, but high fuel consumption offsets this advantage. (Note that Colombia does not have a network for spares and repairs of VW, while Ecuador, Venezuela and Brazil do. Argentina is very expensive for maintenance of any make of car.)

Preparation

Preparing the car for the journey is largely a matter of common sense: obviously any part that is not in first class condition should be replaced. It's well worth installing extra heavy-duty shock-absorbers (such as Spax or Koni) before starting out, because a long trip on rough roads in a heavily laden car will give heavy wear. Fit tubes on "tubeless" tyres, since air plugs for tubeless tyres are hard to find, and if you bend the rim on a pothole, the tyre will not hold air. Take spare tubes, and an extra spare tyre. Also take spare plugs, fan-belts, radiator hoses and headlamp bulbs; even though local equivalents can easily be found in cities, it is wise to take spares for those occasions late at night or in remote areas when you might need them. You can also change the fanbelt after a stretch of long, hot driving to prevent wear (eg after

15,000 km/10,000 miles). If your vehicle has more than one fanbelt, always replace them all at the same time (make sure you have the necessary tools if doing it yourself). If your car has sophisticated electrics, spare "black boxes" for the ignition and fuel injection are advisable, plus a spare voltage regulator or the appropriate diodes for the alternator, and elements for the fuel, air and oil filters if these are not a common type. (Some drivers take a spare alternator of the correct amperage, especially if the regulator is incorporated into the alternator.) Dirty fuel is a frequent problem, so be prepared to change filters more often than you would at home: in a diesel car you will need to check the sediment bowl often, too. An extra in-line fuel filter is a good idea if feasible (although harder to find, metal canister type is preferable to plastic), and for travel on dusty roads an oil bath air filter is best for a diesel car. It is wise to carry a spade, jumper cables, tow rope and an air pump. Fit tow hooks to both sides of the vehicle frame. A 12 volt neon light for camping and repairs will be invaluable. Spare fuel containers should be steel and not plastic, and a siphon pipe is essential for those places where fuel is sold out of the drum. Take a 10 litre water container for self and vehicle. Note that in some areas gas stations are few and far between. Fill up when you see one: the next one may be out of fuel. Some countries have periodic fuel conservation strategies which means you can't get any after a certain hour in the evening, and often not at weekends either.

Security

Apart from the mechanical aspects, spare no ingenuity in making your car secure. Your model should be the Brink's armoured van: anything less secure can be broken into by the determined and skilled thief. Use heavy chain and padlocks to chain doors shut, fit security catches on windows, remove interior window winders (so that a hand reaching in from a forced vent cannot open the window). All these will help, but none is foolproof. Anything on the outside – wing mirrors, spot lamps, motifs etc – is likely to be stolen too. So are wheels if not secured by locking nuts. Try never to leave the car unattended except in a locked garage or guarded parking space. Remove all belongings and leave the empty glove compartment open when the car is unattended. Also lock the clutch or accelerator to the steering wheel with a heavy, obvious chain or lock. Street children will generally protect your car fiercely in exchange for a tip. Be sure to note down key numbers and carry spares of the most important ones (but don't keep all spares inside the vehicle).

Documents

A *carnet de passage* is no longer necessary in any country, but life is much easier with one (see **Additional notes** below). Land entry procedures for all countries – with the exception of Colombia – are simple, though time-consuming, as the car has to be checked by customs, police and agriculture officials. All you need is the registration document in the name of the driver, or, in the case of a car registered in someone else's name, a notarized letter of authorization. Most countries give a limited period of stay, but allow an extension if requested in advance. Of course, do be very careful to keep **all** the papers you are given when you enter, to produce when you leave. Bringing a car in by sea or air is much more complicated and expensive: generally you will have to hire an agent to clear it through customs, expensive and slow. Insurance for the vehicle against accident, damage or theft is best arranged in the country of origin, but it is getting increasingly difficult to find agencies who offer this service. In Latin American countries it is very expensive to insure against accident and theft, especially as you should take into account the value of the car increased by duties calculated in real (ie non devaluing) terms. If the car is stolen or written off you will be required to pay very high import duty on its value. A few countries insist on compulsory third party insurance, to be bought at the border: in other countries it's technically required, but not checked up on (Venezuela seems to be the only country where it is easy to obtain – Ed). Get the legally re-quired minimum cover, not expensive, as soon as you can, because if you should be involved in an accident and are uninsured, your car could be confiscated. If anyone is hurt, do not pick them up (you may become liable). Seek assistance from the nearest police station or hospital if you are able to do so. You may find yourself facing a hostile crowd, even if you are not to blame.

Journey's End

When you finally reach your destination, what happens to the car? Shipping it back is one alternative. From Brazil, Grimaldi line to Genoa is the cheapest: there are also frequent sailings from Montevideo and Buenos Aires to most other destinations. The other alternative is to sell the car. Until now, this has been virtually impossible except in Paraguay, but the economic liberalization in Argentina, Chile and Brazil makes it legal – if not simple – to import cars into those countries. Probably safer not to count on it though, unless you have the sort of car in great demand, like a Mercedes saloon. You can sell anything in Paraguay if you have the time. Legalizing the permanent import of a temporarily imported car costs about 30% of its street value. If you leave it to the buyer to "take care of" obtaining the correct documentation, you should not expect to receive a very favourable price. Dealers are adept at taking advantage of the fact that they can wait, and you cannot, so be prepared for "on – off – on again" dealing.

Car Hire

The main international car hire companies operate in all countries, but they do tend to be very expensive, reflecting the high costs and accident rates. Hotels and tourist agencies will tell you where to find cheaper rates, but you will need to check that you have such basics as spare wheel, toolkit and functioning lights etc. You'll probably have more fun if you drive yourself, although it's always possible to hire a car with driver. If you plan to do a lot of driving and will have time at the end to dispose of it, investigate the possibility of buying a second hand car locally: since hiring is so expensive it may well work out cheaper and will probably do you just as well.

Car Hire Insurance Check exactly what the hirer's insurance policy covers. In many cases it will only protect you against minor bumps and scrapes, not major accidents, nor "natural" damage (eg flooding). Ask if extra cover is available. Also find out, if using a credit card, whether the card automatically includes insurance. Beware of being billed for scratches which were on the vehicle before you hired it.

Additional notes on motoring

A great deal of conflicting information surrounds what documents are required in addition to the vehicle's registration. According to the RAC in the UK there are three recognized documents for taking a vehicle into South America: a *carnet de passages* issued by the Fedération Internationale de l'Automobile (FIA – Paris), a *carnet de passages* issued by the Alliance Internationale de Tourisme (AIT-Geneva), and the *Libreta de Pasos por Aduana* issued by the Federación Interamericana de Touring y Automóvil Clubs (FITAC). The following list gives official requirements, with comments about actual practice: **Argentina** requires a written undertaking that the car will be exported after a given period, either of the *carnets*, or the *libreta* (in practice, nothing is asked for beyond the title document, except at remote border crossings which may demand a *libreta*); **Bolivia**, *libreta* only; **Brazil**, a written undertaking only (nothing asked for); **Chile**, either *carnet*, or the *libreta* (in practice nothing asked for), insurance is obligatory; **Colombia**, either *carnet* or, according to a law of 31.12.1992, you have to purchase a bond on entry to the value of 10% of your vehicle, insurance is necessary; **Ecuador**, neither *carnet* nor *libreta* is required (ask at an embassy in advance); **Paraguay**, either *carnet*, or the *libreta*; **Peru**, either *carnet*, the *libreta* and, for caravans and trailers, an inventory (the consulate in London says that a *libreta* is necessary, but if you cannot obtain one a written declaration that the car will leave Peru, authorized at a Peruvian consulate before leaving your home country, will do instead); **Uruguay**, the *libreta* or the FIA *carnet* only (in practice nothing asked for); **Venezuela**, either *carnet* or the *libreta* (the consulate in London says a *Certificado de uso por turismo* must be completed at a Venezuelan embassy before arrival, no other documents required; in the USA the vehicle's title document must be legalized by a Venezuelan consul, US$100, this, plus title and a letter of intent from your shipper's agent must be taken to US customs at least 2 days before sailing, no *libreta* or *carnet* needed). In view of this confusion, contact the automobile clubs of the countries you intend to drive in and get their advice. In general, motorists in South America seem to fare better with a *libreta* or *carnet de passages* than without it.

The *libreta*, a 10-page book of three-part passes for customs, should be available from any South American automobile club member of FITAC, but in practice it is only available in Venezuela to non-residents (see pages 1519

and 1576 for addresses of the Touring y Automóvil Club). The cost is about US$350, but is more for those who are not members of automobile clubs; about a third of the cost is refundable. The *carnet de passages* is issued only in the country where the vehicle is registered (in the UK it costs £65 for 25 pages, £55 for 10 pages, valid 12 months, either bank indemnity or insurance indemnity, half of the premium refundable value of the vehicle and countries to be visited required), available from the RAC or the AA. In the USA the AAA does not issue the *carnet*, although the HQ in Washington DC may give advice. It is available from the Canadian Automobile Association (1775 Courtwood Crescent, Ottawa, K2C 3JZ, T 613-226-7631, F 613-225-7383) for Canadian and US citizens, cost C$400; full details obtainable from the CAA. For this information thanks go to Paul Gowen, RAC Touring Information Manager, Binka Le Breton and other motorists.

While a normal car will reach most places of interest, high ground clearance is useful for badly surfaced or unsurfaced roads and for fording rivers: 4-wheel drive is recommended for mountain terrain and unmade roads off the beaten track.

If you want to buy a second-hand car, check for corrosion if making the deal in a coastal city and always check, if not change, the full set of tyres.

Shipping a vehicle

From Europe or the USA you can go to Panama and shop around for the best value sailing to whichever port best suits your travelling plans. Alternatively you can ship a vehicle from Europe to Brazil, Uruguay or Argentina. Recommended as good value are Polish Ocean Lines, 10 Lutego, Gdynia, Poland. *Carnet* is necessary; POL agent deals with customs. Departure dates are not scheduled in advance. Vehicles can also be shipped from the USA. You have to get a special exemption in order to be allowed to be carried to Colombia in a non Colombian vessel, which takes time to obtain. Anything left inside the car while it is being shipped will be stolen. As long as your vehicle is not over 2.28m high, it can go in a container, but permission must be obtained for any belongings to remain in the car, and separate insurance for effects purchased. If the car is going ro-ro (drive on), it should be empty of all belongings, unless they are thoroughly secured.

Two books containing much practical information on South American motoring conditions and requirements are *Driving to Heaven*, by Derek Stansfield (available from the author, Ropley, Broad Oak, Sturminster Newton, Dorset DT10 2HG, T/F 01258-472534, £8.85 plus postage, if outside the UK), and the more recent *Central and South America by Road*, Pam Ascanio (Bradt Publications 1996, see **Maps and Guide Books**, below).

MOTORCYCLING

People are generally very amicable to motorcyclists and you can make many friends by returning friendship to those who show an interest in you.

The Machine

It should be off road capable: my choice would be the BMW R80/100/GS for its rugged and simple design and reliable shaft drive, but a Kawasaki KLR 650s, Honda Transalp/Dominator, or the ubiquitous Yamaha XT600 Tenere would also be suitable. Buying a bike in the States and driving down works out cheaper than buying one in the UK. A road bike can go most places an off road bike can go at the cost of greater effort.

Preparations

Many roads in Latin America are rough. Fit heavy duty front fork springs and the best quality rebuildable shock absorber you can afford (Ohlins, White Power). Fit lockable luggage such as Krausers (reinforce luggage frames) or make some detachable aluminium panniers. Fit a tank bag and tank panniers for better weight distribution. A large capacity fuel tank (Acerbis), +300 mile/480 km range is essential if going off the beaten track. A washable air filter is a good idea (K&N), also fuel filters, fueltap rubber seals and smaller jets for high altitude Andean motoring. A good set of trails-type tyres as well as a high mudguard are useful. Get to know the bike before you go, ask the dealers in your country what goes wrong with it and arrange a link whereby you can get parts flown out to you. If riding a chain driven bike, a fully enclosed chaincase is useful. A hefty bash plate/sump guard is invaluable.

Spares

Reduce service intervals by half if driving in severe conditions. A spare rear tyre is useful but you can buy modern tyres in most capital cities. Take oil filters, fork and shock seals, tubes, a good manual, spare cables (taped into position), a plug cap and spare plug lead. A spare electronic ignition is a good idea, try and buy a second hand one and make arrangements to have parts sent out to you. A first class tool kit is a must and if riding a bike with a chain then a spare set of sprockets and an 'o' ring chain should be carried. Spare brake and clutch levers should also be taken as these break easily in a fall. Parts are few and far between, but mechanics are skilled at making do and can usually repair things. Castrol oil can be bought everywhere and relied upon.

Take a puncture repair kit and tyre levers. Find out about any weak spots on the bike and improve them. Get the book for international dealer coverage from your manufacturer, but don't rely on it. They frequently have few or no parts for modern, large machinery.

Clothes and Equipment

A tough waterproof jacket, comfortable strong boots, gloves and a helmet with which you can use glass goggles (Halycon) which will not scratch and wear out like a plastic visor. The best quality tent and camping gear that you can afford and a petrol stove which runs on bike fuel is helpful.

Security

Not a problem in most countries. Try not to leave a fully laden bike on its own. An Abus D or chain will keep the bike secure. A cheap alarm gives you peace of mind if you leave the bike outside a hotel at night. Most hotels will allow you to bring the bike inside. Look for hotels that have a court-

yard or more secure parking and never leave luggage on the bike overnight or whilst unattended.

Documents

Passport, International Driving Licence, bike registration document are necessary. Riders fare much better with a *carnet de passages* than without it. Get your licence endorsed by police in Bolivia.

Shipping

Bikes may be sent from Panama to Colombia by cargo flight (eg CAC). You must drain the fuel, oil and battery acid, or remove the battery, but it is easier to disconnect and seal the overflow tube. Tape cardboard over fragile bits and insist on loading the bike yourself. The Darién Gap is impossible unless you carry the bike. See the Colombia chapter for the *Crucero Express* which carries motorbikes between Panama and Colombia.

Border Crossings

Do not try to cross borders on a Sunday or a holiday anywhere as a charge is levied on the usually free borders in South America. South American customs and immigration inspectors are mostly friendly, polite and efficient. If in doubt ask to see the boss and/or the rule book.

CYCLING

Hallam Murray writes (with recent additions from other cyclists): since the early 1980s, bicycle technology has improved in leaps and bounds. With the advent of Kevlar tyres and puncture-resistant inner tubes it is now theoretically possible to cycle from Alaska to Tierra del Fuego without so much as a single puncture. For the traveller with a zest for adventure and a limited budget there is unlikely to be a finer way to explore. At first glance a bicycle may not appear to be the most obvious vehicle for a major journey, but given ample time and reasonable energy it most certainly is the best. It can be ridden, carried by almost every form of transport from an aeroplane to a canoe, and can even be lifted across one's shoulders over short distances. Cyclists can be the envy of travellers using more orthodox transport, since they can travel at their own pace, explore more remote regions and meet people who are not normally in contact with tourists.

Choosing a Bicycle

The choice of bicycle depends on the type and length of expedition being undertaken and on the terrain and road surfaces likely to be encountered. Unless you are planning a journey almost exclusively on paved roads – when a high quality touring bike such as a Dawes Super Galaxy would probably suffice – a mountain bike is strongly recommended. The good quality ones (and the cast iron rule is **never** to skimp on quality) are incredibly tough and rugged, with low gear ratios for difficult terrain, wide tyres with plenty of tread for good road-holding, cantilever brakes, and a low centre of gravity for improved stability. Although touring bikes, and to a lesser extent mountain bikes, and spares are available in the larger Latin American cities, remember that in the developing world most indigenous manufactured goods are shoddy and rarely last. In some countries, such as Mexico, Chile and Uruguay, imported components can be found but they tend to be extremely expensive. (Shimano parts are generally the easiest to find.) Buy everything you possibly can before you leave home.

Bicycle Equipment

A small but comprehensive tool kit (to include chain rivet and crank removers, a spoke key and possibly a block remover), a spare tyre and inner tubes, a puncture repair kit with plenty of extra patches and glue, a set of brake blocks, brake and gear cables and all types of nuts and bolts, at least 12 spokes (best taped to the chain stay), a light oil for the chain (eg Finish-Line Teflon Dry-Lube), tube of waterproof grease, a pump secured by a pump lock, a Blackburn parking block (a most invaluable accessory, cheap and virtually weightless), a cyclometer, a loud bell, and a secure lock and chain. *Richard's Bicycle Book* makes useful reading for even the most mechanically minded.

Luggage and equipment

Strong and waterproof front and back panniers are a must. When packed these are likely to be heavy and should be carried on the strongest racks available. Poor quality racks have ruined many a journey for they take incredible strain on unpaved roads. A top bag cum rucksack (eg Carradice) makes a good addition for use on and off the bike. A Cannondale front bag is good for maps, camera, compass, altimeter, notebook and small tape-recorder. (Other rec panniers are Ortlieb – front and back – which is waterpoof and almost "sandproof", Mac-Pac, Madden and Karimoor.) "Gaffa" tape is excellent for protecting vulnerable parts of panniers and for carrying out all manner of repairs. My most vital equipment included a light and waterproof tent, a 3 season sleeping bag, an Optimus petrol stove (recommended as it is light and efficient and petrol can be found almost everywhere, but see page 34, **Camping**), a plastic survival bag for storing luggage at night when camping, 4 elastic straps, 4 one-litre water bottles, Swiss Army knife, torch, candle, comprehensive medical kit, money belts, a hat and sunglasses to protect against hours of ferocious tropical sun and small presents such as postcards of home, balloons and plastic badges. A rubber mouse can do wonders for making contact with children in isolated villages.

All equipment and clothes should be packed in plastic bags to give extra protection against dust and rain. (Also protect all documents, etc carried close to the body from sweat.) Always take the minimum clothing. It's better to buy extra items en route when you find you need them. Naturally the choice will depend on whether you are planning a journey through tropical lowlands, deserts, high mountains or a combination, and whether rain is to be expected. Generally it is best to carry several layers of thin light clothes than fewer heavy, bulky ones. Always keep one set of dry clothes, including long trousers, to put on at the end of the day. The incredibly light, strong, waterproof and wind resistant goretex jacket and overtrousers are invaluable. Training shoes can be used for both cycling and walking.

Useful Tips

Wind, not hills is the enemy of the cyclist. Try to make the best use of the times of day when there is little; mornings tend to be best but there is no steadfast rule. In parts of Patagonia there can be gusting winds of 80 kph around the clock at some times of year, whereas in other areas there can be none. Take care to avoid dehydration, by drinking regularly. In hot, dry areas with limited supplies of water, be sure to carry an ample supply. For food, carry the staples (sugar, salt, dried milk, tea, coffee, porridge oats, raisins, dried soups, etc) and supplemented these with whatever local foods can be found in the markets. Give your bicycle a thorough daily check for loose nuts or bolts or bearings. See that all parts run smoothly. A good chain should last 2,000 miles, 3,200 km or more but be sure to keep it as clean as possible – an old toothbrush is good for this – and to oil it lightly from time to time. Always camp out of sight of a road. Remember that thieves are attracted to towns and cities, so when sight-seeing, try to leave your bicycle with someone such as a café owner or a priest. Country people tend to be more honest and are usually friendly and very inquisitive. However, don't take unnecessary risks; always see that your bicycle is secure (most hotels will allow bikes to be kept in rooms). In more remote regions dogs can be vicious; carry a stick or some small stones to frighten them off. Traffic on main roads can be a nightmare; it is usually far more rewarding to keep to the smaller roads or to paths if they exist.

Most towns have a bicycle shop of some description, but it is best to do your own repairs and adjustments whenever possible. In an emergency it is amazing how one can improvise with wire, string, dental floss, nuts and bolts, odd pieces of tin or "Gaffa" tape!

The Expedition Advisory Centre, administered by the Royal Geographical Society, 1, Kensington Gore, London SW7 2AR has published a useful monograph entitled *Bicycle Expeditions*, by Paul Vickers. Published in March 1990, it is available direct from the Centre, price £6.50 (postage extra if outside the UK). (In the UK there is also the Cyclist's Touring Club, CTC, Cotterell House, 69 Meadrow, Godalming, Surrey, GU7 3HS, T 01483-417217, e-mail cycling@ctc.org.uk, for touring, and technical information.)

Most cyclists agree that the main danger comes from other traffic. A rearview mirror has been frequently recommended to forewarn you of vehicles which are too close behind. You also need to watch out for oncoming, overtaking vehicles, unstable loads on trucks, protruding loads etc. Make yourself conspicuous by wearing bright clothing and a helmet.

Ryan Flegal of Los Angeles, California, says that, instead of taking your own expensive bicycle from home with the attendant need for specialized tools and high risks of loss, one can buy a bike in Latin America. "Affix a sturdy rear rack, improvise securing luggage to the bicycle, and go. Carry only a patch kit and wrench to remove the wheel, and rely on the many bike mechanics in the area to do the rest". A steel frame is more durable when heavily laden and can be welded if damaged, unlike aluminium. If undertaking your own maintenance, make sure you know how to do it, and research what tyres you will need, before you go.

RIVER TRANSPORT

Because expanding air services have captured the lucrative end of the passenger market, passenger services on the rivers are in decline. Worst hit have been the upper reaches; rivers like the Ucayali in Peru, but the trend is apparent throughout the region. The situation has been aggravated for the casual traveller by a new generation of purpose-built tugs (all engine-room and bridge) that can handle up to a dozen freight barges but have no passenger accommodation. In Peru passenger boats must now supplement incomes by carrying cargo, and this lengthens their journey cycle. In the face of long delays, travellers might consider shorter "legs" involving more frequent changes of boat; though the more local the service, the slower and more uncomfortable it will be.

Hammocks, mosquito nets (not always good quality), plastic containers for water storage, kettles and cooking utensils can be purchased in any sizeable riverside town, as well as tinned food such as sardines, meat loaf, frankfurters, ham and fruit. Fresh bread, cake, eggs, fruit – papayas, bananas, pineapples, oranges etc – are available in most villages. Cabin bunks are provided with thin mattresses but these are often foul. Replacements can be bought locally but rolls of plastic foam that can be cut to size are also available and much cheaper. Eye-screws for securing washing lines and mosquito nets are useful, and tall passengers who are not taking a hammock and who may find insufficient headroom on some boats should consider a camp-chair. The writer yearned for a cushion.

HM Wams (Amsterdam) endorses the recommendation of taking hammock,

mosquito net and food, adding that in Venezuelan Amazonas hitching rides on boats is possible if you camp at the harbour or police post where all boats must register. Take any boat going in your direction as long as it reaches the next police post. See the special section on the Brazilian Amazon, page 574.

HIKING AND TREKKING

A network of paths and tracks covers much of South America and is in constant use by the local people. In countries with a large Indian population – Ecuador, Peru and Bolivia, for instance – you can walk just about anywhere, but in the more European countries, such as Venezuela, Chile, and Argentina, you must usually limit yourself to the many excellent national parks with hiking trails. Most South American countries have an Instituto Geográfico Militar which sells topographical maps, scale 1:100,000 or 1:50,000. The physical features shown on these are usually accurate; the trails and place names less so. National Parks offices also sell maps.

Hiking and backpacking should not be approached casually. Even if you only plan to be out a couple of hours you should have comfortable, safe footwear (which can cope with the wet) and a daypack to carry your sweater and waterproof (which must be more than showerproof). At high altitudes the difference in temperature between sun and shade is remarkable. The longer trips mentioned in this book require basic backpacking equipment. Essential items are: backpack with frame, sleeping bag, closed cell foam mat for insulation, stove, tent or tarpaulin, dried food (not tins), water bottle, compass. Some but not all of these things are available locally.

When planning treks in the Andes you should be aware of the effects and dangers of acute mountain sickness, and cerebral and pulmonary oedema (see Health, page 47). These can be avoided by spending a few days acclimatizing to the altitude before starting your walk, and by climbing slowly. Otherwise there are fewer dangers than in most cities. Hikers have little to fear from the animal kingdom apart from insects (although it's best to avoid actually stepping on a snake), and robbery and assault are very rare. You are much more of a threat to the environment than vice versa. Leave no evidence of your passing; don't litter and don't give gratuitous presents of sweets or money to rural villagers. Respect their system of reciprocity; if they give you hospitality or food, then is the time to reciprocate with presents.

For trekking in mountain areas, where the weather can deteriorate rapidly (eg in Torres del Paine), trekkers should consider taking the following equipment (list supplied by Andrew Dobbie of Swansea, who adds that it "is in no way finite"): **Clothing**: warm hat (wool or man-made fibre), thermal underwear, T-shirts/shirts, trousers (quick-drying and preferably windproof, never jeans), warm (wool or fleece) jumper/jacket (preferably two), gloves, waterproof jacket and over trousers (preferably Gore-Tex), shorts, walking boots and socks, change of footwear or flip-flops. **Camping Gear**: tent (capable of withstanding high winds), sleeping mat (closed cell – Karrimat – or inflatable – Thermarest), sleeping bag (3-season minimum rating), sleeping bag liner, stove and spare parts, fuel, matches and lighter, cooking and eating utensils, pan scrubber, survival bag. **Food**: very much personal preference but at least two days more supplies than you plan to use; tea, coffee, sugar, dried milk; porridge, dried fruit, honey; soup, pasta, rice, soya (TVP); fresh fruit and vegetables; bread, cheese, crackers; biscuits, chocolate; salt, pepper, other herbs and spices, cooking oil. **Miscellaneous**: map and compass, torch and spare batteries, pen and notebook, Swiss army knife, sunglasses, sun cream, lip salve and insect repellent, first aid kit, water bottle, toiletries and towel.

Maps and Guide Books

Those from the Institutos Geográficos Militares in the capitals (see above) are often the only good maps available in Latin America. It is therefore wise to get as many as possible in your home country before leaving, especially if travelling by land. A recommended series of general maps is that published by International Travel Maps (ITM), 345 West Broadway, Vancouver BC, V5Y 1P8, Canada, T (604) 879-3621, F (604) 879-4521, compiled with historical notes, by the late Kevin Healey. Available are South America South, North East and North West (1:4M), Ecuador (1:1M), The Galapagos Islands (1:500,000), Easter Island (1:30,000), Argentina (1:4M), Rio de Janeiro (1:20,000), Venezuela (1:1.75M), Central America (1:1.8M), Panama (1:800,000), Guatemala and El Salvador (1:500,000), El Salvador (1:375,000), Nicaragua (1:750,000), Honduras (1:750,000), Costa Rica (1:500,000), Belize (1:350,000), Mexico (1:3.3M), Mexico City (1:10,000), Mexico South (1:1M), the Yucatán (1:1M) and Baja California (1:1M). Another map series that has been mentioned is that of New World Edition, Bertelsmann, Neumarkter Strasse 18, 81673 München, Germany, *Mittelamerika*, *Südamerika Nord*, *Südamerika Sud*, *Brasilien* (all 1:4M). For information on Bradt Publications' Backpacking Guide Series (covering Chile and Argentina, Peru and Bolivia, Ecuador, Venezuela), other titles and imported maps and guides, contact 41 Nortoft Road, Chalfont St Peter, Bucks, SL9 0LA, UK, T/F 01494 873478.

A very useful book, highly recommended, aimed specifically at the budget traveller is *The Tropical Traveller*, by John Hatt (Penguin Books, 3rd edition, 1993). **The South American Explorers' Club** is at Avenida Portugal 146 (Casilla 3714), Lima, Peru (T 425-0142), Jorge Washington y Leonidas Plaza, Apartado 17-21-431, Eloy Alfaro, Quito, Ecuador (T 225-228), and 126 Indian Creek Road, Ithaca, NY 14850, USA T (607) 277-0488, e-mail explorer@samexplo.org. (For further details see under Lima and Quito.) Books, maps and travel planning services are available at the US office. The South American Explorers Club is represented in the UK by Bradt Publications.

The Latin American Travel Advisor is

a quarterly news bulletin with up-to-date detailed and reliable information on countries throughout South and Central America. The publication focuses on public safety, health, weather and natural phenomena, travel costs, economics and politics in each country. Annual airmail subscriptions cost US$39, a single current issue US$15, electronically transmitted information (fax or e-mail), US$10 per country. Payment by US$ cheque, MasterCard or VISA (no money orders, credit card payments by mail or fax with card number, expiry date, cardholder's name and signature). Free sample available. Contact PO Box 17-17-908, Quito, Ecuador, international F 593-2-562-566, USA and Canada toll free F (888) 215-9511, e-mail LATA@pi.pro.ec, World Wide Web http://www.amerispan. com/latc/. Information on travel and language schools is available from Amerispan Unlimited, one of several language school brokers in the USA, PO Box 40007, Philadelphia, PA 19106-0513, T (USA and Canada) 800-879-6640, worldwide 215-985-4522, F 215-985-4524, e-mail info@amerispan.com, website http://www. amerispan.com. See also the website http://www.planeta.com of Ron Mader's *El Planeta Platica*: Eco Travels in Latin America.

TRAVELLING WITH CHILDREN

People contemplating overland travel in South America with children should remember that a lot of time can be spent waiting for buses, trains, and especially for aeroplanes. On bus journeys, if the children are good at amusing themselves, or can readily sleep while travelling, the problems can be considerably lessened. If your child is of an early reading age, take reading material with you as it is difficult, and expensive to find. A bag of, say 30 pieces, of Duplo or Lego can keep young children occupied for hours. Travel on trains, while not as fast or at times as comfortable as buses, allows more scope for moving about. Some trains provide tables between seats, so that games can be played. Beware of doors left open for ventilation especially if air-conditioning is not working.

Food

Food can be a problem if the children are not adaptable. It is easier to take biscuits, drinks, bread etc with you on longer trips than to rely on meal stops where the food may not be to taste. Avocados are safe, easy to eat and nutritious; they can be fed to babies as young as 6 months and most older children like them. A small immersion heater and jug for making hot drinks is invaluable, but remember that electric current varies. Try and get a dual-voltage one (110v and 220v).

Fares

On all long-distance buses you pay for each seat, and there are no half-fares if the children occupy a seat each. For shorter trips it is cheaper, if less comfortable, to seat small children on your knee. Often there are spare seats which children can occupy after tickets have been collected. In city and local excursion buses, small children generally do not pay a fare, but are not entitled to a seat when paying customers are standing. On sightseeing tours you should *always* bargain for a family rate – often children can go free. (In trains, reductions for children are general, but not universal.)

All civil airlines charge half for children under 12, but some military services don't have half-fares, or have younger age limits. Children's fares on Lloyd Aéreo Boliviano are considerably more than half, and there is only a 7kg baggage allowance. (LAB also checks children's ages on passports.) Note that a child travelling free on a long excursion is not always covered by the operator's travel insurance; it is adviseable to pay a small premium to arrange cover.

Hotels

In all hotels, try to negotiate family rates. If charges are per person, always insist that two children will occupy one bed only, therefore counting as one tariff. If rates are per bed, the same applies. In either case you can almost always get a reduced rate at cheaper hotels. Occasionally when travelling with a child you will be refused a room in a hotel that is "unsuitable". On river boat trips, unless you have very large hammocks, it may be more comfortable and cost effective to hire a 2-berth cabin for 2 adults and a child. (In restaurants, you can normally buy children's helpings, or divide one full-size helping between two children.)

Travel with children can bring you into closer contact with Latin American families and, generally, presents no special problems – in fact the path is often smoother for family groups. Officials tend to be more amenable where children are concerned and they are pleased if your child knows a little Spanish or Portuguese. Moreover, even thieves and pickpockets seem to have some of the traditional respect for families, and may leave you alone because of it!

Health in Latin America

WITH the following advice and precautions you should keep as healthy as you do at home. Most visitors return home having experienced no problems at all apart from some travellers' diarrhoea. In Latin America the health risks, especially in the lowland tropical areas, are different from those encountered in Europe or the USA. It also depends on where and how you travel. There are clear health differences between the countries of Latin America and in risks for the business traveller, who stays in international class hotels in large cities, the backpacker trekking from country to country and the tourist who heads for the beach. There is huge variation in climate, vegetation and wildlife from the deserts of Chile to the rain forests of Amazonia and from the icy remoteness of Andean peaks, to the teeming capital cities. There are no hard and fast rules to follow; you will often have to make your own judgment on the healthiness or otherwise of your surroundings. There are English (or other foreign language) speaking doctors in most major cities who have particular experience in dealing with locally-occurring diseases. Your Embassy representative will often be able to give you the name of local reputable doctors and most of the better hotels have a doctor on standby. If you do fall ill and cannot find a recommended doctor, try the Outpatient Department of a hospital – private hospitals are usually less crowded and offer a more acceptable standard of care to foreigners.

BEFORE TRAVELLING

Take out medical insurance. Make sure it covers all eventualities especially evacuation to your home country by a medically equipped plane, if necessary. You should have a dental check up, obtain a spare glasses prescription, a spare oral contraceptive prescription (or enought pills to last) and, if you suffer from a chronic illness (such as diabetes, high blood pressure, ear or sinus troubles, cardio-pulmonary disease or nervous disorder) arrange for a check up with your doctor, who can at the same time provide you with a letter explaining the details of your disability in English and if possible Spanish and/or Portuguese. Check the current practice in countries you are visiting for malaria prophylaxis (prevention). If you are on regular medication, make sure you have enough to cover the period of your travel.

Children

More preparation is probably necessary for babies and children than for an adult and perhaps a little more care should be taken when travelling to remote areas where health services are primitive. This is because children can be become more rapidly ill than adults (on the other hand they often recover more quickly). Diarrhoea and vomiting are the most common problems, so take the usual precautions, but more intensively. Breastfeeding is best and most convenient for babies, but powdered milk is generally available and so are baby foods in most countries. Papaya, bananas and avocados are all nutritious and can be cleanly prepared. The treatment of diarrhoea is the same for adults, except that it should start earlier and be continued with more persistence. Children get dehydrated very quickly in hot countries and can become drowsy and uncooperative unless cajoled to drink water or juice plus salts. Upper respiratory infections, such as colds, catarrh and middle ear infections are also common and if your child suffers from these normally take some antibiotics against the possibility. Outer ear infections after swimming are also common and antibiotic eardrops will help. Wet wipes are always useful and sometimes difficult to find in South America, as, in some places are disposable nappies.

MEDICINES AND WHAT TO TAKE

There is very little control on the sale of drugs and medicines in South America. You can buy any and every drug in pharmacies without a prescription. Be wary of this because pharmacists can be poorly trained and might sell you drugs that are unsuitable, dangerous or old. Many drugs and medicines are manufactured under licence from American or European companies, so the trade names may be familiar to you. This means you do not have to carry a whole chest of medicines with you, but remember that the shelf life of some items, especially vaccines and antibiotics, is markedly reduced in hot conditions. Buy your supplies at the better outlets where there are refrigerators, even though they are more expensive and check the expiry date of all preparations you buy. Immigration officials occasionally confiscate scheduled drugs (Lomotil is an example) if they are not accompanied by a doctor's prescription.

Self-medication may be forced on you by circumstances so the following text contains the names of drugs and medicines which you may find useful in an emergency or in out-of-the-way places. You may like to take some of the following items with you from home:

Sunglasses
  ones designed for intense sunlight

Earplugs
  for sleeping on aeroplanes and in noisy hotels

Suntan cream
  with a high protection factor

Insect repellent
  containing DET for preference

Mosquito net
  lightweight, permethrin-impregnated for choice

Tablets
  for travel sickness

Tampons
  can be expensive in some countries in

Latin America

Condoms

Contraceptives

Water sterilising tablets

Antimalarial tablets

Anti-infective ointment eg Cetrimide

Dusting powder for feet etc
containing fungicide

Antacid tablets
for indigestion

Sachets of rehydration salts
plus anti-diarrhoea preparations

Painkillers
such as Paracetamol or Aspirin

Antibiotics
for diarrhoea etc

First Aid kit
Small pack containing a few sterile syringes and needles and disposable gloves. The risk of catching hepatitis etc from a dirty needle used for injection is now negligible in Latin America, but some may be reassured by carrying their own supplies – available from camping shops and airport shops.

Vaccination and immunisation

Smallpox vaccination is no longer required anywhere in the world. Neither is cholera vaccination recognized as necessary for international travel by the World Health Organisation – it is not very effective either. Nevertheless, some immigration officials are demanding proof of vaccination against cholera in Latin America and in some countries outside Latin America, following the outbreak of the disease which originated in Peru in 1990-91 and subsequently affected most surrounding countries. Although very unlikely to affect visitors to Latin America, the cholera epidemic continues making its greatest impact in poor areas where water supplies are polluted and food hygiene practices are insanitary.

Vaccination against the following diseases are recommended:

Yellow Fever

This is a live vaccination not to be given to children under 9 months of age or persons allergic to eggs. Immunity lasts for 10 years, an International Certificate of Yellow Fever Vaccination will be given and should be kept because it is sometimes asked for. Yellow fever is very rare in Latin America, but the vaccination is practically without side effects and almost totally protective.

Typhoid

A disease spread by the insanitary preparation of food. A number of new vaccines against this condition are now available; the older TAB and monovalent typhoid vaccines are being phased out. The newer, eg Typhim Vi, cause less side effects, but are more expensive. For those who do not like injections, there are now oral vaccines.

Poliomyelitis

Despite its decline in the world this remains a serious disease if caught and is easy to protect against. There are live oral vaccines and in some countries injected vaccines. Whichever one you choose it is a good idea to have booster every 3-5 years if visiting developing countries regularly.

Tetanus

One dose should be given with a booster at 6 weeks and another at 6 months and 10 yearly boosters thereafter are recommended. Children should already be properly protected against diphtheria, poliomyelitis and pertussis (whooping cough), measles and HIB all of which can be more serious infections in Latin America than at home. Measles, mumps and rubella vaccine is also given to children throughout the world, but those teenage girls who have not had rubella (german measles) should be tested and vaccinated. Hepatitis B vaccination for babies is now routine in some countries. Consult your doctor for advice on tuberculosis inoculation: the disease is still widespread in Latin America.

Infectious Hepatitis

Is less of a problem for travellers than it used to be because of the development of two extremely effective vaccines against the A and B form of the disease. It remains common, however, in Latin America. A combined hepatitis A & B vaccine is now licensed and will be available in 1997 – one jab covers both diseases.

Other vaccinations:
Might be considered in the case of epidemics eg meningitis. There is an effective vaccination against rabies which should be considered by all travellers, especially those going through remote areas or if there is a particular occupational risk, eg for zoologists or veterinarians.

FURTHER INFORMATION

Further information on health risks abroad, vaccinations etc may be available from a local travel clinic. If you wish to take specific drugs with you such as antibiotics these are best prescribed by your own doctor. Beware, however, that not all doctors can be experts on the health problems of remote countries. More detailed or more up-to-date information than local doctors can provide are available from various sources. In the UK there are hospital departments specialising in tropical diseases in London, Liverpool, Birmingham and Glasgow and the Malaria Reference Laboratory at the London School of Hygiene and Tropical Medicine provides free advice about malaria, T 0891 600350. In the USA the local Public Health Services can give such information and information is available centrally from the Centre for Disease Control (CDC) in Atlanta, T (404) 3324559.

There are additional computerized databases which can be assessed for destination-specific up-to-the-minute information. In the UK there is MASTA (Medical Advisory Service to Travellers Abroad), T 0171 631 4408, F 0171 436 5389, Tx 8953473 and Travax (Glasgow, T 0141 946 7120, ext 247). Other information on medical problems overseas can be obtained from the book by Dawood, Richard (Editor) (1992) *Travellers' Health: How to stay healthy abroad*, Oxford University Press 1992, £7.99. We strongly recommend this revised and updated edition, especially to the intrepid traveller heading for the more out of the way places. General advice is also available in the UK in *Health Information for Overseas Travel* published by the Department of Health and available from HMSO, and *International Travel and Health* published by WHO, Geneva.

STAYING HEALTHY

INTESTINAL UPSETS

The thought of catching a stomach bug worries visitors to Latin America but there have been great improvements in food hygiene and most such infections are preventable. Travellers' diarrhoea and vomiting is due, most of the time, to food poisoning, usually passed on by the insanitary habits of food handlers. As a general rule the cleaner your surroundings and the smarter the restaurant, the less likely you are to suffer.

Foods to avoid: uncooked, undercooked, partially cooked or reheated meat, fish, eggs, raw vegetables and salads, especially when they have been left out exposed to flies. Stick to fresh food that has been cooked from raw just before eating and make sure you peel fruit yourself. Wash and dry your hands before eating – disposable wet-wipe tissues are useful for this.

Shellfish eaten raw are risky and at certain times of the year some fish and shellfish concentrate toxins from their environment and cause various kinds of food poisoning. The local authorities notify the public not to eat these foods. Do not ignore the warning. **Heat treated milk** (UHT) pasteurized or sterilized is becoming more available in Latin America as is pasteurized cheese. On the whole matured or processed cheeses are safer than the fresh varieties and fresh unpasteurized milk from whatever animal can be a source of food poisoning germs, tuberculosis and brucellosis. This applies equally to icecream, yoghurt and cheese made from unpasteurized milk, so avoid these homemade products – the factory made ones are probably safer.

Tap water is rarely safe outside the major cities, especially in the rainy season. Stream water, if you are in the countryside, is often contaminated by communities living surprisingly high in the mountains. Filtered or bottled water is usually available and safe, although you must make sure that somebody is not filling bottles from the tap and hammering on a new crown cap. If your hotel has a central hot water supply this water is safe to drink after cooling. Ice for drinks should be made from boiled water, but rarely is so stand your glass on the ice cubes, rather than putting them in the drink. The better hotels have water purifying systems.

TRAVELLERS' DIARRHOEA

This is usually caused by eating food which has been contaminated by food poisoning germs. Drinking water is rarely the culprit. Sea water or river water is more likely to be contaminated by sewage and so swimming in such dilute effluent can also be a cause.

Infection with various organisms can give rise to travellers' diarrhoea. They may be viruses, bacteria, eg Escherichia coli (probably the most common cause worldwide), protozoal (such as amoebas and giardia), salmonella and cholera. The diarrhoea may come on suddenly or rather slowly. It may or may not be accompanied by vomiting or by severe abdominal pain and the passage of blood or mucus when it is called dysentery.

How do you know which type you have caught and how to treat it?

If you can time the onset of the diarrhoea to the minute ('acute') then it is probably due to a virus or a bacterium and/or the onset of dysentery. The treatment in addition to rehydration is Ciprofloxacin 500 mg every 12 hrs; the drug is now widely available and there are many similar ones.

If the diarrhoea comes on slowly or intermittently ('sub-acute') then it is more likely to be protozoal, ie caused by an amoeba or giardia. Antibiotics such as Ciprofloxacin will have little effect. These cases are best treated by a doctor as is any outbreak of diarrhoea continuing for more than 3 days. Sometimes blood is passed in amoebic dysentery and for this you should certainly seek medical help. If this is not available then the best treatment is probably Tinidazole (Fasigyn) 1 tablet four times a day for 3 days. If there are severe stomach cramps, the following drugs may help but are not very useful in the management of acute diarrhoea: Loperamide (Imodium) and Diphenoxylate with Atropine (Lomotil) They should not be given to children.

Any kind of diarrhoea, whether or not accompanied by vomiting, responds well to the replacement of water and salts, taken as frequent small sips, of some kind of rehydration solution. There are proprietary preparations consisting of sachets of powder which you dissolve in boiled water or you can make your own by adding half a teaspoonful of salt (3.5 gms) and 4 tablespoonsful of sugar (40 gms) to a litre of boiled water.

Thus the lynch pins of treatment for diarrhoea are rest, fluid and salt replacement, antibiotics such as Ciprofloxacin

Water purification

There are a number of ways of purifying water in order to make it safe to drink. Dirty water should first be strained through a filter bag (camping shops) and then boiled or treated. Bringing water to a rolling boil at sea level is sufficient to make the water safe for drinking, but at higher altitudes you have to boil the water for longer to ensure that all the microbes are killed.

There are sterilising methods that can be used and there are proprietary preparations containing chlorine (eg Puritabs) or iodine (eg Pota Aqua) compounds. Chlorine compounds generally do not kill protozoa (eg giardia).

There are a number of water filters now on the market available in personal and expedition size. They work either on mechanical or chemical principles, or may do both. Make sure you take the spare parts or spare chemicals with you and do not believe *everything* the manufacturers say.

for the bacterial types and special diagnostic tests and medical treatment for the amoeba and giardia infections. Salmonella infections and cholera, although rare, can be devastating diseases and it would be wise to get to a hospital as soon as possible if these were suspected.

Fasting, peculiar diets and the consumption of large quantities of yoghurt have not been found useful in calming travellers' diarrhoea or in rehabilitating inflamed bowels. Oral rehydration has on the other hand, especially in children, been a life saving technique and should always be practised, whatever other treatment you use. As there is some evidence that alcohol and milk might prolong diarrhoea they should be avoided during and immediately after an attack.

Diarrhoea occurring day after day for long periods of time (chronic diarrhoea) is notoriously resistent to amateur attempts at treatment and again warrants proper diagnostic tests (most towns with reasonable sized hospitals have laboratories for stool samples). There are ways of preventing travellers' diarrhoea for short periods of time by taking antibiotics, but this is not a foolproof technique and should not be used other than in exceptional circumstances. Doxycycline is possibly the best drug. Some preventatives such as Enterovioform can have serious side effects if taken for long periods.

Paradoxically **constipation** is also common, probably induced by dietary change, inadequate fluid intake in hot places and long bus journeys. Simple laxatives are useful in the short-term and bulky foods such as maize, beans and plenty of fruit are also useful.

HIGH ALTITUDE

Spending time at high altitude in South America, especially in the tropics, is usually a pleasure – it is not so hot, there are no insects and the air is clear and spring like. Travelling to high altitudes, however, can cause medical problems, all of which can be prevented if care is taken.

On reaching heights above about 3,000m, heart pounding and shortness of breath, especially on exertion are a normal response to the lack of oxygen in the air. A condition called acute mountain sickness (*Soroche* in South America) can also affect visitors. It is more likely to affect those who ascend rapidly, eg by plane and those who over-exert themselves (teenagers for example). Soroche takes a few hours or days to come on and presents with a bad headache, extreme tiredness, sometimes dizziness, loss of appetite and frequently nausea and vomiting. Insomnia is common and is often associated with a suffocating feeling when lying in bed. Keen observers may note their breathing tends to wax and wane at night and their face tends to be puffy in the mornings – this is all part of the syndrome. Anyone can get this condition and past experience is not always a good guide: the author, having spent years in Peru travelling constantly between sea level and very high altitude never suffered symptoms, then was severely affected whilst climbing Kilimanjaro in Tanzania.

The treatment of acute mountain sickness is simple – rest, painkillers, (preferably not aspirin based) for the headache and anti sickness pills for vomiting. Oxygen is actually not much help, except at very high altitude. Various local panaceas – Coramina glucosada, Effortil, Micoren are popular in Latin America and mate de coca (an infusion of coca leaves widely available and perfectly legal) will alleviate some of the symptoms.

To **prevent** the condition: on arrival at places over 3,000m have a few hours rest in a chair and avoid alcohol, cigarettes and heavy food. If the symptoms are severe and prolonged, it is best to descend to a lower altitude and to reascend slowly or in stages. If this is impossible because of shortage of time or if you are going so high that acute mountain sickness is very likely, then the drug Acetazolamide (Diamox) can be used as a preventative and continued during the ascent. There is good evidence of the value of this drug in the prevention of soroche, but some people do experience peculiar side effects. The usual dose is 500 mg of the slow release preparation each night, starting the night before ascending above 3,000m.

Watch out for **sunburn** at high altitude. The ultraviolet rays are extremely powerful. The air is also excessively dry at high altitude and you might find that your skin dries out and the inside of your nose becomes crusted. Use a moisturiser for the skin and some vaseline wiped into the nostrils. Some people find contact lenses irritate because of the dry air. It is unwise to ascend to high altitude if you are pregnant, especially in the first 3 months, or if you have a history of heart, lung or blood disease, including sickle cell.

A more unusual condition can affect mountaineers who ascend rapidly to high altitude – **acute pulmonary oedema**. Residents at altitude sometimes experience this when returning to the mountains from time spent at the coast. This condition is often preceded by acute mountain sickness and comes on quite rapidly with severe breathlessness, noisy breathing, cough, blueness of the lips and frothing at the mouth. Anybody who develops this must be brought down as soon as possible, given oxygen and taken to hospital.

A rapid descent from high places will make sinus problems and middle ear infections worse and might make your teeth ache. Lastly, don't fly to altitude within 24 hrs of SCUBA diving. You might suffer from 'the bends'.

HEAT AND COLD

Full acclimatisation to high temperatures takes about 2 weeks. During this period it is normal to feel a bit apathetic, especially if the relative humidity is high. Drink plenty of water (up to 15 litres a day are required when working physically hard in the tropics), use salt on your food and avoid extreme exertion. Tepid showers are more cooling than hot or cold ones. Large hats do not cool you down, but do prevent sunburn. Remember that, especially in the highlands, there can be a large and sudden drop in temperature between sun and shade and between night and day, so dress accordingly. Warm jackets or woollens are essential after dark at high altitude. Loose cotton is still the best material when the weather is hot.

INSECTS

These are mostly more of a nuisance than a serious hazard and if you try, you can prevent yourself entirely from being bitten. Some, such as mosquitos are, of course, carriers of potentially serious diseases, so it is sensible to avoid being bitten as much as possible. Sleep off the ground and use a mosquito net or some kind of insecticide. Preparations containing Pyrethrum or synthetic pyrethroids are safe. They are available as aerosols or pumps and the best way to use these is to spray the room thoroughly in all areas (follow the instructions rather than the insects) and then shut the door for a while, re-entering when the smell has dispersed. Mosquito coils release insecticide as they burn slowly. They are widely available and useful out of doors. Tablets of insecticide which are placed on a heated mat plugged into a wall socket are probably the most effective. They fill the room with insecticidal fumes in the same way as aerosols or coils.

You can also use insect repellents, most of which are effective against a wide range of pests. The most common and effective is diethyl metatoluamide (DET). DET liquid is best for arms and face (care around eyes and with spectacles – DET dissolves plastic). Aerosol spray is good for clothes and ankles and liquid DET can be dissolved in water and used to impregnate cotton clothes and mosquito nets. Some repellents now contain DET and Permethrin, insecticide. Impregnated wrist and ankle bands can also be useful.

If you are bitten or stung, itching may be relieved by cool baths, antihistamine tablets (care with alcohol or driving) or mild corticosteroid creams, eg. hydrocortisone (great care: never use if any hint of infection). Careful scratching of all your bites once a day can be surprisingly effective. Calamine lotion and cream have limited effectiveness and antihistamine creams are not recommended – they can cause allergies themselves.

Bites which become infected should be treated with a local antiseptic or antibiotic cream such as Cetrimide, as should any infected sores or scratches.

When living rough, skin infestations with body lice (crabs) and scabies are easy to pick up. Use whatever local commercial preparation is recommended for lice and scabies.

Crotamiton cream (Eurax) alleviates itching and also kills a number of skin parasites. Malathion lotion 5% (Prioderm) kills lice effectively, but avoid the use of the toxic agricultural preparation of Malathion, more often used to commit suicide.

TICKS

They attach themselves usually to the lower parts of the body often after walking in areas where cattle have grazed. They take a while to attach themselves strongly, but swell up as they start to suck blood. The important thing is to remove them gently, so that they do not leave their head parts in your skin because this can cause a nasty allergic reaction some days later. Do not use petrol, vaseline, lighted cigarettes etc to remove the tick, but, with a pair of tweezers remove the beast gently by gripping it at the attached (head) end and rock it out in very much the same way that a tooth is extracted. Certain tropical flies which lay their eggs under the skin of sheep and cattle also occasionally do the same thing to humans with the unpleasant result that a maggot grows under the skin and pops up as a boil or pimple. The best way to remove these is to cover the boil with oil, vaseline or nail varnish so as to stop the maggot breathing, then to squeeze it out gently the next day.

SUNBURN

The burning power of the tropical sun, especially at high altitude, is phenomenal.

Always wear a wide brimmed hat and use some form of suncream lotion on untanned skin. Normal temperate zone suntan lotions (protection factor up to 7) are not much good; you need to use the types designed specifically for the tropics or for mountaineers or skiers with protection factors up to 15 or above. These are often not available in Latin America. Glare from the sun can cause conjunctivitis, so wear sunglasses especially on tropical beaches, where high protection factor sunscreen should also be used.

PRICKLY HEAT

A very common intensely itchy rash is avoided by frequent washing and by wearing loose clothing. Cured by allowing skin to dry off through use of powder and spending two nights in an airconditioned hotel!

ATHLETES FOOT

This and other fungal skin infections are best treated with Tolnaftate or Clotrimazole.

OTHER RISKS AND MORE SERIOUS DISEASES

Remember that rabies is endemic throughout Latin America, so avoid dogs that are behaving strangely and cover your toes at night from the vampire bats, which also carry the disease. If you are bitten by a domestic or wild animal, do not leave things to chance: scrub the wound with soap and water and/or disinfectant, try to have the animal captured (within limits) or at least determine its ownership, where possible, and seek medical assistance at once. The course of treatment depends on whether you have already been satisfactorily vaccinated against rabies. If you have (this is worthwile if you are spending lengths of time in developing countries) then some further doses of vaccine are all that is required. Human diploid vaccine is the best, but expensive: other, older kinds of vaccine, such as that derived from duck embryos may be the only types available. These are effective, much cheaper and interchangeable generally with the human derived types. If not already vaccinated then anti rabies serum (immunoglobulin) may be required in addition. It is important to finish the course of treatment whether the animal survives or not.

AIDS

In South America AIDS is increasing but is not wholly confined to the well known high risk sections of the population, ie homosexual men, intravenous drug abusers and children of infected mothers. Heterosexual transmission is now the dominant mode and so the main risk to travellers is from casual sex. The same precautions should be taken as with any sexually transmitted disease. The Aids virus (HIV) can be passed by unsterilized needles which have been previously used to inject an HIV positive patient, but the risk of this is negligible. It would, however, be sensible to check that needles have been properly sterilized or disposable needles have been used. If you wish to take your own disposable needles, be prepared to explain what they are for. The risk of receiving a blood transfusion with blood infected with the HIV virus is greater than from dirty needles because of the amount of fluid exchanged. Supplies of blood for transfusion should now be screened for HIV in all reputable hospitals, so again the risk is very small indeed. Catching the AIDS virus does not always produce an illness in itself (although it may do). The only way to be sure if you feel you have been put at risk is to have a blood test for HIV antibodies on your return to a place where there are reliable laboratory facilities. The test does not become positive for some weeks.

MALARIA

In South America malaria is theoretically confined to coastal and jungle zones, but is now on the increase again. Mosquitos do not thrive above 2,500m, so you are safe at altitude. There are different varieties of malaria, some resistant to the normal drugs. Make local enquiries if you intend to visit possibly infected zones and use a prophylactic regime. Start taking the tablets a few days before exposure and continue to take them for 6 weeks after leaving the malarial zone. Remember to give the drugs to babies and children also. Opinion varies on the precise drugs and dosage to be used for protection. All the drugs may have some side effects and it is important to balance the risk of catching the disease against the albeit rare side effects. The increasing complexity of the subject is such that as the malarial parasite becomes immune to the new generation of drugs it has made concentration on the physical prevention from being bitten by mosquitos more important. This involves the use of long sleeved shirts or blouses and long trousers, repellants and nets. Clothes are now available impregnated with the insecticide Permethrin or Deltamethrin or it is possible to impregnate the clothes yourself. Wide meshed nets impregnated with Permethrin are also available, are lighter to carry and less claustrophobic to sleep in.

Prophylaxis and treatment

If your itinerary takes you into a malarial area, seek expert advice before you go on a suitable prophylactic regime. This is especially true for pregnant women who are particularly prone to catch malaria. You can still catch the disease even when sticking to a proper regime, although it is unlikely. If you do develop symptoms (high fever, shivering, headache, sometimes diarrhoea), seek medical advice immediately. If this is not possible and there is a great likelihood of malaria, the treatment is:

Chloroquine, a single dose of 4 tablets (600 mg) followed by 2 tablets (300 mg) in 6 hrs and 300 mg each day following.

Falciparum type of malaria or type in doubt: take local advice. Various combinations of drugs are being used such as Quinine, Tetracycline or Halofantrine. If falciparum type malaria is definitely diagnosed, it is wise to get to a good hospital as treatment can be complex and the illness very serious.

INFECTIOUS HEPATITIS (JAUNDICE)

The main symptoms are pains in the stomach, lack of appetite, lassitude and yellowness of the eyes and skin. Medically speaking there are two main types. The less serious, but more common is Hepatitis A for which the best protection os the careful preparation of food, the avoidance of contaminated drinking water and scrupulous attention to toilet hygiene. The other, more serious, version is Hepatitis B which is acquired usually as a sexually transmitted disease or by blood transfusions. It can less commonly be transmitted by injections with unclean needles and possibly by insect bites. The symptoms are the same as for Hepatitis A. The incubation period is much longer (up to 6 months compared with 6 weeks) and there are more likely to be complications.

Hepatitis A can be protected against with gamma globulin. It should be obtained from a reputable source and is certainly useful for travellers who intende to live rough. You should have a shot before leaving and have it repeated every 6 months. The dose of gamma globulin depends on the concentration of the particular preparation used, so the manufacturer's advice should be taken. The injection should be given as close as possible to your departure and as the dose depends on the likely time you are to spend in potentially affected areas, the manufacturer's instructions should be followed. Gamma globulin has really been superceded now by a proper vaccination against Hepatitis A (Havrix) which gives immunity lasting up to 10 years. After that boosters are required. Havrix monodose is now widely available as is Junior Havrix. The vaccination has negligible side effects and is extremely effective. Gamma globulin injections can be a bit painful, but it is much cheaper than Havrix and may be more available in some places.

Hepatitis B can be effectively prevented by a specific vaccine (Engerix) – 3 shots over 6 months before travelling. If you have had jaundice in the past it would be worthwhile having a blood test to see if you are immune to either of these two types, because this might avoid the necessity and costs of vaccination or gamma globulin. There are other kinds of viral hepatitis (C, E etc) which are fairly similar to A and B, but vaccines are not available as yet.

TYPHUS

Can still occur carried by ticks. There is usually a reaction at the site of the bite and a fever. Seek medical advice.

INTESTINAL WORMS

These are common and the more serious ones such as hookworm can be contracted from walking barefoot on infested earth or beaches.

Various other tropical diseases can be caught in jungle areas, usually transmitted by biting insects. They are often related to African diseases and were probably introduced by the slave labour trade. Onchocerciasis (river blindness) carried by black flies is found in parts of Mexico and Venezuela. Leishmaniasis (Espundia) is carried by sandflies and causes a sore that will not heal or a severe nasal infection. Wearing long trousers and a long sleeved shirt in infected areas protects against these flies. DET is also effective. Epidemics of meningitis occur from time-to-time. Be careful about swimimg in piranha or caribe infested rivers. It is a good idea not to swim naked: the Candiru fish can follow urine currents and become lodged in body orifices. Swimwear offers some protection.

LEPTOSPIROSIS

Various forms of leptospirosis occur throughout Latin America, transmitted by a bacterium which is excreted in rodent urine. Fresh water and moist soil harbour the organisms which enter the body through cuts and scratches. If you suffer from any form of prolonged fever consult a doctor.

SNAKE BITE

This is a very rare event indeed for travellers. If you are unlucky (or careless) enough to be bitten by a venomous snake, spider, scorpion or sea creature, try to identify the creature, but do not put yourself in further danger. Snake bites in particular are very frightening, but in fact rarely poisonous – even venomous snakes bite without injecting venom. What you might expect if bitten are: fright, swelling, pain and bruising around the bite and soreness of the regional lymph glands, perhaps nausea, vomiting and a fever. Signs of serious poisoning would be the following symptoms: numbness and tingling of the face, muscular spasms, convulsions, shortness of breath and bleeding. Victims should be got to a hospital or a doctor without delay. Commercial snake bite and scorpion kits are available, but usually only useful for the specific type of snake or scorpion for which they are designed. Most serum has to be given intravenously so it is not much good equipping yourself with it unless you are used to making injections into veins. It is best to rely on local practice in these cases, because the particular creatures will be known about locally and appropriate treatment can be given.

Treatment of snake bite Reassure and comfort the victim frequently. Immobilize the limb by a bandage or a splint or by getting the person to lie still. Do not slash the bite area and try to suck out the poison because this sort of heroism does more harm than good. If you know how to use a tourniquet in these circumstances, you will not need this advice. If you are not experienced do not apply a tourniquet.

Precautions

Avoid walking in snake territory in bare feet or sandals – wear proper shoes or boots. If you encounter a snake stay put until it slithers away, and do not investigate a wounded snake. Spiders and scorpions may be found in the more basic hotels, especially in the Andean countries. If stung, rest and take plenty of fluids and call a doctor. The best precaution is to keep beds away from the walls and look inside your shoes and under the toilet seat every morning. Certain tropical sea fish when trodden upon inject venom into bathers' feet. This can be exceptionally painful. Wear plastic shoes when you go bathing if such creatures are reported. The pain can be relieved by immersing the foot in extremely hot water for as long as the pain persists.

DENGUE FEVER

This is increasing worldwide including in South and Central American countries and the Caribbean. It can be completely prevented by avoiding mosquito bites in the same way as malaria. No vaccine is available. Dengue is an unpleasant and painful disease, presenting with a high temperature and body pains, but at least visitors are spared the more serious forms (haemorrhagic types) which are more of a problem for local people who have been exposed to the disease more than once. There is no specific treatment for dengue – just pain killers and rest.

CHAGAS' DISEASE (SOUTH AMERICAN TRYPANOSOMIASIS)

This is a chronic disease, very rarely caught by travellers and difficult to treat. It is transmitted by the simultaneous biting and excreting of the Reduvid bug, also known as the Vinchuca or Barbeiro. Somewhat resembling a small cockroach, this nocturnal bug lives in poor adobe houses with dirt floors often frequented by opossums. If you cannot avoid such accommodation, sleep off the floor with a candle lit, use a mosquito net, keep as much of your skin covered as possible, use DET repellent or a spray insecticide. If you are bitten overnight (the bites are painless) do not scratch them, but wash thoroughly with soap and water.

DANGEROUS ANIMALS

Apart from mosquitos the most dangerous animals are men, be they bandits or behind steering wheels. Think carefully about violent confrontations and wear a seat belt if you are lucky enough to have one available to you.

WHEN YOU RETURN HOME

Remember to take your antimalarial tablets for 6 weeks after leaving the malarial area. If you have had attacks of diarrhoea it is worth having a stool specimen tested in case you have picked up amoebas. If you have been living rough, blood tests may be worthwhile to detect worms and other parasites. If you have been exposed to bilharzia (*schistosomiasis*) by swimming in lakes etc, check by means of a blood test when you get home, but leave it for 6 weeks because the test is slow to become positive. Report any untowards symptoms to your doctor and tell the doctor exactly where you have been and, if you know, what the likelihood of disease is to which you were exposed.

The above information has been compiled for us by Dr David Snashall, who is presently Senior Lecturer in Occupational Health at the United Medical Schools of Guy's and St Thomas' Hospitals in London and Chief Medical Adviser to the British Foreign and Commonwealth Office. He has travelled extensively in Central and South America, worked in Peru and in East Africa and keeps in close touch with developments in preventative and tropical medicine.

Section 3
The region

Argentina

HORIZONS

THE LAND

Argentina, excluding the territories claimed in the South Atlantic and Antarctica, is the second largest country in area in South America, equivalent to 29% of Europe. It stretches 4,527 km from N to S and 1,580 km from E to W. Apart from the estuary of the Río de la Plata its coastline is 2,575 km long. Its W frontier runs along the crest of the high Andes, a formidable barrier between it and Chile. Its neighbours to the N are Bolivia and Paraguay and (in the NE) Brazil. To the E is Uruguay. Its far S limit is the Beagle Channel. The country is enormously varied both in types of land and climate. Geographers usually recognize four main physical areas: the Andes, the North and Mesopotamia, the Pampas, and Patagonia.

The Andes includes the whole length of the Cordilleras, low and deeply glaciated in the Patagonian S, high and dry in the prolongation into NW Argentina of the Bolivian Altiplano, the high plateau. South of this is the very parched desert and mountain region S of Tucumán and W of Córdoba. The oases strung along the eastern foot of the Andes – Jujuy, Salta, Tucumán, Catamarca, La Rioja, San Juan, Mendoza and the small town of San Rafael – were the first places to be colonized by the Spaniards.

The North and Mesopotamia contains the vast forested plains of the Chaco and the floodplain and gently rolling land known as Argentine Mesopotamia lying between the rivers Paraná and Uruguay. The Province of Misiones in the NE is actually on the great Paraná plateau. These plains cover 582,750 sq km.

The pampa makes up the heart of the country. These vast, rich plains lie S of the Chaco, E of the Andes, W of the Atlantic and the Río Paraná and N of the Río Colorado. The eastern part, which receives more rain, is usually called the Humid Pampa, and the western part the Dry Pampa. The Pampas stretch for hundreds of kilometres in almost unrelieved flatness, covering some 650,000 sq km.

Patagonia lies S of the Río Colorado – a land of arid, wind-swept plateaux cut across by ravines. In the deep S the wind is wilder and more continuous. There is no real summer, but to compensate for this the winters are rarely severe. Patagonia covers about 780,000 sq km.

Argentina Mainland Only

BOLIVIA · To La Paz · To Tarija · To Santa Cruz
Calama
La Quiaca · Yacuiba
PARAGUAY
Antofagasta
Embarcación
Jujuy
Salta
Metán
3
6
ASUNCIÓN
Formosa
Iguazú
8
Tucumán
RS Peña
Resistencia
Posadas
Santiago del Estero
Corrientes
Catamarca
Paso de los Libres
BRAZIL
7
La Rioja
Uruguaiana
5
Concordia
To Porto Alegre
San Juan
Córdoba
2
Santa Fe
Salto
Paraná
Colón
Paysandú
Mendoza
Río Cuarto
Rosario
Fray Bentos
4
San Luis
URUGUAY
SANTIAGO
San Rafael
BUENOS AIRES
La Plata
MONTEVIDEO
Santa Rosa
Azul
Gen Acha
1
Villa Gesell
9
Bahía Blanca
Mar del Plata
Zapala
Neuquén
Necochea
Temuco
Viedma
San Martín de los Andes
San Antonio Oeste
Atlantic Ocean
Bariloche
Puerto Madryn
Puerto Montt
Esquel
Trelew
10
Comodoro Rivadavia
Perito Moreno
Puerto Deseado
Gob Gregores
San Julián
Calafate
Santa Cruz
Río Turbio
Puerto Natales
Río Gallegos
N
Punta Arenas
Río Grande
11
Ushuaia

Pacific Ocean

C H I L E

0 — 400 km

1	Buenos Aires & the Pampas
2	The Córdoba Region
3	Santiago del Estero, Tucumán, Salta & Jujuy
4	The Cuyo Region: over the Andes to Chile
5	North of Mendoza
6	The Chaco
7	Mesopotamia
8	The Iguazú Falls
9	The Lake District
10	Patagonia
11	Tierra del Fuego

CLIMATE

Climate ranges from sub-tropical in the N to cold temperate in Tierra del Fuego, but is temperate and quite healthy in the densely populated central zone. From mid-Dec to the end of Feb Buenos Aires can be oppressively hot and humid, with temperatures ranging from 27°C (80°F) to 35°C (95°F) and an average humidity of 70%. Beware of the high pollen count in the pollinating season if you have allergy problems. The winter months of June, July and Aug are best for a business visit, though spring weather in Buenos Aires is often very pleasant indeed. The skiing season in Bariloche ends by 30 August. Corrientes and Misiones provinces are wet in Aug and especially September.

HISTORY

The arrival of the Spaniards When, in the early 16th century, the first Europeans came to Argentina, the native Indians had already halted the Inca drive S from Peru through Bolivia into N Argentina. The Spaniard Juan de Solís landed on the shores of the Plata estuary in 1516, but the expedition failed and he was killed. Magellan touched at the estuary 4 years later, but turned S to make his way into the Pacific. In 1527 both Sebastian Cabot and his rival Diego García sailed into the estuary and up the Paraná and the Paraguay. They formed a small settlement, Sancti Spiritus, at the junction of the Carcarañá and Coronda rivers near their confluence with the Paraná, but it was wiped out by the Indians about 2 years later and Cabot and García returned to Spain. 8 years later, in 1535, Pedro de Mendoza, with a large force well supplied with equipment and horses, founded a settlement at Buenos Aires. The natives soon made it too difficult for him; the settlement was abandoned and Mendoza returned home, but not before sending Juan de Ayolas with a small force up the Paraná. Ayolas set off for Peru, already conquered by Pizarro, leaving Irala in charge. It is not known for certain what happened to Ayolas, but in 1537 Irala and his men settled at Asunción, in Paraguay, where the natives were

friendly. There were no further expeditions from Spain to colonize what is now called Argentina, and it was not until 1573 that the settlement at Asunción sent forces S to establish Santa Fe and not until 11 June 1580 that Juan de Garay refounded the settlement at Buenos Aires. It was only under his successor, Hernando Arias de Saavedra (1592-1614), that the new colony became secure. In the meantime there had been successful expeditions into Argentina both from Peru and Chile (see page 118).

The colonial period For 270 years after its foundation Buenos Aires was of little importance. From 1543 all the Spanish territories in South America were governed from Lima, the Vice-Regal capital. Spanish trade was via Lima, Panama and the Caribbean and Spain did not allow Buenos Aires to take part in any overseas trade until 1778; its population then was only 24,203. It was merely a military outpost for Spain to confront the Portuguese settlement at Colonia, across the estuary, and lived, in the main, by smuggling. Even when in 1776 the Viceroyalty of Río de la Plata was formed, it made little difference to Buenos Aires as a capital, for its control of the *cabildos* (town councils) in distant towns was very tenuous. When the British, following Spain's alliance with Napoleon, attacked Buenos Aires in 1806 and again in 1807 before being repulsed by local levies, there was no inkling of its future potential. But the defeat of these attacks, known as the Reconquista, had one important result: a great increase in the confidence of the *porteños* (the name given to those born in Buenos Aires) to deal with all comers, including the mother-country, whose restrictions on trade were increasingly unpopular.

Independence On 25 May 1810, the *cabildo* of Buenos Aires deposed the viceroy and announced that it was governing henceforth on behalf of King Ferdinand VII, then a captive of Napoleon. 6 years later, in July 1816, when Buenos Aires was threatened by invasion from Peru and blockaded by a Spanish fleet in the Río de la Plata, a national congress held at Tucumán declared independence. The declaration was given reality by José de San Martín, who marched an Argentine army across the Andes to free Chile and embarked his forces for Peru, where he captured Lima, the first step in the liberation of Peru.

The formation of the republic When San Martín returned home, it was to find the country rent by conflict between the central government and the provinces. On the one hand stood the Unitarist party, bent on central control; on the other the Federalist party, insisting on local autonomy. The latter had for members the great *caudillos* (the large landowners backed by the *gauchos*) suspicious of the cities. One of their leaders, Juan Manuel de Rosas, took control in 1829. During his second term as Governor of Buenos Aires he asked for and was given extraordinary powers. The result was a 17-year reign of terror which became an international scandal. When he began a blockade of Asunción in 1845, Britain and France promptly countered with a 3-year blockade of Buenos Aires. In 1851 Justo José de Urquiza, Governor of Entre Ríos, one of his old henchmen, organized a triple alliance of Brazil, Uruguay, and the Argentine opposition to overthrow him. He was defeated in 1852 at Caseros, a few kilometres from Buenos Aires, and fled to England, where he farmed quietly for 25 years, dying at Southampton.

Rosas had started his career as a Federalist; once in power he was a Unitarist. His downfall meant the triumph of federalism. In 1853 a federal system was finally incorporated in the constitution, but Buenos Aires refused to join the new federation, which had its capital at Paraná. In 1859 Buenos Aires, under Bartolomé Mitre, was defeated by the federal forces under Urquiza, but 2 years later Buenos Aires defeated the federal forces. Once again it became the seat of the federal government, with Bartolomé Mitre as its first constitutional president. (It was during his term that the Triple Alliance of Argentina, Brazil, and Uruguay defeated Francisco Solano López of Paraguay.) There was another political flare-up of the old quarrel in 1880, ending in the humiliation of the city of Buenos Aires, which was separated from its province and made into a special federal territory; a new provincial capital was founded at La Plata, 56 km to the SE. The conquest at about the same time of all the Indian tribes of the pampas and the S by a young colonel, Julio A Roca was to make possible the final supremacy of Buenos Aires over all rivals.

The 20th century Politically Argentina was a constitutional republic with a very restricted suffrage up to the passage in 1912 of the Sáenz Peña law, which established universal manhood suffrage. From 1916 to 1930 the Unión Cívica Radical (founded in 1890) held power, under the leadership of Hipólito Yrigoyen and Marcelo T de Alvear, but lost it to the military uprising of 1930. Though seriously affected by the world depression of the 1930s, Argentina's rich soil and educated population had made it one of the 10 wealthiest countries in the world, but this wealth was most unevenly distributed, and the political methods followed by the conservatives and their military associates in the 1930s denied the middle and working classes any effective share in their own country's wealth and government.

Perónism and its legacy A series of military coups in 1943-44 led to the rise of Col Juan Domingo Perón, basing his power on an alliance between the army and labour; his contacts with labour were greatly assisted by his charismatic wife Eva (since commemorated in the rock-opera and film 'Evita'). In 1946 Perón was elected President. His government is chiefly remembered by many Argentines for improving the living conditions of the workers. Especially in its early years the government was strongly nationalistic, taking control over the British-owned railways in 1948. Opposition parties were harassed and independent newspapers taken over. Although Perón was easily re-elected in 1951, his government soon ran into trouble: economic problems led to the introduction of a wage freeze which upset the labour unions which were the heart of Peronist support; the death of Evita in 1952 was another blow. In Sept 1955 a military coup unseated Perón who went into exile.

Perón's legacy dominated the period 1955-1973: society was bitterly divided between Peronists and anti-Peronists; the economy struggled; the armed forces, constantly involved in politics, were also divided. These years were marked by an uneasy alternation of three military and two constitutional regimes. The military group which seized power in 1966 was discredited by a deteriorating economy and the emergence of several guerrilla groups in a climate of tension and violence. When it bowed out in 1973, elections were won by the Peronist candidate, Hector Campora. Perón returned from exile in Madrid to resume as President in Oct 1973, but died on 1 July 1974, leaving the Presidency to his widow, Vice-President María Estela Martínez de Perón (his third wife). The subsequent chaotic political situation, including guerrilla warfare, led to her deposition by a military junta, led by Gen Jorge Videla in Mar 1976.

The Dirty War Under the military, guerrilla warfare and the other features of dissidence were repressed with great brutality: about 9,000 people (according to official statistics; human rights organizations believe the total is at least double this) disappeared without trace during the so-called 'dirty war'. Gen Videla was appointed President in 1978 by the military; his nominated successor, Gen Roberto Viola took over for 3 years in Mar 1981 but was replaced by Gen Leopoldo Galtieri in Dec 1981. The latter was in turn replaced in June 1982 by Gen (ret) Reynaldo Bignone.

Return to democracy Confidence in the military ebbed when their economic policies began to go sour in 1980. In 1982-83 pressure for a democratic restoration grew particularly after the South Atlantic conflict with Great Britain in 1982. General elections on 30 October 1983 were won by the Unión Cívica Radical (UCR), with Dr Raúl Alfonsín as president. During 1985 Generals Videla, Viola and Galtieri were sentenced to long terms of imprisonment for their parts in the 'dirty war'. President Alfonsín's popularity gradually waned as his Government failed to solve economic problems.

The Menem years When Alfonsín was defeated by Dr Carlos Saúl Menem of the Partido Justicialista (Peronists) in May 1989, Alfonsín stepped down early because of economic instability. Strained relations between the Peronist Government and the military led to several rebellions, which Pres Menem attempted to appease by pardoning the imprisoned Generals. His popularity among civilians declined, but in 1991-92 the Economy Minister, Domingo Cavallo, succeeded in restoring confidence in the economy and the Government as a whole. After triumphing in Oct 1993 congressional elections at the expense of the UCR, the Peronists themselves lost some ground in April 1994 elections to a constituent assembly. The party to gain most, especially in Buenos Aires, was Frente Grande, a broad coalition of left wing groups and disaffected Peronists. Behind the loss of confidence of these dissident Peronists were unrestrained corruption and a pact in Dec 1993 between Menem and Alfonsín pledging UCR support for constitutional changes which included re-election of the president for a second term of 4 years.

By the 1995 elections, the majority of the electorate favoured stability over constitutional concerns and returned Pres Menem, without recourse to a second ballot. The Peronists also increased their majority in the Chamber of Deputies and gained a majority in the Senate. Menem made his priorities the reduction of joblessness and of corruption, although on neither score did he achieve immediate success. Concurrent with changes at the Finance Ministry and measures to take the economy beyond the 1995 recession (see **Economy** below), labour legislation reform was highly unpopular as it contravened some of Peronism's founding tenets. Menem further had to contend with criticisms from ex-Finance Minister Domingo Cavallo over corruption and links with crime at government level, and with the boost given to the Radicals by that party's victory in the first direct elections for mayor of Buenos Aires in July 1996.

THE TRANSFORMATION OF THE PAMPAS

The pampas, the economic heart of the country, extend fanwise from Buenos Aires for a distance of between 550 and 650 km. Apart from three groups of *sierras* or low hills near Córdoba, Tandil and Bahía Blanca, the surface seems an endless flat monotony, relieved occasionally, in the SW, by sand dunes. There are few rivers. Drinking water is pumped to the surface from a depth of from 30 to 150m by the windpumps which are such a prominent feature of the landscape. There are few species of trees other than those that have been planted, except in the *monte* of the W. There is, in most years however, ample rainfall. It is greatest at Rosario, where it is about 1,020 mm, and evenly distributed throughout the year. The further S from Rosario, the less the rain. At Buenos Aires it is about 940 mm; it drops to 535 at Bahía Blanca, and is only 400 along the boundary of the Humid Pampa. The further S from Rosario, too, the more the rainfall is concentrated during the summer. Over the whole of the pampa the summers are hot, the winters mild, but there is a large climatic difference between various regions: at Rosario the growing season between frosts is about 300 days; at Bahía Blanca it falls to 145 days.

When the Spaniards arrived in Argentina the pampas were an area of tall coarse grasses. The cattle and horses they brought with them were soon to roam wild and in time transformed the Indian's way of life. The only part of the pampa occupied by the settlers was the so-called Rim, between the Río Salado, S of the capital, and the Paraná-Plata rivers. Here, in large *estancias*, cattle, horses and mules in great herds roamed the open range. There was a line of forts along the Río Salado: a not very effective protection against marauding Indians. The Spaniards had also brought European grasses with them; these soon supplanted the coarse native grasses, and formed a green carpet which stopped abruptly at the Río Salado.

The *estancia* owners and their dependent *gauchos* were in no sense an agricultural people, but towards the end of the 18th century, tenants – to the great contempt of both *estanciero* and *gaucho* – began to plant wheat along the Paraná-Plata shore.

The rapidly rising population of Europe during the latter half of the 19th century and the consequent demand for cheap food was the spur that impelled Argentina (as it did the United States and Canada) to occupy its grasslands and take to agriculture. This was made possible by the new machinery and techniques already developed. Roads were, and are, a difficulty in the pampas; the soil lacks gravel or stones for surfacing, and dirt roads become a quagmire in wet weather and a fume of dust in the dry. Railways, on the other hand, were simple and cheap to build. The system grew as need arose and capital (mostly from Britain) became available. The lines in the pampas radiated out fanwise (with intricate intercommunication) from the ports of Buenos Aires, Rosario, Santa Fe and Bahía Blanca. Argentina, unlike most other countries, had extensive railways before a road system was built.

The occupation of the pampas was finally achieved by a war against the Indians in 1878-83 which virtually exterminated them. Many of the officers were given gifts of land of more than 40,000 ha each. The pampas had passed into private hands on the old traditional pattern of large estates.

Cattle products had been the mainstay of Argentine overseas trade during the whole of the colonial period. In the early 19th century wool challenged this supremacy. The occupation of the grasslands did not, at first, alter the complexion of the foreign trade; it merely increased its volume. In 1877, however, the first ship with refrigeration chambers made it possible to send frozen beef to England, but the meat of the scrub cattle was too strong for English taste. As a result, pedigree bulls were imported from England and the upgrading of the herds began. The same process was applied to sheep. But the improved herds could only flourish where there were no ticks – prevalent in the N – and where forage crops were available. Argentina adopted as its main forage crop alfalfa which proved extremely suitable on the pampa. It has since been supplemented with barley, oats, rye, maize, sorghum and oilseeds.

A striking thing about the pampas is the bird life. Flamingoes rise in a pink and white cloud, heron egrets gleam white against the blue sky, pink spoonbills dig in the mud and rheas stalk in the distance. Most fascinating are the oven birds, the *horneros*, which build oven-shaped nests six times as big as themselves on the top of telegraph and fence posts.

The transformation of the pampas has had two profound effects. Because its newly-created riches flowed out and its needs flowed in mainly through Buenos Aires, that port grew from comparative insignificance into one of the great cities in the world. Also, the transformation of the Humid Pampa through immigration, began a process which has made Argentina into a society of predominantly European origin. White immigration was encouraged by the 1853 Constitution and the new political stablity after 1862 encouraged a great wave of settlers from Europe. Between 1857 and 1930 total immigration was over 6 million, almost all from Europe. Italians were by far the most numerous, followed by Spaniards, and then, far behind, groups of other Europeans and Latin Americans.

CULTURE

PEOPLE

In the Federal Capital and Province of Buenos Aires, where almost 40% of the population lives, the people are almost exclusively of European origin. In the far northern provinces, colonized from neighbouring countries, at least half the people are *mestizos* though they form about 15% of the population of the whole country. It is estimated that 12.8% are foreign born and generally of European origin, though there are also important communities of Syrians, Lebanese, Armenians, Japanese and, most recently, Koreans.

Not surprisingly, the traditional image of the Argentine is that of the *gaucho*; *gauchismo* has been a powerful influence in literature, sociology and folklore, and is celebrated each year in the week before the 'Day of Tradition', 10 November.

In the highlands of the NW, in the Chaco, Misiones and in the SW, there are still some indigenous groups. The exact total of the Indian population is unknown; estimates vary from 100,000 to 300,000. As was noted above, the pampas Indians were virtually exterminated in the 19th century; the Indians of Tierra del Fuego are extinct. Surviving peoples include the Wichi and others in Salta and Jujuy provinces (see page 125), various Chaco Indians (see page 186) and tribes related to the Mapuche and Tehuelche nations in the SW. A number of organizations represent indigenous interests, but any legislation, under federal law, has to be enacted separately by each province.

MUSIC AND DANCE

Buenos Aires contains a third of the country's population and its music is the Tango. Indeed to the outside world there is no other Argentine music. Although also sung and played, the Tango was born as a dance just before the turn of the 20th century. The exact moment of the birth was not recorded by any contemporary observer and continues to be a matter of debate, though the roots can be traced. The name 'Tango' predates the dance and was given to the carnivals (and dances) of the black inhabitants of the Río de la Plata in the early 19th century. Elements of the black tradition were taken over by whites, as the black population declined into insignificance. However, the name 'Tango Americano' was also given to the Habanera (a Cuban descendent of the English Country Dance) which became the rage in Spain and bounced back into the Río de la Plata in the middle of the 19th century, not only as a fashionable dance, together with the polka, mazurka, waltz and cuadrille, but also as a song form in the very popular 'Zarzuelas', or Spanish operettas. However, the Habanera led not a double, but a triple life, by also infiltrating the lowest levels of society directly from Cuba via sailors who arrived in the ports of Montevideo and Buenos Aires. Here it encountered the Milonga, originally a Gaucho song style, but by 1880 a dance, especially popular with the so-called 'Compadritos' and 'Orilleros', who frequented the port area and its brothels, whence the Argentine Tango emerged around the turn of the century to dazzle the populace with its brilliant, personalized footwork, which could not be accomplished without the partners staying glued together. As a dance it became the rage and, as the infant recording industry grew by leaps and bounds, it also became popular as a song and an instrumental genre, with the original violins and floorutes being eclipsed by the *bandoneón* button accordion, then being imported from Germany. In 1911 the new dance took Paris by storm and returned triumphant to Buenos Aires. It achieved both respectability and notoriety, becoming a global phenomenon after the First World War. The golden voice of the renowned Carlos Gardel soon gave a wholly new dimension to the music of the Tango until his death in 1935. After losing some popularity in Argentina, it came to the forefront again in the 1940s (1920-50 is considered the real golden age). Its resurgence was assisted by Perón's decree that 50% of all music played on the radio must be Argentine, only to suffer a second, much more serious decline in the face of rock music over the past 2 decades. To see the Tango and Milonga danced in Buenos Aires today, you need to visit one of the clubs or *confiterías* where it is specially featured, see Buenos Aires **Nightclubs and folklore**. Apart from Carlos Gardel, other great names connected with the Tango are Francisco Canaro (Uruguayan), Osvaldo Pugliese and Astor Piazzolla, who has modernized it by fusion with jazz styles (*nuevo tango*). Whilst the majority of Argentine young people will agree that the Tango represents the soul of Buenos Aires, don't expect them to dance it or listen to it. They are more likely to be interested in the country's indigenous rock music.

If the Tango represents the soul of Buenos Aires, this is not the case in the rest of the country. The provinces have a very rich and attractive heritage of folk dances, mainly for couples, with arms held out and fingers clicked or handkerchiefs waved, with the 'Paso Valseado' as the basic step. Descended from the Zamacueca, and therefore a cousin of the Chilean Cueca and Peruvian Marinera, is the slow and stately Zamba, where the handkerchief is used to greatest effect. Equally popular throughout most of the country are the faster Gato, Chacarera and Escondido. These were the dances of the Gaucho and their rhythm evokes that of a cantering horse. Guitar and the *bombo* drum provide the accompaniment. Particularly spectacular is the Malambo, where the Gaucho shows off his dextrous footwork, the spurs of his boots adding a steely note to the rhythm.

Different regions of the country have their own specialities. The music of Cuyo in the W is sentimental and very similar to that of neighbouring Chile, with its Cuecas for dance and Tonadas for song. The NW on the other hand is Andean, with its musical culture closer to that of Bolivia, particularly on the Puna, where the Indians play the *quena* and *charango* and sound mournful notes on the great long *erke*. Here the dances are Bailecitos and Carnavalitos, while the songs are Vidalitas and the extraordinary high pitched Bagualas, the very essence of primeval pain. In the NE provinces of Corrientes and Misiones, the music shares cultural similarities with Paraguay. The Polca and Galopa are danced and the local Chamamé is sung, to the accordion or the harp, the style being sentimental. Santiago del Estero is the heartland of the

Chacarera and the lyrics are often part Spanish and part Quichua, a local dialect of the Andean Quechua language. Down in the Province of Buenos Aires you are more likely to hear the Gauchos singing their Milongas, Estilos and Cifras and challenging each other to a Payada or rhymed duel. Argentina experienced a great folk revival in the 50's and 60's and some of the most celebrated groups are still drawing enthusiastic audiences today. These groups include Los Chalchaleros and Los Fronterizos, the perennial virtuoso singer and guitarist, Eduardo Falú and, more recently, León Gieco from Santa Fe.

THE ECONOMY

Structure of production Argentina is one of the more highly developed countries of the region. It has the third largest gdp in Latin America, but by far the highest per capita income. Wealth traditionally came from farming although agriculture, forestry and fishing now account for only 6% of gdp. Nevertheless, over half of export earnings are generated by farming and food processing. There has been a shift from livestock to crop production since the 1960s. The area sown to oilseeds has risen steeply, now exceeding that of wheat. Although the fertility of the pampas was once so high that fertilizers were unnecessary, overexploitation and soil erosion have made its use essential, increasing the costs of farmers also hit by rising costs, falling commodity prices and lack of cheap credit to invest in modernization. In the 1990s, 150,000-200,000 small and medium sized farms were under severe financial pressure and many faced bankruptcy, leading to a consolidation of land holdings. Cresud, the only landholding company traded on the stock market, increased its holdings from 20,000 to 348,000 ha in 1994-96. Cattle and sheep herds have been reduced because of stiff competition abroad, low wool prices and outbreaks of foot and mouth disease. A vaccination drive started in 1989 has been successful and no further outbreaks have been recorded since 1994, leading farmers to hope that beef import bans imposed by the USA, Japan and Southeast Asian countries might be lifted. Exports of about 450,000 tonnes a year, earning some US$900mn, could double if the bans are lifted. Fishing received a boost in 1993 from an agreement with Britain to share fish resources in the South Atlantic, thereby increasing by 70% Argentina's share of the illex squid catch.

Manufacturing was developed behind high import protection barriers, but these

YPF – from State Company to Oil Magnate

The oil industry was deregulated in 1991 and the state oil company, Yacimientos Petrolíferos Fiscales (YPF) was privatized in 1993, although the Government retains 20%, the employees 10% and provincial governments 11%. YPF is the largest company in Argentina with a market capitalization of US$9bn, and it controls half the domestic oil industry with production, refining and retailing. Exports have risen since the opening in 1994 of an oil pipeline from Neuquén to Concepción in Chile, built by YPF and the Chilean oil company, ENAP, with a capacity of 107,000b/d. YPF and Petrobrás, of Brazil, have a strategic alliance with offshore drilling in the Gulf of Mexico and South Atlantic and are moving into joint downstream activities. In 1995 YPF bought a US-based oil and gas company, Maxus, which has stakes in Venezuela, Bolivia, Ecuador and Indonesia. An agreement with Britain in 1995 opened up the possibility of joint ventures to explore and exploit hydrocarbons in the disputed waters around the Falklands/Malvinas Islands. British Gas and YPF announced their interest in jointly exploring for gas and oil with a 51%/49% stake respectively. The two companies are already partners in the Transgas project to build one of two proposed pipelines to supply Argentine natural gas to Chile.

have now been swept aside. The sector accounts for 26% of gdp and is closely linked with agricultural activity, with food processing and beverages accounting for a quarter of manufacturing output. The regional customs union, Mercosur, opened up a huge market for companies established in Argentina and many food companies have been bought by multinationals. Trade with Brazil has traditionally been biased towards foodstuffs but enterprises in other areas are now growing. Several multinational motor vehicle companies are investing in new plant, many around Córdoba. All plan to sell vehicles to other Mercosur countries as well as within Argentina.

Argentina is self-sufficient in energy and has an exportable surplus of oil, natural gas and hydroelectricity. Hydroelectric potential lies on 10 main rivers: the rivers Paraná and Uruguay in the N where huge joint projects have been built with Paraguay (Yacyretá, Corpus) and Uruguay (Salto Grande), and on rivers in Río Negro and Neuquén provinces. The Government is divesting its stake in electricity generating and will offer its participation to private investors once ratification is secured from the Paraguayan and Uruguayan parliaments. More hydroelectricity generating plants are planned which will be built under concession by private contractors. Argentina has had nuclear power since 1974 when the first stage of the Atucha power station was opened using German technology. Crude oil output is around 785,000 b/d (domestic consumption 485,000 b/d, exports 300,000 b/d) and reserves are to be kept at 10 years' production with more exploration in a US$3bn, 10-year investment programme. The country has more natural gas than oil and reserves are about 560 billion cu m, equivalent to about 30 years' consumption at present rates.

Mining was discouraged by previous administrations, who declared the border region a security zone and closed to foreign investment, but there are substantial mineral deposits in the foothills of the Andes. Investment is now being encouraged by new legislation introduced in 1993. The first major project will be the Bajo de la Alumbrera porphyry copper and gold deposit in Catamarca which is believed to have 752 million tonnes of ore. Mining operations will start in 1997 and production should reach 180,000 tonnes of copper and 640,000 ozs of gold a year. Another copper-gold deposit in Catamarca is Agua Rica, which could be developed into an open pit mine to rival Alumbrera. Both are being developed by Australian and Canadian companies. Lithium deposits at the Salar del Hombre Muerto dry lake bed also in Catamarca are believed to be sufficient for 70 years' production.

Recent trends In the 1980s large fiscal deficits, monetary expansion and a high velocity of circulation caused very high inflation, which was difficult to curb because of structural imbalances in the economy, inadequate levels of investment and inefficiencies and corruption in both the public and private sectors. The Government introduced several stabilization programmes, the first of which was the Austral Plan, named after the currency it introduced, but none was successful. Output and investment contracted as confidence was eroded and the economy became increasingly dollarized. The external debt rose sharply but rescheduling agreements with commercial bank creditors backed by IMF financing facilities all collapsed as policy commitments were not met and payment arrears mounted.

The Menem administration tackled structural economic reform, which initially brought further recession and unemployment. In 1991 it passed a Convertibility Law, fixing the peso at par with the US dollar and permitting the Central Bank to print local currency only if it is fully backed by gold or hard currency. This was the key to achieving price stability; the annual average growth of consumer prices fell from 3,080% in 1989 to 3.9% in 1994 and remained in single figures thereafter. Dozens of state companies were privatized, many using debt reduction techniques. Fiscal surpluses were recorded in 1992-93 and gdp growth rates averaging 7.7% a year were recorded in 1991-94. After a current account surplus in 1990, increasing deficits were recorded in following years, reaching nearly US$10bn in 1994, but these were amply financed by capital inflows and international reserves increased. Imports soared from US$3.7bn in 1990 to US$19.9bn in 1994, while gross domestic investment in the same years rose by 22% to 23% of gdp. In 1993 an agreement was signed with international banks to restructure bank debt by securitizing it into bonds, following the Mexican model of debt or debt service reduction.

Cracks began to appear in the model in the second half of 1994 when a fiscal deficit became apparent. Tax collections fell and current spending rose. The tax structure concentrates on consumption with a high rate of VAT, but the demand side of the economy had been growing only slowly, partly because of rising unemployment as a result of privatizations and streamlined payrolls. The devaluation of the Mexican peso in Dec 1994 created what became known as the 'tequila effect'. Loss of confidence in Mexico spread to other Latin American countries and Argentina suffered a sharp liquidity squeeze as US$8bn in bank deposits, 15% of the total, fled the country. Many banks were merged, yet at 130, there were still too many for the country's deposit base. Unemployment soared to over 18% by May 1995, consumer demand fell sharply, tax collections dwindled and a recession loomed. Riots broke out in parts of the country as provincial governments failed to pay wages for several months.

The Government turned to the IMF, which negotiated a US$7bn rescue package with multilateral lenders. In 1995 exports rose by 33%, as goods were diverted from the weak domestic market, encouraged by high commodity prices and a consumer boom in Brazil, but gdp declined by 2.5%. The recession appeared to be over by the end of the year, though, with industrial production, imports and demand picking up, and unemployment declining, while 90% of bank deposits had returned. A private pension

Argentina: fact file

Geographic
Land area	2,780,400 sq km
forested	18.6%
pastures	51.9%
cultivated	9.9%

Demographic
Population (1996)	34,995,000
annual growth rate (1991-96)	1.2%
urban	86.9%
rural	13.1%
density	12.5 per sq km

Education and health
Life expectancy at birth,	
male	68.2 years
female	71.5 years
Infant mortality rate	
per 1,000 live births (1994)	20.3
Calorie intake as %	
of FAO requirement	109%
Population age 25 and over	
with no formal schooling	5.7%
Literate males (over 15)	96.2%
Literate females (over 15)	96.2%

Economic and Employment
GNP (1994)	US$275,657mn
GNP per capita	US$8,060
Public external debt (1994)	
	US$66,005mn
Tourism receipts (1994)	US$3,970mn
Inflation (annual av 1990-95)	32.2%
Population economically active (1995)	
	14,345,171
Unemployment rate (1996)	17.0%
Military forces	67,300

Source *Encyclopaedia Britannica*

scheme was launched to ease pressure on the bankrupt state scheme as well as raise the savings ratio, reduce dependence on foreign capital and increase investment funds for industry.

In the first half of 1996 the slow rate of recovery had a negative impact on fiscal revenues and the target for the deficit was exceeded. The introduction of new and unpopular austerity measures led to the dismissal of Finance Minister Cavallo, the architect of the 1990s economic restructuring and liberalization programme, for political reasons. His successor, Roque Fernández, formerly president of the central bank, pursued similar economic policies, which provoked strikes. Nevertheless, gdp expanded by 4% in 1996, with the recovery based on investment and exports rather than domestic consumption. Fiscal revenues improved and were to be boosted in 1997 by more privatizations of state enterprises.

GOVERNMENT

The country's official name is La República Argentina (RA), the Argentine Republic. The form of government has traditionally been a representative, republican federal system. Of the two legislative houses, the Senate has 72 seats, and the Chamber of Deputies 257. By the 1853 Constitution (amended most recently in 1994) the country is divided into a Federal Capital (the city of Buenos Aires) and 23 Provinces. Each Province has its own Governor, Senate and Chamber of Deputies. The municipal government of the Federal Capital is exercised by a Mayor who is directly elected. The Constitution grants the city autonomous rule.

Buenos Aires

APART FROM the capital itself, with its museums, theatres, public buildings, parks and shopping, this region contains the Tigre Delta (waterways, lunch spots).

The Río de la Plata, or River Plate, on which Buenos Aires lies, is not a river but an estuary or great basin, 300 km long and from 37 to 200 km wide, into which flow the Ríos Paraná and Uruguay and their tributaries. It is muddy and shallow and the passage of ocean vessels is only made possible by continuous dredging. The tides are of little importance, for there is only a 1.2m rise and fall at spring tides. The depth of water is determined by the direction of the wind and the flow of the Paraná and Uruguay rivers.

The capital has been virtually rebuilt since the beginning of this century and very few of the old buildings are left. In the centre, which has maintained the original lay-out since its foundation, the streets are often very narrow and are mostly one-way. Its original name, 'Santa María del Buen Ayre' was a recognition of the good winds which brought sailors across the ocean.

BASICS *Area*, the capital spreads over some 200 sq km; together with Gran Buenos Aires (including the suburbs in the province of Buenos Aires), the area is 4,326 sq km. The *population* of the Federal Capital itself is about 2.92 million, but the population of greater Buenos Aires is 10.87 million. *Phone code* 01.

NB Extreme humidity and unusual pollen conditions may affect asthma sufferers.

Street numeration: numbers start from the dock side rising from E to W, but N/S streets are numbered from Av Rivadavia, one block N of Av de Mayo rising in both directions. Calle Juan D Perón used to be called Cangallo and MT de Alvear is still referred to by its old name, Charcas.

PLACES OF INTEREST

The heart of the city, now as in colonial days, is the Plaza de Mayo; around it are the historic *Cabildo* (Town Hall) where the movement for independence from Spain was first planned; the Casa Rosada (Presidential Palace); the Municipalidad (City Hall); and the Cathedral. (For a note on the Mothers of the Plaza de Mayo, see page 80.) Within a few blocks are the fashionable church of Nuestra Señora de la Merced and the main banks and business houses.

Running W from the Plaza, the Av de Mayo leads 1½ km to the Congress building in the Plaza del Congreso. Halfway it crosses the wide Av 9 de Julio. The Av 9 de Julio itself, one of the widest in the world, consists of three major carriageways, with heavy traffic, separated in some parts by wide grass borders. In the N the Av 9 de Julio meets the Av del Libertador, the principal way out of the city to the N and W.

North of the Plaza de Mayo is the shopping, theatre and commercial area. The city's traditional shopping centre, C Florida, is the popular down-town meeting

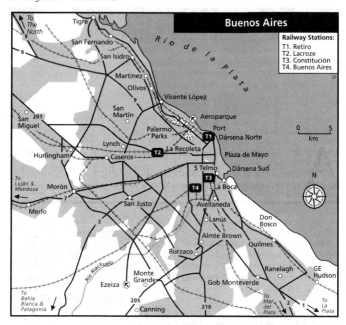

place, particularly in the late afternoon; it is reserved for pedestrians only and the buskers in the 500 block are worth visiting. Another shopping street is Av Santa Fe, which crosses Florida at Plaza San Martín. Av Corrientes is the entertainment centre, a street of theatres, restaurants, cafés and night life. Close by, in C Lavalle (part reserved to pedestrians) and in nearby streets, there are numerous cinemas and many good restaurants.

East of the Plaza de Mayo, behind the Casa Rosada, a broad avenue, Paseo Colón, runs S towards San Telmo and the picturesque old port district known as La Boca, where the Riachuelo flows into the Plata. La Boca is reached by bus 152 from Av L N Alem, or bus 29 from Plaza de Mayo, in the centre, US$0.50. For a tour of La Boca, start at Plaza Vuelta de Rocha, near Av Pedro de Mendoza and Dr Del Valle Iberucea, then walk up Caminito, the little pedestrian street used as a theatre and an art market. Visit the Museo de Bellas Artes de la Boca (see page 78). La Boca, mostly Italian, has its own distinctive life and parts of it are becoming touristy, but the area, with the adjacent industrial and meat-packing suburb of Avellaneda across the high Avellaneda bridge, is generally dirty and run down.

One of the few places which still has late colonial and Rosista buildings is the *barrio* of San Telmo, S of Plaza de Mayo, centred on Plaza Dorrego along the slope which marks the old beach of the Río de la Plata. It is a recognized artistic centre, with plenty of cafés, antique shops and a pleasant atmosphere; and there is a regular Sun morning antiques market at the Plaza Dorrego (see page 91). The 29 bus connects La Boca with San Telmo, and passes the end of C Florida. East of San Telmo on the far side of the docks, the spacious Av Costanera runs along the Plata estuary. The Puerto Madero dock area has been renovated, the 19th century warehouses being turned into restaurants and bars, a popular nightspot. A stretch of marshland reclaimed from the river forms the interesting **Costanera Sur Wildlife Reserve**, where there are many *coypu* (large rodents) and more than 200 species of birds including the rare black-headed duck and the curve-billed reed hunter. The entrance is at Av Tristán Achabal Rodríguez 1550 (reached by buses 4 and 2); it opens daily from 0700-2000 (free, guided tours available at weekends), but much can be seen from the road before then (binoculars useful). There are three trails ranging from 2 km to 6 km long. In summer it is very hot with little shade. For details, contact *Fundación Vida Silvestre*, Defensa 245, p 6, 1075 Buenos Aires, T 331-4864/343-3778.

Principal Public Buildings

Casa de Gobierno on the E side of the Plaza de Mayo, and called the *Casa Rosada* because it is pink, contains the offices of the President of the Republic. It is notable for its statuary, the rich furnishing of its halls and for its libraries. The Museo de los Presidentes is on the lower floors (see under **Museums**). Behind the building, in the semicircular Parque Colón, is a large statue of Columbus.

The **Cabildo**, or old town hall, on the W side of the same Plaza, was put up in 1711 but has been rebuilt several times. In 1940 it was declared a National Monument. See under **Museums**.

Antiguo Congreso Nacional (Old Congress Hall) on the S of the Square, built 1864, is a National Monument. It has been encircled and built over by the Banco Hipotecario. Guided tours Thur, 1500-1700, free.

Palacio del Congreso (Congress Hall) to the SW at the far end of Av de Mayo, of great size and in Greco-Roman architecture, is the seat of the legislature. It contains the Senate and the Chamber of Deputies. There is limited access for the public at sittings announced a week in advance. Passes are given in the Anexo 10 mins before sessions; there they take your passport and give you a ticket for your seat and a pink slip to reclaim your passport. Guided tour in English on Mon,

Tues and Fri at 1100 and 1700 when Congress is not sitting.

Teatro Colón, one of the world's great opera houses, overlooks Av 9 de Julio, with its main entrance on Libertad, between Tucumán and Viamonte. The Colón's interior is resplendent with red plush and gilt; the stage is huge, and salons, dressing rooms and banquet halls are equally sumptuous. The season runs from April to early Dec, and there are concert performances most days. Open daily to visitors (not Sun), guided tours Mon-Fri hourly 0900-1600, Sat 0900-1200, in Spanish, French and English, US$5 (children US$2), from entrance at Viamonte 1180, recommended. Closed Jan-Feb, T 382-6632. Tickets, sold several days before performance, on the C Tucumán side of the theatre. The cheapest seat is US$6 (available even on the same day), and there are free performances most days (Tues-Fri) at 1730 in the Salón Dorado – check programme in the visitors' entrance.

The **Bolsa de Comercio**, built in 1916 is a handsome building containing the stock exchange (entrance 25 de Mayo y Sarmiento).

Churches

Most historic churches apart from the Cathedral are open 0730-1230, 1600-2000.

The **Cathedral**, Rivadavia 437, on the N of Plaza de Mayo, is flanked by the former residence of the Archbishop. On this site was built the first church in Buenos Aires, which after reconstruction in 1677 collapsed in 1753 and the rebuilding was not completed until 1823. The 18th century towers were never rebuilt, so that the architectural proportions have suffered. The tomb (1878) of the Liberator, Gen José de San Martín, is imposing. Masses: Mon-Fri 0900,1100,1230, Sat 1730, Sun 1100,1200,1300. Visiting hours Mon-Fri 0800-1830, Sat 0900-1230, 1700-1930, Sun 0900-1400, 1600-1930.

San Ignacio de Loyola, Alsina y Bolívar 225, built 1710-1734, is the oldest Colonial building in Buenos Aires. It has two lofty towers. Open weekends 1700 (guided tours only).

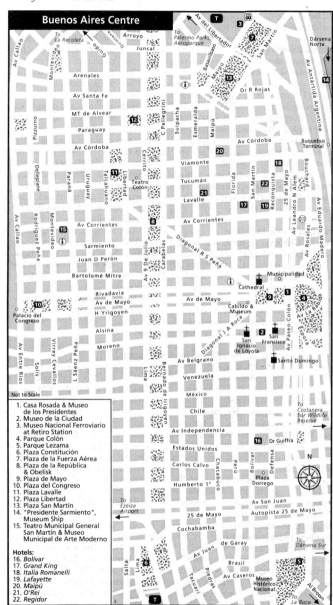

Buenos Aires Centre

To La Recoleta

Av del Libertador

To Palermo Parks, Aeroparque

Dársena Norte

Arroyo

Juncal

Guido

Arenales

Av Santa Fe

MT de Alvear

Paraguay

Av Córdoba

Viamonte

Tucumán

Lavalle

Av Corrientes

Sarmiento

Juan D Perón

Bartolomé Mitre

Rivadavia

Av de Mayo

H Yrigoyen

Alsina

Moreno

Av Belgrano

Venezuela

México

Chile

Av Independencia

Estados Unidos

Carlos Calvo

Humberto 1°

25 de Mayo

Cochabamba

Callao

Montevideo

Rodríguez Peña

Paraná

Uruguay

Talcahuano

Libertad

Cerrito

C Pellegrini

Suipacha

Esmeralda

Maipú

Florida

San Martín

Reconquista

25 de Mayo

Av Leandro N Alem

Av Córdoba

Dr R Rojas

Basavilbaso

Maipú

San Martín

Marcelo T de Alvear

Dárdeno

Av Antártida Argentina

Buquebus Terminal

Diagonal R S Peña

Diagonal J A Roca

Av Paseo Colón

Av de Mayo

Cabildo & Museum

San Ignacio de Loyola

San Francisco

Santo Domingo

Municipalidad

Cathedral

Av La Rábida

To Costanera Sur Wildlife Reserve

Dr Guiffra

Defensa

Bolívar

Perú

Chacabuco

Plaza Dorrego

N

Av San Juan

Autopista 25 de Mayo

de Garay

Brasil

Av Caseros

Museo Histórico Nacional

To Dársena Sur

Al Brown

To La Boca

Av Juan

Tacuarí

Piedras

Salta

To Ezeiza Airport

Lima

Bernardo de Irigoyen

Carabelas

Av 9 de Julio

Solís

Virrey Cevallos

L Sáenz Peña

Av Entre Ríos

Av Callao

Palacio del Congreso

Teatro Colón

Delpilar

Parará

Pizzurno

Not to Scale

1. Casa Rosada & Museo de los Presidentes
2. Museo de la Ciudad
3. Museo Nacional Ferroviario at Retiro Station
4. Parque Colón
5. Parque Lezama
6. Plaza Constitución
7. Plaza de la Fuerza Aérea
8. Plaza de la República & Obelisk
9. Plaza de Mayo
10. Plaza del Congreso
11. Plaza Lavalle
12. Plaza Libertad
13. Plaza San Martín
14. "Presidente Sarmiento", Museum Ship
15. Teatro Municipal General San Martín & Museo Municipal de Arte Moderno

Hotels:
16. Bolívar
17. Grand King
18. Italia Romanelli
19. Lafayette
20. Maipú
21. O'Rei
22. Regidor

San Francisco, Alsina y Defensa, controlled by the Franciscan Order, was built 1730-1754 and given a new façade in 1808.

La Merced, J D Perón y Reconquista 207, was founded 1604 and rebuilt 1760-1769. One of the altars has a wooden figure of Nuestro Señor, carved during the 18th century by an Indian in Misiones. It has one of the few fine carillons of bells in Buenos Aires.

Santo Domingo, Defensa y Belgrano, was founded in 1751. During the British attack on Buenos Aires in 1806 some of Whitelocke's soldiers took refuge in the church. The local forces bombarded it (some of the hits can still be seen on one of the towers); the British capitulated and their regimental colours were preserved in the church. A flame burns over the gate in memory of Gen Belgrano who died nearby. There are summer evening concerts in the church; check times.

El Pilar, Junín 1904, is a jewel of colonial architecture dating from 1732, facing onto the public gardens of the Plaza Recoleta. A fine wooden image of San Pedro de Alcántara, attributed to the famous 17th century Spanish sculptor Alonso Cano, is preserved in a side chapel on the left.

Next to it is the **Cemetery of the Recoleta**, entrance at Junín 1822, not far from Museo de Bellas Artes (see below). It is one of the sights of Buenos Aires (open 0700-1800). "A Doric portico gives on to the main, paved, cypress-lined avenue of a little city of the dead. At the end of the avenue there is a great bronze statue of the resurrected Saviour; on either side, hard up against each other, like houses in a street, there are the family vaults of the Argentine patricians. Every possible style of architecture is represented." GS Fraser, in *News from Latin America*. Evita Perón is buried here; her tomb is marked beside the inscription, Familia Duarte: from the entrance go to the main plaza; turn left and where this avenue meets a main avenue (about 13 'blocks'), turn right; take the 2nd or 3rd passage on the left. On Sat and Sun there is a good craft market near the entrance (1100-1800). The Centro Cultural Ciudad de Buenos Aires alongside the Recoleta cemetery specializes in contemporary local art with many free exhibitions by young artists. Several colectivos: 110, 17; 60 (walk from corner of Las Heras y Junín, 2 blocks); from downtown, eg Correo Central, 61/62, 93, to Pueyrredón casi Av del Libertador, or 130 to Facultad de Derecho.

La Chacarita, another well known cemetery, has the much-visited, lovingly-tended tombs of Juan Perón and Carlos Gardel, the tango singer. It is reached by Subte to the Federico Lacroze station.

Museums, libraries and art exhibitions

NB State and municipal museums and parks are free on Wed. Check opening hours with Tourist Office; many close in Jan or Feb.

Museo de los Presidentes (basement of Casa Rosada), Hipólito Yrigoyen 219. Historical memorabilia, particularly of Former Presidents, 19th century tunnels (open Tues, Wed, Thur 0900-1400, Fri, Sun 1400-1800).

Museo de Bellas Artes (National Gallery), Av del Libertador 1473, T 801-3390. In addition to a fine collection of European works, particularly strong in the 19th century French school, there are 16th and 17th century paintings representing the conquest of Mexico, many good Argentine works including new 19th and 20th century exhibits, and wooden carvings from the Argentine hinterland. Open Tues-Sun 1230-1930, Sat 0930-1930. Entrance US$1 (Thur free), ISIC holders free. Warmly recommended.

The Museo Nacional de Arte Decorativo, Av del Libertador 1902, contains collections of painting, furniture, porcelain, crystal, sculpture; classical music concerts Wed and Thur; open daily except Tues 1400-1900, T 802-6606, US$2, half-price to ISIC holders, closed January. The building is shared with the **Museo Nacional de Arte Oriental**; permanent exhibition of Chinese, Japanese, Hindu and Islamic art, open daily 1500-1900.

Biblioteca Nacional (The National Library), founded in 1810. About 500,000 volumes and 10,000 manuscripts, now housed in futuristic new building at Av del Libertador 1600 y Agüero 2502, T 806-6155, where only a fraction of the stock is available. Cultural events and festivals held here.

Museo Nacional de Historia, Defensa 1600, Parque Lezama, in San Telmo, T 307-4457. Trophies and mementoes of historical events, divided into halls depicting stages of Argentine history. Here are San Martín's uniforms, a replica of his sabre, and the original furniture and door of the house in which he died at Boulogne.

Museo de la Ciudad, Alsina 412, T 343-2123. Permanent exhibition covering social history and popular culture, special exhibitions on daily life in Buenos Aires changed every 2 months, and a reference library open to the public. Open Mon-Fri, 1100-1900, Sun, 1500-1900. Open all year, US$1.

Museo y Biblioteca Mitre, San Martín 336, T 394-8240, preserves intact the household of President Bartolomé Mitre; has coin and map collection and historical archives. Open Mon-Fri 1330-1830, US$1.

Museo de Ciencias Naturales Bernardino Rivadavia, Av Angel Gallardo 470, facing Parque Centenario, T 982-5243. It houses palaeontological, zoological, mineralogical, botanical, archaeological and marine sections. Meteorites from Campo del Cielo on display. Open all year, daily, 1400-1730 (closed holidays), US$0.50. Library, Mon-Fri, 1100-1700.

Museo de la Dirección Nacional del Antártico, Angel Gallardo 470, in the Museo de Ciencias Naturales, Tues, Thur and Sun, 1400-1800. Specimens of flora, fauna and fossils and a library of taped birdsong.

Museo Municipal de Arte Moderno, San Juan 350, with a salon at Av Corrientes 1530, 9th floor: international exhibitions and a permanent collection of 20th century art; open Mon-Fri 1000-2000, Sat and Sun 1200-2000, US$1.50 (US$1 at the salon, Wed free), T 361-1121.

Museo de Arte Moderno Eduardo Sivori, Pasaje de la Infanta Isabel 555, T 774-9452, emphasis on 19th and 20th century Argentine art, Tues-Sun 1200-2000, US$1.

Museo de Bellas Artes de la Boca, Pedro de Mendoza 1835, La Boca, has many works on local life, contemporary Argentine painting, also sculptures and figureheads rescued from ships. Mon-Fri 0800-1800, Sat-Sun 1000-1700, T 301-1080, entrance free.

Museo de la Asociación Evaristo Carriego, Honduras 3784, tango museum of the writer, open Mon-Fri 1300-2000.

Museo de Motivos Populares Argentinos José Hernández, Av Libertador 2373, widest collection of Argentine folkloric art, with rooms dedicated to Indian, colonial and Gaucho artefacts; handicraft sale and library. Open Wed-Fri 1300-1900, Sat and Sun 1500-1900. T 802-7294 for guided visits in English or French. Entrance US$1 (closed in Feb).

Museo de Esculturas Luis Perlotti, Pujol 642, T 431-2825, in the former workshop of this Argentine sculptor, Tues-Fri 1400-1900, Sat/Sun1000-1300, 1400-2000, US$1.

Museo del Instituto Nacional Sanmartiniano, Gral Ramón Castilla and Av A M de Aguado; Mon-Fri 0900-1700. Replica of San Martín's house in exile in Grand Bourg near Paris, T 802-3311 in advance.

Museo del Cabildo y la Revolución de Mayo, Bolívar 65, is the old Cabildo building, converted into a museum in 1940. It contains paintings, documents, furniture, arms, medals, maps, all recording the May 1810 revolution, and memorabilia of the 1806 British attack; also Jesuit art. In the patio is La Posta del Cabildo café and stalls selling handicrafts. Tues-Fri 1230-1900, Sun 1500-1900. T 334-1782 for English tours. Library, Mon-Fri, 1100-1900. Entry free.

Museo Municipal de Cine, Sarmiento 2573, T 952-4598, traces the development of Argentine cinema and contains permanent exhibitions on María Luisa Bemberg and Niní Marshall, Mon-Fri 1000-1830, US$1.

Museo de Arte Hispanoamericano Isaac Fernández Blanco, Suipacha 1422. Contains a most interesting and valuable collection of colonial art, especially silver, in a beautiful colonial mansion. Tues-

Sun, 1400-1900, entry US$2. Thur free; closed January. For guided visits in English or French T 327-0228; guided tours in Spanish Sat, Sun 1600.

Museo y Biblioteca Ricardo Rojas, Charcas 2837 (Tues-Fri 1400-1800). The famous writer Rojas lived in this beautiful colonial house for several decades. It contains his library, souvenirs of his travels, and many intriguing literary and historical curios.

Museo Numismático del Banco Central, San Martín 216, 1st floor, T 394-8411, fascinating, well kept, Tues 1000-1400, Wed and Fri tour at 1400, free, overlooks central foyer, ask guard for directions. Not to be confused with **Museo Numismático e Histórico del Banco Nacion**, B Mitre 326, 1st floor, coins and notes, furniture and historical documents, Mon-Fri 1000-1500, T 342-4041, ext 607.

Fragata Presidente Sarmiento, Av Dávila y Cangallo, Puerto Madero, a sailing ship used as a naval training ship until 1961; now a museum. Open Mon-Fri 0900-2000, Sat-Sun 1000-2200, US$1. Nearby is the **Corbata Uruguay**, the sailing ship which rescued Otto Nordenskjold's Antarctic expedition in 1903. Open daily 0800-2000 all year, US$1.

Bank of London and South America (now Lloyds Bank, BLSA), Bartolomé Mitre y Reconquista, has a miniature museum on its fifth floor. Open during banking hours; the building, designed by SEPRA (Santiago Sánchez Elia, Federico Peralta Ramos, and Alfredo Agostini) and completed in 1963 is worth seeing. Next door is the **Banco de Córdoba**, designed by the brilliant Córdoba architect Miguel Angel Roca, completed in the early 1970s.

Museo Nacional de Aeronáutica, Av Costanera Rafael Obligado 4550, next to Aeroparque/Jorge Newbery airport. Many civil and military aircraft, plus displays of navigational material, documents, equipment, US$3, Tues-Fri 0830-1630, Sun 1400-1900, T 773-0665.

Museo Nacional Ferroviario, Av del Libertador 405, behind Retiro station. For railway fans, locomotives, machinery, documents of the Argentine system's history. Building in very poor condition.

Mon-Fri, 0900-1800, Sat 0900-1200, free, T 325-5353. Archives 1100-1800.

Museo del Teatro Colón, Tucumán 1161, T 382-1430. Documents and objects related to the theatre since 1908. Mon-Fri 0900-1600, Sat 0900-1200, closed in Jan.

Museo Histórico Saavedra (also known as the Museo Histórico de la Ciudad de Buenos Aires, not to be confused with Museo de la Ciudad), Crisólogo Larralde (Republiquetas) 6409, T 572-0746. City history from the 18th century, furniture, arms, documents, jewellery, coins and religious art; daily guided tours. Tues-Fri, 0900-1800, Sun 1400-1800, US$1, closed February.

Museo de la Policía Federal San Martín 353, p 8-9, T 394-6857. Interesting but extremely gruesome forensic section (for strong stomachs only; no one under 15 admitted), Tues-Fri 1400-1800.

Museo Penitenciario Argentino Antonio Ballue, Humberto I 378. Museum of the penal system; Tues-Fri 1000-1200, 1400-1700, Sun 1000-1200, 1300-1700. Entrance US$1

Museo del Teatro Nacional Cervantes, Córdoba y Libertad, history of the theatre in Argentina, Mon-Fri 1430-1800, Sat, Sun 1000-1300, T 815-8881 in advance.

Museo Internacional de Caricatura y Humorismo, Lima 1037, originals of cartoons and caricatures of 20th century, but small international section, admission US$0.50, Mon, Tues, Thur, Fri, 1700-2000, Sat 1200-1700.

Museo de Armas, Av Santa Fe 750, T 311-1071. All kinds of weaponry related to Argentine history, including the 1982 South Atlantic conflict, plus Oriental weapons, Tues-Fri 1400-1930, Sat 1100-1700, Sun 1300-1800, closed 15 Dec-15 Mar, US$1.

Museo de Telecomunicaciones in a magnificent building on the Costanera Sur, Av de los Italianos 851, T 312-5405, Fri, Sat, Sun 1400-1800.

Jewish Museum, Libertad 773, religious objects relating to Jewish presence in Argentina, Tues-Thur 1600-1800.

Museo de Arte Español Enrique Larreta, Juramento 2291, Belgrano (entrance on Av Rafael Obligado). Sat-Sun 1500-1900; Mon, Tues, Fri 1400-1945. Closed Wed, Thur and Jan, US$1. The home of the writer Larreta, with paintings and religious art; T 783-2640 for guided tour in language other than Spanish. Also **Biblioteca Alfonso El Sabio**, Mon-Fri, 1300-1930.

Museo Histórico Sarmiento, Cuba 2079, T 783-7555. Belgrano, the National Congress and presidential offices in 1880; documents and personal effects of Sarmiento; library of his work, Thur-Sun 1500-1900 (2000 in summer).

Museo Etnográfico JB Ambrosetti, Moreno 350, anthropological and ethnographic collections from around the world, including Bolivian and Mapuche silverwork, US$1, Mon-Fri 1400-1800 (1900 on Sat, Sun; closed Feb), T 331-7788.

Parks

Parque Lezama, Defensa y Brasil, originally one of the most beautiful in the city, has an imposing statue of Pedro de Mendoza, who, in 1535, founded the original city, according to tradition on this spot. The park is very lively on Sun.

The **Palermo Parks**, officially known as the Parque Tres de Febrero, with their magnificent avenues are famous for their rose garden, Andalusian Patio, Japanese garden (admission US$2) and the Hipódromo Argentino (the Palermo race course) with seats for 45,000 (Sun, 1500, entry: US$3, senior citizens free). Opposite the parks are the Botanical and Zoological Gardens (the Zoo and Japanese Garden are closed on Mon). Nearby are the Municipal Golf Club, Buenos Aires Lawn Tennis Club, riding clubs and polo field, and the Club de Gimnasia y Esgrima (Athletic and Fencing Club).

The **Planetarium** (just off Belisario Roldán, in Palermo Park), is open Sat and Sun only (1500, 1630, 1800), entry US$5. At the entrance are several large meteorites from Campo del Cielo (see page 187). Reached by Subte line D.

The **Show Grounds** of the Argentine Rural Society, next to Palermo Park, entrance on Plaza Italia, stage the Annual Livestock Exhibition, known as Exposición Rural, in July.

The **Municipal Botanical Gardens**, Santa Fe 2951, entrance from Plaza Italia (take Subte, line D), contain characteristic specimens of the world's vegetation. The trees native to the different provinces of Argentina are brought together in one section. The Gardens, closed at 1800, contain the Museo del Jardín Botánico, T 831-2951, whose collection of Argentine Flora is open Mon-Fri 0700-1600. The Gardens are full of stray cats, fed regularly by local residents.

The **Zoo**, opp the Botanical Gardens, has been privatized and is open Tues-Sun 0930-1830, guided visits available, US$4 entry for adults, children under 13 free.

Plazas

On the Plaza de Mayo, the **Mothers of the Plaza de Mayo** march in remembrance of their children who disappeared during the crisis of the 1970s (their address is H Yrigoyen 1442). The Mothers still march anti-clockwise round the central monument every Thur at 1530, with photos of their 'disappeared' loved-ones pinned to their chests.

The **Plaza San Martín**, has a monument to San Martín in the centre and, at the N end, a memorial with an eternal flame to those who fell in the South Atlantic conflict of 1982.

Other plazas include: the **Plaza de la Fuerza Aérea** (formerly Plaza Británica), with the clock tower presented by British and Anglo-Argentine residents, 'a florid Victorian sentinel, royal crest upon its bosom' (frequently vandalized); the Plaza Canadá (in front of the Retiro Station) in which there is a Pacific Northwest Indian totem pole, donated by the Canadian government; the Plaza Lavalle (see **Markets**, below); the **Plaza del Congreso**, the largest in the city, with a waterfall, floodlit at 2145; Plaza Francia, between Centro Cultural Recoleta and Museo de Bellas Artes, pleasant trees. There is also the great **Plaza de la República**, with a 67m obelisk commemorating the 400th anniversary of the city's founding at the junction between Av Roque Saenz Peña, Av 9 de Julio and Av Corrientes.

LOCAL INFORMATION

● Accommodation

Hotel prices

L1	over US$200	**L2**	US$151-200
L3	US$101-150	**A1**	US$81-100
A2	US$61-80	**A3**	US$46-60
B	US$31-45	**C**	US$21-30
D	US$12-20	**E**	US$7-11
F	US$4-6	**G**	up to US$3

Unless otherwise stated, all hotels in range **D** and above have private bath. Assume friendliness and cleanliness in all cases.

All hotels, guest houses, inns and camping sites are graded by the number of beds available, and the services supplied. The Dirección de Turismo fixes maximum and minimum rates for 1, 2 and 3-star hotels, guest houses and inns, but the ratings do not provide any very useful guidance. 4 and 5-star hotels are free to apply any rate they wish. Hotels in the upper ranges can often be booked more cheaply through Buenos Aires Travel Agencies.

The following list is only a selection; exclusion does not necessarily imply non-recommendation. Rates given below are generally the minimum rates. Room tax is 15% and is not always included in the price. Air conditioning is a must in high summer. Many of the cheaper hotels in the central area give large reductions on the daily rate for long stays. Hotels with red-green lights or marked *Albergue Transitorio* are hotels for homeless lovers (for stays of 1½-2 hrs).

5-star hotels in our L1-2 range: *Alvear Palace*, Av Alvear 1891, T 804-4031, F 804-6110, older-style, nr Recoleta, with roof garden, shopping gallery, elegant, extremely good; *Caesar Park*, Posadas 1232, T 814-5151, F 814-5157, pool, solarium; *Claridge*, Tucumán 535, T 314-7700, F 314-8022, highly rec, but not its restaurant; *Etoile*, R Ortiz 1835 in Recoleta, T 804-8603, outstanding location, rooftop pool, rooms with kitchenette, rec; *Libertador Kempinski*, Córdoba y Maipú, T 322-0032, F 322-9703; *Marriott Plaza*, Florida 1005, T 318-3000, F 318-3008, good restaurant; *Panamericano/Holiday Inn Crowne Plaza*, Carlos Pellegrini 525, T 393-6017, F 348-5250; *Park Hyatt*, Posadas 1088, T 326-1234, F 326-3736; *Sheraton*, San Martín 1225, T 318-9000, F 311-6353, good buffet breakfast.

4-star: L3 *Best Western Confort*, Viamonte 1501, T 814-4917, with breakfast, English spoken, 50% ISIC discount; **L3** *Bisonte*, Paraguay 1207, T 394-8041, F 393-9086, a/c, bar, modern, central, good value; **L3** *Bisonte Palace*, MT de Alvear y Suipacha, T 328-4751, F 328-6476, very good, welcoming; **A1** *Bristol*, Cerrito 286,

T 382-3228, F 382-3384, good breakfast; **A1** *Carsson*, Viamonte 650, T 322-3601, F 332 3551, comfortable, quiet except rooms on street (ending in 17); **L3** *Continental*, Saenz Peña 725, with breakfast, comfortable; **L2** *Crillón*, Santa Fe 796, T 312-8181, comfortable, good breakfast; **L3** *Gran King*, Lavalle 560, T 393 4012/4052, helpful, English spoken; **L3** *Lancaster*, Córdoba 405, T 312-4061, F 311-3021, inc breakfast, expensive laundry service, charming; **L3** *Principado*, Paraguay 481, T 313-3022, F 313-3952, with breakfast, central, helpful; **A3** *Regidor*, Tucumán 451, T 314-9516, F 311-7441, a/c, breakfast inc, rec; **L2** *Regente Palace*, Suipacha 964, T 328 6628, F 328-7460, very good, central, English spoken, buffet breakfast, sports facilities, stores luggage; *Salles*, 9 de Julio/Cerrito y J D Perón, 2 blocks from Obelisco, T 382-0091, F 382-0754, rec.

3-star: **L2** *Camino Real*, Maipú 572, T 322-3162, F 325-9756, pleasant, central; **A2** *City*, Bolivar 160, T 342 6481, F 342-6486, rec; **A3** *Constitución Palace*, Lima 1697, T 305-9020, with breakfast, 30% ISIC discount; **A1** *Deauville*, Talcahuano 1253, T 813-1427, F 814-5732, a/c, restaurant, bar, garage, rec; **A2** *Ecuador*, Alsina 2820, nr Plaza Once, T 956-0533, F 97-9987, rec; **A1** *Embajador*, Pellegrini 1181, T 393-9485, good; **A2** *Eibar*, Florida 328, T 325-0969, with breakfast, quiet, helpful, old fashioned; **A3** *Gran Orly*, Paraguay 474, T/F 312-5344, good location, old fashioned, helpful, good lunches, English spoken, has some rooms for 4, holds mail for guests, arranges tours and taxis, a/c; **A1** *Italia Romanelli*, Reconquista 647, T/F 312-6361, comfortable, rec; **A1** *Liberty*, Corrientes 632, T/F 325-0261, with breakfast, English spoken, luggage stored, various sized rooms; **A3** *Promenade*, M T de Alvear 444, T/F 312-5681, no charge for credit cards, helpful, stores luggage, rec; **A2** *Regis*, Lavalle 813, T 327-2613, F 312-5681, good value, nice atmosphere; **A2** *Sarmiento Palace*, Sarmiento 1953, T 953 3404, comfortable, English spoken, rec; **A2** *Víctory*, Maipú 880, T 314-0655, F 322-8415, a/c, modern, heating, TV, comfortable, luggage storage unreliable; **A3** *Waldorf*, Paraguay 450, T 312-2071, F 312-2079, comfortable, rooms of varying standards, garage, a/c, rec.

2-star: **A3** *Goya*, Suipacha 748, T 322-9269, a/c, quiet, nr Buquebus; **A3** *Gran Hotel de la Paix*, Rivadavia 1187, T 383-7140, old but good, large rooms; **A3** *Gran Hotel Hispano*, Av de Mayo 861, T 342-3472, spacious, pleasant patio, stores luggage, helpful; **A3** *Mundial*, Av de Mayo 1298, T 383-0011, F 383-6318, comfortable; **A3** *Plaza Roma*, Lavalle 110, T/F 311-1679, inc breakfast, rec; **A3** *San Antonio*, Paraguay 372, T 312-5381, nice atmosphere, garden, rec; **A3** *Tres Sargentos*, Tres

Sargentos 345, T 312-6081, secure, new bathrooms, good value; **A2** *Ayacucho Palace*, Ayacucho 1408, T 806-1815, F 806-4467, 10 mins from centre bus 10, very helpful, rec; **B** *Astoria*, Av de Mayo 916, T/F 334-9061, very hospitable.

1-star or below: **A3** *Aguirre*, Aguirre 1041, T 773-5027, safe; **B** *Ceballos Palace*, Virrey Ceballos 261, 2 blocks from Congreso, T 372-7636, safe (next to police HQ); **A3** *Central Córdoba*, San Martín 1021, T/F 312-8524, very central, helpful, quiet, good value; **B** *Europa*, Mitre 1294, T 381-9629, a/c, 10% ISIC discount; **B** *Hispano Argentino*, Catamarca 167, T 304-5835, some rooms with bath, quiet, convenient; **B** *Juncal Palace*, Juncal 2282, T 821-2770, old fashioned, 20% ISIC discount; **A3** *Kings*, Corrientes 623, T 322-8161, F 393-4452, with breakfast, a/c, helpful, top floor rooms have balcony; **B** *Lisboa*, Mitre 1282, T 383-1141, with breakfast, central; **B** *Maipú*, Maipú 735, T 322-5142, popular, hot water, basic, stores luggage, laundry facilities, rec; **A3** *Majestic*, Libertad 121, T 351-949, Subte Lima, colonial-style, good value, inc breakfast; **B** *Marbella*, Av de Mayo 1261, T/F 383-3573, modernized, quiet, breakfast pricey, fans, English spoken, highly rec, no credit cards; **C** *Mediterráneo*, Rodríguez Peña 149, T 476-2852, basic, central, helpful, safe, stores luggage, laundry facilities, rec; **B** *Micki*, Talcahuano 362, T 371-2376, no a/c, basic, good value; **B** *O'Rei*, Lavalle 733, T 393-7186, **C** without bath, basic, central, gloomy, popular; **A3** *Orense*, Mitre 1359, T 476-3173, **C** without bath, with breakfast, fan, laundry and cooking facilities, rec; **B** *Reina*, Av de Mayo 1120, T 381-0547, old fashioned, 20% ISIC discount; **B** *Uruguay*, Tacuarí 83, T 334 3456, central, good value, rec; **A3** *Vedra*, Av de Mayo 1350, T 383-0584, stores luggage, rec; **A3** *Versalles*, Arenales 1394, T 811-5214, W of Av 9 de Julio, basic, no breakfast, fine staircase and mirrors; **B** *Vila Seca*, Av de Mayo 776, T 340-952, basic, helpful, noisy; **C** *Bahía*, H Yrigoyen 3062, hot showers, pleasant, safe, central but noisy, rec;

C *Frossard*, Tucumán 686, T 322-1811, heating; **C** *La Giralda*, Tacuarí 17, T 345-3917, student discounts and for long stays, rec; **C** *Maipú*, Maipú 735, popular, basic; **C** *Sil*, H Yrigoyen 775, T 231-8273, nice but no heating; **C** *Sportsman*, Rivadavia 1426, nr Plaza Congreso, T 381-8021/2, old fashioned, without bath, ISIC discount; **D** *Colonial*, Bolívar 1357, nr Constitución station, IYHA reduction, also dormitories, good kitchen; **D** *Hosp Esterlina*, Mitre 1266, old, rambling, dirty. Longer term accommodation (min 2 weeks) is offered by Juan Carlos Dima, Puan 551 C, T 432-4898, F 432-7101, US$450/month per room, kitchen faciities, English spoken.

In San Telmo: **C** *Bolívar*, Bolívar 886, T 361-5105, good; **D** *Res Carly*, Humberto 1° 464, without bath, fan, quiet, basic, kitchen facilities, good value; **D** *Hotel del Parque*, Defensa 1537, basic.

Youth hostels: *Youth Hostel*, Brasil 675 nr Constitución station, T 362-9133, **E** pp with YHA card (ISIC card accepted), inc breakfast, sheets provided, hot water 24 hrs, basic, rec, no cooking facilities, cheap meals, doors closed 1200-1800 and from 0200, women should be aware that they could attract unwelcome attention nr Constitución station as prostitutes operate there; **E** pp *Del Aguila*, Espinosa 1628, T 581-6663, hot water, cooking and laundry facilities, very good, noisy, membership not necessary (buses 24, 105, 106, 109, 146), highly rec. *Red Argentina de Alojamiento para Jóvenes*, Florida 835, p 3, T 315-1457, F 312-6840, has a network of hostels in the country.

Apartments: contracts are usually for at least 1 year and owners will demand a guarantor or a deposit covering at least 6 months rent (security or cash). One agent is Sr Aguilar, Florida 520, 3°-314, T 322-4074. An agency which arranges sharing apartments (often with senior citizens) is Martha Baleiron, Esmeralda 1066, 5°F, T 311-9944; US$50 fee if an apartment is found, US$10 if not. All agencies should provide contracts which

should be read carefully. To rent flats on a daily basis try *Edificios Esmeralda*, M T de Alvear 842, T 311-3929, inc cleaning; facilities for up to 6 persons. Also *Edificio Suipacha*, Suipacha 1235, T/F 322-6685, and *Aspen Apartment Hotel*, Esmeralda 933, T 313-9011; *Edificio Lemonde*, San Martín 839, T 313-2032, rec; *Res Trianon*, Callao 1869, T 812-3335.

Camping: about 15 km out at Lomas de Zamora, US$3 pp/night, inc swimming pool, 24 hr security, take own drinking water; take bus 141 from Plaza Italia or 28 from Pellegrini to Puente La Noria then No 540 to Villa Albertini which passes the entrance.

● **Places to eat**

'The Buenos Aires Herald' publishes a handy *Guide to Good Eating in Buenos Aires* (with a guide to local wines) by Dereck Foster. There is also *El Libro de los Restaurantes de Buenos Aires*, published annually, describing the city's major restaurants. Eating out in Buenos Aires is very good but is expensive. In 1997 good restaurants were charging US$30 pp and up; more modest places were charging US$20-25 pp. **NB** In many mid to upper range restaurants, lunch is far cheaper than dinner. Lunch or dinner in a normal restaurant cost US$9-12 (cutlet, salad, ¼ of table wine, dessert); a portion at a *comidas para llevar* (take away) place cost US$2.50-3.50. Many cheaper restaurants are *tenedor libre*, eat as much as you like for a fixed price.

The following list, for reasons of space, not quality, gives only those restaurants easily accessible for people staying in the city centre. **In the banking district**, between Av Corrientes and Plaza de Mayo: *Clark's*, Sarmiento 645, in old English outfitter's shop (also at Junín 1777), well cooked food, very expensive, busy, fish and lamb specialities, set lunch very good value; *Bolsa de Comercio*, 25 de Mayo 359, downstairs at the Stock Exchange, good but expensive; *London Grill*, Reconquista 455, British, busy, famous for roast beef and turkey curries, open 0800-1700 only; *El Pulpo*, Tucumán 361, very good seafood (US$30 inc wine); *Sabot*, 25 de Mayo 756, very good business lunches; *Brizzi*, Lavalle 445, business lunches, good and worth the visit; *Blab*, Florida 325, sole, veal, pork specialities, lunchtime only; *La Pipeta*, San Martín 498, downstairs, serving for 30 years, good, noisy, closed Sun; *La Estancia*, Lavalle 941, popular with business people, excellent grills and service, expensive; *La Casona del Nonno*, Lavalle 827, popular, *parrilla* and pasta, not cheap; *ABC*, Lavalle 545, traditional, good value; *El Palacio de la Papa Frita*, Lavalle 735 and 954, Corrientes 1612, Laprida 1339, Maipú 431, 10% discount for ISIC and youth card holders; good value *parrillas* at *La Posada del Maipú*, Maipú 440. *Memorabilia*, Maipú 761, pizzas, bar, music, 20% discount for ISIC cards; *La Rural*, Suipacha 453, rec for *parrillada* and *bife de lomo*, expensive or cheaper *table d'hôte*, English-speaking head waiter is excellent; *Pizzería Roma*, Lavalle 800, cheap and good quality, delicious spicy *empanadas* and *ñoquis*, good breakfasts; *Los Inmortales*, Lavalle 746, specializes in pizza, good, 10% ISIC discount. There are other locations: some serve *à la carte* dishes which are plentiful, and are open from 1500-2000 when most other restaurants are closed.

El Figón de Bonilla, rustic style, L N Alem 673, good, another branch at Junín 1721; *Dora*, L N Alem 1016, huge steaks, get there early to beat the queue; *Los Troncos*, Suipacha 732, good grills, US$18 *menú*; *Catalinas*, Reconquista 875, seafood, very expensive. **A few blocks from this district**: *El Aljibe*, at *Sheraton*, smoked salmon, tournedos Rossini, baby beef; *Dolli*, Av del Libertador 312, nr Retiro, very good food, fairly expensive. La Recova, an area on the 1000 block of Posadas, nr *Hyatt*, has several moderate to expensive restaurants, eg *El Mirasol* and La Tasca de Plaza Mayor, No 1052.

Walking up Av Quintana, you reach Plaza

Recoleta. On Roberto M Ortiz are *Lola*, No 1805, good pasta, lamb and fish but expensive; *La Tasca de Germán*, No 1863, highly rec, European. Cross Guido to: *Gato Dumas*, Junín 1745, expensive but has good fixed price menus; *La Bianca*, Junín 1769, very good value, lunch US$16 pp; *Harper's*, Junín 1773; *Munich Recoleta*, Junín 1871, good steaks, pleasant atmosphere, US$20 pp, no credit cards. Nearby, 2 blocks from Recoleta towards Av Callao, *Au Bec Fin*, Vicente López 1827, reservations needed, open 2000-0200 daily; *Rodi Bar*, López 1900, excellent *bife*.

In the San Telmo area: *Calle de Angeles*, Chile 318, nice setting in an old, covered street, high standards; *La Convención de San Telmo*, Carlos Calvo 375, very good food, tango show; *El Repecho de San Telmo*, Carlos Calvo 242, excellent, expensive, reserve in advance (T 362-5473); *La Casa de Esteban de Luca*, Defensa 1000, very good, good wines. For ice cream, *Sumo*, Independencia y Piedras.

The Costanera Rafael Obligado along the river front (far end of Aeroparque) is lined with little eating places (take taxi, or colectivo 45 from Plaza Constitución, Plaza San Martín or Retiro to Ciudad Universitaria): *El Rancho Inn* is best, try also *Happening*, *La Marea* and *Los Años Locos*, good beef, *parrilla*, cold buffet. *Clo Clo*, La Pampa y Costanera, reservation required. Typical *parrilla* at *Rodizio*, Costanera Norte, opp Balneario Coconor, self-service and waiter service, other branches, eg Av Callao y Juncal, good value, popular.

In Puerto Madero, across the docks from Plaza de Mayo, are *Las Lilas*, Dávila 516, excellent *parrilla*; *Cholila*, Dávila 102, Puerto Viamonte, chic; *Xcaret* Dávila 164; *Mirasol*, No 202, and opp, *Bice*, Dávila 192, mostly Italian, good; *Columbus*, popular (all about US$40 pp inc wine and tip); a bit cheaper (US$30-35) are *Bahía Madero*, Dávila 430, highly rec; branches of *Rodizio* and *Happening*.

Near the Teatro Colón: *Tomo Uno*, Carlos Pellegrini 525 (*Hotel Panamericano*), expensive, trout, mignon, shrimp, home-made pasta, closed Sun; *9 de Julio*, Pellegrini 587, very good value; *Edelweiss*, Libertad 431, tuna steaks, pasta, grill, expensive and famous. **By Congreso**: *Quorum*, Combate de los Pozos 61, behind Congress, popular with politicians. Also nr Congress: *Plaza Mayor*, Venezuela 1399, estancia-style, very popular and, opp, *Campo dei Fiori*, Italian, both rec.

Typical Boca restaurants on Necochea, but check the hygiene. They all serve antipasto, pasta and chicken; no point in looking for beef here. All bands are loud. *La Barca*, Av Pedro de Mendoza, on river bank nr Avellaneda bridge, seafood, rec;

also rec for seafood and good value, *Viejo Puente*, Almte Brown 1499. *El Pescadito*, Mendoza 1483, rec for pasta and seafood.

Other recommendations: *Pepito*, Montevideo 381, very good; *Pippo*, Montevideo 341, large pasta house, simple food, very popular, also at Paraná 356; *Chiquilín*, Montevideo 321, pasta and meat, good value; *Los Teatros*, Talcahuano 350, good (live music 2300-0100); *Nazarenas*, Reconquista 1132, good for beef, expensive, rec; *Ostramar*, Santa Fe 3495 y Julián Alvarez (Subte station Ortiz, then walk back towards town), good quality fish; *El Salmón II*, Reconquista 1014, large portions of good food, not cheap.

Other Italian: *Broccolino*, Esmeralda 776, excellent, very popular, try *pechuguitas*; *Mama Liberata*, Maipú 642, excellent; *Prosciutto*, Venezuela 1212. Three famous *pizzerías* in the centre are on Corrientes: *Banchero*, No 1298; *Las Cuartetas*, No 838, and *Los Inmortales*, No 1369, same chain as above; *Il Gatto*, Corrientes 959, popular and reasonably priced.

International Spanish: *El Imparcial*, H Yrigoyen 1204, and opp, *El Globo*, No 1199, both rec. **Swedish**: food at *Swedish Club*, Tacuarí 147, open to non-members. **Hungarian**: *Budapest*, 25 de Mayo 690, cheap. **British**: *The Alexandra*, San Martín 774, curries, fish and seafood, nice bar, closed in evening.

Oriental: *Nuevo Oriental*, Maipú nr Lavalle, Chinese *tenedor libre*, US$6, good choice; *La China*, J D Perón y Montevideo, *tenedor libre*; *Tsuru*, ground floor of *Sheraton*, authentic Japanese, small, rec.

Vegetarian: *Granix*, Florida 126 and 467 *tenedor libre* US$8, bland but filling, lunchtime Mon-Fri. *Ever Green* is a chain of *tenedor libre* vegetarian restaurants, branches: Paraná 746, Sarmiento 1728 and Cabildo 2979; *La Esquina de las Flores*, Córdoba 1599, excellent value, also good health-food shop; *Los Angeles*, Uruguay 707, US$7 for salad bar, main meal and dessert, rec; *La Huerta II*, Lavalle 895, 2nd floor, *tenedor libre*, US$7, reasonable.

Fast food: *Pumper-nic* is a chain of rather pricey fast food restaurants. Many *McDonalds* in the centre. *The Embers*, Callao 1111, fast food, 10% discount for ISIC and youth card holders.

Cheap Meals Several supermarkets have good, cheap restaurants: *Coto* supermarket, Viamonte y Paraná, upstairs; also *Supercoop* stores at Sarmiento 1431, Lavalle 2530, Piedras y Rivadavia and Rivadavia 5708; *Pizzalandia*, on Brasil (nr Youth Hostel) serves cheap *empanadas*, *salteñas* and pizzas. Good snacks all day and night at Retiro and Constitución railway termini. For quick cheap snacks the markets are rec. The snack bars in underground stations are also cheap. *DeliCity* bakeries, several branches, very fresh pastries, sweets, breads, authentic American donuts; *Biscuit House*, bakery chain, 20 branches, *media lunas*, *empanadas* and breads.

For restaurants with shows, see **Nightclubs and folklore** below.

Tea rooms, cafés and bars: *Richmond*, Florida 468 between Lavalle and Corrientes, genteel (chess played between 1200-2400); well-known are the *Confitería Suiza*, Tucumán 753, and the *Florida Garden* Florida y Paraguay. *Confitería Ideal*, Suipacha 384, old, faded, good service, cakes and snacks, rec. Many on Av del Libertador in the Palermo area. *Café Querandí*, Venezuela y Chacabuco, popular with intellectuals and students, good atmosphere, well known for its Gin Fizz. The more bohemian side of the city's intellectual life is centred on Av Corrientes, between Cerrito and Callao, where there are many bars and coffee shops; *Pub Bar Bar O*, Tres Sargentos 451, good music and prices. *El Molino*, Rivadavia y Callao, popular with politicians, nr Congress, Belle Epoque décor, frequent art sales, good value, self service section. *Café 1234*, Santa Fe 1234, good and reasonable; *Clásica y Moderna*, Callao y Paraguay, bookshop at back, expensive but very popular, jazz usually on Wed night, open 24 hrs. Excellent ice-cream at *Freddo*, de Melo y Callao, or Ayacucho y Quintana. Next door (Quintana y Recoleta) is café *La Biela*, restaurant and *whiskería*, elegant. Also in Recoleta: *Café Victoria*, Ortiz 1865, whiskería/sandwichería, popular; *La Vanguardia*, Montevideo 1671, 30% discount for ISIC card; *Café Rix* and *Hard Rock Café*, both in Paseo del Pilar, ISIC and GO 25 discount; *Henry J Bean*, Junín 1747, ISIC and GO 25 discount. On Lavalle there are *whiskerías* and *cervecerías* where you can have either coffee or exotic drinks. *Barila*, Santa Fe 2375, has excellent confectionery. *Café Tortoni*, Av de Mayo 825-9, delicious cakes, coffee, a haunt of artists, very elegant, over 100 years old, interesting *peña* evenings of poetry and music. On Sat at 2315 it becomes a 'Catedral del Jazz', with Fénix Jazz Band, US$15 entrance. *Café El Verdi*, Paraguay 406, also has live music. *Parakultural New Border*, Chacabuco 1072, mostly avant-garde theatre, popular; *Die Schule*, Alsina 1760, hard rock bar with avant-garde theatre. A 'bohemian, bizarre' bar is *El Dorado*, H Yrigoyen 971. Good bars in San Telmo around Plaza Dorrego, eg *El Balcón de la Plaza*, and on Humberto I. Watch whisky prices in bars, much higher than in restaurants. Most cafés serve tea or coffee plus *facturas*, or pastries, for breakfast, US$2.50-3 (bakery shops sell 10 *facturas* for US$2).

● **Airline offices**
Aerolíneas Argentinas (AR), Paseo Colón 185, T 340-7800, with 4 branches, plus airport offices, reservations T 340-7777, Mon-Fri 0945-1745; **Austral Líneas Aéreas**, L N Alem 1134, T 317-3600; **Líneas Aéreas del Estado** (LADE), Perú 714, T 361-7071, erratic schedules, uninfomed office; **Líneas Aéreas Privadas Argentinas** (Lapa), M T de Alvear 790, T 819-5272 (reservations), or Aeroparque Puente Aéreo section, T 772-9920, cheapest fares to main tourist centres, good service; **Dinar**, R Sáenz Peña 933, T 326-6374, 778-0100; **LAER**, Lavalle 347, p 2B, T 394-5641; **Kaiken**, Almafuerte Travel, Av de Mayo 580, p 6, T 331-0191; **Southern Winds**, Tucumán 1000, T 329-9617; **AeroPerú**, Santa Fe 840, T 311-4115; **Varig**, Carabelas 344, T 329-9200; **Lan Chile**, Paraguay 609 p 1, T 311-5334, 312-8161 for reconfirmations; **Ecuatoriana**, T 312-2180; **United**, M T Alvear 590, T 326-9111; **Lufthansa**, M T Alvear 636, reservations T 319-0600; **Air France**, Santa Fe 963, T 317-4700; **British Airways**, Córdoba 690, T 325-1059; **American**, Santa Fe 881, T 318-1111; **KLM**, Reconquista 559, p 5, T 480-9473.

● **Banks & money changers**
Many shops and restaurants accept US dollar bills. Most banks charge high commission especially on TCS (as much as US$10). Banks open Mon-Fri 1000-1500, be prepared for long delays. US dollar bills are often scanned electronically for forgeries, while TCs are sometimes very difficult to change and you may be asked for proof of purchase. American Express TCs are less of a problem than Thomas Cook. Practices are constantly changing. **Lloyds Bank** (BLSA) Ltd, Reconquista y Mitre, Visa cash advances provided in both US dollars and pesos. It has 10 other branches in the city, and others in Greater Buenos Aires. **Citibank**, B Mitre 502, changes only Citicorps TCs, no commission, also Mastercard; branch at Florida 192. **Bank of America**, JD Perón y San Martín changes Bank of America TCs am only, US$ at very high commission. **Banco Tornquist**, B Mitre 531, Crédit Lyonnais agents, advance cash on visa card. **Deutsche Bank**, B Mitre 401 (and other branches), changes Thomas Cook TCs, also Mastercard, both give cash advances. **Banco Roberts**, 25 de Mayo 258, changes Thomas Cook TCs without commission. Thomas Cook rep, **Fullers**, Esmeralda 1000 y M T Alvear. **American Express** offices are at Arenales 707 y Maipú, by Plaza San Martín, T 312-0900, where you can apply for a card, get financial services and change Amex TCs (1000-1500 only, no commission into US$ or pesos). **Client Mail** in same building, Mon-Fri 0900-1800, Sat 0900-1300. Mastercard ATMs (look for Link-Mastercard/Cirrus) at several locations, mostly **Banco Nacional del Lavoro** inc Florida 40 and Santa Fe y Esmeralda.

There are many *casas de cambio*, some of which deal in TCs. Most are concentrated around San Martín and Corrientes: *Cambio Topaz*, San Martín 1394-1400, 5% commission; *Casa Piano*, San Martín 345-347, changes TCs into pesos or US$ cash for 2-3% commission; *Cambios Trade Travel*, San Martín 967, 3% commission on TCs; *Exprinter*, Suipacha 1107, open from Mon-Fri 1000-1600, Sat closed; *Casa América*, Av de Mayo 959, accepts Thomas Cook TCs. Many *cambios* will exchange US$, TCs for US$ cash at commissions varying from 1.25 to 3%. If all *cambios* closed, try Mercadería de Remate of Aduana, Florida 8, or *Eves*, Tucumán 702, open until 1800. On Sat, Sun and holidays, cash may be exchanged in the *cambio* in some of the large supermarkets (eg *Carrefour*, Paseo Alcorta Shopping Center, open daily 1000-2200). There is no service charge on notes, only on cheques. Major credit cards usually accepted but check for surcharges. General **Mastercard** office at H Yrigoyen 878, open 0930-1800, T 331-1022/2502/2549; another branch at Florida 274 (open 1000-1730). **Visa**, Corrientes 1437, 2nd floor, T 954-3333/2000, for stolen cards. Other South American currencies can only be exchanged in *casas de cambio*.

● **Cultural centres**
British Chamber of Commerce, Corrientes 457; **British Council**, M T de Alvear 590, p 4, T 311-9814/7519, F 311-7747 (open 1000-1200, 1430-1630); **Goethe Institut**, Corrientes 311, German library (open 1300-1900 excluding Wed, and 1000-1400 first Sat of month) and newspapers, free German films shown, cultural programmes, German language courses. In the same building, upstairs, is the German Club, Corrientes 327. **Alliance Française**, Córdoba 946; **USA Chamber of Commerce**, Diagonal R S Peña 567; **US Information Library** (Biblioteca Lincoln), Florida 935, reference and lending library, free, no identification needed, but take passport to become a member, on first 5 days of each month only, fixed address needed (closed Sat/Sun).

Clubs: **American Club**, Viamonte 1133, facing Teatro Colón, temporary membership available; **American Women's Club**, Córdoba 632, p 11; **English Club**, 25 de Mayo 586, T 311-9121, open for lunch only, temporary membership available to British business visitors. The American and English Clubs have reciprocal arrangements with many clubs in USA and UK. **Swedish Club**, Tacuarí 147; **Organización Hebrea Argentina Macabi**, Tucumán 3135, T 962-0947, social and sporting club for conservative Jews.

● **Embassies & consulates**
All open Mon-Fri unless stated otherwise. **Bolivian Consulate**, Belgrano 1670, p 2, T 383-7038, open 0900-1400, visa while you wait, tourist bureau which gives misleading information; **Brazilian Consulate**, Carlos Pellegrini 1363, p 5, open Mon-Fri, 0930-1400, visa takes 48 hrs, T 394-5278; **Paraguayan Consulate**, Viamonte 1851, 0900-1400, T 812-0075; **Peruvian Consulate**, San Martín 691, p 6, T 311-7582, 0900-1400, visa US$5, takes 1 day; **Uruguayan Consulate**, Las Heras 1907, open 1000-1800, T 807-3040, visa takes up to 1 week; **Chilean Consulate**, San Martín 439, p 9, T 394-6582, Mon-Thur 0930-1330, 1530-1830, Fri 0915-1430; **Ecuadorean Embassy**, Quintana 585, p 9 y 19, T 804-6408.

US **Embassy and Consulate Gen**, Av Colombia 4300, T 777-4533/7007, 0900-1730, consulate, visas 0800-1100, calls between 1500 and 1700; **Australian Embassy**, Santa Fe 846 (Swissair Building), T 312-6841, Mon-Thur 0830-1230, 1330-1730, Fri 0830-1315; **Canadian Embassy**, Tagle 2828, T 805-3032; **South African Embassy**, M T de Alvear 590, p 7, T 311-8991/7, Mon-Thur 0900-1300, 1400-1630, Fri 0900-1330; **Israeli Embassy**, Av de Mayo 701, p 10, T 342-1465; **Japanese Embassy**, Paseo Colón 275, p 9 y 11, T 343-2561, 0900-1300, 1430-1800.

Austrian Embassy, French 3671, T 802-1400, 0900-1200; **Belgian Embassy**, Defensa 113-8, T 331-0066/69, 0800-1300; **British Embassy**, Luis Agote 2412/52 (nr corner Pueyrredón y Guido), T 803-7070, open 0915-1215, 1415-1615; **Danish Embassy**, L N Alem 1074, p 9, T 312-6901/6935, 0900-1200, 1400-1600; **Finnish Embassy**, Av Santa Fe 846, p 5, T 312-0600/70, Mon-Thur 0830-1700, Fri 0830-1200; **French Embassy**, Santa Fe 846, p 3, T 312-2409, 0900-1200; **German Embassy**, Villanueva 1055, Belgrano, T 778-2500, 0900-1200; **Greek Embassy**, R S Peña 547, p 4, T 342-4958, 1000-1300; **Irish Embassy**, Suipacha 1380, p 2, T 325-8588, 1000-1230; **Italian Embassy**, Billinghurst 2577, consulate at M T de Alvear 1149, T 816-6132, 0900-1300; **Netherlands Embassy**, edif Buenos Aires, Av de Mayo 701, p 19, T 334-3474, 0900-1200, 1300-1530; **Norwegian Embassy**, Esmeralda 909, p 3 B, T 312-1904, 0900-1430; **Spanish Embassy**, Florida 943 (Consulate, Guido 1760), T 811-0070, 0900-1330, 1500-1730. **Swedish Embassy**, Corrientes 330, p 3, T 311-3088/9 (Consulate, Tacuarí 147, T 342-1422), T 1000-1200; **Swiss Embassy**, Santa Fe 846, p 12, T 311-6491, open 0900-1200.

● **Entertainment**
Cinemas: the selection of films is as good as anywhere else in the world and details are listed daily in all main newspapers. Films are shown uncensored and most foreign films are subtitled.

Tickets best booked early afternoon to ensure good seats (average price US$6, 50% discount Wed and for first show Mon-Fri). Tickets obtainable, sometimes cheaper, from ticket agencies (carteleras), such as **Vea Más**, Paseo La Plaza, Corrientes 1600, local 19 (the cheapest), **Cartelera**, Lavalle 742, T 322 9263, **Teatro Lorange**, Corrientes 1372, T 372-7386, and **Cartelera Baires**, Corrientes 1372, local 25. Many cinemas on Lavalle, around Santa Fe and Callao and in Belgrano (Av Cabildo and environs). Free films at Asociación Bancaria, Sarmiento 337/341, T 313-9306/312-5011/17, once a month (Wed); old films at Cine en la Cinemateca Argentina, Sarmiento 2255, T 952-2170 (half price of other cinemas, plus 20% discount for ISIC holders), and at Sarmiento 2150, T 48-2170. ISIC holders also entitled to discounts at Cine IFT Sala 1, Boulogne Sur Mer 549 (50%). On Sat nights many central cinemas have *trasnoches*, late shows starting at 0100.

Cultural events: the *Luna Park* stadium holds pop/jazz concerts, ballet and musicals, at Bouchard 465, nr Correo Central, T 311-5100, free parking at Corrientes 161. *Teatro Alvear*, Corrientes 1659, T 374-9470, has free concerts Fri at 1300, usually Orquesta de Tango de Buenos Aires. *Tango Week*, leading up to National Tango Day (11 Dec), has free events all over the city, details posted around the city and at tourist offices. *Teatro Municipal Gen San Martín*, Corrientes 1530, organizes many cultural activities of which quite a few are free of charge, inc concerts Sat and Sun evenings, 50% ISIC and GO 25 discount; the theatre's Sala Leopoldo Lugones shows international classic films, Sat-Sun, US$2. Free concerts at ProMusica music shop, Florida 638; schedule in window. *Centro Cultural Gen San Martín*, Sarmiento 1551, and the *Centro Cultural de Recoleta*, Junín 1930, next to the Recoleta cemetery have many free activities. Look for details in main newspapers and weekly paper *La Maga*, US$5 from news stands. **NB** From mid-Dec to end-Feb most theatres and concert halls are closed.

Gay discos: *Bunker*, Anchorena 1170, Fri-Sun, large, loud; *Enigma*, Suipacha 927, Fri-Sat; *Diesel*, Argoz 2424, Fri-Sun. Most gay discos charge US$15-20 entry on door; tickets are much cheaper if bought from bars around Santa Fe y Pueyrredón from 0100.

Jazz: *El Subsuelo*, Perón 1372, good bands featured; *Oliverio*, Paraná 328, excellent live jazz features the great Fats Fernández, Fri-Sat 2330 and 0100; *Café Tortoni*, Av de Mayo 829, T 342-4328, classic tango spot, features the Creole Jazz Band, Fri 2300, 40% ISIC and GO25 discount, also tango concert Fri-Sun 2130, rec.

Music: bars and restaurants in San Telmo district, with live music (usually beginning 2330-2400); *Players*, Humberto I 528 (piano bar); *Samovar de Rasputin*, Iberlucea 1251, Caminito, T 302-3190, good blues, dinner and/or show. Cover charges between US$5 and US$20, or more.

Bailantas are music and dance halls where they play popular styles which for years have been despised as 'low class'. They are now fashionable among the upper classes. A popular place is *Terremoto Bailable*, Paraguay y Thames. **For salsa**: *El Club*, Yerbal 1572, friendly, for all ages, not trendy, all welcome; *La Salsera*, Yatay 961, highly regarded salsa place.

Nightclubs and folklore: Tango: *Casablanca*, Balcarce 668, T 331-4621, very touristy, large coach parties, US$40 pp inc drinks; *Michelangelo*, Balcarce 433, T 334-4321, impressive setting, concert café in an old converted monastery, various types of music inc tango and folklore, Tues-Sun, and *La Ventana*, Balcarce 425, Mon-Sat shows at 2230, T 331-3648/334-1314, very touristy but very good show, US$50 for show, dinner and unlimited wine, through an agency, 20% discount for ISIC and youth card holders, from Asatej office (see **Useful addresses** below); *Querandi*, Peru 302, expensive tango show restaurant. Tango shows also at *La Cumparsita*, Chile 302, T 361-6880, authentic, US$50 for 2 inc wine; *Bar Sur*, Estados Unidos 299, and *Antigua Tasca de Cuchilleros*, Carlos Calvo 319, T 362-3811/28, pleasant surroundings, show US$20, show and dinner, US$32, both in San Telmo. The best affordable tango bars are in La Boca, but it is difficult to find authentic tango for locals, most are tourist-oriented. Good show also at *La Veda*, Florida 1, T 331-6442, average meal with wine and other drinks US$40. *Viejo Buzón*, Corrientes y Rodríguez Peña, good tango, no dinner but plenty of dancing, locals and tourists; *Café Mozart*, Esmeralda 754, tango, jazz, theatre, no dinner; *La Casa de Aníbal Troilo*, Carlos Calvo 2540, good singers and bands, for tourists; *Tango Danza*, J M Moreno 351, Fri, Sat, Sun, from 2200. Also rec are *Café Homero*, J A Cabrera 4946, Palermo; *Mesón Español*, Rodríguez Peña 369, T 35-0516, good folk music show and good food; *Galería Tango Argentino*, Boedo 722 y Independencia, T 93-1829/7527, Wed-Sat, less touristy than others, dinner (usually), show and dancing, has dancers and tango lessons (Mon-Fri, 1800-2100), well-known bands; *Paladium*, San Martín 954, tango/bolero dance hall. Tango lessons at *Champagne Tango*, Rio de Janeiro 387, Tues, Fri, Sun.

Recommended nightclub/discos: inc *Hippopotamus*, Junín 1787, Recoleta, French restaurant (lunch and dinner), fashionable nightclub;

Le Club, small and exclusive, Quintana 111; *Morocco*, H Yrigoyen 851, exclusive, restaurants, ISIC and GO 25 discounts; *Cemento*, Estados Unidos 1238, disco with liveshows, usually hard rock and heavy metal, popular with younger crowds, as are *New York City*, Alvarez Thomas y El Cano, T 552-4141, chic, and *Halley*, Corrientes 2020, heavy metal and hard rock. Some discos serve breakfast for additional charge at entry. Generally it is not worth going to discos before 0230 at weekends. Dress is usually smart.

Also rec: *Bembe*, Niceto Vega 5510, salsa, Fri and Sat, bar opens 2000, dancing from 0100, salsa dance class Fri 2100; *Mama Baker*, Santa Fe 2800; *Cinema*, Córdoba 4633, inside a former cinema; *El Dorado*, H Yrigoyen y 9 de Julio, interesting, different; *El Nacional*, Reconquista 915, in tunnels formerly used for smuggling; *El Angel*, Corrientes 1768 y Callao.

Theatre: about 20 commercial theatres play the year round. There are many amateur theatres. You are advised to book as early as possible for a seat at a concert, ballet, or opera. For ticket agencies, see **Cinemas**, above.

● **Hospitals & medical services**
Innoculations: *Centro Médico Rivadavia*, S de Bustamante 2531 y Las Heras, Mon-Fri, 0730-1900 (bus 38, 59, 60 or 102 from Plaza Constitución), or *Guardia de Sanidad del Puerto*, Mon and Thur, 0800-1200, at Ing Huergo 690, T 334-1875, free, bus 20 from Retiro, no appointment required (typhus, cholera, Mon-Fri 0800-1200; yellow fever, Tues-Thur 1400-1600, but no hepatitis, take syringe and needle, particularly for insulin and TB). Buy the vaccines in *Laboratorio Biol*, Uriburu 159, or in larger chemists. Any hospital with an infectology department will do hepatitis A.

Urgent medical service: (day and night) (**Casualty ward**: *Sala de guardia*). For free municipal ambulance service to an emergency hospital department, T 342-4001/4, 107 (SAME). Public Hospital: *Hospital Argerich*, Almte Brown esq Pi y Margall 750, T 931-5555. *British Hospital*, Perdriel 74, T 23-1081, US$14 a visit; cheap dental treatment at Caseros y Perdriel 76; *German Hospital*, Pueyrredón 1657, between Berutti and Juncal, T 821-4083. Both maintain first-aid centres (*centros asistenciales*) as do the other main hospitals. *French Hospital*, Rioja 951, T 97-1031; *Children's Hospital* (Ricardo Gutiérrez), Bustamante 1399, T 86-5500; *Centro Gallego*, Belgrano 2199, T 47-3061; *Hospital Juan A Fernández*, Cerviño y Bulnes, good medical attention. If affected by pollen, asthma sufferers can receive excellent treatment at the *Hospital de Clínicas José de San Martín*, Córdoba 2351, T 821-6041, US$6/treatment. *Dental Hospital*, Pueyrredón 1940, T 941-5555; *Eye Hospital*, San Juan 2121, T 821-2721.

● **Language schools**
Instituto de Lengua Española para Extranjeros, Lavalle 1619, p 7 C, T/F 375-0730, US$19/hr, groups US$12/hour, rec by individuals and organizations alike, accommodation arranged; *Bromley Institute*, Paraná 641, 1A, T 40-4113, courses in Spanish, Portuguese, French, English, high standards, well-regarded, rec. Free Spanish classes at *Escuela Presidente Roca*, Libertad 581, T 35-2488, Mon-Fri, 1945-2145 (basic level only). Spanish classes also at *Instituto del Sur*, Callao 433, 9 S, T/F 375-0897, individual lessons, cheap; *Estudio Buenos Aires*, San Martín 881, p 4, T 312-8936, owner also lets out rooms; *Link Educational Services*, Arenales 2565, p 5 B, T 825-3017; *Universidad de Buenos Aires*, 25 de Mayo, offers cheap, coherent courses. CEDIC, Reconquista 719, p 11 E, T/F 315-1156, US$16/hr private tuition, US$11/hr in groups, rec. For other schools teaching Spanish, and for private tutors look in *Buenos Aires Herald* in the classified advertisements. Enquire also at Asatej (see **Useful addresses**).

Schools which teach English to Argentines include: *International House*, Pacheco de Melo 2555, British-owned and run; *Berlitz*, Av de Mayo 847; Santiago del Estero 324; *American Teachers*, Viamonte y Florida, T 393-3331. There are many others. Vacancies are advertised in the *Buenos Aires Herald*. Before being allowed to teach, you must offically have a work permit (difficult to obtain) but schools may offer casual employment without one (particularly to people searching for longer-term employment), if unsure of your papers, ask at Migraciones (address below). There are many 'coordinadoras', usually women, who do not have an institute but run English 'schools' out of their homes by hiring native English-speakers and sending them out on jobs. Pay varies between US$10 and 25, depending on where you teach and on negotiation, the pay is usually better than in a fixed institute. Adverts occasionally appear in the *Herald*, but most contacts are by word of mouth.

● **Laundry**
Many dry cleaners and many launderettes, eg Alvear 861, in centre: Junín 15 y Rivadavia, Mon-Sat 0800-2100; Junín 529 y Lavalle; Rivadavia 1340. *Laverap*, Paraguay 888 y Suipacha, Córdoba 466, Local 6, T 312-5460, US$6.50/load (10% discount to ISIC and youth card holders, also at Brasil y Bolívar and Rodríguez Peña 100-200), Arenales 894, Solís nr Alsina (cheaper). The laundry at Brasil 554 costs US$4/load, more for valet service. *Marva*, Perón 2000 y Ayacucho; *Lava Ya*, at Libertad 1290

and 832, Paraguay 888, Moreno 417, H
Yrigoyen 1294 and Esmeralda 577.

● **Libraries**

Fundación Banco Patricios, Callao 312, p 5,
Spanish, English, French and some Italian books,
Mon-Fri 1000-1900, membership
US$15/month. See also Biblioteca Nacional, un-
der **Museums**, and **Cultural and Trade Asso-
ciations**.

● **Places of worship**

(**Non-Catholic**) The *Holy Cross*, Estados Unidos
3150, established by the Passionists; *St John's
Cathedral* (Anglican), 25 de Mayo 282 (services,
Sun 0900 in English, 1030 in Spanish), was built
half at the expense of the British Government and
dedicated in 1831; *St Andrew's*, Belgrano 579, is
one of the 8 Scottish Presbyterian churches. The
American Church, Corrientes 718, is Methodist,
built in 1863, service at 1100; *First Methodist*
(American) Church, Santa Fe 839, Acassuso; *Danish Church*, Carlos Calvo 257.

German Evangelical Church, Esmeralda
162; *Swedish Church*, Azopardo 1422; the
Armenian Cathedral of St Gregory the Illumi-
nator at the Armenian Centre, and the *Russian
Orthodox Cathedral* of The Holy Trinity (Parque Lezama) are interesting.

Synagogue: the most important in Buenos
Aires are the Congregación Israelita en la
República Argentina, Libertad 705 (also has a
small museum), and, the oldest, the Templo
Israelita at Paso 423 (called the Paso Temple),
traditional and conservative. An important orthodox temple is the Comunidad Israelita Orto-
doxa, the seat of the rabbis of Argentina,
Ecuador 530, T 862-2701. The Comunidad Bet-
tel, Av Elcano 3424, and the B'nai Tikvah, Vidal
2049, are for reformed worshippers. Congregación Emanu-El (reformed sect), Tronador
1455, take bus 140 from Av Córdoba to Alvarez
Thomas block 1600, then turn right into Tronador.

● **Post & telecommunications**

General Post Office: Correo Central – now
privatized, Correos Argentinos, Sarmiento y L N
Alem, Mon-Fri, 0800-2000. *Poste Restante* on
1st floor (US$2.25/letter), very limited service on
Sat (closes 1300). Fax service US$5/minute.
Philatelic section open Mon-Fri 1000-1800.
Centro Postal Internacional, for all parcels over
1 kg for mailing abroad, at Antártida Argentina,
nr Retiro station, open 1100 to 1700. Check
both Correo Central and Centro Postal Internacional for *poste restante*.

Telecommunications: the city is split into two
telephone zones, owned by Telecom and Telefónica Argentina. Corrientes 705 (open 0800-
2200) for international phone calls, fax, public

telex in basement; alternatively in Central Post
Office (more expensive), also telex. Other offices
at San Martín 322, on Santa Fe 1841, on
Agüero/Las Heras, and at Lavalle 613. *Fichas* or
cospeles (tokens) for calls in the city from public
telephone boxes cost US$0.50, US$1 for 3, obtained at newspaper stalls, cigarette *kioskos* and
Telecom or Telefónica Argentina offices. Many
phones now use phone cards costing 5 and 10
pesos (break off the corner tab before using), the
cards of the two companies are interchangeable.
International telephone calls from hotels may incur
a 40%-50% commission in addition to government tax of about the same amount. For more
details see **Postage and Telephone Rates** in
Information for travellers.

NB Since privatization, many phone prefixes
in the city have been changed: 34 became 342,
30 – 343, 37 – 383, 38 – 381, 59 – 581, 45 –
476 or 372 depending on location, and 47 –
951. Further changes are likely and will be indicated on the first pages of the phone directory,
or dial 110 to ask the operator.

● **Security**

Buenos Aires is mostly a safe city, but street crime
occurs, especially in the tourist season. Be particularly careful when boarding buses and nr the
Retiro train and bus stations. Beware of
bagsnatching gangs in parks, markets and in the
Subte, especially on Sun: they are not violent,
but particularly skilful. See also **Safety**, page
245, on mustard-spraying gangs; these operate
in main squares and tourist areas. If your passport is stolen, remember to get a new 'entrada'
stamp at the Dirección Nacional de Migraciones.

● **Shopping**

Most shops close lunchtime on Sat. The main,
fashionable shopping streets are Florida and
Santa Fe (especially between 1,000 and 2,000
blocks). Visit the branches of *H Stern*, for fine
jewellery at the *Sheraton* and *Plaza* hotels, and
at the International Airport; *Kelly's*, Paraguay
431, has a very large selection of reasonably
priced Argentine handicrafts in wool, leather,
wood, etc; *Plata Nativa*, Galería del Sol, Florida
860, local 41, for Latin American folk handicrafts; *Campanera Dalla Fontana*, Reconquista 735, leather factory, fast, efficient and
reasonably priced for made-to-measure clothes,
ISIC and GO 25 discount. Good quality leather
clothes factory at Boyacá 2030, T 582 6909 to
arrange time with English speaking owner;
Aida, Florida 670, can make a leather jacket to
measure in 48 hrs; *El Guasquero*, Av Santa Fe
3117, traditionally made leather goods; *Galería
del Caminante*, Florida 844, has a variety of
good shops with leather goods, arts and crafts,
souvenirs, etc; *XL*, in Paseo Alcorta, Alto
Palermo and Alto Avellaneda shopping malls,

for leather goods, ISIC and GO 25 discounts; *Marcelo Loeb*, galería at Maipú 466, for antique postcards from all over the world, not cheap, same galería has several philatelic and numismatic shops. C Defensa in San Telmo is good for antique shops; *Pasaje de Defensa*, Defensa 791, is a beautifully restored colonial house containing small shops; *Casa Piscitelli*, San Martín 450, has a large selection of tapes and CDs. *Galerías Broadway*, Florida 575, for cheap electronic goods, CDs, tapes. For cheap fashion clothes try the area round El Once station; *Mega Sports*, Cabildo 1950, for sports clothing, ISIC and GO 25 discounts.

Shopping malls: Patio Bullrich, between Libertador y Posadas, at Montevideo, entrances on Posadas and at Libertador 750, has boutiques selling high quality leather goods but very expensive. **Alto Palermo**, Col Díaz y Santa Fe, very smart and expensive. **La Plaza Shopping Centre**, at Corrientes 1600, also has a few restaurants. **Paseo Alcorta**, Figueroa Alcorta y Salguero, 4 levels, cinemas, supermarket, stores, many cheap restaurants (take colectivo 130 from Correo Central). **Galerías Pacífico**, on Florida, between Córdoba and Viamonte, is a beautiful mall with fine murals and architecture, many exclusive shops and fast food restaurants in basement. Also good set-price restaurant on 2nd floor and free lunchtime concerts on lowerground floor (details in the press).

Camping equipment: good camping equipment and fuel from *Fugate* (no sign), Gascón 238 (off Rivadavia 4100 block), T 982-0203, also repairs equipment. *Outside Mountain Equipment*, Donado 4660, T 541-2084; *Panamericana y Paraná*, Martínez (Shopping Unicenter, 3rd level). Good camping stores also at Guatemala 5908 and 5451. Camping gas available at Mitre 1111, *Todo Gas*, Paraná 550, and El Pescador, Paraguay y Libertad. Every kind of battery (inc for Petzl climbing lamps) at Callao 373. *Cacique Camping* manufacture camping equipment and clothing, their two shops: Arenales 1435, Barrio Norte, and San Lorenzo 4220, Munro, Provincia Buenos Aires, T 762 0261, F 756 1392, also sell the *South American Handbook*.

Bookshops: many along Av Corrientes, W of Av 9 de Julio, though most have no foreign language sections. Prices are very high for foreign books. Try *Yenny*, No 571, for new English classics (also 9 other branches) and *Distal*, No 913; also *Fausto*, No 1316 and 1243. *ABC*, Av Córdoba 685 and Rawson 2105 in Martínez suburb, good selection of English and German books, also sells *South American Handbook*; *Joyce Proust y Cía*, Tucumán 1545, p 1, T 40-3977, paperbacks in English, Portuguese,

French, Italian; classics, language texts, etc, good prices; *Librería Rodríguez*, Sarmiento 835, good selection of English books and magazines, has another branch on Florida, 300 block; French bookshop at Rivadavia 743; *Librería Goethe*, Lavalle 528, good selection of English and German books. Italian books at *Librería Leonardo*, Av Córdoba 335, also newspapers and magazines; *Liber Arte*, Corrientes 1555, also café, 10% ISIC discount; *Promoteo*, Corrientes 1916, rare books, ISIC discount; *Asatej Bookshop*, Florida 835, p 3° Of 320, T 315-1457, and Santa Fe 2450, Loc 93, sells this *Handbook* 'at the best price' with ISIC discount; *El Ateneo*, Florida 340, basement has good selection of English books, other branches inc Callao 1380; *Kel Ediciones*, MT de Alvear 1369 and Conde 1990 (Belgrano), good stock of English books and sells *South American Handbook*. *Acme Agency*, Suipacha 245, p 1, for imported English books, also Arenales 885. Prices at *Harrods* on Florida are lower than most. *LOLA*, Viamonte 976, 2 p, T 322-3920, Mon-Fri 1200-1900, the only specialist in Latin American Natural History, birdwatching, most books in English; *Librería del Turista*, Florida 937, wide range of travel books inc *South American Handbook*, ISIC and GO 25 discounts.

For used and rare books: *The Antique Bookshop*, Libertad 1236, rec; *Fernández Blanco*, Tucumán 712; *Casa Figueroa*, Esmeralda 970; and *L'Amateur*, Esmeralda 882. Second-hand English language books from *British and American Benevolent Society*, Catamarca 45 (take train to Acassuso). *Aquilanti*, Rincón 79, esp good on Patagonia; *Juan Carlos Pubill*, Talcahuano 353 (ring bell), and from *Entrelibros*, Av Cabildo 2280 and Santa Fe 2450, local 7.

For foreign newspapers try the news stands on Florida, and at kiosk at Corrientes y Maipú.

Every April the Feria del Libro is held at the Centro De Exposiciones, Av Figueroa Alcorta y Pueyrredón, Recoleta; exhibitions, shows and books for sale in all languages.

Camera repairs and film developing: film developing to international standards. *Foto Gráfica*, Perón 1253, for black and white developing; *Photo Station*, Díaz Vélez 5504, T 981-1447, 25% ISIC and GO 25 discount. For developing slides Esmeralda 444, fast service, and *Kinefot*, Talcahuano 244. **Camera repairs**: several good shops on Talcahuano 100-400 blocks. *Horacio Calvo*, Riobamba 183, all brands and variety of rare accessories, rec; fast service at Tacuarí 75; for Olympus cameras, *Rodolfo Jablanca*, Corrientes 2589. German spoken at *Gerardo Föhse*, Florida 890, fast, friendly. Note that some types of camera batteries are unavailable, inc Panasonic CR-32.

Markets: for souvenirs, antiques, etc, **Plaza Dorrego**, San Telmo, with food, dancers, buskers, Sat and Sun 0900-1700, on Humberto I and Defensa, entertaining, not cheap, an interesting array of 'antiques'. **Feria Hippie**, in Recoleta, nr cemetery, big craft and jewellery market, Sat and Sun, good street atmosphere, expensive. **Feria de Las Artes** (Fri, 1000-1700) on Defensa y Alsina. Sat craft, jewellery, etc market, at **Plaza Belgrano**, nr Belgrano Barrancas station on Juramento, between Cuba y Obligado, 1000-2000. Handicraft markets at weekends at Parque Lezama, San Telmo. A secondhand book market is at **Plaza Lavalle** in front of Tribunales, a few English titles (ask around), weekdays only. Plazoleta Santa Fe, Santa Fe and Uriarte (Palermo) old books and magazines, Sat 1200-2000, Sun 1000-2000; plastic arts in the **Caminito**, Vuelta de Rocha (Boca), 1000 2000 summer, 0900-1900 winter. At **Parque Rivadavia**, Rivadavia 4900, around the *ombú* tree, records, books, magazines, stamps and coins, Sun 0900-1300, **Plazoleta Primera Junta**, Rivadavia and Centenera, books and magazines, Sat 1200-2000, Sun 1000-2000. **Parque Patricios**, Caseros entre Monteagudo y Pepiri, 1000-2000, antiques, books, art and stamps. Sat market in **Plaza Centenario**, Díaz Vélez y L Marechal, 1000-2100 local crafts, good, cheap hand-made clothes.

● **Sports**
Aerobics: try the *Le Parc*, San Martín 645, T 311-9191, expensive, though has cheaper branch at Rivadavia 4615, monthly membership required; *Gimnasio Olímpico Cancillería*, Esmeralda 1042, membership required.

Association and rugby football: are both played to a very high standard. Soccer fans should see Boca Juniors, matches Sun 1500-1800 (depending on time of year), Wed evenings, entry US$10 (stadium open weekdays for visits; bus 27), or their arch-rivals, River Plate. Soccer season Sept-May/June, with a break at Christmas. Rugby season April-Oct/November.

Chess: *Club Argentino de Ajedrez*, Paraguay 1858, open daily, arrive after 2000, special tournament every Sat, 1800, with high standards. Repairs for pocket chess computers, T 952-4913.

Cricket: is played at four clubs in Greater Buenos Aires between Nov and March.

Golf: the leading golf clubs are the *Hurlingham, Ranelagh, Ituzaingó, Lomas, San Andrés, San Isidro, Sáenz Peña, Olivos, Jockey, Campos Argentinos* and *Hindú Country Club*. Visitors wishing to play should bring handicap certificate and make telephone booking. Weekend play possible only with a member. Good hotels may be able to make special arrangements. Municipal golf course in Palermo,

open to anyone at any time.

Horse racing: at Palermo, a large, modern racecourse, popular throughout the year. Riding schools at Palermo and San Isidro.

Motor racing: Formula 1 championship racing has been restored: the Gran Premier de la República Argentina is held at the Oscar Alfredo Gálvez autodrome on the outskirts of the city in Mar/April. There are lots of rallies, stock racing and Formula 3 competitions, mostly from Mar to mid-December.

Polo: the high handicap season is Oct to Dec, but it is played all year round (low season April-June). Argentina has the top polo teams. A visit to the national finals at Palermo in Nov or Dec is rec.

Tennis, squash and paddle tennis: are popular. The Argentine Tennis Open is in Nov, ATP tour. There are many private clubs.

● **Tour companies & travel agents**
Tours: a good way of seeing Buenos Aires and its surroundings is by 3-hr tour. Longer tours inc dinner and a tango show, or a gaucho *fiesta* at a ranch (excellent food and dancing, although the gaucho part can be somewhat showy). Bookable through most travel agents, US$50-65. *BAT, Buenos Aires Tur*, Lavalle 1444, T 371-2304, almost hourly departures; *Buenos Aires Vision*, Esmeralda 356, T 394-4682; *Eurotur* (T 312-6170), in English, or *Autobuses Sudamericanos* (TISA), information and booking office at Bernardo de Irigoyen 1370, p 1, Offices 25 and 26, T 307-1956, F 307-8899. Prices range from US$12 to US$60 (20 night time and *estancia* options). For reservations in advance for sightseeing tours, with a 20% court esy discount to *South American Handbook* readers, write to Casilla de Correo No 40, Sucursal 1 (B), 1401 Buenos Aires. In USA T (New York) 212-524-0763, First Class Travel Service Ltd. TISA has other branches in Buenos Aires and publishes *Guía Latinoamericana de Omnibus*, organizes Amerbuspass (T 311-7373 for tickets, or USA 602-795-6556, F 795-8180) for bus travel throughout Latin America. At same address *Transporte Aereo Costa Atlántica* (TACA), passenger charter services to Pinamar, Villa Gesell, Bariloche, T 26-7933. Also *Indiana Cars*, T 307-1956/300-5591, for remise, car hire and taxi service with women drivers.

For river tours of Buenos Aires, Charles Cesaire, Dársena Norte, T 553-4380/314-1780, Sat, Sun, holidays 1500, 1700, 1900, with bar, US$10.

Travel agents: among those rec are *Les Amis*, Santa Fe 810, helpful, efficient; *Exprinter*, Suipacha 1107, T 312-2519, and San Martín 170, T 331-3050, Galería Güemes (especially their

5-day, 3-night tour to Iguazú and San Ignacio Miní; *Furlong*, Esmeralda y M T de Alvear, T 318-3200, T 312-3043, Thomas Cook representatives; *ATI*, Esmeralda 561, mainly group travel, very efficient, many branches; *Turismo Feeling*, L Alem 762, T 311-9422, excellent and reliable horseback trips and adventure tourism; *Versailles*, Callao 257, p 13 N, helpful, friendly; *Giorgio*, Florida y Tucumán, T 327-4200, F 325-4210, also at Santa Fe 1653; *Inti Viajes*, Tucumán 836, T/F 322-8845, cheap flights, very helpful; *Flyer*, Reconquista 621, p 8, T 312-9164, English, Dutch, German spoken, repeatedly rec (details on fishing, polo, *estancias*, motorhome rental); *Eves Turismo*, Tucumán 702, T 393-6151, helpful and efficient, rec for flights; *City Service*, Florida 890 y Paraguay, p 4, T 312-8416/9; *Travel Up*, Maipú 474, p 4, T 326-4648; *Proterra Turismo*, Lavalle 750, p 20 D, T/F 326-2639; *Folgar*, Esmeralda 961, p 3 E, T 311-6937. English is widely spoken.

● **Tourist offices**
National office at Santa Fe 883 with maps and literature covering the whole country. Open 0900-1700, Mon-Fri, T 312-2232, 312-5611. There are kiosks at Aeroparque (Aerolíneas Argentinas section), T 773-9891/05, Mon-Fri, 0830-2000 and Sat 0900-1900, and at Ezeiza Airport, T 480-0224/0011, Mon-Fri 0830-2200.

Municipal office in the **Municipalidad de Buenos Aires**, Sarmiento 1551, p 5, T 374-1251, open Mon-Fri 0930-1730, has an excellent free booklet about the city centre and maps. There are municipally-run tourist kiosks on Florida, junction with Diagonal Roque Sáenz Peña, Mon-Fri 0900-1700 and in Galerías Pacífico, Florida y Córdoba, p 1, Mon-Fri 1000-1900, Sat 1100-1900.

For free tourist information anywhere in the country T 0800-5-0016 (0900-2000)

There are also helpful *Casas de Turismo* for most provinces (open Mon-Fri usually, 1000-1800, depending on office): **Buenos Aires**, Av Callao 237, T 371-7045/7; others on Callao are **Córdoba** (332, T 371-1668, F 476-2615), **Chaco** (322, T 476-0961, F 375-1640), **Mendoza** (445, T/F 371-7301). **Others**: Río Negro, Tucumán 1916, T 371-7066, F 476-2128; **Chubut**, Sarmiento 1172, T/F 382-0822; **Entre Ríos**, Suipacha 844, T/F 328-9327; **Formosa**, H Irigoyen 1429, T 381-7048, F 381-6290; **Mar del Plata**, Santa Fe 1175, T/F 811-4466; Jujuy, Santa Fe 967, p 6, T/F 393-6096; Misiones, Santa Fe 989, T 322-0677, F 325-6197; **Neuquén**, Perón 687, T/F 326-6812; **Salta**, Diagonal R S Peña 933, T 326-1314, F 326-0110; **Santa Cruz**, 25 de Mayo 277, 1st floor, T 343-3653, F 342-1667; **Catamarca**, Córdoba 2080, T/F 374-6891; **Corrientes**, San Martín 333, p 4,

T/F 394-7432; **La Pampa**, Suipacha 346, T/F 326-0511; **La Rioja** Viamonte 749, p 5, T/F 326-1140; **San Juan**, Sarmiento 1251, T 382-5291, F 382-4729; **San Luis**, Azcuénaga 1083, T/F 822-0426; **Santa Fe**, Montevideo 373, p 2, T/F 375-4570; **Santiago del Estero**, Florida 274, T 326-9418, F 326-5915; **Tucumán**, Suipacha 110, T 325-0564; **Tierra del Fuego**, Santa Fe 919, T/F 322-8855; **Villa Gesell**, B Mitre 1702, T/F 374-5098; **Bariloche** hotel, flat and bungalow service in Galería at Florida 520/Lavalle 410, room 116 (cheapest places not listed). Calafate bookings for *Refugio and Autocamping Lago Viedma*, excursions with Transporte Ruta 3 and lake excursions with Empresa Paraíso de Navegación booked from Turismo Argos, Maipú 812, p 13 C, T 392-5460. (For bookings for *Hotel La Loma*, Calafate and further information on the area contact Paula Escabo, Callao 433, p 8 P, T 371-9123.) For tourist information on Patagonia and bookings for cheap accommodation and youth hostels, contact Asatej, see **Useful addresses** below.

On Fri, the youth section of *Clarín* (*Sí*) lists free entertainments; *Página 12* has a youth supplement on Thur called *NO*, the paper lists current events in *Pasen y Vean* section on Fri; also the weekly, free *Aquí Buenos Aires*, the weekly *La Maga* and Sun tourism section of *La Nación* (very informative). *Where in Buenos Aires*, a tourist guide in English, published monthly, is available free in hotels, travel agencies, tourist kiosks on Florida, and in some news stands. The *Buenos Aires Times* is a bilingual monthly newspaper covering tourist topics, available in some hotels. A good guide to bus and subway routes is *Guía Peuser*; there is one for the city and one covering Greater Buenos Aires. Similar guides, *Lumi* and *Guía T*, US$5, are available at news stands, US$10. Also handy is Auto Mapa's pocket-size *Plano guía* of the Federal Capital, available at news stands, US$8, or from sales office at Santa Fe 3117; *Auto Mapa* also publishes an increasing number of regional maps, Michelin-style, high quality. Country-wide maps at Instituto Geográfico Militar, Cabildo 301 (see **Maps** in **Information for travellers**).

● **Useful addresses**
Administración de Parques Nacionales, Santa Fe 680, opp Plaza San Martín, T 311-0303, Mon-Fri 1000-1700, have leaflets on some national parks. Also library (Biblioteca Perito Moreno), open to public Tues-Fri 1000-1700.

Asatej: Argentine Youth and Student Travel Organization, runs a Student Flight Centre, Florida 835, p 3, oficina 320, T 315-1457, F 311-6840; offering booking for flights (student discounts) inc one-way flights at bargains prices, hotels and travel (all payments over US$100 must be in US$ cash); information for all South America, noticeboard for travellers, the *Sleep Cheap Guide* lists economical accommodation in Argentina, Bolivia, Chile, Brazil, Uruguay and Peru, ISIC cards sold (giving extensive discounts; Argentine ISIC guide available here), English and French spoken; also runs the following: *Red Argentino de Alojamiento Para Jovenes*, same address oficina 319, T 315-1457, an Argentine hostal association; *Asatej Travel Store*, oficina 320 and at Santa Fe 2450, p 3, loc 93, selling wide range of travel goods inc *South American Handbook* "at best price".

Oviajes, Uruguay 385, p 8, T 371-6137, e-mail oviajes@redynet.com.ar, also offers travel facilities, ticket sales, information, and issues IYHA, ISIC, ITIC, G025 and FIYTO cards, aimed at students, teachers and independent travellers.

Asociación Ornitológica del Plata, 25 de Mayo 749, T 312-8958, for information on birdwatching and specialist tours, good library.

Central Police Station: Moreno 1550, T 381-8041 (emergency, T 101 from any phone, free).

Comisión Nacional de Museos y Monumentos y Lugares Históricos: Av de Mayo 556, professional archaeology institute.

Migraciones: (Immigration), Antártida Argentina 1365 (visas extended mornings only), T 312-3288/7985/8661, from 1230-1700.

Youth Hostel Association: information for all South America, Talcahuano 214, p 3, T 45-1001 (post code: 1013 Buenos Aires). **NB** A YHA card in Argentina costs US$20, ISIC cards also sold. Secretariat open Mon-Fri 1300-2000. (There are very few hostels nr Route 3, the main road S from Buenos Aires.)

YMCA: (Central), Reconquista 439. **YWCA**: Tucumán 844.

● **Transport**

Local Buses *Colectivos* (city buses) cover a very wide radius, and are clean, frequent, efficient and very fast (hang on tight). The basic fare is US$0.60, US$1 to the suburbs. Have correct coins ready for ticket machine as drivers no longer sell tickets. **NB** The bus number is not sufficient indication of destination, as each number has a variety of routes, but bus stops display routes of buses stopping there and little plaques are displayed in the driver's window. *Guía T* gives routes and livery of all buses and *Lumi* guide gives routes (see above).

Car hire: expensive, with an additional 20% tax. It is difficult to hire cars during holiday periods, best to book from abroad. Use of Avis Car Credit card with central billing in your home country is possible. See also **Information for travellers**. Driving in Buenos Aires is no problem, provided you have eyes in the back of your head and good nerves. Note that traffic fines are high and police increasingly on the lookout for drivers without the correct papers. **Avis**, Cerrito 1527, T 311-1000; **A1 International**, San Luis 3138, T 312-9475; **Budget**, Santa Fe 869, T 311-9870, ISIC and GO 25 discount; **Hertz**, Ricardo Rojas 451, T 312-1317. There are several national rental agencies, eg **AVL**, Av Alvear 1883, T 805-4403; **Ricciard Libertador**, Av del Libertador 2337/45, T 799-8514; **Localiza**, Paraguay 1122, T 314-3999; **Unidas**, Paraguay 864, T 315-0777, 20% ISIC and GO 25 discount. **Motoring Associations**: see page 248 for details of service.

Metro ('**Subte**'): 5 lines link the outer parts of the City to the centre. 'A' line runs under C Rivadavia, from Plaza de Mayo to Primera Junta. 'B' line from central Post Office, Av L N Alem, under Av Corrientes to Federico Lacroze railway station. 'C' line links Plaza Constitución with the Retiro railway station, and provides connections with all the other lines. 'D' line runs from Catedral, under Diagonal R S Peña, Córdoba, Santa Fe and Palermo to Ministro Carranza (5,300 block of Santa Fe). 'E' line runs from Bolívar nr Plaza de Mayo) through San Juan to Plaza de Los Virreyes. Note that three stations, 9 de Julio (Line 'D'), Diagonal Norte (Line 'C') and Carlos Pellegrini (Line 'B') interconnect. The fare is

US$0.45, the same for any direct trip or combination between lines; tokens (*fichas*) must be bought at the station before boarding; buy a few in advance to save time (dollars not accepted). System operates 0530-2215, but some lines close before 2200. Line A, the oldest was built in 1913, the earliest underground in South America. Many of the stations in the centre esp on Line E have fine tile-work designs and pictures which are worth seeing. Some trains date from the early part of the century too. The oldest and nicest station is Perú. Backpacks and luggage allowed. Map available free from stations and from tourist office.

Taxis: are painted yellow and black, and carry *Taxi* flags. Fares are shown in pesos. The meter starts at US$0.96 when the flag goes down; make sure it isn't running when you get in. A charge is sometimes made for each piece of hand baggage (ask first). Tips not usual. Four common taxi driver tricks are 1) to take you on a longer than necessary ride; 2) to switch low-denomination notes for higher ones preferred by the passenger (don't back down, demand to go to the police station); 3) to grab the passenger's baggage and prevent him/her from leaving the taxi (scream for help); 4) to quote 'old' prices for new, eg 'quince' (15) for 1.50 pesos, 'veinte y seis' (26) for 2.60 pesos, etc. If possible, keep your luggage with you. Worst places are the two airports and Retiro; make sure you know roughly what the fare should be before the journey: eg from Aeroparque to: Ezeiza US$32, Congreso US$7, Plaza de Mayo US$6, Retiro US$5, La Boca US$4. Fares double for journeys outside city limits (Gen Paz circular highway). Alberto Pommerenck, T 654 5988, offers reasonable 1/2 day hire, knows suburban leather factories well, good driver.

Remise taxis operate all over the city; they are run from an office, have no meter (but charge about the same as yellow-and-black cabs), and the companies are identified by signs on the pavement. Fares can be verified by phoning the office and items left in the car can easily be reclaimed.

Tram: a green and white old-fashioned street car operates April-Nov on Sat and holidays 1600-1900 and Sun 1000-1300, 1600-1930 (not Easter Sun) and Dec-Mar on Sat and holidays 1700-2000, Sun 1000-1300, 1600-1900 free, on a circular route along the streets of Caballito district, from C Emilio Mitre 500, Subte Primera Junta (Line A) or Emilio Mitre (Line E), no stops en route. Operated by Asociación de los Amigos del Tranvía, T 476-0476.

Air Ezeiza (officially Ministro Pistarini, T 620-0011), the international airport, is 35 km SW of the centre by a good dual carriageway, which links with the Gen Paz circular highway round

the city. The airport has a duty free shop (expensive), exchange facilities (Banco de la Nación, 1.5% commission) and ATMs (Visa and Mastercard), post office (open 0800-2000) and (under the stairs) a left luggage office (US$5/piece). Its hotel, the *Internacional*, is closed for renovation (no other hotels nearby). There is a *Devolucion IVA* desk (return of VAT) for purchases such as leather goods. Airport information, T 480-0217. Reports of pilfering from luggage, to discourage this have your bags sealed after inspection by Your Packet International SA, US$5-10/piece (British Airways insists on, and pays for this for backpacks). Free hotel booking service at Tourist Information desk – helpful, with list of competitively-priced hotels. A display in immigration shows choices and prices of transport into the city. **Airport buses**: 2 companies run special buses to/from the centre: *Manuel Tienda León* (office at customs exit), service to the company office at Santa Fe 790, next to *Hotel Crillon* (T/F 315-0489, F 311-3722, or airport T/F 480-0597/0374 – 24 hrs), 0400, 0500, then every 30 mins till 2030, US$14, return US$25, credit cards accepted. Santa Fe office has check-in desk for AR flights. *San Martín* services from outside Alitalia office, to company office at Santa Fe 887 (next to Secretaría Nacional de Turismo), T 314-4747/3446, Ezeiza 480-9464, 15 mins past each hour, US$11, 10% ISIC and GO 25 discount (will also collect passengers from hotels in centre for no extra charge, book previous day). **Local buses**: No 86 **buses** (white and blue, marked 'Fournier') run to the centre from outside the airport terminal to the right (*servicio diferencial* takes 11/2 hrs, US$4, *servicio común* 21/4 hrs, US$1, coins only no change given) between 0500 and 2400. To travel to Ezeiza, catch the bus at Av de Mayo y Perú, 1 block from Plaza de Mayo – make sure it has 'Aeropuerto' sign in the window as many 86s stop short of Ezeiza. Only one bag is normally allowed and passengers with backpacks may be charged double fare. **Taxis**: both airport ('rojos') and city ('amarillos') taxis are allowed to operate from Ezeiza; they have separate departure points: 'rojos' in front of the central hall, 'amarillos' 50m to the left of the 'Espigón Internacional'. Taxis from centre to Ezeiza US$35-40 but bargain. Fixed-price **remise taxis** can be booked from the Manuel Tienda León counter at Ezeiza, US$49 (inc US$2 toll) payable in advance. Other remises between the city and Ezeiza charge US$30-37. Avoid unmarked cars at Ezeiza no matter how attractive the fare may sound; drivers are adept at separating you from far more money than you can possibly owe them. Always ask to see the taxi driver's licence, if you think you have been cheated, T 343-5001 to complain. If you take an 'amarillo', the Policía Aeronáutica on duty notes down the car's licence and time of departure. **Trains** Local electric trains go to Ezeiza suburb from the Constitución station. The train, marked 'Ezeiza' costs US$0.80, and takes 40 mins. One block from the Ezeiza station, colectivo No 502 goes to the airport, US$0.70, and takes 20 mins.

Aeroparque (Jorge Newbery Airport) 4 km N of the centre nr the New Port, T 771-2071, handles all internal flights, services to Punta del Este and Montevideo and flights from Latin American countries with an intermediate stop in Argentina. The terminal is divided into three sections, one each for AR and Austral and the third, in between, for other airlines. AR section has duty free facilities, tourist information, *confitería*, car rental, Manuel Tienda León office (see below) and luggage deposit (US$3/piece). Exchange: Banco de la Ciudad (Austral section) and Aeromar (between sections), also Visa ATM. No post office or post box. Very expensive and poor quality restaurant upstairs. **Buses** Manuel Tienda León buses to/from centre (see above for address), 0710-2110 every 30 mins, US$5. Local bus 45 runs from outside the airport to the Retiro railway station, then follows Av L N Alem and Paseo Colón to La Boca. Bus 37C goes from Plaza del Congreso to Aeroparque but make sure it has 'Aeroparque' sign, US$0.50. **Remise taxis**: are operated by Universalflet (office in Austral section, T 772-2950) and Manuel Tienda León, US11-13 to centre, US$40 to Ezeiza. Ordinary taxi to centre US$8.

Manuel Tienda León operates buses between Ezeiza and Jorge Newbery airports, stopping in city centre, US$15. AR offer free transfers between Ezeiza and Aeroparque to passengers whose incoming and connecting flghts are both on AR: ask at AR desk for a voucher.

Aerolíneas Argentinas, Austral and Lapa offer daily flights to the main cities, for details see text under intended destination, see also page 247 for the Visit Argentina fare. If travelling in the S, book ahead if possible with LADE, whose flights are cheaper than buses in most cases.

Trains There are 4 main terminals: **Retiro**: really three separate stations (Belgrano T 311-5287; Mitre T 312-6596; San Martín T 311-8704). Services in operation: to Tucumán, Mon and Fri, 1600, returning Thur and Sun, 23 hrs, US$50 pullman, US$36 1st, US$31 tourist (service run by Tucumán provincial government). Suburban services to Tigre, Capilla del Señor, Bartolomé Mitre and Zárate (tickets checked on train and collected at the end of the journey).

Constitución: T 304-0021; frequent services to La Plata (US$1), Ezeiza (US$0.80), Ranelagh (US$0.50) and Quilmes (US$0.90). Also suburban services.(Keep your ticket as you have to show this at your destination.) Service to Bahía Blanca, run by Servicios Ferroviarios Patagónicos, Wed and Sun 0740, US$65 pullman, US$60 1st, US$44 tourist, food mediocre; San Antonio Oeste, US$30, 22 hrs; Mar del Plata 7 times daily from 0100-1830, US$30 pullman, US$19 1st, US$14 tourist; Necochea, Mon, Wed, Fri 2100 (daily in summer), returns Tues, Thur, Sun, US$20.50 pullman, US$16 1st class, US$14 2nd. The Automóvil Club Argentino provides car transporters for its members (see **ACA** in **Information for travellers**).

Federico Lacroze: Ferrocarril Nacional Urquiza (North-Eastern) – T 553-5213. No services except the Tren Histórico: every Sun a Scottish 1888 Neilson steam engine pulls old wooden carriages, either to Capilla del Señor with lunch or a folkloric show at an *estancia* (dep 1000, return 1900), or to Zárate across the Zárate-Brazo Largo bridges over the Paraná river (dep 0900). Prices from US$15-50, T 374-4186, operates in summer only.

Once: Ferrocarril Nacional Sarmiento (Western), T 87-0041/2/3, for services in the province of Buenos Aires.

Buses All long-distance buses leave from terminal at Ramos Mejía y Antártida Argentina (Subte C), behind Retiro station, T for information 314-2323. Information desk on first floor. All offices are on the E side on the ground floor. The passage between the bus station and Retiro is packed with market stalls and is narrow (beware pickpockets), all designed to inconvenience those with luggage (although, as one correspondent points out, this also slows down anyone trying to make a speedy escape with someone else's belongings). There are two left-luggage lockers, tokens from kiosks, US$2.50. Luggage porters charge US$5 per load. The terminal was being redesigned in 1997. Some bus companies charge extra for luggage (illegally). Fares may vary according to time of year and advance booking is advisable Dec-March. Some companies may give discounts, such as 20% to YHA or student-card holders and foreign, as well as Argentine teachers and university lecturers. Travellers have reported getting discounts without showing evidence of status, so it's always worth asking. For further details of bus services and fares, look under proposed destinations.

Hitchhiking: for Pinamar, Mar del Plata and nearby resorts, take bus La Plata to Alpargatas *rotonda* roundabout. For points further S, take bus 96 to Ruta 3 – the Patagonia road. Best to hitch from a service station where trucks stop. The police control point at Km 43 (S) is reported to be friendly and will help to find a lift for you.

For Mendoza try truck drivers at the wine warehouses nr Palermo station (take Subte to Puerto Pacífico, at Buenos Aires at Pacífico train station, at viaduct crossing Av Santa Fe/Av Cabildo; turn left into Av Juan B Justo for the warehouses).

Passenger boats: the *Buenos Aires Herald* (English-language daily) notes all shipping movements. Flota Fluvial del Estado (Corrientes 489, T 311-0728) organizes cruises from Buenos Aires, Dársena Sur (dock T 361-4161/0346) up the Paraná river. South Coast, down to Punta Arenas and intermediate Patagonian ports, served by the Imp & Exp de la Patagonia. Very irregular sailings. For connections with Uruguay, see page 96.

TRAVEL INTO NEIGHBOURING COUNTRIES

● **By Road**

Four branches of the Inter-American Highway run from Buenos Aires to the borders of Chile, Bolivia, Paraguay and Brazil.

To Chile: via Río Cuarto, Mercedes, San Luis, and Mendoza, Total: 1,310 km paved throughout. Direct buses to Santiago, 23 hrs, US$70-75, eg Ahumada, El Rápido Internacional and others, 1,459 km; US$70-75 to Valparaíso or Viña del Mar, TAC, Fénix Pullman Norte, cheaper to book to Mendoza and then rebook. There are also road connections between Catamarca and Copiapó, Bariloche and Osorno and Puerto Montt, and between Salta and Antofagasta.

To Bolivia: via Rosario, Villa María, Córdoba, Santiago del Estero, Tucumán, and Jujuy. Total: 1,994 km. There is no direct bus service from Buenos Aires to La Paz but through connections can be booked (Sudamericanos, T 27-6591, goes via La Quiaca-Villazón, 48 hrs; Atahualpa, T 315-0601, goes via La Quiaca, or Pocitos, daily, then a new ticket to La Paz or Santa Cruz must be bought). Cheapest route to Pocitos is by bus to Tucumán, US$40 and then re-book for Pocitos, US$25.

To Paraguay: via Rosario, Santa Fe, Resistencia, Clorinda and Asunción (via toll bridge). Total: 1,370 km. Buses take 20-22 hrs, with 11 companies (all close to each other at the Retiro bus terminal). You have choice between executive (luxury service, 15 hrs, US$68), *diferencial* (with food, drinks, 18 hrs, US$50) and *común* (without food, but has a/c, toilet, 21 hrs, US$33.50). Also 5 companies to Ciudad del Este, US$30; Caaguazú goes to Villarrica, and Expreso Río Paraná and La Encarnaceña go to Encarnación, US$31. Tickets can be bought up to 30 days in advance.

To drive to Paraguay, 3 main routes: 1) via Rosario, Santa Fe, Resistencia, Clorinda to Asunción; 2) cross the Zárate-Brazo Largo bridges to

Route 12, then head W across Entre Ríos to Paraná and take the tunnel to Santa Fe, or head W across Corrientes to the bridge from Corrientes to Resistencia; 3) via Misiones, San Ignacio Miní and the Iguazú Falls: as for 2), but follow Routes 12 and 14 up the Río Uruguay via Colón and Concordia to Misiones province for Posadas.

To Brazil: to the Iguazú Falls, follow 3) above under **To Paraguay**. On this route you can cross from Paso de los Libres to Uruguaiana in Brazil. Direct buses to Brazil via Paso de los Libres by Pluma (T 313-3901): São Paulo, 40 hrs, US$145, Rio de Janeiro, 45 hrs, US$163; Porto Alegre, US$71; Curitiba, 38 hrs, US$128; Florianópolis, 32 hrs, US$115. To Rio, changing buses at Posadas and Foz do Iguaçu is almost half price, 50 hrs. A third route across the Río de la Plata and through Uruguay is a bit cheaper, not as long and offers a variety of transport and journey breaks. Tickets from Buen Viaje, Córdoba 415, 31-2953, or Pluma, Córdoba 461, T 311-4871 or 311-5986.

To Uruguay: direct road connections by means of two bridges over the Río Uruguay between Puerto Colón and Paysandú and between Puerto Unzué and Fray Bentos (much slower than the air or sea routes given below). '*Bus de la carrera*' (office 65-67 Retiro, T 313-3695) links Montevideo and Buenos Aires, 8½ hrs, US$20. Departure from each city at 1000, 1015, 2200 and 2230, with a *dormibus* at 2230 (US$27), via Zárate-Gualeguaychú-Puerto Unzué-Fray Bentos-Mercedes.

To Peru: Ormeño (T 313-2259) and El Rápido Internacional (T 393-5057) have a direct service to Lima, from Retiro bus station, 3½ days, US$160 inc all meals, one night spent in Coquimbo, Chile (if you need a visa for Chile, get one before travelling), the route is: Mendoza, Coquimbo, Arica, Tacna, Nasca, Ica, Lima.

● **Air, River and Railway Services**

Brazil: daily air services to São Paulo, Rio de Janeiro and other Brazilian cities. No rail connections.

Chile: no passenger rail services, although freight trains run between Salta and Antofagasta. Foreign and national lines fly daily between Buenos Aires and Santiago, 1½-2 hrs.

Bolivia: no passenger rail services from Argentina to connect with the Bolivian lines from La Quiaca to La Paz and Pocitos to Santa Cruz de la Sierra. There are air services to La Paz and Santa Cruz de la Sierra by AR and LAB.

Paraguay: there are daily air services to Asunción by AR and Lapsa. See also Posadas, page 176. Occasional river boats to Asunción from May to Oct, 11 days, bed and private bath, food and nightly entertainment, US$400, reported good. Details from Tamul, Lavalle 388, T 393-2306/1533.

Uruguay: boat connections: 1) Direct to Montevideo, Buquebus, Córdoba 867, T 313-4444, 'Avión de Buquebus' 4 times a day, 0800, 1130, 1500 (1600 Sat), 1930 (Sun 0800, 1600, 1900, 2350), 3 hrs or 2¹⁄₂ hrs by K55 (summer schedule), US$47 tourist class, US$59 1st class one way inc transport from office to port, vehicles US$93.50-103.50, bus connection to Punta del Este, US$10.

2) To Colonia, services by 2 companies: Buquebus (US$17-20 depending on vessel) with bus connection to Montevideo (US$5 extra), 6 a day. Ferrylíneas Sea Cat, Av Córdoba 699, T 394-6800 (port: Dársena Sur, Ribera Este, T 361-4161) at 0815, 1330, 1830 (Mon-Fri), 0730, 1600 (Sat), 0930, 1900 (Sun), US$18, US$25 inc bus to Montevideo, 1 hr to Colonia, total of 4 to Montevideo. Free bus 1 hr before departure from Florida y Córdoba. Ferrylíneas also run a ferry service to Colonia, with connecting bus to Montevideo, 3-hr crossing, US$8, US$15 inc bus to Montevideo. Mon-Thur 0730, 2330, Fri 0730, Sat-Sun 0800. Cars are carried on both services. Sailings may be cancelled in bad weather.

3) From Tigre to Carmelo, boats are operated by Cacciola at 0800,1730 and 2245, 3 hrs, US$11 to Carmelo, and US$18.50 to Montevideo. Cacciola office: Lavalle y Florida 520,oficina 113, T 322-9374/0026 and Estación Fluvial, local 13, Tigre, credit cards accepted. It is advisable to book in advance; connecting bus from offices to port and from Carmelo to Montevideo.

4) From Tigre to Nueva Palmira, Líneas Delta Argentina, from Tigre 0730, 3 hrs, US$14.

Boats and buses heavily booked Dec-Mar, especially at weekends. **NB** No money changing facilities in Tigre, and poor elsewhere. Beware of overcharging by taxis from the harbour to the centre of Buenos Aires. US$3 port tax is charged on all services to Colonia/Carmelo, US$10 port tax in Buenos Aires. Do not buy Uruguayan bus tickets in BsAs; wait till you get to Colonia.

Several airlines fly from Jorge Newbery Airport (Aeroparque) to Colonia 12 mins, US$30. Buy tickets directly at the Lapa or Ausa counters preferably in advance especially at weekends when flights are fully booked. Continue by bus to Montevideo, or special transport connecting with Lapa flight, US$3-4 to Montevideo. Also from Jorge Newbery, shuttle service to Montevideo, known as Puente Aéreo and run by AR and Pluna, daily 0730 and 0910, 40 mins. Book at Jorge Newbery Airport or T 393-5122/773-0440. To Punta del Este, several flights daily 15 Dec-1 Mar with AR, 40 mins, Pluna (out of season, Fri only), and Lapa (Thur-Sun), US$90.

SUBURBS OF BUENOS AIRES

Olivos (*Pop* about 160,000), on the Río de la Plata coast, 20 mins by the Mitre Railway or 40 mins by Bus No 60, is a favourite residential district. The presidential residence is there.

From Olivos station, walk up C Corrientes with its neocolonial architecture and old, shady trees until you reach the river and the Puerto de Olivos, mainly used for construction materials, but there are a marina (private yacht club) and several *parrilladas* (popular). On Sat and Sun a catamaran sails to Tigre, 2 hrs, rec trip past riverside mansions, sailing boats and windsurfers.

San Isidro (*Pop* 80,000), just beyond Olivos, a resort for golf, yachting, swimming, and athletics, is one of the most attractive suburbs on the coast. Fashionable nightlife here, especially along the river bank. There is a magnificent turf racecourse, an attractive central plaza ('hippy' fair at weekends) and fine colonial buildings with a historical museum.

WEST OF THE CAPITAL

TIGRE

Tigre (*Pop* 40,000) on the Delta of the Paraná about 29 km NW, is a popular recreational centre. Regattas are held in Nov and March. The Tigre Boat Club was founded in 1888. There is an excellent fruit and handicrafts market at nearby Canal San Fernando on Sun. North of Tigre are innumerable canals and rivulets, with holiday homes and restaurants on the banks and a profitable fruit growing centre. The fishing is excellent and the peace is only disturbed by motor-boats at weekends. Regular launch services (lanchas) run to all parts of the Delta, including taxi launches – watch prices for these! – from the wharf. Tourist catamarans, run by Interislena (Lavalle 499, T 731-0261, weekends Lavalle 419, T 731-0264) leave from next to the Cacciola dock, Mon-Fri 1330, 1600, 1¹⁄₂ hrs, US$10, different schedule at weekends. Tren de la Costa (see below) also runs luxury catamaran trips. Longer trips (4¹⁄₂ hrs) to the open Río de la Plata estuary are available.

Museums The Museo Naval, Paseo Victorica 602, is worth a visit (open Mon-Fri 0800-1230, Sat and Sun 1400-1800 US$2, 50% ISIC discount). Covers origins and development of Argentine navy. There are also relics of the 1982 South Atlantic war on display outside. **The Museo de la Reconquista**, Castañeda y Liniers, T 749-0090, Wed-Fri 1000-1200, Sat/Sun 14-18, free to ISIC card holders, near the location of Liniers' landing in 1806, celebrates the reconquest of Buenos Aires from the British in 1806-07.

● **Accommodation** There are no good hotels in Tigre itself. On the islands of the Delta: **A3** pp *El Tropezón*, an old inn on Paraná de las Palmas island, inc meals, formerly a haunt of Hemingway, now frequented by affluent *porteños*, highly rec despite the mosquitoes; **A1** *l'Marangatú*, on Río San Antonio, inc breakfast, pool, sports facilities. Delta **Youth Hostel** at Río Luján y Abra Vieja, **F** pp *Canal de San Fernando*, clean, hot showers, table tennis, volleyball, canoes, ask at Talcahuano 214, Buenos Aires. Take all food in advance, there are basic cooking facilities.

● **Places to eat** Restaurants on the waterfront in Tigre across the Río Tigre from railway line; cheaper places on Italia and Cazón on the near side.

● **Transport Trains** By train from Buenos Aires to new Estación Tigre, US$0.65 one way, every 10 mins during peak hours, otherwise every 15 or 20 mins. Alternatively take train from platform 1 or 2 at Retiro station (FC Mitre) to Bartolomé Mitre and change to the Maipú station (the stations are linked) for the new Tren de la Costa, US$1.50 return, US$2 at weekends, every 12 mins, 30 mins' journey. Several stations on this line have shopping centres (eg San Isidro) and the terminus, Estación Delta, will also have a *centro comercial* in 1998, T 732-6200. **Buses** Take No 60 from Constitución: the 60 'bajo' takes a little longer than the 60 'alto' but is more interesting for sightseeing. **Ferries** To Carmelo, Uruguay leave from Cacciola dock (see page 97). Overnight trips to Carmelo (US$72-110 inc accommodation) and 3 day trips to Montevideo (US$118 inc accommodation) are also available from Cacciola.

Martín García island (Juan Díaz de Solís' landfall in 1516) in the Río de la Plata, 45 km N of Buenos Aires, used to be a military base. Now it is an ecological/historical centre and an ideal excursion from the capital, with many trails through the cane brakes, trees and rocky outcrops – interesting birds and flowers. Some of the old buildings have a colonial air. Boat trips daily except Tues and Thur from Tigre at 0800, returning 1700, 3 hrs' journey, US$45 including lunch and guide (US$22 transport only), 2-day trip US$120. Reservations can be made through Cacciola, Florida 520, p 1, Of 113, T 394-5520, who also handle bookings for the inn and restaurant on the island. For bungalow rental: T (0315) 24546.

LUJAN

(*Pop* 30,000; *Phone code* 0323) 66 km W of the capital, Luján is a place of pilgrimage for all devout Catholics in Argentina. An image of the Virgin was being taken from church to church in the area in 1630 by ox cart. The cart got stuck, in spite of strenuous efforts by men and oxen to move it. This was taken as a sign that the Virgin willed she should stay there. A chapel was built for the image, and around it grew Luján. The chapel has long since been superseded by an impressive neo-Gothic basilica with twin towers and stained glass windows and the Virgin now stands on the High Altar. 8 May is her day. Each arch of the church is dedicated to an Argentine province, and the transepts to Uruguay, Paraguay and Ireland. Behind the Cabildo is the river, with restaurants and pleasant river walks and cruises. Luján is a very popular spot at weekends.

Museums Museo Colonial e Histórico, in the old Cabildo building, is one of the most interesting museums in the country. Exhibits illustrate its historical and political development. Wed-Sat 1200-1730, US$1. General Beresford, the commander of the British troops which seized Buenos Aires in 1806, was a prisoner here, and so, in later days, were Generals Mitre, Paz, and Belgrano. Next to it are museums devoted to transport and to motor vehicles and there is also a poor **Museo de Bellas Artes**.

● **Accommodation & places to eat B** *Centro*, Francia 1062, T 20667, without breakfast; **B** *Eros*, San Martín 129, T 20797, F 21265, without breakfast, good beds. Several others around the terminal inc **C** *Venezia*, Alte Brown 100, basic; *City* and *Berlitz*. There are numerous **restaurants** along the river bank and just off the plaza. An excellent one is *L'Eau Vive* on the road to Buenos Aires at Constitución 2112, it is run by nuns, pleasant surroundings.

● **Buses** Bus 52 from Plaza Once, frequent, 2 hrs, US$3.70 or direct service, 1 hr, US$5.50. To **San Antonio de Areco**, 3 a day, US$4, Empresa Argentina, 1 hr.

SAN ANTONIO DE ARECO

(*Phone code* 0326), 113 km NW of Buenos Aires, is an attractive town of single-storey buildings, tree-lined streets and a popular costanera. It is a popular centre for visiting *estancias*. Many handicrafts are sold, mainly *gaucho* objects, ceramics, silver, leather, colonial furniture.

Museo Gauchesco Ricardo Güiraldes, on Camino Güiraldes y Aureliano, is a replica of a typical *estancia* of the late 19th century, containing artefacts associated with gaucho life. Open daily except Tues, 1000-1800. Güiraldes was a writer who described *gaucho* life, his best-known book is *Don Segundo Sombra*.

There is also a local natural history museum, Parque Metri, on Matheu and Moreno. Sub-Dirección de Turismo at Alsina and Lavalle, T 2101.

Día de la Tradición is a *gaucho* festival with traditional parades, games, events on horseback, music and dance, celebrated in the week up to 10 Nov each year (accommodation is hard to find).

● **Accommodation & places to eat B** *San Carlos*, Zapiola y Zerbione, T 22401, ask in advance for meals; **D** *Res Areco*, Segundo Sombra y Rivadavia, T 22166, good, comfortable, 15% ISIC and GO 25 discounts. **Camping:** nr town centre, also *Auto-camping La Porteña*, 12 km from town on the Güiraldes *estancia*, good access roads. Many *parrilladas* on the bank of the Río Areco.

● **Estancias** Day visits can be made to working *estancias* such as *Cina-Cina*, tour inc typical lunch and riding display, rec. Other *estancias* are: *La Bomba*, T 0326-4053; *Los Patricios*, T 0326-3823 and *El Ombú*.

● **Transport** Buses from Buenos Aires: from Plaza Once, 2 hrs, US$4, every hour; also Chevallier from Retiro bus terminal, US$6, 2 hrs.

South of Buenos Aires

THE ATLANTIC coast south of Buenos Aires with its many resorts, including Necochea, Bahía Blanca and, the most famous, Mar del Plata. This region also covers the inland towns of Tandil, Azul and Santa Rosa as well as the hills of the Sierra de la Ventana.

FROM BUENOS AIRES TO MAR DEL PLATA

From Buenos Aires Route 2 runs S, past the coastal city of La Plata, through Chascomús and Dolores to Mar del Plata, the most celebrated Argentine seaside resort.

LA PLATA

La Plata (*Pop* 545,000; *Phone code* 021), on the Río de la Plata 56 km SE of Buenos Aires was founded in 1882 as capital of Buenos Aires province after the city of Buenos Aires had become federal capital. It has a port and an oil refinery. A motorway is being built to link La Plata with Buenos Aires.

Places of interest

The **Muncipalidad**, an Italiante palace, and **Cathedral** ('a magnificent building with a classical Gothic interior') are in the **Plaza Moreno**. From here Av 51 and Av

53 run NE to **Plaza San Martín**, which is bounded by the French-style **legislature** and the Italianate **Casa de Gobierno**. Further NE lies the **Paseo del Bosque**, a large park containing the Museo de Ciencias Naturales, zoological gardens (entry US$2), astronomical observatory and a racecourse. 8 km W of the city is the **República de los Niños**, an interesting children's village with scaled-down public buildings, built under the first Perón administration; take a green microbus 273 or a red and black 518 to República de los Niños from Plaza San Martín. To the N are the **Islas del Río Santiago**, the Yacht Club, Arsenal and Naval Academy. At **Punta Lara**, a holiday resort nearby, there is a small, interesting nature reserve, slide show and tour, open to public Sat-Sun, 1000-1300 and 1400-1800.

Museo de Ciencias Naturales, in the Paseo del Bosque, houses an outstanding collection of extinct animals and artefacts from precolumbian peoples throughout the Americas. There are zoological, botanical, geological, mineralogical, palaeontological and archaeological sections. Free guided tours, weekdays 1400, 1600, Sat/Sun hourly, in Spanish and in English (phone first). Highly recommended, open daily, 1000-1800, US$3, closed 1 Jan, 1 May, 25 Dec.

Local festivals
Foundation of the City, 19 November.

Local information
● **Accommodation**
A3 *Acuarius*, C 3 No 731, T/F 214229, with breakfast, small beds; *Corregidor*, C 26 No 1026, T 256800, 4-star, modern, a/c, snack bar, central, expensive; **A3** *San Marco*, C 54 No 523, T 42249, good.

C *Rex*, Av 44, No 323, T 212703, modern, a/c; **C** *Plaza*, C 44 entre C3 y 4, with bath.

● **Places to eat**
Restaurants rarely open before 2100. *Don Quijote*, Plaza Paso, good value, best in town, can get very crowded; Chinese 'tenedor libre' at *Guinga*, Plaza Paso; *La Linterna*, C 60 y Av 1, upmarket, good value; *El Chaparral*, good *parrillada*, C 60 y C 117 (Paseo del Bosque). Recommended bar, with steak sandwiches, *El Modelo*, C 54 y C5. Best *empanadas* at *La Madrileña*, a hole-in-the-wall on C 60 between Avs 5 and 6. Best bakery is *El Globo*, C 43 y C 5.

● **Entertainment**
Tango and tropical music at *El Viejo Almacén*, on Diagonal 74, C 2. There are free concerts during the summer in the *Teatro Martín Fierro* in the Paseo del Bosque.

● **Tour companies & travel agents**
Turismo San Martín, C 51 between Avs 7 and 8, rec.

● **Tourist offices**
In the Municipality on Plaza Moreno.

● **Transport**
Trains To/from Buenos Aires (Constitución), frequent, US$1.20 (ticket office hidden behind shops opp platform 6).

Buses To Buenos Aires, 1½ hrs, US$3.20, about every 30 mins. From Buenos Aires, from Retiro day and night and from Plaza Constitución, daytime.

CHASCOMUS

(*Pop* 22,200) 126 km from Buenos Aires, on a wide plain on the shores of Lago Chascomús, which covers 3,000 ha and swells greatly in size during the rains. It is an important breeding place for *pejerrey* fish, amateur fishing competitions are held in the winter season. There are a *gaucho* museum, a Regatta Club and bathing beaches.

● **Accommodation**   Four campsites inc Monte Brown, on the far side of the lake (all nicely located, but poor facilities). **Tourist Farm**: 64 km S of Chascomús and 21 km N of Dolores, nr Castelli, **L3** *Estancia Haras La Viviana*, full board, watersports, bird-watching, fishing, horseriding. Contact Haras La Viviana, Castelli, Gaspar Campos 671, Vicente López CP138, Prov Bs As, T 541-791-2406.

DOLORES

(*District pop* 30,000), 204 km from Buenos Aires, was founded in 1818, destroyed by Indians 3 years later, and rebuilt. It is a grain and cattle farming centre. The **Museo y Parque Libres del Sur**, commemorating the revolt of the district against Rosas in the early 19th century, is interesting and well displayed. **Museo de Bellas Artes**, Belgrano 134, Wed-Sun 1000-1700.

● **Accommodation**   **B** *Hotel Plaza*, very pleasant; **B-C** *Avenida* Olavarría 362, T (0245) 7619, 4 blocks from Plaza, ugly but OK. *Parrilladas*, *heladerías* and nightlife on C Buenos Aires.

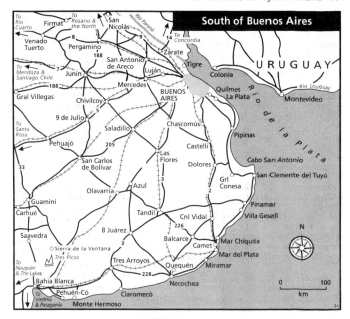

South of Buenos Aires

- **Transport Local Taxi**: taxi stand at Belgrano y Rico, 1 block from plaza, T 3507. **Trains** Station 15 mins from centre, $3\frac{1}{2}$ hrs to Buenos Aires, US\$8. **Buses** To Buenos Aires, 3 hrs, Río de la Plata, Buenos Aires 285, Cóndor/La Estrella, Buenos Aires 300 block.

SAN CLEMENTE DEL TUYU

(Phone code 0252), 107 km E of Dolores, is the nearest Atlantic coastal resort to Buenos Aires. A family resort, it is cheaper than the more fashionable resorts further S. At **Punta Rasa**, 9 km away, there are an old lighthouse and a nature reserve owned by the Fundación Vida Silvestre, which, in summer, is home to thousands of migratory birds from the northern hemisphere.

- **Accommodation** Many places along the promenade, inc **B** *Acuario*, San Martín 444, T 21357, inc breakfast; **C** *Splendid*, C 1 No 2430, T 21316; **C** *Res Bahía*, C 4, between C 1 y C 15, breakfast inc, good. Several campsites.

- **Places to eat** *Restaurante Yo y Vos*, C 4 y C 17, large and cheap portions, friendly, good.

- **Banks & money changers** US dollars can be changed at the **Banco de la Provincia de** Buenos Aires, C 1 y C 4, but TCs are not accepted anywhere in town.

- **Entertainment** 3 km from the centre, nr the harbour (micro bus 500) is **Mundo Marino**, the largest oceanarium in South America (T 0252-21071); attractions include 2 killer whales, dolphins, elephant seals, sea lions and penguins; open daily from 1000, closes 1530 May-Sept, 1630 Mar-April, Oct-Dec, 1800 Jan-February.

- **Buses** To Mar del Plata, frequent, Empresa Costamar, US\$11, 5 hrs. To Buenos Aires, several companies, US\$15-20.

PINAMAR

(Phone code 0254), 89 km S of San Clemente, is a resort with a casino, which is eclipsing Mar del Plata. The water-skiing is good. Fish may be bought on the beach from local fishermen. Tourist office, helpful, is on the main plaza.

- **Accommodation A1** *Playas*, Bunge y de la Sierra, T 82236, F 82226, with breakfast, English spoken. Many, from *Arenas*, Bunge 700, T 82444, 4-star, to *Berlín*, Rivadavia 326, T 82320, 1-star. All hotels fully booked throughout Jan-March. Houses and apartments can be rented from Dec-March: 2-room flats about

US$1,000/month, up to US$5,000 for a mansion. In March rates are halved. **Youth hostel**: Nuestras Malvinas y Sarmiento, T 82908. **Camping**: 3 sites inc *Moby Dick* at Ostende, T 86045, 5 km from beach. On beach at Ostende is *St Tropez*, US$18 (take green *Montemar* bus from terminal).

VILLA GESELL

(Pop 8,700; *Phone code* 0255) 22 km further S, a modern resort with a chocolate factory, fine beaches and over 100 hotels; it has become very popular although less crowded than Mar del Plata.

● **Accommodation** *Terrazas Club*, 4-star, suite accommodation, Av 2 entre C 104 y 105, T 63214; *Colón*, 2-star, 3 blocks from beach at Av 4, C 104, T 62310, restaurant; **B** *Hostería Gran Chalet*, Paseo 105 No 447 y Av 4-5, T 62913, rec; **C** *Bero*, Av 4 y C 141, T 66077, opp bus terminal; **E** pp *Hosp San Hector*, Av 8, No 641, T 62052. Rates for apartment rental as Pinamar. **Camping sites**: many, a few open all year round. **Youth hostel**: *Albergue Camping El Coyote*, Alameda 212 y 306, Barrio Norte, T 68448.

● **Transport Air** With AR and Lapa. **Buses** Direct to Buenos Aires, US$29, Empresa Antón and Río de la Plata, book in advance at weekends. Tourist office at terminal.

MAR DEL PLATA

(Phone code 023), the greatest Argentine resort, dating from the turn of the century, is 130 km further S and 400 km from the capital. There are 8 km of beaches. The normal population is 407,000, but during the summer about 2 million visitors stay there. There are all classes of apartment blocks, boarding houses and lodgings but it is necessary to book in advance between late Dec and mid-Mar (when the night-life continues all night). For the rest of the year the town is fairly quiet and good value.

Places of interest

The most attractive area is around **Playa Bristol**: here are the fine casino (upper floor open to the public), the *Gran Hotel Provincial*, and, behind, the Plaza Colón. Further N is the **Plaza San Martín**, flanked by the attractive cathedral. Southeast of Plaza Colón around C Colón y Gral Alvear at the top of a hill, are some of the more 'eccentric' mansions of the early 20th century inc the Norman style **Villa Ortiz Basualdo**, and the

mock Tudor mansion nearby.

Other beaches include fashionable **Playa Grande**, with its private clubs and the summer estates of wealthy *porteños* and **Playa La Perla**, with moderately priced hotels. At **Punta Iglesia** there is a large rock carving of Florentino Ameghino, the palaeontologist who collected most of the fossils in the museum at La Plata. South of Playa Grande is the port, reached by bus, 15 mins from terminal. There are a large fishing fleet, excursion boats, seafood restaurants and a huge sealion colony (walk along Escollera Sursouthern breakwater).

The wooded municipally-owned **Parque Camet** is 8 km N. It has polo grounds and playing fields. Visits can be paid to the rocky promontory of **Cabo Corrientes** to watch the breakers; to **Punta Mogotes** lighthouse (open Thur 1330-1700); to the **Gruta de Lourdes**, and the **Bosque Peralta Ramos**. Fishing is good all along the coast and *pejerrey, corvina* and *pescadilla* abound; you can charter a private launch for shark fishing.

Museums

Museo de Hombre del Puerto – Cleto Ciocchini, Padre J Dutto 383, Thurs/Fri/Sat 1500-1900, US$2, shows the history of the port and its first Sicilian fishermen. **Museo Municipal de Ciencias Naturales**, Libertad 2999, small but interesting. **Museo Municipal de Arte**, Colón 1189, is housed in the Villa Ortíz Basualdo, which dates from 1909; upper floors of the mansion can be visited, art exhibitions on the ground floor, open weekdays except Wed 1200-1700, Sat/Sun 1400-1900, US$2, free Tues. **Centro Cultural Victoria Ocampo**, Matheu 1851, is housed in the Villa Victoria, a beautiful early 20th century wooden house prefabricated in England, where the famous author spent her summers until her death in 1979; inside are artefacts from her life and temporary exhibition, daily 1400-2000, US$2, ISIC cards US$1. Nearby is the **Villa Mitre**, in the former mansion of a son of Bartolomé Mitre; inside are an ecclectic collection of artefacts inc photos of the city at different points in its history.

Excursions

To the Mar Chiquita, 34 km N, a lagoon joined to the sea by a narrow channel, offering good fishing, yachting, boating and bathing. Also to the Laguna de los Padres and to Balcarce (see below).

Local festivals

10 Feb (Foundation of City); 10 Nov (Day of Tradition); 22 Nov (Sta Cecilia).

Local information

● Accommodation

During summer months it is essential to book in advance. Many hotels open in season only. Out of season, bargain everywhere. 4-star *Provincial*, Blvd Marítimo 2500, T 916376, grand hotel overlooking Playa Bristol; **A1** many 4-star inc *Argentino*, Belgrano y Entre Ríos, also appartments, highly rec; *Astor*, Entre Ríos 1649, T 23051/4, small, no credit cards, 3 mins from beach.

Among the 3-star hotels (**A2**) are: *Benedetti*, Colón 2198, T 30031/2, rec; **A3** *O Sole Mio*, Av Independencia 1277, T 26685, half board, Italian run, highly rec.

Budget accommodation: **B** *Cosmos*, Buenos Aires 2481, T 933544, with breakfast; **B** *Boedo*, Almte Brown 1771, T 24695, hot water, good value, nr beaches (open Jan-Feb only); **B** *Canciller*, Gascon 1639, T 512513, with breakfast; **B** *Sousas*, Alsina y Rawson, T/F 511549, without breakfast; **B** *Piemonte*, Buenos Aires 2447, T 954113, with breakfast, good beds; **C** *Monterrey*, Lamadrid 2627, T 23266, good; **C** *Niza*, Santiago del Estero 1843 (**E** out of season), safe, rec.

Near the bus terminal: **B** *Europa*, Arenales 2735, T 40436, quiet, hot water; **C** *Hosp Paraná*, Lamadrid 2749, T 42825; **C** *Peley*, on Alberti, comfortable, open all year, rec, good value restaurant; **D** pp *Wilton Palace*, Las Heras, T 514456, without breakfast, adequate; **D** pp *Ushuaia*, Gascón 1561, T 510911, with breakfast, pleasant.

Camping: *Pinar de la Serena*, Ruta Provincial 11 y C 3, and other sites, reasonable prices. Several on the road S.

Youth hostel: **D** pp *Pergamino*, Tucumán 2728, T 957927, nr terminal, friendly, clean, small IYHA discount.

Apartment rental: there are many houses and apartments for rent. Monthly rates for summer exclude electricity, gas etc. Flats US$4,200-600, chalets US$550-1,000, houses US$800-1,800. The tourist office has a list of companies.

● Places to eat

Many seafood restaurants nr the fishing port. *El Caballito Blanco*, Rivadavia 2534, excellent, German decor; *Gruta de Capri*, Belgrano 2161, not cheap but excellent value; *La Paella*, Entre Ríos 2025, good. Seafood restaurants in the Centro Comercial Puerto inc *La Caracola*, good but not cheap; *La Piazzetta*, Plaza San Martín, good pasta and salads, vegetarian options; *Teresa*, San Luis 2081, fresh pasta dishes, good value; *Lo de Terri*, Gascón y San Luis, good *parrilla*; *Raviolandia*, Colón y Las Heras, good, cheap, try the seafood with rice. Many *tenedor libre* restaurants of all kinds along San Martín. *Los Inmortales*, Corrientes 1662, good, moderately priced. Good value meals at *La Nueva Glorieta*, Alberti 1821, and *El Nuevo Hispano*, Alberti 1933. Many cheap restaurants along Rivadavia.

● Bars

Marienplatz, Belgrano y Entre Rios, most stylish *confitería* in town, highly rec but expensive; smart bars around C Alem, popular in summer and weekends.

● Banks & money changers

Lloyds Bank, Av Luro 3101. Open 1000-1600, cash advances on Visa. Casas de Cambio **Jonestur**, San Martín 2574 best rates for TCs; **Amex**, Colón 2605, does not cash TCs; **La Moneta**, Rivadavia 2623; **Mar del Plata Cambio**, Buenos Aires 1910; Visa ATM, Santa Fe y Rivadavia.

● Cultural centres

Cultural events: reduced price tickets are often available from *Cartelera Baires*, Santa Fe 1844, local 33 or from *Galería de los Teatros*, Santa Fe 1751. **La Cultura** (formerly Sociedad de Cultura Inglesa), San Luis 2498, friendly, extensive library.

● Entertainment

Casino: open Dec to end-April, 1600-0330; 1600-0400 on Sat. Winter opening, May-Dec, Mon-Fri 1500-0230; weekends 1500-0300. Entrance US$5.

Cinemas: *Cine Arte* at Centro Cultural Pueyrredón, 25 de Mayo y La Rioja, every Mon, US$1.50, followed by discussion; Wed 50% discount at all cinemas.

Discos: most are on Av Constitución.

● Laundry

Laverap, Buenos Aires 2680, Entre Ríos y Rivadavia and Moreno y Corrientes.

● Post & telecommunications

Post Office: Luro 2460, poste restante, also international parcels office (open till 1200). **Telecommunications**: Luro y Santiago del Estero; many *locutorios* around the town.

● **Tourist offices**
Blvd Marítimo 2267, T 41325, open 0800-2000 (later in summer), English spoken, good information, inc bus routes to all sites of interest.

● **Useful addresses**
Immigration Office: Chile y Alberti, open am.

● **Transport**
Air Camet airport, 10 km from town. Many flights daily to Buenos Aires, Austral, Lapa (T 922112) and AR. Southern Winds (T 932121) to Salta, Tucumán and Córdoba. *Remise* taxi from airport to town, mini bus US$3.50.

Trains To Buenos Aires (Constitución) 5¼ hrs, from Estación Norte, Luro 4599, about 13 blocks from the centre. See under Buenos Aires, **Trains** for details. To Miramar, from Estación Sur, J B Justo y Olazábal, daily except Sun, 0500, 1830, 1½ hrs.

Buses Terminal in former railway station at Alberti y Las Heras, central. To **Buenos Aires** 6 hrs, US$26, Micromar, Costera Criolla, also has *coche cama*, Empresa Argentina, Chevallier; to **Miramar** hourly, 45 mins, US$4; El Cóndor and Rápido Argentino to **La Plata**, US$20; La Estrella to **San Martín de los Andes**, US$56; to **Bariloche**, US$60 (none direct, change at Bahía Blanca or Tres Arroyos); to **Bahía Blanca**, only Pampa, 6 daily, US$25, 5½ hrs; to **San Clemente del Tuyú**, Empresa Costamar, frequent, US$11, 5 hrs. To **Puerto Madryn** and **Trelew**, Wed and Sat night. For hitchhiking S, take a colectivo to the monument to El Gaucho.

INLAND FROM MAR DEL PLATA

Picturesque spots reached from Route 226 inland to Balcarce are (19 km) **Laguna de los Padres** (a *reserva provincial*), Sierra de los Padres and (32 km beyond) the **Laguna La Brava**, at the foot of the Balcarce hills.

68 km W of Mar del Plata, is the town of **Balcarce** (*Pop* 28,800), a centre for visits to the Cinco Cerros, five strangely shaped hills. Balcarce is the birthplace of the great racing driver **Juan Fangio**; it has a racing circuit and the **Museo Juan Manuel Fangio** which houses all his racing cars and trophies (C 17 y C 18, open 1100-1800, US$5, recommended). Frequent buses from Mar del Plata. Excellent *parrillas* on the outskirts.

● **Accommodation** **B** *Balcarce*, C 17, T 22055, good.

TANDIL

(*Pop* 125,000; *Phone code* 0293) Beyond Balcarce Route 226 runs 103 km NW to **Tandil**, at the northern end of the Sierra de Tandil, a ridge of hills which run W from the sea into the pampa for 250 km. The air is splendidly clear and refreshing and the Holy Week festivities are outstanding. There is a beautiful lake in the city. Excursions to the Sierra La Aurora.

● **Accommodation & places to eat B** *Plaza*, Gen Pinto 438, T 27160, 3-star, comfortable and quiet; **C** *Kaiku*, Mitre 902, T 23114, basic; **C** *Turista*, 14 de Julio 60, T 22626, 1 star; *Libertador*, Mitre 545, T 22127, central, good value. Recommended restaurant is *El Estribo*, San Martín 759, good atmosphere.

● **Buses** To Buenos Aires, 6 hrs, US$15.

AZUL

(*Pop* about 45,000; *Phone code* 0281) 92 km from Tandil, 264 km SW of Buenos Aires, Azul is a cattle centre with an attractive plaza, a French Gothic-style Cathedral and an ethnographic museum. A good stopping place if driving S from Buenos Aires on Route 3 to Bahía Blanca. The river has been dammed to provide a watersports centre.

● **Accommodation B** *Gran Hotel Azul*, Colón 626, T 22011, excellent cafeteria; **C** *Res Blue*, Mitre 983, T 22742, nr bus station; and others. Municipal campsite, on river bank, hot showers, pleasant.

MAR DEL PLATA TO BAHIA BLANCA

MIRAMAR

(*Pop* 17,500; *Phone code* 0563) lies 53 km SW of Mar del Plata along the coast road. Cheaper than Mar del Plata, the cliffs backing the beach are higher and the surrounding hills more picturesque. There is a fine golf course at *Hotel Golf Roca* and a casino. Immediately S of the city limits is an extensive forest park on the beach, the **Vivero Dunicola**, whose vegetation stays green and blooming throughout the year, despite winter night-time temperatures below freezing. 14 km S, among dunes and black rocks, is Mar del Sur (*Atlantic Hotel*) with good fishing in a lagoon and bathing on the beach.

● **Accommodation** Dozens of hotels and apartments. **B** *Santa Eulalia I*, C 26 No 851, T 20808, friendly but run down; **B** *Villa Cruz*, C 19, No 864, friendly, clean, nr the beach. **Camping:** **F** pp *El Durazno*, 3 km from town, good facilities, shops, restaurant, take bus 501 marked 'Playas'. Many sites, reasonably priced.

● **Tourist offices** On central plaza, has maps.

● **Transport Trains** Ferrobus daily except Sun to Mar del Plata, 0630, 2000. **Buses** To Buenos Aires, Chevallier, Micromar and Costera Criolla, 8 a day, US$31; to Mar del Plata, US$4, Rápido del Sud, Pampa; to Necochea, Pampa.

NECOCHEA

(*Pop* 52,000;*Phone code* 0262), situated about 110 km further SW along the coast, is another famous resort, second only to Mar del Plata. The town is in two parts, with the centre 2 km inland from the seafront area. There is a large Danish community, Danish club and consulate. Its 24 km long beach is one of the best in the country. There is a municipal recreation complex, with a large casino deteriorating in the salt air (open summer daily and winter weekends 2200-0400), various sports facilities, a cinema, discoteque and children's play area. The Parque Miguel Lillo (named after the Argentine botanist) faces the beach, comprising 400 ha of conifers, nature park, swan lake with paddle boats, an amphitheatre, museum and go-cart track. The surroundings are picturesque.

About 3½ km across the mouth of the river from Necochea is **Quequén**, with an excellent beach, good bathing, and pleasant scenery.

● **Accommodation** The Hotel Association is at Av 79 y C 4. Most hotels are in the seafront area from C 2 (parallel with beach) N between Av 71-91. There are at least 100 within 700m of the beach. Most close off-season when it is worth bargaining. **A3** *Hostería del Bosque*, C 89 No 350, entre 8 y 10, T/F 20002, 5 blocks from beach, quiet, upper rooms better, nice bar and garden, parking next door; on plaza, *San Miguel*, C 85 No 301 esq 6, T/F 25155, and *San Martín*, C 6 No 4198 esq 85, T/F 37000, restaurant; **B** *Hostería Necochea*, C 8, No 4365, T 22047, nr beach, open all year; **B** *Doramar*, C 79, No 357, T 25815, family run, helpful; **A3** *Perugia*, C 81, No 288, T 22020, a/c, open

all year; **C** *Hosp Solchaga*, C 62, No 2822, T 25584, excellent; **E** *Hosp Bayo*, C 87, No 363, T 23334. Several in Quequén. The tourist office has a list of apartments for rent. **Camping:** *Río Quequén*, C 22 y Ribera Río Quequén, T 22145; campsites on beach expensive in season.

● **Places to eat** *Rex*, C 62, 'a trip to 1952 Paris', not cheap.

● **Language schools** *Instituto Argentino de Idiomas*, Galería Monviso, local 8, C 62 y 63, rec.

● **Tourist offices** On beach front at Av 79 y Av 2, T 38333, English spoken.

● **Buses** Terminal at Av 47 y C 582, 4 km from the centre; bus 513, 517 from outside the terminal to the beach. Taxi to beach area US$3. To **Buenos Aires**, US$44, La Estrella, El Cóndor and Costera Criolla; to **Mar del Plata**, Pampa US$10; to **Bahía Blanca**, Pampa US$22; to **Tres Arroyos** US$10.

TRES ARROYOS

(*Pop* 85,000;*Phone code* 0983), about 195 km E of Bahía Blanca, is a cattle and wheat growing centre. Many inhabitants are of Dutch origin (Dutch consulate and school). There is also an important Danish colony, with school, club and consulate. A 68 km paved road runs S to the sea at the pleasant little resort of **Claromecó**, with a beautiful beach of dark sand backed by high dunes.

● **Accommodation & places to eat At Tres Arroyos:** inc **A3** *Parque*, Pellegrini 23, T 31350, restaurant, rec; **B** *Alfil*, Rivadavia 140, T 27002, restaurant; *Andrea*, Istilart 228, T 26214, good. *Restaurant Di Troppo*, Moreno 133, good; *Tres Amigos*, Chacabuco 102, popular *parrilla*. **At Claromecó:** several hotels and restaurants. **Camping at Claromecó:** good campsite *Dunamar*, ACA, US$6 pp, hot showers, fire pits and laundry facilities.

● **Buses** Terminal a few blocks from the centre of Tres Arroyos. Buenos Aires-Claromecó, La Estrella, US$40. Tres Arroyos-Claromecó twice daily off season, extra buses from mid-Dec in season. Pampa bus to Mar del Plata 0650, 4½ hrs.

BAHIA BLANCA

(*Pop* 300,000, *Phone code* 091), the most important centre S of Mar del Plata, stands at the head of a large bay at the mouth of the Río Naposta. Bahía Blanca is the centre of an urban area of over a million people, consisting of the city itself, built back from the river front, and five ports at various distances from the city strung along the N bank of the Naposta: Arroyo Pareja and the naval base of Puerto Belgrano at the mouth of the estuary; Puerto Ingeniero White, 23 km inland (reached by buses 500, 501, 504 from the plaza), Puerto Galván, 3½ km beyond, and Cuatreros, 8 km upstream.

Places of interest

The city has some fine buildings especially around the central **Plaza Rivadavia**, notably the ornate Italianate Municipalidad and the French-style Banco de la Nación. There is a modest **Jardín Zoológico** in Parque Independencia, Ruta 3 y Av Pringles, on the outskirts. The **Barrio Inglés** (direction Ingeniero White) is where the foremen and technicians of the port and railway construction teams lived; Brickman St, just past the railway bridge, is a row of late Victorian semi-detached houses. Managers lived at nearby Harding Green.

Museums

Museo Histórico, in the Teatro Municipal, Alsina 425, including sections on the pre-conquest period, the conquest and interesting photos of early Bahía Blanca. Outside is a statue of Garibaldi, erected by the Italian community in 1928. **Museo del Puerto**, Torres y Carrega, Ingeniero White, excellent displays of domesic artefacts from the early 20th century. Serves as a *confitería* on Sun. Bus 500, 504. **Museo de Bellas Artes**, in basement of Municipalidad, Alsina 65, small, free.

Excursions

To the E of Bahía Blanca is an enormous stretch of sandy beaches, developed for visitors (it is usually windy in the afternoon). **Pehuén-Có**, 70 km away (hotel, C, quiet and clean), is an example of the beaches with camping places, well shaded by pine trees (beware of jellyfish when wind is in the S). Signs to it on the main road 24 km from Bahía Blanca. Another fine beach, with hotels and camping places (all closed off season) is **Monte Hermoso**, 106 km, 2 hrs by bus (4 a day in summer, 2 in winter) E of Bahía Blanca. Good cheap meals, several restaurants. (Its hotels are open only Jan-Mar, several camp-

sites – including *Las Dunas*, 30 mins' walk W along the beach, US$3 pp, a friendly spot run by an elderly German couple.)

Local holidays

Sept 24 (Our Lady of Mercy); Nov 10 (Day of Tradition).

Local information

● **Accommodation**

Most hotels charge extra for parking. **A1** *Austral*, Colón 159, T 20241, F 553737, 4-star, restaurant; **A3** *Ameghino*, Valle Encantado 60, T 81098, nr beach; **A3** *ACA Motel Villa Borden*, Av Sesquicentenario, entre Rutas 3 y 35, T 40151, F 21098.

B *Belgrano*, Belgrano 44, T/F 20240/30498, without breakfast, restaurant; *Italia*, Brown 181, T 20121, simple, restaurant; *Muñiz*, O'Higgins 23, T 20021, central; **B** *Barne*, H Yrigoyen 270, T 30864, F 550513, with breakfast, helpful, family run, rec; **B** *Bayón*, Chiclana 487, T 22504, safe; **B** *Victoria*, Gral Paz 82, T 20522, basic, hot water, rec.

C *Chiclana*, Chiclana 370, T 30436, **D** without bath, basic, poor beds; **C** *Del Sur*, 19 de Mayo 75, T 22452, with restaurant, noisy with traffic; **C** *Res Roma*, Cerri 759, T 38500, cheaper without bath; **C** *Hosp Andrea*, Lavalle 88, a/c; **D** *Los Angeles*, Chiclana 367, basic. Other *residenciales* nr railway station, eg **D** *Los Vascos*, Cerri 747, T 29290.

Camping: Balneario Maldonado, 4 km from centre, US$5/tent, US$1 pp, next to petrochemical plant, salt water swimming pool, bus 514 along Av Colón every hour but only when beach is open, ie when sunny and not in evening. Many others.

● **Places to eat**

La Cigala, Cerri 757, very good; *Il Vesuvio*, San Martín 337, good lunch, cheap; *La Casita de Miguel*, San Martín 510, good *comedor*, good food; *Da Sergio*, Gorriti 61, good with large portions, good value; *Café La Bahía*, Chiclana 548, good value, rec; *Bar/Comedor*, Mitre y Casanova, similar. A few good fish restaurants at the harbour, eg *El Royal*. Very good seafood and fish at Ingeniero White. *North Western Café*, Alsina 236, American bar, pizzas, happy hour 1600-1800.

● **Banks & money changers**

Lloyds Bank (BLSA), Chiclana 102; **Citibank**, Colón 58; **Amex**, Fortur, Soler 38, T 26290, *poste restante*, English spoken. *Casas de Cambio*: **Pullman**, San Martín 171, changes US$, TCs to US$ notes, 3% commission on TCs, good rates (closes 1600); **Viajes Bahía Blanca**, Drago 63, good rates. All *casas de cambio* closed at weekends.

● **Laundry**

Laverap, Villarrino 87 and at Perú 122; *Daimar*, Mitre 184.

● **Post & telecommunications**
Post Office: Moreno 34. **Telephones**: O'Higgins 203.

● **Shopping**
Good gaucho shop on Soler, nr Fortur (see above), genuine articles.

● **Tourist offices**
In town hall on main plaza, Alsina 43, Mon-Fri 0800-1200, very helpful.

● **Transport**
Local Bus: US$0.65, but you need to buy *carnets* (cards) from kiosks for 1, 2 or 4 journeys.

Air Comandante Espora, 11 km from centre. Austral and Lapa (T 46566) to **Buenos Aires**. To **Comodoro Rivadavia**, **Río Gallegos** and **Río Grande**, Austral and Kaiken. Lapa and TAN to **Neuquén**.

Trains Station at Av Gral Cerri 780, T 21168. To Buenos Aires daily 2000, 12 hrs, 6/96.

Buses Terminal in old railway station 2½ km from centre at Estados Unidos y Brown, connected by buses 505, 514, 517, no hotels nearby. To **Buenos Aires** frequent, several companies, 10 hrs, US$30-34, shop around; to **Mar del Plata**, Río Paraná, US$25, 5½ hrs; to **Córdoba**, US$44, 12 hrs; to **Neuquén**, 6 a day, 8 hrs, US$20; to **Necochea**, Pampa, 5 hrs, US$22; to **Zapala** 3 daily, 11 hrs, US$25, El Valle; to **Río Colorado** US$8, **Viedma** 3 a day, 4 hrs; to **Trelew**, 3/week, US$32, 12 hrs; to **Río Gallegos**, Don Otto US$80.
    To **Tornquist**, US$4, 0600, 1300, 1720, 1 hrs, last return 2020; to **Sierra de la Ventana** (town) 0600, 2040 (not Sat).

Hitchhiking S or W from Bahía Blanca is possible but not too easy. Most southbound traffic takes Route 22 via Río Colorado. North to Buenos Aires on Route 3 is 'virtually impossible'.

SIERRA DE LA VENTANA

Some 100 km to the N is the **Sierra de la Ventana**, a favourite area for excursions from Bahía Blanca.

The small town of **Tornquist**, 32 km N of Bahía Blanca by Route 33, with an attractive church on the central plaza, is a good starting point (**B** *Gran Central*, Av 9 de Julio, T 091-94005, seedy but friendly; campsite, US$4 pp). The town of Pigue is also recommended as a good base. From Route 33 take Route 76 towards the town of Sierra de la Ventana. After 32 km is the entrance to the **Parque Provincial**, with massive ornate gates from the Tornquist family home. From here it's a 3-hr walk to

the summit of Cerro La Ventana, which has fantastic views from the 'window' in the summit ridge (camping at the base, free, basic facilities, canteen). 5 km further is the forestry station, with audio-visual display, trips to see wild deer, wild horses, guanacos, and on Fri and Sun trips at 0900 to two caves, one an Indian cemetery, the other with petroglyphs (US$0.70). Villa Ventana, 10 km further, is a wooden settlement with excellent teashop, *Casa de Heidi*, and wholefood available from *Jardín de Aylem*. Municipal campsite by river with all facilities.

The town of **Sierra de la Ventana**, further E, is a good centre for exploring the hills. Tres Picos, rising bare and barren from the rich farmlands to 1,070m, is only 6¼ km away. There is a 9-hole golf course, and good trout fishing in the Río Sauce Grande. Excellent tourist information.

● **Accommodation A3** *Provincial*, Drago y Malvinas, T 915025; **D** *La Perlita*, San Martín y Roca, T 915020; **E** pp *Yapay*, Av San Martín nr bus terminal, quiet, rec. **Youth hostel**: *Albergue Sierra de la Ventana* (sleeping bag necessary).

CARHUE

(*Pop* 18,000; *Phone code* 0936), 93 km N of Bahía Blanca by road via Saavedra. Behind the town hall is a museum of the wars against the Indians. Tourist information at bus station. Lago Epecuén, by the town, covers over 40,000 ha and is over 20 times saltier than the sea. No fish can live in the water, which is recommended for chronic rheumatism and skin diseases. There are many hotels and *residenciales* at the lake side. The ghost town of Lago Epecuén, 15 km away, drowned by the lake in 1985, can be visited (unpaved road).

● **Accommodation & services** Hotel *Shalom*, Belgrano 880, T 2503, C, 'eccentric but clean', breakfast extra. Restaurant at bus terminal is reasonable. **Camping**: free site in the beach area, no facilities. Rotary Club site 2 km from Carhué.

Guaminí (*Pop* 3,500), about 38 km by road NE of Carhué, is a pleasant summer hill resort on the shore of Laguna del Monte, not as salty as Lago Epecuén. Accommodation and camping at the lake; *pejerrey* fishing.

Córdoba and the Central Sierras

CORDOBA has some historic, colonial buildings and is an important route centre, especially for road travel to the northwest. It is the Republic's second city. The Sierras de Córdoba contain many pleasant, small resorts in the hills.

FROM BUENOS AIRES TO CORDOBA

There are two main routes: the shorter (713 km) is via Rosario (see page 168) and **Villa María**, an important crossroads where the Rosario-Córdoba highway meets the highway linking central Chile with Paraguay, Uruguay and Brazil. It is a prosperous agricultural town (*Pop* 68,000).

● **Accommodation** B *City*, Buenos Aires 1184, T 20948; C *Alcázar*, Alvear y Ocampo, T 25948, nr bus station, good value.

The longer (835 km) is via San Antonio de Areco, Pergamino, **Venado Tuerto** (154 km; *Pop* 58,000; Country Club; several hotels) and **Río Cuarto** (*pop* 138,000). There is a golf club and a fine old municipal building with a lookout tower worth seeing. In April/May one of the country's biggest motor races is held here.

● **Accommodation** B *Gran*, Sobremonte 725, T 33401, 3-star; C *Alihué*, Sarsfield 58, good value, very friendly, big rooms. Near bus terminal on Sobremonte 100-200 block are three cheap *Residenciales*, *El Ciervo*, *Hosp El Bambi*, *Res Monge*, all **C**. Municipal campsite, *El Verano*.

● **Banks & money changers** Lucero Viajes, Constitución 564, T 33656, only place changing TCs, 3% commission.

● **Buses** To Buenos Aires, US$34, frequent service; to Mendoza, US$24; to Córdoba US$10; to Santiago, Chile, frequent.

North of Río Cuarto Córdoba is 225 km N of Río Cuarto across flatlands and rolling hills. About half-way between the two, the road runs along the retaining wall of the great Río Tercero dam; the artificial lake here is used for recreation. The town of Río Tercero (several hotels) has gained in importance with the development of groundnut plantations and a local military factory.

CORDOBA

(*Pop* 1.2 million; *Alt* 440m; *Phone code* 051), capital of Córdoba Province and Argentina's second city, was founded as early as 1573. The site of the first university in the country, established in 1613 by the Jesuits, it now has two universities. It is an important industrial centre, the home of Argentina's motor industry, and a busy modern city with a flourishing shopping centre.

Places of interest

At the heart of this bustling city is the tranquil **Plaza San Martín**, with a statue of the Liberator. On the W side is the old **Cabildo**, for many years used as the police headquarters. Part is now occupied by tourist offices; inside are 2 patios which form the Casa de la Cultura. Next to it stands the **Cathedral**, the oldest in Argentina, built 1697-1787, with attractive stained-glass windows and a richly-decorated ceiling: see the remarkable cupola. Behind the cathedral is the pleasant Plaza del Fundador, with a statue to the city founder Jerónimo Luís de Cabrera. One of the features of this part of the city is its old churches. Near Plaza San Martín at Independencia 122 is the 16th century **Carmelo convent** and chapel of **Santa Teresa**. The church of **La Compañía**, Obispo Trejos y Caseros, with a simple façade, dates from about 1650; its façade was rebuilt in the 20th century. The barrel vault and cupola of the Capilla Doméstica

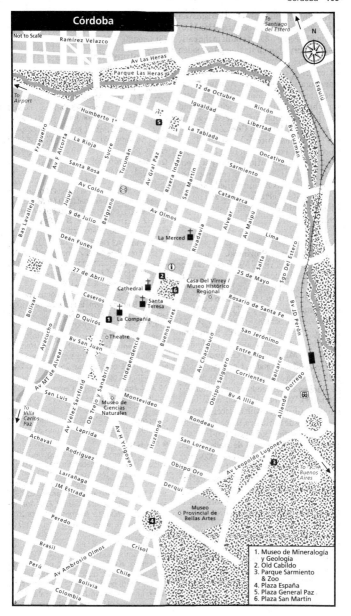

Córdoba

Not to Scale

To Santiago del Estero

N

To Airport

To Villa Carlos Paz

Ramírez Velazco

Av Las Heras

Parque Las Heras

12 de Octubre

Igualdad

Rincón

Libertad

Humberto 1°

La Tablada

Oncativo

Fragueiro

La Rioja

Sucre

Tucumán

Av Gral Paz

Rivera Indarte

San Martín

Sarmiento

Av Alcorta

Santa Rosa

Av Colón

Jujuy

Belgrano

Av Olmos

Catamarca

Alvear

Av Maipú

Lima

9 de Julio

Deán Funes

Rivadavia

La Merced

27 de Abril

Caseros

Cathedral

Santa Teresa

La Compañía

Bolívar

D Quirós

Theatre

Buenos Aires

25 de Mayo

Salta

Sgo Del Estero

Casa Del Virrey / Museo Histórico Regional

Rosario de Santa Fe

San Jerónimo

Bv JD Perón

Ayacucho

Av MT de Alvear

Bv San Juan

Independencia

Sanabria

Av Chacabuco

Entre Ríos

Corrientes

Obispo Salguero

Bv A Illia

Allende

Balcarce

Dorrego

San Luis

Av Vélez Sarsfield

Ob Trejo

Montevideo

Museo de Ciencias Naturales

Achaval

Laprida

Av H Yrigoyen

Ituzaingó

Rondeau

San Lorenzo

Rodríguez

Larrañaga

JM Estrada

Obispo Oro

Derqui

Av Leopoldo Lugones

To Buenos Aires

Peredo

Museo Provincial de Bellas Artes

Brasil

Crisol

Perú

Av Ambrosio Olmos

Chile

Bolivia

Colombia

Esquiú

Bv Guzmán

12 de Octubre

1. Museo de Mineralogía y Geología
2. Old Cabildo
3. Parque Sarmiento & Zoo
4. Plaza España
5. Plaza General Paz
6. Plaza San Martín

of this church, built entirely of Paraguayan cedar, are unique. The basilica of **La Merced** at 25 de Mayo 83, was built in the early 19th century, though its fine gilt wooden pulpit dates from the colonial period. On its exterior, overlooking Rivadavia, are fine murals by local artist Armando Sica. There are some pleasant small 18th century churches with striking bell gables and undulating pediments. The neo-gothic church of the **Sagrado Corazón**, built in 1933, at Buenos Aires e Yrigoyen, is also worth a visit. Further E, at Blvd J D Perón, is the magnificent **Mitre railway station**, dating from the late 19th century, now closed though its beautiful tiled *confitería* is still in use. There is a good **zoo** on Av Lugones, animals in clean spacious environments, US$3.

Museums

Museo Histórico Provincial, in the fine colonial Casa del Virrey Marqués de Sobremonte, Rosario de Santa Fe 218, 1 block E of Plaza San Martín, Tues-Fri 0900-1300, 1500-1900, Sat 0900-1300; **Museo de Ciencias Naturales**, Yrigoyen 115, open Mon-Fri 0800-1900, Sat 0900-1200, good guided tours (in Spanish, entry free, 'interesting skeletons of prehistoric glyptodonts'); **Museo de Mineralogía y Geología** of the Universidad Nacional de Córdoba, V Sarsfield 299, open Mon-Fri, 1400-1600; **Museo de Zoología**, same address, open Mon-Fri 0900-1200, Wed-Fri 1600-1800, many birds but poorly displayed with no labels; **Museo del Teatro y de la Música**, in the Teatro San Martín, V Sarsfield 365, open Mon-Fri 0900-1200; **Museo Provincial de Bellas Artes**, Plaza España, open Tues-Fri 0900-1300, 1500-2000, Sat/Sun 1500-1900, good; **Museo Municipal de Bellas Artes**, Gral Paz 33, open Tues-Fri 0930-1330, 1630-2030, Sat/Sun 1000-2000; **Museo Histórico de la Ciudad**, Entre Ríos 40; **Centro de Arte Contemporáneo**, Parque San Martín; **Museo de Meteorología Nacional**, San Luis 801, open Tues-Fri 0900-1300, 1400-1800, Sat 0830-1230; nearby in Laprida is Argentina's main observatory, open Wed 2000-2200; **Museo de Arte Religioso**, in the convent of Santa Teresa, Independencia 122, Sat 1030-1230.

Local holidays

6 July (Foundation of the City); 30 Sept (St Jerome), 7-10 October.

Local information

● **Accommodation**

More expensive hotels, mainly in the centre: **L3** *Panorama*, Alvear 251, good, pool, central, new; **A3** *Cañada*, Alvear 580, T 37589, good, a/c, restaurant, laundry; **A3** *Windsor*, Buenos Aires 214, T 224012, comfortable, very good.

On Corrientes, **C** *Bristol*, No 64, T 236222, a/c; **C** *Res Mi Valle*, No 586, fan, small, nice, family-run, rec.

On **San Jerónimo**: **A3** *Sussex*, No 125, T 229071, comfortable, roomy, discounts for ACA members; **A3** *Dallas*, No 339, T 46091, with breakfast, parking, a/c, rec; **C** *Corona*, No 574, T 228789, comfortable; **D** *La María*, No 628, parking, good value; **D** pp *Rosa Mística*, No 532, also monthly rates; **D** pp *Res Thanoa*, No 479, T 222807, with bath.

On **Balcarce**: **A3** *Del Sol*, No 144, T 33961, fan, a/c extra, rec, 10% ISIC discount; **B** *Mallorca*, No 73, T 39234, quite clean and nr bus terminal, noisy; **B** *Riviera*, No 74, T 223969, with breakfast, parking; **D** *El Progreso*, No 140, basic.

Other hotels between Plaza San Martín and bus terminal: **B** *Roma Termini*, Entre Rios 687, spotless, welcoming; **C** *Florida*, Rosario de Santa Fe 459, T 26373, rec, some rooms with a/c.

Other hotels: **B** *Garden*, 25 de Mayo 35, T 44739, central, secure, highly rec; **C** *Harbor*, Paraná 126, T/F 217300, without breakfast, good value; **E** pp *Gral Paz*, 25 de Mayo 240, with bath, run down, clean.

A2 *ACA Hotel Dr Cesar C Carman*, Av Sabattini (Ruta 9) y Bajada del Pucará, T 243565, **A1** for non-members, very good.

Camping: Municipal site, Gral San Martín, at the back of the Complejo Ferial (bus 31).

● **Places to eat**

There are numerous grills of all categories on the outskirts of the city, especially in the Cerro de las Rosas district, for meals out-of-doors when the weather is suitable. Many cheap restaurants along San Jerónimo inc *San Carlos*, No 431, good food and service; *Casino Español*, Rivadavia 63, good; *La Mamma*, Alcorta 270, excellent Italian, pricey; *Il Gatto*, Gral Paz y 9 de Julio, great pasta and pizzas, reasonably priced; *Romagnolo*, Perón y San Jerónimo, opp the Mitre railway station, rec; *Betos*, San Juan 494, best *lomitos* in town, parrilla, rec, pricey; *Fancy Café*, Andarte 317, good, cheap; *Firenze*, 25 de Mayo 220, busy, pleasant, traditional café; *Meeting*, 27 de Abril 248, good café; *Sorocabana*, corner of Plaza San Martín, 24-hr café

Excellent fruit juices (*licuados*) at *Kiosco Americano*, Tucumán 185 and at Gral Paz 242. Good *empanadas* at *La Vieja Esquina*, Belgrano y Caseros; *Empanadería La Alameda*, Obispo Trejo nr University, reasonable food, good student atmosphere, best 2200-2400. Icecream at branches of *Dolce Neve* throughout town; *Soppelsa's* ice cream is also highly rec, with several outlets.

● **Airline offices**
Aerolíneas Argentinas and Austral, Colón 520, T 267600; **Lapa**, Caseros 355, T 220188; **Kaiken**, F Alcorta 119, T 244614; **TAN**, Av Colón 119, p 3, T 216458; **Southern Winds**, Av Colón 540, T 241212; **Andesmar**, Av Chacabuco 80, T 217191; **Dinar**, Av Colón 533, T 257886.

● **Banks & money changers**
Lloyds Bank (BLSA), Buenos Aires 23; **Citibank**, Rivadavia 104, poor rates; **Banco Fegin** for Mastercard; **Banco de Galicia** on Sucre for Amex cards. Amex, **Simonelli Viajes**, Alcorta 50, T 26186. Many *cambios* on Rivadavia just off Plaza San Martín; shop around for best rate. Also see **Currency**, page 244, on *bonos*.

● **Cultural centres**
Asociación Argentina de Cultura Británica, San Juan 137, good library, poor reading room, open Mon-Fri 0900-1200, Mon, Wed, Fri 1600-1945, Tues, Thur 1500-1945; **Goethe Institut**, Illia 356, open Tues-Fri 1700-2100.

● **Embassies & consulates**
Consulates: Bolivia, Castro Barros 783, T 732827; **Chile**, Crisol 280, T 609622; **Paraguay**, 9 de Julio 573, T 226388; **Peru**, Poeta Lugones 212, T 603730. **Austria**, J Cortés 636, T 720450; **Italy**, Ayacucho 131, T 221020; **Germany**, Eliseo Conton 1870, T 890809 (Honorary Consul: Carlos Oechsle); **Spain**, Chacabuco 875, T 605013; **Sweden**, Alvear 10, T 240094; **Switzerland**, Entre Ríos 185, L-10, T 226848; **Belgium**, F Posse 2533, T 813298; **Finland**, Chacabuco 716, T 605049.

● **Entertainment**
Cinema: *Teatro Córdoba*, 27 de Abril 275, foreign language films.

Discotheques: several on Av H Yrigoyen, expensive; late night rock music at *Música Pura*, Montevideo 100, Thur-Sat.

Folk music: at *Pulpería El Viejo Rincón*, Dumesnil y Mendoza, excellent music till 0500. **Tango** in *Confitería Mitre*, Mitre railway station, Sun 2130.

● **Hospitals & medical services**
English-speaking doctor, *Ernesto J MacLoughlin*, Centro Asistencial Privado de Enfermedades Renales, 9 de Julio 714, home ·Pérez del Viso 4316, T 814745. Dentist, *Dra Olga Olmedo de*

Herrera, Fco J Muñiz 274, T 804378, daughter speaks English.

● **Language schools**
Comisión de Intercambio Educativo, San José de Calasanz 151, T 243606, offers classes mainly pre-arranged in Germany. (Contact Kommission für Bildungsaustausch, Wrangelstr 122, DW-2000 Hamburg 20.) **Interswop**, Sucre 2828, Alta Cordoba, T 710081, F 220655, organizes stays abroad and language classes (about US$180/week, 25 hrs of classes) and accommodation at about US$10/day, also exchange programmes for any nationality. Applications and details: Interswop, Bornstrasse 16, 20146 Hamburg, Germany, T/F 40-410-8029.

● **Laundry**
Chacabuco 320; **Laverap**, Chacabuco 301, Rivera Indarte 285, and Paraná y Rondeau; **La Lavandería**, Avellaneda 182, local 4; also in bus terminal.

● **Post & telecommunications**
Post Office: Colón 201, parcel service on the ground floor beside the customs office. **Telecommunications**: Telecom, Humberto 1° 510, T 110; Gen Paz 36 and 27 de Abril 27.

● **Shopping**
The main shopping area, with lots of *galerias*, is off Plaza San Martín. Patio Olmos, V Sarsfeld y San Juan, is a large *galería* with varied shops. Handicraft market in Rodríguez y Canada, Sat/Sun. *Librería Blackpool*, Dean Funes 395, for imported English books. Health food shops in *galería* on 27 de Abril opp Plaza Fundador.

● **Tour companies & travel agents**
Carolina, San Jerónimo 270, local 13/14, good value excursions, minimum of 6 people; *El Delfín*, Gral Paz 250, local 140, p 1; **Argentina Turística**, Vélez Sarsfield 30, T/F 234520, rec; **Alexandria**, Belgrano 194, planta alta, T 237421/247503, for budget travel.

● **Tourist offices**
Dirección Provincial de Turismo, Tucumán 360, T 233248. Provincial and municipal tourist offices in the old *Cabildo*, on Plaza San Martín, T 214027. Information office also at bus station, has free maps, extensive information on accommodation and camping in the province, helpful. Tourist Office desk at airport often unmanned. A useful information booklet is the free monthly, *Plataforma 40*, put out by Nueva Estación Terminal de Omnibus de Córdoba (Netoc).

Club Andino: Deán Funes 2100, open Wed after 2100, closed January.

● **Transport**
Local Bus: Municipal buses and electric buses (trolleys) do not accept cash; you have to buy tokens (*cospeles*) or cards from kiosks, normal

US$0.65, *diferencial* US$1.30. **Car hire**: Avis at airport and Corrientes 452, T 227384. **A1**, Entre Ríos 70, T 224867. **Localiza** at airport and Castro Barros 1155, T 747747.

Air   Pajas Blancas airport, 13 km N of city, T 810696, has shops, post office, a good restaurant and a *casa de cambio* (open Mon-Fri 1000-1500). Taxi to airport, US$15. Minibus (*combi*) service between airport and hotels, US$3, run by Turismo Pampa de Achala, Alvear 481, T/F 254773. Alternatively take local bus No 55 from Santa Rosa y Avellaneda (Plaza Colón), allow 1 hr. Several flights to **Buenos Aires** daily, about 1 hr; most major Argentine cities are served by AR, TAN, Kaiken, Southern Winds and Andesmar. International flights to Brazil and Uruguay direct, others via BsAs.

Trains   A tourist train, the Tren de las Sierras, runs in high season only (Holy Week, July, summer), from Rodríguez del Busto station (15 km out of town) to Capilla del Monte. Dep 0830, returns 1530, Tues, Thur, Fri, Sat, Sun depending on demand, US$10 one way, inc taxi transfer from bus terminal to Rodríguez del Busto.

Buses   Large terminal conveniently situated at Blvd Perón 300, T 212073. In the basement are a bank (does not change TCs), post office and phones; the ground floor has booking offices, tourist information and a *casa de cambio*; there are shops and cafés on the first floor and a restaurant, supermarket, laundry and left luggage lockers on the top floor. Very busy at peak travel periods.

To **Buenos Aires**, Ablo, Costera Criolla, Chevalier or Cacorba, 10 hrs, US$30 *común* US$50 *diferencial*: to **Salta** (US$41) and **Jujuy** (US$45), Panamericano, 4 daily, La Veloz del Norte twice, about 12 and 15 hrs. To **Mendoza**, 10 hrs, 6 a day with TAC, slow, 1 daily with Uspallata US$29, avoid La Cumbre; to **Tucumán**, US$30, 8 hrs, about 8 a day, Panamericano has more than other companies; to **Posadas** Expreso Singer, Crucero del Norte (very good buses), 20 hrs; to **Santa Fe**, frequent, 5½ hrs, US$18; to **Trelew** (US$60, 17 hrs), **Comodoro Rivadavia** (US$75, 24 hrs) and **Río Gallegos** (US$100, 36 hrs) Taqsa; to **Mar del Plata** US$45-55; to **La Rioja**, 4 a day, 6½ hrs, US$15; some go on to Catamarca, US$16; to La Rioja-Aimogasta-**Tinogasta**- **Fiambalá** El Cóndor, Tues, Thur, Fri; leaves Tinogasta 1140 arr Fiambalá 1240, returns from Fiambalá same day 1445, from Tinogasta at 1600 (see also page 160). To **Belén** (Catamarca) La Calera, Mon, Wed, Fri, 2100. Cacorba, efficient a/c buses, serve **Villa Carlos Paz** (1 hr, frequent service, every 15 mins), **Cosquín** and **La Falda** in the Sierras de Córdoba.

International services   To **Asunción** (Paraguay) direct, Brújula, 4 times a week, and Cacorba 19 hrs, US$55. To **Montevideo** (Uruguay), US$57, dep 1700, Mon, Wed, Fri and Sun, Encon, 15 hrs. To **Santiago** (Chile), US$32, 16 hrs. To **Lima** (Peru) El Rápido, via Mendoza and Chile, 60 hrs, US$100. To **Pocitos** (Bolivian border) with Panamericano. In general, it is best to travel from Córdoba if you are going N, as it may be hard to get a seat if boarding en route.

SIERRAS OF CORDOBA

Three ranges of undulating hills rise from the pampas, their lower slopes often wooded, particularly in the S. The Sierra Grande, the longest, is in between Sierra Chica to the E and Sierra de Guisapampa and its continuation, the Sierra de Pocho, to the W. The highest peak, Champaquí (2,975m) has a small lake about 2,550m up. The hills run, roughly, for 500 km from N to S; W of Córdoba they are 150 km wide. A network of good roads gives pleasant contrasts of scenery. The region's climate is dry, sunny and exhilarating, especially in winter.

At the foot of the Sierra Chica are large dams to contain the waters of the Río Primero at San Roque, the Río Segundo at Los Molinos and Río Tercero. There are two other large dams in the hills, at Cruz del Eje and La Viña. They provide power and irrigation, and the lakes themselves are attractive. Sailing and fishing are popular.

THE PUNILLA VALLEY

VILLA CARLOS PAZ

(*Pop* 46,000; *Alt* 642m; *Phone code* 0541; 36 km W of Córdoba) On an artificial lake, Lago San Roque, it is the nearest resort to Córdoba and is therefore often crowded. Tours available on amphibian buses as far as the two dams on the lake (US$10); launch trips also available. At the Casa de Gaspar, Miguel Cané and El Redentor, roller-skating and optical illusions, Fri-Sun 1400-1900 out of season. A chair-lift runs (0900-1900) to the summit of the Cerro de la Cruz, which offers splendid views. There is also a museum of meteorites, entry US$2. Bus tours to areas such as Sierra Chica, for those who like snack bars, fun slides and gravity-defying houses.

Excursions North of Villa Carlos Paz, on Route 38, a road branches W to Tanti from where local buses go to Los Gigantes, a paradise for climbers, 2-day treks possible. Club Andino has several *refugios*; details in Villa Carlos Paz.

● **Accommodation** Plenty of hotels, big and small, in all price categories. **C** *El Monte*, Caseros 45, T 22001, F 22993, very good, rec; **C** *Mar del Plata*, Esquiú 47, T 22068, rec; **C** *Villa Carlos Paz Parque*, Santa Fe 50, T 25128, full board available, rec. **Camping**: at ACA site (Av San Martín y Nahuel Huapi, T 22132) and several others inc, **Club de Pescadores**, at lakeside, rec, and **Los Pinos**, rec, Curru Enríquez y Lincoln (open all year). There are many campsites nr the main road through the Punilla Valley, most open Dec-April only.

● **Banks & money changers** Banco de Córdoba, San Martín, accepts US$ cash only.

● **Laundry** San Martín y Libertad.

● **Post & telecommunications Post Office and telephone**: San Martín 190.

● **Shopping Best buys**: leather mats, bags, pottery.

● **Tourist offices** San Martín 400.

● **Buses** To Córdoba every 15 mins in summer, US$2; taxi to/from Córdoba airport, US$10.50. To/from Buenos Aires, Ablo, US$26; also Cacorba, Chevallier, Gen Urquiza.

COSQUIN

From Villa Carlos Paz Route 38 runs N through the Punilla valley to a string of resorts. **Cosquín** (*Pop* 16,400; *Alt* 720m), 26 km from V Carlos Paz, 63 km from Córdoba, on the banks of the Río Cosquín, is known as the National Folklore Capital. It is the site of the most important folklore festival, beginning last week in January. There is also a national *artesanía* festival in the same month; **Museo de Artesanías**, Tucumán 1031. **Museo Camin Cosquín** at Km 760, out of town, minerals and archaeology, recommended.

Take a bus (or walk 2 hrs) to the Pan de Azúcar hill from where there is a good view over the Punilla valley. Chairlift to top (all year round).

● **Accommodation C** *La Serrana*, P Ortiz 740, T 51306, nr bus station; good; **C** *Italia*,

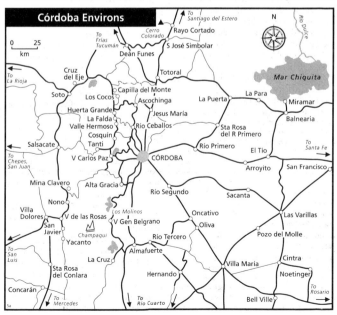

Córdoba Environs

0   25
km

To Santiago del Estero
Río Dulce

Cerro Colorado
Rayo Cortado
S José Simbolar

To Frías
Tucumán
Deán Funes

To La Rioja
Cruz del Eje
Totoral

Soto
Los Cocos
Capilla del Monte
Ascochinga
La Puerta
La Para
Mar Chiquita

Huerta Grande
Jesus María
Miramar

La Falda
Valle Hermoso
Río Ceballos
Sta Rosa del R Primero
Balnearia

Salsacate
Cosquín
Tanti
Río Primero
El Tío
To Santa Fe

V Carlos Paz
CÓRDOBA

To Chepes, San Juan

Mina Clavero
Alta Gracia
Arroyito
San Francisco

Río Segundo
Sacanta
Las Varillas

Nono
Los Molinos
Oncativo
Oliva

Villa Dolores
V de las Rosas
V Gen Belgrano
Pozo del Molle

San Javier
Champaquí
Yacanto
Río Tercero
Cintra

To San Luis
La Cruz
Almafuerte
Villa María
Noetinger

Sta Rosa del Conlara
Hernando
To Rosario

Concarán
To Mercedes
To Río Cuarto
Bell Ville

Ternengo y Vértiz, T 52255, opp bus station, rec; **E** pp **Res Cosquín**, Tucumán y Sabattini, T 51222. Several campsites.

● **Tourist offices** Plaza Próspero Molino; 0700-2100 daily in high season, 0800-2000 daily off season.

● **Buses** To Córdoba, US$2.60, Empresa La Capillense; 1½ hrs, via Carlos Paz or La Calera via the San Roque dam.

LA FALDA

19 km N of Cosquín is **Valle Hermoso** (*Alt* 850m). The old restored chapel of San Antonio is a little gem. Horseriding. A few kilometres N of Valle Hermoso, 82 km from Córdoba, is **La Falda** (*Pop* 30,000; *Alt* 933m; *Phone code* 0548) which is a good touring centre.

Museums Model Railway Museum at **Las Murallas Zoo** at the end of Av 25 de Mayo; **Museo Ambato Arqueológico**, Cuesta del Lago 1467, privately run, well displayed, open Thur-Sun and public holidays 0900-2000, US$0.50.

Excursions Extensive hiking in surrounding hills. 3½ km N by Route 38 is **Huerta Grande**, at 971m, a bathing resort with good fishing and medicinal waters. Round trip excursion to **Cascadas de Olaén** in a spectacular canyon – the water splashes into a small lake full of little fish. On the Pampa de Olaén, there are many quartz mines. To La Candelaria, 53 km W along unpaved roads where there is a Jesuit *estancia* and chapel dating from 1693.

● **Accommodation** About 80 hotels in all categories, all full in Dec-Feb holiday season; La Falda is visited mostly by the elderly, most hotels belong to pension funds. **C** *Res Atenas*, Rosario 329, T 22424, comfortable, rec; **D** *Hostería Los Abrojos*, Goya s/n, Valle Hermoso, T/F 70430, hot water, also full board, sports, excursions; **E** pp *Malvinas*, 2 blocks from terminal, meals available. Houses for rent 1 Mar to 30 Nov on a monthly basis. Various campsites.

● **Places to eat** *El Bochín*, España 117, good, cheap; *Pachamama*, 9 de Julio 160, vegetarian.

● **Banks & money changers** Bancos de la Nación and de Suquía for exchange.

● **Tour companies & travel agents** *Aventura Club*, 9 de Julio 541, T/F 23809, trekking, jeep tours, camping, birdwatching etc. *Wella Viajes*, Av Edén 412, loc 12, T 0548-21380, offers 15% discount to ISIC and youth card holders for trekking, climbing, etc to Cerro Champaquí.

● **Tourist offices** Av España 50 and at bus station.

● **Buses** To Córdoba, US$4, 2 hrs; to Buenos Aires, Cacorba, Cita, US$40.

NORTH OF LA FALDA

La Cumbre (*Alt* 1,141m), 12 km N, offers fine views from the statue of Christ on the hill. Trout streams with good fishing from Nov to April. Swimming, golf, tennis; hang gliding and parapenting nearby at Cuchi Corral. Tourist office in old train station near the bus terminal.

● **Accommodation & places to eat** **A1** *Lima*, Moreno y Dean Funes, with breakfast, T 51727, excellent facilities, pool, quiet; *Victoria*, Posadas s/n, T 51412, charming, small; *La Cumbre Inn*, 9 de Julio 753, T 51736, large and commercial, good views; **C** *Res Peti*, Paz y Rivadavia, good. *Pizza Luis*, Rivadavia 267, rec.

Cruz Chica, 2½ km N of La Cumbre, altitude, 1,067m, is a wealthy residential area with English-style houses and gardens in pine woods. Museo Manuel Mujica Laínez, in former house of Argentine writer, US$3.

Los Cocos, 8 km N of La Cumbre, is a popular mountain resort with three first rate hotels (eg *Blair House*, Av Grierson, T 92147, English-style, recommended) and many holiday houses. Climb up El Mastil and beyond for the views and birds.

CAPILLA DEL MONTE

(*Alt* 979m) 106 km N of Córdoba and set in the heart of the Sierras, is a good centre for exploring this area. Medicinal waters (good baths at La Toma, 4 km), rocks and waterfalls and wide views; El Zapato rock is 'graffiti-ridden', better are Los Mogotes, 3 km from town, reached through Paso del Indio. Excursions in the hills, particularly to Cerro Uritorco, 1,979m, 4 hrs. Walk also to Los Alazanes dam. Many other walks after crossing bridge at La Toma, recommended. You can walk on to the direct dirt road to San Marcos Sierra, 22 km W, known as *capital de la miel* for the quality of its honey; many parakeets and small farmhouses. Along the way you will also get views down to the Cruz del Eje dam. Horse riding costs US$20/half day and there are tours to meditation and 'energy' centres: the location of many sightings of unidentified flying objects, the area is popular for 'mystical tourism'. Tourist office in old railway station, open daily 0830-2030, some English spoken.

- **Accommodation B** *Hosp Italia*, Rivadavia 54, clean, showers, opp bus station. Municipal campsite Calabalumba on the way to Cerro Uritorco, **E**/tent, hot water rec, also cabañas.
- **Buses** To Córdoba, 3 hrs, US$10; to Buenos Aires, many companies, US$38.

NORTH FROM CORDOBA

A road runs N to **Ascochinga** through pleasant little townships such as Villa Allende, Río Ceballos, Salsipuedes and La Granja. At El Manzano, 40 km N of Córdoba, a road branches W to **Candonga**, altitude 810m. The historic church, now a National Monument, was built in 1730 as an oratory of the Jesuit Estancia of Santa Gertrudis.

Santa Catalina, 14 km N of Ascochinga, originally a Jesuit mission founded in 1622 and the most elaborate Jesuit establishment in the Sierras de Córdoba. See the church, begun in 1754, workshops and stone conduits; the families who now use it as a summer home will show you round. Buses from Jesús Maria, twice a day.

- **Accommodation In Río Ceballos**: **D** *La Gloria*, Av San Martín 5495, affiliated to IYHA, warmly rec. Three campsites. Several campsites also at **Salsipuedes**. **In Ascochinga**: **B** *Hostería El Cortijo*, full board only, good value, small swimming pool and river outside, horses for rent, US$1/hr; 5 km walk to Tres Cascadas falls and *balneario*. During winter, open weekends only. Campsite open all year.

JESUS MARIA

From Ascochinga a road runs E for 20 km to **Jesús María** (*Pop* 21,000; *Alt* 533m; 51 km N of Córdoba on Route 9; several hotels). There is a good 18th century Jesuit church and the remains of its once famous winery; in the cloister is an excellent **Museo Jesuítico**, said to be one of the best on the continent (Mon-Fri 0800-1200 and 1400-1900, Sat and Sun 1600-2000). Each Jan there is a gaucho and folklore festival, lasting 10 nights from 2nd week; very popular. Good fishing in winter. Nearby is **Colonia Caroya**, founded by Italian immigrants, where there is an excellent Immigration Museum. Direct bus from Córdoba, US$2, 1½ hrs.

Sinsacate, with an interesting church, is 4 km N of Jesús María. There is also a fine colonial posting inn, now a museum, with long, deep verandah and chapel attached.

At Rayo Cortado, 114 km N of Jesús María, a turning leads W to **Cerro Colorado**, 160 km N of Córdoba, the former home of the Argentine folklore singer and composer Atahualpa Yupanqui. His house, now a museum, can be visited, US$2, ask in the village for the curator. There are more than 30,000 rock paintings by the Comechingones Indians in the nearby Cerro Colorado archaeological park and a small archaeological museum (US$1 entry, includes guide in English or Spanish). There is cheap accommodation with families and camping. Daily bus from Jesús María at 1610.

MAR CHIQUITA

Some 200 km NE of Córdoba, on the S margin of the Chaco and about 320 km SE of Santiago del Estero, Mar Chiquita is an important nature reserve, the feeding area in summer for migratory birds from the northern hemisphere. Fed by the Río Dulce and, in the flood season by two other rivers from the Sierras de Córdoba, the lake has no exit and is naturally salty and warm. There are several islands. On its S shore is the small town of **Miramar**, which is being gradually overwhelmed by the expanding lake. The area is a very popular resort during the summer months; its salt waters are used in the treatment of rheumatic ailments and skin diseases.

NB This Mar Chiquita and Miramar should not be confused with the other Mar Chiquita and Miramar on the Atlantic coast.

- **Accommodation** *Savoy*, San Martín y Sarmiento, cheap, very friendly. **Camping**: *Autocamping Lilly*, Bahía de los Sanavirones.

SOUTHWEST OF CORDOBA

A scenic road SW from Villa Carlos Paz

passes **Ycho Cruz**, by the Río San Antonio (**D** *Hostería Avenida*, with bath; several campsites). Beyond, the road climbs into the Sierra Grande. 7 km N of the village of El Cóndor, a wide trail leads to Quebrada de los Condoritos (6-7 km), with superb landscape and the chance of seeing condors in their easternmost habitat. The road crosses the Pampa de Achala, a huge desert plateau of grey granite, before descending to another chain of resorts. (Bus Córdoba-Ycho Cruz, US$2, Cotap; to El Cóndor US$5.)

MINA CLAVERO

(*Pop* 5,100; *Alt* 915m; *Phone code* 0544), 140 km from Córdoba is a good centre for exploring the high *sierra* and the Traslasierra Valley. There is an interesting museum, **Museo Rocsen**, 13 km S and about 5 km from the village of Nono; the personal collection of Sr Bouchón, it includes furniture, minerals, instruments, animals, open daily 0900 till sunset, US$3. The road S of Nono, near the Embalse Allende (or La Viña), a reservoir surrounded by forests, is lined with hotels and campsites.

● **Accommodation & places to eat** Many hotels, *hosterías* and *hospedajes*. Restaurant *Rincón Suizo*, C Champaquí 1200, serves good pastries; many others. 5 campsites around Mina Clavero, US$3.50-5pp; many others at Cura Brochero and Nono. On the road S of Nono: **D** pp *Castillo Villa La Fontana*, Km 20 between Los Hornillos and Las Rabonas, **E** pp without bath, in beautiful 1920s Italianate palace, attractive gardens, English spoken, cooking and laundry facilities, highly rec.

● **Sports** Horseriding: *Mis Montañas*, at Los Hornillos, Km 22, T 0544-49015, F 0544-94435, German and English spoken.

● **Tourist offices** Municipality, Av San Martín y 25 de Mayo, Plazoleta Merlo, T/F 70171/70241, with information on all accommodation, camping and tourist circuits.

● **Buses** To Córdoba, US$10, 6 a day, 3 hrs; to Buenos Aires, TAC, US$40, 12 hrs; to Mendoza, 8½ hrs, US$26.

CHAMPAQUI

2,884m, the highest peak in the Sierras. It can be reached from Villa de las Rosas, 35 km S of Mina Clavero, or from San Javier, 12 km further S. The latter route goes by Capilla La Constancia, set in a river valley

with pine and nut trees. To the summit takes 8-10 hrs, the descent to La Constancia 4 hrs. Neither route should be attempted in misty weather. A good base is *Vai Kunta*, 5885 Villa de las Rosas, run by Rolf Graf (Swiss), rooms for rent, good food, guiding service. Take any Córdoba-Villa Dolores bus to Villa de las Rosas; at bus station look for the *pizzería* where taxis to Los Molles can be arranged. From Los Molles it's a 2-hr walk to the house.

2 km S of San Javier, at the foot of Champaquí, in a region of woods and waterfalls is **Yacanto**, which has curative waters.

Villa Dolores (*Pop* 21,000; *Alt* 529m), 45 km S of Mina Clavero and 187 km SE of Córdoba, is the southern gateway to this part of the Sierras.

● **Accommodation D** pp *Vila Plaza*, on Plaza, T 21691, without breakfast, parking, poor beds; **D** *Res Champaquí*, F Germán 166, T 22358; **D** pp *Hosp Sonia*, Brizuela 415, T 22938, opp terminal, without breakfast. At Las Tapias, 10 km E is **B** pp *La Posta de Mistal*, T 20893, half board, pool, tennis, restaurant. **Camping**: nearest site at Piedra Pintada, 6 km NE, pleasant village well situated for walks into mountains.

● **Buses** Terminal at Brizuela and Tomás Edison. To Buenos Aires, Chevalier *cama*, US$40, 12 hrs; to San Luis 5¼ hrs; to Córdoba, several companies, US$8-10, 5 hrs; to Mendoza, TAC, US$26, 8 hrs; to Mina Clavero, frequent, US$3, 1½ hrs.

SOUTH FROM CORDOBA

ALTA GRACIA

(*Pop* 39,000; *Alt* 580m; *Phone code* 0547), 39 km SW of Córdoba beside Lago Tajamar, has an interesting colonial church, finished about 1762, open am and after 1700. The buildings housing the **Museo del Virrey Liniers**, on the Estancia de Alta Gracia, were founded in 1588 and taken over by the Jesuits in 1643, open Tues-Fri 0900-1300, 1500-1830, Sat, Sun 0930-1230, 1530-1830, US$1 (all day in summer). There is also the **Museo Manuel de Falla** on Pellegrini Final, closed Mon, entry US$0.30, where the Spanish composer spent his last years. Beautiful views from the Gruta de la Virgen de Lourdes, 3 km W of town.

Excursions The Bosque Alegre and Observatory, 24 km NW, affords good views over Córdoba, Alta Gracia and the Sierra Grande. Open Thur 1600-1800, Sun 1000-1200 and 1600-1800.

● **Accommodation** *Hostería Reina*, Urquiza 229, T 21724, good. Two campsites, one scruffy, the other better (nr golf course) and free in winter.

● **Tourist offices** Tourist office inside clock tower by Lago Tajamar.

● **Buses** To Córdoba, US$1.50, every 15 mins, 1 hr.

VILLA GENERAL BELGRANO

(*Phone code* 0546) The road from Alta Gracia to the Río Tercero dam (79 km S) passes La Serranita, the Embalse Los Molinos and Villa General Belgrano (58 km). A completely German town founded by the surviving interned seamen from the *Graf Spee*, some of whom still live in the town. It is a pleasant resort and a good centre for excursions in the surrounding mountains. Genuine German smoked sausages are sold. Excursions can be made to **La Cumbrecita** a German village 30 km W, where there is Good walking and riding.

Museums Museo Arqueológico Ambrosetti, collection of artefacts from Comechingon Indians, the original inhabitants of the valley; **Museo del Carruaje**, old carriages and cars; **Museo Ovni**, on S outskirts, dedicated to unidentified flying objects.

Local festivals Oktoberfest beer festival in Oct; **Festival de las Tortas y las Masas Vienesas**, around Easter.

● **Accommodation**: **A3** *Bremen*, Route 5 y Cerro Negro, T 61133, restaurant, sports facilities; **A2** *Edelweiss*, Ojo de Agua 295, T 61317, F 61387, pool, excellent food. 2 **Youth Hostels**: **C** *El Rincón*, in beautiful surroundings nr terminal, cooking and laundry facilities, highly rec (reservations: Patricia Mampsey, Casilla 64, T 61323); and at *Estancia Alta Vista*, T 62238, 14 km from town on way to La Cumbrecita, both offer discounts to ISIC and YHA card holders (20% and 25% respectively). **At La Cumbrecita**: **A3** *Cascadas*, T 81015, with pool, tennis etc; **A3** *Panorama*, higher up hill (T 98406); 3 others.

● **Buses** To Córdoba, 2 hrs, US$4, 8 a day; to **Mendoza**, US$28; to **Buenos Aires**, Colta, 1 a day, US$35. To **La Cumbrecita** by taxi (US$33, 1-1½ hrs) or by bus, Sun only.

The Northwest: Santiago del Estero, Tucumán, Salta and Jujuy

THE ROUTE to the major tourist centre of Salta, from where trips can be made into Andean regions, the Quebrada de Humahuaca and the Calchaquí and Cachi valleys. There are prehispanic ruins near Tafí del Valle, Quilmes, Santa Rosa de Tastil and others. This is also a region in which there are a number of Amerindian groups.

The pattern of the land in Northern Argentina, from the crest of the Andes in the W to the Río Paraguay in the E, consists of a high, dry Altiplano rising to a windswept, stony and treeless Puna cut into on its E face by rivers which flow into the Lowlands. This configuration of the land, similar to Bolivia, is carried S into all the NW provinces of Argentina as far S as Tucumán, but the altitudes in Argentina are not so great as in Bolivia, and the whole area not so large. The E running rivers flow into the Chaco; their broad valleys, or *quebradas*, make access to the heights comparatively easy. Between the base of the Puna and the Chaco lie a series of front range hogback hills running roughly from N to S; the lowlands between them are known in Argentina as the *valles*. Tucumán is the southern boundary of this kind of land.

Settlement and economy

The first Spanish expedition from Bolivia entered Argentina in 1542. A little later a better and lower route was discovered – the main route used today – descending from La Quiaca to Jujuy through the Quebrada de Humahuaca, with rugged and colourful mountain ranges closing in on both sides. Along this new route the Spaniards founded a group of towns in the NW: Santiago del Estero (the first), Tucumán, Córdoba, Salta, La Rioja and Jujuy. Mendoza, San Juan and San Luis were all colonized by people who crossed the passes from Chile. All these

colonies were hemmed in by the warlike tribes of the Pampas, and until the war of extermination in 1880 the route from Buenos Aires to Córdoba was often unsafe. The Indians raided frequently for cattle, which they drove S and over the Andes for sale in Chile.

During the whole of the colonial era the trade of the area, mostly in mules, was with Bolivia and Peru rather than with Buenos Aires. The mules were bred mainly in the plains between Rosario, Santa Fe, and Córdoba, and driven finally into Salta for the great fair in Feb and March.

Historically, Tucumán was always important, for the two river routes of the Salado and the Dulce across the dry belt forced the mule traffic to pass through Tucumán on the way to Salta. Tucumán still produces most of Argentina's sugar. Tobacco is a major crop, and an important factor in the NW is the growth of tourism.

- **Recommended reading** Federico Kirbus' *Guía de Aventuras y Turismo de la Argentina* (available at Librería La Rayuela, Buenos Aires 96, Salta and El Ateneo, Florida 340, basement, Buenos Aires).

SANTIAGO DEL ESTERO

(*Pop* 201,000; *Alt* 200m; *Phone code* 085) Founded in 1553 by conquistadores pushing S from Peru, this is the oldest Argentine city. It is 395 km N of Córdoba and 159 km SE of Tucumán.

Places of interest
On the **Plaza Libertad** stand the **Municipalidad** and the **Cathedral** (the fifth on the site). The fine **Casa de Gobierno** is on Plaza San Martín, 3 blocks away. In the convent of **Santo Domingo**, Urquiza y 25 de Mayo, is one of two copies of the 'Turin Shroud', given by Philip II to his 'beloved colonies of America'. On Plaza Lugones is the church of **San Francisco**, the oldest surviving church in the city, founded in 1565. At the back of the church is the cell of San Francisco Solano, patron saint of Tucumán, who stayed in Santiago in 1593. Beyond the church is the pleasant **Parque Aguirre**.

Museums
Museo Arqueológico, Avellaneda 353, containing a large collection of Indian pottery and artefacts from the Chaco, Mon-Fri, 0800-1300, 1400-1900, Sat, 0900-1200, free; **Museo Histórico**, Urquiza 354, Mon-Fri, 0830-1230, 1530-1830, Sat 0900-1200; **Museo de Bellas Artes**, Independencia between 9 de Julio and Urquiza, Mon-Fri, 0900-1300; **Museo Andrés Chazarreta**, Mitre 127, handicrafts.

Local festivals
Carnival in Feb: virtually everything throwable gets thrown by everyone at everyone else.

Local information
● **Accommodation**
A3 *Gran*, Avellaneda e Independencia, T 214400, 4-star; **A3** *Rodas*, Gallo 432, T 218804, safe.

C *Res Emausi*, Av Moreno 600 block, good value; *Santa Rita*, Santa Fe 273, nr bus terminal, basic.

Camping: *Las Casuarinas*, Parque Aguirre.

● **Places to eat**
Restaurant Sociedad Española, Independencia 236, popular, good value; *Centro de Viajes*, Buenos Aires 37, good value lunches; *Mía Mamma*, 24 de Septiembre 16, on Plaza, good restaurant/salad bar, pricey.

● **Banks & money changers**
Banco Francés, 9 de Julio y 24 de Septiembre; Noroeste Cambio, 24 de Septiembre 220, good rates. Amex, El Quijote Paladea Turismo, Independencia 342, T 213207.

● **Tourist offices**
On Plaza Libertad.

● **Transport**
Air Austral to Buenos Aires and Jujuy.

Buses To Buenos Aires, several daily, 12 hrs, US$37, Cacorba, La Unión and Atahualpa; to Resistencia, 3 a day, El Rayo, 9 hrs, US$25, El Rayo, via Quimili and Roque Sáenz Peña (8 hrs); to Córdoba, 12 a day, 7 hrs, US$16; to Tucumán (via Río Hondo) US$8; 4 a day to Salta, US$23, Panamericano, 5½ hrs, and to Jujuy, 7 hrs.

TERMAS DE RIO HONDO
(*Pop* 25,000; *Phone code* 0858), situated 65 km N of Santiago del Estero along the road to Tucumán, is a major spa town. The thermal waters are recommended for blood pressure and rheumatism; good to drink, too, and used for the local soda water. There is swimming (free) in a public pool called La Olla near the bridge which crosses the Río Hondo (see **Camping** below). Tourist office at Pasaje Borges, s/n. The huge Río Hondo dam on the Río Dulce is close by; it forms a lake of 33,000 ha, used for sailing and fishing.

● **Accommodation** There are over 170 hotels, but at national holiday periods, and especially in Aug, accommodation is hard to find, so book well in advance. *Grand Hotel Río Hondo*, Hipólito Yrigoyen 552, T 21195; *Los Pinos*, Maipú 201, T 21043, pleasant; **B** *Ambassador*, Libertad 184, T 21196. **Camping**: Municipal site, Yrigoyen y Ruta 9, nr river bank; *La Olla*, left bank of river; ACA 4 km from town; *El Mirador*, Ruta 9 y Urquiza.

● **Buses** To Santiago del Estero, 1 hr, US$2 and to Tucumán, 2 hrs, US$4; several to Buenos Aires US$38.

TUCUMAN

(*Pop* 400,000; *Alt* 450m; *Phone code* 081), full name San Miguel de Tucumán, was founded by Spaniards coming S from Peru in 1565. Capital of its province, it is the busiest and the most populous city in the N. It stands on a plain, but to the W towers the Sierra de Aconquija. Summer weather can be very hot and sticky.

Places of interest

There are still some colonial buildings left: on the W side of the main Plaza Independencia is the ornate **Palacio de Gobierno**, next is the church of **San Francisco**, with a picturesque façade. On the S side is the **Cathedral**, with an old rustic cross, kept near the baptismal font, used when founding the city. To the S, on C Congreso, is the **Casa Histórica** where, in 1816, the Congress of the United Provinces of Río de la Plata met to draft the country's Declaration of Independence. Tues-Fri 0830-1330,1500-1930, Sat 0830-1300, US$0.40; nightly (not Tues, except in July) at 2030, *son et lumière* programme at Casa Histórica, in garden, adults US$2, children US$1, tickets from tourist office on Plaza Independencia, no seats. Some distance to the W is **Plaza Belgrano**, with a statue to Gen Belgrano, who won a decisive battle against the royalists on this site in 1812.

In the large **Parque Nueve de Julio** (avoid at night) is the house of Bishop Colombres, who introduced sugar cane to Tucumán in the early 19th century (open Tues-Fri 0900-1200, 1730-2030). There are several sugar mills nearby: the easiest to visit is **Ingenio Concepción**, on the outskirts of town, guided tours in Spanish during harvest period only (15 July-early Nov), Mon-Sat, 0930 and 1030, no booking required. Take Aconquija bus for Santo Cristo US$0.60, 15 mins.

Museums

Museo de Antropología y Etnografía, 25 de Mayo 265 in University building, fine collection, Mon-Fri, 0800-1200, 1600-2000. **Museo Folklórico Provincial**, 24 de Septiembre 565, Mon 1730-2030, Tues-Fri, 0900-1230, 1730-2030, Sat, Sun, 1800-2100, free. **Instituto Miguel Lillo**, San Lorenzo y Lillo (30 mins' walk from bus terminal), associated with the natural sciences department of the University, has a small but well-presented museum containing sections on geology and biology with some stuffed animals and a dinosaur skeleton, Mon-Fri, 0900-1200, 1500-1800. **Casa Padilla**, Plaza Independencia, houses a collection of international art and antiques. **Museo Histórico de la Provincia** (Casa de Avellaneda) C Congreso 56, Mon-Fri, 0900-1230, 1700-2000, Sat-Sun, 1700-2000; **Museo Iramaín**, Entre Rios 27, memorial to the sculptor, Mon-Fri, 0900-1900. **Museo de Bellas Artes**, 9 de Julio 48, entre 24 de Septiembre y Alvarez, Tues-Fri, 0900-1300, 1630-2100, Sat-Sun, 0900-1200, 1730-2030.

Excursions

North: **El Cadillal** dam, in the gorge of the Río Sali, 26 km, supplies electricity and water for the city and permanent irrigation for 80,000 ha. There are places to eat, a good ACA campsite, good swimming, and a small archaeological museum at the dam (Sierras y Lagos buses every 1½ hrs approximately, US$1.50, 45 mins, last buses back 1715 and 1945).

South: **Simoca**, 45 km on Route 157, is known as the *capital del sulky* because of the widespread use of sulkies. It has a Sat morning handicrafts and produce market (Posta bus, several, 1½ hrs, US$2.50; essential to get there early).

West: At **Horco Molle**, Km 14 on the edge of the Sierras de Aconquija, is the **Reserva Biológica San Javier**, covering 14,172 ha, with subtropical plants. Bus at 1130 (the only one) returns immediately.

Local holidays

24 Sept (Battle of Tucumán). 29 Sept, San Miguel. 10 Nov, Día de la Tradición.

Local information

● **Accommodation**

L3 *Grand de Tucumán*, Av Soldati 380, T 245000, 5-star, opp Parque 9 de Julio, rooms with even numbers quieter, outstanding food and service, pool (open to non-residents), tennis courts, disco.

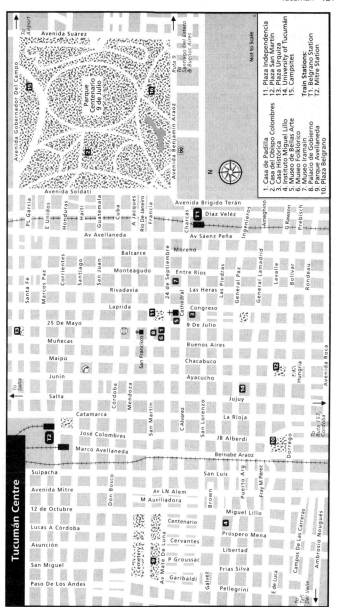

Tucumán Centre

Parque Centenario 9 de Julio

Not to Scale

1. Casa de Padilla
2. Casa del Obispo Colombres
3. Casa Histórica
4. Instituto Miguel Lillo
5. Museo de Bellas Arte
6. Museo Folklórico
7. Museo Iramain
8. Palacio de Gobierno
9. Parque Avellaneda
10. Plaza Belgrano
11. Plaza Independencia
12. Plaza San Martín
13. Plaza Urquiza
14. University of Tucumán
15. Campsites

Train Stations:
T1. Belgrano Station
T2. Mitre Station

A1 *Carlos V*, 25 de Mayo 330, T/F 221972, central, good service, a/c, bar, restaurant, rec; **A2** *Metropol*, 24 de Septiembre 524, T 311180, F 310379, run down, helpful; **A3** *Gran Hotel Corona*, 24 de Septiembre 498 on corner of Plaza Independencia, T 310985, good location and facilities; **A3** *ACA Motel Tucumán*, Av Salta 2080, T 266037; **A3** *Premier*, Alvarez 510, T 310381, a/c, good; **A3** *Colonial*, San Martín 35, T 311523, modern, fan, laundry service, breakfast inc, rec; **A3** *Mayoral*, 24 de Septiembre 364, T 228351, F 310080, 20% discount to *South American Handbook* readers.

C *La Vasca*, Mendoza 281, T 211288, safe, rec; **C** *Casa de Huéspedes María Ruiz*, Rondeau 1824, safe, rec; **C** *Florida*, 24 de Septiembre 610, T 221785, good value, poorly-lit rooms, helpful; **C** *Independencia*, Balcarce, entre San Martín y 24 de Septiembre, with fan, quiet, poor water supply on first floor; **C** *Palace*, 24 de Septiembre 233, rec; **C** *Petit*, Alvarez 765, T 214902, spacious, quiet, without bath, highly rec.

E *Estrella*, Araoz 38, nr terminal, very hospitable.

Camping: avoid the sites in the Parque 9 de Julio. Two roadside camp sites 3 km E and NE of city centre.

● **Places to eat**
There are several popular restaurants and cafés in Parque 9 de Julio and on Plaza Independencia. *El Fondo*, San Martín 848, T 222161, good service, best in town; *Ali Baba*, Junín 380, Arab specialities (Syrian owners), intimate, inexpensive, rec, closed lunchtime; *Adela*, 24 de Septiembre 358, well prepared food, Arab specialities, good value; *La Leñita*, 25 de Mayo 377, expensive, smart, good meat; *La Parrilla de La Plaza*, San Martín 391, excellent, reasonable prices; *Las Brasas*, Maipú 740, good but not cheap; *Augustus*, 24 Septiembre y Buenos Aires, good café; *Pastísima Rotisería*, Mendoza y Laprida and at San Martín 964, good cheap snacks, take out service. *Panadería Villecco*, Corrientes 751, good bread, also 'integral'. In this part of Argentina 'black beer' (eg Salta Negra) is available.

● **Banks & money changers**
American Express, Chacabuco 38, T 217269, does not change cash or TCs, but very helpful; **Noroeste Cambios**, San Martín 775, accepts TCs; **Dinar**, San Martín 645 and 742, cash only, and **Maguitur**, San Martín 763, good rates for cash, accepts TCs. (See note on provincial bonds used as currency, page 244.)

● **Cultural centres**
Alliance Française, Mendoza 255, free events in French; **Instituto Italiano di Cultura**, Salta 60; **Aticana** (North American Centre) inc JF Kennedy Library, Salta 581, open Mon-Fri, 0800-1200, 1700-2100.

● **Entertainment**
Casino: Sarmiento y Maipú, open Fri, Sat, Sun, 2100-0230.

● **Laundry**
Lava Norte, Mendoza 375; *Mi Lavadero*, Ayacucho 115.

● **Post & telecommunications**
Post Office: Córdoba y 25 de Mayo, open 0700-1300, 1600-2000 Mon-Fri, 0800-1300 Sat. **Telecommunications**: Telecom, Maipú 360, open 24 hrs, best after 1900.

● **Shopping**
Artesanía El Cardón, Alvarez 427, excellent handicrafts; *Mercado Artesanal*, at the tourist office in Plaza Independencia, small, but nice selection of lace and leather work. All shops close 1200-1630. There is a lively fruit and vegetable market, *Mercado de Abasto*, at San Lorenzo y Lillo, worth a visit.

● **Tourist offices**
In Plaza Independencia at 24 de Septiembre 484, 0800-1800, 1700-2200. For free tourist information, T 0800-5-8828.

● **Transport**
Local Car hire: Avis, *Hotel del Sol*, Plaza Independencia; **Liprandi**, 24 de Septiembre 524, T 311210/212665; **Movil Renta**, San Lorenzo 370, T 218635/310550, F 310080 and at airport; Localiza, San Juan 959, T 311355. **Car repairs**: Rubén Boss, Av Aconquija 947, rec esp for Volkswagen. **Motorists**: should not park on the street overnight; pay US$5 for garage parking.

Air Airport at Benjamín Matienzo, 15 km from town. Bus for each flight, US$1.50, starts from *Hotel Mayoral*, 24 de Septiembre 364. Taxi US$10. To Buenos Aires, AR, Lapa (T 305530) and Dinar. Andesmar and Southern Winds (T 225554) to Córdoba and Salta (also Lapa and Dinar).

Buses Modern terminal on Av Benjamín Araoz beside a huge shopping complex; to **Cafayate**, 8 hrs, US$20 via Tafí and Santa María, Aconquija, daily at 0600 and 1400; direct to **Salta** (not via Cafayate), 4½ hrs, several daily, eg La Estrella, Veloz del Norte, US$21, 4½ hrs. Plenty of buses to **Jujuy**, eg Veloz del Norte, 0900, 6 hrs.

To **Buenos Aires**, Chevallier, La Estrella, Veloz del Norte, 16 hrs, all with toilet, a/c, bar, video, 3 stops; book in advance; fares US$40-70; to **Mendoza**, La Estrella, US$29, 3 a day (14 hrs), via Catamarca, La Rioja, and San Juan; to **La Rioja**, 7 hrs, US$15. To **Catamarca**, 5 a day with Bosio, plus other lines. To **Santiago del Estero**, US$8; to **Córdoba**, US$30, 7 hrs, many companies. To **Pocitos**, frontier with Bolivia, US$25.

TUCUMAN TO SALTA

THE DIRECT ROUTE

Of the two routes from Tucumán to Salta, via Rosario de la Frontera and Güemes is quicker, but less scenic, than via the beautiful Quebrada de Cafayate.

ROSARIO DE LA FRONTERA

(*Alt* 769m; *Phone code* 0876), 145 km N of Tucumán, is a popular resort (with casino) from June to Sept. 8 km away are sulphur springs.

Excursions About 20 km N is the historical post house, Posta de **Yatasto**, with museum, 2 km E of the main road; campsite. To **El Naranjo**, 19 km, a Jesuit colonial town; church contains images and carvings made by Indians.

● **Accommodation** **A3** pp *Termas*, Route 34, T 81004, full board, rambling place, good food but many rooms without private bath (6 km from bus station, taxi US$7). Baths US$1.50. About 1 km from *Hotel Termas* is *ACA hostería*, T 81143, opp is artificial lake owned by Caza y Pesca Club. **C** *Real*, Güemes 185, T 81067, basic, clean, not all doors close.

● **Buses** To Tucumán, Güemes, Salta and Jujuy, frequent.

North of Rosario, the road continues to Güemes, 148 km, where it forks: Route 34 continues to Jujuy and the Bolivian frontier; Route 9 branches off W, through the mountains to Salta.

PARQUE NACIONAL EL REY

About 80 km N of Rosario de la Frontera, at Lumbreras, a road branches off Route 9 and runs 80 km NE to the Parque Nacional **El Rey**, which extends over 44,160 ha, a wildlife reserve set among 900-1,500m hills with clear streams (good fishing). Vegetation ranges from cloud forest to Chaco type semi-desert. It can also be reached from Salta (196 km) where there is a Park office, España 366, 3rd floor (helpful). Mosquitoes, ticks and chiggers thrive; take lotion.

● **Accommodation** None while *Hostería El Rey* is closed. Camping is free, there are several tent sites, but few facilities. Horse riding.

● **Transport** The access road is poor and fords the river 9 times; passable for ordinary cars except in the wet season. Best time to visit is winter (drier). There is no public transport to the park; ask the park office in Salta about alternatives, or take a tour from an agency, US$50pp for at least 6.

VIA CAFAYATE

TAFI DEL VALLE

46 km S of Tucumán Route 307 branches NW through a gorge with sub-tropical vegetation to **Tafí del Valle**, which is often shrouded in fog caused by clouds entering the valley from the humid lowlands. At Km 27 on this road is a statue to El Indio, with picnic area. Tafí del Valle (*Pop* 3,000, 97 km from Tucumán, not to be confused with Tafí Viejo which is 10 km N of the city) is known to archaeologists as a holy valley of the precolumbian Indian tribes. 10 mins from Tafí is the Capilla Jesuítica y Museo La Banda in the 16th century chapel of San Lorenzo (open Mon-Sat 1000-1600, Sun 900-1200).

10 km S of Tafí del Valle are Dique El Mollar and, nearby, the menhir park of **El Mollar**, with 129 standing stones with engraved designs of unknown significance (collected in the early years of this century from various sites) and good views (best to visit am). Tucumán-Cafayate buses stop on request (see below for tours from Tucumán).

● **Accommodation** **A3** *Hostería ACA*, T 21027, run down, restaurant, garden; **C** *Colonial*, T 21067, nr bus station, closed out of season, no singles; **C** *Atep*, Los Menhires, nr bus terminal, **D** in winter, rec; *Pensión*, opp *Colonial*, in billiard hall, ask in advance for hot water; **E** pp *hostal* run by Celia Correa, nr church, rec. *Luna Huasi*, 200m from town, in former *Estancia Los Cuartos*; 1 km from the town at La Banda is **A1** *La Hacienda Le Pepe*, inc breakfast, English and French spoken, horses for rent. **Camping**: *Autocamping Los Sauzales*, T 21084, run down.

● **Places to eat** *El Rancho de Félix*, rec; *El Portal de Tafí*, good, has video room (movies in summer only); *La Rueda*, at S entrance to village, inexpensive, rec; *Los Faroles*, pleasant cafe. Try local cheese.

● **Estancia** *Estancia Los Cuartos*, T 081-22-6793/0867-21124, offers lunches and activities inc horseriding.

- **Tour companies & travel agents** Tours to El Mollar and Tafí are available from travel agencies in Tucumán, US$15 each for 4 people minimum. For tours throughout the NW from Tafí, contact Margarita and Bruno Widmer, T/F (0867) 21076, highly rec. Off season contact the tourist office to arrange excursions by taxi, US$15 pp.

- **Buses** To/from Tucumán, Aconquija, sit on left-hand side from Tucumán, 4 a day, 3½ hrs, US$9. To **Cafayate** 4 a day, 4 hrs, US$10. Tafí-**El Mollar** daily 1215, returns 1330, US$1.

NORTHWEST OF TAFÍ DEL VALLE

From Tafí the road runs 56 km NW over the 3,040m Infiernillo Pass and through attractive arid landscape to **Amaichá del Valle** which claims 360 sunny days a year. La Pachamama festival at end of pre-Lent Carnival (bus to Tucumán, US$7.) From Amaichá the paved road continues N 15 km to the junction with Route 40.

Santa María (*Pop* 18,000), 22 km S of Amaichá by paved road, is a small town with a little archaeology museum on the plaza (Sarmiento 18). From Santa María Route 40 leads N to Cafayate (55 km) and S to Belén (176 km, see page 160).

- **Accommodation A3** *Plaza*, San Martín 350, T 20309, on plaza, small rooms; **B** *Provincial de Turismo*, San Martín y 1 de Mayo, T 20240, rec, dining room; **C** *Res Alemán*, Quintana 13, T 20226, small rooms, quiet. **Campsite:** Municipal campsite at end of Sarmiento.

- **Buses** To **Tucumán** 6 hrs, 0220, 0800, US$8.50; to **Cafayate**, 4 hrs, El Indio daily at 0700 excluding Thur at 1030, US$10. Empresa Bosio to **Catamarca**, Sat; via Tucumán Sun at 1230, 9 hrs; Cayetano to **Belén** 4 hrs, Mon, Wed, Fri at 0500.

Fuerte Quemado and **Quilmes** From Santa María you can visit Cerro Pintado, 8 km, coloured sandstone mountains, and several archaeological sites: at Fuerte Quemado 15 km N along Route 40; Loma Rica, 18 km; and Ampajango, 27 km S off Route 40. None is as impressive as Quilmes, 37 km N, 5 km along a dirt road off the main Santa María-Cafayate road, 16 km from Amaichá del Valle. There are Inca ruins (dam, village and posting house – *tambo*) with splendid views and interesting cacti (guide 0700-1730, entry US$2). There is also a provincial archaeological museum.

- **Accommodation & services** At Quilmes: **A2** *Parador Ruinas de Quilmes*, T (0892) 21075, at the site, comfortable, underfloor heating in winter, a/c in summer, owners are tapestry and ceramics experts; shop selling good indigenous crafts, particularly textiles; good restaurant, bar and camping facilities.

- **Transport** For a day's visit take 0630 Aconquija bus from Cafayate to Santa María, alight at site, or take 0700 bus from Santa María; in each case take 1100 bus back to Cafayate. Taxi from Cafayate US$60 return.

(*Pop* 8,432; *Alt* 1,660m; *Phone code* 0868) is a clean town, with low rainfall (none Mar-Oct), lying between two ranges of Andean foothills. Surrounded by vineyards, it is home of several renowned *bodegas*. A walk to Cerro San Isidro (3 hrs) takes you to a view of the Aconquija chain in the S to Nevado de Cachi in the N.

Vineyards

The **La Rosa** *bodega* can be visited, Mon-Fri, 0800-1230, 1500-1830, weekends am only, no need to book, 30-min tours and tasting, reached by turning right 500m past the ACA *hostería*; near the cellar is an old water mill which is still in use. **Etchart**, 2 km on Ruta 40 to Tucumán, also has tours (T 21310/2), Mon-Fri 0800-1830. **La Banda**, the oldest *bodega* in the valley (next to ACA *hostería*), is interesting because it is more primitive, English spoken.

Museums

The **Museo de la Vid y El Vino** in an old *bodega* is on Av Güemes, 2 blocks S of the plaza, US$1, very well laid out. **Museo Arqueológico Rodolfo I Bravo**, one block from main plaza, local collection of the late Sr Bravo, pre-Inca funeral urns and 19th century domestic artefacts, US$1.

Local information
● Accommodation

Accommodation is hard to find at holiday periods (especially for a single person).

A3 *Briones*, Toscano 80, main plaza, T 21270, comfortable, with hot water, accepts Amex card; **A3** *Asembal*, Güemes y Almagro, T 21065, nice rooms, good; **A3** *Asturias*, Güemes 158, T 21328, rec; **A3** *Hostería Cafayate* (ACA), T 21296, on N outskirts, modern, quiet

(but cold), colonial-style, covered parking, good food, but restaurant may be closed.
B *Gran Real*, Güemes 128, T 21016, without breakfast, pleasant, rec; **B** *Tinkunaku*, Diego de Almagro 12, 1 block from plaza, rec.

C *Colonial*, Almagro 134, T 21233, charming patio; **E** pp *Confort*, Güemes 232, T 21091, comfortable, member of Red Argentina de Alojamiento para Jóvenes; **C** *La Posta del Rey*, Güemes 415, T 21120; **C** *Pensión Arroyo* (no sign), Niño 160, rec; **C** *Vicano*, Toscana 273, rec; **E** pp *Youth Hostel*, Av Güemes 441, T 21440, small, hot water, stores luggage, tours arranged, English and Italian spoken; another, **E** pp, at Buenos Aires 930, T 239910; **E** pp Rosario 165, T 21098, dormitory style, basic, kitchen. Accommodation in private houses is available.

Campsite: Municipal campsite *Lorohuasi* at S access to town, hot water, swimming pool, well maintained, bungalows for rent, **D** for 4 people; private site N of town, opp ACA *hostería*.

● **Places to eat**
Several good ones on the main plaza: *Cafayate*; *Confitería La Barra*; *El Gordo*; *La Carreta de Don Olegario*, Güemes y Quintana, rec; *El Criollo*, Güemes 254, clean, good, rec; *La López Pereyra*, Güemes 375, good food, friendly. Several *comedores* along Rivadavia (2 blocks N of Plaza), where the locals eat. Only the more expensive restaurants are open late.

● **Banks & money changers**
Banco de la Nación, main plaza, for cash; TCs and credit cards not accepted.

● **Shopping**
Handicrafts: locally woven tapestries are interesting, and very expensive; visit the Calchaquí tapestry exhibition of Miguel Nanni on the main plaza. Also *Platería* of Jorge Barraco, Colón 147, for silver craft work. Oil paintings, woodcarving, metalwork and ceramics by Calixto Mamani can be seen in his art gallery at Rivadavia 452, or contact him at home at Rivadavia 254. Handicrafts in wood and silver by Oscar Hipaucha on main plaza. Pancho Silva and his family have a workshop at 25 de Mayo selling and displaying their own and locals' handicrafts. Souvenir prices are generally high. Local pottery in the *Mercado Municipal de Artesanía* on the main plaza.

● **Tourist offices**
Kiosk on the main plaza.

● **Transport**
Local Rentals: bike hire from Rentavel, Güemes 175 US$2/hr, US$15/day. **Horses**: can be hired from La Florida, Bodega Etchart Privado, 2 km S of Cafayate, or from Tito Stinga (ask in village).

Buses To **Tucumán**, Aconquija, daily 0600, 8 hrs, US$20, also Sat 1500. Alternatively go to Santa María on 1100 El Indio bus, or 0630 Aconquija bus, 2 hrs, US$10, and then take bus to Tucumán; to **Salta** via the Quebrada de Cafayate, El Indio, 4 a day, 4 hrs, US$11 (worth travelling in daylight); to **Angastaco**, El Indio, 1100 daily except Sun, US$4, sit on the right, leaves Angastaco for the return journey at 0630. **Tours** Cafayate can also be visited by organized excursion from Salta, US$40, inc lunch and visit to a *bodega*.

QUEBRADA DE CAFAYATE

Route 68 goes NE from Cafayate to Salta through the gorge of the Río de las Conchas (known as the **Quebrada de Cafayate**) with fascinating rock formations of differing colours, all signposted. The road goes through wild and semi-arid landscapes with many wild birds, including *ñandúes* (rheas). Take the El Indio bus to Salta as far as Los Loros, Km 32, then walk back (and catch a returning bus from Salta); alternatively hire a bike in Cafayate and take it on the 0545 El Indio bus as far as Alemania (84 km) and then cycle back. **NB** The sun is very hot, take lots of water.

North of the Quebrada the road runs through Col Moldes, Cabra Corral (81 km S of Salta), a huge artificial lake; water skiing, fishing, no hotels, one campsite, restaurant and sailing club; **B** *Hostería Cabra Corral*, T 231965, is 4 km from the lake, half board, swimming pool, 'delightful', rec) and El Carril.

VALLES CALCHAQUIES

North of Cafayate Route 40 runs 160 km through the Valles Calchaquíes to Cachi. The road is mainly gravel and can be very difficult after rain, but the views of the Andean-foothill desert country with its strange rock formations and unexpected colours, are fascinating. The population is largely Indian.

SAN CARLOS

(*Alt* 1,710m), a small settlement, about 24 km N of Cafayate, was destroyed four times by Indians. It has a pleasant white church completed 1854, a small archaeological museum. There are artisans' shops and workshops, craft market near church.

● **Accommodation C** *Hostería*, T 218937. Several *hospedajes*. Municipal campsite.

● **Buses** El Indio, on the Salta-Cafayate-Angastaco run, arrive in San Carlos by noon and on the return journey at 0745.

ANGASTACO

North of San Carlos Route 40 enters the Calchaquí valley and climbs to **Angastaco**, 50 km from Salta, 2 km off the main road. The road passes through the spectacular **Quebrada de las Flechas**, remarkable for its formations and colours, 5-10 km S of Angastaco. Small archaeological museum in the civic building. You can sample the local Vino Patero, red or sweet white, in a house close to the river bridge in Angastaco; *vino patero* is supposed to be made by treading the grapes in the traditional manner. Fiesta Patronal Virgen del Valle: second weekend of Dec, with processions, folk music, dancing, rodeos.

● **Accommodation C** *Hostería*, T 222826, negotiable in low season, good, cheap and delicious meals on request, knowledgeable; **F** pp *Res El Cardón*, good, clean, comfortable.

● **Buses** To Cachi and Salta (US$5.50), Fri, 1100 only; daily bus to San Carlos and Cafayate 0545 (Sat and holidays 0630). **Taxi**: to Molinos US$40, ask at police station for address of Orlando López; no transport for hitching.

MOLINOS

From the Angastaco turn-off it is 40 km on a winding road through beautiful and desolate rock formations to **Molinos**. The church, with its fine twin-domed bell-towers, built about 1720, contains the mummified body of the last Royalist governor of Salta, Don Nicolás Isasmendi Echalar. To protect it from visitors plucking its hair, this relic can no longer be viewed by the public. The priest is very knowledgeable about local history. A pleasant walk is down from the church, crossing a creek and then climbing a gentle hill, from which there are good views of Molinos and surrounding country.

● **Accommodation A3** *Hostería Molinos*, T 214871, rec, with breakfast, good meals, in Casa de Isasmendi, which also contains a small museum. *Sra de Guaymas* (known as 'Sra Silvia') runs a restaurant and rents rooms, **E**, basic, clean. There are other rooms to rent around the main plaza.

● **Buses** To Salta via Cachi, Thur, Fri, Sat, Mon

at 0645, also Mon, Thur, Sat at 1315, Marcos Rueda; 2 hrs to Cachi, US$4.50, 7 hrs to Salta. To Angastaco, Thur morning.

CACHI

From Molinos it is 46 km to **Cachi** (Quechua for 'salt'; *Alt* 2,280m), a beautiful little town renowned for its weaving, other crafts and invigorating climate. The church's roof and confessional are made from the wood of the *cardón* cactus. The **Museo Arqueológico** (open Mon-Sat, 0800-1800, Sun, holidays 0900-1200) presents a small but interesting survey of pre-colonial Calchaquí culture, US$1. There are fine views from the Cemetery, 10 mins walk from the village.

The Indian ruins at **Las Pailas**, 18 km W of Cachi, are barely excavated; in themselves, they are not especially impressive but the view is breathtaking, with huge cacti set against snow-topped Andean peaks. They can be reached on foot (4 hrs one way), or by bus from Cachi. Ask for directions or a guide.

● **Accommodation A3** *ACA Hostería Cachi*, T 210001, on hill above the town, good, pleasant; **E** pp *Res Pajarito*, with bath, basic; **E** *Albergue Municipal*, also has good municipal campsite with swimming pool and barbecue pits, on hill at S end of town. **At Cachi Adentro**, 6 km W of Cachi, is the **B** *Hostal Samay Huasi*, a restored *hacienda*, pleasant and helpful owners, heating and hot water at all times; **A1** *El Viejo Molino de Cachi Adentro*, a restored working mill, beautiful views, horse riding, rec, minimum stay 3 days, book in advance, T 8039339, F 4762065 (Bs As), T 213968, F 233122 (Salta); 3 buses a day from Cachi. Hire horses in the village, US$5/hr. Fishing is also possible.

● **Buses** To Salta, 1530 daily (except Wed), also at 0900 Thur, Fri, Sat, Mon, 5 hrs, US$14; to Molinos 1200 daily; El Indio from Cafayate Thur am only, returning Thur pm.

Cachi to Salta Follow Route 40 for 11 km N to Payogasta (new *Hostería*), then turn right to Route 33. This road (gravel) climbs continuously up the Cuesta del Obispo passing a dead-straight stretch of 14 km known as La Recta del Tin-Tin with magnificent views of the **Los Cardones National Park** with the huge candelabra cacti, which grow up to 6m in height. It reaches the summit at Piedra de Molino (3,347m) after 43 km. Then it plunges down through the Quebrada de Escoipe. The road rejoins Route 68 at El Carril, from where it is 37 km back to Salta.

North of Cachi Route 40 continues to San Antonio de los Cobres via **La Poma**, 54 km, a beautiful hamlet (*Alt* 3,015m; *hostería*, **F**) and the Paso Abra de Acay (4,900m, the highest pass in South America negotiable by car; high clearance vehicle advisable; no buses beyond La Poma).

(*Pop* 370,000; *Alt* 1,190m; *Phone code* 087), situated on the Río Arias, in the Lerma valley, lies in a mountainous and strikingly beautiful district. 1,600 km N of Buenos Aires, Salta was founded in 1582 and still possesses a number of fine colonial buildings. Capital of its province, it is a great handicraft centre and the major starting place for tours of the NW.

Places of interest

Follow the ceramic pavement plaques, or get the map from Tourist Office, for an interesting pedestrian tour. The **Cathedral** (open mornings and evenings), on the N side of the central **Plaza 9 de Julio**, was built 1858-1878; it contains the much venerated images of the Cristo del Milagro and of the Virgin Mary, the first sent from Spain in 1592, and has a rich interior mainly in red and gold, as well as a huge late baroque altar. The miracle was the sudden cessation of a terrifying series of earthquakes when the images were paraded through the streets on 15 Sepember 1692. They still are, each September. On the opposite side of the Plaza is the **Cabildo**, built in 1783. The Convent of **San Bernardo**, at Caseros y Santa Fe, was built in colonial style in the mid-19th century; it has a famous wooden portal of 1762. Nuns still live here so the inside of the convent is not open to visitors. **San Francisco** church, at Caseros y Córdoba (1882), rises above the city centre skyline with its magnificent façade and red, yellow and grey coloured tower (open 0700-1200, 1730-2100, in theory).

East of the city centre is the **Cerro San Bernardo** (1,458m), accessible by cable car (*teleférico*), daily except Thurs, 1600-2000, US$6 return, children US$3, from Parque San Martín, fine views. Near the *teleférico* station is a lake where rowing boats can be hired (US$3 for 20 mins). It takes about half an hour to walk back down the hill. Very beautifully set at the foot of the hill is an impressive **statue** by Víctor Cariño, 1931, **to Gen Güemes**, whose *gaucho* troops repelled seven powerful Spanish invasions from Bolivia between 1814 and 1821. A steep path (1,136 steps) behind the nearby Museo Antropológico, with Stations of the Cross, leads to the top of the hill, where there is an old wooden cross, together with restaurant and artificial waterfalls.

Museums

Museo Histórico del Norte, in the Cabildo Histórico, Caseros 549, colonial, historical and archaeological museum, guided tour in Spanish, recommended, Mon-Fri 0930-1330, 1530-2030, Sat/Sun 0930-1330, 1630-2030, US$1. **Museo de Bellas Artes**, Florida 20, Mon-Sat 0900-1300, 1700-2100, Sun 0900-1200, US$0.60 (closed Jan). **Casa Uriburu**, Caseros 421, Tues-Sat, 1000-1400, 1530-1930, US$0.60, has relics of a distinguished *salteño* family. **Museo Folclórico Pajarito Velarde**, Pueyrredón 106. **Museo Antropológico**, Paseo Güemes, behind the statue, contains many objects from Tastil (see page 132), open Tues-Fri 0830-1230, 1430-1830, Sat 1500-1830, Sun 1600-1830, US$1. **Museo de Ciencias Naturales**, in Parque San Martín, has a full display of over 150 regional stuffed birds and an interesting display of armadillos, recommended, open Tues-Sun 1400-2000, US$0.25. **Museo de la Ciudad 'Casa de Hernández'**, La Florida 97, Tues-Sat, 0900-1230, 1600-2030. Check opening times in summer at tourist office; many close then.

Local festivals

15 Sept, Cristo del Milagro (see above); 24 Sept, Battles of Tucumán and Salta. On 16-17 June, folk music in pm and *gaucho* parade in am around the Güemes statue. Salta celebrates Carnival with processions on the four weekends before Ash

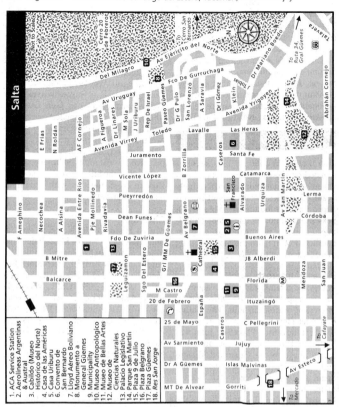

Salta

1. ACA Service Station
2. Aerolíneas Argentinas & Austral
3. Cabildo (Museo Histórico del Norte)
4. Casa de las Américas
5. Casa Uriburu
6. Convento de San Bernardo
7. Lloyd Aéreo Boliviano
8. Monumento a Güemes
9. Municipality
10. Museo Antropológico
11. Museo de Bellas Artes
12. Museo de Ciencias Naturales
13. Palacio Legislativo
14. Parque San Martín
15. Plaza 9 de Julio
16. Plaza Belgrano
17. Plaza Güemes
18. Res San Jorge

Wednesday at 200 in Av Belgrano (seats optional at US$2-4); also Mardi Gras (Shrove Tuesday) with a procession of decorated floats and of dancers with intricate masks of feathers and mirrors. Water is squirted at passers-by and *bombas de agua* (small balloons to be filled with water) are sold for dropping from balconies.

Local information
● Accommodation

Salta is a favourite convention town. Some hotels close for a vacation during the Christmas season until Jan 10, so check. Accommodation is scarce in the last 2 weeks in July because of holidays and around 10-16 Sept because of the celebrations of Cristo del Milagro.

A2 *Salta*, Buenos Aires 1, in main plaza, T 21101/413, 1st class, pool, good restaurant; **A1** *Portezuelo*, Av Del Turista 1, T 310133, F 310133, breakfast extra, some rooms a/c, English, German, French, Italian spoken, pool, helpful, good restaurant, rec; **A2** *California*, Alvarado 646, T 216266, 1 block from main plaza, rec; **A2** *Victoria Plaza*, Zuviría 16, T 310334, expensive but good restaurant, the foyer overlooking the plaza is one of the centres of *salteño* life; **A3** *Colonial*, Zuviría 6, T 310760, a/c, rec, but 1st floor rooms noisy; **A3** *Las Lajitas*, Pasaje Calixto Guana 336, T 233796, modern, good value, ACA reduction, rec; **A3** *Petit*, H Yrigoyen 225, T 213012, pleasant, small, expensive breakfasts, rooms around courtyard with small swimming pool, a/c extra, French spoken; **A3** *Regidor*, Buenos Aires 10, T 222070, English-speaking owner, good value lunch, comfortable.

B *Astur*, Rivadavia 752, T 311305, rec; **B** *España*, España 319, T 217898, central but quiet, simple, rec; **B** *Florida*, Florida y Urquiza 718, T 212133, stores luggage, rec; **B** *Italia*, Alberdi 231, T 214050, next to jazz club/casino, rec; **B** *Res Elena*, Buenos Aires 256, T 211529, quiet, 'charming', safe, try to get there early; **D** pp *Res Crisol*, Ituzaingó 166, T 214462, good meeting place; *Sanyor* San Martín 994, T 214440, laundry facilities.

D pp *Res San Jorge*, Esteco 244 y Ruiz de los Llanos 1164 (no sign), T/F 210443, with or without bath (**E** single), parking, safe deposit, laundry and limited kitchen facilities, central heating, parking, homely, guide for climbing, horse-trekking advice by proprietor, also organizes local excursions by car, good value, highly rec (take buses 3 and 10 from bus station to San Martín y Malvinas); **D** *Casa de familia de María del Toffoli*, Mendoza 915 (about 10 blocks from bus station), T 320813, nice atmosphere, comfortable, roof terrace, cooking facilities, rec, rooms also at Nos 917 and 919, **D-C**, belonging to Sra Toffoli's sisters (reservations at No 917), cosy, highly rec; *Sra Dora de Batista*, Mendoza 947, T 310570, rec, laundry facilities; **E** pp Mendoza 509, no singles; **E** *Hosp Doll*, Pasaje Ruiz de los Llanos 1360 (7 blocks from centre), with bath, safe, rec. Many other cheap hotels nr railway station (eg **E** *Internacional*, Ameghino 651, hot water, basic, with good cheap restaurant), but few nr bus station.

Youth hostel: **E** pp *Backpackers*, Buenos Aires 930, T 314305, bus 12 from bus terminal or 30 mins' walk, **E** pp in dormitories, laundry and kitchen facilities, stores luggage, budget travel information, bar, hot showers, English, Greek and Hebrew spoken, frequently rec. **E** pp *No Me Olvides*, Av de los Pioneros, Km 0.800, shared rooms, cooking facilities, rec. **NB** Do not tempted by touts at the bus station offering convenient accommodation.

Outside Salta: at San Lorenzo, 11 km NW of the centre, **A2** *Hostal Selva Montana*, C Alfonsina Storní 2315, T 921184, luxurious, highly rec; camping and picnicking beside rocky stream and natural woodland. Sibylle Oeschger and Hansruedi Hintermann, T 921080, rent 1 room (**E** pp) and offer horseriding tours, US$24 pp/$1/2$-day. (Hourly bus service from Salta terminal, Empresa Chávez, platform 15, 30 mins, US$1. Bus stops in front of *Quebrada* restaurant (good food, quite expensive). Last bus back about 2330.)

The *Finca San Antonio*, El Carril, T/F 908034, offers accommodation on a farm dating from 1621, pool, horseriding, other activities; **B** pp *Hostería de Chicoana*, in Chicoana, 47 km S, T/F 807003, pool, gardens,

English and German spoken, horses for hire, rec; At **El Bordo**, 45 km E of Salta, Sr de Arias offers luxury accommodation on his finca, L3 pp full board; excursions also arranged. Contact: *Finca El Bordo De Las Lanzas*, 4432 El Bordo, Salta, T 310525.

Camping: Casino Provincial municipal grounds, by river, 300m artificial lake (popular Dec-Feb). Bus 13 to grounds. There is no signposting: leave the city heading S on C Jujuy, after 3 km you will see the Coca Cola plant on your left; turn left before the plant and then take the first road right. Charges US$3/tent plus US$2 pp. Free hot showers available if there is gas (not often), safe, bathrooms run-down, disappointing. At ACA's *Motel Huaico*, Bolivia y P Costas, T 310571. **Municipal Campsite** at Campo Quijano, 30 km W of Salta, at the entrance to Quebrada del Toro gorge, hot showers, bungalows, plenty of room for pitching tents, rec, bus from Salta bus terminal. Camping shops: *HR Maluf*, San Martín y Buenos Aires, and one at La Rioja 995.

● **Places to eat**

El Monumento, Gurruchaga 20 (opp Güemes monument), good food, slow service, good atmosphere, reasonably priced; *Maxims*, Mendoza y Florida, good; *La Posta*, España 476, food and atmosphere both excellent, reasonable prices, highly rec; *El Viejo Jack*, Virrey Toledo 145, good meat dishes, huge portions; *Palacio de la Pizza*, Caseros 459, "best pizza of all anywhere" (Federico Kirbus); *Cantina*, Caseros y 20 de Febrero, pizzas, steaks; *9 de Julio*, Urquiza 1020, excellent lunch; *El Rescoldo*, Caseros 427, cheap lunches, rec; *Green Park*, Caseros 529, good snacks, and milk shakes; *El Mesón de Pepe*, Rivadavia 774, fish specialities, good but pricey. Several good places on Plaza 9 de Julio. Pleasant outdoor restaurants in Parque San Martín, at foot of Cerro San Bernardo; *Sociedad Española*, Balcarce 653, excellent cuisine; *de Pablo*, Mitre 399, excellent set lunch; *Alvarez*, Buenos Aires y San Martín, cafetería style, cheap and good; *Pub Yo Juan*, Balcarce 481, popular, live music at weekends; *Café Van Gogh*, Plaza de Armas, good breakfasts; *Café del Paseo* at Hotel Colonial, Zuviría 6, open 24 hrs, superb breakfast, good value (ask for Té Paseo); *Heladería Gianni*, España 486, ask for copa dell'Amore, excellent coffee; *Cafe Río*, Mitre 40, good breakfasts. Cheap restaurants nr the railway and bus stations, which are also the cheapest places for breakfast. Many restaurants are lunch only, especially on San Martín nr the Municipal Market. Cheapest food is from the numerous *superpanchito* stalls.

● **Airline offices**

Austral, Caseros 475, T 310258; **Lapa**, Caseros

492, T 317080; **Dinar**, Buenos Aires 46, T/F 310606; **Southern Winds**, Buenos Aires 22, T 210808; **Lloyd Aéreo Boliviano**, Buenos Aires 120, T 217753 (will hold luggage and schedule a *colectivo* taxi).

● **Banks & money changers**
Banks, open 0730-1300, do not advance cash against credit cards as all have ATMs. **Banco de la Nación**, Balcarce y España; **Banco Provincial de Salta**, España 526 on main plaza, low commission on TCs; **Banco de Credito Argentino**, Alvaredo 777, for Mastercard and Visa; **Banco Nacional del Lavoro**, Florida y Urquiza, cash on Mastercard; **Banco Roberts**, Mitre 143, good rates, no commission on Amex TCs, changes Thomas Cook TCs; **Amex**, *Chicoana Turismo*, Av Belgrano y Zuviria 255, does not cash TCs. Many *cambios* on España: **Maguitur**, España 666, only cash; **Golden Life**, Mitre 95 (Plaza 9 de Julio), local 1, first floor, best rates for cash. Difficult to buy US$ on cards or TCs. See also **Currency**, page 262, on *bonos*.

● **Cultural centres**
Alliance Française, Santa Fe 20, T 210827.

● **Embassies & consulates**
Bolivia, Dr Mariano Boedo 38, T 223377, open Mon-Fri, 0900-1300 (unhelpful, better to go to Jujuy); **Chile**, Santiago del Estero, T 215757; **Peru**, 25 de Mayo 407, T 310201; **Spain**, Las Heras 1329, T 221420; **Italy**, Alvarado 1632, T 213881; **France**, Santa Fe 20, T 213336; **Germany**, Córdoba 202, T 216525, F 311772, consul Juan C Kühl, who also runs travel agency (see below), helpful; **Belgium**, Pellegrini 835, T 233459.

● **Entertainment**
Music: folk music show and evening meal at *Boliche Balderrama*, San Martín 1126; *Gauchos de Güemes*, Uruguay 750; *Casa Güemes*, España 730. For something less touristy try *Manolo*, San Martín 1296 or *La Casona del Molino*, Luis Burela esq Caseros, T 316079, folk music and *empanadas*. Some bars charge around US$7 pp for music, but don't display charges.

● **Laundry**
Sol de Mayo, 25 de Mayo 755, service wash. *Laverap*, Santiago del Estero 363 (open Sun am) good, fast service, US$6 for one load; *Marva*, Juramento 315; *La Baseta*, Alvarado 1170.

● **Post & telecommunications**
Post Office: Deán Funes 160, between España and Belgrano *poste restante* charges US$1.15/letter. **Telephone**: Belgrano 824, 24 hrs; international calls at Vicente López 146, 0800-1930.

● **Shopping**
Mercado Municipal, corner of San Martín and Florida, for meat, fish, vegetables, *empanadas*,

humitas and other produce and handicrafts, closed 1200-1700 and Sun. Good supermarket, *Disco*, Alberdi y Leguizamon. **Mercado Artesanal** on the outskirts of the city in the Casa El Alto Molino, a late 18th century mansion, at San Martín 2555, T 219195, Mon-Fri 0800-2000, Sat 0900-2000 (sometimes closes in summer) take bus 2, 3, or 7 from Av San Martín in centre and get off as bus crosses the railway line. Excellent range of goods but expensive. Woodcarvings of birds etc from *Tres Cerritas*, Santiago del Estero 202. For objets d'art and costume jewellery made of onyx, visit *Onix Salta*, Chile 1663. *Feria del Libro*, Buenos Aires 83; *Librería Rayuela*, Buenos Aires 96, foreign-language books and magazines; *Plural Libros*, Buenos Aires 220, helpful. Arts and handicrafts are often cheaper in surrounding villages.

● **Tour companies & travel agents**
All agencies charge similar prices for tours (though some charge extra for credit card payments): Salta city US$15; Quebrada del Toro US$18; Cachi US$45; Humahuaca US$50; San Antonio de las Cobres US$75; Cafayate (1 day) US$40; 2-day tour to Cafayate, Angastaco, Molinos, Cachi, US$80. Out of season, tours often run only if there is sufficient demand; check carefully that tour will run on the day you want. *Movitren*, Caseros 431, T 316174, F 311264, for Tren a las Nubes and full programme of tours; *Saltur*, Caseros 525, T 212012, F 311622, very efficient and rec for local tours (no English-speaking guides). *Puna Expediciones*, Braquiquitos 399, T 341875 (well qualified and experienced guide Luis H Aguilar can also be contacted through the *Res San Jorge*), organizes treks in remote areas, US$25 a day inc transport to trekking region, food, porters, highly rec. *Ricardo Clark Expeditions*, Caseros 121, T 215390, specialist tours for birdwatchers, English spoken, books on flora and fauna in several languages sold, highly rec; *Hernán Uriburu*, organizes trekking expeditions, Rivadavia 409, T 310605, expensive but highly professional. *Juan Kühl*, Córdoba 202, T 216525, F 311772 tours by light aeroplane, horseback, caravan, boat, German and English spoken, highly rec, also runs photographic company; *Martin Oliver*, T 321013, F 91052, adventure tourism guide. *Movitrack*, Hostal Selva Montana, Alfonsina Storni 2315, San Lorenzo, Salta, T 921184, F 921433, offer one day safaris in a 4x4 truck, to San Antonio de los Cobres, then N along Route 40 via Salinas Grandes and the Quebrada de Purmamarca to the Quebrada de Humahuaca and thence back to Salta, German, English spoken, dep 0600, 14½ hrs, US$95 plus US$15 for refreshments, 2 or 3 times a week, May-Sept, book in advance direct from

company, not through travel agencies which have their own tours and may tell you trip is full.

● **Tourist offices**

Provincial Tourist Office (Emsatur), Buenos Aires 93 (one block from main plaza). Open every day, except Sun, till 2100. Very helpful, gives free maps. Municipal Tourist office, Buenos Aires 61, closed Sun, helpful, free maps. Both offices arrange accommodation in private houses in high season (July) and can arrange horse-riding, US$50 full day, US$30 ½-day with horses, guide and meals, rec. Office at bus terminal, friendly, no maps.

● **Useful addresses**

Immigration Office: Maipú 35, 0730-1230.

● **Transport**

Local Car hire: very expensive. **Avis**, Alvarado 537, T 216344, rec; **Rent A Car**, Caseros 489 and 221; local companies reported to be cheaper: **ALE**, Caseros 753, T 223469; **López Fleming**, Buenos Aires 33, T 211381, new cars, cheapest, friendly; **Ruiz Moreno**, Caseros 225, in *Hotel Salta*, good cars, helpful; **Renta Autos**, Caseros 400, also good. It may be cheaper and more convenient to hire a taxi for a fixed fee. **Bicycles**: *Pogoni*, España 676, helpful; *Manresa*, Pellegrini 824, imported equipment. Helpful mechanic, *S Fernández*, Urquiza 1051.

Air LAB to **Santa Cruz** (Bolivia) twice a week, once via Tarija, continuing to Cochabamba. Austral, Dinar and Lapa fly to **Bs As** (2 hrs, minimum). Dinar, Lapa, Andesmar and Southern Winds to Tucumán, last 2 companies also to Córdoba and Andesmar to Mendoza. Bus 22 to airport from San Martín; don't be fooled by taxi touts who tell you there is no bus. Taxi from airport to bus station US$9.

Trains Station at 20 de Feb y Ameghino, 9 blocks N of Plaza de Armas, taxi US$2. For details of the Tren a Las Nubes and freight lines to Chile, see below.

Buses Terminal is 8 blocks E of the main plaza (T 214716 for information). Behind terminal serving is a 24 Shell station serving cheap snacks. To **Buenos Aires**, several daily, US$80, 19 hrs (Atahualpa, La Estrella, inc snacks, dinner and breakfast in restaurant, comfortable, rec, 4 daily) US$86 with La Veloz del Norte (20% ISIC discount); to **Córdoba**, 4 a day, 12 hrs, US$41, Expreso Panamericano (T 212460), twice daily, Veloz del Norte; to **Santiago del Estero**, 6 hrs, US$23; to **Tucumán**, 4 hrs, several firms (La Veloz del Norte rec, La Estrella), US$18; to **Puerto Iguazú**, via Tucumán, US$70; to **Mendoza** via Tucumán, several companies, daily, US$52, 20 hrs; to **Embarcación** daily with Atahualpa at 0700, US$14.50; to **Jujuy**, Balut Hnos, or Atahualpa hourly between 0700 and 2300,

'directo', US$6, 1¾ hrs; to **La Rioja**, US$33; to **Belén**, Wed, US$26.

To **Cafayate**, US$11, 4 hrs, El Indio, 4 a day; to **Santa María**, El Indio, 6½ hrs, 0700; to **Cachi**, 5 hrs, US$14, **Angastaco** (dep Thur 1300) and **Molinos** (7 hrs) Marcos Rueda daily (except Tues, Thur) at 1300, unreliable on Sun (sit on left); to **Rosario de la Frontera**, US$5, 2½ hrs. To **San Antonio de Los Cobres**, 5½ hrs, El Quebradeño, Mon-Sat 1600, Sun 1930, US$14. Extra service on Thur 1030 continues to the Tincalayu mining camp (arrives 2140), returning to Salta on Fri 1200, passing San Antonio at 1800. This bus is the only public transport going further into the *puna* than San Antonio.

To **Paraguay**: Salta provides the most reliable cheap land connection between Bolivia and Paraguay. Direct service to Asunción, US$66, 14 hrs, Fri 2030, book through Veloz del Norte. Alternatively travel to **Resistencia**, buses daily 1700, US$40 with La Veloz del Norte (20% reduction for students), Sáenz Peña or Panamericano, 12 hrs, then change. For description of road, see page 186. Salta-**Formosa** with Atahualpa, which provides the quickest route to Asunción (change at Orán), operates only twice weekly because of the state of the road – Wed and Sun at 0630, 12 hrs, US$40.

To **Chile**: Services to Calama, San Pedro de Atacama (both US$45), and Antofagasta (US$50) are run by Géminis, Sat 1600 all year round, arduous 20 hrs to Antofagasta, 16 hrs to Calama. Bus can be caught in San Antonio de los Cobres, book ahead and pay full fare. Tramaca also has services to Calama (US$45), Tues and Fri in winter, plus Sun in summer, at 0700, 12 hrs, via Jujuy (0900) with three meals. Book well in advance, may be difficult to get a reservation, so try just before departure for a cancellation. Be prepared for delays at the frontier and take warm clothes (at night ice sometimes forms on the insides of bus windows), plenty of water, food, a sheet to protect luggage against dust (**NB** Chilean customs will not allow fruit in). This route is usually closed for at least part of the winter and is liable to closure at other periods of the year.

To Bolivia To **La Quiaca**, on Bolivian frontier, about 10 buses daily, Atahualpa, US$27, 11 hrs (via Jujuy, prolonged stop), can be very cold, dusty, not rec, best change to Panamericano in Jujuy. Also Balut, 3 a day, US$23, 7 hrs. To **Orán** (see page 131), 6 hrs, and Aguas Blancas for Bermejo, Bolivia; thence road connection to Tarija. To Yacuiba, via **Pocitos** (Bolivian frontier, see page 142), for Santa Cruz, US$17 with Atahualpa to Pocitos, 7-10 hrs, very full, road paved.

FROM SALTA TO SAN ANTONIO DE LOS COBRES AND CHILE

There is a 900 km long metre-gauge railway from Salta through the little town of San Antonio de los Cobres to Antofagasta, in N Chile.

SAN ANTONIO DE LOS COBRES

(*Pop* 2,200; *Alt* 3,750m; *Phone Code* 087) is a squat, ugly mining town on a bleak, high desert. The inhabitants of this area are Coya Indians. A path leads to La Polvorilla railway viaduct (see below), 3 hrs, ask in town for details.

San Antonio can also be reached by Route 51 from Salta, which is being upgraded. From Campo Quijano it runs along the floor of the Quebrada del Toro (fords) before climbing the Abra Muñano in a long series of steep zig-zags (the section between Santa Rosa de Tastil and *Comedor Alfarcito* is very steep, not suitable for long vehicles).

At Santa Rosa de **Tastil** there are Indian ruins and a small museum (US$0.50), recommended. Basic accommodation next door to the museum, no electricity or heating, take food, water and candles. Take El Quebradeño bus (see below), a tour from Salta, or share a taxi.

● **Accommodation** **A3** *Hostería de las Nubes*, edge of San Antonio on Salta road (T 087-909058, or Bs As 326-0126, Esmeralda 320), modern, inc breakfast, spacious, rec; **E** pp *Hosp Belgrano* (no sign) no heat; **C** pp *Hosp Los Andes*, breakfast extra, very friendly, both on main street and basic. *Res Inti Huasi*, opp the Aduana, T 909995, restaurant. Try the *quesillo de cabra* (goat's cheese) from Estancia Las Cuevas.

● **Transport Trains** On all journeys on this line beware of *soroche* (altitude sickness): do not eat or drink to excess. **The Tren a las Nubes** (Train to the Clouds) runs between Salta and La Polvorilla viaduct. The service operates every other Sat from April to Oct, weather permitting, and on additional days in the high season (July/Aug), depart 0700, return to Salta 2215, US$95, without meals, credit cards not accepted, US$250 from Buenos Aires (planned to run every Sat throughout the year). The train is well-equipped with oxygen facilities and medical staff as well as a restaurant car and snack bar. Explanations are available in English, Spanish, French and Italian. This service is operated privately and cannot be booked through Ferrocarriles Argentinos. Book in advance (especially in high season) through *Movitren*, address under **Salta**, *Veloz del Norte*, Esmeralda 320, p 4, T 326-9623, Bs As, or through any good travel agency. It can be very difficult to book the train from Salta as it is often booked up from Buenos Aires. **Freight trains** still run on the line to Chile,

Railway to the Clouds

👣 The Argentine section of the railway to the Chilean frontier was engineered by Richard Maury, of Pennsylvania, who is commemorated by the station at Km 78 which bears his name. This remarkable project was built in stages between 1921 and 1948, by which time developments in road and air transport had already reduced its importance. No racks were used in its construction. The line includes 21 tunnels, 13 viaducts, 31 bridges, 2 loops and 2 zig-zags. From Salta the line climbs gently to Campo Quijano (Km 40, 1,520m), where it enters the Quebrada del Toro, an impressive rock-strewn gorge. At El Alisal (Km 50) and Chorrillos (Km 66) there are zig-zags as the line climbs the side of the gorge before turning N into the valley of the Río Rosario near Puerto Tastil (Km 101, 2,675m), missing the archaeological areas around Santa Rosa de Tastil. At Km 122 and Km 129 the line goes into 360° loops before reaching Diego de Almagro (3,304m). At Abra Muñano (3,952m) the road to San Antonio can be seen zig-zagging its way up the end-wall of the Quebrada del Toro below. From Muñano (3,936m) the line drops slightly to San Antonio, Km 196. The spectacular viaduct at La Polvorilla is 21 km further at 4,190m, just beyond the branch line to the mines at La Concordia. The highest point on the line is reached at Abra Chorrillos (4,475m, Km 231). From here the line runs on another 335 km across a rocky barren plateau 3,500-4,300m above sea level before reaching Socompa (3,865m).

but they are not supposed to carry tourists. A train leaves Salta Wed only about 1015 for San Antonio, 12 hrs, and Socompa, 26 hrs; tourists are not allowed to board this train, but boarding may be possible in Campo Quijano and Rosario de Lerma, which can be reached by bus from Salta 1800 (ask in the brake van and offer the guard yerba mate, sugar and cigarettes). Long delays are common on this route and you may do the entire journey in the dark. Take food, water and warm clothing. Fare US$35. Beyond Socompa there are irregular freight trains into Chile (Augusta Victoria, Baquedano or Antofagasta): officially the Chilean railway authorities do not permit passengers to travel on this line. To travel on by train or truck may involve a wait of several days. There is no food or accommodation, but try the Chilean customs building.
Buses To Salta, El Quebradeño, daily except Thur and Sat, 5½ hrs, US$14; stops at Santa Rosa de Tastil.

INTO CHILE BY ROAD

The road from San Antonio de los Cobres to San Pedro de Atacama now uses the **Sico Pass** (4,079m), S of the old Huaytiquina Pass (4,200m). The route is well marked. There are no customs or emigration facilities at the border: exit and entry formalities must be completed in San Antonio de los Cobres where the aduana and migration offices are at opposite ends of town. The *gendarme* at San Antonio may be able to advise about road conditions but truck drivers using the route are more reliable. **NB** Hitchhiking across the Andes from here is not recommended. The road on the Argentine side is very good (police checkpoint at Catúa). On the Chilean side continue via Mina Laco and Socaire to Toconao (road very bad between these two points). Police checkpoint in Toconao but customs and immigration in San Pedro de Atacama. Note that fruit, vegetables and dairy products may not be taken into Chile (search 20 km after Paso Sico). Gasoline is available in San Pedro and Calama. Obtain sufficient drinking water for the trip in San Antonio. This is a very beautiful trip: you cross salt lakes with flamingoes and impressive desert. Because of snowfalls, this route may be closed 2-3 times a year, for 2 or 3 days each time.

JUJUY

The direct road **from Salta to Jujuy**, Route 9 via La Caldera and El Carmen, is picturesque with its winding 92 km subtropical stretch, now paved, known as *la cornisa* (huge trees and unexpected plants). The longer road, via Güemes, is the better road for hitchhiking.

San Salvador de Jujuy (pronounced Hoo-hooey) often referred to by locals as San Salvador, is the capital of Jujuy province and is surrounded by partially wooded mountains. The city (*Pop* 182,000; *Alt* 1,260m; *Phone code* 0882) was founded first in 1561 and then in 1575, when it was destroyed by the Indians, and finally established in 1593.

History The province of Jujuy bore the brunt of fighting during the Wars of Independence: between 1810 and 1822 the Spanish launched 11 invasions down the Quebrada de Humahuaca from Bolivia. In Aug 1812 Gen Belgrano, commanding the republican troops, ordered the city to be evacuated and destroyed before the advancing Spanish army. This event is marked on 23-24 Aug by festivities known as El Exodo Jujeño with gaucho processions and military parades.

Places of interest

In the eastern part of the city is the **Plaza Belgrano**, a fine square lined with orange trees. On the S side of the plaza stands the **Casa de Gobierno**, an elaborate French baroque-style palace (open Mon-Fri, 0800-1200, 1600-2000, but not always). On the W side is a colonial **Cathedral** with very fine 18th century images, pulpits, walls and paintings finished about 1746. It has been heavily restored, but in the nave is a superb wooden pulpit, carved by Indians and gilded, a colonial treasure without equal in Argentina. On C Lavalle you can see the doorway through which Gen Lavalle, the enemy of Rosas, was killed by a bullet in 1841, but the door is a copy; the original was taken to Buenos Aires. The **Teatro Mitre** is at Alvear y Lamadrid. In the western part of the city are the **Parque San Martín** and an open space, **La Tablada**, where horses, mules and donkeys used to be assembled in caravans to be driven to the mines in Bolivia and Peru. See the **Palacio de Tribunales** near the river, one of the best modern buildings in Argentina. Streets are lined with bitter-orange trees.

Museums

Museo Histórico Provincial, Lavalle 250, open daily 0830-1230, 1500-2000, including display of colonial art and history of Gen Lavalle; **Museo de Paleontología y Mineralogía**, part of the University of Jujuy, Av Bolivia 2335, Mon-Fri 0800-1300. **Museo de Bellas Artes**, Güemes 956, Mon-Fri, 0800-1200, 1700-1900. **Police Museum**, in the Cabildo, Mon-Fri 1000-1300, 1500-2100, Sat 1000-1230, 1830-2100, Sun 1830-2100; **Museo de la Iglesia San Francisco**, Belgrano y Lavalle, including 17th century paintings from Cusco and Chuquisaca. The **Estación Biológica de Fauna Silvestre**, Av Bolivia 2335, is open to the public on Sun (for private tours on other days, contact Dr Arturo A Canedi, T 25617-25845), very interesting.

Excursions

19 km W of Jujuy is **Termas de Reyes**, where there are hot springs. This resort, with the *Hotel Termas de Reyes* (**A3** with breakfast, or half-board, **A2** full board, run down, restaurant, T 0882-35500), is set among magnificent mountains 1 hr by bus from Jujuy bus terminal, 6 times a day between 0630 and 1945, returning 0700-2040, US$1. US$3 to swim in the thermal pool at the hotel (weekends US$5); municipal baths US$1, open daily 0800-1200 and 1400-1700 (Thur 1400-1700 only). Camping US$5 pp with thermal bath.

Local festivals

Festival on 6 November. El Exodo Jujeño, 23/24 Aug (hotels fully booked).

Local information
● Accommodation

Panorama, Belgrano 1295, T 30183, 4-star, highly-regarded; **A2** *Augustus*, Belgrano 715, T 22668, 3-star, modern, comfortable but noisy; **A3** *Fenicia*, 19 de Abril 427, T 28102, quiet; **A3** *Avenida*, 19 de Abril 469, T 22678, on riverside, with good restaurant (**C** off season, cafeteria only); **A3** *Hostería Posta de Lozano*,

Route 9, Km 18, good restaurant, pools with fresh mountain water, covered parking; **A3** *Sumay*, Otero 232, T 22554, central; **A3** *Alto La Viña*, Route 56, Km 5, T 26588, attractive, swimming pool.

B *Res Los Andes*, Siria 456, T 24315, hot water, a bit prison-like. Opp is **B** *Res San Carlos*, Siria 459, T 22286, modern, some rooms a/c, parking.

Budget Accommodation: **C** *Belgrano*, Belgrano 627, T 26459, old fashioned, hospitable, noisy; **C** *Chung King*, Alvear 627, T 28142, dark, very noisy, many mosquitoes, good restaurant. Near the bus terminal only, **C** *San Antonio*, Lisandro de la Torre (opp), modern, highly rec; **D** *Res Río de Janeiro*, Av José de la Iglesia 1536, very basic, run down; **D** *El Aguila*, Alvear 400, basic.

Camping: *Autocamping Municipal*, US$4/tent, ask for a cheaper rate for one person, 14 km N of Jujuy on Humahuaca road. *Autocamping*, 3 km N outside city at Huaico Chico. Buses 4 or 9 frequent, hot showers (if you remind the staff), clothes washing facilities, very friendly.

● Places to eat

El Cortijo, Lavalle y San Martín, interesting salads, good vegetarian food, reasonably priced; *Sociedad Española*, Belgrano y Pérez, elegant setting, good set price meals; *Bar La Royal*, Belgrano 770, good but expensive; *La Victoria*, Av El Exodo 642, away from centre, good; *Confitería Carena*, Belgrano 899, old-fashioned, good for breakfast; *La Ventana*, Belgrano 751, good cheap menu, good service, à-la-carte menu is expensive; *La Rueda*, Lavalle 320, good food and service, very popular, expensive; *Krysys*, Balcarce 272, excellent atmosphere; *La Pizzería*, Alvear 921, warm welcome, pleasant atmosphere; *Ruta 9*, Costa Rica 968, Barrio Mariano Moreno (take taxi), good local food, Bolivian owners. Cheaper places behind bus terminal on Santiago del Estero and Alem. Very good ice cream at *Helados Xanthi*, Belgrano 515, made by Greek owner. *Opus-Café*, Belgrano 856, good coffee, music and atmosphere. Good bread and cake shop at Belgrano 619. Good sandwiches at *Rada Tilly*, 2 locations on Belgrano.

● Banks & money changers

At banks: Banco de la Provincia de Jujuy, Lavalle, gives cash against Mastercard, no commission, also changes dollars; Amex TCs can only be changed at Banco Quilmes, Belgrano 904, 1% commission while Banco de Galicia, Alvear, charges US$10 commission; nowhere to change Thomas Cook TCs; Horus, Belgrano 722, good rates for cash; Dinar, Belgrano 731. Travel agencies on Belgrano also change cash. If desperate, ask the dueña of the confitería at bus station, rates not too unreasonable. (See note on provincial bonds used as currency, page 244.)

● **Embassies & consulates**
Consulates: Bolivia, Patricinio Argentino 641, T 23156, price of visa should be US$5, pay no more; **Spain**, R de Velasco 362, T 28193; **Italy**, Av Fascio 660, T 23199; **Paraguay**, Tacuarí 430, T 28178.

● **Entertainment**
Chung King, Alvear 627, live music and dancing at weekends.

● **Laundry**
Laverap, Belgrano y Ramírez de Velazco.

● **Post & telecommunications**
Post Office: at Independencia y Lamadrid, in Galería Impulso, Belgrano 775. **Telecom**: Senador Pérez 141, open 0700-0100.

● **Shopping**
Handicrafts are available at reasonable prices from vendors on Plaza Belgrano nr the cathedral; *Regionales Lavalle*, Lavalle 268; *Centro de Arte y Artesanías*, Balcarce 427; *Librería Rayuela*, Belgrano 636; *Librería Belgrano*, Belgrano 602, English magazines and some books; *Farmacia Avenida*, Lavalle y 19 de Abril, 0800-2400.

● **Tour companies & travel agents**
Many along Belgrano: eg *Alicia Viajes*, No 592, T 22541; *Giménez*, No 775, T 2924. All offer tours along the Quebrada de Humahuaca, 12 hrs, US$25. *Be Dor Turismo*, No 860 local 8, 10% for ISIC and youth card holders on local excursions.

For information on bird watching, contact Mario Daniel Cheronaza, Peatonal 38, No 848-830, Viviendas 'El Arenal', Jujuy.

● **Tourist offices**
Belgrano 690, T 28153, very helpful, open till 2000.

● **Useful addresses**
Migración: Antardida 1365

● **Transport**
Air El Cadillal, 32 km SE, T 91505; Tea Turismo vans leave *Hotel Avenida* to meet arrivals, 1 hr, US$4.50. Flights to **Buenos Aires** by Austral. Austral also flies to **Salta**, **Santiago del Estero** and LAB to Tarija twice a week.

Buses Terminal at Iguazú y Dorrego, 6 blocks S of centre. To **Buenos Aires**, US$89, several daily with Balut, La Estrella, La Internacional. Via Tucumán to Córdoba, Panamericano and La Veloz del Norte, daily; **Tucumán** 5 hrs, US$25, and **Córdoba**, 14 hrs US$45; to **Puerto Iguazú**, 2 a week, US$80, 30 hrs. To **Salta** hourly from 0700, 2¾ hrs, US$6. To **La Quiaca**, 6½ hrs, Panamericano (best) and Atahualpa, US$21.50,

road paved only as far as Humahuaca, reasonably comfortable, but very cold at night. To **Humahuaca**, US$7, 3 hrs, sit on left side. To **Orán** daily at 1700; to **Embarcación**, US$7 with Balut, via San Pedro and Ledesma. Jujuy-**Purmamarca-Susques**, leaves Purmamarca at 1330 on Wed and Sat, returning Thur and Sun. To **Tilcara** 1½ hrs, US$5.

To Chile: via the **Jama** pass (*Alt* 4,200m), the route taken by most traffic, including trucks, crossing to northern Chile. In this region, the only accommodation is at **Susques** (*Res La Vicuñita*, opp church, said to be the oldest residencial in NW Argentina, thatched roof, hot water, breakfast), 105 km N of San Antonio de los Cobres on a road through utter desert. Buses from Jujuy to Antofagasta via San Pedro de Atacama and **Calama** (15 hrs), Tramaca, Tues and Fri, US$50 inc cold meal, breakfast; to **Iquique**, Wed and Sat, Panamericano, US$50. Check weather conditions in advance.

NORTH FROM JUJUY: THE ROUTE TO LA QUIACA

NB For drivers heading off main roads in this area, note that service stations are far apart: there are ACA stations at Jujuy, Humahuaca and La Quiaca, and YPF stations at Tilcara and Abra Pampa. Spare fuel and water must be carried.

QUEBRADA DE HUMAHUACA

Route 9, the Pan-American Highway, runs through the beautiful Quebrada, which has a variety of rock colours and giant cacti in the higher, drier parts. In the rainy season (Jan-Mar) ask the highway police about flooding on the roads.

Beyond Tumbaya, where there is a church originally built in 1796 and rebuilt in 1873, a road runs 5 km W to **Purmamarca**, a very popular, picturesque village overlooked by a mountain: seven colours can be distinguished in the rock strata (best seen when sun is in the E). At the entrance to Purmamarca a right turn leads to a new gravel road, which leads through another *quebrada* over the 4,164m Abra Potrerillos to the Salinas Grandes salt flats at about 3,500m on the Altiplano (fantastic views especially at sunset). In the winter months, on both sides of the road, three different ancient

Colonial Churches of the North

🐾 Lovers of old churches will find Salta and Jujuy excellent centres. Franciscan and Dominican friars arrived in the area from Bolivia as early as 1550. The Jesuits about 1585. Some churches can be found along the old Camino de los Incas (now non-existent), eg Susques and Coranzulí. Many more are on or near the Panamericana through the Quebrada de Iturbe. The padres, in the course of two centuries, built simple but beautiful churches, of which about 20 survive. They are marked by crosses on the map on page 118. All of them can be visited by car from Salta or Jujuy, though some of the roads are very rough.

types of salt mining by hand can be seen. From here roads lead SW past spectacular rock formations along the E side of the salt flats to San Antonio de los Cobres and W across the salt flats via Susques to the Paso de Jama and Chile.

● **Accommodation** At Purmamarca: **E** pp *Ranchito del Rincón*, Sarmiento, new, owners Yolanda and Zulma are helpful, highly rec; also 2 rooms in shop, **F** pp, ask at the police station for the address; *comedor* on main square has good, cheap, local food.

About 7 km N of the Purmamarca turning is La Posta de Hornillos, a museum in a restored colonial posting house, of which there used to be a chain from Buenos Aires to the Bolivian border (open, in theory, Wed-Mon 0900-1800, free). 3 km further is **Maimará** (**C** *Pensión La Posta*, the owners' son is a tourist guide and has helpful information, 5 km from Maimará).

TILCARA

22 km N of Purmamarca. The **Museo Arqueológico** here, attached to the University of Buenos Aires, contains a fine collection of precolumbian ceramics from the Andean regions of present day Argentina, Chile and Peru, open Tues-Sun 0900-1200, 1500-1800, highly recommended, US$2, free entry Tues. Admission includes

entry to a reconsruction of a *pucará*, or Inca fortified village, 2 km from the museum, set in botanical gardens containing only high altitude and Puna plants. Beautiful mountain views, recommended. There are excellent craft stalls and shops around the main plaza, selling ponchos, sweaters and wooden items.

Local festivals *Fiestas* on weekends in January.

● **Accommodation** **B** *Turismo*, Belgrano 590, swimming pool, usually dry; **D** *El Antigal*, Rivadavia, pleasant, good restaurant, colonial style, stores luggage, rec; **E** *Hostería La Esperanza*, spacious room, arranges walking tours; **E** *Res Frami*, nr hospital; **E** *Edén*. **Youth hostel: E** *Malka*, San Martín s/n, 5 blocks from plaza, good views, tours offered, kitchen facilities, IYHA affiliated, horse and bike rental, meals provided; also at Radio Pirca, **E** pp, 3 blocks from plaza, use solar energy. **Camping**: Municipal campsite, dirty; *Camping El Jardín*, US$5, clean, hot showers.

● **Places to eat** *Pucará*, good value; *Café del Museo*, good coffee; good value restaurant next to Mercado Municipal.

North of Tilcara there are colonial churches atf Huacalera and Uquía. 2 km before Huacalera, a sundial 20m W of the road gives the exact latitude of the Tropic of Capricorn. At **Huacalera** is the **B** *Hotel Monterrey*, friendly but run down. At **Uquía** church, built 1691, the walls of the naves are hung with 17th century paintings of winged angels in military dress: the so-Called *ángeles arcabuceros*.

● **Accommodation** **B** *Hostal de Uquía*, clean, English spoken.

All along the Quebrada de Humahuaca the pre-Lent carnival celebrations are picturesque and colourful. In Tilcara and Humahuaca pictures of the Passion are made of flowers, leaves, grasses and seeds at Easter and a traditional procession on Holy Thursday at night is joined by thousands.

HUMAHUACA

(*Pop* 4,000; *Alt* 2,940m) 129 km N of Jujuy, dates from 1594 but was almost entirely rebuilt in the mid-19th century. It is an attraction for coach trips from Salta and Jujuy; few tourists stay for more than a couple of hours, but it is an attractive and peaceful centre from which to explore the Quebrada de Humahuaca.

Places of interest

The **church**, **La Candelaria**, originally built in 1631, was completely rebuilt in 1873-80; it has a bell from 1641. A mechanical figure of San Francisco Solano blesses the town from **El Cabildo**, the neo-colonial town hall, at 1200. Overlooking the town is the massive **Monumento a la Independencia Argentina**, weighing 60 tons, built in 1936-50 and sited here because the valley was the scene of the heaviest fighting in the country during the Wars of Independence. There is a good **Feria Artesanal** on Av San Martín (on the far side of the railway line), but avoid the middle of the day when the coach parties arrive.

Museums

Museo La Casa, Buenos Aires 296, next to the post office, open daily 1000-2000, US$3, guided tours in Spanish only, offers a fascinating insight into social customs in the mid-19th century, recommended; **Museo Ramoneda**, Salta y Santa Fe, private collection of contemporary art; **Museo Arqueológico Municipal**, at one side of Independence monument, Mon-Fri 0800-1200, 1400-1700; **Museo Nicasio Fernández Mar**, Buenos Aires, opposite *Hotel de Turismo*, memorial to the sculptor, open daily, free. **Museo Folklórico Regional**, Buenos Aires 435, run by Sixto Vásquez, US$10 including guide.

Excursions

To **Coctaca**, 10 km NE, where there is an impressive and extensive (40 ha) series of pre-colonial agricultural terraces.

Local festivals

2 Feb, La Candelaria.

Local information

● **Accommodation**

C *Provincial de Turismo*, Buenos Aires 650, T 12, run down, poor service, modern building sadly out of keeping with surroundings; **C** *Res Humahuaca*, Córdoba y Corrientes, 1 block N of bus station, some a/c, traditional, rec; **C** *Res Colonial*, Entre Ríos 110, nr bus terminal, T 21007, some windowless rooms, laundry facilities.

Youth hostel: **E** pp *Albergue Humahuaca*, Buenos Aires 447, T 21064, clean, laundry and very limited cooking facilities, cafeteria, cold, special price for ISIC and youth card holders. Offers tours, all with accredited local guides to popular and lesser-known sites, horse riding, trekking, local festivals, also to the Pacific via Lagunas Colorada and Verde (Bolivia) and the Ruta de Che Guevara (Bolivia).

Camping: across bridge by railway station, small charge inc use of facilities.

● **Places to eat**

Most restaurants open only during the day, difficult to find breakfast and the mediocre restaurant at the bus terminal is often the only place open in the evenings. *La Cacharpaya*, Jujuy 295, excellent, pricey, Andean music; *Humahuaca Colonial*, Tucumán 22, good regional cooking, good value, but invaded by coach parties at midday; *El Rancho*, Belgrano s/n, just around the corner from market, lunches only, where the locals eat.

● **Banks & money changers**

Bank. Try the handicraft shops on the main plaza, or the *farmacia* at Córdoba 99. Better rates at Youth Hostel, but best to change elsewhere. Credit cards are not accepted anywhere.

● **Tourist offices**

Kiosk in main plaza in high season.

NORTH OF HUMAHUACA

From Humahuaca Route 9 runs to La Quiaca on the Bolivian border. 20 km N of Humahuaca, at the turn off to Iturbe and Iruya, the paving ends and the road runs across the bleak and barren *puna*.

IRUYA

An unpaved road runs NE from the Panamericana 8 km to **Iturbe** (**F** *Pensión El Panamericano*, basic) and then over the 4,000m Abra del Cóndor before dropping steeply into the Quebrada de Iruya. **Iruya** (*alt* 2,600m), 66 km from Humahuaca, is a beautiful walled village wedged on a hillside. It has a fine 17th century church and Rosario festival on first Sun in October.

It is worthwhile staying in Iruya for a few days; it makes an extremely pleasant and friendly centre for horseback or walking trips (take sleeping bag). At Titiconte 4 km away, there are unrestored pre-Inca ruins (take guide). *Puna Expediciones* (see Salta page 130) runs a 7-day trek, Salta-

Iruya-Nazareno-La Quiaca, walking between Iruya and Nazareno on remote paths where there are no tourists or motor vehicles, sleeping in local schoolhouses; rest of route is by truck.

- **Accommodation & places to eat** F pp *Albergue Belén*, very basic; **F** pp *Hosp Tacacho*, clean, friendly, *comedor*, on the plaza. Food at *Comedor Iruya*.

- **Buses** Daily bus service from Jujuy and Humahuaca to Iturbe by Panamericano, 1400 and 1900, 45 mins; in Yrigoyen you may be able to get a seat on a truck. Empresa Mendoza bus from Humahuaca, 0730, Mon, Wed and Sat, 3½ hrs' journey, US$7 one way, waits 2-3 hrs in Iruya before returning; service varies according to time of year and is suspended in rainy season (esp Feb and Mar) details from *Almacén Mendoza*, Salta y Belgrano, Humahuaca.

Tres Cruces and Abra Pampa

62 km N of Humahuaca on the Panamericana, is Tres Cruces, where customs searches are made on vehicles from Bolivia. **Abra Pampa** *(Pop* 4,000), 91 km N of Humahuaca on the Panamericana, is an important mining centre. 15 km from Abra Pampa is the vicuña farm at Miraflores, the largest in Argentina. Information offered, photography permitted; colectivos go am Mon-Sat Abra Pampa-Miraflores.

- **Accommodation At Tres Cruces**: **E** pp *El Aguilar* (no sign) without bath, clean, basic. **At Abra Pampa**: **F** pp *Res El Norte*, Sarmiento 530, shared room, clean, hot water, good food.

Laguna de los Pozuelos *(Alt* 3,650m) 50 km NW of from Abra Pampa, is a flamingo reserve and natural monument. Bus Mon-Fri 0930, 2 hrs, US$3, dropping you at the park ranger station, 2 km from the Laguna. If driving, the Laguna is 5 km from the road; walk last 800m to reach the edge of the lagoon. Temperatures can drop to -30°C in winter; if camping warm clothing, drinking water and food are essential.

From a point 4 km N of Abra Pampa roads branch W to Cochinoca (25 km) and SW to **Casabindo** (62 km). 'On 15 Aug at Casabindo, the local saint's day, the last and only *corrida de toros* (bullfight) in Argentina is held amidst a colourful popular celebration. The event is called *El Toreo de la Vincha*; in front of the church a bull defies onlookers to take a ribbon and medal which it carries.' The Casabindo church itself is a magnificent building, sometimes called 'the cathedral of the Puna' (Federico Kirbus). La Quiaqueña bus daily on Route 40 from Jujuy to La Quiaca via Casabindo.

LA QUIACA

(Alt 3,442m; *Phone code* 0885), 292 km N of Jujuy, is on the border with Bolivia: a concrete bridge links the town with Villazón on the Bolivian side. Warm clothing is essential particularly in winter when temperatures can drop to -15°C, though care should be taken against sunburn during the day. Most commercial activity has moved to Villazón because everything is much cheaper in Bolivia.

Excursions

Yavi, with the fine church of San Francisco (1690), which has magnificent gold decoration and windows of onyx, is 16 km E of La Quiaca, reached by a good, paved road; taxi available – US$25 return, including 1 hr wait. (Find the caretaker at her house and she will show you round the church, open Tues-Sun 0900-1200 and Tues-Fri 1500-1800.) Opposite the church is the house of the Marqués Campero y Tojo.

At **Santa Catalina**, 67 km W of La Quiaca, along a poor road, there is also a 17th century church. (Bus from Jujuy to Santa Catalina via La Quiaca, 19 hrs, Mon and Fri.)

Local festivals

On the third Sun in Oct the Manca Fiesta, or the festival of the pots, is held here, and the Colla Indians from Jujuy and the Bolivian *altiplano* come, carrying all sorts of pots.

Local information
- **Accommodation**

B *Turismo*, Siria y San Martín, T 2243, rec, modern, comfortable, hot water 1800-2400, heating from 2030-2400 in winter, restaurant.

C *Crystal*, Sarmiento 543, T 2255, run down, hospitable; **C** *Victoria*, opp railway station, good hot showers; *Alojamiento Pequeño*, Av Bolívar 236, cheap, basic; **C** *La Frontera* hotel and restaurant, Belgrano y Siria, downhill from

Atahuallpa bus stop, good.

Camping: is possible nr the control post on the outskirts of town; also at the ACA service station about 300m from the frontier.

● **Places to eat**
Sirio-Libanesa, nr *Hotel Frontera*, good, cheap set meal.

● **Banks & money changers**
No facilities for changing TCs. Rates are better in Villazón.

● **Hospitals & medical services**
There is a good hospital in La Quiaca. *Farmacia Nueva*, ½ block from Church, has remedies for *soroche* (mountain sickness).

● **Transport**
Buses from new terminal, España y Belgrano, luggage storage. Difficult to obtain information in La Quiaca about buses leaving Villazón for points in Bolivia (see page 311 for Villazón); 6-8 buses a day to **Salta** (US$27) via Humahuaca and Jujuy with change in Jujuy (5 hrs to Humahuaca, 6 hrs to Jujuy, 10 hrs to Salta). Panamericano, 5 a day to **Jujuy**, US$21.50, 6½ hrs, some meal breaks, but take own food, as sometimes long delays; cheapest company: Balut, US$23, to Salta. Buses may be stopped and searched for coca leaves; to **Buenos Aires**, via Jujuy, US$89 inc meals, 28 hrs.

FRONTIER WITH BOLIVIA
● **Argentine immigration and customs**
The frontier bridge is 10 blocks from La Quiaca bus terminal, 15 mins' walk (taxi US$2). Offices open 0700-2000 (signature needed from customs officer, who may be out for lunch); on Sat, Sun, and holidays there is a special fee of US$3 which may or may not be charged. Buses arriving outside these hours will have to wait, so check before travelling. You can cross the border at night, without luggage, and your passport will not be stamped.

If leaving Argentina for a short stroll into Villazón, show your passport, but do not let it be stamped by Migración, otherwise you will have to wait 48 hrs before being allowed back into Argentina.

NB Argentine time is 1 hr later than Bolivia.

● **Entering Argentina**
Formalities are usually very brief at the border but thorough customs searches are made 100 km S at Tres Cruces.

● **Bolivian consulate**
Travellers who need a visa to enter Bolivia are advised to get it before arriving in La Quiaca.

SAN PEDRO DE JUJUY
(*Pop* 60,000) is a sugar town, 63 km from Jujuy. The Ingenio La Esperanza, on the outskirts, is a sugar-mill with hospital, housing and a recreation centre.

● **Accommodation B** *Hotel Alex 2*, R Leach 467, T 20269, fan; *Alex I*, Tello 436, T 20299; **E** *Vélez Sarsfield*, V Sarsfield 154, T 20446.

● **Places to eat** Excellent restaurant at *Sociedad Sirio-Libanesa* on the plaza.

● **Buses** To Jujuy, US$2.50, 1½ hrs; to **Embarcación**, Atahuallpa, US$6.50, 2½ hrs.

PARQUE NACIONAL CALILEGUA
Ledesma (formally Libertador Gen San Martín), another sugar town 50 km N of San Pedro, is a base for exploring the **Parque Nacional Calilegua**, an area of peaks and sub-tropical valleys and cloud forest, reached by dirt road from just N of the town. There are over 300 species of bird including the very rare black and chestnut eagle and the red-faced guan as well as condors. Among the 60 species of mammal are tapir, puma, taruca or Andean deer and otters. The best trek is to the summit of Cerro Amarillo (3,720m), 3 days round trip from Aguas Negras. The first park ranger's house is at Agua Negra (Guillermo Nicolossi). (Camping nearby; drinking water from river nearby, and some cooking facilities and tables.) 13 km further along the trail is the 2nd ranger house (Pablo Giorgis), at Mesada de las Colmenas (ask permission at the 1st ranger house to camp here). 10 km from here is the N boundary of the park, marked by an obelisk, and where the most interesting birds can be seen. Best time for visiting is outside the rainy season (Nov-March).

● **Park services** Park headquarters are on San Lorenzo s/n, in Calilegua, 4 km from Ledesma, T (0886) 22046. The park entrance is 10 km along the dirt road (hitching from Ledesma possible), which climbs through the park and beyond to Valle Grande (no accommodation, basic food supplies from shops), 90 km from Ledesma. From here it is possible to walk to Humahuaca and Tilcara (allow at least 3 days; these walks are described in *Backpacking in*

Chile and Argentina by Bradt Publications).
- **Accommodation At Ledesma: E** *Res Gloria*, Urquiza 270, hot water; **E** *Ledesma*, Jujuy 473 just off plaza, large rooms but no keys, local radio station opp so can be noisy.

- **Places to eat** *Sociedad Boliviana*, Victoria 711, where the locals eat.

- **Banks & money changers** On Plaza San Martín, **Banco Roberts** changes dollars at a good rate.

- **Tourist offices** At bus terminal.

- **Transport** Trucks run by Empresa Valle Grande, Libertad 780, leave Ledesma, Tues, and Sat, 0730, 6 hrs if road conditions are good, very crowded, returning Sun and Thur 1000. Check with Sr Arcona (the driver, everyone knows him) in Ledesma whether the truck is going. Weather is unpredictable. Or contact Gustavo Lozano at Los Claveles 358, Barrio Jardín, T 21647, who will contact Angel Caradonna to pick you up.

ROUTES TO BOLIVIA

1. VIA POCITOS

From Ledesma, Route 34 runs NE 244 km, to the Bolivian frontier at Pocitos and Yacuiba (see **Eastern Bolivia**, page 353).

Embarcación (*Pop* 24,000; *Phone code* 0878) lies 101 km NE of Ledesma. 2 km from Embarcación you can walk to the Loma Protestant mission for Matuco and Toba Indians, who sell unpainted pottery.

- **Accommodation & places to eat C** *Punta Norte*, España 277, clean, a/c friendly. Restaurant of *Sociedad Sirio-Libanesa*, **H** Irigoyen and 9 de Julio, cheap and good.

- **Buses** To Orán, 1 hr, US$1.70 on a paved road; to Pocitos change at Tartagal, making sure your ticket is stamped with the next bus time or you won't be allowed on it; to Buenos Aires US$91; to Salta US$14.50, 3 a day. To Formosa daily at 1300, 17 hrs, US$40, Atahualpa, but frequently cancelled; alternative is to take bus to Pichanal, US$1.25, several, change for JV Gonzales, US$10, 1600, and change again for Resistencia, 2215, then take a bus to Formosa and Clorinda.

Tartagal (*Pop* 70,000), 74 km N of Embarcación, is an agricultural centre with a small museum featuring displays on animals of the Chaco and regional folk art. The director, Ramón Ramos, is very informative about the region. Animal masks and pottery are made by Indians nearby at Campo Durán.

- **Accommodation B** *Argentino*, San Martín 54, T 21327, 3-star; **B** *Espinillo*, San Martín 122, T 21007; *Res City*, Alberdi 79, T 21558.

Pocitos, the border town, is 56 km N of Tartagal (**E** *Hotel Buen Gusto*, just tolerable). From Yacuiba, across the border, buses and trains go to Santa Cruz de la Sierra. Customs at Pocitos is not to be trusted (theft reported) and overcharging for 'excess baggage' on buses occurs.

2. VIA AGUAS BLANCAS

At Pichanal, 100 km NE of Ledesma, 16 km before Embarcación, Route 50 heads N to **Orán**, an uninteresting place (*Pop* 34,000).

- **Accommodation B** *Gran Hotel Orán*, Pellegrini 617, T 21214; and several *residenciales*, inc **C** *Res Crisol*, López y Planes, hot water, friendly, rec.

Aguas Blancas on the frontier is 53 km from Orán (no accommodation, nowhere to change money and Bolivianos are not accepted S of Aguas Blancas; restaurants include *El Rinconcito de los Amigos*; also shops). The passport office is open from 0700 to 1200 and 1500 to 1900. Insist on getting an exit stamp. There is no exit tax. Buses run twice daily from Bermejo, across the river (ferry US$0.50), to Tarija (10 hrs). NW of Aguas Blancas is the **Parque Nacional Baritú**, covering a mountainous area of pristine cloud forest. There are no facilities. Ranger post at Los Pozos, NW of the park.

- **Buses** Between Aguas Blancas and Orán buses run every 45 mins, US$2, luggage checks on bus. Direct buses to Güemes, 8 a day, US$10; through buses to Salta, Veloz del Norte and Atahualpa, 3 daily each, US$17.50. From Orán to **Salta**, 7-10 hrs, 6 daily; direct bus to Tucumán at 2130, connecting for Mendoza bus which leaves at 1300; to Jujuy at 1200 daily; to Formosa, US$28, 14 hrs, leaving Tues, Thur, Sat at 0930; to Embarcación, US$3; to Tartagal daily at 0630 and 1800. Note that buses are subject to searches for drugs and contraband and long delays are possible. There is no direct bus from Orán to Asunción, Paraguay; take bus to Embarcación, change for Formosa, then change again for Asunción.

The West: San Luis, Mendoza, San Juan, La Rioja and Catamarca

FROM THE PAMPA to the heights of Aconcagua and the Uspallata Pass, en route to Santiago. Mendoza is a centre of wine making, fruit growing, winter sports (several ski resorts nearby) and climbing.

In the Cuyo region, in the W, there is little rain and nothing can be grown except under irrigation. The two most important oases in this area of slight rainfall are Mendoza itself and San Rafael, 160 km to the S. Of the 15 million ha in Mendoza Province, only 4% are cultivated. Of the cultivated area 40% is given over to vines, 25% is under alfalfa grown for cattle, and the rest under olive groves and fruit trees.

NB No fresh fruit, vegetables or cold meats may be brought into the provinces of Mendoza, San Juan, Río Negro, San Luis or Neuquén.

ROUTE 7 TO SAN LUIS

Junín (*Pop* 63,700; *Phone code* 0362), 256 km W of Buenos Aires across the pampa, is close to lagoons from which fish are taken to the capital. Eva Perón was born near the city.

● **Accommodation A2** *Copahue*, Saavedra 80, T 23390, F 29041, faded, ACA discount;

Embajador, Sáenz Peña y Pellegrini, T 21433.

● **Places to eat** *Paraje del Sauce*, Km 258 on Route 7, picturesque, good food but 'don't stop there if you are in a rush'. *El Quincho de Martín*, B de Miguel y Ruta 7, good.

At **Rufino** (*Pop* 15,300), 452 km from Buenos Aires, is the recommended **L3** *Hotel Astur*, Córdoba 81, C with ACA discount; also at **Laboulaye**, 517 km from Buenos Aires, there are several good and cheap hotels, eg *Victoria*, and **B** *Motel Ranquel Mapu*, Km 489, very good, bottled water supplied.

SAN LUIS PROVINCE

At **Villa Mercedes** (*Pop* 77,000; *Phone code* 0657), the old municipal market (Chacabuco y Mitre) is now an arts and community centre.

● **Accommodation & places to eat** ACA hotel **B** *San Martín*, Lavalle 435, T 22358, restaurant, garages. Cheaper places on Mitre, eg **C** *Res Cappola*, No 1134, rec.

● **Buses** To Buenos Aires US$28.

VILLA MERCEDES TO CORDOBA

Route 8 runs NE to (122 km) Río Cuarto (*Pop* 110,000) in Córdoba province. Route 148 runs N through San José del Morro, near a group of mountains which were originally volcanoes (there is a model in the Museo de Ciencias in Buenos Aires); a lot of rose-quartz can be found here. A short detour W, 70 km NE of San Luis, is La Toma (see below). Route 148 continues N to Villa Dolores (see page 116).

Provincial route 1 parallels Route 148 to the E; a scenic road through a string of pretty villages like Villa Larca, Cortaderas and Carpintería.

Merlo (*Alt* 700m, *Phone code* 0656), almost at the San Luis-Córdoba border, 150 km N of Villa Mercedes, is a small town on the western slopes of the Sierra de Comechingones. It enjoys a fresher climate than the pampas in summer, and the area is being promoted for its rich wildlife, particularly birds. There are many walks and excursions to *balnearios*, waterfalls and other attractions. The tourist office is on the outskirts and the bus station 3 blocks from the main plaza.

8 km N of Merlo is **Piedra Blanca**, a small settlement in attractive surroundings.

● **Accommodation** In Merlo and nearby are many hotels, *hosterías* and *residenciales*. Most in Merlo are along Av del Sol. **A2** *Rincón del Este*, T 75306, 3-star, 5 km from centre, rec; **A1** *Parque*, Av del Sol 821, T 75110, with breakfast, tennis, golf, pool.

● **Tour companies and travel agents** *Valle del Sol*, T 76109, tours to Sierra de las Quijadas US$45 pp, min 6 persons.

● **Buses** Frequent services to San Luis; to Buenos Aires, TAC, Sierras Cordobesas and Chevallier, US$35, 12 hrs; to Villa Dolores 1 hr.

SAN LUIS

About 65 km W of Villa Mercedes, the rolling hills of San Luis begin; beyond there are stretches of woodland.

San Luis, 98 km from Villa Mercedes, is the provincial capital (*Pop* 150,000; *Alt* 765m; *Phone code* 0652). Founded by Martín de Loyola, the governor of Chile, in 1596, it stands at 765m at the S end of the Punta de los Venados hills. The area is rich in minerals including onyx.

Places of interest

Visit the **Centro Artesanal San Martín de Porras**, run by the Dominican fathers, on 25 de Mayo, opp Palacio de Gobierno, where rugs are woven. Open 0700-1300 excluding Sat and Sun.

Excursions

A 'Via Crucis' sculptured in white marble skirts the mountainside at Villa de la Quebrada, 35 km N. Beyond Salto Grande, Salto Colorado and the Gruta de la Virgen de las Flores is El Volcán (12 km; *balneario*, walks, picnics; *Hotel Andrea*) in whose neighbourhood is Cruz de Piedra dam (drives, fishing).

Local information

● **Accommodation**

Several on Pres Illia: **A2** *Quintana*, No 546, T/F 38400, 4-star, best, without breakfast, large rooms, restaurant; **A3** *Aiello*, No 431, T 25609, F 25694, with breakfast, a/c, spacious, garage, rec; **A3** *Gran San Luis*, No 470, T 25049, T 30148, with breakfast, restaurant, pool; **A3** *Gran Hotel España*, No 300, T 37700, F 37707, also cheaper rooms **B**, gloomy but clean; **A3** *Grand Palace*, Rivadavia 657, T 22059, with breakfast, parking, central, spacious, good lunches; *Intihuasi*, La

Pampa 815 (behind Casa de Cultura), spotless, TV, lounge, highly rec (price unknown); **C** *Rivadavia*, Rivadavia 1470, T 22437, without breakfast, good beds, gloomy, opp bus station; next door is **D** *17 de Octubre*, which should be avoided, gloomy, basic, run down; **D** *San Antonio*, Ejército de los Andes 1602, T 22717, without breakfast, restaurant.

16 km from San Luis is **L3** *Hotel Potrero de los Funes*, T (0652) 30125/20889, F 23898 or BsAs 313-4886, F 312-3876 (25 de Mayo 516, p 11), a luxury resort and casino on lake of the same name, sports and watersports, lovely views.

Camping: Rio Volcán, 4 km from town.

● **Places to eat**

Most close at weekends; hotel restaurants are closed Sun, *San Luis'* closes Sat too. *El Cantón de Neuchatel*, San Martín 745, opp Cathedral on main plaza, is open Sun, modest. *Michel*, Lafinur 1361, good food and service.

● **Banks & money changers**

Very difficult to change TCs, try Banco de Galicia, Rivadavia y Belgrano, 1.5% commission.

● **Tourist offices**

Junín, opp Post Office, excellent.

● **Transport**

Bus terminal on Vía España between San Martín y Rivadavia. From BsAs, US$32 (US$37 *coche cama*).

ROUTES The most direct route to Córdoba, is by Route 146 which runs N from San Luis to the W of the Sierras de Córdoba through San Francisco del Monte de Oro, Luján and Villa Dolores. An alternative is Route 20 which runs E through La Toma to meet Route 148 (see above) which follows N to Villa Dolores along the western edge of the Sierras.

THE SIERRAS DE SAN LUIS

Northeast of the city are several ranges of hills, which are becoming more accessible with the building of paved roads. The western edge of the sierras can be visited by taking Route 9 NE from San Luís via Trapiche (**A2** *Hostería Los Sauces*, bus from San Luis, US$4 return) to **Carolina**, where a disused goldmine can be seen. A statue of a gold miner overlooks the main plaza. Near Carolina, at Gruta de Intihuasi, a natural arch forms a cave in which the mummified body of a child was found, estimated to be 8,500 years old. 4WD vehicles can drive up Tomolasta mountain

(2,000m) to see typical San Luis landscapes. From this road the Cuesta Larga descends to San Francisco del Monte de Oro, from where it is possible to follow Route 146 to Villa Dolores.

The central part of the Sierras is best reached by Route 20 to **La Toma**, 70 km E of San Luís, the cheapest place to buy green onyx.

North of La Toma a paved road runs as far as Libertador General San Martín (known as San Martín), 75 km, a good centre for exploring the rolling hills of the northern sierras. From San Martín an unpaved road runs N to reach Route 148.

● **Accommodation In La Toma: C** *Italia*, Belgrano 644, T 21295, hot showers. **In San Martín: E** pp *Hostería San Martín*, with bath and breakfast, meals served, good value, rec.

PARQUE PROVINCIAL SIERRA DE LAS QUIJADAS

This park, 97 km NW of San Luis, can be reached by turning off Route 147 (San Luis to San Juan) at Hualtarán. The area contains interesting geological formations, evidence of dinosaurs and pterosaurs, archaeological remains and flora and fauna of a transitional zone between wooded sierra and open, chaco-type terrain. There are no facilities and no rangers.

MENDOZA

Beyond San Luis Route 7 climbs to almost 1,000m before descending to the valley of the Río Desaguadero, the provincial boundary with Mendoza. **Mendoza**, at the foot of the Andes, is a pleasant city at the centre of an expanding urban area. The city was colonized from Chile in 1561 and named in honour of the then governor of Chile. It was from here that the Liberator José de San Martín set out to cross the Andes, to help in the liberation of Chile. Mendoza was completely destroyed by fire and earthquake in 1861, so today it is essentially a modern city of low dwellings (as a precaution against earthquakes), thickly planted with trees and gardens.

BASICS *Population*: of city 148,000, but with suburbs included, about 600,000. *Alt*: 756m. *Phone code*: 061. 1,060 km from BsAs; 264 km from San Luis. *Annual average temperature*: 19°C (summer 24°; winter 7°). *Annual average rainfall*: 236 mm.

Places of interest

In the centre of the city is the **Parque Independencia**, in the centre of which are the Museo de Arte Moderno and a theatre. On the W side are the *Plaza Hotel*, dating from the 1920s, and next door, the Teatro Independencia. Among the other pleasant squares nearby is the **Plaza España**, attractively tiled and with a mural displaying historical and literary scenes.

On the W side of the city is the great **Parque San Martín** containing watercourses and a 1 km-long artificial lake, where regattas are held, and the **Jardín Zoológico** (US$1). There are views of the Andes (when the amount of floating dust will allow) rising in a blue-black perpendicular wall, topped off in winter with dazzling snow, into a china-blue sky. The park entrance is 10 blocks W of the Plaza Independencia, reached by bus 110 from the centre or the *trolley* from Sarmiento y 9 de Julio. On a hill above the park is the **Cerro de la Gloria**, crowned by an astonishing **monument to San Martín**. There is a great rectangular stone block with bas-reliefs depicting various episodes in the equipping of the Army of the Andes and the actual crossing. In front of the block, San Martín bestrides his charger. An hourly bus ('Oro Negro') runs to the top of the Cerro de la Gloria from the E end of the park, on Av Libertad – it's a long walk (45 mins).

The best shopping centre is **Av Las Heras**, where there are good souvenir, leather and handicraft shops. Av San Martín, the main street, is closed to public transport which passes instead along 9 de Julio and San Juan. **Plaza Pellegrini** (Av Alem y Av San Juan) is a beautiful small square where wedding photos are taken on Fri and Sat nights.

Tours

Official tours of the city are generally poor value. A large sign in Plaza Independencia shows a walking tour which takes about 2 hrs. There is also a bus service (Bus Turístico) which tours the

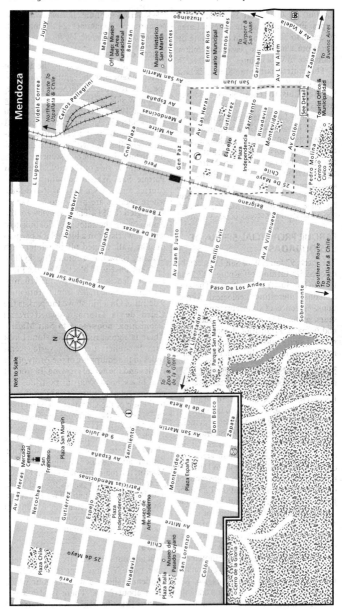

Mendoza

city, with commentary from the driver. There are 14 stops and tourists can alight or join the bus at any point; the US$10 ticket is valid for 24 hrs (the service operates 1000-2000). Stops are clearly marked and the municipal tourist office issues a map. The bus waits for 15 mins at Cerro de la Gloria.

Museums
Museo Histórico San Martín, Av San Martín 1843, containing artefacts from San Martín's campaigns and other items, poorly organized, open Mon-Fri 0900-1200, US$1; **Museo del Pasado Cuyano**, Montevideo 544, large collection including sections on San Martín and history of Mendoza, open Tues-Sat 0930-1230, US$0.50; **Museo de Ciencias Naturales** and **Museo Arqueológico** (in the Ciudad Universitaria), Playas Serranes, Parque San Martín, Tues-Fri 0900-1200, 1400-1800, Sat-Sun 1500-1900; **Museo Municipal de Arte Moderno**, underground (subsuelo) in Plaza Independencia, US$1.50, very small unless there is a special exhibition. The **Acuario Municipal** is underground at Buenos Aires e Ituzaingó, small but worth a visit, US$0.50, open Mon-Fri 1000-1200 and 1530-2000, Sat and Sun same times am. **Museo del Area Fundicional**, Alberdi y Videla Castillo, history of Mendoza, Tues-Sat 0800-1400, 1630-2230, Sun pm only, contains the mummified body of a child found on Aconcagua, US$2, recommended. Across Ituzaingó from the museum are the ruins of the Jesuit church of **San Francisco**, part destroyed in the 1861 earthquake (Ituzaingó y Beltrán).

On the road S of the city to Luján de Cuyo (bus 200, 40 min) is the excellent Museo Provincial de Bellas Artes Emiliano Guiñazu, **Casa de Fader**, dedicated to Argentine artists, surrounded by sculpture in gardens, admission US$1.50, open Tues-Fri 0930-1330, 1500-1900, Sat, Sun 1630-2030, T 960224.

Wine
Wine *bodegas* (wine-making season Mar/April) and fruit preserving; visiting times available from Tourist Office. To *La Colina de Oro* (ex-*Giol*) winery, one of the world's biggest, take 151 bus marked 'Maipú' (every hour, 0900-1230, 1500-1800)from terminal, US$1, but check if winery is open before going, T 972090, short tour, good tasting. Also in Maipú district is *Peñaflor*, on Mitre, T 972388, bus 170 (subheaded 171, 172), tour (in Spanish) and free tasting. *Ruttini*, Coquimbito, Maipú, T 973590, a small bodega, is worth visiting, bus 170, tours 0900-1100, 1600-1800, tasting, Museo del Vino (fascinating), open Mon-Fri 08+00-1100, 1500-1800 (very sales oriented). (In Maipú itself see the lovely square and eat at the *Club Social*, good simple food.) *Bodegas Escorihuela* (bus 'T' G Cruz from centre Belgrano 1188, Godoy Cruz, T 220157), Mon-Fri 0930-1530; *Santa Ana*, Roca y Urquiza, Guaymallén, T 211000, visits 0800-1700; *Chandon*, Ruta Provincial 15, Km 29, T 980830, phone for appointment 0900-1700. The *Toso* bodega at JB Alberdi 808, T 380244, is small, old-fashioned, has excellent wines and an interesting, free guided tour, some tasting, highly recommended. The *Orfila* bodega in San Martín, T (0623) 20637, 40 km E, located in the house of the Liberator, also has a wine museum. Prices at the bodegas have roughly a 100% mark-up from supermarket prices. Many tourist agencies include the bodegas in their ½-day or day-long tours (US$4-8 but these visits are too short, with too few guides and little tasting – only of the cheaper wines, usually in plastic cups).

Excursions
TAC and Uspallata buses run to the hot springs at **Cacheuta**, US$3.15 round trip, US$8 entry (indoor thermal baths for a variety of ailments, for residents only), 45 km to the SW (**L** *Hotel Termas*, T 316085, full board; campsite, T 259000).

About 50 km N of Mendoza are the hot springs at **Villavicencio**, visited by many tourists. Pleasant walks in the area.

Local holidays
18 Jan (Crossing of the Andes); 25 July (Santiago Apóstol); 8 Sept (Virgin of Carmen de Cuyo). The wine vintage festival, **Fiesta de la Vendimia**, is held in the amphitheatre of the Parque San Martín at the end of March. Hotels fill up fast. Prices

rise at this time, and in July (the ski season) and Sept (the spring festival).

Local information

● Accommodation

L3 *Aconcagua*, 4-star, San Lorenzo 545, T 204455, F 311055, good but expensive restaurant, pool, disappointing, tourist advice and bookings available; *Huentala*, Primitivo de la Reta 1007, T 240766, 4-star, good; **L3** *Cervantes*, Amigorena 65, T/F 201782, central, modern.

In our A2-3 range: **A3** *Plaza*, Chile 1124 on main plaza, T/F 233000, elegant but faded, a/c; **A2** *Nutibara*, Mitre 867, T 295428, F 296628, central, a/c, parking, with breakfast, pool, rec; **A3** *Palace*, Las Heras 70, T/F 234200, a/c, with breakfast, good beds, central; *San Martín*, Espejo 435, T 380677, rec; *Vecchia Roma*, España 1615, T 232529 (next door to restaurant of same name), comfortable, safe; **A2** *Balbi*, Las Heras 340, T 233500, F 380626, pool, a/c, nice rooms, helpful; **A3** *Argentino*, Espejo 455, Plaza Independencia, T/F 254000, with breakfast, garage; **A3** *1 de Mayo*, Garibaldi 80, T 204296, highly rec, breakfast inc; **A3** *1° de Mayo*, Garibaldi 82, T 204296, F 204820, good beds, restaurant; **B** *Imperial*, Las Heras 84, T 234671, old fashioned, central, with breakfast; **A3** *Gran Milena*, Babilonia 17, T 202738, with breakfast, small rooms, quiet.

In our price range B: *City*, Gen Paz 95, T 251343, inc breakfast, helpful; *Vendimia*, Godoy Cruz 101, T 250675, F 233099, good; *Petit*, Perú 1419, T 232099, without breakfast, rec; *RJ*, Las Heras 212, T/F 380202, with breakfast, comfortable, helpful, English spoken, rec; *Pacífico*, San Juan 1407, T/F 235444, modern, comfortable, good value; *Milena*, Pasaje Babilonia 17 (off San Juan nr Don Bosco), T 200284, 2-star, nice atmosphere; *Balcarce*, San Martín 1446, T 252579, old fashioned with breakfast; *El Libertador*, España 247, T 290921, good.

In our C range: **D** *Galicia*, Av San Juan 881, nr Av LM Alem, T 202619, gloomy, kitchen facilites, a/c; *San Remo*, Godoy Cruz 477, T 234068, quiet, small roooms, secure parking, highly rec; *Mayo*, 25 de Mayo 1265, T 254424, inc breakfast, good value; *Zamora*, Perú No 1156, T 257537, reasonable.

On Juan B Justo: *Gutelcas*, No 67, T 252811, a/c and heating, good, snack bar; *Ideal*, No 270, T 256842, transport to bus station; *Embajador*, No 365, T 259129, a/c, good value; **C** *Margal*, No 75, T 252013, central, safe, good, with fan.

Necochea, Necochea 541, T 253501, pleasant, cheerful, English spoken; *Res Alberdi*, Alberdi 51, T 234110, family run; *Quijote*, Av San Juan 1407, restaurant; **C** *Escorial*, San Luis 263, T 254777, rec; **E** pp *Res Savigliano*, Palacios

944, T 237746, nr bus terminal, without bath, with breakfast, kitchen facilities, highly rec; **E** pp *Hosp Eben-Ezer*, Alberdi 580, T 312635, quiet, German spoken; **E** pp *El Descanso*, Gral Paz 463; **E** pp *Dam-Sire*, Viamonte 410, nr terminal; **E** pp *Hosp Doña Carmen*, de la Reza 1047 p 1, T 203439, central, good for long stay; **E** pp *Alicia*, Alem 431, T 237799, without breakfast, nr terminal.

Youth hostel: Tirasso 2170, T 263300, **E**, take bus 26B, 'Paraguayo', takes 20 mins, ask driver. *Campamento Base*, Lavalle 2028, Guaymallén, T 457661, **E** pp, buses 52,54, 56 and trolley, cooking and laundry facilities, climbing wall, information on climbing and permits for Aconcagua (phone also given as 240237).

Camping: in Parque Gen San Martín permitted, free. Three campsites at El Challao, open all year, 6 km W of the city centre, reached by colectivo No 110 leaving every hour, *Atsa*, friendly, swimming pool, good service, caters for families, noisy at weekends from disco; *Camping Suizo*, modern with pool, barbeques, hot showers, friendly, rec; *Saucelandia*, at Guaymallén, 9 km E of Mendoza. White gas (*bencina blanca*) can be bought at *Ferretería Alsina*, Catamarca 37.

● Places to eat

Trevi, Las Heras 70, good food and service, rec; *Posta Las Marías*, San Martín 914, English spoken, speciality is roast kid, pricey but good; *Sarmiento*, Av Sarmiento 658 (*parrilla*), good. *Parrillada Arturito*, Chile 1515, good steak, popular with locals; *Montecatini*, Gral Paz 370, wide variety, good food, good value, rec; *Mesón Español*, Montevideo 244, good food and atmosphere, pricey; *Centro Catalá*, San Juan 1437, good fixed menu, rec; *La Reja 14*, San Lorenzo 65, good meat, rec; *Club Alemán*, Necochea 2261, Godoy Cruz, rec; *Comedor Línea Verde*, Montecaseros 1177, vegetarian, *tenedor libre*; *El Dragón de Oro*, Chinese, 25 de Mayo 1553 (nr Las Heras), very good. Ice cream at *Soppelsa*, Las Heras y España and at Paseo Sarmiento, rec. *Sr Cheff*, restaurant/confiteria at *Hotel 1 de Mayo*, Garibaldi 80. *Il Tucco*, Emilio Civit 556, also in centre at Paseo Sarmiento 68, excellent Italian restaurants, reasonable prices; *Boccaduro*, Mitre 1976, *parrilla*, good. Good value, and big 'super pancho' sandwiches in many places, inc *Pizzería Sebastián*, Alem 431; *Pizzería Mi Querencia*, Las Heras 523, good pasta dishes and atmosphere; *Aranjuez*, Lavalle y San Martín, nice café, good meeting place; *Mankie Snack Bar*, Las Heras y Mitre, excellent breakfasts; several good snack bars (known as *carrito* bars): *Tío Paco*, Salta y Alem; *Torombola*, San Juan 1348; *Don Claudio*, T Benegas 744; *El Gran Lomo*, San Martín y Pedro Molina, open 24 hrs, rec. There is a good, cheap café (excellent ice creams) next to the bus station.

● **Airline offices**
Aerolíneas Argentinas and **Austral**, Paseo Sarmiento 82, T 204100; **Lapa**, España 1012, T 291061; **TAN**, España 1012, T 340240; **Dinar**, Paseo Sarmiento 69, T/F 205138; **Southern Winds**, Rivadavia 209, T 204827.

● **Banks & money changers**
Lloyds Bank (BLSA), Gen Gutiérrez 72, cash advance on Mastercard, no commision; **Banco de Crédito Argentino**, España 1168, cash advance on Visa card, high commission; **American Express** agent, Sarmiento 119; **Citibank** Av San Martín 1099, gives US$ cash for cheques. Many *cambios* along San Martín, inc **Exprinter**, No 1198, 2% commision on TCs; **Santiago** No 1199, rec; **Maguitur**, No 1203, 1.5% commision on TCs. *Casas de cambio* open till 2000 Mon-Fri, and some open Sat am.

● **Cultural centres**
Alianza Francesa, Chile 1754; **Instituto Dante Alighieri** (Italy), Espejo 638; **Instituto Cultural Argentino-Norteamericano**, Chile 985; **Instituto Cuyano de Cultura Hispánica** (Spain), Villanueva 389; **Goethe Institut**, Morón 265, Mon-Fri, 0800-1200, 1600-2230, German newspapers, Spanish classes, very good.

● **Embassies & consulates**
Consulates: **Bolivia**, Eusebio Blanco y 25 de Mayo, T 292458; **Chile**, Av Emilio Civit 599, T 255024; **Spain**, Agustín Alvarez 455, T 253947; **Italy**, Necochea y Perú, T 231640; **France**, Houssay 828, T 231542; **Germany**, Montevideo 127, p 1 D6, T 296539; **Finland**, Boulogne Sur Mer 631, T 972388; **Israel**, Olascoaga 838, T 380642.

● **Entertainment**
Casino: 25 de Mayo 1123, daily 2100-0300.
Cinema: *Cine de Arte Eisenchlas*, 9 de Julio 500, Thur-Sun 2200.
Discothèques: *Saudades*, Barraquero y San Martín; *Kalatraba*, Perú 1779.

● **Hospitals & medical services**
Gynaecology: there is a private gynaecological clinic at Gral Paz 445; helpful and relatively inexpensive.

● **Language schools**
Sra Inés Perea de Bujaldon, Rioja 620, T 290429, teaches Spanish to German speakers, rec.

● **Laundry**
Coin-operated laundromat, at corner of San Juan and Rondeau. *Laverap*, Av Colón 547, rec; *La Lavandería*, San Lorenzo 338.

● **Post & telecommunications**
Post Office: Av San Martín y Av Colón, unreliable *poste restante*. **Telephone**: Chile 1584.

● **Shopping**
Mercado Central, Av Las Heras y Patricias Mendocinas, clean, well-stocked, closes 1300-1630. Leather goods good and cheap, try *Alain de France*, Olegario V Andrade 147. English language magazines and *Buenos Aires Herald* usually available from kiosks on San Martín.

● **Sports**
Gymnasium: San Juan y Buenos Aires.
Mountain Climbing: information from Tourist Office. Club Andinista, F L Beltrán 357, Gillén, T 319870. There is a 3-day (Thur-Sat) climbing and trekking expedition via Godoy Cruz and Cacheuta to Cerro Penitentes (4,351m), sleeping in mountain refuge, food inc. See also page 150.

● **Tour companies & travel agents**
Lots, especially on Paseo Sarmiento. *Cuyo Travel*, Paseo Sarmiento 162, 10% discount for ISIC and youth card holders for trekking and climbing on Aconcagua. *Servicios Especiales Mendoza*, Annette Schenker, c/o Hotel Cervantes, Amigorena 65, 5500 Mendoza, F (061) 244721, 240131, or Radio, code 548, 242162/244505, guided tours, many languages spoken, waterskiing on El Carrizal lake, climbing Aconcagua and Andes, trekking and other specialist programmes. *Turismo Cóndor*, 25 de Mayo 1537, T 234019 (also at bus station), rec for tours in and around the city, good guides, Spanish only; *Mylatours*, Paseo Sarmiento 133, T 380717, rec; *Turismo Sepeán*, San Juan 1070, T 204162, friendly and helpful, have branch in Santiago; *Turismo Cultural*, Rivadavia 211, T 242579, helpful; *Ibiza*, Espejo 217, T 258141, helpful and efficient; *Road Runner*, in bus teminal, trekking, horseriding, rafting; *Hunuc Huar Expediciones*, Av España 1340, p 8, oficina 7, and *Huera Pire*, Emilio Civit 320, specialize in assistance to climbers, especially on Aconcagua; *José Orviz*, Juan B Justo 550/536, T/F 256950/380085, guides, mules, transportation and hire of mountain trekking equipment. Many agencies, inc those in the terminal, run tours to the *Cristo Redentor* statue via Puente del Inca, US$28, 12 hrs, only 15 mins at statue.

River rafting in the region is popular; ask agencies for details.

● **Tourist offices**
At airport, T 306484, helpful (frequently closed), at the bus terminal (helpful but limited English spoken), T 259709, at Municipalidad, 9 de Julio 500, T 495185, at San Martín 1143, T 202800, at Paseo Sarmiento/Garibaldi y San Martín, T 201333, central, very helpful, and at Mitre y Las Heras, T 257805. They have a list of reasonable private lodgings and a hotel booking service (**B** range and upwards), and other literature inc

lists of *bodegas* and an excellent free town and province map; the latter is also available at most kiosks.

● **Useful addresses**

Travelling Student, San Martín 1366, Loc 16, T 290029/30.

● **Transport**

Local Carhire: Herbst, in *Hotel Plaza*, Chile 1124, T 289403, reliable vehicles from US$70/day inc mileage and insurance, rec; **Avis**, Rioja 1462, T 255601; **Lis Car**, San Lorenzo 110, T 291416; **Localiza**, at airport and Gutiérrez 453, T 491491; **Al Rent A Car**, San Juan 1012, T/F 304040. **Bicycles**: *El Túnel*, at exit from bus terminal, buys and sells cycles, also repairs, friendly. **Motorcycle repairs**: César Armitrano, Rubén Zarate 138, 1600-2100, highly rec for assistance or a chat; he will let you work in his workshop.

Air El Plumerillo, 8 km N of centre, T 487128, has *casa de cambio* and a few shops. Reached by *remise* taxis (US$7, inc US$1 to enter airport grounds) and bus No 68 from San Juan y Alem which takes you close to the terminal (10 mins' walk); make sure there is an 'Aeropuerto' sign on the driver's window. To **Buenos Aires**: 1 hr 50 mins, with AR, Lapa, Austral and Dinar. National to **Santiago**, daily. Many flights to **Córdoba**; Andesmar serves many northern destinations and Kaiken many in the S. AR, Dinar and Lapa to **San Juan**. TAN flies to **Neuquén**.

Buses Terminal on E side of Av Videla, 15 mins' walk from centre, T 313001, with shops, post office, tourist information and supermarket (open late). To **Bariloche**, Andesmar daily, TAC, 3 a week, US$70, 22 hrs, book well ahead; to **Córdoba**, TAC 5 daily, 9 hrs, US$29; to **San Rafael**, many daily, US$9; to **San Juan** frequent, US$11, 2 hrs (several companies, inc TAC, El Cumbre and Villa del Sur y Media Agua). To **La Rioja** US$25, 10 hrs, 5 a day, 3 companies; similarly to **Catamarca**, 12 hrs, daily, US$25. 6 daily to **Tucumán**, US$29; to **Salta**, Andesmar daily (via Tucumán) at 1300 and 2130, 20 hrs, US$52 (plus 4 other companies). To **Puerto Iguazú** at 1930, Mon, Wed, Sat with Cotal, US$70, 38 hrs; alternatively take daily Villa Marta bus to Santa Fe and change, about 40 hrs inc waiting time. To **Comodoro Rivadavia**, daily with Andesmar, at 2000, US$100, 32 hrs inc 4 meal stops; the Tues and Sat departures continue to Río Gallegos, arriving 1450 Thur. To **Rosario**, US$40, 12 hrs. To **Buenos Aires**, 2nd class US$45, 1st class daily, US$60 (lines inc Chevallier, TAC Coop, Jocoli); luxury service daily at 1800 (Chevallier), US$76 inc meals; via Route 7 (Junín-Mercedes) at 2020, arrive 1205. Dull scenery, and very cold across the Pampas at night. 20% student discount on some routes

(eg Comodoro Rivadavia).

Transport to Chile Turismo cars (Chi-Ar and Nevada) carrying up to 11 passengers (US$27, 5 hrs) and minibuses (5¹/2-6 hrs) do the trip to **Santiago** daily. When booking, ensure that the receipt states that you will be picked up and dropped at your hotel; if not you will be dropped at the bus station. Buses to Santiago daily, several companies, El Rapido, Tur Bus and TAC have been rec, mixed reports on other companies. Most buses are comfortable, 6¹/2-8 hrs, US$20-25, those with a/c and hostess service (inc breakfast) charge more, worth it when crossing the border as waiting time can be a matter of several hours. Also three buses daily to Viña del Mar and 2 to Valparaíso, US$20-25. All companies in same part of Mendoza bus station: shop around. Children under 8 pay 60% of adult fare, but no seat; book at least 1 day ahead. Passport required, tourist cards given on bus. The ride is spectacular. Information at terminal. If you want to return, buy an undated return ticket Santiago-Mendoza; it is cheaper. A taxi Mendoza-Santiago costs about US$90 for 4-5 people. For Chilean side, see Chile, **Santiago and the Heartland** (Section 3), To Buenos Aires across the Andes.

International buses: to **La Serena**, Dec-Mar only. To **Lima**, El Rápido Mon, Wed, Sat 0900. To **Montevideo**, US$66, El Rápido, Tues.

Hitchhiking: between Mendoza and Buenos Aires is quite easy. If hitching to San Juan, take bus No 6 to the airport nr the highway. Hitching from Mendoza to Los Andes (Chile) is easy; go to the service station in Godoy Cruz suburb (also bus No 6), from where all trucks to Chile, Peru and elsewhere leave.

SKI RESORTS

Potrerillos is a charming resort 13 km from Cacheuta, with ski slopes not far away and excellent birdwatching in summer. In summer, you can hike 20 km from Potrerillos to **Vallecito**, a closed ski resort, taking 2 days. On the first you will see desert scenery, blooming cactus flowers, birds and an occasional goat or cow. The second you walk surrounded by peaks, a steep but not difficult climb to the San Antonio refuge, usually open with beds and meals.

● **Accommodations & places to eat**
A1 *Gran Hotel* , T 233000, with meals; ACA campsite; *Restaurant Armando*, rec.

Los Penitentes, a small ski resort 165 km from Mendoza, is named after the majestic mass of pinnacled rocks, passed on the highway to Chile. From their base (easily reached with a guide from Puente del Inca, see below), the higher rocks look like a church and the smaller, sharper rocks below give the impression of a number of cowled monks climbing upwards. At the resort, daily ski hire is US$35, lift pass US$28. Skiing is good with few people on slopes.

● **Accommodation A3-B** *Ayelén*, in middle of village, T 259990, comfortable; **C** *La Taberna del Gringo*, Km 151, Villa Los Penitentes, rec, and others. 5 km from Puente del Inca on the road to Mendoza is **B** *Cruz de Caña* ski club, only open in season, with comfortable dormitories, inc meals, and a good restaurant. The owner organizes trekking expeditions to Plaza de Mulas on Aconcagua; US$50 a day full board during expedition, and US$20/mule.

South of Mendoza, the resort of **Manantiales** is being developed W of Tunuyán (63 km from the city). The best skiing is at Valle de las Leñas, S of San Rafael in the Valle Hermoso (see page 151).

MENDOZA TO CHILE

The route to Chile is sometimes blocked by snow in winter: if travelling by car in June-Oct enquire about road conditions from ACA in Mendoza (San Martín y Amigorena). Officially, driving without snow chains and a shovel is prohibited between Uspallata and the border, but this can be resolved in a friendly way with border police. Both ACA and Chilean Automobile Club sell, but do not rent, chains, but ask at YPF station in Uspallata about chain rental.

USPALLATA

There are two alternates of Route 7, which meet at **Uspallata**, the only settlement of any size between Mendoza and the Chilean frontier. The fully-paved S branch, via Cacheuta and Potrerillos, is wider and better than the N branch, which goes via Villavicencio, after which the road leads up spectacularly to the 3,050m high Cruz del Paramillo. This N branch is still unpaved. 5 km from Uspallata are the ruins of Las Bóvedas, built by the Huarpe Indians under the Jesuits, and an Inca *tam-*

bería; there is a small, interesting museum. They are just off the road which leads to Barreal and Calingasta (see page 155), unpaved for its first part and tricky when the snow melts and floods it in summer. The tourist office in Uspallata keeps unreliable hours.

● **Accommodation A2** *Valle Andino*, Ruta 7, T (0624) 20033, good rooms and restaurant, heating, pool, inc breakfast, ACA discount; **A3** *Hotel Uspallata*, T 20003, nice location, but run down, good service; **C** *Hostería Los Cóndores*, T 20002, good restaurant. **Camping**: municipal site, US$3/tent, hot water.

Beyond Uspallata is a vast, open, undulating plain, wild and bare. On all sides stand the grey, gaunt mountains. On the far side of this plain the valley narrows till Río Blanco is reached, and there the mountain torrents rush and froth into the river. At Punta de Vacas, look left up the Tupungato Valley at the majestic cone of **Tupungato**, one of the giants of the Andes, rising 6,550m. Walking tours in the Tupungato area can be arranged by Quinche Romulo, Alte Brown, Tupungato (a town 73 km SW of Mendoza), T 0622-88029.

PUENTE DEL INCA

(*Alt* 2,718m) 72 km W of Uspallata is a sports resort set among mountains of great grandeur. The natural bridge after which the resort is named is one of the wonders of South America; it crosses the Río Mendoza at a height of 19m, has a span of 21m, and is 27m wide, and seems to have been formed by sulphur-bearing hot springs. Watch your footing on the steps; extremely slippery. There are hot thermal baths just under the bridge, a little dilapidated but a great place to soak you feet. Puente del Inca is the best point for excursions into the higher Andean valleys. Horse treks go to Los Penitentes. Los Horcones, the Argentine customs post, is 1 km E: from here you can visit the green lake of Laguna los Horcones: follow signs to **Parque Provincial Aconcagua**, 2 km, where there is a Ranger station, excellent views of Aconcagua, especially am; free camping, open climbing season only. From here a trail continues to the Plaza de Mulas base camp.

● **Accommodation A3-B** *Hostería Puente*

del Inca, T 380480, less off-season, very pleasant atmosphere, but overpriced and poor service especially in restaurant, more expensive if booked in Mendoza; **E** pp *Parador del Inca*, with breakfast, basic, cheap meals. **Camping**: possible next to the church, if your equipment can withstand the winds.

- **Buses** Expreso Uspallata from Mendoza for Uspallata and Puente del Inca, US$8, 4 hrs, Mon-Fri 0600 and 1000, returning from Puente del Inca 1200 and 1615; local buses also go on from Puente del Inca to Las Cuevas, Expreso Uspallata, US$12 return (**NB** take passport). Also note that buses from Mendoza through to Santiago de Chile do not stop here.

ACONCAGUA

West of Puente del Inca (you can walk along the old railway), on the right, there is a good view of Aconcagua (6,959m), sharply silhouetted against the blue sky. It is the highest peak in the Americas. In 1985, a complete Inca mummy was discovered at 5,300m on the mountain. The mountain was first climbed by Zurbriggen of the Fitzgerald Expedition in 1897.

- **Access & accommodation** Best time for climbing Aconcagua is from end-Dec to February. For trekking or climbing it is first necessary to obtain a permit: 3-day trekking US$15, 5 days' trekking US$30. For climbing a 20-day permit is required (Argentines US$40, foreigners US$80). Permits are sold only at **Dirección de Recursos Naturales Renovables**, Parque Gral San Martín, Mendoza, T 252090. From Mendoza take a bus or colectivo to Puente del Inca. From here mules are available (shop around; large differences in muleteers prices; more economical to travel with a group); you have to pay for 3 days there and back (1 day rest) and for the muleteer and his wages. This only takes you to the base camp at Plaza de Mulas (4,370m), where there is, nearby, the highest hotel in the world (see below), and a rescue patrol, crowded in summer. Also at 4,200m is Plaza de Francia, facing the S face, less crowded in summer. Plaza de Francia is about 25 km from Puente del Inca and can be reached in two stages via Confluencia (camping also available here, rec if pacing yourself). Refugios above this height unserviceable. Take a tent able to withstand 100 mph + winds, and clothing and sleeping gear for temperatures below -40°C. Allow at least 1 week for acclimatization at lower altitudes before attempting the summit (4 days from Plaza de Mulas). Hotel *Plaza de Mulas*, **L3** pp full board, **B** pp without meals, good food, information, medical treatment, recommended, also camping area. In Mendoza you can book *refugio* reservations and programmes which inc

trekking, climbing to the summit, with hotel accommodation or camping, prices from US$990 to US$1,890 for 10 days, T/F Mendoza 61-380383, Nueve de Julio 1126. In Buenos Aires, representation at Proterra Turismo, Lavalle 750, p 20 D, T/F 326-2639.

- **Climbing information** Treks and climbs organized by Sr Fernando Grajales, the famous climber, in *Hostería Puente del Inca*, or at Moreno 898, 5500 Mendoza, Telex 55-154. Information also from Eduardo Enrique Esteban, Emilio Civit 320, Maipú, Mendoza, CP 5515, T/F (61) 973393 and Carlos and Amalia Cuesta, *Los Gateados*, nr Cementerio de los Andinistas, 1 km before Puente del Inca (Dec-Feb, or T Mendoza 391080/290410), rec for details on mules, trekking and climbing. Other guides can be found at the airport in Mendoza and further information from **Dirección de Recursos Naturales Renovables** (see also under Mendoza: **Travel agents**).

LAS CUEVAS AND CRISTO REDENTOR

Las Cuevas (16 km from Puente del Inca) is a neat, modern settlement being developed as a skiing resort (though there is no ski-lift as yet). Beyond Las Cuevas, the road, completely paved, goes through the 4-km El Libertador-Las Cuevas toll road tunnel to Chile (US$2 for cars and VW buses). The old road over La Cumbre pass is now closed to through traffic so that it is no longer possible to go from Mendoza to Santiago via the statue of **El Cristo Redentor** (Christ the Redeemer) at 4,200m. All buses and cars go through the tunnel to Chile, leaving the statue unseen above. It was erected jointly by Chile and Argentina in 1904 to celebrate King Edward VII's decision in the boundary dispute of 1902. It is completely dwarfed by the landscape. (The road from the tunnel to the statue is closed for the season after the first snowfall in April.) To see the statue you must either go on a 12-hr excursion from Mendoza (see above for details) or walk from Las Cuevas, 4½ hrs up, 2 hrs down. You should be in good condition and the weather should be clear.

- **Accommodation & places to eat A3** *Hostería Las Cuevas*, basic, warm rooms, food OK, price inc breakfast and supper. Food available at kiosk at Expreso Uspallata bus stop.

FRONTIER WITH CHILE

● **Argentine immigration**

The Chilean border is beyond Las Cuevas, but all Argentine entry and exit formalities are dealt with at Punta de Vacas, 30 km E of Las Cuevas.

● **Argentine customs**

A new customs post, Ingeniero Roque Carranza has been built near Laguna Los Horcones, nearer Las Cuevas. Customs at the frontier are closed 1200-1400.

● **Crossing by private vehicle**

Car drivers can undertake all formalities in advance at Uspallata while refuelling. Members of ACA need only the *Libreta de Pasos por Aduana*, otherwise you need the *Documento de Exportación* to enter Chile.

● **Chilean consulate**

See under Mendoza. **NB** No visas into Chile are available at the border. Tourist cards are given out on international buses.

● **Hitchhiking**

One can hitchhike, or possibly bargain with bus drivers for a seat, from Punta de Vacas to Santiago, but if one is dropped at the entrance to the tunnel in winter, one cannot walk through. Travellers report that customs men may help by asking motorists to take hitchhikers through to Chile.

SOUTH OF MENDOZA

SAN RAFAEL

(*Pop* 72,200; *Phone code* 0627) lies 273 km SW of San Luis, 242 km S of Mendoza, in an area where irrigation makes possible fruit-growing in large quantities at the foot of the Andes. A road runs W over El Pehuenche pass to Talca (Chile).

Excursions

Two bodegas to visit, *Suter* and *Bianchi* (Monte Caseros y E Civit, recommended). There is a small but interesting natural history museum 6 km SE of town at Isla Río Diamante (Tues-Sun 0800-1200, 1500-1900, free; Iselin bus along Av JA Balloffet); zoo nearby.

Southwest to the **Cañon de Atuel**, a spectacular gorge 20 km long with polychrome rocks. Three buses a day go to the Valle Grande dam at the near end of the canyon, US$3. From here there is no public transport along the road through the gorge to El Nihuel. Around Valle Grande

there is plenty of accommodation and campsites, river rafting and horse riding. Travel agencies in Mendoza run all-day excursions to the canyon.

Local information

● **Accommodation**

C *Kalton*, Yrigoyen 120, T 30047, excellent, safe, good value; and others.

Campsites: 2 sites (one of them ACA) at Isla Río Diamante, 15 km SE.

● **Tourist offices**

Av H Yrigoyen y Balloffet, very helpful. Ask for Aldo or Hector Seguín at España 437 for trekking and climbing information.

● **Transport**

Buses to **Mendoza**, frequent, US$9; to **Neuquén**, US$20.

LAS LEÑAS

182 km SW of San Rafael, a road heads W into the Andes. It passes **Los Molles**, Km 30, where there are thermal springs and accommodation. Opposite Los Molles a *ripio* road leads to the *refugio* of the Club Andino Pehuenche and on 8 km to the **Laguna de la Niña Encantada**, a beautiful little lake and shrine to the Virgin. Further along the Las Leñas road is the **Pozo de las Animas**, two natural pits, both filled with water (the larger is 80m deep); when the wind blows across the holes, a ghostly wail results, hence the name. At the end of Valle Los Molles is **Las Leñas**, 2,250m, a new resort with 33 pistes for good skiing, three T-bars, three ski-lifts (US$35-45/day; equipment hire US$20-24). Beyond Las Leñas the road continues into Valle Hermoso, accessible Dec-Mar only.

● **Accommodation** Three stonebuilt hotels: *Escorpio*, *Acuario* and *Gemini*, T for all 71100, and a disco, shop renting equipment and expensive restaurant. All the hotels are **L2**; for cheaper accommodation you have to stay in Los Molles where there are: **A3** pp *Hostería Lahuen-co*, T/F 0627-27171, full pension, run down, old fashioned; **A3** *Hotel Hualum*, same phone; or in Malargüe.

● **Buses** From San Rafael US$5.30, colectivo US$20; buses from Buenos Aires, 15 hrs, in skiing season only.

MALARGÜE

(*Pop* 8,600; *Phone code* 0627), further S on

Route 40, is developing as a centre for adventure tourism. The **Caverna de las Brujas**, privately owned caves 70 km SW (last 7 km *ripio*, difficult in wet weather), take 2-3 hrs to visit(own vehicle plus guide essential, hire in Malargüe US$20). The **Laguna Llancanelo**, 37 km SE, is one of the main Argentine nesting areas of the Chilean flamingo. The lake is best visited in spring when the birds arrive. Details from the tourist office or the Natural Science Museum. Fishing licences from the Dirección de los Bosques, next to the tourist office.

- **Accommodation A3-B** *Hotel del Turismo*, San Martín 224, T/F 71042, with breakfast, heating, good restaurant, rec; **A3** *El Cisne*, Villegas 278, T 71350, good value, rec; **A2** *Portal del Valle*, Route 40 N, T 71294, F 71811, sauna, pool, restaurant, also suites; **B** *Reyen*, San Martín 938, T/F 71429, with breakfast; **B** *Rioma*, Inalicán 68, T 71065, with breakfast, heating; **B** *Valle Hermoso*, Torres 151, T 71360, F 70470. Several others.

- **Guides & tours** *AGAPE Mendoza*, Asociación Grupo Antropo-Paleonto-Espeleológico; contact Dora de and Héctor Rofsgaard, Beltrán 414, T (0627) 71536. *Karen Travel*, San Martín 1056, T 70342, horseriding, trekking, rafting, excursions; *Turimalal* San Martín 193, T/F 70812, rent out skiing and fishing equipment.

- **Transport Air** Flights with TAN and Tapsa from Mendoza and Neuquén. Also Austral in skiing season. **Buses** TAC and Expreso Uspallata from Mendoza.

NORTH OF MENDOZA

The oases of San Juan, La Rioja and Catamarca between the plains and the Andes. Interesting natural rock formations can be seen, especially Valle de la Luna and Puerta de Talampaya.

Of the three oases in the more arid zone N of Mendoza, San Juan is the most prosperous, wine and olives support La Rioja, but Catamarca is economically depressed.

SAN JUAN

(*Pop* 122,000; *Alt* 650m; *Phone code* 064), 177 km N of Mendoza, was founded 1562 by Don Juan Jufré de Loaysa y Montese and is capital of its namesake province. The city is proud of its sunny climate and clean, tree-lined streets. Nearly destroyed

by a 1944 earthquake, the centre is well laid-out, with a modern cathedral.

Places of interest

The area is famous for its wine, 'to be between San Juan and Mendoza' is an Argentine expression for having drunk too much. One of the country's largest wine producers, *Bodegas Bragagnolo*, on the outskirts of town at Route 40 y Av Benavídez, Chimbas, can be visited (bus 20 from terminal; guided tours daily 0830-1330, 1530-1930, not Sun). **Escuela de Fruticultura y Enología**, Sarmiento 196 (bus going W on Av San Martín), students show visitors round.

Museums

Museo Casa de Sarmiento, Sarmiento y San Martín, open Tues-Sat 0830-1900; birthplace of Domingo Sarmiento (President of the Republic, 1868-1874, also an important historian/educator). **Museo de Ciencias Naturales**, Av San Martín y Catamarca, includes fossils from Ischigualasto Provincial Park (see below), open Mon-Sat, 0830-1230, 1630-2030, Sat 0900-1200, US$0.50. **Museo Histórico Sanmartiniano**, Laprida 96 Este, including the restored cloisters and two cells of the Convent of Santo Domingo. San Martín slept in one of these cells on his way to lead the crossing of the Andes, closed Sun, US$0.40.

Excursions

To the **Museo Arqueológico** of the University of San Juan at La Laja, 20 km N, open Mon-Fri, 0900-1830, Sat, Sun, 1000-1300 (1000-1730 summer) US$2, which contains an outstanding collection of prehispanic indigenous artefacts, including several well-preserved mummies. Inexpensive thermal baths nearby. Bus No 20 from San Juan, 2 a day, but you need to take the first (at 0830) to give time to return.

Vallecito, 64 km E, has a famous shrine to the **Difunta Correa**, an unofficial saint whose infant (according to legend) survived at her breast even after the mother's death from thirst in the desert. During Holy Week, up to 100,000 pilgrims visit the site, some crawling 100m on their knees. See the remarkable collection of personal items left in tribute, including

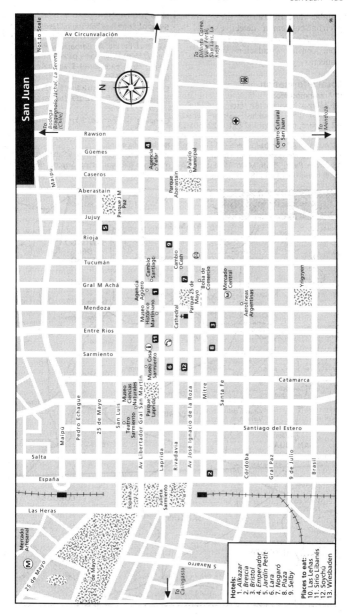

San Juan

Not to Scale

To Bodega Bizagarriolo, Jáchal, La Serena (Chile)

To Bodega Bizagarriolo

To Difunto Correa, Valle Fértil, San Luis, La Rioja

To Mendoza

Centro Cultural o San Juan

Av Circunvalación

Rawson

Güemes

Caseros

Aberastain

Jujuy

Rioja

Tucumán

Gral M Achá

Mendoza

Entre Rios

Sarmiento

Maipú

Pedro Echague

25 de Mayo

Salta

España

Las Heras

Av Circunvalación

Palacio Municipal

Parque Aberastain

Agencia Yafar

Parque J M Paz

Cambio Santiago

Cambio O Cash

Bolsa de Comercio

Mercado Central

Aerolíneas Argentinas

Agencia Agüero

Museo Histórico Martiniano

Parque 25 de Mayo

Cathedral

Museo Casa Sarmiento

Parque Laprida

Museo Ciencias Naturales

Teatro Sarmiento

Av Libertador Gral San Martín

Laprida

Rivadavia

Av José Ignacio de la Roza

Mitre

Santa Fe

Catamarca

Santiago del Estero

Córdoba

Gral Paz

9 de Julio

Brasil

Irigoyen

Mercado Artesanal

25 de Mayo

S Navarro

To Calingasta

Hotels:
1. Alkazar
2. Brescia
3. Bristol
4. Emperador
5. Jardin Petit
6. Lara
7. Nogaro
8. Plaza
9. Selby

Places to eat:
10. Las Leñas
11. Sirio Libanés
12. Soychú
13. Wiesbaden

number plates from all over the world and even one policeman's detective school diploma! (*Res Difunta Correa*). For information, consult Fundación Vallecito at Caucete.

Local information
● Accommodation

A1 *Alkázar*, Laprida 82 Este, T 214965, F 214977, inc breakfast, garage, good; **A2** *Nogaró*, de la Roza 132 Este, T 227501/5, pool, a/c, central, TV, parking (ACA and US AAA discounts); **A3** *Central*, Mitre 131 Este, T 223174, quiet, good beds, welcoming owner; **A3** *Jardín Petit*, 25 de Mayo 345 Este (ACA discount with cash), T 211825, hot water, pricey,

parking next door.

B *Bristol*, Entre Rios 368 Sur, T 222629, a/c, hot water; **B** *Plaza* Sarmiento 344 Sur, T 225179, noisy disco behind; **A3** *Embajador*, Rawson 25 Sur, T 225520, large rooms, pleasant, café, good value. Several residenciales (**B**) along Av España, blocks 100-600 Sur.

C *Jessy-Mar*, Sarmiento 8 Nte, T 227195, small rooms, noisy; **C** *Res 12 de Diciembre*, Sarmiento 272 Norte.

Camping: at Chimbas, 7 km N; 3 sites at Rivadavia, 8 km W.

● Places to eat

Wiesbaden, Circunvalación y San Martín, German-style, pleasant setting; *Soychú*, de la Roza 223 Ote, excellent vegetarian food; *Club Sirio*

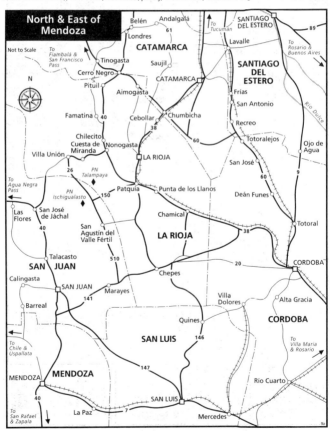

North & East of Mendoza

Not to Scale

To Fiambalá & San Francisco Pass

To Tucumán

Belén Andalgalá SANTIAGO DEL ESTERO

Londres 61 Lavalle 89

CATAMARCA To Rosario & Buenos Aires

Tinogasta Saujil **SANTIAGO DEL ESTERO**

Cerro Negro CATAMARCA

Pituil Aimogasta Frías

Famatina 40 Cebollar Chumbicha San Antonio

38 Recreo

Chilecito Nonogasta 60 Totoralejos Ojo de Agua

Cuesta de Miranda LA RIOJA

Villa Unión San José 60

26 PN Talampaya 9

To Agua Negra Pass 150 Patquía Punta de los Llanos Deán Funes

PN Ischigualasto

Las Flores San José de Jáchal Chamical

40 38 Totoral

San Agustín del Valle Fértil **LA RIOJA**

Talacasto 510 CORDOBA

SAN JUAN Chepes 20

Calingasta SAN JUAN Marayes

141 Villa Dolores Alta Gracia

Barreal **CORDOBA**

Quines To Villa Maria & Rosario

To Chile & Uspallata 146

SAN LUIS

147 Río Cuarto

MENDOZA

MENDOZA

40 SAN LUIS

To San Rafael & Zapala La Paz 7 Mercedes

Libanés 'El Palito', Entre Rios 33 Sur, pleasant decor, good food; *Las Leñas*, San Martín 1670 Ote, *parrilla*, pricey, rec; *El Castillo de Oro*, de la Roza 199 Ote, central, reasonable; *Comedor Central*, de la Roza 171 Este, not luxurious but good *locro* (stew) and *chivito* (goat); *Parrilla Bigotes*, Las Heras e de la Roza, inexpensive 'all you can eat' meat, chicken, salads; *Listo de pollo*, Av San Martín y Santiago del Estero, very good. Many *pizzerias*, *confiterias*, and sidewalk cafés. *Lomoteca San José*, San Martín 179, grills, inexpensive, late night music at weekends; *El Clavel de Oro*, Santa Fe y Entre Ríos, snacks, drinks; *Marilyn Bar*, San Martín y Mendoza, late night drinks.

● **Banks & money changers**
Banks open 0700-1200. **Banco de San Juan**, Mendoza y Rivadavia, for Mastercard advance, no commission. None of the ATMs accept international credit cards. Good rates at **Cambio Santiago**, Gen Acha 52, weekdays until 2100, Sat until 1300; **Cambio Cash**, Tucumán 210 Sur; **Bolsa de Comercio**, Gral Acha 278 Sur.

● **Cultural centres**
Centro Cultural San Juan: Gral Paz 737 Este, concerts and other events.

● **Laundry**
Marva, San Luis y Av Rioja.

● **Shopping**
Mercado Artesanal at Av España y San Luis worth a visit.

● **Sports**
Bicycle repairs: *Ruedas Armado*, San Martín y La Rioja, helpful.

● **Tour companies & travel agents**
Mario Agüero Turismo, Gen Acha 17 Nte, T 220864, tours to Ischigualasto subject to demand, US$50 pp plus US$3 National Park entry fee; *Fascinatur*, Av Lib San Martín 2918 (Ote), Rafael Joliat rec for 4WD treks to remote areas, F 230058, also via Corvalle bus office at terminal. For mountain climbing contact Pablo Schlögl, 543 Haité Este, T 225132, rec as probably the most experienced mountaineer in Argentina.

● **Tourist offices**
Sarmiento Sur 24 y San Martín, helpful, good brochures, open Mon-Sat, 0900-1330, 1430-2100, Sun 0900-1300; also at bus terminal. Arranges tours in summer only. Large-scale provincial maps available at bookshops. **ACA**, 9 de Julio 802 Este, useful information on routes, helpful.

● **Transport**
Local Car hire: Parque Automotor, España y San Martín, T 226018. Cash discount on request. **Localiza**, España 274 (Sur), T 229243.

Air Chacritas Airport, 14 km SE. From **Buenos Aires** with AR (T 220205), Dinar and Lapa (T 216039). AR and Dinar also from Mendoza.

Buses Terminal at Estados Unidos y Santa Fe, 9 blocks E of centre (buses 33 and 35 go through the centre). To **La Rioja**, 9 hrs, US$19, or go via Chepes, 0900 daily US$6, with connecting service from Chepes, Mon, Wed, Sun at 1600, 4 hrs, US$10, **Catamarca** (660 km over secondary roads, US$17, with connection to Salta, US$29), **Tucumán** (3 a day, 13 hrs, Libertador is cheapest), Córdoba, Santa Fe, Mar del Plata, Bahía Blanca and **BsAs** (Autotransporte San Juan, US$47). To **San Agustín** at 1800, US$11. Fifteen departures daily to and from **Mendoza** with TAC and El Cumbre, 2 hrs, US$11, try to sit in the shade (on W side in am, E in pm). Also services to provincial tourist destinations. **To Chile**: only connection with Santiago (Chile) is via Mendoza; catch the TAC bus at 0600, arrives in Mendoza 0830 in time for bus to Santiago.

Crossing to Chile Cars can now cross the Andes via the Agua Negra Pass (4,600) which is spectacular but it is only open Jan to early April; in winter it is closed by snow, in summer it may be closed by rain. No buses take this route. ACA, customs and immigration at Las Flores (see below) informs all the ACA stations in the country of road conditions. It takes approximately 6 hrs from Las Flores in Argentina to Rivadavia in Chile (where the first service station can be found).

Hitchhiking To La Rioja, take route 141 to Chepes (ACA *Hosteria*), then N to Patquía; more traffic on provincial Route 29, a well paved, but less interesting road than that via San Agustín or Jachal (see below).

WEST OF SAN JUAN

Calingasta, 135 km W of San Juan along scenic provincial route 12 (open westbound mornings, eastbound afternoons), lies in the valley of same name (annual cider festival in April).

● **Accommodation B** *Calingasta*, T 22014, remodelled, pool, full board available; **C** *La Capilla*, T 21033, inc breakfast, basic but very clean, family run, the family also sells the TAC bus tickets, and has the only public telephone in the village; municipal campsite.

Barreal, is 40 km S of Calingasta on the road to Uspallata. At El Leoncito (2,348m), 26 km from Barreal there are two observatories (US$3, no public transport; tours can be arranged from San Juan, Av España 1512 Sur, T 213653, or at *Hotel Barreal*) and a nature reserve with a semi-arid environment and interesting wildlife, ranger post at entrance, no facilities.

● **Accommodation A3** *Barreal*, San Martín s/n, T (0648) 41000, reservations through *Nogaró* in San Juan, T 227501, improved and refurbished in 1996, poor restaurant, pool, riding; *Cabañas Alamos-Cordilleranos*, T 41025/41139, on plaza next to *Supermercadito El Angel*; *Cabañas Doña Pipa*, see below; **E** *Hotel Jorge*, clean, very simple; *Posada San Eduardo*, small, most rooms with bath, pleasant and relaxing; accommodation with Sr Patricio Sosa or Sr Cortez; municipal campsite.

● **Places to eat** *Isidoro*, Roca s/n, owned by local baker and sandyacht champion, reasonable, good set meals; food also available at *Mama Rosa*.

● **Tour companies & travel agents Adventure tours**: rafting trips can be arranged in Barreal, contact Sr Eduardo Conterno. Sr Ramón Luis Ossa, physical education teacher at Barreal's high school, runs mule treks into the Andes, crossing the foothills in summer, from 10 to 21 days between Nov and April; he can be reached at *Cabañas Doña Pipa*, Mariano Moreno s/n, 5405 Barreal, Pcia San Juan, T (0648) 41004. The *cabañas* sleep 5, with bath, kitchen, sitting room, comfortable.

● **Buses** From San Juan daily, El Triunfo, 0700, plus Mon, Wed, Fri, Sun at 2030 (return Mon, Wed, Fri, Sun 1330, 1600, Tues, Thur 1400, Sat 1600), 5 hrs, US$11. *Remise* service San Juan-Calingasta-Barreal, US$17 pp, T San Juan 262121 (or 1900-2300 252370), at Pablo D'Marco 5949 (0), Barrio Camus, Rivadavia, San Juan; in Barreal, Sr Pachá, *Restaurante Isidoro*; also Silvio, T San Juan 252370, Barreal 41257, US$14, rec. Omnibus Vitar from Mendoza (Las Heras 494, T 232876) Thur and Sat via Uspallata, continuing to Tamberías and Calingasta (return Fri and Sun); fare Barreal-Calingasta US$7.

Climbing

Mercedario (also El Ligua), 6,770m. No authorization is required, but it is advisable to inform the Gendarmería Nacional at Barreal. From Barreal go to Casas Amarillas on the Río Blanco, about 100 km on a gravel road. It may be possible to hire a Unimog 4 x 4 from the Gendarmería Nacional; guides (*baqueanos*) may also be hired, they can provide mules if necessary. The best time is mid-Dec to end-Feb; the types of terrain encountered are gravel, snow and rock. There is no rescue service. More information is available from Club Andino Mercedario, 9 de Julio 547 Este, 5400 San Juan, or *Antonio Beorchia Nigris*,

director, Ciadam (Research Centre for Andean Archaeology), República del Líbano 2621, 5423 San Juan. **NB** Do not enter this region from Chile, it is illegal.

NORTH OF SAN JUAN

Route 40, the principal tourist route on the E Andean slope, heads N toward Cafayate and Salta, via San José de Jachal. At Talacasto, 55 km from San Juan, route 436 branches toward Las Flores (Km 180) and the Chilean border at Agua Negra pass (4,600m – see above). Alternatively Route 141 runs directly N from Calingasta to Las Flores, a dirt road via Villa Nueva and Tocota, reported scenic but lonely.

At **Pismanta**, 5 km N of Las Flores, the **B** *Hotel Termas de Pismanta*, T 227501, with breakfast, rooms for 120 guests, thermal baths between 38° and 44°C, a large swimming pool, medical attention, bowling, bingo occasionally, covered parking, good value. Reservations in Buenos Aires (Maipú 331) and San Juan (San Martín y Sarmiento); **E** *La Olla*, family run, clean, restaurant. From San Juan, 2 buses daily with TAC, 4 weekly with Empresa Iglesia, also from Mendoza.

San José de Jachal(*Pop* 15,000), 61 km E of Pismanta along a scenic road with several tunnels following the Río Jachal, is a wine and olive-growing centre with many adobe buildings. From here, the undulating Route 40, paved to the La Rioja border, crosses dozens of dry watercourses. It continues unpaved to Villa Unión (see below).

● **Accommodation & places to eat C** *Plaza*, San Juan 545, T 20256; *San Martín*, Juan de Echegaray 387, T 20431. Camping. *El Chato Flores* restaurant, good.

● **Buses** Expreso Argentino bus from San Juan at 0730 arrives at 0940.

EAST OF SAN JUAN

Route 141 runs across the S of the province towards La Rioja province and Córdoba. Just after Marayes (133 km), paved route 510 (poor) goes N 114 km to **San Agustín del Valle Fértil**. There is a municipal swimming pool, and a lake with fishing. Tourist information on the plaza. Local weavers offer ponchos and blankets.

● **Accommodation** *Hostería Valle de la Luna*, Rivadavia s/n, T (0646) 20015-7, new, good, over-looking Dique San Agustín; **D** *Hosp Romero*; **E** pp *Hosp Santa Fe*, with bath, welcoming, rec; private houses also provide lodging.

● **Buses** From San Juan US$9, from La Rioja, Mon-Fri 1215, US$10, 4 hrs.

THE PARKS OF ISCHIGUALASTO AND TALAMPAYA

North of San Agustín, at a police check-point, 56 km by paved road, a side road goes NW for 17 km to the 62,000-ha **Is-chigualasto** Provincial Park, also known as **Valle de la Luna** for its exotic desert landforms, entrance US$5. Here the skeletons of the oldest known dinosaurs have been found (230 million years).

● **Tours & access** All private vehicles must be accompanied by rangers whose knowledge and interest vary greatly; fee US$2 pp. The circular tour, on an unpaved road, lasts 2-3 hrs. Local bus from San Juan Mon and Fri to police check-point and on Sat afternoon, if demand is sufficient. Tours from San Juan, US$50 (not including lunch); from San Agustín US$18 for a guide (ask at tourist office). Rec guide is Barros Lito, US$40 for full day tour of Valle and Talampaya in private car. Taxi to park US$55 (rec if there are 4-5 people), more out of season.

Just beyond the police checkpoint, near Los Baldecitos, paved Route 150 heads E to Patquía and then to La Rioja or Chilecito. From the junction provincial Route 26 heads N to Villa Unión. 58 km N of the junction a paved road goes E to the **Reserva Provincial Talampaya** (open 0800-1630, entrance US$3), another collection of spectacular desert landforms (*Refugio* near the entrance, sleeping bag essential). Herbert Levi writes: "There are 600-year-old petroglyphs with pictures depicting animals. The whole area is said to have been covered with water long ago; now there are two visible strata, the *tarjado* and the *talampaya*. After that one enters a canyon with 'balconies', sheer overhanging walls. Coming out of the canyon there are rocks shaped like a cathedral, a bird, a castle, a chessboard, a monk, and three kings on a camel". Better to visit park in the morning and avoid strong winds in the afternoon. Free campsite next to park administration.

● **Tours & access** Tours follow the dry bed of the Río Talampaya in 4WD vehicles operated by park rangers, 5 tours of different lengths offered, prices per truck, US$30-110, not inc entrance. Tours, arranged through Dirección Provincial de Turismo in La Rioja, or Sr Páez, park director, in Pagancillo, who can also arrange accommodation in the village (eg with **D** pp *Familia Flores*, including breakfast and dinner). Chilecito-San Juan buses pass Talampaya, drop off at Km 144. Patquía-Villa Unión buses pass Pagancillo.

72 km N of Patquía, on Route 38, is the provincial capital of **La Rioja** (*Pop* 106,000; *Phone code* 0822), founded 1592. It is known as 'City of the Orange Trees', but there are also many specimens of the contorted, thorn-studded *palo borracho* tree, whose ripened avocado-like pods release large brown seeds in a kapok-like substance. Despite a major earthquake in 1894, some colonial buildings survive.

Places of interest
The **Convent of San Francisco**, 25 de Mayo/Bazán y Bustos, contains the Niño Alcalde, a remarkable image of the infant Jesus as well as the cell (*celda*) in which San Francisco Solano lived and the orange tree, now dead, which he planted in 1592. To visit the tree when the church is closed, ring the bell at 25 de Mayo 218 next door. At **Los Padrecitos**, 7 km from town, a stone temple protects the remains of the 16th century adobe building where San Francisco converted the Indians of the Yacampis valley. The **Convent of Santo Domingo**, Luna y Lamadrid, dates from 1623. The **Casa González**, a brick 'folly' in the form of a castle, is at Rivadavia 950.

Museums
Museo Folklórico, P Luna 811, Tues-Fri, 0900-1200, 1600-2000, Sat, Sun, 0900-1200, US$1.50; **Museo Arqueológico Inca Huasi**, Alberdi 650, owned by the Franciscan Order, contains a huge collection of fine Diaguita Indian ceramics, open Tues-Fri, 0800-1200, 1500-1900, US$1. **Museo Histórico de la Provincia**, Dávila 87, opening hours variable. **Museo Municipal de Bellas Artes**, Copiapó 253, works by local, national, and foreign artists.

Excursions

Swimming and fishing at Los Sauces dam, 15 km W. Good views of La Rioja from Cerro de la Cruz (1,680m), 12 km W, now a centre for hang-gliding, where condors and falcons may be sighted. To Ischigualasto and Talampaya (via Nonogasta, Cuesta de Miranda and Villa Unión, by private car with guide), costs US$190 for up to 5 people plus entrance fees, departs 0900. To Samay Huasi (see Chilecito, page 158).

Local information

NB Avoid arriving on Sat night as most things are shut on Sun.

● Accommodation

Accommodation can be difficult to find, particularly in the lower price ranges.

A2 *Plaza*, San Nicolás y 9 de Julio, T 25215, rec but street noisy; **A3** *King's*, Quiroga 1070, T 25272; *Libertador*, Buenos Aires 253, T 27474, good value; *Turismo*, Perón y Quiroga, T 25240, offstreet parking.

B *Imperial*, Moreno 345, T 22478, helpful; **B** *Res Petit*, Lagos 427, basic, hospitable.

C *Savoy*, Roque A Luna 14, T 26894, excellent value, hot shower; **C** *Pensión 9 de Julio*, Copiapó y Vélez Sarsfield, rec; **C** *Res Florida*, 8 de Diciembre 524, basic. Tourist Office keeps a list of private lodgings, such as Sra Vera, Dávila 343.

Camping: at Balneario Los Sauces, 13 km W.

● Places to eat

Café Corredor, San Martín y Pelagio Luna, good, cheap; *La Cantina de Juan*, Yrigoyen 190, excellent food, inexpensive; *Il Gatto*, Plaza 25 de Mayo, good pastas and salads; *Club Atlético Riojano*, Santa Fe between 9 de Julio and Buenos Aires, no atmosphere but cheap; good open air *churrasquería* next to *Hotel de Turismo*; *La Casona*, Rivadavia 449, very good and reasonably priced, rec; *Taberna Don Carlos*, Rivadavia 459, good fish and service; *Comedor Sociedad Española*, 9 de Julio 233, excellent pastas, inexpensive; *La Pomme*, Rivadavia y San Martín, open-air terrace, popular meeting place.

● Banks & money changers

US$ cash changed at **Banco de Galicia**, Plaza 25 de Mayo (no commission on Visa cash advance), and **Banco de Crédito**, San Nicolás 476. Cheques difficult to change – try **Banco de la Provincia**, Bazán y Bustos, commission 8%. Better to change plenty before arriving (see note on provincial bonds used as currency, page 244).

● Laundry

Laverap, Av Perón 944.

● Post & telecommunications

Post Office: Perón 258. **Telecommunications**: Perón 764.

● Tour companies & travel agents

Yafar Turismo, Lamadrid 170, tour to Ischigualasto and Talampaya parks.

● Tourist offices

At Perón y Urquiza, T 28834.

● Transport

Air To/from Buenos Aires, AR (T 27257) and Lapa (T 35197); Lapa also Catamarca, AR to Tucumán, Andesmar to Córdoba and Mendoza.

Buses Terminal 7 blocks S of the Cathedral at Artigas y España. To Buenos Aires, Gen Urquiza, US$47, combination Ablo, via Córdoba. To Mendoza (US$25) and San Juan (US$19), La Estrella, Libertador and Andesmar, 8 hrs. To Tinogasta, 0620, 2200, daily, US$11. To Tucumán (US$15), with Bosio and La Estrella. To Salta, Andesmar, 10 hrs, US$33. Also provincial services.

CHILECITO

(*Pop* 20,000), 129 km NW of Patquía, is La Rioja province's second town. Founded in 1715, it has good views of Sierra de Famatina, especially from the top of El Portezuelo, an easy climb from the end of C El Maestro. At Los Sarmientos, 2 km N of town, is the Santa Clara church, dating from 1764. The region is famous for its wines, olives and walnuts.

Museums

Samay Huasi, 3 km S of town, the house of Joaquín V González, founder of La Plata University, open 0800-1200 and 1500-1800, contains the **Museo de Ciencias Naturales, Mineralogía y Arqueología**, pleasant gardens, and good views of Chilecito, the Famatina ridge and connecting valley. **Molino San Francisco y Museo de Chilecito**, at J de Ocampo 63, has archaeological, historical and artistic exhibits, open Mon-Fri 0800-1300, 1400-1900.

Excursions

La Mejicana mine via Santa Florentina road: a cable car system (built 1903) which brought ore 39 km to the railhead at Chilecito is now out of use. The first station has a small historical museum. For treks, and trips to see gold washers at

Famatina or to Talampaya, ask for Carlos de Caro, or enquire at tourist office. To **Famatina** (31 km N), a sleepy hamlet amid nut plantations, *hostería*, restaurants.

Local information
● Accommodation
A3 *Chilecito*, Dr L Martínez y 8 de Julio, T 2201/2, good, no credit cards, safe parking, pool, good restaurant.

B *Riviera*, Castro Barros 133, rec, hot showers.

C *Americano*, Libertad 68, T 8104; **C** *Belsavac*, 9 de Julio y Dávila, T 2877, good but thin walls; **C** *Wamatinag*, Galeria Victoria, W side of Plaza Sarmiento, T 2977, pleasant, best value in town. The Tourist Office has a list of families offering accommodation, but not for singles.

Camping: at Santa Florentina, 6 km NW of Chilecito and Las Talas, 2 km beyond.

● Places to eat
El Gallo, Perón e Illia, excellent. On Plaza Sarmiento are: *Chaplin*, best in town; *Robert Snak Bar*, light meals and drinks; *Vanesa*, good home-made ice-cream; *Toscanini*, Fátima y San Martín, good Italian food, inexpensive; *Ferrito*, Av Luna 661, very good.

● Tour companies & travel agents
For tours in the Reserva Natural Laguna Brava (see below) contact Jorge and Adriana Llanos, T 22171, or Adolfo and Daniel at *Laguna Brava ETV*, T 22348, F 23330.

● Tourist offices
Libertad e Independencia, T 2688, very helpful.

● Transport
Air Líneas Aéreas Riojanas fly **La Rioja**-Chilecito, 20 mins.

Buses To **San Juan**, Tues, Thur, Sat at 2200, arriving 0705; to **Tinogasta** (Catamarca), Mon-Fri, direct at 0700 via route 11, returning same day at 0600; to **La Rioja**, 3 times daily with Cotil, to Villa Unión daily at 1345 with Cotil. Connections with **Catamarca** and **Córdoba** via La Rioja only.

VILLA UNIÓN AND WESTERN LA RIOJA

16 km S of Chilecito, at Nonogasta, partly paved Route 40 heads W climbing through a deep narrow canyon in a series of hairpins to the Cuesta de Miranda (2,010m). After the Cuesta is **Villa Unión**, 92 km from Nonogasta.

● Accommodation **E** *Hosp Paola*, main street opp police station, basic; next door is **E** *Hosp Changuito*, restaurant.

From Villa Unión, excursions can be made by 4WD vehicle to the **Reserva Natural Laguna Brava**, 150 km N. The road goes through Vinchina (several basic *hospedajes*) and Jagüe (entry fee US$10). Further on, as you climb the Portezuelo del Peñón, the salt lake of Laguna Brava becomes visible with some of the mightiest volcanoes on earth in the background. From the left these are the perfect cone Veladero (6,436m), Reclus, Los Gemelos, Pissis (6,882m) the highest volcano in the world, though inactive, and Bonete (6,759m) which is visible from Villa Unión and Talampaya. "Between Bonete and Veladero there is a crater filled by a lake, 5,319m high, until recently believed to be of volcanic origin but now established as having been caused by a meteorite 4 km in diameter. This region is probably one of the last white patches on the maps of the world. Along the route small stone refuges like snailshells can be seen, built in the mid-19th century for the drivers of oxen along this route to Chile. Vicuñas, guanacos and flamingoes may be seen along the route. The building of an international road between La Rioja and Copiapó in Chile will make this area more accessible." (Federico Kirbus) For tours in this area see under Chilecito.

ROUTES From Chilecito, old Route 40, now Route 11, goes via Famatina to Tinogasta. New route 40 goes to Pituil, and on to Salicas and Cerro Negro junction (59 km) with Route 60, the Tinogasta-Aimogasta road. From Cerro Negro it is 38 km SE to **Aimogasta** (national olive festival in May) and another 30 km to turnoff to **Termas Santa Teresita** (**A3** *Hostería Termas Santa Teresita*, T 20445, with breakfast, open air thermal pool, thermal baths in all rooms, good set menu, highly rec, 2 hrs by car from La Rioja.)

30 km S of Aimogasta is **Anillaco**, the birthplace and proposed retirement home of President Carlos Menem. The Menem family *bodega* specializes in white wine. With two hotels (ACA *hostería* and *Los Amigos*) and the proximity of the Señor de la Peña pilgrimage site, 25 km W, Anillaco is becoming a tourist attraction. It is 75 km from La Rioja by Route 75; 115 km by Routes 38 and 9.

CATAMARCA PROVINCE

TINOGASTA AND FIAMBALA

Tinogasta (*Pop* 9,000), a half-Indian former-copper mining town, is in an oasis of vineyards, olive groves, and poplars.

● **Accommodation A3** *Provincial de Turismo*, Romero y Gordillo, T 23911, clean but run down, restaurant; **D** pp *Hostería Novel*, nr airport, friendly.

● **Places to eat** *Persegani*, Tristán Villafañe 373; *Rancho Huairapuca*, on Moreno.

● **Buses** To **Tucumán**, Empresa Gutiérrez, Tues, Fri, Sun 1700, Mon, Tues, Fri, Sun 0615, Fri 0845, US$22; return Tues, Fri, Sun. To **Catamarca** 1700 and 0030 daily; to **La Rioja** 0930, El Cóndor, US$11.

Mountaineering

Tinogasta is the starting point for expeditions to the second highest mountain in South America. Most recent cartography has allowed for some corrections in altitude so that **Pissis** has been confirmed, at 6,882m, as higher than Ojos del Salado (6,879m). To get there take Route 60 which crosses Tinogasta in the direction of the San Francisco pass. Everyone has to register at the police station outside Fiambalá, take passport. Expeditions organized and horse riding with Omar Monuey, La Espiga de Oro, 25 de Mayo 436.

Fiambalá is 49 km N of Tinogasta. Drive or take a taxi from here to **Termas de Fiambalá**, hot springs, 14 km E, temperatures from 30°C to 54°C (make sure taxi fare includes wait and return). The entire province is rich in thermal mineral waters. There are vineyards in the valley. 36 km beyond Fiambalá is Palo Blanco, in the *pre-puna* foothills.

● **Accommodation C** *Hostería Municipal*, good value, also restaurant; small, basic *pensión* (unsigned – ask), nr which is a good restaurant.

● **Buses** Empresa Gutiérrez daily at 1345 to Catamarca via Tinogasta (1500) and Cerro Negro junction (1610), connect with Coop Catamarca bus to Belén (from Catamarca), about 2 hrs by bad road. Also 0530 departure from Fiambalá. 4WD vehicles may be hired for approaching the Pissis-Ojos region; ask at the Intendencia. For transport into the *puna* ask for Sr Jonson Hugo Reynoso (check state of vehicles).

FRONTIER WITH CHILE – PASO SAN FRANCISCO

Fiambalá is the starting-point for the crossing to Chile via Paso San Francisco (4,726m), 203 km NW along a road described as "quite some washboard" (Hannes Scheiner). On the Chilean side roads run to El Salvador and Copiapó. This route is closed by snow between June and Oct; take enough fuel for at least 400 km as there are no service stations from Fiambalá to just before Copiapó.

Londres Turn **W** at Cerro Negro (see **Routes** above) for 2 km, paved route 40 heads N to Londres, founded in 1558 and the second-oldest town in Argentina, named in honour of the marriage of Mary Tudor and Philip II. The town hall displays a glass coat-of-arms of the City of London and a copy of the marriage proposal.

BELEN

(*Pop* 8,800) is 15 km further (paved). The whole district is famous for weavings, ponchos, saddlebags and rugs. There are good views from the new statue of Virgin of Belén at the summit of the path beginning at C Gen Roca, and an interesting archaeological museum, Condor Huasi. Folklore festivals Oct and Christmas. Belén is encircled by mountains, except to the SE; lush vegetation along Río Belén. North of Belén Route 40 runs another 176 km, largely unpaved, to Santa María at Tucumán provincial border (see page 124), and on to Cafayate (page 124).

Excursions To **Villavil** (thermal springs – open Jan-April), inc side trip to Corral Quemado and end of line in Barranca Larga, 19 km N of Villavil, Tues, Thur, Sun at 0800, returns from Villavil at 1830. Sit on right-hand side for best views of impressive canyon and Río Bolsón reservoir.

● **Accommodation & places to eat A3** *Samai*, Urquiza 349, rec; **C** *Turismo*, cheap and good; *Provincial*, dilapidated. Good breakfast at bus terminal; *Restaurant Dalesio*, nr YPF gas station, excellent and cheap; *El Amigazo*, behind church, good.

● **Buses** To Santa María Tues 1330, Fri and Sun 2020; return Tues and Thur 0930, Sun 1945. To **Salta** via Hualfín, Santa María, Cafayate Thur 0600.

Andalgalá (130 km; *Pop* 7,800), is 85 km E of Belén, but best reached by Route 62 which branches N from Route 60, 15 km E of Aimogasta. It is a pleasant town renowned for strong alcoholic drinks. The road, through Saujil, parallels the Salar de Pipanaco on the W and Sierra de Ambato on the E. At Minas Capillitas (N of Andalgalá), rhodochrosite, Argentina's unofficial national stone is quarried; it can be bought at shops around the plaza in Andalgalá.

● **Useful services** *Hostería Provincial*, often full; *Res Galileo*; 3 bus lines to Catamarca.

ROUTES: Belén to Salta via Route 53 (43 on some maps), which branches W off Route 40 at a point 52 km N of Belén. It goes through Villavil (see above) to Antofagasta de la Sierra and San Antonio de los Cobres (petrol available – see page 132). This route is almost impassable in passenger cars after heavy rains, and requires enough fuel for 600 km at high altitudes on unmaintained roads (fill up at Hualfín – thermal springs – 10 km past turnoff to Route 53). Also, the stretch beyond the right turn at Puerto de Corral Quemado is very difficult (37 km of fords), to be avoided in summer rainy season. At Km 87 is Cerro Compo (3,125m), magnificent descent; at Km 99 the road turns right to Laguna Blanca, where there is a small vicuña farm (don't go straight at the junction).

ANTOFAGASTA DE LA SIERRA

(260 km) Together with El Peñón and Laguna Blanca in the *puna*, and Villavil and La Hoyada in the *pre-puna*, this is the main township of NW Catamarca. Around Antofagasta there are lunar landscapes, with salt lakes, and many peaks over 5,000m. Deposits of marble, onyx, sulphur, mica, salts, borates, and gold are present. Wildlife in the sparsely populated region including vicuña, guanaco, vizcacha, flamingoes, foxes and ostriches. No petrol station, but fuel obtainable from *intendencia*. North of Antofagasta the road continues via the Salar de Hombre Muerto to San Antonio de los Cobres. **NB** Petrol/gasoline is rarely available in this region; remember that in the *puna* fuel consumption of carburettor engines is almost double that in the lowlands.

● **Accommodation E** pp *Pensión Darío*, blue door just off main square; *Almacén Rodríguez*, Belgrano y Catamarca, serves meals, inc breakfast.

● **Buses** From Belén on Fri about 1000, arriving 2200, returning Mon 0700, or hire a pickup or hitch.

CATAMARCA

Paved Route 38 runs from La Rioja to the third oasis, **San Fernando del Valle de Catamarca** (*Pop* 89,000; *Alt* 490m; *Phone code* 0833). It is capital of its province, on the Río del Valle, between two S slopes of the Sierra de Aconquija, about 89 km NE of La Rioja, 240 km S of Tucumán. Cattle, fruit, grapes and cotton are the main agricultural products, but it is also renowned for hand-woven ponchos and fruit preserves. Therapeutic mineral springs. There are traces of Indian civilizations, including extensive agricultural terraces (now mostly abandoned), throughout the province. The *Zonda*, a strong dry mountain wind, can cause dramatic temperature increases.

Museums

Instituto Cultural Esquiú, Sarmiento 450, with important archaeological section, open Mon-Fri 0700-1300, 1430-2000, Sat, Sun, am only; **Museo Folklórico**, underground (subsuelo), Paseo Gral Navarro.

Tours

Manzana de Turismo, Roca, primera cuadra, with information, folders, typical handicrafts, visit to the centre where students learn how to make hand-woven rugs. Ask about the *Torres y Campanas* (towers and bells) tour, comprising many old chapels and churches mainly on the way to Las Pirquitas reservoir.

Excursions

To **Dique Las Pirquitas**, 3 hrs with local bus 1A from bus station. Bus stops at *Hostería de Turismo* (with restaurant) at Villa Pirquitas, about 45 mins' walk. Five morning buses from 0700, last returns at 2200. Opening hours Mon-Fri 1000-1900, Sat, Sun and holidays 0830-1900.

Local festivals

Pilgrimages to the church of the Virgen del Valle. In July, regional handicrafts are sold at Festival del Poncho, a *feria* with 4 nights of music, mostly folklore of the NW.

Local information

● Accommodation & places to eat

A3 *Acasti*, Sarmiento 520, T 25001/4, restaurant, ACA discount.

B *Inti Huasi*, República 297, T 24664, ACA discount.

C *Colonial*, República 802, T 23502, no food, rec, welcoming, good value; **C** *Delgado*, San Martín 788, basic; **C** *Suma Huasi*, Sarmiento 547, T 22301, avoid TV lounge and rooms above it, ACA discount.

D *Las Cumbres*, Plaza 25 de Agosto. Many *Residenciales* on Av Güemes. Provincial tourist office has a list of families who rent rooms.

● Places to eat

Sociedad Española, Urquiza 703; *La Cabaña*, Tucumán 1115, has folk dancing. *La Tinaja*, Sarmiento 500 block, excellent, pricey, live music, warmly rec; *Pizzería Maryeli*, Esquiú 521, basic (but good *empanadas*); *Sociedad Italiana*, M Moreno (off Paseo Gen Navarro), pastas, inexpensive; *Comedor Unión Obrera*, Sarmiento 857, good value, speciality *cabrito*; *Parrilla de Adrián*, Güemes block 500, good *asado*; *Montmartre*, Paseo Gen Navarro, good food, reasonably priced; *Marco Polo Bar*, Rivadavia 916, drinks, snacks. Many cheap restaurants along Av Güemes, bars and cafés along Rivadavia (pedestrian street).

● Banks & money changers

Banco de Catamarca, Plaza 25 de Mayo, changes US$ cash but not TCs; *Banco de Galicia* changes TCs, US$10 commission.

● Post & telecommunications

Post Office: San Martín 753, slow, open 0800-1300, 1600-2000. **Telephones**: Rivadavia 758, open 0700-2400, daily.

● Shopping

Catamarca specialities from: *Cuesta del Portezuelo*, Sarmiento 575; *Maica Regionales*, next to Aerolíneas Argentinas; *Casa Valdés*, Sarmiento 586; and *Suma Regionales*, Sarmiento y Esquiú. *Mercado Artesanal*, Urquiza 945, wide range of handicrafts, open 0700-1300, 1400-2000, reached by infrequent colectivo 23 from centre.

● Tour companies & travel agents

Enrique Lovell, at *Huellas Andinas*, T 31930, offers overland tours in 4WD to the Antofagasta de la Sierra region.

● Tourist offices

Sarmiento 450, T/F 22695, open 0800-2000, helpful. In small surrounding towns, go to municipal offices for information and maps.

● Transport

Air AR (office on Sarmiento, next to *Hotel Suma Huasi*, T 24450/24460) and Lapa (Sarmiento 506, T 34772) to/from Buenos Aires and La Rioja.

Buses Good information at bus terminal. To **Tucumán**, 4-5 daily with Bosio, $4^{1}/_{2}$ hrs, US$10, several other companies; road paved, in good condition except for rough stretch at provincial border (Cuesta del Totoral has steep gradients, hairpins, potholes). To **Buenos Aires**, US$50, 2nd class at 2200, 1st class at 1900, daily. To **Belén** via Cerro Negro with Coop Catamarca, returns from Belén daily 1300 (see page 160). Also Belén-Catamarca via Andalgalá; Coop Catamarca via Saujil, Poman, Chumbicha, Tues, Thur 1000, Fri, Sun 1300, about 8 hrs. Catamarca-El Rodeo-Las Juntas daily at 1300, returns from Las Juntas 1700. To **Córdoba**, 5 daily. To **Santiago del Estero**, 1630, US$12. There are several buses daily to Mendoza.

Buses to Santiago del Estero province: a road runs NE to **Lavalle** (towards Santiago del Estero). This 116 km run over the **Cuesta El Portezuelo** (1,980m), offers great views, but is steep and difficult though paved. No bus service over Portezuelo to Lavalle, but a service to Frías, E, and also in Santiago del Estero province – No 9 and not No 18 (which crosses the Totoral), run by Coop de Transportes de Catamarca. Leaves 0500 Tues, Thur, Fri and Sat, arrives at Frías 1000, returns 1400, arrives in Catamarca 1900. From Frías travel to Lavalle.

Catamarca-Frías via Totoral, No 18 Mon, Wed, Fri, Sat 0500, arrives 1030, return 1330, arrives Catamarca 1900. No 14 via El Alto, longer trip, arrives Frías 1045. Catamarca-Lavalle via Totoral, same No 18, leaves Tues, Thur, and Sun 1100, arrives Lavalle 1510.

The Northeast

THIS SECTION begins at the Río de la Plata and ends at the magnificent Iguazú Falls on the Brazilian border. Two routes are followed, the Ríos Uruguay and Paraná, describing the river towns and beaches, and the Jesuit missions near Posadas (in particular San Ignacio Miní). Crossings to Uruguay and Paraguay are also given.

Between the Ríos Uruguay and Paraná lies Argentine Mesopotamia: the provinces of Entre Ríos, Corrientes, and Misiones. The distance between the rivers is 390 km in N Corrientes, but narrows to about 210 km in the latitude of Santa Fe.

The province of Corrientes is marshy and deeply-wooded, with low grass-covered hills rising from the marshes. The normal rainfall is about 2,000 mm, but the rains are not spread uniformly and drain off quickly through the sandy soil. Entre Ríos has plains of rich pasture land not unlike those of Uruguay. Misiones is a hilly strip of land between the Uruguay and the Alto Paraná rivers, 80-100 km wide and about 400 km long; its capital is the river port of Posadas. Its boundary to the N is the Río Iguazú, which here tumbles over the great Iguazú Falls. Misiones is on the Paraná Plateau; much of it is covered with forests of pine and cedar and broad-leaved trees, and the land, with its red soil, is reminiscent of Brazil.

History Mesopotamia was first colonized by Spaniards pushing S from Asunción to reoccupy Buenos Aires; Santa Fe was founded in 1573, Corrientes in 1588. From about 1880 there were Jewish agricultural settlements in Entre Ríos, promoted by Baron Hirsch for victims of pogroms in the Czarist Empire (see 'Los gauchos judíos' by Alberto Gerchunoff). Vestiges of these settlements remain at Domínguez (museum) and Basavilbaso, and across the river in Moisesville (Santa Fe).

Misiones Province was first occupied by the Jesuit Fathers fleeing from the Brazilian Alto-Paraná region with their devoted Indian followers before the slave-hunting Bandeirantes. These missions and their history are described under Posadas (see page 176). The province has attracted immigrants from Eastern Europe, from Paraguay and from the rest of Mesopotamia.

Economy Much of Entre Ríos and Corrientes is still pastoral, a land of large *estancias* raising cattle and sheep. Maize (a gamble in the N) is largely grown in southern Entre Ríos, which is also the most important producer of linseed, citrus fruit and poultry in Argentina. In Corrientes, along the banks of the Paraná between the cities of Corrientes and Posadas, rice and oranges are grown. Misiones is a large producer of *yerba mate*, citrus, tobacco, timber and tung oil.

Climate Winters are mild; summers are hot with rain falling in short, sharp storms. Both Entre Ríos and Corrientes often suffer from summer drought. In Misiones the rainfall is heavy: twice as heavy as in Entre Ríos. The days are hot, and the nights cool.

THE RIO URUGUAY

The Río Uruguay is the eastern boundary of Mesopotamia and forms the western border of the Republic of Uruguay. There are no regular passenger shipping services.

At 193 km from Buenos Aires, the Uruguayan town of Fray Bentos is to the right; there is a bridge (toll US$4) between Fray Bentos and the Argentine town of **Puerto Unzué**, near Gualeguaychú, but pedestrians and cyclists cannot cross it other than on motor vehicles; officials will give lifts on either side (customs formalities take about 10 mins). The river now becomes braided into channels and islands.

GUALEGUAYCHU

Opposite Fray Bentos, on the left, is the mouth of the Río Gualeguaychú; 19 km up is **Gualeguaychú** (*Pop*, 80,000, with quite a large German contingent; *Phone code* 0446) a very pleasant town. Since the opening of the bridges between Zárate and Brazo Largo, the journey time from Buenos Aires, 248 km S, has been reduced and Gualeguaychú has become a popular weekend resort for *porteños*. Airport.

Places of interest and museums

The cathedral was built in 1863. On the river is a promenade and on the opposite bank is the Parque Unzué. **Museo de la Ciudad**, San Luis y Jujuy, in a former mansion built in 1835, US$1; **Museo Arqueológico**, in the Casa de la Cultura, 25 de Mayo 734, with artefacts from indigenous cultures of the Uruguay basin. **Solar de los Haedo**, San José y Rivadavia, in the oldest house in the city, which served as Garibaldi's headquarters when he sacked the city in 1845. Filled with artefacts of the Haedo family, guided tour (Spanish) US$1, Wed-Sat 0900-1145, Fri/Sat also at 1600-1945. **Museo Ferroviario**, Piccini y Rocamora, open air railway museum in the former station.

Local festivals

Lively pre-Lenten Carnival.

Local information

● **Accommodation**

Accommodation is scarce at weekends (when few single rooms are to be found) and during carnival. The tourist office has a list of family accommodation.

A3 *Embajador*, San Martín y 3 de Febrero, T 24414, casino; **A3** *Alemán*, Bolívar 535, T 26153, German-spoken, without breakfast, rec; **A3** *París*, Bolívar y Pellegrini, T 23850, F 26260, with breakfast, fan, restaurant, comfortable; **A2** *Berlin*, Bolívar 733, T/F 25111, German spoken, with breakfast, comfortable.

B *Victoria*, Bolívar 565, T 26469, opp terminal, small rooms, modern, with breakfast.

C *Brutti*, Bolívar 591, T 26048, cleanish, shabby, good value, without breakfast, fan; **C** *Amalfi*, 25 de Mayo 571, T 25677, with breakfast, good beds; **D** *Mayo*, 3 de Febrero y Bolívar, T 27661, uncomfortable beds, with bath.

Camping: *La Delfina* in the Parque Unzué, T 22293; *Costa Azul*, T 23984; *Puerta del Sol*, T 23700, and *Playa Chica*, T 25709, all nr the river; *Ñandubaysal*, 15 km E, T 26009, best.

● **Banks & money changers**

Banco Internacional Cooperativa, 25 de Mayo y Perón, changes cash; Casa de Cambio: Daniel, 3 de Febrero 128.

● **Tourist offices**

Av Costanera y 25 de Mayo, open 0800-2000.

● **Transport**

Bus terminal in centre of town at Bolívar y Chile. To **Fray Bentos**, 1 hr, US$3, 2 a day, ETA. To **Mercedes**, 1½ hrs, US$4, 2 a day; to **Concepción del Uruguay**, **Colón** and **Concordia**; to **Buenos Aires** US$15, 4 hrs, Flechabus and El Rápido, 6 a day each.

CONCEPCION DEL URUGUAY

(*Pop* 65,000; *Phone code* 0442), known locally as Concepción, the first Argentine port of any size on the river is 74 km N of Gualeguaychú. Founded in 1783, it was until 1883 capital of Entre Ríos province.

The old town is centred on Plaza Ramírez. Overlooking the main plaza is the church of the Immaculate Conception which contains the remains of Gen Urquiza.

Museums Museo Casa del Delio Panizza, Galarza y Supremo Entrerriano, in a mansion dating from 1793, containing 19th century furnishings and artefacts; **Museo Don Andrés García**, personal collection, open daily 0900-1200, 1500-1800. **Palacio San José**, Urquiza's former mansion, 35 km W of the town, is now a museum, with artefacts from Urquiza's life and a collection of period furniture, Mon-Fri 0900-1300, 1400-1800, Sat/Sun 0900-1245, 1400-1745, US$1.50, written explanations in

Spanish, French and English (Itape buses to 3 km from the Palacio, US$3, 45 mins), highly rec.

● **Accommodation** B *Res Fiuri*, Sarmiento 779, T 27016, attractive; **C** *Virrey*, González 2075, T 25017, F 25007; **C** *Ramírez*, Martínez 50, T 25106, above bus terminal; **E** *Hosp Los Tres Nenes*, Galarza 1233, nr terminal, good.

● **Places to eat** *El Canguro*, opp terminal, good food, reasonably priced; *Rocamora*, Rocamora y Millán. Bus terminal bar for *tenedor libre* meals.

● **Tourist offices** 9 de Julio 844, T 25820.

● **Buses** Terminal at Rocamora y Martínez (bus 1 to centre or remise, US$1). To **Buenos Aires**, frequent, 4½ hrs, US$15; to **Paraná**, 5 hrs; to **Colón** 45 mins; to **Paysandú** (Uruguay) 1 hr.

COLON

(Pop 15,000) 350 km from Buenos Aires, 45 km N of Concepción del Uruguay, Colón was founded in 1863. The river is more picturesque here with an attractive *costanera* and five sandy beaches, and cliffs visible from a considerable distance; a road bridge links Colón and Paysandú, Uruguay. The town is known for *artesanía* shops along 12 de Abril, and there is a large handicrafts fair at Carnival time (Feb).

● **Accommodation** L3 *Quirinale*, Av Quirós s/n, T 21978, 5-star (with casino); **A3** *Plaza*, 12 de Abril y Belgrano, T 21043, with breakfast, a/c, modern; **A3** *Holimasú*, Belgrano 28, T 21305, F 21303, with breakfast; **B** *Palmar*, Ferrari 285, T 21952, good; **B** *Vieja Calera*, Bolívar 344, T 21139, with breakfast, a/c; **C** *Ver-Wei*, 25 de Mayo 10, T 21972, without breakfast, new ownership. Many **families** rent rooms – the Boujon family, Maipú 430, **C**, good breakfast and other meals extra, rec. Apartments for rent from Sr Ramón Gallo, Av Paysandú, T 472 3280, with kitchen, bathroom, hot showers, close to bus terminal. Several **campsites** along river bank (municipal site, excellent facilities, cheapest).

● **Places to eat** *Comedor El Rayo*, Paysandú 372; *Pizzería Luisa*, San Martín 346; *La Rueda*, San Martín y 3 de Febrero; *Marito*, Gral Urquiza y Andrade.

● **Tourist offices** Av Costanera y Gouchón.

● **Buses** Terminal at Paysandú y Sourigues. To **Buenos Aires**, 4 a day, US$18, 5 hrs; to **Concepción del Uruguay**, Copay and Paccot, 4 a day, 2 on Sun, US$2; to **Concordia**, US$6 (2½ hrs) and **Paraná** daily. To **Córdoba** 4 a week. **To Uruguay**: via the Artigas Bridge (US$4 toll) all formalities are dealt with on the Uruguayan side. Passports are collected on the bus. Easy crossing. Bus to Paysandú, US$3, 45 mins.

PARQUE NACIONAL EL PALMAR

8,500 ha, 51 km N of Colón, on the Río Uruguay, off Route 14: the Park (entrance US$2) contains varied scenery with a mature palm forest, sandy beaches on the Uruguay river, Indian tombs and the remains of an 18th century quarry and port, a good museum and many rheas and other birds. The Yatay palms grow up to 12m and some are hundreds of years old. It is best to stay overnight as wildlife is more easily seen in the early morning or at sunset. Very popular at weekends in summer.

Paraguayan Tea; Indian Tea

Yerba mate (ilex paraguayensis) is made into a tea which is widely drunk in Argentina, Paraguay, Brazil and Uruguay. Traditionally associated with the gauchos, the modern mate paraphernalia is a common sight anywhere: the gourd (*un mate*) in which the tea leaves are steeped, the straw (usually silver) and a thermos of hot water to top up the gourd. It was the Jesuits who first grew *yerba mate* in plantations, inspiring one of the drink's names: *té de jesuitas*. Also used has been *té de Paraguay*, but now just *mate* or *yerba* will do. In southern Brazil it is called *ximarão*; in Paraguay *tereré* when drunk cold with digestive herbs.

In NE Corrientes and in Misiones more Indian tea is now grown than can be absorbed by the internal market. The Indian-tea industry was started by Sir Herbert Gibson, who sent for seed from Assam in 1929; it was sown in Playadito, Corrientes province. Six seeds developed into sturdy bushes. Year after year their seed was given to anyone interested. All Argentina's tea plantations today have their origin in Sir Herbert Gibson's enterprise. Good Indian tea is also grown and sold in Brazil.

● **Access & services** Buses from Colón, 40 mins, US$2.50, will drop you at the entrance and it is easy to hitch the last 6 km to the park administration. Entry US$5. There are camping facilities (US$6 pp, electricity, hot water), a small hotel 8 km N of the Park, with restaurant opposite, and a small shop.

CONCORDIA

(*Pop* 93,800) 104 km N of Colón, a little downriver from Salto, Uruguay, is a prosperous city. The river is impassable for large vessels beyond the rapids of Salto Chico near the city, and Salto Grande 32 km up-river, where there is a large international hydro-electric dam, providing a crossing to Uruguay. Above Salto Grande the river is generally known as the Alto Uruguay. There is excellent fishing in the artificial lake.

Places of interest

In the streets around the main **Plaza 25 de Mayo** there are some fine public buildings. 5 km NE is **Parque Rivadavia**, in the centre of which is the **Palacio San Carlos**, briefly inhabited by Antoine de Saint-Exupéry. The park offers good views of the river and there is also a motor-racing track. To get to the park, take colectivo No 2, 1 block from Plaza 25 de Mayo, to corner of Av Justo and Av Salto Uruguay, from where entrance is 1 block N.

Museums

Museo Regional, Plaza Urquiza, in the Palacio Arruabarrena, local and natural history collections, open 0800-2100 daily, entry free.

Local information
● **Accommodation**

A1 *Salto Grande*, Urquiza 581, T/F 210034, with breakfast, comfortable; **A2** *Palmar*, Urquiza 521, T 216050, F 215020, bright, comfortable, also **B** in older part, with breakfast; **A3** *Federico 1°*, 1° de Mayo 248, T 213323, with fan; **A3** *Centro*, La Rioja y Buenos Aires, T 217776, F 217746, a/c, comfortable, *comedor.*

B *Colón*, Pellegrini 611, T 215510, fan, attractive but run down, poor beds; **B** *Embajador*, San Lorenzo 75, T 213018, nr bus station, neat.

C *Argentino*, Pellegrini 560, T 215767, with bath, old fashioned, nice patio; **C** *Central*, 1° de Mayo 148, T 212842, reasonable, but shared bathrooms not too clean; **C** *Colonial*, Pellegrini 443, T 221448, without breakfast, fan, pleasant; **C** *Concordia*, La Rioja 518, T 216869, with fan, good; **C** *Victoria*, Urquiza next to Esso, 2 blocks from terminal, rec.

Camping: *La Posada de Suárez – Club Viajantes* on Av Costanera nr the park, warmly rec, with good *parrillada* alongside, but beware the cats.

● **Places to eat**

La Estancia, Plaza 25 de Mayo, good value; *Comedor Las Dos Naciones*, Plaza 25 de Mayo y Av 1° de Mayo, good, moderate prices, large portions; *Mafalda*, corner of Plaza Urquiza and Av Entre Ríos, very good home made ice cream and cakes.

● **Banks & money changers**

Banco Río de la Plata, on plaza, no commission on Visa advances; **Casa Julio**, 1 de Mayo, ½ block from plaza; **Casa Chaca**, on plaza.

● **Post & telecommunications**

Post Office: La Rioja y Buenos Aires. **Telephone**: 700 block of San Luis (24 hrs).

● **Tourist offices**

Plaza 25 de Mayo, open 0700-2400 daily, lousy map.

● **Transport**

Buses Terminal 2 km from centre. No 2 bus goes to main plaza. To **Buenos Aires**, 6 daily, US$17, 6½ hrs; to **Córdoba**, US$25 with Expreso Singer, at 2200 and 0300, 9 hrs; to **Paraná** 5 a day, to **Posadas** at 1800 and 2300, with Expreso Singer (8½ hrs, US$32), to **Iguazú** at 1810, 13½ hrs, to **Corrientes** US$11. Bus to **La Paz** (Entre Ríos) – see page 172, 1100, US$10.50, 8 hrs. To **Paso de los Libres** direct, El Recreo 1500 Mon, Sat and several at 0300, US$11, 3½ hrs.

To Uruguay Ferry: take No 4 bus from terminal marked 'Puerto', for ferry crossing to Salto US$3-4, tickets obtainable at a small kiosk, which shuts 15 mins before departure, outside migration in building marked 'Resguardo', 5 departures Mon-Fri, 4 departures Sat, 2 departures (0800 1800) Sun, 20 mins, passengers only. **Bus**: service via Salto Grande dam, Flecha Bus and Chadre 2 a day each, US$3, all formalities on Argentine side, passports checked on bus. **Bicycles**: note that cycles are not allowed to cross the international bridge but officials will help cyclists find a lift.

NORTH OF CONCORDIA

About 153 km upstream from Concordia lies the small port of **Monte Caseros** (*Pop* 18,400; hotels), with the Uruguayan town of Bella Unión, on the Brazilian border, almost opposite.

PASO DE LOS LIBRES

Above Bella Unión, the Alto Uruguay is the boundary between Argentina and Brazil. 96 km above Monte Caseros is **Paso de los Libres** (*Pop* 25,000), with the larger Brazilian town of Uruguaiana opposite: a bridge joins the two. Paso de los Libres was founded in 1843 by Gen Madariaga; it was here that he crossed the river from Brazil with his 100 men and annexed Corrientes province for Argentina. Road (paved) to Paraná.

- **Accommodation A3** *Alejandro I*, Col López 502, T 24100, pool, cable TV, best; **C** *Uruguay*, Uruguay 1252, T 25672, not clean but friendly, good *comedor*; opp is **C** *26 de Febrero*. Near terminal are **C** *Capri*, T 24126, with bath, and several others.

- **Transport Air** Líneas Aéreas Entre Ríos (LAER) flies from Aeroparque, Buenos Aires to Paraná, Gualeguaychú and Concordia with very low fares; enquire at Puente Aéreo desk at Aeroparque. **Buses** Terminal is 1 km from town centre, nr border. To Buenos Aires US$25. **To Brazil**: minibuses run between town and border, US$0.60. No bus service on Sun – taxi charges US$20.

Yapeyú, 58 km N of Paso de los Libres, on the road to Alvear, is the site of a Jesuit mission, famous as the birthplace of the liberator, José de San Martín. Part of the house where he was born is well preserved, and there is an interesting Jesuit Museum.

- **Accommodation B** *San Martín*, next to the *Municipalidad*, T 93120; camping by the river; **B** *Bungalows*, nr river, *cabañas*, good; the Carillo family on the main plaza rent rooms, **E**, good.

BUENOS AIRES TO PARAGUAY: THE RIO PARANA

The only long-distance passenger services up the Río Paraná from Buenos Aires are those to Asunción, Paraguay. Depending on the tide, boats enter the Río Paraná by either the Las Palmas reach of the delta, on which is Zárate, or the Paraná-Guazú reach, on which is Ibicuy.

BUENOS AIRES TO ROSARIO

Route 9 heads NW out of the capital to **Zárate** (90 km; *Pop* 77,000; *Phone code* 0328), on the W bank, an industrial centre with large *frigoríficos* and paper works.

- **Accommodation B** *San Martín*, Amegh-

ino 773, T 22713. *Camping Club La Isla*, on the Paraná Guazú nr the Zárate bridge.

- **Places to eat** *Restaurant La Posta de Correa*, cheap, good service. Along the waterfront are many *parrillas* and restaurants.

- **Buses** From Buenos Aires, Plaza Once, US$3, every 30 mins.

ROUTES The highway continues to Rosario through **San Pedro** (*Pop* 35,500), 50 km further, with many fine campsites on the riverfront, and the grain exporting ports of San Nicolás and Villa Constitución.

North of Zárate, the Paraná de las Palmas and Paraná Guazú rivers, plus the lowlands between, are crossed by the Zárate and Brazo Largo suspension bridges. These beautiful bridges carry rail and road traffic (car toll US$6). Route 14 continues N up the W bank of the Río Uruguay through Gualeguaychú.

ROSARIO

(*Pop* 1 million; *Phone code* 041), largest city in the province of Santa Fe, 320 km N of Buenos Aires, is the third largest city in Argentina It is a great industrial and export centre. The city has a lively cultural scene. It is the home of many popular rock musicians and modern artists and there are good discothèques and theatres. It has a racecourse, two boat clubs and Saladillo Golf Club. The Aero Club is in the suburb of Gral Alvear. Swimming at sandy **Florida beach**, about 8 km N of Rosario. From Oct to early Mar it is warm, and from Dec to the end of Feb uncomfortably hot. Changes of temperature are sudden.

Places of interest

Monument of the Flag, a memorial on the river bank in honour of Gen Belgrano, designer of the Argentine flag, who raised it on this spot for the first time (lifts go to the top); **Parque Independencia**, in the centre of the city, 126 ha, with lakes and monumental gardens. **Cathedral**, 25 de Mayo, in somewhat eclectic style, contains the Virgen of Rosario. A recommended pedestrian tour Called **'Paseo Centenario'** around C Córdoba touches on the interesting buildings and monuments of the 'Golden Days of Rosario' (1880-1950). There are explanation signs.

Museums

Museo Histórico Provincial, Parque Independencia, Mon-Fri 0900-1230, 1400-1730, Sat/Sun 1500-1800; **Museo de Bellas Artes J B Castagnino**, Av Pellegrini 2202, 1,600 paintings, including works by El Greco, Goya and Titian, Tues-Sat 1200-2000, Sun 1000-2000; **Museo de Arte Decorativo Firma y Odilio Estévez**, Santa Fe 748, has some Caravaggios, Goyas and Murillos, Thur-Sun 1500-2000; **Museo Provincial de Ciencias Naturales**, Moreno 750, Tues-Fri 0900-1200, Sat-Sun 1500-1800; **Museo del Paraná y Sus Islas**, Belgrano y La Rioja. Mon, Tues, Thur 0900-1100, Sun 1600-1900.

Excursions

Boat trips to river islands can be made at weekends (eg *Ciudad de Rosario* from Estación Fluvial by the Monument of the Flag, Sat 1730, Sun 1600, 1830), or from Florida beach at any time (US$3-4 river trips; US$100 fishing trips). Canoes can be hired.

28 km N of Rosario is **San Lorenzo** (*Pop* 38,000), with one of the largest chemical works in Argentina. See the restored monastery of San Carlos de Borromeo on the river bank. Nearby is the Campo de la Gloria, where in 1813 San Martín won his first battle in the War of Independence. Visitors are shown a pine tree grown from a cutting of the tree under which the Liberator rested after the battle.

Local holidays

7 Oct (Foundation of the City).

Local information
● Accommodation

A1 *La Paz*, Barón de Mauá 36, T 210905, quiet, rec; **A1** *Presidente*, Av Corrientes 919, T 242854, good; **A1** *Riviera*, San Lorenzo 1460, T 252058, a/c; **A2** *Europeo*, San Luís 1364, T 240382, with breakfast, modern.

B *Colonial*, Maipú 1543, T 219041, with breakfast; **B** *Rosario*, Corrientes 900, T 242170, with breakfast, parking, large rooms, good beds.

C *Río*, Rivadavia 2665, T 396421, pleasant; **C** *Normandie*, Mitre 1030, T 212694, helpful, central.

D *Savoy*, San Lorenzo y San Martín, T 480071, built 1900 and retaining old-fashioned bathrooms, cheap restaurant, good value.

Around terminal: on Santa Fe: **B** *América*, No 3746, T 386584, without breakfast, best value on this street; **B** *Casas*, No 3600, T 304717, without breakfast, a/c, pleasant, rec; **B** *Embajador*, No 3554, T 384188, with breakfst, a/c extra, good; **B** *Nahuel*, No 3518, T/F 397292, with breakfast, gloomy, modern; **B** *Le Nid*, Iriondo 660, T 388762, without breakfast, a/c, modern, pleasant, rec.

Camping: in La Florida, nr the river.

● Places to eat

Don Rodrigo, Sante Fe 968, and *Fénix*, Santa Fe next to Citibank, are both very good. *Doña María*, Santa Fe 1371, good Italian food; *Casa Uruguaya*, Alvear 1125 (T 69320), away from centre, good; *Marialronn*, Santa Fe y Pres Roca, rec for dancing. Along the river are good cheap restaurants and fishing club barbeques, good atmosphere.

● Airline offices

Aerolíneas Argentinas, Santa Fe 1410; **Southern Winds**, Santa Fe 1412, T 249332.

● Banks & money changers

Lloyds Bank (BLSA), La Rioja 1205; **Citibank**, Santa Fe 1101; **First National Bank of Boston**, Córdoba y Mitre. Open 1000-1600. Most banks charge 2% commission on cheques and cash. **Amex**, Grupo 3 de Turismo, Córdoba 1147, T 244415. *Casas de Cambio*: **Transatlántica**, Córdoba 900; **Carey**, Corrientes 802; **Carbatur**, Corrientes 840.

● Entertainment

Café de la Opera, Laprida y Mendoza, bar with cabaret, live music, highly rec, friendly.

● Laundry

Santa Fe 1578.

● Post & telecommunications

Post Office: Córdoba y Buenos Aires. **Telecommunications**: San Luis, between San Martín and Maipú.

● Shopping

Bookshop: *Stratford*, Mitre 726, for imported English books.

● Tourist offices

Belgrano y Buenos Aires, T 495140, Mon-Fri 0800-2000, Sat/Sun 0900-2000, English spoken.

● Useful addresses

Scrivanti, Corrientes 653, p 6, T 253738, for budget travel information.

● Transport

Air Airport at Fisherton, 8 km from centre. Minibus service connects with flights, US$4, to and from hotels and AR office (Transportes Ayolas, Dean Funes 1,525m, T 839863). Taxi or *remise* US$10. Several flights daily to **Buenos Aires** with AR and Austral; Andesmar to **Córdoba** and **Mendoza**.

Buses There are regular bus services to Arroyo Seco, Casilda, Cañada de Gómez, San Lorenzo and other important centres up to 80 km from the city. To **Buenos Aires**, via San Nicolás on Route 9, 4 hrs, or via Pergamino, less frequent, on Route 8 (Chevallier bus every hour, US$20-22; also Ablo, Gen Urquiza, La Unión), NW to **Córdoba** and **Tucumán**. To **Santa Fe**, US$10. To **Mendoza**, US$40. To **Puerto Iguazú**, US$50.

Rosario can be reached from Buenos Aires by Route 8 (marked Córdoba) to Pergamino, and then, following signs, by Route 188, and then 178 to Rosario. This is a better way than lorry-packed Route 9. Hitching to Salta along Route 34 is possible.

Trains The Buenos Aires-Tucumán service stops in Rosario; to Tucuman, US$15, 13 hrs, Mon and Fri.

Ferry To Victoria, in Entre Ríos, which has a municipal campsite.

PARANA

(*Pop* 210,000; *Phone code* 043), capital of Entre Ríos, lies some 180 km above Rosario on the E bank. Founded in 1588, the city was, from 1853 to 1862, the capital of the Republic.

Places of interest

The centre is situated on a hill offering fine views over the river and beyond to Santa Fe. There are many fine buildings; in the centre is the **Plaza Primero de Mayo**, where there are fountains and a statue of San Martín. Around the Plaza are the **Municipalidad**, the **Cathedral**, notable for its portico and its interior, and the **Colegio del Huerto**, seat of the Senate of the Argentine Confederation between 1853 and 1861. The **Casa de Gobierno** at Santa Fe y Laprida has a grand façade. The city's glory is **Parque Urquiza**, to the NW. It has an enormous statue to Gen Urquiza, and a bas-relief showing the battle of Caseros, at which he finally defeated Rosas; also an open-air theatre. There are pleasant walks along the river bank and around the fishing *barrio* of **Puerto Sánchez**.

Museums

Museo de Bellas Artes, Buenos Aires 355; **Museo Histórico**, Buenos Aires y

Laprida, open Tues-Fri, 0700-1300, 1500-2000, Sat, 0900-1200, 1600-1900(winter) 1700-2000 (summer), Sun, 0900-1200.

Local information
● **Accommodation**

There is a shortage of hotel space, especially at peak periods (Semana Santa and July), when the tourist office arranges accommodation with families. There is a greater selection of hotels – at lower prices – in Santa Fe.

A1 *Mayorazgo*, Etchevehere y Córdoba, on Costanera Alta, T 230333, 5-star, with fine view of park and river, has casino and swimming pool; **A2** *Paraná*, 9 de Julio 60, T 231700, with breakfast, pleasant.

C *Bristol*, Alsina 221, T 313961, close to the bus terminal, basic; **C** *Plaza*, San Martín 915, T 210720; **C** *Roma*, Urquiza 1069, with bath, basic, central.

Camping: Balneario Thompson.

● **Laundry**
Laverap, Belgrano 650 and San Juan 273.

● **Tourist offices**
Laurencena y San Martín, T 233677.

● **Transport**
Air Gen Urquiza airport, 12 km from town.

Buses Terminal on Av Ramírez. East across Entre Ríos to **Concordia** on Río Uruguay, 5 a day, 5 hrs. To **Buenos Aires**, US$22.

Travelling between Santa Fe and Paraná The two cities do not face one another, but are 25 km apart and are separated by several islands. From Paraná the Hernandarias tunnel, toll US$2/car, passes under the river to connect with the W bank; from here a road runs 23 km W to Santa Fe across two islands and bridges. Trucks with dangerous loads cross the river by a launch which also carries pedestrians and operates Mon-Sat, 0600-2100, 20 mins' journey, frequency depending on demand from trucks. Frequent bus service between the two cities by Etacer and Fluviales del Litoral, US$2, 1 hr.

SANTA FE

(*Pop* 400,000; *Phone code* 042) a larger city, 165 km from Rosario, is the capital of its province and the centre of a very fertile region. It was founded by settlers from Asunción in 1573, though its present site was not occupied until 1660.

Places of interest

The S part of the city, around the **Plaza 25 de Mayo** is the historic centre. On the

Plaza itself are the majestic **Casa de Gobierno**, built in 1908 in French-style on the site of the historic Cabildo in which the 1853 constitution was drafted. Opposite is the **Cathedral**, with its twin towers capped by blue cupolas. On the E side is the **Colegio de la Inmaculada Concepción**, established by the Jesuits and including the Iglesia de **Nuestra Señora de los Milagros**, dating from 1694, more richly decorated with an ornate dome.

One block S of the plaza is the Iglesia y Convento de **San Francisco** built in 1680. The church has fine wooden ceilings, made from timber floated down the river from Paraguay, carved by indigeneous craftsmen and fitted without the use of nails. Inside are the remains of Estanislao López (see below). The Convent of **Santo Domingo**, a block W of the Plaza at 3 de Febrero y 9 de Julio, has a fine patio and museum; N of the centre at Javier de la Rosa 623, is the modern neogothic style Iglesia de **Nuestra Señora de Guadalupe**, with attractive stained glass windows (open daily 0730-2000, bus 4 from the centre, 20 mins).

Museums

Museo de San Francisco, in the Convent (see above) includes a reconstruction with wax figures of the Constituent Congress of 1852-1853, daily 1000-1200, 1500-1800. **Museo Histórico Provincial**, 3 de Febrero y San Martín, in a building dating from 1680 (one of the oldest surviving civil buildings in the country), includes pieces from the former Jesuit mission of San Javier and artefacts associated with the dictator Rosas and with Urquiza, who overthrew him. There are portraits of both men and of Estanislao López, Rosas's ally who ruled Santa Fe, Tues-Fri 0830-1230, 1430-1900, Sat/Sun 1500-1800. **Museo Etnográfico**, 3 de Febrero y Av Costanera, includes large collection of artefacts from Santa Fe La Vieja (the original site of the city) and items from indigeneous cultures in Santa Fe area, Mon-Fri 0900-1200, 1530-1900, Sat 1530-1830, Sun 1000-1200, 1530-1830. **Museo de Bellas Artes**, Gen López, Tues-Sun 1730-2030, exhibitions of local artists' work.

Local holidays

30 Sept (San Jerónimo); 15 Nov (Foundation of City).

Local information

● **Accommodation**

A1 *Conquistador*, 25 de Mayo 2676, T/F 551195, sauna, pool, gym; **A2** *Río Grande*, San Gerónimo 2586, T 551025, modern, rec; **A2** *Corrientes*, Corrientes 2520, T 592126, with breakfast, garage, restaurant, comfortable; **A2** *Hostal de Santa Fe de la Vera Cruz*, San Martín 2954, T 551740, best, genial, well-kept and run; **A3** *Castellar*, 25 de Mayo y Falucho, T 520141, a/c, parking; **A3** *Suipacha*, Suipacha 2375, T 521135, safe, rec a/c, garage, pleasant.

B *Niza*, Rivadavia 2755, T 522047, very nice, without breakfast, a/c; **B** *Brigadier*, San Luis 3148, T 537387, 2 blocks from bus station, good, a/c, some English spoken, parking; **B** *Emperatriz*, Irigoyen Freire 2440, T 530061, pleasant, good value.

Near the terminal: **A3** *Bertaina*, H Irigoyen 2255, T/F 553068 parking, a/c, good beds, well maintained; **A3** *Zavaleta*, H Yrigoyen 2349, T/F 551840, cafeteria, with breakfast; **B** *Colón*, San Luis 2862, T 545167, **D** without bath, pleasant, large rooms; **B-C** *Royal*, Irigoyen Freyre 2256, T 527359, OK, fan, gloomy; **B-C** *Carlitos*, Irigoyen Freyre 2336, T 531541.

Camping: several sites on the lakes and rivers outside town inc: *Luz y Fuerza*, 7 km N nr Lago Guadalupe; *Cámara del Hogar*, 4 km E on Route 168; 2 sites on Río Colastine, 15 km E on Route 168.

● **Places to eat**

Many good ones, offering excellent meals with good wine. *El Quincho de Chiquito*, Obispo Príncipe y Almte Brown, excellent and good value, classic fish restaurant, huge helpings. Excellent grills inc *surubí* (local fish) at *Gran Parrillada Rivadavia*, Rivadavia 3299. Surubí also at *España*, San Martín 2644. *Baviera San Martín*, San Martín 2941, good salads; *Café de la Paix*, San Martín y Santiago del Estero.

● **Banks & money changers**

Lloyds Bank (BLSA), 25 de Mayo 2501, open 0715-1315; Citibank, San Martín 2609. Amex representative, *Vacaciones Felices*, San Martín 2347. Casas de Cambio: **Camsa**, 25 de Mayo 2466; **Carbatur**, San Martín 2520; **Tourfé**, San Martín 2901, Sat 0830-1230, changes TCs.

● **Laundry**

Servi Rap, Rivadavia 2834 (open Sat 0800-1300); *Laverap*, San Martín 1687.

● **Sports**
Swimming: on river at Guadalupe beach; local bus.

● **Tourist offices**
San Martín 2836 and at the bus terminal: maps, friendly.

● **Transport**
Air Airiport at Sauce Viejo, 17 km from the city. Daily AR flights to and from Buenos Aires, T 599461.

Buses Terminal nr the centre, Gen M Belgrano 2910. To **Córdoba**, US$18, 5 hrs. Many buses to **Buenos Aires** US$19-28; to **Paraná** frequent service US$2, 45 mins; to **Rosario** very frequent, 2½ hrs by autopista, US$10; daily to **Mendoza** (2100), **Posadas**, 12 hrs, US$30, several companies and **Santiago del Estero/Tucumán** (2010). To **Concordia** 4½ hrs, US$16.50. To **Asunción** (Paraguay), daily overnight, La Internacional US$31, común, US$57 diferencial.

Upriver from Santa Fe/Parana On the E bank a road more-or-less parallels the Río Paraná, passing through **La Paz (Entre Ríos)**, a small port (*Pop* 15,200) with regional museum, and **Goya**, the second town of the Province of Corrientes (*Pop* 47,000; several hotels). Across from Goya, joined by vehicle-ferry, is **Reconquista** (*Pop* 34,800; several hotels).

THE IBERA MARSHES

The **Esteros del Iberá (Iberá marshes)** are a nature reserve covering an environment similar to the Pantanal in Mato Grosso, Brazil. Among the species are the endangered aguará-guazú (maned wolf), the marsh deer and the broad nosed caiman. Other interesting species include capybaras, brocket deer, curiyús or yellow ananconda and tegú lizards. About 300 species of bird have been identified, among them the Yabirú (or Juan Grande) stork – the largest stork in the western hemispere, southern screamers and several species of ducks. Trips can be organized through Marcus Moncada, of *Turismo Aventura 4WD*, Junín 1062, Loc 4, Corrientes T/F 33269, from US$75 pp/day, advance booking essential.

Mercedes (140 km E of Goya; *Pop* 20,750) is a good base for visiting the marshes. 27 km S of Mercedes are the strange Ita Pucú rock formations, remnants of a mountain massif long disappeared.

● **Accommodation** *Turismo*, Caaguazú y Sarmiento, T 317; *Plaza*, San Martín 699, T 13, cheapest.

At **Carlos Pellegrini**, 110 km NE of Mercedes (3 buses a week), a new visitors centre to the marshes has been opened (take food, sleeping bag, light, binoculars). Workers at the visitors centre take boat trips in small punts, a recommended way of discovering the wildlife quietly. Bottled water is sold at the main store in the village.

210 km SE of Corrientes, on the edge of the Iberá marshes, is the Estancia of **San Juan Poriahú** (16,500 ha), a wildlife reserve with a superb array of animals and birds. Visitors can explore the *estancia* on horseback, or in pick-ups or tractors. Accommodation is also available; transport from Corrientes US$45.

CORRIENTES

(*Pop* 258,000; *Phone code* 0783), 40 km below the confluence of the Ríos Paraguay and Alto Paraná, was founded in 1588. The 2¾ km Gen Belgrano bridge across the Río Paraná (toll US$1/car) links the city with Resistencia (25 km), from where Route 11 goes N to Formosa and Asunción. East of Corrientes, Route 12 follows the Alto Paraná to Posadas and Iguazú. The river can make the air heavy, moist and oppressive, but in winter the climate is pleasant. The city is capital of Corrientes province and the setting for Graham Greene's *The Honorary Consul*.

Places of interest

The main **Plaza 25 de Mayo** is one of the best preserved in Argentina. On the N side is the police station built in 19th century French style. On the E side is the Italianate **Casa de Gobierno** and on the N is the church of **La Merced**. Two blocks E at Quintana y Martínez is the **Convent of San Francisco**, rebuilt in 1861 (the original dated from the early 17th century). The **Cathedral**, built in 1874 is on Plaza Cabral where there is a statue to the sergeant who saved San Martín's life at the battle of San Lorenzo. The church of **La Cruz de los Milagros** (1897) houses a miraculous cross placed there by the founder of the city, Alonzo de Vera – Indians who tried to burn it were killed by lightning from a cloudless sky. A beautiful walk eastwards, along the Av Costanera, beside the Paraná river leads to **Parque Mitre**, from where there are good views of sunsets over the river. Up river from the bridge to Resistencia, is a **zoo** with animals of the region. Calle Junín is pedestrianized, with restaurants and shops, crowded at night.

Museums

Museo Histórico Regional, 9 de Julio 1044, Tues-Fri 0800-1200, 1600-1800, Sat 0900-1200, US$1; **Museo de Bellas Artes**, San Juan 643, open Tues-Fri, 0800-1200, 1600-2100, Sat, Sun, 0900-1200, 1800-2000; **Museo de Artesanía**, Buenos Aires y Quintana, Mon-Fri, 0730-1200, 1500-2000, Sat 0900-1200, 1600-1900.

Excursions

Northeast along Route 12 are: **Santa Ana de los Guacaras** (20 km), a 17th-century settlement with attractive colonial architecture. The small town of **Paso de la Patria** (38 km) is a paradise for *dorado* fishing (season Aug-Sept), with plenty of bungalows to stay. (*A3 Hostería Don Julián*, T 94021, full board.)

A tiny port on the Alto Paraná, **Itatí** (*Pop* 5,700), is reached by bus (73 km). Here, on 16 July, is held a festival which celebrates jointly the crowning of the Virgin of Itatí (housed in a sanctuary built 1638) and St Louis of France. Thousands of pilgrims arrive on the 16th (when the religious ceremonies begin) from San Luis del Palmar (*Pop* 15,000). *Hospedajes: Antártida, El Promesero, El Colonial*.

Local information
● **Accommodation**
More expensive than Resistencia, **A2** *Gran Hotel Guaraní*, Mendoza 970, T 23663, F 24620, with breakfast, very good, a/c, restaurant; **A3** *Corrientes*, Junín 1549, T 65019, F 65025, with breakfast, a/c, parking, good value, good restaurant; **A3** *Hostal de Pinar*, Martínez y Italia, T 69060, modern, parking, sauna; **A3** *Orly*, San Juan 867, T 27248, with breakfast, a/c, parking; **A3** *San Martín*, Santa Fe 955, T 65004, F 32326, with breakfast, good beds, restaurant, parking.

Cheaper accommodation is difficult to find. In the centre **C** *Robert*, La Rioja 437, basic,

clean, without bath. Several nr the terminal inc **C** *Caribe*, Av Maipú Km 3, T 69045.

Camping: nr bus terminal is *Camping-club Teléfono*, Av Maipú, hot showers or bath, friendly. There is another campsite on the riverbank, go up through Parque Mitre and continue along the road closest to the river; the site is just past the water works.

● **Places to eat**
El Nuevo Balcón, Pellegrini 962, good food, clean, reasonable prices; *Las Brasas*, Av Costanera y San Martín (nr beach). Many others, and various *pizzerías*. Several tea rooms on San Juan, and on Junín. Try local baked delicacy called *chipa*.

● **Banks & money changers**
Banco de la Provincia, 9 de Julio y San Juan, cash advance on Mastercard; Banco de Iberá for cash advance on Visa and Mastercard; Casa de Cambio El Dorado, 9 de Julio 1343.

● **Entertainment**
Nightclubs: *Metal*, Junín y Buenos Aires; *Savage*, Junín y San Lorenzo.

● **Posts & telecommunications**
Post Office: San Juan y San Martín. **Telecommunications**: Pellegrini y Mendoza.

● **Tour companies & travel agents**
Turismo Aventura 4WD, Galería Paseo del Sul, Junín 1062, T 27698, F 33269, Amex. *Quo Vadis*, Carlos Pellegrini 1140, T 23096.

● **Tourist offices**
Plaza Cabral.

● **Transport**
Local Car hire: Avis at *Gran Hotel Guaraní* and airport; only credit cards accepted from foreigners. **Air** Camba Punta Airport, 10 km from city. (Bus No 8 from urban bus terminal at river end of La Rioja.)

Buses To Resistencia US$1.30, Cota, every 15 mins, 40 mins' journey, labelled 'Chaco', leaving from harbour; terminal 5 km S of centre (bus No 6 or 11), US$0.50. To Posadas US$18, 5½ hrs, road paved; to Buenos Aires, US$30, but there are more services from Resistencia to Buenos Aires, Rosario and Santa Fe; to Paso de los Libres, 5 hrs, US$10; to Concordia US$11, Empresa Gualeguaychú, 2 a day; to Asunción (Paraguay) US$18.

RESISTENCIA

(*Pop* 218,000; *Phone code* 0722) the hot and energetic capital of the Province of Chaco, is situated 6½ km up the Barranqueras stream on the W bank of the Paraná. On the Paraná itself is the little port of Barranqueras, about 600 km upstream from

Santa Fe. The city is known as the 'city of the statues', there being over 200 of these in the streets. The local products are cotton, *quebracho* and cattle.

Places of interest

The **Fogón de los Arrieros**, Brown 350, entre López y French, is a famous club frequented by local artists and full of local art and '*objets*' from abroad. It promotes the city's statues. Open to non-members Mon-Sat, 0800-1200, Tues, Wed, Thur only, 2130-0100, US$2.

Museums

Museo Histórico Regional, Donovan 425, Mon-Fri, 0800-1200, 1600-1800, in the Escuela Normal Sarmiento, traces the development of the city; **Museo de Ciencias Naturales**, Pelligrini 802 (former railway station), Mon-Fri, 0830-1230, 1600-2000, Sat 0900-1200; **Museo de Bellas Artes**, Mitre 150, Tues-Sat, 0730-1200, 1500-1900, collection of 19th and 20th century local works; **Museo Regional de Antropología**, Las Heras 727 in the Universidad Nacional del Nordeste, Mon-Fri 0800-1200, 1600-2100; **Museo Del Hombre Chaqueño**, Illia 655, sections on indigenous peoples, European immigration and the fauna of the Chaco; **Museo Policial**, Roca 233, Mon-Fri 0800-1200, 1500-2000, Sat 0800-1200, sections on marijuana and other drugs.

Excursions

To the Parque Nacional Chaco, see page 186.

Local information
● Accommodation

A3 *Colón*, Sta María de Oro 143, T 22862, old fashioned, comfortable; **A3** *Covadonga*, Güemes 182, T 44444, F 43444, small rooms, a/c, *Tabaré* snack bar.

B *Hotel AMCSAPCH* (known as Esmirna), H Irigoyen 83 on corner of Plaza, T 22898, owned by local police, with bath, good, a/c.

C *Alfil*, Santa Maria de Oro 495, T 20882, a/c extra, English spoken; **C** *Celta*, Alberdi 210, T 22986, with bath, basic; **C** *Res San José*, Rawson 304, basic; **C** *Res Alberdi*, Av Alberdi 317, **E** without bath, basic but clean, restaurant, rec.

D *Aragón*, Santiago del Estero 154.

Camping: *Parque Dos de Febrero*, very pretty, nr artificial lake, tent US$3.

● Places to eat

Círculo Residentes Santafecinos, Vadia 150, tasty meals, family style. Try *chupín de surubí*, a sort of bouillabaisse, delightful. *Restaurant Sociedad Italiana*, Yrigoyen 204, excellent cuisine, smart, pricey; *Charly*, Güemes 215, snacks, good breakfast.

● Banks & money changers

Banco del Chaco, Plaza 25 de Mayo, cash only; **Banco de Crédito**, Justo 200 block, cash advance on Mastercard. **Banco de Iberá** changes TCs (3% commission); **Banco Corrientes**, Alberdi 300 block, cash on Visa card; **Cambio El Dorado**, 9 de Julio 201, changes TCs at reasonable rate.

● Laundry

Tokio, Güemes y Brown.

● Post & telecommunications

Post Office: Plaza 25 de Mayo, Mon-Sat, 0700-1200, 1500-2000. **Telecommunications**: Justo y Paz.

● Shopping

Regionales Pompeya, Güemes 154, sells local handicrafts and has an Indian handicraft display. Excellent leather goods at *Chac*, Güemes 160.

● Tour companies & travel agents

Puerto Aventura, Saavedra 557, T/F 32932, very helpful.

● Tourist offices

Justo 135; kiosk in Plaza 25 de Mayo.

● Transport

Local Car hire: Avis, French 701 and at airport. Localiza, Roca 460, T 39255.

Air Airport 8 km from town (no bus). AR (T 22859/25360), Austral (T 45550) and Lapa (T 30201) to/from Buenos Aires; Lapa to Formosa.

Buses To **Corrientes** over the Río Paraná bridge, every 15 mins from Av Alberdi nr Plaza 25 de Mayo, 40 mins, US$1.30. Modern terminal on S outskirts (bus 3 or 10 to centre, US$0.60; remise US$4); to **Buenos Aires** 14 hrs, US$35 several companies, most services overnight; to **Santa Fe**, 8 hrs, US$26; to **Córdoba**, 12 hrs, US$43; to **Formosa** 2½ hrs, US$10; to **Iguazú** US$30; to **Posadas**, 5½ hrs, US$18; to **Tucumán** El Rayo, 1930 and 2200, 12 hrs, US$21; to **Salta** (for connections to Bolivia), Veloz del Norte and Central Sáenz Peña, daily 1700, 14 hrs, US$40. To **Bolivian border at Aguas Blancas/Bermejo**, take bus for Salta, change at Güemes, for direct connection to Orán (Atahualpa buses every 2 hrs or so). To **Clorinda** and Paraguayan border US$14, 5 hrs; to **Asunción** daily, via Formosa, La Internacional, 6½ hrs, US$21.

FORMOSA

(*Pop* 95,000; *Phone code* 0717) the capital of Formosa Province and the only Argentine port of any note on the Río Paraguay, lies 240 km above Corrientes. The surroundings are flat and swampy, the climate and vegetation subtropical. On the opposite side of the river is Isla Alberdi, a Paraguayan duty-free spot, which can be visited only if you have a multiple entry visa.

Museums

Museo Histórico y Regional, 25 de Mayo y Belgrano, Mon-Fri 0730-1200, 1500-1930, entry free, large collection of artefacts with no particular logic.

Local information

● **Accommodation**

A2 *Turismo*, best, San Martín 759, T 26004, best, parking, a/c; **A1** *Colón*, Belgrano 1068, T 26547, noisy, a/c, colour TV, spacious, **B** without a/c, good, inc breakfast.

B *San Martín*, 25 de Mayo 380, T 26769, a/c, with breakfast, run down.

C *Rivas*, Belgrano 1395, T 20499, **E** without bath, cold water, basic, run down; **C** *Colonial*, San Martín 879, T 26345, basic, a/c, parking; **C** *Casa de Familia*, Belgrano 1056, good. Opposite bus terminal is **D** *Hosp El Extranjero*, Gutnisky 2660, T 28676, modern, a/c, with bath, also short stay.

Camping: *Camping Banco Provincial*, Route 11 4 km S, good facilities inc pool, tennis courts, T 29877; *Las Arianas*, 10 km S (turn off Route 11 at El Pucu, Km 6), T 27640.

● **Places to eat**

Ser San, 25 de Mayo y Moreno, good; *Pizzería Italia*, 25 de Mayo y Rivadavia. Also on 25 de Mayo: *El Tono María*, No 55, good Italian food, nice atmosphere, expensive; *Parrillada La Cascada*, No 335.

● **Banks & money changers**

Banks close at noon and there are no *casas de cambio*; buy pesos in Asunción or Clorinda.

● **Tour companies & travel agents**

Turismo de Castro, Brandzen 75, T 34777; *Turinfort*, Moreno 58, T 27011.

● **Tourist offices**

Brandzen 117, T 26502, also at bus terminal very helpful.

● **Transport**

Air El Pucu airport, 7 km N; Austral and Lapa (T 35979) to Buenos Aires.

Buses Modern bus terminal on W outskirts (bus 4 or 11 to/from centre). To **Asunción**, 0400, 0800 and 1730, 3 hrs, US$10.50; easier to go to Clorinda on the border (US$6.50) and then take a micro to Asunción. To **Resistencia**, 6 a day, US$10; to **Buenos Aires** US$41, La Internacional. Bus services to **Embarcación** are frequently cancelled (scheduled daily 1200; do not rely on this as a route to Bolivia, better to go from Resistencia to Salta and then N).

CLORINDA

(*Pop* 40,000; *Phone code* 0718) 137 km N of Formosa, lies almost opposite Asunción (Paraguay). The Puente Loyola crosses to Puerto Falcón, Paraguay (easy border crossing). From Puerto Pilcomayo, close to Clorinda (bus US$0.40) there is is a vehicle ferry service to Itá Enramada (Paraguay), a US$0.65, 20 mins' journey every 20 mins. Clorinda has a banana festival in early October.

● **Accommodation** **B** *Embajador*, San Martín 166, T 21148; **C** *Helen*, San Martín 320, T 21118; **C** *Res 9 de Julio*, San Martín y R Sáenz Peña, T 21221, with a/c; *Res San Martín*, 12 de Octubre 1150, T 21211.

● **Buses** From Argentine end of Puente Loyola: to **Formosa** (10 a day), **Resistencia**, US$14 (4) and **Santa Fe/Rosario/Buenos Aires** (3).

PARQUE NACIONAL RIO PILCOMAYO

50,000 ha, 65 km NW of Clorinda. Flora includes quebrachos, caranday palms and palo borachos. Among the protected species are aguará-guazú, giant anteaters and tapirs. Caimans, tagú lizards, black howler monkeys, rheas and a variety of birds can also be seen. You must be accompanied by *guardaparques*.

● **Access** Buses run to Laguna Blanca, 4 km from the Park Entrance; 3 km further is the *guardaparque* office, nr which camping is permitted.

MISIONES AND IGUAZU

At the confluence of the two rivers above Corrientes the Río Paraguay comes in from the N, the Alto Paraná from the E. The Alto Paraná is difficult to navigate, being shallow in parts, braided in others, its various channels embracing midstream islands. Much rice is grown on its banks.

POSADAS

(*Pop* 141,000; *Phone code* 0752) the main Argentine port on the S bank of the Alto Paraná, is 377 km above Corrientes. The capital of the province of Misiones, it is very hot in summer. The city's centre is **Plaza 9 de Julio**, on which stand the **Cathedral** and the **Gobernación**, in imitation French style. There is a good **Mercado Artesanal** at Alberdi 602 in the Parque Río del Paraguay, 11 blocks N of Plaza 9 de Julio, by the river (Mon-Fri, 0800-1200). A good way of seeing the city is to take the No 7 bus ('Circunvalación') from C Junín. Yerba mate, tea and tobacco are grown in the area. On the opposite bank of the river lies the Paraguayan town of Encarnación, joined to Posadas by the San Roque bridge.

Museums

Museo Regional, Alberdi 606 in the Parque Río del Paraguay, open 0800-1200, 1400-2000, rather neglected; **Museo del Hombre**, Gen Paz 1865, open Mon-Fri, 0700-1300, 1400-1900, housing archaeological pieces from the areas to be flooded by the Yacyretá hydroelectric project and a section on the Jesuit missionary era; **Museo de Ciencias Naturales**, San Luis 384, open Mon-Fri, 0800-1200, 1500-1900, Sat/Sun (summer) 0900-1200, US$1, including sections on the Guaraní, Jesuit missions especially San Ignacio Miní, European colonization and endangered species; **Museo de Bellas Artes**, Sarmiento 1815, open 0700-1230, 1400-1830, entry US$2.

Excursions

87 km W of Posadas is **Ituzaingó** (*Pop* 10,000), a rapidly growing town serving the Yacyretá-Apipé hydroelectric project (all turbines due to be in place by 1998). Buses run to the Relaciones Públicas cen-

tre (free, no stops en route), where a video film is shown and other information given.

● **Accommodation**   Several hotels, eg **A3** *Ituzaingó*, Entre Ríos y Iberá, T 20601; **E** *Hosp Dos Hermanos*, Pellegrini y Posadas, clean, friendly. About 15 km W of Ituzaingó on Ruta Nacional 12, Km 1237, is *Estancia San Gará*, full board **A2** pp, or in dormitory with hammock-style accommodation, **C** pp, inc pool and all excursions into the Iberá marshes, by boat, jeep or on horseback (highly rec); a lovely place with extraordinary hospitality. Book in advance: T 0786-20550, in Posadas 0752-27217, in Buenos Aires, 01-811-1132, F 476-2648 (office at Av Alvear 1668, p 5); ask for owner Sr Pablo Prats. Take any bus between Posadas and Ituzaingó, get off at turning (drivers know it) and walk 1.5 km to the *estancia*.

Local information

NB After alterations to street numbering, all buildings have old and new numbers.

● **Accommodation Posadas**
Best is **A2** *Libertador*, San Lorenzo 2208, T 37601, F 39448, with breakfast, also cheaper rooms for travellers; **A2** *Continental*, Bolívar 314, T 38966, F 35302, comfortable but noisy, restaurant, parking, breakfast; **A2** *Posadas*, Bolívar 1949, T 40888, F 30294, garage, a/c, TV, comfortable, good service, snack bar, laundry, highly rec; **B** *Turismo*, Bolívar 171, T 37401, modern, a/c; **B** *City*, Colón 280, T 33901, a/c, central, good value, good restaurant.

Near bus terminal: **B** *Carioca*, Mitre 2437, T 24113, next to expreso Singer; **C** *Res Misiones*, Azara 382, basic, helpful; **C** *Gran Hotel Misiones*, Líbano y Barrufaldi, T 22777, run down, with breakfast; **B** *Res Marlis*, Corrientes 234, T 25764, German spoken, highly rec; **B** *Le Petit*, Santiago del Estero 1630, T 36031, parking.

C *Res Andresito*, Salta 1743, T 23850, youth hostel style, noisy.

Camping: Municipal campsite on the river, off the road to San Ignacio Miní, electric showers, dirty, shop, reached by buses 4 or 21 from centre.

● **Places to eat**
El Tropezón, San Martín 185, good, inexpensive; *El Encuentro*, San Martín 361, good value; *La Ventana*, Bolívar 1725, excellent; *Restaurant de la Sociedad Española*, La Rioja 1848, good food, popular lunches; *El Estribo*, Tucumán y Ayacucho, good cooking in attractive atmosphere, rec; *La Querencia*, Bolívar 322, on Plaza 9 de Julio, good value, rec; *Pizzería Los Pinos*, Sarmiento y Rivadavia, excellent and cheap; *Pizzería La Grata Alegría*, Bolívar y Junín, good; *Sukimo*, Azara nr San Martín, good for breakfast. The restaurant at San Martín 1788

serves excellent meals, good value. Several cheap places on Mitre nr the bus terminal, nr the market and on the road to the port.

● **Banks & money changers**
Banco de Iberá, Bolívar 1821 (main plaza), changes Amex cheques (4-5% commission); **Banco de La Nación**, Bolívar 1799, opens 0700-1215; **Banco Francés**, San Martín y San Lorenzo, Visa cash advance (am only); **Banco Nacional del Lavoro**, Plaza 9 de Julio, ATM accepts Mastercard and Visa. **Cambio Mazza**, Bolívar 1932 and Buenos Aires 1442, open Sat 0800-1200, TCs accepted. Street money changers on SW corner of Plaza 9 de Julio. If stuck when banks and *cambios* are closed, cross the river to Encarnación and use the street changers.

● **Embassies & consulates**
Consulates: Brazil, Mitre 631, T 24830, 0800-1200, visas issued free, photo required, 90 days given. *Paraguay*, San Lorenzo 179.

● **Entertainment**
Discos: *Los Años 60*, San Lorenzo y Entre Ríos; *Power Bolívar*, San Martín y Jujuy, open 0100-0500 Thur-Sun.

● **Laundry**
Lavemaster, Santiago del Estero y San Lorenzo, efficient.

● **Post & telecommunications**
Post Office: Bolívar y Ayacucho.

● **Tour companies & travel agents**
Viajes Turismo, Colón 1901, ask for Kenneth Nairn, speaks English, most helpful, good tours to Iguazú and local sights. Amex agent, *Express Travel*, Félix de Azara 2097, T 237687.

● **Tourist offices**
Colón 1985 y La Rioja, T 24360, helpful, maps and brochures in English of Posadas, Formosa and Iguazú Falls. Municipal kiosk on Plaza 9 de Julio, open 0800-1200, 1400-2000 daily. Hotel listings for Misiones province.

● **Transport**
Air Gen San Martín Airport, 12 km W, reached by Bus No 8 or 28 from nr bus terminal (ask at kiosk opp terminal) in 20 mins, US$0.45, taxi US$13. To **Buenos Aires**, Lapa (Junín 2054, T 40300) and Austral (Ayacucho 264, T 32889), both once a week via Corrientes; Lapa also to **Iguazú**, Austral to **Formosa**.

Buses Terminal at Uruguay y Mitre. Expreso Singer (Av Mitre 2447, T 24771/2) and Tigre bus terminal is 5 mins' walk from the main bus terminal To **Buenos Aires**, 15 hrs, shop around off season for best deal; Expreso Singer and Tigre-Iguazú each have several buses a day: *común* US$47.50, *diferencial* US$58, *ejecutivo* (with hot meal) US$70; some go via Resistencia, some via Concordia. From the Argentine side of the international bridge bus tickets to Buenos Aires are sold which inc taxi to bus terminal and breakfast. Frequent services to San Ignacio Miní, 1 hr, US$3.50, and Puerto Iguazú, *servicio común* US$16, 7 hrs, *expreso*, US$23, 5 hrs; to **Córdoba** with Singer and Litoral on alternate days at 1200, 19 hrs; to **Corrientes** US$18; to **Formosa**, US$8; to **Tucumán**, La Estrella, Tues, Thur, Sun 1720, 16 hrs, US$28; to **Resistencia**, 6-7 hrs, US$18; to **Concordia**, Expreso Singer, US$32, 2100 daily, 10 hrs; to **Concepción del Uruguay**, Singer, US$29, 11 hrs.

International To **Asunción**, Expreso Singer, daily 1400, 7 hrs, and Empresa Godoy, US$14; to **Montevideo**, a roundabout journey because the main Asunción-Montevideo route passes through Corrientes; alternative is Expreso Singer to the junction for Colón, at Villa San José (ACA hostel, C), local bus to Colón, bus over the bridge to Paysandú, then on to Montevideo. To Brazil via Uruguaiana, Singer, US$10-14, 6 hrs, 3 daily to **Paso de los Libres**, then cross the international bridge. Expreso Singer to **Porto Alegre**, via Oberá, Panambí, Santo Angelo and Carazinho, Tues, Thur, Sun at 1400, arriving 0345 next day.

FRONTIER WITH PARAGUAY

● **Argentine immigration and customs**
On the Argentine side of the bridge to Encarnación. Buses across the bridge (from opp bus terminal every 15 mins, *servicio común* US$1, *servicio diferencial* US$2) do not stop for formalities; alight, keep your ticket and luggage, and catch a later bus.

Pedestrians and cyclists are not allowed to cross; cyclists must ask officials for assistance. The ferry across the river is for locals only.

● **Exchange**
Pesos are accepted in Encarnación, so no need to change them back into dollars.

SAN IGNACIO MINI

63 km E of Posadas is the site of the most impressive Jesuit ruins in the Misiones region. San Ignacio (*Phone code* 0752) is a good base for visiting the other Jesuit ruins and for walking.

San Ignacio was founded on its present site in 1696. The 100m-square, grass-covered plaza, is flanked N, E and W by 30 parallel blocks of stone buildings with 10 small, one-room dwellings in each block. The roofs have gone, but the massive metre-thick walls are still standing ex-cept where they have been torn down by the *ibapoi* trees; each block was surrounded by a roofed gallery. The public buildings, some of them still 10m high, are on the S side of the plaza. In the centre are the ruins of a large church finished about 1724. The masonry, a red or yellow sandstone from the Río Paraná, was held together by a sandy mud. There is much bas-relief sculpture, mostly of floral designs.

200m inside the entrance to the ruins is the **Centro de Interpretación Jesuítico-Guaraní**, or 'Museo Vivo', with representations of the lives of the Guaraníes before the arrival of the Spanish, the work of the Jesuits and the consequences of their expulsion, as well as a fine model of the mission in its heyday; well laid out. **Museo Provincial**, contains a small collection of artefacts from Jesuit reducciones, open 0700-1900 daily. Son et-lumière show at the ruins, 2000 (not Mon or Tues) US$2.50, weekends only out of season, cancelled in wet weather, Spanish only, tickets from museum.

The site is maintained by UNESCO as a National Monument (open 0700-1900, entry US$2.50, US$10 with guide, tip appreciated if the guards look after your luggage). Allow about 1½ hrs for a leisurely visit. Go early to avoid crowds; good birdwatching. There are heavy rains in February. Mosquitoes can be a problem.

Excursions

To the ruins of two other Jesuit missions: **Loreto**, reached by a 3 km dirt road (signposted) which turns off the main road 6 km W of San Ignacio. Little remains other than a few walls, though excavations are in progress. Note the number of old trees with stones encased between their buttresses and main trunk.

● **Accommodation** *Colonial*, at entrance, secluded, recently opened.

Santa Ana, 16 km W, much less well preserved but more extensive in area than San Ignacio. Santa Ana was the site of the Jesuit iron foundry. The ruins are 1½ km along a path from the main road (signposted), entry US$1.

To the house of Horacio Quiroga, the Argentine writer, beautifully secluded, 2 km outside town, entry US$2, recommended. From here the path leads to Puerto Nuevo on the Río Paraná, from where, during summer, boats cross to Paraguay.

Local festivals
30-31 July.

Local information
● **Accommodation & places to eat**
B *Hostería San Ignacio*, T 70064, with breakfast, nice rooms, pleasant grounds; **C** *San Ignacio*, San Martín 823, T 70047, good, *cabañas*; **C** *Hosp El Descanso*, Pellegrini 270, T 70207, modern, quiet, owner speaks German, rec, excellent camping; **F** pp *Hosp Alemán Los Salpeterer*, Sarmiento y Centenario, 100m from bus station, kitchen, nice garden, run down but pleasant, 'pool', camping, rec, English and German spoken, owner Peter Sutter is helpful and has good travel information; **E** *Hosp Italia*, San Martín 1291, artists' house, dormitory style, laundry facilities, rec; **E** pp *Hosp de la Selva*, 5

km S on Route 12, **D** pp with meals, also cabins, horse riding, canoeing and ecological tours, English and German spoken, a good way to experience life on a farm, highly rec, ask at *Rest Don Valentín* (see below) and you will be given a lift there, rec; **D** pp *El Sol*, Chatsa 73, with breakfast, nice garden. *Restaurant Don Valentín*, good and cheap lunches. There are two *comedores* opp the entrance to the ruins. A shop opp the entrance sells huge homemade ice creams for US$2.50.

Camping: outside the ruins in municipal site, cold showers and toilets. Two pleasant sites by small lake about 5 km S of San Ignacio, on Route 12, cold showers only.

● **Transport**
Buses to/from **Posadas** every 30 mins-1 hr, US$3.50, last return bus at 2100; to **Puerto Iguazú**, US$14; to **Buenos Aires**, US$35 inc dinner, 24 hrs, dep 1800 or 1900.

SAN IGNACIO TO PUERTO IGUAZU

Route 12 runs direct NE via Jardín América, 48 km from San Ignacio (*Salto Tabei* campsite 2 km off Route 12, excellent, swimming,

---

The Real Mission

The Jesuits set up their first missions among the Guaraní Indians about 1609, in the region of Guaíra, now in Brazil. The missions flourished: cotton was introduced, the Indians wove their own clothes, dressed like Europeans, raised cattle, and built and sculpted and painted their own churches. But in 1627 they were violently attacked by the slave-hunting Bandeirantes from São Paulo, and by 1632 the position of the missions had become impossible: 12,000 converts, led by the priests, floated on 700 rafts down the Paranapanema into the Paraná, only to find their route made impassable by the Guaíra Falls. They pushed for 8 days through dense virgin forests on both sides of the river, then built new boats and continued their journey. 725 km from their old homes they founded new missions in what is now Paraguay, Argentine Misiones, and Brazilian Rio Grande do Sul. By the early 18th century there were, on both sides of the river, 30 mission villages with a combined population of over 100,000 souls. Only four of these show any signs of their former splendour: San Ignacio Miní, São Miguel (Brazil), and Jesús and Trinidad (Paraguay). (Note Trinidad can also be visited by bus from Posadas. See Paraguay section for details.) At the height of its prosperity in 1731 San Ignacio contained 4,356 people. In 1767, Charles III of Spain expelled the Jesuits from Spanish territory; the Franciscans and Dominicans then took over. After the Jesuits had gone, there was a rapid decline in prosperity. By 1784 there were only 176 Indians at San Ignacio Miní; by 1810, none remained. By order of the Paraguayan dictator Francia, all the settlements were evacuated in 1817, and San Ignacio was set on fire. The village was lost in the jungle until it was discovered again in 1897. In 1943 an agency of the Argentine Government took control. Some of the craft work produced at the settlement can be seen at two museums in Buenos Aires: the Museo Colonial Isaac Fernández Blanco and the municipal Museo de Arte Colonial.

fishing, restaurant, cabins, rec). The main highway continues through **Capioví** (restaurant, *Salto*, and campsite, with a room with beds for budget travellers, pleasant, near Capioví Falls; owner speaks German and English), **Puerto Rico**, 21 km N of Jardín América (hotel, restaurants, poor campsite), and **Montecarlo**, 38 km further N, where there is a zoo and a *yerba mate* packing plant which can be visited. (ACA *hostería*, T 97023, highly recommended; *Hotels Ideal* and *Kayken*, both **C**; good campsite with pool.)

ELDORADO

(*Pop* 14,440; *Phone code* 0751), a prosperous small town 16 km further N, is surrounded by flourishing *mate*, tung, citrus, eucalyptus and tobacco plantations. The ACA office is very helpful and has a large illuminated map of Eldorado and its surroundings. For information on the **Misiones Rainforest Reserve**, contact Daphne Colcombet, T (0751) 21351.

● **Accommodation** **A3** *Hostería ACA*, T 21370, pool, good facilities; **C** *Atlántida*, San Martín 3087, T 21441, a/c, pool, parking, good restaurants, rec; **C** *Esmeralda*, Av San Martín, Km 8, basic; **C** *Ilex*, Av San Martín, Km 9, safe; *Gran Riojano*, Av San Martín 314, T 22217, 5 mins' walk from main road crossing, with restaurant. **Camping**: Municipal site in Parque Schweim, Av San Martín, Km 1, T 2154, free, good.

Near **Wanda**, 42 km further N, at Km 1593, there are two open-cast amethyst and quartz mines which sell gems. There are free guided tours to one of them, Tierra Colorada, daily. Regular buses from Posadas and Puerto Iguazu, then walk 1½ km. Nearby at **Puerto Esperanza** is the **C** pp *Hotel Las Brisas*, Swiss owned, English and German spoken, discount for Swiss nationals. (Buses between Posadas and Puerto Iguazú stop near the mines and the hotel.)

OBERA AND THE INTERIOR OF MISIONES

East of Santa Ana (95 km from Posadas) is **Oberá** (*Pop* 42,000), the second largest town in Misiones. There is a Parque de Naciones, with houses to commemorate the nationalities of all the immigrants who

founded the town (Fiesta Nacional del Inmigrante first week in Oct).

Museums Museo de Ciencias Naturales; ceramics workshops; Criadero de Pájaros Wendlinger (with birds of the region); Serpentario, La Paz (with snakes of Misiones), best visited 1000-1200; and the many tea and mate-leaf drying factories can be visited.

● **Accommodation** *Cuatro Pinos*, Av Sarmiento 853, T 21306, good value; **C** *Real*, opp bus terminal, T 22761, basic, hot showers; *Res Anahi*, Santiago del Estero 36, T 21127, many others; campsite 6 km outside town on road to Santa Ana, with swimming pool and waterfall nearby.

● **Places to eat** *Enqüete* restaurant, Cabeza de Vaca 340, good; excellent *empanadas* at *Bar Terminal* next to bus terminal.

● **Tourist offices** Plazoleta Güemes, Libertad 90, open 0700-1900, Sat 0700-1300, very helpful, lots of maps.

● **Buses** To Posadas, 2 hrs, US$5.50, Expreso Singer; once a day to/from **Iguazú**, 5 hrs.

Route 14 runs NE from Oberá through the heart of Misiones. It passes through **Dos de Mayo** (**C** *Hotel Alex*, clean), **Paraíso** (Maconá falls 82 km away), **San Pedro** and **Tobuna** where there are the Alegría falls.

● **Accommodation** At **Palmera Boca**, 3 km from San Pedro: **C** *American Hotel*, Güemes 670, T 3364, meals served; **C** *Posada Itaroga*, T 0751-70165, a family farm with log houses beside a lake, swimming and rowing boats, inc breakfast, cooking facilities, peaceful, relaxed, rec.

From Tobuna Route 17 heads W to Eldorado through lovely vegetation, or NE to **Bernardo Yrigoyen**, on the Brazilian frontier (**C** ACA *Motel*, T 0751-92026, Ruta Nacional 14, Km 1435, clean, friendly). The direct (dirt) road N from Bernardo Yrigoyen to Puerto Iguazu, 142 km, crosses the National Park of Iguazú, via the quiet attractive villages of Andrecito (**C** *Res Los Robles*, clean, quiet, nice), Cabuneí and San Antonio, offering fine views of rainforest.

● **Buses** There are services to B Yrigoyen from Eldorado and Oberá; from B Yrigoyen local buses run to Iguazú through the national park in dry weather.

THE IGUAZU FALLS

For specific references to the Brazilian side of the Falls, with accommodation and transport links, see Southern Brazil section, the Paraná River. For a general description, local transport arrangements, and specific Argentine references, see below.

The **Iguazú Falls**, on the Argentina-Brazil border 19 km upstream from the confluence of the Río Iguazú with the Río Alto Paraná, are the most overwhelming falls in South America. The main falls are 20m higher than Niagara and about half as wide again. The Río Iguazú (*guazú* is Guaraní for big and *I* is Guaraní for water), which rises in the Brazilian hills near Curitiba, receives the waters of some 30 rivers as it crosses the plateau. Above the main falls the river, sown with wooded islets, opens out to a width of 4 km. There are rapids for $3\frac{1}{2}$ km above the 60m precipice over which the water plunges in 275 falls over a frontage of 2,470m, at a rate of 1,750 cubic metres a second.

Above the impact of the water upon basalt rock hovers a perpetual 30m high cloud of mist in which the sun creates blazing rainbows. Viewed from below, the tumbling water in its setting of begonias, orchids, fern and palms with toucans, flocks of parrots and cacique birds, swifts (*vencejos*) dodging in and out of the very falls, and myriads of butterflies (at least 500 different species), is majestically beautiful, especially outside the cool season (when the water is much diminished, as are the birds and insects). The first European visitor to the falls was the Spaniard Alvar Núñez Cabeza de Vaca in 1541, on his search for a connection between the Brazilian coast and the Río de la Plata.

On both sides of the falls there are National Parks. Transport between the two parks is via the Ponte Tancredo Neves as there is no crossing at the falls themselves. The Brazilian park offers a superb panoramic view of the whole falls and is best visited in the morning when the light is better for photography (entry fee payable in reais only). The Argentine park (which requires a day to explore properly) offers closer views of the individual falls in their forest setting with its wildlife and butterflies, though to appreciate these properly you need to go early and get well away from the visitors areas. Busiest times are holiday periods and on Sun. Both parks have visitors' centres, though the information provided by the Argentine Centre is far superior to that in the Brazilian Centre.

Parque Nacional Iguazú The park covers an area of 55,000 ha. The fauna includes jaguars, tapirs, brown capuchin monkeys, collared anteaters, coatimundi along with a huge variety of birds; among the butterflies are shiny blue morphos and red/black heliconius.

Entry US$5, payable in pesos or dollars only (guests at *Hotel Internacional* should pay and get tickets stamped at the hotel to avoid paying again). Visitors' Centre includes a museum of local fauna and an auditorium for periodic slide shows (on request, minimum 8 people), no commentary, only music; it also sells a good guide book on Argentine birds.

The Garganta del Diablo or Devil's Throat, the most spectacular of the falls, can be visited from Puerto Canoas (reached by bus – see below – or by car, parking US$1). Boats (US$6) link Puerto Canoas with the remains of a series of catwalks (damaged several times by floods, most recently in 1986) which lead to a point above the Garganta, particularly recommended in the evening when the light is best and the swifts are returning to roost on the cliffs, some behind the water (trips by dingy down river from Puerto Canoas to Visitors Centre, 1 hr, US$4, relaxing but not much wildlife).

A trail starting behind the *Hotel Internacional* leads down to the Circuito Inferior and the Río Iguazu ferry to Isla San Martín, ferry leaves on demand, free, 3 mins (may not run in rainy season). A path on the island leads to the top of the hill, where there are trails to some of the less visited falls and rocky pools (take bathing gear in summer to cool off).

Away from the falls are a bird hide overlooking a marsh (Bañado); the Macuco trail, a 4 km-long nature trail in the forest, with a natural pool (El Pozón) fed by a waterfall and good for swimming. Another nature trail leads from the old airstrip, near the start of the Macuco trail, and follows the route of the old road to Puerto Iguazú.

Iguazú Jungle Explorer offer a range of services including Aventura Náutica, a powerboat trip on the river below the falls, US$30, and tours of the jungle by jeep (Spanish only) 'good fun but not a serious nature experience'; these are sold through agencies in Puerto Iguazú as well as direct in the Park. There are also nighttime walking tours between the *Hotel Internacional* and the falls when the moon is

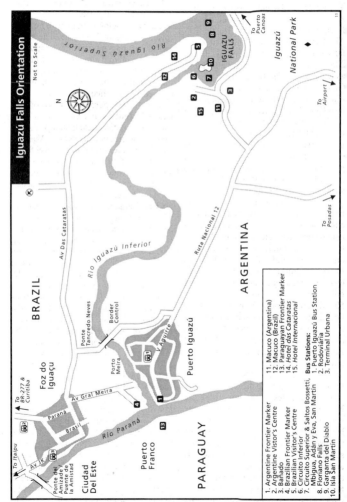

Iguazú Falls Orientation

Not to Scale

BRAZIL

Foz do Iguaçu

Ciudad Del Este

PARAGUAY

Puerto Franco

Puerto Iguazú

ARGENTINA

Iguazú National Park

IGUAZU FALLS

Río Iguazú Superior

Río Iguazú Inferior

Río Paraná

Ruta Nacional 12

Av Das Cataratas

Av Gral Meira

Ponte Tancredo Neves

Border Control

Porto Meira

Ponte del Amizade/ Puente de la Amistad

To Puerto Canoas

To Airport

To Posadas

To BR-277 & Curitiba

To Itaipu

1. Argentine Frontier Marker
2. Argentine Visitor's Centre
3. Bañado
4. Brazilian Frontier Marker
5. Brazilian Visitor's Centre
6. Circuito Inferior
7. Circuito Superior & Saltos Bossetti, Mbigua, Adán y Eva, San Martín
8. Floriano Falls
9. Garganta del Diablo
10. Isla San Martín
11. Macuco (Argentina)
12. Macuco (Brazil)
13. Paraguayan Frontier Marker
14. *Hotel das Cataratas*
15. *Hotel Internacional*

Bus Stations:
1. Puerto Iguazú Bus Station
2. Rodoviária
3. Terminal Urbana

full; on clear nights the moon casts a blue halo over the falls. Mountain bikes and boats can also be hired, US$3 an hour. For serious birdwatching and nature walks with English speaking guide contact Daniel Samay (*Explorador* agency) or Miguel Castelino through the Visitors' Centre, highly rec. Helicopter rides over the falls leave from the Brazilian side, US$50 pp, 7 mins. Apart from disturbing visitors, the helicopters are also reported to present a threat to some bird species which are laying thinner-shelled eggs.

In the rainy season, when water levels are high, waterproof coats or swimming costumes are advisable for some of the lower catwalks and for boat trips. Cameras should be carried in a plastic bag. Wear shoes with good soles, as the rocks can be very slippery in places.

Park information

● Accommodation & food

See under Puerto Iguazú or Foz do Iguaçu. Prices are very similar, though Puerto Iguazú is much safer. Food and drinks are available in the Park but are expensive so best to take your own.

● Transport

Transportes Cataratas buses run every 30-45 mins from Puerto Iguazú bus terminal, stopping at the National Park entrance for the purchase of entry tickets and continuing to Puerto Canoas. Fares US$2 to Visitors' Centre, US$2.50 to Puerto Canoas, payable in pesos, dollars or reais. First bus 0640, last 1700, last return 1900, journey time 30 mins (sometimes erratic, especially when it is wet). There are fixed rates for taxis, US$30, up to 5 people. A tour from the bus terminal, taking in both sides of the Falls, costs US$40. For transport between the Argentine and Brazilian sides see below under Puerto Iguazú.

Motorists visiting the Argentine side from Brazil can park overnight in the National Park, free. Taxis between the border and Puerto Iguazú cost US$15 and between the border and *Hotel Internacional Iguazú* cost US$35. Between Oct and Feb (daylight saving dates change each year) Brazil is 1 hr ahead of Argentina.

PUERTO IGUAZÚ

A small town (*Pop* 19,000; *Phone code* 0757) above the river on the Argentine side; at the far end of Av Tres Fronteras there is a *mirador* overlooking the confluence of rivers Iguazú and Alto Paraná, with several tourist souvenir and crafts stalls.

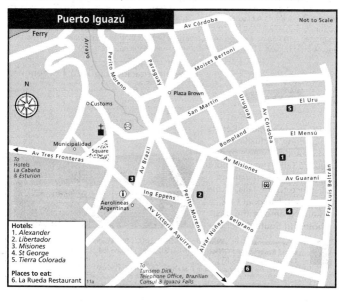

Puerto Iguazú

Not to Scale

Hotels:
1. Alexander
2. Libertador
3. Misiones
4. St George
5. Tierra Colorada

Places to eat:
6. La Rueda Restaurant

Museums

Museo Mbororé, San Martín 231, Mon-Sat 0900-1200, 1600-2000, Sun 1600-2000, US$1, exhibition on Guaraní culture, also sells Guaraní made handicrafts, cheaper than shops.

Local information

● Accommodation

Crowded during summer (Jan-Feb), Easter and July holiday periods and busy at other times of the year. Accommodation is generally expensive. Outside the high season be prepared to shop around and to bargain.

L2-L3 *Internacional Iguazú*, T 21600, 5-star, pool, casino, good restaurants, business facilities, overlooking the falls, rooms with garden views cost less, excellent, check-out can take ages. Reservations at Av Eduardo Madero 1020, Buenos Aires (T 311-4259, or 313-629, in UK through Utell Internacional, in USA T 1-800-Insignia); *Cataratas*, Route 12, Km 4, T 21000, F 21090, 5-star, pool, gymnasium.

A1 *Esturión*, Av Tres Fronteras 650, T 20020, clean, comfortable, swimming pool, good restaurant, reservations at Belgrano 265, p10, Buenos Aires; **A3** *Alexander*, Córdoba 685, T 20249, T 20566, opp bus station, a/c, inc breakfast, pool, rec; **A3** *La Cabaña*, Av Tres Fronteras 434, T 20564, with breakfast, a/c, good, with an older part and a new annexe, swimming pool, rec; **A3** *Las Orquídeas*, Ruta 12, Km 5, T 20472, in the National Park, very comfortable; **A3** *Saint George*, Av Córdoba 148, T 20633, F 20651, with breakfast, comfortable, pool and garden, good, expensive restaurant, **B** in older part, highly rec.

B *Hostería Casa Blanca*, Guaraní 121, T 21320, 2 blocks from bus station, with breakfast, fan, large rooms with phone, rec. Behind *Saint George* is **B** *Hostería Los Helechos*, Amarante 76 (off Córdoba), T 20338, with breakfast, owner speaks German, pleasant, fan, motel-style accommodation, 10% discount for ISIC and YHA card holders, pool; **B** *Gloria*, Av Uruguay 344, pool, quiet; **B** *Libertador*, Bompland 110, T 20416, modern, central, helpful, large bedrooms and public rooms, rooms at back have balconies overlooking garden and swimming pool; **B** *Tierra Colorada*, Córdoba y El Urú 265, T 20649, very good, with fan, trips arranged.

C *Res Lilian*, Beltrán 183, T 20968, 2 blocks from bus terminal, helpful, safe, rec; **C** *Res Río Selva*, San Lorenzo 147, T 21555, laundry facilities, large garden, use of swimming pool, communal barbecue, highly rec; **C** *King*, Aguirre 209, T 20917, pool, hot showers, good value; **C** *Misiones*, Aquirre 304, T 20991, with breakfast, fan; **C** *Res Paquita*, Av Córdoba 158, T 20434, opp bus terminal, nice setting, some rooms with terrace, rec; **C** *Res San Fernando*, Córdoba y Guaraní, T 21429, close to bus station, popular, **D** in low season.

Youth hostel: *Hosp Uno*, Beltrán 116, T 20529, **E** pp with bath, **F** pp dormitory, friendly, clean, rec, tour to Itaipú, Foz de Iguazú and Brazilian side of falls. The Tourist Office has a list of *Casas Familiares* (**E** pp), though it may be reluctant to find private accommodation unless the hotels are full.

Hotel Internacional Iguazú / Argentina

THE FALLS & JUNGLE RESORT

180 rooms' Deluxe Resort offering exclusive and outstanding views of the Iguazú Falls. The only hotel located within walking distance to the falls, at the Iguazú National Park. Ranked among the best hotels in South America.

Reservations: UTELL/INSIGNIA RESORTS USA 1-800-Insignia
Hotel Reservations Office: Fax (54.1) 312.0488 · Phone (54.1) 311.4259
CRS Access Codes: IG or UI
Website: www.iguazufalls.com **E-Mail:** iguazu@impsat1.com

Camping: free site 600m past parking area at Puerto Canoas. Tables, but no other facilities, nearest drinking water at park entrance. Camping sometimes permitted at the school just inside the Park entrance. Municipal campsite in Puerto Iguazú reported 'grim'. Camping El Pindó at the edge of town, charges US$1.60 pp, plus charge for tent and for use of pool, friendly, but very run down. There are also facilities at Complejo Turístico Americano, Km 5, Route 12, T 2782 inc pool (open to non-guests, US$2.50) in pleasant, wooded gardens, but no food; US$3 pp, US$3/car, US$3/tent.

● **Places to eat**
La Rueda, Av Córdoba 28, good food at reasonable prices; *Pizzería Ser*, Victoria Aguirre 453, good pizzas; *Charo*, Córdoba 106, good food, popular with locals, no credit cards; *Don Nicola*, Bompland 555, good; *El Criollito*, Av Tres Fronteras 62, rec; *Casa de Comercio*, Aguirre 327; *Tomás*, Córdoba y Misiones, at bus terminal, open 24 hrs, *tenedor libre*; *Chapa*, behind bus station, cheap, highly rec; *Fechoria*, Ing Eppens 294, good *empanadas*; *Panificadora Real*, Cordoba y Guarani, good bread.

● **Airline offices**
Aerolínas Argentinas, Brasil y Aguirre, T 20194; **Lapa**, Bompland 110, loc 7, T 20214.

● **Banks & money changers**
Three *casas de cambio* opp the tourist office and several on Av Aguirre towards the outskirts of town towards the falls inc **Dick**, changes TCs, at high commission (up to 10%). Kiosk at the bus terminal poor rates. Rates vary so shop around. Alternatively change US$ in Foz do Iguaçu and buy pesos in Puerto Iguazú. Nowhere to get cash on Visa.

● **Tour companies & travel agents**
Turismo Dick, Aguirre 226, T 20778, also in Foz do Iguaçu; *Reinhard Foerster*, Privat Servis, Av Tres Fronteras 335, T 2774, offers naturalists' and birdwatchers' programmes; *Turismo Cuenca del Plata*, Amarante 76, T 20338, offers 10% discount to ISIC and youth card holders on local excursions. Recommended taxi-guide, Juan Villalba, T 20973 (radiotaxi 044), good value, speaks basic English. *Kurtz*, at terminal, T/F 21599, helpful, rec; *Africana Tours*, Esmeralda 358, Buenos Aires T/F 394-1720, are rec for their complete package, by plane or bus, in all tours, hotels and half-board (US$167-598 depending on hotel). Many agencies eg *Flyer Turismo*, run tours from Buenos Aires, starting at US$75 for 1-day.

● **Tourist offices**
Aguirre 396, T 20800, open Mon-Fri 0800-1200, 1500-2000, Sat/Sun 0800-1200, 1630-2000.

● **Transport**
Local Car hire: Avis at airport. Localiza, at airport and Aguirre 279, T 20975. Cars may be taken to the Brazilian side for an extra US$5.

Air There is an Argentine domestic airport nr the Falls, and a Brazilian international airport about half-way between Foz do Iguaçu and the Falls. Taxi between the two airports US$25. Expreso del Valle buses (T 20348) run between Argentine airport and bus terminal to connect with plane arrivals and departures, US$3; check times at Aerolíneas Argentinas office in Puerto Iguazú. Taxis charge US$10 to *Hotel Internacional* and at least US$18 to Puerto Iguazú and US$14 to Foz do Iguazú.

AR and Lapa fly direct to/from Buenos Aires (1 hr 50 mins). For best view on landing, sit on right side of aircraft.

Buses To/from **Buenos Aires**, 21 hrs, Expreso Singer, Expreso Tigre, Expreso Iguazú and other companies daily, US$39-45 *común*, US$65 *cama* (some offer student discounts). It is cheaper to take a local bus to Posadas and then rebook. To **Santiago del Estero**, Wed and Sat at 0130, 20 hrs, Cotal, gives student discount; to **Córdoba**, via Posadas, 23 hrs, US$40, Singer or El Litoral or Cruzero del Norte *semi-cama*; to **Rosario** daily except Thur, US$50; to **Posadas**, stopping at San Ignacio Miní, frequent, 5 hrs, US$23, *expreso*, 7 hrs, US$16 *servicio común*; to **San Ignacio Miní**, US$14 *servicio común*, US$17 *rápido*; to **Resistencia** daily 1430 and 2200, 11 hrs, US$30 (change there for Bolivian border at Aguas Blancas/Bermejo, via Güemes and Orán); to **El Dorado**, 2 hrs, Cotal US$5; to **Salta**, via Tucumán, Tues, Thur, Sun 1100, Itatí, 12 hrs, US$80.

FRONTIER WITH BRAZIL

This crossing via the Puente Tancredo Neves is straightforward. If crossing on a day visit no immigration formalities are required.

Argentine immigration is at the Brazilian end of the bridge. If entering Argentina buses stop at immigration.

● **Brazilian Consulate**
In Puerto Iguazú, Guaraní y Esquiu, 0800-1200.

● **Transport**
Buses leave Puerto Iguazú terminal every 20 mins, US$1.50 but do not wait at the frontier so if you need exit and entry keep your ticket and catch the next bus (bus companies do not recognise each other's tickets).

FRONTIER WITH PARAGUAY

Ferry service from the port in Puerto Iguazú to Tres Fronteras is for locals only (no immigration facilities). Crossing to Paraguay is via Puente Tancredo Neves to Brazil and then via the Puente de la Amistad to Ciudad del Este. Brazilian entry and exit stamps are not required unless you are stopping in Brazil.

● **Paraguayan Consulate**
Bompland 355.

● **Transport**
Direct buses (non-stop in Brazil), leave Puerto Iguazú terminal every 30 mins, US$2, 45 mins, liable to delays especially in crossing the bridge to Ciudad del Este.

THE CHACO

Between the NW highlands and the Río Paraná to the E lies the Argentine Chaco, comprising the entire provinces of Formosa and Chaco, parts of Salta, Santiago del Estero and Santa Fe, and a tiny corner of the province of Córdoba. Its S limit is the Río Dulce valley. It is a sprawling alluvial lowland, rising gradually toward the W, covered by palm savanna and sometimes impenetrable thorn scrub; the birdlife is abundant and interesting.

Climate There are two climatic zones: the Dry Chaco and the Humid Chaco, each with distinct flora and fauna. South America's highest temperatures, exceeding 45°C, have been recorded here, but winters are mild, with an occasional touch of frost in the S. Rain falls mostly in summer, decreasing from E to W.

Numerous **Indian peoples**, who call themselves Wichi, inhabit the Chaco, including the Toba, Mataco, Mocoví and Pilagá.

Economy The Chaco is mostly cattle country, consisting of large *estancias* with low stocking rates. Tannin and cotton are the traditional industries together with sunflowers, maize and sorghum. The iron-hard *quebracho* (axe-breaker) tree, which grows only in the Argentine and Paraguayan Chaco, is the purest known source of tannin. The industry is struggling against competition from synthetic tannin and the huge mimosa plantations in South Africa. The more accessible eastern forests have nearly disappeared; deforestation of all species is proceeding rapidly in the N and W of the province, which produces charcoal for a military steel foundry in Jujuy. Small roadside factories also produce custom furniture.

Towns of the Chaco The most important ones – Resistencia and Formosa – are described under Argentine Mesopotamia. Apart from Roque Sáenz Peña, the only other town of any importance is Santiago del Estero, on the W boundary of the Chaco.

ROQUE SAENZ PENA

Route 16, the main road across the Chaco runs NW from Resistencia to connect with Route 9, the main northern highway, N of Metán and provides the quickest route between Paraguay and NW Argentina. It is mostly paved, several tolls. **Presidencia Roque Sáenz Peña** (*Pop* 75,000; *Phone code* 0714), 160 km NW of Resistencia on Route 16, offers almost no shade for relief from the overpowering summer heat. The Parque Zoológico, 3 km from the centre, is one of the best in the country, containing a wide variety of animals native to the Chaco, as well as a botanical reserve of local species.

● **Accommodation A2** *Gualok*, San Martín 1198, T 20521, inc use of thermal baths (also available to non-residents for a small charge); **A3** *Augustus*, Belgrano 483, T 22809, a/c; *Res Asturias*, Belgrano 402, T 20210, fair; *Res Sáenz Peña*, Sub Palmira 464, T 20320, nr bus station, cheap.

● **Buses** To Buenos Aires, daily 2000, US$40 (from Buenos Aires also daily 2000), La Estrella and La Internacional alternate days; to **Santiago del Estero** and Tucumán, Empresa El Rayo daily; to **Resistencia** (connection for Salta 1700 daily), 2 hrs, US$4.

Central Sáenz Peña has buses at 1100, 1530 and 2000 to the village of **Castelli**, about 100 km N, which has a large Toba Indian community and an *artesanía* shop (**E** *Hotel Guc*, basic).

PARQUE NACIONAL CHACO

Between Resistencia and Sáenz Peña, an ecological island of 15,000 ha, preserves some of the last remaining eastern Chaco forest and savanna. It is a good place to see the region's abundant bird life. Flora includes three species of *quebracho* as well as the palo borracho. The park keeper offers a 1-2-hr walk, explaining the region's plants and animals, rec.

- **Accommodation** Camping facilities, good, free, cold showers, but the nearest supplies are in Capitán Solari, 6 km from the park entrance.
- **Buses** From Resistencia 4 daily, 2½ hrs, US$6, as far as Capitán Solari.

ROUTES ACROSS THE CHACO 31 km NW of Roque Sáenz Peña is **Avia Terai**, where the road forks. Provincial Route 94 goes SW to Gen Pinedo, then continues paved as national Route 89 to Quimilí and Santiago del Estero.

Federico Kirbus tells us that on the border of Chaco and Santiago del Estero provinces on this road is **Campo del Cielo**, a meteorite impact field about 15 km by 4 km where about 5,000 years ago a planetoid broke before landing into 30 main pieces. Some of the meteorites are on display in Buenos Aires (the Rivadavia Museum and the Planetarium), but the largest, 'El Chaco' (33.4 tonnes), is on display at the Campo. Access at Gancedo, where you travel 15 km S to Las Viboras. From Avia Terai, Route 16, heading NW passes through **Pampa del Infierno** to the Santiago del Estero border. In Santiago province the road is good to Los Tigres, then less good to the Salta border. From this border to **Macapillo**, it is straight, well-paved. After Macapillo Route 16 continues to **Joaquín V González**, around which the road is appalling and difficult after rain, then to Ceibalito, El Tunal and on to Route 9. At Ceibalito, 18 km beyond González, an excellent lateral detour leaves Route 16 to connect with provincial Route 5 (passing Parque Nacional Finca El Rey, see page 123) and Route 9 at Lumbreras. The J V González stretch can be avoided by a dust-road detour between just past Macapillo to El Tunal, via Corral Quemado.

- **Useful services** There are service stations at Roque Sáenz Peña, Pampa del Infierno (ACA *Hostería*), Pampa de los Guanacos (good hot, clean and free showers at the YPF station, and good value set dinner at the *comedor* next door), **Taco Pozo** (basic *Hospedaje* ½ block from ACA station), **El Quebrachal** (gaucho festival in late Nov) and J V González (last fuel before Güemes en route to Salta). Fuel cannot be pumped during frequent power cuts. In general, Chaco roads are poor.

The Lake District

THE LAKE DISTRICT contains a series of great lakes strung along the foot of the Andes from above 40° to below 50° in the Los Glaciares National Park area. In the north the western end of these lakes cut deeply into the mountains, their water lapping the forested skirts of some of the most spectacular snow-capped peaks in the world; their eastern ends are contained by the frontal moraines deposited there by the ancient glaciers which gouged out these huge lakes. The water is a deep blue, sometimes lashed into white froth by the region's high winds. The area is good for fishing, watersports, walking, climbing and skiing.

See the Chilean chapter, **The Lake District**, page 760 for map and details of the system of lakes on the far side of the Andes. These can be visited through various passes.

NB Off season, from mid-Aug to mid-Nov, many excursions, boat trips, etc, run on a limited schedule, if at all. Public transport is also limited. For **Fishing**, see page 224.

ROUTES Neuquén is a major stop en route from the E coast to the northern lakes and Bariloche. From Buenos Aires, Route 5 goes via **Chivilcoy** (*Pop* 49,000) and **Pehuajó** (*Pop* 28,500) to **Santa Rosa** (*Pop* 75,000; *Phone code* 0954), capital of La Pampa province, 619 km from Buenos Aires.

● **Accommodation In Santa Rosa**: A2 *Calfucura*, San Martín 695, T 23608, 4-star, no meals, but excellent steak restaurant round the corner; **B** *Hostería Río Atuel*, Luro 256, opp bus terminal, T 22597, very good; **C** *San Martín*, Alsina 101, T 22549, restaurant, garage; **C** *Motel Calden*, Route 35, Km 330, T 24311, good restaurant attached, large rooms.

79 km S of Santa Rosa on Route 35 a road heads 28 km W to **General Acha** after which desert has to be crossed either on Route 20 to Cruz del Desierto and Catriel (no fuel on this stretch), thence on Route 151 to Neuquén, or on Route 152 to Chelforó on Route 22.

Route 22 is the main alternative, direct from Bahía Blanca, cutting across the southern tip of La Pampa to Río Colorado (campsite with all facilities), on the river of the same name. (Bus to Buenos Aires 0100, 11 hrs, US$30.) It then runs through northern Río Negro to **Choele Choel** on the Río Negro itself, 308 km from Bahía Blanca. Large fruit growing areas at Choele Choel and Villa Regina are irrigated from the Río Negro dam. An unbroken series of groves of tall trees shelter the vineyards and orchards.

● **Accommodation Choele Choel**: **B** *ACA Motel* on edge of town, T/F 0946-2394, Ruta Nacional 22, Km 1,006, good restaurant at bus station, and fine modern *Hotel Choele Choel*; several other hotels; free municipal campsite beside Río Negro, shady, excellent, no showers.

NEUQUEN

(*Pop* 90,000; *Phone code* 099) Founded 1904 on the W side of the confluence of the Ríos Limay and Neuquén (223 km from Choele Choel by Route 22), Neuquén is a pleasant provincial capital. It serves both the oilfields to the W and the surrounding fruit orchards. There are also many wine *bode-*

gas nearby. At the Parque Centenario is a *mirador* with good views of the city and the confluence of the rivers, where they become the Negro (be sure *not* to take the bus to Centenario industrial suburb). Facing Neuquén and connected by bridge is Cipolletti, in Río Negro province (*Pop* 43,600) a prosperous centre of the fruit-growing region.

Museums

Museo Histórico Dr Gregorio Alvarez, San Martín 280; **Museo de Ciencias Naturales**, at entrance to airport (as is the Casino); **Museo Provincial Carlos Ameghino**, Yrigoyen 1047, modest but interesting.

Excursions

Paved roads lead 33 km N to the artificial and natural swimming pools at the Ballester dam (take bus marked 'Banda del Medio' from terminal); nearby is artificial Lago Pellegrini, where watersports are held. A narrow-gauge railway with sporadic services runs via Cipolletti to Contralmirante Cordero, 7 km from the dam. All the towns in the valley celebrate the Fiesta Nacional de la Manzana (apples are the main local crop) in the second half of March.

Local information
● **Accommodation**
L3 *del Comahue*, Av Argentina 387, T 480112, 4-star, very good; **A2** *Res Arrayán*, Ruta 22, T 466128, with breakfast, parking, pool; **A3** *Apolo*, Av Olascoaga 361, T 422334, good, but overpriced; *ACA Cipolletti*, Ruta Nacional 22 y Av Luis Toschi, just outside Neuquén, T 71827.

B *Italia*, Justo 782, T 422234; **B** *Huemel*, Tierra del Fuego 335, T 422344.

C *Res Inglés*, San Martín 534, T 422252; **C** *Res Belgrano*, Rivadavia 283, T 424311.

D pp Montevideo 555, nr bus terminal; 13 km S on Zapala road is **A1** *Hostal del Caminante*, T 466118, with pool and garden, popular. Municipal **camping** site nr river, free, local police warn that it's dangerous.

● **Places to eat**
Las Tres Marías, Alberdi 126, excellent. Cheap places on Av Mitre opp bus station.

● **Airline offices**
Austral, Santa Fe 54, T 422409; Lapa, Av Argentina 30, T 438555; TAN, 25 de Mayo 180,

T 423076 (430096 at airport); **Kaiken**, Av Argentina 327, T 471333; **Southern Winds**, Av Argentina 327, T 487248.

● **Banks & money changers**
Pullman, Alcorta 144, T 422438.

● **Post & telecommunications**
Post Office: Rivadavia y Santa Fe.

● **Tourist offices**
San Martín y Río Negro, T 424089, Mon-Fri 0730-2000, Sat 0800-1500.

● **Transport**
Local Car mechanic: Normando Toselli, Mitre 801, Neuquén 8300 (Former South American superbike champion), for cars or motorbikes, highly rec.

Air Airport 7 km W of centre. Taxi US$8. To Buenos Aires, Austral and Lapa; to Bahía Blanca, Lapa. The regional airline TAN flies to many Argentine cities inc Bahía Blanca, Comodoro Rivadavia, Córdoba, Mendoza, Bariloche, San Martín de los Andes and, in Chile, Puerto Montt and Temuco. Kaiken flies to Comodoro Rivadavia, Esquel, Bariloche, Trelew, Ushuaia and Calafate, among others. Southern Winds to Comodoro Rivadavia and Córdoba.

Buses Terminal at Mitre 147. La Estrella/El Cóndor, El Valle and Chevallier to **Buenos Aires** daily US$44, 18½ hrs. Connections with **Copahue**, **Córdoba, San Rafael** (US$20) and **San Martín de los Andes** (US$22, 4 hrs); to **Zapala** daily, 7 hrs; to **Mar del Plata**, US$40, 12 hrs; to **Bariloche**, La Estrella or Chevallier (not El Valle as it stops too often), sit on left; to **Mendoza**, Andesmar, daily, US$46; La Unión del Sud to **Temuco** (Chile) via Zapala all year three times a week, and Ruta Sur twice a week, US$30, 16 hrs.

ROUTES Driving from Neuquén to Bariloche, go via El Chocón hydroelectric lake, Junín and San Martín (both 'de los Andes'), taking Routes 237, 40 and 234; route more attractive than that via Zapala. The most direct road to Bariloche (426 km) is by Route 237, then Route 40, missing Junín and San Martín. The road is fast, skirting the entire length of the reservoir formed by the Ezequiel Ramos Mejía dam. Then it drops over an escarpment to cross the Collón Curá river before following the Río Limay valley to Confluencia (see page 192) and the Valle Encantado.

ZAPALA

Route 22 runs W from Neuquén to **Zapala** (179 km, *Pop* 20,000) through the oil zone at Challacó, Cutral-Có and Plaza Huincul (at the local Carmen Funes municipal mu-

seum, there are the vertebrae of a dinosaur, believed to be the largest that ever lived on Earth; its vertebra are estimated to have weighed 70 kg each; a recovered tibia is 1.60m in length). There is an excellent geology museum (open only to 1300, entry free, closed weekends). Among the collections of minerals, fossils, shells and rocks, is a complete crocodile jaw, believed to be 80 million-years-old. There is an airport and an ACA service station.

The **Parque Nacional Laguna Blanca** 35 km SW of Zapala is known for its animal and bird life (notably black-necked swans), though the areas where most birds can be seen are closed. Small museum, free camping. It can be reached by an unmarked turning off Route 40 about 10 km S of Zapala. The park entrance is 10 km from this turning, and the lagoon lies 4-5 km beyond. No public transport and little traffic makes hitchhiking difficult. Advice may be available at the *guardaparque's* office on Vidal, next to *Hotel Pehuén*, in Zapala.

● **Accommodation A3** *Hue Melén*, Almte Brown 929, T 22407, good value, restaurant; **B** *Coliqueo*, Etcheluz 159, T 21308, opp bus terminal, good; **B** *Nuevo Pehuén*, Vidal y Etcheluz, 1 block from bus terminal, T 21360, rec; **C** *Huinclul*, Roca 313, restaurant; **C** *Odetto's Grill*, Ejército Argentino 455, 2 mins from bus terminal, OK. There is a municipal camping site.

● **Banks & money changers** Banco de la Nación Argentina, good rates, efficient.

● **Buses** To **Bahía Blanca** 3 a day, Alto Valle, 15 hrs, US$25,. El Petróleo bus to **San Martín de los Andes** (5½ hrs) via Junín de los Andes. There is also an overnight Neuquén-Zapala-San Martín bus that comes through Zapala at 0230; same service at 0915 (US$23). To **Bariloche** direct buses about twice a week. To **Temuco** (Chile) all year, several companies at 0500, US$22, 10-12 hrs, as under Neuquén (see above). Also Igi-Llaimi Wed and Fri at 0530, return 0330, twice weekly. Buy Chilean currency before leaving.

NORTH OF ZAPALA

North of Zapala on the Chilean border is the **Reserva Nacional Copahue**, best-known for its thermal baths and volcano of the same name. The **Termas de Copahue** (*Alt* 1,980m) are enclosed in a gigantic amphitheatre formed by mountain walls, with an opening to the East. Accommodation in the town of Copahue (**D** pp *Res Codihue*, T 0948-95031, poor breakfast) 15 km from the Termas. Buses connect Copahue with the winter sports resort of Caviahue which offers horseriding and trekking in summer (accommodation available). There are buses from Neuquén (5 hrs) and Zapala to Copahue; also by road from Mendoza.

Route 40 N via Las Lajas is paved as far as **Chos Malal**, founded as a military fort in 1889 (restored as a historic monument, with Museo Histórico Olascoaga. ACA service station and hotels.

● **Accommodation A3** *Chos Malal*, San Martín 89, T 21469, faded grandeur; on 25 de Mayo, *Hostería El Torreón*, T 21141, No 137, and *Hosp Baal Bak*, No 920, T 21495.

Beyond Chos Malal, Route 40 to Mendoza via Malargüe is more scenic, but slower than the Neuquén-Mendoza route (Nos 151 and 143 via Santa Isabel and San Rafael).

SOUTHWEST NEUQUEN

JUNIN DE LOS ANDES

(*Pop* 7,350; *Phone code* 0944) is 38 km W of Route 40, between Zapala and Bariloche. It is known as the trout capital of Argentina. A short detour from Junín leads to the very beautiful lake of Huechulafquen (bus, Koko, US$6 one way, check return journey with driver).

● **Accommodation L3** *Estancia Huechahue* (reached from the Junín-Bariloche bus), T 91303, English run, comfortable, farmhouse accommodation, horseriding, fishing, river trips; **A3** *Hostería Chimehuín*, Suárez y 25 de Mayo, T 91132, fishing hostelry; **B** *Alejandro I*, Ruta 234, on edge of town, T 91184; **C** *Res Marisa*, Rosas 360, T 91175, cheapest; *Posada Pehuén*, Col Suárez 560, T 91237, good value, charming owners, Rosi and Oscar Marconi, rec. Municipal **campsite**, T 91296.

● **Places to eat** *Ruca Hueney*, Milanesio 641, main plaza, good trout and pasta dishes, rec.

● **Transport Air** Between Junín and San Martín is Chapelco civil airport, served by Austral from Bs As and TAN (T 0972-27872) from Neuquén and Bariloche.

FRONTIER WITH CHILE – THE TROMEN PASS

● **Argentine immigration**
Formalities are carried out at the Argentine side of the Tromen Pass (Chileans call it Mamuil Malal). This route runs through glorious scenery to Pucón (135 km) on Lago Villarrica (Chile). It is less developed than the Huahum and Puyehue routes further S, and definitely not usable during heavy rain or snow (June to mid-Nov). Parts are narrow and steep. (Details of the Chilean side are given under **Puesco**, the Chilean customs post, **The Lake District**, page 771.)

Camping: it is possible to camp in the area (though very windy), but take food as there are no shops at the pass.

● **Transport**
The international bus will officially only pick up people at Tromen but at the discretion of the driver can pick up passengers at Puesco (no hotel) at 0900 and Currarehue stops. Hitchhiking over to the Tromen Pass is difficult. Bus Igi-Llaima, daily Junín de los Andes-Pucón US$26.

LANIN NATIONAL PARK

This beautiful, large park has sparkling lakes, wooded mountain valleys and the snow capped **Lanín Volcano**. Geologically, Lanín (3,768m) is one of the youngest volcanoes of the Andes; it is extinct and one of the world's most beautiful mountains. A 4-hr hike from the Argentine customs post at Tromen pass, where there is a campsite (speak to the *guardaparque* at the border) leads to the *refugio* at 2,400m; from here it is 5 hrs to the summit, not difficult but crampons and ice-axe are essential. Dr González, President of the Club Andino in Junín, can arrange guides and equipment hire. Limited *refugio* space; entry of visitors without tents restricted. Park Administration is in San Martín, on main plaza, helpful but maps poor; entry US$3.

SAN MARTIN DE LOS ANDES

(*Pop* 14,000; *Phone code* 0972), 40 km S of Junín, is a lovely but expensive little town at the E end of Lago Lacar. It is the best centre for exploring **Lanín National Park**. Mirador Bandurrias, 6 km from the centre offers good views. There is excellent skiing on Cerro Chapelco, and facilities for water skiing, windsurfing and sailing on Lago Lacar.

Excursions

The most popular trips by car are to Lagos Lolog, Aluminé, Huechulafquen and Paimún, to a campsite in the shadow of Lanín Volcano (bus from San Martín via Huechulafquen to Paimún, 0800, US$2, Empresa San Martín). Shorter excursions can be made on horseback or by launch. A small road runs W from San Martín along the S edge of Lago Lacar for 10 km to Quila Quina, where there are Indian engravings and a lovely waterfall. Boat trip from San Martín to Quila Quina, 45 mins one way, US$10 return. A good route for cyclists is along Route 234 to Cerro Chapelco, where you can take your bike up the hill in the funicular railway, then back down the paths.

Local information
● **Accommodation**

Single accommodation is scarce. Motel, **L2-L3** *El Sol de los Andes*, very expensive, set above the town (Cerro Cnl Díaz), T 27460, 5-star, shopping gallery, swimming pool, sauna, nightclub, casino, regular bus service to centre of town.

L3-A1 range: *Alihuen Lodge*, Ruta 62, Km 5 (road to Lake Lolog), T 26588, F 26045, inc breakfast, other meals (very good) available, lovely location and grounds, very comfortable, highly rec; *El Viejo Esquiador*, San Martín 1242, T 27690, rec. *La Cheminée*, Roca y Moreno, T 27617, very good, breakfast inc but no restaurant; *La Masia*, Obeid 811, T 27688, very good.

A2 *Turismo*, Mascardi 517, T 27592, rec; *La Raclette*, Pérez 1170, T 27664, 3-star, charming, warm, excellent restaurant, rec; *Posta del Cazador*, San Martín 175, T 27501, very highly rec; **A3** *Hostería Los Pinos*, Almte Brown 420, T 27207 (cheaper low season), German-run, with a/c, breakfast and heating, lovely garden; **A3** *Hostería Anay*, Cap Drury 841, T 27514, central, good value, rec; **A3** *Hostería Las Lucarnas*, Pérez 632, T 27085/27985, English and French spoken; **A3** *Res Peumayén*, San Martín 851, T 27232, with breakfast; **A3** *Villa Bibi*, Díaz 1186, T 72206, with breakfast, comfortable, rec; **A3-B** *Curra-Huincla*, Rivadavia 686, T 27224, modern, rec.

B *Casa Alta*, Obeid 659, T 27456, chalet in rose garden, 'beyond comparison and fantastic'; **B** *Crismallu*, Roca 975, T 27283, F 27583, with breakfast, good value; **B** *Hostería Cumelén*, Elordi 931, T 27304 (or BsAs T 502-3467), hot water, breakfast, rec; **B** *Colonos del Sur*, Rivadavia 686, T 27224, good value; **C** *Vil-*

lalagos, Villegas 717, without breakfast.

Consult Tourist Office for other private addresses, but these are only supplied in high season. Cheapest is **E** pp *Posta del Caminante*, Caballería 1164, summer only, good atmosphere, noisy; **E** pp *La Casa del Trabun*, Elordi 186, T 27755, sleeping bags essential, kitchen facilities. The following offer discounts to ISIC and youth card holders: **E** pp *Hosp Turístico Caritas*, Cap Drury 774, T 27313, run by church, floor space for sleeping bags in summer; *Albergue Universitario Técnico Forestal*, Pasaje de la Paz s/n, T 27618, youth hostel style, and *Hostería Los Pinos* (see above).

Camping: *ACA Camping*, Av Koessler 2176, with hot water and laundering facilities, **F** pp. Pleasant site by the lake at Quila Quina, 27 km from San Martín, with beaches, and another on Lago Lacar at Catritre, 6 km from town.

● **Places to eat**

Try smoked venison, wild boar or trout, at *El Ciervo*, Villegas 724; *Piscis*, Villegas y Moreno, good *parrilla*; *Betty*, San Martín 1203, and *El Peñón*, Calderón, both good. *La Tasca*, Moreno 866, excellent trout and venison, home-baked bread, rec; *Parrilla del Esquiador*, Belgrano 885, reasonable home-cooked food; *Mendieta*, San Martín 713, *parrilla*, popular; *Paprika*, Villegas 568, venison and trout, Hungarian, highly rec; *Jockey Club*, Villegas 657, also good; *Pizzería La Strada*, San Martín 721, good; *Fanfani*, Rodhe 786, has good pasta; *Pocha's*, Villegas y Belgrano, pizzas, friendly; *Tavola del Oso*, Pérez y Villegas, cheap, good; *Las Catalinas*, Villegas 745, excellent value.

● **Banks & money changers**

Banco de la Nación, San Martín 687, cash only; American Express San Martín 1141, T 28453; Andino Internacional, San Martín 876, p 1, only place to change TCs, commission 3%.

● **Laundry**

Laverap, Cap Drury 878, 0800-2200 daily and Villegas 986, cheaper, 0900-1300, 1600-2130 Mon-Fri, 0900-1300 Sat.

● **Sports**

Skiing: there are several chair-lifts of varying capacity on Cerro Chapelco and a ski-tow higher up. Bus from San Martín to slopes, US$7 return. Very good slopes and snow conditions. Lift pass US$20-35, ski hire US$13 a day from *Hostería Villa Lagos*. At the foot of the mountain are a restaurant and base lodge. There are three more restaurants on the mountain and a small café at the top. For information on trout **fishing** or duck and geese **shooting**, contact Logaine and David Denies at *Trails*, Pérez 662, San Martín.

● **Tour companies & travel agents**
Tiempo Patagónico, San Martín 950, T 27113, excursions and adventure tourism, 10% discount to ISIC and youth card holders; also *Pucará Viajes*, San Martín 943.

● **Tourist offices**
Tourist offices at Rosas 790, on main plaza, corner of San Martín, open 0800-2200, very helpful.

● **Useful addresses**
Police station: at Belgrano 611.

● **Transport**
Local   Car hire: Avis, San Martín 998 and at airport. **Localiza** at airport and Villegas 977, T 28876. **A1 Rent a Car** at airport. **Mechanic**: *Taller Fubol 5*, Av San Martín, rec.

Air See under Junín de los Andes above.

Buses Terminal at Gen Villegas 251, good toilet facilities. **Buenos Aires**-San Martín, US$60, daily at 1240 (Chevallier) and 2100 with El Valle. To **Bariloche**, Ko Ko, 3 days a week, 0800, 4 hrs, US$18. To **Villa La Angostura** via Seven Lakes, 3 days a week with La Petroule.

FRONTIER WITH CHILE – THE HUAHUM PASS

This route is open all year round. A road along the N shore of Lago Lacar through the Lanín National Park crosses the border to Puerto Pirehueico. Buses daily at 0600, US$6. Huahum at the W end of the lake has camping and a shop; a boat leaves San Martín at 0930, returns 1800, US$20 (T 27380). For connections from Puerto Pirehueico to Panguipulli and beyond, see Chile chapter, page 773.

● **Transport**
Daily bus to Pirehueico 0900, US$8, 2 hrs.

There are also buses via Junín de los Andes and the Tromen Pass to Pucón and Temuco from mid-Nov to May: Empresa San Martín Mon, Wed and Fri, at 0700, returns from Temuco the following day at 0500, Igi-Llaimi Tues, Thur and Sat at 0600, returns next day at 0630, US$25, 7 hrs, rough journey, sit on the left. From June to mid-Nov, schedules to Temuco are reduced and in winter when Huahum is blocked by snow, there are no buses.

SAN MARTIN DE LOS ANDES TO BARILOCHE

There are two routes S to Bariloche: one, via Lago Hermoso and Villa La Angostura, known as the '**Seven Lakes Drive**', is very

beautiful. (National Park permit holders may camp freely along this route.) From a bridge 7 km S of San Martín, you can see the Arroyo Partido: at this very point the rivulet splits, one stream flowing to the Pacific, the other to the Atlantic. Further S the road passes **Lago Villarino** (*Hostería Lago Villarino*, good food, beautiful setting, camping). Some bus services, however, take a rather less scenic route to **Confluencia** on the paved Bariloche highway (ACA station and a hotel, also motel *El Rancho* just before Confluencia). Neither El Valle buses, 4 a week, nor Ko Ko buses, follow the Seven Lakes Drive. Round trip excursions between San Martín along the Seven Lakes Drive, 5 hrs, are operated by several tour companies.

Villa Traful, beside Lago Traful about half-way between San Martín and Bariloche on a side road, is described as a 'camper's paradise'. There are also hotels on the lake. Marvellous views, fishing (licence needed) excellent. All roads are dirt; drive carefully, avoiding wild cattle!

PARQUE NACIONAL NAHUEL HUAPI

Lago Nahuel Huapi with its surroundings, an area of 7,850 sq km, was set aside in 1903 as a National Park. It contains lakes, rivers, glaciers, waterfalls, torrents, rapids, valleys, forest, bare mountains and snow-clad peaks. Most of the area is covered with abundant vegetation, though it is notably more abundant on the Chilean side, which gets more rain. Many kinds of wild animals live in the region, but they are extremely shy. Bird life, on the other hand – particularly swans, geese and ducks – is seen at any time and everywhere in large flocks.

The outstanding feature of this National Park is the splendour of the lakes. The largest is **Lago Nahuel Huapi** (*Alt* 767m), 531 sq km and 460m deep in places. It is in full view of the snow-covered peaks of the Cordillera and of the forests covering the lower slopes. Towering over the scene is Cerro Tronador. Some 96 km long, and not more than 12 km wide, the lake is very irregular in shape; long arms of water, or *brazos*, stretch far into the land. There are many islands: the largest is **Isla Victoria**, on which stands the forest research station. Trout and salmon have been introduced. Lago Nahuel Huapi is drained eastwards by the Río Limay.

A mere sand bar in one of the northern *brazos* separates Lago Nahuel Huapi from Lago Correntoso, which is quite close to Lago Espejo. Lago Traful, a short distance to the NE, can be reached by a road which follows the Río Limay through the Valle Encantado, with its fantastic rock formations. South of Nahuel Huapi there are other lakes: the three main ones are Mascardi, Guillelmo, and Gutiérrez. The luxury *Hotel Tronador* is on Lake Mascardi, beautiful setting, highly recommended, also camping *La Querencia*. On the shore of Lago Gutiérrez, in a grotto, is the Virgen de las Nieves (Virgin of the Snows).

BARILOCHE

(*Pop* 77,750; *Phone code* 0944), on the S shore of Lago Nahuel Huapi, founded 1898, is the best centre for exploring the National Park. Renowned for its chocolate industry, it is a beautifully-situated town of steep streets, its wooden chalets perched upon a glacial moraine at the foot of Cerro Otto. The place is full of hotels and *hosterías*. To the S lie the heights of the Ventana and the Cerro Colorado (2,135m). The forests are particularly beautiful around May.

The town has experienced phenomenal growth and can be very busy. The best time to visit it is out of season either in the spring or autumn, although the weather is unpredictable. The main road into Bariloche from the E is paved and in good condition.

Places of interest

The **cathedral**, built in 1946, dominates the town; interior unfinished. There is a **belvedere** at the top of Cerro Otto with wide views over the town and the lake and mountain. The **Lido swimming pool** on the lake shore is beautifully sited but somewhat run down. The clock in the **Centro Cívico** has four figures which ro-

tate at noon; photos with St Bernard dogs (including brandy keg) may be taken in the Centro Cívico plaza and on 12 de Octubre above the Lido.

Museums

The **Museo de La Patagonia** in the Centro Cívico has nice collections of stuffed animals and Indian artefacts, open 1000-1200, 1400-1900 Tues-Fri, 1000-1300, Sat US$3; the attached **Biblioteca Sarmiento** is open Mon-Fri, 1100-2200.

Excursions

The resort of **Llao-Llao** (bus No 20, 45 mins, US$2) lies 24 km W along Av Bustillo. Hotels on this road and in the resort are given below. At Km 17.7 on the road to Llao-Llao there is a chairlift to **Cerro Campanario** (0900-1200, 1400-1800 daily, US$10), from the top of which there are fine views of Isla Victoria and Puerto Pañuelo. At Km 18.3 begins the **Circuito Chico**, a 60 km circular route around Lago Moreno Oeste, past Punto Panorámico and through Puerto Pañuelo and Llao-Llao itself. Tour companies do the circuit and it can be driven in half a day (it can also be cycled). It can be extended to a full day: Bariloche-Llao Llao-Bahía López-Colonia Suiza (on Lago Moreno Este)-Cerro Catedral-Bariloche; the reverse direction misses the sunsets and afternoon views from the higher roads, which are negotiable in winter (even snow-covered). The surrounding countryside offers beautiful walking, eg to Lago Escondido on a 3½ km trail off the Circuito Chico. A longer walk is to Cerro López (3 hrs, with a *refugio* after 2); take Colonia Suiza bus (from Moreno y Rolando) and alight at Picada. Longer still is the hike to *refugio Italia* (same bus, but alight at SAC); details of this and 3-5 day continuations from Club Andino.

Boat excursions

A half-day excursion (1300-1830) may be taken from Bariloche to Puerto Pañuelo, then by boat to Isla Victoria. The full-day excursion (0900-1830, or 1300 till 2000 in season) at US$28 includes the Arrayanes forest on the Quetrihue peninsula further N, and 3 hrs on Isla Victoria, picnic lunch advised. It is best to book this trip through an agency, as the boat fare alone is US$21. Some boats going to Arrayanes call first at Isla Victoria, early enough to avoid boat-loads of tourists. All boats are very crowded in season, but operators have to provide seating for all passengers. The Arrayanes forest can also be visited by walking 12 km from Villa La Angostura (see page 199).

Other excursions

For climbing and skiing on Cerros Catedral and Otto, see **Sports** below. A $1/2$-day excursion is possible taking a bus to Virgen de las Nieves on Cerro Catedral, walking 2 km to arrive at beautiful Lago Gutiérrez; walk along lake shore to the road from El Bolsón and walk back to Bariloche (about 4 hrs).

Tours

There are numerous tours: most travel agencies charge the same price. It is best to buy tours on the spot rather than in advance, although they get very booked up in season. Whole-day trip to Lagos Gutiérrez, Mascardi, Hess, the Cascada Los Alerces and Cerro Tronador (3,478m) leaves at 0800, US$29, and involves 1 hr walk to the Black Glacier, interesting but too much time spent on the bus. Catedral and Turisur have a 9-hr excursion, leaving at 0900 (afternoon dep also Dec-Mar), to Puerto Pañuelo, sailing down to Puerto Blest and continuing by bus to Puerto Alegre and again by launch to Puerto Frías (US$19.50). A visit to the Cascada de los Cántaros is made (stay off the boat at the Cascada and walk around to Puerto Blest through beautiful forest, 1 hr, recommended). Several companies run 12-hr minibus excursions to San Martín de los Andes, US$34, through two national parks, passing seven lakes, returning via Paso de Córdoba and the Valle Encantado but these involve 10 hrs on the bus and few stops (taxi for this route US$30 pp).

If staying only 1-2 days in the area the best excursions are to Cerro Tronador the first day, and on the second to Cerro Catedral in the morning and Isla Victoria in the afternoon (possible only Dec-Mar when there are afternoon departures for the island).

Local information
● Accommodation

The most complete listing with map is published by the Oficina Municipal de Turismo, which you are advised to consult if you arrive in the high season without a reservation. It also has a book-ing service at Florida 520 (Galería), room 116, Buenos Aires. Out of season, prices are reason-able, in all ranges, especially if you bargain; in season everything is very expensive. Most hotels outside the town inc half-board, and those in the town inc breakfast. Hotels with lake views normally charge US$3-4 extra/room/day, for the view in high season; the following selection gives lake-view high-season prices where appli-cable.

Hotels on the road to Llao Llao (Av Bustillo): **L2** *Apart-hotel Casablanca*, Km 23.5, T 48117, good, on a peninsula between Lagos Nahuel Huapi and Moreno; **L1** *Hotel Llao-Llao*, Km 25.5, deservedly famous, superbly situated in 'chocolate box' surroundings, fine views (res-ervations: Av Santa Fe 846, p 6, Bs As, T/F 311-3432); **B** *La Caleta*, Km 1.9, bungalows sleeping 4, shower, open fire, excellent value, self-catering, rec, T 25650; **A1** *La Cascada*, Km 6, T 41046, 5-star, rec.

Hotels in Bariloche: **L2** *Bariloche Ski*, San Martín 352, 4-star, T 22913, Telex 18273, good; **L2** *Edelweiss*, Av San Martín 232, 5-star, T 26165, modern, excellent food, enclosed pool, highly rec; **L2** *Lagos de la Patagonia*, San Martín 536, T 25846, 5-star, heated swimming pool.

First class: **A2** *Bella Vista*, Rolando 351, T 22435, large well-appointed rooms with lake view, 2 good restaurants; **A2** *Italia*, Tiscornia 892, new, good breakfast; **B** *Aguas del Sur*, Moreno 353, T 22995/24329, inc excellent 4-course meal and breakfast; **A3** *Colonial*, Quaglia 281, T 26101, helpful, lake views; **A3** *Internacional*, Mitre 171, T 25938, F 20072, reduction for ACA members; **A3** *La Pastorella*, Belgrano 127, T 24656, English and French-spoken, central, rec; **A1** *Nevada*, Ro-lando 250, T 22778, heating, nice room; *Res Tirol*, Pasaje Libertad 175, T 26152, good, Ger-man spoken; **A3** *Ayelén*, same street, No 157, T 23611, 3-star, comfortable, restaurant, rec.

C *Fontán*, Palacios 276, T 29431, pleasant, family-run, good beds; **A3** *Millaray*, Libertad 195, T 21495, good, shower; **B** *Res La Sureña* 432, T 24875, San Martín, 500m W of Civic Centre, helpful; **B** *Hostería Sur*, Beschtedt 101, T 22677; opp is **B** *Res Piuké*, Beschtedt 136, T 23663, German, Italian spoken, rec; **B** *Hos-tería El Ñire*, J O'Connor 94, T 23041, very pleasant, heated, German, English spoken, pre-fers longer-stay visitors, also apartments, rec;

B pp *Hostería El Radal*, 24 de Septiembre 46, T 22551, clean, comfortable, warm, English spoken, **D** pp in low season.

C *Res Premier*, Rolando 263, T 23681, hot showers, English and German spoken, small rooms, rec; **C** pp *Victoria*, Mitre 815, **D** pp without bath, poor beds; **C** *Hostería Güemes*, Güemes 715, T 24785, helpful, rec; **B** *Res Puyehue*,

Elordi 243, T 22196, discount for *SAH* users; **C** *pensión* of Sra Carlota Baumann, Av de los Pioneros 860 (T 29689, F 24502), follow 20 de Febrero uphill for 10-15 mins, kitchen, bath, good breakfast, laundry service, English and German spoken (reported as 20 de Febrero 860, esq 20 de Junio).

D *Godec*, 24 de Septiembre 218, T 23085, run

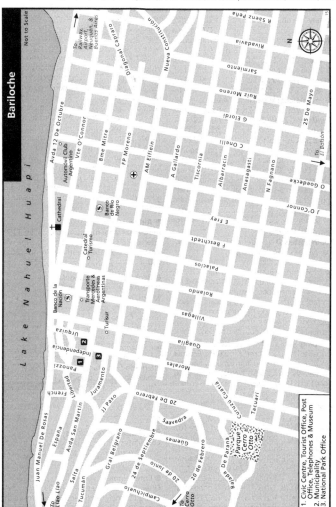

Bariloche

Not to Scale

Lake Nahuel Huapi

1. Civic Centre, Tourist Office, Post Office, Telephones & Museum
2. Municipality
3. National Park Office

down, restaurant (reservations in Buenos Aires T 751-4335); **E** pp *Res No Me Olvides*, Av Los Pioneros Km 1, T 29140, 30 mins walk' from centre or Bus 50/51 to corner of C Videla then follow signs, nice house in quiet surroundings, use of kitchen, camping US$5 pp, highly rec; **E** pp *Res Rosán*, Güemes 691, T 23109 (Sra Arco), repeatedly rec, English and German spoken, cooking facilities, helpful, beautiful garden, camping US$5.

Family accommodation: the tourist office keeps a list. Among those rec are: **C-E** *Familia Dalfaro*, Rolando y Tiscorra (SW corner), quiet; **E** *Pensión Venus*, Salta 571, heating, cooking facilities; **E** pp *Casa Diego*, Elflein 163, T 22556, in dormitory, without breakfast; **E** *Pire-Cuyen*, Anasagasti 840, doubles only; **E** Frey 635, dormitory, cooking and laundry facilities, motorcycle parking; **E** Anasagasti 348; **E** pp *Sra Iris*, Quaglia 526, with bath; **E** *Eloisa Lamuniere*, 24 de Septiembre 71, T 225614, with breakfast, homely, helpful, cooking facilities; **E** pp *Casa Nelly*, Beschtedt 658, T 22295, hot showers, kitchen, camping; **E** pp *Nogarre*, Elflein 58, comfortable, warm, eccentric owner; **D** pp *Lo de Giani*, Elflein, with breakfast; **E** *Mariana Pirker*, 24 de Septiembre 230, T 24873, two 3-bedded apartments with bath and kitchen. Apartments and chalets may also be rented, prices vary enormously according to the season: try C Ruiz 1870, T 26781 (ask for Teo), small but very good.

Youth hostels: **D** pp *Albergue Patagonia Andina*, Morales 564, T 22783, small dormitories, kitchen facilities, information, rec; *Alaska*, T/F 61564, on Av Bustillo, Km 7.5 (buses 10, 20, 21, get off at La Florida), IYHA-affiliated, **D-E** pp, good atmosphere, poor beds, cooking and washing facilities, mountain bikes, pleasant location, English spoken, good information on local treks, book in advance in summer, rec; all offer 10% discount to ISYC and youth card holders.

Camping: list of sites from Tourist Office. Two sites on road to Llao-Llao: *El Yeti*, Km 5.6, rec; *Petunia*, Km 14.9, well protected from winds by trees, hot showers, shop, rec. *Selva Negra*, Bustillo 2500, T 44013, US$8 pp. Shops and restaurants on most sites closed outside Jan-March.

● **Places to eat**
La Marmita, Mitre 329, small, cosy, excellent mixed fondues rec; *El Viejo Munich*, Mitre 102, good meat and fish, rec; *Caza Mayor*, Quaglia y Elflein, game and fish, good but expensive; *La Montaña*, Elflein 49, very good value; *Kandahar*, 20 de Febrero 698, T 24702, excellent, run by Argentine ski champion Marta Peirono de Barber; *Parrilla 1816*, Elflein 167, good meat, rec; *Parrilla La Vizcacha*, Rolando 279, good value, rec; *Cantina Lotito*, Morales 362, very

good *parrillada*, reasonably priced; *Lennon*, Moreno 48, small, good food, reasonably priced, English spoken; *La Jirafa*, Palacios 288, good food, good value; *Simoca*, Palacios 264, inexpensive Tucumán fare; *Familia Weiss*, Palacios 170 (with good delicatessen round corner on Mitre), excellent local specialities. Good pastries and hot chocolate at *Hola Nicolás*, Moreno y Urquiza (see the graffiti-graven tables). *La Rondine*, San Martín 536, Italian, luxurious, good (above *Hotel Panamericano*). *Jauja*, Quaglia 370, good local dishes; *La Andinita*, Mitre 56, rec, pizzas, good value; *Cocodrilo*, Mitre y Urquiza, big choice of good pizzas, good value, take-away service; *Vegetariano*, Elflein y Morales, excellent fixed menu, good value, rec; *Al Dente*, Mitre 370, vegetarian, cheap, good; *Pizzaiola*, Pagano 275, good pizzeria; *La Nueva Estancia*, Elflein y Rolando, good meat and trout, occasional live entertainment; *La Alpina Confitería*, Moreno 98, open fire, reasonably priced, cheese fondue rec, very popular; *Del Turista*, Mitre 231, chocolates, ice cream; *Ermitage*, tea rooms, on road to Llao-Llao at Km 18; *Algunas Frases*, Mitre 211, bar, open 24 hrs. Many good delicatessens with take-away food, inc chicken, pizzas and cheeses, for picnics.

On Av Bustillo are *La Glorieta*, Km 3.8, good; *Patacon Parrilla*, Km 7, excellent; *La Posta del Río*, Km 10, reasonable.

● **Airline offices**
Aerolíneas Argentinas/Austral, Mitre 119 y Villegas, T 23161; **LADE**, Mitre 175; **Lapa**, Villegas 121, T 23714; **Southern Winds**, Mitre 260, T 23704; **TAN**, Villegas 142, T 27889.

● **Banks & money changers**
There are several banks and exchange shops, which buy and sell virtually all European and South American currencies, besides US dollars; Sat is a bad day. **Olano**, Quaglia 238, 2% commission on TCs; **Sudamerica**, Mitre 63; **American Express**, Mitre 387, T 25414, no exchange facilities, sends you to **Banco Nación**, Mitre y Villegas, to buy TCs, but does have emergency cash service. **Banco Integrado Departamental**, O'Connor y 12 de Octubre, for Thomas Cook TCs; **Banco Quilmes**, Mitre 300 block, cash advances on Visa. Beware forged Argentine banknotes. If everything closed try *Kiwanis* (boot rental), Mitre 210, 3% commission.

● **Embassies & consulates**
Consulates: Chile, JM de Rosas 180, friendly, helpful; Germany, Ruiz Moreno 45, T 25695; Switzerland, Quaglia 342, T 26111.

● **Entertainment**
Cinemas: *Arrayanes*, Moreno 39; *Cine Club*, Tues 2115 only, Biblioteca Sarmiento in the Centro Cívico.

● **Hospitals & medical centres**
Clinic: Cruz Azul, Capraro 1216.

● **Laundry**
Marva, San Martín 325, also Beschtedt 166;
Laverap, Rolando 241; *Lavadero del Centro*,
V A O'Connor 716.

● **Post & telecommunications**
Post Office: Centro Cívico (same building as
tourist office). *Poste Restante* US$2.50/letter.
Telecommunications: San Martín e Independencia and Elflein y Frey (3 mins minimum
charge); cheaper from *Hotel Bariloche*, San
Martín 127. Outside the phone office is a telephone with links to several countries (eg UK,
Chile, Japan).

● **Shopping**
The main commercial centre is on Mitre between
the Centro Cívico and Beschtedt; there are lots
of *galerías* here. The products of the local chocolate industry are excellent and are sold by several
shops along Mitre. *Fábrica de Chocolate
Cerro León* on Av 12 de Octubre, nr railway
station. You can watch chocolates being made
at *El Turista*, San Martín 252. 1 block away is
Mamushka, excellent. Very good chocolate at
Estrella Alpina, Villegas 216 or Albarracín 146,
and *Benroth*, Beschtedt 569, and at *Abuela
Goye*, Albarracín 157. Try 'Papas de Bariloche',
the local chocolate speciality. Local wines, from
the Alto Río Negro, are also good. Woollen
goods are rec. Handicraft shops all along San
Martín; some will change money. *Feria Artesanal Municipal*, Moreno y Rolando, rec. *Bur-
ton Cerámica*, 2/3 km on Llao Llao road, Av E
Bustillo 4100, T/F 41102, makes and sells
'Patagonian pottery'. Winter clothing at *Flying
Patagonia*, Quaglia between B Mitre and VA
O'Connor. *Feria Naturista*, Elflein 73, vegetarian and health foods; *Todo* supermarket,
Moreno 319, good selection, cheap.

Bookshop: *Cultura*, Elflein 78, has a good
range of technical books, some in English and
German; *La Barca*, Mitre 131 and *Mileno*,
Quaglia 262, local 19.

● **Sports**
Apart from sailing and boating, there are golf,
mountaineering, walking, birdwatching, skiing,
and fishing (for which you need a permit). Excellent trout fishing Nov-Mar; boat hire arranged
with tackle shops.

Bicycles: may be hired beside the lake in high
season (eg A Carlucci, Mitre 723, US$20/day).
Mopeds from Vertigo Rental, San Martín 594.

Hiking and trekking: before going hiking, buy
moisturizing creams for exposed skin areas and
lips. Horseflies (*tábanos*) frequent the lake
shores and lower areas in summer; lemon juice
is good for keeping them away, but can cause

skin irritation. Club Andino (see below) has
sketch maps of hikes. For horse trekking trips
contact Carol Jones, Casilla 1436 (or through
Hans Schulz – see below under **Tourist Agencies**), US$35 1/2-day, US$60 day trips, spectacular, highly rec. Also *Cumbres Patagonia*, Villegas
222, US$40 for 3 hrs, suitable for all levels of
experience, enjoyable. Or ask at Club Andino
for Valerie, friendly, rec.

Mountain climbing: in the area there is something for every kind of mountaineer. National
Park mountain guides are available but can be
expensive. Book: *Excursiones, Andinismo y Refugios de Montaña en Bariloche*, by Tonek Arko,
available in local shops, US$2, or from the author
at Güemes 691. In treks to *refugios* remember
to add costs of ski lifts, buses, food at *refugio*
and lodging (in Club Andino *refugios*:
US$6/night, plus US$3 for cooking, or US$5 for
breakfast, US$8 for dinner). Take a sleeping bag.
Best information from Club Andino Bariloche,
20 de Febrero 30, open 0900-1200, 1500-2000
Mon-Fri and Sat 0900-1200. The Club arranges
guides; ask for Sr Ricardo, the secretary, who
organizes easy weekend climbs and walks. Its
booklet 'Guía de Sendas y Picadas' gives details
of climbs and it provides maps (1:150,000) and
details of all campsites, hotels and mountain
lodges. The climbing may mean a ride on horseback or a skilled ascent of the slopes of Cerro
Tronador. The Government has built convenient
rest lodges at from 1,000 to 2,000m on the
mountains. Firing, light and food are provided
at these points. Note that at higher levels, winter
snow storms can begin as early as April, making
climbing dangerous.

Skiing: there is good skiing during the winter
season (July to early Oct), supervised by the Club
Andino Bariloche. It is best organized with a tour
company, through whom you can secure discounts as part of an inclusive deal. (Skiing is
cheaper, however, at smaller resorts, such as
Esquel, though more expensive at San Martín
de los Andes.) The favourite skiing slopes are on
Cerro Catedral (several hotels), and a new ski-lift
is to be built higher up, to permit a longer skiing
season. (Hourly bus service with seasonal timetable from Mercedes bus company at Mitre 161,
US$5 return.) There is a cable car (US$10 single,
US$16 return) and a chair lift (US$120 full week,
US$26-32 high season, US$18-22 low – full day)
from the foot of Cerro Catedral to points high
on the ridge. Red and yellow markers painted
on the rock mark a trail, popular in summer, from
the top, which leads to Refugio Frey (well
equipped, blankets, meals, US$5-8, bed US$5
pp) on the edge of a small mountain lake (allow
6 hrs; you can return through the forest to the
ski complex the next day and take a bus back to

Bariloche). The seasonal cable car, with a chair lift from its upper terminal, takes you higher than the main (2-stage) chair lift. Check at tourist info if cable car is running, as everything closes in March. Bus tours from Bariloche to the foot of Cerro Catedral give time for less than 2 hrs on top of the mountain. The only disadvantage at Bariloche is that the snow is unreliable except at the top. There are other skiing slopes 5 km out of Bariloche, on **Cerro Otto** (cable car, US$20 pp; open 0930-1800 Jan, Feb, July, Aug, and 1000-1800 rest of year; free connecting bus service to cable car from Mitre y Villegas, revolving restaurant at top, opens 1000, entry US$3.50, nice *confitería* belonging to Club Andino on Cerro Otto, 20 mins' walk from main *confitería* on summit). Cerro Otto can be reached in 2-3 hrs' walk from the town,rec; take the paved Av de los Pioneros, then switch to the signed dirt track 1 km out of Bariloche (splendid views), or in a minibus which goes every 30 mins from a car park near the National Park headquarters (closed public holidays), between 1400 and 1600, US$7 round trip (local bus US$2.10 return). Also at Piedras Blancas (bus US$7 return); on López (try a car trip, rough road, US$14 for a tour, 1400-1830), Dormilón and La Ventana. Ski hire US$9-16 a day, depending on quality, dearer at Cerro Catedral than in town. Ski clothes can also be rented by the day, at US$1-2/item, from *Kiwanis* sport stores, Mitre 210, or *El Iglú*, Galería Arrayanes II, Rolando 244.

Swimming: in the larger lakes such as Nahuel Huapi and Huechulafquen is not rec, for the water is cold. But swimming in smaller lakes such as Lolog, Lacar, Curruhué Chico, Hermoso, Meliquina, Espejo, Hess and Fonck is very pleasant and the water – especially where the bottom shelves to a shingly beach – can be positively warm.

● **Tour companies & travel agents**
Tour buses pick you up from your hotel. Agencies charge same prices: Circuito Chico US$13, Cerro Catedral US$13, Cerro Tronador US$29, El Bolsón US$29. *Catedral Turismo*, Mitre 399, T 25443/5, F 26215, runs boats to Chile for Peulla-Puerto Montt trip, US$90 one way, rec (10% discount for ISIC and youth card holders on lake crossing to Chile and local excursions); *Turisur*, Quaglia 227, T 26109, organizes trips on lake and on land. *San Carlos Travel*, San Martín, local 19, F 26181/86, birdwatching and other specialist tours, rec; *Limay Travel*, V A O'Connor 710, T/F 20268, English and German spoken; *Rafting Adventure*, San Martín 130, T 32928, for watersports; *Cumbres Patagonia*, Villegas 222, T 23283, F 31835, for rafting, horseriding, trekking, fishing, rec; *Hans Schulz*, Casilla 1017, T 23835/26508 (speaks Spanish, German and English) arranges tours and guides, highly rec;

Tacul Viajes, San Martín 430, T 26321, English spoken, ISIC discount, rec. Arrange trekking with **Sr Daniel José Gorgone**, San Martín 127, DT 0706, T 26181. Rec guide *Daniel Feinstein*, T/F 42259, speaks fluent English, naturalist and mountaineer, very experienced in both Argentina and Chile. **NB** Check what the cost of your tour includes; funicular rides and chair lifts are usually charged as extras. Most agencies now sell excursions which include ride on 'la Trochita' from El Maitén.

● **Tourist offices**
Oficina Municipal de Turismo in Centro Cívico, open daily 0900-2100, Sat 0900-1900. Has full list of city buses, and details of hikes and campsites in the area and is helpful in finding accommodation. The book, *Guía Busch, Turismo y Comercio*, useful, is available free at the Río Negro tourist office in Buenos Aires, but is not free in Bariloche. National Park information (scanty) at San Martín 24, open 0800-2000. Information also from Sociedad Profesional de Guías de Turismo, Casilla de Correo 51, 8400 SC de Bariloche (President: Ama Petroff).

NB Obtain maps and information about the district in Buenos Aires at the National Park Tourist Office at Santa Fe 690, or at the provincial offices (addresses given on page 92); it is hard to obtain these in the provinces themselves. Park wardens are also useful sources of information.

● **Useful addresses**
Immigration Office: Libertad 175.

● **Transport**
Local Car hire: Hertz, Avis, and A1 International, at airport and in town (latter at San Martín 235, T 22582, F 27494); no flat rates, unless reservation made outside Argentina. **Localiza**, at airport and San Martín 570, reliable, helpful, competitive, better km allowance than others. **Guiñazú del Campo**, Libertad 118, good cars, English spoken; **Chapís Car**, Libertad 120, and **Carro's SACI**, Mitre 26, T 25907, out of season open Mon-Fri am only; **Open**, Mitre 382, T/F 26325, are all much cheaper. To enter Chile a permit is necessary, US$50, allow 48 hrs. **Car mechanic**: *Auguen SA*, VA O'Connor 1068, fast, reasonable, highly rec. **Taxis**: *Remise Bariloche*, T 30222; *Auto Jet*, España 11, T 22408. Some drivers speak English or German.

Air Airport, 15 km E of town. Taxi US$10; bus US$3 from AR office (timetable posted in office window). Many flights to **Buenos Aires**, with AR and Lapa (US$109). TAN and Kaiken fly to **Comodoro Rivadavia** and **Neuquén**; TAN also to **San Martín de los Andes** and, in summer only, to **Puerto Montt** (Chile). Kaiken also serves **Mendoza**, **Ushuaia**, **Calafate**, **Esquel** and **Trelew**.

Trains Station 3 km E of centre (booking office closed 1200-1500 weekdays, Sat pm and all Sun), reached by local buses 20 and 21 (US$0.75), taxi US$4-6. Information from the Tourist Office; tickets also available from *Hotel Pagano y Pamozzi*, 3 blocks from Centro Cívico. Train service to **Viedma** only, Tues/Fri 1800, 16 hrs, US$41 pullman, U$28 first. Scenery only interesting between Bariloche and Jacobacci, 4½ hrs.

Buses Terminal next to railway station. Left luggage US$1 per day. Bus company offices: Andesmar, Palacios 240, T 22140; La Estrella, Palacios 246; Mercedes, Mitre 161; TAC, Villegas 147, T26356; Chevallier, Moreno 107, T 23090; Tas Choapa, Moreno 138, T 26663; Cruz del Sur, San Martín 453, T 24163; Don Otto/Bus del Norte, San Martín 283; Ko-Ko, Moreno 107. To **Buenos Aires**, several companies daily, 22½ hrs, US$60-69, Andesmar *coche cama* 21 hrs, US$75; to **Mar del Plata**, Pampa, TAM, or El Rápido, US$60, 20 hrs; to **Bahía Blanca**, TAC, US$55; to **La Plata**, 19 hrs, US$80; to **Mendoza**, US$70, 22 hrs, via Zapala, Buta Ranquil and San Rafael; to **Córdoba**, US$77; to **El Bolsón**, Charter and Empresa Vía Bariloche, 2 hrs, US$10; to **Esquel**, Don Otto, Mercedes, Vía Bariloche, Andesmar; to **Puerto Madryn**, 24 hrs via Esquel (7-hr wait), and Trelew, US$56. To **San Martín de los Andes**, Ko Ko, Mon-Sat 1430, US$18, 4 hrs; to **Junín de los Andes** US$19. To **Neuquén**, US$18 by Transportes Mercedes or daily with La Estrella, 1415, 6½ hrs (a dull journey). No direct bus to **Río Gallegos**; you have to spend a night in Comodoro Rivadavia en route. Don Otto to Río Gallegos US$88. To **Santiago** (Chile), Tues, Fri and Sun, 24 hrs with tea and breakfast served en route. To **Puerto Montt**, see the route to Chile from Bariloche, page 199.

Villa La Angostura is a picturesque town (*Pop* 3,000) 90 km NW of Bariloche on Lago Nahuel Huapi. The port, 3 km from town, is spectacular in summer.

12 km S of the port at the S end of the Quetrihue Peninsula is **Parque Nacional Los Arrayanes**, containing 300 year old specimens of the rare Arrayan tree. Tour boats from Villa La Angostura daily 1500 and 1600, US$12 return. See above for tours by boat from Bariloche; out of season it is more difficult to visit as tour boats only sail if demand is sufficient.

● **Accommodation L2** *Hostería Las Balsas*, T 94308, small, exclusive, high standard, good location; **A3** *Correntoso*, T 94168, has a chalet next door, **B** for 2 bedrooms, shared use of

kitchen and sitting room, luxurious. Cheaper are *La Cabañita* and *Don Pedro* in El Cruce, dirty, both **C**. Ask in the tourist office, opp ACA, for lodgings in private houses, cheaper than hotels. **D-E** *Hostal Nahuel*, member of Red Argentina de Alojamiento para Jóvenes. **Camping**: *El Cruce*, 500m from terminal, US$4 pp, dirty toilets; *ACA Osa Mayor* (2 km along Bariloche road, pleasant, open late Dec to mid-May), *Municipal Lago Correntoso* (Km 87 from Bariloche).

● **Tour companies & travel agents** Turismo Cerro Bayo, Av Arrayanes s/n, of 5, T (0944) 94401/94412, 10% discount for ISIC and youth card holders on ski packages, trekking, rafting, lake and adventure tours.

● **Tourist offices** In bus terminal.

● **Transport** Villa La Angostura can be reached by excursion bus (day trip, 8 hrs) or local bus (at 1900 daily, returning 0800, Transportes Mercedes, US$7) which requires staying overnight. If going on to Osorno (Chile), you can arrange for the bus company to pick you up at La Angostura, US$11 to Osorno. Daily bus at 1700 to San Martín de los Andes.

FRONTIER WITH CHILE
1. The Puyehue pass
A good broad highway, which is paved apart from a 55 km gravel section (difficult in winter) between the two customs posts, goes around the E end of Lago Nahuel Huapi, then follows the N side of the lake through Villa La Angostura. It passes the junction with 'Ruta de Los Siete Lagos' for San Martín at Km 94, Argentine customs at Km 109 and the pass at Km 125 at an elevation of about 1,280m. Chilean customs is at Km 146 in middle of a forest. The frontier is closed at night. It is a 6-hr drive, but liable to be closed after snow-falls.

2. Via Lake Todos Los Santos
The route is Bariloche to Llao-Llao by road, Llao-Llao to Puerto Blest by boat (2½ hrs), Puerto Blest Lago Frías by bus, cross the lake to Puerto Frías (20 mins), then 1½ hrs by road to Peulla. Leave for Petrohué in the afternoon by boat (2½ hrs), cross Lago Todos Los Santos, passing the Osorno volcano, then by bus to Puerto Montt. This route is not recommended in wet or foggy weather. It is also long, tiring and has been criticized as very commercial.

● **Immigration and customs**

The Argentine and Chilean border posts are open every day. The launches (and hence the connecting buses) on the lakes serving the direct route via Puerto Blest to Puerto Montt generally do not operate at weekends; check. There is an absolute ban in Chile on importing any fresh food – meat, cheese, fruit – from Argentina.

Further information on border crossings in the Lake District will be found in the **Chile chapter**.

● **Exchange**

You are strongly advised to get rid of all your Argentine pesos before leaving Argentina; it is useful to have some Chilean pesos before you cross into Chile from Bariloche. Chilean currency can be bought at Puyehue customs at a reasonable rate.

● **Transport**

Four bus companies run services from Bariloche to Osorno (6 hrs), Puerto Montt (7 hrs) and Valdivia, via the Puyehue pass: buses usually leave 0730-0800, there is at least one bus every day from Argentine side and fares range from US$18-25 (US$35 for a 1-day excursion including city tour and Termas de Puyehue). Companies include Bus del Norte, Mercedes, and Tas Choapa (addresses under Bariloche). Sit on left side for best views. You can buy a ticket to the Chilean border, then another to Puerto Montt, or pay in stages in Chile, but there is little advantage in doing this.

Turismo Catedral sells 1 and 2-day crossings to Puerto Montt via roads and lakes (route as stated above). The 1-day crossing costs US$104 + cost of lunch at Peulla (US$18), credit cards accepted; this excursion does not permit return to Bariloche next day. (1 Sept-31 Mar, take own food, buy ticket day in advance, departs 0700). For a 2-day crossing (operates all year round), there is an overnight stop in Peulla. Details about accommodation under Peulla, in **Chile**, page 785. Several tour companies sell this tour, inc transport, board and lodging. Book in advance during the high season. The other agencies sell excursions to Puerto Frías using a Mercedes bus to Puerto Pañuelo, a Turisur boat to Puerto Blest and share a bus and boat to Puerto Frías with excursion groups going on to Chile. Information from Turismo Catedral which owns the exclusive rights to the excursion via the lakes, using their own boats and bus from Puerto Pañuelo to Puerto Frías (Andina del Sud operates with them on the Chilean side).

By car: full-circle from Bariloche can be done by going first via Puyehue to Puerto Montt, returning via Tromen Pass (good road), then Junín and San Martín de los Andes. No cars are taken on the ferry on Lago Todos Los Santos.

SOUTH OF BARILOCHE

The road from Bariloche to El Bolsón is paved for about the first 40 km, after which it becomes narrow and steep with many S bends. It passes the beautiful lakes Gutiérrez, Mascardi and Guillelmo.

Villa Mascardi is the starting point for a 2-day walk from **Pampa Linda** over Paso de los Nubes to Laguna Frías and Puerto Frías on the Chilean frontier. To reach Pampa Linda take the Mercedes bus to Villa Mascardi then hitch the remaining 50 km (the road has a one-way system: up only before 1400, down only after 1600). Register at the Ranger station at Pampa Linda (entry US$5) and ask their advice about conditions (campsite at Ranger Station). The route should only be attempted if there is no snow on the pass (normally passable only between Dec and Feb). From Pampa Linda two other paths lead up Cerro Tronador.

Río Villegas, about 80 km S of Bariloche on the road to El Bolsón, is very beautiful (**D** *Hostería Río Villegas*, pleasant, friendly, restaurant, just outside the gates of the National Park, by the river).

EL BOLSON

130 km S of Bariloche this attractive small town (*Pop* 8,000; *Phone code* 0944) is in beautiful country, with many mountain walks and waterfalls (dry in summer) nearby. As it lies in a hollow at about 300m, it can be very hot in summer. It has good fishing and is fully developed as a tourist resort. Within half an hour's drive are Lagos Puelo (see below) and Epuyén (shops and petrol available). Famous local fruit preserves can be bought at the factories in town. Handicraft market Thur and Sat. The Balneario Municipal is 300m from the town centre, pleasant river swimming.

Excursions

To **Lago Puelo**, about 20 km S in the Parque Nacional Lago Puelo. Regular buses from Av San Martín in El Bolsón go to the lake via Villa Lago Puelo (*Hostería Enebros*, T 99054; *Hostería Lago Puelo*, T 99059; also *cabañas*) where there are a bank, shops and fuel. From here a path runs 12 km W to Chile. Inside the park (free entry) is the *Albergue El Turbio*, T 92523, horse and kayak hire, 10% discount for ISIC and youth card holders (information from *Turismo Translago* in El Bolsón). Good information on the park is available from the wardens at the entrance. *Turismo Translago* excursions from the paying campsite, or from office in town: ½-day trip across the lake to Valle Río Turbio below Cerro Tres Picos, US$15; also to the Chilean border and Lago Interior. Canoes can be rented for US$3/hr to appreciate the beauty of the lake. Use 'Fletes' truck transport to get to more remote treks and campsites. Good walking and climbing on Cerro Piltriquitrón, 6-7 hrs round trip, great views, food and shelter at *refugio*; agencies arrange return transport.

Local information
● Accommodation
Very difficult to find in the high season.

A3 *Cordillera*, San Martín 3210, T 92235, warm; *Motel La Posta*, T 92297, smart (Route 258).

B *Amancay*, San Martín 3217, welcoming; **C** *Hostería Steiner*, San Martín 300, T 92224, pleasant, wood fire, lovely garden; **C** *Familia Sarakoumsky*, San Martín 3003, good; **C** *Salinas*, Rocas 641, T 92396, rec; **D** *Hosp Los Amigos*, Las Malvinas y Balcarce, 2 cabins or camping, breakfast inc, rec (also has cabins and camping 6 km away on Río Azul, good hiking and swimming in river, owners will provide transport); **E** *Campamento Ecológico*, Pagano y Costa del Río, T 92-954, bunks, US$5 camping, hot water, cooking facilities.

Youth hostel: **E** pp *El Pueblito*, 3 km N in Luján, 1 km off Route 258, T 0847, cooking and laundry facilities, shop, open fire; 6 km from town is *La Casona de Odile*, small farm, home cooking, reservations only (Apdo 83, 8430 El Bolsón, Pca Río Negro, T/F 92753). 20 km N of El Bolsón, at Rinconada del Mallín Ahogado (daily bus from El Bolsón) is **A3** *Hostería María y Pancho Kramer*, warmly rec, wholefood meals, hot shower, sauna, swimming pool, chess, volleyball, horseback and trekking excursions to lakes and mountains. At Lago Epuyén, 40 km S of El Bolsón, **E** pp *Refugio del Lago*, with breakfast, also full and half pension; meals with fresh food, tours, trekking, riding, rec, French owned, Sophie and Jacques Dupont, Correo Epuyén, 9211 Chubut, or leave a message, T 0944-99025.

● Camping
Del Sol, Balneario Municipal, **F** pp, pleasant, friendly, cheap food. *La Chacra*, Route 288, 15 mins' walk from town, US$5 pp, hot showers, kiosk, restaurant. *Aldea Suiza* camping site, 4 km N on Route 258, rec, tennis courts, hot showers, good restaurant; *Nokan Cani*, 4 km S on road towards Lago Puelo, pleasant site nr stream, picnic tables, toilets, hot showers, electricity, owner is an acupuncturist, rec; *El Bolsón*, 1 km N of town, clean, rec. The paying campsite (US$5) at Lago Puelo has beautiful views across the lake to Tres Picos, but the walking is limited, expensive shop and café; free campsite also at Lago Puelo. Frequent public transport from El Bolsón.

● Places to eat
Don Diego, San Martín 3217, good; *Ricar-Dos*, Roca y Moreno, good coffee (food less good); *Parrilla Achachay*, San Martín y Belgrano, basic, but reasonable value; *El Viejo Maitén*, Roca 359, good; *Amacuy*, San Mateo 3217, good; *Lustra*, Sarmiento 3212, good value; *Parrilla Las Brasas*, Sarmiento y P Hube, clean, good; *Jauja*, San Martin 2867, great pasta, very friendly, natural ice cream; *Café Bentler*, Güemes y Rivadavia, German run; *El Parador de Olaf*, at Las Golondrinas, Route 258, 6 km S, very good *parrilla* and Scandinavian specialities.

● Banks & money changers
Hotel Cordillera, or *Inmobiliaria Turneo* shop, cash only.

● Sports
Horse riding: Horacio Fernández, Loma del Medio, Apdo Postal 33, El Bolsón, CP 8430; trips of 1 or more days into the mountains, US$20/day, plus US$15 for Horacio and his horse, highly rec for all standards. Cross bridge over Río Azul, follow road to right, at power station turn left, follow path straight ahead and on hill is 'Cabalgatas' sign on left.

● Tour companies & travel agents
Turismo Translago, Perito Moreno 360, T 92523, 10% discount for ISIC and youth card holders on lake excursions to Chilean border and to Valle del Turbio, trekking to Lago Puelo and Lago Plataforma. The local aeroclub (T 92412 or contact via *Hotel Cordillera*) offer spectacular flights over the Andes, US$100 per hr, max 3 passengers.

● Tourist offices
Office on main plaza, open 0900-2000. Sketch maps of the walks in the neighbourhood inc roads that don't exist.

● Transport
Local Car hire: no car hire; best bet is Esquel.

Buses Full-day tours from Bariloche are run by Don Otto and Mercedes, 11 hrs, very crowded and difficult to get on in high season. Also local bus by Mercedes from Bariloche, US$10, 3¼ hrs; Empresa Charter offers 10% to ISIC and youth card holders between Bariloche and El Bolsón.

CHOLILA

situated about 80 km S of El Bolsón, offers superb views of Lago Cholila, crowned by the Matterhorn-like mountains of Cerros Dos and Tres Picos. The ranch where Butch Cassidy, the Sundance Kid and Ethel Place lived between 1901 and 1905 is 13 km N along Ruta 258 and can be visited. A recommended journey for motorists is to spend the night at El Bolsón, enter the Los Alerces park via Cholila and drive right through it to Esquel, travelling the whole length of Lagos Rivadavia and Futalaufquen.

Excursions   Good walk around Lago Mosquito: continue down the road from *El Trébol* past the lake then take a path to the left, following the river. Cross the river on the farm bridge and continue to the base of the hills to a second bridge. Follow the path to the lake and walk between the lake and the hills, crossing the exit river via a suspension bridge just past *El Trébol* – 6 hrs (Nick Saunders and Sarah Jaggs, London W1).

Local festivals   Fiesta del Asado, 3rd week in Jan.

● **Accommodation**   **C** pp *El Trébol*, T/F 98055, with breakfast, comfortable rooms with stoves, meals and half board also available, popular with fishing expeditions, reservations advised, bus stops in village 4 km away; *Hostería El Pedregoso*, at Lago Cholila, 8 km W; *Casa de Te*, Ruta 258 13 km N, with breakfast. **Camping:** **F** pp *Autocamping Carlos Pellegrini*, next to El Trébol; free camping in El Morro park; *Camping El Abuelo*, 13 km S.

ESQUEL

(*Pop* 18,800; *Phone code* 0945), 260 km S of Bariloche, was originally an offshoot of the Welsh colony at Chubut, nearly 650 km to the E. A modern town in a fertile valley, Esquel is known for its tulips, chocolate, jellies and jams. Good walks from the town to Laguna La Zeta, 5 km, nice views, and to Cerro La Cruz, 2 hrs, also good views.

Local information
● **Accommodation**

A2 *Tehuelche*, 9 de Julio 825, T 52421, heating, breakfast, restaurant, some staff speak English; **A3** *Angelina*, Alvear 758, T 52763, good food, warm, run by Italian teacher, highly rec; **C** *Res Esquel*, San Martín 1040, T 52534, helpful, heating, rec; **B** *La Tour D'Argent*, San Martín 1063, T 54612, with breakfast; **B** *Maika*, 25 de Mayo y San Martín, T/F 51466, without breakfast, *confitería*; **C** *Hostería Los Tulipanes*, Fontana 365, T 52748, good rooms and service; **C** *Hostal La Hoya*, Ameghino 2296, T 52473, on road to airport, 1 km (also **C** *Hostería La Hoya* at the Centro Deportivo de Ski at La Hoya itself); **C** *Res Lihuen*, San Martín 820, T/F 52589, without breakfast, English spoken, good value; **C** *Vascongada*, Mitre y 9 de Julio, T 52361, good cheap food; **C** *Huentru Niyeu* (no sign), Chacabuco 606, T 52576, quiet, modern, garage; **D** *Lago Verde*, Volta 1081, T 52251, doubles only, breakfast extra, modern, comfortable, highly rec; **D** pp *Confitería Suiza*, Antártida Argentina 569, T 52727, rooms and apartments, German and English spoken; **C** *Res Huemul*, Alvear y 25 de Mayo, T 52149, without breakfast, good *confitería*; **D** *Res Argentino*, 25 de Mayo 862, T 52237, without breakfast, old fashioned, great bar, restaurant; **C-E** *Sra Helga Hammond*, Antártida Argentina 522, German spoken; **D** *Res El Cisne*, Chacabuco 778, with bath; **E** *Mrs Megan Rowlands' guesthouse* at Rivadavia 330, T 52578, Welsh spoken, rec; **E** *Sra Olga Daher*, Sarmiento 269, quiet. Ask at tourist office for lodgings in private houses. Hotels are often full in February.

Youth hostel: **E** *Lihuen*, San Martín 820, T/F 52589, open all year.

Camping: *El Hogar del Mochilero*, Roca 1028, US$3 pp, laundry facilities, free firewood, rec; *Millalen*, Ameghino 2063, T 56164, good services. Municipal site 5 km from centre on Trevelin road, nr gravel-crushing plant, hot showers, rec. Free campsite at Laguna Z, 5 km along C Fontana. La Colina, on hill overlooking town, Darwin 1400, US$3 pp, hot showers, kitchen facilities, lounge with log fire, highly rec. Those with sleeping bags can go to the Salesian school and sleep in the school classrooms, Dec to Mar; get recommendation from tourist office.

● **Places to eat**

Jockey Club, Alvear 949, reasonably priced; *Ahla Wasahla*, Sarmiento y San Martín, good, cheap, friendly, closed Sun; *Red Fox*, Sarmiento 795 y Alvear, a British-style pub with light, expensive meals, open from 2200, closed Tues; *Don Chichino*, 9 de Julio 964, good, Italian; *Vascongada*, 9 de Julio y Mitre, trout specialities; *Parrilla La Estancia*, 25 de Mayo 541, quite good; *El Mesón*, Rivadavia 1034, reasonable, but slow service; *La Trochita*, Rivadavia 931, *parrilla*, good value; *Parrilla de María*, Rivadavia 1024, popular; *Pizzería Don Pipo*, Fontana 649, good pizzas and *empanadas*; *Atelier*, 25 de Mayo y San Martín, good coffee, cheap, open 24 hrs; *Vestry*, Rivadavia 1065, Welsh tea room. Home made chocolate and the famous local mazard berry liquor is sold at the *Braese Store*, 9 de Julio 1540.

● **Banks & money changers**
Banco de la Nación Güemes y San Martín, accepts TCs, no commission on Mastercard, open 0730-1300; Viajes Sol del Sur, 9 de Julio 1086, accept TCs, open Mon-Fri, 1000-1300; Viasur, 9 de Julio 1027, Amex TCs only.

● **Post & telecommunications**
Post and telecommunications office opp the bus terminal at Fontana y Alvear (open 0800-2000).

● **Laundry**
Laverap, B Mitre 543; *Marva*, San Martín 941, US$10 per load; both 0900-2100 Mon-Sat.

● **Shopping**
Casa de Esquel (Robert Müller), 25 de Mayo 415, wide range of new and second hand books.

● **Sports**
Fishing: in the Arroyo Pescado, US$30 a day.
Skiing: La Hoya, 15 km N, has 7 ski-lifts. For skiing information ask at Club Andino Esquel; bus to La Hoya from Esquel, 3 a day, US$7 return, ski pass US$10-18 depending on season, gear hire US$7 a day.

● **Tour companies & travel agents**
Esquel Tours, Fontana 754, T 52704, and at airport, good for local tours, to Lagos Menéndez and Cisnes. *Fairway Sports and Adventures*, Roca 687, T/F 53380, for trekking, canoeing, *estancias*, horseriding, knowledgeable guides, rec.

● **Tourist offices**
Alvear y Sarmiento, very friendly, can arrange lodgings in private homes. Closed Sat and Sun off-season.

● **Transport**
Local Car hire: Fiocaci, 9 de Julio 740, T 52299/52704; **Esquel Tours**, address above, very good US$60 per day. **Mechanic**: Claudio Peinados, Brown 660, T 53462, highly rec.

Air Airport, 20 km E of Esquel, by paved road, US$14 by taxi. US$2.50 by bus; US$4 by Esquel Tours bus 1 hr before each LADE flight. To **Buenos Aires** with Austral (T 53413/53614), via San Martín de los Andes. Kaiken to Mendoza, Bariloche, Comodoro Rivadavia, Calafate, Ushuaia, Río Gallegos, Río Grande, Trelew and Neuquén.

Trains *La Trochita*: service to El Maitén, Thurs, US$15 one way, return Wed. There is also a *tren turístico* to Nahuel Pan, Mon, Wed, Sat, US$15 return.

Buses From Buenos Aires travel via Bariloche. To **Comodoro Rivadavia** (paved), Don Otto, 4 times a week, US$25 (but usually arrives from Bariloche full in season) or Angel Giobbi, Tues, and Fri 0600, US$25, via Río Mayo. Don Otto to **Bariloche**, US$30, direct. Empresa Mercedes goes daily (9 hrs) to **Bariloche** at 0800, best bus for views (and at 2200), US$28.50. To **El Bolsón**, 5 hrs, US$10. To **Trelew**, US$32, 9 hrs, leaves 0900 Tues, Thur, Sat, and 2200 Mon, Wed, Fri;

La Trochita (The Old Patagonian Express)

Esquel is the terminus of a 402 km branch-line from Ingeniero Jacobacci, a junction on the old Buenos Aires-Bariloche mainline, 194 km E of Bariloche. This narrow-guage line (0.75m wide) took 23 years to build, being finally opened in 1945. It was made famous outside Argentina by Paul Therroux who desribed it in his book *The Old Patagonian Express*. The 1922 Henschel and Baldwin steam locomotives (from Germany and USA respectively) are powered by fuel oil and use 100 litres of water every kilometres. Water has to be taken on at least every 40 km along the route. Most of the coaches are Belgian and also date from 1922. If you want to see the engines you need to go to El Maitén where the workshops are.

Until the Argentine government handed responsibility for railways over to the provincial governments in 1994, regular services ran the length of the line. Since then services have been maintained between Esquel and El Maitén by the provincial government of Chubut. For timetable see under **Esquel**.

In El Maitén there are two hotels, same owner, both overpriced: *Accomazzo*, with good restaurant; **A3** *La Vasconia*, near station, basic. On Thurs a bus for Esquel meets the train in El Maitén, check details first in Esquel.

other bus companies on Av Fontana and Alvear (bus terminal) are Empresa Don Otto, Chubut, Denis. To **Trevelin**, Codao, every hour 0700-2100, US$1. Bus terminal T 52233, also for taxis.

TREVELIN

(Pop 5,000), 23 km SW of Esquel, is an offshoot of the Welsh Chubut colony (see page 208). There is a Welsh chapel (built 1910, closed) and there are tea rooms. The **Museo Regional**, in the old mill (1918) includes artefacts from the Welsh colony and, upstairs, a model of the Futaleufú hydro-electric dam (entry US$2). The **Hogar de Mi Abuelo** is a private park and museum, dedicated to John Evans, one of the first settlers, whose granddaughter acts as a guide, entry US$2. The Nant-y-fall Falls lie 17 km SW on the road to the frontier, entrance US$0.50 pp including guide to all seven falls ($1\frac{1}{2}$-hr walk).

● **Accommodation & places to eat** *Hostería Estefanía*, Perito Moreno s/n, T 8148; *Hosp Trevelin*, San Martín 327, T 8102; *El Chalet*, San Martín y Brown, T 80159, cabins. Grills at *Che Ferrada*, good mixed *parrillada* at *El Quincho*, and several tea rooms offering *té galés* and *torta negra:* eg *El Adobe* on Av Patagonia; *Nain Maggie*, P Moreno 179, rec; *Owen Sea*; *La Cabaña*, 7 km out on the road from Trevelin to Lago Futalaufquen. Municipal campsite nr centre. On the road to Esquel 3 km from Trevelin, signposted on the righthand side, is *La Granja Trevelin*, owned by Domingo Giacci, macrobiotic meals and good Italian cooking, sells milk, cheese and onions; camping, hot water and wc, bungalows US$15 a day; excellent horses for hire.

● **Tourist offices** Good office in central plaza.

PARQUE NACIONAL LOS ALERCES

60 km W of Esquel, the National Park includes larch trees over 1,000 years old and **Lago Futalaufquen**, entry US$5 (even if just passing through on Route 258). The E side of Los Alerces has much the same natural attractions as the Nahuel Huapi and Lanín parks, but is much less developed for tourism. Lago Futalaufquen has some of the best fishing in this huge area (season 15 Nov-Easter).

The park administration is at Villa Futalaufquen, at the southern end of the lake; it has a small museum with displays on the flora and fauna of the park. Nearby are a service station and two expensive supermarkets.

An interesting part of the park can be reached from a separate entrance through Trevelin following the Río Futaleufú, but one can go only 22 km W because of the Futaleufú hydroelectric dam. Behind it is Lago Amutui Quimei, which has swallowed Lago Situación and three others stretching almost to the frontier. Entrance by car to see Futaleufú dam is only allowed at 1500, under police supervision; photography not permitted, except on top of the dam itself. There is no public transport to the dam.

Trekking and tours The W side of Lago Futalaufquen is untouched by tourism, by law. There is good walking eg to Cinco Saltos, and El Dedal. The latter is a 6-hr hike from *Hotel Futalaufquen* up and back, with great views of the lakes and the cordillera from the top. A good information leaflet describing the flora and fauna encountered along the trail up to Cerro Dedal is available at the park headquarters. Regular full day launch trip from Puerto Limonao (reached by early morning minibus) on Lago Futalaufquen (a sheer delight) through Río Arrayanes to windless Lago Verde (2 campsites, one US$3 pp, one free, very crowded in summer, the free campsite is nicely situated and has a small shop; *Camping Agreste Lago Verde* offers 10% discount to ISIC and youth card holders). From there one can walk out to the end of Lago Menéndez, famous for its giant larch trees; a boat on Lago Menéndez leaves at 1400 but book the day before in Esquel, preferably, as it will not leave if there are not enough passengers; arrive early to claim your space, crossing 90 mins. The dock can be reached by a 30-min walk across the bridge between lakes Futalaufquen and Verde. Lovely view of Lago Cisne (Swan Lake) to the NW end of Lago Menéndez. One then walks a 3 km nature trail looking across the Andes to Chile before returning. Tours arranged at Esquel cost US$52 inc boat on Lago Menéndez and a guided tour around the 2 km walk to Lago Cisne. A road connects all the lakes. The tourist office in Esquel has a pamphlet on all the walks in the Park. Guided tours on the dam itself, hourly in season, small fee. **NB** *Refugio Lago Krüger* in the Park offers 10% discount to ISIC and youth card holders, camping and fishing also available.

● **Accommodation On the E side of Lago Futalaufquen**: *Quime Quipán*, T 22272, rec for fishing, closed in winter; **A2** *Hostería Los Tepúes*, simple, rustic, open all year, family bungalow for rent; **A2** *Pucón Pai*, T 3799, good restaurant, rec for fishermen (holds a fishing festival to open the season); open out of season for large groups only; has campsite; next door **C** *Cabañas Tejas Negras*, good facilities for camping. *Cume Hué*, T 2858, also rec for fishing. *Trevelin Lodge*, also specializes in fishing, run by O'Farrell Safaris, organizes tours, whitewater rafting and horse-riding. (Contact Telluride Flyfishers, PO Box 1634, Telluride, Colorado, T 800-828-7547.) Camping at Villa Futalaufquen and at Los Maitenes (US$4pp, hot showers, clean, closed May-Sept), store. **On the W side: L2** *Hotel Futalaufquen* just N of Puerto Limonao, T 2648, rec, especially rooms 2/3 and 4/5 which have balconies overlooking the lake, open all year (no heating in rooms); good walking around the hotel.

● **Transport from Esquel** Bus (Transportes Esquel) to Lago Verde passing along the E side of Lago Futalaufquen at 0800, 1400 and 1830 daily in season (it passes 3 hotels and drives into 2 camp sites).

FRONTIER WITH CHILE – PASO FUTALEUFU

● **Immigration and customs**
The frontier is 70 km SW of Esquel via Trevelin. Campsite (Camping Río Grande) on Argentine side of river. Cross the frontier river by bridge after passing Argentine customs; Chilean customs is 1 km on the other side of river (1 hr for all formalities). At the Futaleufú and Palena border crossings, Argentine border officials only give transit visas: legalize your stay within 10 days either by leaving the country or by renewing your entry stamp at an immigration office.

● **Transport**
From Esquel to Paso Futaleufú, Codao bus Mon, Fri, 0800, 1700, US$4.50, 2 hrs, return departures 1100, 1900. Minibus from Paso Futaleufú to Futaleufú (10 km) US$3. Very little traffic for hitching. (For transport from Futaleufú to Chaitén (Chile) see Chile chapter.) From Esquel to the Palena border crossing, bus Sun, Mon, Wed 1700, Fri 0900, return departures Mon, Tues, Thurs 0700, Fri 1700.

ROUTES South of Esquel, Route 40 is paved through the towns of Tecka and **Gobernador Costa** (**D** *Hotels Jair*, and *Vega*; municipal campsite with all services, US$2) in Chubut province. 34 km S of Gobernador Costa, gravelled Route 40 forks SW through the town of Alto Río Senguer, while provincial Route 20 heads almost directly S for 81 km (ACA petrol station at isolated La Laurita), before turning E towards Sarmiento and Comodoro Rivadavia. At La Puerta del Diablo, in the valley of the lower Río Senguer, Route 20 intersects provincial Route 22, which joins with Route 40 at the town of Río Mayo (see page 219). This latter route is completely paved and preferable to Route 40 for long-distance motorists; good informal campsites on the W side of the bridge across the Río Senguer.

Patagonia

THE VAST, windy, treeless plateau south of the Río Colorado: the Atlantic coast is rich in marine life, most easily seen around Puerto Madryn. In the south of the region is the Parque Nacional de los Glaciares, with journeys on lakes full of ice floes and to the Moreno glacier. In the Chubut Valley is Argentina's Welsh community.

Patagonia is sub-divided into the provinces of Neuquén, Río Negro, Chubut, Santa Cruz and Tierra del Fuego. The area covers 780,000 sq km: 28% of the national territory, but has a population of only 600,000, little over 2.7% of the total population; and 57% of it is urban. Wide areas have less than one person to the sq km, and there are virtually no trees except in the N and the Andean foothills.

Climate and economy

Over the whole land there blows a boisterous, cloud-laden strong wind which raises a haze of dust in summer, but in winter the dust can turn into thick mud. Temperatures are moderated by the proximity of the sea and are singularly mild, neither rising high during the summer nor falling low during the winter. Even in Tierra del Fuego, where the warmest summer months average $10\frac{1}{2}$°C, the winter days' average can reach a high of about 2°C. Make sure you have plenty of warm clothing, and anti-freeze in your car, available locally. In the foothills of the Andes rainfall is high, supporting a line of beech forests which run from Neuquén to Tierra del Fuego. Amounts of rain decline rapidly as you go E and Eastern Patagonia is more or less desert. Deep crevices or canyons intersect the land from E to W. Few of them contain permanent water, but ground water is easily pumped to the surface. The great sheep *estancias* are along these canyons, sheltered from the wind, and in the depression running N from the Strait of Magellan to Lagos Argentino and Buenos Aires and beyond. During a brief period in spring, after the melting of the snows, there is grass on the plateau. Most of the land is devoted to sheep raising. Overgrazing leads to much erosion. Wild dogs, pumas and red foxes are the sole predators of the sheep. Because of the high winds and insufficient rainfall there is little agriculture except in the N, in the valleys of the Colorado and Negro rivers. Some cattle are raised in both valleys where irrigation permits the growing of alfalfa.

Patagonia is rich in extractive resources: the oil of Comodoro Rivadavia and Tierra del Fuego, the little exploited iron ore of Sierra Grande, the coal of Río Turbio, the hydro-electric capacity of El Chocón, plentiful deposits of minerals (particularly bauxite) and marine resources, but their exploitation has been slow. Tourism is opening up too.

In all Patagonia there is only one town – Comodoro Rivadavia – with a population over 100,000. Most of the towns are small ports, which used only to work during the wool-shipping season but have livened up since the local economy began to diversify.

Wildlife

Guanacos and rheas are a common sight: there are also *maras*, Patagonian hares. Along the Patagonian coast there are sea lion and penguin colonies; some protected waters are breeding grounds for the Commerson's dolphin and the grey dolphin. Elephant seals and Southern right whales

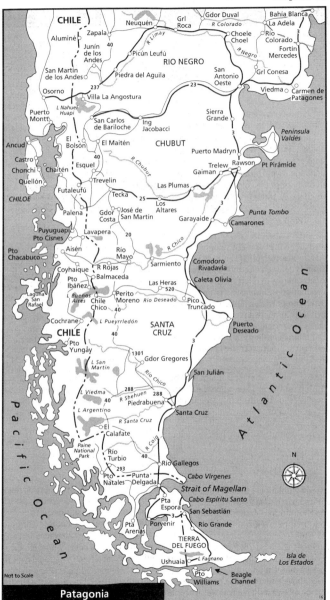

Patagonia

The Welsh Settlement

On 28 July 1865, 153 Welsh immigrants landed at Puerto Madryn, then a deserted beach deep in Indian country. After three weeks they pushed, on foot, across the parched pampa and into the Chubut river valley, where there is flat cultivable land along the riverside for a distance of 80 km upstream. Here, maintained in part by the Argentine Government, they settled, but it was three years before they realized the land was barren unless watered. They drew water from the river, which is higher than the surrounding flats, and later built a fine system of irrigation canals. The colony, reinforced later by immigrants from Wales and from the United States, prospered, but in 1899 a great flood drowned the valley and some of the immigrants left for Canada. The last Welsh contingent arrived in 1911. The object of the colony had been to create a 'Little Wales beyond Wales', and for four generations they kept the Welsh language alive. The language is, however, dying out in the fifth generation. There is an offshoot of the colony of Chubut at Trevelin, at the foot of the Andes nearly 650 km to the W, settled in 1888 (see page 204). It is interesting that this distant land gave to the Welsh language one of its most endearing classics: *Dringo'r Andes* (Climbing the Andes), written by one of the early women settlers.

breed along the coast of Valdés peninsula and the nearby gulfs. The best viewing season is between Oct and April. Further S, particularly in Tierra del Fuego, the Magellan goose (*caiquén*), is one of the most commonly seen of the 152 species of birds (recommended reading, *Aves de Argentina y Uruguay*, available, in English, from main bookshops in Buenos Aires as well as major tourist centres in Patagonia).

Colonization

The coast of Patagonia was first visited by a European late in 1519, when the Portuguese Fernão Magalhães (Magellan), then in the service of Spain, was on his voyage round the world. Early in 1520 he turned W into the strait which now bears his name and there struggled with fierce headwinds until he reached that Sea of Peace he named the Pacific. Later European attempts to settle along the coast were deterred by isolation, lack of food and water and the harsh climate as well as the dour and obdurate local Indians, but these were almost entirely wiped out in the wars of 1879-1883, generally known as the 'Campaign of the Desert'. Before this there had been a long established colony at Carmen de Patagones; it shipped salt to Buenos Aires during the colonial period. There had also been a settlement of Welsh people in the Chubut Valley since 1865 (see box).

After the Indian wars colonization was rapid, the Welsh, Scots and English taking a great part. Chilean sheep farmers from Punta Arenas moved N along the depression at the foot of the Andes, eastwards into Tierra del Fuego, and N to Santa Cruz.

● **Recommended reading** *In Patagonia* by Bruce Chatwin, a good introduction to the area and its people. *Patagonia*, by Metzeltin and Buscaini (Dall' Oglio, Milan). *At Home with the Patagonians*, by George Musters (history of 19th century life of Patagonian Indians), ed John Murray, London 1871/1973. *Argentine Trout Fishing. A Fly Fisherman's Guide to Patagonia* by William C Leitch (ISBN 1-87817-5-06-8)

Communications

Air Main air services are given in the text below. Check for discounts on flights. Prepare for delays in bad weather.

Many air force LADE flights in the region S of Bariloche must be booked in advance from departure point of flight. The planes are small and fly low; passengers miss little of what there is to be seen, highly recommended for those who enjoy flying. The baggage allowance is 15 kg. Flights are often heavily booked ahead, but always check again on the day of the flight if you are told beforehand that it is sold out. LADE tickets are much cheaper for a long flight with stops than buying separate segments. LADE's computer reservation system is linked to Aerolíneas Argentinas, so flight connections are possible between these airlines.

Road The main road, Route 3, which runs near the coast, is paved from Buenos Aires to Río Gallegos. South of this town it is paved as far as Tolhuin, from where it is all weather to Ushuaia. Sometimes passengers going S have to pay for baggage by weight. Many buses do not operate between early April and late October.

The principal roads in Patagonia roughly form an inverted triangle. Route 3 has regular traffic and adequate services. At the southern end, this route enters Chile and crosses the Magellan Straits to Tierra del Fuego by the car ferry at Primera Angostura. The western route (Route 40) zigzags across the moors, is lonely and is good in parts, poor in others (more details given below); there is hardly any traffic except in Dec, Jan and Feb, the tourist season. However, it is by far the more interesting road, with fine views of the Andes and plenty of wildlife as well as the Alerces and Glaciares National Parks. Camping is no problem, and there are good hotels at Esquel, Perito Moreno, Calafate and (in Chile) Coyhaique and Puerto Natales. Third class accommodation also at Gobernador Gregores and Río Mayo. The northern part of the triangle is formed by the paved highway running from Bariloche through Neuquén to San Antonio Oeste.

Many of the roads in Southern Argentina are gravelled. The price of a good windscreen protector varies according to make of car, but can be US$50 in Buenos Aires. For a VW Kombi they are hard to find at a reasonable price. More primitive versions can be bought for much less, or made from wire mesh, wood and string. The best types are the grid-type, or inflatable plastic ones which are made for some standard-type vehicles, the only disadvantage being some loss of visibility. Drivers should also look out for cattle grids (*guardaganados*), even on main highways. They are signed; cross them very slowly. Always carry plenty of fuel, as service stations may be as much as 300

km apart. Fuel prices are very low throughout Patagonia, about half the price of the rest of the country.

Hitchhiking is generally difficult except on Route 3 in spring and summer; camping equipment is useful as long delays can be expected even in the tourist season.

● **NB** In summer hotel prices are grossly inflated (by as much as 100% in Ushuaia, 75% in Calafate); also in some places there may not be enough hotel beds to meet the demand. Camping is increasingly popular, and *estancias* seem hospitable to travellers who are stuck for a bed. Many *estancias*, especially in Santa Cruz province, offer transport, excursions and food as well as accommodation. During Argentine summer holidays (Jan, Feb, Mar) getting a hotel room in Ushuaia, Río Grande, Río Gallegos and Calafate is practically impossible. In this connection, remember that ACA establishments, which charge the same prices all over Argentina, are a bargain in Patagonia and Tierra del Fuego, where all other accommodation is expensive. As very few hotels and restaurants have a/c or even fans, it can get uncomfortably hot in January. TCs are hard to change throughout Patagonia.

NORTHERN PATAGONIA

The upper course of the Río Colorado is the northern limit of Patagonia.

VIEDMA

160 km S of where it reaches the sea (250 km S of Bahía Blanca), about 27 km from the mouth of the Río Negro, is **Carmen de Patagones** (*Pop* 16,000), standing on high ground on the N bank, with **Viedma** (*Pop* 26,000; *Phone code* 0920) the capital of Río Negro Province, across the river, which is spanned by a connecting rail and road bridge, pleasant setting. There is also a frequent ferry service for pedestrians. On a hill behind Patagones a monument commemorates an attack on the twin towns by a Brazilian squadron in 1827. There are three museums, open 1000-1200 only. The swimming is recommended on the Viedma side of the river, where there is a nice shady shore.

Excursions Beautiful beach, El Cóndor, 30 km S of Viedma, 3 buses a day from Viedma in summer, hotel open Jan-Feb, restaurants and shops, free camping on beach 2 km S. 30 km from El Cóndor is the Lobería Punta Bermeja, a sealion colony; daily bus in summer from Viedma; hitching easy in summer.

- **Accommodation & places to eat** At **Viedma**: **B** *Austral*, Villarino 292, T 22019, rec, modern; **C** *Peumayen*, Buenos Aires 334, T 25243; *Restaurant Munich*, Buenos Aires 150, open late. **Camping**: good municipal site 500m after crossing the river on the new road bridge on the right, US$14/tent plus US$4 pp, all facilities inc hot showers, but can be noisy at weekends. Further camping sites on the Río Negro where the main route into Patagonia meets the river (some 170 km from Viedma due NW) with all facilities including a small shop. Additional shops at Gen Conesa, 2 km away. Mosquito repellent needed.

- **Banks & money changers** Travel agency at Namuncurá 78, Viedma, exchanges Amex cheques.

- **Tourist offices** Belgrano 544, p 9, Viedma.

- **Transport Air** From Buenos Aires and Bariloche with Austral (the city is also served by LADE). **Trains** To Bariloche. **Buses** Terminal at C A Zatti y Lavalle about 6 blocks from main plaza. To/from **Buenos Aires** US$45, La Estrella/Cóndor. To **San Antonio Oeste**, US$7.50.

SAN ANTONIO OESTE

Almost due W and 180 km along the coast, on the Gulf of San Matías, is **San Antonio Oeste** (*Pop* 10,000; *Phone code* 0934). 17 km S is a popular seaside resort, **Las Grutas**, developed in the 1960s with good safe beach (the caves themselves are not really worth visiting); bus from San Antonio hourly US$1.30. The whole of Las Grutas closes down in mid-Mar.

- **Accommodation** At **San Antonio**: **B** *Kandava*, Sarmiento 240, T 21430, hot water, good; **C** *Golfo Azul*, simple; **C** *Iberia*, Sarmiento 241, without breakfast, small rooms, but rec; **D** *Betty*, Islas Malvinas 1410, T 22370. In **Las Grutas**: ACA has a *Unidad Turística*, T 97095, with 6-bed rooms, no restaurant. **C** *Tour du Golfe*, Av Bariloche y Sierra Grande, 3 bedrooms, cooking facilities. There are also many good camping sites (eg *La Entrada*, US$5/tent, on edge of town above beach, *AMVI*, clean, nr beach). Seafood restaurants.

- **Transport Trains** lines E to Viedma and W to **Bariloche**. Services: Wed and Sat eve to Bariloche, Wed and Sat 0600 to Viedma. **Buses** North to **Bahía Blanca** and S to **Río Gallegos** and **Punta Arenas** by Transportes Patagónicos;

to **Viedma** 0700 daily, US$7.50; to **Puerto Madryn** and **Trelew**, Don Otto, 0200 and 1530, 4 hrs, US$20; to **Buenos Aires**, US$46 via Bahía Blanca, frequent.

ROUTES From San Antonio Oeste a road runs N 91 km through bush country providing fodder for a few cattle, with a view to the W of the salt flats called Salina del Gualicho, before joining Route 250 which meets the Zapala-Bahía Blanca highway (Route 22) at Choele Choel, 178 km N of San Antonio Oeste (see page 188, and **Road** page 189). Between San Antonio and Puerto Madryn is Sierra Grande (ACA garage and café, camping at rear, no facilities but free hot showers at YPF garage in town), where iron-ore deposits are extracted and piped in solution to an ocean terminal 32 km E.

PUERTO MADRYN AND PENINSULA VALDES

Puerto Madryn (*Pop* about 50,000; *Phone code* 0965), about 250 km S, along Route 3 (paved) in Chubut province, is a port on a wide bay, Golfo Nuevo. The site of the first Welsh landing in 1865, the town was founded in 1886 and named after the Welsh home of the colonist, Jones Parry. The town has a giant alumina plant (visits, Mon 1430, arranged at the tourist office) and fish processing plants. The town is a popular tourist centre, with a casino, skindiving and nature reserves, both close to town and on the nearby Valdés peninsula.

Museums

Museo de Ciencias Naturales y Oceanográfico, Domecq García y J Menéndez, informative and worth a visit, open Tues-Sat 1500-1830, entry US$2, ask to see video.

  Museo de Arte Moderno, Roca 600, daily 1000-1800, US$1.

Local information

- **Accommodation**

Often full in summer, when prices rise; make bookings early. Many smaller places close out of season.

A1 *Península Valdés*, Roca 155, T 71292 4-star, sea view, suites available, sauna, comfortable, rec; **A2** *Bahía Nueva*, Roca 67, T/F 51677, with breakfast, bar, very comfortable; **A3** *Tolosa*, Sáenz Peña 250, T 71850, 3-star, good breakfast; **A3** *Gran Madryn I*, Lugones 40, T 72205, 2-star, good; **A3** *La Posada de Madryn*, Matthews 2951, T 74087, quiet, English spoken, rec; **A3** *Hostal del Rey*, Brown 681, T 71156, on beach, rec, 2-star, breakfast extra, restaurant with fixed price menu; **A3** *Marina*, Roca 7, T 74044, heated, showers, warm, kitchen facilities.

B *Yanco*, Roca 626, T 71581, on beach, without breakfast, nightly entertainment programme, free, has rooms for up to 6; **B** *Muelle Viejo*, Yrigoyen 38, T 71284, opp pier, good restaurant, expensive breakfast, good, quiet; **B** *Res Petit*, Alvear 845, T 51460, quiet, good; **B** *Res La Posta*, Roca 33, T 72422, good, heating, fan, cooking and laundry facilities.

C *Anclamar*, 25 de Mayo 875, T 51509, quiet, rec; **C** *Antiguo/Central*, 28 de Julio 170, T 71742, good, basic, hot water; **C** *Costanera*, Brown 759, T 52800, good value; **C** pp *El Cid*, 25 de Mayo 865, with breakfast, parking; **C** *Español*, 28 de Julio y San Martín, basic, hot water, restaurant, parking, difficult to find; **C** *Hostería Hipocampo*, Vesta 33, helpful; **C** *Res J'os*, Bolívar 75, T 71433, pleasant; **C** *Res Manolo's*, Roca 763, T 72390, breakfast extra, small, quiet, kitchen facilities, homely; **C** *Vaskonia*, 25 de Mayo 43, T 72581, central, good value.

D *Aguas Mansas*, Hernández 51, T 53174, large rooms, kitchen.

E pp *Hosp Santa Rita*, Gob Maiz 370, T 71050, use of kitchen, heating, helpful.

Youth hostel: 25 de Mayo 1136, T 74426, **D** pp dormitory, **C** double room, laundry and kitchen facilities, bike rental, English and French spoken, tours.

Camping: all closed out of season. At Punta Cuevas, 3.5 km S of town, is ACA site with evening hot showers, shop, café, good facilities and shady trees, US$12/tent, but many people camp on beach. There is a swimming pool in the rocks nr the ACA camp site, which gets its water at high tide, very pleasant, and free. Two municipal sites: one at Ribera Sur, 1 km before ACA site on same road along beach (gives student discount). All facilities, very crowded, US$3 pp and US$2/tent for first day. Also room with bunkbeds, **F** pp. Bus from town stops 100m before entrance. The other is N of town at Barrio Brown. Camping out can be interesting as one can watch foxes, armadillos, skunks and rheas roaming around in the evening.

● **Places to eat**

Las Aguilas, M A Zar y Sáenz Peña, rec, large portions, good for seafood; *Don Jorge*, Sáenz

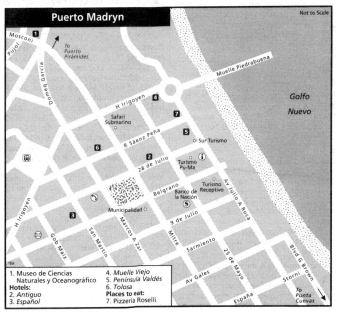

Puerto Madryn

Not to Scale

To Puerto Pirámides

Muelle Piedrabuena

Golfo Nuevo

Mosconi

Pujol

Domec García

H Irigoyen

Safari Submarino

R Sáenz Peña

Sur Turismo

28 de Julio

Turismo Pu-Ma

Belgrano

Turismo Receptivo

Banco de la Nación

Municipalidad

9 de Julio

Marcos A Zar

San Martín

Mitre

Sarmiento

Av Julio A Roca

H Irigoyen

Gob Maiz

25 de Mayo

Blvd G Brown

Storni

Av Gales

España

To Punta Cuevas

1. Museo de Ciencias
   Naturales y Oceanográfico
Hotels:
2. *Antiguo*
3. *Español*

4. *Muelle Viejo*
5. *Península Valdés*
6. *Tolosa*
Places to eat:
7. Pizzería Roselli

Peña y Mitre, *parrilla*, rec; **Cantina El Náutico**, Roca y Lugones, good food, especially fish; *París*, Muelle Piedrabuena, good and reasonably priced; *Pizzería Roselli*, Sáenz Peña y Roca, good, with vegetarian selections; *Quijote*, Belgrano 138, reasonable prices, very good; *Pequeño*, Roca 820, good value; *Barbarians*, 25 de Mayo y 28 de Julio, good coffee. For excellent Welsh afternoon teas, *La Goleta*, Roca 87, 1700-1900. Several local chocolate makers; try *Península* on Roca nr *Turismo Receptivo*; *Café de la Ciudad*, 25 de Mayo y 28 de Julio, very popular.

● **Airline offices**
Aerolíneas Argentinas, 25 de Mayo 150, T 50110; **Lapa**, Belgrano 16, T 50893; LADE office at Roca 119, T 51256.

● **Banks & money changers**
Banks open Mon-Fri 0830-1330 (0800-1300 in summer). **Banco de la Nación**, 25 de Mayo y 9 de Julio, US$10 commission on TCs; **Banco Almafuerte**, 25 de Mayo y Sáenz Peña, 2% commission on TCs; **Banco del Sud**,Sáenz Peña, ATM for Visa; **Banco Provincia Chubut**, 25 de Mayo, changes US$ cash, no commision, Mastercard and Amex ATM. There are no *casas de cambio*, but fair rates from travel agents (eg *Safari Submarino*, address below; go in the morning); **La Moneda**, Roca y 28 de Julio, will exchange large sums, not very good rates. High commission on changing TCs.

● **Entertainments**
Discos: *El Jardín*, Mitre y Sarmiento; *Salsa Discobar*, Brown y 3° Rotonda; *El Rancho*, Brown y 4° Rotonda, American music, small, entry US$10.

● **Laundry**
Laverap, 25 de Mayo 529, 0800-2000, rec.

● **Post & telecommunications**
Post Office: Belgrano y A Maiz. **Telephone**: Roca y 9 de Julio, also fax, 0700-2400; phone and fax at kiosk at Roca 733.

● **Sports**
Puerto Madryn is a diving centre. Tours, inc for those who have never dived before, are organized by several agencies: *Safari Submarino*, Mitre 80, T/F 74110, only one open all year; *Ocean Divers*, Brown entre 1 y 2 Rotundas; *Abismo*, Roca 516, prices inc equipment, US$50 beginners, US$40 experts (less with own equipment) courses on video, photography and underwater communication; PADI instruction US$200. No courses in Jan-February.

● **Tour companies & travel agents**
Several agencies do tours to the Valdés Peninsula, all are for 12 hrs, see below. Prices are fixed by law, but some agencies run larger buses than others. Note that return distances of some tour

destinations are high: Peninsula Valdés 380 km, Punta Tombo 400 km, Ameghino Dam 400 km (last two better from Trelew). The largest agency is *Sur Turismo*, Roca 175, T 73585, ISIC discount; *Safari Submarino*, Mitre 80, Tito Botazzi, small groups, very good, plenty of time at sites (10% reduction to SAH owners) see also under Puerto Pirámides. Other agencies inc: *Receptivo*, Roca 303 y Belgrano, T 51048, Amex agent, weekend and off-season tours, rec; *Pu-Ma*, 28 de Julio 48, T 71482, small groups, rec; *Mar y Valle*, Roca y Belgrano, T 72872, rec; *South Patagonia*, 25 de Mayo 226, small groups; *Coyun Co*, Roca 171, T 51845. *Franca del Sur*, Reconquista 378, T 50710, small groups, Spanish only, rec; *Aquatours*, Muelle Piedrabuena, T 51954, rec.

● **Tourist offices**
Roca 223, T 73029, Mon-Fri 0700-1300, 1500-2100, Sat/Sun 0800-1300,1700-2100 but only Mon-Fri in winter; helpful, has notice board for messages, list of current hotel rates and interesting video on the region.

● **Transport**
Local Car hire: very expensive (US$150/day). Fiorasi, on Sarmiento; **Localiza**, Belgrano 196, T 71660; **Coyun Co**, Roca 171; **Renta Car Patagonia**, Roca 295. **Cycle Hire**: *XT*, Roca 700 block; many other agencies.

Air Daily from Trelew with AR. Airport is 7 km from town, no buses, taxi or *remise* only, US$7-8.

Buses Terminal in old railway station. To **Buenos Aires**, 18 hrs, daily, Don Otto (US$57), La Puntual (US$50), long delays, QueBus (daily except Wed); to **Río Gallegos**, about 20 hrs, Don Otto, 1745 daily US$49, also Andesmar US$58; to **Comodoro Rivadavia**, Don Otto, Andesmar, US$26; to **Bahía Blanca** and Viedma, 12 hrs, US$36; to **Bariloche**, Andesmar daily US$49; to **Córdoba**, US$72, 1900, Tus Tur; to **Caleta Oliva**, US$20, 0700; to **Mendoza**, US$68; Andesmar to **Neuquén**, US$31; to **Santiago** (Chile) via Neuquén, Andesmar, US$89; to **Trelew**, joint service by 28 de Julio and Mar y Valle, approx every 30 mins, US$4.50, 1 hr, driver stops nr entrance to Trelew airport if asked; direct to Trelew airport, Puma, US$5, leaves 1½ hrs before flight and takes arriving passengers back to Puerto Madryn (taxi to airport US$45). Take own food and drink on long trips, regardless of what refreshments you are promised when booking. **Taxis**: outside bus terminal and on main plaza.

For hitching N, try on the industrial estate road, or take a Trelew bus to the main highway then walk 3 km to the service station/truck stop. With luck it is possible to get to Bahía Blanca in 1 day.

NATURE RESERVES

The natural history of the region is most interesting, with elephant seal, sea lion and penguin colonies, breeding grounds for Southern right whales in the Golfo Nuevo and the Golfo San José, fossils in the cliffs, and guanacos, rheas and armadillos in the countryside. Oct-Nov is the time to see the greatest variety of wildlife. Whales can be seen from perhaps as early as June to, at the very latest, end-December. The sea lion breeding season runs from late Dec to late Jan and the penguins are more active in Jan than in Oct-Nov when they are nesting.

The **Punta Loma** sealion reserve is 15 km SE of Puerto Madryn. It is open 0900-1200, 1430-1730; Dec and Jan are the best months. Information and video. Entry US$2. Taxis US$16. Sea-lions can even be seen in Puerto Madryn harbour.

PENINSULA VALDES

The Golfos Nuevo and San José are separated by the Istmo Carlos Ameghino, which leads to Península Valdés. In depressions in the heart of the peninsula are large salt pans; Salina Grande is 42m below sea level. At the entrance to the peninsula, on the isthmus, there is an interesting Visitors' Centre and a conservation officer is stationed here; entry US$5 (US$3 with ISIC card). Near the entrance, Isla de los Pájaros can be seen in Golfo San José. Its seabirds can only be viewed through fixed telescopes (at 400m distance), except for recognized ornithologists who can get permission to visit. The centre for visits to the Peninsula is **Puerto Pirámides** (*Pop* 100), 90 km E of Puerto Madryn. It is from here that whale-watching boat trips depart; sailings are controlled by the Prefectura, according to weather and sea conditions.

At Punta Norte (176 km) at the N end of the Valdés Peninsula, there are elephant seals (breeding season late Sept/early Oct but during the first half of Aug the bull-seals arrive to claim their territory; best seen at low tide); reasonably priced restaurant for meals and snacks. At Caleta Valdés, 45 km S of Punta

Norte you can see penguins and elephant seals at close quarters. At Punta Delgada (at the S of the peninsula) elephant seals and other wildlife can be seen. The beach on the entire coast is out of bounds; this is strictly enforced.

Tours Excursions are organized by tourist agencies in Puerto Madryn (addresses above). Full-day tours take in Puerto Pirámides (with whale-watching in season), plus some, but not necessarily all, of the other wildlife viewing points. Prices are US$25-30 pp plus the entry to the National Park; boat trip to see whales US$20 extra. On all excursions take drink with you, food too if you don't want to eat in the expensive restaurants (binoculars are also a good idea). Most tour companies stay 50-60 mins on location. Tito Bottazzi, T 95050, recommended, can also be contacted via *Safari Submarino* in Puerto Madryn. *Hydro Sports* rents scuba equipment and boats, has a small restaurant, and organizes land and sea wildlife tours (ask for Mariano). Off season tours run when demand is sufficient, usually on Thur and Sun, departing at 0955 and returning at 1730. To avoid disappointment check all excursion dates and opening times in advance.

On the peninsula, the best way to see the wildlife is by car. See above for car hire, a taxi costs US$30 pp for the day. Hitching is very difficult, even at weekends in season. Peninsular roads are all gravel except the road from Puerto Madryn to Puerto Pirámides (tours will not run after heavy rain in the low season).

● **Accommodation & places to eat At Puerto Pirámides: A2** *ACA Motel*, T 72057, poor restaurant, camping; there is also an ACA service station (open daily) with good café and shop; **A3** *Res El Libanés*, T 95007; **C** *Español*, basic but pleasant; *Posada del Mar*, T 95016, restaurant; **A3** pp *Paradise Pub*, T 95030, helpful, rec, good value food and beer, good atmosphere; **B** *Cabañas El Cristal*, T 95033, 4 bed cabañas, rec; municipal campsite by the black sand beach, US$5 pp (free out of season), hot showers in evening only, dirty, busy, get there early to secure a place. Do not camp on the beach: people have been swept away by the incoming tide. **At Punta Delgada: A2** pp *Faro*, T 71910, full board, comfortable, excellent food, rec (reservations at *Hotel*

Península Valdés in Puerto Madryn); there is also a separate restaurant.

● **Shopping** In summer there are several well-stocked shops, but if staying take sun and wind protection and drinking water. There is a shop that sells original Patagonian Indian work.

● **Tourist offices** There is a small tourist office on the edge of Puerto Pirámides, useful information for hikes and driving tours.

● **Buses** Empresa 28 de Julio from Puerto Madryn, Thur, Sun at 1000 returns 1800, US$6.50 each way.

THE CHUBUT VALLEY

RAWSON

(*Pop* 15,000; *Phone code* 0965) the capital of Chubut Province, 7 km from the sea. Above the Ciné Teatro Rawson is the **Museo de la Ciudad**, containing a collection of historical objects and old photos. 5 km down river is Puerto Rawson, and, nearby, Playa Unión, a beach with casino and many restaurants. Tourist Office, 9 de Julio 280.

● **Accommodation** **A3** *Provincial*, Mitre 551, T/F 81400, renovated, comfortable, restaurant; **C** *Res Sampedrano*, Belgrano 744.

● **Places to eat** *La Plaza*, M Moreno y B Vacchina; *Petit Café*, Belgrano y Costa; *Don Ignacio*, 25 de Mayo 251, basic, friendly.

● **Buses** Terminal, Av Antárdida nr 25 de Mayo, but buses to Trelew and La Unión are best caught from the plaza. To Trelew US$2; to Playa Unión US$1, 20 mins.

ROUTES Paved Route 25 runs from Rawson through Trelew, Gaiman (see page 216) and Dolavon to Las Plumas (mind the bridge if driving) and the upper Chubut Valley to Esquel and Trevelin. Spectacular scenery with lots of wildlife.

TRELEW

Pronounced 'TrelAYoo' (*Pop* 61,000; *Phone code* 0965), situated some 20 km up the Río Chubut, is a prosperous town which has lost its Welsh look.

Places of interest

The **Capilla Tabernacle** on Belgrano between San Martín and 25 de Mayo is a red brick chapel dating from 1889. Nearby is another brick building from the same pe-

riod, the Asociación San David. On the road to Rawson, 3 km S is **Chapel Moriah**, the oldest standing Welsh chapel. Built in 1880, it has a simple interior and the graves of many original settlers.

Museums

The **Museo Paleontológico Egidio Feruglio**, 9 de Julio 655, Mon-Fri 0830-1230 1330-2000, Sat 0900-1200, 1400-2100, Sun/holidays 1400-2100, US$5 (ask for leaflet in English), organizes excursions to the Parque Paleontológico Bryn-Gwyn, traces the history of dinosaurs with models made from moulds of dinosaur bones (not all from Patagonia). **Museo Regional**, Fontana y 9 de Julio, 0700-1300, 1400-2000, US$2, displays on indigenous societies, on failed Spanish attempts at settlement and on Welsh colonization; interesting.

Excursions

To Punta Tombo and to the Chubut valley, see below; to the **Florentino Ameghino** dam, 110 km inland on the Río Chubut. The dam covers 7,000 ha with water and irrigates 28,000 ha in the lower Chubut valley, as well as producing electric power. An oasis of cool green trees, recommended for a change of landscape.

Local holidays

28 July (Founding of Chubut); 13 Dec (Petroleum Day).

Local information
● **Accommodation**

L3 *Rayentray*, San Martín y Belgrano, T 34702, pool, expensive but excellent restaurant, helpful, comfortable.

A2 *Centenario*, San Martín 150, T 30042, F 21524, expensive restaurant, Punta Tombo travel agency; **A3** *Libertador*, Rivadavia 31, T 35132, T 20220, without breakfast, good rooms, poor restaurant, quiet, good value; **A3** *Touring Club*, Av Fontana 240, T 33998, excellent, with breakfast.

B *Galicia*, 9 de Julio y Rivadavia, T 33803, F 24273, very warm, without bath; **B** *Res San Carlos*, Sarmiento 758, T 31538, rec; **B** *Res Rivadavia*, Rivadavia 55, T 34472, F 23591, helpful, rec, also cheaper rooms, **D** pp.

C *Res Argentino*, Abraham Matthews 186, T 36134, quiet, good, nr bus terminal; **C** *Hostal Avenida*, Lewis Jones 49, T 34172, nr bus station, lots of character, basic but quiet. Raul G Lerma,

Rucahue 964, T 30208, offers free camping space in garden and local information, speaks English (taxi US$5 or ask at Estrella del Sur Turismo).

Camping: by the river, S of the town on the road to Rawson, on right about 200m beyond the bridge over Río Chubut, US$12, dirty, run-down, beware of mosquitoes; take Rawson bus, No 7 or 25. The site belongs to the Sports Club and has a public swimming pool.

● **Places to eat**

Eulogia Fuentes, Don Bosco 23, good pasta; *El Quijote*, 25 de Mayo 90, good seafood; *Sugar*, 25 de Mayo 247, good *minutas*; *El Mesón*, Rivadavia 588, seafood; *El Marfil*, Italia 42, good, cheap; *La Primera*, Rivadavia y Pasaje Mendoza, excellent *rotisería* and meat, expensive *tenedor libre*; *El Galeón*, San Martín 118, seafood specialities, good; *Cabildo Star*, Roca 76, excellent and cheap pizzas; *Napoli*, Rivadavia y 9 de Julio, old fashioned *confitería*; *Capítulo II*, Roca 393, *tenedor libre*, good and cheap; *La Casa de Juan*, Moreno 360, cosy, good pizzas; *Las Empanadas de Isidro*, Bell 220; *Café Vittorio*, Belgrano 341, good service; café at *Hotel Touring Club*, popular, good coffee.

● **Airline offices**

Austral and **Aerolíneas Argentinas**, 25 de

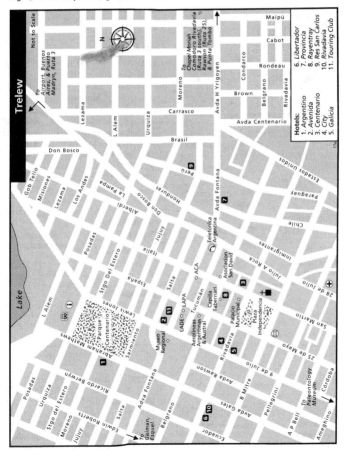

Mayo 33, T 20170; **LADE**, Fontana 227, T 35925; **Lapa**, Fontana 285, T 23438; **TAN**, T 34550.

● **Banks & money changers**
Banco de la Nación, 25 de Mayo y Fontana, accepts Amex and Thomas Cook TCs; **Lloyds Bank** (BLSA), Av 9 de Julio y Belgrano, does not change TCs, cash advance on Visa but will charge for call to verify card; **Banco Provincia del Chubut**, Rivadavia y 25 de Mayo; **Banco del Sud**, 9 de Julio 370, cash advance on Visa, high commission; **Banco Almafuerte**, 9 de Julio 270; *Cambio* at Caja de Ahorro y Seguro, San Martín y Fontana. Banks change currencies before midday only.

● **Post & telecommunications**
Post Office: 25 de Mayo and Mitre. **Telephone**: *Telefónica Fontana*, Fontana 418; *Telefónica Argentina*, Roca nr Fontana; *Los Alerces*, Pellegrini 321, for Fax.

● **Shopping**
Chocolates Patagónicos, Belgrano y Pasaje Mendoza, for local chocolate. *Camping Sur*, Pellegrini 389 for camping equipment.

● **Tour companies & travel agents**
Agencies run tours to Punta Tombo, US$30, Chubut Valley half-day), US$15 Florantino Ameghino, US$30. Tours to Península Valdés are best done from Puerto Madryn. *Sur Turismo*, Belgrano 326-330, organizes good excursions, T 34550; *Estrella del Sur Turismo*, San Martin 129, T 31282, English spoken, rec; *Nievemar*, Italia 20, T 34114; *Punta Tombo Turismo*, San Martín 150, T 20358; and others.

● **Tourist offices**
On ground floor of bus terminal, at airport and in Municipalidad, entrance on San Martín. Free maps, hotel prices and self-guided city tour.

● **Transport**
Local Car hire: expensive. Avis, Localiza and Renta Car Patagonia desks are staffed only at flight arrival times and cars are snapped up quickly. **Localiza**, Urquiza 310, T 35344; **Avis**, Paraguay 105, T/F 34634; **Rent A Car**, San Martín 125, T 20898.

Air Airport 5 km E of centre; taxis about US$8. Local buses to/from Puerto Madryn stop at the airport entrance if asked, turning is 10 mins' walk, US$4.50; AR runs special bus service to connect with its flights. Lapa and AR have flights to/from **Buenos Aires**, **Río Gallegos** and **Ushuaia**. AR also to **Río Grande**; Lapa (and TAN) also to **Comodoro Rivadavia**. Kaiken flies to **Comodoro Rivadavia**, **Ushuaia**, **Río Grande**, **Río Gallegos**, **Esquel**, **Neuquén** (also TAN), **Bariloche** and several other cities; also to **El Calafate** daily, 2 hrs 50 mins, 0830, US$127

one way with overflight of Perito Moreno Glacier.

Buses To Buenos Aires, 4 daily, 21½ hrs US$60; to Bahía Blanca, US$32 daily with Don Otto, 0600, several a week with La Puntual, 0600; to Mar del Plata, changing at Bahía Blanca, US$35 with La Puntual; to Esquel, US$32, 8-12 hrs, Mar y Valle and Empresa Chubut; to Bariloche daily; to Rawson every 15 mins; frequent buses to Gaiman, US$1.15; hourly to Puerto Madryn, US$3.50 with 28 de Julio and Mar y Valle; to Comodoro Rivadavia daily at 2000, and Sun, Wed, Thur and Fri at 1035, US$26, 4 hrs; to Río Gallegos, daily, TAC, 6 hrs, US$55. If **hitching** S from Trelew, take the Rawson bus to the flyover 5 km out of town; there is a junction N of town for Puerto Madryn traffic.

GAIMAN

(*Pop* 4,400) 18 km W of Trelew, is a pretty town of well-built brick houses. It hosts the annual Eisteddfod (Welsh festival of arts) in October. **Museum** in the old railway station, US$1 (open in summer, Mon-Sat 1600-2000, in winter, Tues-Sat 1500-1900, curator Mrs Roberts is 'full of stories'). **El Desafío**, two blocks W of the plaza, is a private theme-park, 16 years work by Sr Joaquín Alonso. It is constructed entirely of rubbish (drinks cans, bottles, piping and wire), a labyrinth of coloured plastic, glass and aluminium with mottos at every turn, US$5, tickets valid 2 months.

● **Places to eat** Welsh teas are served from about 1500 (US$10-12) by several **Tea Rooms**, inc *Casa de Té Gaiman*, Yrigoyen 738, excellent; *Plas y Coed*, Miguel D Jones 123 (oldest, excellent tea 'and enough food for a week', Marta Rees speaks English and is very knowledgeable about the area, highly rec); *Ty Gwyn*, 9 de Julio 111, rec; *Ty Nain*, Yrigoyen 283 (frequented by tour buses, display of historical items); *Ty Te Caerdydd*, Finca 202, 2 km from town, very good, and *Eima*, Tello 571. Small municipal **campsite** beyond Casa de Té Gaiman (poor, no facilities). Most facilities are closed out of season.

Dolavon, is a small town 20 km further W. The main street runs parallel to the irrigation canal built by the settlers; there is a chapel over the canal. The old flour mill at Maipú 61, dates from 1930 and can be visited: key kept in the Municipalidad, Roca 188 (next to Banco Provincial del

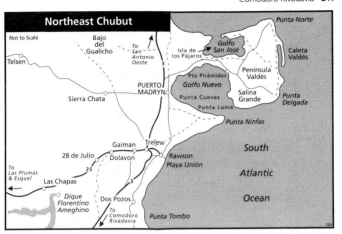

Northeast Chubut

Chubut). Municipal campsite near the service station on the way into town, good facilities, free. Some Trelew-Gaiman buses continue to Dolavon; check at Trelew bus station.

PUNTA TOMBO

This wildlife reserve, 117 km S of Trelew, is the largest breeding ground for Magallenic penguins in Patagonia. It is reached by a well marked road which branches off Route 3, W of Dos Pozos (not shown on ACA map): driving time 1¾ hrs. Park entrance US$5. The wildlife includes guanacos and rheas on the way to the penguin colony, where scavenger birds like chimangos, skuas and kelp gulls can be seen. Season for penguins, Sept-Mar (Jan-Feb is the time when the young are taking to the water); the Reserve closes after March (check date at the Tourist Office). When visits are permitted it is a fantastic experience. You can share a taxi from Trelew (US$30 pp). Trelew and Puerto Madryn travel agencies run tours, spending 30 mins at the site; the fixed fee does not include park entry. About mid-way between Rawson and Punta Tombo, a road leads off Ruta 1 to Isla Escondida (9 km, signed), no facilities, but lovely rock and sand beach with bird and wildlife (badly littered unfortunately); secluded camping

(recommended if visiting the wildlife at Punta Tombo early am).

CAMARONES

275 km S of Trelew and 300 km N of Comodoro Rivadavia. There is a large **penguin colony** 35 km away at Cabo Dos Bahías along a dirt road (US$5, open all year).

● **Accommodation B** *Kau-i-Keuken*, good food, rec, owner runs trips to penguin colony; 2 others, **C**, the one by the power station is not rec. Campsite.

● **Buses** Two a week, US$10, on Mon and Fri from Trelew (Don Otto), book at Uruguay 590, Trelew; bus leaves 0800 from San Martín y Belgrano, arrives 1130, returns to Trelew same day 1600. In Camarones ask the Guardia Fauna on Mon or Fri for a lift, hitchhiking is difficult, but possible at weekends and taxis are unavailable (a private car will charge US$50-60, ask at Busca Vida).

COMODORO RIVADAVIA

(*Pop* 158,000; *Phone code* 0967) the largest city in the province of Chubut, is 387 km S of Trelew. Oil was discovered here in 1907 and about 30% of all Argentina's production comes from wells to the S and W. Renewed interest in the local oil industry is making the town boom. There is an **Oil Museum**, 3 km N in Gral Mosconi (bus No 6 from San Martín y Abasolo). From here southward, prices begin to rise very rapidly, so stock up before reaching Río Gallegos. Good beach at Rada Tilly, 12 km S (buses every 30 mins); walk along beach at low tide to see sealions.

Local holidays
28 July (Founding of Chubut); 13 Dec (Petroleum Day).

Local information
● **Accommodation**
A3 *Austral*, Rivadavia 190, T 32200, noise from traffic but otherwise comfortable, reasonable restaurant; **A3** *Comodoro*, 9 de Julio 770, T 32300, overpriced, restaurant, nightclubs, car rental; **A3** *Res Azul*, Sarmiento 724, T 24874, comfortable, spotless, rec.

C *Colón*, San Martín 341, T 22283, run down, but quiet and safe; **C** *Comercio*, Rivadavia 341, T 22341, old fashioned, dirty, nr bus station, hot showers; **C** *Hosp Belgrano*, Belgrano 546, T 24313, hot water; **C** *Hosp Praga*, España y Sarmiento, shower; **C** *Rada Tilly*, Piedrabuena, in Rada Tilly 5 km S, T 51032, modern; *Motel Astra*, S access of Route 3, T 25394.

Camping: Municipal, 12 km S at Rada Tilly, may be reached by Expreso Rada Tilly bus from town, hot and cold water. There is another, free, campsite at N end of beach, cold water only (watch out for clayslides when it rains).

● **Places to eat**
La Rastra, Rivadavia 384, very good for *churrasco*, but not much else; *Pizzería El Nazareño*, San Martín y España, good. *Bom-Bife*, España 832, good food, inexpensive. Several *rotiserías*, much cheaper, on 400 block of Rivadavia, in municipal market.

● **Airline offices**
Austral, 9 de Julio 870, T 40050; Lapa, Rivadavia 396, T 471685; LADE, Rivadavia 396, T 472400; TAN, T 23855.

● **Banks & money changers**
Lloyds Bank (BLSA), Av Rivadavia 276, Oct-Mar 0700-1300; April-Sept 1200-1800; no exchange transactions after 1000 in summer, 6% commission on TCs, pays US$ cash on TCs but minimum US$300; the Banco de la Nación, San Martín 108, has the best rates on US$ but does not change TCs. Amex agent is *Orbe Turismo Show*, San Martín 488, T 29699, 5% commission for US$, does not change TCs. Several travel agencies also change money inc Roqueta Travel, Rivadavia y Pellegrini, Ceferino, 9 de Julio 852, and CRD Travel, Moreno 844 (TCs accepted).

● **Embassies & consulates**
Consulates: Belgium, Rivadavia 283; Chile, Sarmiento 936; Italy, Belgrano 1053.

● **Post & telecommunications**
Post Office: San Martín y Moreno.

● **Tour companies & travel agents**
Puelche EVT, Rivadavia 527; *Richard Pentreath*, Mitre 952; *San Gabriel* and *Atlas* at San Martín 488 and 263, respectively; *Monitur*, 9 de Julio 948.

● **Tourist offices**
On Rivadavia.

● **Transport**
Local VW dealer: Comercial Automotor, Rivadavia 380, rec. VW concession in Barrio Industrial, Av Irigoyen, also rec. **Car Rental**: Patagonia Car Sur, T 967-26768.

Air Airport, 9 km N. Bus No 6 to airport from bus terminal, hourly (45 mins), US$0.40. Taxi to airport, US$7. To Buenos Aires, Lapa, Dinar and Austral. All major cities S of Córdoba and Mendoza are served by Austral, Lapa, TAN, Kaiken and Andesmar. LADE flies once a week (Wed) Comodoro Rivadavia-Perito Moreno-Gobernador Gregores Calafate/Lago Argentino-Río Gallegos-Río Grande-Ushuaia, and on Mon to Puerto Deseado-San Julián-Gob Gregores-Calafate-Río Turbio-Río Gallegos-Santa Cruz; once a week to Bariloche via Trelew and Viedma, or Trelew and Esquel, or via Esquel, El Maitén and El Bolsón; other services to Neuquén via the Lake District and to Trelew.

Buses Terminal conveniently located in centre; has luggage store, good *confitería* upstairs, lousy toilets, *remise* taxi booth, some kiosks. Services to Buenos Aires daily at 1200 and 2115, 32 hrs, US$108 (same fare on Costera Criolla; also daily with La Estrella/Cóndor at 1335). To Coyhaique (Chile), Angel Giobbi, US$30, 12 hrs, twice a week (Mon and Thur) 0100, June-Sept and 3 a week (Mon, Wed, Fri), 0100, Oct-May (weather permitting), also Turibus, Tues and Sat 0800. Three buses a week to Bariloche, US$55 (Don Otto at 2150, Sun, Tues, Thur, stops at Sarmiento midnight, Esquel at 0600 and for 30 mins at El Bolsón at 0900, arrives 0600 at Bariloche). To Esquel (paved road) direct, Fri 1230, 10 hrs, via Río Mayo, Mon, Thur, 0100, 15½ hrs, to Río Mayo Tues, Thur, Sun, 1700 and 1900, 5½ hrs. In summer buses heading S usually arrive full. To Río Gallegos, Don Otto 2345 daily, and Transportes Patagónica 2200 daily, 11 hrs, US$30. To Puerto Madryn and Trelew, US$26, at 1200. La Unión to Caleta Olivia, hourly, US$3.50. To Sarmiento, US$7, 2½ hrs at 0700, 1300, 1900. To Mendoza, daily at 0130, 20 hrs; to Córdoba, Tues, Fri, Sun, 1200, 33 hrs.

Hitchhiking: there is a truck stop outside Comodoro Rivadavia on Route 3, the road to Bahía Blanca, where you can contact drivers whether heading N or S. Hitch out of the centre on Ruta 3 to 'Astra Km 20', or take any bus going N. Expensive truckdrivers' restaurants along the road; buy food in supermarkets.

FROM COMODORO RIVADAVIA TO CHILE

SARMIENTO

The road to Chile runs inland from Comodoro Rivadavia to (156 km) Colonia Sarmiento (commonly called **Sarmiento**; *Pop* 7,000). Archaeological museum on C Lago Musters, near the large Lago Colhué Huapi, with tourist office next to cathedral, may be closed at weekends.

In the area there are two **petrified forests**, 70,000,000 years old, of fallen araucaria trees, nearly 3m round and 15-20m long: a remarkable sight: the **Bosque Petrificado José Ormachea**, 32 km S of Sarmiento on a gravel road, entry US$5, and the **Víctor Szlapelis** park, some 40 km further SW along the same road (follow signposts, road from Sarmiento in good condition). Taxi, Sarmiento to forests, US$39 (3 passengers), including 1 hr wait, for each extra hour US$9. Hitching is difficult, even in summer. Contact Sr Valero, the park ranger, for guided tours, ask at *Hotel Colón* (see also the *Monumento Natural Bosques Petrificados* below, page 221).

● **Accommodation** B *Hostería Los Lagos*, Roca y Alberdi, T 93046, good, heating, restaurant; E *Colón*, P Moreno 645, restaurant, cheap; B *Lago Musters*, P Moreno y Col, T 93097; *San Martín*, San Martín y P Moreno, cheap, good restaurant; D *Ismar*, Patagonia 248, restaurant; . In Dec-Mar you may be permitted to sleep in the Agricultural School (take sleeping bag) on the road to petrified forest, opp the ACA petrol station. **Camping**: Municipal site 2 km N of centre on Route 24, basic, no shower, US$3 for tent, US$1 pp, beside river.

● **Buses** Overnight services to **Esquel** on Sun, Tues and Thur, stop at Río Mayo, 0630, take food for journey as cafés on route tend to overcharge. Three buses a day to **Comodoro Rivadavia**, 0700, 1300, 1900 and Giobbi buses to Chile leave at 0200. From Sarmiento you can reach Esquel (448 km N along Routes 20 and 40), at the S edge of the Lake District (see page 202).

Hitching along this road is very difficult, even in summer.

Río Mayo (*Pop* 2,260; fuel) is reached by Route 22 (paved) which branches SW 84 km W of Sarmiento. From Río Mayo, a road continues W 114 km to the Chilean frontier at Coyhaique Alto for Coyhaique and Puerto Aisén in Chile.

● **Accommodation** C *Covadonga*, very good; C *Hotel Pingüino*; C *A'Ayones*, T 20044, modern, heating; F pp *San Martín*.

South of Río Mayo Route 40 is paved as far as Perito Moreno (124 km) but there is no public transport and very few other vehicles even in mid-summer. At Km 31 on this road a turning leads W to Lago Blanco (fuel), where there is a small *estancia* community, 30 km from the border with Chile (about 150 km from Río Mayo). No hotel, but police may permit camping at the police post; wild but beautiful place. No public transport to Chile. The road continues to Chile via Paso Huemules and Balmaceda (this route is reported better than Río Mayo to Coyhaique Alto).

● **Buses** The Giobbi buses from Comodoro Rivadavia to Coyhaique, Chile, pass through Río Mayo at 0600 on Mon, Wed and Fri (Mon and Thur, June-Sept), US$14, 6 hrs, but seats are scarce. Mon and Thur at the same hour Giobbi takes Route 40 N from Río Mayo direct to Esquel.

PERITO MORENO

(*Pop* 1,700; *Alt* 400m) is close to Lago Buenos Aires, which extends into Chile as Lago Gen Carrera. Do not confuse it with the famous glacier of the same name on Lago Argentino near El Calafate, nor with nearby **Parque Nacional Perito Moreno**, see below.

● **Accommodation** B *Argentino*, Buenos Aires 1236, dirty, no showers; B *Belgrano*, San Martín 1001, T 2019, with shower, no heating, restaurant, rec; C *Santa Cruz*, on Belgrano, heating, shared bath and hot water. 25 km S on Route 40, B pp *Telken*, sheep station of the Nauta family offers accommodation Oct-April, discounts for families with two children, breakfast inc, other meals extra, English and Dutch spoken. **Camping**: Parque Laguna in town, opp Laguna Cisnes, well shielded, but dirty, US$1.50 pp, US$1 extra for showers, also cabins (slide shows at the tourist office there, information given).

● **Places to eat** *Pipach III*, good pizzas and *empanadas*.

● **Banks & money changers** US$ cash can be exchanged at Banco de la Provincia de Santa Cruz. Better rates from Plácido Treffinger, San Martín opp town hall. Difficult to exchange TCs, though the *Hotel Belgrano* may do so.

● **Transport Air** Airport 7 km E of town, try to hitch as there is only one taxi; El Pingüino flies 3 times a week to **Río Gallegos**, **El Calafate** and **Comodoro Rivadavia**; LADE flies from Perito Moreno to **Río Gallegos** on Wed, check in well in advance. **Road Hitchhikers**: to the S are warned that, outside the tourist season (Jan-mid-Feb), it is usually quicker to head for the coast at Caleta Olivia and go S from there than to take Route 40 via Gobernador Gregores and Piedrabuena.

FRONTIER WITH CHILE – LOS ANTIGUOS

From Perito Moreno Route 43 (paved) runs S of Lago Buenos Aires to **Los Antiguos**, 67 km W, 2 km from the Chilean frontier. (Service station; salmon fishing; annual cherry festival in early Jan.)

● **Accommodation B** *Argentino*, comfortable, restaurant; outstanding municipal campsite, hot showers, 2 km from centre, US$2.50 pp. At Km 29 **A3** *Hostería La Serena* offers accommodation in *cabinas*, 10% reduction to *South American Handbook* readers, good restaurant and organizes trips in both the Chilean and Argentine Lake Districts, open Oct-June; further details from Geraldine des Cressonières, Estancia La Serena, Casilla 87, 9040 Perito Moreno, Santa Cruz. Nearby is Los Chilcas where Indian remains can be found (trout fishing).

● **Transport** To Comodoro Rivadavia, US$20, Co-op Sportsman, from nr *Hotel Argentino*, 1630 daily, 7 hrs, via Perito Moreno and Caleta Olivia, and Empresa La Unión, 0700, 1300 from bar *El Triunfo*. From Los Antiguos Transportes VH buses cross the border by new bridge to Chile Chico, 8 km W, US$3, 45 mins (for routes from Chile Chico to Coyhaique and Puerto Aisén see **Chile**, page 814). Another route to Chile is to follow the roads which go around the N side of Lago Buenos Aires to Puerto Ibáñez. At the roundabout, N edge of town, go straight, on the biggest road (do not follow signs to Puerto Ibáñez); at the police checkpoint, turn right onto a small road. Follow this 75 km and then turn left along N side of Lago Buenos Aires.

SOUTH OF PERITO MORENO

Route 40 is unpaved and rough S of Perito Moreno; at Km 118, a marked road goes directly to the famous **Cuevas de las Manos** (44 km). The series of galleries with 10,000-years-old paintings of human hands and of animals in red, orange, black, white and green, are interesting even for those not interested in rock art. The canyon in which the caves are situated is very beautiful, especially in the evening light (entrance US$3). A ranger lives at the site; he is helpful with information. Camping is permitted but very windy. If it is not busy the ranger may let you sleep inside the park building. No buses, but the tourist office at Perito Moreno can supply names of drivers who can take you there, prices between US$80-100, to be split among a party of visitors.

Corrugated Route 40 is dismal until tiny, forlorn **Bajo Caracoles** (**C** *Hotel Bajo Caracoles*, decent, meals; good grocery store).

92 km S of Bajo Caracoles is the turning off W to Lago Belgrano and Parque Nacional Perito Moreno. 7 km E, along Route 521 is *Hotel Las Horquetas* with a café/bar, and 15 km beyond this is the Tamel Aike village (police station, water). 'Super' grade fuel is available in most places; carry extra, since the only other available source of fuel before Tres Lagos involves a 72-km detour to Gobernador Gregores (see page 223). From the Parque Moreno junction to Tres Lagos, Route 40 improves considerably. At Tres Lagos (accommodation at *Restaurant Ahoniken*, Av San Martín, **E** pp; supermarket, fuel) a road turns off NW to Lago San Martín; nearby is the *Estancia La Maipú*, T 22613, where the Leyenda family offer accommodation, meals, horse riding, trekking and boat excursions on the lake, "real atmosphere of a sheep farming *estancia*" (Santiago de la Vega), reasonable prices.

From Tres Lagos Route 40 deteriorates rapidly and remains very rugged until after the turnoff to the Fitz Roy sector of Parque Nacional Los Glaciares. 21 km beyond is the bridge over Río La Leona, with a hotel which has a bar/café. The remainder of the highway to Calafate, while slow, holds no major problems.

NB It is nearly impossible to hitchhike between Perito Moreno and Calafate. There is no public transport, at any time of year along this road.

PARQUE NACIONAL PERITO MORENO

Midway between Perito Moreno and Gobernador Gregores, at the end of a 90-km spur in bad condition is **Parque Nacional Perito Moreno**, where guanaco and other wildlife roam among a large, interconnected system of lakes below glaciated peaks. The largest of the lakes is Lago Belgrano. Here the mountains are streaked with a mass of differing colours. This is excellent hiking country (ammonite fossils can be found), and a downhill expedition into Chile is possible for intrepid walkers (take all food). On the way to Cerro León is *Estancia La Oriental*, T 0966 2445/2196, guest house and camping site, **D** pp, **A** full board, horses for hire. Good chance of spotting condors here. There are few visitors and no formal facilities, but camping (US$2-4/night) is among the best in South America. The park is situated S of Cerro San Lorenzo, highest peak of the Patagonian Andes. Entrance fee US$5, park ranger has maps and information. There is no public transport into the park but it may be possible to arrange a lift with *estancia* workers from *Hotel Las Horquetas*.

COMODORO RIVADAVIA TO RIO GALLEGOS

CALETA OLIVIA

South of Comodoro Rivadavia, Route 3 continues to **Caleta Olivia** (Km 66; *Pop* 13,000). A good start-point for hitching S, Caleta Olivia is the urban centre for important oilfields. On the central roundabout in front of the bus station is a huge granite monument of an oil driller with the tools of his trade. Local holiday 20 Nov (founding of the city).

- **Accommodation B** pp *Robert*, San Martín 2151, T 61452; **A3 Grand**, Mosconi y Chubut, T 61393; **B Capri**, Hernández 1145, T 61132. Municipal campsite with hot showers nr beach, US$3 pp.

- **Buses** To Río Gallegos, Pingüino, US$34, dep 2100, arr 0900. Many buses to **Comodoro Rivadavia**, 1 hr, US$3.50. To **Calafate**, dep 1400, 5 hrs; to **Perito Moreno** and **Los Antiguos**, 5 hrs, 2 daily.

Fitz Roy, 73 km further S, is named after the captain of Darwin's ship, *Beagle*. Fuel is available. (**B** *Hotel Fitzroy*, good, cheap food, camping sometimes possible.)

The **Monumento Natural Bosques Petrificados**, in a bizarre landscape surrounding the Laguna Grande, has the largest examples of petrified trees. There is a small museum and a 1 km well documented nature walk. Open 1000-2000, no charge but donations accepted; please do not remove 'souvenirs'. There are two unpaved access roads from Route 3: 82 km along provincial route 93 which branches off 22 km S of Fitz Roy; 48 km along provincial route 49 which branches off 86 km S of Fitz Roy. Campsite at *Estancia la Paloma*, 25 km before the entrance.

PUERTO DESEADO

10 km S of Fitzroy Route 281 branches off Route 3 and runs 123 km SE to **Puerto Deseado** (*Pop* 4,100; *Phone code* 0967; airport), at the mouth of the Río Deseado which drains Lago Buenos Aires, far to the W. Founded in 1884, it is the second largest fishing port in Patagonia. The estuary of the Río Deseado is a nature reserve with a colony of Magellanic penguins, the nesting areas of 4 species of cormorants including the unique red legged, and breeding grounds of Commerson's dolphin, which,

Naming the Penguin

It was at Puerto Deseado that a Welshman in Cavendish's expedition of 1586 gave the name of *pengwyn* (white head) to a certain strange-looking bird. It is only fair to mention the opposing theory that the name is derived from a Spanish word, *pingüe*, meaning fat.

with its black and white pattern, is considered one of the most beautiful in the world. Cabo Blanco, 72 km N of Puerto Deseado, is the site of the largest fur seal colony in Patagonia, breeding season Dec-January. Visits can also be made to *Estancia La Madrugada*, accommodation, excursions to sea lion colony and cormorant nesting area, English spoken, highly rec, T 34963 or in Puerto Deseado: Almte Zar 570, T 70204, F 72298.

Local holidays 31 Jan (San Juan Bosco); 9 Oct (Coat of Arms day).

● **Accommodation A3** *Los Acantilados*, Pueyrredón y España, T 70167, beautifully located, ACA discount, poor breakfast; **A3** *Colón*, Almte Brown 450, T 70304, dormitory-style; **A3** *Isla Schaffers*, San Martín y Moreno, T 72246, modern, central; *Albergue Municipal*, Colón y Belgrano, T 70260, dormitory style; several other *residencias*. Municipal campsite, dirty.

● **Places to eat** *El Viejo Marino*, Pueyrredón 224, considered best by locals; *La Casa de Don Ernesto*, San Martín 1245, seafood and *parrilla*; *El Pinguino*, Piedrabuena 958, *parrilla*.

● **Tour companies & travel agents** *Gipsy Tours*, T 72155, F 72142, run by Ricardo Pérez, excursions by boat to Río Deseado reserve, 2 hrs, US$25.

● **Tourist offices** Contact Ricardo Bogetti, Director of Tourism at the Municipalidad, helps, lots of information on excursions.

ROUTES   Inland   Lago Buenos Aires is reached by road in 7 hrs; 280 km to Las Heras, then 177 km to Perito Moreno (see above).

PUERTO SAN JULIAN

(*Pop* 4,480; *Phone code* 0962), founded in 1901 and 268 km S of Fitz Roy, is the best place for breaking the 834 km run from Comodoro Rivadavia to Río Gallegos. There is much wildlife in the area: red and grey foxes, guanacos, wildcats in the mountains, rheas, etc. The main activities are sheep raising for export, fish canning, and production of kaolin and clay. Clay grinding can be seen at Molienda Santa Cruz and ceramics made at the Escuela de Cerámica; good handicraft centre at Moreno y San Martín. There is a regional museum at the end of San Martín on the waterfront.

The cascade of San Julián is formed by two different tides. Punta Caldera is a popular summer beach. The first mass in Argentina was held here after Magellan had executed a member of his crew. Francis Drake also put in here to behead Thomas Doughty, after amiably dining with him. Near San Julián (15 km) is Cabo Curioso beach, with an attractive cave.

Excursions can be made to the *Estancia La María*, 150 km W, which offers transport, accommodation and meals and covers one of the main archeological areas of Patagonia, including a huge canyon with dozens of caves with paintings of human hands, guanacos etc 4,000-12,000 years old, less visited than the Cueva de las Manos. Contact Fernando Behm, Saavedra 1168, T 2328, F 2269.

● **Accommodation A3** *Municipal*, 25 de Mayo 917, T 2300/1, very nice, well-run, good value, no restaurant; **A3** *Bahía*, San Martín 1075, T 3144, modern, comfortable, good value, rec; **A3** *Res Sada*, San Martín 1112, T 2013, nice, hot water, but on busy main road. **B** *Res Sada*, San Martín 1112, T 2013, good rooms, poor breakfast; **C** *Aguila*, San Martín 500 block, sleazy, cheapest in town. Good municipal campsite on the waterfront, US$5 per site plus US$3 pp, repeatedly rec, all facilities, Av Costanera entre Rivadavia y Roca.

● **Places to eat** *Sportsman*, Mitre y 25 de Mayo, excellent value; *Rural*, Ameghino y Vieytes, good, but not before 2100; a number of others. Also bars and tearooms.

● **Banks & money changers** Banco de la Nación, Mitre y Belgrano, and Banco de la Provincia de Santa Cruz, San Martín y Moreno.

● **Post & telecommunications Post Office**: Belgrano y San Martín.

● **Hospitals & medical services Pharmacy**: Del Pueblo on San Martín 570. **Hospital**, Av Costanera entre Roca y Magallanes.

● **Tourist offices** San Martín 581, T 2871.

● **Transport Air** Weekly services (Mon) with LADE to Santa Cruz, Río Gallegos, Puerto Deseado, Gob Gregores, Comodoro Rivadavia, Calafate/Lago Argentino and Río Turbio. **Buses** Transportadora Patagónica comes from Río Gallegos en route to **Buenos Aires** (also Pingüino, 6 hrs, US$14 to/from Río Gallegos); Transportes Staller goes weekly (Sat) to **Lago Posadas** stopping in Gobernador Gregores, *Hotel Las Horquetas*, Bajo Caracoles and Río Blanco. For hitching, walk 5 km to petrol station on Ruta 3.

ROUTES Paved Route 521 runs NW from San Julián to Route 40 along the foothills of the Andes. After 215 km is **Gobernador Gregores** (*Hotel San Francisco*; municipal campsite; good mechanic in town and all grades of fuel available).

PIEDRABUENA AND SANTA CRUZ

Piedrabuena (full name Comandante Luís Piedrabuena, named after the first Argentine settler in Patagonia; *pop* 2,600) on Route 3, is 146 km S of San Julián on the Río Santa Cruz which drains Lago Argentino. From Piedrabuena a paved road heads E 35 km to **Santa Cruz** (*pop* 3,000; airport). Founded in 1878, Santa Cruz was capital of Santa Cruz province until 1904. Outside the town, near the mouth of the Río Santa Cruz is **Punta Quilla**, a major deep water port. South of Piedrabuena is **Monte León**, a provincial nature reserve which includes the Isla Monte León, an important breeding area for cormorants and terns, where there is also a penguin colony and sea lions. There are impressive rock formations and wide isolated beaches at low tide. It is reached by a 22 km dirt road which branches off Route 3 36 km S of Piedrabuena.

● **Accommodation & places to eat** Pie-drabuena: **A3** *ACA Motel*, T 7145, simple, functional but good, warm and nice food; **A3** *Hostería El Alamo*, Lavalle 08, T 7249, quiet, breakfast extra, rec; *Andalucia*, Belgrano Ote 170, hotel and restaurant (good pasta); **C** *Res Internacional*, Ibáñez 99, T 7197, rec; also campsites N of town on Route 3. Several other restaurants. **Santa Cruz: A3** *Hostal de la Ría*, 25 de Mayo 645, T 8038.

ROUTES Inland Provincial Route 9 (1603 on some maps, unpaved, no petrol) from 43 km S of Piedrabuena to Calafate runs along the edge of a plateau with occasional panoramic views across the valley of the Río Santa Cruz below. Then at about 70 km it drops down into the valley itself to follow the river into the hills and to Lago Argentino. Route 288 runs direct from Pie-drabuena to Tres Lagos on Route 40, thence W and S to Lagos Viedma and Argentino. Most traffic to El Calafate goes via Río Gallegos.

RIO GALLEGOS

(*Pop* 75,000; *Phone code* 0966), the capital of Santa Cruz Province, on the estuary of the Río Gallegos, is 265 km S of Santa Cruz. Founded in 1885, it is a centre for the trade in wool and sheepskins and a large military base. There is a deep-water port at Punta Loyola at the mouth of the estuary. It is drab, but has a good shopping centre on Roca. The small Plaza San Martín, 1 block from the post office is well tended, with flower beds and statues.

Museums

Museo Provincial Mario Echevarría Baleta, Moreno 45 entre Zapiola y Roca, has collections of local history, flora, fauna, rock samples (open 0800-1900, weekends 1500-2000); **Museo de los Pioneros**, Alberdi y Elcano in the former house of a Arthur Fenton, a British physician who was one of the early pioneers, free, open 1300-2000.

Excursions

To **Cabo Vírgenes**, 134 km S of Río Gallegos, where a nature reserve protects the second largest colony of Magellanic penguins in Patagonia, entry US$3. The Navy allows visitors to climb up Cabo Vírgenes lighthouse for a superb view. Follow Route 3 then branch off on Route 1 for $3\frac{1}{2}$ hrs (unpaved). You can hitch from this junction with oil workers going to the lighthouse at the cape. Take a taxi to be at the turn off by 0700. Take drinking water. It is possible to arrange return with day trippers from Río Gallegos, or ask at the lighthouse or naval station. 13 km N of Cabo Vírgenes is **Estancía Monte Dinero**, T 22425, where the Fenton family offers accommodation, food and excursions, English spoken, expensive, excellent.

Local holidays

31 Jan; 19 Dec (Foundation Day).

Local information

NB Do not confuse the streets Comodoro Rivadavia with (nearby) Bernardino Rivadavia.

● **Accommodation**

A1 *Costa Río*, San Martín 673, new, comfortable, discounts for ACA members; **A3** *Alonso*, Corrientes 33, T 22414, F 21237, without breakfast, good beds; **A3** *Santa Cruz*, Roca 701, T 20601, with heating, good coffee bar, breakfast; **A3** *Punta Arenas*, Sphur 55, T 22742, in new wing, very comfortable, also **B** in old wing, without breakfast; **A2** *Comercio*, Roca 1302, T/F 22172, with breakfast, good beds, comfortable, restaurant with good fixed-price menu.

B *París*, Roca 1040, T 20111, **C** without bath, old fashioned, poor beds; **B** *Covadonga*, Roca 1214, T 20190, without breakfast, comfortable, rec; **B** *Nevada*, Zapiola y Entre Ríos, T 25990, English spoken, good, parking; **B** pp *Piscis* (no sign), Avellaneda y Magallanes, T/F 20329, owned by army officers' club, without breakfast, good beds, excellent value, rec; **B** *Cabo Vírgenes*, Comodoro Rivadavia 252, T 22141, rec; **B** *Oviedo*, Libertad 746, T 20118, comfortable, kitchen facilities, rec; **C** *Colonial*, Urquiza y Rivadavia, T 22329, cheaper without bath, hot water, heating.

C *Central*, Roca 1127, central, quiet, cold shower, no heating; **C** *Pensión Belgrano*, Belgrano 123, dirty, basic but friendly, good restaurant; **C** *Res Internacional*, Sphur 78, with heating, helpful, but insecure.

D pp *Res Betty*, Alberdi 458, meals, rec. **Private house**: Barrio Codepro II, Casa 71, T 23789, E pp, rec.

NB Accommodation is hard to find in Río Gallegos because of the number of transient workers in town.

Camping: *Camping ATSA* Route 3, en route to bus terminal, US$3 pp + US$1 for tent. Also try the YPF service station.

● **Places to eat**
Plenty and good, some specializing in seafood. Evening meals are hard to find before 2000. *Restaurant Díaz*, Roca 1173, cheap; *Bifería La Vasca*, Roca 1084, snack bar, good value, young crowd, rock music, open till 0300; *El Horneo*, bar of *Club Español*, Roca 862, good meals, cosy, reasonably priced; *Jardín*, Roca 1315, good, cheap, popular; *Club Británico*, Roca 935, good, reasonably priced; *El Palenque*, Corrientes 73, parrilla, rec; *Sociedad Italiana*, Magallanes 69, good; *Café Carrera*, Fagnano y Roca, good but expensive breakfast; *El Herreo*, Roca 1450, good; *Monaco*, Roca y San Martín, good café; *Le Croissant*, Zapiola y Estrada, good bakery.

● **Airline offices**
Aerolíneas Argentinas, San Martín 545, T 20181; **Austral**, Roca 917, T 22038; **Dinar**, San Martín 695; **Lapa**, Estrada 71, T 28382; **TAN**, T 25259.

● **Banks & money changers**
Lloyds Bank (BLSA), Sarmiento 47, open 1000-1600, cash advance on Visa and Mastercard high commission. Many banks on Av Roca inc **Banco de Santa Cruz**, Roca y Errázuriz, fair rates, Mastercard, best rates for TCs, no commission. **Banco Almafuerte**, Roca 990, changes cash. Change TCs here if going to Calafate, where it is even more difficult. **Banco Tierra del Fuego**, changes TCs without commission; **Banco de Crédito Argentino**, quick cash advance on Visa upstairs. **Cambio El Pingüino**, Zapiola 469, may also change European and South American currencies, 7% commission; **Cambio Sur**, San Martín y Roca, often has good rates. **Banco Tierra del Fuego** changes TCs without commission. **Banco de Crédito Argentino**, quick cash advance on Visa upstairs.

● **Embassies & consulates**
Consulates: Chile, Mariano Moreno 136, Mon-Fri, 0900-1300; tourist cards issued at border.

● **Laundry**
El Tumbaito Alberdi y Rawson; *Laverap*, Corrientes 277.

● **Post & telecommunications**
Post Office: Roca 893 and at the airport. **Telephones**: Roca 613.

● **Shopping**
Artesanías Koekén, San Martín 336, leatherwork, woollen goods, local produce; *Artesanías Santacruceñas*, Roca 658; *Tía* department store, Roca 740, good supermarket section; Supermarket *La Anónima*, Roca y España. Most places take a 2-3-hr lunch break.

● **Sports**
Fishing: the S fishing zone inc the Ríos Gallegos, Grande, Coyle, Ewan, San Pablo and Lago Fagnano, nr Ushuaia. It is famous for runs of sea trout. See **Fishing** in **Information for travellers**, page 251.

● **Tour companies & travel agents**
Interlagos, *Pingüino* and *Quebek* at bus terminal and airport offer tours to Calafate and Perito Moreno glacier, US$70, without accommodation.

● **Tourist offices**
Provincial office, Roca 1551, Mon-Fri, 0900-2000, Sat/Sun (summer only) 1000-2000, helpful, English spoken, has list of *estancias*. They will phone round hotels for you. Municipal office in former railway carriage, Roca y San Martín, Mon-Fri 1000-1800, Sat/Sun (summer only) 1000-1300, 1700-2000. Also at airport and bus terminal.

● **Transport**
Local Car rental: Localiza, Sarmiento 237, T 24417; **Eduardo Riestra**, San Martín 1508,

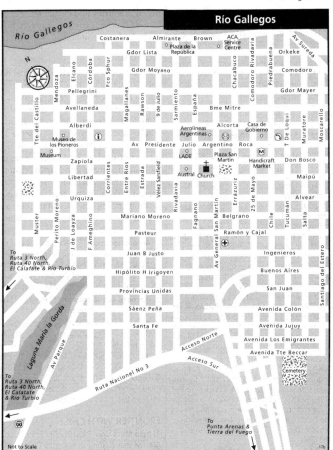

Río Gallegos

Not to Scale

T 21321. Essential to book rental in advance in season. **Car parts and repairs**: *Turbisur*, Corrientes 177, cheapest; *Repuestos Sarmiento*, on Sarmiento, owner very friendly and helpful. **Motorcycle mechanic**: Juan Carlos Topcic, Costa Rica 25, friendly and helpful. **Taxis**: Radio taxi, V Sarsfield y Roca, T 22369. Hiring a taxi for group excursions may be no more expensive than taking a tour bus. *A1*, Entre Ríos 350, T 22453, for taxis and car rental, not cheap.

Air Airport 15 km from town. No buses. Taxi (*remise*) to/from town US$6; hitching from car park is easy. It is permitted to spend the night at the airport prior to early am flights. In summer

make your bookings in advance. AR's Buenos Aires-Auckland-Sydney flight (twice a week) stops at Río Gallegos, but the return journey does not. To/from **Buenos Aires**: AR (direct or via Trelew), Austral (via Bahía Blanca and Comodoro Rivadavia), Lapa (via Trelew or Comodoro Rivadavia), Dinar (via Comodoro Rivadavia). Several flights to **Ushuaia** and **Río Grande** (Tierra del Fuego), direct (AR, always booked, but standby seats available), Austral, Kaiken or Lapa. Kaiken also to **Comodoro Rivadavia**, **Calafate**, **Punta Arenas** and many southern Argentine destinations. LADE (Fagnano 53, T 20316) to **Río Turbio** and Calafate, twice a week, to

Ushuaia and **Comodoro Rivadavia** once a week.

NB Flights may leave early, sometimes up to 40 mins. LADE flights should be booked as far in advance as possible.

Both Pingüino and Interlagos can arrange packages to Calafate inc accommodation and trip to Moreno glacier from their offices at the airport.

Buses Terminal at corner of Route 3 and Av Parque, 3 km from centre (crowded, no left luggage, *confitería*, few toilets, kiosks); taxi to centre US$3, bus US$1 (Nos 1 and 12 from posted stops on Roca).

To **Calafate** via airport, 4-5 hrs, US$20-25, Pingüino and Quebek, very crowded in season; turn up with ticket 30 mins before departure: in winter both companies operate 3 times a week; Pingüino offers 2-night excursion to Calafate, sold at airport only, US$93 in single room, credit cards accepted.

Pingüino daily at 2100 to **Caleta Olivia**, US$30, 11 hrs. To **Trelew** and **Puerto Madryn** daily (18 hrs), US$55. To **Comodoro Rivadavia**, Pingüino, Don Otto and TAC, 10 hrs, US$30. For **Bariloche**, take this bus to Comodoro Rivadavia, then the 2150 Don Otto bus to Bariloche (fare to Bariloche US$88).

To **Buenos Aires**, 36 hrs, Pingüino, Don Otto, TAC, US$70-100. To **Río Turbio**, 4 hrs Pingüino, US$14 (hitching practically impossible); also Ezquerra, US$19. No buses to/from Río Grande. To **El Chaltén**, Burmeister (San Martín 470, T 20293) Mon, Wed, Fri 1500, US$40.

To Chile Buses: to **Puerto Natales**, Pingüino, Tues-Sat, 7½ hrs, US$22. To **Punta Arenas**, Pingüino and others, US$20-22 daily. **By car**: make sure your car papers are in order (go first to Tourist Office for necessary documents, then to the customs office at the port, at the end of San Martín, very uncomplicated). For road details, see Tierra del Fuego sections in Argentina and Chile.

Hitchhiking: to Buenos Aires is possible in about 5-7 days; appearance important; hitching to Tierra del Fuego possible from service station on Ruta 3 at edge of town, trucks stop here for customs check, be there before 0700. To Calafate, from police control outside town.

ROUTES Argentina's longest road, Route 40, ends at Río Gallegos or, more precisely, Punta Loyola; it runs from Bolivia for over 4,667 km. Its last section has been rerouted S of Lago Argentino to follow the Chilean border and go through Río Turbio. The original route, via La Esperanza, forms the majority of the Río Gallegos-El Calafate route (see below). This road (323 km, all paved) is worth while for the number of animals and birds one sees; however, it is flat and subject to strong winds.

RIO TURBIO

(*Pop* 6,000), 257 km W of Río Gallegos and only 30 km from the Chilean town of Puerto Natales, is the site of Argentina's largest coalfield; reserves are estimated at 450m tons. A railway, the most southerly regular line in the world (no passengers) connects it with Punta Loyola. There is a director of tourism, Prof César Cetta, in the municipality on San Martín. Visitors can see Mina 1, where the first mine was opened in the hills; area good for trekking and horse riding. The present mining and industrial area, with the school museum, can also be visited.

● **Accommodation** Hotels almost always full: **A3** *Hostería Capipe*, Dufour (9 km from town, T 91240); **A3** *Gato Negro*, T 91226, also dormitory accommodation **E** pp; **E** pp *Albergue Municipal*, by ski-run in hills, 6 km from town.

● **Places to eat** *Restaurant El Ringo*, nr bus terminal, will shelter you from the wind.

● **Buses** To **Puerto Natales**, 2 companies, US$4, regular. To **Calafate**, Pingüino and Quebek, 6 hrs, US$27. Expreso Pingüino runs daily at 0600 (plus 1300 Tues, Thur, Sat, 6 hrs) in summer or 1300 Wed, Thur, Sat in winter to **Río Gallegos**, but LADE flights are cheaper and avoid the numerous passport checks (airport 15 km from town, taxi US$10 pp).

FRONTIER WITH CHILE

1) Paso Mina Uno: 8 km S of Río Turbio. Open open all year, daytime only. On the Chilean side this runs S to join the main Puerto Natales-Punta Arenas road.

2) Paso Casas Viejas; 33 km S of Río Turbio via 28 de Noviembre. Open all year, daytime only. On the Chilean side this runs E to join the main Puerto Natales-Punta Arenas road.

3) Paso Cancha Carrera: 55 km N of Río Turbio, this is the most convenient crossing for Parque Nacional Torres del Paine. Open Nov-April only. Argentine customs are fast and friendly. On the Chilean side the road continues 14 km to the Chilean border post at Cerro Castillo, where it joins the road from Puerto Natales to Torres del Paine.

EL CALAFATE

El Calafate (*Pop* 3,000; *Phone code* 0902)
on the S shore of **Lago Argentino**, 312 km
NW of Río Gallegos, is a modern town
which has grown rapidly as a tourist centre
for the **Parque Nacional los Glaciares**, 50
km away. The Lago Argentino area is very
popular in Jan-Feb, when booking all
transport in advance is a *must* and accommodation can be difficult to find. The best
months to visit are Oct, Nov and March.
Credit cards are not popular, apart from
hotels, and high commissions are charged.

Places of interest

From the Centro Cívico, visit Capilla
Santa Teresita in Plaza San Martín. Behind it is C Perito Moreno; walk to the top
of the hill for the views of the southern end
of the Andes, Bahía Redonda and Isla
Solitaria on Lago Argentino. Bahía Redonda is a shallow part of the lake just W
of the town centre: it is good for birdwatching in the evenings; in winter when
it freezes, ice-skating and skiing are possible. There is good hill-walking to the S
of the town, while Elephant Hill, W of
Calafate on the road to the Moreno glacier
is good for rock climbing.

Excursions

For the main excursion to the Moreno
glacier, see below. Travel by road to the
most interesting spots is limited and may
require expensive taxis. Tours can be arranged at travel agencies, or with taxi
drivers at the airport who await arrivals.
At **Punta Gualichó**, on the shores of Lago
Argentino 15 km E of town, there are
painted caves (badly deteriorated); 12 km
E of Calafate on the edge of the lake there
are fascinating geological formations
caused by erosion. A recommended walk
is from the Intendencia del Parque, following the new road among cultivated
fields and orchards to **Laguna Nimes**, a
bird reserve, with flamingos, ducks, and

El Calafate & Environs

abundant birdlife. **El Galpón**, 21 km W of Calafate, is an *estancia* offering evening visits (from 1730) featuring walks through a bird sanctuary, displays of sheep shearing and a barbecue as well as horseriding (visits at other times on request), transport arranged, English spoken; in Calafate T/F 91793; BsAs, Av Paseo Colón 221, p 7, T 343-8185, F 334-2669.

An excursion can also be made to **Lago Roca**, 40 km S from Calafate, where there is trout and salmon fishing, climbing, walking, and branding of cattle in summer. Good camping here in wooded area, restaurant.

Local festivals

People flock to the rural show on 15 Feb (Lago Argentino Day) and camp out with much revelry; dances and *asados* (barbecued sides of sheep). There are also barbecues and rodeo etc on Día de la Tradición, 10 November.

Local information
● Accommodation

Many hotels are open only from Oct to April/May.

L2 *Los Alamos*, Moyano y Bustillo, T 91144, F 91186, best, comfortable, very good food and service, extensive gardens, rec; **L3** *Frai Toluca*, C 6 No 1016, T/F 91773/91593 (Buenos Aires T/F 523-3232) good views, comfortable, restaurant; **L3** *Hostería Kau-Yatún*, 25 de Mayo (10 blocks from town centre), T 91059, F 91260, many facilities, old *estancia* house, comfortable, restaurant and barbecues, horse-riding tours with guides; **L3** *El Mirador del Lago*, Libertador 2047, T/F 91176, good accommodation, acceptable restaurant (wines not rec), better not to take half-board.

A1 *Kalker*, V Feilberg 119, T 91073, F 91036, with breakfast, spacious; **A2** *Michelangelo*, Espora y Gob Moyano, T 91045, F 91058, with breakfast, modern, reasonable, good restaurant, accepts TCs (poor rates); **A2** *El Quijote*, Gob Gregores 1191, T 91017, F 91103, rec; **A3** *ACA Hostería El Calafate*, San Martín, T 91004, F 91027, modern, good view, open all year.

B *Amado*, Libertador 1072, T 91134, without breakfast, restaurant, good; **B** *Upsala*, Espora 139, T 91166 F 91075, inc breakfast, good beds, rec; **B** *Cabañas Del Sol*, Libertador 1956, T 91439 (**D** in low season), good meals, highly rec; **B** *Hosp del Norte*, Los Gauchos 813, T 91117, open all year, kitchen facilities, comfortable, owner organizes tours, highly rec; **B** *Paso Verlika*, Libertador

1108, T 91009, F 91279, with breakfast; **A3** *Hostería Schilling*, Paradelo 141, T 91453, with breakfast, nice rooms, poor beds.

B *Kapenke*, 9 de Julio 112, T 91093, inc breakfast, good beds, rec; **A2-3** *La Loma*, Roca 849, T 91016 (Buenos Aires at Av Callao 433, 8a 'P', T/F 371-9123), with breakfast, modern, highly rec, multilingual, restaurant, tea room, spacious rooms, attractive gardens; **B** *Las Cabañitas*, V Feilberg 218, T 91118, cabins, hot water, kitchen and laundry facilities, helpful, rec; **B** *Los Lagos*, 25 de Mayo 220, T 91170, very comfortable, good value, rec; **B** *Hosp Cerro Cristal*, Gob Gregores 989, T 91088, helpful, rec; **C** pp *Cabañas Nevis*, about 1 km from town towards glacier, Libertador 1696, T 91180, for 4 or 8, lake view, full board good value.

Several slightly cheaper hotels but none less than **E** pp, eg **E** pp *Lago Azul*, Perito Moreno 83, T 91419, only 2 double rooms, highly rec; **C** *Hosp Belén*, Los Gauchos 300 y Perito Moreno, T 91028, warm, hot water, cooking facilities, family welcome, highly rec; **C** *Hosp Jorgito*, Gob Moyano 943, T 91323, without bath, basic, cooking facilities, heating, breakfast extra, often full, rec; **E** pp *Hosp Los Dos Pinos*, 9 de Julio 358, T 91271, dormitory accommodation, cooking and laundry facilities, also cabins **C**, and camping **F** pp, arranges tours to glacier, popular; **E** pp *Hosp Buenos Aires*, Buenos Aires 296, 200m from terminal, T 91147, kitchen facilities, helpful, good hot showers, luggage store; **E** pp *Hosp Alejandra*, Espora 60, T 91328, without bath, good value, rec; **D** pp *Youth Hostel Albergue del Glaciar*, Los Pioneros, 200m off Av Libertador, T/F 91243 (reservations in Buenos Aires T 0448-69416, off season only), discount for ISIC or IYHA members, open 1 Oct-31 Mar, kitchen facilities, English spoken, also rooms with bath (**B**) and sleeping bag space (**E** pp), restaurant with good value fixed menu, repeatedly rec, tour agency Patagonia Packpackers, runs tours to Moreno glacier (US$28 pp, constantly rec as good value) and elsewhere, free shuttle service from bus station and airport, Navimag agents, book in advance in summer. **E** pp *Albergue Lago Argentino*, Campaña del Desierto 1050, T 91423, nr bus terminal, dormitory accommodation, limited bathrooms facilites, helpful. Some private houses offer accommodation such as Enrique Rodríguez, Barrio Bahía Redonda, Casa 10, T 91325, **E**, rec; **F** pp *Apartamentos Lago Viedma*, Paralelo 158, T 91159, F 91158, hostel, 4 bunks to a room, cooking facilities. **F** pp *La Cueva de Jorge Lemos*, Gob Moyano 839, behind YPF station, bunk beds, bathroom, showers, kitchen facilities, popular and cheap. If in difficulty, ask at tourist office from which caravans, tents (sleep 4) and 4-berth *cabañas* may be hired, showers extra.

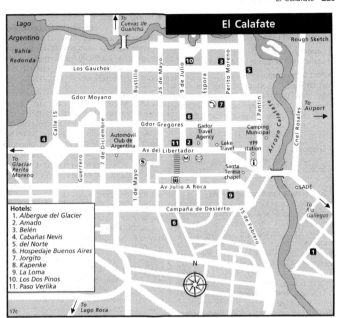

El Calafate

Rough Sketch

Lago Argentino

Bahía Redonda

Los Gauchos

Gdor Moyano

Gdor Gregores

Automóvil Club de Argentina

Av del Libertador

Av Julio A Roca

Campaña de Desierto

To Cuevas de Gualichú

To Airport

Camping Municipal

YPF station

Gador Travel Agency

Lake Travel

Santa Teresa chapel

To Río Gallegos

To LADE

To Glaciar Perito Moreno

To Lago Roca

Santa Teresa chapel

Hotels:
1. *Albergue del Glacier*
2. *Amado*
3. *Belén*
4. *Cabañas Nevis*
5. *del Norte*
6. *Hospedaje Buenos Aires*
7. *Jorgito*
8. *Kapenke*
9. *La Loma*
10. *Los Dos Pinos*
11. *Paso Verlika*

17c

In the Parque Nacional los Glaciares: 40 km W of Calafate on the road to the Moreno glacier: **L3** *Los Notros*, T/F 91437, half-board, spacious, rooms with glacier views, rec (in Buenos Aires: Talcahuano 1457, p 7, T 825-4243, F 815-7645). On the southern shore of Lago Viedma: **L2** *Hostería Helsingfors*, T/F 0966-20719, San Martín 516, Río Gallegos, or BsAs T/F 824-6623/3634, with breakfast, all other meals available, many treks and boat trips available, also riding, sheep-shearing; **E** pp *La Leona*, T 91418, 106 km N of Calafate nr E end of Lago Viedma, without bath, camping. For accommodation in El Chaltén in the northern part of the park see below.

Camping: Municipal campsite behind YPF service station, T 91344/91440, reservations off season 91829 US$4 pp, hot water, security, restaurant, open 1 Oct-30 April. Three campsites in the Park en route to the glacier: *Río Mitre*, nr the park entrance, 52 km from Calafate, 26 km E of the glacier, US$3 pp; *Bahía Escondida*, 7 km E of the glacier, toilets and hot showers, US$3 pp, off season free but no water; unmarked site at Arroyo Correntoso, 10 km E of the glacier, no facilities but nice location and lots of firewood. Take food to all three. Another campsite is *Camping Río Bote*, 35 km, on road to Río Gallegos.

● **Places to eat**
Prices rise during Nov and high season lasts until May. *Pizzería Onelli*, Libertador 1197, reasonable, stays open out of season; *Pizzería Casablanca*, Libertador y 25 de Mayo, good breakfasts; *Michelangelo*, Espora y Gob Moyano, very expensive but magnificent steaks, rec; *Paso Verlika*, Libertador 1108, small, 2 courses with wine US$16, credit cards 10% extra, good value; *Mi Viejo*, Libertador 1111, *parrilla*; *El Rancho*, 9 de Julio y Gob Moyano, large, cheap and good pizzas, popular, free video shows of the glacier, highly rec. Tea rooms: *Maktub*, Libertador 905, excellent pastries, pricey; *Bar Don Diego de la Noche*, Libertador 1603, lamb and seafood, live music, good atmosphere.

● **Airline office**
Sur Turismo, 25 de Mayo 23, T 91266/91854, Kaiken agents.

● **Banks & money changers**
Best to take cash as there are no ATMs and high commission is charged on TCs. **Banco de la Provincia de Santa Cruz**, Libertador, 3% commission on TCs, advances on Visa and Mastercard (17% commission). Travel agencies such as Interlagos change notes; **YPF garage** and **Chocolate El Calafate** and some other shops give good rates for cash; *Albergue del Glaciar*,

5% commision on TCs; **El Pingüino** bus company, 7% commission; the **Scorpio** snack bar in the main street gives good rates.

● **Laundry**
El Lavadero, Libertador 1474, US$8 a load.

● **Post & telecommunications**
Post Office: on Libertador; postal rates much lower from Puerto Natales (Chile) and delivery times much quicker. **Telephones**: run by Cooperativa Telefónica de Cafayate, office on Espora, 0700-0100, also has telex and fax facilities, all services expensive, collect call impossible.

● **Shopping**
Supermarket, Libertad y Perito Moreno, accepts US$ cash. There is a *ferretería* selling white gas for camping.

● **Tour companies & travel agents**
Interlagos, Libertador 1175, tours to Moreno glacier, plenty of time allowed, provide cheapest transport to Fitz Roy (but double check return!), English and Spanish speaking guide, highly rec; *El Pingüino*, in terminal, T 91273; *Los Glaciares*, Libertador 920, T 91159, rec, good value; *Tagle*, Libertador 960; *Tur Aike*, Libertador 1080, T 91436, and *Gador Viajes*, Libertador 900 block; *Upland Goose*, Libertador (1st floor), T 0902-91424, rec; *Hielo y Aventura*, 25 de Mayo, T 91053, organizes 2-hr trek on glacier with champagne US$65, rec. Most agencies charge the same rates for excursions: to the Moreno Glacier US$25 for a trip leaving 0830, returning 1800, without lunch, 3 hrs at glacier; to Lago Roca, at 0930 return 1700, US$25; Cerro Fitz Roy, at 0600 return 1900, US$50, Gualichó caves, 2 hrs, US$16 (see **Excursions**, above). Several hotels also organize tours by minibus inc *Hosp del Norte* and *Albergue del Glaciar*. Jorge Lemos, *Aventrek*, Gob Moyano 839, Aptdo Postal Esp No 7 (9405), El Calafate, Telex Cab pública 86905, runs rec treks with small groups in Glaciares National Park and Fitzroy. Mountain bikes can be hired from Sr Daniel Alvarez, also rec as source of information, at the Mercado Artesanal on Libertador.

● **Tourist offices**
Tourist office in bus terminal. Hotel prices detailed on large chart at tourist office; has a list of taxis but undertakes no arrangements. Helpful staff. Oct-April 0700-2200 daily. For information on the Parque Nacional los Glaciares, park office at Libertador 1302, T 91005, Mon-Fri 0800-1500.

● **Transport**
Air Lago Argentino airport, E of town, with an all-weather runway (though flights may be suspended in severe weather). Kaiken from Río Gallegos, Río Grande, Ushuaia, Bariloche, Esquel, Trelew, Comodoro Rivadavia, Mendoza and Neuquén; LADE twice a week to Río Turbio, US$20, 3 a week in summer to connect with buses to Puerto Natales and Torres del Paine. LADE once a week to Perito Moreno, Río Gallegos and Comodoro Rivadavia. Air fares can be cheaper than buses.

Buses Terminal on Roca, 1 block from Libertador. Journey to **Ushuaia** requires four changes, and ferry, total cost US$43. Interlagos Turismo bus daily at 0800 (summer) or 0915 Tues, Thur, Sat (winter) to **Río Gallegos** and its airport; also Quebek (0900) and El Pingüino daily at 0600 and 1630 (Wed, Fri, Sat, in winter) 4½ hrs, US$20-25, those on this bus going to Chile get off at Güer Aike to catch Pingüino's Gallegos-Río Turbio bus 50 mins later, arriving at 1700. To Río Turbio with Pingüino 4 times a week, 7 hrs, US$27, Quebek, 2 a day, US$24, 4 hrs. To Puerto Madryn, Quebek US$48, 18 hrs. Taxi to Río Gallegos, 4 hrs, US$200 irrespective of number of passengers, up to 5 people.

Direct services to Chile: Cootra to **Puerto Natales** via Río Turbio, several times a week, US$14.50, 7 hrs (rec to book in advance). In summer only Knudsen runs via Cerro Castillo. Travel agencies inc *Albergue del Glaciar* run regular services in summer, on demand in winter, up to US$60, 5 hrs. These connect at Cerro Castillo with buses from Puerto Natales to Torres del Paine (**NB** Argentine pesos cannot be exchanged in the park).

PARQUE NACIONAL LOS GLACIARES

This park, the second-largest in Argentina, extends over 660,000 ha, some 40% of it covered by ice fields (the *hielos continentales*) off which break 13 glaciers which descend into the park to feed two great lakes: Lago Argentino and, further N, Lago Viedma. The Río La Leona, flowing S from Lago Viedma, links the two lakes. The park consists of the southern area around Lago Argentino, the central area between Lago Argentino and Lago Viedma, and the northern area around Mt Fitz Roy. Access to the central area is difficult and there are no tourist facilities.

Ventisquero Moreno

Access to the southern part of the park is from Calafate. At the western end of Lago Argentino (80 km from Calafate) the major attraction is the Ventisquero Perito Moreno, until recently one of the few glaciers in the world that was advancing. It descends to the surface of the water over a 5-km frontage and a height of about 60m. It used to advance across the lake, cutting the Brazo Rico off from the Canal de los Témpanos; then the pressure of water in the Brazo Rico would break up the ice and reopen the channel. Since Feb 1988 this has not occurred, possibly because of global warming. Pieces break off and float away as icebergs. The vivid blue hues of the ice floes and the dull roar as they break away from the snout are spectacular, especially at sunset. Wooden catwalks permit viewing; there is a fine of up to US$500 for leaving the catwalks.

● **Access** From Calafate there are buses by Pingüino and Interlagos. Many agencies also run minibus tours, US$25-28 return (plus US$3.50 park entry) leaving 0800 returning 1800, giving 3 hrs at glacier, book through any agency in Calafate, return ticket valid if you come back next day (student discount available). *Albergue del Glaciar* trips go out by different route passing the *Estancia Anita* and have been repeatedly rec. They also do walking tours on the glacier, book ahead. Taxis, US$80 for 4 passengers round trip. Out of season, trips to the glacier are difficult to arrange, but you can gather a party and share a taxi (remise taxis T 91745/91044); take warm clothes, and food and drink. Ask rangers where

you can camp out of season, no facilities except a decrepit toilet block. Boat trips on the lake are organized by Hielo y Aventura, T 91053, with large boats for up to 60 passengers: 'Safari Náutico', US$20 pp, 1 hr offering the best views of the glacier; or 'Minitrekking', US$67, day trip including 2½ hrs' walk on the glacier, rec, but not for the fainthearted, take your own lunch.

The Upsala Glacier

At the NW end of Lago Argentino, 60 km long and 4 km wide, Upsala Glacier is considered the largest in South America. It can be reached by motor-boat from Punta Bandera, 50 km W of Calafate (check before going that access to the glacier face is possible). The trip also goes to Lago Onelli and glacier (restaurant) and Spegazzini glacier. From the dock on Bahía Onelli to Lago Onelli is an easy 2-km trail done with a guide (in English, German or Spanish) through a lovely southern forest wreathed in bearded moss. Small **Lago Onelli** is quiet and very beautiful, beech trees on one side, and ice-covered mountains on the other. The lake is full of icebergs of every size and sculpted shape.

● **Access** Tour boats usually operate a daily trip to the glacier, the catamaran *Serac*, US$90, or the *Nunatak* (slightly cheaper). The price includes bus fares and park entry fees – pay in dollars and take food. Bus departs 0730 from Calafate for Punta Bandera. 1 hr is allowed for a meal at the restaurant near the Lago Onelli track. Return bus to Calafate at 1930; a tiring day, it is often cold and wet, but memorable. Out of season it is extremely difficult to get to the glacier. Many travel agencies make reservations.

Fitz Roy and El Chaltén

Cerro Fitz Roy (Tehuelche name El Chaltén) and the village of **El Chaltén** (*Phone code* 0962), at its foot, lie 230 km NW of Calafate in the far N of the park, reached by a *ripio* road which branches off Route 40. The Fitz Roy massif towers above the nearby peaks, its sides normally too steep for snow to stick. Chaltén, founded in 1985 is growing rapidly as a centre for trekking (information from National Park office) and climbing. In winter, though there is no transport, cross-country skiing is possible. There are stupendous views: "anyone within 500 miles would be a fool to miss them" (Julian and

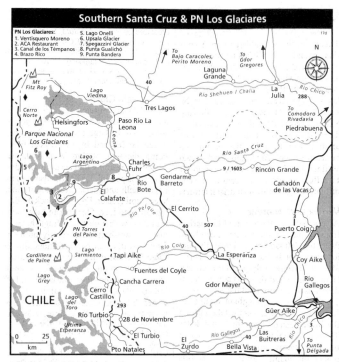

Southern Santa Cruz & PN Los Glaciares

PN Los Glaciares:
1. Ventisquero Moreno
2. ACA Restaurant
3. Canal de los Témpanos
4. Brazo Rico
5. Lago Onelli
6. Upsala Glacier
7. Spegazzini Glacier
8. Punta Gualichó
9. Punta Bandera

Cordelia Thomas). Occasionally at sunrise the mountains are briefly lit up bright red for a few seconds: this phenomenon is known as the 'sunrise of fire' (*amanecer de fuego*).

The **Lago del Desierto**, 37 km N of El Chaltén, is surrounded by forests. Excursions from El Chaltén by *Chaltén Travel* daily in summer; daily boat trips on the lake on *La Mariana II*, 1030, 1330, 1630, 2 hrs, US$30 (details and booking, *Hotel El Quijote*, Calafate).

Día de la Tradición (10 Nov) is celebrated with gaucho events, riding and barbecue (US$5).

● **Accommodation A3** *Fitz Roy Inn*, T 93062 or Calafate 91368, with breakfast, restaurant, also **D** pp in shared cabins; opp is **D** pp *Albergue Patagonia*, T 61564/93019, also dormitory accommodation Fpp, kitchen and laundry facilities, TV and video, book exchange,

accepts TCs, comfortable; **A3** *Posada Lago del Desierto*, T 93010, good beds, *comedor*, Italian spoken, camping US$5pp; **D** pp *Albergue Rancho Grande*, T 93005, small dormitories, good bathrooms, laundry and kitchen facilities, English, Italian, French, German spoken, highly rec, reservations in Chaltén Travel, Calafate, T 91833; **B** pp *Estancia La Quinta*, 3 km from Chaltén, half-board, no heating, prepares lunch for trekkers, rec; **L3** *La Aldea*, T 93040, 5 bed apartments; **D** pp *Casa de Piedra*, T 93015, in shared cabins, also **A1** 4 bed cabins; **D** pp *Cabaña de Miguel*, shared cabins; **D** pp *Cabañas Cerro Torre*, T 93061, built for the Herzog film "El Grito de la Piedra", cabins sleep 4/6, kitchenette; **E** pp *Albergue Los Ñires*, T 93009, small dormitories, also camping US$5pp; **E** pp *Despensa 2 de Abril*, one room, cheapest. **Camping**: *Camping Madsen* (free); *Ruca Mahuida*, T 93018, very helpful, US$6pp, showers, stores gear, rec; two free campsites. A stove is essential for camping as firewood is scarce and lighting fires is prohibited in campsites in the higher parts of the National Park.

Take plenty of warm clothes and a good sleeping bag. It is possible to rent equipment in El Chaltén, ask at park entrance.

● **Places to eat** *La Senyera del Torre*, excellent bread, rec; *Josh Aike*, excellent *confitería*, homemade food, beautiful building, rec; *The Wall Pub*, breakfasts and meals.

● **Shopping** There are several small shops selling food, gas and batteries (*Dispensa 2 de Abril* is said to be cheapest) but buy supplies in Calafate (cheaper and more choice). Sra Isolina bakes the best bread. Fuel is available.

● **Sports Hiking**: trails from Chaltén around the base of the Fitzroy massif are: 1) NW via a good campsite at Lago Capri, wonderful views, to Campamento Río Blanco, and, nearby Campamento Poincenot, 2-3 hrs, from where a path leads up to Lago de los Tres and Lago Sucia, 2-3 hrs return from the camps. From the camps a trail also runs N along the Río Blanco and W along the Río Eléctrico to Lago Eléctrico. 2) W along the Río Fitz Roy to Laguna Torre, beautifully situated at Cerro Torre and fed by Glaciar Torre, 3 hrs. Beware of straying from the paths. A map is essential, even on short walks: the park information centre provides photocopied maps of treks but the best is one published by Zagier and Urruty, 1992, US$10 (Casilla 94, Sucursal 19, 1419 Buenos Aires, F 572-5766) and is available in shops in Calafate and Chaltén. For trekking by horseback with guides: Rodolfo Guerra, T 93020; *El Relincho*, T 93007; *Albergue Los Ñires*, T 93009; prices: Laguna Capri US$20; Laguna Torre, US$25, Río Blanco US$30, Piedra del Fraile US$30, Laguna Toro US$30. **Climbing**: base camp for Fitz Roy (3,375m) is Campamento Río Blanco (see above). Other peaks include Cerro Torre (3,102m), Torre Egger (2,900m), Cerro Solo (2,121m), Poincenot (3,002m), Guillaumet (2,579m), Saint-Exupery (2,558m), Aguja Bífida (2,394m) and Cordón Adela (2,938m): most of these are for very experienced climbers. The best time is mid-Feb to end-Mar; Nov-Dec is very windy; Jan is fair; winter is extremely cold. Permits for climbing are available at the national park information office. Guides are availabe in Chaltén: ask Sr Guerra about hiring animals to carry equipment. Fitz Roy Expeditions, in Chaltén, T 93017/F 91364, owned by experienced guide Alberto del Castillo, organize adventure excursions inc on the Campo de Hielo Continental, highly rec, English and Italian spoken.

● **Transport Mechanic**: ask for Julio Bahamonde or Hugo Masías. **Bus**: daily buses in summer from **Calafate**, 4 hrs, US$25 one way, are run by Chaltén Travel 0800 return departure 1800, Caltur, 0700, return departure 1700, and Los Glaciares, 0800, return departure 1800. Best

to book return before departure during high season. From **Río Gallegos**, Burmeister, Mon, Wed, Fri 1500, US$40, return departures same days. Day trips from Calafate involve too much travelling and too little time to see the area. Some agencies offer excursions eg return travel by regular bus and 1 night accommodation US$79. Off season, travel is difficult: little transport for hitching. Agencies charge US$200 one way for up to 8 people, US$300 return.

EL CALAFATE TO CHILE

On the road trip from Calafate to Punta Arenas it is possible to see guanacos and condors at frequent intervals. About 40 km before reaching the border there are small lagoons and salt flats with flamingos. From Calafate take the almost completely paved combination of provincial Route 11, national Route 40 and provincial Route 5 to La Esperanza (165 km), where there is a service station, campsite and a large but expensive *confitería* (accommodation **D** pp with bath). 90 km SE of Calafate Route 40 takes a rough shortcut which avoids the circuitous La Esperanza route, which is closed in winter. From La Esperanza, gravelled Route 7 heads W to join Route 40 at the Río Coyle. At nearby Fuentes del Coyle, there is a small but acceptable bar/*confitería* with 2-3 rooms for travellers and a Hotel, **D** pp, cold, dirty. The road continues to the border crossing at Cancha Carrera (see above) and then meets the unpaved but good road between Torres del Paine and Puerto Natales (63 km). For bus services along this route see above.

Tierra del Fuego

THE ISLAND at the extreme south of South America is divided between Argentina (east side) and Chile (west). The south has beautiful lakes, woods and mountain scenery, and there is much birdlife to see. Boat trips can be made on the Beagle Channel; there is skiing in winter.

Tierra del Fuego is bounded by the Magellan Strait to the N, the Atlantic Ocean to the E, the Beagle Channel to the S – which separates it from the southern islands – and by the Whiteside, Gabriel, Magdalena and Cockburn Channels etc, which divide it from the islands to the W. Although the island was inhabited by four indigenous groups, all are now extinct. Throughout Tierra del Fuego the main roads are narrow and gravelled. The exceptions are San Sebastián (Argentina)-Tolhuin, which is paved, and the road for about 50 km out of Porvenir (Chile), which is being widened. Part of the S is a National Park: trout and salmon in nearly all the lakes and rivers, and in summer wild geese, ducks, 152 other species of birds, and imported musk rats and beaver. Mar-April is a good time to visit because of the beautiful autumn colours. **NB** Accommodation is sparse and the island is becoming popular among Argentines in summer. Hotel beds and seats on aircraft may begin to run short as early as November. Fruit and meat may not be taken onto the island.

● **Recommended reading** *Tierra del Fuego: The Fatal Lodestone*, by Eric Shipton; *Uttermost Part of the Earth*, by E Lucas Bridges. Available in USA: *Birds of Isla Grande* (Tierra del Fuego) by Philip S Humphrey, and *A Guide to the Birds of South America*, by Rodolphe Meyer de Schauensee. Map of Tierra del Fuego, published by Zagier & Urruty, obtainable in Ushuaia and Buenos Aires.

ROUTES TO TIERRA DEL FUEGO

Via Punta Delgada

There are no road/ferry crossings between the Argentine mainland and Argentine Tierra del Fuego. You have to go through Chilean territory. From Río Gallegos, Route 3 reaches the Chilean frontier at Monte Aymond (55 km approx), passing Laguna Azul (3 km off main road in an old crater; an ibis breeding ground, beautiful colours). For bus passengers the border crossing is very easy; similarly for car drivers if papers are in order (see page 226). 41 km into Chile is **Punta Delgada**, from where a 16 km road goes to the dock for the 30-min ferry-crossing over the Primera Angostura (First Narrows) to **Punta Espora**. Some 40 km S, on Chilean Tierra del Fuego, is Cerro Sombrero, from where the road continues 85 km to Chilean San Sebastián. 14 km E, across the frontier, is Argentine San Sebastián, from where the road is paved to Río Grande (see below). **NB** For details of all transport and accommodation on Chilean territory, see the **Chile** chapter, **Chilean Patagonia**. It is not always possible to cross the Chilean part in 1 day because of the irregularity of the ferry.

VIA PUNTA ARENAS

The alternative ferry crossing is Punta Arenas-Porvenir. The road from Punta Delgada goes on 103 km to the intersection with the Punta Arenas-Puerto Natales road, 54 km before Punta Arenas. 5 km E of Punta Arenas, at Tres Puentes, there is a daily ferry crossing to Porvenir, from where a 225-km road runs E to Río Grande

(6 hrs) via San Sebastián. Border police at San Sebastián will sometimes arrange lifts to Ushuaia or Río Grande. Hitching after San Sebastián is easy. The best way to hitch from Río Gallegos to Punta Arenas is to take any lorry as far as the turn-off for Punta Delgada ferry. Then there is plenty of Chilean traffic from Punta Delgada to Punta Arenas. *Hotel San Gregorio* will put you up if you get stuck near the turn-off.

Entering Argentina from Chile, be firm about getting an entry stamp for as long as you require. Going in the other direction, don't stock up with food in Argentina, as Chilean border guards will confiscate all fruit, vegetable, dairy and meat products coming into Chile.

RIO GRANDE

Río Grande (*Pop* 35,000; *Phone code* 0964), the largest settlement in Tierra del Fuego, is a sprawling modern town in windy, dust-laden sheep-grazing and oil-bearing plains. The oil is refined at San Sebastián in the smallest and most southerly refinery in the world (**A3** *ACA* motel; service station open 0700-2300). The *frigorífico* (frozen meat) plant and sheep-shearing shed in Río Grande are among the largest in South America. Government tax incentives to companies in the 1970s led to a rapid growth in population; the subsequent withdrawal of incentives has produced increasing unemployment and emigration. The gymnasium has free hot showers for men, as has the ACA garage on the seafront. Fill up with gasoline here.

Excursions

To the **Salesian Mission**, 11 km N and the regional museum housed in the original chapel, with Indian artefacts and natural history section, Mon-Sat 1000-1230, 1500-1900, Sun 1500-1900, US$1.50. Afternoon teas, US$3. Nearby is the first parish church of Río Grande. To **Estancia María Behety**, 18 km SW where horses can be hired.

Local festivals

Trout Festival, 3rd Sun in Feb; **Snow Festival**, 3rd Sun in July; **Woodsman Festival**, 1st week of December.

Local information
● Accommodation

Accommodation can be difficult if arriving at night.

A2 *Atlántida*, Belgrano 582, T/F 31914, said to be best, without breakfast, restaurant, parking; **A2** *Posada de los Sauces*, Elcano 839, T/F 30868, with breakfast, good beds, comfortable, good restaurant, bar, rec; **A3** *Los Yaganes ACA*, Belgrano 319, T 30823, F 33897, comfortable, good expensive restaurant; **A3** *Federico Ibarra*, Rosales y Fagnano, T 32485, with breakfast, good beds, large rooms, excellent restaurant; **A3** *Isla del Mar*, Güemes 963, T/F 22883, next to bus terminal, with breakfast.

B *Res Rawson*, Estrada 750, T 25503, F 30352, cable TV, clean, poor beds; **B** *Villa*, San Martín 277, T 22312, without breakfast, very warm; **B** *Hosp Noal*, Rafael Obligado 557, lots of bread and coffee for breakfast, cosy, rec.

C *Hostería Antares*, Etcheverría 49, T 21853; **C** *Avenida*, Belgrano 1001, T 22561.

● Places to eat

Don Rico, Belgrano y Perito Moreno, in ultramodern building in centre, interesting, closed Mon; *La Nueva Colonial*, Rosales 666, home made food, friendly. *Rotisería CAI*, on Moreno, cheap, fixed price, popular with locals.

● Airline offices

Aerolíneas Argentinas, T 22711; **Lapa**, 9 de Julio 747, T 32620; **LADE**, Lasarre 425, T 22968; **Kaiken**, Perito Moreno 937, T 30665; **Aerovías**, 9 de Julio 597, T 30249; **TAN**, T 22885.

● Banks & money changers

Banco de la Nación Argentina, San Martín 200; **Banco del Sud**, Rosales 241, cash advance on Visa; **Superkiosko**, Piedrabuena y Rosales, cash only. Exchange is difficult: if coming from Chile, buy Argentine pesos there.

● Laundry

El Lavadero, P Moreno y 9 de Julio.

● Post & telecommunications

Post Office: Piedrabuena y Ameghino.

● Shopping

La Nueva Piedmontesa, Belgrano y Laserre, 24 hr food store; *Tía* supermarket, San Martín y Piedrabuena, good selection. Food is cheaper than in Ushuaia.

● Tour companies & travel agents

Yaganes, San Martín 641, friendly and helpful.

● Tourist offices

Tourist information at the Municipalidad, on Elano, Mon-Fri.

● **Transport**
Local Car hire: Rent-a-Car, Belgrano y Ameghino, T 22657. **Localiza**, at airport, T 30482. **Car mechanic**: and VW dealer *Viaval SRL*, P Moreno 927.

Air Airport 4 km W of town. Bus US$0.50. Taxi US$5. To **Buenos Aires** AR, daily, 3 hrs 20 mins direct. Austral daily (except Sun) and Lapa daily (except Sat) via Bahía Blanca, Comodoro Rivadavia and Río Gallegos. To **Ushuaia**, AR and Kaiken, daily. LADE also to **Río Gallegos**, 50 mins (book early in summer, 1 a week, Thur), continuing to **Comodoro Rivadavia** via Calafate, Gob Gregores and Perito Moreno. Kaiken flies to **Calafate** daily except Sun; also to **Punta Arenas, Río Gallegos, Bariloche, Trelew** and many other southern destinations.

Buses All buses leave from terminal, Elcano y Güemes. To **Porvenir**, Chile, 5 hrs, Gesell, Wed, Sun, 0800, meticulous passport and luggage control at San Sebastián; to **Punta Arenas**, Chile, via Punta Delgada, 10 hrs, Pacheco, Tues, Thurs, Sat 0730, US$30, Los Carlos, Mon, Fri, 0700, same price. To **Ushuaia**, Tecni Austral, 4 hrs, daily 0730 and 1800, US$21 and Los Carlos, Tues, Sat 1700, sit on right for better views, US$20, stopping at *Hostería El Kaiken*, Lago Fagnano (rec for the view). No buses to Río Gallegos. Very difficult to hitch to Porvenir or N into Argentina (try the truck stop opp the bus terminal or the police post 7 km out of town). Hitching to Ushuaia is relatively easy in summer.

USHUAIA

(*Pop* 30,000; *Phone code* 0901), the most southerly town in Argentina and one of the most expensive, is 234 km SW of Río Grande by a new road via Paso Garibaldi. Situated on the northern shore of the Beagle Channel, named after the ship in which Darwin sailed the Channel in 1832, its streets climb steeply towards snow covered Cerro Martial to the north. There are fine views over the green waters of the Beagle Channel and the snow-clad peaks. The mainstays of the local economy are fishing and tourism.

Museums
The old prison, **Presidio**, Yaganes y Gob Paz, at the back of the Naval Base, houses the **Museo Marítimo**, with models and artefacts from seafaring days; the **Museo Antártico** and, in the cells, the **Museo Penitenciario**, which details the history of the prison. Open daily 1000-1200, 1600-2300, US$3.

Museo Territorial, Maipú y Rivadavia, T 21863, open Mon-Fri 0900-1300, 1630-1930, US$3, small but interesting display of early photos and artefacts of the local Indian tribes, the missionaries and first settlers, as well as natural history section. Known as the 'museum at the end of the world' (you can get a stamp in your passport). Highly rec. The building also contains an excellent library with helpful staff and a post office, open afternoons when the main one is closed.

Museo Fueguino, Gob Godoy, interesting sections on indigenous peoples, videos and library, rec, daily, 1100-1800, free.

Excursions
To **Cerro Martial**, offering fine views down the Beagle Channel and to the N, about 7 km behind the town; to reach the chairlift (*Aerosilla*, US$5) follow Magallanes out of town, allow 1½ hrs. Pasarela and Kaupen run minibus services, several departures daily in summer, US$5 return. In winter the Cerro is inaccessible, even on foot.

Other excursions include: to the **Río Olivia** falls; to **Lagos Fagnano** and **Escondido**. A bus runs to **Puerto Almanza** on the Beagle Channel, 75 km, 4-5 hrs, US$18.

The Estancia **Harberton**, the oldest on the island, now run by descendents of a British missionary, Mr Bridges, offers guided walks through protected forest (not Mon) and tea, in *Manacatush confitería* (T 22742). You can camp. It can be reached by rented car from Ushuaia and by boat. By car, leave Ushuaia on Route 3, after 40 km fork right on Route J, passing Lago Victoria, then 25 km through forest before the open country around Harberton (85 km in all). Some parts of the road are bad; tiring driving, 5 hrs there and back. Agency tours by land cost US$30 plus US$6 entrance; take your own food if not wishing to buy meals at the Estancia. For excursions to Harberton by boat see below. Some tour agencies imply that their excursions go to the Estancia though in fact they only go to the bay; others go by inflatable launch from main boat to shore.

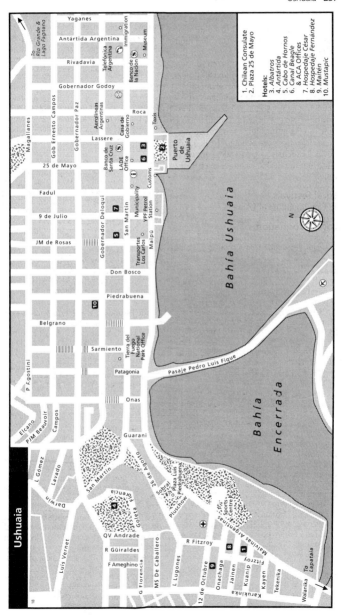

Ushuaia

1. Chilean Consulate
2. Plaza 25 de Mayo

Hotels:
3. Albatros
4. Antártida
5. Cabo de Hornos
6. Canal Beagle & ACA Offices
7. Hospedaje César
8. Hospedaje Fernández
9. Maitén
10. Mustapic

Sea Trips

Excursions can be booked through most agencies. The main trips are: to the sealion colony at Isla de los Lobos, 2 hrs on the *Ana B*, US$35, 4 hrs on the *Tres Marías*, US$40; to Lapataia Bay and Isla de los Lobos, 5 hrs on the *Ezequiel MB*, US$35; to Isla de los Lobos and Estancia Harberton, 6 hrs on the *Luciano Beta*, US$75, Tues, Thurs, Sat; to Isla de los Lobos and the Isla Martillo Penguin colony, 4 hrs on the *Luciano Beta*, US$60. Food and drink on all boats is expensive, best to take your own. Note that the Beagle Channel can be very rough.

Local festivals

12 Oct: Founding of Ushuaia.

Local information

NB Prices double on Dec 12 – the tourist office will help with rooms in private homes and with campsites.

● **Accommodation**

On the road to the Martial Glacier overlooking the city are: **L2** *Las Hayas*, Km 3, T 30710, F 30719, colourful large rooms, pool, and **L1** *del Glacier*, Km 3.5, T 30640, F 30636, modern, casino, pool rooms, shuttle to/from *Hotel Albatros*; **L3** *Tolkeyen*, at the *Luciano Río Pipo* 5 km from town, T 22637, with rec restaurant (see below); **L3** *Albatros*, Lasserre y Maipú, T 30003, F 30666, modern, inc breakfast, good views; **L3** *Ushuaia*, Laserre 933, 1 km N of town, T 30671, F 24217, with breakfast, restaurant, sauna.

A1 *Las Lengas*, Florencia 1722, T 23366, F 24599, superb setting, heating, good dining room; **A2** *Canal Beagle*, Maipú y 25 de Mayo, T 21117, F 21120, restaurant; **A2** *Malvinas*, Deloqui 615, T 22626, F 24482, without breakfast, pleasant, helpful, central heating, rec; **A2** *Cabo de Hornos*, San Martín y Rosas, T 22187, F 22313, comfortable, often full, good value, restaurant not open to non-residents; **A2** *César*, San Martín 753, T 21460, F 32721, comfortable, inc breakfast, rec; **A3** *Fernández*, Onachaga y Fitzroy, T 21192, with breakfast, good beds, overpriced; **B** *Mustapic*, Piedrabuena 238, T/F 23557, multi-lingual owner, breakfast extra, poor beds, great views; **A3** *Posada Fin del Mundo*, Valdez 281, T 22550, family atmosphere, rec.

B *Maitén*, 12 de Octubre 140, T 22745, F 22733, good value, 1 km from centre, no singles, 10% discount for ISIC and youth card holders; **B** *Hostería América*, Gob Paz 1665, T 23358, F 31362, without breakfast, modern;

B *Hostería Alakaluf*, San Martín 146, T 36705, without breakfast, quiet, rec.

D pp *Hosp Torres al Sur*, Gob Paz 1437, T 30745, heating, good atmosphere, kitchen facilities, highly rec; **D** pp *Alojamiento Internacional*, Deloqui 395, 1st floor, T 23483/23622, very basic, scruffy, dormitory, take sleeping bag, no security, good meeting place, changes money; **E** pp *Casa Azul*, Las Primulas 283, Barrio Ecológico, T 34769, floor space; **D** pp *Refugio del Turista*, 25 de Mayo 237, small dormitories with kitchen facilities; **E** pp *Casa del Turista*, Belgrano 236, T 21884, large kitchen, helpful.

Accommodation in private homes: **A3** *Miguel Zapruscky*, Deloqui 271, T 21316, **B** without bath, parking, TV, kitchen, English spoken, rec; **B** *Silvia Casalaga*, Gob Paz 1380, T 23202, without bath, comfortable, heating, breakfast extra, no sign, rec; **B** *María Navarrete*, 25 de Mayo 440, T 23068, without bath or breakfast, cooking facilities; **B** *Familia Cárdenas*, 25 de Mayo 345, T 21954, without bath or breakfast, quiet; **D** pp *Hosp Turístico*, Magallanes 196, good views; **D** pp *Posada de los Angeles*, Paz 1410, good kitchen. List of private accommodation available from the tourist office. Many people offer rooms in private houses at the airport.

At Lago Escondido: **B** *Hostería Petrel*, 54 km from Ushuaia after a spectacular climb through Garibaldi Pass, on the road to Río Grande (bus dep 0900, returns 1500, US$17 return, minimum 4 people), T 33569, trout fishing possible, boat rides, friendly staff.

At Lago Fagnano: **B** *Hostería El Kaiken*, 100 km N of Ushuaia on a promontory, T 92208, also **C** cheaper rooms and bungalows, nice site. Facilities at *Kaiken* and *Petrel* are open all year round. These inns are rec for peace and quiet.

Camping: none in town. East of Ushuaia on Route 3 are: *Ushuaia Rugby Club Camping* (Km 4) US$15/tent, restaurant and good facilities; *Ushuaia Camping Municipal* (Km 8) US$15/tent, toilets, showers; *Camping del Solar del Bosque* (Km 14) US$5pp, hot showers; *Camping Río Tristen*, in the Haruwen Winter Sports complex (Km 36), T/F 24058, US$5/tent, electricity, bar, restaurant. Inside the Parque Nacional Tierra del Fuego (entry fee US$5) is *Camping Lago Roca*, 18 km from Ushuaia, at Lapataia, by forested shore of Lago Roca, with good facilities, dirty, showers (US$3), noisy, reached by bus Jan-Feb, small shop, cafeteria. There are also 4 free sites with no facilities: *Camping Río Pipo*, 10 km from Ushuaia; *Ensenada Camping* 14 km from Ushuaia; *Camping Las Bandurrias* and *Camping Laguna Verde*, both 21 km from Ushuaia.

● **Places to eat**

Barcleit 1912, Fadul 148, cordon bleu cooking at reasonable prices; *Kaupé*, Roca 470, English spoken, excellent food and wine, rec, expensive. Best place to eat lamb is at *Tolkeyen*, Estancia Río Pipo, 5 km from town, meal US$15, taxi US$7; *Barcito Ideal*, San Martín 393, good, cheap, *tenedor libre* US$14, very popular with travellers; *Los Amigos*, San Martín 130, quick service, some cheap dishes; *Volver*, Maipú 37, interesting decor, sea view, good food and service, not cheap; *Quick*, San Martín 130, clean, good service, rec, 10% discount for ISIC card holders; also *Split*, Piedrabuena 238, pizzería, offers same discount, cheap; *Café de la Esquina*, San Martín y 25 de Mayo, rec; *Don Guido Cybercafe*, Godoy 45, surf the net for US$10/hr, also offers mailbox facilities for e-mail, 0800-2400; *Turco*, San Martín 1460, cheapest in town, friendly; *Der Garten*, confitería, San Martín 638, in Galería shopping arcade. *Bidu Bar*, San Martín 898, good music, lunches, good meeting place; excellent homemade chocolate sold at a shop at San Martín 785. *Helados Massera*, San Martín 270-72, good. The coffee bar at the airport is very expensive. Ask around for currently available *centolla* (king crab) and *cholga* (giant mussels). Food and drink (apart from the duty-free items) in Ushuaia are very expensive.

● **Airline offices**

LADE, San Martín 564, T 21123, airport T 21700; **Aerolíneas Argentinas**, Roca 116, T 21218, airport 21265; **Lapa**, Av Malvinas Argentinas 120, T 22150, F 30532; **Kaiken** and **Alta**, San Martín 880, T 32963, or at airport, T 22620/23049; **DAP**, San Martín 626, T 31373; **Lan Chile**, Gob Godoy 169, T 31110.

● **Banks & money changers**

Banks open 1000-1500 (in summer). Useful to have credit cards here as difficult to change TCs and very high commission (up to 10%), but **Banco del Sud**, Maipú 600 block, only place for changing TCs (downstairs). **Banco de la Nación**, Rivadavia y San Martín, only bank which accepts Chilean pesos. Cash advance on Mastercard at **Banco de Tierra del Fuego**, San Martín 1044, accepts Amex TCs. Tourist agencies and the *Hotel Albatros* also give poor rates. *Listus* record shop, San Martín 973, sweet shop next door, or *Caminante* travel agency for better rates for cash.

● **Embassies & consulates**

Consulates: Chile, Malvinas Argentinas y Jainen, Casilla 21, T 21279; **Finland**, Paz y Deloqui; **Germany**, Rosas 516; **Italy**, Yaganes 75.

● **Entertainment**

A popular spot at night is the disco *Siglo* at 9 de Julio y Maipú; other discos are *Barny's*, Antártida Argentina just off San Martín and *Garage*, San Martín 20; *El Ñaupe*, Gob Paz y Fadul, bar with live music.

● **Laundry**

Rosas 139, between San Martín and Deloqui, open weekdays 0900-2100, US$8.

● **Post & telecommunications**

Post Office: San Martín y Godoy, Mon-Fri 0900-1300 and 1700-2000, Sat 0830-1200. **Telephones**: San Martín 1541.

● **Shopping**

Good boots at *Stella Maris*, San Martín 443. **Bookshop** at San Martín y 9 de Julio (Lapataia Arcade). Film is cheaper in Chile. Supermarkets: *Surty Sur* (with clean toilets, San Martín y Onas) and *Sucoop*, Paz 1600. Most things are more expensive than elsewhere but some cheap imported goods, eg electrical equipment and cigarettes.

● **Sports**

Sports Centre on Malvinas Argentinas on W side of town (close to seafront). Ice skating rink at Ushuaia gymnasium in winter (when lagoon is frozen). Beachcombing can produce whale bones.

Fishing: trout. Season 1 Nov-31 Mar, licences US$20/week, US$10/day. Contact Asociación de Caza y Pesca at Maipú y 9 de Julio, with small museum. Fishermen may be interested in visiting the fish hatchery 7 km E of Ushuaia, visiting hours daily 1400-1700. There are brook, rainbow and brown trout and land-locked salmon. Take No 1 bus east-bound on Maipú to the end of the line and continue 2½ km on foot to the hatchery. Birdwatchers will also find this ride rewarding. Fishing excursions to Lago Fagnano are organized by *Yishka*, Gob Godoy 115, T 31535, F 31230.

Skiing, hiking, climbing: contact Club Andino, Solís 50, or *Caminante*. **Skiing**: a downhill ski run (beginner standard) on Cerro Martial. There is another ski run, Wallner, 3 km from Ushuaia, open June-Aug, has lights for night-skiing and is run by Club Andino. The area is excellent for cross country skiing; *Caminante* organizes excursions 'off road'. 20 km E of Ushuaia is Valle Tierra Mayoria, a large flat valley with high standard facilities for cross country skiing, snow shoeing and snowmobiling; rentals and a cafetería; bus am and 1400 from *Antartur*, San Martín 638. The Haruwen Winter Sports complex is 21 km E on Route 3 (Km 36).

● **Tour companies & travel agents**

All agencies charge the same fees for excursions: Tierra del Fuego National Park, 4 hrs, US$19; Lago Escondido, 5 hrs, US$25; Lagos Escondido and Fagnano, 8 hrs, US$30. With 3 or 4 people it is often little more expensive to hire a *remise* taxi. The two largest agencies are: *Rumbo Sur*, San Martín 342, T 30699, runs a range of tours on water and on land and offers a 2-day package to Cafayate, US$150 inc transport and hotel, good value, also organizes bus to ski slope, very helpful; and *Tolkeyen*, 12 de Octubre 150, T 22237, rec. Others include *Antartur*, San Martín 638, T 23240; *All Patagonia*, 25 de Mayo 31, of A, T 24432, F 30707, Amex agent; *Caminante*, Don Bosco 319, T 32723, F 31040, organizes walking, climbing tours and horse riding to suit all levels of experience, provides food, tents, equipment, outdoor clothing, detailed map, very friendly and helpful, English and German spoken, highly rec. Recommended guide: Domingo Galussio, Intervú 15, Casa 211, 9410 Ushuaia, bilingual, not cheap (US$120), rec.

● **Tourist offices**

San Martín 660, T/F (0901) 24550, 'best in Argentina', literature in English, German and Dutch, helpful, English spoken. Large chart of hotels and prices and information on travel and staying at Estancia Harberton. Has noticeboard for messages. Open Mon-Fri 0830-2030, Sat and Sun 0900-2000. **National Park Office**, on San Martín between Patagonia y Sarmiento, has small map but not much information. The **ACA** office on Maipú also has maps and information.

● **Transport**

Local Car hire: Tagle, San Martín y Belgrano, T 22744, good, also **Río Grande**, Elcano 799, T 22571, and **Localiza**, in *Hotel Albatros* and at airport, rec, T 30663.

Air New airport 4 km from town, taxi, US$5 (no bus). Services are more frequent in high season; in winter weather often impedes flights. In the summer tourist season it is sometimes difficult to get a flight out: it may be worth trying Río Grande. Aerolíneas Argentinas (AR) and Lapa to Buenos Aires via Río Gallegos and/or Trelew, all year round, 5 hrs; also Austral continuing BsAs-Río Grande flights. To **Río Grande**, Kaiken US$36, LADE, US$14. Kaiken's services to/from Ushuaia are as for Río Grande. To **Río Gallegos**, LADE once a week US$34, Kaiken, Lapa, AR and Austral US$50-63. LADE to **Comodoro Rivadavia** via Río Grande, Río Gallegos, and Calafate, Gob Gregores and Perito Moreno on Thur (to Calafate only in summer). To **Punta Arenas**, DAP twice a week, US$91; Lan Chile US$95; Alta Mon-Fri US$89.

At the airport ask around for a pilot willing to take you on a 30 mins flight around Ushuaia, US$38 pp (best to go in pm when wind has dropped). Alternatively ask about flights at the tourist office in town. Aerial excursions over the Beagle Channel with local flying club, hangar at airport, 3-5 seater planes, 30 mins: Lago Fagnano, Lapataia and Ushuaia Bay.

Trains A Decauville gauge train for tourists runs along the shore of the Beagle Channel between the Fin del Mundo station, W of Ushuaia and the boundary of the Tierra del Fuego National Park, 4.5 km, 3 departures daily, US$26 (tourist), US$30 (first class), plus US$5 park entrance and US$3 for bus to the station; it is planned to continue to Lapataia. Run by Ferrocarril Austral Fueguino with new locomotives and carriages, it uses track first laid by prisoners to carry wood to Ushuaia; tickets from Tranex kiosk in the port, T 30709. Sit on left outbound.

Buses To Río Grande 4 hrs, Los Carlos, Mon-Fri 0300, US$20 and Tecni Austral, daily 0730, 1800, US$21; to **Punta Arenas**, Los Carlos, Mon-Fri, 0300, 14 hrs, US$58, a comfortable and interesting ride via Punta Delgada. Bus company offices: Los Carlos, *Ticatur Turismo*, San Martín 880, T 22337; Tecni Austral, 25 de Mayo 50, T 23396/23304.

Hitching Trucks leave Ushuaia for the refinery at San Sebastián Mon-Fri; a good place to hitch from is the police control on Route 3.

To Puerto Williams (Chile) No regular sailings. Yachts based at the Club Náutico carry charter passengers in summer, returning the same day; enquire at the Club, most possibilities in Dec because boats visit Antarctica in Jan. Luxury cruises around Cape Horn via Puerto Williams are operated by the Chilean company, *Tierra Austral*, 7/8 days, US$1,260.

To Antarctica: most tourist vessels to Antarctica call at Ushuaia and, space permitting, take on passengers. Enquire at *Rumbo Sur* or other agencies. All agencies charge similar price, US$2,200pp for 8/9 day trip, though prices may be lower for late availability, which are posted in window of *Rumbo Sur*.

PARQUE NACIONAL TIERRA DEL FUEGO

Covering 63,000 ha of mountains, lakes, rivers and deep valleys, the park stretches W to the Chilean frontier and N to Lago Fagnano, though large areas have been closed to tourists to protect the environment. The lower parts are forested; tree species include lenga, ñire and coihue. Fauna include several species of geese including kelp geese, ducks including the beautiful torrent duck, Magellanic woodpeckers and austral parakeets. Introduced species like rabbits, beavers and muskrats, have done serious environmental damage. Near the Chilean frontier beaver dams can be seen and with much luck and patience the beavers themselves. Stand still and down-wind of them: their sense of smell and hearing are good, but not their eye-sight.

There are several beautiful walks; the most popular ones are an interpreted trail along Lapataia Bay, good for birdwatch-ing, a 4 km walk along Lago Roca to the Chilean frontier at Hito XXIV, and a 2½ km climb to Cerro Pampa Alta which offers fine views. Good climbing on Cerro Cóndor, rec. There are no recognized crossing points to Chile. In winter the temperature drops to as low as -12°C, in summer it goes up to 25°C. Even in the summer the climate can often be cold, damp and unpredictable.

● **Access** The park entrance is 12 km W of Ushuaia. Park administration is at **Lapataia Bay**. Entry US$5. In summer buses and minibuses, US$5, to the park are run by several companies: *Pasarela*, Fadul 40, T 21735, leaving from Maipú y Fadul; *Kaupen*, T 34015, leaving from Maipú y 25 de Mayo; and *Eben-Ezer*, T 31133, leaving from San Martín y 25 de Mayo. Timetables vary with demand, tourist office has details. *Cami-nante* also runs a 1 day excursion to the Parque Nacional, including trek, canoeing, *asado* lunch, US$70 inclusive (small groups, book early). Ask at the tourist office about cycling tours in the park, US$65 full day, also 'Eco Treks' available and cultural events. It is possible to hitchhike, as far as Lapataia.

● **Accommodation** See above for **Camping** possibilities.

ISLA DE LOS ESTADOS

Robert T Cook writes: "This long (75 km) and guarded island lies E of Tierra del Fuego. Except for the caretakers of the lighthouse and an occasional scientist few people ever set foot on this cloud-shrouded reserve of Fuegian flora and fauna that no longer exist on the main island. During the 18th and 19th centuries large numbers of ships were wrecked or lost in the treacherous waters surrounding this island. Much gold, silver and relics await salvage." Information and tours from *Rumbo Sur*, San Martín 342, Ushuaia.

Argentina apparently has plans for tour-ist developments in **Antarctica** (accom-modation at Marambio and Esperanza stations). Flights can be arranged in Bue-nos Aires in Jan-Feb through *Surexpress*, Esmeralda 629, 4th floor, T 325-0252. The plane goes to Ushuaia and you take a boat from there. Also try Andy Macfarlane at *Macren Travel*, T 322-7988. Complete trips for US$6,000-8,000 for 11 days can be booked at Corrientes 536, 10th floor, T 394-5399. The National Institute of the Antarctic is at Cerrito 1248, T 816-6313/1689, 0900-1500.

Information for travellers

BEFORE YOU GO

ENTRY REQUIREMENTS

● **Documents**

Check visa requirements in advance. Passports are not required by citizens of neighbouring countries who hold identity cards issued by their own Governments. No visa is necessary for US citizens, British citizens and nationals of other Western European countries, Canada, Bolivia, Brazil, Chile, Panama, Paraguay, Uruguay, Mexico, El Salvador, Nicaragua, Honduras, Costa Rica, Colombia, Ecuador, Peru, Haiti, Barbados, Jamaica, Hong Kong, Malaysia, Israel, Hungary, Poland, Turkey, Croatia, Yugoslavia, Slovenia and Japan, who may stay for 3 months, a period which can be renewed for another 3 (fee US$100) months at the National Directorate of Migration. For all others there are three forms of visa: a business 'temporary' visa (US$28, valid 1 year), a tourist visa (US$28), and a transit visa. Australians, New Zealanders and South Africans need visas. (Australians applying for a visa in London must have a return ticket.) Tourist visas are usually valid for 3 months and multiple entry. If leaving Argentina on a short trip, check on re-entry that border officials look at the correct expiry date on your visa, otherwise they will give only 30 days. Renewing a visa is difficult and can only be done for 30-day periods. Visitors should carry passports at all times; backpackers are particular targets for thorough searches – just stay calm; it is illegal not to have identification handy. When crossing land frontiers, remember that though the migration and customs officials are generally friendly, helpful and efficient, the police at the control posts a little further into Argentina tend to be extremely bureaucratic.

At land borders, 90 days permission to stay is usually given without proof of transportation out of Argentina. If you need a 90-day extension for your stay in Argentina, get a new stamp at the first opportunity. Do not be put off by immigration officials in provincial cities who say that the stamp is not necessary, or too complicated to obtain. You can also leave the country, at Iguazú or to Uruguay, and 90 further days will be given on return. Without a valid stamp you will be fined US$40 on leaving.

NB At Argentine/Uruguayan borders one immigration official will stamp passports for both countries. Argentine immigration and customs officials wear civilian dress. The border patrol, *gendarmería*, in green combat fatigues, operate some borders.

● **Representation overseas**

Australia, 100 Miller Street, Suite 6, Level 30, North Sydney, New South Wales 2060, T 2922-7272, F 2 923-1798; **Belgium**, 225 Avenue Louise B.3, 1050 Brussels, T 2 647-7812, F 2 467-9319; **Canada**, 90 Sparks Street, Suite 620, Ottawa KIP 5B4, T 613 236-2351, F 613 235-2659; **France**, 6 Rue Cimarosa 75116 Paris, T 1 4553-3300, F 1 4553-44633; **Germany**, Wiesenhuettenplatz 26, 8th Floor, 6000 Frankfurt, T 496 923-1050, F 496 923-6842; **Netherlands**, Herengracht 94 1015 BS, Amsterdam, T 2 023-2723/6242, F 2 062-67344; **New Zealand**, 11 Floor, Harbour View Bldg, 52 Quay

Street, PO Box 2320, Auckland, T 9 39-1757, F 9 373-5386; **Spain**, Paseo de la Castellana 53, Madrid 1, Madrid, T 1 442-4500, F 1 442-3559; **UK**, 27 Three Kings Yard, London W1Y 1FL, T 0171 318-1340, F 0171 318-1349; **USA**, 12 West 56th Street, New York 10019, T 212 603-0400, F 212 397-3523.

● **Tourist information**
Addresses of tourist offices are given in the text.

● **Tourist offices overseas**
Delegations abroad: Bonn, Eduardo Piva, Penthouse 1, Suite F, Bldg AmeriFirst, Adenauerallee 52, 5300 Bonn, T 228-222011; New York, López Lecube, 12 West 56 St, NY10019, T 603-0400; Rome, Luis Ruzzi, Via B Ammamati 6, T 963-60-1485; São Paulo, Ruben Eduardo Ali, Av Paulista 2319, Argentine Embassy, F (5511) 881-4063.

● **Specialist tours**
An increasing number of foreign visitors are birdwatchers. Since at least 980 of the 2,926 species of birds registered in South America exist in Argentina, in places with easy access, enthusiasts head for Península Valdés, Patagonia, the subtropical forests in the NW, or the Chaco savannah in the NE. Tours to observe and photograph the animals are led by expert guides. Further details from Asociación Ornitológica del Plata (address under **Buenos Aires**).

● **Maps**
Several series of road maps are available including those of the ACA (see below) and the *Automapas* published by Línea Azul. Topographical maps are issued by the Instituto Geográfico Militar, Cabildo 301, Casilla 1426, Buenos Aires (reached by *Subte* D to Ministro Carranza – or Palermo while Min Carranza is closed for repair – where IGM is one block from station – turn right from station, or take bus 152 from Retiro). 1:500,000 sheets cost US$3 each and are 'years old'; better coverage of 1:100,000 and 1:250,000, but no general physical maps of the whole country or city plans. Helpful staff, sales office accessible from street, no passport required, map series indices on counter, open Mon-Fri, 0800-1300.

HEALTH

Argentina is generally a healthy country to visit, with good sanitary services. In some provinces, like Neuquén and Salta, medical assistance, inc operations, X-ray and medication, is free in provincial hospitals, even for foreigners. Sometimes, though, one must pay for materials. All private clinics, on the other hand, charge. Medicines are more expensive than in Europe (eg US$8.20 for Paracetamol drops for children). Smallpox vaccination no longer required to en-

ter Argentina. If intending to visit the low-lying tropical areas, it is advisable to take precautions against malaria. Chagas' disease (see **Health Information**) is found in NW Argentina. To counter the effects of altitude in the NW, chew coca leaves or take *te de coca* (use of coca is legal, its trade is not). In the S take plenty of sunscreen to prevent burning owing to the thinning of the ozone layer. Certain shellfish from the Atlantic coast are affected once or twice a year by red tide (*Marea roja*), at which time the public is warned not to eat them. Buy seafood, if self-catering, from fishmongers with fridge or freezer. To be certain, soak fish for 30 mins in water with a little vinegar. Cholera presents no problem except in some remote villages on the Bermejo and Pilcomayo rivers in the tropical lowlands of the Salta and Jujuy provinces, where the Mataco and Toba tribes have been affected by the disease. If travelling through this region, use bottled water and take your own food.

MONEY

● **Currency**
– The peso –, which is at par with the dollar, is divided into 100 centavos. Peso notes in circulation: 2, 5, 10, 20, 50 and 100. Coins in circulation: 5, 10, 25 and 50 centavos and 1 peso. It is often difficult to change TCs, particularly at weekends and in the smaller towns. There is a 3% tax on TCs and commissions can be as high as 10% and in banks is generally 4%. Commission can be avoided if you go to a branch of the issuing bank, especially if changing small amounts. TC transactions can take a long time and many forms. TCs are often scrutinized very closely: any variation between signatures can lead to their being refused. It is best to take US$ cash (which is widely accepted, but take only utterly unblemished notes, as dirty or torn notes are usually refused). TCs are generally difficult to change: American Express TCs, which can be changed at the American Express bank in Buenos Aires, are hard to change in N Argentina although the Amex card is widely accepted. Emergency cash from Amex is available only in Buenos Aires and Bariloche. Citibank TCs have been rec; no commission is charged at their own branches around the country. Because of TCs fraud there are periodic crackdowns on particular types; take more than one type to avoid being stuck without funds. Thomas Cook Mastercard TC refund assistance point, 25 de Mayo 195, p 6, Buenos Aires, T 343-8371. Most major towns have exchange shops (*casas de cambio*). Exchange rates are quoted in major newspapers daily. Money remitted to Argentina from abroad is normally paid out in local currency. It is possible

to obtain money from Europe through an express transfer, which takes 2-3 days, and the currency will be subject to tax. For Western Union, T (1) 322-7774. If staying for a long time in Argentina and especially Buenos Aires, you can transfer money from your bank in your home country to a local bank, opening an account in pesos or dollars. Paperwork is not complicated and your money is safe and gaining interest. Check with your bank before leaving.

ATMs are available in Buenos Aires and a few other major cities (known as Cajeros Automáticos). Dollar bills are widely accepted. Visa can be used at Banelco ATMs. Cirrus card can be used at ATMs with Link sign, eg Banco Nacional de Lavoro.

The provinces of Córdoba, Salta, Jujuy, Catamarca and possibly San Juan (1996) issue *bonos* (bonds) which circulate at face value alongside the national currency. Tucumán issues *cheques predatos*. Two warnings: they are not accepted outside the province of issue and even inside province of issue they are not accepted for some transactions, eg trains, long distance buses. Also, they bear redemption dates, after which they are valueless. Try always to use cash in these provinces and pay the exact amount; change may be given in *bonos*.

When crossing a land frontier into Argentina, make sure you have some Argentine currency as there are normally no facilities at the border.

● **Cost of living**

In 1996-97, Argentina was very expensive for the foreign visitor. Budget travellers should allow US$35-40 a day minimum. High costs can be expected for items such as slide film, and clothing as well as basics, although you can save money by camping and preparing your own food. Imported electronic goods are cheap.

● **Credit cards**

American Express, Diners Club, Visa and Mastercard cards are all widely accepted in the major cities and provincial capitals, though less so outside these. There is a 10% surcharge on credit card transactions in many establishments; many hotels offer reductions for cash. Credit cards are readily accepted in all main towns, even in the S, but outside main towns their use is limited. Many service stations accept credit cards (ACA stations only take cards from members; YPF accepts Visa). All shops, hotels and places showing Argencard (head office, H Yrigoyen 878, Buenos Aires, T 331-2088) signs will accept Eurocard and Access, but you must state that these cards are affiliated to Mastercard. Argencard will not permit cash advances on these cards in outlying regions, and is itself very slow in advancing cash. Lloyds Bank, in many cities, handles Mastercard.

● **Value-added tax**

VAT is not levied on most medicines and some foodstuffs but on all other products and services at 21%.

GETTING THERE

BY AIR

● **From Europe**

British Airways (non-stop, 3 times a week) and Aerolíneas Argentinas (AR, via Madrid) each fly from London. Aerolíneas also fly to the following European destinations (with other carriers in parentheses): Frankfurt (Lufthansa); Madrid (Iberia, daily); Paris (Air France); Rome (Alitalia); Zurich (Swiss Air). KLM flies 3 times a week from Amsterdam. Aeroflot flies from Moscow once a week.

● **From North America**

Aerolíneas Argentinas fly from the following US destinations (with other carriers in brackets): Los Angeles (Lan Chile, United); Miami (daily, Lan Chile, American, United); New York (daily, Lan Chile, American, United). American from Dallas daily via Miami, United from Chicago. Canadian Air International fly 5 times a week from Toronto; Aerolíneas fly twice a week from Toronto, once from Montreal. **NB** AR is part of Continental's frequent flier programme.

● **From Australasia and South Africa**

Aerolíneas Argentinas fly from Sydney, Australia, via Auckland, New Zealand, twice a week. On the outward flight from Argentina, Aerolíneas stop at Río Gallegos, but it is difficult to board there in high season. Malaysia Airlines fly twice a week from Johannesburg and Cape Town. South African Airways fly from Johannesburg.

● **From Latin America**

Aerolíneas Argentinas and Lapsa daily from Asunción; AR and Avianca from Bogotá; AR from Caracas; AR from La Paz via Santa Cruz, and LAB direct from Santa Cruz; from Lima, AR (3), Lan Chile, AeroPerú (en route to Cancún); from Montevideo (apart from those given in the Buenos Aires section), AR, Pluna, United and Iberia; frequent flights also to Punta del Este, with many more in holiday season; Ecuatoriana from Guayaquil and Quito (2 a week); from Santiago, Chile, daily with AR and Lan Chile and other Latin American, European and North American carriers on various days. Mexicana, AR, Lan Chile fly from Mexico City.

From Brazil, AR, Transbrasil, Varig and Vasp fly daily from Rio de Janeiro and São Paulo (plus European airlines stopping over at São Paulo); Varig stops over in Porto Alegre. Transbrasil flies daily from Brasília (also Varig), Manaus, São Paulo and Porto Alegre. Transbrasil, Varig and

Vasp from Curitiba and Florianópolis (also AR). Vasp flies daily from Recife and Salvador. See under Brazil, or **Introduction and Hints**, for the Mercosur Air Pass.

BY ROAD

For entering Argentina by automobile see **Motoring, Additional Notes** in **Introduction and Hints**. Tourists can bring into Argentina their own cars, vehicles bought or hired in neighbouring countries for up to 8 months under international documentation. No specific papers are usually required to bring a Brazilian registered car into Argentina.

CUSTOMS

No duties are charged on clothing, personal effects, toilet necessities, etc. Cameras, typewriters, binoculars, radios and other things which a tourist normally carries are duty-free if they have been used and only one of each article is carried. This is also true of scientific and professional instruments for personal use. Travellers may only bring in new personal goods up to a value of US$200 (US$100 from neighbouring countries); the amount of duty and tax payable amounts to 50% of the item's cost. There are red and green divisions at airport customs. Baggage claim tags are inspected at the exit from the customs inspection area.

2 litres of alcoholic drinks, 400 cigarettes and 50 cigars are also allowed in duty-free; for tourists originating from neighbouring countries the respective quantities allowed are 1 litre, 200, 20 and 2 kg. You can buy duty-free goods *on arrival* at Ezeiza airport.

If having packages sent to Argentina, do not use the green customs label unless the contents are of real value and you expect to pay duty. For such things as books or samples use the white label if available.

WHEN YOU ARRIVE

● **Airport information**
Do not send unaccompanied luggage to Argentina; it can take up to 3 days of form-filling to retrieve it from the airport. Paying overweight, though expensive, saves time.

● **Clothing**
Shorts are worn in Buenos Aires and residential suburbs in spring, summer and autumn, but their use is not common outside the capital. Bermuda-type shorts are very fashionable, as are jogging suits. In general, dress tends to be formal (unless casual wear is specified on an invitation) in Buenos Aires and for evening outings to shows, etc. The general standard of dress among Argentines is very high: collar and tie,

with jacket, are very much the standard for men, and women 'should always err on the side of elegance' – David Mackintosh. Men wearing earrings can expect comments, even hostility, in the provinces.

● **Hours of business**
Banks, government offices, insurance offices and business houses are not open on Sat. **Government Offices**: 1230-1930 in the winter and 0730-1300 in summer. **Banks**: generally 1000-1600 but time varies according to the city, and sometimes according to the season. (See under names of cities in text.) **Post Offices**: stamps on sale during working days 0800-2000 but 0800-1400 on Sat. **Shops** are open from about 0900 to 1900, though many close at midday on Sat. Outside the main cities many close for the daily afternoon siesta, reopening at about 1700. 24-hr opening is allowed except on Mon; this applies mainly to restaurants, foodshops, barbers, newspaper shops, art, book and record stores.

Dance halls open at 2300 but don't fill up till after midnight; nightclubs open after midnight. In city centres, cafés and restaurants are busy till after midnight and many evening events, such as lectures, may not start before 2200.

● **Official time**
3 hrs behind GMT.

● **Safety**
Argentina is one of the safest countries in South America but in Buenos Aires and other major cities beware of the common trick of spraying mustard, ketchup or some other substance on you and then getting an accomplice to clean you off (and remove your wallet). If you are sprayed, walk straight on.

NB Never carry weapons, or drugs without prescriptions.

● **Shopping**
Local leather goods in Buenos Aires, eg coats (leather or suede), handbags and shoes. **NB** Leather from the *carpincho* is from the capybara and should not be purchased. A gourd for drinking *yerba mate* and the silver *bombilla* which goes with it, perhaps a pair of *gaucho* trousers, the *bombachas*. Ponchos (red and black for men, all colours for women). Articles of onyx, specially in Salta. Silver handicrafts. Knitted woollens, especially in Bariloche and Mar del Plata.

● **Voltage**
220 volts (and 110 too in some hotels), 50 cycles, AC, European Continental-type plugs in old buildings, Australian 3-pin flat-type in the new. Adaptors can be purchased locally for either type (ie from new 3-pin to old 2-pin and vice-versa).

● **Weights and measures**
The metric system is used.

ON DEPARTURE

● **Airport tax**

US$15 for all international flights, except to Montevideo from Aeroparque, which is subject to US$5 tax; US$3-6, payable only in pesos also for internal flights (US$1.75 in Ushuaia). When in transit from one international flight to another, you may be obliged to pass through immigration and customs, have your passport stamped and be made to pay an airport tax on departure. There is a 5% tax on the purchase of air tickets. Airport tax can be prepaid.

WHERE TO STAY

● **Hotels**

In the beach and inland resorts there are many good hotels and *pensiones*; names are therefore not always given.

● **Camping and youth hostels**

Camping is very popular in Argentina (except in Buenos Aires) and there are sites with services, both municipal, free, and paying private campsites in most tourist centres. Most are very noisy and many are closed off-season. Prices have increased in recent years, though the quality of service is variable. Camping is allowed at the side of major highways and in all national parks (except at Iguazú Falls). Wild camping in deserted areas is possible, but note that in Patagonia strong winds make camping very difficult. Many ACA and YPF service stations have a site where one can camp (usually free) and in general service station owners are very friendly to campers, but ask first. Service stations usually have hot showers. A list of camping sites is available from ACA (labelled for members, but should be easily available) and from the national tourist information office in Buenos Aires, which has a free booklet, *1ra Guía Argentina de Campamentos*; see Autoclub magazine. References to sites will be found in the text. ACA campsites offer discounts to members, and to holders of the International Driving Licence; European automobile clubs' members are allowed to use ACA sites. The Danmark Organization, Junín 1616, p 3, Buenos Aires, T (54-1) 803-3700, has a network of clean, cheap youth hostels throughout Argentina (no age limit, but card needed): in Bariloche, El Bolsón, Pinamar, Calafate and the Tigre Delta. There are few other youth hostels (many open only Feb to Mar), but some towns offer free accommodation to young travellers in the holiday season, on floors of schools or church halls; some fire stations will let you sleep on the floor for free (sometimes men only).

Regular (blue bottle) Camping Gaz International is available in Buenos Aires, at an electrical goods store on Av 9 de Julio, near Teatro Colón, and *Suntime*, Lima 225, Guatemala 5908 (Palermo), Juramento 2452 (Belgrano) and *América Pesca*, Alfredo Pollini Alvear 1461. White gas (*bencina blanca*) is readily available in hardware shops (*ferreterías*). *Camping Center*, Acoyte 1622, Buenos Aires, T 855-0619, rents camping, fishing and backpacking equipment, 5% discount for ISIC holders.

FOOD AND DRINK

● **Food**

National dishes are based in the main upon plentiful supplies of beef. Many dishes are distinctive and excellent; the *asado*, a roast cooked on an open fire or grill; *puchero*, a stew, very good indeed; *bife a caballo*, steak topped with a fried egg; the *carbonada* (onions, tomatoes, minced beef), particularly good in Buenos Aires; *churrasco*, a thick grilled steak; *parrillada*, a mixed grill, mainly roast meat, offal, and sausages, *chorizos* (inc *morcilla*, black pudding to the British, or blood sausage), though do not confuse this with *bife de chorizo*, which is a rump steak (*bife de lomo* is fillet steak). A *choripán* is a roll with a *chorizo* inside. *Arroz con pollo* is a delicious combination of rice, chicken, eggs, vegetables and strong sauce. *Puchero de gallina* is chicken, sausage, maize, potatoes and squash cooked together. *Empanada* is a tasty meat pie; *empanadas de humita* are filled with a thick paste of cooked corn/maize, onions, cheese and flour. *Milanesa de pollo* (breaded, boneless chicken) is usually good value. *Ñoquis* (gnocchi), potato dumplings normally served with meat and tomato sauce, are tasty and often the cheapest item on the menu; they are also a good vegetarian option when served with either *al tuco* or Argentine roquefort (note that most places only serve them on the 29th of the month, when you should put a coin under your plate for luck). *Locro* is a thick stew made of maize, white beans, beef, sausages, pumpkin and herbs. Pizzas come in all sorts of exotic flavours, both savoury and sweet. **NB** Extras such as chips, *puré* (mashed potato), etc are ordered and served separately, and are not cheap. Almost uniquely in Latin America, salads are quite safe. A popular sweet is *dulce de leche* (especially from Chascomús), milk and sugar evaporated to a pale, soft fudge. Other popular desserts are *almendrado* (ice-cream rolled in crushed almonds), *dulce de patata* (sweet potato preserve), *dulce de membrillo* (quince preserve), *dulce de zapallo* (pumpkin in syrup); these *dulces* are often eaten with cheese. *Postre Balcarce*, a cream and meringue cake and *alfajores*, maize-flour biscuits filled with *dulce de leche* or apricot jam, are also very popular. Note that *al natural* in reference to fruit means canned without sugar (fresh fruit is *al fresca*) Croissants (known as *media lunas*) come in two varieties: *de grasa* (dry) and *de mantequilla* (rich and fluffy) Sweets: the Havana brands have been particularly is rec. Excellent Italian-style ice-cream with exotic flavours. For local recipes (in Spanish) *Las Comidas de Mi Pueblo*, by Margarita Palacios, is rec.

Offices close for 2 to 2½ hrs for lunch between 1200 and 1500. Around 1700, many people go to a *confitería* for tea, sandwiches and cakes. Dinner often begins at 2200 or 2230; it is, in the main, a repetition of lunch. Eating out is expensive: the cheapest option is to have the set lunch as a main meal of the day and then find cheap, wholesome snacks for breakfast and supper. Budget travellers should note that especially in Buenos Aires a number of cheaper restaurants are advertised as *tenedor libre* – eat all you want for a fixed price. Those wishing to prepare their own food will find supermarkets fairly cheap for basics.

● **Drink**

Argentine wines (inc champagnes, both charmat and champenoise) are sound throughout the price range. The ordinary *vinos de la casa*, or *comunes* are wholesome and relatively cheap; reds better than the whites. The local beers, mainly lager-type, are quite acceptable. In restaurants wines have become more expensive (up to US$20/bottle for a good quality wine). Hard liquor is relatively cheap, except for imported whisky. *Clericó* is a white-wine *sangria* drunk in summer. It is best not to drink the tap water; in the main cities it is often heavily chlorinated. It is usual to drink soda or mineral water at restaurants, and many Argentines mix it with their cheaper wine, with ice, as a refreshing drink in summer.

GETTING AROUND

AIR TRANSPORT

Internal air services are run by Aerolíneas Argentinas (AR), Austral, Lapa (reliable, cheaper than main airlines), TAN (Transporte Aéreo Neuquén) in the S (book tickets through Austral), Dinar (based in Salta, serving the capital, Mar del Plata and the N, cheap fares), Kaiken (serving Patagonia, Córdoba, Mendoza), LAER (Entre Ríos, Mesopotamia), Andesmar, Southern Winds (both in the N and W) and the army airline LADE (in Patagonia), which provides a good extended schedule with new Fokker F-28 jets. **NB** LADE will not accept IATA MCOs. Deregulation and privatization has permitted the introduction of discounts by the major carriers. Ask at a travel agency. (Even though sometimes offices in various towns may tell you the flights are full, it is usually worth a try out at the airport.)

Some airlines operate during the high season, or are air taxis on a semi-regular schedule. AR and Austral offer discounted, *banda negativa* fares on a limited number of seats on many flights, but reserve well in advance. Lapa and Dinar maintain low fares as long as a flight is not fully booked. All airlines operate standby systems, at half regular price, buy ticket 2-3 hrs before flight. It is only worth doing this off season. *Plan familiar* tickets allow couples to travel with a 25% discount for the spouse. Children under 3 travel free. LADE also operates discount spouse (65%) and children (35%) tickets. If travelling by AR or Austral a long linear distance, eg Río Gallegos-Buenos Aires, but wishing to stop en route, it is cheaper to buy the long flight and pay extra (about US$2) for stopovers. **NB** All local flights are fully booked way in advance for travel in December. Don't lose your baggage ticket; you won't be able to collect your bags without it. Some travellers have rec checking in 2 hrs before flight to avoid being 'bumped off' from overbooking.

Visit Argentina fare Aerolíneas Argentinas sells a Visit Argentina ticket: 4 flight coupons costing US$450, with US$120 for each extra coupon up to a maximum of 8. It is valid for 30 days and must be purchased outside Argentina and in conjunction with an international flight ticket. Note that for children under 2 years Visit Argentina fare is 10% while normally very young children travel free. Austral sell similar tickets (known as Jetpaq) and they are interchangeable (but cannot be used on Inter Austral, its subsidiary). Routing must be booked when the coupons are issued: one change of date and of destination is free (but subsequent changes cost US$50). One stop only is permitted per town; this includes making a connection as many flights radiate from Buenos Aires, journeys to and from the capital count as legs on the airpass, so a 4-coupon pass might not get you very far. If you start your journey outside Buenos Aires on a Sun, when Aerolíneas Argentinas offices are closed, you may have difficulty getting vouchers issued at the airport. If you wish to visit Tierra del Fuego and Lago Argentino it is better fly on the Visit Argentina pass to Río Grande or Ushuaia and travel around by bus or LADE from there than to stop off in Río Gallegos, fly to Ushuaia and thence back to Buenos Aires, which will use 3 coupons. Domestic timetables are given in *Guía Argentina de Tráfico Aéreo* and *Guía Internacional de Tráfico*. It is unwise to set up too tight a schedule because of delays which may be caused by bad weather. Flights between Buenos Aires and Río Gallegos are often fully booked 2 to 3 weeks ahead, and there may be similar difficulties on the routes to Bariloche and

Iguazú. If you are 'wait-listed' they cannot ensure a seat. Reconfirmation at least 24 hrs ahead of a flight is important and it is essential to make it at the point of departure. Extra charges are made for reconfirming LADE flights but they are not high.

LAND TRANSPORT

● Train

On 10 March 1994, the government withdrew its funding for Ferrocarriles Argentinos, handing responsibility for all services to the provinces through which the lines run. Few provinces accepted the responsibility, because of lack of resources. As a result trains now run on only 22,000 of the original 42,000 km of track and most of its is used only by freight services. Surviving passenger services are run either by provincial governments or by the private sector. There are few passenger services outside the Buenos Aires area.

● Road

Most of Argentina is served by about 215,578 km of road, but only 29% are paved and a further 17% improved.

● Bus

Fares are charged at about US$4.50/100 km. Sleeper services from the capital to Mendoza, Córdoba and Bariloche cost US$7/100 km. There are also 'ómnibus truchos' (fake buses), which do not start or end services at bus stations and which have less reliable equipment or timekeeping; they charge less than US$4/100 km (ask at travel agents or hotels). Bus companies may give a 20% student discount if you show an international student card; a YHA card is also useful. The same discount may also be given to foreign, as well as Argentine, teachers and university professors but you must carry documentary proof of your employment. It can be difficult to get reductions between Dec and March. Express buses between cities are dearer than the *comunes*, but well worth the extra money for the fewer stops. When buying tickets at a bus office, don't assume you've been automatically allotted a seat: make sure you have one. Buses have strong a/c, even more so in summer; take a sweater for night journeys. Note that luggage is handled by *maleteros*, who expect payment (theoretically US$1, but in practice you can offer less) though many Argentines refuse to pay.

● Motoring

All motorists are required to carry two warning triangles, a fire-extinguisher, a rigid tow bar, a first aid kit, full car documentation together with international driving licence (for non-residents, but see **Car hire** below), and the handbrake must be fully operative. Safety belts must be worn if fitted. Although few checks are made in most of the country, with the notable exceptions of roads into Rosario and Buenos Aires, checks have been reported on cars entering the country. **NB** Police checks around Buenos Aires can be very officious, even to the point of charges being invented and huge 'fines' demanded. You may not export fuel from Argentina, so use up fuel in spare jerry cans while you are in the country. Always fill up when you can in less developed areas like Chaco and Formosa and in parts of Patagonia as filling stations are infrequent. Diesel fuel 'gas-oil' prices are US$0.27/litre. Octane rating for gasoline ('nafta') is as follows: regular gasoline 83 (US$0.65/litre); super 93 (US$0.78/litre). Unleaded fuel is not widely available but its use is increasing (it is called Ultra SP and costs a little more than super). ACA sells petrol vouchers (*vales de nafta*) for use in ACA stations. Shell and Esso stations are slightly more expensive.

To obtain documents for a resident (holder of resident visa, staying at least 6 months in the country) to take a car out of Argentina, you can go to ACA in Buenos Aires, which may take up to 4 working days, or you can ask for a list of other ACA offices that can undertake the work; take forms with you from Buenos Aires, and papers may be ready in 24 hrs. You will need at least one passport-size photo, which you can have taken at ACA at a fair cost. If the car is not your own (or is hired), you require a special form signed by the owner and witnessed by a notary public. **NB** Non-residents may buy a car in Argentina but are in no circumstances allowed to take it out of the country; it must be resold in Argentina, preferably in the province where it was purchased. Non-residents who take cars into Argentina are not allowed to sell them and will encounter problems trying to leave the country without the vehicle. Third party insurance is obligatory; best obtained from the ACA, for members only.

Most main roads are paved, if rather narrow (road maps are a good indication of quality), and roadside services are good. Road surface conditions vary once one leaves main towns: on the dirt and gravel roads a guard for the windscreen is essential. Most main roads now have private tolls, ranging from US$2 to US$10; tolls are spaced about every 100 km. Secondary roads (which have not been privatized) are generally in poor condition. Sometimes one may not be allowed to reach a border if one does not intend to cross it, stopping eg 20 km from the border.

Automóvil Club Argentino (ACA), Av Libertador Gen San Martín 1850, 1st floor, touring department on 3rd floor, 1425 Buenos Aires, T 802-6061/9, open 1000-1800 (take colectivo

130 from LN Alem and Corrientes down Alem, Libertador and F Alcorta, alight opp ACA and walk 1 block through park; to return take the 130 from corner of Libertador on left as you leave building), office on Florida above Harrod's, 2nd floor, has a travel document service, complete car service facilities, insurance facilities, road information, road charts (*hojas de ruta*-about US$2.35 each to members, if available) and maps (dated with the code letters in the bottom corner – road map of whole country, with service stations and *hosterías* shown, US$4 to members, US$9.50 to non-members, and of each province), a hotel list, camping information, and a tourist guide book sold at a discount to its members and members of other recognized, foreign automobile clubs upon presentation of a membership card. (YPF, the state oil agency, also produces good maps for sale.) **NB** Members of other recognized automobile clubs are advised to check if their club has reciprocity with ACA, thus allowing use of ACA facilities and benefit from lower prices for their rooms and meals at ACA *hosterías*. The Club has service stations, some with parking garages, all over the country. If you are not a member of ACA you will not get any help when in trouble. ACA membership, US$20/month, permits you to pay with Eurocard (Argencard) for fuel at their Service stations, gives 20% discount on hotel rooms and maps, and discounts at associated hotels, and 10% discount on meals.

ACA accommodation comes in 4 basic types: *Motel*, *Hostería*, *Hotel*, and *Unidad Turística*, and they also organize campsites. A *motel* may have as few as 3 rooms, and only 1 night's stay is permitted. *Hosterías* have very attractive buildings and are very friendly. *Hotels* are smarter and more impersonal. All have meal facilities of some kind. Anyone can get in touch with the organization to find out about accommodation or road conditions. **NB** ACA is facing competition from others providing cheaper towing services, and better service stations, so *hosterías* and service stations are closing.

Hitchhikers, as well as motorists, are rec to contact the ACA for its wealth of information.

Touring Club Argentino, Esmeralda 605 and Tucumán 781, p 3, T 392-6742, has similar travel services but no service stations.

● **Motorcycle**
Repairs at Eduardo Olivera, Mecánica Ruben SA, Lavoiser 1187-1674, Sáenz Peña, Buenos Aires, T 757-4285, excellent BMW mechanic with good selection of spares. Juan Carlos Topcic, Costa Rica 25, casa 48, 9400 Río Gallegos, T 0966-23572, all makes.

● **Motorhomes**
Casa Import Trailer, Av Juan de Garay 331,

T 361-5674, sells articles for motorhomes. *Casa Car*, Humberto Primo 236, T 30-0051, rents motorhomes. *Rancho Móvil*, Luis Viale 2821, T 59-9470, is club for motorhome owners; all in Buenos Aires. Porta-Potti toilets are widely sold in Argentina, sometimes under a different name.

● **Car hire**
To rent a small car (for 4 plus luggage) costs from US$40 to US$110 a day, not inc mileage, fuel, insurance and tax (20%); highest prices are in Patagonia. Discounts are available for several days', or weekly rental. Minimum age for renting is 25 (private arrangements may be possible). A credit card is useful. You must ensure that the renting agency gives you ownership papers of the vehicle, which have to be shown at police and military checks. At tourist centres such as Salta, Posadas, Bariloche or Mendoza it may be more economical to hire a taxi with driver, which includes the guide, the fuel, the insurance and the mechanic. Avis offers a good and efficient service with the possibility of complete insurance and unlimited mileage for rentals of 7 days or more, but you should prebook from abroad. No one-way fee if returned to another Avis office, but the car may not be taken out of the country. Localiza, a Brazilian company, accepts drivers aged at least 21 (according to Brazilian rules, but higher insurance). They also offer 4WD vehicles, though only from Buenos Aires. Taking a rented car out of Argentina is difficult with any company. Other companies are given in the text.

If you do not have an international driver's licence, you can get a 3-month licence from Dirección de Transportes de la Municipalidad, Av Roca 5225, Buenos Aires, T 602-6925, Mon-Fri 0800-1300; bring documentation from home.

● **Hitchhiking**
Argentina seems to be getting increasingly difficult for this. Ask at petrol stations. Traffic can be sparse, especially at distances from the main towns, and in Patagonia, which is popular with Argentine hitchhikers. It may be useful to carry a letter from your Consulate. Though they tend to be more reserved in manner than most Latin Americans, Argentines are generally friendly and helpful, especially to foreigners (display your flag, but not the Union Jack).

● **Internal checkpoints**
There are checkpoints to prevent food, vegetable and meat products entering Patagonia, the Western provinces of Mendoza and San Juan, and the Northwestern provinces of Catamarca, Tucumán, Salta and Jujuy. All vehicles and passengers entering these areas are searched and prohibited products are confiscated.

COMMUNICATIONS

● **Language**

Spanish, with variant words and pronunciation. English comes second; French and Italian (especially in Patagonia) may be useful.

The chief variant pronunciations are the replacement of the 'll' and 'y' sounds by a soft 'j' sound, as in 'azure' (though note that this is not done in Mendoza), the omission of the 'd' sound in words ending in '-ado' (generally considered uncultured), the omission of final 's' sounds, the pronunciation of 's' before a consonant as a Scottish or German 'ch', and the substitution in the N and W of the normal rolled 'r' sound by a hybrid 'rj'. In grammar the Spanish 'tú' is replaced by 'vos' and the second person singular conjugation of verbs has the accent on the last syllable eg *vos tenés, podés*, etc. In the N and NW, though, the Spanish is more akin to that spoken in the rest of Latin America.

● **Newspapers**

Buenos Aires dailies: *La Nación, La Prensa, Clarín, La Razón*. Evening paper: *Crónica*. English language daily: *Buenos Aires Herald* (which includes *The Guardian Weekly* free on Sun). Magazines: *Noticias, Gente, Redacción, Mercado, El Gráfico* (sports). The daily, *Página Doce*, is very popular among students and intellectuals. *La Maga* is a weekly cultural review, Wed, US$5. English language magazines: *The Review of the River Plate* (commercial, agricultural, political and economic comment), and *The Southern Cross* (Irish community). German-language weekly, *Argentinisches Tageblatt*, available everywhere, very informative. There is a weekly international edition of *La Nación*, priced in Europe at US$1.30. Write for further information to: La Nación, Edición Internacional, Bouchard 557, 1106 Buenos Aires.

● **Postal services**

Letters from Argentina take 10-14 days to get to the UK and the USA. Rates for letters up to 20 grams: US$0.75 Mercosur, US$1 rest of Latin America, US$1.25 rest of world (add US$2 for *certificado*); up to 150 grams, US$1.50, US$2.25, US$3 respectively.

Small parcels only of 1 kg at post offices; larger parcels from Encomiendas Internacionales, Centro Postal Internacional, Av Antártida Argentina, near Retiro Station, Buenos Aires, and in main provincial cities, about US$40 for 5 kg. Larger parcels must first be examined, before final packing, by Customs, then wrapped (up to 2 kg, brown paper; over 2 kg must be sewn in linen cloth), then sealed by Customs, then taken to Encomiendas Internacionales for posting. Cheap packing service available. Open 1100-1700 on weekdays. Used clothes have to be fumigated before they will be accepted. Having parcels sent to Argentina incurs a customs tax of US$5.75/package. *Poste restante* is available in every town's main post office, fee US$1.

● **Telephone services**

Two private companies operate telephone services, Telecom in the N and Telefónica Argentina in the S. Buenos Aires Federal District and the country as a whole are split roughly in two halves. For the user there is no difference and the two companies' phone cards are interchangeable. For domestic calls public phones operate on *cospeles* (tokens) which can be purchased at news stands (different tokens for local and inland calls). Domestic phone calls are priced at 3 rates: normal 0800-1000, 1300-2200, Sat 0800-1300; peak 1000-1300, Mon-Fri; night rate 2200-0800, Sat 1300-0800 and all day Sun and holidays. Peak is most expensive; night rate is cheapest and at this time also international calls are reduced by 20%. International calls are: rates/minute Uruguay US$0.82; USA, Canada, Brazil, Chile, Paraguay, Bolivia US$1.13 (0.85 each subsequent minute); France, Germany, UK, Spain, Italy US$1.90 (1.43); Japan, Australia, New Zealand US$4.66 (3.50). In main cities there are also privately-run 'Centros de Llamadas', offering a good telephone and fax service. International public phones display the DDI sign (Discado Directo Internacional), DDN (Discado Directo Nacional) is for phone calls within Argentina. Provide yourself with enough tokens or phone cards in Buenos Aires because, in the regions, phone booths exist, but the tokens and cards are not on sale (few phone booths in Patagonia). Most telephone company offices in principal cities have a phone for USA Direct; if they do not, they can direct you to one. BT Chargecard can be used to the UK via the operator. There is frequently a high mark-up on calls made from hotels. No reverse-charge calls to South Africa. It is now easy to call reverse charge to Australia. Operator speaks English. Fax: American Express in Buenos Aires allows card holders to receive faxes at US$1/sheet and to send them at US$8/sheet (to Europe). Telefónica and Telecom send faxes abroad for US$1.23/page, plus cost of the call, and US$1.82/page to receive. (You get charged for sending the fax even if it does not get through.) Communications on the internet are difficult. Some Centros de Llamadas have compatible equipment but static on the lines makes data transmission difficult and you are charged regardless.

NB Owing to modernization, many 2- and 3-digit prefixes are being changed (see page 89).

MEDIA

● **Radio**

English language radio broadcasts can be heard daily on short wave: 0100-0130 on 6060 KHz 49m, 0230-0300 on 11710 KHz 25m, 0430-0500 and 2230-2300 on 15345 KHz 19m; Radiodifusión Argentina al Exterior, Casilla de Correo 555, 1000, Buenos Aires. This is a government station and broadcasts also in Japanese, Arabic, German, French, Italian and Portuguese. Broadcasts by foreign radio stations (inc the BBC) are receivable on short wave.

SPORT

Fishing The three main areas for fishing are the Northern Zone, around Junín de los Andes, extending S to Bariloche; the Central Zone around Esquel; the Southern Zone around Río Gallegos and Río Grande.

The waters of the Lake District are full of fish, and the best time for fishing is at the beginning of the season, that is, in Nov and Dec (the season runs from early Nov to the end of Mar). Among the best are: Lagos Traful, Gutiérrez, Mascardi, Futalaufquen (in Los Alerces National Park), Meliquina, Falkner, Villarino, Nuevo, Lacar, Lolog, Curruhué, Chico, Huechulafquen, Paimún, Epulafquen, Tromen (all in Lanín National Park), and, in the far N, Quillén. In the far S, the fishing in Lago Argentino is also good. The Río Limay has good trout fishing, as do the rivers further N, the Quilquihue, Malle, Chimehuín, Collón-Curá, Hermoso, Meliquina and Caleufú. All rivers are 'catch and release'. They are all in the neighbourhood of San Martín de los Andes. To fish anywhere in Argentina you need a permit, which costs US$10/day, US$30/week, US$100/year. In the Northern Zone forestry commission inspectors are very diligent. For tours arranged from the UK, contact Sport Elite (JA Valdes-Scott), Woodwalls House, Corscombe, Dorchester, Dorset, DT2 ONT.

Walking and skiing Details on outdoor activities in Argentina can be found in *Weekend* (Spanish), good photos and excellent maps. Information on trails in NW Argentina, the Lake District, Patagonia and Tierra del Fuego is given in *Backpacking in Chile and Argentina*, 3rd edition 1994 (Bradt Publications, 41 Nortoft Road, Chalfont St Peter, Bucks, SL9 0LA, UK). Note that Bradt Publications' *South America Ski Guide* (1992) gives details of Argentine ski resorts.

The skiing season is May to end-Oct; best sites are Las Leñas (Mendoza, which has many other small sites), Chapelco, San Martín de los Andes, Bariloche and La Hoya (nr Esquel, cheapest, but shorter runs).

On the basis of treks made with Sr Ramón Ossa of Barreal, Sr Herbert Levi of Buenos Aires recommends the following additions to the organizer's list of recommendations for equipment on any Andean trip: metal drinking mugs, metal containers to prevent tubes of toothpaste etc emptying themselves in mule packs, long underpants to protect against chafing, woollen cap, insect repellent, sunburn cream, laxatives, soap, nylon groundsheet for sleeping bag (depending on weather), portable tent for privacy, and fishing gear for those who prefer catching their own meals (No 3 spoons best for Andean streams – permit required).

HOLIDAYS AND FESTIVALS

The main holiday period, generally to be avoided by business visitors, is Jan-Mar, though some areas, such as Tierra del Fuego, begin to fill up in Nov/December. Winter school holidays, in which travelling and hotels may be difficult, are the middle 2 weeks of July. No work may be done on the national holidays (1 Jan, Good Friday, 1 May, 25 May, 10 June, 20 June, 9 July, 17 Aug, 12 Oct and 25 Dec) except where specifically established by law. There are no bus services on 25 and 31 December. On Holy Thursday and 8 Dec employers are left free to decide whether their employees should work, but banks and public offices are closed. Banks are also closed on 31 December. There are gaucho parades throughout Argentina, with traditional music, on the days leading up to the Día de la Tradición, 10 November. On 30 Dec (not 31 because so many offices in centre are closed) there is a ticker-tape tradition in downtown Buenos Aires: it snows paper and the crowds stuff passing cars and buses with long streamers.

FURTHER READING

Federico B Kirbus has written the highly informative *Guía de Aventuras y Turismo de la Argentina* (with comprehensive English index – 1989), obtainable at El Ateneo, or from the author at Casilla de Correo 5210, 1000, Buenos Aires. Kirbus has also written the *Guía Ilustrada de las Regiones Turísticas Argentinas*, 4 volumes, NW, NE, Centre, S, with about 300 black and white photos, colour pictures and colour plates on Flora and fauna (published by El Ateneo, US$18-21 each); also *La Argentina, país de Maravillas*, Manrique Zago ediciones (1993), a beautiful book of photographs with text in Spanish and English, *Patagonia* (with Jorge Schulte) and *Ruta Cuarenta*, both fine photographic records with text (both Capuz Varela). YPF have published a 6 volume guide in Spanish with extensive maps, good background information, US$10/volume. Also highly rec is the

Pirelli Guide, edited by Diego Bigongiari, US$18, inc map for cultural, historical and nature information. *Nuestros Paisanos Los Indios* by Carlos Martínez Sarasola is an excellent compendium on the history and present of Argentine Indian communities, rec. The Fundación Vida Silvestre (conservation organization and bookshop), Defensa 245/251, has information and books on Argentine Flora and fauna. Field guide to Argentine birds: *Guía para la identificación de las aves de Argentina y Uruguay* by T Narosky and D Yzurieta, with drawings and colour illustrations.

Bolivia

HORIZONS

THE LAND

Bolivia, straddling the Andes, is a land of gaunt mountains, cold desolate plateaux and semi tropical lowlands. In area it is about twice the size of Spain. It is land-locked, with Chile and Peru to the W, Brazil to N and E, and Argentina and Paraguay to the S.

The Andean range is at its widest, some 650 km, in Bolivia. The Western Cordillera, which separates Bolivia from Chile, has high peaks of between 5,800 and 6,500m and a number of active volcanoes along its crest. The passes across it are above 4,000m. To the E of this range lies the bleak, treeless, windswept Altiplano, much of it 4,000m above sea-level. It has an average width of 140 km, is 840 km long, and covers an area (in Bolivia) of 102,300 sq km, or nearly 10% of the country. Its surface is by no means flat, for the Western Cordillera sends spurs into it which tend to divide it into basins. The more fertile northern part is the more inhabited; the southern part is parched desert and almost unoccupied, save for a mining town here and there. Nearly 70% of the population lives on it, for it contains most of the major cities; almost half of the people are urban dwellers.

The Altiplano is a harsh, strange land, a dreary grey solitude except for the bursts of green after rain. The air is unbelievably clear – the whole plateau is a bowl of luminous light. A cold wind blows frequently in the afternoons, causing dust storms.

From the Altiplano rises, to the E, the sharp façade of the Eastern Cordillera. The giant masses of the northern parts of the Eastern Cordillera rise to very great heights in the Cordillera Real to the E of Lake Titicaca: six peaks soar to above 6,000m. The far sides of the Cordillera Real fall away to the NE, very sharply, towards the Amazon basin.

A gently graded passageway runs along the plateau at the foot of the Eastern Cordillera from Lake Titicaca, in the N, to the Argentine frontier, in the S. From Viacha, near La Paz, a railway line runs S along this passageway to Villazón on the Argentine border with connections to Chile (from Uyuni).

Under Spanish rule there were four great trails in use within the country: three of them led through passes in the western Cordillera to the Pacific; the fourth led from La Paz S into Argentina. At the turn of the century, railways replaced the llamas and mules. By far the shortest line is the one from La Paz to Arica (Chile), completed in 1913.

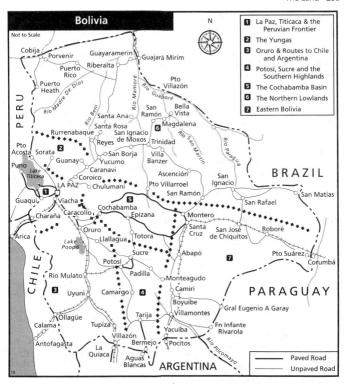

Bolivia

Not to Scale

N

1 La Paz, Titicaca & the Peruvian Frontier
2 The Yungas
3 Oruro & Routes to Chile and Argentina
4 Potosí, Sucre and the Southern Highlands
5 The Cochabamba Basin
6 The Northern Lowlands
7 Eastern Bolivia

PERU

Cobija
Porvenir
Puerto Rico
Puerto Heath
Pto Acosta
Sorata
Puno
Lake Titicaca
Guaqui
Charaña
Viacha
Caracollo

Guayaramerín
Guajará Mirim
Riberalta
Río Madre De Dios
Río Beni
Rurrenabaque
Santa Ana
Santa Rosa
Reyes
Yucumo
San Borja
Guanay
Caranavi
Coroico
Chulumani
LA PAZ
Pto Villarroel
San Ignacio de Moxos
Trinidad
Villa Banzer
Ascención
San Ramón

Pto Villazón
Río Guaporé
Río Mamoré
San Ramón
Bella Vista
Magdalena

BRAZIL
Río San Martín
Río Paraguá
San Ignacio
San Rafael
San Matías

Arica
Caracollo
Oruro
Llallagua
Lake Poopó
Río Mulato
Uyuni
Ollagüe
Calama
Antofagasta

Cochabamba
Epizana
Totora
Sucre
Potosí
Padilla
Camargo
Camiri
Tupiza
Villazón
La Quiaca
Aguas Blancas

Montero
Santa Cruz
San José de Chiquitos
Roboré
Abapó
Monteagudo
Boyuibe
Villamontes
Tarija
Yacuiba
Bermejo
Pocitos

Pto Suárez
Corumbá

PARAGUAY

Gral Eugenio A Garay
Fn Infante Rivarola
Río Pilcomayo

ARGENTINA

CHILE

| | Paved Road |
| | Unpaved Road |

Lake Titicaca

Lake Titicaca, at the northern end of the Altiplano, is an inland sea of 8,965 sq km at 3,810m: the highest navigable water in the world. Its maximum length and breadth are 171 and 64 km, and the greatest known depth is 280m. There are large annual variations between high and low water levels; 95% of the water flowing into it is lost by evaporation, making it more salty than most freshwater lakes. The immense depth of the water keeps the lake at an even all-the-year-around temperature of 10°C. This modifies the extremes of winter and night temperatures on the surrounding land, which supports a large Aymara indian population, tilling the fields and the hill terraces and tending their sheep and llamas.

Wildlife of the Altiplano

Llamas serve as pack animals. They carry up to 22 kg loads up to 20 km a day and yield about 2½ kg of wool when sheared at intervals of from 2-5 years. The alpaca, bred not for work but for wool, belongs to the same group; alpacas have smaller noses, thicker coats and are smaller than llamas. The vicuña, chinchilla and red fox are the main wild animals. The vicuña, an untamed smaller member of the family to which the llama and the alpaca belong, is increasing in numbers in the Reserva Nacional de Fauna Ulla Ulla in the northern Altiplano. It may not be hunted, but its fine silky, tawny coloured wool may be sold.

Agriculture in the Altiplano

The potato and the *oca* (another tuber),

eaten in the dehydrated form of *chuño* and *tunta*, are the main crops. *Quinoa*, a kind of millet, and *cañava*, a smaller and darker grain, are the main cereals; both are extremely nutritious. *Chicha*, the national intoxicant, is brewed from maize (corn). Edible fish (small *boga*, large white-fleshed *pejerrey* and the rainbow and salmon trout with which Lake Titicaca has been stocked) are widely sold in the towns of the Altiplano.

Mining

Since the colonial period mining has been far more important to the economy of the Altiplano than agriculture. In 1545 the Spanish discovered Indian mine workings and vast reserves of silver, tin, bismuth and tungsten in a mountain which they called Cerro Rico (the 'rich hill'). Interested only in silver, they built Potosí at its base, 4,070m above sea level. Today a much more important mining centre is Oruro, 210 km S of La Paz at the base of the Eastern Cordillera, where a low belt of hills supplies tin, copper, silver and tungsten. Nearby are the mines of Huanani, formerly owned by the tin magnate Simón Patiño, and Colquiri. Since the collapse of the world tin market in 1986, most of the other mines in the area have been closed or are now worked as small-scale cooperatives. Lack of investment and the high cost of producing Bolivian tin was a major contributor to the industry's decline. Silver is still mined or extracted from the tailings left by past generations, and variable amounts of lead, bismuth, antimony, tungsten and zinc from pockets in the Cordillera are exported. Large deposits of silver have been found S of the Altiplano, near Lípez, and mines are being reopened, and their tailings reprocessed, two centuries after the Spaniards abandoned them. One of the major new finds is gold, in the far E of the country.

● **Recommended reading** *We Eat the Mines and the Mines Eat Us* by June Nash, New York, 1979; *The Potosí Mita* 1573-1700 by Jeffery Cole, Stanford University Press, 1985; *The Great Tin Crash – Bolivia and the world tin market* by John Crabtree (Latin America Bureau, London, 1987).

THE YUNGAS AND THE PUNA

The heavily forested northeastern slopes of the Cordillera Real are deeply indented by the fertile valleys of the Nor Yungas and Sud Yungas, drained by the Río Beni and its tributaries, where cacao, coffee, sugar, coca and tropical fruits are grown. The problem of transport from here to the consuming centre of La Paz is formidable: the connecting all-weather road, hair-raising in places, climbs 3,430m in 80 km to surmount La Cumbre pass, at 4,725m within 24 km of La Paz.

Further S, from a point just N of Cochabamba the Eastern Cordillera is tilted, not to the NE, but to the E. This part of the Eastern Cordillera rises abruptly in sharp escarpments from the Altiplano, and then flattens out to an easy slope E to the plains: an area known as the Puna. The streams which flow across the Puna are tributaries of the Río Grande flowing NE to the basin of the Amazon, and of the Pilcomayo flowing SE through the Chaco to the Río de la Plata system. They cut increasingly deep incisions as they gather volume until, to the E, the Puna is eroded to little more than a high remnant between the river valleys. These valleys are densely inhabited; a variety of grain crops and fruits is grown. All these semi-tropical mountain valleys are known as Yungas: the generic name is not confined to the valleys of the Provinces of Nor and Sud Yungas to the E of La Paz.

THE LOWLANDS

The lowland tropics, stretching from the foothills of the Eastern Cordillera to the frontiers with Brazil to the NE and E and with Paraguay and Argentina to the SE and S, take up 70% of the total area of Bolivia, but contain only about 20% of its population. In the N and E the Oriente has dense tropical forest. Open plains covered with rough pasture, swamp and scrub occupy the centre. Towards the end of the 18th century this was a populous land of plenty; for 150 years Jesuit missionaries had controlled the area and guided it into a prosperous security. A symbol of their great effort is the cathedral at San José de

Chiquitos: a gem of elegance and dignity. But the Jesuits were expelled in 1767; years of maladministration, spoliation and corruption reduced the area to lethargy.

This once rich land, drained by the Madre de Dios, Beni and Mamoré rivers into the Madeira, a tributary of the Amazon, has been isolated from the rest of the country. It is as difficult to get at from the E as from the W, for there are rapids and falls in the Madeira which limit navigation. In its heart lie the seasonally inundated tropical Llanos de Mojos, ringed in by rain forest or semi-deciduous tropical forest: 230,000 sq km with only 120,000 people. Roads and river connections are being improved; roads link Trinidad with La Paz and Santa Cruz, Guayaramerín and Riberalta with La Paz and Todos Santos and Puerto Villarroel with Cochabamba. Meat is now shipped from Trinidad, capital of Beni Department, and from airstrips in the area, to the urban centres of La Paz, Oruro, and Cochabamba.

The forests and plains beyond the Eastern Cordillera sweep S towards the Río Pilcomayo, getting progressively less rain and merging into a comparatively dry land of scrub forest and arid savanna. The main city of this area is Santa Cruz de la Sierra, founded in the 16th century, now the second city of Bolivia and a large agricultural centre. Here conditions favour the growing of sugar-cane, rice, oil plants and citrus fruit. The plains to the E are mainly used as grazing lands with small areas under cultivation, but in this area are extensive oil, gas, and iron-ore deposits, possibly Bolivia's greatest asset when developed.

CLIMATE

There are four distinct climatic zones: (1) The tropical lowlands; altitude between 150 and 750m; rainfall is high but seasonal (heaviest Nov-Mar, but can fall at any season); large areas suffer from alternate flooding and drought. The climate is hot, ranging from 23° to 25°C in the S and to 27°C in the N. Occasional cold dust-laden winds from the S, the *surazos*, lower the temperature considerably. (2) The Yungas N of La Paz and Cochabamba, among the spurs of the Cordillera; altitude, 750-1,500m; average temperature, 24°C. (3) The Valles, or high valleys and basins gouged out by the rivers of the Puna; average temperature, 19°C. Rainfall in the Yungas valleys is from 700 to 800 mm a year (heaviest Dec-Feb), with high humidity. (4) The Puna and Altiplano; average temperature, 10°C, but above 4,000m may get down to -25°C at night in June-August. By day the tropical sun raises temperatures over 20°C. Rainfall on the northern Altiplano is 400 to 700 mm, much less further S. Little rain falls upon the western plateaux between May and Nov, but the rest of the year can be wet. The period from Dec to Mar is considered the rainy season throughout Bolivia. 1997 saw the worst rainy season for 30 years.

HISTORY

PRE-CONQUEST

At Tiwanaku (Tiahuanaco), near Lake Titicaca, stand the impressive remains of a pre-Inca civilization. The Aymara speaking Indians in this area emerged around 1000 BC into a civilization characterized by massive stone buildings and monuments, exquisite textiles, pottery and metalwork. This phase seems to have been ended abruptly by some unexplained calamity around AD 900 (possibly the failure of the agricultural system). When the Quechua-speaking Incas of Cusco conquered the area around AD 1200, they found the Aymaras at Tiahuanaco living among ruins they could no longer explain. The Aymaras resisted obstinately and were not finally conquered until the latter part of the 15th century in the reign of Inca Túpac Yupangi (1471-93). Even so, they kept their traditional social structures and language, and fought for the Incas under their own leaders. Only religion was formally imposed by the Incas. Kollasuyo, Inca Bolivia, was only a small part of the Inca Empire (and of modern Bolivia) and lasted only about 80 years.

CONQUEST AND AFTER

Francisco Pizarro landed in Peru in 1532. 6 years later Spain conquered Bolivia, and the next year La Plata, now Sucre (still the official capital), was founded. The excellent Inca communications system and economic organization fell into ruin. In 1559 La Plata became capital of the *audiencia* of Charcas, in the Viceroyalty of Peru. As a result of the discovery of silver at Potosí in 1545, Charcas became one of the most important centres of the Spanish colonial economy, sending a constant supply of silver to Spain. By 1610 Potosí, with a population of over 160,000 was the largest city in the Americas, but, as the richest deposits were exhausted and new mines opened in Mexico, Alto Peru, as present day Bolivia was known, went into decline.

Revolutionary movements against Spanish colonial rule began early; there were revolts at La Paz in 1661, at Cochabamba in 1730 and at Sucre, Cochabamba, Oruro and La Paz from 1776 to 1780. In 1809 the University of San Francisco Xavier, at Sucre, called for the independence of all Spain's American colonies. Finally, on 9 December 1824, Simón Bolívar's general, Gen Antonio José de Sucre, won the decisive battle of Ayacucho in Peru and invaded Alto Peru, defeating the Spaniards finally at the battle of Tumusla on 2 April 1825. On 9 February 1825, when he first entered La Paz, Sucre had already promulgated the decree of independence, but his second in command, Santa Cruz, was for retaining links with Peru; Bolívar was in two minds. Sucre had his way and Bolivia was declared independent.

POST INDEPENDENCE

For most of the period since independence, three main features have dominated Bolivian history: the importance of mining; the loss of territory through disputes and wars with neighbouring countries; and chronic political instability. Although silver had been so important in the colonial period, the Bolivian economy has depended for much of this century on exports of tin. The construction of railways and the demand for tin in Europe and the USA (particularly in wartime) led to a mining boom after 1900. By the 1920s the industry was dominated by three entrepreneurs, Simón Patiño, Mauricio Hochschild and the Aramayo family, who exercised great influence over national politics. The importance of mining and the harsh conditions in the isolated mining camps of the Altiplano led to the rise of a militant miners movement.

Bolivian politics have been even more turbulent than elsewhere in Latin America. Although in the 19th century the army was very small, officers were key figures in power-struggles, often backing different factions of the landowning elite. Between 1840 and 1849 there were 65 attempted coups d'etat. The longest lasting government of the 19th century was that of Andrés Santa Cruz (1829-1839), but when he tried to unite Bolivia with Peru in 1836, Chile and Argentina intervened to overthrow him. After the War of the Pacific (1879-1883) there was greater stability, but opposition to the political dominance of the city of Sucre culminated in a revolt in 1899 led by business groups from La Paz and the tin-mining areas, as a result of which La Paz became the centre of government.

Since independence Bolivia has suffered continual losses of territory, partly because of communications difficulties and the central government's inability to control distant provinces. The dispute between Chile and Peru over the nitrate-rich Atacama desert in 1879 soon dragged in Bolivia, which had signed a secret alliance with Peru in 1873. Following its rapid defeat in the War of the Pacific Bolivia lost her coastal provinces. As compensation Chile later agreed to build the railway between Arica and La Paz. Railways traded for valuable territory has been Bolivia's fate. A railway to Yacuiba was Argentina's return for annexing some of the Chaco. When Brazil annexed the rich Acre Territory in 1903, Bolivia was compensated by yet another railway, but this Madeira-Mamoré line never reached its destination, Riberalta, and proved of little use; it was closed in 1972.

There was not even an unbuilt railway

to compensate Bolivia for its next loss. A long-running dispute with Paraguay over the Chaco erupted into war in 1932. Defeat in the so-called Chaco War (1932-1935) resulted in the loss of three quarters of the Chaco (see Paraguay chapter, page 1162).

MODERN BOLIVIA

The Chaco War was a turning point in Bolivian history, increasing the political influence of the army which in 1936 seized power for the first time since the War of the Pacific. Defeat bred nationalist resentment among junior army officers who had served in the Chaco and also led to the creation of a nationalist party, the Movimiento Nacionalista Revolucionario (MNR) led by Víctor Paz Estenssoro. Their anger was directed against the mine owners and the leaders who had controlled Bolivian politics. Between 1936 and 1946 a series of unstable military governments followed. This decade witnessed the apparent suicide in 1939 of one president (Germán Busch) and the public hanging in 1946 of another (Gualberto Villarroel). After a period of civilian government, the 1951 elections were won by the MNR but a coup prevented the party from taking office.

The 1952 revolution

In April 1952 the military government was overthrown by a popular revolution in which armed miners and peasants played a major role. Paz Estenssoro became president and his MNR government nationalized the mines, introduced universal suffrage and began the break-up and redistribution of large estates. The economy, however, deteriorated, partly because of the hostility of the US government. Paz's successor, Hernán Siles Zuazo (president 1956-1964), a hero of the 1952 revolution, was forced to take unpopular measures to stabilize the economy. Paz was re-elected president in 1960 and 1964, but shortly afterwards in Nov 1964 he was overthrown by his vice president, Gen René Barrientos, who relied on the support of the army and the peasants to defeat the miners.

Military rule in the '70s

The death of Barrientos in an air crash in 1969 was followed by three brief military governments. The third, led by Gen Torres, pursued left-wing policies which alarmed many army officers and business leaders. In Aug 1971 Torres was overthrown by Hugo Banzer, a right-wing general who outlawed political parties and trade unions. After Banzer was forced to call elections in 1978, a series of short-lived military governments overruled elections in 1978 and 1979 giving victories to Siles Zuazo. One of these, led by Gen García Meza (1980-1981) was notable for its brutal treatment of opponents and its links to the cocaine trade which led to its isolation by the international community.

Return to democracy and economic stabilization

In Aug 1982 the military returned to barracks and Dr Siles Zuazo assumed the Presidency in a leftist coalition government with support from the communists and trade unions. Under this regime inflation spiralled out of control. The elections of 1985 were won again by Víctor Paz Estenssoro, who imposed a rigorous programme to stabilize the economy. In the elections of 1989, Gonzalo Sánchez de Lozada of the MNR (chief architect of the stabilization programme) failed to win enough votes to prevent Congress choosing Jaime Paz Zamora of the Movimiento de la Izquierda Revolucionaria (MIR), who came third in the elections, as President Aug 1989. Paz had made an unlikely alliance with the former military dictator, Gen (retired) Hugo Banzer (Acción Democrática Nacionalista).

Although Gonzalo Sánchez de Lozada just failed to gain the required 51% majority to win the presidency in the 1993 elections, the other candidates recognized his victory. The main element in his policies was the capitalization of state assets (see page 263, **The Economy**), but as the programme gained pace, so did opposition to it. This and other, far-reaching reforms during Sánchez de Lozada's presidency probably contributed to the electorate giving most votes in 1 June

1997 elections to Banzer and the ADN, rather than to Juan Carlos Durán of MNR. Nevertheless, the ballot's outcome was very close and Banzer had to form alliances to gain the presidency. At the time of going to press this process was unresolved as Banzer preferred a coalition with MIR (3rd in the elections) and fourth-placed Unidad Cívica de Solidaridad, but the USA was opposed to MIR since Jaime Paz Zamora, its leader, and others were *personae non grata* on account of alleged drug links. The final decision would be made in Aug 1997.

CULTURE

PEOPLE

Of the total population some two thirds are Indians, the remainder being *mestizos*, Europeans and others. The racial composition varies from place to place: Indian around Lake Titicaca; more than half Indian in La Paz; three-quarters *mestizo* or European in the Yungas, Cochabamba, Santa Cruz and Tarija, the most European of all. Since the 1980s, regional tensions between the 'collas' (*altiplano* dwellers) and the 'cambas' (lowlanders) have become more marked. Under 40% of children of school age attend school even though it is theoretically compulsory between 7 and 14.

About two-thirds of the population lives in adobe huts, and medical services are sketchy outside the towns and mining camps. Epidemics are comparatively rare on the Altiplano, but malaria, cholera and yellow fever are still problems in the Oriente and Santa Cruz, and hepatitis and Chagas disease (see Health Hints in Introduction) are endemic in the warmer parts of the country.

The most obdurate of Bolivian problems has always been that the main mass of population is, from a strictly economic viewpoint, in the wrong place, the poor Altiplano and not the potentially rich Oriente; and that the Indians live largely outside the monetary system on a self-sufficient basis. Since the land reform of 1952 isolated communities continue the old life but in the agricultural area around Lake Titicaca, the valleys of Cochabamba, the Yungas and the irrigated areas of the S, most peasants now own their land, however small the plot may be. Migration to the warmer and more fertile lands of the E region has been officially encouraged. At the same time roads are now integrating the food-producing eastern zones with the bulk of the population living in the towns of the Altiplano or the W-facing slopes of the Eastern Cordillera.

The highland Indians are composed of two groups: those in the N of the Altiplano who speak the guttural Aymara (an estimated 1 million), and those elsewhere, who speak Quechua, the Inca tongue (3 million – this includes the Indians in the northern Apolobamba region). Outside the big cities many of them speak no Spanish, but knowledge of Spanish is increasing. In the lowlands are some 150,000 people in 30 groups, including the Ayoreo, Chiquitano, Chiriguano, Garavo, Chimane and Mojo. The lowland Indians are, in the main, Guaraní. About 70% of Bolivians are Aymara, Quecha or Tupi-Guaraní speakers. The first two are regarded as national languages, but were not, until very recently, taught in schools, a source of some resentment. There are also about 17,000 blacks, descendents of slaves brought from Peru and Buenos Aires in 16th century, who now live in the Yungas.

The Indian women retain their traditional costume, with bright petticoats (*polleras*), and in the highlands around La Paz wear, apparently from birth, a flattish brown or grey bowler (locally called a *bombín*). In Cochabamba they wear a white top hat of ripolined straw. According to Peter McFarren (*An Insider's Guide to Bolivia*) there are over 100 styles of hat. Indians traditionally chew the coca leaf, which deadens hunger pains and gives a measure of oblivion. Efforts to control the cultivation of coca is one of many sources of friction between the indigenous population and the authorities; others include landlessness, and exploitation of labour. On feast days they drink with considerable application, wear the most sensational masks and dance till they drop.

NB Remember to refer to rural Indians not as 'indios' (an insult) but as 'campesinos' (peasants).

MUSIC AND DANCE

The heart of Bolivia is the 2-mile (3¼ km) high Altiplano and it is the music of the Quechua- and Aymara-speaking Indians of this area that provides the most distinctive Bolivian musical sound. Although there is much that is of Spanish colonial origin in the Indians' dances, the music itself has more Amerindian style and content than that of any other country in South America. It is rare to find an Indian who cannot play an instrument and it is these instruments, both wind and percussion, that are quintessentially Bolivian. The clear sounds of the *quena* and *pinkullo*, the deeper, breathier notes of the *tarka*, *pututo* and *sicuri* accompanied by *huankaré*, *pululu* and *caja* drums can be heard all over the Altiplano, the *charango* (a small, G-stringed guitar) being virtually the only instrument of European origin. The Indian dances are mainly collective and take place at religious fiestas. The dancers wear colourful costumes with elaborate, plumed headdresses and some of them still parody their ex-Spanish colonial masters. Such are the Auqui Auquis and Pakhochos dances. The Khachua dance on the other hand dates from the time of Inca Túpac Yupangi. Other notable dances are the Wititis, Wila Khawani, Jucumaris, Takiri de Kharmisa and Sikuris de Ayata.

The principal popular dances that can be regarded as 'national' in their country-wide appeal are the Cueca and Huayño. The Bolivian Cueca is a close relative of the Chilean national dance of the same name and they share a mutual origin in the Zamacueca, itself derived from the Spanish Fandango. The Huayño is of Indian origin and involves numerous couples, who whirl around or advance down the street, arm-in-arm, in a 'Pandilla'. Other similar, but more regional dances are the Bailecito Chuquisaqueño, Khaluyo Cochabambino, Rueda Tarijeña

from the SE and Carnavalito Cruceño and Taquirari Beniano from the tropical lowlands. Justly celebrated is the great carnival Diablada of Oruro, with its hordes of grotesquely masked devils, a spectacle comparable to those of Rio in Brazil and Barranquilla in Colombia.

The region of Tarija near the Argentine border has a distinctive musical tradition of its own, based on religious processions that culminate with that of San Roque on the first Sun in September. The influence is Spanish, the dance is the Chapaqueada and the musical instruments are the *caña*, *erke* and *violin chapaco*. The first named is an immensely long bamboo tube with a horn at the end, aimed at the sky, on which different 'Toques' are played.

There are many professional folk groups on record, the best known being Grupo Aymara, Los Runas, Los Laris, Los Masis, Kolla Marka and Bolivia Manta, some of which have now established themselves in Europe and North America.

● **Recommended reading** Herbert S Klein, *Bolivia: The Evolution of a Multi-Ethnic Society* (Oxford University Press). Latin American Bureau's *Bolivia in Focus*, on history, culture, politics and economics. *Rebellion in the Veins – political struggle in Bolivia 1952 to 1982*, James Dunkerley (Verso, London, 1984).

THE ECONOMY

Structure of production Bolivia suffers from a rugged terrain, which makes communications difficult, while its landlocked position hinders export development. A history of dictatorships and coup d'états did nothing to improve the living standards of the mostly Indian population, who eked out a living with subsistence farming on the altiplano or down the mines. The restoration of democracy in the 1980s is having a gradual beneficial effect and redistribution of income is a long term goal.

Agriculture is an important sector of the economy, contributing 16% of gdp and employing over a third of the population. Small scale farming of traditional products is in the highlands, where excess produce is sold in local markets. In the E, however, there is very fertile land. The most productive area is in the province of Santa Cruz, where the fluvial plains are extremely rich in nutrients. Here the tropical climate allows two crops a year of soya beans and farmers achieve yields of around 3 tonnes a hectare, compared with 1.5-2 tonnes in neighbouring countries. Bolivian and foreign investors have bought large estates to grow soya and other crops, such as cotton, sunflower and sugar, and agroindustry is booming as processing plants are built. The tropical lowlands of the Chapare region are where some 25,000 families grow the coca leaf on about 50,000 ha. Although growing and chewing coca leaf is legal in Bolivia, almost all the Chapare coca is illegally refined into cocaine and exported. US-funded eradication programmes have been largely unsuccessful. It is believed that about US$350mn a year comes back into the economy from drugs trafficking.

Mining contributes only 10% to gdp, but it is an area of considerable investment and growth. Bolivia is a major producer of tin, antimony, wolfram, bismuth, silver, lead, zinc and gold, while there are large reserves of iron, lithium and potassium. The state mining company, Comibol, closed most of its operations during the recession of the 1980s, forcing unemployment for 23,000 miners. In the mid-1990s all Comibol's deposits, mines, smelters and refineries were put up for sale. Comibol remained as a small operation to administer leasing and joint venture contracts. The 1991 Mining Code allows equal treatment for foreign and national companies and free remittances of profits abroad. Foreigners in joint ventures with Bolivians may now explore and develop the previously prohibited zones within 50 km of borders. Investor interest is considerable, particularly in gold. The Kori Kollo gold mine, near Oruro, is the second largest in Latin America. Total gold output is about 14 tonnes a year, making it a leading export earner. Although Bolivia is one of the largest producers of tin in the world, low prices in the 1980s and 1990s have reduced export

Bolivia: fact file

Geographic

Land area	1,098,581 sq km
forested	53.5%
pastures	24.4%
cultivated	2.2%

Demographic

Population (1996)	7,592,000
annual growth rate (1991-96)	2.4%
urban	57.7%
rural	42.3%
density	6.2 per sq km

Education and Health

Life expectancy at birth,	
male	60.9 years
female	65.9 years
Infant mortality rate	
per 1,000 live births (1990-95)	75.1
Calorie intake as %	
of FAO requirement	88%
Population age 25 and over	
with no formal schooling	23.3%
Literate males (over 15)	87.7%
Literate females (over 15)	71.8%

Economic and Employment

GNP (1994 market prices)	US$5,601mn
GNP per capita	US$770
Public external debt (1994)	
	US$4,113mn
Tourism receipts (1994)	US$135mn
Inflation (annual av 1990-95)	11.9%
Population economically active (1992)	
	2,530,409
Unemployment rate	2.5%
Military forces	33,500

Source Encyclopaedia Britannica.

income. The Cordillera Real is the traditional mining zone for silver and tin, but companies are now looking in the W Cordillera and E towards the Brazilian border where mineral deposits are unexploited. There are iron reserves at El Mutun in Busch province on the border with Brazil, believed to be 40,000 tonnes with 30-50% iron, making it one of the world's largest deposits.

The oil and gas industry provides the Government with its largest single source of income. The state oil and gas company, Yacimientos Petrolíferos Fiscales Bolivianos (YPFB), was the largest company in

Bolivia in 1994 with a workforce of 14,900. YPFB was partly 'capitalized' (see below) in 1996. Bolivia exports natural gas to Argentina worth US$120mn a year, and a joint project with Brazil to build a pipeline to transport initially 8 million cu ft a day of natural gas from the Santa Cruz area to São Paulo will become an even bigger source of foreign exchange in 1998. An agreement has also been signed with Paraguay for a gas pipeline to Asunción. Current proven reserves of gas are 110-170 billion cu m, but exploration in progress is expected to triple those reserves.

Recent trends The recession which afflicted most Latin American countries from 1980 hit Bolivia with six consecutive years of contraction of gdp, accompanied by accelerating inflation, massive and frequent devaluations of the currency and social unrest. Government spending to support key export sectors was hampered by massive public sector deficits and external indebtedness. Economic problems were compounded in 1983 by a severe drought in the Altiplano and floods in the E lowlands, which devastated farming. The resulting food shortages exacerbated existing inflationary pressures and led to hyperinflation with annual rates reaching over 20,000%.

In the mid-1980s the Government introduced severe austerity measures to stabilize the economy, in which price controls were lifted, subsidies removed, public sector wages frozen and a new currency was created, the boliviano, linked to the US dollar in a controlled float. Tax reform was passed, the first of many IMF credits was negotiated, bilateral and multilateral lending began to flow again and steps were taken to buy back at a discount the external commercial bank debt. Inflation came down to 10-20% a year, although unemployment continued to rise and living standards to fall. Nevertheless, by the 1990s growth and employment were recovering.

In 1994 the Government began an ambitious reform programme encompassing fiscal decentralization (Popular Participation Programme), education reform and removing the state from the means of production, aiming to increase investment and savings. The Bolivian divestment scheme, known as 'capitalization', brought no direct revenue to the state. Investors agreed to inject fresh capital into a state-owned company in return for a 50% controlling stake. The other 50% of the shares were distributed to all Bolivians over 18 via a private pension fund scheme, an ambitious proposal in a country where only 5% of the population had bank accounts and savings were negligible. All six state companies, accounting for about 12.5% of gdp, were chosen for capitalization in 1995-96: electricity, telecommunications, air transport, railways, a smelter and several sectors of YPFB. Privatization of Enfe to Chile led to the most violent protests in La Paz in recent years.

GOVERNMENT

The Constitution of 1967 vests executive power in the President, elected by popular vote for a term of 4 years; he cannot be immediately re-elected. Congress consists of two chambers: the Senate, with 27 seats, and the Chamber of Deputies, with 130 seats. There are nine departments; each is controlled by a Delegate appointed by the President.

Bolivia has, in effect, two capitals. Although Sucre is the legal capital, La Paz is in almost all respects the actual capital, being the seat of the Government and of Congress. The Supreme Court, however, still holds its sessions in Sucre.

La Paz

L A PAZ, Lake Titicaca and Mount Illimani are probably the three most familiar sights of Bolivia, set amid high Andean Altiplano and the Cordillera Real. The region around La Paz is known as Little Bolivia, containing snow-peaks, desert and sub-tropical jungle in Coroico, just 3 hours' breathtaking bus-ride away.

The highest capital in the world lies in a steep canyon. Plaza Murillo in the centre, at 3,636m, is about 370m below the level of the Altiplano and the new city of El Alto. Mt Illimani, with its snow-covered peaks (6,439m), towers over the city. One of the best ways to appreciate the setting is from the air. East-west flights pass by Illimani with beautiful views of the summit. The rim of the Altiplano, with El Alto built up to the edge and the old city descending the canyon, is very dramatic. The Spaniards chose this odd place for a city on 20 October 1548, to avoid the chill winds of the plateau, and because they had found gold in the Río Choqueyapu, which runs through the canyon.

BASICS In 1993, the *population* of La Paz was estimated at 1.2 million, over half of it Indian. The mean average *temperature* is 10°C, but it varies greatly during each day, and the nights are cold. It rains almost every day from Dec to Feb, but the sun usually shines for several hours. The rest of the year is mostly clear and sunny. Snow is rare. Beware of *soroche* (altitude sickness), especially if arriving from much lower altitudes by air. *Phone code* 02.

Orientation is relatively simple. A major avenue, changing its name from Av Mcal Santa Cruz to Av 16 de Julio (this section is generally known as Prado) runs SE from Plaza San Francisco down to the Plaza del Estudiante. The business quarter, government offices, central university (UMSA) and many of the main hotels and restaurants are situated in this area. On the hills above Plaza Mendoza are the poorer parts of the city. From the Plaza del Estudiante, Av Villazón and its extensions lead further SE towards the wealthier residential districts, which run from Sopocachi to the bed of the valley at Obrajes, 5 km from the centre and 500m lower than Plaza Murillo. Sopocachi, through which runs Av 6 de Agosto, has many restaurants, discos, bars, etc. The Mercado Sopocachi, on F Guachalla, is good but not cheap. Beyond Obrajes are the upper-class districts of Calacoto and La Florida. The main sports and social clubs are in these districts.

El Alto is now a city in its own right. Apart from the district known as Ciudad Satelite, it is almost 100% indigenous; almost everyone is an emigrant from the countryside. It is growing at 10%/year, reputedly the fastest growing city in South America, compared with 4% growth in the wealthier districts of La

Paz. Costs are much lower than in La Paz, but construction, etc is much more basic. There is a market on Thur and Sun in Av Alfonso Ugarte, more interesting for its size than the items for sale. El Alto is connected to La Paz by motorway (toll US$0.50, cycles free). Buses from Plaza Aguino and Pérez Velasco leave regularly for Plaza 16 de Julio, El Alto.

PLACES OF INTEREST

There are few colonial buildings left in La Paz; probably the best examples are in **Calle Jaén**. Late 19th/early 20th century architecture, often displaying heavy European influence, can be found in the streets around Plaza Murillo, but much of La Paz is modern. The **Plaza del Estudiante** (Plaza Franz Tamayo), or a bit above it, marks a contrast between old and new styles, between the traditional commercial and the more elegant. The **Prado** itself is lined with high-rise blocks dating from the 1960s and 1970s. **Plaza Murillo**, three blocks N of the Prado, is the traditional centre. Facing its formal gardens are the huge, graceful **Cathedral**, the **Palacio Presidencial** in Italian renaissance style, usually known as the Palacio Quemado (burnt palace) twice gutted by fire in its stormy 130-year history, and, on the E side, the **Congreso Nacional**. In front of the Palacio Quemado is a statue of former President Gualberto Villarroel who was dragged into the plaza by an angry mob and hanged in 1946. Across from the Cathedral on C Socabaya is the **Palacio de los Condes de Arana**, see the Museo Nacional del Arte, below. Calle Comercio, running E-W across the Plaza, has most of the stores and shops. On Av Libertador Simón Bolívar (to which Mt Illimani provides a backdrop), is the **Central Market** (called 'Mercado Camacho'), a picturesque medley of Indian victuals and vendors. Further E is the residential district of Miraflores. Another good view of Illimani can be had from the top of the rise on C Illimani.

At the upper end of Av Mcal Santa Cruz is the **Plaza San Francisco** with the church and monastery of San Francisco,

dating from 1549, well worth seeing. The church (opens at 1600) is richly decorated on native religious themes. Its mestizo baroque façade clearly displays how the traditional baroque vine motif is transformed into an array of animals, birds, fruits and plants, while the interior contains huge, square columns and gilt altars on which stand many saints. Indian weddings can be seen on Sat 1000-1200. Behind the San Francisco church a network of narrow cobbled streets rise steeply. Much of this area is a permanent street market. Handicraft shops line the lower part of **Calle Sagárnaga**; further up, from Illampu to Rodríguez and in neighbouring streets, is the local **Rodríguez market**. Turning right on Max Paredes, heading W, is Av Buenos Aires, one of the liveliest streets in the Indian quarter, where small workshops turn out the costumes and masks for the Gran Poder festival. Continuing W along Max Paredes towards the **cemetery district**, the streets are crammed with stalls selling every imaginable item. Transport converges on the cemetery district (for more information see **Buses** below). Do not expect to go anywhere in a hurry in this part of the city. There are good views of Illimani from these heights.

Other churches include **Santo Domingo** (originally the cathedral), Calles Ingavi y Yanacocha, with its decorative 18th-century façade; **La Merced**, on a plazuela at Calles Colón and Comercio; **San Juan de Dios**, on Loayza between Merced and Camacho, with a carved portico; and **San Sebastián**, the first church to be built in La Paz, in Plaza Alonso de Mendoza (named after the church's builder). On **Plaza Sucre** is **San Pedro** church, Av 20 de Octubre y Colombia, built 1720.

A worthwhile walk is to **Mirador Laicacota** on Av del Ejército: one of the delights of La Paz is the change from day to night, when all the lights begin to twinkle on the surrounding hillsides.

MUSEUMS

Museo Nacional de Arte, C Socabaya 432, in the baroque palace of the Condes de

Arana (built 1775), with beautiful exterior and patio, has a fine collection of colonial paintings including many works by Melchor Pérez Holguín, considered one of the masters of Andean colonial art, and also exhibits the works of contemporary local artists. Tues-Fri 0900-1230, 1500-1900, US$0.25, Sat 1000-1300, US$0.50, students US$0.25.

Museo Tiahuanaco (Tiwanaku), or Museo Nacional de Arqueología, go down the flight of stairs by María Auxili church on the Prado: this modern building, simulating the Tiwanaku style, contains good collections of the arts and crafts of ancient Tiwanaku and items from the eastern jungles. It also has a 2-room exhibition of gold statuettes and objects found in Lake Titicaca. Tues-Fri 0900-1230, 1500-1900, Sat 1000-1230, 1500-1830, Sun 1000-1300; US$1.20.

Museo Semisubterráneo, or Templete del Estadio, is in front of National Stadium, with restored statues and other artefacts from Tiahuanaco. It's in a sunken garden and much can be seen from street level. No explanations are given and the statues are being badly eroded by pollution.

Museo Nacional de Etnografía y Folklore, C Ingavi 916, in the palace of the Marqueses de Villaverde, exhibits on the Chipaya and Ayoreo Indians, quite good library adjoining. Mon-Fri 0830-1200, 1430-1830.

The following four museums are included on a single ticket, which costs US$0.75, from Museo Costumbrista. All are open Tues-Fri 1030-1300, 1600-2030, Sat and Sun 1030-1300, with well-displayed items in colonial buildings. All are on C Jaén, a picturesque colonial street with many craft shops, worth seeing for itself.

Museo Costumbrista, Plaza Riosinio, at top of Jaén. Miniature displays depict incidents in the history of La Paz and well-known Paceños. Also has miniature replicas of reed rafts used by Norwegian, Thor Heyerdahl and Spaniard, Kitin Muñoz, to prove their theories of ancient migrations, T 378478.

Museo Casa Murillo, T 375273, was originally the home of Pedro Domingo Murillo, one of the martyrs of the abortive La Paz independence movement of 16 July 1809: a good collection of paintings, furniture and national costumes in a restored colonial house; there is also a room dedicated to herbal medicine (Kallawaya), and two rooms of paintings.

Museo de Metales Preciosos, Jaén 777, well set out with Inca gold artefacts in basement vaults, also ceramics and archaeological exhibits, T 371470.

Museo del Litoral Boliviano, Jaén 789, with artefacts of the War of the Pacific, and interesting selection of old maps.

Casa Museo Marina Núñez del Prado, Ecuador 2034, Mon-Fri, 1000-1300, 1500-1900, Sat, 1000-1300, excellent collection of her sculptures housed in the family mansion.

Museo Tambo Quirquincho, C Evaristo Valle, nr Plaza Mendoza; Tues-Fri, 1030-1300, 1600-2030, Sat-Sun, 1030-1300, US$0.50, Sat free. In a restored colonial building, displaying modern painting and sculpture, carnival masks, silver, early 20th century photography and city plans.

Museo de Historia Natural, C 26, Cota Cota, 30 mins from centre by microbus marked Cota Cota from Plaza San Francisco, open Tues-Sun 1000-1700, US$0.60.

La Paz: Key to map

1. Cathedral; 2. Museo Costumbrista, Museo Casa Murillo, Museo de Metales Preciosos and Museo del Litoral Boliviano; 3. Museo Nacional de Arte; 4. Museo Nacional de Etnografía y Folklore; 5. Palacio Quemado; 6. Parque Prehistórico Tiahuanaco (Museo Semisubterráneo). **Parks and squares:** 7. Plaza Murillo; 8. Plaza del Estudiante/Franz Tamayo; 9. Plaza Mendoza; 10. Plaza Sucre/San Pedro; 11. Plaza Venezuela; 12. Plaza Vicente Eguino; 13. Plaza Velasco; 14. Plaza Riosinio; 15. Plaza Antofagasta; 16. Garita de Lima. **Hotels:** 17. *Continental*; 18. *Copacabana*; 19. *El Dorado*; 20. *España*; 21. *Gloria*; 22. *Libertador*; 23. *Max Inn*; 24. *Milton*; 25. *Panamericano*; 26. *Plaza*; 27. *Presidente*; 28. *Res Rosario*; 29. *Sagárnaga* and *Alem*; 31. *Sucre Palace*; 32. *Viena*; 33. *Hostal Claudia*; 34. *Hostal República*. **Restaurants/Peña:** 35. Casa del Corregidor; 36. Los Escudos.

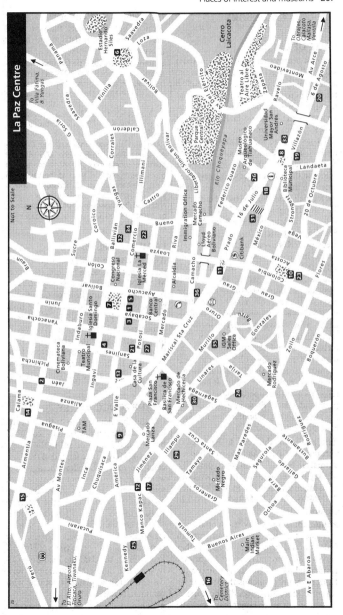

La Paz Centre

Not to Scale

EXCURSIONS

VALLE DE LA LUNA

The best nearby excursion is to Río Abajo and Mallasilla golf course. Through the suburbs of Calacoto and La Florida follow the river road past picnic spots and through some weird rock formations, known as the **Valle de la Luna**, 'Moon Valley'. About 3 km from the bridge at Calacoto the road forks; sharp right leads to the Caza y Pesca Club and Mallasilla golf course. Get out of the minibus (see below) at the turning and walk a few minutes E to the Valle entrance, or get out at the football field which is by the entrance. Take good shoes and water. Just before the Valle are the Aranjuez Forest, the Aniceto Arce cactus gardens (badly eroded) and the *Playa de Aranjuez*, a bathing spot popular for lunch at weekends. Just past the Valle de la Luna and the Mallasilla Golf Course is Mallasa where several small roadside restaurants and cafés have opened; also *Oberland*, T 745040, F 745389, e-mail: wschmid@wara.bol-net.bo, a Swiss-owned, chalet-style restaurant (excellent) and hotel resort (**B** including breakfast buffet), popular at weekends, especially with the expat community: gardens, cabañas, sauna, swimming pool, racket ball, tennis. It has been recommended for superb fondue, raclette, pasta and salads. Book in advance. Also *Los Lobos*, highly recommended for *churrasco* steaks, US$4.50.

The zoo is on the road to Río Abajo, entrance just past Mallasa, well-housed animals in beautiful, wide open park-like setting. The climate in this valley is always much warmer than in the city. Open daily 0900-1700, US$0.40 adults, US$0.20 children.

Achumani is a wealthy residential area; to reach it go up Av Ballivián through Calacoto and turn left at C 22. Further beyond Calacoto and Cota Cota is the new residential zone of Chasquipampa on the Palca road, near which is the Valle de las Animas. Here the eroded landscape is similar to, but much larger than, the Valle

de la Luna and good for walking and picnics. On the way back there are good views of the southern districts and the city above.

- **Transport** To Valle de la Luna and Mallasa: Kombi A, Nos 231 and 273 can be caught on the Prado and pass the Valle de la Luna en route to the Mallasa recreation area, a large weekend excursion area near Mallasa village. If you do not want to walk in the valley, stay on the bus to the end of the line and take a return bus, 2 hrs in all. Alternatively take Micro 11 ('Aranjuez'-large, not small bus) from C Sagárnaga, near Plaza San Francisco, US$0.65, and ask driver where to get off. Most of the local travel agents organize tours to the Valle de la Luna. These are very brief, 5 mins stop for photos in a US$15 tour of La Paz and surroundings; taxis cost US$6. **To Chasquipampa**: take any Kombi or micro marked Ovejuno or Chasquipampa from the Prado.

LA MUELA DEL DIABLO

A gigantic, tooth-shaped rock which can be seen from the Valle de la Luna road; take Micro 'N' from Murillo y Sagárnaga or from the University (last stop Cota Cota), minibus 213 to Rosales, or *trufi* 288 from Cementerio, Plaza Isabel La Católica to Urbanización Pedregal (ask driver where to get off). Cross the river and climb through the village to the cemetery; from there it is 1½ hrs easy climb to the rock. The road continues to Ventilla, the start of the Inca trail.

TO THE ZONGO VALLEY

Pass the abandoned Milluni tin mine, its large roadside cemetery and the colourful but polluted Lago Milluni to the Zongo pass at 4,700m. At the far end of the dam, cross the road and follow the aqueduct which clings to the mountainside with some spectacular drops. After about 45 mins cross the aqueduct and then walk up to reach the base of the Charquini glacier – do not go on the glacier unless you have crampons and are roped. Alternatively continue round for great views of Huayna Potosí. From the dam the road drops almost 3,000m in less than 40 km past various hydroelectric plants – popular with mountain bikers.

- **Transport** Either arrange a jeep through a

The Alacitas Fair

🐾 "It is dedicated to Ekeko, an Indian household god. You can buy plaster images of him at many of the booths. He is a red-nosed cheerfully-grinning little personage laden with an assortment of miniature cooking utensils, coins, balls of wool, tiny sacks of sugar, coffee, salt, rice and flour; a kind of Bolivian Santa Claus. Ekeko is said to bring prosperity and to grant wishes. If you buy a toy house, or a cow, or a sheep at the Alacitas, you will get a real one before the year is out. There are also model motor-cars and planes, for the extreme optimists." (Christopher Isherwood, 'The Condor and the Cows'.) The most popular purchase is miniature dollar bills.

tourist agency for US$70; or go to Plaza Ballivián in El Alto to catch a *camión* at midday Mon, Wed and Fri, US$1, or haggle with drivers of empty minibuses for US$10; or hire a taxi for US$30 for the return trip (make sure the driver knows where he's going); or contact *Refugio Huayna Potosí* which organizes regular transport. If driving, make sure you have your passport and driving documents as there is a police checkpoint immediately before the mine. To get back from the dam if you haven't arranged transport, the truck returns passing the Zongo dam at about midday Tues, Thur and Sat. There are La Paz-bound jeeps and minibuses at irregular intervals during the season.

URMIRI

Take road S towards Oruro, turn left at Urmiri sign at Km 75. To get this far take any bus going to Oruro; lifts from the crossroads are few and far between. A steep scenic descent leads to pool filled by mineral springs and a pleasant basic inn. New owners, *Hotel Gloria* (see below) run transport Tues, Thur and Sun at 0800, US$6, 2½ hrs. Minibuses depart *Hotel Gloria* and return to La Paz same day at 1600. Best time to visit is Tues-Fri, closed Mon, weekends are busy. Room with private pool for 2 or 4 people: **D**, with shared pool, **E**, including breakfast. Book in advance; group discounts. For non-residents entry to pools and sauna US$3; massage US$6, Shiatsu US$10.

LOCAL FESTIVALS

Jan/Feb: the *Alacitas Fair*, from last week of Jan to first week of Feb, in Parque Central up from Av del Ejército, also in Plaza Sucre/San Pedro.

End May/early June: *Festividad del Señor de Gran Poder*, the most important festival of the year, with a huge procession

of costumed and masked dancers. *Fiestas de Julio*, a month of concerts and performances at the Teatro Municipal, offers a wide variety of music, including the University Folkloric Festival. **8 Dec**, festival around Plaza España, not very large, but colourful and noisy. On **New Year's Eve** fireworks are let off and make a spectacular sight; view from higher up. See also page 359 for national holidays and festivals outside La Paz.

LOCAL INFORMATION

Try to arrive in La Paz early in the day as accommodation, especially at the cheaper end of the market, can be hard to find. Prices inc tax and service charge (20% in all).

Hotel prices

L1	over US$200	**L2**	US$151-200
L3	US$101-150	**A1**	US$81-100
A2	US$61-80	**A3**	US$46-60
B	US$31-45	**C**	US$21-30
D	US$12-20	**E**	US$7-11
F	US$4-6	**G**	up to US$3

Unless otherwise stated, all hotels in range **D** and above have private bath. Assume friendliness and cleanliness in all cases.

● **Accommodation**

L3 *Radisson Plaza*, formerly *Hotel La Paz* (still referred to as *Sheraton*), Av Arce 2177, T 316163, F 343391, good 5-star hotel with all facilities, sauna; **L3** *Plaza*, Av 16 de Julio 1789, T 378317, F 343391, excellent, good value restaurant (see below), peña show on Fri; **L3** *Presidente*, Potosí 920 y Sanjines, T 368601, F 354013, inc breakfast, 'the highest 5-star in the world', pool, gymnasium and sauna all open to non-residents, bar, disco, excellent service, comfortable, good food, rec; **L3** *Ritz Aparthotel*, Plaza Isabel La Católica 2478, T 433131, F 433080, 5-star self-catering apartments, inc breakfast.

A1 *El Rey Palace*, Av 20 de Octubre 1947, T 393016, F 367759, inc breakfast, large suites, excellent restaurant, stylish, modern; **A1** *Gran Hotel Paris*, Plaza Murillo esq Bolívar, T 319170, F 372547, inc breakfast, English spoken, elegant restaurant; **A2** *Camino Real*, Ravelo 2123, T 314542, F 365575, self-catering apartments, inc breakfast, parking; **A3** *Gloria*, Potosí 909, T 370010/18, F 391489, central, 2 restaurants, one on top floor with good view, one vegetarian, excellent food and service (see below), rec; **A3** *Libertador*, Obispo Cárdenas 1421, T 351792, F 391225, very good value, good cheap restaurant, helpful, baggage stored, highly rec.

B *Eldorado*, Av Villazón, T 363355, F 391438, with breakfast, safe luggage deposit, secure parking nearby; **B** *Max Inn*, Plaza Sucre 1494, T 374391, F 341720, small rooms, heating, smart, poor service.

C *Hostería Blanquita*, Santa Cruz 242, T/F 352933, 'baroque', inc breakfast, hot showers, comfortable; **C** *Copacabana*, Av 16 de Julio 1802, T 352244, central, restaurant and grill room (lunch only at latter), good service, safe deposit, rooms a bit small, rec; **C** *Hostal Embajador*, Juan de la Riva 1438, T 392079, heating, inc breakfast, German spoken, helpful; **C** *Hostal República*, Comercio 1455 (T 357966), **D** without bath, beautiful old house of former president, warm water, inadequate shared bathrooms, luggage stored, helpful, laundry service, café, very popular with cyclists, usually full, rec, also a separate house is available, sleeps 6, all facilities; **C** *La Joya*, Max Paredes 541, T 324346, F 350959, phone, **D** without bath or TV, modern and comfy, lift, laundry, inc breakfast, free pickup from town centre, close to bus and train station, rec; **C** *Res Copacabana*, Illampu 734, T 367896/375378, hot water, **D** without bath, inc breakfast, changes TCs; **C** *Hostal Rosario*, Illampu 704, T 316156, F 375532, Turisbus travel agency downstairs (see below), **D** without bath, very popular with foreigners, avoid noisier rooms nr foyer, sauna, laundry, excellent restaurant (see below), stores luggage, highly rec; **C** *Sagárnaga*, Sagárnaga 326, T 350252, F 360831, with bath, **D** without, inc basic restaurant, good location, laundry, English spoken, poor service; **C** *Viena*, Loayza 420, T 323572, **E** without bath, beautiful old building with elegant entrance and patio, gloomy rooms, good lunch in restaurant, rec, arrive early, often

full, also Vicuña Tours agency.

D *Andes*, Av Manco Kapac 364, T 323461, **E** without bath, hot water 24 hrs a day, motorcycle parking, discount for IYHA card holders, rec; **D** *Continental*, Illampu 626, T 378226, hot water; **D** *España*, Av 6 de Agosto 2074, T 354643, T/F 342329, hot water, quiet, restaurant; **D-C** *Hostería Claudia*, Av Villazón 1965, T 372917, **E** without bath, secure, rec; **D** *El Alem*, Sagárnaga 334, T 367400, hot water, **F** pp without bath, helpful, secure, laundry, breakfast inc, rec, has helpful travel agency; **D** *Milton*, Illampu y Calderón No 1124, T 368003/353511, F 368388, PO Box 5118, hot water, inc breakfast, laundry, safe parking around corner, popular with travellers, will store luggage, excellent views from roof, good restaurant, rec; **D** *Res La Estancia*, México 1559, T 324308, with breakfast, helpful, good restaurant; **D** *Res Sucre*, Colombia 340, on Plaza San Pedro, T 328414, F355506, cheaper without bath, quiet area, warm water, big rooms, luggage stored, helpful; **D** *Tambo de Oro*, Armentia 367, T 322763, nr bus station, hot showers, helpful and safe for luggage.

E *Alojamiento Illimani*, Av Illimani 1817, T 325948, hot water, quiet and safe, uncomfortable beds, laundry facilities, often full; **E** *Austria*, Yanacocha 531, T 351140, without bath, **F** pp in shared room, hot water, safe deposit, very cosy, good for longer stays, use of kitchen, laundry, TV, very helpful staff, very popular, arrive early, highly rec; **E** *Hostal Latino*, Junín nr Sucre, hot water, motorcycle parking, luggage stored, helpful; **E** *Hostal Yanacocha*, opp Austria, large clean rooms, hot water, secure; **E** *Ingavi*, Ingavi 727, T323645/355178, nice rooms, good value; **E** *La Paz*, Acosta 487, T 322177, quiet, stores luggage, safe, hot showers; **E** *Panamericano*, Manco Kapac 454, T 340810/378370, with hot showers, nr railway station and main bus terminal, helpful, good restaurant, rec; **E** *Res Plaza*, Plaza Pérez Velasco 785, T 322157, nice old building, hot water, **F** without bath, washing and luggage storage facilities, helpful; **E** *Torino*, Socabaya 457, T 341487, hot water on request, **F** without bath, good meeting place but run down, poor beds, dirty, noisy from disco at weekends, top rooms quieter, 2400 curfew, noticeboard, stores luggage, book exchange, bar.

F *Alojamiento Universo*, Inca 575, **G** pp in dormitories, basic, stores luggage, laundry, very popular, usually hot water, motorcycle parking; **F** *Max Paredes*, Max Paredes 660, T 362726, cheaper without bath, modern; **F** *Posada El Carretero*, Catacora 1056, y Pichincha y Sanjinés, T 322233, 5 beds to a room, helpful, hot shower extra, can use kitchen for breakfast, great value; **F** pp *Scala*,

C Unión 425, entre Av América y Chuquisaca, T 350725, hot showers, nice rooms with windows, luggage stored, family-run; **F** *Res Imperial*, Pando, esq Incachaca, hot water 24 hrs, stores luggage, cheap laundry, rec.

Youth Hostel: Asociación Boliviana de Albergues Juveniles, ABAJ, Edif Alborada p 1, of 105, C Juan de la Riva 1406 y Loayza, T 361076/321597, has hostels at *Hostal Duendes*, Av Uruguay 470, T 351125, Casilla 8765, and *Hotel Andes*, Manco Kapac 364, US$3.50 and 3.00 respectively, pp, without breakfast; other hostels around the country are given in the text. To use hostels you must have a Bolivian YHA card, US$2, two photos needed, available from ABAJ, which also sells international cards, US$20.

Camping: no organized site, but Mallasa (Municipal Park, unmarked, turn left at Aldeas Infantiles SOS), Valencia and Palca below the suburb of La Florida have been rec. *Caza y Pesca*, Edif Handal Center, Av Mcal Santa Cruz y Socabaya, *Condoriri*, Sagárnaga 339, T/F 316369, or *Epcot*, Av 6 de Agosto 2190, local 9, T 342424, for camping equipment and camping gas. Kerosene for pressure stoves is available from a pump in Plaza Alexander. Public showers at Duchas La Paz, 20 de Octubre 1677.

● **Places to eat**
Restaurants with international cuisine are to be found mainly on Av 16 de Julio (the Prado), Av 6 de Agosto and Av 20 de Octubre. Service charges and tax of up to 23% are usually inc on the bill but it is customary to leave a tip of 10% anyway.

Av 16 de Julio (street numbers given in brackets): there are many snack bars, inc *Confitería Elis* (1497 and 1800), good lunches, excellent soups, breakfasts and pastries, not cheap, also *Eli's Pizza Express* in same block, English spoken, open daily inc holidays, rec (also at Comercio 914); opp is *Unicornio*, great ice cream, pizza, lunch buffet upstairs; *Patito Pekín* (1687), Chinese, reasonably priced; *California Donuts II* (1695), American-style food, expensive, US$2-10, opens 1230 (*No I* is at Av Camacho 1248, *No III* is on Av Arce); *Utama*, in *Plaza* hotel (1789) excellent salad bar, great value lunch, excellent view, highly rec; *Tokio* (1832), also has tea room and patisserie and rec for *salteñas*, but check prices; *Super 10* (1991 y Villazón), very good, open Sun evenings. On Plaza Estudiante, *Pizza I'Passo II*, good; *Café Ciudad*, 24-hr coffee shop, full menu, change US$ for customers. *Mary's Tee*, nr Plaza Estudiante, for excellent pies and cakes.

South of Plaza del Estudiante and Av Arce: *Andromeda*, Arce 2116, T 354723, European-style and vegetarian, excellent US$3 lunch; *El Batau*, Landaeta 402, T 342518, German owner, Bolivian and international cuisine, rec; *Pizzeria Morello*, Av Arce 2132, good but expensive; excellent buffet Mon and Wed, 2000-2300, at *Radisson Plaza Hotel*, US$5.50, delicious, friendly to backpackers; *Kranky*, Av Villazón 1987, cheap sandwiches, burgers, ice cream, rec; *Mongo's*, Hnos Manchego 2444, nr Plaza Isabela la Católica, T 353914, popular with expats, cable TV for sports, Budweiser, open Mon-Sun, US$4 lunch Mon-Fri 1130-1500, evening meals Mon-Sun 1730-0100, good fish and chips; *Chifa Emy*, Cordero 257, Chinese, good service, takes credit cards; *Rigo's*, Plaza Organo, nr Museo Semisubterráneo, pleasant, good set lunch; *Vienna*, Federico Zuazo 1905, T 391660, German, Austrian and local food, excellent food and service, very popular with Bolivians and foreigners.

In the Sopocachi district: up-market Italian cuisine at *Pronto*, Jauregui 2248, T 355869, Mon-Sat 1830-2230 (below Imprenta Quipus behind 6 de Agosto between Guachalla and Rosendo Gutiérrez), beautiful decor, serves three different types of pasta, popular, good service; *Montesano*, Sánchez Lima 2329, nr Plaza Abaroa, excellent Italian, also fish and steaks. Several restaurants on Belisario Salinas. **On Av 6 de Agosto**: *El Arriero* (No 2535, Casa Argentina), best barbecue with large portions; *Sergiu's Pizza*, No 2036, good; *Mocambo*, 6 de Agosto y Rosendo Gutiérrez 319, Spanish, rec; *Kuchen Stube*, Rosendo Gutiérrez, Edif

VIENNA

RESTAURANT • BAR

European style restaurant offering traditional cuisine and dining amid antiques, old prints and wood.

English and German spoken.

Our kitchen is open
Monday-Friday
12:00-14:00   18:30-22:00
Sundays
12:00-14:30

Federico Zuazo 1905 • Casilla 56
• Tel: 391660 • Fax: 310354
La Paz – Bolivia

Guadalquivír, closed Mon, excellent cakes, coffee and German specialities, also at Mercado 1328, Mon-Fri 0930-1230, 1500-1900. **On Av 20 de Octubre** is *Mamma Mia*, buffet lunch, good Italian restaurant at night; *La Quebecoise*, nr Plaza Abaroa, French Canadian, pleasant atmosphere; *El Gaucho*, No 2041, steakhouse, good. Close to 20 de Octubre: Brazilian *feijoada* on Sat and Sun, at *Ipanema*, Av Ecuador 2139, between Aspiazu and F Guachalla, T 372306, rec, closed Mon; *Gringo Limón*, Plaza Abaroa, delicious; *Filippo*, just off Plaza Abaroa, good *salteñas*; *La Caldera Mágica*, JJ Pérez 322 y 20 de Octubre, nice atmosphere, good lunches, bar.

On the continuation of the **Prado going West**, in Av Mcal Santa Cruz, is *Los Escudos* (Edif Club de La Paz, T 322028/350586), Munich-style bierkeller with fixed 4-course lunch, good *peña* on Fri and Sat nights (2100-0100), US$5 cover charge. *Restaurant Verona*, Colón esq Santa Cruz, economical *plato del día*, popular in the evenings; *La Fiesta*, Santa Cruz 1066, excellent, good lunches, rec; *Tambo Colonial*, in *Res Rosario*, excellent local and international cuisine, rec, *peña* at weekend. On Plaza Velasco is *Kory Punku*, excellent *parrilladas*, cheap and popular, live music some evenings.

On Calle México, running parallel S of the **Prado**: *La Estancia*, No 1553, good *almuerzo*, rec; *Capullito*, No 1490, pleasant café and *confitería*. México continues W as Murillo: at No 1040 is *Casa del Corregidor*, T 353633, centrally heated, Spanish colonial restaurant with Bolivian and European dishes, excellent food, rec; *El Horno*, open Mon-Sat, lunches inc vegetarian, free *peña* at nights (see **Entertainment** below); *Cristal*, No 726, outdoor, quite cheap, good.

On Sagárnaga: *Naira*, next to Peña Naira (No 161 downstairs), good food (see **Entertainment** below); above the Peña, is *Resolana*, often confused with *Naira*, good pizzas and puddings, live jazz most evenings, rec; *El Montañés* (No 323), opp *Hotel Sagárnaga*, open 0700, good American breakfast US$2.50, also homemade dishes; *Imperial*, Sagárnaga 213, 2nd floor, no sign, international vegetarian menu, set lunch US$2, balcony tables, rec. In same area, *El Lobo*, Santa Cruz 441, huge portions, Israeli dishes, good meeting place, noticeboard, very popular; *Los Laureles*, on Evaristo Valle, 4-course lunch rec; *Clávida*, opp train station, excellent set lunch.

In the shopping and business district N of the Prado: there are numerous snack bars and cheap restaurants. *Club de la Prensa*, C Campero, in a pleasant garden, limited menu is typical Bolivian – meat only, in copious quantities – lively company; *Café Club de la Paz*,

Camacho 1202, on the corner where Ayacucho joins Av Mcal Santa Cruz, good tea room, traditional, meeting place for businessmen and politicians, great coffee and cakes; *Café Paris*, in *Gran Hotel Paris*, Plaza Murillo esq Bolívar, good food; *Torino*, at the hotel in Socabaya, excellent set lunch; *Chifa Jardín*, Socabaya 461, good set lunch for US$1.20; *Confitería California*, Potosí 1008, Centro Comercial Cristal, good set lunches US$2.75. Also on Potosí, *Repostería Alemana* (*Nollo*) for breakfasts, *La Kantuta*, in *Hotel Presidente*, No 920, excellent food, good service, *Chez Pierre* (1320), set lunch US$1.20, good; *Rincón Tarijeño La Choza*, good food at reasonable prices; *Hogar Austriaco*, good lunches, pleasant; *Solo Café* (1108), excellent coffee and cappucino (closed lunchtime). On Yanacocha, *La Fregata* (No 525), good value, and *La Tertulia*, nr Ingavi, small, simple, charming, hot drinks and pastries. *Dumbo*, Camacho y Loayza, large portions, good; *Burger Center*, Ayacucho y Camacho, American-run, not cheap but rec; *Wall Street Café*, Camacho 1363 entre Loayza y Colón, good, not cheap, owner speaks English and French; *Confitería Arabesque*, Mercado y Loayza, excellent *café con crema*; *Casa Chang*, Juan de la Riva y Bueno, good set course Chinese meals; *Los Pinochos*, Sanjines 553, excellent cheese empanadas and steaks, large portions, popular café; *La Casa de los Paceños*, Sucre 856, excellent Bolivian food. There are many other snack bars and Chinese restaurants on C Comercio: eg *Salteñería Comercio*, No 1439, excellent *salteñas* and Bolivian food, outdoor seating; *La Diligencia Churrascaría*, No 803, good grill and set meals, rec. On Colón: *Confitería Rivoli*, No 415, small and pleasant snack bar, good and cheap food.

Vegetarian restaurants: *Hotel Gloria*, Potosí 909, buffet lunch, very popular, be there by 1200 for a table, also after 1900 for US$2 and breakfast, closed Sun; *La Huerta*, Plaza Isabel La Católica, Av Arce, p 1, excellent salads, lunchtime and early evening, rec; *Natur Center*, Cañada Strongest 1852, lunches only, closed Sun; *Lila Vatty*, Santa Cruz 266, p 1, good value; *Palacio del Buen Gusto*, 18 de Julio 1698, closed weekends, not cheap.

Burgers: a good chain is *Clap*, Centro Comercial El Patio, Av Arce, C Ayacucho, C Belisario Salinas, another chain is *Denny's*, at Av 16 de Julio 1605.

Comedor Popular, often referred to as *Comedor Familiar*, for strictly limited budgets, cheap but filling local meals around US$0.80-1.50, available at Camacho, Rodríguez and Lanza markets. Bread from street vendors and Cochabamba wholemeal bread (pan integral) sold at the main markets, is rec. Kremrik is a chain of ice-cream parlours, with outlets at Plaza Murillo 542, and on Av Villazón, just off Plaza del Estudiante, good.

The **Calacoto** district situated in The Valley 15 mins S of the city, 'La Zona Sur' (US$0.40 by trufi, US$0.30 by minibus), is home of the resident foreign community. It has international shopping centres, supermarkets stocked with imported items and some of the best restaurants and bars in La Paz. The area begins after the bridge at La Florida where there is an attractive park, Plaza Humbolt – exhibitions of local art work on Sun and a collection of kiosks selling cheap snacks. The main road, Av Ballivián begins at C 8 and continues up the hill to the shopping district of San Miguel on C 21 (about a 20 mins walk). On Av Ballivián: *El Viejo Tonel*, esq C 8, Brazilian restaurant, bar and disco, young crowd; on the left side between C 9 y 10 is *Rumors*, American/Mexican bar, restaurant, excellent music, popular late night place. *Puerto del Sol*, good Chinese on the left, esq C 11; opp is an excellent arts and handicrafts shop, weavings, ceramics, silver etc. Between C 15 y 16 on the left is *The Britannia*, open Tues-Sun from 1700, cosy, popular with regular ex-pat crowd, bar snacks, darts etc, highly rec. Next door is *Abracadabra*, open 7 days for lunch and dinner, ribs, hamburgers and pizza, American owner, rec; the *Ronería* next door is currently the most popular bar in Zona Sur. 5-min walk further up the hill on the right is C 21 (the church of San Miguel is on the corner) which has a huge variety of shops, fast-food cafés, banks and a post office. Back on Av Ballivián, between C 24 y 25 is *Chalet la Suisse* , excellent fondue, steaks, expensive but rec, and almost next door *The Galeon* for excellent seafood. *Zur Mönchsklause*, C 13 y Ovanda Candia, Irpavi, German, open Fri-Sun and holidays, garden, meat dishes and some fish.

● **Airline offices**
Lloyd Aéreo Boliviano (LAB), Camacho 1460, T 367701/7/367718/371020; **Aero Sur**, 16 de Julio 1607, T 371834, F 390457; **British Airways** at Edif Ballivián on C Mercado; **KLM**, Av Arce 2355; **American Airlines**, Av 16 de Julio 1440, Edif Herman, T 372009; **AeroPerú**, Edif Av, 16 de Julio 1490, p 2, T 370002-4; **Aerolíneas Argentinas**, Av 16 de Julio 1479, T 351711/351624; **Ecuatoriana**, T 0800-3001; **Varig**, Av Mcal Santa Cruz 1392, Edif Cámara de Comercio, T 314040, F 391131; **LanChile**, Av 16 de Julio 1566, p 1, T 358377.

● **Banks & money changers**
Citibank, Av 16 de Julio 1434, cashes its own TCs, high commission, will receive money sent from any US bank, but will not advance cash against Ci-

tibank Mastercard. **Banco Industrial**, Av Gral Camacho 1333, open 0830-1700, Sat 1000-1300, good service, changes cash and TCs. Cash advance (in bolivianos) on Visa and Mastercard at **Banco de La Paz** on Prado (limit US$300/day, no commission), **Banco Santa Cruz de la Sierra**, **Banco Mercantil**, Mercado 1124 (good, quick service), **Banco Popular**, **Banco Nacional** and **Banco Boliviano Americano**, Camacho (good, quick service); **Bidesa**, Potosí 1285, good service; **Banco Santa Cruz** branch in Shopping Norte is open Sat pm. **Visa**, Av Camacho 1448, p 11 y 12, T 369975/ 357014, F 354066, for cancelling lost or stolen credit cards. Automatic cash dispensers for Visa and Mastercard can be found at many sites in the city inc Av Camacho 1223, the airport and Shopping Norte shopping centre (look for the sign Enlace – Visa at branches of ATC). **Amex**, Av 16 de Julio 1490, p 5, T 323954/341201.

Exchange houses: Sudamer, Colón 256, good rates also for currencies other than US$, 1.5% commission on TCs into dollars, no commission into bolivianos, frequently rec; **Casa de Cambio Silver**, Mercado 979, 1% commission to change TCs into dollars, good rates; several others around Mercado y Colón. Very few deal in Argentine and Chilean pesos. Street changers on corners around Plaza del Estudiante, Camacho, Colón and Prado, OK rates, always count money in their presence. **NB** If arriving on Fri night, bring bolivianos or US dollars cash as it is difficult to change TCs at the weekend (try *El Lobo* restaurant, which usually changes TCs at any time, good rates, or *Hotel Gloria* which gives good rates for most western currencies). Watch out for forged currency, especially dollars and Chilean pesos.

● **Embassies & consulates**
Argentine Consulate, Sánchez Lima 2103, T 353089/343516, 24 hrs for visa; **Brazilian Consulate**, Av 20 de Octubre, 20-38 Edif Fonconain, Embassy p 11, visa office, p 9, T 352108, 0900-1300, Mon-Fri (visas take 2 days). **Chilean Consulate**, H Siles 5843, esq C 13, Obrajes district, T 785269, open Mon-Fri 0830-1130, visa same day if requested in the morning (take microbus N, A or L from Av 16 de Julio). **Ecuador**, Av 16 de Julio 1440, p 14, T 321208. **Paraguayan Consulate**, Edif Illimani, Av 6 de Agosto, very good visa service, T 322018; **Peruvian Consulate and Embassy**, 6 de Agosto 2190 y C F Guachalla, Edif Alianza, T 353550, 0930-1300, visa costs US$10 in US$ bills, issued same day if you go early; **Venezuelan Embassy and Consulate**, Av Arce 2678, Edif Illimani, p 4, T 375023, consulate open Mon, Wed, Fri 0900-1200 – visas are only given to Bolivian residents, if you need one, get it in your home country.

United States Embassy and Consulate, Av Arce 2780, T 350120/430251, F 359875,

Casilla 425. **Canadian Consulate**, Av 20 de Octubre 2475, Plaza Avaroa, T 375224, Mon-Fri. 0900-1200. **Japanese Embassy**, Rosendo Gutiérrez 497, esq Sánchez Lima, PO Box 2725, T 373151.

Austrian Consulate, Edif Petrolero, p 7, Oficina 1, Av 16 de Julio 1616, T 326601, 1600-1800; **British Embassy and Consulate**, Av Arce 2732-2754, T 433424, F 431073, Casilla 694, Mon-Thur 0900-1200, 1400-1600, Fri 0900-1300, has a list of travel hints for Bolivia, doctors, etc; **Finnish Consulate**, Mercado 1004, c/o Sibo SA, T 350900/367227; **French Consulate**, Av Hernando Siles 5390, esq C 08, Obrajes, T 786114 (take bus No 11 or microbus N, A or L down Av 16 de Julio); **Belgian Embassy** is 1 block from French at No 5290, T 784925; **German Embassy**, Av Arce 2395, T 390850, Mon-Fri 0900-1200; **Italian Embassy**, 6 de Agosto 2575, PO Box 626, T 323597, F 391075; next door is **Danish Consulate**, T 360655/1, F 376380, open 0930-1230; **Netherlands Embassy**, C Rosendo Gutiérrez 481, T 392064, F 391027, PO Box 10509, cellular phone (emergency 012-91173); **Norwegian Consulate**, Av 6 de Agosto 2410, T 322528; **Spanish Consulate**, Av Arce y C Cordero, T 343518; **Swedish Consulate**, Av Arce 2856, Casilla de Correo 852, T 327535, open 0900-1200; **Swiss Embassy**, Av 16 de Julio 1616, p 6, T 353091, F 391462, Casilla 9356, open 0900-1200, 1400-1500; **Israeli Embassy**, Av Mcal Santa Cruz, Edif Esperanza, p 10, T 358676/371287, Casilla 1309/1320.

● **Entertainment**

Best entertainment for visitors are the folk shows (*peñas*), which present the wide variety of local musical instruments. Outstanding show at *Peña Naira* (US$5, inc first drink), Sagárnaga 161, T 325736, every night 2200-0030. Enquire at the *Rumillajta* shop (in the *galería* close to San Francisco church) about future performances by the famous folk group of that name. Good *peña* at *Casa del Corregidor*, C Murillo 1040 (T 363633), dinner show Mon-Thur, no cover charge, Fri and Sat *peña* US$4, colonial atmosphere, traditional music and dance (see also under **Places to eat**); nearby is *La Luna*, Oruro y Murillo, great live bands, contemporary music. See under **Places to eat** for *Los Escudos*. Another *peña* is *Marko Tambo* on C Jaén, US$7 (all inc) repeatedly rec (also sells woven goods). If you wish to learn a live instrument, contact *Academia 'Walisuma'*, Av Apumalla 512, old Cemetery District between José M Asin and José M Aliaga, Pedro Mar teaches bi-lingual courses, English/Spanish, for *quena*, *zampoña* and *charango*.

Good salsa disco at *El Loro en su Salsa*, on Rosendo Gutiérrez on corner of Av 6 de Agosto, open Thur, Fri and Sat pm (salsa lessons at *Gym Cec*, Illampu 868, p 1, T 310158, US$4/hr). *Bar*

Socavón, Aspiazu y 20 de Octubre 2172, Sopocachi, T 353998, has live rock music Thur-Sat, music videos Wed, very popular. On C Belisario Salinas in Sopocachi Bajo, is *Piano Bar*, cosy, with a fireplace, live piano music, good drinks and snacks; and at no 380, *Equinoccio* (T 410653), top live music venue and bar. *Café Montmarte*, Fernando Guachalla, 399 y 20 de Octubre, next to Alliance Française, good French menu, set lunch US$4, bar with live music Thur, Fri, Sat. Excellent jazz at *Marius Club*, Presbitero Medina y Salazar, nr Plaza Avaroa. *Planet – the Funky Nachos Bar*, Prol Ecuador 2638 (Montículo), Wed-Sat from 2100, rock and grunge, Mexican food; *Pig and Whistle*, Goitia 155, serves Guinness and a selection of beers and whiskies; also on Goitia, *La Bodega*, bar with live music, good atmosphere. *Forum Disco*, Victor Sanjínez 2908, a few blocks beyond Plaza España, very popular, good variety of music, US$5 cover charge inc couple of drinks.

Teatro Municipal has a regular schedule of plays, opera, ballet and classical concerts, at Sanjines y Indaburo. Next door is the new **Teatro Municipal de Camera**, a small studio-theatre which shows dance, drama, music and poetry. **Cinemas** show films mainly in English with Spanish subtitles. The excellent Cinemateca Boliviana, Pichincha y Indaburo, is La Paz's art film centre with festivals, courses, etc, US$1.20, students US$0.60. **Casa Municipal de la Cultura 'Franz Tamayo'**, almost opp Plaza San Francisco, hosts a variety of exhibitions, paintings, sculpture, photography, videos, etc, most of which are free. The **Palacio Chico**, Ayacucho y Potosí, in old Correo, operated by the Secretaría Nacional de Cultura, also has exhibitions (good for modern art), concerts and ballet. It is also in charge of many regional museums. Listings available in Palacio Chico.

There are clown and mime shows in Parque del Ejército on Sun, colourful and popular; the Parque Central has a children's amusement park, US$0.20.

● **Hospitals & medical services**

Clínica del Accidentado, Plaza Uyuni 1351, T 328632/321888 offers first aid. Efficient and well run nursing homes include: *Clínica Americana*, Av 14 de Septiembre 78, T 783509; *Clínica Alemana*, 6 de Agosto 2821, T 323023/327521/373676; *Clínica Rengel*, T 390792/8; *Clínica Santa María*, Av 6 de Agosto 2487, not too expensive; *Clínica del Sur*, Av Hernando Siles y C Siete, Obrajes. *Red Cross* opp Mercado Camacho will give inoculations if required, T 323642. *The Methodist Hospital*, 12th block of Obrajes, T 783809 (take 'A' *micro* from the Prado) runs clinic at US$5, telephone for appointment.

Dentists: *Dr Remy Zegarra* at *Hostal Austria*, or home T 212083. *Dr Horacio M Rosso*, Av 20 de Octubre, Edif Guadalquivir, T 354745, his wife speaks German, rec. Also rec: *Dr Benjamín Calvo Paz*, Edif Illimani, Av Arce esq Campos, T 343706, and *Dra Esperanza Aid*, 6 de Agosto 2809, Edif Mercurio, p 3, opp US Embassy, T 431081, both speak English.

Doctors: contact your embassy or the Tourist Office for rec doctor who speaks your language. Check that any medical equipment used is sterilized. *Dr Ricardo Udler*, Edif Mcal de Ayacucho, C Loayza, T 360393/327046, speaks German, rec. *Dr César H Moreno*, Pinilla 274, Edif Pinilla, T 433805/792665 (home), rec. *Dr Eduardo Fernández*, Edif Av, Av 16 de Julio, p 9, T 370385 (surgery)/795164 (home), speaks English, US$30 for consultation, rec.

Health and hygiene: malaria pills and yellow fever vaccination, US$15.50 inc certificate are available at *Centro Piloto de Salva*, Av Montes y Basces, T 369141, about 10 mins walk from Plaza San Francisco, N of the main bus station, rec. *Laboratorio Inti*, Socabaya 266, rec for vaccines (human immunoglobulin, cholera, typhoid, rabies vaccine – but make sure you know precisely how it should be administered). Tampons may be bought at most *farmacias* and supermarkets. The daily paper, *Presencia*, lists chemists/pharmacies on duty (*de turno*). For contact lenses, *Optaluis*, Comercio 1089, well-stocked.

● **Language schools**
Centro Boliviano Americano (address under **Libraries** below) US$140 for 2 months, 1½ hrs tuition each afternoon. *Alliance Française* (see also below); *Instituto de La Lengua Española*, C 14 esq Aviador No 180, Achumani, T 796074, 1-1 lessons US$7/hr, rec. Private Spanish lessons from: Alice, T 783064; William, T 340676/ 812341 and Cecilia T 365428; *María Isabel Daza*, Murillo 1046, p 3, T 360769, US$3/hr, individual or group lessons, speaks English and Danish, rec. For English language teaching try *Pan American English Centre*, Edif Avenida, p 7, Av 16 de Julio 1490, T 340 796, Casilla 5244, native speakers only, minimum stay 3 months; similarly Goethe-Institut, Alliance Française, CBA and foreign schools.

● **Laundromats**
Wash and dry, 6-hr service, at *Gelmi-Lava-Sec*, 20 de Octubre 2019, suite 9, T 352930, helpful service, US$1.40 for 1 kg; *Lavandería Cinco Estrellas*, 20 de Octubre 1714, US$3 for 3 kg. *Limpieza Rosario*, Av Manco Kapac, nr Hotel Andes, US$1/kg, highly rec; *Lavandería Bandel*, Av Mcal Santa Cruz 1032, local 10, T 353563; *Limpieza Finesse*, Illampu 865, good but closed Sat pm.

● **Libraries**
Centro Boliviano Americano (CBA), Parque Zenón Iturralde 121, T 351627/342582 (10 mins walk from Plaza Estudiante down Av Arce), has public library and recent US papers (Mon-Wed 0900-1230, 1500-1930, till 2000 Thur and Fri). *Alliance Française*, F Guachalla 399 y Av 20 de Octubre, T 324075 (open Mon-Fri 1000-1200, 1500-1930), good for French newspapers and magazines. *Goethe-Institut*, Av 6 de Agosto 2118, T 374453 (Mon and Wed, 0900-1200, 1500-2000, Tues and Thur 1500-2000, Fri 0900-1200, 1500-1900), excellent library, recent papers in German, CDs, cassettes and videos free on loan.

● **Places of worship**
Protestant Community Church (inter-denominational), in English, American Co-operative School, C 10, No 7825, Calacoto (T 795639 or 792052). Sunday service at 1100, lots of activities during the week. Anglican-Episcopalian services are held at the Community Church on the 3rd Sun of each month.

Synagogues: C Landaeta 330 (Sat am services only); Colegio Boliviano Israëlito, Cañada Strongest 1846 for Fri service.

● **Post & telecommunications**
Post Office: Correo Central, Av Mcal Santa Cruz y Oruro, Mon-Sat 0800-2200, Sun 0900-1200. Stamps are sold only at the post office. Good philately section on 1st floor. There are a number of shops selling good postcards, etc. Poste Restante keeps letters for 3 months, good service, no charge. Check the letters filed under your surname and first name. Procedure for sending parcels: all is arranged downstairs (office hours only, Mon-Fri 0800-1200, 1430-1830); have contents inspected by customs, then seal parcel with glue, US$1 for each parcel. For mailing prices, see page 359. Don't forget moth balls (difficult to buy – try C Sagárnaga) for textile items. To collect parcels costs at least US$0.50. Express postal service (top floor) is expensive. **DHL**, Av Mcal Santa Cruz 1297; **UPS**, C Batallon Colorados 40, T 361332, F 391072.

Telecommunications: **Entel** T 367474) office for telephone calls is at Ayacucho 267 (the only one open on Sun), and in Edif Libertad, C Potosí. Long wait for incoming calls. Fax also from Ayacucho 267. Many small Entel offices throughout the city, with quicker service. For international and national calls, rather than wait for a booth, buy a phonecard (Bs 5, 10, 20 or 100) and use it in the phones to the left in the main Entel office, also throughout the city, eg Prado. For local calls buy a *ficha* (US$0.10) from the person sitting next to red Entel phone booths; or use a phone in any shop or stall with 'teléfono' sign (US$0.20). You can e-mail online at 6 de Agosto y Salinas, US$1.

● **Shopping**

Look around and bargain first. There are good jewellery stores throughout the city: eg *Joyería Cosmos*, Handal Center, Loc 13, Socabaya y Av 16 de Julio, Inca and Bolivian designs in gold and silver, colonial objects; *Joyería Kings*, Loayza 261, T 328178, F 324147, relocated in 1997 to larger premises, specializing in fine silver. Visit the gold factories for lower prices and special orders. There is inexpensive silver and jewellery in the little cabinets outside Lanza market on Av Santa Cruz. Up Sagárnaga, by the side of San Francisco church (behind which are many handicraft stalls in the Mercado Artesanal), are booths and small stores with interesting local items of all sorts, best value on Sun am when prices are reduced. The lower end of Sagárnaga is best for antiques. At Sagárnaga 177 is an entire gallery of handicraft shops. Upstairs is *Artesanía Sajama*, rec for woollens. *Millma*, Sagárnaga 225, and in *Hotel Radisson*, for alpaca sweaters (made in their own factory) and antique and rare textiles. *Wari* on Sagárnaga will make to measure very quickly, English spoken, prices reasonable; also *Toshy* on Sagárnaga for top quality knitwear. *Artesanía Sorata*, Linares 862, and Sagárnaga 311, 0900-1930, Mon-Sat, specializes in dolls, sweaters and weavings made by a women's cooperative and handmade textiles. For musical instruments: *Rumillajta*, one of the Galería shops adjacent to the San Francisco church entrance; many shops on Sagárnaga/Linares, eg *Sumaj Supay*, No 851, and *Coral* at No 852. Alpaca goods are about 50% more expensive than in Puno. Sweaters are much more expensive than Peru (beware of moths in woollen goods). Handmade clothing for children is good value. Most shops close Sat pm and Sun. See also the 'witchcraft market' on Calles Melchor Jiménez, and Linares, which cross C Santa Cruz above San Francisco, fascinating items for sale.

Artículos Regionales in Plaza del Estudian-

tes is rec. *Suma Ampara*, Av Villazón 1958, wide variety of woven goods, but prices not as low as in street markets. The rec *Casa Fisher* (see Cochabamba **Shopping**) has an outlet in Handal Center, Store No 2, Calles Mcal Santa Cruz y Socabaya, T/F 392948. Antique stores at El Prado 1615, Javier Núñez de Arco downstairs, his father upstairs, nice items, very expensive, also old photographs.

The Indian market is a good place for ponchos and local handicrafts. Many local objects are sold nr Av Buenos Aires, and musical instruments (much cheaper than shops) on C Granier, nr the General Cemetery. At Gallardo 1080, 1 block above Buenos Aires, there is the small workshop of the late master mask-maker, Antonio Viscarra, now run by his daughter and son-in-law. Costume, mask and trinket shops for Gran Poder abound above Buenos Aires. Mercado Camacho, Camacho y Bolívar, is the food market. The Tourist Office has a full list of all markets.

Shopping Norte, Potosí y Socabaya, is a modern mall with restaurants and expensive merchandise. Also try San Miguel in Zona Sur.

Bookshops: large stock of English, French and German books, and US magazines, at *Los Amigos del Libro*, Mercado 1315, also Edif Alameda, Av 16 de Julio (1 block from *Plaza Hotel*) and El Alto airport, rec; they also sell a few tourist maps of the region from Puno to the Yungas, and walking-tour guides. Amigos del Libro will ship books. *Gisbert*, Comercio 1270, books, maps, stationery, will ship overseas, rec. *Multi-Libro*, Loayza 233, T 391896, small, good for maps, politics, religion, psychology etc, open till 2100 Mon-Fri, and am Sat and Sun. *Librería La Paz*, Colón y Balliviân (wide selection of maps). Historian Antonio Paredes-Candia has a kiosk selling rare historical works on Villazón, opp San Andrés University. There are second-hand stalls on Av Ismael Montes and occasional book fairs on the Prado. German

books available at Goethe Institut (see above).

Cycle spares: try the shop at the Velódromo in Alto Irpavi, about 10 km out of town.

Films: any film can be developed at a decent developer. It is normal to get a free film, album or 15 x 21cm print. *Foto Visión*, 6 de Agosto 2044 and other branches, cheap, good prints. *Foto Linares*, Mercado y Loayza, expensive but best for anything out of the ordinary. *Linares* and *Kavlin*, Potosí 1130, develop black and white. *Agfa Centre*, Loayza 250, for slide film, US$4. Fuji and Kodak slide film is more expensive. All slide film should be developed 'solo revelado', ie without mounts because they tend to get scratched, about US$2/film. Cheap Fuji, Kodak or Agfa at street stalls, US$2 for 36, check date. **Repairs** at Av Sánchez Lima 2178 by Rolando Calla C, rec, just ring bell (1400-1700), there is no sign.

Maps: Instituto Geográfico Militar head office is at Estado Mayor Gen, Av Saavedra Final, Miraflores, open 0900-1100, 1500-1700, take passport to purchase maps immediately; or go to Oficina 5, Juan XXIII 100, cul-de-sac off Rodríguez between Murillo y Linares, Mon-Thur 0800-1200 and 1430-1800, Fri 0800-1400. IGM map prices: 1:50,000 topgraphical sheet US$6.70 (photocopy US$4.80); 1:250,000 sheet US$7.65 (copy US$5.75); national communications map (roads and towns) US$6.70; 4-sheet Bolivia physical 1:1,000,000, US$16.25; 4 sheet political 1:1,500,000 US$10.50. Liam P O'Brien has produced a 1:135,000, full colour, shaded relief topographic map of the Cordillera Real, US$10/copy, from 28 Turner Terrace, Newtonville, MA02160, USA (add US$2 for shipping), or from map distributors (Bradt, Stanfords, etc). Walter Guzmán Córdova colour maps of Choro-Takesi-Yunga Cruz, Mururata-Illimani, Huayna Potosí and Sajama, available from bookshops. The German Alpine Club (Deutscher Alpenverien) produces 2 good maps of Sorata-Ancohuma-Illampu and Illimani, best bought before arrival. Senac (the national road service) publishes a Red Vial 1989 map,

which is probably the best, but is still inaccurate, about US$4.50 from the office on 8th floor of Ministerio de Transporte y Communicaciones, Av Mcal Santa Cruz, tall building behind Correo, open till 1800, have to show passport. Also reported as inaccurate are the maps of the Automóvil Club Boliviano. Maps are generally hard to find. They are sold at Ichthus bookshop on the Prado, No 1800; also at Librería La Paz and Amigos del Libro (see page 279). A map and guide of La Paz, in English, is published by Editorial Quipus, Casilla 1696, Calle Jaúregui 2248, T 340062; also Tiwanaku, Sucre and Cochabamba guides. Quipus is also the Poste Restante for South American Explorer Club members.

● **Sports**

Football is popular and played on Wed and Sun at the Siles Stadium in Miraflores (Micro A) and at Cañada Strongest; there are reserved seats.

Golf: Mallasilla, the world's highest course, and Pinos. Non-members can play at Mallasilla on weekdays: club hire, green free, balls, and caddie US$37, the course is empty on weekdays, no need to book; it is in good condition and beautiful.

Snooker/pool: *San Luis*, Edif México, 2do Sótano, C México 1411; *Picco's*, Edif 16 de Julio, Av 16 de Julio 1566, both have good tables and friendly atmosphere.

Tennis: La Paz Tennis and Sucre Tennis.

YMCA sportsground and **gymnasium**: opp the University of San Andrés, Av Villazón, and clubhouse open to the public, Av 20 de Octubre 1839 (table tennis, billiards, etc); regular meetings Tues and Thurs 1930 of a mountaineering group which runs weekend excursions. See also under **Skiing** and **Mountaineering** under **Excursions** below.

● **Tour companies & travel agents**

Crillon Tours, Av Camacho 1223, Casilla 4785, T 374566, F 391039, Email titicaca@wara.bolnet.bo, Web http://www.titicaca.com,with 24-

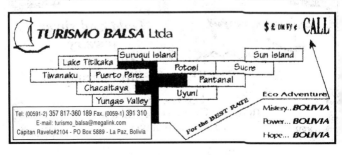

TURISMO BALSA Ltda $ £ DM FF ¢ **CALL**

Suruqui Island   Sun Island

Lake Titikaka   Potosi   Sucre

Tiwanaku   Puerto Perez   Pantanal

Chacaltaya   Uyuni

Yungas Valley   Eco Adventure

For the BEST RATE

Mistery.. **BOLIVIA**
Power... **BOLIVIA**
Hope... **BOLIVIA**

Tel: (00591-2) 357 817-360 189 Fax. (0059-1) 391 310
E-mail: turismo_balsa@megalink.com
Capitan Ravelo#2104 - PO Box 5889 - La Paz, Bolivia

hr ATM for cash on credit cards; in USA, 1450 South Bayshore Dr, suite 815, Miami, FL 33131, T (305) 358-5353, F (305) 372-0054, joint scheduled tours with Lima arranged; see also under **Lake Titicaca**, page 291; *Transturin*, Camacho 1321 esq Colón, T 328560/363654, F 391162, Tx 2301 TRTURIN BV, and Mcal Santa Cruz 1295, p 3, T 342164: these two agencies offer full travel services, with tours ranging from La Paz to the whole country; full details of their Lake Titicaca services will be found on page 293. *Turismo Balsa*, Capitán Ravelo 2104, T 360189/357817, F 391310, and Av 16 de Julio 1650, T 354049, PO Box 5889, city and local tours (rec), see also under **Puerto Pérez**, page 291; *Turisbus*, Illampu 702, Casilla 442, T 369542, F 375532, helpful, trekking equipment rented, agent for Peruvian railways, ENAFER, tickets to Puno and Cusco (US$12 and US$31), also local and Bolivian tours, rec; *Exprinter*, Edif Herrman, Plaza Venezuela (exchange facilities, helpful) to Cusco, US$28, 21 hrs, 3 times a week, via Desaguadero with a stop in Puno; *Magri Turismo*, Av 16 de Julio 1490, p 5, T 323950/341201, F 366309, e-mail: Magri_emete@megalink.com. Amex representative, gives TCs against American Express card, but cannot give cash or exchange TCs, offers all other Amex emergency services and clients' mail, rec for tours in Bolivia, travel services; *Pachamama Tours*, Av Mcal Santa Cruz y Colón, Galería Ed Litoral, subsuelo, of 17, T 322311, rec for tours of La Paz, Tiwanaku, Titicaca, etc, also arranges tours throughout Bolivia; *Diana Tours*, Sagárnaga 328, T 340356/375374/350252, F 360831, some English spoken, tour to Coroico and Tiwanaku, bus to Puno US$12; *Titikaka Tours*, Loayza between Riva and Camacho, good for flights; *Tawa Tours*, Sagárnaga 161 and Rosenda Gutiérrez 701, T 325796, French-run, run jungle tours to their own camp as well as the Salt Lake areas, friendly, good guides (also charter flights

to Europe and USA); *Shima Tours*, Potosí 1310, very helpful, good for flight tickets; *Combi*, Illampu next to *Res Copacabana*, classical tours and transport to Copacabana; *Transamazonas*, Edif V Centenario, p 3, Av 6 de Agosto above lower end of new underpass, T 350411, F 360923, Casilla 14551, German-run, top-end adventure tourism, English, German, French, Spanish spoken; *Fremen*, C Pedro Salazar 537, Plaza Avaroa, T 416336, F 417327, Casilla 9682, e-mail: vtfremen@wara.bolnet.bo own Flotel in Trinidad for jungle cruises in the Beni and Hotel El Puente in the Chapare; *Paititi*, Av 6 de Agosto y Aspiazu, and *Aparthotel Camino Real*, Capitán Ravelo 2123, 0900-1900, T 340108/ 341018/ 353558, F 329625, organizes adventure tours, rec, Javier Palza is helpful and speaks English, German, French, Italian; *Peru Bolivian Tours*, Loayza, Edif Mcal de Ayacucho PB – Of 8, T 363720, F 365845; *America Tours*, Av 16 de Julio 1490, T 328584, F 374204, Casilla 2568, Swiss-Bolivian owned, cultural and ecotourism trips to many parts of the country, English, German, French spoken; *Andes Expediciones*, Plaza Alonso de Mendoza, Edif Santa Ana, p 3, of 314, T 320901/375240, F 392344, treks and mountaineering to many lesser-known and remote destinations, highly rec, manager Bernardo Guarachi is a very experienced mountain guide; also *Carmoar Tours*, C Bueno 159, which is headed by Günther Ruttger (T/F 340633), has information and maps for the Inca Trail to Coroico, rents trekking gear. For information on and arrangement of climbing and adventure tours, *Colibrí*, Sagárnaga 309, see under **Mountaineering** below. *Reinaldo Pou Munt*, Capitán Ravelo 2401, T 327226, Casilla 13632, expensive, offers excellent tours of the city and environs, speaks English and German; *Nuevo Continente*, at *Hotel Alem*, rec for trip to Zongo, Clemente is a good driver, cheap service to airport, very friendly and helpful. Many agen-

cies arrange excursions or travel to Peru (Puno, Cusco, Arequipa), as well as local tours. See also names and addresses under 'Exchange Houses', page 276. *Bracha*, T 327472, has details of and sells tickets for trains from Santa Cruz.

NB Flight tickets can be bought more reliably from airlines than through agencies.

● **Tourist offices**
Information office at the bottom end of Av 16 de Julio (Prado) on Plaza del Estudiante on corner with C México, helpful, English and French spoken, ask here for information on train services, free leaflets, map of La Paz US$2.50. *Dirección Nacional de Turismo*, Edif Ballivián, p 18, C Mercado, T 367463/441. Telephone directories in La Paz have economic and tourist information in English on all the provinces.

● **Useful addresses**
Asociación Boliviana de Agencias de Viajes y Turismo, Edif Litoral, Mcal Santa Cruz 1351, Casilla 3967. **Instituto Nacional de Arqueología de Bolivia**, C Tiwanaku 93.

Immigration: to renew a visa go to Migración Bolivia, Av Camacho 1433 (opp Banco de Santa Cruz), T 379385/370475, Mon-Fri 0900-1200, 1600-1800, fast and efficient.

Tourist Police: Plaza del Estadio, Miraflores, next to *Love City* disco, T 225016, for insurance claims after theft, English spoken, helpful.

YMCA: 20 de Octubre 1839, Casilla 963.

● **Transport**
Local Bus: there are three types of city bus: large Fiat buses run by the city corporation, on fairly limited routes; *micros* (Bluebird-type buses), which charge US$0.18 in the centre, US$0.24 from outside centre; and *Kombis* (minivans), US$0.20/0.34, quicker than *micros*. **Car hire**: cars may be hired direct from **Imbex**, Av Montes 522, T 316895, F 379884, well maintained Suzuki jeeps from US$50/day, inc 100 km free for 4-person 4WD, highly rec; **National**, F Zuazo 1935, T/F 376581, rec; **Rent-a-Car International**, F Suazo 1942, T 357061; **Kolla Motors**, Rosendo Gutiérrez 502, T 341660/351701 who have well-maintained 6-seater 4WD Toyota jeeps, insurance and gasoline extra. **Petita Rent-a-car**, Cañada Strongest 1857-A, T 379182, F 322596, Swiss owners Ernesto Hug and Aldo Rezzonico, rec for well-maintained VW 'beetles' and 4WD jeeps, etc, also offer adventure tours, **Jeeping Bolivia**, German, French, English spoken, rec. Ernesto also has garage for VW and other makes, Av Jaimes Freyre 2326, T 342279, highly rec. **Car Park** on corner of Ingavi and Sanjines, US$1.75 for 24 hrs, safe and central. **Motorcycle rental**: Moto Rent, Av Busch 1255, Miraflores Norte, T 357289, 650 Kawasaki endurance type,

US$50/day unlimited mileage, US$250/week. Motorcycle spares: J Landivar, Av Saavedra 1235, T 329774, F 392427, Honda and other Japanese makes, rec. **Taxis**: normal taxis charge US$0.40 pp for short trips within city limits. *Trufis* are fixed route collective taxis which charge US$0.28-0.40 pp within city limits. Taxi drivers are not tipped. Don't let the driver turn the lights out at night. Radio taxis (eg Alfa T 322427, La Rápida 392323) charge US$1.45 in centre and US$2.80 to suburbs; also good value for tours for 3 people, negotiate price. Eduardo Figueroa, T 786281, taxi driver and travel agent, rec. Adolfo Monje Palacios, in front of *Hotel El Dorado* or T 354384 highly rec for short or long trips. Oscar Vera, Simón Aguirre 2158, Villa Copacabana, La Paz, T 230453, specializes in trips to the Salar de Uyuni and the Western Cordillera, speaks English, rec.

Air El Alto, above La Paz, the highest commercial airport in the world (4,058m) connected to the city by motorway, T 810122/3. A taxi between the centre and airport takes about 30 mins, US$6 to airport, US$5 to centre; current prices, inc luggage, should be on display at the airport exit (enquire at the tourist office in town, or at the airport). Cotranstur minibuses, white with 'Cotranstur' and 'Aeropuerto' written on the side and back, go from Plaza Isabel La Católica, anywhere on the Prado and Av Mcal Santa Cruz to the airport between 0800-0830 to 1900-2000, US$0.55 (allow about 1 hr), best to have little luggage, departures from the airport every 5 mins or so; colectivos from Plaza Isabel La Católica charge US$3.45 pp, carrying 4 passengers. There is a duty-free shop. Bank in international departures hall will change cash, rates OK. To change money when bank is closed, ask at the departure tax window nr information. The international departures hall is the main concourse, with all check-in desks and is the hall for all domestic arrivals and departures. Small tourist office at the Airport, some maps available, English spoken, helpful (when staffed). Bar/restaurant and café (cheaper) upstairs. **Services**: LAB, Aero Sur (T 371833) and TAM fly to the main cities and towns. Fares are comparatively low for internal flights. (For details, see under destinations.) Note that TAM uses the nearby military airport.

Trains The rate of terminal decline of Bolivian railways has accelerated since privatization. Trains are more expensive, slower, and harder to catch than buses and the timetable (when it is met) is outrageously antisocial. La Paz-Oruro and Oruro-La Paz services have been suspended indefinitely, as have services between Potosí and Sucre. For information T 353510/352510/373069. Micros which go to the station are A,

M, N, P, 130, 131, C. The ticket office, at the rear of the building at the N end of main station, opens Mon-Wed 0700, and Fri 0830-1200, but get there at least 2 hrs beforehand.

To **Villazón** (minimum 20 hrs) for Argentina, dep Fri at 1300, *Expreso del Sur*, via Oruro (US$3.60 pullman, US$4.60 salón), Uyuni (US$8.20/9.70), Atocha (US$9.70/11.40), Tupiza (US$11.40/13.30), Villazón (US$13.30/15.30). Book ahead at central station; queue at 0600 on previous day (queuing numbers are given out), take passport. If all train tickets are sold out, go to station 2 hrs before departure for returned tickets, or try Exprinter travel agency, or try and board train anyway and pay the guard.

La Paz-Arica International Railway, 447 km: In the Bolivian section the line climbs to El Alto and then runs SW to Viacha (Km 32) the junction of lines to Antofagasta, Guaqui (freight only) and Villazón. It continues to Corocoro, the copper mining town, crosses the Río Desaguadero at Calacoto (Km 98) and then runs SW to the border at Charaña (Km 208 – see below) a very cold place to change trains or wait for a bus. The mountain peaks visible inc Illimani, Huayna-Potosí, Mururata, and many others. For description of the Chilean part, see Chile, **Iquique**, **Arica and The Far North**. **NB** Chilean pesos can be bought in La Paz at good rates.

There is a Bolivian *ferrobus* service straight through to Arica, on Mon and Fri at 0715, arrives 1935, and Tues and Sat at 1940, US$52 pullman, US$96 *especial*, inc breakfast and lunch, max 20 kg baggage is free, extra charge for excess, worth it for the spectacular scenery, book ticket 1-2 weeks in advance at Estación Central, especially in high season (when extra trains are added). **NB** Service suspended in 1997 after flooding. Alternatively take a train to **Charaña** on Wed from Viacha at 0300, US$3 pullman, then change to a colectivo to Arica, or, on 2nd and 4th Wed of each month a train leaves Charaña at 0930, arriving Arica at 1800 (every Wed Jan-Mar). The return from Charaña to Viacha dep at 1600.

La Paz-Antofagasta, by Antofagasta and Bolivia Railway, 1,173 km, definitely a trip for the adventurous who are impervious to cold at night, or blazing sunshine at tedious daytime border changes. The train is full of contrabandistas, impromptu folk music, and the ride is very rough and subject to long delays. The train starts at Uyuni, running as far as Calama in Chile, then by bus (240 km) to Antofagasta. This route passes through magnificent scenery. For details see under Uyuni **trains** (see page 307).

Buses For information; T 367275/367274; buses to: Oruro, Potosí, Sucre, Cochabamba, **Santa Cruz**, Tarija and Villazón, leave from the main terminal at Plaza Antofagasta (micros 2, M, CH or 130), see under each destination for details. The terminal (open 0700-2300) has a post office, ENTEL, restaurant, luggage store and agencies, such as Turisbus, Diana, Vicuña (cheaper than their offices in town). Touts find passengers the most convenient bus and are paid commission by the bus company.

Buses to **Sorata**, **Copacabana** and **Tiahuanaco** leave only from the Cemetery district. Companies inc Flota Copacabana, Manco Kapac, 2 de Febrero, Ingavi, Trans Perla Andina. To get to the Cemetery district, take any bus or kombi marked 'Cementerio' going up C Santa Cruz (US$0.17); the route is Santa Cruz, Max Paredes, Garita de Lima, Mariano Bautista, Plaza Félix Reyes Ortiz/Tomás Katari (look out for the cemetery arch on your left). On Plaza Reyes Ortiz are Manco Kapac, rec (T 350033) and 2 de Febrero (T 377181) for Copacabana and Tiquina. From the Plaza go up Av Kollasuyo and at the 2nd street on the right (Manuel Bustillos) is the terminal for kombis to Huatajata and Huarina, and buses for Sorata (eg Trans Unificada). Several micros (20, J, 10) and kombis (223, 252, 270, 7) go up Kollasuyo; look for 'Kollasuyo' on the windscreen in most, but not all, cases.

Buses to **Coroico and the Yungas** leave from Villa Fátima (25 mins by micros B,V,X,K, 131, 135, or 136, or *trufis* 2 or 9, which pass Pérez Velasco coming down from Plaza Mendoza, and get off at the service station, C Yanacachi 1434).

International buses: to **Buenos Aires**, daily at 1630, San Roque, T 329769, via Yacuiba, or 1700, San Lorenzo, T 328911, both take 2½ days; also Atahualpa via Yacuiba or La Quiaca/Villazón. Alternatively, go to Villazón and change buses in Argentina. To **Arica** via the frontier at Tambo Quemado and Chungará at 0530 Tues, Fri and Sun, US$29, with Litoral, T 358603 (office No 19 bus terminal), 11 hrs on paved road. Also Géminis once a week, Trans Salvador 3 a week, both US$29, and Transportes Cali, US$22. To Arica via the frontier at Charaña and Visviri in stages (no direct service), Senobus (C Hujutri, 400m from train station in direction of Cementerio), Tues, Fri, Sat evenings (US$11) or (cheaper) El Cariñoso. In Charaña take taxi to Visviri (US$0.65), then bus Tues and Fri, US$7, or colectivo taxi to Arica. It is a beautiful, exhausting trip, but doing it in stages, rather than straight through, involves several waiting at the border, all companies involve several changes of bus, 18 dusty hrs. Military checks can be expected both sides of the frontier. To **Iquique**, Tues, Sat and Sun 1700, US$32, 22 hrs, Litoral. To **Tacna**, also with Litoral, Thur and Sat, 0700, US$20, 10 hrs, road repaired 1996 (there are no

Bolivian customs or immigration at the border for exit stamp, Peruvian entry is given in Tacna). To **Cusco**, Cruz del Sur, 3 a week, US$18, 'not luxurious'. Colectivos and agencies to **Puno** daily with different companies most easily booked through travel agencies, US$13-15.50, 10 hrs. **NB** Of the various La Paz-Puno services, only Transturin does not make you change to a Peruvian bus once over the border. Exprinter/Cruz del Sur, T 362708, go via Desaguadero Tues, Thur, Sat 0800, US$7.20. For luxury and other services to Peru see under **Lake Titicaca** below.

By **Road from La Paz to the Pacific Coast**
There are 2 routes: the shortest and most widely used is the road from La Paz to Arica via border towns of Tambo Quemado (Bolivia) and Chungará (Chile). The majority of Bolivia's imports, inc foreign cars, jeeps and large vehicles from Chile's Pacific sea-ports, Arica and Iquique, are brought to La Paz by truck via this route. From La Paz take the main highway S towards Oruro to **Patacamaya** (104 km – about 1½ hrs from central La Paz on good paved road – 130 km N of Oruro); Sun market, no tourist items; **G** Los Angeles, basic, other cheap accommodation and restaurants. At Patacamaya turn right (W towards the cordillera) at green road sign to Puerto Japonés on the Río Desaguadero (sign only visible coming from La Paz), thence to Tambo Quemado. Take extra petrol (none available after Chilean border until Arica) food and water. The journey is worthwhile for the breathtaking views.

Midway between Patacamaya and Tambo Quemado is the town of Curahuara de Carangas (Alojamiento only, plaza, G, dirty, no electricity). Watch for speed restrictions upon entering town past military school. Possible overnight stop in Sajama Village (4,200m) 22 km E of Tambo Quemado at the foot of Mt Sajama (see **South from La Paz – Excursions from Oruro**). Bolivian customs is at Lagunas, 12 km further on, a popular 'truck-stop'. Petrol available. Restaurant/bar Lagunas offers cheap set menu, helpful, friendly. Owner can usually find accommodation somewhere in the village, US$1, take your own sleeping bag, extra blankets, warm clothing. Facilities are at best very basic; you may well be sleeping on a straw mattress on a dirt floor. No water or electricity, gas lamps or candles are usual. It may be possible for men to sleep at the Puesto Militar, beside the new road, 100m from village. Nights can be bitterly cold and very windy. In the daytime there are spectacular views of nearby snowcapped Mt Sajama.

The Bolivian border control at Tambo Quemado, 10km from Lagunas, consists of 'tránsito' (highway police), immigration, and international police. Approximately US$4.50/'particular' (private non-commercial) vehicle. Check

with Autómovil Club Boliviano, La Paz for any special documents which may be required, depending on the registration of your vehicle. Bolivian vehicles require a Temporary Export Certificate in order to leave Bolivia (to be obtained in La Paz prior to travel), and Temporary Import Certificate approx US$2.50 from customs at Chungará on entering Chile. Best to change a small amount of currency into Chilean pesos in La Paz. Temporary Import/Export Certificates are normally valid 90 days. It is worth double checking all documents inc visa requirements with the Consulate of Chile in La Paz before travelling. From Tambo Quemado there is a stretch of about 7 km of 'no-man's land' before you reach the Chilean frontier at Chungará. Here the border crossing, which is set against the most spectacular scenic backdrop of Lake Chungará and Volcán Parinacota is strictly controlled; open 0800-1200; 1430-1800. Expect a long wait behind lines of lorries; avoid Sun; best to travel midweek. Drivers must fill in 'Relaciones de Pasajeros', US$0.25 from kiosk at border, giving details of driver, vehicle and passengers. Border control consists of Ministry of Agriculture and Livestock (SAG – control of animals entering Chile is rigidly enforced; do not take any fruit, vegetables, or dairy products into Chile), immigration, Customs and Police.

From Chungará the first 50 km section to Putre goes through spectacular Lauca National Park. There are some treacherous bends as the road descends dramatically to sea-level where it meets the Pan Amerian Highway (Route 5) 12 km N of Arica.

An alternative, on which there are no trucks, is to go by good road from La Paz via Viacha to Santiago de Machaco (130 km, petrol); then 120 km to the border at **Charaña** (**G** Alojamiento Aranda; immigration is behind the railway station, only 30-day permit given on entry), very bad road. In Visviri (Chile) there is no fuel, accommodation, bath or electricity, ask for restaurant and bargain price. From Visviri a regular road runs to Putre, then as above.

A variation from Viacha is take the roads which more-or-less follow the railway to Charaña (4WD essential). On this scenic route you pass Comanche (to which excursions are made to see Puya Raimondii plants) and Gen Campero in the Ciudad de Piedra (nr the football field in Gen Campero is a house which lets a room and has water). From Gen Campero roads go to Gen Pérez, Abarao and Charaña. From this route treks can be made S to the mountains towards Sajama and, from Charaña, to Sajama itself.

TREKKING NEAR LA PAZ

● **Maps** All treks in the Cordillera Real are covered by the map of the Cordillera Real, 1:135,000, Liam O'Brien. Takesi, Choro and Yunga Cruz are covered by the Walter Guzmán Córdova 1:50,000 map; see **Maps** above. There are also the IGM 1:50,000 sheets: Takesi Chojlla 6044 IV; Choro Milluni 5945 II, Unduavi 6045 III and Coroico; Yunga Cruz Lambate 6044 II and 6044.

● **Guidebooks** The *Bolivia Handbook* gives greater detail than the following description. See also *Backpacking and Trekking in Peru and Bolivia* (6th edition) by Hilary Bradt (published by Bradt, 1995) and *Trekking in Bolivia* by Yossi Brain (The Mountaineers, Seattle, 1997).

TAKESI (MINA SAN FRANCISCO TO YANAKACHI)

Start at Ventilla (see **Transport** below), walk up the valley for about 3 hrs passing the village of Choquekhota until the track crosses the river and to the right of the road, there is a falling down brick wall with a map painted on it. The Takesi and Alto Takesi trails start here following the path to the right of the wall. The road continues to Mina San Francisco. In the first hour's climb from the wall is excellent stone paving which is Inca or pre-Inca – depending on who you believe – either side of the pass at 4,630m. There are camping possibilities at *Estancia Takesi* and café *Don Pepe*. You also have to pass the unpleasant mining settlement of Chojlla, between which and Yanacachi is a gate where it is necessary to register and often pay a small 'fee'. Yanacachi has a number of places to stay. Buy a minibus ticket on arrival in Yanacachi or walk 45 mins down to the La Paz-Chulumani road for transport. The trek can be done in 1 long day, especially if you organize a jeep to the start of the trail, but is more relaxing in two – or three if you take it really slowly – though you'll have to carry camping kit. Mules can be hired in Choquekhota for US$8 per day plus up to US$8 for the mulateer.

● **Transport** Take a Palca bus from C Venacio Burgoa esq C Boquerón, San Pedro, 0600 during the week, more often at weekends, and get off at Ventilla; or try catching Palca bus from outside *comedor popular* in C Max Paredes above junction with C Rodríguez, daily at 0530, US$1; or

get a Bolsa Negra, Tres Ríos or Pariguaya bus Mon-Sat 0900 from C Gen Luis Lara esq Venacio Burgoa near Plaza Libano, San Pedro (not possible to buy tickets in advance, be there between 0700 and 0800 on the day to ensure ticket). Drivers may not want to take you just to Ventilla so you may have to pay more, eg up to US$2 which is the fare to Chunavi. Alternatively, take any micro or minibus from central La Paz to Chasquipampa or Ovejuyo and then get on any transport going further, most transport goes to Palca, and get off at Ventilla. If there isn't any transport, haggle with drivers of empty minibuses in Ovejuyo; you should be able to get one to go to Ventilla for about US$10. Alternatively, haggle with a radio taxi in La Paz, it should be possible to get one to go to Ventilla for under US$20. The most comfortable way to get to the start of the trek is to hire a jeep from La Paz to Mina San Francisco for US$50 which takes 1½ to 2 hrs.

CHORO (LA CUMBRE TO COROICO)

Immediately before the road drops down from La Cumbre to start the descent to Los Yungas there is a collapsing plastered brick wall on the left which marks the start of the trail. However there is nothing to help you get across the featureless moonscape to the *apacheta* where the trail starts properly. Cloud and bad weather are normal at La Cumbre (4,700m): follow the left hand of the statue of Christ, take a map and compass or guide to get you to the start of the trail which is then well-signposted. The trail passes Chucura, Challapampa (camping possible, US$0.40, wood and beer for sale), the Choro bridge and the Río Jacun-Manini (fill up with water at both river crossings). At Sandillani it is possible to camp in the carefully-tended garden of a Japanese man who keeps a book with the names of every passing traveller. He likes to see postcards and pictures from other countries. There is good paving down to Villa Esmeralda, after which is Chairo (5-star *Hotel Río Selva*), thence to Yolosa. It takes 3 days to trek from La Cumbre to Chairo and a further long day on foot to Coroico, unless you take a truck from Chairo to Yolosa (allegedly at 0600, or hire one if enough people to pay US$2.25 each). From Yolosa it is 8 km uphill to Coroico with regular transport for US$1 pp.

● **Transport** To get to the start take a bus or *camión* from Villa Fátima, but make sure the driver knows you want to get off at La Cumbre. Alternatively, get a radio taxi from central La Paz for about US$16.

YUNGA CRUZ (LAMBATE OR CHUÑAVI TO CHULUMANI)

The best but the hardest of the three 'Inca' trails and therefore less popular so there is less litter and begging. From Chuñavi follow path left (east) and contour gently up. Camping possible after 2 hrs. Continue along the path staying on left hand side of the ridge to reach Cerro Khala Ciudad (literally, Stone City Mountain, you'll see why). Good paving brings you round the hill to join the path from Lambate (this heads uphill for 2 days through Quircoma and then to Cerro Khala Ciudad after which you descend to join the path from Chuñavi). Head N to Cerro Cuchillatuca and then Cerro Yunga Cruz where there is water and camping is possible. After this point water and camping are difficult and normally impossible until you get down to Chulumani. The last water and camping possibilities are all within the next hour, take advantage of them. Each person should have at least two litres of water bottles. There are some clearances on the way down but no water. Starting in Chuñavi saves 2 days' walking and makes the trek possible in 3 days but misses the best bits. Starting in Lambate the trek normally takes 5 days.

● **Buses** Take the Pariguaya bus (see Takesi above) to Lambate or Chuñavi, all other buses stop in Tres Ríos or Bolsa Negra; 6 hrs to Chuñavi by bus, another hour to Lambate.

● **Water purification** Only use iodine-based preparations. Iodine tincture, *iodo* in *farmacias* costs US$0.50: use 5 drops/litre.

MOUNTAINEERING

There are 600 5,000m+ mountains in the Cordillera Real including six at 6,000m or above: Illimani 6,439m, Ancohuma 6,427m, Illampu 6,368m, Chearoco 6,104m, Huayna Potosí 6,088m and Chachacomani 6,000m. A week's acclimatization at the height of La Paz or equivalent is necessary before attempting to climb above 5,000m. Access is easy from the flat Altiplano, but public transport is not always possible. Proper technical equipment, experience and/or a competent guide are essential to cross glaciers and climb snow and ice safely. Do not expect rescue. Conditions are normally excellent during the season May-September.

The most popular peak is **Huayna Potosí**, normally climbed in 2 days, including one night camped on a glacier at 5,600m. To get to the start of the normal route take transport to the Zongo Pass as described in **Excursions** above. The *Refugio Huayna Potosí* organizes regular transport plus guides and porters: contact Dr Hugo Berrios (fluent English and French) at *Hotel Continental*, C Illampu 626 (T 323584, 795936), Casilla 731. The luxury refuge costs US$10 per night, food extra. Do not camp in the Zongo Pass area; there is a major theft problem.

The beautiful 5-peaked **Illimani** overlooks La Paz and the normal route is not technically challenging, but it is high and a 4-day trip. Public transport is difficult and irregular to *Estancia Una* (mules and porters available) where most people start the 4-hr walk-in to first camp at Puente Roto. The only reliable way to avoid paying the US$150 jeep fare (one way) is to get a bus going to Cohoni (pronounced Koni) from C Gral Luis Lara, off C Boquerón in San Pedro, Mon-Sat at 1300 and 1500, 4 hrs, US$2. Mules and porters are available in Cohoni but less readily than from Estancia Una. Day 2 is spent moving up a rock ridge to high camp at Nido de Cóndores where there is no water; take extra fuel for snow melting. A 0300 start to day 3 should see you to the summit, down to Nido de Cóndores and on down to Puente Roto for running water. Day 4, walk out to transport.

Condoriri is a group of 13 mountains, 5,100-5,700m, including Pequeño Alpamayo, which is beautiful and not technically difficult. Non-climbers can go up to Mirador for fantastic views of the surrounding peaks and Huayna Potosí. No public transport, jeep one way US$70 to Tuni dam and then 3-hr walk-in to basecamp (mules available). Alternatives, not recommended: public transport to Milluni (see **Zongo Valley** above) and then walk for 24 km to Tuni, or take a bus/truck/minibus heading N from La Paz (eg to Lake Titicaca or Huarina or Achacachi) to Patamanta (garage on the left) and then walk 20 km+ to Tuni. Established tent guarding system at basecamp which costs from US$1 per tent per day.

● **Recommended reading** *Bolivia – a climbing guide*, by Yossi Brain (The Mountaineers, Seattle, 1997).

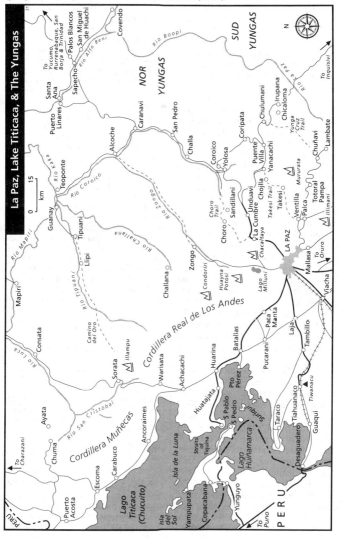

La Paz, Lake Titicaca, & The Yungas

Quimza Cruz: still 'the future of Bolivian mountaineering' because few people make the effort to get there. Rock climbing on granite near Mocaya (6 km after Viloco), beautiful lakeside campsites, snow peaks up to 5,800m, including Gigante Grande, and trekking possibilities, eg Viloco to Mina Caracoles in 2-3 days. It takes a day to get in and another to get out. Buses and trucks go as far as Viloco (no accommodation); from there take a truck to Araca, if you're lucky, 15 km; better from Tallapata. Buses to Viloco dep from C Jorge Carrasco, between C 4 and 5, El Alto, parallel to the Oruro road, Mon, Wed, Thur and Sat at 0700, 10 hrs, US$3.30. Accommodation in Araca at *Hacienda Teneria*, Swiss-style chalet, US$5 pp, German owner can take his jeep to Mocoya, from where it's a 4-hr hike to base camp for the climbs. A jeep can do the drive in under 7 hrs for about US$300 but make sure the driver knows where to go. One driver who does is Vitaliano Ramos (T La Paz 416013). If you have a jeep, the best access is: La Paz-Oruro road to Konani at Km 149 (garage – check everything and fill up tank plus extra containers with petrol) and turn left, then take Quime road to Caxata (55 km); 3 km after Caxata turn left to Rodeo (30 km); from here the road to Viloco (50 km) is very poor but spectacular, often passing the foot of glaciers. Alternatively, take the road to Ventilla then turn off up and left, through Tres Ríos and down to Lambate and then follow the Río Bajo to Araca (dry season only – wet season go via Quime).

For the Western Cordillera with the peaks of Sajama, Parinacota and Pomerape, see under Sajama, page 308, below.

The Cordillera Apolobamba, the N extension of the Cordillera Real, with many 5,000m-plus peaks, can be reached by public transport from La Paz, the main starting out points being **Charazani**, see page 297; bus from C Reyes Cardona, Cemetery district, Wed 1100, US$6, 18-24 hrs, to Pelechuco, also truck at Wed 0630, takes even longer, buy returns Fri 2000.

● **Equipment** The best selections are *Condoriri*, C Sagárnaga 339 (T/F 319369) opp *Hotel Alem*, open Mon to Fri 0930-1300, 1430-2000, Sat 0930-1200. They also do an excellent repair service and rent equipment, José Miranda is rec guide. *Andean Summits*, C Sagárnaga 189, T/F 317497, Casilla 6976, good selection of new camping and climbing gear. Best hire selection is at *Colibrí*, C Sagárnaga 309, T 371936, F 355043, Casilla 7456. The cheapest way to buy kit is from outgoing climbers. CAB has a noticeboard where you can advertise your wares for sale; many adventure travel agencies, inc those mentioned above, will buy secondhand kit.

● **Guidebooks** *Bolivia – a climbing guide*, Yossi Brain (The Mountaineers, Seattle, 1997). A paperback reprint of *La Cordillera Real de los Andes, Bolivia*, by Alain Mesili (Los Amigos del Libro, La Paz, 1984) is available in Spanish.

● **Guides**
Guides must be hired through a tour company. *Club Andino Boliviano*, C México 1638, T 324682, Casilla 5879 (closed Sat) can provide a list of guides. *Dr Hugo Berrios* (see above for contact) is an excellent guide, rec for Huayna Potosí. *Ozono*, Edif Labtec, PB, Av Ballivian y C14, Calacoto, La Paz, T 791786, F 722240, e-mail: bolivia@ozono.bo, British-Bolivian owned agency specializing in mountaineering, trekking, rock climbing and other types of adventure tourism, inc skiing, can also organize radio cover. *Colibrí*, address above, specialize in climbing, with up-to-date information, trips arranged for all levels of experience and adventure tourism in all parts of Bolivia, very helpful, rec, full range of equipment hire. *Colonial Tours*, next to Hostal Austria, provides information and advice on routes, organizes transport. Also recommended, *Ricardo Albert* at Inca Travel, Av Arce 2116, Edif Santa Teresa. *Dr Juan Pablo Ando*, Casillo 6210, T 783495, trained in Chamonix, for mountaineering, rock climbing, trekking and ecological tours.

The *Club de Excursionismo, Andinismo y Camping*, CEAC, helps people find the cheapest way to go climbing, trekking, etc; foreigners may join local groups, T 783795, Casilla 8365, La Paz, or ask at the University or for Catherina Ibáñez at Plaza Tours, Av 16 de Julio 1789, T 378322, F 343301 (she has an information service for CEAC). Each week there is a meeting and slide show.

SKIING

90 mins by car from La Paz (36 km) is **Chacaltaya**, the highest ski run in the world. Season: Dec-April, depending on conditions. Skiing equipment may be hired, and a rope-tow reaches a maximum altitude of 5,221m. The facilities are sub-

standard, emergency services non-existent and the rope-tow should be used with extreme caution. Midweek skiing is not possible unless a group makes prior arrangement with the Club Andino Boliviano (address above). The Club runs its own Sat and Sun excursions (mixed reports). The day trip, beginning at 0730 and returning at 1600, is US$10 for bus ticket, plus US$7 for equipment rental and hook. If you don't go with the club, entry to refuge is US$2; meals and hot drinks at weekends. Out of season the lift only goes if there are 5 or more people. Equipment is very limited, poor quality, queue at once; better take your own. A good tip is to share equipment since, at that altitude, you will need a long break between activities. No one should attempt to ski unless acclimatized at La Paz for at least a week. Sunglasses should block 100% of UV to avoid snowblindness. One can walk to the summit of Chacaltaya for views of Titicaca on one side, La Paz on the other, and Huayna Potosí. Tiring, as it is over 5,000m, but one has most of the day to do the climb. Laguna de Milluni, near Chacaltaya, is a beautiful lake to visit, but do not drink its heavily contaminated water. Take plenty of mineral water when going to the mountains as it's thirsty work in the rarefied air. (Chacaltaya skiing is described in Bradt's *South America Ski Guide*.)

● **Accommodation** For the really hardy, accommodation at the Chacaltaya ski station is free, but take very warm clothes, sleeping bag and bed roll, food and water, as there is no heating, or bedding. Meals are available at the hut at weekends.

● **Transport** Taxi or minibus US$30 (whole car) for a ½-day trip, or similar to the top by rented car costs about US$60, and really only at weekends. However, the trip can be hair-raising, buses carry no chains. Often the buses and tours only go half way. Many agencies do day trips, US$12.50, often combined with Valle de la Luna.

TIAHUANACO (TIWANAKU)

The ruins of Tiahuanako, not far from the village of Tiahuanaco, are 72 km W of La Paz, near the S end of Lake Titicaca.
The road from El Alto (La Paz) is paved and passes through the village of **Laja**

(Laxa), the first site of La Paz, at the junction of the roads between Potosí and Lima and Potosí and Arica. Laja's church was the first cathedral of the region. Its façade is mestizo baroque; the faces of King Ferdinand and Queen Isabella as Indians can be seen on the left bell tower (the right bell tower was built in 1903). The church has a solid silver altar, but is closed to visitors. Simple masses at US$1 available in village. Good views of the Cordillera at the highest point on the road between Laja and Tiahuanaco.

HISTORY

Many archaeologists believe that Tiahuanako existed as early as 1600 BC, while the complex visible today probably dates from the 8th to the 10th centuries AD. The site may have been a ceremonial complex at the centre of an empire which covered almost half Bolivia, S Peru, N Chile and NW Argentina. It was also a hub of trans-Andean trade. The Tiahuanaco civilization's demise, according to studies by Alan Kolata of the University of Illinois, could have been precipitated by the flooding of the area's extensive system of raised fields (*Sukakollu*), which were capable of sustaining a population of 20,000. The Pumapunka section, 1 km S of the main complex may have been a port, as the waters of the lake used to be much higher than they are today. The raised field system is being reutilized in the Titicaca area.

THE SITE

The main structures are: Kalasasaya, meaning 'standing stones', referring to the statues found in that part. Two of them, the Ponce monolith (centre of inner patio) and the Fraile monolith (SW corner), have been re-erected. In the NW corner is the Puerta del Sol, originally at Pumapunku. The split in the top probably occurred in the move. Its carvings, interrupted by being out of context, are thought to be either a depiction of the creator God, or a calendar. The motifs are exactly the same as those around the Ponce monolith. The Templo Semisubterráneo is a sunken temple whose walls are lined with faces, all different, according to some theories depicting states of health, the temple being a house of healing. The Akapana, originally a pyramid, was the largest structure, but is now no more than a hill. At Pumapunku, some of whose blocks weigh up to 100 tonnes, a natural disaster may have put a sudden end to the construction before it was finished.

The entrance ticket to Tiahuanaco costs US$2.50 for foreigners, including entry to museum; the site opens at 0900. There is a small museum at the ticket office. On the other side of the railway from the main site is the Museo Regional Arqueológico de Tiahuanaco, containing a well-illustrated explanation of the raised field system of agriculture. Most of the best statues are in the Museo Tiahuanaco or the Museo Semisubterráneo in La Paz. Locals sell copies of Tiwanaku figures; cheaper here than La Paz. Allow 4 hrs to see the ruins and village.

TIAHUANACO VILLAGE

Tiahuanaco, the present-day village, has arches at the four corners of its plaza, dating from the time of independence. The church, built 1580-1612, used precolumbian masonry. In fact, Tiahuanako for a long while was the 'quarry' for the altiplano.

Local festivals

21 June: at Tiahuanaco, before sunrise, colourful dances, llama sacrifices, etc. In Tiahuanaco village, on the 8th day of carnival (Sun), local carnival, colourful, souvenirs for sale, bargain hard, do not take photographs. Market day in Tiahuanaco is Sun; do not take photos then either.

Local information
● **Accommodation & places to eat**
G pp *Hostal-Restaurant El Puerto del Sol* is the last house on the right leaving the village to La Paz, clean, friendly, great lunch for US$1, owner is very knowledgeable about ruins. There are 3 restaurants on Tiahuanaco's main street serving *almuerzo* and *comida familiar*.

● **Guidebooks in English**
Tiwanaku, by Mariano Baptista, Plata Publishing Ltd, Chur, Switzerland, or *Discovering Tiwanaku* by Hugo Boero Rojo. They are obtainable from Los Amigos del Libro (or 2nd-hand from stalls in

Av Ismael Montes). *Guía Especial de Arqueología Tiwanaku*, by Edgar Hernández Leonardini, a guide on the site, rec. Written guide material is difficult to come by; hiring a good guide costs US$10. Map of site with historical explanation in English (published by Quipus) for sale at ticket office, US$2.50.

● **Transport**
Transportes Ingavi, José María Azin y Eyzaguirre (take any Micro marked 'Cementerio') US$1, 1½ hrs, almost hourly, first dep 0700 (frequency may change according to demand – the earlier you go the better). They are usually full. Tickets can be bought in advance. Taxi for 2 costs about US$25 (can be shared), return, with unlimited time at site (US$40 inc El Valle de la Luna). Some buses go on from Tiahuanaco to Desaguadero; virtually all Desaguadero buses stop at Tiahuanaco, US$0.65. Return buses (last one back 1730-1800) leave from Plaza in village.

Most tours from La Paz cost US$15 return; they stop at Laja and the highest point on the road before Tiahuanaco. Some tours include El Valle de la Luna.

LAKE TITICACA

Lake Titicaca is two lakes joined by the Straits of Tiquina: the larger, northern lake (Lago Mayor, or Chucuito) contains the Islas del Sol and de la Luna at its southern end; the smaller lake (Lago Menor, or Huiñamarca) has several small islands. The waters are a beautiful blue, reflecting the hills and the distant cordillera in the shallows of Huiñamarca, mirroring the sky in the rarified air and changing colour when it is cloudy or raining. Periodically the water level rises, inundating low-lying land, but its size is much reduced from prehispanic times. The trout fished in the lake and served in many restaurants is not native. The local catch is *pejerrey* and *karachi*. Also beginning to be farmed are the Lake's giant frogs, whose legs are served, fried, with chips, in several places. The totora-reed boats are still made, more as museum pieces than for practical purposes. Wood and fibreglass vessels last much longer. A trip on the lake is a must if in the area; boat services are given below.

● **Recommended reading**
Tristan Jones, who crossed South America in his sailing cutter *Sea Dart*, spent over 8 months cruising Lake Titicaca, see his book *The Incredible*

Voyage, Futura Publications. *An Insider's Guide to Bolivia*, by Peter McFarren, gives a good historical background, inc an interesting article about archaeological discoveries in Lake Titicaca, by Johann Reinhard (available in many bookshops and large hotels in La Paz). Reinhard also contributed a chapter on 'Underwater Archaeological Research in Lake Titicaca' to *Ancient America, Contributions to New World Archaeology*, edited by Nicholas J Saunders (Oxford: Oxbow Monograph 24, 1992).

LA PAZ TO COPACABANA

A paved road runs from La Paz to the Straits of Tiquina (114 km El Alto-San Pablo).

PUERTO PEREZ

Puerto Pérez is the closest point to La Paz on Lake Titicaca (72 km, less than 1 hr by car). The road to the port turns off the main road at **Batallas**, a typical Altiplano market town so named because of the final battles between Almagro and Pizarro. The views of the lake and mountains from Puerto Pérez are superb; the sunsets are spectacular, too. The port was the original harbour for La Paz, founded in the 19th century by British navigators as a harbour for the first steam boat on the Lake (the vessel was assembled piece-by-piece in Puno). Colourful fiestas are held on New Year's Day, Carnival (Mon and Tues before Ash Wed), 3 May and 16 July.

● **Accommodation & places to eat A3** *Hotel Las Balsas*, owned and operated by Turismo Balsa (see La Paz **Travel Agents**), T La Paz 357817, F 391310, in a beautiful lakeside setting, with views of the cordillera; all rooms have balcony over the lake. Advertised as 5-star; willing to negotiate out of season; fitness facilities inc pool, massage, jacuzzi, sauna, racket ball; T/F (2) 813226; restaurant expensive, but fixed price lunch or dinner good value at US$12. Nearby on the Plaza is **D** *Hostería Las Islas*, same owners, shared bath, hot water, heated rooms, comfortable, Blue Note jazz bar next door. Turismo Balsa operate boat trips to Suriqui and Kalahuta, and services to Puno and Cusco. Small restaurants in town serve trout.

● **Buses** There is a regular minibus service from La Paz Cementerio district: across from the cemetery, above the flower market, ask for buses to Batallas, price US$0.75.

HUARINA AND HUATAJATA

At **Huarina**, 42 km before Tiquina, a road turns off to Achacachi, Sorata and the road along the E shore of Titicaca to Puerto Acosta. The next town is **Huatajata**, with *Yacht Club Boliviano* (restaurant open to non-members, open Sat, Sun lunch only, sailing for members only) and Crillon Tours International Hydroharbour and *Inca Utama Hotel* (see below). Beyond here is **Chúa**, where there is fishing, sailing and Transturin's catamaran dock (see below). The public telephone office, Cotel, is on the plaza just off the main road.

● **Accommodation & places to eat** In Huatajata, next to Crillon's *Inca Utama*, is *Restaurant Huatajata Utama*, highly rec; then *Inti Raymi*, with boat trips; and others. The restaurants are of varying standard, most lively at weekends and in the high season. Máximo Catari's *Inti Karka* restaurant is on the road (full menu, open 7 days, average prices, good fish), also hotel, a 3-storey building on the waterfront (**F** pp, breakfast extra, basic, shower, water unreliable, some rooms with lake view, ask for extra blankets, T 813212).

Between Huatajata and Huarina (at Km 65 from La Paz) is the **B** *Hotel Titicaca*, T La Paz 374877, F 391225, beautiful views, sauna, pool, good restaurant, very quiet during the week (address in La Paz, Potosí y Ayacucho 1220, p 2).

About 2 km before Chúa is a turning to the right to *La Posada del Inca*, open Sat, Sun and holidays for lunch only, in a beautiful colonial *hacienda*, good trout, average prices.

● **Buses** La Paz-Huatajata/Tiquina, US$0.85, Transportes Titikaka, Av Kollasuyo 16, daily from 0400, returning between 0700 and 1800.

● **Tours 1)** Crillon Tours (address under La Paz **Travel Agents**), run a hydrofoil service on Lake Titicaca with excellent bilingual guides. Crillon's tours stop at the Andean Roots cultural complex at *Inca Utama*: the Bolivian History Museum includes a recorded commentary; a 15-min video precedes the evening visit to the Kallawaya (Native Medicine) museum, where you meet a Kallawaya fortune teller, very interesting. In all seven cultures are represented. The *Inca Utama* hotel has a health spa based on natural remedies; the 60 rooms are comfortable, with heating, electric blankets, good service, bar, good food in restaurant (5-star accommodation, **A1**, reservations through Crillon Tours, T La Paz 374566/350363). Also at Inca Utama is an observatory (*Alajpacha*) with retractable thatched roof for viewing the night sky, a floating restaurant and bar on the lake (*La Choza Nautica*), a new colonial-style tower with 15

de-luxe suites, panoramic elevator and 2 conference rooms. Health, astronomical, mystic and ecological programmes are offered. The hydrofoil trips include visits to Andean Roots complex, Copacabana, Isla del Sol and de la Luna, Straits of Tiquina and past reed fishing boats. See Isla del Sol below for *La Posada del Inca*. Trips can be arranged to/from Cusco and Machu Picchu, hydrofoil and train one way, flight the other; other combinations of hydrofoil and land-based excursions can be arranged (also jungle and adventure tours). Cost is US$173 from La Paz to Puno, US$145 for day excursion from La Paz; fascinating, not least for the magnificent views of the Cordillera on a clear day. All facilities and modes of transport connected by radio.

2) Transturin (see also La Paz **Travel Agents**) run catamarans on Lake Titicaca, either for sightseeing or on the La Paz-Puno route (US$129 La Paz-Copacabana; overnight at *Hotel Titicaca* and tour US$168). From their dock at Chúa, 3-hr trips go to Copacabana, with bar, video, sun deck and music on board. One-night tours to Copacabana are also available. The catamarans are slower than the hydrofoils of Crillon so there is more room and time for on-board entertainment. Transturin runs through services to Puno without a change of bus, and without many of the usual formalities at the border. Transturin has offices in Puno, Jr Libertad, T352771/351316, and Cusco, Av Portal de Panes 109, of 1, T 222332.

ISLANDS OF LAKE HUIÑAMARCA

On **Suriqui** (1½ hrs from Huatajata) you can visit the museum/craft shops of the Limachi brothers (now living at the *Inca Utama* cultural complex) and Paulino Esteban, who helped in the construction, out of totora reeds, of Thor Heyerdahl's *Ra II*, which sailed from Morocco to Barbados in 1970. Heyerdahl's *Tigris* reed boat, and the balloon gondola for the Nasca (Peru) flight experiment (see page 1311), were also constructed by the craftsmen of Suriqui. Reed boats are still made on Suriqui, probably the last place where the art survives. On **Kalahuta** there are *chullpas* (burial towers), old buildings and the uninhabited town of Kewaya. On **Pariti** there is Inca terracing and very good examples of weaving.

● **Boat trips** Máximo Catari (see above) arranges boats to the islands in Lago Huiñamarca, Pariti, Kalahuta and Suriqui: prices, to Suriqui US$22 for 4-5 people, to all 3 islands US$40, 1 hr boat trip US$7.50, sailing boat for 3 US$16 for a day (boat trips rec). Paulino Esteban (see

above) is also rec, contact through Servitur, PO Box 8045, La Paz, T 340060, F 391373. Boats can also be hired in Tiquina for trips to Suriqui, US$3 pp in a group.

From Chúa the main road reaches the E side of the Straits at San Pablo (clean restaurant in blue building, with good toilets). On the W side is San Pedro, the main Bolivian naval base, from where a paved road goes to Copacabana. Vehicles are transported across on barges, US$4. Passengers cross separately, US$0.20 (not included in bus fares) and passports are checked. Expect delays during rough weather, when it can get very cold.

158 km from La Paz, is an attractive little town on Lake Titicaca. It has a heavily restored, Moorish-style cathedral containing a famous 16th century miracle-working Dark Virgin of the Lake, also known as the Virgin of Candelaria, the patron saint of Bolivia.

Places of interest

The cathedral itself is notable for its spacious atrium with four small chapels; the main chapel has one of the finest gilt altars in Bolivia. The basilica is clean, white, with coloured tiles decorating the exterior arches, cupolas and chapels. Vehicles are blessed in front of the church daily, especially on Sun. An *hospicio* (serving now as an almshouse) with its two arcaded patios is worth a visit; ask permission before entering. There are 17th and 18th century paintings and statues in the sanctuary. Entrance at side of Basilica opp Entel; US$0.60, open Mon-Fri, 1100-1200, 1400-1800, Sat and Sun, 0800-1200, 1400-1800, only groups of 8 or more.

On the headland which overlooks the town and port, **Cerro Calvario**, are the Stations of the Cross. On the hill behind the town (Cerro Sancollani) overlooking the lake, roughly SE of the Basilica, is the **Horca del Inca**, two pillars of rock with another laid across them (probably a sun clock rather than a gallows, now covered in graffiti). There is a path marked by white stones. Boys will offer to guide you: fix price in advance if you want their help.

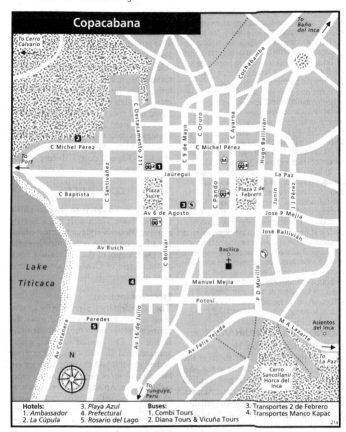

Copacabana

Hotels:
1. *Ambassador*
2. *La Cúpula*
3. *Playa Azul*
4. *Prefectural*
5. *Rosario del Lago*

Buses:
1. Combi Tours
2. Diana Tours & Vicuña Tours
3. Transportes 2 de Febrero
4. Transportes Manco Kapac

21a

Above the Horca, on the other side of the ridge, is the Flecha del Inca, an arrow-shaped hole in a rock. Also close to town is the cemetery at the Asientos (Seats) del Inca. Further from town is **El Baño del Inca**, about 2 km, entrance US$0.60, small museum. Follow C Junín out of town for 1½ km, then head for a large group of eucalyptus trees on hillside 500m away.

Excursions

There is a lovely walk along the lakeside N to Yampupata, 15 km (allow 3½ hrs), through unspoilt countryside. At the village of Sequañe ask for a row boat to Isla del Sol, or José Quispe Mamani who provides a motor launch, plus meals and accommodation.

Copacabana's water supply can be intermittent. Beware of sunburn especially on the lake, even when it does not feel hot. **NB** New arrivals may also be pressurized into paying for 'entry' to the town; the fee is in fact for the sanctuary.

Local festivals

1-3 Feb, *Virgen de la Candelaria*, massive procession, dancing, fireworks, bullfights. Easter, with candlelight procession on Good Friday. **2-5 May**, very colourful; **23**

June, San Juan, also on Isla del Sol; **4-6 Aug**, *La Virgen de Copacabana*. **NB** During these times the town gets very full and hotel prices quadruple.

Local information
● **Accommodation**

C *Playa Azul*, 6 de Agosto, T 320068, full board, rooms OK, but chilly, half-board a possibility, tepid electric showers, water supply and toilets poor, good food; **C** *Res Rosario del Lago*, Rigoberto Paredes between Av Costanera and Av 16 de Julio, same ownership as *Res Rosario*, La Paz, inc breakfast, colonial style, hot water (solar power), Turisbus office, all rooms with lake view, beautifully furnished, rec.

D *Ambassador*, Bolívar y Jauregui, balcony, heater US$2/day, cheaper without bath, rooftop restaurant, great beds, reduction for more than one night or with YHA card, luggage stored for US$2, rec; **D** *La Cúpula*, C Michel Pérez 1-3, T 0862-2029, **E** without bath, bright rooms, sitting room with TV and video, fully-equipped kitchen, library, hot water, book exchange, vegetarian restaurant, great breakfast, offer local tours, run by Amanda and Martin Stratker whose *Centro Cultural Arco y Hamaca* offers painting and sculpting classes and courses in Spanish and English, highly rec; **D** *Prefectural*, **D** pp full board, being refurbished late 1996.

E *Boston*, Conde de Lemos, nr basilica, T 0862-2231, **F** without bath, good, quiet; **E** *Res Sucre*, Murillo 228, T 2080, hot water, with bath, parking, quiet, good cheap breakfast, laundry US$3, offers tours of lake.

F *Alojamiento Aransaya*, Av 6 de Agosto 121, T 229, basic but clean, hot shower but water problems, good trout in restaurant, **F** *Alojamiento Aroma*, Av Jauregui, towards beach, hot showers, helpful and informative owner; **F** *Kota Kahuaña*, Av Busch 15, blue house, hot showers on request, cheap, quiet, some rooms with lake view, rec; **F** *El Turista*, Pando 378, inadequate shower facilities, otherwise rec; **F** *Res Porteña*, by market on Jauregui, safe, rec.

G *Emperador*, C Murillo, behind the Cathedral, popular, laundry service and facilities, shared hot showers, helpful for trips to Isla del Sol, highly rec; **G** *Hostal La Luna*, C José P Mejía, T 2051, hot showers, very comfortable, laundry, breakfast in room on request, changes TCs, can arrange discounts on trips to Isla del Sol, highly rec. Many other residenciales in **F** and **G** categories.

● **Places to eat**

On Plaza 2 de Febrero are *Napolés*, reasonable prices, does vegetarian tortilla, changes money; *Colonial*, decent lunch, good trout. On 6 de Agosto: *Snack 6 de Agosto*, good trout, big portions, some vegetarian dishes, serves breakfast; *Puerta del Sol*, good, excellent trout. Many other restaurants serve decent cheap meals and good trout. Good breakfasts and other meals, especially fish, in the market on C Ayaroa. Very few places open before 0800.

● **Banks & money changers**

Bidesa, same building as *Hotel Playa Azul*, open Wed-Fri 0830-1200, 1430-1700, Sat-Sun 0830-1430. Several *artesanías* on Av 6 de Agosto buy and sell US$ and soles. Many shops (and bank) are closed on Mon and Tues, as they are open on Sun.

● **Post & telecommunications**

Entel: open Sun-Tues 0800-2000, Wed-Sat 0800-2100. **Post Office**: open Mon-Sat 0900-1200, 1400-1800, Sun 0900-1300.

● **Tourist offices**

Tourist Information kiosk on Plaza 2 de Febrero helpful when open. Motorcycles and bicycles can be hired; ask boys at the beach, but bargain.

● **Tour companies & travel agents**

Fremen, Tumusla 0245, T 59392, F 59686.

● **Transport**

Road By car from La Paz to Copacabana (direct), 4 hrs, take exit to 'Río Seco' in El Alto; the road is paved all the way. **Bus**: from La Paz: agency buses charge US$4 and dep La Paz 0800, Copacabana 1330, 4 hrs (Diana Tours, *Hotel Ambassador*, Plaza Sucre; Combi Tours, main plaza, T 2110; Vicuña Tours, C 6 de Agosto, 2 blocks from main plaza, T 2155); public buses US$2.35 plus US$0.20 for Tiquina crossing, several departures daily between 0700-1700 (1730 Sat-Sun with Manco Capac, T 2234, or 350033 in La Paz; 2 de Febrero, T 2233, or 377181, La Paz; both have offices on Copacabana's main plaza and in La Paz at Plaza Reyes Ortíz, opp entrance to cemetery. Note that buses for La Paz are very full on Sun afternoons. 1-day trips from La Paz are not rec as they allow only 1½-2 hrs in Copacabana. Copacabana-**Yunguyo** (Peru), agency buses are Combi, Diana, Vicuña and Turisbus (Av 6 de Agosto), US$3.30-US$4.25 depending on season. For public transport, see **Frontier via Copacabana** below. It is also possible to catch a tour bus to Cusco, usually dep around 1400, tickets US$17-20, change bus in Puno, tour company arranges connection. Bus to **Huatajata**, US$2.10 and to **Huarina**, US$2.50.

ISLA DEL SOL

The site of the Inca creation legend is a short distance by boat from Copacabana. A sacred rock at its NW end is worshipped as the birthplace of Manco Kapac and Mama Huaca, the first Incas. On the E shore near the jetty for Crillon Tours' hydrofoils and other craft is the Fuente del Inca, a pure spring, and Inca steps leading up from the water. A 2-km walk from the landing stage takes one to the main ruins of Pilkokaima (the Sun Gate from the ruins is now kept in the main plaza in Copacabana), a 2-storey building with false domes and superb views, entry US$1.20. Southeast of the Isla del Sol is the **Isla de la Luna** (or Coati), which also may be visited – the best ruins are an Inca temple and nunnery, both sadly neglected.

Local information
● Accommodation
It is worthwhile staying overnight on the Isla del Sol to have the many beautiful walks through villages and Inca terraces, some still in use. It is not possible to see all the sites on the Isla del Sol and return to Copacabana in 1 day; it's 4 hrs on foot from one end of the island to the other. Take camping equipment, all food and water (or water sterilizers), or stay in one of the many basic *posadas* on the island. Most of these are at Yumani, on the S side nr the Inca steps: *La Posada del Inca* is a restored colonial hacienda, owned by Crillon Tours, solar-powered electricity and hot water, with bath, dining room, 2-4 day trekking opportunities, stays linked with hydrofoil itineraries. There are several others, all **G** pp, basic but clean, no electricity or hot water, meals provided US$1-2; *El Imperio del Sol*, is rec as very friendly and comfortable, it is uphill from the school, on the right. Also **G** pp *Albergue Inca Sama*, next to Pilkokaima ruins, sleep on mattresses on floor, good food, also camping in typical tents (contact via *Hotel Playa Azul*, Copacabana, or La Paz T 356566/357817, or Entel office in Yumani T 0811-5006), Sr Pusari, offers boat service from Copacabana and trips to the N of island. Accommodation also at Challa, on the NE coast, **G** pp, on the beach, beer or refrescos for sale; and several places to stay around the Plaza in Challapampa, at the N end of the island.

● Transport
Inca Tours and Titicaca Tours run boats (latter rec); tickets are sold at **La Cúpula** (see **Accommodation**). Boats leave Copacabana at 0815 and leave the island at 1530-1600, arriving back at 1730. With the same ticket you can stay on the island and return another day. Half-day tours and tours which include N and S of Isla del Sol and Isla de La Luna in 1 day are not rec (too short). A tour inc Isla del Sol & La Luna costs US$5 pp.

Tour boats to Isla del Sol often stop only briefly at the jetty by the Fuente del Inca. Crillon's hydrofoils stop for 45 mins.

To hire a rowing boat in Copacabana costs US$4.50/hr.

FRONTIER WITH PERU

There are three routes from La Paz to Puno (see also Peru **Frontier with Bolivia**, page 1336).

ALONG THE WEST SIDE OF LAKE TITICACA

The road and railway (no passengers) go from La Paz 91 km W to **Guaqui**, formerly the port for the Titicaca passenger boats (*Res Guaqui*, nr port, good value, basic, friendly; tiny restaurant on the Plaza de Armas has been recommended). The road crosses the border at **Desaguadero** 22 km further W and runs along the shore of the lake to Puno.

● Bolivian immigration
Just before the bridge. Open 0830-1230 and 1400-2030. 30 days normally given; ask for more if you need it. Get exit stamp, walk a few hundred metres across the bridge then get entrance stamp on the other side. Get visa in La Paz.

● Accommodation & places to eat
G pp *Res San Francisco*, looks OK; also *Hotel Bolivia*, *Alojamiento Avaroa II*, and a couple of very basic places to stay on the Peruvian side. There are several restaurants on both sides of bridge.

● Exchange
Money changers just over the bridge on Peruvian side give reasonable rates.

● Transport
Road unpaved to Tiahuanaco, rough in parts. Buses from La Paz to Guaqui and Desaguadero depart from Ingavi office (José María Asu y Eyzaguirre) 0745 and 1000, US$1.40, 3½ hrs. From Desaguadero to La Paz last bus dep 1700, buses may leave later if enough passengers, but charge a lot more. Frequent buses to Puno until 1930, US$2, 3 hrs.

VIA COPACABANA

From Copacabana an unpaved road leads S to the Bolivian frontier at Kasani, then to Yunguyo. Do not photograph the border area. For La Paz tourist agency services on this route see under International Buses (page 284) and under Lake Titicaca above.

● Bolivian immigration
Border closes at 1900 (Bolivian time). Buses/colectivos stop here and at the Peruvian side; or you can walk, 400m, between the two posts. There should be a statutory 72 hrs period outside Bolivia before renewing a visa but 24 hrs

is usually acceptable. Ask for 90 days on return. 30 days is often given on entering Bolivia, but no problems extending in La Paz. If crossing into Bolivia with a motorcycle, do not be fooled into paying any unnecessary charges to police or immigration.

● **Exchange**
Money can be changed in Yunguyo and soles can be changed in Copacabana (see above).

● **Transport**
Transport does not start till Yunguyo, a further 600m. Colectivo Copacabana-Kasani US$0.50 pp, Kasani-Yunguyo US$0.60 pp. Make sure, if arranging a through ticket La Paz-Puno, that you get all the necessary stamps en route, and ascertain whether your journey involves a change of bus. Note the common complaint that through services La Paz-Puno (or vice versa) deteriorate once the border has been crossed, eg smaller buses are used, extra passengers taken on, passengers left stranded if the onward bus is already full, drivers won't drop you where the company says they will.

ALONG THE EAST SIDE OF LAKE TITICACA

The Peruvian authorities do not officially recognize the road as being a border crossing. Officially, you must get your entry stamp in the Department of Puno, but as this is next to impossible on this route, you will run into difficulties later on. The road passes through Achacachi (see page 303), Ancoraimes (small Sun market), Carabuco (with colonial church), **Escoma**, which has a large Aymara market every Sun morning, and **Kasiri Puerto Acosta**. The area around Puerto Acosta is good walking country and the locals are friendly. From La Paz to Puerto Acosta the road is fine during the dry season (approximately May to October). North of Puerto Acosta towards Peru the road deteriorates rapidly and should not be attempted except in the dry season.

There is an immigration office, but it is advisable to get an exit stamp in La Paz first.

● **Accommodation** G *Alojamiento Espinosa*, basic, friendly, but no restaurants.

● **Buses** La Paz (Cementerio district)-Puerto Acosta, US$3.25, Fri 1130, Sat/Sun 0630. Many trucks travel La Paz-Puerto Acosta on Tues and Fri afternoons. The only transport beyond Acosta is early on Wed and Sat mornings when a couple of trucks go to the markets, some 25 km from Puerto Acosta on the border (no formalities).

ESCOMA TO CHARANAZI

At Escoma a road branches N, roughly parallel with the border, going to Chuma, and to **Charazani** in the Yungas (official name Juan José Pérez; Ulla-Ulla *fiesta*, 16 July; witch doctor; thermal baths, US$1; **G** pp *Hotel Charazani*, good, clean, friendly; 2 restaurants). The road is very scenic, climbing to 4,500m. At the highest point is a sign to the **Reserva Ulla Ulla**, where llamas, alpacas, vicuñas, vizcachas and many birds can be seen, with the backdrop of the Cordillera de Apolobamba. Visitors can stay at the reserve office at La Cabaña, near Ulla Ulla (beds and food available). Camping is possible, ask for the thermal springs, or for permission at farms (payment welcome). Eight park guard posts were due to be opened June 1997, including Charazani, Curva and Pelechuco. Ulla Ulla-Charazani by car 3-4 hrs.

● **Buses** To Charazani depart from 4 blocks above Cementerio in La Paz, Fri, Sat, Sun 0600, US$4.40, 10 hrs, return Sun, Mon, Tues. The road ends at Apolo.

Also in the area is **Iskanwaya**, a major archaeological site on the eastern Andean slopes. A road from the Escoma-Charazani road crosses a 5,000m pass before descending to Aucapata; continue down a very poor jeep track then hike 1 hr down a cactus-filled canyon to the ruin (at about 1,500m). The city stands on two built-up platforms, with delicate walls, plazas, narrow streets, storerooms, niches, pot shards, etc. Admission to the museum in Aucapata is by donation. Great care is needed not to damage this site. Guidebook: *Iskanwaya: la ciudadela que sólo vivía de noche*, Hugo Boero Rojo (Los Amigos del Libro, 1992).

● **Transport** Truck (and rumours of a bus) from Cementerio, La Paz, Fri 0200 to Aucapata, 27 hrs, then walk to ruins. Hire a jeep for US$400 round trip: one driver who knows the way is Oscar Vera, La Paz T 230453. Alternatively take irregular transport from Sorata to Consata, get off above bridge called Boca de Lobo over Río San Cristóbal (which becomes the Llica).

The Yungas

T HE lush forested slopes behind the mountains to the north of La Paz is the main production area of citrus, bananas, coffee and coca leaves for the capital. It is also a favourite retreat for those escaping the Andean chill.

LA PAZ TO THE YUNGAS

The Yungas can be approached either via La Cumbre, NE of La Paz, or by turning off the road which skirts the E shore of Lake Titicaca and crossing the Cordillera to Sorata. The routes join at Caranavi, so a circular route can be made (see map, page 287).

The route NE out of La Paz circles cloudwards over La Cumbre pass at 4,725m; the highest point is reached in an hour; all around are towering snowcapped peaks. Soon after Unduavi the paving ends, the road becomes 'all-weather' and drops over 3,400m to the green semi-tropical forest in 80 km. The roads to Chulumani and Coroico divide just after Unduavi, where there is a *garita* (check point), the only petrol station, but no good place to eat. Note, if travelling by truck from La Paz to the Yungas via La Cumbre, the best views can be seen in May and June, when there is least chance of fog and rain on the heights. It is very cold at La Cumbre and, further down, there are waterfalls at San Juan that baptise open vehicles – be prepared. For the La Cumbre-Coroico hike (Choro), see page 285.

Chulumani (*alt* 1,700m), the capital of Sud Yungas, is an attractive, relaxed little town with beautiful views. Fiesta 24 August.

Excursions

Apa Apa Ecological Park, 8 km away, is the last area of original Yungas forest with lots of interesting wildlife. US$10 park fee including transport and hiking guide; campsite with bathrooms. The road to Irupana (see below) passes the turn-off to the park; ask to get off and walk 15 mins up to *hacienda* of Ramiro Portugal and his wife, Tildi (both speak English); or T 0811-6106 to arrange transport from town; or T (La Paz) 790381, or write to Casilla 10109, Miraflores, La Paz. From Chulumani it is 1½ hrs to **Irupana** (Fiesta 5 Aug; **F** *Hotel Casablanca*, with pool, recommended; several basic, cheap places to stay); bus dep around 1100, US$1, or take any passing truck at the *tránsito*; it can be difficult getting back. Another road to Irupana goes via the ancient village of **Ocabaya**, where the Bolivian revolution began, and passes through **Chicaloma**. Transport from *tránsito* is infrequent; ask around.

Local information
● Accommodation

A3 *Villas San Bartolomé*, 2 km from *tránsito* down Irupana road, arrange hotel transport beforehand if arriving by bus, no taxis, pleasant, superb setting with fabulous views of mountains, swimming pool, can be booked through the *Hotel Plaza*, La Paz, T 378311, Ext 1221 (or Plaza Tours in La Paz).

D pp *La Glorieta*, 30-40 mins walk beyond *Hotel Panorama*, nr top of Loma Linda, spectacular views, shared bath, comfortable, tastefully furnished, restaurant (vegetarian on request), book through Sra Aida de Carrasco at *Hotel Panorama*; **D** *La Hostería*, Junín, nr *tránsito*, T (0811) 6108, **E** without bath, inc breakfast, bar, good restaurant, highly rec; **D** *Panorama*, at top of hill on Murillo, T (0811) 6109, comfortable, garden, restaurant, pool; **D-E** *Res El Milagro*, good views, at entrance to town by *tránsito*, lovely garden with great views.

E *García*, on Plaza Libertad, cheaper without bath, basic, restaurant, noisy at weekends from disco.

G pp *Alojamiento Chávez*, by *tránsito*, shared bath, basic but clean, restaurant.

● **Places to eat**

Don Miguel, just off Junín, on left heading towards Plaza, German-owned, good, fondue speciality, rents comfortable rooms **D** pp full board, with bath and TV; *El Mesón*, on Plaza, good cheap meals. Many cheap places around *tránsito*.

● **Transport**

Buses from La Paz: Trans San Bartolomé, C Ocabaya 435, Villa Fátima (first street on right off Virgen del Carmen, which is first left off Av Las Américas opp YPFB petrol station), T 211674, daily at 0800 and 1230, 4 hrs, US$2.50, return from Plaza daily at 0600 and 1200; Turbus Totai, at top of C Yanacachi, Villa Fátima, T 210607, daily at 0730, 0900, 1100 and 1400 (to Irupana Thur at 0730).

COROICO

The other branch from Unduavi leading to Yolosa, the junction 8 km from Coroico, is steep, twisting, clinging to the side of sheer cliffs, and it is very slippery in the wet. To avoid danger, abide by the rules of the road, especially at weekends. Uphill vehicles always have right of way; downhill must wait or reverse to a passing place. Uphill drives on the cliff side, be it left or right, downhill on the outside.

The little town of **Coroico** is perched on a hill at 1,760m amidst beautiful scenery. The hillside is covered with orange and banana groves; coffee is also grown. One of several good walks is up Uchumachi, the mountain behind El Calvario. Follow the Stations of the Cross by the cemetery, off C Julio Zuazo Cuenca which leads uphill from the plaza. Look

for the red and white antenna behind church; from there it's 1½ hrs uphill. A good local guide is César Argandoña; ask for him in plaza.

Local festivals

There is a colourful 4-day festival on **19-22 Oct**, when accommodation is hard to find. It is great fun, but wait a day or two before returning to La Paz (hung-over drivers). On **2 Nov**, All Souls' Day, the local cemetery is festooned with black ribbons.

Local information
● Accommodation

1 km out of town on road to Caranavi is *El Viejo Molino*, 4-star, with pool, T 0811-6004 (in La Paz, Valmar Tours, T 361076, F 352279).

E pp *Esmeralda*, T 0811-6017, 5 mins uphill from plaza (Casilla 9225, La Paz), cheaper without bath and view, free pick-up service (ring from *Totai Tours*), German owned, English spoken, pool, restaurant, hikes arranged, Visa, Mastercard taken, credit card phones, great views, fantastic hot showers, videos, excellent restaurant, garden, pool, laundry service, best to book ahead, highly rec; **E** *Hostal Kory*, at top of steps leading down from plaza, pool, cheaper without bath (weekly rates available), not always hot water, very helpful, lovely terrace, restaurant, laundry, good beds; **E** *La Casa*, down hill from *Hostal Kory*, hot water, pool, good restaurant (see below); **E** *Lluvia de Oro*, 1 block from church, good value, food rec, cheap, pool, top floor rooms are best; **E-F** *Sol y Luna*, 15-20 mins beyond *Hotel Esmeralda*, dormitory accommodation **G** pp, meals available, Indonesian banquet rec, also 2 *cabañas* for rent with kitchen, **D**, camping US$1 pp, small pool, garden, laundry service, highly rec, reserve through Chuquiago Turismo, Planta Baja, Edif La Primera, Av Santa Cruz 1364, Casilla 4443, La Paz, T 362099/359227.

F pp *La Casa Colonial*, on street uphill from church, shared bath, comfortable, good value; **G** pp *El Cafetal*, beside hospital, French-run, very nice, long walk from town, good value; **G** pp *Hostal Peregrino*, on Julio Zuazo Cuenca, cold water only, restaurant (good soups), good breakfast, nice terrace; on same street is **G** pp *Res de la Torre*, nice garden. Campsite by the small church on the hill overlooking the town (see above). Hotels can be difficult at holiday weekends and, as the area is a popular retreat for the rich from La Paz, prices are higher.

● Places to eat

La Casa German-run, good food and setting, excellent salads, vegetarian dishes, fondue and

raclette for dinner (reserve in advance), wonderful views, rec; the convent opp sells biscuits, peanut butter, wine and coffee liqueurs. *Confitería Claudia Paola*, next to Turbus Totai on plaza, pizza etc, good; *Back-Stube*, next to Hostal Kory, good cakes, muesli, delicious vegetarian lunch and dinner (not Tues), friendly atmosphere. Honey is sold in various places.

● Banks & money changers

No banks. Change TCs at Turbus Totai (poor rates), *Hostal Kory*, or *Hotel Esmeralda* (decent rates).

● Post & telecommunications

Post Office and Tourist Info on plaza. **Entel**, on Sagárnaga next to Flota Yungueña, for international and local calls; **Cotel**, next to church, phones, public TV.

● Transport

From La Paz all companies are on C Yanacachi, beside YPFB station in Villa Fátima: Turbus Totai (T 212391), US$2.50, 3 hrs, 6 daily from 0830-1730 (return to La Paz 0700-1730 daily except Sun); Flota Yungueña (T 212344), 5 daily from 0800-1600; worth booking in advance. Best views on left hand side on the descent to Yungas. Extra services run on Sun. It can be difficult to book journeys to La Paz on holidays and on Sun evenings/Mon mornings (though these are good times for hitching). Trucks and pick-ups from La Paz may drop you at Yolosa, 8 km from Coroico; there is usually transport Yolosa-Coroico, US$1, or you can walk, uphill all the way, 2 hrs. In Coroico trucks leave from the market. Buses, trucks and pick-ups run from Yolosa to **Caranavi**, 3-4 hrs, US$3.25, **Guanay**, 7-8 hrs, US$5.20 and **Rurrenabaque**, daily at 1500 with Yungueña, daily except Sun at 1730, with Turbus Totai, US$8.75, 13-15 hrs, company will take you down to Yolosa to catch bus from La Paz.

Between Coroico and Chulumani is **Coripata** (**F** *Hotel Florida*), beyond which you enter the main coca growing area of N Bolivia. At Puente Villa (**C** *Hotel Tamapaya*, just outside, beautiful setting, with shower, good rooms, swimming pool, recommended) the road joins the Unduavi-Chulumani road. No public transport between Coroico and Chulumani.

CARANAVI

From the road junction at Yolosa the lower fork follows the river NE to **Caranavi**, a very ugly town 164 km from La Paz, 75 km from Yolosa, at times the road follows a picturesque gorge, towards the settled area of the Alto Beni. Market day is Sat; lots of transport in late afternoon.

● **Accommodation** Mainly along Av Mcal Santa Cruz, the main street: **E** *Landiva*, T (0811) 6234, pool; **F** *Caranavi*, rec; **F** *Res Avenida*, basic and cheap; **F** *Alojamiento Capitol*, basic; **G** *Hostal La Paz*, clean, basic.

● **Places to eat** *Paradiso*, cheap; *Tropical*, good set menu and cheap.

● **Buses** From Villa Fátima in **La Paz**; Yungueña daily at 1300, Turbus Totai (T 212526), at 1530, 6-7 hrs; continue to Rurrenabaque. Direct bus **Coroico**-Caranavi on Sun, or you can take a truck, US$2.15. If you want to continue into the Beni Lowlands without going into Caranavi, wait at the checkpoint before the town where all transport has to stop and ask for a ride there.

GUANAY

Some 70 km NW of Caranavi is the gold mining town of **Guanay**, an interesting, friendly place at the junction of the Tipuani and Mapiri rivers.

● **Accommodation** **E** *Panamericana*, helpful, popular with tour groups; **F** pp *Perla Andina*, cold water, rooms on street less hot than those on courtyard, fans in rooms but electricity 1800-2400 only; **F** *Hotel Ritzy*, on main plaza, with mosquito nets; **G** pp *Alojamiento Los Pinos*, opp football pitch, cold water, basic, may arrange exchange of TCs (with commission – cash can be changed with shopkeepers or gold dealers); **G** pp *Estrella Azul*, basic; **G** pp *Pahuichi*, nice restaurant. Camping is possible next to the football field.

● **Places to eat** *Restaurant La Bamba*, opp *Panamericana*, good value, English spoken. Many other eating places on main street have fixed-price meals; one, with courtyard, monkey and parrot, serves excellent value breakfast. Electricity is rationed – every 10 mins or so – and water is available before 1200 only.

● **Transport Road** Buses direct from La Paz; Yungueña and Estrella Azul, about US$8, also trucks, which make frequent stops and diversions. Frequent transport to Caranavi. **River** To Mapiri: from Guanay dock, 3 blocks from plaza, boats leave at 0700 daily, or when full, US$5. Do not rely on cargo boats at other times. En route mines can be seen among the tropical vegetation. Boats go down the Río Beni to **Rurrenabaque** (see page 336), 8-12 hrs, US$11-18 depending on how successfully you negotiate and availability of vessels. Cargo is now carried by road so you have to wait till the boat is full, which can take several days. 'Expreso' boats can be hired from Flota Fluvial, opp *Perla Andina*, US$150-300 depending on size and your ability to bargain. The journey goes through gold mining settlements, then narrow, fertile river banks.

MAPIRI

This ugly mining town on the river of the same name (**G** pp *Alojamiento Porvenir*, best in town) is the starting point for an adventurous route up into the mountains. It goes via Sorata Limitada (a mining town, not to be confused with Sorata) and Santa Rosa to Sorata, thence, completing the Yungas circuit, back to La Paz. The scenery is superb, but the road is narrow, slippery, dangerous and dirty, especially in the rainy season. Try to sit in front with driver; there is usually a carpet to protect passengers against rain, but there is also a lot of dust. Have warm clothing handy for the road crosses the pass at 4,700m before dropping to Sorata.

● **Accommodation & transport** Camionetas run (2 hrs in dry season), to Santa Rosa (*Res Judith*, nice, with pool, wait here for lift to La Paz or Sorata). At Sorata Limitada there are 2 basic *alojamientos*, both **G**, the one beside the football pitch is quieter than the one beside the bar. Camionetas leave for Sorata from Sorata Limitada, US$13, 14 hrs and from Santa Rosa, US$9, 10 hrs.

SORATA

Sorata is a beautiful place, set in a valley at the foot of Illampu, at 2,695m. All around are lovely views and ideal country for hiking and climbing. The plaza, with its trees and, on a clear day, the snow-capped summit of Illampu as a backdrop, is delightful. The market area is near the plaza, ½ block down Muñecas on the right. Market day is Sun; fiesta 14 September.

Local information
● **Accommodation**

C pp *Ex-Prefectural*, at entrance to town, T/F 5201, full board, **E** pp room only, bath, hot water, restaurant, bar, pool, sauna, disco, nice garden, English, French and German spoken, group discounts, arranges treks, rec.

E pp *Copacabana*, 20 mins downhill from the centre (look for the signs), T/F 5042, **F** pp with shared bathroom, good restaurant, nice views.

F *Hostal Panchita*, on plaza, T 5038, shared bath, large rooms, hot water, laundry facilities, good restaurant; **F** pp *Paraíso*, Villavicencio 117, T 5043, with bath, breakfast extra, hot water, smart, restaurant; **F** pp *Res Sorata*, just off plaza, T (0811) 5044, **G** pp with shared bath at the back, huge rooms, some with private bath, hospitable, beautifully-furnished public rooms, excellent restaurant, big garden, laundry facilities, Louis from Quebec has good info and maps on local walks, highly rec.

G pp *San Cristóbal*, Muñecas 350, nr market, basic, shared bath, no single rooms, meals available.

● **Places to eat**
Ristorante Italiana, follow signs from plaza, good Italian cuisine inc vegetarian dishes, homemade ice cream, not cheap but worth it; *La Terraza*, cheap, good breakfast; *Santa Rosa*, on plaza, cheap meals; *El Tigre*, C Ingavi just off plaza, cheap lunches, open late, good value; *Girasol*, plaza at 143, excellent food, rec.

● **Banks & money changers**
Change dollars in shops on plaza displaying signs.

● **Post & telecommunications**
Post Office: on N side of plaza. Two **Entel** offices on plaza (eg *Hostal Panchita*).

● **Shopping**
For handicrafts, *Artesanía Sorata* on plaza, also cashes TCs and accepts them as payment.

● **Transport**
Buses From La Paz with Larecaja and Trans Unificada (both from Kollasuyo in Cemetery district); at least hourly 0630-1330, 5 hrs, US$2; Larecaja has its office on N side of plaza in Sorata; from Sorata 10 deps daily 0500-1430 (more at weekends). Plenty of **trucks** in am from Cemetery district, La Paz, to Sorata. Take your passport for the military checkpoint at Achacachi; don't leave anything on bus when getting off to register.

HIKING AND CLIMBING

The climbing season is end of April to beginning of September. Sorata is the starting point for climbing **Illampu** and Ancohuma (experience and full equipment necessary).

Louis at *Res Sorata* can arrange guides (US$8/day plus food), mules (US$8) and will provide up-to-date information. Club Sorata (at *Hotel Copacabana*) rents equipment and can arrange treks, guides and mules, very expensive; much cheaper to make arrangements yourself (which is permissible, despite claims to the contrary). Bring all equipment if not doing tour with Club Sorata, there is none for hire otherwise.

When trekking in this area avoid glacier melt water for drinking and treat with iodine all other water.

There are lots of walking possibilities. The most popular is to **San Pedro cave**, beyond the village of San Pedro. You can swim in the underground 'lake', though cave is said to be in poor condition. Entry US$0.60, toilets at entrance; a good flashlight is essential; best not to go alone. It is reached either by road, a 12 km walk (2 hrs) each way, or by a path along the Río San Cristóbal (about 3½ hrs one way). Get clear directions before setting out. Take water, at least 1 litre pp, or else take sterilizing tablets and fill up at the tap in San Pedro. Ask for the house selling refrescos in San Pedro.

A highly recommended hike is to Laguna Chillata and Inca Marka, a strenuous full-day walk, climbing from Sorata to 4,207m (either take plenty of water, or a water filter). Go with a guide because this is a sensitive area; the lake is sacred and Inca Marka is a burial place, dating back to the precolumbian Mollu culture. Camping is forbidden; do not touch anything, not even bits of paper, bottles, etc, which may be offerings.

The '**Circuito Illampu**', a 5-7-day high-altitude trek (5 passes over 4,500m) around Mt Illampu, is excellent. It can get very cold and it is a hard walk, though very beautiful with nice campsites on the way. Some food can be bought in Cocoyo on the 3rd day. You must be acclimatized before setting out.

It is also possible to hike from Sorata to Lake Titicaca. It is much cheaper to go to Sorata and ask about trekking there than to book up a trek with an agency in La Paz. See warning in **Hiking**, page 359.

Gold digger's trail

Sorata is the starting point for two treks into the Yungas. The '**Camino del Oro**', a 7-8 days hike to Guanay, rises to 4,741m (Abra Illampu) before going to Ancoma (1½ days from Sorata), then Wainapata, Chusi, 18 hrs from Ancoma (shop), Llipi, 8 hrs from Chusi and Unutulumi (2-3 hrs from Llipi, from here a *camioneta* runs daily to Guanay, US$5, 0930, winding through the many gold-digging towns in the Tipuani valley). After Ancoma it is very hot. The Ancoma-Llipi section is the most interesting, following the Tipuani River, climbing Inca staircases, crossing rivers on precarious plank bridges and going through an Inca tunnel. Very strenuous, not much flat ground for camping.

The Mapiri trail

Built to facilitate the transport of quinine out of the Mapiri area and finished in 1879, the trail goes from Ingenio to Mapiri. The Bolivian army used the trail to get to Acre in 1903, arriving one month too late to prevent Brazil annexing the area, and Colonel Fawcett used it in 1906. It was used by rubber traders until the 1950s and then fell into disuse until reopened by miners looking for gold in 1989. The starting point is Ingenio, 4 hrs from Sorata by pick-up, US$6. As long as the path has been used or cut recently, route finding is straightforward. The main problem is a lack of water along the way. Ask Louis Demers at the Residencial Sorata for more information on this tough 7-8 day trek. From Mapiri, continue to Guanay by boat. Matthew Parris, author of *Inca Kola: a traveller's tale of Peru*, adds: "Your camps must be waterproof and insect-excluding. If you don't like flies, wasps, bees and ants, don't go. Much of your time will be spent crawling along rock-bottomed trenches and under logs. You will be rewarded with parrots, butterflies, flowers, tree-ferns, millions of tons of moss and with unbelievable views over thousands of square miles of near-vertical cloud forest, utterly unpenetrated by man."

SORATA TO LA PAZ

The road to the capital leaves Sorata, descends to the river, crosses a bridge and climbs up the side of the valley. It continues climbing, in a landscape of huge valleys and ridges, to a pass in fields with stone walls and boulders before reaching the openness of the altiplano. Between Warisata and Achacachi is a tremendous marsh, with sheets of water, dykes, farms, cattle, people working the fields and many birds; in the distance snow-capped peaks can be seen.

ACHACACHI

There are good views of Lake Titicaca from the church up the hill from the left side of the plaza (which looks as if it was once prosperous). Interesting Sun market. Fiesta 14 September. The market is behind the main plaza. It is possible to walk to the lake in 1½ hrs.

- **Accommodation & places to eat** None of the three *alojamientos* is clean or welcoming, better stay somewhere else; 2 restaurants.
- **Buses** Plenty of buses to La Paz in the morning, US$1.30; from La Paz to Achacachi every 15 mins from Cemetery district (opp side of Av Kollasuyo from Sorata buses). Achacachi is a good place for connections if coming from Peru to Sorata: from Copacabana take a bus to Huarina, change there for a bus direct to Sorata. Sorata to Peru: take a La Paz bus and get out at Huarina; from there take a bus to Copacabana (best done in the morning).

Oruro and Routes to Chile and Argentina

THE mining town of Oruro with its famous carnival, vast salt-flats, multi-coloured lakes and volcanoes are all found in this remote, starkly beautiful corner of Bolivia which borders Chile and Argentina.

ORURO

Oruro, built at the side of some hills, became famous as a mining town, but there are no longer any working mines. It is, however, an important railway junction and the commercial centre for the mining communities of the altiplano, as well as hosting the country's best-known carnival. (*Pop* 183,422, mostly Indian; *alt* 3,706m; 230 km SE of La Paz; *phone code* 052).

Places of interest

Several fine buildings in the centre hint at the city's former importance, notably the **baroque concert hall** (now a cinema) on Plaza 10 de Febrero and the **Casa de la Cultura** (see below under **Museums**) built as a mansion by the tin 'baron' Simón Patiño. There is a good view of the city from the **Cerro Corazón de Jesus**, near the church of the **Virgen del Socavón**, 5 blocks W of Plaza 10 de Febrero at the end of C Mier. The **zoo** is not really worth a

special visit. The disused **San José mine**, worked for over 450 years for silver, tin and other minerals, lies 3 km W of the city. It can be visited with a permit from Comibol, the state mining company (the Tourist Office will assist; the *Intendencia* of the mine will provide a guide). A 20,000 tonnes-a-year tin smelter nearby at **Vinto** is open to visitors with a permit; apply 24 hrs in advance in Oruro.

Museums

Museo Etnográfico Minero, under the Church of the Virgen del Socavón, W end of C Mier, containing mining equipment and other artefacts from the beginning of the century as well as a 'tío', entry via the church 0900-1200, 1430-1800, US$0.50. **Casa de la Cultura**, Soria Galvarro 5755, formerly one of the Patiño residences, now run by the Universidad Técnica de Oruro, contains European furniture and a coach imported from France, also houses temporary exhibitions, open Mon-Fri 0900-1200, 1430-1800, US$1.45. **Museo Antropológico**, S of centre on Av España (take micro A heading S or any trufi going S) has a unique collection of stone llama heads as well as impressive carnival masks, open Mon-Fri 0900-1200, 1400-1800; Sat/Sun 1000-200, 1500-1800, US$0.75. **Museo Mineralógico**, part of the University (take micro A South to the Ciudad Universitaria), with over 3,000 mineral specimens, open Mon-Fri 0800-1200, 1430-1700.

Local festivals: La Diablada

On the **Sat before Ash Wednesday**, Oruro Carnival stages the *Diablada* ceremony in homage to the miraculous Virgen del Socavón, patroness of miners, and in gratitude to Pachamama, the Earth Mother. The entire procession starts its 5 km route through the town at 0700, reaching the Sanctuary of the Virgen del Socavón at 0400 on Sun. There the dancers invoke her blessing and ask for pardon. The company then proceeds to the Av Cívica amphitheatre, where the dancers perform two masques. Afterwards, the dancers all enter the sanctuary, chant a hymn in Quechua and pray for pardon. The *Diablada* was traditionally performed by Indian miners,

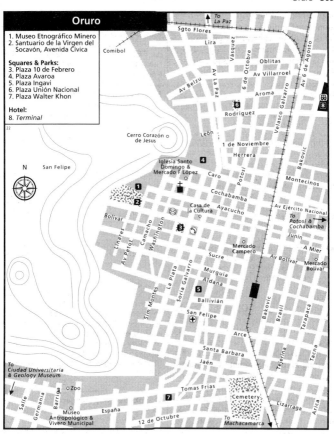

Oruro

1. Museo Etnográfico Minero
2. Santuario de la Virgen del Socavón, Avenida Cívica

Squares & Parks:
3. Plaza 10 de Febrero
4. Plaza Avaroa
5. Plaza Ingavi
6. Plaza Unión Nacional
7. Plaza Walter Khon

Hotel:
8. *Terminal*

but several other guilds have taken up the custom. The Carnival is particularly notable for its fantastically imaginative costumes. The working-class Oruro district known as La Ranchería is particularly famous for the excellence of its costumes.

The *Gran Corso del Carnaval* takes place on the Sun, a very spectacular display. Mon is *El Día del Diablo y del Moreno* in which the Diablos and Morenos, with their bands, compete against each other on Av Cívica in demonstrations of dancing. Every group seems to join in, in 'total marvellous chaos'. The action usually parades out of the amphitheatre, ending up

at the Plaza de Armas. At dusk dancers and musicians go their separate ways, serenading until the early hours. By Tues the main touristic events have ended; *Carnaval del Sur* takes place, with *ch'alla* rituals to invoke ancestors, unite with Pachamama and bless personal possessions. This is also the *día del agua* on which everyone throws water and sprays foam at everyone else (though this goes on throughout carnival; plastic tunics are sold for US$0.20 by street vendors).

The Fri before carnival, traditional miners' ceremonies are held at mines, including the sacrifice of a llama. Visitors may only attend with a guide and permission from Comibol, via the tourist office. The Sun before carnival the groups practise and make their final pledges. **NB** A more detailed description is given in the *Bolivia Handbook*.

● **Seating** Around the Plaza de Armas, along Av 6 de Agosto and on Av Cívica, seats cost US$3 a day, bought from the Alcaldía in the plaza, or whichever business has erected stands outside its building. Seats on Av Bolívar, etc, cost US$2 a day from the shops who built stands. To wander among the dancers you are officially supposed to purchase a professional photographer's ticket for US$15, but amateurs can pay only US$1.50 by showing a small camera and insisting.

● **Accommodation** Must be booked in advance for carnival; hotel prices range from US$15 pp without bath, to US$20 pp with, to US$100 pp/day in the better places. The tourist office has list of all householders willing to let rooms: host and guest arrange the price, at least US$10 pp.

● **Transport** Prices from La Paz triple. Organized day trips from La Paz cost US$50, including transport, food and a seat in the main plaza, departing at 1900 (missing the last 8-9 hrs).

Excursions

To the hot springs at **Obrajes**, 23 km N, where there is the choice of private baths or swimming pool, both hot (not very clean), entry US$1.20. Also springs at Capachos, less good. Free facilities for clothes washing in the natural hot water. Wait at the bus stop at C Caro for the (intermittent) bus to both places, US$0.50 to Capachos. Go early as return transport difficult after 1600. Taxis sometimes make the run. Take picnic lunch. Avoid Sun, when it is very crowded.

Local information

● **Accommodation**

In the centre: **D** pp *Repostero*, Sucre 370 y Pagador, T 50505, hot water, parking; **D** *América*, Bolívar y Pagador, T 60707, **E** without bath, restaurant; **E** *Gran Sucre*, Sucre 510, T 53838, rooms rec in new part, heater on request; **E** *Ideal*, Bolívar 386, T 52863, **F** without bath, basic but clean, poor beds; **E** *Gloria*, Potosí 6059, **F** without bath, basic, hot water, open 24 hrs; **F** *Alojamiento 15 de Octubre*, 6 de Agosto 890, T 40012, without bath, hot showers, safe, good value.

Near the bus terminal: **C-D** *Terminal*, above bus terminal, T 53797, modern, heating, good views, expensive restaurant, dirty, noisy; **D-E** *Lip-*

ton, Av 6 de Agosto 225, T 41538, **F** pp without bath, secure, parking extra, open 24 hrs, good value; **D-E** *Res Verano*, 200m from bus terminal, T 41742, without bath, modern, clean, open 24 hrs; **E** *Bernal*, Brasil 701, opp terminal, T 42468, clean, modern, good value, excellent hot showers; **F** *Bolivia*, Rodríguez 131, T 41047, **F** without bath, hot water, restaurant, open 24 hrs; **F** pp *Res El Turista*, 6 de Agosto 466, T 41888, without bath, unhelpful, safe parking.

Near the railway station: all on Galvarro, **E-F** *Res San Salvador*, No 6325, hot water; **G** pp *Hispano-Americano* No 6392, T 61117, best of the cheapies.

● **Places to eat**

Unicornio, La Plata 5955, 1 block from main plaza, open evenings only, smart, good service, good menu, main dishes around US$4; *Nayjama*, Aldana esq Pagador, best in town, huge portions; *La Casona*, Pres Montes 5970, opp Post Office, good *pizzería*; *Confitería Capri*, Bolívar 749, on plaza, excellent breakfast, bar café, open late; *Club Social Croata*, Junín 729 y Pres Montes, good value lunches; *La Cabaña*, Junín 609, comfortable, smart, good international food, bar, reasonable prices, closed Mon; *Brujas*, Junín y 6 de Octubre, café-concert, open 2100 till late for snacks, bar, live music weekends, good atmosphere, rec; *Mateos*, Bolívar y 6 de Octubre, reasonable prices, also ice cream; *SUM Confitería*, Bolívar esq S Galvarro, good coffee, popular at lunch, open late; *Libertador*, Bolívar 347, excellent set lunch for US$1.50; *Govinda*, 6 de Octubre 6071, excellent vegetarian, lunch US$1.40 Mon-Fri from 1300. *El Huerto*, Bolívar 359, good cheap vegetarian food. Cheap food stalls on Av V Galvarro and Ayacucho.

● **Banks & money changers**

Cash advances on credit cards at **Banco de La Paz**, C Bolívar, US$3.75 authorization charge, Enlace ATM. Enlace also opp Banco Nacional de Bolivia, C La Plata 6153. TCs can be changed at **Banco Boliviano Americano**, 5% commission and at **Banco de Santa Cruz**, Bolívar 670 (also office at Pagador y Caro, open Sat 0900-1200). It is quite easy to change dollars (cash) on the street: good rates on Av V Galvarro, opp train station, or at Ferretería Findel, C Pagador 1491, nr the market (large hardware store), or try Don Ernest at Av V Galvarro 5998, T 60520. Exchange rates are poor in Oruro; up to 5% below the official rate.

● **Embassies & consulates**

German Consulate: at Adolfo Mier y Galvarro.

● **Health**

Public baths: *Duchas Oruro*, 500 block of 6 de Agosto.

● **Laundry**
Alemania, Aldana 280.

● **Post & telecommunications**
Post Office: Presidente Montes 1456. **Entel**: Bolívar, 1 block E of plaza.

● **Shopping**
Reguerín 6 de Octubre 6001 esq Mier, good Diablada dolls and masks. On Av La Paz the 4 blocks between León and Belzu, 48-51, are largely given over to workshops producing masks and costumes for Carnival. There are 3 daily markets, all equally authentic and interesting: *Mercado Bolívar*, nr rail station; *Mercado Campero*, on Mier and Galvarro; *Mercado Fermín López*, on Cochabamba, has an interesting *brujería* section where you can find *curanderos'* magical concoctions.

● **Tour companies & travel agents**
Jumbo Travel, 6 de Octubre 6080, T 55005/55203, efficient. A rec driver and guide is *Juan Carlos Vargas*, T 40333, also rec as tour guide, contact via tourist office.

● **Tourist offices**
Probably the most helpful and informative in Bolivia, at Montes 6072, Plaza 10 de Febrero, T/F 50144, 0800-1200 and 1400-1830 Mon-Fri. Kiosk outside Entel in C Bolívar, open 1000-1200 and 1430-1730 Mon-Fri, 1000-1200 Sat. Colour map and guide (Spanish only), US$1.

● **Transport**
Trains Check in advance which services are running, T 60605. To Uyuni Wed and Sun 1930, US$2.50, 6 hrs. Change at Uyuni for trains to Villazón and Calama. No trains to La Paz, Potosí or Cochabamba. Ticket office opens at 0700, best to be there early.

Buses Bus terminal 10 blocks N of centre at Bakovic and Aroma, T 53535, US$0.20 terminal tax to get on bus. Daily services, first and last buses: to La Paz at least every hour 0400-2200, US$2, 3 hrs; to Cochabamba 0430-2200, US$3, 4½ hrs; to Potosí 0800-1900, US$4, 8 hrs; to Sucre 0900 and 1900, US$6, 12 hrs; to Uyuni 1900, US$5, 9 hrs; to Santa Cruz 0600-1530, US$7, 12 hrs; to Pisiga (Chilean border) 2100-2300, US$6, 5 hrs; to Challapata 0700-1830, US$1.40, 2 hrs; to Llallagua 0630-1900, US$2, 3 hrs. International buses (US$2 to cross border): to Iquique via Pisiga, Trans Jiménez, Tues, Thur and Sat 2200, US$28; Trans Delta Mon and Wed 2230, US$23; to Arica via Tambo Quemado, Trans Salvador, Mon, Tues, Wed and Sun 1000, US$34; Trans Litoral, Tues, Sat and Sun 2200, US$34.

LAGO POOPO

About 65 km S is the **Santuario de Aves Lago Poopó**, an excellent bird reserve on the lake of the same name. Can be visited from Challapata, 120 km S of Oruro on fairly good gravel road; bus dep 0800 and 1430, 2½ hrs, US$1, always full (gas station, basic lodging at main crossing opp former Hotel Potosí, G pp, good beds, basic restaurant); *fiesta* 15-17 July. The lake dries up completely in winter.

LLALLAGUA

Near this mining town, 95 km SE (*alt* 3,881m) is the famous Siglo Veinte, once the largest tin mine (ex-Patiño) in the country. It is now closed, but being worked by small cooperatives (visitors welcome). There is an acute water shortage. Nearby at **Uncia**, Km 102, there are more former Patiño mines and good hot springs; reached by *trufi*, small *alojamiento* near the prison, G, clean, safe, basic, poor restaurants, eat at the market. *Fiesta*: Asunción.

● **Accommodation In Llallagua**: **F** *Hotel Bustillo*; *Santa María*; **G** *Hotel Llallagua*, small beds, no bath, seldom has water, perhaps the best, but not really rec; few restaurants.

● **Buses** Llallagua can be reached by bus from Oruro (Bustillo, 7 a day, Enta 0900, 1700 daily, 3 hrs, US$2.50). Also 1900 from La Paz.

SOUTHWEST FROM ORURO

At Toledo, 38 km SW, there is a colonial church. **Escara**, further SE, is a lovely village with a beautiful plaza; it is a friendly place, has bike rental. From Escara it is only 25 km S to **Chipaya**, 190 km from Oruro, which is less welcoming, the main settlement of the most interesting Indians of the Altiplano. They speak a language closely related to the almost extinct Uru; their distinctive dress and unique conical houses are beginning to disappear as the community changes. This part of the country can be difficult to explore without your own transport (4WD recommended), but there is a daily bus from Oruro to Sabaya, SW of Escara, via Huachacalla; dep 2100, 5 hrs, US$4.50; also transport once a week in either direction from Huachacalla to Chipaya. In Chipaya, the town council charges visitors US$50 for free access and hospitality. For a smaller, or no, contribution you will be much less welcome. There is very little for the visitor to do and it is very cold.

SAJAMA NATIONAL PARK

A 1-day drive to the W is the **Parque Nacional Sajama**, established in 1945 and covering 60,000 ha. The park contains the world's highest forest, consisting mainly of the rare Kenua tree (Polylepis Tarapana) which grows up to 5,200m. The scenery is wonderful and includes views of three volcanoes (**Sajama** – Bolivia's highest peak at 6,530m – Parinacota and Pomerape). The road is now paved. There are restaurants in the park but no fresh food, so take plenty from La Paz. Once you move away from the Río Sajama or its major tributaries, lack of water is a serious problem. In Sajama village (*pop* 500; *alt* 4,200m), Peter Brunnhart (Señor Pedro) and Telmo Nina have a book with descriptions of the various routes to the summit (Telmo Nina keeps the visitors book). Park entry fee US$1; basic accommodation available. It can be very windy and cold at night (good sleeping bag essential; crampons, ice axe and rope are needed for climbing the volcanoes). Mules can be hired, US$6/day. Good bathing in hot springs 5 km N of village, interesting geothermic area 6 km W of village. The Sajama area is a major centre of alpaca wool production.

● **Buses** Take the Litoral La Paz-Arica bus (La Paz 0530 Tues, Fri and Sun; from Arica Mon and Thur 2400), ask for Sajama, pay the full fare. If continuing into Chile (same buses) remember that no meat, dairy products, fruit or vegetables may be taken across the border. This area has become more accessible since the completion of the new asphalted La Paz-Arica highway.

ROUTES A road and railway line run S from Oruro, through Río Mulato, the junction for trains to Potosí, to Uyuni (323 km). The road is sandy, and after rain very bad, especially S of Río Mulato.

UYUNI

Uyuni (*pop* 11,320; *alt* 3,665m; *phone code* 0693), lies near the eastern edge of the Salar de Uyuni. Still a commercial and communication centre, Uyuni was, for much of this century, important as a major railway junction. A giant statue of an armed railway worker, erected after the 1952 Revolution, dominates Av Ferroviaria. Most services are near the station. Water is frequently cut off and may only be available between 0600 and midday. Market Thur, Fri and Sun. *Fiesta* 11 July.

20 km E is **Pulcayo**, on the road to Potosí: a largely abandoned mining town with a railway cemetery and alpaca wool factory (**G** *Hotel Rancho No 1*, without bath, large old rooms, hot water, good meals).

Local information
● **Accommodation**

D *Avenida*, Av Ferroviaria, opp station, T 2078, hot water, **E** without bath in old wing, laundry facilities, motorcycle parking, popular, rec.

E *Magia de Uyuni*, Av Colón between Sucre and Camacho, T 2541, all rooms with bath, inc breakfast.

F *Res Sucre*, C Sucre, clean, basic; **F** *Hostal Tuyupa*, Av Ferroviaria, unlimited hot water, 4 rooms, quiet, cosy.

G pp *Res Urkupiña*, basic and quite clean, hot shower US$0.50.

● **Places to eat**

16 de Julio, Av Arce, opens 0700, not cheap, good meeting place; *Cafetería El Repostero*, good American breakfast US$1.50. *Restaurant-Bar Los Andes*, C Bolívar, good. *Salteñas* go on sale about 0900 daily; cheap meals in market, breakfast for US$0.50.

● **Banks & money changers**

Bidesa, Av Potosí, changes TCs in bolivianos or dollars cash (2% commission). Outside banking hours, try photographer's shop on Av Potosí, changes dollars or Chilean pesos. *Hotel Avenida* changes dollars cash. Tour agencies and some shops accept payment in TCs.

● **Useful addresses**

The **Immigration Office** is at Av Potosí 10, open Mon-Fri 0830-1200 and 1430-1800, for exit stamps if leaving Bolivia via Laguna Verde and Hito Cajón; only issues 30-day stamps, for 90 days go to Potosí. The **tourist office**, Av Potosí 13, is helpful, open Mon-Fri 0830-1200 and 1400-1830, Sat-Sun 0830-1200, T/F 2098; Sr Tito Ponce, a former guide, is very knowledgeable and helpful. Reserva Eduardo Avaroa office is at Potosí esq Sucre, sells excellent colour map and guide to the reserve, US$2.

● **Transport**

Trains Check services on arrival. To Oruro Mon, Tues, Thur and Fri at 0200, US$2.40/US$3.30, 8 hrs. To Villazón, Mon, Tues, Thur and Fri at 0130, US$3/US$3.85, 12 hrs. To Avaroa on Chilean border for connection with train to Calama and then bus to Antofagasta, Mon 0500, US$4, 12 hrs. There is no through train; buy Ollagüe-Calama section after passing the border; pay only in pesos (US$5) which you can buy at the small shop opp water tower in Ollagüe. No money changers on Bolivian side; 1 hr to change trains at Avaroa, then 40 mins to Ollagüe, where Chilean customs take 4-12 hrs. After that it is an uncomfortable 6 hrs to Calama. In Bolivia, seats can be reserved as far as the border 30 mins before train arrives. Restaurant car and waiter service. If taking your own food, eat fresh things first as the Chileans do not allow dairy produce, teabags (of any description), fruit or vegetables to be brought in. All passports are collected and stamped in the rear carriage, they should be ready for collection after 1-2 hrs; queue for your passport, no names are called out.

Buses To **La Paz** with Panasur Wed and Sun 1800, US$9, 13 hrs (Panasur from La Paz bus terminal Tues and Fri 1730). To **Oruro** daily at 1900, US$5, 8 hrs. To **Potosí** 1000, US$4, 6 hrs. To **Sucre** 1000, US$7, 8 hrs. To **Tupiza** Wed and Sun 1000, US$5, 10 hrs. To **Camargo** 1000, US$7, 11 hrs. To **Tarija** 1000, US$12, 14 hrs. To **Challapata** (change for buses to Oruro and La Paz or Potosí), Sat 0530, US$4.

By Road to Chile From Colchani it is about 60 km across to the W shore of the Salar. There are 2 or 3 parallel tracks about 100m apart and every few km stones mark the way; the salt is soft and wet for about 2 km around the edges; get directions from the *Hotel Playa Blanca* near Colchani. There is no real danger of getting lost, especially in the high season, but it is a hard trip and the road is impassable after rain. There is no gasoline between Uyuni and Calama (Chile). It is 20 km from the W shore to 'Colcha K', the military checkpoint. From there a poor gravel road leads 28 km to San Juan, where tour groups spend the night, then the road enters the Salar de Chiguana, a mix of salt and mud which is often wet and soft with deep tracks which are easy to follow. 35 km away is Chiguana, another military post, then 45 km to end of Salar, a few km before the border. This latter part is the most dangerous; very slippery and very little traffic.

To hitch to Chile via Ollagüe, trucks first go N, then across the Salar de Ollagüe. The scenery on this route is amazing and, once in Chile, you will see lakes similar to Lagunas Colorada and Verde. There is nowhere to stay in Ollagüe, but police and border officials will help find lodging and transport for hitchers; change bolivianos into pesos at the blue house.

SALAR DE UYUNI

The salt lake is claimed to be the largest in the world and driving across it is a weird and fantastic experience, especially during June and July when the bright blue skies contrast with the blinding-white salt crust (sunglasses essential).

On its W side, 5 hrs from Uyuni, is **Llica**, capital of Daniel Campos province. Good for llama and other wool handicrafts, but there are no shops or electricity. **F** *Alojamiento Municipal*, basic; Angel Quispe in the plaza has 3 beds; meals available in private houses. Bus from Uyuni 1200 daily, truck 1100.

TOURS TO LAGUNA COLORADA AND LAGUNA VERDE

Laguna Colorada (4,278m), 346 km SW of Uyuni, 10 hrs straight driving over unmarked, rugged truck tracks, is one of Bolivia's most spectacular and most isolated marvels. The shores and shallows of the lake are crusted with gypsum and salt, an arctic-white counterpart to the flaming red, algae-coloured waters (from midday) in which the rare James flamingoes, along with the more common Chilean and Andean flamingoes, breed and live (see *Aves de la Reserva Nacional de Fauna Andina Eduardo Avaroa*, by Omar Rocha and Carmen Quiroga – Museo Nacional de Historia Natural, La Paz 1996 – in Spanish).

The standard outing (see below for operators) lasts 4 days. Day 1: Uyuni to Colchani, from there to the Salar, including a salt-mine visit, lunch on the cactus-studded Isla Pescado, and overnight at a village, eg San Juan, S of the Salar (simple lodging, US$3 pp, electricity 1900-2100, running water). Between Colchani (17 km) and Isla Pescado is **D** *Hotel Playa Blanca* run by Teodoro Colque, built entirely of salt, furniture and all. Day 2: to Laguna Colorada, passing active Volcán Ollagüe and a chain of small, flamingo-specked lagoons. Overnight at Laguna Colorada; demand to stay at Reserva Eduardo Avaroa headquarters US$3 pp, clean, comfortable, modern, quite warm – it's far better than Eustaquio Berna's hut which is also US$3 pp and favoured by the Uyuni agencies. Day 3:

drive past belching geysers at Sol de Mañana (take care not to fall through the crust) and through the barren, surreal landscape of the Pampa de Chalviri at 4,800m, via a pass at 5,000m, to the wind-lashed jade waters of the **Laguna Verde** (4,400m) at the foot of Volcán Licancábur, and back to Laguna Colorada or further. At Aguas Termales Chalviri, between the two lakes, hot springs feed the salty water at about 30°C (hottest early am). *Refugio* at Laguna Verde, US$2, small, mattresses, running water, view of lake. Day 4: Return to Uyuni. A 3-day version eliminates the Salar de Uyuni or Laguna Verde.

● **Tour operators**
Organization of tours from Uyuni is on the whole appalling. Luckily, the staggering scenery makes it worth the effort. Demand a written contract which states a full day by day itinerary, a full meal by meal menu (vegetarians should be prepared for an egg-based diet), what is included in the price and what is not (accommodation is normally not included – add US$3 pp/night). If the tour doesn't match the contract, go back to the operator and demand a refund. If this fails to satisfy, complain to Tito Ponce at the tourism office in Uyuni (see **Useful addresses** above) and then to the Director Regional de Turismo, La Prefectura del Departamento de Potosí, Calle La Paz, Potosí (T 062 27477). The Prefectura recognizes that there is a problem with Uyuni agencies and needs specific information to be able to act.

Trip prices are based on a 6-person group – it is easy to find other people in Uyuni. If there are fewer than 6 you each pay more. The standard 4-day trip (Salar de Uyuni, Lagunas Colorada and Verde) costs US$60-US$220 pp depending on agency and season. There is no refund for leaving to Chile after Laguna Verde. Shorter and longer trips are possible but 4 days in a jeep is as much as most people's bottoms will stand.

Take a good sleeping bag, sunglasses, sun hat, sun protection, lots of warm clothing (the record low recorded in 1996 at Laguna Colorada was -30°C), water bottle, water purification tablets or iodine tincture, lots of film.

Of the 24 agencies in Uyuni (a 50% increase in 2 years), very few can be recommended and even those that can are by no means perfect. Speak to travellers who have just returned from a tour and try the following, all of which are within 50m of each other along Av Ferroviaria and in Plaza Arce: *Tunupa*, Av Arce 15 (T 2099); *Brisa*, Av Ferroviaria 320 (T 2096); *Toñito*, Av Ferroviaria 152 (T/F 2094), change TCs at 3% commission; *Transandino*, Av Arce 2 (T 2132); *Pucara*, Av Arce 4

(T 2055); *Esmeralda*, Av Ferroviara esq Arce (T 2130); *San Cristóbal*, Av Ferroviaria (T 2223). If you can afford it, go with one of the reputable La Paz agencies, eg *Colibrí* or *TransAmazonas*. Agencies in Potosí also organize tours but this mainly involves putting you on a bus to Uyuni where you meet up with one of the Uyuni agencies and get the same quality tour for a higher price.

CROSSING INTO CHILE

If you plan to enter Chile via one of the unattended border crossings in the SW region, you must get an exit stamp at the Bolivian immigration office in Uyuni (Mon-Fri only). The stamp is valid for 3 days, but more than 72 hrs may be permitted if you state the exact date you intend to leave Bolivia. Before issuing the exit stamp, Bolivian immigration requires that you present proof of travel, ie your excursion contract. Most agencies will arrange transport from border to San Pedro for US$10 pp and passport formalities on the morning you are leaving. Buy Chilean pesos in Uyuni.

To **San Pedro de Atacama (Chile)** From Laguna Verde it is 7 km to Hito Cajón, the frontier post with Chile. A further 8 km is La Cruz, the junction with the E-W road between the borax and sulphur mines and San Pedro. There are reports of a daily bus Hito Cajón-San Pedro, but it is much safer to ask tour agencies to arrange transport from Hito Cajón to San Pedro de Atacama (see above and San Pedro de Atacama **Tourist Agencies**, page 725, and **Frontier with Bolivia**). The meteorological station at Laguna Verde will radio for a pick-up from San Pedro. This service costs US$10 pp Hito Cajón-San Pedro. The chance of finding other transport is remote. Adequate, food, water and clothing essential. **Do not underestimate the dangers of getting stuck without transport or lodging at this altitude. Do not travel alone.**

TUPIZA

South of Uyuni, 200 km, is **Tupiza** (*pop* 20,000; *alt* 2,990m), a centre of the silver, tin, lead, and bismuth mining industries. The statue in the main plaza is to Victor

Carlos Aramayo, the founding member of the Aramayo mining dynasty, pre-eminent in the late 19th, early 20th centuries. Chajra Huasi, a palazzo-style, abandoned home of the Aramayo family across the Río Tupiza, may be visited. Local history museum, on 2nd floor of *Casa Municipal de Cultura*, just off plaza, free entry, open late pm. IGM office, for maps, is in the Municipal building. Beautiful sunsets over the fertile Tupiza valley can be seen from the foot of a Christ statue on a hill behind the plaza.

Local information
● **Accommodation & services**

F *Mitru*, Av Chichas, run down, private shower and bath, water unreliable, downstairs rooms preferable, laundry can take 3 days, but still the best, restaurant has good *almuerzo*, but no dinner, annex has snack shop and restaurant, both open for dinner; **F** *Res Valle Hermoso*, Av Pedro Arraya, T 589, hot showers, good, will let you park motorbikes in restaurant; **F** *Centro*, 2 blocks from station, clean, hot water unreliable; **F** *Res My Home*, Abaroa 288, shared bath, hot water, rec; **G** pp *Res Monterrey*, opp railway station, clean, hot water, dirty toilets. *Picantería Las Brisas*, on opp side of river, open Sat and Sun only, large helpings; on C Chorolque nr plaza are, *Los Helechos* and *Il Bambino*, both rec; good ice cream at *Cremelín*, on plaza; *El Flamingo*, good cheap meals; good breakfast at Mercado Negro.

TCs can be changed at *Empresa Bernall Hmnos*, but only in the presence of the owner, good rates; many shops will also change dollars at better rates than in Villazón. Hospital Ferroviário (nr *Hotel Mitru*), Dr Rolando Llano Navarro and staff, very helpful.

● **Transport**

Trains To **Villazon**, Mon/Thur arr 0700 from Oruro, Wed/Sun arr 0845, Fri at 0415, 3 hrs. To **Uyuni** and **Oruro**, Mon, Tues, Thur, Fri, Sat and Sun (Sat continues to La Paz).

Buses To **Villazón** 3 hrs, US$2.50, 1000 and 1500; to **Potosí**, US$5.40, O'Globo at 1000, 8 hrs, Expreso Tupiza daily 2030, US$7.75; to **Uyuni**, US$5.20, 8-10 hrs, poor road. No direct bus to La Paz, only via Potosí. A new road is being built from Uyuni to Atocha. Bad road from Potosí which goes on S to Villazón; often closed in rainy season because road fords the Río Suipacha. Book in advance.

TO SAN VICENTE

Tupiza is the centre of Butch Cassidy and the Sundance Kid country. On 4 November 1908, they held up an Aramayo company payroll N of Salo. (Aramayo *hacienda* in Salo, 1 hr N of Tupiza, still stands. Roadside kiosks serve excellent roast goat, *choclo*, *papas*, soup.) 2 days later they encountered and were killed by a four-man military-police patrol in **San Vicente** (*pop* 400; *alt* 4,500m), 103 km, 4-6 hrs on a good dirt road, NW of Tupiza. Shootout site off main street – ask locals. Cassidy and Sundance are buried in an unmarked grave in the cemetery, but the grave has yet to be found. An investigation of the supposed grave, by the Nova project in 1991, proved negative, but see *Digging Up Butch and Sundance*, by Anne Meadows (New York: St Martin's Press, 1994).

● **Accommodation** Basic *alojamiento* on main street marked 'Hotel'; restaurant 'El Rancho' next-door; several *tiendas* sell beer, soda, canned goods, etc.

● **Tour companies & travel agents** Dr Félix Chalar Miranda, President of the local historical society, offers jeep tours to the hold-up site nr Salo, the escape route and San Vicente; T 467 (office), 509 (home) or contact via *Inquietud* newspaper office at Av Cul Arraya 205. *Tupiza Tours*, Av Chichas 187, T/F (694) 3001, Casilla 67, offer 2-day tours which follow Butch and Sundance's movements in 1908, US$80-100 pp, inc transport, guide, meals and lodging, run by Fabiola Mitru of *Hotel Mitru*; also through *Potosí Tours*, Galería Chuquiago, C Sagárnaga 213, T/F 350870, La Paz, Casilla 11034.

● **Transport** Trucks from Tupiza on Thur early am from Av Chichas nr *Hotel Mitru*. Alternatively hire a vehicle. Fermín Ortega at Taller Nardini, Barrio Lourdes, rec; Don Manuel at *Hotel Mitru* can suggest others, US$30 to US$85 one-way. (Also accessible and a bit closer from Atocha, but fewer vehicles for hire.)

SOUTH TO ARGENTINA

The Argentine border is at **Villazón** (*pop* 13,000; *alt* 3,443m) 81 km S of Tupiza; an unwelcoming place with little to see (2 cinemas). The border area must not be photographed.

Local information
● **Accommodation & places to eat**

D *Res El Cortijo*, 20 de Mayo 338, a few blocks from bus terminal, good value, intermittent hot water, restaurant; **F** pp *Grand Palace*, behind bus terminal, safe; **F** *Hotel Bolivia*, 1 block from border, small rooms, good value breakfast, hot showers extra; **F** *Panamericano*, laundry facilities, rec; **F** *Res Martínez*, ½ block from bus station; well signed, hot water when town's supply is on, basic but well-maintained; **F** *Res 10 de Febrero*, next door, very basic. Restaurants opp bus terminal and on 1st floor of covered market, eg *Repostería*, about US$1 pp. The Mercado Municipal de Vivanderos is nr the frontier, parallel with main street, across the railway.

● **Banks & money changers**

Money changing at **Cambio Porvenir** or other *cambios* on main street, good rates (some take TCs), also at **Cambio Trébol**, shop by border that sells train tickets (see below) but with 6% commission on TCs; **Banco del Estado** does not change TCs. Out of hours try the Ciné Rex. No exchange facilities in La Quiaca.

● **Transport**

Road An improved road goes to Tarija. The road linking Potosí with Villazón via Camargo is in poor condition and about 100 km longer than the better road via Tupiza.

Buses To Potosí several between 0830 and 1830, 10-15 hrs, US$7-8 (terrible in the wet, can take 24 hrs); to **Tupiza**, 0700 and 1500, US$2.50; to **Tarija**, beautiful journey but most buses overnight only, daily at 1900/2000, US$6.50, 6 hrs, very cold on arrival but passengers can sleep on bus until daybreak. From **La Paz**, several companies, 25 hrs, US$17.25 (eg Panamericana and Chicheña, even though buses called 'direct', you may have to change in Potosí, perhaps to another company, eg Villa Imperial), dep La Paz 1830, arrive Potosí 0700, dep Potosí 0830, arrive Villazón 1930; same procedure from Villazón to La Paz. Bus terminal is nr plaza, behind Ciné Teatro Libertador Bolívar, 5 blocks from the border. Taxi to border, US$0.35 or hire porter, US$1, and walk across.

Trains Station about 1 km N of frontier on main road, taxi US$2.35. To **Oruro** (very dusty and cold journey), Mon/Thur 1630, Tues/Fri/Sun 1600, US$7.50, *Expreso del Sur* (continues to La Paz) Sat at 1300, US$15. Train stops at Tupiza, Atocha and Uyuni. The express from La Paz/Oruro connects with a bus to **Tarija**, tickets from railway station. Ticket office opens 0800, long queues.

FRONTIER WITH ARGENTINA

● **Bolivian immigration**

The Bolivian offices open at 0700. Bolivian officials tend to stamp papers in the morning only, so a night in Villazón is usually required; border guards will allow this. This is an easy crossing.

NB Bolivian time is 1 hr earlier than Argentina.

● **Argentine consulate**

In main plaza, Villazón, open Mon-Fri 1400-1700.

Potosí, Sucre and the Southern Highlands

THIS is a region which boasts the World Cultural Heritage sites of Potosí, with its rich mining past and current mining misery, and Sucre, the white city. In the south, Tarija is known for its fruit and wines and its traditions which set it apart from the rest of the country.

POTOSI

Potosí (*pop* 110,000; *alt* 4,070m; *phone code* 062), 551 km SE of La Paz, is the highest city of its size in the world. The climate is often bitterly cold and heating a rare luxury, so warm clothes are essential. It was founded by the Spaniards on 10 April 1545, after they had discovered Indian mine workings at Cerro Rico, which dominates the city.

Immense amounts of silver were once extracted. In Spain 'éste es un Potosí' (it's a Potosí) is still used for anything superlatively rich. By the early 17th century Potosí was the largest city in the Americas, but over the next two centuries, as its lodes began to deteriorate and silver was found elsewhere, Potosí became little more than a ghost town. It was the demand for tin – a metal the Spaniards ignored – that saved the city from absolute poverty. Silver, copper and lead are also mined.

Places of interest

Large parts of Potosí are colonial, with twisting, narrow streets and an occasional great mansion with its coat of arms over the doorway. UNESCO has declared the city to be 'Patrimonio de la Humanidad'. Some of the best buildings are grouped round the Plaza 10 de Noviembre. The old Cabildo and the Royal Treasury – Las Cajas Reales – are both here, converted to other uses. **The Cathedral** (open Mon-Fri 0930-1000, 1300-1500, Sat 0930-1000, guided tour only, US$1) faces Plaza 10 de Noviembre.

The Casa Real de Moneda, or Mint, is nearby, on C Ayacucho (T 22777). Founded in 1572, rebuilt 1759-1773, it is one of the chief monuments of civil building in Hispanic America; entrance US$2, US$1 to take photos. In 30 of its 160 rooms are a museum with sections on armaments and on mineralogy, and an art gallery in a splendid salon on the 1st floor. One section is dedicated to the works of the acclaimed 17th-18th century religious painter Melchor Pérez de Holguín. Elsewhere are coin dies and huge wooden presses which made the silver strip from which coins were cut. The smelting houses have carved altar pieces from Potosí's ruined churches. You cannot fail to notice the huge, grinning mask over an archway between two principal courtyards; its significance is uncertain, perhaps to hide a coat of arms at the time of Independence. Wear warm clothes, as it is cold inside; obligatory guided tours start at 0900 and 1400 sharp, and last for $2\frac{1}{2}$ hrs, Spanish only.

The **Convento y Museo de Santa Teresa** at Chicas y Ayacucho, T 23847 (entry US$2, US$2 to take photos, Mon-Fri 0900-1200, 1300-1800, Sat 0900-1200, but check at Tourist Office, tour in Spanish) has an interesting collection of colonial and religious art, obligatory guide. Among Potosí's baroque churches, typical of the Andean or 'mestizo' architecture of the 18th century, are the **Compañía** (Jesuit) church, on Ayacucho,

with an impressive bell-gable (1700, closed for restoration since 1992); **San Francisco** (Tarija y Nogales) with a fine organ, worthwhile for the views from the tower and roof, museum of ecclesiastical art, underground tunnel system (open 1000-1200 and 1400-1600, Mon-Fri, entry US$1.45, US$2 to take photos); also **San Lorenzo** (1728-1744) with a rich portal, on C Héroes del Chaco, fine views from the tower. **San Martín** on C Hoyos, with an uninviting exterior, is beautiful inside, but is normally closed for fear of theft. Ask the German Redemptorist Fathers to show you around; their office is just to the left of their church. Other churches to visit include **Jerusalén**, close to the *Hotel Centenario*, and **San Agustín** (only by prior arrangement with tourist office) on Bolívar y Quijarro, with crypts and catacombs (the whole city was interconnected by tunnels in colonial times). Tour starts at 1700, US$0.10 admission. From **San Cristóbal**, at Pacheco y Cañete, one gets a fine view over the whole city. **Teatro Omiste** on Plaza 6 de Agosto has a fine façade. The University has a museum with some good modern Bolivian painting (Mon-Fri, 1000-1200, 1500-1700, entrance US$1, C Bolívar, T 22248).

In Potosí, 2,000 colonial buildings have been catalogued. For example, C Quijarro, one of Potosí's best-preserved streets, was, in colonial times, C Ollería – potmakers – and C de los Sombreros. At Quijarro and Omiste is the Esquina de las Cuatro Portadas (four houses with double doors), or Balcón de Llamacancha. There is a fine stone doorway (house of the Marqués de Otavi) in Junín between Matos and Bolívar. Off Junín, see the Pasaje de Siete Vueltas (the passage of the seven turns). At Lanza 8 was the house of José de Quiroz and of Antonio López de Quiroga (now a school). Turn up Chuquisaca from Lanza and after 3 blocks right into Millares; here on the left is a sculpted stone doorway and on the right a doorway with two rampant lions in low relief on the lintel. Turning left up Nogales you come to an old mansion in a little plaza. Turn left along La Paz and 1 block along there is another stone doorway with suns in relief. At La Paz y Bolívar is the Casa

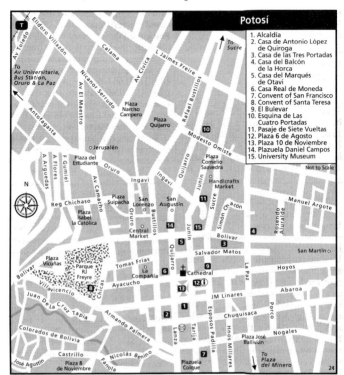

Potosí

1. Alcaldía
2. Casa de Antonio López de Quiroga
3. Casa de las Tres Portadas
4. Casa del Balcón de la Horca
5. Casa del Marqués de Otavi
6. Casa Real de Moneda
7. Convent of San Francisco
8. Convent of Santa Teresa
9. El Bulevar
10. Esquina de Las Cuatro Portadas
11. Pasaje de Siete Vueltas
12. Plaza 6 de Agosto
13. Plaza 10 de Noviembre
14. Plazuela Daniel Campos
15. University Museum

del Balcón de la Horca. Turn left for the Casa de las Tres Portadas.

Local festivals

8-10 Mar is *San Juan de Dios*, with music, dancing, parades etc. In **May** there is a market on C Gumiel every Sun, with lotteries and lots of fun things for sale. On three consecutive Sats at the end of May, beginning of June llama sacrifices are made at the cooperative mines in honour of *Pachamama*; the same occurs on **1 Aug**, the *Ritual del Espíritu*. Other mining festivals are the *Carnaval Minero* and the *Fiesta de los Compadres* in Feb, for decorating El Tío (the Dios Minero) and the workplace. *San Bartolomé*, or the Fiesta de Chutillos, is held from the middle of Aug, with the main event being processions of dancers on the last weekend; Sat features Potosino,

and Sun national, groups. Costumes can be hired in artesanía market on C Sucre. In **Oct**, *Festival Internacional de la Cultura*, in Potosí and Sucre. Potosí is sometimes called the 'Ciudad de las Costumbres', especially at Corpus Cristi, Todos Santos and Carnaval, when special cakes are baked, families go visiting friends, etc.

Local information
● **Accommodation**

Unless otherwise stated hotels have no heating in rooms. **C** *Claudia*, Av Maestro 322, 3-star, T 22242, helpful, modern, highly rec; **C** *Hostal Colonial*, Hoyos 8, a pretty colonial house (T 24809) nr the main plaza, rec, with heating, has names and tel numbers of guides, even if you're not staying there very helpful, very expensive for long-distance phone calls; **C** *Hostal Libertador*, Millares 58, T 27877/24629, Casilla 324, heaters in rooms, quiet, helpful, comfortable, parking, rec; **C** *Hostal Felimar*, Junín 14, T 24357, 2-star, hot water, breakfast, 2 roof-top suites, solar-powered (so no hot water early morning), 1st floor rooms have no exterior windows but warm, quiet.

D *Hostal Santa María*, Av Serrudo 244, T 23255, hot water, comfortable, good cafetería, rec; **D** *Jerusalem*, Oruro 143, T/F 22600, pleasant, helpful, comedor, **E** without bath, parking, laundry; **D** *El Turista*, Lanza 19 (T 22492), also LAB office, helpful, hot showers, breakfast (US$1), good value, rec; **D-E** *San Antonio*, Oruro 136, T 23566, US$2 pp without breakfast, dirty.

E *Central*, Bustillos 1230 y Linares, T 22207, hot shower, breakfast, basic; **E** *Hotel Carlos V*, Linares 42 on Plaza 6 de Agosto, T 25151, breakfast, without bath, occasional hot water, luggage store, late night curfew, rec; **E-F** *Res Sumaj*, Gumiel 10, T 23336, small rooms, double room on top floor good views, hot water 0800-1800, shared bathrooms only, mixed reports; **E** *Res Felcar*, Serrudo 345 y Bustillos, T 24966, **F** without bath, hot water, 0800-1200, popular.

F *Alojamiento El Barquito*, Oruro 7, T 22600, not obviously spotted, good, rustic, rec; **F** *Alojamiento La Paz*, Oruro 262, T 22632, central, basic; **F** *Casa de María Victoria*, Chuquisaca 148, T 22132, clean, stores luggage, popular, laundry facilities, good travel agency, breakfast in courtyard, rec; **F** *Res Copacabana*, Av Serrudo 319, T 22712, individual or shared rooms, restaurant, separate hot showers, will change $ cash, safe car park (owner, Dr Hugo Linares Fuentes will give medical assistance); **F** *Res 10 de Noviembre*, Av Serrudo 181, hot shower, ask for room with window.

G *Alojamiento Ferrocarril*, Av E Villazón 159, T 24294, basic (hot showers US$0.55), close to the railway station.

5 km from Potosí in the village of San Antonio is *Hotel El Tambo*, Km 5 Carretera a Oruro, T 25597, **F** 22985, 3-star, colonial/rustic architecture, 3 restaurants, Bodega Bar, all details from Hidalgo Tours (see below).

● **Places to eat**
Sumaj Orcko, Quijarro 46, excellent, large portions, cheap set lunch, reasonably priced, very popular with travellers, heating, slow service; *Plaza*, Quijarro 38, cheap set lunch, good; *Las Vegas*, Padilla 1, 1st floor, cheap *almuerzos*, dinner more expensive; *The Sky Room*, Bolívar 701, good views of the town and the Cerro, good, slow service; *La Carreta*, Gumiel s/n, excellent, pleasant service, mid-price range; *La Manzana Mágica*, Oruro 239, small but excellent vegetarian, open 0700-2130, lunch US$2; *Kaypichu*, Millares 24, stylish and excellent vegetarian, open 0700-1300 and 1600-2100; *Kivo's*, Quijarro 12, good Italian food, small, cosy; *Coffee Snack El Farol*, Tarija

28, opp San Francisco, high kitsch decor, bohemian atmosphere, popular with artists, open late; *Confitería Cherry's*, Padilla 12 y Linares, good cakes, coffee, burgers, very popular, good breakfast, cheap, rec, open 0800. Other *confiterías*: *Den-Danske Café*, Quijarro esq Matos, opens 1300, main gringo hangout, friendly, good food and music; *UMI Confitería Victoria*, Ayacucho y Bustillos, cheap breakfast, good coffee, owner Benjamin speaks English and German and changes money. Good value food in Mercado Central, between Oruro, Bustillos, Héroes del Chaco and Bolívar; breakfast from 0700, fresh bread from 0600.

● **Banks & money changers**
Banco Nacional, Junín 4-6, exchange for US$ TCs and cash. Many shops on Plaza Alonso de Ibáñez and on Bolívar, Sucre and Padilla display 'compro dólares' signs. Dollar TCs can be changed at Distribuidora Cultural Sud, Matos 19, 3% commission. **Banco Popular**, Bolívar y Sucre, cash withdrawals on Visa.

● **Entertainment**
Cinema: on Padilla and also Bolívar.

Public baths: Sauna Florida, Plaza Chuquimina, nr bus station, open Fri, Sat, Sun, US$1.50 (also has racquetball).

● **Hospitals & medical services**
Clinics: *Clínica Británica*, on Oruro nr *Alojamiento La Paz*, clinics am and pm, English spoken.

● **Laundry**
Limpieza la Veloz, C Quijarro, corner of Mattos, Edif Cademin, and at Camacho 258, US$1.30/kilo.

● **Post & telecommunications**
Post Office: Lanza 3, open Sat till 1900, Sun 0900-1200; unreliable for overseas mail. **Entel**: on Plaza Arce at end of Av Camacho, T 43496; also at Av Universitaria nr bus terminal, and on Padilla, opp *Confitería Cherys*.

● **Shopping**
Mercado Central (see address above) sells mainly food and produce but silver is sold nr the C Oruro entrance. *Mercado Gremial*, between Av Camacho and Oruro, only sells household goods. There is an informal swap market every Fri night at the Plazuela, at Bolívar and Quijarro. *Mercado Artesanal*, at Sucre y Omiste, sells handwoven cloth and regional handicrafts. Some Fri the merchants organize music, food and drink (*ponche*), not to be missed. Almost opp is *Andina*, Sucre 94, for handicrafts and antiques. For musical instruments, Arnaud Gerard (Belgian), workshop *Killay* at the back of Mercado Artesanal, makes beautifully made and tuned pieces, designed to be played, will

make to order, open Mon-Fri, 1700-1930. The best bookshop is at the University, open Mon-Fri, 1000-1200, 1500-1700. Postcards, gifts etc from gift shop at entrance to Post Office.

● **Tour companies & travel agents**
The following have been recommended for a tour of the mines (see also **Guides** below): *Hidalgo Tours*, Junín y Bolívar, T 28293, F 22985, Casilla 310, specialized services within the city and to Salar de Uyuni; *Potosí Tours*, corner of Padilla, on the Plaza, good tours of the city; *Transamazonas*, Quijarro 12, T 27175, F 24796; *Koala Tours*, Ayacucho 5, opp Casa de la Moneda, PO Box 33, T 24708, F 22092; *Turismo Balsa*, Plaza Alonso de Ibáñez, T 26272, English spoken, daily city tours (see also La Paz **Travel Agents**); *Altiplano Tours*, Ayacucho 19, T 25353/ 27299; *Transandino Tours*, Bustillos 1078, T 26787 (see below), also changes TCs at reasonable rates; *Cerro Rico Travel*, Quijarro 8, trips to local village markets, horse and mountain bike hire, trekking.

Some agencies offer trips to the Salar de Uyuni, Laguna Colorada and Laguna Verde (see above page 309) but this is more expensive and time-consuming than excursions to these places from Uyuni. Tours from Potosí cost US$160-180 pp and last 5-6 days. It is essential to get a written contract (a tourist police requirement) and make sure that the guide is approved by the Prefectura.

● **Tourist offices**
Kiosk on Plaza Alonso de Ibáñez (both closed Sat and Sun and unreliable opening times during the week); town maps US$0.40 (English, French, German and Spanish), better than glossy US$0.60 map (Spanish only), helpful. Instituto Geográfico Militar, C La Paz, possible to buy maps, 0900-1200, 1400-1800.

● **Useful addresses**
Migración: at Oruro esq Frías.
Police station: on Plaza 10 de Noviembre.

● **Transport**
Local Bus: within city, US$0.15. **Taxi**: within city limits US$0.50; approx US$1.30/km for longer journeys.

Air Aerosur, Ayacucho 10, T 22088, to La Paz Mon-Sat, 1 hr, also from La Paz. Airport is 5 km out of town on the Sucre road.

Trains Check in advance. To Oruro US$5.20/US$6.45 and La Paz US$8/US$10, Wed and Sun at 1950. **NB** The train to La Paz leaves after the last bus so if the train doesn't show up you'll need to spend the night in Potosí.

Buses The terminal is 20 mins downhill (30 mins uphill) walk or a short taxi or micro ride from the centre of town on Av Universitaria below rail station, T 27354, Entel, Correo, police, B$0.50

terminal tax. When you buy your ticket you check your luggage into the operator's office and it is then loaded directly onto your bus. Daily services: to **La Paz** 0700 and 1830-1930, US$4-US$6, 11 hrs, buscama from Flota Copacabana US$10. To **Oruro** 0630 and 1900, US$4, 7 hrs. To **Cochabamba** 1830, US$6, 12 hrs. To **Sucre** 0630, 0800, 1300, 1700 and 1800, US$3, 3 hrs. To **Santa Cruz** 1900, US$12, 18 hrs. To **Villazón** 0730, 0830, 1800 and 1900, US$4, 11 hrs. To **Tarija** 0700, 1400, 1600 and 1700, US$6, 12 hrs.

Buses to **Uyuni** leave from either side of the railway line (uphill the road is called Av Antofagasta or 9 de Abril, downhill it is Av Universitaria), daily 1130 and 1200, US$5, 6 hrs. (Trans 11 de Julio also run daily buses to Argentina.)

Buses to the thermal baths at **Tarapaya** leave from outside the Chuquimia market on Av Universitaria and from one block higher every 1/2 hr or so 0700-1700, US$0.50, 30 mins.

VISITS TO THE MINES

The state mines in Cerro Rico were closed in the 1980s and are now worked as cooperatives by small groups of miners. A 4 1/2 hrs morning tour to the mines and ore-processing plant involves meeting miners and seeing them at work in medieval conditions. Visitors need to be reasonably fit and acclimatized as parts are very hard going; not recommended for claustrophobics or asthmatics. Guided tours are offered by former miners, who provide essential equipment – helmet, lamp and usually protective clothing (but check when booking). Wear old clothes and take torch and a handkerchief to filter the dusty air. The price of tours is US$10 pp and includes transport. A contribution to the miners' cooperative is appreciated as are medicines for the new health centre (*Posta Sanitaria*) on Cerro Rico. New projects (a radio, drinking water) have been, or will shortly be realized. You should take presents for the miners – dynamite, coca leaves, cigarettes and water.

● **Guides** By law all guides have to work with a travel agency and carry an ID card issued by the Prefectura. Rec are: Eduardo Garnica Fajardo, Hernández 1035, T 22092 (Koala Tours), he speaks English, French and some Hebrew; Koala Tours offer breakfast at 0600, 'plato típico' with llama meat; they also donate 15% of their fee to support on-site health-care facilities (donations can be sent to Eduardo Garnica); Julio César Morales (Victoria Tours, see *Hotel Casa de María Victoria*), speaks English, takes small groups;

Raul Braulio, Millares 147 (Transamazonas Tours), T 25304, experienced, speaks some English, takes only 1 or 2 people; Santos Mamani, Millares 147, T 28212; Marco Mamani, Pacheco 60, T 27299; Geronimo Fuentes and Maria-Esther (Transandino Tours), speak English, small groups; Salustio Gallardo, C Betanzos 231, nr Plaza Minero; Juan Carlos González, Av Japón 10, T 26349 (Turismo Balsa), Spanish spoken only. Efraín Huanca (Hidalgo Tours), friendly and very informative. The size of tour groups varies – some are as large as 20 people, which is excessive.

A good place to freshen up after visiting the mines (or to spend a day relaxing) is **Tarapaya**, where there are thermal baths (public, US$0.30, private, US$0.60; the private baths, higher up, may be cleaner). On the other side of the river from Tarapaya is a 50m diameter crater lake, whose temperature is 30°C, a beautiful spot; take sun protection. Below the crater lake are boiling ponds. Trucks go straight to Tarapaya. Buses, micros and colectivos from market nr train station, Av Antofagasta, US$0.75. Taxi US$7.50 for a group. Last colectivo back to Potosí at 1800.

Caiza, about 2 hrs from Potosí, on a road which forks off the Tarija road at Ingenio Cucho, is at a much lower altitude than Potosí, so is hotter and can provide relief from *soroche*. Cooperatives produce handicrafts in tin and some silver. On 4 Aug, the entry of the Virgen of Copacabana is celebrated with dancing and traditional costumes. For information go to the tourist office in Potosí. *Hotel San Martín de Porres*, nr plaza, clean, restaurant. Two daily buses from Plaza del Minero, Potosí, 1330.

ROUTES Potosí 164 km NE to Sucre The road is fully paved. It passes San Diego (thermal baths, restaurant), Chaqui (pleasant thermal baths, clean, closed Wed; truck or bus from Plaza Uyuni, 1 hr) and goes through **Betanzos** (1 hr, frequent buses from Plaza Uyuni and cemetery, US$0.70; a few *alojamientos*, G, also hotel, E). The Feria de Papas is held within the first 2 weeks of May; folk dances, music and costumes; good market. A few kms away are the famous Umajalanta caves with well-preserved rock paintings.

Sucre 366 km to Cochabamba, via Epizana on the old Santa Cruz-Cochabamba road (see page 334): the first hour out of Sucre is OK, then it is terrible to Epizana. Thereafter the road is paved to Cochabamba.

SUCRE

Founded in 1538 as the city of La Plata, it became capital of the audiencia of Charcas in 1559. Its name was later changed to Chuquisaca. The present name, Sucre, was adopted in 1825 in honour of the first president of the new republic. It is the official capital of Bolivia. In 1992 UNESCO declared the city a 'Patrimonio Histórico y Cultural de la Humanidad'. There are two universities, the oldest dating from 1624. Long isolation has helped it to preserve its courtly charm; by tradition all buildings in the centre are painted in their original colonial white. It is sometimes referred to as La Ciudad Blanca.

BASICS *Pop* 131,769; *alt* 2,790m; *climate* is mild (mean temperature 12°C, 24°C in Nov-Dec and 7°C in June); *phone code* 064.

Places of interest

Plaza 25 de Mayo is large, spacious, full of trees and surrounded by elegant buildings. Among these are the **Casa de la Libertad**, formerly the Assembly Hall of the Jesuit University (open Mon-Fri 0900-1130 and 1430-1830, Sat, 0930-1130, US$1, US$0.40 to take photographs, US$2.65 to use video), where the country's Declaration of Independence was signed. It contains a famous portrait of Simón Bolívar by the Peruvian artist Gil de Castro "... hecho en Lima, con la más grande exactitud y semejanza" – the greatest likeness. Also on the Plaza is the beautiful 17th century **Cathedral**, entrance through the museum in C Ortiz (open Mon-Fri 1000-1200, 1500-1700, Sat 1000-1200, US$2, if door is locked wait for the guide). Worth seeing are the famous jewel-encrusted Virgin of Guadalupe, 1601, works by Viti, the first great painter of the New World, who studied under Raphael, and other church treasures. Four blocks NW of Plaza 25 de Mayo is the modern **Corte Suprema de Justicia**, the seat of Bolivia's judiciary (entry free but must be smartly dressed, leave passport with guard, guide can be found in library). The nearby **Parque Bolívar** contains a monument and a miniature of the Eiffel tower in honour of Bolivia's richest 20th century tin baron,

Francisco Arcandona, who created much of Sucre's latter-day splendour. The obelisk opposite the **Teatro Gran Mariscal**, in **Plaza Libertad**, was erected with money raised by fining bakers who cheated on the size and weight of their bread. Also on this plaza is the **Hospital Santa Bárbara**.

Southeast of the city, at the top of C Dalence, lies the Franciscan monastery of **La Recoleta** (see **Museums**) with good views over the city. Behind the monastery a road flanked by Stations of the Cross ascends an attractive hill, **Cerro Churuquella**, with large eucalyptus trees on its flank, to a statue of Christ at the top. The cemetery is worth a visit, to see mausoleums of presidents and other famous people, boys give guided tours; take C Junín S to its end, 7-8 blocks from main plaza.

Church opening times seem to change frequently, or are simply not observed. **San Miguel**, completed in 1628, has been restored and is very beautiful with Moorish-style carved and painted ceilings, *alfarjes* (early 17th century), pure-white walls and gold and silver altar. In the Sacristy some early sculpture can be seen. It was from San Miguel that Jesuit missionaries went S to convert Argentina, Uruguay and Paraguay (open 1130-1200, no shorts, short skirts or short sleeves). **San Felipe Neri**, church and monastery, neoclassical, attractive courtyard with cloisters. The monastery is used as a school. The church is closed but ask the guide nicely to gain access. The roof (note the penitents' benches), which offers fine views over the city, is only open for an hour between 1600 and 1800 (times change), US$1 entrance with a free guide from Universidad de Turismo office, opposite the convent, at N Ortiz 182. **Santa Mónica** (Arenales y Junín) is perhaps one of the finest gems of Spanish architecture in the Americas, but has been closed to visitors since 1995. **San Francisco** in C Ravelo has altars coated in gold leaf and 17th century ceilings; the bell is the one that summoned the people of Sucre to struggle for independence (open 0700-0930, 1600-1930). **San Lázaro**, Calvo y Padilla, built in 1538, is regarded as the first cathedral of La Plata (Sucre). On the nave walls are six paintings attributed to Zurbarán; it has fine silverwork and alabaster in the Baptistery, open daily for mass 0700-0745.

Museums

These include the University's anthropological, archaeological, folkloric, and colonial collections at the **Museo Universitario Charcas** (Bolívar 698), and its presidential and modern-art galleries (Mon-Fri 0830-1200, 1500-1800, Sat 0830-1200, US$1, photos US$1.50). The **Museo de Santa Clara** (C Calvo 212), displays paintings, books, vestments, some silver and musical instruments (including a 1664 organ); there is a window to view the church; small items made by the nuns on sale, entry US$0.65, Mon-Sat 1000-1130, 1430-1700. The **Museo de la Recoleta**, C Pedro de Anzúrez (Mon-Fri 0900-1130, 1500-1630, US$2 for entrance to all collections, guided tours only), at the Recoleta monastery, notable for the beauty of its cloisters and gardens; the carved wooden choirstalls above the nave of the church are especially fine (see the martyrs transfixed by lances); in the grounds is the Cedro Milenario, a 1,000-year-old cedar. **Museo de Historia Natural**, C San Alberto 156 (Mon-Fri 0830-1200/1400-1800), US$0.50, good displays, recommended. **Caserón de la Capellanía**, San Alberto 413, houses the textile museum run by Antropológicas del Surandino (ASUR), recommended for explanations of Indian groups and their distinctive textiles; Mon-Fri 0830-1200, 1500-1800, Sat 0930-1200, US$1, English and French-speaking guide.

Excursions

To the **Castillo de la Glorieta**, 5 km S on the Potosí road (*trufi* 4 or E from Arce y Siles), the former mansion of the Argandoña family, built in a mixture of contrasting European styles with beautiful painted ceilings and standing in gardens which must once have been delightful (now run down). Restoration is under way after years of military use and neglect. It is in the military compound, US$1, passports surrendered at the gate, open daily 0900-1200, 1500-1700.

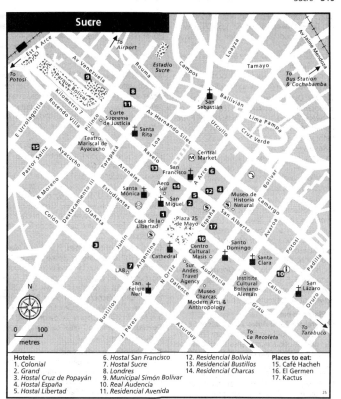

Sucre

Hotels:
1. Colonial
2. Grand
3. Hostal Cruz de Popayán
4. Hostal España
5. Hostal Libertad

6. Hostal San Francisco
7. Hostal Sucre
8. Londres
9. Municipal Simón Bolívar
10. Real Audencia
11. Residencial Avenida

12. Residencial Bolivia
13. Residencial Bustillos
14. Residencial Charcas

Places to eat:
15. Café Hacheh
16. El Germen
17. Kactus

Local festivals

24-26 May: *independence* celebrations, most services, museums and restaurants closed. **8 Sept**: *Virgen de Guadalupe*, 2-day fiesta. **Oct**: *Festival Internacional de la Cultura*, over 2 weeks, shared with Potosí. **21 Sept**: *Día del Estudiante*, music and dancing around main plaza.

Local information
● **Accommodation**

A3 *Real Audiencia*, Potosí 142, T 52809, F 50823, excellent restaurant, modern, rec.

B *Hostal Cruz de Popayán*, Loa 881, T 55156/51706, a beautiful colonial house with interior courtyard, no heating, excellent breakfast served in room or in patio, rec; **B-C** *Colonial*, Plaza 25 de Mayo 3, T 54709/55487,

F 51912, expensive, some rooms noisy, but generally rec, good breakfast.

C-D *Hostal Libertad*, Arce y San Alberto, 1st floor, T 53101/2, spacious comfortable rooms, heating, breakfast and meals in restaurant, highly rec; **C** *Hostal Sucre*, Bustillos 113, T 51411/51928, rooms on patio noisy, great American breakfast for US$2, rec; **C** *Municipal Simón Bolívar*, Av Venezuela 1052, T 51216, restaurant, rec.

D *Grand*, Arce 61, T 52104, F 52461, comfortable, hot showers, inc breakfast in room, good value lunch in *Arcos* restaurant, laundry, safe, rec; **D** *Hostal los Piños*, Colón 502, T 54403, comfortable, hot showers, nice garden, quiet, peaceful, inc breakfast, long way from centre; **D** *Hostal San Francisco*, Av Arce 191 y Camargo, T 52117, **E** without bath, pleasant, meals available, inc breakfast, quiet, comfortable, safe motorcycle parking, large patio, laundry, rec; **D** *Res Charcas*, Ravelo 62, T 53972, **E** without bath, good value breakfast, hot showers, helpful, laundry facilities, will arrange bus to Tarabuco, highly rec; **D-E** *Res Bolivia*, San Alberto 42, T 54346, cheaper without bath, spacious rooms, hot water, breakfast inc, clothes washing not allowed, arranges transport to Tarabuco.

On Av Ostria Gutiérrez (nr bus station): **E** *Alojamiento Austria*, No 518, T 54202, hot showers, good value, restaurant; **F** *Alojamiento Chuquisaca*, No 33, T 54459, shared bathrooms, safe car parking (US$0.50/day). **E** *Res Avenida*, Av H Siles 942, T 51245, hot showers, breakfast extra, laundry, helpful, rec, good Argentine restaurant next door; **E** *Res Bustillos*, Ravelo 158, T 51560, **F** without bath, tiny rooms, hot water, stores luggage.

F *Alojamiento Avaroa*, Loa 419, hot showers, uncomfortable beds, basic but rec; **F** *Alojamiento La Plata*, Ravelo 26, T 52102, without bath, limited shower facilities, basic, nice courtyard, good beds; **F** *Alojamiento El Turista*, Ravelo 118, T 53172, hot showers 0700-1200 only, safe, basic, cheap meals, terrace, doors closed at 2300; **F** *Res Oriental*, San Alberto 43, T 51644, with bath, clean, bit run down but good value, unlockable interior windows, hot water, motorcycle parking.

● **Places to eat**

General and local styles: *Las Vegas* on SE side of Plaza, Nos 36-37, main restaurant and annex (less grand), good, main dishes about US$4, set lunch US$2.35; *La Plaza*, on Plaza 25 de Mayo 33, with balcony, good food and pisco sours, good live music on Fri nights, very popular with locals, set lunch US$2.35; *Kactus*, C España 5, just off main plaza, nice bar and restaurant, pizzas, expensive but highly rec; *El Huerto*, Ladislao Cabrera 86, in beautiful garden, dishes from US$3, highly rec; *Chorizería Los Bajos*, Loa 759, serves special sausages (*chorizo chuquisaqueño*), good, daytime only; *Snack Miriam*, España 136, good *salteñas*; also on España, No 140 is *Snack Lucy*, rec; *La Casona*, Ostria Guitierez 401, nr bus terminal, stylish, *platos típicos*, good value. Good chicken and chips cafés on Camargo between Arce and Loa and on Loa and H Siles. Many fruit juice and snack stalls in the central market; stalls also sell cheap meals (US$0.75-1.40). The local sausages and chocolate are rec.

European styles: *Pizzería Napolitano*, on Plaza 25 de Mayo 30, excellent pizzas (evenings and some lunchtimes) and good home-made ice cream, not cheap; *La Taverne* of the *Alliance Française*, Aniceto Arce 35, ½ block from plaza, closed Sun, French food, also regular films and cultural events, good meeting place; *Piccolíssimo*,

San Alberto 237, very good Italian food, not expensive, popular; *Bibliocafé Sureña*, N Ortiz 30, nr plaza, good pasta and light meals, music opens 1800, closed Mon; *Suizo*, N Ortiz 42, good service, expensive but good, *peña* on Sat, excellent *roesti*, live music some nights; *Kultur-Café Berlin* Avaroa 326, open 1500-2400, good food but limited selection and small portions, German newspapers, *peña* every other Fri, closed Sun (in same building as Instituto Cultural Boliviano Alemán – ICBA), popular meeting place; *Le Repizza*, Calvo 70, very good value lunches, small but good pizzas in evening, rec.

Oriental: *New Hong Kong II*, 25 de Mayo 30, expensive but good, authentic Chinese.

Vegetarian: *El Germen*, Calvo 7, p 2, very good, inc set lunches (US1.60), attractive, elegant with balcony overlooking main plaza, excellent breakfast, US$0.80-1.60, open Mon-Sat 0800-2100, book exchange, German magazines, warmly rec; *Nirvana*, Loa 777, nr Olañeta, open daily for lunch and dinner, good food and atmosphere.

Cafés, etc: *Confitería Palet*, Plaza 25 de Mayo 8, good coffee; *Amanecer*, Pasaje Junín 810-B, German *pastelería*, run by social project supporting disabled children, excellent, opens 1530; *Bunkers*, Ravelo 38, good breakfasts, bar, open 0800 till late; *Café Hacheh*, Pastor Sainz 233, coffee bar, open 1100-2400, art gallery, tasty sandwiches and fresh fruit juices, highly rec; *Salon de Té Las Delicias*, Estudiantes 50, great cakes and snacks, favourite student hangout.

● **Banks & money changers**

Banco Nacional, C España esq San Alberto, cash given on Visa card US$4 commission, good rates for dollars, TCs changed, 2% commission, diagonally opp is **Banco Santa Cruz**, 1% commission for cash on Visa and Mastercard, good rates for cash. Most banks have ATM for cash withdrawal. Travel agencies' rates are good and at *El Arca*, España 134, T 50189, good rates for TCs. Casa de Cambio Ambar, San Alberto 7, T 51339, poor rates for TCs. Stalls at corner of Camargo and Arce buy and sell cash $ as well as Argentine, Chilean and Brazilian currency at good rates. Many shops and street changers on Hernando Siles/Camargo buy and sell $ cash.

● **Cultural centres**

The **Instituto Cultural Boliviano – Alemán** (Goethe Institute), Avaroa 326, Casilla 304, T 52091, shows films, has German newspapers and books to lend (0930-1230 and 1500-2100), runs Spanish, German, Portuguese and Quechua courses and it has the *Kulturcafé Berlin* (see above). Spanish lessons cost from US$3.50 for 45 mins for one person, with reductions the more students there are in the class. The ICBA also runs a folk music *peña* on Fri. **Alianza**

Francesa, Aniceto Arce 35, T 53599, noticeboard on Plaza 25 de Mayo (Casa de Libertad side) announces events. **Centro Boliviano Americano**, Calvo 437, T 51982, library open Mon-Fri 1500-2000 (rec for reference works), rec for language courses. The **Centro Cultural Hacheh** (see address for *Café Hacheh* above), run by Felix Arciénega, Bolivian artist who organizes folk and jazz concerts, conferences, exhibitions and discussions, and is the editor of an art and poetry journal 'Hacheh'. **Casa de la Cultura**, Argentina 65, in beautiful colonial building, presents art exhibitions, concerts, folk dancing etc, open Mon-Sat 0900-1200, 1430-2000.

● **Embassies & consulates**
Germany, Arenales 215, T 54415; **Spain**, Pasaje Argandoña, T 51435; **Italy**, Vice Consul, Dalence 19, T 54280; **Perú**, Avaroa 472, T 55592.

● **Entertainment**
Folklore: **Centro Cultural Masis**, Bolívar 561, T 53403, Casilla 463, promotes the traditional Yampara culture: textiles, ceramics, figurines and music. It offers instruction in Quechua, traditional Bolivian music (3 hrs a week for US\$12 a month, rec) and handicrafts; also musical events and exhibitions. Items are for sale, inc musical instruments to the highest professional standard. Open 1530-2130; contact the director, Roberto Sahonero at the centre Mon, Wed and Fri.

● **Hospitals & medical services**
Doctor: *Dr Gaston Delgadillo Lora*, Colón 33, T 51692, speaks English, French, German, highly rec.
Hospital: *Hospital Gastroenterológico Boliviano-Japonés*, for stomach problems.

● **Laundry**
Laverap, Bolívar 617, quick, US\$2.50 wash and dry. *Lavandería Paola*, Bolívar 543, T 52477, rec.

● **Post & telecommunications**
Post Office: Ayacucho 100 y Junín, open till 2000. *Poste Restante* is organized separately for men and women. **Entel**: España 271, open till 52245.

● **Shopping**
The central market is clean and colourful, wide variety of goods, many stalls selling *artesanía*. A bus from the central market will take you to the *campesino* market. **Artesanías Calcha**, Arce 103, opp San Francisco church, rec, very knowledgeable proprietor. *ASUR*, Antropológicos del Surandino, San Alberto 413, T 23841 (see **Museums** above), weavings from around Tarabuco and from the Jalq'a; weavings are more expensive, but of higher quality than elsewhere. *Charcas*, Camargo 481 y España, high quality hats; *Artesanía Bolivia*, Argentina 31, has a variety of arts and crafts from Tarabuco. Camping gas can be bought at Alberto 25.

● **Sports**
Swimming: pool on Av Venezuela, US\$1 pp.

Tennis: Sucre Tennis Club, Av Venezuela, good clay courts, US\$5 pp inc equipment hire.

● **Tour companies & travel agents**
Sur Andes, N Ortiz 6, T 51983, F 42561, PO Box 736, organizes trekking from half a day to 5 days, inc eg to precolumbian sites such as Pumamachay and the Camino Prehispánico (must take sleeping bag and good shoes, all else provided, but no porters); *Seatur*, Plaza 25 de Mayo 25, T/F 32425, local tours, English, German, French spoken.

● **Tourist offices**
Calle Potosí 102 esq San Alberto, T 55983, good map and guide for sale, US\$2; in the Caserón de la Capellanía/ASUR, but has a different entrance. Check church and museum opening hours. Sub-office at airport, helpful. Tourist information office opp San Felipe Neri, at Nicolás Ortiz 182 (open 0800-1200, 1400-1800 Mon-Fri), is run by students who will show you around tourist sites for free. All offices closed Sat and Sun. For country maps Instituto Geográfico Militar, Dalence, 2, p 1, T 25514, open 0830-1200, 1430-1800, Mon-Fri.

● **Useful addresses**
Car Mechanic: at Camargo 450, rec for Toyotas.
Immigration: Plaza 25 de Mayo, in *Palacio de Gobierno*.

Motorcycle mechanic: Sr Jaime Medina, Motorservi Honda, C René Calvo Arana, T 25484. Will service all makes of machine.

Police radio patrol: T 110 if in doubt about police or security matters.

● **Transport**
Local Taxi: US\$0.55 pp within city limits.

Air LAB and/or Aero Sur fly to La Paz, Cochabamba, Santa Cruz and Tarija, all direct, none daily. Aero Sur, Arenales 204A, T (064) 54895 (Toll free 0800 3030). LAB, Bustillos 127, T 51140/51943 (Toll free 0800 3001). Tucsupaya Airport is 5 km NW of town (T 54445); airport minibus goes from entrance and will drop you off on Siles y Junín, and returns from here, 1½ hrs before flight (not always), US\$0.70, 20-30 mins. Taxi US\$2-3. Trufis No 1 and F go from entrance to H Siles y Loa, 1 block from main plaza, US\$0.55, 25 mins.

Trains Enfe information, T 31115; station is on Plaza Aniceto Arce. No trains to Potosí in 1997.

Buses Terminal is on N outskirts of town, 3 km from centre on Ostria Gutiérrez, T 52029; taxi US$0.65; Micro C or *trufi* No 3. Daily to/from **La Paz** via Cochabamba (19 hrs, US$14), many companies with frequent deps between 0700 and 1700, 3 hrs wait at Cochabamba, very cold at night, Illimani rec and Flota Copacabana bus-cama (first part of road very rough); or via Potosí, US$13 (20-24 hrs) at least 4 companies, dep in am. To **Cochabamba** daily, several companies dep 1800-1830, 10-12 hrs, US$9.75. To **Potosí**, 3 hrs on good paved road; a number of companies have offices in centre of town: Andesbus, Bolívar 621, T 54251/30751, daily 0700 and 1700, US$6.50; Transtur (on Loa, but tickets etc from Sur Andes Travel Agency), all dep from bus terminal; Bustillos dep 1100, US$4. Trans O'Globo goes daily at 0800 to Potosí, continuing to Tupiza (US$12.35) and Villazón (US$13). To Villazón via Potosí daily with Emperador at 0715 and Andesbus at 0700. To **Uyuni**, Americana and Emperador, 0700, 10 hrs, US$9, change buses in Potosí. To **Santa Cruz**, with Bolívar direct Tues, Fri, Sun, dep 1230, 17 hrs; or via Cochabamba, Flota Unificada, highly rec with video, Tues and Fri, 1700, also Mopar, Tues, Fri, Sun (rec) and others, US$13-17, most departures 1130-1300. To **Tarija**, Andesbus' service to Potosí on Mon, Thur and Sat at 0700 continues to Tarija, US$20, 19-20 hrs, daily with Emperador via Potosí at 0715.

TARABUCO

Tarabuco, 3,295m, 64 km by good road SE of Sucre, has a very colourful Indian market on Sun, with local people in traditional dress. It starts around 0930-1000 and is very popular with tourists, but still an enjoyable experience. Those in search of a bargain should have an idea about the quality on offer. **NB** The market is not held at Carnival (when all Tarabuco is dancing in Sucre), Easter Sunday or on a holiday weekend in November.

Local festivals 12 Mar: *Phujllay* independence celebration, very colourful and lively; no one sleeps during this fiesta so no accommodation problems! **Oct**: *Virgen de Rosario*, 1st Sun in October.

● **Accommodation & places to eat** There are at least 2 budget hotels, inc **G** *Res Florida*, basic, cold, dirty, good almuerzo in garden, with music and dancing, good fun; 3 other decent restaurants on plaza and lots of food stalls in market offering tasty local dishes.

● **Transport** Buses (US$2) and trucks (US$1.30) leave from 0630 or when full from Plaza Huallparimachi (take micro B or C from opp Mercado), 2½ hrs journey (or taxi, US$45). Shared *trufi* taxis can be arranged by hotels, with pick-up service, starting at 0700, US$3.25 return. First bus back 1300. AndesBus run tourist service, dep 0800, return 1530, US$6, book at office (address above). Transport more difficult on weekdays; take an early bus and return by truck. Guide to Tarabuco, Alberto from Sucre tourist office, US$45 for a full day in a car for 4 people.

The weavers' villages nearby include **Candelaria** (2 hrs by truck from Tarabuco), Macha (8 hrs from Sucre), **Pocata** (1 hr from Macha), or **Ravelo** (59 km NW of Sucre). At Punilla, on the road to Ravelo, there is a 2½ hrs walk to **Incamachay** where there are precolumbian drawings. Punilla is also where you leave the truck for Challanaca and thence to Potolo, with its distinctive textile designs (red animals on a black or brown background). You can buy direct from the weavers, no stores, but it can be difficult to find them.

● **Transport** To Ravelo: by truck between 0900-1000 from departure point near airport, 3 hrs; *micro*, US$1.65, check at shop at Hernando Siles 843 if it's running, in theory at 0900, return 1600 – trucks back to Sucre invariably full. Trucks to **Potolo** (Thurs and Fri in the dry season) go direct from near Sucre airport; in the wet, you can only get to Challanaca and you walk for 3 hrs to get there.

EAST AND SOUTH OF SUCRE

A main road runs SE from Sucre through Tarabuco, Monteagudo, Camiri and Boyuibe to the frontier with Paraguay at Hito Villazón (not to be confused with the other Villazón on the frontier with Argentina, see above page 311). At Padilla (Km 190, *alt* 2,080m, hotels on plaza), a turn-off heads N 20 km to **Villa Serrano**, where the musician Mauro Núñez lived. A music festival is held on 28-29 December. The journey is beautiful through wild mountains. At **Monteagudo** (Km 323, *alt* 1,138m) there are direct buses to Santa Cruz, twice a week, US$8, 14 hrs. Several basic hotels: **F** *Alojamiento los Naranjos* behind plaza, hot showers, *Alojamiento las Tablitas*, and *Alojamiento Oriental*, both on the main road.

CAMIRI

Further SE at Km 456 is **Camiri** (*pop* 20,000; *alt* 827m), growing rapidly because of nearby oilfields.

● **Accommodation & services** As a garrison town it has several hotels (**E/F** range) inc: **E** *Gran Hotel Londres*, Av Busch 36, motorcycle parking; **F** pp *Res Chaqueña*, C Comercio, clean, good; also restaurants, bars (expensive) and a post office.

● **Transport** Emperador and Andesbus run from Sucre via Monteagudo daily in each direction, at least 20 hrs, US$20. Several minibuses Santa Cruz-Camiri daily, US$10-12, 7-8 hrs. **Road** A paved road heads S from Camiri, through Boyuibe (see below), Villa Montes (see page 327) and Yacuiba to Argentina (see page 353).

CROSSING INTO PARAGUAY

It is possible to drive from Camiri into Paraguay direct in a truck or 4WD, high clearance vehicle, carrying insect repellent, food and water for a week. No help can be relied on in case of a breakdown; a winch is advisable, especially after rain. There are some rivers to ford and although they are dry in the dry season they can be impassable if there is rain in the area. 3 buses a week from Santa Cruz to Asunción via Abapó, Camiri, Boyuibe and Hito Villazón. **Boyuibe**, Km 519, *alt* 817m, the last town in Bolivia (*Hotel Guadalquivir*, or *Hotel Chaqueño* next door, both **F**, both serve meals), is also on regular bus route Tarija- Entre Rios- Villamontes- Santa Cruz. Fuel and water are available, and it is on the Yacuiba railway (rail fare Santa Cruz-Boyuibe: *ferrobus* US$13 and US$10; *rápido* US$5.50 and US$4). Passports are stamped at military checkpoint. If travelling by bus, passports are collected by driver and returned on arrival at Mcal Estigarribia, Paraguay, with Bolivian exit stamp and Paraguayan entry stamp.

750m after the military checkpoint turn left past a large water tower. From then on just follow the most used road; accurate directions may be obtained from the army before leaving Boyuibe. If hitching by bus, at customs post before 0600. It is about 115 km from Boyuibe to the Bolivian border post at Hito Villazón (manned by a Bolivian army unit), very bad road, 3 hrs by bus. You can camp at Hito Villazón, but no food is available, nor is there much water.

The frontier is 12 km E of Villazón at Guaraní and the Paraguayan post is 10 km further E at Fortín Gen Eugenio A Garay. Camping is possible here and for a small contribution the troops may give you use of showers and kitchen. There is a military post (water available) at Fortín Mister Long, about 15 km, further on. "There are long stretches where the road disappears beneath ridges of soft dust; be prepared to spend many hours digging/pushing/pulling your bus out of the countless dust pits in 40° heat" (Simon Watson Taylor, London NW6).

Beyond Fortín Mister Long the road improves through Colonia La Patria and beyond. Entry stamps are given at Mcal Estigarribia where there is a large military base; if you arrive after Fri 1700, you must wait until Asunción and report to immigration there. (For Mcal Estigarribia and the continuation of this route see **Paraguay: The Paraguayan Chaco**.)

TARIJA

ROUTES A road runs S from Potosí to Tarija. At **Camargo**, 186 km from Potosí, accommodation at: **D** *Hotel Cruz Huasa*; **E** *Hostal Las Cañitas*; and a few basic places, **G** pp; also excellent restaurant, *Media Luz*. The vineyards around Camargo produce the country's best singani. The road continues for 182 km to Tarija.

Tarija (*pop* 100,000; *alt* 1,840m; *phone code* 066) was founded 4 July 1574, in the rich valley of the Río Guadalquivir. The city declared itself independent of Spain in 1807, and has a strong cultural heritage. The Indian strain is less evident here than elsewhere in Bolivia. Tarija is a pleasant, small city, with a delightful climate and streets and plazas planted with flowering trees. In **Plaza Luis de Fuentes** there is a statue to the city's founder, Capitán Luis de Fuentes Vargas. The modern Av Las Américas, or **Costanera**, flanks the river.

The best time to visit Tarija is from Jan

onwards, when the fruit are in season. Bolivia's best wines are produced here; see **Excursions** below.

Places of interest

The **Cathedral**, on C La Madrid, is open in the morning and from 1700. **San Francisco** church (La Madrid y Daniel Campos), is beautifully painted inside, with praying angels depicted on the ceiling; note the four evangelists at the four corners below the dome. The library is divided into old and new sections, the old containing some 15,000 volumes, the new a further 5,000. The oldest book is a 1501 *Iliad* incorporating other works. There are also old manuscripts and 19th century photograph albums. To see the library, go to the door at Ingavi 0137 (open 0830-1130, 1530-1730, Sat 0830-1130). Tarija's **university museum**, Trigo y Lema, contains a palaeontological collection (dinosaur bones, fossils, remains of an Andean elephant), as well as smaller mineralogical, ethnographical and anthropological collections; open Mon-Fri 0830-1200, 1430-1800, brochure US$0.65. The **Casa Dorada**, Trigo y Ingavi (entrance on Ingavi), or Maison d'Or, is now the Casa de Cultura (open 0830-1200, 1430-1800, Sat 0900-1200, guided tours only; voluntary donation). This was the house and emporium of importer/exporter Moisés Narvajas and his wife Esperanza Morales, begun in 1886, and has been repainted in original colours, silver and ochre on the outside, cerise, green and dark blue, with white trim, inside. The interior has Italian murals, art nouveau copies on ceiling panels and much gold in the rooms (the photography room contains pictures of Tarijan history and the restoration of the house). It has been described as a superb example of Kitsch decorative art. Near Parque Bolívar (shady, pleasant) is another of Narvajas' houses, the **Castillo de Beatriz**, painted bright blue and white (Bolívar entre Junín y O'Connor; ask the owner if it is possible to visit).

A good view can be had from **La Loma de San Juan**; follow C D Paz to the top of the rise where the buses gather, turn right on the cobbled street, then right through the gate and follow the Stations of the Cross to the top (124 steps up, equestrian statue of Moto Méndez, see **Excursions** below, at the top). On Av Costanera is a pleasant children's park, with open-air theatre, nice gardens, swimming pools and small zoo, US$0.20.

Excursions

The outskirts of the city can be a good place to look for fossils: take a micro or taxi in the direction of the airport. 5 km out of town, before the police control (*garita*), you see lovely structures of sand looking like a small canyon (*barrancos*). Here have been found bones, teeth, parts of saurian spines, etc; things come to the surface each year after the rains. You may have to go a long way from the city.

At **San Jacinto** (8 km, *trufi* from Ingavi y Daniel Campos, by Palacio de Justicia, every 30 mins, 35 mins journey, US$0.45), is a tourist complex beside the lake formed by a dam completed in 1991. At the dam there is a café, several shacks selling food and drink, boats for hire. There is a pleasant, level lakeside walk which can be continued beyond the head of the lake, up the hill to the left (a bit of a scramble to the top) for a good, all-round view. Walk back along the ridge path which descends directly back to the steep ravine which is blocked by the dam (take care on the final descent, in particular do not walk over the cliff where the dam is; keep left, the lake side).

To **San Lorenzo** (15 km, *trufis* from La Loma, top of D Paz, return from San Lorenzo plaza, 45 mins, US$0.40). The road passes Tomatitas river bathing (5 km), and the **Parque Nacional Los Barrancos**, an area of erosion. San Lorenzo's plaza is very pleasant, with palms, oranges and flowers; the church is huge and unadorned. Around the town the land is agricultural; you can walk down to the river (head N and turn right) and ask directions in the fields for the way up the eroded cliffs (45 mins, fine views). Just off the plaza is the Museo Méndez, the house of the independence hero Eustaquio Méndez, El Moto (he lost his right hand, many stories as how it happened). The small museum exhibits his weapons, his bed, his 'testimonio', entry US$0.30, open Mon-Fri 0900-1230, Sat 0900-1200, 1500-1700, Sun 1000-1200. **Los Chorros de Jurina** with natural rock pools, 22 km from Tarija, are 5 km beyond San Lorenzo, you need a guide to walk there (check first if there is water in the falls).

Bodegas

To visit the Aranjuez bodega, ask Sr Milton Castellanos at the Agrochemical shop at Trigo 789. To the Rugero Singani bodega at **El Valle de Concepción**, an appointment must be made with Ing Sergio Prudencio Navarro, Bodegas y Viñedos de la Concepción, Casilla 99, Tarija, La Madrid y Suipacha s/n, T 25040. Ing Prudencio will show visitors round the vineyards and the bodega. To Concepción, 36 km S of Tarija, *trufis* go from Plazuela Sucre every 20-30 mins, US$0.55, return from plaza. The route to Concepción takes the road past the airport, at the *garita* the road forks left to Yacuiba/Pocitos, right to Bermejo. Take the latter and after a while take an unmade road to the right. This area is called Santa Ana. Look on your left for the signposted ex-Russian observatory (a good place to go at night to see the stars). Then you pass the Colonial winery, the Santa Ana bridge and Santa Ana Grande vineyards and the Centro Vitivinicola, Cooperación Española, before reaching Concepción and its plaza filled with bitter orange and ceibo trees.

Local festivals

The city is famous for its colourful *niño* (child) processions. During processions of *San Roque* in a 3-day festival from the first Sun in **Sept** the richly dressed saint's statue is paraded through the streets; wearing lively colours, cloth turbans and cloth veils, the people dance before it as it goes, and women throw flowers from the balconies. Dogs are decorated with ribbons for the day. On the second Sun in **Oct** the flower festival commemorates the *Virgen del Rosario* (celebrations in the surrounding towns are recommended, eg San Lorenzo and Padcaya). Another flower festival takes place in **Easter** week. Also in **Oct**, on two weekends mid-month, there is a *beer festival* on Av de las Américas. Colourful processions take place on **15 April**, *Day of Tarija*.

Santuario Chaguaya, S of El Valle, beyond Padcaya by road, is 60 km S of Tarija. At the fiesta for *La Virgen de Chaguaya*, **15 Aug**, people walk all the way from the city (the pilgrimage route is 45 km). Línea P *trufi* from Plaza Sucre, Tarija, to Padcaya, US$1; bus to Chaguaya and Padcaya from terminal daily, 0700, returns 1700, US$1.35.

Local information

Street numbering: all blocks W of C Colón have a small O before number (oeste), and all blocks E have an E before number (este); blocks are numbered from Colón outwards. All streets N of Av Las Américas are preceded by N.

● Accommodation

A3-B *Victoria Plaza*, on Plaza Luis de Fuentes, T 42700, F 22600, hot water, phone, inc buffet breakfast, laundry service, rec.

B *Grand Hotel Tarija*, Sucre N-0770, T 42684, F 44777, modernized, comfortable, central; **B** *Los Ceibos*, Av Víctor Paz Estenssoro y La Madrid, T 34430, F 42461 (formerly *Prefectural*), inc excellent buffet breakfast, large rooms, phone, mini-bar, good restaurant, outdoor pool and cocktail bar, rec.

D *Hostal Bolívar*, Bolívar E-0265, T 42741, comfortable, hot water, poor breakfast, laundry; **D** *Hostal Carmen*, Ingavi O-0784 y R Rojas, T 43372/44342, shower, good value, some ground floor rooms without exterior windows, good breakfast, sometimes has transport to/from airport, organizes tours of the area, rec; **D** *Hostal Libertador*, Bolívar O-0649, T 44231, phone, sporadic hot water, excellent breakfast extra, family-run, nr cathedral, rec.

E *América*, Bolívar E-0257, T 42627, hot showers, good, run down but quiet, inc small breakfast, good restaurant attached; **E** *Res Rosario*, Ingavi O-0777, **F** without bath, good value, rec.

F *Alojamiento Ocho Hermanos*, Sucre 782, nr main plaza, clean, shared rooms only; **F** *Hostería España*, Alejandro Corrado 0-0546, T 43304, hot showers, pleasant; **F** pp *Res Familiar*, Sucre 656, cheaper without bath, most downstairs rooms without windows.

● Places to eat

Best is *Milano*, in elegant white house at W end of Bolívar where it meets Av Víctor Paz, T 34093, home-made pastas and pizzas around US$2.50, fondue and raclette more expensive, excellent meat, good wine list, rec, annex which houses

Churrasquería, good value. In the evening lots of eating places can be found around the plaza. *La Cabaña de Don Pepe*, N-Campos 0136, nr Av Las Américas, some way from centre, has excellent steaks at reasonable prices; *Cabaña Don Pedro*, in lane off Av Víctor Paz, 1 block W of terminal, good typical food, outdoor patio, moderate prices; *Don Ñato*, 15 de Abril O-0844, good food and service; *Club Social Tarija*, on E side of plaza, pleasant, old-fashioned, excellent *almuerzo* for US$2, rec; *Viejo Bar*, Madrid 0358, on the plaza, good *confitería*, pizzas, ice cream, popular meeting place, bar atmosphere in evening, good food, rec. Also on the plaza: *La Taberna Gatopardo*, pizza, *parrillada* with Argentine beef, hot dogs, snacks, local wines, good value, lively atmosphere; *Pizzería Issabella* and *Fechorías*, good *salteñas* in am, both on W side next to Prefectura; *El Solar*, Campero y V Lema, vegetarian, set lunch, closes 1400; *Chifa Hong Kong*, Ingavi y Gnal Trigo, excellent, US$6 pp, good service; *Pizzería Italia*, C a del Carpo 0-0360, good pasta, reasonable prices, evenings only. For cheap breakfast try the market. Try the local wines, eg Aranjuez, La Concepción, Santa Ana de Casa Real or Kohlberg, the *singani* (a clear brandy, San Pedro de Oro and Rugero are rec labels), also local beer, Astra. **NB** Many restaurants (and much else in town) close between 1400 and 1600.

● **Banks & money changers**
Banco Mercantil de Bolivia, Sucre y 15 de Abril, exchanges cash and gives cash against Visa and Mastercard (US$5 authorization charge). Bidesa, Sucre N-0651, best rates for cash, 2% commission on TCs. *Café Irupana*, Av Domingo Paz 351, charges 3% commission on TCs. Dollars and Argentine pesos can be changed at a number of *casas de cambio* on Bolívar between Campos and Sucre.

● **Embassies & consulates**
German Campero N-0295, helpful; **Argentine** Ballivián N-0699 y Bolívar, T 442273, Mon-Fri, 0830-1230; **Spanish** Ingavi y Méndez.

● **Post & telecommunications**
Post Office: V Lema y Sucre; also at bus terminal. **Entel**: V Lema y D Campos, T 42676; also at terminal.

● **Shopping**
The market is in the block between Domingo Paz, Sucre, Bolívar and Trigo, good basketwork. *Artesanía Juan Gabriel*, Av Domingo Paz y Suipacha, good selection.

● **Sports**
Swimming: Tomatitas, trip of 5 km, popular picnic area (same transport as for San Lorenzo, see above). At lunchtime on Sun in Tomatitas,

many courtyards serve very cheap meals.

● **Tour companies & travel agents**
Internacional Tarija, Sucre 721, T 44446/7 helpful; *Mara Tours*, Gral Trigo 739, T 43490 both helpful. See *Hostal Carmen* above.

● **Tourist offices**
On main plaza in Prefectura, T 31000, very helpful, city map and guide for US$0.20 each.

● **Transport**
Air LAB flies to Santa Cruz, La Paz, Cochabamba, Sucre, Jujuy and Salta. Aero Sur flies daily except Sun to La Paz. Check schedules as they change frequently; also flights are frequently cancelled and/or delayed. TAM fly to/from Tarija. LAB office: Plaza Luis de Fuentes S side next to alcaldía, T 45706. TAM office: La Madrid O-0470, T 45899. Aero Sur office: Ingavi O-0339, T 45820. Taxi to airport, US$1.30 pp or *micro* drops you 2 blocks away. Check hotels have free transport to town, you may have to call them. On arrival at Tarija, reconfirm you return flight immediately. Airport information T 43135.

Buses Daily on the 935-km route Potosí-Oruro-La Paz, dep 0700 and 1700 (26 hrs US$23.25; check which company operates the best buses, eg San Lorenzo has heating). To Potosí (386 km), daily at 1630, US$13.65 with San Lorenzo, San Jorge and Emperador. To Sucre, via Potosí, check if you have to change buses in Potosí. To Villazón, several companies daily deps am and pm, 7 hrs. On Tues, Thur and Sat there is a combined bus/train service to Villazón and La Paz, US$24.50, dep 0700; seat guaranteed on both services. To Santa Cruz, US$19.50, 32 hrs over rough roads, last 140 km from Abapó is paved; via Villamontes, Boyuibe and Camiri; San Lorenzo and Expreso Tarija Mon and Thur at 0730, Sat at 1730, Gran Chaco Thur at 1800; between Entre Ríos and Villamontes is truly spectacular. The new bus station is in the outskirts on Av de Las Américas (30 mins walk from centre, 7-8 mins from airport). Trucks to all destinations dep from Barrio La Loma, 10 blocks W of market.

TO ARGENTINA

The road to Villazón, 189 km, is the shortest route to Argentina; the first 75 km is paved, rest should be paved by end 1997. The alternative route to Argentina via Bermejo is the most easily reached from Tarija, 210 km, the views are spectacular (sit on right); not recommended in the rainy season or a month or so after. The road is quite rough apart from 50 km which are paved. Do not try to cycle. Many uses daily, usually at night, some early am, 4-5 hrs, US$7.75, truck US$4.50. At **Bermejo** (*pop* 13,000; *alt* 415m; at least 3 hotels, 2 *casas de cambio* on main street, thorough customs searches) cross river by ferry to Agua Blanca, Argentina. From Tarija to Yacuiba/Pocitos border is 290 km. Daily buses in am and at night to Yacuiba; from there daily service to Buenos Aires, Salta etc with La Internacional. **NB** Crossing to Argentina, expect up to 4 hrs to pass through customs and immigration. Electronic goods must be entered in your passport for later checks. Also note Bolivia is 1 hr behind Argentina.

VILLAMONTES

Villamontes, 260 km E of Tarija, is renowned for fishing and holds a Fiesta del Pescado in August. It is a friendly town on the edge of the Gran Chaco and is on the road and rail route from Santa Cruz to the Argentine border at Yacuiba. Two roads run E to Paraguay; one follows the Río Pilcomayo SE, the other runs E to Ibibobo; both are only passable in the dry season in high clearance vehicles.

● **Accommodation & services D** pp *Gran Hotel Avenida*, T 2297, F 2412, very clean, a/c, inc breakfast, helpful owner, parking. On street to railway station is **F** *Res Miraflores*, clean, helpful. Good, cheap meals at *La Pascana* and *Chifa Chino*, on plaza, and in market. Entel and TAM office on plaza. Bidesa bank 1 block from plaza.

● **Transport Air** TAM flies to Tarija and Santa Cruz on Sat (T 2135). **Buses** To Tarija via Entre Ríos (280 km, unpaved road, 8 hrs) Thur 0500 and 0600, Sun 0600; via Yacuiba daily at 1700 with Gran Chaco; Expreso Cochabamba daily to Santa Cruz, Sucre, La Paz at 1830; also to Camiri, Tupiza, Villazón.

The Cochabamba Basin

THE fertile foothills surrounding the colonial city of Cochabamba provide much of the country's grain, fruit and coca. Colonial villages and precolumbian sites are also within reach.

It is 394 km from La Paz to Cochabamba by road, now completely paved.

COCHABAMBA

Bolivia's third largest city (*pop* 300,000; *alt* 2,570m; *phone code* 042) was founded in 1571. Its excellent climate (average temperature of 18°C) and the richness of its agriculture, ensured the Cochabamba valley's prosperity as a producer of foodstuffs for the mining areas. Today Cochabamba is an important commercial and communications centre but retains a small-town, rural feel.

Places of interest

At the heart of the old city is the arcaded **Plaza 14 de Septiembre**, with the **Cathedral** dating from 1571, but much added to (open mornings only). Nearby are several colonial churches: **Santo Domingo** (Santiváñez y Ayacucho) begun in 1778 and still unfinished; **San Francisco** (25 de Mayo y Bolívar) 1581, but heavily modernized in 1926; the **Convent of Santa Teresa** (Baptista y Ecuador) original construction 1753; and **La Compañía** (Baptista y

Achá), whose whitewashed interior is completely innocent of the usual riot of late Baroque decoration. From **Plaza Colón**, at the N end of the old town, the wide Av Ballivián (known as **El Prado**) runs NW to the wealthy modern residential areas. To the S of the old town lie the bus and train stations and some of the best produce markets in Bolivia. Overlooking the bus station is the **San Sebastián hill**, offering grand views of the city. From here you can walk to the adjoining **La Coronilla hill**, topped by an imposing monument commemorating the defence of Cochabamba by its womenfolk from Spanish troops in 1812 (beware of robbery). At the E end of Av Heroínas is another hill the **Cerro de San Pedro**, with a statue to Cristo de la Concordia.

Cochabamba was the birth-place of Simón Patiño, the tin baron, who built two houses in the city. One of these, in the centre, is now part of the **Universidad San Simón**; next door on the corner of Calama and Aguirre is his bank, the Banco Mercantil (see the domed interior of the main banking hall). To the N of Plaza Colón at Av Potosí 1450 (T 43137) lies **Palacio de Portales**, the Patiño mansion, now the *Centro Cultural Pedagócico Simón J Patiño*, reached by micro G from Av San Martín. Built in French renaissance style, furnished from Europe and set in 10 ha of gardens inspired by Versailles, the house was finished in 1927 but never occupied; open Mon-Fri 1700 and 1730, and Sat at

1100 for guided tours in Spanish, entrance US$1, don't be late; useful library. There is an excellent art gallery in the basement (open Mon-Fri 1430-1830, Sat 0900-1200, Sun 1000-1200).

Museums

Museo Arqueológico, 25 de Mayo y Heroínas, part of the Universidad de San Simón, Mon-Fri 0900-1200, 1500-1900, Sat 0900-1300, US$1.50, free student guide (Spanish or English) small but interesting display of artefacts including amerindian heiroglyphic scripts and pre-Inca textiles, good 1½ hrs tour. **Museo de la Casa de la Cultura**, 25 de Mayo y Heroínas, Mon-Fri 0900-1200, 1400-1800, free, exhibitions of paintings, occasionally shows films.

Excursions

To the N is **Cerro Tunari**, 5,180m. A road runs to within 300m of the top, usually sprinkled with a little snow. There are beautiful views of the Cochabamba valley from the mountain road which goes into the Parque Tunari from Cala Cala, ending at the lake which supplies drinking water; best in the afternoon. No public transport.

Quillacollo (*pop* 20,000), 13 km W, has a good Sun market but no tourist items; the *campesinos* do not like being photographed. **Fiesta de la Virgen de Urkupiña** lasts 4 days with much dancing and religious ceremony, its date varies each year between June and August. Plenty of transport from Cochabamba, hotels all full throughout the

festivities. Be there before 0900 to be sure of a seat, as you are not allowed to stand in the street. The first day is the most colourful with all the groups in costumes and masks, parading and dancing in the streets till late at night. Many groups have left by the second day and dancing stops earlier. The third day is dedicated to the pilgrimage. (Many buses, micros and *trufis* from Heroínas y Ayacucho, 20 mins, US$0.30.)

2-3 km beyond Quillacollo is a road to the beautiful Pairumani *hacienda*, centre of the Patiño agricultural foundation. Known also as **Villa Albina**, it was built in 1925-32, furnished from Europe and inhabited by Patiño's wife, Albina. The house and Patiño mausoleum may be visited by prior arrangement (T 60082, open Mon-Fri 1500-1600, Sat 0900-1130, Bus 7 or 38, or *trufi* 211 from Cochabamba).

● **Accommodation D-E** *Complejo Planeta de Luz* (hotel ecológico), at Marquina (US$0.65 by bus from Quillacollo, US$10.50 taxi from Cochabamba), PO Box 318, Cochabamba, T 61234, F 91031, hotel, youth hostel (with kitchen, games, reading and dance rooms, music), camping, vegetarian restaurant; it is an ecological Quechua hostal, part of the Movimiento Pachamama Universal; also solar heating, sauna, gardens, pool, natural medicine clinic, tours. Some recent reports indicate undue pressure to join in community activities which are not to everybody's tastes.

The Inka-Rakay ruins, 27 km W of Cochabamba, near Sipe-Sipe: the main attraction is the view from the site of the Cochabamba valley and the mountains ringing the ruins. From Sipe-Sipe to the ruins there is either a 6 km footpath, or a 12 km road with almost no traffic, taking 3 to 4 hrs to walk. It is a beautiful trip, slightly less terrifying on foot than in a vehicle. Start early for it is a full day. Get full directions for the footpath before setting out, or walk there along the road and return by the path (it is easier to find that way). It may be possible to hitch; alternatively hire a guide (Norberto Rojas Mariscal, who runs a shop in the plaza, is recommended, he speaks English). **NB** Take food and plenty of water as there is none available and beware of theft on the footpath. Also worth taking a hat and

sun-block as there is no shade on the path or road. In Sipe-Sipe are *La Cabaña* thermal baths, open all year, with restaurant, good food, book in advance. Bus 245 goes direct from Cochabamba to Sipe-Sipe, also *trufi* 145 (more frequent than bus). From Quillacollo, buses for Sipe-Sipe wait until there are enough passengers.

Tarata, 33 km SE, a colonial town with a traditional arcaded plaza on which stand the church, containing an 18th-century organ and other colonial artefacts (open 0800-1300 daily), the Casa Consistorial, and the Municipalidad. Inside the Franciscan Convent overlooking the town are the remains of the martyr, San Severino, patron saint of the town, more commonly known as the 'Saint of Rain'; festival, on the last Sun of Nov, attracts thousands of people. Large procession on 3 May, day of La Santa Cruz, with fireworks and brass band. Market day Thur (bus US$0.65, 1 hr, frequent, last return 1800, see **Transport** below). Ask for Doña Prima Fernández who sells sweaters at 'amazing prices'; she lives opposite the monastery.

At **Cliza**, 6 km further SE, there is a large Sun market (**G** *Alojamiento*, near bus terminal; see **Transport** below). **Punata**, 48 km E of Cochabamba, has a very lively and colourful market on Tues. Behind the main church, new vehicles are lined up to be blessed by the priest. The local speciality is *garapiña*, a mixture of *chicha* and ice-cream. Beyond Punata, at Villa Rivera, woven wall hangings are produced. At **Arani**, 7 km E of Punata, there is an *artesanía* market on Thur.

Local festivals

Carnival is celebrated 15 days before Lent. Rival groups (*comparsas*) compete in music, dancing, and fancy dress, culminating in El Corso on the last Sat of the Carnival. Drenching from water-throwing is likely the day after Carnival. *Mascaritas* balls also take place in the carnival season, when the young women wear long hooded satin masks. **14 Sept**: *Day of Cochabamba*.

Local information

Street numbering: the city is divided into 4

quadrants based on intersection of Av Las Heroínas running W to E, and Av Ayacucho/Av Libertador Simón Bolívar running N to S. In all longitudinal streets N of Heroínas the letter N precedes the 4 numbers. South of Heroínas the numbers are preceded by S. In all transversal streets W of Ayacucho the letter O (Oeste) precedes the numbers and all streets running E are preceded by E (Este). The first 2 numbers refer to the block, 01 being closest to Ayacucho or Heroínas; the last two refer to the building's number.

● **Accommodation**
L3 *Portales*, Av Pando 1271, T 48700, F 42071, 5-star, swimming pool, a long way from centre.

A1 *Aranjuez*, Av Buenos Aires E-0563, T 41935, F 40158, Casilla 3056, 4-star, rec, 2 blocks from Los Portales, small, colonial style, good restaurant, jazz in the bar, Fri and Sat night; **A2** *Gran Hotel Cochabamba*, Plaza Ubaldo Anze, T 82551, F 42823, beautifully set in the N part of the city (2 blocks from Los Portales at La Recoleta), with garden, swimming pool (guests only) and tennis courts, popular with tour groups, rec. In the city: **A3** *Ambassador*, C España N-0349 (T 48777, F 28778), modern, central and reasonable, good restaurant.

B *Americana*, Av Aroma y Esteban Arce, T 50554, F 50484, fan, helpful, lift, laundry, parking, Rodizio grill next door, good service.

C *Boston*, C 25 de Mayo 0167, T 28530, clean, restaurant, luggage deposit, quiet rooms at back, safe parking, rec; **C** *Ideal*, España N-0329, T 35175, T/F 57930, inc breakfast, restaurant, comfortable, good value; **C** *Unihotel*, Baptista S-0111 Esq Av Heroínas, T 35065, inc breakfast, pleasant, helpful, modern, lift, central.

D *City Hotel*, Jordán E-0341, T 22993, central, inc breakfast, cheaper rooms on upper floors, noisy but modern; **D** *Colonial*, Junín N-0134 entre Colombia y Heroínas, T 21791, with garden and terrace, rooms with big balcony, peaceful, secure, laundry facilities, breakfast served on terrace, highly rec; **D** *Hostal Elisa*, Agustín López, S-0834, T 27846, **E** without bath, good breakfast US$1.25, modern, garden, 2 blocks from bus station, laundry service, very popular with travellers, highly rec; **D** *Hostería Jardín*, Hamiraya N-0248 (entre Colombia y Ecuador), T 47844, **E** without bath, garden, safe car-park, breakfast US$1 extra; **D** *Res Buenos Aires*, 25 de Mayo N-0329, T 29518, **E** without bath, pleasant, clean communal baths.

E *Alojamiento Escobar*, Aguirre S-0749, good value (not to be confused with *Residencial* at Uruguay E-0213); **E-F** *Hostal Florida*, 25 de Mayo S-0583, T 57911, hot water, noisy, popular, laundry service, safe deposit box, breakfast, rec; **E** *Res Copacabana*, Av Arce S-0875 y Brasil,

T 27929, nr bus station, hot showers, motorcycle parking, rec; **E** *Res El Salvador* Montes E-0420, T 27307, with bath, will store luggage, nr market, rec; **E** *Res Familiar*, Sucre E-0554, T 27988, with annex at 25 de Mayo S-0234, T 27986, pleasant, secure, good showers.

F *Res Agustín López*, Agustín López S-0859, T 27250, basic, hot water; **F** *Res Claros*, Av Aroma y Ayacucho, opp bus station, T 24732, hot water only at certain times, small rooms, laundry facilities, OK; **F** *Res Urkupiña*, Av Arce S-0750, T 23502, basic, hot water, shared bath. Many cheap and basic places to stay nr the bus station.

Youth hostel: ABAJ affiliate, **D** *Res Jordán*, C Antesana S-0671, modern, clean, basic. For long-term accommodation, Sra Nora de Durán, Ecuador E-0479, entre 25 de Mayo y San Martín, full board available, good value.

● **Places to eat**
Local and Latin American: *Miraflores*, Av Tarija N-0314, Bolivian food, large, popular, weekend speciality roast pig; *El Caminante*, Arce S-0628, pleasant patio, excellent food inc duck with salad and vegetables; *La Estancia* Anecito Padilla block 7, best steak in town, also grilled fish and chicken (in side street off Plaza Recoleta), also has a salad bar, rec; *Los Troncos*, Junín 0-0942, barbecued meats, stylish, good; *Bufalo*, Torres Sofer, p 2, Av Oquendo N-0654, Brazilian Rodizio grill, all-you-can-eat buffet for US$6, highly rec, great service; *Las Palmeras*, Lanza N-0248, very good food; *Papichín*, Aroma y 25 de Mayo, cheap and friendly, very good chicken and *churrasco*; *Cevichería Arriba Alianza*, Av Oquinda S-06 s/n, highly rec for lovers of Peruvian ceviche, inexpensive; *Acuario Pub*, Ecuador y Hamiraya, superb 4-course self-service meal for US$1.20. Excellent food in Incallacta market for under US$1.

International and European styles: *Suiza*, Av Ballivián 820, T 45485, popular for international cuisine, good value; *BJ*, Av Libertador Bolívar 1580, T 48629, international cuisine, rec; *La Cantonata*, España y Mayor Rocha, Italian, highly rec, though expensive; *Pizzería Don Corleone*, España N-0350, expensive but great pizzas; *Metropolis*, España N-0299, good pasta dishes, huge portions, good value; *Carajillo*, España N-0386, Spanish-style, snacks and drinks, highly rec.

Chinese: *José*, Plaza 14 de Setiembre 0209, popular, not expensive; *Lai-Lai*, Aniceto Padilla 729, rec, also takeaway service; *Chifa Hong Kong*, Hamiraya N-0260, excellent, huge portions, main dishes about US$3.

Vegetarian: *Gopal*, C España 250, Galeria Olimpia, hare-krishna, excellent vegetarian lunch, US$1.60, good spiced bread, and Italian

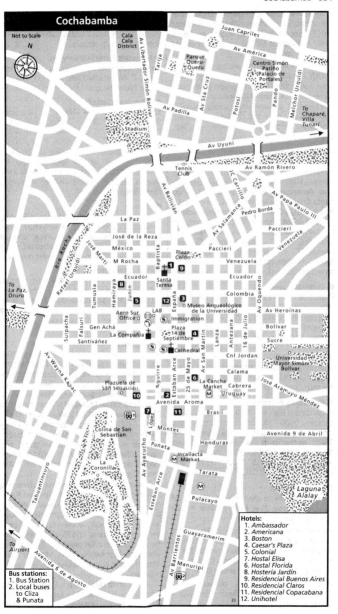

Cochabamba

Not to Scale

N

Cala Cala District

Juan Capriles

Av América

Parque Queru Queru

Centro Simón Patiño (Palacio de Portales)

To Chaparé, Villa Tunari

Av Libertador Simón Bolívar

Tarija

Av Sta Cruz

Potosí

Pando

Melchor Urquidi

Av Padilla

Stadium

Av Uyuni

Tennis Club

Av Ramón Rivero

JC Carrillo

Av Papa Paulo III

Río Rocha

Av Ballivián

La Paz

Pedro Borda

Av Salamanca

Pacciéri

Venezuela

José de la Reza

México

M Rocha

Plaza Colón

Pacciéri

Venezuela

Ecuador

Ecuador

José Martí

Rafael Urquidi

To La Paz, Oruro

Tumusla

Hamiraya

Junín

Santa Teresa

España

Baptista

Colombia

Av Oquendo

Museo Arqueológico de la Universidad

Aero Sur Office

LAB

Immigration

Gen Achá

La Compañia

Plaza 14 de Septiembre

Av Heroínas

Bolívar

Sucre

Suipacha

Falsuri

Santiváñez

Av Wayna Kawac

Aguirre

Cathedral

Av San Martín

Lanza

Antezana

16 de Julio

Cnl Jordan

Universidad Mayor Simón Bolívar

Plazuela de San Sebastián

25 de Mayo

Esteban Arce

La Cancha Market

Calama

Cabrera

Uruguay

José Aramayo Méndez

Colina de San Sebastian

A López

Avenida Aroma

Brasil

Avenida 9 de Abril

La Coronilla

Tahuantinsuyo

Av Ayacucho

Punata

Montes

Honduras

Incallacta Market

Tarata

Laguna Alalay

Esteban Arce

Pulacayo

To Airport

Avenida 6 de Agosto

Guayaramerim

Av Barrientos

Av Manuripi

Bus stations:
1. Bus Station
2. Local buses to Cliza & Punata

Hotels:
1. Ambassador
2. Americana
3. Boston
4. Caesar's Plaza
5. Colonial
6. Hostal Elisa
7. Hostal Florida
8. Hostería Jardín
9. Residencial Buenos Aires
10. Residencial Claros
11. Residencial Copacabana
12. Unihotel

23

in the evenings, pleasant garden, English spoken, closed Sun; *Comedor Naturista*, Ecuador 0-0172, popular and cheap vegetarian; *Snack Uno*, Av Heroínas E-0562, good lunches and dinners inc vegetarian.

General: excellent pastries and ice cream at the *Zurich Tea Room*, Av San Martín Norte 143, open 1500-2000. Good ice-cream parlours on Av Heroínas: *Dumbo* 0440, popular eating and meeting spot, also does cheap meals; *Cristal*, 3 doors away, similar but smaller and quieter; *Unicornio*, Heroínas y Baptista, large, attractive, popular gringo hangout, pricey.

● **Banks & money changers**
Cash on Visa or MasterCard from many banks; no commission on bolivianos. Visa and Mastercard at 'Enlace' cash dispensers at **Banco Boliviano Americano**, Aguirre y Jordán; **Banco Santa Cruz**, 25 de Mayo S-0265; **Banco de La Paz**, Baptista y Gral Achá on main plaza. **Bidesa**, Jordán E-0224, changes TCs, 1% commission for cash dollars or bolivianos, good rates. **Exprint-Bol**, Plaza 14 de Septiembre 252, will change TCs into dollars at 2% commission. Money changers congregate at most major intersections, especially outside Entel, good rates.

● **Cultural centres**
Centro de Cultura El Umbral, España N-0261, video-cinema with good films, theatre with resident company, concerts, dance, art gallery, café with traditional music, library and reading room. **Centro Boliviano Americano**, 25 de Mayo N-0567, T 21288, library of English-language books, open 0900-1200 and 1500-1900; also offers language classes. **Alianza Francesa**, Santiváñez O-0187. **Institut Cultural Boliviano-Alemán**, Sucre E-0693.

● **Embassies & consulates**
Argentina, F Blanco E-0929, T 55859, visa applications 0900-1300; **Brazil**, Edif Los Tiempos Dos, Av Oquendo, p 9, T 55860, open 1400-1800; **Netherlands**, Heroínas 473, *Gitano Tours*, T 28836/29409; **USA**, Av Libertador Bolívar 1724, T 43216, 0900-1200 (will also attend to Britons and Canadians).

● **Entertainment**
Cinemas: on 25 de Mayo opp *Dumbo*; 25 de Mayo y Colombia; 25 de Mayo y Bolívar; and 25 de Mayo y Sucre.

Frequent **concerts** and **plays** at the elegant *Teatro Achá*; more popular stage productions (stand-up comedy, music and dance) at *Tra La La*, Plazuela 4 de Noviembre, opp Chilean consulate, or *Champagne*, C Ballivián 0658.

Discos: *Arlequín*, Uyuni between Plaza Recoleta and stadium; *Reflejos*, Libertador y América, both popular.

Nightlife: is moving to the N area on América between Libertador and Pando. *Wunderbar* in the centre (Antesana 2 blocks from Plaza Colón) good music, darts upstairs.

● **Hospitals & medical services**
Health: Doctor rec by the Tourist Office, *James Koller*, C Baptista N-0386, T 24191, call between 1700-1800.

● **Language classes**
Sra Blanca de La Rosa Villareal, Av Libertador Simón Bolívar 1108, esq Oblitas, Casilla 2707 (T 44298) US$5/45 mins lesson. *Runawasi*, Hinojosa, Barrio Juan XXIII s/n, Casilla 4034 T/F 48923, Spanish and Quechua, also arranges accommodation, rec. *Sra Alicia Ferrufino*, JC Mendoza N-0349, T 81006, US$10/hr, is a rec Spanish teacher; *Patricia Jiménez*, T 92455, Casilla 3968, rec.

● **Laundry**
Superclean, 16 de Julio y Jordán, US$1/kg. *Limpieza Económico*, 16 de Julio entre Venezuela y Paccieri, safe, fast service; also at Women's Prison, Plazuela San Sebastián, good and cheap (possible to visit if you ask guards).

● **Post & telecommunications**
Post Office: Av Heroínas y Ayacucho, next to LAB office (main entrance on Ayacucho); Mon-Sat 0800-1900, Sun 0800-1200. **Entel**: Bolívar y Ayacucho, international phone and Fax (not possible to make AT&T credit card calls), open till 2300, T 25210.

● **Shopping**
Artesanías Casa Fisher, C Ramón Rivero E-0204, opp the Tennis Club, PO Box 3782, T and F 49846, beautiful woollen goods, prices about US$85 locally, US$225-265 in USA. *Fotrama* Cooperative for alpaca sweaters, stoles, rugs, alpaca wool, etc (expensive), run by Maryknoll Mission, factory at Av Circunvalación 0413, T 25468. *Asarti*, Mayor Rocha E-0375, beautiful hand-made and machine-knitted sweaters, can make to order, expensive. For made-to-measure leather goods and alpaca, *Chenza*, 25 de Mayo N-0344, mostly modern designs, highly rec; similarly rec is *Arizona*, Juan Capriles E-0133.

Markets are very good for tourist items and souvenirs. The main market is called San Antonio. La Cancha market (nr railway station) is packed on Wed and Sat with campesinos, 'huge' and well worth a visit'; woollen items are expensive but high quality, US$35-50 for an alpaca sweater. There is a Sat market at Av América y Libertador, best before 0900. Mercado Incallacta is for fruit and vegetables; also sells tourist souvenirs.

A very good **bookshop** is *Los Amigos del Libro*, Av de Heroínas 311 y España, Gral Achá 110, in *Hotel Portales* and *Gran Hotel*

Cochabamba, and in the new Torres Sofer shopping centre, stocks US and English magazines as well as *South American Handbook*. Good city map and guide in colour for US$2.50.

Camera repairs: *Maxell* on Plaza 14 de Setiembre, reasonable prices rec. For developing film *Foto Broadway*, España y Colombia, reasonable prices, inc slide transparencies. *Germán Grunbaum*, 25 de Mayo N-0345, good quality, rec.

Camping equipment: available at shop on 25 de Mayo, just before plaza Colón; wide variety of goods, very helpful owner, speaks English; also Heroínas 225, T 29711. Camping gas available at several shops on Av San Martín.

● **Sports**

Swimming: Tourist complex *El Carmen*, road to Quillacolla, US$2, popular, catch micro on Junín. Pool at Club Social, C Méjico y Plaza Colón (US$1.50), is open to the public. Pool, restaurant at Estancia El Rosedal at Tiquipaya, take bus number 12 from Antesana y Cabrera to end of line. Most are open only at weekend in summer only, check before going.

Tennis: Club de Ténis de Cochabamba admits non-members for US$5/day.

● **Tour companies & travel agents**

Fremen, Tumusla N-0245, T 43827, F 47126, city and local tours, specializes in travel in Bolivian Amazonia, using the *Reina de Enin* floating hotel out of Puerto Varador nr Trinidad; *Tai Tours*, Av Heroínas E-0620, T 51723/21267, adventure tourism. *Turismo Balsa*, Av Heroínas O-0184, T 27065, daily city tours, excursions to Quillacollo, Inca-Rakay, Samaipata, Torotoro, etc, airline reservations (see also under La Paz **Travel agents**).

● **Tourist offices**

Plaza 14 de Septiembre E-0249, T 23364, open Mon-Fri 0900-1200, 1430-1700, helpful, sell city map and guide for US1.25, good service. Also at Jorge Wilstermann airport.

● **Useful addresses**

Immigration Office: Plaza 14 de Septiembre E-0231.

● **Transport**

Local Micros and colectivos, US$0.15; *trufis*, US$0.17; anything marked 'San Antonio' goes to the market. Trufis C and 10 go from bus terminal to the city centre. **Taxis**: about US$0.65 from anywhere to the Plaza; double after dark.

Air Jorge Wilstermann airport. Airport bus is Micro B from Plaza 14 de Septiembre, US$0.40; taxis from airport to centre US$1. Reconfirm all flights (and obtain reconfirmation number) and arrive early for international flights. Several flights daily to/from **La Paz** (35 mins) and **Santa Cruz** (40 mins) with LAB and Aero Sur (book early for morning flights); LAB also to **Sucre , Trinidad** and **Tarija**. See **Information for travellers** for international flights. LAB, Heroínas, between Ayacucho and Baptista, open 0800 (at airport T 50750/50650, opens 0500). Aero Sur, Av Ayacucho S-0170, T 28385.

Buses The main bus terminal is at Av Aroma y Ayacucho. Buses (early am and evening) to **Santa Cruz**, 8-15 hrs, US$9-15; buses take the Chapare route, as opposed to the old mountain road via Epizana (except Cinta de Plata, once a week). See page 334, below. To/from **La Paz** many companies, shop around for best times, services and prices (about US$7.75), by night or day, 7 hrs on paved road. Bus to **Oruro**, US$5.15, 4½ hrs, eg Flota Cometa, 14 a day. To **Potosí**, US$6.75-9.50 via Oruro, several companies. Daily to **Sucre**, US$9.75, 10 hrs, several companies between 1800 and 2015 (Flota Copacabana and Trans Copacabana rec; latter *bus-cama* US$10.40). To Sucre by day; take a bus to Aiquile (see below), then a bus at midnight-0100 passing en route to Sucre (if you want to take a truck in daylight, wait till next day). To **Iquique**, TEPP (Punata) Mon, Wed 1430 via Oruro. Local buses leave from Av Barrientos y Av 6 de Agosto, nr **La Coronilla** for **Tarata**, **Punata** and **Cliza**; Av Oquendo S-0985 (at the edge of Lake Alalay; be careful around this area) to **Villa Tunari**, US$4.50, 4 hrs, several daily; **Chimoré**, US$5.75; **Eterazama**, US$5.75; **Puerto Villarroel**, US$7.75, 6 hrs (from 0800 when full, daily); **Puerto San Francisco**, US$6.50.

TOROTORO NATIONAL PARK

In the province of Potosí is **Torotoro**, a small village best reached from Cochabamba (120 km), set amid beautiful rocky landscape. The village is in the centre of the **Torotoro National Park**, writes Linda Slater, a peace corps worker from Cochabamba. Attractions include caves, a canyon, waterfalls, pictographs, ruins, dinosaur tracks and fossils. Tourist information is available at the national park office in Torotoro. Dinosaur tracks (fossilised?) can be seen by the stream just outside the village. Ask at Santiago, the only shop, for the key to the Umajalanta cave, about 8 km NW of Torotoro; a guide is necessary for both the cave and the dinosaur tracks, US$2.50 pp for whole day.

● **Services** Trucks and *micros* go to Torotoro from Av República y Punata, nr the market in Cochabamba, at 1800 Sun and Thur, US$4, 12 hrs, or a truck also goes from the market at Cliza at about 0800, 10 hrs. Trucks return to

Cochabamba every Mon and Fri. Alternatively, hire a jeep, US$220 for 3 days inc mileage and fuel; quite an adventure. Take your own food as only a limited range is sold at the shop. New *alojamiento* nr bus terminal, **G**, friendly; ask the priest for other places to sleep, rooms are available in locals' homes, cheap and friendly. The village has no electricity.

24-27 July, Fiesta de Santiago; people from surrounding communities congregate here to sing, dance, and drink. **NB** Travel to Torotoro is all but impossible in the wet season (end Nov-May), as flooded rivers wash out roads. Check bus schedules in advance at all times of year.

COCHABAMBA TO SANTA CRUZ

1) **The mountain road**: the 500-km road via the mountains and Epizana to Santa Cruz (page 342) is paved, but the new lowland route is preferred by most transport.

Before the Siberia pass, 5 km beyond Montepunco (Km 119), the 23-km road to Pocona and **Inkallajta** turns off. The Inca ruins, on a flat spur of land at the mouth of a steep valley, are extensive and the main building of the fortress is said to have been the largest roofed Inca building.

• **Accommodation & services** To get there without your own transport, take a micro to the checkpoint 10 km from Cochabamba, then a truck to Km 119, walk towards Pocona then a truck for 15 km, to where a large yellow sign indicates the trail. After approx 10 km the trail divides, take the downhill path and the ruins are a further 2 km. Take food and camping gear. There are several good camping sites. The Cochabamba Archaeological Museum has some huts where visitors can stay, free, but take sleeping bag and food. Water available at nearby waterfall.

Epizana, 13 km beyond Montepunco, Km 128, is the junction for the road to Sucre, 237 km, 6-7 hrs scenic drive, all but the last hour rough, and narrow in parts (*Hotel Urkupiña*, on main road, looks grim; several restaurants; also service stations.) At Km 386 on the road to Santa Cruz is Samaipata (see page 347). 95 km before Samaipata is **Comarapa**, 20 km E of which is the Tambo Mission School, near which is excellent birdwatching (shared accommodation at the school if not already in use, meals at set times, strictly no alcohol; 2 km W is San Isidro with restaurant *El Turista* and a hotel).

EPIZANA TO SUCRE

Totora, on the Sucre road, is a beautiful, unspoiled colonial village. Daily buses from Cochabamba; Pullman Totora (Av Barrientos S-2387, T 29144) at 1600, also at 1430 on Sat; return 0500 Mon-Sat, 1100 Sun. Daily bus to Aiquile at 1600 and to Sucre.

Aiquile, S of Totora and 217 km from Cochabamba, is famous for its wooden *charangos*: *charango* festival in early Nov, ask tourist office; weekend market. Museo Arqueológico Regional, with extensive exhibits on Omereque and Yampara cultures.

• **Accommodation** **F** *Hostal Campero*, Bolívar 960, clean, good food; **F** *Hotel Escudo*, hot shower, comfortable, good food; **F** *Hotel Italia*, OK, good restaurant.

• **Buses** Daily buses from Cochabamba with Trans Campero (Av Barrientos S-2291, 100m past Av 6 de Agosto junction, *trufis* 1, 10, 14, 16, 20 pass in front), daily except Sun at 1300 (Sat 1400), 5 hrs; Flota Aiquile (Av Barrientos S-2365) daily except Sun at 1300.

2) **Via Chapare**: the lowland road from Cochabamba to Santa Cruz runs through Villa Tunari, Sinahota and Chimoré. The road is paved Santa Cruz-Villa Tunari. On this descent to the lowlands, the birdwatching is superb as many types of habitat are traversed.

Villa Tunari (see Cochabamba, **Transport, Buses**, above) is a relaxing place and holds an annual Fish Fair 5 and 6 Aug, music and dancing, delicious meals. Parque Ecoturístico Machía is just outside town offers good trails through semitropical forest; free entry.

• **Accommodation & services A3** *Country Club Los Tucanes*, opp turn-off for *El Puente*, inc breakfast, a/c, 2 swimming pools; **D** *Las Palmas*, T 47554, 1 km out of town, clean, friendly, with pool and good restaurant, rec; **D** *El Puente*, Av de la Integración, with bath in cabins from 2 people to family-size (book in advance at Fremen Travel Agency in Cochabamba or La Paz), to get there continue on the highway through town, cross the second bridge, turn right on the first road to the right, then go 2 km, the turn is clearly marked, the hotel has a beautiful stream and 14 natural pools; **E** *Los Araras*, across bridge on main road to Santa Cruz, T (0411) 4116, large rooms, nice gardens, good breakfast; **F** *La Querencia*, pleasant terrace on river front, .avoid noisy rooms at front, good cheap food, clothes washing facilities. Several other hotels; also restaurants, Entel office, Post office and bank. **In Chimoré**: *Hotel Copacabana*, used by military and prostitutes; water cuts common June-Sept; *Restaurants El Tamarindo*, on right entering village from Cochabamba, and *El Curichi*, on left, mostly for bus passengers, token system, limited menu, but OK. **In Ivirgarzama**: *Hotel El Torero*, very basic; *Restaurant Punata*, 100m from bus station, popular.

The Northern Lowlands

FROM SCRUBBY east lowlands to dense tropical jungle in the north, this is pioneer country: missionaries, rubber tappers and cocaine refiners. Improved roads to Rurrenabaque and Trinidad are opening up the area and wildlife expeditions are becoming increasingly popular.

Bolivia's Northern lowlands, the Cuenca Amazónica, account for about 70% of national territory. Beni department has 53% of the country's birds and 50% of its mammals, but destruction of forest and habitat is proceeding at an alarming rate. A **Beni Biosphere Reserve**, under the auspices of Unesco, has been set up. As much archaeological work is taking place in Beni as in the altiplano; the same efforts to reinstate precolumbian agricultural methods are being made in each zone.

ROUTES There are two main land routes into the northern lowlands: one from La Paz and one from Villa Tunari on the Cochabamba-Santa Cruz road.

CARANAVI TO SAN BORJA

From Caranavi, a road runs N to **Sapecho**, where there is an interesting cocoa cooperative (**E-F** *Alojamiento Rodríguez*, very friendly and pleasant, recently upgraded) and a bridge over the Río Beni. Beyond Sapecho, the road passes through Palos Blancos 7 km from the bridge (Sat market day, several cheap lodgings). The road between Sapecho and Yucumo is now a very good all-weather gravel surface, 3 hrs from Sapecho *tránsito*. There are *hospedajes* (F) and restaurants in **Yucumo**. 550,000 ha of jungle are under cultivation, rice, sugar, corn and fruit being planted. The Chimanes indians are trying to survive the influx of settlers from the altiplano. At Yucumo a road branches NW, fording rivers 21 times on its way to Rurrenabaque.

● **Buses** Yucumo is on the La Paz-Caranavi-Rurrenabaque or San Borja routes. Rurrenabaque-La Paz bus passes through about 1800. If travelling to Rurrenabaque by bus or truck take extra food in case there is a delay for river levels to fall.

SAN BORJA

From Yucumo it is 50 km (1-2 hrs) to **San Borja**, a small, dusty cattle-raising centre with hotels and restaurants clustered near the plaza. This is a coca-growing region and it is unwise for travellers to wander alone inside the Parque Nacional Isiboro in case they are mistaken by coca farmers for DEA agents.

● **Accommodation D-E** *Hostal Jatata*, T 3103, 2 blocks from plaza, modern, comfortable, fans, good snack bar, highly rec; **F** *Trópico*, 1 block from main plaza, clean, rec; **E-F** *Res Manara*, just off plaza, clean, comfortable, some rooms with a/c; **G** *Jaropa*, clean, basic.

● **Places to eat** *Taurus*, good food, cheap; *Club Social*, 2 blocks from plaza, covered open-air restaurant, good *almuerzos*.

● **Banks & money changers** Good rate for dollars at *Joyería San Borja* next to entrance to supermarket round corner from central market.

● **Transport** Flota Yungueña daily except Thur at 1300 to La Paz (19 hrs); also to Rurrenabaque, Santa Rosa, Riberalta, Guayaramerín Thur, Sat, Sun. From San Borja the road goes E to **Trinidad** via San Ignacio de Moxos. There are 5-6 river crossings and, in the wetlands, flamingoes, blue heron and a multitude of waterfowl. The road surface Caranavi-San Borja is very good; San Borja-San Ignacio poor, long stretches are rutted and pot-holed; San Ignacio-Trinidad is good. Gasoline available at Yolosa, Caranavi, Yucumo, San Borja and San Ignacio. Minibuses and camionetas run daily between San Borja and Trinidad throughout the year, about 7 hrs inc 20 mins crossing of Río Mamore on ferry barge. 1 de Mayo daily to San Ignacio (US$8), Trinidad and Santa Cruz at 0850; daily micros and camionetas to Trinidad, US$15, or hitch on a timber truck. Aero Sur flies to Trinidad, daily except Sat.

RURRENABAQUE

Rurrenabaque is a small, picturesque jungle town, on the Río Beni, with San Buenaventura on the opposite bank. Mosquito nets can be bought here much more cheaply than in La Paz. Public swimming pool in town, US$1; Entel office; electricity 1800-2400.

Jungle tours

Agencia Fluvial, at *Hotel Tuichi* runs jungle tours on the Río Tuichi, normally 4 days, but shorter by arrangement, for a group of 5 or more, US$25 pp/day (payable in dollars) inc food, transport and mosquito nets (write to Tico Tudela, Agencia Fluvial, Rurrenabaque). 3 nights are spent in the jungle, learning about plants, survival and the foods of the region. Take swimming costume, insect repellent to ward off sandflies and mosquitoes and a camera. Fluvial also run 3-day 'Pampas Tours' on a boat to Río Yacuma, US$30 pp/day. Fluvial tours can be arranged through *Hotel Tuichi*; recommended guide is Negro. Tico Tudela has opened *Hotel de la Pampa* near Lago Bravo, 2½ hrs from Rurrenabaque. It's a base for visiting Lago Rogagua (birds) and Río Yacuma (anacondas, monkeys, caiman, capybara, pink dolphins, etc). Fully inclusive tours (including meals and accommodation). US$40 pp/day. Pampas tours also with *Ecotour*, office opp *Hotel Berlín*; and *Nahama Tours*, Leo Janko, Av Santa Cruz y Avaroa; both charge US$30 pp/day and are recommended. The jungle is very hot in the rainy season with many more biting insects and far fewer animals to be seen. One day trips are reportedly a waste of time as it takes 3 hrs to reach the jungle. You see far more wildlife on a pampas tour and the weather and general conditions are far more pleasant; season July to October.

Local information

● Accommodation

Most hotels in Rurrenabaque are noisy owing to all night discos.

E *Santa Ana*, **F** without bath, nr plaza, basic, cold water, laundry, pretty courtyard, rec; **E** *Porteño*, cheaper without bath, quite good.

F *Oriental*, on Plaza, **G** without bath, breakfast available, rec; **F** *Rurrenabaque*, safe, cooking and laundry facilities; **F** *Tuichi*, kitchen and laundry facilities, fan.

● Places to eat

Best meals at *Club Social Rurrenabaque*, vegetarian dishes on request. Good ice-cream at *Bambi*, opp Flota Yungueña office, good meeting place; *El Tacuara*, next to *Ecotour*, good. Restaurants facing canoe dock offer good meals for under US$1.

● Banks & money changers

Agencia Fluvial, 5% commission on TCs.

● Transport

Air To and from La Paz with LAB Mon, Wed and Sat. Itemox Express flies from Trinidad to Reyes, 30 km N (lodging, restaurants), a useful alternative to the bus ride.

Road To/from La Paz via Caranavi Mon-Sat with Flota Yungueña and Totai, dep 1200 and 1500, 18-20 hrs, US$8.75. Bus to Riberalta, Tues, Thur, Sat, Sun 2330, 12 hrs, continues to Guayaramerín; trucks also go to Riberalta. To Trinidad, Tues, Thur, Sat, Sun at 2230 with Trans Guaya via Yucumo and San Borja.

River Boats to Guanay, US$16 pp; ask at *Agencia Fluvial* or other tour agencies; take your own food.

From Rurrenabaque an all-weather road leads via **Santa Rosa** (**F** *Hotel Oriental*, changes dollars. *Restaurant and Confitería El Triángulo*, very friendly, recommended) to **Riberalta**.

The charming town (*pop* 60,000; *alt* 175m) is at the confluence of the Madre de Dios and Beni rivers, which together flow into the Mamoré N of Guayaramerín and rather off the beaten track. The whole region attained temporary importance during the natural-rubber boom of the late 19th century. It is a centre for brazil nut production.

Some 25 km away is **Tumi-Chucua** situated on a lovely lake. Nearby are the Nature Gardens. Here you can fish in the lake, good for birdwatching. They also have lots of information on the rainforest, the rubber boom and brazil nut production. Contact Dr Willy Noack, T/F (591) 3 522497 for further information.

Local information

● Accommodation

Ask for a fan and check the water supply.

C-D *Hostal Tahuamanu*, M Hanicke 75, T8006, modern, smart, very comfortable, a/c, inc excellent breakfast, highly rec; **E** *Res Los Reyes*, nr airport, with fan, safe, pleasant but noisy disco nearby on Sat and Sun; **E-F** *Colonial*, Plácido Méndez 1, charming colonial casona, large, well-furnished rooms, nice gardens and courtyard, comfortable, good beds, helpful owners, highly rec.

F pp *Comercial Lazo*, C NG Salvatierra, **D** with a/c, comfortable, laundry facilities, good value; **F-G** *Nor-Oeste*, Av Moreno y Av Molina, T 597, basic rooms, good for budget travellers; **F-G** *Res El Pauro*, Salvatierra 157, basic, shared baths, good café.

● Places to eat

Club Social Progreso, on plaza, good value *almuerzo*. excellent fish; *Club Social Riberalta*, on Maldonado, good *almuerzo* US$3.50, smart dress only; *Quatro Ases*, C Arce, good; *Tucunare*, M Chávez/Martínez, rec. Good lunch at *comedor popular* in market, US$1.50.

● **Banks & money changers**
Banco Internacional de Desarrollo (Bidesa) on Maldonado, changes cash and TCs for $ or bolivianos; also change cash in shops and on street.

● **Transport**
Air Aero Sur, on plaza (T 2798), flies 6 times weekly to Trinidad. Expect delays in the wet season. LAB fly to Guayaramerín, Trinidad, La Paz, Cobija and Cochabamba; office at M Chávez 77, T 2239. TAM flies to Cochabamba, Santa Cruz and La Paz Thur; office Av Suárez/Chuquisaca, T 2646. Check all flight details in advance.

Road Several companies (inc Yungueña) to La Paz, via Rurrenabaque and Caranavi Tues-Sat at 1100, also Tues, Thur, Sat at 1000; US$19.50. To Trinidad with 8 de Diciembre Mon, Wed, Thur, Sat, Sun at 0830, also Trans Guaya daily at 0930, via Rurrenabaque; to Guayaramerín 12 weekly services on Tues, Thur, Sat, Sun at 0630, 1400 and 1700, daily with TransAmazonas at 0730 and 1630; to Cobija on Wed, Fri, Sat at 0900 with 8 de Diciembre, Mon, Thur at 1000 with TransAmazonas. Buses stop in Santa Rosa for meals.

River Cargo boats carry passengers along the Río Madre de Dios, but they are infrequent. There are not many boats to Rurrenabaque.

GUAYARAMERIN

From Riberalta the road continues E, crossing the Río Yata before reaching **Guayaramerín**, a cheerful, prosperous little town (*pop* 35,000) on the bank of the Río Mamoré, opposite the Brazilian town of Guajará-Mirim. It has an important *Zona Libre*. Passage between the two towns is unrestricted; boat trip US$1.65 (more at night).

Local information
● **Accommodation**
B *Esperanza*, Cachuela Esperanza, Casilla 171, reserve through Aero Sur, T 0855 2201, or in La Paz *American Tours*, T 374204, F 328584, eco-friendly.

C *San Carlos*, 6 de Agosto, 4 blocks from port, T 2152/3, with a/c (**D** without), hot showers, changes dollars cash, TCs and reais, swimming pool, reasonable restaurant.

E *Santa Ana*, 25 de Mayo, **F** without bath, close to airport, rec.

F *Litoral*, on 25 de Mayo, nr LAB office, cold water only; **F** *Plaza Anexo*, on Plaza, good value, cold water only, ceiling fan.

● **Places to eat**
All on Plaza: *Made in Brazil*, good coffee; *Gipssy*, good *almuerzo*; *Los Bibosis*, popular with visiting Brazilians. *Only*, 25 de Mayo/Beni, good *almuerzo* for US$2.50, plus Chinese; on road to airport *Heladería Tutti-Frutti*, excellent.

● **Transport**
Air Aero Sur, on plaza (T 2493) to Trinidad. LAB flies to Trinidad, Riberalta, La Paz, Cobija and Cochabamba; office on 25 de Mayo, T 2040. TAM flies to Cochabamba, Santa Cruz and La Paz; office at 16 de Julio (road to airport).

Buses To/from **La Paz**, Flota Yungueña, 5 a week, 36 hrs, US$21.50; to **Riberalta** 2 hrs, US$5.75, 7 deps daily 0700-1730; to **Trinidad** Fri, 30 hrs, US$23; to **Rurrenabaque**, US$16; to **Cobija** 4 a week; to **Santa Cruz** via Trinidad, 1-2 a week, 2½ days. Buses dep from Gral Federico Román.

River Check the notice of boats leaving port on the Port Captain's board, prominently displayed nr the immigration post on the river's bank. Boats up the Mamoré to Trinidad are fairly frequent – a 3-day wait at the most.

FRONTIER WITH BRAZIL
● **Bolivian immigration**
Av Costanera nr port; open 0800-1100, 1400-1800. Passports must be stamped here when leaving, or entering Bolivia.

Entering Bolivia: passports must be stamped at the Bolivian consulate in Guajará-Mirim.

● **Brazilian consulate**
On 24 de Septiembre, Guayaramerín, open 1100-1300; visas for entering Brazil are given here.

● **Banks & money changers**
Exchange money here (TCs at 2% commission in Bidesa bank on plaza) as this is very difficult in the State of Rondônia in Brazil.

COBIJA

The capital of the lowland Department of Pando lies on the Río Acre which forms the frontier with Brazil. It is an unattractive town (*pop* 7,000; *alt* 252m), whose only redeeming feature is the fact that it is a duty-free zone. Shops in centre have a huge selection of imported consumer goods at bargain prices. Brazilians and Peruvians flock here to stock up. The rainy season is Nov to Mar; the rest of the year is dry and hot. Temperatures average 29°C but can reach 40°C, or fall to 15°C when the *surazo* blows. This area has many Brazilian residents. Foodstuffs are much more expensive than in La Paz. Festival 24 September.

Local information
● **Accommodation & places to eat**
D-E *Prefectural Pando*, Av 9 de Febrero, T 2230, inc breakfast, *comedor* does good lunch, poor value, manager Sr Angel Gil, helpful; **F** *Res Frontera*, basic, cheap, fan; **E** *Res Crocodilo*, Av Molina, comfortable, good atmosphere, rooms with fan. *La Esquina de la Abuela*, opp Res Crocodilo, good food, not cheap. Good cheap meals in *comedor popular* in central market.

● **Banks & money changers**
Bidesa Bank on Av 2 de Febrero changes TCs.

● **Hospitals & medical services**
There is an old hospital, a recently built one (Japanese-funded), and the Red Cross.

● **Post & telecommunications**
Post Office: on plaza. **Entel**: on C Sucre, for telephone calls internal and abroad and fax, much cheaper than from Brazil.

● **Transport**
Local Taxis: are very expensive, charging according to time and distance, eg US$10 to the outskirts, US$12 over the international bridge to Brasileia. Besides taxis there are motorbike taxis (much cheaper). Brasileia can also be reached by canoe, US$0.35.

Air Aero Sur, in *Hotel Pando*, T 2230, flies daily except Sun to Trinidad. LAB office on Av Molinos, to Riberalta, Guayamerín, Trinidad and La Paz. TAM office on 2 de Febrero (check schedule).

Buses Flota Yungueña to La Paz via Riberalta and Rurrenabaque Sat at 0700 (check times first, T2318); to Riberalta with several bus companies and trucks, dep from 2 de Febrero, most on Wed, Fri, Sun at 0600; good all-weather surface; 5 river crossings on pontoon rafts, takes 10-11 hrs.

VILLA TUNARI TO THE LOWLANDS

PUERTO VILLARROEL

Another route into Beni Department is via the lowland road between Cochabamba and Santa Cruz. At Ivirgazama, E of Villa Tunari, the road passes the turn-off to **Puerto Villarroel**, 27 km further N, from where cargo boats ply irregularly to Trinidad in about 4-10 days (see below). You can get information from the Capitanía del Puerto notice board, or ask at docks.

● **Accommodation & services** *Hotel Hannover*, no fans, dirty toilets, facilities shared with late night disco; *Alojamiento El Jazmín*, small, helpful, pleasant, meals served; also *Alojamiento Petrolero*. There are very few stores in Villarroel. Sr Arturo Linares at the Cede office organizes boat trips to the jungle – not cheap.

● **NB** As this is coca-growing territory the police advise not to stray from the main road, don't talk to strangers and don't guard or carry other people's luggage.

● **Transport** *Camionetas* go from the junction on the main road to Puerto Villarroel a few times a day, 1 hr, US$1.20. From Cochabamba you can get a bus to Puerto Villarroel (see Cochabamba **Transport**, **Buses**), Puerto San Francisco, or Todos Santos on the Río Chapare.

● **By boat to Trinidad**: Puerto Villarroel is the main port for river transport to the N of Bolivia. The road network is being extended, but many roads can only be used in the dry season. Boats sail between Puerto Villarroel, Trinidad and Guayaramerín, taking passengers. This trip is only for the hardy traveller. In the rainy season when the river is high it takes about 3 to 5 days to Trinidad (45 hrs sailing, but boats stop from sunrise to sunset; US$15 for 3 days and nights inc meals – prices and quality vary); in the dry season, ie between May or June and Aug-Dec, it may last 8 to 10 days (the river is lower, cleaner and there may be more animals to see on the shore – there may be no boats Oct-December). It is another 5 days to Guayaramerín. If you are fussy about food in general, don't make the trip because the kitchen is beyond description and the toilet facilities, too. Take your own drinking water, or water sterilizing tablets as the water served is taken from the river. Supplement the diet with fruit and any other interesting food you can find beforehand. The countryside between Puerto Villarroel and Trinidad is more or less cultivated, with plantations of bananas and cattle ranches. One can see *petas* – small turtles basking in the sun, capibara, river dolphin, jumping fish, now and then monkeys on the beach, and many types of birds. A mosquito net is a 'must', a hammock a good idea, and binoculars for watching the wildlife a useful extra. Bathing in the river is safe.

TRINIDAD

The capital of the lowland Beni Department, founded 1686, is a dusty city in the dry season, with many streets unpaved (*pop* 60,000; *alt* 237m). There are two ports, Almacén and Varador, check which one your boat is docking at. Puerto Varador is 13 km from town on the Río Mamoré on the road between Trinidad and San Borja; cross the river by the main bridge by the market, walk down to the service station by the police checkpoint and take a truck, US$1.70. Almacén is 8 km from the city. The main mode of transport in Trinidad (even for taxis, US$0.40 in city) is the motorbike; rental on plaza from US$2hr, US$8/half day.

Excursions

Hire a motorbike or jeep to go to the river; good swimming on the opposite bank; boat hire US$5. 5 km from town is the Laguna Suárez, with plenty of wildlife; the water is very warm, the bathing safe where the locals swim, near the café with the jetty (elsewhere there are stingrays and alligators). Motorbike taxi from Trinidad, US$1.30.

17 km N is **Chuchini** with the Madriguera del Tigre, an ecological and archaeological centre, accessible by road in dry season and by canoe in wet season. Contact Efrém Hinojoso at C Cochabamba 232 entre Bolívar y Sucre, T 21811; or Edwin Portugal in La Paz, T 341090, T/F 343930; 3 days/2 nights US$210 pp, including accommodation and meals; plenty of wildlife to be seen; also inc **Museo Arqueológico del Beni**, containing human remains, ceramics and stone objects from precolumbian Beni culture, said to be over 5,000 years old. Tours can also be booked through tour agencies in town.

Local information
● **Accommodation**
A2-A3 *Gran Moxos*, Av 6 de Agosto y Santa Cruz, T 22240, inc breakfast, a/c, fridge bar, cable TV, phone, good restaurant, accepts Visa and Mastercard; **A2-A3** *Mi Residencia*, Manuel Limpias 76, T (046) 21529/21376, F 22464, a/c, inc breakfast; **A2-A3** *Mi Residencia II*, Felix Pinto Sancedo y 9 de Abril, quieter and with pool.

B *El Bajío*, Av Nicolás Suárez 520, T 22400/20030, a/c, cheaper with fan, inc breakfast, pool (US$2 for non-residents).

C-D *Monteverde*, 6 de Agosto 76, T 22342/22738, with or without a/c, fridge bar, inc breakfast, owner speaks English, rec.

D *Copacabana*, Tomás Villavicencio, 3 blocks from plaza, T 22811, F 21978, good value, **F** pp without bath; **D-E** *Hostal Triny*, C Sucre 353,

T22613, good value, fan; **D-E** *Paulista*, Av 6 de Agosto 36, T 20018, cheaper without bath, comfortable, good restaurant.

E *Res Oriental*, 18 de Noviembre nr Vaca Díez, T 22534, with bath, good value.

F *Brasilia*, 6 de Agosto 46, T 21685, shared bath, fan, basic.

G pp *Res Palermo*, Av 6 de Agosto 123, T 20472, shared bath, basic, restaurant.

● **Places to eat**
Brasilia, Av 6 de Agosto, good dinner; *Carlitos*, on Plaza Ballivián, rec; *Pescadería El Moro*, Bolívar and 25 Diciembre, excellent fish; also several good fish restaurants in Barrio Pompeya, S of plaza across the river. Good value lunch, US$1.55, at *Jardín Cervecero*, opp *Hotel Monteverde* on Av 6 de Agosto; *Club Social 18 de Noviembre*, N Suárez y Vaca Díez on plaza, good lunch for US$1.35; *La Casona*, on the main plaza, for good pizzas and set lunch, closed Tues; *La Estancia*, on Ibare entre Muibe y Velarde, excellent steaks. Burgers, ice cream and snacks at *Kivón* cafeteria on main plaza; also on plaza, *Heladería Oriental*, good coffee, icecream, cakes, popular with locals. *Balneario Topacare* is a restaurant and bathing resort 10 mins out of town on Laguna Suárez; delicious local specialities, lunch or dinner, beautiful location, excellent bird spotting, favourite spot for locals at weekends. Cheap meals, inc breakfast, are served at the fruit and vegetable market. Try sugar cane juice with lemon – delicious.

● **Banks & money changers**
TCs changed at *Bidesa*, on Vaca Díez nr plaza, 2% commission; **Banco Mercantil**, J de Sierra, nr plaza, changes cash and TCs, cash on Visa. Street changers on 6 de Agosto.

● **Post & telecommunications**
Entel and **Correos** (open daily till 1930) in same building at Av Barace, just off plaza.

● **Tour companies & travel agents**
All on 6 de Agosto: *Tarope Tours*, No 81, T/F 21468, Casilla 351; *Paraíso Travel*, No 138, T/F 20692, Casilla 261, does 'Conozca Trinidad' packages; *Moxos*, No 114, T 21141, Casilla 252, rec; *Fremen*, No 140, F 21834, run speed boat trips along the Mamoré and Iboré rivers and to Isiboro National Park; their *Flotel Reina de Enin* offers tours of more than 1 day, US$70 pp/day, good food. Most agents offer excursions to local *estancias* and jungle tours down river to Amazonia. Most *estancias* can also be reached independently in 1 hr by hiring a motorbike. Note that the more distant parts of Isiboro are at present too dangerous owing to violent disputes between *cocaleros* and the authorities. Tours to Isiboro are very expensive because of the distances involved.

● **Tourist offices**
In Prefectural building on plaza, ground floor, T21722, very helpful, sells guide and city map, US$2.

● **Transport**
Air LAB, at Santa Cruz 324, 20595; to La Paz (daily, direct); to Cochabamba, Santa Cruz, Magdalena, San Joaquín, Cobija, Guayaramerín and Riberalta (check schedules). Aero Sur, Av Barace 51, T 20765/21117; daily to La Paz and Santa Cruz; daily except Sun to Cobija, Guayaramerín, San Borja, and except Sat to Riberalta. TAM, at airport, T 20355, to Baures, Bella Vista, Magdalena and Huacaraje, Riberalta, Guayaramerín, Santa Cruz and La Paz. Itemox Express (Av 6 de Agosto 281, T 22306) has flights to Baures, Huacaraje, Bella Vista, Magdalena, Reyes (nr Rurrenabaque) and Santa Rosa. Airport authority, AASANA, T 20678. Taxi to airport US$1.20.

Buses Several flotas daily to/from La Paz via San Borja and Caranavi, 20-21 hrs, dep 1730, US$17.50 (see also under San Borja, **Transport**). To Santa Cruz (12 hrs in dry season, US$5.80) and Cochabamba (US$11.60), with Copacabana, Mopar and Bolívar at 1700, 1730 and 1800; Trinidad to Casarabe is paved and Santa Cruz to El Puente; good gravel surface on all sections of unpaved road. To Rurrenabaque (US$15.40), Riberalta (US$21.15) and Guayaramerín (US$23), connecting with bus to Cobija; Guaya Tours daily at 1000; road often impassable in wet season, at least 24 hrs to Rurrenabaque. Motorbike taxis will take people with backpacks from bus station to centre for US$0.45; bus station is on Mendoza, between Beni and Pinto, 9 blocks E of main plaza.

River Cargo boats down the Río Mamoré to Guayaramerín take passengers, 3-4 days, assuming no breakdowns, best organized from Puerto Varador (speak to the Port Captain). *Argos* is rec as friendly, US$22 pp, take water, fresh fruit and toilet paper. Ear-plugs are also rec as hammocks are strung over the engine on small boats; only for the hardy traveller.

SAN IGNACIO DE MOXOS

90 km W of Trinidad, known as the folklore capital of the Beni Department. The traditions of the Jesuit missions are still maintained with big *fiestas*, especially during Holy Week; 31 July is the town's patron saint's day, one of the country's most famous and colourful celebrations. 60% of the population are *Macheteros*, who speak their own language.

● **Accommodation** There are a few cheapish *residencias*: **E-F** *Don Joaquín*, on the main plaza, with bath, fan, family atmosphere; **E** *Plaza*, on main plaza, with or without bath, fan, good value, restaurant, rec. Several other basic *alojamientos* on and around plaza. Electricity is supplied in town from 1200 to 2400.

● **Places to eat** Restaurants do not stay open late. *Isireri*, on plaza, good and cheap set lunches and delicious fruit juices; *Casa Suiza*, good European food; *Donchanta*, rec for tasty meat dishes.

● **Buses** Bus Trinidad to San Borja stops at *Restaurant Donchanta* for lunch, otherwise difficult to find transport to San Borja. Minibus to Trinidad daily at 0730 from plaza, also camionetas, check times beforehand.

MAGDALENA

This charming town (*pop* 5,000) NE of Trinidad stands on the banks of the Río Itonama. It was founded by Jesuit missionaries in 1720, made a city in 1911 and is now the capital of the province of Iténez. Beef is the main product of the region and the river is the means of transporting cattle and other agricultural produce. 7 km upriver is the Laguna La Baíqui, popular for fishing. There is an abundance of wildlife and birds in the surrounding area. The city's main festival is on 22 July, Santa María Magdalena, attracting many groups and visitors from all over Beni and beyond.

● **Accommodation & places to eat** **F** *San Carlos*, private toilet, fan, shower and water bed; also **Res** *Iténez* and **F** *Ganerero*; all are modest but clean. Restaurants: *El Gato*, on road off plaza beside church, drinks and nightly dancing; *Heladería Laidi*, 1 block from plaza, simple meals and good juices. Drinking water is available and electricity runs from 1800-2400.

● **Useful information** There is a bank (changes TCs) and an Entel office and Correos on plaza.

● **Transport Air** Itemox Express has daily flights to Trinidad (US$31, in 5-seater); also flights to Bella Vista, Baures and Huacaraje. LAB flies from Trinidad. **Roads** An unpaved road goes to Trinidad via San Ramón, passable only in the dry season. A road to Bella Vista (see below), was due open in 1996.

EAST OF MAGDALENA

Bella Vista on the Río Blanco is considered by many to be one of the prettiest spots in NE Bolivia. Lovely white sandbanks line the Río San Martín, 10 mins paddling by canoe from the boat moorings below town (boatmen will take you, returning later by arrangement; also accessible by motorcycle). Check that the sand is not covered by water after heavy rain. Other activities are swimming in the Río San Martín, canoeing, hunting, good country for cycling.

● **Accommodation & services F-G** *Hotel Cazador*, owner Guillermo Esero Gómez very helpful and knowledgeable about the area, shared bath, provides meals for guests (restaurant to be built). Three well-stocked shops on plaza, but none sells mosquito repellent or spray/coils: many mosquitoes at the beginning of the wet season (apply repellent before leaving the plane). No bank or Entel office. Flights by Itemox Express, no fixed schedule, from Magdalena or Trinidad.

Eastern Bolivia

THE VAST and rapidly developing plains to the east of the Eastern Cordillera are Bolivia's richest area in natural resources. For the visitor, the pre-Inca ruins of Samaipata and the beautiful churches of former Jesuit missions east of Santa Cruz are worth a visit.

SANTA CRUZ DE LA SIERRA

Santa Cruz de la Sierra, capital of the Department of Santa Cruz, is 851 km by road, 552 km by air from La Paz. The city was founded in 1561 by the Spaniard Ñuflo de Chávez, who had come from Paraguay. Until the 1950s Santa Cruz was fairly isolated, but rail and road links ended this isolation. Now there is an ever-increasing flow of immigrants from the highlands as well as Mennonites mostly from USA and Canada and Japanese settlers, such as the Okinawan colony 50 km from Montero, to grow soya, maize, sugar, rice, coffee and other crops, which yield profusely. Cattle breeding and timber projects are also important. The exploitation of oil and gas in the Department of Santa Cruz has greatly contributed to the city's rapid development.

BASICS *Pop* 730,000 (Bolivia's second city); *alt* 437m; *phone code* 03. It is usually hot and windswept from May to August. When the cold *surazo* blows from the Argentine pampas during these months the temperature drops sharply. The rainy season is Dec-February.

Places of interest

The **Plaza 24 de Septiembre** is the city's main square with the **Cathedral** (interesting hand-wrought colonial silver), the Casa de Cultura (see **Museums** below) and the Prefectura set around it. Look for the sloths who live in the trees of the plaza. The Cathedral museum is open Mon and Thur, 1600-1800, and Sun, 1800-2000, entry US$0.75. The heart of the city, with its arcaded streets, retains a colonial air, despite the variety of modern shops and the new building that surrounds it. Five blocks N of the Plaza is **Parque El Arenal**, on an island in the middle of the lake is the Museo Etno-Floklórico (see below). Pleasant residential areas are being developed on the outskirts of town. 5 km out of town on the road to Cotoca are the new **Botanical Gardens** (micro or colectivo from C Suárez Arana, 15 mins).

Museums

Casa de la Cultura, on the plaza, with occasional exhibitions and also an archaeological display; has plays, recitals, concerts and folk dancing. **Museo de Historia Natural** at Av Irala s/n, entre Velasco y Independencia. **Museo Etno-Folklórico**, in the Parque Arenal, entry free, very small collection of artefacts from lowland cultures, the outside is decorated with a mural by the celebrated painter, Lorgio Vaca, and depicts the city's history. *RC Antigüedades*, Bolívar 262, p 2, small Inca, Tiahuanaco and antiques collection.

Excursions

Las Lomas de Arena del Palmar are huge sand-dunes, 20 km to the S. You may be able to get there by taxi, but private transport is best. It may be possible to hitch at weekends, but a 4WD vehicle is normally required.

Cotoca

20 km E of the city is **Cotoca** (20 mins), whose church has a miraculous virgin, associated with which is a religious handicraft tradition (**fiesta** 8 December). Eat

sonzos in the market. Swimming is possible during the wet season in the Río Piray (weekends very crowded), 10 mins by bus from town centre.

Local festivals

Cruceños are famous as fun-lovers and their music, the *carnavalitos*, can be heard all over South America. Of the various festivals, the brightest is **Carnival**, celebrated for the 15 days before Lent: music in the streets, dancing, fancy dress and the coronation of a queen. Beware the following day when youths run wild with buckets and balloons filled with water – no one is exempt. The *mascaritas* balls also take place during the pre-Lent season at *Caballo Blanco*: girls wear satin masks covering their heads completely, thus ensuring anonymity. **International Trade Fair** held each Sept; 24 Sept is a holiday.

Local information

● **Accommodation**

NB Accommodation is relatively expensive here and good value mid and lower-range hotels are hard to find.

L1-L3 *Yotaú*, Av San Martín y James Freyre, T 367799, suites, 5-star, a/c, sauna, all services.

A1 *Cortez*, Av Cristóbal de Mendoza 280, on 2nd Anillo nr the Cristo, T 331234, F 351186, pool, good, a/c, rec for medium or long stays; **A1** *Los Tajibos*, the biggest, Av San Martín 455 in Barrio Equipetrol out of town in 15 acres of lush vegetation, 5-star, T 421000, F 426994, a/c, El Papagayo restaurant good (*ceviche* is rec), business centre, Viva Club Spa has sauna etc, swimming pool for residents only; **A1-A2** *House Inn*, Colón 643, T/F 362323, Casilla 387, 5-star suites, 2 pools, restaurant, a/c, parking, modern, rec; **A2** *Gran Hotel Santa Cruz*, Pari 59, T 348811/348997, F 324194, pool, open to non-residents, fully restored to its 1930s glory, a/c, spacious, rec; **A2** *Las Américas*, 21 de Mayo esq Seoane, T 368778, F 336083, a/c, discount for longer stay, parking, arranges tours and car rental, restaurant, bar, 5-star service, rec.

B *Colonial*, Buenos Aires 57, T 333156, F 339223, a/c, restaurant, comfortable, rec.

C *Bolivia*, Libertad 365, T 336292, modern, comfortable; **C** *Copacabana*, Junín 217, T 339937, **B** with a/c, cheap laundry service, inc breakfast, restaurant; **C** *Mediterráneo*, Vallegrande y Camiri 71, T 338804, F 361344, a/c, fridge, inc breakfast, cheaper with fan.

D *Excelsior*, René Moreno 70, T 325924, inc breakfast, good rooms, good lunches; **D** *Res*

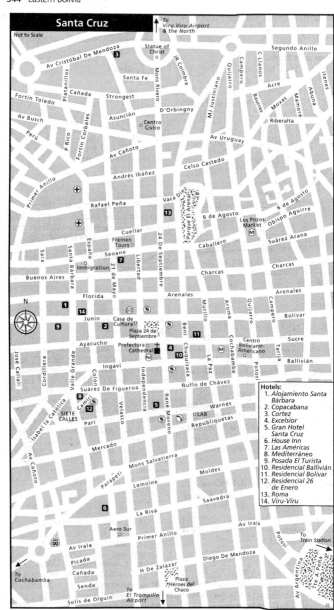

Santa Cruz

Not to Scale

To Viru Viru Airport & the North

Av Cristóbal De Mendoza

Statue of Christ 3

Segundo Anillo

C Llanos
Campero
Quijarro
Acre
Itenes
Albuna
Mamoré
Moxas
Baurres

Santa Fe

Mons Rivero

JR Colmra

MJ Justiniano

Platanillos
Cañada
Strongest

Fortín Toledo

Av Busch
Perú

P Rico
Fortín Corrales

Asunción

D'Orbingny

Centro Cívico

Riberalta

Av Uruguay

Av Cañoto

Andrés Ibáñez

Celso Castedo

Primer Anillo

Rafael Peña

Vaca Die

6 de Agosto

6 de Agosto

Obispo Aguirre

13

Los Pozos Market

Cuellar

Fremen Tours

Caballero

Suárez Arana

Sara

Santa Bárbara

España

Seoane

Immigration

21 de Mayo

Libertad

24 de Septiembre

Charcas

Charcas

7

Buenos Aires

Florida

Arenales

Arenales

Murillo
Aroma
Quijarro
Campero

Bolívar

1

14

Junín

Casa de Cultura

Beni

S

Sucre

Ballivián

N

9

2

Plaza 24 de Septiembre

11

Centro Boliviano-Americano

José Callali

Cordillera

Valle Grande

Ayacucho

Prefectura

Cathedral

Pol

4

10

Chuquisaca

La Paz

Cochabamba

Tarija

Potosí

Ingavi

Colón

Camiri

Suárez De Figueroa

Independencia

René Moreno

Nuflo de Chávez

S

Isabel la Católica

8

12

SIETE CALLES

Pari

Velasco

5

Warnes

LAB

Republiquetas

Av Cañoto

Mercado

Parapetí

Mons Salvatierra

Moldes

Lemoine

Saavedra

6

La Riva

Aero Sur

Primer Anillo

Av Irala

Potosí

To Train Station

Av Irala

Picada

Cañada

Senda

Solis de Olguin

H De Zalazar

Diego De Mendoza

Plaza Héroes del Chaco

To Cochabamba

To El Trompillo Airport

Av Argentina

Fe A Peña

Hotels:
1. Alojamiento Santa Bárbara
2. Copacabana
3. Cortez
4. Excelsior
5. Gran Hotel Santa Cruz
6. House Inn
7. Las Américas
8. Mediterráneo
9. Posada El Turista
10. Residencial Ballivián
11. Residencial Bolívar
12. Residencial 26 de Enero
13. Roma
14. Viru-Viru

Cañada, Cañada 145, nr bus terminal, T 345541, **E** without bath, good; **D** *Res 26 de Enero*, Camiri 32, T 321818, F 337518, **E** without bath, very clean; **D** *Roma*, 24 de Septiembre 530, T 338388, pleasant, good value, helpful; **D** *Viru-Viru* Junín 338, T 322687, inc breakfast, a/c, cheaper with fan, pleasant, rec.

E *Alojamiento San José*, Cañada 136, nr bus terminal, T 328024, hot showers, not great value; **E** *Alojamiento Santa Bárbara*, Santa Bárbara 151, T 321817, hot showers, helpful, will store luggage, rec; **E** *Res Ballivián*, Ballivián 71, T 321960, basic, hot showers, nice patio, rec; **E** *Res Bolívar*, Sucre 131, T 342500, hot showers, some rooms with bath, nice courtyard with hammocks, excellent breakfast US$1, repeatedly rec.

F *Alojamiento Ferrocarril*, Av Capitán Arrien 131, nr train station, T 321061, stores luggage; **F** *Posada El Turista*, Junín 455, good basic room, central, quiet.

● **Places to eat**
La Castañuela, Velasco 308 esq Pari, in beautifully-restored colonial Casona, Spanish restaurant, fine wine list, expensive but good quality; *El Fogón*, Av Viedma 434 and *La Buena Mesa*, Av Cristóbal de Mendoza 538, both excellent for *parrillada* and *churrasquería*, and there are many other barbecue restaurants all around the 2nd Anillo; *Churrasquería El Palenque*, Av El Trompillo y Santos Dumont, good; *Michelangelo*, Chuquisaca 502, excellent Italian, not cheap; *Pizzería Mesón de René*, 24 de Septiembre 285, bright and clean, good; *El Boliche*, Arenales 135, open 1930 onwards, serves good crêpes, expensive. Chinese restaurants inc: *El Patito Pekín*, 24 de Septiembre 307, basic cheap Chinese food (open Sun pm), *Shanghai*, Av 26 de Febrero 77; *Mandarin 2*, Av Potosí 793, both excellent. *Naturcenter*, Arenales 638, vegetarian self service, good value, also at Warnes 138; *Vegetarismo*, Ayacucho 491, p 1, good set lunch. *Español*, Junín y España, popular, cheap, good meals; *Hawaii*, Sucre y Beni, open 0700, good breakfasts and coffee; *La Pascana*, Av Plaza, very popular with tourists and locals, meals, ice-cream and snacks, expensive; *Dumbos*, Ayacucho 247, burgers, great ice-cream and full meals, rec; *Heladería Pastelería Manolo*, 24 de Septiembre 170, good sandwiches, cakes and ice cream, reasonable prices; *Kívon*, Ayacucho 267, highly rec for ice cream, also at Quijarro 409 in Mercado Los Pozos. *Salteñería San Andres*, C Charcas 64, cheap set lunch for US$1. Many cheap restaurants nr the bus terminal on Av Cañoto serving fried chicken. Also on the extension of C 6 de Agosto behind Los Pozos market (daytime). Excellent *empanadas* are sold in the food section of the Los Pozos market. The bakeries on Junín, Los Manzanos and España sell the local specialities: *empanadas de*

queso (cheese pies), *cuñapés* (yuca buns), rice bread and *humitas* (maize pies). Try local speciality *arroz con leche* in markets, only available before 1100.

● **Airline offices**
LAB, Warnes y Chuquisaca, T 344411; **Aero Sur**, Irala/Colón, T 367400; **Varig**, Junín 284, T 391105, open till 1200 on Sat; **AeroPerú**, Beni/Bolívar, T 365385; **American Airlines**, Arenales/Beni, T341314; **Aerolíneas Argentinas**, Edif Banco de la Nación Argentina, on main Plaza, T339776; **Lan Chile**, Libertad 144, T335951; **Iberia**, main Plaza, T 327448.

● **Banks & money changers**
Banco de La Paz, René Moreno y Ballivián, Enlace cash dispenser; **Banco Mercantil**, René Moreno y Suárez de Figueroa, cash advance on Visa, changes cash and TCs; **Banco de Santa Cruz**, Junín 154, bolivianos on Visa and Mastercard, no commission; **Banco Boliviano-Americano**, René Moreno 366 and Colón y Camiri (Siete Calles), Enlace cash dispenser for Visa and Mastercard; **Bidesa**, C Ñuflo de Chávez 150, good for cash and TCs. Banks open 0830-1130, 1430-1730; won't change TCs Sat am. *Casas de cambio:* **Mendicambio** on Plaza 24 de Septiembre will change TCs into dollars at 3% commission; also on main plaza, **Alemana** (changes TCs at 2% commission for $ or bolivianos) and **Sudamer**. **Cambios** can also be found on Libertad, eg **Latina** and **Oriente** in first block. **Magri Turismo**, Ingavi 14, T 345663, 2 blocks from main plaza, the American Express agent doesn't change American Express TCs, but you may have to go there to have cheques certified before a *casa de cambio* will accept them. Street money changers on Plaza 24 de Septiembre and around bus terminal.

● **Cultural centres**
Centro Boliviano Americano, Cochabamba 66, T 342299, library with US papers and magazines, English classes, some cultural events; **Instituto Cultural Boliviano Alemán**, Junín 363, T 329906 (library, films, language courses, etc); **Centro Iberoamericano de Formación**, Arenales 583, T 351311, F 322217, Casilla 875 (concerts, films, art exhibitions, lectures, etc), very good.

● **Embassies & consulates**
Brazil, Av Busch 330, nr Plaza Estudiantes, T 336888, opens at 0830, 24 hrs to process visa applications, reported as unhelpful; **Argentina**, Edif Banco de la Nación Argentina, Plaza 24 de Septiembre, N side, T 347133; **Uruguay**, Moldes 436, T 329317, Mon-Fri 0900-1100; **Paraguay**, Chuquisaca y Ballivián, Edif Oriente, T 36613, colour photo required for visa; **Peru**, Libertad 349, T 368979, p 2, of 213, T 368979; **USA**, Chuquisaca y Ballivián, Edif Oriente, p 3, of 313, T 330725;

Chile, C de Mendoza 441, T327907; **Britain**, Parapetí 28, p 2, T 345682; **France**, Avaroa 70, T 334818; **Netherlands**, Ayacucho 284, p 2, T 334485; **Italy**, Av El Trompillo 476, T 535873; **Switzerland**, Guatemala 245, T 349971; **Denmark**, Km 5½ Carretera al Norte, T 421816, Mon-Fri, 0830-1200, 1430-1800; **Germany**, Av Las Américas 241, T 324825; **Belgium**, Av Cristo Redentor, T 420662.

● **Entertainment**

Discotheques: *Doña Icha*, René Moreno 239, 2 blocks from plaza, Whiskería with 'pub' atmosphere, rec; also good are *Wall Street*, at Chuquisaca 113, and *Dalí Bar de Tapas*, at Beni 222, open 2000.

Check listings in local press for discos and bars.

● **Hospitals & medical services**

Clínica Lourdes, René Moreno 352, T 25518. *Dr Pepe Arzabe Quiroga* has clinic at Cnel Félix Romero 63, T 332970, specialist in tropical diseases.

● **Laundry**

Lavaseco Universal, at Bolívar 426, T 327715, and Beni 747, T 327252, same day service; *Lave Rápido*, Pasaje Callejas 70, side street on Republiquetas, Plaza Callejas, self service.

● **Post & telecommunications**

Post Office: C Junín 146. **Entel**: Warnes 83 (entre Moreno y Chuquisaca), T 325526, local and international calls and fax; change Mon-Fri 0730-2300, Sat, Sun and holidays 0800-2100; also small Entel office at Quijarro 267.

● **Shopping**

Artesanía shops on Libertad and on Plaza 24 de Septiembre y Bolívar. *Artecampo*, Salvatierra esq Vallegrande, T 341843, run by a local NGO, sells handicrafts made in rural communities in department, high quality, excellent value. *RC Limitada*, Bolívar 262, for jewellery and Bolivian gems, the manager also produces and sells good maps of Santa Cruz City and department. *Los Pozos market*, taking up the whole block between 6 de Agosto, Suárez Arana, Quijarro and Campero, is clean, good for midday meals, food aisles serve local and Chinese food, and worth visiting in summer for its exotic fruits. The market is open daily; beware of bag-snatching. There are plenty of smuggled Brazilian goods on sale, exchanged for Bolivian coca. *Bazar Siete Calles*, mainly for clothing, but food and fruit is sold outside, main entrance is in 100 block of Isabel La Católica, also on Camiri and Vallegrande, past Ingavi. There is a fruit and vegetable market at Sucre y Cochabamba. *El Aventurero Caza y Pesca*, Florida 126-130, has absolutely everything you need for fishing, climbing, trekking, or arctic and tropical regions.

Books: *Los Amigos del Libro*, Velasco 37, sells foreign language books and magazines. International magazines and newspapers often on sale in kiosks on main Plaza, eg *Miami Herald*, after arrival of Miami flight.

Film: processing *ABC*, Junín 467 (and Casco Viejo local 5), top quality, 36 prints, plus new film, US$9.50. *Foto Relieve*, Ingaví 256, excellent processing, English spoken.

● **Sports**

Clubs: *Club Las Palmas*, 2½ km on road to Cochabamba, has 18-hole championship golf course and olympic-length pool. *Club de Caza y Pesca*, Av Argentina 317, T 35707, advice on fishing, hunting and safaris.

● **Tour companies & travel agents**

Exprinter, Av Busch 127, T335133; *Magri Turismo*, address under **Banks & money changers**, helpful, rec; *Fremen*, Av Cañoto osq 21 de Mayo, T 338535, F 360265, local tours, also jungle river cruises; *Bracha*, at train station, T 467795, open daily 0830-1230, 1430-1900, for rail tickets to Quijarro and Yacuiba and Empresa Yacyretá buses to Asunción; *Anavin*, 21 de Mayo 208, T 352009, rec; *Amazonas Adventure Tours*, Centro Comercial Cañoto, local 122, T 338350, F 337587, PO Box 2527, operates tours to Perseverancia, a centre for ecotourism and scientific research, in the **Ríos Blanco y Negro Wildlife Reserve**, in the NE jungle. Mario Berndt, *Kayara Tours*, Casilla 3132, home address Tapiosí 113 (nr zoo), T 420340, is highly rec for tours in the high Andes and the lowlands; he is a professional photographer, is knowledgeable about culture, flora and fauna, speaks English, German and Spanish, is safe and attentive. *Selva Tours*, Bolívar 262, T 332725, F 360471, city and area tours, trips to Amboró, Samaipata, Jesuit Missions, gold prospecting; 10-day regional tour inc all the above, airport pick-up, US$165 pp/day, English and German spoken.

● **Tourist offices**

In Prefectura del Departamento, on main Plaza, T 32770, ext 144, need passport for entry; free city map. Also kiosk at airport. *Guía de Santa Cruz*, published by Rede, available in bookshops, gives all details on the city.

● **Useful addresses**

Migración: España 383 esq Seoane, T 36442/332136, Mon-Fri 0830-1200, 1430-1800.

● **Transport**

Local Taxis: about US$1 inside first Anillo, US$1.20 inside 3rd Anillo, fix fare in advance.

Air LAB flies at least twice daily to La Paz and Cochabamba, also daily to Trinidad (book 48 hrs in advance), and to Sucre, Tarija and Puerto

Suárez. Aero Sur flies to La Paz (several daily), and daily to Cochabamba, Trinidad, Puerto Suárez and Sucre. International flights are given in **Information for travellers**, but note that flying is the only straightforward way from Santa Cruz to Paraguay.

The international airport is at Viru-Viru, about 16 km from the town. Information on 181; has Emigration/Immigration office, Entel office, luggage lockers, duty free shop, restaurant (expensive), bank open 0830-1830, changes cash and TCs, withdrawal on Visa and Mastercard (when closed try AASANA desk, where you pay airport tax). Helpful Tourist Information kiosk in Check-In hall, English spoken, free map. Airport bus every 30 mins from the bus terminal, 20 mins (US$0.70). Taxi, US$5-6. From airport take bus to bus terminal then taxi to centre. From Trompillo airport in the S part of the city, flights in small planes to local destinations.

Trains To Puerto Suárez, for Brazil, and Yacuiba, for Argentina, see below.

Buses Bus terminal on corner of Av Cañoto and Av Irala, T 338391 or 340772 (taxi to centre US$1). Daily buses to **Cochabamba** (US$9-15, 10 hrs, sit on left for best views), many *flotas* leave between 0830 and 2030. The only Santa Cruz-Cochabamba bus not to take the lowland route is Cinta de Plata via Epizana, Sun 1700. Direct to **Sucre** daily with Mopar, Unificado, Copacabana and Bolívar at 1700, 12 hrs, US$13-17 (20% discount for students with Copacabana). **Oruro** and **La Paz** 16 hrs direct with Flota Copacabana, US$18.75, 8 a day (plus Bus Cama at 1900, Mon, Thur, Sat, US$36, 19 hrs). To **San Ignacio**, see under **The Chiquitano Jesuit Missions**. To **Yacuiba** and **Tarija**, daily, several companies; 26-32 hrs to Tarija. To **Camiri, Cotoca, Montero**, many colectivos and micros from outside *Hotel España* (US$10-12 to Camiri). To **Trinidad**, several daily, 12 hrs, US$5.80, all dep 1800 or 1830.

ON THE OLD ROAD TO COCHABAMBA

The drive along the Piray gorge and up into the highlands is worthwhile.

SAMAIPATA

The town of Samaipata (*alt* 1,960m; median temperature 24°C) is a popular tourist resort, famous for its plant nurseries (*viveros*), experimental orchards, jams and sweet wines. Local *artesanías* include ceramics. The **Museo Arqueológico Regional** (open daily 0900-1200, 1430-1830, US$1) has a collection of pots and vases with anthropomorphic designs, dating from 200 BC to 200

AD and, most importantly, provides information on the nearby, pre-Inca ceremonial site commonly called **El Fuerte**. This sacred structure consists of a complex system of channels, basins, high-relief sculptures, etc, carved out of one vast slab of rock. Latest research suggests that Amazonian people created it around 1500 BC; there is evidence of subsequent occupations and that it was the eastern outpost of the Incas' Kollasuyo (their Bolivian Empire). El Fuerte is 9 km from the town; 3 km along the highway, then 6 km up a signposted road; 2 hrs' walk one way, or drive to the entrance; entry US$2.

● **Accommodation & places to eat F** *Don Jorge*, Bolívar, T (0944) 6086, shared baths, inc breakfast, clean, hot showers, good beds, patio, good set lunch; **F** *Miny*, T 6151, on highway at entrance to town, with bath, good value; **G** pp *Res Kim*, nr plaza, clean; also *La Víspera*, organic farm/guesthouse, Dutch owners, very peaceful. Many restaurants on and around the plaza, most cheap, but some like *Chancho Rengo*, expensive. *Achira Sierra Resort*, 7 km from town, in Santa Cruz, T 52256 (Igmiri 506, Barrio Urbari, Casilla 1020), cabins, camping, horse riding, sports facilities, restaurant, 6 km from an access point for Amboró National Park (see below).

● **Transport** 24-hr taxi service (T 335067) from Santa Cruz, C Lemoine y Av Cañoto, 2 hrs, US$4 pp for 4 people to village, return by taxi or on any micro or bus passing Samaipata en route to Santa Cruz between 1600-1800. Many buses and micros leave Santa Cruz for Vallegrande, Sucre and other towns in pm, 1600-1800, passing Samaipata; colectivos from C Tundy 70, nr bus terminal, 2 hrs, US$3 pp.

VALLEGRANDE AND HIGUERA

Some 55 km S of the Santa Cruz-Cochabamba road is **Vallegrande**. It has Sun handicraft market and several pleasant, basic places to stay, all **F** or **G**, on or around the plaza; good restaurant on corner of plaza, also several cheap places to eat nr market; Bidesa bank. Flota Bolívar daily buses from Santa Cruz at 1730, 5 hrs, return most days at 0730 and/or 1300. 45 km S from Vallegrande is Pucara; a daily bus dep 0800 from market in Vallegrande; basic accommodation in Pucara. From Pucara there is transport (15 km) to the village of **Higuera**, where Che Guevara was killed. On 8 Oct each year, people gather there to celebrate his memory.

ON THE NEW ROAD TO COCHABAMBA

The new road route to Cochabamba passes through fertile lowland to the NW of Santa Cruz. It goes N through Warnes (note the statue of a man leading an ox-cart-load of bananas at the town entrance), then N to **Montero** (37 km, *pop* 30,000), where sugar and cotton are grown and processed, and on to Puerto Grether, high on the Río Ichilo, a tributary of the Mamoré. It then connects at Todos Santos with the 200-km road to Cochabamba. A non-stop shuttle minibus service leaves Santa Cruz bus station for Montero when full; US$1, 50 mins. The town is named after the Independence hero, Marceliano Montero; the statue to him in the plaza is in the same style as the statue of Bolívar in Santa Cruz, the horse supported by broken cannon.

AMBORO NATIONAL PARK

Buses leave Santa Cruz terminal (also minibuses from Montero) to **Buena Vista**, nr the **Amboró National Park** (180,000 ha) – walk to Cerro Amboró (guide required) recommended. The park is home to butterflies, humming birds, macaws, hoatzin and other native fauna (many of them endangered species). Many biting insects; much wading is required to get around the park (see also below).

● **Access** There is a national park office in Buena Vista (permit free; guide US$7).

● **Accommodation** D *Hotel Amboró*, nr Buena Vista, on the edge of Amboró, T/F 932-2054, Casilla 2097, comfortable, horse riding, guided tours of park; also a few *alojamientos* in Buena Vista.

● **Transport** From Buena Vista: either truck to El Terminal and then walk to the Río Surutú, the park's E boundary, or daily bus to Santa Fe, 0800, then motorcycle taxi to the river, US$5, 1 hr, very rough. At the park guardhouse there are 3 beds (free), take own food. To return ask park guard to radio for a motorcycle taxi.

THE CHIQUITANO JESUIT MISSIONS

Six Jesuit churches survive E of Santa Cruz, San Javier, Concepción, Santa Ana, San Rafael, San Miguel and San José de Chiquitos. All are Unesco World Heritage sites. The first four were built by the Swiss Jesuit, Padre Martin Schmidt, the other two (plus that at San Ignacio de Velasco, which was demolished in 1948, see below) were built by other priests. Besides organizing *reducciones* and constructing churches, for each of which he built an organ, Padre Schmidt wrote music (some is still played today on traditional instruments) and he published a Spanish-Idioma Chiquitano dictionary based on his knowledge of all the dialects of the region. He worked in this part of the then Viceroyalty of Peru until the expulsion of the Jesuits in 1767 by order of Charles III of Spain.

Access to the mission area is by bus or train from Santa Cruz: the simplest is the former, by paved highway N to San Ramón (139 km), then N on a good, all-weather gravel road through San Javier (45 km), turning E here to Concepción (68 km) and San Ignacio. One road continues E to San Matías and the Brazilian border; others head S either through San Miguel, or Santa Ana to meet at San Rafael for the continuation S to San José de Chiquitos. By rail, leave the Santa Cruz-Quijarro train at San José and from there travel N.

SAN JAVIER

The first Jesuit mission in Chiquitos (1691), its church completed by Padre Schmidt in 1752. The original wooden structure has survived more or less intact and restoration was undertaken between 1987 and 1993 by the German Hans Roth. Subtle designs and floral patterns cover the ceiling, walls and carved columns. One of the bas-relief paintings on the high altar depicts Martin Schmidt playing the piano for his Indian choir. The modern town prospers from extensive cattle ranching. Many fine walks in the surrounding countryside; also good for cycling with an all-terrain bike. Local *fiesta*, 3 December.

● **Accommodation & places to eat C** *Gran Hotel El Reposo del Guerrero*, more expensive Sat-Sun, **E** pp with shared bath, inc breakfast, comfortable, T 0963-5022, or Santa Cruz 327830, restaurant, bar; **E** *Alojamiento San Javier*, inc breakfast, hot water, garden, *arte-*

sania shop, good value, rec; **F** *Posada Pinto*, clean, nice, 1 block from plaza. Best restaurant is *Ganadero*, in Asociación de Ganaderos on plaza, excellent steaks; others on plaza.

● **Buses** Many late at night to Santa Cruz and San Ignacio. Micros to Santa Cruz, 4-5 hrs, US$4.85, several between 0700 and 1830.

CONCEPCION

The magnificent cathedral was completed by Padre Schmidt in 1756; it was totally restored by Hans Roth 1975-1982, whose team of European experts had to recreate the building from the crumbling original. The interior of this beautiful church is very fine, with an altar of laminated silver. In front of the church is a bell-cum-clock tower housing the original bells and behind it are well-restored cloisters. The town boasts one of the region's most beautiful plazas; Entel office on the corner; private Centro Médico 1 block away.

● **Accommodation & places to eat B** *Gran Hotel Concepción*, on plaza, T 0964-3031, very comfortable, excellent service, inc buffet breakfast, pool, bar, highly rec; **F** pp *Res Westfalia*, 2 blocks from plaza on same street as Centro Médico, German-owned, nice patio; **F-G** pp *Ganadero*, 1 block from plaza, basic, pleasant, shared bath. *El Buen Gusto*, on plaza, opens early, delicious *empanadas*, snacks, meals; *Club Social Ñuflo de Chávez*, on plaza, excellent value *almuerzos* US$2.30, and breakfast US$1.15. *Don Beto*, 1 block from plaza, good *almuerzo*, popular.

● **Buses** Many buses between Santa Cruz and San Ignacio pass through, about midnight, but drop you at main road, several blocks from plaza; ask around for transport to centre. Flota La Veloz del Norte and 31 del Este micros to San Javier (1½ hrs, US$1) and Santa Cruz (US$5.80) at 0800, 1400 and 1800, from opp *Restaurant Don Beto*.

SAN IGNACIO DE VELASCO

A lack of funds for restoration led to the demolition of San Ignacio's Jesuit church in 1948. A modern replacement contains the elaborate high altar, pulpit and paintings and statues of saints. A museum in the Casa de la Cultura on the plaza has a few musical instruments from the old church. Laguna Guapomó on the outskirts of town is good for swimming, boating and fishing. Entel 2 blocks from plaza.

● **Accommodation & places to eat D** *Plaza*, hot water, inc breakfast, comfortable, good value;

E pp *Casa Suiza*, at the end of C Sucre, 5 blocks W of plaza (taxi US$0.75), small guesthouse run by Horst and Cristina, German and French spoken, full board, excellent food, very comfortable, family atmosphere, hires horses, highly rec; **D** *Palace*, on plaza, inc breakfast, fan, no singles; **E-F** *Guapamó*, Sucre, 2 blocks from market and bus offices, pleasant, restaurant; **F** *31 de Julio*, on plaza, basic, clean; several other cheap lodgings. Several places to eat on the plaza, inc *Pizzería Pauline*, good, US$3-4 per dish; *Snack Marcelito*, good *salteñas*, *Cayoni's Bar*, chicken and burgers; *Riabé*, on Sucre, cheap.

● **Transport Air** TAM on Wed from Santa Cruz, returns Thur, also serves San Matías on the Brazilian border. **Buses** From **Santa Cruz**, Flota Chiquitana, from terminal 1900 daily, 10 hrs, US$6.75; at least 7 other companies, most from C Suárez Arana, Av Uruguay end, en route to San Matías for Brazil, eg Trans Bolivia, at No 332, 2000, and Flota Veloz del Este, No 318, 1800. From San Ignacio: Flota Chiquitano daily at 1800; Trans Velasco at 1900; both from nr market (Trans Brasil at 2030 (office on plaza). To **San Matías** for Brazil (see below), frequent buses Santa Cruz-San Ignacio-San Matías-Cáceres; Trans Velasco and Trans Bolivia dep San Ignacio 0800 and 1800-2100, US$9.70; the final 92 km of road is very poor. To **San José de Chiquitos**, Flota Universal (1½ blocks from plaza on on same street as *Restaurant Pizzería Pauline*, T 2198), Mon, Wed, Fri at 1100 and 1500, Sun at 1000, US$6, 5 hrs, goes via San Miguel and San Rafael. Micros to **Santa Ana** (1 hr, US$1.35) and **San Rafael** (1½ hrs, US$1.95), from market area at 1000 and 1700, returns from San Rafael 1300-1400. To **San Miguel**, from same place at 0800 and 0930-1000, 1 hr, US$1, returns 1245.

SANTA ANA, SAN RAFAEL, SAN MIGUEL

A day trip by taxi from San Ignacio to these villages costs US$35-40 (negotiate).

The church in **Santa Ana** is in fine condition (finished 1755), a lovely wooden building, entirely unrestored. Sr Luis Rocha to show you inside; ask for his house at the shop on the plaza where the bus stops. In a sky-blue house on a corner of the plaza, the lady will prepare a meal for a visiting couple and has a spare room for an overnight stay.

San Rafael's church was completed by Padre Schmidt the year after Santa Ana: beautifully restored with frescoes in beige paint over the exterior (*Alojamiento*, pink house at entrance to village; 2 restaurants on plaza; public phone).

The frescoes on the façade of the church (1754) at **San Miguel** depict St Peter and St Paul; designs in brown and yellow cover all the interior and the exterior side walls. The mission runs 3 schools and workshop; the sisters are very welcoming and will gladly show tourists around. 4 km away is the Santuario de Cotoca, beside a lake where you can swim; ask at *La Pascana* for transport. (**G** pp *Alojamiento y Restaurant La Pascana*, on plaza, basic, cheap meals; just up the hill are 2 other *alojamientos* and Entel.)

SAN JOSE DE CHIQUITOS

The whole of one side of the plaza of this dusty little town is occupied by the superb frontage of the Jesuit mission. The buildings, in Baroque style, are of stone, connected by a wall. They are the restored chapel (1750); the church, unfinished at the expulsion of the Jesuits, with a triangular façade and side walls standing (restoration work in progress); the 4-storey bell-tower (1748); the mortuary (*la bóveda* – 1754), with one central window but no entrance in its severe frontage, behind is a long colonnaded hall.

On Mon, Mennonites bring their produce to sell to shops and to buy provisions. The colonies are 50 km W and the Mennonites, who speak English, German, plattdeutsch and Spanish, are happy to talk about their way of life.

4 km from San José is the **Parque Nacional Histórico Santa Cruz la Vieja**, which includes the ruins of the original site of Santa Cruz (about 1540), a *mirador* giving views over the jungle and, 5 km into the park, a sanctuary. The park's heavily-forested hills contain much animal and bird life; various trails; guides available from the small village in the park (take insect repellent). 2 km past the entrance, at the end of the road at the foot of high hills, is a large swimming pool fed by a mountain stream (open daily, free, no facilities other than changing rooms; take refreshments). The park and pool are best visited by car or taxi because it is a very hot, dusty walk there (allow over 1 hr on foot).

● **Accommodation & places to eat** **E** *Hotel Raquelita*, on the plaza, good, laundry service, restaurant serves good breakfast; **F** *Victoria*, also on plaza, basic; **F** *San Silvestre*, opp train station, basic, good food. Restaurants on plaza inc: *Sombrero e' Sao*, with sidewalk seating under trees, and *Casa e' Paila*, with *artesanías* for sale, both serve good *almuerzo*, not cheap.

● **Services** Electricity is cut from 0200-0630; the town is lighted when trains arrive. Bidesa changes TCs into dollars cash or bolivianos; also Entel and hospital.

● **Transport Trains** Schedule from Santa Cruz as for Quijarro (see **Travel to Brazil**), 8 hrs to San José, US$3.20 by Expreso del Oriente, US$7 by Tren Rápido 1st class, US$5 in 2nd. San José-Santa Cruz trains leave about 8 hrs after departure from Quijarro, check expected arrival time in advance. It is impossible to reserve seats on either service. **Buses** To San Ignacio, Flota Universal, Mon and Fri at 1200, Tues and Sat at 2000, from station area, reserve seat and check time in advance at company's terminal (some distance from town, take taxi), goes via San Rafael and San Miguel, 5 hrs.

TRAVEL TO BRAZIL

There are three routes: two via Puerto Suárez and/or Quijarro, one via San Matías. Puerto Suárez, reached by air, is near Quijarro which is the terminus of the railway from Santa Cruz. On the Brazilian side of the border is Corumbá and the southern Pantanal. San Matías is reached by road from Santa Cruz, with road links to Cáceres, Cuiabá and the northern Pantanal in Brazil.

The populated area by the Brazilian border is made up of several towns which are gradually growing into each other: Puerto Suárez, Puerto Quijarro and Arroyo Concepción. Trade here grew because of increasing prices in Brazil during 1995-1996 and a *Zona Franca* (customs free zone) has been established in the area to encourage development.

PUERTO SUAREZ

Puerto Suárez (*pop* 15,000) on the shore of Laguna Cáceres, a large backwater of the Río Paraguay, was an important commercial port at the beginning of the 20th century, until a dam built by Brazil upriver reduced the water level of the lake and put an end to shipping and the town's prosperity. It is today a friendly, quiet, small town, with a shady main plaza. There is a nice view of the lake from the park at the N end of Av Bolívar. The area around the train station is known as *Paradero*.

Excursions Fishing and photo tours to the Pantanal can be arranged more cheaply than on the Brazilian side. Stewart and Sandra Williams of *Tours Aguas Tranquilas* (inquire at Hotel Frontera Verde) offer airboat trips along small tributaries of the Río Paraguay, which are not accessible with other types of water craft, lots of wildlife, good fishing, US$10 pp/hr (min US$40), US$150 to hire boat for 4 hrs, includes lunch and fishing gear, US$250/7 hrs, max capacity 9, English spoken.

● **Accommodation C** *Frontera Verde*, Vanguardia 24 y Simón Bolívar, T 62468, F 62470, best in town, a/c, **D** with fan, breakfast inc, parking, helpful, English spoken; **C** *Bamby*, Santa Cruz 31 y 6 de Agosto, T 62015, a/c, **D** with fan, cheaper with shared bath, comfortable; **D** *Beby*, Av Bolívar 111, T 62270, a/c, **E** with shared bath and fan; **D** *Ejecutivo*, at S end of Bolívar, T 62267, a/c, parking, cheaper with fan, comfortable; **D** *Roboré*, 6 de Agosto 78, T 62170, fan, **E** with shared bath, basic, restaurant next door; **D** *Sucre*, Bolívar 63 on main plaza, T 62069, a/c, **E** with shared bath and fan, pleasant, good restaurant; **E** *Progreso*, Bolívar 21, shared bath, basic; **E** *Res Puerto Suárez*, Bolívar 105, shared bath, fans, showers, basic. Beware the water, it is straight from the river.

● **Places to eat** *Parillada Jenecherú*, Bolívar nr plaza, grilled meats; opp is *Al Paso*, Bolívar 43, very good value set meals and à la carte, popular; *El Taxista*, Bolívar 100 block, several other small inexpensive restaurants nearby.

● **Banks & money changers** *Supermercado Tocale* changes Bolivianos, reais and US$, cash only. *Banco de la Unión* in Paradero is reported to change TCs.

● **Embassies & consulates** Brazilian Consulate, Santa Cruz entre Bolívar y 6 de Agosto.

● **Post & telecommunications** Post Office: La Paz opp main plaza. **Entel:** La Paz. 3 blocks from Plaza and in Paradero.

● **Shopping** *Supermercado Tocale*, Bolívar next door to *Res Puerto Suárez*, wide selection of Brazilian, Bolivian and imported goods. Several fishing and hunting supply shops.

● **Tour companies & travel agents** *Tours Aguas Tranquilas*, see Excursions above; *R B Travel*, Bolívar 65 by Plaza, T62014, for airline tickets, helpful. Airline offices: *LAB*, La Paz 33, T 62241; *AeroSur*, Bolívar near the Plaza, T/F 62155; *TAM*, C del Chaco s/n, T 62205.

● **Transport Local Taxis**: to Paradero US$1.65; to airport US$2; to Quijarro or the border, US$5 (day), US$6 (night) or US$0.80 pp in a colectivo. **Air** Airport is 6 km N of town, T 62347; airport tax US$2. Daily to Santa Cruz with Aerosur and LAB. TAM to Santa Cruz, continues to Trinidad and La Paz. **NB** Do not buy tickets for flights originating in Puerto Suárez in Corumbá, you will have to pay more. There is an airport immigration office where they will issue Bolivian exit/entry stamps. **Trains** The station for Puerto Suárez is about 3 km from town. It is the first station W of Quijarro. Bracha agent, Bolívar 86, T/F 62577.

PUERTO QUIJARRO

The eastern terminus of the Bolivian railway is at **Puerto Quijarro** (*pop* 15,000), the gateway to Brazil, a town created around the railway station. To coincide with efforts to develop tourism in the Bolivian Pantanal, the town is struggling to improve its infrastructure and image. There have been reports of drug trafficking and related problems in this border area and caution is recommended.

● **Accommodation NB** Water supply is frequently unreliable, try the tap before checking in. Most people prefer to go on to Corumbá where hotels are better. **C** *Santa Cruz*, Av Brazil 2 blocks E of station, T 82113, F 82044, a/c, cheaper with fan, **D** with shared bath, good rooms, nice courtyard, good restaurant, parking, highly rec; **D** *La Frontera*, Rómulo Gómez s/n, 5 blocks from the station on the S side of the tracks, T 82010, fan, parking; **D** *Gran Hotel Colonial*, Av Brazil y Panamá, T/F 82037, a/c, cheaper with fan, **E** with shared bath, good restaurant; **D** *Oasis*, Av Argentina 20, T 82159, a/c, fridge, cheaper with shared bath and a/c, **E** with fan, OK; **D** *Yoni*, Av Brazil opp the station, T 82109, a/c, fridge, **E** with shared bath and fan, comfortable, mosquito netting on windows; **F** *Res Paratí*, Guatemala s/n, shared bath, fan, laundry facilities. On Av Brazil across from the station are: **F** *Alojamiento Urkupiña*, shared bath, basic, unfriendly; **F** *Res Ariane*, T 82122, shared bath, basic, new rooms with bath and a/c; **F** *Vasco de Gamma*, very basic, cheap.

● **Places to eat** The best restaurant in the area is in Arroyo Concepción (see below); owing to poor hygienic conditions, the food stalls by the station and market are best avoided.

● **Banks & money changers** Bolivianos, reais and US$ cash traded along Av Brazil opp the station by changers with large purses sitting in lawn chairs; good rates, but beware of tricks.

● **Tour companies & travel agents** *Santa

Cruz, in hotel of same name, sells Bracha and airline tickets, organizes tours to Pantanal.

● **Post & telecommunications Post Office**: in Puerto Suarez. **Entel**: at the S end of Av Naval, national and international calls, Mon-Sat 0700-2300, Sun 0700-2000; also small office at Guatemala y Brazil nr the station.

● **Shopping**   A duty free zone is at Puerto Aguirre, 700m N of Quijarro; mostly electrical and luxury goods for Brazilian shoppers. Construction of a new, larger, duty free centre started in 1996.

● **Transport Local Taxis**: to the border (Arroyo Concepción) US$0.40 pp; to Puerto Suarez US$0.80 pp or US$5 (day), US$6 (night). **Trains** See below.

BORDER WITH BRAZIL

The Municipality by the border is known as **Arroyo Concepción**.

Going to Brazil: you need not have your passport stamped if you visit Corumbá for the day. Otherwise get your exit stamp at Bolivian immigration (see below), formalities are straightforward. There are no formalities on the Brazilian side, you must get your entry stamp in Corumbá (see page 629); there is also an office at the bus station which is usually closed. Yellow Fever vaccination is compulsory to enter Brazil, have your certificate at hand when you go for your entry stamp, otherwise you will be sent to get revaccinated.

● **Bolivian immigration**
At the border at Arroyo Concepción, blue building on right just before bridge, opens 0700; at Puerto Suárez airport; in San Matías. Passports may be stamped at Santa Cruz station if leaving by train, which may avoid spurious exit charges at Quijarro. Other than the entry/exit tax (see **On departure** in **Information for travellers**), no money has to be paid to anyone at the border.

   NB You can leave Bolivia at Quijarro when the border post is closed, but you have to return from Brazil for a Bolivian exit stamp.

● **Accommodation & places to eat**
The fanciest hotel on either side of the border is in Bolivia, 1½ km from the frontier: **L3** *El Pantanal Hotel Resort & Casino*, T 82089, F 82020, 5 star luxury resort, a/c, buffet breakfast and airport transport included, restaurants, disco, pool, modern buildings on nice grounds, horseback riding, tours to Pantanal and nearby caves; one of the better restaurants in the area is also here: *Pescadería Ceará*, 250m from the border, with excellent fish (moved from Corumbá).

● **Brazilian consulate**
In Santa Cruz (see above). The consulate normally takes 24 hrs to process applications (if you apply at 0900, it may be ready by 1200). A yellow fever certificate is required.

● **Banks & money changers**
Money can be exchanged at the Quijarro border; you will probably only be able to sell bolivianos in Bolivia.

● **Transport**
Air   The simplest way to Brazil is to fly to Puerto Suárez then share a taxi to the border, US$7.50/car. See **Puerto Suárez Transport** above.

Trains   The station in Santa Cruz for the railway to Quijarro is on the eastern edge of the city on C Cochabamba at the Cuarto Anillo, T 348883; No 12 bus to/from the centre, taxi US$1. All trains go via San José de Chiquitos to Quijarro, from where travellers must go by colectivo to the border post (beware overcharging, fare should be US$0.40pp), then by bus to Corumbá. Expreso del Oriente Pullman (all 1st class, a/c, meals available) leaves Santa Cruz Mon and Fri 1415, returning from Quijarro Tues and Sat 1700. Tren Rápido Pullman leaves Santa Cruz Wed and Sun 1350, returning Mon and Thur 1345. Tren Mixto leaves Santa Cruz Mon and Fri at 1915. The journey is scheduled to take 22-24 hrs. It is a mixed train with 3 classes: *Bracha* luxury coaches, a/c, US$22; 1st class – quite basic, US$8; 2nd – bench seats, US$6.50. Take food, drinking water, insect repellent and a torch, whichever class you are travelling. From Mar-Aug take a sleeping bag for the cold; be prepared for delays. Only men are allowed to ride on the roof. It is a monotonous journey through jungle, except for the frequent stops at towns, where the train's arrival is a major event, and for the company of your fellow passengers.

   Tickets may be purchased the day prior to travel, counter opens at 0800, go early because queues form hours before and tickets sell fast. Take passport. Tickets for *Bracha* (see Santa Cruz **Tour companies**, above), can be bought in advance at travel agencies; *Bracha* staff are very friendly and honest, 10% fee, highly rec to avoid queues at the station, also advises on transporting vehicles by rail. Office in Quijarro, T 0976-2325; in La Paz T 327472. At Quijarro station Willy Solís Cruz, T 2204, runs a left-luggage room, speaks English, very helpful, assists with ticket purchases for US$3 (has been known to let people sleep in the luggage room). The Quijarro ticket office sells tickets only on day of departure, open 0700-1600, queuing starts much earlier, it gets crowded, much pushing and shoving, touts resell tickets at hugely inflated prices. Note that times of departure from Quijarro are approximate as they depend on when trains arrive.

Road The road route from Santa Cruz is via San Ignacio de Velasco to San Matías, thence to Cáceres and Cuiabá. See under San Ignacio for bus information. **San Matías** is a busy little town with hotels, restaurants and a bank (Bidesa); TAM flies to/from Santa Cruz and San Igancio; also Servicio Aereo Pantanal daily from Santa Cruz (office at El Trompillo airport, T 531066).

TRAVEL TO PARAGUAY

A road S of Santa Cruz goes through Abapó, Camiri and Boyuibe, from where the route is as given above in **Crossing into Paraguay**, see page 323.

● **Transport**
Buses Empresa Yacyretá twice weekly Santa Cruz-Asunción. In Santa Cruz, at C Cordillera 485, T 349315: Tues, Fri 1300. Tickets can be booked through *Bracha* travel agency.

TRAVEL TO ARGENTINA

From Santa Cruz the route is as for Paraguay to Boyuibe, thence to Villamontes and **Yacuiba** (*pop* 11,000), crossing to Pocitos in Argentina.

● **Bolivian immigration**
The border crossing is straightforward. Passengers leaving Bolivia must disembark at Yacuiba, take a taxi to Pocitos on the border (US$0.40, beware unscrupulous drivers) and walk across to Argentina.

● **Accommodation, places to eat & services**
In Yacuiba: **C** *Hotel París*, Comercio y Campero, T 682-2182, the best; **C** *Monumental*, Comercio 1270, T 682-2088, inc breakfast; **D** *Valentín*, Av San Martín 1462, opp rail station, T 2645, F 2317, **E** without bath, excellent value. Many cheaper places nearby. *Swin*, good food and service; several restaurants also along Av San Martín. Bidesa bank on plaza; also Entel and Correos. Argentine consul at Comercio y Sucre.

● **Transport**
Trains Santa Cruz-Yacuiba Mon and Fri at 0640 and 1540; Yacuiba-Santa Cruz Tues and Sat at 0730 and 1630; US$8 one way. *Bracha* has an office in Yacuiba, T 0682-2772/2525. All details must be verified in advance.

Buses Excellent connections in all directions. To **Santa Cruz**, about 20 companies run daily services, mostly at night, 14 hrs, US$13 (Sra Hidalgo Cortez at Mopar speaks English and is very helpful). To **Tarija**, daily at 0800, 0830 and 1700-1800. To **Villazón**, via Bermejo and Tupiza, at 1800 with Expreso Tarija; also at 2000 with Trans Yacuiba. To **Potosí-Oruro-La Paz**, at 0700 with Trans Yacuiba, and Expreso Tarija at 0830 and 1700. Daily to **Trinidad** and **Sucre** with Flota Copacabana. To **Buenos Aires** and other Argentine destinations daily with Panamericano and Chevallier.

Information for travellers

BEFORE YOU GO

ENTRY REQUIREMENTS

● **Documents**

A passport only is needed for citizens of almost all Western European, North and South American countries, Australia and New Zealand. All are granted 30 or 90 days on entry; if granted 30 you can easily extend to 90 at immigration. Among those countries whose nationals require a visa are the countries of Eastern Europe (except Poland and the Czech Republic), Middle East (except Israel), Africa (except South Africa) and SE Asia (except Japan and the Philippines), the former Soviet Union and the former Yugoslavia, India, Pakistan and Haiti; authorization from the Bolivian Ministry of foreign Affairs is required and can take 3-5 weeks. Those countries which require a visa but not authorization are; Croatia, Cuba, Hungary, South Korea, Malta, Mexico, Panama, Slovenia and Venezuela (takes 1-2 working days). The cost of a visa varies from nationality to nationality. Visas (or permit to stay) can be renewed at any Migración office up to 90 days. After 3 months further renewal is at the discretion of the immigration officer. If refused, leave the country and return. On arrival ensure that visas and passports are stamped with the same, correct date of entry or this can lead to 'fines' later. Business visitors (unless passing through as tourists) are required to obtain a visa from a Bolivian consulate. This costs £35; applicants should check all requirements and regulations on length of stay and extensions in advance.

● **Representation overseas**

Australia, 210 Queen St 5 Floor, Penneys Bldg, Suite 517, Queensland; **Austria**, Doblhoffgasse 316, A-1010 Vienna; **Belgium**, Av Louse N 176 Boite 6, 1050 Brussels; **France**, 12 Ave Du Presidente Kennedy, 75016 Paris 16; **Germany**, Konstantinstrasse N 16, D-5300 Bonn-2; **Italy**, Via Toscana 30 Int 28, 00187 Roma; **Netherlands**, Hacquartraat 4, 1071 SH Amsterdam; **Sweden**, Sveav Gen 31e TR 11134, Estocolmo; **Switzerland**, 2 Rue Du Lyon D'Or 2/do Piso Gusa, CH 1003 Lausanne; **USA**, 3014 Massachusetts Ave NW, Washington DC.

● **Tour Operator**

Amerindia, based in Quito, is a new regional ground operator, who cover Bolivia, Ecuador and Peru (as well as Belize, Costa Rica and Guatemala). It has been created to rediscover the wonders of Latin America. Tours are of the highest quality with experienced guides. Accommodation is in superb lodges. Among tours being offered will be luxury safari-style tents, land rover circuits and yacht charters along the coasts. Further information from Amerindia's head office T (593) 2 439736/469455, F (593) 2 439735, Email amerindi@pi.pro.ec, in UK from Penelope Kellie T (44) 1962 779317, F (44) 1962 779458, Email pkellie@yachtors.u-net.com, in USA T (1) 305 599 9008, F (1) 305 592 7060.

WHEN TO GO

● **Best time to visit**

The best time to visit is May to Nov, the dry season. June-Aug are the coldest months.

HEALTH

Whatever their age, travellers arriving in La Paz by air (too quickly, that is, for a progressive adaptation to the altitude) should rest for half a day, taking very little food and alcoholic drink (drink plenty of non-alcoholic beverages). In Bolivia, do as the Bolivians do: above 3,000m, walk slowly, very slowly uphill. Some of the most notable effects of *soroche* (altitude sickness) are headache, sleeplessness and flatulence; breathlessness lasts much longer than other symptoms. Local remedies are *maté de coca*, *Sorojchi* and *Micoren* capsules (see introductory **Health** section on Altitude sickness). Never go out for the whole day without taking an outer garment: the temperature drops sharply at sunset. Inoculate against typhoid and paratyphoid; take anti-malaria tablets if visiting the lowlands. Visitors should have yellow-fever vaccination when visiting Santa Cruz or the Oriente. A yellow fever vaccination certificate, at least 10 days old, is officially required for leaving the country. Hepatitis is very common. Chagas disease is endemic in the Yungas and other warmer parts of Bolivia (see **Health Hints**, at the beginning of the book). Public hospitals charge five bolivianos for consultation, compared with up to and over US$100 in private hospitals. A good remedy for stomach amoebas is Tinidizol. Contact lens solution is hard to find.

MONEY

● Cost of living

Bolivia is cheaper than most neighbouring countries. Rents, appliances, some clothing, and especially toilet goods and medicines, are high priced. Food, accommodation and transport are not expensive however. Budget travellers can get by on US$30-35 pp a day for 2 travelling together. For basic hotel expect to pay US$3 pp; breakfast US$0.50; *almuerzos* cost from US$2-3.

● Credit cards

Credit cards are commonly used in most cities to obtain cash and for purchases, you should expect to have to show your passport; an extra charge, up to 10%, may be made. American Express is not as useful as Visa, or, to a lesser extent, Mastercard. In La Paz, Cochabamba, Sucre and Santa Cruz automatic cash dispensers displaying the 'Enlace' sign accept Visa (ATC outlets) and Mastercard.

● Currency

The unit of currency is the boliviano (Bs), divided into 100 centavos. There are notes for 200, 100, 50, 20, 10, 5 and 2 (rare) bolivianos, and coins of 2 and 1 boliviano and 50, 20, 10 and 5 (rare) centavos. Bolivianos are often referred to as pesos; expensive items, including hotel rooms, are often quoted in dollars. When changing money, try to get notes in as small denominations as possible and never accept a note with holes or bits missing. Change is often given in forms other than money: eg cigarette, sweet, or razor blade. It is almost impossible to buy dollars at points of exit when leaving or to change bolivianos in other countries. Establishments which change TCs are given in the text; outside major cities it can be impossible. Changing US$ cash presents no problems anywhere. It is not worth trying to change other currencies. All the larger, recognized *casas de cambio* will give US$ cash in exchange for TCs, usually with a commission.

GETTING THERE

BY AIR

● From Europe

Either fly to Lima (see below), to Rio de Janeiro, São Paulo or Buenos Aires for connections, or via Miami.

● From North America

American and LAB from Miami daily to La Paz and Santa Cruz.

● Within South America

From Caracas once a week by LAB. From Lima to La Paz, 12 a week by AeroPerú, or LAB whose flights also go to Cochabamba (4 a week) and Santa Cruz (3 a week). Aero Perú flies Cusco-La Paz daily except Sun, LAB twice a week. LAB flies twice a week Quito-Lima-La Paz-Cochabamba. From Santiago, Iquique and Arica to La Paz, daily by Lan Chile and 4 a week by LAB (daily from Santiago, continuing to Santa Cruz); 4 of LAB's Santiago flights also stop in Cochabamba. From Buenos Aires, 3 direct flights by Aerolíneas Argentinas to La Paz, continuing to Santa Cruz. LAB has 6 weekly flights BsAs-Santa Cruz, one via Montevideo, two continuing to Cochabamba and La Paz. From Asunción, Lapsa and LAB twice a week to Santa Cruz, LAB continuing once to La Paz. Varig flies daily São Paulo-Santa Cruz, 5 times a week Rio de Janeiro-São Paulo-Santa Cruz-La Paz; LAB flies São Paulo-Santa Cruz-Cochabamba-La Paz daily, Rio-São Paulo-Santa Cruz-Cochabamba-La Paz 3 times a week, also from Cuiabá and Manaus to Santa Cruz. LAB flies 3 times a week Bogotá-Santa Cruz and 4 times a week Santa Cruz-Panama City-Mexico City.

BY TRAIN

From Argentina and Chile (see page 282).

BY ROAD

There are 3 routes from Puno (Peru): see **Crossing the Peruvian frontier** in Section 1, above.

From Salta-Jujuy-La Quiaca (Argentina) to Potosí or Tarija.

Alternative routes lead from the Argentine province of Salta via Bermejo or Yacuiba to Tarija or Santa Cruz. Dry weather only.

From Ollagüe (Chile) to Uyuni, see page 309.

From Arica (Chile) via Tambo Quemado or via Visviri (see By Road from La Paz to the Pacific Coast, page 284).

Travel to Paraguay Apart from the journey described on page 323 (also taken by Santa Cruz-Asunción buses), an alternative way of getting to Paraguay is to travel by bus to Salta or Orán (Argentina), then on to Asunción via Resistencia (Argentina).

CUSTOMS

● Duty-free imports

200 cigarettes, 50 cigars and 1 lb tobacco; one opened bottle of alcoholic drink.

WHEN YOU ARRIVE

● Clothing

Visitors to the Altiplano and the Puna should be prepared for the cold at night. The climate in the Eastern Lowlands is tropical. Oruro and Potosí are colder than La Paz; Cochabamba can be very warm.

● Entry tax

Payable when entering by land, US$5.

● Hours of business

Hours of business are normally 0900-1200 (sometimes 1130 in La Paz), and 1400-1800. Sat is a half day. Opening and closing in the afternoon are several hours later in the provinces. Government offices are closed on Sat. Banks 0900-1200, 1400-1630, but closed on Sat.

● Official time

4 hrs behind GMT.

● Security

Bolivian law states that the police may only search bags at a police station, not on the street. Identity must be checked only by immigration officials; see their identity card and verify the date. Insist on going to the police station, or call the uniformed police if in doubt. If at all possible, insist on your right not to show your passport to anyone on the street. If you can get a witness, so much the better.

The procedure for reporting a robbery is to go to the Dpto de Criminalística, or the office for stolen property, in the town where the theft took place. Purchase official paper from the police for them to write the report, then, with patience and politeness, you may get a report costing between US$1.30 and US$5.25.

● Shopping

Best Buys Llama-and alpaca-wool knitted and woven items are at least as good as those from Peru and much cheaper. Ponchos, *mantas*, bags, *chullos* (bonnets). Gold and silverware. Musical instruments such as the *charango* (mandolin traditionally with armadillo-shell sound-box, now usually of wood) and the *quena* (Inca flute), and other assorted wooden items.

● Tipping

Up to 10% in restaurants; in all other cases a tip is given in recognition of a service provided, eg to a taxi driver who has been helpful (an extra Bs 0.50-1), to someone who has looked after a car, carried bags, etc. Usual tip Bs 0.50-1.

● Voltage

Varies considerably. Generally 110 volts, 50 cycles AC in La Paz, 220 volts 50 cycles AC elsewhere, but check before using any appliance. (You may even find 110 and 220 in the same room). US-type plugs can be used in most hotels.

● Work opportunities

See under La Paz **Language schools** for teaching possibilities. Voluntary work at the Hogar Mixto La Paz, Av Arce, nr British Embassy, beside Centro Boliviano Americano.

ON DEPARTURE

● Departure taxes

Tax of US$20, payable in dollars or bolivianos, cash only, is levied on leaving by air (US$30 extra if you have stayed over 3 months). On internal flights a tax of US$1.95 is paid. Tax on airline tickets 18%. On departure by land, there is a US$5 tax.

WHERE TO STAY

● Camping

One can camp almost anywhere in safety, except near settlements (unless unavoidable). Warm sleeping gear essential, even in the lowlands in the winter. Sleeping bags are also useful for getting some sleep on the buses or long distance trains, especially those crossing the Andes. Mosquito nets can be purchased in La Paz, but they are not cheap. Beware sandstorms S of Oruro. Camping gas-style and Epigas cannisters are available in La Paz and all large cities; white gas for Coleman stoves is difficult to find. Kerosene is much easier to find outside La Paz, even in small towns. *Alcohol potable* (meths) is widely available.

● Hotels

Hotels must display prices by law. Throughout Bolivia the cheaper hotels impose their own curfews. In La Paz it tends to be midnight (check) but it can be as early as 2130 in Copacabana. These locking up times are strictly adhered to by hotel keepers. Ask for the hot water schedule, it changes with the season, water pressure, etc. Clothes washing is generally not allowed. Many mid-range hotels will keep money and valuables in the safe if there are no safety-deposit boxes. Cheaper hotels rarely have heating in the rooms. Youth Hostels are not necessarily cheaper: many middle range *residenciales* are affiliated to the IYHA.

FOOD AND DRINK

FOOD

The normal international cuisine is found at most good hotels and restaurants.

Salteñas are meat or chicken pasties (originating from Salta, Argentina, but popular throughout the Andean countries), eaten regularly by Bolivians, mostly in the morning. Some are *muy picante* (very hot) with red chili peppers, but *medio picante* and *poco picante* ones can normally be obtained. *Marraqueta* is bread from La Paz, crusty, with a soft centre; *pan de Batallas* is a sandwich loaf.

In the N lowlands, many types of wild meat are served in tourist restaurants and on jungle tours. Bear in mind the turtles whose eggs are eaten are endangered and that other species not endangered soon will be if they stay on the tourist menu.

NB Bolivian highland cooking is usually very tasty and often *picante*. Local specialities, which visitors should try, inc *empanadas* (cheese pasties) and *humitas* (maize pies); *pukacapas* are *picante* cheese pies. Recommended main dishes inc *sajta de pollo*, hot spicy chicken with onion, fresh potatoes and *chuño* (dehydrated potatoes), *parrillada* (a Bolivian kind of mixed grill), *fricase* (juicy pork dish served with *chuño*), *silpancho* (fried breaded meat with eggs, rice and bananas), *saice*, a dish of minced meat with picante sauce, served with rice, potatoes, onions and tomatoes, *pique macho*, roast meat with chips, onion and pepper, and *ají de lengua*, ox-tongue with chilis, potatoes and *chuño* or *tunta* (another kind of dehydrated potato). The soups are also good, especially a *chairo* soup made of meat, vegetables, *chuño* and *ají* (hot pepper) to which the locals like to add *llajua* or *halpahuayca* (hot sauces always set on restaurant tables) to make it even more *picante*. Fried *vizcacha* is eaten in some places, mostly outside the main towns and cities.

In the lowland Oriente region, the food usually comes with cooked banana and yuca; eg *Pollo Broaster* is chicken with rice, chips, yuca and fried banana. The bread in this region is often sweet with cheese on top, and the rice bread is also unusual.

In the *pensiones* and cheaper restaurants a basic lunch (*almuerzo* – usually finished by 1300) and dinner (*cena*) are normally available. The *comida del día* is the best value, in any class of restaurant. Good cheap and clean breakfasts are served in the markets in most towns (most restaurants do not open very early in the morning). Lunch can also be obtained in many of the modern market buildings in the main towns; eat only what is cooked in front of you. Dishes cooked in the street are not safe. Llama meat contains parasites (similar to those in pork), so make sure it has been cooked for a long time and is hot when you eat it. Be very careful of salads; they may carry a multitude of amoebic life as well as vile green bacteria.

DRINK

The several makes of local beer, lager-type, are recommendable; El Inca is a dark beer, sweet, like a stout; the local hot maize drink, *api* (with cloves, cinnamon, lemon and sugar), should be tried (usually US$0.12), as well as *singani*, distilled from grapes, good, cheap and bracing. *Chuflay* is *singani* and 7 Up or Canada Dry (or whatever carbonated drink is available). Good wines are produced by La Concepción vineyard, near Tarija. *Chicha* is a fermented maize drink, popular around Cochabamba. It is not always alcoholic. In the countryside, look for the white flag outside the houses selling *chicha*. Bottled water, Viscachani, is easily available but make sure the seal is unbroken (rain water is sometimes offered as an alternative); there are also several brands of flavoured mineral water, Cayacayani, La Cabaña, Mineragua. Naturagua is purified water. The local tap water should not be drunk without first being sterilized. Local water purifier is 'Lugol Fuerte Solución', an iodine-based product, US$1.75/small bottle; also *iodo* from *farmacias*, US$0.50. For milk, try sachets of Leche Pil (plain, chocolate or strawberry-flavoured), at US$0.25 each.

GETTING AROUND

AIR TRANSPORT

Internal air services are run by Lloyd Aéreo Boliviano (LAB), Aero Sur and TAM between the main cities and towns. LAB and Aero Sur are generally reliable but TAM much less so.

Boarding passes are issued only at airports; after obtaining one, pay airport tax (see above). LAB offers a 28-day unlimited domestic flight ticket for US$135 for international travellers using LAB (or a foreign carrier with whom LAB may have a pooling arrangement) and must be bought outside Bolivia. Only one stopover per city is allowed, except for connecting flights; note that many flights radiate from La Paz, Santa Cruz or Cochabamba. LAB have 20% discounts for family members if they travel together (take passport); LAB and Aero Sur also offer discounts of 20% to students and passengers over 60; TAM offer 25% discount to students and over 60s. Note that a 'through' flight may require a change of plane, or be delayed waiting for a connecting flight coming from elsewhere. Only on international flights is overnight lodging provided during delays. Insure your bags heavily as they tend to get left around.

NB If your internal flight is delayed keep your baggage with you and do not check it in until the flight is definitely announced. There have been robberies of prematurely checked-in baggage.

LAND TRANSPORT

● Trains

Bolivia has 3,774 km of railway. There are two private railways: Machacamarca-Uncia, owned by the Corporación Minera de Bolivia (108 km) and Uyuni-Pulacayo (52 km) owned by the Empresa Minera Pulacayo. Empresa Nacional de Ferrocarriles (ENFE), was privatized in 1996. Schedules change frequently. Always check departure times in advance. Tickets can be bought in advance.

● Road

The national highway system at the end of 1988 totalled 41,642 km, of which only 4% were paved and under 25% gravel-surfaced. Descriptions of all major roads are given in the text, above. Nearly all Bolivian road surfaces, even the paved sections, are bad, and after flooding or rough weather they are even worse. Even main roads may be closed in the rainy season.

NB On election day no public transport runs whatsoever; only cars with a special permit may be on the road.

● Buses

Buses ply most of the roads (interurban buses are called *flotas*, urban ones *micros*, also minibuses and *trufis*). Reporting time is half an hour before the bus leaves. You should always try to reserve, and pay for, a seat as far as possible in advance and arrive in good time, but substantial savings can be made by buying tickets just before departure as there is fierce competition to fill seats. In the wet season, bus travel is subject to long delays and detours at extra cost. In the dry season journeys can be very dusty. On all journeys, take food and toilet wipes. Bus companies are responsible for any luggage packed on the roof. A small charge is made for use of major bus terminals; payment is before departure.

● Motorists (including motor-cyclists)

For necessary documents, see **Introduction and Hints – Motoring**: motorcyclists may be asked for a *carnet de passages* (*triptico*), but it is not officially necessary. If hiring a car, the company can arrange a 'blanket' driving permit for tourist purposes which is valid for several days and destinations. Tolls vary from US$0.50 to US$2.50 for journeys up to 100 km. In theory, you need an International Driving Permit (and, since a driving licence number is requested, also your national driving licence, or some ingenuity). Just a national licence will do when hiring a car and the rental document usually suffices at police controls. Two authorization certificates are required in La Paz: the first from the Automóvil Club Boliviano, corner of 6 de Agosto and Arce, T/F 372139, and the second from the traffic police at the Comando Departamental, Organismo Operativo de Tránsito, corner of Mcal Santa Cruz and Plaza San Francisco. For hints on high-altitude motoring, see **Introduction and Hints** at front of book.

Take great care when driving at night (it is best not to): cyclists do not usually have lights; truck drivers almost never dip their headlights (keep your own on full beam to make the truck dip his); some truck drivers are drunk, or fall asleep at the wheel; at the slightest sign of danger, pull out of the way. Day or night, watch out for people asleep at the roadside in lowland areas; they tend to lie with head and torso in the road where there are fewer mosquitoes.

Petrol (gasoline) 2 grades: 85 and 92 octane. 85 octane costs US$0.44, super US$0.56; diesel costs US$0.38/litre. Costs are higher in Guayaramerín, Riberalta and Puerto Suárez. Around Lake Titicaca, there are no petrol stations as such, the only two that exist frequently run out. Petrol is sold from the drum in every small village.

● Trucks

Trucks congregate at all town markets, with destinations chalked on the sides. They are normally about half the cost when there is competition. Otherwise they charge what they judge the market will bear and can therefore seem expensive.

COMMUNICATIONS

● Media

In La Paz: morning papers – *Presencia*, daily, the largest circulation, largely Catholic; *La Razón*, *Primera Plana*, *Hoy* and *El Diario* (sensationalist). *Meridiano* (midday): *Ultima Hora*, and *Jornada* (evenings). In Cochabamba – *Los Tiempos*, *Extra*. In Oruro – *La Patria*, mornings (except Mon). *El Día*, *La Estrella del Oriente*, *El Mundo* and *El Deber* are the Santa Cruz daily papers; *Deber* also appears in La Paz and Trinidad. In Sucre, *El Correo*. *Presencia*, *El Diario*, *El Mundo*, *El Mundo* all have good foreign coverage. Weekly: *Nueva Economía*. La Paz papers are on sale in other cities. English language weekly *The Bolivian Times*, published Fri, US$1.50, available in major cities, many local reports (details T 340062, F 390700, address Jauregui 2248, Sopocachi, La Paz, casilla 1696). International papers are available in La Paz. Also, there are about 85 radio stations, a commercial government TV station as well as a university TV service.

● Postal services

Post offices use the post box (casilla) system. Items sent by post should therefore bear, not the street address, but the casilla number and town. Hours are Mon-Sat 0800-2000, Sun 0800-1200. For security, send mail 'certificado'. There is a national and international express post system; special counters and envelopes provided. Air-mail letters to and from Europe take between 5 and 10 days. Letter/postcard up to 30g to Europe US$0.80, to North America US$0.70; letter over 30g to Europe US$2.50, to North America US$1.80. Parcels up to 2 kg can be sent airmail after inspection by customs; to Europe a 2 kg parcel costs US$37, to North America US$26. There is a choice of airmail (which takes 1 week) and APR/SAL (which takes a month). A 5 kg parcel to Europe airmail costs US$62, APR/SAL US$41; to North America airmail US$50, APR/SAL US$35. Parcels are checked by customs officers before being sealed. Several reports of customs officers attempting to charge for inspecting parcels: refuse to pay (politely).

● Telephone services

The national telecommunications company is Entel, which handles all phone, telex and fax services. In the Department of La Paz, Cotel operates local services, alongside Entel. There is now direct satellite communication with Bolivia. Direct calls possible from major cities to Europe, USA, Australia and elsewhere, clear lines, delays minimal; US$2.06/min to Europe and Mexico, US$1.76 to USA and South America, US$3.44 to Australia. BT Chargecard calls available billed to UK. At the La Paz exchange you can pay by credit card and the phone shows the cost as you speak. Outside La Paz you may have to wait a while for an overseas connection, but otherwise there are no problems. Fax to Europe costs US$5/page, to the USA US$3.80, to Australia, New Zealand US$6. Phone calls within city limits are free for private calls; for public phones, coins/fichas or phone cards are necessary. Fichas and phone cards only work in the city in which they are bought.

Direct collect-call numbers: US AT&T 0800 1111, MCI 0800 2222, Sprint 0800 3333, IDB (TRT) 0800 4444; UK BT 0800 0044; Spain Telefónica 0800 0034; Brazil 0800 0055; Chile Entel 0800 0056; Canada Teleglobe 0800 0101; Japan KDD 0800 0081.

SPORT

● Hiking

Various treks are outlined in the text, especially nr La Paz and from Sorata. The Bolivia Handbook gives greater detail. Note that all these trails are remote in parts and that robbery and violent attacks have been made on tourists and Bolivians alike. It is advisable to hike these trails in large, organized groups. Backpacking and Trekking in Peru and Bolivia (1995), published by Bradt Publications, describes 3-9 day hikes in the Cordillera Real within easy reach of La Paz (Bradt Publications also publish South America Ski Guide). Trekking in Bolivia, Yossi Brain (1997), published by The Mountaineers, Seattle. The local tourist office also produces leaflets with sketch maps on walks in the vicinity of La Paz. There are also some excellent guides available through local clubs.

HOLIDAYS AND FESTIVALS

● Public holidays

1 Jan, New Year's Day; Carnival Week, Mon, Shrove Tuesday, Ash Wednesday; Holy Week, Thur, Fri and Sat; 1 May, Labour Day; Corpus Christi (movable); 16 July, La Paz Municipal Holiday; 5-7 Aug, Independence; 12 Oct, Columbus Day; 2 Nov, Day of the Dead; Christmas Day.

● Festivals

In addition to those given in the text: 2 Feb: Virgen de la Candelaria, in rural communities, Copacabana, Santa Cruz. 3 May: Fiesta de la Invención de la Santa Cruz, various parts. 2 June: Santísima Trinidad in Beni Department. 24 June: San Juan, all Bolivia. 29 June: San Pedro y San Pablo, at Tiquina and Tihuanaco. 28 July: Fiesta de Santiago (St James), Altiplano and lake region; Achocalla a convenient place to go to. 16 Aug: San Roque, patron saint of dogs, the animals are adorned with ribbons and other decorations. 1 and 2 Nov: All Saints and All

Souls, any local cemetery. 18 Nov: Beni's Departmental anniversary, especially in Trinidad. For other festivals on the Altiplano enquire at hotels or tourist office in La Paz. Remember that the cities are very quiet on national holidays, but colourful celebrations will be going on in the villages. Beware of water-filled balloons thrown during carnival in most cities – even the coldest. Hotels are often full at the most popular places, for instance Copacabana on Good Friday, worth booking in advance.

FURTHER READING

An Insider's Guide to Bolivia, by Peter McFarren (Fundación Cultural Quipus, Casilla 1696, La Paz, 3rd edition, 1992, US$25) has been recommended, especially for its section on culture. Descubriendo Bolivia, Hugo Boero Rojo (1989), is a tour through the departments of present-day Bolivia, with photographs and road routes (also available in English). Bolivia in Focus, by Paul Van Lindent and Otto Verkaren (Latin American Bureau, London 1984) is a concise study of Bolivian politics, economy, culture and people. Guía Boliviana de Transporte y Turismo (GBT) published monthly at Plaza del Estudiante 1920, T 321027, F 391641, US$6 a month, US$65 a year, gives information on transport, accommodation, restaurants, useful data etc, with town plans, for the whole country.

ACKNOWLEDGEMENTS

For updating this chapter, we are most grateful to Alan Murphy. Our warmest thanks are also due to Yossi Brain, resident correspondent in La Paz and those who helped him: Louis Demers (Residencial Sorata), Ulli Schatz, Oscar Vera, José Velasco, Omar Rocha, Jorge Echalar, Orustva Machado García and Tito Ponce. Thanks also to Darius Morgan and Teresita Reyes of Crillon Tours, Jacques Valleton of Turismo Balsa, Michel Livet of Fremen Tours in La Paz (also Mariel in Cochabamba, Mechy in Santa Cruz and Dora in Trinidad), Amanda and Martin Srätker of La Cúpula, Copacabana; Ingrid Guttentag of Los Amigos del Libro; Fernando at Hotel Esmeralda, Coroico; Saturnino Machaca at La Hostería in Chulumani; Victor Edmundo Salínas of SurAndes) in Sucre, Andy Jackson in Santa Cruz; Horst and Cristina of Casa Suiza in San Ignacio de Velasco. Travellers who have written are acknowledged at the end of the book.

Brazil

HORIZONS

THE LAND

Brazil, the fifth largest country in the world, has the sixth largest population. It is almost as large as the United States of America and its area is nearly half that of South America. For neighbours it has all the South American countries save Chile and Ecuador. Distances are enormous: 4,320 km from N to S, 4,328 km from E to W, a land frontier of 15,719 km and an Atlantic coast line of 7,408 km. Its population is over half that of all South America, and over 65% is under 30 years of age. It was named for the tropical redwood, *pau do brasil*, exported by the first settlers.

Brazil's topography may be divided roughly into five main zones: the Amazon Basin; the River Plate Basin; the Guiana Highlands N of the Amazon; the Brazilian Highlands S of the Amazon; and the coastal strip. The two great river basins account for about three-fifths of Brazil's area.

The river basins

The **Amazon Basin**, in northern and western Brazil, takes up more than a third of the whole country. This basin is plain, broadly based on the Andes and funnelling narrowly to the sea; most of the drained area has an elevation of less than 250m. The rainfall is heavy, for the winds from the NE and SE lose their moisture as they approach the Andes. Some few places receive from 3,750 to 5,000 mm a year, though over most of the area it is no more than from 1,500 to 2,500 mm. Much of the basin suffers from annual floods. The region was covered by tropical forest, with little undergrowth except along the watercourses; it is now being rapidly cut down. The climate is hot and the humidity high throughout the year.

The **River Plate Basin**, in the southern part of Brazil, has a more varied surface

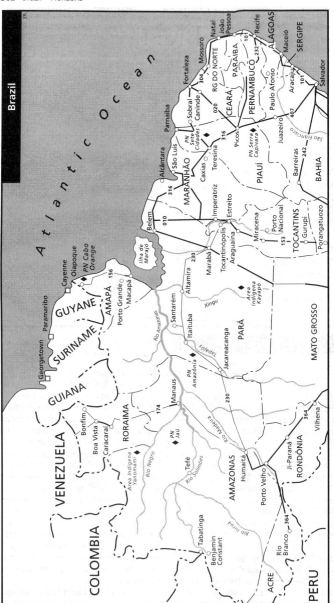

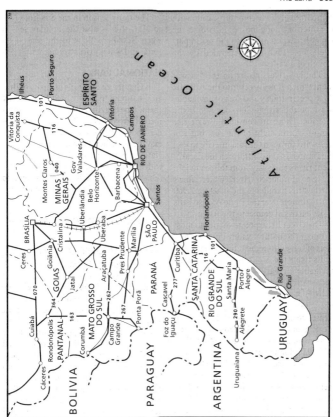

and is less heavily forested than the Amazon Basin. The land is higher and the climate cooler.

Brazil's highlands

Most of the remainder of Brazil's territory is highland. The **Guiana Highlands**, N of the Amazon, are partly forested, partly hot stony desert. Those that face the NW winds get heavy rainfall, but the southern slopes are arid. The rainfall, which comes during the hot season, is about 1,250 mm a year. The summers are hot and the winters cool.

The **Brazilian Highlands** lying SE of the Amazon and NE of the River Plate Basin form a tableland of from 300 to 900m high, but here and there, mostly in SE Brazil, mountain ranges rise from it. The highest peak in southern Brazil, the Pico da Bandeira, NE of Rio de Janeiro, is 2,898m; the highest peak in all Brazil, the Pico da Neblina on the Venezuelan border, is 3,014m.

For the most part the Highlands cascade sharply to the sea. South of Salvador as far as Porto Alegre the coast rises steeply to a protective barrier, the **Great Escarpment**. In only two places is this Escarpment breached by deeply cut river beds – those of the Rio Doce and the Rio Paraíba; and only in a few places does the land rise in a single slope making for comparatively easy communication with the interior. Along most of its course, the Great Escarpment falls to the sea in parallel steps, each step separated by the trough of a valley.

The few rivers rising on the Escarpment which flow direct into the Atlantic do so precipitously and are not navigable. Most of the rivers flow deep into the interior. Those in southern Brazil rise almost within sight of the sea, but run westward through the vast interior to join the Paraná. In the central area the Escarpment rivers run away from the sea to join the São Francisco river, which flows northwards parallel to the coast for 2,900 km, to tumble over the Paulo Afonso Falls on its eastward course to the Atlantic.

The Great Escarpment denies to most of Brazil the natural valley outflows and lines of travel from the interior to the sea. Of its rivers the Amazon alone is directly navigable for a great distance inland.

CLIMATE

The average annual temperature increases steadily from S to N, but even on the Equator, in the Amazon Basin, the average temperature is not more than 27°C. The highest recorded was 42°C, in the dry northeastern states. From the latitude of Recife S to Rio de Janeiro, the mean temperature is from 23° to 27°C along the coast, and from 18° to 21°C in the Highlands. From a few degrees S of Rio de Janeiro to the boundary with Uruguay the mean temperature is from 17° to 19°C. Humidity is relatively high in Brazil, particularly along the coast.

It is only in rare cases that the rainfall can be described as either excessive or deficient: few places get more than 2,000 mm – the coast N of Belém, some of the Amazon Basin, and a small area of the Serra do Mar between Santos and São Paulo, where the downpour has been harnessed to generate electricity. The rainy season in Amazônia is Mar-May, but is getting steadily shorter and less severe, possibly as a result of deforestation. The northeastern droughts are caused by irregular rainfall.

The rainy season in the S is from Dec to Mar; this is also the holiday season when Brazilians flock to the coastal resorts, and when prices are higher.

NATIONAL PARKS

This chapter gives details on many of Brazil's national parks, which are run by Ibama (the Brazilian Institute of Environmental Protection). The Institute is underfunded, often understaffed and visitors may find it difficult to obtain information. National parks are open to visitors, usually with a permit from Ibama. Ecological Stations and Biological Reserves are open to researchers and educational groups, but not tourists.

POLITICAL AND SOCIAL HISTORY

THE PORTUGUESE COLONY

The Portuguese, Pedro Alvares Cabral, landed in Brazil in 1500. He left after a week, shortly followed by Amerigo Vespucci who had been sent to explore further. The first system of government adopted by the Portuguese was a Capitania, a kind of feudal principality – there were 13 of them, but these were replaced in 1572 by a Viceroyalty. In the same year it was decided to divide the colony into two, N and S, with capitals at Salvador and Rio de Janeiro; it was not until 1763 that Rio became the sole capital. The Portuguese crown expected both a personal and a state revenue from its colony.

THE STRUGGLE FOR INDEPENDENCE

300 years under the paternal eye of Portugal had ill-prepared the colonists for independent existence, except for the experience of Dutch invasion (1624 in Salvador, and 1630-1654 in Recife). The colonists ejected the Dutch from Brazil with little help from Portugal, and Brazilians date the birth of their national sentiment from these events. Resentment against Portuguese government and trade intervention led to the **Inconfidência**, the first revolution, masterminded by **Tiradentes** with 11 other citizens of Minas

Gerais. They were unsuccessful (Tiradentes was executed), but when France invaded Portugal in 1807, King João VI was shipped to safety in Brazil, escorted by the British navy. Rio was temporarily declared the capital of the Portuguese Empire. The British, as a price for their assistance in the Portuguese war, forced the opening of Brazil's ports to non-Portuguese trade. King João VI returned to the mother country in 1821, leaving his son, the handsome young Pedro, as Regent. Pedro refused to return control of Brazil to the Portuguese Côrtes (parliament), and on 13 May 1822, by popular request, he agreed to stay and assumed the title of 'Perpetual Defender and Protector of Brazil'. On 7 Sept he declared Brazil's independence with the cry 'Independence or Death' by the Rio Ipiranga; on 12 Oct he was proclaimed constitutional emperor of Brazil, and on 1 Dec he was crowned in Rio de Janeiro.

IMPERIAL BRAZIL

Dom Pedro the First had the misfortune to be faced by a secession movement in the N, to lose the Banda Oriental (today Uruguay) and to get too involved in his complicated love life. Finally, he abdicated as the result of a military revolt in 1831, leaving his 5-year-old son, Dom Pedro the Second, in the hands of a regent, as ruler. On 23 July 1840, the lad, though only 15, was proclaimed of age. Dom Pedro the Second, a strong liberal at heart, promoted education, increased communications, developed agriculture, stamped on corruption and encouraged immigration from Europe. Under his rule the war with the dictator López of Paraguay ended in Brazilian victory. Finally, he declared that he would rather lose his crown than allow slavery to continue, and on 13 May 1888, it was finally abolished by his daughter, Princess Isabel, who was acting as Regent during his temporary absence.

There is little doubt that it was this measure that cost him his throne. Many plantation owners, who had been given no compensation, turned against the Emperor; they were supported by elements in the army and navy, who felt that the Emperor had not given due heed to their interests since the Paraguayan War. On 15 November 1889, the Republic was proclaimed and the Emperor sailed for Europe. 2 years later he died in a second-rate hotel in Paris, after steadfastly refusing a pension from the conscience-stricken revolutionaries. At the time of the first centenary of independence in 1922 the imperial family was allowed to return to Brazil, and the body of Dom Pedro was brought back and buried in the cathedral at Petrópolis.

FROM REPUBLIC TO DICTATORSHIP

The history of the 'Old Republic' (1889-1930), apart from the first 10 years which saw several monarchist rebellions, was comparatively uneventful, a time of expansion and increasing prosperity. Brazil declared war on Germany during both wars and Brazilian troops fought in the Italian campaign in 1944-45. In 1930 a revolution headed by Getúlio Vargas, Governor of Rio Grande do Sul, who was to become known as 'the Father of the Poor' for the social measures he introduced, deposed President Wáshington Luís. Vargas assumed executive power first as provisional president and then as dictator. He was forced to resign in Oct 1945. In 1946 a liberal republic was restored and the following 18 years saw considerable economic development and social advance.

An increase in government instability and corruption prompted the military to intervene in civil affairs. From Mar 1964 until Mar 1985, the military governed Brazil using political repression and torture, yet achieving great economic success (up to 1980). Between 1964-74 average growth was 10% a year but the divide between rich and poor widened. Labour leaders were oppressed, dissenters were jailed and *favelas* mushroomed. Political reform did not occur until 1980 and free elections were not held until 1989.

THE RETURN TO DEMOCRACY

In Jan 1985 a civilian, Tancredo Neves, representing a broad opposition to the military regime, was elected President by the electoral college introduced under the military's 1967 constitution. He was unable, because of illness, to take office: the vice-president elect, Sr José Sarney, was sworn in as acting President in Mar 1985, and in April became President on Sr Neves' death. After complete revision by a Constituent Assembly in 1987-88, Brazil's new constitution of 1988 permitted direct presidential elections in Nov 1989. The elections, held in two rounds, gave Fernando Collor de Melo, of the small Partido da Reconstrução Nacional, 53% of the vote, narrowly defeating his left-wing rival, Luis Inácio da Silva (Lula). Just over half way through his 5-year term, Collor was suspended from office after a landslide congressional vote to impeach over his involvement in corruption. He avoided impeachment by resigning on 29 December 1992. Vice-president Itamar Franco took over, but had scant success in tackling poverty and inflation until the introduction of an anti-inflation package which introduced the real as the new currency.

RECENT DEVELOPMENTS

The success of the **real** plan was the principal reason for its architect, finance minister Fernando Henrique Cardoso, winning the presidential elections of Oct 1994. After trailing Luis Lula da Silva of the Workers Party (PT), Cardoso's popularity grew so rapidly between July and Oct that a second round of voting was not required. Cardoso represented an alliance

of the Brazilian Social Democrat Party (PSDB), the Liberal Front (PFL) and the Labour Party (PTB), which failed to gain a majority in either house of congress. This severely hampered the president's plans to reform the tax and social security systems and the civil service. The government was criticized for its slowness in addressing social problems such as land reform and the violence associated with landlessness; the slave-like working conditions in some agricultural areas; human rights; the demarcation of Indian land. A national plan for human rights was announced in May 1996, but swift congressional approval was not expected.

In all areas, the government's lack of a majority in congress prevented swift progress of any reform. This was best seen in Cardoso's attempt to amend the constitution to allow the president, state governors and mayors to stand for immediate re-election. The amendment was eventually passed in June 1997. The prospect of Cardoso being a candidate would help to advance his reform programme beyond the Oct 1998 elections, but the government had to propose a special 1-year session of congress to unblock civil service and social security reforms languishing before congress since 1994. The measures were viewed as essential for reducing the budget deficit and securing economic stability.

SETTLEMENT AND ECONOMIC HISTORY

The first European settlement was at Salvador da Bahia, and the settlers came mainly from southern Portugal, with its feudal tradition of great estates. For the first few years Portugal, then much concerned with the Orient, paid little attention to Brazil. In about 1507 a second colony was settled at São Vicente, near Santos, and in 1537 a third at Olinda, near Recife. The settlers at São Vicente, who founded the first settlement in the highlands at São Paulo in 1534, were unlike those at Salvador and Recife: they came from the poorer and more energetic N of Portugal. All of them were attracted less by the prospect of earning their living by

self-supporting labour than by opportunities of speculative profit. To do the work they used the primitive Tupi-Guarani Indians, many of whom died from European diseases (see *Red Gold*, by John Hemming). They cohabited freely with the Indians and, later, with slaves imported from Africa to run the huge estates.

Sugar cane had been introduced at São Vicente in 1532, but it was the wealthy settlers of the NE who had the necessary capital to establish the crop and to buy African slaves to work it; the Indian, with a hunting-and-gathering culture, was a disappointment as a labourer. In the matter of sugar, Salvador and Recife had the advantages over São Vicente of being very much nearer home, and of having better ports and easier access to the interior. During the latter half of the 16th and the whole of the 17th centuries, the provinces of Bahia, Pernambuco, and Paraíba were the world's prime source of sugar.

The settlers at São Paulo, envious of the more fortunate NE, sent out expeditions to explore the interior for gold, which had already been found in small quantities in their own streams. These hardy Bandeirantes pushed as far S as Colonia, opposite Buenos Aires, as far W as the Río Paraguay, and N into the area W of the sugar plantations of the NE. In 1698 they struck gold in central Minas Gerais. More was found soon after in central Mato Grosso, and in 1725 in Goiás. Diamonds were discovered in 1729 N of the goldfields of Minas Gerais.

There followed a great gold and diamond rush. The gold boom started early in the 18th century, lasted a 100 years, and then petered out. Minas Gerais was transformed from a wilderness into a well populated agricultural, pastoral, and mining region. It was as an outlet for this area that Rio de Janeiro was developed. Some of the wealth went to create the extraordinarily beautiful city of Ouro Preto, to-day a national monument, and similarly attractive cities like São João del Rei, Mariana, Congonhas do Campo and Diamantina.

Brazil was ready for the next speculation, coffee, introduced about 1720 from French Guyana. Coffee planting began near Rio de Janeiro and at many places round the coast as far as the Amazon, but by 1825 it had mainly been concentrated in the Paraíba valley, W of the capital. From there it spread into São Paulo, where its cultivation attracted a large number of immigrants after 1850.

There have been many other typical Brazilian booms and recessions. The best known is the rubber boom in the Amazon valley; competition from SE Asia wiped it out after 1912. Sugar, coffee, and cocoa were alike the subject of booms. In each case Brazil was challenged by other sources of supply, where more intensive methods of production were applied.

This boom tradition still holds, but it is shifting from agriculture to industry. Nevertheless, a great increase in production and export of manufactured goods has not prevented oases of prosperity being edged by deserts of poverty and wilderness.

CULTURE

PEOPLE

At first the Portuguese colony grew slowly. From 1580 to 1640 the population was only about 50,000 apart from the million or so indigenous Indians. In 1700 there were some 750,000 non-indigenous people in Brazil. Early in the 19th century Humboldt computed there were about 920,000 whites, 1,960,000 Africans, and 1,120,000 Indians and *mestiços*: after 3 centuries of occupation a total of only 4 million, and over twice as many Africans as there were whites.

Modern immigration did not begin effectively until after 1850. Of the 4.6 million immigrants from Europe between 1884 and 1954, 32% were Italians, 30% Portuguese, 14% Spanish, 4% German, and the rest of various nationalities. Since 1954 immigrants have averaged 50,000 a year. There are some 1 million Japanese-descended Brazilians; they grow a fifth of the coffee, 30% of the cotton, all the tea, and are very active in market gardening.

Today the whites and near-whites are about 53% of the population, people of mixed race about 34%, and Afro Brazilians 11%; the rest are either Indians or Asians. There are large regional variations in the distribution of the races: the whites predominate greatly in the S, which received the largest flood of European immigrants, and decrease more or less progressively towards the N.

Most of the German immigrants settled in the three southern states: Santa Catarina, Rio Grande do Sul, and Paraná. The Germans (and the Italians and Poles and other Slavs who followed them) did not in the main go as wage earners on the big estates, but as cultivators of their own small farms. Here there is a settled agricultural population cultivating the soil intensively.

The arid wastes of the Sertão remain largely uncultivated. Its inhabitants are people of mixed Portuguese and Indian origin (*mestiço*); most live off a primitive but effective method of cultivation known as 'slash and burn', which involves cutting down and burning the brushwood for a small patch of ground which is cultivated for a few years and then allowed to grow back.

Though there is no legal discrimination against black people, the economic and educational disparity – by default rather than intent of the Government – is such that successful Afro Brazilians are active almost exclusively in the worlds of sport, entertainment and the arts.

Indigenous peoples

It is estimated that, when the Portuguese arrived in Brazil, there were more than 5 million Indians living in the area. Today there are only about 200,000. Tribal groups number 221; each has a unique dialect, but most languages belong to four main linguistic families, Tupi-Guarani, Ge, Carib and Arawak. A few tribes remain uncontacted, others are exclusively nomadic, others are semi-nomadic hunter-gatherers and farmers, while some are settled groups in close contact with non-Indian society. The struggle of groups such as the Yanomami to have their land demarcated in order to secure title is well-documented. The goal of the Statute of the Indian (Law 6.001/73), for demarcation of all Indian land by 1978, is largely unmet. It was feared that a new law introduced in Jan 1996 would slow the process even further. Funai, the National Foundation for the Support of the Indian, a part of the Interior Ministry, is charged with representing the Indians' interests, but lacks resources and support. There is no nationwide, representative body for indigenous people. Most of Brazil's indigenous people live in the Amazon region; they are affected by deforestation, encroachment from colonizers, small-and large-scale mining, and the construction of hydroelectric dams. Besides the Yanomami, other groups include the Xavante, Tukano, Kreen-Akrore, Kaiapó, Arawete and Arara.

Rural and urban population

The population has historically been heavily concentrated along the coastal strip where the original Portuguese settlers exploited the agricultural wealth, and further inland in the states of Minas Gerais and São Paulo where more recent development has followed the original search for gold, precious stones and slaves. Much of the interior of Pará, Amazonas, Goiás and the Mato Grosso has densities of one person per sq km or less.

The urban population of Brazil increased at rates more than double the overall average rate, until the 1980s, and much of this growth has been concentrated in the larger cities. Internal migration has brought to the cities problems of unemployment, housing shortage, and extreme pressure on services; shanty towns – or *favelas, mocambos, alagados,* according to the region – are an integral part of the urban landscape. But while the NE, because of its poverty, has lost many workers to the industries of the SE, many rural workers from southern Brazil have moved N, drawn by the rapid development of Amazônia, creating unprecedented pressures on the environment.

MUSIC AND DANCE

Perhaps because of its sheer size, Brazil has a greater musical inventory than any other Latin American country, not only reflected in the immense regional spread of folk music but also in its successive waves of urban popular music. The Brazilian expresses him/herself through music and dance to an extraordinary degree and the music covers the whole spectrum from the utmost rural simplicity to the ultimate state-of-the-art commercial sophistication. The far N of the country is virtually in the Caribbean, while the extreme S shares its culture with the Rio de la Plata countries.

The South

In Paraná, Santa Catarina and Rio Grande do Sul, the music is strictly European in origin, rhythm and instrumentation. Rio Grande do Sul shares Gaucho dances such as the Pericom and song styles such as the

Milonga, Trova and Pajada with neighbouring Uruguay and Argentina. The Chula is a competitive dance for men to show off with (comparable to the Argentine Malambo), while the Pexinho is for men and women. The guitar and the accordion are the favourite instruments, also true for Santa Catarina and Paraná, where the names of the dances denote their European origins: Mazurkas, Valsas, Chotes, Polquinhas and Rancheiras. The Chimarrita is a song style that came straight from the Azores. If you are feeling sentimental, you sing a Toada, if energetic, you stamp your feet to a Fandango. Except for the Batuque de Rio Grande do Sul in Porto Alegre, closely related to the Candombe of nearby Montevideo, there is no African influence in the music of this region and none of that classic Brazilian syncopation.

São Paulo, Rio de Janeiro, Minas Gerais

Moving N into São Paulo, we enter an area rich in traditional folk dances and music, with the African admixture beginning to show up. At many religious festivals will be found the Congadas (European 'Moors & Christians', but danced by blacks) and Moçambique (a stick dance for men), while the Samba de Lenço, Fandango and Batuque are recreational dances for one or more couples. The instrumental accompaniment branches out into shakers (the ganzá), drums (caixas and tambores) and above all the guitar (viola). Try the great pilgrimage church at Aparecida do Nte on a Sun. You might well see a group of religious dances. In the hinterland of Rio de Janeiro the Folias de Reis are out on the street from Christmas to Epiphany, singing from house to house, accompanying themselves on the caixa and adufe drums and the guitar, while in the old coastal towns of Paraty and Angra dos Reis are to be found the Dança de Velhos (the old men), performed to the accordion. The Jongo is a dance of African origin for men and women, naturally with a drum accompaniment. And there is hardly need to mention Rio de Janeiro at carnival and its Samba Schools. Further N again, we come to the states of Espíritu Santo, Minas Gerais and Goiás. In colonial Ouro Preto, in Minas, you can hear the old Modinha sung to the Portuguese guitar as a serenade and be transported into the past. Espíritu Santo is home to the Ticumbi, a kind of Congada, danced to the guitar and shakers (chocalhos). Goiás shares with Minas Gerais a very rich heritage of Portuguese derived religious folk song and dance, centred on Folias, Modas and Calangos.

Bahia

Bahia is the heart of African Brazil and a very musical heart it is, born of the Yoruba religion that came with the slaves from what is now Nigeria. The resulting syncretic religion is known as Candomblé in Bahia and the gods or 'Orixás' are worshipped through song, dance and possession in the 'Terreiros', directed by the priests (Pais-de-Santo) and priestesses (Mães-de-Santo). The mainly female adepts, dressed entirely in white, circle gracefully to the background chant of 'Pontos' and the thunderous pounding of the atabaques, the tall drums. The two most revered priestesses are Mãe Olga de Alakêto and Mãe Menininha de Gantois. Similar syncretic African religions are found elsewhere in Brazil. Macumba in Rio, Xangô in the NE and Umbanda all over. Another vital African element in Bahian folk music is the spectacular dance-cum-martial arts form of Capoeira. Bodies whirl and cartwheel around each other to the sound of the berimbau (a one-stringed bow with resonator) and the accompanying chant. Related to the Capoeira is the stick dance Maculelê. Two of the best berimbau groups on record are Camaféu de Oxóssi and the Cordão de Ouro. Bahia has a carnival almost as celebrated as that of Rio and here you can see the Afoxé, a serious religious dance, performed to drums alone.

The North East

North of Bahia is the Nordeste, with music that runs the whole gamut from black African to mediaeval Portuguese. In colonial times the church directed the peoples' musical energies into religious plays, songs and dances and a large number of these are still performed. The Bumba-Meu-Boi is a folk drama in the course of which a bull is killed and then brought back to life. Particularly popular in Piauí and Maranhão, its variants are found as far afield as Amazônia, where it is called the Boi-Bumbá, and Paraná in the far S, where it is known as Boi-Mamão. Also popular along the coast from Ceará to Paraíba is a nautical drama of Portuguese origin called Marujada or Nau Catarineta, a version of Moors and Christians, accompanied by Portuguese guitar (*violão*), drums and the *ganzá* scraper. In Alagoas, Sergipe and Pernambuco we find the sword dance called Reisado, danced after Christmas, the Caboclinhos, who are dressed like Indians and dance with bows and arrows, and the Guerreiros Alagoanos, a mixture of both. The last named are accompanied by the classical northeastern musical group called Terno de Pífanos, with the *pífano* vertical flute, accompanied by *maracas* and *ganzá*. The Banda de Pífanos of Caruaru in Pernambuco can be found on record. Recreational dance music in the Nordeste goes under the generic name of 'Forró', said to be derived from the expression 'For All', because the English companies operating at the turn of the century organized weekend dances for their workmen to which all comers were invited. Four very popular recreational folk dances of this region are the Ciranda (a round dance), the Coco, the Bate-Coxa (where the dancers bump bellies) and the Bambelô. Carnival in Recife, the largest city, is when and where to see the energetic and gymnastic Frevo, danced by young men with an umbrella in their hands, and the very stately and superbly costumed Maracatu dancers, with their queen and king. The Nordeste is equally rich in song styles, notably the Desafios, Emboladas, Cocos and Aboios. The Desafios are performed by so-called Repentistas or Violeiros, who accompany themselves on the Portuguese guitar and whose repertoire includes a large inventory of verse styles. They will sing about individual spectators, who then pay willingly for the compliment. The Emboladas and Cocos are similar, but faster and accompanied solely by tambourines, while the Aboios are haunting songs related to cattle and cattlemen. Repentistas and Emboladores can normally be found at work in markets throughout the region. The premier Repentista is Otacílio Batista do Pajeú, who sang to the Pope during the latter's visit to Brazil.

The music of the Nordeste has also been well propagated by more sophisticated groups that have based themselves on folk roots, such as the Quinteto Violado, Ariano Suassuna's Orchestra Armorial and Cussy de Almeida's Quinteto Armorial, not forgetting the veteran accordionist Luiz Gonzaga and the popular Alceu Valença. As a result of the huge migration of *nordestinos* to the urban S, moreover, it is just as easy to hear this regional music in São Paulo as it is in Recife.

Pará and the Amazon

Finally to Pará and the Amazon in the far N, where the music has been heavily influenced from the Caribbean. The most popular musical genre here is the Carimbó, danced to a Merengue-type rhythm and played on drums, wind or brass (usually the clarinet) and strings, particularly the banjo. Notable performers are Pinduca ('O Rei do Carimbó'), Veriquete and Vieira. It is the last-named who thought up the term 'Lambada' for his particular version of the Carimbó and the spectacular, thigh-entwining dance form introduced to the world in Paris by Karakos and Lorsac in 1988 had already been popular among young people at 'Forrós' throughout the region for some years. The very traditional island of Marajó in the mouth of the Amazon has preserved versions of 18th century dances, such as the Lundú and Chula.

Urban popular music

The vast range of Brazilian regional folk music is only equalled by the chronological depth of its urban popular music, which surges like endless waves on a beach. For the origins we have to go back to Jesuit missions and Portuguese folk music, influenced and blended by African slaves, from which emerged the 19th century Lundús, Polcas and Maxixes that in turn gave way to the romantic and sentimental Choro song genre (from *chorar*, to weep), accompanied by guitar, flute and *cavaquinho* (small guitar), which became all the rage and indeed still has its adepts in Brazil today. Around the turn of the century the instrumentation turned to brass and Rio's urban Samba was born, a birth that was announced by the recording in 1917 of Donga's 'Pelo Telefone'. Names from this early period are Pixinguinha, Sinhô, Heitor dos Prazeres, Ary Barroso, Noel Rosa and of course Carmen Miranda, who took the Samba to Hollywood and the rest of the world. It also became intimately connected with the carnival in the form of Marcha Ranchos and Sambas de Enredo as the first samba schools were formed, of which Salgueiro, Mangueira, Partido Alto, Portela, Mocidade Independente and Beija-Flor are some of the most famous. With the Escolas de Samba came the Batucada or percussion groups playing the *pandeiro* (tambourine), *atabaque* and *tamborim* (drum), *agogô* (cowbell), *reco-reco*, *chocalho*, *afoxê* and *cuíca*. This is the real engine room of Samba. Listen to Lúcio Perrone or Mocidade Independente de Padre Miguel. A new phase was ushered in with an invasion from Bahia and the Nordeste in the early 50s'. From Bahia came Dorival Caymmi, who dropped his fishermen's songs in favour of the Samba, and Luiz Gonzaga, who brought his accordion, *zabumba* drum and *triangulo*, with which to play his Baiãos (his 'Asa Branca' is a classic) and almost put the Samba itself into eclipse for several years. Almost, but not quite, for out of the ashes there soon arose Bossa Nova – white, middle class and silky smooth. Vinícius de Moraes and Tom Jobim were its heroes; 1958 to 1964 the years; Copacabana, Ipanema and Leblon the scene; 'Samba de uma Nota Só', 'A Garota de Ipanema' and 'Desafinado' the songs and Nara Leão, Baden Powell, Toquinho, João Gilberto, Luis Bonfá and Astrud Gilberto the main performers. Stan Getz, the American jazz saxophonist, helped export it to the world. What was now being called MPB (Música Popular Brasileira) then took off in several directions. Chico Buarque, Edu Lobo and Milton Nascimento were protest singers. Out of Bahia emerged 'Tropicalismo' in the persons of Gilberto Gil, Caetano Veloso and his sister Maria Bethânia, Gal Costa, João Gilberto and 'Som Livre'. The words were important, but the rhythm was still there. Brazilian rock also now appeared, with such stars as Roberto Carlos, Elis Regina, Rita Lee, and Ney Mattogrosso. Recently, in turning towards international black consciousness, the Bahianos have mixed Reggae and Samba to produce 'axê'. Still, Samba has survived, although now called 'Pagode' and amazingly, 40% of all Brazilian records sold are of Música Sertaneja, a highly commercialized pseudo-folk genre which is closer to American Country and Western than to most other Brazilian music. Listen to the 'Duplas' of Tonico & Tinoco, Jacó e Jacozinho or Vieira & Vieirinha and you'll see. In the meantime a series of brilliant Brazilian instrumentalists have become international names and often live abroad – Sérgio Mendes, the guitarist Sebastião Tapajós, flautist Hermêto Paschoal, saxophonist Paulo Moura, accordionist Sivuca, percussionists Airto Moreira and Nana Vasconcelos, singer Flora Purim and all-rounder Egberto Gismonti are but a few. On the top of a huge recording industry, we're now a long way from the grassroots and the haunting flute music of the forest Indians.

THE ECONOMY

Structure of production Brazil's economy is the largest in Latin America and the tenth in the world, but its gdp per capita has grown little since 1980 and is less than the average for the whole of Latin America and the Caribbean. It has abundant and varied natural resources, not all of which are fully explored or exploited. The 40 years after 1945 were a period of massive state intervention and industrialization with public sector investment in energy, heavy industry, transport equipment and capital goods, but in the 1990s the country has moved towards a market economy with a smaller role for the state.

Brazil remains a large farming country; processed and unprocessed agricultural products account for about a third of exports and agriculture, forestry and fishing account for 14% of gdp. Brazil is the world's largest producer and exporter of coffee and maintains a dominant position in international markets for soya and orange juice, mostly grown in the state of São Paulo. São Paulo state also produces over half Brazil's harvest of about 300 million tonnes of sugar cane, most of which is distilled into fuel alcohol for cars or electricity generating power plants. Although Brazil used to be the world's largest cocoa grower, with Ilhéus the main area of production, the industry has declined because of underinvestment, fungus and low prices and it is now ranked fourth. Most of Brazil's agricultural land is held by large landowners, with 10% of the farmers owning 80% of the land. Land reform is contentious and has proceeded very slowly with much conflict and violence. Up to 5 million families are believed to want land although only 130,000 were resettled in 1986-94. Holdings must be confirmed unproductive before they can be appropriated for settlement.

The country is richly endowed with metals and other minerals. Brazil has up to a third of the world's iron ore reserves, found mainly in Minas Gerais and certain parts of the Amazon basin, especially the Serra dos Carajás region (Pará). Brazil also exports manganese and produces increasing amounts of tin and copper. In 1996, the state mining company, Companhia Vale do Rio Doce (CVRD), announced a 150-tonne gold find near Carajás, which would make it the largest gold mine in Latin America. It is expected to produce 10 tonnes a year, about 20% of Brazil's present output. The mine is also near Serra Pelada, an open mine which in the 1980s attracted a gold rush of 80,000 *garimpeiros*, wildcat goldminers, but the new one is much deeper and not suitable for being dug by hand. CVRD is one of the world's largest natural resources groups and owns mining and exploration rights worth an estimated US$40bn, including Carajás, where reserves of iron ore are sufficient for 500 years. As well as gold and iron ore, it is

Brazil : fact file	
Geographic	
Land area	8,547.404 sq km
forested	57.7%
pastures	21.9%
cultivated	6.0%
Demographic	
Population (1996)	157,872,000
annual growth rate (1991-96)	1.4%
urban	78.2%
rural	21.8%
density	18.5 per sq km
Education and Health	
Life expectancy at birth,	
male	56.6 years
female	67.3 years
Infant mortality rate	
per 1,000 live births (1995)	57.2
Calorie intake as %	
of FAO requirement	118%
Population age 10 and over	
with no formal schooling	18.1%
Literate males (over 15)	83.3%
Literate females (over 15)	83.2%
Economic and Employment	
GNP (1994 market price)	US$536,309mn
GNP per capita	US$3,370
Public external debt (1994)	US$94,512mn
Tourism receipts (1994)	US$1,925mn
Inflation (annual av 1992-95)	482%
Population economically active (1990)	
	64,467,981
Unemployment rate (1996-registered)	5.9%
Military forces (1995)	295,000

Source *Encyclopaedia Britannica InterAmerican Development Bank*

involved in steel, aluminium, forestry, railways and port and shipping facilities. The Government gradually reduced its stake in CVRD to 51% and the company was sold eventually, amid strong protests and much legal wrangling, to a Brazilian-led consortium.

Industrial production accounts for 36% of gdp and sales of mechanical equipment, cars, chemicals, textiles and other manufactures account for the majority of exports. The steel and vehicle industries are among the top 10 in the world. Brasmotor, a consumer goods conglomerate, is the world's second largest producer of compressors. Ceval and Sadia, two large food processing compa-

Debt – the Rise and ....

During the 1970s large, costly development projects were financed by foreign borrowing. Brazil accumulated the region's largest external debt which became unsustainable in the 1980s. From 1982 annual rescheduling agreements were concluded with creditors, with new money and, in 1983-85, IMF standby facilities. These arrangements did not, however, help to reduce the burden of interest payments and in 1987 Brazil declared a moratorium on interest in order to preserve foreign exchange reserves and halt the net transfer of resources to creditors. The plan failed and a year later reserves were even lower as lenders declined to extend credit. In 1988 Brazil negotiated a financing package from all creditors aimed at restoring its creditworthiness, but by 1989 it had moved back into arrears. In 1992 another IMF standby agreement was made, allowing further debt rescheduling with the Paris Club of creditor governments, but the facility collapsed later in the year. Despite the lack of IMF approval for its economic management, Brazil managed to clinch a deal with its commercial bank creditors to restructure US$49bn of debt in 1994, using so-called Brady bonds as collateral. By 1995 all the collateral for the bonds had been deposited and with reserves of US$40bn, Brazil started to buy back Brady bonds in 1997.

nies, have annual exports of over US$1bn, while Brahma, the largest brewer in Latin America, also exports. The Mercosur free trade area has encouraged exporters to look for markets in neighbouring countries instead of concentrating on the USA and Europe. Privatization, the abolition of price controls and falling tariffs have forced increased efficiency and productivity on to Brazilian companies, which have had to invest in modernization and gear their strategy to coping with competition rather than hyperinflation.

Energy sector development was aimed at substituting local for imported energy. The oil industry was nationalized in 1953 and the state monopoly, Petrobrás, controlled exploration, production, refining and distribution of oil and gas. In 1995, however, Congress voted to end that monopoly and allow private sector companies to compete with Petrobrás. Oil production averages 800,000 b/d; reserves are 10.3 billion barrels, of which 5.1 billion are proven, while gas reserves are 147 billion cu m. Large investments have been made in hydroelectricity, alcohol and nuclear power. A 620-MW nuclear power plant at Angra dos Reis (Rio de Janeiro) came on stream in 1985, but financial restrictions have slowed nuclear and other electricity development. The system's total capacity in 1995 was 52,700MW, but investment was not keeping pace with demand of about 5% a year, so shortages and power cuts periodically affect parts of the country. It is estimated that 10% of homes are not connected to the electricity grid, having improved from 47% in 1970, and some 16% of energy distributed is not paid for because of illegal connections. Constitutional restrictions prevent sweeping privatization, although some states are pursuing sales of their regional utilities. Parts of the state company, Eletrobrás' operations are planned for eventual sale, leaving nuclear power and the Itaipu hydroelectric dam (jointly owned with Paraguay) in state hands. Independent energy producers have been permitted to operate since 1995 but the lack of enabling legislation delayed progress.

Recent trends High inflation in the 1980s and the early 1990s proved intractable as successive governments introduced stabilization programmes with new currencies but limited success. The principal cause of failure was the lack of political will to tackle the structural causes of inflation, namely the public accounts disequilibrium, supply bottlenecks, inefficiencies and corruption in state governments and enterprises, and widespread indexation of wages, prices and financial instruments. It was not until May 1993, with the appointment of Fernando Henrique Cardoso as Finance Minister that a plan was implemented which contained stringent measures to strengthen the public accounts and thus reduce inflation. However, cooperation from powerful political interests was not forthcoming and inflation soared. On 1 July 1994, a new currency, the real, was introduced at par with the US dollar. Inflation immediately plummeted from over 50% a month to less than 2% and while interest rates remained high, the real appreciated. As confidence in the programme grew and price stability led to a rise in real wages, consumer spending also increased. The feelgood factor helped the election of Cardoso to the Presidency. Imports soared while exports were diverted to the domestic market. Investment picked up and gdp rose by 5.7%, the highest growth rate since 1986. By the end of the year Brazil was recording monthly trade deficits for the first time since the mid-1980s. Despite reserves of some US$40bn to support the real, the Mexican financial crisis at the same time brought a bad case of nerves in the financial markets. The Government adjusted the exchange rate regime, introducing a range of floating bands within which the real would range, raised some tariffs to curb imports and imposed emergency measures to balance the budget. Returning the trade account to surplus by mid-1995 proved short-lived as the strong exchange rate continued to encourage imports at the expense of exports. Foreign sales were also restricted by low productivity.

The Government's reform programme encompasses three main areas, all requiring changes to the 1988 Constitution: the responsibilities and spending obligations of the central government to be devolved to local government and the private sector; government revenue to be raised by an overhaul of the tax system; the social security system to be reformed (benefici-aries exceed contributors, costing US$28bn in 1995 compared with US$14bn in 1992). Bills for the reform of the tax and social security systems were sent to Congress, where progress had still not been made by 1997. Privatization was extended to cover energy, transport, telecommunications and mining, while removing some constitutional restrictions on competition, allowing the private sector to compete with or enter into joint ventures with state enterprises such as the oil company, Petrobrás. Priority spending plans have been announced for social spending (particularly health, education and sanitation) and infrastructure (roads, railways, waterways and telecommunications) amounting to US$161bn by the end of the century, some of which will be in joint ventures with the private sector.

GOVERNMENT

Constitution

The 1988 constitution provides for an executive president elected by direct popular vote, balanced by a bicameral legislature (81 seats in the Federal Senate, 513 seats in the Chamber of Deputies) and an independent judiciary. The vote has been extended to 16-year-olds and illiterates. Presidential elections are held every 5 years, with a second round 1 month after the first if no candidate wins an outright majority. Congressional elections are held every 4 years, the deputies being chosen by proportional representation.

Local administration

Each state has a popularly-elected Governor who exercises the executive power, and a Legislative Assembly which legislates on all matters affecting provincial administration and provides for state expenses and needs by levying taxes. Each municipality has a similar structure, with a mayor (*prefeito*), also popularly elected, and a local council (*câmara de vereadores*).

Brasília

T HE PURPOSE-BUILT federal capital of Brazil, with its late 20th century design and its overflow communities, succeeded Rio de Janeiro (as required by the Constitution) on 21 April 1960.

(*Pop* 411,000 (census); 1,600,000 (1992 est); *Alt* 1,150m; *CEP* 7000, *DDD* 061)

Brasília is 960 km away from Rio de Janeiro on undulating ground in the unpopulated uplands of Goiás, in the heart of the undeveloped Sertão.

The Federal District has an area of 5,814 sq km. The climate is mild and the humidity refreshingly low, but trying in dry weather. The noonday sun beats hard, but summer brings heavy rains and the air is usually cool by night. Only light industry is allowed in the city and its population was limited to 500,000; this has been exceeded and more people live in a number of shanty towns located well away from the main city.

History and design

The creation of an inland capital had been urged since the beginning of the last century, but it was finally brought into being after President Kubitschek came to power in 1956, when a competition for the best general plan was won by Professor Lúcio Costa, who laid out the city in the shape of a bent bow and arrow. (It is also described as a bird, or aeroplane, in flight.)

Along the curve of the bow are the residential areas made up of large 6-storey apartment blocks, the 'Super-Quadras'. They lie on either side (E and W) of the 'bow' (the Eixo Rodoviário) and are numbered according to their relation to the Eixo and their distance from the centre. Thus the 100s and 300s lie W of the Eixo and the 200s and 400s to the E; Quadras 302, 102, 202 and 402 are nearest the centre and 316, 116, 216 and 416 mark the end of the Plano Piloto (the official name for the centre). The two halves of the city are referred to as Asa Sul and Asa Norte (the N and S wings). Thus, for example, 116 Sul and 116 Nte are at the extreme opposite ends of the city. Each Super-Quadra houses 3,000 people and has a primary school and playgroup. Each group of four Super-Quadras should have a library, police station, club, supermarket and secondary school. All Quadras are separated by feeder roads, along which are the local shops. There are also a number of schools, parks and cinemas in the spaces between the Quadras (especially in Asa Sul). On the outer side of the 300s and extending the length of the city is the Av W3 and on the outer side of the 400s is the Av L2, both of these being similarly divided into N and S according to the part of the city they are in.

Asa Sul is almost complete and Asa Norte is growing very fast. The main shopping areas, with more cinemas, restaurants and so on, are situated on either side of the old bus station (rodoviária). The private residential areas are W of the

Super-Quadras, and on the other side of the lake.

At right angles to these residential areas is the 'arrow', the 8-km long, 250m wide **Eixo Monumental**. The main N-S road (Eixo Rodoviário), in which fast-moving traffic is segregated, follows the curve of the bow; the radial road is along the line of the arrow – intersections are avoided by means of underpasses and cloverleaves. Motor and pedestrian traffic is segregated in the residential areas.

PLACES OF INTEREST

At the tip of the arrow, as it were, is the **Praça dos Três Poderes**, with the Congress buildings, the Palácio do Planalto (the President's office), the Palácio da Justiça and the Panteão Tancredo Neves. 19 tall Ministry buildings line the Esplanada dos Ministérios, W of the Praça, culminating in two towers linked by a walkway to form the letter H, representing Humanity. They are 28 storeys high: no taller buildings are allowed in Brasília. Where the bow and arrow intersect is the city bus terminal (rodoviária), with the cultural and recreational centres and commercial and financial areas on either side. There is a sequence of zones westward along the shaft of the arrow; a hotel centre, a radio city, an area for fairs and circuses, a centre for sports, the **Praça Municipal** (with the municipal offices in the Palácio do Buriti) and, lastly (where the nock of the arrow would be) the combined new bus and railway station (rodoferroviária) with the industrial area nearby. The most impressive buildings are all by Oscar Niemeyer, Brazil's leading architect.

The **Palácio da Alvorada**, the President's official residence (not open to visitors), with a family of emus on the lawn, is on the the lakeshore. The 80-km drive along the the road round the lake to the dam is attractive. There are spectacular falls below the dam in the rainy season. Between the Praça dos Três Poderes and the lake are sites for various recreations, including golf, fishing and yacht clubs, and an acoustic shell for shows in the open air. The airport is at the eastern end of the lake. Some 395 ha

between the lake and the northern residential area (Asa Norte) are reserved for the Universidade de Brasília, founded in 1961. South of the university area, the Av das Nações runs from the Palácio da Alvorada along the lake to join the road from the airport to the centre. Along it are found all the principal embassies. Also in this area is the attractive vice-presidential residence, the **Palácio do Jaburu**, not open to visitors.

Overview and tours

A fine initial view of the city may be had from the **television tower**, which has a free observation platform at 75m up; also bar and souvenir shop; closes for maintenance on Mon mornings. If the TV tower is closed, the nearby *Alvorada* hotel has a panoramic terrace on the 12th floor (lift to 11th only): ask at reception. A good and cheap way of seeing Brasília is by taking bus rides from the municipal rodoviária at the centre: the destinations are clearly marked. The circular bus routes 106, 108 and 131 go round the city's perimeter. If you go around the lake by bus, you must change at the Paranoá dam; to or from Paranoá Nte take bus 101, 'Rodoviária', and to and from Sul, bus 100, bypassing the airport. Tours, from 1300-1700, start from the downtown hotel area and municipal rodoviária (US$12-20). Many hotels arrange city tours (see also **Tour companies** below).

It is worth telephoning addresses away from the centre to ask how to get there. An urban railway, Metrô, to the SW suburbs is due for completion in 1998.

Official Buildings

Congress is open to visitors Mon-Fri 0930-1130 and 1400-1700 (take your passport), guides free of charge (in English 1400-1600), and visitors may attend debates when Congress is in session (Fri morning). Excellent city views from the 10th floor in Annex 3. The **Palácio do Planalto** may be visited on special occasions only. The guard is changed ceremonially at the Palácio do Planalto on Tues, 0830 and 1730. The President attends if he is available. Opposite the Planalto is the

Supreme Court building, **Supremo Tribunal Federal**. The marvellous building of the Ministry of Foreign Affairs, the **Itamarati**, has modern paintings and furniture and beautiful water gardens (guided visits Mon-Fri at 1600, free). Opposite the Itamarati is the **Palácio de Justiça**, with artificial cascades between its concrete columns, visiting hours Mon-Fri, 0900-1130, 1500-1700.

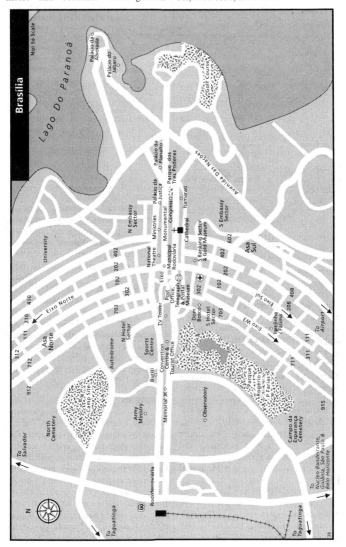

Brasília

Churches

The **Catedral Metropolitana**, on the Esplanada dos Ministérios, a spectacular circular building in the shape of the crown of thorns, is open Tues-Sat, 0830-1130, 1430-1830, T 224 4073. Three aluminium angels, suspended from the airy, domed, stained-glass ceiling, are by the sculptor, Alfredo Scesciatte, who also made the 4 life-sized bronze apostles outside. The baptistery, a concrete representation of the Host beside the cathedral, is connected to the main building by a tunnel (open Suns only). The outdoor carillon was a gift from the Spanish government: the bells are named after Columbus's ships. West of the TV tower on Av W3 Sul, at Quadra 702, is the Sanctuary of **Dom Bosco**, a square building with narrow windows filled with blue glass mosaics, purple at the four corners; the light inside is most beautiful. The **Templo da Boa Vontade**, Setor Garagem Sul 915, lotes 75/76, T 245-1070, is a seven-faced pyramid topped by the world's largest crystal, a peaceful place dedicated to all philosophies and religions (to get there take bus 151 from outside the Centro do Convenções or on Eixo Sul to Centro Médico). Other religious buildings worth seeing are the **Igreja Nossa Senhora de Fátima** church (the Igrejinha) in the Asa Sul at Quadras 307-308, the **Santuário Nossa Senhora de Fátima**, the 'orange caterpillar' on Av W5, Quadra 906, a little S of the Dom Bosco sanctuary, and the chapel (**Ermida**) of Dom Bosco, on the other side of the lake opposite the Alvorada, though the site is not well maintained.

Memorials and military buildings Some 15 km out along the Belo Horizonte road is the small wooden house, known as '**O Catetinho**', in which President Kubitschek stayed in the late 1950s during his visits to the city when it was under construction; it is open to visitors and most interesting. A permanent memorial to Juscelino Kubitschek, the **'Memorial JK'**, contains his tomb and his car, together with a lecture hall and exhibits (open daily 0900-1800, entry US$0.50, has toilets and *lanchonete*). The **Quartel-General do Exército**, Brazilian Army headquarters, designed by Oscar Nie-

meyer, is interesting. The **Panteão Tancredo Neves** is a 'temple of freedom and democracy', built 1985-6 by Niemeyer. It includes an impressive homage to Tiradentes, the precursor of Brazilian independence. **Espaço Lúcio Costa** contains a model of Plano Piloto, sketches and autographs of the designer's concepts and gives the ideological background to the planning of Brasília. The **Monumental Parade Stand** has unique and mysterious acoustic characteristics (the complex is N of the Eixo Monumental, between the 'Memorial JK' and the rodoferroviária). There are remarkable stained glass panels, each representing a state of the Federation, on the ground floor of the Caixa Econômica Federal. **NB** Town clothes (not shorts or minis) should be worn when visiting all the above.

MUSEUMS

Museu Histórico de Brasília Praça dos Três Poderes, really a hollow monument, with tablets, photos and videos; open daily 1000-1800. **Museu de Valores** at the Banco Central exhibits old and new notes and coins and gold prospecting in Brazil; Tues-Fri 1000-1730, Sat 1400-1730. **Museu Postal e Telegráfico da ECT**, Setor Comercial Sul, Ed Apolo, quadra 13 bloco A, stamps, telegraphic equipment, etc; entry, US$0.30, Tues-Fri 0900-1800, Sat 0900-1300. **Museu da Imprensa Nacional**, Setor de Indústrias Gráficas, Quadra 6; bus 152 from municipal rodoviária: admission free; old printing and embossing equipment, etc; open working days 0800-1700.

Sculptures

Brasília is famous for its wealth of modern sculpture. Examples are: 'Cultura' (on the University campus), 'Meteoro' (above the Itamarati water-mirror), and 'Os Candogos', in front of the Planalto, which pays homage to the pioneer workers who built Brasília on empty ground – all by Bruno Giorgi; 'A Justiça' (in front of Palácio da Justiça), the four evangelists in front of the Cathedral and 'As Banhistas' (The Water-Nymphs, above the Alvorada water-mirror) – all by Alfredo Scesciatte; 'Rito dos

Ritmos' (Alvorada gardens), by Maria Martins; and the beautiful 'Sereia' (Mermaid) in front of the Navy Ministry on the Esplanada dos Ministérios. A statue of Juscelino Kubitschek stands above the 'Memorial JK'. A short distance W of here is a huge wooden cross marking the site of the first Mass said in Brasília (3 May 1957), at the city's highest point.

LOCAL HOLIDAYS

Ash Wed; Maundy Thur, half-day; 8 Dec (Immaculate Conception); Christmas Eve.

LOCAL INFORMATION

● **Accommodation**

Hotel prices

L1	over US$200	**L2**	US$151-200
L3	US$101-150	**A1**	US$81-100
A2	US$61-80	**A3**	US$46-60
B	US$31-45	**C**	US$21-30
D	US$12-20	**E**	US$7-11
F	US$4-6	**G**	up to US$3

Unless otherwise stated, all hotels in range **D** and above have private bath. Assume friendliness and cleanliness in all cases.

Prices inc breakfast, but 10% must be added. Weekend discounts of 30% are often available, but must be asked for.

In the **Southern Sporting Sector**, the **L2** *Academia de Tênis*, SCES Trecho 04, Conj 05, Lt 1/B, T 316-6161, F 316-6268, has sports facilities, pools, conference facilities, good restaurant; heavily booked in advance.

In the Southern Hotel Sector: L2 *Nacional*, Quadra 1 bloco A, T 321-7575, F 323-5792, 5-star, pool, expensive, old-fashioned, rec; **A1** *Bristol*, Quadra 4 bloco F, T 321-6162, F 321-2690, 3-star, pool; **A1** *Carlton*, Quadra 5 bloco G, T 224-8819, F 226-8109, 4-star, excellent, pool; **A3** *Planalto*, Quadra 3 bloco A, T 322-1828, F 225-1406, rooms in front noisy, city tours; **A3** *Alvorada*, Quadra 4 bloco A, T 225-3050, F 225-3130, good view from roof terrace, rec.

In the Northern Hotel Sector: L2 *Eron Brasília*, Quadra 5 bloco A, T 321-1777, F 226-2698, 5-star; **A1** *Aracoara*, Quadra 5 bloco C, T 321-9222, F 226-9067, 4-star. The same road gives access to: **A2** *Aristus*, Quadra 2 bloco O, T 223-8675, F 321-5415, good, a/c, TV, phone, money exchange, small restaurant; **A2** *Casablanca*, Quadra 3 lote A, T 321-8586, some rooms noisy; **A2** *Diplomat*, Quadra 2 bloco L, T 225-2010, good value; **A3** *El Pilar*, Quadra 3 bloco F, T 224-

5915, a/c or fan, TV; **C-D** *Mirage*, Quadra 2 lote N, T 225-7150, fan, good, clean, good value; and others. Moderately-priced hotels can be found in the Northern Hotel Sector only.

D *Cury's Solar*, Quadra 707 Sul, Bloco I, Casa 15, T 243-6252 or 244-1899, cramped but helpful, safe, around 30 mins from the centre (Eixo Monumental) along W3 Sul, rec.

E *Pensão da Zenilda*, W3 Sul Quadra 704, Bloco Q, Casa 29, T 224-7532, safe. Teresa Tasso, SQN312-'K'-505, T 273-4844 or 272-4243, offers accommodation in an apartment in the Asa Sul at US$35 for the flat (sleeps 5, kitchen, bath, laundry facilities), excellent value, Teresa gives city tours for US$40, and will collect you at the airport if you phone in advance (bus to flat from centre, 5 mins). Rooms to let (**D-C**) from: Dona Neusa, Av W3 Sul, HIGS 707, Bl I, C15, T 243 6252; Getúlio Valente, warmly rec, Av W3 Sul, HIGS 703, Bl I casa 73, near the TV tower, good, cheap meals available, Portuguese speakers T 226-8507/9639 and Getúlio will pick you up; otherwise, turn right off Av W3 Sul between 703 and 702, then take first left (an unpaved driveway). Nearby is J Araújo, HIGS 703, Bl G, C35, T 226-4059. The tourist office has a list of penses.

The hotels outside the city in **Taguatinga** (take 102 or 106 bus, EIXO, 304 or 306 from rodoferroviária) and Núcleo Bandeirante, though fairly basic, are more economical, but it is difficult to get single rooms. Taguatinga is pleasanter than the Núcleo, which is full of shanties; there are many cheap hotels and restaurants of a reasonable standard, for example: **C** *Colorado*, Setor Hoteleira, Projeção B, T 561-3500, F 351-6637, with bath, fridge, TV, good, in the centre; **D** *Pousada Brasília*, next door at Projeção L, T 562-5055; **D** *Globo*, CNB4, lote 1, T 561-1716, without breakfast, basic; **E** *Solar*, C 7, lote 13, sobreloja, T 563-5660, nr Pão de Açucar Supermarket, basic and clean. Bus 'Estrutural' from Brasília rodoferroviária to Taguatinga Rodoviária where you change, without extra charge to 700 bus which passes, in order: **D** *Camará*, QNE 16, lt 8, T 561-2597 (hourly rentals also); **D** *Palace*, CNB 11, basic, hot water. Bus 700 or 800 (marked 'Eixo') goes from opp Pão de Açucar Supermarket in Taguatinga to old rodoviária in Brasília. Very cheap accommodation in Formosa (see p.382).

Camping: the city's main site is 2 km out, by the Centro Esportivo, nr the motor-racing track, with room for 3,100 campers, mixed reports. Take bus 109 (infrequent) from municipal rodoviária. Água Mineral Parque, 6 km NW of city, direct buses only at weekend; US$1 pp, mineral pool, showers. Associação Brasileira de Camping (Edif Márcia, 12th floor, Setor Comercial Sul, T 225-8768) has two sites: one at Km 19 on the

Belo Horizonte road and one 25 km NE of Brasília at Sobradinho. Camping Clube do Brasil has a site at Itiquira waterfall, 100 km NE of the city, nr Formosa; information from Edif Maristela, room 1214, Setor Comercial Sul, T 223-6561.

● **Places to eat**

The Southern Hotel Sector tends to have more restaurants than the N; there are many cheap places on Av W3 Sul, eg at Blocos 502 and 506. At weekends few restaurants in central Brasília are open. The following are classified by their speciality:

International Cuisine: *Aeroporto*, terrace of international airport, pleasant, very good. Most of the big hotels' restaurants. *Restaurant Gaf*, Centro Gilberto Salomão, Lago Sul (very good, especially meat, and expensive).

For Brazilian food, there are several churrascarias (barbecues), for example *Churrascaria do Lago*, SHTN, Conj 1-A, by Palácio da Alvorada; a number of Brazilian restaurants and some serving Amazonian food.

Seafood: *Panela de Barro*, Galeria Nova Ouvidor, Setor Comercial Sul, Quadra 5.

For European cuisine **Portuguese**: *Cachopa*, Galeria Nova Ouvidor, loja 127; **Spanish**: *O Espanhol*, Av W3 Sul, quadra 506, bloco A; **French**: *Le Français*, Av W3 Sul, quadra 404, bloco B; *La Chaumière*, Av W3 Sul, quadra 408, bloco A. **Italian/Pizzerias**: *Kazebre 13*, Av W3 Sul, quadra 504; *Roma*, Av W3 Sul, quadras 501 and 511, good, quite cheap.

Chinese: *China*, Av W3 Sul, quadra 103 bloco D; *New China*, Av W3 Sul 209, bloco A; *Fon Min*, Av W3 Sul 405; *Fon Pin*, Av W3 Sul 402. **Japanese**: *Nipon*, Av W3 Sul 413 and at 112. Also *El Hadj*, in *Hotel Torre Palace*, Setor Hoteleiro Nte, quadra 4 bloco A, **Arabic**, very good.

Macrobiotic/Vegetarian: *Coisas da Terra*, Av W3 Nte, quadra 703; *Boa Saúde*, Av W3 Nte Quadra 702, Ed Brasília Rádio Center, open Sun-Fri 0800-2000, lunch 1100-1400.

Local: *Bom Demais*, Av W3 Nte, Quadra 706, comfortable, inexpensive, serving fish, beef and rice, etc, live music at weekends (cover charge US$0.50).

Pubs: there are two 'English style' bars: *Gates Pub*, Av W3 Sul 403 and *London Tavern*, Av W3 Sul 409. The *Grenada* bar nr the *Hotel Nacional* has good pavement atmosphere in early evening.

Snack bars: (ie those serving *prato feito* or *comercial*, cheap set meals) can be found all over the city, especially on Av W3 and in the Setor Comercial Sul. Other good bets are the Conjunto Nacional and the Conjunto Venâncio, two shopping/office complexes on either side of the municipal rodoviária, which itself provides the best coffee and *pasteis* in town (bottom departure level). Tropical fruit flavour ice cream can be found in various parlours, eg Av W3 Nte 302. Freshly made fruit juices in all bars.

● **Banks & money changers**

Lloyds Bank, Av W3 Sul, quadra 506, bloco B; **First National Bank of Boston**, Setor Comercial Sul, quadra 6 bloco A; **Citibank**, Edifício Citibank, Setor Comercial Sul; **Banco Francês e Brasileiro**, Av W3 Sul, quadra 506; local banks. Foreign currency (but not always Amex cheques) can be exchanged at these banks and at the branches of: **Banco Regional de Brasília** and **Banco do Brasil**, Setor Bancário Sul, latter also at airport, charge US$20 commission for TCs. **Excel**, Setor Comercial Sul, Subterraneo (currency and Amex cheques), 1045-1630; **American Express**, *Buriti Turismo*, CLS 402 Bloco A, Lojas 27/33, T 225-2686. **Diners Club** office, Av W3 Nte 502. **Mastercard**, for cash against a card, SCRN 502, Bl B, lojas 30 e 31, Asa Nte. Good exchange rates at *Hotel Nacional*. Good exchange rates from hotels with 'exchange-turismo' sign.

● **Cultural centres**

British Council: SCRN 708/709 B1 F No 1/3, T 272-3060, F 272-3455. **Cultura Inglesa**, SEPS 709/908 Conj B, T 243-3065. **American Library**: Casa Thomas Jefferson, Av W4 Sul, quadra 706, T 243-6588. **Aliança Francesa**, Sul Entrequadra 707-907, Bloco A, T 242-7500; **Instituto Cultural Goethe**, Edifício Dom Bosco, Setor Garagem Sul 902, Lote 73, Bloco C, T 224-6773, Mon-Fri, 0800-1200, also 1600-2000, Mon, Wed, Thur.

● **Electric current**

220 volts, 60 cycles.

● **Embassies & consulates**

British: SES, Quadra 801, Conjunto K (with British Commonwealth Chamber of Commerce), or Av das Nações, Caixa Postal 070586, T 225-2710. **USA**: SES, Av das Nações 3, T 321-7272. **Australian**: Caixa Postal 11-1256, SHIS QI-09, Conj 16, Casa 1, T 248-5569 (in residential district, S of the lake). **Canadian**: SES, Av das Nações 16, T 223-7665. **Danish**, Av das Nações 26, CP 07-0484, T 242-8188, open 0900-1200, 1400-1700. **German**: SES, Av das Nações 25, T 243-7466. **Netherlands**: SES, Av das Nações 5, T 321-4769. **Swiss**: SES, Av das Nações 41, T 244-5500; **Austrian**: SES, Av das Nações 40, T 243-3111; **Finnish**: SES, Av das Nações, lote 27, T 242-8555; **Swedish**: Av das Nações 29, Caixa Postal 07-0419, T 243-1444. **Venezuela**: SES, Av das Nações 13, T 223-9325; **Guyana**: SDS, Edifício Venâncio III, 4th floor, sala 410/404, T 224-9229; **Greek**: T 248-1127 248-0920, Shis Q1, 4 Conjunto 1, Casa 18, 704610.

● **Entertainment**

There are three auditoria of the *Teatro Nacional*, the Sala Villa-Lobos (1,300 seats), the Sala Martins Pena (450), and the Sala Padre José

Maurício (120); the building is in the shape of an Aztec pyramid.

The Federal District authorities have two theatres, the *Galpão* and *Galpãozinho*, between Quadra 308 Sul and Av W3 Sul. Concerts are given at the *Escola Parque* (Quadras 507-508 Sul), the *Ginásio Presidente Médici* (Eixo Monumental, nr TV tower), the *Escola de Música* (Av L2 Sul, Quadra 602) and the outdoor *Concha Acústica* (edge of lake in the Setor Hoteleiro Nte). *Planetarium*, on the Eixo next to the TV tower, gives shows Sat and Sun at 1600 and 1700.

Information about entertainment etc is available in two daily papers, *Jornal de Brasília* and *Correio Brasiliense*. Any student card (provided it has a photograph) will get you into the cinema/theatre/concert hall for half price. Ask for 'uma meia' at the box office.

Cinema: there are 15 cinemas in the Plano Piloto; for programme details, T 139, entrance is half price on Wed.

Nightclubs: in Conjunto Venâncio, in Centro Gilberto Salomão and in the main hotels.

● **Post & telecommunications**
Post Office: Poste restante, Central Correio, 70001; SBN-Cj 03, BL-A, Ed Sede da ECT, the central office is in the Setor Hoteleiro Sul, between *Hotels Nacional* and *St Paul*. Another post office is in Ed Brasília Rádio, Av 3 Nte.

● **Shopping**
Shopping complexes include the vast *Conjunto Nacional* on the N side of the rodoviária, the *Conjunto Venâncio* on the S side, the *Centro Venâncio 2000* at the beginning of Av W3 Sul, the *Centro Venâncio 3000* in the Setor Comercial Nte, *Parkshopping* and the *Carrefour* hypermarket just off the exit to Guará, 12 km from centre. For fine jewellery, *H Stern* has branches in the *Nacional* and *Carlton* Hotels and at the Conjunto Nacional and Parkshopping. For handicrafts from all the Brazilian states try *Galeria dos Estados* (which runs underneath the *eixo* from Setor Comercial Sul to Setor Bancário Sul, 10 mins' walk from municipal rodoviária, S along Eixo Rodoviário Sul); for Amerindian handicrafts, *Artíndia* in the rodoviária and at the airport. There is a *feira hippy* at the base of the TV tower every Sat, Sun and holiday: leather goods, wood carvings, jewellery, bronzes. English books (good selection) at *Livraria Sodiler* in Conjunto Nacional and at the airport.

● **Tour companies & travel agents**
Buriti Turismo Ltda, Cls 402, Bloco A, Lojas 27/33, T 225 2686. *Jahjah Turismo*, CRS 504, bloco A, Loja 11, friendly. Many tour operators have their offices in the shopping arcade of the *Hotel Nacional*: *Toscana* has been rec as cheap and good; also *Presmic Turismo*, lojas 33/34,

T 225-5515, full-, half-day and night-time tours (0845, 1400 and 1930 respectively). *Kubitschek Turismo* (Lucas Milhomens – speaks English), T 347-1494, rec for city tour and information. 3-4 hr tours with English commentary can also be booked at the airport by arriving air passengers – a convenient way of getting to your hotel if you have heavy baggage. Some tours have been criticized as too short, others that the guides speak poor English, and for night-time tours, the flood lighting is inadequate on many buildings. Teresa Tasso, T 273-4844, rec; also Otoniel, at airport, T 365-1796, $2^{1}/_{2}$ hrs, US$50.

● **Tourist offices**
At the Centro de Convenções (Detur, helpful, good map of Brasília, open to public 1300-1800 – ask for Eliane, who speaks English, T 321-3318); small stand at rodoferroviária, friendly but not very knowledgeable (open 24 hrs, every day). Tourist office at the Air Terminal is on the international arrival side only, will book hotels, generally helpful; French and English spoken. Detur publishes a book called *Brasília, Coração Brasileiro*, which is full of practical information. **Touring Club do Brasil**, on Eixo, has maps (members only). The information office in the centre of Praça dos Tres Poderes has a colourful map and lots of useful text information. The staff are friendly and have interesting information about Brasília and other places in Goias – only Portuguese spoken. **Maps** 'Comapa', Venâncio 200 business complex, 2nd floor, have expensive maps. 'Didactica', a schoolbook shop in the city rodoviária sell maps of Brazil for US$8.40.

● **Transport**
Car hire: about 9 agencies, inc Budget, Hertz, Locarauto.

Air Frequent daily flights to Rio and São Paulo ($1^{1}/_{2}$ hrs in both cases) and to main cities. Airline offices are in the *Hotel Nacional* building. Bus 102 or 118 to airport, regular, US$0.65, 30 mins. Taxi is US$10 after bargaining, worth it. Left luggage facilities at airport (tokens for lockers, US$0.50). Airport tax US$1.25.

Buses The bus terminal (rodoferroviária) beside the railway station, from which long-distance buses leave, has post office (0800-1700, Sat 0800-1200), telephone and telegram facilities. Bus 131 between rodoviária, the municipal terminal, and rodoferroviária, US$1; taxi rodoferroviária to Setor Hoteleiro Nte, US$7. There are showers (US$0.50). Both bus stations have large luggage lockers. To **Rio**: 17 hrs, 6 *comuns* (US$38) and 3 *leitos* (about US$74) daily. To **São Paulo**: 16 hrs, 7 *comuns* (about US$33) and 2 *leitos* (about US$66) daily (Rápido Federal rec). To **Belo Horizonte**: 12 hrs, 9 *comuns* (US$23) and 2 *leitos* (US$46) daily. To **Belém**: 36 hrs, 4 daily (US$66, Trans Brasília T 233-7589, buses poorly maintained, but no alternative), *leito* (US$132) Tues, Wed and Sat. To **Recife**: 40 hrs. To **Salvador**: 24 hrs, 3 daily (US$45). To **Cuiabá**: 17½ hrs (US$35) daily at 1200 with São Luis. **Mato Grosso:** generally Goiânia seems to be the better place for Mato Grosso destinations. **Barra do Garças:** 0830 and 2000, takes 9 hrs with Araguarina, T 233-7598, US$15.25 return. All major destinations served. Bus tickets for major companies are sold in a subsidiary office in Taguatinga, Centro Ote, C8, Lotes 1 and 2, Loja 1; and at the city rodoviária.

ROUTES From Saída Sul (the southern end of the Eixo) the BR-040/050 goes to Cristalina where it divides; the BR-040 continues to Belo Horizonte and Rio de Janeiro, the BR-050 to Uberlândia and São Paulo (both paved).

Also from Saída Sul, the BR-060 to Anápolis, Goiânia and Cuiabá; from Anápolis the BR-153 (Belém-Brasília) heads N to Belém (paved – for a description of this road, see page 617) and from Goiânia the BR-153 goes S through the interior of the states of São Paulo and Paraná (also paved).

From Saída Norte (the northern end of the Eixo) the BR-020 goes N to **Formosa** (1½ hrs by frequent buses from Brasília, **E** *Hotel Mineiro* and one other, **G**, clean and friendly; cheap restaurants), Barreiras, and after Barreiras on the BR-242 (all paved) to Salvador and Fortaleza. The BR020 is in good condition for 120 km. At Alvorada do Norte (130 km) there are cheap but very basic hotels. **Posse** (295 km) is picturesque (accommodation on Av Padre Trajeiro, inc *Hoki Mundial*, friendly). The road is slow with many potholes until Barreiras.

- **Road distances** in km: Belém, 2,120; Campo Grande, 1,134; Cuiabá, 1,133; Foz do Iguaçu, 1,573; Goiânia, 209; Manaus, 3,490; Recife, 2,220; Rio, 1,148; Salvador, 1,531; São Paulo, 1,015.

DISTRITO FEDERAL

Of the seven *cidades satélites* that contain between them over half the Federal District's population, five are new and two (Brazlândia and Planaltina) are based on pre-existing settlements.

Planaltina

40 km N of the Plano Piloto via Saída Norte (*pop* 50,000), was originally a settlement on the colonial pack route from the mines of Goiás and Cuiabá to the coast.

The old part still contains many colonial buildings and it is a good place for a rural Sun lunch. 5 km outside Planaltina is the Pedra Fundamental, the foundation stone laid by President Epitácio Pessoa in 1922 to mark the site originally chosen for the new capital.

Just before Planaltina, at Km 30 on the BR-020, lies **Águas Emendadas**: from the same point spring two streams that flow in opposite directions to form part of the two great river systems – the Amazon and the Plate. Permission from the biological institute in Brasília is required to visit. At Km 70 is Formosa (see above). Some 20 km N of the town is the Itiquira waterfall (158m high). From the top are spectacular views and the pools at the bottom offer good bathing. It is crowded at weekends. There are four smaller falls in the area. Camping is possible. To get there from the centre of Formosa, follow the signs or ask. The only bus from Formosa to Itiquira leaves at 0730 and returns at 1700.

Cristalina

In the other direction (S), take the BR-040 (Belo Horizonte road) and at Km 104 take a left turn along a dirt road, just after the highway police post, to the Cristalina waterfall (11 km along this road). The town of **Cristalina** (*pop* 24,900) is famous for its semi-precious stones, which can be bought cheaply in local shops. The panning and mining sites amid magnificent rock formations are about 6 km away, an interesting excursion. Small municipal museum R 21 de Abril 156, 0800-1100, 1300-1700, except Tues. **D** *Hotel Goyás*, R da Saudade 41, fan, fridge, OK.

PARQUE NACIONAL DE BRASILIA

Northwest of Brasília, but only 15 mins by car from the centre is the **Parque Nacional de Brasília** (about 28,000 ha), founded in 1961 to conserve the flora and fauna of the Federal Capital. Only a portion of the park is open to the public without a permit. There is a swimming pool fed by clear river water, a snack bar and a series of trails through gallery forest (popular with joggers in early am and at weekends). The rest of the park is rolling grassland, gallery forest and *cerrado* vegetation. Large mammals include tapir, maned wolf and pampas deer; birdwatching is good. Contact Focus Tours, Belo Horizonte (page 431) for birding and nature tours. For information, contact Delegacia Estadual do Ibama, Av W3 Nte, Quadra 513, Edif Imperador, rooms 301-320, or T 233-4055/234-9057.

For information on the State of Goiás, which surrounds the Federal District, see page 613.

State of Rio de Janeiro

THE world-renowned Rio, with its beautiful location, carnival and much more besides (not all of it delightful), plus the hill and beach resorts nearby.

The State of Rio de Janeiro covers 43,305 sq km (the size of Denmark) and in 1991 had a population of 12.6 million, 88% of whom lived in metropolitan areas. The State is Brazil's second-largest industrial producer.

Rio de Janeiro (*Pop* 5,336,180 – 1991 estimate; *CEP* 20000; *DDD* 021) is on the south-western shore of Guanabara Bay, 24 km long and from 3 to 16 km wide. The setting is magnificent. The city sweeps 20 km along a narrow alluvial strip between the mountains and the sea. The combination of a dark blue sea, studded with rocky islands, with the tumbling wooded mountains and expanses of bare grey rock which surround the city is very impressive. Brazilians say: God made the world in six days; the seventh he devoted to Rio (pronounced Heeoo by locals). God's work is now under threat from too many high-rise buildings and failure to maintain or clean the city adequately.

The best known of these rocky masses are the Pão de Açúcar (Sugar Loaf), the highest peak of a low chain of mountains on the fringe of the harbour, and the Corcovado (Hunchback), a jagged peak rising behind the city. There are other peaks, including Tijuca, the tallest point in the foreground, and 50 km away rise the strangely shaped Serra dos Órgãos.

CLIMATE

Rio has one of the healthiest climates in the tropics. Trade winds cool the air. June, July and Aug are the coolest months with temperatures ranging from 22°C (18° in a cold spell) to 32°C on a sunny day at noon. Dec to Mar is hotter, from 32°C to 42°C. Humidity is high. It is important, especially for children, to guard against dehydration in summer by drinking as much liquid as possible. Oct to Mar is the rainy season, and the annual rainfall is about 1,120 mm.

HISTORY

The Portuguese navigator, Gonçalo Coelho, arrived at what is now Rio de Janeiro on 1 January 1502, but it was first settled by the French, who, under the Huguenot Admiral Villegaignon, occupied Lage Island on 10 November 1555, but later transferred to Sergipe Island (now Villegaignon), where they built the fort of Colligny. The fort has been demolished to make way for the Naval College (Escola Naval), and the island itself, since the narrow channel was filled up, has become a part of the mainland. In Jan 1567, Mem de Sá, third governor of Brazil, defeated the French in a sea battle and transferred the Portuguese settlement to the São Januário hill – the Esplanada do Castelo covers the site today. Though constantly attacked by Indians, the new city grew rapidly, and when King Sebastião divided Brazil into two provinces, Rio was chosen capital of the southern captaincies. Salvador became sole capital again in 1576, but Rio again became the southern capital in 1608 and the seat of a bishopric. There was a further French incursion in 1710-11.

Rio de Janeiro was by now becoming the leading city in Brazil. On 27 January 1763, it became the seat of the Viceroy. After independence, in 1834, it was declared capital of the Empire, and remained the capital for 125 years.

PLACES OF INTEREST

Two of the main streets are particularly impressive. The Av Rio Branco, nearly 2 km long and 33m wide, is intersected by the city's main artery, the Av Presidente Vargas, 4½ km long and over 90m wide, which starts at the waterfront, divides to embrace the famous Candelária church, then crosses the Av Rio Branco in a magnificent straight stretch past the Central do Brasil railway station, with its imposing clock tower, until finally it incorporates the palm-lined, canal-divided avenue formerly known as the Av Mangue. Most of the Av Rio Branco's ornate buildings have been replaced by modern blocks; a few remain by Cinelândia and the Biblioteca Nacional. The R do Ouvidor, crossing the Av Rio Branco half way along its length, contains the centre's principal shops. The most stylish shops, however, are to be found in Ipanema, Leblon and in the various large shopping centres in the city (see under **Shopping** below). The Av Beira Mar, with its royal palms, bougainvilleas and handsome buildings, coasting the Botafogo and Flamengo beaches (too polluted for bathing), makes a splendid drive; its scenery is shared by the urban motorway along the beach over reclaimed land (the Aterro), which leads to Botafogo and through two tunnels to Copacabana, described on page 391. Some of the finest modern architecture is to be found along the Av República do Chile, such as the Petrobrás and National Housing Bank buildings, and the new Cathedral.

Churches and religious foundations
Check opening hours before attempting to visit.

The oldest foundation is the convent of the **Ordem Terceiro do Monte do Carmo**, built early in the 17th century, now used as a school on R Primeiro de Março close to Praça 15 de Novembro. Its present church, the Carmo Church in R Primeiro de Março, next to the old cathedral, was built in the 1770s and rebuilt between 1797 and 1826. It has strikingly beautiful portals by Mestre Valentim, the son of a Portuguese nobleman and a slave girl. He also created the main altar of fine

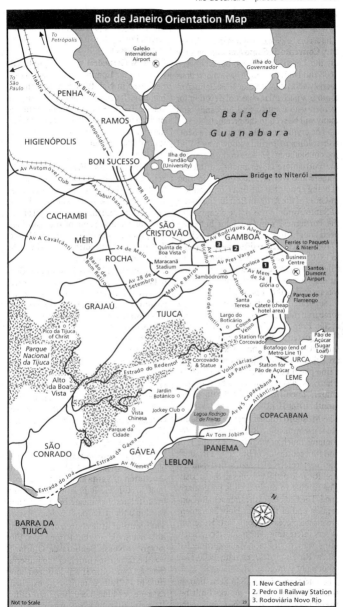

Rio de Janeiro Orientation Map

To Petrópolis

Galeão International Airport

Ilha do Governador

To São Paulo

Itabira

PENHA

Av Brasil

Leopoldina

RAMOS

HIGIENÓPOLIS

BON SUCESSO

Ilha do Fundão (University)

Baía de Guanabara

Bridge to Niterói

Av Automóvel Club

Av Suburbana

BR 101

CACHAMBI

SÃO CRISTOVÃO

Av A Cavalcánti

Av Rodrigues Alves

GAMBOÁ

Ferries to Paquetá & Niterói

MÉIR

24 de Maio

Quinta de Boa Vista

Av F Bicalho

Rio Branco

Business Centre

ROCHA

Barão de Bom Retiro

Maracanã Stadium

Av Pres Vargas

Carioca

Santos Dumont Airport

Av 28 de Setembro

Sambódromo

Av Mem de Sá

GRAJAÚ

Marise Barros

Catumbí

Glória

Parque do Flamengo

Paulo de Frontin

Santa Teresa

Largo do Boticário

TIJUCA

Cosme Velho

Pão de Açúcar (Sugar Loaf)

Pico da Tijuca of Christ

Estação for Corcovado

Botafogo (end of Metro Line 1)

URCA

Parque Nacional da Tijuca

Corcovado & Statue

Voluntárias da Patria

Station for Pão de Açúcar

LEME

Alto da Boa Vista

Jardim Botánico

Av N Capacabana

Atlántica

Vista Chinesa

Jockey Club

Lagoa Rodrigo de Freitas

COPACABANA

Parque da Cidade

SÃO CONRADO

Estrada da Gávea

GÁVEA

Av Tom Jobim

IPANEMA

LEBLON

Estrada do Joá

Av Niemeyer

N

BARRA DA TIJUCA

| 1. New Cathedral |
| 2. Pedro II Railway Station |
| 3. Rodoviária Novo Rio |

Not to Scale

moulded silver, the throne and its chair, and much else.

The second oldest convent is the 17th century **Convento de Santo Antônio**, on a hill off the Largo da Carioca, built between 1608 and 1615. Its church has a marvellous sacristy adorned with blue tiles. Santo Antônio is a particular object of devotion for women who want to find husbands, and many will be seen in the precincts.

The crypt contains the tomb of a Scottish soldier of fortune known as 'Wild Jock of Skelater'. He was in the service of the Portuguese Government during the Napoleonic War, and had the distinction of being appointed the first Commander-in-Chief of the Army in Brazil. The statue of Santo Antônio was made a captain in the Portuguese army after his help had been sought to drive out the French in 1710, and his salary paid to the monastery. In 1810 the statue became a major, in 1814 a lieutenant-colonel, and was granted the Grand Cross of the Order of Christ. He was retired without pay in 1914.

Separated from this church only by some iron railings is the charming church of **São Francisco da Penitência**, built in 1773. Currently closed for renovation but the carving and gilding of walls and altar are superb. In the ceiling over the nave is a fine panel painted by José de Oliveira. There is a museum attached to the church, open first and third Sun of the month, 0700-1000.

The **Mosteiro** (monastery) **de São Bento** (1641); entrance at R Dom Gerardo 68, contains much of what is best in the 17th and 18th century art of Brazil. 'O Salvador', the masterpiece of Brazil's first painter, Frei Ricardo do Pilar, hangs in the sacristy. The carving in the church is particularly good. The Chapels of the Immaculate Conception and of the Most Holy Sacrament are masterpieces of colonial art. The organ is very interesting. The monastery is a few mins' walk from Praça Mauá, turning left off Av Rio Branco. Open daily 0800-1730 (shorts not allowed).

The **Old Cathedral** of São Sebastião, in the R Primeiro de Março, was built between 1749 and 1770. In the crypt are the alleged remains of Pedro Alvares Cabral, the Portuguese explorer (though Santarém, Portugal, also claims to be his last resting-place).

The **New Cathedral**, on Av República do Chile not far from the Largo da Carioca, dedicated in Nov 1976, is a cone-shaped building. Its internal height is 68m, diameter 104m, external height 83m; capacity 5,000 seated, 20,000 standing. The most striking feature is four enormous stained-glass windows (60m high). It is still incomplete.

The Church of **São Francisco de Paula**, at the upper end of the R do Ouvidor, was built in 1759. It contains some of Mestre Valentim's work – the carvings in the main chapel and the lovely Chapel of Our Lady of Victory. Some of the paintings, and probably the ceiling, are by Manuel da Cunha. The beautiful fountain at the back plays only at night.

The Church of **Nossa Senhora da Candelária** (1775-1810), on Praça Pio Dez, at the city end of Av Presidente Vargas, has beautiful ceiling decorations and romantic paintings. It is on the site of a chapel founded in 1610 by Antônio da Palma after he had survived a shipwreck, an event depicted by paintings inside the present dome.

In the R de Santa Luzia, overwhelmed by tall office buildings, is the attractive little church of **Santa Luzia**. When built in 1752 it had only one tower; the other was added late in the 19th century. Feast day: 13 Dec, when devotees bathe their eyes with holy water, considered miraculous.

In the R Primeiro de Março, at the corner of Ouvidor (near the Old Cathedral), is the church of **Santa Cruz dos Militares**, built 1780-1811. It is large, stately and beautiful and has inside been well renovated in a 'light' baroque style.

The beautiful little church on the Glória hill, overlooking the Parque do Flamengo, is **Nossa Senhora da Glória**. It was the favourite church of the imperial family; Dom Pedro II was baptized here. Built in 1791, it contains some excellent examples of blue-faced Brazilian tiling. Its main altar, of wood, was carved by

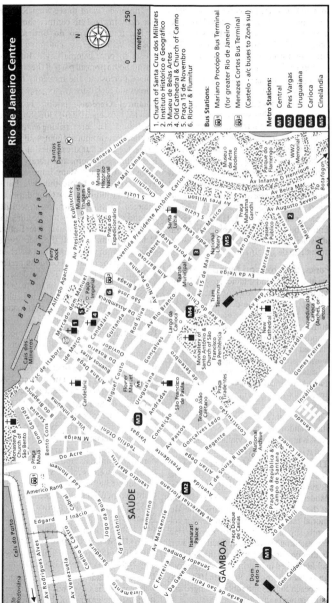

Rio de Janeiro Centre

N

0   250

metres

1. Church of Santa Cruz dos Militares
2. Instituto Histórico e Geográfico
3. Museu de Belas Artes
4. Old Cathedral & Church of Carmo
5. Praça 15 de Novembro
6. Riotur & Flumitur

Bus Stations:

BB1 Mariano Procópio Bus Terminal
(for greater Rio de Janeiro)

BB2 Menezes Cortes Bus Terminal
(Castelo – a/c buses to Zona sul)

Metro Stations:

M1 Central
M2 Pres Vargas
M3 Uruguaiana
M4 Carioca
M5 Cinelândia

Mestre Valentim. The church, open 0900-1200 (only Sat-Sun) and 1300-1700 weekdays, is reached by bus 119 from the centre and 571 from Copacabana. The adjacent museum of religious art is open on application to the priest.

The church of **Nossa Senhora da Penha**, in the N suburb of Penha (early 20th century), is on a bare rock in which 365 steps are cut. This staircase is ascended by pilgrims on their knees during the festival month of Oct; there is a funicular for those unable to do this. Bus 497 from Copacabana, 340 and 346 from centre.

When the Morro do Castelo was levelled to build the Esplanada do Castelo, the old church of **São Sebastião** had to be demolished. Its successor, the Capuchin church of São Sebastião in the R Haddock Lobo, Tijuca, built in 1936, contains the tomb of Estácio de Sá, founder and first Governor of Rio de Janeiro.

Parks, Squares and Monuments

On the Glória and Flamengo waterfront, with a view of the Pão de Açúcar and Corcovado, is the **Parque do Flamengo**, designed by Burle Marx, opened in 1965 during the 400th anniversary of the city's founding, and landscaped on 100 ha reclaimed from the Bay. Behind the War Memorial (see below) is the public yacht marina. In the park are many sports fields and a botanical garden; for children, there are a sailboat basin, a marionette theatre, a miniature village and a staffed nursery. There are night amusements, such as bandstands and areas for dancing. Security in the park is in the hands of vigilante policemen and it is a popular recreation area.

The National War Memorial to Brazil's dead in WW2 (Monumento aos Mortos na Segunda Guerra) and the Museu de Arte Moderna (see page 389) are at the city end of the park, opposite Praça Paris. The Memorial takes the form of two slender columns supporting a slightly curved slab, representing two palms uplifted to heaven. In the crypt are the remains of the Brazilian soldiers killed in Italy in 1944-45. The crypt and museum are open Tues-Sun 1000-1700, but beach clothes and rubber-thonged sandals are not permitted.

Those who want to see what Rio was like early in the 19th century should go by bus to the **Largo do Boticário**, R Cosme Velho 822, a charming small square in pure colonial style. Buses to Cosme Velho from all parts of the city. The square is close to the terminus for the Corcovado rack railway (see page 393).

Botanical Gardens (Jardim Botânico) founded 1808, open 0800-1730 (US$1); well worth a visit. The most striking features are the transverse avenues of 30m royal palms. There are over 7,000 varieties of plants, herbarium, aquarium, and library (some labels are unclear). Many improvements were carried out before the 1992 Earth Summit, including a new Orquidário, an enlarged bookshop, a *lanchonete*, replanting and cleaning up. Visitors needing information in English should ask for Beatriz Heloisa Guimarães, of the Society of Friends of the Garden. Bird-watchers should visit the Botanical Gardens, preferably early in the morning. The Gardens are 8 km from the centre, 140 ha in area; take any bus from the centre, eg 104, to Leblon, Gávea or São Conrado marked 'via Jóquei'. From Copacabana take bus 592.

Parque Laje, near the Jardim Botânico at R Jardim Botânico 414, almost jungle-like, has small grottoes, an old tower and lakes, pleasant. (The Instituto Nacional de Belas Artes is housed in the mansion.) Open daily, 0730-1730, admittance free.

In **Quinta da Boa Vista**, formerly the Emperor's private park, the Palace now houses the Museu Nacional (see page 389).

Jardim Zoológico in the Quinta da Boa Vista, contains Brazilian and imported wild animals, and a fine collection of birds (as well as many 'visitors' – also good for bird-watchers). Open 0800-1800 daily, except Mon (best in the morning), US$2. The gateway is a replica of Robert Adam's famous gateway to Syon House, near London. Near the Zoological Gardens is the Museu de Fauna (see below). Take bus 474 or 472 from Copacabana or Flamengo; bus 262 from Praça Mauá.

Parque da Cidade, a pleasant park a short walk beyond the Gávea bus terminus, was previously the grounds of the home of the

Guinle family, by whom it was presented to the City. Admission free; open Tues-Fri 0730-1730, Sat, Sun and holidays 1100-1700. The proximity of the Rocinha favela means that the park is not very safe. It is advisable to carry a copy of your passport here because of frequent police checks.

Praça da República and **Campo de Santana** is an extensive and picturesque public garden close to the Central Railway station. At Praça da República 197 lived Marshal Deodoro da Fonseca, who proclaimed Brazil a republic in 1889 (plaque). The Parque Júlio Furtado in the middle of the square is populated by agoutis (or gophers), best seen at dusk; there is also a little artificial grotto, with swans.

Passeio Público (turn right at S end of Av Rio Branco) is a garden planted by the artist Mestre Valentim, whose bust is near the old former gateway. Coin and stamp market on Sun, am.

Praça Quinze de Novembro contains the original royal palace (see page 390). Every Sat 0900-1900, flea market; nearby on the waterfront is a Sun antiques market, 1000-1800.

Praça Tiradentes, old and shady, has a statue to D Pedro I. Shops in nearby streets specialize in selling goods for *umbanda* and *macumba* – African-based religion and magic respectively.

Praça Mahatma Gandhi, at the end of Av Rio Branco, is flanked on one side by the cinema and amusement centre of the city, known as Cinelândia. The fountain (1789) by Mestre Valentim in the ornamental garden was moved here from Praça Quinze de Novembro in 1979.

Parque do Catete is a charming small park between the Palácio do Catete (Museu da República) and Praia do Flamengo; it has many birds and monkeys.

Praça Paris, built on reclaimed ground near the Largo da Glória, is much admired for the beauty of its formal gardens and illuminated fountains.

Largo da Carioca, remarkable ensemble of old and new plus the muddle of the street vendors who have occupied the square beween R da Carioca and the Metro.

Museums and other Public Buildings

All museums and the Jardim Botânico are closed over Carnival.

The **Museu Nacional** in the Quinta da Boa Vista has important collections which are poorly displayed. The park surrounding it is dangerous. The building was the principal palace of the Emperors of Brazil, but only the unfurnished Throne Room and ambassadorial reception room on the 2nd floor reflect past glories. In the entrance hall is the famous Bêndego meteorite, found in the State of Bahia in 1888; its original weight, before some of it was chipped, was 5,360 kg. Besides several foreign collections of note, the Museum contains collections of Brazilian Indian weapons, dresses, utensils, etc, of minerals and of historical documents. There are also collections of birds, beasts, fishes, and butterflies. Open 1000-1630, closed Mon; entrance US$3. Buses: 472, 474, 475 from centre, Flamengo and Copacabana, 583 from Largo do Machado. Nearest Metrô São Cristóvão, but thieves operate by park entrance and in the park, taxi to the main door is safer. Some of the collections are open to qualified research students only.

Museu de Fauna also at Quinta da Boa Vista, contains a most interesting collection of Brazilian fauna. Open Tues-Sun 1200-1700.

The **Biblioteca Nacional** at Av Rio Branco 219, was founded in 1810. Its first collection came from the Ajuda Palace in Lisbon, and today it houses over 2 million volumes and many rare manuscripts. Open Mon-Fri 0900-2000, Sat 0900-1500.

Museu Nacional de Belas Artes, Av Rio Branco 199, has about 800 original paintings and sculptures and some thousand direct reproductions. Exhibitions of works by contemporary Brazilian artists from 17th to 20th century. There are several paintings by Cândido Portinari (1903-61), Alberto da Veiga Guignard and Frans Janszoon Post (Dutch 1612-80) who painted Brazilian landscapes in classical Dutch style. Open Tues-Fri 1000-1800; Sat, Sun and holidays 1400-1800; US$1.

Those interested in contemporary art will also visit the former Ministry of Education (Le Corbusier designs modified by Oscar Niemeyer), to see the great murals of Cândido Portinari.

Opposite the Art Museum is the **Teatro Municipal**. Opera and orchestral performances are given here; the small museum that used to be below the theatre is now at R São João Batista 103/105, Botafogo, open 1300-1700 Mon-Fri.

The **Paço Imperial** (former Royal Palace on Praça 15 de Novembro), a beautiful colonial building begun in 1743, has been restored. It has several galleries, one theatre, one cinema, library, the *Bistro* and the *Atrium* restaurants, rec.

The **Museu de Arte Moderna** is a spectacular building at Av Infante D Henrique 85, near the National War Memorial (see page 388). It suffered a disastrous fire in 1978; the collection is now being rebuilt, and several countries have donated works of art. There is also a non-commercial cinema. The collection of contemporary Brazilian art includes very expressive drawings by Cândido Portinari from the 1940s and 50s and drawings and etchings of everyday work scenes by Gregório Gruber, made in the 1970s. Entrance US$1, Tues-Sun 1200-1800.

The **Museu Histórico Nacional** on Praça Rui Barbosa (formerly Praça Marechal Âncora) contains a collection of historical treasures, colonial sculpture and furniture, maps, paintings, arms and armour, silver, and porcelain. The building was once the old War Arsenal of the Empire, part of which was built in 1762. Open Tues to Sun, 1000-1600; Sat, Sun and holidays 1430-1730; admission US$1.20.

Museu da Imagem e do Som, also on Praça Rui Barbosa, has many photographs of Brazil and modern Brazilian paintings; also collections and recordings of Brazilian classical and popular music and a non-commercial cinema Fri-Sun. Open Mon-Fri, 1300-1800.

Museu Naval e Oceanográfico, R D Manoel 15, daily 1200-1630, has large collection of paintings and prints, as well as the display of weapons and figureheads.

Museu do Índio, R das Palmeiras 55, Botafogo, T 286 8799, being partly renovated so there is only a small exhibition. 12,000 objects from many Brazilian Indian groups. There is also a small, well-displayed handicraft shop (shop closes for lunch 1200-1400). Open Mon-Fri 1000-1730. From Botafogo Metrô, it's a 10-min walk; from Catete, bus 571 (Glória-Leblon) which passes R Bento Lisboa and R São Clemente.

The **Chácara do Céu**, or Fundação Raymundo Ottoni de Castro Maia, R Murtinho Nobre 93, has a wide range of art objects and particularly modern painters, including Brazilian. Take Santa Teresa tram to R Dias de Barros, then follow signposts. Open Wed-Sun, Sun 1200-1700, US$1. Castro Maia's former residence, **Museu Açude**, Estrada do Açude 764, Alto da Boa Vista, Tijuca, is also a museum, currently under restoration, T 238-0368.

Museu do Instituto Histórico e Geográfico, Av Augusto Severo 8 (10th floor), just off Av Beira Mar, has an interesting collection of Brazilian products and the artefacts of its peoples. Open Mon-Fri 1200-1700.

The **Museu de Astronomia/National Observatory** (founded 1827) is on São Januário hill, R Gen Bruce 586, São Cristóvão. Hours: Tues-Fri 0900-1700, guided tours 1000-1200; 1400-1600. Visitors advised to call 580-7010 after 1700 to arrange a night viewing.

The **Casa de Rui Barbosa**, R São Clemente 134, Botafogo, former home of the Brazilian jurist and statesman, containing his library and other possessions, is open Tues-Fri 1000-1630, Sat, Sun and holidays 1400-1700. The large garden is also open to the public. Buses 106, 176, 178 from centre; 571 from Flamengo; 591 from Copacabana.

Palácio do Itamarati (Historical and diplomatic Museum), Av Marechal Floriano 196, Centro, Mon, Wed, Fri 1400-1700, with guided tours on the hour, rec.

Museu da República, R do Catete 153, Tues-Fri, 1200-1700, Sat-Sun and holidays 1400-1800 US$1, highly rec. The former palace of a coffee baron, later converted into the presidential seat, until the move to Brasilia, this museum now exhibits historical paintings; the first floor is devoted to the history of the Brazilian republic. You can also see the room where Getúlio Vargas shot himself. Behind the museum is the Parque do Catete.

Museu do Folclore Edison Carneiro, R do Catete 179, not to be missed. Very interesting objects, well selected and arranged. There is a collection of small ceramic figures representing everyday life in Brazil, some very funny, some scenes animated by electric motors. There are fine Candomblé and Umbanda costumes, religious objects, ex-votos. A brochure containing a general description of the objects in English is available at reception. Photography is allowed, but without flash. Tues-Fri 1100-1800 free. Bus 571 from Copacabana, and close to Catete Metrô station.

Museu Carmen Miranda, Tues-Fri 1300-1600, Flamengo park area in front of Rui Barbosa 560 (small display of the famous singer's gowns etc); US$0.30, Sun free, but not always open Sun. **Museu Villa-Lobos**, R Sorocaba 200, Botafogo, Mon-Fri 0930-1730, with instruments, scores, books, recordings. **Capão do Bispo Estate**, Av Suburbana 4616, Del Castilho, Mon-Fri 1400-1700, with archaeological exhibition.

Planetarium, Padre Leonel Franco 240, Gávea, Wed 1830, Sat and Sun at 1530 and 1830; inaugurated in 1970, sculpture of Earth and Moon by Mario Agostinelli. Free *choro* concert Fri at 2100. Buses 176 and 178 from centre and Flamengo; 591 and 592 from Copacabana.

Museu Aeroespacial, Av Marechal Fontenelle 2000, Campo dos Afonsos, Tues-Fri 0900-1600, Sat, Sun and holidays 0930-1600, early Brazilian civil and military aircraft.

Museu Antônio Lago, R Andradas 96, centre, Mon-Fri 1400-1900. Reproduction of historical apothecary's shop.

Amsterdam Sauer Museum, Garcia d'Avila e Visconde de Pirajá 105, reproduction of a Brazilian mine and exhibition of gemstones. Mon-Fri 1000-1700, Sat 0930-1300.

Museu Internacional de Arte Naif do Brasil, R Cosme Velho, 561, Mon-Fri 1000-1900, Sat-Sun 1200-1800, US$5, rec.

Museu do Telefone, R 2 de Decembro, 63, Tues-Sun 1000-1700. The museum exhibits old telephones; on the top floor there is a semi-mechanical telephone exchange from the 1940s plus Getúlio Vargas' golden telephone and a replica of the telephone of Dom Pedro II, rec.

MARACANÃ STADIUM

This is one of the largest sports centres in the world. The football ground has seating capacity for 200,000 spectators. Matches are worth going to if only for the spectators' samba bands; for the best atmosphere try to catch any local derbys between Fluminense, Botafogo, Vasco da Gama or Flamengo. **NB** Agencies charge much more for tickets than at the gate: US$15. It is cheaper to buy tickets from club sites on day before the match (US$10).

● **Transport** Buses 455 from Copacabana; 433 from Flamengo; from Leblon, 464 via Ipanema and Copacabana; also Metrô from Botafogo and centre.

Guided tour of stadium (in Portuguese), US$2.50, and museum, US$0.50, highly rec to football fans. Maracanã is now used only for major games; Rio teams play most matches at their home grounds (still a memorable experience). Hotels can arrange visits to football matches: a good idea on Sun when the metro is closed and buses very full.

THE SUBURBS OF RIO DE JANEIRO

COPACABANA

Built on a narrow strip of land (only a little over 4 sq km) between mountain and sea, **Copacabana** has one of the highest population densities in the world: 62,000 per sq km, or 250,000 in all. Its celebrated curved beach backed by skyscraper apartments is a must for visitors. Tourist police patrol Copacabana beach until 1700.

Copacabana began to develop when the Old Tunnel was built in 1891 and an

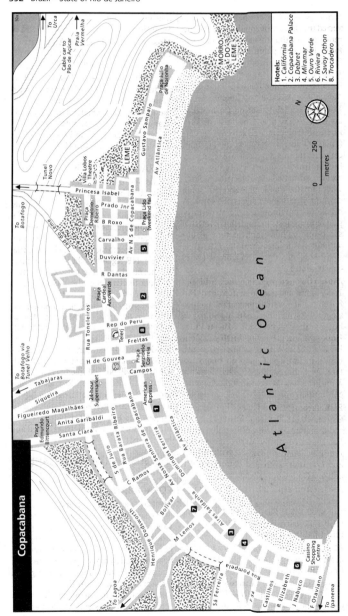

Copacabana

Hotels:
1. California
2. Copacabana Palace
3. Debret
4. Miramar
5. Ouro Verde
6. Riviera
7. Savoy Othon
8. Trocadero

To Urca

Cable car to Pão de Açúcar

Praia Vermelha

Túnel Novo

Villa Lobos Theatre

MORRO DOS LEME

Praça Júlio de Noronha

Gustavo Sampaio

LEME

Av Atlântica

Princesa Isabel

Praça Demétrio Ribeiro

Prado Jnr

B Roxo

Carvalho

Duvivier

R Dantas

Praça Lido (Weekend Fair)

To Botafogo

To Lagoa

Praça Cardeal Arcoverde

Rua Toneleiros

Rep do Peru

Telerj

H de Gouvêa

Freitas

Praça Serzedelo Correia

Campos

Av N S de Copacabana

To Botafogo via Túnel Velho

Tabajaras

Siqueira

Figueiredo Magalhães

Praça Edmundo Bittencourt

Anita Garibaldi

Santa Clara

24-hour Supermarket

American Express

S de Julho

Rua Barata Ribeiro

C Ramos

Av Atlântica

Atlantic Ocean

Henrique Dodsworth

Av Nossa Senhora de Copacabana

Domingos Ferreira

Bolívar

Aires Saldanha

M Lemos

Rua Pompeia

Cassino Shopping Centre

To Ipanema

Sá Ferreira

F Sá

Castilhos

R Elizabeth

J Nabuco

F Otaviano

N

0   250
metres

electric tram service reached it. Weekend villas and bungalows sprang up; all have now gone. In the 1930s the Copacabana Palace Hotel was the only tall building; it is now one of the lowest on the beach. The opening of the New Tunnel in the 1940s led to an explosion of population which shows no sign of having spent its force. Unspoilt Art Deco blocks towards the Leme (city) end of Copacabana are now under preservation order.

There is almost everything in this 'city within a city'. The shops, mostly in Av Copacabana and the R Barata Ribeiro, are excellent; this is the area in which to watch, or participate in, the city's glamorous night life. A fort at the far end of the beach commands the entrance to Rio Bay and prevents a seashore connection with the Ipanema and Leblon beaches. Parts of the military area are now being handed over to civilian use, the first being the Parque Garota de Ipanema at Arpoador, the fashionable Copacabana end of the Ipanema beach.

● **Transport** Buses to and from the city centre are plentiful and cheap, about US$0.40. If you are going to the centre from Copacabana, look for 'Castelo', 'Praça 15', 'E Ferro' or 'Praça Mauá' on the sign by the front door. 'Aterro' means the expressway between Botafogo and downtown Rio (not open Sun). From the centre to Copacabana is easier as all buses in that direction are clearly marked. Aterro bus does the journey in 15 mins.

IPANEMA AND LEBLON

Beyond Copacabana are the beautiful seaside suburbs of **Ipanema** (a good place from which to watch the sunset) and **Leblon**. They are a little less built-up than Copacabana, and their beaches tend to be cleaner. There is now night-time illumination on these beaches and the section in front of the *Caesar Park* hotel is patrolled by the hotel's security staff: this, along with 24-hr video surveillance during the summer season, makes it probably the safest patch of sand in Rio. Backing Ipanema and Leblon is the middle-class residential area of Lagoa Rodrigo de Freitas, by a salt-water lagoon on which Rio's rowing and small-boat sailing clubs are

active; too polluted for bathing. Beyond Leblon the coast is rocky; the Av Niemeyer skirts the cliffs on the journey past Vidigal, a small beach where the *Sheraton* is situated, to the outer seaside suburbs of São Conrado (beach polluted) and Barra da Tijuca (see below). The flat topped Gávea rock can be climbed or scrambled up for magnificent views, but beware snakes.

● **Transport** Buses from Botafogo Metrô terminal to Ipanema: some take integrated Metrô-Bus tickets; look for the blue signs on the windscreen. Many buses from Copacabana to Ipanema (buses 154 and 158 from Flamengo) and Leblon (buses 158, 434 and 488 from Flamengo, continuing to Barra da Tijuca).

SANTA TERESA

A hilly inner suburb SW of the centre, well known as the coolest part of Rio. It boasts many colonial and 19th-century buildings, set in narrow, curving, tree-lined streets. See particularly the Convent (only the outside; the Carmelite nuns do not admit visitors), the Chácara do Céu Museum (see page 390), the Hotel Santa Teresa (the oldest house in the area), Vista Alegre, the R Aprazível, and Largo de Guimarães. Santa Teresa is best visited on the traditional open-sided tram, described on page 408. See also **Security**, below.

CORCOVADO

Corcovado (710m) is the hunch-backed peak surmounted by a 40m high statue of Christ the Redeemer completed in 1931. There is a superb view from the top (sometimes obscured by mist), to which there are a cog railway and a road; both car and train put down their passengers behind the statue – there is a climb of 220 steps to the top, near which there is a café. To see the city by day and night ascend at 1500 or 1600 and descend on the last train, approx 1815. Mass is held on Sun in a small chapel in the statue pedestal. The floodlighting was designed in 1931 by Marconi.

● **Transport** Take a Cosme Velho bus (422, 498 or 497 from Centro or Flamengo) to the cog railway station at R Cosme Velho 513; from Copacabana take No 583, 584 back. Service every 20-30 mins according to demand between 0800 and 1830, journey time 10 mins (cost: US$15 return; single tickets available).

Also, a 206 bus does the very attractive run from Praça Tiradentes (or a 407 from Largo do Machado) to Silvestre (the railway has no stop here now). An active walk of 1 hr will bring one to the top, and the road is shady. (Best done in company.) Coach trips tend to be rather brief, but taxis do wait in front of the station offering tours for US$30 which include Corcovado and Mirante Dona Marta for groups of 3 or more.

PÃO DE AÇÚCAR

The Sugar Loaf (396m) is a massive granite cone at the entrance to Guanabara Bay. The bird's eye view of the city and beaches is very beautiful. There is a restaurant (excellent location, mixed reports on food, closes 1900) and a playground for children on the Morro da Urca, half way up, where there are also shows at night (weekends and Mon, 2200). You can get refreshments at the top.

There are 35 rock routes up the mountain, with various degrees of difficulty (best months for climbing: April to Aug; see **Sports**, below, for climbing clubs).

It is possible to walk or jog on the S side in the military area at the foot.

● **Transport Buses** Bus 107 (from the centre or Flamengo) and 511 or 500 'jardinière', or those marked 'Urca' (from Copacabana) take you to the cable-car station, Av Pasteur 520, at the foot. **Cable car**: Praia Vermelha to Urca: first car goes up at 0800, then every 30 mins (or when full), until the last comes down at 2200. From Urca to Sugar Loaf the first connecting cable car goes up at 0815 then every 30 mins (or when full), until the last leaves the summit at 2200; the return trip costs US$10 (US$5 to Morro da Urca, half-way up). The old cableway has been completely rebuilt. Termini are ample and efficient and the present Italian cable cars carry 75 passengers. Even on the most crowded days there is little queuing.

TIJUCA NATIONAL PARK

The Pico da Tijuca (1,012m) gives a good idea of the tropical vegetation of the interior and a fine view of the bay and its shipping. A 2-3 hr walk leads to the summit: on entering the park at Alto da Boa Vista (open 0600-2100), follow the signposts (maps are displayed) to Bom Retiro, a good picnic place (1½ hrs' walk), passing by the Cascatinha Taunay, Mayrink Chapel (built 1860) and the restaurant *A Floresta*. At Bom Retiro the road ends and there is another hour's walk up a fair footpath to the summit (take the path from the right of the Bom Retiro drinking fountain; not the more obvious steps from the left). The last part consists of steps carved out of the solid rock; look after children at the summit as there are several sheer drops, invisible because of bushes. The route is shady for almost its entire length. The panels painted in the Mayrink Chapel by Cândido Portinari have been replaced by copies and the originals will probably be installed in the Museu de Arte Moderna. Maps of the Park are available.

Other places of interest not passed on the walk to the peak are the Paul and Virginia Grotto, the Vista do Almte and the Mesa do Imperador (viewpoints). Allow at least 5 to 6 hrs for the excursion.

● **Buses** Take a 221 from Praça 15 de Novembro, 233 or 234 bus from the rodoviária or 454 from Copacabana or from Praça Sáenz Pena, Tijuca (reached by Metrô) to Alto da Boa Vista, for the park entrance.

● **Jeep tours** are run by *Rio Jeep Tour*, Atlantic and Forest, daily; contact through travel agencies.

Viewpoints not already mentioned under Tijuca, Corcovado and Pão de Açúcar include the Vista Chinesa (420m), where from a Chinese-style pavilion one can see the inland lake (the Lagoa), Ipanema and Leblon; and the Mirante de Dona Marta (340m) off the Corcovado road, with the same direction of view as the Corcovado, but as it is lower the details can be seen more clearly. There is no public transport to these places.

BARRA DA TIJUCA

This rapidly developing residential area is also one of the principal recreation areas of Rio, with its 20-km sandy beach and good waves for surfing. There are innumerable bars and restaurants, clustered at both ends, campsites (see page 401), motels and hotels: budget accommodation tends to be self-catering. The facilities include Riocenter, a 600,000 sq m convention complex and the huge Barra Shopping and Carrefour shopping centres. The stylish Fashion Mall is opposite the golf club. Hang-gliders jump from the hilltops at weekends.

South of Barra are beaches at Recreio dos Bandeirantes (small, ocean very rough), Prainha (a little cove, good for surfing), and Grumari (very attractive, rustic beach bar), the last two inaccessible by public transport, therefore less crowded and safer. They attract heavy traffic at weekends and this stunning coastal road (the start of the Costa Verde highway) is becoming obliterated by executive housing developments – visit soon, if you can.

The **Autódromo** (motor racing track) is beyond Barra in the Jacarepaguá district. The Brazilian Grand Prix is held here or at Interlagos, São Paulo, alternately in January.

Favela Tour It is possible to visit Vila Canoas, a favela close to São Conrado. This is very interesting and leads to a greater appreciation of Rio and its people. It is best to visit on an organized tour.

FAVELA TOUR

A tour to the Favelas is an illuminating experience if you are looking for a new perspective of Rio and its people. The Tour integrates visitors with local people revealing a whole new vision of the Favelas, changing their reputation of violence and poverty forever.

You will go to the Favela of Vila Canoas, near to the rich São Conrado district, and Rocinha, the largest Favela in Brazil. There you will visit the school, handicraft centre (also supported by the Tour) and other community works. You can bring your camera, and don't be shy; local people will greet you in a friendly manner and enjoy your visit.

Despite their bad reputation, Favelas are safer than most Cariocas believe. However, no matter how brave and adventurous you are, go to a Favela with an organized Tour; Marcelo Armstrong is the pioneer of Favela Tours, you can call him (322-2727, 989-0074 mobile), or contact your Travel Agent.

If you really want to understand this city, don't leave Rio without visiting a Favela.

Try Marcelo Armstrong (T 322 2727 or mobile 989 0074) for a safe, different and interesting experience.

● **Transport** Buses from the Tijuca Forest continue on the 233 or 234 bus (from Praça Sáenz Pena, very good views of São Conrado and Barra), or from the city bus station at R São José, from Santos Dumont airport, bus 591 or 592 from Leme, and from Copacabana via Leblon beach bus 523. Taxi to Zona Sul, US$15 (US$22.50 after midnight). From Botafogo, Glória or Flamengo take bus 179. A comfortable bus, Pegasus, goes along the coast from the Castelo bus terminal to Barra da Tijuca and continues to Campo Grande or Santa Cruz, or take free 'Barra Shopping' bus. Bus 700 from Praça São Conrado (terminal of bus 553 from Copacabana) goes the full length of the beach to Recreio dos Bandeirantes.

PAQUETÁ ISLAND

The island, in Guanabara Bay, is noted for its gigantic pebble shaped rocks, butterflies and orchids. The house of José Bonifácio, the opponent of slavery, may be seen. Horse-drawn carriages may be hired (many have harnesses which cut into the horse's flesh), but they do not stop at the interesting Parque Darke de Mattos. Tour by 'trenzinho', a tractor pulling trailers, US$1.25, or on foot, quieter and free. Bicycles also can be hired. Very crowded at weekends and public holidays, but usually very quiet during the week. Reasonable food and drink prices.

● **Transport** Paquetá Island can be visited by more or less 2-hourly ferry services from Praça 15 de Novembro, none between 1015 and 1300, last back at 1900 (fare US$1.25 by boat, 1 hr, US$6.25 by hydrofoil, 20 mins' journey, which more than doubles its price Sats, Suns and holidays). Bus to Praça 15 de Novembro: 119 from Botafogo; 154, 134, 455, 474 from Copacabana or 415 passing from Leblon via Ipanema.

Other boat trips: Aquatur (T 230-9273), Brazilian Marina Turismo, Camargo (T 275-0643), Passamar, Siqueira Campos 7 (T 236-4136), Greyline (T 274-7146), Soletur (Bay trips Sat and Sun only) and American Sightseeing, Av NS de Copacabana 605, Sala 1204 (T 236-3551). The last three offer a day cruise, inc lunch, to Jaguanum Island (see page 415, under Itacuruçá) and a sundown cruise around Guanabara Bay, also deep-sea fishing expeditions and private charters.

CARNIVAL

Carnival in Rio is spectacular. On the Fri before Shrove Tues, the mayor of Rio symbolically hands the keys of the city to King Momo, a sequinned Lord of Misrule, signifying the start of a five-day party. Imagination runs riot, social barriers are broken, the main avenues are colourfully lit, full of people, and children wear fancy dress. Special bandstands throughout the city are manned for public street-dancing (see local press for where and when) and organized carnival groups, the *blocos carnavalescos*, are everywhere, dancing, drumming and singing.

There are numerous samba schools in Rio, divided into 2 leagues. A school's position in the league determines whether it parades in the Sambódromo (the top schools), or on Av Rio Branco (less spectacular, but free).

Every school presents 3,000-5,000 participants, divided into 40 *alas* (wings) and as many as 30 floats. Each school chooses a theme, then composes a samba, and designs costumes and floats to fit it. The theme must be national (often an element of Brazilian history or a current political topic). The samba song (*enredo*) is a poetic, rhythmic and catchy expression of the theme, which is then developed through the *alas'* floats and costumes. A percussion wing, the *bateria*, maintains a reverberating beat that must keep the entire school, and the audience, dancing frenetically throughout their pageant. Schools are given between 65 and 80 mins to parade, losing points for failure to keep within the limits. Judges award points to each school for components of their procession, such as costume, music and design, and make deductions for lack of energy, enthusiasm or discipline. The best schools are promoted to a higher division, those with fewest points being relegated, as in a football league. Competition is intense. For the winners there is a monetary prize, funded by the entrance fees.

The Carnival parade is the culmination of months of intense activity by community groups, mostly in the city's poorest districts. To understand the traditions of the schools, the meanings of the different parts of the parade, and carnival as a whole, visit the **Museu do Carnaval** in the Sambódromo; although small, it has lots of photographs and the English-speaking staff are very informative (entrance in R Frei Caneca; T 293-9996; Tues-Sun 1000-1700; free). The **Sambódromo**, a permanent site at R Marquês de Sapucaí, Cidade Nova, not far from the centre, is 600m long, with seats for 60,000 people. Designed by Oscar Niemeyer, it handles sporting events, conferences and concerts during the rest of the year; it also houses a public education centre which presently teaches 5,000 children.

Participation Most Samba schools will accept a number of foreigners: you will be charged upwards of US$150 for your costume; your money helps to fund poorer members of the school. You should be in Rio for at least 2 weeks before Carnival (Portuguese speakers can telephone the schools direct). It is essential to attend fittings and rehearsals on time, to show respect for your section leaders, and to enter into the competitive spirit of the event. For those with the energy and the dedication, it will be an unforgettable experience.

Rio's **fancy-dress balls** range from the sophisticated to the wild. The majority of clubs and hotels host at least one. The *Copacabana Palace* hotel's is elegant and expensive (US$250), with costumed mime artists parading on a backlit terrace for the benefit of spectators on the Av Atlântica below; T 255-7070, ext 187 (reservations). The *Scala* club's licentious parties are televised nightly; Av Afrânio de Mello Franco, Leblon, T 239-4448. It is not necessary to wear fancy dress; just join in, although you will feel more comfortable if you wear a minimum of clothing to the clubs (crowded, hot and rowdy). Two of the most famous (both at *Scala*) are the Red & Black Ball (Fri) and the Gay Ball (Tues). Prices vary: from about US$15 pp; US$100 per table for 4; US$750 for a box. Drinks are expensive (beer/soft drink US$3). *Scala* gives free tickets to attractive young women, which their boyfriends then sell outside the entrance: expect to pay about US$15, and check the date. The tourist office has a full list of balls.

The expensive hotels offer special Carnival breakfasts from 0530 at US$10-15, all good; *Caesar Park* (Ipanema) highly rec, wonderful meal, top-floor view of sunrise over beach.

Essential information

● **Attendance**

The Sambódromo parades start at 1900 and last about 12 hrs. Gates (which are not clearly marked) open at 1800. Spectator accommodation comprises seats ('cadeiras') at ground level, terraces ('arquibancadas') and boxes ('camarotes'). The best boxes, which are reserved for tourists and VIPs, sell for around US$1,000 pp. Seats are closest to the parade, but you may have to fight your way to the front. Seats and boxes reserved for tourists have the best view; sectors 4, 7 and 11 are preferred (they house the judging points); 6 and 13 are least favoured, being at the end when dancers might be tired, but have more space. The terraces, while uncomfortable, house the most fervent fans, tightly packed; this is where to soak up the atmosphere (but not take pictures – too crowded). Tickets (maximum 4) are sold through Banco do Brasil or the Banco Meridional in most big cities, and start at about US$40; they are also sold at the Maracanã Stadium box office, but not during Carnival weekend; touts outside will try to sell you places at double the price. Check availability, even if they say all tickets are sold. Samba schools have an allocation of tickets which members sometimes sell off; if you are offered one of these, check its date. Tourist tickets start at US$100; available through Riotur or travel agencies. Taxis to the Sambódromo are negotiable (around US$15) and will find your gate; nearest Metrô is Praça 11: an enjoyable ride in the company of costumed samba school members. Main Metrô and bus routes run all night during Carnival (erratically).

All schools hold a preview of their entire parade in their own neighbourhood, usually the week before Carnival; well worth seeing, admission often free for women, otherwise around US$4, photography OK but don't take valuables; listed in local press under 'ensaios'. It's wise to go by taxi, as most schools are based in poorer districts.

● **Lodging and security**

Visitors wishing to attend the Carnival are earnestly advised to make sure of their accommodation well in advance. Virtually all hotels raise their prices during Carnival, although it should be possible to find a room.

Your property should be safe inside the Sambódromo, but the crowds outside can attract pickpockets: as ever, don't brandish your camera, and take with you only as much money as you need for fares and refreshments (food and drink are sold in the Sambódromo, glass and cans are not allowed if you take your own). It gets hot! Wear as little as possible (shorts or Bermudas and a T-shirt).

● **Samba Schools**

Salgueiro (Andaraí) T 238-5564; Beija-Flor (Nilópolis) T 791-2866; Mangueira (Mangueira) T 234-4129; Estácio de Sá (Cidade Nova) T 293-8944; Imperatriz (Ramos) T 270-8037; Mocidade Independente (Padre Miguel) T 332-5823; Portela (Madureira) T 390-0471; Tradição (Campinho) T 350-5868; União da Ilha (Ilha do Governador) T 396-4951; Vila Isabel (Santa Isabel) T 268-7052; also see local press and Riotur booklet.

● **Sources of information**

Carnival week comprises an enormous range of official contests and events, as well as many unofficial ones. Exhibitions and competitions reach a peak on the Tues; Riotur's guide booklet (also available from better hotels) gives concise information in English; *Veja*, *Manchete* (weekly magazines) and the Jornal do Brasil's *Programa* (Fri) are also invaluable sources: an equally wide programme exists for those looking for entertainment but not wishing to 'play' at Carnival.

Suggested reading: *The Insider's Guide to Rio* (in English; Christopher Pickard, from Rio bookshops); *Samba* (paperback; a personal account by Alma Guillermoprieto, Bloomsbury Press).

● **If you can't be there at Carnival time**

Rehearsals are held at various places from Nov onwards; eg the Portela *escola* at R Arruda Câmara 81, Madureira, late Sat nights. See addresses above. Tour agents sell tickets for glitzy samba shows, which are nothing like the real thing. When buying a Carnival video, make sure the format is compatible (Brazilian format matches the USA; VHS PAL for most of Europe).

● **Carnival dates**

22 Feb 1998; 14 Feb 1999; 5 Mar 2000.

OTHER FESTIVALS

Less hectic than Carnival, but very atmospheric, is the festival of **Iemanjá** on the night of 31 Dec, when devotees of the sea spirit gather on Copacabana, Ipanema and Leblon beaches, singing and dancing around open fires and making offerings, and the elected Queen of the Sea is rowed along the seashore. At midnight small boats are launched as sacrifices to Iemanjá. The religious event is dwarfed, however, by a massive **New Year's Eve party** at Copacabana. The beach is packed as thousands of revellers enjoy free outdoor concerts by big-name pop stars, topped with a lavish midnight firework display. Most crowded in front of *Copacabana Palace Hotel*.

The festival of **São Sebastião**, patron saint of Rio, is celebrated by an evening procession on 20 Jan, leaving Capuchinhos Church, Tijuca, and arriving at the cathedral of São Sebastião. The same evening an *umbanda* festival is celebrated at the Caboclo Monument in Santa Teresa.

LOCAL INFORMATION

● Security

The majority of visitors enjoy Rio's glamour, and the rich variety of experience it has to offer, without any problems. It is worth remembering that, despite its beach culture, carefree atmosphere and friendly people, Rio is one of the world's most densely populated cities. If you live in London, Paris, New York or Los Angeles and behave with the same caution in Rio that you do at home, you will be unlucky to encounter any crime. There is extreme poverty in Rio: most robberies that occur are committed out of desperation. Overseas visitors are an obvious target: simply by having been able to afford the ticket, you are comparatively wealthy. Brazilians can usually tell you are foreign just by the way you carry yourself, but there is no sense in looking as if you have something worth stealing (by wearing expensive clothes, valuable jewellery, a large daypack, or your camera – put it in your shoulder bag, worn in front of you, or buy disposable cameras as often as you need them). If you are unfortunate enough to be threatened, try to remember that the assailant is probably as scared as you are, and will not hurt you if you give him what he's asking for (keep some money easily accessible, just in case). If you see someone having trouble, don't interfere, but try making a lot of noise to frighten the attacker away; if you think you are being followed, go up to a policeman. The streets are not excessively dangerous at night, but if you're going out in your best clothes, don't know the way, or are drunk, it's wisest to get a taxi. All the above advice comes from the **tourist police** (see **Useful addresses** below), who publish a sensible advice leaflet (available from hotels and consulates:

consulates also issue safety guidelines). Officers are helpful, efficient, and multilingual. All the main tourist areas are patrolled. If you have any problems, **contact the tourist police first**.

The following are risky places: the tunnels are not safe to walk through; the city centre on Sun when it is deserted; quiet alleyways; jostling crowds; dark corners. Locals don't walk on the beaches at night: if you must, do not go out of sight of the pavement. The Tijuca forest is best explored with a group of 6 or more, except the stretch between Afonso Vizeu square and Cascatinha which is well policed during the day; the tram (see page 408) attracts pickpockets and Santa Teresa itself is dangerous as a result of *favela* gang warfare; robberies sometimes happen in city buses: don't use them if guarding your property is essential (private 'frescão' buses are more secure). The main bus station is patrolled inside, but uncomfortable outside. If you go to the North Zone at night, use a taxi; wandering around *favelas* at any time of day is both ill-advised and in questionable taste. Street vendors and children working the tables at your bar or restaurant will have been permitted by the management and there is little risk, though children can be light-fingered, so watch your wallet.

It seems that far too many crimes against tourists are the result of thoughtlessness: remember that you are in a busy city, and that the beaches are a pivot of daily life; leaving things unattended on the sand is equivalent to leaving them on Times Square while you go for a walk. We have been asked to advise male readers that all the usual risks apply if hiring prostitutes of either sex (police may well take your companion's side in a dispute over prices – don't argue). The 'red light' districts of the South Zone are unlikely to offend anyone walking about at night, even children or unaccompanied women. Do, however, be suspicious of any club that you are invited into by a stranger (have your drink opened in front of you), and of anyone offering drugs. You have the most to lose when carrying all your belongings and as you go in and out of banks, exchange houses, and expensive shops, so take extra care then. At other times, put your passport, TCs, etc in the hotel safe. Don't take too much out with you, have some sense, and relax.

On all Rio's beaches you should take a towel or mat to protect you against sandflies; in the water stay near groups of other swimmers; there is a strong undertow.

● NB

In early 1997 phone numbers in Rio were being changed. No complete details were available at the time of going to press.

● **Accommodation**

Hotel prices

L1	over US$200	**L2**	US$151-200
L3	US$101-150	**A1**	US$81-100
A2	US$61-80	**A3**	US$46-60
B	US$31-45	**C**	US$21-30
D	US$12-20	**E**	US$7-11
F	US$4-6	**G**	up to US$3

Unless otherwise stated, all hotels in range **D** and above have private bath. Assume friendliness and cleanliness in all cases.

All hotels 2-stars and above in the following list are a/c. A 10% service charge is usually added to the bill and tax of 5% or 10% may be added (if not already inc). Note that not all higher-class hotels inc breakfast in their room rates. The following list begins with expensive hotels and then gives economy establishments, by area.

Centre: well placed for transport, 30 mins from the beaches. Most offices and commerce are located here, but no nightlife, so not a secure area and not rec for tourists.

Flamengo: residential area midway between centre and Copacabana: **L2** *Novo Mundo*, Praia Flamengo 20, T 205-3355, F 265-2369, well rec but noisy; **L3** *Glória*, R do Russel, 632, T 205-7272, F 245-1660, stylish and elegant old building, two swimming pools, highly rec.

Copacabana: the famous seaside residential and commercial area: many hotels on Av Atlântica charge about 30% more for a room with a sea view, but some town-side upper rooms have equally fine views of the mountains. 5-star hotels (**L1-2**): *Copacabana Palace*, Av Atlântica 1702, T 255-7070, F 235-7330, swimming pool, good; *Meridien*, Av Atlântica 1020, T 275-9922, F 541-6447, Air France hotel, world-renowned, but very expensive, pool, rooms small; *Rio Othon Palace*, Av Atlântica 3264, T 521-5522, F 521-6697, pool, very good, as is *Rio Palace*, Av Atlântica 4240, T 521-3232, F 247-1752, all rooms locked by central system at 0130. There are two excellent suites hotels: **L3** *Rio Atlântica*, Av Atlântica 2964, T 255-6332, F 255-6410 with pool, 2 restaurants and other facilities (Swiss management, very high standards) rec; and *Rio Internacional*, Av Atlântica 1500, T 295-2323, F 542-5443, pool.

4-star hotels in Copacabana: there are 4 Othon hotels in this category, all in the **L3-A1** range (some rooms more): *Califórnia Othon*, Av Atlântica 2616, T/F 257-1900, good; *Savoy Othon*, Av Copacabana 995, T/F 521-8282, very central, popular, commercial, quite noisy; *Olinda*, Av Atlântica 2230, T/F 257-1890, also good, and the *Lancaster*, Av Atlântica 1470,

T/F 541-1887, rec, easy to change TCs, non-smoking rooms, helpful management. Next door to the *Lancaster* is *Ouro Verde*, Av Atlântica 1456, T 542-1887, F 542-4597, good value, excellent all round; 3 Luxor hotels: *Luxor Continental*, Gustavo Sampaio 320, T 275-5252, F 541-1946, *Luxor Copacabana*, Av Atlântica 2554, T 235-2245, F 255-1858, *Luxor Regente*, Av Atlântica 3716, T 287-4212, F 267-7693, all good hotels in this range, well-placed. *Leme Palace*, Av Atlântica 656, T/F 275-8080, also good, but poorer location, popular with tour groups; *Rio Roiss*, R Aires Saldanha 48, T 522-1142, F 522-1142, very good, restaurant.

Copacabana 3-stars (A1-A2): *Castro Alves Othon*, Av Copacabana 552, T/F 255-8815, central, very comfortable and elegant, rec; *Debret*, Av Atlântica 3564, T 521-3332, F 521-0899, good, helpful staff, some inner rooms dark; *Plaza Copacabana*, Av Princesa Isabel 263, T 275-7722, F 275-8693, highly rec.

Copacabana 2-stars: **B** *Atlantis Copacabana*, Av Bulhões de Carvalho 61, T 521-1142, F 287-8896, a/c, TV, very good, close to Ipanema and Copacabana beaches; *Biarritz*, R Aires Saldanha 54, T 521-6542, F 287-7640, good, accepts American Express; **B** *Santa Clara*, R Décio Vilares 316, T 256-2650, best rooms at front, quiet, rec; **B** *Toledo*, R Domingos Ferreira 71, T 257-1990, 1 block from beach, good breakfast, single rooms are gloomy, but excellent value; **B** *Acapulco Copacabana*, R Gustavo Sampaio 854, T 275-0022, F 275-3396, a/c, TV, simple, rec.

Ipanema/Leblon: outer seaside residential and commercial area: all the following are good, starting with the most luxurious, **L1** *Caesar Park*, Av Vieira Souto 460, T 287-3122, F 521-6000, pool, beach patrol; **L3** *Marina Palace*, Av Delfim Moreira 630, T 259-5212, F 259-0941, and **L3** *Marina Rio*, Av Delfim Moreira 696, T 239-8844, F 259-0941; **L3** *Praia Ipanema*, Av Vieira Souto 706, T 239-9932, F 239-6889, pool, helpful; **A1** *Sol Ipanema*, Av Vieira Souto, 320, T 267-0095, F 521-6464, rec; **A3** *Ipanema Inn*, Maria Quitéria 27, behind Caesar Park, T 287-6092, F 511-5094, good location; **A3** *Arpoador Inn*, Francisco Otaviano 177, T 247-6090, F 511-5094, only hotel on beach, rec.

São Conrado and further out: spectacular settings, but isolated and far from centre: the first two are luxury hotels with pools: **L1** *Intercontinental*, Av Pref Mendes de Moraes 222 (São Conrado), T 322-2200, F 322-5500; **L1** *Sheraton*, Av Niemeyer 121 (Vidigal), T 274-1122, F 239-5643; **A2** *Atlântico Sul*, Av Sernambetiba 18000 (Recreio), T 437-8411, F 437-8777.

At **Galeão Airport**: **L2** *Luxor Hotel do Aeroporto*, T 398-5960, F 398-3983 (3-star).

Economy hotels: are found mainly in three districts of Rio: Flamengo/Botafogo (best), Lapa/Fátima and Saúde/Mauá. Rates are for doubles, and inc continental breakfast.

Flamengo/Catete: (Residential area between centre and Copacabana, with good bus and Metrô connections.) From the centre, you will come across the hotels in this order: **E** *Opera*, Santa Amaro 75, T 242-3585, recently reopened. On the hillside is Ladeira da Glória: **C** *Turístico*, Ladeira da Glória 30, T 265-1698, inc breakfast, a/c, tourist information provided, mixed reports, some highly favourable. **D** *Victória*, R do Catete 172, with breakfast, hot water, a/c, rec; also on R do Catete: No 233, **D** *Rio Claro*, small rooms, breakfast, a/c, safe, rec; No 160, **D** *Monte Blanco*, breakfast, a/c, radio (try for a room about 1200). To the left is R Silveira Martins: **C** *Inglês*, No 20, T 265-9052, reasonable breakfast. Walking down Praia de Flamengo you will come across the next streets: Ferreira Viana: **A3** *Florida*, No 71/81, T 245-8160, F 285-5777, sauna, pool, safe, quiet, good views, great breakfast, highly rec; **B** *Regina*, No 29, T 225-7280, 2-star, a/c, rooms vary; **D** *Ferreira Viana*, No 58, T 2057396, breakfast, rec; **D** *Unico*, Buarque de Machado 54, T 205-9932, TV, a/c, fridge, rec; also nr Largo do Machado Metrô: **C-D** *Monterrey*, R Artur Bernardes 39, T 265-9899, with fan, TV, some rooms small and poorly lit; at No 29, **D** *Rio Lisboa*, a/c, cheaper rooms without bath, safe, mixed reports – both hotels in this quiet street are family hotels. R Paissandu: No 34, **D** *Venezuela*, very clean, but rooms small and breakfast poor; **B** *Paysandu*, opp *Venezuela* at No 23, T 225-7270, very clean, comfortable and good value. Beyond Largo de Machado: R Gago Coutinho: No 22, **D** *Serrano*, pleasant, helpful; and **B** *Argentina*, Cruz Lima 30, T 225-7233, F 285-4573, best rooms on 5th floor, cheapest on 1st, rec.

Lapa/Fátima: between Lapa and Praça Tiradentes is an inner residential area, less desirable than Flamengo. Parts of this area are deserted from 2200 on. Near Cinelândia Metrô station are a lot of cheap hotels, but many are short stay. In Lapa itself, nr the Arches just beyond Passeio Público, is R Joaquim Silva: No 99, **D** *Marajó*, with breakfast, varied rooms; also **E** *Love's House*, R Joaquim Silva, ask for room with window, safe, respectable, good value. Passing under the Arches you come to Av Mem de Sá (bus 127 from bus terminal): No 85, **E** *Mundo Novo*, a/c. Turning towards Praça Tiradentes is R Resende, No 31, **D** *Estadual*, good; No 35 **D** *Pouso Real*, T 224-2757, good, gay area, rec; **D** *Marialva*, Gomes Freire 430 (nr New Cathedral, convenient for Av Rio Branco, buses etc), 2-star, a/c, breakfast in room, rec. Praça Tiradentes:

D *Rio Hotel*, noisy rooms on Praça, quieter overlooking São Sebastião cathedral, with breakfast (only served in rooms).

Saúde/Mauá: (area between the railway station and the docks): the very cheapest hotels in town are in this area, but it is not too safe at night.

Youth hostels: R Almte Alexandrino 2840, Santa Teresa (*Pousada do Garuda*, T 225-0393/236-1419), Santa Amaro 162, Glória, T 222-8576, noisy; *Chave da Garuda*, Gen Dionísio 63, Botafogo, T 286-0303, US$12, clean, laundry and cooking facilities, superb breakfast, noisy but frequently rec; *Copacabana Praia* (also called *Indy*), R Ten Marones de Gusmão 85, Bairro Peixoto, CEP 22041, T 235-3817/237-5422, US$15, apartments also available from US$30; *Saint Roman*, R Saint Roman 48, Copacabana, T 227-7685; *Copacabana Chalet*, R Pompeu Loureiro 99, T 236-0047, US$23, noisy, nr beach, shops, YHA card not necessary, but you pay a bit more without it. Associations: both at R da Assembleia 10: ALBERJ (for Rio), room 1616, T 531-1302/2234; Federação Brasileira (Brazil), room 1211, T 531-1129. Youth hostels are fully booked between Christmas and Carnival; if intending to stay at this time reserve well in advance.

Remember that 'motels' are mainly for the use of very-short-stay couples.

The city is noisy. An inside room is cheaper and much quieter.

Self-catering apartments: a popular form of accommodation in Rio, available at all price levels: for example, furnished apartments, accommodating up to 6, cost US$240/month in Maracanã, about US$360/month in Saúde, Cinelândia, Flamengo. Copacabana, Ipanema and Leblon prices range from about US$15/day for a simple studio, up to US$2,000 a month for a luxurious residence sleeping 4 to 6. Heading S past Barra da Tijuca, virtually all the accommodation available is self-catering. Renting a small flat, or sharing a larger one, can be much better value than a hotel room. Blocks consisting entirely of short-let apartments can attract thieves, so check the (usually excellent) security arrangements; residential buildings are called *prédio familiar*. Higher floors (*alto andar*) are considered safest.

The following rent apartments in residential blocks: *Hamburg Imobiliária*, Av Copacabana 195, Loja 104, T 542-1446, F 236-4541, German run, specialize in flats, very reasonable, helpful, highly rec, also offer tours at good rates, flights and exchange; *Yvonne Reimann*, Av Atlântica 4.066, Apto 605, T 227-0281/267-0054, rents apartments, all with phone, nr beach, a/c, maid service, English, French, German spoken, all apartments owned by the agency, prices from US$48 up (check if per flat or pp); *Yolanda Thiémard*, Av Prado Junior 165

CO2, T 295-2088, multilingual, good value, rec; *Dona Lígia*, R Ministro Viveiros de Castro 141 apto 101, T 541-6367, speaks English, lower-price apartments. European agent: Mr Peter Corr, Friedrichsplatz 6, D-6816, Mannheim, Germany, T 0049-621-402721, F 0049-6234-801177, rec. 'Apart-Hotels' are listed in the *Guia 4 Rodas* and Riotur's booklet; *Rio Beach*, R Prado Júnior 48, Loja 2, Copacabana, T 547-2395, well-equipped flats for US$18/day and US$400/month; *Copacabana Holidays* at R Barata Ribeiro 90, room 204, Copacabana, T 542-1597/542-1525, and at R Barata Ribeiro 87/ 202, T 255-2016 or 237-1133; *New Rio Home Service*, Visconde de Pirajá 414, sala 522, Ipanema, T 521-2332, F 267-6090, Swed-ish-run, rec; *Mellow Holidays*, R Paula Freitas 45/1101, T 256-5061, have apartments at a range of prices in the Copacabana and Ipanema districts. Agents and private owners advertise in *Balcão* (like *Exchange and Mart*), twice weekly, *O Globo* or *Jornal do Brasil* (daily); under 'Apar-tamentos – Temporada'; advertisements are classified by district and size of apartment: 'va-gas e quartos' means shared accommodation; 'conjugado' (or 'conj') is a studio with limited cooking facilities; '3 Quartos' is a 3-bedroom flat. There should always be a written agreement when renting.

Camping: Camping Clube do Brasil has 2 beach sites at Barra da Tijuca: Av Sernambetiba 3200, T 493-0628 (bus 233 from centre, 702 or 703 from the airport via Zona Sul, US$5 – a long way from the centre), sauna, pool, bar, café,US$12 (half price for members), during Jan and Feb this site is often full and sometimes restricted to members of the Camping Clube do Brasil; a simpler site at Estrada do Pontal 5900, T 437-8400, lighting, café, good surfing, US$6. Both have trailer plots. *Ostal*, Av Sernambetiba 18790, T 437-8350; and *Novo Rio*, at 17.5 km on Rio-Santos road, T 437-6518. If travelling by trailer, you can park at the Marina Glória car park, where there are showers and toilets, a small shop and snack bar. Pay the guards to look after your vehicle.

● **Places to eat**
In Rio, avoid mussels! In 1996, prices were similar to São Paulo, see page 450. While many of Rio's quality hotels offer world-class food and service, they may lack atmosphere and close at midnight. There are much livelier, and cheaper places to eat if going our for an evening meal. Cariocas eat late (2200; later at weekends).

Centre: *Republique*, Pça da República 63 (2nd floor), T 532 4000, chic, designed by architect Chicô Gouveia, good food, expensive (US$50 without wine); *Café do Teatro*, Rio Branco, Teatro Municipal, good food in grand manner, shorts and scruffy gear not admitted; *Fiorino*, Av Heitor Beltrão 126, Tijuca, T 567 4476/567 9189, very good and cheap, rec; *Bistro do Paço*, Praça XV de Novembro 48, Centro, T 252 6353, excellent food, cheap prices, cosy surroundings, fancy place, Swiss run, rec; *Alba Mar*, fish, very good and reasonable, Praça Mal Ancora 184-6; *Rio Minho*, R do Ouvidor 10, for seafood, expensive, old-fashioned, very good. There are several Arab restaurants on Av Senhor dos Pas-sos, also open Sat and Sun. *Luciano*, R das Marrecas 44, all you can eat at buffet, and others on this street. *Salad Market*, Av 13 de Maio 33/c, s/loja, weekday lunches only, US$16/kg; many *lanchonetes* for good, cheap meals in the business sector.

Santa Teresa: *Bar do Arnaudo*, Alm Alexan-drino 316, B, rec; **Lapa**: *Semente*, R Joaquim Silva 138, vegetarian. **Glória**: *Casa da Suíça*, R Cândido Mendes 157, T 252-5182, bar/restau-rant, good atmosphere; several others on this street.

Flamengo and Catete: there are a lot of eating places on R do Catete: *Pastelaria Wong*, No 239, very cheap, good; *Amazônia*, No 234B, downstairs, one-price counter service, upstairs for good, reasonably-priced evening meals, rec; *Catelandia*, No 204, excellent and cheap; *Restaurante e Pizzaria Guanabara*, No 150, excellent value and selection; *Rio Galícia*, No 265, very good pizza, good service; *Machado*, No 286, good Italian food at reasonable prices; *Parmé*, No 311, one of a chain, friendly and reasonable; *No 128*, no name, lunch only, communal tables, rec; *Alcaparra*, Praia do Flamengo 144, elegant Italian, reasonable; *Lamas*, Marquês de Abrantes 18-A, excellent value, good food, great atmosphere, opens late, popular with Brazilian arts/media people, rec; *Alho E Oleo*, R Buarque de Macedo 13, T 205 2541/225 3418, fashionable, pleasant, rec; *Gaúcha*, R das Laranjeiras 114, good.

Botafogo: *Maxim's*, 44th floor of Rio Sul shopping centre, French, closed Sun; *Manolo*, Bambina e M de Olinda, very good value; *Raajmahal*, R Gen Polidoro 29, Indian, reasonable; *Zen Japanese Restaurant*, Praia de Botafogo 228, highly rec.

Copacabana and Leme: the main hotels (see above); most expensive is *Le Saint Honoré* at the *Meridien*, Leme, good food and wonderful view; *Churrascaria Marius*, at Leme end of Av Atlântica, 290-B, all you can eat US$20 with drinks, excellent; *Churrascaria Palace*, R Rodolfo Dantas 16-B, 22 different kinds of meat, very good; *Arataca*, Figueiredo de Magalhães 28, try *carne-de-sol* and *lagosta ao molho*; *A Marisquera*, Barata Ribeiro 232, good seafood; *Ponto d'Encontro* at No 750, Portuguese, try baked *bacalhau*; *Rian*, Santa Clara 8 (international), excellent and reasonable, very popular; *Maximix*, R Siqueira Campos 12, loja A, buffet by weight, opens late, very popular, cheap, rec; *Arosa*, No 110, lanchonete, very good and cheap. *La Tratoria*, Av Atlântica (opp *Hotel Excelsior*), Italian, good food and service very reasonable, rec.

Ipanema: *Il Capo*, Visconde de Pirajá 276, rec; *Banana Café*, Barão da Torre 368, trendy, lively nightclub upstairs after 2400; *Alho e Oleo*, next door, fashionable, friendly, rec; *Porção*, Barão de Torre 218, a very good *churrascaria*, US$8; *Pax Delícia*, Praça Nossa Senhora de Paz, good food, lively crowd; *Amarcord*, R Maria Quitéria 136, T 287 0335, rec; *Mostarda*, Av Epitácio Pessoa 980, not cheap but food excellent, nightclub upstairs, rec. Ipanema is quieter than Copacabana, many nice places round Praça Gen Osório; *Del Mare*, rec, at corner of Prudente de Morais and Vinícius de Morais. *Amarelinho*, R Farme de Amoedo 62, great corner lanchonete with tables outside, fresh food, lunch US$5, friendly, open until 0300, rec. *Casa da Feijoada*, Prudente de Morais 10, serves an excellent *feijoada* all week. Health food at **Restaurante** *Natural*, R Barão de Torre 171. *Delicats*, Av Henrique Dumont 68, good Jewish deli.

Leblon: *Un, Deux, Trois*, R Bartolomeu Mitre 123, very fashionable, restaurant, nightclub; *Antiquarius*, R Aristides Espínola 19, restaurant-cum-antique shop, seafood and international cuisine; *Mediterráneo*, R Prudente de Morais 1810, excellent fish, reasonable prices. In **Jardim Botânico**: *Claude Troisgros*, R Custódio Serrão 62, T 537 8582, elegant French restaurant, rec; *Enotria*, R Frei Leandro 20, T 246 9003, excellent Italian food, service, atmosphere and prices, rec. **Lagoa**: *Mistura Fina*, Av Borges de Medeiros 3207, T 266-5844/537-2844, classy, popular, friendly nightclub upstairs (US$25). **Barra**: *Amarelinho*, Av Ayrton Senna 3000, warmly rec lanchonete, see Ipanema above; *Caffe Milano*, R Rodolfo Amoedo 360, T 494-4671, new, good Italian, US$35 (no credit cards).

Grill or barbecue houses (*churrascarias*) are relatively cheap, especially by European standards. There are many at São Conrado and Joá, on the road out to Barra da Tijuca (see page 394). Look for the 'Churrascaria Rodízio', where you are served as much as you can eat. There are plentiful hamburger stands (literally 'stands' as you stand and eat the hamburger) and lunch counters all over the city. *McDonalds* and *Big Bob's* (similar) can be found at about 20 locations each (Big Mac US$3). *Galetos* are lunch counters specializing in chicken and grilled meat, very reasonable. In the 'shopping centres' there is usually a variety of restaurants and snack bars grouped around a central plaza where you can shop around for a good meal. Most less-expensive restaurants in Rio have basically the same type of food (based on steak, fried potatoes and rice) and serve large portions; those with small appetites, and especially families with children, can ask for a spare plate, and split helpings. *La Mole*, at 11 locations, serves good, cheap Italian food: very popular. *Comida por quilo* is about US$15/kg in Rio. There are many juice bars in Rio with a wide selection. Most restaurants are closed on 24 and 25 December.

Tea rooms: for those who like their teas served English style, the sedate (100 years old in 1994) *Confeitaria Colombo*, R Gonçalves Dias 32 nr Carioca metro station, is highly rec for atmosphere, being the only one of its kind in Rio, with the original Belle Epoque décor, open 0900-1800, lunch available, no service charge so tip the excellent waiters. More modern but similar establishments in some of the main hotels, eg *Pergula*, Copacabana Palace Hotel, Av Atlântica 1702, run by Englishwoman Anne Phillips, Mon to Fri 1400-1700, rec. Also *Casarão*, Souza Lima 37A, Copacabana; *Traiteurs de France*, R Copacabana 386, delicious tarts and pastries, not expensive; *La Bonne Table*, Visc de Pirajá 580 sala 407, Ipanema; *Café de la Paix*, Av Atlântica 1020; *Chá e Simpatia*, Av Atlântica 4240; *Concorde*, Av Prudente de Morais 129.

Bars: wherever you are, there's one near you. A beer costs around US$1.50, but up to US$5 in expensive hotel bars. A cover charge of US$3-7 may be made for live music. Snack food always available. Single drinkers/diners are usually welcome, though you may not remain alone for long unless you stick your nose in a book. Copacabana, Ipanema and Leblon have many beach *barracas*, several open all night. The seafront bars on Av Atlântica are great for people-watching. The big hotels have good cocktail bars (*Copacabana Palace*, poolside, rec); *Alla Zingara*, corner of Min Viveiros de Castro and Belfort Roxo, is friendly. There are only 4 seafront bars in Ipanema: *Barril 1800*, Av Tom Jobim 110, highly rec, nice place to watch the sunset. *A Garota de Ipanema*, R Vinícius de Morais 49, is where the song 'Girl from Ipanema' was written, very lively. Lots more bars opening in districts to the S. *Bar Lagoa*, Av Epitácio Pessoa 1674, Lagoa, rec ('arty crowd', evenings only). *Sobrenatural*, Largo do França, Santa Teresa, free live samba music Wed to Sat. On weekday evenings, Cariocas congregate at the bars around Praça Santos Dumont, Gávea. British ex-pats meet at *Porão*, under the Anglican church hall, R Real Grandeza 99, Botafogo, Fri only.

● **Banks & money changers**
Banks: Lloyds Bank, R da Alfândega 33; Banco Internacional (Bank of America and Royal Bank of Canada), R do Ouvidor 90; Banco Holandês Unido, R do Ouvidor 101; Citibank, R Assembléia 100, changes large US$ TCs into smaller ones, no commission; The First National Bank of Boston, Av Rio Branco 110; many others. Banco do Brasil, there are only 2 branches in Rio which will change US$ TCs, Praia de Botafogo, 384A, 3rd floor (minimium US$200) and central branch R Senador Dantes 105, 4th floor (minimum US$500 – good rates, also changes Argentine pesos, US$10 commission). Banco do Brasil at the International Airport is open 24 hrs a day. Visa cash withdrawals at Banco do Brasil (also TCs) and Bradesco (machines). Citibank advances cash on Eurocard/Mastercard; Mastercard and Cirrus cash machines at Itaú, on Av Atlântica (next to *Copacabana Palace*), R Visconde de Pirajá, close to Pça Gen Osório (Ipanema), and other locations; also at Santos Dumont airport. See **Currency**, page 646.

Money changers: American Express, Av Atlântica 1702, Loja B, *Hotel Copacabana Palace*, T 255-2148/2677, good rates. Most large hotels and reputable travel agencies will change currency and TCs. Copacabana (where rates are generally worse than in centre) abounds with *câmbios*; Euro-

cheques, TCs and currency at *Hamburg Imobiliária*, see **Apartments** above. **NB** Some *câmbios* will change US$ cheques for US$ cash with a 4% commission. These transactions are not strictly legal, so you will have to look around for the *câmbios* that do them.

● **Cultural centres**
The **British Council**, R Elmano Cardim 10, Urca, T 295-7782, F 541-3693. The **British School of Rio de Janeiro**, R Real Grandeza 99. **Sociedade Brasileira de Cultura Inglesa**, Av Graça Aranha 327, and in Copacabana, T 227-0147. **American Chamber of Commerce for Brazil**, Praça Pio Dez 15, 5th floor. **American Society and American Club**, Av Rio Branco 123, 21st floor. **USICA Reference Library**, US Consulate General, Av Presidente Wilson 147. The **American School of Rio de Janeiro**, Estrada da Gávea 132. **Marc Apoio Cultural Contact Center**, PO Box 1736, 20001-970, T/F (21) 275-8605; **German Cultur-Institut** (Goethe), Av Graça Aranha 416, 9th floor; open Mon-Thur 1200-1900, Wed-Thur 1000-1100. **Centro Cultural Banco do Brasil**, R Primeiro de Março 66, free concerts, rec. **Australian Trade Commission**, R Voluntários da Pátria 45, 2°, Botafogo, T 286-7922 (for visas etc you must go to Brasilia).

● **Electric current**
110-220 volts, 60 cycles, AC.

● **Embassies & consulates**
Argentine, Praia de Botafogo 228, T 551-5498, very helpful over visas, 1130-1600; **Uruguay**, Praia de Botafogo 242, 6°, T 553-6030; **Paraguay**, same address, 2nd floor, T 553-2294, visas US$5; **Venezuela**, same address, 5th floor, T 552-2873 (will not issue visas, see under Manaus and Boa Vista).

US Consulate General, Av Presidente Wilson, 147, T 292-7117. **Canada**, R Lauro Müller 116, T 542-9297.

UK, Praia do Flamengo 284, T 553-6850; **Switzerland**, R Cândido Mendes 157, 11° andar, T 221 1867; **German Consulate-General**, R Presidente Carlos de Campos 417, T 553-6777; **France**, Av Pres Antônio Carlos, 58, T 210-1272; **Austria**, Av Atlântica 3804, T 267-5048; **Netherlands**, Praia de Botafogo 242, 7th floor, T 552-9028 (Dutch newspapers here; also at KLM office on Av Rio Branco); **Sweden, Finland and Norway**, Praia do Flamengo 344, 9th floor, T 552-2422; **Denmark**, Av das Américas 3333, Apt 805, T 431-2080.

Israel, Av NS Copacabana 680-C, T 255-5432; **South Africa**, Av Pres Antônio Carlos 607, T 533-0216; **Greece**, T 552-6849, 552-6749, Praia do Flamengo 344/201 22210.

● **Entertainment**
Cinemas: new American releases (with original

soundtrack), plus Brazilian and worldwide films, and classics. A very few give cheaper tickets to students, but not at weekends. See local press. Normal seat price US$4, discount on Wed and Thur.

Nightclubs: Rio nightlife is rich and infinitely varied, one of the main attractions for most visitors. If you are not in Rio for Carnival, it's worth seeing a samba show, cheaper if you pay at the door. *Hotel Nacional* at São Conrado has the most lavish show in town; also *Plataforma I*, R Adalberto Ferreira 32, Leblon, T 274-4022, arrive by 2000, show finishes 2300.

Many young Cariocas congregate in Botafogo for live music. There are free concerts throughout the summer, along the beaches, in Botafogo and at the parks: mostly samba, reggae, rock and MPB (Brazilian pop): information from local press (see below). January sees Hollywood Rock, a vast 3-day open air concert featuring international bands, Praça da Apoteose; there are live concerts every weekend at the Arpoador park, between Copacabana and Ipanema.

Trendiest clubs in 1996-97 (contemporary dance music) were *Le Boy*, Raul Pompéia 94, Copacabana, T 521 0367; *Dr Smith*, R da Passagem 169, Botafogo, T 295-3135, Wed-Sun. *Banana Café*, Barão da Torre 368, Ipanema, T 5211460; *Papillon*, Av Prefeito Mendes de Moraes 222, São Conrado, T 322 2200; *The Basement*, Av NS de Copacabana 1241, new, alternative; also rec is *Torre de Babel*, Visconde de Pirajá (close to hippy market), Sats only; and at the *Jardim Botânico* (weekends). There are dozens of other good clubs, most open Wed-Sun, action starts around midnight, lone women and male-only groups may have trouble getting in.

Canecão is a big, inexpensive venue for live concerts, most nights, see press for listings: R Venceslau Braz 215, Botafogo, T 295-3044.

Rio's famous jazz, in all its forms, is performed in lots of enjoyable venues, see press. The following are sophisticated sit-down places (you have to eat something, budget around US$20 each, comfortable for lone women): *Jazzmania*, Av Rainha Elisabeth, Ipanema, T 227-2447; *Rio Jazz Club*, annexe of *Meridien Hotel*, Av Atlântica, Leme, T 541-9046. Check time of show, usually around 2200.

Gafieiras, for Samba dancing, inc *Elite Club*, R Frei Caneca 4, 1st floor, Centro, T 232-3217; *Estudantinha*, Praça Tiradentes 79, T 232-1149, Thur-Sun: there are many cheaper *gafieiras*: one, enthusiastically rec, under the beach highway at Botafogo. All types of music and entertainment are represented: *Forró da Copacabana*, Av NS de Copacabana 435, has been rec for forró fans (safe, disco upstairs); *Reggae Rock Cafe*, Largo de São Conrado 20, T 322-

4197; *Raizes*, Av Sernambetiba 1120, T 389-6240, for Afro-Brazilian beats.

Copacabana is full of discos where the girls are for hire: biggest and most entertaining is *Help*. Entry charge (US$9) does not inc drink. Music is usually good, trade is low-pressure, women with female friends and a sense of humour can have a lot of fun (but not rec for couples). Sleazier shows are concentrated around Leme, as are gay clubs; many gay clubs also around Lapa (Cinelândia), but good ones exist all over the city. *Stop-Night*, a disco bar at Av Atlântica (nr *Copacabana Palace* hotel) is a popular gay pick-up joint: be careful.

Many people look for Macumba religious ceremonies. Those offered on the night tours sold at hotels are not genuine, and a disappointment. You need a local contact to see the real ones, which are usually held in *favelas* and are none too safe for unaccompanied tourists.

Theatres: there are about 40 theatres in Rio, presenting a variety of classical and modern performances in Portuguese. Seats about US$15; some children's theatre is free.

● **Hospitals & medical services**
Vaccinations at *Saúde de Portos*, Praça 15 de Novembro (international vaccination book and ID required). *Policlínica*, Av Nilo Peçanha 38, rec for diagnosis and investigation. *Hospital Miguel Couto*, Mário Ribeiro 117, Gávea, has a casualty ward (free), but no eye doctors T 274-2121; these can be found at *Hospital Souza Aguiar*, Praça da República III (casuality ward also free), T 296-4114. The *Rio Health Collective* will help you contact an English-speaking doctor: dial 294-0282/325-3327/239-7401; ask for the 'dona da casa'.

Take note of local advice on water pollution; air pollution also occurs.

Dentist: English-speaking, Amílcar Werneck de Carvalho Vianna, Av Pres Wilson 165, suite 811. Dr Djorup, Av Beira Mar Mauro Suartz, R Visconde de Pirajá 414, room 509, T 287-6745, speaks English and Hebrew, helpful.

Public conveniences: there are very few in Rio de Janeiro, but many bars and restaurants (eg Macdonalds) offer facilities; just ask for the 'banheiro' (banyairoo). Good conveniences are to be found in the Shopping Centres.

● **Language courses**
Instituto Brasil-Estados Unidos, Av Copacabana 690, 5th floor, T 255-8332, 8-week course, 3 classes a week, US$200, 5-week intensive course US$260. Good English library at same address. *IVM Português Prático*, R do Catete 310, of 302, T 285-7842, F 285-4979, rec. *Curso Feedback*, branches in Botafogo, Centre, Barra and Ipanema, T 221-1863.

● Laundry

Fénix, R do Catete 214, Loja 20; Praça G Osório, Ipanema. Laundromat at 1216 Av NS de Copacabana; R Barata Ribeiro 662, Copacabana, self-service. In Rio Sul are self-service laundrettes such as *Lavlev*, about US$3-4 for a machine, inc detergent and drying, 1 hr, also at R Buarque de Macedo 43, Catete, R Voluntário da Patria 248, Botafogo, Av Prado Jnr 6313, Copacabana. *Lavlev Flamengo*, RC de Baepinédi 78, or R das Laranjeiras 43, L28.

● Places of worship

Places where worship is conducted other than in Portuguese: **Christ Church**, R Real Grandeza 99, Botafogo (Church of England/American Episcopalian). The British School, for children of 5-16, is nearby. **Chapel of Our Lady of Mercy,** R Visconde de Caravelas 48, Botafogo (Roman Catholic, with primary school). **Union Church:** (Protestant nondenominational) services held at R Parque da Lagoa de Marapendi, CP 37154-CEP 22609 Barra da Tijuca. **International Baptist Church**, R Desembargador Alfredo Russel 146, Leblon. **First Church of Christ Scientist**, Av Marechal Câmara 271, room 301. **Masonic Temple**, in the British School at R da Matriz 76, Botafogo. **Synagogues**, R Pompeu Loureiro 48, Botafogo, T 257-4299; R Barata Ribeiro 489, Copacabana, includes kosher bakery. **Swedish Church**, Igreja Escandinava, Av Rui Barbosa 170, Bloco B 1, 5 And, T 551-6696, open 1300-2200, Sun 1700-2100, will store luggage. **British Cemetery**, R da Gamboa 181, granted to the British community by Dom João, Regent of Portugal, in 1810. It is the oldest cemetery in Rio.

● Post & telecommunications

Post Office: central Post Office, R Primeiro de Março 64, at corner of R do Rosário; Av NS de Copacabana 540, and many other locations; all handle international post. There is a post office at the airport. **Poste Restante**: American Express, Av Atlântica 1702 loja B, Copacabana (for customers), and all large post offices (letters held for a month, rec, US$0.10/letter); Kontik Franstur will forward mail to their branches in Brazil without charge. Federal Express, Av Calógeras 23 (nr Sta Luzia church) T 262-8565, is reliable.

Telephones: international calls at Av Copacabana 540, 2nd floor, international airport, international telephone booths (blue), rodoviária, R Dias da Cruz 192, Méier-4, 24 hrs, 7 days a week, or at Santos Dumont airport, 1st floor (0530-2300). Also at Praça Tiradentes 41, a few minutes' walk from Metrô Carioca. R Visconde Pirajá, 111. Av NS de Copacabana, 540. R do Ouvidor, 60 centro. Larger Embratel offices have telex and fax.

● Shopping

Buy precious and semi-precious stones from reputable dealers. *H Stern* have shops at the airport, and all over Copacabana and Ipanema; they also offer a tour, with head-phone commentary, of their lapidary and designing workshops, on request; *Amsterdam Sauer* offer free taxi rides to their workshops. There are several good jewellery shops at the Leme end of Av NS de Copacabana: *Lido*, R Rodolfo Dantas 26B, T 541-8098, rec. For mineral specimens as against cut stones, try *Mineraux*, Av Copacabana 195, Belgian owner. *Saara* is a multitude of little shops along R Alfândega and R Sen dos Passos (between city centre and Campo Sant'ana) where clothes bargains can be found (especially jeans and bikinis). Little shops on Aires Saldanha, Copacabana (1 block back from beach), good for bikinis and cheaper than in shopping centres. *Malamada*, R da Carioca 13, rec for rucksacks.

Bookshops: for international stock, *Livraria Kosmos*, R do Rosário 155, good shop (in the centre and Av Atlântica 1702, loja 5) and there are many others, eg *Livros Técnicos*, R Miguel Couto 35, wide selection; *Nova Livraria Da Vinci*, Av Rio Branco 185 lojas 2, 3 and 9, all types of foreign books, *SAH* available; *Livraria Argumento*, R Dias Ferreira 417, Leblon, sells imported English books; also branches of *Sodiler* at airports and shopping centres. *Livrarias Siciliano*, Av Rio Branco 156, loja 26, European books, also at NS de Copacabana 830 and branches; French books at No 298. *Unilivros*, Largo do Machado 29C, French and English bestsellers (7 branches); *Livraria Nova Galeria de Arte*, Av Copacabana 291D, international stock. *El Dorado*, Av das Américas 4666, loja 207. Second-hand books also at *Livraria São José*, R Carmo 61 (only a few in English); *Livraria Brasileira*, Av Rio Branco 156, S/Loja 229; Aimée Gilbert, R da Carioca 38 (some in English); *Livraria Antiquário*, Sete de Setembro 207 and in R Pedro I, all in centre. Also on Av Marechal Floriano, nr Av Rio Branco, especially at No 63. On S side of Praça Tiradentes, *Casa dos Artistas* trades in second-hand paperbacks. Second-hand English books at the Anglican church, R Real Grandeza 99, Botafogo.

Cameras and film processing: Kodachrome slide film difficult to get in Rio. For processing, *Flash Studio*, R Visconde de Pirajá 156, expensive; *One Hour Foto*, in the Rio Sul and Barra shopping centres, is rec; *Honório*, R Vinícius de Moraes 146-E, stocks lithium batteries. Nikon camera repairs, *T Tanaka cia Ltda*, Av Franklin Roosevelt 39, of 516, T 220-1127.

Local press: *Balcão*, an advertising newspaper, US$1.50, twice weekly, offers apartments in and around Rio, language lessons, discounted tickets, items for sale, and advertises shops; similar advertisements in the classified sections of *O Globo* and *Jornal do Brasil*, daily. Both dailies have entertainments pages. *O Globo* has a travel section on Thur; the *Jornal do Brasil*'s Friday *Programa* is an essential 'what's-on' magazine, as is the *Rio* supplement to *Veja*, a weekly news magazine (*Veja* publishes similar supplements in other major cities). *Riotur's* monthly booklet listing main attractions; *Rio This Month* (less reliable), free from hotels. *TurisRio's* free magazine about the State of Rio de Janeiro is interesting; if your hotel does not have the above 3 publications, just ask at the reception of one of the larger establishments.

Markets: Northeastern market at Campo de São Cristóvão, with music and magic, on Sun mornings (bus 472 or 474 from Copacabana or centre). Saturday antiques market on waterfront, nr Praça 15 de Novembro (1000-1800), rec, and flea market Sat (0900-1900) in Praça 15; another in Largo da Carioca. Sunday stamp and coin market in Passeio Público. Sunday open-air handicrafts market (hippie fair) at Praça Gen Osório, Ipanema, 0800-1300 or 1400, touristy but fun. Markets on Wed 0700-1300 on R Domingos Ferreira and on Thur, same hours, on Praça do Lido, both Copacabana; also on Thur, good leather and jewellery market on 1 de Março in centre. Sunday market on R da Glória, colourful, cheap fruit, vegetables and flowers; early-morning food market, 0600-1100, R Min Viveiros de Castro, Ipanema. Excellent food and household-goods markets at various places in the city and suburbs (see newspapers for times and places).

Shopping centres: Rio Sul, at Botafogo end of Túnel Novo, Cassino (Copacabana), Norte Shopping (Todos os Santos), Plaza Shopping (Niteroi), Barra on Barra de Tijuca (see page 394). At São Conrado The Fashion Mall is smaller and more stylish.

● **Sports**

There are hundreds of excellent gyms and sports clubs; most will not grant temporary (less than 1 month) membership: big hotels may allow use of their facilities for a small deposit. *Paissandu Athletic Club*, Av Afrânio de Melo Franco 290, Leblon – tennis, bowls, swimming, Scottish dancing, Tues, April-Oct, 2000-2230, may admit non-members. *Jockey Club Racecourse*, by Jardím Botânico and Gávea, meetings on Mon and Thur evenings and Sat and Sun 1400, entrance US$1-2, long trousers required, a table may be booked. Take any bus marked 'via Jóquei'. Betting is by totalizator only. *Sociedade Hípico Brasileiro*, Av Borges de Medeiros 2448, T 246-8090, Jardim Botânico – riding. *Iate Clube do Rio de Janeiro*, Av Pasteur, Urca, T 295-4482 – yachting.

Cycling: tours (hire available) with *Rio Bikers*, R Domingos Ferreira 81, room 201, T 274-5872.

Golf clubs: there are both 18-hole and 9-hole courses at the Itanhangá Golf Club, Jacarepaguá, visiting cards from Av Rio Branco 26, 16th floor. The Gávea club, São Conrado, T 399-4141 and the Teresópolis Golf Club, Estrada Imbuí (Várzea) both have 18 holes. 9 holes at Petrópolis Country Club, Nogueira.

Hang-gliding: with Rejane Reis (US$100), Estrada da Canoa 722, Bl3-201, São Conrado, T 322-6972, F 239-2381. Ultra Força Ltda, Av Sernambetiba 8100, Barra da Tijuca, T 399-3114, 15 mins.

Paragliding: from Leblon beach with Sr Ruy Marra, Brazilian paragliding champion (US$75) T 322-2286 or find him at the beach: "Just fantastic!"

Rock climbing and hill walking: *ECA*, Av Erasmo Braga 217, room 305, T 242-6857/571-0484, personal guide US$100/day, owner Ralph speaks English; *Clube Excursionista Carioca*, also rec for enthusiasts, R Hilário Gouveia 71, room 206, T 255-1348, meets Wed, Fri.

● **Tour companies & travel agents**

American Express, see **Banks & money changers** above; *Roxy*, est 1948, Av Franklin Roosevelt, 71/601, Centro, CEP 20.021-120, T 532-0141, F 532-3165, ask for Michael or Ricardo Werwie who speak English, rec; *Exprinter*, Av Rio Branco, 128; *Manhattan Turismo Ltda*, R da Assembléia 10, GR 3503, Centro, T 242-3779/3064, very helpful, English spoken; *Metropol*, R São José 46, T 5335010, F 5337160, eco, adventure and culture tours to all parts of Brazil; *Tour Brazil*, R Farme de Amoedo 75/605, nr Ipanema, T 521-4461, F 021-521-1056, very good English spoken; *Victor Hummel*, Av Presidente Vargas 290/4, T 223-1262, Swiss-run, rec, T 231-1800. *Marlin Tours*, Av Copacabana 605/1201, T 255-4433, rec, Robin and Audrey speak English. *Quality Travel*, Av NS Copacabana 387, T 235-6888, F 236-6985, helpful with hotel bookings; *Hamburg Imobiliária*, see **Apartments** above, rec; *Hanseatic*, R Sete de Setembro 111/20, T 224 6672, centro, German run (English, French, Portuguese), rec.

Organized trips to Samba shows cost US$50 inc dinner, good but it's cheaper to go independently. Regular sightseeing tours operated by *Gray Line* (294-0393), *American Sightseeing* (236-3551), *Sul América* (257-4235), *Canbitur* (of Copacabana), *Passamar Turismo*, Av Rio Branco 25 (233-8883, 233-4833, 253-1125; also at *Hotel Nacional*). *Adrianotour*, T 208-5103, for guided tours, reservations and commercial services (English, French, German and Spanish spoken). *Sangetur*, Largo do Machado, 29 (Galeria Condor), Loja 39, T 205 0993 or 0245, credit cards only accepted for airplane tickets. *Dantur*, Largo do Machado, 29 (Galeria Condor) Loja 47, T 205 1144, Helena speaks English and is friendly and helpful. *Guanatur Turismo*, R Dias da Rocha 16a, Copacabana, T 235 3275, F 235 3664, sells long distance bus tickets. *Marcelo Niemeyer Armstrong*, Estrada das Canoas 722, Bl 2, apt 125, CEP 22610-210, T 322-2727/989-0074, F 322-5958, offers guided tours of Rio's favelas, safe, different and interesting. Similar tours are offered by Rejane Reis, see **Hang-gliding**, above.

● **Tourist offices**

There are several information centres. **Embratur**, R Mariz e Barros 13, nr Praça da Bandeira, T 273-2212, gives information on the whole country. **Riotur** (for the city of Rio): small, helpful information desk at R da Assembleia 10, 9th floor, has good city maps and a very useful free brochure 'Rioguia' written in both Portuguese and English. More information stands can be found at Pão de Açúcar cablecar station (0800-2000); Marina da Glória, Flamengo; Rodoviária Novo Rio (the bus station – 0600-2400; very friendly and helpful in finding accommodation but has no printed information) and at Copacabana, Av Princesa Isabel 183, T 542 8080 or 8084. Riotur also has a multilingual telephone service operating 24 hrs, T 580-8000. English information service, T 242-8000. **Flumitur** (for the state of Rio de Janeiro) at Rio International Airport, helpful with hotel information and booking, can sometimes arrange discounts, and R da Assembléia 10, 8th floor, very helpful. **Touring Clube do Brasil**, Pres Antônio Carlos 130 and Av Brasil 4294 (out of town) no English spoken. **Centro Cultural Banco do Brasil**, Primeiro Março 66, has a free, computerized information service.

Best guide to Rio, with excellent map, *Guia Quatro Rodas do Rio* in Portuguese and English (the *Guia Quatro Rodas do Brasil*, published annually in Nov also has a good Rio section). Also, *The Insider's Guide to Rio de Janeiro*, an annual guide book by Christopher Pickard, available from Rio bookshops, or enquire at Marlin Tours (T 255-4433). Many hotels provide guests with the weekly *Itinerário* (*Rio This Month*); also see **Local Press**, above.

NB Tourist packs are sold for US$25 at the International Airport – they are completely unnecessary.

Maps: *Guia Rex* street guide. *Guia Schaeffer Rio de Janeiro* is a good map. Maps are also available from Touring Clube do Brasil, newsstands, touring agencies and hotels; Geomapas tourist map is clear. Paulini, R Lélio Gama 75 (outside the entrance of the downtown tram station): topographical and other maps of Brazil and of South America. **NB** Tourist agencies do not normally provide lists of cheap accommodation for travellers; some initiative is required.

● **Useful addresses**

Tourist Police: Av Afrânio de Melo Franco, Leblon (opp Scala nightclub), T 511-5112. Renewal of 90-day visa, US$4.

● **Transport**

Local Buses Good services to all parts, very crowded and not for the aged and infirm during rush hours; buses have turnstiles so awkward if carrying luggage. Hang on tight, drivers living out Grand Prix fantasies. Fare normally about US$0.55. Bus stops are often not marked. The route is written on the side of the bus. Private companies operate a/c fresco buses which can be flagged down practically anywhere: Real, Pegaso, Anatur. They run from all points in Rio Sul to the city centre, Rodoviária and the airports. Fares about US$2 (US$5 to international airport). **Car hire**: Avis, Rio International airport, less helpful than office at Praia do Flamengo 224 (205-5796); **Nobre**, Gustavo Sampaio 826 (275-5297) and Av Princesa Isabel 350 (T 541-4646), Copacabana. **Telecar**, R Figueiredo Magalhães 701 (257-2620).

Many agencies on Av Princesa Isabel, Copacabana. Credit card virtually essential. Recent reports suggest it is cheaper to hire outside Brazil, you may also obtain fuller insurance this way. Remember service stations are closed in many places on Sat and Sun. Road signs are notoriously misleading in Rio, and you can end up in a *favela*. Take care if driving along the Estrada da Gávea to São Conrado as it is possible unwittingly to enter Rocinha, Rio's biggest slum. **Car repairs**: Kyoso Team Mecânico Siqueira Campos, at the entrance to the old tunnel, T 255-0506, a good mechanic who enjoys the challenge of an unusual car, rec. **Taxis**: the fare between Copacabana and the centre is US$9. Between 2300 and 0600 and on Suns and holidays 'tariff 2' is used. Taxis have red number plates with white digits (yellow for private cars, with black digits) and have meters. Smaller ones (mostly Volkswagen) are marked TAXI on windscreen or roof. Make sure meters are cleared and on tariff 1, except at those times mentioned above. Only use taxis with an official identification sticker on the windscreen. Don't hesitate to argue if the route is too long or the fare too much. Radio Taxis are safer but more expensive, eg Cootramo, 270-1442, Coopertramo, 260-2022, Cooper-Transpa, 593-2598, Transcoopass, 278-4888. Luxury cabs are allowed to charge higher rates. Inácio de Oliveira, T 225-4110, is a reliable taxi driver for excursions, only speaks Portuguese, rec. Grimalde, T 267 9812, has been rec for talkative daytime and evening tours, English, Italian, negotiate price. **Trams**: the last remaining tram runs from Largo da Carioca (where there is a museum, open only Fri 0830-1700) across the old aqueduct (Arcos) to Dois Irmãos or Paula Matos in Santa Teresa – historical and interesting, US$0.10. Service is cut in low season. The trams are open sided, do not carry valuables and do not linger at the Santa Teresa end. **Underground railway**: Metrô, good service, clean, a/c and fast. Line 1 operates between Tijuca and Botafogo, via the railway station and Glória; an extension to Arcoverde (Copacabana) is under construction. Line 2, runs from Engenho da Rainha, past the Maracanã stadium to Estácio. An 8.4km extension to Pavunda is being built. Operates 0600-2300, Sun 1400-2000 closed holidays. Fare US$0.60 single (12 tickets US$6); integrated bus/Metrô tickets available. Substantial changes in bus operations are taking place because of the extended Metrô system; buses connecting with the Metrô have a blue-and-white symbol in the windscreen.

Air Rio has two airports. The Santos Dumont airport on Guanabara Bay, right in the city, is used exclusively for Rio-São Paulo shuttle flights (US$300 return), air taxis and private planes. The shuttle services operate every 30 mins throughout the day from 0630 to 2230. Sit on right-hand side for views to São Paulo, other side coming back, book in advance for particular flights. The main airport (Galeão), on Governador Island, some 16 km from the centre of Rio, is in two sections, international and domestic (inc Vasp and Transbrasil's jet shuttle from Rio to São Paulo). Duty-free shops are well-stocked, but not especially cheap. Duty-free at Galeão is open to arrivals as well as departures. Only US dollars or credit cards are accepted on the air-side of the departure lounge.

The a/c '*Alvorada*' bus runs very frequently from the first floor of Galeão to Recreio dos Bandeirantes via the municipal rodoviária and city centre, Santos Dumont Airport, Flamengo, Copacabana, Ipanema and Leblon. Luggage is secured in the hold (receipted), passengers are given a ticket and fares collected during the journey; Zona Sul about US$5. The driver will stop at requested points (the bus runs along the seafront from Leme to Leblon), so it's worth checking a map beforehand so that you can specify your required junction. Returns by same route. A/c taxis (Cootramo and Transcopass) have fixed rates (US$40 Copacabana), buy a ticket at the counter nr the arrivals gate before getting into the car. The hire is for taxi, irrespective of number of passengers. Make sure you keep the ticket, which carries the number to phone in case of difficulty. Check at the Riotur counter before leaving, for folders, maps and advice. Ordinary taxis also operate with the normal meter reading. Do not negotiate with a driver on arrival, unless you are a frequent visitor. Town buses M94 and M95, *Bancários/Castelo*, take a circular route passing through the centre and the interstate bus station.

There are *câmbios* in the departure hall of airport; there is also a *câmbio* on the first floor of the international arrivals area, but it gives worse rates than the Banco do Brasil, 24-hr bank, 3rd floor, which will give cash advances against Visa card (beware 'officials' who say there are no *câmbios* or banks). There is a wider choice of restaurants outside passport control.

Trains There are suburban trains to Nova Iguaçu, Nilópolis, Campo Grande and elsewhere. Buses marked 'E Ferro' go to the railway station. The Silver Train, deluxe, overnight, runs to **São Paulo** daily at 2030, from Barão de Mauá station ('Leopoldina'), T 293-6328; a cabin on the 9-hr journey costs US$100 single.

Buses Rodoviária Novo Rio, T 291-5151 (Av Rodrigues Alves, corner with Av Francisco Bicalho, just past the docks). Some travel agents sell interstate tickets, or will direct you to bus ticket office in centre. Buses run from Rio to all parts of the country; it is advisable to book tickets in advance. Details of journey times and fares are given under destinations throughout the chapter.

International: Asunción, 1,511 km via Foz do Iguaçu, 30 hrs (Pluma), US$53; **Buenos Aires** (Pluma), via Porto Alegre and Santa Fe, 44 hrs, US$163 (book 2 days in advance); **Santiago** de Chile, with Pluma or Gral Urquiza, about 70 hrs.

The main bus station is reached by buses M94 and M95, *Bancários/Castelo*, from the centre and the airport; 126, 127, 136, *Rodoviária/Copacabana*; 170, *Rodoviária/Gávea*; 128, 172, *Rodoviária/Leblon*; these buses pass Botafogo and Flamengo. It has a Riotur information centre, very helpful. Left luggage, US$2.50. The local bus teminal is just outside the rodoviária: turn right as you leave and run the gauntlet of taxi drivers – best ignored. The rodoviária attracts thieves; exercise caution. The a/c Real bus (opp the exit) goes along the beach to São Conrado and will secure luggage. **If you need a taxi collect a ticket**, which ensures against overcharging, from the office inside the entrance (to Flamengo US$13). On no account give the ticket to the taxi driver.

Hitchhiking   To hitch to Belo Horizonte or Brasília, take a C-3 bus from Av Presidente Antônio Carlos to the railway station, cross through the station to a bus station, and catch the Nova Iguaçu bus. Ask to be let off at the Belo Horizonte turn off. For the motorway entrance N and S take bus 392 or 393 from Praça São Francisco.

Roads   Distances in km to some major cities with approximate journey time in brackets: Juiz de Fora, 177 (2¾ hrs); Belo Horizonte, 429 (7 hrs); São Paulo, 434 (6 hrs); Vitória, 519 (8 hrs); Curitiba, 839 (12 hrs); Brasília, 1,148 (20 hrs); Florianópolis, 1,154 (20 hrs); Foz do Iguaçu, 1,500 (21 hrs); Porto Alegre, 1,603 (26 hrs); Salvador, 1,690 (28 hrs); Recife, 2,309 (38 hrs); Fortaleza, 2,861 (48 hrs); São Luís, 3,093 (50 hrs); Belém, 3,187 (52 hrs).

THE STATE OF RIO DE JANEIRO: EAST FROM RIO

NITERÓI

(*Pop* 416,125; *CEP* 24000; *DDD* 021) Founded in 1573, the ex-capital of the State of Rio de Janeiro, is reached across Guanabara bay by bridge or ferries.

Places of interest

On this side of the bay are beaches which, though calm, can be as overcrowded and polluted as those in Rio. The forts on this side of the bay include Santa Cruz (16th century, still a military establishment), Barão do Rio Branco (1633), Gragoatá and Nossa Senhora da Boa Viagem. You should also visit the church of Boa Viagem (1633), built on an island connected to the mainland by a short causeway, a few minutes' walk from Icaraí beach. Nearby, on R Tiradentes, is the **Museu Antônio Parreira**, opens 1300, dedicated to the eponymous artist. The **Museu de Arqueologia de Itaipu** is in the ruins of the 18th century Santa Teresa Convent, and also covers the archaeological site of Duna Grande on Itaipu beach.

Local information
● Accommodation
A2 *Bucsky*, R Cel Tamarindo 150, Praia do Gragoatá, T 717-3322, F 717-3841.

C *Niterói Palace*, R Andrade Neves 134, T 719-2155, F 719-2800; *Icaraí Praia*, R Belisário Augusto 21, T 714-1414, F 710-6142, similar price. Youth Hostel, *AJ Solar dos Díos*, R Santo Eduardo 63, T 709-0686.

● Electric current
110 volts, AC, 60 cycles.

● Entertainment
Clubs: *Rio Cricket*, bus 57 from ferry. *Rio Sailing*, bus 33 marked 'via Froes'.

● Laundry
Lavlev, R Presidente Backer 138.

● Tourist offices
Flumitur information booth to the right of the ferry station.

● Transport
Crossing from Rio Ferry: from the 'barcas' at Praça 15 de Novembro, ferry boats and launches cross every 10 mins to Niterói (20-30 mins, US$0.40). There are also hydrofoils ('aerobarcas') every 10 mins (about 10 mins, US$4.50). Of the frequent ferry boat and hydrofoil services from Praça 15 de Novembro, Rio, the slow, cheaper ferry gives the best views.

Bus/car: the Rio-Niterói bridge (Ponte Costa e Silva) is 14 km long. Toll for cars, US$0.50. (The approach to the bridge is on the elevated motorway from the centre, or via Av Rio de Janeiro, in the Caju district; take Av Rodrigues Alves past the docks.) Bus 999 from the corner of Senador Dantas and Av Beira Mar, Rio, crosses the bridge to Niterói and Icaraí (US$0.75); also 996 and 998 from the Jardim Botânico (all three go to the Rodoviária in Rio).

LOCAL BEACHES

Near the Flumitur office you can take the 33 bus (marked 'via Froes') to the beaches of Icaraí, São Francisco and Jurujuba on the bay, a beautiful ride. Sit on the right-hand side. A few minutes' walk from where the bus route ends at Jurujuba are the attractive twin beaches of Adão and Eva, with lovely views of Rio across the bay. From Praça Gen Gomes Carneiro, take a 38 or 52 bus to Piratininga, Itaipu and Itacoatiara, fabulous ocean beaches and the best in the area, about 40 mins' ride through picturesque countryside (buses leave from the street directly ahead of the ferry entrance, at right angles to coast street). The undertow at Itacoatiara is dangerous, but the beach itself is safe.

LAGOS FLUMINENSES

To the E of Niterói lie a series of salt-water lagoons, the Lagos Fluminenses. Two small lakes lie behind the beaches of Piratininga, Itacoatiara and Itaipu near Niterói, but they are polluted and ringed by mud. The next lakes, Maricá and Saquarema, are much larger; though they are still muddy, the waters are relatively unpolluted, and wildlife abounds in the scrub and bush around the lagoons. At the outlet to the lake of Saquarema (turn right off the main road at Bacaxá) is the holiday village of **Saquarema**. The little white church of Nossa Senhora de Nazaré (1675) is on a green promontory jutting into the ocean. Saquarema is the centre for surfing in Brazil, and the national championships are held here each year in May. Beware of strong currents, though. Mil e Um bus Rio-Saquarema, every 2 hrs 0730-1800, 2 hrs, US$3.60.

The largest lake is **Araruama**, famous for its medicinal mud. The salinity is extremely high, the waters calm, and almost the entire lake is surrounded by sandy beaches, making it very popular with families looking for safe, unpolluted bathing. The major industry of the area is salt, and all around one can see the saltpans and the wind pumps used to carry the water into the pans. At the eastern end of the lake is **São Pedro de Aldeia**, which, in spite of intensive development, still retains much of its colonial charm and has a lovely Jesuit church built in 1723.

The ocean beaches beside these lagoons, except for the sheltered coves of Ponta Negra and Saquarema, are rough and lonely.

- **Accommodation** In the lake district: **Saquarema**: C *Pousada do Holandês*, Av Vilamar 377, at Itaúna beach, highly rec, many languages spoken by Dutch owner and his Brazilian wife (who runs the local day-care centre), good meals – follow the signs, or take a taxi (US$0.80), from Saquarema. Restaurant in Saquarema, *Tem Uma Né Chama Teré*, very good, in main square. There are several in **Araruama** and **São Pedro de Aldeia**. At Ponta Negra are **A3** *Pousada Colonial*, suites and bungalows in this range, inc breakfast, T Rio, 451-6254 for reservations, and **A3** *Solar Tabauna*, T 748-1626, pool, both highly rec. The whole area is perfect for camping; there are campsites (inc Camping Clube do Brasil) at Araruama (close to the *Parque Hotel*) and São Pedro de Aldeia.

- **Transport Road** A very steep road connects the beaches of Itaipu and Itacoatiara with BR-106 (and on to Araruama) via the village of Itaipu-Açu, with beach and good camping. Most maps do not show a road beyond Itaipu-Açu; it is certainly too steep for buses. An alternative to the route from Niterói to Araruama through the lagoons is via Manilla, Itaboraí and Rio Bonito, on the BR-101 and RJ-124; this is a fruit-growing region.

CABO FRIO

(Pop 86,615) 156 km from Rio, is a popular holiday and weekend haunt of Cariocas because of its cool weather, beaches, scenery, sailing and good under-water swimming (but mosquitoes are a problem). The ocean beach is much less frequented than the bay beach. The ruined São Mateus fort nearby was built by the French. There are random car searches for drugs on the road to Búzios.

- **Accommodation** A wide selection, from expensive down to **C** *Jangada*, Granaola 220, nr canal, good breakfast, rec. Youth Hostel, both sexes, open all year to IYHF members (E pp, more for non-members), on R Kubitschek, 1 block from bus station. 3 youth hostels in the area around Cabo Frio rodoviária and one in Arraial do Cabo, at R Joaquim Nabuco 23, nr Praça de Bandeiras (20 mins by bus from Cabo Frio). **Camping**: Clube do Brasil sites at Estrada dos Passageiros, nr town; at Km 135 on the Rio road, 4 km outside town, in Palmeiras; and at Arraial do Cabo on Praia dos Anjos, crowded beach. Also site at Cabo Yacht club.

● **Buses** Rodoviária is 2 km from centre. Bus from Rio every 30 mins, 2½ hrs, US$7.20. To Búzios, from local bus terminus in town centre, every hour, US$1.

BÚZIOS

(*Pop* 26,000; *CEP* 28905; *DDD* 0246) NE of Cabo Frio, an expensive, fashionable resort sprawling with low-rise (but attractive) development. It has 27 sandy coves, best seen by boat (*Queen Lori*, rec), US$22 – schooner trips of 2-3 hrs around the bay are very popular, calm unpolluted waters (superb for windsurfing), beautiful scenery, thriving nightlife. Tourist information office near bus stop. Very crowded during Brazilian holiday season and extremely difficult to get hotel bookings. Notable beaches are: Ossos, close to town; Azeda, very relaxed, topless OK; Geriba, about 2½ km out of town (turn left down the path between two Shell stations – it is marked); Tartaruga, not marked and not developed (take dirt road up small hill opp *Pousada Baer Búzios*); there is a restaurant and snack bar in season.

● **Accommodation** Plenty of good hotels and *pousadas*: eg **A1** *Pousada Happy*, on road to Raza on opp side of crossing to Rio, on beach, inc breakfast, rec, good windsurfing, German owner; **A2** *Pousada Hibiscus Beach*, R 1 No 22, Quadra C, Praia João Fernandes, T/F 23-6221, run by its British owners, 15 nice bungalows, garden, pool, inc breakfast, light meals available, help with car/buggy rentals and local excursions; **A3** *Pousada dos Búzios*, T 231155, a/c, terrace bar with lovely view; all central, rec; **C** *Pousada Casa de Pedra*, Trav Lúcio A Quintanilha 57, T 231499, TV, fridge, safe; **C** *Pousadinha em Búzios*, T 231448, very pretty, friendly; **C** *Bougainville Flats*, T 236501, Estrada Jose Bento Ribeiro Dantas 100 (on the main road that leads to the R de Pedras), comfortable, ceiling fan, fridge, central, rec; **C** *Brigitta's Guest House*, T 236157, R das Pedras 131, 28925-00. Youth hostel: Praia dos Amores, 7 blocks before the 1001 bus from Rio terminates in town centre, T (0246) 23-2422 US$10, rec. Private rooms can be rented in family homes. Camping is allowed but dangerous.

● **Places to eat** Several good restaurants (try the *camarão tropical*) and popular bars (*Chez Michou*, R das Pedras, is reportedly the mecca for trendy travellers).

● **Entertainment Watersports**: there are several agencies selling trips around the Bay of Buzios and its islands. *Buziana* offers a 5-hr trip for US$10 pp, rec; *Casamar*, T 232441 (located

in Rio de Janeiro), a highly professional dive operation offers one day diving trips costing US$25 pp if you bring your own equipment, US$50 pp if you rent equipment, both prices inc 2 bottles of air, Casamar is closed in May and Tues during low season, rec.

● **Transport** Best route from Rio (2 hrs by car) is the paved road towards Macaé, with a paved turnoff to Búzios (1001 bus from Rio, 4-5 a day, 2½ hrs, US$7). Direct road from Cabo Frio (bus 45 mins) is unpaved.

OTHER SEASIDE RESORTS

Continuing to the N, one comes to Barra de São João, **Rio das Ostras** (**C** *Hotel Mirante do Poeta*, T 64-1910, and others) and **Macaé** (**B** *Colonial*, Av Elias Agostinho 140, T 62-5155, helpful, comfortable; **B** *Panorama*, same avenue No 290, T/F 62-4455; **D** *Central*, R Rui Barbosa, nice, good breakfast, secure parking), all containing sheltered coves with good swimming and scuba diving. Macaé is also the supply centre for the offshore oil industry (bus Rio-Macaé 2½-3 hrs, every 30 mins, Mil e Um or Rápido Macaense; bus Macaé-Campos, 1¾ hrs, US$3).

NORTH TO ESPÍRITU SANTO

From Rio and Niterói the BR-101 runs NE past Macaé to Campos. At Km 222 is the **Biological Reserve of Poço das Antas**, the only natural habitat of the *mico-leão*, Golden Lion Tamarin (2 hrs' drive from Rio; it is not open to the general public, for details, Delegacia Estadual do Ibama, Av Pres Antônio Carlos 607-12°, CEP 20.000, Rio de Janeiro).

Campos (*Pop* 368,800) is a busy industrial city, some 276 km (4½ hrs by Mil e Um bus, hourly) from Rio de Janeiro (70 km from Macaé). It stands 56 km from the mouth of the Rio Paraíba, up which coffee planting originally spread to São Paulo state. Coffee is still grown near Campos, though the region is now one of the largest sugar-producing zones in Brazil. Important offshore oil discoveries have been made nearby.

● **Accommodation C** *Palace*, Av 15 de Novembro 143, T 22-7755, F 22-3661; **C** *Planície*, R 13 de Maio 56, T 23-4455; **C** *Terrazo Tourist*, Joaquim Távora 22, T 22-1405, 2-star.

As an alternative to BR-101 to Vitória, one

can take a detour inland, going through São Fidélis, Cambiasca, Itoacara and on to **Santo Antônio de Pádua** (*Pop* 36,330), 130 km from Campos, a pleasant town on the Rio Pomba. (**C** *Hotel das Águas*, a short walk from the centre, in a park with pool, health centre and bottling plant for the local mineral water; **D** *Braga*, in town, good food.) Take road No 393 to Itaperuna, Bom Jesus do Itabapoana and into Espírito Santo, then road No 484 to **Guaçuí** (**E** *Grande Hotel Minas*; *Restaurant Kontiki*, very good), one of the starting points for the Parque Nacional do Caparaó (see page 439). Then take the road 482 to Cachoeira do Itapemirim and the BR-101 (see page 419).

INLAND RESORTS

PETRÓPOLIS

(*Pop* 255,210; *CEP* 25600; *DDD* 0242) A summer hill resort and industrial city, 68 km N of Rio, it is reached by bus along a steep, scenic mountain road. Until 1962 Petrópolis was the 'summer capital' of Brazil; it was founded in 1843 as a summer refuge by Dom Pedro II. Now it combines manufacturing industry (particularly textiles) with floral beauty and hill scenery.

Places of interest

The **Museu Imperial** (Imperial Palace), which seems to express very faithfully what we know of Dom Pedro II's character, is a modest but elegant building, fully furnished and equipped, containing the Crown Jewels and other imperial possessions. It is assiduously well-kept: one might think the imperial family had left the day before one's visit, rather than in 1889. Open Tues-Sun, 1200-1730. Entry US$1.

The Gothic-style **Cathedral**, completed in 1925, contains the tombs of the Emperor and Empress (guide in English, US$0.50).

Museu Ferreira da Cunha, Fernandes Vieira 390 (old road to Rio) shows large collection of arms, open Sat and Sun (groups only; arrange in advance) 0900-1700.

See also the Summer home of air pioneer **Santos Dumont**, showing early inventions. **Palácio de Cristal** in Praça da Confluência, former imperial ballroom and now exhibition centre.

Excursions

Orquidário Binot, R Fernandes Vieira 390 (take bus to Vila Isabel; open Mon-Sat, 0800-1100, 1300-1700), a huge collection of orchids from all over Brazil (plants may be purchased).

Local information
● **Accommodation**
A3 *Casablanca Center*, Gen Osório 28, T 42-2612, F 42-6298; **A3** *Riverside Parque*, R Hermógéneo Silva 522, T 43-2312, F 43-2430.

B *Casablanca*, R da Imperatriz 286, T 42-6662, F 42-5946, good atmosphere in older part, pool, very clean; **B** *Margaridas*, R Bispo Pereira Alves 235, T 42-4686, chalet-type hotel set in lovely gardens with swimming pool, charming proprietors.

Camping: Associação Brasileira de Camping and YMCA, Araras district. Can reserve space through Rio YMCA, T 231-9860.

● **Places to eat**
Churrascaria Majórica, Av do Imperador 754; *Dom Giovanni*, same street, rec; *Bauernstube*, João Pessoa 297.

● **Sports**
Whitewater rafting: at Três Rios, on the junction of rivers Paraibuna, Piabanha and Paraíba do Sul, is arranged by *Klemperer Turismo*, T 43-4052 (also from Rio, T 252-8170), highly rec.

● **Transport**
Buses From Rio every 15 mins throughout the day (US$3.50), Sun every hour, 1½ hrs, sit on the left hand side for best views. Return tickets are not available, so buy tickets for the return on arrival in Petrópolis. 75 mins each way. The ordinary buses leave from the rodoviária in Rio; a/c buses, hourly from 1100, from Av Nilo Peçanha, US$4.25. There is a direct overnight bus from São Paulo.

TERESÓPOLIS

(*Pop* 120,700; *alt* 910m) Near the Serra dos Órgãos, 124 km NE of Rio, it was the favourite summer residence of the Empress Teresa Cristina. Building in recent years has destroyed some of the city's character. See the Colina dos Mirantes hill (30-min steep climb, sweeping view of the city and surroundings, a taxi up is not dear), the Sloper and Iaci lakes, the Imbui and Amores waterfalls, and the Fonte Judith.

Local festivals São Pedro, 29 June, is celebrated with fireworks.

● **Accommodation L3** *São Moritz*, Swiss-style, outside on the Nova Friburgo road, Km 36, T 741-1115, F 741-1135, with meals; **A1** *Montebello*, at Km 17, same road, T/F 742-2116, modern hotel with pool, with 3 meals, rec; **A2** *Alpina*, Parque Imbui, on Petrópolis road, T/F 742-5252; **D** *Várzea Palace*, R Sebastião Teixeira 41, T 742-0878, highly rec. Many cheap hotels in R Delfim Moreira, nr the Praça. **Youth hostel**: Retiro da Inglesa, 20 km on road to Friburgo, Fazenda Boa Esperança (reservations, R Papa Pio XII 50, Jardim Cascata, 25963 Teresópolis). **Camping**: National Park, entrance to Teresópolis from Rio, full facilities; Quinta de Barra, Km 3 on Petrópolis road, T 742-1825; Vale das Choupanas, Km 30 on Rio road.

● **Places to eat** *Taberna Alpina*, Duque de Caxias 131; *Bar Gota d'Água*, Praça Baltasar da Silveira 16 for trout or *feijoada* (small but rec and for *batidas*). Cafeteria in the ABC supermarket, clean and cheap, rec.

● **Banks & money changers** Cash or TCs at Teretur, Trav Portugal 46 (English spoken).

● **Tourist offices** In the bus station, T 742-0999.

● **Buses Rio-Teresópolis**: buses leave every 30 mins from rodoviária. Book the return journey as soon as you arrive at Teresópolis. Fare US$3. From Teresópolis to Petrópolis, every 2 hrs from 0900-2100, US$3.50. **Suggested day trip**: leave Rio 0800 or before (Viação Teresópolis) for the 1¾-hr ride into the mountains to Teresópolis (sit on right side). Upon arrival, buy a ticket right away for Petrópolis (Viação Teresópolis) for the 1200 bus. This gives you 2¾ hrs to wander around. The 90-min drive from Teresópolis to Petrópolis is beautiful. (Sit on left side.) The views on either side are spectacular. Again, upon arrival in Petrópolis, buy your ticket to Rio (Facil or Unica). Take the 1715 bus 'via Quitandinha', and you might catch the sunset over the mountains (in May, June, July, take the 1615 bus). This gives you time to visit most of the attractions listed above.

SERRA DOS ÓRGÃOS

About 30,000 ha of the **Serra dos Órgãos**, so called because their strange shapes are said to recall organ-pipes, are now a **National Park**. The main attraction is the precipitous Dedo de Deus (God's Finger) Peak. There is also the rock formation Mulher de Pedra 12 km out on the Nova Friburgo road, and the Von Martius natural-history museum. The highest point is the Pedra Açu, 2,400m. A path leads up the 2,260m Pedra do Sino, 3-4 hrs' climb. The park is the home of the very rare and

endemic grey-winged cotinga, as well as a number of other cotingas, berryeaters and other rare endemic birds. Anyone can enter the park and hike the trails from the Teresópolis gate, S of the town.

● **Access** Entrance to park, US$1, US$1.65 for the path to the top. A good way to see the Park is to do the Rio-Teresópolis-Petrópolis-Rio circuit; a scenic day trip. Tours of the park with Francisco of *Lazer Tours* are rec, T 742-7616, or find him at the grocery shop on R Sloper 1. Focus Tours of Belo Horizonte (see page 431) offers bird-watching tours.

● **Accommodation** Ibama (T 742-0266/0260) has some hostels, US$5.75 full board, or US$3.75 first night, US$2 thereafter, a bit rough. Camping, US$1.

NOVA FRIBURGO

(*Pop* 166,940; *Alt* 850m) A popular resort during summer months, in a beautiful valley with excellent walking and riding. It was founded by Swiss settlers from Fribourg. Cable car from Praça dos Suspiros 650m up the Morro da Cruz, for view of rugged country.

● **Accommodation A2** *Bucsky*, T 22-5052, F 22-9769, 5 km out on Niterói road, with meals; **A2** *Garlipp*, German-run, in chalets, with meals, at Muri, km 70.5 from Rio, 10 km from Nova Friburgo, T 42-1330, F 42-1444; **B** *Fabris*, Av Alberto Browne 148, T 22-2852, central, TV, hot showers, plentiful breakfast buffet. Under same ownership as *Garlipp* is **B** *Fazenda São João*, T 42-1304, 11 km from *Garlipp* up a side road, riding, swimming, sauna, tennis, hummingbirds and orchids; owner will meet guests in Nova Friburgo or even in Rio. **C** *Everest*, R Manoel António Ventura 75, T 22-7350, comfortable, good breakfasts; **C** *Maringá*, R Monsenhor Miranda 110, T 22-2309, **D** without bath, good breakfast, rec. **Camping** *Camping Clube do Brasil* has sites on Niterói road, at Caledônia (7 km out) and Muri (10 km out). Cambrás site also at Cônego, and private site at Fazenda Sanandu, 20 km out on same road.

● **Buses** From Rio (every hour), 2 hrs, US$5.

THE STATE OF RIO DE JANEIRO: WEST FROM RIO

VOLTA REDONDA

(*Pop* 220,085; *alt* 565m; *CEP* 27180; *DDD* 0243) On a broad bend of the Rio Paraíba,

113 km W of Rio along the railway to São Paulo, **Volta Redonda** has one of the largest steel works in Latin America. The mills are on the river bank and the town spreads up the surrounding wooded and gardened slopes. To visit, apply for a permit from the Companhia Siderúrgica Nacional, Av Treze de Maio 13, Rio de Janeiro (10 days in advance), or locally from the *Bela Vista* hotel. 2½-3 hr visits start at 0900.

● **Accommodation A2** *Bela Vista*, Alto de Boa Vista, on a hill overlooking town, T 43-2022, F 42-4190; **B** *Sider Palace*, R 33 No 10, T 42-0885/1032, F 42-6116; **D** *Embaixador*, Tr LA Félix 36, T 42-3665, 1-star.

● **Buses** From Rio, or minibuses, 2½ hrs, US$3.

MOUNTAIN TOWNS

North of Volta Redonda is **Miguel Pereira**, with an excellent mountain climate; nearby is the Javari lake, a popular recreational spot (**B** *Hotel-Fazendas Javari*, Praça Nações Unidas 35, near town, T 84-3611, restaurant, swimming pool, sports grounds, etc). A tourist train runs 56 km to Conrado on Sat, Sun and holidays, 0945, 3½ hrs, US$18 round trip, beautiful views of mountains, rivers and waterfalls. Further N, and still in the mountains are the university centres of **Vassouras** and **Valença**; both are historical monuments. 35 km from Valença is **Conservatória**, another colonial town. This region can also be reached via the Japeri turn-off on the BR-116 (a beautiful mountain drive).

Some 30 km W of Volta Redonda, in the town of **Resende** (*Pop* 91,575), is the Military Academy of Agulhas Negras. Grounds, with captured German guns of WW2, are open to the public. (Accommodation and restaurants in town.)

● **Buses** From Aparecida do Norte (see page 464), several daily, US$2.50; from Rio, frequent, 1¾ hrs, US$3.60, also from São Paulo and Volta Redonda. From Resende buses go to Barra Mansa (Resendense, 40 mins, US$1.25) where you can change for Belo Horizonte (Util 1230, 8-9 hrs, US$14.50).

In the same region, 175 km from Rio, is the small town of **Penedo** (5 buses a day from Resende) which in the 1930s attracted Finnish settlers who brought the first saunas to Brazil. This popular week-end resort also provides horse riding, and swimming in the Portinho river. (**A3** *Bertell*, T 51-1288, with meals; **C** *Pousada Penedo*, T 51-1309, safe, pool, rec, and others, 2 campsites.)

HILL RESORTS

Some 33 km beyond Penedo (part of road unpaved) is the small village of **Visconde de Mauá** (tourist office closed out of season). There are lots of places offering acupuncture, shiatsu massage, macrobiotic food, etc. Fine scenery and walks, lots of holidaymakers, pleasant atmosphere. There are roads to three other small hill towns: delightful 2 hrs' walk to **Maringá**, to Marumbá and to Mirantão, at about 1,700m, with semitropical vegetation. The Rio Preto, the border between Rio de Janeiro and Minas Gerais states, runs through the region. 6 km up river from Maringá are the Santa Clara falls; between Visconde de Mauá and Maringá is a natural pool in the river (turn left before crossing the bridge). After Marumbá follow signs to Cachoeira Escorrega, a small fall with cold natural swimming pool, 2 km. Horse rental in Visconde de Mauá from Berto (almost opp *Vendinha da Serra*), or Pedro (Lote 10); many places in Maringá.

● **Accommodation** Limited cheap lodgings: enquire at *Vendinha da Serra*, excellent natural food restaurant and store; next door is **F** *Pousada Dona Mariana*, rec, shared bath. *Pousada Beira Rio*, T 54-1801; *Pousada Vale das Hortênsias*, T 54-3030, both provide all meals; rec; ½ km on road to Maringá is *Hotel Turístico*, with handicrafts and homemade food, Italian owner, Nino, and his Brazilian wife, run excursions. Everywhere in town shuts at about 1900, except *Adega Bar*, open till midnight, live music and dancing (Sat only); reasonable pizza, and a restaurant in Lote 10, open till 2200. Youth Hostel, 5 km on road to Maringá. Several **D** hotels, *Bar do Jorge* café; *Forró da Marieta* for forró dancing.

● **Buses** To Visconde de Mauá from Resende, 1500 and 1630, 2 hrs, return 0900-0830, US$1.25. Direct bus Rio-Visconde de Mauá, Cidade de Aço, 0900 daily, plus one in evening, 3½ hrs, US$8.50.

ITATIAIA NATIONAL PARK

Founded 1937 on the Serra de Itatiaia in the Mantiqueira chain of mountains, the park s a few kilometres N of the Via Dutra (Rio-São Paulo highway). The road to it is paved. The town of Itatiaia is surrounded by picturesque mountain peaks and lovely waterfalls. This is a good area for climbing (Pico das Agulhas Negras 2,787m, Pico da Prateleira 2,540m), trekking and bird-watching. The southern masked titi monkey is common, recognizable by its loud hee-haw-like call. Information and maps can be obtained at the park office. Worth seeing are the curious rock formations of Pedra de Taruga and Pedra de Maçã, and the waterfall Véu de Noiva (many birds). The Administração do Parque Nacional de Itatiaia operates a refuge in the park which acts as a starting point for climbs and treks: information on these from Clube Excursionista Brasileira, Av Almte Barroso 2, 8th floor, T 220-3695, Rio. Três Picos wildlife trail near *Hotel Simon*; very difficult to visit park without a car (70 km from *Hotel Simon* to other side), but hotel is helpful. There is a Museum of Flora and Fauna, closed Mon. Entrance to Park, US$1.

● **Accommodation** Basic accommodation in cabins and dormitories is available in the park; you will need to book in season, say 30 days in advance, by writing to Administração do Parque Nacional de Itatiaia, Caixa Postal 83657, Itatiaia 27580-000, RJ, T (0243) 52-1652. **L3** *Simon*, Km 13 park road, T 52-1122, with meals, lovely views, beautifully set, rec; **A2** *Repouso Itatiaia*, Km 11 park road, T 52-1110, F 52-1509, with meals; **A3** *Fazenda da Serra*, Via Dutra Km 151, T 52-1611, with meals; **A3** *Hotel do Ypé*, Km 13 park road, T 52-1453, with meals; **B** *Pousada do Elefante*, 15 mins' walk back down hill from *Hotel Simon*, good food, swimming pool, lovely views, may allow camping; cheap lodging at R Maricá 255, T 52-1699, possibility of pitching a tent on the premises, located close to the National Park. **Camping Clube do Brasil**: site is entered at Km 148 on the Via Dutra.

● **Buses** A bus from Itatiaia, marked *Hotel Simon*, goes to the Park, 1200, returns 1700; coming from Resende this may be caught at the crossroads before Itatiaia. Through tickets to São Paulo sold at a booth in the large bar in the middle of Itatiaia main street.

ENGENHEIRO PASSOS

Further along the Dutra Highway (186 km from Rio) is the small town of **Engenheiro Passos**, from which a road (BR-354) leads to São Lourenço and Caxambu in Minas Gerais (see page 440), passing **Agulhas Negras**. One can climb Agulhas Negras from this side by taking the road from Registro pass (1,670m) to the Abrigo Rebouças refuge, which is manned all year round (take your own food, US$1.25 to stay), at 2,350m.

● **Accommodation** **A2** *Villa Forte*, 1 km from town, T 52-1219, with meals. Nine campsites in the area.

THE NEW RIO-SANTOS HIGHWAY

This section of the BR101, is one of the world's most beautiful highways, hugging the forested and hilly 'Green Coast' SW of Rio. It is now complete through to Bertioga (see page 458), which has good links with Santos and São Paulo. Buses run from Rio to Angra dos Reis, Parati, Ubatuba, Caraguatatuba, and São Sebastião, where it may be necessary to change for Santos. Hotels and *pousadas* have sprung up all along the road, as have expensive housing developments, though these have not spoiled the views. The coast is littered with islands, beaches, colonial settlements and mountain fazendas: the drive should take 7 hrs, but it would be better to break the journey and enjoy some of the attractions.

ITACURUÇÁ

91 km from Rio, a delightful place to visit: there is fine scenery, peace and quiet, with islands off the coast.

The sea is too polluted for bathing, but you can walk along the railway to Castelo where the beach is cleaner. Ilha de Itacuruçá can also be reached from **Muriqui**, a popular beach resort 9 km from Itacuruçá; bathing also in the Véu de Noiva waterfall. The next beach along the coast is Praia Grande.

● **Accommodation** On Ilha de Itacuruçá, is **L2** *Hotel Pierre*, reached by boat from Coroa Grande, N of Itacuruçá on the mainland, 5 mins (boats also go from Itacuruçá); restaurant, bars, sporting facilities. For bookings T/F 788-1560, T Rio 247-8938, or Saveiros Tours, 267-2792. **L3** *Hotel Jaguanum*, Ilha de Jaguanum, Itacuruçá, has apartments and chalets with private bathrooms, full board. There are beautiful walks around the island. Reservations for the hotel inc the boat trip to and from the island (at 1000 and 1700). The only extra is the bus, US$6 return, which picks you up at your hotel. T 235-2893 or 237-5119, in Rio, or enquire at *Sepetiba Turismo*, Av NS de Copacabana 605, s 202.

MANGARATIBA

(*Pop* 17,920) This fishing village half-way from Rio to Angra dos Reis, has muddy beaches, but pleasant surroundings and better beaches outside town, for example Ibicuí, São Brás, Praia Brava, Saco, Guiti and Cação.

● **Accommodation** D *Mendonça*, without breakfast or bath, good; 2 others, more expensive; **F** *Sítio Santo Antônio 12*, T 789-2192, family run, owner Carlito is proud of his shell collection, rec. At Rio das Pedras is *Club Med*, Km 55, Mangaratiba, CEP 23880, RJ, T 021-789-1635, F 021-789-1312.

● **Transport Buses** From Rio Rodoviária 7 a day, US$3. **Ferry** Daily ferry (Conerj) to Ilha Grande island (see below), at 0800 daily, 1½ hrs, highly rec; return ferry Mon, Wed, Fri at 1700, Tues, Thur at 1100, Sat, Sun at 1600. Fare US$3.60. Tues and Thur departures continue to Angra dos Reis. Ferry departures and destinations can be checked at ferry station at Praça Quinze de Novembro, Rio.

ANGRA DOS REIS

Angra dos Reis (*Pop* 85,220; *CEP* 23,900; *DDD* 0243), said to have been founded in 1502, is 197 km SW of Rio by road. A small port with an important fishing and ship-building industry, it has several small bays with good bathing within easy reach and is situated on an enormous bay full of islands. Boat trips around the bay are available, some with a stop for lunch on the island of Jipóia (5 hrs, US$9 pp; boats for hire US$12/hr). Of particular interest are the convent of Nossa Senhora do Carmo, built in 1593, the parish church (1626), the ruins of the Jacuecanga seminary (1797), and the Senhor do Bonfim church (1780).

● **Accommodation** **L3** *Frade*, road to Ubatuba (Km 123 on BR-101, 36 km), T/F 65-1212; **L3** *Porto Aquarius*, Saco de Itapirapuã, T 65-1642, F 65-1766, out of town (access from Km 101 on BR-101, 13 km) lots of facilities, pleasant, helpful staff. At Km 115 on BR-101 is **A2** *Hotel Porto Bracuhy* (T 65-3939) with lots of facilities for watersports, nightly shows and

dancing, restaurant, etc (23 km from Angra dos Reis). **B** *Londres*, R Pompéia 75, T 65-0044, F 65-0511; **B** *Palace*, Carvalho 275, T 65-0032, F 65-2656; **C** *Caribe*, R de Conceição 255, T 65-0033, F 65-3450, central, rec. Youth Hostel at Km 115 on Estrada Rio-Santos.

● **Places to eat** *Taberna 33*, Raul Pompéia 110, good, popular, moderate prices; *Tropicalitá*, Largo do Convento do Carmo.

● **Sports Diving**: *Aquamaster*, Praia da Enseada, US$60 for two dives with drinks and food, take bus marked 'Retiro' from the port in Angra.

● **Transport Trains** The historic *trem da mata atlântica* has been reopened, making the coastal trip to Lidice on weekends only, 1030 (has restaurant car). **Buses** Hourly from Rio's rodoviária, Viação Eval, take the 'via litoral' bus and sit on the left, US$7, 2½ hrs. Tourist information opp the bus station, very good. **Ferry** 2 hrs by boat to Ilha Grande, US$4 one way (Mon, Wed, Fri at 1500, return 1000 – so you have to stay 2 nights; for day trips, go from Mangaratiba).

ROUTES A road runs inland (about 18 km beyond Angra), through Getulândia, to join the BR-116 either just S of Pirai or near Volta Redonda, through nice mountain scenery.

ILHA GRANDE

A 2-hr ferry makes a most attractive trip through the bay to Abraão, on **Ilha Grande**, once an infamous pirate lair, and now occupied principally by fishermen and one of Brazil's larger prisons. Ask in the port at Angra dos Reis for a fishing boat going to Proveta, where you can stay in boat sheds or, if lucky, with a fisherman. It is a beautiful village, from which you can walk through tropical forest on a mountain to Praia do Aventureiro (a day's leisurely walk each way), or go by boat. Take mosquito precautions and register with police post in Abraão.

● **Accommodation** **A1** *Paraiso do Sol* (full board, 2 hrs' walk from Abraão, or hire a boat, reservations, Rio, T 262-1226). Hotel reservations are necessary. Many new *pousadas*: eg **B** *Pousada da Vanda*, T 285-2429, in green surroundings; **C** *Beto's*, T 780-1242, central, rec; **D** *Hotel Ori*, R Prof Lima, rec; **D** *Sonia/Tuti*, R Antonio Moreira 80, T 654512, 5 mins from beach, small house with 2 rooms, rec; **D** *Albatroz*, R das Flores 108, T 627-1730, rec); alternatively you can camp on beaches, or rent a room (E) in Abraão.

PARATY

Beyond Angra dos Reis, the road continues 98 km along the coast, past the nuclear-power plant at Itaorna, to **Paraty** (*Pop* 25,000; *CEP* 23970; *DDD* 0243), a charming colonial town. The centre has been declared a national historic monument in its entirety. It was the chief port for the export of gold in the 17th century and a coffee-exporting port in the 19th century. The opening of the railway from the Paraíba Valley to Rio led to Paraty being effectively isolated until its 'rediscovery' in the 1950s as a tourism and cultural centre. There are four churches: **Santa Rita** (1722) built by the 'freed coloured men' in elegant Brazilian baroque; **NS do Rosário e São Benedito** (1725, rebuilt 1757), R do Comércio, built by black slaves; **NS dos Remédios** (1787-1873, but unfinished), open Mon, Wed, Fri, Sat 0900-1200, Sun 0900-1500, and **NS das Dores** (1800), open Thur 0900-1200, a small chapel facing the sea. The last two were the whites' churches. There is a great deal of distinguished Portuguese colonial architecture in delightful settings. On the northern headland is a small fort, **Forte do Defensor Perpétuo**, 15 mins' walk, pleasant views. Also here is the **Museum of Arts and Popular Traditions**. The town centre is out of bounds for motor vehicles, in spring the roads are flooded, while the houses are above the water level. It is now very popular with tourists at weekends and on holidays.

Excursions

Beaches: **Praia do Pontal**, 10 mins' walk, not very clean; **Praia do Forte** and **Praia do Jabaquara**, worth visiting. **Paraty Mirim**, a small town 27 km away with old buildings and nice beaches, 4 buses a day (3 on Sun).

Fazenda Murycana, an old sugar estate and *cachaça* distillery with a small zoo, excellent restaurant, horse riding. Take Penha/Ponte Branca bus, 4 a day; beware mosquitoes, take repellent and don't wear shorts.

Local festivals

Feb/Mar: *Carnival*. **Mar/April**: *Semana Santa*, religious processions and folk songs. **July**: *Semana de Santa Rita*. **Aug**: *Festival da Pinga, cachaça* fair. **Sept**: *Semana da NS dos Remédios*, processions and religious events. **Sept/Oct**: *Spring Festival of Music*, concerts in front of Santa Rita church; the city is decorated with lights for Christmas, **31 Dec**: *Reveillon*, a huge party with open-air concerts and fireworks (reserve accommodation in advance).

Local information

● **Accommodation**

L3 *Pousada Pardieiro*, R do Comércio 74, T 71-1370, F 71-1139, attractive colonial building with lovely gardens, but always full at weekends, does not take children; **L3** *Pousada do Sandi*, Largo do Rosário 1, T 71-2100, F 71-1236, 18th century building, charming, spacious rooms; **A1** *Pousada Porto Parati*, R do Comércio, T 71-1205, F 71-2111, good value, highly rec; **A1** *Pousada do Príncipe*, Roberto Silveira 289, T 71-2266, F 71-2120, all facilities, pool, highly rec; **A3** *Pousada Mercado do Pouso*, Largo de Santa Rita 43, T/F 71-1114, opp port and Santa Rita, rec; **A3** *das Canoas*, R Silveira 279, T 71-1133, F 71-2005, rec, swimming pool, a/c; **A3** *Pousada do Portal*, Av

Beira-Rio 100, T 71-2221, charming, but some distance from centre, relaxing.

B *Morro do Forte*, R Orlando Carpinelli, T/F 71-1211, lovely garden, good breakfast, pool, German owner Peter Kallert offers trips on his yacht, rec.

C *Pouso Familiar*, R J V Ramos 262, run by Belgian (Joseph Yserbyt) and his Brazilian wife (Lucia), nr bus station, laundry facilities, English, French, German and Flemish spoken, T 71-1475, rec; **C** *Pousada do Corsário*, Beco do Lapeiro 26, T 71-1866, F 71-1319, a/c, TV, fridge, swimming pool, rec; **C** *Solar dos Gerânios*, Praça da Matriz, T/F 71-1550, beautiful colonial building, hard beds, but rec.

D *Marendaz*, R Patitiba 9, T 71-1369, with breakfast, simple, charming; **D** *Pousada Miramar*, Abel de Oliveira 19, T 71-2132, good value, 1 room has own kitchen, rec; **D** *Tia Palminas Lua Nova*, Mal Deodoro s/n, cheap, pleasant, central.

Camping: there is a small Camping Club site on the fine Pontal beach, good, very crowded in Jan and Feb, US$8 pp, T 71-1877. Also at Praia Jabaquara, T 71-2180.

● **Places to eat**
Hiltinho, R Mal Deodoro 233, historical centre, local dishes, excellent seafood, good service; *Corto Maltese*, R do Comércio 130, Italian; *Punto di Vino*, R Mal Deodoro 129, excellent Italian; *Dona Ondina*, R do Comércio 2, by river, family restaurant, good value (closed Mon, Mar-Nov); *Cafe Paraty*, R da Lapa e Comércio, sandwiches, appetizers, light meals, also bar at weekends with live music; *Umoya*, R Com José Luiz, video bar and café, live music at weekends; *Bar Dinho*, Praça da Matriz at R da Matriz, good bar with live music at weekends, sometimes mid-week. Cheaper restaurants are outside the historical centre, mainly on Av Roberto Silveira.

● **Banks & money changers**
Banco do Brasil, Av R Silveira, nr bus station, exchange 1100-1430, ask for the manager.

● **Electric current**
110 volts.

● **Entertainment**
The Puppet Show, R Dona Geralda 327, T 71-1575, Wed, Sat 2100, world-famous puppet show. *Clube Bandeirantes*, for dancing (Fri Brazilian, Sat funk, Sun dance and disco music), popular, entry US$3-5.

● **Post & telecommunications**
Post Office: Rua da Cadeia e Beco do Propósito, 0800-1700, Sun 0800-1200.
Telephones: Telerj for international calls, Praça Macedo Soares, opp tourist office. Local calls from public phones.

● **Tour companies & travel agents**
Paraty Tours, Av R Silveira 11, T/F 71-1327, English and Spanish spoken; *Sol Nascente*, Av R Silveira 58, T/F 71-1536; *Manunguá*, R Domingos Gonçalves de Abreu 3, T 71-2188. All can arrange schooner trips, city tours, trekking in the rain forest and on the old gold trail, visits to Trindade beach, mountain biking, sugar estate visits and transfers. *Narwhal*, T 71-1399, and *Cavalho Marinho*, R da Lapa, T/F 71-2148, offer diving. *Antigona*, Praça da Bandeira 2-Centro Histórico, T/F 71-1349, daily schooner tours, 5 hrs, bar and luncheon on board, rec. *Siberana da Costa*, T 71-1114, and others offer schooner trips in the bay, US$15-US$20, 6 hrs, meals sometimes included, rec.

● **Tourist offices**
Centro de Informações Turísticas, Av Roberto Silveira, nr entrance to historical centre, T 71-2148.

● **Transport**
6 buses a day to **Rio** (241 km, 3¾ hrs, US$15, Eval) and to **Angra dos Reis** (1½ hrs, every 1 hr 40 mins, US$4.20); 2 a day to **Ubatuba** (75 km), **Taubaté** (170 km) and **Guaratinguetá** (210 km); 2 a day to **São Paulo** (304 km, 5½ hrs, US$12, Reunidas, booked up quickly) and São Sebastião.

The coast road continues from Paraty into the State of São Paulo. Another road, rough but scenic, climbs the Serra do Mar to Cunha and Guaratinguetá, also in São Paulo.

Espírito Santo

THE COASTAL state, north of Rio de Janeiro, which has a mountainous interior and a hot, damp seaboard. It is an important grower of coffee. In the north there are large forests containing hardwoods.

CAMPOS TO VITÓRIA

North of Campos (see page 411) is the State of Espírito Santo (*Pop* 2,598,230) with its capital at Vitória. The people are known as Capixabas, after a former Indian tribe. The BR-101 passes 12 km from **Cachoeiro do Itapemirim** (*Pop* 140,400), a busy city on both banks of the fast-flowing Rio Itapemirim; many hotels of all classes.

There is also a coastal route N. Just across the frontier between the states is the resort town of **Marataízes**, with good beaches.

● **Accommodation A2** *Praia*, Av Atlântica 99, T 532-2144, F 532-3515, on beach; **A2** *Saveiros Palace*, Av Miramar 119, T 532-1413, F 532-1285, on beach; **B** *Dona Judith*, Av Lacerda de Aguiar 353, T 532-1436, F 532-1305. **Camping**: Municipal site on Praia do Siri, 10 km from centre; Xodó private site, Av Atlântica, 2 km from centre.

46 km N, at **Anchieta**, is **A3** *Hotel Thanharu Praia*, T 536-1246, F 536-1466, good. Near Anchieta are Praia dos Castelhanos and Praia Iriri, 30 km from Guarapari, served by a regular bus; 2 beaches, beautiful setting, lodging in private houses is possible. A little further N is the fishing village of **Ubu** with **A3** *Pousada Alba Ubu*, R Aleixo Neto 1762, T 361-1320, fully equipped, half board.

GUARAPARI

Further N, 58 km S of Vitória, is **Guarapari** (*Pop* 61,600), whose beaches attract many people seeking cures for rheumatism, neuritis and other complaints, from the radioactive monazitic sands. Information about the sands can be found at the Casa de Cultura, the former seat of the prefeitura, which was built in 1749 (open from 1300), and at the Antiga Matriz church on the hill in the town centre, built in 1585.

Like Marataízes, Guarapari is very crowded mid-Dec to end-February.

● **Accommodation A1** *Porto do Sol*, Av Beira Mar 1, T 361-1100, F 261-2929, Mediterranean style village on rocky point overlooking a calm beach, pool, sauna, etc, rec; **A2** *Atlântico*, Av Edísio Cirne 332, T 261-1237 on beach, rec; **C** *Mariland*, R Silva Mello 98, T 261-0553, nr beach, rec; **C** *Vieira 323*, R Joaquim da Silva, T 261-0185, rec; **C** *do Angelo*, R Pedro Caetano 254, T 261-0230, rec; **C** *Costa Sul*, R Getúlio Vargas 101, breakfast, loads of mosquitoes, otherwise rec; **C** *Bom Jesus*, R Pedro Caetano 156, T 261 1184, breakfast, fan, simple, central, good, rec. **Camping**: Camping Clube do Brasil, Setiba beach, 9 km from centre, T 262-1325. Cambrás site off Vitória highway close to beach, 4 km from centre. Private site nr Cambrás site.

● **Places to eat** *Sonho do Mel*, R Joaquim da Silva Lima, sorvetes, sopas, teâ-room, very good.

● **Buses** Alvorada has separate rodoviária from Itapemirim/Penha, Sudeste, São Gerardo and others. They are close together, 15 mins' walk from the city centre or US$8 by taxi. Penha tickets are sold at *R-Tur Turismo*, in the centre at R Manoel Severo Simões e R Joaquim da Silva Lima where air tickets, free brochures, maps, and hotel addresses can also be obtained. Bus from Vitória, 1 hr with Sudeste, US$2.10. To **Rio** with Itapemirim, 2 a day, US$11.

VITÓRIA

(*Pop* 258,245; *CEP* 29,000; *DDD* 027). Two bridges connect the island on which **Vitória** stands with the mainland. The town is beautifully set, its entrance second only to Rio's, its beaches quite as attractive, but smaller, and the climate is less humid.

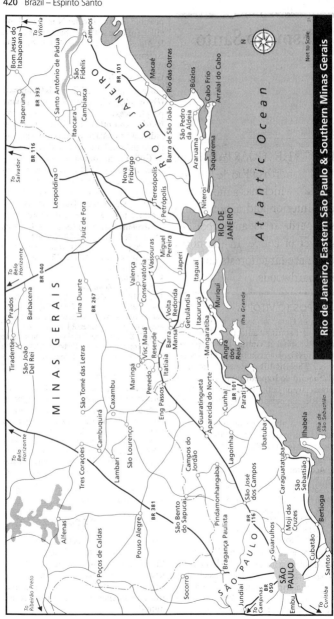

Rio de Janeiro, Eastern São Paulo & Southern Minas Gerais

A rail connection westwards with Minas Gerais transports for export iron ore, coffee and timber. Port installations at Vitória and nearby Ponta do Tubarão have led to some beach and air pollution at places near Vitória, such as Camburi (quite a pleasant beach, though, fair surf).

Places of interest

On Av República is the huge **Parque Moscoso**, an oasis of quiet, with a lake, playground and tiny zoo. The **Teatro Carlos Gomes**, on Praça Costa Pereira, often presents plays, also jazz and folk festivals. The upper, older part of town, reached by steep streets and steps, is much less hectic than the lower harbour area which suffers dreadful traffic problems.

See the mostly ruined, fortified monastery of **Nossa Senhora da Penha**, on a high hill above Vila Velha; the views are superb. The Dutch attacked it in 1625 and 1640. **Vila Velha**, reached by a bridge across the bay, has an excellent beach, but it is built up and noisy: take bus from Vitória marked Vilha Velha; for bigger waves go to Barra do Jucu. There is also a pleasant ferry service to Vila Velha.

Excursions

Visit **Santa Leopoldina** or **Domingos Martins**, both around 45 km from Vitória, less than an hour by bus (2 companies run to the former, approx every 3 hrs). Both villages preserve the architecture and customs of the first German and Swiss settlers who arrived in the 1840s. Domingos Martins (also known as Campinho) has a Casa de Cultura with some items of German settlement (Hotels include **C** *Imperador*, Praça Gerhardt 275, T 268-1115). Santa Leopoldina has interesting museum (open Tues-Sun, 0900-1100 and 1300-1800) covering the settlers' first years in the area.

To **Santa Teresa** (*Pop* 39,365), a charming hill town 2½ hrs by bus from Vitória (US$3.60, beautiful journey). Two hotels, **C** *Pierazzo*, Av G Vargas 115, T 259-1233, **D** *Glebo*, clean, and many restaurants. There is a unique hummingbird sanctuary at the **Museu Mello Leitão**, which is a library including the works of the hummingbird and orchid scientist, Augusto Ruschi. Hummingbird feeders are hung outside the library (open Sat-Sun 1200-1700, at other times with permission). Also the Nova Lombardia National (renamed **Dr Augusto Ruschi**) **Biological Reserve**, a forest rich in endemic bird species. Previous permission must be obtained to visit from Bento Ferreira at Ibama, Av Mal Mascarenhas de Moraes 2487, CP 762, Vitória ES, CEP 29.000.

Local information

● **Accommodation**

A1 *Porto do Sol*, Av Dante Michelini 3957, Praia de Camburi, T 327-2244, F 327-2711, 7 km from centre, overlooking sea; **A3** *Senac Hotel* (Government-run hotel school), luxurious, swimming pool, restaurant, on the ocean at R Bráulio Macedo 417, Ilha do Boi, T 325-0111, F 325-0115.

D *Avenida*, Av Florentino Avidos 350(ish), T 223-4317/0770, with breakfast, rec; **D** *Vitória*, Cais de São Francisco 85, nr Parque Moscoso, excellent restaurant, changes money, rec.

E *Europa*, Sete de Setembro, corner of Praça Costa Pereira, noisy but cheap, good value restaurant (nearby is a good value vegetarian restaurant and a money changer, ask at the hotel). Adequate hotels opp Rodoviária. Hotels located in beach areas, Camburi to the N, Vila Velha to the S, both about 15 mins from city centre.

Youth hostel: R Hugo Viola 135, T 325-6010, take 'Universitário' bus, get off at first University stop.

● **Places to eat**

Mar e Terra opp Rodoviária, good food, live music at night; *Lavacar* and many others at Praia Camburi offer food and live music.

● **Banks & money changers**

Local banks. **Plumatur**, Av Governador Bley 465, Edif Glória, Conj 101 (also tourist information, coffee). **Mastercard**, cash against card, Av Jerônimo Monteiro 1000, Grupo 414/424, Ed Trade Center, Centro.

● **Embassies & consulates**

Danish, R do Sol 141, Sala 210, T 222-4075, open 0900-1300, 1500-1900.

● **Post & telecommunications**

Telecommunications: Embratel, Palácio do Café, Praça Costa Pereira 52.

● **Tourist offices**

Emcatur, Av Getúlio Vargas (corner of Av Jerônimo Monteiro), and at rodoviária (friendly, good free map).

● **Transport**

Trains   Daily passenger service to Belo Horizonte, 14 hrs, US$10 1st class, US$7 2nd, also a very comfortable 'Especial' class.

Buses   Rodoviária is 15 mins' walk W of centre. Rio, 8 hrs, US$14.25 (*leito* 18.50). Salvador, 18 hrs, US$30; Porto Seguro direct 11 hrs with lots of stops, US$20 (also *leito* service); alternatively, take bus to Eunápolis, then change buses which run every hour, US$2. To hitch to Salvador, take a bus to Sara, which is beyond Carapina; alight where the bus turns off to Sara.

NORTH OF VITÓRIA

136 km N of Vitória is **Linhares** (*Pop* 119,500) on Rio Doce, with good hotels and restaurants.

Linhares is close to three **nature reserves**: the **Linhares Reserve** owned by CVRD (the state-owned mining company) is possibly the largest remaining lowland tract of Atlantic forest; permission from the reserve's director must be obtained to visit (very good birdwatching). The **Sooretama Biological Reserve**, NW of the CVRD Reserve, on left of highway, protects tropical Atlantic rain forest and its fauna and birds (it contains several bird species not found in CVRD Reserve). For permission to visit contact Ibama at address above.

The **Comboios Biological Reserve**, just S of Linhares, is designed to protect the species of marine turtles which frequent this coast (for information, contact Ibama).

● *Focus Tours*, Belo Horizonte (page 431) offers 1-week birding and general nature tours combining Museu Mello Leitão, Nova Lombardia, CVRD Reserve and Sooretama; many bird and orchid species are found in these reserves and apparently nowhere else.

CONCEIÇÃO DA BARRA

84 km N of Linhares is **São Mateus**, a pleasant town, 13 km from good beaches (buses). The most attractive beaches in the State, however, are around **Conceição da Barra** (*Pop* 22,290) 242 km N of Vitória. Corpus Christi (early June) is celebrated with an evening procession for which the road is decorated with coloured wood chips.

Itaúnas, 21 km up the coast, is an interesting excursion; the small town has been swamped by sand dunes, so it has been moved to the opposite river bank. There is now a fantastic landscape of huge dunes and deserted beaches. There are a few *pousadas* and a small campsite. Bus from the *padaria* in Conceição da Barra at 0700, returns 1700.

● **Accommodation   Conceição da Barra**, pleasant beach hotels, also **D** *Rio Mar*, Av Dr Mário Vello Silvares, T 762 1228, rec; **D** *Sombra e Água Fresca*, Rodovia Bento Daher 1800, T 762-1206, *pousada*, and campsite, US$3 pp, excellent facilities, many languages spoken, enthusiastically rec; **D** *Caravelas*, Av Dr Mário Vello Silvares 83, T 762-1188, 1 block from beach, basic, shared bathroom, light breakfast, rec. *Camping Clube do Brasil* site with full facilities, Rodovia Adolfo Serra, Km 16, T 762-1346.

Minas Gerais

A STATE with a number of fine colonial cities built during the gold rush in the 18th century, some splendid caves, the Rio São Francisco in the N, and several spas and hill resorts. The capital is Belo Horizonte, the country's first modern planned city, now a major industrial centre.

The inland State of Minas Gerais (*Pop* 15,746,200) somewhat larger than France, is mountainous in the S, rising to the 2,787-m peak of Agulhas Negras in the Mantiqueira range, and in the E, where there is the Caparaó National Park containing the Pico da Bandeira (2,890m). From Belo Horizonte N are undulating grazing lands, the richest of which are in the extreme W: a broad wedge of country between Goiás in the N and São Paulo in the S, known as the Triângulo Mineiro. Being frost-free, Minas Gerais is also a major producer of coffee.

History and economy

Minas Gerais was once described as having a heart of gold and a breast of iron. Half the mineral production of Brazil comes from the State, including most of the iron ore. Diamonds and gold are still found. The easy availability of power and the local agricultural and mineral production has created a large number of metal-working, textile, mineral water, food processing and timber industries.

The colonial cities can easily be visited from Rio or Belo Horizonte; many companies provide tours. The chief glory of the colonial cities is the architecture and, even more, the sculpture of one of the world's great creative artists, 'O Aleijadinho' (see box, page 426).

JUIZ DE FORA

155 km N of Rio by road is the pleasant city of **Juiz de Fora** (*Pop* 378,500; *Alt* 695m; *CEP* 36,100; *DDD* 032). It lies on the Paraibuna river, in a deep valley between the Mar and Mantiqueira mountain chains.

Places of interest

The **Praça da Estação** has good examples of Belle Epoque architecture, the station hall, the hotels *Príncipe* and *Renascença* and the Associação Comercial building. Also see the Portinari mural of tiles in the foyer of Edifício Clube Juiz de Fora; Banco do Brasil building by Oscar Niemeyer, both in R Halfeld where there is also a museum of banking (Mon-Fri 1300-1600) and the French neo-classical Academia de Comércio.

Museums

The **Museu Mariano Procópio**, Mariano Procópio s/n, T 211-1145, in beautiful wooded grounds (open Tues-Sun 1200-1800) has collections dating from Imperial Brazil. There is a **railway museum** at Av Brasil 2001, next to the station; Tues-Sat 0900-1200, 1330-1800.

Excursions

An attractive train journey (25 km) from Estação Mariano Procópio (opp museum, Mon-Sat), runs to South America's first hydro-electric power station at **Matias Barbosa** (return by bus, hourly).

Local information
● **Accommodation**

A1 *Ritz*, Av Rio Branco 2000, T 215-7300, F 215-1892, sauna, pool, parking, takes all credit cards except Amex; **A1** *Center Park*, Av Getúlio Vargas 181, T/F 215-4898, sauna, pool, parking, accepts credit cards; **A3** *Joalpa*, R Afonso Pinto Mota 29, between Avs Rio Branco and G Vargas, T 215-6055, F 215-3446, sauna, pool, parking, credit cards accepted.

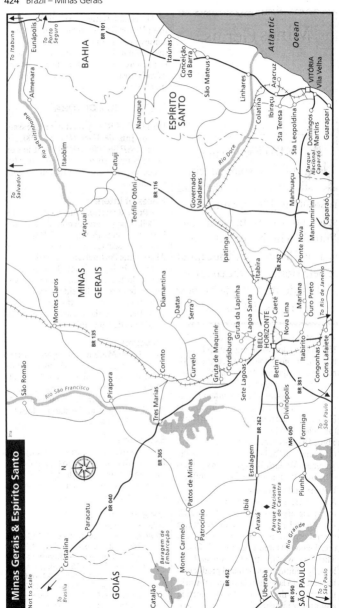

Minas Gerais & Espírito Santo

C *São Luiz*, R Halfeld 360, T 215-1155, art deco lobby, winter garden.

D *Majestic*, R Halfeld 284, T 215-5050, TV, cheaper without bath. Many cheap hotels on Av G Vargas, in E range, mostly short-stay. Take care if walking between Av G Vargas and the railway at night.

● **Places to eat**

Berttu's, R Santo Antônio 572, best in town, *mineira* and international food (about US$20 inc wine); *Cantão Suíço*, R Santa Rita 557/59, good self-service; others on same street and R São João; *Marrakech*, R Espíritu Santo 1081, bar and Arab cuisine; *Barroco*, R Batista de Oliveira 1126, restored cellar with live music, *feijoada* on Sat, good cocktails; *I Due Fratelli*, R São Mateus 144, Italian; *La Belle Bistrot*, R Delfim Moreira 22, French bar/restaurant.

● **Entertainment**

Best nightclub is *Clube Noturno Vila das Tochas*, R Roberto Stigert 4, Bairro São Pedro, crêperie, American bar, dance floor; *Bar do Bené*, Pres Costa e Silva 2305, Bairro São Pedro, friendly pub; *Prova Oral*, R A Braga 210, bar with live music, highly rec. For lots of bars, restaurants, pizzerias and nightlife, visit the Bairro São Mateus, bounded by Av Independência, R São Mateus, R Padre Café, R Mons Gomes Freire with R Manoel Bernardino running down the middle.

● **Shopping**

Priscila Jóias, gold and silver workshop, Galeria Solar, loja 228; many interesting antique shops; plentiful regional foods.

● **Tour companies & travel agents**

Serra Branca, R Aristóteles Braga 186, Cidade Universitária, T 231-1245, local tours and to further afield in Minas Gerais. *Beijaflor*, Shopping Santa Cruz, loja 1148, T 215-0249, French, Italian, some English spoken.

● **Transport**

Air Av Guadalajara, T 233-1089; bus 520 on the hour to centre. Nordeste Linhas Aéreas, T 233-1040, once a day Mon-Fri to São Paulo.

Buses Bus station outside town, Av Brasil 4501, T 215-7696, take bus 630 to town. To/from **Rio**, 19 a day, Útil, US$6, 2¾ hrs (a spectacular trip through mountains and tropical forest); Útil to **Belo Horizonte**, 10 a day, US$8 (Viaçao Útil, T 215-3976, Rodoviária, or in town R Henrique Surerus 22, T 215-6759, Mon-Fri 0800-1800, Sat 0800-1200). To **São João del Rei** via Conselheiro Lafaiete, 6 hrs, US$6.

PARQUE FLORESTAL DE IBITIPOCA

85 km from Juiz de Fora is the **Parque Florestal de Ibitipoca** at 1,760m, which preserves birds, animals and vegetation of the region, plus several quartzite caves and rock formations. Local guide US$10. For guided tours contact Dale Jaume, T (032) 211-7008, US$70 for full day including transport and lunch, US$80 with simple overnight accommodation and breakfast.

● **Access** By unpaved road (4WD rec) from Lima Duarte to Conceição de Ibitipoca. Bus Rio Preto from Juiz da Fora to Lima Duarte, T 221-4461, then seek out Sr Pedro Moreira's taxi, T 281-1200 (Banco do Brasil) or 281-1296 (home); US$18 to Conceiçao and US$23 to the park, one way.

SÃO JOÃO DEL REI

From **Barbacena** (*Pop* 100,050), 103 km on (with an important horse and cattle fair, and a rose festival in Oct), a paved road runs W to the colonial city of **São João del Rei** (*Pop* 72,740; *CEP* 36300; *DDD* 032), at the foot of the Serra do Lenheiro. The streets are paved with fossilized plants: 'almost sacrilegious to walk on them'. A good view of the town and surroundings is from Alto da Boa Vista, where there is a Statue of Christ (Senhor dos Montes). São João del Rei is very lively at weekends.

Places of interest

A fine bridge and three splendid 18th century churches, open most mornings: **Pilar** (the Cathedral, R Getúlio Vargas), the earliest, with rich altars and bright ceiling, and good *azulejos* in choir, and a sacristy with portraits of the Evangelists; **São Francisco de Assis** (1764), Praça Frei Orlando, with two sculptures by Aleijadinho, and others of his school (restoration has removed the plaster from the altars, revealing fine carving in sucupira wood); **Carmo**, Largo do Carmo, designed by Aleijadinho and with interior sculptures by him, very well restored, all in white.

Museums

Near São Francisco is the house of **Bárbara Heliodora** (1759-1819), one of the Inconfidentes (see page 433), which also contains the municipal museum. The **railway museum** (Av Hermílio Alves 366, T 371-2888 see below) is well worth seeing. **Museu de Arte Sacra**, Praça Gastão da Cunha 8, by Cathedral small but recom-

O Aleijadinho

Antônio Francisco Lisboa (1738-1814), the son of a Portuguese architect and a black slave woman, was known as O Aleijadinho (the little cripple) because in later life he developed a maiming disease (possibly leprosy) which compelled him to work in a kneeling (and ultimately a recumbent) position with his hammer and chisel strapped to his wrists. His finest work, which shows a strength not usually associated with the plastic arts in the 18th century, is probably the set of statues in the gardens and sanctuary of the great Bom Jesus church in Congonhas do Campo, but the main body of his work is in Ouro Preto, with some important pieces in Sabará, São João del Rei and Mariana.

mended (Tues-Sun 0900-1700, US$0.50). There are also the **Tancredo Neves Museum**, R Padre José Maria Xavier 7 (weekends and holidays 0900-1700); the **Museu de Arte Regional do Patrimônio Histórico**, in Praça Severiano de Resende (open Tues-Sun, 1200-1730, US$0.50), and a **pewter factory** (with exhibition and shop), Av Leite de Castro 1150, T 371-4422, run by an Englishman, John Somers.

Local festivals

The morning masses on Sun and religious festivals at São Francisco (0915) and Mercês (1030), Praça Br de Hambé, behind and above Pilar, are accompanied by a choir and orchestra who maintain a tradition of over 200 years of local composition.

Local information
● **Accommodation**

In Barbacena: B *Grogotó*, excellent, operated by Senac, T 331-7755, F 32-2234.

In São João del Rei: A3 *Porto Real*, Av Eduardo Magalhães 254, T/F 371-1201, comfortable, good restaurant; **B** *Lenheiro Palace*, Av Pres Tancredo Neves 257, T/F 371-3914, good; **B** *Pousada Casarão*, opp São Francisco church, converted mansion, Ribeiro Bastos 94, T 371-1224, swimming pool, delightful; **C** *Colonial*, Manoel Anselmo 22, T 371-1792, comfortable; **D** *Brasil*, Av Pres Tancredo Neves 395, T 371-2804, lovely colonial house, opp railway station, cheap, rec, no breakfast (*Cafeteria Globo* in the same street, 2 blocks away, is good, though). Cheap *pousadas* in R Marechal Deodoro: *S Benedito*, No 254; *Santa Rita*, No 242, shared rooms.

● **Tourist offices**
In old bus station in São João del Rei.

● **Transport**
Rodoviária is 2 km W of centre of São João. Buses

to **Rio**, 3 daily, 5 hrs, Sun 0800 only, **São Paulo**, 8 hrs, US$12, and **Belo Horizonte**, 3½ hrs. To **Ouro Preto** via Congonhas, US$13, **Juiz de Fora**, US$6, frequent service to Tiradentes.

TIRADENTES

(Originally São José del Rei, renamed in honour of the martyr of the Inconfidência, see page 364; *Pop* 10,220; *CEP* 35325; *DDD* 032) John Parsons writes: The centre of this charming little town, 15 km from São João, with its nine streets and eight churches, at the foot of the green Serra São José, hardly belongs to this century. The town is very busy during Holy Week, when there are numerous religious processions.

Places of interest

The **Santo Antônio** church, first built in 1710, contains some of the finest gilded wood carvings in the country and a small but fine organ brought from Oporto in the 1790s. The reconstructed façade is said to follow a design by Aleijadinho. There is also a sun-dial by him. The charming **Rosário** church has fine statuary and ornate gilded altars; this and **Nossa Senhora das Mercês** have interesting painted ceilings and the latter a notable statue of the Virgin.

At the bottom of the stone paved road which descends from Santo Antônio is the fountain (*chafariz*), installed in 1749, whose water is brought by a stone aqueduct from springs in the forest at the foot of Serra São José. The **museum**, housed where Padre Toledo (another Inconfidente) once lived, exhibits some good pieces of furniture. The simple pilgrimage church of **Santíssima Trindade** is also well worth seeing. See the artists' lithographic printing shop of Largo do Ó. There are attractive walks in the neighbourhood, and a $1\frac{1}{2}$-hr walk to the fountains and pools of Águas Santas.

Excursions

The train on the line between São João del Rei and Tiradentes (13 km) has been in continuous operation since 1881, using the same locomotives and rolling stock, running on 76 cm gauge track, all lovingly cared for. Maximum speed is 20 km per hr: US$2.50 return. Fri, Sat, Sun and holidays, 1000 and 1415, returning 1300 and 1700. Railway museum at the railway station in São João del Rei; open daily 0900-1130, 1300-1700, entrance included in rail fare; there are also a round house which has 16 vintage locomotives in superb condition, an engine shed and a steam-operated machine shop, still working.

Local information
● Accommodation

A1 *Solar da Ponte*, Praça das Mercês (prop John and Anna Maria Parsons) T 355-1255, F 355-1201, atmosphere of country house, inc breakfast and tea, only 12 rooms, fresh flowers in rooms, bar, sauna, garden, swimming pool, light meals for residents only, for larger meals, the hotel recommends 5 local restaurants. Also *Pousada Maria Barbosa*, R Antônio Teixeira Carvalho 134, T 355-1227, pool, very pleasant; *Hotel Wellerson*, R Fogo Simbólico 218, T 355-1226; *Hotel Ponto do Morro das Forras 2*, T/F 355-1342; *Pousada de Laurito*, Direita 187, T 355-1268.

● Places to eat

Local food: *Quinta de Ouro*, Direita 152, rec; *Estalagem*, R Min G Passos 280; *Padre Toledo*, Direita 202. **Italian:** *Donatello*, Direita 205; *Aluarte*, Largo do Ó 1, cheap, garden, sells handicrafts, rec. **Vegetarian:** *Opção Saúdavel*, Av Tiradentes 792, tiny, cheap, rec.

● Tourist offices

In the Prefeitura, R Resende Costa 71.

ROUTES From Belo Horizonte, the shortest road to São João del Rei is via Lagoa Dourada. Just past Lagoa Dourada is the turning (12 km) for **Prados**, a small town 15 km from Tiradentes (local bus, 30 mins) known for its musical and handicrafts traditions, excellent leather clothing, good prices from *Mara e Café*, R Magalhães Gomes 90.

The capital of Minas Gerais is the third largest city in Brazil (*Pop* 2,048,861; *Alt* 800m; *CEP* 3000; *DDD* 031). It is surrounded by mountains, and enjoys an excellent climate (16°-30°C) except for the rainy season (Dec-Mar). It was founded 12 December 1897 and is one of Brazil's fastest growing cities, now suffering from atmospheric pollution.

The industrial area, apart from being the traditional centre of mining and agricultural industries (as well as diamond cutting and precious stones), has steelworks and an automobile industry. The city has a good public transport system (red buses serve central and express routes, yellow circular routes, and blue diagonal routes), and taxis are plentiful, although hard to find at peak hours.

PLACES OF INTEREST

On the **Praça da Assembléia** are three fine modern buildings: Legislative Assembly, church and Banco do Brasil; the **Palácio da Liberdade**, in Praça da Liberdade amid other fine *fin-de-siècle*-style public buildings (every Sun morning and Thur evening an open-air craft market operates here, very good; also a flower market each Fri from 1800 and an antique and occultism market each Sun: at night the fountain is illuminated in a variety of colours); the **Palácio das Artes**, Afonso Pena 1567, which is in the Parque Municipal and contains the Centro de Artesanato Mineiro (craft shop open 0900-1700, Tues-Sun). The **Parque Municipal** (an oasis of green, right in the centre of the city, small amusement park and playground, closed at night and on Mon, except for a small section in the SW corner). **Minascentro** is a convention centre for exhibitions and congresses in the city centre.

MUSEUMS

Museu Mineiro, Av João Pinheiro 342, religious art in old Senate building near centre (open Tues, Wed, Fri 1230-1830, Thur 1500-2100, Sat, Sun 1000-1600);

Museu da Mineralogia Prof Djalma Guimarães, R da Bahia 1149, a Gothic building near the Parque Municipal, with interesting exhibits; **Museu Histórico Abílio Barreto**, R Bernardo Mascarenhas, Cidade Jardim, T 296-3896, in an old *fazenda* which is the last reminder of Belo Horizonte's predecessor, the village of **Arraial do Curral d'el Rey**, built by João Leite da Silva Ortiz in the 18th century, houses most interesting historical exhibits (open 1000-1700 Wed-Mon, take bus 2902 from Av Pena); **Museu da Telecomunicaçao**, Av Afonso Pena 4001, Mangabeiras (open Mon-Fri, 0800-1700); the **railway station**, with museum on 2nd floor showing a model railway and the railway headquarters in a mansion on the hill above the station, with locomotive and railway coach used by Dom Pedro II; **Museu Histórico Natural**, in the Instituto Agronómico, R Gustavo da Silveira 1035, T 461-7666, has a local geological and palaeontological display and good archaeological exhibits (take bus 3803A from Praça Rio Branco).

SUBURBS

8 km from the centre is the picturesque suburb of **Pampulha**, famous for its modern buildings and the artificial lake. Many buildings were designed by Oscar Niemeyer. In Pampulha the glass and marble **Museu de Arte de Belo Horizonte** is at Av Octacílio Negrão de Lima, Km 11 (open 0800-1800 daily); the **Chapel of São Francisco de Assis**, same avenue, Km 12, has interior decorations by the painter Cândido Portinari. There is a bus (not the 4403) from the city centre to the **Jardim Zoológico** (at the far end of the lake from the dam – small selection of birds with some rarities, animals well kept for the most part) that passes the chapel and also the **Mineirão** stadium about ³/₄ km away (the second largest in Brazil after the Maracanã stadium in Rio); bus 2004 goes from Av Afonso Pena to the chapel.

In the southern zone of the city, on the Serra do Curral, the **Parque de Mangabeiras** has a good view of the city, forest trails, sports facilities and snack bars. The natural amphitheatre where the Pope

spoke in 1982 is nearby; there is an iron monument marking the occasion (take bus 2001 from Afonso Pena between Av Amazonas and R Tamóios, closed Mon).

EXCURSIONS

Within easy motoring distance from Belo Horizonte are several of the 400 caves and grottoes for which Minas Gerais is famous. The best and most famous is the **Gruta de Maquiné** with 6 chambers open to visitors, well lit, but hot, 26°C (entry US$2), 126 km NW of Belo (well signposted and with restaurants nearby, which greet potential customers with combined history and menu leaflet; bus at 0915, return at 1500, 3½ hrs, US$4.50). The **Gruta de Lapinha**, almost as good, is only 51 km N of the city (entrance to caves and small museum, US$1, closed Mon); bus at 1015, 1¼ hrs, US$2 one way.

10 km before Lapinha is the town of **Lagoa Santa** (*Pop* 24,890), a weekend resort for Belo Horizonte. The sandy beach on the lake (close to the town centre and bus station) is used for fishing, sunbathing and boating (do not swim, the water is infected with schistosomiasis). Along the beach are bars and restaurants, with more in the nearby main square which also has two small hotels and an interesting modernistic church. The road to Belo Horizonte (½-hourly bus service, US$1) passes Belo Horizonte's international airport. Bus Lagoa Santa-Lapinha every 30 mins. Local bus stop for Lagoa Santa is 2 km downhill from Lapinha caves.

To the NE of the city, a few kilometres off the BR-262, is the **Serra de Piedade**, a high peak giving spectacular views over the surrounding countryside, only accessible by car or special bus service. There are a small chapel and a *churrascaria*.

Turn off the BR-262 (towards Vitória) at Km 73 and go via Barão de Cocais and Brumal to Caraça (120 km), where the seminary, at 1,220m, has been converted into a hotel (B), the site and region highly recommended. Reservations through Instituto São Vicente in Belo, T 031-441-5399 (space is very limited and there is no

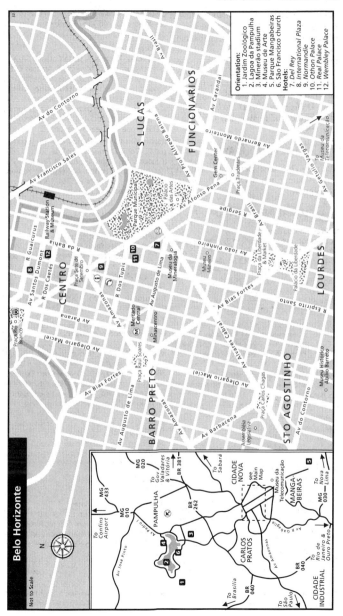

Belo Horizonte

Not to Scale

Orientation:
1. Jardim Zoológico
2. Lagoa da Pampulha
3. Mineirão stadium
4. Museu de Arte
5. Parque Mangabeiras
6. São Francisco church

Hotels:
7. Del Rey
8. International Plaza
9. Normandie
10. Othon Palace
11. Real Palace
12. Wembley Palace

public transport). *Focus Tours* (below) runs tours to the **Caraça Natural Park**, which contains many bird species, some rare, and the endangered masked titi monkey, the common marmoset, the black-capped capuchin and the very rare maned wolf (which the monks feed at dusk). It is possible to stay in Santa Bárbara (**D** *Hotel Karaíbe*; **D** *Sta Inés*, 25 km away on the road to Mariana) and hitch-hike to Caraça.

LOCAL HOLIDAYS

Maundy Thursday; Corpus Christi; 15 Aug (Assumption); 8 Dec (Immaculate Conception).

LOCAL INFORMATION

● **Accommodation**
L2 *Brasilton*, out of town at Km 3.65 on Rodovia Fernão Dias, Contagem, T 396-1100, F 396-1144, very good restaurant; **L3** *Boulevard Plaza*, Av Getúlio Vargas 1640, Savassi district (chic shopping area), T 223-9000, F 225-8438, very nice; **L3** *Othon Palace*, Av Afonso Pena 1050, T 273-3844, F 212-2318, deluxe, excellent, safe deposit boxes, pool on roof, helpful staff.

A1 *Normandie*, R Tamóios 212, T 201-6166, F 222-6133, excellent grill; **A1** *Wembley Palace*, R Espírito Santo 201, T 201-6966, F 224-9946, excellent, central; **A2** *Casa dos Municípios*, R Rio Grande do Nte 1017, Funcionários (Savassi), T 226-5177; **A3** *Estoril*, R Carijós 454, T 201-9322, comfortable, pleasant; **A3** *Itatiaia*, Praça Rui Barbosa 187, T 212-3300, nr railway station, central, a/c, good breakfast.

B *Ambassy*, R Caetés 633, nr bus station, T 201-0222, helpful, English spoken, a/c, noisy, good restaurant; **C** *Continental*, Av Paraná 241, T 201-7944, central, quieter interior rooms rec; **C** *Esplanada*, Av Santos Dumont 304, T 273-5311 (**E** without bath), good restaurant, own garage, good value; **C** *Madrid*, opp rodoviária, rec; **C** *São Salvador*, R Espírito Santo 237, rec.

E *Maciel*, Av Ol Maciel 95, basic. Near rodoviária and in R Curitiba many hotels are for very-short-stay couples, rec: **D** *Magnata*, R Guarani 124, with breakfast, nr rodoviária, good hot shower, safe deposit, rec; **E** *Minas Bahia*, No 173; **E** *São Cristovão*, Av Oiapoque 284, quiet, breakfast. You may spend the night in the rodoviária only if you have an onward ticket (police check at midnight).

Youth hostels: *Pousadinha Mineira*, R Januária 206, T 446-2911, 15 mins from ro-

doviária, rec; *Chalé Mineiro*, R Sta Luzia 288, Sta Efigênia, T 467-1576, attractive, splash pool, highly rec.

● **Places to eat**
Local food: *Tavares*, R Santa Catarina 64, excellent value; *Chico Mineiro*, R Alagoas 626, corner of Av Brasil, local chicken specialities, good, closed Sun; *Santa Felicidade*, R Prof Morais 659 (Funcionários) and da Bahia 1204 (Centro), good; *Arroz com Feijão*, Av Contorno 6510, Av Contorno 7438 and R Antônio de Albuquerque 440, reasonably-priced.

Italian: *Pizzaiolo*, Av Contorno 8495, good for pizzas; *Dona Derna*, R Tomé de Souza 1380 (Funcionários), highly rec; *Buona Távola*, R Sta Rita Durão 309, Funcionários, excellent; *Alpino* (German), Av do Contorno 5761 (Funcionários), good value and popular.

Oriental: *Yun Ton*, Chinese, R Santa Catarina 946, rec. *Kyoto*, Japanese, R Montes Claros, Anchieta, rec.

Vegetarian: *Naturalmente*, Av Andradas 367; *Superbom*, R São Paulo, 971, 1100-1500, Mon to Fri. Many bars and restaurants around Praça Raúl Soares; more on Av Rio de Janeiro. Two rec bars are *Americana*, R Pernambuco 1025; *Janis*, Av Getúlio Vargas 809.

Tea rooms: *Era Uma Vez Un Chalezinho*, R Paraíba 1455; *Tia Clara*, R Antônio de Albuquerque 617.

● **Banks & money changers**
Lloyds Bank, Av João Pinheiro 580; Citibank, R Espírito Santo 871; Banco do Brasil, R Rio de Janeiro 750, Av Amazonas 276; Excel, R Bahia 360, 9th floor, 1000-1630. American Express, Master Turismo, Av Afonso Pena 1967, T 273-3122. Mastercard, cash against card, Banco Meridional, R dos Inconfidentes 1051, 4th floor, Funcionários (for information only), R da Bahia 1255, Centro (for cash); Sr Cláudio, R Espírito Santo 466, 16th floor, office 1608, very good rates. São Paulo Joias, Amazonas 105, good rates. Changing TCs is difficult, but hotels will change them for guests at a poor rate.

● **Electric current**
120-220 AC 60 cycles.

● **Embassies & consulates**
Austrian, R José Américo Cançado Bahia 199, T 333-3622. French, R Prof Antônio Aleixo 843, 5th Floor, T335-5563; Italian, Praça Carlos Chagas 49, 2nd floor, T 335-5394; Netherlands, R Alagoas 1460, 11th floor, T 221-0615; Finland, Av Contorno 6283, sala 604/8, T 227-2725; Denmark, R Prof Jerson Martins 166, T 448 6013, F 261 7561. US: Serviço de Divulgação e Relações Culturais, Av Alvares Cabral 1600, 3rd floor, T 335-3555.

● **Entertainment**

Music school: Av Afonso Pena, opp Palácio das Artes: 'brilliant' classical concerts, entrance free or nominal (US$2).

Nightlife: *L' Apogée*, R Antônio de Alberquerque 729; *Escape*, Av Teresa Cristina 298 for house music; *Pantheon*, Rio Grande do Nte 1470; *Máscaras*, R Sta Rita Durão 667; *Ao Bar*, R Cláudio Manoel 572, Funcionários; *Sausalito*, R Tomé de Souza 912, street café.

● **Hospitals & medical services**

Mater Dei, R Gonçalves Dias 2700, T 335-2200, rec; *Alfredo Balena MedCentre*, R dos Otoni 927, a private hospital. *Dr Ricardo Queiroz Guimarães*, Av Brasil 1474, Funcionários, T 224-2020 for contact lenses and eye problems.

● **Places of worship**

Synagoga Beth Yacou, R Pernambuco 326, T 224-6013; **Presbyterian Church**, R Ceará 1434, T 226-1844; **Baptist Church**, R Joaquim de Figueredo 332, T 384-1322; **Mormon Church**, R Levindo Lopes 214, T 233-7883; **Adventist Church**, R Timbiras 683, T 226-6144.

● **Post & telecommunications**

Post Office with poste restante, Av Afonso Pena 1270. **UPS**: Salima, T 222-9002.

● **Shopping**

Mercado Central, Av Aug de Lima 744, large and clean, open every day. Market for fruit, vegetables, meat and other items at R Santa Catarina e Av Amazonas (nr Praça Raúl Soares). There are huge hypermarkets just outside the city on the highways to Rio and São Paulo. Splendid delicatessen with foreign food and wines – and liquors – *Au Bon Gourmet*, R Tupinambás 187. For gemstones, try *Manoel Bernardes*, R Espírito Santo 835, very reasonable. For music, *Cogumelo*, Av Augusto de Lima 399. *'Hippie fair'* Afonso Pena between R da Bahia and R Guajajaras, Sun mornings. **Food and Antique fair**, Sat, with good home-made food, and Flower market, Fri both at Av Bernardo Monteiro with Av Brasil.

Bookshop: *Daniel Vaitsman*, R Espírito Santo 466, 17th floor, for English language books. Foreign language books at *Livraria Van Damme*, R das Guajajaras 505, also good local and Portuguese selection; *Acaiaca*, R Tamóios 72, good for dictionaries. Used foreign-language books at *Livraria Alfarrábio*, R Tamóios 320.

● **Tour companies & travel agents**

Focus Tours, 14821 Hillside Lane, Burnsville, MN 55306, T 612-892-7830, F 892-0900, e-mail Focus Tours@aol.com, or c/o Regina Caldeira, T/F (031) 296-4506, run by Douglas and Nancy Trent, offer specialized tours all over Brazil and have a special interest in ecology and tours to the Pantanal. Tours in Minas to see a great variety of wildlife. Reliable information and a portion of their profits is used for conservation project in Brazil. *Master Turismo*, Aeroporto Internacional, Suite 45, T 689-2044, and Av Afonso Pena 1967, T 273-3122.

● **Tourist offices**

Belotur (municipal information office), R Tupis 149, 17th floor, T 222-5500; **Turminas**, Av Bias Fortes 50, Praça da Liberdade, T 212-2134, F 201-3942; Praça Sete de Setembro; at rodoviária (particularly polyglot, reasonable free map of centre) ask for the **Guia Turístico** for events, opening times etc, airport (very helpful). **Touring Clube do Brasil**, Av Afonso Pena 1913.

● **Transport**

Local There is a regional, overground metro. **Car hire**: **Nobre**, Confins Airport and Av Francisco Sales 1424, T 227-5700; and others.

Air International airport nr Lagoa Santa, at Confins, 39 km from Belo Horizonte. Taxi to centre, US$24; airport bus, either *executivo* from the exit, US$6, or comfortable normal bus from far end of car park every hr on the $1/2$-hr, US$2.40, both go to/from rodoviária.

Closer to the city is the national airport at Pampulha, which has shuttle services from several cities, inc Rio and São Paulo. Flights, as well as transportation to/from this airport, are cheaper. From airport to town blue bus 1202 leaves across the street from the aiport, 25 mins, US$0.15, bus passes the rodoviária and cheaper hotel district.

Trains To Vitória, daily 0700, tickets sold at 0530, US$10 1st class, US$7 2nd, 14 hrs. *Especial* class also available.

Buses Rodoviária is by Praça Rio Branco at end of Av Afonso Pena (left-luggage lockers, attended service 0700-2200). To **Rio**, 7 hrs, US$14.25 (ordinary), *leito*, US$28.50; to **Brasília**, 10 hrs, 9 a day inc 2 *leitos*, only one leaves in daylight (0800), US$23, *leito* US$46. To **São Paulo**, 10 hrs, US$7.25; route passes the great Furnas reservoir. To **Salvador** US$39, 24 hrs, at 1800 and 1900 daily. **Porto Seguro** 18 hrs, direct, via Nanuque and Eunápolis; **Recife**, US$60; **Belém**, US$91. To **Campo Grande** 2000, with Gontijo, a good route to Bolivia, avoiding São Paulo. All major destinations served. For buses within Minas Gerais, see under destination.

Hitchhiking To Rio or Ouro Preto, take a bus marked 'Shopping', to the shopping centre above Belo Horizonte on the Rio road.

About 120 km NE of Belo Horizonte, the **National Park of Serra do Cipó**, 33,400 sq km of the Serra do Espinaço, has scenic beauty and several endemic plants, insects and birds (the Cipo Canestero – only found outside the park in one small area). There are also several carnivorous plants (Ibama office: Av do Contorno 8121, Cidade Jardim, CEP 30.110-120, Belo Horizonte, T 335-6611).

THE COLONIAL CITIES

The road from Belo Horizonte to the picturesque colonial cities described below follows the Rio das Velhas.

SABARÁ

30 km E of the city is the colonial goldmining (and steel-making) town of **Sabará** (*Pop* 89,680). Sabará is strung along the narrow steep valleys of the Rio das Velhas and Rio Sabará.

Places of interest
Its old churches and fountains, its rambling cobbled streets, its simple houses with their carved doors, and its museum of 18th century gold mining in the **Intendência de Ouro** (built 1732, closed for repairs, 1995) are of great interest. The mineral museum in the **Escola da Minas** is worth a visit.

The other main sights are the **Prefeitura**, in R Pedro II, an old mansion with oratory and main reception room (*salão nobre*); the **Teatro Municipal** (former Opera House) (1770) in the same street, has a fine interior; the portal of the **Casa Azul**, in the same street; the Churches of **Nossa Senhora do Carmo** (1774), with doorway, pulpits and choirloft by Aleijadinho and paintings by Athayde; **Nossa Senhora do Rosário dos Pretos** (left unfinished at the time of the slaves' emancipation); **São Francisco**; **Nossa Senhora da Conceição** (1720) with much gilding, and paintings by 23 Chinese artists brought from Macau; and **Nossa Senhora do Ó**, built in 1698 and showing unmistakable Chinese influence (paintings much in need of restoration), 2 km from the centre of the town (take local bus marked 'Esplanada' or 'Boca Grande'). Also the fountains of Kaquende (1757), and Rosário. *Passeio a Sabará*, by Lúcia

Machado de Almeida, with splendid illustrations by Guignard, is an excellent guide to the place.

Local information
● **Places to eat**
314, Comendador Viana 314, nr main Praça; *Imperial Restaurant/Pizzaria*, in R Pedro II; *Ce Ki Sabe*, R Mestre Caetano 56, rec.

● **Transport**
Bus from Belo Horizonte, US$0.60, 30 mins, from separate part of Belo Rodoviária from main departure hall.

NOVA LIMA

(*Pop* 52,200) About 27 km SE of Belo by a good road, set in eucalyptus forests. Its houses are grouped round the gold mine of Morro Velho, the deepest mine in the Americas. The shaft has followed a rich vein of gold down to 2,591m (not open to tourists). There are interesting carvings by Aleijadinho, recovered from elsewhere, in the (modern) parish church.

At 27 km S along the Belo Horizonte-Rio de Janeiro highway a 68 km road, the Rodovia dos Inconfidentes, branches off to Ouro Preto. On the way (48 km) it passes **Cachoeira do Campo**, which was the centre of the regional mining administration in colonial times: now a sleepy, unspoilt village.

OURO PRETO

(*Pop* 62,485; *Alt* 1,000m; *CEP* 35400; *DDD* 031) The famous former capital of the State was founded in 1711. The city, built on rocky ground, was declared a national monument in 1933. Its cobbled streets wind up and down steep hills crowned with 13 churches. Mansions, fountains, churches, vistas of terraced gardens, ruins, towers shining with coloured tiles, all blend together to maintain a delightful 18th century atmosphere. On 24 June of each year, Ouro Preto again becomes, for that day only, the capital of the state of Minas Gerais. From Oct-Feb the climate is cold and wet.

Places of interest
There is a famous **Escola de Minas** (School of Mining), founded in 1876, in

the fortress-like **Palácio dos Gover-nadores** (1742), facing the main Praça Tiradentes; it has the interesting **Museu de Mineralogia e das Pedras**, a must, the only one open on Mon (1200-1700), but closed Sun. Opposite the Palácio, next to Carmo Church, is the **Museu da Incon-fidência**, a fine historical and art museum which has some drawings by Aleijadinho and the Sala Manoel da Costa Athayde, in an annex (open 1200-1730, entry). **Casa das Contas**, also a museum (open 1230-1700), Sun 0800-1300. All the above US$1. **Casa Guignard**, R Conde de Bobadela 10, displays the paintings of Alberto da Veiga Guignard, open Tues-Sat 0900-1700, Sun 1200-1700, free. The **Mina do Chico Rei**, R D Silvério, open 0800-1700, entrance US$0.75, is not as impressive as some other mines in the area, but is 'fun to crawl about in'; restaurant attached.

In the **Praça de Independência** is a statue of José Joaquim da Silva Xavier, known as Tiradentes, leader of the **Incon-fidentes** (unsuccessful revolutionaries of 1789), regarded in Brazil as the precursor of independence. Another Inconfidente, the poet Tomás Antônio Gonzaga (whose house at R Cláudio Manoel 61 is close to São Francisco de Assis), was exiled to Africa. (Most Brazilians know his poem based on his forbidden love affair; visitors are shown the bridge and decorative fountain where the lovers held their trysts.)

Churches

The following churches are all closed Mon, but are open at following times on other days: **Santa Efigênia** (1720, decorated with gold dust washed out of slaves' hair), Lad Santa Efigênia e Padre Faria, 0800-1200; **Francisco de Assis** (1766-96), Largo de Coimbra (shared ticket with NS Conceição), beautiful interior and exterior with work by both Aleijadinho and Athayde, 0830-1100, 1330-1630 (keep your ticket for admission to the museum); **NS Carmo**, R Brig Mosqueira (museum of sacred art and Aleijadinho sculptures), 1300-1700, shared entry ticket with **NS Pilar** (1733, heavily gilded work of Aleijadinho's father, Manuel Lisboa), 1200-1700; **NS do Rosário**, Largo do Rosário (simple altar, interesting side altars), 1200-1700; **das Mercês e Perdões** (1740-73) R das Mercês, 1000-1400, open in afternoon only. The Antônio Dias parish church, **Nossa Senhora da Conceição** (1722), heavily gilded, contains Aleijadinho's tomb, and a museum devoted to him, Aleijadinho Paróquia, 0800-1130, 1300-1700. There are a number of other churches and chapels. At least two days are needed to see them all; the tourist office on Praça Tiradentes (opens 0800, Portuguese only spoken) and the hotels offer a leaflet showing the opening times; also sells good map for US$2.50. Most of the churches now charge for admission, usually about US$1.50.

Art

Ouro Preto displays many superb baroque carvings, in wood and in soapstone, of the sculptor Aleijadinho. The church of São Francisco de Assis and the façade of the Carmo church are his work, and much else.

The mid-18th century paintings by Mestre Athayde (1732-1827), to be seen in S Francisco de Assis, Sta Ifigênia and elsewhere, are of particular interest: the pigments were obtained from local iron ore and from forest fruits. They are also very fine artistically.

NB In most churches and museums, tourists' handbags and cameras are taken at the entrance and guarded in lockers (visitors keep their own key).

Excursions

The **Cachoeira das Andorinhas**, a nearby waterfall, is reached by taking a bus to Morro de Santana and then walking 25 mins. To walk all the way (N of town) takes 1½ hrs. It may be possible to visit the Zen monastery near the waterfall, apply in advance: Mosteiro Zen Pico de Rajos, Morro de São Sebastião, CP 101, 35400-000, Ouro Preto. The town is dominated by a huge cross, easily reached from the road to Mariana. Lovely sunsets, but don't go alone as it's in a poor district.

Local festivals

Ouro Preto is famous for its Holy Week processions, which in fact begin on the Thur before Palm Sunday and continue (but not every day) until Easter Sunday. The most famous is that commemorating Christ's removal from the Cross, late on Good Friday. Many shops close during this holiday, and on winter weekends. Attracting many Brazilians, Carnival here is also memorable.

Local information
● Accommodation
L2 *Pousada do Mondego*, Largo de Coimbra 38, T 551-2040, F 551-3094, beautifully kept colonial house, rec.

A1 *Grande*, R Sen Rocha 164, T 551-1488, largest hotel in town and the only modern structure, designed by Oscar Niemeyer; **A1** *Luxor Pousada*, Praça Antônio Dias 10, converted colonial mansion, no twin beds, comfortable, T 551-2244, reservations in Rio, T 256-2680, restaurant good; **A1** *Priskar da Barra*, R Antônio Martins 98, T/F 551-2666, good facilities; **A2** *Solar das Lajes*, R Conselheiro Quintiliano 604 (T/F 551-3388), a little way from centre, excellent view, swimming pool, well run.

B *Pouso Chico Rei*, a fascinating old house with Portuguese colonial furnishings, very small and utterly delightful, book in advance, R Brig Mosqueira 90, T 551-1274 (room No 6 has been described as a 'dream'); **B** *Hotel Casa Grande Pousada*, R Conselheiro Quintiliano, 96, T/F 551-4314, TV, fridge, inc breakfast, safe, good views, rec; **B** *Pousada dos Bandeirantes*, R das Mercês 167, T 551-1996, F 551-1962, beautiful views.

C *Pousada Nello Nuno*, R Camilo de Brito 59, T 551-3375, cheaper without bath, charming owner Annamélia speaks some French, highly rec; **C** *Pousada Ouro Preto*, Largo Musicista José dos Anjos Costa 72, T 551-3081, small, laundry facilities, hot showers, English spoken by owner, Gérson Luís Cotta (most helpful), tasty home-made cake, rec; **C** *Hospedária Antiga*, R Xavier da Veiga 3, T 551-2203, a restored colonial house, rec; **C** *Pousada São Francisco de Paula*, 100m from Rodoviária (next to the São Francisco de Paula church), panoramic view, rec.

D *Pousada Ciclo do Ouro*, Felipe dos Santos 241, T 351-4527, laundry facilities, rec; **D** *Pousada Casarão*, R Direita, quiet, shared bathroom, breakfast, rec.

E R Conselheiro Quintiliano 26, Rosana lets rooms, basic, clothes washing; **E** *Hospedaria* of Consuêlo Perdigão, R Pandiá Calógeras 59, Barra, T 551-2318, price pp in shared room, use of kitchen, living room, shared bathroom, very good, English spoken, rec; **E** *Pousada Ouro Preto*, Praça Tiradentes 71, nice, hot water, shared bathroom, rec; **E** *Vermelha Dormitório*, on R Vermelha, T 551-1138, quiet,

shared shower, laundry facilities. Youth hostel in R das Mercês, T 551-3170, accepts student cards as membership. Also try *casas de familia*, reasonably-priced.

Avoid touts who greet you off buses and charge higher prices than those advertised in hotels; difficult to get hotel rooms at weekends and holiday periods. In the low season prices can be negotiated.

Students: may be able to stay, during holidays and weekends, at the self-governing student hostels, known as *repúblicas* (very welcoming, 'best if you like heavy metal music'). Many are closed between Christmas and Carnival.

Camping: Camping Clube do Brasil, 2 km N of city, is quite expensive but very nice.

● Places to eat
Pasteleria Lampião, Praça Tiradentes, good views at the back (better at lunchtime than in evening); *Casa Grande* and *Forno de Barro*, both on Praça Tiradentes, good local dishes; *Café & Cia*, R São José 187, closes 2300, very popular, *comida por kilo* at lunchtime, good salads, juices, rec; *Chafariz*, R São José 167, good local food, all you can eat for US$9; *Calabouço*, good, Conde de Bobadela 132, with an antique shop; *Sobrenatural* on the same street, rec; *Tacho de Ouro Preto*, Conde de Bobadela 76, good lunch buffet, popular; *Casa do Ouvidor*, Conde de Bobadela 42, above De Bernardis jewellery shop, good; *Adega*, R Teixeira Amaral, 1130-1530, vegetarian smorgasbord, US$6, all you can eat, highly rec. Try the local *licor de jaboticaba*. A candlelit bar, *Acaso 85*, Praça Largo Rosário, is not cheap but marvellous for romantics; *Vide Gula*, R Senador Rocha Lagoa, food/kilo, good, friendly atmosphere, rec.

● Banks & money changers
Banco do Brasil, R São José, good rates, also for TCs.

● Electric current
110 volts AC.

● Post & telecommunications
Post Office: on R Direita.

● Shopping
For precious stones, *Videmaju*, owned by Vincente Júlio de Paula, a professor at the School of Mines, sells stones at very good prices from his house at R Conselheiro Santana 175. Buy soapstone carvings at roadside stalls and bus stops rather than in the cities; they are much cheaper. Many artesans sell soapstone carvings, jewellery and semi-precious stones in the square in front of São Francisco de Assis church. Gems are not much cheaper from freelance sellers in Praça Tiradentes than from the shops around

the square, and in the shops themselves, the same quality of stone is offered at the same price – *Brasil Gemas* and *De Bernardis* are rec.

● **Tourist offices**

Praça Tiradentes 41. Enquire here for details of accommodation in *casas de família*, *repúblicas* and other places. The tourist office at the bus station is sometimes open, map US$1.10 from either office.

Guides: Bandeira's *Guia de Ouro Preto* in Portuguese and English (US$3.50 with coloured map, US$1 with black and white one), normally available at Tourist Office. Also available is Lucia Machado de Almeida's *Passeio a Ouro Preto*, US$6 (in Portuguese, English and French). A local guide for a day, Associação de Guias de Turismo, T 551-2655, is more expensive if obtained through Tourist Office (rec guide: Cassio Antunes). *Ourotur* runs a tour of Ouro Preto in a vintage-style bus, 0900 and 1430, from the rodoviária (T 551-2764).

● **Transport**

Buses The rodoviária is above the town nr the São Francisco de Paula church. 10 mins downhill walk to the centre, or a town bus passes every 30 mins; taxis charge exorbitant rates. 11 buses a day from Belo Horizonte (2 hrs), US$4, taxi US$50. Day trips are run. Bus from **Rio**, Útil at 0830 or 2330 (US$18, 7 hrs), return bus to Rio at 2330. Book your return journey to **Belo Horizonte** early if returning in the evening; buses get crowded. There are also buses to **Conselheiro Lafaiete** for connections to Belo Horizonte and Congonhas, and direct to **Congonhas** at 1400 and 1530, or to Rio via Barbacena and Juiz da Fora (direct bus to Rio is often fully booked 2-3 days, or weekends, in advance). Direct bus Ouro Preto to **Vitória** at 2100, US$13, 5½ hrs (connection to Porto Seguro), daily. To **Salvador** with Gontijo (change at Belo Horizonte), 1945, 24 hrs, US$40, buy ticket at Útil desk. Direct bus to **São Paulo**, 1900, 11 hrs, US$24.

MARIANA

(*Pop* 38,115; *Alt* 697m; *CEP* 35420; *DDD* 031) Another old mining city, founded 1696, much less hilly than Ouro Preto, is 12 km E of Ouro Preto on a road which goes on to join the Rio-Salvador highway.

Places of interest

The beautiful old prison on Praça João Pinheiro (**Cadeia**, 1768, now the Prefeitura Municipal); on the same square the **Carmo** church (1784, steatite carvings, Athayde paintings, chinoiserie panelling – closed for repairs since 1992), next to it

is the fine **São Francisco** church (1762, pulpits designed by Aleijadinho, Athayde paintings and tomb, fine sacristy, one side-altar by Aleijadinho, entry, US$0.50) and the old **Palácio dos Governadores** connected with it; the **Museu Arquidiocesano** has fine church furniture, a gold and silver collection, Aleijadinho statues and an ivory cross (R Frei Durão 49, open 0900-1300 except Mon and 1400-1645; entrance US$1, good guide book); **Capela de Santo Antônio**, wonderfully simple and the oldest in town. The **Cathedral**, Basílica de NS da Assunção, built 1711-1760, Praça da Sé, has a wooden German organ (1701), façade by Aleijadinho, beautiful interior and side altars (entry US$0.50). Organ concerts are given on Fri, 1100 and Sun, 1200 (US$5). Between the old prison and São Francisco is a stone monument to Justice, at which slaves used to be beaten. The house of the poet Alphonsus de Guimarães (buried behind the Igreja Santuaria), R Direita 35, is open to visitors: photographs and letters (free). There are viewpoints at the churches of **NS do Rosário**, R do Rosário (1752, with work by Athayde and showing Moorish influence) and **São Pedro dos Clérigos** (built in 1753), Largo de São Pedro. Some people still pan for gold in the river running through the town.

Minas de Passagem

Between Ouro Preto and Mariana is the Minas de Passagem gold mine, dating from 1719. A guided tour visits the old mine workings and underground lake (take bathing suit), entrance US$10, visiting hours 0900-1800, T Ouro Preto 551-1068, Mariana 557-1340/1255. There is a waterfall, Cachoeira Serrinha, where swimming is possible, 30 mins' walk from the bus stop to the mine. Initially you have to walk 100m towards Mariana then ask for directions.

Excursions

24 km N of Mariana (infrequent bus US$0.50), is the small village of Antônio Pereira where the imperial topaz is mined. Tours of an interesting cave with stalactites: pay local children a small fee to show you round.

Local information

● Accommodation

C *Faisca*, R Antônio Olinto 48, T 557-1206, inc breakfast; **C** *Pousada do Chafariz*, R Côn Rego 149, T 557-1492, TV, fridge, parking, breakfast inc, family atmosphere, rec.

D *Providência*, R Dom Silverio 233, T 557-1444, run by nuns, small rooms, pool, quiet.

E *Central*, R Frei Durão 8, on attractive square, pleasant, quiet, rec but avoid downstairs rooms. The modern service station (*posto*) on the highway above the town offers good clean rooms at **E**, with hot showers.

● Places to eat

Papinha della Nonna, D Viçoso 27, Italian, rec. *Portão da Praça*, Praça Gomes Freire 108, excellent, 20% discount given to guests of *Pousada do Chafariz*, rec.

● Tourist offices

Terminal Turístico, 500m beyond rodoviária towards colonial centre, Praça Tancredo Neves, guides' association, small tourist office, map US$1.50. Tourist agency, **Transcolta**, Praça JK, T 557-2056; enquire also at **Embratur**, Praça Tancredo Neves, T 557-1533.

● Transport

Buses leave Ouro Preto from beside the Escola de Minas, for Mariana, US$0.75, all passing Minas de Passagem, US$0.25; bus from Belo Horizonte (via Ouro Preto), US$2, 2¼ hrs. Taxi from Ouro Preto, US$7.80.

CONGONHAS DO CAMPO

(*Pop* 41,070; *Alt* 866m; *CEP* 36404; *DDD* 031) A hill town, it is connected with Ouro Preto by a good road through pleasant farming country (a worthwhile day trip). A paved 3½-km road links with the Rio-Belo Horizonte highway.

The town is dominated by the great pilgrimage church of **Bom Jesus do Matozinho** (1773), which opens at 0815. There is a wide view of the country from the church terrace, below which are six small chapels set in attractive sloping gardens, showing scenes with life-size Passion figures carved by Aleijadinho and his pupils in cedar wood. On the terrace stand the 12 prophets sculpted by Aleijadinho (thought of as his masterpieces). Carved in soapstone with dramatic sense of movement, they constitute one of the finest works of art of their period in the world. Inside the church, as

well as the Room of Miracles, there are paintings by Athayde and the heads of four sainted popes (Gregory, Jerome, Ambrose and Augustine) sculpted by Aleijadinho for the reliquaries on the high altar. (Bus 'Basílica', on the hour from opposite the Rodoviária to Bom Jesus, US$0.40.)

Local festivals Congonhas is also celebrated for its Holy Week processions, which have as their focus the Bom Jesus church. The most celebrated ceremonies are the meeting of Christ and the Virgin Mary on the Tues, and the dramatized Deposition from the Cross late on Good Fri. Pilgrimage season, first half of Sept, draws many thousands.

● Accommodation

D *Colonial*, Praça da Basilica 76, opp Bom Jesus, T 731-1834, good and comfortable, breakfast extra, no showers or toilets in room, blankets only, fascinating restaurant downstairs full of colonial handicrafts and good local food; **E** *Freitas*, R Marechal Floriano 69, T 731-1543, basic. There are handicraft shops selling soapstone artefacts.

● Transport Buses

Rodoviária is 1½ km outside town. To/from **Belo Horizonte**, 1½ hrs, US$3.25, 6 times a day, best to buy a return ticket. To **São João del Rei**, either direct (US$13), or go via Murtinho. Bus to **Ouro Preto**: direct (US$13), or go via Belo Horizonte, Murtinho or Conselheiro Lafaiete.

ROUTES None direct from Rio; you have to change buses at **Conselheiro Lafaiete** (**C** *Rhud's Hotel and Restaurant*, R José Nicolau de Queiroz 11, T/F 721-4199; **B** *Hotel Cupim*, on main Rio road, 18 km, T 721-5022, F 721-5375).

DIAMANTINA

(*Pop* 42,980; *Alt* 1,120m; *CEP* 39100; *DDD* 037) The most remote of these cities is reached from Belo Horizonte by taking the paved road to Brasília. Between Caetanópolis and Paraopeba is the *Flora Eunice* (*Leite ao Pé de Vaca*) snackbar (good toilets) with small private botanic garden and zoo with contented animals, recommended. 19 km beyond Paraopeba is a turning NE to **Curvelo** (a lively town, *Hotel Sagarana*, 5-star, very good; *Restaurant Denise* with sleeping accommodation, on main highway, very clean), beyond which the road passes through the impressive rocky country of the Serra do Espinhaço.

Diamantina, centre of a once active diamond industry founded in 1729, has excellent colonial buildings. Its churches (difficult to get into, except for the modern Cathedral) are not as grand as those of Ouro Preto, but it is possibly the least spoiled of all the colonial mining cities, with carved overhanging roofs and brackets. This very friendly town is in the deep interior, amid barren mountains; it is the birthplace of President Juscelino Kubitschek, the founder of Brasília. His house has been converted into a museum.

After repeated thefts, the diamonds of the Diamond Museum, in the house of Padre Rolim, one of the Inconfidentes have been removed to the Banco do Brasil. *Passeio a Diamantina*, an excellent guide, is written by the author of *Passeio a Sabará*. Diamonds are still sought; see traditional methods at Guinda, 7 km away. Other local industries are the making of Portuguese Arraiolos-style tapestry carpets by hand, at a cooperative in the centre, and etchings on leather.

The house of Chica da Silva, an 18th-century slave who married a rich diamond contractor, is at Praça Lobo Mesquita 266, entry free; Chica has become a folk-heroine among Brazilian blacks.

Excursions

Walk along the **Caminho dos Escravos**, the old paved road built by slaves between the mining area on Rio Jequitinhonha and Diamantina. A guide is essential (ask at the Casa de Cultura – cheap), and beware of snakes. Along the river bank to (12 km) **Biribiri**, a pretty village with an abandoned textile factory. About half-way, swimming pools in the river; opposite them, on a cliff face, animal paintings in red, age and origin unknown. Interesting plant life along the river, and beautiful mountain views.

Local information
● Accommodation

B *Tijuco*, Macau do Melo 211, T 931-1022, best, good food.

D *Dália*, Praça JK (Jota-Ka) 25, T 931-1477, fairly good.

E *JK*, opp rodoviária, with breakfast, clean, friendly; **E** *Pensão Comercial*, Praça M Neves 30, basic. Wild camping nr waterfall just outside town.

● Places to eat

Bar-Restaurant Confiança, R da Quitanda 39, good.*Capistrana*, R Campos Carvalho 36, nr Cathedral square, rec. *Serestas* (serenades) Fri and Sat nights; many young people in bars in Beco da Mota.

● Electric current

110 AC.

● Tourist offices

Depto de Turismo in Casa de Cultura in Praça Antônio Eulálio 53, 3rd floor, pamphlets and a reliable map, also information about churches opening times, friendly and helpful, will arrange free tour of churches with guide who has access to keys (tip guide).

● Transport

Six buses a day to **Belo Horizonte**, via Curvelo, with Pássaro Verde: 2½ hrs to **Curvelo**, US$3.25, to **Belo Horizonte**, US$10.75, 5½ hrs.

SERRO

(*Pop* 19,445; *CEP* 39150; *DDD* 037) 92 km by paved road from Diamantina and reached by bus from there or from Belo Horizonte is this unspoiled colonial town on the Rio Jequitinhonha. It has six fine baroque churches, a museum and many beautiful squares. It makes *queijo serrano*, one of Brazil's best cheeses, being in the centre of a prosperous cattle region. The most conspicuous church is **Santa Rita**, on a hill in the centre of town, reached by steps. On the main square, by the bottom of the steps, is the **Carmo**, arcaded, with original paintings on ceiling and in choir. The town has two large mansions: those of the **Barão de Diamantina**, now in ruins, and of the **Barão do Serro** across the river, beautifully restored and used as the town hall and Casa de Cultura; there are old mine entrances in the hillside behind the courtyard.

Just by the Serro turnoff is the town of **Datas**, whose spacious church (1832) decorated in red and blue, contains a striking wooden image of Christ with the crown of thorns.

● Accommodation C *Pousada Vila do Príncipe*, T 941-1485, very clean, in an old mansion at R Antônio Honório Pires 38, contains its own museum, the artist Mestre Valentim is said to

have been born in slave quarters; other cheap hotels.

● **Places to eat** *Itacolomi*, Praça João Pinheiro 20, fair; *Churrascaria Vila do Príncipe* on R A H Pires.

NORTH OF BELO HORIZONTE

THE RIO SAO FRANCISCO

Some 240 km NW of Belo Horizonte is a lake five times as large in area as Rio de Janeiro bay, formed by the **Três Marias** dam on the upper reaches of the São Francisco river. The town (*Pop* 21,410) is at the lake's northern end.

PIRAPORA

North of Três Marias is the terminus for boat journeys on the Rio São Francisco (see also page 529). The cutting down of trees, in part as fuel for the boats, and the low rainfall in recent years, has greatly reduced the flow. The town itself (*Pop* 46,230; *CEP* 39270; *DDD* 037) is a tourist attraction because of the falls in the river which make for excellent fishing. The fishermen use punt-like canoes. The sandy river beaches are used for swimming. The riverboats' grotesque figureheads, *carrancas*, are made in the workshops of Lourdes Barroso, R Abaeté 390.

● **Accommodation B** *Pirapora Palace*, on Praça Melo Viana (7 blocks W and 1 block S of Rodoviária), T 741-1330, ask for room on garden, safe; **C** *Canoeiras*, Av Salmeron 3, T 741-1946, used by river-tour parties; **C** *Daila*, Praça JK 13, with breakfast but without bath; **D** *Grande*, R da Quitanda 70, with bath but without breakfast.

● **Places to eat** *Lá em Casa*, 'meals by the kilo, huge *caipirinhas* US$0.50, excellent value'.

Passenger services on the river have been discontinued. Masters of cargo boats in the port may permit passage. The regular stops are at Januária (famous for Brazil's reputed best *cachaça*) and Bom Jesus da Lapa (a pilgrimage centre with a church built in a grotto inside a mountain, but a very poor town; hotels inc **B** *Hansão das Pedras*, **C** *Real*, **F** *Brasília*; a choice of bars on the river beach). Between Pirapora and Januária is the colonial town of **São Fran-**

cisco, with many attractive houses and a good handicraft market in the town hall; the boats do not always stop there.

● **Tours** Of the two remaining wood-burning stern-wheel boats, allegedly built for Mississippi services in the 1860s and imported from the USA in 1922 to work on the Amazon, one, the *Gaiola*, has been restored for tourist-agency use. An expensive weekly trip (starting Sun) is made downriver visiting various ports as far as São Francisco, organized in Belo Horizonte by *Unitour* (Av Tupis 141) or *Mangabeira Turismo* (R Goitacases 71, 8th floor).

ROUTES Northern Minas to Bahia: take a bus from Pirapora or Diamantina to **Montes Claros**, a pleasant town with many hotels (eg **E** *Giovanni*, close to rodoviária, clean, modern), restaurants and cinemas. Then bus Montes Claros-Almenara (12 hrs), Almenara-Salto da Divisa (2½ hrs; hotel facing bus station), then take a bus to Porto Seguro.

An alternative route to Bahia is the daily 1000 bus to Vitória da Conquista (see page 514, Gontijo line US$13); interesting journey through hilly country, pine and eucalyptus plantations, and many remote towns.

EASTERN MINAS

Eastern Minas Gerais is a centre of semi-precious stone processing and crystal carving, and also contains the Serra do Caparaó, where are found several of Brazil's highest mountains. The two principal towns, Governador Valadares and Teófilo Otôni, are both on the BR-116 inland Rio-Salvador road, and both have good connections with Belo Horizonte. Only through *Focus Tours* (see Belo Horizonte, page 431) can the private Caratinga Biological Station be visited, 880 ha of mountainous, inland Atlantic forest which is home to four rare primates: the muriqui (formerly called the woolly spider monkey, the largest primate in the Americas and the largest mammal endemic to Brazil), the black-capped capuchin, the brown howler monkey and the buffy-headed marmoset. Also at the station are brown-throated, three-toed sloths and an incredible array of birds. The primates and many of the birds are not bothered by human presence. Entrance fee is US$20 pp per day.

GOVERNADOR VALADARES

A modern planned city (*Pop* 230,490; *Alt* 170m; *CEP* 35100; *DDD* 0332), 324 km from Belo Horizonte, 5½ hrs by bus (US$9.50, US$19 *leito*), is a good place to break the Belo Horizonte-Salvador journey. It is a centre of semi-precious stone mines and lapidation, as well as for the cut-crystal animals one finds in tourist shops all around Brazil.

Excursions To the top of the Pico de Ibituruna, 960m.

- **Accommodation A3** *Governador Palace*, Av Minas Gerais 550, T 271-7474, F 271-4750; **B** *Panorama*, Mal Floriano 914, T 221-7833; **B** *Real Minas*, Praça Serra Lima 607, T 271-6751. Many **F** hotels nr bus station.

- **Places to eat** Main hotels; *JB*, R Bárbara Heliodora 384, rec.

- **Transport Air** Airport is on the BR-381, 6 km from the city centre with flights to Belo Horizonte and Ipatinga.

TEÓFILO OTÔNI

(*Pop* 140,640; *Alt* 335m; *CEP* 39800; *DDD* 033) 138 km from Governador Valadares, this is a popular buying spot for dealers of crystals and semi-precious stones, with the best prices in the state.

- **Accommodation C** *Lancaster*, R Frei Gonzaga 142, T 522-3131; **C** *Presidente*, Av Getúlio Vargas 183, good breakfast, laundry facilities; **D** *Pousada Tio Miro*, R Dr Manoel Esteves 389, T 521-4343, relaxed atmosphere, rec.

- **Transport** Buses to Porto Seguro via Nanuque (can break Belo Horizonte-Salvador journey here; **F** *Hotel Minas*, at rodoviária, adequate, and others nearby).

CAPARAÓ NATIONAL PARK

In the park are the Pico da Bandeira (2,890m), Pico do Cruzeiro (2,861m) and the Pico do Cristal (2,798m). The park features rare Atlantic rainforest in its lower altitudes and Brazilian alpine on top. From the park entrance (small fee) it is 6 km on a poorly-maintained road to the car park at the base of the waterfall. From the hotel (see below) jeeps (US$20 per jeep) run to the car park at 1,970m (2½ hrs' walk), then it's a 3-4-hr walk to the summit of the Pico da Bandeira, marked by yellow arrows; plenty of camping pos-

sibilities all the way up, the highest being at Terreirão (2,370m). This is good walking country. It is best to visit during the dry season (April-Oct). It can be quite crowded in July and during Carnaval. Contact via Caixa Postal 17, alto Jequitibá, MG, CEP 36976-000, T 255, via operator on 101, Alto do Caparaó.

- **Accommodation C** *Caparaó Parque*, 2 km from park entrance, 15 mins' walk from the town of Caparaó, nice, T (032) 741-2559. Ask where **camping** is permitted in the park. In **Manhumirim**: **E** *São Luiz*, good value, but *Cids Bar*, next door, Travessa 16 do Março, has better food.

- **Access** Caparaó National Park is 49 km by paved road from Manhuaçu (about 190 km S of Governador Valadores) on the Belo Horizonte-Vitória road (BR-262). There are buses from Belo Horizonte, Ouro Preto or Vitória to **Manhumirim** (pop 27,625), 15 km S of Manhuaçu. From Manhumirim, take a bus direct to Caparaó, 0930, 1630 US$0.80, or to Presidente Soares (several, 7 km), then hitch 11 km to Caparaó. By car from the BR-262, go through Manhumirim, Pres Soares and Caparaó village, then 1 km further to the *Hotel Caparaó Parque*.

THE SPAS OF SOUTHERN MINAS GERAIS

Some 240 km SW of Belo is the huge lake formed by the Furnas dam. It can be seen from the BR-381 road to São Paulo.

The popular spas are easily reached by road and in some cases by air from Rio de Janeiro and São Paulo; Dec-Mar is the high season.

POÇOS DE CALDAS

(*Pop* 110,150; *Alt* 1,180m; *CEP* 37700; *DDD* 035) The city is sited on the crater of an extinct volcano in a mountainous area on the SW border of the state. It is 272 km from São Paulo, 507 km from Rio and 510 km from Belo Horizonte. Venetians from Murano settled here and established a crystal-glass industry. The resort, a traditional honeymoon centre, has thermal establishments for the treatment of rheumatic, skin and intestinal diseases; you need a local doctor's certificate to use these facilities. Excursions include the Véu das Noivas with its three waterfalls illuminated at night; the tall statue of Cristo

Redentor (*alt* 1,678m), which can be reached by cable car; Pedra Batão, an 80m granite rock; and the Japanese teahouse at the Recanto Japonês. Hippie fair every Sun in Praça Pedro Sanches. Festivals include Carnival, São Benedito ending on 13 May, and the Festival de Música Popular Brasileira (Festa UAI, 2nd half of Aug). Excellent climate.

● **Accommodation** Some 80 hotels and pensions. **A1** *Palace*, Praça Pedro Sanches, T 722-1392, old fashioned but well run, with sulphur baths. The following are **E** pp and good: *Real*, R Minas Gerais 390, T 721-4152; *Virginia*, R Minas Gerais 506, T 722-2694.

● **Places to eat** Local specialities: smoked cheese, sausages, sweets and jams (try squash-and-coconut).

● **Banks & money changers** Meridional, R Prefeito Chagas, 138, for Mastercard cash.

● **Transport Air** Airport. A **monorail** runs down the main avenue, Av Fco Sales, to the cable car station. **Buses** Rodoviária 3 km from centre. **Rio**, 8 hrs, US$11.50; **São Paulo**, 4$^{1}/_{2}$ hrs, US$6.60.

HILL RESORTS NEAR TRES CORAÇÕES

8 km E of BR381 is **Tres Corações** (*Pop* 57,040; *DDD* 035), also in southern Minas but not a spa. It is the birthplace of Pelé, the legendary football star (statue). Reached by daily buses from Rio, São Paulo and Belo Horizonte.

● **Accommodation D** *Italian Palace*, Av Dep R Azeredo 1009, T/F 232-2112; **E** *Capri*, Av Getúlio Vargas 111, T 231-1427. Good food at *Hotel Cantina Calabresa*, R J Bento de Carvalho 65, T 231-2108.

There are two daily buses to (35 km, US$1.80, 2 hrs) **São Tomé das Letras**, a beautiful hilltop village, one of the five highest places in Brazil (*Pop* 5,710; *Alt* 1,291m). A traditional quarry town, it has some charming old-style buildings with frescoed 17th-century church and many caves in surrounding hills. Cave inscriptions have lent the town a mystical reputation, attracting 'new age' visitors, very popular at weekends. Waterfalls: Cachoeira de Eusebiose, 4 km; Véu de Noiva 8 km.

● **Accommodation & places to eat** *Hospedaria do Gê*, R Gabriel Luis Alves 28;

restaurant opp, *Das Letras*, both rec. **Other resorts Pocinhos de Rio Verde**, a friendly hill resort, bus 1 hr; *Hotel Bosque das Fontes*, rec, at entrance to town, chalets, camp sites, restaurant, low cost steam and mineral baths; *O Portal*, R Armando Vilela 7, camping, good signage on offer; lake, horses and many trails. Rainy season Oct-March. Downhill, on road to Sobrachinha is the quiet community of **Harmonia**, 'new age', cheap vegetarian food, clean accommodation (**E** pp); *Hospedaria dos Sonhos I* and *II*, T 237 1235, restaurant, swimming pool, sauna, television in rooms, rec.

OTHER HYDRO RESORTS

São Lourenço (*Pop* 29,510; *Alt* 850m; *CEP* 37470; *DDD* 035) is easily accessible from Rio de Janeiro (5-6 hrs by bus) or São Paulo (6-7 hrs by bus). There is a splendid park, tennis, boating, swimming, a flying field, and fishing from the Ilha dos Amores in a lake ringed by gardens and forests. Its rich mineral waters are used in the treatment of stomach, liver, kidney and intestinal complaints. The famous carbo-gaseous baths are unique in South America. There is a grand ride through fine scenery to the Pico de Buqueré (1,500m). On Sat and Sun a tourist train goes to São Lourenço from Cruzeiro (São Paulo state), 0900, US$15 including guide and snack.

The waters at **Caxambu** (*Pop* 19,470; *Alt* 900m; *CEP* 37440; *DDD* 035), N of São Lourenço, are used for treating stomach, kidney and bladder diseases, and are said to restore fertility. They seemed to work for Princess Isabel, daughter of Dom Pedro II, who produced three sons after a visit. The little church of Santa Isabel da Hungária stands on a hill as a thank-offering. The mountains and forests around are very beautiful. View over the city from Morro Caxambu, 1,010m. Excellent hotels.

Lambari (*Pop* 16,080; *Alt* 900m; *CEP* 37480; *DDD* 035) is 56 km W of Caxambu. The Parque das Águas has seven springs and a swimming pool. There are boat trips on the Lago Guanabara. Casino. **Cambuquirá** (*Pop* 11,600; *Alt* 946m; *CEP* 37420; *DDD* 035) is a little N of Lambari by road, very popular.

374 km W of Belo Horizonte is **Araxá** (*Pop* 69,860; *Alt* 970m) in the Minas Triangle, with thorium and radio-active waters, sulphur and mud baths. Airport.

● **Accommodation A1** *Grande de Araxá*, luxury, 8 km away, T 661-2011; **A3** *Colombo*, same location, T 661-3016, F 661-5367; *Pinto*, Pres O Maciel 284, T 661-2551.

From Araxá, BR-262 heads W to **Uberaba** (120 km; *Pop* 210,800; *Alt* 700m; *CEP* 38100; *DDD* 034), also in the Minas Triangle on the Rio da Prata, 718 km from São Paulo. It is an important road junction on the direct highway between São Paulo and Brasília and serves a large cattle raising district. At the beginning of May each year the Rural Society of the Minas Triangle holds a famous cattle and agricultural exhibition at Uberaba. Several hotels and restaurants. Bus from Belo Horizonte, US$11.50 (leito US$23), 7 hrs.

About 100 km N of Uberaba is **Uberlândia** (*Pop* 366,710; *CEP* 38400; *DDD* 034), founded in 1888 as São Pedro do Uberabinha; good communications by air and road (buses to Brasília, 6 hrs, US$9; to Belo Horizonte, 9 hrs, US$14.50, to São Paulo, US$15.25). **D** *Hotel Nacional*, Higino Guerra 273, T 235-4983, opp rodoviária, with view (cheaper without), shower and breakfast; many others, also restaurants. In the rodoviária is a helpful tourist information kiosk.

SERRA DA CANASTRA NATIONAL PARK

South of Araxá is the **Serra da Canastra National Park**, in which the Rio São Francisco rises. It is a cool region (temperatures in May and June average 18°C), best reached from Piumhi, on state road 050, 267 km SW of Belo Horizonte. (Ibama, address as for Serra do Cipó, above.)

The State of São Paulo

THE state is the industrial heart of Brazil, with much agriculture too; the city is the financial centre. The metropolis does have much of cultural interest in the way of museums, and the famous Butantã Snake Farm. On the coast there are many fine beaches, although pollution is a problem; inland there are hill resorts.

The State of São Paulo (*Pop* over 31,000,00), with an area of 247,898 square km, is larger than the states of New York and Pennsylvania together and about the same size as Great Britain and Northern Ireland. A narrow zone of wet tropical lowland along the coast rises in an unbroken slope to the ridge of the Great Escarpment – the Serra do Mar – at from 800 to 900m above sea level. The upland beyond the Great Escarpment is drained westwards by the tributaries of the Rio Paraná. The broad valleys of the uplands are surmounted by ranges of low mountains; one such range lies between the São Paulo basin and the hinterland of the state. West of the low mountains between the basin and the rest of the state lie the uplands of the Paraná Plateau, at about 600m above the sea. One of the soils in this area is the terra roxa, the red earth in which coffee flourishes. When dry it gives off a red dust which colours everything; when wet it is sticky and slippery. There is ample rainfall in São Paulo State; indeed, the highest rainfall in Brazil (3,810 mm) is over a small area between Santos and São Paulo; at São Paulo itself it is no more than 1,194 mm. Temperatures on the plateau are about 5°C lower than on the coast, but it is only S of the latitude of Sorocaba that frosts occur and then not frequently. Temperatures are too low for coffee in the São Paulo basin itself, but the State produces, on average, about 7 million bags a year.

Between 1885 and the end of the century a boom in coffee and the arrival of large numbers of Europeans transformed the State out of all recognition. By the end of the 1930s there had arrived in São Paulo State a million Italians, half a million each of Portuguese and immigrants from the rest of Brazil, nearly 400,000 Spaniards and nearly 200,000 Japanese. It is the world's largest Japanese community outside Japan. Today the State produces some 20% of Brazil's agricultural output and 65% (40% in São Paulo city alone) of its industrial production. São Paulo provides 33% of the total exports of Brazil and takes 40% of the total imports.

SÃO PAULO

São Paulo (*Pop* 10,998,000 – metropolitan population est 19,000,000; *Alt* 730m; *CEP* 01000; *DDD* 011) is 429 km from Rio de Janeiro, and is connected with it by air, the Via Dutra highway, and the Central do Brasil railway. It is the most populous city in South America and the continent's leading industrial centre. Visitors find the characteristic sharp changes of temperature troublesome and even Paulistanos seem to catch cold often. (Incidentally, one differentiates between Paulistas – inhabitants of the State – and Paulistanos – inhabitants of the city.) The amount of air pollution can be exasperating: in dry weather eyes and nose are continually troubled.

HISTORY

São Paulo was founded in 1554 by two Jesuit priests from São Vicente, Blessed José Anchieta and Padre Manuel Nóbrega, as a mission station. The original settlement, was at the Pátio do Colégio in the centre of the city, where a copy of Anchieta's original church has been built, using one of the surviving mud-packed walls of the original 16th century structure (open Tues-Sun, 1300-1700).

Until the 1870s it was a sleepy, shabby little town known as 'a cidade de barro' (the mud city), as most of its buildings were made of clay and packed mud. The city was transformed architecturally at the end of the 19th century when wealthy landowners began to invest in São Paulo as a financial and residential centre. The main reasons for the city's development lie in its position at the focus of so much agricultural wealth, and the availability of plentiful hydro-electric power. Nowadays, it covers more than 1,500 sq km – three times the size of Paris; short-sighted planning policies in the 1980s contributed to the loss of innumerable historical buildings and green areas.

DISTRICTS

The shopping, hotel and restaurant centre embraces the districts of Av São Luís, Praça da República, and R Barão de Itapetininga. The central commercial district, containing banks, offices and shops, is known as the Triângulo, bounded by R Direita, Quinze de Novembro, São Bento and Praça Antônio Prado, but it is rapidly spreading towards the Praça da República. R Augusta begins close to Av São Luís, extends as far as **Avenida Paulista**, and continues beyond into one of the most affluent areas, Jardins. Both sides of R Augusta have a variety of shops, snackbars and restaurants, but the Jardins side contains the more exclusive boutiques and fashion houses, while the part which leads to the centre is a rather curious but colourful mix of seedy bars, saunas and 5-star hotels. Avenida Paulista, once the home of coffee barons and São Paulo's

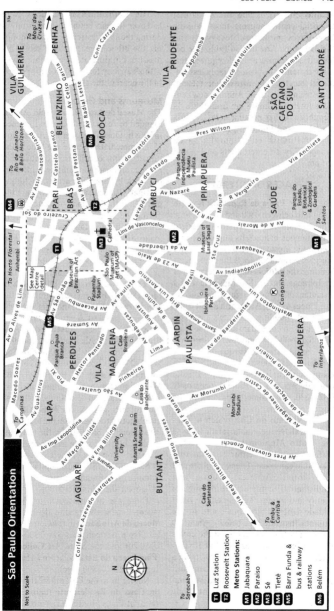

São Paulo Orientation

Not to Scale

T1 Luz Station
T2 Roosevelt Station
Metro Stations:
M1 Jabaquara
M2 Paraiso
M3 Sé
M4 Tietê
M5 Barra Funda &
bus & railway
stations
M6 Belém

wealthy citizens, is now Brazil's largest financial centre housing most banking head offices (most consulates as well), and the Museu de Arte de São Paulo (see below). It is becoming a new downtown area, more dynamic, but considerably less colourful than the old centre with its maze of pedestrianized streets. Another new centre is Av Faria Lima, 8 km from Praça da República. Other popular areas are Vila Madalena and Pinheiros; in the latter is Espaço Paulista on Depto La Cerda Franco 87, with entertainers on Fri and Sat pm.

PLACES OF INTEREST

The park in **Praça da República** is worth going into between 0800 and 1400 on Sun: birds, trees and Brazilians in all their variety, and a famous handicrafts fair; on Sat pm there is live music, and stalls sell sweets and salgados. Near the Praça is the city's tallest building, the **Edifício Itália** on the corner of Av Ipiranga and Av São Luís. There is a restaurant on top and a sightseeing balcony (see **Places to eat**). Also worth a visit is the **Martinelli building**, the city's first skyscraper, R Líbero Badaró and Av São João, Mon-Sat, 0900-1600, entry to 26th floor, free. Two central parks are **Parque da Luz**, Av Tiradentes (110,000 sq metres) and **Siqueira Campos** (Parque Trianon), Peixoto Gomilde 949 and Av Paulista, open daily 0700-1830, a welcome green area in the busiest part of the city.

The **Viaduto do Chá**, which bridges the central avenue, Anhangabaú, leads to the **Teatro Municipal**, one of the few distinguished 19th-century survivals that São Paulo can boast. The Av Paulista and the 'jardins' América, Paulista and Paulistano still contain some mansions of beauty and interest and are on the 702U Cidade Universitária bus route to the Butantã Institute (see below). About 10 mins' walk from the centre of the city is the old **Mercado Municipal** at R Cantareira 306 (open Mon-Sat 0400-1600); a new Mercado Municipal has been built in the outskirts. The **Biblioteca Municipal** is surrounded by a pleasant shady garden.

The **Cathedral's** foundations were laid over 40 years before its inauguration during the 1954 festivities commemorating the 4th centenary of the city. This massive building in neo-Gothic style, with a capacity for 8,000 worshippers, is in the heart of the city.

Museums and Galleries

The **Museu de Arte de São Paulo** (MASP, founded by Assis Chateaubriand, opened in 1968 by Queen Elizabeth II, Av Paulista 1578, immediately above the 9 de Julho tunnel) has major collections of European painters and sculptors, and some interesting work by Brazilian artists, including Portinari. Particularly interesting are the pictures of the NE done by Dutch artists during the Dutch occupation (1630-54): the exotic tropical landscapes have been made to look incredibly temperate. (Exhibitions vary, not all the artists above may be on view.) Temporary exhibitions are held in the basement. Entrance US$5 (free on Thur), Tues-Fri 1300-1700, Sat-Sun 1400-1800 (nearest metro is Paraíso on the N-S line, or MASP-Trianon on the new line, or bus 805A from Praça da República). The **Museu de Arte Brasileira** is at R Alagoas 903, Pacaembu, entrance free, Tues-Fri 1400-2200, Sat-Sun 1300-1800, houses collections of Brazilian artists such as Portinari, Anita Malfatti and Brecheret. Here also there are copies of Brazilian sculptures, including those of Aleijadinho. The **Museu de Arqueologia e Etnologia** is on the fourth and fifth floors of Bloco D in the students resident blocks (known as Crusp) in the main Arts Complex of the Universidade de São Paulo (USP), bus stop before the entrance to the Butantã Institute (see page 447); open Tues-Fri 0900-1700.

There are two museums on Av Tiradentes, near the Jardim da Luz, the **Museu de Arte Sacra** in the Convento da Luz, No 676 (open Tues-Sun 1300-1700, US$0.20) and the **State Art Collection** (**Pinacoteca do Estado**) at No 141 (open Tues-Sun 1300-1800, free).

Not far from the Butantã Institute are the **Casa do Bandeirante** (being renovated) at Praça Monteiro Lobato, the re-

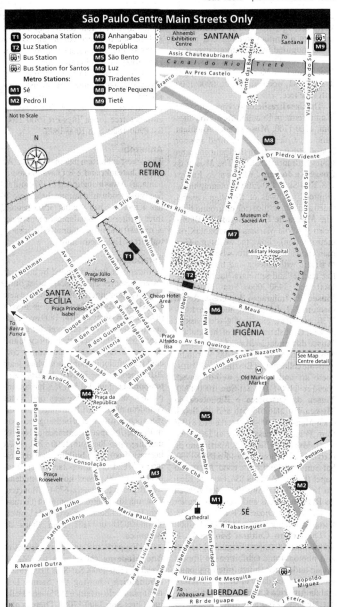

São Paulo Centre Main Streets Only

T1 Sorocabana Station
T2 Luz Station
🚌1 Bus Station
🚌2 Bus Station for Santos

Metro Stations:
M1 Sé
M2 Pedro II
M3 Anhangabau
M4 República
M5 São Bento
M6 Luz
M7 Tiradentes
M8 Ponte Pequena
M9 Tietê

constructed home of a pioneer of 400 years ago; and the **Casa do Sertanista**, a museum of Indian folklore and handicrafts mounted by the famous expert on the Indians, Orlando Villas Boas, at Av Prof Francisco Morato 2200, Caxingui, T 211-5341, open Tues-Sun, 0900-1700, entrance free.

The **Casa Brasileira**, Av Faria Lima 774, is a museum of Brazilian furniture, Tues-Sun, 1300-1700. **Museu Padre Anchieta**, Pátio do Colégio, is a restored mission house, with items from the Jesuit era, same hours, entrance US$0.50. The **Museu da Imagem e do Som** (MIS) is at Av Europa 158, Tues-Sun 1400-2200, photographic exhibitions, archives of Brazilian cinema, video and music, nice café on ground floor. The **Museu de Lasar Segall**, R Alfonso Celso 362, Vila Mariana (near Santa Cruz metro station), shows the works of a German expressionist painter who emigrated to Brazil, with cinema and library, holds free courses and seminars, Tues-Fri 1430-1800, Sat 1430-2000, Sun 1430-1830. **Museu da Imigração Japonesa**, R São Joaquim 381, Liberdade, Tues-Sun 1330-1730, excellent, nice roof garden, ask at desk for English translation of the exhibits. **Museu da Fundação Maria Luisa e Oscar Americano**, Av Morumbi 3700, Morumbi, a private collection of Brazilian and Portuguese art and furniture, well-displayed, Tues-Fri 1100-1700, Sat-Sun 1000-1700. **Museu da Discoteca e Biblioteca da Música**, R Catão 611, 5th and 6th floors, open Mon-Fri, 0900-1300 (take bus 819 P from Praça Princesa Isabel to Lapa district). **Museu do Telefone**, Martiniano de Carvalho 851, Paraíso, Tues-Fri 0900-1730, Sat-Sun 1400-1800, quite good. **Museu do Papel** (Paper), R Mauá 836, casa 25, Tues-Fri 1330-1700, Sat-Sun 1000-1400. **Museu do Relógio** (clocks and watches), rec for enthusiasts, Av Diógenes R de Lima 2333, Pompéia, Mon-Fri 0800-1130, 1300-1700.

The **Centro Cultural São Paulo**, R Vergueiro 1000 (metro Vergueiro) has art and photographic exhibitions, a library, music and dance shows (often regional) and films; open daily until 2200. **Memorial da América Latina**, designed by Oscar Niemeyer, built in Mar 1989, at Av Mário de Andrade 664, next to Barra Funda metro station, relief map of Central and South America under a glass floor in the section which houses a permanent exhibition of handicrafts from all over Latin America, library of photographs, books, magazines, newspapers and films shown on video, very impressive, restaurant; at weekends there are free concerts, entrance free (open Tues-Fri 0900-2100, Sat 0900-1800, Sun 1000-1800).

Anhembi

The largest exhibition hall in the world (Av Assis Chateaubriand e R Olava Fontoura, Santana), it was inaugurated in 1970 and all São Paulo's industrial fairs are held there. It has a meeting hall seating 3,500 people, three auditórios, 24 conference rooms (*salas de reunião*) and two restaurants. It's a short walk from Tietê metro station.

Ibirapuera

In Ibirapuera Park (designed by architect Oscar Niemeyer and landscape artist Burle Marx) is the architecturally impressive new **Legislative Assembly**. There is also a **planetarium** (shows at 1600-1800 weekends and holidays, during the week for groups only, T 544-4606); a velodrome for cycle and motor-cycle racing; an all-aluminium covered stadium for indoor sports which seats 20,000 people. The **Museu de Arte Contemporâneo**, founded in 1963, has an important collection of Western and South American modern art. The collection is divided between the Bienal building, 3rd floor, in Parque Ibirapuera (entrance at back of building, open Tues-Sun, 1200-1700, closed holidays, free) and a building at R da Reitoria 109, Cidade Universitária, open Wed-Sun 1000-1700, closed holidays, students free. Buses to Ibirapuera, 675-C (Monções) from Ana Rosa metro station; 6414 (Gatusa) from Praça da Bandeira; to Cidade Universitária 702U or 7181 from Praça da República.

In this park, too, are the museums of **Arte Moderna** (Modern Art – MAM, Tues-Fri 1300-1900, Sat-Sun 1100-1900), **Aeronáutica** (showing the Santos Dumont plane; closed since 1995), and **Folklore** (Tues-Sun 1400-1700). There is also a unique display of nativity scenes and scenes of the life of Christ. (Concerts held at Christmas-time.) At the entrance is a majestic monument to the Bandeirantes, or pioneers.

Every odd-numbered year the São Paulo Bienal at Ibirapuera has the most important show of modern art in Latin America, open from beginning of Sept till November.

Shopping centres

Typical of modern development are the huge Iguatemi, Ibirapuera and Morumbi **shopping centres**. They include luxurious cinemas, snack bars and most of the best shops in São Paulo. On a humbler level are the big supermarkets of El Dorado (Av Pamplona 1704) and Pão de Açúcar (Praça Roosevelt, near the *Hilton*); the latter is open 24 hrs a day (except Sun).

CITY EXCURSIONS

The large municipal stadium in the **Pacaembu** valley, a residential district, is built on Olympic lines in an area of 75,500 sq metres. It holds nearly 70,000 spectators. Besides the flood-lit football ground including athletics field and basketball court, there are also a covered gymnasium, open-air and covered tennis courts, an illuminated 50m long swimming pool, and a great hall for receptions and rallies. There is a larger stadium holding 100,000 people in **Morumbi**, another residential district. Motor racing fans might like to visit the Morumbi cemetery, last resting place of Ayrton Senna; take 6291 bus to Rua Prof Benedito Montenegro.

The palatial **Jockey Club** racecourse is in the Cidade Jardim area with easy access by bus (Butantã from República, among others). Race meetings are held on Mon, Wed and Thur at 1730 and Sat and Sun at 1500.

The Butantã Snake Farm and Museum, Av Dr Vital Brasil 1500, Pinheiros, on the university campus, is the most popular tourist attraction. The snakes are milked for their poison six times a day but you may not witness this; the antidotes made from the venom have greatly reduced deaths from snakebite in Brazil. It also deals with spider and scorpion venom, has a small hospital and is a biomedical research institute. Open daily from 0900-1700 (except Mon), entrance US\$1.50. Informative museum; details in English and Portuguese. From Praça da República take bus marked 'Butantã' or 'Cidade Universitária' (Nos 701U or 792U) along Av Paulista, and ask to be let out at Instituto Butantã.

Parque da Independência, in the suburb of Ipiranga, contains the famous Ipiranga Monument to commemorate the declaration of Brazilian independence; beneath the monument is the Imperial Chapel, with the tomb of the first emperor, Dom Pedro I, and Empress Leopoldina (open Tues-Sun, 1300-1700). Take bus 4612 from Praça da República. The **Casa do Grito**, the little house in which Dom Pedro I spent the night before his famous cry of Ipiranga – 'Independence or Death' – is preserved in the park (open Tues-Sun 0930-1700). The **Museu Paulista**, housed in a huge palace at the top of the park, has old maps, traditional furniture, collections of old coins and of religious art and rare documents, and a department of Indian ethnology. Behind the Museum is the **Ipiranga Botanical Garden**. Open Tues-Sun and holidays, 0900-1700. Take bus 478-P (Ipiranga-Pompéia for return) from Ana Rosa. There is a *son et lumière* show on Brazilian history in the park on Wed, Fri and Sat evenings at 2030.

Parque do Estado (Jardim Botânico), out at Água Funda (Av Miguel Estefano 3687), has a vast garden esplanade surrounded by magnificent stone porches, with lakes and trees and places for picnics, and a very fine orchid farm worth seeing during the flowering season, Nov-December. Over 32,000 different kinds of orchids are cultivated. Open Tues-Fri, 0900-1130, 1230-1700, Sat-Sun 0900-1600. The astronomical observatory nearby is open to the public Thur afternoons. Take metro to São Judas on Jabaquara line, then bus.

Zoological Gardens, Av Miguel Estefano 4241, near the Jardim Botânico, have a large variety of specimens in an almost natural setting of about 35 ha of forest. Open 0900-1700, admission US$0.45 (bus 4742, 'Jardim Celeste', from São Judas). There is a wild-life park, **Simba Safari**, nearby, admission US$0.80 per pedestrian, US$3 pp with a car (children under 11 free), open Tues-Fri 1000-1630, Sat-Sun 0900-1630 (1730 in summer).

Parque Água Branca (Av Água Branca 455) has beautiful gardens with specimens of tropical plants, Brazilian birds and wildlife. Pavilions house a well stocked aquarium, a zoo, and exhibitions of food produce.

In Tremembé, a little beyond Cantareira, 30 mins from the down-town area, is the **Horto Florestal** (R do Horto, in Parque Estadual da Cantareira, 7,900 ha), containing examples of nearly every species of Brazilian woodland flora, 15 km of natural trails, museum with exhibits of regional flora and fauna, view of São Paulo from Pedra Grande on the right of entrance to the park (admission US$0.80, daily, 0700-1730).

Miraporanga Botanical and Wildlife Sanctuary in the foothills of the Serra do Mar, is 1 hr's drive from São Paulo city centre. It has a vast collection of orchids, carnivorous and aquatic plants, waterlily pools, a lake and 20 glasshouses. It also contains armadilloes, deer and other mammals, monitor lizards and a variety of hummingbirds, T Sr Samuel Jorge de Mello, 816-0817, weekends 476-6716 for information and prices.

Santo Amaro Dam (Old Lake), is 3 km from the centre of Santo Amaro suburb. This is a popular boating resort with several sailing clubs and many attractive cottages along the shore. There is a bus (30 min) from São Paulo to Santo Amaro.

Interlagos (Av Interlagos, T 577-0522), which have an 18-km motor-racing circuit, is São Paulo's lake resort on the Santo Amaro dam. It can be reached from Santo Amaro by bus. Close to the track, where the Brazilian Grand Prix takes place every second year, usually in Feb, is the 32-km long **Guarapiranga** artificial lake with good restaurants and several luxurious sailing and sports clubs (Av Guarapiranga 575, open 0600-1700 daily). Camping Clube do Brasil site. Guarapiranga is less polluted than the other artificial lake, Billings, which also has restaurants.

Pico de Jaraguá (1,135m) the highest peak in the neighbourhood, gives good views of Greater São Paulo on a fine day. Lots of hang gliding here at weekends; reached from Km 18 on the Campinas highway (Via Anhanguera) by a good road through Taipas and Pirituba.

Embu (*Pop* 138,520), 28 km from São Paulo, is a colonial town which has become a centre for artists and craftsmen. On Sun afternoons there is a large and popular arts and crafts fair (0900-1800). Buses from close to the Largo de Pinheiros, São Paulo, or Santo Amaro bus.

LOCAL HOLIDAYS

25 Jan (Foundation of City). Note that during carnival most museums and attractions are closed.

LOCAL INFORMATION

● **Accommodation**

Hotel prices

L1	over US$200	**L2**	US$151-200
L3	US$101-150	**A1**	US$81-100
A2	US$61-80	**A3**	US$46-60
B	US$31-45	**C**	US$21-30
D	US$12-20	**E**	US$7-11
F	US$4-6	**G**	up to US$3

Unless otherwise stated, all hotels in range **D** and above have private bath. Assume friendliness and cleanliness in all cases.

NB Hotels in our **L1** range can exceed US$300 a night. Among the most luxurious (corporate rates available), all with swimming pools, nightclubs and convention halls, are the **L1** *Brasilton*, R Martins Fontes 330, T 258-5811, F 258-5812; **L1** *Caesar Park*, R Augusta 1508, T 253-6622, F 288-6146; **L1** *Della Volpe Garden*, R Frei Caneca 1199, T 285-5388, F 288-8710, rec; **L1** *Grand Hotel Cà d'Oro*, R Augusta 129, T 236-4300, F 236-4311; **L1** *Hilton*, Av Ipiranga 165, T 256-0033, F 257-3137; **L1** *Holiday Inn Crowne Plaza*, R Frei Caneca 1360, T 253-2244, F 251-3121, 5-star, central, small swimming pool, very comfortable; **L1** *Hotel Deville*, Av Monteiro Lobato s/n, Guarulhos, T 6468-0400, F 6464-0594, comfortable, excellent food, nr airport; **L1** *Maksoud Plaza*,

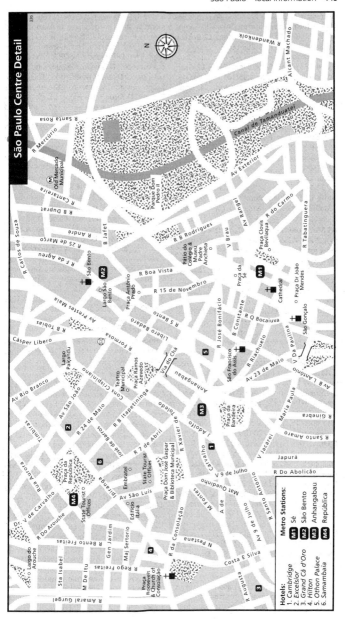

São Paulo Centre Detail

Metro Stations:
M1 Sé
M2 São Bento
M3 Anhangabau
M4 República

Hotels:
1. Cambridge
2. Excelsior
3. Grand Cã d'Oro
4. Hilton
5. Othon Palace
6. Samambaia

Alameda Campinas 150, T 253-4411, F 253-4544; **L1 Mofarrej Sheraton**, Alameda Santos 1437, T 253-5544, F 280-8670 (rec); **L2 Bristol**, R Martins Fontes 277, T 258-0011, F 231-1265; **L2 Eldorado Boulevard**, Av São Luís 234, T 214-1833, F 256-8061 (excellent); **L2 Gran Corona**, Basílio da Gama 95/101, T 214-0043, F 214-4503, convenient, comfortable, good services, warmly rec; **L3 Linson**, R Augusta 440, Consolação, T 256-6700, F 258-5371, all apartments with double bed, kitchenette, sitting room, bath, TV security system, restaurant, pool; **L3 Othon Palace**, R Líbero Badaró 190, T 239-3277, F 37-7203; **L3 Planalto**, Cásper Líbero 117 (Varig-Tropical chain), T 230-7311, F 227-7916, secure, helpful, good service, good dining room; **L3 Samambaia**, R Sete de Abril 422, T 231-1333 (discounts for cash and at weekends); **L3 San Juan**, Aurora 909, nr Praça da República airport bus terminal, T 250-9100, rec. A residential hotel, rec for longer stays, is **A1 Metropolitan Plaza**, Alameda Campinas 474, T 287-4855, F 285-3158. There are many other Aparthotels which are rec for longer stays. **Service-Flat Monterey**, Alameda Itu 265, Jardim Paulista, T 285-6111, F 283-3247, has been rec for longer stays, safe parking, comfortable accommodation; **A3 Banri**, R Galvão Bueno 209, T 270-8877, F 278-9225, good, nr metro station Liberdade (Japanese quarter).

There are scores of cheaper hotels, of which we include a selection: **C Continental**, R Vitória 223, safe, highly rec; **C Itamarati**, Av Vieira de Carvalho 150, T 222-4133, 1/2 block from Praça da República, good location, safe, highly rec; **C Itauna**, Av Rio Branco 280, well furnished, rec; **C Las Vegas**, R Vitória 390 (corner Av Rio Branco)rec; **C Lincoln**, Av Rio Branco 47, excellent breakfast, safe, rec; **C Joamar**, José de Barros, Centro, in the pedestrian area, hot showers, safe, TV, room service; **C Natal**, R Guaianazes 41, T 220-6722, very well rec; **C Ofir**, R dos Timbiras 258, T 223-8822, stores valuables but not money, big rooms, TV, well equipped, good value; **C Plaza Marabá**, Av Ipiranga 757, T 220-7811, rec; **C Riviera**, Av Barão de Limeira 117, T 221-8077, excellent value, highly rec; **C S Sebastião**, 7 de Abril 364 (T 257-4988/255-1594), rec; **C Serrano**, R Gago Coutinho 22, T 285-3233, warmly rec.

D Metro, R Vergueiro 1563, nr Paraíso, T 549-8531, without breakfast, quiet, convenient. In Av São João: **B Cineasta**, No 613, T 222-5533, a/c; **C Central**, No 288, **D** without shower, good, helpful, central; many others in the district.

Take the metro to Luz station and in the block behind the old Rodoviária, off Av Rio Branco, there are scores of cheap hotels with prices ranging from E to C: R Santa Ifigênia: **C Uai**, No 66, pleasant, rooms on street are good, rec; **D Aliança**, R Gral Osório 235, corner of Sta Ifigênia, nice; **D Luanda**, No 348, with breakfast, English-speaking owner, helpful, rec; **D Trinidade**, No 737, good value. R dos Gusmões: **D Galeão**, No 394, safe, helpful, hot showers; **D Itaipu**, No 467, good; **D Lepanto**, R Cásper Líbero 359, shower, TV; **D Lima**, Ipiranga 770, rec; **D Tatuí**, Praça Princeza Isabel 171 (on corner of Av Duque de Caxias, 2 blocks from old bus station), clean with bath. **NB** The red light district is in the blocks bounded by RR Santa Ifigênia, dos Andradas, dos Gusmões and Av Ipiranga, and is definitely not rec for women travelling alone. The whole area around Av Rio Branco is rather seedy and not entirely safe late at night.

E Casa do Politécnico, R Afonso Pena 272, cheap accommodation; **E São José**, Alameda Barão de Piracicaba 221, without breakfast, basic.

Youth hostels: at R Mariz e Barros 350, Vila Santa Eulália (bus 4491 from Parque Dom Pedro in the centre), F, cooking and washing facilities, good fruit and vegetable market directly across R Ricardo Jafet on Tues. YHA for membership, 15 de Novembro e Av São João – office in centre, about US$5 a year. Also Magdalena Tagliaferro, Estrada Turística do Jaguará 651, Km 18, via Anhanguera, 05173 São Paulo (T 229-3787/3011); **Sampa City**, R dos Franceses 100, T/F 288-1592, 500m from Brigadeiro metro station, US$6.50, and **Bela Vista**, R João Passalacqua 181, T 607 3662, US$7 rec.

Camping: list of sites can be obtained from Camping Clube do Brasil, R Minerva 156, Perdizes (T 864-7133).

● **Places to eat**
Apart from the international cuisine in the first-class hotels, here are a few recommendations out of many (the average price of a meal in 1996 was US$20-30 in trattorias, US$40-60 in 1st class places rising to US$100 in the very best restaurants; remember that costs can be cut by sharing the large portions served.

The best (by all accounts): **Bassi**, R 13 de Maio 334, T 34-2375, Bela Vista, for meat; **Don Curro**, R Alves Guimarães 230, T 852-4712, Piaheiros, closed Mon, for seafood, especially paella; **Le Bistingo**, Al Franca 580, T 289-3010; **Massimo**, Al Santos 1826, T 284-0311, international cuisine; **Antiquarius**, Al Lorena 1884, T 282-3015, Portuguese; **La Tambouille**, Av 9 de Julho 5925, Itaim Bibi, T 883-6276, French and Italian, closed Mon, reserve in advance.

French: **L'Affiche**, R Campos Bicudo 141, small, intimate, décor inc owner's collection of antique French posters; **La Casserole**, Largo do Arouche 346 (centro), best known bistro in São Paulo, closed Mon (US$40-60 pp). **Marcel**, R da Consolação 3534, sensational soufflés.

German: *Jucalemão*, R Álvaro Rodrigues 320; *Arnold's Naschbar*, R Pereira Leite 98, Sumarezinho, *Eisbein peruruca*, rec; *Bismarck* (excellent draught beer) and *Paprika* (very reasonable), on Av Ibirapuera 3178 and 573 respectively.

Greek: *Zorba*, R Henrique Monteiro 218.

Hungarian: *Hungaria*, Al Joaquim Eugênio de Lima 776, Jardins, old world décor, expensive; *Hungaria Express*, Av Jaú 310, cheap.

Italian: *San Genovese*, R Bela Cintra 1849, very reasonable, US$29 pp, *salada Lellis* is a must, and fresh squid in batter; *Famiglia Mancini*, R Avanhandava 81, Bela Vista, excellent, salads and cold dishes, always queues between 2000-2400; *Gigetto*, Avanhandava 63, for pasta, reasonable prices; *Trattoria del Sargento*, Al Pamplona 1354, Jardim Paulista, popular; *Da Fiorella*, R Bernardino de Campos 294, Brooklin (closed Mon and Sun pm), top quality vegetarian pasta; *Don Cicillio*, Praça Tomás Morus 185, Perdizes, homecooking in traditional surroundings; *Via Veneto*, Al Barros 909, Sta Cecília, for pasta and meat, very popular; *La Trattoria*, R Antônio Bicudo 50, Pinheiros, closed Mon, midweek until 1900, Fri, Sat till 0100, reasonably priced food, *strozzapreti* a must; *La Farina*, Av Ipiranga 924, for cheap pasta, popular. Many Italian restaurants in Bela Vista/Bixiga area, especially R 13 de Maio; rec pizzerias are *Torre do Bixiga*, 13 de Maio 848, *Capuano*, R Consarrão 416, *Margherita*, Al Tietê 255.

Portuguese: *Abril em Portugal*, R Caio Prado 47, reasonable; *Bocage*, Al Joaquim Eugênio de Lima 1377.

Russian: *Samovar*, R Baronesa de Bela Vista 602, Aeroporto, typical shows at weekends, closed Sun.

Swiss: *Chamonix*, Al Lorena 1052, and *Le Jardin Suisse*, Al Franca 1467, both in Jardim Paulista, expensive, very good.

Arabic: *Almanara*, reasonable, Av São João 1155 (Centro), Oscar Freire 523 (Cerqueiro César), R Basilio da Gama 70 and Av Vieira de Carvalho 109 (Consolação), Al Itú 1564, Jardim Paulista, mainly Lebanese, high standard, not cheap; *Bambi*, Al Santos 59, cheapish; *Rubayat*, Av Vieira de Carvalho 116, Al Santos 86 and Av Faria Lima 583, excellent meat, fixed price meals.

Indian: *Govinda*, R Princesa Isabel 379, expensive.

Oriental: (Japanese tends to be expensive) *Sino-Brasileiro*, R Alberto Torres 39 (Perdizes); *Iti Fuji*, Al Jaú 487, typical Japanese; *Sushigen*, Av Brig Luis Antônio 2367, Lojas 13 and 14, for *sushi* and *sashimi* but a bit overpriced; *Komazushi*, same street No 2050, Loja 7, reasonably priced; *Korea House*, Galvão Bueno 43 (Liberdade). *Kar Wua* Chinese restaurant, at R Mourato Coelho 30, highly praised. Many other Chinese and Japanese restaurants in Liberdade, the Japanese quarter, where there is a Japanese food market in the square by the metro station.

Vegetarian: almost always the cheapest option in São Paulo. *Sattva*, R da Consolação 3140; *O Arroz de Ouro*, Largo do Arouche 42-44 (shop as well, central); *Cheiro Verde*, Peixoto Gomilde 1413, Jardins, more expensive than most; *Nutri Som*, R 9 Júlio 160, rec; *Intergrão*, R Joaquim Antunes 377, macrobiotic; *Delícia Natural*, Av Rio Branco 211 (4th floor), corner Av Ipiranga, lunch only; *Sabor Natural*, same building, 1st floor, lunch only; *Folhas e Raizes*, Líbero Bádaro 370, buffet lunch US$3.20; *Saúde Sabor*, São Bento 500, lunch only; *Vegetaliano*, D Sampaio 155, Sto Amaro, Italian vegetarian. 'Vida Integral' newspaper gives details of all health food restaurants and stores in São Paulo.

General: *Terraço Itália*, on top of Edifício Itália (Ipiranga e São Luis), 41 floors up, fixed price lunch and other meals, dancing with excellent band and superb view (minimum consumption charge of US$10 to be allowed to see the view), US$85 pp inc wine in dancing part, US$65-70 otherwise, dress smartly; *Mexilhão*, R 13 de Maio 626, Bela Vista, seafood; *Paulista*, João Moura 527, Pinheiros, top quality meat, popular; *Dinho's Place*, Al Santos 45 and Largo do Arouche 246, Fri seafood buffet, also meat, US$45, has daily bargains; *Mate Amargo*, Av Pompéia 1603, *churrascaria*, live music, rec; *Paddock*, Av São Luís 258 and Av Faria Lima 1541, traditional fare, excellent *feijoada*; *Um, Dois, Feijão e Arroz*, Praça de Sé 42 and R Ipiranga 940, modest but very good traditional food; *Novo Olido*, Largo do Arouche 193, closed Sat, regional dishes from interior of São Paulo; *Bolinha*, Av Cidade Jardim 53 for *feijoadas* (on Wed and Sat); *Oxalá*, Tr Maria Antônia 72, just off Consolação, Bahian specialities at modest prices; *Bronx*, R Haddock Lobo 1576, very reasonable traditional home cooking.

McDonalds and other fast food chains can be found all over the city as well as many other not quite so fast, but infinitely more interesting alternatives. *Frevinho Lanches*, R Augusta 1563, famous for its *beirute* (speciality of São Paulo), as well as many other toasted sandwiches with pitta bread; *Baguette*, Consolação 2426, nr Paulista, opp Belas Artes cinema, for sandwiches, especially lively around midnight; *Absolute*, Al Santos 843, best hamburgers in town; *Rock Dreams*, Al Tietê 580, for hamburgers and sandwiches; *Restaurante do MASP*, Av Paulista 1578, in basement of museum, reasonably priced, often has live music; *Casa da*

Fogazza, R Xavier de Toledo 328 and R 7 de Abril 60 (both close to Praça da República), Calzone, with different fillings, juices, rec.

Bars and cafés: *Ritz*, Al Franca 1088, Jardins, always lively, predominantly gay clientèle; *Riviera*, R da Consolação 2450, traditional haunt of students and 'counter' revolutionaries since early 60s, noisy, a bit rough but kept under control by surly waiters. *Café com Arte*, R Oscar Freire 1051 (Jardins), small coffee shop, 1000-2000 (later weekends); *Fran's Café*, open 24 hrs, Av Paulista 358; R Heitor Penteado 1326 (Sumaré); R Haddock Lobo 586; Estac Alameda Lorena 1271 (Jardim Paulista); *Café do Bixiga*, 13 de Maio 76 and lots of others in Bixiga/Bela Vista area with live music, eg *Café Piu Piu* (closed Mon) and *Café Pedaço*, at 13 de Maio 134 and 140. Bixiga is traditionally known as the 'Bohemian' area and bars here are usually cheaper than Jardins and Pinheiros areas. *Euro Bar*, R Min José Geraldo R Alkimin 2338, quiet; *Baguette*, good breakfasts, R Consolação 2426 (Consolação) and R 13 de Maio (Bela Vista); in Itaim Bibi: *Hard Rock Café*, R Brigadeiro Haroldo Veloso 707, fake but still sells the T-shirts; *Blue Note Jazz Bar*, Av São Gabriel 558, as the name describes.

● **Banks & money changers**

Banks: opening hours vary from bank to bank, but most are open between 1000-1630. Many national and international banks, most on R 15 de Novembro, Av Paulista, Av Brig Faria Lima and R Líbero Badaró. **Banco do Brasil**, R 7 de Abril, nr República will accept payment orders from overseas but with a US$30 charge and payment in reais. **Citibank**, Av Ipiranga 855, or Av Paulista 1111 (T 576-2211) will receive money from abroad (US$20 charge, takes 5 days). **Banco Mercantil de São Paulo**, Av Paulista 1450, for cash advances on Access/Mastercard; **Mastercard**, cash against card, R Campo Verde 61, 4° andar, Jardim Paulistano; also at: **Banco Meridional**, R Boa Vista 200; **Banorte**, Avenida Paulista 2421. Thomas Cook/Mastercard TC refund assistance point: R Haddock Lobo 337, 2 andar, 01414 São Paulo, T 259-3022. **Western Union** at Banco Itamarati, T 0800-11-9837.

Money changers: many *câmbios* nr Praça da República; none nr rodoviária or Tietê hotels. **American Express**, Al Santos 1437 (*Hotel Mofarrej Sheraton*) T 284-2515 and Kontik Franstur (address below) very helpful; **Exprinter**, Barão de Itapetininga 243, also deals in foreign currencies (cash only). **Avencatur**, Av Nações Unidas 1394, Morumbi, changes TCs, Deutschmarks, good rates. **Interpax**, Praça da República 177, loja 13, changes cash but not cheques; **Amoretur**, Praça da República 203, will change cheques. Most travel agents on Av São Luís change TCs and cash at good rates.

● **Cultural centres**

British Chamber of Commerce of São Paulo, R Barão de Itapetininga 275, 7th floor; Caixa Postal 1621, T 255-0519. **British Council**, R Maranhão 416, Higienópolis, Caixa Postal 1604, T 826-4455, F 66-3765, library at R Dep Lacerda Franco 333, Pinheiros, T 814-4155. **Sociedade Brasileira de Cultura Inglesa**, Av Higienópolis 449, has cinema (films US$1.50). **American Chamber of Commerce for Brazil**, R Formosa 367, 29th floor, T 222-6377. **American Library**, União Cultural Brasil-Estados Unidos, R Col Oscar Porto 208, T 287-1022. **Goethe-Instituto**, R Lisboa 974, T 280-4288 (open Mon-Thur 1400-2030). **Instituto Hans Staden**, R Cons Crispiniano 53, 12th floor. See under **Entertainment** for Alliance Française Theatre.

● **Education**

There are three universities: the official university of São Paulo, the Pontifical Catholic University, and the Mackenzie University. The official University of São Paulo is situated in the Cidade Universitária (buses from main bus station), beyond Pinheiros. There are a number of architecturally interesting buildings plus the museums mentioned above. They have courses available to foreigners, inc a popular Portuguese course, registry is through the Comissão de Cooperação Internacional, R do Anfiteatro 181, Bloco das Colméias 05508, Cidade Universitária, São Paulo.

● **Electric current**

110-220 volts AC, 60 cycles.

● **Embassies & consulates**

Argentine, Av Paulista 1106, T 284-1355 (open 0900-1300, very easy to get visa here); **Bolivian**, R da Consolação 37, 3rd floor (open 0900-1300), T 255-3555; **Chilean**, Av Paulista 1009, T 284-2044; **Paraguayan**, Av São Luís 50, 10th floor, T 255-7818; **Peru**, R Laplace 739, T 531-0943; **Uruguayan**, R Teixeira da Silva 660, T 884-8474; **Venezuelan**, R Veneza 878, T 887-4583.

American, R Padre João Manuel 933, T 881-6511; **Canadian**, Av Paulista 854, 5th floor, T 287-2122; **British**, Av Paulista 1938, 17th floor, Caixa Postal 846, T 287-7722; **Irish**, Av Paulista 2006, 5th floor, T 287-6362; **Danish**, R João Tibiriçá 900, T 831-9799, open 0900-1200, 1300-1700, Fri until 1400 only; **German**, Av Brig Faria Lima 1383, 12th floor, T 814-6644; **Swiss**, Av Paulista 1754, 4th floor, Caixa Postal 30588, T 289-1033; **Austrian**, R Augusta 2516, 10th floor, T 282-6223; **French**, Av Paulista 1842, 14th floor, T 287-9522; **Swedish**, R Oscar Freire 379, 3rd floor, T 883-3322 (Caixa Postal 51626); **Dutch**, Av Brig Faria Lima 1698, T 813-0522; **Greek**, Av Paulista 2073, 23rd floor, T 251-0675.

● Entertainment

The **Teatro Municipal** (magnificent interior) is used by visiting theatrical and operatic groups, as well as the City Ballet Company and the Municipal Symphony Orchestra who give regular performances. There are several first-class theatres: **Aliança Francesa**, R Gen Jardim 182, T 259-0086; **Itália** (Av Ipiranga 344, T 257-3138; **Cacilda Becker** (R Tito 295, T 864-4513); **Paiol** (R Amaral Gurgel 164, T 221-2462); **Ruth Escobar** (R dos Ingleses 209, T 251-4881), among others. Free concerts at **Teatro Popular do Sesi**, Av Paulista 313, at midday, under MASP (Mon-Sat); see also **Museums** above. The biggest cinema is reckoned to be the *Marabá*, Av Ipiranga 757, which has 1665 seats. In cinemas entrance is usually half price on Wed; normal seat price is US$2.50.

See *Ilustrada* selection of *Folha de São Paulo* for listings of concerts, theatre, museums, galleries and cinema. *Veja São Paulo* of weekly news magazine *Veja* lists bars, restaurants, clubs and shows as well as the above.

Nightclubs: São Paulo is teeming with clubs catering to most preferences. We list a small section:

Disco bars: Entrance/cover charges US$5-10: *Banana-Banana Café*, Av 9 de Júlio 5872 (Itaim Bibi), closed Mon; *HB Club*, R Cardeal Arcoverde 2958 (Pinheiros), closed Sun, bar, snooker, and informal dance lessons; test your new skills at *Blen-Blen*, packed weekends, live Latin bands; *Cervejaria Continental*, packed, mixed music, R dos Pinheiros 1275 and R Haddock Lobo 1573.

Clubs: entrance US$5-20 which may inc a drink: *Columbia* upstairs, R Estados Unidos 1570, lively; *Hell's Club* downstairs, opens 0430, techno, wild; *Cha-Cha-Cha*, R Tabapuã 1236, closed Mon, no Brazilian music, art on walls, candles, gay and straight; *Balafon*, R Sergipe 160, Wed-Sun, small, Afro-Brazilian; *Reggae Night*, Av Robert Kennedy 3914, Thur-Sun, outdoors on lakeside; *Limelight Industry*, R Franz Schubert 93, pop hits, Japanese restaurant upstairs; *Plataforma 1*, Av Paulista 424, dinner and folkloric show, very touristy but extremely popular.

● Hospitals & medical services

Doctors: (English-speaking) *Edwin Castello*, José Maria Lisboa 861, s/104, T 884-9132; *Ruy Silva*, Conselheiro Brotero 1505, No 64, T 67-2470; *Wilson Frey*, Barão de Jaceguai 1103, T 241-4474. *Christel Schlúnder*, R Alvares de Azevedo 127, Santo Amaro, T 247-5963, German speaking and for children. Also *Samaritans' Hospital*, R Conselheiro Brotero 1486, T 825-1122.

Emergency and ambulance: T 192, no charge. **Fire**: T 193.

● Places of worship

St Paul's Anglican (Episcopal) Church, R Comendador Elias Zarzua 1231, Santo Amaro, T 246-0383. **Igreja Metodista**, Av Liberdade 659, T 278-5895. **Adventist**, R Jaguá 88, T 279-8206. **Presbyterian**, R Néstor Pestanha 106, T 255-6111. **Mormon Church**, Av Prof Francisco Morato 2430, T 570-2483. **Synagogue** Congregação Shalom, R Comendador Elias Zarzur 568; Israelita Paulista, R Antonio Carlos 553. **Templo Budista**, Av do Cursino 753, T 63-4015. **Lutheran church**, Av Rio Branco 34. **Swedish Church**, Igreja Evangelica Luterana Escandinava, R Job Lane 1030, T 247 88 29.

● Post & telecommunications

Post Office: Correio Central, Praça do Correio, corner Av São João and Prestes Máia, T 831-5222. Booth adjoining tourist office on Praça da República, weekdays only 1000-1200, 1300-1600, for letters and small packages only. *UPS*, Brasinco, Alameda Jaú 1, 1725, 01420 São Paulo, T 852-8233, F 853-8563; *Federal Express*, Av São Luiz 187, is reliable.

International Telephone: R 7 de Abril 295, nr Praça da República. **Telecommunications**: Embratel, Av São Luís 50, and Av Ipiranga 344.

● Security

Beware of assaults and pickpocketing in São Paulo. Thieves often use the mustard-on-the-back trick (see **Introduction and Hints, Security**). The areas around Luz station, Praça da República and Centro are not safe at night, and visitors should not enter *favelas*.

● Shopping

Souvenirs from *Mimosa*, Joaquim Nabuco 275, Brooklin Paulista; *Artdinda*, R Augusta 1371, loja 119 (Galeria Ouro Velho); *Coisarada*, R Tabapuã 390, Itaim Bibi (T 881-4810); *Casa dos Amazonas*, Av São Luis 187, Galeria Metrópole, loja 14; *Ceará Meu Amor*, R Pamplona 1551, Loja 7, good quality lace from the NE. *H Stern*, jewellers, at Praça da República 242, R Augusta 2340 and at Iguatemi, Ibirapuera and Morumbi shopping centres and main hotels; designer jewellery, *Our Collection*, R São Benedito 1747, Alto da Boa Vista.

Open air markets: **'Hippy' fair**, Praça da República, daily 0800-1400, very varied, many tourists, good selection of inexpensive fossils, Bahian food, lots of artists, items from Peru and Bolivia; **'Oriental' fair**, Praça da Liberdade Sun pm, good for Japanese snacks, plants and some handicrafts, very picturesque, with remedies on sale, tightrope walking, gypsy fortune tellers, etc. Below the Museu de Arte de São Paulo, an **antiques** market takes place on Sun, 0800-1700. There are **flea markets** Suns in the main square of the Bixiga district (Praça Don Orione) and in Praça Benedito Calixto in Jardim América. São Paulo is relatively cheap for film and clothes (especially shoes). The **Ceasa flower market** should not be missed, Av Doutor Gastão Vidigal 1946, Jaguaré, Tues and Fri 0700-1200. **Handicraft market** at Praça Campos de Bagatelle, Sun 0800-1300.

Bookshops: *Livraria Cultura*, Av Paulista 2073, loja 153, Conjunto Nacional, new books in English; *Livraria Freebook*, R da Consolação 1924, T 259-1120, ring bell for entry, wide collection of art books and imported books in English; *Livraria Triângulo*, R Barão de Itapetininga 255, loja 23, Centro and *Ilco*, Barão do Triúnfo 371, Brooklin Paulista, books in English; *Livraria Kosmos*, Praça Dom José Caspar 134, loja 30, international stock. In various shopping malls *Livrarias Saraiva* and *Laselva* (also at airports) sell books in English; *Livraria Alemã*, R Laplace 159, Brooklin; *Librairie Française*, R Barão de Itapetininga 275, 6th floor, wide selection; *Letraviva*, Av Rebouças 2080, Mon-Fri 0900-1830, Sat 0900-1400, specializes in books and music in Spanish; *Book Centre*, R Gabus Mendes 29 loja 5, Consolação area books in English and German; *Duas Cidades*, R Bento Freitas 158, nr República, good selection of Brazilian and Spanish American literature; *Cinema Elétrico*, R Augusta 973, Centro, and *Sola Cinemateca*, R Fradique Coutinho 361, sell postcards and books on cinema and art.

Camera repairs: Canon and other makes: *Cine Camera Service*, R Cons Crispiniano 97, 2nd floor.

● **Sports**
The most popular is association football. The most important matches are played at Morumbi and Pacaembu grounds. For nature trails, etc, Free Way, R Leôncio de Carvalho 267, Paraíso, T 285-4767/283-5983.

Golf courses: about half an hour's drive from the centre there are 18-hole golf courses at the São Paulo Golf Club, Praça Dom Francisco Souza 635, in Santo Amaro, in beautiful surroundings; Clube de Golf de Campinas, Via Anhanguera, Km 108, Campinas; Clube de Campo São Paulo and Guarapiranga Golf e Country, both at Reprêsa Guarapiranga, Estrada Paralheiros, Km 34; São Fernando Golf Club, Estrada de Cotia, Km 29; a lakeside club at Km 50 on the Santos road.

9-hole courses at São Francisco Club, Estrada de Osasco, Km 15; Anglo Sports Center, Barretos; International golf club, Via Dutra Km 232, Guaratinguetá.

● **Tour companies & travel agents**
Woehrle Turismo, R do Tesouro 47, CEP 01013, T 37-7594, USA T (011) 532-1105, helpful, German spoken; *Lema Turismo*, Av Marquês de Itú

837, personalized excursions, Marta Schneider speaks 8 languages, inc Hungarian; *AmEx* office in *Hotel Sheraton Mofarrej*, Al Santos 1437, T 284-3515; *Kontik-Franstur* (American Express representative), R Marconi 71, T 259-4211; *Student Travel*, Estados Unidos 153, T 887 4242; *Audiotur* (ask for Janice Kawasake), Estados Unidos 627, T 887-3400, gives information about trains; *Ambiental Viagens e Expedições*, Av Brig Faria Lima 1684-S/L 40, Jardim Paulista, T 814-8809, English and Spanish spoken, helpful, rec for trips to less well known places; *Terra Expedições*, Osmar e Valdir, R Silva Jardim 429, Sta Terezinha, Santo André, CEP 09250, T 446-3381/447-3535, rec for motocycle tours and information, Spanish and Italian spoken (English improving). Visits to coffee fazendas (May-June) and round trips into the surrounding country are organized by the travel agencies.

● **Tourist offices**
Praça da República (very helpful, most regularly open), Praça da Sé and Liberdade metro entrances, Praça Dom José Gaspar (corner Av São Luís), R Augusta esq Av Paulista, R Barão de Itapetininga, nr Teatro Municipal; excellent free map at all these offices. Office at Guarulhos airport is helpful. For information on São Paulo State, Praça Antônio Prado 9, 6th floor, Av São Luís 115. Tours of the city costing US$17 leave tourist office at Praça da República every 30 mins Tues-Sat from 0900 to 1700 and Sun 0900-1600; there are 8 different itineraries visiting places of cultural interest. Each tour lasts approximately 3 hrs, tickets and full programme from tourist office in Praça da República, T 267-2122, ext 627/640, Mon-Fri, CMTC tours by metro on Sat-Sun from 0900-1000, 1400-1500 from Praça da Sé; information at Praça da Sé, T 229-3011. Tourist offices have free magazines in Portuguese and English: *Where* and *São Paulo This Month* (also available from most travel agencies and better hotels). Also rec is Quatro Rodas *Guia de São Paulo*.

Maps: of São Paulo in train timetables at newsstands (US$3.50), and in the monthly tourist guide published by the Prefeitura (US$0.70 – poor map but good for what's on). Also obtainable from the tourist offices, the rodoviária (upstairs), the better hotels, American Express and H Stern, the jeweller. Map shops: *Mapolândia*, 7 de Abril 125, shop 40; **Metrópole Mapas**, Av São Luís 153, Loja 1 (Galeria Metrópole). 2 private map producers: Geo Mapas, R Líbero Badaró 336, CEP 01008, T 259-2166 (40% discount for volume purchases, excellent 1988 1:5,000,000 map of Brazil, town maps), and Editorial Abril, R do Cartume 769, Bl G, 11° andar, Lapa, CEP 05066-900, T 831-0599, F 831-0599 ext 2270.

● **Useful telephone numbers**

Police: T 228-2276; Radio Patrol, T 190. Federal Police, Av Prestes Maia 700, open 1000-1600 for visa extensions.

● **Transport**

Local City buses and taxis: buses are normally crowded and rather slow, but clean. Maps of the bus and metro system are available at depots, eg Anhangabaú. Taxis display cards of actual tariffs in the window (starting price US$3.20). For 'especial taxis', dearer but fewer hassles, T 223-1975 (Tele Taxi), call out charge US$1, calls not accepted from public phones.

Metro: the first in Brazil, began operating in 1975. It has two main lines intersecting at Praça de Sé: N-S from Santana to Jabaquara; E-W from Corinthians Itaquera to Barra Funda (the interchange with Fepasa and RFFSA railways and site of the São Paulo and Paraná Rodoviária. A third line runs from Clínicas in the W, along Av Paulista, to Ana Rosa in the S, joining the Jabaquera line at Paraíso and Ana Rosa. The system is clean, safe, cheap and efficient; it operates from 0500-2400. Fare US$0.60, book of 10 tickets US$5; backpacks are allowed. Combined bus and metro ticket are available, eg to Congonhas airport.

Motorcycle repairs: BMW São Paulo, R Funchal 551, CEP 04551, São Paulo, T 820-8633, few parts but helpful and they have all BMW motorcycle special tools; can order parts from Miami. Imported spares and tyres at Edgar Soares & Cia, R General Osorio 663.

Air There are air services to all parts of Brazil, Europe, North and South America from the international airport at Guarulhos, also known as Cumbica, Av Monteiro Lobato 1985, T 945-2111 (30 km from the city). Varig has its own, new terminal for international flights, adjoining the old terminal which all other airlines use. Money exchanges open 0800-2200 daily, post office, etc, 2 information booths.

The local airport of Congonhas, 14 km from the city centre, is used for the Rio-São Paulo shuttle, some flights to Belo Horizonte and Vitória and private flights only, T 536-3555.

From Guarulhos there are airport taxis which charge US$36 on a ticket system (go to the second booth on leaving the terminal and book a Co-op taxi at the Taxi Comum counter, the best value). Fares from the city to the airport are US$40-US$45 and vary from cab to cab. Emtu bus service every 30 mins to Guarulhos from Praça da República (NW side, corner of R Arouche), US$8.50, very comfortable (in airport buy ticket at booth in Domestic Arrivals); the same company runs services from Guarulhos to Tietê (hourly), Congonhas airport (hourly 0600-2200) and Av Paulista (hourly 0600-0700 from airport to 2100, passing in front

of, or nr many major hotels on its route to the city: *Bristol*, *Brasilton*, *Cá d'Oro*, *Caesar Park*, *Della Volpe*, *Crowne Plaza*, *Sheraton*, *Maksoud Plaza*). Cheap buses from Bresser and Jabaquara bus terminals to Guarulhos, without luggage space, usually crowded. Inter-airport bus US$12. There are about 400 flights/week to Rio de Janeiro (US$300 return). All airline offices in triangle formed by Av São Luís, Av Ipiranga and R da Consolação.

Air freight: Varig will send anything, anywhere, but involves some red tape.

Trains Railways are being privatised and as a result many long distance passenger services have been withdrawn including services to Campo Grande, Corumbá and Brasília via Campinas. São Paulo has four stations: **1)** **Estaço da Luz**, T 681-3039/3062, for commuter trains between NW and SE of São Paulo, on the former Santos a Jundiaí Railway. There is also a Metro stop here.

2) **Barra Funda**, T 702-1100/1400, handles commuter destinations on the former Sorocabana and former Santos a Jundiaí railway lines. All long distance trains (second class coaches only) to Pres Prudente (about 15 hrs), Campinas, São José do Rio Preto (overnight train sometimes carries a sleeper) and Marilia. Connections via Campinas to Ribeirão Preto, Uberlândia and Araguari. Departures also to Santos, at weekends 0820, arr Santos 1205, return – in the dark – 1700 (superb scenery). Also from this station, on a special platform, departs the Silver Train to **Rio de Janeiro**, daily, 2030, T 825-7022 (office R Cap Mor Gonçalo Monteiro 6), US$100 with meals. Also Metro station at Barra Funda.

3) **Júlio Prestes station**, T 220-8862, for commuter services to the W on the former Sorocabana metre gauge railway; 4) **Roosevelt**, T 942-1132, for commuter trains to E on former Central do Brasil and Santos a Jundiaí railways.

Buses To get to the main rodoviária (T 235-0322), take the metro to Tietê, very convenient. Left luggage US$0.80/day/item. You can sleep in the bus station after 2200 when the guards have gone; tepid showers US$2.50. Bus to centre, US$0.80. Buses to the interior of São Paulo state, all state capitals and international buses (see next paragraph): to **Rio**, 6 hrs, every 30 mins, US$20 (*leito*, 40), special section for this route in the rodoviária, request the coastal route via Santos ('via litoral') unless you wish to go the direct route; to **Florianópolis**, 9 hrs (US$23); to **Porto Alegre**, 18 hrs, US$37 (*leito*, 82); **Curitiba**, 6 hrs, US$8 (*leito*, 16); **Belo Horizonte**, 10 hrs, US$7.25; buy ticket and get on bus at Terminal Bresser (Metro Bresser, T 692-5191); **Salvador**, 30 hrs, US$58 (*leito*, 116); **Recife**, 40 hrs, US$80 (*leito*, 160); **Cuiabá**, 24 hrs, US$50;

Porto Velho, 60 hrs (or more), US$108; **Brasília**, 16 hrs, US$33 (*leito*, 66); **Foz do Iguaçu**, 16 hrs, US$39; **São Sebastião**, 4 hrs US$7.80 (say 'via Bertioga' if you want to go by the coast road, beautiful journey but few buses take this route). To **Santos**, US$3 (there is a bus station for Santos and São Vicente at the southern end of the Metro line, at Jabaquara, buses from here leave every 5 mins, taking about 50 mins). There are two other bus terminals, Barra Funda, T 235-0322 or 66-4682 (same as metrô and rail station), to cities in southern São Paulo state and many destinations in Paraná; Bresser, T 299-0177 (Cometa) or 267-7411 (Transul), for destinations in Minas Gerais.

To **Montevideo**, via Porto Alegre, with TTL, departs 2200, 31 hrs, US$79, cold a/c at night, plenty of meal stops, bus stops for border formalities, passengers disembark only to collect passport and tourist card on Uruguayan side. To **Buenos Aires**, Pluma, 36 hrs, US$145; to **Santiago**, Pluma or Gral Urquiza (both start from Rio), 56 hrs, US$110 (leito US$220), Chile Bus, Av Paulista 1009, SL 1909, T 251-5388, or Terminal Tietê, T 267-6239, US$107 (poor meals, but otherwise good, beware overbooking); to **Asunción** (1,044 km), 18 hrs with Pluma or RYSA, US$41 (leito US$82); to **Puerto Suárez** (Quijarro, Bolivia), 22 hrs.

ROUTES   To take the beautiful coast road to Rio, take the Via Anchieta to the Guarujá turn, before Guarujá take Bertioga turn and you're on the Santos-Rio highway. Motorists leaving the ring road for Curitiba and Iguaçu should follow Regis de Bittencourt signs. To hitch to Rio, take the metro to Ponte Pequeno, then a bus to Guarulhos, alighting where the bus turns off the Rio road for Guarulhos.

CAVERNS OF THE VALE DO RIBEIRO

The caves are SW of the state capital, W of the BR-116; among the best known as the 8-km **Gruta da Tapagem**, or Caverna do Diabo (Devil's Cave – as huge 'as a cathedral' with well-lit formations), 45 km from Eldorado Paulista; open 0800-1100, 1200-1700; bar and toilets.

43 km from Caverna do Diabo is **Caverna de Santana**, 10 km from the town of Iporanga; it has 5.6 km of subterranean passages and three levels of galleries.

● **Access** **Iporanga** is the most convenient town for visiting both sets of caves; it is 64 km W of Eldorado Paulista, 42 km E of Apiaí, on the SP-250, 257 km SW of São Paulo.

A suitable stopping place for visiting the caves area is **Registro** (*Pop* 48,860) on BR-116, in the heart of the tea-growing region, populated mainly by Japanese Brazilians. (C *Lito Palace Hotel*, Av J Banks Leite 615, T 21-1055, F 21-4470; **F** *Hotel Brasília*, R Brasília, round corner from rodoviária, no breakfast, shower, clean, airy; good *Churrascaria* next to bus station; international telephone exchange in town centre).

● **Transport** Bus to Eldorado Paulista from Santos or São Paulo, US$4.75, 4-5 hrs, then hitchhike on banana trucks; alternatively, tourist buses run from both cities; most traffic on Sat and Sun. From Curitiba, change buses at Jacupiranga on the BR-116 for Eldorado Paulista.

THE COAST OF THE STATE OF SÃO PAULO

SANTOS

(*Pop* 428,525; *CEP* 11000; *DDD* 0132) 63 km SE of São Paulo and 5 km from the open sea, **Santos** is the most important Brazilian port. (Over 40% by value of all Brazilian imports and about half the total exports pass through it.) It is reached from Rio by a direct highway (see pages 415 and 458). Although best known for its commerce, Santos is also a holiday resort, with magnificent, but polluted, beaches, and views. The port is approached by the winding Santos Channel; at its mouth is an old fort (1709). A railway and the Anchieta and Imigrantes highways run to São Paulo. A free-port zone for Paraguay, 1,930 km by rail or road, has been established. A few kilometres outside the city there is an important industrial area round the steelworks, oil refinery and hydroelectric plant at Cubatão.

The island upon which the city stands can be circumnavigated by small boats. The city has impressive modern buildings, wide, tree-lined avenues, and wealthy suburbs.

Places of interest

The streets around **Praça Mauá** are very busy in the daytime, with plenty of cheap shops. In the centre, an interesting building is the **Bolsa Oficial de Café**, in R 15 de Novembro. The night-life is best in the **Gonzaga** area which has the large hotels.

There are many monuments: in Av Ana Costa to commemorate the brothers Andradas, who took a leading part in the movement for independence; in the Praça Rui Barbosa to Bartolomeu de Gusmão, who has a claim to the world's first historically recorded airborne ascent in 1709; in the Praça da República to Bras Cubas, who founded the city in 1534; and in the Praça José Bonifácio to the soldiers of Santos who died in the Revolution of 1932. **Museu do Mar**, R República do Equador 81. In the eastern district of José Menino are the orchid gardens in the **Praça Washington** (flowering Oct-Feb). There is an open-air cage containing humming-birds of 20 different species and the park is a sanctuary for other birds.

Excursions

The **Ilha Porchat**, a small island reached by a bridge at the far end of Santos/São Vicente bay, has beautiful views over rocky precipices, of the high seas on one side and the city and bay on the other. At the summit is a splendid nightclub, the *Top House Restaurante e Discoteca*. No entrance fee but there is a minimum charge of US$10.

To **Alto da Serra**, the summit of the forest-clad mountain range; magnificent views. The return journey can be done in under 2 hrs by road.

Monte Serrat At the summit there is a semaphore station and look-out post which reports the arrival of all ships in Santos harbour. There is also a quaint old church, dedicated to Nossa Senhora da Monte Serrat, said to have performed many miracles. The top can be reached on foot or by funicular. Seven shrines have been built on the way up; annual pilgrimages are made by the local people. Fine views.

Local holidays

26 Jan (Foundation of Santos); Good Fri; Corpus Christi.

Local information
● Accommodation

A2 *Mendes Plaza*, Av Floriano Peixoto 42, T 37-4243, F 4-8253; **A2** *Parque Balneário*, complex at the centre of Gonzaga, Ana Costa 555, T 34-7211, F 4-0475, with shopping centre.

Beach front hotels on Av Pres Wilson: **B** *Atlântico*, No 1, T 37-8823, F 37-8837, good value; **B** *Avenida Palace*, No 10, T 4-1166; **B** *Maracanã Santos*, No 172, T 37-4030; **B** *Indaiá*, Av Ana Costa 431, T 4-1134. Many cheap hotels nr the Orquidário Municipal (Praça Washington), 1-2 blocks from the beach.

● Places to eat

Cibus, Av Vicente de Carvalho 1, beach end, considered the best; *Hong Kong Palace*, Av Conselheiro Nébias 288 (Chinese); first class *Pizzaria Zi Tereza*, Av Ana Costa 449; *Churrascaria Tertúlia*, Av Bartolomeu de Gusmão 187, T36-1461.

● Banks & money changers

Banks: Banco Holandês Unido, Citibank, Banco do Brasil, all on R 15 de Novembro; **First National Bank of Boston**, Praça Visc de Mauá 14. Banks open: 1000-1630.

Money changers: Casa Faro, R 15 de Novembro, 80 & 260; **Casa Bancária Branco**, Praça de República 29; **Gonzaga**, R Galeão Carvalhal 52/4.

● Electric current

220 AC 60 cycles.

● Embassies & consulates

British, R Tuiuti 58, 2nd floor, Caixa Postal 204, T 33-6111/34-6656. **Danish**, R Frei Gaspar 22, 10th floor, 106, CP 726, T 235 5165, F 232 8752, open 1000-1100, 1500-1700.

● Places of worship

All Saints Church: Praça Washington 92, José Menino. Services in English held every Sun.

● Post & telecommunications

Telecommunications: Embratel, Largo Senador Vergueiro 1 and 2.

● Sports

Golf courses: two 9-hole courses: Santos Golf Club, Av Pérsio de Queiroz Filho, São Vicente; Guarujá Golf Club (see below).

● Tourist offices

Praça dos Expedicionários 10, 10th floor; booths at Aquarium (Av Bartolomeu de Gusmão, Ponta da Praia), rodoviária, Casa do Café, Orquidário Municipal.

● Transport

Local Taxis: all taxis have meters. The fare is a fixed charge of US$0.50 plus US$0.20/km. Taxi, Gonzaga to bus station, US$4.

Trains The British-built Santos a Jundiaí up the hill to São Paulo is one of the railway wonders of the world; it passes through Cubatão and then, running on toothed tracks up the escarpment, interesting hill scenery. The schedule for weekend passenger services is given under São Paulo. From Ana Costa station, a mixed train may be taken to Embu Guaçu from where there is a bus to São Paulo.

Buses For most suburbs buses start from Praça Mauá, in the centre of the city. There are buses to **São Paulo** (50 mins, US$2.40) at intervals of approximately 15 mins, from the rodoviária nr city centre. Express cars also run to São Paulo at regular intervals. Fare, US$4.50 each way, per passenger. (The two highways between São Paulo and Santos are sometimes seriously crowded, especially at rush hours and weekends.) To **Rio** (Normandy company, 6 a day, 7½ hrs, US$20, leito at 2230, US$40); to Rio along the coast road is via São Sebastião (US$12, change buses if necessary), Caraguatatuba and Ubatuba.

GUARUJÁ

(*Pop* 206,750) There is a strong undertow on nearly all the Guarujá beaches; the Jequiti-Mar beach (officially called Praia de Pernambuco) is the safest. The beaches are built-up and polluted.

● **Accommodation & services** Turn left in centre of Guarujá and drive less than 1 km to **L2** *Delphin Hotel* and its restaurant *La Popote* at the beginning of the long Praia da Enseada, Av M Stéfano 1295, T 86-2111, F 86-6844. Close by, at Av M Stéfano 999, is **L2** *Casa Grande Hotel*, luxury, in colonial style, with clean beach, T/F 86-2223. Facing sea is the luxurious **A1** *Ferraretto Hotel*, R Ribeiro 564, T 86-1112 (nightclub, swimming pool). Camping Clube do Brasil site at Praia do Perequê (where the best fish restaurants are), nr municipal nursery. Good *churrascaria* opp rodoviária. The *Jequiti-Mar* holiday complex, 8 km beyond Guarujá on the road to Bertioga, is extremely attractive, T 53-3111, F 53-2325. There are private beaches (excellent swimming and boating), fine fishing grounds, and chalet accommodation, **A1-3**; excellent restaurant, 2 nightclubs; open each weekend and every night from Dec to Mar, in the holiday season. 2 km further N is a beach where fishing boats land their catch – a number of good seafood restaurants line the seafront.

● **Transport** The route from Santos to the resort of Guarujá is along Av Conselheiro Nébias to the seafront, continuing along the beach to the Guarujá ferry (every 10 min, free for pedestrians) at Ponta da Praia. On the other side proceed as far as Enseada das Tartarugas (Turtle Bay). During the season and weekends there is a long delay at the Ponta da Praia vehicle ferry; to avoid this take the ferry on foot and get the bus on the Guarujá side; motor boats also cross for US$0.10. Trolleybus from Praça Mauá in Santos to the ferry, then buses.

BEACHES EAST OF SANTOS: BERTIOGA AND SÃO SEBASTIÃO

There are good sea-food restaurants on the road to **Bertioga**, an overcrowded place, where the fort of São João houses the João Ramalho museum (bus Guarujá-Bertioga, 1 hr, US$0.30). (Hotels: **A3** *Marazul*, Av Tomé de Souza 825, good seafood restaurant; restaurants include *Zezé e Duarte*, same street No 10.) The coastal road beyond Bertioga is paved, and the Rio-Santos highway, 1-2 km inland, provides a good link to São Sebastião. Going NE, the beaches are Praia de Bertioga, Praia São Lourenço, Praia Guaratuba and Praia Boracéia (campsite, meals served).

Beyond Boracéia is **Camburi**, surrounded by the Mata Atlântica. The sea is clean and good for bathing and watersports, including surfing. You can walk on the Estrada do Piavú into the Mata Atlântica to see streams, vegetation and wildlife (bathing in the streams is permitted, but use of shampoo and other chemicals is forbidden). 5 km from Camburi is Praia Brava, 45 mins' walk through the forest, camping and nude bathing possible.

● **Accommodation** There are a number of good hotels and restaurants: **A2** *Pousada da Rosa*, R das Rosas 139, T 0124-651412, **B** in low season, with breakfast, pool.

● **Transport** 3 daily buses from São Paulo, 160 km, en route to São Sebastião/Ilhabela; US$6.

30 km beyond Boracéia is **Maresias**, a fashionable place for surfers. Several hotels in town. *Mr Harris Jazz Bar*, rec.

From Maresias it is 21 km to **São Sebastião** (*Pop* 32,845; *CEP* 11600; *DDD* 0124). There is a **Museu de Arte Sacra** in the chapel of São Gonçalo in the town centre. Tourist Office: Av Dr Altino Arantes 174, friendly and helpful except regarding Ilhabela. The beaches within 2-3 km of São Sebastião harbour are polluted; others, Barra do Una, Boiçucanga, Praia da Balcia, are clean and inviting. Ilhabela tends to be expensive in season, when it is cheaper to stay in São Sebastião.

● **Accommodation A2** *Arrastão*, T 62-0099, most facilities; **B** *Recanto dos Pássaros*, Porto Grande, T 52-2046; **B-C** *Hotel Roma*, on the main square, T 52-1016, excellent, warmly rec; **D** *Bariloche*, R Três Bandeirantes 133, basic but clean. Non-members can stay in the *Camping Clube do Brasil* grounds for US$4 a night. 6 km S of São Sebastião is *Camping do Barraquecaba Bar de Mar de Lucas*, hot showers, English spoken, cabins available, rec. Halfway between Bertioga and São Sebastião, on the Praia de Juqueí beach, are **L3** *Encanto da Praia*, with dinner, on the hill leading to Barra da Una, rec.

• **Transport Buses** Two buses a day from Rio, 0830 and 2300, to Rio 0600 and 2330, heavily booked in advance; 4 a day from **Santos**, 4 hrs, US$12; buses from **São Paulo** (US$8) run inland via São José dos Campos, unless you ask for the service via Bertioga, only 2 a day. Free **ferry** to Ilhabela (4 hrs by bus from Santos, 3 a day, US$6).

ILHA DE SÃO SEBASTIÃO (ILHABELA)

The island of São Sebastião, known popularly as Ilhabela, is of volcanic origin, roughly about 390 sq km in area. Its highest peak, Morro do Papagaio, rises 1,300m above sea-level, often obscured by mist; the slopes are densely wooded. Most of the flatter ground is given over to sugar-cane. In the 19th century illegal slave traders used the island.

The only settled district lies on the coastal strip facing the mainland, the Atlantic side being practically uninhabited except by a few fisherfolk. The place abounds in tropical plants and flowers, and many fruits grow wild, whose juice mixed with cachaça and sugar makes as delicious a cocktail as can be imagined.

A 50-km return journey on foot over the hump of the island down towards the Atlantic, sometimes through dense tropical forest following the old slave trail, requires a local guide. There is a rough road to the Atlantic side, but it is very difficult to drive. The terraced Toca waterfalls amid dense jungle close to the foot of the 970m Baepi peak give cool freshwater bathing (entry, US$0.50); other beautiful waterfalls can be reached on foot. In all shady places, especially away from the sea, there abounds a species of midge known locally as *borrachudos*. A locally sold repellant (Autan) keeps them off for some time, but those allergic to insect bites should remain on the inhabited coastal strip. There is a small hospital (helpful) by the church in town.

ILHABELA

No alterations are allowed to the frontage of the main township, **Ilhabela** (*Pop* 9,500). It is very popular during summer weekends; at such times it is very difficult to find space for a car on the ferry. It is, however, a nice place to relax on the beach, with good food and some good value accommodation.

Places of interest Visit the old **Feiticeira** plantation, with underground dungeons. The road is along the coast, sometimes high above the sea, towards the S of the island. You can go by bus, taxi, or horse and buggy. *Gipsy Tur*, T 72-1518, helpful.

Pedras do Sino (Bell Rocks) These curious seashore boulders, when struck with a piece of iron or stone, emit a loud bell-like note. Campsite nearby.

Bathing On the mainland side it is not recommended because of oil, sandflies and jelly fish on the beaches and in the water. **Praia dos Castelhanos**, reached by a rough road over the island (no buses), is recommended.

• **Accommodation L2** *Ilhabela*, Av Pedro Paulo de Morais 151, T 72-1083, F 72-1031, good breakfast, rec; next door is **L3** *Itapemar*, T 72-1329, F 72-1329, windsurfing equipment rented. **A3** *Pousada dos Hibiscos*, Av PP de Morais 714, T 72-1375, good atmosphere, swimming pool, rec; others in this price range and several other less expensive hotels in B-C range, mostly on the road to the left of the ferry. *Camping Porto Seguro*, T 72-9147, accessible by 2-hourly bus from Ilhabela.

• **Places to eat** *Perequê*, Av Princesa Isabel 337, reasonable. *Farol*, Av Princesa Isabel 1634, Perequê, good, especially seafood, rec.

• **Transport Buses** A bus runs along the coastal strip facing the mainland. **Ferry** Passenger ferry every 2 hrs; stops at Perequê and Ilhabela; car ferry runs through the night and serves Perequê only (fare for cars is US$7 weekdays, double at weekends).

NORTH OF SÃO SEBASTIÃO

On the Santos-Rio road, is São Francisco, good beaches. Further on is **Caraguatatuba** (*Pop* 52,915) with 17 good beaches to the NE and SW (several hotels, popular at weekends, good restaurants and campsites). Direct buses to Caraguatatuba from Rio de Janeiro, São Paulo and Santos; direct buses from São Paulo do not use the coast road. Further E is **Lagoinha**, 34 km W of Ubatuba, with chalets and sailing boats for hire. Exotic birdlife and forest.

UBATUBA

(*Pop* 47,295; *CEP* 11680; *DDD* 0124) In all, there are 72 beautiful beaches, quite spread out (Grande, just S, and one 6 km N of Ubatuba are rec; Iperoig, Itaguá and Saco da Ribeira are officially designated polluted). There is also a yacht haven. The area gets very crowded at Carnival time as people from Rio come to escape the crowds in their city. Jewellery market on beach, Sats.

● **Accommodation** At all holiday times it is expensive, with no hotel less than US$15 and camping costing US$8. **A1** *Saveiros*, Praia do Lázaro T 42-0172, pool, restaurant, English spoken; **A2** *Solar das Águas Cantantes*, Praia do Lázaro, T 42-0178, reached by local bus, swimming pool, restaurant; **C** *Xaréu*, JH da Costa 413, T 32-1525, central nr beach, quiet, rec; **C-D** *Jangadeiro*, Av Abreu Sodre (15 mins' walk from centre, cross bridge, next to beach), good value; *Mauricio*, Av Abreu Sodré 607, nr Praia do Perequê-Açu, has cheap rooms, clothes washing possible; *Pousada do Page*, T 32-4515, breakfast, on beach, rec. **Camping**: two Camping Clube do Brasil sites at Maranduba and Perequê-Açu beaches.

ROUTES The road from São Sebastião is paved, so a journey from São Paulo along the coast is possible, 5 buses daily. 25 km S of Ubatuba at Baia Fortaleza is *Refúgio de Corsário*, T 43-1126, C and up, a clean quiet hotel on the water front, sailing and swimming, a good place to relax. Ubatuba is 70 km from Parati (see page 417), several buses daily, on the hour, from *Lanchonete Nice*, near rodoviária. If driving from Ubatuba along the coast to Rio, one can stop for lunch at Porto Aquarius, where there is a cave and hotel in a beautiful setting (not cheap). Direct buses from Rio (US$12), São Paulo and Santos.

PARQUE NACIONAL SERRA DA BOCAINA

Straddling the border of São Paulo and Rio de Janeiro states is the **Parque Nacional Serra da Bocaina**, which rises from the coast to heights of over 1,900m, encompassing three strata of vegetation (Ibama, T 021-294-6497, or 0125-77-1225).

SOUTHWEST FROM SANTOS

It is 50 km beside the Praia Grande to **Itanhaém** (*Pop* 33,210) with its pretty colonial church and semi-ruined Convento da Conceição on a small hill. There are several good sea-food restaurants along the beach, hotels and camping (many more 29 km away at Peruíbe beach, including: **B** *Vila Real*, Av Anchieta 6625, T 458-2797 breakfast, shower). There are many attractive beaches here, and hot springs with medicinal mud. The whole stretch of coast is completely built up with holiday developments. The beaches of Praia Grande and Itanhaém were officially declared polluted in 1990. Frequent buses from Santos US$1.50, 1 hr.

IGUAPE AND ILHA COMPRIDA

Further S is the town of **Iguape** (*Pop* 27,890; *DDD* 0138) founded in 1538. Typical of Portuguese architecture, the small municipal museum is housed in a 16th century building. It has a market, hotels and restaurants. Opposite Iguape is the northern end of the **Ilha Comprida** with 86 km of beaches (some dirty and disappointing). The island has good restaurants, hotels, supermarket – fresh fish is excellent. At the southern end **Cananéia** (*Pop* 9,905) is more commercialized than Iguape; it has several hotels (from **C**).

● **Accommodation** At **Iguape**: **B** *Alpha*, R São Lourenço 14, T 842-1270, incl breakfast, hot shower, parking; **C** *Silvi*, R Ana Cândida Sandoval Trigo 515, T 41-1421, with breakfast, good; **C** *Rio Verde*, R Antônio José de Morais 86, T 41-1493, good rooms but humid; *Camping Clube do Brasil* site 15 km from Iguape; other sites on Ilha Comprida, inc *Britânia*, US$10 for 2, good, clean, friendly.

● **Transport** Buses To Iguape: from São Paulo, Santos, or Curitiba, changing at Registro (see above). **Sea** A continuous ferry service runs from Iguape to Ilha Comprida (passengers free; cars at a small charge); buses run until 1900 from the ferry stop to the beaches. From Iguape it is possible to take a boat trip down the coast to Cananéia and Ariri. Tickets and information from Dept Hidroviário do Estado, R Major Moutinho 198, Iguape, T 41-1122. It is a beautiful trip, passing between the island and the mainland. Ariri has no road connections; there is a hostel, E, run by the shipping line.

TOWNS IN THE STATE OF SÃO PAULO

About 13% of Brazil's population lives within 200 km of São Paulo city, a circle which includes 88 municipalities. Four of them – the big ABCD towns – sharing a population of over a million, are Santo André, São Bernardo, São Caetano and Diadema; they have many of the largest industrial plants. There are some 70 cities in the State with populations of over 50,000 and São Paulo is linked with all of them by road, and several of them by railway.

NORTHWEST OF SÃO PAULO

An important broad-gauge railway (formerly Santos a Jundiaí, now CPTM), runs from Santos to São Paulo and across the low mountains which separate São Paulo city from the interior to its terminus at **Jundiaí** (*Pop* 312,520; *CEP* 13200; *DDD* 011), 58 km from São Paulo, which has textile factories and other industries. The district grows coffee and grain and there is an annual Grape Festival.

● **Accommodation C** *Grande Hotel*, R do Rosário 605, T 434-5355, with good restaurant.

CAMPINAS

Campinas (*Pop* almost 1 million; *CEP* 13100; *DDD* 0192), an industrial centre 88 km from São Paulo by the fine Via Anhanguera highway, is important as a clearing point for coffee. The Viracopos international airport is 11 km from Campinas, which also has its own airport.

Places of interest

See the fine cathedral, old market, colonial buildings, several museums (including Arte Contemporânea, Arquidiocesano, Carlos Gomes and, in the Bosque de Jequitibás, Histórico and Folclore), arts centre (noted symphony orchestra; the city is the birthplace of the 19th century Brazilian composer Carlos Gomes), and the modern university outside the city. Visits can be made to the Agricultural Institute to see all the aspects of coffee. A tourist tram operates in Parque Taquaral.

Local information
● **Accommodation**

L2 *Royal Palm Plaza* Praça Rotatória 88, T 2-9085, F 2-7085; **L2** *Solar das Andorinhas*, a health farm with pool, sauna, horses, sports, etc 18 km outside city on the Mogi-Mirim road, with meals, T 39-4411, F 39-5899.

A1 *Savoy*, R Regente Feijó 1064, T 32-9444, F 2-9207.

B *Opala Avenida*, Av Campos Sales 161, T 8-4115, F 31-6983, central; **B** *Parati Palácio*, R Bernardino de Campos 426, T 32-0395/8368, German spoken, rec; **B** *Hotel IPE*, R Bernardino de Campos 1050, T 31 7746, rec.

● **Places to eat**

Bar Restaurante Barão, Barão de Jaguará 1381 and *Churrascaria Gaúcha*, Av Dr Campos Sales 515, excellent for Brazilian food. *Nutrir*, R Dr Quirino 1620, vegetarian, very good value. *Sucão*, R Benjamin Constant 1108, good variety of juices; *Pastelaria do Sr Júlio*, R de 13 Maio 143, friendly, helpful, cheap, rec.

● **Entertainment**

Nightlife on weekends is busy around the Centro de Convivência, Praça Imprensa Fluminense, in city centre. There are cinemas in the city centre and the Iguatemi and Galleria shopping centres.

● **Places of worship**

Community Church: services in English at School of Language and Orientation, R Eduardo Lane 270.

● **Shopping**

Bookshops: *Pontes Editores*, R Dr Quirino 1223, has English books; second-hand at *Sebo Comércio*, R Bareto Leme 1265, and *O Livrão*, R B Jaguara 936, Loja 11.

● **Transport**

Trains A metre-gauge line, connecting with the broad-gauge former Paulista at Campinas, serves the northeastern part of the state. It goes through Ribeirão Preto to Uberlândia and Araguari in the Triângulo de Minas Gerais. Three trains a day to São Paulo and one daily to Araguari via Ribeirão Preto. 25 km from Campinas, at Jaguariúna, is a railway preservation group with steam engines and wagons; hourly bus from Campinas US$1, or take the steam train itself from Campinas (station behind Carrefour, Anhumas, reached by town bus), Sat and Sun, T 53-6067 for schedule. Tourist train once Sat a month to Peruibe, 0700, 6 hrs, run by Pettená-Tur.

Buses To São Paulo, US$3, Ribeirão Preto and Araguari; to Rio de Janeiro, 7 hrs, US$11.50.

AROUND CAMPINAS – SERRA NEGRA

(*Pop* 21,660; 78 km NE of Campinas) A

very pleasant spa town and summer holiday resort in the mountains at 1,080m, 145 km from São Paulo. There are a *balneário* and a small zoo.

20 km from Serra Negra is the even better-known spa town of **Lindóia** (*Pop* 4,665), whose still waters are bottled and sent all over Brazil.

● **Accommodation L2** *Rádio Hotel*, Serra Negra, T 92-3311, very nice indeed, and several others of a good standard.

Americana (*Pop* 142,580) is 42 km from Campinas in an area settled by Confederate refugees from the S of the USA after the Civil War. Most of the original settlers soon returned to the States, but some stayed, and there are still reminders of their occupation. A visit to the cemetery reveals an unusual number of English surnames.

RIBEIRÃO PRETO

(*Pop* 430,805; *Alt* 420m; *CEP* 14100; *DDD* 016) The centre of a rich coffee-growing district, the town also has a steel industry. It is a distribution centre for the interior of São Paulo State and certain districts in Minas Gerais and Goiás. Products: coffee, cotton, sugar, grain and rice. It is 300 km from São Paulo by rail via Campinas or paved road (4 hrs by bus); airport.

● **Accommodation L3** *Holiday Inn*, R Alvares Cabral 1120, T 625-0186, F 635-1279; **A3** *Stream Palace*, R Gen Osório 850, T 636-0660, F 636-7834, with TV; **B** *Umuarama Recreio*, Praça dos Cafeeiros 140, T 637-3790, 6 km from centre, very pleasant, pool, gardens.

Barretos Some 115 km NW of Ribeirão Preto is where, in the third week in Aug, the **Festa do Peão** is held. This is the biggest annual rodeo in the world. Trips from the UK are run by *Last Frontiers*, Swan House, High St, Long Crendon, Bucks, HP18 9AF, T/F 01844-208405.

WEST OF SÃO PAULO

SOROCABA

(*Pop* 377,270; *Alt* 540m; *CEP* 18100; 110 km W of São Paulo, **Sorocaba** is an important centre for industrial and agricultural products. The climate is temperate. There are railway workshops, extensive orange

groves and packing house installations. Communications with São Paulo are better by road than by rail; the Castello Branco highway passes nearby.

● **Accommodation B** *Terminus*, Av Gen Carneiro 474, T 21-6970; **D** *Manchester*, R 15 de Novembro 21, basic, friendly.

SÃO PAULO TO BAURU

There is a picturesque paved road along the Tietê valley from São Paulo to Bauru, via the colonial towns of **Pirapora de Bom Jesus** (*Pop* 7,935), a popular place of pilgrimage, in a most attractive setting on both sides of the river, and **Itu** (*Pop* 106,870), founded by the Bandeirantes in the 17th century (hotels; campsites in the vicinity). The beautiful falls of Salto de Itu, 8 km N, are flanked by a park and a textile mill.

Bauru (*Pop* 260,380; *CEP* 17100; *DDD* 0142) was founded at the end of the last century. The town is used by Paulistanos as a weekend resort.

● **Accommodation** Hotels in all price ranges up to **A3**; the cheaper ones are nr the rodoviária and the railway station.

● **Transport** One train a day to São Paulo and Panorama (via Marília). Connections on to Campo Grande must be made by bus.

Marília (*Pop* 151,760), W of Bauru, is a pleasant clean town with a good hotel, **A3** *Sun Valley Park*, R Aimorés 501, T/F 33-5944, friendly.

Ourinhos (*Pop* 76,900), founded in 1924, is 95 km S of Marília near the border with Paraná state. It is surrounded by sugar cane plantations. A possible stop-over on the road from São Paulo to Foz do Iguaçu or Campo Grande, it is on the railway which runs to Presidente Epitácio (see page 496) on the Paraná river. **Accommodation C** *Pousada Ourinhos*, R Mons Córdova 333, T 22-5898, good value; **D** *Comercial*, R Amornio Prado 38, friendly.

Further W is **Presidente Prudente** (*Pop* 165,450), another useful place to make bus connections for Campo Grande, Porto Alegre, São Paulo, Ribeirão Preto, 9 hrs. The train from São Paulo does not connect with the 2nd class train to Presidente Epitácio on the Rio Paraná. You must stay overnight. **A1** *Hotel Aruá*, Av

Marcondes 1111, T 22-4666, F 22-0765, doubles better than single rooms; **D** *Hotel Alves* opp rodoviária, clean, nice but noisy.

NORTHEAST OF SÃO PAULO

CAMPOS DO JORDÃO

(*Pop* 36,850; *Alt* 1,710m; *CEP* 12460; *DDD* 0122) A mountain resort between Rio de Janeiro and São Paulo in the Serra da Mantiqueira, it is prettily set in a long valley. The climate is cold and dry in winter and cool in summer, a great relief from the coastal heat and humidity.

Places of interest

Palácio Boa Vista, 4 km from Abernéssia Centre, Governor's residence and museum, open Wed, Sat, Sun, 1000-1200, 1400-1700; **Pedra do Baú** (1,950m), to get there take a bus to São Bento do Sapucaí at 0800 or 1500, then walk to Paiol Grande and then on an unmarked path to the Pedra. Return buses from São Bento at 0915 and 1615. Near Paiol Grande is the small waterfall of **Cachoeira dos Amores**. **Pico do Itapeva** (2,030m) and **Imbiri** (1,950m) command a beautiful view of the Paraíba valley; see also **Morro do Elefante** (chairlift available); **Gruta dos Crioulos**; nature reserve at **Horto Florestal** (20 km), signposted from chairlift station, very pretty – go in the morning to avoid crowds; lots of streams with bridges, waterfalls nearby. Campos do Jordão is a popular place for hikers; most of the roads leading off the main avenue lead to quiet areas with nice views, eg up Av Dr Antônio Nicola Padula, turn left 500m past Refúgio na Serra for waterfalls and Pico do Itapeva. The villages of **Emílio Ribas** and **São Cristóvão** are connected by a railcar which runs frequently, US$0.15.

Local information
● **Accommodation**

Book accommodation in advance if going June/July. Many hotels inc *Toriba*, Av E Diederichsen, T 62-1566, F 63-2793; *Vila Inglesa*, Sen R Simonsen, T 63-1955, F 63-2699; *Refúgio Alpino*, Av Roberto Simonsen 885, T 63-1660, and others at Capivari.

B *Refugio na Serra*, Av Dr Antônio Nicola Padula 275, T 63-1330, comfortable, good breakfast, very helpful owners (some English spoken), rec.

Camping: *Clube do Brasil* site in the Descansópolis district, T 63-1130.

Youth hostel: R Diogo de Carvalho 86, T 229-3787/3011, ramal 286; membership card and permission from Tourist Office in the rodoviária required.

● **Places to eat**

Sole Mio, Av Dr Emilio Lang 485 (on road to Horto Florestal), Italian, big portions; *Baden Baden*, R Djalma Forjaz 93, German, good.

● **Shopping**

There are plenty of chocolate shops, also jams and cheese for sale. Stalls on main square Thur-Sun sell local produce.

● **Transport**

Road There are now two routes from São Paulo; either take the new Airton Senna tollway, Carvalho Pinto tollway and then new road from Taubaté, or the 87 km paved road from São José dos Campos, 100 km from São Paulo, then the Presidente Dutra (BR-116) highway. By car it takes about 3 hrs from São Paulo, 6 to 7 from Rio.

Trains Railcars make round trips between Campos do Jordão and Santo Antônio do Pinhal, in season, six times a day, out of season (Oct-Nov, Mar-April) at 1310 only, a bit bumpy, but beautiful views (sit on the right on the way there, left coming back): hills, valleys, tight corners. The train is very crowded even though you are assigned a seat; fare US$1.50 (buy ticket in advance, and get return immediately on arrival in San Antônio; watch your belongings on board). Whole trip takes about 3 hrs: 1 hr each way on train, 40 mins-1 hr in Santo Antônio (not much on offer there: a few snack bars, nice views, statue of Madonna and Child).

Buses From São Paulo, US$6, 3 hrs; from Rio, changing at São José dos Campos, US$9.50.

ROUTES The short road down to **Pindamonhangaba**, starting from the paved road 24 km SW of Campos do Jordão, is paved (5 buses daily, 50 mins). Railcar to 'Pinda' out of season, leaves 1705 Mon-Thur and weekends, from Pinda 0600 Tues-Fri, 0930 weekends (no service during high season, when all cars are used on Campos do Jordão-San Antônio route). There is a local railcar service within 'Pinda' (very crowded but cheap). From 'Pinda' buses run to **São Paulo** and to **Aparecida do Norte**, 1030, US$2.

APARECIDA DO NORTE

(*Pop* 35,060) Nearer to Rio than the Pindamonhangaba turn, just off the BR-116, is Brazil's chief place of pilgrimage and the seat of its patron saint, Nossa Senhora Aparecida. This small black image of the Virgin is said to have been taken by a fisherman from the nearby Río Paraíba, and quickly acquired a miraculous reputation. It is now housed in a huge modern basilica in Romanesque style on top of a hill, with the clean white-walled, red-roofed town below.

Southern Brazil: Rio Grande do Sul

THIS consists, from south to north, of the three states of Rio Grande do Sul, Santa Catarina and Paraná. Rio Grande do Sul is gaúcho (cowboy) country; it is also Brazil's chief wine producer. Throughout the south European settlement, especially from Germany, heavily influences cultural and agricultural activity. The coast offers a variety of beaches and scenery while in the far west is one of Latin America's major natural attractions, the Iguaçu falls, and one of its largest manmade constructions, the Itaipu dam.

The conformation of the land is not unlike that further N; the Great Escarpment runs down the coastal area as far as Porto Alegre, receding from the coast in a wide curve between Paranaguá and Florianópolis. South of Tubarão to the borders of Uruguay the hills of southern Rio Grande do Sul, which never rise higher than 900 to 1,000m, are fringed along the coast by sand bars and lagoons.

In southern Rio Grande do Sul, S and W of the Rio Jacuí (draining into the Lagoa dos Patos) there are great grasslands stretching as far as Uruguay to the S and Argentina to the W. This is the distinctive land of the *gaúcho*, or cowboy (pronounced ga-oo-shoo in Brazil), of the flat black hat, of *bombachas* (the baggy trousers worn by the *gaúcho*), of the poncho and *ximarão* (or *mate* without sugar), the indispensable drink of southern cattlemen. There are many millions of cattle, sheep and pigs, and some 75% of all Brazilian wine comes from the state. Its population (who all call themselves

gaúchos) now number over 9 million. The *gaúcho* culture is increasingly developing a sense of distance from the African-influenced culture of further N. This separationist strain was most marked in the 1820s and 1830s when the Farroupilha movement, led by Bento Gonçalves, proclaimed the República Riograndense in 1835. The subsequent war with the federal government ended with the Treaty of Ponche Verde in Feb 1845.

There are three sharply contrasted types of colonization and land owning in Rio Grande do Sul. During the colonial period, wars with the Spaniards of Uru-

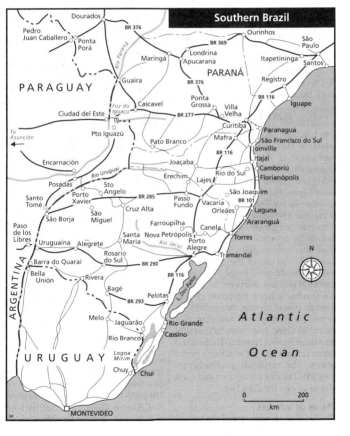

guay were frequent, and the Portuguese government brought into the grasslands of the S a number of military settlers from the Azores; these soldiers intermarried with the Brazilian herdfolk in the area. In the colonial period, also, the Jesuits built several settlements to acculturate the local Indians; relics of this process include the impressive ruins of the **Sete Povos das Missões Orientais** (São Borja, São Nicolau, São Luiz, São Lourenço, São Miguel, São João, Santo Ângelo).

At São Leopoldo, N of Porto Alegre, a group of Germans were settled in 1824 on their own small farms, and during the next 25 years over 20,000 more were brought into the area by the Brazilian Government. The Germans concentrated on rye, maize, and pigs. Between 1870 and 1890, settlers from northern Italy arrived, bringing viticulture with them, and settled N of the Germans at Alfredo Chaves and Caxias do Sul.

PORTO ALEGRE

(*Pop* 1,262,630; *CEP* 90000; *DDD* 051) The capital of Rio Grande do Sul, lies at the confluence of five rivers (called Rio Guaíba, although it is not a river in its own right) and thence into the great freshwater lagoon, the Lagoa dos Patos, which runs into the sea. The fresh-water port, one of the most up-to-date in the country, handles ocean-going vessels up to 7,000 tonnes and 4.87m draught. Porto Alegre is the most important commercial centre S of São Paulo and one of the most heavily industrialized cities in Brazil. Standing on a series of hills and valleys on the banks of the Guaíba, it has a temperate climate through most of the year, though the temperature at the height of summer can often exceed 40°C and drop below 10°C in winter. Mosquitoes are plentiful. The business centre juts out into the water on a promontory. The surrounding suburbs are pleasant. The city's many bars and clubs cluster around the Zona Norte.

Places of interest

The older residential part of the town is on a promontory dominated previously by the **Palácio Piratini** (Governor's Palace), the imposing modern **cathedral**, and the two high white towers of the old church of **Nossa Senhora das Dores**, but Governor and God have now been utterly dwarfed by the skyscraper of the **Assembléia Legislativa**. The streets in the centre are famous for their steep gradients.

Do not miss that section of the **R dos Andradas** (R da Praia) that is now permanently closed to traffic. It is the city's principal outdoor meeting place, the main shopping area, and by around 1600 it is jammed full of people.

The **Parque Farroupilha** (called Parque Rendação) is a fine park near the city centre. The interesting cathedral of the **Anglican-Episcopal church** of Brazil, the **Jardim Zoológico do Estado** near São Leopoldo (bus US$0.80), the **Botanic Gardens** (Bairro Jardim Botânico, bus 40 from Praça 15 de Novembro) and the **Cidade Universitária** are worth a visit. The **Mercado Público** is next to the Prefeitura, in the centre of town. In the **Cidade Baixa** quarter are the colonial **Travessa dos Venezianos** (between RR Lopo Gonçalves and Joaquim Nabuco) and the **house of Lopo Gonçalves**, R João Alfredo 582, which houses the Museu de Porto Alegre, free, 0900-1700 Tues-Sun. The 5-km wide Rio Guaíba lends itself to every form of boating and there are several sailing clubs. Boat trips leave from Av Mauá opp the Ministério da Fazenda, US$3.50, 1 hr. **Ipanema beach**, on the southern banks of the river, offers spectacular sunsets. A good view of the city, with glorious sunsets, may be had from the **Morro de Santa Teresa** (take bus 95 from the top end of R Salgado Filho, marked 'Morro de Santa Teresa TV' or just 'TV').

A visit to Varig's installations and workshops is worth while. Varig's museum, R Augusto Severo 851 e 18 de Novembro 800, São João, is open Tues-Fri and 0900-1300 Sun. *Cervejaria Brahma*, Av Cristovão Colombo 545, offers tours of its brewery (but not Dec-Mar).

Museums

Museu Júlio de Castilhos, Duque de Caxias 1231, has an interesting historical collection (Tues-Sun 0900-1700), and there is the **Museu do Trem** in the old railway station of São Leopoldo, decrepit but interesting exhibits: entrance free, Mon-Fri 1400-1800, sometimes closed Mar-Nov. **Museu de Arte do Rio Grande do Sul**, Praça Senador Florêncio (Praça da Alfândega), Tues 1000-2100, Wed-Sun 1000-1700, entry free, is interesting. **Museu Antropológico**, R Carlos Chagas 55, T 225-0624, Mon-Fri 0830-1200, 1400-1700, good.

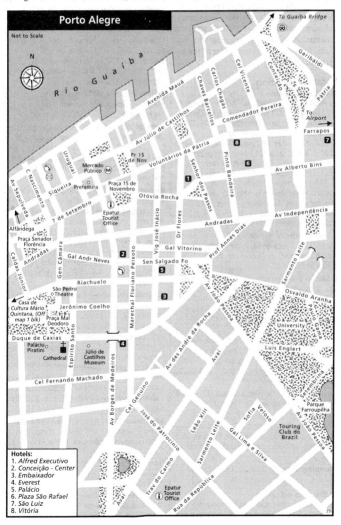

Porto Alegre

Not to Scale

To Guaíba Bridge
To Airport

Rio Guaíba

Hotels:
1. *Alfred Executivo*
2. *Conceição - Center*
3. *Embaixador*
4. *Everest*
5. *Palácio*
6. *Plaza São Rafael*
7. *São Luiz*
8. *Vitória*

Local festivals

The main event is on 2 Feb (local holiday), the festival of **Nossa Senhora dos Navegantes** (Iemanjá), whose image is taken by boat from the central quay in the port to the industrial district of Navegantes. **Semana Farroupilha**, celebrating *gaúcho* traditions in parades in traditional style, main day 20 Sept. The **Carnival** parade takes place in Av A do Carvalho, renamed Av Carlos Alberto Barcelos (or Roxo) for these 3 days only, after a famous carnival designer.

Local information

● **Accommodation**

L2 *Plaza São Rafael*, Av Alberto Bins 514, T 221-6100, F 221-6883; *Conceição-Center*, Av Senador Salgado Filho 201, T 225-7774, good; **L3** *Alfred Executivo*, Av Otávio Rocha 270, T 221-8966; **L3** *Embaixador*, Jerônimo Coelho 354, T 228-2211, 4-star, comfortable, unexciting restaurant; **L3-A1** *Ritter*, Largo Vespasiano J Veppo 55, T 228-4044, 221-8155, F 228-1610, conveniently located opp rodoviária, good service, English, French, German, fine restaurant, bar, small pool, rec; **L3** *Continental*, next door (No 77, T 225-3233, F 228-5024), all facilities, high standards, rec.

A1 *Porto Alegre Residence*, R Des André da Rocha 131, T 225-8644, large rooms, TV, a/c, rec; **A2** *Everest*, R Duque de Caxias 1357, T 228-3133.

B *São Luiz*, Av Farrapos 45, T 228-1722, spotless, good service, but nr rodoviária so a bit noisy; **B** *Terminaltur*, opp rodoviária, next to *Continental* No 125, T 227-1656, a/c, breakfast, heating, small rooms and tiny bathrooms, not too comfortable.

C *Palácio*, Av Vigário José Inácio 644, central, hot water, rec; **C** *Açores*, R dos Andradas 885, T 221-7588, central, cramped but friendly; **C** *Savoy*, Av Borges de Medeiros 688, T 224-0511, good value.

D *Curitibano*, R Dr Barros Cassal 82, T 228-2343, rec; **D** *Uruguay*, Dr Flores 371, simple, rec.

Hotels in the area around R Garibáldi and Voluntários da Patria between Av Farrapos and rodoviária are overpriced and used by 'working' girls.

Camping: Praia do Guarujá, 16 km out on Av Guaíba.

● **Places to eat**

Many good ones. *Gaúcho* cooking features large quantities of meat, while German cuisine is also a strong influence. Regional farm (*campeiro*) food, now a dying art, uses plenty of rice, vegetables, and interesting sauces. Vegetarians might try some of the *campeiro* soups or casseroles, otherwise stick to Italian restaurants or *churrascaria* salad bars.

German: *Sociedade Germânia*, Av Independência 1269, 6th floor, T 222-9094, Sat night dinner-dance, reasonable, closed Mon, Sat lunch, Sun eves, rec; *Hannover*, Av C Colombo 2140 (Floresta), T 222-7902, inexpensive, closed Mon, rec; *Chopp Stübel*, R Quintino Bocaiúva 940, T 332-8895, closed Sun, rec; *Wunderbar*, R Marquês do Herval 5981, T 222-4967, opens 2000-0400, very busy, rec (both in Moinhos de Vento).

Italian: *Pizzeria 4 Climas*, Av Vigario José Inácio 695; *Spaguetti Express*, Centro Comercial Nova Olária, Lima e Silva 776, good.

General: *Mosqueteiro*, Estádio Olímpico (belongs to football club); *Komka*, Av Bahia 1275 (San Geraldo), T 222-1881, reasonable, rec; *Chalé da Praça 15*, Praça 15 de Novembro, average food but rec for early evening drinks and snacks.

Regional: *Recanto do Tio Flor*, Av Getúlio Vargas 1700 (Menino Deus), T 233-6512, *comida campeira*, reasonable, rec; *Pulperia*, Tr do Carmo 76 (Cidade Baixa), T 227-1172, inexpensive, music, opens to 0400, closed Sun lunch; *Porky's*, Av Cristóvão Colombo 1971 (Floresta), T 222-7552, serves wild boar and buffalo, closed Sun, rec; *Farroupilha*, Fernando Machado 973 (corner of Borges de Medeiros), delicious *prato feito* US$3.

Churrascarias: all rec: *Gauchão* at Rodoviária, inexpensive, live entertainment nightly; *Santo Antônio*, R Dr Timotéu 465 (Moinhos de Vento), T 222-3541/ 222-3138, more expensive; *Zequinha*, Av Assis Brasil 1294 (Passo D'Areia), T 341-8157, with regional dances; *Galpão Crioulo*, Parque Maurício Sirotsky Sobrinho (in park, Cidade Baixa), T 226-8194, show and dancing; *Moinhos de Vento*, R Dona Laura 424, T 331-1847, closed Sun pm; *Capitão Rodrigo*, Av Alberto Bins 514 (in *Plaza São Rafael* hotel), T 221-6100, closed Mon.

Vegetarian: (Mon-Fri, lunch only) *Ilha Natural*, R Gen Câmara 60, self service, cheap; also try *Associação Macrobiotica*, R Mal Floriano 72, T 225-4784, weekdays only.

Bars: (beer and sandwiches, music) *Cía Sandwiches*, Getúlio Vargas 1430; *João de Barro*, R da República 546, Cidade Baixa, good jazz; *Sgt Peppers*, Dona Laura 329. There is a pleasant bar at the *Casa de Cultura Mário Quintana*, R dos Andradas 736.

● **Banks & money changers**

Exchange on Av Borges de Medeiros, good rate, cash only. **Platino Turismo**, Dos Andrades e Av Borges de Medeiros (only one to change TCs, Amex, but 6% less than cash), **Exprinter**, Sen Salgado Filho 247 (best for cash); **Mastercard**, cash against card, R 7 de Setembro 722, 8th floor, Centro; for other addresses consult tourist bureau brochure. **Lloyds Bank**, R Gen Câmara 249 (open 1000-1630). **Banco do Brasil**, Uruguai 185, 9th floor (open 1000-1500), good rates for TCs. **Bradesco**, Praça Senador Florêncio, Visa machine.

● **Cultural centres**

Sociedade Brasileira da Cultura Inglesa, Praça Mauricio Cardoso 49, Moinhos de Vento. **Instituto Goethe**, 24 de Outubro 122 (open Mon-Fri, 0930-1230, 1430-2100), occasional concerts, bar rec for German *Apfelkuchen*.

● **Electric current**

110-120 AC 50 cycles.

● **Embassies & consulates**

Argentine, R Prof Annes Dias 112, 1st floor, T 24-6799/6810/6786. **Uruguayan**, R Siquera Campos 1171, 6th floor, T 224-3499. **US**, Genuino 421, corner of Medeiros, T 226-4288. **British**, R Itapeva 110, Sala 505, Edif Montreal Bairro D'Areia, T 41-0720; **Austrian**, R 7 de Setembro 1069, conj 1714, Caixa Postal 1771, T 2460 77/85. **Danish**, Av Ipiranga 321, 5th floor, Bairro Menino Deus, Caixa Postal 500, T 231 7344, F 233 6158, open 0800-1200, 1400-1800. **Finnish**, R Comendador Azevedo 224, T 222-7188.

● **Entertainment**

The old Hotel Majestic has become the **Casa de Cultura Mário Quintana**, at R dos Andrades 736: this is a lively centre for the arts, with exhibitions, theatre etc. Plays by local and visiting companies at the theatres of **São Pedro** (opp Government Palace) free noon and late afternoon concerts Sat, Sun, art gallery, café, and **Leopoldina** (Av Independência). **Centro de Tradição Gaúcha** has *gaúcho* shows every Sat, starting at 2200.

Nightclubs: *Crocodillo's*, 24 de Outuoiro (Auxiliadora), disco, rec. *Descretu's*, Venâncio Aires 59, gay club, shows at 0230. *Gaúchos* congregate at late-night bars. Popular in 1996-97 were: *Amsterdam*, Av Nilo Peçulha 1690 (3 Figueras), 1900-0200, closed Sun, sophisticated; *Best Bier*, Av C Colombo 3000, esq R Germano Petersen Júnior (Higienópolis), Mon-Fri 1800-0100, weekends 2000-0200, mixed crowd, live music, choice of ambiences; *Barong*, R Mostadeiro 517, T 222-1663, Balinese style, Indian snack food, varied music, closed Sun.

● **Laundry**

Several along Av Andre da Rocha inc *Lavanderia Lav-Dem*, No 225, US$1.70/kg wash and dry.

● **Language courses**

Portuguese and Spanish, Matilde Dias, R Pedro Chaves Barcelos 37, apto 104, T 31-8235. US$10 for 90 mins, rec.

● **Post & telecommunications**

Post: R Siqueria Campos 1100, Centro, Mon-Fri 0800-1700, Sat 0800-1200. *UPS*: T 43-4972/42-4602 (Alvaro).

Telecommunications: Embratel, R Siqueira de Campos 1245, T 41233.

● **Security**

The market area in Praça 15 de Novembro and the bus terminal are dangerous at night; thefts have been reported in Voluntários da Pátria and Praça Parcão.

● **Shopping**

H Stern jewellers at Shopping Center Iguatemi and international airport. The Praia de Bello shopping centre, claimed to be the largest in Latin America, is a US$1.50 taxi ride from town. There is a street market (leather goods, basketware, etc) in the streets around the central Post Office. Good leather goods sold on the streets. Sun am handicraft and bric-a-brac market (plus sideshows) Av José Bonefácio (next to Parque Farroupilha). Very good food market.

Bookshops: *Livraria Kosmos*, R dos Andradas 1644 (international stock); *Livraria Lima*, Borges de Medeiros 539; *Livraria Londres*, Av Osvaldo Aranha 1182, used books in English, French and Spanish and old *Life* magazines; *Papyrus*, R dos Andrades e Caldos Jnr, cheap English books; *Livres e Artes* bookstall in book market, Praça Senador Florêncio, English books.

● **Sports**

Weights and aerobics at *Academia do Parcão*, 24 de Outuoiro 684.

Golf: Porto Alegre Country Club, Av Líbero Badaró, 18 holes, closed to non-members. Several 9-hole courses in nearby towns.

Swimming: from the beaches nr or in the city is forbidden because of pollution. See **Beaches**, below.

● **Tour companies & travel agents**

Several tour companies offer trips to Foz do Iguaçu and Ciudad del Este, overnight journey each way (12 hrs in Paraguay). 3-day trips with 1 night's hotel accommodation, US$56 including sightseeing (time at the falls may be limited). See Turismo section in 'Zero Hora' classifieds (Thur, Sat, Sun) for tour companies' ads.

● **Tourist offices**
Epatur, Travessa do Carmo 84 (head office), 0830-1800, maps and literature, helpful. **Setur**: Salgado Filho airport, friendly; interstate bus station, very helpful (free city maps). **CRTur** (Companhia Riograndense de Turismo), R dos Andradas 1137, 6th floor. A monthly booklet is available. City bus tour US$6, regional tour US$18, Spanish or Portuguese only. Enjoyable boat tours (daytime or evening) on the *Cisne Branco* and *Noiva do Caí*, information from hotels. **Touring Clube do Brasil**, Av João Pessoa 623.

● **Transport**
Local First-class minibuses (*Lotação*), painted in a distinctive orange, blue and white pattern, stop on request. Safer and pleasanter than normal buses, fare about US$1. There is also a **metrô** service, the Trensurb, from the southern terminal at the Mercado Modelo (station beside the market) going as far N as Sapucaia do Sul. The second station serves the rodoviária and the fifth the airport (10 mins), 0500-2300, single journey US$0.50.

Air International airport, Salgado Filho, 8 km from the city, connected to the centre by train (see above). There are daily flights to many Brazilian cities, Buenos and Montevideo.

Buses The terminal on Av Mauá with Garibáldi has good facilities, inc a post office and long-distance telephone service until 2100. A regular bus runs from the rodoviária to the airport, also the Trensurb metrô service (see above), just outside. There are 2 sections to the terminal; the ticket offices for interstate/international destinations are adjacent to the regional ticket office. Regional ticket windows are very busy – ask for travel information at the very helpful booth on the station concourse. To **Rio**, US$50 (*leito* 113), 24 hrs; **São Paulo**, US$37 (*executivo* 45, *leito* 82), 18 hrs; **Brasília**, US$69, 33hrs; **Uruguaiana**, US$17, 8 hrs; **Florianópolis**, US$15, 7 hrs with Viação São Cristóvão (beware of overbooking and of stopping buses – eg Santo Anjo – on this route); **Curitiba**, US$26, 11 hrs; **Rio Grande**, US$11.50, 8/day, 0600 to 2000, 4½ hrs. **Foz do Iguaçu**, US$36, 15 hrs. Very many other destinations. To **Cascavel** (Paraná) for connections to Campo Grande, Cuiabá and Porto Velho: daily except Sat with Aguia Branca, 21 hrs, or Unesul, 19 hrs. To **Jaguarão** on Uruguayan border at 2400, 6 hrs, US$10.50.

International buses: to Montevideo, with TTL (daily 1700 and 2000, US$40, US$63 *leito*; see page 475), alternatively take bus to border town of Chuí at 1200 daily, 7½ hrs, US$22, then bus to Montevideo (US$11-12). *Leito* to **Punta del Este** (Uruguay), departs Fri 2100, arriving Sat 0700. Ouro e Prata operates a 2-3 times weekly service to Salto and Paysandú (Uruguay), via Santana do Livramento/Rivera. To **Asunción** with

Unesul at 1900, Tues, Fri, 18 hrs via Foz do Iguaçu. **Santiago**, 0800 Mon. There are bus services to **Buenos Aires**, US$71, 19 hrs (depending on border) with Pluma, 1700 daily (*leito*, 1715 Mon), route is Uruguaiana, Paso de los Libres, Entre Ríos and Zárate. For Misiones (Argentina), take 2100 bus (not Sat) to Porto Xavier on Río Uruguay, 11 hrs, US$20, get exit stamp at police station, take a boat across to San Javier, US$2, go to Argentine immigration at the port, then take a bus to Posadas (may have to change in LN Além). **NB** Take your passport when purchasing international bus tickets.

ROUTES Good roads radiate from Porto Alegre, and Highway BR-116 is paved to Curitiba (746 km). To the S it is paved (though some stretches are in poor condition), to Chuí on the Uruguayan frontier, 512 km. In summer visibility can be very poor at night owing to mist, unfenced cows are a further hazard. The paved coastal road to Curitiba via Itajaí (BR-101), of which the first 100 km is a 4-lane highway, is much better than the BR-116 via Caxias and Lajes. The road to Uruguaiana is entirely paved but bumpy.

BEACHES

The main beach resorts of the area are to the E and N of the city. On the road N, 112 km from Porto Alegre, is **Osório** (*Pop* 36,775) a pleasant town near sea and lakes, with, **E** *Big Hotel*, good.

TRAMANDAÍ AND TORRES

The towns of **Tramandaí** (126 km, *Pop* 20,070) and **Torres** (209 km, *Pop* 37,505) have the most popular beaches, with lots of luxury and other hotels, motels, bars, restaurants, and other standard seaside amenities. To celebrate independence in 1836, a cavalcade of horses reaches Torres on 16 Sept from Uruguay. Hotels tend to be very full during the summer season.

Between the two resorts are the resorts (heading S to N) of **Atlântida**, **Capão da Canoa**, **Arroio Teixeira** and **Arroio do Sal** (**D** *Hotel D'Itália*, Av Assis Brasil 11, T 09, on beach, highly rec; *Casa da Sogra*, good food).

● **Accommodation** At Tramandaí: **C** *São Jorge*, F Amaral 19, T 661-1154, quiet, rec. Many more. **At Torres**: many, inc **A1** *Dunas da Praia*, on beach, T 664-1011, F 664-2080; **A3** *A Furninha*, R Joaquim Porto 281, good service, T 664-1655, F 664-1437; **B** *Grande*

Hotel Torres, R Júlio de Castilhos 124, T 664-1887, balcony and breakfast; **C** *Central*, Borges de Medeiros 296, T 664-2580, good breakfast; **C** *Salth*, Borges de Medeiros 209, T 664-1881, good Dec-Feb; **C** *Pousada Brisa do Mar*, R Julio de Castilhos, T 664 2019, good breakfast, rec; **C** *Oceano Hotel*, Av Barão do Rio Branco 400, T 664 1154, rec; **E** *São Domingo Youth Hostel* in a school building, Júlio de Castilhos 875, T 664-1865, clean. **Camping**: there are fully equipped campsites at both towns, and camping is also allowed on some beaches.

- **Places to eat** *Bom Gosto*, Rio Branco 242, churrascaria; *Sol Macrobiótico*, J Castilhos 746, good cheap vegetarian with a cosy, personal atmosphere.

- **Banks & money changers** In Torres, **Banco do Brasil** and at Rodoviária.

ROUTES There is a paved road from Torres and Tramandaí (mostly prohibited to trucks) along the coast to Quintão, giving access to many beaches. A track continues to Mostardas, thence along the peninsula on the seaward side of the Lagoa dos Patos to São José do Norte, opposite Rio Grande. There is accommodation in **Palmares do Sul** (across the peninsula from Quintão) and Mostardas. South of Mostardas is **Tavares** on the **Lagoa do Peixe**, a national park, which is a resting place for migrating birds (details from Praça Luís Martins 30, Mostardas, CEP 96270-000, T 051-673-1464). The road to the park is called the Estrada do Inferno. In Tavares, the red house on the Praça is a hotel, no sign, rec; several buses a week Tavares – São José do Norte (130 km) and several daily to Porto Alegre.

SÃO LOURENÇO DO SUL

Another popular beach area is S of Porto Alegre, around Cassino, near Rio Grande (see page 474). 40 km to the S (towards Rio Grande) begins the Costa Doce of the Lagoa dos Patos; noted bathing points are Tapes, Barra do Ribeiro, Arambaré, **São Lourenço do Sul** and Laranjal. São Lourenço is a good place to enjoy the lake, the beaches, fish restaurants and watersports. The town hosts a popular 4-day festival in March.

- **Accommodation** At São Lourenço do Sul is *Hotel Vilela*, R Almte Abreu 428, family hotel, clean, friendly. Good **camping** facilities nearby, at Reponte by the beach.

Inland is the pleasant Serra Gaúcha, the most beautiful scenery being around the towns of **Gramado** and **Canela**, about 130 km from Porto Alegre. There is a distinctly Bavarian flavour to many of the buildings in both towns. In spring and summer the flowers are a delight, and in winter there are frequently snow showers. This is excellent walking and climbing country among hills, woods, lakes and waterfalls. In both towns it is difficult to get rooms in the summer/Christmas. Local crafts include knitted woollens, leather, wickerwork, and chocolate.

GRAMADO

(Pop 22,045) The town has two fine parks, Parque Knorr and Lago Negro, and Minimundo, a collection of miniature models.

- **Accommodation** **L3** *Serra Azul*, R Garibáldi 152, T 286-1082, F 286-3374; **A1** *Ritta Höppner*, R Pedro Candiago 305, T 286-1334, in cabins which have TV and fridge, very good value, friendly, good breakfasts, German owners, pool and miniature trains in grounds; **A2** *Pequeno Bosque*, R Piratini 486, T 286-1527, fridge, good breakfast, located in wood close to Véu da Noiva waterfall; **A3** *Pousada Zermatt*, A Acorsi e R da Fé, T 286-2426, rec; **B** *Luiz*, Senador Salgado Filho 432, T 286-1026, good breakfast; **B** *Parque*, Leopoldo Rosenfeldt 818, T 286-1326, bungalows, good breakfast, maid will do laundry reasonably; **C** *Dinda*, R Augusto Zatti 160, T 286-1588, one of the cheapest; *Planalto*, Borges de Medeiros 2001, T 286-1210, opp rodoviária, clean and friendly; a private house in this street, No 1635, rents rooms, rec.

- **Places to eat** *Nápoli*, Av Borges de Medeiros 2515, good Italian; *Lancheira*, R Garibáldi 321, cheap and good. Coffee shop, *Tia Nilda*, das Hortênsias 765. *Pyp* yoghurt factory, Av S Diniz 1030, has snack bar serving health food sandwiches and yoghurt. The local speciality is *café colonial*, a 5 o'clock meal of various dishes, inc meats, rec at *Café da Torre*, das Hortênsias 2174. Visitors should also sample hot *pinhões* (nuts from the Paraná pine) and *quentão* (hot red wine, cachaça, ginger, cloves, sugar and cinnamon, often topped with *gemada* – beaten egg yolks and sugar).

- **Banks & money changers** Banco do Brasil, R Garibáldi esq Madre Verónica.

- **Tourist offices** Corner of Borges de Medeiros and Col Diniz, Gramado (2 blocks from Rodoviária, no English spoken) and on main square in Canela, good maps and hotel lists.
- **Transport** Frequent bus service to Canela, 10 mins.

CANELA

(*Pop* 24,375; *DDD* 054) 6 km from Canela is the **Parque Estadual do Caracol**; a well-marked nature trail leads to the foot of the falls, which are 130m high (allow $1\frac{1}{2}$ hrs of daylight), and to smaller falls above Caracol. From the high point at Ferradura, 7 km from the park, there is a good view into the canyon of the Rio Cai. Good views also from Morro Pelado, follow signs from behind the town (nice walk through forest).

- **Accommodation L2** *Laje de Pedra*, Av Pres Kennedy Km 3, T 282-1530, F 282-1532, all amenities; **A1** *Vila Suzana Parque*, Theoboldo Fleck 15, T 282-2020, chalets, heated pool attractive; **C** *Bela Vista*, R Oswaldo Aranha 160, T 282-1327, nr rodoviária, good breakfasts; **C** *Canela*, Av Osvaldo Aranha, 223, T 282 2774, breakfast, English speaking staff, rec; *CNEC*, youth hostel, R Melvin Jones 151, T 282-1134; **D** *Central*, Av Júlio de Castilhos 146, safe, rec; **D** pp *Pousada do Viajante*, R Ernesto Urbani 132, kitchen facilities, rec, T 282-2017. **Camping**: *Camping Clube do Brasil*, 1 km from waterfall in Parque do Caracol, 1 km off main road, signposted (6 km from Canela); excellent honey and chocolate for sale here, highly rec. *Sesi*, camping or cabins, $2\frac{1}{2}$ km outside Canela, T (054) 282-1311/1697, clean, restaurant, rec.
- **Electric current** 220 volts AC.
- **Transport** Several buses daily Canela-Caxias do Sul, 2 hrs, US$3. From Florianópolis, you have to go via Porto Alegre.

PARQUE NACIONAL DE APARADOS DA SERRA

80 km from São Francisco de Paula (38 km E of Canela, 117 km N of Porto Alegre) is the **Parque Nacional de Aparados da Serra**, where the major attraction is the 7.8-km canyon, known locally as the Itaimbezinho (check in advance if open – Ibama, R Miguel Teixeira 126, Cidade Baixa, Caixa Postal 280, Porto Alegre, CEP 90050-250, T 225-2144). Here, two waterfalls cascade 350m into a stone circle at the bottom. There is a free campsite and a restaurant, which has a few rooms, in the

park. From the restaurant one can walk to the canyon of Malacara. For experienced hikers (and with a guide) there is a difficult path to the bottom of Itaimbezinho. One can then hike 20 km to Praia Grande in Santa Catarina (see page 477). As well as the canyon, the park and surrounding region have several bird specialities. Red-legged Seriema, a large conspicuous bird, can be seen on the way to the park, and there are two fox species.

- **Access & accommodation** Tourist excursions, mostly at weekends, from **São Francisco de Paula** (hotel: **A1** *Veraneio Hampal*, RS-235 road to Canela, Km 73, T 644-1363). At other times, take a bus to Cambará, get off at the crossroads, from where it is 15 km to the park – walk or hitchhike if you're lucky. *Pousadas* in Cambará: **C** *Mirão*, R Benjamin Constant, breakfast, rooms and apartments, rec; **D** *Fortaleza*, with bath; **F** *São Jorge*.

NOVA PETRÓPOLIS

24 km W of Gramado (bus US$0.65) is another city (*Pop* 16,715) with strong German roots. Nova Petrópolis has a Parque do Imigrante, an open-air museum of German settlement. North of Nova Petrópolis is **Jammerthal**, a valley in the Serra Gaúcha with German farms, many of whose inhabitants still speak German (go to Joanete and walk from there).

- **Accommodation** Nova Petrópolis hotels inc *Recanto Suiço*, Av 15 de Novembro 2195, T 281-1229, on Parque dos Imigrantes, 3-star; *Petrópolis*, R Steglich 81, T/F 281-1091; *Veraneio Schoeller*, RS-235, Km 8.5, T 281-1778, 1-star; youth hostel *Bom Pastor*, at Km 14, Linha Brasil RS 235, T 281 1195 ext 14.

CAXIAS DO SUL

(*Pop* 290,970; *CEP* 95100; *DDD* 054) 122 km from Porto Alegre is the centre of the Brazilian wine industry. Caxias' population is principally of Italian descent, and it is an expanding and modern city. Vines were first brought to the region in 1840 but not until the end of the century and Italian immigration did the industry develop.

Places of interest

The church of **São Pelegrino** has paintings by Aldo Locatelli and 5m-high bronze doors sculptured by Augusto Murer. Good

municipal museum at R Visconde de Pelotas 586 (open Tues-Sat, 0800-1200, 1400-1800), with displays of artefacts of the Italian immigration. Jan-Feb is the best time to visit.

Excursions

Caxias do Sul's festival of grapes is held in Feb-March. Many *adegas* accept visitors (but do not always give free tasting). Good tour and tasting (6 wines) at *Adega Granja União*, R Os 18 de Forte 2346. Visit also the neighbouring towns of **Farroupilha**, **Bento Gonçalves** and **Garibáldi** (*Pop* 25,900); dry ski slope and toboggan slope – equipment hire, US$2.50/hr. A good *adega*, with free tasting, is *Cooperativa Viti Vinícola Emboaba Ltda*, in Nova Milano (bus to Farroupilha, then change – day trip).

A restored steam train leaves Bento Gonçalves Sat at 1400 for Carlos Barbosa; called 'a rota do vinho' (the wine run), it goes through vineyards in the hills. US$25 round trip, including wines, with live band; reserve in advance through *Giodani Turismo*, R Emy H Dreher 197, T 451-2788.

Local information
● **Accommodation**

Caxias do Sul: **L3** *Alfred Palace*, R Sinimbu 2302, T/F 221-8655 (also **A1** *Alfred* at No 2266); **L3** *Samuara*, 10 km out on RS-122, road to Farroupilha, T 227-2222, F 227-1010.

A1 *Cosmos*, 20 de Setembro 1563, T/F 221-4688; **A1** *Volpiano*, Ernesto Alves 1462, T 221-4744, F 221-4445; **A3** *Itália*, Av Júlio de Castilhos 3076, T/F 225-1177.

D *Peccini*, R Pinheiro Machado 1939, shared bath, good breakfast; **D** *Pérola*, corner Ernesto Alves and Marquês de Herval (No 237), good value; **D** *Hotel Praça*, R Cândido Mendes 330, T 521-3782, good. Hotels fill up early pm.

At Farroupilha: **D** *Don Francesco*, R Dr J Rossler 88, T 261-1132, 2-star.

At Bento Gonçalves: **B** *Dall'Onder*, R Emy Hugo Dreher 197, T/F (054) 451-3555; **C** *Vinocap*, R Barão do Rio Branco 245, T 452-1566.

At Garibáldi: **A3** *Pietá*, João Pessoa 1728, T 262-1283.

Camping: *Palermo*, 5 km out on BR-116 at Km 118, T 222-7255. At Garibáldi, Camping Clube do Brasil, estrada Gen Buarque de Macedo Km 4.

● **Places to eat**

Good restaurants inc *Cantina Pão e Vino*, R Ludovico Cavinato 1757, Bairro Santa Catarina,

Caxias; *Dom Rafael*, Praça Rui Barbosa.

● **Tourist offices**
Kiosk in Praça Rui Barbosa.

SOUTH OF PORTO ALEGRE

PELOTAS

(*Pop* 289,495; *CEP* 96100; *DDD* 0532) On the BR-116, 266 km S of Porto Alegre, 56 km N of Rio Grande, **Pelotas** is the second largest city in the State of Rio Grande do Sul, on the left bank of the Rio São Gonçalo which connects the Lagoa dos Patos with the Lagoa Mirim. It has an array of shops and pleasant parks.

Within a radius of 60 km, there are numerous excursions to the farms of settlers of German descent in the hilly countryside. 5 km from Taím there is an ecological station with a small museum of regional animals; some accommodation for interested visitors.

● **Accommodation B** *Estoril*, R Gen Osório 718, T 25-2411, a/c, reasonable. **B** *Rex*, Praça Pedro Osório 205, T 22-1163, friendly, dowdy.

D *Grande*, Praça Pedro Osório 51, T 25-8139/6659, 'wonderful colonial hotel', some rooms with electric shower.

Camping: Municipal camp site on coast N of town, take bus Z3 from centre, superb site, fresh fish in village 2 km away.

● **Banks & money changers** Banco do Brazil will change TCs. It is difficult to change money at weekends.

● **Transport Air** One plane a day Mon-Fri to Porto Alegre and Rio Grande. **Buses** Rodoviária is far out of town, with bus every 15 mins to centre. Frequent daily buses to **Porto Alegre**, 244 km (US$8.50, 3-4 hrs, paved road); **Rio Grande**, 90 mins (paved but in poor condition) buses stop at Praça 20 de Setembro; **Jaguarão**, on frontier with Río Branco, Uruguay (police post for passport checks 3 km before the Maná bridge, customs at the bridge), paved; and inland to **Bagé** and other towns. The road to the Uruguayan frontier at Chuí (paved), has international bus service, but only a couple of daily buses Pelotas-Chuí. TTL bus services (Montevideo-Porto Alegre) stop at the bus station for Montevideo, US$30-46 (RR Chile and Venezuela); tickets must be purchased from agency during day. Bus service to Buenos Aires via Uruguaiana. From Bagé, where there is a police post, the Uruguayan company Núñez runs buses 3 times a week to Melo, via Aceguá. Good direct road NW to Iguaçu via **São Sepé** (**C** *Trevo Parque Hotel*, a/c, very friendly), Santa Maria (see page 475) and São Miguel mission ruins (see below).

RIO GRANDE

(*Pop* 172,435; *CEP* 962000; *DDD* 0532) At the entrance to the Lagoa dos Patos, 274 km S of Porto Alegre, **Rio Grande** was founded in 1737. The city lies on a low, sandy peninsula 16 km from the Atlantic Ocean. Today it is the distribution centre for the southern part of Rio Grande do Sul, with significant cattle and meat industries.

During the latter half of the 19th century Rio Grande was an important centre, but today it is a rather poor town, notable for the charm of its old buildings. (**Museu Oceanográfico**, US$0.50, 0900-1100, 1400-1700 daily, interesting, 2 km from centre; bus 59 or walk along waterfront.) At Praça Tamandaré is a small zoo.

Excursions

To **Cassino**, a popular seaside town on the Atlantic Ocean, 24 km, over a good road.

The breakwater (the Barra), 5 km S of Cassino, no bus connection, through which all vessels entering and leaving Rio Grande must pass, is a tourist attraction. Barra-Rio Grande buses, from E side of Praça Ferreira pass the Superporto. Very good fishing. The coastline is low and straight, lacking the bays to the N of Porto Alegre; unfortunately the beach is used as a roadway. One attraction is railway flat-cars powered by sail, settle the price in advance; the railway was built for the construction of the breakwater.

Local information
● Accommodation

A1 *Charrua*, R Duque de Caxias 55, T 32-8033, rec, good value; **B** *Europa*, R Gen Neto 165, main square, T 32-8133; **D** *Paris*, R Marechal Floriano 112, T 32-8944, old, charming.

At Cassino: **B** *Atlântico*, Av Rio Grande, 387, T 36-1350, special rates for students; **B** *Marysol*, Av Atlântica 900, T 36-1240, nr beach. Private campsite on Av 33, on the way out to Rio Grande. Camping Clube do Brasil site nr town.

● Places to eat
Recanto Doce, Silva Paes 370, cheap; *China Brasil*, R Luís Loréa 389, good but not cheap;

Pescal, Mal Andréa 389, for fish, fairly expensive; *Caumo's*, Dr Nascimento 389, good churrascaria; *Jensen*, Al Abreu 650, nr rodoviária, good and cheap; *Bar Brejeiro*, Andrades 193, jazz upstairs; *Tia Laura*, 29 km from town on BR-392 N to Pelotas, excellent, specializes in home cooking and *café colonial*.

● Embassies & consulates
British, R Francisco Marques 163, Caixa Postal 455, Centro, 96-200 Rio Grande, T 32-7788. **Danish**, R Mal Floriano 122, CP 92-96200, T 532-32-4422, open 0800-1200, 1330-1800.

● Post & telecommunications
Telecommunications: Embratel, R Andrade Neves 94.

● Tourist offices
R Riachuelo, on the waterfront, behind the Câmera de Comércio and beneath the Hidroviária; good map and information.

● Transport
Buses Frequent daily buses to and from Pelotas (56 km), Bagé (280 km), Santa Vitória (220 km), and Porto Alegre (US$11.50, 4½ hrs). To Itajaí, 14 hrs, US$24. All buses to these destinations go through Pelotas. Road to Uruguayan border on Chuí is paved, but the surface is poor (5 hrs by bus, at 0700 and 1430, US$7.75). Bus tickets to Punta del Este or Montevideo at *Bentica Turismo*, Av Silva Paes 373, T 32-1321/32-1807.

Sea Boat trip across mouth of Lagoa dos Patos, to pleasant village of São José do Norte, US$0.30, every hour from Porto Velho.

WESTERN RIO GRANDE DO SUL

JESUIT MISSIONS

328 km NW of Porto Alegre is **Passo Fundo**, 'the most *gaúcho* city in Rio Grande do Sul', so much so that the town's square boasts a statue of a maté gourd and bombilla – otherwise not much of interest (*Pop* 147,215; several hotels).

West of here are the Sete Povos das Missões Orientais (see page 466). The only considerable Jesuit remains in Brazilian territory (very dramatic) are at **São Miguel** (church, 1735-45, and small museum), some 50 km from **Santo Ângelo** (*Pop* 76,375). At São Miguel there is a *son et lumière* show, weekdays at 2000, weekends at 1930, but ends too late to return to Santo Ângelo. *Gaúcho* festivals often held on Sun afternoons, in a field near the Mission (follow the music).

● **Accommodation At Santo Ângelo**: *Hotel Turis*, R Antônio Manoel 726, T (55) 312-4055, helpful, rec; **D** *Maerkli*, Av Brasil 1000, rec; other cheap central hotels near old railway station. **At São Miguel**: **D** *Hotel Barichello*, highly rec, **E** *Hotel Nova Esperança*, behind bus station, without breakfast.

Rail and road to the W and SW of Rio Grande do Sul go through **Santa Maria** (*Pop* 217,565).

● **Accommodation A1** *Hotel Itaimbé Palace*, R Venâncio Aires 2741, T 222-1144, F 221-2051; **E** *Jantzen*, R Rio Branco, central, noisy on disco nights; *Imperial*, R Manoel Ribas 1767, near station, clean, garden; **E** *Popular*, also near station, clean amenities, not so rooms, basic; fruit and vegetable market Sat am R 13 de Maio.

TO URUGUAY: INLAND ROUTES

Santana do Livramento
The southern interior of the state is the region of the real *gaúcho*. Principal towns of this area include **Santana do Livramento** (*Pop* 80,215). Its twin Uruguayan city is Rivera. Duty free shopping.

All one need do is cross the main street to Rivera, but by public transport this is not a straightforward route between Brazil and Uruguay; Uruguayan immigration is 2 km from the border. For motorists there are 3 customs offices in Santana do Livramento, about 30 mins needed for formalities. Banco do Brasil on Av Sarandí; best rates for Amex TCs at *Val de Marne*.

● **Accommodation A3** *Jandaia* R Uruguai 1452 T 242-2288, rec; **A3** *Portal*, Av Tamandaré 2076, T 242-2533, garage, clean, rec; **D** *Uruguaiana*, close to bus station. **Youth hostel: F** *Hotel Palace*, R Manduca Rodrigues 615, with breakfast, single rooms available, old and grimy.

● **Transport** Bus to Porto Alegre, 2 daily, 7 hrs, US$18; 3 daily to Urugaiana (4 hrs, US$8.50), services also to São Paulo and other destinations). Rodoviária is at Gen Salgado Filho e Gen Vasco Alves.

Uruguaiana: frontier with Argentina
In the extreme W are **Uruguaiana** (*Pop* 117,460), a cattle centre 772 km from Porto Alegre, and its twin Argentine town of Paso de los Libres, also with a casino. A 1,400m bridge over the Rio Uruguai links the two cities.

● **Brazilian immigration & customs**
At the end of the bridge, 5 blocks from the main praça; exchange and information in the same building. Exchange rates are better in the town than at the border.

● **Accommodation**
A1 *Hotel Glória*, R Domingos de Almeida 1951, T 412-4422, good; **D** *Palace*, Praça Rio Branco, without breakfast. *Fares Turis Hotel*, Pres Vargas 2939, T/F 412-3358, may let you leave your bags while you look around town.

● **Transport**
Taxi or bus across the bridge about US$3.50. Buses connect the bus stations and centres of each city every 30 mins; if you have to disembark for visa formalities, a following bus will pick you up without extra charge. There are bus services to Porto Alegre.

● **To Uruguay from Uruguaiana**
Planalto buses run from Uruguaiana via Barra do Quaraí/Bella Unión (US$4.50) to Salto and Paysandú in Uruguay.

COASTAL ROUTE TO URUGUAY: CHUÍ

The Brazilian border town is **Chuí** (*pop* 20,060); its Uruguayan counterpart is Chuy.

● **Brazilian immigration**
Immigration (and tourist caravan) is about 2½ km from the border, on Av Argentina, road to Pelotas. All buses, except those originating in Pelotas, stop at customs on both sides of the border; if coming from Pelotas, you must ask the bus to stop for exit formalities. International buses, eg TTL from Porto Alegre, make the crossing straightforward: the company holds passports; hand over your visitors card on leaving Brazil and get a Uruguayan one on entry. Have luggage available for inspection. Make sure you get your stamp, or you will have trouble leaving Brazil.

● **Entering Brazil**
From Uruguay, on the Uruguayan side, the bus will stop if asked, and wait while you get your exit stamp (with bus conductor's help); on the Brazilian side, the appropriate form is completed by the rodoviária staff when you purchase your ticket into Brazil. The bus stops at Polícia Federal (Av Argentina) and the conductor completes formalities while you sit on the bus. Also, if entering by car, fill up with petrol in Brazil, where fuel is cheaper.

● **Accommodation**
C *Turismo* Av Rio Branco 1078, T 63-1431; **D** *San Francisco*, Av Colombia e R Chile,

shower, restaurant; on R Chile, **D** *Itaipú*, No 1169, 1 block from rodoviária, shower; *Hospedagem Roberto* at No 1631; **E** *Pensão* in private house at No 767.

● **Exchange**

Change all remaining Uruguayan pesos into *reais* before leaving Uruguay since not even black marketeers in Brazil want them. Note that you cannot obtain US$ cash in Brazil.

● **Post & telecommunications**

Post Office: Av Uruguay, between Colombia and Argentina (Chuí).

Telephones: corner of R Chile and Av Argentina.

● **Transport**

Rodoviária on R Venezuela. Buses run from Chuí to **Pelotas** (6-7 daily, US$10, 4 hrs), **Rio Grande** (0700, 1400, 5 hrs, US$7.75) and **Porto Alegre** (1200, 2400, 7½ hrs, US$22); also from Chuí to **Santa Vitória** nearby, where there are a few hotels and rather quicker bus services to the main cities.

Santa Catarina

FURTHER up the coast, in Santa Catarina (*Pop* 4,536,435), a group of Germans settled at Lajes in 1822. In 1848 a new German-speaking settlement was founded at Blumenau. The Germans spread inland over the mountains from the port of São Francisco to Joinville (censuses have revealed that some isolated families still speak only German, understanding little Portuguese). The Italians came later. Over northern Rio Grande do Sul and Santa Catarina the vast majority of people today can trace their origin to these immigrants.

In Santa Catarina, a state of smallholdings, the farmer owns his land and cattle: the familiar European pattern of mixed farming worked by the family. 60% of the population is rural. There is coal in the S, and flourishing food processing (notably poultry and soyabean) and knitted textile industries. Itajaí and São Francisco do Sul are the main ports, handling 90% of the trade. Except for the summer months of

Jan and Feb, the beaches of Santa Catarina are pleasant and uncrowded.

TUBARÃO AND THE SOUTH OF THE STATE

Just across the border from Rio Grande do Sul (but not on the main highway – BR101) is **Praia Grande** (hotel, E, and churrascaria, just off praça, good and cheap). Buses from Praia Grande go to **Araranguá** (*Pop* 48,220), on the BR101, 13 km from which is the beautiful beach of **Arroio do Silva**.

● **Accommodation** D *Hotel Scaini Palace*, T/F 22-1466, good food, rec; *Hotel Paulista*, R Dionizio Mondardo No 58, T/F 26-1244. *Bar Nabar*, Av Getulio Vargas 970, T 526 1290, cheap drinks, English speaking owners, live music, close to beach, rec.

Some 75 km N of Araranguá is the coalfield town of **Tubarão** (*Pop* 95,060). Inland from the main road are the coalfields of Criciúma and Içara, with good beaches nearby.

Termas do Gravatal can be visited from Tubarão (one first class hotel, and two others: **E** *Petit Village*, a/c, mineral pool, good value, quiet, good food.)

About 60 km inland from Tubarão is **Orleães**. Its museum has an original water-powered workshop and sawmill, complete with waterwheel. It dates from the original settlers (late 19th century), and is still in working order. To get there one must get off the bus at the junction about 3 km from the town.

SÃO JOAQUIM

Buses from Tubarão go inland to Lauro Müller, then over the Serra do Rio do Rastro (beautiful views of the coast in clear weather) to **Bom Jardim da Serra** which has an apple festival every April. The road continues to **São Joaquim** (*Pop* 22,285;*Alt* 1,360m). The highest town in Southern Brazil, it regularly has snowfalls in winter; a very pleasant town with an excellent climate. From São Joaquim NE over Pericó to Urubici is unpaved. These roads go around the **Parque Nacional de São Joaquim** (33,500 ha) in the Serra Geral. It has canyons containing sub-tropical vegetation, and araucaria forest at higher lev-

els. There is no bus (local Ibama office, T 0482-22-6202, Secretaria de Turismo de São Joaquim, T 0492-33-0258).

● **Accommodation In São Joaquim** *Nevada* (expensive meals) and **D** *Maristela* (good breakfast), both on R Manoel Joaquim Pinto, 213 and 220 respectively (5 mins' walk from Rodoviária). Camping Clube do Brasil site.

● **Transport** Bus to **Florianópolis** 0830 and 2230, 7½ hrs, US$9.50. To **Caxias do Sul**, 4½ hrs, US$7.25.

LAGUNA

386 km NE of Porto Alegre, 15 km from Tubarão, is the small fishing port of **Laguna** (*Pop* 44,825;*DDD* 0486), in southern Santa Catarina. At Laguna is the **Anita Garibáldi Museum**, containing documents, furniture, and the personal effects of the Brazilian wife of the hero who fought in the 1840s for the independence of Rio Grande do Sul and later helped to unify Italy (US$0.10). Laguna's beach, 2 km from the centre, is not very good, but 16 km away (by ferry and road) are beaches and dunes at **Cavo de Santa Marta**. Also from Laguna, take a Lagunatur or Auto Viação São José bus to **Farol** (infrequent, US$0.85). You have to cross the mouth of the Lagoa Santo Antônio by ferry to get to Farol; look out for fishermen aided by dolphins (*botos*). Here is a fishing village with the alleged third oldest lighthouse in the world (Farol Santa Marta) – guided tours available (taxi, US$10, not including ferry toll). It may be possible to bargain with fishermen for a bed.

● **Accommodation** *Hotel Laguna Tourist*, Praia do Gi, 4 km, T 44-0022, F 44-0123, first class; **B** *Turismar*, Av Rio Grande do Sul 207, T 44-0024, F 44-0279, view over Mar Grosso beach, TV; several others, medium-priced, **C** *Hotel Farol de Santa Marta*, T 44-0370; **D** *Grande*, opp post office, without breakfast; **E** *Recanto*, close to bus terminal, basic.

● **Transport** Buses to/from Porto Alegre, 5½ hrs, with Santo Anjo Da Guarda; same company goes to Florianópolis, 2 hrs.

Another 32 km to the N of Laguna is the port of **Imbituba** (*Pop* 30,975) where there is a carbo-chemical plant, from which air pollution is very bad. The rail link between Imbituba and Tubarão is one of the busiest steam services in South America (freight only apart from an occasional tourist steam train on Sun, probably summer only). There are good beaches (particularly those near Garopaba and Araçatuba), and bus services to Porto Alegre.

FLORIANÓPOLIS

124 km N of Laguna is **Florianópolis** (founded in 1726, *Pop* 254,945; *CEP* 88000; *DDD* 0482), capital of the State, on the Ilha de Santa Catarina joined to the mainland by two bridges, one of which is Ponte Hercílio Luz, the longest steel suspension bridge in Brazil (closed in 1994). The newer Colombo Machado Salles bridge has a pedestrian and cycle way beneath the roadway. It is a port of call for coastal shipping, 725 km from Rio de Janeiro and 420 from Santos. The natural beauty of the island, beaches and bays make Florianópolis a popular tourist centre (only Jan and Feb are very crowded and expensive). The southern beaches are usually good for swimming, the E for surfing, be careful of the undertow.

Places of interest

The **Cathedral** on Praça 15 de Novembro has a life-size sculpture in wood of the flight into Egypt, originally from the Austrian Tyrol. **Forts** include the **Santana** (which houses a **Museu de Armas de Policia Militar**), **São José da Ponta Grossa** (at the N end of the island) and **Nossa Senhora da Conceição** (at the S end). There are three other museums, the **Museu Histórico** in the old Palácio Cruz e Souza, on Praça 15 de Novembre (1000-2000, Tues-Fri, 1000-1800 Sat-Sun), the **Museu de Antropologia** at the Federal University (0900-1700 Mon-Fri 1300-1800 Sat-Sun) and the **Museu do Homem Sambaqui** at the Colégio Catarinense, R Esteves Júnior 159 (open 0800-1100, 1400-1700, Mon-Sat). There is a look-out point at **Morro da Cruz** (take Empresa Trindadense bus, waits 15 mins). Carnival is recommended as beautiful.

Excursions

Excursions can be made on the mainland to the hot springs at **Caldas da Imperatriz** (41°C) and **Águas Mornas** (39°C); at the former are two spa hotels (**B** *Caldas da Imperatriz*, including meals and baths, built in 1850 under the auspices of Empress Teresa Cristina, houses public baths; from **A3** *Plaza Caldas da Imperatriz*, with baths, swimming pools, very well appointed), at Águas Mornas, the **A1** *Palace Hotel* is on the site of the springs, baths open to public Mon-Fri am only. Boat trips can be made from Florianópolis in the bay, T 22-1806, from US$4.50.

See below for a description of the island.

Local information

NB All Florianópolis phone numbers have been changed from 6 to 7 digits. We give new ones where available.

● **Accommodation**

L3 *Florianópolis Palace*, R Artista Bittencourt e R dos Ilhéus 26, T 222-9633, F 223-0300, best, a/c, rec.

A1 *Ivoram*, Av Hercílio Luz 652, T 224-5388, F 224-5890, discount in low season; **A3** *Royal*, Trav João Pinto 34, T 222-2944, F 222-2537, good.

C *Veleiro*, R Silva Jardim 234, T 224-6622, with breakfast, a/c, rec, pier for yachts, 10 mins from bus station, take Cidade Universitária bus.

Within 10 mins' walk of the rodoviária: **A3** *Querência Palace*, R Jerônimo Coelho 95, T 224-2677, F 222-3874, highly rec; **A3** *Diplomata Hotel*, T 224 4455, F 222 7082, Av Paulo Fontes 1210, very good views, R Felipe Schmidt, **A1** *Faial*, No 603, T 224-2766, F 222-9435, good restaurant; **D** *Cacique*, No 53, good, good value but rooms vary; **B** *Baia Sul*, R Tiradentes 167, T 223-2269, F 224-0810, nr Praça 15 de Novembro, a/c, safe, inc breakfast, rec; **B** *Felippe*, 1 block from 15 de Novembro at R João Pinto 25, good, small rooms, 10% off to Youth Hostel members.

On the mainland: **B** *Bruggeman*, R Santos Saraiva 300, T 244-2344, F 244-2045 (bus 236 or 226 from Terminal Urbano do Aterro), motel-type rooms and 2-star accommodation; several cheaper places in same street; **C** *Oasis*, R Gral L Bittencourt 201, T 244-2440, breakfast, good (take bus 201 from here to bus terminal); **D** *Carvalho*, Fúlvio Adduci 184-186, good views, rec. There are plenty of cabins and apartments for rent in the city and on the island outside the Jan-Feb season.

Youth hostels: on the island: Ilha de Santa Catarina, R Duarte Schutel 59, T 223-1692, rec, cooking facilities, breakfast extra, low rates for IYHA cardholders, US$4/night); Barra da Lagoa

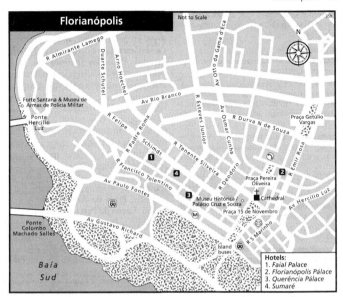

Florianópolis

Hotels:
1. Faial Palace
2. Florianópolis Pálace
3. Querência Pálace
4. Sumaré

(T 222-6746) and Fortaleza da Barra (T 232-0169), both on Estrada Geral da Barra da Lagoa; Praia do Campeche (T 222-6746) and Praia dos Ingleses (T 222-6746 also).

Camping: *Camping Clube do Brasil*, São João do Rio Vermelho, N of Lagoa da Conceição, 21 km out of town; also at Lagoa da Conceição, Praia da Armação, Praia dos Ingleses, Praia Canasvieiras. 'Wild' camping allowed at Ponta de Sambaqui and Praias Brava, Aranhas, Galheta, Mole, Campeche, Campanhas and Naufragados. 4 km S of Florianópolis, camping site with bar at Praia do Sonho on the mainland, beautiful, deserted beach with an island fort nearby. 'Camping Gaz' cartridges from *Riachuelo Supermercado*, on R Alvim e R São Jorge.

● **Places to eat**

Manolo's, R Felipe Schmidt 71, nr centre, good, but not cheap. *Lindacap*, R Felipe Schmidt 1132 (closed Mon), rec, good views. *Pim-Pão*, R Marechal Deodoro, good cheap breakfast, lunches; *Don Pepé Pizza*, R Heitor Luz e Rafael Bandeira, giant helpings; *Papparella*, Almirante Lamego 1416, excellent giant pizzas. Shrimp dishes are good everywhere. *Polly's*, Praça 15 de Novembro 151, 1st floor, good food and service, reasonable prices; *Macarronada Italiana*, Av Rubens de Arruda Ramos 2258, Beira Mar Norte, good. *Churrascaria Ataliba*, Av Irineu Bornhausen 14, excellent rodízio.

Vegetarian: *Vida*, R Visconde Ouro Preto 62 (closed Sun); *La Cucina*, R Padre Roma 73, buffet lunch, Mon-Sat, pay by weight – good, vegetarian choices, rec.

● **Banks & money changers**

Banco do Brasil, R dos Ilheus, poor service; **Banco do Estado de São Paulo**, Tenente Silveira 55; **Banco Estado de Santa Catarina**, Trajano 33, cheques and cash. **Lovetur**, Av Osmar Cunha 15, Ed Ceisa and **Centauro Turismo** at same address. Money changers on R Felipe Schmidt.

● **Electric current**
220 volts AC.

● **Post & telecommunications**

Post Office: Praça 15 de Novembro 5, T 222-3188.

Telecommunications: Telesc, Praça Pereira Oliveira 20, T 223-3700 (interstate and international telephones).

● **Tour companies & travel agents**
Ilhatur Turismo e Cambio Ltda, R Felipe Schmidt, 303 Sobreloja, T 224 6333.

● **Tourist offices**
Head office: Portal Turístico de Florianópolis (Setur), at the mainland end of the bridge, 0800-2000 (Sat, Sun 0800-1800); Praça 15 de Novembro, 0800-1800 (2200 in high season),

reliable for leaving messages; at rodoviária and airport, 0700-1800 (0800 Sat, Sun); maps available, free.

● **Transport**
Local Car hire: Auto Locadora Coelho, Felipe Schmidt 81, vehicles in good condition.

Air Daily flights to all main cities; also flights on weekdays from many southern Brazilian cities. International flights from **Buenos Aires** daily (several at weekends); once a week from Montevideo.

Buses Rodoviária at the E (island) end of the Ponte Colombo Machado Salles; the Terminal Urbano do Aterro for the island nearby, is on R Proc A Gomes between R Paulo Fortes and R Antônio Luz, 2 blocks from Praça 15 de Novembro. Regular daily buses to **Porto Alegre** (US$15, 7 hrs), **São Paulo**, 9 hrs (US$23, *leito* US$60), **Rio**, 20 hrs (US$31 ordinary, 62 *leito*), **Brasília** (3 a week at 0300, US$43); to **Foz do Iguaçu** (US$20, continuing to Asunción US$30), to most other Brazilian cities.

International buses: Montevideo, US$55, daily 0815, by TTL. **Buenos Aires**, US$115, Pluma, buses very full in summer, book 1 week in advance. The coastal highway (BR-101) is preferred as an alternative to the congested inland BR-116; it runs close to Florianópolis but it is bad in places and has many lorries.

ILHA SANTA CATARINA

There are 42 beaches around the island almost all easily reached by public buses: northern beaches from the Terminal Urbano do Aterro, southern beaches from the nearby Praça 15 de Novembro (schedules from Tourist Office). Buses (US$0.15-0.35) run hourly to virtually every place on the island.

To **Lagoa da Conceição** for beaches, sand dunes, fishing, church of NS da Conceição (1730), market every Wed and Sat, post office, boat rides on the lake. Tandem hang gliding, *Lift Sul Vôo Livre*, T 32-0543.

Across the island at **Barra da Lagoa** is a pleasant fishing village and beach, lively in the summer season, with plenty of good restaurants, which can be reached by 'Barra da Lagoa' bus (US$1, every 30 mins from Terminal Urbano, platform 5, or *seletivo* vans, US$1). The same bus goes to beaches at **Mole** (good for walking) and at **Joaquina** (surfing championships in January).

There is a pleasant fishing village at **Ponta das Canas**, walk 1 km to Praia Brava for good surfing, and the beach at **Canasvieiras** is good. Also in the N of the island, is **Praia dos Ingleses** (bus 602). Other northern beaches: Jureré, Daniela and Forte (with fort and beautiful views).

On the W side, N of the city, you can visit the 'city of honey bees' with a Museo da Apicultura, closes 1600 Sat, and the Church of Sto Antônio Lisboa; take Trinidadense bus 331 or any bus going N, to the turn off, on the way to Sambaqui beach and fishing village.

In the S of the island are **Praia de Campeche**, 30 mins by bus from Florianópolis, **Praia da Armação** with, just inland, **Lagoa do Peri** (a protected area). Further S is **Pantano do Sul**, an unspoilt fishing village. Praia dos Naufragados and Fora beaches: take bus to Caieira da Barra do Sul and take 1-hr walk through fine forests.

● **Accommodation Lagoa da Conceição**: E *Pousada Zilma*, R Geral da Praia da Joaquina 279, T 232-0161, quiet, safe, rec; Ricardo, R Manoel S de Oliveira 8, CEP 88062, T 32-0107, rents self-contained apartments, can arrange houses also, rec; restaurant: *Oliveira*, R Henrique Veras, excellent seafood dishes. **At Barra da Lagoa**: A3 *Cabañas Verde Limão*, on the beach, small cabins with bath, fan, fridge; A3 *Pousada 32*, on beach, comfortable apartments, helpful; C *Mini-Hotel Caiçara*, good, nr beach; C *Pousada Floripaz*, Estrada Geral (across hanging bridge at bus station, take bus 403 from terminal municipal), T 232-3193, book in advance, safe, family run, helpful owners, will organize tours by boat and car on island, highly rec; D *Pousada-Lanchonete Sem Nome*, Praia do Moçambique, in 4-bunk rooms, bathrooms separate, kitchen, laundry, rec; E *Albergue do Mar*, basic, good for lone travellers; *Pousada Sol Mar* operates as a youth hostel but only 2 bathrooms for all; *Camping da Barra*, T 32-3199, beautiful site clean, helpful owner; restaurant: *Meu Cantinha*, R Orlando Shaplin 89, excellent seafood. **At Joaquina**: A1 *Hotel Cris*, T 32-0380, F 32-0075, luxurious, rec. **At Ponta das Canas**: B *Hotel Moçambique*, T/F 66-1857, in centre of village, noisy at weekends; houses to let from Frederico Barthe, T 66-0897. **At Praia dos Ingleses**: B *Sol e Mar*, T 62-1211, excellent, rec. **At Praia de Campeche**: *Hotel São Sebastião da Praia*, T/F 37 4247/4066, resort hotel on splendid beach, offers special monthly rate April to Oct, excellent value; *Natur Campeche Hotel Residencial*, T 37-4011, 10 mins walk from beach. **Near Pantano do Sul**: **B** *Pousada dos Tu-**canos*, Estrada Geral da Costa de Dentro 2776, T 237-5084, Caixa Postal 5016, English, French, Spanish spoken, spacious bungalows in garden setting, excellent organic food, very highly rec;

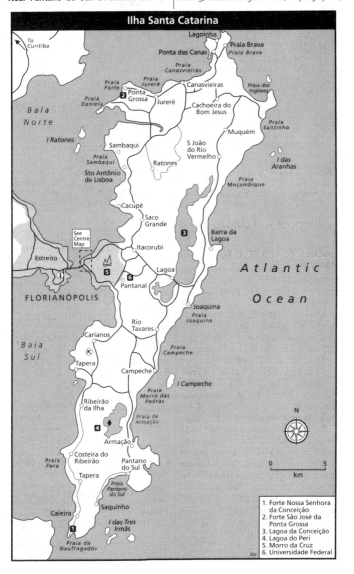

Ilha Santa Catarina

To Curitiba

Lagoinha

Ponta das Canas
Praia Brava
Praia Brava

Praia Canasvieiras

Praia Forte
Praia Jureré
Ponta Grossa
Canasvieiras
Praia dos Ingleses

Praia Daniela
Jureré

Cachoeira do Bom Jesus

Bahía Norte

I Ratones

Sambaqui
S João do Rio Vermelho
Muquém
Praia Santinho

Ratones
I das Aranhas

Praia Sambaqui

Sto Antônio de Lisboa
Praia Moçambique

Cacupé

Saco Grande

See Centre Map
Itacorubi
Barra da Lagoa

Estreito
Lagoa

FLORIANÓPOLIS
Pantanal

Atlantic Ocean

Bahía Sul
Joaquina
Praia Joaquina

Rio Tavares
Praia Campeche

Carianos

Tapera
Campeche

I Campeche

Ribeirão da Ilha
Praia Morro das Pedras

Praia da Armação

Armação

Costeira do Ribeirão
Pantano do Sul

Praia Fora
Tapera

Praia Pantano do Sul

Caieira
Saquinho

I das Tres Irmãs

Praia da Naufragados

N

0   5
km

1. Forte Nossa Senhora da Conceição
2. Forte São José da Ponta Grossa
3. Lagoa da Conceição
4. Lagoa do Peri
5. Morro da Cruz
6. Universidade Federal

take bus to Pantano do Sul, walk 6 km or telephone and arrange to be picked up by German owner.

LAGES

West of Florianópolis, 212 km by paved road, is **Lages** (formerly spelt Lajes; *Pop* 150,865; *DDD* 0492) a convenient stopping place on BR-116 between Caxias do Sul and Curitiba. The route can also be done on poorer roads via São Joaquim (see above), which is perhaps the most interesting journey in the State, with scenery changing as the road climbs out of coastal forest (3 buses a day run on the main road in summer, 1 in winter, 5 hrs, via Alfredo Wagner, otherwise go via Blumenau). Bus station is 30 mins' walk SE of centre.

● **Accommodation** **B** *Grande*, R João de Castro 23, T/F 22-3522, good; **C** *Presidente*, Av Pres Vargas 101, T 22-1058. Others nr rodoviária. Voltage 220 AC.

NORTH OF FLORIANÓPOLIS

BEACHES: PORTO BELO TO CAMBORIÚ

On the coast N of Florianópolis there are many resorts. They include **Porto Belo** (*Pop* 9,700), a fishing village on the N side of a peninsula settled in 1750 by Azores islanders, with a calm beach and a number of hotels (eg *Baleia Branca*, T 69-4011, with camping) and restaurants (bus Florianópolis – Porto Belo with Praiana or Biguaçu, 8 daily, 3 on Sun). West of Port Belo is **Praia de Perequê** (Hotels: **E** *Tati*, T 69-4363, across from beach, and **E** *Blumenauense*, with bath and breakfast, on beach, T 69-4208). Around the peninsula are wilder beaches reached by rough roads: Bombas (2 hotels), Bombinhas (*Pousada do Arvoredo*, T 69-4355, up on a hill), Mariscal, and, on the southern side, Cantinho (**B** *Pousada Zimbros*, T 69-4225, cheaper off season, on beach, sumptuous breakfast, restaurant, highly rec, spear fishing guide).

Balneário Camboriú (*Pop* 25,715; 86 km) once beautiful, now has 4 blocks of concrete jungle behind the beach, which is very safe. From 15 Dec to end-Feb it is very crowded and expensive; the resort is

popular with Argentines. Beto Carrero World is an imitation of Disney World. A few kilometres S, at Lojas Apple, there is a museum, zoo and aquarium; and at Meia Praia, which is quieter and cleaner than Camboriú. Pinho beach, 15 km out of the city, is one of Brazil's few legal nudist beaches; 2 campsites and a small hotel. Between Itajaí and Camboriú is the beautiful, deserted (and rough) beach of Praia Brava. Note that from mid-July to mid-Aug it can be chilly.

● **Accommodation** From Mar-Nov it is easy to rent furnished apartments by the day or week (try Bom Pastor agency, Av Brasil 1861, T 0473-66-0769, reliable). There are a great many hotels, restaurants and campsites. **D** *Jaitur*, opp the rodoviária, with hot water, safe, rec.

● **Buses** From Florianópolis, Joinville and Blumenau. TTL buses Montevideo-São Paulo stop here at about 1800, a good place to break the journey (US$58 from Montevideo).

ITAJAÍ

100 km up the coast N of Florianópolis by the paved BR-101 is the most important port in Santa Catarina at the mouth of the Rio Itajaí (*Pop* 119,585; *CEP* 88300; *DDD* 0473). It is well served by vessels up to $5\frac{1}{2}$m draught, and is the centre of a district largely colonized by Germans and Italians. Airport. You can walk to Cabeçudas beach, which is quiet and small.

Resorts N of Itajaí include Piçarras, with sandy beaches interspersed with rocky headlands (ideal for fishing), and **Barra Velha** (**D** *Hotel Mirante*, good, cheap restaurant, and 2 dearer hotels).

● **Accommodation** **A1** *Marambaia Cabeçudas*, at Cabeçudas beach, best, 6 km out of town, T 44-0999; **C** *Grande*, R Felipe Schmidt 44, T 44-0968, good value. Recommended bar, *Trudys*, on riverfront at end of main street, a good place for changing cash.

● **Embassies & consulates** Finnish Consulate, R Almte Tamandaré 100, T 44-6511.

BLUMENAU

There is a 61 km paved road to **Blumenau** (*Pop* 211,175; *CEP* 89100; *DDD* 0473), 47 km up the Rio Itajaí. It is in a prosperous district settled mostly by Germans; the city is a notable textile centre. A clean, beach, offers special monthly rate April to Oct, excellent value; *Natur Campeche Hotel Residencial*, T 37-4011, 10 mins walk from beach. **Near Pantano do Sul**: **B** *Pousada dos Tu-* *canos*, Estrada Geral da Costa de Dentro 2776, T 237-5084, Caixa Postal 5016, English, French, Spanish spoken, spacious bungalows in garden setting, excellent organic food, very highly rec;

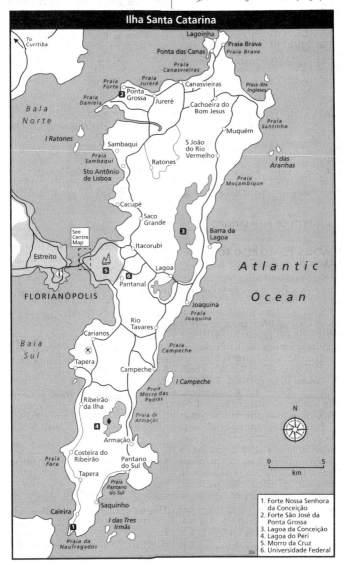

Ilha Santa Catarina

To Curitiba

Lagoinha
Ponta das Canas
Praia Brava
Praia Brava
Praia Canasvieiras
Praia Forte
Praia Jurerê
Ponta Grossa
Canasvieiras
Praia das Inglêses
Praia Daniela
Jurerê
Cachoeira do Bom Jesus

Baía Norte

I Ratones
Sambaqui
S João do Rio Vermelho
Muquém
Praia Santinho

Praia Sambaqui
Sto Antônio de Lisboa
Ratones
I das Aranhas

Praia Moçambique

Cacupé
Saco Grande
Itacorubi
Barra da Lagoa

See Centre Map

Estreito
Lagoa

FLORIANÓPOLIS

Pantanal

Atlantic

Ocean

Joaquina
Praia Joaquina

Rio Tavares

Baía Sul

Carianos
Tapera
Praia Campeche

Campeche

I Campeche

Praia Morro das Pedras

Ribeirão da Ilha
Praia da Armação

Armação

Costeira do Ribeirão
Pantano do Sul

Praia Fora

Tapera

Praia Pantano do Sul

Caieira
Saquinho
I das Tres Irmãs

Praia da Naufragados

N

0   5
km

1. Forte Nossa Senhora da Conceição
2. Forte São José da Ponta Grossa
3. Lagoa da Conceição
4. Lagoa do Peri
5. Morro da Cruz
6. Universidade Federal

35a

take bus to Pantano do Sul, walk 6 km or telephone and arrange to be picked up by German owner.

LAGES

West of Florianópolis, 212 km by paved road, is **Lages** (formerly spelt Lajes; *Pop* 150,865; *DDD* 0492) a convenient stopping place on BR-116 between Caxias do Sul and Curitiba. The route can also be done on poorer roads via São Joaquim (see above), which is perhaps the most interesting journey in the State, with scenery changing as the road climbs out of coastal forest (3 buses a day run on the main road in summer, 1 in winter, 5 hrs, via Alfredo Wagner, otherwise go via Blumenau). Bus station is 30 mins' walk SE of centre.

● **Accommodation B** *Grande*, R João de Castro 23, T/F 22-3522, good; **C** *Presidente*, Av Pres Vargas 101, T 22-1058. Others nr rodoviária. Voltage 220 AC.

NORTH OF FLORIANÓPOLIS

BEACHES: PORTO BELO TO CAMBORIÚ

On the coast N of Florianópolis there are many resorts. They include **Porto Belo** (*Pop* 9,700), a fishing village on the N side of a peninsula settled in 1750 by Azores islanders, with a calm beach and a number of hotels (eg *Baleia Branca*, T 69-4011, with camping) and restaurants (bus Florianópolis – Porto Belo with Praiana or Biguaçu, 8 daily, 3 on Sun). West of Port Belo is **Praia de Perequê** (Hotels: **E** *Tati*, T 69-4363, across from beach, and **E** *Blumenauense*, with bath and breakfast, on beach, T 69-4208). Around the peninsula are wilder beaches reached by rough roads: Bombas (2 hotels), Bombinhas (*Pousada do Arvoredo*, T 69-4355, up on a hill), Mariscal, and, on the southern side, Cantinho (**B** *Pousada Zimbros*, T 69-4225, cheaper off season, on beach, sumptuous breakfast, restaurant, highly rec, spear fishing guide).

Balneário Camboriú (*Pop* 25,715; 86 km) once beautiful, now has 4 blocks of concrete jungle behind the beach, which is very safe. From 15 Dec to end-Feb it is very crowded and expensive; the resort is popular with Argentines. Beto Carrero World is an imitation of Disney World. A few kilometres S, at Lojas Apple, there is a museum, zoo and aquarium; and Meia Praia, which is quieter and cleaner than Camboriú. Pinho beach, 15 km out of the city, is one of Brazil's few legal nudist beaches; 2 campsites and a small hotel. Between Itajaí and Camboriú is the beautiful, deserted (and rough) beach of Praia Brava. Note that from mid-July to mid-Aug it can be chilly.

● **Accommodation** From Mar-Nov it is easy to rent furnished apartments by the day or week (try Bom Pastor agency, Av Brasil 1861, T 0473-66-0769, reliable). There are a great many hotels, restaurants and campsites. **D** *Jaitur*, opp the rodoviária, with hot water, safe, rec.

● **Buses** From Florianópolis, Joinville and Blumenau. TTL buses Montevideo-São Paulo stop here at about 1800, a good place to break the journey (US$58 from Montevideo).

ITAJAÍ

100 km up the coast N of Florianópolis by the paved BR-101 is the most important port in Santa Catarina at the mouth of the Rio Itajaí (*Pop* 119,585; *CEP* 88300; *DDD* 0473). It is well served by vessels up to 5½ m draught, and is the centre of a district largely colonized by Germans and Italians. Airport. You can walk to Cabeçudas beach, which is quiet and small.

Resorts N of Itajaí include Piçarras, with sandy beaches interspersed with rocky headlands (ideal for fishing), and **Barra Velha** (**D** *Hotel Mirante*, good, cheap restaurant, and 2 dearer hotels).

● **Accommodation A1** *Marambaia Cabeçudas*, at Cabeçudas beach, best, 6 km out of town, T 44-0999; **C** *Grande*, R Felipe Schmidt 44, T 44-0968, good value. Recommended bar, *Trudys*, on riverfront at end of main street, a good place for changing cash.

● **Embassies & consulates** Finnish Consulate, R Almte Tamandaré 100, T 44-6511.

BLUMENAU

There is a 61 km paved road to **Blumenau** (*Pop* 211,175; *CEP* 89100; *DDD* 0473), 47 km up the Rio Itajaí. It is in a prosperous district settled mostly by Germans; the city is a notable textile centre. A clean,

The State of Paraná

THE Italians were first in Paraná, but apart from a few Germans most of the later settlers were of Slavonic origin – Poles, Russians, Ruthenians and Ukrainians.

Paraná is now the leading producer of wheat, rye, potatoes and black beans, but its population, 8,415,660, no longer expands as quickly as it did, partly because of the displacement of rural workers following the uprooting of coffee plants in the more frost-prone areas and the turning of the land over to cattle. The recent boom crop, soya, also employs fewer workers throughout the year than coffee.

CURITIBA

Capital of Paraná state (*Pop* 1.3 million; *Alt* 900m; *CEP* 80000; *DDD* 041), a modern city on the plateau of the Serra do Mar. It has won a prize as one of the 3 cleanest cities in Latin America.

Places of interest

A panoramic view can be had from the telecommunications tower, **Telepar**. The commercial centre is busy R 15 de Novembro (old name: R das Flores), which has a pedestrian area where there are Sat morning painting sessions for children. Another pedestrian area is behind the cathedral, near Largo da Ordem, with sacred art museum, flower clock and old buildings, very beautiful in the evening when the old lamps are lit – nightlife is concentrated here. Art market Sat morning in Praça Rui Barbosa, and on Sun morning in Praça Garibáldi (rec), beside the attractive Rosário church. The **Centro Cívico** is at the end of Av Dr Cândido de Abreu, 2 km from the city centre: a monumental group of five buildings dominated by the **Palácio Iguaçu**, headquarters of the state and municipal governments. In a patio behind it is a relief map to scale of Paraná. The **Bosque de João Paulo II** behind the Civic Centre contains the Polish immigrants' museum: both are worth a visit. In contrast to the Civic Centre is the old municipal government building in French Art Nouveau style, now housing the Museu Paranaense in Praça Generoso Marques. Nearby, on Praça Tiradentes, is the **Cathedral** (1894). The most popular public park is the **Passeio Público**, in the heart of the city (closed Mon); it has a little zoo, a network of canals with boats, and a small aquarium.

On the NE edge of the city is **Parque do Barigui**, take bus 450 'São Braz' from Praça Tiradentes. Near the shores of Lagoa Bacacheri on the northern edge of the city (R Nicarágua 2453) is an unexpected Egyptian temple – the Brazilian centre of the Rosicrucians – visits can be arranged – take Santa Cândida bus to Estação Boa Vista, then walk). 4 km E of the rodoferroviário, the **Jardim Botânico** is worth visiting. There are three modern **theatres**, the **Guaíra** for plays and revues (also has free events – get tickets early in the day), one for concerts and ballet, and the **Teatro Paiol** in the old arsenal.

Museums

Museu Paranaense, Praça Generoso Marques (open Tues-Fri 1000-1800, other days 1300-1800, closed first Mon of each month). **Museu David Carneiro**, on R Comendador Araújo 531, Sat, 1400-1600. **Museu Guido Viário**, R São Francisco 319, painter's house, Tues-Fri 1400-1830; **Museu de Arte Contemporânea**, R D Westphalen 16 (Tues-Fri 0900-1900, Sat-Sun 1400-1900). **Casa Andersen**, R Mateus Leme 336, house of painter, open Mon-Fri, 0900-1200, 1400-1800. **Arte**

Paranaense, R Dr Keller 289, new, in restored house, Mon-Fri 1000-1800. **Museu do Expedicionário** (WW2 Museum), Praça do Expedicionário, open daily 0800-1800; **Museo do Automóvel**, Av Cândido Hartmann 2300 (Sat 1400-1800, Sun 1000-1200, 1400-1800), all worth a visit.

Excursions

20 km W of Curitiba (at Km 119) on the road to Ponta Grossa is the **Museu Histórico do Mate**, an old water-driven mill where mate was prepared (free admission).

The beautiful **Ouro Fino** estate (34 km W) is open to the public every day except Mon, Dec-Mar, and every second Sun the rest of the year. The nearest bus stop is 16 km away at Campo Largo, so car is the best way to get there. Advance permission needed, from R Silva Jardim 167, Curitiba, T 232-7411, or phone Ouro Fino (041) 292-1913.

Local holidays

Ash Wednesday (half-day); Maundy Thursday (half-day); 8 Sept (Our Lady of Light).

Local information
● **Accommodation**

The majority of Curitiba telephone numbers have been altered during the installation of a new exchange, and many are likely to change again in 1997. We have updated numbers where possible.

L2 *Bourbon*, Cândido Lopes 102, T 322-4001, F 322-2282, most luxurious in centre, newly restored; **L2** *Grand Hotel Rayon*, R Visconde de Nacar 1424, T 800-8899, rec; **L3** *Slaviero Palace*, Sen Alencar Guimarães 50, T 322-7271, F 222-2393, central.

The following, in our categories **L3-A1**, are rec: *Caravelle Palace*, R Cruz Machado 282, T 322-5757, F 223-4443, first class; *Del Rey*, Ermelino de Leão 18, T/F 322-3242, good restaurants; *Lancaster*, R Voluntários da Pátria 91, T 223-8953, F 233-9214, tourist class; *Ouro Verde*, R Dr Murici 419, T 322-5454, F 225-6165, standard class.

In the **A2-A3** categories: *Curitiba Palace*, R 15 de Novembro 950, T 223-5282, F 225-2224, central, airy modern hotel with vast rooms, 24-hr restaurant, pool, great value, highly rec; *Tibagi*, Cândido Lopes 318, T 223-3141, F 234-4632, central, business hotel; *Tourist Universo*, Praça Gen Osório 63, T 322-0099, Sky TV, good restaurant, rec.

B *Climax*, R Dr Murici 411, T 224-3411, F 225-6165, good value, popular; **C** *Novo Roma*, R Barão do Rio Branco 805, T 224-2117, cheaper without bath, rec.

D *Cervantes*, R Alfredo Bufrem 66, T 222-9593, amazing breakfast, rec; **D** *Hotel Laron*, R Barão de Rio Branco, basic, rec; **D** *Regência*, R Alfredo Bufrem 40, T 223-4557, with breakfast, excellent.

F *Solar*, Jaime Reis 445, basic but adequate.

There are good hotels in the vicinity of the Rodoferroviária, but the cheaper ones are close to the wholesale market, which operates noisily throughout the night (there are many hotels so don't settle for a bad one), those listed are **A3-C** unless stated otherwise: *Condor*, Av 7 de Setembro 1866, T 262-0322, a/c, breakfast, rec; *Costa Brava*, R Francisco Torres 386, T 262-7172, restaurant, well rec; *Doral*, Mota 1144, T 222-1060, frigobar, good breakfast; *Filadélfia*, Gen Carneiro 1094, T 264-5244, good breakfast, 4 blocks from station through market; *Jaraguá*, Av Pres A Camargo, T 362-2022, F 264-7763, noisy, good breakfast, rec; *Maia*, Av Pres Afonso Camargo 360 block, quiet; on same street **D** *Cristo Rei*, basic; **C** *Inca*, R João Negrão 370, German spoken, good; same street *La Rocha*, No 528, basic; *Itamarati*, Tibagi 950, T 222-9063, fan, garage, good breakfast, showers can be dangerous; *Nova Lisboa*, Av 7 de Setembro 1948, with breakfast, bargain for cheaper rates without breakfast, rec.

Apart Hotel: **C** *King's*, Av Silva Jardim 264, T 223-5953, good, secure, highly rec.

Youth hostels: **F** *Casa dos Estudantes*, Parque Passeio Público, N side, with student card, 4 nights or more; **F** *Casa do Estudante Luterano Universitario*, R Pr Cavalcanti, T 223-8981, good. For information on youth hostels in Paraná state write to: Associação Paranaense de Albergues de Juventude, Av Padre Agostinho 645, Curitiba PR, CEP 80.410.

Camping: *Camping Clube do Brasil*, 16 km, BR-116, direction São Paulo.

● **Places to eat**

Ile de France (French), Praça 19 de Dezembro 538; *Matterhorn*, Mateus Leme 575, centre (Swiss); *A Sacristia*, R João Manuel 197, restaurant, pizzeria, bar, very good; *Oriente*, R Ebano Pereira 26 (1st floor), excellent, huge Arab lunch; *Salão Italiano*, R Padre G Mayer 1095, Cristo Rei, good Brazilian and Italian food; *Cantina do Eisbein*, Av dos Estados 863, Água Verde, owner Egon is friendly, duck specialities highly rec (US$15 for 2). Local and Italian food and local red wine in nearby Santa Felicidade (10 km out of town on road to Ponta Grossa), eg *Madalosso*, Av Manoel Ribas 5875, enormous

Italian self-service, allegedly the 2nd largest in world, cheap, rec, and **Dom Antônio**, same street No 6121, excellent.

Japanese: *Mikado*, R São Francisco 126, good, vegetarian, lunch only; *Nakaba*, R Nunes Machado 56, huge set meal under US$10.

Vegetarian: (most closed at night) *Vherde Jante*, R Pres Faria 481, very good, US$2.85 (open in evening); *Super Vegetariano*, R Pres Faria 121, Cruz Machado 217, R Dr Murici 315, lunch and dinner Mon-Fri, very good and cheap (buffet US$1.35). *Greenland*, Av Garibáldi 18

rec; *Panini*, R da Glória 307, rec for buffet lunches (US$4 with meat; US$2.50 vegetarian) in a charming house.

Kisco, 7 de Setembro nr Tibagi, good, huge *prato do dia*, US$4, friendly. Cheap food also nr old railway station and a good meal in the bus station. Close to the Rodoferroviária is the market, where there are a couple of *lanchonetes*. Hot sweet wine sold on the streets in winter helps keep out the cold.

Bars: at R Visconde de Nacar is the *Rua 24 Horas*, an indoor street full of bars and cafés,

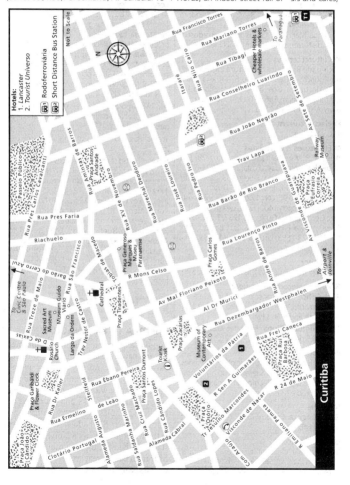

open all night. *Francis Drake*, Alameda Dr Muricy 1111, pub; *London Pub*, São Francisco 294, rec.

● **Banks & money changers**
Banco Noroeste, 15 de Novembro 168, advances on Eurocard/Master Card. ABN/AMRO, Dutch bank, Av Cândido Abreu 304, Centro Cívico, T 252-2233, changes TCs, also arranges money transfer from Netherlands, paid in *reais* (2-3 days). Triangle Turismo Travel, Praça Gen Osório 213, cash and TCs; Diplomata, R Presidente Faria 145 in the arcade. Transoceânica, R Mal Deodoro 532, English and German spoken; Sydney Turismo, R Marechal Deodoro 301. Credicard, cash with Mastercard, R Saldanha Marinho 1439, Bigorrillo; Bradesco, R XV de Novembro, Visacard machine.

● **Cultural centres**
Sociedade Brasileira de Cultura Inglesa (British Council), R Gen Carneiro 679 (Caixa Postal 505). Instituto Goethe, R Schaffenberg, nr Military Museum, Mon-Thur 1500-1900, Library, Mon-Tues till 2130.

● **Electric current**
110 v 60 cycles.

● **Embassies & consulates**
Austria, R Marechal Floriano Peixoto 228, Edif Banrisul, 17 andar, Caixa Postal 2473, T 224-6795; Danish, R Prof Francisco Ribeiro 683, Caixa Postal 321, T 843 2211, F 843 1443; Dutch, R Mal Floriano Peixoto 96, conj 172, T 222-0097, consul Tony Bruinjé, open 1400-1700, except emergencies; German, Av J Gualberto 1237, T 252-4244; Swiss, Av Mal F Peixoto 228, Edif Banrisul, conj 1104/5T 223-7553; Uruguayan, R Vol da Pátria 475, 18th floor.

● **Laundry**
R C Laurindo 63, next to theatre, US$3 for 5 kg.

● **Post & telecommunications**
Post Office: main post office is at Marechal Deodoro 298; post offices also at R 15 de Novembro and R Pres Faria.

Telecommunications: Embratel, Galeria Minerva, R 15 de Novembro. UPS, T 262-6180.

● **Shopping**
Curitiba is a good place to buy clothes and shoes. *H Stern* jewellers at Mueller Shopping Centre. Bookshop: *O Livro Técnico*, Shopping Itália, R João Negrão e Mal Deodoro.

● **Sports**
Golf: Graciosa Country Club, Av Munhoz da Rocha 1146: 9 holes.

● **Tourist offices**
Guía Turística de Curitiba e Paraná, annual, US$4, on sale at all kiosks, has been rec. Paranatur has booths at Rodoferroviária and at

airport, helpful, English spoken, but no maps. Free maps from R Ebano Pereira 187, 5th floor. Free weekly leaflet, *Bom Programa*, available shops, cinemas, paper stands etc.

● **Useful addresses**
Visa extensions: Federal police, Dr Muricy 814, 1000-1600.

● **Tour companies & travel agents**
BMP Turismo Passagens e Servicos Ltd, R Brigadeiro Franco, 1845, T 224 7560.

● **Transport**
Local The city has a very efficient bus system (US$0.60); all bus stops have maps. Express buses on city routes are orange: eg from centre (Praça Rui Barbosa) take Leste bus marked 'Villa Oficinas' or 'Centenário' for Rodoferroviária (combined bus and railway station). A tourist bus, US$3 (rec), stops at the Botanic Garden, the Opera, the University and other sites; 4 stops permitted.

Rodoferroviária at end of Av 7 de Setembro (bus to centre US$0.15).

Air Two airports: Afonso Peña (21 km away) for international and national flights; Bacacheri for national flights.

Trains Passenger trains to Paranaguá, see below.

Buses Short-distance bus services (up to 40 km) begin at old bus station at R João Negrão 340. Frequent buses to São Paulo (6 hrs, US$8; *leito* 17) and Rio de Janeiro (12 hrs, US$42 *executivo*). To Foz do Iguaçu, 10 a day, 10 hrs, US$30; Porto Alegre, 10 hrs; Florianópolis, 4½ hrs; good service to most destinations in Brazil. Pluma bus to Buenos Aires US$128 and to Asunción US$32. TTL runs to Montevideo, 26 hrs, US$66, 0340 departure (*semi-cama*). If travelling by car to Porto Alegre or Montevideo, the inland road (BR-116) is preferable to the coastal highway (BR-101).

LONGER EXCURSIONS

CURITIBA TO PARANAGUÁ

Popular expeditions during the summer are by paved road or rail (4½ hrs) to Paranaguá. The railway journey is the most spectacular in Brazil. There are numerous tunnels with sudden views of deep gorges and high peaks and waterfalls as the train rumbles over dizzy bridges and viaducts. Near Banhado station (Km 66) is the waterfall of Véu da Noiva; from the station at Km 59, the mountain range of **Marumbi** can be reached: see below.

● **Transport** This railway is under threat of

closure, T 322-9585 for details. A modern a/c railcar (the Litorina, also called the *automotriz*) leaves Curitiba at 0900 Tues, Thur and at weekends during the summer and in July, arriving in Paranaguá at 1130, returning at 1500 (US$8 each way, reserved seats bookable 2 days in advance; recorded commentary in Portuguese, French, Spanish and English) and stops at the viewpoint at the Santuário da NS do Cadeado and at Morretes (only a few minutes). Out of season, the Litorina only runs at weekends. There is also a 'normal' service at 0730 (Tues Thur and weekends in high season, Sun only in low season,) arriving at 1030 and returning to Curitiba at 1600 (US$5 one way); sandwiches, chocolate and drinks for sale on board. Avoid the front coach. Sit on the left-hand side on journey from Curitiba. Remember that in winter part of the ordinary train's journey is in the dark (also, on cloudy days there's little to see on the higher parts). The train is usually crowded on Sat and Sun. Many travellers recommend returning by bus (1½ hrs, buy ticket immediately on arrival, US$5.20), if you do not want to stay 4½ hrs. A tour bus meets the train and offers a tour of town and return to Curitiba for US$6.

ANTONINA AND MORRETES

You can also visit **Antonina** (a port, not on main route, *Pop* 17,055) and **Morretes** (on main route, *Pop* 13,130), two sleepy colonial towns which can be reached by bus on the old Graciosa road, which is almost as scenic as the railway. 14 km N of Morretes is the beautiful village of **São João de Graciosa**, 2 km beyond which is a flower reserve. The Graciosa road traverses the **Marumbi** range for 12 km, with 6 rest stops with fire grills, shelters and camping. Marumbi is very beautiful; you can also hike the original trail which follows the road and passes the rest-stops. Take food, water and plenty of insect repellent.

● **Accommodation At Morretes:** **C** *Nhundiaquara*, in town centre, well located but hot and cramped, good restaurant; good restaurants in town (try *barreado*, beef cooked for 24 hrs, especially good in the two restaurants on the river bank, highly rec) and a river beach.

● **Transport** Buses from Paranaguá to Morretes at 1830, US$1.25, to Antonina, stopping en route at Morretes, 6 a day (US$2). 12 buses daily Morretes-Curitiba US$2; 20 buses a day Curitiba-Antonina.

PARANAGUÁ

(*Pop* 107,585; *CEP* 83200; *DDD* 041) Chief port of the state of Paraná and one of the main coffee-exporting ports, **Paranaguá** was founded in 1585, 268 km S of Santos. It is on a lagoon 29 km from the open sea and is approached via the Baia de Paranaguá, dotted with picturesque islands. Paranaguá is a free port for Paraguay.

Places of interest

The **fort of Nossa Senhora dos Prazeres** was built in 1767 on a nearby island; 1-hr's boat trip. The former Colégio dos Jesuitas, a fine baroque building, has been converted into a **Museu de Arqueológia e Artes Populares** (Tues-Sun 1200-1700; entrance US$1). Other attractions are a 17th century fountain, the church of **São Benedito**, and the shrine of **Nossa Senhora do Rocio**, 2 km from town. There are restaurants and craft shops near the waterfront. The part of town between the waterfront, railway station and new bus station has been declared a historic area.

Excursions

Cruises on Paranaguá Bay by launch, daily from Cais do Mercado.

Matinhos (*Pop* 11,315) is invaded by surfers in Oct for the Paraná surf competition; several cheap hotels, inc *Bolamar* (**E**, basic, cheapest) and *Beira Mar*. Four camp sites in the vicinity. Bus from Paranaguá at 1000, 1400 and 1615, US$1. 8 km S is Caiobá, at the mouth of a bay the other side of which is **Guaratuba** (*Pop* 17,990 less built up than Caiobá). The ferry between the two towns is frequent, beautiful crossing, free for pedestrians, US$1.50 for cars. Both towns have hotels; also camping at Guaratuba, where restaurant *Sol Nascente*, R Vicente Machado 967, is superb.

Local information
● **Accommodation**

A3 *Portofino*, Av Atlântica s/n, T/F 458-1488, Balneário Portofino, very nice.

C *Auana*, R Correia de Freitas 110, T 422-6531, good value, rec.

D *Karibe*, F Simas 86, T 422-1177, good value; **D** *Litoral*, R Correia de Freitas 66, without breakfast, comfortable.

Camping: *Arco Iris* at Praia de Leste, on the beach, 29 km S of Paranaguá, 30 mins.

● **Places to eat**

Bobby's, Faria Sobrinho 750, highly rec, esp for seafood. *Danúbio Azul*, 15 de Novembro 91, good, not cheap, view of river; *Aquarius*, Av Gabriel de Lara 40, good but not cheap seafood; there are cheap restaurants in the old market building, and plenty of cheap ones nr the markets on the waterfront; the *Yacht Club*, beyond *Danúbio Azul* is impressive and has a good bar.

● **Banks & money changers**

Banco do Brasil, Largo C Alcindino 27; **Câmbio**, R Faria Sobrinho, for cash.

● **Tourist offices**

Tourist information kiosk outside railway station.

● **Transport**

All buses operated by Graciosa. To **Curitiba**, US$5.20, many, 1½ hrs (only the 0745 in either direction and the 1545 to Curitiba take the old Graciosa road); direct to **Rio** at 1915, 15 hrs, US$38.50.

ILHA DO MEL

On the island, which is an ecological reserve (no cars permitted), well-developed for tourism, there are two beach villages, 5 km apart. From Praia dos Encantados to Nova Brasília there are boats (US$10, or US$2 pp if more than 5), or you can walk on a track (1½-2 hrs) or follow the coast, walking in the sea. From Nova Brasília, a 20-min walk leads to El Farol for good views. Praia dos Encantados is more suitable for swimming than Brasília. The beaches, caves, bays and hill walks are beautiful. 4 hrs' walk from the villages is an old Portuguese fort. In summer and at holiday times the island is very crowded with an active nightlife and *Forró* dancing (eg *Forró Zorro*, Praia dos Encantados, Thur-Sun, lively, popular); at other times it is very quiet.

● **Accommodation** Camping is possible on the more deserted beaches (good for surfing). At Praia dos Encantados, one can camp or rent a fisherman's house – ask for *Valentim's Bar*, or for Luchiano; behind the bar is *Cabanas Dona Maria*, shared showers, cold water; food available if you ask in advance. At Praia Nova Brasília, *Pousada Portal*, T 978-3534, with breakfast, good. *Pousadinha*, on road to Praia do Farol, excellent breakfast, delightful rooms, good beds, fan, bath, mosquito nets, staff speak various languages; *Pousada Praia do Farol* or

Estalagem Ancoradouro, both with breakfast; *Estalagem Pirata*, Nova Brasília, wonderful house on beach, music, easy atmosphere, run by Roberto and Darlene, all accommodation is **D-E**. If camping, watch out for the tide, watch possessions and beware of the *bicho de pé* which burrows into feet (remove with a needle and alcohol) and of the *borrachudos* (discourage with Autan repellent).

● **Places to eat** *Lanchonete Paraíso*, nice meeting place, good food and music, more expensive restaurant next door to *Forró Zorro*, Restaurant *Toca do Abutre*, 1 km from Nova Brasília, Praia do Farol, and bar *Barbeira*.

● **Electricity** On the island 1000-0200.

● **Transport** Ferries to Ilha do Mel, take bus to Pontal do Sul (many daily, direct from/to Curitiba, 1 hr, US$2), then wait for a bus to the ferry, US$2; if one does not leave soon, take a taxi or walk; turn left out of the bus station and go 25m to main road, turn right for 1½ km and bear left along a sandy road for 2 km to fishermen's houses from where a ferry runs (US$3). Alternatively, go the small harbour in Paranaguá and ask for a boat to Ilha do Mel, 2-3 hrs, US$5 one way (no shade). Make sure the ferry goes to your chosen destination (Nova Brasília or Encantados are the developed areas; ferries to the S go to an area with only a camping site, 2-3 hrs' walk to Nova Brasília at low tide only). Ferries return from Ilha do Mel to Pontal do Sul at 0745, 1000, 1300, 1645.

VILA VELHA

On the road to Ponta Grossa is **Vila Velha**, now a national park, 97 km from Curitiba: the sandstone rocks have been weathered into most fantastic shapes. The Lagoa Dourada, surrounded by forests, is close by. Nearby are the Furnas, three water holes, the deepest of which has a lift (US$1 – not always working) which descends almost to water level (the same level as Lagoa Dourada); entrance US$0.20. The park office is 300m from the highway and the park a further 1½ km (entrance – also to Furnas, keep the ticket – US$2 – opens at 0800).

● **Accommodation** *Camping Clube do Brasil* site nr Vila Velha, 85 km from Curitiba.

● **Transport** Take a bus from Curitiba to the Parque Nacional, not to the town 20 km away. Princesa dos Campos bus from Curitiba at 0730 and 0930, 1½ hrs, US$4.75 (return buses pass park entrance at 1500 and 1700), but often full; it may be advisable to go to Ponta Grossa and return to Curitiba from there).

Bus from Vila Velha at 1310, 1610 and 1830,

US$1, 4½ km to turn-off to Furnas (another 15 mins' walk) and Lagoa Dourada (it's not worth walking from Vila Velha to Furnas because it's mostly uphill along the main road). Allow all day if visiting all 3 sites (unless you hitch, or can time the buses well, it's a lot of walking).

PONTA GROSSA

About 117 km from Curitiba the road inland reaches **Ponta Grossa** (*Pop* 233,515; *CEP* 84100; *DDD* 0422, 895m). It now calls itself the 'World Capital of Soya'. Roads run N through Apucarana (hotels, campsites) and Londrina to São Paulo, and S to Rio Grande do Sul and the Uruguayan border.

● **Accommodation A2** *Vila Velha Palace*, R Balduino Taques 123, T 25-2200, F 24-4348; **C** *Planalto Palace*, R 7 de Setembro 652, T 25-2122, plain and clean; **C** *Scha Fransky*, R Francisco Ribas 104, T 24-2511, very good breakfast; almost next door, same street No 162, is **D** *Central*, with fan and basin; **D** *Gravina*, R Col Bittencourt 92, T 24-0503, with bath; **E** *Esplanada*, in bus station (quiet, however), with bath and breakfast, safe; **F** *Luz*, basic, nr railway station; **F** *Casimiri*, next door, often full.

● **Places to eat** *Casa Verde*, nr the *Central*, lunch only, rec; there are cheap restaurants nr the railway station.

● **Transport** Bus Princesa dos Campos to **Curitiba**, 6 a day, 2 hrs, US$7; same company to **Iguaçu**, 4 daily, 11 hrs, US$14.50. To **Vila Velha** at 0700 and 0900 (return bus at 1800).

If driving from Curitiba to Foz do Iguaçu (or vice versa), **Guarapuava** makes a useful stopover town (258 km from Curitiba, 389 km from Foz); **C** *Hotel América*, excellent value, and others. A number of bus services from Paraná state to Porto Alegre (Aguia Branca, Unesul) and to Campo Grande, Cuiabá and Porto Velho (Eucatur) commence at **Cascavel** (*Pop* 218,410) further S on the Curitiba-Iguaçu road (hotels: **B** *Grand Prix*, Av Brasil 5202, safe, good breakfast, parking; **D** *Príncipe*, Av Brasil, good; and others).

NORTHWEST PARANÁ

In Alto Paraná in the extreme NW of the State, connections have traditionally been with São Paulo rather than with Curitiba. In 1930 four Japanese and two Germans arrived in **Londrina** (*Pop* 388,330), developed by a British company. Today it is a city with skyscrapers, modern steel and glass cathedral, and wide streets; small museum at Sergipe e Rio de Janeiro.

Maringá (*Pop* 239,930, about a third Japanese) is 80 km W of Londrina, founded in 1947. There is a small conical cathedral; Parque Ingá is shady, with a Japanese garden.

● **Accommodation Londrina**: **C** *Coroados*, Sen Souza Naves 814, T 23-7690, standard; **C** *Triúnfo*, R Prof João Cândido 39, T 23-5054, laundry, restaurant; **E** *Cravinho*, R Minas Gerais 88, clean, friendly. **Youth hostel**: R Gomes Carneiro 315, centro Esportivo Moringão. **Maringá**: **D** *Hotel Fatima*, Av Brasil 224 2321, with breakfast, clean, hot shower, TV.

● **Transport** Londrina and Maringá are good points for connections between the S (Porto Alegre), Foz do Iguaçu and Mato Grosso do Sul (Campo Grande). Bus Londrina-Porto Alegre takes 22 hrs; to Campo Grande 11 hrs, via Presidente Prudente (see page 462). Londrina-Ponta Grossa, US$8.50, 5½ hrs.

THE PARANÁ RIVER

IGUAÇU FALLS

In the extreme SW of the State, on the Argentine frontier, are the **Iguaçu Falls**, 32 km from the Falls is the city of Foz do Iguaçu.

For a detailed description of the Falls as a whole, and the Argentine side in particular, together with maps and an account of road links between the Argentine and Brazilian sides and Paraguay, **see the Argentine chapter**.

If one has the time, first visit the Brazilian side to get some idea of the size and magnificence of the whole, and take introductory photographs in the morning, and then cross to the Argentine side to see the details. This can all be done in a day, starting at about 0700, but the brisk pace needed for a rapid tour is exhausting for the non-athletic in the heat. Sunset from the Brazilian side is a worthwhile experience.

A 1½ km paved walk runs part of the way down the cliff near the rim of the Falls, giving a stupendous view of the whole Argentine side (the greater part) of the falls. It ends up almost under the powerful Floriano Falls; a new catwalk leads right to the edge of one of the lower waterfalls, giving impressive views of the 'Devil's Throat' from below. Waterproof clothing can be hired although it is not absolutely necessary. An elevator (from 0800) hoists the visitor to the top of the Floriano Falls (US$0.50) and to a path leading to Porto Canoa, if there is a queue it is easy and quick to walk up. A safari, Macuco, near the falls, costs US$30 for a guided tour (AMEX accepted), but it is better on the Argentine side. Helicopter – US$50/head – min 2 people, lasts 7 mins, departing from *Hotel das Cataratas*. (There is pressure for the helicopter rides to stop: the noise is seriously disturbing the wildlife – altitude has been increased, making the flight less attractive.) There is a small museum 10 km from the Falls (1 km from park entrance is a side road to the museum, look for sign 'Centro de Visitantes' near the Polícia Militar post) and opposite it are some steps that lead down the steep slope to the river bank. Beautiful walk. It can be misty early in the morning at the Falls. Entry to the Brazilian side of the Falls is US$5, payable in *reais* only at the National Park entrance. If possible, visit on a weekday when the walks are less crowded.

● **Access** From Foz do Iguaçu, Dois Irmãos buses (from local bus station – *Terminal Urbana* – on Av Juscelino Kubitschek, opp Infantry Barracks) marked 'Cataratas' run to the falls every hour at weekends, holidays and in high season, Mon-Fri, past airport and *Hotel das Cataratas*: schedule is usually 0800 to 1800, journey takes 40 mins; Transbalan buses marked 'Parque Nacional', every 30 mins, stop at the park entrance, take a 'Cataratas' bus the rest of the way (this works out more expensive). Buses of either route can also be picked up at any of the stops on Av Juscelino Kubitschek. Buses return 0700-1800, US$1 one way, payable in *reais* only. The driver waits at the Park entrance while passengers purchase entry tickets. (The taxi fare is US$6, plus US$2.50 for each hour of waiting.) The tours of the Falls organized by the various hotels have been recommended in preference to taxi rides. If visiting Brazilian side from Puerto Iguazú by bus, ask driver to let you off shortly after the border at the roundabout for road to the falls (BR 469), where you can get another bus.

To the Argentine side: buses between Foz do Iguaçu and Puerto Iguazú (Argentina) run half-hourly from the Terminal Urbana, crossing the frontier bridge; 20 mins' journey, no stops for border formalities (Pluma and Tres Fronteiras companies, tickets interchangeable between the two, US$2). There are many advantages in staying in Foz and commuting to the Argentine side (better and cheaper hotels and restaurants, for example). If you decide to stay in Brazil, do not rely on spending *reais* in Argentina; they are accepted, but at very poor rates. It is better to change dollars into pesos for the day, which is easily done at Puerto Iguazú bus station or nearby before taking the bus to the Falls. A poorer rate for pesos is given in Brazil. **NB** Be sure you know when the last bus departs from Puerto Iguazú for Foz (usually 1900) and remember that in summer Argentina is an hour earlier than Brazil. Combined tickets to Puerto Iguazú and the Falls cost more than paying separately; when returning from Puerto Iguazú, ask to be let off in Foz. Taxi Foz-Argentina US$33, US$45 to *Hotel Internacional Iguazú*. Crossing the frontiers in a private vehicle, if only intending to visit the National Park, presents no problems.

● **Frontier crossings** Be sure to get a stamp on your passport if intending to stay in Brazil, but if going nowhere other than Iguaçu there is no need for citizens of countries requiring visas to have one. There is an entry tax on the Brazilian side for car passengers only, not for bus passengers. If driving into Brazil insist on visiting customs. You must get entry papers for your car here or you'll have serious problems later.

There are Brazilian immigration offices on the Brazilian sides of the bridges into Paraguay and Argentina; if you are just visiting Ciudad del Este or Puerto Iguazú and the Argentine side of the Falls and returning to Brazil the same day, you must take your passport; no need to have it stamped. If you do have your passport stamped when leaving Brazil, you must get a new stamp when re-entering. There are Brazilian customs patrols looking for undeclared goods on the roads past the frontier. Note that if entering or leaving a country and you have to visit customs and immigration, buses won't wait; take a taxi instead.

See under **Transport** below for crossing to Paraguay.

FOZ DO IGUAÇU

(*Pop* 188,190; *CEP* 85890; *DDD* 045) A rapidly developing and improving town, with a wide range of accommodation and good communications by air and road with the main cities of southern Brazil, and with Asunción, Paraguay.

Excursions

From Foz, you can make an excursion to the 12,600-megawatt **Itaipu** dam, the largest single power station in the world, which Brazil and Paraguay have built nearby. The dam is 8 km long. The power house 1½ km. Paraguay does not use all its quota of power so this is sold to Brazil, which powers all of Southern Brazil and much of Rio, São Paulo and Minas Gerais from Itaipu. The Paraguayan side may also be visited from Ciudad del Este. Santa Helena on Lake Itaipu, has an artificial beach and relaxing leisure park, US$2.50.

• **Tours of Itaipu** Bus marked Canteira da Obra from Terminal Urbana (stand 50 Batalhão) goes every 40 mins to the Public Relations office at the main entrance (US$0.35), Conjunto C-via Norte or via Sul bus goes more frequently to within 250m. Visits are free, but in groups only, a film in Portuguese or English is shown (half of which is about protecting animals and the environment) and then the dam is visited (one stop for taking photos); ask in reception if you may see turbines. Several tours daily between 0800 and 1600 (closed between 1100 and 1400). 300m before Public Relations is the Eco Museum, about the Itaipú dam, free visit with guide, rec (closed Sun). The 'executive' bus and agency tours are an unnecessary expense. If it's sunny, go in the morning as the sun is behind the dam in the afternoon and you will get poor photographs.

Good reports on the **Parque das Aves** bird park, entrance US$8, at Rodovia das Cataratas Km 10.5, just before the falls. To book a guided tour, T 523-1007. Several other excursions, by bus or boat, into the surrounding countryside, enjoyable, book with a reputable company. **Fishing** for dourado and surubi with Simon Williams at Cataratas Iate Club, Av Gen Meira, Km 5, T 523-2073.

Local information
● Accommodation
On a height directly overlooking the Falls, 32 km from Foz, is the **L1** Hotel das Cataratas, T 523-2266, F 574-1688 (but 40% discount for holders of the Brazil Air Pass) highly rec, an attractive colonial-style building with nice gardens and a swimming pool. Much wildlife can be seen in the grounds at night and early am. Check exchange rate if paying in dollars. Non-residents can have US$27.50 meal here (midday and evening buffets, or else wait 45 mins for à-la-carte dishes), dinner (churrasco) with show.

Many out-of-town hotels on the Falls road state their address as kilometres from Foz. On road to Falls (Rodovia das Cataratas) are **L2** Bourbon, all facilities, excellent buffet dinner, open to non-residents (US$12), Km 2.5, T 523-1313, F 574-1110; **L3** Colonial (Km 16.5), T 574-1777, F 76-1960, nr airport, swimming pool, fine location; **A1** Carimã (Km 16), T 523-1818, F 574-3531, 3-star, very good value, a/c, pool, restaurant, bars, rec; **A3** Panorama (Km 12), good value, pool, T 23-1200, F 574-1490; many others.

In 1994, many street numbers were changed. Both old numbers (lower) and the new higher ones were still in use. We have altered numbers where known: bear changes in mind when looking for your hotel. If you know which hotel you wish to stay in (there are over 180), note that touts may say it no longer exists, or quote room rates below what is actually charged. There is a scam in which children will escort you to a cheap hotel, receiving commission for doing so. Your luggage is then stolen from the hotel. In high season (eg Christmas-New Year), you will not find a room under US$15.

L2 Internacional, Almte Baroso 345, T 523-1414, F 574-5201, good.

A1 Continental Inn, Av Paraná 485, T/F 574-4122, good restaurant; **A1** Salvatti, R Rio Branco 651, T 523-1121, F 574-3674, all a/c (with restaurant and cinema); **A2** Rafahin, Mal Deodoro 984, T 523-1213, F 523-2007, good restaurant, pool, well spoken of; **A2** Suiça, Av Felipe Wandscheer 3580, Swiss manager, helpful, pool; **A3** Foz Presidente, R Marechal Floriano 1851, T 523-2318, F 574-5155, shower, a/c, restaurant, swimming pool, trips arranged to Falls, inc breakfast, convenient for buses, rec.

On Av Brasil: **A1** Bogari Palace, No 106, T 523-2243, F 523-1125, excellent restaurant, swimming pool; **A3** Foz do Iguaçu, No 97, T 574-4455, F 574-1775, good, expensive laundry, will look after luggage; **B** City, No 938, T 574-2074, fan, hot water; **C** O Astro, No 660, T 72-3584, OK, a/c; **C** Dani Palace, No 509, comfortable, good buffet breakfast; **D** Ortega, No 1140, T 574-1288, good breakfast.

In R Rebouças: **C** Minas, No 641, T 574-5208, basic, hot water, safe, no breakfast; **D** German Pension, No 1091, T 574-5603, rec; **D** Pietá, No 84, T 574-5581, pool, good breakfast, car and guide, rec; **D** Piratini, No 101, hot showers, shabby but rec; **E** Trento, No 665, T 574-5111, a/c, noisy but rec; **E** Pousada Verde Vale, No 335, T 574-2925, youth hostel style, cramped but popular, buses to Falls stop outside.

B Estoril, Av República Argentina 694, T 523-1233, F 523-2311, breakfast, pool, TV, rec.

C *Bastos*, Castelo Branco 931, T 574-5839, a/c, secure, helpful, rec; **C** *Hotel Tarobá*, R Tarobá 1048, T 574-3670 or 574-3890, helpful, good breakfast, rec; **C** *Luz*, Almte Barroso, T 573-1891, nr Rodoviária, rec; **C** *Patt's Hotel*, R Marechal Floriano Peixoto, 1368, T 574-2507, good breakfast, a/c, TV, rec; **C** *Pousada da Laura*, R Naipi 671, T/F 572-3374, secure, Spanish, English, Italian and French spoken, excellent; **C** *San Remo*, Kubitschek e Xavier da Silva 467, T 572-2956, good breakfast, a/c, rec.

D *Hospedaria Britos*, Santos Dumont e Xavier da Silva, shared shower, large breakfast, good value; **D** *Hospedaria Janice*, Santos Dumont 1222, very helpful; **D** *Piratini*, R Rui Barbosa 237, T 523-3370, hot showers, good breakfast, safe, rec; **D** *Pousada Evelina Navarrete*, R Irlan Kalicheski 171, Vila Yolanda, T/F 574-3817, lots of tourist information, English, French and Spanish spoken, helpful, good breakfast and location, nr Av Cataratas on way to the Falls, warmly rec; **D** *Pousada Pôr do Sol*, R Santos Durmont 41, T 574-3122, family-run, helpful, rec.

E *Holiday*, Xavier da Silva 1407, T 574-5948,

good, breakfast; **E** *Maria Schneider*, Av Jorge Schimmelpfeng 483, T 574-2305, German spoken; **E** *Senhor do Bonfim*, Almte Barroso 6, breakfast, fans, hot water, family atmosphere, not very secure, convenient for the Cataratas bus which departs from the TTU square 4 blocks away. Many hotels have a minibus service to the airport for guests for a small fee and also offer excursions to Falls. **E** *Paudimar*, Remanço Grande, nr airport, T 574-5503, pool, soccer pitch, quiet, breakfast, out of town but will arrange pick up from bus terminal, highly rec.

Camping: (pretty cold and humid in winter). By National Park entrance *Camping Clube do Brasil*, 17 km from Foz, US$10 pp a night (half with International Camping Card), swimming pool, clean; park vehicle or put tent away from trees in winter in case of heavy rain storms, no restaurants, food there not very good, closes at 2300. *Camping Ecológico*, Fazenda São João Batista (W Keller), T 574-1794, 8 km from Foz, turn left just before park entrance, basic, nice scenery, dormitory and space for tents. Camping not permitted by hotel and Falls. Sleeping in car inside the park also prohibited.

Hotels:
1. *Bogari*
2. *Continental Inn*
3. *Foz do Iguaçu*
4. *Internacional*
5. *Lanville*
6. *Pousada Verde Vale*
7. *Salvatti*

Terminal Urbana
Rodoviária (off map)

Foz do Iguaçu

● **Places to eat**

Many open till midnight, most accept a variety of currencies. *Rafain*, Av das Cataratas, Km 6.5, with Paraguayan harp trio, good *alcatra* (meat), excellent buffet, but expensive; *Rafain Center*, Rebouças 600 block, next to *Minas Hotel*, a collection of food stalls for different tastes and budgets, with live music and dancing 2000 to 0200, lively, rec; *Calamares*, No 686, all you can eat buffet US$5, closes 2300, rec; *Santos De-lavy*, Av J Kubitschek 393, Argentine owner, cheap and friendly; *Ali Baba*, No 998, very good Arabic food; *Churrascaria Bufalo Branco*, R Rebouças 530, all you can eat for US$17, good salad bar; *Churrascaria Cabeça de Boi*, Av Brasil 1325, large, live music, buffet US$9, also for coffee and pastries; *Cantina*, Av Rodrigues 720, buffet, all you can eat, rec; *Clarks*, No 896, excellent food, reasonable; *El Club Caxos*, No 249, cheap; *Scala*, Santos Dumont e Xavier da Silva, good atmosphere and value.

● **Banks & money changers**

Rates are bad in Foz and it is very difficult to exchange on Sun, but quite possible in Paraguay where US dollars can be obtained on credit cards. There are plenty of banks and travel agents on Av Brasil: **Banco do Brasil**, good rates for TCs (note that you cannot obtain US dollars in Brazil); **Bradesco**, No 1192, cash advances on Visa.

● **Electric current**

110 volts a/c.

● **Embassies & consulates**

Argentina, ER Bianchi 26, T 74-2877/2969, open 0800-1300; **Paraguay**, Bartolomeu de Gusmão 480.

● **Entertainment**

Discotheque Whiskadão with three different dance halls, Alm Barroso 763, reasonable, lively at weekends. There is a cinema on Barão do Rio Branco, US$2.50, films over $1\frac{1}{2}$ hrs are cut.

● **Hospitals & medical services**

There is a free 24-hr clinic on Av Paraná, opp Lions Club. Few buses: take taxi or walk (about 25 mins). Ask for Sra Calça: friendly and helpful. Her son speaks English.

● **Post & telecommunications**

Post Office: Praça Getúlio Vargas 72, next to Tourist Office.

International phone: calls from the office on Rui Barbosa.

● **Security**

At bus terminals watch out for pickpockets who pose, with a coat over their arm, as taxi drivers. Taxis are only good value for short distances when you are carrying all your luggage.

● **Tour companies & travel agents**

Beware of overcharging for tours by touts at the rodoviária. There are many travel agents on Av Brasil. *Dicks Tours* is said to change up to US$100/day, 10% charge, and has been rec for its all-day tour to the Brazilian side of the Falls, to Paraguay (Ciudad del Este) and to the Itaipú dam. Recommended guides, *Wilson Engel*, T 574-1367, friendly, flexible. Ruth Campo Silva, *STTC Turismo Ltda*, Hotel Bourbon, Rodovia das Cataratas, T 574-3557; *Chiderly Batismo Pequeno*, R Almte Barroso 505, Foz, T 574-3367.

● **Tourist offices**

Praça Getúlio Vargas 56; **Paranatur**, very help-ful, Almte Barroso 1300, T 574-2196; **Turifon**, Jorge Sanways 576, T 523-5222. Kiosk on Av Brasil, by Ponte de Amizade (helpful), will book hotels. Airport tourist information is also good, open for all arriving flights, gives map and bus information. Helpful office, free map, at ro-doviária, English spoken. A newspaper, *Triplice Fronteira*, carries street plans and other tourist information. *Kunda Livraria Universitária*, R Almte Barroso, T 523-4606, for guides and maps of the area, books on the local wildlife, novels etc in several languages inc French and English. There is a help line number, 1516.

● **Transport**

Air The Iguaçu international airport has daily flights from Río, São Paulo, Curitiba and other Brazilian cities. Taxis to town from the Brazilian airport 18 km from Foz charge a fixed rate of US$20, rates posted on the walls at airport; Dois Irmãos town bus for US$0.50, first at 0530, does not permit large amounts of luggage (but back-packs OK). Varig office in Foz: Av Brasil 821, T 523-2111; staff speak foreign languages; Vasp, T 574-2999. Money exchange is on the 1st floor and a small commission is charged.

Buses Rodoviária, Av Costa e Silva, 4 km from centre on road to Curitiba; bus to centre, Anel Viario, US$0.35. Book departures as soon as pos-sible. Foz is reached by buses from **Curitiba** (Su-lamericana, 9-11 hrs, paved road, US$30), from Guaíra via Cascavel only (5 hrs, US$9.50), and from **São Paulo** (15 hrs, about US$39 with Pluma, *executivo* US$51). To **Campo Grande**, 15 hrs by Maringá company (3 hrs to Cascavel, and 12 from there to Campo Grande) 17 hrs by Medianeira company direct, US$32.50, 1700, rec; to **Brasília**, 26 hrs, 1800, US$50; to **Rio** 22 hrs, several daily, US$37 (*leito* 74). **Buenos Aires**, Pluma daily 1630, 18 hrs, US$45. It is cheaper to go to **Posadas**, Argentina, via Paraguay.

Travel To/From Paraguay Paved road from Asunción: Nuestra Señora, Rysa, Pluma and Unesul ply the route, US$15. From Ciudad del

Este, take a bus to the Ponte de Amizade (Friendship Bridge, Brazilian post open until 0200, pay US$2 in dollars, guaraníes or reais at the Paraguayan end), pass Brazilian Customs and take Ponte-Cidade bus to Terminal Urbana where buses go to the Falls or to Argentina. Bus Foz-Ciudad del Este, US$0.60. Do use the buses to cross no-man's-land.

GUAÍRA

In the far NW of the state, also on the Rio Paraná, were the tremendous waterfalls known in Brazil as Sete Quedas (the Seven Falls), and in Spanish Latin America as the Salto de Guaíra; they were drowned by the filling of the lake behind the Itaipu dam in 1982. **Guaíra** (*Pop* 30,965, about 130 km N of Iguaçu), is 4 km from the lake (US$2.50 one way, return taxi up to US$12, or walk). Entrance to park US$0.35; small museum 3 blocks from Guaíra rodoviária, 0800-1100 and 1400-1700.

A luxury passenger vessel, the *Epitácio Pessoa*, sails twice monthly (weekly during holiday periods) from Guaíra to **Presidente Epitácio** (*Pop* 34,740) in São Paulo state, on Sat at 1100, arrives at Pres Epitácio at 2200 Sun. It returns Wed 1700, arriving in Guaíra at 1900 Thur. Bookings should be made in advance with: **Comércio e Navegação Alto Paraná Ltda**, Praça da República 177, Loja 15, São Paulo, T 259-8255, Tx 011-32400. Passages can also be purchased (subject to space available) at the office by the port in Presidente Epitácio, and in Guaíra from Ernst Mann, **Americatur**, R Alvorada 253. Alternatively it may be possible to obtain passage on a cargo boat.

● **Accommodation**   Near the rodoviária: **C** *Palace Hotel*, Rui Barbosa 1190, T 42-1325; **D** *Majestic*, opp rodoviária, with or without bath, with breakfast, good; **D** *Sete Quedas*, Otávio Tosta 385, with breakfast and sandwich lunch, not too clean; and others.

Presidente Epitácio Hotel: E *Itaverá*, Curitiba 622, good value, nr station.

● **Places to eat**   *O Chopão*, Otávio Tosta 69, pleasant.

● **Transport Buses** Guaíra-Campo Grande: buy a ticket (US$32) at the Guaíra rodoviária, take ferry to Ponta Porã, then bus to Mondo Novo, change bus there for Campo Grande; morning and night bus, 12 hrs in all. There is a bus service between **Curitiba** and Guaíra, US$23, 10 hrs; bus to **São Paulo**, US$30, 16 hrs (same fare from Pres Epitácio); Guaíra to **Presidente Epitácio**, US$3.50. Other destinations inc **Iguaçu** (bumpy, but interesting) 5 hrs or may be cancelled in the wet, US$9.50.

FRONTIER WITH PARAGUAY

● **Immigration & transport**
There is an hourly passenger ferry service from Porto de Lanchas and Porto Guaíra to Paraguayan side, US$0.60, and hourly car ferry from Porto Guaíra (US$4 for car with 2 people). The car ferry runs until 1800 (Brazilian time); customs and immigration for documentation close at 1700. There is a time change when you cross the Paraná. The area is intensively patrolled for contraband and stolen cars, ensure that all documentation is in order.

Bahia

S ALVADOR, the capital of Bahia, is one of Brazil's most historic cities, with a wealth of colonial architecture. It is also dubbed 'Africa in exile': the mixture of African and European finds its most powerful expression in Carnival. The state's coast has many fine beaches, particularly in the south around Porto Seguro. Inland is the harsh Sertão, traversed by the Rio São Francisco.

Bahia is the southernmost of the nine states of the northeastern bulge of Brazil. The other eight are Sergipe, Alagoas, Pernambuco, Paraíba, Rio Grande do Norte, Ceará, Piauí, and Maranhão. They cover 2.6 million sq km and contain a third of Brazil's people. The birthrate is the highest in Brazil, but so is the infant mortality rate. The average annual income from subsistence farming is deplorably low. Despite the misery, both regional and state loyalty remain ineradicable.

The nine states may be roughly divided into three contrasting parts. One is the sugar lands of the Zona da Mata along the coast between Salvador (Bahia) and Natal, where the rainfall can be depended upon. This was the first part of Brazil to be intensively colonized; hence the wealth of 16th century buildings and the density of old settlements. Inland from the Zona da Mata is the Zona do Agreste, with less rainfall, but generally enough for cattle raising. Inland again is the true interior, the Sertão, where rainfall cannot be depended upon; there is a little agriculture where water allows it but the herding of goats, and occasionally cattle, is more important. There are few blacks here; the inhabitants are mostly of Portuguese-Indian stock, one of the most distinctive in Brazil. They are known as *sertanejos* until drought forces them to emigrate, when they become *flagelados*, the scourged ones.

When there is rain, food in the zone is plentiful and varied. But in the years of drought, when the hot dry winds from Africa scorch the earth, the effects can be tragic. Migration towards the coast and the southern towns begins, and the people are exposed to castigation of yet another sort: exploitation by grasping labour contractors. But at the first news that there is rain, the *flagelado* heads for home.

The main export crops of the NE are sugar, cotton and cacao. Sugar and cotton have long been in decline, and now the southern states grow more than half of the Brazilian total. But cacao is grown almost entirely in southern Bahia, inland from the port of Ilhéus.

Some of Brazil's main oilfields are in the State of Bahia; there are also offshore wells in the coastal waters of Alagoas, Sergipe and Rio Grande do Norte.

SALVADOR

(*Pop* 2 million; *CEP* 40000; *DDD* 071) The capital of the state of Bahia. It is the third largest city in Brazil (it is often called Bahia, rather than Salvador). The population of the state is 14 million in an area about that of France.

CLIMATE

It rains somewhat all the year but the main rainy season is between May and September. The climate is pleasant and the sun is never far away. Temperatures range from 25°C to 32°C, never falling below 19° in winter.

Salvador stands on the magnificent Bahia de Todos os Santos, a sparkling bay dotted with 38 islands. The bay is the largest on the Brazilian coast covering an area of 1,100 sq km. Rising above the bay on its eastern side is a cliff which dominates the landscape and, perched on top, are the older districts of Salvador with buildings dating back to 17th and 18th centuries.

HISTORY

The bay was discovered by Amérigo Vespucci on 1 November 1501, All Saints Day. The first Governor General, Tomé de Sousa arrived on 23 March 1549 to build a fortified city to protect Portugal's interest from constant threats of Dutch and French invasion. Salvador was the capital of Brazil until 1763 at which stage it was the most important city in the Portuguese Empire after Lisbon, ideally situated in a safe, sheltered harbour along the trade routes of the New World.

African presence The city's first wealth came from the cultivation of sugar cane and tobacco, the plantations' workforce coming from the W coast of Africa. For three centuries Salvador was the site of a thriving slave trade and this major influx is responsible for Salvador being described as the most African city in the Western Hemisphere. The influence permeates the city: food sold on the street is the same as in Senegal and Nigeria, Bahian music is fused with pulsating African polyrhythms, men and women nonchalantly carry enormous loads on their heads, fishermen paddle dug out canoes in the bay, the pace of life is a little slower than elsewhere. The pulse of the city is *candomblé*, an Afro-Brazilian religion in which the African deities of Nature, the Goddess of the sea and the God of creation are worshipped. These deities (or *orixás*) are worshipped in temples (*terreiros*) which can be elaborate, decorated halls, or simply someone's front room with tiny altars to the *orixá*. *Candomblé*

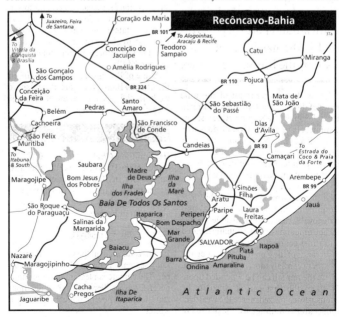

Salvador Orientation

1. Campo Grande
2. Centro Administrativo de Bahia
3. Ferry Terminal
4. Forte de Santo Antônio
5. Iguatemi Shopping Centre
6. Monte Serrat
7. Nossa Senhora da Penha
8. Nosso Senhor do Bomfim
9. See area of detail map

ceremonies may be seen by tourists – but not photographed – on Sun and religious holidays. Contact the tourist office, Bahiatursa, or see their twice monthly calendar of events.

Modern Salvador Salvador today is a city of 15 forts, 166 Catholic churches, 1,000 *candomblé* temples and a fascinating mixture of old and modern, rich and poor, African and European, religious and profane. It is still a major port exporting tropical fruit, cocoa, sisal, soya beans and petrochemical products. Its most important industry, though, is tourism; after Rio it is the second largest tourist attraction in the country, very popular with Brazilian tourists who see Bahia as an exotic destination. It is mostly a rundown, poor and dirty city, but most visitors feel that the richness of its culture is compensation enough for any problems they encounter.

PLACES OF INTEREST

The centre of the city is divided into two levels, the Upper city (or Cidade Alta) where the Historical Centre lies, and the Lower city (Cidade Baixa) which is the commercial and docks district. The two levels are connected by a series of steep hills called *ladeiras*. The easiest way to go from one level to the other is by the *Lacerda* lift which connects Praça Municipal (Tomé de Sousa) in the Upper city with Praça Cairu and the famous Mercado Modelo. There is also the Plano Inclinado Gonçalves, a funicular railway which leaves from behind the Cathedral going down to Comercio, the commercial district.

Centro Histórico

There is much more of interest in the Upper city. From Praça Municipal to the Carmo area 2 km N along the cliff is the **Centro Histórico** (Historical Centre), now a national monument and also protected by Unesco. It was in this area that the Portuguese built their fortified city and where today stand some of the most important examples of colonial architecture in the Americas. The historic centre is undergoing a massive restoration programme funded by the Bahian state government and UNESCO. The colonial houses have been painted in their original pastel colours. Many of the bars have live music which spills out onto the street on every corner. Patios have been created in the open areas behind the houses with open air cafés and bars. Artist ateliers, antique and handicraft stores have brought new artistic blood to what was once the bohemian part of the city. Many popular traditional restaurants and bars from other parts of Salvador have opened new branches in the area.

Praça Municipal, Praça de Sé and Terreiro de Jesus

Dominating the **Praça Municipal** is the old **Paço Municipal** (Council Chamber – 1660), while alongside is the **Palácio Rio Branco** (1918), once the Governor's Palace now the headquarters of Bahiatursa, the state tourist board. Leaving it with its panoramic view of the bay, R Misericôrdia goes N passing the **Santa Casa Misericôrdia** (1695 – see the high altar and painted tiles) to **Praça da Sé**. This square with its mimosa and flamboyant trees leads into **Terreiro de Jesus** (under reconstruction until 1997), a picturesque square named after the church which dominates it. Built in 1692, the **church of the Jesuits** became the property of the Holy See in 1759 when the Jesuits were expelled from all Portuguese territories. The façade is one of the earliest examples of Baroque in Brazil, an architectural style which was to dominate the churches built in the 17th and 18th centuries. Inside, the vast vaulted ceiling and 12 side altars in Baroque and Rococco frame the main altar completely leafed in gold. The tiles in blue, white and yellow in a tapestry pattern are also from Portugal. It houses the tomb of Mem de Sá. The church is now the city Cathedral; open Tues to Sun, 0800-1100, 1500-1800; parts are currently being renovated. Across the square is the church of **São Pedro dos Clérigos** which is beautifully renovated, while alongside is the church of the **Ordem Terceira de São Domingos** (Dominican Third Order), open in the morning US$0.25, which has a beautiful painted wooden ceiling.

São Francisco

Facing Terreiro de Jesus is Praça Anchieta and the church of **São Francisco**. Its simple façade belies the treasure inside. The entrance leads to a sanctuary with a spectacular painting on the wooden ceiling, by local artist José Joaquim da Rocha (1777). The main body of the church is the most exuberant example of Baroque in the country. The cedar wood carving and later gold leaf was completed after 28 years in 1748. The cloisters of the monastery are surrounded by a series of blue and white tiles from Portugal. The church is open 0800-1115 and 1400-1700 (entry to cloisters US$0.20, church free). Next door (and with the same opening hours, entry US$0.20) is the church of the **Ordem Terceira de São Francisco** (Franciscan Third Order – 1703) with its façade intricately carved in sandstone. Inside is a quite remarkable Chapter House with striking images of the Order's most celebrated saints.

Largo do Pelourinho

Leading off the Terreiro de Jesus is R Alfredo Brito, a charming, narrow cobbled street lined with fine colonial houses painted in different pastel shades. This street leads into the **Largo do Pelourinho** (Praça José Alencar), which was completely renovated in 1993. Considered the finest complex of colonial architecture in Latin America, it was once the site of a pillory where slaves were publicly punished and ridiculed. It was also the site of the slave market. After the cleaning of the area, new galleries, boutiques and restaurants are opening, and at night the Largo is lively, especially on Tues (see **Nightlife** below). **Nosso Senhor Do Rosario Dos Pretos** church, the so-called Slave Church, dominates the square. It was built by former slaves, with what little financial resources they had, over a period of 100 years. The side altars honour black saints. The painted ceiling is very impressive, the overall effect being one of tranquillity in contrast to the complexity of the Cathedral and São Francisco. A small entrance fee is charged.

At the corner of Alfredo Brito and Largo do Pelourinho is a museum to the work of Jorge Amado (**Casa da Cultura Jorge Amado**, mainly photos, book covers and a lecture room, Mon-Fri 0900-1800), who lived in, and set many of his books, in this section of the city. A good way to get a feel of the city and its people is to read *Dona Flor and her two husbands*. The Carmo Hill is at the top of the street leading out of

Largo do Pelourinho. The **Carmo** (Carmelite Third Order) church (1709) houses one of the sacred art treasures of the city, a sculpture of Christ made in 1730 by a slave who had no formal training, Francisco Xavier das Chagas, known as O Cabra. One

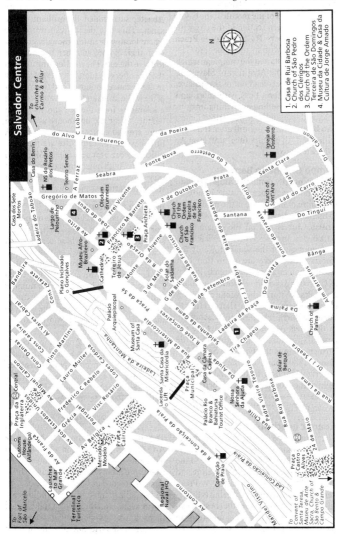

Salvador Centre

To churches of Carmo & Pilar

1. Casa de Rui Barbosa
2. Church of São Pedro dos Clérigos
3. Church of the Ordem Terceira de São Domingos
4. Museu da Cidade & Casa da Cultura de Jorge Amado

of the features of the piece is the blood made from whale oil, ox blood, banana resin and 2000 rubies to represent the drops of blood. Opening hours are 0800 to 1200 and 1400 to 1730, entry US$0.30.

South of the Praça Municipal

In the direction of the mouth of the bay, is the more modern section of the city with many skyscrapers. R Chile leads to **Praça Castro Alves**, with its monument to Castro Alves, who started the campaign which finally led to the Abolition of Slavery in 1888. Two streets lead out of this square, Av 7 de Setembro, busy with shops and street vendors selling everything imaginable, and, parallel to it, R Carlos Gomes. **São Bento** church (rebuilt after 1624, but with fine 17th century furniture) is on Av 7 de Setembro.

Campo Grande to Barra

Both eventually come to **Campo Grande** (also known as Praça Dois de Julho). In the centre of the square is the monument to Bahian Independence, 2 July 1823. The British Club is just off the square on R Banco dos Ingleses. Av 7 de Setembro continues out of the square towards the Vitória area. There are some fine 19th century homes along this stretch, known as Corredor da Vitória (Vitória Corridor). From Praça Vitória, the avenue continues down Ladeira da Barra (Barra Hill) to **Porto da Barra**. The best city beaches are in this area. Also in this district are the best bars, restaurants and nightlife. A little further along is the **Forte de Santo Antônio**, 1580, built on the spot where Amérigo Vespucci landed in 1501. It is right at the mouth of the bay where Bahia de Todos Os Santos and the South Atlantic Ocean meet.

Atlantic beach suburbs

The promenade leading away from the fort and its famous lighthouse is called Av Oceânica, which follows the coast to the beach suburbs of Ondina, Amaralina and Pituba. The road is also called Av Presidente Vargas, but the numbering is different. Beyond Pituba are the best ocean **beaches** at Jaguaripe, Piatã and Itapoan (take any bus from Praça da Sé marked Aeroporto or Itapoan, about 1 hr). En route the bus passes small fishing colonies at Amaralina and Pituba where *jangadas* can be seen. A *jangada* is a small raft peculiar to the northeastern region of Brazil used extensively as well as dug out canoes. Near Itapoan is the **Lagoa do Abaeté**, surrounded by brilliant, white sands. This is a deep, fresh water lake where local women traditionally come to wash their clothes and then lay them out to dry in the sun. The road leading up from the lake offers a panoramic view of the city in the distance, the coast, and the contrast of the white sands and fresh water less than a kilometre from the sea and its golden beaches. Near the lighthouse at **Itapoan** there are two campsites on the beach. A little beyond the campsites are the magnificent ocean beaches of Stella Maris and Flamengo, both quiet during the week but very busy at the weekends. Beware of strong undertow at these beaches.

Bomfim and Itapagipe

See also the famous church of **Nosso Senhor do Bomfim** on the Itapagipe peninsula in the suburbs, whose construction began in 1745; it draws endless supplicants (particularly on Fri and Sun) offering favours to the image of the Crucified Lord set over the high altar; the number and variety of ex-voto offerings is extraordinary. The processions over the water to the church on the third Sun in Jan are particularly interesting.

Also on the Itapagipe peninsula is a colonial fort on **Mont Serrat** point, and at Ribeira the church of **Nossa Senhora da Penha** (1743). The beach here has many restaurants, but the sea is polluted (bus from Praça da Sé or Av França).

MUSEUMS

The city has 27 museums. The **Museu de Arte Contemporânea**, converted from an old estate house and outbuildings off Av Contorno, is only open for special exhibitions. The good restaurant (*Solar do Unhão*) is still there, and the buildings are worth seeing for themselves (take a taxi there as access is dangerous).

Museu de Arte Sacra is in the 17th

century monastery and church of Santa
Teresa, at the bottom of the steep Ladeira
de Santa Teresa, at R do Sodré 276 (off R
Carlos Gomes). Many of the 400 carvings
are from the Old World, but a number are
local. Among the reliquaries of silver and
gold is one of gilded wood by Aleijadinho.
Open Mon-Fri 0700-1800, US$0.40. The
collection of treasures which used to be
in the Casa de Calmon, Av Joana Angélica
198, are well worth a visit. Opposite is
Tempostal, a private museum of postcards, open Tues-Sat, 1000-1130, 1400-
1600, at R do Sodré 276 (proprietor,
Antônio Marcelino do Nascimento).

Museu do Carmo, in the Convento do
Carmo, has a collection of icons and co-
lonial furniture, open Mon-Sat 0800-
1200,   1400-1800,   Sun   0800-1200,
US$0.10; see the carving of Christ by
Francisco Xavier das Chagas (see above).

Museu Abelardo Rodrigues, Solar
Ferrão, Pelourinho (R Gregório de Mattos 45, open Mon-Fri 1000-1200, 1400-
1700, closed Tues, Sat-Sun 1100-1700), is
another religious art museum, with objects from the 17th, 18th, and 19th centuries, mainly from Bahia, Pernambuco and
Maranhão. **The Pelourinho Renovation
Exhibition**, R Gregório de Matos (next
door), pictures showing houses before
and after the renovation.

Museu Afro-Brasileiro, in former Faculty of Medicine building, Terreiro de Jesus, open Mon-Sat, 0900-1700, US$1,
comparing African and Bahian Orixás
(deities) celebrations, beautiful murals and
carvings, highly rec. **Museu Arqueológico
a Etnográfico**, in the basement of the same
building, archaeological discoveries from
Bahia (stone tools, clay urns etc), exhibition on Indians from the Alto Rio Xingu
area (artefacts, tools, photos) rec. Medical
museum in same complex.

Casa do Benin, below NS do Rosario
dos Pretos, shows African crafts, photos,
video show on Benin and Angola, open
Tues-Sat 1000-1800.

Museu da Cidade, Largo do Pelourinho, arts and crafts, old photographs,
entrance free, Tues-Fri 1000-1800, Sat,
Sun, 1300-1700. From the higher floors of
the museum you can get a good view of
the Pelourinho.

Museu Costa Pinto, Av 7 de Setembro
2490, US$2, daily 1430-1800, is a modern
house with collections of crystal, porcelain, silver, furniture etc. It also has the
only collection of *balangandãs* (slave
charms and jewellery), highly rec.

Museu de Arte da Bahia, Av 7 de
Setembro 2340, Vitória, Tues-Fri 1400-
1900, Sat-Sun 1430-1830, US1, interesting
paintings of Brazilian artists between 18th
and early 20th century. The **Museu
Geológico do Estado** is at Av 7 de Setembro 2195, Vitória, open Mon-Fri 1330-1830.

Museu Hidrográfico, Forte de Santo
Antônio (Tues-Sat 1300-1800 US$1); re-
cently restored and housed in the upper
section of the fort, fine views of the bay
and coast, rec.

36 km from the city is the **Museu do
Recôncavo** (Museu do Vanderlei do
Pinho) in the old Freguesia mill – 1552
(open Tues, Thur and Sun 0900-1700), in
which one can find artefacts and pictures
of three centuries of the economic and
social life of this region. The Casa Grande
e Senzala (the home of the landowner and
the combined dwelling and working area
of the slaves) is still intact. It is a peaceful
way to spend an afternoon, but difficult
to get to by public transport, the museum
is near the town of São Francisco do
Conde, 7 km from main highway.

NB Many guides offer their services in
museums, but their English is poor and
their expectations of a tip high.

LOCAL HOLIDAYS

6 Jan (Epiphany); Ash Wednesday and
Maundy Thursday, half-days; 2 July (Independence of Bahia); 30 Oct; Christmas
Eve, half-day. An important local holiday
is the **Festa do Nosso Senhor do Bomfim**;
it takes place on the second Sun after
Epiphany, but the washing or *lavagem* of
the Bomfim church, with its colourful parade, takes place on the preceding Thur
(usually mid-Jan). The **Festa da Ribeira**
is on the following Mon. Another colourful festival is that of the fishermen of Rio
Vermelho on 2 Feb; gifts for Yemanjá,
Goddess of the Sea, are taken out to sea in a

procession of sailing boats to an accompaniment of *candomblé* instruments. The Holy Week processions among the old churches of the upper city are also interesting.

The **pre-Carnival festive season** begins towards the end of Nov with São Nicodemo de Cachimbo (penultimate Sun of Nov), then comes Santa Bárbara (4 Dec), then the Festa da Conceição da Praia, centred on the church of that name (open 0700-1130 normally) at the base of the Lacerda lift. (8 Dec is the last night – not for those who don't like crowds!) The last week of Dec is the Festa da Boa Viagem in the lower city; the beach will be packed all night on the 31st. On 1 Jan is the beautiful boat procession of Nosso Senhor dos Navegantes from Conceição da Praia to the church of Boa Viagem, on the beach of that name in the lower city. The leading boat, which carries the image of Christ and the archbishop, was built in 1892. You can follow in a sailing boat for about US$1; go early (0900) to dock by Mercado Modelo. A later festival is São Lázaro on the last Sun in January.

CARNIVAL IN BAHIA

Carnival officially starts on Thur night at 2000 when the keys of the city are given to the Carnival King 'Rei Momo'. The unofficial opening though is on Wed with the Lavagem do Porto da Barra, when throngs of people dance on the beach. Later on in the evening is the Baile dos Atrizes, starting at around 2300 and going on until dawn, very bohemian, good fun. Check with Bahiatursa for details on venue, time etc (see under Rio for carnival dates).

Carnival in Bahia is the largest in the world and it encourages active participation. It is said that there are 1½ million people dancing on the streets at any one time.

There are two distinct musical formats. The **Afro Blocos** are large drum based troupes (some with up to 200 drummers) who play on the streets accompanied by singers atop mobile sound trucks. The first of these groups was the Filhos de Gandhi (founded in 1949), whose participation is one of the highlights of Carnival. Their 6,000 members dance through the streets on the Sun and Tues of Carnival dressed in their traditional costumes, a river of white and blue in an ocean of multicoloured carnival revellers. The best known of the recent **Afro Blocos** are Ilê Aiye, Olodum, Muzenza and Malê Debalê. They all operate throughout the year in cultural, social and political areas. Not all of them are receptive to foreigners among their numbers for Carnival. The basis of the rhythm is the enormous *surdo* (deaf) drum with its *bumbum bumbum bum* anchorbeat, while the smaller *repique*, played with light twigs, provides a crack-like overlay. Ilê Aiye take to the streets around 2100 on Sat night and their departure from their headquarters at Ladeira do Curuzu in the Liberdade district is not to be missed. The best way to get there is to take a taxi to Curuzu via Largo do Tanque thereby avoiding traffic jams. The ride is a little longer but much quicker. A good landmark is the Paes Mendonça supermarket on the corner of the street from where the bloco leaves. From there it's a short walk to the departure point.

The enormous **trios eléctricos** 12m sound trucks with powerful sound systems that defy most decibel counters, are the second format. These trucks, each with its own band of up to 10 musicians, play songs influenced by the **afro blocos** and move at a snail's pace through the streets, drawing huge crowds. Each **Afro Bloco** and **bloco de trio** has its own costume and its own security personnel who cordon off the area around the sound truck. The **bloco** members can thus dance in comfort and safety.

The traditional Carnival route is from Campo Grande (by the *Tropical Hotel da Bahia*) to Praça Castro Alves near the old town. The **blocos** go along Av 7 de Setembro and return to Campo Grande via the parallel R Carlos Gomes. Many of the trios no longer go through the Praça Castro Alves, once the epicentre of Carnival. The best night at Praça Castro Alves is Tues (the last night of Carnival) when the famous 'Encontro dos trios' (Meeting of the Trios) takes place. Trios jostle for position in the square and play in rotation until the dawn (or later!) on Ash Wednesday. It is not uncommon for major stars from the Bahian (and Brazilian) music world to make surprise appearances.

There are grandstand seats at Campo Grande throughout the event. Day tickets for these are available the week leading up to Carnival. Check with Bahiatursa for information on where the tickets are sold. Tickets are US$10 (or up to US$30 on the black market on the day). The blocos are judged as they pass the grandstand and are at their most frenetic at this point. There is little or no shade from the sun so bring a hat and lots of water. Best days are Sun to Tues. For those wishing to go it alone, just find a friendly *barraca* in the shade and watch the blocos go by. Avoid the Largo da Piedade and Relogio de São Pedro on Av 7 de Setembro: the street narrows here creating human traffic jams.

The other major centre for Carnival is Barra to Ondina. The **blocos alternativos** ply this route. These are nearly always **trios electricos** connected with the more traditional blocos who have expanded to this now very popular district. Not to be missed here is Timbalada, the drumming group formed by the internationally renowned percussionist Carlinhos Brown.

Recommended Blocos Traditional Route (Campo Grande): *Mel*, T 245-4333, Sun, Mon, Tues; *Cameleão*, T 336-6100, Sun, Mon, Tues; *Pinel*, T 336-0489, Sun, Mon, Tues; *Internacionais*, T 242-6211, Sun, Mon, Tues; *Cheiro de Amor*, T 336-6060, Sun, Mon, Tues. **Afro Blocos**: *Ilê Aiye*, T 241-4969, Sat, Mon; *Olodum*, T 321-5010, Fri, Sun. **Blocos Alternativos**: *Timbalada*, T 248-3412, Fri, Sat; *Nana Banana*, T 235-0113, Fri, Sat; *Melomania*, T 245-4570, Fri, Sat.

Prices range from US$180 to US$450. The quality of the **bloco** often depends on the act that plays on the **trio**. See **Music in Bahia**, below.

CULTURE

The Bahianas – black women who dress in traditional 18th century costumes – are street vendors who sit behind their trays of delicacies, savoury and seasoned, made from the great variety of local fish, vegeta-bles and fruits.

See Capoeira, a sport developed from the traditional foot-fighting technique introduced from Angola by African slaves. The music is by drum, tambourine and *berimbau*; there are several different kinds of the sport. If you want to attempt Capoeira, the best school is Mestre Bimba in Terreiro de Jesus, at R Francisco Muniz Barreto 1. Classes are held in evenings (if you want to get the most out of it, knowledge of Portuguese is essential). There are two more schools in Forte de Santo Antônio behind Pelourinho, but check addresses at the tourist office. Exhibitions take place in the Largo do Pelourinho, very picturesque, in the upper city (cost: US$2). You can also see the experts outside the Mercado Modelo on most days, around 1100-1300, and at Campo Grande and Forte de Santo Antônio on Sun afternoons; they often expect a contribution. Negotiate a price before taking pictures or demands may be exorbitant. At the Casa da Cultura at Forte de Santo Antônio there is also free live music on Sat night.

MUSIC IN BAHIA

The best time to hear and see artists and groups is during carnival but they are also to be seen outside the carnival period. Olodum, Ilê Aiye, Muzenza and Araketu are the most famous of the numerous drumming troupes where up to 100 drummers form the powerful rhythms for the sweet melodies. For Olodum and Ilê Aiyê, see **Nightlife** below.

Artists and bands using electronic instruments and who tend to play in the *trios elêctricos* draw heavily on the rich rhythms of the drumming groups creating a new musical genre known as *Axé*. The most popular of such acts is Daniela Mercury, following the steps to internationals stardom of Caetano Veloso, Maria Bethânia, João Gilberto, Gilberto Gil. Other newer, interesting acts are Margareth Menezes who has travelled extensively with David Byrne. Gerónimo was one of the first singer/songwriters to use the wealth of rhythms of the Candomblé in his music and his song 'E d'Oxum' is something of an anthem for the city. Other artists worth investigating are Roberto Mendes, Carlinhos Brown and his vibrant drumming group Timbalada. The most famous of the trio bands are Chiclete com Banana, Banda Mel, Banda Beijo and Banda Reflexus.

All of the above have albums released and you can find their records easily in most record stores. See **Shopping in the Pelourinho**, below. Also try *Billbox* in the Shopping Barra on the third floor.

EXCURSIONS

From the lower city the train (Trem do Leste) leaves Calçada for a 40 min journey through the bayside suburbs of Lobato, Plataforma (canoes and motor boats for Ribeira on the Itapagipe peninsula), Escada (17th century church), Praia Grande, Periperi and Paripe (take bus for 17th century church at São Tomé de Paripe). The train runs Mon-Fri only; the same trip can be made by bus, less picturesquely.

LOCAL INFORMATION

● **Accommodation**

Hotel prices

L1	over US$200	L2	US$151-200
L3	US$101-150	A1	US$81-100
A2	US$61-80	A3	US$46-60
B	US$31-45	C	US$21-30
D	US$12-20	E	US$7-11
F	US$4-6	G	up to US$3

Unless otherwise stated, all hotels in range **D** and above have private bath. Assume friendliness and cleanliness in all cases.

A 10% service charge is often added to the bill. Check which credit cards are accepted. All have swimming pools.

Luxury hotels: **L2** *Enseada das Lajes*, Av Oceânica 511, Rio Vermelho, T 336 1027, family run, 9 rooms in what used to be a private house, antique furniture, excellent pieces of art, wonderful setting, 2 mins beach. **L3** *Bahia Othon Palace*, Av Oceânica 2456, Ondina, T 247 1044, F 245 4877, 5-star, nice rooms and views, excellent swimming pool, next to beach; **L3** *Hotel da Bahia* (Tropical), Praça 2 de Julho 2, Campo Grande, F 321 9725, refurbished, well-run, owned by Varig, convenient for city centre, daily courtesy bus to beach, swimming pool, sauna, fitness centre, beauty parlour; **L3** *Marazul*, Av 7 de Setembro

3937, Barra, T 336 2110, F 235 2121, 4-star, on seafront, heartily rec, good discounts for longer stays; **L3** *Meridien*, R Fonte do Boi 216, Rio Vermelho, 5-star, T 248 8011, F 248 8902, well-run, ocean views, no beach, nothing within walking distance so taxis must be used. **L3** *Ondina Apart Hotel*, Av Oceânica 2400, Ondina, T 203 8000, 5-star, self-contained apts, on beach, highly rec; **L3** *Sofitel* (Quatro Rodas), R da Passargada, Farol de Itapoan, T 249 9611, F 249 6946, 5-star, a complete resort hotel 22 km from city centre, extensive grounds, peaceful but plenty of activities available eg golf, tennis, etc, shuttle bus to city centre.

A1 *Itapoan Praia*, Jardim Itapoan, Placafor, T 249 9988, F 248 7111, 3-star, 20 km from centre nr excellent beaches; **A1** *Ondina Praia*, Av Oceânica 2275, Ondina, T 336 1033, F 247 9434, 3-star, nr beach; **A1** *San Marino*, Av Oceânica 889 Barra, T 336 4363, 3-star, on ocean.

Centre: (includes old city and main shopping area): **B** *Palace*, R Chile 20, T 243 1155, F 243 1109, rec; **D** *Chile*, opp, big rooms, some have harbour view; **B-C** *Imperial*, Av 7 de Setembro 751, Rosario, T 321 3389, a/c, helpful, breakfast, rec; **C** *Pousada da Praça*, Ruy Barbosa 5, T 321 0642, breakfast not inc, rooms with and without bath, rec; **C** *Pousada do Boqueirão*, R Direita do Santa Antônio 48, T/F 241 2262, family run, beautiful house overlooking the bay, relaxed atmosphere, most European languages spoken, great food, especially breakfast, highly rec; **D** *Internacional*, R da Faisca 88, T 243 6151, convenient, good value; at no 13, **D** *Paris*, T 321 3922, a/c rooms more expensive, shared showers, breakfast, restaurant in same building, rec; **D** *São Bento*, Largo de São Bento 3, T 243 7511, good cheap restaurant. Cheaper hotels on Av 7 de Setembro: **D-E** *São José*, No 847, T 321 4928, safe, rec; **E** *Pousada Pampulha*, No 76, 1st floor, São Pedro, T 243 1240, breakfast, restaurant, laundry service; **F** *Madrid*, No 186, Mercês, T 321 9505, very cheap and basic, damp, not too secure; **F** pp *Pousada*, No 2349, warmly rec. **F** *Joana Angélica* in street of same name, helpful, no breakfast.

There are many hotels nr the Praça da Sé. The following have been rec: **C** *Pelourinho*, R Alfredo Brito 20, T 321 9022, run down but central and charismatic; **D** *Solara*, R José Alencar 25, Largo do Pelourinho, T 321 0202, with shower, toilet, breakfast, laundry facilities; **D** *Themis*, Praça da Sé 398, Ed Themis, 7th floor, T 243 1668, fan, wonderful views over bay and old city, rec restaurant with French chef; Spanish is spoken in all of the following: **D-E** *Ilheus*, Ladeira da Praça 4, 1st floor, T 243 2329, breakfast; **E** *Vigo*, R 3 de Maio 18, with bath and breakfast (**F** without), fairly clean and safe.

Campo Grande/Vitória: this is a much quieter area, still central and convenient for museums: **B** *Bahia do Sol*, Av 7 de Setembro 2009, T 336 7211, F 336 7776, comfortable, safe and frigo-bar in room, family run, good breakfast and restaurant, rec; **D** *Caramuru*, Av Sete de Setembro 2125, Vitória, T 336 9951, breakfast, safe parking, rec; **D** *Do Forte*, R Visc de São Lourenço 30, Campo Grande, T 321 6915, breakfast, bath; **D** *Santiago* at No 52, breakfast, bath, T 245 9293.

Santo Antônio: quiet residential district NE of Pelourinho, **A3** *Pousada das Flores*, R Direita de Santo Antônio 442, T 2431836, nr Santo Antônio fort, Brazilian/French owners, only one suite with bath, excellent breakfast, beautiful old house, highly rec.

Barra: the best location to stay in: it is safe, has good beaches (but the sea may be polluted), is a short bus ride from the centre, has good restaurants in all price ranges and good nightlife (but note that the bars around Porto da Barra have become meeting places for prostitutes and European tourists). On Av 7 de Setembro: **B** *Barra Turismo*, No 3691, Porto da Barra, T 245 7433, breakfast, a/c, fridge, on beach, rec; **C** *Porto da Barra*, No 3783, Porto da Barra, T 247 7711, some rooms very small, on beach; **C** *Pousada Malu*, No 3801, T 237 4461, small, with breakfast, on beach; **C** *Villa da Barra*, No 3959, Porto da Barra, T 247 7908, F 247 9667, chalets in front of the beach, English spoken, rec. **B** *Barra Praia*, Av Alm Marqués do Leão 172, Farol da Barra, T 235-0193, a/c, one street from beach, rec; **C** *Enseada Praia da Barra*, R Barão de Itapoá 60, Porto da Barra, T 235 9213, breakfast, safe, money exchanged, accepts credit cards, laundry bills high otherwise good value, nr beach; **C** *Seara Praia*, R Belo Horizonte 148, Barra Av, T 235 0105, good breakfast; **D** *Bella Barra*, R Afonso Celso 439, T 237 8401, a/c, rec; **D** pp *Pousada do Porto*, R Barão de Sergy 197, T 247 8228, hostel in beautiful turn-of-the-century house, breakfast, nr beach, convenient, English spoken, can get cramped but highly rec; **E** *Pousada da Carmen Simões*, R 8 de Dezembro 326, safe, helpful; **E** *Pousada Marcos*, Av Oceânica 281, T 235 5117, youth hostel style, great location nr lighthouse, very busy, many notices in Hebrew for potential travelling companions, good value, rec. Also rooms to let in private apartment, rec, from Gorette, R 8 de Dezembro 522, Apt 002, T 237-3584.

Atlantic Suburbs: this is the modern suburban area built along the coast from Ondina to Itapoan stretching for 20 km towards the airport. The best beaches are in this area. **A3** *Catharina Paraguaçu*, R João Gomes 128, Rio Vermelho, T 247 1488, charming, small, colonial-style,

tastefully decorated, rec; **A3** *Mar A Vista*, R H C Ribeiro 1, Ondina, T 247 3866, rec, nr beach; **A3** *Ondina Plaza*, Av Pres Vargas 3033, Ondina, T 245 8188, a/c, pool, good value, on beach, rec. Two in Pituba: **B** *Paulus*, Av Otávio Mangabeira, T 248 5722, a/c, pool; **D** *Pituba*, Av Manoel Dias da Silva 1614, T 248 5469, no breakfast. Two nr excellent beach, in Placaford: **B** *Praia Dourada*, R Dias Gomes 10, T 249 9639, a/c, rec; **B** *Praia dos Coqueiros*, Av Otavio Mangabeira 25, Placaford, T 249 9828, a/c, rec. In Itapoan: **A3** *Praia da Sereia*, Av Dorival Caymmi 14, T 249-4523, F 249-4550, very good, pool, safe; **B** *Grão de Areia*, Loteamento Jardim Piatã, Quadra 25, Lote 23/24, T 249 4818, a/c, pool, nr good beach; **B** *Pousada de Itapoan*, Av D Caymmi, V dos Ex Combatentes, Quadrá 1, Lote 3, T 249 9634, **D** without bath, excellent breakfast, good value, laundry, parking; **C** *Europa*, R Genibaldo Figueiredo 53, T 249 9344, breakfast; **D** *Pousada Glória*, R do Retiro 46, T 249 1503, no breakfast, nr beach.

A1 *Solar Diana*, Av Yemanjá, R U, Lote 16, Jardim Armação, nr Convention Center, T 231 1017, F 231 7927, sophisticated, small, most European languages spoken, highly rec; **A3** *Portal Da Cidade*, Av Antônio Carlos Magalhães 4230, next to rodoviária, T 371 0099, a/c, pool.

Apart Hotels: these are self-contained apartments with fully equipped kitchen and a/c, with all the facilities of a hotel, which can be rented by the day; standards are generally high. *Jardim Paraiso*, Av Dunas 259, Itapoan, T 249 3397, pool, nr beach; *Bahia Flat*, Av Pres Vargas 235, Barra, T 336 4233, on beach, pool, sauna; *Barra Apart Service*, R Marquês de Caravelas 237, Barra, T 247 5844; *Flat Jardim de Alá*, Av Otavio Mangabeira 3471, Armação, T 371 5288, beautiful location by beach, pool, sauna, rec; *Manhattan Residence Service*, R Maranhão 445 Pituba, T 248 9911, pool, gym, popular with business visitors; *Parthenon Farol da Barra Flat*, Av Oceânica 409, Barra, T 336 6722, pool, sauna, on beach, rec; *Pituba Apart Hotel*, R Paraíba 250, Pituba, T 240 7077, pool, sauna; all in A1-A3 range rec; *Lucia Arleo*, R Miguel Bournier, 59-Ap 203, 237-2424, specially furnished apartments nr the beach, rec.

Youth hostels: Albergues de Juventude, E-F pp inc breakfast but cheaper if you have a YHA membership card. In Pelourinho: **D** *Albergue das Laranjeiras*, R Inácio Acciolli 13, T/F 321-1366, independent hostel, with breakfast, cooking facilities, English spoken, warmly rec; *Albergue Solar*, R Ribeiro dos Santos 45-47, T 241 0055; **E-F** *Pousada Jamayka*, same street, monthly rates available in low season; *Albergue do Peló*, same street No 5, T 242 8061; *Pousada do Passo*, No 3, T 321-3656, highly rec. *Casa Grande*, R Minas Gerais, 122, Pituba, T 248 0527; *Albergue da Barra*, R Florianopolis 134, Jardim Brasil, Barra, T 247 5478, good location.

Pensionatos are places to stay in shared rooms (up to 4 persons/room); part or full board available. Houses or rooms can be rented for US$5-35 a day from Pierre Marbacher, R Carlos Coqueijo 68A, Itapoan, T 249 5754 (Caixa Postal 7458, 41600 Salvador), he is Swiss, owns a beach bar at R K and speaks English. At Carnival it's a good idea to rent a flat; the tourist office has a list of estate agents (eg José Mendez T 237 1394/6). They can also arrange rooms in private houses, however caution is advised as not all householders are honest.

Camping: *Ecológica*, nr the lighthouse at Itapoan, take bus from Praça da Sé direct to Itapoan, or to Campo Grande or Barra, change there for Itapoan, about 1 hr, then 30 mins' walk: bar, restaurant, hot showers, highly rec. *Camping de Pituaçu*, Av Prof Pinto de Aguiar, Jardim Pituaçu. Sea bathing is dangerous off shore nr campsites.

● **Places to eat**

Bahian cuisine: is spiced and peppery. The main dish is *moqueca*, seafood cooked in a sauce made from coconut milk, tomatoes, red and green peppers, fresh coriander and *dendê* (palm oil). It is traditionally cooked in a wok-like earthenware dish and served piping hot at the table. Served with *moqueca* is *farofa* (manioc flour) and a hot pepper sauce which you add at your discretion, it's usually extremely hot so try a few drops before venturing further. The *dendê* is somewhat heavy and those with delicate stomachs are advised to try the *ensopado*, a sauce with the same ingredients as the *moqueca*, but without the palm oil.

Nearly every street corner has a Bahiana selling a wide variety of local snacks, the most famous of which is the *acarajé*, a bean dumpling fried in palm oil. To this the Bahiana adds *vatapá*, a dried shrimp and coconut milk paté (also delicious on its own), fresh salad and hot sauce (*pimenta*). For those who prefer not to eat the palm oil, the *abará* is a good substitute. *Abará* is steamed, wrapped in banana leaves. The Bahianas are being given lessons on hygiene, but seek local advice on which are safest.

Three good Bahianas are *Chica*, at Ondina beach (on street at left side of *Mar A Vista Hotel*), *Dinha* at Largo da Santana (very lively late afternoon), serves *acarajé* until midnight, extremely popular, and the one in front of *Tiffany's* restaurant on R Barão de Sergy at Porto da Barra. Bahians usually eat *acarajé* or *abará* with a chilled beer on the way home from work or the beach at sunset.

Another popular dish is *Xin-Xin de Galinha*, chicken on the bone cooked in *dendê*, with dried shrimp and squash.

Pelourinho (Historical Centre): *Cantina da Lua*, Terreiro De Jesus, open daily, popular but hangers-on can sometimes be a nuisance; *El Mesón*, Alfredo Brito 11 (upstairs), open Mon-Sat, 1100-2330, Sun 1800-2330, good seafood, meat, English spoken; *Pizzaria Micheluccio*, Alfredo Brito 31, best pizzas in Pelourinho, open daily 1200 till late, rec (T 321 5884). *Senac*, Praça José Alencar 8/Largo do Pelourinho, state run catering school, a selection of 40 local dishes, buffet, lunch 1130-1530, dinner 1830-2130, all you can eat for US$16, inconsistent quality but very popular, folkloric show Thur-Sat 2030, US$5. *Casa do Benin*, Praça José Alencar 29, Afro-Bahian restaurant, great surroundings, try the shrimp in the cashew nut sauce, closed Mon, open 1200-1600, 1900-2300, expensive but highly rec. *Bar Banzo*, Praça José Alencar 6 (upstairs) Mon-Sat 1100 to 2300, Sun 1800 to 2300, reasonably priced, good view of streetlife in Largo do Pelourinho below, friendly, good music. *Celina*, R dos Passos nr Casa do Benin, good, cheap, popular with locals.

Atelier Maria Adair, R J Castro Rabelo 2, specializing in coffees and cocktails, owner Maria is a well known artist whose highly original work is on display, rec. Good wholemeal snacks and juices at *Saúde Brasil*, No 16, open daily 0900-2330, rec; *Dona Chika-Ka*, No 10, 1100-1500 and 1900-0200, good local dishes. Open gates beside *Dona Chika-Ka* lead to an open square (known locally as Quadra 2M) with many bars and restaurants. On the next block down is *Tempero da Dadá*, R Frei Vicente 5, open daily 1130 till late, closed Tues, the best Bahian cuisine in the Pelourinho, owners Dadá and Paulo are genial hosts, extremely popular, try the *bobó de camarão* (shrimp in yam sauce) and the shrimp *moqueca* served with *pirão* (thick manioc gravy), highly rec. Next door is *Mustafá*, No 07, open 1200-2400 except Sun 1200-1500, closed Tues, Middle Eastern dishes, try the *mezze*, a selection of starters and main dishes, enough for two people. Across the street is *Abará da Ró*, specializing in *acarajé* and *abará*, popular late afternoon and early evening.

Uauá, R Gregório de Matos 36 (upstairs), 1130-1500 and 1900-2330, closed Tues, excellent northeastern cuisine, try the *carne de sol* (sun-dried beef), very reasonably priced, highly rec. *Casa da Gamboa*, R João de Deus 32, 1st floor, 1200-1500 and 1900-2400, closed Mon.

Good *feijoada* at *Alaíde do Feijão*, R Fransisco Muniz Barreto 26, open daily 1100-2400. Also at *da Dinha* on Praça José Alencar 5, Mon-Sat 0800-2000; *Encontro dos Artistas*, R Ribeiro do Santos 10, Passo – Pelourinho, vegetarian food, cheap, rec.

Between Historical Centre and Barra: at Praça Da Sé, *Café Brasil*, good breakfast; also *Hotel Themis* (see above). *Bar Padrão*, R José Gonçalves, nr Praça Da Sé, rec. There are some good snack bars on Av 7 de Setembro; *Nosso Cantinho*, nr *Hotel Madrid*, good value; *Kentefrio*, No 379, the best, clean, counter service only, closed Sun, rec; *Casa D'Italia*, corner of Av 7 and Visconde de São Lourenço, reasonable prices, good service; *Grão de Bico*, No 737, very good vegetarian. Another good vegetarian restaurant is *Nutrebem*, Av Joana Ângélica 148. *Casa Da Gamboa*, R da Gamboa, beautifully located in old colonial house overlooking the bay, good reputation, open Mon to Sat 1200-1500 and 1900-2300, not cheap. *Manjur*, R Banco dos Ingleses 20, Campo Grande, good, friendly, vegetarian dishes, 0900-1900, great view of bay. An excellent Japanese restaurant is *Gan*, Praça A Fernades 29, Garcia, intimate atmosphere, Tues-Sun 1900 till midnight, rec. The best churrascaria in Salvador is *Baby Beef*, Av AC Magalhães, Iguatemi, top class restaurant, excellent service, extremely popular, not expensive, highly rec, open daily 1200-1500 and 1900-2300.

At the bottom of the Lacerda Lift is Praça Cairu and the famous *Mercado Modelo*: on the upper floor of the market are two very good restaurants, *Camafeu De Oxossi* and *Maria De São Pedro*, both specializing in Bahian dishes, great atmosphere, good view of the port, daily 1130 till 2000, Sat lunchtime particularly busy. Opposite Mercado Modelo, the Paes Mendonça supermarket self-service counter is good value, 1100-1500, 1st floor. At the base of the Lift is *Cinquenta Saladas*, not only salads, very reasonable. On Av Contorno, *Solar Do Unhão*, beautiful manor house on the edge of the bay, lunch and dinner with best folklore show in town, expensive. *Juárez*, Mercado de Ouro, Comércio, good steaks, cheap, rec.

Barra section: *Xangai*, Av 7 de Setembro 1755 (Vitória), Chinese, reasonable; *Nan Hai*, No 3671, good Chinese, lunch and dinner (Porto da Barra); good cheap snacks at Goethe Institute and American Institute; *Tiffany's*, Barão do Sergy 156, 1900-2400, French, rec; on same street are *Alface e Cia*, wide range of salads and juices; *Via Brera* No 162, T 247-6973, upmarket Italian; *Unimar* supermarket, good cheap meals on 2nd floor.

Near the lighthouse at the mouth of the bay (Farol Da Barra area) there are a number of good fast food places: *Micheluccio*, Av Oceânica 10, good pizza, always busy, rec; next door is *Baitakão*, good hamburger and sandwiches. *Mon Filet*, R Afonso Celso 152, good steaks, pastas, open 1830 till midnight; on same street, *Pastaxuta*, pizza, pasta, reasonable prices, and a number of other good cheap restaurants, eg

Maná, opens 1100 till food runs out, different menu each day, closed sun, owner Frank speaks a little English; also *Luar da Barra*, No 447. Shopping Barra has good cheapish places to eat, *Pizza e Cia* on ground floor, good selection of fresh salads, also good pizzas, good value, rec; opp is *Perini*, great ice cream, chocolate, savouries and cakes; *Saúde Brasil*, on the top floor (L3), for very good wholefood snacks, cakes and a wide variety of juices, rec. The best Bahian restaurant in the area is *Frutos Do Mar*, R Marquês de Leão 415. A very good vegetarian restaurant is *Rama*, R Lord Cochrane, great value. *Don Vitalone*, D M Teixeira 27, nr lighthouse, off seafront, excellent Italian, open daily for lunch and evening meal, highly rec.

In Ondina: *Double Gula* in *Mar A Vista Hotel*, for excellent meat. Further along Av Oceânica towards the Rio Vermelho district is *Sukiyaki*, No 3562, excellent Japanese, open 1200-1500, 1900 till midnight, not cheap, rec. *Extudo*, Largo Mesquita 4, T 237-4669, good varied menu, lively bar at night, attracts interesting clientele, open 1200-0200, closed Mon, not expensive, rec. *Manjericão*, R Fonte do Boi (the street leading to *Meridien Hotel*), excellent wholefood menu, Mon-Sat 1100-1600, highly rec. *Philippe Camarao*, same street, bar and restaurant, specializes in shrimp dishes, expensive. *Marisco*, at Paciência Beach nearby, good seafood, 1100-1500, 1800-2100, good value.

There is an interesting fish market at Largo Da Mariquita with a number of stalls serving food from noon until the small hours, clean, good atmosphere, popular with locals. A good kiosk is *Riso e Nega* (kiosk with green tables), friendly, good basic food; nearby is *Brisa*, R Augusto Severo 4, Mon-Sat 1100-1500, excellent wholefood restaurant, small, simple, cheap, owner Nadia is very friendly.

Further along Avenida Oceânica at Jardim Armação: *Yemanjá*, 20 minute taxi ride from centre, excellent Bahian seafood, open daily from 1130 till late, very typical, always busy, reasonably priced, good atmosphere, highly rec. Nearby is *Tamboril*, busy seafood restaurant, 1200-1600 and 1900-2400. *Deutsches Haus*, Av Otávio Mangabeira 1221, good German cooking. Highly rec for Bahian cuisine is *Bargaço*, open daily 1200-1600 and 1900-2400, great selection of starters, oyster, lobster, fresh water shrimp, crab meat, etc, expensive but worth it.

A Porteira at Boca do Rio specialises in northeastern dishes inc *carne de sol*, 1200-1600 and 1800-2300, seafood dishes also served. *Casquinha De Siri* at Piatã beach, daily from 0900, live music every night, cover charge US$2, very popular. The beaches from Patamares to Itapoan are lined by *barracas*, thatched huts serving chilled drinks and freshly cooked seafood dishes, ideal for lunch and usually very cheap. Try *Ki-Muqueca*, Av Otávio Mangabeira 36 (Av Oceânica), for large helpings of excellent Bahian food in attractive surroundings. At Itapoan the road goes left towards the airport along Av Dorival Caymmi. *Restaurant Uauá*, Av Dorival Caymmi 46, open Thur to Sun. Fri and Sat are very busy with forró dancing till 0400.

● **Banks & money changers**

Don't change money on the street (see below) especially in the Upper City where higher rates are usually offered. Changing at banks can be bureaucratic and time-consuming. Banks are open 1000-1600. All major banks have exchange facilities but these are only available at selected branches. **Citibank**, R Miguel Calmon 555, Comércio, centre, good rates, will change large denomination TCs into smaller ones with a commission. **Lloyds Bank**, R Miguel Calmon 22, Comércio. **Banco Econômico**, R Miguel Calmon 285, Comércio is the American Express representative (also in Ondina, under *Ondina Apart Hotel*). Visa at **Banco do Brasil**, Av Estados Unidos 561, Comércio, in shopping centre opp Rodoviária (also a *câmbio* here), at the airport (open 0830-1530 and 1600-2100 Mon-Fri and 0900-1600 Sat, Sun and holidays); branches in Barra, R Miguel Bournier 4; in Shopping Barra and in Ondina. Mastercard at **Credicard**, 1st floor, Citibank building, R Miguel Calmon 555, Comércio. **Carlos**, Bazaar Colon, Praça Anchieta 17, in front of São Francisco church in the old city gives good rates, but doesn't always accept TCs (will require passport when he does). **Figueiredo**, opp *Grande Hotel da Barra* on Ladeira da Barra will exchange cash at good rates. If stuck, all the big hotels will exchange, but at poor rates. **Banespa**, Av dos Estados Unidos, changes TCs without commission.

● **Cultural centres**

British Club, Inglesa 20B, just off Campo Grande. **Cultura Inglesa**, R Plínio Moscoso 357, Jardim Apipema. **Associação Cultural Brasil-Estados Unidos**, Av 7 de Setembro 1883, has a library and reading room with recent US magazines, open to all, and at No 1809 on the same avenue is the German **Goethe Institut**, also with library and reading room.

● **Embassies & consulates**

British Vice-Consulate, Av Estados Unidos 4, Salas 1109/1113, Ed Visc de Cairu, Caixa Postal 38, Comércio, T 243-9222, Mon-Fri, 0800-1200, 1400-1730. **USA**, Av Antônio Carlos Magalhães, Ed Cidadella Center 1, Sala 410, Itaigara, T 358 9166, Mon-Fri, 1430-1630. **Germany**, R Lucaia 281, Rio Vermelho, T 247 7106, Mon-Fri 0900-1200. **Austria**, R Alm Marquês do Leão 46, Apto 33, Barra, T 247 6013, Mon,

Wed, Fri 1400-1700. **Belgium**, Centro Empresarial Iguatemi, Bloco B, Sala 809, Iguatemi, T 358 9542, Tues and Thur 1430-1800, Fri 0900-1200. **Denmark**, Av Sete de Setembro 3959, Barra, T 247 9667, Mon-Fri 0900-1200, 1400-1700. **Spain**, R Marechal Floriano 21, Canela, T 336 9055, Mon-Fri 0900-1300. **Finland**, C Portinari 19, Barra, T 247 3312, Mon-Fri 1000-1600, closes for lunch. **France**, Trav Francisco Gonçalves 1, Sala 805, Comércio, T 371-0410, Mon-Fri 0800-1130. **Holland**, R Lauro Miller 8, Sala 503, T 241 7645 Mon-Fri 0800-1130, 1400-1730. **Italy**, Av Sete de Setembro 1238, Mercês, T 321-8335, Mon, Wed, Fri, 0900-1100, 1500-1700. **Norway and Sweden**, R Quintino de Carvalho 153, Apto 601, Jardim Apipema, T 247 0528, Mon-Fri 0800-1200. **Portugal**, Praça Piedade, Gabinete Português de Leitura, T 241-1633, Mon-Fri 0800-1400. **Switzerland**, Av Tancredo Neves 3343, 5th floor, sala 507, T 371 5827.

● **Electric current**

110-220 AC, 60 cycles.

● **Entertainment**

Nightlife: in the historical centre, there is live music on the streets on Tues and Sun evening (especially the first and last Tues of the month) and Fri and Sat nights (particularly lively, especially in the summer months). *Pagôde*, a samba style from Rio, is played in the Pelourinho Square in front of the Casa de Jorge Amado. The main attraction is the rehearsal of the Olodum drummers on Tues; these are the most innovative of the carnival drumming groups and have attracted much attention after being featured on Paul Simon's 1990 album, *Rhythm of the Saints*. They rehearse in an open space known as the Quadra behind Teatro Antônio Miguel on R João de Jesus from 1900-2300, tickets on sale from 1700, US$4, buy tickets in advance from Casa do Olodum on R Gregório de Matos and go early. They also rehearse on Sun in Largo de Pelourinho from 1800-2300, but these rehearsals can be very crowded (at both, beware pickpockets and fights, police use tear gas to quell trouble). Other drumming groups, Levado do Pelô and Primeiro Odum de Dida (a drumming group of girls), play for free on Tues at the same time as Olodum in the Largo do Pelourinho. Ilê Ayê, plays every Sat from 2200 in Forte Santo Antônio de Carmo. It is recommended to get as close as the crowds permit by taxi at night.

Araketu, a fusion of samba and African rhythms, rehearses in R Chile on Fri night; very popular, US$12. Live jazz every Wed night in summer months at Praça Teresa Batista, behind the Sebrae building (entry free). A good bar on the square is *Oratório*. The *Cailleur Bar* across the street leads onto the Praça Pedro Arcanjo.

The best night here is Sat, when a local big band under the baton of the great local musician Fred Dantas plays to a packed square. Check with Bahiatursa for details on both squares.

Good bars are *Atelier Maria Adair* (see above), *Casa do Olodum*, *Estação Pelô* and *Bar Do Reggae* and *Alamabique Cachaçaria*, all on R João de Deus, the latter has a great selection of cachaças from all over Brazil, watch out for the steep stairs, especially after a few cachaças! Also good is *Café Impresso*, R João de Deus 3, interesting clientele, rec. Many bars on the Quadra 2M (see above), *Dom Crepe*, *Habeas Copos* are very busy. There is often live music in this square. *Cafelier*, R Inacio Acciolli 16 and *Bar Museum* next door, both good 'artcafés'. Good café and great chocolate at *Cailleur*, R Gregório de Matos 17, open daily 0930-2100, bar service continues till 0100. Popular disco is *Gueto*, R Alfredo Brito, plays techno mainly, but does vary.

Barra section: *Mordomia Drinks*, Ladeira Da Barra, enter through narrow entrance to open air bar with spectacular view of the bay, very popular. Most Barra nightlife happens at the Farol da Barra (lighthouse). R Marquês de Leão is very busy, with lots of bars with tables on the pavement: *Habeas Copos*, R Marquês de Leão 172, famous street side bar, very popular; also *Aladim*, *Bali*, *Ponte de Safena* and *Psicoanalista*, all busy. In the next street, R Afonso Celso, is *Casco Grosso*. *Barril 2000*, on Av Oceânica, is very busy, with live music (MPB – popular Brazilian music) at weekends; *Barra Vento 600*, popular open air bar on the beach front.

Further along the coast at Ondina is the *Bahia Othon Palace Hotel* with a good disco called *Hippotamus*, busy at weekends. In **Rio Vermelho** district are *Rio de Janeiro Bar*, Largo Mesquita, small bar attracting bohemian clientele, few tables, most people drink in the street, Thur-Sat, 1900-0300. *Vía Brasil*, rooftop bar in *Bahia*

Park Hotel, Largo da Mariquita, open Wed-Sun 2130-0300, live music, cover charge. In same square, *Bar Canoa* at the *Meridien Hotel* has live music every night, jazz, popular Brazilian music, cover charge US$6, 2100 till 0100. Dancing at *Carinhoso*, Av Otávio Mangabeira, T 248-9575; *Champagne* at *Salvador Praia Hotel*, T 245-5033; *New Fred's*, Av Visc de Itaboraí 125, T 248-4399 (middle-aged market, singles bar). *Bell's Beach* disco at Boca Do Rio, open Tues to Sat 2200-0400, up-market, expensive; *Concha Acústica*, Ladeira da Fonte (behind Teatro Castro Alves, Campo Grande), concerts every weekend with best Brazilian musicians, Rock, MPB, mainly during summer months, usually very cheap, open air, good venue.

Theatres: *Castro Alves*, at Campo Grande (Largo Dois de Julho), frequent concerts; *Teatro da Gamboa*; *Teatro Vila Velha*; *Senac*; *Instituto Cultural Brasil-Alemanha* (ICBA); *Teatro Santo Antônio*, part of the Escola de Teatro da Universidade Federal da Bahia; *Teatro de Arena*.

● **Hospitals & medical services**

Clinic: Barão de Loreto 21, Graça. *Dr Argemiro Júnior* speaks English and Spanish. First consultation US$40, second free. *Dr Manoel Nogueira* (from 1000-1200), Av Joana Angélica 6, T 241-2377, English-speaking.

Doctors: German-speaking doctor, *Dr Josef Stangl*, R Conselheiro Pedro Luiz 179, Rio Vermelho, T 237-1073.

Medical: yellow fever vaccinations free at Delegação Federal de Saúde, R Padre Feijó, Canela. Ensure that a new needle is used. Israeli travellers needing medical (or other) advice should contact *Sr Marcus* (T 247-5769), who speaks Hebrew.

● **Language classes**
Casa do Brasil, R Milton de Oliveira 231, Barra, T 245-5866.

● **Laundry**

Lavandería Lavalimpo, R do Pilar 31, Comércio, Mon-Sat 0800-1800. *Lavandería Comficha*, Av Doutora Praquer Fries, Porto da Barra, automatic, reasonable.

● **Post & telecommunications**

Post Office: main post office and poste restante is in Praça Inglaterra, in the Lower City, open Mon-Fri 0800-1700, Sat 0800-1200. Other offices at Praça da Sé in Ed Associação Bahiana de Imprensa on R Guedes de Brito 1, T 240-6222; R Alfredo Brito 43, Mon-Sat 0800-1700, Sun 0800-1200, has philatelic section; Rodoviária, Mon-Sat 0800-1800 (till 1200 on Sun); airport; Barra and Iguatemi Shopping Malls (Mon-Fri); Av Princesa Isabel, Barra, and R Marquês de Caravelas; in Ondina by the hotels there is a booth by the beach next to *Ondina Apart Hotel*.

Telecommunications: Embratel, R do Carro 120. Telebahia has branches at Campo da Pólvora, on R Hugo Baltazar Silva (open 0700-2200 daily), Barra and Iguatemi Shopping Centres (Mon-Fri 1000-2200 and Sat 0900-2000), airport (daily 0700-2200) and rodoviária (Mon-Sat 24 hrs and Sun 0700-2200).

● **Security**

Be very careful of your money and valuables at all times and in all districts. Avoid the more distant beaches out of season, when they are empty (eg Itapoan, Piatã, Placafor); on Sun they are more crowded and safer. At night, the area around and in the lifts and buses are unsafe. On no account change money on the streets; this is a guaranteed way to be robbed. Leave valuables securely in your hotel (inc wristwatch and cameras if possible: disposable cameras are widely available), particularly at night. Carry a small amount of money that you can hand over if you are threatened. One is warned not to walk down any of the links between the old and new city, especially the Ladeira de Misericôrdia, which links the Belvedere, near the Lacerda lifts, with the lower city. The promenade behind the Barra lighthouse can be dangerous at night. Should a local join you at your table for a chat, leave at once if drugs are mentioned. The civil police are reported to be very sympathetic and helpful and more resources have been put into policing the old part of the city, which is now well-lit at night. Police are little in evidence after 2300, however.

● **Shopping**

H Stern jewellers at *Hotels Meridien*, *Othon* and *Bahia*, also at Barra and Iguatemi Shopping centres. The Barra and Iguatemi shopping centres are big, modern and a/c with big department stores. Quality *artesanato* at the 3 official FIEB-SESI shops: Av Tiradentes 299 (Bonfim); Av Borges dos Reis 9 (Rio Vermelho); Av 7 de Setembro 261 (Mercês).

Shopping in Pelourinho: the major carnaval *afro blocos* have boutiques selling tee-shirts etc. *Boutique Olodum*, on Praça José Alencar, *Ilê Aiyê*, on R Fransisco Muniz Barreto 16 and *Muzenza* next door. On the same street is *Modaxé*, a retail outlet for clothes manufactured by street children under the auspices of the Projeto Axé, expensive but these are the trendiest T-shirts in town. Also on this street at No 18 is *Brazilian Sound*, latest in Brazilian and Bahia music, CDs mainly. Another good record store is *Mini Som* in nearby Praça da Sé, wide collection in a very small store, has a good collection of older recordings upstairs (watch the steep steps); more than willing to let you hear the records before buying.

Instituto Mauá, R Gregorio de Matos 27 (T 321 5638), open Tues-Sat 0900-1800, Sun 1000-1600, good quality Bahian handicrafts at fair prices, better value and better quality for traditional crafts than the Mercado Modelo. A similar store is *Loja de Artesanato do SESC*, Largo Pelourinho (T 321 5502), Mon-Fri 0900-1800 (closed for lunch), Sat 0900-1300.

Trustworthy, reliable jewellery stores are *Lasbonfim* (T 242 9854) and *Simon* (T 242 5218), both in the Terreiro de Jesus. They both have branches in the nearby Carmo district. Excellent hand-made lace products at *Artesanato Santa Barbara*, R Alfredo Brito 7. For local art the best stores are *Atelier Portal da Cor*, Ladeira do Carmo 31 (T 242 9466), run by a cooperative of local artists, Totonho, Calixto, Raimundo Santos, Jô, good prices, rec. Also across the street at *Casa do Indio*, Indian artefacts and art, restaurant and bar open here till late, good surroundings. Also good *naif* art at *Koisa Nossa* on R Alfredo Brito 45. Good wood carvings next door by a cooperative of sculptors, Palito and Negão Barão being the most famous. Hand-made traditional percussion instruments (and percussion lessons) at *Chez Lua*, Alfredo Brito 27, made by percussionist Dilson Lua. Also percussion lessons at *Oficina de Investigação Musical*, Alfredo Brito 24 (T 321 0339), Mon to Fri, 0800-1200 and 1300-1600. *Shopping do Pelô*, R Francisco Muniz 02 (T 321 4200), is run by SEBRAE, the Brazilian small business authority, open daily until 1800, stalls with varied goods, clothes, jewellery etc.

Bookshops: *Livraria Brandão*, R Ruy Barbosa 104, Centre, T 243 5383, secondhand English, French, Spanish and German books. *Livraria Civilizaçao Brasileira*, Av 7 de Setembro 912, Mercês, and in the Barra, Iguatemi and *Ondina Apart Hotel* shopping centres have some English books; also *Graúna*, Av 7 de Setembro 1448, and R Barão de Itapoan 175, Porto da Barra, many English titles; *Livraria Planeta*, Carlos Gomes 42, loja 1, sells used English books. The bookshop at the airport has English books and magazines.

Markets: the **Mercado Modelo**, at Praça Cairu, lower city, offers many tourist items such as wood carvings, silver-plated fruit, leather goods, local musical instruments. Lace items for sale are often not handmade (despite labels), are heavily marked up, and are much better bought at their place of origin (eg Ilha de Maré, Pontal da Barra and Marechal Deodoro, see page 536). Cosme e Damião, musical instrument sellers on 1st floor, has been rec, especially if you want to play the instruments. Bands and dancing, especially Sat (but very much for money from tourists taking photographs), closed at 1200 Sun. Photograph exhibition of the old market in basement. (Many items are often cheaper on the Praça da Sé.) Largest and most authentic market is the **Feira de São Joaquim**, 5 km from Mercado Modelo along sea front: barkers, trucks, *burros*, horses, boats, people, mud, all very smelly, every day (Sun till 1200 only), busiest on Sat morning; interesting African-style pottery and basketwork; very cheap. (Car ferry terminal for Itaparica is nearby.) **Iguatemi Shopping Centre** sells good handicraft items, it is run by the government so prices are fixed and reasonable; similarly at Instituto Mauá, Porto da Barra. Every Wed from 1700-2100 there is a **handicrafts fair** in the 17th century fort of Santa Maria at the opp end of Porto da Barra beach. On Fri from 1700-2100, there is an open air market of handicrafts and Bahian food in **Porto da Barra**, a popular event among the local young people. Daily market of handicrafts in Terreiro de Jesus in the old city from 1100-1800. Mosquito nets from *Casa dos Mosquiteiros*, R Pedro Sá 6F, Calçada, T 226 0715.

Photography and repairs: *Pepe*, R da Ajuda, ed Triúnfo, 1st floor, Centre. *Maxicolor*, R Estados Unidos (Mercado Modelo), for cut-price developing. *Fotocolor*, R da Misericórdia 3, rec place for slide film. *Gil Filmes*, R da Misericórdia 5, rec for Fujichrome and Ektachrome (well priced).

Videotapes: *HAL Video Produçoes*, R da Paz, 1 (nr Largo da Graça), T 235-7946, copies produced for US$15/tape or US$20 inc new tape, transcodificação (Brazilian NTSC – European PAL system) US$25; *Videovic*, Vitória-Centre, Av Centenário 2883, opp Shopping Barra, copying and transcodificação US$28-35.

● **Tour companies & travel agents**
Bus tours are available from several companies: *LR Turismo*, *Itaparica Turismo*, *Bahia Tours* and *Alameda Turismo*: city tour (US$25 pp), Bahia by Night includes transport to *Moenda* restaurant, show and dinner (US$45 pp). All day boat trip on

Bahia de Todos Os Santos from 0800-1700 inc visit to Ilha dos Frades, lunch on Itaparica (US$10 extra) US$35 pp. *Tatur Turismo*, Av Antônio Carlos Magalhães 2573, Ed Royal Trade, Sala 1308, Salvador 40280-200, T 358-7216, F 351-7216, run by an Irishman, specializes in Bahia, gives private guided tours and can make any necessary travel, hotel and accommodation arrangements, rec. They are represented in the USA by Brazil Nuts, 1150 Post Rd, Fairfield, CT 06430, T (203) 259-7900, F 259-3177. *Submariner*, R de Paciência 223, Rio Vermelho, T 237-4097, hire diving equipment, friendly. *Kontik-Franstur Viagens e Turismo Ltda*, R da Argentia 1, Terreo Comércio, POB 973, T 242-0433. *Turitravel*, Av Centenário 2883, Ed Vitória Center, Sala 1106, T 245 9345 or 237 4596, helpful, English spoken.

● **Tourist offices**
(With lists of hotels and accommodation in private homes) **Bahiatursa**, Palácio Rio Branco (see above), R Chile on Praça Municipal, open 0800-1830, Mon-Fri, English and German spoken, helpful. Visitors can obtain weekly list of events and itineraries (on foot or by car) planned by the city, well worth doing. Map, US$2, good; offices have noticeboard for messages. Also at R Francisco Muniz Barreto 12, Historical Centre, T 321 2463, open daily 0830-1930; at rodoviária (good, English spoken); airport (T 204-1244, open daily 0800-2000), friendly (but inefficient); in the Mercado Modelo (T 241-0242, Mon-Fri 0800-1800, Sat 0800-1200); Porto da Barra (T 247-3195, Mon-Fri, 0800-1800, Sat-Sun 0800-1200). Also details of travel throughout State of Bahia. Phone 131 0600-0030 for tourist information in English. **Emtursa**, at airport, T 377 2262, Mon-Sat 0800-2200, has good maps. **Maps** from Departamento de Geografia e Estatística, Av Estados Unidos (opp Banco do Brasil, lower city): also from newsstands inc airport bookshop, US$1.50.

● **Useful addresses**
Immigration: (for extensions of entry permits), Polícia Federal, Av O Pontes 339, Aterro de Água de Meninos, Lower City, T 321-6363, open 1000-1600. Show an outward ticket or sufficient funds for stay, visa extension US$11.

Tourist Police: R Gregório de Matos 16.

● **Transport**
Local Bus: local buses US$0.35, *frescões* (or *executivos*) US$1.60. On buses and at the ticket-sellers' booths, watch your change and beware pickpockets. To get from the old city to the ocean beaches, take a 'Barra' bus from Praça da Sé to the Barra point and walk to the nearer ones; the Aeroporto *frescão* (last 2130) leaves Praça da Sé, passing Barra, Ondina, Rio Vermelho, Amaralina, Pituba, Costa Azul, Armação, Boca do Rio, Jaguaripe, Patamares, Piatã and Itapoan,

before turning inland to the airport. The glass-sided Jardineira bus goes to Flamengo beach (30 km from the city) following the coastal route; it passes all the best beaches; sit on right hand side for best views. It leaves from the Praça da Sé daily 0730-1930, every 40 mins, US$1.50. For beaches beyond Itapoan, take the frescão to Stella Maris and Flamengo beaches. These follow the same route as the Jardineira. During Carnival, when most streets are closed, buses leave from Vale do Canela (O Vale), nr Campo Grande. **Car rental**: Avis, Av Sete de Setembro 1796, T 237-0155, also at airport, T 377-2276 (toll free 0800-118066); **Budget**, Av Presidente Vargas 409, T 237-3396; **Hertz**, R Baependi, T 245-8364, **Unidas**, Av Oceânica 2456, Ondina, T 336 0717. If renting a car check whether credit card or cash is cheapest. National Car Rentals allow decision at the end of the rental. **Hitchhiking**: out of Salvador, take a 'Cidade Industrial' bus from the rodoviária at the port; it goes on to the highway. **Taxi**: Taxi meters start at US$0.60 for the 'flagdown' and US$0.15/100m. They charge US$15/hr within city limits, and 'agreed' rates outside. Taxi Barra-Centro US$3 daytime; US$4 at night. Watch the meter, especially at night; the night-time charge should be 30% higher than daytime charges. Teletaxi (24-hr service), 321-9988.

Air Daily flights to all the main cities. Nordeste Regional Airlines, Av Dom João VI 259, Brotas T 244 3355 has daily flights to Porto Seguro and several flights a week to destinations in the interior of Bahia. Dois de Julho Airport is 32 km from city centre. Buses from airport to Centre Aeroporto-Campo Grande US$0.35, at least 1 hr. Special *Executivo* bus Aeroporto-Praça da Sé along the coast road for hotels, US$1.30. Special taxi (buy ticket at airport desk) US$30; taxis airport to city are controlled by certain drivers. From the city to airport is less restricted, but still can be expensive.

Trains See **Excursions**, above.

Buses Rodoviária is 5 km from city with regular services to centre (US$0.30); bus RI or RII, 'Centro-Rodoviária-Circular'; in centre, get on in lower city at foot of Lacerda lift; buses also to Campo Grande; journey can take up to 1 hr especially in peak periods. Executive bus, quicker, from Praça da Inglaterra (in front of MacDonalds), Comércio, runs to Iguatemi Shopping Centre, weekdays only, from where there is a walkway to the rodoviária (take care in the dark, or a taxi, US$10). To **Recife**, US$25 (*leito*, 47), 13 hrs, 4 a day and 1 *leito*, Itapemirim, T 388-0037, all at night; plenty to **Rio** (28 hrs, US$50, *leito* 115, Itapimirim, good stops, clean toilets, rec), **São Paulo** (30 hrs), US$58, *leito* US$116 (0815 with Viação Nacional, 2 in pm

with São Geraldo, T 533-0188), to **Fortaleza** 19 hrs, US$44 at 0900 with Itapemerim; **Ilhéus** 7 hrs, Aguia Branca, T 533-1515, *comercia* US$14, *expresso* US$17, *executivo* US$19, *leito* US$28, several; **Belo Horizonte**, Gontijo T 358-7448, at 1700, US$40, São Geraldo at 1800 US$39. **Foz do Iguaçu**, 52 hrs, US$65. There are daily bus services to **Brasília** along the fully paved BR-242, via Barreiras, 3 daily, 23 hrs Paraíso, T 358-1591, US$45. Frequent services to the majority of destinations; a large panel in the main hall of the terminal lists destinations and the relevant ticket office.

ROUTES To Rio can do the trip on the BR-116 highway in 3 days, stopping at **Vitória da Conquista** (524 km from Salvador), a busy town with large market Mon-Sat, and a man-made lake with fountains and waterfalls: **C** *Hotel Livramento*, Praça Barão do Rio Branco, T 424-1906, with restaurant, and **F** *Tel-Aviv Palace*, good breakfast, one block from final stop of urban bus from rodoviária; also Camping Clube do Brasil site at Km 831 (bus to Salvador, 8 hrs, US$10; to Lençóis – change at Bominal – 8 hrs); Teófilo Otôni, 946 km, or Governador Valadares, 1,055 km (see page 439), and Leopoldina (1,402 km). Fairly good hotels are also available in **Jequié** (*Itajubá*, *Rex*, and motels), and basic ones in Milagres. Stopovers on the BR-101 coastal road can be made at Vitória and Itabuna (or Ilhéus), and there are many other towns on or near the coast.

ISLANDS IN THE BAY

From Ribeira (see **Excursions**) a small boat goes 25 km to **Ilha da Maré** between 0900 and 1100, connecting the island's villages of Itamoaba, Praia Grande and Santana (US$1); boat returns next day from Santana at 0400-0500. Santana is a centre for lace making, Praia Grande for basket-weaving. None of the villages has a hotel, but there are restaurants and bars and camping is possible. From São Tomé de Paripe, near the naval base at Aratu, irregular boats go to **Ilha dos Frades**, sparsely populated, no electricity, one *pousada* (**C** *Ponta de Nossa Senhora de Guadalupe*, beachfront, T Salvador 245-8536). The beach is busy lunchtimes with excursions from Salvador, but otherwise is quiet, good snorkelling.

ITAPARICA

Across the bay from Salvador lies the island of **Itaparica**, 29 km long and 12 km wide. The town of Itaparica is very picturesque, with a fair beach in the town, and well worth a visit. Take a bus or kombi by the coast road (Beira Mar) which passes through the villages of Manguinhos, Amoureiras and Ponta de Areia. The beach at Ponta de Areia is one of the best on the island and is very popular. There are many *barracas* on the beach, the best and busiest is *Barraca Pai Xango*, always very lively.

In Itaparica there are many fine residential buildings from the 19th century, plus the church of São Lourenço, one of the oldest in Brazil, a delightful walk through the old town. During the summer months the streets are ablaze with the blossoms of the beautiful flamboyant trees. The beaches at Mar Grande are fair but can be dirty at times. There are many *pousadas* in Mar Grande and the nearby beaches of Ilhota and Gamboa (both to the left as you disembark from the ferry).

From Bom Despacho there are many buses to other towns such as Nazaré das Farinhas, Valença (see below) and also **Jaguaribe**, a small, picturesque colonial port. Both of these towns are on the mainland connected by a bridge on the SW side of the island, turn off between Mar Grande and Cacha Pregos (bus company is Viazul). There are good beaches across the bay on the mainland, but a boat is needed to reach these (US$8.25).

Local information
● Accommodation

A good simple *pousada* at Amoureiras is **C** *Pousada Pé na Praia*, good breakfast, good sized rooms, English and French spoken (T 831 1389).

There is a popular **Club Med** on the island (Fazenda Boca do Rio, 44470 Vera Cruz, Bahia, T 071-833-1141, F 071-241-0100). There are few *pousadas* in the town. The best is **L3** *Quinta Pitanga* (T 831 1554), beautifully decorated by the owner Jim Valkus, 3 suites and 2 singles, beachfront property, a retreat, excellent restaurant, expensive but highly rec, accepts day visitors. **A1** *Grande Hotel da Itaparica* (Av Beira Mar, T 831 1120); **C** *Pousada Santa Rita*, and **E** *Restaurant/Pousada Cantinha da Ilha*;

C *Pousada Icarai*, charming, good location.

In Mar Grande: A3 *Pousada Arco Iris*, Estrada da Gamboa 102, T 833 1130, magnificent building and setting in mango orchard, expensive, good if slow restaurant, *Manga Rosa*, rec. They have camping facilities next door, shady, not always clean. **C** *Pousada Estrela do Mar*, Av NS das Candeias 170 (T 833 1108), good rooms, fan or a/c, rec. **E** *Pousada Samambaia*, same street, No 61, good breakfast, French spoken, rec. **C** *Lagoa e Mar*, R Parque das Dunas, 01-40, T/F 823-1573, very good breakfast, spacious bungalows, swimming pool, 200m to beach, restaurant, helpful, highly rec; **C** *Pousada Scórpio*, R Aquárius, T 823-1036, breakfast, beach, swimming pool, simple rooms, weekend restaurant, rec; **C** *Água no Toco*, Av Atlántica, T 823-1190, 20m to beach, restaurant, weekend busy, rec; **C** *Pousada Sonho do Verão*, R São Bento 2, opp *Pousada Arco Iris*, chalets and apartments, cooking facilities, French and English spoken, T 833 1616. Like other *pousadas* they rent bicycles (US$3/hr); they also rent horses (US$5/hr). Near the church in the main square is the **C** *Pousada Casarão da Ilha*, T 833 1106, spacious rooms with a great view of Salvador across the bay, swimming pool, a/c, rec.

At Gamboa B *Hotel Pousada Ponta Caieira* (T 833 1080), beachfront, take bus to Gamboa and it's a 5-min walk to the *pousada*, quiet.

At Aratuba there is an excellent hostel, *Albergue da Juventude*, F (for students) – E, on the beach, shady, rec.

At Cacha Pregos: *Club Sonho Nosso*, T 837 1040 or 226 1933, very clean huts on clean beach, good service, collect you from anywhere on the island – also Bom Despacho Kombis stop in front of entrance, 5-min walk, rec; **D** *Pousada Cacha Pregos*, next to the supermarket, with fan, bath, no breakfast, good, T 839 1594. Also **C** *Pousada Babalú*, T 837-1193, spacious bungalows, frigobar, fan, good breakfast, rec.

● Places to eat

Good restaurants in Mar Grande are *Philippe's Bar and restaurant*, Largo de São Bento, French and local cuisine, information in English and French. *O Pacífico* is peaceful. *Restaurant Rafael* in main square for pizzas and snacks. Also pizzas at *Bem Me Quer*, opp *Pousada Samambaia* down alley. There are many Baianas selling *acarajé* in the late afternoon and early evening in the main square by the pier.

● Transport

Ferry The island is reached from the main land by two ferries. The main passenger ferry leaves for Bom Despacho from São Joaquim (buses for Calçada, Ribeira stop across the road from the ferry terminal; the 'Sabino Silva – Ribeira' bus passes in front of the Shopping Barra). The first ferry from Salvador leaves at 0600 and, depending on demand, the ferries leave at intervals of 45 mins. Last ferry from Salvador is at 2230. Returning to Salvador the first ferry is at 0515 and the last one is at 2230. During the summer months the ferries are much more frequent. Enquiries at the Companhia de Navegação Bahiana (CNB), T 321 7100 from 0800 to 1700. One way ticket for foot passengers Mon-Fri US$0.80, Sat-Sun US$1.20.

Mar Grande can be reached by a smaller ferry (Lancha) from the Terminal Marítimo in front of the Mercado Modelo in Salvador. The ferries leave every 45 mins and the crossing takes 50 mins, US$0.45.

Road From Bom Despacho there are many buses, kombis and taxis to all parts of the island. The best beaches are at Ponta de Areia, Mar Grande (US$0.50 by kombi), Berlinque, Aratuba and Cacha Pregos. Kombi and taxis can be rented for trips around the island but be prepared to bargain, US$20-30 for a half-day tour.

Tours of the Bay

Small boats for trips around the bay can be hired privately at the small port by the Mercado Modelo called Rampa do Mercado. A pleasant trip out to the mouth of the bay should take 1½ hrs as you sail along the bottom of the cliff. When arranging to hire any boat ensure that the boat is licensed by the Port Authority (Capitânia dos Portos) and that life-jackets are on board. The Companhia de Navegação Bahiana (T 321 7100) sails 5 times a week to **Maragojipe** on the Rio Paraguaçu to the W (see under **The Recôncavo** below). The trip takes 3 hrs. It sails across the bay and then up the valley of the river. There are some very beautiful views along the trip. The ship makes two stops along the way, at Barra do Paraguaçu and at Mutuca where locals row out to the ship in dug outs to disembark passengers. A good trip would be to continue to Cachoeira by bus from Maragogipe and return to Salvador the following day. Departure from Salvador from Terminal Turístico in front of the Mercado Modelo Mon-Thur 1430 (1530 in summer). Fri departure is at 1130. Departure Maragogipe Mon-Thur 0500 and Fri 0830, US$3.

American yachtsman Steve Lafferty is highly rec for enjoyable sailing trips, US$120 a day for up to 4 people: R do Sodré 45, apt 301, T 241-0994.

NAZARE DAS FARINHAS

(*Pop* 25,940) 60 km inland from Itaparica, and reached over a bridge by bus from **Bom Despacho**. This 18th-century town is celebrated for its market, which specializes in the local ceramic figures, or *caxixis*. There is a large market in Holy Week, particularly on Holy Thursday and Good Friday. 12 km from Nazaré (taxi US$5.50, also buses) is the village of **Maragojipinha**, which specializes in making the ceramic figures. Bus from Salvador, 1530, takes 5 hrs.

FEIRA DE SANTANA

(*Pop* 405,690) 112 km NW of Salvador on both the coastal BR-101 and the inland BR-116 roads to Rio, the centre of a great cattle breeding and trading area; its Mon market, known as Feira do Couro (leather fair), said to be the largest in Brazil, attracts great crowds to its colourful display of local products. The permanent Artesanato market in the centre has a bigger selection, including leather, than the Mon market. Bus every 30 mins from Salvador, 2 hrs, US$3. (Rodoviária has a wall of painted tiles made by Udo-Ceramista, whose workshop is Brotas, Av Dom João VI 411, Salvador.)

● **Accommodation A1** *Luxor*, BR-116 Sul, Km 437, T 221-5922; **C** *Flecha*, about 20 km away at Km 171 BR-101, T 221-5999; several cheap ones in Praça da Matriz and nr the rodoviária, which is quite nr the centre; **C** *Senador*, R Senador Quintino 10, rec, Bahian restaurant in same street, No 259, *Panela de Barro*, good.

THE RECÔNCAVO

The area around Salvador, known as the Recôncavo Baiano, was one of the chief centres of sugar and tobacco cultivation in the 16th century.

Leaving Salvador on the Feira road, at Km 33 one forks left on the BR-324 to the **Museu do Recôncavo Vanderlei de Pinho** (see page 503). Further W, round the bay, is **São Francisco do Conde**, 54 km from Salvador, with a church and convent of 1636 and the ruins of Don Pedro II's agricultural school, said to be the first in Latin America.

At 60 km from Salvador the BA-026 road branches off the BR-324 to Santo Amaro, Cachoeira and São Félix.

SANTO AMARO DA PURIFICAÇÃO

73 km from Salvador is **Santo Amaro da Purificação** (*pop* 54,145) an old sugar centre sadly decaying, noted for its churches (often closed because of robberies), municipal palace (1769), fine main square, house of the poet and singer Caetano Veloso and ruined mansions including Araújo Pinto, former residence of the Barão de Cotegipe. Other attractions include the splendid beaches of the bay, the falls of Vitória and the grotto of Bom Jesus dos Pobres. Festivals in Jan and Feb (Santo Amaro and NS da Purificação) are interesting. Craftwork is sold on the town's main bridge. No good hotels or restaurants.

3 km beyond Santo Amaro on BR-420, turn right onto BA-878 for **Bom Jesus dos Pobres**, a small, traditional fishing village with a 300-year history. One good hotel: **B** *Água Viva*, T (075) 696 1178, reservations (Salvador 071) 359 1132, beach front, chalets or apartments, a/c or fan, good breakfast and restaurant, on one of the oldest farms in the region, good beach, rec. Bus from Salvador rodoviária 4 a day (Camurjipe), US$3.75.

CACHOEIRA AND SÃO FÉLIX

At 54 km from Santo Amaro, and only 4 km from the BR-101 coastal road, are the twin towns of **Cachoeira** (Bahia's 'Ouro Preto', *pop* 28,255), and **São Félix** (*pop* 12,095) on either side of the Rio Paraguaçu below the Cachoeira dam. Cachoeira, recently declared a national monument, was twice capital of Bahia: once in 1624-5 during the Dutch invasion, and once in 1822-3 while Salvador was still held by the Portuguese. It was the birthplace of Ana Néri, known as 'Mother of the Brazilians', who organized nursing services during the Paraguayan War (1865-70). There are beautiful views from above São Félix.

Places of interest Cachoeira's main buildings are the **Casa da Câmara e Cadeia** (1698-1712), the **Santa Casa de Misericórdia** (1734 – the hospital, someone may let you see the church), the 16th-century **Ajuda** chapel (now containing a fine collection of vestments), and the Convent of the **Ordem Terceira do Carmo**, whose church has a heavily gilded interior. Other churches: the **Matriz** with 5m-high *azulejos*, and **Nossa Senhora da Conceição do Monte**. Beautiful lace cloths on church altars. All churches are either restored or in the process of restoration. Tourist office in the Casa de Ana Néri. Craftwork in ceramics and wood readily available. The Danneman cigar factory can be visited to see hand-rolling in progress.

Excursions 6 km from Cachoeira, on the higher ground of the Planalto Baiano, is the small town of Belém (turning 2½ km on road to Santo Amaro). Church and seminary of Carmo. It is a healthy spot where people from Salvador have summer homes.

Maragojipe (*pop* 38,800) a tobacco exporting port 22 km SE of Cachoeira along a dirt road (BA-123), can also be reached by boat from Salvador. See the old houses and the church of São Bartolomeu, with its museum. The main festival is São Bartolomeu, in August. Good ceramic craftwork.

The tobacco centre of Cruz das Almas can also be visited, although transport is poor.

Local festivals São João (24 June) 'Carnival of the Interior' celebrations inc dangerous games with fireworks, well-attended by tourists; Boa Morte (early Aug); a famous *candomblé* ceremony at the Fonte de Santa Bárbara on 4 December.

● **Accommodation In Cachoeira: B** *Pousada do Convento de Cachoeira* (run by Bahiatursa), T 725-1716, in newly restored 16th-century convent, good restaurant; *Pousada do Guerreiro*, 13 de Maio 14, T 724-1203, no restaurant; **E** *Santo Antônio*, nr the rodoviária, basic, safe, laundry facilities, rec; **E** *Colombo*, nr the river, basic, meals available, rec. *Youth Hostel*, Av Parnamirim 417, T 268-4844/3390.

● **Places to eat** *Cabana do Pai Thomaz*, 25 de Junho 12, excellent Bahian food, good value, also an hotel, **D** with private bath and breakfast;

Recanto de Oxum, nearby, *Gruta Azul*, Praça Manoel Vitorino, lunch only; *Do Nair*, R 13 de Maio, delicious food and sometimes Seresta music. **São Félix**: *Xang-hai*, F, good, cheap food, warmly rec. Try the local dish, *maniçoba* (meat, manioc and peppers).

- **Transport** Buses from Salvador (Camurjipe) every hour or so; Feira Santana 2 hrs US$1.70.

INLAND FROM SALVADOR

ROUTES   Motorists to Brasília can save a little time by taking the ferry to Itaparica, book in advance to avoid long queues, and then going across country to Itaberaba for the BR-242 highway. The journey can be broken at Itaberaba, Lençóis (see below), or Ibotirama on the Rio São Francisco; at Barreiras on the Rio Grande, where buses stop for 2-3 hrs; or at Posse or Alvorada do Norte (Goiás). All have hotels of varying quality. The road is paved from Salvador to Brasília, but it is reported poor between Salvador and Lençóis and full of potholes between Barreiras and Alvorada do Norte.

LENÇOIS

400 km W of Salvador on the BR-242 is **Lençois** (*pop* 7,590; *DDD* code 075), a historical monument and a colonial gem, founded in 1844 because of diamonds in the region. There are still some *garimpeiros*. In the town, *Artesanato Areias Coloridas*, R das Pedras, owned by Tourino, is the best place for local sand paintings made in bottles. These are inexpensive and fascinating to see being done. They will make one as you wait. For ceramic work, the best is *Jota*, who has a workshop which can be visited. Take the steps to the left of the school near the *Pousada Lençóis*. His work is very original, rec. Mon am market is rec. It is difficult to change money in Lençóis.

Local information
● Accommodation
A3 *Pousada de Lençóis*, T 334-1102, with breakfast, swimming pool, rec.

B *Canto de Águas*, Av Senhor dos Passos s/n, T 334-1154, F 334-1188, comfortable, good location, swimming pool, a/c or fan, good service, rec; **B** *Estalagem Alcino e Silvinha*, R Gen Vieira de Morais 139, T 334-1171, **D** pp shared bath, beautiful, restored 19th-century house, superb breakfast, highly rec; **B** Zé Carlos and

Lia Vieira de Moraes have 2 excellent chalets in their huge garden at the entrance to the town, R Gen Viveiros 187, T 334 1151, English spoken, good breakfast (he is a keen birdwatcher and an authority on the region, she makes excellent jams).

C *Pousada do Parque*, BR-242, T 334-1173, quiet, by first bridge before town; **C** *Pousada Village Lapão*, nearby, chalets of various size, quiet, T 334-1117.

D *Pousada dos Duendes*, R do Pires s/n, T/F 334 1229, shared bath, with breakfast, run by Olivia Taylor, Englishwoman who can arrange tours and treks from 1 to 11 days and more; **D** *Pousalegre*, R Boa Vista 95, T 334-1124, with good regional breakfast, safe, hot showers, good vegetarian restaurant; **D** *Reposada*, R Boa Vista, next door, good breakfast, safe, rec; **D** *Tradição*, R José Florêncio, T 334-1120, breakfast, fridge, mosquito net, pleasant.

E *Bicho de Mata*, contact in Salvador 240-4337, Alto da Estrele s/n (nr Zion Reggae Bar), quiet, relaxed, good breakfast, highly rec; **E** *Casa de Hélia*, R das Pedras 102, t 334 1143, English and some Hebrew spoken, good facilities, renowned breakfast, rec.

Two campsites, one 2 km before Lençóis, one in the town centre (friendly, rec). There are also houses to rent in the town. Most of these are basic, with cooking and washing facilities. Juanita in R do Rosário rents rooms with access to washing and cooking facilities, US$3.50 pp. Isabel rents a house on the main square in front of the Correios, US$4 pp without breakfast.

● Places to eat
Lajedo, good food with good view of town, popular meeting place at night; *Goody*, R da Rodaviária s/n, good simple cooking, reasonably priced. A busy local bar is *Ynave*, with live music on weekends. The busiest spot at weekends is *Amigo da Onça*, R José Florêncio, nr municipal market, lambada, forró and samba-reggae until the small hours, good fun.

● Post & telecommunications
Communications: Telebahia, open daily 0800-2200.

● Tour companies & travel agents
Reliable tour company: *Pé de Trilha Turismo Aventura*, Praça Horácio de Matos s/n, T/F 334-1124, nr Banco do Brasil, guiding, trekking, rents camping equipment, etc, can make reservations for most of the *pousadas* in the Chapada Diamantina (see below), represented in Salvador by Tatur Turismo (071-358-7216, F 071-351-7216). A reliable guide is Edmilson (known locally as Mil), who can be found at Sectur; he knows the region extremely well and is very knowledgeable. Roy Funch, the ex-director of

the Chapada Diamantina National Park, is an excellent guide and can be found at his craft shop, *Funkart*, in the main square. Another rec guide to Chapada Diamantina is João (contact at *Pousalegre*, above), experienced and knowledgeable on biology and geology, group tours, US$30 (eg to Gruta do Lapão, 6 people; Cachoeira da Fumação and Capão, 8 people, US$13 extra for food, 3-day tour).

● **Tourist offices**
Sectur, nr *Pousada Lençois*, open daily 0800-1200, 1400-1800. Also on Praça Oscar Maciel, next to the church across the river from town, T 334-1121. There are many guides offering their services at most *pousadas*, about US$18; most of them are very young.

● **Transport**
Paraíso bus from **Salvador** 0730, 1200 and 2200, US$14 (bus goes to Seabra, 80 km beyond Lençois, make sure driver knows you want to go to Lençois); **Feira de Santana**, returns at 0900, 2100; buses also from Recife, Ibotirama, Barreiras or **Brasília**, 16 hrs, US$22.

PARQUE NACIONAL DA CHAPADA DIAMANTINA

Lençois is the headquarters of the **Parque Nacional da Chapada Diamantina** (founded 1985), which contains 1,500 sq km of mountainous country, with a similar geology to the Guayana Highlands of Venezuela but on a smaller scale, an abundance of endemic plants, waterfalls, large caves (take care, and a strong torch, there are no signs and caves can be difficult to find without a guide), rivers with natural swimming pools and good walking tours. Information, T (075) 332-2175, or Ibama, Av Juracy Magalhães Jr 608, CEP 40295-140, Salvador, T (071) 240-7322.

Excursions near Lençois and in the Chapada Diamantina Near the town, visit the **Serrano** with its wonderful natural pools in the river bed, which give a great hydro massage. A little further away is the **Salão de Areia**, where the coloured sands for the bottle paintings come from. **Ribeirão do Meio** is a 45-min walk from town; here locals slide down a long natural water shute into a big pool (it is best to be shown the way it is done and to take something to slide in).

Gruta do Lapão, 3 hrs from Lençois, guide essential, is in quartz rock and therefore has no stalagmites. Some light rock climbing is required. **Cachoeira da Primavera**, two very pretty waterfalls close to town, rec. **Cachoeira Sossego**, 2 hrs from town, a 'picture postcard' waterfall, swimming in pool, rec.

Morro de Pai Inácio, 30 km from Lençois, has the best view of the Chapada, rec at sunset (bus from Lençois at 0815, 30 mins, US$0.75). In the park is the **Cachoeira da Fumaça** (or Smoke Waterfall, also called **Glass**), 384m, the highest in Brazil. To see it, go by car to the village of **Capão** and walk 2½ hrs. The view is astonishing; the updraft of the air currents often makes the water flow back up creating 'smoke' effect. To get to the bottom is an amazing 3-day walk (enquire at *Pousada dos Duendes* in Lençois).

Other excursions are: **Lapa Doce**, a cave with fine stalagmites and stalactites, 70 km, **Andaraí**, 101 km, and the diamond ghost town of **Igatu**, a further 14 km on the other side of the Rio Paraguaçu. There is a bridge across the river. The town has a good *pousada*. A good day trip from Lençois is to **Poço Encantado** (23 km SE of the Chapada itself, 55 km from Andaraí), a mountain cave with a lake of crystal clear water, 60m deep, very spectacular, known locally as the 8th wonder of the world. From April to Aug, the sunlight enters the cave from the mountain side, hits the water and is dispersed into the colours of the spectrum. A visit is highly recommended and can be followed by a trip to Igatu on the return to Lençois. Southeast of the park is **Mucujé** (*Hotel Mucujé*, opp rodoviária, good food, basic, take mosquito coils), lovely walks among hills or along Rio Paraguaçu. Buses from Mucujé to Seabra run Tues, Thur, Sat at 0500; frequent service from there to Lençois and Palmeiras.

● **Accommodation In Capão**: **C** *Candombá*, good breakfast, excellent food, homegrown vegetables, run by Claude and Suzana (Claude speaks French and English and guides in the region); F (075) 332 2176, or through Tatur Turismo in Salvador (address above); **D** *Pousada Verde*, at entrance to town, very good breakfast, rec; **E** *Pouso Riacho do Our*, friendly, rec; **E** *Tatu Feliz*, no breakfast.

● **Transport** From Salvador you can get a bus to Chapada Diamantina, US$11, 3 times daily, last bus from Salvador departs 2200 arrives 0430 via Alto Paraiso. **NB** Book in advance. Local guides can often arrange transport to the more remote excursions, certainly this is possible when groups are involved.

SOUTH FROM SALVADOR

VALENÇA

271 km from Salvador, on an asphalted road, is this small, attractive town (*pop* 66,785), at the mouth of the Rio Una. Two old churches stand on rising ground; the views from Nossa Senhora do Amparo are recommended. The town is in the middle of an area producing black pepper, cloves and *piaçava* (used in making brushes and mats). Other industries include the building and repair of fishing boats (*saveiros*). The Rio Una enters an enormous region of mangrove swamps. The main attraction of Valença is the beaches on the mainland (Guabim, 14 km N) and on the island of Tinharé. Avoid touts at the rodoviária; better to visit the friendly tourist office opposite the rodoviária.

● **Accommodation** **B** *Rio Una*, R Maestro Barrinha, T 741-1614, swimming pool; **C** *Guabim*, Praça da Independência, T 741-1110, modest, rec, good *Akuarius* restaurant; next door, **D** *Rafa*, large rooms, well rec; **E** *Tourist Hotel*, Mal Floriano 167, good; **E** *Valença*, R Dr H Guedes Melo 15, T 741-1807, comfortable, good breakfast, rec.

● **Transport** Long-distance buses run from the new rodoviária, Av Maçônica, T 741-1280, while the old one is for local buses. Eight buses a day to/from **Salvador**, 5 hrs, US$9, Camarujipe (T 071 358-0109) and São Jorge companies; São Jorge to **Itabuna**, 5 hrs, US$7, very slow. For the shortest route to Valença, take the ferry from São Joaquim to Bom Despacho on Itaparica island, from where it is 130 km to Valença via Nazaré das Farinhas (see page 431). To/from Bom Despacho on Itaparica, Camarujipe and Águia Branca companies, 16 a day, 1 hr 45 mins, US$4.

TINHARÉ AND MORRO DE SÃO PAULO

Tinharé is a large island separated from the mainland by the estuary of the Rio Una and mangrove swamps, so that it is hard to tell which is land and which is water. The best beaches and *pousadas* are at Morro de São Paulo.

Morro de São Paulo is very popular in summer, situated on the headland at the northernmost tip of the island, lush with ferns, palms and birds of paradise, dominated by the lighthouse and the ruins of a Dutch colonial fort (1630). The village has a landing place on the sheltered landward side, dominated by the old gateway of the fortress. From the lighthouse a path leads to a ruined lookout with cannon, which has panoramic views. The place is expensive Dec-Mar, crowded at holiday times, but cheaper during the rest of the year. All roads are unmade, but beaches are good. Fish can be bought from the fishermen in summer, or borrow a pole and catch your own at sunset. Secondhand books (English, German, and others) sold at the back of the craft shop: the bearded owner will trade 2 for 1 if he's in the mood.

Galeão is another village in the island, but has no beach, only mangrove swamps. The church of São Francisco Xavier looks imposing on its hill.

Local information
● **Accommodation**
In **Morro de São Paulo**: *Pousada da Tia Glória*, quiet; next door is **D** *Pousada da Praça*, fan, rec. There are many cheap *pousadas* and rooms to rent nr the fountain (Fonte Grande) but this part of town is very hot at night, eg **E** pp *Pousada Mare Sol*, simple, rec. Senhora Preta rents rooms E, ask at quay; **D** *Pousada Village da Ponte*, R da Fonte Grande, T in Salvador 071-248 2699, a/c, fridge, fan, rec; **E** pp *Pousada Trilha do Riacho*, without breakfast, fan; **D** pp *Pousada Escorregue no Reggae*, with breakfast, reggae played all day, rec. Highly rec are **C** *Pousada Porto da Cima* (200m past **D** *Pousada Casarão*) chalets with fans; **C-D** *Pousada Gaúcho*, huge breakfast, shared bath. A little further along and up some steep steps to the left is **B** *Pousada Colibri*, cool, always a breeze blowing, excellent views, only six apartments, Helmut, the owner, speaks English and German, highly rec.

Beach hotels: the beaches on Morro de São Paulo are at the bottom of the main street where one turns right on to the first beach (Primeira Praia). **B** *Pousada Vistabela*, owner Petruska is extremely welcoming, good rooms, those to the front have good views and are cooler, all

have fans, hammocks, rec, T (073) 254 1272;
C *Pousada Farol do Morro*, all rooms with sea
view, cool, T (071) 243 4144, F 243 4207;
D *Pousada Ilha da Saudade*, good breakfast,
simple; **C** *Pousada Ilha do Sol*, good views, rec.
On second beach (Segunda Praia) is **C** *Pousada
Oxum*. On third beach (Terceira Praia) is
B *Pousada Gaimu*, 14 rooms, in lush tropical
setting, secluded (T 071-321 1936). Nearby is
B *Pousada Fazenda Caeira*, large grounds, private, well stocked library with snooker and other
games, T (075) 741 1272, both of these are rec;
Hotel Ville Gaignon, 5-star, swimming pools,
games rooms, convention rooms, etc. On fourth
beach (Quarta Praia) is **C** *Pousada Catavento*.

● **Places to eat**

Restaurant Gaúcho for good, reasonably
priced, typical regional cooking. *Ebano* offers a
good varied menu. *Belladonna* on the main
street is a very good Italian restaurant with great
music, a good meeting point; owner Guido
speaks Italian, English and French and a willing
source of information on the Morro; open daily
from 1800 till the small hours, rec. Across the
street in a very good pizzeria called *Pizzas!*, rec.
Casablanca is a good simple restaurant, open
daily till late. Good breakfasts at *Doceria da
Paula* on main street and at *Pousada
Natureza*, nr church, US$5. The second beach
is the liveliest with many beach huts offering
cool drinks, meals etc. *Barraca Caita* opens till
late with good music, dance music at weekends.
They have snorkelling equipment for hire, popular meeting point, potent cocktails! Another
barraca is *Ponto da Ilha* alongside. There are
many other barracas on the third beach but a
short walk to the fourth beach is *Barraca da
Piscina*, good swimming in front, good ambience, dominos, draughts etc, reasonable seafood menu, open till late during summer
months; *Comida Natural*, on main street,
comida a kilo, good juices, rec. *Bahiana*, main
square, good food, rec.

● **Transport**

From Salvador, a direct ferry service sails from
the Terminal Marítimo in front of the Mercado
Modelo to Morro de São Paulo (*Lancha Execu-
tiva*): daily in high season, Fri, Sat, Sun in low
season, 0830, returns 1730, US$30 one way,
2½ hr trip. Also, the *Bonanza III* from Rampa
do Mercado Modelo, US$15, daily at 1300, 4
hrs, T 226-7523 (Salvador), 783-1062 (Morro de
São Paulo). Part of the trip is on the open sea,
which can be rough.

Boats (US$1.50) leave every day from Va-
lença for Galeão (1½ hrs), Gamboa (1½ hrs)
and Morro de São Paulo (1½ hrs).

Boats to the Morro leave from the main bridge
in Valença 5 times a day (signalled by a loud
whistle). The fare is US$2.50. Only buses be-
tween 0530-1100 from Salvador to Valença
connect with ferries. Private boat hire can be
arranged outside these times. A responsible
local boatman is Jario, T (075) 741 1681; he can
be contacted to meet travellers arriving at the
rodoviária for transfer to the Morro. He also
offers excursions to other islands, especially
Boipeba, a small simple fishing village with lovely
beaches on the island of the same name, just S of
Tinharé. Overnight excursions to this village are
possible; **A1-2** *Pousada Tassimirim*, T/F (071) 972-
4378 (R Com Madureira 40, 45400-000 Valença),
bungalows, bar, restaurant, inc breakfast and dinner, secluded; **D** pp *Pousada Tropical*, lunch available, highly rec; **D** *Pousada Luar das Águas* (T 741
2238), simple, good. Regular boat from Valença,
weekdays 1000-1230 and 1500-1700, 3-4 hrs.

ITACARÉ

On the coast, S toward Ilhéus, is the picturesque fishing village of **Itacaré**. It is a
beautiful area with a protected beach with
crystal-clear water to the right of town;
across the river there are beaches with
good surfing.

● **Accommodation C** *Pousada Litoral*, R de
Souza 81, 1 block from where buses stop, owner
João Cravo speaks English and can organize
tours to out of the way beaches, hiring fishing
boats, etc, rec; **C** *Sage Paint*, owned by a Cuban
Ana Cubana, ocean-front *pousada*, showers,
outings organized to nearby beaches etc, rec.

● **Transport** Buses to **Ilhéus**, 3-4 hrs,
US$4.75; to **Salvador**, change at Ubaituba (3
hrs, US$2), Ubaituba-Salvador, 6 hrs, US$9.50,
several daily.

ILHÉUS

(*Pop* 223,350; *CEP* 45660; *DDD* 073) Near
the mouth of the Rio Cachoeira, 462 km S
of Salvador, the port serves a district which
produces 65% of all Brazilian cocoa. Shipping lines call regularly. A bridge links the
Pontal district (airport) to the mainland.
The town is the scene of the famous novel
by Jorge Amado, *Gabriela, Clove and Cinnamon*. The local beaches are splendid, but
the central beach is polluted.

Places of interest

Among the churches to visit are **Nossa
Senhora da Vitória**, in Alto da Vitória,
built in 17th century to celebrate a victory
over the Dutch; **São Jorge**, in city centre;

and the cathedral of **São Sebastião** on sea shore; **Santana**, in Rio de Engenho, is one of the oldest in Brazil.

Excursions

Buses run every 30 mins to **Itabuna** (32 km; *pop* 185,180), the trading centre of the rich cocoa zone (also many lumber mills). Ceplac installations at Km 8 on the Itabuna-Ilhéus road show the whole processing of cocoa. Tours of cocoa plantations can be arranged through the *Ilhéus Praia* hotel; Jorge Amado's novel *The Violent Lands* deals with life on the cocoa plantations. Bus from Salvador, $6^{1}/_{2}$ hrs, US$8.50. The paved BA-415 links Itabuna to Vitória da Conquista (275 km) on the BR-116.

The **beaches** between Ilhéus and Olivença are good, eg Cururupe, and frequent buses run to Olivença. For the good beaches at Pontal, take 'Barreira' bus and get off just past *Hotel Jardim Atlântico*. Hot baths (*balneário*) 18 km away, are reached by Viação São Jorge or Canavieiras buses.

Local festivals

Include Festa de São Sebastião (17-20 Jan), Carnival, Festa de São Jorge (23 April), Foundation day, 28 June, and Festa do Cacau (Oct).

Local information

● **Accommodation** in Ilhéus

A3 *Hotel Barravento* on Malhado beach, R NS das Graças, T 231-3223, ask for the penthouse – usually no extra charge, inc breakfast and refrigerator; **A3** *Ilhéus Praia*, Praça D Eduardo (on beach), T 231-2533, pool, helpful, rec; **A3** *Pontal Praia*, T 231-3033, Praia do Pontal, swimming pool.

C *Britânia*, T 231-1722, R 28 de Junho 16, and at No 29 **D** *San Marino*, T 231-3668. **D** *Pousada Kazarão*, Praça Coronel Pessoa 9, no breakfast, noisy; **D** *Pousada Sol Atlântico*, Av Lomanto Júnior, 1450, Pontal T 231-8059, outside city but frequent buses passing, good view over bay, fan, TV, balcony.

Plenty of cheap hotels nr municipal rodoviária in centre; **E** *Hotel Atlântico Sul*, R Bento Berilo 224, Centro, T 231 4668 or 8051, good bar/restaurant, rec.

Campsite: *Estância das Fontes*, 19 km on road S to Olivença, cheap, shady, rec.

In Itabuna: of the hotels, the **A3** *Itabuna Palace* (Av Cinquentenário 1061, T/F 211-1233, restaurant) is probably the best; also **B** *Príncipe*,

R Miguel Calmon 234, T 211-3272, and **C** *Lord*, Quintino Bocaiúva 1017, T/F 211-1233.

● **Places to eat**

Os Velhos Marinheiros, Av 2 de Julho, on the waterfront, rec; *Come Ben*, nr Praça Cairu, cheap and good; *Vesúvio*, Praça D Eduardo, next to Cathedral, made famous by Amado's (see above), now Swiss-owned, very good but pricey; *Nogar*, Av Bahia 377, close to the sea, good pizzas and pasta. Local drink, *coquinho*, coconut filled with cachaça, only for the strongest heads! Also try *suco de cacau* at juice stands.

● **Tourist offices**

Situated on beach opp Praça Castro Alves (a few minutes from cathedral), friendly, maps US2, rec.

● **Transport**

Buses Rodoviária is 4 km from centre on Itabuna road, but Itabuna-Olivença bus goes through centre of Ilhéus. Several daily to **Salvador**, 7 hrs, US$14-19 (*leito* US$28, Expresso São Jorge); 0620 bus goes via Itaparica, leaving passengers at Bom Despacho ferry station on the island – thence 50-mins ferry to Salvador. To **Itacaré**, 4 hrs, US$4.75; to **Eunápolis**, 7 hrs, US$6, this bus also leaves from the central bus terminal. Other destinations also served; local buses leave from Praça Cairu. Insist that taxi drivers have meters and price charts.

PORTO SEGURO

About 400 km S of Ilhéus on the coast is the old town of **Porto Seguro** (*pop* 34,520; *CEP* 45820; *DDD* 073). Building is subject to controls on height and materials, in keeping with traditional Bahian styles (colonial or Indian). In the area are remains of original Atlantic coastal forest, with parrots, monkeys, marmosets and snakes.

It was N of the site of Porto Seguro that Cabral first landed on 22 April 1500; a cross marks the supposed site of the first mass in Brazil on the road between Porto Seguro and Santa Cruz Cabrália. A tourist village, Coroa Vermelha, has sprouted at the site, 20 mins by bus to the N, with souvenir shops selling Pataxó-Tupi Indian items, beach bars, hotels and rental houses, all rather uncoordinated. From the roundabout at the entrance to Porto Seguro take a wide, steep, unmarked path uphill to the historical city (**Cidade Histórica**), three churches (NS da Misericórdia-1530, NS do Rosário-1534, and NS da Pena-1718), the former jail and the cross; a small, peaceful place with lovely gardens and panoramic views.

There are *borrachudos*, little flies that bite feet and ankles in the heat of the day; coconut oil keeps them off; at night mosquitoes can be a problem (but there is no malaria, dengue or yellow fever).

Excursions

Guided tours of the area with BPS, at the Shopping Centre, T 288-2373. *Companhia do Mar* (Praça dos Pataxós, T 288-2981) does daily trips by schooner to coral reefs off the coast. The most popular is to Recife de Fora, with good snorkelling; leaves daily 1000, returns 1630, about US$18, US$3 extra for snorkelling gear. 10 mins N of Coroa Vermelha, **Santa Cruz Cabrália** is a delightful small town with a splendid beach, river port, a 450-year old church with a fine view, and several hotels (eg *Pousada Xica da Silva* near bus stop, cheap, nice, good restaurant *Coqueiro Verde* – try *pitu*, a kind of crayfish). Across the river (dugout US$1) is Santo André, a small village on the ocean, also with a beach and inns. Hourly buses from Santa Cruz to Porto Seguro (23 km). Schooner trips to the reef also from Santa Cruz.

Local information
● Accommodation

The town is a popular holiday resort – prices rise steeply Dec-March. In all the towns below, long-stay rates can be negotiated, especially in low season.

A3 *Porto Seguro Praia*, 3 km N of city on coast road, T 288-2321, F 288-2069; *Cabanas do Tio João*, BR-367, Km 64, 2 km N of Porto Seguro, T 288-2315, a/c, pool, English and French spoken, rec.

B *Estalagem Porto Seguro*, R Mal Deodoro 66, T 288-2095, old colonial house, a/c, fan, rec; **B** *Pousada Albatroz*, Av dos Navegantes 600, a/c, pool, rec, T 288-2394, F 288-2047; **B** *Pousada Casa Azul*, 15 de Novembro 11, T 288-2180, English spoken, good, swimming pool; **B** *Pousada Coqueiro Verde*, R 'A' No 01, T 288-2621, F 288-2623, a/c, pool, sauna; **B** *Pousada do Cais*, Portugal 382, T 228-2111, colonial house on sea-front, good; several others on same street; **B** *Pousada Gaivota*, Av dos Navegantes 333, T/F 288-2826, a/c, pool, sauna; **B** *Pousada Pirata*, R Mal Deodoro 249, excellent breakfast, rec; **B** *Pousada Solar da Praça*, Praça da Bandeira, a/c, good seafront

location; **B** *Vela Branca*, Cidade Histórica, T 288-2316, top of cliff, good.

C *Chica da Silva*, Av dos Navegantes 94, T 288-2280, family run; **C** *Pousada Aquarius*, R Pedro Alvares Cabral 176, T 288-2738, fan, English, French, Italian spoken, rec; *Pousada Coral*, R Assis Chateaubriand 74, T 288-2630, good breakfast, fan; **C** *Pousada Las Palmas*, Praça Antônio Carlos Magalhães 102, Centro, T 288 2643, 281 1179, highly rec; **C** *Pousada Saveiros*, Av Navegentes 151, T 288-2122, good breakfast, will change TCs; **D** *Mar Azul* at No 109, rec; **D** *Pousada do Frances*, Av 22 de Abril 180, T 288 2469, a/c, TV, with breakfast, rec. On Av Getúlio Vargas, without breakfast unless shown: **C** *Pousada da Praia*, No 153, T 228 2908, a/c, fridge, showers, rec; **C** *Pousada Raizes*, Praça dos Pataxós 196, T 288-2198, fan, rec; same square No 278 is **C** *Pousada Travessia*, T 288-2616, with good breakfast; **C** *Pousada Mar e Sol*, No 223, T 228-2137, safe, filtered drinking water, very helpful manager (who teaches *lambada*), highly rec; **D** *Pousada Peixinho*, No 228, attractive; **D** *Pousada Coroa Vermelha*, No 12, T 288-2132, good.

D *Porto Brasília*, Praça Antônio Carlos Magalhães 234, with breakfast, **E** without; *Pousada Navegantes*, Av 22 de Abril 212, T 288-2390, rec; **D** *Pousada Vera Cruz*, Av 22 de Abril 100, T 288-2162, with bath, good breakfast, clean.

Some good, cheap *pousadas* on R Mal Deodoro at the port: **D** *Estalagem da Yvonne*, No 298, with breakfast, more with a/c, T 288-2045; **D** *Pousada de Sagres*, R 15 de Novembro, T 288-2031, with good breakfast, family run; **D** *Pousada Sonho Meu*, same street No 86, with breakfast, fan, good; **E** house of Luisiana Silva Mercedes, No 214, T 288-1137.

Outside Dec-Feb rooms with bath and hot water can be rented for about US$150/month.

Camping: *Camping dos Marajas*, Av Getúlio Vargas, central; *Camping Gringa*, Praia do Cruzeiro, T 288-2076, US$2.50 pp/night, laundry, café, pool, excellent; *Camping do Sitio*, R da Vala, mosquitoes can be a problem here.

● Places to eat

Cruz de Malta, R Getúlio Vargas 358, good seafood; *Preto Velho*, on Praça da Bandeira, à la carte or self-service, good value; also good value is *Hall of Hunger*, R Rui Barbosa 194, home cooking here from 1200 to 2200, cheap; good breakfast at *Pau Brasil*, Praça dos Pataxós, and *Club dos Sem Casa*, R Pedro Alvares Cabral 185, open 0800-2100, good, cheap lunches here also. On Praça Pataxós: *do Japonês*, No 38, excellent value with varied menu, open 0800-2300, rec; *Ponto do Encontro*, No 106, good simple food, owners rent rooms, open 0800-2400; *Prima Dona*, No 247, Italian, good. *Anti-Caro*, R Assis Chateaubriand 26, good, rec, also antique shop, good atmosphere. *Churras-caria do Maça*, R Mal Deodoro 342, open 1500-2400, very good meat restaurant, try *picanha*, enough for 3 people, not expensive; *Les Agapornis*, Av dos Navegantes 180, wide selection of crêpes and pizzas; *Tres Vintens*, Av Portugal 1246, good imaginative seafood dishes, rec; *Ninõ*, 22 de Abril 100, good pizzas; *Vida Verde*, R Dois de Julho 92, good vegetarian, open 1100-2100 except Sun, T 288 2766, rec.

● **Banks & money changers**
Banco do Brasil, Av 22 de Abril e Av Carlos Alberto Paracho, Dec-Mar for exchange 1800-2200, but not Sun. Good rates in the new shopping centre, nr Banco do Brasil; good rates at *Agência do Descobrimento*, Av Getúlio Vargas, lower rate for TCs, also arranges flight tickets and house rental. Rates are not as good as in the big cities.

● **Entertainment**
Porto Seguro is famous for the *lambada* (see **Music and Dance**). The best place to see it is at *Boca da Barra* at Praia do Cruzeiro. Instructors are on hand from 1800-2000, then the locals take the floor until the small hours. No entry charge, not to be missed, nightly throughout the year. The strong local liqueur, *guarachaça*, a mixture of guaraná and cachaça, keeps the dancers going during the long hours. Another place to see *lambada* is **Lambaporto**, busy only at weekends.

A good bar for live music is *Porto Prego* on R Pedro Alvares Cabral, small cover charge. *Sotton Bar*, Praça de Bandeira, is lively. There are lots of bars and street cafés on Av Portugal.

● **Post & telecommunications**
Telephones: Telebahia service post, Praça dos Pataxós beside ferry terminal, open daily 0800-2200, cheap rates after 2000.

● **Sports**
Diving equipment, Portomar Ltda, R Dois de Julho 178, also arranges diving and snorkelling trips to the coral reefs offshore, professional instructors.

● **Tourist offices**
Casa de Lenha, Praça Visconde de Porto Seguro, nr port, has basic information, is keen to sell tours.

● **Transport**
Local Rentals: Car hire, Itapoan, Av Portugal 1350, T 288-2710; **motorcycles**, Lupa Motos, Praça dos Pataxós, T 288-2868, expensive, heavy deposit required; **bicycles**, Oficina de Bicicleta, Av Getúlio Vargas e R São Pedro, about US$10 for 24 hrs; also at Praça de Bandeira and at Dois de Julho 242.

Air Nordeste Sat and Sun from Rio, direct 2 hrs 15 mins with 2 stops; Nordeste on same days from Belo Horizonte and Salvador; Rio Sul daily to Salvador and São Paulo; Vasp once a week to São Paulo and Belo Horizonte, twice to Salvador.

Buses From Porto Seguro: **Salvador** (Água Branca), daily, 12 hrs, US$37, once a day each service; **Vitória**, daily, 11 hrs, US$20; **Ilhéus**, daily 0730, 5½ hrs, US$12; **Eunápolis**, 1½ hrs, US$2. For **Rio** direct (São Geraldo), leaving at 1745, US$43 (*leito* 60), 18 hrs, from Rio direct at 1600, or take 1800 for Ilhéus and change at Eunápolis. To **Belo Horizonte** daily direct. To **São Paulo** direct, 1045, 25 hrs, not advisable, very slow, much better to go to Rio then take Rio-São Paulo express. Other services via Eunápolis (those going N avoid Salvador) or Itabuna (5 hrs, US$10). (For the routes from Vitória see page 419 and from Belo Horizonte page 431). At Brazilian holiday times, all transport N or S should be booked well in advance. There is new rodoviária, with reliable luggage store and lounge on 3rd floor, on the road to Eunápolis, 2 km from the centre, regular bus service (30 mins) through city to the old rodoviária near port. For local trips a taxi is an economic proposition for two or more passengers wishing to visit various places in 1 day.

ARRAIAL DA AJUDA

Across the Rio Buranhém S from Porto Seguro (10 mins, US$0.25, ferries take cars day time only, every 30 mins day and night), and a further 5 km (US$0.45 in bus), is the village of **Arraial da Ajuda**; about 15 mins' walk from the beach (better for camping than Porto Seguro). Pilgrimage in Aug to the shrine of Nossa Senhora da Ajuda (interesting room in church, full of ex-voto offerings – fine view from behind church). Ajuda has become very popular with 'younger' tourists and there are many *pousadas*, bars and small shops. Known as a 'hippie' resort: drugs are said to be widely available, but easily avoided. Parties almost every night, on the beach or in the *Broadway*. At the *Jatobar* bar the *lambada* is danced, on the main square, by the church (opens 2300 – *pensão* at the back is cheap, clean and friendly). There is also a *capoeira* institute; ask for directions. At Brazilian holiday times it is very crowded and, with the coastline up for sale, it may become overdeveloped in a few years. The beaches, several protected by coral reef, are splendid, for instance Pitinga, Lagoa

Azul and Mucugê. Porto Belo or Sta Cruz Cabrália buses go to the beaches frequently from the port.

● **Accommodation B** *Ivy Marey*, nr centre on road to beach, T 875-1106, 4 rooms and 2 bungalows, showers, nice décor, good bar, French/Brazilian owned, rec; nearby *Le Grand Bleu*, T 875-7272, same French owner, similar prices, good *pizzaria*, rec; **B** *Pousada das Brisas*, T 875-1033, panoramic views, English, German, French and Spanish spoken; **B** *Pousada Canto d'Alvorada*, on road to Ajuda, T 875-1218, in season, D out of season, Swiss run, 7 cabins, restaurant, laundry facilities; **B** *Sole Mio*, T 875-1115, just off beach road leading from ferry to Arraial, different French owners, English spoken, laid back, 4 chalets, excellent *pizzaria*, rec; **C** *Pousada Caminho do Mar*, T 875-1099, English spoken, rate depending on season, owners very informative and helpful, also highly rec; **C** *Pousada Erva Doce*, T 875-1114, good restaurant, well appointed chalets, highly rec; **C** *Pousada Natur*, run by German environmentalist, rec, English spoken T 288-2738; **C** *Thaina Plage*, highly rec, reserved in São Paulo, T 011-533-5898, or in Paris T 43-26-31-41, and **C** *Pousada Torrorão*, between village and beach, T 875-1260, restaurant, rec; **C** *Pousada Tubarão*, R Bela Vista, beyond the church on the right, T 875-1086, good view of the coastline, cool, good restaurant, rec; **C** *Vila do Beco*, beautiful garden, good value; **D** *Pousada Aberta Mar*, on road to beach, good breakfast; **D** *Pousada Flamboyant*, pleasant, good breakfast, rec; **D** *Pousada Flor*, on square, T 875-1143, owner Florisbela Valiense takes good care of female guests, warmly rec; **D** *Pousada Gabriela*, R Projetada s/n – cep 45820, T 875-1237, with breakfast, rec; **D** *Pousada Le Cottage* (across ferry from Porto Seguro, but before Ajuda, T 875-1029), French owner, Sr Georges, C in chalet; **D** *Pousada do Paulista*, with breakfast, fan, laundry facilities, rec; **D** *Pousada Vento Sul*, Caminho da Praia, T 875-1294, hammocks, ocean view; **E** *Pousada Mangaba*, on way to the beach, bath, laundry facilities, without breakfast, rec; **E** *Pousada Nova Esperança*, nearby, without breakfast, bath, rec; **E** *Pousada Tamarind*, on Praça Brigadeiro Eduardo Gomés, nr church, without breakfast, bath; **E** *Pousada Tio Otto*, without breakfast, alongside church. **NB** Above prices are high season prices unless otherwise stated. **Camping**: *Praia*, on Mucugê Beach, good position and facilities, US$1 pp/night; *Chão do Arraial*, 5 mins from Mucugê beach, shady, good snack bar, also hire tents, rec. Also *Camping do Gordo*, on left shortly after leaving ferry, on beach but beach is not as good as Mucugê.

● **Places to eat** *São João*, nr the church, is the best typical restaurant; *Robin Wood*, opp police station, garden/restaurant, fresh food, excellent value, US$5, rec; *Asa Branca*, R Santa Rita, very good *carne de sol de picanha*; *Manda Brasa*, on Broadway, good *prato feito*, cheap; also on Broadway, *Spaghetti Point*, good, US$3; *Le Gourmet*, R São João, good international cuisine, specialise in French dishes, not cheap, rec; *Mão na Massa*, an excellent Italian restaurant, behind the church, rec; also rec is *Varanda Grill*, good grilled fish, meat and chicken; *Paulinho Pescador*, open 1200-2200, excellent seafood, also chicken and meat, English spoken, good service, *bobó de camarão* highly rec. *Café das Cores*, on way to the beach, good cakes and snacks, expresso coffee. Two good 'barracas' on Pitinga beach are *Bar da Pitinga* and *Bar do Genésio*, fresh fried fish, shrimp etc.

● **Post & telecommunications Telephone**: Telebahia has a service post on the main square, open 0800 until 2200.

TRANCOSO

25 km to the S of Porto Seguro and 15 km from Ajuda is **Trancoso**, reached by bus, 5 a day (US$0.60, 50 mins, last returns at 1630, more buses and colectivos in summer), by colectivo, hitchhiking or by walking along the beach; the road bridges are not safe, bus passengers alight and walk across. This simple village, with its beautiful beaches (some nude), is popular with Brazilian tourists and many Europeans have built or bought houses there. There are good restaurants around the main square. From the end of Praça São João there is a fine coastal panorama. Trancoso has a historic church. Colectivos run from Trancoso to Ajuda (US$1.90). Between Ajuda and Trancoso is the village of Rio da Barra. Caraiva with beautiful beaches, no electricity, can be reached by boat, 4 hrs from Porto Seguro, by bus from Trancoso 2 hrs, two daily. The sandy road from Trancoso is a difficult drive, ending at the river which must be crossed by boat. There are *pousadas* and restaurants with electricity generators, but no exchange facilities.

● **Accommodation A3** *Hotel de Praça*, games room, good breakfast (T São Paulo 211-2239); **B** *Pousada Calypso*, good apartments, comfortable, rooms at lower price also available, good library, German and English spoken, rec (T Rio 267-3741); **C** *Caipim Santo*, to the left of main square, with breakfast, the best restaurant in Trancoso (natural cuisine), rec; **C** *Posada*

Canto Verde, with breakfast, restaurant only in high season, rec (T 0242-43-7823). Also on main square, **C** *Gulab Mahal*, oriental style, lovely garden, vast breakfast, highly rec; **C** *Pousada do Bosque*, on the way to the beach, English, German and Spanish spoken, with breakfast, camping facilities also available, good value; **E** *Pousada Terra do Sol*, without breakfast, good, rec. About 500m inland away from main square (known as the 'quadrado') lies the newer part of Trancoso (known as the 'invasão') with two good value *pousadas*: **D** *Pousada Quarto Crescente*, English, German, Dutch and Spanish spoken, cooking facilities, laundry, helpful owners, library, highly rec, about 15 mins from beach; **D** *Luna Pousa*, further along on the left, with breakfast, well ventilated, only 4 rooms, rec. There are many houses to rent, very good ones are rented by Clea who can be contacted at *Restaurant Abacaxi* on main square on right. You can leave a message for any one of the above mentioned *pousadas* by calling the Telebahia service post 867-1116, most people in town check there for messages daily.

● **Places to eat** *Urano*, just before the main square is rec, good portions; *Rama* has also been rec; *Abacaxi* on main square does good breakfasts, light snacks and very good crêpes; *Galub Mahal* for Eastern dishes; good breakfast also at *Pé das Frutas*, *Maré Cheia* next door good simple dishes. Good ice cream at *Tão Vez*. Apart from restaurants which serve breakfast most others open at 1500 until 2200 or so.

PARQUE NACIONAL DE MONTE PASCOAL

South of Porto Seguro, reached by a paved access road from the BR-101 16 km N of Itamaraju, is the **Parque Nacional de Monte Pascoal** (buses from Itamaraju at 0600 on Fri, Sat, Sun and Mon only) set up in 1961 to preserve the flora, fauna and birdlife of the coastal area in which Europeans made landfall in Brazil (Caixa Postal 076, CEP 45830-000 Itamaraju, T 073-281-2419). The Pataxó Indian reservation is located at Corombau village, on the ocean shore of the park. Corombau can be reached by schooner from Porto Seguro. A small luxury resort has been built at Corombau.

CURUMUXATIBA

From Itamaraju (93 km S of Eunápolis) the coastal towns of **Curumuxatiba** (**D** *Pousada Guainamby*, R Bela Vista, CEP 45983, Ger-

man and Brazilian owned, small, clean, comfortable chalets, good views to long beach, good breakfast and fish and Italian meals, rec) and Prado. Also reached from Itamaraju is the *Jacotoka* holiday village, which offers diving, surfing and riding in a tropical paradise. US$50/day, reservations at 7 de Setembro 149, Porto Seguro, T 288-2291, F 288-2540; it can also be reached by boat from Porto Seguro.

CARAVELAS

Further S still, 130 km S of Porto Seguro, a charming little town (*pop* 21,650), rapidly developing for tourism, but a major trading town in 17th/18th centuries. It had a rail connection to Minas Gerais. Caravelas is in the mangroves; the beaches are about 10 km away at Barra de Caravelas (hourly buses), a fishing village.

● **Accommodation A1** *Marina Porto Abrulhos*, on beach front, very luxurious; **C** *Pousada Caravelense*, 50m from rodoviária, T 297-1182, TV, fridge, good breakfast, excellent restaurant, rec; **D** *Shangri-la*, Barão do Rio Branco 216, bath, breakfast. **At Barra de Caravelas: C** *Pousada das Sereias*, French-owned; **E** *Pousada Jaquita*, use of kitchen, big breakfast, bath, airy rooms, owner is Secka who speaks English; some food shops, restaurants and bars.

● **Tourist offices** Helpful tourist information at **Ibama Centro de Visitantes**, Barão do Rio Branco 281.

● **Useful services** Teresa and Ernesto (from Austria) organize boat trips (US$40/day), jeep and horse hire (turn left between bridge and small supermarket). 'Alternative' beach holidays (organic vegetarian food, yoga, meditation, other activities) with Beky and Eno on the unspoilt island of Coçumba, rec; contact *Abrolhos Turismo*. Banco do Brasil does not change money (Praça Dr Imbassahi); on same square, No 8, *Abrolhos Turismo* rents diving gear and arranges boat trips.

● **Transport** Buses to Texeira de Freitas (4 a day), Salvador, Nanuque and Prado.

Prado (*pop* 20,000) has some 16th-century buildings and beautiful beaches N and S. It is 200 km S of Porto Seguro. The proprietors of the *Casa de Maria*, R Seis, Novo Prado, T (073) 298-1377, claim to serve the best breakfast in the region. **D** *Pousada Talipe* (1125 Central Ave, 23rd St, Los Alamitos, T 555 6539, USA), friendly, good breakfast, rec.

PARQUE NACIONAL MARINHO DOS ABROLHOS

John Raspey writes: The **Parque Nacional Marinho dos Abrolhos** is 70 km E of Caravelas: 5 small islands (Redonda, Siriba, Guarita, Sueste, Santa Bárbara), and several coral reefs. The archipelago is administered by Ibama, and a navy detachment mans a lighthouse on Sta Bárbara, which is the only island that may be visited. Permission from Parque Nacional Marinho dos Abrolhos, Praia do Kitombo s/n, Caravelas, Bahia 45900, T (073) 297-1111, or Ibama, Av Juracy Magalhães Jr 608, CEP 40295-140, Salvador, T (071) 240-7322. The islands and surrounding reefs are home to goats, birds, whales, fish, turtles and giant fire corals. Darwin visited them in 1830. A master authorized by the Navy to take tourists is Mestre Onofrio Frio in Alcobaça, Bahia, T (073) 293-2195. Tours also available from *Abrolhos Turismo*, see above, Caravelas, T 297-1149 (about US$170 for a slow 2½ day tour by *saveiro*). 1-day tours in a faster boat (US$100) from Abrolhos or the Marina Porto Abrolhos.

NORTH FROM SALVADOR

The paved BA-099 coast road from near the airport is known as the Estrada do Coco (Coconut Highway, because of the many coconut plantations) and for 50 km passes some beautiful beaches. The best known from S to N are Ipitanga (with its reefs), Buraquinho, Jauá, Arembepe, Guarajuba, Itacimirim, Castelo Garcia D'Ávila (with its 16th century fort) and Forte. Buses serve most of these destinations. The Estrada do Coco was extended in 1994 to the state of Sergipe. The road is called the Linha Verde (Green Line), because of the concern to disturb the environment as little as possible.

AREMBEPE

Some 50 km to the N of Salvador this former fishing village is now a quiet resort. There is an 'alternative' village of palm huts, 30 mins' walk along the beach, behind the sand dunes, café and swimming. Best beaches 2 km N of town. *Pousada da Fazenda* on the beach, thatched huts, good seafood, not cheap; **E** *Pousada*; and restaurant *Mar Aberto*, T 824-1257, rec, food very good, English and French spoken; Verá's restaurant, try *pastel de banana*. Bus from Terminal Francês, Salvador, every 2 hrs, 1½ hrs, US$1.20, last one back at 1700; or from Itapoan.

PRAIA DO FORTE

The fishing village, 80 km N of Salvador, takes its name from the castle built by a Portuguese settler, Garcia D'Ávila, in 1556. He built the fortification to warn the city to the S of enemy invasion. Garcia D'Ávila was given a huge area of land, from Praia do Forte to Maranhão, on which he made the first farm in Brazil. He who brought the first head of cattle to the country, he cleared the virgin Atlantic forest and brought the first coconut and mango trees to Brazil. Praia do Forte is now a tranquil resort with a strong emphasis on preservation of the local flora and fauna. Inland from the coast is a *restinga* forest, which grows on sandy soil with a very delicate ecosystem. Near the village is a small *pantanal* (marshy area), which is host to a large number of birds, caymans etc. Birdwatching trips on the *pantanal* are rewarding. The Tamar Project was set up to preserve the sea turtles which lay their eggs in the area. Praia do Forte is now the headquarters of the national turtle preservation programme and is funded by the Worldwide Fund for Nature. There is a visitors centre at the project.

● **Accommodation** (Prices rise steeply in summer season.) Most hotels are in the **A1** price range. It may prove difficult to find cheaper accommodation. *Praia do Forte Resort Hotel*, apartment with seaview, very good sports facilities, 4 swimming pools, watersports equipment for hire, T 832-2333/835-1111, F 832-2100; *Pousada Praia do Forte*, 18 chalets in peaceful setting, more private than larger *Resort Hotel*, rec, T 835-1410, F 876-1050; *Pousada Solar da Lua*, R do Forte, T 876-1029, good location, spacious rooms; *Pousada Sobrado da Vila*, on main street, T 876-1088, F 235-7886, pleasant, good value restaurant; *Pousada Tatuapara*, T 876-1015, friendly; **B** *Pousada João Sol*, R da Corvina, T 876-1054, owner speaks English, Spanish and German, good, rec, only 6 apts, great breakfast; **B** *Pousada Canto da Sereia*, R da Corvina, with fan, good breakfast; **B** *Pousada Sol Nascente*, on street parallel to main street, good, bath, frigobar, fan, breakfast; **C** *Tia Helena*, Helena being the motherly proprietor who provides an excellent meal and enormous breakfast, nice rooms, price reduced to US$20/night for 3 day stay, highly rec. Two-bedroom apartments at *Solar dos Arcos*, on beach, US$90, with pool, gardens, lawns, warmly rec.

● **Places to eat** *Bar Da Souza*, on the right as you enter the village, best seafood in town, open daily, live music at weekends, highly rec, reasonably priced; *Brasa Na Praia*, specializes in grilled seafood and meat, open daily, peaceful setting, rec; *La Crêperie*, excellent crêpes, Tues to Sun, good music, popular, owner Klever very friendly, highly rec; *Pizzaria Le Gaston*, good pizza and pasta, also good home made ice-creams, open daily. There are many other restaurants in the village: good ones inc *Pousada Solar Da Lua*, open daily until late, *Nora*, on main street, and *Restaurant Tropical*.

● **Tour companies & travel agents Tours**: *Odara Turismo*, in the *Resort Hotel*, T 876-1080, F 876-1018, imaginative tours to surrounding areas and outlying villages and beaches using 4WD vehicles. They are very friendly and informative, rec. The owners, Norbert and Papy, speak English and German. Praia do Forte is ideal for windsurfing and sailing owing to constant fresh Atlantic breezes.

● **Transport** Buses to Praia do Forte from Salvador (US$2.50): Santa Maria/Catuense leaves 5 times daily from rodoviária, 1½ hrs.

TO THE SERGIPE BORDER

The Linha Verde runs for 142 km to the Sergipe border, the road is more scenic than the BR-101, especially near Conde. There are very few hotels or *pousadas* in the more remote villages. The most picturesque are **Imbassaí**, Subaúma, **Baixios** (very beautiful, where the Rio Inhambupe meets the sea) and **Conde**. Sítio do Conde on the coast, 6 km from Conde, has many *pousadas*, but the beaches are not very good. Sítio do Conde is a good base to explore other beaches at Barra do Itariri, 12 km S, at the mouth of a river (fine sunsets). The road passes unspoilt beaches (the best are Corre Nu and Jacaré). You can also go to Seribinha, 13 km N of Sítio do Conde (the road goes along the beach through coconut groves and mangroves; at

Seribinha are beach huts serving cool drinks or food, one *pousada* reported on beach). The last stop on the Linha Verde is **Mangue Seco**. Access from Sergipe is by boat or canoe on the Rio Real from Pontal (10 min crossing). A steep hill rising behind the village to tall white sand dunes offers a superb view of the coastline. The encroaching dunes have caused the mangrove to dry up. Bus Salvador-Conde (São Luis, T 071 358-4582), 3 a day, 4 on Fri, US$7.50.

● **Accommodation & places to eat Imbassaí: A3** *Pousada Caminho do Mar*, T/F 832-2499, 12 bungalows with a/c, restaurant, German run; **C** *Pousada Imbassaí*, T 235-3599, chalets and apartments of varying sizes; **B** *Pousada Anzol de Ouro*, T 971-9025, reservations, T/F 243-2614, 12 chalets, ventilation, swimming pool; **B** *Pousada Lagoa da Pedra*, T 971-7095, reservations 359-3512/245-2506, large grounds, a little English spoken, friendly. **Subaúma: B** *Pousada da Praça*, simple, clean. **Sítio do Conde: A3** *Hotel Praia do Conde*, T (075) 429-1229, reservations (071) 321-2542, a/c, pool; **C** *Pousada Oasis*, T (075) 421-2397, simple; **C** *Pousada Beira Mar*. Cheaper are **D** *Pousada do Boliviano* and **E** *Pousada de Dona Dulce*. **Restaurants**: *Bar e Restaurante Zeca*, typical dishes; *Pizzaria Marcos*; *Restaurante Harmonioso*. **Mangue Seco**: **B** *Pousada Mangue Seco*, T (071) 359-8506, in main square, fan; further away, left from boat landing, 15 mins' walk, **B** *Pousada Village Mangue Seco*, T (071) 241-7355, swimming pool, fan. Seafood restaurants at boat landing.

INLAND, NORTH FROM SALVADOR

MONTE SANTO AND CANUDOS

About 270 km N of Feira da Santana, and 38 km W of Euclides da Cunha on the direct BR-116 road to Fortaleza, is the famous hill shrine of **Monte Santo** in the Sertão, reached by 3½ km of steps cut into the rocks of the Serra do Picaraça (about 45 mins' walk each way - set out early). This is the scene of pilgrimages and great religious devotion during Holy Week. The shrine was built by an Italian who had a vision of the cross on the mountain in 1765. One block N of the bottom of the stairs is the Museu do Sertão, with pictures from the 1897 Canudos rebellion.

Canudos itself is 100 km away at the junction of the BR-116 and BR-235 (direct buses from Salvador); religious rebels led by the visionary Antônio Conselheiro defeated three expeditions sent against them in 1897 before being overwhelmed. These events are the theme of two great books: *Os Sertões* (Rebellion in the Backlands) by Euclides da Cunha, and *La Guerra del Fin del Mundo* (The War of the End of the World) by the Peruvian Mario Vargas Llosa. The Rio Vaza Barris, which runs through Canudos has been dammed, and the town has been moved to Nova Canudos by the dam. Part of the old town is still located 10 km W.

● **Accommodation** **D** *Grapiuna*, Praça Monsenhor Berenguer 401, T 275-1157, cheaper without bath, downstairs, rec; **E** *Santa Cruz*, opp Banco do Brasil, shared bath, basic but clean; pleasant bars. At Euclides da Cunha, on the BR-116 39 km from Monte Santo, are *Hotel Lua*, simple and *Hotel Conselheiro*.

PARQUE NACIONAL DE PAULO AFONSO

Part of the northern border of Bahia is the Rio São Francisco; on the opposite bank are Pernambuco and Alagoas. From Salvador, the BR-110 runs N to the river at Paulo Afonso; the road is paved for all but 30 km between Cícero Dantas and Antas. At Jeremoaba, 41 km further N, BR-235 heads W to Canudos; 110 km, 76 km N of Jeremoaba is the **Parque Nacional de Paulo Afonso**. The Falls of **Paulo Afonso**, once one of the great falls of the world but now exploited for hydroelectric power, are 270 km from the mouth of the São Francisco river, which drains a valley 3 times the size of Great Britain. There are 2,575 km of river above the Falls to its source in Minas Gerais. Below the Falls is a deep, rock gorge through which the water rushes. The national park is an oasis of trees and the lake amid a desert of brown scrub and cactus. The best time to visit the Falls is in the rainy season (Jan-Feb); only then does much water pass over them, as almost all the flow now goes through the power plant. The best view is from the northern (Alagoas) bank. The Falls are in a security area; admission from 0800 only by car or taxi and only with a guide. Go to the tourist information office in the centre of the town and sign up for a tour of the hydroelectric plant, 2 hrs, US$6/car.

● **Accommodation** **A3** *Grande Hotel de Paulo Afonso* (a/c, TV, pool, T 281-1914) and a guest house (apply for room in advance) at the Falls. The town of Paulo Afonso (pop 86,560) is some distance from the Falls, reached by bus from Salvador, by paved road from Recife, bus, 7 hrs, US$8, or from Maceió (306 km) via Palmeira dos Índios, partially paved. **C** *Belvedere*, Apolônio Sales 457, T 281-1814, a/c, swimming pool and **C** *Palace*, T 281-1521, a/c, swimming pool, 'best value in town', next door. Plenty of restaurants.

● **Shopping** Handicrafts (embroidery, fabrics) from Núcleo de Produção Artesanal, Av Apolônio Sales 1059.

TRAVEL ON THE RIO SÃO FRANCISCO

PETROLINA AND JUAZEIRO

The river is navigable above the Falls from above the twin towns (linked by a bridge) of Juazeiro, in Bahia, and Petrolina, in Pernambuco, thriving towns compared to many on the upper São Francisco. Navigation is possible as far as Pirapora in Minas Gerais, linked by road to the Belo Horizonte-Brasília highway (see page 438).

Like Pirapora, **Petrolina** (pop 174,970) is famous for the production of *carrancas* (boat figureheads, mostly grotesque) of wood or ceramic. Petrolina has its own airport and close to this is the small Museu do Sertão – relics of rural life in the NE and the age of the 'coronéis' and the bandit Lampião.

Juazeiro (pop 128,380) is the poorer of the two cities. Market on Fri and Sat.

● **Accommodation** & **places to eat Petrolina**: **D** *Pousada da Carranca*, BR-122, Km 4, T 961-3421; **E** *Hotel Newman*, Av Souza Filho 444, T 961-0595; **E** *Espacial*, EF Leste Brasileiro Km 2. *Restaurante Panorâmico*, the only one on the river front, is good. **Juazeiro**: *Grande Hotel*, R Pititinga, T 811-2710, *Vitória*, T 811-2712, and *União* (rec) and *Oliveira*, the last two in R Conselheiro Saraiva. **B** *Hotel Pousada de Juazeiro*, 6 km S on BR-407, T 811-2820, a/c, pool, restaurant, bar, pleasant. Unique restaurant known as the *Vaporzinho* is high and dry on the river front, a side-wheel paddle steamer (poor food), the *Saldanha Marinho*, built at Sabará in 1852.

● **Transport** For information on river transport T Juazeiro (075) 811-2465.

ROUTES The BR-253 runs W from Canudos to Juazeiro, alternatively, from Salvador go to Feira de Santana, take the paved BR-324, then the BR-407, which continues through Petrolina to Picos in Piauí (see page 566) junction for Fortaleza or Teresina. On the BR-407, 124 km S of Juazeiro is **Senhor do Bonfim** (*pop* 83,260), a busy market town with lots of life (also banks and post office).

The Northeast: Sergipe and Alagoas

THE EIGHT northeastern states are generally poor economically, but are neither poor historically (see Recife, Olinda, São Luís), nor culturally (eg 'Forró' and other musical styles, many good museums, lacework, ceramics). There is a multitude of beaches: those in established resorts tend to be polluted, but you don't have to travel far for good ones, while off the beaten track are some which have hardly been discovered.

Climate South of Cabo São Roque (Rio Grande do Norte) there is abundant rainfall, but in Pernambuco the zone of ample rain stretches only 80 km inland, though it deepens southwards. São Luís in Maranhão also gets plenty of rain, but between eastern Maranhão and Pernambuco lies a triangle, with its apex deep inland, where the rainfall is sporadic, and occasionally non-existent for a year. Here the tropical forest gives way to the *caatinga*, or scrub forest bushes which shed their leaves during drought.

History There was a brief period of colonization from northern Europe in the NE, when the Dutch West India Company, based at Recife, controlled some seven captaincies along the coast. They gained control in 1630, when Portugal was subject to Spain. After 1640, when Portugal freed itself, the colonists fought the Dutch, finally expelling them in 1654.

247 km N of Salvador, on BR-101, almost midway between the Sergipe-Bahia border and Aracaju is **Estância**, with pleasant hotels: **E** *Turista*, and **E** *Dom Bosco*, opposite, slightly cheaper, bath and breakfast. The town boasts a small Jorge Amado museum and the June festival of São João. Many buses stop at the Rodoviária, which is on the main road.

ARACAJU

(*Pop* 401,245; *CEP* 49000; *DDD* 079) Capital of Sergipe (*state pop* 1,492,400), 327 km N of Salvador, founded 1855, it is a clean and friendly town. It stands on the S bank of the Rio Sergipe, about 10 km from its mouth.

Places of interest

In the centre is a group of linked, beautiful parks: **Praça Olímpio Campos**, in which stands the cathedral, **Praça Almirante Barroso**, with the Palácio do Governo, and **Praças Fausto Cardoso** and **Camerino**. Across Av Rio Branco from these two is the river. The streets are clean (parts of Laranjeiras and João Pessoa in centre reserved for pedestrians). There is a handicraft centre, the **Centro do Turismo**, open 0900-1300, 1400-1900, in the restored Escola Normal, on Praça Olímpio Campos; the stalls are arranged by type (wood, leather, etc). The commercial area is on Ruas Itabaianinha and João Pessoa, leading up to R Divina Pastora and Praça General Valadão. At R Itabaianinha 41 is the **Instituto Geográfico e Histórico de Sergipe** (Mon-Fri 0800-1200, 1400-1700).

Beaches

A 16-km road leads to the fine **Atalaia** beach: oil-drilling rigs offshore. Beaches continue S down the coast. There is an even better beach, **Nova Atalaia**, on Ilha de Santa Luzia across the river, reached by boat from the Hidroviária (ferry station), which is across Av Rio Branco from Praça General Valadão. Boats cross the river to **Barra dos Coqueiros** every 15 mins (US$0.25); the boats at a quarter past the hour combine with a bus to Nova Atalaia (US$0.35). Buses return to Barra on the hour. Services are more frequent at weekends, when it is very lively. The river at Barra dos Coqueiros is busy with fishing and pleasure craft.

Excursions

15 km NW from Aracaju is **Laranjeiras** (*pop* 15,600), reached by São Pedro bus, from old rodoviária in centre, 30 mins-1 hr. A small pleasant town, with a ruined church on a hill, it has three museums (Museu Afro-Brasileiro, Centro de Cultura João Ribeiro, and Sacro in the Conceição church), and the 19th century Capela de Sant'Aninha with a wooden altar inlaid with gold. **C** *Pousada Vale dos Outeiros*, rec.

70 km W of Aracaju is **Itabaiana**, which has a famous gold market on Sat.

Local festivals

On 8 Dec there are both Catholic (Nossa Senhora da Conceição) and Umbanda religious festivals.

Local information
● **Accommodation**

In Atalaia (Velha) there are many hotels and aparthotels, mostly mid-to-high priced.

L2 *Parque dos Coqueiros*, Atalaia beach, R F R Leite Neto 1075, T 243-1511, F 243-2186, large pool, luxurious, attractive, only hotel on beach; **A1** *Beira Mar*, Av Rotary, T 243-1921, F 243-1153; **D** *Pousada da Praia*, R Niceu Dantas 667, T 223-1700. At Atalaia Nova is the **A2** *Da Ilha*, T 262-1221, F 262-1359.

In the centre: **A2** *Palace de Aracaju*, Praça Gen Valadão, T 224-5000, 3-star, a/c, TV, fridge, central, restaurant, pool, parking; **A2** *Grande*, R Itabaianinha 371, T 211-1383, F 222-2656, a/c, TV, fridge, central, *Quartier Latin* restaurant; **B** *Aperipê*, R São Cristóvão 418, T 211-1880, central, a/c, phone, fridge, restaurant; **A3** *Serigy*, R Santo Amaro 269, T 211-1088, same management and facilities, comfortable; **C** *Brasília*, R Laranjeiras 580, T 224-8022, good value, good breakfasts, rec; **C** *Oásis*, R São

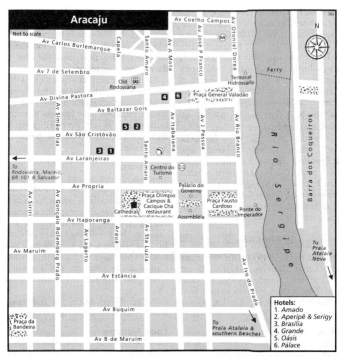

Aracaju

Not to scale

Av Carlos Burlemarque

Av 7 de Setembro

Old Rodoviária

Av Divina Pastora

Av Baltazar Gois

Av São Cristóvão

Av Laranjeiras

To Rodoviária, Maceió, BR 101 & Salvador

Av Propria

Palácio do Governo

Praça Olímpio Campos & Cacique Chá restaurant

Cathedral

Av Itaporanga

Av Maruim

Praça Fausto Cardoso

Assembléia

Ponte do Imperador

To Praia Atalaia Nova

Av Estância

Av Buquim

Praça da Bandeira

Av B de Maruim

To Praia Atalaia & southern beaches

Av Coelho Campos

Av José P Franco

Av Otoniel Dorea

Ferry

Terminal Hidroviário

Praça General Valadão

Rio Sergipe

Barra dos Coqueiros

Centro do Turismo

Hotels:
1. Amado
2. Aperipê & Serigy
3. Brasília
4. Grande
5. Oásis
6. Pálace

Cristóvão 466, T 224-2125, with good breakfast, hot water, fair, a bit tatty; **D** *Amado*, R Laranjeiras 532, a/c (less with fan), laundry facilities; **E** *Turista*, R Divina Pastora 411, noisy, mosquitoes, no hot water or breakfast, friendly. **F Youth Hostel**, T 223-2802, on road to Atalaia (take bus Os Campos, from Centre), no card needed, clean, friendly; new **youth hostel**, R Braulio Costa 675, with pool, rec.

Camping: *Camping Clube do Brasil* site at Atalaia Velha beach.

● **Places to eat**
Very many in Atalaia; on Av Oceânica try *Chapéu de Couro*, No 128, rec; *Cantinha da Bahia*, No 180, rec for fresh crab. In town, there is a good bar and restaurant, *Cacique Chá*, in the cathedral square, lively at weekends; also on Praça Olímpio Campos is *Rancho Gaúcho*, No 692, quite good, very friendly; *Bar e Lanchonete Dom Qui Chopp*, Laranjeiras opp Telergipe, popular.

● **Post & telecommunications**
Post Office: Laranjeiras and Itabaianinha.

Telephones: Telergipe, Laranjeiras 296, national and international calls until 2200.

● **Shopping**
Artesanato interesting: pottery figures and lace particularly. Fair in Praça Tobias Barreto every Sun. Municipal market is a block N of the Hidroviária.

● **Tourist offices**
Bureau de Informaçes Turísticas de Sergipe, R 24 Horas, T 224-5168, very friendly, helpful, abundant leaflets. In the centre, go to **Aracatur**, R Maruim 100, Sala 10, T 224-1226, which has leaflets and maps such as *Aracaju no bolso* and *Onde?*, helpful, English spoken.

● **Transport**
The rodoviária for interstate buses is 4 km from the centre, linked by local buses from the adjacent terminal (buy ticket before going on to the platform). Bus 004 'T Rod/L Batista' goes to the centre, US$0.25; look for route plates on the side of buses and at termini in town. The old bus terminal in town is at Santo Amaro e Divina Pastora, Praça João XXIII; buses from here to new

rodoviária, Laranjeiras and São Cristóvão (45 mins, US$0.70). Buses to the rodoviária also can be caught at the terminal nr the Hidroviária and from Capela at the top of Praça Olímpio Campos.

To **Salvador**, 6-7 hrs, 11 a day with Bonfim, US$13.50, executive service at 1245, US$18, saves 1 hr. To **Maceió**, US$12 with Bonfim. Many coastal destinations served; also Vitória (US$44), Rio (US$60), São Paulo, Belo Horizonte (US$50).

SÃO CRISTÓVÃO

(*Pop* 41,300) The old state capital of Sergipe, SW of Aracaju on the road to Salvador, was founded in 1590 by Cristóvão de Barros. It is the fourth oldest town in Brazil. Built on top of a hill, its colonial centre is unspoiled, the majority of buildings painted white with green shutters and woodwork. (No hotels, but families rent rooms near the rodoviária at the bottom of the hill.)

Places of interest Worth visiting are the **Museu de Arte Sacra e Histórico de Sergipe** in the **Convento de São Francisco** (open Tues-Sun 0800-1800), and the **Museu de Sergipe** in the former **Palácio do Governo**, both on Praça de São Francisco. Also on this square are the churches of **Misericórdia** (1627) and the **Orfanato Imaculada Conceição** (1646, permission to visit required from the Sisters). On Praça Senhor dos Passos are the churches of **Senhor dos Passos** and **Terceira Ordem do Carmo** (both 1739), while on the Praça Getúlio Vargas (formerly Praça Matriz) is the **Igreja Matriz Nossa Senhora da Vitória** (all are closed Mon). Also worth seeing is the old **Assembléia Legislativa** on R Coronel Erundino Prado. Outdoor arts festival in second half of October.

● **Transport** Buses (São Pedro) from Aracaju, from old rodoviária in centre, see above. A tourist train runs between Aracaju and São Cristóvão each Sat and Sun, 0900, 3½ hrs.

The Rio São Francisco marks the boundary between Sergipe and Alagoas. The BR-101 between Aracaju and Maceió – the next port to the N – is paved, crossing the São Francisco by bridge between Propriá and Porto Real do Colégio.

Another crossing can be made by boat from **Neópolis** in Sergipe, to **Penedo** (*pop* 40,665) in Alagoas, near the mouth of the Rio São Francisco.

Penedo is a charming town, with a nice waterfront park, Praça 12 de Abril, with stone walkways and walls. Originally the site of the Dutch Fort Maurits (built 1637, razed to the ground by the Portuguese), the colonial town stands on a promontory above the river. Among the colonial architecture, modern buildings such as the Associação Commercial and *Hotel São Francisco*, both on Av Floriano Peixoto, do not sit easily.

Places of interest

On the Praça Barão de Penedo is the neoclassical **Igreja Matriz** (closed to visitors) and the 18th century **Casa da Aposentadoria**. East and a little below this square is the Praça Rui Barbosa, on which are the **Convento de São Francisco** (1783 and later) and the church of **Santa Maria dos Anjos** (1660). As you enter, the altar on the right depicts God's eyes on the world, surrounded by the three races, one Indian, two negroes and the whites at the bottom. The church has fine *trompe-l'oeil* ceilings (1784). The convent is still in use. Guided tours are free. The church of **Rosário dos Pretos**, on Praça Marechal Deodoro, is open to visitors, while **Nosso Senhor da Corrente** (1764), on Praça 12 de Abril, and **São Gonçalo Garcia** (1758-70) on Floriano Peixoto are closed, the latter for restoration to its façade. Also on Floriano Peixoto is the pink **Teatro 7 de Setembro** of 1884; between it and the old covered market are fruit and vegetable stalls. The **Casa de Penedo**, at R João Pessoa 126 (signs point the way up the hill from F Peixoto), displays photographs and books on, or by, local figures.

River traffic

Very few of the long two-masted sailing vessels that used to cruise on the river can be seen now, although there are plenty of smaller craft. Boats can be rented at the waterfront for excursions to the river islands, the mouth of the river and to beaches (eg Praia do Peba).

Local information

● Accommodation

C *Pousada Colonial*, Praça 12 de Abril 21, T 551-2677, *luxo* and suite have phone, TV and fridge, suites have a/c, spacious, good cheap restaurant, front rooms with view of Rio São Francisco; **C** *São Francisco*, Av Floriano Peixoto, T 551-2273, standard rooms have no a/c, others have a/c, TV, fridge, rec except for poor restaurant.

E *Turista*, R Siqueira Campos 143, T 551-2237, with bath, fan, hot water, rec.

F *Impérial*, Av Floriano Peixoto, basic.

● Places to eat

Forte da Rocheira, R da Rocheira (take either of the alleys running W off the hill between Praças Barão de Penedo and 12 de Abril, turn right), good food, especially *ensopada de jacaré* (alligator stew); continue along the cliff walkway to the riverside for *Churrascaria O Scala*, at the end of R 15 de Novembro.

● Banks & money changers

Banks open 0830-1300. *Banco do Nordeste do Brasil* on Av F Peixoto; *Banco do Brasil* and *Bradesco* on Av Duque de Caxias, opp Bompreço. *Restaurant e Bar Lulu*, Praça 12 de Abril, will change cash if conditions suit the owner, fair rates.

● Post & telecommunications

Post Office: Av Floriano Peixoto, opp *Hotel Imperial*.

Telephones: Telasa on Barão de Penedo.

● Shopping

Daily market on streets off Av Floriano Peixoto. Good hammocks. Ceramics for sale outside Bompreço supermarket on Av Duque de Caxias.

● Tourist offices

Tourist office in Casa da Aposentadoria, Praça Barão de Penedo (if open).

● Transport

Buses 451 km from **Salvador** (US$16, 6 hrs, by daily bus at 0600, book in advance), at same time for **Aracaju** (US$8.50); buses S are more frequent from Neópolis, 6 a day (0630-1800) to Aracaju, 2 hrs, US$5. 115 km from **Maceió**, 5 buses a day in either direction, US$5-6, 3-4 hrs. One bus to **São Paulo** daily, 1500, 2 a day to **Recife**, 0700, 2100. The Penedo rodoviária is on Av Duque de Caxias, behind Bompreço, little information; timetables posted in *Pousada Colonial*.

Ferries Frequent launches for foot pasengers and bicycles across the river to Neópolis, 25 mins, US$0.35. The dock in Penedo is on Av Duque de Caxias, below Bompreço. The ferry makes three stops in Neópolis, the second is closest to the rodoviária (which is near the Clube Vila Nova, opp Texaco station). Also half-hourly car ferry (US$1; take care when driving on and off).

(Pop 527,440; *CEP* 57000; *DDD* 082) The capital of Alagoas state *(pop* 2,513,000) is about 287 km NE of Aracaju by road, and 244 km S of Recife. It is mainly a sugar port, although there are also tobacco exports and a major petrochemical plant. A lighthouse stands in a residential area of town (Farol), about one km from the sea. The commercial centre stretches along the seafront to the main dock and climbs the hills behind. Alagoas is one of the poorest and least developed states, but Maceió is a friendly city with a low crime rate.

Places of interest

Two of the city's old buildings, the **Palácio do Governo**, which also houses the Pierre Chalita museum (see below), and the church of **Bom Jesus dos Mártires** (covered in tiles), are particularly interesting. Both are on the Praça dos Martírios (or Floriano Peixoto). The recently restored **cathedral**, Praça Dom Pedro II, is also interesting. The Associação Comercial has a museum on R Sá e Albuquerque, Jaraguá, near the sea, in a beautiful, though deteriorating building.

Museums

Instituto Histórico e Geográfico, R João Pessoa 382, T 223-7797, good small collection of Indian and Afro-Brazilian artefacts. **Fundação Pierre Chalita**, Praça Floriano Peixoto 49, centre, T 223-4298, Alagoan painting and religious art. **Museu do Folclore Theo Brandão**, Praça Sinimbu 206, centre. All closed Sat and Sun.

Lagoa do Mundaú

This lagoon, whose entrance is 2 km S at **Pontal da Barra**, limits the city to the S and W: excellent shrimp and fish at its small restaurants and handicraft stalls; a nice place for a drink at sundown. Boats make excursions in the lagoon's channels.

Beaches

Beaches fronting the old city, between Salgema terminal and the modern port area (Trapiche, Sobral) are too polluted for swimming. Beyond the city's main dock the beachfront districts begin; within the city, the beaches are posher the further from the centre you go. The first, going N, is Pajuçara where there is a nightly craft market. At weekends there are wandering musicians and entertainers and patrols by the cavalry on magnificent Manga Larga Marchador horses. There are periodic *candomblé* and *axé* nights and rituals to the

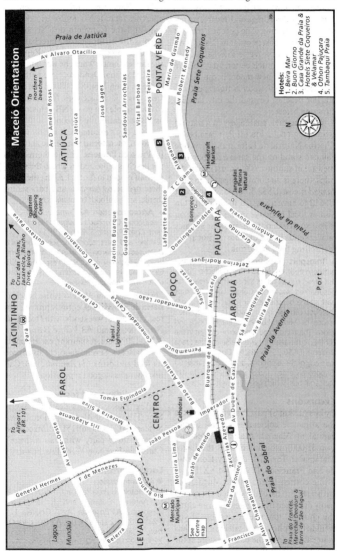

Maceió Orientation

Hotels:
1. Beira Mar
2. Buon Giorno
3. Casa Grande da Praia & Hotel Siete Coqueiros
4. Othon Pajuçara
5. Tambaqui Praia & Velamar

goddess Iemanjá. Next is Ponta Verde, then Jatiúca, Cruz das Almas, Jacarecica (9 km from the centre), Guaxuma (12 km), Garça Torta (14 km), Riacho Doce (16 km), Pratagi (17 km) and Ipioca (23 km). Jatiúca, Cruz das Almas and Jacarecica are all good for surfing. The beaches, some of the finest and most popular in Brazil, have a protecting coral reef a kilometre or so out. Bathing is much better 3 days before and after full or new moon, because tides are higher and the water is more spectacular. For beaches beyond the city, see **Excursions** below.

Jangadas take passengers to a natural swimming pool 2 km off Pajuçara beach (Piscina Natural de Pajuçara), at low tide you can stand on the sand and rock reef (beware of sunburn). You must check the tides, there is no point going at high tide. *Jangadas* cost US$2.50 pp/day (or about US$12 to have a *jangada* to yourself). On Sun or local holidays in the high season it is overcrowded, take mask or goggles (at weekends lots of *jangadas* anchor at the reef selling food and drink).

● **Transport** Taxis from town go to all the northern beaches (eg 30 mins to Riacho Doce), but buses run as far as Ipioca. The Jangadeiras bus marked 'Jacarecica-Center, via Praias' runs past all the beaches as far as Jacarecica. From there you can change to 'Riacho Doce-Trapiche', 'Ipioca' or 'Mirante' buses for Riacho Doce and Ipioca. These last three can also be caught in the centre on the seafront avenue below the Praça Sinimbu (US$0.25 to Riacho Doce). To return take any of these options, or take a bus marked 'Shopping Center' and change there for 'Jardim Vaticana' bus, which goes through Pajuçara.

Excursions

By bus (22 km S) past Praia do Francês to the attractive colonial town and former capital of Alagoas, **Marechal Deodoro** (*pop* 31,000), which overlooks the Lagoa Manguaba. The 17th century **Convento de São Francisco**, Praça João XXIII, has a fine church (Santa Maria Magdalena) with a superb baroque wooden altarpiece, badly damaged by termites. You can climb the church's tower for views, but if you want to take photos you will have to collect your camera from the baggage store at the entrance. Adjoining it is the **Museu de Arte Sacra**, open Tues-Sun, 0900-1700, US$0.30 (guided tours available, payment at your discretion). Also open to visitors is the Igreja **Matriz de NS da Conceição** (1783). Remains of other 18th century churches include NS do Rosário, do Amparo and the Convento do Carmo. The town is the birthplace of Marechal Deodoro da Fonseca, founder of the Republic; the modest house where he was born is on the R Marechal Deodoro, close to the waterfront, open Mon-Sat, 0800-1700 (entry free). Good local lacework. *Restaurant São Roque*, simple but good. **NB** Schistosomiasis is present in the lagoon.

On a day's excursion, it is easy to visit the town, then spend some time at beautiful **Praia do Francês**. The northern half of the beach is protected by a reef, the southern half is open to the surf. Along the beach there are many *barracas* and bars selling drinks and seafood; try *agulhas fritas*.

● **Accommodation A2** *Cumaru*, T 231-2223, 3-star, good; **C** *Pousada Bougainville e Restaurant Chez Patrick*, T 231-1079, a/c, TV, pool, seafood and international cooking, very nice; **D** *Pousada Le Baron*, T 235-3061, on road from beach to highway, good; **D** *O Pescador*, T 231-6959, with restaurant. Recommended **restaurant** *Panela Mágica*; several others.

Further out from Maceió is the beach of **Barra de São Miguel**, entirely protected by reef, crowded at weekends, with *Pousada da Barra*, good, and **A3** *Village Barra Hotel*, T 272-1207, pool, restaurant, excursions to other beaches. Several good, cheap *barracas* for food and drink (*da Amizade*, rec). Carnival here has a good reputation.

Local holidays and festivals

27 Aug (Nossa Senhora dos Prazeres); 16 Sept (Freedom of Alagoas); 8 Dec (Nossa Senhora da Conceição); 15 Dec (Maceiofest, 'a great street party with *trios elêctricos*'); Christmas Eve; New Year's Eve, half-day.

Local information
● **Accommodation**
Many hotels on Praia Pajuçara, mostly along Av Dr Antônio Gouveia and R Jangadeiros Alagoanos. **A1** *Enseada*, Av A Gouveia 171, T 231-4726, F 231-5134, rec; **A1** *Pajuçara Othon*, R Jangadeiros Alagoanos 1292, T 231-2200, F 231-5499; **A2** *Sete Coqueiros*, Av A Gouveia 1335, T 231-8583, F 231-7467, 3-star,

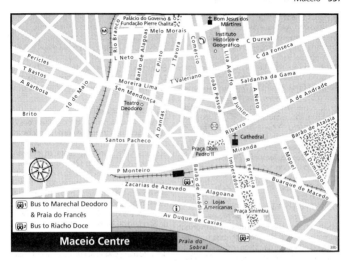

Bus to Marechal Deodoro
& Praia do Francês

Bus to Riacho Doce

Maceió Centre

Praia do Sobral

a/c, TV, phone, popular restaurant; pool; next door is the smaller **B** *Velamar*, T 231-5888, a/c, TV, fridge, safes in rooms.

Many good *pousadas* R Jangadeiros Alagoanos, one block back from the beach (it can be hard to find a room during the Dec-Mar holiday season, when prices go up): **B** *Laguna Praia*, No 1231, T 231-6180, highly rec; **B** *Maceió Praia*, No 3, T 231-6391, highly rec; **B** *Pousada Sete Coqueteiros*, No 123, T 231-5877, rec; **B** *Verde Mar*, No 1, a/c, hot water, TV, T 231-2669, very good; **C** *Buongiorno*, No 1437, T 231-7577, F 231-2168, a/c, fridge, English-speaking owner, helpful; **D** *Casa Grande da Praia*, No 1528, T 231-3332, a/c and TV, cheaper without, rec; *Amazona*, No 1095, great breakfast; **D** *Costa Verde*, No 429, bath, fan, good family atmosphere, English, German spoken, rooms on 1st floor are best, T 231-4745; **D** *Pousada Maramar*, No 343, bright, some rooms with sea view, exchange library; **D** *Pousada Quinta Pruma*, No 597, T 231-6065. On Antônio de Mendonça: **D** *Pousada Rex*, No 311, T 231-4358, helpful, highly rec (esp the breakfast); **D** *Pousada Shangri-La*, No 1089, T 231-3773, safe. *Mandacaru*, Almte Maranenhas 85, 2 corners from beach, safe, good value.

At Ponta Verde beach: **A1** *Tambaqui Praia*, R Eng Mário de Gusmão 176, T 231-0202, a/c, TV, phone, restaurant; **C** *Dos Corais*, R H Guimarães 80, helpful; **C** *Hotel do Mar*, Av R Kennedy 1447, T 231-3171, good; **D** *Baleia Azul*, Av Sandoval Arroxeias 822, a/c, fridge, TV;

D *Sol de Verão*, R Eng Mário do Gusmão 153, **E** in small rooms without bath; **D** *Pousada Bela Vista*, Av Eng Mario de Gusmão, 1260, T 231 8337, well situated, excellent breakfast, a/c, TV, rec.

Further from centre, **L2** *Matsubara*, on Cruz das Almas beach, T 231-6178, F 235-1660, pool, tennis, all facilities, rec; **D** *Hospedaria de Turismo Costa Azul*, Av João Davino and Manoel Gonçalves Filho 280, T 231-6281, shower, fan, English spoken, discounts over a week.

C-D *Pousada Cavalo Marinho*, R da Praia 55, Riacho Doce (15 km from centre), facing the sea, T 235-1247, F 235-3260, use of bicycle, canoes and body boards inc, hot showers, German and English spoken, tropical breakfasts, Swiss owner, very highly rec (nearby is *Lua Cheia*, good food and live music at night).

In the centre: **A1** *Beiriz*, R João Pessoa 290, T 221-1080, comfortable, pool; **C** *Parque*, Praça Dom Pedro II 73, T 221-9099, a/c; **D** *Pousada Sol e Mar*, Av Rosa da Fonseca s/n, T 221-2615, helpful owners, safe, rec; **E** *Golf*, R Prof Domingos Moeda 38A (nr the Cathedral), clean. Cheap hotels (mostly without windows) in R Barão de Atalaia. Owing to pollution, few visitors now stay on Avenida or Sobral beaches.

Youth hostel: **F** *Nossa Casa*, R Prefeito Abdon Arroxelas 177, T 231-2246.

Camping: there is a Camping Clube do Brasil site on Jacarecica beach, T 235-3600, a 15-min taxi drive from the town centre. Camping Pajuçara at Largo da Vitória 211, T 231-7561, clean, safe, food for sale, rec.

● **Places to eat**

Ao Lagostão, Av Duque de Caxias 1348, seafood, fixed price (expensive) menu; *Pizzeria Sorrisa*, Av Alagoana e J Pessoa Imperator, very cheap, good food, popular with Brazilians; *Bar das Ostras*, R Cruzeiro do Sul 487, Vergel do Lago, expensive but good. Vegetarian: *O Natural*, R Libertadora Alagoana (R da Praia) 112; *Nativa*, Osvaldo Sarmento 56, good views. *Spettus*, Av R Kennedy 1911, Ponta Verde, *churrascaria rodizio*. Many good bars and restaurants in Pajuçara: rec places on Av Antônio Gouveia are: *Paraíso*, No 631, vegetarian, open late; *O Dragão*, No 21, Chinese; *Comes e Bebes*, No 981, Italian and Arabic, good, take-away service; *Tempeiro Paulista*, No 1103, typical food, good service, cheap. *Massarella*, Jangadeiras Alagoanas 1255, Italian, small, good. *Mello's Bar*, R Epaminondas Gracindo 194, excellent food and value. The beaches for 5 km from the beginning of Pajuçara to Cruz das Almas in the N, are lined with *barracas* (thatched bars) providing music, snacks and meals until midnight (later at weekends). Vendors on the beach sell beer and food during the day: clean and safe. At Ponto da Barra, on the lagoon side of the city, *Alípio*, and many others. Local specialities include oysters, *pitu*, a crayfish (now becoming scarce), and *sururu*, a kind of cockle. Local ice cream, *Shups*, rec.

● **Banks & money changers**

Banco do Brasil, etc. Open 1000 to 1500. Good rates at **Banespa**. **Banorte**, cash against Mastercard, R de Comercio, 306, Centro. **Banco Meridional**, cash against Mastercard, Praça Dom Pedro II, 95, Centro.

● **Electric current**

220 volts AC, 60 cycles.

● **Entertainment**

Teatro Deodoro, Praça Marechal Deodoro, in centre; *Cinema São Luiz*, R do Comércio, in centre; *Arte 1* and *2* Pajuçara and Iguatemi shopping centre; the other cinemas tend to be fleapits; *Bar Chapéu de Couro*, José Carneiro 338, Ponto da Barra, is a popular music bar for young people.

Nightlife: is relaxed and varied. Popular *barracas* are *Bar Lampião* (or *Tropical*) and *Ipaneminha* on Pajuçara (Brazilian pop), and *Fellini* on Ponta Verde (varies: good blues and jazz). There are nightclubs to suit most tastes; *Calabar*, in Pajuçara, for *forró* and *lambada*, *Lambadão* at Cruz das Almas (excellent *lambada*, weekends only).

● **Post & telecommunications**

Post Office: R João Pessoa 57, centre, 0700-2200.

Telecommunications: R do Comércio 508, almost opp Bandepe. Small Telasa office on Pajuçara beach, opp *Othon* hotel. Also at rodoviária.

● **Tourist offices**

Ematur, Duque de Caxias 2014, Centro, T 221-8987. Also at airport and rodoviária (latter not always open). Helpful, has good maps and leaflets. The municipal tourist authority is **Emturma**, R Saldanha da Gama 71, Farol, T 223-4016; information post on Pajuçara beach, opp *Hotel Solara*.

● **Transport**

Local Bus: Frequent buses, confusingly marked, serve all parts of the city. Bus stops are not marked, best to ask where people look as if they are waiting. The 'Ponte Verde/Jacintinho' bus runs via Pajuçara from centre to rodoviária, also take 'Circular' bus (25 mins Pajuçara to rodoviária, the stop in Pajuçara is opp the petrol station by Bompreço supermarket); 'Feitosa' also goes to the rodoviária, by a different route. See also **Beaches**, above. Buses and kombis to Marechal Deodoro, Praia do Francês and Barra de São Miguel leave from R Barão de Anádia, outside the ferroviária, opp *Lojas Americanas*: bus US$0.50, kombi US$0.55 to Marechal Deodoro, 30 mins, calling at Praia do Francês in each direction. Last bus back from Praia do Francês to Maceió at 1800.

Air 20 km from centre, taxi about US$15. Buses to airport from nr *Hotel Beiriz*, R João Pessoa 290 or in front of the Ferroviária, signed 'Rio Largo'; alight at Tabuleiro dos Martins, then 7-8 mins' walk to airport, bus fare US$0.50. Tourist flights over the city.

Trains The ferroviária is in the centre, R Barão de Anádia 121. 5 trains a day, Mon-Sat, from 0630-1855 to Rio Largo (35 km, US$0.12), via Fernão Velho, Satuba and Utinga. Worth taking in one direction at least since it passes the Lagoa Mundaú, through places where buses do not go.

Buses Rodoviária is 5 km from centre, on a hill with good views and cool breezes. Luggage store. Take bus marked 'Ouro Preto p/centro' or see above (taxi quicker, US$3.50) to Pajuçara. Bus to **Recife**, 10 a day, 3½ hrs express (more scenic coastal route, 5 hrs) US$10; to **Aracaju**, US$12, 5 hrs (potholed road); to **Salvador**, 10 hrs, 4 a day, US$27 (*rápido* costs more). Buses to most large cities including Belém, Fortaleza, Brasília, Belo Horizonte, Rio, São Paulo.

NORTH TO PERNAMBUCO

There are many interesting stopping points along the coast between Maceió and Recife. At **Paripueira**, 40 mins bus ride from Maceió (Rodoviária), the beach is busy only during high season. **Barra de Santo Antônio**, 45 km N, is a busy fishing village, with a palm fringed beach on a narrow peninsula, a canoe-ride away; boats also go to the Ilha da Croa; many beautiful beaches nearby.

● **Accommodation & places to eat** E *São Geraldo*, simple, very clean, restaurant; *Pousada Buongiorno* in Maceió has 6 modest rooms to rent in a farmhouse, bathrooms but no electricity, many fruit trees (T Maceió 231-7577, F 231-2168); accommodation can be found through local people. *Peixada da Rita*, try prawns with coconut sauce, rec for local seafood; *Estrela Azul*, more expensive, good, popular with tourists.

Pernambuco

RECIFE

About 244 km N of Maceió and 835 km N of Salvador is **Recife** (*pop* 1,290,150; *CEP* 50000; *DDD* 081), founded on reclaimed land by the Dutch prince Maurice of Nassau in 1637 after his troops had burnt Olinda, the original capital. It is the capital of Pernambuco State (*pop* 7,110,000). The city centre consists of three portions, Recife proper, Santo Antônio and São José, and Boa Vista and Santo Amaro. The first two are on islands formed by the rivers Capibaribe, Beberibe and Pina, while the third is made into an island by the Canal Tacaruna, which separates it from the mainland. The centre is always very busy by day; the crowds and the narrow streets, especially in the Santo Antônio district, can make it a confusing city to walk around. Recife has the main dock area, with commercial buildings associated with it. South of the centre is the residential and beach district of Boa Viagem, reached by bridge across the Bacia do Pina. Olinda, the old capital, is only 6 km to the N (see page 547).

PLACES OF INTEREST

Churches

The best of them are the churches of **Santo Antônio do Convento de São Francisco** (1606; beautiful Portuguese tiles), in the R do Imperador, and adjoining it the **Capela Dourada** (Golden Chapel, 1697, the finest sight of all, Mon-Fri 0800-1130 and 1400-1700, Sat 0800-1130: US$0.15, no flash photography; it is through the Museu Franciscano de Arte Sacra, entry

Recife Orientation

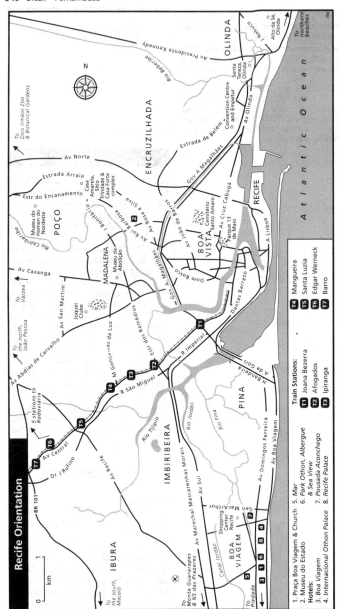

Train Stations:
T1 Joana Bezerra
T2 Afogados
T3 Ipiranga
T4 Mangueira
T5 Santa Luzia
T6 Edgar Werneck
T7 Barro

1. Praça Boa Viagem & Church
2. Museu do Estado

Hotels:
3. Boa Viagem
4. Internacional Othon Palace
5. Mar
6. Park Othon, Albergue & Sea View
7. Pousada Aconchego
8. Recife Palace

0 1 km

US\$1); **São Pedro dos Clérigos** in São José district (1782), for its façade, its fine wood sculpture and a splendid *trompe-l'oeil* ceiling, open Tues-Fri 0800-1200, 1400-1630, Sat 0800-1000; **Santo Antônio** (1753), in Praça da Independência, rebuilt in 1864, open daily 0800-1200 and Mon-Fri 1400-1800, Sun 1700-1900; **Conceição dos Militares**, R Nova 309 (1708), grand ceiling and a large 18th century primitive mural of the battle of Guararapes (museum next door), open Mon-Fri, 0700-1130, 1330-1600, Sat 0730-1100; **Nossa Senhora do Carmo**, Praça do Carmo (1675), open Mon-Sat 0800-1200, 1400-1800, Sun 1000-1100, 1900-2000; **Madre de Deus** (1706), in the street of that name in the district of Recife, with a splendid high altar, and sacristy, Mon-Fri 0800-1100, Sun 1000-1100; the **Pilar Church** (1680), R do Pilar, Recife district; the **Divino Espírito Santo** (1642), the original church of the Jesuits, Praça 17 in Santo Antônio district, Mon-Fri 0730-1630, Sat 0730-1200; **S José do Ribamar** (19th century), in São José, open Thur only. There are many others. Most of them are closed to visitors on Sun because of services.

14 km S of the city, a little beyond Boa Viagem and the airport, on Guararapes hill, is the historic church of **Nossa Senhora dos Prazeres**, open daily 0800-1700. It was here, in 1648-9, that two Brazilian victories led to the end of the 30-year Dutch occupation of the NE in 1654. The church was built by the Brazilian commander in 1656 to fulfil a vow. Boa Viagem's own fine church dates from 1707.

Other attractions

Forte do Brum (built by the Portuguese in 1629, before the founding of Recife), is an army museum – open Tues-Fri 1000-1700, Sat-Sun 1400-1700. **Forte das Cinco Pontas** (with **Museu da Cidade do Recife** – cartographic history of the settlement of Recife – open Mon-Fri 1300-1800, Sat-Sun 1400-1800, free), built by the Dutch in 1630 and altered by the Portuguese in 1677. The two forts jointly controlled access to the port at the northern and southern entrances respectively. The first Brazilian printing press was installed in 1706 and Recife claims to publish the oldest daily newspaper in South America, *Diário de Pernambuco*, founded 1825. The building is on the Praça da Independência.

The artists' and intellectuals' quarter is based on the **Pátio de São Pedro**, the square round São Pedro dos Clérigos. Folk music and poetry shows in the square on Fri, Sat and Sun evenings and there are pleasant little restaurants, with good atmosphere, at Nos 44, 46 and 47, and No 20 *Caldeira de Cana e Petisqueira Bangüê*. The square is an excellent shopping centre for typical NE craftware (clay figurines are cheapest in Recife). Not far away is the **Praça do Sebo**, where the city's second-hand booksellers concentrate; this Mercado de Livros Usados is off the R da Roda, behind the Edifício Santo Albino, near the corner of Av Guararapes and R Dantas Barreto. Visit the city markets in the São José and Santa Rita sections.

The former municipal prison has now been made into the **Casa da Cultura** (open Mon-Sat 0900-1900, Sun 1400-1800), with many cells converted into art or souvenir shops and with areas for exhibitions and shows (also public conveniences). Local dances such as the ciranda, forró and bumba-meu-boi are held as tourist attractions on Mon, Wed and Fri at 1700 (T 241-2111 to check in advance). Among other cultural centres are Recife's three traditional **theatres**, **Santa Isabel** (Praça da República, open to visitors Mon-Fri 1300-1800), **Parque** (R do Hospício 81, Boa Vista, restored and beautiful, open 0800-1200, 1400-1800) and **Apolo** (R do Apolo 121, open 0800-1200, 1400-1700).

Boa Viagem is the finest residential and hotel quarter. The 8 km promenade commands a striking view of the Atlantic, but the beach is crowded at weekends and not very clean. During the Jan breeding season, sharks come close to the shore. Go fishing on *jangadas* at Boa Viagem with a fisherman. The main square has a good market Sat, with forró dancing. Bus from centre, take any marked 'Boa Viagem'; from Nossa Senhora do Carmo, take buses marked 'Piedade', 'Candeias' or 'Aeroporto' – they go on Av Domingos

Ferreira, two blocks parallel to the beach, all the way to Praça Boa Viagem (at Av Boa Viagem 500). Back to centre take buses marked 'CDU' or 'Setubal' from Av Domingos Ferreira.

MUSEUMS

The **Museu do Homem do Nordeste**, Av 17 de Agosto 2223, Casa Forte (open Tues-Sun, 1100-1700, entry US$1), comprises the **Museu de Arte Popular**, containing ceramic figurines (including some by Mestre Alino and Zé Caboclo); the **Museu do Açúcar**, on the history and technology of sugar production, with models of colonial mills, collections of antique sugar bowls and much else; the **Museu de Antropologia**, the **Nabuco Museum** (at No 1865) and the modern museum of popular remedies, **Farmacopéia Popular**. Take the 'Dois Irmãos' bus (check that it's the correct one, with 'Rui Barbosa' posted in window, as there are two) from in front of the Banorte building near the post office on Guararapes, 30 mins' ride 10 km outside the city to the **zoo** (US$0.20, not very good) and **botanical gardens**; it passes the museum complex, and together with the zoo they make a pleasant day's outing. It is easier to get to the museum complex by taxi.

The **Museu do Estado**, Av Rui Barbosa 960, Graças (closed am on Sat and Sun, and all day Mon), has excellent paintings by the 19th-century landscape painter, Teles Júnior. **Museu do Trem**, Praça Visconde de Mauá, small but interesting, especially the Henschel locomotive (open Tues-Fri 0900-1200, 1400-1700, Sat 0900-1200, Sun 1400-1700). **Museu de Imagem e Som**, R da Aurora 379, Boa Vista, open Mon-Fri 0900-1200, 1400-1800.

EXCURSIONS

Any bus going S of Boa Viagem passes the **Ilha do Amor**; ask a fisherman to row you out to it and collect you at a set time, US$2.50. Walk across the island (10 mins) to the Atlantic side for a fine, open, uncrowded beach. Take care here as it is a little isolated. About 30 km S of Recife, beyond Cabo, is the beautiful and quiet **Gaibu** beach (take bus 'Centro do Cabo' from airport, frequent buses – 20 mins – from Cabo), *Pousada Beto Qualhado*; rooms, E, at *Oliver y Daniel*, Av Laura Cavalcante 20, German, very relaxed, cheap restaurants; 1 km on foot from Gaibu is **Praia Calhetas**, which is very nice. **Itapuama** beach is even more empty, also reached by bus from Cabo. **Cabo** (*pop* 121,000), Pernambuco's main industrial city, has interesting churches and forts and a Museu da Abolição, and at nearby Suape are many 17th-century buildings and a biological reserve. **Porto de Galinhas**, further S still, is a beautiful beach, reached by bus from Cais de Santa Rita, Recife US$2, via the town of Nossa Senhora do Ó, 2 hrs, 0900, 1230, 1530 (not Sun), 0740 Sun only, take 0900 since others don't allow enough time; last back at 1600, packed out. It has cool, clean water, and waves. **A1** *Solar Porto de Galinhas*, T 325-0772, F 325-1331, on beach, many facilities, beautiful place; *pousada* of Dona Benedita in the street where the bus stops, very basic, clean; several other hotels and *pousadas*; food at *Rang Bem* in same street as *Benedita*. Further S (80 km from Recife) are the beaches of **Barra do Sirinhaém**, with little tourist development as yet, 3 hotels including **E** *dos Cataventos*; fishermen make trips to offshore island (good views).

Carpina (*pop* 71,950), 54 km from Recife, is well known for its carnival and for the traditional Epiphany festival early in Jan, and also for the carpets made in the nearby village of Lagoa do Carro. There is a historical museum. Hotels (**A3** *Pousada das Acácias*, BR-408, Km 77, T 621-0594; **C** *São João da Escócia*, Av João Alfredo 136, T 621-0365) and restaurants. **Tracunhaém** (*pop* 13,700), is a peaceful town where fine ceramics are made; there are two interesting early 19th-century churches. It is just N of Carpina, on to the road to Nazaré da Mata.

LOCAL HOLIDAYS

1 Jan (Universal Brotherhood). 12-15 Mar, parades to mark the city's foundation. 24 June (São João), celebrated with bonfires and fireworks, see also below. 16 July (Nossa Senhora do Carmo, patron saint of the city). 8 Dec (Nossa Senhora da Conceição).

Recife

1. Church of Espíritu Santo
2. Church of Santo Antônio
3. Conceição dos Militares
4. Diário de Pernambuco
5. Nossa Senhora do Rosário dos Pretos
6. Palácio do Campo das Princesas (Governor's Palace)
7. Pátio de São Pedro & São Pedro dos Clérigos
8. Praça da Independencia
9. Praça da República
10. Praça do Sebo
11. Santo Antônio do Convento de São Francisco
12. Teatro de Santo Isabel
Hotels:
13. *Hotel Recife Plaza*

🚌1 Buses to Itamaracá & Igarassu
🚌2 Buses to Porto da Galinhas
🚌3 Buses to Boa Viagem

Carnival

The carnival groups dance at the doors of all the churches they pass; they usually go to the Church of Nossa Senhora do Rosário dos Pretos, patron saint of the slaves (R Estreita do Rosário, Santo Antônio), before proceeding into the downtown areas. A small car at the head bears the figure of some animal; it is followed by the king and queen under a large, showy umbrella. The *bahianas*, who wear snowy-white embroidered skirts, dance in single file on either side of the king and queen. Next comes the *dama do passo* carrying a small doll, or *calunga*. After the *dama* comes the *tirador de loas*: he chants to the group which replies in chorus, and last comes a band of local percussion instruments.

Still flourishing is the dance performance of the *caboclinhos*. The groups wear traditional Indian garb: bright feathers round their waists and ankles, colourful cockades, bead and animal teeth necklaces, a dazzle of medals on their red tunics. The dancers beat out the rhythm with bows and arrows; others of the group play primitive musical instruments, but the dance is the thing: spinning, leaping, and stooping with almost mathematical precision.

There is a *pre-carnavalesca* week, followed by the main days Sun to Tues; on the Sat the *bloco* 'Galo da Madrugada' officially opens carnival (wild and lively), see local press for routes and times. The groups taking part are *maracatu, caboclinhos, trocas, blocos, ursos, cabloclos de lança, escolas de samba* and *frevo*. Usually they start from Av Conde da Boa Vista and progress along R do Hospício, R da Imperatriz, Ponte da Boa Vista, Praça da Independência, R 1° de Março and R do Imperador. During Carnival (and on a smaller scale throughout the year) the Casa de Cultura has frevo demonstrations where visitors can learn some steps of this unique dance of Pernambuco (check press for details of 'Frevioca' truck and frevo orchestras during Carnival in the Pátio de São Pedro). The best place to see the groups is from the balconies of *Hotel do Parque*. Information from Casa de Carnaval, office of Fundação da Cultura de Recife, Pátio de São Pedro, lojas 10-11.

Festivais Juninos

In the June *festas* of São João and São Pedro, the forró is danced. This dance, now popular throughout the NE, is believed to have originated when the British builders of the local railways held parties that were 'for all'.

LOCAL INFORMATION

● Accommodation

(For Olinda hotels, see page 549.)

Hotel prices

L1	over US$200	L2	US$151-200
L3	US$101-150	A1	US$81-100
A2	US$61-80	A3	US$46-60
B	US$31-45	C	US$21-30
D	US$12-20	E	US$7-11
F	US$4-6	G	up to US$3

Unless otherwise stated, all hotels in range **D** and above have private bath. Assume friendliness and cleanliness in all cases.

Hotels in the **centre**: **A3** *Recife Plaza*, R da Aurora 225, T 231-1200, Boa Vista, 3-star, overlooking the Rio Capibaribe, every comfort, highly rec, fine restaurant (very popular lunchtime); **B** *4 de Outubro*, R Floriano Peixoto 141, Santo Antônio, T 424-4477, 4 standards of room, hot water, TV, phone, a/c.

In the cheaper categories: **D** *América*, Praça Maciel Pinheiro 48, Boa Vista, T 221-1300, 2-star, with a/c (cheaper without), front rooms pleasanter, quiet; **D** *Lido*, R do Riachuelo 547, T 222-4660, good breakfast, hot water, rec; **D** *Nassau*, Largo do Rosário 253, T 224-3977/3520, hot showers, but a bit noisy (breakfast only, served on 7th floor, with a balcony overlooking the city); **E** *Interlaine*, R do Hospício 186, T 222-3762, good value in town centre, highly rec; **E** *Parque*, R do Hospicio 51, inc breakfast, good view, good value, rec; **E** *Recife*, R do Imperador 310, T 224-0799, cheaper without bath, central, OK but grubby.

Hotels on or near the beach in Boa Viagem: **L2** *Mar*, nr beach at R Barão de Souza Leão 451, T 341-5433, F 341-7002, 5-star; 2 *Othon* hotels: *Praia*, Av Boa Viagem 9, T/F 465-3722, and *Park*, R dos Navegantes 9, T 465-4666, F 465-4767; **L2** *Recife Palace*, Av Boa Viagem 4070, T 325-4044, F 326-8895, 5-star; **A1** *Do Sol*, No 978, T 326-7644, F 326-7166, 4-star; **A2** *Savaroni*, No 3773, T 325-5077, F 326-4900, 4-star, good, pool; **A3** *Aguamar Praia*, R dos Navegantes 492, T 326-4604, a/c, TV, safe, good breakfast; **A3** *Arcada*, Av Cons Aguiar 3500, T 326-9922, F 326-9622, hotel, fondue restaurant and travel agency with exchange; **A3** *Casa Grande e Senzala*, Av Conselheiro Aguiar 5000, T/F 341-

0366, 3-star; *Castelinho Praia*, No 4520, T 326-1186, F 465-1150, 3 stars, pool, bar, restaurant; **A3** *Recife Monte*, R Petrolina e dos Navegantes 363, T 326-7422, F 326-2903, good value, rec; **B** *Pousada da Praia*, Alcides Carneiro Leal 66, T 326-7085, a/c, fridge, TV, safe, rooms vary (some tiny), helpful; **B** *Setúbal*, R Setúbal 932, T 341-4116, helpful, good breakfast; **B** *Uzi Praia*, Av Cons Aguiar 942, T 325-2741, a/c, rec; **C** *Pousada Aconchego*, Félix de Brito 382, T 326-2989, F 326-8059, 3 levels of tariff, a/c, pleasant, swimming pool, good meals, safe is closed on Sun and in evening, English-speaking owner, will collect you from the airport; **C** *Praia Mar*, Av Boa Viagem 1660, T 326-6905, small, rec; **C** *200 Milhas*, No 865, T 326-5292, safe, highly rec; **C** *Sea View*, R Navegantes 101, T 326-5891, Dutch-owned (Dutch, English, French spoken), a/c, small, rec; **D** *Guest House Pousada*, Luis Marquês Teixeira 155, T 341-0559, a/c, secure, proprietor Ricardo Teixeira is a Sevagtur guide, helpful, English and German spoken, rec; **D** *Solar da Tia Cléo*, R Joaquim Carneiro da Silva 48, T 326-3460/1090, no sign outside, fans, family atmosphere, fine garden, English spoken, rec.

Youth hostels: E *Albergue do Mar 81*, R dos Navegantes 81, T 326-2196, cheaper for IYHA members, good breakfast and atmosphere; **E** *Albergue Mandacaru*, R Maria Carolina 75, T 326-1964, stores luggage, English and German spoken, good breakfast, rec; *Maracatus do Recife*, R Maria Carolina 185, T 326-1221, good breakfast, pool, clean, safe, friendly, membership not needed, rec. Membership information from Associação Pernambucano de Albergues da Juventude (APEAJ), from Empetur (see below – take 2 photos).

Paulo Bezerra de Mello, DHL, R do Riachuelo 201, T 221-2000, rents an apartment for 3 at Boa Viagem, rec. Hotels in the Santa Rita area are not rec as this area is dangerous at night.

During Carnival and for longer stays at other times, private individuals rent rooms and houses in Recife and Olinda; Lins Turismo has listings as does the *Diário de Pernambuco*, or ask around the streets of Olinda. This accommodation is generally cheaper, safer and quieter than hotels. Many hotels sell 5-day Carnival packages (at high prices), which you must take regardless of the length of time you wish to stay. Shop around.

● **Places to eat**
There are many good restaurants, at all prices, in the city, and along beach at Boa Viagem.

City: *Leite* (lunches only), Praça Joaquim Nabuco 147/53 nr Casa de Cultura, old and famous, good service, smart (another branch in Boa Viagem, at Prof José Brandão 409). *Le Buffet*, R do Hospício 147-49, good, helpful, English-speaking owner;

Fuji (Japanese), No 354, economical, good tofu dishes; *Lisboa á Noite*, Hospício nr Conde da Boa Vista, good, reasonable, open Sun evenings (unlike many); *Tivoli*, R Matias de Albuquerque, Santo Antônio, lunches downstairs, a/c restaurant upstairs, good value; *Galo D'Ouro*, Gamboa do Carmo 83, rec, good value; at No 136, *Casa de Tia*, lunch only, must arrive by 1215, try *cosido*, a meat and vegetable stew, enough for 2, highly rec. *O Vegetal*, R Cleto Campelo e Av Guararapes (2nd floor) behind Central Post Office, lunch only, highly rec, closed Sat-Sun. *Casa dos Frios*, da Palma 57, loja 5, delicatessen/sandwich bar, salads, pastries etc, very good.

Boa Viagem: Main hotels. *Maxime*, Av Boa Viagem 21, is where the locals eat seafood; *O Porção*, Av Domingos Ferriera 4215, very good rodizio and salad bar, expensive; *Oficina da Massas*, No 2232, Italian; pizzas at *Mr Pizza*, Av Cons Aguiar 3553 and *Fiorentino*, R Laete Lemos 60 (another branch at Av Bernardo Vieira de Melo 4738, Candeias); *Mediterráneo*, R Setúbal, 100m from *Hotel Setúbal*, Italian, pasta, fish, reasonable, rec; *Shangai Palace* (Chinese), Av Domingos Ferreira 4719, excellent, plenty of food, another branch at Av Boa Viagem 5262; *China Especial*, Av Domingos Ferreira 3470, good value, large helpings; *Futuba*, R Mauoel de Brito 44, a tiny side street towards beach from Av Conselheiro Aguiar 1313, Japanese, good; *Chinés*, Herculano Bandeiro 875, Pina (just after bridge, on Boa Viagem side), good value, another branch at Av Bernardo Vieira de Melo, Piedade; *Prá Vocês*, Av Herculano Bandeira 115, Pina (town end of Boa Viagem beach), good but pricey seafood; *Boa Opçion* on the corner of Barão de Souza Leão and Av Domingos Ferreira, cheap, delicious local specialities, open for lunch and dinner, food/kilo, rec; *Snack Bar Flamingo*, Av Cons Aguiar 542, good hamburgers and ice cream; *Churrascaria o Laçador*, R Visconde Jequitinhonha 138, good meat, superb salads of all kinds, rec.

Be careful of eating the local small crabs, known as *guaiamum*; they live in the mangrove swamps which take the drainage from Recife's *mocambos* (shanty towns).

Bars: the Graças district, W of Boa Vista, on the Rio Capibaribe, is popular for bars and evening entertainment. Recommended is *Depois do Escuro*, R da Amizade 178, Graças, but there are many others. *Shoparia*, 2 doors from *Maxime* restaurant, rec for beer and atmosphere, live rock music after 2200; *Highlander*, English pub at Av Domingos Ferreira 2222, Boa Viagem.

● **Banks & money changers**
Banks open 1000-1600, hours for exchange vary between 1000 and 1400, sometimes later. **Banco do Brasil**, next to shopping centre, Boa

Viagem (Visa), US$20 commission, very helpful. In Boa Viagem, **Banorte** branches on Avs Domingos Ferreira and Cons Aguiar. **Mastercard**, cash against card, Av Cons Aguiar 3924, Boa Viagem. **Banco Meridional**, cash against Mastercard, Av Rio Branco, 155, Centro, **Lloyds Bank**, R do Fogo 22. Moneychanger hangs out at *Casa dos Frios* deli, R da Palma corner with Guararapes. **Edifício Bancomércio**, 3rd floor, R Matias de Alberquerque 223, takes cash and TCs. *Restaurante Leite*, Praça Joaquim Nabuco 147/53, good rates for TCs and cash.

● **Embassies & consulates**
British, Domingos Ferreira 222, sala 203, Boa Viagem, T 326 3733, open 0800-1130. **Danish**, Av M de Olinda 85, Ed Alberto Fonseca 2°, CP 3450030, T 224-0997, open 0800-1200, 1400-1800. **Swiss**, Av Rio Branco 4880, loja 32, Boa Viagem, T 326-3144. **Swedish**, Av Marquês de Olinda 126, sala 101, T 326-3144. **Finnish**, Av Conde da Boa Vista 708. **German**, Dantas Barreto 191, Edif Santo Antônio, 4th floor, T 424-3488. **French**, Av Dantas Barreto 1186, 18th ° floor, T 224-7421. **US**, Gonçalves Maia 163, Boa Vista, T 221-1412.

● **Cultural centres**
British Council, Domingos Ferreira 4150, Boa Viagem, CP 6104, T 272-3060, F 272-3455, 0800-1500, reading room with current English newspapers, very helpful. **Instituto Brasileiro Alemã**, R do Sossego 364. **Alliance Française**, R Amaro Bezerra 466, Derby, T/F 222-0918.

● **Electric current**
220 volts AC, 60 cycles.

● **Entertainment**
Discotheques: tend to be expensive and sophisticated – best of these are in Casa Forte. Best times are around midnight on Fri or Sat. Take a taxi.

Recife Ballet: shows in the Recife/Olinda Convention Center, US$10, traditional dances in full costume, rec.

The following have live regional music: *O Catedral da Seresta*, R Real da Torre 1435, Bairro Torre, T 228-0567; *O Pirata*, Av 17 de Agôsto 1738, Bairro Casa Forte; *Maria Bonita*, R Jack Ayres s/n, Boa Viagem, T 325-5402. Also visit a typical northeastern 'Forró' where local couples dance to typical music, very lively especially on Fri and Sat: several good ones at Candeias.

● **Laundry**
Av Conselheiro Aguiar 1385, Boa Viagem.

● **Places of worship**
Church: Episcopalian, R Carneiro Vilela 569.

● **Post & telecommunications**
Post Office: including poste restante, Central Correios, 50001, Av Guararapes 250 (or American Express, R Félix de Brito 666, T 465-5000 for poste restante). In Boa Viagem, Av Cons Aguiar e R Cel Sérgio Cardim.

Telecommunications: Embratel, Av Agamenon Magalhães, 1114, Parque Amorim district, T 221-4149; also Praça da Independência. Telpe, Av Cons Aguiar e R Padre Carapuceiro, closes 1200 on Sun. **International telephones**: R Diário de Pernambuco, 38 (closes 2230); also at airport (first floor), noisy.

● **Security**
Opportunistic theft is unfortunately common in the streets of Recife and Olinda (especially on the streets up to Alto da Sé). Keep hold of bags and cameras, and do not wear a watch. The police in Olinda are reported to be far less helpful than those in the city.

● **Shopping**
Markets: permanent craft market in **Casa da Cultura** (see above); prices for ceramic figurines are lower than Caruaru (see below). Mercado São José (1875) for local products and handicrafts. **'Hippy fair'** at Praça Boa Viagem, on the sea front, life-sized wooden statues of saints (a good meeting place is the *Bar Lapinha* in the middle of the square). Sat craft fair at **Sítio Trindade**, Casa Amarela: during the feast days of 12-29 June, fireworks, music, dancing, local food. On 23 April, here and in the Pátio de São Pedro, one can see the *xangô* dance. Herbal remedies, barks and spices at Afogados market.

Bookshops: *Livraria Brandão*, R da Matriz 22 (used English books and some French and German) and bookstalls on the R do Infante Dom Henrique. *Livro 7*, a huge emporium with a very impressive stock, R Sete de Setembro 329. *Sodiler* at Guararapes airport has books in English, newspapers, magazines. *Livraria do Nordeste*, between cells 118 and 119, Ralo Leste, Casa da Cultura, for books in Portuguese on the NE. *Livraria Nordeste*, R Imperatriz 43, Boa Vista. A great local character, *Melquísidec Pastor de Nascimento*, second-hand bookseller, at R Bispo Cardoso Aires, 215; also has a second-hand stall at Praça do Sebo (see page 541).

● **Sports**
Golf: Caxangá Golf & Country Club, Av Caxangá 5362: 9 holes.

● **Tour companies & travel agents**
Trilhas, T 222-6864, rec for ecologically oriented excursions; *Souto Costa Viagens e Turismo Ltda*, R Felix de Brito Melo 666, T 465-5000, and Aeroporto de Guararapes.

● **Tourist offices**
Empetur (for the State of Pernambuco), main office, Centro de Convenções, Complexo Ro-

doviário de Salgadinho, T 241-2111, F 241-9011, between Recife and Olinda, branch at airport – 24 hrs (will book hotels, helpful but few leaflets, English spoken). Maps available, or can be bought at newspaper stands in city; also sketch maps in monthly guides *Itinerário Pernambuco* and *Guia do Turista*.

Hours of opening of museums, art galleries, churches etc are published in the *Diário de Pernambuco*.

● **Transport**

Local Bus: city buses cost US$0.35; they are clearly marked and run frequently until about 2230. Many central bus stops have boards showing routes. On buses, especially at night, look out for landmarks as street names are written small and are hard to see. Integrated bus-**metrô** (see **Train** below) routes and tickets (US$0.75) are explained in a leaflet issued by CBTU Metrorec, T 251-5256. See below for buses to Olinda and other destinations outside the city. Trams run in the city centre. Taxis are plentiful; fares double on Sun.

Air The principal international and national airlines fly to Guararapes airport, 12 km from the city. For international flights see **Information for travellers**, page 646. Internal flights to all major cities. Bus to airport, No 52, US$0.60, 30 mins from NS do Carmo, or 'Aeroporto' from city centre and Av Domingos Ferreira, Boa Viagem (US$0.25, 10 mins). Tourist taxis at the airport cost US$5 to Boa Viagem, while ordinary taxis picked up on the main road cost about US$1 less. There is a bank desk before customs which gives much the same rate for dollars as the moneychangers in the lobby.

Trains Commuter services, known as the **Metrô** but not underground, leave from the central station; they have been extended to serve the rodoviária (frequent trains, 0500-2300, US$0.25). If going to Boa Viagem from the rodoviária, get off the Metrô at Joanna Bezerra (20 mins from rodoviária) and take a bus or taxi (US$5.25) from there.

Buses The rodoviária, mainly for long-distance buses, is 12 km outside the city at São Lourenço da Mata (it is called Terminal Integrado dos Passageiros, or TIP, pronounced 'chippy'). T 455-1999/1503. There is a 30-mins metrô connection to the central railway station, entrance through Museu do Trem, opp Casa da Cultura, 2 lines leave the city, take train marked 'Rodoviária'. From Boa Viagem a taxi all the way costs US$18, or go to Joana Bezerra Metrô station and change there. Bus US$0.60, 1 hr, from centre or from Boa Viagem. The train to the centre is much quicker than the bus. Real Alagoas bus tickets (for Maceió and Aracaju) also sold at Cais de Santa Rita (opp EMTU) and

Fruir Tur, Av Segismundo Gonçalves 487, Carmo, Olinda.

To **Salvador**, 13 hrs, 4 a day (all at night) US$32 (1 *leito*, 64); 12 hrs to **Fortaleza**, US$34, and 4 hrs to **Natal** US$11. To **Rio**, 50 hrs; to **São Paulo**, 40 hrs; to **São Luís**, 28 hrs, Progresso at 1430 and 1945, US$48.50; to **Belém**, 34 hrs (Boa Esperança bus rec). Good roads N to **João Pessoa** (buses every 30 mins, US$3.60), Natal and Fortaleza, W to Arcoverde and Caruaru (US$4.75, 2 hrs). South to **Maceió**, US$10, 3½ hrs (express), 6 hrs (slow), either by the main road or by the coast road daily 'via Litoral'. Efficient service to most Brazilian cities, last bus leaves at 2400.

Buses to the nearby destinations of Igarassu (every 15 mins) and Itamaracá (every 30 mins) leave from Av Martins de Barros, in front of *Grande Hotel*; to Olinda, see below; those to beaches beyond Olinda from Av Dantas behind the post office. To Cabo (every 20 mins) and beaches S of Recife from Cais de Santa Rita.

OLINDA

(*Pop* 340,675; *CEP* 53000; *DDD* 081) 6 km N of Recife is the old capital, founded in 1537 and named a 'Patrimônio da Humanidade' by Unesco in 1982. A programme of restoration, partly financed by the Netherlands government, was initiated in order to comply with the recently conferred title of National Monument. Despite adoption by Unesco and the Dutch, the need for restoration and cleaning has grown.

Places of interest

Of particular interest are: on R São Bento, the **Prefeitura**, once the palace of the viceroys, and the monastery of **São Bento**, founded 1582 by the Benedictine monks, restored 1761, the site of Brazil's first law school and the first abolition of slavery (paintings, sculpture, furniture; the monastery is closed to anyone without written permission to visit); the convent of **Santa Teresa** (1687), Av Olinda 570; the **Convento de São Francisco** (1585), with splendid woodcarving and paintings, superb gilded stucco, and azulejos, in Capela de São Roque (entry US$1); the church of **NS das Neves**, Ladeira de São Francisco (visits permitted only with prior written application); the **Igreja da Misericórdia**, built 1540, R Bispo Coutinho, fine tiling and gold work, and Académia Santa Gertrudes; the **Cathedral** (1537), Alto da Sé,

Olinda

Not to scale

To
Nossa Senhora
do Monte

do Sarapião

Farol

Av Mons Fabricio

São João

do Bonsucesso

Misericórdia /
Académia
Santa
Gertrudes

Museu de
Arte Sacra

NS das Graças /
Seminário

Cathedral,
Alto da Sé

São
Francisco

To
northern
beaches

São Miséricórdia /

Bispo Coutinho

São João
Batista

Museu
Regional

Amparo

das Bertiogas

Ladeira da Sé

São Francisco

T A lfredo T S

do Sol

Flor da Manhã

Praia de São Francisco

da Floresta

Cel Joaquim Cavalcante

Biordas 4 Cantos

do Bonfim

Prudente de Morais

da Palha

Liberdade

Bus stops /
Praça do Carmo

Pousada dos
Quatro Cantos

Bernardo Vieira

7 de Setembro

Carmo

Av Joaquim Nabuco

13 de Maio

Museu de Arte
Contemporaneo

Henrique Dias

São Bento

Seguro

Balcão
Mourisco /
Praça João
Alfredo

Vasconcelos

Dr J Gonçalves

Bico de
São
Pedro

Prefeitura

10 de Novembro

Av Segismundo Gonçalves

Manoel Borba

Atlantic

Ocean

15 de Novembro

São Bento

N

Santos Dumont

Mercado
Eufrásio
Barbosa

To
Recife

the first church to be built in the city, of simple and severe construction; the **Graças** church (seminary) built 1582, also in Alto da Sé; **São João Batista dos Militares** (1581), R da Saudade, the only church not burnt by the Dutch; **Nossa Senhora do Monte**, built early 16C; the **Carmo** church (1588) overlooking Praça Carmo (under restoration, guides may be able to get you in), and the colonial public fountain, the **Bica de São Pedro**, R Joaquim Cavalcanti. None of the historic buildings has fixed opening hours.

There are some houses of the 17th century with latticed balconies, heavy doors and pink stucco walls, including a house in Moorish style at Praça João Alfredo 7, housing the *Mourisco* restaurant.

There is a colony of artists and excellent examples of regional art, mainly woodcarving and terracotta figurines, may be bought in the Alto da Sé, the square on top of the hill by the cathedral, or in the handicraft shops at the **Mercado da Ribeira** (the former slave market), R Bernardo Vieira de Melo (Vieira de Melo gave the first recorded call for independence from Portugal, in Olinda in 1710). Handicrafts are also sold at good prices in the Mercado Eufrásio Barbosa, by the junction of Av Segismundo Gonçalves and Santos Dumont, Varadouro; the bars serve good value meals. There is a **Museu de Arte Sacra** in the former Palácio Episcopal (1696) at Alto da Sé 7, open Mon-Fri, 0700-1300. At R 13 de Maio 157, in the 18th-century jail of the Inquisition, is the **Museu de Arte Contemporânea** (Tues-Fri 0900-1700, Sat-Sun 1400-1700). The **Museu Regional**, R do Amparo 128, is excellent (same hours).

Guides

Guides with identification cards wait in Praça do Carmo. They are former street children and half the fee for a full tour of the city (about US$20) goes to a home for street children. If you take a guide you will be safe from mugging which, unfortunately, occurs (see below). If in doubt about this system, ask at the *Pousada Flor da Manhã*.

Beaches

The beaches close to Olinda are reported to be seriously polluted. Those further N from Olinda, beyond Casa Caiada, are beautiful, usually deserted, palm-fringed; at **Janga**, and **Pau Amarelo**, the latter can be dirty at low tide (take either a 'Janga' or 'Pau Amarela' bus). At many simple cafés you can eat *sururu* (clam stew in coconut sauce), *agulha frita* (fried needle-fish), *miúdo de galinha* (chicken giblets in gravy) and *casquinha de carangueijo* (seasoned crabmeat and *farinha de dendé* served in crabshells). Visit the Dutch fort on Pau Amarelo beach; small craft fair here on Sat nights. Near the fort is *Bar Lua Cheia*, which has music and dancing.

Local festivals

At Olinda's **carnival** thousands of people dance through the narrow streets of the old city to the sound of the Frevo, the brash energetic music which normally accompanies a lively dance performed with umbrellas. The local people decorate them with streamers and straw dolls, and form themselves into costumed groups to parade down the R do Amparo; Pitombeira and Elefantes are the best known of these groups. Foundation Day is celebrated with 3 days of music and dancing, 12-15 Mar, night time only.

Local information

NB Olinda has been severely afflicted by rapidly-worsening poverty, the effects of which are perhaps more noticeable in this attractive and comparatively prosperous area. Please exercise caution, and sympathy.

● Accommodation

At Casa Caiada, Av José Augusto Moreira 2200 (T 431-2955, F 431-0670), is **L2** *Quatro Rodas* with swimming pool, excellent restaurant, tennis courts, gardens, very good.

A3 *Pousada dos Quatro Cantos*, R Prudente de Morais 441, in a converted mansion, very good, highly rec, prices rise to L2 for 5-night package during Carnival, T 429-0220, F 429-1845, sometimes has live entertainment, expensive restaurant.

B *Cinco Sóis*, Av Min Marcos Freire 633, Bairro Novo, T 429-1347, a/c, fridge, hot shower, parking; **B** *Marolinda*, Av Min Marcos Freire (Beira Mar) 1615, Bairro Novo, T 429-1699, F 326-6934, 2-star, rec, rooms at front very noisy at weekends; **B** *Pousada São Francisco*, R do Sol 127, T 429-2109, F 429-4057, comfortable, pool, rec, modest restaurant; **B** *Quatorze Bis*, Av Beira Mar 1414, T 429-0409, helpful, run by Dutchman; **B-E** *Pousada d'Olinda*, P João Alfredo 178, T/F 439-1163, happy, warmly rec, 10% discount with *South American Handbook*, 5 luxury a/c apartments, 2 colonial suites, 16 rooms with shared bath, two communal rooms with good view, pool, breakfast, other meals if requested in advance, English, French, German and Spanish spoken.

C *Circular do Bonde*, Av Min Marcos Freire 223, T 429-3485, shared bath, sea views, communal breakfast, garage, pool, rec; **C** *Oh! Linda Pousada*, Av Min Marcos Freire 349, Bairro Novo, T 439-2116, rec.

D *Hospedaria do Turista*, Av Beira Mar 989, excellent, T 429-1847; **D** *São Pedro*, Praça Cons João Alfredo 168, T 429-2935, cosy, helpful, laundry, Danish run, English spoken, rec; **D-E** *Flor da Manhã*, R São Francisco 162, T 429-2266, good food, beautiful views, safe, multilingual, consistently rec.

E *Albergue da Olinda*, R do Sol 233, T 429-1592, reasonable, popular with gringos, suites with bath and communal bunk rooms, clothes washing facilities, discounts for IYHA members, highly rec.

Several **youth hostels**: *Portalinda*, Av Min Marcos Freire (Beira Mar) 295, Bairro Novo, T 429-3198; **E** *Cheiro do Mar*, No 95, T 429-0101, more expensive for non-members, very good small hostel with some double rooms (room No 1 is noisy from disco), cooking facilities, ask driver of 'Rio Doce/Piedade' or 'Bairra de Jangada/Casa Caiada' bus (see below) to drop you at Albergue de Juventude on sea front; *Palanquim*, Prof Cândido Pessoa 1833, Bairro Novo, T 429-0101; **E** *Do Bomfim*, R do Bomfim 115, Carmo, T 429-1674, more for non-members, safe, breakfast, cooking and laundry facilities. **NB** Hotels on R do Sol and in Bairro Novo are below the old city and on the roads heading N.

At Carnival, the price of accommodation rises steeply. Houses or rooms may be rented at this time for 5-10 days.

Camping: *Olinda Camping*, R Bom Sucesso 262, Amparo, T 429-1365, US$5 pp, space for 30 tents, 5 trailers, small huts for rent, quiet, well-shaded, town buses pass outside, rec.

● **Places to eat**
Mourisco, R João Alfredo 7, calm and pleasant, discotheque attached; *Samburá*, Av Min Marcos Freire 1551 (with terrace) rec to try *caldeirada* and *pitu* (crayfish), also lobster in coconut sauce or daily fish dishes, very good; on Av Beira Mar, *Ouriço*, local food good; *Gouiaba*, charcoal grill, facing sea, good value, rec; *Cantinho da Sé 305*, lively, good view of Recife, views just as good and prices lower upstairs; *O Rei do Vatapá*, on seafront nr Praça do Carmo, good, quite cheap; *Tony*, 2 blocks from Praça do Carmo towards Recife, good, reasonable; *Chin Lee*, excellent Chinese food; many others, mostly for fish. The traditional Olinda drinks, *Pau do Índio* (which contains 32 herbs) and *Retetel*, are both manufactured on the R do Amparo. In Olinda also try *tapioca*, local dish made of manioc with coconut or cheese.

● **Entertainment**
At Janga beach on Fri and Sat, you can join in a *ciranda* at the bar-restaurant *Ciranda de Dona Duda*. For the less active, there is the *Casa da Seresta*, also in Janga on the beach side of the main road. On Praça do Carmo is *Clube Atlântico*, a forró dance hall. *Capoeira* is practised on Sun at about 1800 in the Mercado da Ribeira.

Beginning at dusk, but best after 2100, the Alto da Sé becomes the scene of a lively street fair, with arts, crafts, makeshift bars and barbecue stands, and impromptu traditional music; even more animated at Carnival.

● **Post & telecommunications**
Post Office: in Santa Tereza, nr Santa Tereza church, on way out of Olinda to Recife.

● **Tour companies & travel agents**
Viagens Sob O Sol, Prudente de Moraes 424, T 429-3303/432-5109, 24 hrs, transport offered to all parts, any type of trip arranged, contact Mauro and Felipe. *FruirTour*, Av Segismundo Gonçalves, close to Praça do Carmo, bus tickets sold, rec.

● **Tourist offices**
Secretaría de Turismo, R do Sol 127, Carmo, T 429-1039.

● **Transport**
From Recife: take any bus marked 'Rio Doce', No 981 which has a circular route around the city and beaches, or No 33 from Av NS do Carmo, US$0.60 or 'Jardim Atlântico' from the central post office at Siqueira Campos; from Boa Viagem, take bus marked 'Piedade/Rio Doce' or 'Bairra de Jangada/Casa Caiada' (US$0.65, 30 mins). Change to either of these buses from the airport to Olinda: take 'Aeroporto' bus to Av Domingos Ferreira, Boa Viagem, and ask to be let off; and from the Recife Rodoviária: take the metrô to Joana Bezerra station and then change. In all cases, alight in Praça do Carmo. Taxis between Olinda and Recife put their meters onto higher rates at the Convention Centre (between the two cities), best to start a journey either way there (taxi to Recife US$6, US$10.75 to Boa Viagem at night).

BIOLOGICAL RESERVES

For information on Pernambuco's two reserves, contact Ibama, Av 17 de Agosto 1057, Casa Forte, CEP 50.000, Recife. They are **Saltinho**, which preserves some of the last vestiges of Atlantic Forest in the NE, and **Serra Negra**, which has some of the last remaining forest at higher altitude in the interior.

IGARASSU

(Pop 79,400) 32 km N of Recife on the road to João Pessoa, Igarassu has the first church built in Brazil (SS Cosme e Damião), the Livramento church nearby, and the convent of Santo Antônio with a small museum next door. The church of Sagrado Coração is said to have housed Brazil's first orphanage. Much of the town (founded in 1535) has been declared a National Monument; it is an attractive place, with a number of colonial houses and Brazil's first Masonic hall. Hotel: **A2** *Fazenda Praia da Gavoa*, Estrada do Ramalho (Nova Cruz), T 543-0110, F 541-1088; Camping Clube do Brasil has site nearby at Engenho Monjope, an old sugar estate, now a historical monument (it is 3 km before Igarassu coming from Recife – bus US$0.65 – alight at the 'Camping' sign and walk 5-10 mins, T 543-0528). Igarassu buses leave from Av Martins de Barro, Recife, 45 mins, US$0.70.

ITAMARACA

North of Igarassu you pass through coconut plantations to Itapissuma, where there is a bridge to **Itamaracá** island, where, the locals say, Adam and Eve spent their holidays (so does everyone else on Sun, now). It has the old Dutch Forte Orange; an interesting penal settlement with gift shops, built round the 1747 sugar estate buildings of Engenho São João, which still have much of the old machinery; charming villages and colonial churches, and fine, wide beaches. Buses from Recife (Av Martins de Barros opp *Grand Hotel*, US$0.75, very crowded) and Igarassu.

Excursions Pleasant trips by *jangada* to Coroa do Avião, a recently-formed sandy island (developing wildlife, migratory birds) with rustic beach bars, crossing (US$2 return) from Forte Orange, S of Igarassu bridge; Praias do Sossego and da Enseada, quiet, some bars but relatively undiscovered, crossing 3 km N of Itamaracá town, rec for sun worshippers.

Further N again, 2 hrs from Recife by bus, is **Pontas de Pedra**, an old fishing village, nice beach, fishing and diving expeditions, lots of bars; try **C** *Pousada Calanda*, R do Meio 269, T 626-0500.

● **Accommodation A2** *Itamaracá Parque*, Estrada do Forte, T 544-1030; **B** *Caravela*, Praça João Felipe de Barros Dias, T 544-1130, good restaurant, on beach, rec; **B** *Pousada Itamaracá*, R Fernando Lopes 205, T 544-1152, pool rec, some minutes from beach; **C** *Santa Ina*, on main square, with good restaurant, *Barretinha*; **D** *Pousada Jaguaribe*, R Rios 355 (close to bus terminal), close to beach, fans and mosquito nets in all rooms, kitchen, laundry facilities, swimming pool.

● **Places to eat** Those with a car and above budget means should have lunch and a swim at **Porto Brasílis**, a restaurant at tiny, hidden, charming Vilha Velha (T 081-543-0366 for reservation); allow all afternoon. There is good, relaxing music, fine artefacts and furnishings and a majestic panorama.

GOIANA

(*Pop* 64,060; *CEP* 55900; *DDD* 081) On the Recife-João Pessoa road; founded 1570, this is an important towns for ceramics. Visit the workshop of Zé do Carmo, opposite the *Buraco do Giá* restaurant (excellent seafood; owner has tame crab which will offer you a drink), R Padre Batalha 100. (**D** *Hotel Dois Irmãos*, in town centre.)

Places of interest Carmelite church and monastery, founded 1719, impressive but poorly restored; Matriz do Rosário, only open for 1800 mass, Soledade convent (1755); Amparo church with sacred art museum; Misericórdia church (1723).

At the Pernambuco-Paraíba border, a 27 km dirt road goes to the fishing village of **Pitimbu**, with *jangadas*, lobster fishing, surf fishing, lobster-pot making. No tourist facilities but camping is possible; food from *Bar do Jangadeiro*. Bus from Goiana, US$0.60.

WEST OF RECIFE

85 km W of Recife is **Gravatá** (*pop* 60,000), known as the Switzerland of Pernambuco for its scenery and good hill climate.

CARUARU

(*Pop* 250,000) 130 km W of Recife. The paved road there passes through rolling hills, with sugar cane and large cattle fazendas, before climbing an escarpment. As the road gets higher, the countryside becomes drier, browner and rockier. Caruaru is a busy, modern town with a big Fri to Sun market: a combination of the *feira da Sulanca* (clothes), *feira do Gado* (livestock), *feira da Troca-Troca* (barter market), and *feira de Antigüidades* (antiques). A separate site, *Feira do Artesanato*, across the river for leather goods, ceramics, hammocks and basketware, although now disappointingly tourist-oriented, is open daily. See the hand-painted textiles of Sr Valério Cristóvão, R 13 de Maio 94, 1st floor; he is very helpful and his work depicts local history. The little clay figures (*figurinhas de barro*) originated by Mestre Vitalino, and very typical of the NE, are a local speciality; many local potters live at Alto da Moura 6 km away, where a house once owned by Vitalino is open, but has no examples of his work. Bus, 30 mins, bumpy, US$0.35.

Local festivals 22 Dec-2 Jan, Festa de Comércio; 18-22 May, city's anniversary;

São João, June, huge *forró* festival; 15-22 Aug, folklore week; carnival; Semana Santa; Sept, Micaru; Oct, Vaquejada (Brazilian cross between rodeo and bull fighting), biggest in the NE.

● **Accommodation A1** *Do Sol*, Cidade Alta, T 721-3044, F 721-1336 (3-star) on hill outside town, good restaurant, pool; **B** *Grande Hotel São Vicente de Paulo*, Av Rio Branco 365, T 721-5011, bar, restaurant, laundry, a/c, pool, TV; *Trevo*, opp rodoviária, and *Village*, on road to Recife from rodoviária, 3 km out, T 721-5974, food rec. Cheap *hospedarias* around central square, Praça Getúlio Vargas; **C** *Central*, R Vigario Freire 71, T 721-4669, good breakfast, in centre, rec; **C** *Centenário*, 7 de Setembro 84, T 722-9011, good breakfast, in town centre, rec.

● **Transport** Rodoviária is 4 km from town; buses from Recife stop in the town centre. Alight here and look for the *Livraria Estudantil* on the corner of Vigario Freire and R Anna de Albuquerque Galvão. Go down Galvão, turn right on R 15 de Novembro to the first junction, 13 de Maio; turn left, cross the river to the Feira do Artesanato. Bus from centre, same place as Recife bus stop, to Rodoviária, US$0.20. Many buses from TIP in **Recife**, 2 hrs express, US$4.75, also *comum*. Bus to **Maceió**, 0700, 5 hrs, US$5.50. Bus to **Fazenda Nova** 1030, 1 hr, US$2, returns for Caruaru 1330.

FAZENDA NOVA AND NOVA JERUSALEM

During Easter Week each year various agencies run package tours to the little country town of **Fazenda Nova**, 23 km from Caruaru. Just outside the town is **Nova Jerusalém**, where for the week up to Easter Sun, an annual passion play, suggested by Oberammergau's, is enacted. The site is one third the size of the historic quarter of Jerusalem, with 12 permanent stages on which scenes of the Passion are presented; the audience moves from one to another as the story unfolds. Performances begin at 1800, lasting around 3 hrs.

● **Accommodation In Fazenda Nova**: *Grande*, Av Poeta Carlos Penha Filho, T 732-1137, best; and others.

GARANHUNS

Good roads via Caruaru or Palmares run to the city of **Garanhuns** (*pop* 113,470), 243 km SW of Recife. Its claims to be the best holiday resort in the NE are attributed to its cool climate – it stands at 890m, and has an average temperature of 21°C – its mineral waters and its beautiful landscapes and parks.

● **Accommodation A2** *Tavares Correia*, Av Rui Barbosa 296, T 761-0900, 4-star; **B** *Petrópolis*, Praça da Bandeira 129, T 761-0125. **Camping**: *Camping Treze*, BR-432, Km 105.

Arcoverde (*pop* 54,150), about 126 km W of Caruaru (bus 2½ hrs, US$3), is a market town in the Sertão, market every Sat, cool at night. Hotels: **C** *Grande Majestic*, Av Cel Japiassu 326, T 821-1175 (fair), with breakfast; **E** *Dormitório O Barão*, clean.

TRIUNFO

(*Pop* 28,900) About 200 km W of Arcoverde via Serra Talhada is a delightful small town in Serra de Borborema, good climate, with great variety of crops, flowers and fruits. There are also a sugar mill that can be visited (Engenho Boa Esperança), waterfalls, sounding rocks, the convent of São Boaventura, and the Museu do Cangaça, showing the lives and relics of the traditional bandits of the Nordeste.

● **Accommodation B** *Pousada Baixa Verde*, R Manoel Paiva dos Santos 114, T 846-1103, nice rooms, good breakfast; **B** *Hospedaria Santa Terezinha* (Centro), abundant and good meals; **D** *Pousada Baixa Serote*, superb breakfast, highly rec.

● **Transport** Two buses daily to and from Recife (6½ hrs).

FERNANDO DE NORONHA

A small archipelago 345 km off the NE coast declared a Marine National Park in 1989 (T Parnamar 081-619-1210). Only one island is inhabited. It is part of the state of Pernambuco administered from Recife. The islands were discovered 1503 and were for a time a pirate lair. In 1738 the Portuguese built the Forte dos Remédios, later used as a prison in this century; remains still exist as well as a semi-deserted village nearby. Many locals are now dependent on tourism and most food is brought from the mainland; prices are about double. Repellent is not available for the many mosquitoes. The island, which is dominated by a 321m peak, has many unspoilt beaches, interesting wildlife and fishing; scuba-diving and snorkelling are excellent. It is now prohibited to swim with the dolphins but they can be seen from the beach. Take sufficient *reais* as dollars are heavily discounted. The time is 1 hr later than Brazilian Standard Time. Entry to the island has been limited to 120 tourists per day because of the serious problems of energy and water supply.

Tours

Boat trips and jeep tours around the island are available; also possible to hire a jeep or beach buggy. You can hitch everywhere as everyone stops. Scuba-diving is organized by *Águas Claras* (T 619-1225, US$50) in the hotel grounds, staff are regarded as entertaining but unqualified; 2 dives (with superannuated equipment).

Local information
● **Accommodation**

The only hotel, *Pousada Esmeralda*, T 619-1355, is expensive and none too comfortable. Large a/c apartments at *Solar dos Ventos* (full board) have been rec, ask for 'o capitanão'. Overpriced packages from mainland travel agents usually place visitors in the *Esmeralda*. Beware of similar packages at lower prices in other 'pousadas' because they turn out to be rooms in family homes. Independent travellers can go much cheaper as many local families rent out rooms with full board, US$20 pp/day. The best known is that of Suzanna and Rocha, rooms with fan and bathroom, but they never refuse a reservation and farm people out to other families with much inferior levels of accommodation. Vanilda across the street has been highly rec.

● **Places to eat**

There is only one restaurant, called *Ilha Encantado*, nr the hotel.

Bars *Bar da Vila* in the village of Remédios, only open in the daytime; *Bar Idade* on the Conceição beach, daytime only with loud rock music; *Mirante Bar*, nr the hotel, with spectacular view over Boldró beach, has loud music and at night is an open-air disco and the only nightlife on the island.

● **Transport**

Air Three flights daily from Recife, 4 on Sat and Sun, some flights via Natal, on 13 and 17 seater planes by Nordeste, T 341-3187, 1 hr 40 mins. An entry fee of US$13 a day is payable at the airport.

Paraíba

JOÃO PESSOA

It is a bus ride of 2 hrs through sugar plantations over a good road from Recife (126 km) to **João Pessoa** (*pop* 497,215; *CEP* 58000; *DDD* 083), capital of the State of Paraíba (*pop* 3,200,620), on the Rio Paraíba. Ocean-going ships load and unload at Cabedelo (see **Excursions**).

PLACES OF INTEREST

The old monasteries are worth seeing, and the 18th century church of **São Francisco** is a beauty (open 0800-1700). At São Francisco is an excellent cultural centre with a magnificent collection of colonial and popular artefacts. This is also the best point to see the sun set over the forest. Other tourist points include the **Casa da Pólvora**, an old gunpowder store which has become the city museum; the city parks; and trips on the Rio Paraíba. See the booklet *Relíquias da Paraíba*, by Padre Antônio Barbosa.

The beachfront stretches from Ponta do Seixas (S) almost to Cabedelo (N); main areas are Tambaú, Cabo Branco, Manaira and Bessa. All are urban beaches, cleaner the further you go N or S from **Tambaú**, which is 7 km from the city centre. Take a taxi or bus (No 510 'Tambaú' from outside the rodoviária, alight at *Hotel Tropical*). Cabo Branco club on Tambaú beach, open to visitors: good food, beautiful views.

EXCURSIONS

14 km S down the coast is the **Cabo Branco** lighthouse at Ponta do Seixas, the most easterly point of continental Brazil and South

America; there is a panoramic view from the cliff top over the palm-lined beaches below. Take bus 507 'Cabo Branco' from outside the rodoviária and get out at last stop; hike up to the lighthouse. the **Fundação José Américo de Almeida**, Av Cabo Branco 3336, Cabo Branco, on the esplanade, should be visited by those interested in modern literature and politics; it is in the former house of the novelist and sociologist.

At **Cabedelo** (*pop* 28,925), 18 km by road or rail, are the impressive walls of the 17th-century fortress of Santa Catarina. If you take a Cabedelo bus and alight at Jacaré, about 12 km from João Pessoa, there is an excellent beach with food stalls at weekends. In Jacaré, where the yachts tie up, is a bar run by an Englishman.

LOCAL INFORMATION

● **Accommodation**
Central hotels: D *Aurora*, Praça João Pessoa 51, T 241-3238, with a/c, rec; D *Guarany*, R Almeida Barreto 181 e 13 de Maio, T 241-2161 (more with a/c and TV), safe, good value, good breakfast; D *Pedro Américo*, Praça Pedro Américo, 109 (no breakfast on Sun); cheap hotels nr the old rodoviária, eg E *São Pedro*, R Irineu Pinto 231, basic. *Villa Mare Apartment Hotel*, Av Nego 707, T 226-2142, apartments for 2 or 3 people, US$600/month, helpful, rec.

Also in Tambaú: L3 *Tropical Tambaú*, Av Alm Tamandaré 229, Tambaú, T 226-3660, F 226-2390, comfortable, good service, rec; B *Costa Bela Praia*, Av Négo 131, T 226 1570, rec, small; B *Sol-Mar*, Rui Carneiro 500, T 226-1350, F 226-3242, pool, superb restaurant, highly rec; D *Gameleira*, Av João Maurício 157, T 226-1576, good breakfast, dirty, noisy at night.

At Cabo Branco: *Pousa das Águas*, Praia do Cabo Branco, T 226-5103/7268, seafront.

Youth hostels: on Av das Trincheiras, at Palácio dos Esportes, T 221-7220/1, and R Bezerra Reis 82, T 226-5460/1988.

● **Places to eat**
Two good restaurants on Tambaú beach are *Adega do Alfredo* (Portuguese) and *Wan Li* (Chinese); *Pescador*, nr Cabo Branco lighthouse.

● **Banks & money changers**
Banco do Brasil, nr Praça João Pessoa, 3rd floor, helpful. Banco Meridional, cash against Mastercard, R Duque de Caixas, 454, Centro.

● **Electric current**
220 volts AC, 60 cycles.

● **Shopping**
Mercado de Artesanato, Centro de Turismo, Almte Tamandaré 100, Tambaú.

● **Post & telecommunications**
Telecommunications: Embratel, R das Trincheiras 398.

● **Tourist offices**
PBTUR, Centro de Turismo, Almte Tamandaré 100, Tambaú, at Rodoviária and airport. For information, T 1516.

● **Transport**
Air Airport for internal services.

Buses Rodoviária is 10 mins from centre; luggage store. To **Recife**, every 60 mins, US$3.60, 2 hrs. To **Natal**, every 2 hrs, US$6, 3 hrs; to **Fortaleza**, 4 daily, 16 hrs, US$18.

CAMPINA GRANDE

(*Pop* 326,155) Known as the 'Porta do Sertão', this rapidly growing centre for light industry and an outlet for goods from most of the NE is 120 km from João Pessoa (bus 2 hrs). There is a museum of modern art, and another of the cotton industry. Most genial climate. Near Campina Grande is Lagoa Seca, where figures in wood and sacking are made.

● **Accommodation** *Rique Palace Hotel* (excellent) is on the top floors of the tallest building in town, Venâncio Neiva 287, T 341-1433: the restaurant is on the 11th floor. B *Ouro Branco*, João Lourenço Porto 20, T 341-2929, F 322-5788. Many nr old rodoviária.

WEST OF CAMPINA GRANDE

The main highway, still paved, leads on through **Patos** (*pop* 81,300, **E** *Hotel JK*) to Ipaumirim (Ceará).

Here a left turn leads to the twin towns of **Crato** (*pop* 90,360) and **Juazeiro do Norte** (Ceará, *pop* 173,300), oases of green in the dry Sertão. Mosquitoes can be a problem at night. Juazeiro do Norte is a small pilgrimage town; it was the home of Padre Cícero, one of the unofficial saints of the NE. A statue to him stands in the Logradouro do Horto, a park overlooking the town; either take the pilgrim trail up the hill or go by bus.

● **Accommodation** C *Panorama*, R Sto Agostinho 58, T 511-2399, F 511-2173, good value; D *Vieira*, corner of R São Pedro and R Santo Antônio, with bath and breakfast; D *Municipal*, Praça P Cícero, T 511-2299, rec.

Rio Grande do Norte

There are many beautiful fishing villages along the coast heading N from João Pessoa, often difficult to reach. One of the most popular is **Baía Formosa** in Rio Grande do Norte (daily bus from Natal, 2½ hrs). No hotel; ask in town for accommodation in fishermen's houses.

The people of the state of Rio Grande do Norte are called 'Potiguares' after an Indian tribe that now resides at Jacaré de São Domingos, municipality of Rio Tinto in neighbouring Paraíba state.

NATAL

(*Pop* 606,540; *CEP* 59000; *DDD* 084) Capital of Rio Grande do Norte (*pop* 2,413,620), on the estuary of the Rio Potengi, about 180 km to the N of João Pessoa. Its setting is very scenic.

PLACES OF INTEREST

The old part of the city is called **Cidade Alta**. The main square, the **Praça João Maria**, oblong in shape, has the old cathedral (restored 1996) at one end and a fine modern bank building at the other. (The modern cathedral is on Av Marechal Deodoro.) The city is centred on the Av Rio Branco. The church of **Santo Antônio**, R Santo Antônio in the centre, dates from 1766, and has a fine, carved wooden altar and a sacred art museum. The **Museu Câmara Cascudo**, Av Hermes de Fonseca 1440 (T 212-2795), has exhibits on archaeological digs, Umbanda rituals and the petroleum industry (open Tues-Fri, 0800-1100, 1400-1600, Sat 1000-1600, US$1.40). The **Forte dos Reis Magos** (16th-century) on the coast at Rocas is open Tues-Sun 0900-1700; between it and the city is a military installation. It is possible to walk along the beach to the fort, or to go in a tour, or by taxi; it is worth it for the views (entry US$1.40). The **Marine Research Institute** at the Praia da Areia Preta can be visited; bus marked 'Areia Preta' from Av Rio Branco. At Mãe Luiza is a lighthouse with beautiful views of Natal and surrounding beaches (take city bus marked Mãe Luiza; get key from the house next door).

Beaches

Natal has excellent beaches: **Ponta Negra**: many hotels (see below). It is 20 mins by bus from centre; pleasant and 'quaint' atmosphere (not safe to wander alone on the dunes as there are robberies). Some beaches are on the far side of the Potengi river, for example Redinha and **Genipabu** – where you can toboggan down the sanddunes – reached by direct bus from old Rodoviária, last bus back from Genipabu at 1830. Few people are there from June-October. You can hire buggies to drive on the dunes for US$50-100 (depending on destination) a day, or by the hour, these are making the most popular beaches very noisy. More beautiful beaches to the S: Pirangi, Tabatinga, **Búzios**. Litoral Sul bus from rodoviária follows coastline, US$1. The friendly village of **Pipa** lies 80 km S of Natal. It has lovely beaches and several *pousadas*. Hotels arrange transport to the stunning bay N of the village, visited most mornings by dolphins. (Bus to Pipa from Natal Rodoviária Nova daily 0830, 1515, return 0500, 1600, US$3.50.)

Excursions

At **Pirangi**, 25 km S, or 30 mins by bus from new rodoviária, is the world's largest cashew-nut tree (*cajueiro*); branches springing from a single trunk cover an area of some 7,300 sq metres. From Natal (Viação Campos), US$0.60, 5 times a day from 0630 to 1815, 3 on Sun, 0730, 0930, 1645; the snack bar by the tree has schedules of buses back to Natal. A number of good beaches and attractive villages may be found along this coast. North of Natal are extensive cashew plantations.

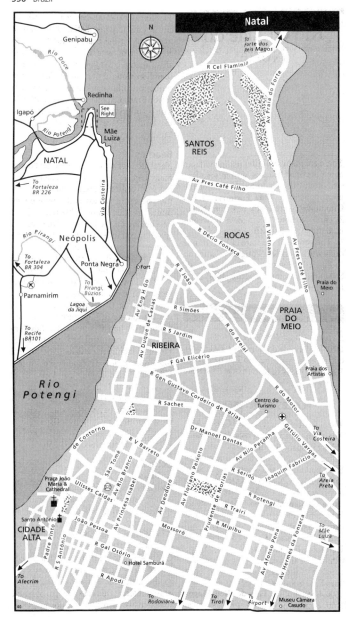

Natal

N

To Forte dos Reis Magos

R Cel Flamínio

Av Praia do Forte

SANTOS REIS

Av Pres Café Filho

R Décio Fonseca

ROCAS

R Vietnam

Av Pres Café Filho

R S João

R Simões

Praia do Meio

Av Eng H Go

Av Duque de Caxias

R S Jardim

R do Areial

PRAIA DO MEIO

Fort

RIBEIRA

F Gal Elicério

R Gen Gustavo Cordeiro de Farias

Praia dos Artistas

R Sachet

Centro do Turismo

R do Motor

Rio Potengi

de Contorno

R V Barreto

Dr Manoel Dantas

Av Nilo Peçanha

Getúlio Vargas

To Via Costeira

São Tomé

Av Rio Branco

R Serídó

Joaquim Fabricio

To Areia Preta

Praça João Maria & Cathedral

Ulisses Caldas

Av Princesa Isabel

Av Deodoro

Av Floriano Peixoto

Prudente de Morias

R Trairi

R Potengi

Santo Antônio

CIDADE ALTA

Padre Pinto

R S Antônio

João Pessoa

Mossoró

R Mipibu

To Mãe Luiza

R Gal Osório

Hotel Samburá

Av Afonso Pena

Av Hermes da Fonseca

To Alecrim

R Apodi

To Rodoviária

To Tirol

To Airport

Museu Câmara Casudo

Inset map:

Genipabu

Rio Dorce

Redinha

Igapó

Rio Potengi

See Right

Mãe Luiza

NATAL

To Fortaleza BR 226

Via Costeira

Neópolis

Rio Pirangi

To Fortaleza BR 304

Ponta Negra

To Pirangi, Búzios

Parnamirim

Lagoa da Jiqui

To Recife BR101

40

Local festivals

In mid-Oct there is a country show, **Festa do Boi**, bus marked Parnamirim to the exhibition centre, it gives a good insight into rural life. Mid-Dec sees **Carnatal**, a lively 4-day music festival with dancing in the streets.

Local information

● **Accommodation**

L3 *Marsol Natal*, Via Costeira 1567, Km 7, Parque das Dunas, T/F 221-2619, 3-star; Via Costeira is a good place to stay, but hotels mostly in **A1-A3** range: eg *Barreira Roxa Praia*, T/F 222-1093, 5 km from the centre, helpful, good; *Imirá Plaza*, Costeira 4077, T 211-4105, F 211-5722, on beach, pool, tennis, rec.

B *Oássis Swiss*, R Joaquim Fabrício 291, Casa 08, Petrópolis, T/F 202-2455, Swiss-owned, a/c, cheaper with fan, pool, massive breakfasts, exceptional value; **B** *Praia do Sol*, Av Pres Café Filho 750, Praia do Meio, T/F 211-4562, opp beach, renovated, quiet, a/c, TV, rec; **B** *Samburá*, R Prof Zuza 263, T 221-0611, rec.

C *Parque das Dunas*, T 202-1820, R João XXIII 601 (take Bus 40, alight at Farol, 40 mins from centre), excellent breakfast, safe.

D *Beira Mar*, Av Pres Café Filho, Praia dos Artistas, T 222-4256, on the beach front, with breakfast, but no a/c, small, good value, popular; **D** *Farol*, Av Gouv Silvio Pedrosa 174 (on beach), T 222-4661, a/c; **D** *Le Bateau*, Praia de Areia Preta, on beach front, helpful, good breakfast, English and French spoken; **D** *Pousada Marina*, at No 860, T 222-0678, a/c, TV, fridge, 'lovely'; **D** *Pousada Terra do Sol*, Av Pres Café Filho, 11, Praia dos Artistas, T 211 4878, noisy, arranges good Passeio de Buggy, rec.

E *Casa Grande*, R Princesa Isabel 529, T 211-4895, with a/c, **F** without bath, good breakfast, pleasant, excellent value, rec; **E** *Fenícia*, Av Rio Branco 586, T 222-1366 (more with a/c), with breakfast and shower, English spoken; **E** *Flat*, R 31 de Março, Morro de Careca, T 219 2541, breakfast, fridges in rooms, fans, hot showers and a nice garden, warmly rec; **E** *Natal*, Av Mar Floriano Peixoto 104, English spoken; *Bom Jesús*, Av Rio Branco 384, good value, popular; **E** *Pousada Zur Kurve*, Av Silvio Pedrosa 97, good breakfast, safe, rec; *Papa Jerimum*, R Rodrigues Dias 445, Praia do Meio, English spoken, rec.

Beach hotels   At Ponta Negra: **C** *Maria Bonita 2*, T 236-2941, rec; *Caminho do Mar*, R Des HH Gomes 365, nr Ponta Negra beach, T 219-3363; **C** *Ponta Negra*, R Des João V da Costa 8896, T 219-3264, pool, rec; **C** *Pousada do Mar*, T 236-2509, pool; **D** *Pousada Porta*

do Sol, R Francisco Gurgel 9057, T 236 2555, room with bar, TV, excellent breakfast, pool, steps down onto beach, good value, rec. Also restaurants.

At Genipabu: **A3** *Aldeia*, Caixa Postal 274, T 225-2011, has 5 luxury bungalows and a restaurant;   **D** *Mar-Azul*,   T   225-2065; **E** *Pousada Porta Alberta*, on beach, good breakfast.

At Buzios: **C** *Balneário Rio Doce*, pool, games, highly rec; **C** *Pousada da Lagosta*, rec. Other *pousadas* and bars.

At Pipa: **F** *Pousada do Pipa*, French-owned, highly rec, good food, good music, bath in room; **D** *Tropical*, good food, rec.

Youth hostels: head office of Associação Potiguar de Albergues da Juventude, Av Deodoro 249, Petrópolis, T 221-3751, open 1300-1730. All **D** pp: *Lua Cheia*, Av Estrela do Mar 2215, Conj Algamar, Ponta Negra, T 236-3696; *Verdes Mares*, R das Algas 2166, Conj Algamar, T 236-2872; *Ladeiro do Sol*, R Valentin de Almeida 10, Praia dos Artistas, T 221-5361. *Meu Canto*, R Mandel Dantas 424 Petrópolis, CEP 59012-270, T 211 3954, highly rec.

Camping: *Camping Clube do Brasil* site at Sítio do Jiqui, expensive. Vale das Cascatas, Ponta Negra beach, swimming pool, leisure facilities.

● **Places to eat**

Casa de Mãe, R Pedro Afonso 153 (Petrópolis), regional food, rec; *Bom Demais*, R Princesa Isabel No 717-C, cheap, good; *Thin-San*, Av Hermes da Fonseca 890, Tirol, Chinese, quite good, not expensive. *Tereré*, Estrada de Pirangi 2316, *rodizio*, and *Camarões*, Via Costeira 2610, seafood, both Ponta Negra; *Mamma Italia*, Av Gov Silvio Pedrosa 43, Praia de Areia Preta. Vegetarian (with shop): *A Macrobiótica*, Princesa Isabel 524. For snacks try the stalls on Praia do Meio, there are also various restaurants along the beach road nearby, where itinerant musicians play. Try the restaurants between Praias dos Artistas and da Areia Preta (eg *Calamar*). *Chaplin*, Av Pres Café Filho 27 (Praia dos Artistas), good seafood.

● **Banks & money changers**

Cash advances against Visa card at **Banco do Brasil**, Av Rio Branco 510.

● **Electric current**

220 volts AC, 60 cycles.

● **Entertainment**

Dance is an important pastime in Natal. The *Casa da Música Popular Brasileira* has dancing on Fri and Sat night and Sun from 1700, very popular. Daily shows also at *Mandacaru*, Av do Jiquí 21, Neopolis, T 217-3008 (US$8) and *Zás-Trás*, R Apodi 500, Tirol, T 222-6589; many other enjoyable venues where visitors are encouraged to join in.

● **Post & telecommunications**
Telecommunications: Embratel, Av Duque de Caxias 99, T 221-2209. International phone calls, Telern, R João Pessoa e Princesa Isabel.

● **Shopping**
Centro de Turismo (a converted prison with wide variety of handicraft shops, art gallery and antique shop, good view), R Aderbal de Figueiredo s/n, off R General Cordeiro, Petrópolis; *Centro Municipal de Artesanato*, Praia dos Artistas, daily 1000-2200.

● **Tourist offices**
Rodoviária and airport.

● **Transport**
Air Augusto Severo, 15 km from centre; flights to Belém, Brasília, Cuiabá, Fernando de Noronha, Fortaleza, Manaus, Recife, Rio, Salvador, São Paulo and other cities. Bus every 30 mins from old rodoviária nr centre US$0.65, taxi US$25.

Buses Rovoviária, with luggage store, is about 6 km out of town, bus 'Cidade de Esperança Av 9', 'Areia Preta via Petrópolis' or 'Via Tirol' to centre. To **Recife**, 4 hrs, US$11; to **Fortaleza**, 8 hrs, US$18; to **Maceió**, buses both direct and via Recife, US$30; to **João Pessoa**, US$6, 3 hrs.

ROUTES The state has three main paved roads radiating from Natal: S to João Pessoa and Recife, SW to Caicó and W to Mossoró and Fortaleza. Between **Caicó** (*pop* 50,660) and **Mossoró** (*pop* 191,960; **A3** *Hotel Termas*, comfortable, with a hot, mineral water pool system, each pool on a terrace, with temperatures ranging from 54°C at the top to 30°C at the bottom; there are cheaper alternatives) there is a turning to **Patu** with its huge basilica on a hillside, with passable 'hotels', rather primitive. Bus Mossoró-Aracati (Ceará) at 0800 with Emp Nordeste, 2 hrs, US$2.

Ceará

ARACATI AND CANOA QUEBRADA

From Mossoró the main road, BR304, enters Ceará and continues about 50 km to **Aracati** (*pop* 60,710; important Carnaval).

10 km from Aracati is the fishing village **Canoa Quebrada** on a sand dune, famous for its *labirinto* lacework and coloured sand sculpture, for sand-skiing on the dunes, for the sunsets, and for the beaches. To avoid jiggers (*bicho de pé*), it is best to wear shoes. Nowhere to change money except Banco do Brasil in Aracati.

Beyond Canao Quebrada is **Majorlândia**, reached by paved road from the main highway. A very nice village, with many-coloured sand dunes (used in bottle pictures) and a beach; the arrival of the fishing fleet in the evening is an important daily event. 4-5 km S along the beach is the village of Camo.

● **Accommodation Aracati**: **B** *Hotel Litorânea*, R Cel Alexandrino 1251, T 421-1001, a/c, **D** with fan, nr rodoviária. **Canoa Quebrada**: **C** *Pousada Ma Alice*, fan, safe; **D** *Pousada Alternativa*, with or without bath, central, rec; **D** *Pousada Cultural*, basic but nice; **D** *Pousada Lagos*, at entrance to town, 4 rooms, quiet; **C** *Pousada do Rei*, fan, highly rec; 2 rooms **D** behind *Sol de Manha* café on main-street, with shower, good breakfast in the café; **D** *Tenda do Cumbe*, at end of road on cliff, thatched huts, restaurant, warmly rec; also on cliff above beach, **D** *Pousada Ao Nascer do Sol*, shower, hammocks for rent; villagers will let you sling your hammock or put you up cheaply (Veronica is rec, European books exchanged; Sr Miguel rents good clean houses for US$10 a day). **Youth hostel**: *Lua Estrela*, R Nascer do Sol 106, T 421-1401, restaurant and café. **Majorlândia**: **D** *Apartamento Beira Mar*, on beach; **D** *Pousada e Restaurante Requinte*, 100m before beach on main road, airy rooms, use of kitchen, rooms with or without bath, rec.

● **Places to eat** **Canoa Quebrada**: bars and restaurants, vegetarian food in *Espácio Cultural*, cheap seafood (don't drink the water); *Casaveide*, good food – Chinese, Mexican and typical Brazilian, good atmosphere, cards and darts available, good music.

● **Transport** Bus Natal-Aracati via Mossoró, 6 hrs, US$13; Fortaleza-Aracati, 174 km, São Benedito bus 11 a day, US$6.35; 4 a day Fortaleza-Majorlândia, US$6.55. Aracati-Canoa Quebrada from Gen Pompeu e T João Paulo, US$1; taxi US$6. Canoa Quebrada-Fortaleza US$6.50.

MORRO BRANCO

87 km from Fortaleza (too far for a day trip) is **Morro Branco** (4 km from Beberibe – bus from Aracati, 2 hrs), with spectacular beach, craggy cliffs and beautiful views. *Jangadas* leave the beach at 0500, returning at 1400-1500. Beach buggies and taxi for hire, Marambaia can be visited, some accommodation. Very crowded at holiday times.

● **Accommodation** **A1** *Praia das Fontes*, T 338-1179, F 338-1269, luxurious, rec; **C** *Recanto Praia*, good breakfast, rec; **D** *Cabana do Morro*, *Pousada do Morro*, mosquitoes, fan and shower, both with pool; **D** *Novo*, noisy at weekends; **D** *Pousada Sereia*, on the beach, good breakfast, highly rec; **E** *Rosalias'*, with use of kitchen, 50m from bus stop, strongly rec; or you can rent fishermen's houses; meals can also be arranged at beach-front bars (try *O Jangadeiro*). Double room at **E** *Bar São Francisco*, or 7-room house for rent.

● **Transport** São Benedito bus from Fortaleza, US$3.60; 2½ hrs, 4 a day. To get to Natal, take 0600 bus to Beberibe, then 0800 bus (only one) to Aracati, US$1, then on to Natal.

BEACHES SE OF FORTALEZA

Further up the coast is **Caponga** beach. A 30-min walk S along the deserted white-sand beach leads to a river mouth, offering a combination of fresh-and salt-water bathing. *Jangadas* set sail in the early morning (arrangements can be made to accompany fishermen on overnight trips); there is a fish market on the beach. Weekend houses now being built here.

● **Accommodation** Accommodation at *Caponga Praia*, on the beach front, simple rooms and good meals, **D** *Mon Kapitan*, on the square, very helpful, good restaurant.

● **Transport** Direct bus from Fortaleza (2 a day) or take a bus from Fortaleza to Cascavel

(80 mins, US$1.50) then a bus from Cascavel (20 mins, US$0.45).

40 km before Fortaleza, along the coast, is **Prainha**, a fishing village and weekend resort near the town of Aquiraz (bus terminal in Fortaleza opp Escola Normal at 1430 and 1700, return 1530 and 1800). You can see *jangadas* coming in daily in the late afternoon. The beaches are clean and largely empty.

● **Accommodation** **C** *Prainha Solex Hotel*, R Pericich Ribeiro 5, T 361-1000/01/02, ramal 156.7, pool, comfortable; also **C**, the *pousada*, nr rodoviária, no name and no breakfast, owner lives on beach, noisy but clean.

● **Places to eat** Good fish restaurant, *O Leonção*, on same street as *pousada*. There are several small, cheap and good restaurants, where it is possible to see displays of the Carimbó, one of the N Brazilian dances.

FORTALEZA

(*Pop* 1,758,335; *CEP* 60000; *DDD* 085, 088 outside metropolitan Fortaleza) Capital of the State of Ceará, **Fortaleza** is about 520 km from Natal, NW along the coast (population of Ceará state 6,353,345). It is 1,600 km by road from Belém and 885 km from Recife. There are fair dirt roads throughout the State, and paved roads W to São Luís and SE to Recife; the federal highway S to Salvador (BR-116) is now largely paved but much is in poor condition.

Places of interest

A fine tourist centre in the old prison on the waterfront (Av Senador Pompeu 350) includes the **Museu de Arte e Cultura Populares** (open Mon-Fri, 0800-1800, Sat 0800-1400, Sun 0800-1200, most interesting), shops and restaurants. Other museums: **Museu Histórico e Antropológico do Ceará**, R São Paulo (next to Praça dos Lees in the centre), (Mon-Fri 1000-1800, Sat 0900-1500; take bus marked 'Dom Luís'); **Museu de Minerais**, R Sen Pompeu 350 (open Mon-Fri, 0800-1800, Sat 0800-1400, Sun 0800-1200). Also visit **Forte Nossa Senhora da Assunção**, originally built by the Dutch, Av Alberto Nepomuceno, open daily 0800-1100, 1400-1700. The mausoleum of President Castelo Branco (1964-67), next to the state government building, may be vis-

Fortaleza

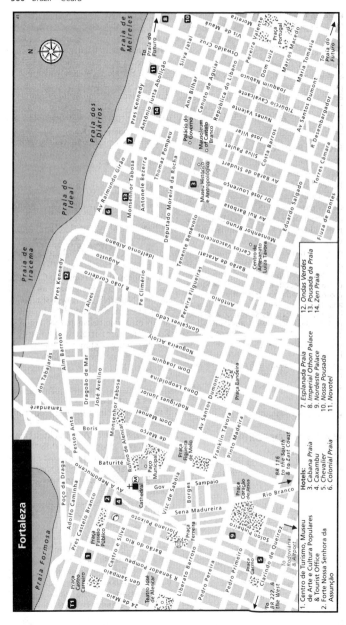

1. Centro de Turismo, Museu
   de Arte e Cultura Populares
   & Tourist Office
2. Forte Nossa Senhora da
   Assunção

Hotels:
3. Cabana Praia
4. Caxambu
5. Chevalier
6. Colonial Praia
7. Esplanada Praia
8. Imperial Othon Palace
9. Nordeste Palace
10. Nossa Pousada
11. Novotel
12. Ondas Verdes
13. Pousada da Praia
14. Zen Praia

ited, Av Barão de Studart 505, daily 0800-1800. The new **cathedral**, in gothic style but built in concrete, stands beside the new **Mercado Central**, open Mon-Fri 0700-1800, Sat 0800-1600, Sun 0800-1200; it has beautiful stained glass windows.

Beaches

Beaches are fine (take bus marked 'P Futuro' from Praça Castro Carreira, 'Praia Circular' bus which does a circular route to Praia Futuro, or bus marked 'Caça e Pesca', which passes all SE beaches on its route), and you can watch the boats coming in before sundown with their catch. The majority of high class hotels are on the beach from Praia de Iracema (which is the most popular beach, though now unsuitable for swimming; in the evenings everyone promenades along this beach). Other beaches not suitable for bathing are Diarios, Meireles, Volta da Jurema and Mucuripe all to the SE. **Praia do Futuro** is 8 km to the SE (no natural shade), many vendors. **Iguape** beach is recommended, but is at the end of a 90-min bus ride – São Benedito bus marked 'Iguape' from R Domingos Olimpio, esq Agunabi (trips on *jangadas* for US$8.50). Northwest of the centre is **Praia Barra do Ceará**, 8 km, where the Ceará river flows into the sea. **Praia de Icaraí** 22 km to the NW is under development. Beyond Icaraí, 12 km, is **Cumbuco**, a lively beach, dirty in high season, bars, buggies, horse riding, dunes which you can snowboard down into a rain water lake, palm trees; *Teto do Praia*, cooking facilities, on beach, *jardineira* bus from Av Pres Kennedy and other points in Fortaleza, US$2.

Local holidays

6 Jan (Epiphany); Ash Wed; 19 Mar (São José); Christmas Eve; New Year's Eve, half-day.

A festival takes place at Praia de Mucuripe on the last Sun in July, during which the traditional *jangada* (raft) races take place. On 15 Aug, the local Umbanda *terreiros* (churches) celebrate the Festival of Iemanjá on Praia do Futuro, taking over the entire beach from noon till dusk, when offerings are cast into the surf. Well worth attending (members of the public

may 'pegar um passo' – enter into an inspired religious trance – at the hands of a *pai-de-santo*). Beware of pick-pockets and purse-snatchers.

Local information

NB The road which runs along the sea front (Av Pres Kennedy) is often known as Av Beira Mar. Many new hotels and apartment blocks have been built along this stretch.

● **Accommodation**

L2 *Marina Park*, Av Pres C Branco 400, T 252-5253, F 253-1803, huge new luxury leisure complex with all facilities, modern mooring for yachts at reasonable prices, day rates available for non-residents, strongly rec; **L3** *Beira Mar*, on Meireles beach, Av Pres Kennedy, T 244-9444, F 261-5659, swimming pool; **L3** *Colonial Praia*, 4-star, R Barão de Aracati 145, T 211-9644, F 252-3501, pleasant grounds and big pool, laundry service (10 mins' walk from Av Kennedy); **L3** *Novotel*, Av Pres Kennedy 2380, T 244-9122, F 261-2793.

A1 *Imperial Othon Palace*, 5-star, Av Pres Kennedy 2500, T 244-9177, F 224-7777, beach front location (rec *feijoada* on Sat); *Nordeste Palace*, R Assunção 99 in centre, T 221-1999, large rooms, good value; **A2** *Pousada Jardim*, Idelfonso Albano 950, T 231-7991, no sign outside, by Iracema beach, nice garden, excursions arranged, many languages spoken, warmly rec, 20% discount to *SAH* users; **A2** *Samburá Praia*, Av Pres Kennedy 4530, T 263-1999, F 263-2177, cheaper than most beach hotels.

B *Apart-hotel Aquidabá*, Av Raimundo Girão 630, T 226-1405, at beginning of Praia Iracema, 20 mins' walk from centre, with bath, pool and bar, quiet; **B** *Cabana Praia II*, at R João Lourenço 441 (T 261-1399) and No I at Av Rui Barbosa 555, T 261-4954, both small; **B** *Caxambu*, General Bezerril 22 (T 231-0339), a/c, with breakfast, central (opp Cathedral, in market area); **B** *Paraíso da Praia*, R dos Pacajus 109, T 231-3387, Iracema, small, on beach, helpful, good *trattoria* next door; **B** *Pousada d'Antonietta*, Carlos Vasconcelos 660, T 224-3454, quiet, 5 mins from beach, buses nearby; **B** *Pousada da Praia*, Av Mons Tabosa 1315, Iracema, 2 blocks from beach, a/c, also cheaper rooms, fan, rec, bus stop for centre outside.

C *Ondas Verdes*, Av Pres Kennedy 934, T 226-0871, fan, TV, rec; **C** *Passeio*, R Dr João Moreira 221, fan, good breakfast, safe, storage, good value; **C** *Pousada Central*, Av Dom Manuel, nr Costa Barrios, T 252-5040, good value; **C** *Pousada Village Mar e Sol*, R Idelfonso Albano 614, Praia Iracema, T 252-3206, with or without bath, rec.

D *Chevalier*, Av Duque de Caxias 465, T 231-4611, with fan, pleasant; **D** *Pousada Vida da Praia*, José Vilar 252, T 244-6444, in Aldeota district, safe, helpful, English spoken; **D** *Pousada Tropicália*, Almte Barroso 617, T 244-4019, laundry, kitchen, English-run, rec.

On Av Abolição, Meireles, **C** *Zen Praia*, No 1894, rec; **D** *Nossa Pousada*, No 2600, T 261-4699, without bath, nr beach, helpful.

Several hotels along R Senador Pompeu, eg **D** *Universo*, at No 1152, without breakfast, may rent by the bed (ie single sex clients 3 to a room), smokers not welcome, some rooms have mosquito nets. Try student houses on Av Universitários, cheap or even free.

E *Pousada Abril em Portugal*, Av Almte Barroso 1006, with bath, breakfast, fan, good value, rec.

Youth hostel: *Albergue Praia de Iracema*, Av Al Barroso 998, T 252-3267, US$12 for members, US$20 for non-members, good location, mixed reports; another at R Rocha Lima 1186, Aldeota, T 244-1850.

Camping: *Barra Encantada*, Praia do Barro Preto, 42 km, T 244-1916 (office Av Barão de Studart 2360, s 1607); *Fazenda Lago das Dunas*, Uruaú (115 km away), T 244-2929.

● **Places to eat**
Several good fish restaurants at the eastern part of Av Presidente Kennedy, where the boats come ashore between 1300 and 1500. At Praia de Iracema, good outdoor nightlife and a collection of cafés on the beach serve good fast food and great coffee; rec on Av Kennedy are: *Alfredo* (good fish), No 4616, and, next door, No 4632, *Peixada do Meio*. *Colher de Pau*, R Federico Borges e R Ana Bilhar, rec, in Varjota district (others here, too). Italian are *La Trattoria* (see above), *Sandras*, Av Eng Luis Vieirra 555, Praia do Futuro, lobster has been specially rec, as has *Francés-Italiano*, Av Desem Moreira 155. *Parque Recreio*, Rui Barbosa 2727, good churrasco. Good Chinese: *HongKong*, Av Pres Kennedy 4544, Mucuripe. Japanese: *Mikado*, Av Barão de Studart 600. On same avenue, *Plato*, No 2360, Aldeote, revolving restaurant, expensive. Vegetarian: *Alivita*, Barão do Rio Branco 1486, good for fish, lunch only, Mon-Fri; *Céu da Boca*, R Franklin Távora 136, lunch and 1800-2000 Mon-Fri, good and inexpensive; *Fonte de Saúde*, R Pedroi 339, excellent vegetarian food, sold by weight, and a wide range of fruit juices; *Belas Artes*, Major Facundo 82, just up from Passeio Público, good. Cheap meals at railway station. Emcetur restaurant, *Xadrez*, in old prison, good atmosphere, open to 2400, reported safe to 2100. *Tropical* ice cream parlour, several branches, try *murici* and other Amazonian flavours. *Espaço Cultural Diogo Fontenelle*, R Gustavo Sampaio 151, art

gallery and bar with live music, rec. Many good bars and clubs along the beach. *El Mirante*, on a hill with spectacular views, has many lively bars and restaurants, accessible by bus or taxi (rec at night).

● **Banks & money changers**
Banco do Nordeste, Major Facundo 372, a/c, helpful, rec; and other national banks. Open 0900-1630. Banco Excel, R Major Facundo 322, T 211-1834, sells TCs on Amex card; TCs exchanged and cash with Visa at Banco do Brasil, R Barão do Rio Branco 1500, also on Av Abolição. Exchange at Tropical Viagens, R Barão do Rio Branco 1233, T 221-3344, English spoken; Libratur, Av Abolição 2794, rec; ACCtur has exchange booths for dollars (cash and TCs) throughout the city. Rudy Constantino has automatic exchange machines, eg Av Virgílio Távora 150, for several currencies.

● **Electric current**
220 volts AC, 60 cycles.

● **Embassies & consulate**
Danish, R Inácio Capelo 50, T 228-3399, Caixa Postal 34, open 0800-1800; Honorary British Consulate, Annette de Castro, Edson Queiroz Building, esq Av Desembargador Moreira e Av Antônio Sales. French, R Bóris 90, T 254-2822.

● **Entertainment**
Forró is danced at the *Pirata* club, Praia de Iracema, rec; *Clube dos Vaqueiros*, out on the BR-116 S, Wed 2230; *Mucuripe Club*, on Beira Mar, popular. *Chico do Caranguejo*, Praia do Futuro, lively bar, Thur nights, rec. *Bar Mirabilis*, R Barão de Aracati 142, nr *Hotel Colonial*, German and Swiss newspapers and sports results.

Theatre: *Teatro José de Alencar*, nr railway station in centre, built 1810, building contains also newer theatre built 1910, T 252-2324.

● **Hospitals & medical services**
Instituto Dr José Frota, R Barão do Rio Branco 1866, T 255-5000, rec public hospital. R Vicente Leite 631, English-speaking doctor.

● **Laundry**
Laundromat, Av Aboliço 3038.

● **Post & telecommunications**
Post Office: Praça Ferreira in centre. Parcels must be taken to Receita Federal office at Barão de Aracati 909, Aldeota (take 'Dom Luiz' bus).
Telecommunications: Embratel, Av Pontes Vieira 1554. International calls from Emcetur hut on Iracema beach and from Teleceará offices (R João Moreira esq R Floriano Peixoto). Public phones take phone cards.

● **Security**
Tourists should avoid the Serviluz favela between the old lighthouse (Av Vicente de Castro)

and Praia do Futuro; the favela behind the railway station; the Passeio Público at night; Av Abolição at its eastern (Nossa Senhora da Saúde church) and western ends. Generally, though the city is safe for visitors.

● **Shopping**

Fortaleza has an excellent selection of textiles which are among the cheapest in Brazil, and some handicrafts. The local specialities are lace (some hand-made) and embroidered textile goods; also hammocks (US$3-20) on R Conde Deu, fine alto-relievo wood carvings of NE scenes, basket ware and clay figures (*bonecas de barro*). Bargaining is OK at the **Mercado Central** in the Praça da Sé, and the **Emcetur tourist market** in the old prison (more expensive). Leather, lacework and cashew nuts at the Mercado Central are excellent. Every night (1800-2300), there are stalls along Av Pres Kennedy (the beach), lively, fair prices. *Cearart*, Av Santos Dumont 1589, is good but expensive. Clothes boutiques along Monsenhor Tabosa between Senador Almino and João Cordeiro.

● **Sports**

Golf: The Ceará Golf Club has 9 holes.

● **Tour companies & travel agents**

Lavila, Rui Barbosa 1055, T 261-4777, rec; tour to Jericoacoara by *Pousada Ondas Verdes*, rec (US$90); *Lafuente Turismo*, Av Senador Virgílio Tavora 496, T 244 8558.

● **Tourist offices**

Emcetur, in ex-municipal prison, helpful, has maps (sometimes), enquire about beach tours. Open 0700-1800, Sun 0700-1200, T 1516. **Foptur** municipal offices, Praça Ferreira, Av Beira Mar (Praça de Iracema), airport and Av Santos Dumont 5335, T 252-1444.

● **Transport**

Local Car hire: beach buggies rentable from *Junna's Buggy*, Av Abolição 2480, T 244-7872.

Air Direct flights to major cities. Flights from Europe with Varig and Transbrasil, see page 646. Bus 404 from airport to Praça José de Alencar, US$0.65, taxis US$10. The airport is nr the rodoviária; to be rebuilt in 1997.

Trains Tourist trains run on Sat to Croatá, plus bus trip to Praia da Lagoínha, US$30, and on Sun to Baturité, plus bus to the mountains (Pacotí, Estância das Flores), dep 0710, US$40, book in advance through *Turistar* at station, T 212-3090/2456, cellular 982-4675.

Buses Rodoviária 6 km from centre, bus from Av Gral Sampaio marked 'Aguanambi' 1 or 2, or 'Bairra de Fátima-Rodoviária' bus from Praça Coração de Jesus, US$0.35 (and others); no luggage store, only lockers. The 'Expresso Guan-

abara' runs daily to **Recife** (12 hrs, US$34, 4 daily), book early for weekend travel; also **Rio de Janeiro**, 48 hrs, US$86 (*leito* 110), **São Paulo**, 48 hrs, US$88 (*leito* 176); **Jericoacoara** daily 0900, 2100, US$14, 7 hrs; **Natal**, 5 daily, US$18, 8 hrs; **Salvador**, daily 2000, US$44, 21 hrs and many other cities. **Belém** US$58, 5 buses a day, 23 hrs (2 companies, Exp Timbira also sells Belém-Manaus boat tickets). **Piripiri**, for Parque Nacional de Sete Cidades, US$12, 9 hrs, a good stop en route to Belém.

To hitch to Teresina, take a bus W to the BR-222, the Teresina road.

INLAND EXCURSIONS

The Serra de Maranguape with tropical growth and distant views back to the city is 30 km inland from Fortaleza. The pilgrimage centre of **Canindé** may be visited, 108 km SW of Fortaleza, 3-hr bus ride from the rodoviária (office 21, Viação Nova Esperança). Large modern church on hill with carved baptistery doors, many ex-votos, interesting dry-land vegetation along route. (Hotels: *Plaza*, by basilica, food OK; *Santo Antônio*). Another inland town, **Baturité**, can be seen, 3 hrs from rodoviária (office 45) by Redenção bus, mornings only, also a tourist train round trip Sun.

NORTHWEST OF FORTALEZA

2 hrs NW of Fortaleza by bus is **Paracuru** (*pop* 20,940), a fishing port which is being developed as Ceará's carnival city (restaurant *Ronco do Mar*, good fish dishes, also *Balança do Mar* and a pizzaria; breakfast at Dona Luci's *sitio*, No 25 in the market; *Boca do Poço* bar has *forró* at weekends). It has some lovely deserted white sand beaches with good bathing, and the people are very friendly. Some 7 hrs from Fortaleza, passing lovely Lagoinha and Fleixeras beaches, is the sleepy fishing village of **Almofala**, served by many buses. There is electricity, but no hotels or restaurants, although locals rent hammock space and cook meals. Bathing is better elsewhere, but the area is surrounded by dunes and is excellent for hiking along the coast to explore beaches and lobster-fishing communities. In Almofala, the church with much of the town was covered by shifting sands and remained covered for 50 years, reappearing in the 1940s.

JERICOACOARA

Nestled in the dunes 165 km before the border with the state of Piauí is the fishing community of **Jericoacoara**. It is popular with travellers and Brazilians, crowded Jan to March. The visitor is rewarded with towering sand dunes, deserted beaches with little shade, cactus-covered cliffs rising from the sea, and a chance to savour village life, although it is becoming ever more geared to tourism. Electricity depends on generators. There is forró nightly.

● **Accommodation A3** *Avalon*, R Principal, with fan, pleasant, crêpes in restaurant; **A3** *Hippopotamus*, with pool; **A3** *Matusa*, pool and bar; **B** *Isalana*, R São Francisco, light and shower; **C** *Casa do Turismo*, T (088) 621-0211, jericoacoara@secrel.com.br, nice cabins, information, tours, bus tickets, exchange. **On R do Forró: C** *Isabel*, light and shower, rec; on R São Francisco, **D** *Acoara*, by beach, gas lamps; **D** *Pousada Paraiso*, friendly, clean; **F** *Natur*, basic, hammocks, friendly. Also rec: **C** *Capitão Tomáz*, on beach, good, apart from breakfast; **D** *Posada Renata*, 500m from beach, bath, patio with hammocks, breakfast, English, Italian and German spoken; *Recanto das Araras*, clean, good breakfast, friendly, washing facilities, nr beach; **D** *do Coqueiro*, **E** *Por do Sol*, basic, good value, with bath.

● **Places to eat** There are several restaurants serving vegetarian and fish dishes: *Acoara do Jèrico*, reasonable; *Alexandre, Isabel*, both on beach, good seafood, pricey; *Samambaia*, R Principal, good value; *Pizza Banana*, R Principal, good; *Senzala*, same street, nice Italian; *Cantinha da Masa*, R do Forró, good; pasta and pizza at *Casinha da Barra*; *Espaço Aberto* also rec for breakfast. Several shops sell basic provisions, so camping is possible. *Restaurante Central*, in Jijoca, is rec; *Sorrisa de Natureza* cheap, tasty food, rec.

● **Entertainment Nightlife** is interesting: Forró nightly in high season at R do Forró, Wed-Sat in low season. Action moves to the bars when forró has stopped. *Bar Barriga da Lua* and *Pizza Reggae*, opp forró.

● **Transport** Horses can be hired to visit beautiful lagoons, but the animals may be badly treated. A *jardineira* (open-sided 4x4 truck) meets Redenção bus from/to Fortaleza, at Jijoca de Cruz: 1½ hrs, US$1.75, from Jijoca at 1400, 0200, from Jericoacoara at 0600, 2200. At other times pick-ups can be hired in Jijoca. If coming from Belém, go via Sobral (US$47, 20 hrs), where you change for Jijoca. A direct journey

from Fortaleza on a 2 or 3-day tour is possible in a VW Kombi, book through an hotel or T 244-5974, Maria do Carmo. You can also get there by boat 'seasickness guaranteed', or bus from **Camocim** (a little further W; **F** *Hotel Lusitania*). Take a truck from Camocim to Guriú where hammock space can be found. The village musician sings his own songs in the bar. Walk 4 hrs, or take boat across the bay to Jericoacoara. Many other marvellous beaches in this region; some like Nova Tatajuba, recently discovered, with simple *pousadas*; others like Maceió, also reached from Camocim, an unspoilt paradise.

WEST TO PIAUÍ

The road to Sobral and Teresina, BR-222, is paved, but in poor condition between Tianguá and Alto Alegre. **Sobral** (*pop* 127,450), the principal town in western Ceará and well-known for straw hats, has **C** *Hotel Visconde*, 10 mins from rodoviária, friendly, good breakfast, and **D** *Francinet's Hotel, Hotel Vitória*, cheap good lunch buffet, rec. At **Tianguá**, 311 km from Fortaleza on the Teresina road, is **B** *Serra Grande* hotel, all amenities, good (bus from Fortaleza US$9, from Belém, US$32.50).

UBAJARA NATIONAL PARK

The Ubajara caves in the **Ubajara National Park** are 18 km off the road to Teresina, on a good paved road, 3 km from Ubajara town. A cablecar descends the cliff to the cave entrance, 0830-1630, US$4.40. Lighting has been installed in the nine caverns of the complex, but a torch and spare batteries may be useful. Ibama office at the park entrance, 5 km from the caves; not always helpful (reported closed in 1996), T 634-1388. There is a 3-km cobbled path from the cablecar (take drinking water). The views of the *sertão* from the upper cablecar platform are superb, beautiful walks among forest and waterfalls and old sugar-mills scattered around the plateau. To walk all the way up to the top of the plateau takes 14 hrs; if you want to do this take plenty of water, from the trail entrance the walk is 3 hrs.

● **Accommodation** Nearby is the **C** *Pousada Neblina*, T 634-1270, in beautiful cloud forest, with swimming pool, rustic campground

S$1.25), with breakfast and private shower
without breakfast) restaurant open 1100-
000, meals rec; opp is **F** *Pousada Gruta da
bajara*, with bath, rustic, restaurant, rec. Near
e park, at Sítio Santana (ask taxi driver for 'Sítio
Alemão'), is the coffee plantation of *Herbert
ein*, on which there are 3 small chalets, D,
armly rec, with full facilities, excursions, bicycle
re offered (postal address Caixa Postal 33, CEP
2.350, Ubajara, Ceará), if chalets are full the
eins accommodate visitors at their house.

Ubajara town (*pop* 23,350), 2 hotels; **C** *Le
illage*, on Ibiapina road, T 634-1364, restau-
nt, pool, sauna, good value; **D** *Ubajara*, R
vêncio Luís Pereira 370, T 634-1261, small
staurant. Most restaurants US$10, big meals
the old market cost US$3. An interesting Sun
orning market sells produce of the *sertão*.
uses to Fortaleza.

rateús South of Sobral is a remote town
op 66,635), paved road all the way to
ortaleza, with the **D** *Crateús Palace Ho-
l*, very reasonable and clean, with break-
st. Good restaurant, *Churrascaria
equena Cabana*, at back of hotel. Bus
rvice from Crateús over very bad road
Teresina, every 2 days.

Piauí

PARNAÍBA

Between the states of Maranhão and Piauí
runs the Rio Parnaíba. Near the river
mouth is the anchorage of Luís Correia,
where ships unload for final delivery by
tugs and lighters at **Parnaíba** (*pop* 127,990;
CEP 64200; *DDD* 086) 15 km up river, the
collecting and distributing centre for the
trade of Piauí: tropical products and cattle.
There is a regular connection here to
Tutóia, for boats across the Parnaíba delta
(see page 567).

Beaches
Beaches at Luís Correia, which with Parnaíba has radioactive sands. Some 15 km
from Parnaíba is Pedra do Sal: dark blue
lagoons and palm trees. At Lagoa de
Portinho there are bungalows, a bar and
restaurant and it is possible to camp; canoes for hire.

● **Accommodation B** *Cívico*, Av Gov Chagas
Rodrigues, T 322-2470, with a/c, good breakfast, rec; **E** *Rodoviária*, and other basic hotels
in the centre.

TERESINA

(*Pop* 598,450; *CEP* 64000; *DDD* 086)
About 435 km up the Rio Parnaíba, is the
capital of the State of Piauí (*pop* 2,581,055),
possibly the poorest in Brazil. There are
paved road and rail connections (freight
only) with the neighbouring state capitals.
The city itself is reputed to be the hottest
after Manaus (temperatures rise to 42°C).

Places of interest
The **Palácio de Karnak** (the old governor's palace), just S of Praça Frei Serafim,
Mon-Fri 1530-1730; it contains litho-
graphs of the Middle East in 1839 by

David Roberts RA. **Museu do Piauí**, Praça Mal Deodoro, Mon-Fri 0800-1730, Sat, Sun, 0800-1230, US$0.60. There is an interesting **open market** by the Praça Mal Deodoro and the river is picturesque, with washing laid out to dry along its banks. The market is a good place to buy hammocks, but bargain hard. Every morning along the river bank there is the **troca-troca** where people buy, sell and swap; an under-cover complex (**Mercado Central do Artesanato**) has been built at R Paissandu 1276 (Praça Dom Pedro II), open daily 0800-2200 (not weekends). Most of the year the river is low, leaving sandbanks known as *coroas* (crowns).

Local information
● Accommodation
A1 *Luxor Hotel do Piauí*, T 222-4911, F 222-4171, and *Teresina Palace*, Paissandu 1219, T 222-2770.

B *Sambaíba*, R Gabriel Ferreira 230-N, 2-star, T 222-6711, central, good; **B** *São José*, João Cabral 340, T 223-2176, F 223-2223, reasonable restaurant.

E *Fortaleza*, Felix Pacheco 1101, Praça Saraiva, T 222-2984, fan, basic, rec; many cheap hotels and *dormitórios* around Praça Saraiva; **E** *Grande*, Firmino Pires 73, very friendly and clean. Many cheap ones in R São Pedro and in R Alvaro Mendes; **E** *Glória*, at 823 (clean, best), blocks 800 and 900 on each street.

● Places to eat
For fish dishes, *Pesqueirinho*, R Domingos Jorge Velho 6889, in Poty Velho district. Many eating places in Praça Dom Pedro II.

● Banks & money changers
Try *Alda Tur*, R A de Abreu 1226. Larger hotels may be helpful.

● Shopping
Supermarket on Praça Marechal Deodoro 937, clean, good, fresh food. Local handicrafts include leather and clothes.

● Tourist offices
Piemtur, R Alvaro Mendes 2003, Caixa Postal 36, information office at R Magalhães Filho s/n (next to 55 N, English spoken); kiosks at rodoviária and airport.

● Transport
Air Flights to Fortaleza, Brasília, Rio de Janeiro, São Paulo, Goiânia, São Luís.

Buses The bus trip from Fortaleza is scenic and takes 9 hrs (US$12.25, *leito* US$24.50). There are direct buses to Belém (16 hrs, US$20), Recife

(16 hrs, US$30) and to São Luís (7 hrs, US$9.50).

ROUTES A road, very bad, leads inland to Porto Franco and **Imperatriz** on the Belém-Brasília highway (see page 571); daily bus takes 26-40 hrs for the trip to Imperatriz (US$17), depending on the state of the road; these buses are very crowded. Another main road, runs SE to *Picos* (*pop* 78,425; **E** *Hotel Picos*, basic, but a/c); from there a good road runs via Salgueiro (many *pousadas*) to Recife (800 km) and another to **Petrolina**, on the River São Francisco opposite the Bahian town of Juazeiro (see page 529).

PARQUE NACIONAL DE SETE CIDADES
Some 190 km NE of Teresina and 12 km from Piracuruca is the interesting 20-sq km Parque Nacional de **Sete Cidades** with its strange eroded rock formations, just off the Fortaleza-Teresina road. From the ground it looks like a medley of weird monuments. The inscriptions on some of the rocks have never been deciphered; one theory suggests links with the Phoenicians, and the Argentine Professor Jacques de Mahieu, considers them to be Nordic runes left by the Vikings. There is plenty of birdlife, and iguanas, descending from their trees in the afternoon. If hiking in the park, beware of rattlesnakes. Ibama provides a free bus, returns 1700, or else walk (takes all day, very hot, start early). Ibama, Av Homero Castelo Branco 2240, Teresina, CEP 64048-400, T 232-1142. Small booklet with sketch map (not really good enough for walking), entrance US$1.40. There are camping facilities (US$2) and two natural swimming pools, although several years of drought have lowered their water level drastically. Local food is limited and monotonous: bring a few delicacies, and especially fruit. Guided tours with *Tropicália Turismo*, Piracuruca, T (086) 343-1347. 50 km away Pedro Segundo is a good place to buy opals.

● **Accommodation** 6 km from the park entrance is the hotel **B** *Fazenda Sete Cidades* with private bath, swimming pool, good restaurant and bicycle or horse transport (it is at Km 63 on BR-222, T (086) 261-3642); also has a free pick-up to the park (and a most unpleasant zoo). In the park is an Ibama hostel, T 343-1342, **F** rooms with bath, pleasant, good restaurant natural pool nearby, camping, rec. **Hotels in Piripiri**: 26 km away (*Pop* 63,015), **F** *Dos Viajantes*, basic and clean; *Piripiri*, both nr bus offices and behind the church. Exchange at the bank only. Piripiri is a cheap place to break the Belém-Fortaleza journey.

● **Transport** A free bus service leaves the Praça in Piripiri (in front of Telpisa office), at 0700, passing *Hotel Fazenda Sete Cidades* at 0800, reaching the park 10 mins later; return at 1630, or hitchhike. Taxi from Piripiri, US$14, or from Piracuruca, US$18. Bus Teresina-Piripiri and return, throughout the day 2$^1/_2$ hrs, US$3.50. Bus São Luís-Piripiri, 1200, 1630, 2130, 10 hrs, US$12. Several daily buses Piripiri-Fortaleza, 9 hrs, US$12. Bus Piripiri-Ubajara (see above), marked 'São Benedito', or 'Crateús', 2$^1/_2$ hrs; US$3.60, first at 0700 (a beautiful trip).

OEIRAS

In the S of the state, some 300 km S of Teresina, is **Oeiras** (*pop* 51,890) old capital of Piauí, where the state government is restoring some of the old buildings, such as the bishop's palace and the church of Nossa Senhora da Vitória.

PARQUE NACIONAL SERRA DA CAPIVARA

About 500 km S of Teresina is the **Capivara National Park** a 130,000 ha park established in 1979 and now on the Unesco World Heritage list. Some 30,000 prehistoric rock paintings have been found dating to between 6,000 and 12,000 years ago. Excavations by Brazilian and French archaeologists have uncovered fossilized remains of extinct animals such as the sabre-toothed tiger. The area is good for hiking, but there is very little infrastructure. Access is from São Raimundo Nonato on the BR 324, or from Petrolina in Pernambuco. Taxi from Petrolina airport will cost about US$200 one way. For further information contact Dr Niéde Guidon, Fumdham Parque Nacional, R Abdias Neves 551, CEP 64770-000 São Raimundo Nonato, Piauí, T 582 1612, F 582 1656.

Maranhão

MARANHÃO state (*pop* 4,922,340) is about the size of Italy; its land is flat and low-lying, with highlands to the S. The Atlantic coastline – a mass of sandbanks and creeks and sandy islands on one of which stands São Luís – is 480 km long. A quarter of Maranhão is covered with *babaçu* palms, the nuts and oil of which are the state's most important products. Rice comes a poor second. There are salt pans along the coast. The huge Boa Esperança hydroelectric plant on the Parnaíba river now floods the State with energy, and some petroleum has been discovered.

The main road from Teresina passes through the Maranhense town of Caxias, which has a good churrascaria, *Selva do Braz* (Av Central 601), live music in the evening.

Crossing the Parnaíba delta, which separates Piauí from Maranhão, is possible by boat arriving in **Tutóia**: an interesting trip through swamps sheltering many birds. Trucks from Tutóia go to Barreirinhas, gateway to the Parque Nacional dos Lençois Maranhenses, a vast protected area of sand dunes with rare birds and other wildlife (see below).

SÃO LUÍS

São Luís (*pop* 695,780; *CEP* 65000; *DDD* 098), the capital and port of Maranhão state, founded in 1612 by the French and named for St Louis of France, is about 560 km W of Fortaleza (1,080 km by road) and 400 km SE of Belém (830 km by road) in a region of heavy tropical rains, but the surrounding deep forest has been cut down to be replaced by *babaçu* palms. The city stands upon São Luís island between the bays of São Marcos and São José. The urban area extends to São Francisco island, connected with São Luís by three bridges. An old slaving port, the city has a large black population and has retained much African culture.

Places of interest

The old part, on very hilly ground with many steep streets, is still almost pure colonial. Part of it, known as the Reviver, has been restored with generally splendid results: the damp climate stimulated the use of ceramic tiles for exterior walls, and São Luís shows a greater variety of such tiles than anywhere else in Brazil, in Portuguese, French and Dutch styles. The commercial quarter (R Portugal, also called R Trapiche) is still much as it was in the 17th century; best shopping area is R de Santana near Praça João Lisboa.

The **Palácio dos Leões** (Governor's Palace – closed since Jan 1995), has beautiful floors of dark wood (*jacarandá*) and light (*cerejeira*), marvellous views from terrace. The restored **Fortaleza de Santo Antônio**, built originally by the French in 1614, is on the bank of the Rio Anil at Ponta d'Areia. The **Fonte do Ribeirão**, Largo do Ribeirão, was begun in 1796.

The **Fábrica Canhamo**, a restored factory houses an arts and crafts centre, near Praia Grande. The **Centro da Creatividade Odylo Costa Filho**, Praia Grande, is an arts centre with theatre, cinema, exhibitions, music, etc, with a bar and café, a good

meeting place. Near the Travessa Ladeira there is live music at night.

Churches

The best colonial churches are the **Cathedral** and the churches of **Carmo**, **São João**, **Rosário**, and **Santana**. On Largo do Desterro is the church of **São José do Desterro**, finished in 1863, but with some much older parts.

Museums

The **Cafua das Mercês**, R Jacinto Maia 43, is a museum housed in the old slave market (open Mon-Fri 1330-1700), well worth the effort to find it: a small building opposite the Quartel Militar. Also visit the Casa dos Negros, next door. The **Museu Histórico e Artístico do Estado**, in a fine early 19th century mansion (complete with slave quarters) at R do Sol 302, closed for renovation (since Jan 1995). Also on the R do Sol is the **Teatro Artur Azevedo** (1816). **Museu de Artes Visuais**, Av Portugal 289, shows ceramics and post war art (Mon-Fri 0800-1300, 1600-1800, US$0.65 entry).

Excursions

Calhau is a huge beach, 10 km away, excellent *Churrascaria Pavan*; **Ponta D'Areia** is nearer to São Luís but more crowded. An hour's bus ride from São Luís is **Raposa**, a fishing village built on stilts; another fishing village is **Ribamar**, a 30-min bus ride from São Luís, from in front of the market.

Local festivals

On 24 June (São João), the Bumba-Meu-Boi, see **Music and Dance**: for several days before the festival street bands parade, particularly in front of the São João and São Benedito churches. There are dances somewhere in the city almost every night in June. In Aug, São Benedito, at the Rosário church. Festival in Oct, with dancing, at Vila Palmeira suburb (take bus of same name).

Local information

● **Accommodation**

L2 *Quatro Rodas*, 8 km from centre **on Calhau beach**, T 227-0244, F 227-4737, excellent with all facilities; **L2** *Vila Rica*, 5-star, Praça D Pedro II, T 232-3535, F 222-1251, central, many

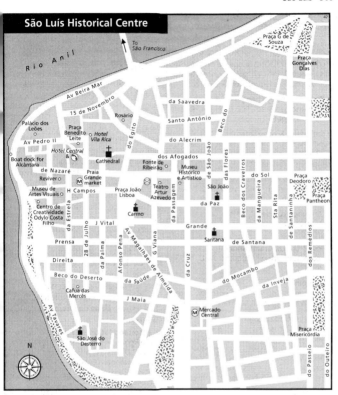

São Luís Historical Centre

To São Francisco

Rio Anil

Praça G de Souza

Praça Gonçalves Dias

Av Beira Mar

15 de Novembro

da Saavedra

Rosário

Santo Antônio

do Egito

do Alecrim

Palácio dos Leões

Av Pedro II

Praça Benedito Leite

Hotel Vila Rica

Hotel Central

Cathedral

Fonte de Ribeirão

dos Afogados

Museu Histórico e Artístico

de São João

das Flores

do Sol

Praça Deodoro

Boat dock for Alcântara

Reviver

de Nazaré

Praia Grande market

Museu de Artes Visuais

Centro de Creatividade Odylo Costa Filho

H Campos

Praça João Lisboa

Teatro Artur Azevedo

São João

da Paz

Beco dos Craveiros

da Mangueira

Sta Rita

Praça Pantheon

da Estrela

J Vital

Carmo

da Passagem

Grande

de Santaninha

dos Remédios

Prensa

28 de Julho

da Palma

Afonso Pena

Av Magalhães de Almeida

G Viana

Santana

de Santana

Praça Misericórdia

Direita

Beco do Deserto

da Saúde

da Cruz

do Mocambo

da Inveja

Cafua das Mercês

Av Tavares

J Maia

Mercado Central

São José do Desterro

do Passeio

do Outeiro

N

amenities, rec. **At Ponta d'Areia**: **A1** *Praia Mar*, T 227-4477, on the beach, 5-star, all amenities, opp *São Francisco*, T 227-1155.

C *Deodoro*, R de Santaninha 535, T 222-1196, good; **C** *Pousada Colonial*, R Afonso Pena 112, T 232-2834, in beautiful restored, tiled house, rec; **C** *São Marcos*, Saúde 178, T 232-3763, restored colonial house, a/c, family-run, rec.

D *Lord*, R Nazaré 258, T 222-5544 facing Praça Benedito Leite, comfortable, rec, good breakfast. Many cheap hotels in R das Palmas, very central, and R Formosa; **D** *Pousada Solar do Carmo*, Praça João Lisboa 400, T 222-2455, pleasant, light and airy, excellent food; **E** *Estrela*, R da Estrela 370, Centro (T 222-1083), noisy, not too clean, safe; **E** *Lusitano*, R da Palma 220 (also called R Dr Herculano Parga), with breakfast, cheaper without bath, cheaper still without window; **E** *Pousada da Praia*, R dos Magistrados 10, helpful owner, mosquitoes.

● **Places to eat**

Solar do Ribeirão, R Ribeirão 141, T 222-3068, good buffet lunch and seafood, good value but not cheap, regional cuisine, closed Sat pm and Sun; *La Bohème*, R Isaac Martins 48, very good food, live music, expensive, popular; *Candelabro*, R do Egito, very expensive but excellent international cuisine; *Base de Edilson*, R Paulo Kurger de Oliveira 31, shrimp only, excellent; *Hibiscus* Av dos Franceses, and *Tia Maria*, Av Nina Rodrigues (Ponta d'Areia), seafood, rec; *Base do Germano*, Av Wenceslau Bras in Canto da Fabril district, excellent *caldeirada de camarão* (shrimp stew). *Tia Dadi*, Praça Manuel Beckman, Beira Mar Centre, good regional dishes; *Beiruth Self Service*, Av Castelo Branco 751-B, T 227 8447, rec; *Senac*, R Nazaré (next to hotel *Lord*), tourism school restaurant, good local cuisine in a beautifully restored mansion; *Seu Nacib*, R do Trapiche 260, opp Museu de Artes Visuais, kilo restaurant, excellent; *Kanto Lanches*, Nazaré y de Palma, cheap snacks, friendly. *Base da Lenoca*, R Don Pedro II 187, good view, seafood, big portions; *Naturalista Alimentos*, R do Sol 517, very good, natural foods shop and restaurants, open till 1900. Said to be more choice in new São Francisco district, just across bridge, eg *Oriental*, Av Pres Castelo Branco 47, good Chinese. Try the local soft drink called *Jesús* or *Jenève*.

● **Banks & money changers**
TCs at Banco do Brasil, Praça Deodoro; BFB, R do Sol 176; **Agetur**, R do Sol 33.

● **Embassies & consulates**
Denmark, R do Sol 141, Ed Colonial, Sala 210, T 222-4075, open 0900-1300, 1500-1900. French, R do Passeio 495, centro, T 222-7412.

● **Hospitals & medical services**
Clínica São Marcelo, R do Passeio 546, English speaking doctor.

● **Language courses**
Portuguese lessons: Sra Amin Castro, T 227-1527, rec.

● **Post & telecommunications**
Telecommunications: Embratel, Av Dom Pedro II 190.

● **Shopping**
Funai shop at R do Sol 371. *Centro do Artesanato* in main street of São Francisco suburb.

● **Tourist offices**
Maratur, R Djalma Dutra 61-A, also at R Isaac Martins 141, Centro, Av dos Franceses, good information on walks in city. **Taguatur** and **Babaçu Viagens**, both in R do Sol shopping gallery, good. Town maps from agencies and office in Praça João Lisboa, opp post office.

● **Transport**
Air Internal flights only. 15 km from centre; buses ('São Cristovão') to city until midnight, US$0.40.

Trains Three trains a week on Carajás railway to Parauapebas, 13½ hrs, 890 km, leave São Luís 0800, Mon, Wed, Fri, return 0800, Tues, Thur, Sat (crowded, take own food); for station take 'Vila Nova' or 'Anjo da Guarda' bus.

Buses Rodoviária 12 km from centre on airport road, 'Rodoviária via Alemanha' bus to centre (Praça João Lisboa), US$0.20. Bus to Fortaleza, US$24, 4 a day, 18 hrs. Also to Recife, US$48.50, 25 hrs, all other major cities and local towns.

ROUTES To Belém: direct paved road via **Santa Inês** (convenient stopping place, **D** *Pousada San Antonio*, on street with same name, breakfast; **E** *Hotel Novo Horizonte*, nr rodoviária, with bath) and **Alto Bonito**, in reasonable condition (sometimes washed out but still passable – fascinating swamp-

lands), with petrol stations not far apart (about 9 hrs driving with stop for lunch). There is a bus service 13 hrs, US$22. Transbrasiliana at 1900 and 2000 (no *leito*).

ALCÂNTARA

Some 22 km away by boat is **Alcântara** (city *pop* 4,000, municipality 19,620) the former state capital, on the mainland bay of São Marcos. Construction of the city began at the beginning of the 17th century and it is now a historical monument. There are many old churches (eg the ruined **Matriz de São Matias**) and colonial mansions (see the **Casa**, and **Segunda Casa, do Imperador**, also the old cotton barons' mansions with their blue, Portuguese tiled façades) the traditional pillory, the **Pelourinho**, in the Praça Gomes de Castro, also a small museum in the square (US$0.20) and the **Forte de São Sebastião** (1653) now in ruins. See also the **Fonte de Mirititiva**. Canoe trips to **Ilha do Livramento**, good beaches, good walking around the coast (can be muddy after rain), mosquitoes after dark. A rocket-launching site has been built nearby. Principal festival: **Festa do Divino**, at Pentecost (Whitsun).

● **Accommodation B** *Pousada do Mordomo Régio*, R Grande 134 (T 337-1197 or São Luís 227-0110), TV, refrigerator, good restaurant; **C** *Estalagem Enseada do Guará*, at Praia da Baronesa, bungalows with showers, good restaurant; **C** *Pousada do Pelourinho*, Praça Gomes de Castro 55, T 337-1150, breakfast, good restaurant, communal bathroom, rec. Ask for hammock space or rooms in private houses, friendly but no great comfort; provide your own mineral water.

● **Places to eat** *Bar do Lobato*, on the praça, is pleasant, with good, simple food, fried shrimps highly rec. The restaurants are not cheap (about US$15 per meal).

● **Banks & money changers** Banco do Estado do Maranhão, R Grande 76, exchanges US$ cash and TCs.

● **Post & telecommunications** Post Office, R Direita on Praça Matriz, T 337-1155. **Telecommunications**: Telma, just off main square (0700-2200 daily).

● **Transport** Ferries cross the bay daily, leaving São Luís dock or from São Francisco district at about 0700 and 0930, returning from Alcântara about 0815 and 1600: check time and buy the ticket at the *hidroviária* (W end of R Portugal,

ão Luís) the day before as departure depends on
he tides. The journey takes 90 mins, return US$15,
worth paying extra for 'panorámica' seat. Sea can
be very rough between Sep and Dec. Old wooden
boats the *Newton Bello* and *Mensageiro da Fé*
leave São Luís at 0630 and 1600 returning at 0730
(1 1/2 hrs, US$5 return). There are sometimes
catamaran tours bookable through tour operators
in São Luís, meals not included.

PARQUE NACIONAL LENÇÓIS MARANHENSES

To the E of São Luís, on the Atlantic Coast
is the **Parque Nacional Lençóis Maranhenses**, 155,000 ha of beaches, lakes and
dunes, with very little vegetation and
largely unstudied wildlife. For information, phone the Ibama office, T 221-
2125/2776, or *Baluz Turismo*, T 222-6658,
or *Jaguarema Turismo*, T 222-4764.

IMPERATRIZ

On the Eastern bank of the Rio Tocantins,
at Maranhão's western border with Tocantins, is **Imperatriz** (*pop* 276,450), a city
serving a large cattle region. To get to the
ferry across the river, go along R Luís
Domingues, which runs parallel to Av
Getúlio Vargas.

• **Accommodation B** *Poseidon*, R Paraíba
740, T 721-4466, central, best, a/c, TV, swimming pool, rec; **D** *Anápolis*, BR-010, Km 1345,
T 721-2255, opp rodoviária, a/c, fridge, swimming pool; a lot of cheap hotels nr rodoviária.

• **Entertainment** There is a good, expensive
discotheque at Beira Rio, N of the ferry crossing,
Fly Back Disco Club; it has two dance floors,
one fast, one slow (for couples only).

• **Post & telecommunications Telephone
Office**: on R Rio Grande do Norte, a side street
off Av Getúlio Vargas, nr *Hotel Poseidon*.

ROUTES Lying on the Belém-Brasília
highway, Imperatriz has bus connections
with both cities; there is a slow, crowded bus
service to Teresina. To get to Marabá on the
Transamazônica, you can either take a
Transbrasiliana bus direct, 7-10 hrs (starting
on the Belém highway, the bus then turns W
along a poorer road, passing finally through
destroyed forest, new fazendas and unplanned cities), or, a faster route, involving
taking a ferry across the river in the early
morning (0600-0700) to catch a pick-up on
the other side, takes about 5 hrs, but is more
expensive.

Northern Brazil

BRAZILIAN Amazônia,
from the mouth of the
great river to the Co-
lombian and Peruvian borders.
The cities of Belém, Santarém
and Manaus are described, together with river travel between
and excursions into the jungle.
Also dealt with are the land and
water routes to Venezuela and
the Guianas.

Northern Brazil consists of the states of
Pará, Amazonas, Amapá and Roraima. The
states of Rondônia and Acre are dealt with
under Section 10, Southern Amazônia.

Brazilian Amazônia

The area is drained by the Amazon, which
in size, volume of water – 12 times that of
the Mississippi – and number of tributaries has no equal in the world. At the base
of the Andes, far to the W, the Amazonian
plain is 1,300 km in width, but E of the
confluences of the Madeira and Negro
rivers with the Amazon, the highlands
close in upon it until there is no more than
80 km of floodplain between them. Towards the river's mouth – about 320 km
wide – the plain widens once more and
extends along the coast southeastwards
into the state of Maranhão and northwards
into the Guianas.

Brazilian Amazônia, much of it still
covered with tropical forest, is 56% of the

national area. Its jungle is the world's largest and densest rain forest, with more diverse plants and animals than any other jungle in the world. It has only 8% of Brazil's population, and most of this is concentrated around Belém (in Pará), and in Manaus, 1,600 km up the river. The population is sparse because other areas are easier to develop; the rainfall is heavy, the humidity high and the climate hot; and the soil, as in all tropical forest, is poor.

Successive governments have made strenuous efforts to develop Amazônia. Roads have been built parallel to the Amazon to the S (the Transamazônica), from Cuiabá (Mato Grosso) northwards to Santarém (Pará), and NE from Porto Velho through Humaitá to the river bank opposite Manaus. Some maps show a road N of the Amazon, marked Perimetro (or Perimetral) Norte; this road does not exist, never has and probably never will. Agricultural settlements are being established along these roads; major energy and mining projects for bauxite and iron ore are bringing rapid change. Much environmental damage has been caused to the region by gold prospectors (*garimpeiros*), especially by their indiscriminate use of mercury. The most important cause of destruction, however, has been large scale deforestation to make way for cattle ranching.

There is a gradually growing awareness among many Brazilians that their northern hinterland is a unique treasure and requires some form of protection. Most recently, much attention has been focused on ecotourism as a potentially non-destructive source of income for the region.

Anyone interested in the Amazonian development programme and its ecological, social, economic and political effects should read Richard Bourne's masterly *Assault on the Amazon* (London, Gollancz, 1978), *Dreams of Amazonia*, by Roger D Stone (Penguin, 1986), or *Amazon* by Brian Kelly and Mark London (Harcourt Brace Jovanovich, New York, 1983). *The Fate of the Forest* by Suzanne Hecht and Alexander Cockburn (Penguin, 1991) has also been rec.

ALONG THE TRANSAMAZÔNICA

The Transamazônica, about 5,000 km in length, represents the greater part of a direct road connection between Brazil's furthest E and furthest W points. It skirts the southern edge of the Amazonian plain, linking Estreito (junction with the Belém-Brasília highway, N of Araguaína, see page 617), Marabá (on the Tocantins river), Altamira (on the Xingu), São Luís do Tapajós, near Itaituba (on the Tapajós) Jacarèacanga, Humaitá (on the Madeira) Rio Branco, and Japim, in the far W of the State of Acre. The road was officially opened in Dec 1973. Parts of it have been paved, but the harsh climate and inadequate maintenance have caused much deterioration. Some sections are often totally intransitable throughout the rainy season (eg Santarém to the Belém-Brasília Highway). Others may require 4WD and winch. There are stretches with regular truck traffic and scheduled bus services but as conditions are constantly changing detailed local inquiry is essential before heading out. Also ensure that you have sufficient *reais* for your journey.

MARABÁ

Near **Marabá** (*pop* 121,815; *alt* 84m), are beaches on the Rios Tocantins and Itacaiúnas, best June-October. With the filling of the Tucuruí dam the town has been moved; even so it suffers from flooding There is a bridge across the Tocantins at Marabá. There are essentially three parts of Marabá: Marabá Velha (also called Marabá Pioneira), Marabá Nova, and Cidade Nova. The distance between Marabá Nova and Velha is about 2.5km. A good travel agent is *IBR Travel* on the main street of Marabá Velha. Banco do Brasil will not cash TCs; parallel market in larger stores, eg *Supermercado Bato Logo*.

Excursions The **Serra Pelada** gold mines are now worked by heavy machinery. This massive excavation was the scene of much human misery (and some fabulous fortunes). Bus to Km 6, change there to Serra Pelada bus (US$3, 3 hrs, last bus back 1400). 11 km before the town is a police post: search for weapons and alcohol (forbidden); second search at the airport 2 km from the mine. No prior permission is needed to visit the mines.

● **Accommodation B** *Vale do Tocantins*, Folha 29, Cidade Nova, 7 km, T 322-2321, modern, restaurant, travel agency; of similar standard are **B** *Itacaiúnas*, nearby, T 322-1715, and *Del Príncipe*, Av Mal Rondon 95, Cidade Nova, T 324-1175; **C** *Dallas*, Nova Marabá, next to rodoviária, rec; **C** *Bahia*, Nova Marabá, also next to the rodoviária; **C** *Plaza*, Folha 32, Quadra 10, Lote 06, T 322 1610/1611/1612, fan, quiet, helpful, very good breakfast, some English spoken, rec; **E** *Serra de Ouro*, all of wood, shower; others nr rodoviária.

● **Places to eat** *Kome Aki no Chikão*, Av Antônio Maia 997, central, a/c, modest, 1200-1500, 1800-2300 (in theory); *Bambu*, Pedro Carneiro 111, Cidade Nova, 3 km, mainly fish, clean, good value, 1100-1500, 1800-2300. Good *Churrascaria* in main square nr public TV set; juice bars and *Disco Tony* discotheque; *Lanchonete Domino*, opp rodoviária, rec.

● **Transport Air** Airport in Cidade Nova, 3 km. There are no direct flights to Altamira or Santarém, only via Belém with Brasil Central or Varig. Brasil Central flies to several local destinations, eg São Luís, Imperatriz. **Buses** Rodoviária in Nova Marabá, 4 km on PA-150, T 321-1892. Buses leave daily for **Belém** (654 km, paved), for **Santarém** (34 hrs) and many daily for **Imperatriz** (7-10 hrs, US$9.50, there is also a pick-up to the bank of the Tocantins opp Imperatriz, 5 hrs, but more expensive, US$12); buses can be caught going S at **Tocantinópolis**, opp Porto Franco on the Belém-Brasília road. Also a bus can be taken to **Araguaína**, 12½ hrs, US$19; bus Marabá-**Goiânia** (change at Araguaína) US$48. Bus to **Santa Inês** (Maranhão, on Belém-Teresina road), 19 hrs, US$23. Transbrasiliana bus to **Altamira** daily, 1300 (if road is passable) 15 hrs, US$38; direct to **Rio** US$60, **São Paulo** US$52. On these bus trips take plenty of food and drink – local supplies are expensive. From rodoviária to **Railway Station** take coletivo bus US$0.31 from opp the rodoviária to 'Km 6' (a kind of suburb of Marabá), then another coletivo bus US$0.31 to the Estação Ferrovia. The coletivos are not frequent but are crowded. Alternatively taxis, which can be shared cost US$11 from railway station to town. **River Boat**: trips to Belém (24 hrs) and Santarém (18 hrs).

CARAJÁS MINE

Companhia Vale Rio Doce (CVRD) operates the very impressive iron mine at **Carajás** (the largest mineral development in Brazil) which looks like a giant red hole in a green jungle. The ore is almost pure iron oxide and is therefore extremely profitable. It is ground, washed and shipped to São Luis by trains up to 2 km long, without further treatment or chemical processing. Apart from iron other metals like manganese are also mined by the CRVD in the area. To get into Carajás (checkpoint 35 km from the project), you must have a permit, available from CVRD in Marabá, São Luís, São Paulo or Rio: Av Graça Aranha 26, 16°, andar, Centro, Rio 20030000 – attention Dr Hugo Mourão (hotel bookings handled here too); apply in advance and have a good reason. **Parque Zoo-Botânico** is a very pleasant zoo with local animals, and like everything else in the region is run by CVRD. The animals have very spacious, quasi-natural cages. There is a lot to see including a small shop with Funai articles from the local indians.

37 km before the mine is **Parauapebas**. Originally intended as a temporary settlement for the Carajás construction workers, it is now a big city and still growing. Both cities however are expensive, especially Carajás. In the dry season, summer, there are frequent bush fires in the region, ignited mainly as *fazendeiros*. The old part of Parauapebas is where the colorful fruit-market, shops and banks are situated and is very busy.

● **Accommodation Parauapebas**: **B** *Almaribe*, T 346 1048, very pleasant, manager Alipio speaks excellent English, some French and German, safe, a/c, refrigerator, TV, good breakfast, restaurant, gym machines, good atmosphere, highly rec; **D** *Ouro Verde*, Rio Verde district nr market, basic, cheap, rec. *Florida Bar*, T 346 1038, has good cocktails and food, the friendly owner Neuma speaks good Austrian/German, opens from 2000 closed Mon, Tues, rec. *Pit Dog*, on main street, has fast food and live music, rec.

● **Transport Air** There are flights to Carajás from Belém, Marabá and Tucuruí. **Trains** Parauapebas is the final station of the Carajás railway line. To Marabá, dep 1930, 2 hrs, US$1.55. To São Luís, see page 570. **Buses** There are 8 daily buses to Marabá between 0545 and 1900. There is 1 daily bus to Conceição de Araguaia. Direct buses from Rio, São Paulo and Vitória to Parauapebas with Aguia Branca. Plenty of Transbrasiliana buses daily Marabá-**Carajás**, 4-5 hrs, US$5.75. Military Police check for weapons and drugs at Curianópolis.

OTHER TOWNS IN THE TRANSAMAZONICA

The Transamazônica crosses the Rio Xingu at Favânia, 41 km E of **Altamira**, a busy, booming Amazônian town with many gold dealers (*pop* 120,565). A road is being paved 46 km N to the fishing village of Vitória on the lower Xingu, from which boats go to Belém; a good place to watch the *garimpeiros* working below the last rapids. No organized trips but a boat can be hired, US$25/day, for a trip up the Xingu which is highly rec. Many animals. The area is an Assurine Indian reservation and it is not allowed to enter villages; buy food in Altamira.

● **Accommodation & places to eat** C *Alta Palace*, Av Tancredo Neves 3093, bar/restaurant, a/c, good, T 515-2057; **D** *Pae e Filho*, simple, rec; **D** *Requinte*, rec; **D** *Lisboa*, Lindolfo Aranha 405, a/c, TV, good value, slightly better than **D** *Imperatriz*, R Beto Somez nr market, bath, a/c, rec; good *churrascos* and shopping in the market; *Restaurante Casa Grande*, R Anchieta, centre, good *churrascos*, cheap, 1130-1430, 1930-2330; *Restaurante Esquina*, next to hotel *Lisboa*, good *sucos*, closed Sun, rec.

● **Transport Air** The airport is 8 km from centre, no bus, exchange is difficult; flights to Belém, Santarém, Cuiabá and other Amazon destinations. **Buses** Rodoviária on Av Perimentral, T 515-1879, no left luggage.

Rurópolis (Presidente Medici) lies at the junction of the Transamazônica and the Santarém highway. Hotel run by Incra.

Itaituba, a *garimpeiro* town (malaria present), is the jumping-off place for the **Amazônia National Park**; see Father Paul Zoderer, who may help to arrange a visit, at church on waterfront – nearest Ibama information, T (091) 224-5899/2621. (**C** *Hotel Central Plaza*, rec; **E** *Hotel 3 Poderes*, clean, friendly, rec.)

● **Transport** The Transbrasiliana company has a rodoviária on the Rio Tapajós, nr the ferry docks. Bus to Marabá, about 34 hrs, US$30. Bus to Santarém via Rurópolis, 11 hrs, US$20.

In **Humaitá** (*pop* 38,755) there are several basic hotels on the eastern edge of town: **D** *Hotel Macedonia*, fan, shower and restaurant. The Soltur rodoviária is in the centre.

● **Transport** There is very little traffic on the Transamazônica from Humaitá E to Itaituba

(1,028 km); local drivers may give lifts. A ferry crosses the Rio Aripuanã at Vila do Carmo. The road is good for about 350 km from Humaitá, then it deteriorates badly. It is hilly, narrow, and the jungle usually grows over the side of the road. Bus to **Apuí** (**F** *Hotel Goaino*, basic) 458 km, about 12 hrs, US$23, bus to Jacarèacanga erratic service, US$30 when running, another 232 km (the town is 8 km off the highway). One must stay overnight and catch the Transbrasiliana bus to Itaituba (24 hrs, schedule erratic, US$14.50, the bus is replaced occasionally by a truck). **D** *Hotel São Cristóvão*, with good restaurant, or try the filling station on the Transamazônica near the Jacarèacanga turn-off, for hammock space. Travel times depend on the weather conditions, the condition of the bus, and whether the driver decides to stop somewhere for the night. Flights Jacarèacanga-Itaituba cost US$90; boat, not daily, ticket from filling station, US$25, 11/2 days, very basic, hammock space only. 70 km before Itaituba there are rapids, rest of journey by pickup, US$10.

UP THE AMAZON RIVER

The Amazon system is 6,577 km, long, of which 3,165 km are in Brazilian territory. Ships of up to 4-5,000 tons regularly negotiate the Amazon for a distance of about 3,646 km up to Iquitos, Peru. Distances upstream from the river mouth to Manaus in nautical miles are:

Belém	80
Narrows (entrance)	225
Narrows (exit)	330
Garupa	334
Prainha	452
Santarém	538
Óbidos	605
Parintins	694
Itacoatiara	824
Manaus	930

RIVER TRANSPORT IN AMAZONIA

Although air service is widespread throughout the region, and road transport is gradually increasing, rivers remain the arteries of Amazônia for the transport of both passengers and merchandise. The two great ports of the region are Belém, at the mouth of the Amazon, and Manaus at the confluence of the Rio Negro and Rio Solimões. Manaus is the hub of river transport, with regular shipping services E to Santarém and Belém along the lower Amazon, S to Porto Velho along the Rio Madeira, W to Tabatinga (the border with Colombia and Peru) along the Rio Solimões, NW to São Gabriel da Cachoeira along the Rio Negro, and N to Caracaraí (for Boa Vista) along the Rio Branco. There is also a regular service connecting Belém and Macapá, on the N shore of the Amazon Delta, Santarém and Macapá, as well as Santarém and Itaituba S along the Rio Tapajós. All of the above services call at many intermediate ports and virtually every village has some form of riverboat service.

The size and quality of vessels varies greatly, with the largest and most comfortable ships generally operating on the Manaus – Belém route; acceptable conditions can be found, however, on some boats to almost all destinations. Since the introduction of more stringent government control in 1991 (see **Health** below), there is less overcrowding, better hygiene, better food, and friendlier service. Many of the larger ships offer a/c berths and even suites with double beds and private bath, in addition to first class (upper deck) and second class (lower deck) hammock space (on many routes this distinction does not apply). Most boats have some sort of rooftop bar serving drinks and snacks (generally overpriced).

Riverboat travel is not a substitute for visiting the jungle. Except for a few birds and the occasional dolphin, little wildlife is seen. However it does offer an insight into the vastness of Amazônia and a chance to meet some of its people.

Extensive local inquiry and some flexibility in one's schedule are indispensable for river travel as schedules change frequently. The following are some suggestions on how to choose a riverboat. Refer to the appropriate city sections for details of port facilities in each.

Whenever possible, see the vessel yourself and have a chat with the captain or business manager to confirm departure date and time, length of voyage, ports of call, price, etc. Inspect cleanliness in

the kitchen, toilets and showers. All boats are cleaned up when in port, but if a vessel is reasonably clean upon arrival then chances are that it has been kept that way throughout the voyage. You can generally arrange to sleep onboard a day or two before departure and after arrival, but be sure to secure carefully your belongings when in port. If you take a berth, lock it and keep the key even if you will not be moving in right away. If you are travelling hammock class, board ship at least 8 to 12 hrs before sailing in order to secure a good spot (away from the toilets and the engine). Be firm but considerate of your neighbours as they will be your intimate companions for the duration of the voyage. Always keep your gear locked. Take some light warm clothing, it can get chilly at night in the hammock area.

Compare fares for different ships. As a general rule of thumb they will be about half of the prevailing one-way airfare, including all meals. (Drinks not included. Many ships sail in the evening and the first night's supper is not included.) Empty cabins are sometimes offered to foreigners at reduced rates once boats have embarked. Payment is usually in advance. Insist on a signed ticket indicating date, vessel, class of passage, and berth number if applicable.

All ships carry cargo as well as passengers and the amount of cargo will affect the length of the voyage because of weight (especially when travelling upstream) and loading/unloading at intermediate ports. All but the smallest boats will transport vehicles, but these are often damaged by rough handling. Insist on the use of proper ramps and check for adequate clearance. Vehicles can also be transported aboard cargo barges. These are usually cheaper and passengers may be allowed to accompany their car, but check about food, sanitation, where you will sleep (usually in a hammock slung beneath a truck), and adequate shade.

The following are the major shipping routes in Amazônia giving a selection of vessels and indicating intermediate ports, average trip durations, and fares. Not all ships stop at all intermediate ports.

There are many other routes and vessels providing extensive local service. All fares shown are one-way only and include all meals unless otherwise stated. Information is identical for the respective reverse voyages (except Belém-Manaus, Manaus-Belém).

● **Boat services**
Belém-Manaus via Breves, Almeirim, Prainha, Monte Alegre, Curua-Uná, Santarém, Alenquer, Óbidos, Juruti, and Parintins on the lower Amazon. 5 days upriver, 4 days downriver, including 18 hr stop in Santarém, suite US$500 upriver, 400 down, double berth US$300 upriver, 260 down, hammock space US$85 upriver, 75 down, vehicle US$320 small car, US$420 combi usually including driver, other passengers extra; motorcycle US$100. *Nélio Correa* is best on this route. *São Francisco* is largest, new and modern but toilets smelly. *Cisne Branco* of similar quality. *Cidade de Bairreirinha* is the newest on the route, a/c berths. *Lider II* has good food and pleasant atmosphere. *Enasa* has 1 sailing/week 2000 Thur, US$54 pp inc meals.

Belém-Santarém, same intermediate stops as above. 2 days upriver, 1½ days downriver, fares berth US$200, hammock US$61. All vessels sailing Belém-Manaus will call in Santarém and there are others operating on only the Belém-Santarém route.

Santarém-Manaus, same intermediate stops as above. 2 days upriver, 1½ days downriver, fares berth US$100, hammock US$30. All vessels sailing Belém-Manaus will call in Santarém and there are others operating only the Santarém-Manaus route, including: *Cidade de Terezinha III* and *IV*, good. *Miranda Dias*, family run and friendly.

Belém-Macapá (Porto Santana) non-stop, 24 hrs on large ships, double berth US$120, hammock space US$30 pp, meals not included but can be purchased onboard (expensive), vehicle US$100, driver not included. *Silja e Souza* (Wed) is best. *Almirante Solon* (Thur, Sat) is state run, slightly cheaper, crowded and not as nice. Same voyage via Breves, 36 to 48 hrs on smaller riverboats, hammock space US$25 pp inc meals. *ENAL* (Sat); *Macamazónia* (every day except Thur), slower and more basic; *Bartolomeu I* of Enavi, food and sanitary conditions OK, 30 hrs; *JK I, II, III, Cidade de Santarém* all others, none too clean.

Macapá (Porto Santana)-Santarém via Vida Nova, Boca do Jari, Almeirim, Prainha, and Monte Alegre on the lower Amazon (does not call in Belém), 2 days upriver, 1½ days downriver, berth US$150, hammock US$48.

Santarém-Itaituba along the Rio Tapajós, 24 hrs.

Manaus-Porto Velho via Borba, Manicoré, and Humaitá on the Rio Madeira. 4 days upriver, 3½ days downriver (up to 7 days when river is low), double berth US$200, hammock space US$79 pp. Recommended boats are *Almirante Moreira II*, clean, friendly owner; *Lord Scania*, recently refurbished (1996), friendly; *Ana Maria VIII*, modern; *San Antonio da Borda*, clean, friendly, good meals.

Manaus-Tefé via Codajás and Coari, 24 to 36 hrs, double berth US$80, 1st class hammock space US$30 pp, 2nd class hammock space US$25 pp. *Capitan Nunes* is good. *Jean Filho* also OK. Note that it is difficult to continue W from Tefé to Tabatinga without first returning to Manaus.

Manaus-Tabatinga via Fonte Boa, Foz do Mamaria, Tonantins, Santo Antônio do Ica, Amataura, Monte Cristo, São Paulo de Olivença and Benjamin Constant along the Rio Solimões. Up to 8 days upriver (depending on cargo), 3 days downriver, double berth US$250, hammock space US$75 pp. *Voyagers, Voyagers II* (T 236-3782) rec; *Almirante Monteiro, Avelino Leal,* and *Capitão Nunes VIII* all acceptable, *Dom Manoel,* cheaper, acceptable but overcrowded.

Manaus-Caracaraí (for Boa Vista) along the Rio Branco, 4 days upriver, 2 days downriver, many sandbars, impassable during the dry season. Now that the BR-174 (Manaus-Boa Vista road) has been improved and remains open almost all year, river service is erratic.

Manaus-São Gabriel da Cachoeira via Novo Airão, Moura, Carvoeiro, Barcelos, and Santa Isabel do Rio Negro along the Rio Negro. Berth US$240, hammock US$80, leaves from São Raimundo dock, N of main port.

● **What to wear**
Light cotton or poplin clothing for the day and at night put on a sweater or coat, for it gets quite cold. Wear long trousers. Leather sandals fall apart in the wet, rubber ones are better, but proper shoes or boots are best for going ashore: there are many foot-attacking parasites in the jungle. (2 pairs of trainers, so you always have a dry pair, is a good idea.) Also take a hat and rain gear, such as a poncho with hood.

A hammock is essential on all but the most expensive boats; often too hot to lie down in cabin during day. Light cotton hammocks seem to be the best solution. Buy a wide one on which you can lie diagonally; lying straight along it leaves you hump-backed. A climbing carabiner clip is useful for fastening hammocks to runner bars of boats. It is also useful for securing baggage making it harder to steal.

● **Health**
There is a danger of malaria in Amazônia. Mos-

quito nets are not required when in motion as boats travel away from the banks and too fast for mosquitoes to settle, though repellent is a boon for night stops. From April to Oct, when the river is high, the mosquitoes can be repelled by Super Repelex spray or K13. A yellow-fever inoculation is strongly advised; it is compulsory in some areas and may be administered on the spot with a pressurized needle gun. In response to the 1991 cholera outbreak, hygienic conditions are much improved. The larger ships must have an infirmary and carry a health officer. There are regular sanitary inspections at all ports of call. All drinking water is now treated (usually by adding chlorine bleach), but taking your own mineral water is a good idea. Micropur brand water purification tablets are available in Belém pharmacies.

● **Food**

Ample but monotonous, better food is usually available to cabin passengers. Meal times can be chaotic. Fresh fruit is a welcome addition; also take plain biscuits, tea bags, seasonings, sauces and jam. Fresh coffee available; most boats have a bar of sorts. Plates and cutlery may not be provided. Bring your own plastic mug as drinks are served in plastic beakers which are jettisoned into the river. A strong fishing line and a variety of hooks can be an asset for supplementing one's diet; with some meat for bait, piranhas are the easiest fish to catch. Negotiate with the cook over cooking your fish. The sight of you fishing will bring a small crowd of new friends, assistants, and lots of advice – some of it useful.

In Amazônia Inevitably fish dishes are very common, including many fish with Indian names, eg pirarucu, tucunaré, and tambaqui, which are worth trying. Also shrimp and crab dishes (more expensive). Specialities of Pará include duck, often served in a yellow soup made from the juice of the root of the manioc with a green vegetable (jambú); this dish is the famous pato no tucupi, highly rec. Also tacaca (shrimps served in tucupi), vatapá (shrimps served in a thick sauce, highly filling, simpler than the variety found in Salvador), maniçoba (made with the poisonous leaves of the bitter cassava, simmered for 8 days to render it safe – tasty). Caldeirada, a fish and vegetable soup, served with pirão (manioc puree) is a speciality of Amazonas. There is also an enormous variety of tropical and jungle fruits, many unique to the region. Try them fresh, or in ice creams or juices. Avoid food from street vendors.

● **Exchange**

Facilities are sparse in Amazônia: banks and exchange can be found in Belém, Macapá, Santarém and Manaus. Small amounts of US$ cash can usually be exchanged in many other towns, but some boat captains will not take US$ dollars.

Belém (do Pará – Pop of city 1,246,435, of state 5,084,725; CEP 66000; DDD 091), founded in 1616, 145 km from the open sea and slightly S of the equator, is the great port of the Amazon. It is hot (mean temperature, 26°C), but frequent showers freshen the streets.

Places of interest

There are some good squares and fine buildings. There was much renovation of public places in 1985-87, and a building boom in the early 1990s sent up many new apartment towers. The largest square is the **Praça da República**; the main business and shopping area is along the wide Av Presidente Vargas leading to the river and the narrow streets which parallel it. The neo-classical **Teatro da Paz**, one of the largest theatres in the country, has free concert and theatre performances (recently restored, open Mon-Fri 0800-1200, 1400-1800, tours cost US$0.50).

Visit the **Cathedral** (1748) with several remarkable paintings (closed Tues-Fri 1130-1400, Sun 1200-1600, all day Mon), and directly opposite the 18th-century **Santo Aleixandre** church (now being restored) noted for its wood carving. The 17th-century **Mercês** church (1640), near the market, is the oldest church in Belém; it forms part of an architectural group known as the Mercedário, the rest of which was heavily damaged by fire in 1978 and is being restored. The **Basilica of Nossa Senhora de Nazaré** (1909), built from rubber wealth, is an absolute must for its beautiful marble and stained glass windows (closed 1200-1500, Mon-Fri). The **Lauro Sodré palace**, praça Dom Pedro II, a gracious 18th-century Italianate building, contains Brazil's largest framed painting, 'The Conquest of Amazônia' by de Angelis (Mon-Fri 0800-1200, 1400-1800). The **Palácio Antônio Lemos, Museu da Cidade** and **Prefeitura**, closed Mon, downstairs old views of Belém, upstairs historic rooms, beautifully renovated, furniture, paintings etc, well explained.

The Belém market, known as **'Ver-o-**

Peso' (see the weight), now has lots of gift shops selling charms for the local African-derived religion, *umbanda*; the medicinal herb and natural perfume stalls are also interesting. It is one of the most varied and colourful markets in South America; you can see giant river fish being unloaded around 0530, with frenzied wholesale buying for the next hour. The area around the market swarms with people, including many armed thieves and pickpockets. In the old town, too, is the **Forte do Castelo**, which you can enter on request; the site also contains the *Círculo Militar* restaurant (entry US$1; drinks and *salgadinhos* served on the ramparts from 1800 to watch the sunset, restaurant is good). At the square on the waterfront below the fort the *açaí* berries are landed nightly at 2300, after picking in the jungle (*açaí* berries ground up with sugar and mixed with manioc are a staple food in the region).

The **Bosque Rodrigo Alves**, Av Almte Barroso (0900-1700 closed Mon), is a public garden (really a preserved area of original flora), with a small animal collection; yellow bus marked 'Souza' or 'Cidade Nova' – any number – 30 mins from 'Ver-o-Peso' market, also bus from Cathedral. The **Museu Emílio Goeldi**, Av Magalhães Barata 376, takes up a city block and consists of the museum proper (with a fine collection of Marajó Indian pottery, an excellent exhibition of Mebengokre Indian lifestyle), a zoological garden (including manatees), and botanical exhibits including Victoria Régia lilies; open Tues-Sat 0900-1200, 1400-1700, all day Sun, closed Mon, and Wed and Fri pm. Entry US$1, additional charges for specialist areas, now renovated. Take bus from the Cathedral. The **Murucutu ruins**, an old Jesuit foundation, are reached by the Ceará bus from Praça da República, through an unmarked door on the right of the Ceará bus station.

Excursions

Travel agents offer short and longer visits to the rivers and jungle (Ciatur's ½ day trip, US$25, rec). A passenger ferry (*foca*) to the small town of Barcarena makes an interesting ½ day trip, departures from Ver-o-Peso, US$1. A return trip on the ferry from Ver-o-Peso to **Icaoraci** provides a good view of the river. Several restaurants here serve excellent seafood; you can eat shrimp and drink coconut water and appreciate the breeze coming off the river. The nearest beach is at **Outeiro** (35 km) on an island near Icoaraci, about an hour by bus and ferry (the bus may be caught near the Maloca, an Indian-style hut near the docks which serves as a nightclub). To visit the ceramics workshops where marajoara and tapajônica wares are made, take the bus from Av Presidente Vargas to Icoaraci (1 hr). Open all week but best on Tues-Fri. Artisans are friendly and helpful, will accept commissions and send purchases overseas. A further bus from Icoaraci to Outeiro takes 30 mins. Further N is the island of **Mosqueiro** (86 km) now accessible by toll bridge (US$0.20) and an excellent highway, with many beautiful sandy beaches and jungle inland. It is popular at weekends when traffic can be heavy (also July) and the beaches can get crowded and polluted. Buses Belém-Mosqueiro every hour from rodoviária, US$1.45, 80 mins.

● **Accommodation & places to eat** Many hotels and weekend villas at the villages of Mosqueiro and Vila; rec (may be full weekends and July). **C** *Farol*, on Praia Farol, 1920s architecture in good repair, small restaurant, good views; **C** *Marésia*, Praia de São Francisco, on beach, pool, helpful owner, agree prices for excursions in advance; **C** *Murumbira*, on Praia Murumbira, pool, restaurant. Restaurants at Mosqueiro: in *Hotel Ilha Bela*, Av 16 de Novembro 409, rec for fish, no evening meals; highly rec at Praia Chapeu Virado is *Marésia*. *Sorveteria Delícia*, Av 16 de Novembro, good local fruit ice creams, owner buys dollars. Camping is easy.

Local holidays

Maundy Thursday, half-day; 9 June, Corpus Christi; 15 Aug, accession of Pará to independent Brazil; 7 Sept, Independence Day, commemorated on the day with a military parade, and with a students' parade on the preceding Sun (am); 30 Oct, half-day; 2 Nov, All Souls' Day; 8 Dec, Immaculate Conception; Christmas Eve, half-day.

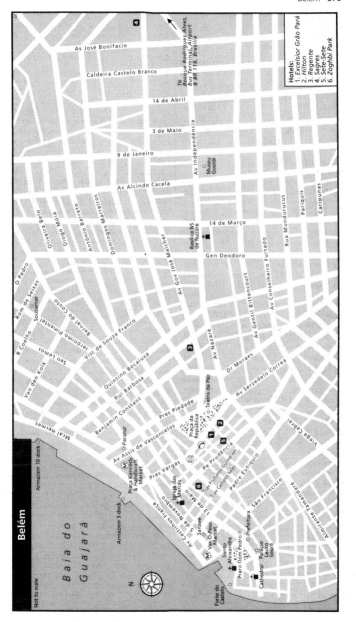

Belém

Baía do Guajará

Not to scale

N

Armazem 10 dock

Armazem 3 dock

Forte do Castelo

Santo Alexandre

Praça Dom Pedro II

Palácio Lauro Sodré

Cathedral

Av Castilhos França

Sanave

Ver-O-Peso Market

5 de Novembro

Prefeitura

São Francisco

Amirante Tamandaré

13 de Maio

Igreja das Mercês

Praça Kennedy & Handicraft Market

Av Assis de Vasconcelos

Av Paratur

Pres Vargas

Trav Frutuoso Guimarães

Trav Campos Sales

Padre Eutiquio

Pe Prudência

Viega Cabral

Mcal Hermes

Benjamin Constant

Rui Barbosa

Quintino Bocaiuva

Visc de Souza Franco

Jerônimo Pimentel

Bernalo do Couto

Sen Lemos

Van den Kolk

R Coelho

Rom de Seixas

Souzamar

D Pedro

Oliveira Belo

Diogo Móia

Antônio Barreiro

Domingos Marreiros

Av Gov José Malcher

Av José Malcher

Pres Piedade

Praça da República

Teatro da Paz

Av Nazaré

Dr Moraes

Av Serzedelo Correa

Av Gentil Bittencourt

Av Conselheiro Furtado

Rua Mundurucus

Pariquis

Caripunas

14 de Março

Gen Deodoro

Basílica NS de Nazaré

Av Independência

Museu Goeldi

Av Alcindo Cacela

9 de Janeiro

3 de Maio

14 de Abril

Caldeira Castelo Branco

Av José Bonifacio

To Bosque Rodrigues Alves, Bus Terminal, Airport & BR 316, Brasília

Hotels:
1. Excelsior Grão Pará
2. Hilton
3. Regente
4. Sagres
5. Sete-Sete
6. Zoghbi Park

Círio, the Festival of Candles in Oct, is based on the legend of the Nossa Senhora de Nazaré, whose image was found on the site of her Basilica around 1700. On the second Sun in Oct, a procession carries a copy of the Virgin's image from the Basilica to the cathedral. On the Mon, 2 weeks later, the image is returned to its usual resting-place. There is a Círio museum in the crypt of the Basilica, enter at the right side of the church; free. (All hotels are fully booked during Círio.)

Local information
● Accommodation

L2 *Hilton*, Av Pres Vargas 882, T 223-6500, F 225-2942, swimming pool, sauna, restaurants (the *Açaí* is rec for regional dishes and others, Sun brunch, desserts, expensive); **L2** *Novotel*, Av Bernardo Sayão 4808, T 229-8011, F 229-8709, a/c, swimming pool, unprepossessing neighbourhood, far from centre (take Universidade bus).

A2 *Cambará*, 16 de Novembro 300, esq Tamandaré, T 224-2422, a/c, good, mosquitoes; **A3** *Vanja*, Av Benjamin Constant 1164, T 222-6688, F 222-6709, good service, inexpensive rooftop restaurant, pool, rec; **A3** *Verde Oliva*, Boaventura da Silva 1179 (T 224-7682), 10 mins from centre, a/c, TV, good value, rec; *Regente*, Av Gov José Malcher 485, T 241-1222, F 224-0343, 3-star, modest, comfortable, good breakfast.

B *Itaoca*, Av Pres Vargas 132, T 241-3434, F 241-0891, a/c, new, charming, inc breakfast.

C *Novo Avenida*, No 404, T 222-9953, central, some rooms better than others, no backpackers, good breakfast; **C** *Vidonho*, R O de Almeida 476, T 242-1444, a/c, fridge, shabby, abundant breakfast, in a side street.

D *Plaza*, Praça da Bandeira, T 224-2800, 2-star, a/c, fridge, restaurant good value, take care in this area, especially at night; **D** *São Geraldo*, R Padre Prudêncio 56, T 223-7800, central, rec; **D** *Sete-Sete*, Trav 1 de Março 677, T 242-7730, F 224 2346, comfortable, with breakfast, rec; **D** *Ver-o-Peso*, Castilhos Franco 208, T 224-2267, opp Ver-o-Peso market, rooftop restaurant, TV and fridge in room, rec.

E *Central*, Av Presidente Vargas 290 (T 222-3011), under same ownership as *Vidonho*, with a/c (**F** without bath), some rooms noisy, but comfortable, good meals, a must for art-deco fans (one reader suggests checking doors for peep-holes), rec. **E** *Vitória Régia*, Frutuoso Guimarães 260, T 224-2833, F 224-3475, with breakfast, more with a/c, bath, fridge (**F** without), refurbished, safe, rec; next door is **E** *Fortaleza*, Frutuoso Guimarães

276, very basic (will put you in contact with ferry agent) rec. Many cheap hotels close to waterfront, none too safe. Near the rodoviária, all OK, all **E**, *Akemi*, *Duas Irmãs*, *Real*.

Camping: nearest at Mosqueiro, 86 km away.

● Places to eat

All the major hotels have good but expensive restaurants. *Círculo Militar* rec for Belém's best Brazilian food and situation in the grounds of the fort with view over river (good choice, try *filete na brasa*, expensive). *Churrascaria Rodeio*, Rodovia Augusto Montenegro Km 4, excellent meat, salad bar, reasonable prices; *Augustos*, Av Almte Barroso 493, past rodoviária, a/c, good food, reasonable prices, piano music; *Cristal*, R Benjamin Constant e R dos Mundurucus, very good, nice décor, expensive; *Roxy Bar e Restaurante*, Av Sen Lemos 231, delicious dishes named after Hollywood stars, pleasant, nice music, no a/c, open late, reasonable prices; *Casa Portuguesa*, R Manoel Barata 897, good, inexpensive; *Lá em Casa*, Av Gov José Malcher 247, try *menu paraense*, good cooking, fashionable, expensive; *Okada*, R Boaventura da Silva, past R Alcindo Cacela, Japanese, excellent, try 'Steak House', various types of meat, rice and sauces, vegetables, all you can eat, also try *camarão à milanesa com salada*, good prices; *Miako*, Travessa 1 de Março 766, behind Praça de República (very good medium-priced oriental food), rec; *Germania*, R Aristides Lobo 604, Munich-style, mid price, rec; *Pizzaria Napolitano*, Praça Justo Chermont 12 (in particular pizzas and Italian dishes); *Cantina Italiana*, Benjamin Constant 1401, very good Italian, enthusiastically rec; *Chez Jacques*, R Silva Santos 102 (behind Hilton), delicious French food: knock on the window to enter, and check bill carefully.

Vegetarian: *Nectar*, Av Gentil Bittencourt, Travessa P Eutíquio 248, pedestrian zone, good, lunch only. *Casa dos Sucos*, Av Presidente Vargas, Praça da República, serves 41 types of juice (including Amazonian fruits) and delicious chocolate cake (vegetarian restaurant upstairs, rec for lunches).

Specially rec are some very good snack-bars (mostly outdoors in Belém) where you can buy anything up to a full meal, much cheaper than restaurants: *Charlotte*, Av Gentil Bittencourt 730, at Travessa Quintino Bocaiuva, for best *salgadinhos* in the city, also good desserts, very popular. Many buffet-style restaurants along R Santo Antônio pedestrian mall and elsewhere in the *Comércio* district, generally lunch only, good variety, pay by weight, prices average US$4/kg. *Bar do Parque*, next to Municipal Theatre, excellent place for meeting local people, the more flamboyant stroll here after 2100. *Cosanostra Café*, Trav Benjamin Constant 1507, 'pub' atmosphere, a/c, internet service, expensive. There are also many street and market vendors, who, although they should be viewed with care, often sell delicious local food.

● **Banks & money changers**
Banco do Brasil, Av Presidente Vargas (nr *Hotel Central*), good rates, and other Brazilian banks (open 0900-1630, but foreign exchange only until 1300). **Banco de Amazônia** (Basa), on Pres Vargas, gives good rates for TCs (Amex or Citicorp only), but does not change cash. **American Express**, R Gen Gurjão e Av Vargas, No 676, also representative office in *Hilton Hotel*, helpful. **Mastercard**, cash against card, Trav 14 de Março 1155, Nazaré. *Casas de câmbio*: **Carajás**, Av Pres Vargas 762, Galeria da Assambléia Paraense, Loja 12, also at Pres Vargas 620; **Casa Francesa**, Trav Padre Prudêncio 40; **Monopólio**, Av Pres Vargas 325, térreo do Ed Palácio do Rádio; **Turvicam**, Av Conselheiro Furtado 1558A, also at Av Pres Vargas 640, Loja 04; **Banorte**, R Cons João Alfredo 331 Centro; **Meridional**, R Santo Antonio 273, Centro; **Loja Morpho**, Presidente Vargas 362. *Hilton*, *Central* (cash only), *Ver-o-Peso* (cash and cheques, reasonable rates) and *Victória Régia Hotels*. French francs are readily available, but rates vary markedly between different *câmbios* and change rapidly.

● **Electric current**
110 AC, 60 cycles.

● **Embassies & consulates**
Venezuelan, opp French Consulate, Av Pres Pernambuco 270, T 222-6396 (Venezuelan visa takes 3 hrs, costs US$30 for most nationalities, but we are told that it is better to get a visa at Manaus; latest reports indicate that a yellow fever vaccination certificate is not required but best to check in advance – see also **Health** below). **British**, Robin Burnett, Ed Palladium Centre, room 410/411, Av Gov José Malcher 815, T 222-8470, open at 1130; **Swedish**, R Santo Antônio 316, mailing address Caixa Postal 111, T 222-4788, open 1600-1800; **French**, Av Pres Pernambuco 269, T 224-6818 (also for French Guiane; South Africans must apply in South Africa); **German**, Trav Piedade 651, sala 201, T 222-5634/5666; **Finnish**, Rodovia Arthur Bernardes 1393, Bairro Telégrafo, T 233-0333; **Danish** (Consul Arne Hvidbo), R Senador Barata 704, sala 1503, T 223-5888 (PO Box 826); **US**, Av Oswaldo Cruz 165, T 223-0800.

● **Entertainment**
Eskapuli, Rodovia Augusto Montenegro, huge dance hall with various types of music, live and recorded, frequented by all age groups, open Wed-Sat from 2200 (take a radio taxi for safety), no a/c, dress informally; *Bar Teatro Maracaibo*, Av Alcindo Cacela 1289, informal place with live Brazilian popular music, moderate prices; *Rhinos*, Av Nazaré 400, good discotheque, also

Pink Panther, R Aristedes Lobo 92.

● **Hospitals & medical services**
Health: a yellow fever certificate or inoculation is mandatory. Best to get yellow fever vaccination at home (always have your certificate handy) and avoid the risk of recycled needles. Medications for malaria prophylaxis are not sold in Belém pharmacies. You can theoretically get them through the public health service, but this is hopelessly complicated. Such drugs are sometimes available at pharmacies in smaller centres, eg Santarém and Macapá. Bring an adequate supply from home. *Clínica de Medicina Preventativa*, Av Bras de Aguiar 410 (T 222-1434), will give injections, English spoken, open 0730-1200, 1430-1900 (Sat 0800-1100). *Hospital Ordem Terceira*, Trav Frei Gil de Vila Nova 2, doctors speak some English, free consultation but a bit primitive. British consul has a list of English-speaking doctors.

● **Post & telecommunications**
Post Office: Av Presidente Vargas 498, but international parcels are only accepted at Post Office on the praça at the corner of Trav Frutuoso Guimarães e R 15 de Novembro, next door to NS das Mercês (hard to find).

Telecommunications: telegrams and Fax at the Post Office, Av Presidente Vargas. For phone calls: Telepará, Av Presidente Vargas.

● **Shopping**
Shopping in Av Presidente Vargas; also try the Indian handicrafts shop at Praça Kennedy, set in a garden with Amazonian plants and animals. *Parfumaria Orion*, Trav Frutuoso Guimarães 268, has a wide variety of perfumes and essences from Amazonian plants, much cheaper than tourist shops. Belém is a good place to buy hammocks, look in the street parallel to the river, 1 block inland from Ver-o-Peso. Bookshop with English titles in arcade next to *Excelsior Hotel* on Av Pres Vargas.

Camera repairs: *Neemias Teixeira Lima*, R Manoel Barata 274, Sala 211, T 224-9941.

● **Tour companies & travel agents**
Ciatur, Av Presidente Vargas 645, T 224-1993, good half-day tour on water and in forest and 32-hr trip to Marajó. *Gran-Para Turismo Ltda*, *Hilton Hotel*, Av Presidente Vargas 882 LJ8, T 224-2111.

● **Tourist offices**
Municipal office, **Detur**, in airport and Rodoviária. Hotel reservations made, including low-priced hotels. Map, US$1, from rodoviária bookshop. **Paratur**, Praça Kennedy on the waterfront, by the handicraft shop, helpful, many languages spoken; has a good map of Belém in many languages (but some references are incorrect). Town guidebook, US$2.75.

● **Useful information**

Police: for reporting crimes, R Santo Antônio e Trav Frei Gil de Vila Nova. To avoid crime, take sensible precautions and stay out of dark corners.

● **Transport**

Air Bus 'Perpétuo Socorro-Telégrafo' or 'Icoaraci', every 15 mins from Prefeitura, Praça Felipe Patroni, to airport, 40 mins, US$0.30. Taxi to airport, US$10 (ordinary taxis cheaper than Coop taxis, buy ticket in advance in Departures side of airport). Airport has a hotel booking service but operated by, and exclusive to, 5 of the more expensive hotels, discounts offered. Twice weekly flights N to **Miami** by Varig, S to **Brasília** and other Brazilian cities, and W to **Santarém** and **Manaus**. To **Paramaribo**, and **Cayenne** 3 times weekly. Air France, R Boaventura Da Silva 1457, T 223-7547/7928. Surinam Airways, R Santo Antônio 432, Edif Antonio Velho, 4th floor, English spoken, helpful with information and documentation. Travellers entering Brazil from Guyane may need a 60-day visa (takes 2 days) before airlines will confirm their tickets.

Buses The rodoviária is at the end of Av Gov José Malcher 5 km from centre, take Aeroclube, Cidade Novo, No 20 bus, or Arsenal or Canudos buses, US$0.35, or taxi, US$5 (day) US$7 (night) (at rodoviária you are given a ticket with the taxi's number on it, threaten to go to the authorities if driver tries to overcharge). It has a good snack bar and showers (US$0.10). Regular services to all major cities. There are direct buses from Belém to Marabá (16 hrs) on the Transamazônica, Transbrasiliana US$16, then change to Santarém. Direct bus Belém-Santarém once a week (US$75, more expensive than by boat and can take longer). To **São Luís**, 2 a day, 13 hrs, US$22, interesting journey through marshlands.

River services To **Santarém, Manaus,** and intermediate ports (see **River Transport in Amazônia**, page 574). The larger ships berth at Portobrás/Docas do Pará (the main commercial port) either at Armazém (warehouse) No 3 at the foot of Av Pres Vargas, or at Armazém No 10, a few blocks further N (entrance on Av Marechal Hermes esq Av Visconde de Souza Franco). The guards will sometimes ask to see your ticket before letting you into the port area, but tell them you are going to speak with a ship's captain. Ignore the touts who approach you. Smaller vessels (sometimes cheaper, usually not as clean, comfortable or safe) sail from small docks along the Estrada Nova (not a safe part of town). Take a Cremação bus from Ver-o-Peso.

To **Macapá (Porto Santana).** *Silja e Souza* of Souzamar, Trav Dom Romualdo Seixas corner R Jerônimo Pimentel, T 222-0719, and *Almirante Solon* of Sanave (Serviço Amapaense de Navegação, Castilho Franca 234, opp Ver-o-Peso, T 222-7810). ENAL, T 224-5210; *Macamazônia*, R Castilho Franca (see **River Transport in Amazônia**, page 574). There is a desk selling tickets for private boats in the rodoviária; some hotels (eg *Fortaleza*) recommend agents for tickets. Purchase tickets from offices 2 days in advance. Smaller boats to Macapá also sail from Estrada Nova.

Hitchhiking Going S, take bus to Capanema, 3½ hrs, US$3.80, walk ½ km from rodoviária to BR-316 where trucks stop at the gas station.

ROUTES A good asphalted road, BR-316, leads E out of the city. A branch goes N to the coast town of Salinópolis, some 223 km, at the extreme end of the eastern part of the Amazon Delta. Various paved roads branch off: 118 km out of Belém the BR-010 turns right, paved highway S to Brasília (2,120 km). Straight on, the road leads to Bragança, the centre of an early, unsuccessful, attempt in the 1900s to transfer population to Amazônia. At **Capanema** (**E** *Hotel São Luís*, good), 54 km before Bragança, the BR-316 for São Luís, Teresina, Fortaleza and Recife branches right.

Tomé-Açu South of Belém on the Rio Acará-Mirim, affords a view of life on a smaller river than the Amazon; 3 buses a day from Belém, US$8.75. **E** *Hotel Las Vegas*, owner Fernando is very friendly. Boat back to Belém on Sun at 1100, arriving 1800, US$7.50.

MARAJÓ

The world's largest river island (a claim disputed by the Bananal): flooded in rainy Dec-June, it provides a suitable habitat for the water buffalo, said to have swum ashore after a shipwreck. They are now farmed in large numbers (try the cheese and milk). It is also home to many birds, crocodiles and other wildlife, and has several good beaches. It is crowded at weekends and in the July holiday season. The island was the site of the precolumbian Marajoaras culture.

Ponta de Pedras

Boats leave Belém (near Porto do Sal, seat US$3.60, cabin US$38 for 2, 5 hrs) most days for **Ponta de Pedras** (**E** *Hotel Ponta de Pedras*, good meals, buses for Souré or Salvaterra meet the boat). Bicycles for hire

(US$1/hr) to explore beaches and the interior of the island. Fishing boats make the 8 hr trip to Cachoeira do Arari (one hotel, E) where there is a Marajó museum. A 10 hr boat trip from Ponta de Pedras goes to the Arari lake where there are two villages, Jenipapo (one *pousada*, E) built on stilts, forró dancing at weekends, and Santa Cruz which is less primitive, but less interesting (a hammock and a mosquito net are essential). There is a direct boat service to Belém twice a week.

Soure

A ferry from Belém to **Soure** (*pop* 17,200), 'capital' of the island, sails weekends only departing from the old Enasa dock near the Ver-o-Peso market (4 hrs, US$5). There is a ferry from the 'escalinha' at the end of Av Pres Vargas to Porto do Cámara (3 hrs US$10). Then take a bus to Salvaterra and ferry to Soure. Boats return from Cámara at 0800 and 1100. There is a 'taxi-plane' service to Soure. There are fine beaches, Araruna (2 km – take supplies and supplement with coconuts and crabs, beautiful walks along the shore), do Pesqueiro (bus from Praça da Matriz,1030, returns 1600, eat at *Maloca*, good, cheap, big, deserted beach, 13 km away) and Caju-Una (15 km). Small craft await passengers from the Enasa boats, for Salvaterra village (good beaches and bars: seafood), US$12, 10 mins, or trips bookable in Belém from Mururé, T 241-0891, **B** *Pousada das Guarãs* (on beach, well-equipped), or *Hotel Marajó*, T 741-1396 (Belém 225-2880), cheaper.

● **Accommodation & services Soure**: **D** *Cosampa*, Travessa 14, T 229-3928, hot showers, free transfer from docks; **D** *Soure* (3a R, Centro: walk straight on from Enasa dock, then take 3rd street on left), a/c, basic; **D** *Waldeck*, Trav 12, T 741-1414, only 4 rooms; *Pousada Marajoara*, and **E** *Pousada Parque Floresta*, nearby, good meals; **F** *Pensão* at 2a R 575 (*Bar Guarani*), simple, rec. *Canecão*, Praça da Matriz, sandwiches, meals, rec. Changing money is only possible at very poor rates. Take plenty of insect repellent.

SALINÓPOLIS

(*Pop* 22,688) This seaside resort with many small places where you can eat and drink at night by the waterfront, and fine sandy beach nearby (buses and cars drive on to the beach), is a peaceful place mid-week. Best during holiday month of July. Atalaia, opposite Salinópolis, is pleasant, reached by taxi (US$10) or with a fisherman.

● **Accommodation C** *Atalaia*, on island of Atalaia, 15 km from Salinópolis, T 724-1122, simple, beautiful setting, reserve in advance, take a taxi; **C** *Solar*, Av Beira Mar s/n, with bath, best in town, good restaurant; **D** *Jeanne d'Arc*, with breakfast; **E** *Salinas*, on beach.

● **Places to eat** *Bife de Ouro* opp filling station, simple, but excellent fish and shrimp, always crowded for lunch; *Gringo Louco*, further out than Atalaia (take taxi or hitch), at Cuiarana beach, follow signs, gringo owner serves good, unusual dishes, and some 'wild' drinks known as 'bombs', popular.

● **Transport** Buses 4 hrs from Belém on good road, US$5.50.

AMAPÁ

Rubber was almost the only product of Amapá until the 1950s, when manganese was discovered 150 km NW of Macapá. A standard-gauge railway, 196 km long, the only one in Brazil, has been built from the mining camp to Porto Santana, from which there is an excellent road. Other products are gold, coal, timber and agricultural. The state is one-quarter the size of France but with only 289,050 inhabitants. Malaria is rampant in the state; the illiteracy rate is 85%; smuggling goes on in a big way. The mining area – Icomiland (*pop* 4,000) – is a startling exception: swimming pools, football fields, bowling alleys, supermarkets, dance halls, movies, a healthy oasis in the wilderness.

MACAPÁ

There are ferries and daily flights from Belém to **Macapá** (*pop* 179,610; *CEP* 68900; *DDD* 096), the capital of Amapá on the northern channel of the Amazon Delta. It used to be decrepit but is now improving, particularly along the riverfront. Macapá was declared a customs free zone in Jan 1993.

Places of interest

Each brick of the **Fortaleza de São José**

do Macapá, built 1764, was brought from Portugal as ballast. The Fortaleza is used for concerts, exhibits, and colourful festivities on the anniversary of the city's founding, 4 February. In the handicraft complex (**Núcleo de Produção Artesanal**), Av Azárias Neto e Av JM Lombaerd, T 222-3681, daily 0800-1200, 1500-2000, craftsmen produce their wares onsite. A feature is pottery decorated with local manganese ore, also woodcarvings and leatherwork. **São José Cathedral**, inaugurated by the Jesuits in 1761, is the city's oldest landmark.

The riverfront has been landscaped with trees, lawns and paths. It is a very pleasant place for an evening stroll. There are food and drink kiosks, and a nice lively atmosphere. The main avenue along the river is closed to vehicles on weekends. The pier (*trapiche*) is decaying, but is still a lovely spot for savouring the cool of the evening breeze, or watching sunrise over the Amazon. There is a monument to the equator, **Marco Zero** (take Fazendinha bus from Av Mendonça Furtado). The equator also divides the nearby football stadium in half, aptly named O Zerão. South of these, along the road to Fazendinha, are the **zoo** and **botanical gardens**. **Fazendinha** itself is a popular local beach, very busy on Sun.

Excursions
Lagoa dos Indios, 4 km W of the city along the Duque de Caxias road is a lake with snowy egrets and water buffaloes. Also fishing and swimming. **Curiau**, a town 8 km from Macapá, is inhabited by the descendants of African slaves who have maintained many of the customs of their ancestors. Analogous to the Bush Negroes of Suriname, but apparently the only such village in Brazil.

Local festivals
Marabaixo is the traditional music and dance of the state of Amapá, festival held 40 days after Easter.

Local information
● **Accommodation**
A1 *Ekinox*, R Jovino Dinoá 1693, T 222-4378, F 223-7554, central, a/c, helpful, excellent res-

taurant, highly rec; **A1** *Novotel*, French-owned, Av Azarias Neto 17, on waterfront, T 223-1144, F 231-1115, small, 4-star, all rooms a/c, swimming pool, rec.

D *Amapaense Palace*, R Tiradentes 109, T 222-3366, F 222-0703, 2-star, a/c, cold showers, comfortable; **D** *Santo Antônio*, Av Coriolano Jucá 485, T 222-0226, nr main square, fan, good breakfast extra; **D** *Tropical*, Av Antônio Coelho de Carvalho 1399, 20 mins from centre, 1-star, T 223-4899, cheaper without a/c, rec.

E *Kamilla*, Av Padre JM Lombaerd, behind *Novotel* tennis courts, with fan and bath. The following are 10 mins' walk from port and from Praça São José (where bus from Porto Santana stops): **E** pp *Mara*, R São José 2390, with bath, a/c, TV, fridge, good, breakfast; **E** *Mercúrio*, R Cândido Mendes, 1300 block (no sign), T 223-4123.

● **Places to eat**
Kamilla, below hotel of same name, good buffet, pay by weight. Another buffet *Kilo's*, Hamilton Silva 1398, T 223-1579, elegant, overpriced; *O Boscão*, Hamilton Silva 997, no sign, quite good; *O Paulistano*, Av Henrique Galúcio 412, a/c, good; *Churrascaria Tropeiro*, Av Pres Vargas 450; *Pizza San Carlos*, Cândido Mendes 1199, good for lunch; *Lennon*, good pavement café, no meals, at R Gen Rondon esq IC Nunes. Excellent ice cream, eg *Sorveteria Santa Helena*, Av Feliciano Coelho 1023, Bairro do Trem; *Sorveteria Macapá*, R São José 1664, closer to centre.

● **Banks & money changers**
Banco do Brasil, Av Independência 250, cash and TCs. *Câmbios* (cash only): *Lantur*, Cândido Mendes 1085, *Casa Francesa*, on same street, *Monopólio*, Av Isaac Alcoubre 80. Both US$ and French francs can be exchanged here. Best to buy francs in Belém if heading for Guyane as câmbios in Macapá are reluctant to sell them and they are more expensive and hard to obtain at the border.

● **Embassies & consulates**
For French consular agent, ask taxi drivers or at *Novotel*; visas are not issued for non-Brazilians. Only French and Portuguese spoken.

● **Post & telecommunications**
Post Office: Praça da Bandeira.

● **Useful addresses**
Ibama, R Hamilton Silva 1570, Santa Rita, CEP 68.900, Macapá.

● **Transport**
Local Car rentals: National, Av Independência 30, nr Praça Beira Rio, T 223-2799, at airport 231-4799. Localiza, Alameda Serrano, T 223-2799. Locauto, Av Pres Vargas 519, T 222-1011/1511.

Air Varig, office on R Cândido Mendes 1039,

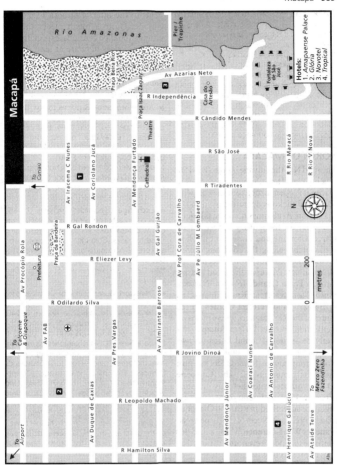

Macapá

Rio Amazonas

Pier / Trapiche

Praça Beira Rio

Av Azarias Neto

Casa do Artesão

R Independência

R Cândido Mendes

Praça Isaac Zagury

Theatre

R São José

Cathedral

R Tiradentes

To Curiaú

Av Iracema C Nunes

Av Coriolano Jucá

Av Mendonça Furtado

Av Gal Gurjão

Av Prof Cora de Carvalho

Av Pe Júlio M Lombaerd

R Rio Maracá

R Rio V Nova

N

R Gal Rondon

R Eliezer Levy

Praça da Bandeira

Prefeitura

Av Procopio Rola

200

0

metres

R Odilardo Silva

Av Almirante Barroso

To Curiaú

To Cariaene & Oiapoque

Av FAB

R Jovino Dinoá

Av Pres Vargas

Av Mendonça Junior

Av Coaraci Nunes

Av Antonio de Carvalho

To Marco Zero Fazendinha

R Leopoldo Machado

Av Duque de Caxias

To Airport

R Hamilton Silva

Av Henrique Galúcio

Av Ataíde Teive

Fortaleza de São José

Hotels:
1. Amapaense Palace
2. Glória
3. Novotel
4. Tropical

T 223-1755, flies to Cayenne, Paramaribo, Belém and other Brazilian cities.

Sea Shipping service: most ships now dock at Porto Santana, 30 km from Macapá (frequent buses US$0.55, shared taxis US$3.60 pp), however some smaller vessels still arrive at the pier in Macapá itself. This pier is also used when all of Porto Santana's dock space has been occupied by ore freighters.

To Belém, *Silja e Souza* of Souzamar, R São José S of cathedral, and *Almirante Solon* of Sanave (Serviço Amapaense de Navegação, Av Azárias Neto, Praça Beira Rio). Both ships operate twice a week (see **River Transport in Amazônia**, page 574). Purchase tickets from offices 2 days in advance. Also smaller boats.

There is also regular direct service to **Santarém**, not going via Belém.

Buses To **Oiapoque**: Estrela de Ouro has its office on the main square, in front of the cathedral; it leaves daily at 2000. Cattani, office on Nunes between São José and Cándido Mendes, leaves daily at 0630. Journey time about 12 hrs (dry season) with several rest stops, 14-24 hrs in rainy season. Both leave from opposite Polícia Técnica, 30 mins from centre, take bus 'Jardim' and get out at Polícia Técnica. Fare US$40. The Oiapoque bus does not go into Amapá or Calçoene and it is therefore very inconvenient to break the trip at these places. Bus fare to Amapá and Calçoene US$25, 7 hrs, daily at 0700.

Pickup **trucks** (office Av Pres Vargas between São José and Tiradentes, can reserve in advance) run daily to various locations throughout Amapá, crowded on narrow benches in the back, or pay more to ride in the cab. Despite posted schedules, they leave when full. To Oiapoque at 0800, 10-12 hrs, US$40 cab, US$25 in back. To Lourenço at 0900.

NORTH OF MACAPÁ

The road N to the Guyane border (BR-156) is being paved and although precarious in places, it is open throughout the year with buses and pickups operating even in the wet season. At all times however, take food and water for the journey as services are scarce. Gasoline and diesel (not alcohol) are available along the road but drivers should take extra fuel from Macapá.

North of Macapá the road passes through **Porto Grande** (*Recanto Ecológico Sonho Meu*, resort at Km 108, Macapá T 234-1298) and **Ferreira Gomes** on the shores of the Rio Araguari, where the pavement ends. Further on are **Amapá** (formerly the territorial capital; **D** *Tourist Hotel* and one other, clean, comfortable, one block from square towards docks, turn right, 2nd house on left) and **Calçoene** (**D** government-owned hotel by bus stop, expensive food in adjoining canteen; sleeping space advertized in a café on Oiapoque road, very cheap). North of Calçoene a road branches W to **Lourenço**, whose gold fields continue to produce even after various decades of prospecting.

FRONTIER WITH GUYANE

The main road continues N across the Rio Caciporé and on to the border with French Guyane at **Oiapoque**, on the river of the same name. It is 90 km inland from Cabo Orange, Brazil's northernmost point on the Atlantic coast. 7 Km to the W is Clevelândia do Norte, a military outpost and the end of the road in Brazil.

Oiapoque is remote, with its share of contraband, illegal migration, and drug trafficking. It is also the gateway to gold fields in the interior of both Brazil and Guyane. Quite a rough place, and the visitor should be cautious, especially late at night. Prices here are at least double those of anywhere else in Brazil, but still lower than in neighbouring Guyane. The **Saut Maripa** rapids can be visited, 20 mins upstream along the Oiapoque River.

- **Accommodation & places to eat D** *Government Hotel*, at E end of riverfront, now privately operated, refurbished, best in town, restaurant; **E** *Kayama*, on riverfront street above Taba office, with fan, 1 room has private bath, good. Another **F** next door, basic. **F** *Sonho Meu*, one street back from river, basic. *Restaurant Paladar Drinks*, one block up from river, very expensive. There are several cheap hotels (**F**) along the waterfront.

- **Exchange** It is possible to exchange US$ and *reais* to francs, but dollar rates are low. Visa users can withdraw *reais* at Bradesco, exchanging these to francs. Gold merchants, some shops, and one *câmbio* in the market will sell *reais* for US$ or French francs, but are reluctant to sell francs. Rates are even worse in St-Georges. Best to buy francs in Belém, or abroad.

- **Transport Buses** Estrela de Ouro leaves for Macapá from the waterfront, daily at 1000, 12 hrs (dry season), 14-24 hrs (wet season), US$40, also Cattani. Pickup **trucks** depart from the same area when full, US$40 in cab, US$25 in the back. **Sea** Occasional cargo vessels to Belém or Macapá (Porto Santana). **Crossing to Guyane**: motorized canoes cross to St-Georges de L'Oyapock, 10 mins downstream, F20 pp, slightly cheaper in *reais*, bargain. There is no vehicle ferry and no bridge. There is no road from St-Georges to Cayenne, you must fly or take a boat (details given on page 1630). While awaiting flights to Cayenne it is much cheaper to wait on the Brazilian side. Polícia Federal for Brazilian exit stamp is on the road to Calçoene, about 500 meters back from the river.

BELÉM TO MANAUS

A few hours up the broad river the region of the thousand islands is entered. The passage through this maze of islets is known as 'The Narrows'. The ship winds through 150 km of lanes of yellow flood with equatorial forest within 20 or 30m on both sides. In the Furo Grande the vessel rounds a hairpin bend almost touching the trees, bow and stern.

On one of the curious flat-topped hills

after the Narrows stands the little stucco town of **Monte Alegre**, an oasis in mid-forest (airport; some simple hotels, **E**). Lagoon cruises to see lilies, birds, pink dolphins; boat trips to ancient cave paintings; village visits (US$25-40 per day), rec guide lives next door to a small brown and white hotel near the end of terrace at E side of docks.

SANTARÉM

(*Pop* 265,105; *CEP* 68100; *DDD* 091) 2-3 days upstream on the southern bank, the city stands at the confluence of the Rio Tapajós with the Amazon, half-way between Belém and Manaus. It was founded in 1661, and is the third largest town on the Brazilian Amazon. Its attractive colonial squares overlooking the waterfront. There is a road southwards to Cuiabá (Mato Grosso), meeting the Transamazônica at Rurópolis (see page 574), and the city is the jumping off point for gold prospectors in the Mato Grosso territories to the south.

Places of interest

The yellow Amazon water swirls alongside the green-blue Tapajós; the **meeting of the waters**, in front of the market square, is nearly as impressive as that of the Negro and Solimões near Manaus. A small **museum** in the old city hall on the waterfront, downriver from where the boats dock, has a collection of ancient Tapajós ceramics, as well as various 19th century artefacts and publications. The unloading of the fish catch between 0500 and 0700 on the waterfront is interesting. There are good beaches nearby on the Rio Tapajós.

Excursions

To **Alter do Chão**, a friendly village on the Rio Tapajós, at the outlet of Lago Verde; Saivé Festival in 2nd week of July, rec. Hotel (**D**), comfortable; *Pousada* near the church, quiet, clean; luxury hotel to be built shortly; *Restaurant Mongote*, Praça 7 de Setembro, good fresh fish, huge portions; *Lago Verde*, try *calderada de tucunaré*; good swimming in the Tapajós from the beautiful, clean beach. From Santarém: bus stop on the square opposite Mercado Modelo, very close to *Hotel Plaza*, US$0.70, about 1 hr, timetable at hotel reception desk.

Local information
● Accommodation

A *Tropical*, Av Mendonça Furtado 4120, T 522-1533, F 522-2631, swimming pool, friendly but run down, 4 km from centre, taxi US$5.

B *Brasil Grande Hotel*, Trav 15 de Agosto 213, T 522-5660, family-run, with restaurant; **B** *Santarém Palace*, close to city centre, Rui Barbosa 726, T 523-2820, good.

C *Central Plaza*, Praça Rodrigues dos Santos 877, with fan, run-down, friendly; **C** *City*, Trav Francisco Correia 200, T 522-4719, a/c, frigo-bar, good, will collect from airport.

D *Brasil*, Travessa dos Mártires 30, inc breakfast, communal bath, good food, good service; **D** *Greenville*, Av Adriano Pimenal 44, T 522-5820, good bathroom facilities and balcony view across the river.

E *Horizonte*, Travessa Lemos 737, clean.

● Places to eat

Mascotinho bar/pizzeria, on riverfront, popular, good view; *Storil*, Travessa Turiano Meira, 2 blocks from Rui Barbosa, good fish, live music, takes credit cards; *Ritz*, Praça do Pescador, good; *Lanchonete Luci*, Praça do Pescador, good juices and pastries; *Sombra do Jambeiro*, Trav 15 de Novembro, Norwegian-owned bar and lanchonete, excellent meals.

● Banks & money changers

It is very difficult to change dollars (impossible to change TCs anywhere), try *Farmácia Java*, opp *Coruá-Una Turismo*, 15 de Novembro, or **Ouro Minas**, a gold dealer, Travessa dos Mártires, close to Banco do Brasil on Av Rui Barbosa (next to *Santarém Palace Hotel*); also try travel agencies. Cash withdrawals on Visa at *Banco do Brasil*.

● Hospitals & medical services

Dr Ihsan Youssef Simaan, T 522-3886/3982, speaks English and Spanish.

● Tour companies & travel agents

Gil Serique, Praça do Pescador 131, T 522-5174, English-speaking guide, rec. *Coruá-Una Turismo*, 15 de Novembro 185-C, T 522-6303/7421 offers various tours, Pierre d'Arcy speaks French, rec. *Tapam Turismo*, Travessa 15 de Agosto, 127 A, T 522 3037/1946/2334, rec. *Amazon Tour*, Travessa Turiano Meira, 1084, T 522 1098, the owner Steve Alexander is a very friendly, helpful man who can give you lots of hints what to do. He also organizes excursions for groups to remote areas which are quite expensive, rec. *Santarém Turismo*, in *Hotel Tropical* (above), owned by Perpétua and Jean-Pierre Schwarz (speaks French), friendly, helpful, also quite expensive group tours (for a group of 5 US$50/day pp), rec.

● **Transport**

Air 15 km from town. Internal flights only. Varig office, R Siqueira Campos, block between Travessas 15 de Agosto and 15 de Novembro. Buses to centre or waterfront. From centre bus leaves in front of cinema in Rui Barbosa every 80 mins from 0550 to 1910, or taxis (US$12 to waterfront). The hotels *Tropical* and *New City* have free buses for guests; you may be able to take these.

Buses Rodoviária is on the outskirts, take 'Rodagem' bus from the waterfront nr the market, US$0.25. Santarém to **Itaituba**, 11 hrs, US$20; to **Marabá** on the River Tocantins (via Rurópolis and Altamira), 36 hrs (if lucky; can be up to 6 days), US$80, with Transbrasiliana. Also to **Imperatriz**, 46 hrs, US$54, office on Av Getúlio Vargas and at rodoviária. Enquire at rodoviária for other destinations. (Beware of vehicles that offer a lift, which frequently turn out to be taxis.) Road travel during the rainy season is always difficult, often impossible.

Shipping services To Manaus, Belém, Macapá, Itaituba, and intermediate ports (see **River Transport in Amazônia**, page 574). Most boats, in particular the smaller ones, dock at the waterfront by the centre of town, but at times they may dock at the Cais do Porto, 4 km W, take 'Circular' or 'Circular Externo' bus. Check both places for departures to your destination. Also local service to **Óbidos, Oriximiná, Alenquer,** and **Monte Alegre** (US$10, 5-8 hrs).

BELTERRA AND HENRY FORD

37 km S from Santarém on a dirt road is **Belterra** (*pop* about 8,000), where Henry Ford established one of his rubber plantations, in the highlands overlooking the Rio Tapajós. Ford built a well laid-out new town; the houses resemble the cottages of Michigan summer resorts. Many of the newer houses follow the white paint with green trim style. The town centre has a large central plaza that includes a band stand, the church of Santo Antônio (circa 1951), a Baptist church and a large educational and sports complex. A major hospital, which at one time was staffed by physicians from North America, is now closed. Ford's project was unsuccessful: now the rubber forest is in bad condition. (**E** *Hotel Seringueira*, with about 8 rooms and pleasant restaurant.)

Fordlândia was the Ford Motor Company's first rubber plantation, founded in 1926. *Hotel Zebu*, in old Vila Americana (turn right from dock, then left up the hill);

one restaurant, two bars and three shops on town square. There is a little pebble beach N of the town. Km 83, South of Santarém on BR 163, there is a section of the **Floresta Nacional do Tapajós** which has a vehicle track running due W through it; beautiful rainforest which can be entered with permission from Ibama if accompanied by one of their guides. It is well worth a visit if only to see the butterflies.

● **Transport** Bus from Santarém to Belterra (from unmarked *Café Amazonas*, Travessa Moraes Sarmento between Rui Barbosa and São Sebastião), 1000 and 1230, Mon-Sat, return 1300 and 1530, US$2, about 2 hrs. **NB** 1 hr time difference between Santarém and Belterra so if you take the 1230 bus you'll miss the 1530 return bus. Boats from Santarém to Itaituba may stop at Fordlândia if you ask (leave Santarém 1800, arrive 0500-0600, US$12 for 1st class hammock space); ask the captain to stop for you on return journey, about 2300.

Óbidos (*Pop* 42,195), 110 km up-river from Santarém, is a picturesque and clean city with many beautiful, tiled colonial buildings. It is located at the narrowest and deepest point on the river. For many kilometres little is seen except the wall of the great Amazonian forest. Small airport.

The next city upstream, Manaus was at one time an isolated urban island in the jungle. It is the collecting-point for the produce of a vast area which includes parts of Peru, Bolivia and Colombia. There is superb swimming in the natural pools and under falls of clear water in the little streams which rush through the woods, but take locals' advice on swimming in the river; electric eels and various other kinds of unpleasant fish, apart from the notorious *piranhas*, abound and industrial pollution of the river is growing.

Until recently Manaus' only communications were by river and air. A road SW to Porto Velho, which is already connected with the main Brazilian road system, has been completed, but officially closed since 1990. Another, not yet fully paved, has been built due N to Boa Vista, from where other roads reach the Venezuelan and Guyanese frontiers.

Manaus (*pop* 1,010,560; *CEP* 69000; *DDD* 092) is the capital of the State of Amazonas, the largest in Brazil (1.6 million sq km), which has a population of 2.1 million. Though 1,600 km from the sea, it is only 32m above sea-level. The average temperature is 27°C. The city sprawls over a series of eroded and gently sloping hills divided by numerous creeks (*igarapés*).

Manaus is building fast; 20-storey modern buildings are rising above the traditional flat, red-tiled roofs. It was the first city in South America to instal trams, but they have now been replaced by buses.

Places of interest

Dominating the centre is a **Cathedral** built in simple Jesuit style on a hillock; nothing distinguished inside or out. Nearby is the main shopping and business area, the tree-lined Av Eduardo Ribeiro; crossing it is Av Sete de Setembro, bordered by ficus trees. The area between Av Sete de Setembro and the rear of *Hotel Amazonas* is now reserved to pedestrians. There is a modern air-conditioned theatre.

The main attractions are the **Botanic Gardens**, the well stocked public library, and the legendary Opera House, the **Teatro Amazonas**, completed in 1896 during the great rubber boom following 17 years of construction and rebuilt in 1929. It seats 685 people; for information on programmes, T 622-2420 (open Mon-Sat 0900-1600, 20-min guided tour US$6 but same price to attend a concert). Another interesting historic building is the **Mercado Adolfo Lisboa**, commonly known as the Mercado. It was built in 1902 as a miniature copy of the now demolished Parisian Les Halles. The wrought ironwork which forms much of the structure was imported from Europe and is supposed to have been designed by Eiffel. There is a curious little church, the **Igreja do Pobre Diabo**, at the corner of Avs Borba and Ipixuna in the suburb of Cachoeirinha; it is only 4m wide by 5m long, and was built by a worker (the 'poor devil' of the name); take Circular 7 Cachoeirinha bus from cathedral to Hospital Militar.

The remarkable **harbour installations**, completed in 1902, were designed and built by a Scottish engineer to cope with the up to 14m annual rise and fall of the Rio Negro. The large passenger ship floating dock is connected to street level by a 150m-long floating ramp, at the end of which, on the harbour wall, can be seen the high water mark for each year since it was built. When the water is high, the roadway floats on a series of large iron tanks measuring 2½m in diameter. The material to build the large yellow **Alfândega** (customs building) near the harbour was brought block by block from Scotland as ballast. Tourists can visit the docks 0730-2000 daily.

Museums

Museu do Índio, kept by the Salesian missionaries: this interesting museum's collection includes handicrafts, ceramics, clothing, utensils and ritual objects from the various Indian tribes of the upper Rio Negro, R Duque de Caxias (nr Av 7 Setembro); excellent craft shop, rec; open Mon-Fri 0800-1200 and 1400-1700, Sat 0800-1130, closed Sun, T 234-1422, US$3; **Museu do Porto de Manaus**, contains various historical items, documents, letters, diaries and charts, R Vivaldo Lima 61 (nr Harbour); open Mon-Sat 0700-1100 and 1300-1700, Sun 1200-1700, T 232-0096; **Museu Tiradentes**, kept by the Military Police, holds selected historical items and old photographs, Praça da Polícia; open Mon 1400-1800, Tues-Fri 0800-1200 and 1400-1800, T 234-7422; **Museu de Minerais e Rochas** has a large collection of minerals and rocks from the Amazon region, Est do Aleixo 2150; Mon-Fri 0800-1200 and 1400-1800, T 236-1582; **Museu do Homem do Norte** reviews the way of life of the Amazonian population; social, cultural and economic aspects are displayed with photographs, models and other pieces, Av 7 de Setembro 1385 (nr Av J Nabuco), Mon-Thur 0900-1200, 1300-1700, Fri 1300-1700, T 232-5373, US$1; **Instituto Geográfico e Histórico do Amazonas**, located in a fascinating older district of central Manaus, houses a museum and library of over 10,000 books which thoroughly document Amazonian life through the ages, R Bernardo Ramos

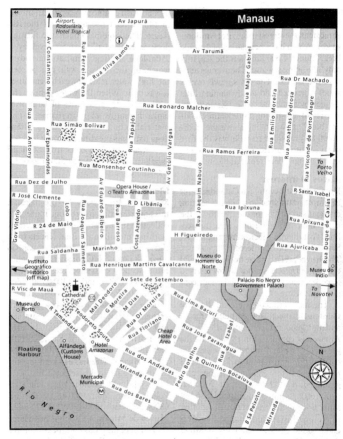

Manaus

117 (nr Prefeitura); open Mon-Fri 0800-1200, T 232-7077, US$0.20; **Museu de Ciências Naturais da Amazônia**, has a pavilion with insects and fish of the region, Est Belém s/n (difficult to get to, 'São José-Acoariquarape/Tropolis' bus 519 to Conjunto Petro, then 2 km walk, best take a taxi), US$3.50, Tues-Sun 0900-1700, T 244-2799. The **Centro Cultural Chaminé**, R Isabel, near R Q Bocaiuva bridge, has occasional art exhibitions mounted in a restored water treatment works, built by the British in 1896. **Jardim Botânico 'Chico Mendes'**

(Horto Municipal). The botanical gardens contain a collection of plants from the Amazon region. Av André Araujo s/n (Buses 'Aleixo', 'Coroado'). Daily 0800-1200 and 1400-1700.

Zoo Run by CIGS, the Brazilian Army Unit specializing in jungle survival. About 300 Amazonian animals are kept in the Gardens (reported run-down with small cages). Est Ponta Negra 750 (no sign). Bus 120 or 207 (marked 'Ponta Negra'), US$0.45, every 30 mins from R Tamandaré, opp cathedral in centre, alight 400m past the 1st Jungle Infantry

Barracks (a big white building), look for the sentries. Open 0800-1700. Entrance for foreigners, US$0.75, free on Sun. Small zoo also at *Hotel Tropical*, see below. **Instituto Nacional de Pesquisas Amazonas** (INPA), Estrada de Aleixo, at Km 3, not far from the Natural Science Museum (any bus to Aleixo), has named trees and manatees (best seen Wed and Fri at 0830 when water is changed), caimans and giant otters; worth a visit and good for birdwatchers.

Excursions

Meeting of the waters About 15 km from Manaus is the confluence of the yellow-brown Solimões (Amazon) and the blue-black Rio Negro, which is itself some 8 km wide. The two rivers run side by side for about 6 km without their waters mingling. Tourist agencies run boat trips to this spot (US$50). The simplest route is to take a taxi or No 617 'Vila Buriti' bus to the Careiro ferry dock, and take the car ferry across. The ferry goes at 0700 returning 0900, and 1500 returning 1830 (approx). Small private launches cross, 40 mins journey, about US$12/seat, ask for the engine to be shut off at the confluence, you should see dolphins especially in the early morning. Alternatively, hire a motorized canoe near the market (US$15 approx; allow 3-4 hrs to experience the meeting properly). A 2-km walk along the Porto Velho road from the Careiro ferry terminal will lead to a point from which Victoria Regia water lilies can be seen in April-Sept in ponds, some way from the road.

Manacapura A typical Amazon town, 84 km on AM-070 by bus, 4 daily, US$5, 2 hrs including ferry crossing. A small market town on the Solimões W of Manaus, with three basic hotels, and *Il Maccarone* pizzeria, Av Eduardo Ribeiro 1000.

Araça A village on the Rio Mamori, 3 hrs by No 11 bus from Rodoviária in the direction of Castanho; the journey includes the ferry at the confluence of the Negro and Solimões (fare to Araçá US$0.85, bus leaves 0600 and 1100). Canoes can be hired. Plenty of wildlife close at hand. 3 buses a day return to Manaus.

Local holidays

6 Jan (Epiphany); Ash Wednesday, half-day; Maundy Thursday; 24 June (St John); 14 July; 5 Sept; 30 Oct; 1 Nov, All Saints Day, half-day; Christmas Eve; New Year's Eve, half-day.

Feb: **Carnival** dates vary – 5 days of Carnival, culminating in the parade of the Samba Schools (see below). 3rd week in April: **Week of the Indians**, Indian handicraft, talks, photographic exhibition, various localities. Second fortnight of Aug: this is reported to be second only to Carnival. In Sept: **Festival de Verão do Parque Dez**, second fortnight, summer festival with music, fashion shows, beauty contests, local foods, etc, Centro Social Urbano do Parque Dez; **Festival da Bondade**, last week, stalls from neighbouring states and countries offering food, handicrafts, music and dancing, SESI, Est do Aleixo Km 5. 8 Dec: **Processão de Nossa Senhora da Conceição**, from the Igreja Matriz through the city centre and returning to Igreja Matriz for a solemn mass.

Carnival in Manaus

Carnival in Manaus has spectacular parades in a sambadrome modelled on Rio's, but with 3 times the capacity. Tourists may purchase grandstand seats, but admission at ground level is free (don't take valuables), with every samba school member guaranteed entrance.

NB Manaus time is 1 hr behind Brazilian standard time (2 hrs behind during Oct-Mar when the rest of Brazil is on summer time).

Local information
● Accommodation

Hotel prices			
L1	over US$200	**L2**	US$151-200
L3	US$101-150	**A1**	US$81-100
A2	US$61-80	**A3**	US$46-60
B	US$31-45	**C**	US$21-30
D	US$12-20	**E**	US$7-11
F	US$4-6	**G**	up to US$3
Unless otherwise stated, all hotels in range **D** and above have private bath. Assume friendliness and cleanliness in all cases.			

10% tax and service must be added to bills. There is a hotel booking service at the airport.

The Zona Franca is reported to be safer than the area around Av Joaquim Nabuco.

L1-L2 *Tropical*, Praia de Ponta Negra, T 658-5000, F 658-5026, a lavish, 5-star Varig hotel 20 km outside the city (taxi to centre, US$20), very expensive, 30% discount with a Varig air pass, *Restaurant Tarumã* open for dinner only, *churrascaria* by pool, 24-hr coffee shop, open to well-dressed non-residents, take minibus from R José Paranaguá in front of Petrobras building esq Dr Moreira, US$6 return, 0830, 0930, 1130 to Hotel, 1200, 1400, 1500, 1800 to town, or take Ponta Negra bus, US$0.35, then walk. Hotel collects guests from the airport. It is rarely full, except in Jan-Feb. Parkland setting, wave pools, small zoo with animals in small cages, beach with new dock, departure point for many river cruises, glossy nightclub Thur-Sat, tennis. Exchange at official rate only. Also away from centre, **L2** *Novotel*, Av Mandii 4 in the Industrial Area, 4-star, luxurious, T 663-1213/3323, F 611-3721, pool, US$1.75 taxi ride from centre; **A2** *Da Vinci*, R Belo Horizonte 240, 3 km from centre, T 663-1213/3323, F 611-3721, pool.

Central hotels: L3 *Best Western*, Marcílio Dias 217/225, T 622-2844, F 233-5984, some rooms a/c, expensive for what is offered, with good breakfast, good service; has a cheaper annex; **L3** *Amazonas*, Praça Adalberto Vale, T 622-2233, F 622-2064, 4-star, the ground floor is not rec, but rooms are reasonable, hot water, a/c; opposite is **A1** *Ana Cassia Palace*, expensive, R dos Andradas 14, T 622-3637, F 622-4812. A highly rec Aparthotel is **L3** *St Paul*, R Ramos Ferreira 1115, T 622-2131/36, F 622-2137, best in town, suites with bath, kitchen, living room, has pool, gym and sauna. **A2** *Mônaco*, R Silva Ramos 20, T 622-3446, F 622-3637, 3-star, rooms have good view, pleasant (some rooms noisy), rooftop restaurant/bar, delicious breakfast; **C** *Premier*, Av Eduardo Ribeiro 124, T 234-0061, some rooms with TV and fridge, good value; **R** *Sulista*, R Pedro Botelho, a/c, breakfast, safe, friendly restaurant, good value, rec; **D** *Janelas Verdes*, Leovegildo Coelho 216, T 233-1222, a/c, small, quiet (except Sun), safe, rec; **D** *Dona Joana*, R dos Andradas 553, T 233-7553, a/c, good value, insecure; **D** *Especial*, Av Pres Vargas 198, T 234-0389, a/c, fridge, inc breakfast; **D** *Neide*, opp rodoviária, with fan, rec; **D** *Hospedaria Turística 10 de Julho*, Dez de Julio 679, T 232 6280, a/c, rec; **E** *Cheap*, R dos Andradas, safe; **E** *Jangada*, R dos Andradas 473, basic, breakfast, cooking facilities, cheap, rec.

In R G Moreira (Zona Franca): B *Internacional*, No 168, T 234-1315, F 234-5396, 2-star, a/c, central, coffee most of the day, good exchange rates; **B** *Rey Salomão*, No 119, T 234-7374, breakfast; **B** *Central*, No 202,

T 232-7887, some a/c, quiet; **B** *Nacional*, No 59, T 233-0537, fridge, a/c, safe.

In Av Joaquim Nabuco (by no means a safe area): **D** *Ideal*, No 491, a/c, **E** with fan, bath, pleasant, modern, free coffee, bar; **E** *Arteiro*, No 471, T 622-1343, nr corner with R Lima Bacuri, with a/c or fan, large rooms with bath; **E** *Aurora*, No 120, T 234-5121, with bath, a/c, noisy TV in front rooms, good, simple breakfast; **E** *Luz*, No 779, above a gym, singles only; **E** *Manauara*, No 129, with bath, a/c, fridge, coffee all day, has TV; **E** *Pensão Sulista*, No 347, breakfast, clean, outside showers, parking, rec; **E** *Rio Branco*, No 484, T 233-4019, rec, avoid damp rooms on ground floor, safe, laundry facilities, a/c, popular, highly rec; **E** *Jangada*, No 473, cooking allowed, laundry facilities, very basic, fan, without bath. Other cheaper places in same area: **E** *Turístico*, R Miranda Leão 356, basic, popular; **E** *Hospedaria Olinda*, R L Coelho y J Paranaguá, rec, has soccer evenings.

NB When taking a taxi from the airport, insist on being taken to the hotel of your choice, and not to the one which pays the driver commission.

10 km E of the city is the small but growing town of **Iranduba**, cheaper than Manaus and with a good beach. **D** *Hotel Verdes Matas*, T 367-1133, rec. Easy bus ride from Manaus, includes ferry crossing.

Camping: there are no campsites in or nr Manaus; it is difficult to find a good, safe place to camp wild.

● **Places to eat**

Novotel serves a rec *feijoada completa* on Sat; *Tropical Hotel*, see above; *Canto da Peixada*, R Emílio Moreira 1677 (Pça 14), T 234-3021, superb fish dishes, lively atmosphere, unpretentious, close to centre; *La Barca*, R Recife 684, wide variety of fish dishes, classy, popular, often has live music; *São Francisco*, Blvd Rio Negro 195, 30 mins' walk from centre (or bus 705), in Educandos suburb, good fish, huge portions, highly rec; *Panorama* next door, No 199, T 624-4626, also good for fish, balcony overlooking river, cheap, highly rec. *Caçarola*, R Maués 188, Cachoeirinha, T 233-3021, very good local fish dishes (take a taxi); Japanese at *Miako*, R São Luís 230, also *Suzuran*, Blvd Álvaro Maia 1683, Adrianópolis, good, closed Tues, take taxi; *Búfalo*, churrascaria, Joaquim Nabuco 628, all you can eat (high quality); *Fiorentina* R José Paranaguá 44 (Praça da Polícia), Italian, very good, half price on Sun; *Esquina do Lanche*, Paranaguá e Dr Moreiro, good, cheap; *Fiorella*, R Pará 640, good Italian; *Olinda*, Pedro Botelho 93, nr Miranda Leão, good regional dishes, *caldeirada*, rec; *Frangolandia*, Joaquim Nabuco nr 7 de Setembro, good grill. *Chapaty*, Saldanho Marinho 429B; also R Costa Azevedo

105, vegetarian, closed pm. *Mandarim*, Av Eduardo Ribeiro 650, Chinese, all you can eat lunches US$5, closed Sun; *Schnaps bar and restaurant*, R Recife 1005, Casa 17-A, typical German, friendly, evenings only, closed Sun; *Skina dos Sucos*, E Ribeiro e 24 de Maio, rec for juices; pizzeria next door also good; *Casa do Guaraná*, R Marcílio Dias, marvellous juices mixed with *guaraná*; *Casa dos Sucos*, 7 de Setembro between Joaquim Nabuco and G Vargas, regional fruit juices and snacks; *Maté Amargo*, R Saldanha Marinho 603, good buffet, all you can eat; *Veneza*, Av Getúlio Vargas 570, good Sat *feijoada*; *Floresta*, R dos Andradas 335, friendly, English-speaking, good vegetables; *Jangada Bar*, opp *Hotel Amazonas*, good for snacks; good, but expensive snacks in *Hotel Amazonas* itself; *Alemã*, cafeteria, R José Paranaguá/Praça da Polícia, good for juices, sandwiches; *Sorveteria Glacial*, Getúlio Vargas 161 and other locations, highly rec for ice cream. *Restaurante Natalia*, Av Epaminondas s/n, downtown, with garden, has Pagode music and dancing on Fri nights. Many restaurants close on Sun nights and Mon. City authorities grade restaurants for cleanliness: look for A and B. Good juice bars along Av Joaquim Nabuco, try *cupuaçu*.

The fishing catch is brought to the waterfront between 2300-0100, including the giant *pirarucu*.

● **Banks & money changers**
Banco do Brasil, R Marechal Deodoro (5th floor) and airport changes dollars cash, 8% commission, Visa withdrawals at Pça Dom Pedro II (in front of docks), efficient; many local banks, open 0900-1600. Most offices shut afternoons; foreign exchange operations 0900-1200 only, or close even as early as 1100. **Banco Meridional**, 7 de Setembro 691 (minimum drawing limit on Mastercard is US$100 as opposed to US$200 in other banks). Thomas Cook cheques changed by **Banespa** (good rates, cheques and cash). **Bamerindus**, R Marcílio Dias 196, TCs only, good rates, fast and friendly service; **Banco Amazonas**, R Henrique Martins Cavalcante, good rates; **Credicard**, Av Getúlio Vargas 222 for Mastercard and Diner's cash advances. **American Express** for money transactions and mail, Selvatur, Praça Adalberto Valve, T 622-2577, adjacent to *Hotel Amazonas*. Cash at main hotels; Sr Lima, R Quintino Bocaiúva 189, Sala 34; *Câmbio Cortez*, 7 de Setembro e Getúlio Vargas, converts TCs into US$ cash at 3-5% commission. Do not change money on the streets.

● **Electric current**
110 volts AC; some hotels 220 volts AC, 60 cycles.

● **Embassies & consulates**
Most open am only. **Peruvian**, Conjunto Morada do Sol/ R KL Casa 6, Aleixo, T 642-1646 F 642 1083 0800-1300. **Colombian**, R Dona Libânia 62, nr opera house, T 234-6777, double check whether a Colombian tourist card can be obtained at the border. **Venezuelan**, R Ferreira Pena 179, Cep 60,010,140, T 233 6004, F 233 0481, 0800-1400; everyone entering Venezuela overland needs a visa, the requirements are: 1 passport photo, an onward ticket and a yellow fever certificate (check with a Venezuelan consulate in advance for changes to these regulations). **Bolivian**, the consulate is now apparently run from a restaurant, *Los Palmas*, R Rio Jauari.

British, Eduardo Ribeiro 520, Sala 1202, T 622-3879. **United States**, Geral Recife 101, T 234 4546 (office hours) and 232 1611 (outside office hours); will supply letters of introduction for US citizens. **Spain**, R Monsenhor Coutinho, T 234-0842; **Dutch**, R M Leão 41, T 234-8719/223-6874; **Austria**, Av Eduardo Ribeiro 500, 1st floor; **Italy**, R Belo Horizonte 240, T 611-4877; **Japanese**, R Ferreira Pena 92, T 234-2521; **Danish**, R M Leão 45, T 622-1356, also handles **Norway; Finnish**, T 234-5084; **Belgium**, 13 qd D conj Murici, T 236-1452; **Portugal**, R Terezina 193, T 234-5777.

● **Entertainment**
For *Teatro Amazonas*, see above. *Spectrum*, R Lobo D'Almada 322, very young. Cachoeirinha has a number of bars offering music and dancing, liveliest at weekends. The *Tropical Hotel's* nightclub attracts Manaus's wealthy citizens on Thur-Sat, as does its bingo club; nearby Ponta Negra beach becomes extremely lively late on weekend nights and during holidays; *Kalamazon Night Club*, Km 12 on Torquato Tapajós road, T 651-2797, Wed-Sat, all kinds of music, disco; *Studio 5* disco, R Contorno, Distrito Industrial, T 237-8333; *Clube de Samba*, R Manicoré.

Cinema: 6 screens at the new Amazonas shopping centre, bus Cidade Nova 5, or 204, 207, 208, 307. Most foreign films are shown with original soundtrack and Portuguese sub-titles. Afternoon performances are rec as long queues often form in the evenings.

● **Hospitals & medical services**
Hospital of tropical medicine, Av Pedro Teixeira (D Pedro I), T 238-1711, treatment free, some doctors speak a little English. Take 'Dom Pedro' bus from rodoviária, about a 20-min ride.

● **Laundry**
Lavlev Blvd Alvaro Maia 1400.

● **Post & telecommunications**
Post Office: main office including poste restante in Marechal Deodoro. On the first floor is the philatelic counter where stamps are sold, avoiding the long queues downstairs. Staff don't speak English but are used to dealing with

tourists. For airfreight and shipping, Alfândega, Av Marones Santa Cruz (corner of Mal Deodoro), Sala 106. For airfreight and seamail, Correio Internacional, R Monsenhor Coutinho e Av Eduardo Ribeiro (bring your own packaging). **UPS** office, T 232-9849 (Custódio).

Telephone: TeleAmazon, R Guilherme Moreira, 326 e 7 de Setembro; Av Getúlio Vargas, 950 e R Leo Malcher.

● **Security**
Manaus is a good deal safer than the big cities of southern Brazil, but the usual precautions against opportunist crime should be taken (see **Information for travellers**).

● **Shopping**
Bookshops: *Livraria Nacional*, R 24 de Maio, stocks some French books, the *Livraria Brasília* has some English books.

Markets and souvenirs: go to the *Mercado Adolfo Lisboa* (see above) early in the morning when it is full of good quality regional produce, food and handicrafts, look out for *guaraná* powder or sticks, scales of *pirarucu* fish (used for manicure), and its tongue used for rasping *guaraná* (open daily 0500-1800). In Praça da Saudade, R Ramos Fereira, there is a Sun *Festa de Arte* from 1700; try prawns and calaloo dipped in *tacaca* sauce. In the Praça do Congresso, Av E Ribeiro, there is a very good Sun craftmarket. See the two markets nr the docks, best in the early morning. The *Central Artesanato*, R Recife s/n, nr Detran, has local craftwork. *Casa de Beija-Flor*, in the *Hotel Tropical*, good. *Selva Amazônica*, Mercado Municipal, for wood carvings and bark fabric. Ponta Negra beach boasts a small 'hippy' market, very lively at weekends; for hammocks go to R dos Andradas where there are many shops. Since Manaus is a free port, the whole area a few blocks off the river front is full of electronics shops. Note that all shops close at 1400 on Sat and all day Sun.

Photographic: highly rec for camera repairs: *Oficina Kawasky*, R Floriano Peixoto, enter via passage next to Casa do Chave; film processing at *Studio Universal*, R 24 de Mai 146, cheap, good quality.

● **Sports**
For **swimming**, go to Ponta Negra beach by Soltur bus for US$0.35, though beach virtually disappears beneath the water in April-Aug; popular by day and at night with outdoor concerts and samba in the summer season. Good swimming at Bolívar Falls in the Rio Tarumã, where lunch is available, shade, crowded at weekends; take Tarumã bus from R Tamandaré or R Frei J dos Inocentes, 30 mins, US$0.35 (very few on weekdays), getting off at the police checkpoint on the road to Itacoatiara.

Cycling Bicycle repairs: 3 shops on R Com Clementino, nr Av Alvaro Maia.

● **Tour companies & travel agents**
Agencia Selvatur Ltda, Praça Adalberto Vale s/n, T 622-2577. *Tucumaré Turismo*, R Henrique Martins, T 234-5071, will give information and make reservations.

● **Tourist offices**
Emamtur, Praça 24 de Outubro, R Tarumã 379 helpful, 0730-1330, weekdays only, at Teatro Amazonas, corner of Eduardo Ribeiro, and airport. Town map from *Hotel Amazonas* or from Amazon Explorers. *Guide Book of Manaus*, US$3, available from *Hotel Amazonas* and other places, in English, useful. *A Notícia*, newspaper, lists local entertainments and events. *Mananara Guia*, a very detailed Manaus street index and guide, is available from news kiosks, US$18.

● **Useful addresses**
Police: take bus from *Hotel Amazonas* to Kissia Dom Pedro for Polícia Federal post, people in shorts not admitted.

● **Transport**
Air International flights: Varig to Miami and Orlando (twice) and Mexico City once a week; LAB to La Paz, Santa Cruz and Miami. Ecuatoriana to Quito and Guayaquil. To the Guyanas, connection must be made in Belém. Transbrasil to Buenos Aires daily (3 stops). Make reservations as early as possible, flights may be full. Do not rely on travel agency waiting lists; go to the airport 15 hrs early and get on the airport waiting list. Varig, M Dias 284, T 622-3161, English spoken, helpful; LAB, T 232-7701; Vasp, T 622-1141/3470; Transbrasil, T 622-3738.

Internal flights: There are frequent internal flights with Varig, Vasp and Transbrasil.

The taxi fare to or from the airport is US$12, fixed rate, buy ticket at airport and in most hotels; or take bus 306 marked Aeroporto Internacional from R Tamandaré nr cathedral, US$0.45, or 1107 from Ed Garagem on Av Getúlio Vargas. No buses 2200-0700. (Taxi drivers often tell arrivals that no bus to town is available, be warned!) It is sometimes possible to use the more regular, faster service run by the *Tropical Hotel*; many tour agenices offer free transfers without obligation. Check all connections on arrival. **NB** Check in time is 2 hrs in advance. Allow plenty of time at Manaus airport, formalities are very slow. The restaurant serves good à la carte and buffet food through the day. It is possible to sleep on the airport observation deck if catching an early morning flight. Local flights leave from airport terminal 2: make sure in advance of your terminal.

Buses Manaus rodoviária is 5 km out of town at the intersection of Av Constantino Nery and R Recife; take local bus from centre, US$0.45, marked 'Aeroporto Internacional' or 'Cidade Nova' (or taxi, US$7.50). Local buses to Praça 14 or airport leave from opposite Hotel Amazonas; take airport bus and alight just after Antártica (factory) or take local bus to Ajuricaba.

ROUTES To **Itacoatiara**, 285 km E on the Amazon, with Brazil-nut and jute processing plants (bus service 8 a day, 4 hrs); now paved route AM-010, 266 km, through Rio Preto da Eva.

The road N from Manaus to Boa Vista (770 km) is described on page 600. Hitchhiking with truckers is common, but not recommended for women travelling alone. To hitch, take a Tarumã bus to the customs building and hitch from there, or try at 'posta 5', 2 km beyond rodoviária.

The Catire Highway (BR 319) from Manaus to Porto Velho (868 km), has been officially closed since 1990, several bridges are out, and there is no repair in sight. The alternative for drivers is to ship a car down river on a barge, others have to travel by boat (see below).

Shipping To Santarém, Belém, Porto Velho, Tefé, Tabatinga (for Colombia and Peru), Caracaraí (for Boa Vista), São Gabriel da Cachoeira, and intermediate ports (see **River Transport in Amazônia**, page 574). Almost all vessels now berth at the first (downstream) of the floating docks which is open to the public 24 hrs a day. Bookings can be made up to 2 weeks in advance at the ticket sales area by the port's pedestrian entrance (bear left on entry). The names and itineraries of departing vessels are displayed here as well as on the docked boats themselves; travellers still recommend buying tickets from the captain on the boat itself. The port is relatively clean, well organized, and has a pleasant atmosphere.

ENASA (the state shipping company) sells tickets for private boats at its office in town (prices tend to be high here). A few local boats and some cargo barges still berth by the concrete retaining wall between the market and Montecristi.

NB See introduction to **Up the Amazon River** section on **Health**. Departures to the less important destinations are not always known at the Capitânia do Porto, Av Santa Cruz 265, Manaus. Be careful of people who wander around boats after they've arrived at a port: they are almost certainly looking for something to steal.

Immigration For those arriving by boat who have not already had their passports stamped (eg from Leticia), the immigration office is on the first of the floating docks next to the tourist office. Take the dock entrance opposite the cathedral, bear right, after 50m left, pass through a warehouse to a group of buildings on a T section.

TOURS

There are many different kinds of tours: 'luxurious', which are comfortable but 'set up' for tourists; some aiming at seeing lots of animals, and others at seeing how the people in the jungle live. Be sure to ascertain in advance the exact itinerary of the tour, that the price includes everything (even drink and tips), that the guide is knowledgeable and he himself will accompany you, and that you do not want to kill anything rare. Ensure that others in your party share your expectations and are going for the same length of time. Choose a guide who speaks a language you can understand. A shorter tour may be better than a long, poor one. Packaged tours, booked overseas, are usually of the same price and quality as those negotiated locally. **NB** Guides must be officially registered with Embratur and must carry an identity card. It is potentially very dangerous to go with an unofficial guide. Do not employ freelance guides touting at the airport or the river port. Wait until you get to your hotel, seek advice on reputable companies there, then book direct with the company itself. Ask for a detailed, written contract.

Flights over the jungle give a spectacular impression of the extent of the forest. Bill Potter, resident in Manaus, writes: "opposite Manaus, near the junction of the Rio Negro and the Rio Solimões, lies the **Lago de Janauri**, a small nature reserve. This is where all the day or half-day trippers are taken usually combined with a visit to the 'meeting of the waters'. Although many people express disappointment with this area because so little is seen and/or there are so many 'tourist-trash' shops, for those with only a short time it is worth a visit. You will see some birds and with luck dolphins. In the shops and bars there are often captive parrots and snakes. The area is set up to receive large numbers of tourists, which ecologists agree relieves pressure on other parts of the river. Boats for day trippers leave the harbour constantly throughout the day, but are best booked at one of the larger operators such as Amazon Explorers or Selvatour. Remember that in the dry season, 1-day tours may not offer much to see if the river is low."

Those with more time can take the longer cruises and will see various ecological environments, but bear in mind that most tour operators will make a trip up the Rio Negro because it is easier to navigate, generally calmer and there are many fewer biting insects. There is also much less animal life in general, so to see any patience and luck are needed. To see virgin rainforest a 5 day trip by boat is needed. On the Rio Solimões there is more wildlife, but you are less likely to see anything because you'll be constantly fighting the mosquitoes and sandflies.

Another alternative is to go up river to one of the jungle hotels. From the base, you can then take short trips into the forest or along the river channels.

Taking a transport boat from Manaus is not a substitute for a tour as they rarely get near to the banks and are only interested in getting from A to B as quickly as possible.

Generally, between April and Sept excursions are only by boat; in the period Oct-Mar the Victoria Regia lilies virtually disappear. Fishing is best between Sept and Mar (no flooding). If using a camera, do remember to bring a fast film as light is dim.

Prices vary. The recommended companies charge within the following ranges: 1 day, US$30-60; 2 days, US$100-150; 4 days, US$200-250; longer, specialized, or more luxurious excursions will cost significantly more. It is more economical to incorporate the meeting of the waters in a longer trip than to make a separate excursion.

● **Tour companies & travel agents** *Amazon Explorers Manaus Ltda*, run by Manoel (Bebê) Barros, R Quintino Bocaiúva 189, T 232-3052 his day's tour including 'meeting of the waters', Lago do Janauari and rubber collecting and lunch has been highly rec by most users (US$70); 32-hr trips, require a minimum of 4 people; other tours available. Boat *Amazon Explorer* available for hire at about US$230/day. Next door is *Swallows and Amazons*, R Quintino Bocaiúva 189, andar 1, Sala 13, T/F 622-1246 (or Box 771, Eastham, Mass 02642, T 508-255-1886, F 508-240-0345, e-mail: winstonsc@aol.com), Mark and Tania

Aitchison, wide range of riverboat tours and accommodation (up to 9 days). *Transamazona Turismo*, Leonardo Malcher 734, T 622-4144 (reservations through South American Turismo, Av NS de Copacabana 788, T 255-2345, 22050 Rio de Janeiro), for parties of 10 or less offers a 3-days-plus stay at *Amazon Lodge*, a floating lodge on Lagoa Periquitão, 80 km from Manaus, or *Amazon Village*, an hotel on dry land, rec. *Ariaú Jungle Tower*, Rio Amazonas Turismo, at Hotel Mônaco, R Silva Ramos 41, T 234-7308, 35 km from Manaus on a side channel of the Rio Negro, jungle hotel with observation tower and a walkway across a swamp, trips to Anavilhanas islands in groups of 10-20, rec. The better hotels also arrange tours (ask for Joe Sears in *Hotel Tropical*) and so do *Selvatur* (office in *Hotel Amazonas* T 622-2577), Rio Negro trip, 0800-1500, with lunch at *Janaurylândia* floating hotel. *Exotic Amazon Tours*, Av 7 de Setembro 1367A; *Queiroz Tours*, Av Joaquim Nabuco 681, sala 02, T 233 3354. *Safari Ecológico*, Av Marechal Câmara 160, Sala 621, Caixa Postal 3321, CEP 20.010, Rio de Janeiro, T (021) 240-6785, has been rec for its ecological tours. (Manaus address: R Monsenho Coutinho 119, T 233-6910, bookings also through Carretour du Brésil, Paris; Brazil Nuts, Fairfield CT, USA; Jolivac, Montreal.) All tours are accompanied by guide, scientific adviser and doctor. The **Amazon Monkey Jungle**, 30 mins up Rio Tarumã from the Rio Negro confluence, is part of a new *Amazon Ecopark* initiative where many monkey species are treated and rehabilitated in natural surroundings. For day tours T 234-0939 The Living Rainforest Foundation, which administers the ecopark, also offers educational jungle trips and overnight camps (bring own food). Entrance US$15.

● **Guides** There appears to be an endless supply of guides. Those listed below have been rec by travellers in 1996, but bear in mind that different tourists have different expectations and recommendations can change: for trips or the Amazon and Rio Negro, *Moacir Fortes*, R Miguel Ribas 1339, Santo Antônio, Manaus, T 232-7492 or through Amazônia Expeditions Ltd, Houston, T (713) 660-8115 (has his own 19m boat *Amazônia Expedition*), he speaks English and German. Also *Gerry Hardy*, very warmly rec, contact through Chris at *Hotel Rio Branco*, or T 237-6981, Chris, who charges up to 30% commission, also deals with Elmo de Morais López, Carlos Colares (see below), and *Carlos Grandes Perez*, enthusiastically rec. Carlos Grandes Perez can also be contacted through the *Hotel Turístico* at Lad da Glória in Rio de Janeiro, and *Hotel Nunes*, Porto Velho, T 069-221-1389. *Elmo de Morais López*, R Henrique Martins 364, Centro, T 233-8927, speaks English, German, Spanish, Italian, French, rec for 2-5 day tours, 2-4 people, sleeping in hammocks (Elmo works for agencies as well). *Amazon Wild*, R Quintino Bocaiúva 425, T 233-9308, mixed reports, rec guides Cláudio Gonzaga and Robert, speaks English and French, Anselmo Oliveira (T 233-3106); *Francisco da Silva*, T 625-1905, has his own boat, rec. *Albuquerque Turismo*, A Tarumã 418, T/F 234 7961, native guide Ricardo, guiding since 1974, specific tours, medium-sized boat, biology and ecology studies the Rio Negro primary forest and expeditions to the Upper Rio Negro indian tribes, US$50/day inc food and all equipment.

Thérèse Aubreton, director of *Alternatur Amazônia*, R Costa Azevedo 9, sala 203, works with Carlos Jorge Damasceno (see below) to provide ecologically sensitive tours away from the usual routes, T 232-5541, F 233-5941. For those prepared to spend around 10 days in the interior on a real expedition, contact *Carlos Colares*, Av Atlântica 91, Raiz, 69.000 Manaus, T 237-1961, Telex 092-165 XPMNA, or PO Box 360, who conducts private excursions, with fishing, hunting and exploring in the more remote regions of the Rio Negro. Carlos Colares speaks good English. A colleague of his, *Sebastião Dimas*, also rec, can be reached at R Elisabeth 6, Bairro de Flores. Similar tours arranged by *Sabrina Lima de Almeida*, R Boa Esperança 6, T 237-7359, Portuguese speaking only, rec. *Agência Amazones Indian Turismo*, R dos Andradas 335, T 233-3140, Indian guides Soares and Cristôvão who speak Portuguese and Spanish, cheap, mixed reports. Serious deep jungle exploration with an ecological slant and visits to remote historical and Indian settlements: *Carlos Jorge Damasceno*, Jaguar, R Belém 1646, Cachoeirinha, T 234-0736; multilingual, very highly rec. *The Global Heritage*, Av Joaquim Nabuco 337, Sala 204, Centro, tour operator Sandro Gama speaks English, rec. *Green Planet Tours*, R Isabel 239, T 633-3303, rec guide Cláudio Gonzala, friendly, helpful and serious, 2 days in motor canoe US$80/day, 3 days in boat US$50/day, rec. *Amazônia Expeditions*, Caixa Postal 703, 69000, T/F 671-2731, Cellular 981-2652, highly rec. *Iaratur*, city office, R Mundurucús, 90, Centro, T 232-2949, 4/3 night tours, overnight in the jungle 3 days US$210, rec. Zequinho (T 624-2362), who lives a half-hour boat ride from Araça, has been recommended, as has Pedro 'Rocky' (T 237-1710).

● **Birdwatching** Many kinds of birds can be seen in and around the grounds of the *Hotel Tropical*. Sloths and monkeys may also be seen. For further information contact Moacir Fortes

TEFÉ

(*Pop* 26,000) Approximately halfway between Manaus and the Colombian border. The waterfront consists of a light sand beach; waterfront market Mon am; the nuns at the Franciscan convent sell handicrafts and embroidery; there are three small hotels and five pensions (**D** *Anilce*, Praça Santa Teresa 294, clean, a/c, do not leave valuables in your room, very helpful; *Hotel Panorama*, rec, good restaurant, the restaurant *Au Bec d'Or* by the port, French/Amazonian cuisine). Airport with connection to Manaus. If travelling on to Tabatinga, note that Manaus-Tabatinga boats do not usually stop at Tefé. You must hire a canoe to take you out to the main channel and try to 'flag down' the approaching ship.

BENJAMIN CONSTANT

(*Pop* 15,000) On the frontier with Peru, with Colombian territory on the opposite bank of the river.

● **Accommodation & services** Several hotels, inc, **B** *Benjamin Constant*, beside ferry, all rooms a/c, some with hot water and TV, good restaurant, arranges tours, postal address Apdo Aéreo 219, Leticia, Colombia; *Mar Azur*, a/c, friendly; **D** *Benjamin*, very basic; **D** *Márcia Maria*, with bath, a/c, fridge, clean, friendly, rec; **E** *Hotel São Jorge*, rec, meals available; **E** *Hotel Lanchonete Peruana*, good food. Eat at *Pensão Cecília*, or *Bar-21 de Abril*, cheaper. Clothes shop on road reaching to port (left hand side) changes US$ cash.

● **Shipping** Boat services from Manaus, 7 days, or more; to Manaus, 4 days, or more.

TABATINGA

(*Pop* 27,950) 4 km from Leticia (Colombia). The Port Captain in Tabatinga is reported as very helpful and speaking good English. **NB** The port area of Tabatinga is called Marco. Hammock (good) will cost US$15 in Tabatinga (try Esplanada Teocides) or Benjamin Constant. Mosquito net for hammock essential if sailing upstream from Tabatinga;

much less so downstream.

● **Accommodation & places to eat** *Hotel Martins*, good but expensive; **D** *Residencial Aluguel Pajé*, with bath, fan, clean; **D** *Solimões*, run by the military – close to the airport – with breakfast, other meals available if ordered in advance, excellent value, clean – some taxi drivers are unaware that this hotel accepts non-military guests, but there is a VW colectivo minibus from the barracks to town centre, harbour and Leticia; excellent *Tres Fronteiras* restaurant.

● **Banks & money changers** It is difficult to change TCs in Tabatinga (try *Casa Branca*, *Casa Verde* or *Casa Amarela* on main road, or general manager of the main shopping centre), and far harder to purchase Peruvian soles than in Leticia. Good rates found at *Câmbio Cortez*, Av da Amizade 2205 (nr Banco do Brasil).

● **Transport** Airport to Tabatinga by minibus, US$0.75.

THE BRAZILIAN/COLOMBIAN/ PERUVIAN FRONTIER

It is advisable to check all requirements and procedures before arriving at this multiple border. As no foreign boat is allowed to dock at the Brazilian, Colombian and Peruvian ports, travellers should enquire carefully about embarkation/disembarkation points and where to go through immigration formalities. If waiting for transport, the best place for accommodation, exchange and other facilities is Leticia, Colombia.

● **Brazilian immigration**
Entry and exit stamps are given at the Polícia Federal, 10 mins' walk from the Tabatinga docks, opp *Café dos Navegantes* (walk through docks and follow road to its end, turn right at this T-junction for 1 block to white building), Mon-Fri 0800-1200, 1400-1800; also at airport, open Wed and Sat only. Proof of US$500 or onward ticket may be asked for. There are no facilities in Benjamin Constant. One-week transit in Tabatinga is permitted.

In this frontier area, carry your passport at all times.

If coming from Peru, you must have a Peruvian exit stamp and a yellow fever certificate.

NB When crossing these frontiers, check if there is a time difference (eg Brazilian summer time, usually mid-Oct to mid-Feb).

● **Colombian consulate**
Near the border on the road from Tabatinga to Leticia, opp *Restaurant El Canto de las Peixadas*

(0800-1400). Tourist cards are issued on presentation of 2 passport photos.

● **Transport**
Travel between Tabatinga and Leticia is very informal; taxis between the two towns charge US$3 (more if you want to stop at immigration offices, exchange houses, etc; beware of tax drivers who want to rush you, expensively over border before it 'closes'), or US$0.80 in a colectivo (more after 1800).

Boats From Manaus to Benjamin Constant normally go on to Tabatinga, and start from there when going to Manaus. Boats usually wait 1-2 days in both Tabatinga and Benjamin Constant before returning to Manaus; you can stay on board. Tabatinga and Leticia are 1½-2 hrs from Benjamin Constant (ferry/recreio US$2.50, much quicker by speedboat, US$13).

For information on boats to/from Manaus, see Manaus **Shipping** and **River Transport in Amazônia**.

● **Colombian immigration**
DAS, C 9, No 8-32, T 27189, Leticia, and at the airport. Exit stamps to leave Colombia by air or overland are given only at the airport. If flying into Leticia prior to leaving for Brazil or Peru, get an exit stamp while at the airport. Check both offices for entry stamps before flying into Colombia.

Entering Colombia To enter Colombia you must have a tourist card to obtain an entry stamp, even if you are passing through Leticia en route between Brazil and Peru (the Colombian consul in Manaus may tell you otherwise; try to get a tourist card elsewhere). The Colombian Consular Office in Tabatinga issues tourist cards. 24-hr transit stamps can be obtained at the DAS office. If visiting Leticia without intending to go anywhere else in Colombia, you may be allowed to enter without immigration or customs formalities (but TCs cannot be changed without an entry stamp).

● **Colombian customs**
No customs formalities for everyday travel between Leticia and Tabatinga.

● **Consulates**
Brazilian, C 11, No 10-70, T 27531, 1000-1600, Mon-Fri, efficient, helpful; onward ticket and 2 black-and-white photos needed for visa (photographer nearby); allow 36 hrs. **Peruvian**, Cra 11, No 6-80, T 27204, F 27825, open 0830-1430; no entry or exit permits are given here.

● **Transport**
Travel between Colombia and Brazil and Peru is given above and below respectively. Travel from/into Colombia is given under Leticia.

● **Peruvian immigration**

At the border, immigration for entry/exit formalities is at Aguas Verdes, opposite Leticia/Tabatinga. Every boat leaving Peru stops here. There is also an immigration office in Iquitos, where procedures for leaving can be checked.

● **Consulates**

Brazilian and Colombian consulates are in Iquitos.

● **Exchange**

At Islandia (see below).

● **Transport**

Boats sail from Iquitos to a mud bank called Islandia, on the Peruvian side of a narrow creek a few metres from the Brazilian port of Benjamin Constant (11-36 hrs downstream, depending on the speed of the boat). Passengers leaving Peru must visit immigration at Aguas Verdes when the boat stops there. For entry into Brazil, formalities are done in Tabatinga; for Colombia, in Leticia. Boats to Peru leave from Islandia, calling at Aguas Verdes (2-3 days upstream to Iquitos). There is a fast boat service twice a week from Tabatinga to Iquitos, 11/2 days, US$150. Tickets from office next to *Hotel Estrela*.

Boats between Iquitos and Brazil are listed under Iquitos.

UP THE RIO NEGRO

It is possible to get a launch from Manaus up the Rio Negro; see **River Transport in Amazônia**, see page 574. There are hardly any villages of more than a few houses; these places are important in terms of communications and food resources. It is vital to be self-sufficient in food and cash and to be able to speak Portuguese or have a Brazilian guide. **Nova Airão**, on the W bank of the Negro, is about 2 days upstream. It has a large boat-building centre at the S end, and a fish and vegetable market at the N end. Ice and bread can also be purchased here. It has a telephone (from which international calls can be made – after a fashion).

Nova Airão is the starting point for the **Parque Nacional Jaú** (Ibama office in Manaus, BR-319, Km 01, Distrito Industrial, Caixa Postal 185, CEP 69.000, T 237-3721).

Moura is about 5 days upstream from Manaus; it has basic medical facilities and the military base has an airstrip (only usable Sept to Dec) and telecommunications. About a day further upstream is **Carvoeira**, almost opposite the mouth of the Rio Branco; vibrant festival in the first week of August. More than a day beyond is **Barcelos**, with an airstrip (Hotel *Oasis*, German spoken; *Macedo*).

A great distance further upstream is **São Gabriel da Cachoeira**, from where you can continue to Venezuela (see Venezuela section). In São Gabriel, Tom Hanly, an Irish Salesian brother, is helpful, friendly and informative. Hotels: **E** *Valpes*; another (better class) on the island, restaurant, rec, shops, 2 banks, no exchange, beautiful white beaches and, in the river, rapids for 112 km. São Gabriel is near the **Pico de Neblina National Park** (Pico de Neblina is the highest mountain in Brazil, 3,014m, Ibama office in Manaus, see above).

Cargo boats ply to **Cucuí** at the Brazil/Colombia/Venezuela border, also twice-weekly bus, US$2.50 (1 hotel, ask for Elias, no restaurants). From Cucuí daily boats to Guadalupe (Colombia), infrequent boats to Santa Lucía (Venezuela).

Many of the **gold prospectors** (*garimpeiros*) expelled from the Yanomami reserves in Roraima have begun to move W to the middle and upper reaches of the Rio Negro, bringing conflict and destruction in their wake. Get detailed local information and exercise considerable caution if travelling to this region.

THE RIO BRANCO

About 2 days up the Rio Branco is **Santa Maria de Boiaçu**, a village with a military airstrip (in use in July and Aug), very basic medical facilities and an indirect radio link with Manaus. Three small shops sell basic necessities (frequently closed), and several tiny, but lively churches. The Rio Branco is yellowish in colour, and less acidic than the Negro. Biting insects and their associated diseases are more prevalent outside the wet season. The river is better for fishing, though, and there is more wildlife to see.

CARACARAÍ

River traffic on the Rio Branco connects Manaus with **Caracaraí**, a busy port with modern installations. It is also on the the Manaus-Boa Vista road (see below). If this road is washed out, the Rio Branco is the only route through to Venezuela. The river banks are closer, so there is more to see than on the Amazon and stops in the tiny riverside settlements are fascinating.

● **Accommodation & places to eat** D *3 Irmãos*, behind rodoviária, clean, rec; **E** *Caracaraí*, down street from rodoviária, friendly but dirty; *Sorvetería Pizzaria Lidiany*, rec.

● **Banks & money changers** Silas in the Drogaria on S side of town will change dollars.

● **Transport** Buses from Caracaraí to Boa Vista costs US$6, 3 hrs. **NB** The Perimetral Norte road marked on some maps from Caracaraí E to Macapá and W to the Colombian frontier does not yet exist; it runs only about 240 km W and 125 km E from Caracaraí, acting at present as a penetration road. **Shipping** In the rainy season, April-Sept, river transport is quite easy to arrange (bargain for your fare, and sling your hammock under a truck); empty trucks offer cheaper fares for cars, talk to the drivers; 96 hrs upstream, 48 down, take water or purifying treatment.

MANAUS TO VENEZUELA AND GUYANA

The road which connects Manaus and Boa Vista (BR-174 to Novo Paraíso, then the Perimetral, BR-210, rejoining the BR174 after crossing the Rio Branco at Caracaraí, ferry during daylight hours) is regularly maintained. Paving of the entire route was due for completion in 1997. The road is fully paved from Caracaraí to Boa Vista. There are service stations with toilets, camping, etc, every 150-180 km, but all petrol is low octane. Until paving is complete, drivers should take a tow cable and spares, and bus passengers should prepare for delays in the rainy season. At Km 100 is Presidente Figueiredo, with shops and a restaurant. About 100 km further on is a service station (road paved to here, Jan 97) at the entrance to the Uaimiri Atroari Indian Reserve, which straddles the road for about 120 km. Private cars and trucks are not allowed to enter the Indian Reserve between sunset and sunrise, but buses are exempt from this regulation. Nobody is allowed to stop within the reserve at any time. At the northern entrance to the reserve there are toilets and a spot to hang your hammock (usually crowded with truckers overnight). At Km 327 is the village of Vila Colina with *Restaurante Paulista*, good food, clean, can use shower and hang hammock. At Km 359 there is a monument to mark the equator. At Km 434 is the clean and pleasant *Restaurant Goaio*. Just S of Km 500 is *Bar Restaurante D'Jonas*, a clean, pleasant place to eat, you can also camp or sling a hammock. Beyond here, large tracts of forest have been destroyed for settlement, but already many homes have been abandoned.

Boa Vista has road connections with the Venezuelan frontier at Santa Elena de Uairen (237 km, paved, the only gasoline 110 km S of Santa Elena) and Bonfim for the Guyanese border at Lethem. Both roads are open all year.

BOA VISTA

(*Pop* 142,815; *CEP* 69300; *DDD* 095) Capital of the extreme northern State of Roraima (*pop* 215,790), it is 759 km N of Manaus. Mount Roraima, after which the Territory is named, is possibly the original of Sir Arthur Conan Doyle's 'Lost World'. There is swimming in the Rio Branco, 15 mins from the town centre (too polluted in Boa Vista), reachable by bus only when river is low. This town has a modern functional plan, which often necessitates long hot treks from one function to another. South of town is an industrial estate; NW is a new government district. Interesting modern cathedral; also a museum of local Indian culture (poorly kept). Under heavy international pressure, the Brazilian government expelled some 40,000 gold prospectors (*garimpeiros*) from Yanomami Indian Reserves in the W of the state of Roraima in the early 1990s. The economic consequences were very severe for Boa Vista, which went from boom to bust. An increase in cattle ranching in the area has not taken up the slack.

Local information

● **Accommodation**

Generally expensive.

A1 *Aipana Plaza*, Praça Centro Cívico 53, T 224-4800, F 224-4116, modern, good service; **A1** *Uiramutam*, Av Cap Ene Garcez 427, T 224-9912.

C *Eusêbio's*, R Cecília Brasil 1107, T 224-0300, always full, book ahead, demand single if on your own, very good restaurant, swimming pool, free transport to rodoviária or airport, rec. **D** *Beija-Flor*, Av Nossa Sra da Consolata 939 W, Bairro, T 224 8241, F 224 8270, inc breakfast, nr rodoviária, run by a Belgian Jean and his Brazilian wife Néia, highly rec; *Colonial*, Ajuricaba 532, T 224-5190, nr Consolação church, a/c with breakfast; **D** *Roraima*, Av Cecília Brasil e Benjamin Constant, rec, restaurant opp is also rec. **D** *Três Nações*, Av Ville Roy 1885, T 224-3439, close to rodoviária, some rooms a/c, refurbished, basic, often rec.

E *Joelma*, Av NS da Consolata, corner of Av Gulana S Vincento, T 224-5404, with bath, nr rodoviária; **E** *Lua Nova*, R Benjamin Constant 591, without a/c, more expensive with, English spoken, noisy, seedy, often full; **E** *Monte Líbano*, Benjamin Constant 319 W, without a/c, dearer with a/c (bus from rodoviária to centre passes by); **E** *Brasil*, next door at No 331, W nr

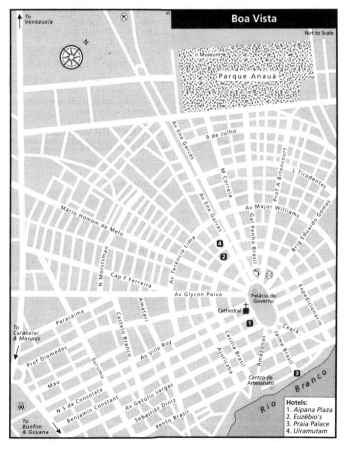

Boa Vista

Not to Scale

To Venezuela

Parque Anauá

Museum

9 de Julho

Av Ene Garcés

M Correia

L Tiradentes

Prof A Bitencourt

Av Ene Garcés

Av Major Williams

Gal Penha Brasil

Brig Eduardo Gomes

Mário Homem de Melo

Av Terencio Lima

N Morstsman

Cap F Ferreira

4

2

Expedicionário

Av Glycon Paiva

Palácio do Governo

Cathedral

1

Paracaima

Amatari

Castelo Branco

To Caracaraí & Manaus

Prof Diomedes

Av Ville Roy

Surumu

Cecília Brasil

Ajuricaba

Amazonas

Ceará

Jaime Brasil

Mau

Branco

To Bonfim & Guyana

NS da Consolata

Benjamin Constant

Av Getúlio Vargas

Sebastião Diniz

Bento Brasil

Centro de Artesanato

3

Rio

Branco

Hotels:
1. Aipana Plaza
2. Euzébio's
3. Praia Palace
4. Uiramutam

Drogafarma, good meals (do not confuse with dirty, overpriced *Hotel Brasa* in same street); at Av Ville Roy 1906-24 Carlos Alberto Soares lets a room, warm shower, rec; **F** *Terraço*, Av Cecília Brasil 1141, without bath, noisy, friendly; and **E** *Universo*, No 997, only 4 rooms, with bath, rec.

Camping: Rio Caaumé, 3 km N of town (unofficial site, small bar, clean river, pleasant).

● **Places to eat**
Senzala, Av Castelo Branco 1115, where the town's high society eats; *Café Pigalle*, R Cecília Brasil, just off central square, next to *Eusêbio's*, good food, drinks and atmosphere, open till all hours; *Góndola*, Benjamin Constant e Av Amazonas, good; *Vila Rica*, R Ville Roy, nr rodoviária, good cheap lunch. Snacks at *Top Set*, Av Jaime Brasil, *Catequeiro*, Araújo Filho e Benjamin Constant, rec *prato feito*.

● **Banks & money changers**
US$ and Guyanese notes can be changed in Boa Vista. TCs and cash in **Banco do Brasil**, Av Glycon Paiva 56, 1000-1300 (minimum US$200). There is no official exchange agency and the local rates for bolívares are low: the Banco do Brasil will not change bolívares. Best rate for dollars, **Casa Pedro José**, R Araújo Filho 287, T 224 4277, also changes TCs and bolívares; *Timbo's* (gold and jewellery shop), on corner of R Cecília Brasil e Av Getúlio Vargas, will change money.

● **Hospitals & medical services**
Yellow fever inoculations are free at a clinic nr the hospital.

● **Tourist offices**
Tourist information at rodoviária. **Tour Guide**: boat trips on Rio Branco and surrounding waterways (jungle, beaches, Indian reservations), *Acqua*, R Floriano Peixoto 505, T 224-6576. Guide Elieser Rufino is rec.

● **Transport**
Air To and from São Paulo, Brasília and Manaus; confirm flights before reaching Boa Vista as they are fully booked. Aircraft maintenance, baggage checking and handling are unreliable. No left luggage, information or exchange facilities at airport. Bus 'Aeroporto' from centre is US$0.40. Taxi to rodoviária, US$9, to centre US$12, 45 mins' walk.

Buses (See also Border Crossings below.) Rodoviária is on town outskirts, 3 km at end of Av Ville Roy; taxi to centre, US$5, bus US$0.45, 10 mins (marked '13 de Setembro' or 'Joquey Clube' to centre). Local bus terminal is on Av Amazonas, by R Cecília Brasil, nr central square. Note that it is difficult to get taxi or bus to rodoviária in time for early morning departures; as it's a 25-min walk, book a taxi the previous

evening. To Manaus, by União Cascavel, US$56, 18 hrs, 0830 and 1330, can be very crowded, (leaves 1730, 1800 from Manaus), advisable to book because sometimes buses are fully booked days in advance, but extra buses may run when scheduled service is full, check times. Buses often run late, and the night bus has to wait up to 4 hrs for the Rio Branco ferry. **Boa Vista-Caracaraí** US$6, 3 hrs. União Cascavel to **Bonfim**, 1700, Mon, Wed, Fri, 2 hrs, returning next morning, US$5.

Hitchhiking To Santa Elena, Venezuela, is not easy; either wait at the bridge and police checkpoint on the road to the border, or try to find a Venezuelan driver on the square. Hitching from Boa Vista to Manaus is fairly easy on the many trucks travelling S; try from the service station nr the rodoviária. You may have to change trucks at Caracaraí. At the ferry crossing over the Rio Branco there is usually a long queue of waiting hikers; try to arrange a lift on the ferry. Truck drivers ask approx half the bus fare to take passengers in the cab (bargain), much cheaper or free in back. The view from the truck is usually better than from the bus and you can see the virgin forest of the Indian Reserve in daylight. Take some food and water.

FRONTIER WITH VENEZUELA

● **Brazilian immigration and customs**
Border searches are thorough and frequent at this border crossing.

● **Entering Brazil**
Ensure in advance that you have the right papers for entering Brazil before arriving at this frontier. It may be possible to get your passport stamped in Manaus, but you may be fined.

● **Venezuelan consulate**
Av Benjamin Constant 525E, Boa Vista, T (095) 224-2182, open Mon-Fri 0830-1300, but may close earlier. Everyone who crosses this border must have a visa for Venezuela; current procedure is take filled out visa form, two photos and deposit slip from Banco do Brasil (US$30) to Venezuelan consulate, be prepared to wait an hour, but it may be possible to get visa at border; check requirements in advance. There is also a Venezuelan consulate in Manaus which issues 1-year, multiple entry visas (see page 593).

● **Accommodation & exchange**
On the Brazilian side there are a basic hotel, *Pacaraima Palace*, a guest house, camping possibilities and a bank.

● **Transport**
Buses leave Boa Vista rodoviária at 0700 and 0830 for Santa Elena de Uairén, stopping at all checkpoints, US$13.70, 4-6 hrs, take water. It is

possible to share a taxi. Through tickets to Ciudad Bolívar are sold, but are more expensive than paying separately.

FRONTIER WITH GUYANA

The main border crossing between Brazil and Guyana is from Bonfim, 125 km NE of Boa Vista, to Lethem. The towns are separated by the Rio Tacutu, which is crossed by small boats for foot passengers; vehicles cross by pontoon, or can drive across in the dry season. The river crossing is 2½ km from Bonfim, 1.6 km N of Lethem. Formalities are generally lax on both sides of the border, but it is important to observe them as people not having the correct papers may have problems further into either country.

There is another border crossing at Laramonta from where it is a hard, but rewarding walk to the Guyanese town of Orinduik.

● **Brazilian immigration**
At Polícia Federal (closed for lunch): from rodoviária in Bonfim take a taxi, obtain exit stamp, then walk to the river. Once across, keep to the right, on the road to the airport; the first enclosed building on your right is the police station for entry stamps for Guyana.

● **Brazilian customs**
At Ministério da Fazenda checkpoint, before entering Bonfim; jeeps from here charge US$1 to immigration.

● **Guyanese consulate**
There is no consul in Boa Vista, so if you need a visa for Guyana, you must get it in São Paulo or Brasília (see Guyana **Documents** in **Information for travellers**).

● **Accommodation & places to eat**
D *Bonfim*, owned by Mr Myers, who speaks English and is very helpful, fan, shower; **E** *Blessing*; *Frontera*; *Domaia*. There is a café at the rodoviária, opp the church, whose owner speaks English and gives information; *Restaurante Internacional*, opp rodoviária, on other side from church; another restaurant a bit further from the rodoviária serves good food. English-speaking teacher, Tricia Watson, has been helpful to bewildered travellers. Electricity is officially turned off between 2200 and 0700; take a torch or candles.

● **Exchange**
Reais can be changed into G$ in the shop at Brazilian immigration post; exchange rates in Bonfim are not as good as in Lethem. Boa Vista is best.

● **Transport**
Buses Boa Vista-Bonfim daily 1500, return daily 0600, US$5; colectivos charge US$18; T Bonfim 2290 for a car to take you, US$50. Weekly jeep Boa Vista-Laramonta US$30.

Ferry To cross the river, yell 'boat' and a motor boat will come to ferry you, US$0.25 (no boats at night).

Southern Amazônia

RONDÔNIA and Acre, frontier areas, not just between Brazil and Peru and Bolivia, but also between the forest and colonization. Much of Rondônia, now colonized, has been deforested. Acre is still frontier country with great expanses of forest in danger of destruction.

Rondônia, with a population of 862,000 in 1985, which had reached 1,130,400 in 1991, is the focus of experimental agriculture, with attendant colonization. At the same time, much of the state is reserved for Indians and national forests.

The Rio Madeira on which Porto Velho, the state capital stands, is one of the Amazon's major tributaries. The four main rivers which form it are the Madre de Dios, rising a short distance from Cusco (Peru); the Beni, coming from the southern Cordillera bordering Lake Titicaca; the Mamoré, rising near Sucre, Bolivia; and the Guaporé, coming out of Mato Grosso, in Brazil.

PORTO VELHO

(*Pop* 296,400; *CEP* 78900; *DDD* 069) **Porto Velho** stands on a high bluff overlooking a curve of the Rio Madeira. The city prospered during the local gold and timber rush but this has slowed.

Places of interest

At the top of the hill, on Praça João Nicoletti, is the **Cathedral**, built in 1930, with beautiful stained glass windows; the **Prefeitura** (town hall) is across the street. The principal commercial street is Av Sete de Setembro, which runs from the railway station and market hall to the upper level of the city, near the rodoviária. The centre is hot and noisy, but not without its charm, and the port and old railway installations are interesting. There is a **Geological Museum** at the old railway yards, known as Praça Madeira Mamoré. (See page 607 for the Madeiro-Mamoré railway.) A neoclassical **Casa do Governo** faces Praça Getúlio Vargas, while Praça Marechal Rondon is spacious and modern. There are several viewpoints overlooking the river and railway yards: **Mirante I** (with restaurant) is at the end of R Carlos Gómes; **Mirante II** (with a bar and ice cream parlour), at the end of R Dom Pedro II. There is a clean fruit and vegetable market at the corner of R Henrique Dias and Av Farqhuar and a dry goods market 3 blocks to the S, near the port.

Excursions

The Cachoeira de Santo Antônio, rapids on the Rio Madeira, 7 km upriver from Porto Velho, is a popular destination for a swim during the dry season; in the rainy season the rapids may be underwater and swimming is dangerous. Access is by boat, taking a tour from Porto Cai N'Água, 1 hr; or by train on Sundays (see Madeira-Mamoré Railway, below); or by bus, take city bus No 102, *Triângulo*, which runs every 50 mins from the city bus terminus or from bus stop on R Rogério Weber, across from Praça Marechal Rondon. Gold dredges may be seen working near Porto Velho, ask around if interested.

Local information

NB Malaria is common; the drinking water is contaminated with mercury (from gold panning). With rising unemployment, crime has increased in the city and outside. Caution is recommended in the evenings and even during the day nr the railway station and port.

● **Accommodation**
L3 *Vila Rica*, Av Carlos Gomes 1616, T/F 224-3433, tower block, flashy but efficient, restau-

rant, pool, sauna; **A1** *Rondon Palace*, Av Gov Jorge Teixeira corner Jacy Paraná, away from the centre, T/F 223-3422, a/c, fridge, restaurant, pool, travel agency; **A3** *Selton*, Av Brasília 2323, T 221-7535, F 221-2900, a/c, fridge, TV, restaurant, central, rec; **B** *Central*, Tenreiro Aranha 2472, T 224-2099, F 223-2302, a/c, TV, fridge, rec.

On Av Carlos Gomes: **A3** *Novo*, No 2776, nr rodoviária, T 221-4284, a/c, fridge, TV, parking, comfortable; **E** *Erica*, opp rodoviária, convenient but short-stay; much better is **E** *Líder*, nr rodoviária, honest, reasonably clean, fan, coffee, rec for new arrivals; **D-E** *Karme (Tía Carmen)*, No 2995, T 221-7910, very good, honest, good cakes in *lanche* in front of hotel, highly rec. From rodoviária, take bus No 301 'Presidente Roosevelt' (outside *Hotel Pontes*), which goes to railway station at riverside, then along Av 7 de Setembro as far as Av Marechal Deodoro, passing: **C** *Pousada da Sete*, No 894, T 221-8344, a/c, cheaper with fan, **D** with shared bath; **D** *Guaporé Palace*, No 927, T 221-2495, a/c, restaurant; **D** *Sonora*, No 1103, fan, laundry facilities; **D** *Cuiabano*, No 1180, T 221-4080, good, a/c, cheaper with fan, **E** with shared bath, fan, no breakfast, rec; **D** *Nunes*, No 1195, T 221-1389, fan, basic; **E** *Sonora*, No 1209, bath, fan, basic, not too clean; **E** *Laira*, Joaquim Nabuco, just off 7 de Setembro, good, cheap.

● **Places to eat**

Churascaria Natal, Av Carlos Gomes 2783, good meat and chicken; *Assados na Brasa*, Carlos Gomes 2208, similar; *Mister Pizza II*, Carlos Gomes e José de Alencar, good. *Almanara*, R José de Alencar 2624, good authentic Lebanese food, popular, not cheap, rec; *Chá*, Av Pres Dutra 3024, by kilo buffet, pricey. A number of good restaurants around the intersection of Dom Pedro II and Av Joaquim Nabuco: *Champagne*, rec for pizzas, and a good Chinese; J Nabuco 2264, oriental food; *Bella Italia*, J Nabuco 2205, Italian, pizza and *comida caseira*. Many *lanches* in town: rec are *Petiskão*, Av 7 de Setembro e Joaquim Nabuco, excellent juices; *Panificadora Popular*, Av Mal Deodoro between 7 de Setembro e Dom Pedro II, good juices and soups; *Xalezinho*, opp, for an even bigger bowl of soup. *Banana Split*, Av 7 de Setembro, popular, good by the kilo meals; also *Sorvette Pinguim* for ice creams. Avoid eating much fish because of mercury contamination.

● **Banks & money changers**

Banks in mornings only; **Banco do Brasil**, Dom Pedro II 607 e Av José de Alencar, cash and TCs with 2% commission, min commission US$10, min amount exchanged US$200. *Marco Aurélio Câmbio*, R José de Alencar 3353, T 223-2551, quick, efficient, poor rates, Mon-Fri 0900-1500.

Parmetal (gold merchants), R J Nabuco 2265, T 221-1566, cash only, good rates, open Mon-Fri 0730-1800, Sat 0730-1300. Local radio news and papers publish exchange rates. Difficult elsewhere in Rondônia.

● **Electric current**

110 volts AC, Guajará-Mirim also, elsewhere in Rondônia 220 volts.

● **Hospitals & medical services**

Dentist: at Carlos Gomes 2577; 24-hr clinic opp.

● **Laundry**

Lavanderia Marmoré, Pinheiro Machado 1455b.

● **Post & telecommunications**

Post Office: Av Pres Dutra 2701, corner Av 7 de Setembro.

Telephones: Teleron, Av Pres Dutra 3023 e Dom Pedro II, 0600-2300 daily.

● **Shopping**

Bookshop *Livraria da Rose*, Av Rogério Weber 1967, opp Praça Mal Rondon, exchanges English paperbacks; Rose, the proprietor, speaks English, friendly; other bookshops nearby. Indian handicrafts at *Casa do Índio*, R Rui Barbosa 1407 and *Casa do Artesão*, Praça Madeira-Mamoré, behind the railway station, open Thur-Sun 0800-1800. Hammocks more expensive than in Manaus. *Supermercado Maru*, 7 de Setembro e Joaquim Nabuco. Camping supplies and gas at *Casa do Pescador*, J Nabuco e Pinheiro Machado. Film developing at 7 de Setembro e José de Alencar.

● **Transport**

Local Car hire: Silva Car, R Almte Barroso 1528, Porto Velho, T 221-1423/6040, US$50/day.

Air Airport 8 km W of town, take bus marked 'Aeroporto' (last one between 2400-0100). Daily flights to many Brazilian cities.

Buses Rodoviária is on Jorge Teixeira between Carlos Gomes and Dom Pedro II. From town take 'President Roosevelt' bus No 301 (if on Av 7 de Setembro, the bus turns at Av Mal Deodoro); 'Aeroporto' and 'Hospital Base' (No 400) also go to rodoviária. Health and other controls at the Rondônia-Matto Grosso border are strict. To break up a long trip is much more expensive than doing it all in one stretch. Bus to **Humaitá**, US$8, 3 hrs; to **São Paulo**, 60-plus hrs, US$108; to **Cuiabá**, 23 hrs, US$63, expensive food and drink is available en route. To **Rio** US$142, 72 hrs; **Belo Horizonte** US$99, 44 hrs; **Curitiba** US$137, 52 hrs; **Fortaleza** US$175, 72 hrs. To **Guajará-Mirim**, see below. To **Rio Branco**, Viação Rondônia, 5 daily, 8 hrs, US$19. Daily bus with Eucatur from **Cascavel** (Paraná, connections for Foz do Iguaçu) via

Maringá, Presidente Prudente, Campo Grande and Cuiabá to Porto Velho (Porto Velho-Campo Grande 36 hrs, US$94). To **Cáceres** for the Pantanal, 18 hrs, US$52. Hitching difficult, try the gasoline stations on the edge of town. There is no bus service to **Manaus** as the road remains closed (1997).

Road To Cuiabá (BR-364 – Marechal Rondon Highway), 1,450 km, fully paved; see below and page 636; Rio Branco, 544 km, BR-364, poorly paved; N to Humaitá (205 km) on the Madeira river, BR-319, paved, connecting with the Transamazônica, BR-230 (frequently closed, ascertain conditions before travelling). The BR-319 from Humaitá to Manaus is closed indefinitely. Road journeys are best done in the dry season, the second half of the year.

River services See **River Transport in Amazônia**, page 574. Passenger service from *Porto Cai N'Água* (which means 'fall in the water', watch out or you might!), for best prices buy directly at the boat, avoid touts on shore. The Rio Madeira is fairly narrow so the banks can be seen and there are several 'meetings of waters'. Shipping a car: São Matheus Ltda, Av Terminal dos Milagros 400, Balsa, takes vehicles on pontoons, meals, showers, toilets, cooking and sleeping in car permitted. Wait at the Capitânia do Porto in the centre of town for a possible passage on a cargo boat; these boats leave from the Porto Bras docks, down river from Porto Velho. **NB** From Manaus to São Paulo is cheaper by boat Manaus-Porto Velho, then bus to São Paulo, than by flying direct or by boat to Belém then bus.

Boats usually call at Humaitá (paved road and regular bus service from Porto Velho, see above, 1st class hammock Humaitá-Manaus US$61), Manicoré (see below), Novo Aripuanã, Borba and Nova Olinda. Passengers can disembark or embark at these ports, if that is your intention confirm the itinerary beforehand; if embarking at an intermediate port you will not have your choice of hammock space.

6 days a week a boat leaves at 1800 for Manaus from Manicoré, at the confluence of the Rios Madeira and Manicoré, two nights and 1 day's journey, food included; boats from Porto Velho to Manicoré on Mon, Wed and Sat (1800, arr 0200, but you can sleep on the boat), connecting with Manicoré-Manaus boats (a rec boat is *Orlandina*). **Manicoré** (*pop* 37,810) is a pleasant town; the Praça de Bandeira is at the corner of Av Getúlio Vargas and Av Pedro Tinoco (one block to left of road that goes up from the dock). **E** *Hotel Silviani*, 4 blocks left from Praça on Av Vargas, just before the big church; *Restaurant Tapuia*, 1 block from Praça in opp direction to river on Av Tinoco; slow but good restaurant at floating dock. Fruit market on Av Vargas.

THE BR-364

A result of the paving of BR-364 is the development of farms and towns along it; cattle ranches can be seen all along the road, with least population density in the S between Pimenta Bueno and Vilhena. From Porto Velho S, the towns are: **Ariquemes** (202 km from Porto Velho; *pop* 65,899; *CEP* 78930; *DDD* 069; buses hourly from 0600, 3-4 hrs, Banco do Brasil); Nova Vida (200 km), Jaru (257 km), Ouro Preto d'Oeste (297 km).

● **Accommodation Ariquemes**: **E** *Valérius Palace*, Av T Neves 3113, T 535-3311, *Ariquemes*, Av Cap Sílvio 1141, T 535-2200, a/c, fridge, parking. About 250 km S of Porto Velho it is possible to stay on a working *fazenda*, the *Rain Forest Lodge Rancho Grande* at Caixa Postal 361, Ariquemes, Rondônia 78. 914, F (069) 535-4301 (reservations and tours can be arranged through Focus Tours, Belo Horizonte). Not cheap but rec, esp for butterfly lovers. About 450 bird species and numerous mammals can be seen on the 20 km of trails. Harald Schmitz speaks English, German and Spanish, highly rec.

Ji Paraná (376 km; *pop* 106,457; *DDD* 069; *CEP* 78960; bus to Porto Velho, US$23, 16 hrs; to Cuiabá, 15 hrs, US$47), on the shores of the Rio Machado. It is a pleasant town with a small riverside promenade, which has several bars, lively at night; there is swimming at the river, beware of the current; a telegraph museum is on Av Marechal Rondon.

● **Accommodation A2** *Transcontinental*, R J Guerra 258, centre, T 422-1212, F 422-2064, a/c, TV, fridge, restaurant, pool, overlooking the river, rec; **A3** *Vitória Regia*, R Júlio Guerra 172, centre, T 422-1432, a/c, fridge, TV, parking, view of the river; **B** *Plaza*, R Martins Costa 336, across the bridge from the centre, T 422-2524, a/c, fridge, TV, parking; **D** *Nova Era*, Av Marechal Rondon 1845, 2 blocks from the rodoviária, with bath, a/c, TV, cheaper with fan, parking, good value, rec; **E** *Sol Nascente*, R Dr Osvaldo 101, accross the bridge from the centre, T 421-1997, with *churrascaria*; *Casablanca*, R Padre Rohl 465, centre, T 421-5894, with bath, a/c, fridge, TV, cheaper with fan; cheap hotels in front of rodoviária are filthy – not rec.

Further SE are **Cacoal** (481 km; *pop* 74,691; *DDD* 069; *CEP* 78975), **Pimenta Bueno** (440 km; *pop* 50,000), with a gasoline station, rodoviária (both with hotels), and **Vilhena** on the Rondônia-Mato

Grosso border (*pop* 41,452; *DDD* 069; *CEP* 78995), 704 km from Porto Velho (bus US$42, 11 hrs); 752 km from Cuiabá (bus US$34, 11 hrs), a good place to break the Cuiabá-Porto Velho trip.

● **Accommodation Vilhena**: hotels in the centre, **A2** *Mirage*, Av Mcal Amarantes 3536, T/F 321-2166, a/c, TV, fridge, parking, pool, on the main commercial street; **C** *Comodoro*, Av Cap Castro 3663, T/F 321-1244. In Nova Vilhena ('Circular' bus to the centre), nr the rodoviária, are: **A3** *Diplomata*, R Francisco Tildre 63, T 321-3173, F 321-3233, a/c, fridge, TV, pool; **B** *Santa Rosa Palace*, R Dal Toé 191, T 321-3900, a/c, fridge, TV, parking, **C** with fan; **D** *Vitória*, at No 117, T 321-3918, with fan, cheaper with shared bath, parking; on Av Sabino Bezerra de Queiroz are: **B** *Campinense*, No 5227, T/F 321-3156, fan, parking, **E** with shared bath, good value, rec; **B** *Nacional*, No 5363, T 321-3952, a/c, TV, fridge, **C** with fan, parking; **C** *Rover Pálace*, No 5423, T/F 321-2253, with fan, TV, parking, simpler rooms D; **D** *Luz*, No 5341, T/F 321-1825, with fan, parking, good value; **D** *Rodoviário*, No 5537, T 321-3785, with fan, **E** with shared bath, basic, run down. Restaurants, on Av Sabino Bezerra de Queiroz by the rodoviária are *Tókio*, at No 5489 for oriental food and *Bom Papão II*, No 5261, good *comida caseira*.

At the Mato Grosso state border proof of yellow-fever inoculation is required: if no proof, new shot.

PACAÁS NOVOS NATIONAL PARK

The **Pacaás Novos National Park**, 765,800 ha, lies W of the BR-364; it is a transitional zone between open plain and Amazonian forest. Details from Ibama, T (069) 223-2599/3597, Porto Velho; also enquire here about the Jaru Biological Reserve in the E of the State.

On the Rio Guaporé is the Guaporé Biological Reserve, in which is the Forte Príncipe da Beira, begun in 1777 as a defence of the border with Bolivia. The fort, which is being restored, can be reached from Costa Marques (20 km by road), which is some 345 km by unpaved road W of **Rolim de Moura**. This unplanned town (*pop* 110,000) has several hotels, including **B** *Transcontinental*; it is 40 km W of Pimenta Bueno.

THE MADEIRA-MAMORÉ RAILWAY

Porto Velho was the terminus of the Madeira-Mamoré railway of 367 km (closed 1971), Brazil's price to Bolivia for annexing the Acre territory in the rubber boom. During construction, it cost a life for every 100 sleepers, 6,208 in all, earning it the nickname 'the devil's railroad'. The line, built 1907-12, by-passed the 19 rapids of the Madeira and Mamoré rivers, and gave Bolivia an outlet of sorts to the Atlantic. It was supposed to go as far as Riberalta, on the Rio Beni, above that river's rapids, but stopped short at Guajará Mirim. It still runs the 16 km from Porto Velho, past the Madeira river rapids at Santo Antônio, to Bananeiras. Woodburning steam trains, built in 1925 in Philadelphia, use a narrow-gauge track. The line works all week but tourist excursions are on Sun only, departures at 0800, 1115 and 1430, returning at 0915, 1500 and 1600, US$3 return, crowded with people going to bathe at the falls during the dry season – good fun; there are dolphins at Santo Antônio. The roundhouse, recently restored, has two other antique locomotives on display, Mr Johnson at the station speaks English.

GUAJARA MIRIM

From Porto Velho, the paved BR-364 continues 220 km SW to **Abunã** (**E** *Hotel Thalita*; **E** *Dormitório Oliviera*), where the BR-425 branches S to Guajará Mirim. 9 km E of Abunã is a ferry crossing over the Rio Madeira, where it receives the waters of the Rio Abunã. The BR-425 is a fair road, partly paved, which uses the former rail bridges (in poor condition). It is sometimes closed Mar-May. Across the Mamoré from Guajará Mirim is the Bolivian town of Guayaramerín, which is connected by road to Riberalta, from where there are air services to other Bolivian cities. **Guajará Mirim** (*Pop* 32,530; *DDD* 069) is a charming town. The **Museu Municipal** is at the old Guajará Mirim railway station beside the ferry landing; interesting and diverse, highly rec. An ancient stern wheeler plies on the Guaporé; 26-day, 1,250 km trips (return) can be made on the Guaporé from Guajará Mirim to

Vila Bela (see page 642) in Mato Grosso, fare includes food.

● **Accommodation** **B** *Jamaica*, A Leopoldo de Matos 755, T 541-3721, F 541-2007, a/c, fridge, parking; **B** *Lima Palace*, Av 15 de Novembro 1613, T 541-3521, F 541-2122, a/c, fridge, parking; *Central Palace*, Av Marechal Deodoro 1150, T 541-2610, rec; **C** *Mini-Estrela*, Av 15 de Novembro 460, T 541-2399, a/c, parking; **D** *Chile*, Av Q Bocaiuva, good value, inc breakfast, rec; **E** *Fénix Palace*, Av 15 de Novembro 459, T 541-2326, higly rec; **E** *Mamoré*, R M Moraes, T 541-3753, clean, friendly. **Youth hostel**: Av 15 de Novembro, Centro Deportivo Afonso Rodrigues, T 541-3732. There is a basic *dormitório*, **E**, opp rodoviária.

● **Places to eat** Best is *Oasis*, Av 15 de Novembro 464, rec (on main dishes 10% service charge is added); *Lanchonates*, self-service, good value, rec.

● **Banks & money changers** Banco do Brasil (foreign exchange am only). *Loja Nogueira*, Av Pres Dutra, esq Leopoldo de Matos (cash only). There is no market in Brazil for bolivianos.

● **Post & telecommunications** Post Office: on Av Pres Dutra. **Telephone**: office on Av B Ménzies 751.

● **Transport** Buses from Porto Velho to Guajará Mirim, 5½ hrs or more depending on season, 8 a day with Viação Rondônia, US$18. Taxi from Porto Velho rodoviária, US$25 pp for 4-5, 3 hrs, leaves when full.

FRONTIER WITH BOLIVIA

● **Brazilian immigration**
Brazilian exit/entry stamps from Polícia Federal, Av Pres Dutra 70, corner of Av Q Bocaiuva, T 541-2437.

● **Bolivian consulate**
Av C Marquês 495, T 541-2862, Guajará Mirim; visas are given here.

● **Transport**
Speedboat across the Mamoré River (border), US$1.50, 5-min crossing, operates all day, tickets at waterside; ferry crossing for vehicles, T 541-3811, Mon-Sat 0800-1200, Mon-Fri 1400-1600, 20-min crossing.

ACRE

NB Rio Branco time is 1 hr behind Porto Velho and Manaus time; this means 2 hrs behind Brazilian Standard Time.

This intriguing state, rich in natural beauty, history and the *seringueiro* culture, is still very much off the beaten track. The area is beginning to develop its considerable tourist potential for adventure tourism and historians as links are opened up with neighbouring Peru and Bolivia.

RIO BRANCO

From Abunã, the BR-364 continues W in excellent condition, 315 km to **Rio Branco** (*pop* 195,943; *CEP* 69900; *DDD* 068) the capital of the State of Acre (*pop* 417,440). During the rubber boom of the late 19th Century, many *Nordestinos*, migrated to the western frontier in search of fortune. As a result, the unpopulated Bolivian territory of Acre was gradually taken over by Brazil and formally annexed in the first decade of the 20th century. In compensation, Bolivia received the Madeira-Mamoré railroad, as described above. In 1913, Rio Branco became capital of the new Território Federal do Acre, which attained statehood in 1962. The main industries remain rubber and *castanha* (Brazil nut) extraction, but timber and ranching are becoming increasingly important and improved road access is putting the state's tropical forests at considerable risk. Despite improved air and road links, Rio Branco remains at the 'end of the line', a frontier outpost whose depressed economy, high unemployment and prevalent drug-running make the city unsafe at night, and some caution is advised at all hours.

Places of interest

The Rio Acre is navigable upstream as far as the Peru and Bolivia borders. It divides the city into 2 districts called Primeiro (W) and Segundo (E), on either side of the river. In the central, Primeiro district are **Praça Plácido de Castro**, the shady main square; the **Cathedral**, NS de Nazaré, along Av Brasil; the neoclassical **Palácio Rio Branco** on R Benjamin Constant, across from Praça Eurico Gaspar Dutra. Two bridges link the districts. In the Segundo district is the **Calçadão da Gameleira**, a pleasant promenade along the shore, with plaques and an old tree marking the location of the original settlement. The airport and rodoviária are in the Segundo district. There are several large parks in the city; the **Horto Forestal**, popular with joggers, in Vila Ivonete (1° distrito), 3 km N of the centre ('Conjunto Procon' or 'Vila Ivonete' city-buses), has native amazonian trees, a small lake, walking paths and picnic areas; the **Parque Zoo-Botânico**, on the UFAC campus (1° distrito), is 5 km from the centre, along BR-364.

Museums

Museu da Borracha (Rubber Museum), Av Ceará 1177, Mon-Fri 0900-1800, Sat-Sun 1600-2000, in a lovely old house with a tiled façade, has information about the rubber boom, archaeological artefacts, a section about Acreano Indians, documents and memorabilia from the annexation and a display about the Santo Daime doctrine (see excursions below), rec. **Casa do Seringueiro**, Av Brasil 216, corner of Av Getúlio Vargas, has a good exhibit on rubber tappers and on Chico Mendes in particular; the Sala Hélio Melo has a display of Melo's paintings, mainly on the theme of the forest.

Excursions

8 km SE of town, upriver along the Rio Acre is **Lago do Amapá**, a U-shaped lake good for boating and watersports; access is by river or by land via route AC-40. 2 km beyond along the AC-40 is **Praia do Amapá**, a bathing beach on the Rio Acre; there is an annual arts festival here in September. Excursions can be made to **rubber plantations** and rubber extraction areas in native forest (*seringais nativos*). 13 km from Rio Branco is **Colônia Cinco Mil** (access along AC-10), a religious centre of the followers of the Santo Daime doctrine: its members (many originally from outside Acre and Brazil) live a communal life, working in agriculture and producing crafts made of latex; the religion centers around the use of *Ayahuasca*, a hallucinogenic potion adopted from local Indians. Visitors are usually welcome, but enquire beforehand.

Local information
● Accommodation

There are few economical hotels in the centre, but a reasonable selection of these by the rodoviária.

In 1° distrito (W bank): **L3** *Pinheiro Palace*, Rui Barbosa 91, T 224-7191, F 224-5726, a/c,

pool, rec; **A2** *Inácio Palace*, R Rui Barbosa 72, T 224-6397, F 224-5726, fridge, TV, overpriced, fair restaurant; **A3** *Rio Branco*, R Rui Barbosa 193, T 224-1785, F 224-2681, by Praça Plácido de Castro, a/c, fridge, TV, nice but simple.

B *Triângulo*, R Floriano Peixoto 727, T 224-9265, a/c, TV, fridge, restaurant; **C** *Albemar*, R Franco Ribeiro 99, T 224-1938, a/c, fridge, good breakfast, good value, rec.

D *Xapurí*, Nações Unidas 187, T 225-7268, shared bath, fan, basic, 15 mins' walk from centre.

In 2° distrito (E bank), **in Cidade Nova by the rodoviária**: **A3** *Rodoviária*, R Palmeiral 268, T 224-4434, a/c, fridge TV, D with shared bath, fan, good value; **C** *Skina*, Uirapuru 533, T 224-0087, a/c, fridge, TV, fan; **D** *Nacional*, R Palmeiral 496, T 224-4822, fan, both cheaper with shared bath.

Youth hostel: Fronteira Verde, Trav Natanael de Albuquerque, 2° distrito, T225-7128.

● Places to eat

Kaxinawa, Av Brasil at corner of Praça Plácido de Castro, best in town for Acreano regional food; *Pizzaria Tutti Frutti*, Av Ceará 1132, accross from Museu da Borracha, pizzas, ice cream, not cheap; *Casarão*, Av Brasil 310, next to telephone office, good food and drink; *Churrascaria Triângulo*, R Floriano Peixoto 727, as much charcoal-grilled meat as you can eat, rec; *Remanso do Tucunaré*, R José de Melo 481, Bairro Bosque, fish specialties; *Anexos*, R Franco Ribeiro 99, next door to *Albemar Hotel*, popular for meals and drinks. A local delicacy is *tacacá*, a soup served piping hot in a gourd (*cuia*), it combines manioc starch (*goma*), cooked *jambú* leaves which numb the mouth and tongue, shrimp, spices and hot pepper sauce; rec from Sra Diamor, Boulevar Augusto Monteiro 1046, Bairro 15 in the 2° distrito (Bus Norte-Sul from the centre), other kiosks in town, ask around. For ice cream *Sorveteria Arte Sabor*, Travessa Santa Inés 28, corner Aviario, 1° distrito, 15 mins' walk from the centre, excellent home made ice cream, many jungle fruit flavours, highly rec; *Sorvete & Cia*, Av Brasil 394, ice cream by kilo and fix it yourself hot dogs.

● Post & telecommunications

Post Office: on corner of R Epaminondas Jacome and Av Getúlio Vargas.

Telephone: Teleacre, Av Brasil between Mal Deodoro and Av Getúlio Vargas, long delays for international calls.

● Shopping

Market: 1° distrito, off R Epaminondas Jacome.

● Tour companies & travel agents

Nilce's Tour, R Quintino Bocaiúva 20, T/F 223-

2611, for airline tickets, helpful, 15 mins' walk from the centre; *Serra's Tur*, R S Coelho 372, T 224-4629; *Inácio's Tur*, R Rui Barbosa 91, at *Hotel Pinheiro*.

● **Tourist offices**

DETUR/AC, Departamento de Turismo, Av Getúlio Vargas 659, Centro, T 224-3997, ramal 20, part of the Acre Secretaria de Indústria e Comércio.

● **Transport**

Local Car hire: prices for car rentals with the nationwide agencies are higher in Acre than in other states; **Interlocadora**, Rodovia AC-40, Km 0, 2° distrito, T 224-7041; **Localiza**, T 224-7746; **Unidas**, T 224-5044.

Air The airport is on AC-40, Km 1.2, in the 2° distrito. Taxi from the airport to the centre US$20 flat rate, but going to the airport the meter is used, which usually comes to less. By bus, take 'Norte-Sul' or 'Vila Acre'. Flights with Varig daily to **Porto Velho**, Manaus, Brasília, São Paulo, Cuiabá and Campo Grande; once a week to **Cruzeiro do Sul**. Ote Redes Aéreas T 223-2390 (airport), 224-2830 (manager, Pasco at home), operates a twin engine Bandeirante with capacity for 18, to **Puerto Maldonado**, Peru, irregular departures (1-3/week), US$100 (payable in US$ cash or *reais*), a 1 hr interesting flight over the jungle; Puerto Maldonado office, González Prada 360, T 571-656; the Polícia Federal are at the airport for exit/entry stamps when these international flights operate. Airport tax is US$6.

Buses Rodoviária on Av Uirapuru, Cidade Nova, 2° distrito (E bank); city bus 'Norte-Sul' to the centre. To **Porto Velho**, Viação Rondônia, 5 daily, 8 hrs, US$19. To **Guajará Mirim**, daily with Rondônia at 1130 and 2200, 5-6 hrs, US$17; or take *Inácio's Tur* shopping trip, 3/week. To **Brasiléia** with Acreana, daily at 0600, 1115 and 1300, 5 hrs in the wet season, faster in the dry, US$17, continuing to **Assis Brasil** in the dry season only.

ROUTES From Rio Branco the BR-364 continues W (in principle) to Cruzeiro do Sul and Japim, with a view to reaching the Peruvian frontier further W when completed; it is hoped that it will be continued by the Peruvians to Pucallpa. It is very difficult to get from Rio Branco to Cruzeiro do Sul by road because there is no bus service, and the occasional truck goes mainly in the dry season; the road is frequently impassable (it is open, on average, 20 days a year).

WEST OF RIO BRANCO: CRUZEIRO DO SUL

(Pop 66,600) An isolated Amazonian town on the Rio Juruá in western Acre; cheap excursions can be made on the river, for example to the village of Rodrigues Alves (2-3 hrs, return by boat or by road, 15 km). In the jungle one can see rubber-tapping, and collecting the latex into 'borrachas' which weigh up to 45 kg.

● **Accommodation & places to eat D** *Savonne*, next to cathedral, rec; **E** *Novo do Acre*, rec, a/c; **E** *Flor de Maio*, facing river, showers, full board available. Several other hotels and restaurants.

● **Banks & money changers** Money changing is very difficult.

● **Transport Air** Besides the scheduled Varig flight to Rio Branco, air taxis go to Rio Branco (Tavaj) and Pucallpa (Tasa). In rainy season, **river** transport to Manaus is possible.

FRONTIER WITH PERU AND BOLIVIA

The BR-317 from Rio Branco heads S and later SW, parallel to the Rio Acre; it is paved as far as **Xapuri** (the location of the Fundação Chico Mendes in memory of the environmentalist and union organizer murdered in 1989); one very basic lodging and two restaurants. The road continues to **Brasiléia** (three buses daily to Rio Branco, 5 hrs in the wet, US$17, three hotels, two basic lodgings, several restaurants, Polícia Federal give entry/exit stamps), opposite the Bolivian town of Cobija on the Rio Acre. It is possible to stay in Epitaciolândia (**D** *Hotel Kanda*, 5 mins walk from police post) and cross border into Bolivia early in the morning. Road ends at Assis Brasil where the Peruvian, Bolivian and Brazilian frontiers meet. Across the Rio Acre are Iñapari (Peru), border crossing difficult, even out of wet season, and Bolpebra, Bolivia. Bus service operates only in the dry season beyond Brasiléia to Assis Brasil, access in the wet season is by river. In **Assis Brasil**, there are two hotels (one basic but clean, friendly, E), two restaurants, some shops, a bank which does not change US dollars (the hotel owner may be persuaded to oblige). You get between Iñapari and Assis Brasil by wading across the river. **NB** There is no Polícia Federal in the village, get entry/exit stamps in Brasiléia.

The Centre-west

T HE so-called Centre-West (*Centro-Oeste*) of Brazil, occupied by the states of Goiás, Mato Grosso and Mato Grosso do Sul (divided from Mato Grosso in 1977), was the most isolated part of the nation until President Vargas' 'Drive to the West' in the 1940s (when many of the Xingu Indian tribes were first contacted).

Today Goiás, with an area of 364,714 sq km and 4,024,550 inhabitants, is one of Brazil's most rapidly-developing frontier agricultural areas, producing coffee, soya and rice, most of Brazil's tin and tungsten, and raising beef on the country's largest cattle ranches. The Federal District of Brasília was subtracted from its territory in 1960, which was further split in half in 1990 to form the new state of Tocantins in the N (see page 617). Old colonial mining towns in the state sprang from gold rushes which began in 1722, as Paulistas and Bandeirantes pushed out from Minas Gerais in search of precious stones and new mineral wealth. The eroded Brazilian Plateau, clothed in woodland savannah and varying from 600m to 900m in height, ripples across the S of the state; most of its rivers flow N to feed the Araguaia and Tocantins rivers. Elsewhere, the climate is sub-tropical, with distinct wet and dry seasons.

GOIÂNIA

(*Pop* 920,840; *CEP* 74000; *DDD* 062) Just off the BR-060, 209 km SW of Brasília: the second (after Belo Horizonte) of Brazil's planned state capitals, Goiânia was founded in 1933 and replaced Goiás Velho as capital 4 years later. In general, commercial and industrial sectors are to the N, with administration in the centre and residential zones to the south.

Places of interest

The unremarkable **Metropolitan Cathedral**, corner Ruas 14 e 19, stands two blocks E of the Praça. Walk due N on broad Av Goiás to see the painted walls of the **Projeto Galeria Aberta**; many city buses are also painted with eye-catching designs.

It is a spacious city, with many green spaces and well-lit main avenues, ornamented with plants, radiating out from the central **Praça Cívica**, on which stand the Government Palace and main Post Office. 1½ km out along the Av Araguaia (which runs diagonally NE from the Praça) is the shady **Parque Mutirama**, with recreational and entertainment facilities and a planetarium (Sun sessions at 1530 and 1630); there is also a pleasant **Parque Zoológico**, Av Anhangüera, some distance W of the main square, with good zoo, zoological museum, playground, lake and sports fields (park open Tues-Sun 0900-1830).

Museums

Museu Antropológico do UFG on the Praça Universitária (1 km E of Praça Cívica) with wide-ranging ethnographic displays on the Indians of the Centre-West (Mon-Fri 0900-1700), **Museu de Ornitologia**, Av Pará 395 (Sétor Campinas), with more than 8000 stuffed birds and animals from many countries (open 0900-1900, except Mon). Just off the Praça Cívica is the **Museu Estadual 'Zoroastro Artiaga'**, Praça Dr P L Teixeira 13, with a collection of local handicrafts, religious objects, animals and Indian artefacts.

Excursions

To the thermal springs at Cachoeira Dourada (240 km S on the Paranaíba

River), the fantastic rock formations of the Serra das Galés at **Paraúna** (160 km SSW off BR-060) and a host of delightful, colonial mining villages within 2 hrs' drive on good (often paved) roads. Travel agents in town can arrange day tours, eg *Turisplan Turismo*, R 8 No 388, T 224-1941 (which also sells regular bus tickets).

Local information
● Accommodation
Av Anhangüera, on which many hotels are located, runs E-W 4 blocks N of the Central Plaza; it is busy and noisy.

L3 *Castro's Park*, Av Rep do Líbano 1520, Setor Ote, T 223-7766, F 225-7070, warmly rec.

A1 *Papillon*, Rep do Líbano 1824, T 223-8511, F 223-8381, good; *Umuarama*, R 4 No 492, T 224-1555, F 224-1673, good; **A3** *Cabiúna Palace*, Av Parnaíba 698 (close to Parque Mutirama), T/F 224-4355, good value; **A3** *Karajás*, Av Goiás e R 3, T 224-9666, F 229-1153, 3 blocks N of Praça, convenient and comfortable.

B *Augustus*, Praça Antônio Lizita 702, T 224-1022, F 224-1410, good; **B** *Vila Rica*, Anhangüera 3456, T 224-0500, F 225-0551, 2-star Embratur hotel, a/c, convenient.

Cheaper (**C-D**) are: *Príncipe*, Anhangüera 2936 e Av Araguaia, T 224-0085, fans, good value; *Paissandú*, Av Goiás 1290 e R 55, T 224-4925, fans, 6 long blocks N from Praça; *Hotel del Rey*, R 8 No 321, T 225-6306, good location on pedestrian mall, fans, good value; *Rodoviária*, opp bus station, safe, cheap, good.

Several cheap hotels (**D-E**) nr the rodoviária: eg *Star*, R 68 No 537, basic, interesting clientele; *Itaipú*, R 29A No 178 at the old rodoviária (Setor Aeroporto), T 212-4055; *J Alves*, opp rodoviária. Northwest of the rodoviária are many cheap *dormitórios*.

Camping: at *Itanhangá* municipal site, Av Princesa Carolina, 13 km, attractive wooded location, reasonable facilities, US$5.50 pp.

● Places to eat
Goiânia is much cheaper for eating than Brasília, and the variety of eating places is too wide to list here. Many *churrascarias*, eg *Boi na Brasa*, on Praça Germano Roriz (the first large square due S of Praça Cívica on R 84), open 1100-0100, and the more expensive *Lancaster Grill*, R 89 No 117, a/c, live music; *Le Steak*, Av 85 No 352, excellent, a/c, good atmosphere, expensive by Brazilian standards; *Fim de Tarde*, Av 85 No 301, good meat dishes (inc *picanha* and *kibe*, Arabic appetizer) and beer, open from 1700; *Costeleria do Marcão*, Av 31 de Março, past Praça do Cruzeiro, best ribs in Goiás, rec, open

from 1700; *Bom Gourmet*, Av 85 No 1676, for meat and chicken dishes, very good, seats on street or in a/c room. Varied menu at *Cliff Piano Bar e Restaurante*, R 23 No 72, esq Av Rep do Líbano, expensive, nice atmosphere, highly rec. *Palatinum*, in *Hotel Augustus*, Italian, very good, elegant, a/c, piano music. Good array of restaurants and watering holes around the Praça Tamandaré (Ruas 8 e 5, just beyond the Bosque dos Buritis, 1 km W of Praça Cívica), including *Modiglianni* for good pizzas.

Vegetarian: *Arroz Integral*, R 93 No 326 (1100-1400, 1800-2100, self-service), or *Naturalmente Natural*, R 15 No 238, 1 block from the cathedral. Many small eating places nr the rodoviária, which also has good food at low prices.

For **regional specialities** try the *Centro de Tradições Goiánas*, R 4 No 515 (above the Parthenon Centre), rice and fish cuisine. *Piquiras*, Av Rep do Líbano 1758 (nr *Castro's Hotel*) and R 139 s/n, Setor Marista, try the appetizer *pastelzinho de piquí* (a regional fruit used in many traditional Goiás dishes). Street stands (*pamonharias*) sell *pamonha* snacks, tasty pastries made with green corn, sweet, savoury, or *picante*/spicy; all are served hot and have cheese in the middle, some include sausage. Rec are: *Pomonharia 100*, R 101 esq R Dr Olinto Manso Pereira, behind the Forum, Setor Sul; *Frutos da Terra*, Av Perimetral 669, for home delivery T 233-1507/281-4049; *Pura*, Av 83 No 193, Setor Sul. Local meat pies (*empadões de Goiás*) are also delicious.

Bars and dancing: Goiânia is famous for its street bars, some with live music. *People Club* and *Académia da Birita*, R 7 No 1000, Secrote Ote, dance club, bar and restaurant, very popular, Thu, Fri, Sat pm; *Cave Bar*, Av 85, Caravelo Center, entrance through back of Center, access by narrow R 85C, on left, small pub, nice drinks and decor, foreign owner Gisela, good soft music; *Café Madrid*, R 101, No 353, Setor Sul, behind the Forum, a/c, bar and restaurant, best *paella* in Goiânia, famous for *margaritas*, live music (MPB, saxophone groups), open daily from 2100. Av Ricardo Paranhos, Setor Sul, is full of bars and crowds of young people after 2000.

● Banks & money changers
National banks. Travel agents will exchange cash, poor rates for TCs.

● Shopping
Ceramic, sisal and wooden handicrafts from *Centro Estadual do Artesanato*, Praça do Trabalhador (0800-1800); Sun handicrafts markets at the Praça Cívica (am) and Praça do Sol (pm). The latter starts after 1530, until 2100, known as the Honey Fair as all types of honey are sold; also good for a Sun snack, with many sweets and tarts sold along the street. Two

shopping centres: *Flamboyant*, the largest, is some way from the centre (take a bus); *Bougainville*, nr R 9, Setor Marista, newer; both have cinemas, snack bars.

● **Sports**

Many sporting facilities throughout Goiânia, visitors welcome; for sunbathing, swimming and water skiing go to the Jaó Club (T 261-2122), on reservoir nr the city.

● **Tourist offices**

Goiastur, the state tourist agency, on 3rd floor of Serra Dourada football stadium in Jardim Goiás; friendly staff but remote and difficult to get to. Extensive information, maps and bus routes in *Novo Guía Turístico de Goiás*, readily available at news stands, US$2.25.

● **Useful addresses**

Immigration Office: R 235, Setor Universitário.

● **Transport**

Air Santa Genoveva, 6 km NE off R 57 (T 207-1288). Daily flights to main cities and many provincial centres. Several car hire firms at the airport. Taxi from centre US$6. Varig, Av Goiás 285, T 224-5040; Vasp, R 3 No 569, T 223-4266.

Buses Huge new rodoviária on R 44 No 399 in the Norte Ferroviário sector, about a 40-min walk to downtown (T 224-8466). Buses 'Rodoviária-Centro' (No 404) and 'Vila União-Centro' (No 163) leave from stop on city side of terminal, US$0.80; No 163 goes on to the Praça Tamandaré. To **Brasília**, 207 km, part divided freeway, at least 15 departures a day, 2½ hrs, US$7.80, and **São Paulo**, 900 km via Barretos, US$36, 14½ hrs, *leito* services at night. To **Goiás Velho**, 136 km, hourly from 0500, 2½ hrs, US$7.20; **Campo Grande**, 935 km, 4 services daily, 18 hrs, US$38-39. Pirenópolis 0700 and 1700, 2 hrs, US$7.50. To **Cuiabá** (Mato Grosso), 916 km on BR-158/070 via Barra do Garças, or 928 km on BR-060/364 via Jataí (both routes paved, most buses use the latter route), 4 buses a day, US$30, 15-16 hrs, continuing to Porto Velho (Rondônia) and Rio Branco (Acre) – a very trying journey indeed. At Iporá, 200 km W of Goiânia on BR-158, there is a good hotel. At **Rio Verde** (*pop* 95,895), on the BR-060 some 240 km W of Goiânia, are several possible hotel stops on the way to Cuiabá, **D** *Rio Verde Palace*, R Gusmão 599, and **D** *Vitória*, Praça 5 de Agosto, a/c, are the best of a poor lot.

ANÁPOLIS

(*Pop* 239,050; *CEP* 77100; *DDD* 062) A busy trading centre 57 km nearer Brasília; accommodation is cheaper than the capital and more convenient than Goiânia. The **Centro de Gemologia de Goiás**, Quadra 2, Módulo 13, Daia, about 10 km

out on the Brasília highway (near the Embratel tower), has a fine collection of gemstones, library, sales and valuation courses, will show visitors how real and synthetic gemstones are distinguished, open Mon-Fri 0730-1630.

● **Accommodation** **B** *Estância Park*, in parkland setting 6 km NE, T 324-7624, F 324-1226, pool, tennis, minizoo, etc, best in town; *Príncipe*, R Eng Portela 165, T 324-0611, F 324-0936, and *Itamaraty*, R Manoel d'Abadia 209, T 324-4812, both **C** and comfortable. Many cheap ones around the rodoviária (Av Brasil-Norte), eg **D** *Serra Dourada*, Av Brasil 375, T 324-0051, restaurant, parking, fans, good value. *Restaurante Caiçara*, 14 de Julho 905, serves good *churrascos*.

● **Transport** At Anápolis the BR-153 (Brasília-Belém) turns N and begins the long haul (1964 km) through Tocantins, Maranhão and Pará to Belém, a bumpy, monotonous trip of 35 hrs or more, US$60. There are regular bus services to Pirenópolis (66 km N).

GOIÁS VELHO

(*Pop* 27,780) The former state capital, 144 km NW of Goiânia, is a picturesque old gold-mining town (founded 1727 as Vila Boa) with narrow streets, seven baroque churches and many well-preserved 18th-century colonial mansions and government buildings.

Places of interest

The oldest church, **São Francisco de Paula** (1761), Praça Alves de Castro facing the Market, is undergoing restoration. There is a good view of the town from **Santa Bárbara** church (1780) on the R Passo da Pátria. Also worth visiting are: the **Museu da Boa Morte**, in the colonial church of the same name (a small, but interesting collection of old images, paintings, etc). The **Museu das Bandeiras** is in the Casa da Câmara e Cadeia (old town hall and prison), by the colonial fountain. The old **Government Palace** is next to the red-brick Cathedral in the main square. The **Palácio Conde dos Arcos**, Praça Castelo Branco (across from the Cathedral), still has its original 1755 furniture on display (Tues-Sat 0800-1700, Sun 0800-1200). Most churches and museums are closed on Mon. The **Mercado Municipal** (18th century) is next to the rodoviária, $\frac{1}{2}$ km W of the central Praça do Coreto.

Local festivals

The streets of Goiás Velho blaze with torches during the solemn *Fogaréu* processions of Holy Week, when hooded figures re-enact Christ's descent from the cross and burial.

Local information

● **Accommodation**

B *Vila Boa*, 1 km SE on the Morro do Chapéu do Padre, T 371-1000, pool, bar, restaurant, a/c, good views, rec.

D *Araguaia*, Av Ferreira de Moura (the road into town from the S), T 371-1462, best budget place, fans, comfortable, rec; similar is the nearby *Serrano* (no phone), parking, bar.

Camping: attractive, well-run *Cachoeira Grande* campground, 7 km along the BR-070 to Jussara (nr the tiny airport), with bathing place and snack bar. More basic site (*Chafariz da Carioca*) in town by the river.

● **Places to eat**

Dona Maninha, R Dom Cândido, regional food, good value.

● **Shopping**

Centro de Tradições Goianas, in *Hotel Vila Boa*, and (cheaper) *Associação dos Artesãos de Goiás*, at the Rosário Church and in the Municipal Market, for local crafts; many types of sugary sweets can be purchased direct from the bakeries.

● **Transport**

Regular bus services to Goiânia (2½ hrs), Aruanã, Barra do Garças and Jussara.

PIRENÓPOLIS

This lovely colonial silver-mining town (*Pop* 25,010; *Alt* 770m) in the red hills of Goiás, 122 km due W of Brasília, was founded in the same year as Goiás Velho and declared a National Heritage Site in 1989; as the nation's unofficial silver capital, shopping for jewellery and related items here is unsurpassed.

Places of interest

The **Igreja Matriz NS do Rosário** is the oldest church in the state (1728), but that of **Nosso Senhor de Bonfim** (1750-54), with three impressive altars and an image of the Virgin brought from Portugal, is the most beautiful. A museum of religious art

is housed in the church of **NS de Carmo** (daily 1300-1700), and another displays regional historical items, the **Museu Família Pompeu** (R Mestre Propício 29, open only 1300-1500, not Mon). The **Theatro de Pyrenópolis** on R Com Joaquim Alves is a testament to turn-of-the-century optimism Pirenópolis was the birthplace of José Joaquim da Veiga Valle, the 'Aleijadinho of Goiás', many of whose works are in the Boa Morte museum in Goiás Velho. **Fazenda Babilônia**, 25 km SW by paved road, is a fine example of an 18th-century sugar *fazenda* now a small museum, original mill, no public transport.

Local festivals

Festa do Divino Espírito Santo, 45 days after Easter (Pentecost), is one of Brazil's most famous and extraordinary folkloric/religious celebrations, lasting 3 days, with medieval costumes, tournaments, dances and mock battles between Moors and Christians, a tradition held annually since 1819.

Local information

● **Accommodation**

A3 *Hotel Fazenda Quinta da Santa Bárbara*, in garden setting at R do Bonfim 1, T 331-1304, all facilities inc *Restaurante Brasília*; **A3** *Pousada dos Pirineus*, Chácara Mata do Sobrado, Bairro do Carmo, T 331-1345, a/c, TV, restaurant, bar, 2 pools, gym, tennis and other sports, boat hire.

C *Pousada das Cavalhadas*, Praça da Matriz, T 331-1261, central, fans, fridges in rooms, best of the budget choices.

More basic are: **D** *Rex*, also on the Praça da Matriz, T 331-1121, 9 sparse rooms, small restaurant; *Pousada Tavares*, *Pensão Central* and *Dormitório da Geny* are all **E** and mostly for the desperate. All accommodation is filled during the Festa (see above) and even the downtown municipal camping site beside the Rio das Alvas overflows; better to visit from Brasília at this time.

CALDAS NOVAS

(*Pop* 24,060; *CEP* 76940; *DDD* 062) 187 km SE of Goiânia, a thermal resort with good hotels and camp sites with hot swimming pools. There are three groups of springs within this area: Caldas Novas, Fontes de Pirapetinga (7 km from the town) and Rio Quente (29 km from the town, bus from Caldas Novas); water temperatures are 37-51°C.

● **Accommodation** 48 in all. Very fashionable is **L2** *Hotel Turismo* (5-star) – *Pousada do Rio Quente* (4-star) complex at Rio Quente, T 452-1122, F 452-1177, or F São Paulo 282-5281, T 852-5733, or Brasília 224-7166, breakfast and lunch, transportation to main pools and recreation facilities inc in price, other extras paid for with hotel's own currency, good hotel, accommodation in main buildings or chalets. (The *Turismo* has a private airstrip.) **L3** *Parque das Primaveras*, R do Balneário, T 453-1355, F 453-1294, rec by locals; **C** *Serra Dourada*, Av Correia Neto 574, T 453-1300, rec; **E** *Imperial*, nr Rodoviária, clean, friendly. **Camping**: at Esplanada, and *Camping Clube do Brasil* site on the Ipameri road, 1 km from the centre. Many other 'Clubes e Campings', all with snack bars, eg *Tropical*, 2 sites in town, and *Berro d'Água*, Bairro do Turista, rec.

● **Places to eat** *Caminho do Natural*, R José Borges 550 vegetarian, good, but expensive.

● **Transport** Many buses from Goiânia; best reached from Morrinhos on BR-153 (Goiânia-São Paulo). Daily bus from Morrinhos US$1, 30 mins.

CHAPADA DOS VEADEIROS

Goiás has two major National Parks. In the elevated region 200 km N of Brasília is popular **Chapada dos Veadeiros** (US$0.60 fee). The main attractions are a number of high waterfalls complete with palm-shaded oases and natural swimming pools, and the varied wildlife: capibara, rhea, tapir, wolf, toucan, etc (Ibama R 219 No 95, Setor Universitário, 74605-800 Goiânia, T 062-224-2488, or T 061-646-1109).

● **Access** The park is reached by paved state highway 118 to Alto Paraíso de Goiás, then gravel road W towards Colinas for 30 km where a sign marks the turnoff (just before the village of São Jorge). Buses Brasília-Alto Paraíso 1000 and 2200, US$6; occasional local buses Alto Paraíso-São Jorge, inc 1600 departure, 5-km walk to park entrance.

● **Accommodation** There is a small hotel (**E**) by the rodoviária in Alto Paraíso and a very basic *dormitório* in São Jorge (take sleeping bag or hammock), but camping in the park is the most pleasant option, about US$2/night and busy on weekends in the best visiting season (May-Oct).

EMAS NATIONAL PARK

In the far SW of the state, covering the watershed of the Araguaia, Taquari and Formoso Rivers, is the small **Emas National Park**, 110 km S of Mineiros (*pop* 33,600) just off the main BR-364 route between Brasília and Cuiabá (112 km beyond Jataí).

Douglas Trent of Focus Tours writes: "The near 132,868 ha of undulating grasslands and 'campo sujo' cerrado forests host the world's largest concentration of termite mounds. They provide a surreal setting for large numbers of pampas deer, giant anteater and greater rhea, or 'ema' in Portuguese. Maned wolf are frequently seen roaming the grasses in search of tinamou and other prey. The park holds the greatest concentration of blue-and-yellow macaws outside Amazônia, and blue-winged, red-shouldered and red-bellied macaws can also be seen. (There are many other animals and birds.) A pair of bare-faced currasow, white-woodpeckers, streamer-tailed tyrants and other showy birds visit the park HQ building daily.

Along with the grasslands, the park supports a vast marsh on one side and rich gallery forests on the other. The crystal clear waters of the Rio Formosa pass right by the headquarters and wander through the park. Many have compared this park with the African savannas. As many of the interesting mammals are nocturnal, a spotlight is a must."

● **Access** The park is most easily reached from Campo Grande (approx 6 hrs by car, compared with about 20 hrs from Goiânia, paved road poor). The road to the National Park is now paved; there is no regular transport but tour operators can organize 4WD trips. The São José monastery, Mineiros, can arrange the necessary permission to visit, turn left out of rodoviária and walk ½ km along dirt road (or from Ibama, as above, also from Secretaria de Turismo, Praça Cel Carrijo 1, T 661-1551). A 4-day, 3-night visit to the Park can be arranged through agencies (eg Focus Tours, Belo Horizonte, see page 431).

● **Accommodation In Mineiros**: are **C** *Pilões Palace*, Praça Alves de Assis, T 661-1547, restaurant, comfortable; and **D** *Boi na Brasa*, R Onze 11, T 661-1532, no a/c, good *churrasco* restaurant attached; next door **E** *Mineiros Hotel*, with bath and huge breakfast, good lunch, rec. Camping within the park costs about US$2 pp and there is simple, dormitory accommodation at the park headquarters; kitchen and cook available but bring own food.

THE RIO ARAGUAIA: WEST AND NORTH OF GOIÂNIA

Brazilians are firmly convinced that the 2,630-km-long Rio Araguaia is richer in fish than any other in the world; a visit to the 220-km stretch between Aruanã and the Ilha do Bananal during the fishing season is quite an experience. As the receding waters in May reveal sparkling white beaches, thousands of Brazilian and international enthusiasts pour into the area, intent on getting the best camping spots. As many as 400 tent 'cities' spring up, and vast quantities of fish are hauled in before the phenomenon winds down in Sept, when the rivers begin to rise again and flood the surrounding plains.

● **Access** Without Brazilian contacts, the traveller's best way of experiencing this annual event is with one of the specialist tour operators; rec are *Transworld*, R 3 No 560, Goiânia, T 224-4340 (one week group trips in a 'botel' out of Aruanã to Bananal), and *KR International Travel*, R Mexico 11-Gr 1701, Rio de Janeiro, T 210-1238, ex-Peace Corps manager, good for info on the Centre-West region. Boats (US$10-25 an hour) and guides can also be hired in Aruanã, Britânia, Barra do Garças or **Porto Luís Alves** (**A1** *Pousada do Jaburu*, including meals; **A3** *Pousada do Pescador*, a/c, access to boats and guides), guide Vandeir will arrange boat trips to see wildlife, take food and water. Interesting walks in surrounding jungle with Joel, ask at the hotel.

● **Health** Yellow-fever vaccination is rec for the region. *Borrachudos*, tiny biting insects, are an unavoidable fact of life in Central Brazil in June and July; repellent helps a little.

ARUANÃ

The Araguaia is most readily accessible from **Aruanã** (*pop* 5,400) a port 165 km NW of Goiás Velho by paved highway, which sees little excitement outside the winter fishing season (when its comfortable hotels are booked out for months). Boats can be rented to visit some of the beautiful lakes and beaches nearby. Buses from the rodoviária serve Araguapaz, Britânia and Goiânia. The Brazilian Canoeing Championships are also held along the river in July.

● **Accommodation & places to eat A2** *Recanto Sonhado*, on river at end of Av Altamiro Caio Pacheco (2 km), T 376-1230, self-service restaurant, boutique, inc lunch (reservations can be made through T 062-241-7913 in Goiânia); **C** *Araguaia*, Praça Couto Magalhães 53 (opp the docks), T 376-1251; both have pools, a/c, and meals available; restaurants in town rather poor, but try *Columbia*, R João Artiaga 221 (opp Municipal Stadium), clean, good menu. The official campground is a 20-min boat ride away on Ilha Redonda, but open (and full) only in July.

BARRA DO GARÇAS

A direct dirt road (250 km, via Jussara) and a more circuitous paved route through Iporá (340 km) connect Goiás Velho with Aragarças (on the Goiás side) and **Barra do Garças** (on the Mato Grosso side of the Araguaia). Barra (*pop* 45,600) is the pleasanter of the two and has the better facilities, including several banks and hotels. 6 km E of Barra on the road to Araguaiana is **Parque Balneário das Águas Quentes**, with thermal pools (42°C), river bathing and recreational opportunities. The abrupt 600m-high Morro do Cristo (10 km) gives a wide view over the Araguaia and surrounding country.

Local festivals A *Festival de Praia* is held locally in July: fishing tournaments, displays, boat races, etc.

● **Accommodation** In Barra do Garças: **C** *Esplanada Palace*, R Waldir Rabelo 81, T 861-2515, a/c, safe parking; various **D-E** hotels along Av Min João Alberto, eg *Novo Mundo*, *Presidente* and *Avenida*, all clean and a/c. *Churrascarías* also on this avenue and nr the bridge (eg *Del Fronteyra*, live music, 1100-1400, 1900-2200); pleasant river beach with bars and snacks; campsite on island in river; nighttime entertainment by the port. In Aragarças: (4 km) is the new **A1** *Hotel Toriuá Park*, T 861-2232, pool, minizoo, own launch, lakeside location rec.

● **Transport** Buses to Barra to/from São Paulo direct, 20 hrs, US$30; to São Felix do Araguaia at 2000, US$24, arrives early afternoon, wildlife may be seen in early am.

ROUTES If heading for the Pantanal, note that BR-070 from Barra to Cuiabá is in poor condition after the turn to Poxoréo; better to go to Rondonópolis, either for Cuiabá or Campo Grande.

The road N to Marabá (BR-158), paralleling the Araguaia on the Mato Grosso and Pará side, leaves Barra do Garças and runs 140 km to **Xavantina** (*pop* 13,000) on the Rio das Mortes, the famous 'River of Deaths' which once marked the territorial boundary of the intractable Xavante Indians. The road is paved for a further 310 km to Alô Brasil, then marginal dirt (465 km) to beyond the Pará state border; it is again paved for the remaining 650 km to Marabá via Redenção and Xinguara (see below).

● **Accommodation** (on BR-158, in Mato Grosso): At **Xavantina**: is **E** *Hotel Xavantina*, basic but nothing better; *Churrascaria Arca de Noé*, highly rec. At **Água Boa** (*pop* 16,570), 76 km N of Xavantina, are **C** *Palace* and *Manga Rosa*, good churrascaria.

On the other (E) side of the Araguaia, the Brasília-Belém highway (BR-153) runs N through the heart of Goiás and Tocantins states.

TOCANTINS

The new state of Tocantins (277,321.9 sq km; *pop* 920,135) is technically an Amazonian state, the boundary of the Norte region running along the border between it and Goiás.

TOWNS IN TOCANTINS

Miracema do Tocantins is the provisional capital until the purpose-built **Palmas** is complete (*pop* in 1993, 6,000, mostly government personnel and construction workers). The small town of **Gurupi** on the BR-153, 90 km N of the Tocantins border, has been rec as a pleasant place to break the journey. Hotel (E) near the rodoviária. Entry to the Bananal is not permitted from here.

At **Fátima**, on the BR-153, a paved road heads **E** 52 km to a new bridge over the Rio Tocantins to **Porto Nacional** (*pop* 43,225). From here a road runs N to Palmas, 55 km, a few kilometres from the village of Canela (which is opposite Molha – ferry across the Tocantins). Porto Nacional has 3 habitable hotels, 3 restaurants, an airport with regional flights, 7 banks, the regional hospital and a small rodoviária on Praça do Peso Boiadeiro. The church of Nossa Senhora das Mercês (1903) is on the main square; a regional festival of N Sra das Mercês is on 24 September. 2-hr boat trips up the Tocantins from the old ferry port go the Carreira

Comprida rapids and island beaches (best May-Sept).

77 km upriver from Palmas, on the W bank, **Miracema do Tocantins** (*pop* 20,850) has 5 hotels, an airport, sightseeing at nearby Cachoeiras do Lajeado Grande and a 24-hr ferry to Tocantínia on the E bank. From the BR-153 to Miracema is 23 km.

At **Guaraí** the road forks, one branch continuing W into Pará, then turning N to Marabá on the Transamazônica. The other branch goes to Araguaína, whereafter the BR-226 goes to Estreito in Maranhão, from where the BR-010 runs N through Imperatriz to Belém. A pleasant overnight stop on the road to Araguaiana is the hilly town of **Uruaçu**, cheap hotels near rodoviária.

ARAGUAÍNA

(*Pop* 103,395) In Tocantins, on the Brasília-Belém road (Brasília, 1,102 km; Belém 842 km; Imperatriz, 174 km); several hotels near rodoviária including **D** *Esplanada*, may have to share a room, friendly, clean, fan, no breakfast, good; *Líder*, *São Jorge*, *do Norte* and *Goiás* (all **E**).

● **Transport Air** Rio Sul **flights** daily from Brasília, Imperatriz, Uberaba and São Paulo. **Buses** Bus leaves Araguaína for Marabá 0700 and 1400. Ordinary bus to Goiânia takes 24 hrs: try to get an express. If travelling to Belém or Brasília by bus, reservations are not normally accepted: be at the terminal 2 hrs before scheduled departure as buses tend to leave early; as soon as bus pulls in, follow the driver to the ticket counter and ask if there are seats. Brasília 1200, 2400, US$36 (22 hrs). Buses also to Santarém.

TO CONCEIÇÃO DO ARAGUAIA

Off the Brasília-Belém road are fast-developing frontier regions between the lower Araguaia and Xingu rivers. Kevin Healey writes: There is now a soaring concrete bridge spanning the Araguaia just S of Conceição do Araguaia, which is the only bridge across the Araguaia between Barra dos Garças and Marabá.

North and W of Conceição are many new townships and ranches. Places like **Redenção** (*pop* 54,365) and Xinguara are raw, dusty and not very salubrious for tourists, especially at night. At **Xinguara** (*pop* 40,315 already) is the **E** *Hotel Rio Vermelho*, not too bad.

CONCEIÇÃO DO ARAGUAIA

The town (*pop* 54,490) has a frontier atmosphere, although mudhuts are being replaced by brick: cowboy hats, battered Chevrolet pick-ups, skinny mules and a red light district. Airport 14 km SW. Conceição would be a useful base for visiting the Ilha do Bananal.

● **Accommodation & places to eat** The best hotel is the **B** *Taruma Tropical* (T 421-1205), pool, conference centre, garage, sauna, frigobars, expanded restaurant, clean and functioning bathrooms, a/c – when it works; the hotel is well patronized by ranchers and absentee landowners from Brasília; also *Marajoara*, Av JK 1587, T 421-1220, some a/c, safe parking, breakfast; *Araguaia*, R Couto de Magalhães 2605, breakfast, both small, overpriced. Best place to eat is *Café Taboquinha*, Av Francisco Vitor, well-prepared fish, open 1200-1500, 1800-2300.

ILHA DO BANANAL

Douglas Trent, of Focus Tours, Belo Horizonte (who arrange tours, see page 431), writes:"**Bananal** is the world's largest river island, located in the state of Tocantins on the northeastern border of Mato Grosso. The island is formed by a division in the S of the Rio Araguaia and is approximately 320 km long. The entire island was originally a national park (called **Parque Nacional Araguaia**), which was then cut in half and later further reduced to its current size of 562,312 ha (of an original 2 million). The island and park are subject to seasonal flooding and contain several permanent lakes. The island, and especially the park, form one of the more spectacular wildlife areas on the continent, in many ways similar to the Pantanal. The vegetation is a transition zone between the *cerrado* (woody savanna) and Amazon forests, with gallery forests along the many waterways. There are several marshlands throughout the island.

The fauna is also transitional. More than 300 bird species are found here, including the hoatzin, hyacinthine macaw, harpy eagle and black-fronted piping guan. The giant anteater, maned wolf, bush dog, giant otter, jaguar, puma, marsh deer, pampas deer, American tapir, yellow anaconda and South American river turtle also occur here. The island is flooded most of the year, with the prime visiting (dry) season being from June to early Oct, when the beaches are exposed. Unfortunately, the infrastructure for tourism aside from fishing expeditions (the island is a premier spot for big fish) is very limited.

Permission to visit the park should be obtained in advance from Sr Levi Vargas, Director of the Park, Ibama, R 219, No 95, Setor Universitário, 74605-800 Goiânia."

Local information
● **Accommodation & access**
Access to the park is through the small but pleasant town of **Santa Teresinha** (*pop* 8,900) which is N of São Felix (see below), and is the gateway to the park. A charming hotel is the **A3** *Bananal*, Pça Tarcila Braga 106, CEP 78395 (Mato Grosso), with full board. There is room only for 10; reserve well in advance, either by mail, allowing several months for the mail to get through, or by phoning the town's telephone operator, asking the hotel to call you back and hoping that you hear from them.

There is some simple accommodation for scientists at the park, which can sometimes be reserved at the address above or from IBDF, the National Parks department in Brasília. Bring your own food and bedding, and the severely underpaid but dedicated staff would appreciate any extra food or financial help, although it will not be solicited. A boat to the park can be lined up at the *Hotel Bananal*.

Bananal can be visited from São Félix do Araguaia – see below (with permission from Funai in the town) by crossing the river to the Carajá village of **Santa Isabela de Morra** and asking to see the chief, who can tell you the history of the tribe. The island can be crossed from São Félix to **São Miguel de Araguaia** by taking an 8-hr trip (contact the *Bar Beira*). From São Miguel a 5-hr bus trip brings you to **Porangatu** (**E** *Hotel Mauriti*, shower, restaurant) on the Belém-Brasília highway.

SÃO FÉLIX DO ARAGUAIA

São Félix do Araguaia (*pop* 14,365) is a larger town with more infrastructure for fishing than Santa Teresinha. Many Carajás indians are found in town; a depot of their handicrafts is between the *Pizzaria* and *Mini Hotel* on Av Araguaia. Mosquito nets are highly recommended: high incidence of malaria.

Tours Many river trips available for fishing or to see wildlife. Juracy Lopes, a very experienced guide, can be contacted through *Hotel Xavante*; he has many friends, including the chief and council, in Santa Isabela (see above). Morning or afternoon trips to the village or to see wildlife, cost US$15 for 2; longer trips can be made to the meeting of the waters with the Rio das Mortes, or spending a night in the jungle sleeping in hammocks. *Icuyala* is recommended, T (062) 223-9518 (Goiâna), excellent food, drink, and service, US$100/day, independent visitors also welcomed. Fazenda owners may invite you as their guest – do not abuse this privilege, and remember to take a gift.

● **Accommodation & places to eat** A very simple hotel with the best view in town is the **D** *Mini Hotel Araguaia*, Av Araguaia 344, T (065) 522-1154, inc breakfast. They have a/c rooms, not rec, electricity is turned off at night and the closed-in room gets very hot. Rec is **D** *Xavante*, Av Severiano Neves 391, T 522-1305, a/c, shower, frigobar, excellent breakfast, delicious *cajá* juice, Sr e Sra Carvalho very hospitable rec. A good restaurant is the *Pizzaria Cantinho da Peixada* on Av Araguaia, next to the Texaco station, overlooking the river: the owner, Klaus, rents rooms, E, better than hotels, T 522-1320, he also arranges fishing trips rec. *Bar Paralelos* has live music.

● **Transport Air** Access to both Santa Teresinha and São Félix is by Brasil Central/TAM flights, and to São Félix by bus from Barra do Garças, see above. The air service is unreliable and, as the planes hold just 15 passengers, it is common to get held over for a day or two. There is a daily Votec flight from São Felix to Belém, stopping at Redenção, Tucumã, and many other places. **Buses** Rodoviária is 3 km from centre and waterfront, taxi US$3; buses to Barra do Garças at 0500, arr 2300, or 1730, arr 1100 next day; also to Tucumã, 6-8 hrs, and to São José do Xingu, 10 hrs. No buses to Marabá. In Sta Teresinha look out for a man in a yellowish taxi who kindly offers a free ride and then tries to collect outrageous sums from foreigners. There are legitimate taxis available – use them.

Mato Grosso do Sul and Mato Grosso

TO THE west of Goiás are the states of Mato Grosso and Mato Grosso do Sul, with a combined area of 1,231,549 sq km and a population of only about 3.8 million, or about three persons to the sq km. The two states are half covered with forest, with a large wetland area (230,000 sq km) called the Pantanal (roughly west of a line between Campo Grande and Cuiabá, between which there is a direct road), partly flooded in the rainy season (see page 629).

Cattle ranching is very important, with over 21 million head of beef cattle on 16 million ha of free range pasture in Mato Grosso do Sul alone. The Noroeste Railway (passenger service indefinitely suspended) and a road run across Mato Grosso do Sul via Campo Grande to Porto Esperança and Corumbá, both on the Rio Paraguai; much of the road is across the wetland, offering many sights of birds and other wildlife.

CAMPO GRANDE

(*Pop* 565,620; *CEP* 79100; *DDD* 067) Capital of the State of Mato Grosso do Sul (*pop* 1,778,500). It was founded in 1899 and became state capital in 1979 when Mato Grosso do Sul separated from Mato Grosso. It is a pleasant, modern city. Because of the *terra roxa* (red earth), it is called the 'Cidade Morena'.

Places of interest

In the centre is a shady park, the **Praça República**, commonly called the Praça do Rádio after the Rádio Clube on one of its corners. Three blocks W is **Praça Ari Coelho**. Linking the two squares, and running through the city E to W, is Av Afonso Pena; much of its central reservation is planted with yellow ypé trees. Their blossom covers the avenue, and much of the city besides, in spring. The city also has a great many mango trees, consequently it is very leafy. The **Parque dos Poderes**, a long way from the centre, extends for several hectares; as well as having the Palácio do Governo and state secretariats, it has a small zoo for the rehabilitation of animals from the Pantanal (phone the Secretaria do Meio Ambiente to visit), lovely trees and cycling and jogging tracks.

Museums

Museu Dom Bosco (Indian Museum), R Barão do Rio Branco 1843 (open daily 0700-1100, 1300-1700, US$0.50, T 383-3994), is a superb museum with the following collections: exhibits from the 5 Indian groups with which the Salesian missionaries have had contact in the 20th century: the Bororó, from the region between Bolivia to the border with Goias and between the Rio Garças and Rio das Mortes; the Moro, from Paraguay and Bolivia; the Carajá, from the shores of the Rio Araguaia, including Ilha do Bananal; the Xavante, from central Brazil beyond Rio das Mortes, and tribes of the Rio Uaupés in Amazônia, all with explanatory texts; fossilized shells, malacology (shells), entomology, 2,800 stuffed birds, 7-8,000 butterflies, mammals, minerals and 'monstruos' (2-headed calves, etc). Each collection is highly rec. **Museu do Arte Contemporâneo**, Mal Rondón e Calógeras, modern art from the region, open Mon-Fri 0900-1700, Sat 0900-1200, free.

Local information

NB The important street in the centre, R Marechal Cândido Mariano Rondon, is called either Marechal Rondon, or Cândido Mariano.

● **Accommodation**

L2 *Exceler Plaza*, Av Afonso Pena 444, T 721-0102, F 721-5666, 4-star, very good, luxury, art gallery, pool, tennis, all-you-can-eat business lunches; **L2** *Campo Grande*, R 13 de Maio 2825, T 384-6061, F 724-8349, central, a/c, luxury, cash discounts; **L3** *Buriti*, Av A M Coelho 2301, T/F 384-2211, a/c, fridge, pool, sauna, parking, restaurant.

A1 *Concord*, Av Calógeras 1624, T 384-3081, F 382-4987, very good, swimming pool, a/c, mini bar; **A1** *Vale Verde*, Av Afonso Pena 106, T 721-3355, a/c, mini bar, restaurant, pool, rec; **A3** *Advanced*, Av Calógeras 1909, T 721-5000, F 725-7744, a/c, fridge, **B** with fan, modern; **A3** *Fenícia*, Av Calógeras 2262, T 383-2001, F 383-2862, a/c, mini bar, TV; **A3** *Paris*, Av Costa e Silva 4175, T 787-1795, F 725-7744, a/c, mini bar, **C** with fan.

C *Americano*, R 14 de Julho 2311 e Marechal Rondón, T 721-1454, a/c, fridge, cheaper with fan, a bit run down, friendly; by Praça Ari Coelho are **C** *Pousada LM*, R 15 de Novembro 201, T 383-3300, fan, fridge, also rents by the month; and **D** *Central*, R 15 de Novembro 472, T 384-6442, fan, basic, cheaper with shared bath.

Near the rodoviária (not safe at night): **A3** *Internacional*, Allan Kardec 245, T 384-4677, F 721-2729, a/c, fridge, **B** with fan, modern, pool; on Dom Aquino are **A3** *Iguaçu*, No 761, T 384-4621, F 721-3215, a/c, fridge, **B** with fan, modern, pleasant, rec; **A3** *Palace*, No 1501, T 384-4741, a/c, fridge, **B** with fan, some rooms small; **B** *Nacional*, No 610, T 383-2461, a/c, cheaper with fan, **C** with shared bath; **B** *Village Palace*, No 802, T 724-1954, a/c, fridge, **C** with fan; **B** *Saigali*, Barão do Rio Branco 356, T 384-5775, a/c, mini bar, parking, cheaper with fan, comfortable, rec; **C** *Cosmos*, Dom Aquino 771, T 384-4270, fan, good value; **C** *Novo*, J Nabuco 185, T 721-0505, without breakfast, good value, rec; **C** *Turis*, Allan Kardec 200, T 382-7688, a/c, cheaper with fan, **D** in basement; **C** *Rocha*, Barão do Rio Branco 343, 1 block from rodoviária, T 7256874, without breakfast, fan, parking; **D** *Vânia*, Marechal Rondón 1004, T 384-2338, fan, cheaper with shared bath, laundry, rec; **D** *Santa Inês*, Afonso Pena 1413, T 724-2621, fan, comfortable, cheaper with shared bath; **D** *Pamella*, J Nabuco 245, T 724-3209, shared bath, fan, buffet restaurant; **F** *Paiva*, R Dom Aquino 523, TV, shower. There

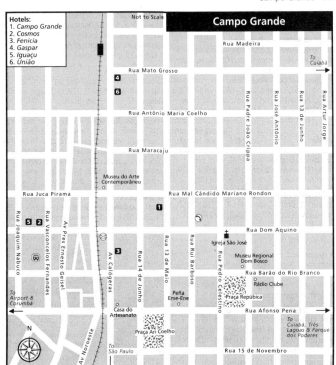

Hotels:
1. Campo Grande
2. Cosmos
3. Fenícia
4. Gaspar
5. Iguaçu
6. União

Not to Scale

Campo Grande

Rua Madeira

To Cuiabá

Rua Mato Grosso

Rua Antônio Maria Coelho

Rua Padre João Crippa

Rua José Antônio

Rua 13 de Junho

Rua Artur Jorge

Rua Maracaju

Museu do Arte Contemporáneo

Rua Juca Pirama

Rua Mal Cándido Mariano Rondon

Rua Dom Aquino

Rua Joaquim Nabuco

Rua Vasconcelos Fernandes

Av Pres Ernesto Geisel

Av Calógeras

Rua 14 de Junho

Rua 13 de Maio

Rua Rui Barboso

Rua Pedro Celestino

Igreja São José

Museu Regional Dom Bosco

Rua Barão do Rio Branco

Rádio Clube

Praça República

Rua Afonso Pena

Peña Eme-Ene

Casa do Artesanato

Praça Ari Coelho

To São Paulo

To Airport & Corumbá

N

To Cuiabá, Três Lagoas & Parque dos Poderes

Rua 15 de Novembro

46a

is a wide variety of hotels in the streets around the rodoviária; leave bags in the *guarda volumes* and shop around.

Near the railway station: **B** *Gaspar*, Av Mato Grosso 2, T/F 383-5121, opp station, a/c, fridge, **C** with fan, ask for quiet room, good breakfast, comfortable; next door is **C** *União*, Calógeras 2828, T 382-4213, cheaper with shared bath, good breakfast, ask for quiet room; **D** *Continental*, R Maracaju 229, 2 blocks from railway, 5 from rodoviária, comfortable, German owner; **D** *Esperança*, R Dr Temistocles 93, 1 block from station, hot and cold showers, basic, no a/c or fan, restaurant, very helpful; **D** *Caçula*, Calógeras 2704, T 721-4658, fan, cheaper with shared bath, basic, hot showers, laundry.

● **Places to eat**

Churrascarias: *Vitório*, Av Afonso Pena 1907, live music evenings; *Terracus Gaúcho*, at rodoviária, huge meal; *Campo Grande*, Av Calógeras 2199, good value; *Nossa Querência*, Av Afonso Pena 1267, rodizio, good value and quality, nr rodoviária, 2-for-1 special in evenings, rec. **Comida caseira**: *Carinca*, SE corner of main square, modern, clean, good plain food; *Bandeirantes*, Dom Aquino 803, good and economical; *Papa Gula*, Dom Aquino 1761, central, good value meals and snacks; *Restaurante da Gaúcha*, Allan Kardek 238, nr rodoviária.

Oriental: *Hong Kong*, R Maracaju 131, centre, good Chinese food, also a legal outlet for *jacaré* meat, closed Mon.

Other: *Cafeteria Lojas Americanas*, Marechal Rondón 1336, in a supermarket, and *Meio Kilo* opp, good value buffet; *El Café*, R Dom Aquino 1248, rec. *Nutre Bem*, vegetarian, Pedro Celestino 1696, good. Plenty of good, cheap places in R Barão de Rio Branco, eg *Maracaju*. *Confidência Mineira*, 14 de Julho 945, Mineiro food and 49 types of *cachaça* on sale, open daily, shows Sun and Tues.

Regional specialities include *caldo de piranha* (soup), *chipa* (Paraguayan cheese bread), sold on the streets, delicious when hot, and the local liqueur, *pequi com caju*, which contains *cachaça*.

● **Banks & money changers**
Banco do Brasil, 13 de Maio e Av Afonso Pena, open 1000-1500, commission US$10 for cash, US$20 for TCs, regardless of amount exchanged; **Banco Francês Brasileiro**, Marechal Rondon 1672, open 1000-1200 and 1330-1430, US$ cash and TCs, no commission; **Overcash Câmbio**, R 13 de Maio 2892, open Mon-Fri 1000-1600, poor rate for TCs, 7% commission to change TCs to US$ cash; **Campo Grande Câmbio**, R 13 de Maio 2484, open Mon-Fri 0930-1630, cash only; **Origem & Destino Câmbio**, R Dom Aquino 1682, cash only, fair rates. On weekends, try: *Hotel Fenícia*, 10% commission on TCs, check notes carefully.

● **Embassies & consulates**
Bolivia, R Dom Aquino 1353, T 382-2190; **Paraguay**, R João Crippa 1065, T 721-4430.

● **Entertainment**
See below for *Peña Eme-Ene*.

● **Hospitals & medical services**
Yellow and Dengue fevers are both present in Mato Grosso do Sul. There is a clinic at the railway station, but it's not very hygienic, best to get your immunizations at home.

● **Post & telecommunications**
Post Office: on corner of R Dom Aquino e Calógeras 2309 and Barão do Rio Branco corner Ernesto Geisel, both locations offer fax service, US$2.10/page within Brazil.

Telephone: TELEMS, R Dom Aquino 1805, between P Celestino and Rui Barbosa, open 0600-2200 daily.

● **Shopping**
The *Casa do Artesão*, Av Calógeras 2050 e Av Afonso Pena, open Mon-Fri 0800-1800, Sat 0800-1200, has a good collection of native crafts, Indian jewellery and arrows on sale. *Eme-Ene*, Av Afonso Pena 2303, T 382-2373, regional handicrafts, open 0700-1900, Sat 0700-1700, Sun 0800-1200, good, has a *peña* (folk music show) each Wed at 2100, rec; *Arte do Pantanal*, Av Afonso Pena 1743, regional crafts. A local speciality is Os Bugres da Conceição, squat wooden statues covered in moulded wax. There is a market (Feira Livre) on Wed and Sat.

Bookshop: R 15 de Junho e R Dom Aquino, highly rec, English spoken, will exchange English books.

● **Tour companies & travel agents**
Vox Tour, R Cândido Mariano 1777, T 3843335, F 725-8663, English and Spanish spoken, helpful; *Tainá Turismo*, R Sete de Setembro 1966, T 384-6544, F 384-2510; *Im-*

pacto, R Padre João Crippa 1065, sala 101, T 382-5197, T/F 724-3167, Pantanal and Bonito tour operators and wholesalers, helpful; *Origem e Destino*, R Dom Aquino 1682, T 721-1430, F 721-1470, English, French and Spanish spoken.

● **Tourist offices**
Tourist information from the state run *Casa do Turismo*, R Arthur Jorge 622, by Parque Belmar Fidalgo, T/F 724-5104, friendly, helpful. Maps and books for sale at the municipal *Centro de Informação Turística e Cultural*, Av Noroeste 5140 corner Afonso Pena, housed in Pensão Pimentel, a beautiful mansion built in 1913, also has a data base about services in the city and cultural information. Another office on R Barão do Rio Branco between 14 de Junho and 13 de Maio, helpful. Kiosk at airport.

● **Transport**
Local Car hire: Laredo, R Dom Aquino 1878, T/F 382-2984; on Av Afonso Pena are: **Localiza**, No 318, T 382-8786, T (airport) 763-1401; **Hertz**, No 2620, T 383-5331; **Locagrande**, No 466, T 721-3282, F 721-3282; **Unidas**, No 829, T 384-5626, F 384-6115, T (airport) 763-2145. Daily rates from US$37.

Air Daily flights to most major cities. Airport tax US$6.50. City bus No 158, 'Popular' stops outside airport. Taxi to airport, US$6. Banco do Brasil at airport exchanges dollars. Post office, fax and phones in same office. Safe to spend the night at the airport.

Trains The railway station is on Av Calógeras, 8 blocks from the bus terminal. There are no passenger services.

Buses Rodoviária is in the block bounded by Ruas Barão do Rio Branco, Vasconcelos Fernandes, Dom Aquino and Joaquim Nabuco, T 383-1678, all offices on 2nd floor; at the V Fernandes end are town buses, at the J Nabuco end state and interstate buses. In between are shops and *lanchonetes*. 8 blocks' walk from Praça República; cinema in rodoviária, US$1.20. (Taxi to rodoviária, US$3.60.) Campo Grande has good connections throughout the country: **São Paulo**, US$36, 14 hrs, 9 buses daily, 1st at 0800, last at 2400, 3 *leito* buses US$71. **Cuiabá**, US$25, 10 hrs, 12 buses daily, *leito* at 2100 and 2200 US$48. To **Brasília**, US$46, 23 hrs at 0900 and 1900. To **Goiânia**, São Luís company 1100, 1630, 1900, 2300, 15 hrs on 1900 service, US$39, others 24 hrs, US$1 cheaper. **Rio de Janeiro**, US$50, 21 hrs, 4 buses daily, *leito* at 1745 US$100. **Corumbá**, with Andorinha, 8 daily from 0600, 6 hrs, US$24. Campo Grande-Corumbá buses connect with those from Rio and São Paulo, similarly those from Corumbá through to Rio and São Paulo. Good connections to all major cities. **Ponta Porã**, 5 hrs, 9 buses daily, US$10. **Dourados**, 4 hrs, 14 daily (Queiroz), US$9. Beyond Dourados is Mundo Novo, from where buses go to Ponta Porã (0530) and to Porto Frajelli (very frequent); from Mundo Novo ferries for cars and passengers go to Guaíra for US$0.50. Twice daily direct service to **Foz do Iguaçu** (17 hrs) with Integração, 1200, 1600, US$32.50; same company goes to Cascavel, US$23. To **Pedro Juan Caballero** (Paraguay), del Amambay company, 0600, US$10. Amambay goes every Sunday morning to **Asunción**.

CAMPO GRANDE TO SÃO PAULO

The Campo Grande-São Paulo journey can be broken at **Três Lagoas** (*pop* 68,070), 9½ hrs from São Paulo (motorway) and 6 hrs from Campo Grande by paved highway BR-262 (buses dep Campo Grande.

16 km E of Três Lagoas is the massive **Jupiá** Dam on the Rio Paraná, which can be visited with prior permission (T 521-2753) on weekends and holidays only, 0800-1800.

Further N are other hydroelectric dams, most impressive of which is at **Ilha Solteira** (50 km, several hotels and good fish restaurants on São Paulo state side); guided tours at 1000 and 1500 weekends and holidays. Excellent swimming is to be had at **Praia Catarina**, with bars, playground and kiosks (6 km). Overlooking the river 35 km S of Ilha Solteira is restored **Fort Itapura**, built during the War of the Triple Alliance, with beach and restaurants nearby.

● **Accommodation & places to eat** B *Três Lagoas*, Av Rosário Congro 629, T 521-2500, a/c, best; **C** *Regente Palace*, R Paranaíba 580, a/c, good value; **E** *Novo*, Av Antônio de Souza Queiroz, nr rodoviária. *Restaurant Casarão*, R Munir Tomé 30, good selection; *Boi na Brasa*, Av Antônio Trajano 487, for *churrascos*. rec.

● **Buses** Campo Grande-Três Lagoas 0800, 1200, 2230, US$15.75, an interesting journey, 'especially for cattle farmers'.

CAMPO GRANDE TO PARAGUAY

DOURADOS

The paved road from Campo Grande to the Paraguayan frontier at Ponta Porã passes through **Dourados** (224 km; *pop* 135,780; *alt* 430m), the supply centre of a developing agricultural region carved from the red *sertão*, in large part by Japanese immigrants. Apart from a couple of pleasant parks and lakes for swimming there is little of note for the traveller.

● **Accommodation & places to eat** B *Alphonsus*, Av Pres Vargas 603, T 421-5211, F 421-9178, best; **C** *Figueira Palace*, R Toshinobu Katayama 553, T 421-5611, a/c, pleasant; **C** *Bahamas*, R Cândido da Câmara 750, T 421-4714, a/c, simpler but excellent value. *Restaurante Boxexa*, R Araújo 780, good pizzas; *Churrascaria Guarujá* (No 595 same street) for *churrascos* in enjoyable surroundings.

● **Transport Air** Scheduled flights to Marília, Ponta Porã, Pres Prudente and São Paulo from the small airport (10 km). **Buses** Good bus connections for Campo Grande, Ponta Porã, Mundo Novo, and Presidente Prudente and Maringá to the E of the Rio Paraná.

PONTA PORÃ

The highway continues 115 km to **Ponta Porã** (*pop* 55,830), separated from Pedro Juan Caballero in Paraguay only by a broad avenue. With paved streets, good public transport and smart shops, Ponta Porã is decidedly more prosperous than its neighbour, although Brazilian visitors flock across the border to play the casino and buy cheaper 'foreign' goods. At the **Parque das Exposições**, by the rodoviária, an animal show is held each October.

● **Accommodation** B *Porta do Sol Palace*, R Paraguai 2688, T 431-3341, F 431-1193, a/c, pool, very nice; B *Guarujá*, R Guia Lopes 63, T 431-1619, rec; opp is **C** *Barcelona*, maze-like building, a/c, restaurant, pool; **C** *Alvorada*, Av Brasil 2977, T 431-5866, good café, close to post office, good value but often full; **C** *Internacional*, R Internacional 1267, T 431-1243, **D** without a/c, hot water, good breakfast, rec; **E** *Dos Viajantes*, across park opp railway station, very basic. Brazilian hotels inc breakfast in tariff, Paraguayan ones do not.

● **Places to eat** *Top Lanches*, beside *Hotel Barcelona*, cheap and friendly. *Chopão*, R Mal Floriano 1877, good food at reasonable prices. *Comabem*, R 7 de Setembro, nr Casas Pernambucanas on Av Mariscal Floriano for burgers and pizzas.

● **Banks & money changers** Banco do Brasil changes TCs. Several *cambios* on the Paraguayan side. Many in the centre of town (but on Sun change money in hotels).

● **Electric current** 220 volts AC.

● **Transport Air** Services to São Paulo, Dourados, Marília and Pres Prudente. **Trains** The station is some 8 blocks from the centre, take 'Ferroviária' bus (US$1); no passenger trains. **Buses** To Campo Grande: 9 a day from 0100-2130, 4 hrs, US$9; the rodoviária is 3 km out on the Dourados road ('São Domingos' bus, taxi US$5).

FRONTIER WITH PARAGUAY

There are no border posts between the two towns and people pass freely for local visits.

● **Brazilian immigration**
The Brazilian Federal Police office (for entry/exit visas) is on the 2nd floor of the white engineering supply company building at R Marechal Floriano 1483, T 431-1428, open weekdays 0730-1130, 1400-1700.

● **Paraguayan consulate**
The two nations' consulates face each other on R Internacional (border street) a block W of Ponta Porã's local bus terminal; some nationalities require a visa from the Paraguayan consul (next to *Hotel Internacional*), open only 0800-1200 Mon-Fri. **Check requirements carefully**, and ensure your documents are in order: without the proper stamps you will inevitably be sent back somewhere later on in your travels.

● **Transport**
Taking a taxi between offices can speed things up if pressed for time; drivers know border crossing requirements; US$7.

BONITO

The municipality of **Bonito** in the Serra do Bodoquena yields granite and marble and is clad in forest. (*Town pop* 16,388; *CEP* 79290; *DDD* 067; distance from Campo Grande 248 km.) The area's main attractions are in its rivers and caves (the formations are comparable to those found in the Lagoa Santa region of Minas Gerais). There are spectacular walks through mountains and forest; wildlife includes birds, rheas, monkeys, alligators and anaconda. Most excursions require authorization; this is not an obstacle to those with their own transport but as there is no public transport, those without a car will need to use an agency (see below). Bonito has become very popular with Brazilian vacationers, especially during Dec-Jan, Carnival, Easter, and July (at these times advance booking is essential). Prices are high. The wet season is Jan-Feb; Dec-Feb is hottest, July-Aug coolest.

Local attractions: Caves

The first cave to be opened is **Lagoa Azul**, 26 km from Bonito. Lagoa Azul has a lake 50m long and 110m wide, 75m below ground level. The water, 20°C, is a jewel-like blue as light from the opening is refracted through limestone and magnesium. Prehistoric animal bones have been found in the lake. The light is at its best Jan-Feb, 0700-0900, but is fine at other times. A 25-ha park surrounds the cave. You must pay a municipal tax, US$5; if not using your own transport, a car for 4 costs US$20. Also open is **NS Aparecida cave**, which has superb stalactites and stalagmites; no tourism infrastructure.

River excursions

The **Balneário Municipal** on the Rio Formoso (7 km on road to Jardim), with changing rooms, toilets, camping, swimming in clear water, plenty of fish to see (strenuous efforts are made to keep the water and shore clean), US$2. **Horminio** waterfalls, 13 km, eight falls on the Rio Formoso, suitable for swimming; bar and camping, entry US$0.15. **Rafting** on the Rio Formoso: 12km, 2½ hrs, min 4 people, US$15 pp, a mixture of floating peacefully downriver, swimming and shooting 4 waterfalls, lifejackets available; arranged by *Hapakany Tour* and many other agencies, see below. The **Aquário Natural** is one of the **springs of the Rio Formoso**; to visit you must have authorization from *Hapakany Tour*; you can swim and snorkel with 5 types of fish (US$25). Do not swim with suntan oil on. Other tours are: from the springs of the Rio Sucuri to its meeting with the Formoso (permission from *Hapakany* or *TapeTur*), about 2 km of crystal-clear water, with swimming or snorkelling, birdwatching, very peaceful; **Aquidaban**, a series of limestone/marble waterfalls in dense forest; **Rio da Prata** a spring with underground snorkelling for 2 km, very beautiful. The **fishing** season is from 1 Mar to 31 October. In late Oct, early Nov is the *piracema* (fish run), when the fish return to their spawning grounds. Hundreds can be seen jumping the falls.

NB Bonito's attractions are nearly all on private land and must by visited with a guide. Owners also enforce limits on the number of daily visitors so, at busy times, pre-booking is essential.

Local information
● **Accommodation**

A1 *Zagaia Resort*, Rodovia Bonito-Três Morros, T/F 255-1280, luxurious, pool, L1 full board including tours; **A2-B** *Pousada Olho d'Água*, just outside Bonito, Km 1 on road to Três Morros, T 255-1430, F 255-1470, accommodation in cabins, inc breakfast, fan, showers with solar-heated water, fruit trees, fresh vegetables, small lake, own water supply, horse riding, bicycles, rec.

B *Palace Hotel Gemila*, R Luis da Costa Leite 2085, fan, hot water, laundry; **B** *Tapera*, on hill above Shell station on road to Jardim, T 255-1700, fine views, cool breezes, a/c, comfortable, good.

C *Bonanza*, R Cel Pilad Rebuá (main street) 628, T 255-1315, F 255-1235, suites and family rooms available, a/c, frequently rec, opp is parking lot, with bar from 1800, darts and *churrascaria* on Fri; *Canaã*, Pilad Rebuá 1293, T 255-1255, parking, TV, a/c, fridge, phone, restaurant and *churrascaria*.

D *Pousadinha da Praça*, Pilad Rebuá 2097, T 255-1135, 2-4 bedded rooms (latter cramped), fan, hot water.

E pp *Pousada Muito Bonito*, Pilad Rebuá 1448, T/F 255-1645, with bath, or rooms with bunkbeds, nice patio, clean, excellent, helpful owners, inc breakfast, also with tour company (Mario Doblack speaks English, French and Spanish), warmly rec. Also on Rebuá at 1800, is a hostal **F**, owned by the Paraiso tour agency, T 255-1477, shared bath, rec.

Camping: at *Ilha do Padre*, 12 km N of Bonito, very pleasant, no regular transport (Hapakany's raft trip ends here), T/F 255-1430; 4 rustic cabins with either 4 bunk beds, or 2 bunks and a double, US$10 pp, youth hostel with two sets of 12 beds, US$6 pp, same price for camping, toilets, showers, clothes washing, meals available, bar, electricity, lots of trees, can swim anywhere, to enter the island for a day US$3. Managers are Henrique Ruas and Jane Tatoni. Camping also at *Poliana* on Rio Formosa, 100m past Ilha do Padre, very pleasant.

● **Places to eat**

Tapera, Pilad Rebuá 480, T 255-1110, good, home-grown vegetables, breakfast, lunch, pizzas, meat and fish dishes, opens 1900 for evening meal; *Comida Caseira*, Luis da Costa Leite e Santana do Paraiso, good local food, lunch and dinner, not open Sun pm; *Verdo-Frutos e Sucos Naturais*, Pilad Rebuá 1853, next to *Bonanza* car park, good juices and fruits.

● **Banks & money changers**

Banco do Brasil, for Visa; some hoteliers may change money.

● **Post & telecommunications**

Post Office: on R Cel Pilad Rebuá.

Telephones: on Santana do Paraiso.

● **Tour companies & travel agents**

There are 13 agencies and 54 guides in Bonito who accompany visitors to the private sites. Sérgio Ferreira Gonzales, R Cel Pilad Rebuá 628, T 255-1315 (opp *Bonanza*), is an authority on the caves, rec. *Hapakany Tour*, Pilad Rebuá 628, T 255-1315, F 255-1235, Jason and Murilo, for all local tours, rec. *TapeTur*, next to *Tapera* restaurant, guides, information, tours, clothes shop, also rec. For information in English and French, contact Henrique Ruas, T/F 255-1430, see *Ilha do Padre* or *Pousada Olho d'Água* above.

● **Transport**

Rodoviária is on edge of town. From Campo Grande, US$15, 5½-6 hrs, 1500, returns at 0530. Bus uses MS-345, with stop at Autoposto Santa Cruz, Km 60, all types of fuel, food and drinks available. For Aquidauana, take Campo Grande bus. Bus Corumbá-Miranda-Bonito-Jardim-Ponta Porã, Mon-Sat, leaves either end at 0600, arriving Bonito 1230 for Ponta Porã, 1300 for Miranda; can change in Jardim (1400 for 1700 bus) or Miranda (better connections) for Campo Grande; fare Corumbá-Bonito US$18. Also connections on 1230 route in Bela Vista at 2000 for Asunción and Coronel Oviedo. Ticket office opens at 1200.

ROUTES The road to **Jardim** is paved. In Jardim, which has a wide, tree-lined main street, there is a rodoviária for Cruzeiro do Sul buses. A few blocks uphill is *Panificadora Massa Pura*, clean and bright, and other eating places.

From Bonito there is a road to **Porto Murtinho** where a boat crosses to Isla Margarita in Paraguay (entry stamp available on the island). Hotels **E** *Eldorado*, friendly, clean, good food; **E** *Beira Rio*, basic; and others; 2 *lanchonetes*, *Churrascaria Gaspão*. Elia, taxi driver, will change money.

● **Buses** From Jardim: to Campo Grande 0730, 1300, 1700 and 2 in middle of night, US$10.15; Aquidauana 0730 and 1700; Bonito (US$5), Miranda and Corumbá at 1130; Dourados 0600; Bela Vista (Paraguayan border) 0200, 1030, 1500, 1930; Porto Murtinho 0010 and 1530 (bus from Bonito connects); Ponta Porã 0600, 1500; Sun only at 1400 to São Paulo.

CAMPO GRANDE TO CORUMBÁ AND BOLIVIA

BR-262 is paved most of the way from Campo Grande to Corumbá and the Bolivian border, rail service along this route was suspended indefinitely in 1995. It is best to make this journey during the day, to take advantage of marvellous scenery.

AQUIDAUANA

131 km W of Campo Grande, just N of the road is **Aquidauana** (*pop* 39,300, several daily buses from Campo Grande). BR-412 heads S from here to Jardim, with connections to Paraguay (see above). Also turn S here for one route to Bonito. The Ibama-controlled *jacaré* farm, *Olhos d'Água*, is not open to visitors. Aquidauana is a gateway to the Pantanal (see below), excursions in fishing boats negotiable around US$42 pp a day, or via *Chalanatur*, T 241-3396, 6-day trips rec.

● **Accommodation** *Fazenda Toca da Onça*, see page 632; take taxi, owner also has a camp site. In town, several hotels around railway station, inc **E** *Fluminense*, with fan and breakfast, a/c more expensive; **E** *Lord*, R Manoel Antônio Paes de Barros 739, 79200, T 241 1857, shared bathroom in single room own in double room, rec.

● **Places to eat** *O Casarão (grill)*, R Manoel Paes de Barros 533, T 241 2219, rec.

● **Tour companies & travel agents** *Buriti Viagens e Turismo Ltda*, R Manoel Paes de Barros 720, 79200, T 241 2748, rec; *Lucarelli Turismo Ltda*, R Manoel Paes de Barros 552, T 241 3410, rec; *Cordon Turismo*, R Búzios, Cep 79003-101, T 384 1483, organizes fishing trips into the Pantanal, rec; *Panbratur*, R Estevão Alves Correa 586, T/F 241-3494, tour operator in southern Pantanal.

77 km further W is **Miranda** (*pop* 14,255), another entrance to the Pantanal (see also below for hotels, etc). Here too is a *jacaré* farm, *Granja Caimã*, which is open to visitors, US$1 entry. A road heads S to Bodoquena and on to Bonito. Bus Campo Grande-Miranda, 7 a day with Expresso Mato Grosso, US$8.50, and others. The Campo Grande-Corumbá road crosses the Rio Miranda bridge (two service stations before it) then carries on, mostly paved to cross the Rio Paraguai.

CORUMBÁ

(*Pop* 89,585; *CEP* 79300; *DDD* 067) Situated on the S bank by a broad bend in the Rio Paraguai, 15 mins from the Bolivian border, the city offers beautiful views of the river, great for photography, especially at sunset.

Climate

Hot and humid (70%); cooler in June-July, very hot from Sept-January. It has millions of mosquitoes in Dec, Jan and Feb, but is a pleasant place nevertheless.

Places of interest

There is a spacious shady **Praça da Independência** and the port area is worth a visit. Av General Rondon between Frei Mariano and 7 de Septembro has a pleasant palm lined promenade which comes to life in the evenings. The **Forte Junqueira**, the city's most historic building, which may be visited, was built in 1772. In the hills to the S is the world's greatest reserve of manganese, now being worked. Corumbá is the best starting point for the southern part of the Pantanal, with boat and jeep trips and access to the major hotel/farms.

The combination of economic hard times since 1994 and drug-running make the city unsafe late at night.

Local festivals

2 Feb, **Festa de Nossa Senhora da Candelária**, Corumbá's patron saint, all offices and shops are closed. 24 June, **Festa do Arraial do Banho de São João**, fireworks, parades, traditional food stands, processions and the main event, the bathing of the image of the saint in the Rio Paraguai. 21 Sept, Corumbá's anniversary, include a Pantanal fishing festival held on the eve.

Local information

● **Accommodation**

A1 *Internacional Palace*, R Dom Aquino 1457, T/F 231-6852, a/c, fridge, pool, sauna, parking, cafe; **A2** *Nacional Palace*, R América 936, T 231-6868, F 231-6202, a/c, fridge, good pool, parking; **A2** *Santa Mônica*, R Antônio Maria Coelho 345, T 231-3001, F 231-7880, a/c, good restaurant, pool; **A3** *Carandá*, R Dom Aquino

47, T 231-2023, a/c, fridge, pool, good, helpful, restaurant; **A3** *Laura Vicuña*, R Cuiabá 775, T 231-5874, F 231-2663, a/c, fridge, **B** for simpler room, parking, modern, rec.

B *City*, R Cabral 1031, T 231-4187, between rodoviária and centre, a/c, **C** with fan, cheaper with shared bath, parking; **B** *Premier*, R Antônio Maria Coelho 389, T 231-4937, small rooms, a/c; **B** *Salette*, R Delamaré 893, T 231-3768, F 231-4948, a/c, safe, **C** with bath and fan, **D** with shared bath and fan, rec; **B** *Santa Rita*, Dom Aquino 860 (unsigned), T 231-5453, a/c, **C** with fan, noisy, overpriced, good meals in restaurant.

C *Angola*, R Antônio Maria 124, T 231-7233, a/c, **D** with fan, restaurant; **C** *Beira Rio*, R Manoel Cavassa 109, T 231-2554, a/c, cheaper with fan, by the port, popular with fishermen; **C** *Copacabana*, R Cuiabá 926, **D** with shared bath, basic; **C** *Lincoln*, R 15 de Novembro 205, T 231-4483, a/c, parking; **C** *Nelly*, Delamaré 902, T 231-6001, F 231-7396, a/c, **D** with shared bath and fan, good breakfast; **C** *Timoneiro*, R Cabral 879, T 231-5530, between rodoviária and centre, a/c, **D** with fan, cheaper with shared bath.

D *Campus*, R Antônio João 1333, fan, cheaper with shared bath, good value; **D** *Lisboa*, R 13 de Junho 720, T 231-7727, a/c, cheaper with fan, small rooms; **D** *Roboré*, R Dom Aquino 587, shared bath, small rooms, basic. **Near the**

rodoviária are: **D** *Beatriz*, R Porto Carreiro 896, T 231-7441, fan, cheaper with shared bath, small rooms, basic; **D** *Internacional*, R Porto Carreiro 714, T 231-4654, shared bath, fan, basic, simple breakfast, owner organizes fishing trips; **D** *Londres*, Joaquim Murtinho 1021, T 231-6717, good value, private bath, fan.

E *Esplanada*, opp railway station, cold shower, basic; *Irure*, R 13 de Junho 776, small and clean; **E** *Pousada Pantaneira*, R Ladário 271, T 231-5313, private house, friendly proprietor Dona Joana, fan, **D** with private bath, popular, often full, rec; **E** pp *Pousada Pantaneira*, Frei Mariano 1335, T/F 231-3934, with same name as above but different owner and atmosphere, dormitories with shared bath and cooking facilities, linen not supplied, basic, popular, not too clean, Swiss owner Claudine also organizes camping tours (see *Colibri Pantanal Safari*).

Youth hostel: R Antônio Maria Coelho 677, T 231-2305, dorms, rec, the owner, Sr Pontis, organizes jungle trips, cheaper for a group, negotiate price.

Outside town: **A3** *Gold Fish*, Av Rio Branco 2799, T 231-5106, F 231-5433, on river front, 4 km on the road to Ladário, a/c, fridge, pool; **A3** pp full board *Porto Vitória Régia*, 12 km from Corumbá past Ladário, on the river front, a/c, pool, restaurant, boats, camping area; **B** *Pousada do Cachimbo*, R Allan Kardec 4,

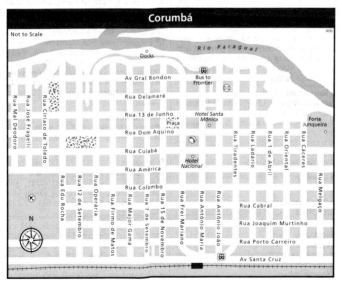

T 231-3910, on the way to the Bolivian border, a/c, fridge, country setting by the river, gardens, pool; **B Paraíso do Pantanal**, Cunha Couto 1532, Ladário, T/F 231-5394, a/c, fridge, pool, restaurant, tours organized.

● **Places to eat**
Several rec restaurants in R Frei Mariano: *Churrascaria Gauchão*, No 879, good value; *Tarantella*, No 780, Italian; *Barril de Ouro*,No 556, good; *Drink's*, No 564, economical set meals; *Peixaria do Lulú*, R Antônio João 410, good fish; *Churrascaria Rodéio*, 13 de Junho 760, very good, lunchtime buffet, rec; *Churrascaria Paladar*, R Antônio M Coelho 577, rodízio; *Viva Bella*, R Arthur Mangabeira 1 (behind Clube Corumbaense 1 block from Gen Rondon), fish, meat, pizza, home made pastas, drinks, magnificent views over the river especially at sunset, live music Wed-Sat, opens at 1700, good food and atmosphere, rec; *Pastina Nostra*, Av Gen. Rondon 1189, Italian and international; *Cacharas's*, Av Gen Rondon 1191, fish specialities, open evenings and weekends; *Restaurante Peixaria Galpão*, R 13 de Junho 797, meat and fish; *Soba-Yá*, R Delamaré 1181, Chinese, opens at 1900; *Trivial*, R 15 de Novembro 148, Centro, good, reasonably-priced buffet, rec; *Almanara*, R America 964 next to *Hotel Nacional*, good Arabic food; on the waterfront you can eat good fish at *Portal do Pantanal*; lots of open-air bars on the river front. Bolivian snacks in *'Sslato*, R Dom Aquino. Lanchonetes tend to overcharge – check prices. Many good ice-cream parlours: *Cristal*, R 7 de Setembro e Delamaré, rec.

Local specialities include *peixadas corumbaenses*, a variety of fish dishes prepared with the catch of the day; as well as ice cream, liquor and sweets made of *bocaiúva*, a small yellow palm fruit, in season Sept-February.

● **Banks & money changers**
Banco do Brasil, R 13 de Junho 914, Mon-Fri 1100-1600, for cash, US$3 commission per US$100 TCs. Câmbio Mattos, R 15 de Novembro 140, Mon-Fri 0800-1700, good rates for US$ cash, 5% commission on TCs; Câmbio Rau, R 15 de Novembro 212, Mon-Fri 0800-1700, Sat 0900-1200, cash only, good rates.

● **Laundry**
Apae, R 13 de Junho 1377, same day service.

● **Post & telecommunications**
Post Office: main at R Delamaré 708 (has fax service) branch at R 15 de Novembro 229.

Telephone: Telems, R Dom Aquino 951, nr Praça da Independência, open 0700-2200 daily. To phone Quijarro/Puerto Suárez, Bolivia, it costs slightly more than a local call, dial 214 + the Bolivian number.

● **Shopping**
Shops tend to open early and close by 1700. *Pro-Sol, Casa do Artesão*, R Dom Aquino Correa 405, in a converted prison, open Mon-Fri 0800-1200 and 1400-1800, Sat 0800-1200, good selection of handicrafts and a small bookshop, friendly staff but high prices. *CorumbArte*, Av Gen Rondon 1011, for good silk-screen T shirts with Pantanal motifs. *Livraria Corumbaense*, R Delamaré 1080 for state maps.

Supermarkets: *Ohara*, Dom Aquino corner Antônio João; *Frutal*, R 13 de Junho 538, open 0800-2000.

● **Tour companies & travel agents**
Corumbá has many travel agencies selling tours to the Pantanal; we list some. For more information see page 633: *Mutum Turismo*, R Frei Mariano 17, T 231-1818, F 231-3027, for airline tickets, tours, helpful; *Pantanal Tours/Sairú Turismo*, R M Cavassa 61, T 231-4683, F 231-2523, fishing trips, agents for *Cabexy I and II*, luxurious floating hotels, day trips on land, US$55 pp, river trips US$15 pp/3 hrs, happily rec; *Pantanal Service*, R Dom Aquino 700, T/F 231-5998, fishing and photo trips by boat, agents for *Hotel Porto Vitória Régia*; *Corumbatur*, Antônio M Coelho, T/F 231-1532, combined Pantanal/Bonito tours; *JMS Turismo*, R M Cavassa 215, T 231-5235, small fishing boats for rent US$60/day for 3 persons, minivans for trips to Bolivia US$10 pp; *Pérola do Pantanal*, R M Cavassa 255, T 231-1470, F 231-6585, river and land tours, good 1-day river tour with *Lancha Pérola*; *Taimã*, R Antônio M Coelho 786, T/F 231-6696, river trips, flights over Pantanal, airline tickets; *Pantur*, R América 969, T 231-4343, F 231-6006, tours, agents for *Hotel Fazenda Xaraés* in Nhecolândia; *Receptivo Pantanal*, R Frei Mariano 502, T 231-5795, helpful (1-day tour US$50, 3-day US$100, 4-day US$130).

● **Tourist offices**
Emcotur, R America 969, T 231-6996, municipal tourist office, for general information and city maps.

● **Transport**
Local Car hire: Localiza, airport and R Frei Mariano 51, T 231-6379, F 231-3741, daily rates from US$90 (unlimited km), weekly from US$540; Unidas, R Frei Mariano 633, T/F 231-3124.

Air Daily flights to Campo Grande, TAM and Pantanal (much cheaper); TAM also to Cuiabá, daily, Londrina and São Paulo (via Campo Grande). See **Bolivia**, **Section 5**, for flights between Puerto Suárez and Santa Cruz. There is a flight to Santa Cruz, Bolivia, with Aerosul or travel overland to Asunción and fly from there.

Buses The rodoviária is on R Porto Carreiro at the S end of R Tiradentes, next to the railway station. Andorinha services all points east. To **Campo Grande**, 7 hrs, US$24, 13 buses daily, between 0630 hrs and midnight, interesting journey ('an excursion in itself') – take an early bus to see plentiful wildlife, connections from Campo Grande to all parts of Brazil. To **São Paulo** direct, 22 hrs, US$58, 1100 and 1500, confirm bus times in advance as these change(T 231-2033). To **Rio** direct, 28 hrs, US$72, daily 1100. Cruzeiro do Sul operates the route S to the Paraguayan border. To **Ponta Porã**, 12 hrs, US$36, via Bonito (6 hrs, US$18) and Jardim (9 hrs, US$22), Mon-Sat at 0600; ticket office open 0500-0600 only, at other times call T 231-2383. City bus to rodoviária from Praça da República. **Taxis**: are extortionate.

River Shipping The *Acuri*, a luxury vessel, sails between **Cáceres** and Corumbá, once a week, US$600 including return by air. (See page 641, under Cáceres.)

FRONTIER WITH BOLIVIA

Over the border from Corumbá are Arroyo Concepción, Puerto Quijarro and Puerto Suárez. From Puerto Quijaro a 650-km railway runs to Santa Cruz de la Sierra. There is a road of sorts.

● **Brazilian immigration**

Immigration and emigration formalities are constantly changing so check procedure in advance. You need not have your passport stamped to visit Quijarro or Puerto Suárez only for the day. Otherwise, get passport stamped by Brazilian Polícia Federal at their main office, Praça da República, next door to the NS da Candelária church, T 231-5848, open 0800-1730 (knock after hours). If exiting Brazil merely to obtain a new visa, remember that exit and entry must not be on the same day.

Entering Brazil If you arrive in Brazil without a yellow fever vaccination certificate, you may have to go to R 7 de Setembro, Corumbá, for an inoculation.

● **Bolivian consulate**

R Antônio Maria Coelho 852, Corumbá, Mon-Fri, 0700-1100, 1500-1730, Sat and Sun closed. Check **Documents** in **Bolivian Information for travellers** for requirements. A fee is charged to citizens of those countries which require a visa. A yellow fever vaccination certificate is required.

● **Exchange**

Money changers at the border and in Quijarro offer same rates as in Corumbá.

● **Transport**

Leaving Brazil, take Canarinho city bus marked Fronteira from port end of R Antônio Maria Coelho to Bolivian border (15 mins), walk over the bridge to the Bolivian border post (blue building), go through formalities, then take colectivo to Quijarro or Puerto Suárez.

When travelling from Quijarro, take a taxi or walk to the Bolivian border to go through formalities. Just past the bridge, on a small side street to the right is the bus stop for Corumbá, it goes to Praça da República, US$0.50, every 45 min between 0630 and 1915, don't believe taxi drivers who say there is no bus. Taxi to centre US$10. Find a hotel then take care of Brazilian formalities at Polícia Federal, address above.

Trains Services to **Santa Cruz** in Bolivia, from Quijarro, the Bolivian frontier station, are given on page 352. The schedule of each appears to change frequently so check on arrival in Corumbá. Tickets may be booked through travel agencies, which charge higher prices than if booked direct. If purchasing your own ticket, you must do so in Quijarro on day of departure, except for the luxury *Bracha* coach (from travel agents only). Go as early as possible (it may be best to stay in Quijarro to get a good place in the queue).

PANTANAL

This vast wetland, measuring 230,000 sq km between Cuiabá, Campo Grande and the Bolivian frontier, is one of the world's great wildlife preserves. Parts spill over into neighbouring Bolivia and Paraguay, and the entire area has been opened up to tourism. The water in the Pantanal is not stagnant, a gentle gradient ranging for 1 to 3 cm/km, from N to S, keeps it flowing in that direction, hence during the wet season flooding gradually advances southwards. The region is drained by the São Lourenço, Cuiabá, Piquiri, Taquari, Aquidauana, Miranda and Apa rivers, all of which are tributaries of the Rio Paraguai.

Flora and fauna

Similar in many ways to the Amazon basin, though because of the more veldt-like open land, the wildlife can be viewed more easily than in the dense jungle growth. Principal life seen in this area is about 300 species of birds, including the hyacinth macaw, jabiru stork (the *tuiuíu*, almost 1.2m tall), plumbeous ibis, both blue-throated and red-throated piping guans and roseate spoonbill. There are some 230 varieties of fish, from the giant *pintado*, weighing up to 80 kilos, to the tiny, voracious *piranha*. Fishing here is exceptionally good (best May-Oct). Animal life is represented among others by giant and collared anteaters, 4 species of opossum, 5 armadillo species, black-tailed marmoset, black howler monkey, maned wolf, South American coati, southern and giant river otters, ocelot, margay, jaguarundi, puma, 3 peccary species, marsh deer and two other species, yellow anaconda and the ubiquitous *capivara*, a species of giant aquatic guinea-pig. Probably the most impressive sight is the *jacaré* (Yacare Caiman). The extraordinary thing is that man and his domesticated cattle thrive together with the wildlife with seemingly little friction. Local farmers protect the area jealously.

Ecology and conservation

Only one area is officially a national park, the **Parque Nacional do Pantanal Matogrossense** in the municipality of Poconé, 135,000 ha of land and water, only accessible by air or river. (Permission to visit at Ibama, R Rubens de Mendonça, Cuiabá, CEP 78008-000, T 644-1511/1581.) Hunting in any form is strictly forbidden throughout the Pantanal and is punishable by 4 years imprisonment. Fishing is allowed with a licence (controlled by Ibama, issued by Banco do Brasil, enquire at travel agents); it is not permitted in the spawning season or *piracema* (Oct 1 to Feb 1 in Mato Grosso do Sul, Nov 1 to Mar 1 in Mato Grosso). Like other wilderness areas, the Pantanal faces important threats to its integrity. Agrochemicals and *garimpo* mercury washed down from the neighbouring *planalto* are a hazard to wildlife. Visitors must share the responsibility of protecting the Pantanal and you can make an important contribution by acting responsibly and choosing your guides accordingly: take out your rubbish, don't fish out of season, don't let guides kill or disturb fauna, don't buy products made from endangered species, don't buy live birds or monkeys, and report any violation of these norms to the authorities.

The International Union for the Conservation of Nature is concerned at the amount of poaching, particularly of jacaré skins, birds and capivaras. The Forestry Police have built control points on all major access roads to the Pantanal. Biologists interested in research projects in the area should contact the Coordenador de Estudos do Pantanal, Departamento de Biologia, Universidade Federal do Mato Grosso do Sul, Caixa Postal 649, Campo Grande, CEP 79070-900, T (067) 787-3311 ext 2113, F (067) 787-5317.

Climate

There are two distinct seasons. In the rainy season (Dec-Mar, wettest in Feb), most of the area floods, mosquitoes abound, and cattle crowd on to the few islands remaining above water. In the southern part, many wild animals leave the area, but in the N, which is slightly higher, the animals do not leave. An ordinary vehicle should be able to manage the Transpantaneira out of Cuiabá throughout most of the year, but in the wet season you should be prepared to get stuck, and muddy, pushing your car from time to time. The dry season (July to Oct) is the nesting and breeding season. The birds form vast nesting areas, with hundreds and thousands crowding the trees creating an almost insupportable cacophony of sounds; the white sand river beaches are exposed, *jacarés* bask in the sun, and *capivaras* frolic amid the grass.

In winter (June-Aug), temperatures fall to 10°, warm clothing and covers or sleeping bag are needed at night, but it's very hot and humid during summer.

Wear long sleeves and long trousers and spray clothes as well as skin with insect repellent (less of a problem July-Aug). Take insect repellent from home as mosquitoes, especially in the N Pantanal, are becoming immune to local brands.

Access

The Pantanal is not easy or cheap to visit. The best starting points are Corumbá, Cuiabá, and to a lesser extent Campo Grande, from where one finds public transport all around the perimeter, but none at all within. Wild camping is possible if you have some experience and your own transport. Remember that the longer you stay and the further you go from the edges (where most of the hotels are located), the more likely you are to see rare wildlife.

From Corumbá there is access to the Pantanal by both road and river, offering a variety of day trips, luxury house boat excursions, and connections to many surrounding *fazendas*. Along the road from Corumbá to Campo Grande (BR-262), are Miranda and Aquidauana, both important gateways to various fishing and tourist lodges. The BR-163 which connects Campo Grande and Cuiabá skirts the E edge of the Pantanal; Coxim, 242 Km N of Campo Grande offers access via the Rio Taquari but few facilities. From Cuiabá there is year-round road access to Barão de Melgaço and Poconé, both of which can be starting points for excursions. The Transpantaneira Highway runs S from Poconé to Porto Jofre, through the heart of the Pantanal, providing access to many different lodges, but does not have any bus service. Finally Cáceres, 215 Km W of Cuiabá at the NW corner of the Pantanal, offers access along the Rio Paraguai to one of the least developed parts of the region.

Tourist facilities in the Pantanal currently cater to four main categories of visitors. **Sports fishermen** usually stay at one of the numerous speciality lodges scattered throughout the region, which provide guides, boats, bait, ice and other related amenities. Bookings can be made locally or in any of Brazil's major cities. **All-inclusive tours** combining air and ground transportation, accommodations at the most elaborate *fazendas*, meals, guided river and land tours, can be arranged from abroad or through travel agencies in Brazil's gateway cities. This is the most expensive option. **Moderately priced tours** using private guides, camping or staying at more modest *fazendas* can be arranged locally in Cuiabá (where guides await arrivals at the airport) or through the more reputable agencies in Corumbá. **The lowest priced tours** are offered by independent guides in

Corumbá, some of whom are unreliable and travellers have reported at times serious problems here (see below). For those with the barest minimum of funds, a glimpse of the Pantanal and its wildlife can be had on the bus ride from Campo Grande to Corumbá, by lodging or camping near the ferry crossing over the Rio Paraguai (Porto Esperança), and by staying in Poconé and day-walking or hitching S along the Transpantaneira. Whatever your budget, take binoculars.

How to choose a guide

A tour of the Pantanal could be the highlight of your travels, so it is best to do some research before contracting a guide. Many budget travellers en route to or from Bolivia make Corumbá their base for visiting the Pantanal. Such tourists are often approached, in the streets and at the cheaper hotels, by salesmen who speak foreign languages and promise complete tours for low prices. They then hand their clients over to agencies and/or guides, who often speak only Portuguese, and may deliver something quite different. Some travellers have reported very unpleasant experiences and it is important to select a guide with great care anywhere. By far the best way to do so, is to speak with other travellers who have just returned from a Pantanal tour. Most guides also have a book containing comments from their former clients. Do not rush to sign up when first approached, always compare several available alternatives. Discuss the planned itinerary carefully and try to get it in writing (although this is seldom possible). Do not pay everything in advance of departure, and try to deal directly with agencies or guides, not salesmen (it can be difficult to tell who is who). Always get an itemized receipt. Bear in mind that a well-organized 3-day tour can be more rewarding than 4 days with an ill-prepared guide. There is fierce competition between guides who provide similar services, but with very different styles. Although we list a few of the most reputable guides below, there are other good ones and most economy travellers enjoy a pleasant if spartan experience. Remember that travellers must shoulder part of the responsibility for the current chaotic guiding situation in Corumbá. Act responsibly and don't expect to get something for nothing. (See also Corumbá guides section.)

Camping allows you to see the wildlife at its greatest period of activity – dawn and dusk but protection against mosquitoes is essential. Care should also be taken to avoid dangerous animals: snakes (especially in the rainy season), piranhas (especially in the dry season), killer bees and the larger *jacarés*. The inexperienced are cautioned not to strike out on their own.

● **Further reading** The Pantanal: Brazil's Forgotten Wilderness, Vic Banks (Sierra Club Books, 1991, 730 Polk St, San Francisco, CA 94100).

Local information
● **Accommodation**

There are many lodges with fair to good accommodation, some only approachable by air or river; most are relatively expensive. One option is to hire a car and check accommodation for yourself: in June-Sept, especially July, it is necessary to book accommodation in advance. Following is a list of some of those presently operating:

From Campo Grande: L1 full board *Pousada São Francisco*, 135 km from Aquidauana in the Rio Negro area of Nhecolândia, accessible only by air during the wet, with bath, fan, screening, horseback riding, price inc transport, meals, tours, bookings through *Impacto Turismo*, Campo Grande, T/F (067) 724-3167; **L1** full board *Refúgio Ecológico/Caimã*, 36 km from Miranda, 236 km from Campo Grande, first class, full board, excursions, T (067) 242-1102, or 725-5267, or São Paulo 246-9934; **L3** full board *Pousada Aguapé*, Fazenda São José, 59 km N of Aquidauana, 202 km from Campo Grande, farmhouse hotel, screened rooms, some with a/c, pool, horse riding, boat trips, trekking, meals and tours inc, bookings through *Impacto Turismo*, as above; **L3** full board *Hotel Fazenda Carandá*, 60 km from Aquidauana, cabins, a/c, full board, horses, boat trips on Rio Aquidauana, bookings through *Panbratur*, Aquidauana, T/F (067) 241-3494; **A1** *Cabana do Pescador*, 65 km from Aquidauana on the Rio Miranda, T (067) 241-3697, access by Bonito bus from Campo Grande (see page 624), fishing lodge, inc breakfast; **A1** *Fazenda Salobra*, T (067) 242-1162, 6 km from Miranda, 209 km from Corumbá, 198 from Campo Grande, is rec, with bath, inc all meals, tours, boat rentals and horses are extra; it is by the Rio Salobra (clear

water) and Rio Miranda, with birds and animals easily seen. Take bus from Campo Grande to Miranda, and alight 50m from the bridge over Rio Miranda, turn left for 1,200m to the Fazenda. **A1** *Pousada Caiman*, US$620 for 3 nights, everything inc, airport pickup/drop-off, boats, trucks, horses, day and night hikes, great guides, excellent food, pool, highly rec. *Fazenda Rio Negro*, 13,000 ha farm on the shores of the Rio Negro, farm house dating to 1920, tours, horses, fishing, bookings through Panbratur, Aquidauana, T/F as above; *Pousada Mangabal*, in Nhecolândia, farm setting, horses, tours, walks, bookings through Panbratur, Aquidauana, T/F as above; *Pousada Toca da Onça*, 10 km from Aquidauana on the shores of the Rio Aquidauana, cabins, a/c, restaurant, boats, bookings through Panbratur, Aquidauana, T/F as above. **B** *Pousada Águas do Pantanal*, Av Afonso Pena 367, Miranda, T/F (067) 242-1314, F 242-1242, contact Fátima or Luis Cordelli, very good, good food, restaurant serves jacaré legally (closed in Feb/96). There is a good campsite 30 km past Miranda. Alternatively, hire a car in Corumbá and drive to Miranda, but note that the dirt road is bad after rain (consequently not much traffic and more wildlife can be seen). Car with driver can be hired at Salobra for US$25. There are several camping possibilities along the shores of the Rio Aquidauana including *Camping Baía*, 50 km from Aquidauana, on a bay on the river, trees for shade, boats; *Pequi Camping*, 48 km from Aquidauana, with toilets, electricity; *Camping Itajú*, sandy beach, cabins, lanchonete, shower, electricity, boat rental.

Another access to the Pantanal from the E is **Coxim** (pop 28,276; DDD 067; CEP 79400; 242 Km N of Campo Grande) on the BR-163, half way between Campo Grande and Rondonópolis; it sits in a green bowl, on the shores of the Rio Taquari; the area has great potential for tourism, but there are no official tours to the Pantanal, a great place if you have your own boat. **Accommodation A3** Coxim, 4 km S of town, T 291-1480, F 291-1479, a/c, fridge, TV, restaurant; **A3** Santa Ana, R Miranda Reis on the river bank, T 291-1602 cabins for 4, pool; **C** Santa Teresa, 5 km S of town, T 291-2215, F 291-1289, with bath, fan; Piracêma, by the bridge over the Rio Taquari, with restaurant; Sinhazino, N of the Taquari bridge; there are several simpler hotels in town.

From Corumbá: 1 day river trips available on river boats with a capacity of 80 passengers, US$15 half-day; US$30 full day, inc transfers and hot fish meal. Smaller boats US$15 pp for 3 hrs. Tickets at travel agents and by port. Boats may be hired, with fishing tackle and guide, at the port (US$100/day, up to 3 people, in season only). Cattle boats will on occasion take passengers on their round trips to farms in the Pantanal, but take your own food – it is not always possible to disembark. Ask at Bacia da Prata, 10 mins out of Corumbá on the Ladário bus.

Lodges: **L1** full board *Pousada do Pantanal*, T (067) 231-5797, 125 km from Corumbá nr the Campo Grande road at Fazenda Santa Clara (still a working cattle ranch), very comfortable, easy access by bus, reservations from all agencies in Corumbá; US$190 pp for 3 days/2 nights, minimum 2 persons, good food (but drinks not inc), with horseback, car and boat excursions, guides inc, canoes, simple fishing gear, motor boats for rent (try bargaining in the off-season for reduced rates). **L1** full board *Hotel Fazenda Xaraés*, T (067) 231-6777, Rio Abobral, 130 km from Corumbá, luxurious, a/c, pool, restaurant, horses, boats. **A2** *Fazenda Santa Blanca*, on the Rio Paraguai, 15 mins by boat S of Porto Esperança (where the BR-262 crosses the Rio Paraguai), full board, good kayak excursions, horse riding, information from R 15 de Novembro 659, 79300 Corumbá, T 231-1460, or *Flins Travel* (Walter Zoss), R do Acre 92, 6th floor, 602, CEP 20081, Rio de Janeiro, T (021) 253-8588/0195 or *Safari Fotográfico*, R Frei Mariano 502, Corumbá, T 231-5797. *Fazenda Leque*, Roberto Kassan (contact through R América 262, Corumbá, T 231-1598), take mosquito coils, unlimited use of horses and boats, on small lake behind the farm, good food, plenty of wildlife to be seen. *Pousada Do Castelo*, 3 hrs by boat from Corumbá, T (067) 231-5151. The going rate for a 3-day camping photo safari by jeep is US$70-80 pp for 4-6 people; US$80-90 pp for 4 days. Fishing trips in luxurious floating hotels for 8 (eg *Tuiuiú* T/F 231-2052 and *Cabexy II* from *Pantanal Tours*, Corumbá – must be booked in advance), US$1,200-2,000/day, minimum 5 days. Hotels specializing in fishing, all reached from Corumbá by road: **L2** full board

Pesqueiro da Odila, on the Rio Paraguai, reservations from Belo Horizonte T (031) 221-4003, a/c, fridge, restaurant. **L3** full board *Porto Morrinho*, on the Rio Paraguai, T 231-1360, a/c, fridge, TV, pool. **L3** full board *Pesqueiro Tarumã*, Rio Paraguai, 65 km from Corumbá, Corumbá office at R M Cavassa 109, T/F 231-4771. **L3** full board *Pesqueiro Paraiso dos Dourados*, 72 km from Corumbá, Rios Paraguai e Miranda, Corumbá office at R Antônio João, T/F 231-3021, a/c, fridge, tours. **L3** *Pantanal Park*, 20 min by boat from Porto Esperança (where the BR 262 crosses the Rio Paraguai), with a/c, restaurant. **A1** *Pesqueiro Cabana do Lontra*, including meals T (067) 383-4532, 180 km from Aquidauana on the Corumbá road.

● **Tour companies & travel agents**
Travel agents in Corumbá: some of Corumbá's many agencies are listed on page 628. Tours out of Corumbá are of 3-4 days, costing between US$50-90 (includes all food, accommodation and transport). Travel is in the back of a pick-up (good for seeing animals), up to a maximum of 6. Accommodation is in a hammock under a palm thatch on a *fazenda*. Food can be good. If you want flushing toilets, showers or luxury cabins, approach an agency. Guides provide bottled mineral water (make sure enough is carried), but you must take a hat, sun screen and mosquito repellent. Some guides go to *fazendas* without permission, have unreliable vehicles, or are inadequately equipped, so try to check their credentials.

Guides will generally not make the trip with fewer than 5 people, so if you have not already formed a group, stay in touch with several guides (most important during Mar-Oct, when fewer tourists are around). Decide on your priorities: try to ensure that your guide and other group members share your ideas.

We list below those guides who have received positive reports from travellers: *Natureza Tours*, Durvanil Pereira Rodrigues, R

Dom Aquino 255, T 231-1218, 2-4 day trips to his own family *fazenda*, including boat trip, fishing, horse riding, cheap but very good; *Colibri Pantanal Safari*, run by Claudine (Swiss) out of one of the *Pousadas Pantaneiras*, popular; *Green Track*, R Ladário 271, rec; *Tucantur*, at *Hotel Londres*, Corumbá, 3-5 day trips; *Katu*, R Dom Aquino 220, T 231-1987, rec; *Gil Tours*, R Porto Carrero 612, T 231-1772, guide Elísio Rodríguez da Silva, rec. There are many other guides not listed here; lots have received criticisms (some repeatedly) from correspondents. There may be others on whom we have received no feedback.

TO THE PANTANAL FROM CUIABÁ

The Transpantaneira Highway, built in 1976, was originally projected to connect Cuiabá with Corumbá but currently goes only as far as Porto Jofre on the Rio Cuiabá. Work has been suspended indefinitely because of difficulties, costs and ecological considerations.

POCONÉ

A paved road turns S off the main Cuiabá-Cáceres road to **Poconé** (*pop* 31,190; *DDD* 065; *CEP* 78175; 102 km from Cuiabá), which was founded in 1781. It is known as the Cidade Rosa. Until 1995 there was much *garimpo* activity north of town and many slag heaps can be seen from the road.

- **Accommodation & places to eat** E *Pousada Pantaneira*, good restaurant, clean and simple, on Transpantaneira, T 721-1220, to hitchhike to Pixaim or Porto Jofre (see below), start at 0600 outside the hotel; E *Hotel Joá*, with bath, basic, acceptable, car parking; also on the Transpantaneira just S of town are *Aurora do Pantanal* T 721-1339 and *Hotel Santa Cruz*. *Three Poderes Restaurant*, R Beri, cheap good food; *Doce e Mel*, Praça Matriz, pleasant café serving good sweets and coffee.

- **Transport Buses** From Cuiabá US$7.65 by TUT, T 322-4985, 6 a day between 0600 and 1900. Poconé has a 24-hr **gas station** with all types of fuel, but closed on Sun.

From Poconé the Transpantaneira runs 146 km S to Porto Jofre (just a gas station, gasoline and diesel, but no alcohol available). At the entrance to the Pantanal, there is a gate across the road where drivers are given a list of rules of conduct. The road is of earth, in poor condition, with ruts, holes and many bridges that need care in crossing. Easiest access is in the dry season (July-Sept), which is also the best time for seeing birds and, in Sept, the trees are in bloom. In the wet, especially Jan-Feb, there is no guarantee that the Transpantaneira will be passable. The wet season, however, is a good time to see many of the shier animals because more fruit, new growth and other high calorie foods are available, and there are fewer people. Campos de Jofre, about 20 km N of Porto Jofre is said to be magnificent between Aug and Oct, with very large concentrations of birds and animals. In Poconé one can hitch (not much traffic, bumpy, especially in a truck) to Porto Jofre, or hire a vehicle in Cuiabá. You will get more out of this part of the Pantanal by going with a guide; a lot can be seen from the Transpantaneira in a hired car, but guides can take you into *fazendas* and will point out wildlife. Recommended guides in Cuiabá are listed below. Although there are gas stations in Pixaim and Porto Jofre, they are not always well stocked, best to carry extra fuel.

PIXAIM

63 km from Poconé is **Pixaim** (2 hrs in the dry, up to 5 in the wet season), a bridge across the Rio Pixaim, where there are two hotels, with a fuel station (all types available, check that the pump is set to zero) and a tyre-repair shop (*borracheria*).

- **Accommodation In Pixaim and The Transpantaneira: A2** *Pousada Pixaim*, built on stilts, T 721-1899, full board (meals also available separately), 10 rooms with a/c or fan, mosquito-netted windows, hot water, electricity 24 hrs, pleasant setting, boat trips – US$30/hr with driver, camping possible US$10/tent or free if you eat in the restaurant, rec, bookings through *Faunatur* in Cuiabá. On the opp bank of the Rio Pixaim is **A1** *Hotel Beira Rio*, T/F (065) 321-9445, modern cabins, 35 rooms for 3-6 people, with full board, fan, clean, hot water (also family-size apartments with a/c), good home-grown food, in radio contact with office on R Barão de Melgaço in Cuiabá, camping possible, boat rental with driver US$30/hr; **A2** *O Pantaneiro*, full board, 6 rooms with 2-3 bunk beds each, bath, simple, owned and operated by *pantaneiros* (reservations through *Focus Tours*, Belo Horizonte, see page 431, or through *Faunatur* in Cuiabá), about 45 km from Pixaim, not as far S as **L3** *Hotel Fazenda Santa Rosa*, 150 km from Poconé, in Porto Jofre, with full board, no electricity, an old *fazenda*, refurbished in 1996, occasional water problems, river trips not inc and expensive, breakfast-eating parrot (reservations through *Focus Tours*, Belo Horizonte).

L2 *Pousada Araras*, Km 30 on Transpantaneira, 10 rooms with bath, rec, pool, good food, home-made *cachaça*, book through *Expeditours* in Cuiabá; **A1** *Hotel-Fazenda Cabanas do Pantanal*, 142 km from Cuiabá, 50 km from Poconé by the Rio Pixaim, on the northern edge of the Pantanal, 10 chalet bedrooms with bath, restaurant, boat trips (few in dry season), horse-riding, fishing, helpful proprietor and staff, everything except boat trips and bar drinks inc in price (booking: *Confiança*, Cuiabá). **L2** *Sapé Pantanal Lodge*, Caixa Postal 2241 – CEP 78020.970, Cuiabá, T (065) 322-3426, F 361-4069, 14 rooms, 4-day, 3-night all-inclusive programme US$500, fishing, wildlife observation and photography excursions, holder of the Embratur 'Ecológico Especial' classification and FEMA (Environmental Bureau) Green Stamp. A complete programme includes road transport from Cuiabá airport to Barão de Melgaço (wet season), or Porto Cercado (dry season) with onward river transportation (2 hrs and 1½ hrs respectively), and return; full board; outboard powered boats with experienced guides at guests' disposal during entire stay; optional trekking and horse riding in dry season, paddling in wet; English, French, Spanish spoken. *Sapé* is closed 20 Dec-31 Jan, highly rec.

BARÃO DE MELGAÇO

130 km from Cuiabá (TUT bus at 0730 and 1500, US$6.50) on Rio Cuiabá, **Barão de Melgaço** is reached by two roads: the shorter, via Santo Antônio de Leverger, unpaved from Sto Antônio to Barão (closed in the wet season), or via São Vicente, longer, but more pavement. The way to see the Pantanal from here is by boat down the Rio Cuiabá. Boat hire, for example from *Restaurant Peixe Vivo* on waterfront, up to US$85 for a full day; or enquire with travel agencies in Cuiabá. The best time of day would be sunset, but it would need some organizing to be in the best part at the best time, without too much boating in the dark. Protect against the sun when on the water. Initially the river banks are farms and small habitations, but they become more forested, with lovely combinations of flowering trees

(best seen Sept-Oct). After a while, a small river to the left leads to the Baia and Lakes Chacororé and Sia Mariana, which join each other. Boats can continue beyond the lakes to the Rio Mutum, but a guide is essential because there are many dead ends. The area is rich in birdlife and the waterscapes are beautiful.

● **Accommodation** In the town are *Barão Tour Hotel*, apartments with a/c, restaurant, boat trips and excursions (T Cuiabá 322-1568, or Melgatur), and, much humbler, *NS do Carmo Hotel* on the waterfront, and *Pousada e Lanchonete Francisco de Asis* on main road down to waterfront. *Mercadinho do Povo* minimarket sells provisions, including cheap hats. **Hotels reached from Barão de Melgaço**: on Sia Mariana are *Pousada do Barão*, 6 chalets with bath, swimming pool, 1st class, boat and trekking expeditions (book through Melgatur); *Restaurant Flamingo*, simple food, rooms, camping with permission, popular with fishermen; one other restaurant. Barão de Melgaço is also the starting point for the *Pousada Passargada*, programmes from 3 days up, full board, boat, car and trekking expeditions, transport from Barão de Melgaço, owner speaks English, French and German, food excellent, highly rec, closed Dec to Feb; reservations in Barão de Melgaço on riverside, through *Nature Safaris*, Av Mal Rondon, Barão de Melgaço, or Av NS de Copacabana 330, Rio de Janeiro, CEP 22020, T 235-2840, F 236-5285. Much cheaper if booked direct with the owner, Maré Sigaud, Mato Grosso, CEP 786807, *Pousada Passargada*, Barão de Melgaço.

● **Tour companies & travel agents in Cuiabá**: *Confiança*, Mariano 434, T 321-4142, very helpful travel agency, tours to Pantanal are expensive. Also rec *Expeditours*, Av Gov Ponce de Arruda 670, T 381-4959/5674, sightseeing, fishing trips for 4-5 days by boat; *Anaconda*, R Comandante Costa 649, T 624-4142, F 624-6242, tour operators for Pantanal, Chapada dos Guimarães and Southern Amazonia, Pantanal day tour as far as Pixaim US$60 pp, 2 day US$155 pp, 3 day US$210, day tour to Chapada or Águas Quentes US$50 pp, Amazon trips to Alta Floresta/Rio Cristalino region US$100 pp/day + airfare; *Ametur*, R Joaquim Murtinho 242, T 624-1000, very helpful, good for air tickets; Adriana Coningham of *Ararauna Turismo Ecológica*, R Barão de Melgaço, highly rec. All these agencies arrange trips to the Pantanal; for longer or special programmes, book in advance. *Focus Tours* of Belo Horizonte (see page 431) specializes in tours in this part of the Pantanal and, starting from Cuiabá, to the southern Amazon, with bases at Alta Floresta and on the Rio Cristalino (see page 642).

Recommended guides (in alphabetical order): Sérgio Alves, F 623-5258, speaks English, bird-watching and other tours; Djalma dos Santos Moraes, R Arnaldo Addor 15, Coophamil, 78080 Cuiabá, T/F 625-1457, US$100 pp/day, rec. Laércio Sá, *Fauna Tour*, Real Palace Hotel, Praça Ipiranga 102, CEP 78020-600, T/F 321-5375 (Attn Faunatours) or Av Beira Rio, Quadra 28, Casa 21, CEP 78.065-780, has own car, well-informed, helpful, speaks English, Spanish and Italian, 2 day Pantanal tours US$140 pp, 3 day US$190 pp (inc transport, accomodation, meals, trekking, horse riding, boat trips, fishing) can arrange longer tours and camping (Aug-Oct) on request, also excursions to Chapada dos Guimarães, rec. Joel Souza, can be contacted at the airport, speaks English well, checklists for flora and fauna provided, will arrange all transport, farm accommodation, fishing, horse riding, trekking, night excursions (US$140 for 2-night tours). Most guides await incoming flights at airport; compare prices and services in town if you don't wish to commit yourself at airport.

CUIABÁ

(*Pop* 435,647, unofficially much larger; *alt* 165m; *CEP* 78000; *DDD* 065) **Cuiabá**, the capital of Mato Grosso state (*pop* 2,020,580) on the Rio Cuiabá, an upper tributary of the River Paraguai, is in fact two cities: Cuiabá on the E bank of the river and Várzea Grande, where the airport is, on the W. It is very hot; coolest months for a visit are June, July, and Aug, in the dry season. It has a number of squares and is known as the *Cidade Verde* (green city).

PLACES OF INTEREST

Cuiabá has an imposing government palace and other fine buildings round the green **Praça da República**. On the square is the **Cathedral**, with a plain, imposing exterior, two clock-towers and, inside, coloured-glass mosaic windows and doors. Behind the altar is a huge mosaic of Christ in majesty, with smaller mosaics in side chapels. Beside the Cathedral is another leafy square, **Praça Alencastro**. On **Praça Ipiranga**, at the junction of Avs Isaac Póvoas and Ten Cel Duarte, a few blocks W of the central squares, there are market stalls and an iron bandstand from Hud-dersfield. On a hill beyond the square is the church of **Bom Despacho** (closed for restoration, 1996). In front of the Assembléia Legislativa, Praça Moreira Cabral, is a point marking the **Geogedesic Centre of South America** (see also under Chapada dos Guimarães, below).

MUSEUMS

Museus de Antropologia, História Natural e Cultura Popular, in the Fundação Cultural de Mato Grosso, Praça da República 151, US$0.50, historical photos, documents, furniture, one room of religious art, contemporary art gallery, stuffed fauna, stones and woods from the region, Indian items and weapons, archaeological finds and pottery, open Mon-Fri 0800-1730. **Museu de Arte Sacra**, beside Bom Despacho church. **Museu de Pedras**, US$2 entry, Galdino Pimentel 195, Mon-Fri 0800-1100 and 1300-1700, exhibits stones from the Chapada dos Guimarães. At the entrance to Universidade de Mato Grosso, 10 mins by bus from the centre, is the **Museu do Índio/Museu Rondon** (by swimming pool), small, well-displayed exhibits. Carrying on along the road through the campus, signed on the left before a right turn in the road, is the **Zoológico**, open 0800-1100, 1330-1700 (closed Mon), free; the jacaré, capivara, tortoise and tapir pen can be seen at any time, but best early am or late pm, also has coatis, otters, emu, monkeys, peccaries, birds, etc. Opposite the zoo is the theatre.

EXCURSIONS

The **Águas Quentes** hot springs, 86 km (9 km S of the BR 163, 77 km E of Cuiabá) can be visited; **L3** *Hotel Águas Quentes* at the springs, all meals inc, reservations through *Hotel Mato Grosso Palace*, address below, T 624-6637. The waters fill pools of 42° and 36° C; no buses go there, arrange transport through *Hotel Mato Grosso Palace*.

LOCAL INFORMATION

NB The port area is best avoided, even in daylight.

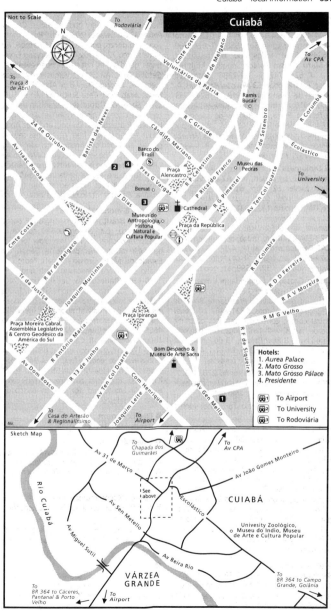

Cuiabá

Not to Scale

N

To Rodoviária

To Av CPA

To Praça 8 de Abril

Cmte Costa

Voluntários da Pátria

Br de Melgaço

Ramis Bucair

R Corumbá

R C Grande

Cândido Mariano

Ecolástico

24 de Outubro

Batista das Neves

7 de Setembro

Av Isaac Póvoas

Banco do Brasil

Praça Alencastro

R Celestino

Museu das Pedras

To University

2 4

Pres G Vargas

R Ricardo Franco

R G Pimenel

Bemat

J Dias

3

Cathedral

Av Ten Col Duarte

Cmte Costa

R Br de Melgaço

Museus do Antropologia, História Natural e Cultura Popular

Praça da República

R M Coimbra

Tr da Justiça

R D D Ferreira

R A V Moreira

Joaquim Murtinho

R M G Velho

Praça Ipiranga

Praça Moreira Cabral, Assembléia Legislativo & Centro Geodésico da América do Sul

R Antônio Maria

Bom Despacho & Museu de Arte Sacra

R F de Siqueira

Av Dom Bosco

R 13 de Junho

Av Ten Col Duarte

Com Henrique

Joaquim Leite

Av Gen Melo

To Casa do Artesão & Regionalíssimo

To Airport

1

Hotels:
1. *Aurea Palace*
2. *Mato Grosso*
3. *Mato Grosso Pálace*
4. *Presidente*

🚌₁ To Airport

🚌₂ To University

🚌₃ To Rodoviária

Sketch Map

To Chapada dos Guimarães

To Av CPA

Av 31 de Março

Av João Gomes Monteiro

Rio Cuiabá

Av Sen Metello

See above

Ecolástico

CUIABÁ

Univesity Zoológico, Museu do Índio, Museu de Arte e Cultura Popular

Av Miguel Sutil

Av Beira Rio

VÁRZEA GRANDE

To BR 364 to Cáceres, Pantanal & Porto Velho

To Airport

To BR 364 to Campo Grande, Goiânia

● **Accommodation**
L2 *Eldorado Cuiabá*, Av Isaac Póvoas 1000, T 624-4000, F 624-1480, very smart; **L2** *Global Garden*, Av Miguel Sutil 5555, T 6241660, F 6249966, a/c, fridge, pool, bar, restaurant; **L3** *Mato Grosso Palace*, Joaquim Murtinho 170, T 624-7747, F 321-2386, 4-star, a/c, fridge, central, good; **L3** *Novotel Paiaguas*, Av Rubens de Mendonça 1718, T 624-5353, F 322-2910, a/c, fridge, pool, sauna, restaurant; **L3** *Taiamã Plaza*, Av Rubens de Mendonça 1184, Bosque de Saúde, T/F 624-1490, 3-star, very good, pool, excellent breakfast; **L3** *Veneza Palace*, Av Cel Escolástico 738, T 321-4847, F 322-5212, 3-star, rec.

A2 *Diplomata*, Av João Ponce de Arruda 686, T 682-2942, by airport, rec; **A2** *Las Velas*, Av Filinto Müller 62, opp airport, T 6823840, F 6823734, pool, good value; **A3** *Aurea Palace*, Gen Melo 63, T 322-3377, pleasant rooms, restaurant, swimming pool, good; **A3** *Almanara*, Av Cel Escolástico 510, T 323-1244, F 323-2049, with a/c, fridge; opp but less good is **A3** *Bandeirantes*, at No 425, T 321-0920, F 624-5363, a/c, fridge, SE of centre; **B** *Abudi Palace*, No 259, T 322-7399, a/c, good.

B *Mato Grosso*, R Comandante Costa 2522, T 321-9121, 2-star, a/c, cheaper with fan, good restaurant, good value; **B** *Presidente*, Barão de Melgaço e Av G Vargas, T 321-6162, on a busy central corner, convenient but lots of traffic outside, a/c, **C** with fan, fridge, cheaper with shared bath; **B** *Real Palace*, 13 de Junho 102, Praça Ipiranga, T 321-5375, F 611-1141, large rooms, some with a/c, good breakfast.

C *Samara*, R Joaquim Murtinho 270, T 322-6001, central, with bath, hot shower, fan, basic but good, cheaper with shared bath.

E *Lagunas*, Av Gen Melo 166, small rooms, basic.

By the rodoviária, on Jules Rimet are: **A3** *Skala Palace*, at No 26, T 322-4347, with a/c, fridge, restaurant, smart lobby, front rooms noisy; **B** *Brazil*, No 20, T 621-2703, a/c, fridge, parking, **D** with fan, cheaper with shared bath, ground floor rooms are best; **C** *Ipanema*, s/n, T 621-3069, a/c, **D** with fan, cheaper with shared bath, good value, good breakfast, rec; **C** *Grande*, No 30, T 621-3852, a/c, **D** with fan, cheaper with shared bath, basic; **E** *Modelo*, No 221, fan, basic; **D** *União*, R Poxoréu 13, T 621-1589, fan, basic; **E** with shared bath, basic; others in same area.

● **Places to eat**
Bierhaus, Isaac Póvoas 1200; *Tio Ari*, R Comandante Costa 770, buffet with a wide variety of vegetarian and a few meat dishes, good quality and value, rec; *Sachimi*, Av Isaac Póvoas across

from *Eldorado Hotel*, Japanese. *O Choppão*, Praça 9 de Abril, very good, popular; *Cacalo Peixaria*, Av Lavapés 203, Santa Rosa, traditional fish dishes, popular, good; *Salambô*, Av 31 de Março 720, across from *Shopping Goiabeiras*, good buffet, not cheap, open evenings; *Getúlio Grill*, Av Getúlio Vargas 1147, meat specialties; *Cedros*, Praça 8 de Abril 750, Goiabeiras, Arab food; *Casa Suíça*, Av Miguel Sutil 4200, Swiss food, trout. Restaurants in the city centre are closed at night, try Av Getúlio Vargas, between Praças Santos Dumont and 9 de Abril, about 10 mins' walk from centre, has several popular pizza and other restaurants, also along Isaac Póvoas in the same direction (NW). On Av CPA are many good restaurants and small snack bars. There are several restaurants and lanchonetes on R Jules Rimet across from the rodoviária, *Paladar*, at No 60, good value, rec.

● **Banks & money changers**
Banco do Brasil, Av Getúlio Vargas e R Barão de Melgaço, commission US$10 for cash, US$20/transaction for TCs, very slow for TCs, but best rates; fewer people at **Banco do Estado de Mato Grosso** (Bemat), Pedro Celestino s/n, Praça Alencastro, cash and TCs, 1000-1500; **Banespa**, Av Getúlio Vargas 240, cash and TCs, min transaction US$500, 1000-1330. The following travel agents or gold dealers change cash only at poor rates (generally open Mon-Fri): *Mattos-Tur*, R Cândido Mariano 465; *Goldmine*, R Cândido Mariano 400, 0800-1600; *Ourominas*, R Cândido Mariano 401, 0800-1700, may change on Sat 0800-1200 if cash is available, enquire first, T 624-9400; *Portobello*, R Comandante Costa 555, 0900-1600. It is difficult to get cash advances on credit cards especially Mastercard, for Visa try Banco do Brasil or Bradesco.

● **Electric current**
110 volts AC, 60 cycles.

● **Entertainment**
Cuiabá is quite lively at night, bars with live music and dance on Av CPA; *Tucano* bar/restaurant, Av CPA, beautiful view, rec. Four cinemas in town.

● **Post & telecommunications**
Post Office: main branch at Praça da República, fax service.

Telecommunications: Telemat, R Barão de Melgaço 3209, 0700-2200, also at rodoviária, 0600-2130, international service.

● **Shopping**
Handicrafts in wood, straw, netting, leather, skins, Pequi liquor, compressed *caju* fruit, compressed *guaraná* fruit (for making the drink), Indian objects on sale at airport, rodoviária, craft

shops in centre, and daily market, Praça da República, interesting. The *Casa de Artesão*, Praça do Expedicionário 315, T 321-0603, sells all types of local crafts in a restored building, rec. Fish and vegetable market, picturesque, at the riverside.

● **Tourist offices**

Secretaria de Desenvolvimento do Turismo, **Sedtur**, Praça da República 131, next to post office building, T/F 624-9060, Mon-Fri, 0700-1800. Good maps, friendly, helpful regarding general information, hotels and car hire, some English and Spanish spoken. **Ramis Bucair**, R Pedro Celestino 280, is good for detailed maps of the region.

● **Transport**

Local Buses Many bus routes have stops in the vicinity of Praça Ipiranga. To/from airport, see below; bus 501 or 505 (Universidade) to University museums and zoo (ask for 'Teatro') from Av Ten Cel Duarte by Praça Bispo Dom José, a triangular park just E of Praça Ipiranga. To rodoviária, No 202 from R Joaquim Murtinho behind the cathedral, about 20 mins. **Car hire**: **Unidas**, Av Isaac Póvoas 720, T 682-4062; **Nobre**, at airport, T 381-1651; **Localiza**, Av Dom Bosco 963, T 6247979; **Atlântida**, Av Isaac Póvoas, T 623-0700.

Air Airport in Várzea Grande, T 682-2213. By air to most major cities. No bank at airport; there is a post office and a Turimat office (not always open). Taxi to centre US$10-15, bus US$0.40 (take any white Tuiuiú bus, name written on side, in front of airport to Av Ten Cel Duarte; to return take 'Aeroporto' bus from Praça Ipiranga).

Buses Rodoviária is on R Jules Rimet, Bairro Alvorada, N of the centre; town buses (see above) stop at the entrance. Comfortable buses (toilets) to **Campo Grande**, 10 hrs, US$25, 12 buses daily, *leito* at 2000 and 2100, US$48. To **Goiânia**, 14 hrs, US$30; direct to **Brasília**, 24 hrs, US$37, *leito* US$59. To **Porto Velho**, 6 União Cascavel buses a day, US$63, 21 hrs. Andorinha 1700 bus São Paulo-Cuiabá connects with Porto Velho service. Several to **São Paulo**, eg Motta, US$50. To **Barra do Garças**, Xavante 0800, 1300 and 2030, US$17, also Barattur. Connections to all major cities.

ROUTES There is a paved road to Campo Grande (712 km); the 2,400 km BR-364 road from Brasília to Porto Velho and Rio Branco passes through Cuiabá; it is paved all the way between Brasília, Cuiabá (1,133 km) and is in good condition, but between Cuiabá and Porto Velho (1,450 km) there are many pot-holes. Service stations often provide free hot showers and the *prato comercial* is a cheap meal. The more direct road to

Brasília through Barra do Garças and Goiás Velho (the BR-070) is paved also. Several paved feeder roads connect the BR-070 and BR-364.

CHAPADA DOS GUIMARÃES

68 km NE of Cuiabá lies one of the oldest plateaus on earth. The pleasant town of **Chapada dos Guimarães** (*pop* 13,416; *DDD* 065; *CEP* 78195), the main population centre, is a base for many beautiful excursions in this area; it has the oldest church in the Mato Grosso, **NS de Santana** (1779), a bizarre blending of Portuguese and French baroque styles, and a huge spring-water public swimming pool (on R Dr Pem Gomes, behind the town). Formerly the centre of an important diamond prospecting region, today Chapada is a very popular destination for Cuiabanos to escape the heat of the city on weekends and holidays.

The Chapada is an immense geological formation rising to 700m, with rich forests, curiously-eroded rocks and many lovely grottoes, peaks and waterfalls. A **National Park** has been established in the area just W of the town, where the **Salgadeira** tourist centre offers bathing, camping and a restaurant close to the Salgadeira waterfall. The beautiful 85m **Véu da Noiva** waterfall (Bridal Veil), 12 km before the town near Buriti (well-signposted, ask bus from Cuiabá to let you off), is reached by a short route, or a long route through forest. Other sights include the **Mutuca** beauty spot, **Rio Claro**, the viewpoint over the breathtaking 80m-deep **Portão do Inferno** (Hell's Gate), and the falls of **Cachoeirinha** (small restaurant) and **Andorinhas**. 8 km E of town is the **Mirante do Ponto Geodésico**, a monument officially marking the Geodesic Centre of South America, which overlooks a great canyon with views of the surrounding plains, the Pantanal and Cuiabá's skyline on the horizon; to reach it take R Fernando Corrêa E, drive 8 km then turn right at the 'Centro Geodésico' sign. Continuing E, the road goes through agricultural land and later by interesting rock formations including a stone bridge and stone cross; 45 km from Chapada you reach the access for

Caverna do Francês or Caverna Aroe Jari ('the dwelling of the souls' in the Bororo language), a sandstone cave over 1 km long, the second largest in Brazil; it is a 2-km walk to the cave, in it is Lagoa Azul, a lake with crystaline blue water, a good place for a dip. Other excursions are to the **Cidade de Pedra** rock formations, 25 km from town along the road to the diamond prospecting town of Agua Fria, nearby is a 300m wall formed by the Rio Claro and 60 km from town, are the **Pingador** and **Bom Jardim** archaeological sites, caverns with petroglyphs dating back some 4,000 years. The Chapada dos Guimarães is one of the most scenic areas of Brazil and retains much of the mystery attributed to it for centuries. In the 1920s Colonel Fawcett was told of many strange things hidden in its depths, and an unusual local magnetic force which reduces the speed of cars has been documented. The birdwatching is very good and mammals, such as puma, giant river otter and black-tailed marmoset, live here.

Tours Hiring a car in Cuiabá is the most convenient way to see many of the scattered attractions, although access to several of them is via rough dirt roads which may deteriorate in the rainy season; drive carefully as the area is prone to dense fog. Hitchhiking from Chapada town to the National Park is feasible on weekends and holidays, but expect crowds at the swimming holes. Travel agencies in Chapada and Cuiabá offer expensive tours to all the sights. The Secretaria de Turismo e Meio Ambiente office, R Quinco Caldas 100, near the praça, provides a useful map of the region and organizes tours; José Paulino dos Santos is a guide working with this office (weekdays 0800-1100, 1300-1800, T 791-1245). Rec tours with Jorge Belfort Mattos from *Ecoturismo Cultural*, Praça Dom Wunibaldo 464, T/F 791-1393; he speaks English and knows the area well; several 4- to 6-hr itineraries from US$20-56 pp (min 4 people or prices increase). Also with Cássio Martins of *AC Tour*, R Tiradentes 28, T 791-1122, who often waits at the rodoviária. 4 hr tours are about US$20 pp, min 5 persons; 7-8 hr tours, US$25 pp, min 5; horseback day tour,

US$25 pp, min 2; an 8-10 km hike with a guide, US$20 pp, min 2; bicycle tour with guide, US$20 pp, min 2. Tours from Cuiabá cost US$35-40 pp.

Local festivals The **Festival de Inverno** is held in last week of July, and **Carnaval** is very busy. Accommodation is scarce and expensive at these times.

● **Accommodation A1** *Pousada da Chapada*, 2 km out on Cuiabá road (MT 251, Km 63), T 791-1171, F 791-1299, a/c, fridge, **A2** with fan, very comfortable, restaurant, bar, pool, sports facilities, parking; **A3** *Turismo*, R Fernando Corrêa 1065, a block from rodoviária, T 791-1176, F 791-1383, a/c, fridge, **B** with fan, restaurant, very popular, German-run; **B** *Estância San Francisco*, at the entrance to town from Cuiabá (MT 251, Km 61), T 791-1102, F 791-1537, on 42 ha farm with 2 lakes, a/c, fridge, said to have the best breakfast in town fresh from the farm; **B** *Rio's Hotel*, R Tiradentes 333, T 791-1126, a/c, fridge, **C** with fan, cheaper with shared bath, good breakfast, rec; **B** *Chapadense*, R Ver José de Souza 535, T/F 791-1410, a/c, fridge, **C** with fan, restaurant serves *comida caseira*; **C** *Pousada Bom Jardim*, Praça Bispo Dom Wunibaldo s/n, T 791-1244, fan, comfortable, parking, good breakfast, rec; **D** *São José*, R Ver José de Souza 50, T 791-1152, fan, cheaper with shared bath and no fan, hot showers, basic, good, owner Mário sometimes runs excursions; **D** *Dormitório*, R Tiradentes s/n, basic, no fan, cheaper with shared bath. **Camping: E** pp *Aldeia Velha*, in the Aldeia Velha neighbourhood at the entrance to town from Cuiabá, T 322-7178 (Cuiabá), fenced area with bath, hot shower, some shade, guard; Salgadeira, unorganized camping 16 km from town at the tourist centre, watch your belongings.

● **Places to eat** *Nivios*, Praça Dom Wunibaldo 631 for good regional food; *Fogão da Roça*, Praça Dom Wunibaldo 488, comida Mineira, generous portions, good quality, rec; *O Mestrinho*, R Quinco Caldas 119, meat, regional dishes, rodízio at weekends; *Choppada* (*O Chopp da Chapada*), R Cipriano Curvo s/n nr praça, drinks and meals, regional dishes, live music at weekends; *Trapiche*, R Cipriano Curvo 580, pizza, drinks, regional dishes; *O Mestrinho*, *Peixaria Serrano*, R Dr Pem Gomes 505 (nr pool), fish specialities and *comida caseira*, cheaper than those nr the praça; *Veu da Noiva*, R Dr Pem Gomes 524, regional dishes, fish in season (*piracema* fishing ban 1 Oct-1 Mar). *Pequi* is a regional palm fruit used to season many foods; *arroz com pequi* is a popular rice and chicken dish.

- **Post & telecommunications** Post Office: R Fernando Corrêa 848.
- **Shopping** Crafts, indigenous artefacts, sweets and locally-made honey from *Casa de Artes e Artesanato Mato Grossense* (Praça Dom Wunibaldo). Regional sweets from *Doceria Olho de Sogra*, Praça Dom Wunibaldo 21. João Eloy de Souza Neves is a local artist, his paintings, music and history about Chapada (*Chapada dos Guimarães da descoberta aos dias atuais*) are on sale at *Pousada Bom Jardim*.
- **Transport** Seven departures daily to and from Cuiabá (Rubi, 0700-1900, last back to Cuiabá 1800), 1½ hrs, US$4.

CÁCERES AND TO BOLIVIA

River trips from Cuiabá to Corumbá are very difficult since boats on the Cuiabá river are few and irregular. You can sometimes get to Corumbá by river from **Cáceres** (*pop* 77,821; *DDD* 065; *CEP* 78200), on the banks of the Rio Paraguai, 200 km W of Cuiabá, very hot but clean and hospitable. The city has many well mantained 19th century buildings, painted in pastel colours. The Municipality runs the **Museu Histórico de Cáceres** (R Antônio Maria by Praça Major João Carlos). The main square, Praça Barão de Rio Branco, has one of the original border markers from the Treaty of Tordesillas, which divided South America between Spain and Portugal; it is pleasant and shady during the day. In the evenings, between Nov and Mar, the trees are packed with thousands of chirping swallows (*andorinhas*), beware of droppings; the square is surrounded by bars, restaurants and ice cream parlours and comes to life at night. The city is known for its many bicycles as most people seem to get around on two wheels. Until 1960, Cáceres had regular boat traffic, today it is limited to a few tour boats and pleasure craft. The beautiful Serra da Mangabeira is about 15 km E, crossed by the road from Cuiabá; the town is also at the edge of the Pantanal. Vitória Regia lilies can be seen N of town, just across the bridge over the Rio Paraguai along the BR-174. There are archaeological sites on the river's edge N of the city.
Local festivals Piranha Festival, mid Mar; International Fishing Festival in mid Sept; annual cattle fair.

- **Accommodation A2** *Turbo*, Av São Luiz 1399 by BR 070, T 223-1984, luxury, a/c, fridge, restaurant, pool; **A2** *Ipanema*, R Gen Osório 540, T 223-1177, F 223-1743, with a/c, fridge, garage, good restaurant; **A3** *Comodoro*, Praça de Caxias 561, T 223-2078, a/c, fridge; **A3** *Caiçaras*, R dos Operários 745, corner R Gen Osório, T 223-3187, F 223-2692, a/c, **B** without fridge and TV, pleasant, modern, parking; **B** *Fênix*, R dos Operários 600, T 223-1027, F 221-2243, fridge, a/c, comfortable; **B** *Rio*, Praça Major João Carlos 61, T 223-3387, F 223084, a/c, **C** without fridge, TV, **D** with shared bath, fan; **C** *Charm*, Col José Dulce 405, T/F 223-4949, a/c, **D** with shared bath, friendly; nr the rodoviária are: **C** *Capri*, R Getúlio Vargas 99, T 223-1711, a/c, comfortable; **C** *13 de Junho*, R 13 de Junho s/n, T 223-3871, a/c, pleasant; **C** *Gasparin*, Av Sangradouro 162, T 223-4579, a/c, fridge, cheaper with fan; **D** *União*, R 7 de Setembro 340, fan, **E** with shared bath, basic, good value; **D** *Rio Doce*, R 7 de Setembro, a/c, cheaper with shared bath, good value; **E** *Santa Terezinha*, R Tiradentes 485, with fan, breakfast, not clean. Many other cheap hotels.
- **Places to eat** *Corimbá* on riverfront, fish specialities, good, not cheap; *Bistecão*, R General Osório 977, meat, opens erratically; *Kaskata*, floating restaurant at the end of R Coronel José Dulce, by the port, nice setting, fish and *jacaré* specialties, fanciest in town, expensive; *Gulla's*, R Col José Dulce 215, buffet by kilo, good quality and variety, rec; *Hispano*, Praça Barão de Rio Branco 64, buffet by kilo; *Kaskata Pizzaria*, R Col José Dulce 250, pricey; *Panela de Barro*, R Frei Ambrósio 34, nr rodoviária, *comida caseira*.
- **Banks & money changers** Casa de Câmbio Mattos, Comandante Bauduino 180, next to main praça, changes cash and TCs at good rates.
- **Post & telecommunications**: Praça Barão de Rio Branco s/n.
- **Tour companies & travel agents** *Cáceres*, Av Getúlio Vargas 408, T 223-1428, F 223-2440, fishing and photo tours to Pantanal, boat rentals, Cláudio Duarte helpful guide; *Pantanal Tour*, R Com Farías 180, T 223-1200, boat rentals, fishing trips, tickets; *Vereda Turismo*, R Padre Cassemiro 1121, T 223-4360, tours, boat rentals, fishing.
- **Shopping** *Náutica Turismo*, R Bom Jardim 119A, by the waterfront, for fishing/camping supplies and boat repairs.
- **Transport** Local Car hire: Localiza, Padre Cassemiro 640, T 223-4562. **Buses** Colibrí/União Cascavel buses Cuiabá-Cáceres, US$13.50, many daily before 0630-2400 (book in advance, very crowded), 3½ hrs. **River** The *Acuri*, a luxury tourist vessel, sails to

Corumbá, 1 week cruise including return by air from Corumbá to Cuiabá US$600 pp. For information on other boat sailings, ask at the Capitânia dos Portos, on the corner of the main square at the waterfront. If possible phone in advance to Cáceres, Posto Arrunda, 221-1707 to find out if any boats are going. Also Portobrás on the outskirts at the waterfront (T 221-1728). In the dry season there are practically no boats to Corumbá. At the waterfront you can hire a boat for a day trip, US$5/hr/pp, min 3 people; on holidays and some weekends there are organized day trips on the river.

FRONTIER WITH BOLIVIA

An unpaved road runs from Cáceres to the Bolivian border at San Matías.

● **Brazilian immigration**
Polícia Federal, R Coronel Farías, Cáceres, for exit and entry formalities.

● **Transport**
Buses To San Matías, Transical-Velásquez, Mon-Sat at 0630 and 1500, Sun 1500 only (return at same times), US$4, 3 hrs; connecting service to Santa Cruz, US$23.50, 24 hrs in the dry season, 30 hrs or more in the wet; Trans Bolivia to San Matías, Sun, Mon, Fri at 1500, Tues, Wed, Thur and Sat at 0700.

ROUTES A journey along the Porto Velho road from Cáceres (BR-174, 364) demonstrates the amount of development and deforestation along Brazil's 'Far West' frontier, see page 606. At **Pontes e Lacerda** (**A3** *Verona Palace Hotel*, T 266-1507, a/c, restaurant, pool; also 2 dormitories by rodoviária) a side road goes to **Vila Bela** on the Rio Guaporé, which used to be the capital of Mato Grosso. It has a ruined church, cannon balls lying around, and is very interesting.

OUTLYING DISTRICTS OF MATO GROSSO: NORTH

The road due N from Cuiabá to Santarém (1,777 km) has been completed and is all-weather, through **Sinop** (*pop* 41,057), with a branch W to **Colíder** (*pop* 31,155), and **Alta Floresta** (*pop* 68,217; *DDD* 065; *CEP* 78580): daily bus from Cuiabá with São Luís at 2000, 12 hrs, US$46. Outside

Alta Floresta, the *Cristalino Jungle Lodge*, on the Cristalino river, is a basic lodge, with shared baths, in a very rich and well-preserved section of southern Amazônia. Many rare mammals are found here (including the short-eared dog), as well as five species of macaw, harpy eagle and a few hundred other bird species. *Anaconda Operators* in Cuiabá run tours to *Cristalino Jungle Lodge*, US$100 pp/day plus airfare (US$200 return); *Focus Tours* of Belo Horizonte can also make reservations or arrange guided tours.

● **NB** When travelling N of Cuiabá, yellow fever vaccination is obligatory; if you do not have a certificate, you will be (re)vaccinated.

● **Accommodation Sinop: C** *Italian Palace*, Av das Figueras 493, T 531-2109, restaurant, bar, sauna. **Alta Floresta: B** *Floresta Amazônica*, Av Perimetral Ote 2001, T 521-3601, F 521-3801, in park, lovely views, pool, sports, all facilities; **C** *Pirâmide Palace*, Av do Aeroporto 445, T 521-2400, a/c, fridge, restaurant; **D** *Grande Hotel Coroados*, R F 1 118, T 521-3022, not too well kept but has a/c, pool and bar.

SOUTHEAST: RONDONÓPOLIS

From **Rondonópolis** (*pop* 125,110), about 215 km SE of Cuiabá on the road to Goiânia, a paved road branches southwards to Campo Grande and thence to the western parts of the State of São Paulo.

● **Accommodation** Many hotels, **A1** *Novotel*, R Floriano Peixoto 711, T 421-9355, F 421-9322, a/c, fridge, pool; **A2** *Guarujá*, R Fernando Corrêa 624, T/F 421-8611, a/c, fridge; **A2** *Thaani*, Av Amazonas 472, T 4219288, a/c, fridge, pool; **A3** *Nacional*, R Fernando Corrêa 978, T 421-3245, F 421-4848, a/c, fridge; **D** *Dormitório Beija Flor*, nr rodoviária.

● **Transport Air** For internal flights. **Buses** From Rondonópolis, **Brasília**, US$23, 14½ hrs; **Goiânia**, US$19, 11 hrs; **Campo Grande**, US$9.50, 6½ hrs; **Presidente Epitácio**, US$7.75; **Presidente Prudente**, US$11.50. Beware of overbooking on Viação Motta buses.

Information for travellers

BEFORE YOU GO

ENTRY REQUIREMENTS

● Documents

Consular visas are not required for stays of up to 90 days by tourists from Western European or South American (except Guyana) countries, Finland, Slovenia, Morocco, Costa Rica, Bahamas, Barbados, Trinidad and Tobago, South Africa, and the Philippines. For them, only the following documents are required at the port of disembarkation: valid passport (or *cédula de identidade* for nationals of Argentina, Chile, Paraguay and Uruguay); and a return or onward ticket, or adequate proof that you can purchase your return fare, subject to no remuneration being received in Brazil and no legally binding or contractual documents being signed. Some consulates (eg Frankfurt and London) insist that your passport be valid for at least 6 months from date of entry. Venezuelan passport holders can stay in Brazil for 60 days on filling in a form at the border. (Some consulates, eg Santiago, ask to see an onward ticket: persistence, adequate money and showing a credit card may overcome this.) 90-day renewals are easily obtainable, but only at least 15 days before the expiry of your 90-day permit, from the Polícia Federal: the procedure is, give your name, passport data and Brazilian address to the clerk, who will type this on the form for extension (US$0.50); take this to a bank; pay US$10 tax; then return to Polícia Federal who will stamp the extension in your passport after they have seen onward flight tickets and receipt from the bank for the tax;

sometimes proof of sufficient funds for your continued stay is requested. Some points of entry refuse entry for longer than 30 days, renewals are then for the same period, insist if you want 90 days. For longer stays you must leave the country and return (not the same day) to get a new 90-day permit. If you overstay your visa, or extension, you will be fined US$7/day, with no upper limit. After paying the fine to Polícia Federal, you will be issued with an exit visa and must leave within 8 days. If you cannot pay the fine you must pay when you next return to Brazil.

Visas US and Canadian citizens and people of other nationalities, and those who cannot meet the requirements above, *must* get a visa before arrival, which may, if you ask, be granted for multiple entry. Visa fees vary, eg free for USA (but £16 processing fee), £32 for Canadians, £40 for Japanese and Russians; for most others a tourist visa costs £16: prices from Brazilian consulate, London, April 1997. Do not lose the emigration permit they give you when you enter Brazil. Leaving the country without it, you may have to pay up to US$100 pp.

Officially, if you leave Brazil within the 90-day permission to stay and then re-enter the country, you should only be allowed to stay until the 90-day permit expires. Usual practice, though, is to give another 90-day permit, which may lead to charges of overstaying if you apply for an extension.

You must always carry identification when in Brazil; it is a good idea to take a photocopy of the first 5 pages of your passport, plus that with your Brazilian immigration stamp, and leave your passport in the hotel safe deposit. Always keep an independent record of your passport details. In Rio it is a good idea to register with your consulate to expedite document replacement if yours gets lost/stolen.

● **Vaccinations**

Vaccination against smallpox is no longer required for visitors, but proof of vaccination against yellow fever is necessary if you are visiting Amazônia and the Centre-West, or are coming from countries with Amazonian territories, eg Bolivia, Colombia, Ecuador, Peru. It is strongly recommended to have a yellow fever inoculation before visiting northern Brazil since those without a certificate will be inoculated on entering any of the northern and centre-western states. Although yellow fever vaccination is free it might be administered in unsanitary conditions. Poliomyelitis vaccination is required for children from 3 months to 6 years. If you are going to Amazônia, or to other low-lying forested areas, malaria prophylaxis is advised (this can be difficult to obtain in some areas – the local name for paludrine is doroprim) and water purification tablets are essential. Dengue fever is now endemic in Brazil, and Rio is one of the worst places: protect yourself against mosquitoes. Sporadic outbreaks of cholera have occurred in the Amazon region and on the NE coast (eg Recife), but numbers have been in the tens, rather than the hundreds. Drink only sterilized water. Also, in the Amazon basin, sandflies abound; take a good repellent and get inoculations against hepatitis and typhoid.

Yellow fever (see page 642) and some other vaccinations can be obtained from the Ministério da Saúde, R Cais de Pharoux, Rio de Janeiro. Less common vaccinations can be obtained at Saúde de Portos, Praça 15 de Novembro, Rio de Janeiro. It is reported that shots of immunoglobulin against hepatitis are not screened against Aids, which is widespread.

● **Representation overseas**

Canada, 2000 Mansfield, Suite 1700, Montreal H3A 3AS, T 514-0499; **Denmark**, Ryvangs Alle 24, 21 Copenhagen, T 20-6478; **France**, 34 Cours Allert IER, 75008 Paris, T 4225-9250; **Germany**, Stephanstrasse 3, 4 Stock, 6000 Frankfurt, T 290709; **UK**, 32 Green St, London WIY 4AT, T 0171-499-0877, consulate at 6 St Albans St, London SW1Y 4SQ, T 0171-930-9055; **USA**, 630 Fifth Ave, 27 Floor, New York NY 10111, T 212 916-3251/3200; **USA**, 8484 Wilshire Blvd, Suites 730-711, Los Angeles, California, T 213 651-2664.

● **Tourist information**

All Brazil's States, and most cities and towns have their own tourist information bureaux. They are not usually too helpful regarding information or cheap hotels. It is also difficult to get information on neighbouring states. *Quatro Rodas*, a motoring magazine, publishes an excellent series of maps and guides in Portuguese and English from about US$10. Its *Guia Brasil* is a type of Michelin Guide to hotels, restaurants (not the cheapest) sights, facilities and general information on hundreds of cities and towns in the country, including good street maps. These guides can be purchased at street newspaper vendors throughout the country. Quatro Rodas Guides may be bought in Europe from Distribuidora Jardim, Quinta Pau Varais, Azinhaga de Fetais, Camarate 2685, Lisbon, Portugal, T Lisbon 947-2542. In USA: Lincoln Building, 60 East 42nd St, Suite 3403, New York, NY 10165, T 557-5990/3, F 983-0972. Note that telephone yellow pages in most cities (but not Rio) contain good street maps which, together with the Quatro Rodas maps, are a great help for getting around.

Many of the more expensive hotels provide locally-produced tourist information magazines for their guests. Travel information can be very unreliable and it is wise to recheck details thoroughly.

WHEN TO GO

● **Best time to visit**

The best time for a visit is from April to June, and Aug to Oct, inclusive. Business visitors should avoid from mid-Dec to the end of Feb, when it is hot and people are on holiday. In these months hotels beaches and means of transport tend to be crowded. July is a school holiday month.

Conditions during the winter (May to Sept) are like those of a N European summer in Rio de Janeiro (including periods of rain and overcast skies), but more like a N European autumn in São Paulo and the southern states. Summer-weight woollens can be worn without discomfort in winter in Rio de Janeiro (temperatures vary at this season from 14°C to the high 20s), but further S something heavier is often required. It can get very cold in the far S. In São Paulo, which is in the Highlands, light-weight clothing is only required in the summer; the climate can be treacherous, however, with large temperature changes in a brief space of time. It can get surprisingly cold S and W of Rio and on high ground anywhere in Brazil, at night warm clothes are needed. The season of heavy rains is from Nov to Mar in Rio and São Paulo, Jan to April in the N, and from April to Aug around Recife.

Summer conditions all over the country are tropical, but temperatures of 40°C are comparatively rare. On the coast there is a high degree of humidity. The luminosity is also very high sunglasses are advisable.

HEALTH

Be very careful about bathing in lakes or slow rivers anywhere in Brazil: harmful parasites abound (including the snails that carry schistosomiasis – this disease is rampant in Minas Gerais and most of central Brazil). South of the Amazon beware of *borrachudos*, small flies with a sharp bite that attack ankles and calves; coconut oil deters them. Water should not be drunk from taps unless there is a porcelain filter attached or unless you have water sterilizing tablets ('Hydrosteril' is a popular local brand); there is mineral water in plenty and excellent light beer, known as 'chopp' (pronounced 'shoppi'), and soft drinks. For those who have been in Brazil for a while, *água gelada* (chilled water) is usually safe to drink, being filtered water kept in a refrigerator in most hotels, restaurants and stores. Avoid ice in cheap hotels and restaurants; it is likely to be made from unfiltered water. Colestase is the recommended local treatment for upset stomachs.

Brazilians are famous for their open sexuality: appearances can be deceptive, however, and attitudes vary widely. To generalize, the coastal cities are very easy-going, while in smaller towns and the interior, traditional morals are strictly enforced. Aids is widespread, commonly transmitted by heterosexual sex, and tolerance of male homosexuality is diminishing. You should take reliable condoms with you, even if you are sure you won't be needing them. The primary means of HIV infection in Brazil is now heterosexual sex. Local condoms are reported not to be reliable.

Tampons are available, as are Hydrocare contact lens products (expensive).

● **Medical facilities**

An excellent hospital, supported by the American and British colonies in São Paulo, is Hospital Samaritano, R Conselheiro Brotero 1486, São Paulo (T 51-2154). If staying in Brazil for any length of time, it is rec to take out Brazilian health insurance; Banco Econômico and Citibank are reported to provide good advice on this matter.

MONEY

● **Banks**

Banks open between 1000-1600 or 1630 Mon-Fri.

● **Banks & money changers**

Banks in major cities will change cash and TCs. For the latest exchange rate, see tables nr end of book. If you keep the exchange slips, you may convert back into foreign currency up to 50% of the amount you exchanged. This applies to the official markets only; there is no right of reconversion unless you have an official exchange slip. The parallel market, found in travel agencies, exchange houses and among hotel staff, was of no benefit compared with bank rates in 1997. TCs are a safer way to carry your money, but rates for cheques are usually lower than for cash and they are less easy to change, commission may be charged. In 1996-97, many banks (especially the Banco do Brasil) were charging up to US$20 for TC transactions. Many banks may only change US$300 minimum in cash, US$500 in TCs. Dollars cash are becoming more frequently used for tourist transactions and are also useful for those places where TCs cannot be changed and for when the banks go on strike: damaged dollar notes may be rejected. Parallel market and official rates are quoted in the papers and on TV news programmes.

● **Cost of living**

Since the introduction of the *real* in July 1994, prices for residents and visitors have increased. Eating in smart restaurants is very costly. While hotel accommodation has risen steeply in price since 1995, budget hotels have responded by cutting extras, cramming more beds into rooms, etc. A cheap room will cost about US$12. Shopping prices are equivalent to Europe. Hotel price categories and transport fares in this chapter reflect the appreciation of the *real*, but travellers may find variations as the *real* fluctuates within the floating exchange rate system introduced in 1995. Prices are higher in Amazônia than elsewhere.

● **Credit cards**

Credit cards are widely used; Diners Club, Mastercard, Visa and American Express are useful. Mastercard/Access is accepted by Banco Econômico, Banco Meridional and Banco Real. Overseas credit cards need authorization from São Paulo, this can take up to 2 hrs, so allow plenty of time if buying air tickets. Mastercard and Diners are equivalent to Credicard, and Eurocheques can be cashed at Banco Alemão (major cities only). Banco Bradesco handles the international Visa automatic teller machine (ATM) network, Visa cash advances also at Banco do Brasil (in case of lost or stolen cards T 000-811-933-5589). Some of Banco Itaú's ATMs give cash withdrawals on Mastercard/Cirrus, but not as common as Visa ATMs. Both Bradesco and Itaú have machines at airports, shopping centres and major thoroughfares; Banco 24 Horas machines, at similar locations, operate with Amex, Diners, Boston and Citibank among others. Credit card transactions are charged at the tourist official rate. Cash advances on credit cards will only be paid in *reais* at the tourist rate, incurring a 1½% commission. Banks in small remote places may still refuse to give a cash advance: if you have run out of cash and TCs, try asking for the manager ('gerente'). Automatic cash dispensers are now common in Brazil: it's worth remembering your PIN number since queues can be extremely long.

● **Currency**

The unit of currency is the *real*, R$ (plural *reais*) introduced on 1 July 1994. By Mar 1997 the official rate for the *real* was R$1.05 = US$1. Any amount of foreign currency and 'a reasonable sum' in *reais* can be taken in; residents may only take out the equivalent of US$4,000. Notes in circulation are: 100, 50, 20, 10, 5 and 1 *real*; coins 1 *real*, 50, 25, 10, 5, 2 and 1 centavo.

Money sent to Brazil is normally paid out in Brazilian currency, so do not have more money sent to Brazil than you need for your stay in the country itself. It is relatively easy and quick to have money sent, especially from accounts in the US. Always quote the 'routing' number of the receiving bank. To open a bank account in Brazil, you need to have a visa valid for more than one year. In most large cities Citibank will hold US personal cheques for collection, paying the day's tourist dollar rate in *reais* with no charge. Banco do Brasil offers the same service with small charge. From the UK the quickest method of having money sent is Swift Air. Tourists cannot change US$ TCs into US$ notes (though some exchange houses will do this illegally), but US$ TCs can be obtained on an American Express card (against official policy).

GETTING THERE

BY AIR

● **From Europe**

Varig Brazilian Airlines flies from London to Rio and São Paulo 5 times a week. British Airways flies nonstop twice a week from London Gatwick to both São Paulo and Rio. Brazil is also connected to the principal cities of Europe by Aerolíneas Argentinas, Air France, Alitalia, Air Portugal (TAP), Iberia, KLM, LAN Chile, Lufthansa, Swissair and Varig. Varig flies to Salvador and Fortaleza from Milan, Rome and Paris. There are also flights with Varig to Recife from Lisbon (also TAP), Madrid, Milan and Rome. Vasp flies to Athens Barcelona, Brussels and Zurich to Brazil. Transbrasil now flies from London Gatwick to Rio, São Paulo and Porto Alegre via Recife and Salvador and from Vienna and Amsterdam to Rio and São Paulo.

● **From USA**

Brazil is connected to the USA direct by Varig, Transbrasil, American Airlines, United Airlines and Vasp (LA-Rio and São Paulo, Miami-São Paulo and Rio). The cheapest route is probably from Miami.

There are also daily flights from the USA to Belo Horizonte with United and American.

● **From Latin America**

All South American capitals are connected by air services to São Paulo and Rio. Bogotá, 2 a week to both Rio and São Paulo (Varig, Avianca); Caracas, 5 weekly to Rio and São Paulo (Varig); La Paz, 4 weekly to São Paulo, via Santa Cruz (Varig, Lloyd), 3 to Rio; Lima, 3 to Rio and 6 to São Paulo (Varig, Aero Peru); Quito/Guayaquil, 2 a week to Rio, 4 a week to São Paulo (Ecuatoriana); there are daily flights to São Paulo with connections to Rio from: Asunción (Varig, American, Lapsa); Santiago (several carriers and flights daily); Montevideo (Pluna, Varig); Buenos Aires (several daily). Paramaribo, twice a week by Surinam Airways to Belém via Cayenne. If buying a ticket to another country but with a stopover in Brazil, check whether two tickets are cheaper than one.

From Mexico City there are 6 flights a week to São Paulo and 3 to Rio (Varig) and 1 flight a week from San José, Costa Rica to Rio (Varig, Lacsa).

Varig and Aerolíneas Argentinas operate the Mercosur Airpass, in conjunction with other carriers in Brazil, Argentina, Uruguay and Paraguay. Valid for a minimum of 7 and a maximum of 30 days, the pass is for a maximum of 8 flight coupons, no more than 4/country. At least two countries must be included; rerouting is not permitted. The airpass is available to all international return ticket holders travelling by air into the participating countries. Passes are price-banded according to mileage flown and fares range from US$225 to US$870. Varig also has an extensive 'Stopover' programme which gives reduced rates on transfers and hotel rooms in many cities in Brazil and throughout South America (plus San José, Costa Rica).

● **From elsewhere**

Varig and South African Airways fly between São Paulo and Johannesburg 4 times a week. There are 5 weekly flights between both Tokyo/São Paulo and Seoul/São Paulo, and 2 weekly flights between Bangkok/São Paulo and Hong Kong/São Paulo. Middle East Airlines have weekly service from Beirut and Abidjan to São Paulo. Airline tickets are expensive in Brazil, buy internal tickets with *reais* (you can pay by credit card). External tickets must be paid for in dollars.

NB Regulations state that you cannot buy an air ticket in Brazil for use abroad unless you first have a ticket out of Brazil.

BY ROAD

To drive in Brazil you need either a translation of your home driving licence, or an international licence. There are agreements between Brazil and all South American countries (but check in the case of Bolivia) whereby a car can be taken into Brazil (or a Brazilian car out of Brazil) for a period of 90 days without any special documents; an extension of up to 90 days is granted by the customs authorities on presentation of the paper received at the border, this must be retained; this may be done at most customs posts and at the Serviço de Controle Aduaneiro, Ministério da Fazenda, Av Pres A Carlos, Sala 1129, Rio de Janeiro.

For cars registered in other countries, the requirements are proof of ownership and/or registration in the home country and valid driving licence (international or from home country). It is better to cross the border into Brazil when it is officially open because an official who knows all about the entry of cars is then present. The motorist should in any case insist on getting the correct paper 'in accordance with Decree No 53.313/63', or he/she might find it impossible to get the 90-day extension. You must specify which border station you intend to leave by, but application can be made to the Customs to change this.

BY SEA

For shipping lines that carry passengers to Brazil, see **Introduction and Hints**. **NB** There is an 8% tax on international shipping-line tickets bought in Brazil.

CUSTOMS

Clothing and personal articles are free of import duty. Such articles as cameras, movie cameras, portable radios, tape-recorders, typewriters and binoculars are also admitted free if there is not more than one of each. Tourists may also bring in, duty-free, 12 bottles of alcohol, 400 cigarettes, 25 cigars, 280 grams of perfume, up to 10 units of cosmetics, up to 3 each of any electronic item or watch, up to a total value of US$500. Duty free goods may only be purchased in foreign currency.

WHEN YOU ARRIVE

● Clothing

Fashions are provocative, and while women are advised to dress in the local style, this can have unnerving effects. It is normal to stare and comment on women's appearances, and if you happen to look different or to be travelling alone, you will undoubtedly attract attention. You are very unlikely to be groped or otherwise molested: this is disrespectful, and merits a suitable reaction. Be aware that Brazilian men can be extraordinarily persistent, and very easily en-

couraged; it is safest to err on the side of caution until you are accustomed.

In general, clothing requirements in Brazil are less formal than in the Hispanic countries. It is, however, advisable for men visiting restaurants to wear long trousers (women in shorts may also be refused entry), trousers and jackets or pullovers in São Paulo (also for cinemas). As a general rule, it is better not to wear shorts in official buildings, cinemas, inter-state buses and on flights.

● Conduct

Men should avoid arguments or insults (care is needed even when overtaking on the road); pride may be defended with a gun. Gay men, while still enjoying greater freedom than in many countries, should exercise reasonable discretion.

Colour The people of Brazil represent a unique racial mix: it is not uncommon for the children of one family to be of several different colours. Individuals are often described by the colour of their skin (ranging through several shades of brown), and 'white' can refer to people who would not necessarily be thought white in Europe or North America. Generally speaking, the emphasis is on colour rather than racial origins.

Racial discrimination is illegal in Brazil. There is, however, a complex class system which is informed both by heritage and by economic status. This effectively discriminates against the poor, who are chiefly (but by no means exclusively) black due to the lack of inherited wealth among those whose ancestors were servants and slaves. Some Brazilians might assume that a black person is poor, therefore of low status. Black visitors to the country may encounter racial prejudice. We have also received a report from a black North American woman who was the subject of sexual advances by non-Brazilian, white tourists. Black women travelling with a white man may experience some problems, which should disappear with the realisation that your partnership is not a commercial arrangement. A surprising number of Brazilians are unaware that black Europeans exist, so you could become the focus of some curiosity.

Brazilian culture is rich in African influences. Those interested in the development of Afro-Brazilian music, dance, religion, arts and cuisine will find the whole country N of São Paulo fascinating, and especially the cities of Bahia and São Luís which retain the greatest African influences. Black Pride movements are particularly strong in Bahia. Further reading: *Samba* by Alma Guillermoprieto, paperback, Bloomsbury Press; *Towards the Abolition of Whiteness* by David Roediger, Verso, £11.95 (a sociological study of how 'colour' is determined by economic status, mostly in the USA and UK).

● **Hours of business**

Hours of business are 0900-1800 Mon to Fri for most businesses, which close for lunch some time between 1130 and 1400. Shops are open on Sat till 1230 or 1300. Government departments are open from 1100-1800 Mon to Fri. Banks 1000-1500, but closed on Sat.

● **Official time**

Brazilian standard time is 3 hrs behind GMT; of the major cities, only the Amazon time zone, Manaus, Cuiabá, Campo Grande and Corumbá are different, with time 5 hrs behind GMT. The State of Acre is 4 hrs behind GMT. Clocks move forward 1 hr in summer for approximately 5 months (usually between Oct and Feb or Mar) but times of change vary. This does not apply to Acre.

The days of the week are: segunda feira (Mon), terça feira (Tues), quarta feira (Wed), quinta feira (Thur), sexta feira (Fri), sábado (Sat), domingo (Sun).

● **Police**

There are 3 types of police: Polícia Federal, civilian dressed, who handle all federal law duties, including immigration. A subdivision is the Polícia Federal Rodoviária, uniformed, who are the traffic police. Polícia Militar is the uniformed, street police force, under the control of the state governor, handling all state laws. They are not the same as the Armed Forces' internal police. Polícia Civil, also state-controlled, handle local laws; usually in civilian dress, unless in the traffic division.

● **Safety**

Personal safety in Brazil has deteriorated of recent years, largely because of the economic recession, and crime is increasing. Some recommend avoiding all large cities; the situation is far less insecure in smaller towns and in the country. The police are reported to be charging for documents reporting crimes if these are required quickly.

Apart from the obvious precautions of not wearing jewellery (wear a cheap, plastic *digital* watch), do not camp or sleep out in isolated places and if you are hitchhiking, never accept a lift in a car with two people in it. Money belts are safer than bags for your valuables. Consider buying clothing locally to avoid looking like a gringo. If you are held up and robbed, it is worth asking for the fare back to where you are staying. It is not uncommon for thieves to oblige. Do carry some cash, to hand over if you are held up. Do not leave valuables in hotel rooms, except where a safe is provided. Hotel safe deposits are generally (but not always) secure. If you cannot get a receipt for valuables in a hotel safe, seal the contents in a plastic bag and sign across the seal. Always photocopy your passport, air ticket and other documents, make a record of TC and credit card numbers and keep them separately from the originals. Leave another set of records at home. Never trust anyone telling 'sobstories' or offering 'safe rooms', when looking for a hotel, always choose the room yourself. Take only your towel and lotion to the beach, tuck enough money for your cold drinks into your trunks/bikini bottom. A few belongings can safely be left at a bar. Ted Stroll of San Francisco advises, "remember that economic privation has many Brazilians close to the edge, and that they are probably as ashamed of exploiting you as you are angry at being exploited". The corollary is be generous to those who give you a good deal. Travellers are most vulnerable when carrying baggage, if possible take a taxi, but don't leave the driver in the car with your bags.

● **Shopping**

Gold, diamonds and gemstones throughout Brazil. Innovative designs in jewellery: buy 'real' at reputable dealers (best value in Minas Gerais); cheap, fun pieces from street traders. Interesting furnishings made with gemstones, marble; clay figurines from the NE; lace from Ceará; leatherwork; strange pottery from Amazônia; carvings in soapstone and in bone; tiles and other ceramic work, African-type pottery and basketwork from Bahia. Many large hotel gift shops stock a good selection of handicrafts at reasonable prices. Brazilian cigars are excellent for those who like the mild flavours popular in Germany, the Netherlands and Switzerland. Recommended purchases are musical instruments, eg guitars, other stringed, and percussion instruments.

Excellent textiles: good hammocks from the NE; other fabrics; design in clothing is impressive, though unfortunately not equalled by manufacturing quality. Buy your beachwear in Brazil: it is matchless. For those who know how to use them, medicinal herbs, barks and spices from street markets; coconut oil and local skin and haircare products (fantastic conditioners) are better and cheaper than in Europe, but known brands of toiletries are exorbitant. Other bad buys are film (including processing), cameras and any electrical goods (including batteries). Sunscreen, sold in all department stores and large supermarkets, is expensive.

As a rule, shopping is easier, quality more reliable and prices higher in the shopping centres (mostly excellent) and in the wealthier suburbs. Better prices at the small shops and street traders; most entertaining at markets and on the beach. Bargaining (with good humour) is expected in the latter.

● Tipping
Tipping is usual, but less costly than in most other countries, except for porters. Restaurants, 10% of bill if no service charge but small tip if there is; taxi drivers, none; cloakroom attendants, small tip; cinema usherettes, none; hairdressers, 10-15%; porters, fixed charges but tips as well; airport porters, about US$0.50/item.

● Weights and measures
The metric system is used by all.

● Working in Brazil
Work-permit restrictions are making it harder to find work as an English language teacher than it used to be, though many people do it unofficially and leave Brazil every 90 days in order to re-enter as tourists. One's best bet would be in a small language school. Or advertise in the Press.

ON DEPARTURE

● Airport tax
The equivalent of about US$20 is charged for international flights and, for internal flights, US$7-US$10 depending on the class of airport. It must be paid on checking in, in reais or US$. Tax is waived if you stay in Brazil less than 24 hrs.

WHERE TO STAY

● Accommodation
The best guide to hotels in Brazil is the *Guia Brasil Quatro Rodas*, with good maps of towns. Motels are specifically intended for very short-stay couples: there is no stigma attached and they usually offer good value (the rate for a full night is called the *pernoite*), though the decor can be a little unsettling. The type known as *hotel familiar*, to be found in the interior – large meals, communal washing, hammocks for children – is much cheaper, but only for the enterprising. *Pousadas* are the equivalent of bed-and-breakfast, often small and family run, although some are very sophisticated and correspondingly priced. Usually hotel prices include breakfast; there is no reduction if you don't eat it. In the better hotels (our category B and upwards) the breakfast is well worth eating: rolls, ham, eggs, cheese, cakes, fruit. Normally the *apartamento* is a room with a bath; a *quarto* is a room without bath. The service stations (*postos*) and hostels (*dormitórios*) along the main roads provide excellent value in room and food, akin to truck-driver type accommodation in Europe, for those on a tight budget. The star rating system for hotels (5-star hotels are not price-controlled) is not the standard used in North America or Europe. For information about Youth Hostels contact Federação Brasil Albergues Juventude, R da Assembleia 10, room 1211, T 531-1129, Rio de Janeiro; its brochure provides a full list of good value accommodation. Also see the Internet Guide to Hostelling which has list of Brazilian youth hostels: http://www.hostels.com/br.html. Low-budget travellers with student cards (photograph needed) can use the Casa dos Estudantes network. Leave rooms in good time so frigobar bills can be checked; we have received reports of overcharging in otherwise good hotels.

Business visitors are strongly recommended to book accommodation in advance, and this can be easily done for Rio or São Paulo hotels with representation abroad. Varig has a good hotel reservation service, with discounts of up to 50% for its passengers.

NB Taxi drivers will try to take you to the expensive hotels, who pay them commission for bringing in custom. Beware!

● Camping
Members of the Camping Clube do Brasil or those with an international campers' card pay only half the rate of a non-member, which is US$10-15 pp. The Club has 43 sites in 13 states and 80,000 members. For enquiries, Camping Clube do Brasil, Divisão de Campings, R Senador Dantas 75° andar (T 262-7172), Rio de Janeiro. It may be difficult to get into some Camping Clube campsites during the high season (Jan-Feb). Private campsites charge about US$5 pp. For those on a very low budget and in isolated areas where there is no camp site, service stations can be used as camping sites (Shell stations rec); they have shower facilities, watchmen and food; some have dormitories; truck drivers are a mine of information. There are also various municipal sites; both types are mentioned in the text. Campsites often tend to be some distance from public transport routes and are better suited to those with their own transport. Never camp at the side of a road; wild camping is generally not possible.

Good camping equipment may be purchased in Brazil and there are several rental companies. Camping gas cartridges are easy to buy in sizeable towns in the S eg in HM shops. *Guia de Camping* is produced by Artpress, R Araçatuba 487, São Paulo 05058; it lists most sites and is available in bookshops in most cities. Quatro Rodas' *Guia Brasil* lists main campsites. Most sizeable towns have laundromats with self service machines. *Lavanderias* do the washing for you but are very expensive.

FOOD AND DRINK

FOOD

The most common dish is *bife (ou frango) com arroz e feijão*, steak (or chicken) with rice and the excellent Brazilian black beans. The most famous dish with beans is the *feijoada completa*: several meat ingredients (jerked beef, smoked sausage, smoked tongue, salt pork, along with spices, herbs and vegetables) are cooked with the beans. Manioc flour is sprinkled over it, and it is eaten with kale (*couve*) and slices of orange, and accompanied by glasses of *aguardente* (unmatured rum), usually known as *cachaça* (booze), though *pinga* (drop) is a politer term. Almost all restaurants serve the *feijoada completa* for Sat lunch (that means up to about 1630). Bahia has some excellent fish dishes (see note on page 508); some restaurants in most of the big cities specialize in them. *Vatapá* is a good dish in the N; it contains shrimp or fish sauced with palm oil, or coconut milk. *Empadinhas de camarão* are worth trying; they are shrimp patties, with olives and heart of palm. A mixed grill, including excellent steak, served with roasted manioc flour (*farofa*; raw manioc flour is known as *farinha*) goes under the name of *churrasco* (it came originally from the cattlemen of Rio Grande do Sul), normally served in specialized restaurants known as *churrascarias* or *rodizios*; good places for large appetites. Minas Gerais has two splendid special dishes involving pork, black beans, *farofa* and kale; they are *tutu á mineira* and *feijão tropeiro*. A white hard cheese (*queijo prata*) or a slightly softer one (*queijo Minas*) is often served for dessert with bananas, or guava or quince paste. Meals are extremely large by European standards; if your appetites are small, you can order, say, one portion and one empty plate, and divide the portion. However, if you are in a position to do so tactfully, you may choose to offer the rest to a person with no food (many Brazilians do – observe the correct etiquette) alternatively you could ask for an *embalagem* (doggy bag) or get a take away called a *marmita* or *quentinha*, most restaurants have this service but it is not always on the menu. Many restaurants now serve *comida por kilo* where you serve yourself and pay for the weight of food on your plate. Unless you specify to the contrary many restaurants will lay a *coberto opcional*, olives, carrots, etc, costing US$0.50-0.75. **NB** The main meal is usually taken in the middle of the day; cheap restaurants tend not to be open in the evening. **Warning** Avoid mussels, marsh crabs and other shellfish caught nr large cities: they are likely to have lived in a highly polluted environment. In a restaurant, always ask the price of a dish before ordering.

For vegetarians, there is a growing network of restaurants in the main cities. In smaller places where food may be monotonous try vegetarian for greater variety. We list several. Most also serve fish. Alternatives in smaller towns are the Arab and Chinese restaurants.

There is fruit all the year round, ranging from banana and orange to mango, pawpaw, custard-apple (*fruta do conde*) and guava. One should try the *manga de Ubá*, a non-fibrous small mango. Also good are *mora* (a raspberry that looks like a strawberry), *jaboticaba*, a small black damson-like fruit, and *jaca* (jackfruit), a large yellow/green fruit.

The exotic flavours of Brazilian ice-creams should be experienced. Try *açaí, bacuri, biribá, buruti, cupuaçu* (not eveyone's favourite), *marimari, mucajá, murici, pajurá, pariri, patuá, piquiá, pupunha, sorva, tucumã, uxi* and others mentioned below under 'drinks'.

If travelling on a tight budget, remember to ask in restaurants for the *prato feito* or *sortido*, a money-saving, excellent value table-d'hôte meal. The *prato comercial* is similar but rather better and a bit more expensive. *Lanchonetes* are cheap eating places where you generally pay before eating. *Salgados* (savoury pastries), *coxinha* (a pyramid of manioc filled with meat or fish and deep fried), *esfiha* (spicey hamburger inside an onion-bread envelope), *empadão* (a filling – eg chicken – in sauce in a pastry case), *empadas* and *empadinhas* (smaller fritters of the same type), are the usual fare. In Minas Gerais, *pão de queijo* is a hot roll made with cheese. A *bauru* is a toasted sandwich which, in Porto Alegre, is filled with steak, while further N has tomato, ham and cheese filling. *Cocada* is a coconut and sugar biscuit.

DRINK

Imported drinks are expensive, but there are some fair local wines. Chilean and Portuguese wines are sometimes available at little more than the cost of local wines. The beers are good and there are plenty of local soft drinks. *Guaraná* is a very popular carbonated fruit drink. There is an excellent range of non-alcoholic fruit juices, known as *sucos*: *caju* (cashew), *pitanga, goiaba* (guava), *genipapo, graviola* (= *chirimoya*), *maracujá* (passion-fruit), *sapoti* and *tamarindo* are rec. *Vitaminas* are thick fruit or vegetable drinks with milk. *Caldo de cana* is sugar-cane juice, sometimes mixed with ice. Remember that *água mineral*, available in many varieties at bars and restaurants is a cheap, safe thirst-quencher (cheaper still in supermarkets). Apart from the ubiquitous coffee, good tea is grown and sold. **NB** If you don't want sugar in your coffee or *suco*, you must ask when you order it. *Água de côco* or *côco verde* (coconut water from fresh green coconut) cannot be missed in the Northest.

Among the better wines are Château d'Argent, Château Duvalier, Almadén, Dreher, Preciosa and Bernard Taillan. The red Marjolet from Cabernet grapes, and the Moselle-type white Zahringer have been well spoken of. It has often been noticed that a new *adega* starts off well, but the quality gradually deteriorates with time; many vintners have switched to American Concorde grapes, producing a rougher wine. Greville Brut champagne-type is inexpensive and very drinkable. A white-wine *Sangria*, containing tropical fruits such as pineapple and papaya, is worth looking out for. The Brahma, Cerpa and Antárctica beers are really excellent, of the lager type, and are cheaper by the bottle than on draught. Buying bottled drinks in supermarkets, you may be asked for empties in return.

Some genuine Scotch whisky brands are bottled in Brazil; they are very popular because of the high price of Scotch imported in bottle; Teacher's is the most highly regarded brand. Locally made gin, vermouth and campari are very good. The local firewater, *aguardente* (known as *cachaça* or *pinga*), made from sugarcane, is cheap and wholesome, but visitors should seek local advice on the best brands; São Francisco, Praianinha, Maria Fulô, '51' and Pitu are rec makes. Mixed with fruit juices of various sorts, sugar and crushed ice, *cachaça* becomes the principal element in a *batida*, a delicious and powerful drink; the commonest is a lime batida or *batida de limão*; a variant of this is the *caipirinha*, a *cachaça* with several slices of lime in it, a caipiroska is made with vodka. *Cachaça* with Coca-Cola is a *cuba*, while rum with Coca-Cola is a *cuba libre*.

GETTING AROUND

AIR TRANSPORT

Because of the great distances, flying is often the most practical option. Internal air services are highly developed, but very expensive. The larger cities are linked with each other several times a day. A monthly magazine, *Guia Aeronáutico*, gives all the timetables and fares. All national airlines – Varig, Vasp and Transbrasil – offer excellent service on their internal flights. Between 2200 and 0600, internal flights cost 30% less than daytime flights. (Ask for the *vôo coruja*.) On some flights couples can fly for the price of one-and-a-half. A 30% discount is offered on flights booked 7 days or more in advance. Similar discount on flights at airports

a few hours before a domestic flight. It is well worth enquiring in detail. Double check all bookings (reconfirm frequently) and information given by ground staff as economic cutbacks have led to pressure on ground service (but not to flight service).

Varig, Vasp and Transbrasil offer good value 21-day airpasses. The Varig airpass covers 3 zones: from US$490 for 5 flights to all cities, with a maximum of 4 coupons available for US100 each; US$350 Central South with no extra coupons available; and US$290 North East (Varig sells 'linking' flights from São Paulo or Rio to the North East for US$150 return). Routes must be specified before arrival. Both Varig and Transbrasil require an itinerary to be specified and reserved at time of purchase. Amendments may be made once prior to commencement of travel and once after at US$30 per time. The Varig pass is only available to travellers arriving in Brazil with Varig or the foreign airlines with which they share the route (eg it is available to TAP passengers who start their journey in Lisbon, but not London). The Transbrasil airpass, also divided into 3 zones, is available to individuals arriving on the services of other carriers as well as their own. The Vasp airpass costs US$440 and is available to anyone arriving in Brazil on a Vasp flight. All airpasses must be purchased outside Brazil, no journey may be repeated and none may be used on the Rio-São Paulo shuttle. Make sure you have two copies of the airpass invoice when you arrive in Brazil; otherwise you will have to select all your flights when you book the first one. Remember that domestic airport tax has to be paid at each departure. Hotels in the Tropical and Othon chains, and others, offer discounts of 10% to Varig airpass travellers; check with Varig, who have a hotel reservation service. Promotions on certain destinations offer a free flight, hotel room, etc; enquire when buying the airpass. We have been told that it is advisable for users of the airpasses to book all their intended flights in advance or on arrival in Brazil, especially around summer holiday and Carnival time. Converting the voucher can take some hours, do not plan an onward flight immediately, check at terminals that the airpass is still registered, faulty cancellations have been reported. Cost and restrictions on the airpass are subject to change. An alternative is to buy an internal flight ticket which includes several stops.

Small scheduled domestic airlines operate Brazilian-built *Bandeirante* 16-seater prop-jets into virtually every city and town with any semblance of an airstrip. **NB** Internal flights often have many stops and are therefore quite slow. Most airports have left-luggage lockers (US$2 for 24 hrs). Seats are often unallocated on internal flights: board in good time.

LAND TRANSPORT

● Train

There are 30,379 km of railways which are not combined into a unified system. Brazil has two gauges and there is little transfer between them. Two more gauges exist for the isolated Amapá Railway and the tourist-only São João del Rei line. There are passenger services in the state of São Paulo and between São Paulo and Rio. More and more services are being withdrawn.

● Motoring

Though the best paved highways are heavily concentrated in the SE, those serving the interior are being improved to all-weather status and many are paved. Brazil has over 1.65 million km of highways, of which 150,000 km are paved, and several thousand more all-weather. Most main roads between principal cities are paved. Some are narrow and therefore dangerous. Many are in poor condition.

Any foreigner with a passport can purchase a Brazilian car and travel outside Brazil if it is fully paid for or if permission is obtained from the financing body in Brazil. Foreigners do not need the CPF tax document (needed by Brazilians – you only have to say you are a tourist) to purchase a car, and the official purchase receipt is accepted as proof of ownership. Sunday papers carry car advertisements and there are second-hand car markets on Sun mornings in most cities – but don't buy an alcohol-driven car if you propose to drive outside Brazil. It is essential to have an external intake filter fitted, or dust can rapidly destroy an engine. VW Combi vans are cheapest in Brazil where they are made, they are equivalent to the pre-1979 model in Europe. Be sure to travel with a car manual and good quality tools, a VW dealer will advise. There are VW garages throughout the continent, but parts (German or Latin American) are not always interchangeable. In the main, though, there should be no problems with large components (eg gears). If a lot of time is to be spent on dirt roads, the Ford Chevrolet pickup is more robust. A letter in Spanish from your consul explaining your aims and that you will return the vehicle to Brazil can make life much easier at borders and checkpoints. Brazilian cars may not meet safety regulations in N America and Europe, but they can be easily resold in Brazil.

● Bus

There is no lack of transport between the principal cities of Brazil, mostly by road. Ask for window seats (*janela*), or odd numbers if you want the view. Brazilian bus services have a top speed limit of 80 kph (buses are supposed to have governors fitted). They are extremely comfortable (many have reclining seats), stopping fairly frequently (every 2-4 hrs) for snacks; the cleanliness of these *postos* is generally good, though may be less so in the poorer regions. Standards of comfort on buses and in *postos* vary from line to line, which can be important on long journeys. Buses only stop at official stops. Take something to drink on buses in the N. The bus terminals are usually outside the city centres and offer fair facilities in the way of snack bars, lavatories, left-luggage stores ('guarda volume'), local bus services and information centres. *Leito* buses ply at night between the main centres, offering reclining seats with foot and leg rests, toilets, and sometimes in-board refreshments, at double the normal fare. For journeys over 100 km, most buses have chemical toilets. Air conditioning can make *leito* buses cold at night, so take a blanket or sweater (and plenty of toilet paper); on some services blankets are supplied. Some companies have hostess service. Bus stations for interstate services and other long-distance routes are usually called *rodoviárias*. Buy bus tickets at rodoviárias (most now take credit cards), not from travel agents who add on surcharges. Reliable bus information is hard to come by, other than from companies themselves. It is not easy to sell back unused bus tickets. Some bus companies have introduced a system enabling passengers to purchase return tickets at point of departure, rather than individual tickets for each leg. Buses usually arrive and depart in very good time; you cannot assume departure will be delayed. In the SE and S a *Horário de Ônibus* is available at *rodoviárias* (not available for N or NE). Many town buses have turnstiles which can be inconvenient if you are carrying a large pack. Urban buses normally serve local airports.

● Car hire

It is essential to have a credit card in order to hire in Brazil; four agencies accept TCs, dollars cash may not be accepted, but *reais* cash may qualify for a discount. Check insurance carefully, as few policies give full cover, unless purchased outside Brazil. Avis is found only in the major cities and has only a time-and-mileage tariff. National, ie Localiza, is represented in many places, often through licencees; connected with Inter-Rent/Europcar in Europe, will accept credit cards from InterRent/Europcar and offers unlimited mileage if booked in advance from Europe on a fixed US$ rate. Compare prices of renting from abroad and in Brazil. If you intend to hire a car for a long time, buying and reselling a vehicle within Brazil may be a reasonable alternative (see above).

NB It is virtually impossible to buy premium grades of petrol/gasoline anywhere. With alcohol fuel you need about 50% more alcohol than regular gasoline. Larger cars have a small extra tank for 'gasolina' to get the engine started; remember to keep this topped up. Fuel is only 85 octane (owing to high methanol content), so be prepared for bad consumption and poor performance and starting difficulties in non-Brazilian cars in winter. Diesel fuel is cheap and a diesel engine may provide fewer maintenance problems. Service stations are free to open when they like. Very few open during Carnival week.

● **Hitchhiking**

Information on hitchhiking (*carona* in Portuguese) suggests that it is difficult everywhere; drivers are reluctant to give lifts because passengers are their responsibility. Try at the highway-police check points on the main roads (but make sure your documents are in order) or at the service stations (*postos*).

● **Taxis**

Taxi meters measure distance/cost in 'taxi units' (UT), not *reais*. Taxi units are converted into *reais* with a price list. In many cities this list is taped to the side window of the taxi; in others the driver has the list. Be sure that the list is not a photocopy. The original either has colours inset on the black and white, or, if black and white only, is laminated. Whether or not you see the conversion sheet, you can work out the price by knowing the *real* value of each UT. This rate will either be posted near the meter in the front window, or written on the bottom of the conversion sheet. The rate varies from city to city, but is consistent within each city. At the outset, make sure the meter is cleared and shows tariff 1, except 2300-0600, Sun, and in Dec when 2 is permitted. Check that the meter is working, if not, fix price in advance. The radio taxi service costs about 50% more but cheating is less likely. Taxis have a 40% surcharge on Sun. Taxi services offered by smartly-dressed individuals outside larger hotels usually cost twice as much as ordinary taxis. If you are seriously cheated note the number of the taxi and insist on a signed bill, threatening to go to the police; it can work.

SEA

Clipper Voyages, Albany House, Suite 404, 324/326 Regent St, London, W1R 5AA, T 0171 436 2931, has a 122-passenger expedition cruise ship which sails the Amazon and parts of the Brazilian coast.

COMMUNICATIONS

● **Language**

The language is Portuguese. Efforts to speak it are greatly appreciated and for the low-budget traveller, Portuguese is essential. If you cannot lay your tongue to 'the language of the angels', apologize for not being able to speak Portuguese and try Spanish, but note that the differences in the spoken languages are very much greater than appears likely from the printed page and you may well not be understood: you will certainly have difficulty in understanding the answers.

One important point of spelling is that words ending in 'i' and 'u' are accented on the last syllable, though (unlike Spanish) no accent is used there. This is especially important in place names: Parati, Iguaçu. Note also that 'meia' (half) is frequently used for number 6 (ie half-dozen). Audioforum, Microworld House, 2-6 Foscote Mews, London W9 2HH, T 0171-266 2202 does cassette courses on Brazilian Portuguese (US$195/£155 and US$245/£165), orders by mail or phone with credit card no. There are Brazilian tutors in most cities (in London, see *Time Out* and *Leros*, the Brazilian magazine, for advertisements).

● **Postal services**

Postal charges are high: the overseas rate for letters, aerogrammes and postcards is the same. Air mail takes 4 to 6 days to or from Britain or the US; surface mail takes some 4 weeks. 'Caixa Postal' addresses should be used when possible. All places in Brazil have a post code, *CEP*; these are given in the text. Postes restantes usually only hold letters for 30 days. You can buy charge collected stamps, Compravenda de Francamento (CF) for letters only, to be paid on delivery. The Post Office sells cardboard boxes for sending packages internally and abroad (they must be submitted open); pay by the kilo; you must fill in a list of contents; string, official sellotape is provided in all post offices. Franked and registered (insured) letters are normally secure, but check that the amount franked is what you have paid, or the item will not arrive. Aerogrammes are most reliable. It may be easier to avoid queues and obtain higher denomination stamps by buying at the philatelic desk at the main post office. Poste Restante for Amex customers is efficiently dealt with by the Amex agents in most large towns. Courier services such as DHL, Federal Express and UPS (rec) are useful, but note that they may not necessarily operate under those names.

● **Telephone services**

There is a trunk-dialling system linking all parts: for the codes see DDD in the text, or look in the telephone directory. There are telephone boxes at airports, post offices, railway stations, hotels, most bars, restaurants and cafés, and in the main cities there are telephone kiosks *for local calls only* in the shape of large orange shells, for which *fichas* can be bought from bars, cafés and newsvendors; in Rio they are known as *orelhões* (big ears). Phone cards are available from telephone offices, newstands, post offices and some chemists. Public boxes for intercity calls are blue; there are boxes within main telephone offices for international calls, make sure you buy a card worth at least 100 international units. Collect calls within Brazil can be made from any telephone – dial 9, followed by the number, and announce your name and city. Local calls from a private phone are normally free. International phone calls are priced on normal and cheaper rates, depending on time of day. Check with the local phone company. Peak rate to Europe is US$4/minute, to USA US$3. There is a 40% tax added to the cost of all telephonic and telegraphic communications, which makes international service extremely dear. Local phone calls and telegrams, though, are quite cheap. **NB** Brazil is now linked to North America, Japan and most of Europe by trunk dialling (DDI). Codes are listed in the telephone directories. Embratel operates Home Country Direct, available from hotels, private phones or blue public phones to the following countries (prefix all numbers with 00080); Argentina 54, Australia 61, Bolivia 13, Canada 14, Chile 56 (Entel), 36 (Chile Sat), 37 (CTC Mundo), Denmark 45, France 33, Israel 97, Italy 39, Japan 81 (KDD), 83 (ITJ), 89 (Super Japan), Holland 31, Norway 47, Portugal 35, Spain 34, Sweden 46, UK 44 (BT Direct), USA 10 (AT&T), 12 (MCI), 16 (Sprint), 11 (Worldcom), Uruguay 59, Venezuela 58. For collect calls from phone boxes (in Portuguese: 'a cobrar'), dial 107 and ask for the *telefonista internacional*. No collect calls available to New Zealand. To use the telephone office, tell the operator which city or country you wish to call, go to the booth whose number you are given; make your call and you will be billed on exit. Not all offices accept credit cards.

Fax services operate in main post offices in major cities, or from private lines. In the latter case the international fax rates are as for phone calls; from the post office the rates are US$3-4/page within Brazil, US$10.50 to Europe and US$9 to the USA. To receive a fax costs US$1.40.

ENTERTAINMENT

● **Newspapers**

The main **Rio** papers are *Jornal do Brasil*, *O Globo*, and *Jornal do Commércio*. **São Paulo** Morning: *O Estado de São Paulo*, *Folha de São Paulo*, *Gazeta Mercantil* and *Diário de São Paulo*. Evening: *Jornal da Tarde*, *A Gazeta*, *Diário da Noite*, *Ultima Hora*.

● **Radio**

English-language radio broadcasts daily at 15290 kHz, 19m Short Wave (Rádio Bras, Caixa Postal 04/0340, DF-70 323 Brasília).

HOLIDAYS AND FESTIVALS

National holidays are 1 Jan (New Year); 3 days up to and including Ash Wed (Carnival); 21 April (Tiradentes); 1 May (Labour Day); Corpus Christi (June); 7 Sept (Independence Day); 12 Oct, Nossa Senhora Aparecida; 2 Nov (All Souls' Day); 15 Nov (Day of the Republic); and 25 Dec (Christmas). The local holidays in the main cities are given in the text. Four religious or traditional holidays (Good Friday must be one; other usual days: 1 Nov, All Saints Day; 24 Dec, Christmas Eve) must be fixed by the municipalities. Other holidays are usually celebrated on the Mon prior to the date.

ACKNOWLEDGEMENTS

This chapter has been updated by Steve Collins to whom we are most grateful. We are also grateful to Robert and Daisy Kunstaetter (Quito), who sent new information on the NE, and John Gledson (Liverpool) for a detailed review of the chapter. Travellers who wrote to the *Handbook* are acknowledged at the end of the book.

Chile

HORIZONS

Chile is smaller than all other South American republics save Ecuador, Paraguay, Uruguay and the Guianas. Its territory is a ribbon of land lying between the Andes and the Pacific, 4,329 km long and, on average, no more than 180 km wide. Of this width the Andes and a coastal range of highland take up from a third to a half. There are wide variations of soil and vast differences of climate; these are reflected in the density of population and the occupations of its people.

THE LAND

In the extreme N Chile has a frontier with Peru running 10 km N of the railway from the port of Arica to the Bolivian capital of La Paz. Its eastern frontier – with Bolivia in the far N and with Argentina for the rest of its length – is along the crest of the Andes, gradually diminishing in height from Santiago southwards to the southern seas, where the Strait of Magellan lies, giving access to the Atlantic. Chile's western and southern coastline is 4,500 km long.

Down the whole length, between the Andes and the coastal range, there runs a valley depression, though it is less well defined in the N. North of Santiago transverse ranges join the two massifs and impede transport, but for 1,044 km S of the capital the great longitudinal valley stretches as far as Puerto Montt. South of Puerto Montt the sea has broken through the coastal range and drowned the valley, and there is a bewildering assortment of archipelagos and channels.

From N to S the country falls into five sharply contrasted zones:

A The first 1,250 km from the Peruvian frontier to Copiapó is a rainless hot desert of brown hills and plains devoid of vegetation, with a few oases. Here lie nitrate deposits and several copper mines.

B From Copiapó to Illapel (600 km) is semi-desert; there is a slight winter rainfall, but great tracts of land are without vegetation most of the year. Valley bottoms are here cultivated under irrigation.

C From Illapel to Concepción is Chile's heartland, where the vast majority of its people live. Here there is abundant rainfall in the winter, but the summers are perfectly dry. Great farms and vineyards

Chile

1. Santiago &
   The Heartland
2. Valparaíso &
   Viña del Mar
3. From Santiago
   to La Serena
4. North of La Serena
5. Antofagasta, Calama
   & San Pedro
6. Iquique, Arica &
   The Far North
7. South through
   The Central Valley
8. The Lake District
9. Chiloé
10. Archipelagic Chile
11. Chilean Patagonia

cover the country, which is exceptionally beautiful.

D The fourth zone, between Concepción and Puerto Montt, is a country of lakes and rivers, with heavy rainfall through much of the year. Cleared and cultivated land alternates with mountains and primeval forests.

E The fifth zone, from Puerto Montt to Cape Horn, stretches for 1,600 km. This is archipelagic Chile, a sparsely populated region of wild forests and mountains, glaciers, fjords, islands and channels. Rainfall is torrential, and the climate cold and stormy. There are no rail links S of Puerto Montt, but the Carretera Austral now provides almost unbroken road access for more than 1,000 km S of that city. Chilean Patagonia is in the extreme S of this zone.

A subdivision of the fifth zone is Atlantic Chile – that part which lies along the Magellan Strait to the E of the Andes, including the Chilean part of Tierra del Fuego island. There is a cluster of population here raising sheep and mining coal. Large offshore oilfields have now been discovered in the far S, and the area is developing rapidly.

National parks

Chile has an extensive system of protected natural areas, 7 million ha in all. The areas, managed by Conaf (the Corporación Nacional Forestal), are divided into 30 national parks, 36 forest reserves and 10 natural monuments. Of the 76 areas, 46 have public access, and details of the majority are given in the text.

HISTORY

A century before the Spanish conquest the Incas moved S into Chile from Peru, crossing the desert from oasis to oasis at the foot of the Andes. They reached the heartland and conquered it, but were unable to take the forest S of the Río Maule; there the fierce Mapuches (Araucanians) held them. In 1535-37 Diego de Almagro, at the head of a 100 Spaniards and some thousands of Indians, took the Inca road from Peru S to Salta and across the Andes. Many of the Indians perished, but the heartland was reached; bitterly disappointed at not finding gold they returned to Peru. The next *conquistador*, who took the desert road, was Pedro de Valdivia; he reached the heartland in 1541 and on 12 Feb founded Santiago. Reinforced by fresh colonists from Peru and Spain, Valdivia pushed S into Mapuche land and founded a number of forts. Valdivia was killed in 1553 and the Mapuches soon overran all the Spanish settlements apart from the town to which he had given his name. The Mapuches were fearsome opponents; they soon mastered the use of horses and were effective guerrilla fighters. In 1598 they began a general offensive which destroyed most of the Spanish settlements S of the Río Biobío. The Spanish were forced to create a special frontier army and to build a string of forts along the Biobío. For the rest of the colonial period the Spanish presence S of the river was limited to the coastal fortress of Valdivia and the Island of Chiloé.

In addition to constant wars against the Mapuches, the colonial period was marked by internal dissensions, particularly between the landowners and the priests who strongly objected to a system of Indian serfdom. There were also natural disasters in the form of earthquakes and tidal waves which wiped out cities again and again. From the end of the 16th century British and French pirates frequented the coasts. For most of the colonial period, Chile formed part of the Viceroyalty of Peru; it was controlled from Lima, and trade was allowed only with Peru. This led to uncontrolled smuggling and by 1715 there were 40 French vessels trading illegally along the coast. It was not till 1740 that trading was allowed between Chile and Spain.

In 1810 a group of Chilean patriots, including Bernardo O'Higgins – the illegitimate son of a Sligo-born Viceroy of Peru, Ambrosio O'Higgins, and a Chilean mother – revolted against Spain. This revolt led to 7 years of war against the occupying troops of Spain – Lord Cochrane was in charge of the insurrectionist navy – and in 1817 Gen José de San Martín crossed the Andes with an army from Argentina and helped to gain a decisive victory. O'Higgins became the first

head of state: under him the first constitution of 1818 was drafted. But there was one thing which was dangerous to touch in Chile: the interests of the dominant landed aristocracy, and O'Higgins's liberal policies offended them, leading to his downfall in 1823. A period of anarchy followed, but in 1830 conservative forces led by Diego Portales restored order and introduced the authoritarian constitution of 1833. Under this charter, for almost a century, the country was ruled by a small oligarchy of landowners.

After 1879 Chilean territory was enlarged in both N and S. During the 1870s disputes arose with Boliva and Peru over the northern deserts which were rich in nitrates. Although most of the nitrates lay in Bolivia and Peru, much of the mining was carried out by Anglo-Chilean companies. In the ensuing war (War of the Pacific, 1879-1883) Chile defeated Peru and Bolivia, mainly because her stronger navy gave her control over the sea and even allowed her to land troops in Peru and occupy Lima. Chile gained the Bolivian coastal region as well as the Peruvian provinces of Tarapacá and Arica and for the next 40 years drew great wealth from the nitrate fields.

In the S settlers began pushing across the Río Biobío in the 1860s, encouraged by government settlement schemes and helped by technological developments including repeating rifles, telegraph, railways and barbed wire. At the end of the War of the Pacific the large Chilean army was sent to subdue the Mapuches who were confined to ever-diminishing tribal lands. The territory was then settled by immigrants – particularly Germans – and by former peasants who had fought in the North.

The rule of the Right was challenged by the liberal regime of President Arturo Alessandri in 1920. Acute economic distress in 1924, linked to the replacement of Chilean nitrates with artificial fertilizers produced more cheaply in Europe, led to army intervention and some reforms were achieved. The inequalities in Chilean society grew ever sharper, despite the maintenance of political democracy, and gave rise to powerful socialist and communist parties. President Eduardo Frei's policy of 'revolution in freedom' (1964-70) was the first concerted attempt at overall radical reform, but it raised hopes it could not satisfy. In 1970 a marxist coalition assumed office under Dr Salvador Allende; the frantic pace of change under his regime polarized the country into Left- and Right-wing camps. Gradually increasing social and economic chaos formed the background for Allende's deposition by the army and his death on 11 September 1973. After the overthrow of President Allende, Chile was ruled by a military president, Gen Augusto Pinochet Ugarte, and a 4-man junta with absolute powers. In its early years particularly, the regime suppressed internal opposition by methods which were widely condemned. Despite economic prosperity and efforts to make the regime more popular, Pinochet's bid for a further 8 years as president after 1989 was rejected by the electorate in a plebiscite in 1988.

As a result, presidential and congressional elections were held in 1989. A Christian Democrat, Patricio Aylwin Azócar, the candidate of the Coalition of Parties for Democracy (CPD, or Concertación), was elected President and took office in March 1990 in a peaceful transfer of power. The CPD won 71 of the 120 seats in the Chamber of Deputies, but only 22 seats in the 47-seat Senate, its majority wiped out by nine seats held by Pinochet appointees, who could block constitutional reform. Gen Pinochet remained as Army Commander although other armed forces chiefs were replaced. The new Congress set about revising many of the military's laws on civil liberties and the economy. In 1991 the National Commission for Truth and Reconciliation published a report with details of those who were killed under the military regime, but opposition by the armed forces prevented mass human rights trials. In Dec 1993 presidential elections resulted in the election of the Christian Democrat Eduardo Frei, son of the earlier president, but in congressional elections held at the same time the Concertación failed to achieve the required two-thirds majority in Congress to reform the constitution, replace heads of the armed forces and end the system of designated senators. In Aug 1995, Frei presented bills to make the necessary constitutional reforms to these non-elected powers. He also proposed that investigations continue into the disappearance of some 500 political prisoners in the 1970s. On both issues the military and their political allies appeared to have sufficient support to prevent government success, contrary to public opinion and despite some opposition members favouring reform. In municipal elections in Oct 1996, the Concertación candidates gained 56% of the vote nationwide while the Unión por el Progreso opposition won 33%. The results were seen as indicators as to the outcome of the Dec 1997 congressional elections. Nevertheless, the Concertación was defeated in a congressional vote in June 1997 to reform the constitution when the Senate, for the third time, rejected the abolition of the nine non-elected senators.

CULTURE

PEOPLE

There is less racial diversity in Chile than in most Latin American countries. Over 90% of the population is *mestizo*. There has been much less immigration than in Argentina and Brazil. The German, French, Italian and Swiss immigrants came mostly after 1846 as small farmers in the forest zone S of the Biobío. Between 1880 and 1900 gold-seeking Serbs and Croats settled in the far S, and the British took up sheep farming and commerce in the same region. The influence throughout Chile of the immigrants is out of proportion to their numbers: their signature on the land is seen, for instance, in the German appearance of Valdivia, Puerto Montt, Puerto Varas, Frutillar and Osorno.

There is disagreement over the number of indigenous people in Chile. The Mapuche nation, 95% of whom live in the forest land around Temuco, between the Biobío and Toltén rivers, is put at 1 million by Survival International, but much less by other, including official, statistics. There are also 15,000-20,000 Aymara in the northern Chilean Andes and 2,000 Rapa Nui on Easter Island. A political party, the Party for Land and Identity, unites many Indian groupings, and legislation is proposed to restore indigenous people's rights.

The population is far from evenly distributed: Middle Chile (from Copiapó to Concepción), 18% of the country's area, contains 77% of the total population. The Metropolitan Region of Santiago contains, on its own, about 39% of the whole population.

The rate of population growth per annum is slightly under the average for Latin America. The birth rate is highest in the cities, particularly of the forest zone. The death rate is highest in the cities. Infant mortality is highest in the rural areas.

Since the 1960s heavy migration from the land has led to rapid urbanization. Housing in the cities has not kept pace with this increased population; many Chileans live in slum areas called *callampas* (mushrooms) on the outskirts of Santiago and around the factories.

MUSIC AND DANCE

At the very heart of Chilean music is the Cueca, a courting dance for couples, both of whom make great play with a handkerchief waved aloft in the right hand. The man's knees are slightly bent and his body arches back. It is lively and vigorous, seen to best advantage when performed by a Huaso wearing spurs. Guitar and harp are the accompanying instruments, while handclapping and shouts of encouragement add to the atmosphere. The dance has a common origin with the Argentine Zamba and Peruvian Marinera via the early 19th century Zamacueca, in turn descended from the Spanish Fandango. For singing only is the Tonada, with its variants the Glosa, Parabienes, Romance, Villancico (Christmas carol) and Esquinazo (serenade) and the Canto a lo Poeta, which can be in the form of a Contrapunto or Controversia, a musical duel. Among the most celebrated groups are Los Huasos Quincheros, Silvia Infante with Los Condores and the Conjunto Millaray. Famous folk singers in this genre are the Parra Family from Chillán, Hector Pávez and Margot Loyola. In the N of the country the music is Amerindian and closely related to that of Bolivia. Groups called 'Bailes' dance the Huayño, Taquirari, Cachimbo or Rueda at carnival and other festivities and precolumbian rites like the Cauzulor and Talatur. Instruments are largely wind and percussion, including *zampoñas* (pan pipes), *lichiguayos*, *pututos* (conch shells) and *clarines*. There are some notable religious festivals that attract large crowds of pilgrims and include numerous groups of costumed dancers. The most outstanding of these festivals are those of the Virgen de La Tirana near Iquique, San Pedro de Atacama, the Virgen de la Candelaria of Copiapó and the Virgen de Andacollo.

In the S the Mapuche nation, the once greatly feared and admired 'Araucanos', who kept the Spaniards and Republicans at bay for 400 years, have their own songs, dance-songs and magic and collective dances, accompanied by wind instruments like the great long *trutruca* horn, the shorter *pifilka* and the *kultrun* drum. Further S still, the island of Chiloé, which remained in the hands of pro-Spanish loyalists after the rest of the country had become independent, has its own unique musical expression. Wakes and other religious social occasions include collective singing, while the recreational dances, all of Spanish origin, such as the Vals, Pavo, Pericona and Nave have a heavier and less syncopated beat than in central Chile. Accompanying instruments here are the *rabel* (fiddle), guitar and accordion.

THE ECONOMY

Structure of production Chile is endowed with a diversified environment, allowing the production of all temperate and Mediterranean products. Traditional crops, such as cereals, pulse, potatoes and industrial crops (sugarbeet, sunflowerseed and rapeseed) account for about a third of the value added of agriculture, and vegetables for a quarter. Fruit growing has grown rapidly and fresh fruit now accounts for over US$1bn in exports a year, making fruit the second most important earner after copper. Another area of expansion is forestry; timber and wood products make up the third place in exports. More than 80% of the 1.6 million ha of cultivated forest is planted with insignis radiata pine, a species which in Chile grows faster than in other countries. However, native forest has been declining rapidly, partly because of demand by wood chippers. Chile is the most important fishing nation in Latin America and the largest producer of fishmeal in the world. Industrial consumption absorbs about 93% of the fish catch; fresh fish and fish products contribute about 10% of merchandise exports. Salmon farming is being expanded.

The dominant sector of the economy is mining. Chile has been the world's largest producer of copper since 1982 and also produces molybdenum, iron ore, manganese, lead, gold, silver, zinc, sulphur and nitrates. Chile has a quarter of the world's known molybdenum ore reserves and is believed to have around 40% of the world's lithium reserves. Mineral ores, most of which is copper, account for half of total export revenue. Fluctuations in world prices for minerals can have a great impact on the balance of payments. Foreign investment is the driving force in mining, which has averaged almost US$900mn a year in the 1990s in exploration and mine development. By 2000 output of copper will be 4 million tonnes a year, over 40% of world production, of which 1.4 million tonnes will be produced by the state company, Codelco, from its five mines, Chuquicamata, El Teniente, Salvador, Andina and Radomiro Tomic (to come on stream in 1998). Privately owned, high-tech mines or joint ventures are responsible for most of the expected growth, the largest being Escondida, which produces 800,000 tonnes a year (1997).

Chile is fortunate in possessing reserves of oil, natural gas and coal, and abundant hydroelectricity potential. Almost all the country's hydrocarbon reserves are in the extreme S, on Tierra del Fuego, in the Strait of Magellan and the province of Magallanes. Natural gas is likely to be piped across the Andes from Argentina from 1997. Two pipelines are planned and up to six new gas-fired power plants may be built in 1998-2002, reducing electricity costs and pollution around Santiago if coal-fired plants are closed.

Manufacturing activity is mostly food processing, metalworking, textiles, footwear and fish processing. The sector has been vulnerable to changes in economic policy: nationalization during the Allende administration in the early 1970s; recession brought about by anti-inflation policies in the mid-1970s; increased competition resulting from trade liberalization in the early 1980s and greater exports together with import substitution in the mid-1980s. The contribution of manufacturing to total gdp fell from 25% in 1970 to 17% in 1994, but its share of exports rose and the sector grew by over 6% a year in the 1990s.

Recent trends The policies used to bring inflation down from over 500% at the end of 1973 to less than 10% by end-1981 resulted in fiscal balance but an overvalued currency. Freeing the exchange rate in 1982 caused renewed inflation; this was restricted by tight monetary control and a lower public sector borrowing requirement which caused a severe recession and contraction in gdp. IMF help was sought following a sharp fall in international commercial lending in 1982 and a decline in Chile's terms of trade. In the 1980s Chile negotiated several debt refinancing packages and reduced its foreign debt through schemes which converted debt into equity in Chilean companies. Renewed growth in debt in the 1990s was offset by rising gdp and exports which meant that the debt:gdp ratio fell from 94% in 1985 to an estimated 40% in 1995, while the debt service ratio declined from 48% to about 15% in the same period.

Chile: fact file

Geographic

Land area	756,626 sq km
forested	22.0%
pastures	18.2%
cultivated	5.7%

Demographic

Population (1996)	14,376,000
annual growth rate (1991-96)	1.5%
urban	85.8%
rural	14.2%
density	18.9 per sq km

Education and Health

Life expectancy at birth,	
male	71.5 years
female	77.4 years
Infant mortality rate	
per 1,000 live births (1993)	13.1
Calorie intake as %	
of FAO requirement	106%
Population age 25 and over	
with no formal schooling	5.7%
Literate males (over 15)	81.3%
Literate females (over 15)	80.9%

Economic and Employment

GNP (1994 market prices)	US$50,051mn
GNP per capita	US$3,170
Public external debt (1994)	US$17,611mn
Tourism receipts (1994)	US$833mn
Inflation	
(annual av 1990-95)	13.8%
Population economically active (1994)	
	5,568,100
Unemployment rate	6.1%
Military forces	89,700

Source *Encyclopaedia Britannica*

The Government follows anti-inflationary policies, accompanied by structural adjustment and reform. Privatization has been widespread, although certain key companies such as Codelco remain in state hands. Privatizing the pension system and corporate savings have doubled domestic savings to 27% of gdp. Pension funds now manage assets of US$25bn, about 40% of gdp. Rising investor confidence has brought economic growth every year since the mid-1980s and the Chile model has been held up as an example for other debtor countries to adapt to their own needs. Unemployment has fallen and progress is being made in reducing poverty with increased public spending on health and education. Infant mortality dropped from 33 per thousand in 1980 to 14.3 per thousand in 1992; the literacy rate rose from 90.8% to 95.3% in the same period and the percentage of malnourished children fell from 8.8% in 1982 to 5.3% in 1993.

GOVERNMENT

The pre-1973 constitution was replaced, after a plebiscite, on 11 March 1981. This new constitution provided for an 8-year non-renewable term for the President of the Republic (although the first elected president was to serve only 4 years), a bicameral Congress and an independent judiciary and central bank. In Feb 1994, the Congress cut the presidential term of office from 8 years to 6. Congress is composed of a 120-seat Chamber of Deputies and a 47-seat Senate, eight of whose members are nominated, rather than elected. In 1974 the country was divided into 13 regions, replacing the old system of 25 provinces.

The Santiago Region

THE CAPITAL and its surroundings, from north of the Río Aconcagua to the Río Maipo; within easy reach are several vineyards and Andean ski resorts.

From a third to half of the width of the area is taken up by the Andes, which are formidably high in the northern sector; at the head of the Río Aconcagua the peak of Aconcagua (in Argentina), the highest in the Americas, rises to 6,964m. The region suffers from earthquakes. There is a mantle of snow on the mountains: at Aconcagua it begins at 4,300m. The lower slopes are covered with dense forests. Between the forest and the snowline there are alpine pastures; during the summer cattle are driven up to these pastures to graze.

The coastal range, over 2,130m high, takes up another third of the width. It is lower here than in the northern desert, but the shoreline is unbroken; it is only at Valparaíso and San Antonio that good harbourage is to be found.

Between the coastal range and the Andes lies the Central Valley; rivers cross it at right angles and cut their way to the sea through narrow canyons in the coastal highland.

Nearly 70% of the people of Chile live in the comparatively small heartland. The rural population density in the area is exceptional for Latin America: it is as high as 48 to the square km to the S of Santiago.

Climate

There is rain during the winter in the heartland, but the summers are dry. The rain increases to the S. On the coast at Viña del Mar it is 483 mm a year, but is somewhat less inland. Temperatures, on the other hand, are higher inland than on the coast. There is frost now and then, but very little snow falls.

Temperatures can reach 33°C in Jan, but fall to 13°C (3°C at night) in July. Days are usually hot, the nights cool.

SANTIAGO

Santiago, founded by Pedro de Valdivia in 1541, is the fifth largest city in South America and one of the most beautifully set of any, standing in a wide plain. The city is crossed from E to W by the Río Mapocho, which passes through an artificial stone channel, 40m wide, spanned by several bridges. Public gardens are filled with flowers and kept in good order. The magnificent chain of the Andes, with its snow-capped heights, is in full view for much of the year, rain and pollution permitting; there are peaks of 6,000m about 100 km away. More than half the country's manufacturing is done here; it is essentially a modern capital, full of skyscrapers, bustle, noise, traffic and smog (tables for which are published in the daily papers, as are the registration numbers of those cars which are not allowed into the city each day).

BASICS *Pop* almost 5 million; *Alt* 600m; *Phone code* 02.

PLACES OF INTEREST

The centre of the old city lies between the Mapocho and the Av O'Higgins, which is usually known as the **Alameda**. From the **Plaza Baquedano** (**Plaza Italia**), in the E of the city's central area, the Mapocho flows to the NW and the Av O'Higgins runs to the SW. From Plaza Baquedano the C Merced runs due W to the **Plaza de Armas**, the heart of the city; it lies 5 blocks S of the Mapocho.

Around the Plaza de Armas On the eastern and southern sides of the Plaza de Armas there are arcades with shops; on the northern side is the Post Office and the Municipalidad; and on the western side the Cathedral and the archbishop's palace. The **Cathedral**, much rebuilt, contains a recumbent statue in wood of San Francisco Javier, and the chandelier which lit the first meetings of Congress after independence; it also houses an interesting museum of religious art and historical pieces. In the **Palacio de la Real Audiencia** on the Plaza de Armas is the Museo Histórico Nacional (see **Museums**, below). A block W of the Cathedral

The Santiago Region

Mt Cupula

Mt Colorado

Putaendo

Termas de Jahuel

Mt Aconcagua

Puenta de Lanca

Puente de Vacas

San Felipe

Santa María

Redentor Tunnel

Portillo

Los Penitentes

Río Aconcagua

Mt Penitente

To Valparaíso

Los Andes

Río Blanco

Chacabuco Tunnel

Mt San Emeteri

Mt Olivares

ARGENTINA

Termas de Colina

Santuario de la Naturaleza Yerba Loca

Mt El Polomo

Colina

La Parva

El Colorado

Mt Yupungato

Farallones

Mt Piuquenes

To Valparaíso

Lo Prado Tunnel

SANTIAGO

Maipú

San Bernardo

Peñaflor

Puente Alto

Lagunillas

Mt Marmolejo

To San Antonio

Pomaire

Pirque

San José de Maipo

Parque Nacional El Morado

Río Mapocho

El Molocotón

San Alfonso

Lo Valdés

Mt San José

Reserva Nacional Río Clarillo

Río Maipo

El Volcán

Termas de Colina

Mt Manantial Redondo

0   10
Km

Mt Cabeza de Novillo

To Rancagua

30a

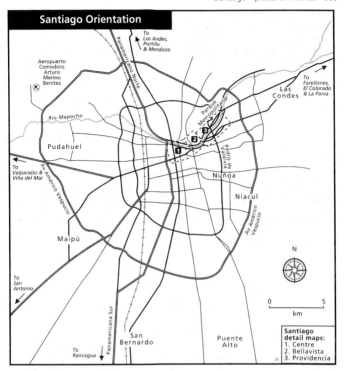

Santiago Orientation

To Los Andes, Portillo & Mendoza

Aeropuerto Comodoro Arturo Merino Benitez

To Farellones, El Colorado & La Parva

Las Condes

Río Mapocho

Parque Metropolitano

Pudahuel

Pedro de Valdivia

To Valparaíso & Viña del Mar

Av Américo Vespucio

Ñuñoa

Niacul

Maipú

Av Américo Vespucio

To San Antonio

N

0   5
km

To Rancagua

Panamericana Sur

San Bernardo

Puente Alto

31

Santiago
detail maps:
1. Centre
2. Bellavista
3. Providencia

is the **former Congress** building now occupied by the Ministry of Foreign Affairs (the new Congress building is in Valparaíso). Nearby are the law courts. At C Merced 864, close to the Plaza de Armas, is the **Casa Colorada**, built in 1769, the home of the Governor in colonial days and then of Mateo de Toro, first President of Chile. It is now the Museum of the History of Santiago. From the Plaza de Armas Paseo Ahumada, a pedestrianized street lined with cafés runs S to the Alameda 4 blocks away, crossing Huérfanos, which is also pedestrianized.

Four blocks N of the Plaza de Armas is the interesting **Mercado Central**, at 21 de Mayo y San Pablo. The building faces the Parque Venezuela, on which is the Cal y Canto metro station, the northern terminus of Line 2, and, at its western end,

the former **Mapocho Railway Station**, now a cultural centre. If you head E from Mapocho station, along the river, you pass through the Parque Forestal (see below), before coming back to Plaza Baquedano.

Along the Alameda The Av O'Higgins runs through the heart of the city for over 3 km. It is 100m wide, and ornamented with gardens and statuary: the most notable are the equestrian statues of Generals O'Higgins and San Martín; the statue of the Chilean historian Benjamín Vicuña MacKenna who, as mayor of Santiago, beautified Cerro Santa Lucía (see **Parks and Gardens** below); and the great monument in honour of the battle of Concepción in 1879.

From the Plaza Baquedano, where there is a statue of Gen Baquedano and the Tomb of the Unknown Soldier, the

Alameda skirts, on the right, Cerro Santa Lucía, and on the left, the Catholic University. Beyond the hill the Alameda goes past the neo-classical **Biblioteca Nacional** on the right, Moneda 650 (temporary exhibitions). Beyond, on the left, between C San Francisco and C Londres, is the oldest church in Santiago: the red-walled church and monastery of **San Francisco**. Inside is the small statue of the Virgin which Valdivia carried on his saddlebow when he rode from Peru to Chile. South of San Francisco is the Barrio París-Londres, built in 1923-1929, now restored and pedestrianized. Two blocks N of the Alameda on C Agustinas is the **Teatro Municipal**. A little further W along the Alameda, is the **Universidad de Chile**; the **Club de la Unión** is almost opposite. Nearby, on C Nueva York is the **Bolsa de Comercio**.

One block further W is the Plaza de la

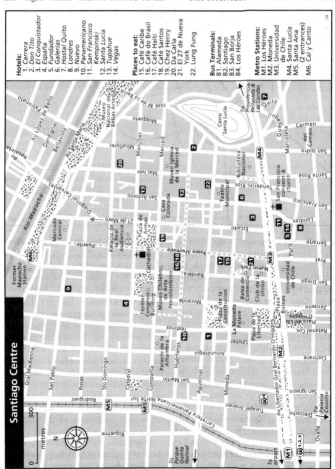

Hotels:
1. Carrera
2. Don Tito
3. El Conquistador
4. España
5. Fundador
6. Galerías
7. Hostal Quito
8. Londres
9. Nuevo
10. Panamericano
11. San Francisco
12. Santa Lucía
13. Tupahue
14. Vegas

Places to eat:
15. Café Caribe
16. Café de Brasil
17. Café Haiti
18. Café Santos
19. Chez Henry
20. Da Carla
21. El 27 de Nueva York
22. Lung Fung

Bus Terminals:
B1. Alameda
B2. Santiago
B3. San Borja
B4. Los Héroes

Metro Stations:
M1. Los Héroes
M2. Moneda
M3. Universidad de Chile
M4. Santa Lucía
M5. Santa Ana (2 entrances)
M6. Cal y Canto

Santiago Centre

Libertad. To the N of the Plaza, hemmed in by the skyscrapers of the Centro Cívico, is the **Palacio de la Moneda** (1805), the Presidential Palace containing historic relics, paintings and sculpture, and the elaborate 'Salón Rojo' used for official receptions (guided visits only with written permission from the Dirección Administrativa – 3 weeks notice required). Although the Moneda was damaged by air attacks during the military coup of 11 September 1973 it has been fully restored. In front of the Palace is the statue of former President Arturo Alessandri Palma. (Ceremonial changing of the guard every other day, 1000, never on Sun; Sun ceremony is performed Mon.)

The Alameda continues westwards to the **Planetarium** (Av O'Higgins 3349, T 776-2624, US$2.50) and, opposite it on the southern side, the railway station (Estación Central or Alameda). On Av Matucana, running N from here, is the very popular **Parque Quinta Normal** (see below). About 7 blocks W of the Estación Central are the major bus terminals.

Lastarria and Bellavista Between the Parque Forestal, Plaza Baquedano and the Alameda is the **Lastarria** neighbourhood (Universidad Católica metro). For those interested in antique furniture, objets d'art and old books, the area is worth a visit, especially the **Plaza Mulato Gil de Castro** (C José V Lastarria 305). Occasional shows are put on in the square. Nearby, on Lastarria, are the **Jardín Lastarria**, a cul-de-sac of craft and antique shops and, at the corner with Merced, the Instituto Chileno-Francés (see below).

The **Bellavista** district, on the N bank of the Mapocho from Plaza Baquedano at the foot of Cerro San Cristóbal (see below), is the main focus of nightlife in the old city. Around C Pío Nono are restaurants and cafés, theatres, entertainments, art galleries and craft shops (especially those selling lapis lazuli).

Providencia East of Plaza Baquedano, the main E-W axis of the city becomes **Avenida Providencia** which heads out towards the residential areas, such as Las Condes, at the eastern and upper levels of the city. It passes through the neighbourhood of Providencia, a modern area of shops, offices and restaurants around Pedro de Valdivia and Los Leones metro stations, which also contains the offices of Sernatur, the national tourist board. At Metro Tobalaba it becomes Avenida Apoquindo.

PARKS AND GARDENS

Cerro Santa Lucía, bounded by C Merced to the N, Av O'Higgins to the S, Calles Santa Lucía and Subercaseaux, this cone of rock rises steeply to a height of 70m. It can be climbed from the Caupolicán esplanade, on which, high on a rock, stands a statue of that Mapuche leader, but the ascent from the northern side of the hill, where there is an equestrian statue of Diego de Almagro, is easier. There are striking views of the city from the top (reached by a series of stairs), where there is a fortress, the Batería Hidalgo (closed to the public). Even on smoggy days, the view of the sunset is good; the Cerro closes at 2100. It is best to descend the eastern side, to see the small Plaza Pedro Valdivia with its waterfalls and statue of Valdivia. The area is famous, at night, for its gay community.

Parque O'Higgins lies about 10 blocks S of Av O'Higgins. It has a small lake, playing fields, tennis courts, swimming pool (open from 5 Dec), an open-air stage, a discothèque, the racecourse of the Club Hípico, an amusement park, *Fantasilandia* (admission US$7, unlimited rides, open at weekends only in winter, and not when raining), kite-fighting contests on Sun, good 'typical' restaurants, craft shops and museums detailed below. Cars are not allowed in the Parque.

● **Access Metro** Line 2 to Parque O'Higgins station. **Bus** from Parque Baquedano via Avs MacKenna and Matta.

North of the Estación Central on Av Matucana y D Portales is the **Quinta Normal**, founded as a botanical garden in 1830. It contains four museums, see below.

Parque Forestal lies due N of Santa Lucía hill and immediately S of the Mapocho. The Museo Nacional de Bellas

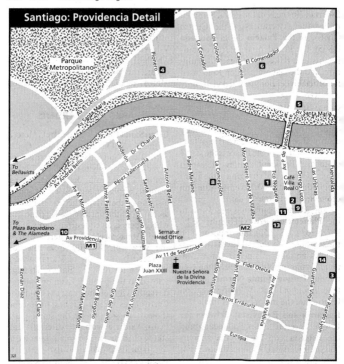

Santiago: Providencia Detail

Artes is in the wooded grounds and is an extraordinary example of neo-classical architecture (details below). **Parque Balmaceda** (Parque Gran Bretaña), E of Plaza Baquedano, is perhaps the most beautiful in Santiago (the Museo de los Tajamares is here).

The sharp, conical hill of **San Cristóbal**, forming the **Parque Metropolitano**, to the NE of the city, is the largest and most interesting of the city's parks. There are two entrances: from Pío Nono in Bellavista and further E from Pedro de Valdivia Norte. On the summit (300m) stands a colossal statue of the Virgin, which is floodlit at night; beside it is the astronomical observatory of the Catholic University which can be visited on application to the observatory's director. Near the Bellavista entrance is a zoo, which has an excellent collection of animals which are well-cared for (open 1000-1300, 1500-1800 Tues-Fri, 1000-1800 Sat, Sun and holidays). Further E in the Tupahue sector there are terraces, gardens, and paths; in one building there is a good, expensive restaurant (*Camino Real*, T 232-1758) with a splendid view from the terrace, and an Enoteca (exhibition of Chilean wines: you can taste one of the three 'wines of the day', and buy if you like, though prices are higher than in shops). Nearby is the Casa de la Cultura which has art exhibitions and free concerts at midday on Sun. There are two good swimming pools: one at Tupahue; the other, Antilen, can be reached from the road that starts below the Enoteca. East of Tupahue are the Botanical Gardens, with a collection of Chilean native plants, guided tours available.

● **Access By funicular**: every few minutes

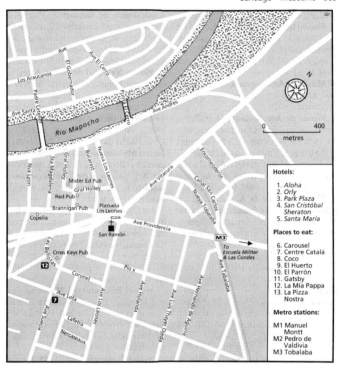

Hotels:

1. Aloha
2. Orly
3. Park Plaza
4. San Cristóbal
   Sheraton
5. Santa María

Places to eat:

6. Carousel
7. Centre Catalá
8. Coco
9. El Huerto
10. El Parrón
11. Gatsby
12. La Mia Pappa
13. La Pizza
    Nostra

Metro stations:

M1 Manuel
   Montt
M2 Pedro de
   Valdivia
M3 Tobalaba

from Plaza Caupolicán at the northern end of C
Pío Nono, stopping on its way at the Jardín
Zoológico, US$2 in week, US$2.25 weekends
1000-1900 Mon-Fri, 1000-2000 Sat and Sun
(closed for lunch 1330-1430). Fares: from Plaza
to zoo US$2.40 (easily walked); from zoo to San
Cristobal US$3.20. **By teleférico** from Estación
Oasis, Av Pedro de Valdivia Norte via Tupahue
to San Cristóbal near the funicular's upper station, 1030-1900 at weekends, 1500-1830
weekdays except Tues (in summer only),
US$2.80. A combined funicular/teleférico ticket
is US$6. An open bus operated by the teleférico
company runs to San Cristóbal and Tupahue
from the Bellavista entrance with the same
schedule as the teleférico itself. To get to Tupahue at other times you must take the funicular
or a taxi (or walk to/from Pedro de Valdivia metro
station, about 1 km). **By taxi** either from the
Bellavista entrance (much cheaper from inside
the park as taxis entering the park have to pay
entrance fee), or from metro Pedro de Valdivia.

MUSEUMS

NB Almost all museums are closed on
Mon and on 1 November.

Museo Histórico Nacional, Plaza de
Armas 951, in the former Palacio de la
Real Audiencia, covers the period from
the Conquest until 1925; Tues-Sun,
1000-1730, US$1.

Museo de Santiago, Casa Colorada,
Merced 860, history of Santiago from the
Conquest to modern times, excellent displays and models, guided tours; Tues-Sat,
1000-1800 (US$1.50), Sun and holidays,
1000-1300.

**Museo Chileno de Arte Precolom-
bino**, Bandera 361, in the former Real
Aduana, representative exhibition of objects from the precolombian cultures of
Central America and the Andean region,
highly rec; Tues-Sun 1000-1800, US$1.25,

Booklet, US$0.35.

Museo Iglesia de la Merced, MacIver 341, colonial religious art and archaeological collection from Easter Island; Tues-Fri 1000-1300, 1500-1800, Sat 1000-1300, US$1.

Museo de Arte Sagrado, in the Cathedral, Mon and Fri only, 0930-1230, 1530-1830, free.

Museo de Arte Colonial, Londres 4, beside Iglesia San Francisco, religious art, includes one room with 54 paintings of the life of St Francis; in the cloisters is a room containing Gabriela Mistral's Nobel medal; also a collection of locks; Tues-Sat 1000-1800, Sun 1000-1400, US$1.

The Palacio de la Alhambra, Compañía 1340 corner of Amunátegui, is a national monument sponsored by the Society of Arts; it stages exhibitions of paintings as well as having a permanent display; Mon-Fri 1100-1300, 1700-1900, T 80875.

Palacio Cousiño, C Dieciocho 438, 5 blocks S of the Alameda, a large mansion in French rococo style with a superb Italian marble staircase. Owned by the Municipalidad, it is open as a museum; Tues-Fri 0930-1330, 1430-1700, Sat, Sun and holidays 0930-1330, US$3. Guided tours only, in Spanish, English and Portuguese, visitors have to wear cloth bootees to protect the floors.

In the Parque Quinta Normal are: **Museo Nacional de Historia Natural**, which has exhibitions on zoology, botany, mineralogy, anthropology, ethnography and archaeology; Tues-Sun 1000-1745, US$0.80. **Museo Ferroviario** containing 13 steam engines built between 1884 and 1953 (Tues-Fri, 1000-1215, 1400-1700, Sat, Sun and holidays, 1100-1330, 1500-1830, US$1, free to those over 60, photography permit, US$2.50). **Museo Ciencia y Tecnología**, US$1, same hours as **Ferroviario**. **Museo Artequín**, nearby on Av Portales in the Chilean pavilion built for the 1889 Paris International Exhibition, containing prints of famous paintings and activities and explanations of the techniques of the great masters, rec, daily 1000-1800, US$1.25.

In Lastarria and Bellavista are: **Museo**

Arqueológico de Santiago, in Plaza Mulato Gil de Castro, Lastarria 307, temporary exhibitions of Chilean archaeology, anthropology and precolombian art; Mon-Fri 1030-1400, 1530-1900, Sat, 1030-1400, free.

Museo Nacional de Bellas Artes, in the Parque Forestal, has a large display of Chilean and foreign painting and sculpture; contemporary art exhibitions are held several times a year (Tues-Sat 1000-1800, Sun and holidays 1100-1800, US$0.70). In the W wing of the building are the **Museos de Arte Popular Americano**, a collection of N and S American folk art, and **de Arte Contemporáneo** (neither is on full view as the wing is awaiting renovation).

La Chascona, F Márquez de la Plata 0192, T 777-8741, the house of the poet Pablo Neruda and now headquarters of the Fundación Pablo Neruda. Open daily except Mon, 1000-1300, 1500-1800, US$2 guided visits only, English guides can be booked (see page 699).

Museo Tajamares del Mapocho, Parque Balmaceda, Av Providencia 222, an exhibition of the 17th and 18th century walls built to protect the city from flooding by the river, and of the subsequent canalization; Tues-Sat 1000-1800, Sun 1000-1330.

Museo Benjamín Vicuña MacKenna, Av V MacKenna 94, recording the life and works of the 19th century Chilean historian and biographer; occasional exhibitions.

In the Parque O'Higgins are: **Museo del Huaso**, a small, interesting collection of criollo clothing and tools; Tues-Fri 1000-1300, 1430-1715, Sat, Sun and holidays 1000-1800, free. **Acuario Municipal** at Local 9, Tues-Fri 1000-2000 (till 2100 Sat, Sun, holidays – small charge). **Museo de Insectos y Caracoles**, Local 12, a collection of indigenous items, same hours as the aquarium but open till 2200 at weekends and holidays.

Museo de la Escuela Militar, Los Militares 4500, Las Condes, with displays on O'Higgins, the Conquest, the Pacific War and a room devoted to the medals of Gen Pinochet (not on general display so ask), Mon-Fri 1000-1130, 1530-1830, Sat 0930-1430, Sun 1430-1800, free.

Museo Ralli, Sotomayor 4110, Vitacura, collection of works by modern European and Latin American artists, including Dali, Chagall, Bacon and Miró; Tues-Sun 1100-1700, free.

Museo de Artes Decorativos, Casas Lo Matta, Av Pdte Kennedy 9350, Vitacura, a beautiful museum containing Don Hernán Garcés Silva's bequest to the nation: antique silverplate from South America and Europe, 16th-18th century Spanish colonial and European furniture, 15th century Books of Hours, housed in an 18th century country mansion. Guided tours available; by bus, take Intercomunal No 4 from Mapocho station, or take a taxi; in either case ask to be let out at 'Casas lo Matta'.

Museo Aeronáutico, Camino a Melipilla 5100, Cerrillos Airport, Tues-Sun 1000-1700, displays on space exploration, worth a visit.

EXCURSIONS

To **Maipú**, a suburb 10 km SW of Santiago where a monument marks the site of the Battle of the Maipú, 5 April 1818, which resulted in the final defeat of the Spanish royalist forces in mainland Chile. Nearby is the **National Votive Temple of Maipú**, of fine modern architecture and stained glass; interesting (open daily 0800-2100, also daily mass at 1830, 1730 Sat, 1000-1400, 1600-2000 Sun and religious holidays), and so is the attached **Museo del Carmen** of carriages, furniture, clothing and other colonial and later items, Sat 1600-2000, Sun and holidays, 1100-1400, 1600-2000. Bus from Teatinos y O'Higgins, 45 mins.

LOCAL FESTIVALS

During Nov there is a free art fair in the Parque Forestal on the banks of the Río Mapocho, lasting a fortnight. In Oct or Nov there are a sumptuous flower show and an annual agricultural and industrial show (known as Fisa) in Parque Cerrillos. Religious festivals and ceremonies continue throughout Holy Week, when a priest ritually washes the feet of 12 men.

The image of the Virgen del Carmen (patron of the Armed Forces) is carried through the streets by cadets on 16 July.

LOCAL INFORMATION

● Accommodation

Hotel prices			
L1	over US$200	L2	US$151-200
L3	US$101-150	A1	US$81-100
A2	US$61-80	A3	US$46-60
B	US$31-45	C	US$21-30
D	US$12-20	E	US$7-11
F	US$4-6	G	up to US$3

Unless otherwise stated, all hotels in range **D** and above have private bath. Assume hot water, friendliness and cleanliness in all cases.

Check if breakfast and 18% tax is included in the price quoted (if foreigners pay in US$ cash or with US$ TCs, the 18% IVA/VAT should not be charged; if you pay by credit card, there is usually a 10% surcharge).

Expensive hotels In the Providencia area: **L1** *San Cristóbal Sheraton*, Santa María 1742, T 233-5000, F 223-6656, best in town, good restaurant, good buffet lunch, and all facilities, also *Sheraton Towers*, slightly cheaper; **L1** *Park Plaza*, Ricardo Lyon 207, T 233-6363, F 233-6668, good; **L3** *Presidente*, Eliodoro Yáñez 867, T 235-8015, F 235-9148, almost at Providencia, good value and good location; **A1** *Aloha*, Francisco Noguera 146, T 233-2230/7, F 233-2494, helpful, good restaurant; **A1** *Santa María*, Santa María 2050, T 232-6614, F 231-6287, excellent, small, good breakfast, other meals good value, highly rec; **A1** *Orly*, Pedro de Valdivia 27, metro Pedro de Valdivia, T 232-8225, also smaller, cheaper rooms, comfortable; **A1** *Torremayor*, Ricardo Lyon 322, T 234-2000, F 234-3779, modern, good service, good location; **A2** *Posada del Salvador*, Eliodoro Yáñez 893, T 235-9450, F 251-8697, metro Salvador.

In Las Condes: L1 *Hyatt Regency Santiago*, Av Kennedy N 4601, T 218-1234, F 218-2279, superb, beautifully decorated, highly rec; **A1** *Montebianco*, Isidora Goyenechea 2911, T 233-0427, F 233-0420, small, smart motel; **A2** *Manquehue*, Esteban Dell'Orto 6615, T/F 2128862, very good; **A1** *Parinacota*, Av Apoquindo 5142, T 246-6109, F 220-5386, 4-star, small, all services, no pool.

In the central area: L1 *Carrera*, Teatinos 180, T 698-2011, F 672-1083, enormous rooms, pool, rooftop restaurant (good buffet lunch); **L1** *El Conquistador*, Miguel Cruchaga 920, T/F 696-5599, and **L1** *Galerías*, San Antonio

65, T 638-4011, F 639-5240, excellent, welcoming; **L1** *San Francisco Kempinski*, O'Higgins 816, T 639-3832, F 639-7826, Lufthansa affiliated, 5-star, good; **L2** *Fundador*, Paseo Serrano 34, T/F 632-2566, helpful, good value; **L2** *Holiday Inn Crowne Plaza*, O'Higgins 136, T 638-1042, F 633-6015, all facilities, also good, spacious, a/c (book through travel agent for better rates); **L3** *Hostal del Parque*, Merced 294, opp Parque Forestal, T 639-2694, F 639-2754, comfortable, quiet, rec.

A1 *Tupahue*, San Antonio 477, T 638-3810, F 639-5240, excellent, welcoming; **A2** *Ducado*, Agustinas 1990, T 696-9384/672-6739, F 695-1271, with breakfast, rec, secure parking; **A2** *Panamericano*, Teatinos 320 y Huérfanos, T 672-3060, F 696-4992, comfortable, serves popular business lunch between 1230 and 1530; **A3** *City*, Compañía 1063, T 695-4526, F 695-6775, old-fashioned, rec; **A3** *Conde Ansúrez*, Av República 25, T 699-6368, F 671-8376, metro República, convenient for central station and bus terminals, helpful, safe, luggage stored; **A3** *Don Tito*, Huérfanos 578, T 639-1987, good service, excellent breakfast, English spoken; **A3** *Libertador*, O'Higgins 853, T 639-4212, F 633-7128, helpful, rec, stores luggage, good restaurant, bar, roof-top pool; **A3** *Majestic*, Santo Domingo 1526, T 695-8366, F 697-4051, with breakfast, pool, English spoken; rec; **A3** *Monte Carlo*, Subercaseaux 209, T 633-9905, F 633-5577, at foot of Santa Lucía, modern, restaurant, with heating, stores luggage; **A3** *Santa Lucía*, San Antonio 327 y Huérfanos, p 4, T 639-8201, garage 2 blocks away, comfortable, small, quiet restaurant.

Mid-price hotels In the centre: **B** *Imperio*, O'Higgins 2879, T 689-7774, F 689-2916, nr central station, good restaurant, parking; **B** *Principado*, Arturo Burhle 015, just off Vicuña MacKenna 1 block S of Plaza Baquedano, T 635-3879, F 222-6065, convenient location, very nice; **B** *Lira*, Lira 314, T 222-2492, F 634-3637, excellent; **B** *Turismo Japón*, Almte Barroso 160, T 698-4500, convenient location, intermittent hot water, helpful, good breakfast, manager speaks English, best rooms at top, rec; **B** *Res Alicia Adasme*, Moneda 2055, T 696-0787, with breakfast; **B** *Santa Victoria*, Vicuña MacKenna 435, T 634-5753, quiet, small, safe, family run, rec; **B** *Vegas*, Londres 49, T 632-2514, F 632-5084, large comfortable rooms, good breakfast; **B** *Hostal Quito*, Quito 36, T 639-9918, F 639-7470, without breakfast, central, also apartments; **B** *Hostal Vía Real*, Marín 066, T 635-4676, F 635-4678, charming, helpful, small, TV, laundry, rec; **C** *Res Alemana*, República 220 (no sign), T 671-2388, Metro

República, pleasant patio, central, heating on request, good cheap meals available, rec; **C-D** *Res Londres*, Londres 54, T/F 638-2215, former mansion, large old-fashioned rooms and furniture, few singles, no heating, English spoken, very popular, rec repeatedly (often full by 0900); **C-D** *París*, C París 813, T 639-4037, no singles, quiet, good meeting place, good value, luggage store, also short-stay.

Cheaper hotels In the Centre: **D** *Hostal Aula Magna*, Vergara 541, T 698-0729, laundry facilities, Metro Toesca; **D** *Res del Norte*, Catedral 2207, T 696-9251, inc breakfast, safe, large rooms, convenient, credit cards accepted; **D** pp *San Patricio*, Catedral 2235, T 695-4800, **E** pp without bath, with breakfast, safe, good value; **D** *Maury*, Tarapacá 1112, T 672-5889, F 697-0786, safe, meals, English and French spoken; **E** *Indiana*, Rosas 1339, T 714-251, convenient for buses to centre, very basic; **E** pp *Nuevo*, Morandé y San Pablo, T 671-5698, simple but OK, central, erratic hot water, safe, basic, poor beds, use of kitchen (no utensils), cable TV, popular, good meeting place; **E** pp *Olicar*, San Pablo 1265, quiet, rec.

Convenient for bus terminals and Estación Central: near Metro Republica are: **D** *Res Mery*, Pasaje República 36, off 10 block of República, T 696-8883, big green building down an alley, quiet, rec; **E** *Alojamiento Diario*, Sanfuentes 2258 (no sign), T 699-2938, shared rooms, safe, kitchen facilities; **E** pp Sazie 2107, T 672-2269, basic. Elsewhere: **C** *Elisa*, Manuel Rodríguez 140, T 695-6464, quiet; **C** *Res Los Andes Midi*, Unión Americana 134, huge rooms with ancient furniture, basic, laundry facilities, noisy; **E** *Res Sur*, Ruiz Tagle 55, meals available. On N side of Alameda opp bus terminals: **F** pp Federico Scotto 130, T 779-9364, use of phone and fax, good meals, cooking facilities, often full; **E** pp Federico Scotto 079, T 7766484, with breakfast, helpful, luggage stored; **E** pp Huérfanos 2842, T 681-4537, kitchen, laundry, dormitory accommodation.

North of the Plaza de Armas near Mapocho Station: **D** pp *Res Miraflores*, Riquelme 555, T 696-3961, with breakfast, safe, meals available, rec; **D** *Res Amunátegui*, Amunátegui 652. Several on Gral MacKenna 1200 block, all very basic inc **D** *San Felipe*, No 1248, T 713816, secure, cheap laundry service, kitchen, noisy (second floor quieter), luggage stored; **E** *Ovallino*, Gral MacKenna 1477 y San Martín, secure; **E** pp *Casa Andina*, Recoleta 895, T 737-2831, cheap, across the river from Cal y Canto Metro. **NB** Morandé, Gen MacKenna, San Martín and San Pablo are in the red light district.

Family accommodation: travellers can find good accommodation in comfortable family guesthouses through *Amigos de Todo el Mundo*, Av Pdte Bulnes, Paseo, 285, dept 201, Casilla 52861 Correo Central, T 672-6525, F 698-1474, Sr Arturo Navarrete, prices from US$16 with breakfast, other meals extra, monthly rates available, also transport to/from airport, rec; **E** pp *Alberto and Paola Peirario*, Chapultepec 5657, T 218-2101, F 204-4652, minimum 5 days, Spanish classes; also **E** pp *Sra Marta*, same address depto 401, T 779-7592, similar; **E** pp *Sra Lucía*, Catedral 1029, p 10, dept 1001, T 696-3832, central, safe, cooking facilities, basic; **E** pp *Sra Fidela*, San Isidro 261, Apt H, T 222-1246, shared bathroom, breakfast, rec; **D** *Casa Paxi*, Llico 968, T 522-9947, F 521-6328, 1 block from Metro Departamental, washing machine, gardens, quiet; **D** *Sra Marta*, Amengual 035, Alameda Alt 4.400, T 779-7592, lado Norte (metro Ecuador), good, hospitable, kitchen facilities, motorcycle parking; **E** *Sra Eliana Zuvic*, Almte Latorre 617, T 696-8700, Metro Toesca, hot water, nice atmosphere, highly rec; **D** pp *Alicia Bravo*, Artemio Gutiérrez 1328, T 556-6620, with breakfast, helpful, not very central, rec.

Longer stay accommodation: see the classified ads in *El Mercurio*, flats, homes and family *pensiones* are listed by district, or in *El Rastro* (weekly), or try the notice board at the tourist office. In furnished apartments, if you want a phone you may have to provide an *aval*, or guarantor, to prove you will pay the bill, or else a huge deposit will be asked for. Estate agents handle apartments, but often charge 1/3 of the first month's rent as commission, while a month's rent in advance and 1 month's deposit are required. Rec apartments are *Edificio San Rafael*, Miraflores 264, T 633-0289, F 222-5629 US$29 a day single, US$46 a day double, minimum 3 days, US$600 a month, very central.

Youth hostels: **E** pp Cienfuegos 151, T 671-8532, F 672-8880, e-mail histgoch@entelchile.net (5 mins from metro Los Héroes), modern, satellite TV, no cooking facilities, cafeteria, laundry facilities, parking, highly rec; **E** pp *Res Gloria*, Almte Latorre 447, T 698-8315, Metro Toesca, clean, popular, meals, difficult to use kitchen. Information from Youth Hostal Association, Hernando de Aguirre 201, of 602, Providencia, T/F 233-3220 (worth getting a list of YH addresses around the country as these change). Supplies student cards (2 photos required and proof of student status, though tourist card accepted), US$11.

Camping: S of Santiago nr Puente Alto (take Av J Pedro Alessandri S to Las Vizcachas and La Obra where there is a small park on left side of road). Excellent facilities about 70 km from Santiago at Laguna de Aculeo, called *Club Camping*

Maki: inc electricity, cold water, swimming pool, boat mooring, restaurant, but only available to members of certain organizations. An alternative site is *El Castaño* camping (with casino), 1 km away, on edge of lake; very friendly, café sells fruit, eggs, milk, bread and kerosene; good fishing; no showers, water from handpump.

● **Places to eat**
In The Centre: many places in the centre close early in the evening: after 2200 it is better to try Bellavista or Providencia. In addition to those at the main hotels and those in Parque O'Higgins: **Mainly local food**: *Chez Henry*, on Plaza de Armas, expensive restaurant and delicatessen at Alameda 847, which is highly rec; also in Plaza de Armas, *Faison d'Or*, good *pastel de choclo*, pleasant place to have a drink and watch the world go by; *Torres*, O'Higgins 1570, traditional bar/restaurant, good atmosphere, live music at weekends; *Silvestre*, Huérfanos 956, open 0800-2400, good buffet-style; *Mermoz*, Huérfanos 1048, good for lunches; *Bar Nacional No 1*, Huérfanos 1151 and *Bar Nacional No 2*, Bandera 317, good restaurants, popular, local specialities; *Guima*, Huérfanos y Teatinos, good, reasonable prices, good value *almuerzo*; *Café Dante*, Merced 801 y San Antonio, for *pastel de choclo*, lunchtime only; *Bar Central*, San Pablo 1063, typical food, rec; *Fra Diavolo*, París 836 (nr *Res Londres*), lunches only, local and Italian, excellent food and service, popular; *Verdijo*, Morandé 526, noisy, cheap and popular; *El Lugar de Don Quijote*, café, and *Parrilladas de Don Quijote*, restaurant, good, Morandé y Catedral; *Círculo de Periodistas*, Amunátegui 31, p 2, unwelcoming entrance, good value lunches, rec; *Los Adobes de Argomedo*, Argomedo 411 y Lira, hacienda-style, good Chilean food and floor show inc cueca dancing, salsa and folk, Mon-Sat, only place in winter which has this type of entertainment on a Mon.

Seafood: *El 27 de Nueva York*, Nueva York 27, central, pricey, good; *Savory Tres*, Ahumada 327, good but limited choice and closed evenings. Some of the best seafood restaurants are to be found in the Mercado Central (by Cal y Canto metro; lunches only), or at the Vega Central market on the opp bank of the Mapocho.

Oriental: *Guo Fung*, Moneda 1549, rec; *Lung Fung*, Agustinas 715, delicious food, pricey, excellent fixed price lunch, large cage in the centre with noisy parrots; *Pai Fu*, Santa Rosa 101, good; *Kam Thu*, Santo Domingo 771, nr San Antonio, good, large helpings; all Chinese. *Izakaya Yoko*, Merced 456, good, Japanese, rec.

Others: *Nuria*, MacIver 208, wide selection, US$20 plus; *Da Carla*, MacIver 577, Italian food, good, expensive; and *San Marco*, 2 doors away, better still; *Casa Suiza*, Huérfanos 648, good

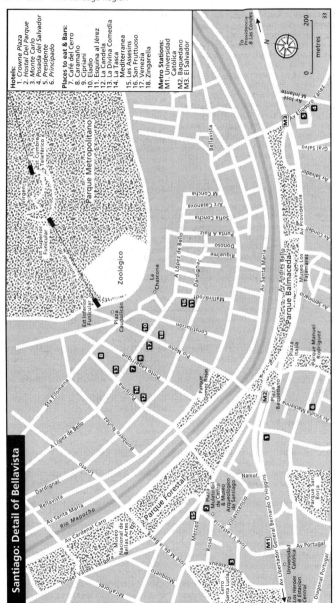

Santiago: Detail of Bellavista

Hotels:
1. Crowne Plaza
2. Hostal Del Parque
3. Monte Carlo
4. Posada del Salvador
5. Presidente
6. Principado

Places to eat & Bars:
7. Café del Cerro
8. Caramaño
9. Cipriani
10. Eladio
11. Esquina al Jerez
12. La Candela
13. La Divina Comedia
14. La Tasca
15. Mediterranea
16. Les Assesins
17. San Fruttuoso
18. Venezia
19. Zingarella

Metro Stations:
M1. Universidad Católica
M2. Baquedano
M3. El Salvador

Swiss food; *Les Assassins*, Merced 297, French, very good, highly rec.

In Lastarria and Bellavista: many, inc *La Pergola de la Plaza* in Plaza Mulato Gil de Castro; better and close by are *Quiche Lorraine* in the Instituto Chileno-Francés, Lastarria 345, highly rec for food, drink and ambience; *Gatopardo*, Lastarria 192, good value and *R*, highly rec. *Café Universitario*, Alameda 395 y Subercaseaux (nr Sta Lucía), good, cheap *almuerzos*. Many restaurants/bars on Pío Nono inc: *Venezia*, huge servings, good value; *Zingarrella*, Italian, good; *Los Ladrillos*, popular, lively, and *La Maviola*, speciality pizzas. On Pinto Lagarrigue: *Café del Cerro*, No 192, T 778-308, with live music (check *El Mercurio* for programme), door charge, highly rec; *Cipriani*, No 195, pasta, elegant atmosphere, US$25-30, top class; *Picoroco*, No 123, good seafood. On López de Bello: *Al Mazzat*, No 82, Arab dishes, good; *El Otro Sitio*, No 53, excellent food, elegant not cheap. On Purísima: *Caramaño*, No 257, good seafood, reasonably priced, ring doorbell, rec; *Les Copains*, No 65, French, good food; *La Tasca Mediterránea*, No 153, good food, rec; *La Divina Comida*, No 215, Italian with 3 rooms – Heaven, Hell and Purgatory, highly rec. On Mallinkrodt: *La Esquina al Jérez*, No 102, excellent Spanish; *San Fruttuoso*, No 180, Italian, rec.

In Providencia: on Av Providencia: *El Parrón*, No 1188, *parrilladas*, rec, the local dice game of 'dudo' is played in the bar; *Lomit's*, No 1980, good; *Gatsby*, No 1984, American food; as-much-as-you-can-eat buffet and lunch/dinner, snack bar open till 2400, tables outside in warm weather, good.

Italian: *La Pizza Nostra*, Av Las Condes 6757, pizzas and good Italian food, real coffee, pricey, also at Av Providencia 1975 and Luis Thayer Ojeda 019; *da Renato*, Mardoqueo Fernández 138 (metro Los Leones), good. *La Mía Pappa*, Las Bellotas 267, very popular lunches.

Others: *Olé Olé*, Guardia Vieja 136, Spanish, good food, wide selection; *Coco*, La Concepción 236, good seafood, expensive, rec, reservation advised; *Centre Catalá*, Av Suecia 428 nr Lota, good, reasonably-priced; *Carrousel*, Los Conquistadores 1972, French, very good, nice garden, over US$20.

In Las Condes: many first-class restaurants, inc grills, Chilean cuisine (often with music), French cuisine and Chinese. This area tends to be more expensive than central restaurants. *Seriatutix*, Av Condes 5137, restaurant and disco, live music, café, great atmosphere; *La Tasca de Altamar*, Noruega y Linneo, good seafood, reasonably priced. On Vitacura: *Delmónico*, No 3379, excellent, reasonably priced; *El Madroñal*, No 2911, T 233-6312, excellent, booking essential;

Praga, No 3917, Czech. On Isadora Goyenechea: *Pinpilinpausha*, No 2900, good; *Martín Carrera*, No 3471, good nouvelle cuisine; *Taj Mahal*, No 3215 (Metro El Golf), T 232-3606, only Indian in Santiago, expensive but excellent. On El Bosque Norte: *München*, German, No 204, rec; *Coco Loco*, No 215, good, US$20-30. On Av Las Condes: *La Estancia*, No 13810 (US$20-25), *La Querencia*, No 14980, a bit cheaper, both good; *Santa Fe*, No 10690, excellent Mexican.

Eating on a budget: it is difficult to eat cheaply in the evening apart from fast food, so budget travellers should make the *almuerzo* their main meal. In the centre cheap lunches from several *fuentes de soda* along Av Santa Rosa between the Alameda and C París. Also: *Casino La Bamquita*, San Martín 75, popular with locals. *Food Garden*, in *galería* at Estado/Ahumada and Huérfanos/Agustinas, p 2, is collection of fast food kiosks, good resting place.

Vegetarian: *El Huerto*, Orrego Luco 054, Providencia, T 233-2690, rec, open daily, live music Fri and Sat evenings, varied menu, very good but not cheap, popular; *Rincón Vegetariano*, Monjitas 558, cheap fixed price lunches, good, juices, rec, closes 1800.

● **Cafés & bars**

For good coffee try *Café Haití*, *Café Brasil* and *Café Caribe*, all on Paseo Ahumada and elsewhere in centre and Providencia. Note that almost all hotel bars are closed on Sun.

In the centre: *Bucaneros*, Morandé 564, good value lunches and snacks; *Café Paula*, several branches, eg Estado at entrance to Galería España, excellent coffee and cake, good breakfast, also on San Antonio opp the Teatro Municipal. *Café Colonia*, Maclver 133, rec; *Café Santos*, Huérfanos 830, popular for 'onces' (afternoon tea); *La E*, San Pablo 1310, good coffee; *Bon Bon Oriental*, Merced 345, superb Turkish cakes; *Cafetería Berri*, Rosal 321, live music at weekends; *Tip-Top Galetas* rec for freshly baked biscuits, branches throughout the city, eg Merced 867.

In Bellavista and Lastarrria: *Café de la Dulcería Las Palmas*, López de Bello 190, good pastries and lunches; several on Purísima 100-200, inc *La Candela*. *El Biógrafo*, Villavicencio 398, bohemian style, rec.

In Providencia: *Geo Pub*, Encomenderos 83, owner Francisco Valle speaks English, pub and expensive restaurant with travel films once a week in winter, music occasionally, popular with travellers; rec; *Villa Real*, Pedro de Valdivia 079, rec. Many on Av Providencia inc: *Phone Box Pub*, No 1670, T 496627; *El Café del Patio*, next door, student hang-out; *Salón de Té Tavelli*, Drugstore precinct, No 2124, rec.

Golden Bell Inn, Hernando Aguirre 27, popular with expatriates; *Cross Keys Pub*, Las Bellotas 270 local 5 (opp *La Mia Pappa*), nr Los Leones metro, with darts, pints, etc, good value. Many other good bars nearby on Av Suecia inc *Mr Ed*, No 1552; *Brannigan Pub*, No 35, good beer, live jazz; *Red Pub*, No 29.

In Las Condes: *El Vikingo*, Rotunda Atena, good atmosphere, cheap; *Café Iguana*, Av Vitacura y La Tranquera; *El Metro* and *Country Village*, Av Las Condes y Estoril; further E on Av Las Condes at Paseo San Damián are several popular bar-restaurants inc *Tequila* and *Mississippi*.

For snacks and ice cream: several good places on Av Providencia inc *Coppellia*, No 2211, *Bravissimo*, No 1406, and *El Toldo Azul*, No 1936.

● **Airline offices**

LanChile, sales office: Agustinas 640, Torre Interamericana, T 699-0505; reservations T 632-3211; **Ladeco**, Huérfanos 1157, T 698-2233 and Pedro de Valdivia 0210, T 251-7204; **National Airlines**, Huérfanos 725, p 3, B, T 633-9288/632-2698; **Aerovías DAP**, Luis Thayer Ojeda 0180, of 1304, Providencia, T 334-9658, F 334-5843; **Alta**, Las Urbinas 30, T/F 244-1777; **British Airways**, Isidora Goyenechea 2934, Oficina 302, T 601-8614, 232-9560 (for confirmation); **Aerolíneas Argentinas**, Moneda 756; **Varig**, Miraflores, between Agustinas and Moneda, T 639-5976; **Aero Perú**, Fidel Oteiza 1953, p 5, T 274-3434; **Ecuatoriana** T 671-2334; **Lacsa**, Av Providencia 2083, Oficina 22, T 233-6400; **Iberia**, Bandera 206, T 698-1716; **KLM**, San Sebastián 2839, Oficina 202, T 233-0011; **Aeroflot**, Agustinas 640, Local 5, T 632-3914; **South African Airlines**, Moneda 970, p 18, next to Lufthansa (T 698-6490); **Swiss Air**, Estado 10, p 10.

● **Banks & money changers**

Banks, open from 0900 to 1400, but closed on Sat. Official daily exchange rates are published in *El Mercurio* and *La Epoca*. **Banco Central de Chile**, Ahumada entre Huérfanos y Agustinas, demands the minimum of formalities, but may charge commission. **Banco O'Higgins**, Bandera 201, changes TCs into dollars with commission on transactions between US$100-1,000. **Citibank**, Ahumada 40.

Casas de Cambio (exchange houses) in the centre are mainly situated on Agustinas and Huérfanos. **Exprinter**, Agustinas 1074, good rates, low commission; **Cambios Andino**, Ahumada 1062; **Teletour**, Guardia Vieja 55; **Afex**, Moneda 1160, good rates for TCs; **Intermundi**, Moneda 896. In Providencia several around Av Pedro de Valdivia, eg at Gral Holley 66, good rates; and **Mojakar**, Pedro de Valdivia 072. All major currencies can be bought or sold. Some

casas de cambio in the centre open Sat am (but check first). Normally there is no commission on TCs though rates may be lower.

American Express, Agustinas 1360 (Turismo Cocha, Av El Bosque Norte 0430, Providencia, for travel information and mail collection), no commission (can change TCs into dollars – no limit). Mastercard at **Fincard**, Alameda 1427, T 698-4260, 2465/7, 3855, 7229, offers its full range of services (even lost or stolen cards are replaced in a couple of days); open 24 hrs. Thomas Cook/Mastercard agent, **Turismo Tajamar**, Orrego Luco 23, T 231-5112. For Cirrus ATMs go to Banco Santander and Banco de Santiago and other banks with Redbank sign. Visa at **Banco Concepción**, Huérfanos y Bandera, but beware hidden costs in 'conversion rate', and **Banco Osorno**, Av Providencia y Pedro de Valdivia, no commission. For stolen or lost Visa cards go to **Transbank**, Huérfanos 777, p 3.

Unless you are feeling adventurous avoid street money changers (particularly common on Ahumada and Agustinas): they will usually ask you to accompany them to a *Casa de Cambio* or somewhere more obscure. Rates for such transactions are no better and the passing of forged notes and mugging are reported.

● **Cultural centres**

Instituto Chileno Británico de Cultura, Santa Lucía 124, T 638-2156, 0930-1900, except 1330-1900 Mon, and 0930-1600 Fri, has British papers in library (also in Providencia, Darío Urzúa 1933, and Las Condes, Renato Sánchez 4369), runs language courses; **British Chamber of Commerce**, Suecia 155-c, Providencia, Casilla 536, T 231-4366; **British Council**, Eliodoro Yáñez 832, nr Providencia, T 223-4622. The British community maintains the **British Commonwealth Society** (old people's home etc), Alessandri 557, T 223-8807, and the interdenominational Santiago Community Church, at Av Holanda 151 (Metro Tobalaba), Providencia, which holds services every Sun at 1045.

Instituto Chileno Francés de Cultura, Merced 298, T 639-8433, in a beautiful house; **Instituto Chileno Alemán de Cultura**, Goethe-Institut, Esmeralda 650, T 638-3185; **German Chamber of Commerce**, Ahumada 131. **Instituto Chileno de Cultura Hispánica**, Providencia 927; **Instituto Chileno Italiano de Cultura**, Triana 843; **Instituto Chileno Israeli de Cultura**, Moneda 812, oficina 613; **Instituto Chileno Japonés de Cultura**, Providencia 2653, oficina 1902.

Instituto Chileno Norteamericano de Cultura, Moneda 1467, T 696-3215, good for US periodicals, cheap films on Fri; also runs language courses and free Spanish/English language exchange hours (known as Happy Hours) which are a good way of meeting people. (Ask also about Mundo Club which organizes excursions and social events.)

Instituto Cultural del Banco del Estado de Chile, Alameda 123, regular exhibitions of paintings, concerts, theatrical performances; **Instituto Cultural de Providencia**, 11 de Septiembre 1995 (Metro Pedro de Valdivia), art exhibitions, concerts, theatre; **Instituto Cultural Las Condes**, Apoquindo 6570, nr beginning of Av Las Condes, also with art exhibitions, concerts, lectures, etc.

● **Embassies and consulates**

Embassies: **Argentina**, Miraflores 285, T 633-1076; Consulate Vicuña MacKenna 41, T 222-6853, Australians need letter from their embassy to get visa here, open 0900-1400 (visa US$25, free for US citizens), if you need a visa for Argentina, get it here or in the consulates in Concepción, Puerto Montt or Punta Arenas, there are no facilities at the borders; **Bolivia**, Santa María 2796, T 232-8180 (Metro Los Leones), open 0930-1400; **Brazil**, Alonso Ovalle 1665, T 698-2347, p 15, visas issued by Consulate, MacIver 225, p 15, Mon-Fri 1000-1300, US$10 (visa takes 2 days); take: passport, 2 photos, ticket into and out of Brazil, photocopy of first 2 pages of passport, tickets, credit card and Chilean tourist card; **Panama**, Del Inca 5901, T 220-8286 (open 1000-1330); **Paraguay**, Huérfanos 886, Oficina 514, T 639-4640, consulate open 0900-1300 (2 photos and copy of first page of passport required for visa); **Peru**, Andrés Bello 1751, T 232-6275 (Metro Pedro de Valdivia).

United States, Andrés Bello 2800, T 232-2600, F 330-3710; **Consulate**, T 710133, Merced 230 (visa obtainable here); **Canada**, Nueva Tajamar 481, p 12, T 362-9660 (prints a good information book).

Australia, Gertrudis Echeñique 420, T 228-5065, 0900-1200; **Israel**, San Sebastian 2812, T 246-1570; **Japan**, Av Providencia 2653, p 19; **New Zealand**, Isadora Goyenechea 3516, Las Condes, T 231-4204; **South Africa**, Av 11 de Septiembre 2353, Edif San Román, p 16, T 231-2862.

Austria, Barros Errázuriz 1968, p 3; **Belgium**, Av Providencia 2653, depto 1104, T 232-1071; **United Kingdom**, El Bosque Norte 0125 (Metro Tobalaba), Casilla 72-D, T 231-3737, F 231-9771, will hold letters, open 0900-1200; **Denmark**, Santa María 0182, T 737-6056; **Finland**, Sótero Sanz de Villalba 55, Oficina 71, T 232-0456; **France**, Condell 65, T 225-1030; **Germany**, Agustinas 785, p 7 y 8, T 633-5031; **Italy**, Clemente Fabres 1050, T 223-2467; **Netherlands**, C Las Violetas 2368, T 223-6825, open 0900-1200; **Norway**, Vespucio Norte 548, T 228-1024; **Spain**, Av Providencia 329, p 4, T 40239; **Sweden**, 11 de Septiembre 2353, Torre San Ramón, p 4, Providencia, T 231-2733, F 232-4188; **Switzerland**, Av Providencia 2653, Oficina 1602, T 232-2693, open 1000-1200 (metro Tobalaba).

● **Entertainment**

Cinemas: 'Ciné Arte' (quality foreign films) is very popular and a number of cinemas specialize in this type of film: *El Biógrafo*, Lastarria 181; *Alameda Cultural Centre*, Av Providencia 927, *Casa de Extensión Universidad Católica*, O'Higgins 390, T 222-1157; *Espaciocal*, Goyenechea y Vitacura; *Tobalaba*, Av Providencia 2563, and others, full details are given in the press. Try also Goethe Institut, and Instituto Chileno-Francés (addresses above). Other cinemas tend to show 'sex, violence and war'. Seats cost US$3-5 with reductions on Wed (elsewhere in the country the day varies).

Discotheques: *Gente*, Apoquindo 4900, also *Baltas*, Av Las Condes 10690, both expensive, but good. *El Baile*, López de Bello, Bellavista. *Maestra Vida*, Pío Nono 380. Many more, mainly in the Providencia and Las Condes areas.

Nightclubs: some of the restaurants and cafés which have shows are given above. Listings are given in *El Mercurio*, or *La Epoca*. Clubs in Bellavista are cheaper and more down market generally than those in Providencia. *La Cucaracha*, Bombero Núñez 159 (Bellavista), is very popular, floorshow at 2330, US$3.50 cover charge, orchestras, dancing. *Varadero*, on Pío Nono, good. Several tango clubs inc *Club Troilo*, Cumming 795, cheap, unpretentious (tango classes 1800-2000, Fri and Sun). *El Tucano Salsateca*, Pedro de Valdivia 1783, p 4, Wed-Sun 2200-0600, fashionable. *Peña Nano Parra*, San Isidro 57, good folk club, cheap.

Theatres: *Teatro Municipal*, Agustinas y San Antonio, stages international opera, concerts by the Orquesta Filarmónica de Santiago, and the Ballet de Santiago, throughout the year; on Tues at 2100 there are free operatic concerts in the Salón Claudio Arrau; tickets range from US$5.60 for a very large choral group with a symphony orchestra, and US$7 for the cheapest seats at the ballet, to US$80 for the most expensive opera seats. Some cheap seats are often sold on the day of concerts. *Teatro Universidad de Chile*, Plaza Baquedano, is the home of the Orquesta y Coro Sinfónica de Chile and the Ballet Nacional de Chile; prices from US$1.25-3.50 for concerts to US$1.25-13.50 for ballet.

Free classical concerts are sometimes given in San Francisco church in summer; arrive early for a seat.

There are a great number of theatres which stage plays in Spanish, either in the original language or translations. *Santiago Stage* is an

English-speaking amateur drama group. Outdoor rock concerts are held at the *Estadio Nacional*, Av Unión Latino Americana (metro of same name), at the Teatro Teletón, Rosas 325 (excellent sound system), and elsewhere. Theatres and events are listed in *El Mercurio* and *La Época*. The most comprehensive listings appear in *El Mercurio's Wikén* magazine on Fri.

● **Hospitals & medical services**
Emergency Pharmacy: Portugal 155, T 382439.

Hospitals: emergency hospital at Marcoleta 377 costs US$60. If you need to get to a hospital, it is better to take a taxi than wait for an ambulance. For yellow fever vaccination and others (but not cholera), *Hospital San Salvador*, J M Infante 551, T 225-6441, Mon-Thur 0800-1300, 1330-1645; Fri 0800-1300, 1330-1545. Also *Vaccinatoria Internacional*, Hospital Luis Calvo, MacKenna, Antonio Varas 360. *Clínica Central*, San Isidro 231, T 222-1953, open 24 hrs, German spoken. *Clínica Alemana*, Vitacura 5951, Las Condes, German and English spoken (bus 344 from centre). Physician: Dr Sergio Maylis, T 232-0853 (1430-1900). Dentist: Antonio Yazigi, Vitacura 3082, Apto 33, T 487962, English spoken, rec. Dr Torres, Av Providencia 2330, Depto 23, excellent, speaks English.

● **Language schools**
Centro de Idiomas Bellavista, Dominica 25, T 777-5933/227-7137, offers Spanish in groups or individually and organizes accommodation. *Escuela de Idiomas Violeta Parra*, Ernesto Pinto Lagarrigue 362A, Recoleta-Barrio Bellavista, T/F 229-8246, courses aimed at budget travellers, information programme on social issues, arranges accommodation and visits to local organizations and national parks. Many private teachers, inc Carolina Carvajal, T 623-8405, highly rec, and Patricia Vargas Vives, Monitor Araucano 0680, Depto 25AC, Providencia, T 777-0595, qualified

and experienced (US$12.50/hr). Lucía Araya Arévalo, Puerto Chico 8062, Villa Los Puertos, Pudahuel, T 236-0531, speaks German and English. Patricio Ríos, Tobalaba 7505, La Reina, T 226-6926, speaks English, rec.

● **Laundry**
Wet-wash places in the centre: at Agustinas 1532, also *Nataly*, another at Bandera 572, at Catedral y Amunátegui and *Lava Fácil*, Huérfanos 1750, Mon-Sat 0900-2000, US$4/load. There are plenty of dry-cleaners, eg Merced 494. Nearby, just S of Metro Universidad Católica there are several, inc *American Washer*, Portugal 71, Torre 7, local 4, US$3, open 0900-2100 inc Sun, can leave washing and collect it later, also at Monjitas 650. Wet wash laundries in Providencia inc *Marva*, Carlos Antúñez 1823 (Metro Pedro de Valdivia), wash and dry US$8; Av Providencia 1039, full load, wet wash, US$5, 3 hrs; *Laverap*, Av Providencia 1600 block; Manuel Montt 67. At the corner of Av Providencia and Dr Luis Middleton there are several self-service dry cleaners (Metro Pedro de Valdivia, 11 de Septiembre exit).

● **Places of worship**
American Presbyterian Church, Iglesia San Marcos, Manquehue Norte 1320, Los Hualtatas, service in English Sun 0915; **Anglican Church**, Holanda 151 (service 1030); **Synagogues**, Tarapacá 870, T 393872, and Las Hortensias 9322, T 233-8868.

● **Post & telecommunications**
Telephones: Compañía de Teléfonos de Chile, Moneda 1151, closed Sun. International phone calls also from: Entel, Huérfanos 1133, Mon-Fri 0830-2200, Sat 0900-2030, Sun 0900-1400, calls cheaper 1400-2200; Fax upstairs. Fax also available at CTC offices, eg Mall Panorámico, 11 de Septiembre, 3rd level (phone booths are on level 1). There are also CTC phone offices at

some metro stations, La Moneda, Escuela Militar, Tobalaba, Universidad de Chile and Pedro de Valdivia for local, long-distance and international calls. There are also phone boxes in the street from which overseas calls can be made. International telex service, Bandera 168. Local calls 50 pesos, only 50 peso coins accepted. **Internet services**: *Café Virtual*, Av B O'Higgins 145, T 638-6846, www.cafe-virtual.cl, cybercafe, good food too; *Interdata* in Apumanque shopping centre rents computer time by the hour; another place above *Geo Pub*.

Post Office: Plaza de Armas (0800-1900), poste restante well organized (though only kept for 30 days), US$0.20, passport essential, list of letters and parcels received in the hall of central Post Office (one list for men, another for women, indicate Sr or Sra/Srta on envelope); also has philatelic section, 0900-1630, and small stamp museum (ask to see it). Another office at Moneda 1155. If sending a parcel, the contents must first be checked at the Post Office; paper, tape etc on sale; open Mon-Fri 0800-1900, Sat 0800-1400.

● **Security**

Like all large cities, Santiago has problems of theft. Pickpockets and bagsnatchers, who are often well-dressed, operate especially on the Metro and around the Plaza de Armas. The Cerro Santa Lucía area is reported to be dangerous even in daytime.

● **Shopping**

El Almacén Campesino, Purísima 303, Bellavista, is a cooperative association in an attractive colonial building, selling handicrafts from all over Chile, inc attractive Mapuche weavings, wood carvings, pottery (best bought in Pomaire, 50 km away, see page 686) and beautiful wrought copper and bronze. Prices are similar to those in similar shops in Temuco. Ask about shipping. The gemstone lapis lazuli can be found in a few expensive shops in Bellavista but is cheaper in the arcades on S side of the Plaza de Armas and in the **Centro Artesanal Santa Lucía** (Santa Lucía metro, S exit) which also has a wide variety of woollen goods, jewellery, etc. *Amitié*, Ricardo León y Av Providencia (Metro Los Leones); *Dauvin Artesanía Fina*, Providencia 2169, Local 69 (Metro Los Leones) have also been rec. *H Stern* jewellery shops are located at the *San Cristóbal Sheraton*, *Hyatt Regency* and *Carrera* hotels, and at the International Airport. *Cema-Chile* (Centro de Madres), Portugal 351 and at Universidad de Chile metro stop, *Manos Chilensis*, Portugal 373, *Artesanías de Chile*, Varas 475, *Artesanía Popular Chilena*, Av Providencia 2322 (nr Los Leones metro), and *Artesanía Chilena*, Estado 337, have a good selection of handicrafts. *Talleres Solidarios*, de la Barra 456, small selection. Antique stores in

Plaza Mulato Gil de Castro and elsewhere on Lastarria (Merced nr).

Beside and behind the Iglesia de los Dominicos, on Av Nueva Apoquindo 9085, is **Los Graneros del Alba**, or *El Pueblo de Artesanos*, open daily except Mon, 1130-1900; all types of ware on sale, classes given in some shops, interesting. *Restaurant El Granero* is here. To get there, take a No 326 or 327 bus from Av Providencia, marked 'Camino del Alba'; get out at the children's playground at the junction of Apoquindo y Camino del Alba, at the foot of the hill leading up to the church, and walk up.

Mercado Central, between Puente y 21 de Mayo by the Río Mapocho (Cal y Canto metro) is excellent but quite expensive; there is a cheaper market, the *Vega Central*, on the opp bank of the river. There are other craft markets in an alleyway, 1 block S of Av B O'Higgins between A Prat and San Diego, on the 600 to 800 blocks of Santo Domingo (inc pieces from neighbouring countries) and at Pío Nono y Santa María, Bellavista. The shopping arcade at the Central Station is good value, likewise the street market outside. Cheap clothes shops in the city, eg on Bandera esp 600 block, are good for winter clothes for travellers who need them (look for sign Ropa Europea). There is a flea market at Franklin y Santa Rosa on Sun am and a good outside fruit market at Puente 815, by *Frutería Martínez*. There is an antique fair on Sun (1000-1400) in the summer and a Fiesta de Quasimodo on the first Sun after Easter at Lo Barnechea, 30 min by bus from Santiago. Parque Arauco is a large modern shopping mall in Las Condes on Av Kennedy, nr Metro Escuela Militar.

Bookshops: book prices tend to be high compared with Europe. *Librería Albers*, Vitacura 5648, Las Condes, T 218-5371, F 218-1458, and 11 de Septiembre 2671, Providencia, T 232-7499 (Spanish, English and German – good selection, cheaper than most, helpful, also German and Swiss newspapers); *Librería Catalonia*, Huérfanos 669; *Feria Chilena del Libro*, Huérfanos nr McIver, and in Drugstore precinct, Providencia 2124; *Librería Inglesa*, Huérfanos 669, local 11, and Pedro de Valdivia 47, Providencia, T 231-9970, good selection of English books, sells *South American Handbook*. *South American Way*, Apoquindo 6856, Las Condes, T 211-8078, sells books in English. There are many bookshops in the Pedro de Valdivia area on Av Providencia. Second-hand English books from *Librería El Patio*, Av Providencia 1652, Metro Pedro de Valdivia; exchange for best deal. Also, from Henry at Metro Los Leones, and *Books*, next to *Phone Box Pub*, Av Providencia 1670 (the artist's shop in same precinct sells attractive cards). *Librairie Française*, books and newspapers, Estado 337. *Gutenberg Lafourcade* *y Cía*, Jardín Lastarria 307, antiquarian book-shop, other good antiquarian bookshops on Merced around the corner from Lastarria, eg *América del Sur Librería Editorial*, No 306, *Libros Antiguos El Cid*, No 344. Many stalls on Paseo Ahumada/Huérfanos sell foreign newspapers and journals.

Camera repairs and film: *Harry Müller*, Ahumada 312, Oficina 402, not cheap but good and fairly quick, rec; speaks German and English. For Minolta and Canon repairs, *TecFo*, Nueva York 52, p 2, T 695-2969, rec. Many developers on Ahumada offer 24-hr service of varying quality (some develop, but do not mount, slides, slow service). *Tecnofoto*, Ahumada 131, p 7, Oficina 719, T 672-5004, efficient. *Prontofoto*, Ahumada 264, T 672-1981 good quality and cheap; *Moretto*, Merced 753, cheap and good. *Black Box*, Gral Flores 229 (Metro Mannel Montt), highly rec. For camera batteries and other spares try *Fotocenter*, Ahumada y Huérfanos.

Camping equipment: standard camping gas cartridges can be bought at *Fabri Gas*, Bandera y Santo Domingo, or *Unisport*, Av Providencia 2503. *Reinaldo Lippi*, Grenado 566 (nr Santa Lucía hill), T 639-1180, F 639-9169, makes tents, sleeping bags, back packs, etc, sells secondhand kit, and does repairs, most helpful. Camping goods from *Club Andino* and *Federación de Andinismo* (see page 680 below): expensive because these articles are imported. *Lomas*, Santa Rosa y 10 de Julio, good selection of sleeping bags, helpful. Good sleeping bags from *Fuc*, Rengo 1670 (off M Montt), T 225-8862. For packs also try Sr Espinosa, San Martín 835. Repair of camping stoves at *Casa Italiana*, Tarapacá 1120. For second hand equipment try Luz Emperatriz Sanhuela Quiroz, Portal de León, Loc 14, Providencia 2198 (Metro Los Leones).

● **Sports**

Bicycles: for parts and repairs *Importadora Caupolicán*, San Diego 863, T 697-2765, F 696-1937, wide range, helpful. Ask for Nelson Díaz 'a walking encyclopaedia' on bikes.

Chess: *Chess Club*, Alameda O'Higgins 898, Mon-Sat 1800, lively.

Football: main teams inc Colo Colo who play at the Estadio Monumental (reached by any bus to Puente Alto; tickets from Cienfuegos 41), Universidad de Chile (Estadio Nacional, Grecia 2001, T 239-2212) and Universidad Católica who play at San Carlos de Apoquindo, reached by bus from Metro Escuela Militar.

Other sports: **Running**: the Hash House Harriers hold runs every other week; information through the British Embassy and Consulate. **Tennis**: Club de Tenís Jaime Fillol, Rancho Melnichi, Par 4. **Bowling**: Bowling Center, Apo-

quindo 5012. **Gymnasium**: Gimnasio Alicia Franché, Moneda 1481, T 696-1681, aerobics and fitness classes (women only); another at Huérfanos 1313, T 671-1562. **Tai Chi** and other martial arts: Raul Tou-Tin, Irarrázaval 1971, T 204-8082. **Cricket**: Sat in summer at Club Príncipe de Gales, Las Arañas 1901 (bus from Tobalaba metro).

Racecourses: Club Hípico, every Sun and every other Wed afternoon (at Viña del Mar, Jan-Mar); Hipódromo Chile every Sat.

Skiing and climbing: Club Andino de Chile, Enrique Foster 29, ski club (open 1900-2100 on Mon and Fri). **Federación de Andinismo de Chile**, Almte Simpson 77A (T 222-0888, F 222-6285), open daily (frequently closed Jan/Feb); has a small museum; library (weekdays except Wed 1930-2100); shop selling guides and equipment. **Escuela Nacional de Montaña** (ENAM), at same address, T 222-0799, holds seminars and courses. It has the addresses of all the mountaineering clubs in the country. It has a mountaineering school. **Club Alemán Andino**, El Arrayán 2735, T 242-5453, open Tues and Fri, 1800-2000, May-June. Also try **Skitotal**, Apoquindo 4900, Oficina 32,33,43, T 246-0156, for 1-day excursions. Equipment hire is much cheaper in Santiago than in ski resorts. Sunglasses are essential. For ski resorts in the Santiago area see below page 686.

Skiing and climbing equipment: *Mountain Service*, Portal de León, Metro Los Leones, English spoken, tents, stoves, clothing, equipment rental, rec; at same address, Sra Lucy, also rec; *Panda Deportes*, Paseo Las Palmas 2217 (Metro Los Leones), T 232-1840.

Swimming Pools: Tupahue (large pool with cafés, entry US$9 but worth it) and Antilen, both on Cerro San Cristóbal, open daily in summer except Mon 1000-1500 (check if they are open in winter, one usually is). In Parque O'Higgins, 1330-1830 summer only, US$3. Olympic pool in Parque Araucano (nr Parque Arauco Shopping Centre, Metro Escuela Militar), open Tues-Sat 0900-1900 Nov-March.

● **Tour companies & travel agents**

Wagons-Lits Cook, Carmencita, Providencia, T 233-0820, rec; *Turismo Cocha* (American Express representatives with mail service), El Bosque Norte 0430, PO Box 191035, Providencia, Metro Tobalaba, T 230-1000. *Passtours*, Huérfanos 886, Oficina 1110, T 639-3232, F 633-1498, many languages spoken, helpful, rec; *Viamonte* 1160, Local 19, T/F 696-7829, for all services, German, English, French, Italian and Portuguese spoken, helpful, repeatedly rec; *Selectours*, Agencia de Viajes, Las Urbinas 95, Providencia, T 252-0201/334-2637, F 234-2838; *All Travels*, Huérfanos

1160, local 10, T 696-4348, good for flight tickets; *Asatej Student Flight Centre*, Av Providencia 2594, Oficina 426, T 232-5388, 334-5166/7, F 233-3220, for cheap flights and youth travel; *Patagonia Connection SA*, Fidel Oteíza 1921, Oficina 1006, Providencia (Metro Pedro de Valdivia), T 225-6489, F 274-8111, for cruises to Patagonia; *Eurotur*, Huérfanos 1160, local 13, for cheap air tickets to Europe; *Blanco*, Pedro de Valdivia near Av Providencia, good for flight information and exchange; *Rapa-Nui*, Huérfanos 1160, specializes in trips to Easter Island; *Turismo Grace*, Victoria Subercaseaux 381, T 693-3740, good service. For local tours: *Ace Turismo*, O'Higgins 949, T 696-0391, city tour, US$12 for 1/2 day. *Maysa*, Paseo Ahumada 6, Of 43, T/F 696-4468, good tours of bodegas and Valparaíso, US$35.

For adventure tours and trekking: *Sportstours*, Teatinos 330, p 10, T 696-8832/698-3058, German-run, helpful, 5 day trips to Antarctica (offices also at Hotels *Carrera* and *San Cristóbal*); *Altue Expediciones*, Encomenderos 83 P 2, Las Condes, T 232-1103/233-2964, F 233 6799, for wilderness trips inc tour of Patagonia, rec (above *Geo Pub*). Climbing and adventure tours in the Lake District and elsewhere, *Antu Aventuras*, Casilla 24, Santiago, T 271-2767, Tx 440019, RECAL CZ. *Andescape*, Santa Beatriz 84A, Providencia, T/F 235-5225, useful for information on Torres del Paine. *Azimut 360*, Monte Carmelo 360, Dept 36, T 777-2375, highly rec, low prices; *Mountain Service*, Ebro 2805, Las Condes, T 242-9723, F 234-3438, rec for climbing trips; *Racies*, Plaza Corregidor Zañartu 761, cultural tours, inc Robinson Crusoe Island and Antarctica, T/F 638-2904. *Turismo Grant*, Huérfanos 863, Oficina 516, T 639-5524, helpful, English spoken; *Patagonia Chile*, Constitución 172, Bellavista, T 351871, offer mountain trips, river rafting, trekking. *Turismo Cabo de Hornos*, Agustinas 814, Of 706, T 6338481, F 6338480, for DAP flights and Tierra del Fuego/Antarctica tours. *Andina del Sud*, Bombero Ossa 1010, p 3, Of 301, T 697-1010, F 696-5121, for tours in the Lake District. Ask at *Hotel Maury*, address above, for tours with Fernández (Tony), who speaks English, inc riding, rafting and barbecue, US$50 pp, rec. For skiing in the Santiago area see below page 686.

Turismo Joven, Suecia Norte 0125, T 232-9946, F 334-3008, E-mail turjoven@mailent. rdc.cl, youth travel services for young people and students for travel, studies, leisure with links in Latin America and worldwide.

● **Tourist offices**

Servicio Nacional de Turismo (Sernatur – the national tourist board), Av Providencia 1550 (Casilla 14082), T 236-1416, Tx SERNA CL 240137, between metros Manuel Montt and Pedro de Valdivia, next to Providencia Municipal Library, open Mon-Fri 0900-1900, Sat 0900-1300. English and German spoken and maps (road map US$1.50), brochures and posters are available. Good notice board. Ask for the free booklet, *Paseos en Santiago* (City Walks in Santiago), which is very useful for those with time to explore on foot. Kiosk on Ahumada nr Agustinas (erratic opening times). Information office also at the airport, open 0900-2100 daily. **Municipal Tourist Board**, Casa Colorada, Merced 860, T 336700/330723, offers walking tours of the city, Wed 1500, or from kiosk on Paseo Ahumada. **NB** Many tourist offices outside Santiago are closed in winter, so stock up on information here.

Excellent road maps (US$1.75) and information may be obtained from the **Automóvil Club de Chile**, Vitacura 8620, T 212-5702/3/4, F 229-5295 (Metro P de Valdivia then bus to Vitacura, or a US$6 taxi ride from the centre), which also gives discounts to members of affiliated motoring organizations; open Mon-Fri 0845-1815, Sat 0900-1300, very helpful. Geophysical and topographical maps (US$11) are available from **Instituto Geográfico Militar**, Dieciocho 369, T 698-7278, 0900-1800 Mon-Fri (0900-1400 in Feb, may be closed Jan). The **Guía Caminera** (1991) gives roads and city plans, US$8.75 (not wholly accurate). The collection of maps at the Biblioteca Nacional may be photocopied; very useful for climbing.

Conaf (Corporación Nacional Forestal), Presidente Bulnes 259, oficina 206 (main office at No 285), T 696-0783/699-2833, publishes a number of booklets and has documents and maps about the national park system that can be consulted or photocopied (not very useful for walking). **CODEFF** (Comité Nacional Pro-Defensa de la Fauna y Flora), Sazie 1885, T 696-1268, can also provide information on environmental questions.

● **Useful addresses**

Immigration: Ministerio del Interior, *Extranjería* section, Moneda 1342, T 672-5320, Mon-Fri 0900-1330.

Policia Internacional: for lost tourist cards, etc, Santo Domingo y MacIver.

● **Transport**

Local Buses and taxis: destinations and fares of all buses are marked clearly on the front. There are three kinds of buses: the small fast kind called *liebres* (hares) which cost US$0.50 a ride; the regular buses at US$0.30, and the large buses marked Expreso, at US$0.40. Taxis (black with yellow roofs) are abundant, and not expensive, with a minimum charge of US$0.40, plus US$0.12/200m. Taxi drivers are permitted to charge more at night, but in the day time check that the meter is set to day rates. At bus terminals,

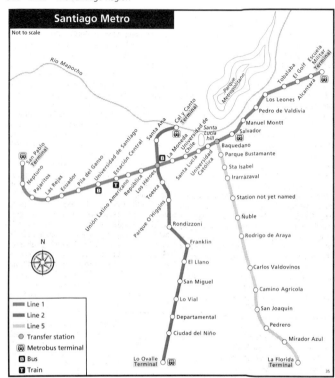

Santiago Metro

Not to scale

Río Mapocho

San Pablo Terminal
Neptuno
Pajaritos
Las Rejas
Ecuador
Unión Latino Americano
Universidad de Santiago
Estación Central
República
Los Héroes
Toesca
Santa Ana
Cal y Canto Terminal
La Moneda
Universidad de Chile
Santa Lucía hill
Santa Lucía
Universidad Católica
Baquedano
Salvador
Manuel Montt
Pedro de Valdivia
Los Leones
Tobalaba
El Golf
Alcántara
Escuela Militar Terminal
Parque Metropolitano

Parque Bustamante
Sta Isabel
Irarrázaval
Station not yet named
Ñuble
Rodrigo de Araya
Carlos Valdovinos
Camino Agrícola
San Joaquín
Pedrero
Mirador Azul
La Florida Terminal

Parque O'Higgins
Rondizzoni
Franklin
El Llano
San Miguel
Lo Vial
Departamental
Ciudad del Niño
Lo Ovalle Terminal

N

Legend:
▓▓▓ Line 1
▓▓▓ Line 2
▓▓▓ Line 5
◯ Transfer station
🚌 Metrobus terminal
Ⓑ Bus
Ⓣ Train

35

drivers will charge more – best to walk a block and flag down a cruising taxi. Large blue taxis do not have meters. Avoid taxis with more than one person in them especially at night. There are also colective taxis (*colectivos*) on fixed routes to the suburbs, US$0.70. For journeys outside the city arrange the charge beforehand. The private taxi service which operates from the bottom level of *Hotel Carrera* has been rec (same rates as city taxis), as has Radio Taxis Andes Pacífico, T 225-3064/2888; similarly Rigoberto Contreras, T 638-1042, ext 4215, available at *Holiday Inn Crowne Plaza*, but rates above those of city taxis.

Car hire: prices vary a lot so shop around first. Hertz, Avis and Budget available from airport. **Hertz**, Andrés Bello 1469, T 225-9328, and airport, T 601-9262, has a good network in Chile and cars are in good condition. **Avis**, La Concepción 334, T 495-757, poor service reported. **Seelmann**, Antonio Varas 1472, of 156, T 225-2138, F 285-3222. **Automóvil Club de**

Chile car rental, Marchant Pereira 122, Providencia, T 274-4167/6261, discount for members and members of associated motoring organizations. A credit card is usually asked for when renting a vehicle. Tax of 18% is charged but usually not included in price quoted. If possible book a car in advance. Remember that in the capital driving is restricted according to licence plate numbers; look for notices in the street and newspapers.

Metro: the first line of the underground railway system runs W-E between San Pablo and Escuela Militar, under the Alameda, and the second line runs N-S from Cal y Canto to Callejón Ovalle. The connecting station is Los Héroes. Line 5, from Baquedano S to La Florida opened in April 1997. The trains are fast, quiet, and very full. The first train is at 0630 (Mon-Sat), 0800 (Sun and holidays), the last about 2245. Fares vary according to time of journey; there are 3 charging periods: high 0715-0900, 1800-1900, US$0.45; medium 0900-1800, 1930-2100 and weekends, US$0.40; low 0630-0715, 2100-2230, US$0.25. The simplest solution is to buy a *boleto valor*, US$5; a charge card from which the appropriate fare is deducted. Metrobus services connect with the metro at Lo Ovalle for southern Santiago and at Escuela Militar for Vitacura, Las Condes and Apoquindo.

Motorcycles: small BMW workshop, Av San Camilo 185, Sr Marco Canales. BMW car dealer *Frederic*, Av Portugal, has some spares. Also tyre shops in this area. BMW riders can also seek help from the *carabineros* who ride BMW machines and have a workshop with good mechanics at Av Rivera 2003.

Air International and domestic flights leave from Arturo Merino Benítez Airport at Pudahuel, 26 km NW of Santiago. There are two terminals: domestic and international. Airport information T 601-9709. On arrival get entry card from desk at entrance to arrivals hall before proceeding to immigration, otherwise you will be set back. The international terminal is more modern and has most facilities, inc bank and Afex *cambio* (better rates, but not as good as in town), Sernatur office which will book accommodation and a fast-food plaza. The domestic terminal has a few shops, but they are very expensive, as are the bar and restaurant. Buy your wine etc in town. Left luggage US$2.50/bag/day.

Airport taxi, about US$15 but bargain hard and agree fare beforehand: more expensive with meter. Taxi to airport is much cheaper if flagged down in the street rather than booked by phone. Frequent bus services to/from city centre by 2 companies: *Tour Express* (Moneda 1529, T 671-7380) US$2.50, first bus from centre 0530, last from airport 0030; and *Centropuerto* (T 601-9883/695-8058), US$1.50, first from centre 0600, last from airport 2330. Buses leave from outside airport terminal and, in Santiago, from Moneda y San Martín calling at Plazoleta Los Héroes (near the yellow 'Línea 2' sign), Estación Central and the Terminal Santiago. (Beware the bus marked *Aeropuerto* which stops 2 km short of the Airport). *Empresa Turismo Bar-C* from your house or hotel to airport (or vice-versa), any time day or night, T 246-3600/1 for reservation (cheaper than taxi). *Empresa Navett*, Av Ejército Libertador 21 (nearest metro Los Héroes), T 695-6868 has a round-the-clock service, US$7. For schedules of domestic flights from Santiago, see under destinations.

Accommodation nearby at **B** pp *Hacienda del Sol y La Luna*, 4 Hijuela 9978, Pudahuel, T/F 601-9254, English, German, French spoken, rec.

Trains All trains leave from Estación Central at Alameda O'Higgins 3322. The line runs S to Rancagua, San Fernando, Curicó, Talca, Linares, Parral and Chillán, thereafter services go to 1) **Concepción**, 2) **Puerto Varas** (for Puerto Montt) via **Temuco**, with a bus connection to **Valdivia**. Schedules change with the seasons, so you must check timetables before planning a journey. See under destinations for fares and notes on schedules. *Expreso* services do not have sleepers; some *rápidos* do (in summer *rápidos* are booked up a week in advance). *Dormitorio* carriages were built in Germany in 1930's, bunks (comfortable) lie parallel to rails, US-Pullman-style (washrooms at each end, one with shower-bath – often cold water only); an attendant for each car; bar car shows 3 films – no cost but you must purchase a drink ticket in advance. There is also a newer, *Gran Dormitorio* sleeping car (1984), with private toilet and shower, US$10 extra for 2, rec. For the *expresos* there are no reservations (get your ticket the morning of the day the train leaves and sit on the train as soon as you can get on; otherwise you'll stand for the whole journey). Free hot water supplied, so take own mug and coffee. Also a car-transporter service to Chillán, Temuco and Puerto Montt. Trains are still fairly cheap and generally very punctual, although 1st class is generally more expensive than bus; meals are good though expensive. Check for family, senior citizen and student discounts. Trains can be cold and draughty in winter and spring. There are also frequent local *Metrotren* services to Rancagua. Booking offices: for State Railways, Alameda O'Higgins 853 in Galería Hotel Libertador, Local 21, T 632-2801, Mon-Fri 0830-1900, Sat 0900-1300; or Metro Escuela Militar, Galería Sur, Local 25, T 228-2983, Mon-Fri 0830-1900, Sat 0900-1300; central station, open till 2230, T 689-5718/689-1682. For Calama-Uyuni, contact Tramaca, Ahumada 11, Of 602, T 698-5536. Left luggage office at Estación Central.

A steam train runs tourist services between Santiago and Los Andes, 5-hrs' journey, T 698-5536 for details.

Buses There are frequent and, good, interurban buses to all parts of Chile. (**NB** Many leave early because of tight competition: arrive at bus station early.) Check if student rates are available (even for non-students), or reductions for travelling same day as purchase of ticket; it is worth bargaining over prices, especially shortly before departure and out of the summer season. Also take a look at the buses before buying the tickets (there are big differences in quality among bus companies); ask about the on-board services, many companies offer drinks for sale, or free, and luxury buses have meals and wine, colour videos, headphones. Reclining seats are common and there are also *salón cama* sleeper buses. A new Backpackers Bus takes in all parts of Chile. Based in Talca, T 094 525680, F 071 224611. Fares from/to the capital are given in the text. On Fri evening, when night departures are getting ready to go, the terminals are murder.

There are four bus terminals: 1) Terminal de Buses Alameda, which has a modern extension called Mall Parque Estación, O'Higgins 3712, metro Universidad de Santiago; all Pullman-Bus and Tur-Bus services go from here. 2) Terminal de Buses Santiago, O'Higgins 3878, one block W of Terminal Alameda, T 791-385, metro Universidad de Santiago; services to southern destinations; poorly organized. 3) Terminal San Borja, O'Higgins y San Borja, 1 block W of Estación Central, 3 blocks E of Terminal Alameda, metro Estación Central (entrance is, inconveniently, via a busy shopping centre); separate sections for buses to Region 5, inc Valparaíso and Viña del Mar and services to northern destinations; booking offices and departures organized according to destination. Left luggage US$1.50 per piece/day. 4) Terminal Los Héroes on Jiménez, just N of the Alameda, metro Los Héroes, has booking offices of about 10 companies for N and S routes as well as some international services. Varmontt buses, who run an expensive service to Puerto Montt, have their own terminal at Av 21 de Septiembre 2212 (office on 2nd floor), metro Los Leones.

See the note under **Taxis** about not taking expensive taxis parked outside bus terminals. Also, do not change money at the bus terminals; if coming from Argentina, try to get some Chilean pesos before you arrive.

International buses Most services leave from Terminal Santiago, though there are also departures from Terminal Los Héroes.

Short distance: there are frequent services through the Cristo Redentor tunnel to **Mendoza** in Argentina, 6-7 hrs, US$20-25, many companies, departures around 0800, 1200 and 1600. Touts approach you in Terminal Santiago. There are also collective taxis from the same terminal and from the 800/900 blocks of Morandé (Chi-Ar taxi company, Morandé 890, rec; Chile-Bus, Morandé 838; Cordillera Nevada, Morandé 870, T 698-4716), US$27, 5 hrs, shorter waiting time at customs.

Long distance: to Buenos Aires, US$70-75, 22 hrs (TAC and Ahumada rec); to **Montevideo**, most involving a change in Mendoza, eg El Rápido, or Tas Choapa, 27 hrs, inc meals, US$90; to **Córdoba** direct, US$32, 18 hrs, several companies inc Turbus, Tas Choapa and TAC (El Rapido not rec); to **San Juan**, TAC, Tas Choapa, US$20; to **Bogotá** US$200, 7 days; to **Caracas** (Tues and Fri 0900) US$230; to **Lima**, Ormeño, 51 hrs, US$70, it is cheaper to take a bus to Arica, a colectivo to Tacna (US$4), thence bus to Lima. Services also to **São Paulo** and **Rio de Janeiro** (eg Chilebus, Tues, Thur, Sat, US$100, 52 hrs); **Asunción** (4 a week, 28 hrs, US$75); **Guayaquil** and **Quito**. Tramaca, runs a *combinación* service which links with the train from Calama to **Uyuni** in Bolivia. Géminis goes on Tues to **Salta**, Argentina, changing in Calama.

Hitchhiking To Valparaíso, take Metro to Pajaritos and walk 5 mins to W – no difficulty. Or, take bus 'Renca Panamericana' from MacIver y Monjitas. To hitch S, take Metro to Estación Central, then Buses del Paine to C Borja as far as possible on the highway to the toll area, about US$1, 75 mins. To hitch N take blue Metrobus marked 'Til-Til', frequent departures from near the Mercado Central as far as the toll bridge (*peaje*), 40 mins, US$60, then hitch from just beyond the toll-bridge. To Buenos Aires (and Brazil) take a bus to Los Andes, see page 688.

Shipping Navimag, Av El Bosque Norte 0440, T 203-5030, F 203-5025, for services from Puerto Montt to Puerto Natales and viceversa. **Transmarchilay**, Agustinas 715, Oficina 403, T/F 633-5959, for services between Chiloé and the mainland, ferry routes on the Carretera Austral and on Lago General Carrera. M/n *Skorpios*: Augusto Leguía Norte 118, Las Condes,

T 231-1030, F 232-2269 for luxury cruise out of Puerto Montt to Laguna San Rafael. Transmarchilay also sail to the Laguna San Rafael in summer. Check shipping schedules with shipping lines rather than Sernatur. **Patagonia Connection SA**, Fidel Oteíza 1921, Oficina 1006, Providencia (Metro Pedro de Valdivia), T 225-6489, F 274-8111, for services Puerto Montt-Coyhaique/Puerto Chacabuco-Laguna San Rafael.

DAY-TRIPS AND ACTIVITIES OUTSIDE SANTIAGO

45 km NE of Santiago, the **Santuario de la Naturaleza Yerba Loco** covers 39,000 ha, ranging from 900 and 5,500m. Park administration is at Villa Paulina, 4 km N of Route G21, reached by a dirt road. From here a 4 hour walk leads N to Casa de Piedra Carvajal, which offers fine views. Further N are two hanging glaciers, La Paloma and El Altar. Open Sept to April (small entrance fee).

Termas de Colina, 43 km N, an attractive, popular spa (915m): take a bus from Cal y Canto metro station to the town of Colina (hourly in summer only, 40 mins), then another to the military base 1½ km from town. From here a rough road leads through beautiful countryside 6 km to **L3** *Hotel Termas de Colina*, T 844-1408, modern, thermal baths, beautiful swimming pool (closed Fri), formal restaurant; facilities open to public: swimming pool US$6 (crowded at weekends), thermal baths US$10; last return bus at 1900. On the walk to the hotel do not take photos or even show your camera when passing the military base. Taxi from Colina to the hotel, US$6.

CAJON DEL MAIPO

Southeast of Santiago, in the Upper Maipo valley (Cajón del Maipo) are a number of resorts including: **San José de Maipo**, some 50 km from the capital, particularly beautiful in spring. The mountain town of **Melocotón** is 6 km further S, and **San Alfonso**, 4 km on. The walk from San Alfonso to the *Cascada de las Animas* is pleasant; ask permission to cross the bridge at the campsite (see below) as private land is crossed.

● **Accommodation San José: E** *Alojamento Inesita*, Comercio 301, good. **San Alfonso: B** *Posada Los Ciervos*, with breakfast and bath, **A** full board, good; **C** *Res España*, clean, comfortable, restaurant, also others; campsite at the *Comunidad Cascada de las Animas*, T 251-7506, also rents cabins (**C** for 4, hot water, cooking equipment etc) sauna, horseriding.

● **Transport** Buses leave Santiago from Metro Parque O'Higgins, Av Norte-Sur, or W side of Plaza Ercilla, every 30 mins to San José, US$2, 2 hrs.

31 km further SE is **El Volcán** (1,400m); there are astounding views, but little else (the village was wiped away in a landslide). **NB** If visiting this area or continuing further up the mountain, be prepared for military checks: passport and car registration numbers may be taken. From El Volcán the road (very poor condition) runs E to the warm natural baths at **Baños Morales**, open from Oct, entry to baths, US$1. 12 km further E up the mountain are **Baños Colina**, not to be confused with Termas de Colina, see above; hot thermal springs, entry US$5, horses for hire. This area is popular at weekends and holiday times, but is otherwise deserted.

● **Accommodation & places to eat** At **Baños Morales: D** *Pensión Díaz*, friendly, good food, excellent café in the village, serving homemade jam, it closes at Easter for the winter; **C** pp *Refugio Baños Morales*, full board, hot water; **D** pp *Res Los Chicos Malos*, comfortable, fresh bread, good meals; free campsite. 14 km E of El Volcán, just after Baños Morales, **B** pp *Refugio Alemán Lo Valdés*, stone-built chalet accommodation, full board, own generator, good food, rec, a good place to stay for mountain excursions, open all year. A splendid region which deserves the journey required to get there. At **Baños Colina: D** pp *Res El Tambo*, full board; restaurant, also camping. No shops so take food (try local goats cheese).

● **Transport** Buses from Metro Parque O'Higgins, to El Volcán 3 daily (US$2) and to Baños Morales daily in Jan/Feb, weekends only in March and Oct-Dec, at 0700, US$4, 3 hrs, returns at 1800; buy return on arrival to ensure seat back; alternatively, hitch back to Santiago on quarry lorries.

North of Baños Morales, **Parque Nacional El Morado** is reached by a turning off the main road from Puente Alto. It covers an area of 3,000 ha of the valley of the Río Morales, including the peaks of

El Morado (5,060m) and El Mirador del Morado (4,320m), and El Morado glacier. Administration is in Baños Morales. Park open Oct-April. Entry US$2.50.

POMAIRE

A little town 65 km W of Santiago, where pottery can be brought and the artists can be observed at work. The area is rich in clay and the town is famous for its cider in the apple season and Chilean dishes; highly rec: *Restaurant San Antonio*, welcoming.

● **Transport** From Santiago take the Melipilla bus from C San Borja behind Estación Central metro station, every few minutes, US$1 each way, Rutabus 78 goes on the motorway, 1 hr, other buses via Talagante take 1 hr 25 mins (alight at side road to Pomaire, 2-3 km from town, colectivos every 10-15 mins – these buses are easier to take than the infrequent, direct buses).

VISITS TO VINEYARDS

The Maipo Valley is considered by many experts to be the best-wine producing area of Chile. Several vineyards in the Santiago area can be visited. *Cousiño-Macul*, Av Quilin on E outskirts of the city, offers tours Mon-Fri, phone first T 238-2855. *Concha y Toro* at Pirque, near Puente Alto, 40 km S of Santiago, T 850-3168, short tour (Spanish, English, French, German, Portuguese), Mon-Sat and Sun pm, free entry. Take 'La Puntilla' bus from Metro O'Higgins, 1 hr, US$1, asking to be dropped at Concha, or colectivo from Plaza Italia, US$2.50. The *Undurraga* vineyard at Santa Ana, SW of Santiago, T 817-2346, also permits visits with prior reservation only, 0930-1200, 1400-1600 on weekdays (tours given by the owner-manager, Pedro Undurraga). Take a Melipilla bus (but not Rutabus 78) to the entrance. *Viña Santa Carolina*, Rodrigo de Araya 1341, in Nuñoa, offers tours at weekends.

SKIING

There are six main ski resorts near Santiago, four of them around the mountain village of Farellones, 51 km E of the capital. All have modern lift systems, international ski schools, rental shops, lodges, mountain restaurants and first aid facilities. The season runs from June to Sept/Oct, weather per-mitting, although some resorts have equipment for making artificial snow. Altitude sickness can be a problem, especially at Valle Nevado and Portillo: avoid overexertion on the first day or two.

Farellones, situated on the slopes of Cerro Colorado at 2,470m and reached by road in under 90 mins, was the first ski resort built in Chile. Now it is more of a service centre for the three other resorts, but it provides affordable accommodation, has a good beginners area and is connected by lift to El Colorado. Popular at weekends, it has several large restaurants. It offers beautiful views for 30 km across 10 Andean peaks and incredible sunsets. Daily ski-lift ticket, US$30; a combined ticket for all four resorts is also available, US$40-50 depending on season. 1-day excursions are available from Santiago, US$5; enquire Ski Club Chile, Goyenechea Candelaria 4750, Vitacura (N of Los Leones Golf Club), T 211-7341.

● **Accommodation** *Motel Tupungato* (Candelaria Goyenechea 4750, Santiago, T 218-2216), **A3** pp *Refugio Club Alemán Andino* (address under **Skiing and Climbing**, above), hospitable, good food; *Colorado Apart Hotel* (Av Apoquindo 4900, Oficina 43, Santiago, T 246-0660, F 246-1447); *Posada Farellones*, highly rec.

● **Transport** Buses from Santiago leave from front of Omnium building, Av Apoquindo, 4 blocks from Escuela Militar Metro, daily at 0830, essential to book in advance, US$7. It is easy to hitch from the junction of Av Las Condes/El Camino Farellones (petrol station in the middle): take a Las Condes bus from C Merced almost to the end of the line.

El Colorado, 8 km further up Cerro Colorado, has a large but expensive ski lodge at the base, offering all facilities, and a mountain restaurant higher up. There are 9 lifts giving access to a large intermediate ski area with some steeper slopes. A good centre for learning to ski. Lift ticket US$37.

● **Accommodation** *Edificio Los Ciervos* and *Edificio Monteblanco*, in Santiago, San Antonio 486, Oficina 151.

La Parva, 6 km further E at 2,816m, is the upper class Santiago weekend resort with 12 lifts, 0900-1730. Accommodation is in a chalet village and there are some good bars in high season. Good intermediate to advanced skiing, not suitable for beginners. Lift ticket, US$40; equipment rental, US$10-15 depending on quality.

In summer, this is a good walking area.

● **Accommodation** *Condominio Nueva Parva*, good hotel and restaurant, reservations in Santiago: Roger de Flor 2911, T 220-8510/206-5068. Three other restaurants.

Valle Nevado, 16 km from Farellones, owned by Spie Batignolles of France. It offers the most modern ski facilities in Chile. There are 25 runs accessed by 8 lifts. The runs are well prepared and are suitable for intermediate level skiers and beginners. There is a good ski school and excellent hell skiing is offered. Lift ticket US$30 weekdays, US$42 weekends.

● **Accommodation** **L1** *Hotel Valle Nevado*, and more; *Hotel Puerta del Sol; Condominium Mirador del Inca*; 6 restaurants. *Casa Valle Nevado*, Gertrudis Echeñique 441, T 206-0027, F 228-8888.

Portillo, 2,855m, is 145 km N of Santiago and 62 E of Los Andes near the customs post on the route the Argentina. One of Chile's best-known resorts, Portillo is near the Laguna del Inca, 5½ km long and 1½ km wide; this lake, at an altitude of 2,835m, has no outlet, is frozen over in winter, and its depth is not known. It is surrounded on three sides by accessible mountain slopes. The runs are varied and well prepared, connected by 12 lifts, two of which open up the off-piste areas. This is an excellent family resort, with highly regarded ski school. Cheap packages can be arranged at the beginning and out of season. Lift ticket US$35, equipment hire US$22.

There are boats for fishing in the lake; but beware the afternoon winds, which often make the homeward pull 3 or 4 times as long as the outward pull. Out of season this is another good area for walking, but get detailed maps before setting out.

● **Accommodation** **L2** *Hotel Portillo*, cinema, night club, swimming pool, sauna and medical service, on the shore of Laguna del Inca; accommodation ranges from lakefront suites, full board, fabulous views, to family apartments, to bunk rooms without or with bath (much cheaper, from C up), parking charges even if you go for a meal, jacket and tie obligatory in the dining room, self-service lunch, open all year. Reservations, Roger de Flor 2911, T 231-3411, F 699-2575, Tx 440372

PORTICZ, Santiago; **L3** *Hostería Alborada*, inc all meals, tax and service. During Ski Week (last in Sept), about double normal rate, all inclusive. Reservations, Agencia Tour Avión, Agustinas 1062, Santiago, T 72-6184, or C Navarro 264, San Felipe, T 101-R. Cheaper accommodation can be found in Los Andes but the road is liable to closure due to snow.

● **Places to eat** Cheaper than the hotels are *Restaurant La Posada* opp *Hotel Portillo*, open evenings and weekends only; and *Restaurant Los Libertadores* at the customs station 1 km away.

● **Transport** Except in bad weather, Portillo is easily reached by taking any bus from Santiago or Los Andes to Mendoza; you may have to hitch back.

Lagunillas, 67 km SE of Santiago in the Cajón del Maipo, 17 km E of San José de Maipo (see above for details of transport to San José de Maipo). Accommodation in the lodges of the Club Andino de Chile (bookings may be made at Ahumada 47, Santiago). Tow fee US$20; lift ticket US$25; long T-bar and poma lifts; easy field. Being lower than the other resorts, its season is shorter, but it is also cheaper.

FROM SANTIAGO TO ARGENTINA

The route across the Andes via the Redentor tunnel is one of the major crossings to Argentina. Before travelling check on weather and road conditions beyond Los Andes. See under Santiago, **International Buses**. Route 57 runs N from Santiago through the rich Aconcagua Valley, known as the Vale of Chile. North of Llaillay, at Km 69, the road forks, the W branch going to San Felipe, the E to Los Andes.

San Felipe (*Pop* 42,000; *Alt* 635m; *Phone code* 034), the capital of Aconcagua Province, is 96 km N of Santiago and 128 km NE of Valparaíso. It is an agricultural and mining centre with an agreeable climate. Part of the Inca highway has been discovered in the city.

● **Accommodation** **C** *Hostería San Felipe*, Merced 204, T 510508.

Termas de Jahuel, high in the Cordillera (1,190m), is 18 km by road from San Felipe. The mountain scenery includes a distant view of Aconcagua (**L2** *Termas de Jahuel*, T 511-240 or Santiago 393-810, thermal pool, tennis courts).

LOS ANDES

(*Pop* 30,500; *Alt* 730m; *Phone code* 034), 16 km SE of San Felipe and 77 km N of Santiago, is situated in a wealthy agricultural, fruit-farming and wine-producing area, but is also the site of a large car assembly plant. There are monuments to José de San Martín and Bernardo O'Higgins in the Plaza de Armas, and a monument to the Clark brothers, who built the Transandine Railway to Mendoza (now disused). Good views from El Cerro de la Virgen, reached by a trail from the municipal picnic ground on Independencia (1 hr).

Museums Museo Arqueológico de los Andes, O'Higgins y Santa Teresa, recommended, 1030-1300, 1500-1830, entry US$1. Opposite is the museum of the former Carmelite Convent of Santa Teresa.

● **Accommodation A1** *Baños El Corazón*, at San Esteban, T 421371, with full board, use of swimming pool but thermal baths extra, take bus San Esteban/El Cariño (US$0.50); **B** *Plaza*, Esmeralda 367, T 421929, good but restaurant expensive; **B** *Central*, Esmeralda 278, T 421275, reasonable; **E** *Alameda*, Argentina 576, T 422403, without bath; **F** pp *Res Maruja*, Rancagua 132; **F** pp *Estación*, Rodríguez 389, T 421026, cheap restaurant; **F** *Valparaíso*, Sarmiento 160.

● **Banks & money changers** Cambio Inter at *Plaza Hotel*, good rates, changes TCs.

● **Post & telecommunications Telephones**: CTC, O'Higgins 405.

● **Tourist offices** On main plaza, opp post office. Automóvil **Club de Chile**, Chacabuco 33, T 422790.

● **Transport Trains** Rail service to Viña del Mar and Valparaíso (see under **Valparaíso**). **Buses** To Santiago US$2.50. To Mendoza (Argentina) Tas Choapa, Fenix Pullman Norte, Cata and Ahumada. **Hitchhiking** Over the Andes possible on trucks from Aduana building in Los Andes.

The road to Argentina follows the Aconcagua valley for 34 km until it reaches the village of **Río Blanco** (1,370m), where the Ríos Blanco and Juncal meet to form the Río Aconcagua. East of Río Blanco the road climbs until Juncal where it zig-zags steeply through a series of 29 hairpin bends at the top of which is Portillo (see **Skiing** above).

● **Accommodation** *Hostería Luna*, 4 km W of Río Blanco, good value, helpful, good food;

Hostería Guardia Vieja, 8 km E of Río Blanco, expensive but untidy, campsite.

● **Transport To Río Blanco**: buses run daily from Los Andes; from Santiago, Ahumada, at 1930 daily, direct, 2 hrs, US$2.

FRONTIER WITH ARGENTINA: LOS LIBERTADORES

The Redentor tunnel, 4 km long, is open from 0800-1800 Chilean time, toll US$3. The old pass, with the statue of Christ the Redeemer (**Cristo Redentor**), is 8 km beyond the tunnel on the Argentine side. On the far side of the Andes the road descends 203 km to Mendoza.

● **Immigration & customs**
The Chilean border post is at Portillo. Bus and car passengers are dealt with separately. There may be long delays during searches for fruit, meat and vegetables, which may not be imported into Chile. All luggage entering Chile is X-rayed; remove all camera film before boarding bus as hand-luggage is not X-rayed.

● **Exchange**
Casa de Cambio in customs building in Portillo.

Valparaíso and Viña del Mar

PACIFIC BEACHES close to the capital include the international resort of Viña del Mar and a variety of others. On the same stretch of coast are the ports of Valparaíso and San Antonio.

Climate This coastline enjoys a Mediterranean-style climate; the cold sea currents and coastal winds produce much more moderate temperatures than in Santiago and the central valley. Rainfall is moderate in winter and the summers are dry.

VALPARAISO

Valparaíso (*Pop* 277,000; *Phone code* 032) capital of V Región (Valparaíso), 90 km W of Santiago, is the principal port of Chile, and an important naval base. With the construction of the new Congress building, it is also the seat of the Chilean parliament. The city is situated on the shores of a sweeping bay and on a crescent of hills behind. Seen from the ocean, it presents a majestic panorama: a great circle of hills is backed by the snow-capped peaks of the distant Cordillera.

History

Founded in 1542, Valparaíso became, in the colonial period, a small port used for trade with Peru. It was raided by pirates at least seven times in the colonial period.

The city prospered from independence more than any other Chilean town. It was used in the 19th century by commercial agents from Europe and the United States as their trading base in the southern Pacific and became a major international banking centre as well as the key port for shipping between the northern Pacific and Cape Horn. Its decline was the result of the development of steam ships which stopped instead at the coal mines around Concepción and then the opening of the Panama Canal in 1914. Since then it has declined further owing to the development of a container port in San Antonio, the shift of banks to Santiago and the move of the middle-classes to nearby Viña del Mar.

Little of the city's colonial past survived the pirates, tempests, fires and earthquakes of the period, but a remnant of the old colonial city can be found in the hollow known as El Puerto, grouped round the low-built stucco church of La Matriz. Most of the principal buildings date from after the devastating earthquake of 1906 (further serious earthquakes occurred in July 1971 and in March 1985) though some impression of its 19th century glory can be gained from the banking area of the lower town and from the mansions of wealthy merchants.

Places of interest

There are two completely different cities. The lower part, known as **El Plan**, is the business centre, with fine office buildings on narrow streets strung along the edge of the bay. Above, covering the hills ('cerros'), is a fantastic agglomeration of fine mansions, tattered houses and shacks, scrambled in oriental confusion along the narrow back streets. Superb views over the bay are offered from most of the 'cerros'. The lower and upper cities are connected by steep winding roads, flights of steps and 16 *ascensores* or funicular railways dating from the period 1880-1914. The most unusual of these is **Ascensor Polanco** (entrance from C Simpson, off Av Argentina a few blocks SE of the bus station), which is in two parts, the first of which is a 160m horizontal tunnel through the rock, the

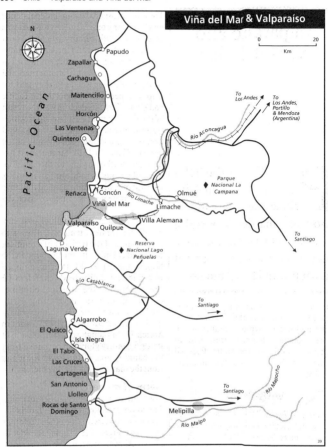

Viña del Mar & Valparaíso

second a vertical lift to the summit on which there is a *mirador*. Note that the lower entrance is in a slum area which is unsafe: do not go alone and do not take valuables.

The old heart of the city is the **Plaza Sotomayor**, dominated by the former **Intendencia** (Government House), now used as the Regional Naval Headquarters. Opposite is a fine statue to the 'Heroes of Iquique' (see page 755). The passenger quay is 1 block away (handicraft shops on quay) and nearby is the railway station, from which passenger services run on the metropolitan line to Los Andes. The streets of El Puerto run on either side from Plaza Sotomayor. C Serrano runs NW for 2 blocks to the Plaza Echaurren, near which stands the church of **La Matriz**, built in 1842 on the site of the first church in the city. Further NW, along Bustamante lies the Plaza Aduana from where there is an *ascensor* to the bold hill of **Cerro Artillería**, crowned by the huge Naval Academy and a park.

Southeast of Plaza Sotomayor Calles

Prat, Cochrane and Esmeralda run through the old banking and commercial centre to Plaza Aníbal Pinto, the most attractive square in Valparaíso around which are several of the cities oldest bars. Further E is the Plaza de la Victoria with the Cathedral; S of the Plaza on Cerro Bellavista and reached by C Molina is the Museo al Cielo Abierto, a collection of 20 murals on the exteriors of buildings. E of Plaza de la Victoria, reached by following C Pedro Montt is Plaza O'Higgins (flea market on Sat mornings), which is dominated by the imposing new **Congreso Nacional**.

To the W of **Cerro Artillería** the Av **Playa Ancha** runs to a stadium, seating 20,000 people, on Cerro Playa Ancha. Avenida Altamirano runs along the coast at the foot of Cerro Playa Ancha to **Las Torpederas**, a picturesque bathing beach. The **Faro de Punta Angeles**, on a promontory just beyond Las Torpederas, was the first lighthouse on the W Coast; you can get a permit to go up. On another high point on the other side of the city is the **Mirador de O'Higgins**, the spot where the Supreme Dictator exclaimed, on seeing Cochrane's liberating squadron: 'On those four craft depends the destiny of America'.

The New Year is celebrated by a firework display on the bay, which is best seen from the Cerros.

Museums

Museo Municipal de Bellas Artes, with Chilean landscapes and seascapes and some modern paintings, housed in Palacio Baburizza, Paseo Yugoeslavo (free), open Tues-Sun 1000-1800; take Ascensor El Peral from Plaza Justicia, off Plaza Sotomayor.

Museo del Mar Almirante Cochrane, housing collection of naval models built by local Naval Modelling Club, good views over port, Tues-Sun 1000-1800, free, take Ascensor Cordillera from C Serrano, off Plaza Sotomayor, to Cerro Cordillera; at the top, Plazuela Eleuterio Ramírez, take C Merlet to the left.

Museo Naval, in the old Naval Academy on Cerro Artillería, Paseo 21 de Mayo, naval history 1810-1880, includes exhibitions on Chile's two naval heroes, Lord Cochrane and Arturo Prat, Tues-

Sun 1000-1800, US$0.35 (take Ascensor Artillería from Plaza Aduana).

Museo de Historia Natural and **Galería Municipal de Arte**, both in 19th-century Palacio Lyon, Condell 1546, Tues-Fri 1000-1300, 1400-1800, Sat/Sun 1000-1400.

Museo La Sebastiana, Pasaje Collado 1, Av Alemania, Altura 6900 on Cerro Florida, T 256606, former house of Pablo Neruda (see also his house at Isla Negra below), Tues-Sun 1030-1430, 1530-1800 (closes 1700 June-Aug), US$2 (take Verde Mar Bus O or D along Av Alemania).

Casa Mistral, Higueras 118, exhibition dedicated to life and work of Gabriela Mistral, Tues-Sun 1000-1330, 1530-1930.

Sightseeing

Launches run trips in summer around the harbour from Muelle Prat, 30 mins, US$1.20, to Playa Las Torpederas and to Viña del Mar; other boats for hire for fishing. **NB** Don't photograph naval ships or installations. The **Camino Cintura**/Av Alemania is the only road which connects all the hills above Valparaíso; it affords constantly changing views, perhaps the best being from Plaza Bismark. No 9 'Central Placeres' bus gives a fine scenic drive over the hills to the port; also bus 'Mar Verde' (O) from Av Argentina near the bus terminal to Plaza Aduana.

Excursions

The **Reserva Nacional Peñuelas**, covering 9,260 ha surrounding the artificial Lago Peñuelas, is situated SE of Valparaíso near the main road to Santiago (Route 68 – Valparaíso-Santiago buses pass the entrance). Much of the park is covered by mixed forest and shrubs. Access is permitted for walking and fishing; administration at park entrance, about 30 km from Valparaíso.

Laguna Verde, 18 km S of Valparaíso, is a picturesque bay for picnics, reached by a 2-hr dusty walk over the hills. Bus No 3, marked 'Laguna Verde' from Victoria y Rancagua, hourly.

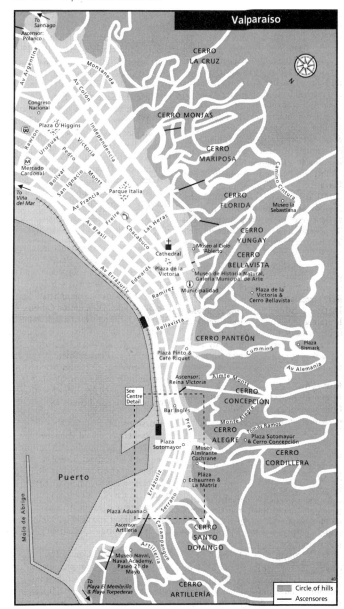

Valparaíso

To Santiago
Ascensor: Polanco

CERRO LA CRUZ

Av Argentina

Montaneda

Av Colón

Congreso Nacional

Plaza O'Higgins

Rawson
Uruguay
Victoria
Independencia
Pedro Montt
Bolívar
San Ignacio

CERRO MONJAS

CERRO MARIPOSA

Mercado Cardonal

To Viña del Mar

Av Francia

Parque Italia

Av Brasil
Freire
Las Heras
Chacabuco

CERRO FLORIDA

Camino Cintura

Museo la Sebastiana

CERRO YUNGAY

CERRO BELLAVISTA

Cathedral

Museo al Cielo Abierto

Av Erràzuriz
Edwards

Plaza de la Victoria

Museo de Historia Natural, Galería Municipal de Arte

Ramírez

Municipalidad

Plaza de la Victoria & Cerro Bellavista

Bellavista

CERRO PANTEÓN

Cumming

Plaza Bismark

Av Alemania

Plaza Pinto & Café Riquet

Ascensor: Reina Victoria

Almte Montt

CERRO CONCEPCIÓN

Bar Inglés

Prat

Monte Alegre

CERRO ALEGRE

Tomás Ramos

Plaza Sotomayor & Cerro Concepción

Plaza Sotomayor

Museo Almirante Cochrane

CERRO CORDILLERA

Puerto

Molo de Abrigo

Plaza Echaurren & La Matriz

Errázuriz

Plaza Aduana

See Centre Detail

Serrano

Ascensor: Artillería

CERRO SANTO DOMINGO

Carampangue

Artillería

Museo Naval, Naval Academy, Paseo 21 de Mayo

To Playa El Membrillo & Playa Torpederas

CERRO ARTILLERÍA

Circle of hills
Ascensores

Local information

● Accommodation

B *Prat*, Condell 1443, T 253081, scruffy entrance but comfortable rooms, central, restaurant; under same management is **B** *Condell*, Pirámide 557, T 212788, similar.

C *Lancaster*, Chacabuco 2362, with breakfast; **C** *Reina Victoria*, Plaza Sotomayor 190, T 212203, **D** on top floors, without bath, with breakfast, poor beds, run down.

D *Res Dinamarca*, Dinamarca 539 (from Plazuela Ecuador – just S of Condell y Bellavista – take any micro marked 'Cárcel'; or climb 10 mins up Av Ecuador), good value, also short stay, parking, serves full breakfast and snacks; **D** *Garden*, Serrano 501, T 252776, use of kitchen; **D** *Res Lily*, Blanco Encalada 866, T 255995, 2 blocks from Plaza Sotomayor, safe (despite no locks on doors); **D** *Enzo and Martina Tesser*, Av Quebrada Verde, T 288873, with breakfast, German spoken (reached by bus 1); **D** pp *María Pizarro*, Chacabuco 2340, Casa No 2, T 230791, lovely rooms, central, quiet, kitchen, highly rec; her neighbours, Francisca Escobar and Guillermo Jones, Chacabuco 2326, T 214193, also rent rooms, same price, equally rec, English spoken.

E pp *Res Mi Casa*, Rawson 310, nr bus terminal, basic, fleas, also has rooms at Yungay 2842, quiet; **E** pp *Sra Mónica*, Av Argentina 322, Casa B, T 215673, 2 blocks from bus terminus; **E** pp *Sra Silvia*, Pje La Quinta 70, Av Argentina, 3 blocks from Congress, T 216592, quiet, kitchen facilities, rec; **E** pp *Sra Anita*, Higuera 107, Cerro Alegre, with good breakfast, wonderful views. Many of the 'cheap' hotels in the Chacabuco area are for short-term occupation only. Youth hostel office at Edwards 695, p 3, will extend membership; nearest hostel in Viña del Mar.

● Places to eat

Al Galeone D'Oro, Independencia 1766, Italian, not cheap but good; *Tentazione*, Pedro Montt 2484, good, cheap; *La Parrilla de Pepe*, Pedro Montt 1872, good food and service; *Hamburg*, O'Higgins 1274, German management, German beer, beware of overcharging; *Del Mónico*, Prat 669, good, cheap lunches, popular; *La Rotunda*, Prat 701, good food; *Nantón*, Brasil 1368, Chinese, good. Around the market there are lots of cheap lunch restaurants, specialising in seafood inc *Los Porteños*, Valdivia 169, very good. At Caleta Membrillo, 1 km NW of Plaza Sotomayor there are several good fish restaurants inc *Club Social de Pescadores*, Altamirano 1480, good; opp are *San Pedro*, shabby but friendly and *El Membrillo*, more expensive. Other good places for lunch: *Nahuel*, Donoso 1498, popular, cheap; *Mesón del Lord*, Cochrane 859; *Bambú*, Pudeto 450, vegetarian.

Cafés and bars: two traditional bar/restaurants on Plaza Aníbal Pinto are: *Riquet*, comfortable, expensive, good coffee and breakfast, rec; *Cinzano*, popular. *Bar Inglés*, Cochrane 851 (entrance also on Blanco Encalada), good food and drink, traditional, rec, not cheap; *Westfalia*, Cochrane 847, coffee, breakfasts, vegetarian lunches; *Café do Brasil*, Condell 1342, excellent coffee, juices, sandwiches; *Turri*, Templemann 147, on Cerro Concepción, T 259196, overlooking port, good food and service.

● Airline offices

LanChile, Esmeralda 1048, T 251441; Ladeco, Blanco Encalada 951, T 216355.

● Banks & money changers

Banks open 0900 to 1400, but closed on Sat. Good rates at **Banco de Santiago**, Prat 816, and **Banco de Crédito e Inversiones**, Cochrane 820; **Fincard** (Mastercard), Esmeralda 1087; **Exprinter**, Prat 887 (the building with the clocktower at junction with Cochrane), good rates, no commission on TCs, open 0930-1400, 1600-1900; **Inter Cambios**, Errázuriz esq Plaza Sotomayor, good rates; **Gema Tour**, Esmeralda 940; **New York**, Prat 659, good rates for cash; **Afex**, Cochrane 828. When *cambios* are closed, street changers operate outside *Inter Cambios*.

● Cultural centres

Instituto Chileno-Norteamericano, Esmeralda 1069, shows foreign films.

● Embassies & consulates

British Consul, Blanco Encalada 725, oficina 26, T 256117, Casilla 82-V; Argentine Consul, Cochrane 867.

● Entertainment

Proa Al Canaveral, Errázuriz 304, good seafood restaurant downstairs, pleasant bar upstairs with dancing from 0100, poetry reading on Thur; several popular bars on Ecuador, some with live music and small entry charge.

● Laundry

Las Heras 554, good and cheap

● Post & telecommunications

Telecommunications: VTR Telecommunications, Cochrane 825; CTC, Esmeralda 1054 or Pedro Montt 2023; Entel, Condell 1491.

● Security

Robbery is common in El Puerto and around the *ascensores*, especially on Cerro Santo Domingo.

● Shopping

Bookshop: *Librería Universitaria*, Esmeralda 1132, good selection of regional history; many others.

● Tourist offices

In the Municipalidad building, Condell 1490, Oficina 102, open Mon-Fri 0830-1400, 1530-

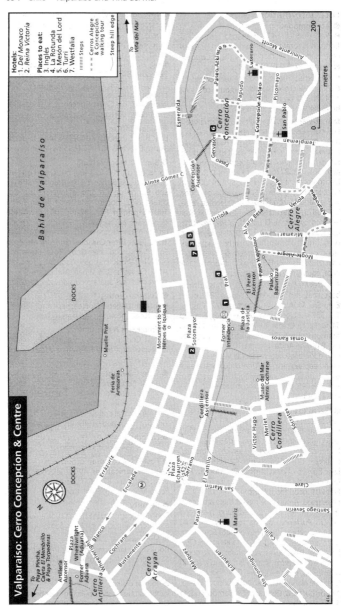

Valparaíso: Cerro Concepción & Centre

Hotels:
1. *Del Monaco*
2. *Reina Victoria*

Places to eat:
3. Inglés
4. La Rotunda
5. Mesón del Lord
6. Turri
7. Westfalia

|||||| Steps

▪ ▪ ▪ Cerros Alegre & Concepción walking tour

⌇⌇⌇⌇ Steep hill edge

To Viña del Mar

Bahía de Valparaíso

DOCKS

DOCKS

Feria de Artesanías

Muelle Prat

Monument to the Héroes de Iquique

Plaza Sotomayor

Former Intendencia

Plaza de la Justicia

Plaza de la Justicia

Museo del Mar Almte Cochrane

Tomás Ramos

El Peral Ascensor

Palacio Baburizza

Paseo Yugoslavo

Monte Alegre

Cerro Alegre

Miramar

Álvaro Besa

Urriola

Concepción Ascensor

Almte Gómez C

Esmeralda

Cerro Concepción

Paseo Atkinson

Lutherano

Papudo

Pilcomayo

Concepción Abtao

San Pablo

Templeman

Gervasoni

paseo

Galos

Navarro

Almirante Montt

Prat

Cochrane

Blanco

Serrano

Plaza Echaurren

Esmeralda

Cordillera Ascensor

Cerro Cordillera

Victor Hugo

Merlet

Socrates

Clave

San Martín

El Castillo

Pascal

La Matriz

Márquez

Echaurren

Bustamente

Cochrane

Wheelwright (Aduana)

Plaza Wheelwright (Aduana)

Artillería Ascensor

Cerro Artillería

Former Aduana

Cerro Arrayán

Santiago Severin

Calle

Sto Domingo

To
Playa Prncha
Caleta El Membrillo
& Playa Torpederas

N

metres
0   200

1730. Kiosks at bus terminal (good map available), helpful, open 0900-1300, 1530-1930 (closed Thur, Apr-Nov), Muelle Prat, open Nov-March 1030-1430, 1600-2000, and in Plaza Victoria, open 1030-1300, 1430-2000 Nov-March.

● **Useful addresses**

YMCA: (Asociación Cristiana de Jóvenes), Blanco Encalada 1117. **YWCA**: (Asociación Cristiana Feminina), Blanco 967. **Valparaíso Seamen's Institute**: Blanco Encalada 394.

● **Transport**

Local Buses: US$0.20 within city limits. **Funiculares**: US$0.30. **Taxis**: are more expensive than Santiago: a short run under 1 km costs US$1.

Trains Regular service on Merval, the Valparaíso metropolitan line between Valparaíso, Viña del Mar, Quilpué, Limache, Quillota, La Calera, Llaillay, San Felipe and Los Andes (and intermediate stations); to Viña del Mar every 15-30 mins, trains that run the entire route are 1800 daily, 1430 Mon-Fri (not holidays), 0805, Sat, Sun and holidays, fare to Los Andes US$1.50, 3 hrs. *El Porteño* tourist train runs on Sun, 1 Jan-28 Feb and on most public holidays.

Buses Terminal is on Pedro Montt 2800 block, corner of Rawson, 1 block from Av Argentina; plenty of buses between terminal and Plaza Sotomayor. Excellent and frequent service to Viña del Mar, 25 min, US$0.25 from Plaza Aduana, passing along Av Errázuriz; colectivos to Viña US$0.40. To Santiago, 2 hrs, US$3-4, shop around, frequent (book on Sat to return to the capital on Sun); to Concepción, 11 hrs, US$12; to Puerto Montt, 17 hrs, US$18; to La Serena, 8 hrs, US$10; to Calama, US$35; to Arica, US$40, Fénix *salón cama* service, US$50. To Argentina: to Mendoza, 4 companies, 6-7 hrs, US$25; to Córdoba, US$40.

If driving to Santiago the main road passes through two tunnels, toll of US$3.25 paid at the first, but this can be avoided by turning off onto the old road over the mountains about 1 km before the tunnel; there is another toll just before the start of the motorway, 56 km from Santiago.

Hitchhiking To Santiago is easy from the service station on Av Argentina.

PARQUE NACIONAL LA CAMPANA

Route 62 runs through Viña del Mar, climbs out of the bay and goes through Quilpué (Km 16) before reaching the Aconcagua Valley at **Limache** (Km 40). 8 km E is Olmué, N of which is **Parque Nacional La Campana**, which covers 8,000 ha and includes Cerro La Campana (1,828m) which Darwin climbed in 1836 and Cerro El Roble (2,200m). There are

extensive views from the top of these Cerros, but a guide may be necessary because there are a number of ascents, some of which are very difficult. Much of the park is covered by native woodland. Near Ocoa there are areas of Chilean palms (*kankán*), now found in only two locations in Chile.

● **Access** There are three entrances: at Granizo, reached by paved road from Olmué, 5 km E; at Cajón Grande, reached by unpaved road which turns off the Olmué-Granizo road; at Palmar de Ocoa to the N reached by unpaved road (10 km) leading off the Pan-American Highway between Hijuelas and Llaillay. There is no public transport to the park.

VIÑA DEL MAR

(*Phone code* 032), 9 km NE of Valparaíso via Route 68 which runs along a narrow belt between the shore and precipitous cliffs. This is one of South America's leading seaside resorts. 6 km further N along the coast is the more exclusive resort of **Reñaca**.

Places of interest

The older part is situated on the banks of a lagoon, the Marga Marga, which is crossed by bridges. Around Plaza Vergara and the smaller Plaza Sucre to its S are the **Teatro Municipal** (1930) and the exclusive **Club de Viña**, built in 1910. The municipally owned **Quinta Vergara**, formerly the residence of the shipping entrepreneur Francisco Alvarez, lies two blocks S. The grounds are superb and include a double avenue of palm trees. The **Palacio Vergara**, in the gardens, houses the Museo de Bellas Artes and the Academia de Bellas Artes. Part of the grounds is a children's playground, and there is an outdoor auditorium where concerts and ballet are performed in the summer months, and in Feb an international song festival is held. (Tickets from the Municipalidad).

Further W on a headland overlooking the sea is **Cerro Castillo**, the summer palace of the Presidents of the Republic: its gardens can be visited. Just N, on the other side of the lagoon is the **Casino**, built in the 1930s and set in beautiful gardens, US$6 to enter, jacket and tie for men required (open all year).

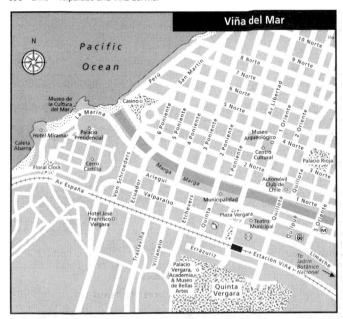

The main beaches, Acapulco and Mirasol are located to the N but S of Cerro Castillo is Caleta Abarca, also popular. Beaches may be closed because of pollution. The coastal route N to Reñaca provides lovely views over the sea. East of the centre are the **Valparaíso Sporting Club** with a racecourse and playing fields. North of here in the hills are the Granadilla Golf Club and a large artificial lake, the **Laguna Sausalito**, adjacent to which is the Estadio Sausalito (home to Everton soccer team, among many other sporting facilities). It possesses an excellent tourist complex with swimming pools, boating, tennis courts, sandy beaches, water skiing, restaurants, etc. Entry US$2.50, children under 11, US$1.75; take colectivo No 19 from C Viana.

Museums

Museo de la Cultura del Mar, in the Castillo Wulff, on the coast near Cerro Castillo, contains a collection on the life and work of the novelist and maritime historian, Salvador Reyes, Tues-Sat 1000-1300, 1430-1800, Sun 1000-1400.

Museo de Bellas Artes, Quinta Vergara, Tues-Sun 100-1400, 1500-1800, US$0.25.

Palacio Rioja, Quillota 214, built in 1906 by a prominent local family and now used for official municipal receptions, ground floor preserved in its original state, open to visitors 1000-1400, 1500-1800, Tues-Sun, rec.

Museo Sociedad Fonk, C 4 Norte 784, archaeological museum, with objects from Easter Island and the Chilean mainland, including Mapuche silver, open Tues-Fri 1000-1800, Sat-Sun 1000-1400, entry US$0.20. An Easter Island statue stands on the lawn between the railway and the beach just beyond Caleta Portales, between Viña del Mar and Valparaíso.

Centro Cultural, Libertad 250, holds regular exhibitions.

Excursions

The **Jardín Botánico Nacional**, formerly the estate of the nitrate entrepreneur Pascual Baburizza, now administered by Conaf, lies 8 km SE of the city. Covering 405 ha, it contains over 3,000 species from all over the world and a collection of Chilean cacti but the species are not labelled. Take bus 20 from Plaza Vergara, entry US$1.

Local festivals

El Roto, 20 Jan, in homage to the workers and peasants of Chile.

Local information

● **Accommodation**

Many in **L3-A3** range, some with beach.

L3 *San Martín*, San Martín 667, T 689191, with breakfast.

A2 *Alborada del Mar*, San Martín 419, T 975274, tastefully decorated; **A2** *Español*, Plaza Vergara 191, T/F 685145, phone and *Restaurante Colonial*; **A2** *José Francisco Vergara*, von Schroeders 392, T 626022, has garden houses for up to 5; **A3** *Res Offenbacher Hof*, Balmaceda 102, T 621483, rec; **A3** *Monte Carlo*, V MacKenna 136, 6 km N in Reñaca, T 830397, very modern, comfortable.

B *Balia*, von Schroeders 36, T 978310, F 680724, phone, parking; **B** *Petit Palace*, Paseo Valle 387, T 663134, small rooms, good, central, quiet; **B** *Quinta Vergara*, Errázuriz 690, T 685073, large rooms, beautiful gardens, rec.

C *Capric*, von Schroeders 39, T 978295, good value, **E** pp IYHA card holders; **C** *El Escorial*, 4 Norte 535, T 907919, with breakfast, shared bath, central; *Res Victoria*, Valparaíso 40, T 977370, without bath, with breakfast, central; **C** *Villamar*, 2 Poniente 440, T 974404, with breakfast; **C** *Res Villarica*, Arlegui 172, good.

D *Res Blanchart*, Valparaíso 82, T 974949, with breakfast, good service; **D** *Res Familiar*, Batuco 147; **D** *Res France*, Montaña 743, safe, helpful; **D** *Sra Nalda*, 2 Norte 849 (Pasaje Klamer), T 970488, good garden, cooking facilities, rec; **D** *Res Tajamar*, Alvarez 884, opp railway station, old-fashioned, central, huge rooms, atmospheric; **E** pp von Schroeders 151, T 971861, safe, helpful. There are a great many more places to stay inc private accommodation (E pp). Out of season furnished apartments can be rented through agencies (with commission). In season it is cheaper to stay in Valparaíso and commute to the Viña beaches.

Camping: *Camping Reñaca*, Santa Luisa 401, expensive, dirty, also cabins.

Motels: several at Reñaca.

Youth hostels: **E** pp *Res La Montaña*, Agua Santa 153, T 622230, for YHA card holders, with breakfast, other meals available, dingy, dirty bathroom, no cooking facilities, also family rooms; **E** pp *Lady Kinnaird Hostal*, 1 Oriente 1096, T 975413, YWCA, central, English spoken, women only, highly rec. See also *Hotel Capric* above.

● **Places to eat**

At hotels. *Cap Ducal*, Marina 51, expensive; *Raul*, Valparaíso 533, live music; *Casino Chico*, Valparaíso y von Schroeders, Chilean and international dishes; *Panzoni*, Pasaje Cousiño 12-B, good lunches, Italian; *Machitún Ruca*, San Martín 529, excellent. *Pizzería Mama Mía*, San Martín 435, good, reasonably priced; *Armandita*, San Martín 501, parrilla, large portions, good service; *El Encuentro*, San Martín 477, fish, very good; *Las Gaviotas*, 14 Norte 1248, Chilean meat dishes, not expensive, live music. Many restaurants on Av Valparaíso, try in the Galerías (arcades), eg *Café Big Ben*, No 469, good coffee, good food; *Alster*, No 225, expensive; *Samoiedo*, No 637, confitería, grill and restaurant. Several pleasant restaurants and cafés along the renovated Muelle Vergara inc *La Mía Pappa*, Italian, good lunches and evening buffets. *Centro Vital*, Av Valparaíso 376, vegetarian, excellent lunches.

In Reñaca: *El Pancho*, Borgoño 16180, excellent seafood and service; *Anastassia*, Borgoño 15000, excellent international menu, expensive; *Rincón Marino*, Borgoño 17120, good seafood, pricey; *Hotel Oceanic*, Borgoño, T 830006, very good, expensive.

● **Banks & money changers**

Many *casas de cambio* on Arlegui inc **Afex**, No 641 (open 0900-1400 Sat); **Cambio Norte**, No 610; **Cambio Andino** No 644; also in the tourist office; **Fincard** (Mastercard), Ecuador 259.

● **Cultural centres**

Instituto Chileno-Británico, 3 Norte 824, T 971061; **Instituto Chileno – Norteamericano de Cultura**, 3 Norte 532, T 662145; **Casa Italia** (cultural centre, consulate, restaurant), Alvarez 398; **Goethe Institut**, El Salto, 20 mins from town; **Instituto Chileno-Francés**, Alvarez 314, T 685908.

● **Entertainment**

Discotheques: *Topsy Topsy*, Santa Luisa 501 and *La Cantina del Cocodrilo*, Av San Martín, both in Reñaca, expensive, rec; *El Gato de la Luna*, Arlegui 396, good bar, live music and dancing.

● **Post & telecommunications**

Telephone: CTC, Valparaíso 628; Global Telecommunications/Entel, 15 Norte 961.

● **Shopping**

Market: at intersection of Av Sporting and river, Wed and Sat.

● **Tourist offices**
Valparaíso 507, Of 303, T 882285. Arrangements may be made at the Tourist Office for renting private homes in the summer season. **Automóvil Club de Chile**: 1 Norte 901, T 689509.

● **Transport**
Local Car hire: Euro Rent-A-Car, in *Hotel O'Higgins*, clean cars, efficient.

Air Ladeco Santiago-Viña del Mar (to naval airfield nr Concón), several daily, 10 mins, US$15, T 978210; National T 883505; Alta, Av Libertad 22, local 1, T 692920, F 692917.

Trains Services on the Valparaíso Metropolitan line (Merval) stop at Viña (details under Valparaíso).

Buses Terminal at Av Valparaíso y Quilpué. To Santiago, US$3-4, 2 hrs, frequent, many companies, heavily booked in advance for travel on Sun afternoons, at other times some buses pick up passengers opposite the train station; to La Serena, 6 daily, 8 hrs, US$10, to Antofagasta, 20 hrs, US$35.

RESORTS NORTH OF VIÑA DEL MAR

North of Viña del Mar the coast road runs through Las Salinas, a popular beach between two towering crags, Reñaca and Cochoa, where there is a large sealion colony 100m offshore, to Concón. There is also a much faster inland road, between Viña del Mar and Concón.

Concón, on the southern shore of a bay at the mouth of the Río Aconcagua, is 18 km N of Viña del Mar. Main attractions: tennis, bathing, fishing, and riding. Main eyesore: an oil refinery (not visible from beach; some pollution). Near the Concón beach there is a pelican colony.

● **Accommodation L2** *Hostería Edelweis*, Borgoño 19200, T 903600, modern cabins, comfortable, sea views, inc breakfast, excellent food in attached restaurant, German spoken, highly rec; **D** *Cabañas Koala Place*, Los Pescadores 41, T 813026, one-night stays unwelcome.

● **Places to eat** Good seafood *empanadas* at bars; *Vista al Mar*, Borgoño 21270, T 812-221, good fish restaurant, good value; *Don Chico*, Borgoño 21410, good seafood; *Mirador Cochoa*, Borgoño 17205, good, pricey.

Quintero (*Pop* 16,000) another 16 km N of Concón, is a fishing town situated on a rocky peninsula with lots of small beaches.

● **Accommodation A2** *Yachting Club*, Luis Acevedo 1736, T 930061; **D** *Isla de Capri*, 21 de Mayo 1299, T 930117, pleasant, sea views; **D** *Monaco*, 21 de Mayo 1530, T 930939, run down but interesting, good views. A number of *residenciales*.

Horcón (also known locally as Horcones) is set back in a cove surrounded by cliffs, a pleasant small village, mainly of wooden houses. On the beach hippies sell cheap and unusual jewellery and trinkets. Vegetation is tropical with many cacti on the cliff tops. It is best avoided in Jan-Feb when it is packed out.

● **Accommodation B** *El Ancla*, cabañas, pleasant; **C** *Cabañas* on Playa Cau Cau, good; **C-B** *Aranciba*, **D** without bath, pleasant gardens, good food, rec; also rooms in private houses; no campsite but camping possible at private houses.

● **Places to eat** *El Ancla* rec; *Reina Victoria*, cheap, good.

Further N is **Maitencillo** (*Pop* 1,200), with a wonderful long beach. Just to the S is the tourist complex of Marbella. 14 km beyond is **Zapallar** (*Pop* 2,200) a fashionable resort. A hint of its former glory is given by a number of fine mansions along Av Zapallar. At Cachagua, 3 km S a colony of penguins may be viewed from the northern end of the beach.

● **Accommodation A1** *César*, T 711313, very nice; **A3** *Isla Seca*, T 711508, small, pool, good restaurant; good, reasonably-priced food in *Restaurant César* (different management from hotel), on seafront; no *residenciales*, no campsite.

Papudo (*Pop* 2,500), 10 km further N, was the site of a naval battle in Nov 1865 in which the Chilean vessel *Esmeralda* captured the Spanish ship *Covadonga*. Following the arrival of the railway Papudo rivalled Viña del Mar as a fashionable resort in the 1920s but it has long since declined.

● **Accommodation D** *Moderno*, Concha 150, T 711496; **D'** *Peppino*, No 609, T 711482; many more.

● **Transport** Buses from Valparaíso and Viña del Mar: To **Concón** bus 9 or 10 (from Av Libertad between 2 and 3 Norte in Viña), US$0.50; to **Quintero** and **Horcón**, Sol del Pacífico, every 30 mins, US$1, 2 hrs; to **Zapallar** and **Papudo**, Sol del Pacífico, 4 a day (2 before 0800, 2 after 1600), US$3.

RESORTS NEAR THE MOUTH OF THE RIO MAIPO

SAN ANTONIO

(*Pop* 74,742; *Phone code* 035), 112 km S of Valparaíso and 113 km from Santiago near the mouth of the Río Maipo, is a commercial centre for this part of the coast. It is a container and fishing port and is the terminal for the export of copper brought by rail from El Teniente mine, near Rancagua. Nearby to the S are two resorts: **Llolleo** (4 km), famous for the treatment of heart diseases, and 7 km further **Rocas de Santo Domingo**, the most attractive and exclusive resort in this area with 20 km of beaches and a golf course.

Museums Museo Municipal de Ciencias Naturales y Arqueología, Av Barros Luco, Mon-Fri 0900-1300, 1500-1900.

● **Accommodation At San Antonio**: **C** *Jockey Club*, 21 de Mayo 202, T 31302, best, good views, restaurant; **D** *Colonial*, Pedro Montt 196. **At Llolleo**: **D** pp *Oriente*, Inmaculada Concepción 50, T 32188; *Res El Castillo*, Providencia 253, T 373821. **At Santo Domingo**: **B** *Rocas de Santo Domingo*, La Ronda 130, T 231348; no cheap accommodation – try Llolleo.

● **Banks & money changers** Casa Amarilla, Av Centenario 176, will also change pesos into dollars.

● **Transport** Buses to **Valparaíso**, Pullman Bus, every 45 mins until 2000, US$2; to **Santiago**, Pullman Bus, every 20 mins, US$2.

CARTAGENA

(*Pop* 10,318), 8 km N of San Antonio, is the biggest resort on this part of the coast. The centre is around the hilltop Plaza de Armas. To the S is the picturesque Playa Chica, overlooked by many of the older hotels and restaurants; to the N is the Playa Larga. Between the two a promenade runs below the cliffs; high above hang old houses, some in disrepair but offering spectacular views. Cartagena is a very popular resort in summer, but out of season it is a good centre for visiting nearby resorts; there are many hotels and bus connections are good.

● **Accommodation D** *Biarçitz*, Playa Chica, T 32246; **D** *La Bahía*, Playa Chica, T 31246; **D** *Violeta*, Condell 140, T 234093, swimming pool, good views; **E** pp *El Estribo*, just off Plaza de Armas, with breakfast, basic, cheap *comedor*; **E** pp *Res Carmona*, Playa Chica, T 212199, small rooms, basic, good value.

NORTH OF CARTAGENA

There are several small resorts including **Las Cruces, El Tabo** and **El Quisco**, a small fishing port with 2 beautiful white beaches (crowded during Chilean holidays).

● **Accommodation At Las Cruces**: **C** *La Posada*, T 233520, with breakfast, good bird-watching. **At El Tabo**: **C** *Hotel El Tabo*, T 33719, quite nice, and *Motel El Tabo*, T 212719, next door; 2 cheap and basic campsites. **At El Quisco** (accommodation generally expensive): **C** *Motel Barlovento*, T 481030; *Residenciales* 100-200m from beach in **C** range, eg *Res Oriental*, T 481662, with breakfast, good; **D** pp *Cabañas del Irlandés Volador*, Aguirre 277, T 473464; **D** *Res Julia*, Aguirre 0210, T 481546, quiet, good value, rec; **D** *Cabañas Pozo Azul*, Capricornio 234, SE of town, quiet. Several on Dubournais (main street) inc **D** *El Quisco*, No 166, with breakfast, open weekends only, with excellent seafood restaurant.

4 km S of El Quisco in the village of **Isla Negra** is the beautifully-restored **Museo-Casa Pablo Neruda**. Bought by Neruda in 1939, this house, overlooking the sea, was his writing retreat in his later years. It contains artefacts gathered by Neruda from all over the world. It is open for guided tours in Spanish, English or French (last two only after 1500), Tues-Sun 1015-1230, 1500-1800, in summer 1000-1745, US$2, T 035-212284 for opening hours or to book English guide (see also his house, La Chascona, under Santiago **Museums**, and La Sebastiaña, under Valparaíso **Museums**). Tours from Santiago, departing at 0900 from Plaza de Armas (Compañía y Ahumada), cost US$23.75 and include seaside resorts, T 232-2574.

● **Accommodation B** *Hostería Santa Elena*, beautiful building and location, restaurant, some rooms damp and gloomy.

29 km N of Cartagena, **Algarrobo** is the largest resort N of Cartagena and the most chic, with its large houses, yacht club and marina. From Playa Canelo there are good views of pelicans and boobies on an offshore island (no entry). In summer there are boat tours round the island from the jetty.

- **Accommodation** **C** *Costa Sur*, Alessandri 2156, T481151; **D** *Uribe*, behind *Costa Sur*, T 481035, pleasant, quiet; **D** *Vera*, Alessandri 1521, with breakfast, good; **E** pp *Res San José*, Av Principal 1598, basic, no hot water.

- **Transport** Buses to Santiago, Pullman Bus, every 20 mins, 2 hrs, US$3, stopping in Cartagena and the resorts along the coast (but not San Antonio). Services to San Antonio by Empresa de Buses San Antonio (frequent, last bus around 2000) and Empresa Robles.

From Santiago to La Serena

THE CHIEF INTEREST lies along the coast; the land becomes less fertile as you go further North. The largest resort is La Serena, from where access can be made to the pisco-producing Elqui Valley and to one of the world's major astronomical centres.

From the Río Aconcagua to the Río Elqui is a transitional zone between the fertile heartland and the northern deserts. The first stretch of the Pan-American Highway from Santiago is inland through green valleys with rich blue clover and wild artichokes. North of La Ligua, the Highway mainly follows the coastline, passing many beautiful coves, alternatively rocky and sandy, with good surf, though the water is very cold. The valleys of the main rivers, the Choapa, Limarí and Elqui, are intensively farmed using irrigation to produce fruit and vegetables. Elsewhere the vegetation is characteristic of semidesert (dry scrub and cactus), except in those areas where condensation off the sea provides sufficient moisture for woods to grow.

Rainfall is rare and occurs only in winter. On the coast the average temperature is 14°C; the interior is dry, with temperatures averaging 16-17°.

- **Driving** See page 739 for list of service stations between Santiago and the Peruvian border.

From Santiago to La Serena

To Antofagasta

La Serena
Río Elqui
Coquimbo
Río Turbio
Vicuña
Juntas
Paihuano
Pasto Salado (4,843m)
de los Bañado
Monte Grande
Incaguasi (4,843m)
Guanaqueros
Andacollo
El Tololo
Pisco Elqui
Paso del Agua Negra
Tongoy
Monumento Nacional Pichasca
Cerra de la Laguna (4,902m)
To Rodeo (Argentina)
Colorado (5,151m)
Embalse Recoleta
Parque Nacional Fray Jorge
Ovalle
Río Limari
Termas de Socos
Valle del Encanto
Embalse La Paloma

Pacific Ocean

Embalse Cogotí

ARGENTINA

Illapel
Río Illapel
Salamanca
Río Choapa
Los Vilos
Vizcachar (1,968m)
Loma Blanca (1,868m)
Morado (4,114m)
Pichidangui
Río Quillimari
Jorquera (3,743m)
Los Molles
Río Petorca
La Ligua

To Los Andes & Mendoza (Argentina)

N

0   30
Km

Viña del Mar
Valparaíso

SANTIAGO

Chile: From Santiago To Arica

Tacna
Arica → Putre/ Parinacota / La Paz
195
Pisagua — 77 — Camiña
38
52   80
Iquique — 74 — Mamiña
249   43   37 — Pica
210
Tocopilla — 73   70 — Chuquicamata
16
192 — Calama
188   115 — San Pedro De Atacama
13
Antofagasta
264
Taltal — 25
121 — 117 — El Salvador
Chañaral — 93
Caldera
74 — Copiapó
150
Vallenar
198
Coquimbo — 9 — La Serena
18
Tongoy — 89 — Ovalle
37
156
59 — Illapel
Los Vilos
119
Viña Del Mar / Valparaíso — 110 — Los Andes/ Mendoza
120
Santiago

1000

LOS VILOS

Los Vilos (*Pop* 9,422; *Phone code* 051), 216
km N of Santiago, is a former mineral port,
now a small seaside resort with frequent
launches to Isla de Los Huevos, in the bay,
and, 5 km S, Isla de Los Lobos where there
is a colony of seals. 26 km S is **Pichidangui**
(*phone code* 053), with a beautiful beach.
Los Molles, 10 km S of Pichidangui, is
where many wealthy residents of Santiago
have their summer homes. There are two
small hotels.

- **Accommodation Los Vilos**: **C** *Hostería
Arrayán*, Caupolicán 1, T 541005; **C** *Lord Willow*, Hostería 1444, T 541037, overlooking
beach and harbour, with breakfast, pleasant,
parking, weekend disco next door; **D** *Bellavista*, Rengo 20, T 541073, with breakfast, without bath; **F** pp *Res Angelica*, Caupolicán 627,
central, warm water, restaurant attached, expensive camping (US$13/site). The *American
Motel* is right on the highway, Km 224,
T 541020, and is a convenient stopping place
between Viña del Mar or Santiago and La
Serena, quite good. **In Pichidangui**: *Motel El
Bosque*, El Bosque s/n, T 541182, rec; **B** *Motel Pichidangui*, Francis Drake s/n, T 594010,
swimming pool; **C** *Puquen*, 2 Poniente s/n,
attractive, good value; various other hotels
and *pensiones* in every price range. **Camping**: two good sites in Pichidangui, US$10 in
season, bargain for lower price off season.

- **Places to eat** In Los Vilos *Restaurant
Costanera*, good views over ocean, good
meals, expensive.

- **Transport** Only 1 bus daily Pichidangui-San-
tiago, but N-S buses (eg Inca Bus) on the Highway pass 3 km from the towns.

Illapel (*Pop* 18,900) 59 km NE of Los
Vilos, lies in the basin of the Río Choapa.
A commercial centre for the valley, it has
Museo Casa de la Cultura, on O'Higgins.

OVALLE

(*Pop* 53,000; *Alt* 200; *Phone code* 053) 412
km N of Santiago, lies inland in the valley
of the Río Limarí, a fruit, sheep-rearing,
and mining district. Market days are Mon,
Wed, Fri and Sat, till 1600; the market
(*feria modelo*) is on Benavente. The town is
famous for its *talabarterías* (leather workshops) and for its products made of locally-
mined lapis lazuli. Southeast of the city, at
the confluence of the Ríos Grande and

Huatulame, is the Paloma reservoir, the
largest in Chile.

Museums

Museo del Limarí, Independencia 329,
open Tues-Sun 1000-1600, displays on petroglyphs and a good collection of Diaguita
ceramics and other artefacts.

Excursions

The **Monumento Nacional Valle del Encanto**, about 22 km SW of Ovalle, is a most
important archaeological site. Artefacts
from hunting peoples from over 2,000
years ago have been found but the most
visible remains date from the Molle culture (700 AD). There are over 30 petroglyphs as well as great boulders,
distributed in 6 sites. Camping facilities.

- **Access** Mon-Fri 0900-1300, 1500-1900,
Sat 0900-1300, 1500-1800, Sun 1000-1300,
US$1). No local bus service; you must take a long
distance bus and ask to be dropped off – 5 km
walk to the valley; flag down a bus to return.

Termas de Socos, 35 km SW of Ovalle on
the Pan-American Highway, has fine
thermal springs (entrance US$5), a good
hotel (**A2**, T Ovalle 621373, Casilla 323)
and a campsite (US$10 per tent, but bar-
gain) nearby. Bus US$2.

Parque Nacional Fray Jorge, 90 km W
of Ovalle and 110 km S of La Serena at
the mouth of the Río Limarí, the Park
is reached by a dirt road leading off the
Pan-American Highway. It contains
original forests which contrast with
the otherwise barren surroundings.
Receiving no more than 113 mm of
rain a year, the forests survive because
of the almost constant covering of fog.
Open Sat, Sun and public holidays
only, entry 0830-1600, last departure
1800, US$4; visits closely controlled
owing to risk of fire. Waterproof clothing essential. Round trip in taxi from
Ovalle, US$30, Abel Olivares Rivera,
T Ovalle 620352, rec.

Monumento Nacional Pichasca, 47
km NE of Ovalle at an altitude of 1,350,
reached by an unpaved and largely winding road. It contains petrified tree trunks,
archaeological remains, including a vast
cave with vestiges of ancient roof paintings, and views of gigantic rock forma-

tions on the surrounding mountains. Open 0830-1700, US$3. Daily bus from Ovalle to Río Hurtado passes the turn off (to San Pedro) about 42 km from the city. From here it is 3 km to the park and about 2 km more to sites of interest.

Local information
● Accommodation
D *Res Bristol*, Araucano 224, pleasant spacious building, restaurant. On Libertad: **D** *Francia*, No 231, T 620828, pleasant, restaurant; **D** *Roxy*, No 155, T 620080, patio, *comedor*, highly rec; **E** *Venecia*, No 261, T 620968, safe, rec; **E** *Res Socos*, Socos 22, T 624157, quiet, family run, rec. For cheaper accommodation try **G** *Res Lolita*, Independencia 274, **F** with bath, basic, rec.

● Places to eat
Club Social, V MacKenna 400 block, excellent fish dishes though pricey; *Club Social Arabe*, Arauco 255, spacious glass-domed premises, limited selection of Arab dishes, good but not cheap; *El Quijote*, Arauco 294, intimate atmosphere, good seafood, inexpensive; *Alamar*, Santiago 259, excellent seafood, good value. Good value *almuerzos* at *Casino La Bomba*, Aguirre 364, run by fire brigade. For drinks and snacks try *Café Caribe Express*, V MacKenna 241; *Yum Yum*, V MacKenna 21, good, cheap, lively; *D'Oscar Bar*, Plaza de Armas; *Pastelería Josti*, Libertad 427. *Club Comercial*, Aguirre 244 (on plaza), open Sun.

● Tourist offices
Two kiosks on the Plaza de Armas. **Automóvil Club de Chile**, Libertad 144, T 620011, very helpful, overnight parking.

● Transport
Buses to **Santiago**, several, 6½ hrs, US$7; to **La Serena**, 12 a day, 1¼ hrs, US$2; to **Antofagasta**, US$20.

ANDACOLLO
The good inland road between Ovalle and La Serena makes an interesting contrast to Ruta 5 (Panamericana), with a fine pass and occasional views of snow-capped Andes across cacti-covered plains and semi-desert mountain ranges. 61 km N of Ovalle a side road runs 44 km SE (last 20 km very bad) to **Andacollo** (*Pop* 10,216; *Alt* 1,050m). This old town, in an area of alluvial gold washing and manganese and copper mining, is one of the great pilgrimage sites in Chile. In the enormous **Basilica** (1893), 45m high and

with a capacity of 10,000, is the miraculous Virgen del Rosario de Andacollo. The Fiesta Grande from Dec 23 to 27 (most important day Dec 26) attracts 150,000 pilgrims. The ritual dances date from a pre-Spanish past. Colectivos run to the festival from C Benavente, near Colocolo, in La Serena, but 'purists' walk (torch and good walking shoes essential). There is also a smaller festival, the Fiesta Chica on the first Sun of October.

● Accommodation
No hotel, but some *pensiones*; during the festival private houses rent beds and some let you pay for a shower

● Transport
To **Ovalle** colectivo, US$2.40; bus, US$1.70.

COQUIMBO

(*Pop* 106,000; *Phone code* 051) 84 km N of Ovalle and on the same bay as La Serena, this is a port of considerable importance. It has one of the best harbours on the coast and major fish-processing plants. The city is strung along the N shore of a peninsula. Most of the commercial life is centred on 3 streets which run between the port and the steep hillside on which are perched many of the poorer houses. On the S shore of the peninsula lies the suburb of Guayacán, with an iron-ore loading port, a steel church designed by Eiffel and an English cemetery. Nearby is **La Herradura**, 2½ km from Coquimbo which has the best beaches.

Museums
In 1981 heavy rain uncovered 39 ancient burials of humans and llamas which had been sacrificed; they are exhibited in a small museum in the Plaza Gabriela Mistral.

Local information
● Accommodation
Generally much cheaper than in La Serena.

B *Lig*, Aldunate 1577, T 311171, comfortable, good value, nr bus terminus; **C** *Prat*, Bilbao y Aldunate, T 311845, comfortable, pleasant; **C** *Iberia*, Bandera 206, p 8, T 671-4510, rec; **D** *Punta del Este*, Videla 170, T 312768, nice rooms; **E** *Claris*, Aldunate 669, run-down, old-fashioned, rambling hotel with bar and *comedor*, live music on Fri and Sat, popular with sailors; **E** *Mi Casa*, Varela 1653, good value. Several hotels in La Herradura, inc **C** *Hotel La*

Herradura, Costanera 200, T 321320.

Camping: *Camping La Herradura*, T 312084.

● **Places to eat**

Lots of good fish restaurants inc *Sal y Pimiento del Capitán Denny*, Aldunate 769, one of the best, pleasant, old-fashioned, mainly fish, US$12-20 pp; *La Picada*, Costanera nr statue of O'Higgins, pricey; *Crucero*, Aldunate 1326; *La Barca*, Ríos y Varela, modest; and *La Bahía*, Pinto 1465, good value. Several good seafood restaurants (known as *pensiones*) at the municipal market, Melgarejo entre Bilbao y Borgoño (*El Callejón* rec). *Mai Lai Fan*, Av Ossandón 1, excellent Chinese, rec; *Tavola Calda*, Bilbao 451, good Italian, good value.

● **Post & telecommunications**

Telephones: CTC, Aldunate 1633.

● **Tour companies & travel agents**

Ingservitur, Los Lirios 300, Coquimbo, T 313821, F 312943, varied programme of tours, inc Parque Nacional Fray Jorge (see page 702), depending on demand.

● **Tourist offices**

Kiosk in Plaza de Armas (open summer only).

● **Transport**

Buses leave from the terminal at Varela y Garriga. To **La Serena**, every few mins, US$0.30. To **Guanaqueros**, US$0.80, 45 mins, and to **Tongoy**, US$1, 1 hr, with Ruta Costera, frequency varies according to day (more on Sun) and season. Colectivos US$1.40 and US$1.70 respectively.

RESORTS SOUTH OF COQUIMBO

At **Totoralillo**, 12 km south there are good beaches, ideal for swimming. **Guanaqueros**, 37 km S, is a fishing village with beaches (**D** *Hotel La Bahía*, simple). A further 13 km S is **Tongoy** (*Pop* 3,350), an old fishing port occupying the whole of a small peninsula. It is now a rapidly growing resort: to the S the Playa Grande is 14 km long; to the N the Playa Socos is 4 km in length.

● **Accommodation Tongoy: A1-B** *Hotel Yachting Club*, Costanera 20, T 391154, good; **A2** *Panorámico*, Mirador 455, T 391944, inc breakfast, all rooms with view of bay and fishing boats, excellent; **E** *Plaza*, on main square, T 391184; several basic *residenciales*.

● **Places to eat** Try the *marisquerías* nr the fishing port, excellent value. *Restaurant El Buque*, Puesto 17 on seafront, nr fishing harbour, fish and meat with superb sauces, good service, highly rec.

La Serena (*Pop* 120,000; *Phone code* 051), 12 km N of Coquimbo, 473 km N of Santiago, is the capital of IV Región (Coquimbo). Built on a hillside 2 km inland from Bahía de Coquimbo, it is an attractive city and major tourist centre.

History

La Serena was founded by Juan de Bohón, aide to Pedro de Valdivia, in 1544, destroyed by Diaguita Indians in 1546 and rebuilt by Francisco de Aguirre in 1549. The city was sacked by the English pirate Sharpe in 1680. In the colonial period the city was the main staging-post on the route N to Peru. In the 19th century the city grew prosperous from copper-mining; the present-day layout and architectural style have their origins in the 'Plan Serena' drawn up in 1948 on the orders of Gabriel González Videla, a native of the city.

Places of interest

Around the attractive Plaza de Armas are most of the official buildings, including the Post Office, the **Cathedral** (built in 1844 and featuring a carillon which plays every hour) and the **Casa González Videla**, now the Museo Histórico Regional (see below). There are 29 other churches, several of which have unusual towers. **San Francisco**, Balmaceda y de La Barra, built 1586-1627, has a barroque façade and faces a small plaza with arcades. **Santo Domingo**, half a block from the Plaza de Armas, built 1755 is fronted by a small garden (Museo de Arte Religiosa in the church).

La Recova, the new market, at Cienfuegos y Cantournet, includes a large display of handicrafts and, upstairs, several good restaurants. On the W edge of the old city is the **Parque Pedro de Valdivia**, which includes a children's zoo and the Parque Japonés, open daily 1000-2000, US$1.25.

Av Francisco de Aguirre, a pleasant boulevard lined with statues and known as the **Alameda**, runs from the centre to the coast, terminating at the **Faro Monumental**, a neo-colonial mock-castle (US$0.45 entry). A series of beaches stretch from here to Peñuelas, 6 km S, linked by the Av del Mar. Many apartment blocks, hotels,

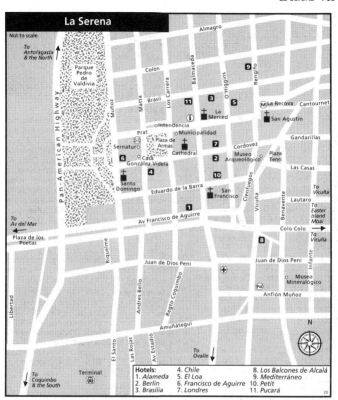

La Serena

Not to scale

To
Antofagasta
& the North

Parque
Pedro
de
Valdivia

Almagro

Colón

Pan-American Highway

Muñoz

Matta

Los Carrera

Balmaceda

O'Higgins

Regrifo

9

Brasil

11 3 5

i La
Merced

M La Recova Cantournet

San Agustín

Intendencia

Prat Municipalidad

Sernaturo Plaza de
Armas

Cathedral

Casa
González Videla

6 4

Santo
Domingo

Gandarillas

Cordovez

7

2 Museo
Arqueológico

Plaza
Tenri

Las Casas

To
Vicuña

Eduardo de la Barra

10

San
Francisco

Av Francisco de Aguirre

Cienfuegos

Vicuña

Benavente

Lautaro

To
Easter
Island
Moai

To
Av del Mar

Plaza de los
Poetas

Colo Colo

To
Vicuña

8

Libertad

Riquelme

Andres Bello

Regto Coquimbo

Juan de Dios Peni

Juan de Dios Peni

Infante

Pol

Museo
Mineralógico

Anfión Muñoz

N

Amuñátegui

El Santo

Las Rojas

Av Estadio

To
Ovalle

To
Coquimbo
& the South

Terminal

Hotels:
1. Alameda
2. Berlín
3. Brasilia
4. Chile
5. El Loa
6. Francisco de Aguirre
7. Londres
8. *Los Balcones de Alcalá*
9. *Mediterráneo*
10. *Petit*
11. *Pucará*

20

cabañas and restaurants have been built along this part of the bay.

Museums

Museo Histórico Regional in the Casa González Videla on the Plaza de Armas, including several rooms on the man's life. Open Tues-Sat 0900-1300, 1600-1900, Sun 1000-1300, US$0.60, ticket also valid for **Museo Arqueológico**, Cordóvez y Cienfuegos, outstanding collection of Diaguita and Molle Indian exhibits, especially of attractively decorated pottery; open Tues-Sat 0900-1300, 1600-1900, Sun 1000-1300, US$0.30. **Museo Mineralógico** in the University of La Serena, A Muñoz between Benavente and Infante (for geologists, open Mon-Fri 0930-1200, free).

Local information

Note that O in front of an address indicates West of the centre and E indicates East.

● Accommodation

Accommodation in the centre of town is expensive. Route 5 from La Serena to Coquimbo is lined with cheaper accommodation, from hotels to *cabañas*, and restaurants. There are no buses along Av del Mar, but it is only ½ km off Route 5. The tourist office in the bus terminal has accommodation information, helpful. Do not be pressurized into choosing rooms at the bus station; there is much more choice than touts would have you believe.

L3 *El Escorial I*, Colón 617, T 224793, F 221433, good; **L3** *Los Balcones de Alcalá*, Av de Aguirre 452, T 225999, F 211800, comfortable; **L3** *Mediterráneo*, Cienfuegos 509, Casilla 212, T 225837, inc good breakfast, rec.

A2 *Francisco de Aguirre*, Córdovez 210, T 222991, with breakfast, shower, good rooms, reasonable restaurant; **A2** *Pucará*, Balmaceda 319, T 211966, F 211933, with breakfast, modern, quiet; **A3** *Berlín*, Córdovez 535, T 222927, F 223575, safe, efficient, rec.

C *Londres*, Córdovez 550, T 214673, **D** without bath, restaurant, old fashioned; **C** *Hostal Croata* Cienfuegos 248, T/F 224997, **D** without bath, with breakfast, laundry facilities, patio, hospitable; rec; **C** *Hostal Del Mar*, Cuatro Esquinas 0680 (nr beach), T 225816, also *cabañas*.

D *Alameda*, Av de Aguirre 450, T 213052, run down, comfortable; **D** *Hostal Santo Domingo*, Bello 1067, 10 mins' walk from bus station, with breakfast, highly rec; **D** *Lido*, Matta 547, T 213073, good; **D** *Res Chile*, Matta 561, T 211694, basic, small rooms, hot water am only; **D** *El Cobre*, Colón y Matta, large rooms, spotless, highly rec; **D** Edith González, Los Carrera 885, T 221941, cooking and laudry facilities, central, rec, also owns **D** Pení 321; **D** *Res El Loa*, O'Higgins 362, with shower, good inexpensive home cooking, friendly; **D** *Res Petit*, de la Barra 586, T 212536, hot water; **D** *Turismo 2000*, Lautaro 960, T 215793, bargain; **D** Lautaro 880, rec; **D** *Gabriela Matos*, Cienfuegos 230 p 2, T 214588, in beautiful old building, use of kitchen, helpful, rec; **D** *Casa del Turista*, Colón 318, back rooms better, laundry facilities, helpful.

E pp *Gregoria Fernández*, Andrés Bello 979A, T 224400, highly rec, good beds, 3 blocks from terminal, excellent breakfast; **E** *Rosa Canto*, Cantournet 976, T 213954, hot water, kitchen, comfortable, family run, rec; **E** pp Las Rojas 21, T 215838, nr terminal, use of kitchen; also *María's Casa*, No 18, highly rec; **E** pp *Alejandro Muñoz*, Brasil 720, T 211619, with breakfast and toilet, good showers, nice garden, central, English and French spoken, helpful, rec; **E** pp *Ana Jofre*, Rgto Coquimbo 964 (entre Pení y Amunátegui), T 222335, kitchen facilities, nr terminal, rec; **E-F** *Res Americana*, Bello 859 nr terminal, basic, cold water.

F pp unnamed *Residencial* at Av de Aguirre 411, in dormitories.

Youth Hostel: E pp *Res Limmat*, Lautaro 914, T/F 211373, with breakfast, central, patio, tours offered, English and German spoken, IYHA reduction, rec.

Motels: A1 *Canto del Agua*, Av del Mar 5700, T 242203, F 241767, very good, pleasant cabins; **A3** *Les Mouettes*, Av del Mar 2500, T 225665, F 226278, good restaurant, inc breakfast, rec; **B** *Cabañas Los Papayos*, Huerto 66, 2 km S of city (Vista Hermosa bus), much cheaper out of season, 2 bedroom cabins, rec, pool, gardens; **B** *La Fuente*, Av del Mar 5665, T 245755, F 541259, appartments, cable TV,

parking, very good; several more motels along the beach.

Camping: *Camping Peñuelas*, Los Pescadores 795, T 313818. *Maki Payi*, 153 Vegas Norte, T 213628, about 5 km N of La Serena, nr sea, rec, self-contained cabins available. *Hipocampo*, 4 km S on Av del Mar (take bus for Coquimbo and get off at Colegio Adventista, US$2.50 pp by Playa El Pescador), T 214276.

● **Places to eat**

El Granero, Colón 360, excellent steaks, reasonably priced; *Club Social*, Córdovez 516, p 1, unpretentious but excellent value; *El Rincón Colonial*, Córdovez 578, good fish; *Hotel La Serena*, Córdovez 610, good meat. *Ciro's*, Av de Aguirre 431, T 213482, old-fashioned, good lunch, rec; *El Cedro*, Prat 572, Arab cuisine, expensive; *Mesón Matías*, Balmaceda 1940, excellent Spanish, elegant, expensive but highly rec; *La Mía Pizza*, O'Higgins 460, Italian, good value, inexpensive (branch on Av del Mar in summer); *Pastissima Limitado*, O'Higgins 633, Italian, very good; *Mai Lai Fan*, Córdovez 740, good Chinese, reasonably priced; *Salón Las Tejas*, Av de Aguirre 395, cheap, local dishes; *Chopería Don Antonio*, Vicente Zorrilla 837-9, 20m from *La Recova* market, good value.

Several good cafés: *Tito's*, O'Higgins y Córdovez, popular meeting place; *Café do Brasil*, Balmaceda 461, good coffee; *Casa Miró*, Balmaceda 265, good for coffee and late evening drinks; *Café La Crêperie*, O'Higgins y de la Barra, crêpes, light meals, occasional live music; *Bocaccio*, Prat y Balmaceda, good cakes, modern, smart, popular; *Café del Patio*, Prat 470, sandwiches, cakes and coffee, English spoken, rec.

● **Airline offices**

LanChile, T 225981; **Ladeco**, Córdovez 484, T 225753; **National**, Eduardo de la Barra 435, T 214460, F 232808; **Alta**, Los Carrera 515, T 212832, F 215671.

● **Banks & money changers**

Fincard (Mastercard), Balmaceda 383, Local 217, Mon-Fri 0900-1400, 1600-2030. Banco Concepción, O'Higgins 529, Visa. **Casas de Cambio: La Reconquista**, in a *galería* on Córdovez between Balmaceda and O'Higgins, excellent rates; US$100 **Money Exchange**, Prat 645, Mon-Fri 0900-1400, 1600-2100, Sat 0900-1400; **Viajes Val**, Prat 540 (open Sat 1100-1400); **Serena Cambios** at bus terminal and airport, open 1100-2300 daily; **Cambio Colonial**, Caracol Colonial, Balmaceda 460, good rates, changes TCs (another *cambio* in the basement, building closed 1400-1600). If heading N note that La Serena is the last place to change TCs before Antofagasta.

● **Laundry**

Ro-Ma, Los Carrera 654, open 0900-1300,

1600-2000; another at Balmaceda y Brasil.

● **Post & telecommunications**
Telecommunications: long distance calls from Cordóvez 446 and La Recova market. Entel, Prat 571. CTC administration on Plaza de Armas sells *Turistel*. **Cyber café**: Matta 611.

● **Shopping**
La Recova handicraft market, though many items imported from Peru and Bolivia; *Cema-Chile*, Los Carrera 562; *Las Brisas* supermarket, Cienfuegos y Cordóvez, food not as cheap as in *La Recova*.

● **Tour companies & travel agents**
Gira Tour, Prat 689, T 223535; *Turismo Elquitur*, Los Carrera 594, T 227875. See also *Ingservitur* under Coquimbo, above.

● **Tourist offices**
Main **Sernatur** office in Edificio de Servicios Públicos (next to the Post Office on the Plaza de Armas), T 225138, open Mon-Fri 0900-1300, 1500-1700 (0830-1800 in summer). Kiosks at bus terminal (summer only) and at Balmaceda y Prat (open in theory Mon-Sat 1100-1400, 1600-1900), helpful. **Automóvil Club de Chile**: Eduardo de la Barra 435, T 225279.

● **Transport**
Local Bicycle repairs: *Green Go Club*, Panamericana Norte y Av de Aguirre, T 224454, North American run, good parts, information on local cycle routes. **Buses:** City buses US$0.25. **Car hire:** Hertz, Av de Aguirre 0225, T 225471/226171; Budget, Av de Aguirre 0240; Daire, Prat 645, T 226149, rec, good service; Oceanic, Av de Aguirre 062, T 214007, good value; Dollar, O'Higgins 672, T 225714, good value; Oceanic, Av de Aguirre 0240, good service. **Taxis:** US$0.75 + US$0.10/every 200m.

Air Aeropuerto Gabriela Mistral, 5 km E of the city. Ladeco flies to **San Juan**, Argentina, in summer only. To **Santiago** and **Copiapó**, Lan Chile, Ladeco, National and Alta.

Buses Bus terminal, El Santo y Amunátegui (about 8 blocks S of the centre). Buses daily to **Santiago**, several companies, 7-8 hrs, US$17-24; to **Arica**, US$30; to **Calama**, US$29, 16 hrs. To **Valparaíso**, 7 hrs, US$10; to **Caldera**, 7 hrs, US$10; to **Antofagasta**, 11 hrs, several companies, US$20 (Flota Barrios *cama* US$38), and to **Iquique**, 17 hrs, US$25; to **Vicuña**, Frontera Elqui, Av Perú y Esmeralda, frequent service, 1 hr, US$2; *colectivo* to Vicuña, Empresa Nevada del Sol de Elqui, Domeyko 550, T 21450, others from Av Aguirre y Balmaceda, US$2.50; to **Pisco Elqui**, Vía Elqui, 4 a day from terminal, US$3, but other services run along Av Amunátegui outside terminal; to **Coquimbo**, bus No 8 from Av Aguirre y Cienfuegos, US$0.30, every few minutes.

OBSERVATORIES

The La Serena area is one of the astronomical centres of the world, with three observatories:

El Tololo at 2,200m, 89 km SE of La Serena in the Elqui Valley, 51 km S of Vicuña, belongs to Aura, an association of US and Chilean universities. It possesses the largest telescope in the southern hemisphere, seven others and a radio telescope. It is open to visitors by permit only every Sat 0900-1200, 1300-1600; for permits (free) write to Casilla 603, La Serena, T 051-225-415, then pick your permit up before 1200 on the day before (the office is at Colina Los Pinos, on a hill behind the new University – personal applications can be made here for all three observatories). During holiday periods apply well in advance; at other times it is worth trying for a cancellation the day before. They will insist that you have private transport; you can hire a taxi, US$33, but you will require the registration number when you book.

La Silla at 2,240m, 150 km NE of La Serena, belongs to ESO (European Southern Observatory), financed by 8 EU countries, and comprises 14 telescopes. Open first Sat of the month, 1430-1730; registration in advance in Santiago essential (Alonso de Córdoba 3107, Santiago, T 228-5006/698-8757) or write to Casilla 567, La Serena, T 224-527. From La Serena it is 114 km N along Route 5 to the turn-off (**D** *Posada La Frontera*, cabañas), then another 36 km.

Las Campanas at 2,510m, 156 km NE of La Serena, 30 km N of La Silla, belongs to the Carnegie Institute, has 4 telescopes and is altogether a smaller facility than the other two. It is open without permission every Sat 1430-1730, T 224680/211254, or write to Casilla 601, La Serena. Follow Route 5 to the same junction as for La Silla, take the turning for La Silla and then turn N after 14 km. La Silla and Las Campanas can be reached without private transport by taking any bus towards Vallenar (2 hrs, US$3.25) getting out at the junction (*desvío*) and hitch from there.

● **Tours** Travel agents in La Serena and Coquimbo inc Ingservitur and Gira Tour, receive tickets from the observatories and arrange tours (to Tololo US$22 pp), though you may need to reserve several days in advance in holiday periods. Taxi-drivers will also do these trips: eg Cecilia Cruz, T 222529 (mobile 09-551-0579), rec, US$63 to La Silla.

THE ELQUI VALLEY

The valley of the Río Elqui is one of the most attractive oases in this part of northern Chile. There are mines, orchards, orange groves and vineyards. The road up the valley is paved as far as Varillar, 24 km beyond Vicuña, the capital of the valley. Except for Vicuña, most of the tiny towns have but a single street. The Elqui Valley is the centre of *pisco* production: of the nine distilleries in the valley, the largest is Capel in Vicuña. Huancara, a delicious liqueur introduced by the Jesuits, is also produced in the valley.

VICUÑA

(*Pop* 7,716; *Alt* 610m; *Phone code* 051) 66 km E of La Serena, this small, clean, friendly, picturesque town was founded in 1821. On the W side of the plaza are the municipal chambers, built in 1826 and topped in 1905 by a medieval-German-style tower – the Torre Bauer – imported by the German-born mayor of the time. Also on the plaza is the Iglesia Parroquial, dating from 1860. Tourist office on Plaza de Armas. There are good views from Cerro La Virgen, N of town. The Capel Pisco distillery is 1½ km E of Vicuña, to the right of the main road; guided tours (in Spanish) are offered Dec-Feb, Mon-Sat 0930-1200, 1430-1800, Sun 1000-1230; Mar-Nov, Mon-Fri 0930-1200, 1430-1800, Sat 1000-1230, free; no booking required.

Museums Museo Gabriela Mistral, C Gabriela Mistral y Riquelme (open Tues-Sat 0900-1300, 1500-1900, Sun 1000-1300, entry US$0.40); next door is the house where the poet was born.

● **Accommodation L3** *Hostería Vicuña*, Sgto Aldea 101, T 411301, F 411144, swimming pool, tennis court, excellent restaurant; **A2** *Yunkai*, O'Higgins 72, T 411195, F 411593, cabañas for 4/6 persons, pool, restaurant. On Gabriela Mistral: **C** *Valle Hermoso*, No 706, T 411206, comfort-

able, parking, rec; **D** *Sol del Valle*, No 743, vineyard, restaurant; **E** *Hostal Michel*, No 573, large gardens; **E** *Res Moderna*, No 718, full board available, no hot water, nothing modern about it, but quiet, very nice; **E** pp *Res Mistral*, No 180, restaurant, basic, hot water. **Camping**: *Camping y Piscina Las Tinajas*, E end of Chacabuco, swimming pool, restaurant.

● **Places to eat** Mainly on G Mistral: *Club Social de Elqui*, No 435, very good, attractive patio, good value *almuerzo*; *Mistral*, No 180, very good, popular with locals, good value *almuerzo*; *Halley*, at No 404, good meat dishes, also *chopería*, swimming pool (US$5 pp); *Yo Y Soledad*, No 364, inexpensive, good value.

● **Transport** Buses to **La Serena**, about 10 a day, most by Frontera Elqui, first 0800, last 1930, 1 hr, US$2, *colectivo* from Plaza de Armas US$2.50; to **Santiago** via La Serena, Expreso Norte at 1145 and 2200; to **Pisco Elqui**, 4 a day, Vía Elqui and Frontera Elqui, 1 hr, US$2.

From Vicuña the road continues up the valley another 18 km to Rivadavia where it divides: the main route (Route 41) winding through the mountains to the Argentine frontier at Agua Negra (see below). At Juntas there is a turning to Baños del Toro and the Mina el Indio. The other branch of the road runs through Paihuano (camping) to Monte Grande, where the schoolhouse where Gabriela Mistral lived and was educated by her sister is now a museum. The poet's tomb is situated 1 km out of town. (Buses from the plaza in Vicuña.) Here the road forks, one branch leading to El Colorado. Along this road are several Ashram places. The other branch leads to **Pisco Elqui**, an attractive town with a shady plaza. Here there are 2 *pisco* plants with another outside town.

● **Accommodation C** *Carillón*, pool, also cabanas (B); **E** pp *Hosteria de Don Juan*, with breakfast, fine views, noisy; **E** *El Elqui*, hot shower, good restaurant, rec, not always open; *Las Vegas* campsite, **F** pp *Sol de Barbosa*, also camping; **G** pp *Camping El Olivo*, small restaurant, pool, excellent facilities. Well-stocked supermarket one block from the plaza.

● **Useful information** CODEFF, the environmental organization, has an office on the outskirts of town.

● **Transport** Buses to La Serena, US$3, via Vicuña.

FRONTIER WITH ARGENTINA: PASO AGUA NEGRA

Paso Agua Negra (4,775m) is reached by unpaved road from Rivadavia, 18 km E of Vicuña.

● Immigration

Chilean immigration and customs at Juntas, 84 km W of the frontier, 88 km E of Vicuña. Open 0800-1700; US$2/vehicle, 1700-2200, Jan-April only.

● Accommodation

Basic accommodation at Huanta (Guanta on many maps) Km 46 from Vicuña,G, clean,ask for Guillermo Aliaga. Huanta is the last chance to buy food.

● Transport

No public transport. El Indio mine transport may give lifts to Juntas.

North of La Serena

THE northern desert begins beyond the mining and agro-industrial centre of Copiapó.

North of the Río Elqui, the transitional zone continues to Copiapó. Thereafter begins the desert, which is of little interest, except after rain. Then it is covered with a succession of flowers, insects and frogs, in one of the world's most spectacular wildlife events. Rain, however, is rare: there is no rain in summer; in winter it is light and lasts only a short time. Annual precipitation at Copiapó is about 115 mm. Drivers must beware of high winds and blowing sand N of Copiapó.

The Huasco valley is an oasis of olive groves and vineyards. It is rugged and spectacular, dividing at Alto del Carmen, 30 km E of Vallenar, into the *Carmen* and *Tránsito* valleys. There are *pisco* distilleries at Alto del Carmen and San Félix. A sweet wine known as Pajarete is also produced.

VALLENAR

(*Pop* 42,725; *Alt* 380; *Phone code* 051; airport) the chief town of the Huasco valley, is 194 km N of La Serena. The **Museo del Huasco**, Sgto Aldea y Alonso de Ercilla, contains historic photos and artefacts from the valley (Tues-Fri 1030-1230, 1530-1900; Sat-Sun 1000-1230). At the mouth of the river, 56 km W, is the pleasant port of **Huasco** (cheap seafood restaurants near the harbour).

Excursions

To **Freirina**, 36 km W of Vallenar, easily reached by colectivo. Founded 1752, Freirina was the most important town in the valley, its prosperity based upon the nearby Capote goldmine and on later discoveries of copper. On the main plaza are the Municipalidad (1870) and the Santa Rosa church. No accommodation.

To the **Humbolt Penguin Natural Reserve** on Isla Chañaral, where, besides penguins, there are seals, sea lions, a great variety of seabirds and, offshore, a colony of grey dolphin. Turn off the Pan-American Highway at Domeyko, 51 km S where an unpaved road turns W for Caleta Chañaral. Permission to visit must be sought from Conaf in Caleta Choros.

Local information
● Accommodation
L3 *Hostería Vallenar*, Ercilla 848, T 614538, excellent, pool, Hertz car hire office, restaurant reputed to be among the best in Chile; **B** *Cecil*, Prat 1059, T 614071, rec; **B** *Real*, Prat 881, T 613963, parking; **C** *Vall*, Aconcagua 455, T 611226, parking, rec; **D** *Res La Oriental*, Serrano 720, T 613889, parking, rec; **D** *Viña del Mar*, Serrano 611, T 611478, comedor. Several residenciales.

● Places to eat
Bavaria, Santiago 678, good, not cheap; *El Fogón*, Ramírez 944, for meat dishes, almuerzo good value; *Shanghai*, Ramírez 1267, Chinese; cheap places along S end of Av Brasil.

COPIAPO

The valley of the Río Copiapó, generally regarded as the southern limit of the Atacama desert, is an oasis of farms, vineyards and orchards about 150 km long.

Copiapó (*Pop* 100,000; *Alt* 400m; *Phone code* 052), capital of III Región (Atacama), 144 km N of Vallenar, 60 km inland, is an important mining centre. Founded in 1744, Copiapó became a prosperous town after the discovery in 1832 of the third largest silver deposits in South America at Chañarcillo (the mine was closed in 1875). The discoverer, Juan Godoy, a mule-driver, is commemorated at Matta y O'Higgins. The wealth from Chañarcillo helped finance the first railway line in South America, linking Copiapó to Caldera (1851).

Places of interest

The **Cathedral**, on Plaza Prat, dates from 1851. **San Francisco**, 5 blocks W of the Plaza, built in 1872 (the nearby convent is from 1662) is a good example of a 19th century construction using Oregon Pine and Guayaquil cane. **Belén**, Infante nr Yerbas Buenas, a colonial Jesuit church, was remodelled in 1856. The **Santuario de la Candelaria**, 3 km SE of the centre, is the site of two churches, the older built in 1800, the other in 1922; inside the latter is the Virgen de la Candelaria, discovered in the Salar de Maricunga in 1788. The wealth of the 19th century mining families is reflected in the **Villa Viña de Cristo**, built in Italian renaissance style, $1\frac{1}{2}$ km N of the centre on Freire.

Museums

Museo Mineralógico, Colipí y Rodríguez, 1 block E from Plaza de Armas; Mon-Fri 1000-1300, 1500-1900, Sat 1000-1300, US$0.50, the best in Chile. Many ores shown are found only in the Atacama desert. **Museo Regional del Atacama**, Atacama y Rancagua, entrance US$0.75 (free on Sun), interesting. Open Mon-Sat 0900-1245, 1500-1830, Sun 1000-1245. The museum at the **railway station** is dull, but the Norris Brothers steam locomotive and carriages used in the inaugural journey between Copiapó and Caldera in 1851 can be seen at the Universidad de Atacama about 2 km N of the centre on C Freire.

Excursions

To the **Centro Metalúrgico Incaico**, a largely reconstructed Inca bronze foundry, 90 km SE up the Copiapó valley by paved road. By public transport: take Casther bus, 0845, to Valle del Cerro, US$1.50, 2 hrs and get off at Valle Hermoso (foundry is 1 km walk from main road). Return buses pass about 1400 and 1600.

Local festivals
Fiesta de la Candelaria, first Sun in Feb.

Local information
● Accommodation
A2 *Hostería Las Pircas*, Av Kennedy s/n, T 213220, bungalows, pool, dining room, out of town; **A2** *San Francisco de la Selva* Los Carrera 525, T 217013, modern.

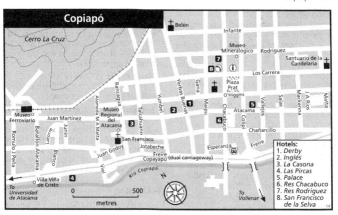

Copiapó

Hotels:
1. Derby
2. Inglés
3. La Casona
4. Las Pircas
5. Palace
6. Res Chacabuco
7. Res Rodriguez
8. San Francisco de la Selva

C *Derby*, Yerbas Buenas, 396, T 212447; **C** *Inglés*, Atacama 337, T 212797, old-fashioned, spacious; **C** *Palace*, Atacama 741, T 212852, patio, pleasant, parking; **C** *La Casona*, O'Higgins 150, T 217277/8, tours organized; **C** *Marcoan*, Yumbel 351, T 211397, modern.

E pp *Res Chacabuco*, C Chacabuco 271, T 213428, nr terminal, quiet; **E** *Res Nuevo Chañarcillo*, Rodríguez 540, T 212368, without bath, comfortable, rec; **E** *Res Rodríguez*, Rodríguez 528, T 212861, basic, good *comedor*, rec; **E** *Res Rocío*, Yerbas Buenas 581, T 215360, good value, attractive patio, rec.

● **Places to eat**
La Carreta, on Carretera de Copayapu, 5 km S, ranch-style, very good meat and fish; *Bavaria*, on main plaza, good but not cheap. *Chifa Hao Hua*, Colipi 340, good Chinese; *Pampas*, Maipú y Atacama, smart, pleasant.

● **Banks & money changers**
Fincard (Mastercard), Chacabuco 389, Mon-Fri 0900-1400, 1630-1930, Sat 1030-1300. Banco Concepción, cash advance on Visa.

● **Post & telecommunications**
Telephones: CTC, Atacama 566.

● **Tour companies & travel agents**
Exploration and Adventure Tour, Rodríguez 771, T 212459, organizes a wide range of excursions.

● **Tourist offices**
Los Carrera 691, N side of Plaza de Armas, T 212838, helpful.

● **Transport**
Local Car hire: Hertz at Copayapu 173, T 211333. **Cycle repairs**: *Biman*, Atacama

360B, T/F 217391, excellent.

Air LanChile, O'Higgins 640, T 213512, daily to/from Santiago, also to El Salvador; National (Colipi 350, T 218951) direct to La Serena and on to Santiago.

Buses Terminal 3 blocks from centre on Freire y Chacabuco. To **Santiago** US$15, 12 hrs; to **La Serena** US$7, 5 hrs; to **Caldera**, US$2, 1 hr.

FRONTIER WITH ARGENTINA: PASO SAN FRANCISCO

Paso San Francisco is reached either by unpaved road NE from Copiapó,via the Salar de Maricunga and Laguna Verde or by an unpaved road SE from El Salvador: the two roads join near the Salar de Maricunga, 96 km W of Paso San Francisco. Officially open all year, this crossing is liable to closure in winter. On the Argentine side a poor road continues to Tinogasta (suitable only for 4WD vehicles).

● **Chilean immigration and customs**
Near the Salar de Maricunga, 100 km W of the frontier, open 0830-1830; US$2/vehicle charge for crossing Sat, Sun and holidays.

Ojos del Salado

Ojos del Salado, believed to be the third highest peak in the Americas, is situated S of the pass; its height is now thought to be 6,864m (although the latest Chilean IGM map says 6,879m – 1994; it seems to depend which side of the border you are on).

● **Climbing** Ojos del Salado is best climbed between Jan and March. Access is by a road turning off the main Chile-Argentina road at *Hostería Murray* (burned down). Base camp for the climb is at the Argentine frontier post (4,500m). There are 2 refugios: *Atacama* (4-6 beds) at 5,200m and *Tejos* (better, 12 beds) at 5,700m. From the latter it is 10-12 hrs' climb to the summit, approx grade 3. The climb is not very difficult, except the last 50m, which is moderate climbing on rock to the crater rim and summit. Water is available at *Hostería Murray* but it may be advisable to carry it from Copiapó. Large quantities must be taken on the ascent. Guides and equipment can be hired in Copiapó: try Rubén E Rubilan Cortés, O'Higgins 330, T 216535 and others (US$450-600). Permits are required: obtainable free from the Dirección de Fronteras y Límites, Ministerio de Relaciones Exteriores, p 5, Bandera 52, Santiago, T 671-4210, F 697-1909 (or from the Municipalidad in Copiapó, which will fax Santiago).

NORTH FROM COPIAPO

There are two alternative routes N: W to Caldera and then N along the coast to Chañaral, 167 km; the inland route via Diego de Almagro and then W to meet the Pan-American Highway near Chañaral, 212 km.

CALDERA

(*Pop* 12,000; *Phone code* 052), 73 km W of Copiapó, is a port and terminal for the loading of iron ore. **Iglesia de San Vicente** (1862) on the Plaza de Armas was built by English carpenters working for the railway company.

Bahía Inglesa, 6 km S of Caldera, 6 km W of the Highway, is popular with Chileans for its beautiful white sandy beaches and unpolluted sea (very expensive and can get crowded Jan-Feb and at weekends). It was originally known as Puerto del Inglés after the visit in 1687 of the English 'corsario', Edward Davis.

● **Accommodation In Caldera**: **B** *Hostería Puerta del Sol*, Wheelwright 750, T 315205, inc tax, cabins with kitchen, view over bay; **C** *Costanera*, Wheelwright 543, T 316007, takes credit cards, simple rooms; **A3** *Portal del Inca*, Carvallo 945, T 315252, cabins with kitchen, English spoken, restaurant not bad, order breakfast on previous night; **D** *Res Fenicia*, Gallo 370, T 315594, eccentric owner, rec. **In Bahía Inglesa**: cheaper to stay in Caldera in summer. **B** *Los Jardines de Bahía Inglesa*, Av Copiapó, *cabañas*, T 315359, open all year,

good beds, comfortable; *Camping Bahía Inglesa*, Playa Las Machas, T 315424, **B**/tent site, fully equipped *cabañas* for up to 5 persons, **A3**. *El Coral* restaurant has some cabins **C**, T 315331, Av El Morro, overlooking sea, good seafood, groups welcome, open all year.

● **Places to eat In Caldera**: *Miramar*, Gana 090, at pier, good seafood. *El Pirón de Oro*, Cousiño 218, good but not cheap.

● **Transport** Buses to Copiapó and Santiago, several daily; to Antofagasta, US$18, 7 hrs; to travel N, it may be better to take a bus to Chañaral (Inca-bus US$2), then change. Hourly buses between Bahía Inglesa and Caldera; taxis and colectivos US$1, all year; frequent micro service Jan-Feb US$0.25.

CHAÑARAL

The valley of the Río Salado, 130 km in length, less fertile or prosperous than the Copiapó or Huasco valleys, is the last oasis S of Antofagasta.

Chañaral (*Pop* 12,000, *Phone Code* 052), a neglected looking town with wooden houses perched on the hillside at the mouth of the Salado, is 93 km N of Caldera and 968 km N of Santiago. In its heyday it was the processing centre for ore from the nearby copper mines of El Salado and Las Animas, but it is now a base for visits to beaches and the Parque Nacional Pan de Azúcar.

● **Accommodation B** *Hostería Chañaral*, Miller 268, T 480055, excellent restaurant; **C** *Mini*, San Martín 528, T 480079, good value restaurant; **D** *Nuria*, Costanera 302, good; **D** *Jiménez*, Merino Jarpa 551, without bath, patio with lots of birds, rec, restaurant good value; **E** *La Marina*, Merino Jarpa 562, basic.

● **Places to eat In** hotels; *Rincón Porteño*, Merino Jarpa 567, good and inexpensive. *San Remo*, Torreblanca, good seafood; *Restaurante de los Pescadores*, in La Caleta, good fish, cheap, rec.

● **Tourist offices** Kiosk on the Pan-American Highway at S end of town (closed, winter). If closed, go to Municipalidad.

● **Transport** Bus terminal Merino Jarpa 854. Frequent services to Antofagasta US$11, 5 hrs, and Santiago.

PARQUE NACIONAL PAN DE AZUCAR

The park, N of Chañaral, consists of the Isla Pan de Azúcar on which Humboldt penguins and other sea-birds live, and some 43,700 ha of coastal hills rising to 900m. There are fine beaches (popular at weekends in summer). Fishermen near the Conaf office offer boat trips round Isla Pan de Azúcar to see the penguins, US$25, though these are sometimes visible from the mainland. **NB** There are heavy fines for driving in 'restricted areas' of the park.

Wildlife Vegetation is mainly cacti, of which there are 26 species, nourished by frequent sea mists (*camanchaca*). After rain in some of the gullies there are tall purple lilies. The park is home to 103 species of birds as well as guanaco and foxes.

● **Park information** Two entrances: N by good secondary road from Chañaral, 28 km to Caleta Pan de Azúcar; from the Pan-American Highway 45 km N of Cañaral, along a side road 20 km (road in parts deep sand and very rough, 4WD essential). Bus from Chañaral library 0730-0800, return 1800, US$2.50, but check if it's running; taxi US$20, or hitch a lift from fishermen at sunrise.

● **Conaf** office in Caleta Pan de Azúcar, maps available; park entry US$6, camping, US$10, no showers, take all food.

EL SALVADOR

(*Pop* 10,437; *Alt* 2,300) is a modern town, built near one of the biggest copper mines in Chile, 129 km E of Chañaral in the valley of the Río Salado, reached by a road which branches off the Pan-American Highway 12 km E of Chañaral. Further E by unpaved road is the **Salar de Pedernales**, 30,000 ha of saltflats at an altitude of 3,350m.

● **Accommodation** *Hostería El Salvador*, Potrerillos 003, T 472492; *Camino del Inca*, El Tofo 333, T 472311; *Res Linari*, Potrerillos 705.

● **Transport Air** Lan Chile from Santiago and Copiapó (T 052-121-2590). **Buses** Pullman Bus daily to Santiago.

TALTAL

(*Pop* 9,000; *Phone code* 055) 146 km N of Chañaral, this is the only town between Chañaral and Antofagasta, a distance of 420 km. Along Av Prat are several wooden buildings dating from the late 19th century when Taltal prospered as a mineral port of 20,000 people. It is now a fishing port with a mineral processing plant. **Museo Arqueológico**, on Av Prat. 72 km N is the Quebrada El Médano, a gorge with ancient rock-paintings along the upper valley walls.

● **Accommodation C** *Hostería Taltal*, Esmeralda 671, T 101, excellent restaurant, good value *almuerzo*; **C** *Verdy*, Ramírez 345, T 105, **E** without bath, spacious, restaurant, rec; **E** *San Martín*, Martínez 279, T 88, without bath, good *almuerzo*; **E** *Viña del Mar*, Serrano 762.

● **Places to eat** *Caverna*, Martínez 247, good seafood; *Club Social Taltal*, Torreblanca 162, excellent, good value.

● **Transport** Buses to Santiago 2 a day; to Antofagasta Tramaca, TurBus and Ramos, US$5.

77 km E of Taltal, and some 175 km S of Antofagasta, is Agua Verde, a fuel station and fruit inspection post.

Antofagasta, Calama and San Pedro

ANTOFAGASTA and Calama are export and service centres respectively for the copper industry in the area. Calama is also the starting point for one of the rail journeys to Bolivia. Around San Pedro de Atacama (which has remains of Atacameño culture) are superb Andean landscapes; San Pedro itself is growing increasingly as a tourist centre.

The next two sections deal with the 1,255 km between Copiapó and Arica, a desert without vegetation, with little or no rain. The inhospitable shore is a pink cliff face rising to a height of from 600 to 900m. At the bottom of the cliff are built the towns, some of considerable size. The far from pacific Pacific often makes it difficult to load and unload ships. The nitrate fields exploited in this area lie in the depression between Taltal and Pisagua. Major copper deposits are mined in the Cordillera.

Life in the area is artificial. Water has to be piped for hundreds of kilometres to the cities and the nitrate fields from the Cordillera; all food and even all building materials have to be brought in from elsewhere.

There is some difference of climate between the coast and the interior. The coast is humid and cloudy; in the interior the skies are clear. The temperatures on the coast are fairly uniform; in the interior there is often a great difference in the temperature between day and night; the winter nights are often as cold as -10°C, with a cruel wind.

ANTOFAGASTA

(*Pop* 185,000; *Phone code* 055) 1,367 km N of Santiago and 699 km S of Arica, **Antofagasta** is the largest city in Northern Chile. It is the capital of the Second Region and is a major port for the export of copper from Chuquicamata. It is also a major commercial centre and home of two universities. The climate is delightful (apart from the lack of rain); the temperature varies from 16°C in June/July to 24°C Jan/Feb, never falling below 10°C at night.

Places of interest

In the main square, **Plaza Colón**, is a clock tower donated by the British community. **Paseo Prat**, which runs SE from Plaza Colón, is the main shopping street. Two blocks N of Plaza Colón, near the old port, is the **Ex-Aduana**, built as the Bolivian customs house in Mejillones and moved to its current site after the War of the Pacific. Opposite are the former **Capitanía del Puerto** (now occupied by the Fundación Andrés Sabella, which offers occasional workshops on weaving, painting, etc) and the **ex-Resguardo Marítimo** (now housing Digader, the regional coordinating centre for sport and recreation). East of the port are the buildings of the **Antofagasta and Bolivia Railway Company** (FCAB) dating from the 1890s and beautifully restored, but still in use and difficult to visit. The former main square of the **Oficina Vergara**, a nitrate town built in 1919 and dismantled in 1978, can be seen in the campus of the University of Antofagasta, 4 km S of the centre (bus 3 or 4). Also to the S on a hill (and reached by Bus B) are the ruins of **Huanchaca**, a Bolivian silver refinery built after 1868 and closed in 1903.

Museums

Museo Histórico Regional, in the former Aduana, Balmaceda y Bolívar, Tues-Sat 1000-1300, 1530-1830, Sun 1100-1400, US$0.80, children half-price, fascinating new displays (many in Spanish only) on life on land and in the oceans, development of civilization in South America, minerals, human artefacts, rec.

Museo Geológico of the Universidad Católica del Norte, Av Angamos 0610, inside the university campus, open Mon-Fri, 0830-1230, 1500-1800, free (colectivo 3 or 33 from town centre).

Excursions

The fantastic cliff formations and symbol of the Second Region at **La Portada** are 16 km N, reached by minibuses from Latorre y Sucre (US$2 return) or any bus for Mejillones from the Terminal Centro. Taxis charge US$11. Hitching is easy. From the main road it is 2 km to the beach which, though beautiful, is too dangerous for swimming; there is an excellent seafood restaurant (*La Portada*) and café (open lunch-time only). A number of bathing beaches are also within easy reach.

Juan López, 38 km N of Antofagasta, is a windsurfers' paradise (Hotel *La Rinconada*, T 268502; *Hostería Sandokan*, T 692031). Buses at weekends in summer only, also minibuses daily in summer from Latorre y Sucre. For those with their own transport, follow the road out of Juan López to the beautiful cove at Conchilla. Keep on the track to the end at Bolsico. The sea is alive with birds, including Humboldt penguins, especially opposite Isla Santa María.

Local festivals

29 June, *San Pedro*, patron saint of the fishermen: the saint's image is taken out by launch to the breakwater to bless the first catch of the day. On the last weekend of Oct, the foreign communities put on a joint festival on the seafront, with national foods, dancing and music.

Local information

● **Accommodation**

A1 *Nadine*, Baquedano 519, T 227008, F 265222, bar, café, parking, etc; opp is **A2** *Ancla*, Baquedano 508, T 224814, F 261551, bar, restaurant, exchange; **A2** *Antofagasta*, Balmaceda 2575, T/F 268259, garage, swimming pool, lovely view of port and city, run down, after breakfast (discount for Automóvil Club members), beach; **A2** *Diego de Almagro*, Condell 2624, T 268331, good for the money but a bit tatty; **A3** *Colón*, San Martín 2434, T 261851, F 260872, with breakfast, quiet.

B *Pieper*, Sucre 509, T 263603, modern, warmly rec; **B** *San Marcos*, Latorre 2946, T 251763, modern, comfortable, parking, avoid rooms at the back (loud music), overpriced; **B** *San Martín*, San Martín y Bolívar, T 263503, parking, safe; **B** *Tatio*, Grecia 1000, T 247561, modern, out of old town on the beach, has buses converted into caravans, **D**, beautiful views, acts as youth hostel, no cooking facilities.

C *Latorre*, Latorre 2450, T 221886, pleasant; **C** *San Antonio*, Condell 2235, T 268857, helpful, modern but noisy from bus station.

D *Res La Riojanita*, Baquedano 464, T 268652, basic, old-fashioned, hot water on demand, noisy; **D** *Res El Cobre*, Prat 749, T 225162, central, noisy, basic; **D** *Res O'Higgins*, Sucre 665, T 267596, big, old, dirty, no hot water; **D** *Rawaye*, Sucre 762, T 225399, without breakfast, basic, hot water am only, no towels; **D** *Res Toconao*, Bolívar 580; **E** pp *Brasil*, Bolívar 568.

Camping: to the S on the road to Coloso are: *Las Garumas*, Km 9, T 247758, US$10 for tent (bargain for lower price out of season), US$15 for cabins; cold showers and beach (reservations Av Angamos 601, casilla 606). *Rucamóvil*, Km 13, T 231913 and 7 *cabañas*, T 221988. Both open year-round, expensive. To the N are: *La Gruta*, Km 12 and *La Rinconada*, Km 30, off road to Mejillones, between La Portada and Juan López, T 261139.

● **Places to eat**

Marina Club, Av Ejército 0909, good fish and seafood dishes, expensive but worth it; *Tío Jacinto*, Uribe 922, good seafood; *El Arriero*, Condell 2644, good service, good set lunch otherwise pricey, live music; *Bavaria*, Ossa 2428, excellent meat and German specialities, not cheap; *Flamingo*, Condell y Baquedano, rec; *D'Alfredo*, Condell 2539, pizzas, good; *Chicken's House Center*, Latorre 2660, chicken, beef and daily specials, open till 2400; *Casa Vecchia*, O'Higgins 1456, good value. *Café Bahía*, Prat 452, and *Café Caribe*, Prat 482, good coffee, open 0900; *Piccolo Mondo*, Condell 2685, expresso coffee, snacks, drinks, open 0930, good; ice cream at *Fiori di Gelatto*, Baquedano 519, in *Hotel Nadine*, highly rec. Many eating places in the market; *Chico Jaime* above the market, surrealistic decor, seafood, *almuerzo* US$3, mixed reports; good reports of *El Mariscal* in same

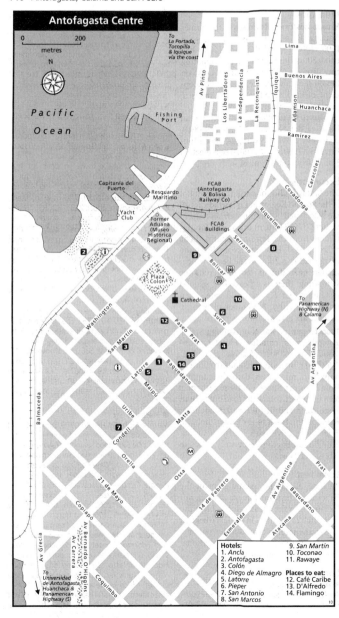

Antofagasta Centre

0 ____ 200
metres

N

Pacific
Ocean

To
La Portada,
Tocopilla
& Iquique
via the coast

Lima

Buenos Aires

Huanchaca

Ramirez

Av Pinto

Los Libertadores

La Independencia

La Reconquista

Iquique

Adamson

Caracoles

Covadonga

Fishing
Port

Capitania del
Puerto

Resguardo
Maritimo

Yacht
Club

Former
Aduana
(Museo
Histórica
Regional)

FCAB
(Antofagasta
& Bolivia
Railway Co)

FCAB
Buildings

Serrano

Riquelme

8

2

9

Bolivar

Plaza
Colón

Cathedral

10

To
Panamerican
Highway (N)
á Calama

6

Sucre

12

Paseo Prat

4

Washington

San Martin

3

Latorre

1

Baquedano

14

13

11

5

Maipú

Av Argentina

Uribe

Matta

Balmaceda

7

Condell

Orella

M

Ossa

21 de Mayo

14 de Febrero

Av Argentina

Prat

Baquedano

Esmeralda

Atacama

Copiapó

Av Grecia

Av Bernardo O'Higgins

Av Carrera

Coquimbo

To
Universidad
de Antofagasta,
Huanchaca &
Panamerican
Highway (S)

Hotels:
1. Ancla
2. Antofagasta
3. Colón
4. Diego de Almagro
5. Latorre
6. Pieper
7. San Antonio
8. San Marcos
9. San Martín
10. Toconao
11. Rawaye

Places to eat:
12. Café Caribe
13. D'Alfredo
14. Flamingo

area. Good cheap lunches at *El Rincón de Don Quijote*, Maipú 642. Good fish restaurants in *terminal de pescadores*; also at Coloso, 8 km S nr the Playa Amarrilla (take your own wine). *Chez Niko's*, Ossa 1951, restaurant, bar, bakery, *pasteleria*, good pizzas, *empanadas* and bread. *Chifa Pekín*, Ossa 2135, Chinese, smart, reasonable prices.

● **Airline offices**
LanChile, Washington 2552, T 265151; **Ladeco**, Washington 2589, T 269170, F 260440; **National**, Latorre 2572, T 224418, F 268996; **Alta**, Balmaceda 2584, T 226089, F 282202.

● **Banks & money changers**
Banco de Concepción, Plaza Colón for Visa. **Banco Edwards**, Prat 461, TCs changed at high commission. **Fincard**, Prat 431, for Mastercard. Foreign money exchange (all currencies and TCs) is best at *Hotel Ancla* (address above), open all day every day. **NB** Impossible to change TCs S of Antofagasta until you reach La Serena.

● **Embassies & consulates**
Bolivia, Grecia 563, Oficina 23, T 225010; **France and Belgium**, Baquedano 299, T 268669.

● **Entertainment**
Discotheques: *Con Tutti*, Grecia 421; *Popo's*, Universidad de Chile (far end from town); *Parador 63*, Baquedano 619, disco, bar-restaurant, live shows, good value.

Theatre: *Teatro Municipal*, Sucre y San Martín, T 264919, modern, state-of-the art; *Teatro Pedro de la Barca*, Condell 2495, run by University of Antofagasta, occasional plays, reviews.

● **Laundry**
París, Condell 2455, laundry and dry cleaning, expensive, charges per item; *Laverap*, 14 Febrero 1802.

● **Post & telecommunications**
Post Office: on Plaza Colón, 0830-1900, Sat 0900-1300.
Telephones: Entel Chile, Baquedano, 753; CTC, Condell 2529.

● **Shopping**
Galería del Arte Imagen, Uribe 485, sells antiques inc artefacts from nitrate plants.

Bookshop: *Librería Universitaria*, Latorre 2515, owner Germana Fernández knowledgeable on local history; opp is *Multilibro*.

Market: Municipal market, Matta y Uribe.

● **Sports**
Swimming: Olympic pool at Condell y 21 de Mayo, US$1.20, open till 1800, best in am.
Sauna: Riquelme y Condell.

Tennis: Club de Tenis Antofagasta, Angamos 906.

● **Tour companies & travel agents**
Many inc *Tatio Travel*, Latorre 2579, T 263532, Tx 225242 TATIO CL, English spoken, tours arranged for groups or individuals, highly rec. *Turismo Cristóbal* in *Hotel Antofagasta*, helpful. *Turismo Corssa*, San Martín 2769, T/F 251190, rec. Alex Joseph Valenzuela Thompson, Edif Bulnes, Sucre 220, p 4, Oficina 403, T 243322/F 222718, Aptdo Postal 55, offers to guide German speakers around the area.

● **Tourist offices**
Maipú 240, T 264044, Mon-Fri 0830-1300, Mon-Thur 1500-1930, Fri 1500-1930; kiosk on Balmaceda nr *Hotel Antofagasta* Mon-Fri 0930-1300, 1530-1930, Sat/Sun 0930-1300, kiosk at airport (open summer only). **Automóvil Club de Chile**: Condell 2330, T 225332.

Customs agent: Luis Piquimil Bravo, Prat 272, oficina 202, excellent, fast service, efficient.

● **Transport**
Local Car rental: Rent-a-Car, Prat 810, T 225200; **Avis**, Prat 272, T 221668; **Budget**, Prat 206, T 251745; **Hertz**, Balmaceda 2566 (T 269043), offer city cars and jeeps (group D, Toyota Landcruiser) and do a special flat rate, with unlimited mileage; **Felcar**, 14 de Febrero 2324, T 224468, English spoken.

Air Cerro Moreno Airport, 22 km N. Taxi to airport US$7, but cheaper if ordered from hotel. LanChile, Ladeco and National fly daily to Santiago, Iquique and Arica.

Trains The journey to Bolivia starts from Calama (see below) – tickets from Tramaca, Uribe 936 or in Calama.

Buses No main terminal; each company has its own office in town (some quite a distance from the centre). Buses for **Mejillones** and **Tocopilla**, operated by Barrios, Tramaca, Camus and others, depart from the Terminal Centro at Riquelme 513. Minibuses to Mejillones leave from Latorre 2730. Bus company offices: Tramaca, Uribe 936, T 223624; Flota Barrios, Condell 2764, T 268559; Géminis, Latorre 3099, T 251796; Fénix Pullman Norte, San Martín 2717; Incatur, Maipú 554; Turis Norte, Argentina 1155; Libac, Argentina 1155; Pullman Bus, Latorre 2805, T 262591; Chile-Bus (to Argentina and Brazil) and Tur-Bus, Latorre 2751. To **Santiago**, 18 hrs (Flota Barrios, US$60, *cama* inc drinks and meals); 30% reduction on Inca, Tramaca and Géminis buses for students, but ask after you have secured a seat; many companies: fares US$35-40, book 2 days in advance. If all seats to the capital are booked, catch a bus to **La Serena** (13 hrs, US$20, or US$38 *cama* service), or **Ovalle**, US$20, and re-book. To **Valparaíso**, US$35. To **Arica**, US$16 (Tur-Bus), 13½ hrs, Tramaca, US$18. To **Chuquicamata**,

US$6, frequent, 3 hrs. To **Calama**, several companies, US$5, Tramaca, 3 hrs; to **San Pedro de Atacama**, Turbus at 0800, Tramaca and Pullman direct service 1100 or go via Calama. Direct to **Copiapó** on Thur and Sat at 2230, US$10.50. Frequent buses to **Iquique**; US$13, 8 hrs.

Buses to Salta, Argentina Géminis, Wed, US$50, 22 hrs; via Calama, San Pedro and Paso Sico, immigration check at San Pedro de Atacama, then on to high Cordillera and to San Antonio de los Cobres (Argentine customs) all year round, although April-Sept dependent on weather conditions. Also Atahualpa/Tramaca joint service in summer only, Tues, Fri 0700 via Calama, San Pedro, Paso Sico and Jujuy US$50, student discount if you are persistent. Book in advance for these services, take food and as much warm clothing as possible. There is nowhere to change Chilean pesos en route. These services can be picked up in San Pedro, but book first in Calama or Antofagasta and notify bus company.

Hitchhiking If hitching to Arica or Iquique try at the beer factory a few blocks N of the fish market in Av Pinto, or the lorry park a few blocks further N. If hitching S go to the police checkpoint/restaurant/gas station La Negra, about 15 km S of the city.

MEJILLONES

(*Pop* 5,500; *Phone code* 055), 60 km N of Antofagasta, this little fishing port stands on a good natural harbour protected from westerly gales by high hills. Until 1948 it was a major terminal for the export of tin and other metals from Bolivia: remnants of that past include a number of fine wooden buildings: the Intendencia Municipal, the Casa Cultural (built in 1866) and the church (1906), as well as the Capitanía del Puerto.

● **Accommodation A2** *Costa Del Sol*, M Montt 086, T 621590, 4-star, new; **D** *Res Marcela*, Borgoño 150, pleasant; **F** *Res Elisabeth*, Latorre 440, T 621568, basic, restaurant. No campsite but wild camping possible on the beach.

● **Places to eat** *Juanito*, Las Heras 241, excellent *almuerzo*; *Sion-Ji*, Latorre 718, Chinese, good value.

North from Antofagasta There are two routes from Antofagasta N to Iquique. 1) Along the Pan-American Highway via Baquedano and Carmen Alto (Km 98), the turning to Calama. **María Elena** (*Pop* 7,700; *Alt* 1,250m) and **Pedro de Valdivia**

(*Pop* 8,600), the two nitrate mines in Chile still functioning, are situated off a turning at Km 167. The **Museo Arqueológico y Histórico**, on the main plaza in María Elena, has exhibits on prehispanic cultures.

● **Transport** Buses to Iquique 6 hrs, US$10.

2) Along the coast road from Antofagasta and Mejillones to Tocopilla, 187 km N, is paved all the way, but with no fuel N of Mejillones. The route runs at the foot of 500m cliffs, behind which are mountains which are extensively mined for copper, often by *piqineros* (small groups of self-employed miners).

Reminders of the area's mining past can be seen at several points, principally the ruins of **Cobija** (127 km N), founded in 1825 as Bolivia'a main port. A prosperous little town handling silver exports from Potosí, it was destroyed by an earthquake in 1868 and again by a tidal wave in 1877 before losing out to the rising port of Antofagasta. Adobe walls, the rubbish tip (right above the sea) and the wreckage of the port are all that remains. The atmospheric ruins of port of Gatico are at Km 144. About 5 km further N there is an amazing ransacked cemetery.

There are good, weekend beach resorts at Hornitos (88 km N of Antofagasta) and Poza Verde (117 km N).

TOCOPILLA

(*Pop* 24,600; *Phone code* 055) is 187 km N of Antofagasta via the coastal road and 365 km via the Pan-American Highway. The town is dominated by a thermal power station, which supplies electricity to the whole of northern Chile, and by the port facilities used to unload coal and to export nitrates and iodine from María Elena and Pedro de Valdivia. There is a sports stadium and two good beaches: Punta Blanca (12 km S) and Caleta Covadonga. Tocopilla Yacht Club, 45 km S, has a good beach, restaurant and bar. There is also fine deep sea fishing if you can find a boat and a guide.

● **Accommodation On 21 de Mayo:** **C** *Chungará*, No 1440, T 811036, comfortable, rec; **C** *Vucina*, No 2069, T 811571, modern,

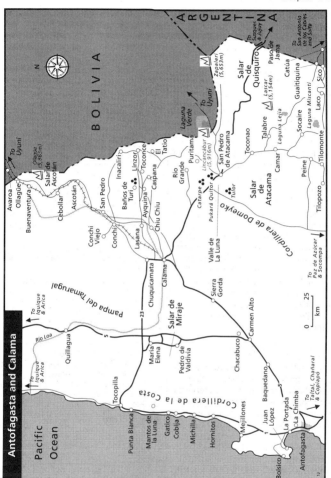

good restaurant; **C** *Casablanca*, No 2054, T 813222, F 813104, helpful; **D** *Hostería Bolívar*, Bolívar 1332, T 812783, modern, helpful, meals, highly rec; **E** *Hostal Central*, Aníbal Pinto 1241; **F** *Res La Giralda*, 21 de Mayo 1134.

● **Places to eat** *Club de la Unión*, Prat 1354, good *almuerzo*, cheap; *Kong Jong*, 21 de Mayo 1833, reasonable value, Chinese; *El Pirata*, 21 de Mayo 1999, *parrilladas*. Good seafood at the Muelle Pesquero opp the old wooden clock tower.

● **Transport** Buses to **Antofagasta** 8 a day, several companies inc Barrrios, Tramaca and Camus, US$3, 2½ hrs; to **Iquique**, by bus and minibus along coastal road, Barrios, Tramaca and Turisnorte, 4 hrs, US$7, frequent. To **Chuquicamata** and **Calama**, Camus, 2 a day, 3 hrs, US$5. No direct services to **Santiago**, go via Antofagasta or take Tramaca or Flota Barrios to Vallenar or La Serena and change. Bus company offices are on 21 de Mayo.

ROUTES East of Tocopilla a good paved

road runs up the narrow valley 72 km to the Pan-American Highway. From here the road continues E in a very bad state (requires careful driving) to Chuquicamata.

81 km N of the crossroads is **Quillagua** (customs post, all vehicles and buses are searched) and 111 km further is the first of three sections of the **Reserva Nacional del Tamarugal**. In this part are the **Geoglyphs of Pintados**, some 400 figures on the hillsides (3 km W of the highway). Beyond the Reserve are Pozo Almonte and the turn-off for Iquique. The second part of Tamarugal is near La Tirana (see page 733), the third 60 km N of Pozo Almonte.

The coastal road from Tocopilla N to Iquique, 244 km, offers fantastic views of the rugged coastline and tiny fishing communities. The customs post at Chipana-Río Loa (90 km N) searches all vehicles for duty-free goods; long delays. Basic accommodation is available at San Marcos, a fishing village, 131 km N. At Chanaballita, 184 km N there is a hotel, cabañas, camping, restaurant, shops. There are also campsites at the former salt mining town of Guanillos, Km 126, Playa Peruana, Km 129 and Playa El Aguila, Km 160.

CALAMA

(*Pop* 106,970; *Alt* 2,265m; *Phone code* 055), lies 202 km NE of Antofagasta in the oasis of the Río Loa. Initially a staging post on the silver route between Potosí and Cobija, it has grown in this century as a commercial and residential centre for nearby Chuquicamata. It is an expensive modern town.

Calama can be reached from the N by a poor road via Chuquicamata, or, from the S, by a paved road leaving the Pan-American Highway 98 km N of Antofagasta at Carmen Alto (petrol and food). This road passes many abandoned nitrate mines (*oficinas*).

Places of interest

2 km from the centre on Av B O'Higgins is the **Parque El Loa** (open 1000-1800 daily), which contains a reconstruction of a typical colonial village built around a reduced-scale reproduction of Chiu Chiu church. Nearby in the park is the **Museo**

Arqueológico y Etnológico, with an exhibition of pre-hispanic cultural history (open Tues-Fri 1000-1330, 1430-1800, Sat-Sun 1100-1830; colectivos 4, 5, 6 or 18 from the centre).

Local information
● **Accommodation**

L3 *Lican Antai*, Ramírez 1937, T 341621, with breakfast, good service and good restaurant, TV, phone, safe, rec.

A1 *Park*, Camino Aeropuerto 1392, T 319900, F 319901, 233-8509 in Santiago, first class, swimming pool, popular, bar and restaurant, rec; **A1** *Quitor*, Ramírez 2116, T 314159, good but overpriced; **A2** *Alfa*, Sotomayor 2016, T 342565, comfortable; **A2** *Hostería Calama*, Latorre 1521, T 341511, comfortable, good food and service; **A3** *Mirador*, Sotomayor 2064, T/F 340329, **D** without bath, helpful, rec.

B *Casablanca* on Plaza, Sotomayor 2160, T 312966.

C *Res John Keny*, Ecuador 1991, T 211430, modern, parking; **C** *Hostal Coco*, Sotomayor 2215, hospitable.

D *El Loa*, Abaroa 1617, T 311963, English spoken; **D** *Res Splendid*, Ramírez 1960, T 211841, **E** without bath, good; **D** *Genesis*, Granaderos 2148, T 212841, nr Tramaca and Geminis bus terminals, kitchen, rec; **D** *Res Toño*, Vivar 1973, T 211185, next to Kenny bus, basic.

E *Universo*, Sotomayor 1822, T 313299, hospitable; **E** *Res El Tatio*, P L Galo 1987, T 212284, basic, noisy, reasonable; **E** pp *Capri 2*, Ramírez 1880, basic, safe; **E** *Los Andes*, Vivar 1920, T 341073, renovated, good beds, noisy; **E** *Luxor*, Vargas 1881, T 310292 basic, safe; **E** *Claris Loa*, Granaderos 1631, T 311939, quiet, good beds.

● **Places to eat**

Bavaria, Sotomayor 2095, modern, good coffee and delicatessen, open early morning; *Club Croata*, Abaroa 1869 (Plaza de Armas), serves good set lunches and evening meals. Good, cheap lunches at *Hotel Quitor*, *Comedor Camarino*, Latorre 2033, *Lascar*, Ramirez 1917, and in the market. *Mariscal JP*, Félix Hoyos 2127, good seafood. Good ice cream at *Fior di Gelato*, Plaza de Armas.

● **Banks & money changers**

Rates are generally poor especially for TCs. *Banco de Crédito e Inversiones*, Latorre, good rates, no commission (US$100 minimum); *Banco Osorno* (Visa), Sotomayor; *Fincard* (Mastercard), Latorre 1763, p 1, Mon-Fri 0900-1400, 1600-2000, Sat 1100-1300. *Casa de Cambio*, Sotomayor 1818, Mon-Fri, 0830-1400, 1500-1900 (closes 2300 for passengers

The slow train to Oruro

The line between Calama and Oruro in Bolivia is the only section of the old Antofagasta and Bolivia Railway line still open to passenger trains. It is a long slow journey but well worthwhile for the scenery. The journey is very cold, both during the day and at night (-15°C). From Calama the line climbs to reach its highest point at Ascotán (3,960m); it then descends to 3,735m at Cebollar, skirting the Salar de Ascotán. Chilean customs are at Ollagüe, where there is a delay of 5-6 hrs while an engine is sent from Uyuni. The train is searched at Bolivian customs at Avaroa and passengers are required to disembark at both border posts for passport-control. There are money changers at Ollagüe and Avaroa. From the border the line runs NE to Uyuni, 174 km, crossing the Salar de Chiguana and running at an almost uniform height of 3,660m. Uyuni is the junction with the line S to the Argentine frontier at Villazón. Río Mulato is the junction for Potosí, but it is much quicker to travel by bus from Uyuni.

on train to Bolivia). Money changers selling Bolivian money outside the railway station. At weekends try Tramaca or Morales Moralitos bus offices or *farmacias* (poor rates).

● **Embassies & consulates**
Bolivian Consulate, Sr Reynaldo Urquizo Sosa, Bañados Espinoza 2232, Apdo Postal 85, T 341976, open (in theory only) 0900-1230, 1530-1830, Mon-Fri, helpful.

● **Laundry**
Laverap, Félix Hoyos y Abaroa; *París*, Vargas 2178 and Latorre 1955; *Universal*, Antofagasta 1313 (cheapest).

● **Post & telecommunications**
Post Office: Granaderos y V Mackenna, 0830-1300, 1530-1830, Sat 0900-1230, will not send parcels over 1 kg.
Telecommunications: CTC, Abaroa 1756; Entel, Sotomayor 2027.

● **Shopping**
Supermarkets, *El Cid*, Vargas 1942, *El Cobre*, Vargas 2148; market at Antofagasta between Latorre and Vivar.

● **Tour companies & travel agents**
Several agencies run 1-day and longer tours to the Atacama region, inc San Pedro; these are usually more expensive than tours from San Pedro and require a minimum number for the tour to go ahead. Reports of tour quality are increasingly mixed – poorly maintained vehicles and poor guides. Those with positive recommendations inc: *Talikuna*, Gral Velázquez 1948, T 212595; *Turismo El Sol*, Abaroa 1796, T 210152; *Desierto Diferente*, Sotomayor 2261, T 315111; *Nativa*, Avaroa 1780, T 319834, F 340107; *Livia Tours*, Vivar 1960, T 211664, rec for their 3-day desert tour; *Moon Valley*, Sotomayor 1814, T/F 317456, very helpful, excursions, cycle rental.

● **Tourist offices**
Latorre 1689, T 211314. Map of town, helpful. Open Mon-Fri 0900-1300, 1430-1900 Sat-Sun (summer only) 0900-1300. **Automóvil Club de Chile**, Av Ecuador 1901, T 342770.

● **Transport**
Local Car hire: Comercial Maipo SA, Balmaceda 3950, T 212204; **Hertz**, Latorre 1510, T 341380; **Avis**, Latorre 1512, T 319797; **Maxso**, Abaroa 1930, T 212194; **Budget**, Granaderos 2925, T 341076. A 4WD jeep (necessary for the desert) costs US$87-118 a day. Rates are sometimes much lower at weekends. A hired car or taxi, shared between several people, is an economic alternative for visiting the Atacama region. **NB** Car hire is not available in San Pedro de Atacama.

Air LanChile (Latorre 1499, T 341477/ 341494), daily, and Ladeco (Ramírez 1858, T 312626/ 315183), to Santiago, via Antofagasta. Taxi to town US$6 (courtesy vans from Hotels *Calama*, *Alfa* and *Lican Antai*).

Trains To Uyuni and Oruro (Bolivia), weekly service, Wed 2300: Calama-Ollagüe fare US$5. You have to change trains at the border, then pay US$4 to Uyuni, where you change again for any onward journey. Book seats in advance (passport essential) from Tramaca in Calama (Sotomayor 1961) or in Antofagasta. (The 2 offices sell tickets for different carriages and do not know of reservations made at the other office). Catch the train as early as possible: although seats are assigned, the designated carriages may not arrive; passengers try to occupy several seats (to sleep on) but will move if you show your ticket. Sleeping bag and/or blanket essential. Restaurant car; food is also available at Ollagüe and Río Mulato (only for the conditioned).

Buses No main terminal, buses leave from

company offices: Tramaca, terminal at Granaderos 3048 (colectivo 1A from centre), office at Sotomayor 1961; Frontera, Antofagasta 2041, T 318543; Géminis, terminal Antofagasta 2239, office Sotomayor y Balmaceda; Kenny Bus, Vivar 1954; Flota Barrios, Ramírez 2298; Tur Bus at Sotomayor y Balmaceda. To **Santiago** 23 hrs, US$35-40; to **Arica**, Tramaca, Géminis or Tur Bus overnight, US$18-20, 8 hrs, or change in Antofagasta; to **Valparaíso/Viña del Mar**, US$35; to **Iquique**, 8 hrs, US$14.50, overnight only (Geminis rec, Kenny Bus not rec). To **La Serena**, usually with delay in Antofagasta, 15 hrs, US$29. To **Chuquicamata** (see below). For services to **San Pedro de Atacama** and Toconao, see below; to **Antofagasta**, 3 hrs, several companies, eg Tramaca, hourly on the half-hour till 2130, US$5.

To Argentina Géminis services from Iquique and Antofagasta to **Salta** call at Calama, details above, book well in advance, US$45, 22 hrs (Géminis service can also be picked up in San Pedro but book in Calama and tell the booking office). Also Tramaca, service from Antofagasta, dep Mon and Fri 1000, US$45, via Jujuy.

NB Remember that between Oct and March, Chilean time is 1 hr later than Bolivian.

CHUQUICAMATA

(*Pop* 13,000; *Alt* 2,800m; *Phone code* 055), 16 km N of Calama, is a clean modern town serving the world's largest open-cast copper mine, employing 9,000 workers and operated by Codelco (the state copper corporation). Everything about Chuquicamata is huge: the pit from which the ore is extracted is 4 km long, 2 km wide and 630m deep; the giant trucks, with wheels over 3.5m high, carry 225 ton loads and work 24 hrs a day; in other parts of the plant 60,000 tons of ore are processed a day. Guided tours in Spanish (by bus, also in English if enough people) leave from the office of Chuqui Ayuda (a local children's charity) near the entrance at the top end of the plaza, Mon-Fri 1000 (though less frequently in low season – tourist office in Calama has details), 1 hr, US$2.50 donation, be there by 0915. Register in good time in the café near the entrance at least 30 mins in advance. Passport essential. No filming permitted, but photographs may be taken at specified points in the tour.

● **Places to eat** Cheap lunches available at the *Club de Empleados* and at *Arco Iris* both facing the bus terminal.

● **Transport** From Calama: yellow colectivo taxis (marked 'Chuqui') from the corner of the main plaza, US$0.75. Buses to **Arica** at 2200 (weekends at 2300), US$16, 9 hrs; to **Antofagasta**, 10 a day, US$6; to **Iquique**, US$14; to **Santiago**, US$28, 24 hrs.

NORTH ALONG THE RIO LOA

Near Calama there are several small towns and villages in the valley of the Río Loa. **Chiu Chiu** (*Pop* 300, *Alt* 2,500m), 33 km E of Calama, was one of the earliest centres of Spanish settlement in the area. The church of **San Francisco**, dating from 1611, has roof beams of cactus and walls over 1m thick. Nearby is a unique, perfectly circular, very deep lake, called Chiu Chiu or Icacoia. Ancient rock carvings are to be found a few kilometres N in the Río Loa valley.

At **Lasana** (*Pop* 800) 8 km N, there are the ruins of a pre-Incaic *pukará*, a national monument, with explanatory tablets (soft drinks and beer on sale). At **Conchi**, 25 km N of Lasana, there is a spectacular view from the bridge over the Río Loa, but it is a military zone, so no photographs allowed. Access to the river is by side tracks, best at Santa Bárbara; interesting wildlife and flower meadows, trout fishing in season (permit from Gobernación in Calama).

From Chiu Chiu a road runs to Ollagüe, 240 km N on the Bolivian frontier. There is a *carabinero* checkpoint at Ascotán, the highest point of the road at 3,900m. North of Ascotán the road becomes worse, especially where it crosses the Salares de Ascotán and Ollagüe (ask at Ascotán or Ollagüe before setting out about the conditions, especially in Dec/Jan or Aug). There are many llama flocks along this road and flamingoes on the salares. **NB** The desert to the eastern side of the road is extensively covered by minefields.

NB There is no petrol between Calama and Uyuni in Bolivia. If really short try buying from the *carabineros* at Ollagüe or Ascotán, the military at Conchi or the mining camp at Buenaventura. The only real answer is to take enough.

OLLAGÜE

(*Pop* 200; *Alt* 3,690m) 198 km N of Calama on the dry floor of the Salar de Ollagüe, surrounded by a dozen volcanic peaks of over 5,000m. Police and border officials will help find lodging. There is one bus a week to Calama. Ollagüe can be reached by taking the Calama-Uyuni train (see above) but, if you stop off, you will have to hitch back as the daily freight trains are not allowed to carry passengers. (Hitching is difficult but the police may help you to find a truck.)

A 77-km spur railroad of metre gauge runs to the copper mines of Collahuasi, and from there one can reach the highest mine in the world: the Aucanquilcha, at 5,580m. From the mine you can scramble to the summit of Aucanquilcha at 6,176m, superb views. High clearance vehicle needed to drive to the mine. The highest passenger station on this spur is Yuma, at 4,400m.

At this altitude nights are cold, the days warm and sunny. Minimum temperature at Ollagüe is -20°C, and at the mine, -37°C. There are only 50 mm of rain a year, and water is very scarce.

FRONTIER WITH BOLIVIA: OLLAGÜE

Open 0800-2100; US$2 per vehicle charge for crossings 1300-1500, 1850-2100. A bad unmade road from Ollagüe runs into Bolivia (see **Bolivia**, page 309).

SAN PEDRO DE ATACAMA

is 103 km SE of Calama by a paved road. There is no fuel, food or water along this road. At Paso Barros Arana (Km 58) there is an unpaved turning to the left which leads through interesting desert scenery to the small, mud-brick village of Río Grande. Look out for vicuñas and guanacos on the pass. The main road skirts the Cordillera de la Sal about 15 km from San Pedro. Spectacular views of sunset over to the Western Cordilleras. The old unmade road to San Pedro turns off the new road at Km 72 and crosses this range through the Valle de La Luna (see **Excursions** below), but should only be attempted by 4WD vehicles. This road is partly paved with salt blocks.

San Pedro de Atacama is a small town (*Pop* 1,600; *Alt* 2,436m; *Phone code* 055) more Spanish-Indian looking than is usual in Chile, now attracting large numbers of visitors. Both Diego de Almagro and Pedro de Valdivia stopped in this oasis.

Places of interest

The **Iglesia de San Pedro**, dating from the 17th century, has been heavily restored (the tower was added in 1964). The roof is made of cactus; inside, the statues of Mary and Joseph have fluorescent light halos. Nearby, on the Plaza, is the **Casa Incaica**, the oldest building in San Pedro.

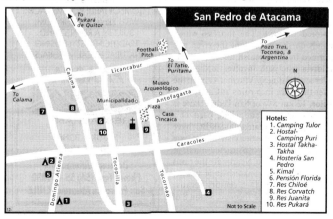

San Pedro de Atacama

To Pukará de Quitor

Football Pitch

To El Tatio, Puritama

Licancabur

To Calama

Calama

Museo Arqueológico

Municipalidad

To Poza Tres, Toconao, & Argentina

N

Antofagasta

Plaza

Casa Incaica

Caracoles

Domingo Atienza

Tocopilla

Toconao

Not to Scale

Hotels:
1. *Camping Tulor*
2. *Hostal-Camping Puri*
3. *Hostal Takha-Takha*
4. *Hostería San Pedro*
5. *Kimal*
6. *Pensión Florida*
7. *Res Chiloé*
8. *Res Corvatch*
9. *Res Juanita*
10. *Res Pukará*

Museums

Museo Arqueológico, the collection of Padre Gustave Paige, a Belgian missionary who lived in San Pedro between 1955 and 1980, is now under the care of the Universidad Católica del Norte (Mon-Fri, 0800-1200, 1500-1900; Sat, and Sun, 1000-1200, 1500-1800; summer, Mon-Fri 0900-1200, 1400-1800, Sat-Sun 1000-1200, 1400-1800, entry US$4). It is a fascinating repository of artefacts, well organized to trace the development of prehispanic Atacameño society. Labels on displays are good and there is a comprehensive booklet in Spanish and English. There is no heating nor electricity: wear warm clothing even in warm weather and visit when sunlight is strongest.

Excursions

The **Valle de la Luna**, 12 km W of San Pedro, with fantastic landscapes caused by the erosion of salt mountains, is crossed by the old San Pedro-Calama road. Although buses on the new Calama-San Pedro road will stop to let you off where the old road branches off 13 km NW of San Pedro (signposted to Peine), it is far better to travel from San Pedro on the old road, either on foot (allow 3 hrs there, 3 hrs back; no lifts), by bicycle or by car. The Valle is best seen at sunset (provided the sky is clear). Take water, hat, camera and torch. Also consider spending the night to see the sunset (take warm clothes and plenty of water).

3 km N of San Pedro along the river is the **Pukará de Quitor**, a pre-Inca fortress restored in 1981. The fortress, which stands on the W bank of the river, was stormed by the Spanish under Pedro de Valdivia (the path involves fording the river several times). A further 4 km up the river there are Inca ruins at Catarpe. At **Tulor**, 12 km SW of San Pedro, there is an archaeological site where parts of a stone-age village (dated 500-800 BC) have been excavated; worth a visit on foot (you can sleep in two reconstructed huts), or take a tour, US$5 pp. Nearby are the ruins of a 17th century Spanish-style village, abandoned in the 18th century because of lack of water. For Toconao, 37 km S of San Pedro, see below.

Local information

San Pedro has electricity in the evening (until 2300/2400), but take a torch (flashlight) for walking at night. *Residenciales* supply candles, but better to buy them in Calama beforehand. Accommodation is scarce in Jan/Feb and expensive. Drink bottled water as the local supply is not drinkable.

● **Accommodation**

L3 *Hostería San Pedro*, on Solcor, T 11, reserve in advance, swimming pool (residents only), petrol station (leaded fuel only), tents for hire, cabins, hot water, electricity am-1200 and 1800-2300, restaurant (good lunch) and bar, rec, no credit cards or TCs; **C** *Kimal*, Atienza y Caracoles, T/F 55-851030, good.

D *La Quinta Adela*, Toconao; **D** *Res Corvatch*, Antofagasta s/n, T 87, good rooms, good beds, German spoken highly rec; **D** *Res Juanita*, on the plaza, T 39, hot water on request, restaurant, rec; **D** *Hostal Takha-Takha*, on Caracoles, T 38 (F camping), very small rooms, some tents for rent; **D** *Res Andacollo*, Tocopilla 11, T 6, basic, laundry facilities, cheap restaurant; **D** *Res*

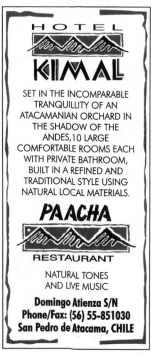

Licancábur, Toconao, T 7, cooking facilities,safe, good.
E pp *Pensión Florida*, Tocopilla, temperamental hot water, basic, laundry facilities, poor beds;
E pp *Pukará*, Tocopilla 28, cold water, basic;
E pp *Res Chiloé*, Atienza, T 17, good meals, laundry facilities, good beds, safe, popular; **F** pp *Res Solcor*, Atienza, dormitory accommodation; **E** pp *Camping Tulor*, off Atienza, T 27, good food, camping **F** pp, rents camping equipment, laundry facilities, rec; **E** pp *Hostal-Camping Puri*, Caracoles s/n, T 49, restaurant, quiet, camping **F**, rental of camping and climbing gear.

● **Places to eat**
Best food in town at *Hostería San Pedro*. On Caracoles are *Estaka*, good set lunches and evening meals, popular; *Tambo Cañaveral*, live music at weekends, own generator, open late. Apart from these try *Residenciales: Juanita*, good set lunch and evening meal; *Andacollo. Chañar Luminoso*, Caracoles, good coffee and juice. *Sonchek*, coffee, fruit juice, vegetarian dishes, also motorbikes for hire US$5/hr; *Chapaka*, sells health foods, bread, muesli.

● **Banks & money changers**
Cambio Atacama, Caracoles, open daily, poor rates, changes TCs, but often closed, best to change elsewhere. If stuck try *Hostería San Pedro* (worse rates still), or *Hostal Takha-Takha*.

● **Post & telecommunications**
Post Office: Granaderos y MacKenna sells excellent postcards.
Telephone: CTC, Caracoles y Gabriela Mistral; Entel on the plaza.

● **Sports**
Climbing: San Pedro is a good centre for climbing Mt Lincancábur (5,916m) and other peaks on the Chile/Bolivia border. Allow at least 8 hrs to climb Lincancábur and 4 hrs to descend. Take plenty of water and your passport and hire a 4WD vehicle in Calama.

Horse riding: *Galopea*, run by Eleanor Merrill and Roberto Plaza Castillo ('Guatita'), guided horseback tours, US$5/hr, speak 6 languages, ask in post office.

Swimming Pool: *Piscina Oasis*, at Pozo Tres, 3 km SE, open all year 0500-1730 daily (except Mon). US$1.50 to swim, sometimes empty; enquire before walking there. Camping US$3 and picnic facilities, very popular at weekends.

● **Tour companies & travel agents**
About 10 agencies, most charging the same rates and organizing joint tour groups. Agencies inc: *Nativa*, Toconao, T 44, rec; *Cosmo Andino Expediciones*, Caracoles s/n, T/F 340107, English, German, French and Dutch spoken, book exchange in the above languages, wide selection, owner Martin Beeris (Martín El Holandés), rec; *Atacama Inca Tour*, Toconao s/n, T 34, F 52, rec; *Desert Adventure*, Caracoles s/n; opp is *Merakopp*, rec; *Pachamama*, Toconao, rec; *Ochoa*, Toconao, Spanish only, rec; *Turismo Colque*, Caracoles s/n, T 851109; *Antai*, Caracoles s/n, English and French spoken, also sells handicrafts, rec; *Cactus* offers horseriding with good guides to Valle de la Luna and other sites. Tours are also run by several *Residenciales*. Usual tour rates: to Valle de la Luna (best at sunset) US$6; to Toconao and the Salar de Atacama (best at sunset) US$12; to El Tatio (begin at 0400) US$18 (take swimming costume and warm clothing), but shop around as different rates may be available. These run most days in season, subject to demand at other times.

Turismo Colque run tours to Laguna Verde, Laguna Colorado, Uyuni and other sites in Bolivia, 3 days, changing vehicles at the border as the Bolivian authorities refuse permits for Chilean tour vehicles, US$65 pp, take own food and water and obtain passport stamps before departure.

Before taking a tour, check that the agency has dependable vehicles (4WD land-cruisers are best), suitable equipment (eg oxygen for El Tatio), a guide who speaks English if so advertised, and that the company is recognized by the municipality. An Asociación de Operadores Turísticos de San Pedro de Atacama has been formed. Report any complaints to the municipality.

● **Transport**
Local Bicycle hire: from several places inc *Takha-Takha*; *Dada Atacama*, US$2.50/hr, US$10-12 a day; *Pangea*, Caracoles, English spoken, also cycle repairs. **Car hire**: is impossible. Try Calama. Pick up truck with 4WD best. Agency authorization essential to take a hired car into Bolivia.

Buses From Calama: two companies, both from Balmaceda y Sotomayor, opp railway station. Frontera, 6 a day from **Calama** (Frontera in San Pedro at Licancabur s/n). Also Turbus, same price, 1½ hrs. Fare US$2.50 one way. Frequencies vary with more departures in Jan/Feb and some weekends, fewer out of season. Book in advance to return from San Pedro Sun pm. Frontera also run to Toconao. Géminis buses from Iquique and Antofagasta to Salta (Argentina) stop in San Pedro on Wed and Sat – book in Calama, Iquique or Antofagasta.

FRONTIER WITH BOLIVIA: HITO CAJON

Hito Cajón is reached by a poor road E from San Pedro, 45 km. From the frontier it is 7 km N to Laguna Verde.

● **Immigration**
Chilean immigration and customs in San Pedro, open 0900-1200, 1400-1600. Incoming vehicles and passengers are searched for fruit and vegetables.

● **Bolivian consulate**
See under Calama.

● **Transport**
There are reports of a daily bus service from San Pedro to Hito Cajón to meet tour vehicles from Uyuni, US$10 pp. At Hito Cajón you may be able to find space in a tour vehicle (about US$20 to Uyuni). *Nativa* will take people to the frontier, US$120/vehicle.

FRONTIER WITH ARGENTINA: PASO DE JAMA AND PASO SICO

The Paso de Jama (4,200m) is reached by an improved road, suitable for all vehicles, which continues on the Argentine side to Susques and Jujuy. This is more popular than the Laguna Sico route but note but there is no accommodation in Susques.

Laguna Sico (4,079m) is reached by poor road which runs S and E of San Pedro, 207 km via Toconao. On the Argentine side this road continues to San Antonio de los Cobres and Salta.

● **Immigration**
Chilean immigration and customs in San Pedro. Incoming vehicles are searched for fruit.

● **Crossing by private vehicle**
Check road conditions before setting out as Paso de Jama can be closed by heavy rain in summer and blocked by snow in winter.

● **Transport**
For bus services from Antofagasta, Calama and San Pedro to Jujuy and Salta see above.

NORTH OF SAN PEDRO

El Tatio

(*Alt* 4,500m), the site of geysers, is a popular attraction. From San Pedro it is reached by a maintained road which runs NE, past the Baños de Puritama (28 km), then on a further 94 km. The geysers are at their best 0630-0830, though the spectacle varies: locals say the performance is best when weather conditions are stable. A swimming pool has been built nearby. There is a workers' camp which is empty apart from one guard, who will let you sleep in a bed in one of the huts, G pp, take food

and sleeping bag. From here you can hike to surrounding volcanoes if adapted to altitude. There is no public transport and hitching is impossible. If going in a hired car, make sure the engine is suitable for very high altitudes and is protected with antifreeze; 4WD is advisable. If driving in the dark it is almost impossible to find your way: the sign for El Tatio is N of the turn off. Tours arranged by agencies in San Pedro and Calama. **NB** People have been killed or seriously injured by falling into the geysers, or through the thin crust of the mud.

There are three alternatives from El Tatio to Calama: 1) Direct, on an atrocious track, to **Caspana** (**G** pp at village stores, basic), beautifully set among hills with a tiny church dating from 1641 and a museum with interesting displays on Atacameño culture, and then W along the valley of the Río Salado.

2) North via Linzor to Inacaliri and the Ojo de San Pedro saltflat. Follow the road along the Río San Pedro Valley and cross the Río Loa at Conchi. The Río San Pedro has been a route for herders and silver caravans for centuries and there are many sites of interest, although access is on foot.

3) North from El Tatio to Linzor and then W to **Toconce**, which has extensive prehispanic terraces set among interesting rock formations. Between Toconce and Caspana to the S are valleys of pampas grass with llama herds. If visiting Toconce, check in with the *carabineros* in the square. From Toconce follow the road W to Calama via Lasana and Chiu Chiu. For details on Conchi, Lasana and Chiu Chiu, see page 722 above.

20 km W of Toconce is **Ayquina**, in whose ancient church is enshrined the statue of the Virgin of Guadalupe. Her feast-day is 8 Sept, when pilgrims come from far and wide. There is day-long group dancing to Indian rhythms on flute and drum. Towards sunset the Virgin is carried up a steep trail to a small thatched shrine, where the image and the people are blessed before the dancing is renewed at the shrine and all the way back to the village.

6 km N of Ayquina are the luke-warm thermal waters of the **Baños de Turi** and the ruins of a 12th-century *pukará* which was the largest fortified town in the Atacama mountains. Southwest of Ayquina is **Cupo**, which has a *fiesta* on 19 Mar (San José). Between this village and Turi is a large, ruined prehispanic settlement at **Paniri** with extensive field systems, irrigation canals (including aqueducts) and a necropolis. Some of the fields are still in use. The area around Cupo is one of the best for seeing the Atacama giant cactus (*Notocereus atacamensis*). Flamingos can be seen on the mudflats.

SOUTH OF SAN PEDRO

From San Pedro to Toconao, 37 km S, the road (well-surfaced) runs through groves of acacia and pepper trees. There are many tracks leading to the wells (*pozos*) which supply the intricate irrigation system. The groves of trees are havens for wildlife especially rheas (ñandu) and Atacama owls.

About 4 km before you reach Toconao, there are some vehicle tracks heading E across the sand. They lead to a hidden valley 2 km from the road where there is a small settlement called **Zapar**. Here are some well-preserved pre-hispanic ruins on the rocky cliffs above the cultivated valley. The sand is very soft and 4WD is essential.

Toconao, with some 500 inhabitants is on the eastern shore of the Salar de Atacama. All houses are built of bricks of white volcanic stone, which gives the village a very characteristic appearance totally different from San Pedro. The 18th century church and bell tower are also built of volcanic stone. East of the village is an attractive oasis called the Quebrada de Jérez. The quarry where the stone (*sillar*) is worked can be visited, about 1½ km E (the stones sound like bells when struck). Worth visiting also are the vineyards which produce a unique sweet wine, and the tree-filled gorges with their hidden fields and orchards.

- **Accommodation** Three basic *residenciales* – ask around in the village. **Camping**: possible along the Quebrada de Jérez.

- **Transport** Yusmar buses daily from San Pedro, 1300, return 1645, US$1.30.

SALAR DE ATACAMA

South of Toconao is one of the main entrances to the Salar de Atacama, 300,000 ha, the third largest expanse of salt flats in the world. Rich in minerals including borax, potassium and an estimated 40% of world lithium reserves, the Salar is home to the pink flamingo and other birds (though these are usually only visible at a distance). The air is so dry that you can often see right across the Salar. Entry is controlled by Conaf in Toconao, US$1.50.

Three areas of the Salar form part of the **Reserva Nacional de los Flamencos**, which is in 7 sectors totalling 73,986 ha and administered by Conaf in San Pedro. From Toconao the road heads S through the scenic villages of **Camar** (where handicrafts from cactus may be bought) and **Socaire** (which has domesticated llamas, knitwear for sale). 20 km S of Socaire is the beautiful **Laguna Miscanti** (*Alt* 4,350m) where wildlife abounds; 3 types of flamingo may be seen: Andean, Chilean (white and pink, no black) and James (small, with yellow legs). After Socaire the road goes on to the mine at Laco (one poor stretch below the mine), before proceeding to Sico, which has replaced the higher, more northerly Guaytiquina pass (4,295m, also spelt Huaytiquina) to Argentina.

10 km S of Toconao the old road branches E towards Guaytiquina. In a deep *quebrada* below Volcán Láscar is the small agricultural settlement of **Talabre**, with terracing and an ancient threshing floor. Above the *quebrada* is an isolated, stone-built cemetery. Large flocks of llamas graze where the stream crosses the road below the Láscar volcano (5,154m). After a steep climb, you reach the **Laguna Lejía** (4,190m), where flamingos abound. You then pass through the high plains of **Guaytiquina** (4,275m), where only a few herdsmen are found. This crossing is not open for road traffic to Argentina.

67 km S from Toconao, on a road that runs along the eastern edge of the Salar de Atacama is the attractive village of **Peine**, which is the site of the offices of

the lithium extraction company. There is also a pool filled by thermal springs where you can swim. Woollen goods and knitwear are made here. To the E of the village lies a group of beautifully coloured hills (colours best at sunset) with good views over the Salar de Atacama.

From Peine a road (64 km) crosses the Salar de Atacama; it joins a road which runs from San Pedro down the W side of the Salar and continues S to Pan de Azúcar, an abandoned railway station. Here it meets the road which leads from the Pan-American Highway, 50 km S of Antofagasta via the modern copper mine of La Escondida to Socompa on the Argentine border. Between Pan de Azúcar and Socompa (poor road) is Monturaqui, the source of the green onyx which is much used for carving in northern Chile.

FRONTIER WITH ARGENTINA: SOCOMPA

● **Immigration**

Chilean immigration is at Socompa. The Chilean side is open 0800-2200. On the Argentine side the road carries on to San Antonio de los Cobres and Salta. Argentine immigration is at San Antonio de los Cobres.

● **Crossing with a private vehicle**

US$2 is charged for crossing between 1300-1500 and 1860-2100.

Iquique, Arica and The Far North

THE continuation of the desert zone to the Peruvian border. The main cities are Iquique and Arica; between them are old mineral workings and even older geoglyphs. Large areas of the Andean highland have been set aside as national parks.

The Atacama Desert extends over most of the Far North. The Cordillera de la Costa slowly loses height N of Iquique, terminating at the Morro at Arica: from Iquique North it drops directly to the sea and as a result there are few beaches along this coast. Inland the central depression (*pampa*) 1,000-1,200m is arid and punctuated by salt-flats S of Iquique. Between Iquique and Arica it is crossed from E to W by four gorges. East of this depression lies the *sierra*, the western branch of the Andes, beyond which is a high plateau, the *altiplano* (3,500m-4,500m) from which rise volcanic peaks. In the *altiplano* there are a number of lakes, the largest of which, Lago Chungará, is one of the highest in the world.

The coastal strip and the *pampa* are rainless; on the coast temperatures are moderated by the Pacific Ocean, but in the *pampa* variations of temperature between day and night are extreme, ranging from 30°C to 0°C. In the *sierra* temperatures are lower, averaging 20°C in summer and 9°C

Far North

PERU

To La Paz

To Tacna

Visviri 6

Putre

Parinacota 3

Paso Tambo Quemado 2

Arica

Poconchile

Rio Lluta

Relén

Parque Nacional Lauca 4 5 1

Tignamar

Tignamar Viejo

Rio Azapa

Reserva Nacional Las Vicuñas

Guallatiri

BOLIVIA

Codpa

Monumento Natural Salar de Surire

Rio Camarones

Tranque de Caritaya

Surire

Salar de Surire

Cuya

Parque Nacional Volcán Isluga

British Cemetery

Camiña

Colchane 7

Isluga

Pisagua

9

Giant of the Atacama

Cariquima

Chusmisa 8

Tarapacá

Huara

Mamiña

Humberstone

Iquique

La Tirana

Pica 9

Matilla

Geoglifos de Pintados

Pacific Ocean

N

0   30
km

Mountains:
1. Guallatiri   (6,060m)
2. Parinacota (6,342m)
3. Pomerape   (6,282m)
4. Acotango   (6,050m)
5. Capurata   (5,990m)
6. Tacora   (5,988m)
7. Isluga   (5,530m)
8. Alto Toroni (5,982m)
9. Sections of Reserva Nacional Pampa Del Tamarugal

——— Paved Roads
——— Unpaved Roads

5A

in winter. The *altiplano* is much colder, temperatures averaging 10°C in summer and -5°C in winter. Both the *sierra* and the *altiplano* receive rain in summer.

IQUIQUE

Iquique (*Pop* 145,139; *Phone code* 057), the capital of I Región (Tarapacá) and one of the main northern ports, is 492 km N of Antofagasta. The name of the town is derived from the Aymara word *ique-ique*, meaning place of 'rest and tranquillity'. The city is situated on a rocky peninsula at the foot of the high Atacama pampa, sheltered by the headlands of Punta Gruesa and Cavancha. The city, which was partly destroyed by earthquake in 1877, became the centre of the nitrate trade after its transfer from Peru to Chile at the end of the War of the Pacific.

A short distance N of town along Amunátegui is the Free Zone (Zofri), a giant shopping centre selling mainly imported electronic goods: it is worth a visit (much better value than Punta Arenas), good for cheap camera film (Fuji slide film available)(open Mon-Sat 0900-1330, 1630-2000). Collective taxi from the centre US$0.35. Limit on tax free purchases US$650 for foreigners, US$500 for Chileans.

Places of interest

In the centre of the old town is **Plaza Prat** with a clock tower and bell dating from 1877. On the NE corner of the Plaza is the **Centro Español**, built in Moorish style by the local Spanish community in 1904; the ground floor is a restaurant, on the upper floors are paintings of scenes from Don Quijote and from Spanish history. On the S side of the Plaza is the **Teatro Municipal**, built in 1890; the façade features 4 women representing the seasons. Three blocks N of the Plaza is the old **Aduana** (customs house) built in 1871; in 1891 it was the scene of an important battle in the Civil War between supporters of President Balmaceda and congressional forces. Part of it is now the **Naval Museum**. Along C Baquedano, which runs S from Plaza Prat, are the attractive former mansions of the 'nitrate barons', dating from between 1880 and 1903. The finest of these is the **Palacio Astoreca**, Baquedano y O'Higgins, built in 1903, subsequently the Intendencia and now a museum.

Sealions and pelicans can be seen from the harbour. There are cruises from the passenger pier, US$2.65, 45 mins, minimum 10-15 people.

Museums

Museo Naval, Sotomayor y Baquedano, focussing on the Battle of Iquique, 1879 (see page 755), open Tues-Sat 0930-1230, 1430-1800, Sun and holidays 1000-1300, entry US$0.50. **Museo Regional**, Baquedano 951, containing an archaeological section tracing the development of prehispanic civilizations in the region and a section devoted to the Nitrate Era which includes a model of a nitrate *oficina* and the collection of the nitrate entrepreneur, Santiago Humberstone, open Mon-Fri 0830-1300, 1500-1900, Sat 1030-1300, Sun (in summer) 1030-1300, US$0.50. **Palacio Astoreca**, Baquedano y O'Higgins, fine late 19th century furniture and exhibitions of shells, open Tues-Sun 1000-1300, 1600-2000, entry free.

Excursions

To **Humberstone**, a large nitrate town, now abandoned, at the junction of the Pan-American Highway and the road to Iquique. Though closed since 1961, you can see the church, theatre, *pulpería* (company stores) and the swimming pool (built of metal plating from ships' hulls). Entry US$2.50, guided tours Sat-Sun, leaflets available. Nearby are the ruins of three other mining towns: Santa Laura, Peña Chica and Keryma, all of which can be visited. All four form the **Museo Arqueológico Industrial**; details from Salitreras Nebraska, T 751213, or Las Encinas 6141, Vitacura, Santiago, T 218-4161. Transport to/from Iquique: take any bus to/from Arica or Antofagasta, or a colective taxi for Pozo Almonte from Sgto Aldea y Barros Arana, US$2.

To Pintados (see page 734) take any bus S, US$2.50, and walk from the Pan-American Highway then hitch back or flag down a bus. Many other sites around Iquique, including the Giant of the Atacama (see page 734), are difficult to visit without a vehicle. Hire a car and drive S along the Pacific coast to see sealions, fishing villages and old salt mines, including the ghost town of Guanillos.

Local festivals
See below under La Tirana.

Local information
● Accommodation
Accommodation is scarce in the weeks before Christmas as many Chileans visit Iquique to shop in the Zofri.

L3 *Hostería Cavancha*, Los Rieles 250, T 431007, 4-star, S of city, on water's edge.

A2 *Atenas*, Los Rieles 738, T 431100, F 424349, good service and food, rec; **A2** *Playa Brava*, Los Rieles 2503, T 431167, with breakfast, good; **A2** *Primeras Piedras*, street of same name, T 421358, 3 km from city, good food; **A3** *Tamarugal*, Tarapacá 369, T 424365, central, modern, good restaurant.

B *Durana*, San Martín 294, T 412511, helpful; **B-C** *Inti-Llanka*, Obispo Labbé 825, T 412511, helpful.

C *Barros Arana*, Barros Arana 1330, T 412840, modern, good value; **C** *Camino del Mar*, Orella 340, T 420465, restored building, simple; **C** *Hostal Cuneo*, Baquedano 1175, T 428654, modern, pleasant; **C** *Phoenix*, Aníbal Pinto 451, T 421315, with breakfast, old but pleasant, noisy juke box.

D *Res Condell*, Thompson 684, T 423079, good; **D** *Plaza*, Plaza Prat, T 414268, pleasant; **D** *Res Nan-King*, Thompson 752, T 423311, good value; **D** *Hostal América*, Rodríguez 550, T/F 427524, nr beach, good value; **D** *Hostal San Francisco*, Latorre 990, OK but noisy; **D** *Res José Luis*, San Martín 601, spacious; **D** *Res Marclaud*, Juan Martínez 753, rec, motor-cycle parking.

E *Playa*, Gral Hernán Fuenzalida 938, T 22911, small; **E** *Res Araucano*, San Martín 777, T 420211, cooking facilities, grubby, noisy; **D** *Res Li Ming*, Barros Arana 705, T 421912, good value; **E** *Res Sol del Norte*, Juan Martínez 852, T 421546, cold water, basic, small rooms.

F pp *Hosp Tarapacá*, Tarapacá 1348, T 426040, no hot water; **F** pp *Centenario*, Amunátegui 845.

Camping: no site but wild camping possible on La Brava beach. Equipment: *Tunset*, in Zofri; *Lombardi*, Serrano 447.

● Places to eat
Club de la Unión, Plaza Prat, roof terrace, good views, good, not cheap; *Centro Español*, Plaza Prat, good meals well served in beautiful building, expensive; *José Luis*, Serrano 476, pleasant atmosphere, good value *almuerzo*; *Bavaria*, Wilson y Pinto, good but not cheap; *Rapa Nui*, Amunátegui 715, good, cheap, local food; *Grecia*, Thompson 865, cheap but good; *Balcón*, Lynch 656, snacks, live music; *Pizzería D'Alfredo*, Vivar 631, expensive, good coffee; *Italianissimo*, Edificio España, Vivar y Latorre, very good coffee. Several good, inexpensive seafood restaurants (eg *Bucanero*) can be found on the second floor of the central market, Barros Arana y Latorre; opp the bus terminal, on the wharf, are fish restaurants which sell good, cheap lunches. *El Rey del Pescado*, Bulnes y Juan Martínez, good and cheap seafood dishes; also *El Pescado Frito*, Bulnes y Juan Martínez, large portions. *Chifa Fu-Wa*, Barros Arana 740, Chinese.

Cafés: *Salón de Té Chantilly*, Tarapacá 520; *Café Diana*, Vivar 836; *Pinina*, Ramírez y Tarapacá, juices, ice-cream; *Samoa Grill*, Bolívar 396, good coffee and snacks.

● Airline offices
LanChile, Aníbal Pinto 641, T 414378; **Ladeco**, San Martín 428, T 413038; **National**, Galería Lynch, Local 1-2, T 427816, F 425158.

● Banks & money changers
National banks. **Fincard** (Mastercard), Serrano 372, open Mon-Fri 0900-1400, 1600-1800. Difficult to change TCs in town. Best rates for TCs and cash at *casas de cambio* in the Zofri.

● Embassies & consulates
Consulatas: Bolivia, Serrano Pasaje Alessandri 429, p 2, Of 300, Mon-Fri 0930-1400; **Peru**, Los Rieles 131, T 431116.

● Language schools
Academia de Idiomas del Norte, Ramírez 1345, T 411827, F 429343, Swiss run, Spanish classes and accommodation for students.

● Laundry
Bulnes 170, expensive; Obispo Labbé 1446.

● Post & telecommunications
Post Office: Correo Central, Bolívar 458. **Telecommunications**: CTC, Serrano 620, Ramírez 587; Entel, Gorostiaga 287; Diego Portales 840; Telegrams at TelexChile, Lynch y San Martín. **NB** Correos, Telex/Telefax and Entel all have offices in the Plaza de Servicios in the Zofri.

● Sports
Bathing: beaches at Cavancha just S of town centre, good, and Huaiquique, reasonable, Nov-March. Restaurants at Cavancha. Piscina Godoy, fresh water swimming pool on Av Costanera at Aníbal Pinto and Riquelme, open pm, US$1.

Fishing: equipment: *Ferretería Lonza*, Vivar 738; *Ferretería La Ocasión*, Sgto Aldea 890; fishing for broadbill swordfish, striped marlin, yellowfin tuna, oceanic bonito, Mar till end of August.

● **Tour companies & travel agents**
Iquitour, Lynch 563, Casilla 669, T 422009, no English spoken, tour to Pintados, La Tirana,

Humberstone, Pica, *etc*, 0900-1900, lunch inc, a lot of time spent eating and bathing; *Lirima*, Baquedano 1035, rec; *Taxitur*, Sgto Aldea 791, 5-6 hr tour to local sites, maximum 5 passengers.

● **Tourist offices**
Aníbal Pinto 436, T 411523; open Mon-Fri, 0830-1300, 1500-1800, little information, poor

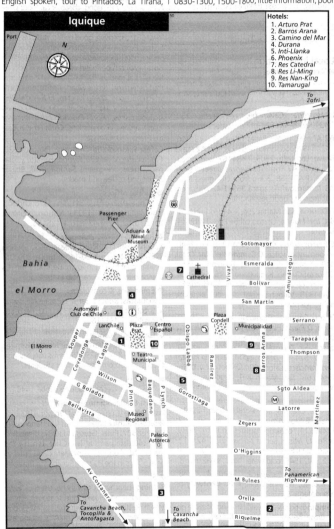

Iquique

Hotels:
1. Arturo Prat
2. Barros Arana
3. Camino del Mar
4. Durana
5. Inti-Llanka
6. Phoenix
7. Res Catedral
8. Res Li-Ming
9. Res Nan-King
10. Tamarugal

maps. **Automóvil Club de Chile**: Serrano 154, T 426772.

● **Transport**
Local Car hire: expensive: **Hertz**, Souper 650, T 426316. **Continental**, Thompson 159, T/F 411426; **J Reategui**, Serrano 1058-A, T 429490/446079; **GP Car Rental**, O'Higgins 179. **Mechanic**: Sergio Cortez, *Givet*, Bolívar 684, highly rec for motorcycles. In the Zofri there is a wide range of motorcycle tyres.

Air Diego Aracena international airport, 35 km S at Chucumata, T 424577. Taxi from outside *Hotel Prat*, Plaza Prat, US$3, T 426184. Airport bus to city centre, US$2. LanChile, Ladeco and National all fly daily to Arica, Antofagasta and Santiago.

Buses Terminal at N end of Patricio Lynch (not all buses leave from here); bus company offices are nr the market on Sgto Aldea and B Arana. All luggage is searched for duty-free goods before being loaded onto buses; all southbound buses are then searched again, at Quillagua on the Pan American Highway and at Chipana on the coastal Route 1. To **Arica**, buses and colectivos, frequent, US$8, 4½ hrs; to **Antofagasta**, US$13, 8 hrs. To **Calama**, 8 hrs, US$14.50, Kennybus not rec. To **Tocopilla** along the coastal road, buses and minibuses, several companies, 4 hrs, US$7; to **La Serena**, 17 hrs, US$25; to **Santiago**, 28 hrs, several companies, US$30 (US$50 for Barrios *salón cama*).

International buses: Géminis (Obispo Labbé y Sotomayor) to **La Paz** (Bolivia) via Oruro, Thur and Sat 2300, 22 hrs, US$37; also Litoral, Esmeralda 974, T 423670, Tues, Sat, Sun 2300, US$37. To **Oruro** via Colchane/Pisiga, Trans Jiménez 3 a week, US$28, and Trans Delta twice a week, US$23. To **Salta** (Argentina) via Calama and San Pedro, Géminis, once a week, US$50; Tramaca twice a week to Jujuy via Paso de Jama, US$50.

ROUTES AROUND IQUIQUE

Iquique lies 47 km W of the Pan-American Highway; 5 km S of the junction is Pozo Almonte (*Pop* 4,000). Note that the rainy season in this area is mainly in January.

MAMIÑA

(*Pop* 430; *Alt* 2,750m) 74 km (first 54 km paved) from Pozo Almonte, has thermal springs and a mud spring (Baño El Chino; open 0930-1300). There are ruins of a prehispanic *pukurá* (fortress) and a church, built in 1632, the only colonial Andean church in Chile with two towers. Electricity till 2230.

● **Accommodation C** pp *Termas de Salitre*, full board, thermal pool in each room, electricity till midnight, swimming pool open 0930-1300; **B** *Termal La Coruña*, T 796298, good, nice views; **C** *Tamarugal*, T 424365, thermal pool in each room; **D** *Res Sol de Ipla*, cheapest, 2 others; *cabañas* to let and campsite.

● **Transport** Minibuses from Iquique leave B Arana y Latorre, Mon-Sat 1600; from Mamiña, 0800; Sun from Iquique 0930, from Mamiña 1600, US$4.50.

La Tirana (*Pop* 550; *Alt* 995m) is famous for a religious festival to the Virgen del Carmen, held from 10 to 16 July, which attracts some 80,000 pilgrims. Over 100 groups dance night and day, starting on 12 July. All the dances take place in the main plaza in front of the church; no alcohol is served. Accommodation is impossible to find, other than in organized camp sites (take tent) which have basic toilets and showers. It is 10 km E of the Pan-American Highway (70 km E of Iquique), turn-off 9 km S of Pozo Almonte.

Matilla (*Alt* 1,160m) 38 km E of La Tirana, is an oasis settlement founded in 1760. Its church (1887) is built of blocks of borax. Nearby is a **Museum** in the Lagar de Matilla, used since around 1700 for fermenting wine (open daily 0900-1700, key from the kiosk in the plaza).

Pica (*Pop* 1,767; *Alt* 1,325m) 4 km NE of Matilla, was the most important centre of early Spanish settlement in the area. Most older buildings date from the nitrate period when it became a popular resort. The town is famous for its pleasant climate, its citrus groves and its two natural springs, the best of which is Cocha Resbaladero (open 0700-2000 all year, snack bar, beautiful pool, entry US$0.70).

● **Accommodation & places to eat D** *Resbaladero*, Ibáñez 57, T 741316, full pension, good pool; **D** *San Andrés*, Balmaceda 197, T 741319, with large breakfast, parking; **E** *El Tambo*, Ibáñez 60, T 741320, old fashioned, good restaurant; also *cabañas* for rent. Campsite at *Camping Miraflores*, T 741333. *Restaurant Palomar*, Balmaceda 74, excellent *almuerzo*.

● **Transport** Buses from Iquique operated by Santa Rosa, Latorre 937, daily 0930, 2 hrs; from Pica 1800, US$3. Several companies (Flonatur, Sgto Aldea 790; Julia, B Arana 965) operate minibuses from Iquique. There are two roads to Pica: La Tirana-Pica is paved; the other, Salar de Pintados-Pica, is unpaved and quite rough.

FROM IQUIQUE TO THE BOLIVIAN FRONTIER

At Huara, 33 km N of Pozo Almonte, a road turns off the Pan-American Highway to **Colchane**, 173 km NE on the Bolivian frontier at Pisiga (open 0800-1300, 1500-1800 daily). At Km 13 the road passes, on the right, the **Giant of the Atacama**, 86m high, reported to be the largest geoglyph in the world (best viewed from a distance).

At Km 23 a road branches off S to **Tarapacá** (*Alt* 1,350m), capital of the Peruvian province of Tarapacá until 1855, now largely abandoned. From Km 25 the road is unpaved. At **Chusmisa** (*Alt* 3,650m), 3 km off this road at Km 77 there are thermal springs: the water is bottled and sold throughout northern Chile. Basic accommodation is available.

● **Transport** Colchane can be reached by Kennybus from Iquique, once a week, returns after 2 hrs. Géminis bus from Iquique to La Paz and Jiménez and Delta to Oruro also pass through Colchane.

PARQUE NACIONAL VOLCAN ISLUGA

Northwest of Colchane, the park covers 174,744 ha at altitudes above 2,100m with some of the best volcanic scenery in northern Chile. The village of **Isluga**, near the park entrance, 6 km NW of Colchane, has an 18th century Andean walled church and bell tower. Wildlife varies according to altitude but includes guanacos, vicuñas, llamas, alpacas, vizcachas, condors and flamingoes.

● **Park information** Park Administration at Enquelga, 10 km N of the entrance, but *guardaparques* are seldom there. There is a campsite at Aguas Calientes, 2 km S of Enquelga.

NORTH TOWARDS ARICA

The Pan-American Highway runs across the Atacama desert at an altitude of around 1,000m, with several steep hills which are best tackled in daylight (at night, sea mist, *camanchaca*, can reduce visibility).

At Zapiga, 80 km N of Pozo Almonte, there is a crossroads: one branch leads W for 41 km to **Pisagua** (*Pop* 200), formerly an important nitrate port, now a small fishing village. Several old wooden buildings here are National Monuments. The fish restaurants make a pleasant stop for a meal. Mass graves dating from just after the 1973 military coup were discovered near here in 1990.

Camiña (*Pop* 500; *Alt* 2,400m), a picturesque village in an oasis, lies 67 km E of Zapiga along a poor road (deep sand and dust).There is a basic hostal. 45 km further NE is the Tranque de Caritaya, a dam which supplies water for the coastal towns set in splendid scenery with lots of wildlife and interesting botany (especially *llareta*). From here mountain roads lead across the Parque Nacional Volcán Isluga to Colchane.

At Km 57 N of Huara there is a British cemetery dating from 1876. The **Geoglifos de Chiza** (sign-posted, to left, and easily accessible), Km 121, can be seen from the highway. At Km 172 a road runs E to **Codpa**, an agricultural community in a deep gorge with interesting scenery. From Codpa poor roads lead N and E through **Tignamar** and Belén to Putre. **Belén** (*Alt* 3,240), a tiny village founded by the Spanish in 1625, was on the silver route between Potosí and the coast. It has two colonial churches.

ARICA

(*Pop* 174,064; *Phone code* 058) Chile's most northerly city, 19 km S of the Peruvian border, built at the foot of the Morro headland, fringed by sand dunes. The Andes can be clearly seen from the anchorage.

It is an important port and route-centre. About half the legal trade of Bolivia passes along a 448 km railway from La Paz. The road route to La Paz via Tambo Colorado is now paved and an oil pipeline also runs to La Paz. Arica is frequented for sea-bathing by Bolivians as well as the locals. A 63 km railway runs N to Tacna in Peru. Regrettably there are indications that Arica is also becoming a key link in the international drugs trade. There are large fishmeal plants and a car assembly factory.

Places of interest

The **Morro**, with a good view from the park on top (10 mins' walk by footpath from the southern end of Colón), was the scene of a great victory by Chile over Peru in the War of the Pacific on 7 June 1880.

At the foot of the Morro is the Plaza Colón with the cathedral of **San Marcos**, built in iron by Eiffel. Though small it is beautifully proportioned and attractively painted. It was brought to Arica from Ilo (Peru) in the 19th century, before Peru lost Arica to Chile, as an emergency measure after a tidal wave swept over Arica and destroyed all its churches. Eiffel also designed the nearby **Aduana** (customs house) which is now the Casa de la Cultura (open Mon-Sat 1000-1300, 1700-2000.) Just N of the Aduana is the La Paz railway station; outside is an old steam locomotive (made in Germany in 1924) once used on this line. In the station is a memorial to John Roberts Jones, builder of the Arica portion of the railway, and a small museum (key at booking office).

Museums

Museo Histórico y de Armas, on the summit of the Morro, containing weapons and uniforms from the War of the Pacific.

Excursions

To the Azapa valley, E of Arica, by yellow colectivo from P Lynch y Chacabuco, US$1. At Km 13 is the **Museo Arqueológico de San Miguel**, part of the University of Tarapacá, containing an important collection of mummies from the Chinchorro culture, reputed to be the oldest collection in the world, as well as sections on Andean weaving, basketwork and ceramics (open Mon-Fri 0830-1300, 1500-1800, Sat, Sun, and holidays 1200-1800, Latin Americans US$1, others US$4, worth a visit). In the forecourt of the museum are several boulders with precolumbian petroglyphs. On the road between Arica and San Miguel images of humans and llamas ('stone mosaics') can be seen to the S of the road. On the opposite side of the valley at San Lorenzo are the ruins of a *pukará* (pre-Inca fortress) dating from the 12th century.

To the **Lluta valley**, N of Arica along Route 11, bus from MacKenna y Chacabuco, 4 a day: At Km 14 and Km 16 there are ancient images of llamas and humans on the hillside. The road continues through the Lauca National Park and on to Bolivia.

Local festivals

Fiestas for the *Virgen de las Peñas* at the Santuario de Livircar in the Azapa Valley are held on the first Sun in Oct and a lesser festival on 7-9 Dec (on 8 Dec the festival moves to Arica). Take a bus from Av Chacabuco y Vicuña Mackenna, then walk 12 km from where it stops to the sanctuary. The Dec festival is not particularly outstanding but it takes place in a part of the valley not normally accessible.

Local information

● **Accommodation**

NB In this area, *pensión* means restaurant, not hostel.

L3 *Arica*, San Martín 599, T 254540, F 231133, best, price depends on season, good value, good and reasonable restaurant, other services expensive, about 2 km along shore (buses No 7, 8, frequent), tennis court, pool, lava beach (not safe for swimming), good breakfast, poor water supply; **L3** *El Paso*, bungalow style, pleasant gardens, swimming pool, Gen Velásquez 1109, T 231965, with breakfast, good food; **L3** *San Marcos*, Sotomayor 382, T 232970, F 254815, helpful, restaurant, parking.

A1 *Saint Georgette*, Camino a Azapa 3221, T 221914, F 223830, 5-star, pool, tennis court, restaurant, bar; **A2** *Azapa*, Sánchez 660, Azapa, T 222612, attractive grounds, several km from centre, also cheaper cabins, restaurant; **A2** *Central*, 21 de Mayo 425, T 252575, central, nicely decorated; **A3** *Savona*, Yungay 380, T 232319, comfortable, quiet, highly rec.

B *Diego de Almagro*, Sotomayor 490, T 224444, F 221248, helpful, comfortable, parking, rec, stores luggage; **C** *Lynch*, Lynch 589, T 231581, D without bath, pleasant but poor beds, rec, parking; **C** *Res América*, Sotomayor 430, T 254148, hospitable, central.

D *Hostal 18 de Septiembre*, 18 de Septiembre 524, T 251727, good, breakfast; **D** *Res Blanquita*, Maipú 472, T 232064, pleasant; **D** *Res Caracas*, Sotomayor 867, T 253688, TV, breakfast; **D** *Res Chungará*, Lynch 675, T 231677, without bath, also meals; **D** *Res Ecuador*, Juan Noé 987, T 251573, noisy, helpful, meals available; **D** *Res Las Condes*, Vicuña Mackenna 628, T 251583, helpful, rec; **D** *Res Real*, Sotomayor

578, T/F 253359, helpful, rec; **D** *Pensión Donoso*, Baquedano y Maipú, downstairs with bath, gloomy, **E** upstairs without bath, bright.

E *Casa Blanca*, Gen Lagos 557, modern, rec; **E** *Hostal Raissa*, San Martín 281, T 251070, without bath, with breakfast; **E** *La Posada*, 21

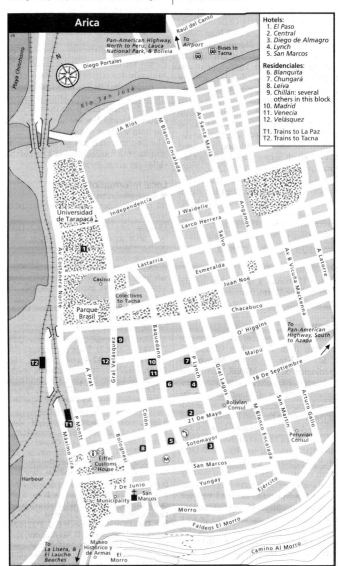

Arica

Hotels:
1. El Paso
2. Central
3. Diego de Almagro
4. Lynch
5. San Marcos

Residenciales:
6. Blanquita
7. Chungará
8. Leiva
9. Chillán: several others in this block
10. Madrid
11. Venecia
12. Velásquez

T1. Trains to La Paz
T2. Trains to Tacna

de Mayo 186, small rooms, good beds, central, without bath; **E** *Res Española*, Bolognesi 340, T 231703, central, basic, quiet; **E** *Res Las Vegas 120*, Baquedano 120, T 231355, basic, dark rooms, safe, central; **E** *Res Leiva*, Colón 347, T 232008, without bath, French spoken, cooking facilities, motorcycle parking with difficulty; **E** *Res Madrid*, Baquedano 685, T 231479, without bath, good value but poor beds, reductions for IYHA cards; **E** *Res Maipú*, Maipú 479, T 252157, basic, safe.

On Velásquez are: E *Res El Sur*, Maipú 516, small rooms, basic; **E** Gloria Martínez, pasaje 7, Población Juan Noé, T 241971, helpful; **E** *Res Ine'sa*, No 725, T 231609, comfortable, breakfast available, kitchen, laundry, good; **E** *Res Valencia*, No 719, T 253479, cooking and laundry facilties, motorcycle parking, rec; **E** *Res Velásquez*, No 685, T 231989, central, basic. **E** pp Raul del Canto 947, nice, nr bus terminal; **E** pp Sra Leony Vidiella, Gonzalo Cerda 1030, close to bus terminal, with breakfast, cooking facilities, safe, tepid water, English spoken; **E** *Res Venecia*, Baquedano 739, T 252877, spotless, small rooms, rec; **F** pp Sra Eliana, Arteaga 50, T 232304, with breakfast, luggage stored, laundry facilities, rec. In Jan-Feb the municipality supplies cheap basic accommodation, ask at the tourist office.

Camping: *Gallinazos*, at Villa Frontera, 15 km N, T 232373, full facilities, pool; *El Refugio de Azapa*, 3.5 km from Arica, T 227545.

● **Places to eat**
Acuario, Máximo Lira, Terminal Pesquero, for food and atmosphere, expensive; *El Rey del Marisco*, Maipú y Colón, seafood, pricey, rec; *Maracuyá*, San Martín 0321, seafood, splendid location on the coast, pricey; plenty of seafood lunch places in the market; *Los Aleros del 21*, 21 de Mayo 736, rec for seafood and service; *Don Floro*, V MacKenna y Chacabuco, steaks; *Snack Suceso Inn*, 18 de Septiembre 250, good set meal and coffee; *Casanova*, Baquedano 397, excellent but not cheap; *Yuri*, Maipú 500, good service, cheap, rec; *Bavaria*, Colón 613, expensive, with delicatessen and expresso coffee, repeatedly rec; *Govinda*, Bolognesi 430, vegetarian, good value lunches, repeatedly rec; *Scala*, 21 de Mayo 201, excellent fruit juices; *Carpaccio*, Velásquez 510, restaurant and bar, live music from 2330 Wed-Sat; *El Tambo*, in Poblado Artesanal, Hualles 2025, for lunches, folk music and dancing on Sun; *La Picá del Muertito*, San Miguel de Azapa at entrance to cemetery, not far from the Museo Arqueológico, typical *norteño* food. Several good Chinese restaurants inc *Si Lom*, Sotomayor 593; *Chin Huang Tao*, Lynch 317. Several places for cheap breakfasts and set meals on Baquedano 700 block. *Casino de Bomberos*, Colón 357, at fire station, good value *almuerzo*; *Schop*, 18 de Septiembre 240, cheap sandwiches.

● **Airline offices**
LanChile, 21 de Mayo 341, T 251641; **Ladeco**, 21 de Mayo 443, T 252021; **Lloyd Aéreo Boliviano**, on Sotomayor, T 251472; **AeroPerú**, Colón 367, T 232852; **National**, 21 de Mayo 627, T 253447, F 251283.

● **Banks & money changers**
Many money changers on 21 de Mayo and its junction with Colón, some accept TCs but with high commision. **Banco Santander**, 21 de Mayo, cash on Visa, no commission; **Fincard** (Mastercard), 21 de Mayo 252, Mon-Fri 0900-1400, 1600-1730, only pesos given, at varying rates. *Casas de Cambio*: **Inter-Santiago** and **Cambio Fides**, Shopping Centre del Pacífico, Diego Portales 840; **Daniel Concha**, Chacabuco 300; **Sol y Mar**, Colón 610; **Tacora**, 21 de Mayo 171, good rates for cash; **Yanulaque**, 21 de Mayo 175, which stays open until 2000 but closes all day Sun. Most large hotels also change cash. Rates for TCs are generally poor, you may even get better rates in the street.

● **Embassies & consulates**
Consulates: **Brazil**, Las Margaritas 717, Pob Prat, T 231142; **Bolivia**, 21 de Mayo 575, T 231030; **Peru**, San Martín 220, T 231020.

Denmark, 21 de Mayo 399, T 231399; **Germany**, 21 de Mayo 639, T 231551, open 0900-1300; **Italy**, San Martín y Chacabuco, T 229195; **Norway**, 21 de Mayo 399, T 231298; **Spain**, Santa María 2660, T 224655; **United Kingdom**, the only one in Chile N of Valparaíso, and Instituto Chileno – Británico de Cultura (library open Mon-Fri 0900-1200, 1600-2100), Baquedano 351, T 231960, Casilla 653.

Instituto Chileno-Alemán de Cultura, 21 de Mayo 816; **Instituto Cultural Chileno Norteamericano**, San Marcos 581.

● **Entertainment**
Cinemas: *Colón*, 7 de Junio 190, T 231165; *Cine Arte Universidad*, University Campus, T 251813.

Discotheques: 3 S of town along front, also *Sunset* and *Swing*, both 3½ km out of town in the Valle de Azapa, 2300-0430 weekends (taxi US$3).

Theatre: *Teatro Municipal de Arica*, Baquedano 234, new, wide variety of theatrical and musical events, exhibitions, rec.

● **Hospitals & medical services**
Dentist: *Juan Horta Becerra*, 18 de Septiembre 1154, T 252497, speaks English; *Rodrigo Belmar Castillo*, 18 de Septiembre 1051, T 252047.

Health: *Dr Juan Noé*, 18 de Septiembre 1000, T 231331 (T 232242 for urgent cases).

● **Laundry**

Lavandería La Moderna, 18 de Septiembre 457, per item, expensive; *Niko's*, Prat 466, US$2.50/kilo, fast; *Americana*, Lynch 260, T 231808.

● **Post & telecommunications**

Post Office: Prat 375. To send parcels abroad, contents must be shown to Aduana (under main post office) on weekdays, except Tues, between 1500 and 1700. Your parcel will be wrapped, cheaply, but take your own carton.

Telephones: Entel-Chile, 21 de May 345, open 0900-2200; CTC, Colón 430 and at 21 de Mayo 211; VTR Telecommunications, 21 de Mayo 477, telex, fax, telegrams.

● **Shopping**

Poblado Artesanal, Plaza Las Gredas, Hualles 2025 (take bus 2, 3 or 7): local 2, expensive but especially good for musical instruments; *Mercado Central*, Sotomayor, between Colón and Baquedano, mornings only. *Feria Turística Dominical*, Sun market, W end of Chacabuco extending S on Av Costanera Norte, good prices for llama sweaters. Fruit, vegetable and old clothes market at Terminal Agropecuario at edge of town; take bus marked 'Terminal Agro'. Arica, as a duty free zone, is an important centre for cheapish electronic goods for Bolivian and Peruvian shoppers. Supermarket at San Martín y 18 de Septiembre.

● **Sports**

Bathing: Olympic pool in Parque Centenario, Tues-Sun, US$0.50; take No 5A bus from 18 de Septiembre. The best beach for swimming is Playa Chinchorro, N of town. Buses 7 and 8 run to beaches S of town – the first two beaches, La Lisera and El Laucho, are both small and mainly for sunbathing. Playa Brava is popular for sunbathing but not swimming (dangerous currents). Strong currents also at Playa Las Machas which is popular with surfers. Good surfing also beyond seawall at Club de Yates.

Golf: 18-hole course in Valle de Azapa, open daily except Mon.

Tennis: *Club de Tenis Centenario*, Av España 2640, open daily.

● **Tour companies & travel agents**

Jurasi, Bolognesi 360 A, T 251696, will hold mail, helpful, good city tour; *Huasquitur*, Sotomayor 470, T 223875, helpful, English spoken, will cater for individual itineraries, rec for flights; *Vicuña Tour*, 18 de Septiembre 399, oficina 215, T 253773, F 252404, rec; *Globo Tour*, 21 de Mayo 260, T 232807, F 231085, very helpful; *Aricamundi*, Prat 358, T 252263, F 251797, for airline tickets; *Latinorizons*, O'Higgins 440, T/F 250007, specializes in tours to Lauca National Park, small groups in 4WD

Landcruiser; *Parinacota Expeditions*, Lynch 731, T 251309, excellent day tour to Lauca, Arica city tour, archaeological tours of Azapa Valley. Agencies charge similar prices for tours: Valle de Azapa US$12; city tour US$10; Lauca National Park, see page 740. Alex Figares, Casilla 2007, T/F 231643, rec as guide, speaks English.

● **Tourist offices**

Sernatur, Prat 375, p 2; open Mon-Fri 0830-1330, 1500-1900, T 232101. Very helpful, English spoken, good map; Kiosk on 21 de Mayo between Colón and Baquedano, open Mon-Fri, 0830-1300, 1500-1900; **Automobile Club** Chacabuco 460, T 252678; **Conaf**, Av Vicuña MacKenna 820, T 250570, closed weekends (take Colectivo 1).

● **Transport**

Local Bus: buses run from C Maipú, US$0.25. Collective taxis on fixed routes within city limit, US$0.30 pp (US$0.50 pp after 2000). **Car hire**: Hertz, *Hotel El Paso*, Gen Velázquez 1109, T 231487; **Budget**, 21 de Mayo 650, T 252978; **Klasse**, Velásquez 762, Loc 25, T 254498; **American**, Gen Lagos 559, T 252234; **GP**, Copacabana 628, T 252594; **Viva**, 21 de Mayo 821, T 251121; 4WD and antifreeze are essential for Lauca National Park.

Motoring **Automóvil Club de Chile**: Chacabuco 469, T 237780. **Car insurance**: at Dirección de Tránsito; may insist on car inspection. **Car service**: Shell, Panamericana Norte 3456; Esso, Portales 2462; Autocentro, Azola 2999, T 241241. **Bicycle parts**: *Bicicletas Wilson*, 18 de Sept 583, also Portales 1479.

Air Airport 18 km N of city at Chacalluta, T 222831. Taxi to town US$9, collective taxi US$4-5 pp from Lynch y 21 de Mayo. Flights: to La Paz, LanChile and LAB; to Santiago, Ladeco (via Iquique and Antofagasta), LanChile (via Iquique or Antofagasta), and National (via Iquique or Antofagasta). Book well in advance. To Lima, AeroPerú and others from Tacna (Peru), enquire at travel agencies in Arica.

Trains To La Paz (Bolivia): direct ferrobus services leave Arica Tues and Sat at 0830, also on Mon and Fri, 12 hrs, US$52 (in clean US$ bills only) inc breakfast, lunch and drinks up to lunchtime (extra food and drinks sold). Book well in advance in Jan-Mar, tickets from the station at 21 de Mayo 93, T 232844; agent is *Waskitours*, Sotomayor 417. Baggage allowance, 20 kg plus hand luggage (luggage is weighed and searched at the station). Local trains run to the frontier towns of Visviri (Chile) and Charaña (Bolivia) every other Tues (every Tues in Jan-Mar) at 2300, 9 hrs, US$12 1st class, US$7 2nd class; from Charaña a service runs at 1600 to Viacha, 32 km from La Paz, US$3 pullman. Check details in advance. On all journeys, take plenty of warm clothing; long delays, particularly at the frontier are common. Search for fruit, vegetables and dairy products at Arica station for passengers arriving from Bolivia.

The line from Arica skirts the coast for 10 km and passes into the Lluta Valley, whose vegetation is in striking contrast with the barrenness of the surrounding hills. From Km 70 there is a sharp rise of 2,241m in 42 km through a series of tunnels. At Puquíos station, Km 112, the plateau is reached at 4,168m. The line continues through Col Alcérreca (Km 140) and Villa Industrial (Km 165), before reaching its highest point at General Lagos (4,247m). In the distance can be seen the snowcapped heights of Tacora, Putre, Sajama, and their fellows. The frontier station of Visviri is at Km 205, with a customs house. Beyond, the train enters Bolivia and the station of Charaña. In summer a tourist train runs from Arica to Col Alcérreca and back on Sun, 0800, returning to Arica 2100.

See below for trains to Tacna, Peru.

Buses Bus terminal at Av Portales y Santa María, T 241390, bus or colectivo No 8 or 18 (US$0.15, or US$0.30), taxi to centre US$2 (terminal tax US$0.25). All luggage is carefully searched for fruit prior to boarding and again at Cuya on the Pan American Highway. Bus company offices at bus terminal. Local services: Flota Paco (La Paloma), Germán Riesco 2071 (bus U from centre); Humire, P Montt 662, T 231891; Martínez, 21 de Mayo 575, T 232265; Bus Lluta, Chacabuco y V Mackenna.

To **Antofagasta**, US$18, 10 hrs. To **Calama** and **Chuquicamata**, 12 hrs, US$18-20, several companies, between 2000 and 2200; to **Iquique**, frequent, US$8, 4½ hrs, also collective taxis, several companies, all with offices in the terminal; to **Santiago**, 28 hrs, a number of companies, eg Carmelita, Ramos Cholele, Fénix and Flota Barrios US$40-45, also *salón cama* services, run by Fichtur, Flota Barrios, Fénix and others, US$75, Tramaca rec (most serve meals and the more expensive, the more luxurious; student discounts available); to **La Serena**, 18 hrs, US$30; to **Viña del Mar** and **Valparaíso**, US$40, also *salón cama* service, US$50.

International buses: to **La Paz**, Bolivia, Internacional Litoral, Chacabuco 454, T 254702, Mon, Thur and Sat, 0600, US$34, no food; service via border towns of Chungará (Chile) and Tambo Quemado (Bolivia, 8-10 hrs, take food and water). Also Géminis, Wed 0800, US$34, some food, via Huara and Challapata (Bolivia); Transalvador, Av Santa María, Mon, Tues, Wed, Fri 2300, US$34; Cali, Puerto Montt y Maipú, US$27. To **Salta** (Argentina), Géminis, Tues 2130, US$50, connects at Calama next day with Antofagasta-Salta service. Computerized

booking ensures seat reservation; passport details required, book in advance.

Motorists It is illegal to take fruit and dairy products S of Arica: all vehicles are searched at Cuya, 105 km S, and at Huara, 234 km S. **Service stations** between the Peruvian border and Santiago can be found at: Arica, Huara, Iquique, Pozo Almonte, Oficina Vitoria, Tocopilla, Oficina María Elena, Chuquicamata, Calama, Carmen Alto, Antofagasta, La Negra, Agua Verde (also fruit inspection post), Taltal, Chañaral, Caldera, Copiapó, Vallenar, La Serena, Termas de Soco, Los Vilos, and then every 30 km to capital.

Hitchhiking Not easy to hitch S: try the Terminal Agropecuario (trucks leave Mon, Thur and Sat before 0700) and the Copec station opp (bus from Arica marked 'Agro').

By road to Bolivia There are 2 routes:
1) Via Chungará (Chile) and Tambo Quemado (Bolivia). This, the most widely used route, begins by heading N from Arica on the Pan-American Highway (Route 5) for 12 km before turning right (E towards the cordillera) on Route 11

Travelling in the Northern Altiplano

"In all of the mountain areas of the N of Chile, it is important to note that weather and road conditions are very variable. The *carabineros* and military are very active trying to control the borders with Bolivia and Argentina, so they know about the conditions and are quite willing to tell, but only if asked. Some frontier areas are closed to visitors.

If you plan to stay in the mountains for any length of time, take small gifts for the locals, such as tea, sugar, coffee, salad oil, flour, or a few litres of fuel. Drivers should carry a tow-rope to assist other drivers. It is often possible to get people to bake bread etc for you, but you need to supply flour, yeast and salt. If you are planning to do much cooking, then a good pressure cooker is indispensible (remember water boils at only 90°C at these altitudes). You may also have problems with kerosene stoves; petrol ones, though rather dangerous, are much more reliable."

Dr Lyndsey O'Callaghan.

towards Chungará via Putre and Lauca National Park (see below). This road is now paved to La Paz, estimated driving time 6 hrs.

2) Via Visviri (Chile) and (Charaña) Bolivia, following the La Paz-Arica railway line. This route should not be attempted in wet weather.

FRONTIER WITH PERU: CHACALLUTA

● **Immigration**

Open 0800-2400; a fairly uncomplicated crossing.

NB Between Oct and Mar Chilean time is 1 hr later than Peruvian, 2 hrs later Oct to Feb or Mar, varies annually.

● **Crossing by private vehicle**

US$2/vehicle is charged for crossing 1300-1500, 1850-2400 and on Sat, Sun, holidays. Drivers entering Chile are required to file a form, *Relaciones de Pasajeros*, giving details of passengers, obtained from a stationery store in Tacna, or at the border in a booth near Customs. You must also present the original registration document for your car from its country of registration. The first checkpoints outside Arica on the road to Santiago also require the *Relaciones de Pasajeros* form. If you can't buy the form, details on a piece of paper will suffice or you can get them at service stations. The form is *not* required when travelling S of Antofagasta.

● **Exchange**

Facilities at the frontier but reported better rates in Tacna.

● **Transport**

Local Collective taxis: run from the W end of C Noé and company offices in Arica to **Tacna**, US$4 pp, 1½ hrs, drivers take care of all the paperwork. Four companies: Chile Lintur, Baquedano 796, T 232048; Chasquitur, Chacabuco 320, T 231376; San Marcos, Noé 321, T 252528; Colectivo San Remo, Chacabuco 350, T 251925. Bus from the terminal, US$2, also Taxibus, 2 hourly, US$4. For Arequipa it is best to go to Tacna and catch an onward bus there.

Trains Services for passengers to Tacna leave Arica 3 times a week, US$1.60, 2½ hrs, from the station at Máximo Lira 889, T 231115. In Tacna there is a customs check at the station but no immigration facilities.

FRONTIER WITH BOLIVIA: VISVIRI

● **Immigration**

Open 0800-2400. Chilean formalities at Visviri, Bolivian formalities at Charaña, 10 km E.

● **Crossing with a private vehicle**

US$2/vehicle charge for crossing 1300-1500, 1850-2100 and Sat, Sun and holidays.

● **Transport**

Buses from Arica to Visviri, Tues and Fri, 1000, 2200, US$7 from Puerto Montt y Maipú. Collective taxi from Arica US$10. In Visviri take a jeep across the border to Charaña. Bus from Charaña to La Paz, US$11, 7 hrs.

PARQUE NACIONAL LAUCA

The Parque Nacional Lauca, 176 km E of Arica stretching to the frontier with Bolivia, is one of the most spectacular National Parks in Chile. Acess is easy as the main Arica-La Paz road runs through the park and is paved. On the way, at Km 90 there is a pre-Inca *pukará* (fortress) and a few kilometres further there is an Inca *tambo* (inn). During the rainy season (Jan and Feb) roads in the park may be impassable; check in advance with Conaf in Arica.

Situated at over 3,200m (beware of soroche unless you are coming from Bolivia), the park covers 137,883 ha and includes numerous snowy volcanoes including 10 peaks of over 6,000m, two large lakes (Cotacotani and Chungará) and lava fields at Cotacotani. The park contains over 120 species of bird, resident or migrant, as well as camelids, vizcacha and puma. A good base for exploring the park and for acclimatization is **Putre** (3,500m), a scenic village, 15 km before the entrance with a church dating from 1670 and surrounded by terracing dating from pre-Inca times, now used for cultivating alfalfa and oregano. From here paths provide easy walking and great views.

At **Parinacota** (4,392m), at the foot of the Payachatas volcano, there is an interesting 17th century church – rebuilt 1789 – with frescoes and the skulls of past priests. Local residents knit alpaca sweaters, US$26 approx; weavings of wildlife scenes also available. Weavings are sold from a tin shed with an orange roof opposite the church. From here an unpaved road runs N to the Bolivian frontier at Visviri (see above). From the Conaf hut you can climb Guane Guane, 5,300m, in 2-3 hrs, ask the wardens. 20 km SE of Parinacota is **Lago Chungará**, at 4,600m, a must for its views of the Parinacota, Sajama and Guallatire volcanoes and for its varied wildlife. From here it is about 10 km to the Bolivian frontier at Tambo Quemado. About 30 km S of Parinacota by road is Choquelimpie, the highest gold mine in the world, with an attractive colonial church in the precinct.

Park information
● Accommodation

At Putre: **A2** *Hostería Las Vicuñas*, T 228564, bungalow-style, heating, good restaurant, does not accept TCs, US$ cash or credit cards; *Res La Paloma*, hot showers, no heating, good food; **E** pp *Res Rosamel*, pleasant, hot water, restaurant; **F** pp *Res Oasis*, basic, no showers, good restaurant; Conaf also rent out 2 rooms, **E** pp basic, no heating. **Camping**: Sra Clementina Cáceres, blue door on C Lynch, allows camping in her garden.

At **Chucuyo**: a village 30 km E of Putre, there are two shops/restaurants, both of which have rooms to let, no showers.

In **Parinacota**: accommodation at the local school, **G** pp, rec.

There are three Conaf refuges in the park, but check in advance with Conaf in Arica that they are open: at **Parincota** (there is supposed to be oxygen for those suffering from soroche, but it is often not available), at **Lago Chungará**, and at **Las Cuevas** (emergencies only, no tourist facilities); the first two have cooking facilities, but no heating, US$12 pp, sleeping bag essential, take your own food, candles and matches. Camping US$12 tent. Advance booking rec. On arrival in Putre you are supposed to register with Conaf. Maps of the park (unreliable) are sometimes available from Conaf in Arica and from the tourist office.

● Banks & money changers
No facilities; buy pesos in Arica.

● Shopping
Food is available in Putre, which has several stores, 2 bakeries and where several private houses sell fresh produce. Fuel is much more expensive than in Arica but available in Putre from the Cali and Paloma supermarkets and from **ECA**, a government subsidized market on the plaza (cheapest). No food is available outside Putre.

● Tours companies & travel agents
Tours: *Birding Altoandino*, Baquedano 299 (Correo Putre) T 56-58-300013, F 56-58-222735, run general tours and specialist bird-watching tours to remote areas of the park and to the Salar de Surire and Parque Nacional Isluga; English spoken, owner is an Alaskan biologist. *Turismo Taki*, is located in Copaquila, about 45 km W of Putre, 100 km E of Arica: restaurant, camping site and excursions to nearby *pucarás*, Inca *tambo* and cemetery, good local food, English and Italian spoken.

One-day tours are offered by most travel agencies in Arica (addresses above), daily in season, according to demand at other times, US$23 pp with breakfast and light lunch; but some find the minibuses cramped and dusty. Shop around carefully. You spend all day in the bus and, if not acclimatized, you will suffer from soroche. You can leave the tour and continue on another day as long as you ensure that the company will collect you when you want (tour companies try to charge double for this). For 5 or more, the most economical proposition is to hire a vehicle.

● Transport
Flota Paco buses (known as La Paloma) leave Arica for Putre daily at 0645, 4 hrs, US$4, returning Sun/Wed 1200, otherwise 1300; Jurasi collective taxi leaves Arica daily at 0700, picks up at hotels, T 222813, US$6.50. Bolivia Litoral bus from Arica to La Paz also runs along this route (charges full Arica-La Paz fare). Martínez buses run to Parinacota Tues and Fri. Bus to La Paz from Putre crossroads (about 1½ km from town), twice a week, US$22.50, buy ticket and get schedule from *Supermercado*

Cali, can arrange collection from Lago Chungará.

Hitching back to Arica is not difficult; you may be able to bargain on one of the tour buses. Trucks from Arica to La Paz rarely give lifts, but a good place to try is at the Poconchile control point, 37 km from Arica. Most trucks for Bolivia pass Parinacota between 0700-1100.

FRONTIER WITH BOLIVIA: CHUNGARA

● **Immigration**
Open 0800-2100; US$2/vehicle crossing 1300-1500, 1850-2100 and Sat, Sun and holidays. Long delays are reported at this crossing.

● **Transport**
For details of through buses between Arica and La Paz see above under Arica.

RESERVA NACIONAL LAS VICUÑAS

South of Lauca is the beautiful **Reserva Nacional Las Vicuñas** at 4,300 to 5,600m. Be prepared for cold, skin burns from sun and wind, etc; there is no public transport. A high clearance vehicle is essential and, in the summer wet season, 4WD: take extra fuel. Administration is at **Guallatiri**, reached by turning off the Arica-La Paz road onto the A147 2 km after Las Cuevas, where there is also a Conaf office. Open Mar-November.

MONUMENTO NATURAL SALAR DE SURIRE

The same road leads into the **Monumento Natural Salar de Surire** (4,200m), which is open for the same months and for which the same conditions apply. Administration is in **Surire**, 45 km S of Guallatiri and 129 km S of Putre. This can be reached by getting a ride in a borax truck; these run every day between July and Nov from Zapahuira (a road junction between Bolivia and Arica).

● **Accommodation** At Surire there is a Conaf *refugio*, 4 beds, very clean, prior application to Conaf in Arica essential. Campsite at Polloquere, 16 km S of Surire, no facilities.

South through the Central Valley

ONE of the world's most fruitful and beautiful countrysides, with the snowclad peaks of the Andes delimiting it to the east, the Central Valley contains most of Chile's population. It is a region of small towns, farms and vineyards, with several protected areas of natural beauty. To the south are the major city of Concepción, the port of Talcahuano and the main coal-mining area.

This section covers three of the administrative regions of Chile, Regions VI, VII and VIII. The Central Valley is a wide depression between the Andes to the E and the Cordillera de la Costa to the West. Five major rivers cross the Central Valley, cutting through the Coastal Range to reach the Pacific: from N to S these are the Ríos Rapel, Mataquito, Maule, Itata and Biobío. Of these the Biobío, one of the three largest rivers in Chile, is the most important.

ROUTES Road and railway run S through the Central Valley; the railway has been electrified from Santiago to just S of Temuco. Along the road from Santiago to Temuco there are several modern motels. From Santiago to San Javier (S of Talca), the highway is dual carriageway, with two tolls of US$3 to

South through the Central Valley

50

pay. The highway between Santiago and Rancagua is dangerous for cyclists (inattentive truck drivers).

RANCAGUA

(*Pop* 167,000; *Phone code* 072), the capital of VI Región (Libertador Gen Bernardo O'Higgins), lies 82 km S of Santiago, on the Río Cachapoal. Founded in 1743, it is a service and market centre.

Places of interest

At the heart of the city is an attractive tree-lined plaza, the **Plaza de los Héroes**, and several streets of single-storey colonial-style houses. In the centre of the plaza is an equestrian statue of O'Higgins. The **Merced** church, 1 block N, several times restored, dates from 1758. The **Museo Histórico**, Estado y Ibieta, housed in a colonial mansion, contains collections of religious art and late 19th century furniture. The main commercial area lies along Av Independencia which runs W from the plaza towards the bus and rail terminals.

Excursions

To the thermal springs of **Cauquenes**, 28 km E, reached by colectivo from Rancagua market (**A3** *Hotel Termas de Cauquenes*, T 297226, excellent, gardens, rec).

The battle of Rancagua

Rancagua was the scene of an important battle during the Wars of Independence. On 1-2 October 1814 Bernardo O'Higgins and his 1,700 Chilean patriots were surrounded in the centre of the town by 4,500 Royalist (pro-Spanish) troops. O'Higgins, who commanded his forces from the tower of the Merced church, managed to break out and escape. Defeated, he was forced into exile in Argentina, while the Royalists reestablished control over Chile. Plaques in the centre of Rancagua mark the sites of the battle and a diagram in the Plaza de los Héroes shows the disposition of the troops.

Local festivals

National Rodeo Championships, at the end of March (plenty of opportunities for purchasing cowboy items).

Local information

● **Accommodation**

B *Aguila Real*, Brasil 1055, T 222047, inc breakfast; **B** *Rancagua*, San Martín 85, T 232663, F 241155, quiet, secure parking, rec. **C** *España*, San Martín 367, T 230141, cheaper without bath, central, pleasant. Many hotels do not accept guests before 2000, or may charge you double if you arrive in the afternoon.

● **Places to eat**

Café Haiti, Paseo Independencia 690, p 2, lively at night; *Bravissimo*, Astorga 307, for ice cream; *Lasagna*, W end of Plaza, for bread and *empanadas*.

● **Banks & money changers**

Afex, Av Campos 363, for US$ cash; **Fincard**, Av Campos 376, Mon-Fri 0900-1400, 1530-1930, Sat 1000-1300, for Mastercard.

● **Tourist offices**

Germán Riesco 277, T 230413, helpful, English spoken. **Automóvil Club de Chile**: Ibieta 09, T 239930.

● **Transport**

Trains Main line services between Santiago and Concepción and Chillán stop here. Also regular services to/from Santiago on Metrotren, 1¼ hrs, 10-13 a day, US$2.

Buses Main terminal at Ocarrol y Calvo; local buses leave from the Terminal de Buses Regionales, just N of the market. Frequent services to **Santiago**, US$3, 1 hr 10 mins.

East of Rancagua

The **El Teniente** copper mine, one of the biggest in the country, 67 km E, can only be visited by prior arrangement with Codelco. Nearby, on a private road above El Teniente, is the small **Chapa Verde** ski resort, owned by Codelco, but open to the public in season. It can only be reached by mine-transport bus (from Del Sol shopping centre, daily 0900, weekends in season every 15 mins between 0800 and 0930). Equipment can be hired, no accommodation, lift tickets US$18 weekdays, US$25 weekends, obtainable only from resort office in Del Sol shopping centre.

SAN FERNANDO

(*Pop* 44,500; *Alt* 460m; *Phone code* 072) **San**

Fernando stands on the Río Tinguiririca 51 km S of Rancagua. Founded in 1742, it is capital of Colchagua Province and a service town for this fertile valley. From San Fernando a road runs E towards the Cordillera and divides: the northern branch (75 km) runs to the **Termas del Flaco** (*Alt* 1,720m), near the Argentine frontier (poor campsite, *cabañas* and hotels, but open only in summer when it attracts large numbers of visitors); the southern branch goes to the resort of **Sierra Bellavista**, a private *fundo* where many Santiago businessmen have holiday houses. Rodeos in Oct and November.

Excursions **Los Lingues** is a private *hacienda* 20 km NE of San Fernando, 126 km S of Santiago, where, it is said, the best horses in Chile are bred. Visits can be arranged to the 17th century house, a gift of the King of Spain. One-day tours including transport, rodeo and lunch are available, also accommodation with extra charge for breakfast or full board, very expensive (the Hacienda is a member of the French Hotels et Relais et Chateaux). Contact: Hacienda Los Lingues, Torre C de Tajamar, Of 205, Santiago, T 235-2458/5446/7604, F 235-7604, Tx 346060 LINGUES CK. To 6060 LINGUE.

- **Accommodation** On Av Rodríguez: **C** *Español*, No 959, T 711098; **D** *Marcano*, No 968, T 714759; **E** *Imperio*, No 770, T 714595, with bath; **D** *Pérez*, No 1028, T 713328, without bath.

PICHILEMU

(*Pop* 6,827) 120 km W of San Fernando (road 86 km paved), **Pichilemu** is a coastal resort with a great many hotels and *residenciales* and several beaches, including the Punta Los Lobos beach, where international surfing competitions are held.

- **Accommodation** **B** *Chile-España*, Ortúzar 255, T 841270, helpful, excellent restaurant, good value; **C** *Rex*, Ortúzar 34, T 681003, good breakfast, good value; **E** *Bahía*, Ortúzar 262, with breakfast. **Camping**: Campsites, US$15/site.

- **Transport** Andimar bus to **Santiago**, 4 hrs, US$5.50.

CURICO

(*Pop* 103,919; *Alt* 200m; *Phone code* 075) 54 km S of San Fernando and 192 km from Santiago, **Curicó** lies between the Ríos Lontué and Teno. Founded in 1744, it is the only town of any size in the valley.

Places of interest

In the **Plaza de Armas** there are fountains and a monument to the Mapuche warrior, Lautaro, carved from the trunk of an ancient beech tree. There is a steel kiosk, built in New Orleans in 1904, which is a national monument. The church of **San Francisco** (1732), also a national monument, partly ruined, contains the 17th century Virgen de Velilla, brought from Spain. At the junction of Carmen and Av San Martín is the imposing **Iglesia del Carmen**. The fine, broad and tree-lined Av Manso de Velasco leads to **Parque Balmaceda**, in which is a bust of the poet, Gabriela Mistral. Overlooking the city, the surrounding countryside and with views to the distant Andean peaks is **Cerro Condell** (100m); it is an easy climb to the summit from where there are a number of walks.

Excursions

To the **Torres wine bodega**, 5 km S of the city: take a bus for Molina from Henríquez y O'Higgins and get off at Km 195 on the Pan-American Highway, open 0900-1300, 1500-1800, no organized tour, Spanish only, worthwhile.

Local information
- **Accommodation**

B *Luis Cruz Martines*, Prat 301 y Carmen, T 310552, breakfast extra, overpriced; **C** *Comercio*, Yungay 730, T 312442, rec; **D** *Res Rahue*, Peña 410, T 312194, basic, meals, annex rooms have no ventilation; **D** *Res Central*, Av Prat, 2 blocks from station, good value; **E** *Prat*, Peña 427, T 311069, pleasant patio, laundry facilities; **E** *Res Colonial*, Rodríguez 461.

- **Places to eat**

El Fogón Chileno, Yungay 802, good for meat and wines; *American Bar*, Yungay 647, coffee, small pizzas, good sandwiches, pleasant atmosphere, open early am to late pm inc weekends, rec; *Café-Bar Maxim*, Prat 617, light meals, beer and wine. *Club de la Unión*, Plaza de Armas, good; *Centro Italiano Club Social*, Estado 531, good, cheap meals.

● **Banks & money changers**
Fincard, Carmen 498, for Mastercard. Casa de Cambio, Merced 255, Local 106, no TCs.

● **Laundry & dry cleaners**
Limpiabien, Prat 454 (and other branches), quick, efficient.

● **Post & telecommunications**
Telephones: CTC, Peña 650-A.

● **Tourist offices**
Tourist information supplied by the Mayor's secretary, Gobernación building, p 2, Plaza de Armas, helpful, has street map. **Automóvil Club**

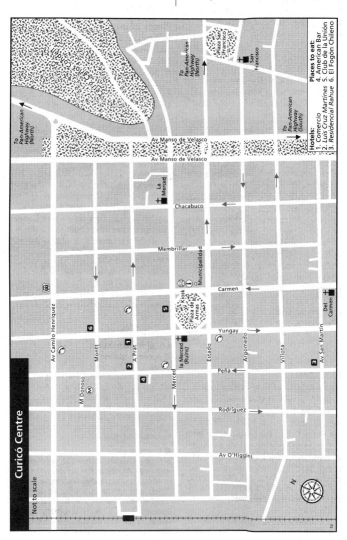

Curicó Centre

Not to scale

Places to eat:
4. American Bar 5. Club de la Unión 6. El Fogón Chileno

Hotels:
1. Comercio 2. Luis Cruz Martines 3. Residencial Rahue

de Chile: Chacabuco 759, T 311156. **Conaf**: Gobernación, p 1, Plaza de Armas.

● **Transport**
Trains Station is at the end of Prat, 4 blocks W of Plaza de Armas, T 310028. To/from Santiago, 5 a day, US$4 *económico*, US$5 *superior*. To/from Concepción 1 a day.

Buses Companies have their own terminals for interprovincial destinations. Local buses, inc to coastal towns, from Terminal Rural, O'Higgins y Prat, 1 block E of railway station. Many southbound buses by-pass Curicó, but can be caught by waiting outside town. To **Santiago** US$3, 3 hrs; to **Temuco**, LIT and Tur Bus, US$7.

ROUTES There is a toll (US$3) on the Longitudinal Highway S of Curicó. The city has a good road connection with Argentina, via Paso Vergara (Paso del Planchón, 92 km from Curicó) to San Rafael (transport schedules from Turismo Bucalemu, Yungay 621).

Area de Protección Radal Siete Tazas

The park is in 2 sectors, one at Radal, 65 km E of Curicó, the other at Parque Inglés, 9 km further E. At Radal, the Río Claro flows through a series of seven rock bowls (the *siete tazas*) each with a pool emptying into the next by a waterfall. The river then passes through a canyon, 15m deep but only 1½m wide, which ends abruptly in a cliff and a beautiful waterfall. The park is open Oct to March. Administration is in Parque Inglés.

● **Accommodation D** *Hostería La Flor de la Canela*, at Parque Inglés, inc breakfast, T 491613, good food, highly rec, camping, open summer only. **Camping**: campsites near entrance, dirty.

● **Transport** Buses from Molina, 26 km S of Curicó to the Park, on Tues and Thur 1700, returning Wed and Fri 0800. Daily bus from Curicó in summer, 1545, 4½ hrs, returns 0745 (Sun 0700, returns 1900).

WEST OF CURICO

From Curicó a road runs W to the mouth of the Río Mataquito and the popular resort of **Iloca**. Another resort, **Llico**, is N of Iloca, reached either by a coastal route or by an unpaved inland road which branches off at Hualañe (Km 74).

● **Accommodation D** *Res Atlántida 2000*, nr beach, good restaurant, bar, friendly, discount for *South American Handbook* readers; **D** *Pensión Chile*, rooms with bath have hot water, cheap meals.

● **Transport** Buses, from Terminal Rural in Curicó daily, 3 hrs.

Lago Vichuquén, surrounded by pine forest, is 114 km W of Curicó, just E of Llico. It is very popular with the wealthy and with water-sports enthusiasts. **Reserva Nacional Laguna Torca**, just N of Lago Vichuquén, 604 ha, is a natural sanctuary for over 80 species of birds, especially black-necked swans and other water fowl. Administration is 4 km E of Llico; campsite nearby. Open Sept-April. Take any bus from Curicó to Llico and get out near Administration.

TALCA

(*Pop* 160,000; *Phone code* 071) 56 km S of Curicó (258 km from Santiago, all dual carriageway). The most important city between Santiago and Concepción it is a major manufacturing centre and the capital of VII Región (Maule). Founded in 1692, it was destroyed by earthquakes in 1742 and 1928.

Places of interest

Just off the Plaza de Armas at 1 Norte y 2 Oriente is the **Museo O'Higginiano** (open Tues-Sat, 0915-1245, 1500-1845, US$1) located in a colonial mansion which belonged to Juan Albano Pereira, tutor to the young Bernardo O'Higgins who lived here between the ages of 4 and 10. The house was later the headquarters of O'Higgins' Patriot Government in 1813-14 (before his defeat at Rancagua). In 1818 O'Higgins signed the declaration of Chilean independence here: the room (Sala Independencia) is decorated and furnished in period style. 8 km SE is **Villa Huilquilemu**, a 19th century hacienda, now part of the Universidad Católica del Maule, housing four museums, of religious art, handicrafts, agricultural machinery and wine.

Local information
● **Accommodation**
On the Panamericana Sur, Km 250, are **A3** *Cabañas Entre Ríos*, T 223336, F 220477 (Santiago: San Antonio 486, of 132, T 633-3750, F 632-4791), very good value, excellent breakfast, pool, very helpful owner, highly rec. **A3** *Plaza*, 1 Poniente 1141, T 226150, good

commercial standard; **C** *Amalfi*, 2 Sur 1265, T 225703, old-fashioned, central; **D** *Alcázar*, 2 Sur 1359, breakfast and meals available, rec; **D** pp *Cordillera*, 2 Sur 1360, T 221812, F 233028, nr bus terminal.

● **Banks & money changers**
Edificio Caracol, Oficina 15, 1 Sur 898, for US$ cash; Fincard (Mastercard), 1 Sur 826.

● **Post & telecommunications**
Post Office: 1 Oriente s/n.
Telephones: CTC, 1 Sur 1156 and 1 Sur 835.

● **Tourist offices**
1 Poniente 1234, T 233669. **Automóvil Club de Chile**: 1 Poniente 1267, T 223-2774.

● **Transport**
Trains Station at 2 Sur y 11 Oriente, T 226254. To **Santiago**, 5 a day, US$5; to **Concepción**, 1 a day, to **Temuco** 1 a day.

Buses Terminal at 12 Oriente y 2 Sur. To **Chillán**, frequent service, US$2; also frequent to **Constitución**, 2 hrs, US$1.20.

EAST OF TALCA

A road from Talca runs 175 km SE along **Lago Colbún** and up the valley of the Río Maule, passing through some of the finest mountain scenery in Chile to reach the Argentine frontier at Paso Pehuenche.

● **Accommodation** *El Colorado*, on N shore of Lago Colbún, T/F 221750; **C** pp *Centro Portezuelo*, at Quinamávida, S of Lago Colbún on the road to Linares, T 09-7520510, full board, large *estancia* offering forest trails, beaches, English spoken, highly rec.

VILCHES

63 km E of Talca, is the starting point for the climb to the volcanoes Quizapu and Descabezado (3,850m). For walks on Descabezado Grande and Cerro Azul (ice axe and crampons needed) contact recommended guide Carlos Verdugo Bravo, Probación Brilla El Sol, Pasaje El Nickel 257, Talca (Spanish only).

The **Area de Protección Vilches** 2 km from Vilches, covers 16,684 ha and includes three peaks, several small lakes, the Piedras Tacitas, a stone construction supposedly made by the aboriginal inhabitants of the region, and a visitors' centre. The administration is 1 km from the *Hotel Altos de Vilches* (closed).

● **Accommodation C** pp *Hostería Rancho Los Canales*, with breakfast, use of kitchen,

good food, log cabins C for 4 people, hospitable, pool, knowledgeable family (postal address: Casilla 876, Talca).

● **Transport** Two buses a day, US$1.50, 2-2½ hrs, leave Talca 1300 and 1650, leave Vilches 0700 and 1730.

FRONTIER WITH ARGENTINA: PASO PEHUENCHE

Paso Pehuenche (2,553m) is reached by unpaved road SE from Lago Colbún (see above). On the Argentine side the road continues to Malargüe and San Rafael. The border is open Dec-Mar 0800-2100, April-Nov 0800-1900.

CONSTITUCION

(*Pop* 28,748) lies W of Talca at the mouth of the Río Maule and is reached by road (89 km) from San Javier. Founded in 1794, it is an industrial town with naval shipyards and a cellulose factory; fishing is also important. Its main attraction is as a seaside resort. The beach, an easy walk from the town, is surrounded by very picturesque rocks. There are good views from Cerro Mutrún, at the mouth of the river (access from C O'Higgins).

● **Accommodation A2** *Hostería Constitución*, Echeverría 460, T 671450, best; **C** *Avendaño*, O'Higgins 681, pleasant patio, restaurant, safe; **D** *Res Urrutia*, Freire 238, inc breakfast, some rooms gloomy, laundry facilities; **D** *Res Fadiz*, Bulnes nr bus terminal, laundry facilities; other *residenciales* in Freire 100-300 blocks, Portales 300 block and Rengifo 300 block. Book in advance Jan-March.

SOUTH OF CONSTITUCION

A paved road runs along the coast to **Curanipe**, 83 km S, which has a beautiful beach.

● **Accommodation C** *Pacífico*, Comercio 509, T 495903, pleasant; several others; municipal campsite.

Nearby there are two **Reservas Nacionales: Los Ruiles**, off the road E to Cauquenes, covers 45 ha of native forest and flowers. Open Oct-March; daily buses from Constitución or Cauquenes. **Federico Albert**, on the coast ½ km N of Chanco, covers 145 ha of dunes and forest planted in experiments to control the shifting sand. It has a visitors' centre and campsite; open Oct-March.

This area can also be reached from **Parral**, 88 km S of Talca on the Pan-American Highway, the birthplace of the Nobel Prize-winning poet Pablo Neruda. The road goes through Cauquenes.

CHILLAN

(*Pop* 146,000; *Alt* 118m; *Phone code* 042), 150 S of Talca, capital of Ñuble province and a service centre for this agricultural area. Following an earthquake in 1833, the site was moved slightly to the NW, though the older site, Chillán Viejo, is still occupied. Further earthquakes in 1939 and 1960 have ensured that few old buildings have survived. Chillán was the birthplace of Bernardo O'Higgins (Arturo Prat, Chile's naval hero, was born 50 km away at Ninhue).

Places of interest

Northwest of the Plaza O'Higgins, in the **Escuela México**, at Av O'Higgins between Vega de Saldías and Gamero, donated to the city after the 1939 earthquake, are murals by the great Mexican artists David Alvaro Siqueiros and Xavier Guerrero which present allegories of Chilean and Mexican history. The **San Francisco** church, 3 blocks NE of the Plaza, contains a **museum** of religious and historical artefacts. The modern **Cathedral** on the Plaza O'Higgins is designed to resist earthquakes. The **Mercado y Feria Municipal** (covered and open markets) sells regional arts and crafts and has many cheap, good restaurants, serving regional dishes; open daily, Sun until 1300. In **Chillán Viejo** (SW of the centre) there is a monument and park in honour of O'Higgins; it has a 60m long mural depicting his life (an impressive, but sadly faded, mosaic of various native stones), and a **Centro Histórico y Cultural**, with a gallery of contemporary paintings by regional artists (park is open 0900-1300, 1500-1900).

Museums

Museo Naval Arturo Prat, Collin y I Riquelme, contains naval artefacts and models Chilean vessels, Tues-Fri 0930-1200, 1500-1730.

Excursions

27 km SW of Chillán is **Quinchamalí**, a little village famous for the originality of its craftsmen in textiles, basketwork, black ceramics, guitars and primitive paintings (all on sale in Chillán market).

Local information
● Accommodation

A2 *Isabel Riquelme*, Arauco 600, T 213663.

B *Cordillera*, Arauco 619, on Plaza de Armas, T 215221, 3-star, small, all rooms with heating, good; **B** *Rucamanqui*, Herminda Martín 590 (off Plaza de Armas), T 222927, spartan; **B** *Floresta*, 18 de Septiembre, 268, quiet, old fashioned.

C *Quinchamalí*, El Roble 634, T 223381, central, quiet, heated lounge; **C** *Nevado de Chillán*, O'Higgins 497, T 221013, **D** without bath, good value.

D *Libertador*, Libertad 85, T 223155, large rooms; **D** *Real*, Libertad 219, T 221827, good; these two are a few minutes' walk from the railway station and are much better than the closer hotels such as **E** *Bahía*, opp station, no hot water, basic, good restaurant below; **D** *Res Su Casa*, Cocharcas 555, T 223931, inc breakfast, parking; **D** *Claris*, 18 de Septiembre 357, T 221983, 2 blocks from plaza, good value, rec; **E** *Hosp Sonia Segui*, Itata 288, T214879, good breakfast, small rooms, run down.

● Places to eat

Centro Español, Plaza de Armas, separate bar with snacks, excellent; *Fuente Alemana*, Arauco 661, for *churrasco*, reasonable; *Café París*, Arauco 686, expresso coffee, fine restaurant upstairs, rec; *Club Comercial*, Arauco 745, popular at lunchtime, good value *almuerzo*, popular bar at night; *Quick Lunch*, El Roble 610, open 0800-2400 for good value meals with good service; *Arco Iris*, Plaza de Armas, vegetarian, lunches only, excellent; *O'Higgins*, O'Higgins y Libertad, good value; *Jai Yang*, Libertad 250, good Chinese; *La Copucha*, 18 de Septiembre y Constitución, inexpensive meals and sandwiches; *Café Madrid*, 5 de Abril 608, good for coffee; *La Masc'a*, 5 de Abril 544, excellent cheap meals, *empanadas de queso*, drinks, rec. In Chillán Viejo, *Los Adobes*, on Parque O'Higgins, good food and service, reasonable prices. The Chillán area is well-known for its *pipeño* wine (very young) and its *longanizas* (sausages).

● Banks & money changers

Both **Banco de Concepción** and **Banco Sudamericano** give poor rates. Better rates at *Casa de Cambio*, Constitución 550, or *Café París* on Arauco (ask for Enrique Schuler). **Fincard** (Mastercard), El Roble 553.

● **Language schools**

Interswop JB Turismo, Constitución 633, Of 03, T 223526, F 210744, offers exchange programmes with opportunities for work and language courses, US$180 for 25 hrs study. Also **travel agency**. (Address in Germany: Bornstrasse 16, 20146 Hamburg, T/F 40-410-8029.)

● **Tourist offices**

In Gobernación building on main plaza, central courtyard, left-hand gallery; street map of city, leaflets on skiing, Termas de Chillán, etc. **Automóvil Club de Chile**: O'Higgins 677, T 212550.

● **Transport**

Trains Station, Brasil opp Libertad, 5 blocks from plaza, T 222424. To **Santiago**, 2 daily, 5½ hrs, *salón* US$7-7.35 depending on the service, *económico* US$5-5.35.

Buses Long distance buses leave from Constitución y Brasil (opp railway station). Local buses leave from Maipon y Sgto Aldea. To **Santiago**, 7 hrs, US$7.50; to **Concepción**, every 30 mins.

TERMAS DE CHILLAN

82 km E of Chillán by good road (paved for the first 50 km) 1,850m up in the

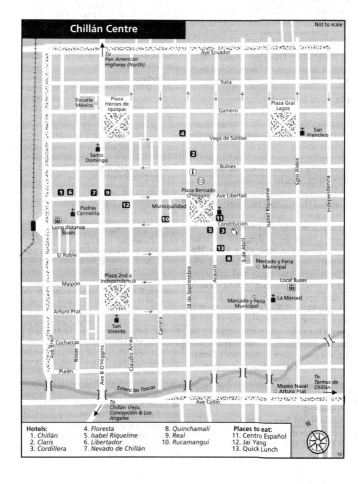

Chillán Centre   Not to scale

Hotels:
1. Chillán
2. Claris
3. Cordillera
4. Floresta
5. Isabel Ríquelme
6. Libertador
7. Nevado de Chillán
8. Quinchamali
9. Real
10. Rucamangui

Places to eat:
11. Centro Español
12. Jai Yang
13. Quick Lunch

Cordillera are thermal baths and, above, the largest ski resort in southern Chile. There are two open air thermal pools (officially for hotel guests only) and a health spa with jacuzzis, sauna, mud baths etc. Suitable for families and beginners and cheaper than centres nearer Santiago, the ski resort is to be expanded in 1997 with a new luxury hotel and more lifts. Season: middle Dec to the end of March. Lift pass US$30/day, US$20/half-day. Information from Chillán Ski Centre, Barros Arana 261, or from Libertador 1042. Equipment hire also from Chillán Ski Centre (about US$25 pp).

● **Accommodation** Ski Club de Chile has a tourist centre with hotel (full board, T 223887 Chillán, Casilla 247, office at Arauco 600, or Santiago T 251-5776, Av Providencia 2237, locales 42-4). At Las Trancas on the road to the Termas, 70 km from Chillán are **A2 Hotel Los Pirineos**, T 293839, and **A2 Parador Jamón, Pan y Vino**, 18 de Septiembre 661, oficina 23, T 492241, Casilla 22, Chillán (Don Emilio Chamorro), arranges rec horse riding expeditions. *Cabañas* also available in the village. **Camping**: 2 km from the slopes.

● **Transport** Ski buses run from Libertador 1042 at 0800 and from Chillán Ski Centre, subject to demand, US$30 (inc lift pass). Taxi US$30 one way, 1½ hrs. At busy periods hitching may be possible from Chillán Ski Centre.

ROUTES From Chillán there are various road routes to Concepción: (1) W to Tomé then S along the coast through Penco; (2) along the Longitudinal Highway to Bulnes, where a branch road goes SW to Concepción; or to Cabrero from where there is a paved road W to Concepción.

CONCEPCION

(*Pop* 326,784; *Phone code* 041) the capital of VIII Región (Bío-Bío), 15 km up the Biobío river and 516 km from Santiago, is the third biggest city in Chile. The most important city in southern Chile, it is one of the country's major industrial centres; to the S are coalfields and an important forestry area. Talcahuano, Chile's most important naval base is 15 km N.

Founded in 1550, Concepción became a frontier stronghold in the war against the Mapuche after 1600. Destroyed by an earthquake in 1751, it was moved to its present site in 1764.

The climate is very agreeable in summer, but from April to Sept the rains are heavy; the annual average rainfall, nearly all of which falls in those 6 months, is from 1,250 to 1,500 mm.

Places of interest

In the attractive Plaza de Armas at the centre are the **Intendencia** and the **Cathedral**. It was here that Bernardo O'Higgins proclaimed the independence of Chile on 1 January 1818. Every Feb in the **Parque Ecuador** (on Victor Lamas, at the foot of Cerro Caracol), there is a craft fair. At the edge of the park is the Galería de la Historia (see below).

Cerro Caracol can easily be reached on foot starting from the statue of Don Juan Martínez de Rozas in the Parque Ecuador, arriving at the Mirador Chileno after 15 mins. From here it is another, 20 mins climb to **Cerro Alemán**. The Biobío and its valley running down to the sea lie below. On the far side of the river you see lagoons, the largest of which, **San Pedro**, is a watersport centre. On the city side, among cypress trees, is the modern **Barrio Universitario**. A stroll through the grounds, which are beautifully kept with geese, ducks, swans, hummingbirds and a small enclosure with *pudu-pudu* (miniature deer) is recommended.

Concepción is linked with Talcahuano, by two good roads, half-way along one of which is the Club Hípico's racetrack. Races are held on Sun and holidays. A branch road leads to good beaches, including Tomé (see below), Las Escaleras (a private club) and Ramuntcho.

Museums

Museo de Concepción, near Barrio Universitario, Tues-Sat 1000-1300, 1400-1700, Sun 1430-1730; entrance US$0.50; interesting on history of the Mapuche nation. The **Galería de la Historia**, Lincoyán y V Lamas, is an audiovisual depiction of the history of Concepción and the region; upstairs is a collection of Chilean painting, Mon 1500-1830, Tues-Fri 1000-1330, 1500-1830, Sat/Sun 1000-1400, 1500-1930, free. The **Casa del Arte**, Roosevelt y Larena, contains the University art collection; the entrance hall is dominated by *La Presencia de América Latina*, by the Mexican Jorge González Camerena, (1965) an impressive allegorical mural depicting Latin American history. Open Tues-Fri 1000-1800, Sat 1000-1600, Sun 1000-1300, entry free, explanations are given free by University Art students. There is another fine mural in

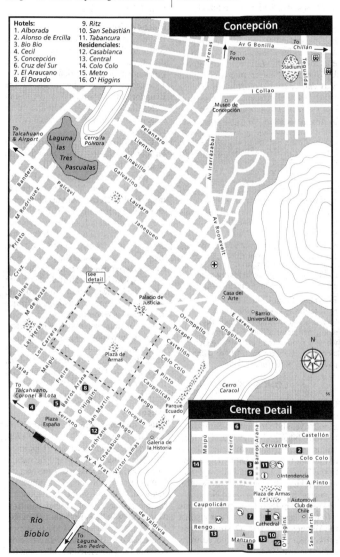

Hotels:
1. *Alborada*
2. *Alonso de Ercilla*
3. *Bio Bio*
4. *Cecil*
5. *Concepción*
6. *Cruz del Sur*
7. *El Araucano*
8. *El Dorado*
9. *Ritz*
10. *San Sebastián*
11. *Tabancura*

Residenciales:
12. *Casablanca*
13. *Central*
14. *Colo Colo*
15. *Metro*
16. *O' Higgins*

the entrance hall of the railway station, *The History of Concepción* by Gregorio de la Fuente.

To the **Museo y Parque Hualpen**, a house built around 1885 (now a national monument) and its gardens; it contains beautiful pieces from all over the world, 2 hr visit, rec (open Tues-Sun 0900-1230, 1400-1800, free). The park also contains Playa Rocoto, which is at the mouth of the Río Biobío. Take a city bus to Hualpencillo from Freire, ask the driver to let you out then walk 40 mins, or hitch. You have to go along Av Las Golondrinas to the Enap oil refinery, turn left, then right (it is signed).

To the **Museo Stom**, SE of Concepción, at Progreso 156, in Chiguayante, T 362014, Mapuche artefacts.

Local information
● Accommodation
A1 *Alborada*, Barros Arana 457, Casilla 176, T 242144, good; **A1** *Eldorado*, Barros Arana 348, T 229400, F 231018, comfortable, central, cafetería, parking; **A2** *Concepción*, Serrano 512, T 228851, F 230948, central, comfortable, heating, English spoken, rec; **A3** *San Sebastián*, Rengo 463, T 244529, F 243412, with breakfast, parking.

B *Casablanca*, Cochrane 133, T 226576, **C** without bath; **B** *Ritz*, Barros Arana 721, T 226696, reasonable; **B** *Tabancura*, Barros Arana 790, p 8, T 238348, highly rec. **C** *Cecil*, Barros Arana 9, T 226603, nr railway station, formerly great hotel, with breakfast, quiet, highly rec.

C *Res Antuco*, Barros Arana 741, flats 31-33, T 235485, rec; **C** *Res San Sebastian*, Barros Arana 741, flat 35, T 242710, F 243412, rec, reductions for IYHA (both of these are entered via the Galería Martínez); **C** *Res Metro*, Barros Arana 464, T 225305, without bath.

E pp *Pablo Araya*, Salas 643-C; **E** *Silvia Uslar*, Edmundo Larenas 202, T 227449, good breakfast, quiet, comfortable. *El Naturista* restaurant lets out 2 rooms, **E** pp, central. Good budget accommodation is hard to find.

● Places to eat
El Rancho de Julia, Barros Arana 337, Argentine *parrillada*; *Piazza*, Barros Arana 323, good pizzas; *Rincón de Pancho*, Cervantes 469 (closed Sun), excellent meat, also pasta and congrio, good service and ambience; *Novillo Loco*, Portales 539, good, efficient service. *Le Château* Colo Colo 340, French, seafood and meat, expensive, closed Sun. Oriental: *Yiet-Xiu*, Angol 515, good, cheap; *Chungwa*, Barros Arana 270. *Big Joe Saloon*, O'Higgins 808, just off plaza, popular at lunchtime, closed Sun am but open in pm, good breakfasts, vegetarian meals, snacks and pizzas. *Saaya 1*, Barros Arana 899, excellent *panadería/pastelería/rotisería*, highly rec. Vegetarian: *El Naturista*, Barros Arana 244, good fresh juices, soups and other dishes, closes 1800, highly rec. Several *fuentes de soda* and cafés on Caupolicán nr the Plaza de Armas inc: *Fuente Alemana*, No 654, rec; *Café El Dom*, No 415, and *Café Haití*, No 515, both open Sun am, good coffee; *Royal Pub*, O'Higgins 790, a posh snack bar; *Nuria*, Barros Arana 736, very good breakfasts and lunches, good value; *QuickBiss*, O'Higgins entre Tuscapel y Castellón, salads, real coffee, good service, good lunches; *Treinta y Tantos*, Prat 356, nice bar, good music, wide selection of *empanadas*, rec; good breakfasts and lunches at the market.

● Airline offices
LanChile, Barros Arana 541, T 25014/240025; **Ladeco**, Barros Arana y Lincoyán, T 248824; **National**, Barros Arana 348, T 246710; **Alta**, Caupolicán 246, T 223371, F 223173; **Aerolíneas Argentinas**, O'Higgins 650, Of 602.

● Banks & money changers
Several *cambios* in Galería Internacional, entrances at Barros Arana 565 and Caupolicán 521: **Cambios Fides**, local 58, good rates for TCs; **Inter-Santiago**, local 31, T 228914; **Afex**, local 57, no commision on TCs. **Fincard** (Mastercard), O'Higgins 412, open 24 hrs. Banks such as **Banco Concepción** (which handles Visa) charge high commision on TCs.

● Cultural centres
Alliance Française, Colo Colo y Lamas, library, concerts, films, cultural events; **Chilean-British Cultural Institute**, San Martín 531 (British newspapers, library); **Chilean-North American Institute**, Caupolicán 301 y San Martín, has library; **Chileno-Italiano**, Barros Arana.

● Embassies & consulates
Argentina, San Martín 472; **United Kingdom**, Dr John F Pomeroy, Castellón 317, T 225655, Casilla 452.

● Laundry
Lincoyán 441; *Lavandería Radiante*, Salas 281, open 0900-2030, very good; *American Cleaning*, Freire 817.

● Post & telecommunications
Post Office: O'Higgins y Colo Colo.
Telephones: CTC, Colo Colo 487, Angol 483. Entel, Barros Arana 541, Caupolicán 567, p 2; Colo Colo 487.

● **Shopping**

Main shopping area is N of Plaza de Armas. *Galería Internacional*, Caupolicán y Barros Arana is worth a visit (*El Naturista* vegetarian restaurant has a shop here at local 22). The market has excellent seafood, fruit and vegetables. *Las Brisas* supermarket, Freire y Lincoyán.

● **Tour companies & travel agents**

South Expeditions, O'Higgins 680, p 2, oficina 218D, T/F 232290, rafting and trekking expeditions, 1 and 2-day programmes.

● **Tourist offices**

Aníbal Pinto 460 on plaza, T 227976. Information on the more expensive hotels and *residenciales*. **Automóvil Club de Chile**: O'Higgins 630, Of 303, T 245884, for information and car hire (T 222070). **Codeff** (Comité Nacional pro Defensa de la Fauna y Flora), Caupolicán 346, Oficina E, p 4, T 226649.

● **Transport**

Local Bicycle repairs: *Martínez*, Maipú y Lincoyán, very helpful. **Car hire**: Hertz, Prat 248, T 230152; **Budget**, Arana 541, T 225377. Automóvil Club de Chile, Caupolicán 294, T 2250939.

Air Airport N of the city, off the main road to Talcahuano. In summer, flights daily to and from Santiago (fewer in winter) and connections to Temuco, Puerto Montt and Punta Arenas. Airlines run bus services to the airport from their offices, leaving 1 hr before flight, US$2.50, also meet flights. Taxi US$8.

Trains Station at Prat y Barros Arana, T 226925. Regular daily train to/from **Santiago**, plus Rápido del Bío Bío overnight service, 9 hrs; *salón* US$20, upper bunk US$30, lower bunk US$39; *departamento* US$80. Also local services to Laja and Yumbel. Booking offices at the station and at Galería Alessandri, Aníbal Pinto 478, local 3, T 225286.

Buses Main long distance terminal, known as Terminal Collao, 2 km E, on Av Gen Bonilla, next to athletics stadium. (To the city centre take a Bus marked 'Hualpencillo' from outside the terminal and get off in Freire, US$0.40, taxi US$4.) Tur Bus, Línea Azul and Buses Bío Bío services leave from Terminal Camilo Henríquez 2 km NE of main terminal on J M García, reached by buses from Av Maipú in centre. To **Santiago**, 8½ hrs, US$10; to **Valparaíso**, 9 hrs, US$12; to **Loncoche**, 7 hrs, US$6.50; to **Puerto Montt** several companies, US$15, about 12 hrs; to **Pucón**, 8 hrs, US$8; to **Valdivia**, 9 hrs, US$10; to **Los Angeles**, US$2.50. Best direct bus to **Chillán** is Línea Azul, 2 hrs, US$2. For a longer and more scenic route, take the Costa Azul bus which follows the old railway line, through Tomé, Coelemu and Ñipas on to Chillán (part dirt-track,

takes 5½ hrs). Services to **Coronel** (US$0.45), **Lota**, **Lebu**, **Cañete** and **Contulmo** are run by J Ewert (terminal next to railway station on Prat) and Los Alces (terminal at Prat y Maipú). To **Talcahuano** frequent service from Plaza de Armas (bus marked 'Base Naval'), US$0.20, 1 hr, express US$0.30, 30 mins.

NORTH OF CONCEPCION

A road runs N from Concepción along the coast through the suburbs of **Penco**, Km 12, and **Lirquén**, Km 15, a small, old, pretty town of wooden houses with a beach (walk along railway to reach it). Plentiful cheap seafood for sale. **Tomé**, 13 km further N, is a small town set in a broad bay with long beaches.

Dichato, 9 km further N along a hilly road offering fine views, is a beautiful fishing village and has the oceanographic centre of the University of Concepción. In summer it is a busy holiday resort. Private Museo del Mar, by Benjamín Ortega, interesting, free. Take a local bus to the tiny village of Cocholgüe.

● **Accommodation & places to eat** In Penco: **D** *Hotel La Terraza*, T 451422, **E** *Hosp Miramar*, good, and *Casinoriente*, good seafood restaurant. In Tomé: **D** *Hotel Roxy*, Sotomayor 1077, T 650729, and **E** *Linares*, Serrano 875, T 651284. 7 km before Tomé, on a hill, is *El Edén*, restaurant, bar and *cabañas*, D. In Dichato: **A3** *Chamaruk*, Daniel Vera 912, T 683022, **C** without bath; pleasant; **A2** *Manantial*, on seafront, T 683003; **B** *Kalifa*, Casimiro Vera 766, T 681027, restaurant; **C** *Chicki*, Ugalde 410, T 683004, **D** without bath; **E** pp *Res Santa Inés*, República 540, without bath; *albergue* in the school in summer.

● **Transport** Línea Azul and Costa Azul buses from Concepción pass through all these villages, which can also be reached cheaply by collective taxi.

TALCAHUANO

(*Pop* 244,000) Situated at the neck of a peninsula, **Talcahuana** has the best harbour in Chile. It is Chile's main naval station and an important commercial and fishing port.

Places of interest The **Huáscar** (see box), is in the naval base and can be visited, Tues-Sun 0900-1130, 1400-1700, US$1.25. Photography is permitted, but passports must be handed in at the main

The Huáscar

At the outbreak of the War of the Pacific the Chilean navy blockaded Iquique, then an important Peruvian nitrate port. On 21 May 1879, the Peruvian Navy's huge ironclad, the *Huáscar*, and the smaller *Independencia* reached Iquique to lift the siege. Chile sent out two small wooden ships, the *Covadonga* and the *Esmeralda*, under Captain Arturo Prat to challenge them. Prat fought with ferocity. When his damaged vessel, the *Esmeralda*, was rammed by the *Huáscar*, Prat called upon his men to follow him, boarded the enemy and continued fighting until he was killed. Chile later captured the *Huáscar* at the battle of Angamos near Mejillones, on 8 October 1879.

gate. On Península Tumbes is **Parque Tumbes**, owned by Codeff: paths lead along the coast, no services, no admission charge (details from Codeff office in Concepción).

● **Places to eat** *Benotecas*, on seafront, a row of four restaurants sharing one window facing the harbour, superb fish and seafood in each one, rec, reasonable prices. *La Aguada*, Colón 912, shellfish dishes; *Domingo Lara*, Aníbal Pinto 450, seafood specialities, excellent.

SOUTH OF CONCEPCION

South of the Biobío is the **Costa del Carbón**, the main coal producing area of Chile, linked with Concepción by road and bridge. Between Concepción and Lota are the Lagunas San Pedro Chica (swimming) and Grande (watersports), just across the Río Biobío. Nearer Lota are Playa Negra (small, few people, black sand) and Playa Blanca (bigger, bars, cafés, crowded, white sand, free campsite), both on the Bahía de Coronel.

LOTA

(*Pop* 52,000) 42 km S of Concepción, **Lota** is the site of the most important coalmine in Chile, now state-owned, formerly the property of the Cousiño family. In the church on the main plaza you can see a virgin made of coal.

The **Parque de Lota**, covering 14 ha on a promontory to the W of the town, was the life's work of Isadora Cousiño. Laid out by English landscape architects in the last century, it contains plants from all over the world, ornaments imported from Europe, romantic paths and shady nooks offering views over the sea, and peafowl and pheasants roaming freely. (Admission US$1.25,

no picnicking; open 1000-1800 daily, till 2000 in summer.)

The Coalmine, the tunnels of which run almost entirely under the sea can be visited. Guided tours (Spanish only) Tues-Sat 1000, 3 hrs (minimum party of 5) US$13 pp, meet at the Park entrance, tiring but highly rec. Advance booking advisable, T 876362 Anexo 204, or at Tourist Office in Concepción from whom further details can be obtained. Ask to see the mining museum before you leave.

● **Transport** Buses to **Concepción**, 1½ hrs, US$0.50. Many buses by-pass the centre: catch them from the main road.

South of Lota the road runs past the seaside resort of **Laraquete** where there are miles of golden sands. At Carampangue, Km 24, it forks, one branch running W to **Arauco** (*Pop* 12,000), the site of two cellulose factories.

● **Accommodation   In   Laraquete**: **D** *Laraquete*, on Gabriela Mistral, main street, small rooms, baths in poor repair; **D** *Hostería El Quinto*, helpful, basic, good breakfast. Several *residenciales* close to beach; campsite nr beach. **In Arauco: B** *Hostería Arauco*, P de Valdivia 80, T 551131. **D** *Plaza*, Chacabuco 347, T 551265.

LEBU

(*Pop* 20,000; *Phone code* 041) a fishing port and coal washing centre, lies at the mouth of the Río Lebu 149 km S of Concepcíon and is the capital of Arauco province. There are enormous beaches to both N and S, popular on summer weekends: 3 km N at Playa Millaneco are caves with steep hills offering good walks and majestic views.

● **Accommodation A1** *Hostería Millaneco*, T 511540, T 511904 at Playa Millaneco, *cabañas* sleep 7, good restaurant; rec; **C** *Cen-*

tral, Pérez 183, T 511904, parking, rec; **D** pp *Gran*, Pérez 309, T 511939, **E** pp without bath, old fashioned, *comedor*; **E** *Res Alcázar*, Alcázar 144, with breakfast, cold water.

CAÑETE

(*Pop* 15,642; *Phone code* 041) A small town on the site of Fort Tucapel where Pedro de Valdivia and 52 of his men were killed by Mapuche warriors in 1553.

Museums Museo Mapuche de Cañete, 3 km S on the road to Contulmo, in a modern building inspired by the traditional Mapuche *ruca*; includes Mapuche ceramics and textiles. Behind the museum is a reconstruction of a *ruca*. Open 0930-1230, 1400-1830, daily in summer, closed Mon in winter. Entry US$0.75.

● **Accommodation C** *Alonso de Ercilla*, Villagrán 641, T 611974; **D** *Derby*, Mariñán y Condell, T 611960, without bath, basic, restaurant; **D** *Nahuelbuta*, Villagrán 644, T 611073, pleasant, parking; **E** *Comercio*, 7° de la Línea, T 611218, very pleasant, rec; **E** *Gajardo*, 7° de la Línea 817 (1 block from plaza), without bath, old fashioned, pleasant.

● **Places to eat** *Don Juanito*, Riquelme 151, very good, rec by the locals; real coffee at *Café Nahuel*, off the plaza.

● **Transport** Buses leave from 2 different terminals: J Ewert, Inter Sur and Thiele from Riquelme y 7° de la Línea, Jeldres, Erbuc and other companies from the Terminal Municipal, Serrano y Villagrán. To **Santiago**, Inter Sur, daily, 12 hrs; to **Purén**, US$1.50; sit on right for views of Lago Lanalhue; to **Concepción**, 3 hrs, US$2.50; to **Lebu** US$1.50; to **Angol** US$3.50; to **Tirúa**, Jeldres, frequent and J Ewert, 3 a day, 2 hrs, US$2.

Tirúa, at the mouth of the Río Tirúa, is 78 km S of Cañete (3 *hospedajes*, **E**; buses from Cañete). The island of **Mocha** lies 32 km offshore. Most of the island's 800 inhabitants live around the coast, the interior being of forests. The main settlement is La Hacienda where accommodation is available with families. Transport from Tirúa: ferry daily 0600, US$14; plane US$56 (ask the police to radio the plane which is based on Mocha).

Lago Lanalhue

The lake, S of Cañete, is surrounded by forested hills from which there has been extensive logging. Much less popular than the Lake District, this area offers good opportunities for walking. A road runs S from Cañete along the N side of the lake to Contulmo at its southern end. Playa Blanca, 10 km N of Contulmo, is a popular beach in summer (take any bus between Contulmo and Cañete).

Contulmo (*Pop* 2,000; *Alt* 31m) is a sleepy village at the foot of the Cordillera which hosts a Semana Musical (music week) in January. The wooden Grollmus House and Mill are 3 km NW along the S side of the lake. The house, dating from 1918, has a fine collection of every colour of *copihue* (the national flower) in a splendid garden. The mill, built in 1928, contains the original wooden machinery. From here the track runs a further 9 km N to the *Posada Campesina Alemana*, an old German-style hotel in a fantastic spot at the water's edge. The **Monumento Natural Contulmo**, 8 km S and administered by Conaf, covers 82 ha of native forest.

● **Accommodation In Contulmo**: **E** pp *Central*, Millaray 131, without bath, no sign, very hospitable. **On the lake: A3** *Posada Campesina Alemana*, open Dec-Mar, poor beds, own generator, fish come to hotel steps to be fed by guests, details from Millaray 135 in Contulmo; **B** *Hostal Licahue*, 4 km N towards Cañete (Casilla 644, Correo Contulmo) T Santiago 273-8417, with breakfast, also full board, attractively set overlooking lake, pool, highly rec, also *cabañas*, **A1**, sleep 8, on far side of lake (connected by boat). **Camping at Playa Blanca**: *Camping Elicura*, clean, rec, US$6; *Camping Playa Blanca*, clean; *Camping Huilquehue*, 15 km S of Cañete on lakeside.

● **Transport** Buses to **Concepción**, Thiele, US$4.50, 4 hrs; to **Temuco**, Thiele and Erbuc, US$4; to **Cañete**, frequent, US$1.

Puren (*Pop* 7,572) 20 km further S, is reached by crossing the Cordillera through dense forest (do this journey in daylight). Located in a major logging area, Purén was a key stronghold of the Chilean army in the last campaign against the Mapuche (1869-1881); there is a full-scale reconstruction of the wooden fort. **Lumaco**, 21 km SE, is the site of a major Mapuche festival, the Piedra Santa (20 Jan).

● **Accommodation D** *Hotel Tur*, Dr Garriga 912, T 22, good; *Central Hotel*, on the plaza, meals excellent, rooms in tourist season only.

LOS ANGELES

(*Pop* 93,000; *Alt* 133m; *Phone code* 043) situated on the Pan-American Highway 110 km S of Chillán, is the capital of Bío-Bío province. Founded in 1739 as a fort, it was destroyed several times by the Mapuche. It has a large Plaza de Armas and a good daily market.

Local information

● Accommodation

A3 *Mariscal Alcázar*, Lautaro 385 (Plaza de Armas), T 311725; **B** *Gran Hotel Müso*, Valdivia 230 (Plaza de Armas), T 313183, good restaurant open to non-residents; **C** *Winser*, Rengo 138, overpriced, otherwise OK; **C** *Res Santa María*, Plaza de Armas, TV, good beds.

Private house at Caupolicán 651, E, large breakfast, good value; opp is another, also No 651, basic, cheaper. **E** pp *Res Winser*, Colo Colo 335, T 323782, small rooms. 10 km N is **D** pp *Casa de familia/Cabañas El Rincón*, Panamericana Sur Km 494, Cruce La Mona 1 km E, T (09) 441-5019, F 043-317168, Elke and Winfried Lohmar, beautiful property beside a small river, restful, South American and European cuisine, inc vegetarian (**B** pp full board), tours arranged, English, French, German and Spanish spoken, highly rec (to publish *Backpackers Best of South Chile* in Sept 1997); *Antukelen*, Camino Los Angeles-Santa Bárbara-Ralco, 62.7 km SE on the Alto Bío-Bío, reservations Siegfried Haberl, Casilla 1278, Los Angeles, T 09-450-0210, camping, showers, German, English and French spoken, vegetarian food and other natural attractions; Spanish classes; *cabañas*, natural therapy centre and excursions to be developed in 1997.

● Places to eat

El Arriero, Colo Colo 235, T 322899, good *parrillas* and international dishes; *Di Leone*, Colón 265, good lasagna; *Julio's Pizzas*, Colón 542 and *Rancho de Julio*, Colón 720, excellent *parrilla*. *Bavaria*, Colón 357, good.

● Banks & money changers

Banco Santander, Colón 500, Mastercard; Banco Concepción, Colón 300; Banco Sudamérica, Valdivia 276.

● Language schools

El Rincon, Casilla 940, T 4415019, recently opened by Elke and Winfried Lohmar, promises 5 hrs tuition Mon-Fri, accommodation, excursions.

● Post & telecommunications

Post Office: on Plaza de Armas.

Telephones: CTC, Paseo Quilpué, or Valdivia 326; Entel, Colo Colo 393.

● Tourist offices

Proto-Turismo, Edif Cámara Comercio No 24, beside Lautaro 267. **Conaf**, Ercilla 936, 0900-1300. **Automóvil Club de Chile**: Villagrán y Caupolicán, T 322149.

● Transport

Long distance bus terminal on NE outskirts of town, local terminal at Villagrán y Rengo in centre. To **Santiago**, 9 hrs, US$12; to **Viña del Mar** and **Valparaíso**, 10 hrs, US$14; 4 daily to **Concepción**, US$2.50, 2¼ hrs; to **Temuco**, US$4, hourly; to **Curacautín**, daily at 0600, 3 hrs, US$4.

SALTO EL LAJA

25 km N of Los Angeles, is a spectacular waterfall in which the Río Laja plunges 47m over the rocks. It costs a few pesos to enter and walk up to the falls, or to walk on the hotel side.

● Accommodation
A3-B *Motel Salto del Laja*, address: Casilla 562, Los Angeles, T 321706, F 313996 with fine restaurant, 2 swimming pools and chalet-type rooms on an island overlooking the falls; nearby are *Camping Los Manantiales*, T 323606, and Motels *El*

Pinar and *Los Coyuches*.

● **Transport** Buses (Bus Bío-Bío) from Los Angeles, US$1, 30 mins – frequent; to Chillán, frequent, US$2.

PARQUE NACIONAL LAGUNA DE LAJA

93 km E of Los Angeles by a road which runs past the impressive rapids of the Río Laja, the park is dominated by the Antuco volcano (2,985m), which is still active, and the glacier-covered Sierra Velluda. The Laguna is surrounded by stark scenery of scrub and lava. There are 46 species of birds including condors and the rare Andean gull.

● **Access** Take a bus from Los Angeles (ERS Bus, Villagrán 507) to Abanico (**E** pp *Hostería del Bosque*, restaurant, also good campsite), 20 km past Antuco (US$1.35, 2 hrs, weekdays 5 daily, 2 on Sun and festivals, last return 1730), then 4 km to park entrance (details from Conaf in Los Angeles, Ercilla 936, 0800-1300, 1430-1800 Mon-Fri).

● **Accommodation** *Cabañas y Camping Lagunillas*, T 314275 (or Caupolicán 332, oficina 2, Los Angeles T 323-1066) 50m from the river, 2 km from park entrance, open all year, restaurant, poor campsite US$2.50 pp. Camping not permitted on lake shore. 21 km from the lake is the *Refugio Chacay* offering food, drink and bed (**B**, T Los Angeles 222651, closed in summer); two other *refugios*: *Digeder*, E, and Universidad de Concepción, both on slopes of Volcán Antuco, for both T Concepción 229054, office O'Higgins 740. Nearby is the Club de Esquí de los Angeles with two ski-lifts, giving a combined run of 4 km on the Antuco volcano (season, May-Aug).

SOUTH OF LOS ANGELES

The Pan-American (or Longitudinal) Highway (Ruta 5) runs via Collipulli (campsite), Victoria, Púa and Lautaro to Temuco.

ANGOL

(*Pop* 39,000; *Alt* 71m; *Phone code* 045) Capital of the Province of Malleco, **Angol** is reached by paved roads from Collipulli and Los Angeles. Founded by Valdivia in 1552, it was seven times destroyed by the Indians and rebuilt. The church and convent of **San Beneventura**, NW of the attractive Plaza de Armas, built in 1863,

became the centre for missionary work among the Mapuche. **El Vergel**, founded in 1880 as an experimental fruit-growing nursery, now includes an attractive park and the **Museo Dillman Bullock** with precolumbian Indian artefacts (open daily 0830-1300, 1500-1800, US$1, 5 km from town, colectivo No 2).

● **Accommodation** Several in town. **D** pp *La Posada*, at El Vergel, T 712103, full board; **D** *Res Olimpia*, Caupolicán 625, T 711162, good; **D** pp *Casa Matriz*, Caupolicán 579, T 711711, with breakfast, good food; **E** *Casa de Huespedes*, Dieciocho 465, with breakfast.

● **Tourist offices** O'Higgins s/n, across bridge from bus terminal, T 711255, excellent.

● **Transport** Bus to Santiago US$6.50, Los Angeles, US$1.20, or Collipulli. To Temuco, Trans Bío-Bío, frequent, US$2.50.

Parque Nacional Nahuelbuta

Situated in the coastal mountain range at an altitude of 800-1,550m, the park covers 6,832 ha of forest and offers views over both the sea and the Andes. Open all year (snow June-Sept). Although the forest includes many species of trees, the araucaria is most striking; some are over 2,000 years old, 50m high and 2m in diameter. There are also 16 species of orchids. Fauna include pudu deer, Chiloé foxes, pumas, black woodpeckers and parrots. There is a Visitors' Centre at Pehuenco, 5 km from the entrance, open summer only 0800-1300, 1400-2000.

● **Access** Bus to Vegas Blancas (27 km from Angol) 0700 and 1600 daily, return 0900 and 1600, 1½ hrs, US$1.20, get off at *El Cruce*, from where it is a pleasant 7 km walk to park entrance (entry US$2.50). Rough maps are available at the park entrance for US$0.25. **Conaf**, Prat 191, p 2, Angol, T 711870.

● **Accommodation Camping**: nr Visitors' Centre, US$9 – there are many free campsites along the road from *El Cruce* to the entrance.

The Lake District

Y ET MORE beautiful scenery: a variety of lakes, often with snow-capped volcanoes as a backdrop, stretch southwards to the salt water fjords which begin at Puerto Montt. There are a number of good bases for exploring (Valdivia has the added attraction of colonial forts a river trip away) and many national parks.

The land and people

South from the Río Biobío to the Gulf of Reloncaví the same land formation holds as for the rest of Chile to the N: the Andes to the E, the coastal range to the W, and in between the central valley. The Andes and the passes over them are less high here, and the snowline lower; the coastal range also loses altitude, and the central valley is not as continuous as from Santiago to Concepción. The climate is cooler; the summer is no longer dry, for rain falls all the year round, and more heavily than further N. The rain decreases as you go inland: some 2,500 mm on the coast and 1,350 mm inland. This is enough to maintain heavy forests, mostly beech, but agriculture is also important; irrigation is not necessary. The farms are mostly medium sized, and no longer the huge *haciendas* of the N. The characteristic thatched or red tiled houses of the rural N disappear; they are replaced by the shingle-roofed frame houses typical of a frontier land rich in timber. The farms raise livestock, fruit and food crops, and timber is a major industry.

Between parallels 39° and 42° S is found one of the most picturesque lake regions in the world. There are some 12 great lakes of varying sizes, some set high on the Cordillera slopes, others in the central valley southwards from Temuco to Puerto Montt. Here, too, are imposing waterfalls and snowcapped volcanoes. Anglers revel in the abundance of fish, the equable climate, and the absence of troublesome insects (except for enormous horseflies, *tavanos*, between mid-Dec and mid-Jan – do not wear dark clothes). Out of season many facilities are closed, in season (from mid-Dec to mid-Mar), prices are higher and it is best to book well in advance, particularly for transport. It is a peaceful area, with fewer tourists than across the border in the Argentine lake district.

About 20,000 **Mapuches** live in the area, more particularly around Temuco. There are possibly 150,000 more of mixed blood who speak the Indian tongue, though most of them are bilingual.

Crossing to Argentina There are four main routes from the Chilean Lake District to Argentina: 1) The Tromen Pass, from Pucón and Curarrehue to Junín de los Andes (see page 190); 2) the Huahum Pass, from Panguipulli via Choshuenco and Lake Pirehueico to San Martín de los Andes (see page 773); 3) The Puyehue Pass, from Osorno and Entrelagos via the Parque Nacional Puyehue to Bariloche (see page 780); 4) The Lakes Route, from Puerto Montt or Osorno via Ensenada, Petrohue and Lago Todos Los Santos to Bariloche (see page 793).

TEMUCO

(*Pop* 225,000; *Alt* 107m; *Phone code* 045) founded in 1881 after the final treaty with the Mapuches, lies 679 km S of Santiago. The city is the capital of IX Región (Araucanía) and one of the fastest growing commercial centres in the south.

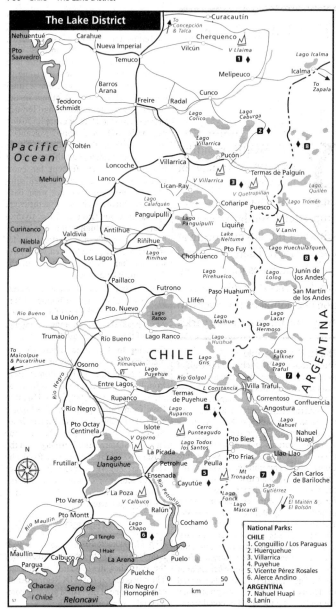

The Lake District

National Parks:
CHILE
1. Conguillio / Los Paraguas
2. Huerquehue
3. Villarrica
4. Puyehue
5. Vicente Pérez Rosales
6. Alerce Andino

ARGENTINA
7. Nahuel Huapi
8. Lanín

Places of interest

The city centre is the Plaza Aníbal Pinto, around which are the main public buildings including the cathedral and the municipalidad. On the plaza itself is a small Sala de Exposiciones. The **cattle auctions** in the stockyards behind the railway on A Malvoa, Thur mornings, are interesting; you can see the *huasos*, or Chilean cowboys, at work. There are also cattle sales at the Feria Agroaustral, just outside Temuco on the road to Nuevo Imperial, on Fri (take bus 4 from C Rodríguez), auction starts at 1400, and at Nuevo Imperial, 35 km away, on Mon and Tues. The **Municipal Cultural Centre** at the intersection of Balmaceda, Caupolicán and Prat houses the municipal library, a theatre, and art galleries. Temuco is the Mapuches' market town and you may see some, particularly women, in their typical costumes in the produce market next to the railway station (Lautaro y Pinto). Mapuche textiles, pottery, woodcarving, jewellery etc are also sold inside and around the **municipal market** in centre of town (corner of Aldunate and Diego Portales – it also sells fish, meat and dairy produce), but these are increasingly touristy and poor quality. The *Casa de la Mujer Mapuche*, Gen MacKenna 83, T 233886, F 236141, sells the textiles made by a co-operative of 135 Mapuche weavers; all items are 100% wool with traditional designs. Also highly recommended is the *Casa de Arte Mapuche*, Matta 25-A, T 213085, Casilla 1682, for information on Mapuche arts and crafts speak to the director Rayen Kvyeh. There is a good view of Temuco from **Cerro Ñielol**, a park (entry US$1), where there is a fine collection of native plants in the natural state, including the national flower, the *copihue rojo*. There is also a bathing pool (US$0.40) and a restaurant (open 1200-2400). On Cerro Ñielol is also La Patagua, the tree under which the final peace was signed with the Mapuches in 1881.

Museums

Museo de la Araucanía, Alemania 84, devoted to the history and traditions of the Mapuche nation, with a section on German settlement. Open Tues-Sat 0800-1300, 1500-1800; Sun 1000-1400, US$1.

Parque Museo Ferroviario, Av Barros Arana 3 km N of centre, contains 15 railway engines under restoration.

Excursions

To **Chol Chol**, a country town 30 km NW by unpaved road, providing a pleasant trip through Mapuche country. The trip traverses rolling countryside with panoramic views. Nearer Chol Chol, a few traditional round *rucas* can be seen. Daily buses from Terminal Rural, Huincabus 1 hr, 4 times between 1100 and 1800, US$0.60.

Local information

NB Do not confuse the streets Vicuña MacKenna and Gen MacKenna.

● **Accommodation**

A1 *Nuevo Hotel de la Frontera*, Bulnes 726, T 210718, inc breakfast, excellent; **A2** *Bayern*, Prat 146, small rooms, helpful; **A2** *Apart Hotel Don Eduardo*, Bello 755, T 215554, parking, suites with kitchen, rec; **A3** *C'Est Bayonne*, Vicuña MacKenna 361, T 235510, F 714915, with breakfast, modern, German and Italian spoken.

B *Continental*, Varas 708, T 238973, F 233830, popular with business travellers, colonial-style, excellent restaurant, the bar is popular in pm, cheaper rooms without bath, rec; **B** *Turismo*, Claro Solar 636, T 210583, nr main plaza, restaurant, good value, **C** without bath, good service, IYHA reductions.

C *Oriente*, M Rodríguez 1146, T 233232, rec.

D *Hosp Adriane Becker*, Estebáñez 881, without bath, good breakfast, basic; **D** *Alba Jaramillo*, Calbuco 583, T 240042, by Av Alemania, with breakfast; **D** *Hosp Aldunate*, Aldunate 187, T 213548, cooking facilities, also **E** dormitory accommodation; **D** *Hostal Austria*, Hochstetter 599, T 247169, excellent, breakfast; **D** *Casa Blanca*, Montt 1306 y Zenteno, T 212740, good breakfast, rec; **D** *Casa de huéspedes Centenario*, Aldunate 864, with breakfast; **D** *Flor Acoca*, Lautaro 591, breakfast; **D** *Hosp Millarey*, Claro Solar 471, simple, basic; **D** *Hostal Montt*, Manuel Montt 965, T 211856, parking; **D** *Rupangue*, Barros Arana 182, helpful, good value. The following are in our **D** or **E** pp range: on Av Alemania, Sra Veronica Kiekebusch, T 247287 (house number unknown), with breakfast, quiet, rec, buses No 1 or 9 from rural bus terminal; No 035, large rooms, use of kitchen, pleasant; Las Heras 810, without breakfast, basic; Blanco Encalada 1078, T 234447, use of kitchen, rec; Bulnes 1006 y O'Higgins, good double rooms, above drugstore, ask for house key otherwise access limited to shop hours; on Claro Solar, No 151, with breakfast; Gen MacKenna 46, Jan-Mar only; other private houses in same street; on Rodríguez, No 1311, meals served; No 1341, *Res Temuco*, T 233721; Zenteno 486 (Sra Ruth Palominas), T 211269, rec; **E pp** Zenteno 525, without breakfast, large rooms, poor beds but good value; **E** *Res Ensueño*, Rodríguez 442; **E** *Hosp González*, Lautaro 1160, p 2, safe, rec; **E** San Martín 01760 (Sra Egla de González), T 246182, with breakfast. Accommodation in private houses, category **D**, can be arranged by Tourist Office. Other *residenciales* and *pensiones* can be found in the market station area.

Camping: *Camping Metrenco*, 10 km S on Route 5.

● **Places to eat**

Café Marriet, Prat 451, Local 21, excellent coffee; on Bulnes: *Dino's*, No 360, good coffee; *Il Gelato*, No 420, delicious ice cream; *Julio's Pizza*, No 778, wide variety, not cheap; *Centro*

Español, No 483; *Della Maggio*, No 536, good coffee and light meals. *D'Angelo*, San Martín 1199, good food, pleasant, pricey. For cheap lunches try eastern end of C Lautaro or inside the municipal market. *Pront Rapa*, Aldunate 421, for take-away lunches and snacks, rec; *Ñam-Ñam*, Portales 802, pizzas, sandwiches etc, good; *Café Artesanía Raíces Indoamericanas*, Manuel Montt 645, T 232434, specializes in Mapuche dishes, good coffee, adjoining shop sells handicrafts and textiles. *La Cumbre del Cerro Ñielol* (dancing), on top of Cerro Ñielol.

● **Airline offices**

LanChile, Bulnes 667, T 211339; Ladeco, Prat 565, Local 102, T 214325; National, Claro Solar 780, Local 7, T 215764; Varig, MacKenna 763, T 213120; TAN, T 210500.

● **Banks & money changers**

Good rates for TCs at Banco Osorno and

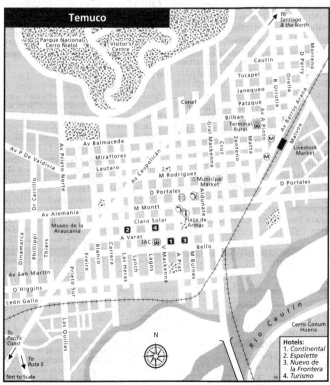

Temuco

Hotels:
1. Continental
2. Espelette
3. Nuevo de la Frontera
4. Turismo

Global both on Plaza de Armas; also Turcamb, Claro Solar 733; Christopher Money Exchange, Prat 696, Oficina 419; also at Bulnes 202; Inter-Santiago, Bulnes 443, local 2. All deal in dollars and Argentine pesos. Fincard (Mastercard), Claro Solar 922. Banco Concepción (for Visa), M Montt 901; Banco de Chile, Varas 818, rec for money transfers by Switch.

● **Embassies & consulates**
Netherlands, España 494, Honorary Consul, Germán Nicklas, is friendly and helpful.

● **Laundry**
Caupolicán 110, Nos 4 and 5, open 0900-2100 daily, good, cheap, quick; Portales 1185, expensive; automatic at M Montt between Las Heras and Lynch

● **Post & telecommunications**
Post Office: Portales 839.
Telephones: Centro de Llamadas CTC, A Prat just off Claro Solar and plaza, Mon-Sat 0800-2400, Sun and holidays 1030-2400. Entel, Bulnes 303, daily 0830-2200.

● **Shopping**
Cameras: Ruka, Bulnes 394, helpful, owner speaks German.
Crafts: best choice in the indoor municipal market at Aldunate y Portales.
Supermarket: Las Brisas, Carrera 899; Frutería Las Vegas, Matta 274, dried fruit (useful for climbing/trekking).

● **Tourist offices**
Bulnes 586, T 211969. Open 0830-2030, all week in summer, 0900-1200, 1500-1800 Mon-Fri in winter. Also at Balmaceda y Prat. **Automóvil Club de Chile**: Varas 687, T 213949. **Conaf**: Bilbao 931, T 234420.

● **Transport**
Local Car hire: Hertz, Las Heras 999, T 235385. Budget, Lynch 471, T 214911; Automóvil Club de Chile, Varas 687, T 213949 and at airport; Puig, Portales, 779; Fatum, Varas 983, T 234199; Euro, MacKenna 426, T 210311, helpful, good value.

Air Manquehue Airport 6 km from the city. LanChile, Ladeco, Avant and National to Santiago. LanChile and Ladeco to Osorno and Valdivia; National to Puerto Montt and once a week to Punta Arenas; TAN flies to Neuquén, Argentina.

Trains Station at Barros Arana y Lautaro Navarro, T 233416. To Santiago: 2 a day, 12 hrs: fares económico US$16, superior/salón US$22 (depending on service), sleeper US$24, double compartment, restaurant car expensive. To Osorno and Puerto Montt daily in summer 0850, 9 hrs. Ticket office at Bulnes 582, T 233522, open Mon-Fri 0900-1300, 1430-1800, Sun 0900-1300 as well as at station.

Buses No long-distance bus terminal – buses leave from company offices. Buses to neighbouring towns leave from Terminal Rural, Pinto y Balmaceda. Bus company offices: Igi Llaima and Narbus, Barros Arana y Miraflores; Erbuc, Miraflores y Bulnes; LIT, San Martín y Bulnes; Cruz del Sur, V MacKenna 671; JAC, MacKenna y Andrés Bello; ETTA, Longitudinal Sur and Thiele, V MacKenna 600 block, nr Varas; Power, Bulnes 174; Pangui Sur, Miraflores 871.

Buses to Santiago US$16; to Curacautín, Erbuc, US$2, 7 daily, 2¾ hrs; to Lonquimay, Erbuc, 4 daily, 5½ hrs, US$3; to Laguna Captren, Erbuc, Mon and Fri 1645, 4 hrs, US$3; to Contulmo, US$4, 2 hrs, Cañete, US$4 and Lebu, Erbuc and Thiele; Cruz del Sur, 3 a day to Castro, 10 a day to Puerto Montt (US$9, 5½ hrs), to Valdivia US$4; to Osorno US$6; to Villarrica and Pucón many between 0705 and 2045, 1½ hrs, US$3, and 2 hrs, US$3.50; to Coñaripe, 3 hrs, and Lican Ray, 2 hrs; to Panguipulli, Power and Pangui Sur at 0730, 3 hrs, US$2; Pangui Sur to Loncoche, Los Lagos, Mehuin in summer only; to Concepción, Bío Bío, US$5, 4½ hrs; to Arica, US$55 or US$70 cama; to Antofagasta, US$45.

Buses to Argentina: JAC from Terminal Rural to Junín de los Andes (US$25), San Martín de los Andes (US$25) and Neuquén (US$30), Wed and Fri 0400; also Igi Llaima and San Martín 3 a week each to San Martín, US$25. Nar Bus from Terminal Rural to San Martín and Neuquén, Mon-Fri (San Martín buses go via Villarrica and Pucón when the Tromen Pass is open); Ruta Sur, Miraflores 1151, to Zapala (US$22) and Neuquén (US$28),via Paso Pino Hachado, Wed and Sat 0400; La Unión del Sud, Miraflores 1285, same destinations Wed, Fri and Sat. Fénix (address above) to Buenos Aires and Mendoza.

ROUTES South of Temuco The Longitudinal Highway (Ruta 5) runs from Loncoche (81 km S of Temuco, good place for hitching) through Lanco to Paillaco and Osorno. At San José de la Mariquina, a road branches off Ruta 5 to Valdivia, 42 km from the Highway (bus Lanco-Valdivia, Chile Nuevo, US$0.85, 4 a day, fewer at weekends). The road from Valdivia to Ruta 5 going S is not in very good condition; the Highway is rejoined near Paillaco.

Coastal resorts near Temuco

Carahue (Pop 8,000), 55 km W by paved road is built on the site of the Spanish colonial city of Imperial which was destroyed by the Mapuche (accommodation available). **Puerto Saavedra**, about 30 km further, S of the mouth of the Río Imperial, lies behind a black volcanic sandspit. It comprises three distinct towns: administrative, the fishing port and the tourist area. A ferry crosses the river to Nehuentue, on the N bank, from where there are fine views of the bay.

● **Accommodation** D pp *Boca Budi*, T (09) 453-2107, good rooms, excellent seafood, excursions to Indian villages; **E** Sra Rita Sandoval Muñoz, Las Dunas 01511, lovely, knowledgeable; many *hosterías* in D-E category.

● **Transport** Buses to Temuco (Terminal Rural), Nar Bus, 3 a day, 3¼ hrs, US$2.50.

Lago Budi is the only inland, salt-water lake in Chile. Over 130 species of water bird, including black-necked swans, visit it. On the E shore 40 km by road S of Carahue is **Puerto Domínguez**, a picturesque little fishing town. On the W shore is Isla Huapi (also spelt Guapi), a peninsula with a Mapuche settlement of traditional thatched houses (*rucas*) and fine views of both the lake and the Pacific. Ideal for camping.

● **Transport Buses** to Puerto Domínguez from Temuco, 3 hrs. **Ferries** The *Carlos Schalchli* ferry leaves Puerto Domínguez for Isla Huapi, Mon and Wed 0900 and 1700, returning 0930 and 1730, free, 30 mins. Ferry to Isla Huapi also from about 10 km S of Puerto Saavedra.

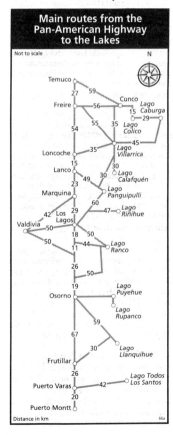

Main routes from the Pan-American Highway to the Lakes

Not to scale

N

Temuco
59
27
Freire — 56 — Cunco
Lago Caburga
15
29
55 35 Lago Colico
54
45
Lago Villarrica
Loncoche — 35
15 30 Lago Calafquén
Lanco
23 49
Marquina 60 Lago Panguipulli
42 29 47 — Lago Riñihue
Los Lagos
Valdivia 50
18 50 Lago Ranco
11 44
26 50
19 Lago Puyehue
Osorno
Lago Rupanco
59
67
30 Lago Llanquihue
Frutillar
26 Lago Todos Los Santos
Puerto Varas 42
20
Puerto Montt
Distance in km 66a

EAST OF TEMUCO

CURACAUTIN

(*Pop* 12,737; *Alt* 400m) is small town situated 84 km NE of Temuco (road paved for the first 57 km) and 56 km SE of Victoria by paved road. Its main industry is forestry (there are several sawmills); it is a useful centre for visiting the nearby national parks and hot springs.

● **Accommodation** D pp *Plaza*, Yungay 157, T 56, main plaza, restaurant good but pricey; **E** pp *Res Rojas*, Tarapacá 249, without bath, good meals, rec; **E** pp *Turismo*, Tarapacá 140, T 116, good food, comfortable, best value; **E** pp Rodríguez 705 (corner of plaza) with breakfast, kitchen facilities. *Camping Trahuilco*, 3 km S, expensive.

● **Transport** Bus terminal on the plaza. Buses to/from Temuco and Los Angeles.

HOT SPRINGS EAST OF CURACAUTIN

Termas de Manzanar, indoors, 18 km E of Curacautín (US$5, open all year) are reached by bus from Temuco and Victoria. The road passes the Salto del Indio (Km 14), and Salto de la Princesa, just beyond Manzanar.

● **Accommodation** B *Termas*, also simple rooms with bath; **E** *Hostería Abarzúa*, simple.

The **Termas de Río Blanco**, hotel, hot springs and mud baths, are 32 km SE at 1,046m on the slopes of the Sierra Nevada and near Lago Conguillío (bus to Conguillío National Park – see page 765 below – only at 1800).

The beautiful pine-surrounded **Termas de Tolhuaca** (open 1 Nov-30 April) are 35 km to the NE of Curacautín by unpaved road, or 57 km by unpaved road from just N of Victoria (high clearance 4WD essential).

● **Accommodation A2** *Termas de Tolhuaca*, with full board, inc use of baths and horse riding, very good, T 164, Casilla 48 Curacautín, or T Temuco 220975; **E** pp *Res Roja*, food, camping nr the river, good.

2 km N of the Termas is the **Parque Nacional Tolhuaca**, including the waterfalls of Malleco and Culiebra, and two lakes, Laguna Malleco and Laguna Verde. Superb scenery and good views of volcanoes from Cerro Amarillo. Park administration is near Laguna Malleco (open Dec-April), with a campsite nearby.

Reserva Nacional Malalcahuello-Nalcas

Situated NE of Curacautín, this 31,305 ha park is on the slopes of the **Lonquimay volcano** which is a popular ski resort (season May-Nov). It is much less crowded than nearby Parque Nacional Conguillio. The volcano begun erupting on Christmas Day 1988; the new crater is called Navidad. To see it, access is made from Malalcahuello, 15 km S and half-way between Curacautín and Lonquimay town. The teacher at Malalcahuello school charges US$10 for transport to and from the volcano; Sra Naomi Saavedra at *Res Los Sauces* also arranges lifts. The Reserve is also a popular centre for fly-fishing: Sr Jorge Vio, at the ski lodge provides information.

● **Accommodation** *Res Los Sauces*, **D** pp full board, or **E** pp with use of kitchen, hot water, good value; there is also a Conaf lodge. Accommodation is also available at the Centro de Ski Lonquimay, 10 km from the bus stop, **B** pp with breakfast, full board also available, free camping, open all year, ski pass US$17.

● **Transport** Bus Erbuc from Temuco, US$2 to Malalcahuello, 4 a day, 4 hrs, 5½ to Lonquimay town, US$3.

PARQUE NACIONAL CONGUILLIO

The park, 80 km E of Temuco, is one of the most popular in Chile, but is deserted outside Jan/Feb and weekends. In the centre is the 3,050m **Llaima volcano**, which is still active (the western side of the crater was completely blown out in 1994 and it began erupting again in Mar 1996). There are two large lakes, Laguna Verde and Laguna Conguillio, and two smaller ones, Laguna Arco Iris and Laguna Captrén. North of Laguna Conguillio rises the snow covered Sierra Nevada, the highest peak of which reaches 2,554m.

Wildlife This is the best place in Chile to see araucaria forest which used to cover an extensive area in this part of the country. Other trees include cypresses, lenga and cinnamom. Birdlife includes the condor and the black woodpecker.

Climbing Llaima Crampons and ice-axe are essential. Climb NE from *Guardería Captrén*. Allow 5 hrs to ascend, 2 hrs to descend. Information on the climb is available from Sr Torres at *Guardería Captrén*.

Walking There is a range of trails, from 1 km to 22 km in length. Details are available from Park administration or Conaf in Temuco.

Skiing Llaima ski resort, one of the prettiest in Chile, reached by poor road from Cherquenco, 30 km W (high clearance vehicle essential).

● **Park Information** Administration and information, open Nov-June, at Laguna Arco Iris, Laguna Captrén and at Truful-Truful. Out of season administration is at the western entrance. There is a Visitors' Centre at Laguna Captrén, open Dec-March. Entry US$4.

● **Access** There are three entrances:
1 From Curacautín, N of the park: see **Transport** below.
2 From **Melipeuco**, 13 km S of the southern entrance at Truful-Truful.
3 From Cherquenco to the W entrance near the Llaima ski resort. It is then a 2-3 day hike around Volcán Llaima to Laguna Conguillio, dusty, but beautiful views of Laguna Quepe, then on to the Laguna Captrén *guardería*.

● **Accommodation** In the park, **Laguna Captrén**: campsite US$20/site inc firewood but no other facilities. **Laguna Conguillio**: campsite (US$15/tent, hot water, showers, firewood), cheaper campsite (*camping de mochileros*, US$5 pp); *cabañas* (**A3** summer only, sleep 6, no sheets or blankets, gas stove, and café/shop). In Melipeuco: **E** *Germania*, Aguirre 399, basic, good food; **E** *Pensión Hospedaje*, Aguirre 729, more spacious, rec; **C** *Hostería Hue-Telén*,

Aguirre 15, Casilla 40, T 693032 to leave message, good restaurant; free municipal campsite; also *Camping Los Pioneros*, 1 km out of town on road to the park, hot water. *Restaurant Los Troncos*, Aguirre 352, rec. Buy supplies in Temuco or Melipeuco: much cheaper than the shop in the park.

● **Transport** To the northern entrance: Bus from Temuco Terminal Rural, Nar Bus, 5 daily, 0900-1830, 4 hrs, US$1.30, ask driver to drop you at the road fork, 10 km from park entrance, last back to Temuco at 1630. Bus from Curacautín to Laguna Captrén, Erbuc, Mon and Fri, 1730, summer only, otherwise Erbuc at 1830, Mon and Fri, to bus stop 10 km from Laguna Captrén, 1 hr, US$1. In summer it's easy to hitch. To the western entrance: Daily buses from Temuco to Cherquenco, from where there is no public transport to the park. Transport can be arranged from Melipeuco into the park (ask in grocery stores and *hospedajes*, US$25 one way). For touring, hire a 4WD vehicle in Temuco.

FRONTIER WITH ARGENTINA: PASO PINO HACHADO

Paso Pino Hachado (1,884m) can be reached either by unpaved road, 77 km SE from Lonquimay or by unpaved road 103 E from Melipeuco. On the Argentine side this road continues to Zapala.

● **Chilean immigration & customs**
In Liucura, 22 km W of the frontier, open Dec-Mar 0800-2100, April-Nov 0800-1900. Very thorough searches and 2-3 hr delays reported.

● **Transport**
Buses from Temuco to Zapala and Neuquén use this crossing: see under Temuco.

FRONTIER WITH ARGENTINA: PASO DE ICALMA

Paso de Icalma (1,298m) is reached by unpaved road, 53 km from Melipeuco. On the Argentine side this road continues to Zapala.

● **Chilean immigration**
Open Dec-Mar 0800-2100, April-Nov 0800-1900.

VILLARRICA

Wooded Lago Villarrica, 21 km long and about 7 km wide, is one of the most beautiful in the region, with snow-capped Villarrica volcano (2,840m) to the SE. The town of **Villarrica** (*Pop* 36,000; *Alt* 227m;

Phone code 045), pleasantly set at the extreme SW corner of the lake, can be reached by a 63-km paved road SE from Freire (24 km S of Temuco on the Pan-American Highway), or from Loncoche, 54 km S of Freire, also paved. Founded in 1552, the town was besieged by the Mapuche in the uprising of 1599: after three years the surviving Spanish settlers, 11 men and 13 women, surrendered. The town was refounded in 1882. There is a **Museo Histórico**, Pedro de Valdivia y Zegers.

Local festivals
Festival Cultural Mapuche, with market, usually in second week of Feb; enquire at the Santiago or Temuco tourist office.

Local information
● **Accommodation**

A3 *Hotel El Ciervo*, Gen Koerner 241, T 411215, German-run, beautiful location, pool, rec; **A3** *Yachting Club*, San Martín 802, T 411191, pleasant, terraced gardens, pool, restaurant, boating and fishing, cheaper rooms in motel annex; **A3** *Hostería la Colina*, Ríos 1177, overlooking town, T 411503, Casilla 382, run by North Americans, with breakfast, great gardens, good service, good restaurant, highly rec; **A3** *Hotel y Cabañas El Parque*, 3 km out of Villarrica on Pucón road, T 411120, Casilla 65, lakeside with beach, tennis courts, with breakfast, good restaurant set meals, highly rec.

B *Hostería Kiel*, Gen Koerner 153, T 411631, **D** off season, lakeside, good; **B** *Cabañas Traitraico*, San Martín 380, T 411064, 100m from lake, cabins sleep 6, TV, heating, kitchenette, parking; **B** *Hostería Bilbao*, Henríquez 43, T 411452, small rooms, pretty patio, good restaurant.

C *Rayhuen*, Pedro Montt 668, T 411571 (B in summer), good restaurant, good breakfast, lovely garden, rec.

D *Yandaly*, Henríquez 401, T 411452, small rooms, good, also restaurant, rec; **D** *Fuentes*, Vicente Reyes 665, T 411595, basic, restaurant; **D** *Res Villa Linda*, Valdivia 678, T 411392, basic, good restaurant.

E pp *Res Victoria*, Muñoz 530, cooking facilities; **E** pp Vicente Reyes 854, nr JAC terminal, good breakfast, poor bathroom facilities. Rooms in private homes, all **E** pp, inc several in Francisco Bilbao; Eliana Castillo, No 537; *La Torre Suiza*, No 969, T 411213, Swiss-run, highly rec; Urrutia 407, large breakfast, kitchen; Matta 469, cooking facilities.

Youth hostel: **E** pp *Res San Francisco*, Julio Zegers 646, shared rooms.

Camping: 2 sites just outside town on Pucón

road, *Los Castaños*, T 65-250183, and *du Lac*, quiet, but buy supplies at *Los Castaños* which is cheaper. Many more on S side of Lake Villarrica, see under Pucón (below). Summer houses available in Dec-February.

● **Places to eat**

Club Social, P de Valdivia 640, good; *El Rey de Mariscos*, Letelier 1030, good seafood; several good and cheap places for seafood in the market; *Rapa Nui*, V Reyes 678, good and cheap, closed Sun; *Café 2001*, Henríquez 379, coffee and ice-cream, good.

● **Banks & money changers**

Banco de Osorno changes TCs; *Casa de Cambio*, O'Higgins 210, poor rates for TCs; *Cristophe Exchange*, Valdivia 1061, good rates for TCs.

● **Laundry**

Lavandería y Lavaseco Villarrica, Andrés Bello 348, T 411449.

● **Post & telecommunications**

Post Office: Muñoz y Urrutia, open 0830-1230, 1400-1800 (Mon-Fri), 0830-1230 (Sat). **Telephones**: Entel, Reyes 721. CTC, C Henríquez 430.

● **Tourist offices**

Valdivia 1070; information and maps (open all day all week in summer).

● **Transport**

Buses to **Santiago**, 10 hrs, US$15-20. To **Pucón**, in summer every 30 mins, 40 mins' journey, US$1; to **Valdivia**, JAC, US$3.50, 3 a day, 2½ hrs; daily service to **Panguipulli** at 0700, US$2, scenic ride; to **Coñaripe** (US$1.50) and **Liquiñe** at 1600 Mon-Sat, 1000 Sun; to **Temuco**, JAC, US$3; to **Loncoche** (road and railway junction), US$1.50. **NB** JAC has 2 terminals: long distance at Bilbao y Muñoz, next to the main terminal, local is opp the main terminal.

To **Argentina** at 0615 on Tues, Thur and Sat with Empresa San Martín (Av A Muñoz 417) and at 0730 on Mon, Wed and Fri with Igi-Llaima, US$12, but if the Tromen pass is blocked by snow buses go via Panguipulli instead of Pucón.

PUCON

(*Pop* 8,000; *Alt* 280m; *Phone code* 045) **Pucón** is on the southeastern shore of Lago Villarrica, 26 km E of Villarrica. The major tourist centre on the lake, it is a pleasant town with a good climate. The black sand beach is very popular for swimming and watersports. Between 15 Dec to 15 Mar it is crowded and expensive; off season it is very pleasant but many places are closed. Apart from the lake,

other attractions nearby include whitewater rafting and winter sports (see **Skiing** below). The town is scheduled for major development, with plans to build on La Península and around La Poza, the yacht harbour.

Places of interest

There is a pleasant walk to **La Península** for fine views of the lake and volcano, pony rides, golf, etc (private land owned by an Apart-Hotel, you must get permission first). There is another pleasant *paseo*, the **Otto Gudenschwager**, which starts at the lake end of Ansorena (beside *Gran Hotel Pucón*) and goes along the shore. Launch excursion from the landing stage at La Poza at the end of O'Higgins at 1500 and 1900, US$4 for 2 hrs. There is a large handicraft centre where you can see spinning and weaving in progress.

Excursions

2-km walk N along the beach to the mouth of the Río Pucón, with views of the volcanoes Villarrica, Quetrupillán and Lanín. To cross the Río Pucón: head E out of Pucón along the main road, then turn N on an unmade road leading to a new bridge, upstream from the old ferry crossing to La Reducción de Quelhue, near the N bank. From here there are pleasant walks along the N shore of the lake to Quelhue and Trarilelfú, or NE towards Caburga, or up into the hills through farms and agricultural land, with views of three volcanoes and, higher up, of the lake.

Local information
● **Accommodation**

In summer, Dec to Feb, add 20% to hotel prices; at this time rooms may be hard to find – plenty of alternatives (usually cheaper) in Villarrica. Off-season it is often possible to negotiate for accommodation.

L1 *Antumalal*, luxury class, 30m above the shore, 2 km from Pucón, T 441011, F 441013, very small, picturesque chalet-type, magnificent views of the lake (breakfast and lunch on terrace), lovely gardens, excellent, with meals, open year round, good beach, swimming pool and good fishing up the river; state owned **L3** *Gran Pucón*, Holzapfel 190, T 441001, half board, L2 full board, restaurant, shabby, disco, sports centre; **L3** *Interlaken*, Caupolicán, on lakeside 10 mins from town, T 441276,

F 441242, Swiss run, chalets, rec, water skiing, golf, pool, TCs changed, credit cards not accepted (open Nov-April), no restaurant.

A2 *Gudenschwager*, Pedro de Valdivia 12, T 441904, classic Bavarian type, views over lake, volcano and mountains, attentive staff, comfortable, excellent restaurant (open in summer only); **A2** *Hostería El Principito*, Urrutia 291, T 441200, good breakfast, rec; **A3** *La Posada*, Valdivia 191, T 441088, cheaper without bath, full board available, also spacious cabins (**C** low season).

C *Hosp La Casita*, Palguín 555, T 441712, laundry and kitchen facilities, English and German spoken, large breakfast, garden, motorcycle parking, ski trips, Spanish classes, **D** off season, rec; **C** *La Tetera*, Urrutia 580, T 441462, with breakfast, German and English spoken, book swap, warmly rec; **C** *Salzburg*, O'Higgins 311, T 441907, with breakfast, rec, German spoken, some rooms with view over volcano (possible to borrow crampons); **C** *Turista*, O'Higgins 136, T 441153 (**D** low season), good.

D *Hosp De La Montaña*, O'Higgins 472, T 441267, good value, TV, central, restaurant, next to JAC buses; **D** *Hostería Milla Rahue*, O'Higgins 460, T 441904, good inexpensive restaurant, convenient for JAC; **D** *Res Lincoyán*, Av Lincoyán, T 441144, cheaper without bath, comfortable; **D** *Hosp Gerlach*, Palguín 460, kitchen facilities, helpful.

D *Hostería ¡école!*, Urrutia 592, T 441675, F 441660, inc breakfast, run by Ancient Forest International, good vegetarian and fish restaurant, ecological shop, forest treks, information.

Accommodation in private houses, all **D** or **E** pp unless stated: Familia Acuña, Palguín 233 (ask at *peluquería* next door), without breakfast, kitchen and laundry facilities, dirty, good meeting place. On Lincoyán: Juan Torres, No 445, T 441248, poor bathrooms, noisy, cooking facilities; *El Refugio*, No 348, with breakfast,

good; *Hosp Sonia*, No 485, T 441269, hot showers, use of kitchen, meals; No 815, cooking facilities (information on climbing Villarrica); **F** pp Irma Torres, No 545, with breakfast, cooking facilities; **F** pp No 565, safe, quiet, rec, cooking facilities; next door is *Casa Eliana* (Pasaje Chile 225, T 441851), kitchen facilities, highly rec; **E** Adriana Molina, No 312, with breakfast, helpful; **F** pp, No 630, T 441043, kitchen facilities, good value; *Hosp Cherpas*, Fresia 161, T 441089, kitchen facilities, warm; *Hosp Graciela*, Pasaje Rolando Matus 521 (off Av Brasil), good food and atmosphere; Irma Villena, Arauco 460, rec; *Perú 720*, use of kitchen, helps organize excursions; **F** pp Roberto y Alicia Abreque, Perú 170, basic, noisy, popular, kitchen and laundry facilities, information on excursions; **E** pp *Casa Richard*, Uruguay 539, behind service station on the edge of town, basic, cooking facilities, rec; **E** pp *Casa de Mayra*, Brasil 485, helpful; many other families have rooms, especially on Calles Perú, Uruguay and Paraguay – look for the signs or ask in bars/restaurants.

Camping: buy supplies in Villarrica (cheaper). There are so many establishments along the lake's southern shore that you cannot get to the water's edge unless staying in one: close to Pucón are *La Poza*, 300m out of town on road to Villarrica, **E** pp, all facilities; **D** pp *Saint John*, 2 km, T 441165/92, Casilla 154, open Dec-Mar, also *hostería*. Camping is also possible in gardens, US$2.50 pp with use of bathroom. On the road to Tromen Pass, *Cabañas El Dorado*, US$18 for 2, good site, poorly maintained. Cheaper sites en route to Caburga. **Camping equipment:** *Eltit*, O'Higgins y Fresia; *Mawinda*, Ansorena 485.

● **Places to eat**

Pizzería Che Thomas, Palguín 465, good value, small place run by Jorge; *El Fogón*, O'Higgins 480, very good; *El Refugio*, Lincoyán 348, some vegetarian dishes, expensive wine; *Le Demago*,

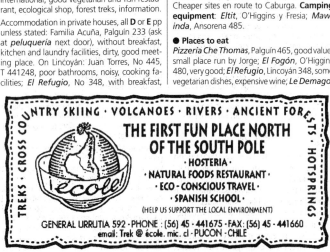

Lincoyán 361 (plus *Pub Naf-Naf*); *Carnes Orlando*, bar/restaurant/butcher's shop, Ansorena nr Urrutia; *Club 77*, O'Higgins, excellent trout; *Puerto Pucón*, on Fresia, Spanish, stylish; *Pastelería Suiza*, next to *Hostería Suiza*, O'Higgins 116, good; *Café de Brasil*, Fresia 477, for real coffee; *Holzapfel Backerei*, Clemente Holzapfel 524, German cafe, rec; *La Tetera*, Urrutia 580, wide selection of teas, good coffee, snacks, see **Accommodation**; *Bar de Julio Parra*, Ansorena 370, English-style pub.

● **Banks & money changers**
Many *casas de cambio* on O'Higgins, poor rates. Big supermarket on O'Higgins changes TCs.

● **Laundry**
Fresia 224; Colo-Colo 475 and 478.

● **Post & telecommunications**
Post Office: Fresia 813.
Telephone: CTC, Gen Urrutia 472; Entel, Ansorena 299.

● **Shopping**
Large supermarket on O'Higgins.

● **Sports**
Fishing: Pucón and Villarrica are celebrated fishing centres, for the lake and the very beautiful Lincura, Trancura and Toltén rivers. Local tourist office will supply details on licences and open seasons etc. Some tourist agencies also offer fishing trips, US$12-20.

Hiking: to the Cañi Forest Sanctuary, overnight hikes are rec; enquire at *Hostería ¡école!*

Horse riding: horse hire US$5/hr.

Watersports: water-skiing, sailing, windsurfing at the beach by *Gran Hotel* and La Poza beach end of O'Higgins (more expensive than hotel, not rec); hotel rates: waterskiing US$10 for 15 mins, Laser sailing US$11/hr, sailboards US$6/hr, rowing boats US$3/hr.

Whitewater rafting: is very popular in high season only; many agencies offer trips (see below), basic course: US$9; advanced US$30.

● **Tour companies & travel agents**
Travel agents: on O'Higgins: *Sol y Nieve* (esq Lincoyán, also at *Grán Hotel Pucón*), excellent guides, frequently rec; *Altue*, No 371, *Nacional Travel Club*, No 323, *Trancura*, No 211, T 441959/441189 (good guides and equipment, some English spoken, rec); *Apumanque*, No 412, T 441085, poor equipment, good guides. All arrange trips to thermal baths, trekking to volcanoes, whitewater rafting, etc (prices: whitewater rafting and riding, see above; climbing Villarrica, US$40-45, 12 hrs, equipment provided; mountain bike hire from US$5/hr to US$20/day; tours to Termas de Huife, US$20 inc entry). Shop around: prices vary at times, quality of guides and equipment variable.

Sergio Catalán, T 441269 (office) or 441142, Gerónimo Alderete 192, tours, excursions and taxi service all year round. For falls, lakes and *termas* it is cheaper, if in a group, to flag down a taxi and bargain.

● **Tourist offices**
Sernatur, Caupolicán y Brasil, very helpful, ask here about all types of accommodation. Municipal Tourist Office at O'Higgins y Palguín provides information and sells fishing licences (US$1/month).

● **Transport**
Local Bicycle hire: *Taller el Pollo*, Palguín 500 block and *Trancura*, O'Higgins 261, US$20/day. Try also travel agencies, eg *Sol y Nieve* and *Andean Sports Tour* on O'Higgins. **Car hire**: Hertz, Fresia 220, US$65 for cheapest car (inc tax, insurance, and 200 km free); same prices/day at *Gran Hotel*. **Taxis**: Cooperative, T 441009.

Buses No main terminal: each company has its own terminal: JAC, O'Higgins 480, T 441923; LIT, O'Higgins y Palguín; Cordillera, Av Miguel Ansorena nr O'Higgins.

JAC to Villarrica, **Temuco** (frequent, US$3, 2 hrs, *rápido* US$3.50, 1 hr) and **Valdivia** (US$4.50); for **Puerto Montt** go to Valdivia and change; to **Santiago**, 10 hrs, US$18-25, many companies, Power cheapest (and least comfortable), overnight only; daytime go via Temuco; *cama* service by Tur-Bus. Colectivos to Villarrica from O'Higgins y Palguín. **Buses to Argentina**: Buses from Temuco to Junín pass through Pucón, fares are the same as from Temuco.

PARQUE NACIONAL VILLARRICA

The park has three sectors: Villarrica Volcano, Quetrupillán Volcano and the Puesco sector which includes the slopes of the Lanín Volcano on the Argentine frontier. Each sector has its own entrance and ranger station.

The **Villarrica** volcano, 2,840m, 8 km S of Pucón (entry US$6) can be climbed up and down in 8-9 hrs (go in summer when days are longer), good boots, iceaxe and crampons, sunglasses, plenty of water and sun block essential. Beware of sulphur fumes at the top – take a cloth mask moistened with lemon juice.

● **Access** Entry is permitted only to groups with a guide and to individuals who can show proof of membership of a mountaineering club in their own country. Several agencies offer excursions, US$40-50 (plus park entry) including guide, transport to park entrance and hire of equipment (no reduction for those with their own equipment); at the park entrance equipment is checked; entry is refused if the weather is poor. Note that travel agencies will not start out if the weather is bad: establish in advance what terms apply in the event of cancellation and be prepared to wait a few days. Bargain for cheaper rate (US$30 pp for groups). Guides, see above under **Tour companies & travel agents**. Also Alvaro Martínez, Cristóbal Colón 430; Juan Carlos, at Oliva's *pensión*, or his pool room on main street, rec. Many others, all with equipment; ask for recommendations at the tourist office. Crampons, ice axe, sunglasses can be rented for US$4/day from the *Taller El Pollo* bicycle shop (address above).

● **Accommodation** There is a refuge without beds 4 km inside the Park, insecure and in desperate need of renovation. Campsite with drinking water, toilets, below refuge.

Skiing The Pucón resort, owned by the *Gran Hotel Pucón*, is on the eastern slopes of the volcano, reached by a badly maintained track, 35 mins. The lodge offers equipment rental (US$15/day, US$82/week), ski instruction, first aid, restaurant and bar as well as wonderful views from the terrace. Lift ticket US$12 full day, US$18 weekends; season is July to November. Information on snow and ski-lifts (and, perhaps, transport) from *Gran Hotel Pucón*. Good for beginners; more advanced skiers can try the steeper areas.

LAGOS CABURGA AND COLICO

Lago Caburga (spelt locally Caburgua) is a very pretty lake in a wild setting 25 km NE of Pucón, is unusual for its beautiful white sand beach (other beaches in the area are of black volcanic sand). The E and W shores of the lake are inaccessible to vehicles. The N shore can be reached by a road from Cunco via the N shore of **Lago Colico**, a more remote lake N of Lago Villarrica. The village of Caburga, at the southern end is reached by a turning off the main road 8 km E of Pucón. Around Caburga the shore is lined with campsites. Rowing boats may be hired US$2/hr. Just off the road from Pucón, Km 15, are the **Ojos de Caburga**, beautiful pools fed from underground, particularly attractive after rain (entry US$0.50).

● **Accommodation Caburga**: **B** *Hostería Los Robles*, 3 km from village, lovely views,

good restaurant; campsite, T 236989, expensive in season, but cheap out of season. No shops, so take own food. **Colico**: **A2** *Trailanqui*, on riverbank 20 km W of Lago Colico, luxury, also suites and cabañas with kitchens. Booking: Trailanqui, Portales 812A, Temuco, T/F 045-214915. **Camping**: 2 sites about half way along N shore of Colico: *Quichelmalleu*, Km 22 from Cunco, T 573187; *Ensenada*, Km 26, T 221441.

● **Transport** To Caburga: taxi day trips from Pucón, US$25 return. Cordillera bus departs 1230 for Caburga, returns 1400, 2nd bus (in summer only) leaves 1700 and returns next morning (US$1 single), but there are colectivos or you can try hitching. If walking or cycling, turn left 3 km E of Pucón (sign to Puente Quelhue) and follow the track for 18 km through beautiful scenery, rec.

PARQUE NACIONAL HUERQUEHUE

East of Lago Caburga, the park includes steep hills and at least 20 lakes, some of them very small (the shapes of many of these are constantly changing). Entrance and administration are near **Lago Tinguilco**, the largest lake, on the western edge. From the entrance there is a well-signed track N to three beautiful lakes, Lagos Verde, Chico and Toro (private car park, US$0.50, 1½ km along the track). The track zig-zags up (sign says 5 km, but worth it) to Lago Chico, then splits left to Toro, right to Verde. From Toro you can continue to Lago Huerquehue and Lago de los Palos (camping).

● **Access** Park entrance is 7 km (3 uphill, 3 down, 1 along Lago Tinquilco) from Paillaco, which is reached by a dirt road (dusty in dry weather, very slippery after rain) which turns off 3 km before Caburga. Entry US$2. The park is open officially only Jan-Mar, but you can get in at other times. Warden very helpful; people in the park rent horses and boats. Take your own food.

● **Accommodation** At the park entrance there are two campsites, US$8. 1½ km before the park entrance, two German speaking families, the Braatz and Soldans, offer accommodation, **E** pp, no electricity, food and camping (US$6); they also rent rowing boats on the lake; Nidia Carrasco Godoy runs a *hospedaje* in the park, T 09-443-2725, **E** pp, with breakfast, hot water, camping.

● **Transport** JAC bus from Pucón to Paillaco, 1½ hrs, US$1, Mon-Fri 1230, 1700, Sat/Sun 1600, returns immediately.

Hot Springs South of Huerquehue

South of the Huerquehue Park on a turning from Pucón – Caburga road there are **Termas de Quimey-Co**, about 29 km from Pucón, campsite, 2 cabins and *hostería* (*centro turístico* under construction), new, less ostentatious or expensive than **Termas de Huife** (*Hostería Termas de Huife*, T 441222, PO Box 18, Casilla), Km 33, US$8, including use of one pool, modern, pleasant (taxi from Pucón, US$23 return with taxi waiting, US$16 one way).

Reserva Forestal Cañi, S of Parque Nacional Huerquehue and covering 74,000 ha, is a private park containing some of the oldest araucaria trees in Chile. From its highest peak, El Mirador, five volcanoes can be seen. For further information, including visiting arrangements, contact the *Hostería íecole!* in Pucón.

THE ROUTE TO ARGENTINA

From Pucón a road runs SE via Curarrehue to the Argentine frontier. At Km 18 there is a turning S to the **Termas de Palguín**. There are many hikeable waterfalls in the area; eg Salto China (spectacular, entry US$0.60, restaurant, camping); Salto del Puma (US$0.60) and Salto del León (US$1.25), both spectacular and 800m from the Termas.

● **Accommodation A1** *Termas*, address, Casilla 1D, Pucón, T 441968, full board, B in small huts with bath, run down, poor food, German-speaking owner, cool swimming pool, baths US$6. Nearby is the **D** *Rancho de Caballos*, rooms, *cabañas* and camping, good food, horse riding (write to Cristina Bonninghoff, *Rancho de Caballos*, Casilla 142, Pucón).

● **Transport** From Pucón take Bus Regional Villarrica from Palguín y O'Higgins at 1100 to the junction (10 km from Termas); last bus from junction to the Termas at 1500, so you may have to hitch back. Taxi rates as for Huife.

Near Palguín is the entrance to the **Quetrupillán** section of the Parque Nacional Villarrica (high clearance vehicle necessary, horses best), free camping, wonderful views over Villarrica Volcano and six other peaks. Ask rangers for the route to the other entrance.

At Km 23 on the Curarrehue road a turning leads to **Termas de San Luis**,

entry US$12.50, small hotel, 30 mins' walk to Lago del León (reached by Pucón-Curarrehue bus).

From Curarrehue the road turns S to Puesco and climbs via **Lago Quellelhue**, a tiny gem set between mountains at 1,196m to reach the frontier at the Mamuil Malal or Tromen Pass. To the S of the pass rises the graceful cone of Lanín volcano. On the Argentine side the road runs S to Junín de los Andes, San Martín de los Andes and Bariloche.

● **Chilean immigration & customs**
At Puesco, open Dec-Mar 0800-2100, April-Nov 0800-1900, US$2/vehicle at other times.

● **Accommodation**
Conaf campsites at Puesco and 5 km from the frontier near Lago Tromen, free, no facilities.

● **Transport**
Daily bus from Pucón, 1800, 2 hrs, US$2.

LAGO CALAFQUEN

Dotted with small islands, Lago Calafquén is a popular tourist destination. **Lican-Ray** (*Pop* 1,700; *Alt* 207m) 30 km S of Villarrica on a peninsula on the N shore, is the major resort on the lake. Boats can be hired from the beach (US$1.50 an hour). Although very crowded in season, most facilities close by the end of March. 6 km to the E is the river of lava formed when the Villarrica volcano erupted in 1971.

● **Accommodation A3** *Refugio*, Canadian-owned, on Playa Grande, open all year, Travellers' Exchange Library for English-language books; **E** pp *Res Temuco*, G Mistral 515, good; **E** Hugo Linolilli 235; several motels, *hosterías* and camping sites (eg *Camping Las Gaviotas*, 3 km E).

● **Places to eat** *Café Ñaños*, Urrutia 105, very good, reasonable prices, helpful owner. Also on Urrutia, *Restaurant-Bar Guido's*, good value.

● **Transport** Buses from Villarrica, 1 hr, US$1, several daily in summer from Villarrica (JAC – 7 a day, 3 on Sun – and García, Reyes y Henríquez, also frequent colectivos, US$0.60); in Jan-Feb, there are frequent direct buses from Santiago and Temuco; to Panguipulli, Mon-Sat 0730.

Coñaripe (*Pop* 1,253), 21 km SE of Lican-Ray at the eastern end of Lago Calafquén, is another popular Chilean tourist spot. Its setting, with a black sand beach surrounded by mountains, is very beautiful. There is a good walk from the left-hand side of the beach back through the fields to Coñaripe. From here a road around the lake's southern shore leads to Lago Panguipulli (see below) and offers superb views over Villarrica volcano.

● **Accommodation** D *Antulafquen*, homely; **E** pp *Hosp House*, with breakfast; **E** pp good *hospedaje* in bus terminal building, good meals; cheap campsites nr private houses (closed off season).

● **Transport** Buses to Panguipulli, 3 a day, US$1 and Villarrica US$1.50.

From Coñaripe a road runs SE over the steep Cuesta Los Añiques offering views of tiny **Lago Pellaifa**. The **Termas de Coñaripe**, with 4 pools, accommodation, restaurant, cycles and horses for hire, are at Km 16, 2 km from the lakeshore. Further S at Km 32 are the **Termas de Liquiñe** (hotel, **B** pp, cabins, restaurant, hot swimming pool, small native forest; accommodation in private houses, **E** pp; **F** *Hosp La Casona*, T 045-412085, Camino Internacional, hot shower, good food, comfortable; tours from Lican-Ray in summer, US$17, 0830-1830 with lunch). 8 km N of Liquiñe is a road going SW (20 km) along the SE shore of **Lago Neltume** to meet the Choshuenco-Puerto Fuy road (see below).

FRONTIER WITH ARGENTINA: PASO CARIRRIÑE

Paso Carirriñe is reached by unpaved road from Termas de Liquiñe. It is open 15 Oct-31 August. On the Argentine side the road continues to San Martín de los Andes.

LAGO PANGUIPULLI

The lake is reached by paved road from Lanco on the Pan-American Highway or unpaved roads from Lago Calafquén. A road leads along the beautiful N shore, wooded with sandy beaches and cliffs. Most of the S shore is inaccessible by road. **Panguipulli** (*Pop* 8,326; *Alt* 136m), at the NW corner of the lake in a beautiful setting, is the largest town in the area. The streets are planted with roses: it is claimed that there are over 14,000. The **Iglesia Parroquial**, built by the Swiss Padre Bernabé, is in Swiss style; its belltower contains three bells from Germany. Fish-

ing excursions on the lake are recommended.

Local festivals Last week of Jan, *Semana de Rosas*, with dancing and sports competitions.

● **Accommodation** *C Hostería Quetropillán*, Etchegaray 381, T 348, comfortable, food; **D** *Central*, good breakfast, rec; **E** pp *Res La Bomba*, quiet; **E** pp private house opp *Quetropillán*, beautiful garden; **E** pp Etchegaray 464, for longer stays, good breakfast; **E** pp Sra Pozas, Pedro de Valdivia 251, laundry extra; **E** pp Olga Berrocal, JM Carrera 834, small rooms; **E** pp Eva Halabi, Los Ulmos 62, T 483, good breakfast. **Camping**: *El Bosque*, P Sigifredo, US$7.50/site, clean, hot water; Municipal campsite 1½ km outside town, US$5 with all facilities, rec (closes at end-Feb); free camping on lakeside at Panguipulli possible.

● **Places to eat** *Didáctico El Gourmet*, restaurant of professional hotel school, excellent food and wine, pricey but high quality; *Café de la Plaza*, O'Higgins 816, good food and coffee; *Café Central*, M de Rosas 880, good cheap lunches, expensive evening meals; several cheap restaurants in O'Higgins 700 block.

● **Banks & money changers In Panguipulli**: Banco de Crédito e Inversiones; Casa de Cambio, M de Rosas. Some shops accept US$ cash. Rates poor, TCs not accepted anywhere.

● **Tourist offices** In plaza next to police station.

● **Transport** Bus terminal at Gabriela Mistral y Portales. To Santiago daily at 1845, US$20; to Valdivia, frequent (Sun only 4), several lines, 2 hrs, US$3; to Temuco frequent, Power and Pangui Sur, US$2, 3 hrs; to Puerto Montt, US$5; to Calafquén, 3 daily at 1200, 1545 and 1600; to Choshuenco 1530, 1630 (reported as 0700 and 1100) US$2, 2½ hrs; to Puerto Fuy, 1800, 2½ hrs; to Coñaripe (with connections for Lican-Ray and Villarrica), 4 a day, 1½ hrs, US$2; to Neltume, Choshuenco, Puerto Fuy 1200, dep Puerto Fuy 1700 (means you can visit Huilo Huilo falls – see below – and return same day).

Choshuenco (*Pop* 622) lies 23 km E of Panguipulli at the eastern tip of the lake. To the S is the **Reserva Nacional Mocho Choshuenco** (7,536 ha) which includes two volcanoes: Choshuenco (2,415m) and Mocho (2,422). On the slopes of Choshuenco the Club Andino de Valdivia has ski-slopes and three *refugios*. This can be reached by a turning from the road which goes S from Choshuenco to Enco at the E end of Lago Riñihue (see page 773). Southeast of Choshuenco a road leads to Lago Pirehueico, via the impressive waterfalls of **Huilo Huilo**, where the river channels its way through volcanic rock before thundering down into a natural basin. The falls are 3 hrs' walk from Choshuenco, or take the Puerto Fuy bus and get off at *Alojamiento Huilo Huilo*, Km 9 (1 km before Neltume) from where it is a 1½-hr walk to the falls.

● **Accommodation In Choshuenco** **D** *Choshuenco*, run down, good meals; various hosterías, inc **D** *Hostería Rayen Trai* (former yacht club), Maria Alvarado y O'Higgins, good food, open all year, rec; *Restaurant Rucapillan*, lets out rooms. **Camping**: on the beach. **In Neltume**: **E** *Pensión Neltume*, meals. **At Huilo Huilo**: **E** pp *Alojamiento Huilo Huilo*, basic but comfortable and well situated for walks, good food, highly rec.

● **Buses** To Panguipulli 0645 and 0700.

LAGO PIREHUEICO

A long, narrow and deep lake, surrounded by virgin *lingue* forest, is totally unspoilt except for some logging activity. There are no roads along the shores of the lake, but two ports: **Puerto Fuy** (*Pop* 300) at the N end 21 km SE of Choshuenco, and **Puerto Pirehueico** at the S end. The two ports can be reached by a road from Neltume which links Puerto Pirehueico and the Argentine frontier crossing at Paso Huahum.

● **Accommodation In Puerto Pirehueico and Puerto Fuy**: beds available in private houses inc the white house near bus terminal, very basic **F** pp. **Campsite**: Puerto Fuy on the beach (take your own food).

● **Transport Buses** Daily Puerto Fuy to Panguipulli, 3 daily, 3 hrs, US$3. **Ferries** From Puerto Fuy across the lake to Puerto Pirehueico US$3, 2-3 hrs. A beautiful crossing (to take vehicles reserve in advance at the *Hotel Quetropillán* in Panguipulli). Schedule varies according to season (Tues and Thur 0700 out of season).

FRONTIER WITH ARGENTINA: PASO HUAHUM

Paso Huahum (659m) is a 4-hr walk from Puerto Pirehueico. On the Argentine side the road leads to San Martín de los Andes and Junín de los Andes.

● **Chilean immigration**
Open summer 0800-2100, winter 0800-2000.

VALDIVIA

(*Pop* 110,000; *Phone code* 063), 839 km S of Santiago by road, lies at the confluence of two rivers, the Calle Calle and Cruces which form the Río Valdivia. It is set in rich agricultural land receiving some 2,300 mm of rain a year and is the capital of Valdivia province. To the N of the city is a large island, Isla Teja, where the Universidad Austral de Chile is situated.

Valdivia was one of the most important centres of Spanish colonial control over Chile. Founded in 1552 by Pedro de Valdivia, it was abandoned as a result of the Mapuche insurrection of 1599 and the area was briefly occupied by Dutch pirates. In 1645 it was refounded as a walled city, the only Spanish mainland settlement S of the Río Biobío. The coastal fortifications at the mouth of the river also date from the 17th century. They were greatly strengthened after 1760 owing to fears that Valdivia might be seized by the British, but were of little avail during the Wars of Independence: overnight on 2 February 1820 the Chilean naval squadron under Lord Cochrane seized San Carlos, Amargos and Corral and turned their guns on Niebla and Mancera which surrendered the following morning. From independence until the 1880s Valdivia was an outpost of Chilean rule, reached only by sea or by a coastal route through Mapuche territory. From 1849 to 1875 Valdivia was a centre for German colonization of the Lake District and a comparatively small number of German and Swiss colonists settled in the city, exerting a strong influence on architecture and on the agricultural methods, education, social life and customs of the area.

Places of interest

On the tree-lined, shady **Plaza de la República**, a new cathedral is under construction. A pleasant walk is along **Avenida Prat** (or **Costanera**), which follows the bend in the river, from the bus station to the bridge to Isla Teja, the boat dock and the riverside market. On **Isla Teja**, near the library in the University, are a **botanic garden** and **arboretum** with trees from all over the world. **Lago de los Lotos** in Parque Saval on the island has beautiful blooms in Nov, entry US$0.30.

Museums

Museo Austral, on Isla Teja, run by the University, contains cartography, archaeology, history of German settlement (including cemetery), local Indian crafts, etc. Open Tues-Sun, 1000-1300, 1500-1800, US$1.

Excursions

The district has lovely countryside of woods, beaches, lakes and rivers. The vari-

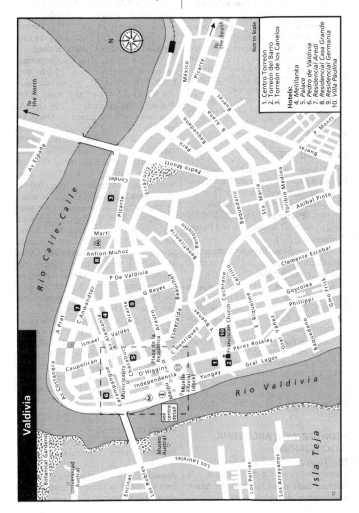

Valdivia

Not to Scale

1. Centro Torreón
2. Torreón del Barro
3. Torreón de los Canelos

Hotels:
4. Melillanka
5. Palace
6. Pedro de Valdivia
7. Residencial Aredi
8. Residencial Casa Grande
9. Residencial Germania
10. Villa Paulina

ous rivers are navigable and there are pleasant journeys by rented motor boat on the Ríos Futa and Tornagaleanes around the Isla del Rey. Among the waterways are countless islands, cool and green.

The **Santuario de la Naturaleza Río Cruces**, flooded as result of the 1960 earthquake, where lots of bird species are visible, can also be visited; tours by boat. *Isla del Río*, daily 1415, 6 hrs, US$15 pp.

Local festivals

Semana Valdiviana, in mid Feb, culminates in Noche Valdiviana on the Sat with a procession of elaborately decorated boats which sail past the Muelle Fluvial. Accommodation is scarce at this time.

Local information
● **Accommodation**

L3 *Pedro de Valdivia*, Carampangue 190, T/F 212931, good; **A3** *Melillanca*, Alemania 675, T 212509, F 222740, rec; **A2** *Naguilán*, Gen Lagos 1927, T 212851/52/53, F 219130, quiet, pool, good restaurant; **A2** *Villa del Río*, España 1025, T 216292, F 217851, restaurant expensive, rents apartments with kitchen; **A3** *Palace*, Chacabuco y Henríquez, T 213319, F 219133, good, comfortable; **A3** *Villa Paulina*, Yerbas Buenas 389, T/F 216372, pool.

B *Hostal Centro Torreón*, P Rosales 783, T 212622, with breakfast, without bath, old German villa, nice atmosphere, car parking; **B** *Hosp Pérez Rosales*, Pérez Rosales 1037, T 215607, **E** pp without bath, modern, small rooms, good beds, overpriced.

C *Hosp Turístico*, Henríquez 747, T 222574, **E** pp without bath, lovely villa in large gardens, large rooms, kitchen and laundry facilities, English spoken, highly rec.

Around the bus terminal: on Picarte, **C** *Hostal Montserrat*, No 849, T 215410, with breakfast, comfortable, highly rec; **D** *Res Germania*, No 873, T 212405, with breakfast, poor beds, German spoken, IYHA reductions, lovely garden; **E** pp *Hostal del 900*, No 953, with breakfast, good value, heated lounge; **D** *Hosp Elsa Martínez*, No 737, T 212587, highly rec; several others. On A Muñoz, outside terminal: **E** pp No 345, with breakfast; **E** pp No 353, breakfast, rec. On C Anwandter: **E** pp *Hostal Casa Grande*, No 880, T 202035, attractive old house, laundry facilities, highly rec; **E** *Hosp Aredi*, No 624, Casa 2, T 214162, with breakfast, good value, *comedor*; **B** *Hostal La Terraza*, No 624, Casa 4, T 212664, with breakfast, very comfortable, lovely views, parking; **E** pp *Hosp Andwandter*,

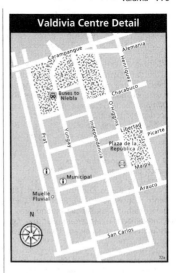

No 482, hot water; **F** pp No 490, without breakfast, use of kitchen.

Other, cheaper accommodation: **D** *Prat*, Prat 595, T 222020, with good breakfast; **D** *Unión*, Prat 514, T 213819, central, good value; **E** pp, Gen Lagos 874, T 215946, with breakfast, old German house, pleasant family atmosphere, rec; **E** pp *Hostal Cochrane*, Cochrane 595, with breakfast; **E** pp Riquelme 15, T 218909, with breakfast, good value; **E** pp *Ana María Vera*, Beauchef 669, T 218542, good breakfast; **E** pp García Reyes 658, T 212015, Mario and Marcela, with breakfast, helpful, English and German spoken, use of kitchen, rec; Sra Paredes, García Reyes 244, **D** with breakfast, rec; **G** pp *Albergue Juvenil*, García Reyes s/n, off Picarte, Jan/Feb only.

Campsite: Camping Centenario, in Rowing Club on España, **E**/tent, overlooking river. Also in Parque Saval. White gas impossible to find, other than in pharmacies/chemists.

● **Places to eat**

Centro Español, Henríquez 436, good, lunch US$3.50; *Sociedad Protectora de EECC*, Independencia y Libertad, good seafood; *La Calesa*, Yungay 735, Peruvian and international, music, art gallery, pier, highly rec; *Dino*, Maipú y Rosales, good coffee; *Palace*, Arauco y P Rosales, popular, good atmosphere, expensive; *Pizzerón*, Henríquez 314, cheap, good, popular; *Delicias*, Henríquez 372, rec for meals and cakes, real coffee (open Sun am); *Selecta*, Picarte 1093, pleasant, excellent fish and meat, not cheap; *Shanghai*, Andwandter y Muñoz, pleasant Chinese, reasonably priced. *Fértil Provincia*, San Carlos 169, café, bookshop, cultural events, good meeting place, rec; *Café Haussmann*, O'Higgins 394, good tea and cakes; *Café Express*, Picarte 764, real coffee; several restaurants on the Costanera facing the boat dock, good food and atmosphere: *Bar Olimpia*, Libertad 28, always full, 24 hrs, cheap, good meeting point; *Entrelagos*, Pérez Rosales 622, ice cream and chocolates. Bakery: *La Baguette*, Libertad y Yungay, French-style cakes, brown bread, repeatedly rec.

● **Banks & money changers**
Banco del Estado at Arauca y Camilo Henríquez (huge commission on TCs). Good rates for cash at **Banco Osorno**, P Rosales 585, **Banco Concepción** (Visa), Picarte 370, will change cash and TCs. **Banco Santiago**, Arauco e Independencia, Mastercard. **Turismo Cochrane**, Arauco y Caupolicán. **Fincard** (Mastercard), Picarte 334, Mon-Fri 0900-1400, 1500-1930, Sat 0900-1330. *Casa de Cambio* at Carampangue 325, T 213305, open 0800-2100 Mon-Fri, 0930-1800 Sat, 0930-1400 Sun; *Turismo Austral*, Arauco y Henríquez, Galería Arauco, accepts TCs.

● **Laundry**
Au Chic, Arauco 436; *Lavazul*, Chacabuco 300, slow. Coin laundry *Lavamatic*, Schmidt y Picarte (Mon-Sat 0930-2030); *Manantial*, Henríquez 809, T 217609.

● **Shopping**
Supermarket: *Hiper-Unico*, Arauco 697.

Film: *Fotoquideon*, Picarte 417, for developing.

● **Sports**
Clubs: Santa Elvira Golf Club (9 holes); tennis, sailing, motor, and rowing clubs like Phoenix on Teja Island.

● **Tour companies & travel agencies**
Paraty Club, Independencia 640, T 215585; for excursions to Corral and Niebla, try the kiosks along the Muelle Fluvial.

● **Tourist offices**
Prat 555, by dock, T 213596. Good map of region and local rivers, list of hotel prices and examples of local crafts with artisans' addresses. Helpful kiosk in bus terminal, mainly bus information. **Conaf**: Ismael Váldez 431. **Automóvil Club de Chile**: Caupolicán 475, T 212378, also for car hire.

● **Transport**
Car hire: Hertz, Aguirre Cerda 1154, T 218316; Turismo Méndez, Gral Lagos 1249, T 233205.

Air LanChile (Arauco 159, of 201, T 213042) and Ladeco (Caupolicán 579, local 18, T 213392) to/from Santiago every day via Temuco.

Trains Station at Ecuador 2000, off Av Picarte, T 214978. To **Santiago**, one a day, 14 hrs, bus Valdivia-Temuco 2¾ hrs, then change to train.

Buses Terminal at Muñoz y Prat, by the river. To **Santiago**: several companies, 13 hrs, most services overnight, US$12-17 (TurBus good) *salón cama* US$45; Pullman daily to and from central and southern towns. Half-hourly buses to **Osorno**, 2 hrs, several companies, US$5; to **Llifén**, 4 a day, US$2.50; to **Panguipulli**, US$3, Empresa Pirehueico, about every 30 mins, US$3; many daily to **Puerto Montt**, US$7, 3 hrs; to **Puerto Varas**, 2 hrs, US$6; to **Frutillar**, US$4, 3 hrs; to **Villarrica**, by JAC, 6 a day, 2½ hrs, US$3.50, continuing to Pucón, US$4.50, 3 hrs. Frequent daily service to Riñihue via Paillaco and Los Lagos.

To Argentina: to Bariloche via Osorno, 10 hrs, Bus Norte, US$20, and Tramaca; to **Zapala**, Igi-Llaima, Mon, Thur, Sat, 2300, change in Temuco at 0200, arrive Zapala 1200-1500, depending on border, US$34.

COASTAL RESORTS NEAR VALDIVIA

At the mouth of the Río Valdivia there are attractive villages which can be visited by land or by river boat. The two main centres are Niebla on the N bank and Corral opposite on the S bank.

Niebla, 18 km from Valdivia is a resort with seafood restaurants and accommodation. To the W of the resort is the Fuerte de la Pura y Limpia Concepción de Monfort de Lemus, on a promontory. Partially restored in 1992, it has an interesting museum on Chilean naval history. Entry US$0.75, Sun free, open daily in summer 1000-1900, closed Mon in winter. Tourist information and telephone office nearby.

● **Accommodation** D *Hostería Riechers*; *Cabañas Fischers*, **C** per cabin, 2 campsites; **E** *Santa Clara*; *Las Delicias*, with restaurant with 'a view that would be worth the money even if the food weren't good', also *cabañas* and camping.

Los Molinos, 6 km further round the coast is a seaside resort set among steep wooded hills (campsite, lots of seaside restaurants)

CORRAL

A fishing port with several good restaurants (eg *Español*, Av 6 de Mayo, good seafood), is 62 km by road from Valdivia. The Castillo de San Sebastián, with 3m wide walls was defended by a battery of 24 guns. It has a museum and offers a view upriver to Volcán Llaima in the distance, entry US$2.50. 3 km further N along the coast is the Castillo San Luis de Alba de Amargos in poor condition.

In midstream, between Niebla and Corral is **Isla Mancera** a small island, fortified by the Castillo de San Pedro de Alcántara, which has the most standing buildings. The island is a pleasant place to stopover on the boat trips, but it can get crowded when an excursion boat arrives. (**C** *Hostería Mancera*, T/F 216296, open Dec-Mar, depending on weather, no singles, phone first: water not drinkable, electricity due to be connected in 1997).

- **Accommodation E** *Res Mariel*, Tarapacá 36, T 471290, modern, good value.

San Carlos, 4 km N along the coast from Corral is the site of the ruins of the Castillo de San Carlos. The coastal walks W and S of here are splendid.

- **Accommodation E** *Hostería Los Alamos*, a delightful hideout for those seeking a quiet life.

- **Transport** The tourist boats (*Neptuno* or *Calle-Calle*) to Isla Mancera and Corral, offer a guided half-day tour (US$20 with meals – cheaper without) from the Muelle Fluvial, Valdivia (behind the tourist office on Av Prat 555), 1330 daily. The river trip is beautiful, but you can also take a bus to Niebla from Chacabuco y Yungay, Valdivia, roughly every 20 mins between 0730 and 2100, 30 mins, US$0.75 (bus continues to Los Molinos), then cross to Corral by boat, frequent, US$1. There are occasional buses from Valdivia to Corral.

Further N is **San José de la Mariquina**, 42 km from Valdivia on the Río Cruces. A further 27 km NW **Mehuin** is reached. A popular resort and fishing port with a long beach (lovely walks). **A3-B** *Hotel El Nogal*, T 63 451352, pool, sauna, bikes, boat trips to local islands. Bus from Valdivia 2 hrs, US$2, on paved road.

INLAND FROM VALDIVIA

A beautiful, unpaved road runs 61 km E from Valdivia along the Río Calle Calle to **Los Lagos**, at the junction with the Pan-American Highway.

- **Accommodation D** *Roger*, Lynch 42, T 261, disco on Sat, rec; *Turismo Tell*, 10 km E, cabañas and campsite, T 09-653-2440, English, French and German spoken; 2 buses a day in summer.

Lago Riñihue, 39 km further E, has no road around its northern edge and the road around the southern shore from Riñihue to Enco is closed (except to jeeps in summer only). **Riñihue**, a beautiful but very small and isolated village at the western end of the lake, is worth a visit.

- **Accommodation B** *Hostería Huinca Quinay*, 3 km E of Riñihue, T 461347, F 461406, cabañas, restaurant; **E** *Restaurant del Lago* (no meals). Campsite by the lake.

LAGO RANCO

Around this large, island-starred lake is a road, terrible (lots of mud and animals, including oxcarts), but worth taking to see an older lifestyle, the beautiful lake, waterfalls and sunsets on the distant volcanoes. (If walking, beware the numerous guard dogs in the area.) There is excellent fishing on the S shore and several hotels organize fishing expeditions.

From the N the lake can be reached from the Longitudinal Highway from Los Lagos or from a point 18 km S of Los Lagos, 11 km N of Paillaco. These two roads join and meet the road around the lake some 5 km W of **Futrono**, the main town on the northern shore. From the S access is from La Unión, which is bypassed by the Longitudinal Highway.

Llifén, 22 km from Futrono, is a picturesque place on the eastern shore. From Llifén, a visit can be paid to **Lago Maihue**, 33 km further E, the S shore of which is covered by native forests. From Llifén the road continues via the Salto de Nilahue (Km 14) to **Riñinahue**, Km 23, at the SE corner of the lake and **Lago Ranco**, Km 47, an ugly little town on the S shore, which has a museum with exhibits on Mapuche culture. On the western shore is **Puerto Nuevo** (hotel of same name, **A1**, very good, watersports, fishing on the Río Bueno). Further N, 10 km W of Futrono is **Coique** with the best beach on the lake.

● **Accommodation Around the lake in Futrono**: there are *hosterías* and **F** pp in the Casa Parroquial. **In Llifén A1** *Huequecura*, Casilla 4, T 09-653-5450, inc meals and fishing services, good restaurant; **B** *Hostería Chollinco*, 3 km out of town on the road towards Lago Maihue, T 0638-202, limited electricity, swimming pool; **C** *Hostería Lican*, T 09-653-5315, F Valdivia 218921; 4 campsites in the vicinity, eg at Chollinco. **In Riñinahue**: **A3** *Hostería Riñinahue*, Casilla 126, T 491379, organizes fishing expeditions. **In Lago Ranco**: *residenciales*, houses to let in summer.

● **Transport** Cordillera Sur bus from Valdivia to Llifén, twice daily, once Sun; from Osorno to Lago Ranco, Empresa Ruta 5, 6 daily.

OSORNO

(*Pop* 114,000; *Phone code* 064), 921 km from Santiago and 105 km N of Puerto Montt, was founded in 1553, was abandoned in 1604 and was refounded by Ambrosio O'Higgins and Juan MacKenna O'Reilly in 1796. It later became one of the centres of German immigration; their descendants are still of great importance in the area.

Places of interest

On the large **Plaza de Armas** stands the modern, concrete and glass cathedral, with many arches, repeated in the tower, itself an open, latticed arch with a cross superimposed. West of the centre on a bend overlooking the river is the **Fuerte María Luisa**, named after the Spanish queen much painted by Goya, built in 1793, restored 1977, with only the river front walls and end turrets standing. East of the main plaza along MacKenna are a number of late 19th century mansions built by German immigrants, now preserved as National Monuments.

Museums

Museo Histórico Municipal, Matta 809. Entrance in Casa de Cultura, US$1; Mon-Fri 1000-1230, 1430-1800, also Sat 1000-1300, 1500-1800 and Sun 1500-1800 in summer. Includes displays on natural history, Mapuche culture, refounding of the city and German colonization.

Excursions

Drive or take bus (US$0.60, frequent) N of Osorno to Río Bueno, celebrated for its scenery and for fishing, to La Unión, and to **Trumao**, a river port on the Río Bueno.

The sea beaches at **Maicolpue** (60 km from Osorno – **D** *Hostería Müller*, on the beach, good service, rec, campsite) and **Pucatrihue** are worth a visit in the summer (daily bus service).

Local information

● **Accommodation**

L3 *Del Prado*, Cochrane 1162, T 235020, pool, garden, good meals, well-located, charming.

A1 *Waeger*, Cochrane 816, T 233721, PO Box 802, F 237080, 4-star, restaurant, comfortable, rec; **A2** *Gran*, O'Higgins 615, T 233990, F 239311, cable TV, comfortable; **A3** *Inter-*

Lagos, Cochrane 515, T 234695, F 232581, with breakfast, garage, restaurant; **A3** *Pumalal*, Bulnes 630, T 243520, F 242477, with breakfast, modern, airy; **A3** *Res Riga*, Amthauer 1058, T 232945, pleasant, highly rec but heavily booked in season; **A3** *Eduviges*, Eduviges 856, T/F 235023, spacious, quiet, attractive, gardens, also *cabañas*, rec.

B *Millantúe*, Errázuriz 1339, T 242072, opp bus terminal, with breakfast, parking; **B** *Res Hein*, Cochrane 843, T 234116, **C** without bath, old-fashioned, spacious, family atmosphere; **B** *Res Bilbao*, Bilbao 1019, T 236755, F 321111 and *Res Bilbao II*, MacKenna 1205, T 242244, with breakfast, parking, restaurant.

D *Amunátegui* 520, nr bus terminal, good; **D** *Germania*, Rodríguez 741, no hot water, cooking facilities; **D** *Res Ortega*, Colón y Errázuriz, 1 block from bus terminal, parking, basic, toilet facilities limited; others nr bus terminal: at A Pinto 1758, **E** inc breakfast and hot water, T 238024.

E pp *Res Sánchez*, Los Carrera 1595, use of kitchen, noisy on ground floor, with breakfast; **E** pp *Hosp de la Fuente*, Los Carrera 1587, basic; **E** pp Colón 844, with breakfast.

F pp *Res Carillo*, Angulo 454, basic; *Silvane*, Errázuriz y Lastarria, T 234429, fairly basic. Private houses at Germán Hube, pasaje 1, casa 2, población Villa Dama, **E** pp, use of kitchen, rec.

Camping: Municipal site at S entrance to city, open from Jan only, free.

● **Places to eat**

Peter's Kneipe, M Rodríguez 1039, excellent German restaurant, not cheap; *Dino*, Ramírez 898, on the plaza, restaurant upstairs, bar/cafeteria downstairs, good. *Los Troncos*, Cochrane 527, good pizzas, French spoken; *Chung Hwa*, Freire 543, Chinese, good value set menus; *Casa del Atillo*, MacKenna 1011, good food and service, pleasant atmosphere, rec; *La Paisana*, Freire 530, Arab specialities, not cheap; *Waldis*, O'Higgins next to *Gran Hotel*, good coffee; *Travels* in bus terminal for cheap snacks. Bakery at Ramirez 977 has good wholemeal bread.

● **Banks & money changers**

Fincard for Mastercard, MacKenna 877, Mon-Fri 0900-1400, 1530-1900, Sat 0930-1330. For good rates try *Cambio Tur*, MacKenna 1010, T 4846; *La Frontera*, Ramírez 949, local 5 (Galería Catedral); if stuck try *Travels* bar in bus terminal.

● **Laundry**

Prat 678 (allow at least a day).

● **Post & telecommunications**

Post Office: O'Higgins 645, also Telex.
Telephone: Ramírez at central plaza and Juan MacKenna y Cochrane.

● **Shopping**

Reinares and Thone, Ramírez 1100, for good fishing gear.

● **Sports**

Skiing: *Club Andino* O'Higgins 1073, for advice on possibilities.

● **Tourist offices**

Provincial government office, on Plaza de Armas, O'Higgins s/n, p 1, left, T 234104. **Automóvil Club de Chile**: Bulnes 463, T 232269, information and car hire.

● **Transport**

Air LanChile, Matta 862, T 236688, Ladeco, MacKenna 975, T 234355; both operate daily flights Osorno-Santiago, via Temuco.

Trains Station at MacKenna 600, T 232992. Daily train to/from Santiago (18 hrs).

Buses Main terminal 4 blocks from Plaza de Armas at Errázuriz 1400. Left luggage open 0730-2030. Bus from centre, US$0.30. To **Santiago**, frequent, US$16, *salón cama* US$25, 16 hrs; to **Valparaíso** and **Viña del Mar**, Tas Choapa, US$25; to **Arica**, Tas Choapa, US$55; to **Concepción**, US$12; to **Temuco**, US$6; to **Pucón** and **Villarrica**, Tur Bus, frequent, US$6; to **Valdivia**, frequent, 2 hrs, several companies, US$5; to **Frutillar**, US$2.50, **Llanquihue**, **Puerto Varas** and **Puerto Montt** (US$5) services by Varmontt every 30 mins; to **Puerto Octay**, US$1.50, Vía Octay company 6 daily between 0815-1930 (return 0800-1930) Mon-Sat, 5 on Sun between 0800 and 2000 (4 return buses); to **Punta Arenas**, US$60-75, Cruz del Sur, Turisbus, Eurobus and Bus Norte, all twice a week.

Local buses to **Lago Ranco**, **Entre Lagos**, **Puyehue** and **Aguas Calientes** leave from the Mercado Municipal terminal, 1 block W of the main terminal. To Lago Ranco, 6 a day from 0810, Empresa Ruta 5, 2 hrs, US$1.50; to Entre Lagos frequent services in summer, Expreso Lago Puyehue and Buses Puyehue, 45 mins, US$1, reduced service off-season; some buses by both companies also continue to Aguas Calientes (off-season according to demand) 2 hrs, US$2; in summer there are also services Maicolpué on the coast if demand is sufficient.

ROUTES From Osorno Route 215 runs E to the Argentine frontier at the Puyehue Pass via the S shore of Lago Puyehue, Anticura and the Parque Nacional Puyehue.

LAGO PUYEHUE

(*Alt* 207m) is about 47 km E of Osorno, surrounded by relatively flat countryside. At the western end is **Entre Lagos** (*Pop* 3,358) and the **Termas de Puyehue** are at the eastern end (entry US$15 pp, 0900-2000).

• **Accommodation & places to eat In Entre Lagos**: **C** *Hosp Vista Hermosa*, with breakfast; **D** *Hostería Entre Lagos*, Ramírez 65, lake view, T 647225; **D** *Villa Veneto*, Gral Lagos 602, T 647203; **D** pp *Hosp Millarey*, with breakfast, excellent; *Restaurant Jardín del Turista*, very good; *Pub del Campo*, highly rec restaurant, reasonable prices. **On the S lakeshore**: *Chalet Suisse*, Ruta 215, Km 55 (Casilla 910, Osorno, T Puyehue 647208, Osorno 064-234073), *hostería*, restaurant with excellent food; a few kilometres beyond, *Hosp y cabañas* at Almacén Valenciana; **B** *Posada Puntillo*, at Shell station, Km 62, before **A1** *Motel Ñilque*, T Santiago 231-3417, or (0647) 218, cabins, half-price May-Oct, fishing trips, watersports, car hire. **B** *Hostería Isla Fresia*, located on own island, T 236951, Casilla 49, Entre Lagos, transport provided. **At the Termas**: **L2-A1** pp *Gran Hotel Termas de Puyehue*, T 232157, F 371272 (cheaper May to mid-Dec) 2 thermal swimming pools (one indoors, very clean), well maintained, meals expensive, in beautiful scenery, heavily booked Jan-Feb (postal address Casilla 27-0, Puyehue, or T Santiago 231-3417); accommodation also in private house nearby, **E** pp full board. **Camping**: *Camping No Me Olvides*, Km 56, US$10; *Playa Los Copihues*, Km 56.5 (hot showers, good), all on S shore of Lake Puyehue; *Camping Playa Puyehue*, Km 75.

• **Transport Buses** Bus 2½ hrs, schedule under Osorno **Buses**; buses do not stop at the lake (unless you want to get off at *Gran Hotel Termas de Puyehue* and clamber down), but continue to Aguas Calientes.

PARQUE NACIONAL PUYEHUE

The Park, E of Lago Puyehue, stretches to the Argentine frontier. On the E side are several lakes and there are two volcanic peaks: **Volcán Puyehue** (2,240m) in the N (access via a private road US$2.50) and **Volcán Casablanca** (also called Antillanca, 1,900m). Park administration is at Aguas Calientes, 4 km S of the Termas de Puyehue; there is also a ranger station at Anticura. Leaflets on walks and attractions are available.

At **Aguas Calientes** there is an open air pool with very hot thermal water beside the Río Chanleufú, open 0830-1900, US$1.50, children US$1, and a very hot indoor pool, open Mon-Fri (in season only) 0830-1230, 1400-1800, Sat, Sun and holidays (all year) 0830-2030, US$5, children US$3.

From Aguas Calientes the road contin-

ues 18 km SE to **Antillanca** on the slopes of Volcán Casablanca, past three small lakes and through forests. This is particularly beautiful, especially at sunrise, with the snow-clad cones of Osorno, Puntiagudo and Puyehue forming a semicircle. The tree-line on Casablanca is one of the few in the world made up of deciduous trees (southern beech). From Antillanca it is possible to climb Casablanca for even better views of the surrounding volcanoes and lakes, no path, 7 hrs return journey, information from Club Andino in Osorno.

Skiing Attached to the *Hotel Antillanca* is one of the smallest ski resorts in Chile; there are 3 lifts, ski instruction and first aid available. Skiing quality depends on the weather: though rain is common it often does not turn to snow.

In the Anticura section of the park, NE of Aguas Calientes, are three waterfalls, including spectacular 40m wide **Salto del Indio**.

• **Accommodation** A *Hotel Antillanca*, T 235114, inc free mountainbiking and parapenting, at foot of Volcán Casablanca, excellent restaurant/café, with pool, sauna, friendly club-like atmosphere. **Camping**: *Chanleufu*, in Aguas Calientes, with hot water, US$25/site, cabañas (**A3** in season, **C** off season) T 236988, a small shop – better to take your own food, and an expensive café; *Los Derrumbes*, 1 km from Aguas Calientes, no electricity, US$20/site. Conaf *refugio* on Volcán Puyehue, but check with Conaf in Anticura whether it is open.

• **Transport** See under Osorno for buses. No public transport from Aguas Calientes to Antillanca; try hitching – always difficult, but it is not a hard walk.

FRONTIER WITH ARGENTINA: PASO PUYEHUE

● **Chilean immigration**
Open second Sat in Oct-second Sat in Mar 0800-2100, otherwise 0800-1900. The Chilean frontier post is at **Anticura**, 22 km W of the border (*Hostería y Cabañas Anticura*; *Camping Catrue*).

NB This route is liable to closure after snow.

● **Crossing by private vehicle**
For vehicles entering Chile, formalities are quick (about 15 mins), but includes the spraying of tyres, and shoes have to be wiped on a mat; pay US$2 to 'Sanidad' and US$1.25 at the docu-

ments counter. Passage will be much quicker if you already have Chilean pesos and don't wait to change at the border.

● **Transport**
To Anticura, bus at 1620 from Osorno, 3 hrs. Several bus companies run daily services from Puerto Montt via Osorno to Bariloche along this route (see under Puerto Montt for details). Although less scenic than the ferry journey across Lake Todos Los Santos and Laguna Verde (see page 785) this crossing is cheaper, more reliable and still a beautiful trip.

Lago Rupanco

This lake is very beautiful and much less developed than most of its neighbours. A 40 km dirt road runs along the S shore, passing through the village of **Piedras Negras**. At the western end, **El Paraíso** is reached by a 13 km road from Entre Lagos, while the S shore is best reached from the Osorno-Puerto Octay road, turning E after 33 km.

● **Accommodation El Paraíso** Hostería y Cabañas El Paraíso, T 236239. **In Piedras Negras:** Hostería El Islote 7 km E. **Camping:** several sites inc at Piedras Negras. **A3** Hacienda Rupanco, lodging with full board, also camping, on the largest milk-producing farm in Chile, horseriding, fishing, rafting, canoeing and sailing on Lago Rupanco. The main entrance is off the Osorno-Puerto Octay road.

● **Transport** Buses from Osorno to Piedras Negras from either Minimarket El Capricho, MacKenna y Colón, or Estacion Viejo (old railway station), leaves 1645, 1545 on Sat, returns from Piedras Negras 0700.

LAGO LLANQUIHUE

The lake, covering 56,000 ha, is the second largest in Chile. Across the great blue sheet of water can be seen two snowcapped volcanoes: the perfect cone of Osorno (2,680m) and the shattered cone of Calbuco (2,015m), and, when the air is clear, the distant Tronador (3,460m).

The largest towns, Puerto Varas, Llanquihue and Frutillar are on the western shore, linked by the Pan-American Highway. There are roads around the rest of the lake: that from Puerto Octay E to Ensenada is very beautiful, but is narrow with lots of blind corners, necessitating speeds of 20-30 kph at best in places (see below).

PUERTO OCTAY

(Pop 2,000; Phone code 064), 56 km SE of Osorno, is a small town at the N tip of the lake in a beautiful setting. Founded by German settlers in 1851, the town enjoyed a boom in the late 19th century when it was the northern port for steamships on the lake. The church and the enormous German-style former convent survive from that period. 3 km S along an unpaved road is the Peninsula of **Centinela** with a launch dock and watersports. From the headland are fine views of the volcanoes and the Cordillera of the Andes; a very popular spot in good weather (taxi US$2.50 one way).

Museums Museo el Colono, Independencia 591, with displays on German colonization, open Tues-Sun 0900-1300, 1500-1900, Dec-Feb only; another part of the museum, housing agricultural implements and machinery for making chicha, is just outside town on the road to Centinela.

● **Accommodation & places to eat**
B Haase, Pedro Montt 344, T 193, with breakfast, attractive old building; **C** Posada Gubernatis, Santiago s/n, lakeside, comfortable; **E** pp Hosp La Naranja, Independencia 361, without bath, with breakfast, restaurant; **E** pp Hosp Fogón de Anita, 1 km out of town, T 34523, good breakfast; **F** pp Hosp Raquel Mardorf, Germán Wulf 712, with enormous breakfast, comfortable, owners have Restaurante La Cabaña at No 713, good; Restaurante Baviera, Germán Wulf 582, cheap and good. **Camping:** El Molino, beside lake, US$5 pp, rec. **Centinela:** Hotel Centinela, T Santiago 234-4010, sadly neglected, meals available, also has cabañas; **E** pp Hostería La Baja, Casilla 116, T 391269, beautifully situated at the neck of the peninsula, with breakfast and bath. **Camping:** Municipal site on lakeside, US$15/site.

● **Tourist offices** Pedro Montt s/n, T 276, open Dec-Feb daily 0900-2100.

● **Transport** Buses to **Osorno** 7 a day; to **Frutillar** (1 hr), Puerto Varas (2 hrs) and Puerto Montt (3 hrs) Thaebus, 8 a day; to **Las Cascadas** (see below) Mon-Fri 1700, return next day 0600. Bus to Ensenada 0600, daily in season, less frequent out of season.

East of Puerto Octay 10 km E of Puerto Octay is Playa Maitén, 'highly recommended, nice beach, marvellous view to the Volcán Osorno, no tourists'. 24 km further on is **Las Cascadas**, surrounded by picturesque agricultural land, old houses and German cemeteries.

- **Accommodation** *Centro de Recreación Las Cascadas*, T 235377; **E** *Hostería Irma*, on lake, 2 km past Las Cascadas, run by Tres Marías, attractive, good food, very pleasant. Several farms on the road around N and E side of the lake offer accommodation, look for signs. **Camping**: *Centro de Recreación Las Cascadas* and Villa Las Cascadas picnic area (free); at Playa Maitén, rec.

FRUTILLAR

(*Pop* 5,000; *Phone code* 065) About halfway along the W side of the lake, **Frutillar** is divided into Alto Frutillar, with a railway station, just off the main highway, and Bajo Frutillar beautifully situated on the lake, 4 km away. (Colectivos run between the two towns, 5 mins, US$0.50.) Bajo Frutillar is possibly the most attractive – and expensive – town on the lake. At the N end of the town is the **Reserva Forestal Edmundo Winckler**, run by the Universidad de Chile, 33 ha, with a guided trail through native woods.

Museums Museo Colonial Alemán, including watermill, replicas of two German colonial houses with furnishings and utensils of the period, a blacksmith's shop (personal engravings for US$5), and a *campanario* (circular barn with agricultural machinery and carriages inside), gardens and handicraft shop. Open daily 0930-1900 summer, Tues-Sun 0930-1400, 1530-1800 winter, US$2.

Local festivals In late Jan to early Feb there is a highly-regarded classical music festival (accommodation must be booked well in advance).

- **Accommodation North of Frutillar Bajo**: **L3** *Salzburg*, T 421589 or Santiago 2061419, excellent, country style, restaurant, sauna, mountain bikes, arranges tours and fishing; *Hostal Cinco Robles*, Casilla 100, T 421351, with breakfast, other meals on request, parking. In Frutillar Bajo: **B** *Casona del 32*, Caupolicán 28, T 421369, Casilla 101, with breakfast, comfortable old house, central heating, English and German spoken; **C** *Hosp El Arroyo*, Philippi 989, T 421560, with breakfast, highly rec; **C-D** *Hosp Costa Azul*, Philippi 1175, T 421388,

mainly for families, good breakfasts; also on Philippi: **C** *Winkler*, No 1155, T 421388, discount to YHA members, cabins, rec; **D** pp *Hosp Vivaldi*, No 851, T 421382, Sra Edith Klesse, quiet, comfortable, excellent breakfast and lodging, also family accommodation, rec; **D** *Las Rocas*, No 1235, T 421397, with breakfast; **D** *Residenz/Café am See*, No 539, good breakfast; **C** No 451, T 421204, good breakfast; **D** *Hosp Trayén*, No 963, T 421346, basic; **E** pp *Hosp Kaisersseehaus* (Viola Herbach), No 1333 (Casilla 13, T 421387), good, cheap food, welcoming, English, German, Spanish spoken, poor beds; **D** *Pérez Rosales* 590, excellent breakfast. In Frutillar Alto: **D** *Faralito*, Winkler 245, cooking facilities (owner can be contacted at shop at Winkler 167, T 421440).Several along Carlos Richter (main street). Cheap accommodation in the school in Frutillar Alto, sleeping bag required. **Camping**: *Playa Maqui*, 7 km N of Frutillar, T 421139, fancy, expensive; *Los Ciruelillos*, 2 km S, T 9123, most services. Try also Sr Guido González, Casa 3, Población Vermont, T 421385, G pp, rec.

Places to eat *Club Alemán*, Av Philippi 747, good but not cheap, hostile to backpackers; *Bar Restaurant* upstairs at the Fire Station, *Bomberos*, best value, open all year, memorable painting caricaturing the firemen in action. *Bierstube*, Varas, open 1600-2400. Many German-style cafés and tea-rooms on C Philippi (the lakefront) eg *Salón de Te Frutillar*, No 775. *Der Volkladen*, O'Higgins y Philippi, natural products, chocolates and cakes, natural cosmetics. Budget travellers should eat at *Kaisersseehaus* (see **Accommodation**) 'and explode'.

Useful services Toilet, showers and changing cabins for beach on O'Higgins. *Cema-Chile* shop, Philippi y O'Higgins.

Tourist offices On lakeside opp *Club Alemán*, helpful; *Viajes Frutillar*, Richter y Alissandre in Alto Frutillar, run tours.

Transport Buses to Puerto Varas (US$0.75) and Puerto Montt (US$1.25), frequent, Varmontt and Full Express; to Osorno, Varmontt 1¼ hrs, US$3; to Puerto Octay, Thaebus, 6 a day. Most buses leave from opp the Copec station in Alto Frutillar.

PUERTO VARAS

(*Pop* 16,000; *Phone code* 065) This beauty spot is only 20 km N of Puerto Montt. In the 19th century, it was the southern port for shipping on the lake. The Catholic church, built by German Jesuits in 1918, is a copy of the church in Marieenkirche in the Black Forest. North and E of the

Gran Hotel Puerto Varas (1934) are German style mansions dating from the early 20th century. **Parque Philippi**, on top of the hill, is pleasant; walk up to *Hotel Cabañas del Lago* on Klenner, cross the railway and the gate is on the right.

Excursions

Puerto Varas is a good base for trips around the lake. On the S shore two of the best beaches are Playa Hermosa (Km 7) and Playa Niklitschek (entry fee charged). **La Poza**, at Km 16, is a little lake to the S of Lago Llanquihue reached through narrow channels overhung with vegetation; **Isla Loreley**, an island on La Poza, is very beautiful (frequent boat trips); a concealed channel leads to yet another lake, the Laguna Encantada. At Km 21 there is a watermill being converted into a museum.

Buses from Puerto Montt run every day on the southern side of the lake between Puerto Varas and Ensenada, in the S-eastern corner of the lake, continuing to Ralún, Cochamó and Río Puelo (see below). In summer, buses go daily from Puerto Montt and Puerto Varas in the morning to Ensenada, Laguna Verde, Petrohué Falls and Lago Todos Los Santos, US$7, good value.

Local information

● **Accommodation**

Accommodation is expensive, it is cheaper to stay in Puerto Montt.

L3 *Los Alerces*, Pérez Rosales 1281, T 233039, 4-star hotel, with breakfast, cabin complex, attractive.

A1 *Colonos del Sur*, Del Salvador 24, T 233369, F 233394, good views, good restaurant, tea room; **A1** *Cabañas del Lago*, Klenner 195, T 232291, F 232707, on Phiippi hill overlooking lake, spacious rooms with good breakfast, restaurant with superb views; also self-catering cabins sleeping 5 (good value for groups), heating, sauna; **A1** *Antonio Varas*, Del Salvador 322, T 232375, F 232352, very comfortable; **A2** *Bellavista*, Pérez Rosales 60, T 232011, F 232013, cheerful, rec, restaurant, overlooking lake; **A3** *Cabañas Ayentemo*, Pérez Rosales 1297, comfortable cabins, T/F 232270; **A3** *Licarayén*, San José 114, T 232305, F 232955, overlooking lake, comfortable, 'enthusiastically rec', book in season, **C** out of season, 'the perfect place for bad weather or being ill'.

B *Merlín*, Walker Martínez 584, T/F 233105, quiet, excellent restaurant, highly rec; **C** *El Greco*, Mirador 134, T 233388, modern, good; **B** *Hosp Loreley*, Maipo 911, T 232226, rec, homely, quiet.

D María Schilling Rosas, La Quebrada 752, rec; **D** pp *Hosp Las Carmelas*, Imperial y Rosario, excellent, helpful, good meals, lends books inc some in English, highly rec; **D** pp *Cabañas Amancay*, Martínez 564, with breakfast, German spoken, rec; **D** pp Andrés Bello 321, nice atmosphere, good breakfast; **D** *Res Alemana*, San Bernardo 416, T 232419, with breakfast, without bath; **D** *Hosp Don Raúl*, Salvador 928, laundry and cooking facilities, rec, camping **F** pp; **C** Imperial 8 (opp *Motel Trauco*), good breakfast, good views, highly rec; other family *hospedajes* on same street inc **D** *Hosp Imperial*, No 653, T 232451, inc breakfast, central, rec; **F** pp Pío Nono 489, T 233172, with breakfast; **E** pp Elsa Pinto, Verbo Divino 427; **E** *Hosp Ellenhaus*, Martínez 239, T 233577, use of kitchen, lounge, hospitable, highly rec.

Camping: on S shore of Lago Llanquihue starting at Puerto Varas: Km 10, Playa Hermosa, T Puerto Varas 8283, Puerto Montt 252223, fancy, rec, take own supplies. Km 11, Playa Niklitschek, full facilities; Km 20, Playa Venado; Km 49, Conaf site at Puerto Oscuro, beneath road to volcano, very good.

● **Places to eat**

Donde El Gordito, downstairs in market, immense portions, very popular, good value; *Domino*, Del Salvador 450, good, cheap; *Café Danés*, Del Salvador 441, good coffee and cakes; *El Amigo*, San Bernardo 240, large portions, good value. At the Puerto Chilo end of Pérez Rosales are *Costa Azul*, No 01071, rec and *Ibis*, No 1117, warmly rec. *Café del Turismo*, next to Cruz del Sur office, cheap, good.

● **Banks & money changers**

Turismo Los Lagos, Del Salvador 257 (Galería Real, local 11), open daily 0830-1330, 1500-2100, Sun 0930-1330, accepts TCs, good rates. Banco Osorno, Del Salvador 399, good rates.

● **Laundry**

Del Salvador 553.

● **Post & telecommunications**

Post Office: San José y San Pedro.
Phone Office: Del Salvador y Santa Rosa.

● **Shopping**

VYH Meistur Supermarket, Walker Martínez, good selection, reasonably priced.

● **Sports**

Fishing: the area around Puerto Varas is popular for fishing. A licence costs US$2.50 a year, obtainable from the Municipal offices.

Cycle hire: *Travel Art*, Imperial 0661, T 232198, but check equipment carefully.

● **Tour companies & travel agents**
Andina del Sud, Del Salvador 243, T 232511, operate 'lakes' trip to Bariloche, Argentina via Lago Todos los Santos, Peulla, Cerro Tronador (see under Puerto Montt, **To Argentina**), plus other excursions, good. Also *Eco Travel*, Av Costanera s/n, T 233222, *Aqua Motion*, Imperial 0699, T/F 232747, for trekking, rafting and climbing, German and English spoken, good equipment; several others. Most tours operate in season only (1 Sept-15 April).

● **Tourist offices**
Del Salvador 328, T 232402, F 233315, 0900-2100 in summer, helpful, find cheap accommodation; also art gallery.

● **Transport**
Trains To Santiago daily, 1600, details under Puerto Montt.

Buses Varmontt terminal, San Francisco 500 block. To **Santiago**, Varmontt, Igi Llaima and others, US$20; to **Puerto Montt**, 30 mins, Varmontt and Full Express every 15 mins, US$0.50; same companies, same frequency to Frutillar (US$0.75, 30 mins) and **Osorno** (US$3.50, 1¼ hrs); to **Valdivia** US$6. To **Bariloche**, Andina del Sud, see above. Minibuses to Ensenada and Petrohué leave from San Bernardo y Martínez, Buses JM and Varastur.

ENSENADA

47 km E of Puerto Varas, beautifully situated at the SE corner of Lago Llanquihue and a good centre for excursions. A half-day trip is to Laguna Verde, about 30 mins from *Hotel Ensenada*, along a beautiful circular trail behind the lake (take first fork to the right behind the information board), and then down the road to a campsite at Puerto Oscuro on Lago Llanquihue. The site is quiet and secluded, a good spot for a picnic.

● **Accommodation** **A2** *Hotel Ensenada*, Casilla 659, Puerto Montt, T 232888, olde-worlde, good food (closed in winter), good view of lake and Osorno Volcano, runs tours, hires mountain bikes (guests only); also *hostal* in the grounds, cooking facilities, cheaper. **B** *Hosp Ensenada*, T 8278, excellent breakfast, **D** off-season, rec; **C** *Hostería Los Pumas*, 3 hrs up the hill, also highly rec, in season only; about 2 km from town is **C** *Pucará*, also with good restaurant; **C** *Ruedas Viejas*, T 312, for room, or **D** in cabin, about 1 km W from Ensenada, IYHA reductions, basic, damp, restaurant; **C** *Hosp Arena*, on same road, with breakfast, rec; **D** *Cabañas Brisas del Lago*, T 252363, chalets for

6 on beach, good restaurant nearby, highly rec for self-catering, supermarket next door; **D** *Moteles Hostería*, with breakfast, poor service, comfortable; **D** *Hosp Opazo*, with breakfast, **E** pp *Hosp* above Toqui grocery, cheapest in town, basic, quiet, hot water, use of kitchen, beach in the back yard, rec. **Camping**: *Camping Montaña*, opp *Hotel Ensenada*, US$10, fully equipped, highly rec; also at Playa Larga, 1 km beyond *Hotel Ensenada*, US$10 and at Puerto Oscuro, 2 km N, US$8.

● **Places to eat** *Canta Rana* rec for bread and *kuchen*; *Ruedas Viejas*, the cheapest; most places closed off season, a few pricey shops; take your own provisions.

● **Tour companies & travel agents Guide**: Ludwig Godsambassis, owner of *Ruedas Viejas*, who works for *Aqua Motion* in season, works independently as a guide out of season and is very knowledgeable.

● **Transport** Minibuses run from Puerto Varas, frequent in summer (see above). Hitching from Puerto Varas is difficult.

Volcan Osorno

North of Ensenada, can be reached either from Ensenada, or from a road branching off the Puerto Octay-Ensenada road at Puerto Klocker, 20 km SE of Puerto Octay.

Climbing Weather permitting, *Aqua Motion* (address under Puerto Varas) organize climbing expeditions with local guide, transport from Puerto Montt or Puerto Varas, food and equipment, US$150 pp payment in advance (minimum group of 2, maximum of 6 with 3 guides) all year, setting out from the *refugio* at La Burbuja. *Aqua Motion* check weather conditions the day before and offer 50% refund if climb is abandoned due to weather. From La Burbuja it is 6 hrs to the summit. Conaf do not allow climbing without a guide and insist on 1 guide to every two climbers. Only experienced climbers should attempt to climb right to the top, ice climbing equipment essential.

● **Accommodation** The Club Andino Osorno (address under Osorno) has three shelters (US$3 pp): to the N at La Picada (20 km SE of Puerto Klocker) at 950m; to the S at *Las Pumas*, 12 km from Ensenada at 900m, with plenty of beds and cooking facilities, very friendly guards (apply at the Oficina de Turismo de Osorno); also to the S, 1.5 km from Ensenada at 1,200m **Refugio Teski Club**, E, bunk accommodation, restaurant and bar, sleeping bag useful, bleak site above the tree line; a good base for walking.

PARQUE NACIONAL VICENTE PEREZ ROSALES

Lago Todos los Santos is a long irregularly shaped sheet of water, the most beautiful of all the lakes in southern Chile. The waters are emerald green; the shores are deeply wooded and several small islands rise from its surface. In the waters are reflected the slopes of Volcán Osorno. Beyond the hilly shores to the E are several graceful snow-capped mountains, with the mighty Tronador in the distance. To the N is the sharp point of Cerro Puntiagudo, and at the northeastern end Cerro Techado rises cliff-like out of the water. The ports of **Petrohué** at its western and **Peulla** at its eastern ends are connected by boat. Trout and salmon fishing are excellent in several parts including Petrohué.

There are no roads round the lake and the only scheduled vessel is the Andino del Sud service with connections to Bariloche (Argentina), but private launches can be hired for trips. Isla Margarita, the largest island on the lake, with a lagoon in the middle, can be visited (in summer only) from Petrohué, boats by Andino del Sud leave 1500, US$30.

Petrohué, 16 km NW of Ensenada, is a good base for walking. The **Salto de Petrohué** (entrance, US$1.50) is 6 km (unpaved) from Petrohué, 10 km (paved) from Ensenada (a much nicer way from Petrohué). Near the falls is a snackbar; there are also two short trails, the Senderos de los Enamorados and Carileufú.

Peulla, is a good starting point for hikes in the mountains. The Cascadas Los Novios, signposted above the *Hotel Peulla*, are stunning once you have climbed to them. Good walk also to Laguna Margarita, 4 hrs, take water.

On the S shore of Lago Todos Los Santos is the little village of **Cayutué**, reached by hiring a boat from Petrohué, US$30. From Cayutué it is a 3-hr walk to Laguna Cayutué, a jewel set between mountains and surrounded by forest. Good camping and swimming. From here it is a 5 hr hike S to Ralún on the Reloncaví Estuary (see below). This is part of the old route used by missionaries in the colonial period to travel between Nahuel Huapi in Argentina and the island of Chiloé. It is now part of a logging road and is good for mountain bikes.

The park is infested by *tavanos* in Dec and Jan: cover up as much as possible with light-coloured clothes which may help a bit.

Park Administration Conaf office in Petrohué with a visitors centre, small museum and 3D model of the park. There is a *guardaparque* office in Puella.

● **Accommodation At Petrohué: A2** *Hostería Petrohué*, T/F 258042, with bath, excellent views, log fires, cosy; owner, Franz Schirmer, a former climbing guide, can advise on activities around the lake; **A3** *Fundo El Salto*, near Salto de Petrohué, run by New Zealanders, mainly a fishing lodge, good home cooking, fishing trips arranged, Casilla 471, Puerto Varas; **E pp** *Familia Küschel* on other side of river (boat across), with breakfast, meals available, electricity only 3 hrs in pm, dirty, noisy, poor value, camping possible. Albergue in the school in summer. Conaf office can help find cheaper family accommodation. There is a shop with basic supplies in the village. **At Peulla: A1** *Hotel Peulla*, PO Box 487, Puerto Montt, T 253253 (inc dinner and breakfast, direct personal reservations A3, PO Box 487, Puerto Montt, cheaper out of season), beautiful setting by the lake and mountains, restaurant and bar, good but expensive meals, cold in winter, often full of tour groups (tiny shop at back of hotel); **D pp** *Res Palomita*, 50m W of Hotel, half board, family-run, simple, comfortable but not spacious, separate shower, book ahead in season, lunches; accommodation is also available with local residents: Elmo and Ana Hernández Maldonado (only house with a balcony), **D** with breakfast, use of kitchen, helpful. Small shop in Andino del Sud building but best to take your own food. **Camping**: at Petrohué on far side beside the lake, US$4/site, no services (local fishermen will ferry you across, US$0.50). At Peulla, opp Conaf office, US$1.50. Good campsite 1¾ hrs' walk E of Peulla, take food.

● **Transport Minibuses** from Puerto Varas to Ensenada continue to Petrohué, frequent in summer.

The **boat** between Petrohué and Peulla costs US$25 day return or one way (book in advance); it leaves Petrohué at 1030, Peulla at 1500 (not Sun, 2½ hrs – most seating indoors, no cars carried, cycles free), commentaries in Spanish, English and German plus loud music. This connects with the Andina del Sud tour bus between

Puerto Montt and Bariloche (see under Puerto Montt). Local fishermen make the trip across the lake, but charge much more than the public service.

FRONTIER WITH ARGENTINA: PASO PEREZ ROSALES

● **Chilean immigration**

In Peulla, 30 km W of the frontier, open summer 0800-2100, winter 0800-2000.

NB It is impossible to do this journey independently out of season as then there are buses only as far as Ensenada, there is little traffic for hitching and none of the ferries takes vehicles.

RELONCAVI ESTUARY

The Reloncaví estuary, the northernmost of Chile's glacial inlets, is recommended for its local colour, its sealions, dolphins and its peace.

Ralún, a small village at the northern end of the estuary, is 31 km SE from Ensenada by a paved road along the wooded lower Petrohué valley. The road continues, unpaved, along the E side of the estuary to Cochamó and Puelo. In Ralún there is a village shop and post office, with telex.

● **Accommodation E** pp *Restaurant El Refugio* rents rooms; **E** pp *Navarrito*, restaurant and lodging; **F** pp *Posada Campesino*, simple, without breakfast; the *Hotel Ralún*, at S end of the village, which burnt down in 1992, has cabins.

● **Transport** Bus from Puerto Montt, 5 a day, Bohle, between 1000 and 1930, 4 on Sat, return 0700-1830, US$2. Also bus from Ensenada daily, US$1.

Cochamó, 17 km S of Ralún on the E shore of the estuary, is a pretty village, with a fine wooden church similar to those on Chiloé, in a striking setting, with the estuary and volcano behind.

● **Accommodation D** *Cochamó*, T 212, basic but clean, often full with salmon farm workers, good meals, rec, and a large number of *pensiones* (just ask), eg **E** pp *Mercado Particular Sabin*, Catedral 20, next to *Hotel*; **E** pp Sra Flora Barrientos offers floorspace in her bar/restaurant/drugstore, same street No 16; **E** pp *Restaurant Copihue*; **E** pp *Res Gato Blanco*; cheapest accommodation at Catedral 2, by the pier (floor only). *Camping Los Castaños*, T 214 (Reservations Casilla 576, Puerto Montt).

● **Places to eat** *Reloncaví*, next to *Hotel*;

Donde Payi opp church.

● **Trail Horseriding** *Campo Aventura* (Casilla 5, Correo Cochamó) T/F 065-232910, in Valle Río Cochamó, offer accommodation at their base camp 2 km S of Cochamó (**E** pp, kitchen, sauna, camping) and at their other base in the valley of La Junta. Specialize in horseback and trekking expeditions between the Reloncaví Estuary and the Argentine frontier, 2-10 days (in Europe, PO Box 111945, 86044 Augsburg, Germany).

● **Transport** Bus Fierro to Ralún, Ensenada, Puerto Varas and Puerto Montt, 3 daily; to Puelo 2 daily

The **Gaucho Trail** E to Paso León on the Argentine frontier was used in the colonial period by indians and Jesuit priests and later by gauchos. The route runs along Río Cochamó to La Junta, then along the N side of Lago Vidal, passing waterfalls and the oldest surviving Alerce trees in Chile at El Arco, 3-4 days by horse, 5-6 days on foot, depending on conditions (best done Dec-Mar). From the border crossing at Paso León it is a 3-hr walk to the main road to San Carlos de Bariloche.

Puelo, further S, on the S bank of the Río Puelo, is a most peaceful place (ferry crossing); lodging is available at the restaurant (F pp) or with families – try Roberto and Olivia Telles, simple, no bath/shower, meals on request, or Ema Hernández Maldona; two restaurants.

● **Transport** Buses Fierro services from Puerto Montt, Mon-Sat 1230 and 1600, Sun 0900, 1500 (from Puerto Varas 30 mins later). Daily buses from Cochamó Mon-Sat 0800 and 1730, Sun 1130 and 1700. In summer boats sail up the Estuary from Angelmó. Tours from Puerto Montt US\$30. Off season the *Carmencita* sails once a week, leaving Puelo Sun 1000 and Angelmó Wed 0900 (advisable to take warm clothes, food and seasickness pills if it's windy).

PUERTO MONTT

(*Pop* 110,139; *Phone code* 065) The capital of X Región (Los Lagos), 1,016 km S of Santiago, was founded in 1853 as part of the German colonization of the area. Good views over the city and bay are offered from outside the Intendencia Regional on Av X Region. The port is used by fishing boats and coastal vessels, and is the departure point for vessels to Puerto Chacabuco, Laguna San Rafael and for the long haul S to Punta Arenas. A paved road runs 55 km SW to Pargua, where there is a ferry service to Chiloé.

Places of interest

The **Iglesia de los Jesuitas** on Gallardo, dating from 1872, has a fine blue-domed ceiling; behind it on a hill is the **campanario** (clock tower). The little fishing port of **Angelmó**, 2 km W, has become a tourist centre with many seafood restaurants and handicraft shops (reached by Costanera bus along Portales and by collective taxi Nos 2, 3, 20 from the centre, US\$0.30pp).

Museums

Museo Regional Juan Pablo II, Portales 997 near bus terminal, local history and a fine collection of historic photos of the city; also memorabilia of the Pope's visit. Open daily 1030-1800, US\$0.50.

Excursions

Puerto Montt is a popular centre for excursions to the Lake District. **Chinquihue**, W of Angelmó, has many seafood restaurants, with oysters as a speciality. There is a bathing beach with black sand (polluted) at **Pelluco**, 4 km E of Puerto Montt (accommodation including *cabañas*; several good seafood restaurants, including *Pazos*, best *curanto* in Puerto Montt, rec). The wooded

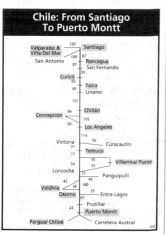

Chile: From Santiago To Puerto Montt

Valparaíso & Viña Del Mar — Santiago
San Antonio — Rancagua
San Fernando
Curicó
Talca
Linares
Concepción — Chillán
Los Angeles
Victoria — Curacautín
Temuco
Villarrica/ Pucón
Loncoche — Panguipulli
Valdivia — Entre Lagos
Osorno
Frutillar
Puerto Montt
Pargua/ Chiloé — Carretera Austral

Isla Tenglo, reached by launch from An- gelmó (US$0.30), is a favourite place for picnics. Magnificent view from the summit. The island is famous for its *curantos*, a local dish. **Isla Guar** may also be visited by boat from Angelmó (1600, 2 hrs); boat returns from the other end of the island at 0730. Accommodation, if lucky, at the church; best to camp.

West of Puerto Montt the Río Maullín, which drains Lago Llanquihue, has some attractive waterfalls and good fishing (salmon). The little fishing village of **Maullín**, founded in 1602 (**B** *Motel El Pangal*, 5 km away, T 244), at the mouth of the Río Maullín, is worth a visit. South- east of here, on the coast, is Carelmapu; 3 km away is an excellent beach, Playa Brava. **Calbuco**, centre of the fishing in- dustry (*Restaurant San Rafael*, rec) with good scenery, is on an island linked to the mainland by a causeway. It can be visited direct by boat or by road (the old coast road from Puerto Montt is very beautiful).

Local information
● Accommodation
Accommodation is expensive in season, much cheaper off season. Check Tourist Office.

L3 *Vicente Pérez Rosales*, Varas 447, T 252571, with breakfast, excellent restaurant, seafood, tourist and climbing information, rec; **A1** *O'Grimm*, Gallardo 211, T 252845, F 258600, with breakfast, cosy restaurant with occasional live music, central; **A2** *Burg*, Pedro Montt y Portales, T 253813, modern, central heating, centrally located, good, interesting tra- ditional food in restaurant; **A1** *Club Presi- dente*, Portales 664, T 251666, F 251669, 4-star, with breakfast, very comfortable, also

suites, rec; **A1** *Don Luis*, Urmeneta y Quillota, T 259001, F 259005, heating, very good; **A3** *Montt*, Varas y Quillota, T 253651, **C** with- out bath, good value, good restaurant; **A3** *Raysan*, Benavente 480, T 256151, helpful; **A2** *Viento Sur*, Ejército 200, T 258701, F 258700, excellent, good restaurant, sauna, gym, excellent views; **A3** *Millahue*, Copiapó 64, T 253829, F 253817, and apartments at Benavente 959, T/F 254592, with breakfast, modern, good restaurant.

B *Colina*, Talca 81, T 253813, restaurant, bar, car hire, rec; **B** *Le Mirage*, Rancagua 350, T 255125, F 256302, with breakfast, small rooms; **B** *El Candil*, Varas 177, T 253080, attractive.

C pp *Hostal Pacifico*, J J Mira 1088, T 256229, **D** pp without bath, with breakfast, cable TV, parking, comfortable, rec; **C** *Res Embassy*, Valdivia 130, T 253533, **E** pp without bath, stores luggage, rec; **C** pp *Res Urmeneta*, Urme- neta 290, T 253262, **D** pp without bath, com- fortable, rec, IYHA reductions; **C** pp *Res La Nave*, Ancud y Varas, T 253740, **E** pp without bath, pleasant, inexpensive restaurant.

Near the bus terminal: C *Hosp Polz*, J J Mira 1002, T 252851, with breakfast, warm, good beds, rec; **D** *Res El Turista*, Ancud 91, T 254767, with and without bath, with break- fast, comfortable, rec; **D** *Res Punta Arenas*, J J Mira 964, with breakfast, basic; **E** pp *Casa Gladis*, Ancud y Mira, dormitory style, kitchen and laundry facilities, crowded; **E** pp *Hosp Leti- cia*, Lota 132, basic, safe, cooking facilities, rec; **E** pp *Res Central*, Lota 111, T 257516, use of kitchen, rec; **E** pp *Goecke* 119, T 266339, with breakfast, cooking facilities, poor bathroom.

Near the Plaza de Armas: D *Res Calipso*, Urmeneta 127, T 254554, without bath, IYHA accepted; **D** *Res La Alemana*, Egaña 82, T 255092, with breakfast, German spoken, run down; in C Huasco: **E** pp No 16, with breakfast, basic; **E** pp No 126, rec; **E** pp No 130, hot

showers, cooking facilities, rec; **E** pp Sr Raúl Arroyo, Concepción 136, T 262188 (go to the 'inland' end of Concepción, turn right to end of alley), with breakfast, basic, crowded, run down, poor kitchen and bathroom facilities, English spoken, also has a cabaña 3 km away, sleeps 10; **D** Varas 840, basic, inc breakfast.

Other cheaper accommodation: **D** *Casa Haraldo Steffen*, Serrano 286, T 253823, with breakfast, 15 mins' walk from centre, small rooms, run down, only 1 bathroom; **D** pp *Alda González*, Gallardo 552, T 253334, **E** pp without bath, with breakfast, cooking facilities,

popular; **F** pp *El Tata*, Gallardo 621, floor space, very basic, popular, packed in summer; **D** Aníbal Pinto 328, with breakfast, popular, laundry facilities, 10 mins' walk from centre, rec; **E** pp, Balmaceda 300, with breakfast; **E** pp Balmaceda 283, hospitable; **E** pp Balmaceda y Vial, reached by steep path behind Balmaceda 283, good breakfast, safe, rec; **E** pp *Vista Hermosa*, Miramar 1486, with bath, quiet, helpful; **E** pp Trigal 309, T 259923, use of kitchen, with breakfast; **E** pp *Casa Perla*, Trigal 312, T 262104, with breakfast, French, English spoken, helpful, meals, Spanish classes offered off season rec; **E** pp *Hosp*

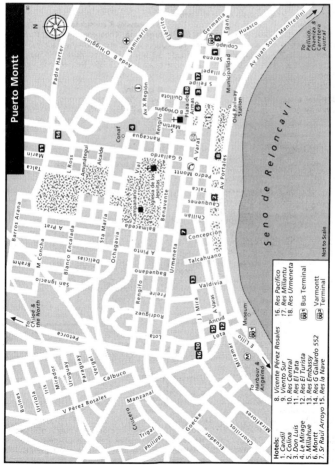

Puerto Montt

Seno de Reloncaví

Not to Scale

Hotels:
1. Candil
2. Colina
3. Leon Luis
4. Le Mirage
5. Millahue
6. Montt
7. Sr Raúl Arroyo
8. Vicente Pérez Rosales
9. Viento Sur
10. Res Central
11. Res El Tata
12. Res El Turista
13. Res Embassy
14. Res G Gallardo 552
15. Res La Nave
16. Res Pacífico
17. Res Millantu
18. Res Urmeneta

Bus Terminal
Varmontt Terminal

Reina, Trigal 361, family run, welcoming; **E** pp Bilbao 380, T 256514, comfortable; **E** pp Sra María Oyarzo, Subida Miramar 1184, T 259957, inc breakfast, basic (no heating, hot water next door), good beds; **E** pp *Res Emita*, Miraflores 1281, inc breakfast with homemade bread, safe; **D** pp *Suiza*, Independencia 237, with breakfast, German spoken; on Petorca: **E** pp No 119, T 258638, rec; **E** pp *Hosp Montesinos*, No 121, T 255353, with breakfast, rec; **E** pp Colo Colo 1350, T 263342, with good breakfast.

Camping: *Camping Municipal* at Chinquihue, 10 km W (bus service), open Oct-April, fully equipped with tables, seats, barbecue, toilets and showers. Small shop, no kerosene. *Camping Anderson*, 11 km W, American run, hot showers, private beach, home-grown fruit, vegetables and milk products. *Camping Los Alamos*, T 256067, 13 km W, nice views, poor services, stray dogs, US$17/site; *Camping Metri*, 30 km W on Carretera Austral, T 251235, Fierro bus, $2/tent.

● **Places to eat**
Embassy, Ancud 106, very good, pricey; *Club de Yates*, Juan Solers/n, excellent, extensive seafood; *Centro Español*, O'Higgins 233, expensive but very good; *Super Yoco*, Quillota 259, good value; *Kiel*, Capilla 298, excellent food and atmosphere, not cheap; *Club Alemán*, Varas 264, old fashioned, good food and wine; *Café Real*, Rancagua 137, for *empanadas*, *pichangas*, *congrio frito*, and cheap lunches; *Costa de Reloncaví*, Portales 736, good, moderate prices; *Café Central*, Rancagua 117, good atmosphere, meals and pastries. *Dino*, Varas 550, restaurant upstairs, snacks downstairs (try the lemon juice). *Don Pancho*, by the sea, in railway station, good. *Di Napoli Pizzas*, Gallardo 119, limited choice; *Café Amsel*, Pedro Montt y Portales, superb fish but not cheap; *Plato's*, Portales 1014, Galería Comercial España, cheap, good; also in the Galería is *El Rinconcito*, a good bar. *Super Dragon*, Benavente 839, Chinese, not cheap. Excellent and cheap food at bus terminal (all credit cards accepted). In **Angelmó**: many small seafood restaurants in the old fishing port, very popular, lunches only, ask for *té blanco* (white wine – they are not legally allowed to serve wine); *Asturias*, Angelmó 2448, limited menu, often rec.

Bakery: *La Estrella*, Varas 984, self-service, good. Local specialities inc *picoroco al vapor*, a giant barnacle whose flesh looks and tastes like crab, and *curanto*.

● **Airline offices**
LanChile, San Martín 200, T 253141/253315; Ladeco, Benevente 350, T 253002; National, Benevente 505, T 258277, F 250664; Aerosur, Urmeneta 149, 252523; TAN, T 250071; Don Carlos, Quillota 127, T 253219.

● **Banks & money changers**
Impossible on Sun (but try *Hotel Pérez Rosales*). For Visa try **Banco Concepción**, Pedro Montt y Urmeneta, good rates. **Banco Osorno**, Varas y Garrardo, good for Visa cash, but does not change TCs. Commission charges vary widely. Good rates at **Galería Cristal**, Varas 595, **El Libertador**, Urmeneta 529-A, local 3, and **Turismo Latinoamericano**, Urmeneta 531; *Travellers* travel agent in Angelmó (address below) has exchange facilities. **Fincard** (Access), Varas 437. **La Moneda de Oro** at the bus terminal exchanges Latin American currencies (Mon-Sat 0930-1230, 1530-1800). Obtain Argentine pesos before leaving Chile.

● **Embassies & consulates**
Argentina, Cauquenes 94, p 2, T 253996, quick visa service; **Germany**, Varas y Gallardo, p 3, of 306, Tues/Wed 0930-1200; **Spain**, Rancagua 113, T 252557; **Netherlands**, Seminario 350, T 253428.

● **Laundry**
Center, Varas 700; *Lavatodo*, O'Higgins 231; San Martín 232; *Unic*, Chillán 149; *Yessil't*, Edif Caracol, Urmeneta 300; *Nautilus*, Av Angelmó 1564, cheaper, good service; also in *Las Brisas* supermarket. Laundry prices generally high (US$7 for 3 kg).

● **Post & telecommunications**
Post Office: Rancagua 120, open 0830-1830 (Mon-Fri), 0830-1200 (Sat).
Telephone Office: Pedro Montt 114 and Chillán 98. **Entel**: A Varas entre Talca y Pedro Montt.

● **Shopping**
Woollen goods and Mapuche-designed rugs can be bought at roadside stalls in Angelmó or on Portales opp the bus terminal. Prices are much the same as on Chiloé, but quality is often lower. Supermarkets: *Las Brisas* opp bus terminal, very good, open 0900-2200 daily; *Mondial*, 2 blocks W is cheaper with better selection. *Libros*, Portales 580, small selection of English novels, also maps.

● **Sports**
Aerial Sports: Felix Oyarzo Grimm, owner of the *Hotel O'Grimm* can advise on possibilities, esp parachuting.

Fishing: Luis Wellman, at the *Hotel Don Luis* is very knowledgeable about fishing in the area.

Gymnasium: Urmeneta 537.

Sailing: two Yacht Clubs in Chinquihué: Marina del Sur (MDS), T/F 251958, modern, bar and restaurant, sailing courses, notice board for crew (*tripulante*) notices. MDS Charters office (also Santiago T/F 231-8238) specializes in cruising the Patagonian channels. Charters US$2,200-

8,500/week depending on size of boat. Club de Desportes Náuticas, founded by British and Americans in 1940s, more oriented towards small boat sailing, windsurfing, water sports.

● **Tour companies & travel agents**

Andina del Sud, very close to central tourist kiosk, Varas 437, T 257797, sells a daily tour at 0830 (not Sun) to Puerto Varas, Parque Nacional V Pérez Rosales, Petrohué, Lago Todos los Santos, Peulla and back (without meals US$27, with meals US$37), and to other local sights, as well as skiing trips to the Osorno volcano (see below for trip to Bariloche); *Travellers*, Av Angelmó 2456, PO Box/Casilla 854, T 262099, F 258555, e-mail gochile@chilepac.net, close to 2nd port entrance and Navimag office, open Mon-Fri 0900-1330,1500-1830, Sat 0900-1400 for booking for Navimag ferry *Puerto Edén* to Puerto Natales, Osorno volcano trips and other excursions, money exchange, flights, also sells imported camping equipment and runs computerized tourist information service, book swap ('best book swap S of Santiago'), map display, TV, real coffee, English-run, rec; *Petrel Tours*, San Martín 167, of 403, T/F 255558, rec. Many other agencies. Most offer 1-day excursions to Chiloé and to Puerto Varas, Isla Loreley, Laguna Verde, and the Petrohué falls: both these

tours are much cheaper from bus company kiosks inside the bus terminal, eg Bohle, US$15 to Chiloé, US$11 to the lakes.

● **Tourist offices**

Sernatur is in the Intendencia Regional, Av Décima Región 480 (p 3), Casilla 297, T 254580/256999, F 254580, Tx 270008. Open 0830-1300, 1330-1730 Mon-Fri. Ask for information on Chiloé as this is often difficult to obtain on the island. Also kiosk on Plaza de Armas run by the municipality, open till 1800 on Sat. Town maps available, but little information on other places. Telefónica del Sur and Sernatur operate a phone information service (INTTUR), dial 142 (cost is the same as a local call). Dial 149 for chemist/pharmacy information, 148 for the weather, 143 for the news, etc. The service operates throughout the Tenth Region. **Conaf**: Ochogavia 458, but cannot supply details of conditions in National Parks. **Automóvil Club de Chile**: Esmeralda 70, T 252968.

● **Transport**

Local Car hire: Hertz, Varas 126, T 259585, helpful, English spoken; **Automóvil Club de Chile**, Ensenada 70, T 254776, and at airport. Others are **Avis**, Egaña 64, T 256575 and at airport; **Budget**, San Martín 200 and at airport; **Dollar** (*Hotel Vicente Pérez Rosales*), Varas 447;

First, Varas 437; **Formula Uno**, Santa María 620, T 254125, highly rec; **Autovald**, Portales 1330, T 256355, cheap rates; **Travicargo**, Urmeneta 856, T 257137/256438; **Automotric Angelmó**, Talca 79, cheap and helpful. **Famas**, Portales y Gallardo, helpful, good value, has vehicles that can be taken to Argentina.

Air El Tepual Airport, 13 km NW of town. ETM bus from terminal 1½ hrs before departure, US$2. To Santiago at least 2 daily flights by LanChile, Ladeco, National and Avant. To Punta Arenas, LanChile, Ladeco, National and Avant daily; in Jan, Feb and Mar you may well be told that flights are booked up; however, cancellations may be available from the airport. National also flies to Concepción and Temuco. Flights to Bariloche and Neuquén (Argentina), TAN, twice a week, 40 mins. To Balmaceda, LanChile and Ladeco, daily. To Coyhaique, LanChile daily. Don Carlos flies to Chaitén, 1115 and 1515 Mon-Fri, Sat 1115 (fares under Chaitén), and runs regular charters for 5 passengers to Bariloche, Chaitén, and Coyhaique. Alta to Chaitén and to Balmaceda, Puerto Natales (3 hrs, US$70, highly rec for views) and Punta Arenas. Aerosur, also flies to Chaitén, daily except Sun and to Futaleufú and Palena on Tues and Fri.

Trains New station under construction at Alerce, 10 km N of town. Old station at San Felipe 50, T 254908, functions only as ticket office (0830-1130, 1300-1700). Daily service in summer to **Santiago** departs from Puerto Varas, 1600, Rápido with 1930s German-built sleepers, 19 hrs. Seats: *turista* US$21, *salón* US$35; sleepers: US$44 lower bunk, US$59 upper bunk, US$130 double compartment, bicycles US$10, restaurant car, car transporter, book 3 days in advance, but 2 weeks in advance in high season

Buses Terminal on sea front at Portales y Lota, has telephones, restaurants, *casa de cambio* (left luggage, US$1/item for 24 hrs). Varmontt has its own terminal at Copiapó y Varas, but Varmontt buses also call at main terminal. To **Puerto Varas** (US$0.50), **Llanquihue**, **Frutillar** (US$1.25) and **Osorno** (US$5) every 30 mins, Varmontt and Full Express. To **Ensenada** and **Petrohué** Buses JM at least 3 a day. To **Pucón**, US$7. To **Santiago**, express 15 hrs, US$18-25, *cama* US$68, Tur-Bus, very good, 14 hrs, Tas Choapa *Royal Class* US$33; to **Punta Arenas**, Austral, Turibus, Queilen/Cidher and Buses Punta Arenas, between 1 and 3 times a week, US$60-75 depending on company, departing either 0800 or 1100 (bus goes through Argentina via Bariloche – take US$ cash to pay for meals etc in Argentina), 32-38 hrs; book well in advance in Jan-Feb and check if you need a multiple-entry Chilean visa; also book any return

journey before setting out; to **Temuco** US$9, to **Valdivia**, US$7; **Concepción**, US$15. For services to Chiloé, see page 797.

Buses to Argentina via Osorno and the Puyehue pass Daily services to Bariloche on this route via Osorno, US$20-25, 6-10 hrs, are run by Cruz del Sur, Andesmar, Turismo Lanín (not rec), Tas Choapa and Bus Norte. Tas Choapa services also run to Mendoza, Buenos Aires, Montevideo and Rio de Janeiro. Out of season, services are reduced. Buy tickets for international buses from the bus terminal, not through an agency. If intending to return by this route, buy an open return ticket as higher fares are charged in Argentina. Book well in advance in Jan and February. Hitchhiking on this route is difficult and may take as long as 4 days. For the route to Argentina via Lago Todos Los Santos see below.

Motoring: when driving N out of Puerto Montt (or out of Puerto Varas, Frutillar, etc), look for signs to 'Ruta 5'.

Boat hire: Lucinda Cárdenas, Manuel Montt Pasaje 7, Casa 134, Angelmó, for trips around the harbour or to Tenglo island.

Shipping offices in Puerto Montt: **Navimag** (Naviera Magallanes SA), Terminal Transbordadores, Angelmó 2187, T 253318, F 258540; **Skorpios 1** and **2** of **Constantino Kochifas C**, Angelmó 1660 y Miraflores (Castilla 588), T 252619, Tx 370161 NATUK CL; **Transmarchilay Ltda**, Angelmó 2187, T 254654, F 253683; **Patagonia Connection**, Portales 872, T 259790.

TO ARGENTINA VIA LAGO TODOS LOS SANTOS

This popular route to Bariloche, involving ferries across Lago Todos Los Santos, Lago Frías and Lago Nahuel Huapi is outstandingly beautiful whatever the season, though the mountains are often obscured by rain and heavy cloud. The route is via Puerto Varas, Ensenada and Petrohué falls (20 mins stop) to Petrohué, where it connects with catamaran service across Lago Todos Los Santos to Peulla. Lunch stop in Peulla 2 hrs (lunch not inc in fare: *Hotel Peulla* is expensive, see page 785 for alternatives). Chilean customs in Peulla, followed by a 2 hr bus ride through the Paso Pérez Rosales to Argentine customs in Puerto Frías, 20 min boat trip across Lago Frías to Puerto Alegre and bus from Puerto Alegre to Puerto Blest. From Puerto Blest it is a beautiful 1½ hr catamaran trip along

Lago Nahuel Huapi to Puerto Panuelo, from where there is a 1 hr bus journey to Bariloche (bus drops passengers at hotels, camping sites or in town centre). Out of season this trip is done over 2 days with overnight stay in Peulla, add about US$89 to single fare for accommodation in *Hotel Peulla*. (Baggage is taken to *Hotel Peulla* automatically but for alternative accommodation see under Peulla above.)

● **Transport** The route is operated only by Andino del Sud (address above). Bus from company offices daily at 0800; the fare is US$104 one way. Note that the trip may be cancelled if the weather is poor; there are reports of difficulty in obtaining a refund. Try both Puerto Montt and Puerto Varas offices if you want to take the Andina del Sud trip in sections.

SEA ROUTES SOUTH OF PUERTO MONTT

Taxi from centre to ferry terminal, US$2. All shipping services should be checked in advance; schedules change frequently.

To Puerto Natales

The dramatic 1,460 km journey first goes through Seno Reloncaví and Canal Moraleda. From Bahía Anna Pink along the coast and then across the Golfo de Peñas to Bahía Tarn it is a 12-17 hrs sea crossing, usually rough. The journey continues through Canal Messier, Angostura Inglesa, Paso del Indio and Canal Kirke (one of the narrowest routes for large shipping). The only regular stop is made off Puerto Edén (1 hr S of the Angostura Inglesa), where there are 3 shops, with scant provisions, one off-licence, one café, but no hotel or camping facility, nor running water. Population is 180, plus 5 *carabineros* and the few remaining Alacaluf Indians. It is, though, the drop-off point for exploring Isla Wellington, which is largely untouched, with stunning mountains. If stopping here, take all food; maps (not very accurate) are available in Santiago.

Navimag's *Puerto Edén* sails **to Puerto Natales** every 8 days, taking 4 days and 3 nights; the fare ranges from US$160 pp economy (inc meals) to US$660 pp in various classes of cabin (also inc meals); 10% discount on international student cards in cabin class only. Payment by credit card

or foreign currency generally not accepted. Economy class accommodation is basic, in 24-berth dormitories and there is limited additional space for economy class passengers when weather is bad. Apart from videos, entertainment on board is limited. Economy class and cabin passengers eat in separate areas. Some report good food, others terrible. Standards of service and comfort vary, depending on the number of passengers and weather conditions. Take seasickness tablets.

Another Navimag vessel, the *Amadeus*, carries cargo between Puerto Montt, Puerto Chacabuco and Puerto Natales, with a few passengers, same price as cheaper cabins on the *Puerto Edén*, no fixed timetable.

● **Booking** Economy class can only be booked, with payment, through Navimag offices in Puerto Montt and Puerto Natales. Economy tickets are frequently sold just before departure. Cabin class can be booked in advance through *Travellers* in Puerto Montt or Puerto Natales (see **Tour companies**, above), through Navimag offices in Puerto Montt, Puerto Natales and Punta Arenas, or through Cruceros Australis (Navimag parent company) in Santiago. All of these have their own ticket allocation: once this is used up, they have to contact other offices to request spare tickets. Book well in advance for departures between mid-Dec and mid-Mar especially for the voyage S (Puerto Natales to Puerto Montt is less heavily booked). It is well worth going to the port on the day of departure if you have no ticket. Note that departures are frequently delayed – or even advanced.

To Puerto Chacabuco
● **Shipping services**

The roll on/roll off vehicle ferry m/n *Evangelistas* of Navimag, runs twice weekly to Puerto Chacabuco (80 km to W of Coyhaique), usually Wed and Sat, returning from Puerto Chacabuco on the following day. From end-Dec to mid, or end-Mar the schedule changes to include a Sun-Tues trip from Puerto Chacabuco to Laguna San Rafael, so Pto Montt to Pto Chacabuco is Wed and Sat, but return to Pto Montt is Tues and Thur. The cruise to Puerto Chacabuco lasts about 24 hrs. First class accommodation includes 2 cabins with bath (US$125-250 depending on which cabin and number of occupants); tourist class, 14 bunks (about US$145 double); and third class, 400 reclining seats (US$68, type 'B', US$40, type 'A'). Fare to Laguna San Rafael US$155-220, reclining seat, or US$285-510 in cabin. First class reservations must be made in advance at the Santiago offices (see page 684). There is a small canteen; long queues if the boat is full. Food is expensive so take your own.

The *Colono* of Transmarchilay sails to Puerto

Chacabuco on Tues and Fri between 1 Jan and early Mar, 26 hrs; passengers US$24-164 pp, vehicles US$165. Transmarchilay also runs a ferry service on the route Quellón (Chiloé)-Chaitén-Puerto Montt-Chaitén-Quellón (see under Quellón and Chaitén for details). Over-booking and long delays reported.

To Laguna San Rafael
● **Shipping services**
The m/n *Skorpios 1* and *2* of Constantino Ko-chifas C leave Pto Montt on Sat at 1100 for a luxury cruise with stops at Puerto Aguirre, Me-linka, Laguna San Rafael, Quitralco, Castro (each ship has a slightly different itinerary) and returns to Puerto Montt on Fri at 0800. The fare varies according to season, type of cabin and number of occupants: a double ranges from US$465 (low) to US$660 (high) on *Skorpios 1* and from US$770 (low) to US$1,100 (high) on *Skorpios 2*, which is the more comfortable of the two. It has been reported that there is little room to sit indoors if it is raining on *Skorpios 1*, but generally service is excellent, the food superb and at the glacier, you chip your ice off the face for your whisky. (After the visit to San Rafael the ships visits Quitralco Fjord where there are thermal pools and boat trips on the fjord.)

Patagonia Connection SA, Fidel Oteíza 1921, Oficina 1006, Providencia, Santiago, T 225-6489, F 274-8111, operates *Patagonia Express*, a catamaran which runs from Puerto Chacabuco to Laguna San Rafael via Termas de Puyuhuapi, see page 808. Tours lasting 4 to 6 days start from Puerto Montt and include the catamaran service, the hotel at Termas de Puyuhuapi and the day excursion to Laguna San Rafael. High season 20 Dec-20 Mar, low season 11 Sept-19 Dec and 21 Mar-21 April. High season fares for a 4-day tour from US$940, all inclusive, highly rec.

Other Routes
The m/n *Bohemia* makes 6 day/5 night trips from Puerto Montt to Río Negro, Isla Llancahué, Baños Cahuelmó and Fiordo Leptepu/Coman, US$545-720 pp depending on season (Antonio Varas 947, T 254675, Puerto Montt).

See also under Chaitén for passenger services on Terminales Marítimos Chilenos.

Chiloé

THE CULTURE of Chi-loé has been strongly influenced by isolation from Spanish colonial currents, the mixture of early Spanish settlers and Mapuche indians and a dependence on the sea. Religious and secular architecture, customs and crafts, combined with delightful landscapes, all contribute to Chiloé's uniqueness.

Land and climate
The island of **Chiloé** is 250 km long, 50 km wide and covers 9,613 sq km. Thick forests cover most of the western side. The hillsides in summer are a patchwork quilt of wheat fields and dark green plots of potatoes. Most of the population of 116,000 live on the sheltered eastern side.

The West coast, exposed to strong Pacific winds, is wet for most of the year. The sheltered east coast and the offshore islands are drier, though frequently cloudy.

History
The original inhabitants of Chiloé were the Chonos, who were pushed S by the Mapuches invading from the N. The first Spanish sighting was by Francisco de Ulloa in 1553 and in 1567 Martín Ruiz de Gamboa took possession of the islands on behalf of Spain. The small Spanish settler population divided the indigenous population and their lands between them. The

rising of the Mapuche after 1598 which drove the Spanish out of the mainland S of the Río Biobío left the Spanish community on Chiloé (some 200 settlers in 1600) isolated. Much of Chiloé's distinctive character derives from its 200 years of isola-

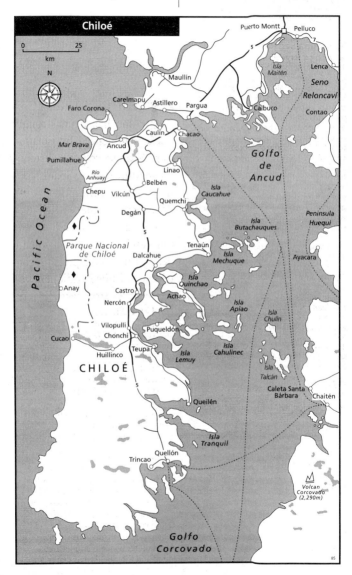

tion from the mainstream of Spanish colonial development and from the presence
of the Jesuits, who first arrived in 1608.
During the 17th century Chiloé was
served by a single annual ship from Lima.
Following a violent earthquake in 1646 the
Spanish population asked the Viceroy in
Lima for permission to leave, but this was
refused.

The islanders were the last supporters
of the Spanish Crown in South America.
When Chile rebelled the last of the Spanish Governors fled to the island and, in
despair, offered it to Britain. Canning, the
British Foreign Secretary, turned the offer down. The island finally surrendered to
the patriots in 1826.

The availability of wood and the lack of
metals have left their mark on the island.
Some of the earliest churches were built
entirely of wood, using wooden pegs instead of nails. These early churches often
displayed some German influence as a result of the missionary work of Bavarian
Jesuits. Two features of local architecture
often thought to be traditional are in fact
late 19th century in origin. The replacement of thatch with thin tiles (*tejuelas*)
made from alerce wood, which are nailed
to the frame and roof in several distinctive
patterns, and *palafitos* or wooden houses
built on stilts over the water.

The island is also famous for its traditional handicrafts, notably woollens and
basket ware, which can be bought in the
main towns and on some of the off-shore
islands, as well as in Puerto Montt.

Although the traditional mainstays of the
economy, fishing and agriculture, are still
important, salmon farming has become a
major source of employment. Seaweed is
harvested for export to Japan. Tourism
provides a seasonal income for a growing
number of people. Nevertheless, the relatively high birth rate and the shortage of
employment in Chiloé have led to regular
emigration.

Transport to Chiloé

Regular ferries cross the straits of Pargua
between **Pargua**, 55 km SW of Puerto
Montt on the mainland, and **Chacao** on
Chiloé.

● **Buses** From Puerto Montt, frequent, US$2,
1 hr, though most buses go right through to
Ancud (3½-4 hrs) and Castro. Transport to the
island is dominated by Cruz del Sur, who also
own Trans Chiloé and Regional Sur and have
their own ferries. Cruz del Sur run frequent
services from Puerto Montt to Ancud and Castro, 6 a day to Chonchi and Quellón; their fares
are highest (Trans Chiloé lowest but sell out
quickly) but in busy periods they are faster (their
buses have priority over cars on Cruz del Sur
ferries). Fares from Puerto Montt: to Ancud,
Cruz del Sur US$5.75, Trans Chiloé US$4.50;
to Castro, Cruz del Sur US$7.50, Trans Chiloé
US$6; to Chonchi, US$7, Quellón, US$9. There
are direct bus services from Santiago, Osorno,
Valdivia, Temuco and Los Angeles to Chiloé.
Buses drive on to the ferry (passengers can get
out of the bus). **Ferries** About 24 crossings a
day, 30 min crossing, operated by several companies inc Transmarchilay and Cruz del Sur; all
ferries carry buses, private vehicles (cars US$10
one way) and foot passengers (who travel free).

ANCUD

(*Pop* 23,148; *Phone code* 065), lies on the N
coast of Chiloé 30 km W of the Straits of
Chacao at the mouth of a great bay, the
Golfo de Quetalmahue. Founded in 1767
to guard the shipping route around Cape
Horn, it was defended by two fortresses,
the Fuerte San Antonio and Fuerte Ahui
on the opposite side of the bay.

Places of interest

The port is dominated by the **Fuerte San
Antonio**, built in 1770, the site of the
Spanish surrender of Chiloé to Chilean
troops in 1826. Close to it are the ruins of
the **Polvorín del Fuerte** (a couple of cannon and a few walls). 1 km N of the fort is
a secluded beach, **Arena Gruesa**. 2 km E
is a **Mirador** offering good views of the
island and across to the mainland.

Museums

Near the Plaza de Armas is the **Museo
Regional** (open summer daily 1100-1900,
winter Tues-Fri 0900-1300, 1430-1830, Sat
1000-1330, 1430-1800, US$1), with an in-
teresting collection on the early history of
Chiloé as well as replicas of a traditional
Chilote thatched wooden house and of the
small sailing ship *Ancud* which, in 1843,
sailed to the Straits of Magellan to claim
the Peninsula for Chile.

Excursions

To **Faro Corona**, the lighthouse on Punta Corona, 34 km W, along the beach, which, though unsuitable for swimming, offers good views with interesting birdlife and dolphins. To **Pumillahue**, 27 km SW, and **Mar Bravo** on W coast, bus 1230 Mon-Fri. Near Pumillahue (bus daily 0700, details from tourist office) there is a penguin colony: hire a fishing boat to see it, US$2.50 pp.

Local information

● Accommodation

A1 *Hostería Ancud*, San Antonio 30, T/F 622340/622350, overlooking bay, attractive, very comfortable, helpful, restaurant; **A3** *Galeón Azul*, Libertad 751, T 622567, F 622543; **A3** *Lydia*, Pudeto y Chacabuco, T 622990, F 622879, with bath, **B** without bath, poor beds, small rooms, overpriced; **A3** *Lacuy*, Pudeto 219 near Plaza de Armas, T/F 623019, with breakfast, restaurant, rec; **A3** *Montserrat*, Baquedano 417, T/F 622957, with breakfast, good views, attractive.

B *Cabañas Las Golondrinas*, end of Baquedano at Arena Gruesa, T 622823, superb views, with kitchenette; **B** *Hostería Ahui*, Costanera 906, T 622415, with breakfast, modern, good views; **B** *Polo Sur*, Costanera 630, T 622200, good seafood restaurant, not cheap, avoid rooms overlooking disco next door; **B** *Res Weschler*, Cochrane 480, T 622318, **D** without bath, view of bay; **B** *Res Germania*, Pudeto 357, T/F 622214, **C** without bath, parking, comfortable; **C** *Madryn*, Bellavista 491, T 622128, also meals.

D *Caleta Ancud*, Bellavista 449, good breakfast, good restaurant; **D** *Hosp Alto Bellavista*, Bellavista 449, T 622384, with sleeping bag on floor much cheaper; **D** *Hosp Capri*, Ramírez 325, good breakfast; **D** *Hosp Alinar*, Ramírez 348, hospitable; **D** *Hosp Santander*, Sgto Aldea 69, **E** without bath, rec; **D** *Res MaCarolina*, Prat 28, with breakfast; **E** pp Edmundo Haase Pérez, Ramírez 295, with breakfast, basic, good value; **E** pp Elena Bergmann, Aníbal Pinto 382, use of kitchen, parking; **E** pp Pudeto 331, T 622535, without bath, old fashioned; **E** pp Lautaro 947, T 2980; **E** pp Familia Reuter-Miranda, Errázuriz 350, T 622261, good breakfast, spacious, opp Cruz del Sur terminal, rec; Errázuriz 395, T 622657, without bath; **F** pp Pudeto 619, with breakfast. In summer the school on Calle Chacabuco is used as an *albergue*.

Camping: *Arena Gruesa* at N end of Baquedano; *Playa Gaviotas*, 5 km N; *Playa Larga Huicha*, 9 km N, E per site, bath, hot water, electricity.

● Places to eat

Seafood restaurants in market area. On Pudeto: *Carmen*, No 159, Chilean cooking, *pasteles*; *Coral*, No 346, good, not cheap; *Jardín*, No 263, good local food, not cheap; *Lydia*, No 254, Chilean and international. *Macaval*, Chacabuco 691; *El Trauco*, Blanco y Prat, seafood excellent, highly rec; *La Pincoya*, next to harbour, good seafood; *El Cangrejo*, Dieciocho 155, seafood highly rec; *Hamburguería*, Av Prat, much better than name suggests, good seafood; *Mar y Velas*, Serrano 2, p 2, beautiful views, good food.

● Post & telecommunications

Post Office: On corner of Plaza de Armas at Pudeto y Blanco Encalada.
Telephone: Plaza de Armas, open Mon-Sat 0700-2200.

● Tour companies & travel agents

Turismo Ancud, Pudeto 219, Galería Yurie, T 2235, Tx 297700 ANCD CL; *Paralelo 42*, T 28, T 2458, F 2656, rec for tours to the Río Chepu area, inc 2-day kayak trips, guide Carlos Oyarzun (also at *Res MaCarolina*) rec.

● Tourist offices

Sernatur, Libertad 665, T 622665, open Mon-Fri 0900-1300, 1430-1800.

● Transport

Buses Cruz del Sur, Trans Chiloé and Regional Sur use the terminal at Errázuriz y Los Carrera; local buses leave from municipal terminal at Pedro Montt 538 though a new terminal is under construction on the E outskirts at Aníbal Pinto y Marcos Vera. To **Castro**, US$3, frequent (see below), 1½ hrs. To **Puerto Montt**, 2 hrs, Cruz del Sur 10 a day, Trans Chiloé 3 a day, Varmontt 3 a day from *Hotel Polo Sur*. To **Quemchi** via the coast 2 hrs, US$1.50.

Shipping Transmarchilay Libertad 669, T 622317/622279, Tx 375007 MARCHI CK.

Longer excursions

Chepu, on the coast SW of Ancud, famed for its river and sea fishing, is a base for exploring the drowned forest and river environment of the Río Chepu and its tributaries, inhabited by a wide range of birds. (It is also the entrance to the N part of the Parque Nacional Chiloé, see under Cucao.) At **Río Anhuay** (also known as **Puerto Anhuay**) there is a camping site and *refugio*. From here it is a 1½ hr walk to Playa Aulén which has superb forested dunes and an extinct volcano.

Activities Boat trips can be organized in Río Anhuay to Laguna Coluco, 1 hr up the Río Butalcura (a tributary of the Río Chepu). Longer trips, navigating the Ríos Grande, Carihueco and Butalcura usually start further inland and finish at Río Anhuay, 2 days, arrange in Ancud (*Paralello 42* rec). This area offers great opportunities for horse-riding with long beaches for galloping. Try Sr Zuñipe or Sr Uroa (rec), US$5 per hr (ask at the *refugio* in Río Anhuay).

● **Access** From Route 5, 26 km S of Ancud by a 24 km dirt road. Alternatively there is a 2 day coastal walk from Ancud: you can take the daily bus to Pumillahue (0700, return 1330) or hitch. The route is difficult to follow so take food for 3 days and wear light-coloured clothes in summer to protect against *tavanos*. No public transport.

ANCUD TO CASTRO

There are two routes: direct along Route 5, the Pan-American Highway, crossing rolling hills, forest and agricultural land, or via the E coast along upaved roads passing through small farming and fishing communities. The two main towns along the coastal route, Quemchi and Dalcahue, can also be reached by roads branching off Route 5.

Quemchi (*Pop* 2,000) 68 km S of Ancud via Route 5, is a quiet town with long beaches (basic accommodation).

Dalcahue (*Pop* 2,300), 74 km S of Ancud, is more easily reached from Castro, 30 km further S. It is one of the main ports for boats to the offshore islands, inc Quinchao and Mechuque. The wooden church on the main square dates from the 19th century. The market is on Sun, from 0700 to 1300; good quality. Tourist kiosk in season. Tenaún, 40 km E of Dalcahue, is an interesting fishing village with a good 18th-century church.

● **Accommodation & places to eat** D/E *La Feria*, Rodríguez 17, T 641293, without bath, basic; **D/E** *Res Playa*, Rodríguez 9, basic; **E** *Hosp Puteman*, Freire 305, T 330, basic; **E** *Res San Martín*, San Martín 1, T 641207, basic, also meals. *Restaurant La Dalca*, Freire 502, good food and service, rec.

● **Transport** Buses to Castro, hourly, 40 mins, US$1. Also collective taxis.

QUINCHAO

On the island of Quinchao the main settlement is **Achao**, a quiet, pretty fishing village with a market. Its wooden church, built in 1730 and saved by a change of wind from a fire which destroyed much of the town in 1784, is a fine example of Chilote Jesuit architecture. The original construction was without use of nails. There is a small museum, entry US$1.

● **Accommodation D** *Plaza*, Plaza de Armas, T 661283, with breakfast, good; **D/E** *Hosp Chilhue*, Zañartu 021, without bath, with breakfast; **D** pp *Hosp Achao*, Serrano 061, T 661373, good; **E** pp *Hosp Sao Paulo*, Serrano 52, basic, poor beds; **D** pp *Hostería La Nave*, Prat y Aldea, T 661219, **E** pp without bath, with breakfast, restaurant with fine views over bay.

● **Places to eat** *Arrayan*, Zañartu 19; *Restaurant Central*, Delicias, simple, cheap, good; *Restaurant Mar y Velas*, on waterfront, good fish, cheap, rec.

● **Tourist offices** Serrano y Progreso (Dec-Mar only).

● **Transport Ferry**: from Dalcahue, frequent, free for pedestrians and cyclists.

The island of **Mechuque**, E of Dalcahue, has one village and offers splendid walking country. (**Accommodation** with the schoolteacher's son or with Sra Dina del Carmen Paillacar, **E**, good meals, rec.)

● **Transport Boat**: from Dalcahue, dep Tues and Thur 1330, return Mon and Wed 1000, 2½ hrs, US$2.50 one way.

CASTRO

(*Pop* 20,000; *Phone code* 065) the capital of Chiloé lies 88 km S of Ancud on a fjord on the E coast. Founded in 1567, the centre is situated on a promontory, from which there is a steep drop to the port.

Places of interest

On the Plaza de Armas is the large **Cathedral**, strikingly decorated in lilac and orange, with a splendid wood panelled interior, built by the Italian architect, Eduardo Provosoli in 1906. S of the Plaza on the waterfront is the **Feria**, or Mercado Municipal de Artesanía, where local woollen articles (hats, sweaters, gloves) can be found. *Palafitos* can be seen on the northern side of town and by the bridge over the

Río Gamboa. There are good views of the city from **Mirador La Virgen** on Millantuy hill above the cemetery.

Museums

Museo Regional on Esmeralda, opp *Hotel La Bomba*, contains history, folklore, handicrafts and mythology of Chiloé and photos of the 1960 earthquake, open summer Mon-Sat 0930-2000, Sun 1030-1300; winter Mon-Sat 0930-1300, 1500-1830, Sun 1030-1300; **Museo de Arte Moderno**, near the Río Gamboa, in the Parque Municipal, about 3 km NW of the centre, reached by following C Galvarino Riveros up the hill W of town, T 632787, F 635454 (open 1000-2000).

Excursions

To **Puntilla Ten Ten** and the Peninsula opposite Castro, a pleasant walk through woods and fields, 2 hrs round trip, turn off Route 5, 2 km N of town.

Local information

● **Accommodation**

A1 *Unicornio Azul*, Pedro Montt 228, T 632359, F 632808, good views over bay, comfortable, restaurant; **A2** *Cabañas Centro Turístico Nercón*, 5 km S, T 632985, with heating, restaurant, tennis court; **A3** *Hostería Castro*, Chacabuco 202, T 632301, F 635668, with breakfast, good restaurant, attractive building, wonderful views; **A3** *Cabañas Truyen*, 5 km S of Castro, B off season, lovely views; **A2** *Gran Alerce*, O'Higgins 808, T 632267, heating, helpful, breakfast, also has *cabañas* and restaurant 4 km S of Castro.

B *Casita Española*, Los Carrera 359, T 635186, heating, TV, parking, rec; **B** *Chilhue*, Blanco Encalada 278, T 632956, good; **C** *Quinta Niklitschek*, Panamericana Norte 331 (3 km N), T 632137, better inside than out; **C** *Costa Azul*, Lillo 67, T 632440, **D** without bath.

On San Martín (convenient for bus terminals): **D** *Res Mirasol*, No 815, basic, noisy; **E pp** *Hosp Chiloé*, No 739, breakfast, rec; **E pp** *Hosp Angie*, San Martín 747, small rooms, pretty; **E pp** *Hosp Guillermo*, No 700; **E pp** *Res Capullito*, No 709, quiet; **F pp** No 879, with big breakfast, central, highly rec; **F pp** Lidia Low, No 890, with good breakfast, warm showers, use of kitchen; **E pp** No 581, helpful.

Other Budget accommodation: **D** *Hilton*, Ramírez 385, good value, breakfast; **E pp** *Hosp* of Jessie Toro, Las Delicias 287, good breakfast, helpful, spacious, good bathrooms, also cabins

warmly rec; **D** *La Bomba*, Esmeralda 270, T 632300, without bath, cheaper on 3rd floor, good value, good 3 course *menú*; **E pp** *Casa Blanca*, Los Carrera 300, inc breakfast, modern, warm; **D** *Los Carrera* 658, no sign, with breakfast, rec; **E pp** *Res La Casona*, Serrano 488, above TV shop, with breakfast, rec; **E** *Serrano* 407, breakfast, warm water; **D** *Res El Gringo*, Lillo 51, without bath, good views, overpriced; **E pp** *Eyzaguirre* 469, comfortable, rec; **E pp** María Zuñiga, Barros Arana 140, T 635026, inc breakfast, comfortable, cooking facilities, secure, rec; **E pp**, Freire 758, breakfast, good value; **E pp** O'Higgins 415, Dpto 41, quiet; **E pp** O'Higgins 865, hospitable; **E pp** Chacabuco 449, good beds, quiet, water only warm; **D** *Hosp Sotomayor*, Sotomayor 452, T 632464, with breakfast, quiet, small beds; **E pp** *Hospedaje El Mirador*, Barros Arana 127, T 633795, good breakfast; **F pp** *Hosp Polo Sur*, Barros Arana 169, T 635212, safe, cooking facilities, wonderful views. Basic accommodation Dec-Feb in the Gimnasio Fisical, Freire 610, T 632766, **F** with breakfast.

Camping: *Camping Pudú*, Ruta 5, 10 km N of Castro, T 635109, showers with hot water, sites with light, water, children's games. Several sites on road to Chonchi.

● **Places to eat**

Palafito restaurants near the Feria Artesanía on the waterfront offer good food and good value, inc *Brisas del Mar*, *Mariela* and *La Amistad*; *Gipsy*, O'Higgins 548, Chinese; *Sacho*, Thompson 213, good sea views, clean; *Don Camilo*, Ramírez 566, good food, not expensive, rec; *Pizzería La Nona*, Serrano 380, good pizzas, welcoming staff; *Stop Inn Café*, Prat y Chacabuco, good coffee; *Chilo's*, San Martín 459, good lunches; *El Curanto*, Lillo 67, seafood inc *curanto*, rec. *Maucari*, Lillo 93, good seafood, not expensive. In the market, try *milcaos*, fried potato cakes with meat stuffing; also *licor de oro*, like Galliano; *La Brújula del Cuerpo*, Plaza de Armas, good coffee, snacks; breakfast before 0900 is difficult.

● **Banks & money changers**

Banco del Estado de Chile, Plaza de Armas, accepts TCs (at a poor rate). BCI, Plaza de Armas, Mastercard and Visa ATM. Better rates from Julio Barrientos, Chacabuco 286, cash and TCs.

● **Hospitals & medical services**

Doctor: *Muñoz de Las Carreras*, near police station, surgery 1700-2000 on weekdays, rec.

● **Laundry**

Lavandería Adolfo, Blanco Encalada, quick, reasonably priced.

● **Post & telecommunications**
Phone Office: Latorre 289. **Entel**: O'Higgins entre Gamboa y Sotomayor.
Post Office: on W side of Plaza de Armas.

● **Shopping**
See above for market. Cema-Chile outlet on Esmeralda, opp *Hotel La Bomba*. *Libros Chiloé*, Blanco Encalada 204, books in Spanish on Chiloé. Cassettes of typical Chilote music are widely available.

● **Sports**
Bicycle hire: San Martín 581.

● **Tourist offices**
Kiosk on Plaza de Armas opposite Cathedral; **Conaf** in Gamboa behind the Gobernación building.

● **Tour Companies and travel agents**
Pehuén Expediciones, Thompson 229, T 635254; *Chiloé Tours*, Blanco Encalada 318, T 635952; *Turismo Queilén*, Gamboa 502, T 632776 good tours to Chonchi and Chiloé National Park. *LanChile* agency, Thompson 245. **Ladeco** agency on Serrano, opp *Hosteria Castro*. *Transmarchilay* agency at Suzuki Car Hire, San Martín y Blanco Encalada. Local guide Sergio Márquez, Felipe Moniel 565, T 632617, very knowldegeable, has transport. Tour prices: to Parque Nacional Chiloé US$25, to Mechuque US$37.

● **Transport**
Local Buses: frequent services to Chonchi, choose between buses (Cruz del Sur, Queilén Bus and others), minibuses and collective taxis (from Esmeralda y Chacabuco). Arroyo and Ocean Bus both run to Cucao, 1 a day off season, 0945 and 1600 in summer, US$2. To Dalcahue frequent services by Gallardo and Arriagada, also collective taxis from San Martín 815. To Achao via Dalcahue and Curaco de Vélez, Arriagada, 4 daily, 3 on Sun, last return from Achao 1730. To Puqueldón on the island of Lemuy, Gallardo, Mon-Fri 1315, US$2. To Quemchi, 2 a day, 1½ hrs, US$2.50; to Quellón, Regional Sur and Trans Chiloé, frequent; to Queilén, Queilén Bus; to Quemchi, 2 a day, Queilén Bus.

Buses leave from 2 terminals: Cruz del Sur, T632389, Trans Chiloé and Arriagada from Cruz del Sur terminal on San Martín behind the cathedral. Other services leave from the Municipal Terminal, San Martín, 600 block (2 blocks further N). Frequent services to Ancud and Puerto Montt by Cruz del Sur and Trans Chiloé. Cruz del Sur also run to Osorno, Valdivia, Temuco, Concepción and Santiago. Bus Norte to Ancud, Puerto Montt, Osorno and Santiago daily; to Punta Arenas, Tur Bus, Ghisoni and Austral.

CHONCHI

(*Pop* 3,000; *Phone code* 065) is a picturesque fishing village 25 km S of Castro. From the plaza Calle Centenario, with several attractive but sadly neglected wooden mansions, drops steeply to the harbour. Fishing boats bring in the early morning catch which is carried straight into the nearby market. The wooden church, on the plaza, was built in 1754, remodelled in neo-classical style in 1859 (key from handicraft shop next door). There is another 18th century church at Vilopulli, 5 km N.

Museums Museo de las Tradiciones Chonchina, Centenario 116, artefacts donated by local families reflecting life in the early 20th century.

● **Accommodation A3** *Posada Antiguo Chalet*, Irarrazával, T 671221, **B** in winter, charming, beautiful location, very good; **B** *Cabañas Amankay*, Centenario 421, T 671367, homely, kitchen facilities, rec; **C** *Hosteria Remis*, Irarrazával 27, T 671271, **E** without bath, lovely position on waterfront, good food, rec; **D** *Hosp Chonchi*, O'Higgins 379, T 671288, full board available, good value, rec; **D** *Esmeralda By The Sea*, on waterfront 100 m E of *Restaurant La Costanera*, T 671328 (Casilla 79), with breakfast, attractive, welcoming, English spoken, boat trips offered, information, highly rec; **D** *Huildin*, Centenario 102, T 671388, without bath, old fashioned, good beds, also *cabañas* **D** with superb views, parking; **D** *Hosp Mirador*, Alvarez 198, with breakfast, rec; **E** pp Alvarez 891, noisy, good breakfast; **E** *Res Turismo*, Andrade 299, T 257, without bath, with breakfast; **E** Baker at Andrade 184.

● **Places to eat** *La Parada*, Centenario 133, good selection of wines, often closes evenings, rec; *El Alerce*, Aguirre 106, excellent value; *La Quila*, Andrade 183. Cheapest place for lunch is *La Costanera*, on waterfront.

● **Banks & money changers** Nicolás Alvarez, Centenario 429, cash only.

● **Shopping** Handicrafts from *Opdech* (Oficina Promotora del Desarrollo Chilote), on the waterfront, and from the *parroquia*, next to the church (open Oct-March only).

● **Tourist offices** Kiosk on the main plaza in summer.

● **Transport** Buses and taxis to Castro, frequent, US$0.75, from main plaza. Services to Quellón and Queilén from Castro and Puerto Montt also call here.

Lemuy (*Pop* 4,200), an island, 97 sq km, with one main village, **Puqueldón**, lies offshore opposite Chonchi and offers many good walks along quiet unpaved roads through undulating pastures and woodland.

● **Accommodation E** pp *Restaurant Lemuy* and *Café Amancay*, without bath, good.

● **Transport Buses** Once a day from Castro. **Ferry** service from Puerto Huicha, 4 km S of Chonchi, approx every 30 mins, foot passengers free (from here it is 8 km to Puqueldón).

Queilén, 46 km by unpaved road SE of Chonchi, is a pretty fishing village with long beaches and wooden pier.

● **Accommodation & places to eat F** pp *Pensión Chiloé*, without bath, basic; *Restaurant Melinka*, friendly.

● **Transport** Buses to Castro, Queilén Bus, 6 a day, 4 on Sat, 3 on Sun, 2 hrs, US$2.50.

CUCAO

From Chonchi an unpaved road leads W to **Cucao**, 40 km, one of two settlements on the W coast of Chiloé. At Km 12 is Huillinco, a charming village on Lago Huillinco (**E** pp *Residencia*, good food, or stay at the Post Office). At Cucao there is an immense 15 km beach with thundering Pacific surf and dangerous undercurrents.

● **Accommodation & places to eat E** pp *Hosp Paraíso*; **E** pp *Posada Cucao*, with breakfast, meals; **E** pp with full board or *demi-pension* at *Provisiones Pacífico* (friendly, good, candles provided, no hot water), Sra Boreuel or with Sra Luz Vera, next to school, meals and good homemade bread, rec; **E** pp *Casa Blanca*, with breakfast. **Camping**: several campsites inc *Parador Darwin*, check prices carefully first. *Las Luminarias* sells excellent *empanadas de machas* (*machas* are local shell fish).

● **Transport** For buses from Castro see above; in season as many as 4 buses a day, last departure 1600, reduced service off-season; hitching is very difficult.

PARQUE NACIONAL CHILOE

The Park, which is in 3 sections, covers 43,057 ha. Much of the park is covered by evergreen forest. The northern sector, covering 7,800 ha, is reached by a path which runs S from Chepu (see page 798). The second section is a small island, Metalqui, off the coast of the N sector. The southern

sector, 35,207 ha, is entered 1 km N of Cucao, where there is an administration centre (limited information), small museum and guest bungalow for use by visiting scientists (applications to Conaf via your embassy). Park entry US$2.50. No access by car. Maps of the park are available. (**NB** *Refugios* are inaccurately located.)

A path runs 3 km N from the administration centre to Laguna Huelde (many camp sites) and then N a further 12 km to Cole Cole (*refugio*, key kept at Conaf office at entrance, free camping, dirty) offering great views, best done on horseback (return journey to/from Cucao 9 hrs by horse). The next *refugio* is at Anay, 9 km further N across the Río Anay (crossed by ferry, US$10). There are several other walks but signposting is limited. Many houses in Cucao rent horses at US$2.50/hour, US$22/day. If you hire a guide you pay for his horse too. Horseflies are bad in summer (wear light clothing).

QUELLON

(*Pop* 7,500; *Phone code* 065) 92 km S of Castro. There are pleasant beaches nearby at Quellón Viejo (old wooden church), Punta de Lapa and Yaldad. The launch *Puerto Bonito* sails 3 times daily in summer from the pier, US$12.50 to tour the bay passing Punta de Lapa, Isla Laitec and Quellón Viejo. A trip can also be made to Chaiguao,11 km E, where there is a small Sun morning market; horses can be hired US$2.50/hr. Also kayaks with a guide, US$2.50/hr; camping US$3.50.

Museo de Nuestros Pasados, Ladrilleros 215, includes reconstructions of traditional Chilote house and mill; **Museo Municipal**, on Gómez García.

● **Accommodation A1** *Golfo Corcovado*, Vargas 680, T 681528, F 681527, overlooking town, fine views, very comfortable, English spoken; **B** *Melimoyu*, P Montt 369, T 681250, good beds, parking; **D** *Playa*, P Montt 427, T 681278, with breakfast, without bath; **E** pp *Leo Man*, P Montt 445, T 681298, without bath, pleasant, good value; **E** pp *El Chico Leo*, Aguirre Cerda 20, T 681567, without bath, basic; **C/D** *Res El Tráfico*, P Montt 115, **E** pp without bath, with breakfast, parking; **E** pp *Hosp La Paz*, La Paz 370, with breakfast, hot water; **F** pp *Las Brisas*, P Montt 555, T 681413, without bath, basic; **F** pp *Turino Club Deportes*, La Paz 24, floor space and camping, cold water, kitchen facilities, basic, open Dec-Feb only. *Albergue*, Ladrilleros, nr Carrera Pinto, **G** pp locals, **F** pp foreigners; dormitory accommodation. At Punta de Lapa, 7 km W are: *Leo Man*, chalets and *cabañas*; *Cabañas y Camping Las Brisas*.

● **Places to eat** *Rucantú* on waterfront, good food, good value; *El Coral*, 22 de Mayo, good, reasonably priced, superb views; *Fogón Las Quilas*, La Paz 053, T 206, famous for lobster, rec; *Hotel Leo Man* serves good coffee, pleasant *comedor*; *Nuevo Amanecer*, 22 de Mayo 201, cheap, clean.

● **Banks & money changers** Banco del Estado, US$12 commission on TCs, credit cards not possible, no commision on US$ cash.

● **Tourist offices** Kiosk on the park, open mid-Dec to mid-March. Ask about *hospedajes* not listed in their information leaflet.

● **Transport Buses** To Castro, 2 hrs, frequent, Cruz del Sur, US$4, Trans Chiloé US$3; also services to Ancud and Puerto Montt. **Ferries**: in summer only (2 Jan-8 Mar), the Transmarchilay ferry *Pincoya* sails to Chaitén on the mainland, Mon and Wed 1600, return departure Wed and Sat 0900, 5 hrs crossing, US$70-80 per car, US$11 pp. The ship continues from Chaitén to Puerto Montt. The *Pincoya* also sails from Quellón to Puerto Chacabuco Sat 1600, all year round, 18 hrs, cars US$110, passengers US$20-27. If you take this ferry when heading S you miss a large section of the Carretera Austral; if you wish to see the Carretera's scenery, take the ferry to Chaitén. From 15 Mar to 29 Dec ferries go only from Pargua to Chaitén and Puerto Chacabuco. **Transmarchilay** office, Pedro Montt 451, Quellón, T 681331. Enquire first, either in Santiago or Puerto Montt.

South from Puerto Montt: the Carretera Austral

CONSTRUCTION of the Carretera Austral has opened up the impressive landscapes of this wet and windy region of mountains, channels and islands. The main town is Coyhaique. A boat journey, either as a means of access, or for viewing the glacier at Laguna San Rafael gives an equally magnificent, but different perspective.

Land and climate

A third of Chile lies to the south of Puerto Montt, but its land and climate are such that, until recently, it has been put to little human use: less than 3% of the country's population lives here.

South of Puerto Montt the sea has broken through and drowned the central valley between the Andes and the coastal mountain range. The higher parts of the latter form a maze of islands, stretching for over 1,000 km and separated from the coast by tortous fjord-like channels. It is fortunate for shipping that this maze has a more or less connected route through it: see page 794.

The Carretera Austral: Puerto Montt to Puerto Cisnes

Not to scale

Puerto Montt
Parque Nacional Andino Alerce
La Arena
Puelche
Río Negro/ Hornopirén
Parque Nacional Hornopirén
Isla Llancahué
Fiordo Reñihue
Fiordo Leptepu
Leptepu
Fiordo Largo
Caleta Gonzalo
Golfo de Corcovado
Santa Barbara
Chaitén
Amarillo
Lago Espolón
Futaleufú
To Esquel
Río Yelcho
Puerto Cárdenas
Lago Yelcho
Puerto Ramirez
Villa Santa Lucía
Palena
To Route 40
Río Palena
La Junta
Reserva Nacional Rosselot
Río Figueroa
Lago Rosselot
Lago Risopatrón
Lago Verde
To Route 40
Termas de Puyuhuapi
Puyuhuapi
Parque Nacional Queulat
To Route 40
Parque Nacional Isla Magdalena
Río Cisnes
Puerto Cisnes
Villa Amengual
Canal Puyuguapi
Reserva Nacional Lago Las Torres
Lago Las Torres
To Coyhaique

ARGENTINA
N

90

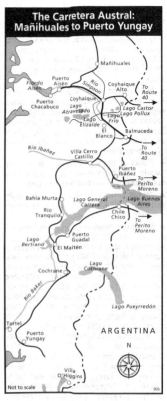

The Carretera Austral: Mañihuales to Puerto Yungay

Mañihuales
Fiordo Aisén
Puerto Aisén
Río Simpson
Coyhaique Alto
To Route 40
Puerto Chacabuco
Coyhaique
Lago Atravesado
Lago Castor
Lago Pollux
Lago Frío
Lago Elizalde
El Blanco
Balmaceda
Río Ibáñez
Villa Cerro Castillo
To Route 40
Puerto Ibáñez
To Perito Moreno
Bahía Murta
Lago General Carrera
Lago Buenos Aires
Río Tranquilo
Chile Chico
To Perito Moreno
Lago Bertrand
Puerto Guadal
El Maitén
Cochrane
Lago Cochrane
Río Baker
Lago Pueyrredón
Tortel
ARGENTINA
N
Puerto Yungay
Villa O'Higgins

Not to scale

90b

The Andes are much lower than further N and eroded by glacial action: towards the coast they rise in peaks; inland they form a high steppe around 1,000m. To the S of Coyhaique are two areas of high land covered by ice and glaciers, known as *campos de hielo* (ice fields).

Five main rivers flow westwards: from N to S these are the Futaleufú or Yelcho, the Palena, the Cisnes, the Simpson or Aisén and the Baker. The latter, 370 km long, is the third longest river in Chile. Only the Cisnes and the Simpson are entirely in Chile, the other three being largely fed from Argentina. The three largest lakes in this region, Lago Gen Carrera (the largest in Chile), Lago Cochrane and Lago O'Higgins are also shared with Argentina.

There is no real dry season. On the offshore islands and the western side of the Andes annual rainfall is over 2,000 mm. Westerly winds are strong especially in summer. Temperatures vary little between day and night. Inland on the steppelands the climate is drier and colder. Jan and Feb are probably the best months for a trip to this region.

Economy Potatoes and cereals are among the major crops, while sheep farming is more important than cattle. Chile Chico and the shores of Lago Gen Carrera enjoy a warm microclimate which allows the production of fruit. Fishing is an important source of employment in the inland channels. Wood is used for construction and in towns such as Coyhaique and is in such demand in winter for fuel that it costs as much as petrol. It is also increasingly exported, often as woodchips.

The **Carretera Austral** can be divided into three major sections: Puerto Montt-Chaitén (242 km) with 2-3 ferry crossings (see below); Chaitén-Coyhaique (435 km); and Coyhaique-Puerto Yungay (421 km). It is described on Chilean maps as a "camino ripio" (paved with stones). Most of the villages along the Carretera are of very recent origin and consist of a few houses which offer accommodation and other services to travellers. Although tourist infrastructure is growing rapidly, motorists should carry adequate fuel and spares, especially if intending to detour from the highway itself, and should protect their windscreens and headlamps. Unleaded fuel is available as far S as Cochrane. Cyclists should note the danger of stones thrown up by passing vehicles.

PUERTO MONTT TO CHAITEN

This section of the Carretera Austral, 242 km, includes two ferry crossings. Before setting out, it is imperative to check when the ferries are running and, if driving, make a reservation: do this in Puerto Montt, rather than Santiago, at the Transmarchilay office, Angelmó 2187, T 254654. The alternative to this section is by ferry from Puerto Montt or Quellón to Chaitén.

The road (Ruta 7) heads E out of Puerto Montt, through Pelluco and after an initial rough stretch follows the shore of the beautiful Seno Reloncaví passing the southern entrance of the Parque Nacional Alerce Andino.

PARQUE NACIONAL ALERCE ANDINO

The park contains one of the best surviving areas of alerce trees, some over 1,000 years old (the oldest is estimated at 4,200 years old). Wildlife includes pudú, pumas, vizcachas, condors and black woodpeckers. There are four ranger posts: at Río Chaicas, Lago Chapo, Sargazo and at the N entrance. There are basic *refugios* at Río Pangal, Laguna Sargazo and Laguna Fría and camping sites at Río Chaicas and the N entrance. Very little information at ranger posts; map available from Conaf in Puerto Montt.

● **Access** There are two entrances: 2.5 km from Correntoso (35 km E of Puerto Montt) at the northern end of the park and 7 km E of Lenca (40 km S of Puerto Montt) at the southern end.

● **Transport** To N entrance: take Fierro or Río Pato bus to Correntoso (or Lago Chapo bus which passes through Correntoso), several daily except Sun, then walk. To S entrance: take any Fierro bus to Chaicas, La Arena, Contau and Hornopirén, US$1.50, getting off at Lenca sawmill, then walk (signposted).

46 km from Puerto Montt (allow 1 hr), is the first ferry at **La Arena**, across the Reloncaví Estuary to Puelche.

● **Ferries** 30 mins, US$4.65 for a car, 7 crossings daily. Ferry leaves Puelche for La Arena 45 mins before it returns from La Arena. Arrive at least 30 mins early to guarantee a place; buses have priority. Roll-on roll-off type operating all year.

Río Negro (*Pop* 1,100) also called **Hornopirén** after the volcano above it, is 58 km S of Puelche. From here you catch the second ferry, to Caleta Gonzalo. At the mouth of the fjord is **Isla Llancahué**, good for hiking in the forests amid beautiful scenery. *Hotel Termas de Llancahué* charges C pp full board (excellent food), hot spring at the hotel. To get there, make arrangements by phoning 0965-38345. The hotel will send an open boat for you; the 1 hr crossing affords views of dolphins and fur seals. Efforts are under way to preserve areas of ancient emerald araucaria and alerce forest E of Volcán Hornopirén, coordinated by Ancient Forest International and Codeff, the Chilean environmental organization.

● **Accommodation** Electricity 1900-0100. *Cabañas* at Copec service station; **B** *Perlas del Reloncaví*, pleasant, good restaurant, English and German spoken, highly rec; **D** pp *Holiday Country*, on the road to Pichanco, hot shower, restaurant, and the *Hornopirén*, at the water's edge, next to the sawmill, highly rec, T Puerto Montt 255243.

● **Transport Buses** Fierro run daily 0800 and 1500 from Puerto Montt. There are no buses S from Río Negro. **Ferries** Río Negro – Caleta Gonzalo, Transmarchilay, Wed 1600, Thur-Sun 1500, 5 hrs (may be much longer if the ferry cannot dock in rough weather). Going N the ferry leaves Caleta Gonzalo at 0900, Mon, Thur, Fri, Sat, Sun. Fare for vehicles over 4m US$88, under 4m US$75, passengers US$14, bicycles, US$9. Ferry operates Jan/Feb only and can be very busy; there can be a 2-day wait to get on the ferry. The Río Negro-Caleta Gonzalo trip may also use two ferry stages, the first, from Pichanco up the Fiordo Leptepu, passing a narrow channel in which the German light cruiser *Dresden* hid from the British fleet in 1915. The crew was protected by the local German community. The second stage, after a 10 km stretch of road from Leptepu to Fiordo Largo, crosses the Fiordo Reñihue to Caleta Gonzalo.

South of Caleta Gonzalo there is a steep climb on a coarse gravel surface to Laguna Blanca. Caleta Santa Bárbara, a black sand beach with nice camping and swimming, is at Km 48. (**NB** Do not camp close to the water.) It is a further 12 km to Chaitén.

CHAITEN

(*Pop 3,258; Phone code 065*) The capital of Palena province, **Chaitén** is important as a port for ferries to Puerto Montt and Quellón. There are good views over the Corcovado Bay from the Costanera. Fuel is available.

● **Accommodation A2** *Mi Casa*, Av Norte, T 731285 – on a hill – rec, comfortable, or **E** in youth hostel, negotiable, the owners prefer you to eat in their restaurant; **B** *Hostería Schilling*, Corcovado 230, T 731295, on waterfront, with heating (check if hot water is turned on), no restaurant; **D** *Continental*, Juan Todesco 18, T 731312, no heating nor private bath, but good meals, very helpful, rec; **D** *Hostería Los Alerces*, Av Norte s/n, F 731266, restaurant; **D** *Res Astoria*, Corcovado 442, T 731263, with breakfast, without bath, bar downstairs; **E** pp *Hosp Lo Watson*, Ercilla 580, use of kitchen; **E** pp *Casa Rita*, Rivero y Prat (**F** pp for floor space, **F** pp for camping), use of kitchen, open all year, heating, rec; **E** pp Corcovada 466, family atmosphere, hot shower extra; **E** pp Martín Ruiz, Carretera Austral 1 km N, inc breakfast, nice views; **E** pp *Hosp Recoba*, Libertad 432, T 731390, with breakfast, good meals. *Los Arrayanes* campsite 4 km N, with hot showers and close to sea, good.

● **Places to eat** *Flamengo*, Corcovado, T 314, excellent, popular; *Mahurori*, Inde-

pendencia 141.

● **Sports Fishing**: there is excellent fishing nearby, especially to the S in the Ríos Yelcho and Futaleufú and in Lagos Espolón and Yelcho. Fishing licences are sold at the Municipalidad.

● **Tour companies & travel agents** *Chaitur*, in bus terminal, helpful.

● **Transport Air** Flights Puerto Montt-Chaitén-Puerto Montt with Don Carlos, Juan Todesco 42, T 275, 1220 and 1600, Mon-Fri, 1220 on Sat. Also Aerosur daily except Sun, and Aero Chaitén, US$38. **Buses** Arteturr (Av Costanera) runs microbuses between Chaitén and Coyhaique, 3 a week in summer, Wed and Sat off-season (US$30, 12-14 hrs). The service depends very much on demand and in winter especially may not run all the way (ie only to La Junta). On the full service, the bus stops overnight in La Junta in winter but only briefly in summer. Other stops on request, but it is easier to go right through than pick up a bus on route. Similar services by Transportes San Rafael, Mon and Thur 1200, and B and V Tours (Libertad 432) summer only. Hitching the whole route takes about a week, but you must be prepared for a day's wait if you find yourself out of luck. **Ferries** Port about 1 km from town. The Transmarchilay ferries *Pincoya* and *Mailen* run between Chaitén, Puerto Montt and Quellón on Chiloé: sailings for Puerto Montt are on Mon 2200, Mon 2400, Thur 0900 and Fri 0900, 11 hrs; from Puerto Montt to Chaitén Tues 1200, Tues 1400, Thur 2200 and Fri 2000. Fares to Puerto Montt US$100/car over 4m, US$88 under 4m, US$16/deck passenger, seat US$20, bunk US$31, bicycle US$11. To Quellón Wed and Sat 0900 in Jan-early March, otherwise Sat 0900 only, fares under Quellón. The Navimag ferry *Alejandrina* sails between Chaitén and Puerto Montt, no bunks, no fixed schedule. Check in advance for exact times; office Av Corcovado 266, T 731272. There is also a ferry to Puerto Montt for trucks, Ro-Ro *Mercedes*, Terminales Marítimos Chilenos, which will also take passengers but with no shelter, standing only, unless someone lets you get in their vehicle, once a week (twice a week Jan-Feb), 12 hrs, US$8. Office is in a hardware store (*ferretería*) on Juan Todesco, T 731333; in Puerto Montt, Chorillos y Pudeto, T 257259.

CHAITEN TO COYHAIQUE

This section of the Carretera Austral, 422 km, runs through small villages and passes through the Parque Nacional Queulat; roads branch off E to the Argentine frontier and W to Puerto Cisnes.

Puerto Cárdenas, 46 km S of Chaitén, is on the northern tip of **Lago Yelcho**, a beautiful lake on Río Futaleufú surrounded by hills and frequented by anglers. The *Isla Monita Lodge* offers packages for anglers and non-anglers on a private island in the lake, as well as fishing in many nearby locations; contact *Turismo Grant*, PO Box 52311, Santiago, T 639-5524, F 633-7133. Further S at Km 60, a path leads to **Ventisquero Yelcho** (2 hrs' walk).

● **Accommodation** Two *residenciales* inc **C** *Res Yelcho*, full board available; *Cabañas Cavi*, 7 km S on lakeshore, also camping, cafeteria.

The Argentine frontier is reached in two places, Futaleufú and Palena by a road which branches off at **Villa Santa Lucía** (Km 81), where there are 30 houses, a military camp, one small shop and bread is available from a private house. The road to the border is single track, gravel, passable in a regular car, but best with a good, strong vehicle; the scenery is beautiful. At **Puerto Ramírez** at the southern end of **Lago Yelcho** the road divides: the N branch runs along the valley of the Río Futaleufú to **Futaleufú** and the southern one to Palena. **Lago Espolón**, W of Futaleufú, reached by a turning 41 km NE of Villa Santa Lucía, is a beautiful lake in an area enjoying a warm microclimate: 30°C in the day in summer, 5° at night. The lake is warm enough for a quick dip but beware of the currents. There are *cabañas* (**E** pp) and a campsite; Aníbal, who owns the campsite, sells meat, bread, beer and soft drinks and will barbecue lamb. The Río Futaleufú and Lago Espolón provide excellent fishing (ask for the Valebote family's motorboat).

● **Accommodation At Villa Santa Lucía:** several places on main street: at No 7 (Sra Rosalía Cuevas de Ruiz, basic, meals available), No 13 (breakfast extra) and No 16 (not bad), all F pp, none has hot water. **At Puerto Ramírez:** *Hostería Río Malito*, rooms, camping, fishing. **At Futaleufú:** **D** *Res Carahue*, O'Higgins 322, T 221; **E** pp *Hotel Continental*, Balmaceda 597, T 222, basic, rec, cheap restaurant. **At Palena:** *La Frontera*, T 741240; *Res La Chilenita*, T 258633.

● **Transport Air** Aerosur flights from Chaitén to Futaleufú, Tues and Fri, US$62. **Buses** A microbus runs from Chaitén to Futaleufú on Tues, at least.

FRONTIER WITH ARGENTINA: FUTALEUFU

● **Chilean immigration**
In Futaleufú, 9 km W of the frontier. Allow 1½ hrs for formalities. The border is at the bridge over the Río Grande.

NB Only transit visas for Argentina are issued, which can cause problems. You must either leave within 10 days or renew your entry stamp at an immigration office

● **Entering Chile**
Continue from Futaleufú towards Puerto Ramírez, but outside Ramírez, take the unsigned right turn to Chaitén (left goes to Palena)

● **Exchange**
Change money in Futaleufú (poor rates); nowhere to change at the border.

● **Transport**
From Futaleufú a bus runs to the border, Tues and Fri 1300, 1300 approx, US$3, 30 mins (ask at the small grey store, Kitty, at the school corner on Balmaceda).

FRONTIER WITH ARGENTINA: PALENA

● **Chilean immigration**
At Palena, 8 km W of frontier.

NB Only transit visas are issued (see above under Futaleufú crossing).

● **Accommodation**
Several *pensiones* in Palena.

● **Transport**
Expreso Yelcho bus from Chaitén twice a week, US$12, 5½ hrs.

LA JUNTA

(*Pop* 736) A drab, expensive village at the confluence of Río Rosselot and Río Palena, 151 km S of Chaitén. **Lago Rosselot**, surrounded by forest in the **Reserva Nacional Lago Rosselot**, 9 km E of La Junta, can be reached by a road which continues E, 74 km, to Lago Verde and the Argentine frontier.

● **Accommodation C** *Hostería Valdera*, Varas s/n, T 314105, inc breakfast, very good value; **C** *Cabañas Espacio Tiempo*, T 314141, restaurant, fishing expeditions; **E** pp *Copihue*, Varas 611, T 314140, few rooms, without bath, good meals, changes money at very poor rates; **D** *Café Res Patagonia*, Lynch 331, T 314115, good meals, limited bathrooms.

● **Banks & money changers** If desperate to change money try the hotels, but bargain hard.

• **Transport** Fuel is available. Buses to Coyhaique, Artetur (Diego Portales 183), US$14.30, twice a week, also Transaustral twice a week US$15.

PUYUGUAPI

From La Junta the Carretera Austral runs S along the W side of Lago Risopatrón, to Puyuguapi (also spelt Puyuhuapi; *Pop* 500; *phone code* 068), 45 km further S at the end of the Puyuguapi Channel. The village was founded by four Sudeten German families in 1935. The famous carpet factory can be visited. 18 km SW, accessible only by boat, are **Termas de Puyuhuapi**, several springs with 40°C water filling three pools near the beach (baths cost US$15 pp, children under 12 US$10, take food and drink). Sr Alonso runs day-trips from Puyuguapi, US$30.

• **Accommodation L3-A1** *Hotel Termas de Puyuhuapi* (price depends on season and type of room), inc use of baths and boat transfer to hotel, full board US$40 extra, good restaurant, rec. For reservations: *Patagonia Connection SA*, Fidel Oteíza 1921, Oficina 1006, Providencia, Santiago (Metro Pedro do Valdivia), T 223-6489, F 274-8111 or directly at the *Hotel Termas de Puyuhuapi*, T 325 103. (See also under Puerto Montt **Shipping**.) Boat schedule from jetty, 2 hrs' walk from town, 0930, 1000, 1200, 1230, 1830, 1900, residents only, US$3 each way, 10 mins crossing. **A3** *El Pangue*, 17 km N on Lago Risopatrón, T/F 325128, cheaper off season, *cabañas*, camping, restaurant; **B** *Res Alemana*, Otto Uebel 450, T 325118, a large wooden house on the main road, comfortable, highly rec; **C** pp *Hostería Ludwig*, on the road S, T 325131, excellent, often full; **E** pp *Hosp El Pino*, Hamburgo s/n, T 325117, homemade bread; **E** pp *pensión* of Sra Leontina Fuentes, Llantureo y Circunvalación, good breakfast for US$1; **E** pp *Res Elizabeth*, Llantureo y Henríquez, inc breakfast; **E** pp *pensión* at Tureo 18. **A3** *Cabañas Fiordo Queulat* (T Coyhaique 233302), rec. There is a dirty campsite by the sea behind the general store. The store is behind the service station, which sells fuel until 1930.

• **Places to eat** *Café Rossbach* with limited menu, not cheap, excellent salmon. 2 bars.

• **Transport** Bus transport out of Puyuguapi is very scarce. Artetur (O'Higgins 039, T 325101) to Coyhaique and La Junta twice a week, to Chaitén once a week (Tues), Transaustral twice a week to Coyhaique.

Parque Nacional Queulat lies N and E of Puyuguapi and is, according to legend,

the site of the rich town of Césares. In the N of the park is **Lago Risopatrón**; 24 km S of Puyuguapi, is the beautiful Ventisquero Colgante (hanging glacier), with the Salto del Cóndor waterfall a further 29 km S. Boat trips can be made on Lago Risopatrón and Laguna Tempano. Administration is in the Conaf office in La Junta; entry US$1.

• **Accommodation A3** *Cabañas El Pangue*, at N end of Lago Risopatrón, F 325128, also camping; *Cabañas Lago Queulat*, on Seno Queulat, campsite nearby, US$3.50.

PUERTO CISNES

59 km S of Puyuguapi, a road branches W and follows the Río Cisnes 35 km to **Puerto Cisnes** (*Pop* 1,784) at the mouth of the river. Fuel is available.

The Río Cisnes, 160 km in length, is recommended for rafting or canoeing, with grand scenery and modest rapids except for the horrendous drop at Piedra del Gato; there is a 150m cliff at Torre Bright Bank. Good camping in the forest.

• **Accommodation B** *Manzur*, E Dunn 75, T 346453, *cabañas*; **D** pp *Hostal Michay*, Mistral 112, T 346462; **D** pp *Res El Gaucho*, Holmberg 140, T 346483, with breakfast, dinner available, welcoming, hot water; *pensión* at Carlos Condell y Dr Steffen, **D** pp, with breakfast, hot shower.

• **Transport** Buses Wed and Sun at 1100 to Coyhaique with Litoral, 5½ hrs, US$14, Trans Mañihuales daily US$14, Colectivos Basoli 2 a week, US$12.

89 km S of Puyuguapi is Villa Amengual (accommodation, food); at Km 92 a road branches E, 104 km to La Tapera and to the Argentine border. Chilean immigration is 12 km W of the frontier, open daylight hours only. On the Argentine side the road continues to meet up with Ruta 40, the N-S road at the foot of the Andes.

The **Reserva Nacional Lago Las Torres**, at Km 98, includes the wonderful Lago Las Torres, which offers good fishing and a small Conaf campsite.

Villa Mañihuales (*Pop* 1,339) at Km 148 is near the **Reserva Forestal Mañihuales**; the forests were largely destroyed by forest fires in the 1940s, but the views are good. Entry US$1.

● **Accommodation** There are at least 3 *pensiones*, inc **E** pp *Pensión Bienvenido*, with restaurant; **E** pp *Villa Mañihuales*, breakfast, *cabañas* **A** (both right-hand side of road going S at southern end).

● **Transport** Bus to Coyhaique, Trans Mañihuales, one a day except Sun.

13 km S of Villa Mañihuales the road forks W to Puerto Aisén, E to Coyhaique. At Villa Ortega on the Coyhaique branch, the *Restaurant Farolito* takes guests, E pp, rec.

COYHAIQUE

(*Pop* 36,367; *Phone code* 067) 420 km S of Chaitén in the broad green valley of the Río Simpson. Founded in 1929, it is the administrative and commercial centre of the XI Region. It provides a good base for hiking, skiing and, especially, fishing excursions.

Places of interest

On the pentagonal plaza stand the Cathedral, the Intendencia, the Liceo San Felipe Benicio and a handicraft market. The **Museo Regional de la Patagonia Central** in the Casa de Cultura, Baquedano 310 (US$0.75, Tues-Sun 0900-1300, 1500-2000), contains photos of early settlers, history, paleontology, fauna and archaeology, good. If arriving from the airport, look left from the bridge over the Río Simpson the **Piedra del Indio**, a rock outcrop which looks like a face in profile.

Excursions

To the **Reserva Nacional Coyhaique**, 5 km NW off the Carretera Austral, which covers 2,150 ha of mixed forest. Park administration is at the entrance (US$1; 2 campsites and a *refugio*).

Southwest to **Lagos Atrevesado** (20 km) and **Elizalde** which offers good fishing, yachting and camping. Southeast to **Lagos Frío**, **Castor** and **Pollux**, all of which offer good fishing. At El Fraile, 29 km SE near Lago Frío, there is skiing: there are 5 pistes and 2 lifts, cafeteria, equipment hire (season June to Sept). The **Monumento Natural Dos Lagunas**, 21 km E on the Coyhaique Alto road, is a small park which includes Lagos El Toro and Escondido. Entry US$1; camping US$12 per site.

Local information
● **Accommodation**

In summer rooms are in very short supply; the tourist office has a full list of all types of accommodation, but also look out for notices in windows (several on Baquedano and Almte Simpson).

A2 *Los Ñires*, Baquedano 315, T 232261, with breakfast, comfortable, parking; **A2** *Cabañas La Pasarela*, T 234520, Km 1.5 Carretera a Aisén, good atmosphere, *comedor*; **A2** *Cabañas Río Simpson*, T 232183, Km 3 road to Pto Aysén, cabins for 5, or 2, fully-equipped, horse hire, fishing; **A3** *Cabaña Abedules*, 18 de Septiembre 463, F 232396, at Plaza Angol, price/cabin for 5, heating, kitchen, TV, suitable for families; **A3** *Austral*, Colón 203, T 232522, English spoken, tours arranged, rec.

B *Cabaña San Sebastián*, Freire 554, T 231762, with breakfast; **B** *Res El Reloj*, Baquedano 444, T 231108, with restaurant.

C *Licarayen*, Carrera 33A, T 233377 (Santiago T 743-1294) with breakfast, rec; **C** *Res Puerto Varas*, Serrano 168, T 233689, without bath, check which of the bathrooms has hot water, restaurant and bar, basic, tatty.

D pp *El Serrano*, Serrano 91, T 235522, with breakfast, rec.

E pp *Hosp* at Baquedano 20, T 232520, Patricio y Gedra Guzmán, room in family home (also 3 flats), use of kitchen, breakfast with homemade bread, tent sites with bathroom and laundry facilities down by the river, English spoken, most hospitable, rec; **D** *Hosp Hermina Mansilla*, 21 de Mayo 60, with breakfast, highly rec; **F** pp *Res Navidad*, Baquedano 198, T 235159, without bath or breakfast, *comedor*, hot showers, use of kitchen; **E** pp *Hosp Pierrot*, Baquedano 130, T 221315, with breakfast, quiet. Several cheap places on Av Simpson, eg **E** *Casa El Fondo*, No 417, good; **E** pp *Los Cuatro Hermanos* Colón 495, T 232647, without breakfast (more with); **E** pp Baquedano 274, small rooms, very good; **E** pp *Hosp Lautaro*, Lautaro 532, T 231852, comfortable, kitchen facilities, large rooms, rec. Youth hostel in summer at one of the schools (it changes each year), F pp with sleeping bag.

Camping: at Baquedano 20, see above. There are many camping sites in Coyhaique and on the road between Coyhaique and Puerto Aisén, eg at Km 1, 2 (*Camping Alborada*, US$8.50, T 231014, hot shower), 24, 25, 35, 37, 41, 42 (*Camping Río Correntoso*, T 232005, US$15/site, showers, fishing, Automobile Club discount) and 43. Sernatur in Coyhaique has a full list of all sites in XI Región.

● **Places to eat**
Loberías de Chacabuco, Barroso 553, good

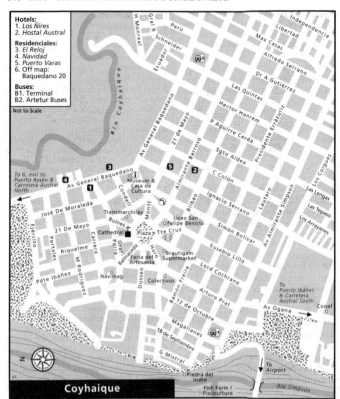

Coyhaique

Hotels:
1. Los Ñires
2. Hostal Austral

Residenciales:
3. El Reloj
4. Navidad
5. Puerto Varas
6. Off map: Baquedano 20

Buses:
B1. Terminal
B2. Arteturo Buses

Not to Scale

seafood, slow service; *La Olla*, C Parra entre Riquelme y Moraleda, popular, good lunches; *Café Oriente*, 21 de Mayo y Condell 201, good bakery, tea; *Café Kalu*, Prat 402, set meals, hamburgers; *Café Ricer*, Horn 48, good; *Cafetería Alemana*, Condell 119, nice, excellent cakes and coffee, vegetarian dishes; *Lito's*, Lautaro 147, next to Bus Terminal, good food and atmosphere; *Casino de Bomberos*, Gen Parra 365, wide range, cheap. A good bar is *Pub*, 12 de Octubre 361, nice atmosphere and music; around the corner is *Bar West*, Western style.

● **Airline offices**
LanChile, Gen Parra 215, T 231188; Ladeco, Dussen y Prat 188, T 231300; Don Carlos, Cruz 63, T 231981.

● **Banks & money changers**
Banco Osorno, Prat 340, T 232214, for cash advance on Visa, and **Turismo Prado**, 21 de Mayo 417, T/F 231271, both accept TCs. **Banco Santander**, Condell 100, Mastercard ATM. For dollars TCs and Argentine pesos **Lavaseco** on Gen Parra. **Fincard** (Mastercard), Prat 340, local 1, T 233026, Mon-Fri 0900-1400, 1530-1900, Sat 0930-1330; at same address, oficina 208, *El Libertador*, T 233342.

● **Language schools**
Baquedano International Language School, Baquedano 20, at *Hosp* of Sr Guzmán (see **Accommodation** above), T 232520, F 231511: US$300/week course inc lodging and all meals, 4 hrs a day person-to-person tuition, other activities organized at discount rates.

● **Laundry**
Lavamatic, Bilbao 198; *QL*, Bilbao 160; *Universal*, Gen Parra 55; *Lottie*, Baquedano 1259.

● **Post & telecommunications**
Post Office: Cochrane 202, open Mon-Fri 0830-1230, 1430-1800, Sat 0830-1200.
Telephone Office: at Barroso 626, open till 2200, opens on Sun about 0900.

● **Shopping**
Feria de Artesanía on the plaza; *Cema-Chile* on plaza, between Montt and Barroso. Large well-stocked supermarkets: *Brautigam*, Horn, Prat y Bilbao; *Central*, Magallanes y Bilbao, open daily till 2230; 2 small ones on Prat, Nos 480 and 533, open Sun. Food, especially fruit and vegetables, is more expensive than in Santiago but cheaper than Argentina.

● **Tour companies & travel agents**
Turismo Prado, address in **Banks & money changers** above; *Expediciones Coyhaique*, Bolívar 94, T/F 232300. Both offer tours of local lakes and other sights, arrange Laguna San Rafael trips, etc; *Prado* does historical tours, while *Expediciones* does fishing trips and excursions down the Río Baker. *Turismo Queulat*, 21 de Mayo 1231, T/F 231441, trips to Queulat glacier, adventure and nature tourism, fishing, etc. *Exploraciones Lucas Bridges*, E Lillo 311, Casilla 5, T/F 233302, e-mail lbridges@entelchile.net, small group adventure trips, rec. *Res Serrano*, C Serrano, organizes trips to Lago Elizalde and Lago Atrevesado, US$15 pp. *Aventura*, Bilbao 171, T 234748, offers rafting; *45 Sur*, 12 de Octubre 253, T 234599, horseriding, good value; *Alex Prior*, T 234732, for fly fishing. Tours only operate in season.

● **Tourist offices**
Sernatur, Bulnes 35 (Casilla 601); municipal office at Museo Regional, T 232100, F 231788. Conaf: office, Ogana 1060. Maps (photocopies of 1:50,000 IGM maps) from Dirección de Vialidad on the square.

● **Transport**
Local Bicycle rental: *Figón*, Simpson y Colón, check condition first. Bicycle spares from several shops on Simpson. **Car hire: Automóvil Club de Chile**, Bolívar 254, T 231649, rents jeeps and other vehicles. **Budget**, Parra 215; **Traeger-Hertz**, Baquedano 457; **Economy**, Carrera 339, T 233363, cars may be taken across Argentine border and may be returned to a different office; **Automundo AVR**, Bilbao 509. 4WD rec for Carretera Austral. Buy fuel in Coyhaique, several stations. **Taxis**: US$5 to airport (US$1.65 if sharing); fares in town US$1.35. 50% extra after 2100. Colectivos congregate at Prat y Bilbao, average fare US$0.50.

Air Airport, Tte Vidal, about 5 km SW of town (inc a steep climb up and down to the Río Simpson bridge). Served by local airlines; larger planes use Balmaceda (see below). Air taxi to visit glaciers, US$350 (5 passengers), also to southern archipelagic region. Don Carlos to Chile Chico (Tues, Thur, Sat), and Cochrane (Wed, Fri, 45 mins, rec only for those who like flying, with strong stomachs, or in a hurry).

Buses Terminal at Lautaro y Magallanes; most buses leave from here, but not all. Bus company offices: Turibus, Baquedano 1171, T 231333; Transaustral, Baquedano 1171, T 231333; Don Carlos, Subteniente Cruz 63, T 232981; Litoral, Baquedano e Independencia, T 232903; Artetur, Baquedano 1347, T 233768, F 233367; Transportes San Rafael, 18 de Sept 469, T 233408; B and V Tours, Simpson 1037.

To/from **Puerto Montt**, via Bariloche, all year, Turibus, Tues and Fri 1600, US$28.50, with connections to Osorno, Valdivia, Temuco, Santiago and Castro, often heavily booked. To **Puerto Aisén**, Transaustral, 4 a day, 5 on Sun, La Cascada (T 231413), 4 daily, and Don Carlos taxi-bus, US$3, 8 a day, 3 on Sun; to **Puerto Chacabuco**, Transaustral Thur and Sun, La Cascada 3 times daily, US$3.25. **Puerto Cisnes** daily with Litoral, Tues and Sat at 1130, or Colectivos Basoli, T 232596, Thur and Sun 1200, US13. There are daily buses to **Mañihuales**, Trans Mañihuales (daily 1700) and Litoral. To **Balmaceda** and **Puerto Ibáñez**, Buses Ruta Sur, T 232788.

To **Puerto Ibáñez** on Lago Gen Carrera, colectivos (connect with *El Pilchero* ferry to Chile Chico) from *El Gran Calafate*, C Prat, 3 hrs, book the day before, US$7; to Bajada Ibáñez, Aerobus from bus terminal, Mon, Wed, Fri 1000, return next day, US$5.45, and Pudú, T 231000/6, Tues and Sat 0815.

Buses on the **Carretera Austral** vary according to demand: N to **Chaitén**, with Artetur, Wed 0700, US$30, overnight stop in La Junta, extra service on Sat in summer, in winter may go only as far as La Junta, US$14.30. Similar service by Transportes San Rafael, Mon and Thur 0900 in summer, 11 hrs, US$30, Transaustral, Tues and Sat 0900 and B and V Tours. Transaustral goes to La Junta via Puyuguapi, US$15, Tues and Sat. To Puerto Montt, Tues and Fri US$35. South to **Cochrane** Pudú, at terminal, T 231008, Don Carlos and Río Baker Taxis (T 231051), all 3 times a week, charging US$23, 10-12 hrs.

To Argentina: options are given below and under Balmaceda, Chile Chico and Cochrane. Many border posts close at weekends. If looking for transport to Argentina it is worth going to the local Radio Santa María, Bilbao y Ignacio Serrano, and leaving a message to be broadcast.

Shipping: Transmarchilay, 21 de Mayo 147, T 231971, Tx 377003 MARCHI CK. **Navimag**, Ibáñez 347, T 233306, F 233386.

FRONTIER WITH ARGENTINA: COYHAIQUE ALTO

On the Argentine side the road leads through Río Mayo and Sarmiento to Comodoro Rivadavia.

● **Chilean immigration**

At Coyhaique Alto, 43 km E of Coyhaique, 6 km W of the frontier, open May-Aug 0800-2100, Sept-April 0700-2300.

● **Transport**

To **Comodoro Rivadavia**, Empresa Giobbi, Coyhaique bus terminal, T 232067, Tues, Thur, Sat 0830, US$30, 12-13 hrs, also service by Turibus, 2 a week.

PUERTO AISEN

The paved road between Coyhaique and Puerto Aisén passes through **Parque Nacional Río Simpson**, which has beautiful waterfalls, good views of the river and very good fly-fishing. Administration is at the entrance; campsite near the turning to Santuario San Sebastián US$5.

Puerto Aisén (*Pop* 13,050; *Phone code* 067) is 57 km W of Coyhaique and 426 km S of Chaitén, at the meeting of the rivers Aisén and Palos. They say it rains 370 days a year here. Formerly the region's major port, it has been replaced by Puerto Chacabuco, 15 km to the W. There are few vestiges of the port left, just some boats high and dry on the river bank when the tide is out and the foundations of buildings by the river, now overgrown with fuchsias and buttercups. To see any maritime activity you have to walk a little way out of town to Puerto Aguas Muertas where the fishing boats come in.

A new bridge over the Río Aisén and a paved road lead to **Puerto Chacabuco**; a regular bus service runs between the two. The harbour is a short way from the town.

There is a good walk N to Laguna Los Palos, 2 hrs from Puerto Aisén. In season the *Apulcheu* sails regularly to **Termas de Chiconal**, about 1 hr from Puerto Chacabuco, offering a good way to see the fjord, US$28, take own food.

Local festival of folklore, 2nd week in November.

● **Accommodation** Hard to find, most is taken up by fishing companies in both ports. Unless otherwise stated, services are in **Puerto** Aisén. **D** *Plaza*, O'Higgins 237, T 332784, without breakfast; **D** *Res Aisén*, Av Serrano Montaner 37, T 332725, good food, full board available; **D** *Roxy*, Aldea 972, T 332704, large rooms, highly rec, restaurant; **E** pp unnamed *hospedaje* at Serrano Montaner 471, T 332574, very pleasant and helpful, rec; **E** pp *Yaney Ruca*, Aldea 369, T 332583. No campsite but free camping easy. In **Puerto Chacabuco**: **A2** *Parque Turístico Loberías de Aisén*, Carrera 50, T 351115, F 351188, accommodation overpriced, best food in the area, climb up steps direct from port for drink or meal overlooking boats and mountains before boarding ferry; **D** *Moraleda*, O'Higgins, T 331155. No other places to buy food or other services.

● **Places to eat** *Gastronomía Carrera*, Cochrane 465, large, very good, popular.

● **Banks & money changers** Banco de Crédito, Prat, for Visa; Banco de Chile, Plaza de Armas only changes cash, not TCs.

● **Post & telecommunications** Post Office: on other side of bridge from Plaza de Armas. **Telephone Office**: on S side of Plaza de Armas, next to *Café Rucuray*, which posts boat information.

● **Tourist offices** In Municipalidad, Prat y Sgto Aldea, 1 Dec to end-Feb only, helpful.

● **Transport Buses** to Puerto Chacabuco, La Cascada on Serrano Montaner, to left of Sgto Aldea (main street) walking away from Plaza de Armas, 6 a day between 0800-1730, 30 mins, US$1, return 0830-1800; colectivo US$1.50 pp. La Cascada to **Coyhaique**, 4 a day between 0830-1900 (Sun and holidays between 0845 and 1930), US$3, 1½ hrs; Transaustral, Sgto Aldea 348, 4 a day; Don Carlos taxi-bus, 8 a day, US$3. Transaustral and La Cascada have daily buses between Coyhaique and Puerto Chacabuco. **Ferries** Transmarchilay's *Colono* runs from Puerto Chacabuco via the Canal Moraleda to Puerto Montt, Mon 1400 and Wed 2200, 26 hrs, all year service (fares under Puerto Montt); meals are available. From Jan to early March the ship also makes an excursion from Puerto Chacabuco to Laguna San Rafael each Sat at 2100, returning Mon 0800 (fares, inc food, US$105-225 pp, ranging from economy class to cabin). Transmarchilay's *Pincoya* sails to Quellón on Chiloé Sun 1600, all year round (fares under Quellón) stopping at Melinka and Puerto Aguirre. Navimag's *Evangelistas* sails each Thur and Sun from Puerto Chacabuco to Puerto Montt, taking about 24 hrs (fares under Puerto Montt, the *pionero* seats are quite spacious and comfortable and there is a cafeteria selling burgers, sandwiches, soft drinks, beer, hot beverages, etc); it too diverts from its schedule in summer to run a 5-day trip to Laguna San Rafael, leaving Sat, from US$250. See under Puerto Montt **Shipping** for *Patagonia Express*. **Shipping Offices: Agemar**, Tte Merino 909, T 332716, Puerto Aisén; **Navimag**, Terminal de Transbordadores, Puerto Chacabuco, T 351111, F 351192; **Transmarchilay**, Av O'Higgins s/n, T 351144, Puerto Chacabuco. It is best to make reservations in these companies' offices in Puerto Montt, Coyhaique or Santiago (or, for Transmarchilay, in Chaitén or Ancud). For trips to Laguna San Rafael, see below; out of season, they are very difficult to arrange, but try Edda Espinosa, Sgto Aldea 943, or ask at *Restaurant Yaney Ruca* or *Restaurant Munich*.

SOUTH OF COYHAIQUE

The southernmost section of the Carretera Austral, 443 km, currently ends at Puerto Yungay. Branch roads run off to Balmaceda and Puerto Ibáñez and Chile Chico on Lago General Carrera. The section around the W of Lago Gen Carrera is reckoned by some to be the most spectacular.

El Blanco (Km 35) is a hamlet with *pensión* at *Restaurant El Blanco* (or **F** pp *El Nuevo* – breakfast extra) and shop. At Km 41 a branch road runs E to **Balmaceda** on the Argentine frontier at Paso Huemules (no accommodation). Chilean immigration is open May-July 0800-2100, Sept-April 0700-2100.

● **Transport Air** Balmaceda airport is used by LanChile, Ladeco and National for flights from Santiago via Puerto Montt for Coyhaique. Taxi from airport to Coyhaique, 1 hr, US$6, minibus US$4.50. **Buses** Daily to Coyhaique, 0800, US$1.70.

LAGO GENERAL CARRERA

Straddling the frontier, Lago General Carrera (Lago Buenos Aires in Argentina), covers 2,240 sq km. Sheltered from the prevailing W winds by the Campo de Hielo Norte, the region prides itself in having the best climate in Southern Chile with some 300 days of sunshine; much fruit is grown as a result especially around Chile Chico. Rainfall is very low for this area. The main towns, Puerto Ibáñez on the N shore and Chile Chico on the S, are connected by a ferry, the *Pilchero*. There are two alternative routes to Chile Chico: through Argentina or on the Carretera Austral which runs W around the lake.

Puerto Ibáñez (*Pop* 800), the principal port on the Chilean section of the lake, is reached by taking a branch road, 31 km long, from the Carretera Austral 97 S of Coyhaique. There are some fine waterfalls, the Salto Río Ibáñez, 6 km N.

● **Accommodation E** pp *Ibáñez*, Bertrán Dixon 31, T 423227 clean, warm, hot water; **D** *Hostería Doña Amalia*, Bajada Río Ibáñez. Fuel (sold in 5 litre containers) available at Luis A Bolados 461 (house with 5 laburnum trees outside).

● **Transport Minibus**: to Coyhaique, 2½ hrs, US$7. There is a road to Perito Moreno, Argentina, but no public transport. **Ferries** The car ferry, *El Pilchero*, sails between Puerto Ibáñez and Chile Chico, 4 times a week. Fares for cars US$33, for passengers US$3.50, 2¾ hr crossing, bicycles US$2.50. Number of passengers limited to 70; reservations possible (Sotramin, Portales 99, Coyhaique, T 234240). Buses and jeeps meet the ferry in Puerto Ibáñez for Coyhaique. The *Chelenco* has regular sailings, carrying vehicles only (passengers stay in their cars), schedules and fares from 21 de Mayo 417, Coyhaique, T/F 233367.

From the turning to Puerto Ibáñez the Carretera Austral goes through Villa Cerro Castillo (Km 8) which has a small supermarket and three *residenciales* (inc one at Aguirre Cerda 35, **D** with good meals). The **Reserva Nacional Cerro Castillo** nearby, is named after the fabulous mountain (2,675m), which looks like a fairytale castle, with pinnacles jutting out of thick snow. The park includes several other peaks in the northern wall of the Río Ibáñez valley. *Guardería* on the Senda Ibáñez, opp Laguna Chinguay, open Nov-Mar, camping US$4. The Carretera climbs out of the valley, passing the aptly-named Laguna Verde and the Portezuelo Cofré. It descends to the boggy Manso valley, with a good campsite at the bridge over the river, watch out for mosquitoes.

Bahía Murta, 5 km off the Carretera, lies at Km 198, on the northern tip of the central 'arm' of Lago General Carrera. From here the road follows the lake's western shore; the colour of the water is an unbelievable blue-green, reflecting the mountains that surround it and the clouds above.

● **Accommodation E** pp *Res Patagonia*, Pasaje España; **E** pp *Hostería Lago Gen Carrera*, Av 5 de Abril, welcoming, excellent meals, also has cabin with own stove; free camping by lake, good view of Cerro Castillo.

Río Tranquilo, Km 223, is where the buses stop for lunch: fuel is available at the ECA store from a large drum (no sign).

● **Accommodation D** pp *Res Los Pinos*, 2 Oriente 41, basic; **D/E** pp *Cabañas Jacricalor*, 1 Sur s/n; **E** pp *Res Carretera Austral*, 1 Sur 223.

El Maitén, Km 273, is at the SW tip of Lago Gen Carrera: here a road branches off E along the S shore of the lake towards Chile Chico (see below). South of El Maitén the Carretera Austral becomes steeper and more bendy (in winter this stretch, all the way to Cochrane, is icy and dangerous). **Puerto Bertrand**, Km 284, is a good place for fishing. Nearby is a sign to the Nacimiento del Río Baker: the place where the Río Baker is reckoned to begin.

● **Accommodation A3** *Hostería Campo Baker; Casa de Huéspedes*, dormitory accommodation; one small shop.

Beyond the road climbs up to high moorland, passing the confluence of the Rios Neff and Baker, before winding into Cochrane. The scenery is splendid all the way; in the main the road is rough but not treacherous. Watch out for cattle on the road and take blind corners slowly.

South Coast of Lago Gen Carrera At **Puerto Guadal**, 10 km E of El Maitén, there are shops, a post office and petrol.

● **Accommodation & places to eat E** pp *Hostería Huemules*, Magnolia 382, T 411212, with breakfast, good views; **E** pp *Res Maitén*, Las Magnolias. *Restaurant La Frontera*, Los Lirios y Los Pinos.

Further E are the villages of Mallín Grande and **Fachinal** (people will let you stay for free if you have a sleeping bag). Parts of this road were built into the rock face, giving superb views, but also dangerous, unprotected precipices.

CHILE CHICO

(*Pop* 2,200) A quiet, friendly but dusty town on the lake shore which has an annual festival at end-January.

● **Accommodation B** *Hostería de la Patagonia*, Camino Internacional s/n, full board, excellent food, English, French and Italian spoken, trekking, horse-riding and white-water rafting (Casilla 91, Chile Chico, XI Region,

T 411337, F 411444), rec; **E** pp *Casa Quinta No me Olvides/Manor House Don't Forget Me*, *hospedaje* and camping, Camino Internacional s/n, cooking facilities, warm, bathrooms, hot showers, honey, eggs, fruit and vegetables for sale, rec, tours arranged to Lago Jeinimeni and Cueva de las Manos; **E** pp *Plaza*, O'Higgins y Balmaceda, basic, rec; **E** pp *Hosp Don Luis*, Balmaceda 175, meals available. **Camping**: free campsite at Bahía Jarra, 15 km E.

● **Places to eat** Apart from *Residenciales*: *Cafetería Elizabeth y Loly* on Plaza serves coffee and delicious ice-cream and cakes. Supermarket on B O'Higgins.

● **Banks & money changers** It is very difficult to change dollars (*Café Elizabeth y Loly* changes dollars at bank rate in small amounts); change Argentine pesos in shops and cafés on main street (very poor rates).

● **Tourist offices** On O'Higgins; ask here or at the Municipalidad for help in arranging tours.

● **Transport Minibuses**: are run by 3 companies along the S side of the lake between Chile Chico and Puerto Guadal, up to 3 times a week each, US$9. These connect in Puerto Guadal with Pudú service for Cochrane. Minibus to Coyhaique, frequency varies, US$9, 2¾ hrs. Flights to/from Coyhaique (see above).

FRONTIER WITH ARGENTINA: CHILE CHICO

● **Chilean immigration**
open Sept-April 0700-2300, May-Aug 0800-2100.

● **Transport**
Minibuses run from Chile Chico to Los Antiguos on the Argentine side, US$3, ¾ hr inc formalities, ask around for times; from here connections can be made to Perito Moreno and to Caleta Olivia on the coast.

Reserva Nacional Lago Jeinimeni

J M Bibby (The Wirral) writes: "60 km S of Chile Chico lies the **Reserva Nacional Lago Jeinimeni**, covering breathtaking snow-capped peaks, impressive cliffs, waterfalls, small glaciers and Lakes Jeinimeni and Verde. The reserve contains huemul deer, pumas and condors. Activities include fishing for salmon and rainbow trout, trekking and rowing. A good map is essential. Entrance fee US$1, camping US$2.75 (take all your requirements). Access only between Nov and Mar owing to high river levels. Lifts may be possible from Chile Chico: try Juan

Núñez, Hernán Trizzando 110, for a lift on a timber truck, or ask in the Conaf office."

The country to the S and W of Chile Chico, with weird rock formations and dry brush-scrub, provides good walking for the mountaineer.

COCHRANE

(*Pop* 2,000) 343 km S of Coyhaique, **Cochrane** sits in a hollow on the Río Cochrane. It is a simple place, sunny in summer, good for walking and fishing. The **Reserva Nacional Lago Cochrane**, which surrounds Lago Cochrane, 12 km E, includes a few surviving huemules (deer). Campsite at Playa Vidal. Northeast of Cochrane is the **Reserva Nacional Tamango**, with lenga forest and guanaco, foxes and lots of birds including woodpeckers and hummingbirds. It is inaccessible in the four winter months. Ask in the Conaf office on the square (T 422164) about visiting because some access is through private land and tourist facilities are rudimentary, entry US$1. The views from the reserve are superb, over the town, the nearby lakes and to the Campo de Hielo Norte to the west.

● **Accommodation** **B** pp *Hostería Wellmann*, Las Golondrinas 36, T 522171, comfortable, warm, good meals, rec; **D** pp *Res Rubio*, Tte Merino 04, T 522173, Sra Elva Rubio, very nice, breakfast inc, lunch and dinner extra; **E** pp *Res Austral Sur*, Sra Sonia Salazar, Prat s/n, T 522150, breakfast inc, also very nice; **D** *Residencia Cero a Cero*, Lago Brown 464, T 522158, with breakfast, welcoming. In summer it is best to book rooms in advance. **Camping**: ask for Washington Baez, speaks English.

● **Places to eat** *Belén*, Esmeralda 301; *Café* at Tte Merino 502.

● **Transport** Bus company agencies: Pudú at *Botillería Los Ñadis* on Tte Merino; Don Carlos, *Res Austral Sur*; Río Baker Taxis, Río Colonia. All run 3 buses a week to Coyhaique, US$23. To Vagabundo on the Río Baker (102 km, 21 km from Puerto Yungay) Los Ñadis, Los Helechos 490, T 522196, and Acuario 13, several weekly, Tues departure connects with launch to Tortel. Los Ñadis also goes to San Lorenzo, on the Río del Salto close to Argentine border. Petrol is available, if it hasn't run out, at the Empresa Comercial Agrícola (ECA) and at the Copec station. Horses can be hired for excursions in the surrounding countryside, ask around, eg at *Hostería Wellmann*.

To Argentina: 17 km N of Cochrane, a road through Villa Chacabuco and Paso Roballos (78 km), enters Argentina and continues to Bajo Caracoles); no public transport, road passable in summer but often flooded in spring. If hitching, allow a week.

SOUTH OF COCHRANE

The Carretera Austral has been constructed a further 122 km S of Cochrane to Puerto Yungay, with 50 km of the final stretch to Villa O'Higgins completed. En route, it bypasses **Tortel** (*pop* 403), a village built on a hill at the mouth of the Río Baker. It has no streets, no proper plan, only wooden walkways ('no hay ni una bicicleta'). It trades in wood with Punta Arenas and fishes for shellfish (such as *centolla* and *loco*). From here you can hire a boat to the **Glaciar Jorge Montt**; contact Don Juan Nahuel by leaving a phone message at the Municipality in Tortel or by Radio Santa María in Coyhaique or Cochrane. Three day trip, US$250, take sleeping bag, also one day trips.

● **Accommodation** Ask for Doña Berta Muñoz, **D** pp full board. "Expect fresh mutton meals and if you are squeamish about seeing animals killed don't look out of the window when they butcher the 2 lambs a day on the front porch." Carrie Wittner.

● **Transport Air** Don Carlos five-seater plane (every Wed from Cochrane, US$12, book well in advance). **Land** By horse, mountain bike or on foot, several days journey from Cochrane on a good track by the Río Baker (several river crossings by boat). **Boat** From Vagabundo, 1½-2½ hrs, book in advance. Hire of private boat, US$85. Or by kayak down the Río Baker.

PARQUE NACIONAL LAGUNA SAN RAFAEL

Some 150 nautical miles S of Puerto Aisén is the **Laguna San Rafael**, into which flows a glacier, 30m above sea level, and 45 km in length. It calves small icebergs, carried out to sea by wind and tide. The thick vegetation on the shores, with snowy peaks above, is typical of Aisén. The glacier is one of a group of four that flow in all directions from Monte San Valentín. This icefield is part of the **Parque Nacional Laguna San Rafael** (1.74 million ha), regulated by Conaf.

Park entry fee is US$4.65. At the glacier there is a small ranger station which gives information; a pier and two paths have been built. One path leads to the glacier. The rangers are willing to row you out to the glacier in calm weather, a 3-hr trip.

Robert af Sandeberg (Lidingö, Sweden) describes this journey as follows: "The trip in the rowboat is an awesome venture. At first it is fairly warm and easy to row. Gradually it gets colder when the wind sweeps over the icy glacier (be sure to take warm clothes – a thick sweater, and waterproof jacket are rec – Ed). It gets harder to row as small icebergs hinder the boat. Frequently somebody has to jump onto an icefloe and push the boat through. The glacier itself has a deep blue colour, shimmering and reflecting the light; the same goes for the icebergs, which are an unreal, translucent blue. The glacier is very noisy; there are frequent cracking and banging sounds, resembling a mixture of gun shots and thunder. When a hunk of ice breaks loose, a huge swell is created and the icebergs start rocking in the water. Then great care and effort has to be taken to avoid the boat being crushed by the shifting icebergs; this is a very real danger."

In the national park are puma, pudú (miniature deer), foxes, dolphins, occasional sealions and sea otters, and many species of bird. Walking trails are limited (about 10 km in all) but a lookout platform has been constructed, with fine views of the glacier.

● **Transport** The only way there is by plane or by boat: Air Taxi from Coyhaique (Don Carlos), US$110 each if party of 5; some pilots in Puerto Aisén will fly to the glacier for about US$95, but many are unwilling to land on the rough airstrip. The glacier is best seen from the sea: the official cruises are: *Skorpios I* and *II* (see under Puerto Montt); Navimag's *Evangelistas* and Transmarchilay's *Colono* (see under Pto Chacabuco); *Patagonia Express* a catamaran which runs from Puerto Chacabuco to Laguna San Rafael via Termas de Puyuhuapi, in tours lasting 4-6 days, from Puerto Montt over Coyhaique including the catamaran service, the hotel stay at Termas de Puyuhuapi and the day excursion to Laguna San Rafael (see page 795); *Pamar*, Pacheco Altamirano 3100, T 256220, Puerto Montt, Sept-Mar only; Compañía Naviera Puerto Montt has 2 vessels: the *Quellón*, with 6-day, 6-night tours to the Laguna from Puerto Montt via various ports and channels (US$900 not inc flight from Santiago); Puerto Montt, Diego Portales 882, T/F 252547; Puerto Chacabuco T 351106. *Odisea* and *Visun*, motorized sailing boats, Dec to Mar, in Santiago, Alameda B O'Higgins 108, local 120, T 633-0883, in Puerto Aisén, Sgto Aldea 679, T 332908, 6-day trips from Puerto Chacabuco to Laguna San Rafael. Private yachts can be chartered in Puerto Montt for 6-12 passengers to Laguna San Rafael. Local fishing boats from Chacabuco/Puerto Aisén take about 18-20 hrs each way, charging the same as the tourist boats. Ask for Jorge Prado, or Sr Ocuña at the port; Andino Royas, Cochrane 129; Justiniano Aravena, Dr Steffen 703; Rodrigo Azúcar, Agemar office, T 332716. **NB** These unauthorized boats may not have adequate facilities; check with the Gobernación Marítima in Puerto Aisén that the boat is licensed for the trip.

Chilean Patagonia

THE GLACIAL regions of southern Patagonia and Chilean Tierra del Fuego. Punta Arenas and Puerto Natales are the two main towns, the latter being the gateway to the Torres del Paine and Balmaceda national parks. In summer, a region for climbing, hiking, boats trips and the southernmost crossings to Argentina.

Land and climate

Magallanes (XII Región), which includes the Chilean part of Tierra del Fuego, has 17.5% of Chile's total area, but it is inhabited by under 1% of Chile's population.

In summer the weather is most variable, with temperatures seldom rising above 15°C. In winter snow covers the country, except those parts near the sea, making many roads more or less impassable, except on horseback. Strong, cold, piercing winds blow, particularly during the spring, when they may exceed 100 km an hour. The dry winds parch the ground and prevent the growth of crops, except in sheltered spots and greenhouses. When travelling in this region, protection against the sun's ultraviolet rays is essential.

For much of this century, sheep breeding was the most important industry, before being replaced after 1945 by oil.

Although oil production has ceased, large quantities of natural gas are now produced and coal is mined near Punta Arenas. Sheep farming continues to be important: about 50% of all Chilean sheep are in the Magallanes region. Tourism is growing rapidly, making an increasingly important contribution to the area's economy.

PUNTA ARENAS

(*Pop* 110,000; *Phone code* 061) The most southerly city in Chile, and capital of XII Región, 2,140 km S of Santiago, lies on the eastern shore of the Brunswick Peninsula facing the Straits of Magellan at almost equal distance from the Pacific and Atlantic oceans. It is a centre for the local sheep farming and fishing industries and exports wool, skins, and frozen meat. It is also the home of La Polar, the most southerly brewery in the world. Although it has expanded rapidly, particularly in recent years, it remains tranquil and pleasant. Several new hotels have been built in response to increased tourism. Good roads connect the city with Puerto Natales, 247 km N, and with Río Gallegos in Argentina. Punta Arenas has certain free-port facilities; the Zona Franca is 3½ km N of the centre, on the righthand side of the road to the airport. **NB** Calle Pedro Montt runs E-W, while Calle Jorge Montt runs N-S.

Places of interest

Around the **Plaza Muñoz Gamero** are a number of former mansions of the great sheep ranching families of the late 19th century. See the **Palacio Sara Braun**, which dates from 1895. In the centre of the plaza is a statue of Magellan with a mermaid and 2 Fuegian Indians at his feet. According to local wisdom those who rub the big toe of one of the Indians will return to Punta Arenas. Just N of the plaza on C Magallanes are the **Palacio Braun Menéndez** (see below) and the **Teatro Cervantes** (now a cinema): the interiors of both are worth a visit. Further N, at Av Bulnes 929, is the **Cemetery**, even more fantastic than the one at Castro (Chiloé), with a **statue of Indiecito**, the little Indian

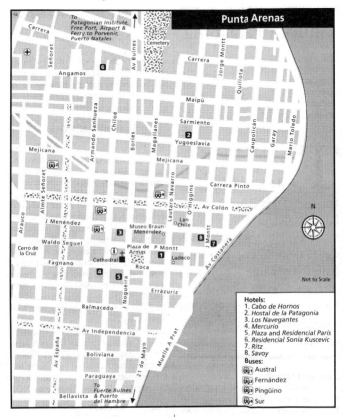

Punta Arenas

Hotels:
1. Cabo de Hornos
2. Hostal de la Patagonia
3. Los Navegantes
4. Mercurio
5. Plaza and Residencial París
6. Residencial Sonia Kuscevic
7. Ritz
8. Savoy

Buses:
1. Austral
2. Fernández
3. Pingüino
4. Sur

Not to Scale

(now also an object of reverence, bedecked with flowers, the left knee well-rubbed, NW side of the cemetery), cypress avenues, and many memorials to pioneer families and victims of shipping disasters (open 0800-1800 daily).

East of the Plaza Muñoz Gamero on C Fagnano is the **Mirador Cerro de La Cruz** offering a view over the city. Nearby on Waldo Seguel are two reminders of the British influence: the **British School** and **St James' Church** next door. The **Parque María Behety**, S of town along 21 de Mayo, features a scale model of Fuerte Bulnes and a campsite, popular for Sun picnics.

Museums

Museo Regional Salesiano Mayorino Borgatello, in the Colegio Salesiano, Av Bulnes 374, entrance next to church, covering history of the indigenous peoples, sections on local animal and bird life, and other interesting aspects of life in Patagonia and Tierra del Fuego, excellent. Tues-Sat 1000-1200 and 1500-1800, Sun 1500-1800, hours change frequently (entry US$1.25). **Museo de Historia Regional Braun Menéndez**, Magallanes 949, off Plaza de Armas, T 244216, located in the former mansion of Mauricio Braun, built in 1905, recommended. Part is set out as room-by-room regional history, the rest of the house is furnished (guided tours in Spanish only). Closed Mon, otherwise open 1100-1600 (summer) and 1100-1300 (winter, entry US$1), free booklet in English. The **Instituto de la Patagonia**, Av Bulnes Km 4 N (opp the University), T 244216, has an open air museum with artefacts used by the early settlers, pioneer homes, a naval museum and botanical gardens. Outdoor exhibits open Mon-Fri 0800-1800, indoor pavillions: 0830-1115, 1500-1800. **Naval and Maritime Museum**, Pedro Montt 981, open Mon-Fri 0930-1230, 1500-1800, Sat 1000-1300, 1500-1800.

Excursions

The **Reserva Forestal Magallanes**, 7 km W of town and known locally as the Parque Japonés, extends over 13,500 ha and rises to 600m. There is a self-guided nature trail, 1 km, free leaflet. The 14 km road through the woods, passes several small campgrounds. From the top end of the road a short path leads to a lookout over the Garganta del Diablo (Devil's Throat),

a gorge formed by the Río de las Minas, with views over Punta Arenas and Tierra del Fuego. From here a slippery path leads down to the Río de las Minas valley and thence back to Punta Arenas. Administration at Conaf in Punta Arenas. *Turismo Pali Aike* offers tours to the park, US$ 3.75 pp.

Local information

● **Accommodation**

Most hotels include breakfast in the room price. Hotel prices are substantially lower during winter months (April-Sept).

L2 *Hotel José Nogueira*, Plaza de Armas, Bories 959 y P Montt, in former Palacio Sara Braun, T 248840, F 248855, beautiful loggia, good food, lovely atmosphere, rec; **L3** *Cabo de Hornos*, Plaza Muñoz Gamero 1025, T/F 242134, rec; **L3** *Finis Terrae*, Colón 766, T 228200, F 248124, modern, some rooms small but all very nice, safe in room, rooftop café/bar with lovely views, parking; **L3** *Isla Rey Jorge*, 21 de Mayo 1243, T 222681, F 248220, modern, pleasant, pub downstairs; **L3** *Los Navegantes*, José Menéndez 647, T 244677, F 247545; **L3** *Tierra del Fuego*, Colón 716, T/F 226200, good breakfast, parking, rec, *Café 1900* downstairs.

A2 *Hostería Yaganes,* Camino Antiguo Norte Km 7.5, T 211600, F 211948, cabins on the Straits of Magellan, nice setting; **A1-A2** *Apart Hotel Colonizadores,* Colón 1106, T 243578, F 244499, fully furnished apartments (2 bedrooms **A1**, 1 bedroom **A2**) discounts for long stay; **A3** *Hostal de la Patagonia,* O'Higgins 478, T 241079, **B** without bath, good breakfast, excellent; **A3** *Hostal Carpa Manzano,* Lautaro Navarro 336, T/F 248864, rec; **A3** *Cóndor de Plata,* Colón 556, T 247987, F 241149, very good; **A3** *Mercurio,* Fagnano 595, T/F 242300, good restaurant and service, rec; **A3** *Plaza,* Nogueira 1116, p 2, T 241300, F 248613 (**B** without bath), pleasant, good breakfast.

B *Savoy,* Menéndez 1073, T 241951, F 247979, pleasant rooms but some lack windows, good place to eat; **B** *Ritz,* Pedro Montt 1102, T 224422, old, cosy, rec; **C** *Res Central,* No 1 España 247, T 222315, No 2 Sanhueza 185, T 222845, **D** without bath, comfortable; **B** *Chalet Chapital,* Sanhueza 974, T 242237, F 225698 (cheaper without bath), comfortable, doubles only, welcoming; **B** *Hostal de la Avenida,* Colón 534, T 247532, good breakfast, safe, rec.

C *Albatros,* Colón 1195, T 223131, without bath, good; **C** *Res Sonia Kuscevic,* Pasaje Darwin 175 (Angamos altura 550), T 248543, popular, IYHA accepted, with breakfast, heating, parking.

D *Casa Dinka,* Caupolicán 169, T 226056, with breakfast, use of kitchen, noisy, very popular; **D** pp *Res Roca,* Roca 1038, T 243903, without bath; **D** pp *Res Rubio,* España 640, T 226458, helpful. Accommodation available in many private houses, usually E pp, ask at tourist office; **D** *Hosp Lodging,* Sanhueza 933, T 221035, good value, heating, modern; **D** *Sra Carolina Ramírez,* Paraguaya 150, T 247687, hot water, safe motorcycle parking, meals, rec.

E pp Caupolicán 99, T 222436, with breakfast; **E** pp *Casa Deportista,* O'Higgins 1205, T 225205, F 243438, cheap meals, cooking facilities, dormitory style, noisy; **E** pp *Casa Roxas,* Angamos 971, very good, with bath; **E** pp *Hostal Paradiso,* Angamos 1073, T 224212, with bath, breakfast, parking, use of kitchen, rec; **E** pp *Backpackers' Paradise,* Carrera Pinto 839, T 222554, F 226863, popular, large dormitories, cooking facilities, limited bathroom facilities, good meeting place, luggage store, rec; **E** pp *Sra Lenka,* José Miguel Carrera 1270, heating, use of kitchen, rec; **E** *Nena's,* Boliviana 366, T 242411, with breakfast, highly rec; **E** pp, España y Boliviana, T 247422, without bath, use of kitchen; **E** Sanhueza 750, homely, rec.

F pp *Alojamiento Prat,* Sgto Aldea 0520, rec; **F** pp Sanhueza 712, T 225127, basic, use of kitchen; **F** pp Bellavista 577, dormitory accommodation, kitchen, hot showers.

Camping: in Reserva Forestal Magallanes (no public transport, see **Excursions** above). *Camping Pudú,* 10.5 km N on Route 9, G pp, pleasant, good facilities.

● **Places to eat**

Main hotels: good value set lunches and dinners at *Cabo de Hornos,* excellent restaurants at *Los Navegantes* and *José Nogueira.*

Many places closed on Sun. *El Mercado,* Mejicana 617, open 24 hrs, reasonably-priced set lunch, expensive a la carte; *Centro Español,* Plaza Muñoz Gamero 771, above Teatro Cervantes, large helpings, limited selection, reasonably priced; *El Mesón del Calvo,* Jorge Montt 687, excellent, pricey; seafood at *Sotitos,* O'Higgins 1138, good service and cuisine, rec; *La Mama,* Sanhueza 700 block, little Argentine-style pasta house, rec; *Lucerna,* Bories 624, excellent meat, reasonably priced; *Dino's Pizza,* Bories 557, cheap, good, big pizzas; *Café Garogha,* Bories 817, open Sun pm, busy at night, smoky; *Bianco's Pizza,* Bulnes 1306, excellent pizzas; *El Quijote,* Lautaro Navarro 1087, good sandwiches, highly rec; *Asturias,* Lautaro Navarro 967, good food and atmosphere; *Venus,* Pedro Montt 1046, good food, service and atmosphere, reasonable prices; *La Casa de Juan,* O'Higgins 1021, Spanish food; *El Estribo,* Carrera Pinto 762, good grill, also fish; *Yaganes,* Camino Antiguo Norte Km 7.5, beautiful setting, weekend buffet; *Golden Dragon,* Colón 529, Chinese, good, expensive; *La Terraza,* 21 de Mayo 1288, sandwiches, empanadas and beer, cheap and good; *La Taberna del Club de la Unión,* Plaza Muñoz Gamero y Seguel, for drinks. For economic set lunches several along Chiloé: *Restaurant de Turismo Punta Arenas,* No 1280, good; *Los Años 60 The Mitchel,* No 1231, also serves beer and 26 varieties of sandwiches, open 24 hrs; *Parrilla Apocalipsis,* Chiloé esq Balmaceda; *Carioca,* Menéndez 600 esq Chiloé, parrilla, snacks and beer; *Lomit's,* Menéndez 722, cheap snacks and drinks, open when the others are closed; *Kiosco Roca* (no sign), Roca 875, early morning coffee. Cheap fish meals available at stalls in the *Cocinerías,* Lautaro Navarro S of the port entrance. Excellent *empanadas,* bread and pastries at *Pancal,* 21 de Mayo 1280; also at *La Espiga,* Errázuriz 632; excellent pastries at *Casa del Pastel,* Carrera Pinto y O'Higgins. Lobster has become more expensive because of a law allowing only lobster pots. *Centolla* (king crab) is caught illegally by some fishermen using dolphin, porpoise and penguin as live bait. There are seasonal bans on *centolla* fishing to protect dwindling stocks, do not purchase *centolla* out of season. At times *centolla* fishing is banned if the crabs are infected with a disease which is fatal to humans. If *marea roja* (red tide) occurs, bivalve shellfish must not be eaten. Mussels should not be picked along the shore owing to pollution and the *marea roja*.

● **Airline offices**
LanChile, Lautaro Navarro 999, T 241232, F 222366; **Ladeco**, Lautaro Navarro 1155, T/F 241100/223340. **National**, Bories 701, T 221634. **Aerovías DAP**, O'Higgins 899, T 223340, F 221693, open 0900-1230, 1430-1930; **Kaiken**, Magallanes 974, T 242134 ext 106, F 241321.

● **Banks & money changers**
Banks open Mon-Fri 0830-1400. *Casas de cambio* open Mon-Fri 0900-1230, 1500-1900, Sat 0900-1230; outside business hours try *Buses Sur*, Colón y Magallanes, kiosk at *Garogha Café*, Bories 817 and the major hotels (lower rates). **Fincard** (Mastercard), Pedro Montt 837, T 247864, Mon-Fri 0900-1400, 1530-1730. **Banco Concepción**, Magallanes y Menéndez, for Visa. **Banco O'Higgins**, Plaza de Armas, changes TCs, no commission. Argentine pesos can be bought at *casas de cambio*. Good rates at *Cambio Gasic*, Roca 915, Oficina 8, T 242396, German spoken; *La Hermandad*, Lautaro Navarro 1099, T 243991, excellent rates, US$ cash for Amex TCs; *Sur Cambios*, Lautaro Navarro 1001, T 225656 accepts TCs. *Kiosco Redondito*, Mejicana 613 in the shopping centre, T 247369.

● **Embassies & consulates**
Argentina, 21 de Mayo 1878, T 261912, open 1000-1400, visas take 24 hrs, US$25; **Brazil**, Arauco 769, T 241093; **Belgium**, Roca 817, Oficina 61, T 241472; **Britain**, Roca 924, T 247020; **Denmark**, Colón 819, Depto 301, T 221488; **Holland**, Sarmiento 780, T 248100; **Finland**, Independencia 660, T 247385; **Germany**, Pasaje Korner 1046, T 241082, Casilla 229; **Italy**, 21 de Mayo 1569, T 242497; **Norway**, Independencia 830, T 242171; **Spain**, J Menéndez 910, T 243566; **Sweden**, Errazúriz 891, T 224107.

● **Entertainment**
Discotheques: discos in the city centre often have a young crowd: *Gallery*, J Menéndez 750, T 247555; *Yordi*, Pedro Montt 937; *Borssalino*, Bories 587. On the outskirts of town, to the S: *Club Boulevard*, Km 5.5, T 265807; *Torreones*, Km 5.5, T 261985; *Salsoteca*, Km 5. To the N: *Drive-In Los Brujos*, Km 7.5, T 212600; *Salsoteca*, Km 6.

Nightlife: *The Queen's Club*, 21 de Mayo 1455. Lots of *Whiskerias*.

● **Hospitals & medical services**
Dentists: *Dr Hugo Vera Cárcamo*, España 1518, T 227510, rec; *Rosemary Robertson Stipicic*, 21 de Mayo 1380, T 22931, speaks English.

Hospitals: *Hospital Regional Lautaro Navarro*, Angamos 180, T 244040, public hospital, for emergency room ask for *La Posta*; *Clínica Magallanes*, Bulnes 01448, T 211527, private clinic.

● **Laundry**
Lavasol, the only self-service, O'Higgins 969, T 243067, Mon-Sat 0900-2030, Sun (summer only) 1000-1800, US$6/machine, wash and dry, good but busy; *Lavaseco Josseau*, Carrera Pinto 766, T 228413; *Lavanderia Limpec*, 21 de Mayo 1261, T 241669.

● **Post & telecommunications**
Post Office: Bories 911 y J Menéndez, Mon-Fri 0830-1930, Sat 0900-1400.

Telecommunications: for international and national calls and faxes (shop around): *CTC*, Nogueira 1106, Plaza de Armas, daily 0900-2200, and Roca 886, loc 23, daily 0900-2030; *Entel*, Lautaro Navarro 957, Mon-Fri 0830-2200, Sat-Sun 0900-2200; *Telex-Chile/Chile-Sat*, Bories 911 and Errázuriz 856, daily 0830-2200, also offers telex and telegram service. *VTR*, Bories 801, closed Sat afternoon and Sun. For international calls and faxes at any hour *Hotel Cabo de Hornos*, credit cards accepted, open to non-residents.

● **Shopping**
For leather goods and sheepskin try the Zona Franca; quality of other goods is low and prices little better than elsewhere; Mon-Sat 1030-1230, 1500-2000 (bus E or A from Plaza de Armas; many colectivo taxis; taxi US$3). Handicrafts at *Pingüi*, Bories 404, *Artesanía Ramas*, Independencia 799, *Chile Típico*, Carrera Pinto 1015, *Indoamérica*, Colón y Magallanes and outdoor stalls at the bottom of Independencia, by the port entrance. **Supermarkets**: *Listo*, 21 de Mayo 1133; *Cofrima*, Lautaro Navarro 1293 y Balmaceda, *Cofrima 2*, España 01375; *Marisol*, Zenteno 0164.

Cameras: wide range of cameras but limited range of film, from Zona Franca. *Foto Arno*, Bories 893, for Kodak products. *Foto Sánchez*, Bories 768, for Fuji film and *Fotocentro*, Bories 789, for Agfa: all have same day print-processing service.

Chocolate: hand made chocolate from *Chocolatería Tres Arroyos*, Bories 448, T 241522 and *Chocolatería Regional Norweisser*, José Miguel Carrera 663, both good.

● **Sports**
Golf: 9-hole golf course 5 km S town on road to Fuerte Bulnes.

Skiing: Cerro Mirador, only 9 km W from Punta Arenas in the Reserva Nacional Magallanes, the most southerly ski resort in the world and one of the few places where one can ski with a sea view. Transtur buses 0900 and 1400 from in front of *Hotel Cabo de Hornos*, US$3, return, taxi US$7. Daily lift-ticket, US$7; equipment rental, US$6 per adult. Mid-way lodge with food, drink and equipment. Season June to Sept, weather permitting. Contact the Club Andino, T 241479, about crosscountry skiing facilities. Also skiing at Tres Morros.

● **Tour companies & travel agents**
Turismo Lazo, Angamos 1366, T/F 223771, wide range of tours, highly rec; *Turismo Aventour*, J Nogueira 1255, T 241197, F 243354, English spoken, helpful, good, specializes in fishing trips, organize tours to Tierra del Fuego. *Turismo Comapa*, Independencia 840, T 241437, F 247514, tours to Torres del Paine, Tierra del Fuego and Isla Magdalena, also trips to the Falklands/Malvinas, charter boats to Cape Horn; *Turismo Runner*, Lautaro Navarro 1065, T 247050, F 241042, adventure tours; *Arka Patagonia*, Ignacio Carrera Pinto 946, T 248167, F 241504, all types of tours, rafting, fishing, etc; *Turismo Pehoé*, Av Colón 782, T 244506, F 248052, organizes tours and hotels, enquire here about catamaran services; *Turismo Aonikenk*, Magallanes 619, T 228332, rec; *Turismo Pali Aike*, Lautaro Navarro 1129, T 223301; *El Conquistador*, Menéndez 556, T 222896, rec; *Turismo Viento Sur*, Fagnano 565, T/F 225167, for camping equipment; *Operatur Patagonica*, Pedro Montt 966, T 240513, F 241153, good for Torres del Paine, biking and trekking; *Turismo Patagonia*, Bories 655 local 2, T 248474, F 247182, specializes in fishing trips. And others. Most organize tours to Torres del Paine, Fuerte Bulnes and *pingüineras* on Otway sound: shop around as prices vary; Sr Mateo Quesada, Chiloé 1375, T 222662, offers local tours in his car, up to 5 passengers.

In-Tur is an association of companies which aims to promote tourism in Chilean Patagonia. The members are *Arka Patagonia, Turismo Aventour, Turismo Pehoé, Turismo Runner, Aerovías DAP* and *Hostería Las Torres* (in the Parque Nacional Torres del Paine). The head office is at Errázuriz 840, p 2, Punta Arenas, T/F 229049, which should be contacted for information. See **Bus services**, below, for In-Tur's SIB bus to Torres del Paine.

● **Tourist offices**
Sernatur, Waldo Seguel 689, Casilla 106-D, T 241330, at the corner with Plaza Muñoz Gamero, 0830-1745, closed Sat and Sun. Helpful, English spoken. Kiosk on Colón between

Bories and Magallanes Mon-Fri 0900-1300, 1500-1900, Sat 0900-1200, 1430-1730, Sun (in the summer only) 1000-1230. Turistel Guide available from kiosk belonging to *Café Garogha* at Bories 831. **Conaf**, Menéndez 1147, p 2, T 223841, open Mon-Fri.

● **Transport**
NB All transport is heavily booked from Christmas through to March: advance booking strongly advised.

Local Car hire: Hertz, Colón 798 and Carrera Pinto 770, T 248742, F 244729; **Australmag**, Colón 900, T 242174, F 226916; **Autómovil Club**, O'Higgins 931, T 243675, F 243097, and at airport; **Budget**, O'Higgins 964, T 241696; **Internacional**, Sarmiento 790-B, T 228323, F 226334, rec; **Willemsen**, Lautaro Navarro 1038, T 247787, F 241083, highly rec; **Lubac**, Magallanes 970, T/F 242023/247060; **Todoauto**, España 0480, T 212492, F 212627. **NB** You need a hire company's authorization to take a car into Argentina. **Car repair**: *Automotores del Sur*, O'Higgins 850, T 224153. **Taxis**: ordinary taxis have yellow roofs. Collective taxis (all black) run on fixed routes, US$0.25 for anywhere on route. Reliable service from *Radio Taxi Austral*, T 247710/244409.

Air Carlos Ibáñez de Campo Airport, 15 km N of town. Bus service by Austral Bus, J Menéndez 565, T 247139, T/F 241708, between the airport and Plaza Muñoz Gamero scheduled to meet flights, US$2.50. LanChile, DAP and Ladeco have their own bus services from town, US$2.50; taxi US$10. The airport restaurant is good. To **Santiago**, LanChile, Ladeco, DAP and National daily US$220, via Puerto Montt (sit on right for views), some National flights also stop in Concepción. When no tickets are available, go to the airport and get on the standby waiting list. To **Porvenir**, Aerovías DAP daily at 0815 and 1750, return 0830 and 1750 (US$20), plus other irregular flights, with Twin-Otter and Cessna aircraft. (Heavily booked with long waiting list so make sure you have your return reservation confirmed.) Military (FACh) flights approx twice a month to Puerto Montt US$30, information and tickets from airforce base at the airport, Spanish essential, T 213559; need to book well in advance. It is very difficult to get space during the summer as all armed forces personel and their families have priority over civilians.

Services to Argentina: To Ushuaia, Aerovías DAP twice a week, also Kaiken in summer (schedules change frequently). To Río Grande, Kaiken 5 a week. Reserve well in advance from mid-Dec to February.

Buses Company offices: Pingüino, Sanhueza 745, T 242313, F 225984; **Fernández**, Almte Señoret y Carrera Pinto; **Ghisoni**, Lautaro Navarro 975, T 223205; **Pacheco**, Colón 900,

T 242174; **Bus Sur**, Colón y Magallanes, T 244464; **Austral Bus**, Menéndez 565, T 247139, T/F 241708. **Los Carlos**, Plaza Muñoz Gamero 1039, T 241321. **Turibus**, Errázuriz 932, T/F 225315. **Gesell**, José Menéndez 556, T 222896. Bus timetables are printed daily in *La Prensa Austral*.

Bus services: buses leave from company offices. To **Puerto Natales**, 3½ hrs, Fernández, Austral Bus, and Buses Sur, several every day, last departure 1800, US$6. *In-Tur* (see **Tour companies**, above) runs a twice daily circuit Punta Arenas-Puerto Natales-Torres del Paine in minibuses with snack, English-speaking guide and inc National Park entry; service runs mid-Oct to mid-April. Turibus, Queilen/Cidher, Buses Punta Arenas and Austral have services through Argentina to **Osorno**, **Puerto Montt** and Castro. Fares: to Puerto Montt or Osorno US$60-75 (US$49 off season) 36 hrs; to Castro US$67-83; Turibus continues to **Santiago**, US$95 (US$60 in winter), 46 hrs.

To **Río Gallegos**, Argentina, Pingüino daily 1200, return 1300; Ghisoni, daily except Fri, 1000; Mansilla Fri 1000, Magallanes Tour, Tues 1000. Fares US$20-22, officially 5 hrs, but can take up to 8, depending on customs, 15 mins on Chilean side, up to 3 hrs on Argentine side, inc 30 mins lunch at Km 160. All customs formalities now undertaken at the border, but ask before departure if this has changed (taxi to Río Gallegos US$130). To **Río Grande**, Hector Pacheco, Mon, Wed, Fri 0730 via Punta Delgada, return Tues, Thur and Sat, 0730, 10 hrs, US$30, heavily booked. To **Ushuaia** via Punta Delgada, Los Carlos, Tues and Sat, 0700, return Mon and Fri, 0300, 14 hrs, US$48, book any return at same time. Alternatively, Tecni Austral runs daily from Río Grande to Ushuaia at 0730 and 1800, 4 hrs, US$20.

Ferries   For services to Porvenir (Tierra del Fuego), see page 831.

Shipping Offices Navimag, Av Independencia 830, T 224256, F 225804; **Comapa** (Compañía Marítima de Punta Arenas), Independencia 830, T 244400, F 247514.

Shipping Services   For Navimag services Puerto Montt – Puerto Natales, see under Puerto Montt (confirmation of reservations is advised). Visits to the beautiful fjords and glaciers of Tierra del Fuego are highly rec. Comapa runs a once a fortnight 22-hr, 320-km round trip to the fjord d'Agostino, 30 km long, where many glaciers come down to the sea. The luxury cruiser, *Terra Australis*, sails from Punta Arenas on Sat via Ushuaia and Puerto Williams; details from Comapa. Advance booking (advisable) from Cruceros Australis SA, Miraflores 178, p 12, Santiago, T 696-3211, F 331871. Government

supply ships are rec for the young and hardy, but take sleeping bag and extra food, and travel pills. All tickets on ships must be booked in advance Jan-February.

● **To the Falkland Islands/Islas Malvinas**
Punta Arenas is now the main South American link with the islands. Aerovías DAP (address above) fly the following schedule: depart Santiago Wed 1300, arrive Punta Arenas 1600, dep 1700, arrive Mt Pleasant, Falklands/Malvinas 1815; depart Mt Pleasant Thur 1530, arrive Punta Arenas 1700, depart 1800, arrive Santiago 2100, all year. Book well in advance.

● **To Puerto Williams**
For details of sea and air service, see page 833.

● **To Antarctica**
Other than asking in agencies for possible free berths on cruise ships, the only possibility is with the Chilean Navy. The Navy itself does not encourage passengers, so you must approach the captain of the vessel direct. Spanish is essential.

● **Overland to Argentina**
From Punta Arenas there are 3 routes to Calafate and Río Gallegos: 1) NE via Route 255 and Punta Delgada to the frontier at Kimiri Aike and then along Argentine Route 3 to Río Gallegos. 2) N along Route 9, turning 9 km before Puerto Natales for Dorotea (good road) and then NE via La Esperanza (fuel, basic accommodation). 3) Via Puerto Natales and Cerro Castillo on the road to Torres del Paine joining the road to La Esperanza at Paso Cancha.

Longer Excursions

56 km S, **Fuerte Bulnes** is a replica of the wooden fort erected in 1843 by the crew of the Chilean vessel *Ancud* to secure Chile's southernmost territories after Independence. Nearby is Puerto Hambre. Tours by several agencies, US$12. At the intersection of the roads to Puerto del Hambre and Fuerte Bulnes, 51 km S of Punta Arenas, is a small marker with a plaque of the Centro Geográfico de Chile, ie the midway point between Arica and the South Pole.

53 km S, covering 18,814 ha, **Reserva Forestal Laguna Parrillar** has older forest than the Magallanes Reserve and sphagnum bogs. There is a 3-hr walk to the tree-line along poorly-marked paths. (No public transport, radio taxi US$60.)

60 km N of Punta Arenas, **Otway Sound** is the site of a small colony of Magellanic penguins which can be visited (Nov-Mar only). Visitors are only

allowed to see the penguins at a distance (there are a fence and bird-hides). Patience is required to see the birds since they nest in burrows underground, in the late afternoon they can be seen by the beach where screens have been built to facilitate viewing. Rheas and skunks can also be seen. Tours by several agencies, US$12, entry US$4; taxi US$35 return.

Isla Magdalena

A small island 25 km NE, is the location of the **Monumento Natural Los Pingüinos**, a colony of 150,000 penguins. Deserted apart from the breeding season (Nov-Jan), the island is administered by Conaf. Magdalena is one of a group of three islands (the others are Marta and Isabel), visited by Drake, whose men killed 3,000 penguins for food.

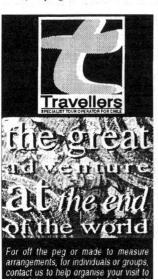

Travellers
SPECIALIST TOUR OPERATOR FOR CHILE

the great adventure at the end of the world

For off the peg or made to measure arrangements, for individuals or groups, contact us to help organise your visit to this fabulous part of the world.

Fax :+ 56 - 65 - 258555
e - mail : gochile@chilepac.net

Avenida Angelmó 2456
P.O. Box/Casilla 854. Ph. + 56 - 65 - 262099
http://www.chilepac.net/~travellers
Puerto Montt, Chile

- **Transport** Boat with Comapa (address above): Tues, Thur, Sat, 0800 (Dec-Feb), 2 hrs each way, with 2 hrs on the island, returns 1400, coffee and biscuits served, US$60, rec.

North from Punta Arenas

From Punta Arenas a gravel road runs N to Puerto Natales; beside it, the southbound lane is paved. Fuel is available in Villa Tehuelches, 100 km from Punta Arenas.

- **Accommodation** Along this road are several hotels, inc **B** *Hostal Río Penitente*, Km 138, T 331694, in an old *estancia*, rec; **C** *Hotel Rubens*, Km 183, T 226916, popular for fishing; *Hostería Llanuras de Diana*, Km 215, T 248742, F 244729 (Punta Arenas), T 411540 (Puerto Natales) hidden from road, highly rec; **C** *Hostería Río Verde*, Km 90, E off the highway on Seno Skyring, T 311122, F 241008, private bath, heating.

PUERTO NATALES

(*Pop* 15,000; *Phone code* 061) 247 km N of Punta Arenas and close to the Argentine border at Río Turbio. It stands on the Ultima Esperanza gulf amid spectacular scenery and is the jumping-off place for the magnificent Balmaceda and Torres del Paine national parks. Very quiet in the winter, packed with tourists in the summer.

Museums

Museo De Agostini, in the Colegio Salesiano at Padre Rossa 1456, 1 room, Tierra del Fuego fauna, free. **Museo Histórico Municipal**, Bulnes 285, Tues-Sun 1500-1800.

Excursions

A recommended walk is up to **Cerro Dorotea** which dominates the town, with superb views of the whole Ultima Esperanza Sound. Take any bus going E and alight at the jeep track for summit (Km 9.5).

The **Monumento Natural Cueva Milodón** (50m wide, 200m deep, 30m high), 25 km N, contains a plastic model of the prehistoric ground-sloth whose bones were found there in 1895. Evidence has also been found here of occupation by early Patagonian humans some 11,000 years ago. (Free camping once US$4 entrance fee has been paid.)

- **Transport** Buses J and B regular service US$7.50; taxi US$15 return or check if you can

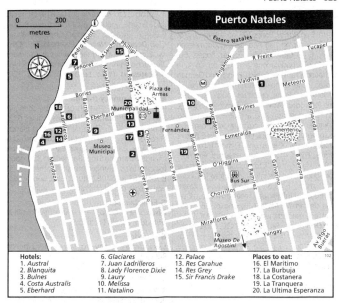

Puerto Natales

Hotels:		
1. Austral	6. Glaciares	12. Palace
2. Blanquita	7. Juan Ladrilleros	13. Res Carahue
3. Bulnes	8. Lady Florence Dixie	14. Res Grey
4. Costa Australis	9. Laury	15. Sir Francis Drake
5. Eberhard	10. Melissa	
	11. Natalino	

Places to eat:
16. El Maritimo
17. La Burbuja
18. La Costanera
19. La Tranquera
20. La Ultima Esperanza

get a ride with a tour; both Adventur and Fernández tour buses to Torres del Paine stop at the cave.

Local information
● Accommodation

In season cheaper accommodation fills up quickly after the arrival of the *Puerto Edén* from Puerto Montt. Most prices include breakfast.

L3 *Eberhard*, Pedro Montt 58, T 411208, F 411209, excellent views, restaurant; **L3** *Costa Australis*, Pedro Montt 262, T 412000, F 411881, modern, good views, popular cafeteria.

A1 *Palace*, Ladrilleros 209, T 411134, good food, overpriced; **A1** *Juan Ladrilleros*, Pedro Montt 161, modern, good restaurant, T 411652, F 412109, rec; **A2** *Glaciares*, Eberhard 104, T 412189, F 411452, new, snack bar; **A2** *Hostal Sir Francis Drake*, Phillipi 383, T/F 411553, good views, snack bar, rec; **A3** *Hostal Lady Florence Dixie*, Bulnes 659, T 411158, F 411943, modern, rec; *Martín Guisinde*, Carlos Bories 278, T 412770, F 412820, phone, TV, tourist information, parking, pub, restaurant, new.

B *Blanquita*, Carrera Pinto 409, quiet, rec; **B** *Hostal Melissa*, Blanco Encalada 258, T 411944; **B** *Natalino*, Eberhard 371, T 411968 (tours to Milodón Cave arranged); **C** without bath, parking.

C *Hostal Los Antiguos*, Ladrilleros 195 y Bulnes, T/F 411488, without bath, pleasant; **C** *Res Carahue*, Bulnes 370, T 411339, with breakfast, laundry facilities, nice; **C** *Bulnes*, C Bulnes 407, T 411307, with breakfast, good, stores luggage.

D *Lago Sarmiento*, Bulnes 90, T 411542, some rooms with heating, good dinners; **D** *Res Sutherland*, Barros Arana 155, with and without bath, welcoming, kitchen facilities.

E pp *Hosp La Chila*, Carrera Pinto 442, use of kitchen, welcoming, luggage store, bakes bread, rec; **E** pp *María José*, Magallanes 646, cooking facilities, helpful; **E** pp *Hostal Famatina*, Ladrilleros 370, T 412067; **E** pp *Hosp GammalMilodón*, El Roble 650, T 411420, cooking and laundry facilities, evening meals, tours; **E** pp *Los Inmigrantes*, Carrera Pinto 480, good breakfast, kitchen facilities, luggage store, rec; **E** pp *Res El Mundial*, Bories 315, T 412476, large breakfast, use of kitchen, good value meals, luggage stored, rec; **E** pp *Tierra del Fuego*, Bulnes 29, clean, family of Juan Osorno, stores luggage, good; **E** pp *Casa de familia Bustamante*, Bulnes 317, T 411061, good breakfast, helpful, luggage store, rec; **E** pp *Casa de familia Dickson*, Bulnes 307, T 411218, good breakfast, helpful, cooking and laundry facilities, rec; **E** pp *Pensión Ritz*, Carrera Pinto 439, full pension available; **E** pp *Res Temuco*, Ramírez 310, T 411120, reasonable, good food, clean; **E pp** *Hosp Laury*, Bulnes 222, with breakfast, cooking and laundry facilities, warm; **E pp** *Bories*, Bories 206, hostel type, use of kitchen, sleeping bag necessary, good meeting place; **E pp** *Casa Cecilia*, Tomás Rogers 60, T/F 411797, backpackers' annexe **F pp**, cooking and laundry facilities, English, French and German spoken, rents camping equipment, information on Torres del Paine, organizes tours, highly rec; **E pp** *Patagonia Adventure*, Tomás Rogers 179, T 411028, dormitory style, and private rooms, use of kitchen, breakfast, English spoken, camping equipment for hire, book exchange, rec; **E Niko's** (Gladys, Paola, Carlos and Franco Nicolás), E Ramírez 669, F 412810, with breakfast, very hospitable, family-run, kitchen facilities, luggage store, good meals, rec, information, travel arrangements made; **E pp** Sra Bruna Mardones, Pasaje Don Bosco 41 (off Philippi), meals on request; **E pp** *Casa de familia Alicia*, M Rodríguez 283, with breakfast, spacious, luggage stored, helpful, rec; **E pp** *Don Bosco*, Padre Rossa 1430, good meals, use of kitchen, helpful, rec, motorcycle parking, luggage store; **E-F pp** Sra Teresa Ruiz, Esmeralda 463, good value, warm, cheap meals, quiet, rec, tours to Torres del Paine arranged; **F pp** *Res Lago Pingo*, Bulnes 808, T 411026, basic, breakfast extra, laundry, use of kitchen, stores luggage; **F pp** private house at Magallanes 1, cheap meals.

North of Puerto Natales are: **L3-A2** *Cisne de Cuello Negro*, a former guest house for meat buyers at the disused meat packing plant, T 411498 (Av Colón 782, Punta Arenas, T 244506, F 248052), reasonable, excellent cooking, rec, 5 km from town at Km 25 nr Puerto Bories; **A2** *Patagonia Inn*, Km 26 N, reservations *Hotel Cabo de Hornos*, T/F 242134, Punta Arenas, restaurant; **C** *Hotel 3 Pasos*, 40 km N, T 228113, simple, beautiful. In Villa Cerro Castillo, 63 km N: **B** *Hostería El Pionero*, T/F 411646, country house ambience, good service. **NB** Hotels in the countryside open only in summer months: dates vary.

● **Places to eat**
Don Alvarito, Blanco Encalada 915, hospitable; *El Marítimo*, Pedro Montt 214, seafood and salmon, good views, popular, slow service; *Mari Loli*, Baquedano 615, excellent food, good value; *La Ultima Esperanza*, Eberhard 354, rec for salmon, seafood, enormous portions, not cheap but worth the experience; *La Costanera*, Bories y Ladrilleros, good food, superb views; *Andrés*, Ladrilleros 381, excellent, good service; *La Burbuja*, Bulnes 371, huge portions, reasonably priced; *Tierra del Fuego*, Bulnes 29, cheap, good, slow service; *Café Josmar*, Yungay 743, only cafe open every day, packed lunches sold for boat trips; *Nuria*, Bulnes 186, good value, family-run; *Centro Español*, Magallanes 247,

reasonable; *La Frontera*, Bulnes 819, set meals and à la carte, good value; *La Tranquera*, Bulnes y Blanco Encalada, popular. Cheap meals at *Club Deportivo Natales*, Eberhard 332. *Cristal*, Bulnes 439, good sandwiches and salmon; *Tío Cacho*, Phillipi 553, pizzas and sandwiches; *Delicatessen Pollo Loco*, Baquedano 330, T 411393, good, does packed lunches, rec.

● **Banks & money changers**
Poor rates for TCs, which cannot be changed into US$ cash. **Banco O'Higgins**, Bulnes 633, Mastercard, ATM. *Casas de cambio* on Blanco Encalada 226 (Andes Patagónicos) and 266 (Enio América) where Argentine pesos can be changed. **Cambio Stop**, Baquedano 380, good for cash (also arranges tours). Another two at Bulnes 683 and 1087 (good rates; also Argentine pesos); others on Prat. Shop around.

● **Entertainment**
Discos: *El Cielo*, Esmeralda y Ramírez; *Milodón*, Blanco Encalada.

● **Laundry**
Lavandería Papaguayo, Bulnes 518; *Liberty*, Bulnes 513, or try Sra María Carcamo (at Teresa Ruiz's *Hospedaje* at 1000-1200, 1800-2200), good service, more expensive.

● **Post & telecommunications**
Post Office: Eberhard 417, open Mon-Fri 0830-1230, 1430-1745, Sat 0900-1230.
Telephones: CTC, Blanco Encalada 23 y Bulnes, phones and fax.

● **Shopping**
Supermarket: *El Favorito*, Bulnes 1008; 24 hr supermarket Bulnes 300 block; markets good; food prices variable; cheaper in Punta Arenas.

● **Sports**
Camping equipment: *Patagonia Adventures*, see **Hotels** above; *Casa Cecilia*, Tomás Rogers 54, German, French and English spoken, imported gear, also for sale, rec; *Patagonia Adventures*, Tomás Rogers 179. Check all equipment and prices carefully. Average charges, per day: tent US$6, sleeping bag US$3-5, mat US$1.50, raincoat US$0.60, also cooking gear, US$1-2. (**NB** Deposits required: tent US$200, sleeping bag US$100.) Camping gas is widely available in hardware stores, eg at Baquedano y O'Higgins and at Baquedano y Esmeralda.

Fishing: tackle for hire at *Andes Patagónicos*, Blanco Encalada 226, T 411594, US$3.50/day for rod, reel and spinners; if you prefer fishing with floats, hooks, split shot, etc, take your own. Other companies up to 5 times as expensive.

● **Tour companies & travel agents**
Turis Ann, Tomás Rogers 255, T/F 411411, very helpful, accommodation arranged, tours, equipment hire; *San Cayetano*, Eberhard 145,

411112; *Michay*, Baquedano 388, T 411149/411957 (Pedro Fueyo rec); *Andescape*, Pedro Montt 308, next to harbour, T 412592; *Knudsen Tours*, Encalada 284, T 411531, rec; *Onas*, Bulnes 453, T 412707 (Casilla 78); *Servitur*, Pratt 353, T 411028; *Turismo Zalej*, Bulnes 459, rec, T 412260, F 411355. Patricio Canales, Eberhard 49, rec as a good guide; *Turismo Cabo de Hornos*, Pedro Montt 380; *Turismo Tzonka*, Carrera Pinto 626, T 411214. Reports of the reliability of agencies, especially for their trips to Torres del Paine National Park, are very mixed. It is better to book tours direct with agents in Puerto Natales than through agents in Punta Arenas.

Several agencies offer tours to the Perito Moreno glacier in Argentina, 1 day, US$70 without food or park entry fee. The agencies are reluctant to let tourists leave the tour in Calafate and continue into Argentina.

● **Tourist offices**
Offices in kiosk on waterfront, Av Pedro Montt y Phillipi; maps for US$1 from Eberhard 547. **Conaf**: Carrera Pinto 566.

● **Transport**
Local Bicycle hire: *Onas*, Bulnes 453, US$10 a day; also try *Hotel Eberhard*. **Bicycle repairs**: *El Rey de la Bicicleta*, Arauco 779, good, helpful. **Car hire**: Andes Patagónicos, Blanco Encalada 226, T 411594, helpful, US$85/day inc insurance and 350 km free; **Todoauto**, Bulnes 20, T 412837, US$110/day for high clearance vehicle, others US$80/day, or US$85 with driver. Hire agents can arrange permission to drive into Argentina, but this is expensive and takes 24 hrs to arrange. **Mechanic**: Carlos González, Ladrilleros entre Bories y Eberhard, rec.

Air Alta from Puerto Montt, fine views, 3 hrs, US$50, a rec alternative to the ferry. (In late 1996, Alta was planning a Puerto Natales-Calafate service.)

Buses To **Punta Arenas**, several daily, 3½ hrs, US$6. Bus Fernández, Eberhard 555, T 411111, Bus Sur, Baquedano 534, T 411325 and Austral Bus, Baquedano y Valdivia, T 411415. Book in advance. To **Coyhaique** via Calafate, Urbina Tours, 4 days, US$120 (Nov-March). Out of season the only service to rest of Chile: Austral Bus, Tues to Pto Montt, US$150, book days in advance.

To Argentina: to **Río Gallegos** direct, Bus Sur, US$22, Tues and Thur 1830 and El Pingüino, Wed and Sun 1200, US20; hourly to **Río Turbio**, Lagoper, Baquedano y Valdivia, and other companies, US$4, 2 hrs (depending on Customs – change bus at border). To **Calafate**, Cootra via Río Turbio, several times a week, US$14.50, 7 hrs, or more direct service via Cerro Castillo with

Knudsen, summer only. Otherwise travel agencies run several times a week depending on demand, 5 hrs, US$60, shop around, reserve 1 day ahead.

Shipping See page 793 on services from Puerto Montt. Navimag office: Pedro Montt 262 Loc B, Terminal Marítimo, T/F 411421.

FRONTIER WITH ARGENTINA

There are three crossing points:

1) PASO CASAS VIEJAS

16 km E of Puerto Natales. On the Argentine side the road continues to a junction, with alternatives S to Río Turbio and N to La Esperanza and Río Gallegos.

● **Chilean immigration**
Open all year 0800-2000.

2) VILLA DOROTEA

16 km NE of Puerto Natales. On the Argentine side this joins the Río Turbio-La Esperanza road.

● **Chilean immigration**
Open all year daytime only.

3) CERRO CASTILLO

65 km N of Puerto Natales on the road to Torres del Paine. On the Argentine side, Paso Cancha Carrera (14 km), the road leads to La Esperanza and Río Gallegos.

● **Chilean immigration**
open 0830-1200, 1400-2000, Nov-March or April only.

● **Accommodation**
2 *hospedajes* in Cerro Castillo.

PARQUE NACIONAL BERNARDO O'HIGGINS

Usually referred to as the **Parque Nacional Monte Balmaceda**, the park is at the N end of Ultima Esperanza Sound and can be reached by sea only. Two boats *21 de Mayo* and *Alberto de Agostini* sail daily from Puerto Natales in summer and on Sun only in winter (minimum 10 passengers), when weather conditions may be better with less cloud and rain, US$43 (US$38 off season). After a 3-hr journey up the Sound, the boat passes the Balmaceda Glacier which drops from the eastern slopes of Monte Balmaceda

(2,035m). The glacier is retreating; in 1986 its foot was at sea level. The boat docks 1 hr further N at Puerto Toro, from where it is a 1-km walk to the base of Serrano Glacier on the N slope of Monte Balmaceda. On the trip dolphins, sea-lions (in season), black-necked swans, flightless steamer ducks and cormorants can be seen.

Bookings through *Andes Patagónicos* (address above) or other agencies, expensive lunch extra, take own food, drinks available on board. Take warm clothes, hat and gloves.

PARQUE NACIONAL TORRES DEL PAINE

145 km NW of Puerto Natales and covering 181,414 ha, this national park is a 'must' for its wildlife and spectacular scenery. In the centre of the park is a granite *massif* from which rise the *Torres* (Towers) and *Cuernos* (Horns) of Paine, oddly shaped peaks of over 2,600m. The valleys are filled by beautiful lakes at 50m to 200m above sea level. There are 15 peaks above 2,000m, of which the highest is Cerro Paine Grande (3,050m). On the W edge of the Park is the enormous *Campo de Hielo Sur* icecap; 4 main glaciers (*ventisqueros*), Grey, Dickson, Zapata and Tyndall, branch off this and drop to the lakes formed by their meltwater. Two other glaciers, the Francés and Los Perros descend on the W side of the central *massif*.

The scenery in the Park is superb, with constantly changing views of fantastic peaks, ice-fields, vividly coloured lakes of turquoise, ultramarine and grey and quiet green valleys. The park enjoys a micro-climate especially favourable to wildlife and plants: there are 105 species of birds including 18 species of waterfowl and 11 birds of prey. Particularly noteworthy are condors, black-necked swans, rheas, kelp geese, ibis, flamingos and austral parrots. There are also 25 species of mammals including *guanaco*, hares, foxes, *huemules* (a species of deer), pumas and skunks. Over 200 species of plants have been identified. The Park is open all year round, although snow may prevent access in the winter: warmest time is Dec-Mar, although it can be wet and windy. I is also more crowded at this time. Oct-Nov can be very nice. In winter there can be good, stable conditions and well-equipped hikers can do some good walking.

Torres del Paine has become increasingly popular with foreigners and Chileans alike: in 1996 it received 51,000 visitors, most during the summer. Despite the best efforts to manage this large influx of visitors rationally, their impact is starting to show. Litter has become a problem especially around the *refugios* and camping areas. Please take all you rubbish out of the park and remember that toilet paper is also garbage.

The park is administered by Conaf the Administration Centre is in the S o the park at the N end of Lago del Tord (open 0830-2000 in summer, 0830-1230 1400-1830 off season). The Centre provides a good slide show at 2000 on Sat and Sun and there are also exhibitions, but no maps or written information to take away For information (in Spanish) on weather conditions phone the Administratior Centre (T 691931). There are six range stations (*guarderías*) staffed by ranger (*guardaparques*) who give help and advice and will also store luggage (except at Laguna Amarga where they have no room). Rangers keep a check on the whereabouts of all visitors: you are re quired to register and show your passpor when entering the park. You are also re quested to register at a ranger station before setting off on any hike. There are entrances at Laguna Amarga, Lago Sarmiento and Laguna Azul. Entry for foreigners: US$12 (proceeds are shared between all 35 Chilean National Parks) climbing fees US$800. Allow a week to 10 days to see the park properly.

Warning It is vital not to underestimate the unpredictability of the weather (which can change in a few minutes), nor the arduousness of some of the stretches on the long hikes. Rain and snowfall are heavier the further W you go, and bad weather sweeps off the *Campo de Hielo Sur* without warning. It is essential to be properly equipped against cold, wind and rain. The only means of rescue are on horseback or by boat; the nearest helicopter is in Punta Arenas and high winds usually prevent its operation in the park.

Hikes

There are about 250 km of well-marked trails. Visitors must keep to the trails: cross-country trekking is not permitted. **NB** The times indicated should be treated with caution: allow for personal fitness and weather conditions.

El Circuito The most popular hike is a circuit round the Torres and Cuernos del Paine: it is done either anticlockwise starting from the Laguna Amarga *guardería* or clockwise from the administration centre. From Laguna Amarga the route is N along the W side of the Río Paine to Lago Paine, before turning W to follow the Río Paine to the S end of Lago Dickson. From here the path runs along the wooded valley of the Río de los Perros before climbing steeply to Paso John Gardner (1,241m, the highest point on the route), then dropping to follow the Grey Glacier SE to Lago Grey, continuing to Lago Pehoé and the administration centre. There are superb views, particularly from the top of Paso John Gardner.

It normally takes 5-6 days. Lone walkers are not allowed on this route and camping gear must be carried. The circuit is often closed in winter because of snow. The longest lap is 30 km, between Refugio Laguna Amarga and Refugio Dickson (10 hrs in good weather), but the most difficult section is the very steep slippery slope between Paso John Gardner (1,241m) and *Campamento Paso*. The major rivers are crossed by footbridges, but these are occasionally washed away.

The Valley of the Río del Francés From *Refugio Pehoé* this route leads N across undulating country along the W edge of Lago Skottberg to *Campamento Italiano* and then follows the valley of the Río del Francés which climbs between (to the W) Cerro Paine Grande and the Ventisquero del Francés and (to the E) the Cuernos del Paine to *Campamento Británico*. Allow 2½ hrs from Refugio Pehoé to *Campamento*

Italiano, 2½ hrs further to *Campamento Británico*. The views from the *mirador* above *Campamento Británico* are superb.

To Lago Pingo From *Guardería Grey* (18 km W by road from the Administration Centre) follow the Río Pingo, via *Refugio Pingo* and *Refugio Zapata* (4 hrs), with views S over Ventisquero Zapata (plenty of wildlife, icebergs in the lake) to reach the lake (5 hrs from *Guardería Grey*). Ventisquero Pingo can be seen 3 km away over the lake.

To the base of the Torres del Paine From *Refugio Laguna Amarga* the route follows the road W to *Hostería Las Torres* before climbing along the W side of the Río Ascensio via *Campamento Chileno* to *Campamento Las Torres*, close to the base of the Torres and near a small lake. Allow 1½ hrs to *Hostería Las Torres*, then 2 hrs to *Campamento Chileno*, 2 hrs further to *Campamento Torres* where there is a lake: the path is well-marked, but the last 30 mins is up the morraine; to see the towers lit by sunrise (spectacular but you must have good weather), it's well worth humping camping gear up to *Campamento Torres* and spending the night. 1 hr beyond *Campamento Torres* is the good site at *Campamento Japonés*.

To Laguna Verde From the administation centre follow the road N 2 km, before taking the path E over the Sierra del Toro and then along the S side of Laguna Verde to the *Guardería Laguna Verde*. Allow 4 hrs. This is one of the easiest walks in the park and may be a good first hike.

To Laguna Azul and Lago Paine This route runs N from Laguna Amarga to the W tip of Laguna Azul, from where it continues across the sheltered Río Paine valley past Laguna Cebolla to the *Refugio Lago Paine* at the W end of the lake. Allow 8½ hrs.

Equipment

A strong, streamlined, waterproof tent is preferable to the *refugios* and is essential if doing the complete circuit. Also essential are protective clothing against wind and rain, strong waterproof footwear, compass, good sleeping bag, sleeping mat, camping stove and cooking equipment. In summer take shorts and sun-screen also. Equipment is checked at the entrance. Take your own food: the small shops at the Andescape *refugios* (see below) and at the *Posada Río Serrano* are expensive and have a limited selection. Note that rats and mice have become a major problem around camping sites and the free *refugios*. Do not leave food in your pack (which will be chewed through): the safest solution is to hang food in a bag on wire. Maps (US$3), are obtainable at Conaf offices in Punta Arenas or Puerto Natales. Most maps are unreliable but the one produced by Sociedad Turística Kaonikén, US$5, has been recommended as more accurate than the Conaf map (available at *Nandú Artesanía* at port end of Bulnes).

Park information
● Accommodation

Hotels: **L1** *Hotel Explora*, luxurious and comfortable, at Salto Chico on edge of Lago Pehoé, T 411247, offering spectacular views, pool, gym, tours (reservations: Av Américo Vespucci 80, p 7, Santiago, T 228-8081, F 208-5479); **L3** *Hostería Pehoé*, T 411390, 60 rooms, private facilities, cheaper off season, 5 km S of Pehoé ranger station, 11 km N of park administration, on an island with spectacular view across the Lake to Cerro Paine Grande and Cuernos del Paine, good meals (reservations: *Turismo Pehoé* in Punta Arenas or Antonio Bellet 77, office 605, T 235-0252, F 236-0917, Santiago); **L3** *Hostería Las Torres*, head office Lautaro Navarro 1125, Punta Arenas, T/F 222641, modern conveniences, separate restaurant, English spoken at reception, horse-riding, transport from Laguna Amarga ranger station, rec; **L3** *Hostería Lago Grey*, T/F 227528, or Punta Arenas T/F 241042/248167, good food, on edge of Lago Grey (reservations through *Arka Patagonia* or *Turismo Runner* in Punta Arenas); **A1** *Hostería Estancia Lazo*, on the E edge of the park, 8 cabins beautifully situated on Laguna Verde with spectacular views, comfortable, excellent food, very highly rec (reservations: *Operatur Patagónia SA*, Av Colón 568, T/F 61-221130/240056, Punta Arenas); **A2** pp *Posada Río Serrano*, an old *estancia*, some rooms with bath, some without, nr park administration, with expensive but good restaurant and a shop (reservations advisable: run by *Turismo Río Serrano*, Prat 258, Puerto Natales, T 410684).

Refugios: **F** pp *Refugio Lago Toro*, nr administration centre, run by Conaf, hot showers, cooking facilities, good meeting place, sleeping bag and mattress essential, no camping, open summer only – in the winter months another more basic (free) *refugio* is open nr administration centre. The following are run by Andescape (addresses under Puerto Natales and Santiago): *Refugio Lago Pehoé*, on the NE arm of Lago Pehoé; *Refugio Grey*, on the eastern shore of Lago Grey; *Refugio Lago Dickson*; all **D** pp, modern, closed in winter until 10 Sept, clean, with dormitory accommodation (sheets not provided) hot showers (US$2 for non-residents) cooking and laundry facilities, meals served, kiosk with basic food and other supplies, rental of camping equipment, campsite (US$3 pp). **D** pp *Refugio Las Torres*, is owned by *Hostería Las Torres*, meals served.

In addition there are 6 free *refugios*: Zapata, Pingo, Laguna Verde, Laguna Amarga, Lago Paine and Pudeto. Most have cooking areas (wood stove or fireplace) but Laguna Verde and Pingo do not. These are now in very poor condition and are very crowded in summer (rangers know how many people are on each route and can give you an idea of how busy *refugios* are).

Camping: in addition to sites at the Andescape *refugios* there are the following sites: *Camping Serón* and *Camping Las Torres* (at *Hostería Las Torres*) both run by Estancia Cerro Paine, US$4, hot showers; *Camping Los Perros*, run by Andescape, US$3 pp, shop and hot showers; *Camping Lago Pehoé* and *Camping Serrano*, both run by Turismo Río Serrano (address above), US$20/site at former (max 6 persons, hot showers) and US$15/site at latter (max 6 persons, cold showers, more basic); *Camping Laguna Azul*, hot showers, **D**/site. Free camping is permitted in seven other locations in the park: these sites are known as *campamentos*. Fires may only be lit at organized *camping* sites, not a *campamentos*. The *guardaparques* expect people to have a stove if camping. (**NB** These restrictions should be observed as forest fires are a serious hazard.) Beware mice, which eat through tents. Equipment hire in Puerto Natales (see above).

● Boat trips
From *Hostería Grey* at the S end of Lago Grey to the Grey Glacier, minimum 8 passengers, US$25 inc refreshments, 2-3 hrs, a stunning trip. From *Refugio Lago Pehoé* to *Refugio Pudeto*, US$12 one way daily, from Pudeto 1030, 1600, from Pehoé 1200, 1530, 1 hr, in high season reserve in advance at the *refugios* at either end or at *Turismo Tzonka* in Puerto Natales. Off-season, radio for the boat from *Refugio Pehoé*.

● Transport
Car hire: hiring a pick-up from Budget in Punta Arenas is an economical proposition for a group (up to 9 people): US$415 for 4 days. If driving

there yourself, the road from Pto Natales is being improved and, in the Park, the roads are narrow, bendy with blind corners, use your horn a lot; it takes about $3^1/_2$ hrs from Pto Natales to the administration, 3 to Laguna Amarga. Petrol available at Río Serrano, but fill up in case. **Horse hire**: Baquedano Zamora, Blanco Encalada 226, Puerto Natales, T 411592.

Buses San Cayetano, Servitur and JB Buses (addresses above) run daily bus services to the park from Puerto Natales leaving between 0630 and 0800, returning between 1300 and 1500, $3^1/_2$ hrs' journey, US$8.75 one way, US$12.50 open return (return tickets are not interchangeable between different companies, buy single ticket), from early Nov to mid April. See also under Punta Arenas **Buses** for the daily In-Tur minibus service from Punta Arenas. Buses pass *Guardería Laguna Amarga* at 1030, *Guardería Pehoé* at 1130, arriving at Admin at 1230, leave Admin at 1400 (in high season the buses fill quickly so it is best to board at the Administration). All buses wait at *Refugio Pudeto* until the 1430 boat from *Refugio Lago Pehoé* arrives. Travel between two points within the park (eg Pudeto-Laguna Amarga) US$1.25. At other times services by travel agencies are dependent on demand: arrange return date with driver and try to arrange your return date to coincide with other groups to keep costs down. Luis Díaz has been rec, about $12 pp, min 3 persons.

From Torres del Paine to Calafate (Argentina): services from Puerto Natales (see above); alternatively take a bus from the park to Cerro Castillo (106 km S of administration centre) then catch Knudsen direct service to Calafate, operates summer only.

Tours Several agencies in Puerto Natales including Servitur, *Scott Tours* and *Luis Díaz* offer 1-day tours by minibus, US$37.50 (some travellers report that these are a waste of time as you need to stay overnight to appreciate the park). José Torres of *Sastrería Arbiter* in C Bulnes 731

(T 411637) rec as guide. *Enap* weekend tours in summer cost US$45 including accommodation and meals. *Buses Fernández* offer 2-day tours, US$132 and 3-day tours (which includes trip to the Balmaceda Glacier) US$177. Before booking a tour check carefully on details and get them in writing: increasingly mixed reports of tours. Many companies who claim to visit the Grey Glacier only visit Lago Grey (you see the Glacier in the distance). Taxi costs US$80 per day, run by *Zalej* (Arturo Prat 260), but may be cheaper if you catch him when he's going to the Park anyway. After mid-Mar there is little public transport (ask *San Cayetano*) and trucks are irregular.

Onas Turismo (address under Puerto Natales **Tour companies**) runs trips from the Park down the Río Serrano in dinghies to the Serrano glacier and from there, on the *21 de Mayo* or *Alberto de Agostini* tour boats to Puerto Natales, US$90 pp all inclusive. Book in advance.

TIERRA DEL FUEGO

The largest island off the extreme S of South America, Tierra del Fuego is surrounded by the Magellan Strait to the N, the Atlantic Ocean to the E, the Beagle Channel to the S – which separates it from the southern islands – and by the Whiteside, Gabriel, Magdalena and Cockburn channels etc, which divide it from the islands situated to the W. The western side belongs to Chile and the eastern to Argentina. It produces most of Chile's oil.

Ferries to Tierra del Fuego
There are two ferry crossings to Tierra del Fuego.

Punta Arenas to Porvenir The *Melinka*, sails from Tres Puentes (5 km N of Punta

Arenas, bus A or E from Av Magallanes, US$1; taxi US$3) at 0930 daily except Mon in season, less frequently off season, 2½ hr crossing (can be rough and cold), US$6 pp, US$5 per bike, US$30 per vehicle. Return from Porvenir 1400 (1700 Sun). Timetable dependent on tides and subject to change: check in advance. Reservations essential especially in summer (at least 24 hrs in advance for cars), obtainable from *Agencia Broom*, Bulnes 05075, T 218100, F 212126. The ferry company accepts no responsibility for damage to vehicles on the crossing.

Punta Delgada to Punta Espora This crossing is via the *Primera Angostura* (First Narrows), 170 km NE of Punta Arenas. There are several crossings a day; schedules vary with the tides. Price US$1 pp (cycles free) and US$14 per car, one way. The ferry takes about 4 trucks and 20 cars; before 1000 most space is taken by trucks. There is no bus service to or from this crossing. If hitching, this route is preferable as there is more traffic.

● **Accommodation** In Punta Delgada: **E** pp *Hotel El Faro*; **C** *Hostería Tehuelche*, T 061-694433 at Kamiri Aike 17 km from port, with restaurant.

PORVENIR

(*Pop* 4,500, several hundred from former Yugoslavia; *Phone code* 061) is the only town in Chilean Tierra del Fuego. There is a small museum, the **Museo Fernando Cordero Rusque**, Samuel Valdivieso 402, with archaeological and photographic displays on the Onas.

● **Accommodation** Porvenir: **A2** *Los Flamencos*, Tte Merino, T 580049, best; **C** *Central*, Phillippi 298, T 580077; **C** *Rosas*, Phillippi, T 580088, heating, restaurant and bar, rec; **E** pp *Res Colón*, Damián Riobó 198, T 580108, also full board; **C** *España*, Santos Mardones y Croacia, good restaurant with fixed price lunch; *Res Los Cisnes*, Soto Salas 702, T 580227; **E** pp *Res* at Santos Mardones 366 (**D** with full board), heaters in rooms, good. **Elsewhere in Chilean Tierra del Fuego**: at Cerro Sombrero, 46 km S of Primera Angostura: **E** pp *Hostería Tunkelen*, rec; **F** *Pensión del Señor Alarcón*, good; *Posada Las Flores*, Km 127 on the road to San Sebastián, reservations via *Hostal de la Patagonia* in Punta Arenas; *Refugio Lago Blanco*, on Lago Blanco, T Punta Arenas 241197. For accommodation at San Sebastián see below.

● **Places to eat** *Croacia Club* does wholesome and reasonable lunch (about US$5), also *Restaurante Puerto Montt*, Croacia 1169, for seafood, rec. Many lobster fishing camps where fishermen will prepare lobster on the spot.

● **Banks & money changers** At *Estrella del Sur* shop, Santos Mardones.

● **Transport Air** From Punta Arenas – weather and bookings permitting, Aerovías DAP, Oficina Foretic, T 80089, Porvenir, fly daily except Sun at 0815 and 1730 to Porvenir, return at 1000 and 1930, US$20. Heavily booked so make sure you have your return reservation confirmed. **Buses On Tierra del Fuego** 2 a week between Porvenir and Río Grande (Argentina), Tues and Sat 1400, 5 hrs, Transportes Gessell, Duble Almeyda 257, T 580488, US$20 heavily booked, buy ticket in advance, or phone; Río Grande-Porvenir, Wed and Sun 0800. **Ferries** Terminal at Bahía Chilota, 7 km W, see above for details. From bus terminal to ferry, taxi US$6, bus (if running) US$1.50. **Motorists** All roads are gravel. Fuel is available in Porvenir, Cerro Sombrero and Cullen. **Hitchhiking** Police may help with lifts on trucks from Porvenir to Río Grande; elsewhere is difficult as there is so little traffic.

FRONTIER WITH ARGENTINA: SAN SEBASTIAN

The only legal frontier crossing between the Chilean and Argentine parts of Tierra del Fuego is 142 km E of Porvenir. On the Argentine side the road continues to Río Grande.

NB There are two settlements called San Sebastián, one on each side of the frontier but they are 14 km apart; taxis are not allowed to cross.

NB Argentine time is 1 hr ahead of Chilean time, March-October.

● **Entering Chile**
No fruit, vegetables, dairy produce or meat permitted.

● **Accommodation**
E pp *Hostería de la Frontera*, in the annex which is 1 km away from the more expensive main building.

● **Transport**
Minibus from Porvenir to San Sebastián, US$14. For transport between Porvenir and Río Grande, see above.

PUERTO WILLIAMS

(*Pop* 1,500; *Phone code* 061) is a Chilean naval base on **Isla Navarino**, S of the Beagle Channel. Situated about 50 km E of Ushuaia (Argentina) at 54° 55' 41" S, 67° 37' 58" W, Puerto Williams is the most southerly place in the world with a permanent population. It is small, friendly and remote (it suffered a serious fire in 1994). The island is totally unspoilt and beautiful, with a chain of rugged snowy peaks, magnificent woods and many animals, including large numbers of beaver which were introduced to the island and have done a lot of damage.

Excursions

Sights include beaver dams, cascades, the Villa Ukika, 2 km E of town, the place where the last descendants of the Yaganes people live, and the local *media luna* where rodeos are held. For superb views, climb Cerro Bandera (3-4 hrs round trip, steep, take warm clothes). No equipment rental on island; buy food in Punta Arenas.

Museums

Museo Martín Gusinde, known as the *Museo del Fin del Mundo* ('End of the World Museum') is full of information about vanished Indian tribes, local wildlife, and voyages including Charles Darwin and Fitzroy of the *Beagle*, a 'must'. Open 1000-1300, 1500-1800 (Mon-Thur); 1500-1800 (Sat-Sun), Friday closed (subject to change). Admission US$1.

Local information

● **Accommodation**

A3 *Hostería Walla*, on the edge of Lauta bay, T 223571, 2 km out of town (splendid walks), very hospitable, good food; **E** pp *Res Onashaga* (run by Señor Ortiz – everyone knows him), cold, run down, good meals, helpful, full board available; **D** pp *Pensión Temuco*, Piloto Pardo 224, also half board, comfortable, hospitable, good food, hot showers, rec; you can also stay at private houses. You can camp nr the *Hostería*: collect drinking water from the kitchen.

● **Airline offices**

Aerovías DAP, LanChile, Ladeco in the centre of town.

● **Post & telecommunications**

Post Office: closes 1900

Telephone: CTC, Mon-Sat 0930-2230, Sun 1000-1300, 1600-2200). **Telex**.

● **Tourist offices**

Near the museum (Closed in winter). Ask for details on hiking. Maps available.

● **Transport**

Air From Punta Arenas by air, Aerovías DAP (details under Punta Arenas) on Mon and Fri 1400, Wed 0830, return Mon and Fri 1800, Wed 1000, US$64 single. Book well in advance; 20 seater aircraft and long waiting lists (be persistent). The flight is beautiful, with superb views of Tierra del Fuego, the Cordillera Darwin, the Beagle Channel, and the islands stretching S to Cape Horn. Also army flights available (they are cheaper), but the ticket has to be bought through DAP.

Ferries No regular sailings from Ushuaia (Argentina).

Boats from Punta Arenas: *Ferry Patagonia* (Austral Broom), once a week, US$48 inc food, 36 hrs. The *Navarino* leaves Punta Arenas in 3rd week of every month, 12 passengers, US$150 pp one way; contact the owner, Carlos Aguilera, 21 de Mayo 1460, Punta Arenas, T 228066, F 248848 or via *Turismo Pehoé*. The *Beaulieu*, a cargo boat carrying a few passengers, sails from Punta Arenas once a month, US$300 return, 6 days.

Boat trips: ask at the yacht club on the off chance of hitching a ride on a private yacht. Luxury cruises around Cape Horn are run by *Tierra Austral* for US$800, 6 days. Captain Ben Garrett offers recommended adventure sailing in his schooner *Victory*, from special trips to Ushuaia to cruises in the canals, Cape Horn, glaciers, Puerto Montt, Antarctica in Dec and January. Write to Victory Cruises, Puerto Williams (slow mail service); Fax No 1, Cable 3, Puerto Williams; phone (call collect) asking for Punta Arenas (Annex No 1 Puerto Williams) and leave message with the Puerto Williams operator.

The Chilean Pacific Islands

T WO NATIONAL park possessions in the Pacific: Juan Fernández Islands, a little easier to reach (and leave) now than in Robinson Crusoe's time, and the unique Easter Island.

JUAN FERNANDEZ ISLANDS

The land
(*Pop* 500) Situated 667 km W of Valparaíso, this group of small volcanic islands is a national park administered by Conaf. The islands are named after João Fernández, the first European to visit in 1574. There are three islands, Robinson Crusoe, the largest, which was the home (1704-09) of Alexander Selkirk (the original of Defoe's *Robinson Crusoe*), Alejandro Selkirk and Santa Clara, the smallest. Selkirk's cave on the beach of Robinson Crusoe is shown to visitors. The only settlement is San Juan Bautista, a fishing village of simple wooden frame houses, located on Bahía Cumberland on the N coast of Isla Robinson Crusoe: it has a church, schools, post office, and radio station. The islands are famous for *langosta de Juan Fernández* (a pincerless lobster) which is sent to the mainland.

Climate
The islands enjoy a mild climate and the vegetation is rich and varied. Fauna includes wild goats, humming birds and seals. The islands were declared a UN World Biosphere Reserve in 1977. Best time for a visit: Oct-March. **Take insect repellent**.

Places of interest
The remains of the **Fuerte Santa Bárbara**, the largest of the Spanish fortresses, overlook San Juan Bautista. Nearby are the **Cuevas de los Patriotas**, home to the Chilean independence leaders, deported by the Spanish after the Battle of Rancagua. South of the village is the **Mirador de Selkirk**, the hill where Selkirk lit his signal fires. A plaque was set in the rock at the look-out point by British naval officers from HMS *Topaze* in 1868; nearby is a more recent plaque placed by his descendents. Selkirk, a Scot, was put ashore from HMS *Cinque Ports* and was taken off 4 years and 4 months later by a privateer, the *Duke*. The Mirador is the only easy pass between the N and S sides of the island. Further S is the anvil-shaped **El Yunque**, 915m, the highest peak on the island, where Hugo Weber, a survivor from the *Dresden*, lived as a hermit for 12 years. (The *Dresden* was a German cruiser, cornered by two British destroyers in Bahía Cumberland in 1915; the scuttled *Dresden* still lies on the bottom and a monument on the shore commemorates the event.) The only sandy beach on Robinson Crusoe is **Playa Arenal**, in the extreme SW corner, 2 hrs by boat from San Juan Bautista.

Each Feb, a yachting regatta visits the islands; setting out from Algarrobo, yachts sails to Isla Robinson Crusoe, thence to Talcahuano and Valparaíso. At this time Bahía Cumberland is full of colourful and impressive craft, and prices in restaurants and shops double for the duration. (Thomas G Lammers, Department of Botany, University of Miami.)

Local information
● **Accommodation**
C pp *Hotel Selkirk*, good food, full board A pp, rec (T Santiago 531-3772); **A3** *Hostería Robinson Crusoe*, full board, plus 20% tax, about 1 hr walk from the village; **A1** *Daniel Defoe Hotel*, at Aldea Daniel Defoe (T Santiago 531-3772); *Hostería Villa Green*, good. Lodging with villagers is difficult.

● **Banks & money changers**
There are no exchange facilities. Only pesos and US$ cash accepted. No credit cards, no TCs.

● **Transport**
Air Air taxi daily in summer (subject to demand) from Santiago (Los Cerrillos airport, US$395 round trip), by Transportes Aéreas Isla Robinson Crusoe, Monumento 2570, Maipú, Santiago, T 531-4343, F 531-3772, and by Lacsa, Av Larraín 7941, La Reina, Santiago, T 273-4354, F 273-4309; also from Valparaíso. The plane lands on an airstrip in the W of the island; passengers are taken by boat to San Juan Bautista (1½ hrs, US$2 one way).

Sea The boat service, about every 3 weeks from Valparaíso on the *Río Baker* and *Charles Darwin*, is for cargo and passengers, modest accommodation, 36-hr passage; *Agentur*, Huérfanos 757, oficina 601, T 337118, Santiago. *Pesquera Chris*, Cueto 622, Santiago, T 681-1543, or Cochrane 445 (near Plaza Sotomayor), Valparaíso, T 216800, 2 week trips to the island (5 days cruising, a week on the island); from US$200 return. No fishing or cargo boats will take passengers.

EASTER ISLAND

Easter Island (Isla de Pascua, Rapa Nui; *phone code* 108) is just S of the Tropic of Capricorn and 3,790 km W of Chile; its nearest neighbour is Pitcairn Island.

The land
The island is triangular in shape, 24 km across, with an extinct volcano at each corner. The original inhabitants called the island Te Pito o te Henua, the navel of the world. The population was stable at 4,000 until the 1850s, when Peruvian slavers, smallpox and emigration to Tahiti (encouraged by plantation-owners) reduced the numbers. Now it is about 2,800, of whom about 500 are from the mainland, mostly living in the village of Hanga Roa. About half the island, of low round hills with groves of eucalyptus, is used for horses and cattle, and nearly one-half constitutes a National Park (entry US$11, payable at Orongo). The islanders have preserved their indigenous songs and dances, and are extremely hospitable. Tourism has grown rapidly since the air service began in 1967. Paid work is now more common, but much carving is still

done. The islanders have profited greatly from the visits of North Americans: a Canadian medical expedition left a mobile hospital on the island in 1966, and when a US missile-tracking station was abandoned in 1971, vehicles, mobile housing and an electricity generator were left behind.

Climate
Average monthly temperatures vary between 15-17°C in Aug and 24°C in Feb, the hottest month. Average annual rainfall is 1,100 mm. There is some rain throughout the year, but the rainy season is Mar-Oct (wettest in May). The tourist season is from Sept to April.

History
It is now generally accepted that the islanders are of Polynesian origin. Thor Heyerdahl's theories, as expressed in *Aku-Aku, The Art of Easter Island* (New York: Doubleday, 1975), are less widely accepted than they used to be, and South American influence is now largely discounted (see below).

European contact with the island began with the visit of the Dutch admiral, Jacob Roggeven, on Easter Sunday 1722, who was followed by the British James Cook in 1774 and the French Le Perouse in 1786. The island was annexed by Chile in 1888.

Places of interest
The unique features of the island are the 600 (or so) *moai*, huge stone figures up to 9m in height and broad in proportion. One of them, on Anakena beach, was restored to its (probably) original state with a plaque commemorating Thor Heyerdahl's visit in 1955. Other *moai* have since been re-erected.

A tour of the main part of the island can be done on foot, but this would need at least 2 days, either camping at Anakena or returning to Hanga Roa and setting out again the next day. To see more, hire a horse or a vehicle. From Hanga Roa, take the road going SE past the airport; at the oil tanks turn right to Vinapu, where there are two *ahu* and a wall whose stones are joined with Inca-like precision. Head

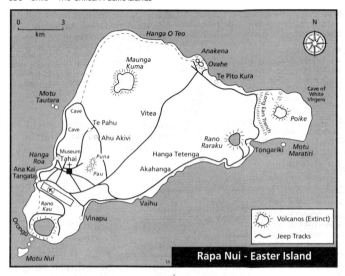

Rapa Nui - Easter Island

back NE along the S coast, past Vaihu (an *ahu* with eight broken *moai*; small harbour); Akahanga (*ahu* with toppled *moai*); Hanga Tetenga (1 toppled *moai*, bones can be seen inside the *ahu*), Ahu Tongariki (once the largest platform, damaged by a tidal wave in 1960, being restored with Japanese aid). Turn left to Rano Raraku (20 km), the volcano where the *moai* were carved. Many statues can be seen. In the crater is a small lake surrounded by reeds (swimming possible beyond the reeds). Good views.

The road heads N past 'the trench of the long-ears' and an excursion can be made to Poike to see the open-mouthed statue that is particularly popular with local carvers (ask farmer for permission to cross his land). On Poike the earth is red; at the NE end is the cave where the virgin was kept before marriage to the victor of ceremonies during the birdman cult (ask directions). The road along the N coast passes Ahu Te Pito Kura, a round stone called the navel of the world and one of largest *moai* ever brought to a platform. It continues to Ovahe. At Ovahe, there is a very attractive beach with pink sand and some rather recently carved faces and a cave.

From Ovahe, one can return direct to Hanga Roa or continue to Anakena, site of King Hotu Matua's village and Thor Heyerdahl's landing place. From Anakena a coastal path of variable quality passes interesting remains and beautiful cliff scenery. At Hanga o Teo, there appears to be a large village complex, with several round houses, and further on there is a burial place, built like a long ramp with several ditches containing bones. From Hanga o Teo the path goes W then S, inland from the coast, to meet the road N of Hanga Roa.

A 6-hr walk from Hanga Roa on the W coast passes Ahu Tahai (a *moai* with eyes and top knot in place, cave house, just outside town). Two caves are reached, one inland appears to be a ceremonial centre, the other (nearer the sea) has 2 'windows' (take a strong flashlight and be careful near the 'windows'). Further N is Ahu Tepeu (broken *moai*, ruined houses). Beyond here you can join the path mentioned above, or turn right to Te Pahu cave and the seven *moai* at Akivi. Either return to Hanga Roa, or go to Puna Pau crater (2 hrs), where the topknots were carved (good views from the three crosses at the top).

Rano Kau, S of Hanga Roa, is another important site to visit; one finds the curious Orongo ruins here. The route S out of Hanga Roa passes the two caves of Ana Kai Tangata, one of which has paintings. If on foot you can take a path from the Orongo road, just past the Conaf sign, which is a much shorter route to Rano Kau crater. 200m below is a lake with many reed islands. On the seaward side is Orongo, where the birdman cult flourished, with many ruined buildings and petroglyphs. Out to sea are the 'bird islets', Motu Nui, Motu Iti and Motu Kao. It is very windy at the summit; good views at sunset, or under a full moon (it is easy to follow the road back to Hanga Roa in the dark).

In Hanga Roa is Ahu Tautira, next to a swimming area marked out with concrete walls and a breakwater (cold water). Music at the 0900 Sun mass is 'enchanting'. Museum near Tahai, US$6, most objects are reproductions because the genuine articles were removed from the island, but it has good descriptions of island life. There is a cultural centre next to the football field, with an exhibition hall and souvenir stall.

Local festivals

Tapati, or *Semana Rapa Nui*, end-Jan/beginning-Feb, lasts about 10 days. Dancing competitions, singing, sports (horse rac-

---

The cultural development of Easter Island

"Far from being the passive recipient of external influences, Easter Island shows the extent of unique development possible for a people left wholly in isolation. It is believed to have been colonized from Polynesia about AD 800: its older altars (*ahu*) are similar to those of (French) Polynesia, and its older statues (*moai*) similar to those of the Marquesas Islands. The very precise stone fitting of some of the *ahu*, and the tall gaunt *moai* with elongated faces and ears for which Easter Island is best known were later developments whose local evolution can be traced through a comparison of the remains. Indigenous Polynesian society, for all its romantic idylls, was competitive, and it seems that the five clans which originally had their own lands demonstrated their strength by erecting these complex monuments. The *moai* were sculpted at the Rano Raraku quarry and transported on wooden rollers over more or less flat paths to their final locations; their red topknots were sculpted at and brought from the inland quarry of Puna Pau; and the rounded pebbles laid out checkerboard fashion at the *ahu* all came from the same beach at Vinapu. The sculptors and engineers were paid out of the surplus food produced by the sponsoring family: Rano Raraku's unfinished *moai* mark the end of the families' ability to pay. Over several centuries from about AD 1400 this stone work slowed down and stopped, owing to the deforestation of the island caused by roller production, and damage to the soils through deforestation and heavy cropping. The birdman cult represented at Orongo is a later development after the islanders had lost their clan territoriality and were concentrated at Hanga Roa, but still needed a non-territorial way to simulate inter-clan rivalry." David Bulbeck, Adelaide.

The central feature of the birdman cult was an annual ceremony in which the heads of the lineages, or their representatives, raced to the islets to obtain the first egg of the sooty tern (known as the Manutara), a migratory seabird which nests on Motu Nui, Motu Iti and Motu Kao. The winning chief was named Bird Man, Tangata Manu, for the following year. It appears that, in the cult, the egg of the tern represented fertility, although it is less clear what the status of the Tangata Manu actually was. The petroglyphs at Orongo depict the half-man, half-bird Tangata Manu, the creator god Make Make and the symbol of fertility, Komari.

ing, swimming, modified decathlon), body-painting, typical foods (lots of small booths by the football field), necklace-making, etc. Only essential activities continue outside the festival.

Recommended Reading There is a very thorough illustrated book by J Douglas Porteous, *The Modernization of Easter Island* (1981), available from Department of Geography, University of Victoria, BC, Canada, US$6. See also Thor Heyerdahl's work, details above; *Easter Island, Earth Island*, by Paul Bahn and John Flenley (Thames and Hudson, 1992) for a comprehensive appraisal of the island's archaeology. *Islas Oceánicas Chilenas*, edited by Juan Carlos Castillo (Ediciones Universidad Católica de Chile, 1987), contains much information on the natural history and geography of Juan Fernández and Easter Islands.

Anyone continuing into Polynesia or Melanesia from Easter Island will find David Stanley's *South Pacific Handbook* (Moon Publications Inc, PO Box 3040, Chico, CA 95927, USA, F 1-916-345-6751) a useful guidebook.

Local information

Time zone: Easter Island is always 2 hrs behind the Chilean mainland, summer and winter time.

● Accommodation

The accommodation list at the airport information desk only covers the more expensive places. Flights are met by large numbers of hotel and *residencial* representatives but it is cheaper to look for yourself. Note that room rates, especially in *residenciales* can be much cheaper out of season and if you do not take full board. Unless it is a particularly busy season there is no need to book in advance; mainland agencies make exorbitant booking charges.

L3 *Hanga Roa*, Av Pont, inc all meals (120 beds), no credit cards, T 223299 (Santiago 633-9130, F 639-5334); **L3** *Iorana Hotel*, Ana Magara promontory, 5 mins from airport, T 223312 (Santiago 633-2650), excellent food, convenient for visiting Ana Kai Tangata caves.

A1 *Easter Island*, Policarpo Toro, Hanga Roa, breakfast and dinner (excellent restaurant), good service, nice garden, T 223294, or Santiago 211-6747; **A1** *Otai*, Te Pilo Te Henua, T 223250, comfortable, family run, rec; **A1** *Victoria*, Av Pont, T 223272, helpful owner arranges tours; **A1** *Topo Ra'a*, Atamu Kekena,

T 223223, 5 mins from Hanga Roa, very good, helpful, excellent restaurant; **A3** *Cabañas Taha Tai*, 2 houses beyond *Ana Rapu* on C Apina, new, fan, fridge, use of kitchen, inc breakfast and airport pick-up; **A3** *Poike*, Petero Atamu, T 223283, homely, hot water.

C *Vai Moana*, 3 blocks from museum, 2 from Tahai, 5 mins from main street, owner Edgar Hereveri, T 100626, F 100105, cabañas with shared bath, good meals, French and English spoken, rec.

Homes offering accommodation and tours (rates ranging from US$18 to US$35, inc meals): **A1** *Res Pedro Atán*, T 223329, full board, Policarpo Toro; **A1** *Res Apina Nui*, Hetereki, T 223292 (C low season, but bargain), good food, helpful, English spoken; Yolanda Ika's **A2** *Res Taire Ngo Oho*, T 223259, with breakfast, rec, modern; Krenia Tucki's **A2** *Res Kai Poo*, Av Pont, small, hot water; **A2** *Res Hanga Roa Reka*, T 223276, full board, good, camping; María Georgina Hucke, of Tiki Tours, **B** with half board, rec; *Res El Tauke*, Te Pito Te Henua s/n, T 223253, same rates as *Hanga Roa Reka*, excellent, airport transfers, tours arranged; *Res Taheta One One*, T 223257, same rates, motorbike rental; **B** *Res Tahai*, Calle-Rei-Miro, T 100395, with breakfast, **A2** full board, nice garden, rec; **B** pp *Res Holiday Inn*, T 223337, half board, excellent food, hot water, rec; **C** Anita and Martín Pate's guesthouse, opp hospital in Hanga Roa, half board in high season, less low season, good food; **D** pp *Res Taniera*, T 223290, also camping, horses; **D** pp María Cecilia Cardinale, nr Tahai Moai, half board, speaks English and French, excellent food, camping; **D** María Goretti, rooms with breakfast, camping; **C** pp *Ana Rapu*, C Apina, T 223540, F 223318, inc breakfast, evening meal US$7, camping US$10, comfortable, family-run, hot water (except when demand is heavy), English spoken, popular; **C** pp *Res Viaka Pua*, Simón Paoa, Hanga Roa, T 223377, full board, comfortable, rec. **A3** Emilio and Milagrosa Paoa, with full board, rec accommodation and tours. From **F** pp *Mara Villa*, Sara Tuki Tepano, popular, welcoming, sometimes organizes barbecues.

Camping: free in eucalyptus groves near the Ranger's house at Rano Raraku (with water tank), and at Anakena, no water, make sure your tent is ant-proof. Officially, camping is not allowed anywhere else, but this is not apparently strictly enforced. Many people also offer campsites in their gardens, US$5-10 pp (see above), check availability of water first; some families also provide food. Several habitable caves around the coast: eg between Anakena beach and Ovahe. If you must leave anything behind in a cave, leave only what may be of use to other campers, candles, oil, etc, certainly not rubbish. **NB** Camping gas is expensive and of poor quality. Camping equipment can be hired from a shop on Av Policarpo Toro, US$50/day for everything.

● **Places to eat**

Mama Sabina, Av Policarpo Toro, clean, welcoming; *Ave Rei Pua*, limited menu, good; *Tarake* near municipal market (which does not sell food); *Pizzería*, opp post office, moderately priced. Several others. *Le Pecheur*, French run, unfriendly, expensive; *Kona Koa*, not cheap but good. Most *residenciales* offer full board. Coffee is always instant. Beware of extras such as US$3 charge for hot water.

● **Banks & money changers**

Best done in Santiago. Bank next to Entel, open 0900-1200 daily, charges US$18 commission on changing TCs, but you can change as many TCs for this fee as you like (and they can be in different names). Cash can be exchanged in shops, hotels, etc, at about 5% less than Santiago. Good rates on Amex TCs at Sonoco service station. Amex TCs also changed by Kia-Koe Land Operator, *Hanga Roa Hotel*. Prices are often quoted in dollars, but bills can be paid in pesos. Amex credit cards are accepted on the island, but cannot be used to obtain cash (but enquire at Sonoco service station), similarly Visa; Mastercard can be used to get cash.

● **Entertainment**

Discotheques: there are three in Hanga Roa: *Maitiki* (open daily), E side of town, with pool table; *Toroko*, near harbour (open Thur-Sat), US$1.25, and *Piditi*, near airport (open Thur-Sat). Action begins after 0100. Drinks are expensive: a bottle of pisco costs US$9, canned beer US$2.

● **Hospitals & medical services**

There is a 20-bed hospital as well as 2 resident doctors, a trained nurse and 2 dentists on the island.

● **Post & telecommunications**

Post Office: 0900-1700; only sends packages up to 1 kg.

Telephones: phone calls from the Chilean mainland are subsidized, at US$0.35/minute. Calls to Europe cost US$10 for 3 mins, cheap rate after 1400.

● **Shopping**

On Av Policarpo Toro, the main street, there are lots of small shops and market stalls (which may close during rain) and a couple of supermarkets, cheapest *Kai Kene* or *Tumukai*. Local produce which can be found free (but ask) inc wild guava fruit, fish, 'hierba luisa' tea, and wild chicken.

Food, wine and beer are expensive because of freight charges, but local fish, vegetables, fruit and bread are cheap. Average prices: coffee/tea US$0.50, meals about US$7.50, snacks US$1, bread US$3/kg, beer/cola US$1.50 in most bars and restaurants. Bring all you can from the mainland, but not fruit. Vegetarians will have no problems on the island.

Handicrafts: wood carvings, stone moais, best bought from the craftsmen themselves, such as Antonio Tepano Tucki, Juan Acka, Hipolito Tucki and his son (who are knowledgeable about the old culture). The expensive municipal market, left of church, will give you a good view of what is available – no compunction to buy. The airport shop is expensive. Good pieces cost between US$30 and 150. Souvenirs at *Hotu Matuu's Favorite Shoppe* are good, quite expensive, designs own T-shirts, fixed prices; also sells music. There is a *mercado artesanal* next to the church and people sell handicrafts at Tahai, Vaihu, Rano Raraku and Anakena. Bargaining is only possible if you pay cash. Bartering items such as shampoo, shoes, T-shirts, is common.

● **Sports**

Hiking: allow at least a day to walk the length of the island, one way, taking in all the sites. It is 5 easy hrs from Hanga Roa to Rano Raraku (camp at ranger station); 5 hrs to Anakena (camp at ranger station, but ask first). You can hitch back to Hanga Roa, especially at weekends though there are few cars at other times. Anyone wishing to spend time exploring the island would be well-advised to speak to Conaf first (T 223236); they also give good advice on special interests (biology, archaeology, handicrafts, etc). **Horseback**: the best way to see the island, provided you are fit, is on horseback: horses, US$15-20 a day. A guide is useful. Try Emilio Arakie Tepane, who also leads horseback tours of the island (Spanish only) T 504.

● **Tour companies & travel agents**

Mahinatur Ltda, vehicle reservations in advance. Their guide, Christian Walter, is rec; *Kia-Koe*, at *Hanga Roa Hotel*, *Schmidt Osterinsel Reisen*, office in *Hanga Roa Hotel*, T 223600, F 223532, English, French and German spoken, offers tours around the island and to caves, both US$15. Maps are sold on Av Policarpo Toro for US$15-18, or at the ranger station at Orongo for US$10. LanChile office on Av Policarpo Toro provides tours of the island (inc during stopovers). Many agencies, *residenciales* and locals arrange excursions around the island, eg: *Aku-Aku Tours*, Krenia Tucki of *Res Kai Poo*, Michel Fage, Fernando and Marcelo León (Pai Tepano Rano, rec), Hugo Teave (good English, well-informed, polite), Charles Wilkins (*Mahinatur Ltda*), English-born guide, rec, as is Victoriano

Giralde, *Kia-Koe Tours*. Some go in jeeps, others will accompany tourists in hired vehicles (eg US$130 for 8), prices up to US$30 pp/day. The English of other tour guides is often poor.

● **Transport**

Local There is one taxi and in summer a bus goes from Hanga Roa to Anakena on Sun at 0900, returning pm (unreliable). **Vehicle rental**: a high-clearance vehicle is better-suited to the roads than a normal vehicle. If you are hiring a car, do the sites from S to N since travel agencies tend to start their tours in the N. Jeep hire at **Sunoco service station**, Vaihu, T 223325 or 223239, on airport road, US$10/1 hr, US$20/4 hrs, US$50/day. **Hertz**, opp airport, US$50/day. Many other vehicle hire agencies on the main street. Chilean or international driving licence essential. There is no insurance available, drive at your own risk (be careful at night, many vehicles drive without lights). **Motorbike rental**: about US$40 a day inc gasoline (Suzuki or Honda 250 rec because of rough roads). Rentals from Av Policarpo Toro, T 223326. **Bicycles**: some in poor condition, are available for rent for US$20 on main street or from *residenciales*, or you can buy a robust one in Santiago (LanChile transports bikes free up to a limit of 20 kg) and sell it on the island after 4 days.

Transport to Easter Island Air LanChile fly 4 days a week in high season (Sat, Sun, Tues, Thur), 2 days a week low season (Sun, Thur) 3 hrs 25 mins. Return to Santiago is Mon, Tues, Fri and Sat (Mon, Fri out of season). Most flights continue to Papeete, Tahiti. LanChile office on Av Policarpo Toro, T 223279, reconfirm flights here – imperative; do not fly to Easter Island unless you have a confirmed flight out (planes are more crowded to Tahiti than back to Santiago) and reconfirm your booking on arrival on the Island. For details of LanChile air passes which inc Easter Island and which must be purchased outside Chile, see **Information for travellers**. The fare in 1997 was US$898 return. Special deals may be available on flights originating outside Chile. Get to airport early and be prepared for a scramble for seats. Students studying in Chile eligible for 30% discount. If flying to, or from Tahiti, check if you can stay over till another flight or even if there is time for sightseeing before the flight continues – US$10 stop-over sightseeing tours can be arranged (in either case it won't be long enough to take it all in properly). Don't take pesos to Tahiti, they are worthless in French Polynesia. The airport runway has been improved to provide emergency landing for US space shuttles. **Airport tax**: flying from Santiago to Easter Island incurs the domestic tax of US$8; if flying to Tahiti without stopping on Easter Island you pay the international departure tax of US$18. The airport tax for international flights from Easter Island to Tahiti is US$5.

Sea There are no passenger services to Easter Island. Freight is brought by sea 3 times a year.

Information for travellers

BEFORE YOU GO

ENTRY REQUIREMENTS

● **Documents**

Passport (valid for at least 6 months) and tourist card only are required for entry by all foreigners except citizens of New Zealand, Guyana, Haiti, Kuwait, African countries, Cuba and some ex-Communist countries, who require visas. It is imperative to check visa requirements before travel. These details were correct in Jan 1997 according to the Chilean Consul in London, but regulations change. National identity cards are sufficient for entry by citizens of Argentina, Brazil, Colombia, Paraguay, and Uruguay. Tourist cards are valid for 90 days (except for nationals of Greece, Indonesia and Peru where their validity is 60 days); they can be obtained from immigration offices at major land frontiers and Chilean airports; you must surrender your tourist card on departure and it is essential that you keep it safe. If you wish to stay longer than 90 days (as a tourist), you must buy a 90-day extension from the Departamento de Extranjería (address under Santiago **Useful addresses**); it costs US$100. To avoid this, make a day-trip to Argentina and return with a new tourist card. An onward ticket is officially required but is seldom asked for. Tourist card holders are not allowed to change their status to enable them to stay on in employment or as students: to do this you need a visa, obtained from a Chilean consulate. On arrival you will be asked where you are staying in Chile. For some nationalities a visa will be granted within 24 hrs upon pro-duction of an onward ticket, for others (eg Guyana), authorization must be obtained from Chile. For visitors from New Zealand, single or multiple entry visa costs US$45. For other nationalities who need a visa, a charge is made, but it varies from country to country. Note that to travel overland to or from Tierra del Fuego a multiple entry visa is essential since the Argentine-Chilean border is crossed more than once (it is advisable to get a multiple entry visa before arriving, rather than trying to change a single entry visa once in Chile). A student card is sometimes useful for obtaining discounts on buses, etc. Student cards can be obtained from Hernando de Aguirre 201, of 602, Providencia and cost US$8, photo and proof of status required.

● **Tourist information**

The national secretariat of tourism, *Sernatur*, has offices throughout the country (addresses are given in the text). City offices provide town maps, leaflets and much useful information. A rec guide book is *Turistel*, published annually in three parts, *Norte*, *Centro*, and *Sur*, sponsored by the CTC telephone company, with information and a wealth of maps covering the whole country and neighbouring tourist centres in Argentina (eg Mendoza, San Martín de los Andes, Bariloche), in Spanish only. Each volume costs between US$11-15, depending where you buy it, but buying the whole set is better value; they can be found in CTC offices, bookshops, but best of all in the news stands in the centre of Santiago. Turistel also publishes a *Mapa rutero* annually, US$4 from news stands and a guide to camping US$9. The publisher is Impresora y Comercial Publiguías SA. **Conaf** (the Corporación Nacional Forestal see page 681) publishes a series of illustrated booklets in Spanish/English on Chilean trees, shrubs and flowers, rec, as well as **Juventud, Turismo y Naturaleza**, which lists National Parks, their facilities and the flora and fauna of each. Ancient Forest International, Box 1850, Redway, CA 95560, T/F 707-323-3015, USA, can be contacted regarding Chilean forests. Bird-lovers will appreciate *Guía de Campo de Las Aves de Chile*, by B Araya and G Millie.

WHEN TO GO

● **Best time to visit**

The best time for a visit to Santiago is between Oct and April when fine weather is almost assured, but business visits can be made any time during the year. During the holiday season, between mid Dec and early March, it is sometimes difficult to make appointments.

HEALTH

Tap water is fairly safe to drink in the main cities but bottled water is safer away from the larger centres. Hotels and restaurants are usually clean. Inoculation against hepatitis and typhoid is a wise precaution. Hepatitis type B inoculation is unavailable.

Tampons are available but expensive.

MONEY

● **Currency**

The unit is the peso, its sign is $. Notes are for 500, 1,000, 5,000 and 10,000 pesos and coins for 1, 5, 10, 50 and 100 pesos. There is a shortage of change so keep a supply of small denomination coins.

● **Cost of living**

Shops throughout Chile are well stocked and there is a seasonal supply of all the usual fruits and vegetables. Milk in pasteurized, evaporated, or dried form is obtainable. Chilean tinned food is dear. Food is reasonable, but food prices vary tremendously. Santiago tends to be more expensive for food and accommodation than other parts of Chile. Slide film is very expensive, much cheaper in Bolivia.

In 1996-97 the average cost for a traveller on an economical budget was about US$280/week. Cheap accommodation in Santiago costs over US$10 pp while N and S of the capital rates are US$7-12 pp. Breakfast in hotels, if not inc in price, is about US$2 (instant coffee, roll with ham or cheese, and jam). *Alojamiento* in private houses (bed, breakfast and often use of kitchen) costs US$7-10 pp (bargaining may be possible). Southern Chile is more expensive between 15 Dec and 15 March.

● **Banks & money changers**

Travellers' cheques are accepted at reasonable rates if exchanging them for pesos, rates are better in Santiago than in most other places and this has become more difficult in most towns apart from Arica, Antofagasta and Puerto Montt. TCs can be changed into dollars in Santiago, but is much more difficult elsewhere: check if a commission is charged as this practice seems to vary. Even slightly damaged US dollar notes may be rejected for exchange. Exchange shops (*casas de cambio*) are open longer hours and often give slightly better rates than banks. It is always worth shopping around. Rates tend to get worse as you go N from Santiago. Official rates are quoted in *El Economista* and *El Mercurio*.

Prices may be quoted in US dollars; check if something seems ridiculously cheap. Remember that foreigners who pay with US dollars cash or TCs are not liable for VAT.

The easiest way to obtain cash is by using ATMs (in major cities) which operate under the sign Redbank; they take Cirrus, Visa and Mastercard and permit transactions up to US$250. Diners' Club, Visa and Mastercard are common in Chile (Bancard, the local card, is affliated to the last two), offices can be found in most cities and will give cash against the cards: Fincard handles Mastercard and Banco Concepción takes Visa, but American Express is less useful (use in American Express banks does not incur commission). US dollars cash are very rarely given against cards or cheques. For Western Union, T (02) 696-8807.

GETTING THERE

BY AIR

● **From Europe**

To Santiago: British Airways from London via Rio or São Paulo (3 times a week); Air France from Paris (3 per week); from Madrid LanChile and Iberia (4 a week each); KLM from Amsterdam (3), Lufthansa (3) and LanChile from Frankfurt (4 a week), Alitalia from Rome (2) and Aeroflot from Moscow (2). Connections from Europe can be in Buenos Aires.

● **From North America**

American Airlines fly daily from Miami, direct. LanChile also has daily flights from Miami. Also from Miami, United flies daily and AeroPerú via Lima. From New York, United and Lan Chile. From Los Angeles there are flights with LanChile via Mexico City and Lima, Lacsa via Mexico City, San José and Lima, and Mexicana via Mexico City and Bogotá. From Dallas with American. From other US cities, connect with LanChile flights in Miami, New York or Los Angeles. CP

Air have 2 flights per week from Toronto (changing planes in São Paulo).

● **Transpacific routes**

LanChile flies once or twice a week, depending on season, between Tahiti (making connections from Japan, Australia and New Zealand) and Santiago; they stop over at Easter Island. Air New Zealand and LanChile have a cosharing agreement on weekly flights between Auckland, Sydney and Santiago. For excursion fares between Australia/New Zealand and Chile, the stopovers at Easter Island now carry a surcharge of about US$125.

● **Within Latin America**

To/from Buenos Aires (about 75/week) by LanChile, Aerolíneas Argentinas, Air France, Alitalia, KLM, Swissair, American, or Avianca (many depart at the same time, check carefully); from Mendoza by Aerolíneas Argentinas or National. From Montevideo (8 per week) by LanChile and Pluna; from Asunción 6 times a week by National, 4 days a week with Lapsa; from Rio de Janeiro with British Airways (once) and Iberia direct (4 a week), Lan Chile, or Varig via São Paulo; from São Paulo non-stop by LanChile, Varig, British Airways; from La Paz 5 per week by Lloyd Aéreo Boliviano (LAB) and daily with LanChile (LAB also from Cochabamba twice a week and Santa Cruz 2 a week, LanChile 3 a week from Santa Cruz); from Caracas, LanChile; from Lima (23/week) by Aeroperú, Lacsa, United and LanChile; from Bogotá (12) by Avianca, Mexicana and Lan Chile; from Ecuador, LanChile, Tame and Saeta non-stop from Guayaquil; Saeta and Tame start in Quito.

To Arica and Iquique, from La Paz and Santa Cruz by LAB and LanChile. National flies from Arequipa to Arica and Iquique, also to Iquique from Asunción.

● **Overland From Neighbouring Countries**

By land: Roads connect Santiago with Mendoza, and Osorno and Puerto Montt with Bariloche, in Argentina. Less good road connections N and S of Santiago are described in the main text. The main route connecting northern Chile with Bolivia (Arica-La Paz) is paved. Other routes are poor. Note that any of the passes across the Andes to Argentina can be blocked by snow from April onwards.

Four international railways link Chile with its neighbours. There are two railways to Bolivia: between Arica and La Paz (448 km), and from Antofagasta via Calama to La Paz; and one to Peru: Arica-Tacna. Between Chile and Argentina there is only one line now in operation, between Antofagasta and Salta, in the Argentine NW. There is no international passenger service on this line.

CUSTOMS

● **Duty free allowance**

500 cigarettes, 100 cigars, 500 grams of tobacco, 3 bottles of liquor, camera, and all articles of personal use. Fruit, vegetables, meat, flowers and milk products may not be imported. It has been reported that bringing a video recorder into Chile involves a great deal of paperwork.

NB There are internal customs checks for all travellers going S on leaving the First Region (ie for duty-free goods from the Zofri free zone in Iquique).

WHEN YOU ARRIVE

● **Entry tax**

A US$20 entry tax is charged on all US citizens, valid until expiry of passport.

● **Clothing**

Warm sunny days and cool nights are usual during most of the year except in the far S where the climate is like that of Scotland. Ordinary European medium-weight clothing can be worn during the winter (June to mid-Sept). Light clothing is best for summer (Dec to Mar), but men do not wear white tropical suits. Chileans are very fashion-conscious. Dress well though conservatively: practical travel clothing makes you stick out as a foreigner.

● **Hours of business**

Banks: 0900-1400, but closed on Sat. Government offices: 1000-1230 (the public is admitted for a few hrs only). Business houses: 0830-1230, 1400-1800 (Mon to Fri). Shops (Santiago): 1030-1930, and 0930-1330 Sat.

● **Law enforcement**

Officers are Carabineros (brown military uniforms), who handle all tasks except immigration. Investigaciones, in civilian dress, are the detective police who deal with everything except traffic. Policia Internacional, a division of Investigaciones, handle immigration.

● **Official time**

GMT minus 4 hrs; minus 3 hrs in summer. Clocks change from mid-Sept or Oct to early March.

● **Shopping**

There is an excellent variety of handicrafts: woodwork, pottery, copperware, leatherwork, Indian woven goods inc rugs and ponchos in the S. VAT is 18%.

● **Tipping**

10% in restaurants and a few pesos in bars and soda fountains. Railway and airport porters: US$0.10 a piece of luggage. Cloakroom attendants and cinema usherettes: US$0.05. Taxi-drivers are not tipped.

● **Voltage**
220 volts AC, 50 cycles.

● **Weights & measures**
The **metric** system is obligatory but the quintal of 46 kilos (101.4 lb) is used.

ON DEPARTURE

● **Airport & other taxes**
7,500 pesos, or US$18.25 for international flights; US$8 for domestic flights. There is a tourist tax on single air fares of 2%, and 1% on return fares beginning or ending in Chile; also a sales tax of 5% on all transport within Chile.

WHERE TO STAY

● **Accommodation**
On hotel bills service charges are usually 10%, and VAT on bills is 18%. Prices increase in January. **If you pay in dollars cash or TCs, you do not have to pay VAT**. Dollar rates posted in hotels should not include VAT; peso rates should by law. Whether or not the 18% is added to bills in hotel restaurants that are signed and charged to the hotel bill depends on the policy of the establishment. When booking in make certain whether meals are included in the price or only breakfast or nothing at all, and don't rely on the posted sheet in the bedroom for any prices. It is often worth asking for a discount, especially out of season. Particularly in North and Central Chile breakfast is likely to be coffee and bread or toast. In more popular tourist destinations, especially in the S, large numbers of families offer accommodation: these are usually advertised by a sign in the window; people often meet buses to offer accommodation. If you are looking for a motel, ask for a *motel turístico*; most motels are short stay.

● **Camping**
Camping is easy but no longer cheap at official sites. A common practice is to charge US$10 for up to 5 people, with no reductions for fewer than 5. 'Camping Gaz International' stoves are rec, since green replaceable cylinders are available in Santiago (white gas – *benzina blanca* – is available in hardware shops; for good value try the *Sodimac* chain of DIY stores). Copec run a network of 33 'Rutacentros' along Ruta 5 which have showers, cafeterias and offer free camping. Free camping is also available at many filling stations.

● **Youth hostels**
There are youth hostels throughout Chile; average cost about US$5-8 pp. Although some hostels are open only from Jan to the end of Feb, many operate all year round. The IYHA card is usually readily accepted. In summer they are usually crowded and noisy, with only floor space available. Chilean YHA card costs US$4. An additional stamp costing US$4 enables you to use the card in Argentina, Uruguay and Brazil. IYHA card costs US$15. These can be obtained from the Asociación Chilena de Albergues Turísticos Juveniles, Hernando de Aguirre 201, of 602, Providencia, Santiago, T/F 233-3220; together with a useful guidebook of all Youth Hostels in Chile, *Guía Turística Chilena de los Albergues Juveniles*. In summer there are makeshift hostels in many Chilean towns, usually in the main schools.

FOOD AND DRINK

FOOD

A very typical Chilean dish is *cazuela de ave*, a nutritious stew containing large pieces of chicken, potatoes, rice, and maybe onions, and green peppers; best if served on the second day. *Valdiviano* is another stew, common in the S, consisting of beef, onion, sliced potatoes and eggs. Another popular Chilean dish is *empanadas de pino*, which are turnovers filled with a mixture of raisins, olives, meat, onions and peppers chopped up together. *Pastel de choclo* is a casserole of meat and onions with olives, topped with a maize-meal mash, baked in an earthenware bowl. *Humitas* are mashed sweetcorn mixed with butter and spices and baked in sweetcorn leaves. *Prieta* is a blood sausage stuffed with cabbage leaves. A normal *parrillada* or *asado* is a giant mixed grill served from a charcoal brazier. The *pichanga* is similar but smaller and without the brazier. *Bistek a lo pobre* (a poor man's steak) can be just the opposite: it is a steak topped by a fried egg, mashed potatoes, onions and salad.

What gives Chilean food its personality is the seafood. The delicious *congrio* fish is a national dish, and *caldillo de congrio* (a soup served with a massive piece of conger, onions and potato balls) is excellent. A *paila* can take many forms (the *paila* is simply a kind of dish), but the commonest are made of eggs or seafood. *Paila Chonchi* is a kind of bouillabaisse, but has more flavour, more body, more ingredients. *Parrillada de mariscos* is a dish of grilled mixed seafood, brought to the table piping hot on a charcoal brazier. Other excellent local fish are the *cojinoa*, the *albacora* (swordfish) and the *corvina*. Some shellfish, such as *loco* (known to Australians as abalone) and mussels may be periodically banned because they carry the disease *marea roja* (which is fatal in humans). *Cochayuyo* is seaweed, bound into bundles, described as 'hard, leathery thongs'. The *erizo*, or sea-urchin, s also commonly eaten. *Luche* is dried seaweed, sold as a black cake, like 'flakey bread pudding' to be added to soups and stews.

Avocado pears, or *paltas*, are excellent, and play an important role in recipes. Make sure whether vegetables are included in the price for the main dish; menus often don't make this clear. Always best, if being economical, to stick to fixed-price *table d'hôte* meals or try the local markets. A *barros jarpa* is a grilled cheese and ham sandwich and a *barras luco* is a grilled cheese and beef sandwich. *Sopaipillas* are cakes made of a mixture which includes pumpkin, served in syrup (traditionally made in wet weather). Ice cream is very good; *lúcuma* and *chirimoya* are highly rec flavours.

Lunch is about 1300 and dinner not before 2030. *Onces* (Elevenses) is tea taken at 1700, often accompanied by a snack. The cocktail hour starts at 1900. Waiters are known as *garzón* – never as *mozo*. Good, cheap meals can usually be found in Centros Españoles or Casinos de Bomberos. By law restaurants have to serve a cheaper set meal at lunchtime; it is called *co-lación* and may not be included on the menu.

Coffee is generally instant except in expresso bars including popular chains of cafés such as *Café Haiti*, *Café Brasil* and *Dino*, found in major cities. Elsewhere specify *café-café, expresso*. The soluble tea should be avoided, but tea-bags are widely available. If you order '*café*, or *té, con leche*', it will come with all milk; to have just a little milk in either, you must specify that. After a meal, instead of coffee, try an *agüita* – hot water in which herbs such as mint, or aromatics such as lemon peel, have been steeped. There is a wide variety, available in sachets, and they are very refreshing.

DRINK

The local wines are very good; the best are from the central areas. The bottled wines are graded, in increasing excellence, as *gran vino*, *vino especial* and *vino reservado*. Champagne-style wines are also cheap and acceptable. A small deposit, US$0.30, is charged on most wine bottles. Beer is quite good and cheap (about US$0.75, plus US$0.75 deposit in shops); the draught lager known as *Schop* is good; also try Cristal Pilsener or Royal Guard in the central regions and Escudo and Polar in the S. Malta, a brown ale, is rec for those wanting a British-type beer.

Good gin is made in Chile. Reasonably good brandy, *anís* and crème de menthe are all bottled in Chile. *Pisco* is worth sampling, especially as a 'Pisco Sour' with grapefruit or lemon juice. *Manzanilla* is a local liqueur, made from *licor de oro* (like Galliano); *crema de cacao*, especially Mitjans, has been rec. Two popular drinks are *vaina*,

a mixture of sherry, egg and sugar and *cola de mono*, a mixture of *aguardiente*, coffee, milk and vanilla served very cold at Christmas. *Chicha* is any form of alcoholic drink made from fruit; *chicha cocida* is 3-day-old fermented grape juice boiled to reduce its volume and then bottled with a tablespoonful of honey. Cider (*chicha de manzana*) is popular in the S. *Chicha fresca* is plain apple juice. *Mote con huesillo*, made from wheat hominy and dried peaches, is very refreshing in summer.

GETTING AROUND

AIR TRANSPORT

Most flights of LanChile, Ladeco and National, between Santiago and major towns and cities, are given in the text. Two new airlines, Alta and Avant, fly the length of the country, the former linking smaller cities. Try to sit on the left flying S, on the right flying N to get the best views of the Andes.

LanChile and Ladeco offer a 21-day 'Visit Chile' ticket; 5 prices: US$300, valid for Santiago and northern Chile, or Santiago and southern Chile; US$550 for all mainland Chile; Pacific 1, US$812, Santiago-Easter Island-Santiago; Pacific 2, US$1080, valid for a trip to Easter Island and either northern Chile, or southern Chile; Pacific 3, US$1,290 for all mainland Chile and Eastern Island. It must be purchased abroad in conjunction with an international ticket and reservations made well ahead since many flights are fully booked in advance. Rerouting charge US$30. Booked destinations can be left out so it is worth including as many destinations as possible. The airpass is not interchangeable between airlines. It is also possible for the route Santiago – Antofagasta – Arica – Santiago to take a coupon ticket which allows greater flexibility. **NB** Book well in advance (several months) for flights to Easter Island in Jan-February. Check with the airlines for matrimonial, student and other discounts. Both LanChile and Ladeco sell out-price tickets (up to 50% off) either as part of special promotions or to stand-by passengers (though the availability of standby fares is often denied). Note that with some fares on National, Alta and Avant it is as cheap to fly long distance as take a *salón cama* bus. **NB** You have to confirm domestic flights at least 24 hrs before departure.

LAND TRANSPORT

● Train

There are 6,560 km of line, of which most are state owned. Most of the privately owned 2,130 km of line are in the desert N, where the northern terminal is Iquique. The main gauge on the

Valparaíso and southern lines is 5-ft 6 in (1.676m). Passenger services in the S go as far as Puerto Montt. Passenger services N of the Valparaíso area have ceased except for the international routes to La Paz. The Ferrocarriles del Estado publish an annual *Guía Turística*, available in various languages from the larger stations.

Trains in Chile are moderately priced, and not as slow as in other Andean countries, but dining car food is expensive. Student discounts are given on *económico* and *salón* fares, but not on sleepers. There is a railway information office at O'Higgins 853 (at end of arcade), Santiago, for all lines except the Antofagasta-Bolivia (Ahumada 11, Oficina 602, T 698-5536). English spoken.

● **Roads**

About one-half of the 79,293 km of roads can be used the year round, though a large proportion of them is unimproved and about 12,685 km are paved. The region round the capital and the Central Valley are the best served.

The Pan-American (Longitudinal) Highway, Ruta 5, from Arica through Santiago to Puerto Montt and recently extended by the Carretera Austral beyond Cochrane to within 30 km of its terminus, is vital to the Chilean economy and is paved to Puerto Montt.

● **Bus**

Buses are frequent and on the whole good. Apart from holiday times, there is little problem getting a seat on a long-distance bus. *Salón-cama* services run between main cities (TurBus and Tramaca highly rec). Generally avoid back seats near toilet due to smell and disruption of passing passengers. *Salón-cama* means 25 seats, *semi-cama* means 34 and *Salón-ejecutivo* means 44 seats. Stops are infrequent. Prices are highest between Dec-Mar and fares from Santiago double during the Independence celebrations in September. Since there is lots of competition between bus companies, fares may be bargained lower, particularly just before departure. Students and holders of IYHA cards may get discounts, amount varies, but not usually in high season. Most bus companies will carry bicycles, but may ask for payment (on TurBus payment is mandatory).

● **Motoring**

Car drivers require a *Relaciones de pasajeros* document, available at borders, and must present the original registration document of their vehicle, as must motor cyclists. Insurance is obligatory and can be bought at borders. See also **Motoring** in **Introduction and Hints**. The Carta Caminera from the Dirección de Vialidad is the most detailed road map (series of 26) but is only available at Vialidad, Marsende y Alameda, Santiago. Reasonable road maps may also be obtained from the Automóvil Club de Chile, Av Vitacura 8620, Santiago; or other regional offices. You will find several individual maps provide much greater detail than the Club's road atlas. Members of foreign motoring organizations may join the Automóvil Club de Chile (US$58/3months), and obtain discounts at hotels. Town maps from the Automóvil Club and Copec service stations. Shell publish a *Guía caminera y turística de Chile*. The *Turistel* Guides are very useful for roads and town plans, but note that not all distances are exact and that the description 'ripio' (gravel) usually requires high clearance; 'buen ripio' should be OK for ordinary cars. Hydrographic maps from Instituto Hidrográfico, Malgarejo 59, Valparaíso. Gasoline (sold in litres) costs the equivalent of US$2.40 a gallon; it becomes more expensive the further N and further S you go. Unleaded fuel, 93 octane, is available at many service stations, but less frequently outside Santiago and not in the Atacama region. Unleaded 95 and 97 octane are less common. Diesel fuel is widely available. Service stations are frequently reluctant to accept credit cards. Often when they advertise that they accept credit cards, they refuse to do so: always ask beforehand. In Santiago car parts available from many shops on C 10 de Julio. For car and motorcycle tyres try Serranos 32, reported to be the best stock in South America.

Carabineros are strict about speed limits: Turistel maps mark police posts, make sure you are not speeding when you pass them. Car drivers should have all their papers in order and to hand since there are frequent checks, but fewer in the S. When driving in the S (on the Carretera Austral particularly), and in the desert N, always top up your fuel tank and carry spare petrol/gasoline. Car hire companies may not have fuel cans. These are obtainable from some supermarkets but not from service stations. Tyres need to be hard-wearing (avoid steel belt); it is rec to carry more than one spare and additional inner tubes.

For motorcyclists the following shops in Santiago have been rec: *Calvín y Calvín*, Av Las Condes 8038, T 224-3434, run by Winston Calvín, friendly, helpful, speaks English, knows about necessary paperwork for buying bikes, Honda and Yamaha parts and service; *Solo Moto*, Vitacura 2760, T 2311178, English spoken, service and parts for Honda and Yamaha; *Moto Service*, Vitacura 2715, new and second-hand Honda and Yamaha dealer; *Guillermo de Freitas Rojas* (Willy), C Félix Mendelson, 4740-Santiago, T 521-1853, excellent BMW mechanic; *Miebacc*, Doble Almeda 1040, Nunoa, T 2237533, for BMW parts and service. Mechanics, etc outside Santiago are given in the text.

● **Car hire**

Many agencies, both local and international, operate in Chile. Vehicles may be rented by the day, the week or the month, with or without unlimited mileage. Rates quoted do not normally include insurance or 18% VAT. Make sure you know what the insurance covers, in particular third-party insurance. Often this is only likely to cover small bumps and scratches. Ask about extra cover for a further premium. If you are in a major accident and your insurance is inadequate, your stay in Chile may well be prolonged beyond its intended end. A small car, with unlimited mileage costs about US$500 a week in high season, a pick-up much more. In some areas rates are much lower off-season. (At peak holiday times, eg Independence celebrations, car hire is very difficult.) Shop around, there is much competition. Note that the Automóvil Club de Chile has a car hire agency (with discounts for members or affiliates) and that the office has regional delegation. **NB** If intending to leave the country in a hired car, you must obtain an authorization from the hire company, otherwise you will be turned back at the frontier. When leaving Chile this is exchanged for a quadruple form, one part of which is surrendered at each border control. (If you plan to leave more than once you will need to photocopy the authorization.)

● **Taxis**

Taxis have meters, but agree beforehand on fares for long journeys out of city centres or special excursions. A 50% surcharge is applied after 2100 and on Sun. Taxi drivers rarely know the location of any streets away from the centre. There is no need to tip unless some extra service, like the carrying of luggage, is given. Collective taxis are often little more expensive than buses.

● **Hitchhiking**

Hitchhiking is easy and safe, but in some regions traffic is sparse.

● **Skiing**

Bradt Publications' *South America Ski Guide*, 1992, gives thorough coverage of all Chile's ski areas.

BOAT

Shipping information is given in the text under Santiago and all the relevant southern ports. Local newspapers are useful for all transport schedules.

COMMUNICATIONS

● **Language**

The local pronunciation of Spanish, very quick and lilting, with final syllables cut off, can present difficulties to the foreigner.

● **Postal services**

Airmail takes 3-4 days from the UK. Seamail takes 8-12 weeks. There is a daily airmail service to Europe with connections to the UK. Poste restante only holds mail for 30 days, then returns it to sender. Lista de Correo in Santiago, Central Post Office, is good and efficiently organized. Rates: letters to Europe/North America US$1.20, aerogrammes US$0.75. To register a letter costs US$0.75. Surface mail rates for parcels to Europe: Less than 1 kg US$14; 1-3 kg US$18; 10 kg US$30.

● **Telephone services**

National and international calls have been opened up for competition. In May 1996 there were eight main companies (*portadores* carriers) offering competing rates (widely advertised). Callers choose companies by dialling an access code before the city code. Access codes: Entel 123; CTC Mundo 188, CNT (Telefónica del Sur – in Regions X and XI) 121: VTR 120; Chilesat 171; Bell South Chile 181; Iusatel Chile 155 (under new ownership, Jan 1997); Transam Comunicaciones 113. For international calls you dial the company code, then 0, then the country code. International calls are cheap. Ask which carrier has the best links with the country you wish to call (eg for making collect calls); for instance CTC is good for phoning Germany.

Telephone boxes can be used to make local and long-distance calls, for making collect calls and receiving calls. Although it is possible to make international calls from these phones, in practice it may be easier to go to a company office. Telephone boxes have been programmed to direct calls via one carrier: to make a local call, simply dial the number you require and pay the rate charged by the carrier who owns the booth, US$0.20-0.30/minute. To make an inter-urban call, dial '0' plus the area code (DDD) and the number; if you wish to select a carrier, dial its code, then the area code (leaving out '0'), then the number. The area codes given in the text include '0'; omit this if selecting a carrier. To make an international call from a carrier's booth without choosing a different company, dial '00' before the country code. Yellow phones accept only 50 peso coins. Blue phones accept pre-paid phone cards costing 5,000 pesos (*tarjeta telefónica*); available from kiosks. On phone cards, only the time of the call is charged rather than the normal 3 min minimum. There are special phones for long-distance domestic calls which accept credit cards (Mastercard and Visa). Entel has strategically-placed, self-dialling phones, which are white. Users press a button and are instantly connected with the operator from their own country.

To send a fax abroad costs US$4-5, depending on the company. There is also a charge for receiving a fax. VTR also operate telex services. Amex Card holders can often use telex facilities at Amex offices free of charge.

MEDIA

● **Newspapers**
Santiago daily papers *El Mercurio, La Nación* (state-owned), *La Epoca* (liberal/left), *La Segunda, La Tercera* and *La Quarta. Las Ultimas Noticias. The Latest Daily News* is an English language paper, published daily except Mon, in Santiago, with international news and tourism details. Also in English is *The News Review*, published twice weekly. *Condor*, weekly in German.

Weekly magazines; *Hoy, Qué Pasa, Ercilla.* Monthly: *Rutas* (official organ, Automobile Association).

● **Television**
TV channels include TVUC (Universidad Católica) on Channel 13, the leading station; TVN (government operated) on Channel 7; Megavisión (private) on Channel 9 and La Red (private) on Channel 4.

SPORT

Sernatur will give all the necessary information about sport.

Skiing Season from June to Sept/Oct, weather depending. For information write to: La Federación de Ski de Chile, Casilla 9902, Santiago.

Horse racing is popular and meetings are held every Sun and on certain feast days at Viña del Mar, Santiago and Concepción throughout the year; horse riding and rodeo are also popular.

Fishing Santiago and Valparaíso residents fish at the mountain resort of Río Blanco. Some of the world's best fishing is in the Lake District, but this region is very popular. Better still, and rela-

tively less-heavily fished, are the lakes and rivers S of Puerto Montt: Lago Yelcho, Río Futaleufú, Río Yelcho, the rivers and lakes S of Chaitén to La Junta, around Coyhaique and around Cochrane. The licence required can be got from the local police or such angling associations as the Asociación de Pesca y Caza, which gives information on local conditions, or Sernap, San Antonio 427, p 8, Santiago, open Mon-Fri 0900-1400, US$2 a year. Check with Sernatur on closed seasons. Outside Chile, all information can be obtained from Sport Elite Ltd, Woodwalls House, Corscombe, Dorchester, Dorset, UK, DT2 0NT, T 093589-1477, F 093589-1797 (Major J A Valdes-Scott).

Other popular sports are football and basketball. Viña del Mar has a cricket ground; on Sat there are polo matches at Santiago.

HOLIDAYS AND FESTIVALS

1 Jan, New Year's Day; Holy Week (2 days); 1 May, Labour Day; 21 May, Navy Day; 15 Aug, Assumption; 18, 19 Sept, Independence Days; 12 Oct, Discovery of America; 1 Nov, All Saints Day; 8 Dec, Immaculate Conception; 25 Dec, Christmas Day.

ACKNOWLEDGEMENTS

For updating this chapter, our warmest thanks are due to Charlie Nurse, who visited Patagonia in early 1997. He would like to thank for their assistance and hospitality: Adrian Turner (Puerto Montt); Werner and Cecilia Ruf-Chaura, Casa Cecilia, Puerto Natales; Helen Fell, Arka Patagonia, Punta Arenas; Arturo Aliaga Mancilla, Turismo Comapa, Punta Arenas; Manuel and Ximena Fernández and family and their relatives, Sra Leontina VDA de Standen and family, and Sr Luis Pineda and family, all in Santiago.

Colombia

HORIZONS

Colombia is the fourth largest country in South America. It has coast lines on both the Caribbean (1,600 km) and the Pacific (1,306 km). Nearly 55% of the area is almost uninhabited lowland with only 4% of the population; the other 96% are concentrated in the remaining 45%, living for the most part in narrow valleys or isolated intermont basins, or in the broad Caribbean lowlands. The population is infinitely varied, ranging from white, Indian, and black to mixtures of all three.

THE LAND

The 620,000 sq km of almost uninhabited land in Colombia lie E of the Eastern Cordillera. Near the foot of the Cordillera the plains are used for cattle ranching, but beyond is jungle. Islands of settlement in it are connected with the rest of the country by air and river, for there are no railways and very few roads.

In the populous western 45% of the country four ranges of the Andes run from S to N. Between the ranges run deep longitudinal valleys. Of the 14 main groups of population in the country, no less than 11 are in the mountain basins or in the longitudinal valleys; the other three are in the lowlands of the Caribbean.

THE PACIFIC COAST

The first 320 km along the Pacific coast N from the frontier with Ecuador to the port of Buenaventura is a wide, marshy, and sparsely inhabited coastal lowland. Along the coast N of Buenaventura runs the Serranía de Baudó. East of this range the forested lowlands narrow into a low trough of land; E of the trough again rise the slopes of the Western Cordillera. The trough (the Department of the Chocó) is drained southwards into the Pacific by the Río San Juan, navigable for 200 km, and northwards into the Caribbean by the Río Atrato, navigable for 550 km. The climate is hot and torrential rain falls daily. The inhabitants are mostly black.

THE CORDILLERAS

From the borders of Ecuador two ranges of mountains, the Western Cordillera and the Central Cordillera, run N for 800 km to the Caribbean lowlands. Five peaks in the Western Cordillera are over 4,000m but none reaches the snowline. The Central Cordillera, 50-65 km wide, is much higher; six of its peaks, snow clad, rise above 5,000m and its highest, the volcano cone of Huila, is 5,439m. Apart from the peaks, mostly inactive volcanoes, there are large areas of high undulating plateaux dissected by deep river gorges giving spectacular scenery. There are narrow ribbons of soil along some of the rivers.

Between the two ranges, as they

emerge from Ecuador, lies a valley filled in the S to a height of 2,500m by ash from the volcanoes. Further N between these two ranges lies the Cauca valley; in its northern 190 km, roughly from Popayán N past Cali to Cartago, there is an important agricultural region based on a deep

	Colombia
1	Bogotá
2	Bogotá to Cúcuta
3	The North Coast and Islands
4	Up the Magdalena River
5	The Central Cordillera: Medellín and Manizales
6	The Cauca Valley
7	Popayán, Tierradentro and San Agustín
8	The Llanos and Leticia
9	Southern Colombia

bed of black alluvial soil which yields as many as five crops a year. This valley, which is at a height of about 1,000m and up to 50 km wide, is drained northwards by the Río Cauca. Cali, the second city, is the business centre of the valley, and a road and railway run from Cali over a low pass of less than 1,500m in the Western Cordillera to Buenaventura. Sugar cane was the great crop of this valley in colonial times, but has now been varied with tobacco, soya, cotton, pineapple, and every other kind of tropical fruit. There is still some cattle raising. Coffee is grown on the Cordillera slopes above 600m.

At Cartago the two Cordilleras close in and the Cauca valley becomes a deep gorge which runs all the way to the Caribbean flatlands. In the Cordillera Central, at an altitude of 1,540m, is the third largest city and industrial centre in Colombia: Medellín. Much of the coffee and 75% of the gold comes from this area. North of Medellín the Cordillera Central splits into three ranges, separated by streams flowing into the Caribbean.

Near Latitude 2°N, or about 320 km N of the Ecuadorean border, the Eastern Cordillera, the longest of all, rises and swings N and then NE towards Venezuela. About Latitude 7°N it divides; one branch becomes the western rim of the Maracaibo basin and the other runs E into Venezuela, to the S of the Maracaibo basin.

Between this Eastern Cordillera and the Central Cordillera runs the 1,600 km long Río Magdalena, with the Caribbean port of Barranquilla at its mouth. There are more intermont basins in the Eastern Cordillera than in the others. Some of its peaks rise above the snow line. In the Sierra Nevada del Cocuy (just before the Cordillera divides) there is a group of snowy peaks, all over 5,200m; the highest, Ritacuba Blanca, reaches 5,493m. The basins are mostly high, at an altitude of from 2,500 to 2,750m. In the Lower Magdalena region the river banks are comparatively deserted, though there are a few clearings made by the descendants of black slaves who settled along the Magdalena after their emancipation. There

are oilfields in the valley, particularly at Barrancabermeja.

In a high basin of the Eastern Cordillera, 160 km E of the Río Magdalena, the Spaniards in 1538 founded the city of Bogotá, now the national capital. The great rural activity here is the growing of food: cattle, wheat, barley, maize and potatoes.

Roads run N from Bogotá to the basins of Chiquinquirá and Sogamoso, over 160 km away. Both are in the Department of Boyacá, with Tunja, on a mountain between the two, as capital. Both basins, like that of Bogotá, produce food, and there are emerald mines at Muzo, near Chiquinquirá.

There are other basins in the N of the Eastern Cordillera: in the Departments of Santander and Norte de Santander at Bucaramanga and Cúcuta, and a small one at Ocaña. Movement into these basins by Europeans and *mestizos* did not take place until the 19th century, when chinchona bark (for quinine) rose into high demand. By 1885 this trade was dead, but by that time coffee was beginning to be planted. In Bucaramanga coffee is now the main crop, but it has been diversified by cacao, cotton and tobacco, all grown below the altitude suitable for coffee.

There is one more mountain group in Colombia, the Sierra Nevada de Santa Marta, standing isolated from the other ranges on the shores of the Caribbean. This is the highest range of all: its snow-capped peaks rise to 5,800m within 50 km of the coast.

THE CARIBBEAN LOWLANDS

To the W of this Sierra, and N of where the Central and Western Cordilleras come to an end, lies a great lowland which has three groups of population on its Caribbean shores; at Cartagena, Barranquilla and Santa Marta. The rivers draining this lowland (the Magdalena, Sinú, Cauca, San Jorge and César) run so slowly that much of the area is a network of swamps and lagoons with very little land that can be cultivated. Indeed the whole area E of the channel of the Magdalena is under water at most times of the year. When the floods come, large areas of the land W of the Magdalena – the plains of Bolívar – are covered too, but during the dry season from Oct to Mar great herds of cattle are grazed there.

NATIONAL PARKS

Colombia has 43 National Nature Parks (RNN) and Flora and Fauna Sanctuaries (SFF). They vary in size from the tiny island of Corota in the Laguna de la Cocha near the border with Ecuador to large areas of forest in the eastern lowlands. All the significant mountain areas are National Parks including the Sierra Nevada de Santa Marta, El Cocuy, El Nevado de Huila, Los Nevados (Tolima and Ruíz) and Puracé. There are 14 on or near the Caribbean and Pacific coasts.

All except the smallest parks have one or more centres staffed with rangers (*guardaparques*) which often offer information and guidance for visitors. Most, however, are remote with difficult access and few facilities. Because Colombia's parks are virtually free of 'tourism', they are of particular interest to those looking for unspoilt natural surroundings. Admission charges are high and are based on high and low seasons. High season is: weekends, June-July, Dec-Jan, public holidays, Semana Santa.

The parks' service is the responsibility of the Unidad Administrativa Especial del Sistema de Parques Nacionales Naturales (UAE) at the Ministerio del Medio Ambiente (Ministry of the Environment) referred to in this guide as 'MA'. Their main office for information is in the Caja Agraria building at Cra 10, No 20-30, p 8, Bogotá, T 283-0964, F 341-5331. They publish a National Parks guide, attractive and informative, US$10 (pay in Tesorería on the 7th floor, collect book on the 2nd floor). Information on individual parks and the entry charges is available on the 8th floor. Permits to visit the parks are obtainable here and at the many MA offices near the parks themselves (see text). If you intend to visit the parks, this is a good place to start and ask for up-to-

date details. Information is also available on possibilities to work as volunteer rangers, minimum 30 days, maximum 90: Juan David Herrera, office on 8th floor, very helpful.

Other useful address: Ecotourism office, Cra 13, No 93-40, T 623-3508, open Mon-Fri 0800-1700, Dra Sara Hernández. *Fundción FES*, C5, No 6-05, Cali, or C19, No 22-64 (María Cristina Benevides), Pasto, T (92) 884-5933, F 884-4706 (Cali) for information on private reserves in Nariño. *Red de Reservas Naturales de la Sociedad Civil*, C23N, No 6AN-43, p 3 (Amparo Casasfranco, coordinadora administrativa), Cali, T 661-2581, F 660-6133, e-mail: resnatur@mafalda.univalle. edu. co, also for private reserves around the country. *Organización Nacional de Indígenas de Colombia* (ONIC), C13, No 4-38, Bogotá, T 284-2168, very helpful on indigenous peoples and access to their communities. *Instituto Colombiano de Antropología* (ICAN, C8, No 8-87, T 333-0535, Mon-Thur 0830-1630, Fri 0830-1230, also very helpful.

HISTORY

Before the coming of the Spaniards the country was occupied by Indians, most of whom were primitive hunters or nomad agriculturists, but one part of the country, the high basins of the Eastern Cordillera, was densely occupied by Chibcha Indians who had become sedentary farmers. Their staple foods were maize and the potato, and they had no domestic animal save the dog; the use they could make of the land was therefore limited. Other cultures present in Colombia in the precolumbian era were the Tairona, Quimbaya, Sinú and Calima. Exhibits of their and the Chibcha (Muisca) Indians' gold-work can be seen at the Gold Museum in Bogotá (see page 865).

SPANISH COLONIZATION

The Spaniards sailed along the northern coast as far as Panama as early as 1500. The first permanent settlement was by Rodrigo de Bastidas at Santa Marta in 1525. Cartagena was founded in 1533. In 1536, Gonzalo Jiménez de Quesada (who wrote a full account of his adventures) pushed up the Río Magdalena to discover its source; mounting the Eastern Cordillera in 1536, he discovered the Chibchas, conquered them, and founded Santa Fe de Bogotá in 1538. In the meantime other Spanish forces were approaching the same region: Pizarro's lieutenant, Sebastián de Belalcázar, had pushed down the Cauca valley from Ecuador and founded Pasto, Popayán and Cali in 1536. Nicolás de Federmann, acting on behalf of the Welser financiers of Germany, who had been granted a colonial concession by Charles V, approached from Venezuela. Belalcázar reached Bogotá in 1538 and Federmann got there in 1539. As in Peru, the initial period of settlement was one of strife between contending *conquistadores*. The royal Audiencia de Santa Fe set up in 1550 gave the area a legislative, judicial and administrative entity. In 1564 this was followed by a presidency of the kingdom of Nueva Granada controlling the whole country and Panama, except Belalcázar's province of Popayán. The Presidency was replaced in 1718 by a viceroyalty at Bogotá which controlled the provinces now known as Venezuela as well; it was independent of the Viceroyalty of Peru, to which this vast area had previously been subject.

INDEPENDENCE FROM SPAIN

The movement towards independence from Spain was set going in 1794 by a translation into Spanish by the *criollo* Antonio Nariño of the French Declaration of the Rights of Man. The movement was given point and force when, in 1808, Napoleon replaced Ferdinand VII of Spain with his own brother Joseph. The New World refused to recognize this: there were several revolts in Nueva Granada, culminating in a revolt at Bogotá and the setting up of a *junta* on 20 July 1810. Other local *juntas* were established: Cartagena bound itself to a *junta* set up at Tunja. Late in 1812 the young Bolívar, driven out of Venezuela, landed at Cartagena. In a brilliant campaign in 1813 he pushed up the Magdalena to Ocaña, and from there to Cúcuta, and obtained permission from the *junta* at Tunja to advance into Venezuela. In 90 days

he marched the 1,200 km to Caracas over mountain country, fighting six battles, but he was unable to hold Caracas and withdrew to Cartagena in 1814.

Napoleon fell in 1815, and the Spanish Government immediately set about reconquering, with some success, Venezuela and New Granada. Gen Pablo Morillo took Cartagena after a bitter siege of 106 days (Bolívar had withdrawn to Jamaica) and was later "pacifying" Bogotá with a "Reign of Terror" by May 1816.

Bolívar had by now assembled an army of Llaneros, fortified by a British legion recruited from ex-servicemen of the Peninsular wars, in Venezuela at Angostura (now Ciudad Bolívar). In the face of incredible difficulties he made a forced march across the Andes in 1819. After joining up with Francisco de Paulo Santander's Nueva Granada army, he defeated the royalists at the battle of the Swamps of Vargas in July and again at Boyacá on 7 August. He entered Bogotá 3 days later.

GRAN COLOMBIA

Bolívar reported his success to the revolutionary congress sitting at Angostura, and that body, on 17 December 1819, proclaimed the Republic of Gran Colombia, embracing in one the present republics of Venezuela, Colombia, and Ecuador. A general congress was held at Cúcuta on 1 January 1821, and here it was that two opposing views which were to sow such dissension in Colombia first became apparent. Bolívar and Nariño were for centralization; Santander, a realist, for a federation of sovereign states. Bolívar succeeded in enforcing his view for the time being, but Gran Colombia was not to last long; Venezuela broke away in 1829 and Ecuador in 1830. The remaining provinces were named Nueva Granada; it was not till 1863 that the name Colombia was restored.

COLOMBIA'S CIVIL WARS

Almost from its inception the new country became the scene of strife between the centralizing pro-clerical Conservatives and the federalizing anti-clerical Liberals.

From 1849 the Liberals were dominant during the next 30 years of insurrections and civil wars. In 1885 the Conservatives imposed a highly centralized constitution which was not modified for over 100 years. A Liberal revolt in 1899 turned into a civil war, "the War of the Thousand Days". The Liberals were finally defeated in 1902 after 100,000 people had died. It was in 1903 that Panama declared its independence from Colombia, following US pressure.

After 40 years of comparative peace, the strife between Conservatives and Liberals was reignited in a little-publicized but dreadfully bloody civil war known as *La Violencia* from 1948 to 1957 (some 300,000 people were killed). This was ended by a unique political truce, decided by plebiscite in 1957 under which the two political parties supported a single presidential candidate, divided all political offices equally between them, and thus maintained political stability for 16 years. In 1978 the agreement was ended, though some elements of the coalition were allowed to continue until 1986. Sr Belisario Betancur, the Conservative president from 1982-86, offered a general amnesty to guerrilla movements in an attempt to end violence in the country. Following an initial general acceptance of the offer, only one of the four main guerrilla groups, the FARC, upheld the truce in 1985-7. In May 1986, when the Liberal candidate, Sr Virgilio Barco, won the presidential elections, FARC's newly-formed political party, the Unión Patriótica (UP), won 10 seats in congress; the Liberal party took the majority. Right-wing groups refused to accept the UP and by the beginning of 1990, 1,040 party members had been killed in 5 years. During the campaign for the 1990 presidential both the Liberal Party and the UP presidential candidates, Luis Carlos Galán and Bernardo Jaramillo, were assassinated.

Peace talks between the government and the Coordinadora Guerrillera (CG, an umbrella group representing all the insurgent factions) collapsed, to be followed in 1992-93 by several indecisive, but destructive offensives on the part of both the guerrillas and the armed forces.

THE NARCOTICS TRADE

In Medellín and Cali, two cartels transformed Colombia's drugs industry into a major force in worldwide business and crime. Their methods were very different: Medellín being ostentatious and violent, Cali much more low-key. In 1986, President Barco instigated an international effort to bring them to justice, but opposition to extradition of suspects to the USA stymied progress. Pablo Escobar, the alleged leader of the Medellín drugs cartel, who had surrendered under secret terms in 1991, escaped from custody in July 1992. Despite a multi-million dollar reward offered for his recapture and renewed conditional offers of surrender, he remained at large until his death in Dec 1993.

Having won the presidential elections held on 27 May, 1990, César Gaviria Trujillo (Liberal), took up the candidacy of the murdered Luis Carlos Galán, appointed a coalition government made up of Liberals from rival factions, Conservatives and the M-19 leader. As a result of the reform of the Constitution in 1991, a further general election was held in Oct 1991 (although not due until 1994), and the Liberals retained a majority in the Senate and the House of Representatives. Voter turnout was low, but many small parties, including M-19 and the indigenous National Indian Organization gained representation in Congress.

The Gaviria government was unable to stem violence, whether perpetrated by drug traffickers, guerrillas or common criminals. Not surprisingly, this was one of the issues in the 1994 election campaign, in which Ernesto Samper (Liberal) defeated Andrés Pastrana (Conservative). The main thrust of Samper's programme was that Colombia's current economic strength should provide resources to tackle the social deprivation which causes drug use and insurgency. He placed much emphasis on bringing the FARC and ELN guerrillas to the negotiating table and on public spending on social welfare. Most impetus was lost during 1995-97, in the wake of revelations that Samper's election campaign had received about US$6mn from the Cali cartel. Some ministers resigned, others were arrested and jailed for complicity. The debate over Samper's awareness of the funding lasted until June 1996, almost overshadowing the capture or surrender of most of the leading Cali drug lords. That Congress voted to absolve Samper of all knowledge of the money may have eased the domestic political crisis, but it created new problems. The USA having decided in Mar 1996 to decertify (remove) Colombia from its list of countries making progress against drugs trafficking, dismissed Congress's ruling and denied Samper the right to a US visa. To Colombia's consternation, the US Congress again decertified the country in Mar 1997, not least because the Cali cartel bosses were continuing their business from prison having been given light sentences. Whatever progress was being made to eradicate drugs plantations and stocks, the denial of US aid through decertification permitted little scope for the establishment of alternative crops. Many rural communities were therefore left without means of support. At the same time, the level of violence around the country remained high, with FARC and ELN still active.

CULTURE

PEOPLE

The regions vary greatly in their racial make-up: Antioquia and Caldas are largely of European descent, Pasto is Indian, the Cauca Valley and the rural area near the Caribbean are African or *mulato*. No colour bar is legally recognized but it does exist in certain centres. Population figures of cities and towns in the text refer to the 1993 census.

The birth and death rates vary greatly from one area to the other, but in general infant mortality is high. Hospitals and clinics are few in relation to the population. About 66% of the doctors are in the departmental capitals, which contain about half of the population, though all doctors have

to spend a year in the country before they can get their final diploma.

An estimated 400,000 tribal peoples, from 60 ethnic groups, live in Colombia. Groups include the Wayun (in the Guajira), the Kogi and Arhauco (Sierra Nevada de Santa Marta), Amazonian indians such as the Witoto, the nomadic Nukak and the Ticuna, Andean indians and groups of the Llanos and in the Pacific Coast rain forest. The diversity and importance of indigenous peoples was recognized in the 1991 constitutional reforms when indians were granted the right to two senate seats; the National Colombian Indian Organization (ONIC) won a third seat in the Oct 1991 ballot. State recognition and the right to bilingual education has not, however, solved major problems of land rights, training and education, and justice.

EDUCATION

Education is free, and since 1927 theoretically compulsory, but many children, especially in rural areas, do not attend. There are high standards of secondary and university education, when it is available.

MUSIC AND DANCE

No South American country has a greater variety of music than Colombia, strategically placed where the Andes meet the Caribbean. The four major musical areas are (a) the mountain heartland (b) the Pacific coast (c) the Caribbean coast and (d) the Llanos or eastern plains.

The mountain heartland

The heartland covers the Andean highlands and intervening valleys of the Cauca and Magdalena and includes the country's three largest cities, Bogotá, Cali and Medellín. It is relatively gentle and sentimental music, accompanied largely by string instruments, with an occasional flute and a *chucho* or *carángano* shaker to lay down the rhythm. The preferred instrument of the highlands and by extension Colombia's national instrument, is the *tiple*, a small 12-stringed guitar, most of which are manufactured at

Chiquinquirá in Boyacá. The national dance is the Bambuco, whose lilting sounds are said to have inspired Colombian troops at the Battle of Ayacucho in 1824. It is to be found throughout the country's heartland for dancing, singing and instrumentalizing and has long transcended its folk origins. The choreography is complex, including many figures, such as la Invitación, Los Ochos, Los Codos, Los Coqueteos, La Perseguida and La Arrodilla. Other related dances are the Torbellino, where the woman whirls like a top, the more stately Guabina, the Pasillo, Bunde, Sanjuanero and the picaresque Rajaleña. Particularly celebrated melodies are the "Guabina Chiquinquireña" and the "Bunde Tolimense". The following fiestas, among others, provide a good opportunity of seeing the music and dance:- La Fiesta del Campesino, ubiquitous on the first Sun in June, the Fiesta del Bambuco in Neiva and Festival Folklórico Colombiano in Ibagué later in the month, the Fiesta Nacional de la Guabina y el Tiple, held in Velez in early Aug, the Desfile de Silleteros in Medellín in the same month and Las Fiestas de Pubenza in Popayán just after the New Year, where the Conjuntos de Chirimía process through the streets.

The Pacific coast

On Colombia's tropical Pacific coast (and extending down into Esmeraldas, Ecuador) is to be found some of the most African sounding black music in all South America. The Currulao and its variants, the Berejú and Patacoré, are extremely energetic recreational dances and the vocals are typically African-style call- and-response. This is the home of the *marimba* and the music is very percussion driven, including the upright *cununo* drum plus *bombos* and *redoblantes*. Wakes are important in this region and at these the Bundes, Arrullos and Alabaos are sung. Best known is the "Bunde de San Antonio". The Jota Chocoana is a fine example of a Spanish dance taken by black people and tuned into a satirical weapon against their masters. The regional fiestas are the Festival Folklórico del Litoral at Buenaventura in July and San Francisco de Asís at Quibdó on 4 August. Quibdó also features a "Fiesta de los Indios" at Easter.

The Caribbean coast

The music of Colombia's Caribbean lowlands became popular for dancing throughout Latin America more than 30 years ago under the name of "Música Tropical" and has much more recently become an integral part of the Salsa repertory. It can be very roughly divided into 'Cumbia' and 'Vallenato'. The Cumbia is a heavily black influenced dance form for several couples, the men forming an outer circle and the women an inner one. The men hold aloft a bottle of rum and the women a bundle of slim candles called "espermas". The dance probably originated in what is now Panama, moved E into Cartagena, where it is now centred and quite recently further E to Barranquilla and Santa Marta. The most celebrated Cumbias are those of Ciénaga, Mompós, Sampués, San Jacinto and Sincelejo. The instrumental accompaniment consists of *gaitas* or *flautas de caña de millo*, backed by drums. The *gaitas* ("male" and "female") are vertical cactus flutes with beeswax heads, while the *cañas de millo* are smaller transverse flutes. The most famous conjuntos are the Gaiteros de San Jacinto, the Cumbia Soledeña and the Indios Selectos. Variants of the Cumbia are the Porro, Gaita, Puya, Bullerengue and Mapalé, these last two being much faster and more energetic. Lately Cumbia has also become very much part of the Vallenato repertoire and is therefore often played on the accordion. Vallenato music comes from Valledupar in the Department of Cesar and is of relatively recent origin. It is built around one instrument, the accordion, albeit backed by *guacharaca* rasps and *caja* drums. The most popular rhythms are the Paseo and the Merengue, the latter having arrived from the Dominican Republic, where it is the national dance. Perhaps the first virtuoso accordionist was the legendary "Francisco El Hombre", playing around the turn of the century. Today's best known names are those of Rafael Escalona, Alejandro

Durán and Calixto Ochoa. In April the Festival de la Leyenda Vallenata is held in Valledupar and attended by thousands. Barranquilla is the scene of South America's second most celebrated Carnival, after that of Rio de Janeiro, with innumerable traditional masked groups, such as the Congos, Toros, Diablos and Caimanes. The Garabato is a dance in which death is defeated. Barranquilla's carnival is less commercialized and more traditional than that of Rio and should be a "must" for anyone with the opportunity to attend. Other important festivals in the region are the Corralejas de Sincelejo with its bullfights in Jan, La Candelaria in Cartagena on 2 Feb, the Festival de la Cumbia in El Banco in June, Fiesta del Caiman in Ciénaga in Jan and Festival del Porro in San Pelayo (Córdoba). To complete the music of the Caribbean region, the Colombian islands of San Andrés and Providencia, off the coast of Nicaragua, have a fascinating mix of mainland Colombian and Jamaican island music, with the Calypso naturally a prominent feature.

The Llanos

The fourth musical region is that of the great eastern plains, the so-called Llanos Orientales between the Ríos Arauca and Guaviare, a region where there is really no musical frontier between the two republics of Colombia and Venezuela. Here the Joropo reigns supreme as a dance, with its close relatives the Galerón, the slower and more romantic Pasaje and the breathlessly fast Corrido and Zumba que Zumba. These are dances for couples, with a lot of heel tapping, the arms hanging down loosely to the sides. Arnulfo Briceño and Pentagrama Llanera are the big names and the harp is the only instrument that matters, although normally backed by *cuatro*, guitar, *tiple* and *maracas*. Where to see and hear it all is at the Festival Nacional del Joropo at Villavicencio in Dec.

THE ECONOMY

Structure of production Colombia has varied natural resources and an economic structure which is no longer dependent on any one commodity. Agriculture is the major employer, providing about 13% of gdp and about half of total legal exports. The traditional crops are coffee, flowers, sugar cane, bananas, rice, maize and cotton. Colombia is the leading producer of mild Arabica coffee and second to Brazil in world production. Diversification since 1984 and disease have reduced output, but exports of coffee still amount to about a fifth of total exports, depending on world prices. About 1 million ha are planted to coffee in the central Andes and production is around 11-12 million bags a year. Flowers, mostly grown near Bogotá because of ease of access to the airport, are exported mainly to the USA. Expansion has been so successful that Colombia is the second largest exporter of cut flowers in the world. Bananas are grown on the tropical lowlands, about 56 million boxes from around Urabá and 30 million around Santa Marta, while sugar cane is grown in the Cauca valley.

Manufacturing contributes 19% of gdp, with farming activities such as food processing, drink and tobacco accounting for about a third of the sector's value added. Textiles and clothing are also important and provide an outlet for homegrown cotton. Other major industries include chemicals, transport equipment, cement, metalworking and paper.

The most dynamic sector of the economy in the 1980s was mining, with average annual growth rates of 18%, although rates in the 1990s have declined. Mining (coal, nickel, emeralds, gold and platinum) now accounts for about 16% of total exports. Coal reserves are the largest in Latin America, which partial surveys have put at 16.5 billion tonnes. The largest deposits are in the Cerrejón region, where a huge project mines and exports steam coal from a purpose built port at Bahía de Portete. A mine at La Loma (César Department) and deposits in the Chocó are also being developed with railways and ports for export markets. With the exception of a few major projects, mining of precious metals is concentrated in the hands of small scale producers with little technology or organization. Much of their output remains outside the

Colombia: fact file

Geographic
Land area	1,141,568 sq km
forested	22.0%
pastures	18.2%
cultivated	5.7%

Demographic
Population (1996)	35,652,000
annual growth rate (1991-96)	1.7%
urban	70.3%
rural	29.7%
density	31.2 per sq km

Education and Health
Life expectancy at birth,	
male	69.7 years
female	75.4 years
Infant mortality rate	
per 1,000 live births (1995)	26.9
Calorie intake as %	
of FAO requirement	115%
Population age 25 and over	
with no formal schooling	15.3%
Literate males (over 15)	86.7%
Literate females (over 15)	85.9%

Economic and Employment
GNP (1994 market prices)	
	US$58,935mn
GNP per capita	US$1,620
Public external debt (1994)	
	US$14,615mn
Tourism receipts (1994)	US$794mn
Inflation (annual av 1990-95)	24.9%
Population economically active (1985)	
	9,558,000
Unemployment rate	4.3%
Military forces	146,300

Source *Encyclopaedia Britannica*

formal economy. Colombia is a major producer of gold, platinum and emeralds, which have traditionally dominated the sector. Mining of precious metals, including silver, is primarily in the Department of Antioquia and El Chocó; huge gold deposits have also been discovered on the borders of the Departments of Cauca and Valle, while others have been found in the Guainía, Vaupés and Guaviare regions near the Brazilian border.

Since 1990 oil has vied with coffee for the position of top export earner. Traditionally, oil production came from the Magdalena basin, but these are older fields which are running down. The discovery of the Caño Limón field near Arauca raised output to around 450,000 b/d. The Cusiana and Cupiagua fields, in the Llanos, came into full production in 1995 and average output in 1996 was 630,000 b/d. Cusiana also has substantial reserves of gas. Another field, Coporo, with reserves estimated at possibly 1.3 billion barrels, is due in production in 1998-99. Investment is taking place to double oil output, build refineries, petrochemical plants and pipelines, although guerrilla attacks make operating in Colombia costly for foreign oil companies. In 1997 the oil and gas fiscal regime was being amended to attract more foreign investors.

Despite abundant hydrocarbons, some 78% of installed generating capacity is hydroelectric. Three quarters of the nation's hydroelectric potential is in the central zone, where 80% of the population live, giving hydroelectricity a natural advantage over thermal power, but after a severe drought in 1992 the Government encouraged the construction of several thermal plants, due to come on stream in 1998-99. Rationing may have to be reimposed in 1997 if there is not sufficient rainfall. Demand is forecast to grow annually by over 6% and there are plans to increase total capacity from 10,380MW to 13,000MW by 2000. 10 power stations, which generate 3,445MW, are to be privatized under a 1994 law. Two use coal, four gas and four hydro-power. With privatization and new private sector power plants, up to two thirds of generating capacity could be privately owned by the end of the 1990s.

Recent trends Current account surpluses in the late 1970s during a coffee price boom were turned into large deficits in the first half of the 1980s because of lower export receipts and rapidly rising imports. However, Colombia was able to avoid having to reschedule its foreign debt and took steps to adjust its external accounts. The devaluation of the peso was speeded up, reinforced by import restrictions and export incentives. The fiscal accounts were also turned around and the public sector deficit was reduced while economic growth remained positive throughout and per capita income increased. The World Bank and the IMF endorsed the Colombian economic strategy and commercial banks continued to lend to the country to refinance loans falling due. The Gaviria Government accelerated the economic opening of the country and liberalized financial, investment, foreign exchange and tax legislation. High real interest rates encouraged capital inflows and economic stability encouraged foreign investors.

President Samper's 1995-98 development plan emphasized spending on the social sector and productive infrastructure (with private sector involvement) to help combat poverty. The means of achieving this included decentralization; departmental and municipal governments received a larger slice of current revenue, most of which was spent on health, education and sanitation. However, the transfer of responsibilities to the regions, as ordered by the 1991 Constitution, has lagged behind the transfer of revenues, resulting in a growing fiscal imbalance and inflationary pressures. In 1996 and early 1997, these pressures were not relieved by the combination of uncertainty surrounding the government's links with drugs, guerrilla activity and strikes. To help finance military counter-insurgency, funds were raised through compulsory war bonds. In Jan 1997 a state of economic emergency was called to raise US$800mn in fiscal revenue, but in Mar the Constitutional Court rejected it, saying the budget deficit (US$4bn at end-1996) was chronic, not extraordinary. When, in Feb 1997, Samper yielded to demands for 20% pay rises for public sector workers and for a commission to study privatization plans, it became clear that not only was he behind schedule on his election programme, but also that his negotiating position had been seriously eroded.

GOVERNMENT

Senators and Representatives are elected by popular vote. The Senate has 102 members, and the Chamber of Representatives has 163. The President, who appoints his 13 ministers, is elected by direct vote for a term of 4 years, but cannot succeed himself in the next term. Every citizen over 18 can vote. The 1886 Constitution was reformed by a Constituent Assembly in 1991.

Administratively the country is divided into 23 Departments, 4 Intendencias, 5 Comisarias, and the Special District of Bogotá.

Liberty of speech and the freedom of the press are in theory absolute but in practice more limited. The language of the country is Spanish. Its religion is Roman Catholicism. There is complete freedom for all other creeds not contravening Christian morals or the law.

Bogotá

T HE capital, with its wealth of museums and historic buildings, and nearby towns for a weekend excursion out of the city.

The full name of the capital of the Republic is Santa Fé de Bogotá. The plateau on which it stands is known as La Sabana de Bogotá.

BASICS *Pop* 6.3mn, 1993; *Alt* 2,650m; *Area* 1,587 sq km; *Av temp* 14°C (58°F); *Phone code* 01.

Visitors should not be too active for the first 24 hrs. Some people get dizzy at Bogotá's altitude. Be careful with food and alcoholic drinks for the first day also.

The Calles (abbreviated 'C', or 'Cll') run at right angles across the Carreras ('Cra' or 'K'). It is easy enough to find a place once the address system, which is used throughout Colombia, is understood. The address Calle 13, No 12-45 would be the building on Calle 13 between Carreras 12 and 13 at 45 paces from Carrera 12; however transversals (Tra) and diagonals (Diag) can complicate the system. The Avenidas, broad and important streets, may be either Calles (like 19) or Carreras (like 14). Av Jiménez de Quesada, one of Bogotá's most important streets, owes its lack of straightness to having been built over a river-bed. Similarly, C 7, further S, is also over a river bed, the Río Agustín. Part of Carrera 7, one of the main shopping streets and several other main streets, are now closed to motor traffic on Sun and holidays when joggers, cycles, roller skates and skateboards take over.

CENTRAL BOGOTA

The central part of the city is full of character and contrasts: La Candelaria is the historic centre, occupying the area to the S of Av Jiménez de Quesada and N of Cra 10. There is some modern infill but many of the houses are well preserved in colonial style, of 1 or 2 storeys with tiled roofs, projecting eaves, wrought ironwork and carved balconies. The churches, museums and palaces are concentrated around and above the Plaza Bolívar. There are also many intriguing cobbled streets further out from this nucleus. Some hotels are found in this part, more along the margins, eg Av Jiménez de Quesada. The streets are relatively uncrowded and safe; care should be exercised after dark. West of Cra 10 and S of C 6 is seedier; the streets accommodate market stalls.

Downtown Bogotá, the old commercial centre with shops, offices and banks, runs in a band northwards from Av Jiménez de Quesada. It is a thorough mix of styles including modern towers and run down colonial and later buildings, together with a few notable ones. This commercial hub narrows to a thin band of secondary shops extending between Cra 7 and Av Caracas to around C 60. The streets are full of life; they are also paralyzed by traffic and laden with fumes much of the time. The pavements can be very congested too, particularly Cra 7 and

Av 19. Many of the budget hotels and some of the better ones are found in this area, which is rated as low to moderate risk.

The area in which to exercise most caution is generally SW of Av Caracas. Away from the centre, the whole of the S of the city should be avoided unless there were specific reasons for a visit.

MONSERRATE

There is a very good view of the city from the top of **Monserrate** (3,210m), the lower of the two peaks rising sharply to the E. It is reached by a funicular railway and a cable car. The new convent at the top is a popular shrine. At the summit, near the church, a platform gives a bird's-eye view of the city's tiled roofs and of the plains beyond stretching to the rim of the Sabana. Sunrise and sunset can be spectacular. Also at the top are several restaurants, including *Casa San Isidro*, French menu, seafood, fireplace, spectacular view, Mon-Sat 1200-2400, expensive but good, and a snack bar. The Calle del Candelero, a reconstruction of a Bogotá street of 1887, has plenty of street stalls. Behind the church are popular picnic grounds.

● **Access and security** The fare up to Monserrate is US$4 adult return (US$2 child). The funicular normally works only on Sun and holidays (expect to have to queue for an hour if you want to go up before about 1400, and for coming down); the cable car operates 0600-2400 daily. A good time to walk up is Sat or Sun about 0500, before the crowds arrive. There are enough people then to make it quite safe and you will catch the sunrise. The path is dressed stone and comfortably graded all the way up with refreshment stalls at weekends every few metres. It takes about 1¼ hrs up (if you don't stop). On no account walk down in the dark. Although the area is reportedly safer than it used to be, it is still best not to go alone. On weekdays, it is not recommended to walk up and especially not down. You should also take a bus or taxi to the foot of the hill Mon-Fri and, at all times, from the bottom station into town. There are usually taxis waiting by the footbridge across the road. The walk up to Guadalupe, the higher peak opposite Monserrate, is said to be more dangerous and not recommended at any time.

At the foot of Monserrate is the **Quinta de Bolívar**, C 20, No 3-23 Este, T 284-6519 a fine colonial mansion, with splendid gardens and lawns. There are several cannons

captured at the battle of Boyacá. The house, once Bolívar's home, is now a museum showing some of his personal possessions and paintings of events in his career. (Open 0900-1700, Tues-Sun, expected to reopen after renovations in mid 1997.)

OLD CITY

The Plaza Bolívar, contemporary with the city's foundation, is at the heart of the city; around the Plaza are the narrow streets and mansions of the **Barrio La Candelaria**. The district is popular as a residential area and has an artists' community.

Places of interest

Each place is described under the numeral for it in the street map of Bogotá on page 865.

1. **Plaza Bolívar**, with a statue of the Liberator at its centre. On the eastern side is the **Palacio Arzobispal**, with splendid bronze doors. To one side of it is the colonial **Plazuela de Rufino Cuervo**. Here is the house of Manuela Sáenz, the mistress of Bolívar. On the other side is the house in which Antonio Nariño printed in 1794 his translation of "The Rights of Man" which triggered off the movement for independence.

See the **Casa del Florero** or **Museo 20 de Julio** in a colonial house on the corner of Plaza Bolívar with C 11. It houses the famous flower vase that featured in the 1810 revolution and shows collections of the Independence War period, including documents and engravings and some fine portraits of Simón Bolívar. Entry fee US$1, open Tues-Sat, 0900-1615, Sun 1000-1515. On the northern side of the Plaza is the **Corte Suprema de Justicia**, wrecked in a guerrilla attack in 1985. A new Corte Suprema de Justicia is under construction.

2. The **Catedral**, rebuilt in 1807 in classical style. Notable choir loft of carved walnut and wrought silver on the altar of the Chapel of El Topo. Several treasures and relics; small paintings attributed to Ribera; the banner brought by Jiménez de Quesada to Bogotá, in the sacristy. There is a monument to Jiménez inside the Cathedral. In one of the chapels is buried

Gregorio Vásquez Arce y Ceballos (1638-1711), by far the best painter in colonial Colombia. Many of his paintings are in the Cathedral, which is closed for restoration, 1997.

3. The beautiful chapel of **El Sagrario**, built end of the 17th century. Several paintings by Vásquez Arce.

4. **Alcaldía Mayor de Bogotá**.

5. The **Capitolio Nacional**, an imposing building with fine colonnades (1847-1925). Congress sits here.

6. The colonial church of **Santa Clara**; religious museum and concert hall.

7. **San Ignacio**, Jesuit church built in 1605. Emeralds from the Muzo mines in Boyacá were used in the monstrance. Paintings by Gregorio Vásquez Arce.

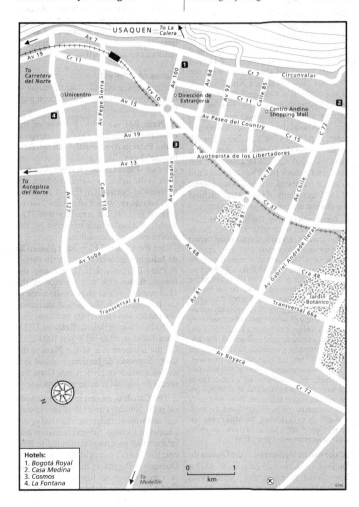

Hotels:
1. *Bogotá Royal*
2. *Casa Medina*
3. *Cosmos*
4. *La Fontana*

8. The **Palacio de San Carlos**, where Bolívar lived. He is said to have planted the huge walnut tree in the courtyard. On 25 September 1828, there was an attempt on his life. His mistress, Manuela, thrust him out of the window and he was able to hide for 2 hrs under the stone arches of the bridge across the Río San Agustín (now C 7). Santander, suspected of complicity, was arrested and banished.

The **Museo de Arte Colonial**, across from the Palacio de San Carlos (Carrera 6, No 9-77) is one of the finest colonial buildings in Colombia. It belonged originally to the Society of Jesus, and was once the seat of the oldest University in Colombia and of the National Library. It has a splendid collection of colonial art and paintings by Gregorio Vásquez Arce, all kinds of utensils, and two charming pat-

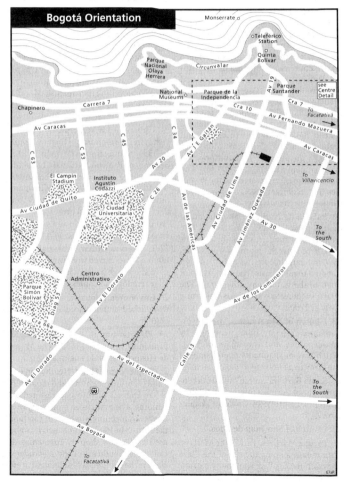

Bogotá Orientation

ios. Open Tues to Fri 1000-1700; Sat and Sun 1100-1700. Entry fee US$0.40 for adults; students US$0.20. (This is also closed for renovations, 1997.)

9. Church of **María del Carmen**, with excellent stained glass and walls in bands of red and white.

10. **Teatro Colón**, C 10, No 5-32 (operas, lectures, ballets, plays, concerts, etc), late 19th century with lavish decorations.

11. The **Casa de la Moneda** (Mint), built in 1720, is at C 11, No 4-93. The courtyard is worth seeing. Open Mon-Sat 1000-1800, Sun and holidays, 1000-1600, US$1. In the same street, No 4-14, is the Banco de la República's Biblioteca de Luis Angel Arango, one of the best endowed and arranged in South America, with three reading rooms, research rooms, art galleries on the 1st and 3rd floors and, the best, across the street. There is also a splendid concert hall. There are exhibitions and regular concerts (free on Mon pm, US$0.75 on Sun am, and full-price on Wed, student tickets at US$0.75). The architecture is impressive and the lavatories are recommended. There is a good cafeteria on the 6th floor.

12. **Palacio de Nariño** (1906), the presidential palace. Spectacular interior, fine collection of modern Colombian paintings. Free tours Sat morning with guide, 0930 in Spanish, 1000 in English, though not on a regular basis (enquire). It is not open to the public any other time. The guard is changed – full-dress uniform – daily at 1700.

13. Church of **San Agustín**, strongly ornamented (1637). Fine paintings by Vásquez Arce and the Image of Jesus which was proclaimed Generalísimo of the army in 1812.

14. **Santa Bárbara** church (mid-16th century), one of the most interesting colonial churches. Paintings by Gregorio Vásquez Arce.

15. Church of **San Juan de Dios**.

16. **Parque Mártires** (Park of the Martyrs) with monument, on the site of the Plaza in which the Spanish shot many patriots during the struggle for independence.

17. **Palacio de Comunicaciones** (postal and telegraph), built on the site of the colonial church of Santo Domingo.

18. The **Banco de la República**, next to Parque Santander. Next to the Bank is the wonderful **Museo del Oro** (see page 865). In Parque Santander there is a bronze statue of Santander, who helped Bolívar to free Colombia and was later its President.

19. **Gobernación de Cundinamarca**, almost as imposing as the Capitolio. Corinthian style.

20. **San Francisco** church (mid-16th century), with paintings of famous Franciscans, choir stalls, a famous ornate gold high altar (1622), and a fine Lady Chapel with blue and gold ornamentation. The remarkable ceiling is in Spanish-Moorish (*mudéjar*) style. Try to see this church when fully illuminated.

21. Church of **La Veracruz**, first built 5 years after the founding of Bogotá, rebuilt in 1731, and again in 1904. In 1910 it became the Panteón Nacional e Iglesia de la República. José de Caldas, the famous scientist, was buried along with many other victims of the 'Reign of Terror' under the church. It has a bright white and red interior and a fine decorated ceiling. Fashionable weddings are held here.

22. **La Tercera Orden**, a colonial church famous for its carved woodwork along the nave and a high balcony, massive wooden altar reredos, and confessionals.

23. **Las Nieves**, colonial church, has been demolished and replaced by a modern church.

24. **Planetarium**, in Parque de la Independencia, open 1100-1630. (The Museo de Historia Natural is next door.)

25. **Tequendama Hotel**. Nearby (on Cra 7 and C 26) are the church and monastery of San Diego, a picturesque, restored old building. The Franciscan monastery with fine *mudéjar* ceiling was built in 1560 and the church in 1607 as its chapel. It is now used as a crafts shop by Artesanías de Colombia. Southeast of the *Tequendama Hotel* is the Biblioteca Nacional, with entrance on C 24.

Museums

All closed on Mon. In addition to those mentioned above:

Museo del Oro (the Gold Museum), is in the splendid premises of the Banco de la Republica at the Parque de Santan-

Bogotá

26. Museo de Arqueologia
27. Museo de Arte y Tradiciones Populares
28. Colegio Mayor de Nuestra Señora del Rosario
29. Corporación Nacional de Turismo
30. Airmail Office / Avianca
31. Ministerio del Medio Ambiente

1 - 25. See Text

der (Cra 6, No 15-82, T 342-1111, see No 18 on map). This collection is a 'must', for it is unique. There are no less than 30,000 pieces of precolumbian gold work in the total collection most of which are shown here. The rest are in other **Museos de Oro** sponsored by the Banco de la Republica throughout Colombia. Open Tues to Sat 0900-1630; Sun and holidays, 0900-1200 (people in shorts not allowed). Charge, US$1.50. There are tours and films in Spanish and English, enquire for times. Do not miss the Salón Dorado, a glittering display inside an inner vault.

The ancient gold objects discovered in Colombia were not made by the primitive technique of simple hammering alone, but show the use of virtually every technique known to modern goldsmiths.

Museo Nacional, on Cra 7, No 28-66, the Panóptico, T 342-5925, an old prison converted into a museum (to the NE of the map), founded by Santander in 1823. Its top floor houses a fine art section, comprising national paintings and sculptures. Open Tues-Sat 0900-1700, Sun 1000-1600, US$0.60 (pensioners free).

Museo de Arte Moderno, C 24, No 6-00, entry US$0.60, half price for students (open Tues-Sat 1000-1900, Sun 1200-1800), good café. If you want to photograph in the museum you must obtain permission from the office.

Museo de Historia Natural, C 26 y Cra 7, T 238-6309, open Tues-Sun, and holidays, 1000-1700 (see map, No 24).

Museo Mercedes de Pérez, formerly the Hacienda de El Chicó, a fine example of colonial architecture, is at Cra 7, No 94-17. It contains a world-wide collection of mostly 18th century porcelain, furniture, paintings, etc. Open Tues-Sun, 0930-1230, 1430-1700.

Museo de Arte y Tradiciones Populares is at Cra 8, No 7-21 in an old monastery and exhibits local arts and crafts. It has a shop, selling handicrafts at higher prices than Artesanías de Colombia, and a reasonably-priced bar and restaurant (dishes typical of different regions of Colombia served in colonial setting, usually with regional traditional music). Open 0830-1730, Mon-Sat. Entry fee US$0.50.

Museo Siglo XIX, Cra 8, No 7-93, founded by the Bancafé, has a collection of 19th-century paintings, clothes and furniture. Open Tues-Sat 0830-1730. US$0.30.

Museo Arqueológico (belonging to the Banco Popular) is a fine and extensive collection of precolumbian pottery, in the restored mansion of the Marqués de San Jorge, Cra 6, No 7-43, T 282-0760. The house itself is a beautiful example of 17th century Spanish colonial architecture. US$1.80 entry. Open Tues-Sat 0800-1200, 1300-1600, Sun 1000-1300.

Museo Militar, C 10, No 4-92, history of Colombian armed forces and good collection of weapons, T 281-3086, Tues-Fri 0900-1230, 1400-1530, Sat 0900-1330, US$0.60.

Casa-Museo Jorge Eliécer Gaitán, C 42, No 15-52, is former residence of the populist leader whose assassination in April 1948 triggered the infamous 'Bogotazo', at the outset of La Violencia.

Instituto Nacional de Investigaciones Geológico-Mineras has a library and pleasant museum at Diagonal 53, No 34-53. Entrance US$0.10.

Museo de los Niños, Cra 48, No 63-97, T 225-9058, natural sciences explained for children, created by Sra Ximena Rosas with funding from industry, Tues-Fri 0830-1600, Sat, Sun, holidays 0900-1600.

Museo Colsubsidio, C 26, No 25-42, exhibitions of contemporary artists.

Casa de Poesía Silva, C 14, No 3-41, T 286-7510, museum, bookshop and audio room/library with readings of almost every Spanish-speaking author. Tapes can be bought in the bookshop at about US$10. Also there are lectures and poetry readings.

NORTH BOGOTA

North of C 68 is an expanding band of wealthy suburbs, shopping malls and classy restaurants. The best hotels are scattered through this area, which is regarded as relatively safe.

Places of interest

In the link between Central and North Bogotá, is the **Universidad Nacional** (about 13,000 students), which is housed in the Ciudad Universitaria shown on the orientation map. The oldest centres of learning are in the old centre: oldest of all is the Colegio Nacional de San Bartolomé (C 10, No 6-57), in the same block as the Chapel of El Sagrario (3 on map), founded 1573. The second oldest, founded on 18 December 1653, is the Colegio Mayor de Nuestra Señora del Rosario (C 14, No 6-25); its beautiful colonial building is well worth a look (you can buy a good cheap lunch at the cafeteria; it is not far from the Gold Museum).

There is an interesting and well organized **Jardín Botánico**, José Celestino Mutis, Cra 66, No 56-84. It has a collection of over 5,000 orchids, plus roses, gladioli and trees from all over the country (see map).

Short excursions from Bogotá

If you have a car, drive round the Av Circunvalar for splendid views. For longer excursions, see the end of this section.

Local information

NB Potholes in both roads and pavements can be very deep: avoid them, especially when it is wet.

● **Accommodation**

Hotel prices

L1	over US$200	**L2**	US$151-200
L3	US$101-150	**A1**	US$81-100
A2	US$61-80	**A3**	US$46-60
B	US$31-45	**C**	US$21-30
D	US$12-20	**E**	US$7-11
F	US$4-6	**G**	up to US$3

Unless otherwise stated, all hotels in range **D** and above have private bath. Assume friendliness and cleanliness in all cases.

Book hotels in advance whenever possible. IVA tax of 16% is charged by middle and more expensive hotels and is additional to the bill but included in our price classification.

Hotels in North Bogotá, Calles 76 and upwards: **L1** Bogotá Royal, Av 100, No 8A-01, T 218-9911, F 218-3362, excellent; **L1** Bogotá Plaza, C 100, No 18A-30, T 621-7088, F 218-4050, good restaurant, Atrium; **L1** Charleston, Cra 13, No 85-46, T 257-1100, F 218-0605, handsome building, close to restaurants and clubs; **L1** Victoria Regia, Cra 13, No 85-80, T 616-0202, F 610-3516, PO Box 250-718, superior rooms and suites, all services, pool, restaurant;

L1 La Fontana, Av 127, No 21-10, T 274-7868, F 216-0449, distinctive, very good (Los Arcos restaurant in hotel, superb, elegant); **L1** Hacienda Royal, C 114, No 6A-02, T 612-1666, F 620-0958, CCH Santa Bárbara, very well-appointed; **L1** Los Urapanes, Cra 13, No 83-19, T 218-1188, F 218-9242, very pleasant, smart, smaller hotel; **L2** La Bohème, C 82, No 12-35, T 617-1177, F 618-0003, well-equipped rooms, attractive, good location, but noisy outside; **L2** Cosmos 100, C 100, No 21 A-41, great view, good breakfasts, T 257-4000, F 257-1035, rec; **L2** El Belvedere, Tr 18, No 100-16, T 257-7700, F 257-0331, inc breakfast, modern, very good value, excellent restaurant Balmoral; **L2** Meliá Santafé, C 116 (Av Pepe Sierra), No 17-64, T 629-0029, F 629-0039, small, luxurious; **L3** Dann Carlton, Av 15, No 103-60, T 635-0010, F 635-0189, new 1996; **L3** Portón 84, C 84, No 7-65, T 616-4006, F 616-3905, very good, excellent restaurant, offer free health insurance for stay; **L3** Richmond Suites, C 93, No 18-81, T 616-7121, convenient, quiet, excellent rooms.

A2 Rincón del Chicó, C101, No 13-32, T 214-7371, hot water, safe, family atmosphere, helpful, good restaurant; **A2** Apartamentos 82, Cra 14, No 81-34, T 256-6751, self catering flatlets, good service, pleasant, safe, rec.

C Hostal Moreno, Transversal 33 No 95-28, T 257-9127, meals available, house taxi driver, nearby frequent bus service to centre, safe for left luggage, quiet, comfortable, hot water, good value, highly rec.

Between Calles 31 and 75: **L1** Casa Medina, Cra 7, 69A-22, T 217-0288, F 212-6668 (in the French 'Relais et Châteaus' chain), nice interior, chic; **L2** Orquidea Royal, Cra 7, No 32-16, T 287-0788, F 288-7169, restaurant, pool; **A1** Centro Internacional, Cra 13A, No 38-97, T 288-5566, F 288-0850, popular, good location; **A2** Fiesta Avenida, Av Caracas, No 47-28, T 285-3407, safe, restaurant, rec; **A2** Las Terrazas, C 54A, No 3-12, 2-star, T 255-5777, "rustic charm", pleasant, nice view of city; **A3** Hostal Linden, C 36, No 14-39, T 287-4239, central, small, 2 rooms with kitchenette, credit cards accepted.

C Casa Berlinesa, C 45A, No 21-40, T 232-8504, German and English spoken, full breakfast available.

D La Cabaña, C 58, No 9-55, safe, good value; **D** Hospedaje Turístico 61, C 61, No 10-18, T 217-0383, OK, discounts for stays over 3 days, also has short-stay section.

In Central Bogotá (Av Jiménez de Quesada up to Calle 31): **L1** Tequendama, Cra 10, No 26-21, T 286-1111, F 282-2860, restaurant serves excellent ajiaco, good for breakfast; **L3** Bacatá, C 19, No 5-20, T 283-8300, F 281-7249, downtown on busy street, cheaper at weekends, worth asking at other times, restaurant not rec; **L3** *Dann*, C 19, No 5-72, T 284-0100, F 282-3108, very helpful; **L3** *Del Parque*, C 24, No 4-93, T 284-2200, F 283-2315, good commercial hotel.

A3 *Del Duc*, C 23, No 9-38, T 334-0080, good French restaurant; **A3** *El Virrey*, C 18, No 5-56, T 334-1150, modern, good value restaurant, rec; **A3** *Santa Mónica*, Cra 3, No 24-11, T 242-8080, a/c, comfortable, good location, rec; **A3** *San Diego*, Cra 13 y C 24, T 284-2100, large rooms, good value, accepts credit cards but not Amex TCs.

B *La Sabana*, C 23, No 5-23, T 284-4830, F 284-6552, central, quiet, English spoken, small restaurant, Visa accepted; **B** *Los Cerros*, C19, No 9-18, T 334-0711, pleasant, good restaurant; **B** *Quiratama*, C 17, No 12-44, T 282-4515, F 341-3246, very nice rooms, good service; **B** *Regina*, Cra 5, No 15-16, T 334-5137, good; **C** *Príncipe de Viena*, C 19, No 15-35, T 342-0090, big old rooms, laundry service, bar, restaurant.

D *Italia*, Cra 7, No 20-40, convenient, safe, T 334-6629, hot water, TV lounge, laundry, safe, rec.

E *Hollywood*, C 18, No 8-68, small rooms with bath; **E** *Panamerican*, C 15, No 12-70, T 242-1802, good, with bath, helpful; **E** *Regis*, C 18, No 6-09 (also known as *Residencias María*), C with shower, sometimes hot water, old-fashioned, run down but safe, safe parking for car or motorcycle; **E** *Virgen del Camino*, C 18A, No 14-33, quiet, safe, T 282-4450.

In Old Bogota, La Candelaria to Av Jiménez de Quesada: **L3** *Nueva Granada*, Av Jiménez, No 4-77, T 286-5877, F 284-5465, inc breakfast, discount for longer stays, relaxed atmosphere, parking.

A1 *Dann Colonial*, C 14, No 4-21, T 341-1680, F 334-9982, with breakfast, laundry, popular with groups, safe parking; **A3** *La Hostería de la Candelaria*, C 9, No 3-11, T 342-1727, Aptdo Aéreo 15978, quiet and relaxed, charming patio, restaurant (Café Rosita), suite with good view of old Bogotá, dinner available if ordered in am, good for longer stays, mixed reports 1997.

B *San Sebastian*, Av Jiménez 3-97, T 336-2193, F 282-9825, spacious rooms, restaurant.

C *Ambala*, Cra 5, No 13-46, T 286-3751, good value, central; **C** *Avenida Jiménez*, Av Jiménez, No 4-71, T 243-6685, helpful, sauna, safe; **C** *Residencia Dorantes*, C 13, No 5-07, T 334-6640, cheaper without bath, hot water, high ceilings, 1950s décor, most rooms with good view of Monserrate, reasonable, safe, rec; **C** *Santa Fe*, C 14, No 4-48, T 342-0560, F 342-1879, good service, quiet, safe, good restaurant, popular with locals, good value, rec.

D *Internacional*, Cra 5, No 14-45, T 341-8731, cheaper without bath, hot water, excellent kitchen, good value, safe deposit, popular with Israelis (specify the address, there are several other hotels with similar names).

E *Platypus*, C 16, No 2-43, T 341-2874, pleasant, kitchen facilities, hot water, free coffee, informative owner, very good book exchange, excellent travellers guest house, highly rec; **E** *Residencia Aragón*, Cra 3, No 14-13, T 342-5239/284-8325, safe, honest, hot water, will store luggage, parking facilities, warmly rec.

There are any number of small, unregistered hotels and *hostales* in other parts of the city, many of which are cheap, some of which are clean. However, such areas may be regarded from time to time as unsafe for tourists and are remote from places of interest.

Private vehicles should be parked in lockable, guarded parqueaderos.

Youth Hostel Association: Alcom, Apdo Aéreo 3220, Cra 7, No 6-10, behind Presidential Palace, safe area, T 280-3041/280-3202, F 280-3460; IYHA member, has a full list of 16 hostels around the country. There is a hostel at this address with 90 beds, US$4.50 pp members, US$5.50 non-members/night, lunch available US$2, 1200-1500. Ask for full information at Alcom. Reservations for all hostels must be made through Prosocial, Bogotá 16, No 33-29, T 285-9296/285-9351, 0800-2000.

● **Places to eat**

16% value-added tax may be charged. For hotel restaurants, see above.

Recommended restaurants in **North Bogotá** (C 76 and above) include: *El Arko de los Olivos*, Tr 22, C 122-13, new, rustic style, excellent cooking; *La Fragata*, C 100, No 8A-55, 12th floor of World Center, revolving; also at Cra 13 No 27-98 and Diag 127A, No 30-26, L1, expensive, excellent fish; *La Academia de Golf*, Cra 15, No 85-42, and Cra 15, No 102-20, international, very good; *La Bodega Marina*, Cra 11A, No 93A-46, Cra 9, No 81-49, and 2 other branches, superb; *Longaniza*, C 93, No 16-53, very good; *Le Petit Bistrot*, C 76, No 10-28, excellent French cuisine; *Il Giardino*, C 93, No 18-25, Italian; *Il Piccolo Caffe*, Cra 15, No 96-55, pasta etc, very good quality; *Las Tapas*, Av 19, No 114-13, Spanish bar-restaurant; *Zeukadi*, C 82, corner of Cra 11, fire lit at 2200, candlelight, rec; *Na Zdarovia*, Cra 14, No 80-71, Russian, very good, same owners; *Tandoor*, Cra 11, No 84-53, good Indian; *Viva Villa*, C 82, No 12-70, Mexican, good food, rec; *Casa de Cultura de México*, Cra 14, No 80-44, good Mexican food on second floor; *El Mondongo y Algo Más*, Cra 11, No 97A-38, local food; *El Buque*, Cra 18 y C 101, seafood, excellent; *Fulanitos*, C 81, No 9-13, good Valle Cauca food, friendly atmosphere; *Fridays*, C 82, No 12-18, US$10-12, superb value, rec; *Le Bilbouquet*, C 83, No 12-19, excellent French, nice atmosphere, rec; *L'Epicurien*, Cra 30, No 89-56, French chef, 1960 décor, very good, rec; *Il Pomeriggio*, Cra 11 y C82 in Centro Andino, popular, good atmosphere, expensive – the place to see and be seen; *Welcome*, Cra 14, No 80-65, Japanese, good cooking supervised by perfectionist owner; *Hatsuhana*, Cra 13, No 93A-27, Japanese. In these restaurants meals cost from US$20/25 to US$40.

Tony Roma's, C 86A, No 13A-10, good quality food and excellent service; *Café Oma*, several locations, inc Cra 15, No 82-58, Av 19, No 118-78, Cra 5, No 14-71, and airport Muelle Nacional local 2-33, good food and coffee, nice atmosphere but relatively expensive, open till 0100; *Café y Crepes*, Cra 16, No 82-17, T 236-2905, good food, good atmosphere, climbers meet here; *Houston*, Cra 17, No 93-17, very popular, US-style; *Di Lucca*, Cra 13, No 85-32, T 236-73-01, freshly made pasta, excellent cooking, open daily 1200-2400.

Central Bogotá (note that in the colonial centre very little is open after 2000 any day of the week): *Refugio Alpino*, C 23, No 7-49, is an excellent international restaurant; *Casa Vieja*, Av Jiménez 3-73, traditional Bogotá food, live music, also at C 116, No 20-50 in North Bogotá and 2 other branches; *Eduardo*, C13, No 8-66, T 243-0118, good business restaurant upstairs, more popular downstairs; *Doña Herta*, C 19, No 8-61, the best goulash in town, friendly, Swiss owned; *Tierra Colombiana*, Cra 10, No 27-27, good, expensive food, evening floor show; *Cafetería Romana*, Av Jiménez, No 6-65, all meals, very clean, reasonable pasta, but excellent, expensive breakfast menu; its sister restaurants *Sorrento* (C 14, No 6-64) and *Salerno*, Cra 7, No 19-48, good value; *Pizzería El Sol de Napolés*, C 69, No 11-58, T 249-2186, small, cozy, excellent antipasto; *Chalet Suizo*, Av 22, No 39A-48, delicious fondues and good steaks. For excellent, inexpensive Arab food, *Ramses*, Cra 7, No 18-64, open to 2200. *Bambú*, Cra 7 y C 61/62, good Chinese, reasonable prices; *El Patio*, Cra 4A, No 27-86, T 282-6141, and *Il Caffe*, next door, both under same management, good Italian, rec.

Punta Roja, Cra 7 y C 22, good value, open 24 hrs; *Punto Rápido*, Cra 7, No 19-49, self service, good meals, reasonable, 24 hrs service; *Salón Fontana*, C 14, No 5-98, busy, good, inexpensive; *La Tienda de Don Zoilo*, Cra 4, No 19-56, student pub, good food, friendly atmosphere, rec; *Crepes y Waffeles*, restaurant chain, good value; also *La Boliche*, C 27, No 5-64, Italian and good crepes; *Empanadas La 19*, Av 19, No 8-56, good, cheap meals and

snacks; *Café l'Avenir*, C 11, No 2-98, French style, crèpes a speciality, pleasant atmosphere, useful notice-board, 1000-2200, rec; *Andante ma non Troppo*, Cra 2, No 10-92, Italian specialities, good comida US$3, Mon-Sat 1200-1500; *Los Secretos del Mar*, Cra 5, No 13-20, fish, good; *Pittaline*, Cra 11, No 66-55, Israeli food, good snacks etc; *Empanadas Don Camillo*, Cra 4, No 12-15, excellent filled *arepas*, warmly rec; *Cafetería Salon Fontana*, C 14, No 5-98, excellent busy breakfast place, try their *almojabanas*, rec. A cheap 2-course meal can be had in the cafetería of the Ley and Tía supermarkets. For the traveller on a budget, *bandeja* (the local *plato del día*) can cost US$2-2.50 for a 2-course meal.

Vegetarian: *La Berenjena*, C 19, No 34-37, highly rec, lunch US$2.50; *El Champiñon*, Cra 8, No 16-36, 2 other branches, good vegetarian lunches; *Lotus Azul*, C 15, Cra 6, good quality and good value; vegetarian food excellent at Cra 8, No 11-19, nr Plaza Bolívar; *Samovares*, Cra 11, No 69-63 (lunch only, fixed menu, nice atmosphere), also Cra 11, No 67-63 and Av Caracas No 32-64. *El Integral Natural*, Cra 11, No 95-10, health food shop with a few tables at street level, restaurant downstairs.

Tea rooms: (Pastelerías) *Panadería Florida*, Cra 7, No 20-82, also has good pastries and is the place to try *chocolate santafereño*; *La Espiga*, Cra 15 esq C 82, and other locations, excellent bread and pastries.

● Airline offices

The *Avianca* office is at Cra 7, No 16-36, T 295-4611/243-1613, airport 413-8295; **SAM**, Cra 10, No 27-91, T 286-8402, airport 413-8868; **Satena**, Centro Tequendama, Cra 10 y C27, T 286-2701, airport 413-8158, military airline, not best for comfort and delays. Most airlines, local and international, have offices in both Central and North Bogotá. Many international airline offices are closed on Sat and Sun. See page 983 for procedure to obtain refunds on unused tickets.

● Banks & money changers

Banks: everywhere in Bogotá where there is commercial activity. Some head offices are grouped around the Avianca building at the corner of Plaza San Francisco, others have recently moved to North Bogotá on or nr C 72. **Banco Anglo Colombiano**, Cra 8, No 15-46/60, T 334-5088, and 18 local agencies, will cash Thomas Cook and Amex TCs (US$100 min, 0900-1300, passport will be stamped), will give advances against Visa, and will accept sterling, good rates. **Banco Unión Colombiana** (Cra 10, No 26-55 – after 1000, take passport, not a copy) and other banks (eg **Banco Popular**, **Bancafé**, Edif Centro de Comercio Internacional, C 28, No 13A-15/53, cash machines accept Visa; **Banco del Occidente**) will in theory change TCs, but obtaining cash against a credit card is best (your passport will be photocopied). **Credibanco**, Visa, C 72, No 6-12, T 312-4400; **Banco Industrial de Colombia** (BIC), Cra No 24-89, p 43, T 284-1656, Mastercard agency, gives good rates for TCs. See **Hours of Business** and **Currency** in **Information for travellers**.

Money changers: American Express, Tierra Mar Aire Ltda, edif Bavaria Torre B, Local 126, Cra 10, No 27-91, T 283-2955, does not change TCs, but will direct you to those who do. Also very helpful in replacing lost Amex TCs provided you have full details, have a police report of the loss and preferably proof of purchase. Other offices at C 92, No 15-63, T 218-5666 and Cra 8 y C 15 are helpful. **International Money Exchange**, Cra 7, No 32-29, open Mon to Fri till 1600, check all transactions carefully; opp at *Hotel Orquidea Real*, you can exchange on Sat. Also exchange at Av 19, No 15-35. **Exprinter**, Av Jiménez y Cra 6. Inside you can only get pesos and no TCs are exchanged, but the black market operates on the pavement outside, or try the kiosk right there; Peruvian and Ecuadorean currencies available (rates generally little different from official rates). **Cambios Country**, Western Union agents, Cra 11, No 71-40, Of 201, T 346-6788, several other city offices, good rates, speedy service; **Orotur**, Cra 10, No 26-05 (very small, below *Hotel Tequendama*) is quick and efficient, cash only; **Money Point**, Cra 10, No 27, in Centro Internacional, unit 161, good rates, take passport photocopy. Other *cambios* on Av Jiménez de Quesada, between Cras 6 and 13, and in the N of the city. On Sun exchange is virtually impossible except at the airport.

● **Cultural centres**
British Council, C 87, No 12-79, T 236-3976 has a good library and British newspapers; **Centro Colombo Americano**, C 109A, No 17-10, T 215-6697, English and Spanish courses, rec; **Alianza Colombo-Francesa**, Cra 3, No 18-45, T 341-3082 and Cra 7, No 84-72, T 236-8605, films in French, newspapers, library monthly bulletin etc; **Goethe Institut**, Cra 7, No 81-57, T 255-1843; **Biblioteca Luis Angel Arango**, C 11, No 4-14, see under No 11 on map.

● **Embassies & consulates**
Venezuelan Consulate, Av 13, No 103-16, T 256-0587, hours of business 0900-1230, 1300-1500, visas cost US$30, but allow 3 days (they will tell you to get your visa at the border, which may not be easy; it is hard to persuade them to give visas to overland travellers); **Ecuadorean Embassy**, C 89, No 13-07, T 257-0066; **Brazilian Embassy**, C 93, No 14-20, T 218-0800; **Peruvian Consulate**, Cra 10, No 93-48, T 218-0133; Bo-

livian Embassy, Tr 12, No 119-95, Apto 101, T 215-3274; **Panamanian Consulate**, C 92, No 7-70, T 257-5067; Mon-Fri, 0900-1300; **Costa Rican Consulate**, Cra 15, No 102-25, Mon-Fri 0900-1300, T 256-6007; **Guatemalan Consulate**, Transversal 29A, No 139A-41, T 258-0746, Mon-Fri, 0900-1200, visa takes 48 hrs, US$10 (cash only), one photo, one airline ticket (does not have to be return), tourist visa free for Canadians, takes 48 hrs; **Mexican Embassy**, C 82, No 9-25, T 256-6121; **El Salvador Embassy**, Cra 9, No 80-15, T 212-5932.

US Embassy, Cra 50, Av El Dorado (mailing address: Apdo Aéreo 3831, Bogotá 1, DE), T 315-0811, consulate/visas, T 315-1566. **Canadian Embassy**, C 76, No 11-52, T 313-1355, open 0800-1630 (mailing address: Apdo Aéreo 53531, Bogotá 2, DE).

British Embassy, C 98, No 9-03, p 4, T 621-0670, postal address: Apdo Aéreo 4508; **German Embassy**, Cra 4, No 72-35, p 6, T 212-0511; **French Embassy**, Cra 11, No 93-12, T 618-0511; **French Consulate**, Cra 7, No 38-99, T 285-4311; **Belgian Embassy**, C 26, No 4A-45, p 7, T 282-8901; **Dutch Embassy**, Cra 13, No 93-40, T 611-5080; **Finnish Consulate**, Cra 7, No 35-33, p 7, T 212-6111; **Norwegian Consulate**, Cra 13, No 50-78, Oficina 506, T 235-5419; **Swedish Embassy**, C 72, No 5-83, T 255-3777; **Danish Consulate General**, Cra 10, No 96-29, of 611, T 610-0887, 0900-1300 Mon-Thur, 0900-1200 Fri; **Swiss Embassy**, Cra 9, No 74-08, oficina 1101, T 255-5280, open Mon-Fri 0900-1200; **Italian Consulate**, C 93B, No 9-92 (Apdo Aéreo 50901), T 218-6680; **Israeli Embassy**, Edif Caxdac, C 35, No 7-25, p 14, T 232-0764; **Japanese Embassy**, Cra 9A, No 99-02, p 6, T 618-2800.

● **Entertainment**
Cinema: *Cinemateca Distrital*, Cra 7, No 22-79. The *Museo de Arte Moderno* shows different films every day, all day. Foreign films old and new are shown on weekend mornings at 1030 in commercial cinemas and there are many small screening rooms which run the occasional feature. Consult *El Espectador* or *La Prensa*, and handbills all over town for what is on; frequent programme changes. Admission, US$3.

Gay bars: *Adonis*, C 33 y Cra 13A; *Alex*, C 22 y Cra 7, expensive drinks.

Nightlife: there are many popular bars, discos etc in the Cra 15, C 82 region, known as the Zona Rosa. Also many popular bars and dancing places on Cra 5 with C 25, relatively safe area. Try *El Viejo Almacén*, Cra 5 y C 13-14, run by an aged Argentine lady who plays 78 tango records and sells reasonably priced beer and *aguardiente* (on Fri and Sat only). *Disco del*

Teatro de Candelaria, C 15 between Cras 4 and 5, good atmosphere especially Fri and Sat. **Sauna**: Los Andes, Cra 4, No 16-29, good service, open daily 1000-2200. Sauna San Diego, Cra 7 nr C 25, massage, turkish bath and sauna rec.

Theatre: many of the theatres are in the Candelaria area. *Teatro Colón* details on page 864. *Teatro Libre de Bogotá*, C 62, No 10-65, T 217-1988; *Nacional*, C 71, No 10-25, T 235-8069; *La Candelaria*, C 12, No 2-59, T 281-4814; *Teatro Popular de Bogotá*, C 5, No 14-71, T 342-1675.

● **Hospitals & medical services**

Cruz Roja Nacional, Av 68, No 66-31, T 250-661/231-9027/231-9008, open 0830-1800; *Instituto Nacional de Salud*, Av El Dorado y Cra 50, for vaccinations, T 222-0577; *Centro Médico La Salud*, Cra 10, No 21-36, p 2, T 243-1381/282-4021; *Walter Röthlisberger y Cía Ltda*, C 26, No 13-37, T 283-6200, imports medicines, inc Vivotif for typhoid and gamma globulin, and stores medicines correctly, trade prices. Embassies will advise on doctors, dentists, etc. *Profamilia*, C 34, No 14-46, for contraceptives. *Clínica Marly*, C 50, No 9-67, T 287-1020 (bus runs along Cra 4-14) and *Clínica del Country*, Cra 15, No 84-13, T 257-3100, are well-equipped private hospitals. *Dr Arturo Corchuelo* at C 89, No 12-21, T 218-8710, rec for orthopaedic problems; *Clínica Barraquer*, Av 100, No 18A-51, internationally known eye clinic.

● **Language courses**

The best Spanish courses are in the *Universidad Nacional* (see map) US$180 for 2 months, 8 hrs/week, or *Universidad de los Andes*, US$300, 6 weeks and *Pontificia Universidad Javeriana*, Centro Latino Americano de Relaciones Humanas e Interculturales, Cra 10, No 65-48, T 212-3009. Accommodation with local families can be arranged. Most other schools in Yellow Pages offer one-to-one private tuition at US$10/hr.

If coming from abroad, make sure you have a student visa, preferably before you arrive, if not, from DAS in Bogotá, before starting the course. You may not study on a tourist visa.

● **Laundry**

Ask in your hotel, or locally. *Burbujas*, Edif Procoil, Av 19, No 3A-37, open Mon-Sat 0730-1930, manager speaks English.

● **Post & telecommunications**

Post: main airmail office and foreign *poste restante* in basement of Ed Avianca, Cra 7, No 16-36, open 0730-1900 Mon to Fri, 0730-1800 Sat, closed Sun and holidays (*poste restante* 0730-1800, Mon-Sat, letters kept for only a month, bureaucratic, US$0.40/letter). Parcels by air, contact Avianca. To send film abroad pay for recorded delivery, use regulation envelope and get glue from counter 15.

International telephone calls: from several Telecom offices in centre of Bogotá (eg C 12 y Cra 8, C 23, No 13-49, in the *Tequendama Hotel*/Centro Internacional complex); all close within 30 mins of 2000. Purchase of phone cards rec if you are using call boxes.

● **Security**

As in any city of this size, take care not to tempt thieves by careless display of money or valuables. Also, anyone approaching you with questions, offers to sell something or making demands, may well be a thief or a con-artist.

The Judicial Unit for Tourism (Tourist police) offers 24-hr service for tourists at Cra 7, No 27-42, T 283-4930 or 334-2501. If you are robbed of documents, contact police at C 46 y Cra 14, of valuables, police at C 40, No 8-09.

● **Shopping**

16% value-added tax on all purchases. *Artesanías de Colombia* (state-owned), Almacén San Diego, in the old San Diego church, Cra 10, No 26-50, Claustro de Las Aguas, next to the Iglesia de las Aguas, Cra 3A, No 18-60, has good selection of folk art and crafts. A street market on Av Jiménez and Cra 14 (Av Caracas) sells cheaper *ruanas*, blankets, leatherware, etc. Mercado de Pulgas (fleamarket) on Cra 7/C 24, in car park beside *Museo de Arte Moderno*, on Sun afternoons and holidays (on no account wander around here other than on Sun).

Galerías Cano, Ed Bavaria, Cra 13, No 27-98 (Torre B, Int 1-19B), Unicentro, Loc 218, Airport, sell textiles, pottery as well as gold and gold-plated replicas of some of the jewellery on display in the Gold Museum; *Galería Alfred Wild*, C 82, No 12-35, has excellent but pricey drawings and paintings.

The pavements and cafés along Av Jiménez, below Cra 7, Parque de los Periodistas, and C 16 and Cra 3, are used on weekdays by emerald dealers. Great expertise is needed in buying: bargains are to be had, but synthetics and forgeries abound. *La Casa de la Esmeralda*, C 30, No 16-18, wide range of stones; *Joyas Verdes Ltda*, Cra 15, No 39-15 also. Other jewellery shops in the *Hotel Tequendama*. See *H Stern's* jewellery stores at the International Airport, and Tequendama Hotel.

Shopping centres: *Unicentro*, Cra 15, No 123-30 (take 'Unicentro' bus from centre, going N on Cra 10 – takes about 1 hr). *Centro Granahorrar*, Av Chile (C 72), No 10-34; *Metropolis*, Av 68, No 75A-50 (with *Exito* supermarket opp), *Hacienda Santa Bárbara*, Cra 7 y C 116, *Bulevar Niza*, Cra 52, No 125A-59, *Centro Comercial Andino*, Cra 12 entre C 82 y C 83 (nr *Hotel La Bohème*).

Heavy duty plastic for covering rucksacks etc, is available at several shops around C 16 and Av Caracas; some have heat sealing machines to make bags to size.

Bookshops: *Librería Aldina*, Cra 7, C 70-80, most helpful on books and Bogotá alike, excellent stock of English-language books inc this *Handbook*, open 0930-1930, Sat 0930-1700, Sun 1000-1400; *Oma*, Cra 15, No 82-58 T 256-5621 (and other branches), good art and literature books, international newspapers, also sells this *Handbook*, open late inc Sun; *Librería Nacional*, Cra 7, No 17-51 (has small selection of English novels); *Librería Francesa*, Cra 8, No 63-45, also imports English books. Similarly *Libros y Discos*, Cra 15, No 82-58, also sells *Footprint* Handbooks. *Librería Lerner*, Av Jiménez, No 4-35 and C 92, No 15-23, T 236-0580 (specializes in 'libros colombianos'); *Librería Buchholz*, Cra 7, No 27-68 (opp *Hotel Tequendama*), also at C 59, No 13-13 (Chapinero), most books in Spanish, useful advice in a number of languages; *Sociedad Colombiana de Arquitectos*, Cra 6, No 28-85, good bookstore on ground floor; *Ateneo*, C 82, No 13-19, in the N of the city, good selection of Colombian titles, knowledgeable staff; *Panamericana*, Cra 7, No 14-09, disorganized, but has some guidebooks and maps. Books in Colombia are generally expensive.

Maps: the best current map of Bogotá is by Cartur, scale 1:25,000, 1994, and of Colombia, Mapa Vial de Colombia by Rodríguez, scale 1:2,000,000, also 1994, about US$4 each.

You may have to try several bookshops. Hiking, topographical, town and general maps, also a good new (1996) road atlas of the country (*Hojas de ruta*) from Instituto Geográfico Agustín Codazzi, Av Ciudad de Quito y C 45, T 368-3666, F 368-0998 who also have a relief map of the country: Mapa Vial y Turístico, 1:1,500,000, 1995, US$5.80. The topographi-

cal details of the walking maps are generally accurate, but trails and minor roads less so. They are open 0900-1500, maps are mainly from US$2.50 to $6 and you pay at the Bancafé next door. There is a library open to 1630 and refreshments available at lunchtime.

Esso road maps from some service stations, US$2.

Photography: *Foto Japón*, branches all over the city, gives free film, branch at Cra 7, No 50-10, develops slides in 1 hr. *Poder Fotográfico*, Cra 5, No 20-70, T 342-4130, for good developing in 2-3 hrs.

● **Sports**

Bull fighting: on Sat and Sun during the season, and every 2-3 weeks for the rest of the year, at the municipally owned Plaza de Santamaría, nr Parque Independencia. In season, the bulls weigh over 335 kg; out of season they are "comparatively small and unprofessional". (Local bullfight museum at bullring, door No 6.) **Boxing matches** are held here too.

Football: tickets for matches at El Campín stadium can be bought in advance at *Cigarrería Bucana*, C 18, No 5-92. It is not normally necessary to book in advance, except for the local Santa Fe-Millonarios derby, and of course, internationals. Take a cushion, matches Sun at 1545, Wed at 2000.

Hiking: Sal Si Puedes hiking group arranges walks every weekend and sometimes midweek on trails in Cundinamarca, and further afield at national holiday periods eg Semana Santa; very friendly, welcomes visitors. Hikes are graded for every ability, from 3 km to 4-day excursions of 70 km, camping overnight. The groups are often big (30-60), but after the preliminary warm-up exercises, and the Sal Si Puedes hymn, the regime relaxes and it is possible to stray from the main group. Reservations should be made and paid for a week or so in advance at Cra 7, No 17-01, offices

640 and 641, T 283-9086 or 341-5854, open 0800-1200 and 1400-1800, or contact Justo Alfonso Gamboa, Diagonal 123, No 50-30, Bogotá, T 283-9980 office, 253-6228 home.

Horse races: at Hipódromo los Andes, on Autopista Norte Km 21, races at 1400 (entrance US$1 and US$0.35), and at the Hipódromo del Techo, in the SW, on Sat, Sun and public holidays.

● **Tour companies & travel agents**

Recommended: *Tierra Mar Aire*, Cra 10, No 27-91, T 288-2088, is Amex agent, has several offices around town eg Santa Bárbara: Av 15, No 118-34, T 629-0274 and does city tours from *Hotel Tequendama* (T 286-1111). *Interamerican Tours*, C 17, No 6-57 very helpful arranging flights to Central America via San Andrés. *Viajes Chapinero*, Av 7, 124-15, T 612-7716, F 215-9099, with branches at C63, No 13-37, Chapinero, and Cra 40C, No 57-08, bloque A1, manager David Krech, helpful with information in English. *Eco-Guías*, Cra 3, No 18-56A, Of 202, T 334-8042, T/F 284-8991, E-mail: ecoguias@openway.com.co; Luis Enrique La Rotta and Nadia Diamond, specialize in ecotourism, climbing, trekking, riding and tourism on coffee *fincas*, highly rec.

● **Tourist offices**

Corporación Nacional de Turismo (CNT), C 28, No 13A-59, admin offices at C 28, No 13A-15, T 413-8202/9830, Edif Centro de Comercio Internacional (the name at the top of the building is Bancafé), Mon-Fri, 0830-1300, 1400-1700, closed Sat and Sun, take identification; they can give you information on safety and have maps of major cities available (though mostly out of date), and will tell you where to go to get detailed information. Tourist police kiosk outside *Hotel Tequendama*, nr bridge on Cra 7. Municipal tourist office, **Instituto Distrital de Cultura y Turismo**, C 10, No 3-61, T 286-6555 (also at bus terminal, T 295-4460). **Alcaldía Mayor**, C 14 y Cra 3, helpful, sells booklets, posters, T-shirts etc. **Corporación Cultura y Turismo de Cundinamarca**, C 16, No 7-76, T 242-8587, for details of towns around Bogotá. The **Coordinadora de Turismo de Bogotá** (Cra 13, No 27-95) has daily tours of the city with interpreters. For information on 24-hr chemists (pharmacies), events, attractions, etc, T 282-0000.

MA, the National Parks Office: full details in **Introduction, National Parks**. Regional office for Amazonia and Orinoquia, Cra 10, No 20-30, T 283-3009, F 243-3091.

● **Useful addresses**

DAS: Immigration office, Cra 27, No 17-85, open 0730-1530; **Dirección de Extranjería** (for renewing entry permits): C 100, No 11B-27, open Mon-Thur 0730-1600, Fri 0730-1530.

T 610-7371 (División de Extranjería) or 277-6666 (emergency). DAS will not authorize photocopies of passports; look in Yellow Pages for notaries, who will.

Emergency numbers: **Ambulance**: T 125; **Fire**: T 119; **Red Cross**: 132.

● **Transport**

Local Bus: buses stop (in theory) by 'Paradero' boards; otherwise flag buses down. Bus fares are from US$0.30 up, depending on length of route and time of day. Most buses have day/night tariff advertised in the window. *Busetas* charge a little more. There are some 'super-executive' routes with plush seats, at US$0.45. Fares are a bit higher at night and on holidays. Urban buses are not good for sightseeing because you will be standing as likely as not. **Car rental**: **Dollar Rent-a-Car**, airport and Diag 109, No 14-61, T 612-8295; **Hertz**, at airport, and at Cra 10, No 26-35, T 284-1445; **Avis**, C 99, No 11-26, T 610-4455, and at airport; **Arrencar**, Trans 17, No 121-12, T 214-1413, F 620-3359, good value. **Taxis**: have meters; insist that they are used. Starting charge, US$0.50. Average fare from North Bogotá to the centre US$3.50. Check before taking your first taxi if there are any additional charges above what the meter states eg: night charge or legal surcharge after recent fare increases (a list of legal charges should be posted in the taxi). At busy times, empty taxis flagged down on the street may refuse to take you to less popular destinations. Radio taxis are rec for safety and reliability; when you call the dispatcher gives you a cab number, confirm this when it arrives (eg Proturismo T 223-2111; Taxis Libres, T 231-1111; also 311-1111 and 222-2222 are radio taxi fleets). Taxis are relatively cheap, so it is worthwhile taking one if you are carrying valuables, or at night. Tipping is not customary, but is appreciated. If you are going to an address out of the city centre, it is helpful to know the section you are going to as well as the street address, eg Chicó, Chapinero (ask at your hotel). See also under **Airport** and **Buses** below.

Air The airport at El Dorado has the world's second largest landing field. There are two terminals, the Puente Aéreo terminal (T 413-8103) being 1 km before the main terminal (T 413-9500) on Av El Dorado. Frequent buses run between the two. Avianca international flights use both terminals (usually Miami and New York). Puente Aéreo is more comfortable but there is not as much duty-free shopping. **You must check which terminal your flight will use**. 'Tourist Guide' policemen have white armbands. The main terminal is being slowly modernized. The departure areas with the usual duty-free shops are of a high standard and comfortable. Free Colombian coffee inside the customs area, between gates 2 and 3. Many snack bars and restaurants on 1st floor. International calls can be made from Telecom on 1st floor, credit cards accepted; post office in main arrivals lounge. Exchange rates are marginally lower than in the city, but pesos cannot be changed back into dollars at the airport without receipts. Airport bank changes TCs, but is not open at holiday times. When closed, ask airport police where to change money. Allow 2 hrs for checking in and security. There is no baggage deposit nor, at time of writing, tourist information.

The taxi fare from airport to city is a fixed charge, US$8, more at night and early am. Make sure you get a registered taxi, normally yellow, found at right (from inside) side of main terminal or Avianca terminal (drivers try to overcharge all the same). Unofficial taxis not advisable. Use only uniformed porters. There are colectivos (US$1 plus luggage pp) from airport to centre; also buses in the daytime, US$0.25 (not easy with bulky luggage and they may refuse to take you). You have to cross eight busy lanes of traffic to get a bus into town, and negotiate two drainage ditches. In the city centre buses and black and red colectivos can be picked up on Av 19, anywhere between Cras 3 and 10 at which they turn right for the airport; colectivos can also be taken from the corner of C 13 (Av Jiménez de Quesada) and Av 14 (Av Caracas); buses marked 'Aeropuerto' or 'Universitaria Dorado'; colectivos marked 'Aeropuerto'. Check with your hotel for the best way to the airport. Watch belongings inside and outside airport, especially at night.

For internal flights, which serve all parts of the country, see page 987. For most domestic shuttle flights to Medellín/Montería, Cali/Pasto, and Barranquilla, go to Puente Aéreo terminal. Sometimes, flights are overbooked, so check in well in advance.

Trains Long distance services were suspended in 1992. There are no passenger services at present from Bogotá (La Sabana) station at C 13 y Cra 20 except a tourist steam train which runs on Sun at 0730 calling at Usaquén, C 110, Transversal 10, in the N of the city (see map) at 0830, going N to Nemocón (1140), returning at 1430 and back in Bogotá Usaquén at 1715 and La Sabana at 1800. Cost: adult US$14, child up to 10, US$8. Information, Turistrén Ltda, Transversal 17 A, No 98-17, T 257-1459. Tickets should be bought in advance here, at La Sabana station or from travel agents.

Buses There is a long-distance bus terminal, Terminal de Transportes, nr Av Boyacá (Cra 72) between El Dorado (Av 26) and Av Centenario (C 13). There is also access from Cra 68. Exact address C 33 B, No 69-59, T 295-1100. The terminal is divided into modules serving the 4 points of the

compass; each module has several bus companies serving similar destinations. If possible, buy tickets at the ticket office before travelling to avoid overcharging. **Fares and journey times are given under destinations below.** If you are travelling N, enquire if the bus company has a pick-up point on the Autopista del Norte around C 160. Velotax busetas are slightly quicker and more expensive than ordinary buses, as are colectivos, which go to several long-distance destinations. To get to the terminal take bus marked 'Terminal' from 'Terminal Transportes' bus stop at corner of Av Jiménez de Quesada and Cra 15, or *buseta* on Cra 10 before *Hotel Tequendama*. At night take a colectivo taxi from Av 13 y Av Caracas, US$0.45 (no buses). To get into town take buses marked 'Centro' or 'Germania' at the terminal: the buses go through the W of the city, then E on C 13, turning right on Cra 14, closest to the centre (from this junction the 'Germania' bus goes up to the centre and La Candelaria). A *buseta* runs from Cra 68 to the terminal and back. Taxi around US$3.50, depending on destination, surcharge at night, passengers are given a computer slip showing the cab's registration number and the exact fare (avoid the unofficial taxis, normally touting for particular hotels). The terminal is well-organized and comfortable, but, as usual, watch out for thieves who are also well organized – we have an increasing number of reports of baggage thefts. Free self-service luggage trolleys are provided. There are shops and restaurants. There are showers at the terminal (between Nos 3 and 4), US$0.50, soap and towel provided.

Buses to Venezuela: it is better not to buy a through ticket to Caracas with Berlinas de Fonce as this does not guarantee a seat and is only valid for two Venezuelan companies; moreover no refunds are given in Cúcuta. Ideally, if you have time, make the journey to Cúcuta in two stages to enjoy the scenery to the full. Bus connections from San Antonio de Táchira in Venezuela to Caracas are good.

EXCURSIONS SOUTHEAST FROM BOGOTA

To the SE of Bogotá is **Choachí**, an attractive village set in a valley, where there are hot springs (good food at *El Colonial*, 1½ blocks from main square). Flota Macarena bus, several a day. Transoriente also go there from Av 6A, No 15-48, T 243-5599, every 15 mins, US$2 (take a taxi to the terminal in Bogotá, don't walk). A turnoff from the Choachí road goes to the Santuario de San Francisco, with better views of Bogotá than from Monserrate.

EXCURSIONS SOUTHWEST FROM BOGOTA

The Simón Bolívar Highway runs from Bogotá to Girardot (see page 929); this 132 km stretch is extremely picturesque, running down the mountains.

About 20 km along this road from the centre of Bogotá is Soacha, now the end of the built-up area of the city. A right fork here leads past the Indumil plant to the **Chicaque Parque Natural**, a privately owned 300 ha park, principally cloud forest between 2,100m and 2,700m on the edge of the Sabana de Bogotá. It is a popular spot for walkers and riders at weekends with good facilities for day visitors and a new Swiss style *refugio*, opened in mid-1997, about 1 hr down the trail from the entrance, which provides meals and accommodation for 70 or so costing US$25-30/day including meals. Park open daily 0800-1600, entrance US$3. Take a bus to Soacha and ask for continuing transport to the Park. If driving, there is a better route via Mosquera on the Honda road, left towards La Mesa and in 11 km left again on the road to Soacha. The park sign is 6 km along this road.

Salto de Tequendama

Take the exit from the Giradot Highway marked El Colegio to **Salto de Tequendama** (5 km), where the water of the Río Bogotá or Funza falls 132m over the lip of the Sabana; the water is dirty with sewage but the falls are still a spectacular sight though the smell can be most unpleasant. The site is in an amphitheatre of forest-clad hill sloping to the edge of a rock-walled gorge. There is a good bus service from Bogotá (31 km).

8 km beyond the falls is the **Zoológico Santa Cruz**, a private collection of local animals, birds and reptiles. It is open daily, 0900-1700 US$2. Further along the road to El Colegio is Bellavista. Turn right here for **Santandercito**, a charming village in steeply wooded countryside. In its own grounds nearby is **A1-A2** *Alto de la Palma*, T (91)847-3807, cheaper mid-week, a remarkable republican style house, recently remodelled, popular with English speaking Colombian residents for weekend breaks, pool, riding, run by a dedicated English owner, Simon Humber, excellent restaurant, genuine English breakfasts, warmly recommended.

FUSAGASUGA

After the Tequendama Falls turning is **Fusagasugá** (*Pop* 58,215; *Alt* 1,740m) which lies in a rich wooded valley famous for its fruits, its good climate and Sun market. Splendid orchids can be seen in the Jardín Luxemburgo (best flowering Nov-Feb but it is a long walk out of town) and in the Jardín Clarisa; pleasant garden also at the Casa de la Cultura. There are bathing spots on the Río Sumapaz.

- **Buses** From Bogotá, Autos Fusa and Cootransfusa, US$1.20.

Down the main road from Fusagasugá is El Boquerón, below which is a spectacular rock overhang known as El Nariz del Diablo (Devil's Nose), near which is a side road left to **San Bernardo**, a pretty little town. The cemetery has a macabre attraction; looking through a window near the central 'altar' you see mummified figures, including a woman and child, assembled in the dimly lit cellar, entry US$0.25. Off this road go right about 10 km to **Pandi** where there is a park with ancient stones. Nearby, on the road to Icononzo, is a famous natural bridge in a spectacular and very deep gorge through which runs the Río Sumapaz. This can also be reached from the road to San Bernardo (above) by turning right 3 km short of the village. Bus: from Fusagasugá to San Bernardo, 1½ hrs.

MELGAR

A popular weekending place, near Girardot, for Bogotanos who like a little warmth. There are three tolls between Bogotá and Melgar (not always manned). For those driving S towards Neiva there is a new bypass avoiding Girardot.

- **Accommodation** There are lots of hotels in the area most of which have swimming pools; it is best to try whichever you like the look of and move on to another if it is full; there are also camping sites and the state-subsidized Cafam vacation centre, best visited in mid-week. There are good places to stop for snacks and meals, often with good family facilities, eg *Parador Las Villas*, near the Girardot bypass.

EXCURSIONS NORTHWEST FROM BOGOTA

The Sabana de Bogotá is dotted with white farms and groves of eucalyptus. The road passes through two small towns, Fontibón and Madrid. **Fontibón**, 10 km from Bogotá, has a good colonial church, and about 3 km outside the town are stones with Indian pictographs; nearby, on the road from the old Techo airport to Bogotá, there are replicas of San Agustín statues.

Facatativá (*pop* 61,590) is 40 km from Bogotá. Some 3 km from Facatativá, on the road to the W, is the park of Piedras de Tunja, a natural rock amphitheatre with enormous stones, numerous Indian pictographs and an artificial lake. A road goes SW from Facatativá to Girardot through **Tocaima** (*pop* 8,520), a small, attractive holiday town (several hotels). A road runs through beautiful mountain country, via La Mesa, to Mosquera on the road between Madrid and Fontibón. This is a good alternative to the Simón Bolívar highway from Girardot to Bogotá.

VILLETA

71 km from Facatativá **Villeta** (*pop* 12,465) is a popular weekend resort for Bogotanos. Not far away are the waterfalls of Quebrada Cune. On the road to Bogotá is *Balneario El Descanso*, swimming pool, safe parking. Near the centre is *Llamarade* restaurant, good value; many good ice-cream parlours around the square; also hotels. The road continues to Honda (see page 928), half way to which is **Guaduas**; in the main square is a statue of the liberator Policarpa Sala Varrieta, and a delightful colonial hotel. Public swimming pool; Sun market. Best local dish is *quesillos*. Bus to Honda, US$1.45, 1 hr. The surrounding countryside is beautiful, including waterfalls at Versalles (10 km).

EXCURSIONS NORTH FROM BOGOTA

Interesting day trips can be made to the attractive rolling antiplano, leaving Bogotá on the Autopista del Norte (extension of Av 13), or on the parallel Carretera del Norte (the old road, extension of Av 7). On the latter, once out of Bogotá, there are many old fincas and good typical restaurants. The two roads join at Km 24 at La Caro where a road leaves left (W) to Chía and Zipaquirá. At this junction is the 'castle' of Rodríguez Gacha with a sinister history connected to this drug baron. By contrast, there is opposite the graceful colonial bridge over the Río Bogotá, now preserved and bypassed by the road to Chía.

CHIA

Typical Sun market (bus from Av Caracas, Bogotá US$0.30). On the way there you pass through Fonqueta, where tapestries are made. Walk, or take a bus to La Barbanera church on a hill overlooking the Sabana de Bogotá. Good restaurant just outside Chía, *Andrés Carne de Res*, good music, good atmosphere, good food from 1600.

ZIPAQUIRA

From Chía (via Cájica, *pop* 15,315, pleasant town with good shopping for ponchos and carpets) to **Zipaquirá** (*pop* 62,130), centre of a rich cattle farming district, and famous for its rock salt mine, which has been exploited for centuries. The church in the attractive central Plaza is also worth a visit for its stonework (despite its external appearance, it has a modern interior).

The original underground cathedral, constructed by miners inside the huge main salt mine, was dedicated in 1954 to Nuestra Señora del Rosario (patron saint of miners). Continuing deterioration made the whole cave unsafe and it was closed. A remarkable, new salt cathedral was opened on 16 December 1995 (entry US$7, including 1¼ hrs guided tour, car park US$1); it is 500m from, and 58m below, the old salt cathedral, open Tues-Sun 1000-1600, Sun mass at 1200, admission by ticket. The entrance to the cave is in hills about 20 mins' walk W of the town. There is an information centre at the site. There is an interesting **Museo**

Quevedo Zornozo, C 3, No 7-69, which displays musical instruments and paraphenalia including the piano of General Santander. Open Tue-Fri 0930-1200, 1400-1600, Sat-Sun 0900-1700, US$1.

● **Accommodation C-D** *Hostería del Libertador*, Vía Catedral de Sal, T 852-6846, F 852-6851, restored colonial mansion, nr the mine, good food; **E** *Hotel Colonial*, C 3, No 6-57, T 852-2690, showers, nice. Restaurants on main square, *El Mesón del Zipa*, good, cheap food; *Asadero Colonial*, C 5 y Cra 7, good food, arepas, bandejas.

● **Buses** From Bogotá: many from Cra 30 (Av Ciudad de Quito), marked 'Zipa', Flota Alianza, or others, US$0.80 each way, 1¼ hrs. The Zipaquirá bus station is 15 mins' walk from the mines and cathedral. Zipaquirá can also be reached from Tunja (see page 878), by taking a Bogotá-bound bus and getting off at La Caro for connection to Zipaquirá, US$2.40. Leave plenty of time for the return journey as it can be difficult to stop Bogotá-Tunja buses at La Caro. It can also be difficult to get on a bus from Zipaquirá going N towards Villa de Leiva.

15 km NE of Zipaquirá, at **Nemocón**, there are salt mines (now closed) and a church. There is a small but interesting **Museo de Sal** on the plaza, which includes history of the salt industry in the time of the Chibcha Indians, US$1. Restaurant, *El Colonial*, 100m from the station. A side (dirt) road connects with the Bogotá-Cúcuta highway.

A steam-hauled *tren turístico* runs on Sun from Bogotá to Zipaquirá and Nemocón. See under Bogotá, **Train**.

Continuing N from Zipaquirá towards Chiquinquirá, the road crosses a high ridge with some impressive mountain scenery. 48 km N of Zipaquirá is **Ubaté**, the cheese-making centre of the Sabana. Good restaurant, *La Rueda* in Plaza Catedral, trout from local lakes a speciality. The main road continues past the **Laguna de Fúquene** (Devil's Lake) now about 4,850 ha of water with four cultivated islands. In times past the lake was much more extensive as can readily be seen as the road follows the old shore line. Thence to Chiquinquirá, see page 882.

Bogotá to Cúcuta

THE main road route from Bogotá to Venezuela has some beautiful stretches. It passes through, or near, several colonial towns and gives access to the Sierra Nevada del Cocuy, excellent climbing and hiking country.

A 618-km road runs NE from Bogotá to Cúcuta, near the Venezuelan border, through Tunja, Moniquirá, Barbosa, Socorro, San Gil, Bucaramanga and Pamplona. It is good most of the way. The road out of Bogotá is the *autopista* to La Caro (see page 876), then follow Tunja signs.

From La Caro, the road goes through rich agricultural country with many crops including fruit and flowers. At Km 32.5 is the Alpina Yogurt factory and the Parque Puerto de Sopó with artificial lake. At **Sopó** itself there is an image of the Saviour which has appeared in an eroded stone; the paintings of angels in the church are very strange and worth seeing (ask at the Casa Cural for entry to church – give a tip). 2 km E of the main road is **Sesquilé**, several restaurants, no accommodation. On your right beyond the town is the large Tominé lake and dam. There is a campsite on the lakeside.

GUATAVITA

The modern town of **Guatavita Nueva** (75 km from Bogotá, 17 km from Sesquilé), was built in colonial style when the old town of Guatavita was submerged by the reservoir. The original inhabitants were unwilling to stay in the new town, so it is now a weekend haunt for Bogotanos and tourists. Cathedral, artisan workshops and small bull-ring for apprentices to practise Sun afternoons; two small museums, one devoted to the Muisca Indians and the other to relics of the old Guatavita church, including a delightful Debain harmonium (Paris 1867). Sun market best in morning, before Bogotanos get there. Julio A Martínez at the tourist information booth can find accommodation for visitors; he speaks English.

Laguna de Guatavita (also called Lago de Amor by locals) is where the legend of El Dorado originated. The lake is a quiet, beautiful place; you can walk right round it close to the water level, 1½ hrs, or climb to the rim of the crater in several places. Opinions differ on whether the crater is volcanic or a meteorite impact, but from the rim at 3,100m there are extensive views over the varied countryside.

● **Access** Bus Bogotá-Guatavita Nueva (Flota Valle de Tenza, Cra 25, No 15-72, rec; Flota Aguila, Cra 15 No 14-59), US$1.45, 2-3 hrs, departures 0730, 0800 and 0930; last return bus at 1730. You can walk (2-3 hrs) or ride (US$7/horse) from Guatavita Nueva to the lake. An easier approach is from a point on the Sesquilé-Guatavita Nueva road (the bus driver will let you off at the right place) where there is a sign "via Lago Guatavita". Nearby, on the main road, are good places to eat at weekends. There is a good campsite nearby. From the main road

to the lakeside the road is paved as far as a school, about half way. Follow the signs. This road and subsequent track can be driven in a good car to within 300m of the lake where there is a car park and good restaurant, *Hostería Caminos a El Dorado*, open at weekends.

Beyond Sesquilé, the main road goes through **Chocontá** (*pop* 13,650), 88 km from Bogotá, the route is across the western slopes of the Eastern Cordillera to Tunja, 137 km from Bogotá.

BOYACA DEPARTMENT

TUNJA

Capital of Boyacá Department, **Tunja** (*pop* 113,945; *alt* 2,820m) stands in an dry mountainous area. The climate is cool: mean temperature, 12°C. When the Spaniards arrived in what is now Boyacá, Tunja was aleady an Indian city, the seat of the Zipa, one of the two Chibcha kings. It was refounded as a Spanish city by Gonzalo Suárez Rendón in 1539. The city formed an independent Junta in 1811, and Bolívar fought under its aegis during the campaign of the Magdalena in 1812. 6 years later he fought the decisive battle of Boyacá, nearby (see below).

Places of interest

Churches The most remarkable colonial building is the church of **Santo Domingo**, a masterpiece begun in 1594; the interior is covered with wood most richly carved. Another is the **Santa Clara**

The Gilded Man

The basis of the El Dorado (Gilded Man) story is established fact. It was the custom of the Chibcha king to be coated annually with resin, on which gold dust was stuck, and then to be taken out on the lake on a ceremonial raft. He then plunged into the lake and emerged with the resin and gold dust washed off. The lake was also the repository of precious objects thrown in as offerings; there have been several attempts to drain it (the first, by the Spaniards in colonial times, was the origin of the sharp cut in the crater rim) and many items have been recovered over the years. The factual basis of the El Dorado story was confirmed by the discovery of a miniature raft with ceremonial figures on it, made from gold wire, which is now one of the most prized treasures of the Museo de Oro in Bogotá. Part of the raft is missing; the story is that the gold from it ended up in one of the finder's teeth! (Read John Hemming's *The Search for El Dorado* on the subject.)

chapel (1580), now the hospital of San Rafael, with some fine wood carving. The church of **Santa Bárbara** is full of colonial woodwork, and in the nearby parish house are some notable religious objects, including silk embroidery from the 18th century. Also impressive is the church of **San Ignacio**.

Museums The **house of Don Juan de Vargas** is a museum of colonial Tunja, entry US$0.25 includes guided tour in several languages, 0800-1200, 1300-1800. The **Casa del Fundador Suárez Rendón**, Plaza de Bolívar, is one of the few extant mansions of a Spanish *conquistador* in Colombia (1539-43); peaceful courtyard with fine view of valley through gateway; museum open Wed-Sun; see the unique series of plateresque paintings on the ceilings. There are some fine colonial buildings on Plaza de Bolívar opposite the Cathedral. In **Parque Bosque de la República** is the adobe wall against which three martyrs of the Independence were shot in 1816. Ask the tourist police guarding these buildings for information.

Excursions

The battle of Boyacá was fought about 16 km S of Tunja, on the road to Bogotá. On the bridge at Boyacá is a large monument to Bolívar. Bolívar took Tunja on 6 August 1819, and next day his troops, fortified by a British Legion, the only professional soldiers among them, fought the Spaniards on the banks of the swollen Río Boyacá. With the loss of only 13 killed and 53 wounded they captured 1,600 men and 39 officers. Only 50 men escaped, and when these told their tale in Bogotá the Viceroy Samao fled in such haste that he left behind him half a million pesos of the royal funds. There is now a huge modern restaurant overlooking the site.

On a hillside outside Tunja is the carved rock throne of the Chibcha king, the Zipa; ask for directions from the Tourist Office.

Local festivals

During the week before Christmas, there is a lively festival with local music, traditional dancing and fireworks.

Local information
● Accommodation

A3 *San Ignacio Plaza*, C 18 No 10-51, T 437583, F 423472, modern, pleasant; **A2** *Boyacá Plaza*, C 18, No 11-22, T 401116, F 427635, inc breakfast, parking, good; **A1** *Hunza*, C 21A, No 10-66, T 424111 (Bogotá 347-0099), F 424119, modern, breakfast inc, good restaurant, pool, sauna.

B *Conquistador*, C 20, No 8-92, T 431465, F 423534, corner of Plaza de Bolívar, 22 traditional rooms round courtyard, nice restaurant, good; **B** *Hostería San Carlos*, Cra 11, No 20-12, T 423716, colonial style, interestingly furnished, good restaurant, highly rec.

C *San Francisco*, Cra 9, No 18-90, T 426645, 3rd floor, on Plaza de Bolívar nr cathedral.

E *Americano*, Cra 11, No 18-70, hot water, attractive lobby; **E** *Dux*, next to *Lord*, nice creaky old hotel, good rooms, cold water, good value; **E** *Lord*, C 19, No 10-64, small rooms, hot water, run down; **E** *Saboy*, C 19, No 10-40, nice covered patio, family run.

F *Colonial*, Cra 8, No 20-40, safe; **F** *Imperial*, C 19, No 7-43, basic, use of kitchen. Area around bus station said not to be safe at night (eg **F** *Bolívar Príncipe*).

● Places to eat

San Ricardo, C 19, No 8-38, good; *Surtipan*, C 20, No 12-58, good cakes and coffee; *Estar de Hunzahúa*, C 20, No 11-20 (2nd floor), good value, rec; *Pollo Listo* Cra 11, No 19-30, good; *Santo Domingo*, Cra 11, No 19-66, good; *Americano*, Cra 11, 18-70, light meals; *Café Imperial*, C 20, No 9-14, good coffee and cakes until late; *Doña Cecilia*, Cra 8, No 18-18, good *comida corriente*. **Fast food**: many fast food, pizza etc outlets in the pedestrianized streets nr Plaza de Bolívar.

● Shopping

Market, nr Plaza de Toros on outskirts of town, open every day (good for *ruanas* and blankets). Fri is main market day.

● Tourist offices

In Casa del Fundador, Plaza de Bolívar, helpful. Also try 'Fondo Mixto' Cámera de Comercio building C 21, No 10-52. Information on Boyacá: tourist office adjacent to the *Hotel Hunza*.

● Transport

Bus station is a steep 500m down from city centre. From **Bogotá** 2½-4½ hrs, US$6, **Duitama**, Cotrans, and others. To **Bucaramanga**, hourly, 7½ hrs, US$17.

VILLA DE LEIVA

About 40 km W over the mountain divide is the colonial town of **Villa de Leiva** (also spelt Leyva, *pop* 3,310). To reach it from Bogotá, turn left at the Boyacá monument, or go through Tunja. The two roads join and you must turn right at Sáchica for the final 6 km to Villa de Leiva.

The town dates back to the early days of Spanish rule, but unlike Tunja, it has been declared a national monument so will not be modernized. The first president of Nueva Granada (see page 853), Miguel Venero de Leiva, lived in the town.

Places of interest

Two **colonial houses** should be visited: the house in which Antonio Nariño lived (Cra 9, No 10-39, open Tues-Sun 0900-1230, 1400-1800) – he translated the *Rights of Man* into Spanish – and the building in which the first Convention of the United Provinces of New Granada was held, C 13 y Cra 9, on corner of plaza. Also worth a visit is the restored birthplace of the independence hero Antonio Ricaurte (Cra 8 y C 5). A **palaeontological museum** is 15 mins' walk N of the town on Cra 9, interesting and well displayed, US$0.75. On the Plaza Mayor is the **Casa-Museo Luis Alberto Acuña**, housing fascinating examples of Acuña's work (recommended, US$1, extra to take photographs). The **Monasterio de las Carmelitas** has one of the best museums of religious art in Colombia, open Sat and Sun 1400-1700. Part of the monastery is the **Iglesia del Carmen** and the **Convento**, all worth a visit.

Excursions

The mountains around Villa de Leiva abound in fossils. 5 km along the road to Santa Sofía can be seen the complete fossil of a dinosaur now housed in a room, entry US$0.50, look for road signs to **El Fósil** (0800-1200, 1300-1600, Thur 1300-1600). 2 km from El Fósil along this road is the turning for (1 km) the archaeological site of **El Infiernito**, where there are several huge carved stones believed to be giant phalli and a solar calendar (0900-1200, 1400-1700, closed Mon, US$0.50). 6 km after the Infiernito turning is the Monas-

tery of **Ecce-Homo** (founded 1620); note the fossils on the floor at the entrance. There are buses from Villa de Leiva at 0645, 0930 and 1345, going to Santa Sofía, US$0.50; it's 30 mins to the crossing, then a 2-km walk to the monastery. Beyond Santa Sofía is La Cueva de Hayal, a cave set in beautiful scenery. A tour of most of these attractions leaves the plaza at 0930, Sat/Sun, US$6, recommended.

20 km from Villa de Leiva, there is a left turn for the **Iguaque National Park** (3 km) run by MA: interesting oak woods, flora, fauna and several lakes. There are guided paths and a marked trail to Lake Iguaque, a walk of $2\frac{1}{2}$ hrs. Entrance US$0.70, students US$0.55, cars US$1.35; tourist centre with accommodation for 60; restaurant with good food at reasonable prices. The most likely day for a lift is Sat, market day, but there is a daily bus at 0700 from Villa de Leiva to the turn off to the Park. It returns at 1300. (Camping is allowed, safe.)

Local festivals

Virgin del Carmen, 13-17 July annually. In Aug (check dates) an international kite festival is held in the Plaza Major and a festival of light is held every year in mid-December. Market day is Sat, held in the Plaza del Mercado (not the Plaza Major).

Local information

NB The town tends to be full of visitors at weekends and bank holidays and is generally expensive. On Mon and Tues many places are closed. The houses are closed Mon-Fri out of season, but the trip is worth while for the views and for long, peaceful walks in the hills.

● **Accommodation**

L3 *Hospedería Duruelo*, C 13, No 2-88, T 320222, modern colonial style, beautiful views, nice gardens, also conference hotel, good food; **L3** *Plazuela de San Agustín*, Cra 9, No 13-25, T 320286, well appointed hotel, nicely decorated.

A1 *El Molino la Mesopotamia*, C del Silencio (top of Cra 8), T 320235, a beautifully restored colonial mill, 10% rebate for booking 10 days ahead, excellent home cooking, beautiful gardens, a memorable hotel, rec; **A2** *Mesón de la Plaza Mayor*, Cra 10, No 12-31, T 320425 (T 218-7741 Bogotá), beautifully restored *hospedaría*; **A2** *Hospedaje El Mesón de Los Virreyes*, Cra 9, No 14-51, T 320252, good restaurant; **A2** *Hostería Los Frayles*, C 8, No 9-38, T 320296, colonial décor, 5 mins walk from the centre.

Villa de Leiva

B *Hospedaria El Marquéz de San Jorge*, C 14, No 9-20, T 320240, colonial mansion, beautiful courtyard, parking; **B** *Los Llanitos*, C 9, No 12-31, T 256-1643 (Bogotá), 5 mins' walk from main plaza, quiet, hot water, good food; **B** *Mesón La Candelaria*, next to Molino de Mesopotamia, T 230534, 8 rooms, family atmosphere, Spanish cuisine.

D *Hospedaje El Sol de la Villa*, Cra 8, No 12-28, T 320-224, safe, hot shower, very good breakfast, cooking facilities on request, good value, rec; **D-E** *Hostería La Roca*, C 13, No 9-54, pleasant, with some rooms overlooking main square and reasonable breakfast, attractive tiled courtyard and garden, noisy at night because of bar music.

Booking essential during holidays, and advisable at weekends (try bargaining Mon-Thur).

Camping: MA's *Vivero*, 15 mins walk N of plaza on road to Arcabuco (just before palaeontological museum), nice place with bathroom, warm shower, ask for Juan; also Los Olivares nr village of Sáchica, 4 km from Villa de Leiva (no services). Ask for advice on other sites at the Tourist office.

● Places to eat
Nueva Granada, C 13, No 7-66, good value,

friendly, owner Jorge Rodríguez, plays classical guitar music on demand; *El Parrillón de los Caciques*, Cra 9, No 9-05, nr bus station, good value, open till 2000, rec; *El Estar de la Villa*, C 13, No 8-89, good; *El Rincón Bachue*, Cra 9, C 15, interesting decoration with a china factory behind; *Giorgio*, C 12 between Cra 8 and 9, Italian, good atmosphere, reasonable prices; *Casa Blanca*, C 13, No 7-16, good juices, and *comida corriente*, open till 2100, rec; *Tienda de Teresa*, Cra 10, 13-72, good breakfasts; *Café y que Café*, C 12, No 8-88, excellent *tinto*; *Zarina Galeria Café*, C 14, No 7-67, antique décor, good.

● Post & telecommunications
Post Office: in Telecom building, C 13, No 8-26.

● Shopping
The shops in the plaza and the adjoining streets have an excellent selection of Colombian handicrafts and offer many bargains.

● Tour companies & travel agencies
Guías & Travesías, Cra 8A, No 11-59, T 320359, arranges trips throughout the region, guides for Iguaque National Park, Enrique Maldonado, Director, very helpful.

● **Tourist offices**
Cra 9, No 13-04 just off the plaza, open Tues-Sun 0800-1200, 1400-1800, local maps US$0.25, gives advice on cheaper accommodation. Director Nelly Delgado and the staff are most helpful.

● **Transport**
Station in 8th block of Cra 9. It is rec to book the return journey on arrival. Buses to **Tunja**, 1 hr, US$2.50 with Flota Reina or Valle de Tenza. To **Bogotá** via Tunja, takes 4 hrs, US$6, several companies, and via Zipaquirá and Chiquinquirá, US$6.70. Colectivo taxis leave the bus station in Tunja for **Villa de Leiva** every hour, US$3, and return from the main plaza. To **Ráquira** busetas at 0730, 0800, 1740, 1930 US$1, taxi, US$2.50. Bus at 1000 from Leiva to **Moniquirá** (see page 885) connects with bus to Bucaramanga, thus avoiding Tunja.

Ráquira

At **Ráquira** locals make mainly earthenware pottery in several workshops in and around the village. The ceramics, among the best-known in Colombia, are sold in about 10 shops on the main street. Apart from kitchen and houseware items, there are many small ornaments and toys to enjoy. The craftsmen are happy for you to watch them at work.

● **Accommodation & places to eat** Two good hotels, **B** *Nequeteba*, T 320461, converted and renovated colonial house, pool, restaurant, craft shop, helpful owner, parking, and **D** *Norteño*, nice and clean (both on plaza). At weekends it is possible to eat at the Museo de Arte y Tradiciones Populares. Market day Sun.

About 7 km along a very rough road, which winds up above Ráquira affording spectacular views, is a beautiful 16th-century monastery, the **Convento de la Candelaria** (1604). On the altar of the fine church is the painting of the Virgen de La Candelaria, dating from 1597, by Francisco del Pozo of Tunja. The painting's anniversary is celebrated each 1 Feb, in addition to 28 Aug, the saint's day of San Agustín. Next to the church is the cloister with anonymous 17th-century paintings of the life of San Agustín (open daily 0900-1200, 1300-1700, US$1.20 with a guided tour which includes a simple but interesting museum). Among other things, they sell a delicious honey to help finance the monastery. **C** *Parador La Candelaria*, adjoining monastery, picturesque, good food.

● **Transport Roads** From Villa de Leiva, take the continuation S of Cra 9 past the bus station out of town to Sáchira, turn right to Sutamarchan and Tinjaca and left at Tres Esquinas for Ráquira, a further 5 km. The road from Tres Esquinas continues to Chiquinquirá. **Buses** Ráquira is best reached from Tunja, 1 hr US$1.70, although there are direct buses from Bogotá (Rápido El Carmen), 0545, 0715, US$6, 6 hrs, returning 1330). Last bus to Tunja 1330. If stuck after 1330, walk 5 km to Tres Esquinas, where buses pass between 1530-1630, mostly going E. There are busetas from Villa de Leiva.

CHIQUINQUIRÁ

134 km by road from Bogotá, and 80 km from Tunja **Chiquinquirá** (*pop* 32,585; *alt* 2,550m) is on the W side of the valley of the Río Suárez. It is a busy commercial centre and the focus of a large coffee and cattle region. In Dec thousands of pilgrims honour a painting of the Virgin whose fading colours were restored by the prayers of a woman. The picture is housed in the imposing **Basílica**, but the miracle took place was in what is now the **Iglesia de la Renovación**, Parque Julio Flores. In 1816, when the town had enjoyed 6 years of independence and was besieged by the Royalists, this painting was carried through the streets by Dominican priests from the famous monastery, to rally the people. The town fell, all the same.

Local festivals Special celebrations at Easter and on 26 Dec, the anniversary of the miracle.

● **Accommodation B** *Gran*, C 16 No 6-97, T 263700, comfortable, secure, good restaurant, parking; **B** *Sarabita*, C 16, 8-12, T 262068, business hotel, pool, sauna, restaurant, building is a national monument; **C** *Real Muisca*, C 16, No 9-22, bar, restaurant; **D** *Moyba*, Cra 9, No 17-53, facing square, cheaper without bath, dingy; **F** *Residencias San Martín*, Cra 9, No 19-84, basic. Many others.

● **Places to eat** *El Escorial*, Parque Julio Flores, good but expensive; *Plaza 17*, C 17, No 11-45, nr basilica, good. Plenty of reasonable places to eat around and nr Parque Julio Flores.

● **Shopping** The shops display the toys made locally: some ceramics painted in gay colours and others white and porous as they come from the kiln; also pottery items from Ráquira; tops and teetotums and other little things carved from tagua nuts which come from the Chocó and Amazonas; orange-wood balls to catch on a stick; the most durable tambourines in the world; shining, brightly coloured gourds; diminutive 9-stringed guitars on which children try the first measures of the *bambuca*. Along the S side of the Basilica are several shops specialising in musical instruments, perhaps the best is across the square, Almacén El Bambuco, Cra 11, No 17-96.

● **Buses** To Villa de Leiva 1¾ hr, US$2.70 (see page 879). To **Tunja**, 3 hrs, US$4; to **Zipaquirá**, US$4.30; to **Bogotá**, 2½ hrs, US$5 (last returns at 1730); all from bus station.

A poor road, dangerous in the rainy season, runs 80 km SW to **Muzo** (*pop* 5,000; *alt* 600m; 3 fair hotels), on the banks of the Río Carare. 16 km away a famous open-cast emerald mine has been worked since 1567, and long before that by the Muzo tribe of Indians. You can visit the mine; check at your hotel.

ROUTES From Tunja there are two possible routes to Cúcuta; the main road, almost entirely paved, goes via Bucaramanga, but the other heading NE via Duitama and Málaga, rejoining the main road at Pamplona, is also interesting, though there are few filling stations N of Duitama.

NORTHEAST OF TUNJA

41 km along the road NE of Tunja is **Paipa**, noted for the popular **Aguas Termales** complex 3 km to the SE. The baths and the neighbouring **Lago Sochagota** are very popular with Colombians and increasingly so with foreign tourists. The facilities are open daily 0600-2200, basic entrance US$5, children US$3. From Paipa there is a minibus service, US$0.50, a taxi costs US$1, or you can walk in 45 mins. There are innumerable hotels on the main street of Paipa (Cra 19)and on the approach road to the Aguas Termales.

7 km beyond the *Aguas Termales* on a winding hilly paved road is the **Pantano de Vargas**, the site of the battle on 25 July 1819 between the forces of Bolívar and the Spaniards. A huge bronze sculpture commemorates the event. Regular minibuses run to Paipa and Duitama for about US$0.50, taxis US$3.

15 km beyond Paipa is **Duitama**, known for basket weaving, where there is the interesting tourist complex Punta Larga.

(**E** *Isobel*, Cra 18, No 18-60, clean, quiet; many others nearby.) Bus Duitama to Bucaramanga at 0900, 9 hrs, US$11; to Málaga at 0800, sit on right side for best views, 6 hrs.

SOGAMOSO

At Duitama turn right and follow the valley of the Río Chicamocha for **Sogamoso**, a large, mainly industrial town. This was an important Chibcha settlement, and a **Parque Arqueológico** has been set up on the original site. A comprehensive museum describes their arts of mummification, statuary, and crafts, including gold working (Tues-Sun 0900-1300, 1400-1800, US$1.50 adults, US$0.80 children). Cafeteria near the entrance and camping possible in the grass car park opposite, with permission.

● **Accommodation A2** *Tobacá*, C 13, No 10-68, T 715316, central, parking, restaurant; **A3** *Sogamoso Real*, Cra 10, No 13-11, T/F 706856, 1 block behind central plaza, business hotel, all facilities, conference rooms; **B** *Litavira*, C 12, No 10-30, T 702585, F 705631, discounts at weekends, breakfast inc, cable TV, private parking, good value; **D** *Bochica*, C 11, No 14-33, T 704140, comfortable rooms, hot water, TV, good value. Many hotels nr bus station eg **F** *Hostal Aranjuez*, basic, safe, very helpful, **F** *Residencia Embajador*, secure, rec; **G** *Residencia El Terminal*, basic, safe. Several reasonable restaurants nr the centre, one of the best is *Susacá*, Cra 16, No 11-35, T 702587, open 1200-2100, specialties include trout, good *comida*, large portions, good value rec.

● **Buses** To Bogotá, 4½ hrs, US$8.50; to Yopal, US$5, 4 hrs, several daily.

LAGO DE TOTA

The main road S of Sogamoso climbs quite steeply to the continental divide at El Crucero at 3,100m. At this point, the main road continues to Yopal. Turn right for Lago de Tota (3,015m), ringed by mountains. Virtually all round the lake, onions are grown near water level, and the whole area has an intriguing 'atmosphere' of pine, eucalyptus and onion. **Aquitania**, is the principal town on the lake. There are plenty of food shops and a bright, restored church with modern stained glass windows. Above the town is a hill (El Cumbre) with beautiful views.

• **Accommodation Aquitania**: **F** *Residencia Venecia*, C 8, No 144, clean, basic, reasonable. Numerous restaurants inc *Luchos*, *Tunjo de Oro* and *Pueblito Viejo* together on corner of plaza. **Lakeside**: **A3** *Hotel Genesis* (from where main road reaches lake, turn right 4 km), hotel rooms, cabañas for 4 to 10 people (**D** pp), geared for watersports and fishing, T 615-8711 (Bogotá). On the main road continue 2 km (turn left at junction), **A2** *Camino Real*, Km 20 via Sogamoso a Aquitania, T 700684, on the lake, pleasant public rooms, colourful gardens, boat slipway, boats for hire; **A1** *Pozo Azul*, 3 km further, in a secluded bay on the lake, T 257-6586 (Bogotá), also cabins up to 6, suitable for children, comfortable, full range of water sport facilities, good food. 3 km before Aquitania is **A3** *Hotel Santa Inez*, Km 29 Sogamoso-Aquitania, T 794199, also cabins, good position on lake, boats for hire/fishing, good food, helpful. At Playa Blanca, SW corner of lake, is *Las Rocas Lindas* campground, with bath and hot water, 2 cabins for 7, one for 8, boats for hire, dining room, bar, fireplaces, rec, friendly.

• **Buses** From Sogamoso, US$1.10, 1 hr; bus from Bogotá (Rápido Duitama), via Tunja and Sogamoso, goes round the lake to Aquitania, passing Cuitiva, Tota and the *Rocas Lindas*.

Yopal (*pop* 10,000), 4 hrs from the El Crucero (see above), is capital of the Intendencia of Casanare in the Llanos. The road passes through *páramo* and virgin cloud forest. Direct buses from Sogamoso and Bogotá (US$13).

NORTHEAST OF SOGAMOSO

9 km NE of Sogamoso is **Tópaga**, with a colonial church, unusual topiary in the plaza and the bust of Bolívar to commemorate the battle of Peñón of 11 July 1819. Beyond Tópaga is **Mongua**, a pleasant colonial town, with churches worth visiting.

Turn S before Topagá to **Monguí**, which has recently earned the title of "most beautiful village of Boyacá province". The upper side of the plaza is dominated by the basilica and convent. There are interesting arts and crafts shops in all directions. Walk down Cra 3 to the Calycanto Bridge, or up C 4, to the Plaza de Toros. A recommended excursion is E of Monguí with particularly fine *frailejones* and giant wild lupins in the **Páramo de Ocetá**.

• **Accommodation C** *Hostal Calycanto*, pink house next to the bridge, lovely setting, restaurant (but give advance notice); **E** *La Cabaña*, chalet on road beyond river (cross brige, turn left), basic but comfortable, food if advised, information from Miriam Fernández at *Cafetería La Cabaña* next to the Municipality. Several restaurants round the plaza; *Taller de Arte Colonial*, Cra 3, coffee and snacks.

• **Tourist offices** In Municipality building on Plaza, Janeth Téllez, T 782050, very helpful, local craftwork eg leather and wool items sold, can arrange excursions and will advise about guides.

• **Transport** Bus office on plaza. To **Bogotá**, Libertadores daily at 0730 and 1600, US$9, 4½ hrs. To **Sogamoso**, every ½-hr by buseta, US$0.75, 45 mins.

The road NE of Duitama to Málaga passes Belén and **Soatá** (*Residencias Colonial*, excellent, good restaurant; **D** *Hotel Turístico*, swimming pool) before descending again to the now very dry, spectacular valley of the Río Chicamocha.

SIERRA NEVADA DEL COCUY

By the bridge over the Río Chicamocha at **Capitanejo** is the turning to the very attractive **Sierra Nevada del Cocuy** in the Eastern Cordillera. The Sierra extends in a half circle for 30 km, offering peaks of rare beauty, lakes and waterfalls. The flora is particularly interesting. Everyone wears ponchos, rides horses and is very friendly. The area is good for trekking and probably the best range in Colombia for rock climbers. The most beautiful peaks are Cocuy (5,100m), Ritacuba Negro (5,200m), Ritacuba Blanco (5,330m) and El Castillo (5,100m). The main towns are to the W of the Sierra. The centre for climbing the main peaks is **Guicán**, a friendly place about 50 km E of Capitanejo. The other main town is **Cocuy** (tourist office on Cra 3, No 8-06, run by Pedro Moreno). See page 985 for security advice and ask locally before going into the mountains.

Hiking and climbing Above Guicán: from the López house (see below, **Accommodation**) it is 3 strenuous hrs' walk on a clear trail to the snowline on Ritacuba Blanco. Rope and crampons recommended for the final section above 4,800m. This would also be the best base for the 2-3 day walk round the N end of the Sierra and into Ratoncito valley, which is surrounded by snow-capped mountains. A milk truck ('el lechero') leaves Guicán between 0600 and 0700 via Cocuy for La Cruz, 1 hrs' walk below the cabins, arriving 1100, getting back to Guicán around 1230, a rough but interesting ride. Guicán is 1-1½ hrs' drive by jeep from the mountains, so it is recommended to stay higher up (jeep hire about US$17 from José Riaño or 'Profe' in Guicán).

Above Cocuy there is no formal accommodation, although you can sleep at the unoccupied Hacienda La Esperanza (8 hrs from Guicán) and may be able to get food at the house below La Esperanza. It is best to camp and take your own food. La Esperanza is the base for climbing to the Laguna Grande de la Sierra (7 hrs round trip), a large sheet of glacier-fed water surrounded by five snow-capped peaks, and also for the 2-day walk to the Laguna de la Plaza on the E side of the Sierra, reached through awesome, rugged scenery. Between Cocuy and La Esperanza is Alto de la Cuera where you can stay at El Himat meterological station for US$5, basic, including 2 meals. There is a fine walk from here to Lagunillas, a string of lakes near the S end of the range (5 hrs there and back). Permission to camp can easily be obtained from the friendly people. Sketch maps available in Cocuy from the tourist office. It takes 8-10 days to trek from one end to the other through a central rift, but equipment (crampons, ice axe, rope etc) is necessary. Be prepared for unstable slopes and rockfalls, few flat campsites and treacherous weather. The perpendicular rock mountains overlooking the Llanos are for professionals only. The best weather is from Dec to April.

● **Accommodation** In **Capitanejo** are several hotels where the bus stops: F *Residencias El Oasis*, G *Residencia El Córdobes*, *Residencia El Dorado* and *Villa Del Mar*, and more on the parque on block below bus stop, all are basic. There are three hotels in **Guicán**: F *Hotel La Sierra*, good, owner 'Profe' (Orlando Corea) has good maps of the region, informative visitors' book for trekkers, meals available; F *Las Montañas*, basic, but pleasant, meals available, laundry facilities, overlooks main plaza, thin walls; F *Del Norte*, on opposite corner. At *Las Montañas*, Teresa Cristancho or Jorge Ibáñez can arrange a stay in **Cabinas Kanwara** at 3,920m, about 1,000m above Guicán, **E**, restaurant, 9 beds, well furnished, open fires, electrically-heated showers; or camping (US$1.25), horse rental (US$4.55/day) and guide service inc, with Dionisio and Berthilda López at the last house before the Nevado on Ritacuba Blanco, highly rec. In **Cocuy**: E *Gutiérrez*, friendly, hot water, meals, laundry facilities; F *Residencia Cocuy*, cold water, meals, laundry.

● **Buses** 6 buses a day Bogotá-Cocuy, 2 with Tricolor, 2 with Paz de Río, 1 Libertadores and 1 Gacela, either 0300 or 0400 or between 1000-1800, 13 hrs, US$12; Paz de Río or Libertadores Capitanejo-Cocuy at 0400 and 1200, US$2.15, to **Guicán**, 3-4 hrs, US$2.75, Libertadores Tunja-Cocuy/Guicán 0730, 10 hrs, US$9.75. From Guicán buses leave at 0400, 1600 and 1800 for **Capitanejo**, **Duitama** (US$6.15), **Paipa** (9 hrs, US$6.65) and points N. For points N, or to get to this area from the N, change at Capitanejo. From Capitanejo 3 buses a day to Bucaramanga, 4 to Cúcuta.

MALAGA

The area around **Málaga** (Santander Department), 35 km N of Capitanejo, is very picturesque: pretty red-tiled villages, riders in ponchos and cowboy hats, and mountains (some covered in flowering trees). The roads are twisty but spectacular. There are several hotels, **E** and **F**, eg *Príncipe*, nr main square, shared bathroom, good meals, rec, and restaurants, eg *La Riviera*, Cra 8, No 13-61, good food.

● **Buses** Good services to Duitama (6 hrs), Bucaramanga (6-7 hrs, US$6) and Pamplona.

ROUTES From Málaga to Pamplona is a beautiful, but hard journey. To Bucaramanga is another spectacular trip through the mountains, but the road is not good and is very tortuous.

SANTANDER DEPARTMENT

The main road from Tunja goes N to **Moniquirá** (64 km) 1,650m (still in Boyacá Department), a pleasant place to stay. Hotels (all on central plaza) **D** *Mansión*, good; **E** *Clara Luz*, OK; **E** *Casablanca*, with swimming pool; **F** *Tairona*. 10 km beyond is **Barbosa** in the Department of Santander (**E** *Hotel Príncipe*, with bath; youth hostel at *Parador Turístico Barbosa*; *El Palacio del Pollo*, good, simple roadside restaurant).

SOCORRO

The road (toll at Santana, US$0.40) goes NE for 84 km to **Socorro** (*pop* 23,020), with steep streets and single storey houses set among graceful palms. It has a singularly large and odd stone church. Daily market.

At Socorro, in 1781, began the peasant *comuneros*, revolt against poverty. It was led at first by a woman, Manuela Beltrán, and then, when other towns joined, by Juan Francisco Berbeo. They marched as far as Zipaquirá; rebel terms were accepted by the Spaniards, and sworn to by the Bishop of Bogotá, but when they had returned home troops were sent from Cartagena and there were savage reprisals. Another woman from Socorro, Antonia Santos, led guerrillas fighting for independence and was captured and executed by the Spaniards in 1819; her statue is in the main square. The Casa de Cultura museum (opening hours vary according to season) has disappointingly little information on these local heroines, but is still worth a visit.

● **Accommodation & places to eat C** *Tamacara*, C 14, No 14-15, T 273517, swimming pool; **E** *Colonial*, Cra 15, good, TV; **F** *Venezia*, shower, dining room, nice old rooms, good value. *Panadería Imperial*, C 14 y Cra 13, good meals, simple; *La Gran Parrilla*, C 9, Cra 15, good steaks.

BARICHARA

From Socorro, a road leads N and W to Barrancabermeja (see page 927). 21 km along, there is a dirt track off to **Barichara** (*pop* 7,175; *alt* 1,336m), a beautiful colonial town founded in 1714 and designated as a national monument. A better road connects Barichara to San Gil. Among Barichara's places of historical interest, is the house of the former president Aquiles Parra (the woman next door has the key). An interesting excursion is to **Guane**, 9 km away by road, or 1½ hrs delightful walk by trail, where there are many colonial houses and an archaeological museum in the priest's house, collection of coins and a mummified woman (admission, US$0.25). The valley abounds with fossils. There are buses from Barichara, but not every day. Another interesting trip

is to the waterfall Salto de Mica, a 30-min walk along a trail following the line of cliffs near Barichara.

● **Accommodation D** *Santa Barbara*, C 5, No 9-12, T 7163, old colonial house, quiet, pool, all meals available; **D** *Corata*, Cra 7, No 4-02, charming courtyard, restaurant and lovely cathedral views, rec; **F** *Posada Real*, Cra 7, No 4-78, restaurant. You can make reservations in Bogotá, at Cra 16A, No 79-61, T 610-3425. Ask at the Casa de Cultura about staying in private homes.

● **Places to eat** *La Casona*, C 6, Cras 5-6, cheap, good food; *Bahía Chala*, nr the central plaza, goat-meat speciality.

Another 20 km N of Barichara is **Zapatoca**, a town which at one time controlled the traffic between highland Santander and the Magdalena. Local products include juicy sweets (*cocadas*) and *pauche*, a balsa type wood painted and carved into many forms. There is also a small museum. Local excursions to the Cuevas del Nitro and to a natural swimming pool with waterfall, Pozo del Ahogado. There are buses to Bucaramanga, 2 hrs, US$4.20.

SAN GIL

About 21 km beyond Socorro, NE on the main road to Bucamaranga, is **San Gil**, a colonial town with a good climate, which has El Gallineral, a riverside spot whose beautiful trees are covered with moss-like tillandsia. (Entrance US$0.50.) Good view from La Gruta, the shrine overlooking the town (look for the cross).

Excursions 1 hr S of San Gil on the road to Duitama, is **Charalá**, which has a beautiful plaza with a statue of José Antonio Golán, leader of the 1781 Comunero revolt. Also an interesting church and Casa de la Cultura; very attractive lush scenery. **E** *Hotel El Refugio*, with bath, safe. Bus San Gil-Charalá, US$1.

● **Accommodation** Roadside hotels are noisy. **E** *Alcantuz*, Cra 11, No 10-15, T 3160, free coffee, good location, pleasant; **E** *Residencia Abril*, Cra 10, C 8, T 3381, secure parking, relatively quiet; **E** *Residencias Señorial*, C 10, No 8-14, T 4442, pleasant, quiet; **F** *Victoria*, nr bus terminal, with bath; **G** *San Gil*, C 11, Cra **F** with bath, upstairs rooms are preferable, basic. Between Socorro and San Gil, there are *Balneario Campestre El Raízon*, swimming pool, showers, restaurant, car campers allowed and a few small rooms, and **B** *Cabañas Mesón de Cuchicute*, nr Pinchote.

● **Places to eat** *Central*, C 10, No 10-70, good and cheap; *La Mama*, Cra 9, good vegetarian; *Antojos*, Cra 9, No 11-19, good juices; *La Palma*, opp *Residencias Abril*, rec; open air restaurant in Parque Gallineral, good in evening, music at weekends.

● **Transport Air** Flights to Bogotá. **Buses** Bus station 5 mins out of town by taxi on road to Tunja. Bus to **Bogotá**, US$7.20; to **Bucaramanga**, US$3.50, 2½ hrs; to **Barichara** from C 12, US$1, 1 hr.

12 km from San Gil on the main road N to Bucaramanga is Curití noted for handicrafts in fique (agave sisal). About 28 km N of San Gil, a little off the road, is the picturesque village of **Aratoca**, with a colonial church. 10 km further on, the descent from the heights along the side of a steep cliff into the dry Río Chicamocha canyon, with spectacular rock colours, is one of the most dramatic experiences of the trip to Cúcuta, but, if driving, this is a demanding and dangerous stretch.

BUCARAMANGA

Bucaramanga (*pop* 464,585), 420 km from Bogotá, is the capital of Santander Department. The city was founded in 1622 but was little more than a village until the latter half of the 19th century. The city's great problem is space for expansion. Erosion in the lower, western side topples buildings over the edge after heavy rain. The fingers of erosion, deeply ravined between, are spectacular. The metropolitan area has grown rapidly because of the success of coffee, tobacco and staple crops.

BASICS *Pop* 464,585; pop of metropolitan area 782,345; *Alt* 1,018m; *Av max temp* 30°C; *Av min temp* 19.4°C. *Rainfall* is about 760 mm, and *humidity* is high (68% to 90%). *Phone code:* 97.

Places of interest

The **Parque Santander** is the heart of the modern city, while the **Parque García Rovira** is the centre of the colonial area. Just off Parque García Rovira is the **Casa de Cultura**. **Casa Perú de la Croix**, C 37, No 11-18, is a beautiful colonial mansion (closed, temporarily it is hoped, since

1989). The **Club Campestre** is one of the most beautifully set in Latin America. There is an amusement park, **Parque El Lago**, in the suburb of Lagos I, SW of the city on the way to Floridablanca. On the way out of the city NE (towards Pamplona) is the **Parque Morrorico**, well-maintained with a fine view. There is a sculptured Saviour overlooking the park, a point of pilgrimage on Good Friday.

Museums

Museo de Arte Moderno, C 37, Cra 26, US$0.20. Also **Casa de Bolívar**, C 37, No 12-15, interesting (Mon-Fri, 0900-1200, 1400-1700, entry US$0.15).

Excursions

The suburb of **Floridablanca**, 8 km SW, has the famous El Paragüitas gardens (also known as the Jardín Botánico), belonging to the national tobacco agency. The gardens open at weekends 0800-1100, 1400-1700; US$0.25. There are plenty of buses: take the Cotandra bus (US$0.30) from Cra 22, Bucaramanga, either Florida Villabel which goes by El Paragüitas, or Florida Autopista (continuation of Cra 33) which goes direct to the square in Florida and you have to walk about a kilometre. Toll on road to Floridablanca, US$0.20.

Lebrija (*pop* 19,130), 17 km to the W, is in an attractive plain. **Rionegro** (*pop* 28,415) is a coffee town 20 km to the N with, close by, the Laguna de Gálago and waterfalls. One fine waterfall is 30 mins by bus from Rionegro to Los Llanos de Palma followed by a 2-hr walk through citrus groves towards Bocas. Complete the walk along a railway to the Bucaramanga-Rionegro road. **Girón** (*pop* 75,155) a tobacco centre 9 km SW of Bucaramanga on the Río de Oro, is a quiet and attractive colonial town, filled with Bumangueses at weekends, with a beautiful church. The buildings are well preserved and the town unspoilt by modernization. By the river are *tejo* courts and popular open air restaurants with *cumbia* and *salsa* bands; in the square at weekends, sweets and *raspados* (crushed ice delights) are sold.

● **Accommodation & places to eat B** *San Juan de Girón*, outside town on road from Bucaramanga, T 466430, swimming pool, restaurant uninspired; **F** *Río de Oro*β, in centre, but make sure you get a lock for the door. Restaurants: *Mansión del Fraile* on the plaza, in a beautiful colonial house, good food – Bolívar slept here on one occasion, ask to see the bed; *La Casona*, C 28, No 27-47, rec, try their 'fritanga gironesa'. Take the bus from Cra 15 or 22 in Bucaramanga, US$1.75.

In **Piedecuesta**, 18 km SE of Bucaramanga (bus from Cra 22, US$0.45, 45 mins, hotel: **F** *Piedecuesta*, good, safe). Here you can see cigars being hand-made, furniture carving and jute weaving – cheap, hand-decorated *fique* rugs can be bought. There are frequent buses to all these dormitory towns for the city; a taxi costs US$6. Corpus Christi processions in these towns in June are interesting.

Local festivals
The annual international piano festival is held here in mid-Sept in the Auditorio Luis A Calvo at the Universidad Industrial de Santander, one of the finest concert halls in Colombia. The university is worth a visit for beautiful grounds and a lake full of exotic plants and alligators.

Local information
● **Accommodation**
A2 *Chicamocha*, C 34, No 31-24, luxury, a/c, swimming pool (non guests US$1.50); **A2** *Bucarica*, C 35 y Cra 19, T 301592, F 301594, spacious, on main plaza, good restaurant and snack bar; **A3** *Ruitoque*, Cra 19, No 37-26, T 334567, F 302997, a/c, hospitable.

D *El Pilar*, C 34, No 24-09, T 453147, hot water, quiet, good service and food, rec; **D** *D'León*, C 56, No 21-49, T 436998, parking.

E *Tamana*, Cra 18, No 30-31, **F** without bath, rec.

Wide variety of hotels on C 31, between Cras 18-21. **E** *Las Bahamas*, S of the Central Plaza, opp Copetran terminal, good value; **E** *Residencias San Diego*, Cra 18, No 15-71, T 434273, quiet, good; **E** *Nutibara*, C 55, No 21-42, shower, fan; **F** *Residencias Tonchala*, C 56, No 21-23, with bath, good; **F** *Residencias Amparo*, C 31, No 20-29, with bath; **F** *Hostal Doral*, C 32, No 21-65, with bath, family business, safe, several nice tiny rooms but varying reports. **NB** Since Bucaramanga is the site for numerous national conventions, it is sometimes hard to find a room.

● **Places to eat**
La Casa de Spagheti, Cra 27, No 51-18, cheap and good. Pizzas at: *Piz Pan Pum*, Cra 33, No 31-107 (next to Cinema Rivera); *Tropical*, C 33,

No 17-81; *Los Notables*, Cra 18, C 34/35, pleasant, good breakfast; *Fonda*, C 33, No 34-42, good, cheap, vegetarian; *Zirus*, C 56, No 30-88, friendly, owner speaks a little English; *Super Pizza*, Centro Comercial Cabecera (pizza by the slice, hamburgers, etc).

Vegetarian: *Maranatha*, Cra 24, No 36-20, good lunches and dinners, reasonable prices; *Govinda*, Indian vegetarian, Cra 20, No 34-65, excellent lunch; *Energía y Vida*, C 35, No 12-47, good lunch US$1.50. *Berna*, C 35, No 18-30, best pastries in town. Try the *hormigas calonas* (large black ants), a local delicacy mainly eaten during Holy Week (sold in shops, not restaurants).

● **Banks & money changers**
Banco Anglo Colombiano, Cra 19 No 36-43, and 4 agencies. Banco Industrial Colombiano, by Parque Santander, will cash Thomas Cook and Amex TCs. Long queues (cheques and passports have to be photocopied). Many other banks. Cash changed at *Distinguidos*, C36, No 17-52 local 1A33.

● **Entertainment**
Discotheques: several on road to Girón and on Cra 33/35. Worth taking a look at: *Barbaroja*, Cra 27, No 28, a *salsa* and *son* bar set in a renovated red and white, gothic-style mansion, happy hour 1700-1800.

● **Shopping**
Camping equipment: *Acampemos*, C 48, No 26-30, last place in Colombia to get camping gas cartridges before Venezuela.

Handicrafts: in Girón (expensive – see above) and typical clothing upstairs in the food market, C 34 y Cras 15-16. Similar articles (*ruanas*, hats) in San Andresito. *Feria de artesanías* in first 2 weeks of Sept, usually nr the Puerta del Sol.

● **Tourist offices**
On main plaza in *Hotel Bucarica* building, C 35 y Cra 19, friendly and knowledgeable, T 338461 (closed 1200-1400). City maps free. **MA**, Cra 29, No 41-25, T 458309, Dr Armando Rodríguez Ochoa.

● **Transport**
Local Most taxis have meters; beware of overcharging from bus terminals. Buses charge US$0.35.

Air Palonegro, on three flattened hilltops on other side of ravine S of city. Spectacular views on take-off and landing. Daily Avianca flights to Bogotá (also Aces and Aero República), Barranquilla, Cartagena and Medellín. Taxi, US$4; colectivo, US$1. Buses are scarce despite the fact that some bus boards say "Aeropuerto" (direction 'Girón/Lebrija' from Diagonal 15). Avianca, T 426117; Aces T 349595; Aero República T 433384.

Road To the Magdalena at Barrancabermeja, 174 km; to Cúcuta, 198 km; to Bogotá, 420 km; to Medellín, 1,010 km; to Santa Marta, 550 km, all paved. **Bus**: the terminal is on the Girón road, with cafés, shops, a bank and showers. Taxi to centre, US$1.50; bus US$0.35. To **Bogotá**, 8-11 hrs, US$18 (Pullman) with Berlinas del Fonce, Cra 18, No 31-06 (this journey is uncomfortable, there are no relief stops, and it starts off hot and ends cold in the mountains, be prepared); Expreso Brasilia, C 31, Cra 18-19, T 422152, runs to Bogotá but they sell tickets only 30 mins before departure; Copetran, C 55, No 17B-57, recommended for advance bus reservations, has 3 classes of buses to Bogotá inc Pullman, 10 hrs, and to **Cartagena**, US$30, 13 hrs, leaving at 1930 daily; **Tunja**, 7½ hrs, US$17; **Valledupar**, 8 hrs, US$20; **Barranquilla**, 10 hrs (US$25 first class with Copetran); **Santa Marta**, 9 hrs, maybe more according to season, US$22 with Copetran; to **Pamplona**, Copetran, 3 a day, US$4.50 (Pullman), US$3.50 (*corriente*); **Cúcuta**, 6 hrs, US$5 (Pullman), Berlinas buses often arrive full from Bogotá, Copetran US$6 and colectivo US$7.20. The trip to Cúcuta is spectacular in the region of Berlín (see below). **Barrancabermeja**, 3 hrs, US$2.30, a scenic ride with one rest stop permitted; this road is paved. To **El Banco** on the Río Magdalena, US$15, several companies, direct or change at Aguachica. Hourly buses to **San Gil**, US$3.50. To **Berlín**, US$1.20. Other companies with local services to nearby villages on back roads, eg the colourful folk-art buses of Flota Cáchira (C 32, Cra 33-34) which go N and E.

The road (paved but narrow) runs E to Berlín, and then NE (a very scenic run over the Eastern Cordillera) to Pamplona, about 130 km from Bucaramanga.

BERLÍN

Berlín is an ideal place to appreciate the grandeur of the Eastern Cordillera and the hardiness of the people who live on the *páramo*. The village lies in a valley at 3,100m, the peaks surrounding it rise to 4,350m and the temperature is constantly around 10°C, although on the infrequent sunny days it may seem much warmer. There is a tourist complex with cabins and there are several basic eating places. Camping (challenging but rewarding) is possible with permission. At the highest point on the road between Bucaramanga and Berlín, 3,400m, is a café where you can camp on the covered porch. They have a friendly woolly dog.

PAMPLONA

(*Pop* 43,645; *Alt* 2,200m) Few modern buildings have as yet broken the colonial harmony of this city. Founded in the mountains in 1548, it became important as a mining town but is now better known for its university.

Places of interest

Cathedral in the spacious central plaza. The earthquake of 1875 played havoc with the monasteries and some of the churches: there is now a hotel on the site of the former San Agustín monastery, but it may still be possible to visit the ex-monasteries of San Francisco and Santo Domingo. The **Iglesia del Humilladero**, adjoining the cemetery, is very picturesque and allows a fine view of the city.

Museums

Museum of **religious art** at C 5 y Cra 5. **Casa Colonial** archaeological museum, C 6, No 2-56, open Tues-Sat, 0900-1200, 1400-1800; Sun, 0900-1200, "a little gem". **Casa Anzoátegui**, Cra 6, No 7-48, museum of the Independence period; one of Bolívar's generals, José Antonio Anzoátegui, died here in 1819, at the age of 30, after the battle of Boyacá. The state in NE Venezuela is named after him.

Local festivals

Renowned Easter celebrations.

Local information

● **Accommodation**

C *Cariongo*, Cra 5, C 9, T 682645, very good, excellent restaurant, US satellite TV (locked parking available).

E *Residencia Doran*, Cra 6, No 7-21, **F** without bath, large rooms, good meals; **E** *Imperial*, Cra 5, No 5-36, T 682571, on main plaza, large rooms, hot water, safe, restaurant.

F *Llanos*, C 9 y Cra 7, shared bath, cold water, motorcycle parking, rec; **F** *Orsua*, on main plaza, cheap, good food. Hotel accommodation may be hard to find at weekends, when Venezuelans visit the town.

● **Places to eat**

El Maribel, C 5, No 4-17, cheap lunch; *La*

Casona, C 6, No 6-57, limited but good menu;
Las Brazas, next door, good, cheap; *La Garza
de Oro*, C 6, No 5-46, good; *El Gran Duque*,
on main plaza, student-run, good music; *El
Rincón Paisa*, also on main plaza, good; *Portal
Alemán*, C 7 y Cra 6, good meals, especially
breakfasts; *Angelitas*, C 7 y Cra 7, good coffee;
Piero's Pizza, C 9 y Cra 5, good.

● **Banks & money changers**
At banks, or try the store at C 6, No 4-37, where
"Don Dolar" will change cash and TCs; **Banco
de Bogotá**, on the main plaza, gives Visa cash
advances.

● **Post & telecommunications**
Post Office Cra 6 y C 6, in pedestrian passage.
Telecom: C 7 y Cra 5A.

● **Shopping**
Pamplona is a good place to buy *ruanas*. Good
indoor market.

● **Tourist offices**
C 5 y Cra 6, on main plaza (believed temporarily
closed 1997). Maps available at Instituto
Geográfico, Banco de la República building on
the main street.

● **Transport**
Buses to **Bogotá**, US$18, 13-16 hrs; to **Cúcuta**,
US$3, 2½ hrs; to **Bucaramanga**, US$4.50, 4 hrs,
great views; to **Málaga** from main plaza, 5 a day
from 0800, 6 hrs, US$3.75; to **Tunja**, US$10.75,
12 hrs (leaving at 0600). To **Berlín**, US$2.10.

Cúcuta and the Road to Independence

🐾 Cúcuta, because it is the gateway
of entry from Venezuela, was a focal point
in the history of Colombia during the wars
for independence. Bolívar captured it after his lightning Magdalena campaign in
1813. The **Bolívar Column** stands where
he addressed his troops on 28 February
1813. At **El Rosario de Cúcuta**, a small
town of 8,000 inhabitants 14½ km from
Cúcuta on the road to the frontier, the
First Congress of Gran Colombia opened
on 6 May 1821. It was at this Congress
that the plan to unite Venezuela, Ecuador,
and Colombia was ratified; Bolívar was
made President, and Santander (who was
against the plan) Vice-President. (Santander was born at a *hacienda* near El Rosario
which is now being developed as a tourist
centre.)

CUCUTA

It is a run of 72 km from Pamplona through
sparsely populated country, descending to
Cúcuta (*pop* 525,465; *alt* 215m; *phone code*
975), capital of the Department of Norte
de Santander, and only 16 km from the
Venezuelan frontier. It was founded 1734,
destroyed by earthquake 1875, and then
rebuilt, elegantly, with the streets shaded
by trees, and they are needed for it is hot:
the mean temperature is 29°C. Coffee is
the great crop in the area, followed by
tobacco. There are also large herds of cattle. The **cathedral**, Av 5 between C 10 and
11, is worth a visit. Note the oil paintings
by Salvador Moreno. The **international
bridge** between Colombia and Venezuela
is SE of the city.

Excursions

Just short of the border is the small town
of **Villa del Rosario**, where the Congress
met which agreed the constitution of Gran
Colombia in the autumn of 1821, one of
the high points of the the career of Simón
Bolívar. The actual spot where the documents were signed is now a park beside
which is the **Templo del Congreso**, in
which the preliminary meetings took
place. Also nearby is the **Casa de Santander**, where General Santander, to whom
Bolívar entrusted the administration of
the new Gran Colombia, was born and
spent his childhood. There is also an archaeological museum with interesting relics from NE Colombia, including Tairona,
Muisca and Guarne artifacts, open Tue-
Sat 0800-1200, 1400-1800, Sun 0900-1330.

Local information
● **Accommodation**
A3 *Tonchalá*, C 10, Av 0, T 712005, good restaurant, swimming pool, a/c, airline booking
office in hall.

C *Casa Blanca*, Av 6, No 14-55, T 721455,
F 722993 good, reasonable meals, rec; **C** *Lord*,
Av 7, No 10-58, T 713766, a/c, nice rooms, good
restaurant and service, safe.

D *Amaruc*, Av 5, No 9-73, T 717625, F 721805,
with fan, no hot water; **D** *Cacique*, Av 7, No
9-66, T 712652, F 719484, a/c, cold showers
only, reasonable.

E *Flamingo*, Av 3, No 6-38, T 712190, fan, with
bath, noisy.

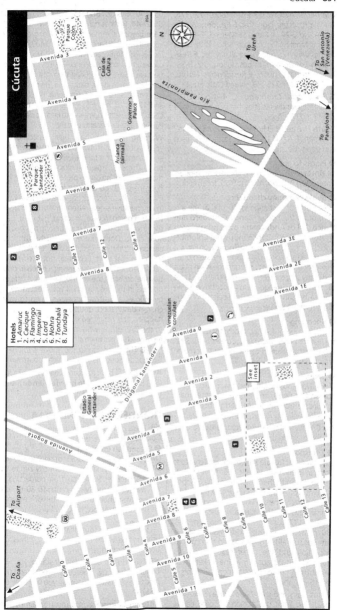

Cúcuta

Hotels
1. Amaruc
2. Cacique
3. Flamingo
4. Imperial
5. Lord
6. Nohra
7. Tonchalá
8. Tundaya

Parque Colón

Avenida 3

Casa de Cultura

Avenida 4

Governor's Palace

Avenida 5

Avantca (airmail)

Avenida 6

Parque Santander

Avenida 7

Avenida 8

Calle 10
Calle 11
Calle 12
Calle 13

To Ureña
To San Antonio (Venezuela)
To Pamplona

Río Pamplonita

Avenida 3E
Avenida 2E
Avenida 1E

Venezuelan consulate

Avenida 0

Avenida 1

See inset

Avenida 2

Avenida 3

Estadio General Santander

Diagonal Santander

Avenida 4

Avenida Bogotá

Avenida 5

Avenida 6

To Airport

Avenida 7

Avenida 8

To Ocaña

Calle 0
Calle 1
Calle 2
Calle 3
Calle 4
Calle 5
Calle 6
Calle 7
Calle 8
Calle 9
Calle 10
Calle 11
Calle 12
Calle 13

Avenida 9

Avenida 10

Avenida 11

N

F *Imperial*, Av 7, No 6-28, T 712866, F 726376, with bath, secure, highly rec; **F** *Residencia Leo*, Av 6A, No 0-24 N, Barrio La Merced, T 41984, run by family Mogollón de Soto, with bath, clothes washing, free coffee all day, rec; **F** *Residencia Los Rosales*, nr bus station, C 2, 8-39, fan, with bath, good; **F** *Residencias Nohra*, C 7, No 7-52, T 725889, shared bath, quiet.

G *Residencia Zambrano*, C 4, No 11E-87, breakfast, laundry facilities, family run by Cecilia Zambrano Mariño.

Youth Hostel: at El Rosario de Cúcuta in *Hotel El Saman*, T 700411, with bar, restaurant, disco and pools. Details from Alcom in Bogotá.

● **Places to eat**
La Brasa, Av 5, C 7, good *churrascos*, modest prices; *Don Pancho*, Av 3, No 9-21, local menus.

● **Banks & money changers**
Good rates of exchange in Cúcuta, at the airport, or on the border. **Banco Ganadero** and **Banco de Los Andes** nr the plaza will give cash against Visa cards. **Banco Industrial Colombiano** changes TCs; **Banco de Bogotá**, on Parque Santander, advances on Visa. There are money changers on the street all round the main plaza and many shops advertise the purchase and sale of bolívares. Change pesos into bolívares in Cúcuta or San Antonio – difficult to change them further into Venezuela.

● **Shopping**
A good range of leather goods: try C 10, Av 8 for leather boots and shoes. *Cuchitril*, Av 3 No 9-89, has a selection of the better Colombian craft work.

● **Tourist offices**
C 10, No 0-30, helpful, has maps, etc. At bus station (1st floor), and at airport. Other maps obtainable from **Instituto Geográfico**, Banco de la República building, in the main plaza.

NB Cúcuta and the surrounding area is a great centre for smuggling. Be careful.

● **Transport**
Air Airport at Cúcuta for Colombian services to Bogotá (daily with Avianca, SAM and Aero República) and other Colombian cities. Airport 10 mins by taxi from the town and the border, US$2. It is cheaper to buy tickets in Colombia than in advance in Venezuela. Avianca, C 13, No 5-09, T 717758. Also at San Antonio, Venezuela (30 mins) for Venezuelan domestic lines. At latter, be sure all baggage is sealed after customs inspection and the paper seals signed and stamped. **NB** Do not buy airline 'tickets' from Cúcuta to Venezuelan destinations, all flights go from San Antonio.

Buses Bus station: Av 7 and C 0 (a really rough area). Taxi from bus station to town centre,

US$2.40. Bus to **Bogotá**, hourly, 17-24 hrs, US$21.40, Berlinas del Fonce (has own terminal, 2 km beyond the main terminal along continuation of Diagonal Santander) 1000, 1400, 2 stops, inc 15 mins in Bucaramanga (US$2.50 extra for *cochecama*), or Bolivariano, 20 hrs. There are frequent buses, even during the night (if the bus you take arrives in the dark, sit in the bus station café until it is light). To **Cartagena**, Brasilia 1800 and 1930, 18 hrs, US$35. To **Bucaramanga**, US$5, 6 hrs, with Copetran and Berlinas del Fonce Pullman, several departures daily.

Warning Travellers have been reporting for years that the bus station is overrun with thieves and conmen, who have tried every trick in the book. This is still true. You must take great care, there is little or no police protection. On the 1st floor there is a tourist office for help and information and a café/snack bar where you can wait in comparative safety. Alternatively, go straight to a bus going in your direction, get on it, pay the driver and don't let your belongings out of your sight. Don't put your valuables in bus company 'safety boxes'. Make sure tickets are for buses that exist; tickets do not need to be "stamped for validity". For San Cristóbal, only pay the driver of the vehicle, not at the offices upstairs in the bus station. If you are told, even by officials, that it is dangerous to go to your chosen destination, double check. If the worst happens, the victimized should report the theft to the DAS office, who may be able to help to recover what has been stolen.

NB The exception to the above is the new Berlinas del Fonce terminal, which is much safer.

ROUTES There are good roads to Caracas (933 km direct or 1,046 km via Mérida), and to Maracaibo (571 km).

FRONTIER WITH VENEZUELA

NB There is a 1-hr time difference between Colombia and Venezuela.

● **Colombian immigration**
DAS, Av Primera, No 28-55, open 0800-1200, 1400-2000 daily. Take bus from city centre to Barrio San Rafael. Shared taxi from border US$1, will wait for formalities, then US$0.80 to bus station. Women should not visit this office alone.

DAS also at airport, which will deal with land travellers.

Exit and entry formalities handled at DAS office in the white house before the international border bridge.

NB If you do not obtain an exit stamp, you will be turned back by Venezuelan officials and the next time you enter Colombia, you will be fined US$7.50.

Entering Colombia You must obtain both a

Venezuelan exit stamp and a Colombian entry stamp at the border. Without the former you will be sent back; without the latter you will have problems with police checks, banks and leaving the country. You can also be fined.

Air travellers All Colombian formalities can be undertaken at the airport.

● **Colombian customs**
Aduana office on the road to the airport (small sign); has a restaurant.

● **Leaving Colombia by private vehicle**
Passport must be stamped at DAS in town and car papers must be stamped at Aduana on the road to the airport. The same applies for those entering Colombia.

● **Venezuelan consulate**
Av 0, C 8, Cúcuta, T 713983/712107, open 0800-1300, Mon-Fri. All overland visitors to Venezuela need a visa and tourist card, obtainable from here or the Venezuelan Embassy in Bogotá (which may send you to Cúcuta). Requirements: 2 passport photographs; proof of transportation out of Venezuela, with date (not always asked for in Cúcuta); proof of adequate funds sometimes requested. In Cúcuta (1996), pay US$30 in pesos for visa at a bank designated by the consulate, then take receipt to consulate. Apply for visa at 0800 to get it by 1400. You may need a numbered ticket to get served. If you know when you will be arriving at the frontier, get your visa in your home country.

● **Transport**
From Cúcuta: bus to **Caracas**; San Cristóbal, US$1.20 (Bolivariano), colectivo US$2.40; **San Antonio**, taxi US$7.20, bus and colectivo from C 7, Av 4, US$1.

On any form of transport which is crossing the border, make sure that the driver knows that you need to stop to obtain exit/entry stamps etc. You may be asked to pay extra, or alight and flag down a later colectivo.

Just to visit San Antonio de Táchira, no documents are needed.

The North Coast and the Islands

CARIBBEAN Colombia, very different in spirit from the highlands: the coast stretches from the Darién Gap, through banana plantations, swamplands and palm plantations to the arid Guajira. The main resorts are Cartagena, which is also steeped in colonial history, and Santa Marta, near which is the Tairona national park with precolombian remains and the unique Sierra Nevada de Santa Marta coastal range.

Climate
The climate is much the same for the whole area: the heat is great – ranging from 26° to 36°C and there is a difference of only 2° between the hottest and coolest month. From Nov to Mar the heat is moderated by trade winds.

People
Character, like climate, seems to change in Colombia with the altitude. The *costeños* (the people of the coast) are gayer and more light-hearted than the more sober people of the highlands. The coastal people talk very fast, slurring their words and dropping the final s's.

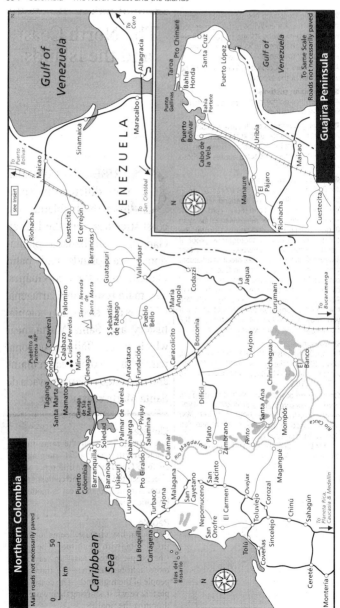

CARTAGENA

Cartagena (*pop* 661,830; *phone code* 95), steeped in history, is one of the most interesting towns in South America. An arm of the river, 145 km long, canalized in 1650 by Spain – the Canal del Dique – from Calamar to Cartagena allows free access for ships from the up-river ports.

History

Cartagena was founded by Pedro de Heredia on 13 January 1533. There were then two approaches to it, Bocagrande, at the northern end of Tierra Bomba island – this was a direct entry from the Caribbean – and Boca Chica, a narrow channel at the S leading to the great bay of Cartagena, 15 km long and 5 km wide. (Bocagrande was blocked after Admiral Vernon's attack in 1741 – see below.) The old walled city lies at the N end of the Bahía de Cartagena. To the W is the Caribbean Sea and to the N and E are lakes and lagoons.

Fortifications Cartagena was one of the storage points for merchandise sent out from Spain and for treasure collected from the Americas to be sent back to Spain. A series of forts protecting the approaches from the sea, and the formidable walls built around the city, made it almost impregnable.

Entering Boca Chica by sea, the island of Tierra Bomba is to the left. At the tip of a spit of land is the fortress of **San Fernando**. Opposite it, right on the tip of Barú island, is the **Fuerte San José**. The two forts were once linked by heavy chains to prevent surprise attacks by pirates. North of Barú island stretches Manga island, much larger and now an important suburb. At its northern end a bridge, **Puente Román**, connects it with the old city. This approach was defended by three forts: **San Sebastián del Pastelillo** built between 1558 and 1567 (the Club de Pesca has it now) at the northwestern tip of Manga Island; the fortress of **San Lorenzo** near the city itself; and the very powerful **Castillo San Felipe de Barajas** inland on San Lázaro hill, 41 m above sea-level, to the E of the city. Building began in 1639 and it was finished by

1657. Under the huge structure are tunnels lined with living rooms and offices. Some are open and lighted; visitors pass through these and up to the top of the fortress. Baron de Pointis, the French pirate, stormed and took it, but Admiral Vernon failed to reach it (see box). Entrance fee US$5 (half price for students and Colombians). Guide US$1.50 for 1 to 5 people. Open daily 0800-1800.

Yet another fort, **La Tenaza**, protected the walled city from a direct attack from the open sea. The huge encircling walls were started early in the 17th century and finished by 1735. They were on average 12m high and 17m thick, with 6 gates. They contained, besides barracks, a water reservoir.

Independence Cartagena declared its independence from Spain in 1811. A year later Bolívar used the city as a jumping-off point for his Magdalena campaign. After a heroic resistance, Cartagena was retaken by the royalists under Pablo Morillo in 1815. The patriots finally freed it in 1821.

Places of interest

The old walled city was in two sections, inner and outer. Much of the wall between the two was razed some years ago. Nearly all the houses are of 1 or 2 storeys. The houses in **El Centro** were occupied by the high officials and nobility. **San Diego** (the northern end of the inner town) was where the middle classes lived: the clerks, merchants, priests and military. The artisan classes lived in the 1-storey houses of **Getsemaní** in the outer city. Today, the streets of the inner city are relatively uncrowded; budget hotels and restaurants are sprinkled thinly throughout the area. Immediately adjoining is the downtown sector, known as **La Matuna**, where vendors crowd the pavements and the alleys between the modern commercial buildings. Several middle range hotels are in this district, between Avs Venezuela and Urdaneta Arbeláez. South of the latter is Getsemaní, where many colonial buildings survive; the greatest concentration of budget hotels and restaurants is here. Just under a kilometre from the old city, along an ocean boulevard, **Bocagrande** is a spit

The Sacking of Cartagena

In spite of its daunting outer forts and encircling walls Cartagena was challenged again and again by enemies. Sir Francis Drake, with 1,300 men, broke in successfully in 1586, leading to a major reconstruction of the ramparts we see today. Nevertheless the Frenchmen Baron de Pointis and Ducasse, with 10,000 men, beat down the defences and sacked the city in 1697. But the strongest attack of all, by Sir Edward Vernon with 27,000 men and 3,000 pieces of artillery, failed in 1741 after besieging the city for 56 days; it was defended by the one-eyed, one-armed and one-legged hero Blas de Lezo, whose statue is at the entrance to the San Felipe fortress.

of land crowded with hotel and apartment towers.

The old city streets are narrow. Each block has a different name, a source of confusion, but don't worry: the thing to do is to wander aimlessly, savouring the street scenes, and allow the great sights to catch you by surprise. Our map is marked with numerals for the places of outstanding interest. The most attractive streets have been given a star (*). Most of the "great houses" can be visited. Churches generally open to the public at 1800.

The numbers stand for the following places:

1. The **Puente Román**, which leads from the island of Manga into Getsemaní.
2. The chapel of **San Roque** (early 17th century), near the hospital of Espíritu Santo.
3. In an interesting plaza, the church of **Santísima Trinidad**, built 1643 but not consecrated till 1839. North of the church, at number 10, lived Pedro Romero, who set the revolution of 1811 going with his cry of "Long Live Liberty".
4. The monastery and church of **San Francisco**. The church was built in 1590 after the pirate Martin Côte had destroyed an earlier church built in 1559. The first Inquisitors lodged at the monastery. From its courtyard a crowd surged into the streets claiming independence from Spain on 11 November 1811. Handicrafts are sold in the grounds of the monastery, good value, fixed prices. The Iglesia de la Tercera Orden is now the **Teatro Colón**.

Immediately to the N is **Plaza de la Independencia**, with the landscaped **Parque del Centenario** just off it. At right

angles to the Plaza runs the **Paseo de los Mártires**, flanked by the busts of nine patriots executed in the square on 24 February 1816 by the royalist Morillo when he retook the city. At its western end is a tall clock tower. Through the tower's arches (the main entrance to the inner walled city) is

5. The **Plaza de los Coches**. Around almost all the plazas of Cartagena arcades offer refuge from the tropical sun. On the W side of this plaza is the famous **Portal de los Dulces**, a favourite meeting place.
6. **Plaza de la Aduana**, with a statue of Columbus and the **Palacio Municipal**.
7. Church of **San Pedro Claver** and Monastery, built by Jesuits in 1603 and later dedicated to San Pedro Claver, a monk in the monastery, who was canonized 235 years after his death in 1654. He was called the Slave of the Slaves (El Apostol de los negros): he used to beg from door to door for money to give to the black slaves brought to the city. His body is in a glass coffin on the high altar, and his cell and the balcony from which he sighted slave ships are shown to visitors. Entry, US$0.60. Guides charge US$2. Open daily 0800-1800.
8. **Plaza de Bolívar** (the old Plaza Inquisición), modest, and with a statue of Bolívar. On its W side is
9. The **Palacio de la Inquisición**, established in 1610, but the building dates from 1706. The stone entrance with its coats of arms and well preserved and ornate wooden door is very notable. The whole building, with its balconies, cloisters and patios, is a fine example of colonial baroque. There is a modest historical museum at the Palacio, and a library. Entry

US$0.75; good historical books on sale. Open Mon-Fri, 0800-1130, 1400-1700.

10. The **Cathedral**, in the NE corner of Plaza de Bolívar, begun in 1575 and partially destroyed by Francis Drake. Reconstruction was finished by 1612. Great alterations were made between 1912 and 1923. A severe exterior, with a fine doorway, and a simply decorated interior. See the guilded 18th century altar, the Carrara marble pulpit, and the elegant arcades which sustain the central nave.

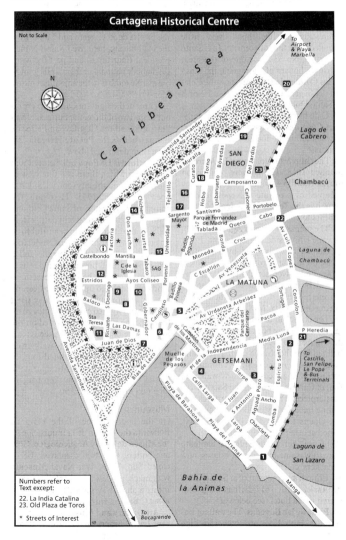

Cartagena Historical Centre

Not to Scale

Caribbean Sea

Numbers refer to Text except:

22. La India Catalina
23. Old Plaza de Toros

* Streets of Interest

11. Church and convent of **Santa Teresa**, founded 1609.

12. The church and monastery of **Santo Domingo**, built 1570 to 1579 and now a seminary. The old monastery was replaced by the present one in the 17th century. Inside, a miracle-making image of Christ, carved towards the end of the 16th century, is set on a baroque 19th century altar. Most interesting neighbourhood, very little changed since the 16th century. In C Santo Domingo, No 33-29, is one of the great patrician houses of Cartagena, the **Casa de los Condes de Pestagua**, now the Colegio del Sagrado Corazón de Jesús. North of Santo Domingo, at

13. C de la Factoria 36-57 is the magnificent **Casa del Marqués de Valdehoyos**, now containing a Tourist Office; open to visitors.

14. The church and convent of **La Merced**, founded 1618. The convent – a prison during Morillo's reign of terror – is now occupied by a private university, and its church is the **Teatro Municipal**, but now appears to be in disrepair.

15. The monastery of **San Agustín** (1580), now the Universidad de Cartagena. From its chapel, now occupied by a printing press, the pirate Baron de Pointis stole a 500-pound silver sepulchre. It was returned by the King of France but the citizens melted it down to pay their troops during the siege by Morillo in 1815.

16. The church of **Santo Toribio de Mongrovejo**. Building began in 1729. In 1741, during Admiral Vernon's siege, a cannon ball fell into the church during Mass and lodged in one of the central columns; the ball is now in a recess in the W wall. The font of Carrara marble in the Sacristy is a masterpiece. There is a beautiful carved ceiling (*mudéjar* style) above the main altar. Opens for Mass at 0600 and 1800, closed at other times.

17. **Casa del Consulado** (C Sargento Mayor) was one of the great houses, now a teachers' college.

18. Church and monastery of **Santa Clara de Assisi**, built 1617-21, has been converted into a hotel (see below).

19. **Plaza de las Bóvedas**. The walls of Las Bóvedas, built 1799, are some 12m high and from 15 to 18m thick. From the rampart there is a grand view of the harbour. At the base of the wall are 23 dungeons, now containing tourist shops. Both a lighted underground passage and a drawbridge lead from Las Bóvedas to the fortress of La Tenaza on the sea shore.

20. **Casa de Núñez**, just outside the walls of La Tenaza in El Cabrero district opposite the Ermita de El Cabrero and 5 mins from the old bullring; here lived Rafael Núñez, president (four times) and poet (he wrote Colombia's national anthem). His grandiose marble tomb is in the adjoining church. Mon-Fri 0800-1200, 1400-1800.

Three of the sights of Cartagena are off our map. Two of them, the Fortress of San Fernando and the Castillo San Felipe de Barajas, across the **Puente Heredia** (21) have been described above.

The third is **La Popa** hill, nearly 150m high, from which there is a fine view of the harbour and the city (entry US$1.10); open daily 0800-1745. Here are the church and monastery of Santa Cruz and restored ruins of the convent dating from 1608. In the church is the beautiful little image of the Virgin of La Candelaria, reputed a deliverer from plague and a protector against pirates. Her day is 2 February. For 9 days before the feast thousands of people go up the hill by car, on foot, or on horseback. On the day itself people carry lighted candles as they go up the hill. The name was bestowed on the hill because of an imagined likeness to a ship's poop. It is dangerous to walk up on your own; either take a guided tour, or take a public bus to Teatro Miramar at the foot of the hill (US$0.50), then bargain for a taxi up, about US$2.50.

Museums

On the opposite side of the Plaza de Bolívar to the Palacio de la Inquisición, is the **Museo del Oro y Arqueológico**. Gold and pottery, very well displayed; US$1, closed Sun. There is a **Naval Museum** with maps, models and display of armaments a short way towards the city wall along C Baloco, entry US$0.75.

Art Gallery and Museum, contemporary Latin American paintings, Banco

Ganadero, Plaza de la Aduana. Nearby is the **Museo de Arte Moderno** (open Mon-Fri, 0900-1200, 1500-1800, Sat, 1000-1200), opposite the San Pedro Claver church.

Beaches

Take a bus S from the clocktower, taxi US$1.50, or walk to Bocagrande. Thousands of visitors flock to this beach with its resort atmosphere. Sand and sea can be dirty. You will also be constantly hassled.

Marbella beach is an alternative, just N of Las Bóvedas. This is the locals' beach, and therefore quieter during the week than Bocagrande and is good for swimming, though subject at times to dangerous currents.

The Boca Chica beach, on Tierra Bomba island, is also none too clean. Boats leave from Muelle Turístico, the departure point is the tourist office. The round trip can take up to 2 hrs each way and costs about US$12. *Ferry Dancing*, about half the price of the faster, luxury boats, carries dancing passengers. Boats taking in Boca Chica and the San Fernando fortress include *Alcatraz*, which runs a daily trip from the Muelle Turístico.

Boats to the Islas del Rosario (see below) may stop at the San Fernando fortress and Playa Blanca on the Isla de Baru for 1 hr. You can bargain with the boatman to leave you and collect you later. Take food and water since these are expensive on the island. Playa Blanca is crowded am, but peaceful after the tour boats have left. There are several restaurants on the beach, the best *La Sirena* run by Carmen 'La Española' (care: there are other Carmens around!), good food, hammocks for hire US$3.50. You can also reach Playa Blanca by taking the bus to Pasacaballo, crossing the Canal de Dique by canoe and thence by truck or jeep to the beach; if walking, 2½ hrs in all. If staying the night at Playa Blanca in cabañas or tents, beware of ferocious sandflies. **NB** Pay for boat trips on board if possible, and be certain that you and the operator understand what you are paying for.

Local festivals

La Candelaria, see La Popa, above; *Independence* celebrations, 2nd week of Nov: men and women in masks and fancy dress roam the streets, dancing to the sound of *maracas* and drums. There are beauty contests, battles of flowers and general mayhem. This festival tends to be wild and can be dangerous. *Caribbean Music Festival* for several days in Mar, groups from all over the Caribbean region and beyond perform salsa, reggae, etc; loud and fun. There is a *film festival* in either Mar or April. Avianca offices everywhere have details of festival dates.

Local information

● **Accommodation**

On **Bocagrande** beach, 10 mins by bus from city: at the extreme tip is **L1-2** *Cartagena-Hilton*, El Laguito, T 665-0666, F 665-0661 (Apto Aéreo 1774, best equipped); **L2** *Del Caribe*, Cra 1, No 2-87, T 665-0155, F 665-3707, colonial style with newer annexes, comfortable, a/c, stylish, nice grounds, swimming pool in the (expensive) restaurant; **L3** *Capilla del Mar*, C 8, Cra 1, T 665-1140, F 665-5145, resort hotel, good French restaurant, swimming pool on top floor, no connection with restaurant of same name 500m away.

A2-3 range: *Casa Grande*, Av 1A, No 9-126, pleasant small hotel on beach, hot water, tropical garden, restaurant, owner speaks English, a/c, cheaper with fan only; *Costa del Sol*, Av 1 y C 9A, T 665-0866, tower with rooftop pool, very comfortable; **A2** *Flamingo* Av San Martín No 5-86 (cheaper in low season), T 665-0301, a/c, good breakfast inc, helpful, pleasant, eat on the terrace, parking, rec.

C *India Catalina*, Cra 2, No 7-115, T 665-5392, very good, a/c, safe (acts as youth hostel); **C** *Playa*, Av 2, No 4-87, T 665-0552, a/c, open air bar, restaurant, swimming pool, noisy disco next door; **C** *Residencias Internacional*, Av San Martín 4110, T 665-0675 (D in low season), small rooms, a/c, cold water, uncomfortable beds, convenient location; **D** *Leonela*, Cra 3, 7-142, T 665-4761, quiet, comfortable; **D** *La Giralda*, Cra 3, No 7-166, T 665-4507, fan, a/c dearer; **E** *Residencia Punta Canda*, C 7 between Cras 2 and 3, reasonable; **F** *La Sultana*, Av San Martín, No 7-44, pleasant atmosphere. On Cra 3, there are plenty of small, pleasant **D** *residencias*, for instance *Mary*, No 6-52, T 665-2822, small, respectable, and No 5-29, cheaper in low season.

In La Matuna: C *Del Lago*, C 34, No 11-15, T 665-3819, more for a/c, phone, no singles, reasonable restaurant, laundry, credit cards accepted, no parking; **D** *Montecarlo*, C 34, No 10-16, T 664-5835, more with a/c, good value, good laundry next door, fair restaurant; **D** *San Felipe*, Cra 9, No 13-72, T 664-5439, central, close to old city, big café.

In Old City: **L2** *Santa Clara*, Cra 8, No 39-29, T 664-6070, F 664-8040, French Sofitel group, magnificently restored 16th century convent, French, Italian and Colombian restaurants, all services, rec; **D** *Hostal Baluarte*, Media Luna No 10-81, T 664-2208, fan, converted colonial house, family run, helpful, will arrange day trips, well-priced restaurant; **D** *Hostal Santo Domingo*, C Santo Domingo, No 33-46, basic but quiet, well located, rec; **D** *Veracruz*, C San Agustín, No 6-15, opp San Agustín church (more with a/c), safe, helpful but noisy disco on ground floor; **E** *Doral*, Media Luna, No 10-46, T 664-1706, nice, fan, large rooms but avoid ground floor, safe courtyard where you can park cycles/motorbikes, noisy at night and bad water problems; **E** *Suiza*, opp *Doral* on Media Luna, new 1996, German owner, good food; **E** *Holiday*, Media Luna, No 10-47, T 664-0948, fan, quiet, pleasant courtyard, luggage store, hot water, rec; **E** *Familiar*, C del Guerrero, No 29-65, nr Media Luna, T 664-8374, safe, fan, space for bike or motorcycle, use of kitchen, laundry facilities, good value; **E** *Punta Arena*, opp *Familiar*, family run; **F** *Viena*, San Andrés, No 30-53, T 664-6242, run by Patrick Vercoutere, Belgian, clean, safe, cooking facilities, washing machine, book exchange, excellent value, rec, profits help street children; **F** *Media Luna*, Media Luna y Centenario, without bath, good value; **F** *Monterrey*, Camellón de los Mártires (opp the clocktower 'prison cell'), central, good Colombian meals in restaurant; **F** *Residencias Venecia*, C del Guerrero No 29-108, some rooms with fan, garden, washing facilities, secure; **F** *Tropicana*, Plaza Independencia, run down but helpful. The following are used frequently, but recently none has received good reports (ie insecure, poor value); **F** *El Refugio*, C Media Luna, No 10-35; **F** *Hostal Valle*, C Media Luna, No 10-15, some rooms with bath, free coffee, discounts for long stay, check the room before taking. Many cheap hotels on C Media Luna are brothels; area not advisable for women on their own. *Turístico Margie*, Av 2A, 63-175, Crespo district, convenient for airport, walking distance to old city (or bus), family-run, modern.

On the road to the airport are several hotels and *pensiones*, particularly at Marbella beach, eg **D** *Bellavista*, Av Santander, fans, nice patio, English-speaking owner, Enrique Sedó, secure, nice atmosphere, rec for longer stays; right behind is **F** *Mirador del Lago*, large rooms, fan.

NB Hotel prices rise for high season, 1 Nov-31 Mar, and June-July. From 15 Dec to 31 Jan they rise by as much as 50% (ie increase Bocagrande hotels by at least a letter in our range at this time; in town nothing is below E, but price increases are not so steep); hotels tend to be heavily booked right through to March.

Camping: on the beach is not secure. Vehicle parking overnight possible at the Costa Norte Beach Club, 2 km NE on coast beyond the airport, US$4/night.

● **Places to eat**

Bocagrande: *Nautilus*, Cra 3, good, seafood, other branches, facing the statue of La India Catalina and on road to airport in Marbella; *Capilla del Mar*, rec, seafood. *Italia*, Av San Martín 7-55, good Italian, excellent ice-creams and sorbets; *Palacio de las Frutas*, Av San Martín y C 6, good *comida corrida*; *La Fonda Antioqueña*, Cra 2, No 6-161, traditional Colombian, nice atmosphere. Good reasonably priced food in the chain restaurants: *Crepes y Waffles*, *Pizza por Metro* and *La Loca*.

Away from Bocagrande: *Pacos*, good bar/restaurant on Plaza Santo Domingo; *El Zorba*, Plaza Fernández, small, cosy, good music. On C Quero, close to *Zorba*, *La Tablada*, arty, usually good music, basic, gay bar at night; *Mesón Taurino*, No 9-23, good, cheap; *Dalmacia*, C Santo Domingo, just off square, charming, run by a Croatian, rec, closes 2000; *La Crepería*, Plaza de Bolívar 3-110, excellent salads, fruit drinks, crêpes, gets busy around 1230; *Nuevo Mundo*, Media Luna nr plaza, Chinese, big portions, good typical menu, cheap, good value; *Café-Galería Abaloa*, C Espíritu Santo, No 29-200, Gatsemaní, quiet, cultural ambience, books, music etc, drinks, breakfasts, also has 3 cheap rooms; *Café del Casa Santísimo*, C Santísimo No 8-19, T 664-3316, quiet, attractive, good salads and sandwiches; *Le Bistrot de L'Alianza*, Parque Fernando Madrid No 37-34, French, good food, excellent crêpes; *El Koral*, next to *Hotel Doral*, Media Luna, good, cheap; *El Ganadero*, also on Media Luna, good value; *Bucarest*, Marbella, next to *Hotel Bellavista*, for seafood and juices. Many restaurants around Plaza Independencia have good value meals, eg *Fonda El Socorro*, C Larga on Plaza Independencia. Several Chinese restaurants in the old city, eg *Wing-Wah*, C Ayos, rec; *Dragón de Oro*, C Venezuela, good, inexpensive; *El Diamante*, C de la Soledad, large helpings, good; *Jumbo*, C Tabaco, good Chinese and local food, *churrasco*, large portions, reasonable prices.

Vegetarian: *Tienda Naturista*, C Quero 9-09, good cheap vegetarian; *Govinda*, Plaza de los Coches 7-15, good set meal US$2.50; *Girasoles*, C de Quero y C de los Puntales, good vegetarian; *Panadería La Mejor*, Av Arbeláez, good for breakfast, fine wholemeal bread, coffee, yoghurt, expensive.

At cafés try the *patacón*, a biscuit made of green banana, mashed and baked; also in Parque del Centenario in early morning. At restaurants ask for *sancocho* a local soup of the day of vegetables and fish or meat. Also try *obleas* for a snack, biscuits with jam, cream cheese, or caramel fudge, and *buñuelos*, deep-fried cheese dough balls.

● **Banks & money changers**
Banco Unión Colombiana, Av Venezuela (C 35) No 10-26, La Matuna, changes American Express and Thomas Cook TCs up to a maximum of US$300, without commission; **Banco Industrial**, good rates for TCs; **Bancafé**, gives money on Visa cards, both on Av Venezuela. **Banco Sudameris**, opp conference centre at harbour, for Visa cash advances. There are many *cambios*; many in the arcade at Torre Reloj and adjoining streets change Amex TCs; also *Caja de Cambio Caldas*, Av San Martín, No 4-118, Bocagrande, and on the corner of Plaza de los Coches, downtown. Be sure to count the pesos yourself before handing over your dollars. Never change money on the street. **American Express** (Tierra Mar Aire), Bocagrande, Cra 4, No 7-196, is a travel agency downstairs, and gives cash against credit cards upstairs. TCs can be changed Sat am (arrive early) at **Joyería Mora**, Román 5-39, and at El Portal nearby, in the old city.

● **Embassies & consulates**
Venezuelan, Edif Los Ejecutivos, Cra 2, Bocagrande, open to 1500, possible to get a visa the same day (US$30): you need onward ticket, two photos, but ensure you get a full visa not a 72-hrs transit unless that is all you need; **Canadian Honorary Consul** (for emergencies only), C de la Inquisición con Santo Domingo, esq, No 33-08, Apto 201; **Danish**, Cra 10, No 5-68; **Finnish**, Av San Martín, Centro Comercial Bocagrande, p 3, 308, T 665-7672; **Norwegian Consulate**, Edif Banco Central Hipolecario, La Matuna, T 665-4639; **Panamanian Consulate**, C 69, No 4-97, T 666-2079.

● **Entertainment**
Discos: good discos in Bocagrande eg *La Escollera*, also in Old City, Parque La Marina, upmarket, in stately building. Bar *La Muralla* on the city wall W of Plaza Bolívar, open at night only, live music at weekends, romantic, but drinks expensive; for salsa, *Quiebra Canto*, C Media Luna at Parque Centenario, nice atmosphere.

● **Language schools**
Enysys, Plaza Fernández de Madrid, No 36-123, p 2, T 664-3951, also offers English for Colombians and other courses, rec.

● **Places of worship**
Anglican Church, C Ricuarte, services in English can be arranged.

● **Post & telecommunications**
Post Office: beside Avianca office Edif Los Andes, Plaza de La Aduana.

Telecom: Av Urdaneta Arbeláez nr corner of C 34; long distance phones behind this building; long distance also in Bocagrande.

● **Security**
Carry your passport, or a photocopy, at all times. Failure to present it on police request can result in imprisonment and fines. Generally, the central areas are reported safe and friendly (although Getsemaní is less secure), but should you require the police, there is a station in Barrio Manga.

Beware of drug pushers on the beaches, pickpockets in crowded areas and bag/camera snatchers on quiet Sun mornings. At the bus station, do not be pressurized into a hotel recommendation different from your own choice. On the street, do not be tempted by offers of jobs or passages aboard ship: jobs should have full documentation from the Seamen's Union office; passages should only be bought at a recognized shipping agency.

● **Shopping**
A good selection of *artesanías* at *Compendium* on Plaza Bolívar, but in general (except for leather goods) shopping is much better in Bogotá. Handicraft shops in the Plaza de las Bóvedas are good but expensive. Woollen *blusas* are good value; try the *Tropicano* in Pierino Gallo building in Bocagrande. Also in this building are reputable jewellery shops. *H Stern* has a jewellery shop in the Pierino Gallo shopping centre and at the *Hilton Hotel*. *Centro Comercial Getsemaní*, C Larga between San Juan and Plaza de la Independencia, a large new shopping centre has many establishments. *Magali París*, Av Venezuela y C del Boquete, is an a/c supermarket, with cafetería. Good badges for backpacks from the shops along the wall of the old prison.

Bookshop: *Librería Bitacura*, Av San Martín 7-187, English and Spanish books, second hand exchange, run by friendly lady.

Markets: there is a new market out of town, which is disappointing; bus from Av Urdaneta Arbeláez. The fish market is in the SE suburbs of the old city.

● **Sports**
Bullfights and cockfights: the former take place mainly in Jan and Feb in the new Plaza de Toros on Av Pedro de Heredia away from the centre; the old, wooden Plaza de Toros (no 23 on the map) is a fine structure, but is no longer in use. Cockfights are held throughout the year on Sat, Sun and holidays. On Sat and Mon at

1500 cockfighting takes place at the Gallerita Popular de la Quinta and on Sun at 1600 at Club Gallístico Pedro Rhenals in El Bosque.

Watersports: *Yachting*: *Club Náutica*, on Isla Manga across the Puente Román, good for opportunities to crew or finding a lift to other parts of the Caribbean. Windsurf rental, Bocagrande, US$6.50/hr. **Diving**: *Eco Buzos*, Marina Todomar, Cra 2 No 15-346, Bocagrande, T 665-5449, F 665-5960, 2 dives inc all equipment US$75, snorkelling US$35, also snacks and drinks; *La Tortuga Dive Shop*, Edif Marina del Rey, 2-23 Av del Retorno, Bocagrande, T 665-6995, 2 dives US$70. Faster boat, which allows trips to Isla Baru as well as Los Rosarios, same price at *Hotel Caribe Dive shop*, though discounts are sometimes available if you book via the hotels, enquire. Recompression chamber at the naval hospital, Bocagrande.

● **Tourist offices**

Empresa Promotora de Turismo de Cartagena, Av Blas de Lezo, Ed Muelle de los Pegasos, T 665-1843; also in Parque Flanagan, Bocagrande, T 665-4987, and at the airport, who will call cheaper hotels (all 3 open 0700-1900 daily, allegedly). Town plan for US$0.20. CNT, Calle de la Factoría, Casa del Marqués de Valdehoyos, Cra 3, No 36-57, T 664-7015/9, open daily till 1730, US$0.25 to tour the house. Recommended guide, Fernando Vargas Osorio, C de Magdalena, No 7-52.

DAS: just beyond Castillo San Felipe, behind the church (ask), Plaza de la Ermita (Pie de la Popa), T 666-4649, helpful. DAS passport office is in C Castelbondo, nr Plaza de la Artillería.

● **Transport**

Local Bus: within the city large buses (with no glass in windows) cost US$0.50. **Car rental**: National and Hertz at airport; Avis at *Hilton Hotel*. **Taxis**: from Bocagrande to the centre US$1.50; for airport, see below. Try to fix price before committing yourself. A horse-drawn carriage can be hired for US$10, opp *Hotel El Dorado*, Av San Martín, in Bocagrande, to ride into town at night (romantic but rather short ride).

Air Crespo, 1½ km from the city, reached by local buses from Blas de Lezo, SW corner of inner wall. Bus from airport to Plaza San Francisco US$0.50. Taxi to Bocagrande US$4, to town US$1.55 (official prices). Tourist information desk gives list of taxi prices. Good self-service restaurant. No exchange facilities. Daily flights to all main cities. SAM (T 665-5500) and Avianca (T 665-6102) offices both in Plaza de la Aduana. From Dec to Mar all flights are overbooked – even reconfirming and turning up 2 hrs early doesn't guarantee a seat; don't book a seat on the last plane of the day.

Buses New bus terminal is 30 mins from town, taxi US$3-4, or take city buses 'Terminal de Transportes'. Pullman bus from Cartagena to **Medellín** 665 km, US$35 (Brasilia, or Rápidos Ochoa, slightly cheaper, rec). Several buses a day, but book early (2 days in advance at holiday times), takes 13-16 hrs. The road is now paved throughout, but in poor condition. To **Santa Marta**, US$9.10 (with Brasilia, C 32, No 20D-55), 4 hrs, also cheaper lines, US$7.20. To **Barranquilla** US$5 with Transportes Cartagena, 3 hrs, or US$6 with Expreso Brasilia Pullman or La Costeña, US$4, 2 hrs. To/from **Bogotá** via Barranquilla and Bucaramanga with Expreso Brasilia pullman or Copetran, 8 a day, US$48, may take 21-28 hrs, depending on number of check-points. To **Magangué** on the Magdalena US$8.50, 4 hrs with Brasilia; to **Mompós**, Unitransco, 0530, 12 hrs inc ferry crossing from Magangué, US$9.50. To **Valledupar** with Expreso Brasilia, pullman US$10 (with a 30 mins stop in Barranquilla), for Sierra Nevada and Pueblo Bello. To **Riohacha**, US$12. Bus to **Maicao** on Venezuelan frontier US$16.75 (with Expreso Auto Pullman, Expreso Brasilia at 2000, or Unitrasco), 12 hrs; the road is in good condition, except for 30 km.

Shipping: there are modern wharves. It is possible to ship a car from Cartagena to Panama. For Cartagena-Colón (Panama) ferry service, see page 905. Two other companies which will ship vehicles to Panama: Hermann Schwyn, Edif Concasa, 10th floor, T 664-7450, and Mundinaves, Cra 53, No 64-72, of 301, T 645-4691. There are boats leaving most days for points S along the coast, for example to Turbo cargo boats take 24 hrs, all in cost about US$25 pp, and up the Río Sinú to Montería and the Atrato as far as Quibdó. For the trip to Quibdó see page 940.

Environs of Cartagena

The little fishing village of **La Boquilla**, NE of Cartagena, is near the end of a sandy promontory between the Ciénaga de Tesca and the Caribbean, about 20 mins past the airport. There is a good beack nearby, busy at weekends but quiet during the week. On Sat and Sun nights people dance the local dances. Visit the mangrove swamps nearby to see the birds. Golf courses are under development here.

● **Accommodation & transport** A luxury hotel has been built nearby, **A1** *Las Americas Beach Resort*. Also **E** *Los Morros* (clean, good food) and campsite, good, clean, showers, restaurant and small market, tents rented with mattresses. Go there by taxi, US$3 (there is a reasonable bus service).

On the coast, 50 km NE is **Galerazamba**, no accommodation but good local food. Nearby are the clay baths of Volcán del Totumo, in beautiful surroundings. The crater is about 25m high and the mud lake, at a comfortable temperature, 30m across and reputed to be over 500m deep. A bathe will cost you US$2, masseurs available for a small extra fee. Bus from Cartagena to Galerazamba, US$1.50.

ISLAS DEL ROSARIO

The National Park of **Corales del Rosario** embraces the archipelago of Rosario (a group of 30 coral islets 45 km SW of the Bay of Cartagena) and the mangrove coast of the long island of Baru to its furthest tip. Isla Grande and some of the smaller islets are easily accessible by day trippers and those who wish to stay in one of the hotels. Permits are needed for the rest, US$10. The islands represent part of a coral reef, low-lying, densely vegetated and with narrow strips of fine sand beaches. Rosario (the largest and best conserved) and Tesoro both have small lakes, some of which connect to the sea. There is an incredible profusion of aquatic and bird life. An Aquarium in the sea is worth visiting, US$3, not included in boat fares. Many of the smaller islets are privately owned.

Apart from fish and coconuts, everything is imported from the mainland, fresh water included. *Hotel del Caribe* in Bocagrande has scuba lessons in its pool followed by diving at Islas del Rosario, US$230 and up. Diving permit from MA costs US$31.

● **Access** Travel agencies and the hotels offer launch excursions from the Muelle Turístico, leaving 0800-0900 and returning 1600-1700, costing from US$10 to US$25, lunch included; free if staying at one of the hotels. Book in advance. Rec are Excursiones Roberto Lemaitre, C 8, No 4-66, Bocagrande, T 665-2872 (owner of *Club Isla del Pirata*). They have the best boats and are near the top end of the price range. *Yates Alcatraz* are more economical; enquire at the quay. For five or more, try hiring your own boat for the day and bargain for around US$10 pp.

● **Accommodation A2** pp *Club Isla del Pirata*, mainland booking office at C 8, No 4-66, Bocagrande, T 665-2873, F 665-2862, complex occupies a tiny islet in the archipelago, inc meals, add 16% tax; **L3** pp *San Pedro de Majagua*,

mainland office at Cra 5, No 8-59, Bocagrande, T 665-2745, F 665-2745, inside *Restaurant Capilla del Mar*, under the same ownership, complex occupies part of Isla Grande, in the Rosario archipelago, price inc meals. *Casa Blanca*, white with arched windows, former family home, converted to luxury 5-star hotel.

SOUTH OF CARTAGENA

The highway S towards Medellín goes through **Turbaco**, 24 km (Botanical Garden, 1½ km before village on the left, student guides), **Malagana**, 60 km (**G** *Res Margarita*, fan, basic) and **San Jacinto**, 90 km (**F** *Hospedaje Bolívar*, no sign, at turn off by petrol station, simple, showers, parking, good food at *El Llanero* next door; bus from Cartagena US$5), where local craft work, eg hand woven hammocks are made: try *Artesanías Clauli*, 60m beyond petrol station.

10 km before San Jacinto is **Los Colorados National Park** (turn left towards the Río Magdalena just after San Juan Nepomuceno). Pleasant, if neglected park, good forest walking, main attraction the colorado monkeys – but you need to walk 2 hrs into the hills to reach their habitat.

SINCELEJO

The capital of Sucre Department is a cattle centre 193 km S of Cartagena (*pop* 148,420). The town is hot, dusty and power cuts are common.

Local festivals The dangerous bull-ring game in Jan is similar to the San Fermín festivities in Pamplona, Spain, in which bulls and men chase each other. At Eastertime there is the 'Fiesta del Burro' where they dress up donkeys and prizes go to the best and the funniest. A big party for 3 days.

● **Accommodation B** *Marsella*, C 21, No 23-59, T 820729; **D** *Majestic*, Cra 20, No 21-25, T 821872; **D** *Ancor*, Cra 25, No 20A-45, T 821125; **E** *Panorama*, Cra 25, 23-108, a/c; **E** *Santander*, corner of Plaza Santander, with bath, balconies, good restaurant, *La Olla*, opp.

35 km from Sincelejo, on the coast, is **Tolú**, a fast developing holiday town popular for its offshore islands and diving. A good trip is by boat 3 hrs to Múcura island in the Islas de San Bernardo, about

US$15. If camping, take your own supplies. Trips to the mangrove lagoons also recommended. A good agency is *Mar Adentro*, Av La Playa 11-30, T 885481, daily tours to San Bernardo Islands 0800, back 1600, including aquarium on Isla Palma.

● **Accommodation & places to eat A3** *Alcira*, Av La Playa 21-151, T 885016, less off-season, a/c, TV, pleasant; **C** *Ibabama*, Av La Playa 19-45, T 885159, comfortable, a/c, patio, restaurant; **E** *Darimar*, C 19, nr Unitransco bus station, with bath, fan; **F** *El Turista*, Av La Playa, basic, restaurant, best value. Many others. *El Zaguán Paisa*, on Plaza, good *comidas*, open late. Other places to eat nearby eg *Cafetería* on corner of Plaza, good cakes.

● **Transport** Tolú can be reached by *colectivo* from Sincelejo, or direct from Cartagena, several morning buses, 4 hrs, US$7; also service to Medellín with Rápido Ochoa and Brasilia 1100 and 1800, 10 hrs, US$24.

There are better beaches at **Coveñas**, 20 km further SW (several *cabañas* on the beach and hotels). This is the terminal of the oil pipeline from the oilfields in the Venezuelan border area. Buses and *colectivos* from Tolú.

SOUTH OF SINCELEJO

The main road from Sincelejo passes **Planeta Rica** (127 km) and **Caucasia** (194 km), a convenient stopping place between Cartagena and Medellín. Visit the Jardín Botánico (entry US$0.25).

● **Accommodation** 11 km before Caucasia is *Parador Chambacú* (T 226946), with campsite; next door is the **C** *Mesón del Gitano* (T 94-328-1882); **F** *Residencia Bonaire*, good, quiet, TV in lounge. In Caucasia: *Auto Hotel*, Cra 2, No 22-43, T 226355, best, quiet, heavily booked; **D** *Colonial*, Cra 2, No 20-68, T/F 822-7461, pleasant, a/c, cheaper with fan, good view of river, rec for value; **D** *Yen*, nr market, a/c, cheaper with fan; **E** *Residencias San Francisco*, Cra 49 y C 45, with bath, good value; **F** *Del Río*, with bath, close to bus station, free morning coffee but avoid front rooms on street; **F** *Residencia El Viajero*, Cra 2, No 23-39, nr centre, quiet, fan.

● **Buses** From Caucasia to Medellín US$11, 7 hrs; to Cartagena US$17 (Brasilia, 6 hrs), US$15 (Rápido Ochoa), US$10 (2nd class, 17 hrs).

50 km S of Caucasia is **Taraza** (**G** *Residencia Magdalena*, fan, parking at the Mobil station, basic, but noisy bar). About half way between Caucasia and Medellín is **Valdivia** with a spectacular bridge over the Cauca. The road continues to Yarumal (see page 938).

MONTERÍA

Montería (*municipal pop* 266,850), capital of Córdoba Department, on the E bank of the Río Sinú, can be reached from Cartagena by air, by river boat, or from the main highway to Medellín. (Bus from Cartagena – dual carriageway almost completed, US$11, 5 hrs, with Brasilia, has own terminal in Montería, or colectivo, US$10, also 5 hrs.) It is the centre of a cattle and agricultural area. It has one fine church, picturesque street life and extremely friendly people. Average temperature: 28°C.

● **Accommodation A3** *Sinú*, Cra 3, C 31 y 32, T 823355, F 823980, a/c, swimming pool, TV, restaurant; **D** *Alcázar*, Cra 2, No 32-17, T 824900, comfortable, restaurant; **F** *Brasilia*, good value; **F** *Residencias Imperial*, Cra 2; many cheap dives around.

67 km W of Montería, on the coast, is **Arboletes** a small quiet town with nearby mud lake of volcanic origins. You can 'swim' in the mud lake, then wash off in the ocean, 100m away.

● **Accommodation & places to eat E** *Ganadero*, fan, bath, good beds; **E** *Aristi*, very clean but small windows; **F** *Julia*, on the main square, no private bathrooms. Other accommodation along the beach. *Guido's* restaurant is probably the best.

● **Buses** 4 a day to Turbo, 5-6 hrs, US$5.40, 10 a day to Montería, 3 hrs, US$2.40.

An unmade road continues to Turbo (see below), **Chigorodó** (**F** *Residencial Tobi*, fan), **Dabeiba**, 186 km S of Turbo (**F** *Residencia Diana*, on main street, simple, helpful), **Cañasgordas** (**G** *Doña Concha*, private bath, modern, good value), Antioquia (see page 938) and Medellín. Scenic, but a long, bumpy ride.

COLOMBIA TO PANAMA

TURBO

On the Gulf of Urabá is the port of **Turbo**, now a centre of banana cultivation, which is booming. It is a rough frontier community. **Before going to Turbo, or contemplating crossing Darién by land, please see**

Notes and Cautions below.

● **Accommodation D** *Castillo de Oro*, best, reliable water and electricity, good restaurant; **D** *Playa Mar*, good, but somewhat run down; **D** *Sausa*, running water in early morning only, helpful owners, pleasant dining room; **F** *Residencia Sandra*, good; **F** *Residencia Turbo*, good; **F** *Residencia Marcela*, quiet, secure, best value; **G** *Residencia El Golfo*, good; in Playa district: *Miramar*, *Rotitom*, both **D**.

● **Banks & money changers** No banks are open for exchange of TCs on Mon or Tues; try exchanging money in stores.

● **Transport** Buses from Cartagena and from Medellín (6 a day, a gruelling 17 hrs, US$12; to Montería, 8 hrs, US$9, bad road, several army checkpoints). Boats are available to Cartagena and up the Río Atrato to Quibdó, but services are intermittent and unreliable.

FRONTIER WITH PANAMA

There are various routes involving sea and land crossings around or through the **Darién Gap**, which still lacks a road connection linking the Panamanian Isthmus and South America. Detailed descriptions of these routes are given in the *Mexico and Central American Handbook* (although in the direction Panama-Colombia). While maps of the region are available, there is no substitute for seeking informed local advice. In all cases, it is essential to be able to speak Spanish.

● **Colombian immigration**
DAS Office: at the Postadero Naval, Cra 13 between Cs 101 and 102, Turbo, open 0800-1630. If going from Colombia to Panama via Turbo you should get an exit stamp from the DAS office. There is also a DAS office in Capurganá (see below), opp *Hotel Uvita*, and a Panamanian consultate, but best not to leave it that late. If leaving Colombia, check the facts at any DAS office.

NB Colombian pesos are impossible to change at fair rates in Panama.

● **Entering Colombia**
Arriving from Panama, go to the DAS in Turbo for your entry stamp. Panamanian immigration at Puerto Obaldía is sometimes obstructive (all baggage will be checked for drugs, adequate funds for your stay may have to be shown – US$400, TCs or credit card; a ticket out of Panama is required, although a ticket from another Central American country may do).

NB If travelling from Panama to Colombia by coastal boat or land, we strongly advise you to aim for Turbo (or Buenaventura) and obtain your entry stamp from the DAS office there. Travellers who have requested entry stamps at other DAS offices have been fined or accused of illegal entry. A police stamp is no substitute.

● **Transport**
Colombia to Panama The simplest way is to fly from Barranquilla, Bogotá, Cali, Cartagena, Medellín or San Andrés. **Sea**: the ferry service from Cartagena to Colón (Cristóbal), Panamá that commenced in Dec 1994, was suspended in Nov 1996. The reasons are not clear, and hopes are expressed in Colombia and Panamá that it will be restarted in the near future. At the time of writing, information was available at: T 286-3050 (Bogotá), or T 660-7722 (Cartagena). In Panama City, T 263-3323, F 263-3326, and Colón, T 441-6311.

Given this new and uncertain situation, we can only recommend that you enquire on the spot in Cartagena and in Colón if you wish to transport a vehicle between the two countries. Foot passengers have always had the possibility to travel, *ad hoc*, on reputable cargo boats, but you must arrange with the captain the price and destination before departure. Small, irregular boats may well be contraband or arms runners; if a passenger on one you will be in trouble if stopped and, even if not stopped, will have difficulty in obtaining the necessary entry stamp.

CROSSING DARIEN: CARIBBEAN SIDE

On the Caribbean side, the starting point is Turbo from where boats sail to Acandí, 3 hrs, Capurganá and Zapzurro (all in Colombia) and Puerto Obaldía (Panama). **Acandí** *(pop about 7,000)*, has several *residencias*, eg **F** *Central*, safe; **G** *Pilar*; **F** *Acandí*, OK. Most have their own electricity generators. A little further N is **Capurganá**, now a small tourist resort with several hotels: **B** *Calipso*, a/c, good facilities; **D** *Náutico*, cabins; **E** *Uvita*, with bath, safe, by harbour; and cheaper accommodation. Across the Panamanian border, **E** *Residencial Cande* in Pto Obaldía is good, with meals.

● **Transport** Boats normally leave Turbo at 0900 daily, US$25, via Capurganá. Enquire for the best passage. There are also cargo boats from Cartagena to Capurganá which take passengers, 30-50 rough hrs, US$25-30, take hammock. From Puerto Obaldía (see above on immigration), boats to Colón, planes to Panama City (daily except Sun).

Overland from Turbo Two main alternative routes cross the central Gap to Paya, from where there is a well-trodden route to Yaviza: Paya-Pucuro, 6 hrs on foot; Púcuro-Boca de Cupe, by dugout, US$20-50; Boca de Cupe-Pinogana, also by dugout, US$15 pp, plus a walk, 2 hrs in all; Pinogana-Yaviza, walk and ferries/dugouts. From Yaviza (one hotel, **E** *Tres Américas*, basic) buses can be caught to Panama City, US$15, 10-14 hrs,

road subject to wash-outs.

One route to Paya: take a boat from Turbo across the Gulf of Urabá into the Río Tarena to Unguía, **F** *Residencias Viajero*, with bath; **G** *Doña Julia*, also with bath. Also basic restaurants. From here it is 3-4 hrs to the frontier, then 3 hrs to the Río Paya. You then hike down the Río Paya through dense jungle to Paya itself (about 12 hrs). Do not attempt the

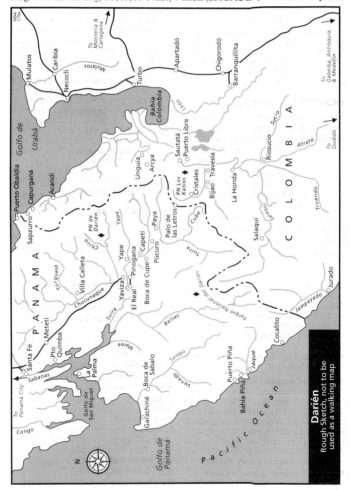

Darién

Rough Sketch, not to be used as a walking map

Unguía-Paya route without a guide.

The other main route to Paya: motorboat from Turbo across the Bahía de Colombia, through the Great Atrato Swamp and up the Río Atrato, with much birdlife to be seen (US$10 if scheduled, US$130 to hire a boat). At Travesía, also called Puente América, at the confluence of the Río Cacarica, you can buy limited provisions. There is a restaurant and rooms to stay in Travesía. From Travesía you go by another boat to Bijao (3 hrs, up to US$120). **NB** Both Travesía and Bijao are very expensive places to buy supplies, but worse still they have become anti-gringo. From Bijao you have to get by boat to Cristales in the Los Katíos National Park; the Inderena rangers may take you for up to US$100/boat. At Cristales there is an Inderena hut; 7-8 hrs through the Park on foot is Palo de las Letras, the frontier stone, from where it is 4-6 hrs to Paya. A guide is strongly recommended. It is best to take 2 days for this section. You can approach this route from Quibdó down the Río Atrato to Travesía (see Section 6). Get your Panamanian entry stamp in Boca de Cupe, Púcuro or Yaviza (enquire: it can be very difficult to get an entry stamp anywhere before Panama City on this route; try at every opportunity as hikers have been detained in the capital for not having an entry stamp. It may help to prove you have adequate funds for your stay).

LOS KATÍOS NATIONAL PARK

To visit the park, go first to the MA office in Turbo, where all necessary information is available. The office is 1 km along the road to Medellín. Because of violence and guerrilla activity in the region, MA discourages entry; if you insist you must sign a disclaimer.

The Katíos National Park, extending in Colombia to the Panamanian border, contains several waterfalls: Tilupo, 125m high; the water cascades down a series of rock staircases, surrounded by orchids and fantastic plants. This is 6 hrs return trip. A 5-hr trip passing through splendid jungle is required for two other fine waterfalls, the Salto de La Tigra and Salto de La Tendal. A full day's hike goes to Alto de Limón for a fine view of primary forest. You can stay overnight in a hut. Also in the park are the Alto de la Guillermina, a mountain behind which is a strange forest of palms called "mil pesos", and the Ciénagas de Tumaradó, with red monkeys, waterfowl and alligators.

● **Park information** The National Park can be reached by boat from Turbo most days, charging US$8. The boats, normally going up the Atrato to Riosucio, or beyond, will leave you at the MA headquarters of the Park in Sautatá. Ask in Turbo harbour when they are leaving. You should have a permit from MA in Turbo for the Park, or you can pay in the park. Arrange your return trip Sautatá – Turbo with the park guide at Sautatá beforehand. Boats do not normally stop. The Park can be visited with mules from the MA headquarters in Sautatá (cabins US$5.50 pp, or rangers may offer free space for your hammock, very friendly). Food can be ordered half a day in advance.

CROSSING DARIEN: PACIFIC SIDE

On the Pacific side, crossing into Panama involves travel by both boat and on foot, the quantity of each depending on the route chosen.

● **Transport** One sea route is from Bahía Solanó (see page 942) or Juradó in Chocó Department. Canoes go from both towns to Jaqué, 50 km N of the Colombian border (Juradó-Jaqué 1½ hrs, US$20), from where you can take a boat to Panamá City, 12 hrs, or fly, or fly to La Palma, capital of Darién in Panama (one *pensión* **F**, English spoken). Launches and dugouts go from La Palma to Puerto Lardo on the Río Sabanas, from where it is a 2-hr walk (or hitch on a truck) to Santa Fe on the Panamá-Yaviza road. (Bus Santa Fe-Panamá 6-8 hrs). Alternatively from La Palma take a boat to Puerto Quimba, then transport to Metetí, from where a bus can be taken to Panama City. Transport out of Jaqué is frustrating; you must obtain a DAS stamp in either Turbo or Buenaventura, without it you will have problems in Jaqué or Panama City.

Notes and cautions

Latest information from Colombia (mid 1997) is that armed groups, hostile to travellers including tourists, are particularly active in the NW corner of Colombia which includes the area on the Colombian side of the border. If information has not improved before you set out to cross Darién by land either way, you

are advised not to go. This warning includes visits to Los Katíos National Park and the road S of Turbo to Dabeiba.

Assuming the security situation is favourable and you are properly equipped, we suggest you follow these points of advice: 1) travel only in the dry season; 2) travel with a reliable companion or two; 3) hire at least one Indian guide, but do it through the village *corregidor*, whose involvement may add to the reliability of the guide he selects (budget up to US$12/day/guide and his food); 4) travel light and move fast.

Dr Richard Dawood, author of *Travellers' Health: How to Stay Healthy Abroad*, and photographer Anthony Dawton, crossed the Darien Gap at the end of the wet season (Nov). We include an abbreviated version of Dr Dawood's health recommendations for such a journey: **Heat** Acclimatization to a hot climate usually takes around 3 weeks. It is more difficult in humid climates than in dry ones, since sweat cannot evaporate easily, and when high humidity persists through the night as well, the body has no respite. Requirements for salt and water increase dramatically under such conditions. We had to drink 12 litres/day to keep pace with our own fluid loss on some parts of the trip.

In hot countries it is always essential to drink beyond the point of thirst quenching, and to drink sufficient water to ensure that the urine is consistently pale in colour.

Salt losses also need to be replaced. Deficiency of salt, water, or both, is referred to as heat exhaustion; lethargy, fatigue, and headache are typical features, eventually leading to coma and death. Prevention is the best approach: add salt to all fluids, one quarter of a level teaspoon (approximately 1 gram) per pint – to produce a solution that is just below the taste threshold. Salt tablets, however, are poorly absorbed, irritate the stomach and may cause vomiting.

Sun Overcast conditions in the tropics can be misleading. The sun's rays can be fierce, and it is important to make sure that all exposed skin is constantly protected with a high factor sun screen –

preferably waterproof for humid conditions. A hat is also essential.

Food and water Much caution is needed with food hygiene to prevent diarrhoea. Carry your own supplies and prepare them carefully. In the villages, oranges, bananas and coconuts are available. The freshly baked bread is safe, as is the rice.

Purify water with 2% tincture of iodine carried in a small plastic dropping bottle, 4 drops to each litre – more when the water is very turbid – wait 20 mins before drinking. This method is safe and effective. Alternatively, use a water purifying pump based on a ceramic filter. There are several on the market. It takes about a minute to purify a litre of water. When water is cloudy, eg after rain, pumps are less effective and harder work. It is worth travelling with a suitable antidiarrhoeal medication such as Arret.

Malaria Drug resistant malaria is present in the Darien area, and antimalarial medication is essential. Free advice on antimalarial medication for all destinations is available from the Malaria Reference Laboratory, T 0891-600-350 in the UK. An insect repellent is also essential, and so are precautions to avoid insect bites.

Insects Beside malaria and yellow fever, other insect-borne diseases such as dengue fever and leishmaniasis may pose a risk. The old fashioned mosquito net is ideal if you have to sleep outdoors, or in a room that is not mosquito-proof. An insecticide spray is valuable for clearing your room of flying insects before you go to sleep, and mosquito coils that burn through the night giving off an insecticidal vapour, are also valuable.

Ticks The currently favoured method of removing ticks is to ease the head gently away from the skin with tweezers.

Vaccinations A yellow fever vaccination certificate is required from all travellers arriving from infected areas, and vaccination is advised for personal protection.

Immunization against hepatitis A and typhoid are strongly advised. In addition, all travellers should be protected against tetanus, diptheria and polio.

Attacks by dogs are relatively common: the new rabies vaccine is safe and effective, and carrying a machete for the extra purpose of discouraging animals (and warding off snakes) is advised.

You can get some food along the way, but take enough for at least 5 days. Do take, though, a torch/flashlight, and a bottle of rum, or present of equal worth for the ranger at Cristales.

Wet season travel is not impossible, but with heavy rain every afternoon, the rivers are full and dangerous, and there is mud beyond belief making progress painfully slow.

NORTHEAST FROM CARTAGENA

The main Cartagena-Barranquilla road goes via Sabanalarga (50 km before Barranquilla) and Baranoa. A spectacular bridge over the Río Magdalena gives a fine view of Barranquilla and the river.

BARRANQUILLA

Barranquilla (*pop* 1.09 million; *phone code* 953), is Colombia's fourth city. It lies on the western bank of the Río Magdalena, about 18 km from its mouth, which, through deepening and the clearing of silted sandbars, makes it a seaport (though less busy than Cartagena or Santa Marta) as well as a river port.

Places of interest

Barranquilla is a modern industrial city with a colourful, polluted central area near the river, and a good residential area in the NW, beyond C 53. The principal boulevard is **Paseo Bolívar**. The church of **San Nicolás**, formerly the Cathedral, stands on Plaza San Nicolás, the central square, and before it is a small statue of Columbus. The new **Catedral Metropolitana** is at Cra 45, No 53-120, opposite Plaza de la Paz. There is an impressive statue of Christ inside by the Colombian sculptor, Arenas Betancourt. The commercial and shopping districts are round the Paseo Bolívar, a few blocks N of the old Cathedral, and in C Murillo. The vibrant **market** is between Paseo Bolívar and the river, the

so-called Zona Negra on a side channel of the Magdalena. Good parks in the northern areas include **Parque Tomás Suri Salcedo** on C 72. Stretching back into the northwestern heights overlooking the city are the modern suburbs of El Prado, Altos del Prado, Golf and Ciudad Jardín. There are five stadia in the city, a big covered coliseum for sports, two for football and the others cater for basketball and baseball. The metropolitan stadium is on Av Murillo, outside the city.

Museums

Small **archaeological** collection, C 68 No 53-45 (Mon-Fri 0900-1200, 1400-1700), with big physical relief map on front lawn. Also, **Museo Romántico**, Cra 54, No 59-199, history of Barranquilla.

Zoo

There is a well-maintained zoo with some animals not often seen in zoos, but many are in small cages, C 77, Cra 68 (bus 'Boston/Boston' or 'Caldes/Recreo'), US$0.60, 0830-1200, 1400-1800. All the trees are labelled.

Excursions

Regular buses from Paseo Bolívar and the church at C 33 y Cra 41 to the attractive bathing resort of **Puerto Colombia**, 19 km (US$0.60, 30 mins). Beach clean and sandy, water a bit muddy. South along the Magdalena to the little town of Palmar de Varela. On this road, 5 km from the city, is the colonial town of **Soledad** (*pop* 16,000); around the cathedral are old narrow streets.

Local festivals

Carnival, lasting 4 days, with parades, floats, street dancing and beauty contests, is one of the best in Latin America (22 February 1988).

Local information
● **Accommodation**

L2 *El Prado*, Cra 54, No 70-10, T 450111, F 450019, some distance fron the centre, best, the social centre, swimming pool and tennis courts, good restaurant, sauna, original 1920s building is national monument, new annex behind; **L3** *Dann Barranquilla*, Cra 51B, No 79-246, T 560731, F 455079, highrise, in Altos del Prado.

A3 *Royal*, Cra 54, No 68-124, T 565533, good service, swimming pool, modern. **B** *Apartotel*,

Cra 44, No 70-242, T 561213, a/c, parking, large rooms.

C *Capricornio*, Cra 44B, No 70-201, T 340244/565045, good service, a/c.

D *Canadiense*, C 45, No 36-142, fan, noisy but convenient for bus station 2 blocks away; **D** *Villa Venecia*, C 61, No 46-41, T 414107, TV, a little noisy but rec.

E *Diplomático*, Cra 38, No 42-60, with bath, fan, TV room, laundry facilities, cafeteria; **E** *Victoria*, C 35, No 43-140, downtown, large, scruffy rooms with fan.

F *California*, C 32 y Cra 44, pleasant but about to fall down, enjoy the chickens; **F** *Horizonte*, C 45 y Cra 44, with bath, quiet, fan, safe. **NB** Hotel prices may be much higher during Carnival. Watch for thieves in downtown hotels.

● **Places to eat**
La Puerta de Oro, C 35, No 41-100, central, a/c good for meals (inc breakfast); *El Huerto*, Cra 52, No 70-139, good vegetarian; *Jardines de Confucio*, Cra 54, No 75-44, good Chinese food, nice atmosphere; various Lebanese with belly-dancers; several Chinese and *pizzerías*. Many places, for all tastes and budgets, on C 70 from *Hotel El Prado* towards Cra 42; at C 70 y 44B are several *estaderos*, bars with snacks and verandas.

● **Banks & money changers**
Banco Anglo Colombiano, C 34, No 44-43, and 3 agencies; **Banco Internacional de Colombia**, cash against Mastercard. *Casa de cambio* El Cacique, C 34, No 43-108, T 326392, reliable.

● **Embassies & consulates**
Venezuelan, C 70, No 53-74 (Centro Financiero El Prado, 4° piso), T 580048/582832, 0800-1500 (take 'Caldas/Recreo' or 'Boston/Boston' bus), visa issued same day, but you must be there by 0915 with photo and US$30 cash; onward ticket may not be requested; **US**, Centro Comercial Mayorista, C 77, No 68-15, opp zoo (Apdo Aéreo 51565), T 457088 or 457181 (visas obtainable only in Bogotá); **British**, Cra 44, No 45-57, T 326936; **German**, C 80, nr Vía 40 (ask for Herr Schnabel); **Norwegian**, C 72, No 57-33, T 581043; **Dutch**, Cra 42H, No 85-33, T 341282; **Spanish**, C 51, No 37-64, T 313694; **Finnish**, Vía 40 de las Flores, Cementos del Caribe, T 350080.

● **Post & telecommunications**
Post Office: in Plaza Bolivar.

● **Shopping**
Bookshop: *Librería Nacional*, Cra 53, No 75-129, English, French and German books.

Market: San Andrecito, or 'Tourist Market', Vía 40, is where smuggled goods are sold at very competitive prices; a good place to buy film. Picturesque and reasonably safe. Any taxi driver will take you there.

● **Tour companies & travel agents**
Tierra Mar Aire, Amex agent, C 74, No 52-34, very helpful for flights to Central America.

● **Tourist offices**
Tourist information at main hotels and at C 72, No 57-43, of 401, T 454458 or 336658. CNT is at Cra 54, No 75-45, T 454458. **Maps**: from Instituto Agustín Codazzi, C 36, No 45-101.

● **Useful addresses**
DAS: C 54, Cra 43.
Police: (for declarations of theft, etc), Policia F2, C 47 y Cra 43.

● **Transport**
Local Taxis: within the town cost US$1.25 (eg downtown to northern suburbs).

Air Ernesto Cortissoz airport is 10 km from the city. City bus from airport to town, US$0.15 (US$0.20 on Sun). Taxi to town, US$4.50 (taxis do not have meters, fix fare in advance). To town, take only buses marked 'centro' from 200m to right when leaving airport; the bus to the airport (marked Malambo) leaves from Cra 44 up C 32 to Cra 38, then up C 30 to Airport. Taxi to Cartagena, US$40. Avianca (C 72, No 57-79, T 454355).

Buses Most bus companies operate from C 34 and Cra 45 (Brasilia and Copetran at C 45 y Cra 35: Brasilia links all N coast towns and S as far as Bogotá, rec a/c buses). To **Santa Marta**, US$3.25, Pullman (less in non-a/c, Cooliber-tador), about 2 hrs, also direct to Santa Marta's Rodadero beach; to **Valledupar**, 4½ hrs, US$6; to **Montería**, US$11, 8 hrs; to **Medellín** by Pullman, 16 hrs; to **Bucaramanga**, US$25 with Copetran, a/c, first class, departures at 1130 most days, 9 hrs; to **Bogotá**, 20-24 hrs, US$25 direct; to **Caucasia**, US$10.75, 11 hrs. To **Maicao**, US$10.75, 5 hrs (with Brasilia, every 30 mins from 0100-1200); to **Cartagena**, 3 grades of bus, 3 hrs (US$5 with Transportes Cartagena, US$6 with Expreso Brasilia, by Brasilia Van Tours mini-bus, from their downtown offices as well as the bus terminals), 2 hrs by colectivo.

Shipping See Warning under Cartagena (page 901) regarding jobs and passages aboard ship. If shipping a car into Barranquilla allow 2 days to complete all paperwork to retrieve your car from the port, unless you have a *carnet de passages*, which opens all doors and dispenses with all other paperwork.

SANTA MARTA

Santa Marta (*municipal pop* 279,960) is the capital of Magdalena Department. The third Caribbean port, it is 96 km E of Barranquilla, at the mouth of the Río Manzanares. It is best reached from Bar-

Santa Marta

Main Streets Only

Punta de Betín

← Isla El Morro

Bahía de Santa Marta

N

To Taganga

Terminal Marítimo

Customs

Casa de la Aduana Museum

Parque Bolívar

Convento de Santo Domingo & Tourist Office

Avianca

Cathedral

Parque Santander

Parque San Miguel

To Rodadero, Airport & Ciénaga

To Riohacha & PN Tairona

0   150
metres

Hotels:
1. Andrea Doria
2. Residencias Miramar
3. Sompallón
4. Yuldama

---

ranquilla by the paved road along the coast, which passes salt pans and skirts an extensive and most interesting lagoon, the Ciénaga de Santa Marta (see below). There is a paved road S to Bucaramanga (see page 887) and Bogotá.

Santa Marta lies on a deep bay with high shelving cliffs. The climate ranges seasonally from hot and trying to hot but pleasant in Feb and Mar; occasionally one can see snow-clad peaks of the Sierra Nevada to the E, less than 50 km away. The city's promenade offers good views of the bay and is lined with restaurants, accommodation and nightlife. The main shops and banks are on Cra 5.

History

Santa Marta was the first town founded (1525) by the *conquistadores* in Colombia.

Founder: Rodrigo de Bastidas. Most of the famous sea-dogs – the brothers Côte, Drake and Hawkins – sacked the city in spite of the two forts built on a small island at the entrance to the bay. It was here that Simón Bolívar, his dream of Gran Colombia shattered, came to die. Almost penniless he was given hospitality at the *hacienda* of San Pedro Alejandrino, see below. He died on 17 December 1830, at the age of 47, and was buried in the Cathedral, but his body was taken to the Pantheon at Caracas 12 years later.

Beaches

Sandy beaches stretch from the Simón Bolívar airport to Punta Aguja across the Rodadero de Gaira and the little fishing villages of Villa Concha, surrounded by meadows and shady trees, and Taganga (see below). A jutting rock – the Punta de Betín – rises from the sea in front of the city and is topped by a lighthouse. Rugged Isla del Moro, 3 km off Santa Marta, completes the panorama. Playa El Rodadero is the most fashionable and tourist-oriented part of Santa Marta, though it lies some distance W of the city (local bus service, taxi, US$1.80). Many of the buses coming from Barranquilla and Cartagena stop at Rodadero on the way to Santa Marta. There is also a dirty, unsafe beach with a seaside promenade close to the centre of town.

Museums

Casa de la Aduana, C 14 y Cra 2, displays an excellent archaeological collection, including precolombian gold artefacts; visit recommended before going to Ciudad Perdida. Open Tues-Sat, 0800-1200, 1400-1800, Sun 0800-1200, during the tourist season, Mon-Fri, 0800-1200, 1400-1800, the rest of the year; entry US$1.

Quinta de San Pedro Alejandrino, 5 km SE of the city: the simple room in which Simón Bolívar died with a few of his belongings can be seen, and other paintings and memorabilia of the period are on display; US$2.50, open daily 0900-1700; take a bus or colectivo from the waterfront, Cra 1 C, to Mamatoca and ask for the Quinta, US$0.25.

Tours

Launches leave Rodadero beach every hour for the Aquarium, modest, not as good as the one at Islas del Rosario, US$3 return (includes admission), last boat back 1600. From the Aquarium, it's a 10-min walk to Playa Blanca where swimming is less crowded than elsewhere – food available at the beach. Small Indian figures are sculptured at José Pertuz, C 38, up the hill beyond Cra 17. They cut stone with traditional instruments and will chisel animals etc to order. They are sold on Rodadero beach. Punta Betín, behind harbour, marine eco-system research centre run by Colombian and German universities. Ask for details at the Tourist Office.

Local information
● **Accommodation**

In town: Av Rodrigo de Bastidas (Cra 1) has several seaside holiday hotels while Cra 2 and connecting Calles have many budget *residencias* in our E range.

A3 *Yuldama*, Cra 1, No 12-19, T 210063, F 214932, probably best in the city, a/c, reasonable food.

D *Bermuz*, C 13, No 5-16, T 210004. F 213625, good, also good vegetarian restaurant; **D** *Costa Azul*, C 17, No 2-09, T 232036, some rooms with a/c, fan, windows into courtyard, rec; **D** *Saratoga*, C 11, No 2-29, T 210644, a/c, less with fan, average, plain; **D** *Sompallón*, Cra 1, No 1 B-57, T 237195, modern, with *pizzería* and *casa de cambio*; **D** *Hostal Yuldama*, C 12, No 2-70, T 230057, a/c, cheaper without, modern, plain, safe deposit, rec.

E *Andrea Doria*, C 18, No 1C-90, T 234329, with bath and fan; **E** *Park*, Cra 1, No 18-67, T 211215, F 211574, on sea front, with shower, fan, reasonable, phone, popular with young Colombians; **E** *Residencial Familiar*, C 10 C No 2-14, bath, family-run, good breakfast, cooking facility, highly rec; **E** *Hotel Residencias Yarimar*, Cra 1A, No 26-37, fan, noisy; **E** *Residencia Nueva Granada*, C 12, No 3-19, large courtyard, quiet; **E** *Residencias Altamar*, C 10C, No 1C-68, safe; **E** *Residencias Bahía Blanca*, Cra 1, No 11-13, T 234439, private shower, fan, safe deposit, will store luggage, rec; **E** *Residencia Jomar*, Cra 2, No 18-22, fan, quiet, will store luggage.

F *Miramar*, C 10C, No 1C-59, "gringo hotel", tends to be crowded, robberies have often been reported, and be warned this is a dump, its popularity only because it is cheap, motorbike parking, restaurant, 2 blocks from railway station and beach, can arrange trips; not to be confused with **D** *Hotel Residencias Miramar*, Cra 1C, No 18-23, a/c, tidy, cheap, safe, no drugs, nice atmosphere.

Youth Hostel: *Hotel Nabusimake*, details from Alcom in Bogotá.

At Rodadero Bay: **L2** *Irotama*, Km 14, between airport and Rodadero Bay, T 218021, all inclusive, has bungalows; **A3** *La Sierra*, Cra 1, No 9-47, T 227960, F 228198, overlooking ocean, restaurant and cafeteria; **A2** *Arhuaco*, Cra 2, No 6-49, T 227234, 200m from beach, quiet, pool, bar; **A2** *Santamar* (Travelodge), 8 km from Rodadero towards airport, price is pp all inclusive (about half the price low season), T 218486, or 1-800-255-3050 toll free; **A2** *Tamacá*, Cra 2, No 11A-98, T 227015, direct access to beach, fair rooms, good service, fine pool; **A2** *Yuldama Rodadero*, Cra 3, No

10-40, T 229252, F 229232, a/c, pool, sauna. **B** *Mar Azul*, Cra 3, No 5-146, a/c, also has apartments.

C *El Rodadero*, C 11, No 1-29, T 227262, F 227371 swimming pool, English-speaking manageress, very helpful; **C** *La Riviera*, Cra 2, No 5-42, Apdo Aéreo 50-69, small, safe, a/c; **C** *Residencias Edmar*, Cra 3, No 5-188, T 227874, a/c, cafeteria, welcoming.

D *Tucuraca*, Cra 2, No 12-04, T 227493, fan, will store luggage; **D** *Valladolid*, Cra 2, No 5-67, T 227465, good value, large rooms, helpful, rec.

For groups of 4 or more, ask about apartments for short rent in the new buildings.

● **Places to eat**
In town: *Yarimar*, Cra 1A, No 26-37, good seafood; *El Gran Wah Yuen*, C 14, No 3-74, good Chinese *à la carte* and *comida corriente*, plenty of fresh vegetables; *Cafetería del Calle*, Cra 3A, No 16-26, good *empanadas*. Restaurant opp Telecom (C 13, Cra 5), good menu and vegetarian dishes.

At Rodadero Bay: *Pincho*, Cra 2, No 6-30, good food, moderate prices; *El Pibe*, C 6, No 1.26, steaks, Argentine run; *Pez Caribe*, Cra 4, No 11-35, sea food. There are also fast food restaurants and very good juice kiosks along the seafront.

● **Banks & money changers**
Change money at **Banco de Occidente**, good rates for Mastercard. **Banco Industrial Colombiano**, C 13 y Cra 5 for Amex TC exchange, but in am only. **Amex** office Tierra del Mar, C 15, No 2-60, T 33497. *Casas de cambio* in 3rd block of C 14, many others on this street. In Rodadero, Apto 201, Cra 1, No 9-23. Santa Marta is a good place to change pesos with Venezuelan bolívares.

● **Laundry**
Lavandería Paraíso, C 14, No 8C-47.

● **Security**
The N end of town, beyond the railway station, and areas nr, especially S of, Rodadero beach are very dangerous and travellers are advised not to go there alone. If you arrive by bus, beware taxi drivers who take you to a hotel of their choice, not yours. Also beware of 'jungle tours', or 'boat trips to the islands' sold by street touts.

● **Sports**
Diving: diving shops operate at Rodadero: *Buceo y Salvamento*, Edif Libertador, Cra 2 y C8 local 13, p 2, T 228179, 2 dives US$44 inc equipment; *Tienda de Buceo*, C 10 y Cra 2, Ed Playa Blanca, local 3, sells good equipment, but for trips sends you to *Pro-Buzos de Colombia*, C 14 No 9-170, Santa Marta, T 236383, 2 dives US$55, PADI certification US$150. There are many dive shops in Taganga: *Scuba Sport*,

Apdo 1275, T 217228, English and German spoken, offers bed and breakfast, 2 dives US$50; *Oceano Scuba Club*, Frente a la Playa, T 230325 (also at Carrera 44 No 70-56, Barranquilla, T 340857); *Centro de Buceo*, T 232422, 2 dives US$45, English spoken. You must check that a fully qualified dive master is present.

● **Tourist offices**
Tourist office in the former Convent of Santo Domingo, now Casa de Cultura, Cra 2, No 16-44, T 35773, open office hours Mon-Fri (has library and art exhibitions). There is also an office at Rodadero, C 10, No 3-10. **MA** office, C 12, No 16D-05, T 203116, F 204506, Urb Riascos, and at the Quinta de San Pedro Alejandrino. **Turcol** which arranges trips (details in text), Cra 1, No 22-77. **DAS Office**, C 27 y Cra 8.

● **Transport**
Air Simón Bolívar, 20 km from city; bus, US$0.25, taxi from Santa Marta, US$8.50, from Rodadero, US$3. During the tourist season, get to the airport early and book well ahead. Avianca, Cra 3A, No 17-09, T 210276.

Buses Terminal S of the city, towards Rodadero, taxi US$1.50 to centre, minibus US$0.30; US$3 to Rodadero. To **Bogotá**, 22 hrs, US$45, 4 a day; coming from the capital check that if the bus is continuing to Barranquilla, you will be dropped in Santa Marta, not short of it. Copetran to **Bucaramanga** about 9 hrs (US$22). Journey time will be affected by the number of police checks. There is a good meal stop at Los Límites. Buses to **Barranquilla**, 2 hrs (US$3.25); to **Cartagena**, 4-5 hrs (US$7.20, or US$9.10, Brasilia). To **Riohacha** US$3.45, 3 hrs to **Maicao**, US$9 a/c at 0500, also cheaper non a/c, 4-5 hrs. There are 3 buses a day (Brasilia) direct to **Rodadero Beach** from Barranquilla, taking 2 hrs and costing US$1.80. They return to Barranquilla at 1300, 1530 and 1730.

Port Without a *carnet de passages*, it can take up to 4 working days to get a car out of the port, but it is usually well guarded and it is unlikely that anything will be stolen. (See also under **Motorcycles** in **Information for travellers**.)

CIENAGA DE SANTA MARTA

All types of water birds, plants and animals may be seen in this large lagoon. Cutting off the egress to the sea to build the coast road caused an ecological disaster. A National Environment Programme, funded with the help of IDB, is working to reopen the canals and restore the area's fish and vegetation. On the E shore of the lagoon is **Ciénaga** (*pop* 75,000 – see **Music and dance** for festival). Cotton, bananas, tobacco and cacao are grown in the area.

Santa Marta Environs

Aracataca, 60 km S of Ciénaga and 7 km before Fundación, is the birthplace of Gabriel García Márquez, fictionalized as Macondo in some of his stories (notably *Cien años de soledad*). His home, called a museum, may be seen in the backyard of La Familia Iriarte Ahumada; ask for directions. There are *residencias* (**G**), but it is better to stay in **Fundación**. Banana growing in the area has now been replaced almost entirely by African palm plantations.

● **Accommodation** *Caroli*, Cra 8, No 5-30, best; **F** *Fundación* (**E** with a/c); **E** *Centro del Viajero*, with a/c, good value; others in this price range.

● **Buses** Ciénaga-Fundación, US$1; Fundación-Aracataca, US$0.20; an all weather road W from Fundación goes to Salmina on the Río Magdalena, ferry to Puerto Giraldo 0500-1800, then road to Sabanalarga, bus Fundación-Barranquilla, US$4.20.

TAGANGA

Close to Santa Marta (minibus US$0.30, taxi US$2.50, 10 mins) is the fishing village and beach of **Taganga**. Swimming good, especially on Playa Grande, 25 mins' walk round coast, but thieving is common there. Taganga is quiet during week, but trippers from Santa Marta pour in on Sun.

● **Accommodation A2** *La Ballena Azul*, most attractive, comfortable, restaurant, also run boat tours to secluded beaches, ask Mauricio about tours, horses for hire (postal address: Apdo Aéreo 799, Santa Marta, T 54-216668, F 54-217580, e-mail ballena@red-net.net.co); **B** *Bahía*, C 2, No 1-35, T 217620, overlooking bay, breakfast served on balcony, hospitable; **D** *Playa Brava*, fan or a/c, quiet, basic beds; **E** *El Delfín*, fan, basic. Joselito Guerra on the beach, **G** for hammock space, may charge for use of kitchen, secure for luggage. Restaurants expensive, but a good one is *Tibisay*, seafood.

Minca

A dirt road leads SE from Santa Marta through Mamatoco to a television relay centre on the high foothills of the Sierra Nevada, and on to Vistanieves. About 20 km along this road is **Minca**, at about 600m, surrounded by forests and coffee fincas. **E** *Hospedaje Las Piedras*, C de las Piedras on the banks of the Río Gaira, opened 1996, some rooms with bath, hot water, meals available, local excursions, mountain bikes and horses for hire. Also two hotels locally, *Sierra Nevada* and *Torcorama*. Regular jeeps leave market in Santa Marta for Minca, 40 mins.

TAYRONA NATIONAL PARK

The park extends from N of Taganga for some 85 km along the coast. The wild coastal woodland is beautiful and mostly unspoilt. You will see monkeys, iguanas and maybe snakes. In the wet, the paths are very slippery. The park is closed at times, check with MA in Santa Marta before visiting.

The entrance is at the E end of the park, 35 km from Santa Marta; it opens at 0800 (entry US$10). If you arrive earlier, you may be able to pay at the car park just before **Cañaveral**, 1 hr's walk into the park from the gate. 40 mins W of Cañaveral on foot is **Arrecifes**, from where it is 15 mins' walk to Rancho Viejo, then $1\frac{1}{2}$ hrs on a clear path to the archaeological site of **Pueblito**. A guided tour around the site is free, every Sat or as arranged, with a park guard. Other Tayrona relics abound. At Pueblito there are Indians; do not photograph them. From Pueblito you can either return to Cañaveral, or continue for a pleasant 2 hrs walk to Calabazo on the Santa Marta-Riohacha road. A circuit Santa Marta, Cañaveral, Arrecifes, Pueblito, Calabazo, Santa Marta in 1 day is arduous, needing a 0700 start at least.

It is advisable to inform park guards when walking in the park. Wear hiking boots and beware of bloodsucking insects. Take your own food and water, but no valuables as robbery is common. You may be able to hire donkeys for the Arrecifes-Pueblito stretch, US$5 each way, but watch them as these animals eat everything. Generally, there is litter everywhere along the main trails and around the campsites.

Beaches Bathing is not recommended near Cañaveral as there is often heavy pounding surf and the tides are treacherous, but the beach is less crowded and cleaner than Rodadero. 5 km E of Cañaveral are splendid, deserted sandy beaches; you have to walk there, but take care as the park borders drug-growing areas. 15-20 mins' walk left along the beach at Arrecifes (sea dangerous on this beach) is La Piscina, a beautiful, safe natural swimming pool, excellent snorkelling.

● **Lodging and camping At Cañaveral**: cabins for 4-6 persons, US$78-107/night pp (high season, 65-91 low, MA price), great views over sea and jungle, good restaurant. Campsite US$39/tent; has facilities, but only one restaurant with a tiny store, take all supplies; attractive site but plenty of mosquitoes. Beware of falling coconuts and omniverous donkeys. **At Arrecifes**: one campsite charges US$2.50 for tent, US$1.50 for hammock space, US$2 to hire hammock, US$3 for hut, fresh water shower and toilets; the other site is cheaper, with no electricity or showers. 3 restaurants of which *El Paraíso* is the most expensive; also a basic shop and guardroom for gear, soft drinks available. On the path to Pueblito there is a campsite at **Cabo** where the path turns inland, small restaurant and hammocks for hire; there are other camping and hammock places en route. You must obtain permission from MA to camp in the park if you are not staying at Cañaveral; this is normally forthcoming if you specify where you intend to stay. There is nowhere to stay at Pueblito.

● **Transport** To get to the park entrance, take a minibus from the market in Santa Marta, Cra 11 y C 11, about US$1, 45 mins, or go to the Riohacha road police checkpoint (taxi US$1 or bus to Mamatoca) and catch a bus there. Tourist bus from *Hotel Miramar* in Santa Marta daily at 1030, US$12 inc park entrance but not food. This hotel also arranges tours for US$80-100, very interesting but little care is taken over waste disposal. Other hotels help in arranging tours, but there is no need to take guides (who charge US$20 or more pp for a day trip). A boat can be hired in Taganga to go to Arrecifes, about 2 hrs along the scenic coast, US$80 for 8.

Beyond Cañaveral, along the coast, is **Palomino**. Tours can be arranged from there to Indian villages taking up to 6 days, cost around US$32/day. Enquire at Turcol in Santa Marta.

CIUDAD PERDIDA

Ciudad Perdida, discovered in 1975, was founded near the Río Buritaca between 500 and 700 AD and was surely the most important centre of the Tayrona culture. It stands at 1,100m on the steep slopes of Cerro Corea, which lies in the northern part of the Sierra Nevada de Santa Marta. The site covers 400 ha and consists of a complex system of buildings, paved footpaths, flights of steps and perimetrical walls, which link a series of terraces and platforms, on which were built cult centres, residences and warehouses. Juan Mayr's book, *The Sierra Nevada of Santa Marta* (Mayr y Cabal, Apdo Aéreo 5000, Bogotá), deals beautifully with the Ciudad Perdida.

Archaeologists and army guards will ask you for your permit (obtainable in Santa Marta, MA, Turcol or ask at tourist office). Ciudad Perdida is a National Park: it is strictly forbidden to damage trees and collect flowers or insects. Note also that there are over 1,200 steps to climb when you get there.

• **Access** One week trips organized by the tourist office and Turcol in Santa Marta (addresses above) cost US$250pp all inclusive: price includes mules, guide and food, 3 days' hike there, 1 day at site, 3 days back. Ask at hotels in Santa Marta (eg *Hotel Miramar*) or Taganga, or at Santa Marta market (Cra 11 y C 11) for alternative tours. Prices depend on the services required. If you are prepared to shop around and cook and carry your supplies and belongings, a tour could cost you less. Recommended guides: Frankie Rey, known to German tourists as 'die graue Eminenz', very knowledgeable, or Edwin Rey (ask at the tourist office about them), Donaldo, Wilson Montero, Edilberto Rey and Jairo García, who lives at the *Residencia Miramar*, in Santa Marta. There are many unscrupulous guides about, checking with the Tourist Office is recommended. If you want to see rainforest on the trek, insist on going via La Tagua (more beautiful, but more strenuous). A circuitous route to the site can be arranged through *Hotel La Ballena Azul* (above). It costs about US$250 pp for the 6-day round trip, all inclusive. Its advantage is that it avoids all settlements, especially in the drug-growing lower valleys and Kogi villages which may not welcome foreigners. Toyota jeeps go up to La Tagua (about 3 hrs), where it is possible to rent mules and pay local guides (but see above). You need to take a tent or a hammock and mosquito net (probably supplied by the guide), a good repellent, sleeping bag, warm clothing for the night, torch, plastic bags to keep everything dry, and strong, quick drying footwear. Check conditions, especially information on river crossings, and ensure you have adequate food, water bottle and water purifying tablets before you start. Try to leave no rubbish behind and encourage the guides to ensure no one else does. You can reach Ciudad Perdida by helicopter from Santa Marta in about 20 mins. Ask at Helicol, at the airport, at Tourist Office in Santa Marta, or at Aviatur, Edif Centro Ejecutivo, p 2, Santa Marta, T 213840, 15 days advance booking may be required. Price: about US$350 there and back with a 3 hr stay.

SANTUARIO LOS FLAMENCOS

The **Santuario de Fauna y Flora Los Flamencos** is 95 km E of Santa Marta and 25 km short of Riohacha. There are several small and two large saline lagoons (Laguna Grande and Laguna de Navío Quebrado), separated from the Caribbean by sand bars. The latter is near Camarones (colectivo from Riohacha, new market) which is just off the main road. 3 km beyond Camarones is "La Playa", a popular beach to which some colectivos continue at weekends. The two large lagoons are fed by several intermittent streams which form deltas at the S point of the lakes and are noted for the flamingoes which normally visit between Oct and Dec, ie during the wet season when some fresh water enters the lagoons. The birds are believed to migrate to and from the Dutch Antilles, Venezuela and Florida. Across Laguna de Navío Quebrado is a warden's hut on the sand bar, ask to be ferried across by local fishermen or the Park guards. The locals survive, after the failure of the crustaceans in the lagoons, on tourism and ocean fishing. There are several bars/restaurants and two stores on the beach.

RIOHACHA

Riohacha (*pop* 130,000), capital of Guajira Department, 160 km E of Santa Marta, is a port at the mouth of the Río César: low white houses, concrete streets, no trees or hills. It was founded in 1545 by Nicolás Federmann, and in early years its pearling industry was large enough to tempt Drake to sack it (1596). Pearling almost ceased during the 18th century and the town was all but abandoned. At the weekend, Riohacha fills up, and bars and music spring up all over the place. The sea is clean, despite the red silt stirred up by the waves.

Local information
● Accommodation
B *Arimaca*, C 1 y Cra 9, T 273481. **D** *Gimaura* (state-owned), Av La Playa, T 272266, inc breakfast, helpful, rec, they allow camping in their grounds, with outside shower.

E *Hostal Plaza*, C 2, No 9-74, pleasant, one block from sea and central plaza, two from Venezuelan consulate; **E** *International*, Cra 7, No 12A-31, patio, free iced water, rec.

F *Residencia Yalconia*, Cra 7, No 11-26, T 73487, private bath, safe, helpful, half way between beach and bus station. Near the bus station are: **F** *Panorama*, Cra 5, C 13/14; **F** *Tamiti*, opp *Panorama*; **F** *Tropical*, C 15, Cra 5/6.

● Places to eat
Glennpy, Av La Marina, S end, good, especially for fish. Many small restaurants along sea-front.

● Banks & money changers
Banco de Colombia, Cra 8, No 3-09; Banco de Bogotá, Cra 7, between C 2/3, for Visa.

● Embassies & consulates
Venezuelan: Cra 7, No 3-08 (hours 0900-1300, and closed from 1500 Fri to 0900 Mon). With two passport photographs, photocopy of passport and an exit ticket with date most can get a visa on the same day, if you get there early, but be prepared for an interview with the consul himself; visas cost US$30 and should not be a transit visa, valid for 72 hrs only. Travellers report it is easier to get a Venezuelan visa in Barranquilla.

● Post & telecommunications
Post Office: C 2, Cra 6/7. **Avianca** for airmail, C 7, No 7-104, T 273624, also airline ticket agency. Telecom, C 15/Cra 10, T 272528.

● Shopping
Good hammocks sold in the market. For mantas and other local items: *La Casa de la Manta Guajira*, Cra 6/C 12, be prepared to bargain; *Rincón Artesanal Dicaime*, C 2, No 5-61, T 273071; *Ojo de Agua*, C 2/Cra 9.

● Tour companies & travel agents
Guajira Tours, C 3, Cra 6-47, T 273385; *Administradores Costeños*, C 2, No 5-06, T 273393; *Guajira Viva*, agency in *Hotel Arimaca*, T 270607. All do tours to El Pájaro, Musichi, Manaure, Uribia and Cabo de Vela, leaving about 0600, 12-hr trip, US$40 pp, min 4 people.

● Tourist offices
Cortguajira, Cra 7/C 1, Av La Marina, T 272482, F 274728, well organized.

● Useful addresses
DAS Office (immigration): C 5, No 4-48, T 272407, open 0800-1200, 1400-1800.

● Transport
Air Airport José Prudencio Padilla is S of the town towards Tomarrazón.

Buses Main terminal is on C 15 (Av El Progreso)/Cra 11. (It is best to travel from Riohacha in a luxury bus, early am as these buses are less likely to be stopped and searched for contraband.) Some colectivos for Uribia and the NE leave from the new market 2 km SE on the Valledupar road.

ROUTES South of Riohacha on an alternative road to Maicao and the Venezuelan frontier is **Cuestecita** (*Hotel Turismo*; *Restaurant La Fogata*), where you can turn SW to **Barrancas**, one of the largest coal mines in the world – El Cerrejón.

VALLEDUPAR

Continuing on this road, which takes you either round the Sierra Nevada to Barranquilla and Santa Marta via Fundación (see above) or S to Bucaramanga, you come to **Valledupar**, capital of César Department (*municipal pop* 247,940). Valledupar claims to be the home of the *vallenato* music (see **Music and dance**). You can change money at *casas de cambio* on C 16.

Local information
● Accommodation
A3 *Vajamar*, Cra 7, No 16A-30, T 725121, pool, expensive food; **A3** *Sicarare*, 2-star, Cra 9, No 16-04, T 722137; cheaper 2-star hotel is **B** *Kurakata*, C 19C, No 7-96, T 724425; **F** *Residencia El Triunfo*, C 19, No 9-31, with bath, small rooms, fan, clean, good; next door is *Hotel/Restaurant Nutibara*, excellent cheap meals and breakfast, excellent fruit juices; several other hotels in this street.

● Transport
Air To Bogotá, Barranquilla and Bucaramanga.

Bus From Santa Marta, 6 hrs, from Cartagena, US$10 (with Expreso Brasilia); to Barranquilla, 4$\frac{1}{2}$ hrs, US$6; to Bucaramanga, 8 hrs US$20: a paved road runs S through Codazzi to the Santa Marta-Bucaramanga highway, Curumaní (*Hotel Himalaya*) and Aguachica.

THE SIERRA NEVADA DE SANTA MARTA

The Sierra Nevada, covering a triangular area of 16,000 sq km, rises abruptly from the sea, or from lowlands which nowhere reach over 300m above sea-level. "Indeed, the N slope is one of the most striking anywhere, lifting from the Caribbean to 5,800m snow peaks in about 45 km, a gradient comparable with the S face of the Himalaya, and unequalled along the world's coasts. The interior is made up of some eight E-W ranges with their intervening valleys. The lower parts of these interior valleys are flanked by forests – the homes of Indians as well as of pumas, jaguars, and a variety of snakes and birds – but for the most part the Sierra is almost lunar in its sterile grandeur, bleak *páramos* leading to naked crag and scree and glacier, where only an occasional questing condor moves. In the rocky heart of the area are a large number of small, beautiful lakes, many in cirques." – Frank F Cunningham, in an excellent illustrated article on exploring the Sierra in *The Geographical Magazine*. Hikes in the Sierra go through villages, valleys alive with butterflies, flowers and waterfalls, and to the lakes and the snowfields and summit of Pico Colón at 5,800m. The rainy season in these mountains ends Nov; Jan is best month for a visit.

The Indians of the Sierra do not take kindly to being photographed without permission. (Do not leave litter or disrespect the Indians' sacred grounds; stay on paths and do not stray on to private land.) They like to be given seashells which can be ground into powder and mixed with coca leaves. Learning a few words of their language can work wonders.

● **Access** Before leaving for the Sierra Nevada, check with MA, ONIC and ICAN in Bogotá (see page 852), the Fundación Pro-Sierra Nevada, Edif Los Bancos 502, Santa Marta, T 214697, F 214737, for information and guidance on what permits are required. It may be necessary to obtain a safe-conduct pass from Dra Eva Alonso at the Casa Indígena (45 mins out of town) in Valledupar if you are going further than San Sebastián.

● **Accommodation & transport** From Valledupar one route is along the Guatepuri valley. Another route is by jeep from Valledupar, Cra 7A, C 18, Nos 37-55, to Pueblo Bello, 2 hrs US$2 (less, 1 hr, from turn off main road to Pueblo Bello). In **Pueblo Bello** (**F** *Hotel El Encanto*, good meals US$1, friendly, but poor beds, hot, small, dark; **F** *Los Ensueños*, friendly, clean), enquire for jeeps to **San Sebastián de Rábago** (also called **Nabusimake**), the central village of one of the four tribes of Indians living in the Sierra, the Arhuacos (jeeps leave 0700-0800, 2-2½ hrs, US$3 to US$6 depending on conditions, dreadful road). It is set in beautiful surroundings and is the epitome of an Indian village with stone, thatched roof houses and local costumes. Ask for El Salto, a 2-hr walk, guide US$4.50 (not really needed). Jeep drivers may be able to arrange for you to stay on a farm; Doña Inés rec, **F** (arrange price on arrival), clean, friendly, good food. Also recommended is Ñoco, a mestizo who has lived in the valley for over 30 years; he has floor space, free camping (cold). Camping is also permitted in the valley.

● **Trekking** Very limited as the Arhuacos will not allow access deep into the Sierra. Climbing is not permitted (1997). Ñoco (see above) can arrange mules for trips (US$8.50/mule inc guide/day). Ñoco himself occasionally acts as guide if he is free (he runs a grocery store); he is very knowledgeable. Also recommended is Ricardo Olarté, C 22, No 16-61 Santa Marta, T 203413, who will arrange transport, food, accommodation for treks in the Sierra Nevada region and has a very good relationship with the local Indians. Before hiking in the Sierra, visitors must get permission from the Arhuaco chief in San Sebastián (at the police HQ); a charge may be made for whatever walk you are allowed to do, this ranges from US$7 to US$15. **NB** Information in mid 1997 indicates that no permissions are being granted at present to go into the high Sierra, but day trips with guides or on your own are permitted provided you report back the same day: for this, no charge is made. Walking upstream along the Río San Sebastián from the village is rec. There is plenty of drinking water, but Pueblo Bello is the only place to stock up with food. A tent is necessary for trekking (though not applicable in present circumstances). The best place for maps is Bogotá. Trekking tours to the Nevada de Santa Marta can be arranged in the Santa Marta area, check with the Tourist Office.

GUAJIRA PENINSULA

Beyond Riohacha to the E is the arid and sparsely inhabited **Guajira Peninsula**. The Indians here collect dividivi, tend goats, and fish. They are Guajiros, and of special interest are the coloured robes worn by the women. Sunsets in the Guajira are magnificent.

To visit a small part of the Peninsula take a bus from Riohacha (twice a day from the Indian market) to Manaure, US$2.40, 3 uncomfortable hrs through fields of cactus but offering fine views of flamingoes and other brightly coloured birds. **Manaure** is known for its salt flats SW of the town. If you walk along the beach past the salt works, there are several lagoons where flamingoes congregate. 14 km from Manaure in this direction is **Musichi**, an important haunt of the flamingoes, sometimes out of the wet season. From Manaure there are *busetas* to **Uribia** (US$1) and thence to Maicao. You can get *busetas* from Uribia to Puerto Bolívar (from where coal from El Cerrejón is exported) and from there transport to **Cabo de Vela**, where the lagoons seasonally shelter vast flocks of flamingoes, herons and sandpipers. It costs about US$3 from Uribia to Cabo de Vela. There are fine beaches.

● **Accommodation In Manaure**: G *Hotel Flamingo*; at **Uribia**: one basic *residencia*, no running water. **In Cabo de Vela**: a basic but friendly, Indian-run hotel, *El Mesón* (rooms, hammock veranda, showers, good meals – excellent fried fish), or sling a hammock at *El Caracol* where there is an expensive restaurant (better value next door at *La Tropicana* if you order food in advance). Also Conchita will hire out a large hut, hammocks for up to 5, cook food with prior request, along the coast, ask anyone.

MACUIRA NATIONAL PARK

Towards the NE tip of the Guajira peninsula is the Serranía de Macuira, a range of hills over 500m which create an oasis of tropical forest in the semi-desert. Moisture comes mainly from clouds which form in the evening and disperse in the early morning. Its remoteness gives it interesting flora and fauna and Indian settlements little affected by outsiders. To reach the area, you must travel NE from Uribia either round the coast past Bahía Portete, or direct across the semi-desert, to Nazareth on the E side of the park. There are no tourist facilities anywhere nearby and no public transport though trucks may take you from the Bahía Portete area to Nazareth, 6-8 hrs (if you can find one). You may be able to arrange

a trip in Riohacha, try Guajira Tours. Eco-Guias in Bogotá arrange trips here from time to time.

NB The Guajira peninsular is not a place to travel alone, parties of 3 or more are recommended. If going in your own transport, check on safety before setting out. Also remember it is hot, it is easy to get lost, there is little cover and very little water. Locals, including police, are very helpful in giving lifts.

MAICAO

The paved Caribbean coastal highway runs direct from Santa Marta to Riohacha, thence, paved to Maicao.

Maicao is full of Venezuelan contraband and is still at the centre of the narcotics trade. Its streets are unmade; most commercial premises close before 1600 and after 1700 the streets are unsafe.

Local information
● **Accommodation**

D *Maicao Juan Hotel*, Cra 10, C 12, T 8184, the only safe one; several others on Cra 10 and elsewhere; no reports.

● **Transport**

Buses to **Riohacha**, US$1.35; **Santa Marta** (Expreso Occidente), US$9; **Barranquilla**, last one at 1600, US$10.75. **Cartagena**, US$16.75. Colectivos, known as "por puestos" in Venezuela, Maicao-Maracaibo, US$5 pp, or infrequent microbus, US$3.30, very few buses to Venezuela after midday. Brasilia bus company has its own security compound: non-passengers are not allowed in (you can change money, buy bus tickets and food before journey). *Por puestos* wait here for passengers to Maracaibo; very easy transfer.

FRONTIER WITH VENEZUELA
● **Colombian immigration**

At the border. Entering Colombia by *por puesto* make sure the driver stops at the Colombian entry post. If not you will have to return later to complete formalities.

With all the right papers, border crossing is easy.

● **Venezuelan consulate**

There is now no Venezuelan Consul in Maicao. You must get a visa in Barranquilla, Cartagena or Riohacha. Entering Venezuela, everyone travelling overland should have a visa; a transit visa only will suffice if you have a confirmed ticket to a third country within 3 days.

SAN ANDRES AND PROVIDENCIA

Colombia's Caribbean islands of the San Andrés and Providencia archipelago are 480 km N of the South American coast, 400 km SW of Jamaica, and 180 km E of Nicaragua. This proximity has led Nicaragua to claim them from Colombia in the past. They are small and attractive, but very expensive by South American standards. Nevertheless, with their surrounding islets and cays, they are a popular holiday and shopping resort.

Being a customs-free zone, San Andrés is very crowded with Colombian shoppers looking for foreign-made bargains. Although alcoholic drinks are cheap, essential goods are extremely costly, and electronic goods are more expensive than in the UK.

The People

The original inhabitants, mostly black, speak some English, but the population has swollen with unrestricted immigration from Colombia. There are also Chinese and Middle Eastern communities. The population in 1992 was about 41,580 and is now estimated at 65,000.

Culture and festivals

20 July: independence celebrations on San Andrés with various events. Providencia holds its carnival in June.

San Andrés and Providencia are famous in Colombia for their music, whose styles include the local form of calypso, soca, reggae and church music. Concerts are held at the Old Coliseum (every Sat at 2100 in the high season); the Green Moon Festival is held in May. There is a cultural centre at Punta Hansa in San Andrés town (T 25518).

SAN ANDRES

San Andrés is of coral, some 11 km long, rising at its highest to 104m. The town, commercial centre, major hotel sector and airport are at the northern end. A picturesque road circles the island. Places to see, besides the beautiful cays and beaches on the eastern side, are the Hoyo Soplador (South End), a geyser-like hole through which the sea spouts into the air most surprisingly when the wind is in the right direction. The W side is less spoilt, but there are no beaches on this side. Instead there is The Cove, the island's deepest anchorage, and Morgan's Cave (Cueva de Morgan, reputed hiding place for the pirate's treasure) which is penetrated by the sea through an underwater passage. At The Cove, the road either continues round the coast, or crosses the centre of the island back to town over

San Andrés

Not to Scale

Punta Norte
Johnny Cay
Bahía Sardinas
Punta Hansa
Roca del Pescador
SAN ANDRES
Punta Paraíso
Bahía de San Andrés
Bahía Baja
El Acuario
Loma Alta
Haynes Cay
Cueva de Morgan
Lagoon
Cayo Rocoso
Punta Evans
San Luis
Sound Bay
Bahía El Cove
Smith Channel
Monte Derecho
La Piscinita
Elsie Bay Channel
Hoyo Soplador
Punta Sur

N

La Loma, on which is a Baptist Church, built in 1847.

Marine life and watersports

Diving off San Andrés is very good; depth varies from 3 to 30m, visibility from 10 to 30m. There are three types of site: walls of seaweed and minor coral reefs, large groups of different types of coral, and underwater plateaux with much marine life. 70% of the insular platform is divable.

Diving trips to the reef: *Buzos del Caribe*, Centro Comercial Dann, T 23712, offer diving courses and equipment hire; *Sharka Dive Shop*, T 25940, on the coast 10 mins from town, PADI advanced certificate course, US$250.

For the less-adventurous, take a morning boat (20 mins, none in the afternoon) to the so-called Aquarium (US$3 return), off Haynes Key, where, using a mask and wearing sandals as protection against sea-urchins, you can see colourful fish. Snorkelling equipment can be hired on San Andrés for US$4-5, but it is better and cheaper on the shore than on the island.

Pedalos can be rented for US$4/hr. Windsurfing and sunfish sailing rental and lessons are available from Bar Boat, road to San Luis (opp the naval base), 1000-1800 daily (also has floating bar, English and German spoken), and Windsurf Spot, *Hotel Isleño*, T 23990; water-skiing at Water Spot, *Hotel Aquarium*, T 23117, and Jet Ski. From Tominos Marina there are boat trips around the island. Bay trips for 2 hrs cost US$8.75, for 4 hrs US$17.50, including 3 free rum-and-cokes.

Beaches and cays

Boats go in the morning from San Andrés to Johnny Key with a white beach and parties all day Sun (US$3 return, you can go in one boat and return in another). Apart from those already mentioned, other cays and islets in the archipelago are Bolívar, Albuquerque, Algodón/Cotton (included in the Sunrise Park development in San Andrés), Rocky, the Grunt, Serrana, Serranilla and Quitasueño.

On San Andrés the beaches are in town and on the eastern coast. Perhaps the best is at San Luis and Bahía Sonora/Sound Bay.

Local information
● **Accommodation**

NB Some hotels raise their prices by 20-30% on 15 Dec.

A1 *Aquarium*, Av Colombia 1-19, T 23120, F 26174, all suites; **A1** *Casablanca*, Av Colombia y Costa Rica, T 25950, central, food; **A1** *Casa Dorada*, Av Las Américas, T 24008, salt water washing, reasonable food; *Decamerón*, road to San Luis Km 15, book through *Decamerón Cartagena*, T 655-4400, F 653-738, all-inclusive resort, pool, a/c, TV, good restaurant, rec; **A2** *Cacique Toné*, Av Colombia, No 5-02, T 24251, deluxe, a/c, pool, on sea-front; **A2** *El Isleño*, Av de la Playa 3-59, T 23990, F 23126, 2 blocks from airport, in palm grove, good sea views; **A2** *Royal Abacoa*, Av Colombia No 2-41, T 24043, good restaurant; **A3** *Bahía Sardinas*, Av Colombia No 4-24, T 23793, across the street from the beach, a/c, TV, fridge, good service, comfortable, no swimming pool; **A3** *El Dorado*, Av Colombia No 1A-25, T 24057, a/c, restaurant, casino, swimming pool; **A3** *Verde Mar*, Av 20 de Julio, T 25525, quiet, a/c, rec; **A3** *Viña del Mar*, Av de la Playa, 3-189, T/F 24791/28298, spacious rooms, close to beach and centre, bargain for a good price.

B *Capri*, Av Costa Rica No 1A-64, T 24315, a/c, good value.

C *Nueva Aurora*, Av de las Américas No 3-46, T 23811, fan, pool, restaurant.

D *Coliseo*, Av Colombia No 1-59, T 23330, noisy, good restaurant; **D** *Olga and Federico Archibold*, C de la Bodega Marlboro, No 91-18, T 25781, have 3 self-contained apartments, modern; **D** *Residencias Hernando Henry*, Av de las Américas 4-84, T 26416, restaurant, fan, good value, often full, on road from airport; also nr the airport, *Residencia Restrepo*, 'gringo hotel', Av 8 nr airport, noisy ('share a room with a Boeing 727'—till midnight), much cheaper than others, **E**, or less for a hammock in the porch, but you get what you pay for, the accommodation is in a poor state and the grounds are a junkyard, not rec. Opposite *Restrepo* is a tobacco/paper shop whose owner rents a/c apartments with kitchen, etc, **D**.

● **Places to eat**

Oasis (good), Av Colombia No 4-09; *El Zaguán de los Arrieros*, Av 20 de Julio (50m after cinema), good food and value; *Fonda Antioqueña Nos 1 and 2*, on Av Colombia nr the main beach, and Av Colombia at Av Nicaragua, best value for fish; *Sea Food House*, Av 20 de Julio, at Parque Bolívar, good cooking, not expensive, second floor terrace; excellent fruit juices at *Nueva China*, next to *Restrepo*, reasonable Chinese; *Fisherman's Place*, in the fishing cooperative at N end of main beach, very good, simple. Cheap fish meals can be bought at San Luis beach.

● Banks & money changers

Banco Industrial Colombiano, Av Costa Rica; **Banco de Bogotá** will advance pesos on a Visa card. **Banco Occidente** for Mastercard. Many shops will change US$ cash; it is impossible to change TCs at weekends.

● Tourist offices

Av Colombia No 5-117, English spoken, maps.

● Transport

Local Buses cover the eastern side of the island all day (15 mins intervals), US$0.30 (more at night and on holidays). **Taxis**: round the island,

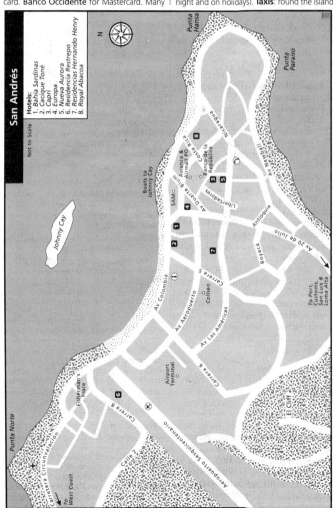

San Andrés

Hotels:
1. Bahia Sardinas
2. Cacique Toné
3. Capri
4. Europa
5. Nueva Aurora
6. Residencia Restrepo
7. Residencias Hernando Henry
8. Royal Abacoa

Not to Scale

US$8; to airport, US$3.50; in town, US$0.60; *colectivo* to airport, US$0.50. **Train**: a 'tourist train' (suitably converted tractor and carriages) tours the island in 3 hrs for US$4.50. **Vehicle rental**: bicycles are easy to hire, eg opp *El Dorado Hotel* – usually in poor condition, choose your own bike and check all parts thoroughly (US$1.10/hr, US$6/day); motorbikes also easy to hire, US$8 for min 2 hrs. Cars can be hired for US$15 for 2 hrs, with US$6 for every extra hour.

Air The airport is 15 mins' walk to town. All airline offices in town, except Aces at airport. Flights to most major Colombian cities with Avianca, Aces, Aero República and SAM (you can arrange a stop-over in Cartagena, which is good value). SAM also flies to Guatemala City, San José (also Aero Costa Rica) and Panama City. **NB** Panama, Costa Rica and Honduras all require onward tickets which cannot be bought on San Andrés, can be in Cartagena. (There are Panamanian and Costa Rican consulates in San Andrés.) For advice on purchasing tickets to Colombia via San Andrés, see page 985. The SAM office in San Andrés will not issue officially one way tickets to Central America. You buy a return, and SAM office on the mainland will refund once you show an onward ticket. The refund (less 15%) may not be immediate. However travellers report that you can purchase a one-way ticket at the SAM desk at the airport. Sun flights are always heavily booked, similarly July-Aug, Dec-January. If wait-listed, don't give up hope. Fares are changing all the time, so for best value, shop around both in Colombia and in Central America.

Ship Cruise ships and tours go to San Andrés; there are no other, official passenger services by sea. Cargo ships are not supposed to carry passengers to the mainland, but many do. If you want to leave by sea, speak only to the ship's captain. (Any other offer of tickets on ships to/from San Andrés, or of a job on a ship, may be a con trick.) The sea crossing takes 3-4 days, depending on the weather. In Cartagena, ships leave from the Embarcadero San Andrés, opposite the Plaza de la Aduana.

Boat Cooperativa de Lancheros, opp *Hotel Abacoa*.

PROVIDENCIA

Providencia, commonly called Old Providence (4,500 inhabitants), 80 km back to the N-NE from San Andrés, is 7 km long and is more mountainous than San Andrés, rising to 610m. There are waterfalls, and the land drops steeply into the sea in places. Superb views can be had by climbing from Casabaja/Bottom House or Aguamansa/Smooth Water to the peak. There are relics of the fortifications built on the island during its disputed ownership. Horse riding is available, and boat trips can be made to neighbouring islands such as **Santa Catalina** (an old pirate lair separated from Providencia by a channel cut for their better defence), and to the NE, Cayo Cangrejo/Crab Cay (beautiful swimming and snorkelling) and Cayos Hermanos/Brothers Cay. Trips from 1000-1500 cost about US$7 pp. Santa Catalina is joined to the main island by a wooden bridge. On the W side of Santa Catalina is a rock formation called Morgan's Head; from the side it looks like a man's profile.

On Providencia the three main beaches are Bahía Manzanillo/ Manchincal Bay, the largest, most attractive and least developed, Bahía del Suroeste/South West Bay and Bahía Agua Dulce/ Freshwater Bay, all in the SW.

Like San Andrés, it is an expensive island. There is no bank: exchange rates

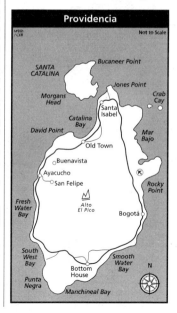

Providencia

Not to Scale

SANTA CATALINA

Bucaneer Point

Jones Point

Morgans Head

Crab Cay

Santa Isabel

Catalina Bay

David Point

Mar Bajo

Old Town

Buenavista

Ayacucho

San Felipe

Alto El Pico

Rocky Point

Fresh Water Bay

Bogotá

South West Bay

Smooth Water Bay

Bottom House

Punta Negra

Manchineal Bay

N

from shops and hotels are poor, or use credit cards. The sea food is good, water and fresh milk are generally a problem. English is widely spoken. Day tours are arranged by the Providencia office in San Andrés, costing US$30 inclusive. SAM flies from San Andrés, US$35, 25 mins, 6 times a day, bookable only in San Andrés. (Return flight has to be confirmed at the airport, where there is a tourist office.) Boat trips from San Andrés take 8 hrs, but are not regular.

Local information
● **Accommodation**

Most of the accommodation is at Freshwater (Playa Agua Dulce): **B** *Cabañas El Recreo* (Captain Brian's, T 48010); **A1** *Cabañas El Paraíso*, T 26330, a/c, TV, fridge; **B** *Cabañas Aguadulce Miss Elma's*, T 481600, rec for cheap food; also *Morgan's Bar* for fish meals and a good breakfast. On Santa Catalina is the German-owned *Cabañas Santa Catalina*, friendly, use of small kitchen. Several houses take in guests. Camping is possible at Freshwater Bay.

Up the Río Magdalena

THE old waterway from the Caribbean, now superseded by road and air, leads from Barranquilla to the limit of navigation at Girardot. The route passes snow-capped volcanoes and *tierra caliente* weekend resorts before climbing to the river's upper reaches entering Huila Department.

THE LOWER MAGDALENA

The Magdalena is wide but shallow and difficult to navigate because of surface eddies, and there are little whirlpools over submerged rocks. Away to the NE in the morning, one can see the high snow-capped peaks of the Sierra Nevada de Santa Marta. Passenger travel by the lofty paddle boats on the river has come to an end, though the adventurous traveller may still find an occasional passage by cargo paddle boat. In general the only way of getting from one place to the other along the river is by motor launch (*chalupa*). The river trip from the N coast (bus to Magangué) to Puerto Berrío or Puerto Boyacá and thence by bus to Bogotá can be completed in about 4 days.

Insect repellents should be taken, for mosquitoes are a nuisance. Guerrilla activity has been reported in the Magdalena

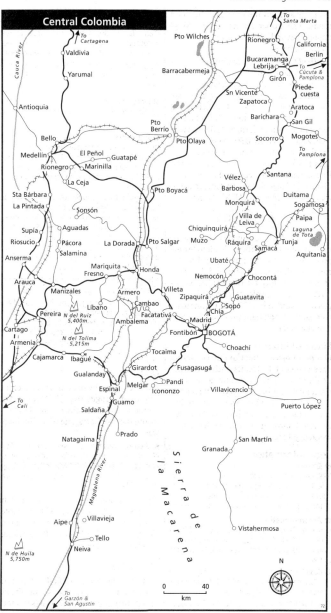

Central Colombia

Cauca River

To Cartagena

Valdivia
Yarumal

Antioquia

Bello
Medellín
El Peñol Guatapé
Rionegro Marinilla
La Ceja

Sta Bárbara
La Pintada
Sonsón

Supía
Aguadas
Riosucio Pácora
Anserma Salamina

Arauca
Mariquita
Fresno Honda
Manizales
Pereira N del Ruiz Líbano Cambao
5,400m Armero
Cartago N del Tolima Ambalema
Armenia 5,215m
Cajamarca Ibagué
Gualanday
To Espinal Melgar
Cali Guamo Icononzo Pandi
Saldaña
Natagaima Prado

Aipe Villavieja
Tello
N de Huila Neiva
5,750m

To Garzón & San Agustín

Pto Wilches
Rionegro California
Berlín
Bucaramanga
Barracabermeja Lebrija To
Girón Cúcuta & Pamplona
Sn Vicente Piede-
Zapatoca cuesta
Barichara Aratoca
Pto San Gil
Berrío Socorro Mogotes
Pto Olaya To
Pamplona
Santana
Vélez Santana
Barbosa
Pto Boyacá Monquirá Duitama
Villa de Sogamosa
Chiquinquirá Leiva Paipa
Muzo Ráquira Laguna
La Dorada Pto Salgar Samacá de Tota Tunja
Ubaté Aquitania
Nemocón Chocontá
Villeta Guatavita
Zipaquirá Sopó
Facatativá Chía
Madrid
Fontibón BOGOTÁ
Tocaima Choachí
Girardot Fusagasugá
Villavicencio
Puerto López

San Martín
Granada

S
i
e
r
r
a
d
e
l
a
M
a
c
a
r
e
n
a

Vistahermosa

Magdalena River

0   40
km

N

valley away from the river and the main roads. The upper reaches of the Magdalena, beyond Neiva, are dealt with on pages 963-968.

South of Calamar, the terminus of the Canal del Dique, is Tenerife, where Bolívar had his first victory in the Magdalena campaign. At **Zambrano** (96 km; *pop* 8,210, **E** *España*, with bath, good), a cattle and tobacco centre, there is a road W to the N-S Cartagena-Medellín road at El Carmen de Bolívar, jeep from Zambrano, US$0.30. On the opposite (E) shore is Plato from where another road goes 108 km through to the Santa Marta-Bucamaranga road across the flat flood plain of the Magdalena valley. Chalupa from Zambrano to Mompós, US$5, 2½ hrs.

MOMPOS

Near Pinto the river divides: the eastern branch, silted and difficult, leads to Mompós (also written Mompóx) (*pop* 10,810): cattle farming and tobacco, and the scene of another victory for Bolívar: "At Mompós", he said, "my glory was born." Mompós was founded in 1537 and, thanks to its comparative isolation, preserves its colonial character.

Places of interest

Old buildings are the Casa de Gobierno, once a home of the Jesuits, and the Colegio de Pinillos. There are 7 churches and the Easter celebrations are said to be among the best in Colombia. The cemetery has considerable historical interest. The town is well known in Colombia for hand-worked gold jewellery.

Local information
● **Caution**
Malaria is endemic in the surrounding countryside. If staying overnight, mosquito nets and/or coils are a must. Drinking fruit juices is not rec nr the river, glasses may be washed in river water.

● **Accommodation**
C *Hostal Doña Manuela*, C Real del Medio (Cra 2), 17-41, T 55620, a converted colonial house, quiet and peaceful, restaurant is the best in town.

D *Residencias Aurora*, shower, fan, good meals, bargaining possible; **D** *Residencias Unión*, C 18, No 3-43, with fan.

E *San Andrés*, Cra 2, No 18-23, T 855886,

modern, with bath, fan, TV, central, restaurant; **E** *Residencias Villas de Mompós*, 500m E of Plaza Tamarindo, family run, free coffee; **E** *Posada de Vinney*, opp *Doña Manuela*, shared bath, modern, above medical practice.

F *Residencias Solmar*, C Cra 18-22, nr main square, basic, but you are welcomed with a "tinto".

● **Places to eat**
El Galileo, next to the Plaza, good *comida corriente*.

● **Transport**
Buses From Cartagena with Unitransco (0530, returns 0700), daily, 12 hrs, US$9.50, otherwise take Brasilia bus to **Magangué** 4½ hrs, US$8.50. Buses also go to **Barranquilla** and **Sincelejo**.
To **Valledupar** and **Santa Marta**, either go from El Banco (see below), or cross the river at **Talaigua** (between Mompós and Magangué, *carritos* leave Mompós early am) to **Santa Ana**. Buses leave Santa Ana 0700 for Santa Marta and Valledupar, first 2½ hrs unpaved, then paved; US$8 to Valledupar. For Sierra Nevada alight at Pueblo Bello crossroads.

NB Most *chalupas* and buses run in the morning. There is little public transport after 1400.

River From Magangué you have to take a *chalupa* (launch) either direct to Mompós, 2 hrs, US$3.30, or to Bodega, ¾ hr, and thence by jeep or taxi 1½ hrs, US$2. You can also reach Mompós in 2 hrs US$4 by *chalupa* from El Banco to the SE.

MAGANGUE

Most vessels go by the western arm of the loop to **Magangué** (*pop* 61,265), the port for the savannas of Bolívar. A road runs W to join the N-S Cartagena-Medellín highway.

● **Accommodation** 5 hotels inc **D** *Hans Burchardt*, a/c, fridge; 10 *residenciales*, cheapest *Londres*, *Brasil* or *Hotel Medellín*, all **G** pp. Few places to eat, *Terraza*, to the left of plaza, reasonable.

Upstream from Magangué, the Río San Jorge, 379 km long, 240 km of it navigable, comes in from the Western Cordillera. Further up, the Río Cauca, 1,020 km long, comes in from the far S.

EL BANCO

At **El Banco** (*pop* 10,250), 420 km from Barranquilla, the river loops join. This is an old, dirty and beautiful town (see under

Music and dance for festival). Along the river front are massive stone stairways. The Cordilleras are in the distance, a blue range on either side of the valley. Egrets, various species of heron, ringed kingfishers much in evidence.

● **Accommodation** **D** *Central*, nr church, modern, fan; **E** *Continental*, nr jeep terminal; **E** *Casa del Viajero*, C 8, colour TV, fan, bath, safe; **F** *Colonial*, 1 block from harbour, with bath and fan; **G** pp *Residencia Ocaña*, basic, noisy; **G** *Residencia Edén*, C 9, free coffee; about a dozen others.

● **Transport Buses** Daily buses from El Banco to Bucaramanga, US$15, Cúcuta and Valledupar. Bus from Cartagena 0800, US$8. Don't get conned into taking an expensive boat across the river instead of the bus ferry. **River** *Chalupa* service El Banco-Barrancabermeja with Cootransfluviales, 0800, 7 hrs, US$16, trip rec.

Continuing upriver are the small towns of **Puerto Boca, Tamalameque** (basic *residencia* and restaurant), La Gloria, **Gamarra** (*pop* 3,700), San Pablo and **Puerto Wilches** (*pop* 5,600). All are connected by launch.

To the E of the river is the main road from the coast to Bucaramanga and, eventually, Bogotá. 100 km N of Bucaramanga at San Alberto, a new road has been completed which runs comparatively close to the Magdalena some 400 km to Honda. This is now by far the fastest road from the capital to the Caribbean.

BARRANCABERMEJA

Some 30 km above Puerto Wilches and 30 km from this new road is **Barrancabermeja** (or more commonly Barranca – *pop* 135,955), so called because of the reddish-brown oil-stained cliffs on which it stands. It is an important oil refining centre. It is also a warm, humid place with an interesting indoor market.

Local information
● **Accommodation**
C *Achue*, Cra 17, No 9-12, T 222500, a/c, restaurant, safe.

F *Hostal Real*, opp station, hot water, pleasant owner, safe (locked day and night), restaurant, good value; **F** *Residencias Ferroviario*, with bath, opp railway station; **F** *Santa Fe*, in town, pleasant; many more around the train station and in town. A shop at C 19, Avs 18 y 19 sells good bread and muesli.

● **Banks & money changers**
Banco de Bogotá will change TCs.

● **Transport**
Air 10 mins by taxi from centre, 2 daily flights to Bogotá, Aces.

Trains To Medellín, daily 0500, US$10-12, 15 hrs.

Buses Bucaramanga, 3 hrs, US$2.30; Medellín, 1045, US$17.

River Boat: *Chalupa* to Puerto Boyacá, 0845, 6 hrs, US$12. Several daily to El Banco, 7 hrs, US$15.

PUERTO BERRIO

(*Pop* 25,200) On the W bank 100 km above Barrancabermeja and 756 km from Barranquilla, this is the river port for Medellín and Antioquia Department. A railway from Medellín runs down the slopes of the Cordillera Central and over a low pass to Puerto Berrío, where it connects with the Bogotá-Santa Marta line.

● **Accommmodation & places to eat** **E** *Hotel Magdalena*, pleasant, on a hilltop nr river; **F** *Residencias El Ganadero*, with bath, modern, with ceiling fans. Many others. *La Buena Mesa*, good big meals; *Heladeria Joi*, good ice-cream and sundaes.

● **Transport** Train to **Santa Marta** and **Medellín**, check if trains are running at **Grecia** station, 4 km from the town (taxi service only). There is an airport with flights to Medellín.

UPRIVER FROM PUERTO BERRIO

Puerto Boyacá (75 km; **B** *Palagna*, a/c, large pool, good restaurant, TV, good value; also several *residencias*); there has been guerrilla activity in the area.

● **Transport Buses** Rápido Tolima has regular buses to Honda (3 hrs, US$2.70) on the Medellín-Bogotá highway. **River** To Puerto Berrío US$4.10.

La Dorada (*pop* 56,220), a further 76 km, on the W bank, linked by a bridge from **Puerto Salgar**, on the E bank. The Medellín-Bogotá crosses here.

● **Accommodation** La Dorada: **F** *Rosita*, C 17, No 3-28, T 72301, with bath, pleasant, rec; others nr railway station; youth hostel at *Centro Vacacional La Magdalena*, 3 km from La Dorada – details from Alcom in Bogotá – *Parador Turístico* next door. **Puerto Salgar**: **G** *Residencia Antioquia*, with fan.

• **Transport** Bus to **Bogotá** via Honda (see next section), 5 hrs, US$8.50; to **Medellín** US$12.

The Lower Río Magdalena navigation stops at La Dorada as there are rapids above, as far as Honda. There are no passenger services S of Puerto Boyacá. The Upper Magdalena is navigable as far as Girardot (see below).

THE UPPER MAGDALENA

HONDA

Honda (*pop* 25,481; *av temp* 29°C; *alt* 230m) on the W bank of the river, is 32 km upstream from La Dorada (149 km from Bogotá).

Places of interest It is a pleasant old town with many colonial houses. It has an interesting indoor market and a small museum. The streets are narrow and picturesque, and the town is surrounded by hills. El Salto de Honda (the rapids which separate the Lower from the Upper Magdalena) are just below the town. Several bridges span the Ríos Magdalena and the Guali, at whose junction the town lies. In Feb the Magdalena rises and fishing is unusually good. People come from all over the region for the fishing and the festival of the Subienda, as the season is called.

• **Accommodation**   C *Campestre El Molino*, 5 km from Honda on Mariquita road, T 3130, swimming pools, fans in rooms; C *Ondama*, C 17 y 13A, T 3565, swimming pool; D *Club Piscina*, Cra 12, No 19-139, T 3273, fan, swimming pool, arranges safe parking, rec; E *Residencias Las Mercedes*, with bath.

• **Places to eat** *La Cascada*, overlooking river, good. There is a row of good cheap restaurants across the Río Magdalena bridge in Puerto Bogotá.

• **Buses** From **Bogotá** by Velotax US$4.80, and Rápido Tolima, US$3, 4 hrs. **Manizales**, US$3.60. Rápido Tolima run ½-hourly buses to **La Dorada** (1 hr), and beyond, to **Puerto Boyacá** (3 hrs), US$2.70. The Bogotá-Medellín highway passes round the town.

MARIQUITA

West from Honda a paved road goes to **Mariquita** (21 km; *pop* 13,000), in fruit-growing country, and **Fresno** (a further 30 km), the heart of a coffee growing area. The road continues up the slopes of the Central Cordillera to Manizales (83 km).

Mariquita (founded 1551) has several old houses and buildings: a mint, the viceroy's house, the parish church. Here José Celestino Mutis lived for 8 years during his famous Botanic Expedition towards the end of the 18th century (he and his helpers accumulated a herbarium of 20,000 plants, a vast library, and a rich collection of botanical plates and paintings of native fauna, now held in Madrid).

• **Accommodation**   C *Las Acacias*, on Armero road, T 522016; D *San Felipe*, 8 km from Mariquita on Armero road, good, pool, restaurant with slow service; and others; campsites.

• **Buses**   From Honda, Rápido Tolima, US$0.35, 30 mins; same company to Manizales.

From Mariquita the road turns S to (32 km) **Armero**, which was devastated by the eruption of the Nevado del Ruiz volcano (see page 946) in Nov 1985. Over 25,000 people were killed as approximately 10% of the ice core melted, causing landslides and mudflows. (Armero can be reached by colectivo from Honda; nearest lodging at **Lérida**, 12 km S.)

IBAGUE

The main road from Armero goes direct for 88 km to **Ibagué**, capital of Tolima Department. It is a large city (*pop* 386,425; *alt* 1,250m), lying at the foot of the Quindío mountains. It is cooler here (22°C) than in the valley.

Places of interest

Parts of the town are old: see the Colegio de San Simón and the market. The Parque Centenario is pleasant. The city specializes in hand-made leather goods (there are many good, cheap shoe shops) and a local drink called *mistela*. There is an excellent Conservatory of Music.

Local festivals

National Folklore Festival, third week of June. The Departments of Tolima and Huila commemorate San Juan (24 June) and SS Pedro y Pablo (29 June) with bullfights, fireworks, and music.

Local information
● Accommodation
A3 *Ambala*, C 11, No 2-60, T 610982, F 633490, TV, pool, restaurant.

D *Ambeima*, Cra 3, No 13-32, T 634300;
D *Farallones*, C 16, No 2-88, good, fan, and opp **D** *Cordillera*, also good.

E *Bolívar*, C 17 y Cra 4, good, TV; **E** *Bram*, C 17 y Cra 4, convenient, secure, insect-free, cold water; **E** *Residencia Puracé*, opp Tolima bus station; nearby **F** *La Paz*, C 18, No 3-119, free tinto in am.

F pp *Montserrat*, C 18, Cra 1 y 2, quiet, rec; **F** *Boston*, nr bus station, basic.

● Places to eat
24-hr restaurants inc *Punto Rojo*, in the shopping precinct on Cra 3, good lunch; *El Espacio*, Cra 4, No 18-14, large helpings, good value. Vegetarian, *Govinda*, Cra 2 y C 13.

● Tourist offices
Cra 3, between Cs 10 and 11; helpful; closed Sat and Sun. The Instituto Geográfico Agustín Codazzi has an office at C 14A, No 3-14, p 3, for maps.

● Transport
Bus terminal is between Cras 1-2 and C 19-20. Tourist police at terminal helpful. To **Bogotá**, US$8 Expreso Palmira 0915, 4 hrs; also buses to **Pereira**, **Cali** and **Popayán**. To **Neiva**, US$7.

NEVADO DEL TOLIMA

Just outside, on the Armenia road, a dirt road leads to the slopes of the **Nevado del Tolima**, southernmost 'nevado' in the **Parque Nacional Los Nevados**. Gerhard Drekonja of Vienna writes: For climbing the Nevado del Tolima (5,215m) go from Ibagué to Juntas and El Silencio (2 hrs by train if running). From there 30 mins walk to the fabulous natural thermal waters of El Rancho (simple sleeping accommodation and food available). The climb starts from El Rancho. It takes 8 to 10 hrs to the top; equipment (crampons and pica) indispensable. The final climb has to be done at sunrise because clouds and mist invariably rise around 0800. From the top is a breathtaking view across the other snowcapped mountains of the Cordillera Central.

● Information and guides
Admission US$10, car US$4, camping US$32 (US$25 low season). For information contact Cruz Roja Colombiana in Ibagué, Zona Industrial El Papayo, near the E entrance to the city, T 646014, who can put you in touch with a climbing group,

Asociación Tolimense de Montañistas y Escaladores. Helpful guides are: Claus Schlief, who speaks German and English; Manolo Barrios, who has some Himalayan experience and is well rec, ask for information at the Cruz Roja; Fernando Reyes, Cra 11, No 1-21, Barrio Alaska, Ibagué, T 639027, who will take you rock or ice climbing on Tolima at about US$15/day. He can also arrange accommodation, supply equipment and make and repair backpacks.

The Quindío Pass, 3,350m (commonly called *La Línea* after the power lines that cross the mountains here) is on the road to Armenia, 105 km W of Ibagué across the Cordillera Central. At night, fog, reckless drivers and stray animals make the pass hazardous. On the E side of the Pass is **Cajamarca**, a friendly town in a beautiful setting at 1,900m (**G** *Residencia Central*; *Nevado*, both on same street). *Bar El Globo*, on the corner of the main plaza worth a visit, excellent coffee from an ancient *Aguila Roja* machine, and notice the instruction above the pool tables "*Por favor no limpia las manos sobre las mesas*". Interesting market on Sun.

GIRARDOT

79 km E of Ibagué is **Girardot** (*pop* 80,040; *alt* 326m), on the Upper Magdalena. The road from Ibagué runs through **Gualanday** (accommodation; restaurants), joining the highway from Bogotá at **Espinal**, an important agro-industrial town (*pop* 42,780; **B** *Hotel Yuma*, T 4323; **F** *Hotel Bucaros*, central, with bath, restaurant, 1 hr by bus from Ibagué.

At Girardot, the climate is hot and there are heavy rains. Bogotanos come down here at weekends to warm up. Here the navigation of the Upper Magdalena ends, although in dry weather boats cannot get this far. Large cattle fairs are held on 5-10 June and 5-10 December. Launch rides on the river start from underneath the bridge. A 1-hr trip to Isla del Sol is recommended (US$9).

● Accommodation
A2 *El Peñón*, on site of former *hacienda* just outside town, Cra 16, No 79-31, T 34981, fashionable bungalow complex, casino, huge swimming, lake, price/bungalow; **B** *Bachué*, Cra 8, No 18-04, T 34791, modern, large cooled pool, excellent, a/c, restaurant; **D** *Nuevo Río*, Cra 10, No 16-31, TV, fan, res-

taurant, laundry, English and German spoken;
D *Los Angeles*, on main plaza, rec; **E** *Miami*,
Cra 7, No 13-57, large rooms, fan, good, central
location safe. Opp new bus terminal, **F** *El Cid*,
with fan and **F** *Maroti*; **F** *Rincón*, C 19, No
10-68, balcony, fan.

● **Shopping** There is a 2-storey market, at its
best in early morning but nevertheless good all
day, and another good market on Sun mornings.

● **Buses** To Bogotá, 132 km, US$7, 3½ hrs;
to Neiva, US$3, 3½ hrs. To Fusagasugá, US$2.

South of Girardot the highway and the
Río Magdalena continue to Neiva. Coffee
and tobacco are grown on the slopes, and
cattle are raised in the valley. 35 km S of
Girardot is **Guamo** (*pop* 13,340). Just before Guamo is a marked turn off to **La
Chamba**, where internationally famous
pottery is made and sold.

A pretty spot is the reservoir located
near **Prado**, Tolima, 25 km E of Saldaña;
it is well signposted. There is a dirt road
for the last 12 km past Purificación, where
you cross the Magdalena. Buses can be
caught in Bogotá, Ibagué and all intermediate towns. The pretty part of the lake is
hidden from the end of the road and must
be seen from a boat. Take an official boat
trip from the mooring-point down the
slope at the end of the road (food is available here). Swimming is good and the
water is warm, but wading is not advisable because of the fresh-water stingray.

● **Accommodation At Guamo**: *Lemayá*,
Cra 8 y C 9, T 270230; modern, swimming pool,
best in region. **At Prado**: cheap hotels; basic
restaurants. **At the Lake**: government hotel,
B in cabin, **D** in room, pleasant; free camping
on shore.

37 km before Neiva you can turn left,
cross a fence, and see the **Piedra Pintada
de Aipe**, a stone not in fact painted but
carved by precolumbian Indians with designs akin to the shapes of some of the
pieces in the Museo del Oro at Bogotá.

About 50 km N of Neiva is a small area
(300 sq km) of scrub and arid eroded red
soil known as the **Tatacoa** desert, with
large cacti, isolated mesas and unusual
wildlife. Bus from Neiva to Villavieja,
near the Río Magdalena, and the Neiva-
Bogotá highway at Aipe daily 1030, 1½
hrs, US$2. Contact Nelson Martínez
Olaya, an official tourist guide at the

Restaurant La Tatacoa, Villavieja, Cra 4,
No 7-32, for 4/5 hr walks through the
desert. There is also a museum showing
prehistoric finds in the area. You can cross
the Magdalena by motorized canoe near
Villaviejo for US$0.75.

NEIVA

The capital of Huila Department, **Neiva**
(*pop* 248,000; *alt* 470m) was first founded
in 1539, when Belalcázar came across the
Cordillera Central from Popayán in quest
of El Dorado. It was soon after destroyed
by the Indians and refounded in 1612. It
is now a pleasant, modern city on the E
bank of the Río Magdalena.

Places of interest
There is an interesting monument to the
struggles for independence by the riverside. There are rich coffee plantations
around Neiva, for here the valley bottom
is high enough to be in the coffee zone.
The cathedral was destroyed by earthquake in 1967. There is a large and colourful market every day. Tourist information
is given at the cultural centre with museum and gallery on the main square.

Local festivals
18 to 28 June, when the Bambuco Queen
is elected: folklore, dances and feasting.

Local information
● **Accommodation**
B *Anayaco*, C 8, No 3-26, T 713044, a/c, TV;
B *Sulicam*, Cra 3, No 5-51, T 713062,
F 710159, restaurant; **B** *Tumburagua*, C 5A,
No 5-40, T 729165, rec.

C *Hostería Matamundo*, in old *hacienda* 3
km from centre, on road to Garzón and San
Agustín, T 727778, a/c, swimming pool, restaurant, disco.

D *Americano*, Cra 5, No 8-67, T 729240,
swimming pool; **D** *Plaza*, C 7, No 4-62,
T 723980, swimming pool, fan, pleasant, restaurant, disco.

E *Central*, Cra 3, No 7-82, meals, nr market,
good value, rec.

F *Residencias Astoria*, C 6, No 1-41, shared
bath, big rooms; **F** *Residencia Magdalena*, C
1A Sur, No 8A-57, T733586, close to new bus
station, restaurant.

● **Places to eat**
Hostería Los Cerros, C 11, No 32-39; *El*

Caimo, C 8, No 7A-22; *Los Gauchos*, Cra 15, No 5-12; *Neiva Viejo*, C 9, No 6-49; *Heladería La Pampa*, Pasaje Camacho 8, excellent juices.

● **Banks & money changers**
Banco Industrial, nr Parque Santander, will change US$ cash and TCs.

● **Tourist offices**
Inderena, C 10, No 6-61, T 722580 (Sra María Cristina Sánchez).

● **Transport**
Air La Marguita, 1½ km from city. Aires flies from **Bogotá** daily; also Medellín, Cali, Ibagué, Florencia, Leguizamo and Puerto Asís. Taxi to bus terminal about US$0.85 (overcharging probable).

Buses New bus station out of town; bus from the centre leaves from the old terminal (Cra 2, Cs 5 y 6). To **Bogotá** (331 km, paved road), 5½ hrs, US$10.50. Regular bus service with Autobuses Unidos del Sur, Cootranshuila (0600) and Coomotor to **San Agustín**, US$6, 5½ hrs (US$5.40 by colectivo). To **Garzón**, US$3.60; to **Pitalito**, US$5. To **La Plata**, for Tierradentro, US$5. To **Espinal**, 3 hrs, US$2.40, good road except for stretch between Aipe and Nataguima. To **Pasto**, US$10.75; to **Popayán**, US$9.25, ordinary bus at 0330, 1000, 1500, 1930, 11 hrs poor road; to **Florencia**, US$7.80. To **Ibagué** at 1200, US$7.

    Warning At the bus stations, both off and on buses, in Neiva, Garzón and especially Pitalito, theft is rife.

South of Neiva lie the plains of Huila Department, arid, but still capable of supporting cattle, dominated by the snow-capped Nevado del Huila to the NW (see page 961).

Antioquia and Chocó

MEDELLIN, the capital of Antioquia Department, is a major industrial centre yet, for all the factories and commerce, the surrounding countryside is green, mountainous (but much is cultivated) and pleasant. From the Cordillera Central to the Pacific stretches Chocó Department, thickly wooded, mountainous and undeveloped, but rewarding to explore.

The Central Cordillera lies W of the Río Magdalena. In it are several of the most important cities in Colombia: Medellín, the second largest city in the country, Manizales, Pereira and Armenia. The last three are in the heart of the coffee growing area and are covered in the next section.

HISTORY AND SETTLEMENT

The town of Santa Fé de Antioquia was founded in 1541, but the Spaniards, eager for gold, were not interested in the hinterland, which was then very sparsely inhabited by nomadic Indians who made very poor agricultural labourers. But during the 17th century a new wave of settlers came to Colombia from Spain; many of them were Jewish refugees who were deliberately seeking isolation, and found it in the little valley of the Río Aburrá, where they founded the city of Medellín in 1616. Rather than *conquistadores*, they were farmers with their families, intermarrying very little with either Indian or black. They divided the land into small farms which they worked themselves, living on the food they themselves produced. Their only exports were a little gold and silver from their streams.

In the early 19th century the settlement began to expand, particularly to the S. The settlers occupied all the cultivable land on the western side of the Central Cordillera and Manizales, 120 km S, was founded in 1848.

It was coffee, introduced in the Magdalena valley about 1865, that brought stability to this expansion. They were slow to adopt it, none being exported from Antioquia before the end of the century. The 1914-18 war suddenly gave a fillip to the industry: within 20 years the Departments of Antioquia and Caldas were producing half the coffee of Colombia, and, together with Quindío and Risaralda, they are by far the most important producers today. The industrialization of Medellín followed the coffee boom. There has been little immigration since the original settlement, but the natural growth in population has been extraordinary. Antioquia is considered by many to be the cultural heartland of Colombia. Its residents, referred to as "Paisas", are renowned for their distinctive accent and customs.

MEDELLIN

Medellín (*pop* 1.7mn; *alt* 1,487m; *phone code* 94), capital of Antioquia Department, is set in a comparatively narrow valley surrounded by forbidding mountain barriers in nearly all directions. Its climate is generally warm and pleasant though it is often cloudy and rain can come at any time. Medellín is one of the main industrial cities of Colombia, and seethes with energy. The first looms arrived in 1902. Today the city produces more than 80% of the textile output of the country, and tex-

tiles account for only half its industrial activity. Other major local industries are brick making, leather goods and plastics. A fine new Metro gives easy communication across the expanding city. In the S, El Poblado has become an up-market residential area and many companies have moved their headquarters there from the centre. The best hotels and restaurants are in or near El Poblado. Around Cra 70 and C 44 are busy commercial and entertainment sectors with many new hotels, shopping centres and the huge Atanasio Girardot sports stadium nearby.

Places of interest

For your first general view of the city, take the Metro. Most of the track in the centre is elevated. You will notice three prominent hills in the Aburrá valley: **Cerro Nutibara** (across the river from Industriales station), where there are a stage for open air concerts, sculpture park, miniature Antioquian village (known as Pueblito Paisa), souvenir shops and restaurants; **Cerro El Volador** (seen as the Metro turns between Universidad and Caribe stations), tree covered and the site of an important Indian burial ground; and **Morro El Salvador** (to the E of Alpujarra station) with a cross and statue on top, now mostly built over and not recommended for visits.

Medellín is well-laid-out. The old colonial buildings have nearly all disappeared, but there are still some 17th century churches left: the old Cathedral on Parque Berrío and the churches of **San Benito**, **La Veracruz**, and **San José**. The new **Cathedral of Villanueva** (Catedral Metropolitana), built between 1868 and 1931, one of the largest brick buildings in the world, is on Parque Bolívar, an attractive place with a statue of Bolívar. Three 18th century churches survive: **San Ignacio**, in Plaza San Ignacio, **San Juan de Dios**, and **San Antonio**. The city's commercial centre, **Villanueva**, is interesting for its blend of old and modern architecture, including many skyscrapers. There is a fine sculpture, **Monumento a la Vida**, next to the Edif Seguros Suramericana on C 50, where exhibitions of work by leading South American artists are held on

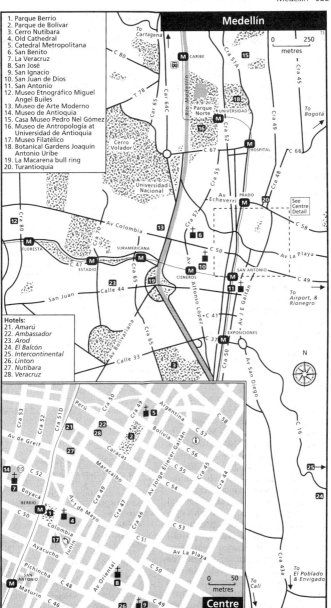

1. Parque Berrío
2. Parque de Bolívar
3. Cerro Nutibara
4. Old Cathedral
5. Catedral Metropolitana
6. San Benito
7. La Veracruz
8. San José
9. San Ignacio
10. San Juan de Dios
11. San Antonio
12. Museo Etnográfico Miguel Angel Builes
13. Museo de Arte Moderno
14. Museo de Antioquia
15. Casa Museo Pedro Nel Gómez
16. Museo de Antropología at Universidad de Antioquia
17. Museo Filatélico
18. Botanical Gardens Joaquín Antonio Uribe
19. La Macarena bull ring
20. Turantioquia

Hotels:
21. Amarú
22. Ambassador
23. Arod
24. El Balcón
25. Intercontinental
26. Linton
27. Nutibara
28. Veracruz

the ground floor. There are many other sculptures in the city – one collection not to be missed is the works of Fernando Botero, Colombia's leading contemporary artist, in Parque San Antonio between C 44/46 and Cra 46 including the 'Torso Masculino' (which complements the female version in Parque Berrío), and the 'Bird of Peace' which was severely damaged by a guerilla bomb in 1996. At the request of the sculptor, it has been left unrepaired as a symbol of the futility of violence. In the centre, Pasaje Junín (Cra 49) is closed to traffic from Parque de Bolívar to Parque San Antonio (C 46).

Botanical and Zoological Gardens

Joaquín Antonio Uribe gardens, Cra 52, No 73-298, near the campus of the University of Antioquia, which include an orchid garden, are open daily, 0900-1730, US$0.50 entrance (some of the plants are named); there is a restaurant, pleasant but not cheap. The **Zoológico Santa Fe**, at C 77 y Cra 68, is mainly of South American animals and birds (admission US$0.80). In the zoo grounds is the **Museo Santa Fe** (closed Mon and Tues), an extra US$0.20 to enter. Also visit **El Ranchito**, an orchid farm between the towns of Itagüí and La Estrella (entry US$0.50; April to June is the best time to visit).

Museums

Museo Etnográfico Miguel Angel Builes, Cra 81, No 52B-120, has an extensive collection of artefacts housed in a beautiful new building. The **Museo de la Madre Laura**, Cra 92, No 33B-21, has a good collection of indigenous costumes and crafts from Colombia, Ecuador and Guatemala. **Museo El Castillo**, C 9 Sur, No 32-260, formerly a landowner's home, has interesting objects and beautiful grounds; entry US$1.20; take bus to Loma de los Balsos, El Poblado (US$0.07), then walk 1 km up the hill until you see the road lined with pine trees to the right. Open 1300-1700, closed Sun. The **Museo de Antioquia**, Cra 53 y C 52, opp main post office, shows contemporary pictures and sculptures, including works by Fernando Botero, US$1 (guides free). **Museo de Arte**

Moderno, Cra 64B, No 51-64, small collection, open Tues-Fri, 0900-1300, 1500-1800 (foreign films 2-3 a week). **Casa Museo Maestro Pedro Nel Gómez**, Cra 51B, No 85-24, T 233-2633, house of the contemporary painter and sculptor (closed during school holidays). **Museo Antropológico** at University of Antioquia, C 67, No 53-108 (new campus), also has exhibitions of modern art, free. **Museo Filatélico**, on 4th floor of Banco de la República building. Most museums are closed on Mon. **Biblioteca Pública Piloto para América Latina**, Cra 64, No 52-32, T 230-2382, art and photo exhibitions, authors reading their own work, foreign films.

Local festivals

Flower fair (Feria de las Flores/Desfile de Silleteros) is held annually in the first week of Aug, with parades and music. The flowers are grown at Santa Elena in the Parque Ecológico de Piedras Blancas, 14 km from Medellín (bus from Plaza Las Flores).

Local information

NB In our listings, we give the Calle and Carrera numbers for easy reference. Unlike other Colombian cities (except central Cartagena), most streets are named, and locally these are normally used. Refer to the maps which show both numbers and names.

● **Accommodation**

South of centre, in or near Poblado: **L2** *Intercontinental*, C 16, No 28-51, Variante Las Palmas, T 266-0680, F 266-1548, the best, some distance from the city, excellent; **L2** *Poblado Plaza*, Cra 43A, No 4 Sur 75, T 268-5555, F 268-6949, also excellent.

A1 *El Balcón*, Cra 25, No 2-370, nr *Intercontinental*, in Transversal Superior, T 268-2511, beautiful view of the city, good meals.

West of centre, near stadium: **L3** *Lukas*, Cra 70 No 44A-28, T 260-1761, F 260-3765, best hotel in sector; **L3** *Florida*, Cra 70, No 44B-38, T 260-4900, F 260-0644, new, smart, expensive but negotiable.

A2 *Arod*, C 44, No 69-80, T 260-1427, F 260-1441, small, secure, 1½ km from centre, basement parking, rec; **A2** *Imperio*, Cra 70, No 45E-117, T 250-0311, 2 min from Metro, price negotiable, opened 1997.

In centre: **L3** *Nutibara* (casino and swimming pool), C 52A, No 50-46, T 231-9111, F 231-3713, best in centre; *Residencias Nutibara*, annex facing hotel of same name, slightly cheaper with all the same facilities.

A1 *Amaru*, Cra 50A, No 53-45, T 511-2155, F 231-0321, central, quiet, good, expensive restaurant with excellent service; **A1** *Ambassador*, Cra 50, No 54-50, T 511-5311, F 513-5311, breakfast inc, in connection with **A1** *Veracruz*, Cra 50, No 54-18, T 511-5511, F 231-0542, with bath, swimming pool, very good, restaurant on 11th floor gives fine view over city; **A1** *Gran*, C 54, 45-92, T 513-4455, F 381-0068, with breakfast, some cheap offers, pool.

B *Horizonte*, Cra 47 No 49A-24, T 511-6188, good and popular restaurant; **B** *Mariscal*, Cra 45, No 46-49, T 251-5433, hot shower, good service.

C *Cannes*, Cra 50, No 56-17, T 242-7329, well run; **C** *Casa Blanca*, Cra 45, No 46-09, T 251-5211, small restaurant, safe but noisy.

D *Linton*, Cra 45, No 47-74, T 217-0847, TV, safe parking nearby US$0.50/night, central; **D** *Comercial*, C 48, No 53-94, hot water available in some rooms, best on top floor, doors barred to all but residents after 1800, good meals; **E** *Residencias Doris*, Cra 45, No 46-23, T 251-2245, family run, clean sheets every day, laundry facilities, locked night and day, good value, rec; **E** *Gómez Córdoba*, Cra 46, No 50-29, good value, renovated, safe, central; **E** *Romania*, Av Echeverri, C 58, No 50-46, with bath, a bit noisy.

● **Places to eat**
In or near El Poblado: *Frutos del Mar*, Cra 43B, No 11-51, good seafood; *La Crèperie*, opp (No 11-88), French; on Av Poblado (Av 43A): *Café Le Gris*, Centro Comercial Oviedo (Cra 43A No 6 Sur-15), good upmarket dishes; *Aguacatala*, Cra 43A, No 7 Sur-130 (an old country house with patio and wandering musical trio, *comida típica*, quiet surroundings), and similar, *La Posada de la Montaña*, Cra 43-B, No 16-22, excellent Colombian food, very attractive setting, rec; *Carbón*, Variante a las Palmas, Km 1 T 262-5425, good grills, good view over city, live music at weekends; *Frutas de mi Tierra*, also Variante a las Palmas, extraordinary fruit salads; *Hato Viejo*, opp *International Hotel*, good service, local dishes, large portions, free snacks with drinks, good value.

West of centre: *Manhattan*, Cra 70, No 42-39, good international; *Asados La 80*, Cra 81, No 30-7, very good, large steaks; *El Palacio China*, Circular 4, No 74-69, good Chinese, reasonable prices; *La Llanera*, Cra 70, Circular 1-36, local dishes, good quality. Plenty of cheap local restaurants and fast food outlets in the Cra 70 area.

In the centre: apart from the hotels, there are few of the better restaurants in the centre.

Exceptions are: *Palazzetto D'Italia*, C 54, No 43-102, excellent Italian, reasonable prices, rec; *Trigo y Miel*, C 53, No 43-54, very good vegetarian, set lunch US$3.50, rec; *El Viejo Vapor*, Cra 43, No 53-19, café, bar, artist clientèle, good meeting place, set lunch US$3. Good local food at *Don Edoardo*, Cra 45, No 48-57, central, modest prices. Many vegetarian restaurants, eg *Govinda*, C 51 No 52-17; *Crepes y Waffles*, Cra 36, No 10-54, good; *Paracelso*, C 51 y Cra 45, big, tasty, cheap meals, open 1100-1600. There are several cheap, round-the-clock cafés in the vicinity of Cra Junín between Maturín and Amador. Many good, cheap restaurants on Cra 49 (eg *La Estancia*, No 54-15). Excellent pastries at *Salón de Té Astor*, Cra 49, No 53-39, a delightful traditional tea house. Also in Pasaje Junín are two upstairs bar/cafés, *Boulevard de Junín* and *Balcones del Parque*, both good for refreshments while watching Medellín in action below.

● **Bars**
Bar Berlín 1930, C 10, No 41-65, attractive, low level music, snooker table; *Bar Blue Rock*, C 10, No 40-20, popular.

● **Banks & money changers**
There are banks everywhere in the three business zones. Most of the major banks have ATMs, many will accept international cards. Some banks, eg **Banco Anglo Colombiano**, C 50, No 51-14 in the centre and Diagonal 47, No 15S-31 in Poblado, will cash Amex TCs with passport and purchase voucher, and give cash at the counter against credit and debit cards. **Banco Industrial de Colombia**, in Poblada, cash against Mastercard, Amex, good rates for TCs and cash. **Banco de Colombia** accepts Visa cards. Banks are increasingly opening later and on Sat. Main hotels will cash TCs for residents when banks are closed, but at less favourable rates.

● **Embassies & consulates**
British, Cra 49, 46A, Sur-103, Envigado, T 331-8625, F 331-0046, very helpful, take a taxi and phone for directions as it's hard to find; **Danish**, C 49, No 50-21, Of 1904, T 216-5161; **German**, Cra 43F, No 17-419; **French**, Cra 52, No 14-200, Of 204, T 235-8037 F 265-7291; **Panamanian**, C 10, No 42-45, Of 233, T 268-1157; **Venezuelan**, C 32B, No 69-59, T 351-1614, F 351-1909. **NB** The **Venezuelan** consul will not issue visas.

● **Entertainment**
Cinema: free foreign films daily at Universidad de Medellín or Universidad de Antioquia.

Discotheques: in central hotels, and in El Poblado. Also many discos and popular dance halls on C 50, between Cras 65 and 75, and Cra 70, between C 36 and C 44, also in Envigado, nr Plaza Envigado. For a dark, underground and lively young place, try *Puf*, *Britania* or *Bartolomé* next to each other on autopista Palmas, Km 5. Couples only allowed in to many discos.

Music: monthly concerts by the Antioquia Symphony Orchestra. Band concerts and other entertainments in the Parque Bolívar every Sun. Universidad de Medellín theatre has monthly tango shows. Tango also at *Vos...Tango-Show*, C 34, No 66A-13, diagonal al Super Ley de Unicentro, T 265-9352, US$10.

● **Hospitals & medical services**

There is a clinic with free consultations and basic treatment in the airport buildings.

● **Post & telecommunications**

Post Office: main airmail office in Avianca building, Cra 52, No 51A-01, Mon-Sat, 0700-2200, has *poste restante*. Also, Avianca post office in the Colseguros building Cra 46, C 53/54.

Telecommunications: Pasaje Junín and on corner of C 49 and Cra 50.

● **Security**

Travellers should take the same safety precautions as they would in any large city, particularly at night. It is, nevertheless, a friendly place.

● **Shopping**

Poor selection of handicraft shops in the city, but there are *artesanía* shops on the top of Cerro Nutibara and there is a small handicrafts market at C 52 nr Cra 46 with many hippy stalls. **Mercado San Alejo**, Parque Bolívar, open on the first Sat of every month except Jan, and before Christmas it is there Sat and Sun (handicrafts on sale at good prices). Good shopping generally around Parque Bolívar. Many of the textile mills have discount clothing departments attached where good bargains can be had; ask at your hotel. *Aluzia Correas y Cinturones*, Oviedo Shopping Center, Poblado, Unicentro Medellín, also in Bogotá, for an incredible selection of belts, US$15-40. *La Piel*, at C 53, No 49-131, has an excellent selection of leather goods at very reasonable prices. *Supermarket Exito* (Cra 66, No 49-01, C 10, No 43E-135, Poblado) is reasonable for cheap leather bags. There are several shopping centres.

Bookshops: *Librería Continental*, Cra 50 y C 52; *Librería Científica*, C 51, No 49-52, T 231-4974, large selection, some foreign books; *La Anticuaria*, C 49, No 47-46, T 511-4969, antique and secondhand books, inc in English, helpful; *Centro Colombo Americano*, Cra 45, No 53-24, T 513-4444, good selection of books in English for sale (inc *Footprint Handbooks*).

Maps: virtually nothing in the bookshops. Reasonable map of the city centre from Fomento y Turismo (see Tourist Offices). Local and national maps from Instituto Geográfico Agustín Co-

dazzi in Fundación Ferrocarril building, Cra 52, No 14-43, office in the basement.

Photography: for developing, *Almacenes Duperly* (several branches, eg C 52, No 46-28), good quality. **Camera repairs**: *Clínica de Cámeras*, Centro Coltejer, Local 120.

● **Sports**

Bullfights: at the bull-ring of La Macarena, C 44 and Cra 63, in Feb; cheapest US$14, usually fully booked.

Sports complex: Estadio Atanasio Girardot, Cra 74, C 50, football, baseball, velodrome etc. Next to the *Estadio* Metro station.

● **Tour companies & travel agents**

Marco Polo, C 48, No 65-94, T 230-5944, very helpful, owner speaks some English; *Tierra Mar Aire* (American Express agents), C 52, No 43-124, T 513-0414, helpful; *Realturs*, Cra 46, No 50-28, T 511-6000, good.

● **Tourist offices**

Fomento y Turismo de Medellín, C 57 No 45-129, T 254-0800, for information on the city, run by Fabiola Montes whose staff will help you. **Turantioquia**, Cra 48, No 58-11, T 291-1111, good information on Antioquia and owns 2 good hotels in the Department.

MA: Cra 76, No 49-92, T 422-0883.

● **Useful addresses**

DAS, C 19, No 80A-40 in Belén la Nubia section, T 341-5900 ; **Tourist Police** at airport, T 287-2053; local police T 112.

● **Transport**

Local Metro: 2 lines: A from Niquía to Itagüí, B from San Javier to San Antonio, where they intersect. One journey (anywhere on the system) US$0.35, 2 US$0.65, 10 US$3. **Taxis**: they have meters, make sure they are used.

Air José María Córdova, 28 km from Medellín by new highway, and 13 km from Rionegro; *Presto* restaurant, shops, Telecom, Fax service, no left luggage, but Turantioquia may oblige. Taxi to town US$16 (fixed), colectivo US$4, *buseta* to centre, US$3, frequent service, about 1 hr: sit on right going to town. To go to the airport catch *buseta* or colectivo in small road behind *Hotel Nutibara*. To Rionegro, bus US$0.20, taxi US$10.20.

By air to **Bogotá**, 45 mins with Avianca (Cra 52, No 51A-23, T 511-3099), SAM, Aces or Aero República (cheapest), several daily. Also to many other Colombian cities. There is also a small municipal airport, Olaya Herrera, non-jets only, 10 mins by taxi with flights to Quibdó (3 flights daily, US$33), Bahía Solano, Pereira etc.

Trains For long-distance travel to Barrancabermeja, a train leaves daily 0645, US$10 or US$12 one way, 12-15 hrs (running 1997). No trains running at present beyond Puerto Berrío to Bogotá or beyond Barranca to Santa Marta, but check. A tourist train to and from Cisneros runs at weekends and holidays, leaving Medellín at 0800 and Cisneros at 1600, return trip US$11.80 or US$13. For information call Terminales de Transportes del Norte, T 267-7756, or go to the station itself, Metro to Caribe on line A, cross to the bus terminal and go to the ground floor where there is a booth by the tunnel entrance to the railway platforms.

Buses The terminal for long-distance buses going N and E is **Terminal del Norte** at Cra 64 (Autopista del Norte) y Transversal 78, about 3 km N of the centre, with shops, cafeterias, left luggage (US$0.50/day) and other facilities. Quite safe. Bus service to city centre, US$0.30, buses to station from C 50, marked: "Terminal de Transporte", or better, by Metro to Caribe. To/from **Bogotá**, 9-12 hrs, US$20, every 40 mins or so, with 5 companies; to **La Dorada**, US$12. To **Caucasia**, US$11, 7 hrs. To **Cartagena**, 17-20 hrs, or 12 hrs, by Pullman bus, US$35 (take food with you, the stops tend to be at expensive restaurants); road paved throughout but poor. To **Barranquilla**, 16 hrs by Pullman, US$40. To **Sincelejo**, 9½ hrs, US$23. To **Turbo**, US$17 with Gómez (the best), 14 hrs.

For buses going S, **Terminal del Sur**, Cra 65, C 10, alongside the Olaya Herrera airport, for information, T 285-9157. Take a bus No 143 (marked "Terminal del Sur") from C 53 along Cra 54, or the Metro to Poblado on Línea A, but you will need a taxi for the remaining 2 km to the bus station. To **San Agustín**, Rápidos Tolima, 0600, US$45. Frequent buses for **Cali** US$22, 10-12 hrs. Frequent buses to **Manizales**, 6 hrs US$10, by Empresa Arauca. To **Cartago**, 7 hrs, Flota Magdalena, US$12. To **Pereira**, 8 hrs, US$14 by Flota Occidental Pullman. To **Popayán**, US$30, 12 hrs, Flota Magadalena at 1400 and 1800. To **Ipiales**, US$40, 22 hrs, Expreso Bolivariano (takes Visa). To **Quibdó**, 11-13 hrs, US$16.

MAIN ROADS FROM MEDELLIN

SOUTHEAST FROM MEDELLIN

The new Medellín-Bogotá highway is totally paved, but between Medellín and Honda the road through the Cordillera is subject to landslides in wet weather. At **Guarne** (22 km), is the Hipódromo Los Comuneros, with horse races on Sat and Sun, US$1, great atmosphere.

On the main road at **Marinilla**, 46 km from Medellín, a road N goes 25 km to **El Peñol**, a precipitous, bullet-shaped rock which towers above the surrounding hills and the Embalse del Peñol reservoir. It has been eroded smooth, but a spiral staircase has been built into a crack from the base to the summit (entry US$1, parking US$1). At the summit is a snackbar with fine views (meals at holiday times only). Bus to the rock and to the pretty town of **Guatapé** with Cía Fco López, from Terminal del Norte, Medellín, US$2.70; **E** *La Florida*, on main plaza, T 825-3600, good restaurant, and several other places to stay on the lakeside. Plenty of restaurants, one of the best is *La Tienda de Toño* on the lakeside, *asados*, trout, *bandeja*, good view, pleasant, recommended. Bus back to Medellín may have to be caught in the town of Peñol Nueva which replaced the old town submerged by the reservoir (take a colectivo from Guatapé or the rock).

RIONEGRO

39 km SE of Medellín and 5 km from the airport is the town of **Rionegro**, in a delightful valley of gardens and orchards. The **Casa de Convención** (where the 1863 Convention took place) is now an archive museum, entry US$0.50. The cathedral, with its gold and silver altar, deserves a visit. A museum of religious artefacts is behind the altar (entry US$0.25); it includes a virgin's robe with 300,000 pearls. There are colourful processions in Easter Week.

● **Accommodation D** *Liborio Mejía*, Cra 50, No 46-91, T 271-0804, hot water, good; **E** *Casa Vieja*, Cra 51, No 48-68, small, good; **E** *Casaloma*, Cra 46, No 41-68, with bath, safe, hot water; **E** *Dorado*, Cra 50, No 46-124, OK.

● **Places to eat** *Las Abedules*, C 48, No 50-51, good *ajiaco* US$3, rec; *Los Cheffs*, C 49, No 50-41, central plaza, good; *Doña Bertha* Cra 51, No 48-66, *comida* US$1.70, OK. Many other places to eat in and nr the plaza.

● **Transport** Buses from Medellín, from Terminal del Norte via Santa Elena, US$1.40, 1½ hrs, every 30 mins or so. Others from Terminal del Sur. Also colectivos from C 49/Cra 42, US$2.50, 45 mins. To El Peñol from Rionegro, take a colectivo to Marinilla from nr market, US$0.60.

There are many interesting pottery and ceramics factories in the Rionegro area, hardly mechanized, as well as leather working; they welcome visitors and explain the processes. 10 km from Rionegro (15 mins by colectivo, leave when full from plaza, US$0.75; buses every 2 hrs, US$0.30) is **Carmen de Viboral**, well-known for its fine pottery; there are several factories just N of the market place.

Near Rionegro on the road to El Retiro is **Fizebad**, an old estate house, restored with original furniture and artefacts, and a display of flowering orchids (entry US$2.50). Many roadside stalls sell typical Colombian snacks: clotted cream, strawberries, *arequipe*, fruits and juices. Near El Retiro is the attractive Tequendamita Falls with a good restaurant nearby. In **El Retiro** itself has a small colonial church and an even older chapel which is seldom open; ask for the caretaker. (To Fizebad, catch a La Ceja or El Retiro bus.) The scenery is splendid and one can see typical Antioquian life.

From Marinilla, the new road to Bogotá continues to Puerto Triunfo on the Río Magdalena.

The old Bogotá road continues to **La Ceja**, 16 km from Rionegro; any of the surrounding hills affords an excellent view of the area.

• **Accommodation & places to eat D** *Turin*, C 19, No 21-55, T 553-1316, nr plaza, small rooms, hot water, cheaper rooms available, laundry facilities, good value; **D** *Primavera*, Cra 20, No 20-61, cheaper without bath or TV, uncomfortable beds, small rooms; youth hostel at *Centro Vacacional La Montaña*, details from Alcom in Bogotá. Several restaurants inc *Pollos Mario*. Bus to Medellín, US$1.50.

At **Sonsón**, 121 km from Medellín, the Casa de los Abuelos is an old house with many historical objects, inc a printing press which produces a weekly newspaper (**F** *Tahami*, very good value, and *Imperio*).

NORTH FROM MEDELLIN

To Cartagena, 665 km: 10 km N is the industrial town of **Bello** (*pop* 260,360), where a hut in which Marcos Fidel Suárez, president 1918-1922, was born, is covered in glass for its preservation. The main road follows the Río Medellín for 25 km to El Hatillo where it turns left to climb past Don Matías and the Río Grande dam (2

hotels, several restaurants), and over the Alto Matasano, to **Yarumal** (132 km; *pop* 23,515), a friendly town in a cold mountain climate (fine views from Parroquia La Merced; many *hosterías* on the main plaza and C Caliente. The road goes on via Valdivia and Caucasia to Cartagena.

Crossing the Río Medellín and continuing down the valley from El Hatillo leads to Barbosa and **Cisneros**, where there is a park and waterfalls, and where the tourist train from Medellín terminates at weekends. The first locomotive to cross the Magdalena is displayed here. There are at least 7 *residencias* in town and many restaurants. The road continues to cross the Magdalena at Puerto Berrío.

NORTHWEST FROM MEDELLIN: ANTIOQUIA

The road to Turbo leads from Cra 80 NW, winding up to Alto de Boquerón, 22 km from the city (good views). 57 km from Medellín is **San Jerónimo**, with two holiday centres on the main road.

A further 23 km along is the crossing of the Río Cauca and Santa Fé de **Antioquia** (to give it its full name) just W of the river. It was founded as a gold mining town by the Spaniards in 1541, the first in the area, and still retains its colonial atmosphere, with interesting Christmas/New Year fiestas. Until 1826 it was the capital of the Department, and retains much of its character; it was given National Monument status in 1960.

The fine old Cathedral is worth seeing, as is the church of Santa Bárbara. There is a small museum next to this church. There is an interesting wooden bridge, the Puente de Occidente, 300m long, 3 km downstream from the (new) steel bridge, ask for directions or take a taxi.

• **Accommodation A3** *Hostal de la Villa*, Cra 10, No 8-36, T 853-1097, with full board, pool, fan; **C** *Mariscal Robledo*, Cra 12, No 9-70, T 853-1111, **B** with refrigerator and TV, full holidays and most weekends, swimming pool, good restaurant with excellent buffet lunch US$6, rec; **D** *Hostal del Viejo Conde*, C 9, 10-56, T 853-7091, cheaper without bath, restaurant rec; **D** *El Mesón de la Moneda*, Cra 11, No 9-31, with breakfast, pleasant; **F** *Dally*, C 10, No 8-50, basic. On the road between the centre and the bridge: **B** *Hostería Mis Ancestros*, C 9, No 1-192, T 853-1657, F 853-2499, pool, jacuzzi etc, new (1996); **A1** *Hostería Real*, 2 km from town, T 853-1048, full board, good food, pool; **A2** *Lago Antioquía*, 3 km from town, T 853-1154, holiday hotel with many facilities, close to the river, plane at entrance crashed into the lake behind the hotel in 1992. There is good food in the hotels and nr the main square, eg *Los Faroles*, Cra 11, No 9-33.

● **Buses** The bus station is on the road to Turbo at the N end of Cras 9 and 10. To **Medellín** US$3 (Socurabá or Transporte Sierra), 2½ hrs. To **Turbo**, US$14, 8 hrs, every 2 hrs or so.

SOUTHWEST FROM MEDELLÍN

At **Envigado**, now a suburb 10 km S of Medellín, craftsmen have for generations turned out the traditional *antioqueño* pouch called a *carriel*, carried by the men. Now used for money, its original use was for coffee samples (**D** *Las Antillas*, C 44B Sur No 36-04, Barrio La Paz, T 331-3969. Several Chinese restaurants, C 36S/Cra 43). 12 km S of Envigado is Caldas, famous for its ceramics and the interesting wood altar in its cathedral.

ROUTES There are three ways to Manizales: 1) 57 km S of Medellín on the main road is **Santa Bárbara** (*alt* 1,857m), on a green hill top, providing stunning views in every direction of coffee, banana and sugar plantations, orange-tiled roofs and folds of hills. (**E** *Centenario*, C Santander, 1 block from plaza, T 846-3085; **F** *Hotel Palomares*, on main plaza, good; restaurants and cafés on main plaza, as is the large church; bus to Medellín, US$1.20.)

A further 26 km is **La Pintada** (camping; hotels **E** *Mi Rey*, T 846-4008, OK; **E** *La Montaña*, with bath; **G** *Residencia Cosina*, basic, fan, mosquitos, restaurant). Here the road crosses the Río Cauca, then splits. To the left an unpaved road runs through Aguadas, Pácora and **Salamina** (**F** *Res Puerto Nuevo*, opp bus office, clean, good meals), all perched on mountain ridges. At Aranzazu, paving begins for the 51 remaining km to Manizales.

2) The main road, all paved, goes through **Supía**, a pleasant town 140 km S of Medellín (**F** *Hotel Mis Ninietas*, near plaza, unsigned, with bath, clean). 13 km further is **Riosucio**, another delightful town with fine views and a large colonial church

(many restaurants, bars and shops). At Anserma the road turns E to Manizales via Arauca.

Shortly after Caldas, a road to the right (W) descends through Amagá to cross the Cauca at Bolombolo. From here, follow the river S to the next bridge where a dirt road climbs up 18 km to **Jericó**, an interesting Antioquian town with a large cathedral, several other churches, two museums and a good view from *Morro El Salvador* above the town.

3) If instead of following the Cauca upstream from Bolombolo you take the right fork at Peñalisa, you can keep to the valley of the Río San Juan for 19 km to Remolino where the road again divides, right for Quibdó and left for **Andes**, a busy town (several places to stay and to eat, all on Cra 50/51; attractive waterfalls in the neighbourhood), and **Jardín**, 16 km SE of Andes. This typical Antioquian village is surrounded by cultivated hills. There is a small museum in the Casa Cultura with paintings and local artifacts, and a bank that accepts Visa cards.

● **Accommodation & places to eat** **E** *Jardín*, on plaza, T 855-5651, with bath, hot water, restaurant, balcony overlooking plaza, good value; several *residencias* on or nr plaza. Also on plaza: restaurants, cafés and bars, eg *Restaurante Zodiaco*, good.

● **Transport** Buses to **Medellín** (Terminal Sur), 4 hrs. To **Riosucio**, 3 hrs, US$4.40.

The road continues S to Riosucio (see above) through good walking country.

To Quibdó This road continues from Remolino for 17 km through coffee, tobacco and pineapple plantations to **Bolívar**, in the centre of the coffee region where the evening's entertainment is to watch the local horsemen and women showing off their riding skills around the plaza. **E** *Residencias Bahía*, the best available; *Guillo's* restaurant nearby, good.

CHOCO

Stretching like a ribbon between the Cordillera Occidental and the Pacific Coast, from Panama to Valle del Cauca, Chocó is one of Colombia's least developed and most beautiful departments. It is also one of the rainiest regions on earth ('dry season': Dec to Mar). In the northern ¾ of the department, the mountain ranges of the Serranía de Los Saltos and Serranía del Baudó rise directly from the ocean to reach a height of about 500m. The scenery of pristine rainforest descending the mountain slopes to the sea is spectacular. The principal transport routes are along the Pacific coast from Buenaventura in the S and up the Río Atrato from the Gulf of Urabá and Cartagena to the N. The Ríos Baudó and San Juan flow to the Pacific in the S of the department. Road access is via two unpaved routes across the Cordillera Occidental, one from Medellín via Bolívar, just described, the other from Pereira to the SE via La Virginia and Pueblo Rico.

Chocó is very sparsely populated. The coastline is dotted with fishing villages whose inhabitants, although also of African origin, are culturally distinct from the Caribbean Afro-Colombians. Inland along the rivers are Indian communities, whose lifestyle is based on hunting, fishing, and subsistence farming. Along the Río San Juan, in the S, there is much gold prospecting around the towns of Tadó and Istmina.

The construction of a road to the mouth of the Río Tribugá, where a deep sea port and industrial complex is planned as an alternative export terminal for coffee to Buenaventura represents a serious threat to Chocó's unique environment.

Malaria, yellow fever, and dengue remain endemic throughout Chocó, and the appropriate precautions (prophylaxis, vaccination, mosquito nets, etc) are recommended.

QUIBDÓ

Quibdó is on the eastern bank of the Río Atrato. Prices are higher here than in central Colombia, but they are higher still in the coastal villages, so it is a good place to get supplies. Despite its frontier town appearance, Quibdó is one of the safest cities in Colombia.

There is an interesting mural in the cathedral. Hordes of birds fly in to roost at dusk and there are magnificent sunsets. A good place to view them is the permanently moored boat which houses

the civil defence authority (bright orange roof, take insect repellent). The large Jorge Isaacs auditorium is used for cultural activities (see under **Music and dance** for festivals).

● **Accommodation** E *Cristo Rey*, bath, fan, safe; E *Del Río*, good, with bath, safe, free coffee, its restaurant, *Club Naútico* on 2nd floor has an excellent bar, good food and views; F *Dora Ley*, cheaper without bath, fan, rooms vary in quality, meals; F *Pacífico*, good rooms and beds; F *Residencia Darién*, Cra 4, No 26-68, T 712997, bath, fan, space to park motorcycle; F *Oriental*, no private showers, quiet, charming elderly proprietor.

● **Places to eat** *El Paisa*, Cra 4, No 25-54, excellent; *Chopán* bakery, good pastries and coffee.

● **Banks & money changers** Banco de Bogotá, cash against Visa, other banks do not change money. *Restaurant El Paisa*, *Farmacia Mercedes*, and a few shopkeepers sometimes change US$ cash, but rates are poor. Best to buy pesos in larger centres before arriving.

● **Useful addresses DAS Office**: C 29, Cra 4. No entry or exit stamps.

● **Transport Air** Aces and Avianca fly daily to Medellín; Aces also to Bogotá, Bahía Solano and Nuquí. **Buses** Transportes Ochoa to Medellín via El Carmen and Bolívar, 5 daily, 10-12 hrs, US$7.50 regular, US$16 luxury coach. Transportes Arauca to Manizales via Tadó, Pueblo Rico, La Virginia and Pereira, Tues, Thur, Sat, Sun at 0600, 14-17 hrs, US$14. Flota Occidental along same route to Pereira, daily at 0700, 8-10 hrs, US$9.60. Occasional buses to Cali, US$14 otherwise change at La Virginia. Bus to Bogotá US$24. Local service to Santa Cecilia and Tadó. **River** From Buenaventura up the Río San Juan to Istmina and on by road; services infrequent. Irregular cargo service down the Río Atrato to Turbo and Cartagena takes passengers. Cost to Turbo US$26, food included; to/from Cartagena US$40-53, 4 days, take drinking water. Deal directly with boats. Also 20-seater open boats, 7 hrs to Turbo, about US$30. The lower Atrato was a very dangerous area in 1997 (guerrillas, kidnappings, drug running). Much caution and detailed advance inquiry are strongly rec.

QUIBDÓ TO MANIZALES

The road to Manizales begins in a very poor state, very slow, and you can be stuck in mud for hours. Most is through pure jungle with colourful butterflies, waterfalls and few people. 60 km S is Las Animas where there is a turning E to cross the San

Juan, reaching **Tadó** (8 km from Las Animas), with a silver-fronted church. **E** *Hotel Macondo*, very basic but restaurant OK; **E** *Residencias Confort*, without bath, clean, friendly; good café/bar on corner of plaza. After crossing into Risaralda Department, the road improves before reaching the Cauca Valley.

TOWNS ALONG THE PACIFIC COAST

NUQUI

On the Gulf of Tribugá, surrounded by estuaries and virgin beaches, **Nuquí** is gaining popularity among Colombian sports fishermen and vacationers. A number of luxury homes have been built nearby. To the S lies the wide curve of Playa Olímpica and the fishing village of Pangui (cross first estuary by canoe, the second at low tide or swim). To the N is the even smaller hamlet of Tribugá, a splendid beach and the proposed site of a deep sea port (see above).

● **Accommodation** Along the beach at the N end of town, fully booked during the holiday period, are **C** *Playa del Mar* and **D** *Rosio del Mar*, cabins with bath. **E** *Doña Jesusita*, at S end of town, basic. Felipe and Luz Largacha will sometimes rent rooms in their home (along main street S of town centre), **F**, basic. On Playa Olímpica, Guillermo and Doralina Moreno, run a small hotel, **E/F** range, shared bath, pleasant. You can also pitch your tent in their coconut grove for a small fee, hammock not recommended because of heavy rains and vicious sandflies at night (mosquito net rec, repellent a must). Meals available if arranged in advance.

● **Places to eat** Several small restaurants on road to airport serving mostly fish. Shops are well stocked with basic goods, prices somewhat higher than in Quibdó.

● **Transport Air** By air from Quibdó (20 min) and Medellín (50 mins). Aces flies on Mon, Wed, Fri, and Sun; SAM from Medellín only, same days. **Overland** Construction is continuing on a road from Las Animas (see above) to Nuquí and the port planned for Tribugá. At present, it is a strenuous 3-day trek along a jungle trail from the roadhead, through several Indian villages, to Nuquí. **Sea** There are launches S to Arusi (Mon, Wed, Fri), and N to El Valle (Tues, Thur, Sat), as well as occasional coastal vessels (small fuel barges) to Buenaventura.

EL VALLE

50 km N of Nuquí along the coast, **El Valle** has the best bathing and surfing beaches in the area. El Almejal, N of town, is the best. The entrance to El Valle's harbour is very tricky at ebb tide and many boats have been swept onto the rocks here.

● **Accommodation** Several large but simple tourist complexes at El Almejal, with rooms and cabins (**D/E** range), as well as bars and restaurants (deserted on weekdays off-season). **A1** *Cabañas El Almejal*, cabins with private bath, the best, full board, reservations T Medellín 230-6060. Between El Valle and El Almejal is **F** *Cabinas Villa Maga*, safe, family run.

● **Transport Road** A rough road runs 18 km from El Valle to Bahía Solano (passes by airport before town). Jeeps leave every morning, 1 hr ride, US$2.50, tickets can be purchased 1 day in advance. **Sea** There are launches S to Nuquí on Tues, Thur and Sat, and three times a week to Buenaventura.

ENSENADA DE UTRIA NATIONAL PARK

Between Nuquí and El Valle this **National Park** was created in 1985 to preserve several unique aquatic and terrestrial habitats. Day trips may be arranged from El Valle or Nuquí, and special permits are sometimes granted for longer stays by MA in Bogotá. The ranger welcomes volunteers to help in clearing rubbish from the beaches and other tasks (also best arranged in advance from Bogotá).

The park is named for a large inlet (*ensenada*) at its centre, which is home to two varieties of whales, corals, needlefish, and many other aquatic species. Motorboats are not allowed past the park headquarters, located half-way up the inlet, and the area is best appreciated if you paddle through in a canoe (try to rent or borrow). The surrounding hillsides are covered with pristine rainforest and there are several magnificent white sand beaches.

● **Access** Boats hired from El Valle take 45 mins and cost approximately US$12 return, from Nuquí 1½ hrs, US$24. Boats will not leave when the sea is too rough, which may be for several days. The launch which runs from Nuquí to El Valle can sometimes (depending on tides) leave you at Playa Blanca, a small island near the park boundary. Here Sr Salomon Caizamo has a simple restaurant and rents space for one or two tents (a nice spot). The park headquarters are 5 mins away by motorboat and you can generally hitch a ride with fishermen or park employees. There are also a road and trail leading through the jungle from El Valle to the head of the inlet (9 km, 4-5 hrs, can be very muddy), but you must arrange for a boat to pick you up as it is not possible to reach the park headquarters on foot.

● **Accommodation** At the park headquarters and visitors centre is a display of whale bones and other exhibits, plus a small restaurant. There are simple but comfortable accommodation for about 15 people in a guest house (camping prohibited) and an outdoor kitchen with a wood stove. Fresh fish can sometimes be purchased, but all other provisions should be brought from town. Mosquito nets are essential for protection against insects and vampire bats. Across the inlet from the headquarters is a private research station run by Fundación Natura as a base for biologists.

BAHIA SOLANO

Also known as Ciudad Mutis, it lies on a large bay set against jungle covered hills. As a resort, it gets quite busy during holiday periods when prices rise. The bay is rather muddy and there are no beaches by the town itself. Good bathing beaches may be reached by launch or by walking about 1½ hrs at low tide (eg Playa Mecana. Be sure to return before the tide rises or you will be stranded).

● **Accommodation & places to eat B** *Balboa* T (816) 27074, best in town, pool, boat service to bathing beaches; **E** *Bahia*, in same street as Satena office, with fan and private bath, good restaurant; **F** *Hostal del Mar*, across the street, run by Estelle and Rodrigo, good, excursions arranged. Several others. Two youth hostels, ask at Alcom in Bogotá. Good food at *Las Delicias* and at the restaurant run by Señora Ayde nr the *Balboa* hotel.

● **Transport** Daily flights from Medellín (Aces); 4 a week with SAM. Aces also flies 3 times a week from Quibdó. There is daily jeep service to El Valle (see above). Occasional coastal cargo vessels N to Juradó and S to Buenaventura.

La Zona Cafetera and the Cauca Valley

MODERN and colonial cities line both the fertile western slopes of the Cordillera Central which is the centre of Colombia's coffee production, and the narrow Cauca valley, whose focus is Cali, the country's southern industrial centre. From here the Pacific port of Buenaventura is reached.

LA ZONA CAFETERA

The Department of Caldas until 1965 contained what are now the Departments of Quindío and Risaralda. The three departments are generally known as the "Zona Cafetera". Much of the land here is between the critical altitudes for coffee of 800m-1,800m, and has the right balance of rain and sunshine.

MANIZALES

Manizales (*pop* 378,890; *alt* 2,153m; *phone code* 968) can be reached from the capital by a road (309 km) passing through Facatativá and Honda; or through Girardot to Ibagué, then over the high crest of the Quindío pass via Armenia. The city is dominated by its enormous (still unfinished) concrete Cathedral and the Nevado del Ruiz volcano, which erupted so catastrophically in Nov 1985.

The city rides its mountain saddle uncompromisingly, the houses falling away sharply from the centre of the city into the adjacent valleys. The climate is extremely humid (average temperature is 17°C, and the annual rainfall is 3,560 mm), encouraging prodigious growth in the flowers that line the highways to the suburbs N and S. Frequently the city is covered in cloud. The best months of the year are from mid-Dec through to early March. The city looks down on the small town of Villa María, "the village of flowers", now almost a suburb.

Places of interest

Several earthquakes and fires have destroyed parts of the city over the years, so the architecture is predominantly modern with high-rise office and apartment blocks. Traditional architectural styles are still seen in the suburbs and the older sections of the city. The departmental government building, the Gobernación, opposite the Cathedral in the Parque Bolívar, is an imposing example of neo-colonial architecture; the bull-ring is an impressive copy of the traditional Moorish style. Chipre, a recreational park, provides a good view of the city (well-visited on Sun); El Tanque, near Chipre, is another vantage point.

Museums

Banco de la República, Cra 23, No 23-06, gold and anthropology museum open during banking hours, classical music every afternoon in the Bank. **Universidad de Caldas**, natural history museum with good selection of butterflies, moths and birds; open every day from 0800 to 1200 and 1400 to 1800 (take a 'Fátima' bus to the University). **La Galería del Arte**, Av Santander at C 55, exhibitions of work by local artists, pictures can be bought.

Local festivals

Early in Jan the Fair and Coffee Festival is held, with bullfights, beauty parades and folk dancing.

Local information

● Accommodation

NB In Jan, during the fiesta, hotel prices are grossly inflated.

A2 *El Carretero*, C 36, No 22-22, T 840225, good but slow restaurant, business clientèle, comfortable; **A2** *Las Colinas*, Cra 22, No 20-20, T 842009, 3-star, 2 bars, good restaurant, very comfortable.

C *Villa Kempis*, Cra 23, No 19-22, T 830187, on road to Pereira, about 2 km past bull-ring, old religious retreat house, beautiful view over the valley, very quiet, hot water am only, restaurant and bar, good food at moderate prices.

D *Europa*, Av Centenario, No 25-98, T 822253, nr the bull-ring, restaurant for breakfast only, comfortable; **D** *Rokasol*, C 21, No 19-16, T 823307, nr bus station so noisy, hot water, good restaurant.

E *Tamá Internacional*, C 23, No 22-43, T 832594, next to Cathedral, with bath, meals, noisy; **E** *Residencias Avenida No 2*, C 21, No 20-07, T 835251, with bath, safe; **E** *Residencias Avenida No 3*, C 19, No 16-35, T 844130, opp bus terminal, bath, quiet, safe, rec; next door is **E** *California*, No 16-37, T 824217, modern, laundry facilities, safe, car parking, good.

F *Consol No 4*, Cra 20, No 21-10, large rooms; **F** *Marana*, C 18, No 17-34, T 843872, 1 min from bus station, bath, hot water only am; **F** *Residencias Caldas*, Cra 19, No 22-45, nr bus station, US$1 surcharge on holidays, hot water, quiet, but not too clean; **F** *Residencias Margarita*, C 17 between Cras 22 and 23, quieter on 2nd floor, good, safe, private parking opp US$0.75/night; **F** *Residencias Nueva York*, C 20, No 20-17, hot water, clothes-washing facilities, some bar noise in front but rec; several **F** range hotels around C 18, Cra 22-23.

● Places to eat

Las Redes, Cra 23, No 75-97, predominantly sea food, good but pricey; *Las Brasas*, Cra 23, No 75A-65, good grill and *comida típica*; *Fonda Paisa*, Cra 23, No 72-130, nice local dishes with local Andean music; *Casa Kena*, Cra 23, No 72-49, good Italian, fresh pasta daily, Caruso recordings; *La Suiza*, Cra 23, No 26-57, good fruit juices and cakes; unnamed restaurant with pink façade on Cra 23 nr C 31, economical, huge portions, highly rec; *Caballo Loco*, Cra 61, No 23-07, good; another with the same name at C 21, No 23-40 is mainly a bar but serves expensive pizzas; *El Ruiz*, Cra 19, No 22-25, filling 3-course meal.

● Banks & money changers

Banco Anglo Colombiano, Cra 22, No 17-04, and other banks. Exchange not possible Sat and Sun.

● **Entertainment**

Theatre: Teatro de los Fundadores is a modern cinema-theatre auditorium. Interesting wood-carved mural by Fernando Botero, who also has murals in the entrance hall of the Club Manizales and *Hotel Las Colinas*. Events held here and at other locations during Theatre Festival in first 2 weeks of September. Free films at the Universidad de Caldas on Wed at 1700. Good way to meet students.

● **Tourist offices**

Plaza Bolívar, opp Cathedral, T 848124, good, helpful.

For visits to coffee *fincas*, see page 948.

● **Useful addresses**

DAS Office: Cra 23 y C 24.

● **Transport**

Air Aces flies to Bogotá (also Avianca), Medellín, and Cali.

Road To Medellín, see above. Manizales-Honda-Bogotá: all paved but in poor condition. The road climbs to 3,000m, with most superb scenery and little traffic. First accommodation is in Padua, then Fresno (cheap hotels), Mariquita and Honda (see page 29).

Buses New terminal with good restaurant, C 19 between Cras 15 and 17. Buses to **Medellín**: Autolegal via Neira and Aguadas, 6 hrs, US$5.40; Empresa Arauca via Anserma, 10 hrs, 1st class US$10; colectivo to Medellín, US$10.25. Bus to **Bogotá**, Expreso Bolivariano Pullman, US$12, 9 hrs; 7½ hrs by Flota El Ruiz *buseta*, US$13.50. To **Honda**, US$3.60 (Expreso Bolivariano). **Cali** by bus Expreso Palmira or Expreso Trejos, hourly, 7 hrs, US$11 ordinary; Pullman 6 hrs, US$13. To **Cartago**, 4 hrs, every 20 mins, US$1.50; **Pereira**, Expreso Palmira, Expreso Trejos, ½-hourly, 1½ hrs, excellent road, beautiful scenery, US$2.50 ordinary. **Armenia**, Expreso Palmira, 3 hrs, US$4. To **Quibdó**, Transportes Arauca, via Pereira, La Virginia, Pueblo Rico and Tadó, Mon, Wed, Fri, Sat 0600, 14-17 hrs, US$14.

LOS NEVADOS

Parque Nacional Los Nevados: The park comprises 58,000 ha and straddles the departments of Caldas, Quindío, Risaralda, and Tolima. To Nevado del Ruiz (5,399m) with a vehicle, either take the Bogotá road from Manizales, then a branch road to a viewpoint (22 km). La Esperanza is the point to leave the main road for excursions towards the volcano. An alternative route follows the road to Villa María for 6 km, turning left to Barrio La Enea and continuing on an unpaved road for 22 km to Termales del Ruiz at 3,500m. 5 km further on, this road meets the road coming from La Esperanza. Turning right, and continuing 2 km brings you to Las Brisas (small restaurant). You can walk from Las Brisas down to Manizales in a day, stopping along the way at the Termales del Ruiz, ask about short cuts.

Past Las Brisas the road forks. To the left it continues over enormous landslides caused by the 1985 Nevado del Ruiz eruption to the village of Ventanas (a very scenic drive) and on to Murillo in the department of Tolima. To the right it climbs steeply for 1 km to reach the **park entrance and visitors' centre** at 4,050m. The turnoff (left) to Nevado del Ruiz is 10 km beyond the park entrance and one can drive to within 2 km of the snow line. On foot from 4,050m to the summit takes 6 to 7 hrs if you are acclimatized. At 4,800m, near the foundations of a large shelter (destroyed by fire before the eruption), there is a basic hut, no water, no beds nor any facilities, ask at the entrance if it is open. From here, it is about 3 hrs to the summit. An authorized guide is obligatory if you wish to climb from the snowline to the crater. Another excellent climb nearby is La Olleta (4,850m), the ash cone of an extinct volcano. You can descend into the crater, but note your route well as fog can obliterate landmarks very quickly. The principal road continues (S) below the Nevados del Cisne and de Santa Isabel between which you can visit the Laguna Verde, but you will need a special permit. 20 km further along the road and 39 km beyond the turnoff to Nevado del Ruiz is Laguna del Otún at the southern end of the park, trout fishing and camping with permission of MA.

● **Park information** You must check in advance if entry to the park is permitted. For information in Manizales contact MA, C 23, No 55-05, T 854581; or the tourist office in Manizales, which organizes day trips to Nevado del Ruiz at weekends (US$16 1 day, leave 0800, return via hot pools); a recommended guide is Javier Echavarria Carvajal, T Manizales 740116. See under Pereira, page 946, for access from that city and under Ibagué, page 929, for **Nevado de Tolima**. Visitors to the park should come prepared for cold damp weather, and remember to give yourselves time to acclimatize to the altitude. Maps of the area are available at the Instituto Geográfico in Manizales, just behind the Club Manizales on Carrera 24.

● **Accommodation A2** *Hotel Termales del Ruiz*, comfortable, with restaurant and good thermal pools on premises. You can camp at Las Brisas, but it is very cold, you will need a good sleeping bag, but beautiful surroundings. 4 km from the park entrance is the new *Chalet Arenales* at 4,150m run by Carlos Alberto, **D** pp inc sleeping bag, food, hot showers, cooking facilities, good atmosphere, crowded at weekends. You can stay at the *Refugio El Cisne*, a small farm at 4,200m nr Laguna Verde (see above), where a farmer lets you sleep in his warehouse (very cold, but less so than outside) for US$3.50 and offers you milk and coffee.

● **Transport** If you do not have a car, it is still possible to reach Las Brisas and the park entrance with a milk truck that leaves the Celema dairy in Manizales, Cra 22, No 71-97, between 0500 and 0600 daily US$3, returning in the early afternoon, or the Rápido Tolima bus at 1430 from the Terminal in Manizales to Murillo goes through Las Brisas, US$3, 2 hrs.

22 km SW of Manizales is **Chinchiná** (**F** *Hotel Pielroja*, basic, but clean), followed by **Santa Rosa de Cabal**, 15 km away and 12 km from Pereira. A 11-km road branches E off to **Termales de Santa Rosa**, where waters from a hot spring cascade down a mountain into a swimming pool, entry US$4.50 (busy at weekends; **A1** *Hotel Resort*, rooms from 1 to 6 persons, restaurant, bar and cafeteria, information T 641309 and in Santa Rosa de Cabal). There are also cold showers fed from a natural spring. Bus Pereira-Santa Rosa, US$0.50; then bargain for a jeep ride, about US$1.50 pp, to the springs (an afternoon excursion is better value than a 1-night package).

PEREIRA

Capital of Risaralda Department, 56 km SW of Manizales, **Pereira** (*pop* 412,135; *alt* 1,476m) stands within sight of the *Nevados* of the Cordillera Central. After a severe earthquake on 5 February 1995, some buildings have been rebuilt. Others, like the Palacio Municipal on the corner of Plaza Bolívar, are awaiting a decision on whether to pull down or repair.

Places of interest

It is a pleasant modern city, founded in 1863, with a cathedral on the central **Plaza Bolívar**, drab and unimpressive from the outside but with an elegant interior. In the plaza there is the striking sculpture of a nude Bolívar on horseback, by Rodrigo Arenas Betancur. There are three other principal parks: the most picturesque is the Parque del Lago, with an artificial lake; a fountain is illuminated several times a week. (Good Christmas illuminations, too.) There is a lively market.

Zoo and gardens

Adjacent to the airport is the Matecaña zoo though mostly in poor condition. A feature is the "ligre", a cross between a lion and a tiger. There are also many birds. Entry US$1.50. Bus from town centre to zoo, US$0.25. The Tzobota orchid gardens, S of the city, can also be visited.

Local information

● **Accommodation**

L3 *Meliá Pereira*, Cra 13, No 15-73 (T 350770/353970, F 350675, Apdo Aéreo 4050), restaurant, bars, swimming pool, well appointed top hotel, tourist service in lobby.

A1 *Soratama*, Cra 7, No 19-20, T 358650, F 250014, on Plaza Bolívar, restaurant, parking; **A2** *Gran*, C 19, No 9-19, T 359500, inc breakfast, older hotel, good restaurant, bar, travel agency, well managed, rec; **A3** *Marandúa*, Cra 8, No 14-73, T 357131/356192, F 334081, central, rec.

B *Calle Royal*, Cra 8, No 16-13, T 359577, hot water, comfortable, simple; **B** *Cataluña*, C 19, No 8-61, T 354527, 2 floors up, hot water, spacious, a bit gloomy.

C *Royal*, C 16, No 7-56, T 352501, 2 floors up, hot water, rec.

D *El Hotel*, C 25, No 7-10, T 352217, on Parque del Lago, hot water, hospitable; **D** *Residencias Minerva*, C 18 between Cra 8 and 9, central, safe, TV; **D-E** *Ocmara*, Cra 9, No 19-25, cheaper without bath/breakfast, fan, secure, hot water, cable TV, rec.

F *Los Reyes*, C 4, No 16-23, efficient, good value.

Youth hostel: *Centro Vacacional Viejo Caldas*, 10 mins by car from Pereira, details from Alcom in Bogotá.

● **Places to eat**

El Vitral, C 17, No 6-60, international food, very good; *Wall Street*, Edif Antonio Correa, Cra 7, No 18-21, Local 215, business lunches, good;

Naturista No 2, C 19, No 5-73, good; *Pastelería Lucerna*, C 19, No 6-49, large coffee shop, fountain/garden, good cakes, snacks, icecream, clean; *Banana Rosse*, C 16, No 7-30, good local dishes, *bandeja paisa* US$5, *menú* US$3.20; *El Galeón*, C 20, No 8-29, *menú* US$2.50, good.

There are several good restaurants on the Av 30 de Agosto (the road W to the airport), inc *Kisses Parilla*, good steaks. Also, past the *Hotel Meliá* on the Av Circunvalar going E, No 6-55, *Mi Ciudad*, good meat dishes and on the same road at C 5, La Terraza, *Pizza Piccolo*, good Italian food, excellent pizzas, rec.

● **Banks & money changers**
Banco Anglo Colombiano, Cra 7, No 18-70, Suite 201, changes Amex TCs with purchase receipt, cash against most credit cards, good rates, open 0800-1130, 1400-1600. Few other banks take TCs but many have cash machines, some of which take foreign cards, check. Many other banks in the centre. *Casas de cambio* change cash and some exchange TCs but check at what time of day: several around Cra 9/C 18.

● **Tour companies & travel agents**
Tierra Mar Aire, Av Circunvalar No 14-60, T 356565, general travel agency, good service; *Eco Sueños*, C 25, No 6-57, T 339955, trips arranged to Ucumari Park, Los Nevados etc, Manager: Soraya Quintana, very helpful and a fully qualified guide, rec; *David's Tours*, Cra 15, No 14-06, T 340850.

● **Tourist offices**
Tourist information at Compañía Regional de Turismo de Risaralda, Centro Comercial Alcides Arévalo, C 19 y C 6, Of 308, T 356427; Oficina de Fomento al Turismo, Cra 7, No 19-28, Of 403, T 357132/357172, F 267684, Head of Promotions, and very helpful is Dr Humberto García Ramires. Corporación Autónomo Regional de Risaralda (Carder), C 24, No 7-29, pisos 4-5, T 354152, for information and permission to visit local National Parks.

● **Transport**
Air Matecaña airport is 5 km to the S, bus, US$0.25. Aces (T 242237), SAM and Avianca (T 358509) flights to and from **Bogotá**, Aces to Medellín, US$71.

Buses New bus terminal, clean, with shops, outside city centre. Bus to **Armenia**, 1 hr, US$2.50, a beautiful trip; to **Cali**, US$9.75, 4½ -5 hrs, buses by night, take colectivo by day, same price; to **Medellín**, 8 hrs, US$14; **Manizales**, US$2.50, 1½ hrs; to/from **Bogotá**, US$11, 7 hrs (route is via Girardot, Ibagué and Armenia).

Route to Chocó A nice ride can be taken through the heart of coffee country along the road NW to Tadó and Quibdó. The Río Cauca is crossed before **La Virginia** (**F** *Hotel New York*, Cra 9, No 7-45, several others). The road then climbs the eastern slopes of the Cordillera Occidental to reach **Pueblo Rico** (basic hotels and restaurants). The many *veredas cafeteras* with their colourfully painted balconies decorated with flowers and the mountain scenery along the way are beautiful.

UCUMARI PARK

From Pereira, a 2 to 4-day excursion to the beautiful **Ucumari Park** is recommended. This is one of the few places where the Andean spectacled bear survives. Above 4,000m in the park are spectacular *fraílejón* plants. Permission to visit must be obtained from Carder (see above under **Tourist offices**). There is excellent camping, US$2 pp or US$25 for three good meals and room for the night at the *Pastora* refuge. Here Andean bears are kept in a compound in natural surroundings (you won't see them anywhere else in the park). From *La Pastora* it is a 1-2 day hike to Laguna de Otún through beautiful scenery of changing vegetation (see page 944).

Hikes can be made to the **Nevado del Ruiz** (see also page 928 and page 944). Take a chiva from Pereira at 0900 daily, additional chivas at weekends, to **El Cedral** (1½ hrs – return at 1630), then walk 2 hrs to the MA *refugio* through lush forest. Reservations for the *refugio* must be made in advance at Carder. Enquire there if a guide, eg Wilson Cardona or Soraya Quintana, is available for tours to the volcano. Camping is possible in the park, check with the rangers.

PEREIRA TO ARMENIA

A 44 km road runs through the heart of the *Zona Cafetera*. Above 2,000m forest provides communities such as **Filandia** with wood products as a livelihood.

Closer to Armenia, turn off the main road at the *Posada Alemana* and go E for 9 km to **Salento**, well into the foothills of the Cordillera. This small town is brightly painted with an attractive plaza. Up Cra 6 (continuation of the N side of the plaza) is a 250-step climb, 14 stations of the cross to measure your progress, to an outstanding viewpoint, overlooking the upper reaches of the Quindío and Cardenas rivers known as the Corcora valley, one of the finest views in Colombia. It is a popular weekend resort for Colombians for walking, riding and trekking but quiet during the week.

● **Accommodation & places to eat A3** *Mis Bohios*, on road to Corcora Valley (see below), **A2** with 3 meals, good facilities; **B** *La Posada del Café*, Cra 6, No 3-08, T 593012, breakfast, pleasant patio; **D** *El Caseron*, Cra 6, No 2-46, T 593090, pleasant atmosphere, cooking facilities, good restaurant with trout specialities; *El Fogata de Salento*, Cra 3, Esq Las Colinas, T 593248, good food; *Café Patacón y Trucha*, on Plaza, good fish. There are other places to eat and to stay, ask around, but make arrangements early in the day.

● **Tourist offices** For information about the area, contact Fundación Herencia Verde, C Real (Cra 6), No 2-15, Salento, T 967 593142 or in Cali, C 4 Oeste, No 3A-32, T 880-8484, F 881-3257. Trips can be arranged with guides and extended to the Parque Nacional de los Nevados and Nevado del Tolima.

Valle de Corcora

The centre of the Cocora valley is 12 km up from Salento along a rough track, jeeps take about 40 mins. Here there are three restaurants (*Las Orillas*, *Las Palmas* and *Bosque de Corcora*) all serving food at weekends, check in Salento during the week. 5 km beyond Cocora at 2,770m is the **Acaime Natural Reserve** with a visitor centre, ponies for hire, accommodation for 20 and a small restaurant. There are lots of humming birds, cloud forest and the most important area of wax palm (the national tree).

Above Acaime there are many trails into the high mountains, with day long treks to peaks such as **Morro Gacho** 3,450m or **Alto Español** 3,480m, and 3-4 day expeditions to **Paramillo del Quindío** 4,700m and **Nevado del Tolima** 5,221m.

ARMENIA

Quindío Department of which **Armenia** is capital (*pop* 231,745; *alt* 1,838m; mean temperature 19°C) is reached from Ibagué

by the Quindío pass (see page 929). The city was founded in 1889. To reduce its dependence on coffee, many new agricultural crops and activities are developing.

Places of interest

The central **Plaza de Bolívar** is dominated by the tall Quindío administration building and the striking modern cathedral. The facade is triangular in shape with a tall bell tower on the right. Inside, the nave continues the form and leaves a light airy feeling, accentuated by the fine modern stained glass. The plaza has two bronze sculptures, a conventional Bolívar by Roberto Henau Buritacá, and a fine example of Rodrigo Arenas Betancur's work, the **Monumento al Esfuerzo**.

Museums

The **Museo Quimbaya** is on the edge of town on the road to Manizales (take a city bus or taxi); fine collection of ceramics and gold pieces from the Quimbaya culture, well-displayed.

Local information
● **Accommodation**

A2 *Internacional*, C 20, No 14-56, T 414898, central, restaurant, full service hotel.

B *Palatino*, C 21, No 14-49, T 412740, central, inc breakfast, restaurant, bar, comfortable.

C *Mariscal Sucre*, Cra 17, No 18-33, T 410867/410876, discounts possible, hot water, modern.

E *Cordillera*, Cra 19, No 15-41, T 453722, good parking across the street; **E** *Imperial No 2*, Cra 19, C 21, central, safe, good but sometimes noisy; **E** *Moderno Aristi*, C 18, No 19-67, with bath, hot water.

F *Aymora*, Cra 19, opp *Nueva York*, safe, private bath, radio; **F** *Imperial*, C 21, No 17-43, T 441967, safe, rec; **F** *Pensión Nueva York*, Cra 19, No 23-52, basic but clean.

● **Places to eat**

La Fogata, Av Bolívar (Cra 14), No 14N-39, international menu; *Sierra Dorada*, Cra 14, No 1-160, seafood; *El Portón Quindiano*, C 17, No 15-40, T 451060, also at C 19, No 14-47, local dishes, good; *Frisby*, Cra 16, No 20-22, good pizza or fried chicken; *Cafetería Punto Rojo*, C 21, No 17-36, open 24 hrs.

Vegetarian: *Manjar*, C 18, No 15-52 and *Rincón*, Cra 16, No 18-28, closed Sun.

● **Tourist offices**

Tourist information at **Corporación de Fo-**

mento y Turismo, C 20, No 15-31, T 449441; **Corporación Autónomo Regional de Quindío** (CRQ), Caja Agraria Building, C 17, No 18-20, piso 4,5 y 6, for information on parks and natural reserves. Excellent map of Paramillo del Quindío and Nevado de Tolima, scale 1:40,000, available.

● **Transport**

Air El Edén, 13 km from city. Fog often makes air services unreliable.

Buses Terminal 15 blocks from centre. To **Ibagué**, US$3. To/from **Bogotá**, hourly, 9 hrs, US$13. To **Neiva**, Flota Magdalena, 0100, 0400, 2230, US$11. **Cali**, Expreso Bolivariano, US$10.50, 3 hrs, frequent service.

Parque Nacional del Café

12 km NW of Armenia is **Montenegro**, near which is the **Parque Nacional del Café**, near Pueblo Tapao. There are restaurants, a botanical garden, ecological walks, a Quimbaya Indian cemetery, a tower with a fine view and an interesting museum which covers all aspects of the origins, cultivation, marketing and consumption of coffee. The park is open Tues-Sun, 0900-1600, US$3, children US$2, parking US$1, T (967) 524174, F 536095. Take a bus (US$0.35), or colectivo (US$0.45) from Armenia to Montenegro and then a jeep marked 'Parque' (US$0.25) or taxi (US$2) to the entrance.

Staying on coffee farms

The decline of coffee prices since 1992 has had a significant effect on the Colombian coffee *finca*. Coffee is still by far the most important agricultural product of the area, but there has been a good deal of diversification into other crops as varied as flowers, asparagus and even bamboo. Recently, the idea caught on to open the farms to tourism. No two *fincas* are the same – they range from beautiful historic country mansions to modest accommodation. Urban Colombian families are increasingly spending their holidays in such places and this is being broadened to include foreign visitors. For information on the possibilities, contact travel agents (*Eco-Guias* in Bogotá is specially recommended), the coffee industry, which has an organization specially concerned with this endeavour: Cordicafe, C 73, No 8-17, P 6, Bogotá, T 345-6600, Ext 791, with offices in Armenia, T (967) 44209, and

Pereira, T (963) 358709, and the tourist office in Armenia will also advise on visits to coffee farms. To see the full process of coffee growing in Caldas, apply to the Comité Departmental de Cafeteros de Caldas, Cra 22, No 18-21, T 841700; recommended.

THE CAUCA VALLEY

From Pereira and Armenia roads runs W to Cartago, at the northern end of the rich Cauca Valley, which stretches S for about 240 km but is little more than 30 km wide. The road, the Panamericana, goes S up this valley to Cali and Popayán, at the southern limit of the valley proper. There it mounts the high plateau between the Western and Central Cordilleras and goes through to Ecuador.

Two roads go from Armenia to the Panamericana. A newer, direct road with heavy traffic, joins the highway 8 km S of Zarzal. The slower old road emerges 9 km further S. Before it drops into the Cauca Valley is **Caicedonia**, near which is a coffee finca owned by Dolly and Umberto Samin de Botero, T 458530, who will show you around their plantations, make arrangements first. Further on is **Sevilla**; C *Hotel Sevilla*, good, C 49, No 49-70, T 6434; others cheaper.

CARTAGO

Cartago (*pop* 98,640), about 17 km SW of Pereira, is on a small tributary of the Río Cauca before it takes to the gorge separating the two *cordilleras*.

   Founded in 1540, it still has some colonial buildings, particularly the very fine Casa de los Virreyes. Visit the cathedral, with the cross apart from the main building.

● **Accommodation** Around Plaza Bolívar: D *Don Gregorio*, Cra 5, No 9-59, T 627491, swimming pool, a/c; F *Río Pul*, Cra 2, No 2-146, fan and bath, rec. Many others in area around bus terminals (Cra 9) and railway station (Cra 9 y C 6); F *Central*, Cra 6, No 11-51, safe, good parking; F *Casa Turista*, Cra 6 y C 11, fan.

● **Places to eat** *Mullipán*, Cra 6 y C 12, good cheap *meriendas*; *El Portal*, Cra 6 y C 11, good *churrascos*.

● **Banks & money changers** Banco Popular, and Bancafé in Plaza Bolívar will exchange cash, but not TCs.

● **Post & telecommunications** Post Office: on Plaza Bolívar.

● **Buses** To Cali, US$4.20, 3½ hrs; to Armenia, US$1.75, 2-3 hrs; to Pereira, US$0.50, 45 mins; to Medellín, US$12, 7 hrs.

36 km S of Cartago is **La Victoria** (the Panamericana bypasses it to the E), a pleasant, small colonial town with a shady plaza (**F** *Hotel Turista*, family atmosphere, one block from the plaza; several restaurants).

13 km S is Zarzal. After the Armenia road junction is Andalucía (30 km – *Balneario Campestre*, car camping). 18 km S of Andalucia is **Tuluá** (**G** *Mariscal Sucre*, clean, fan and vegetarian restaurant *Vivamejor*, Cra 26, No 31-64, good).

BUGA

23 km S again this colonial city (*pop* 87,450) was founded in 1650. Its modern Cathedral contains the image of the Miraculous Christ of Buga to which pilgrimages are made.

Excursions On the road to Buenaventura, before the Río Cauca, is the **Laguna de Sonso Reserve**, which is good for birdwatching.

● **Accommodation** B *Guadalajara*, C 1, No 13-33, T 282611, swimming pool, rec, cabins for families, excellent restaurant, self-service cafeteria; *residencias* around Cathedral usually good value. **G** *Res Palermo*, C 9, No 9-82, T 72552, with bath.

● **Buses** To Cali, US$1.80. Toll 22 km S of Buga, US$0.50.

CALIMA

If you take the road from Buga to Buenaventura you come to the manmade **Lago Calima**. Many treasures of the Calima culture are said to have been flooded by the lake, when the dam was built. The northern route round the lake goes through **Darién** at 1,500m with an archaeological museum, open Tues-Fri 0800-1700, Sat-Sun 1000-1800, with good displays of Calima and other Colombian cultures.

● **Accommodation** A1 *Los Veleros*, T (92)

661-3701 (Cali), swimming pool; **E** *Darién*, cold showers, good; **E** *Sulevar*, cold showers, restaurant, parking; also cabins available at a Centro Náutico on the lakeside. Camping possible nr the village. Taking the southern route round the lake, 42 km from Buga is the **D** *Hotel del Lago Calima* set in very pleasant surroundings on the edge, no swimming pool, but some brave people swim in the lake, which is about 16°C.

● **Tourist offices** At C 10, No 6-21.

● **Transport** Direct buses from Buga, 2 hrs, and Cali, 4 hrs.

PALMIRA

47 km S from Buga is **Palmira** (*pop* 189,485) with a College of Tropical Agriculture. The best road S is from Palmira through Candelaria and Puerto Tejada, avoiding Cali, to Popayán; paved, straight, not much traffic.

● **Accommodation** B *Las Victorias*, Cra 32 Via a Candelaria, T 272-2666; **E** *Pacífico No 1*, C 30, No 32-55, T 272-5633, with bath, simple but nice; **F** *Residencias Belalcázar*, C 30, No 31-29, T 272-3782, **G** without bath, good value; many other cheap places.

● **Places to eat** *Ricuras*, C 30, No 32-16, good local dishes.

● **Transport** Bus to Cali, 29 km SW, US$0.55, Transportes Palmira, terminal on C 30, nr Cra 33.

At La Manuelita, 5 km N of Palmira, is a famous sugar estate. Beyond La Manuelita any of 3 roads running E will reach, in 12 km, the fine restored colonial *hacienda* of **El Paraíso**, where the poet Jorge Isaacs (author of *María*, a Colombian classic) lived and wrote. Entry US$0.50; there is a café. 9 km from El Paraíso is a **Museo del Caño** (sugar cane museum) in the Hacienda Piedechinche (open 0930-1600, closed Mon; admission, US$0.20). Tours of Piedechinche and Hacienda El Paraíso are arranged by Comercializadora Turística Ltda, Cra 4, No 8-39, local 101, Cali (US$12, including transport, entrance fee, guided tour and lunch). Bus to El Paraíso from Palmira, Cra 25 y C 26, 2 before 1230, US$0.65, 30 mins, return after 1500. There is no public transport connection between the two *haciendas*, so you must walk or arrange a taxi.

CALI

Cali, capital of Valle del Cauca Department, is the second largest city in Colombia, set in an exceptionally rich agricultural area producing sugar, cotton, rice, coffee and cattle.

BASICS *Pop* 1.78mn; *alt* 1,030m; *av temp* 25°C, hot and humid at mid-day but a strong breeze which blows up about 1600 and makes the evenings cool and pleasant; *phone code* 02.

It was founded in 1536, and until 1900 was a leisurely colonial town. Then the railway came, and Cali is now a rapidly expanding industrial complex serving the whole of southern Colombia. South of Cra 10 are many 1- and a few 2-storey houses, tiled and wide-eaved. Through the city runs the Río Cali, a tributary of the Cauca, with grass and exotic trees on its banks.

Places of interest

The church and monastery of **San Francisco**: inside, the church has been renovated, but the 18th century monastery has a splendidly proportioned domed bell-tower. From the 18th century church of **San Antonio** on the Colina de San Antonio there are fine views. Cali's oldest church, **La Merced** (C 7, between Cras 3 and 4), has been well restored by the Banco Popular. The adjoining convent houses two museums: **Museo de Arte Colonial** (which includes the church) and the **Museo Arqueológico** with precolumbian pottery (US$1). More Indian pottery can be seen in the **Sociedad de Mejoras Públicas**, across the street from La Merced; this collection belongs to the Universidad del Valle. Another church worth seeing is **La Ermita**, on the river between Cs 12 and 13.

The city's centre is the **Plaza de Caicedo**, with a statue of one of the independence leaders, Joaquín Caicedo y Cuero. Facing the square are the **Cathedral**, the **Palacio Nacional** and large office buildings. Across the river, which is 2 blocks from the Plaza de Caicedo, is the Centro Administrativo Municipal (CAM) and the main post office.

On one overlooking mountain, from which the best views are obtained, there is a statue of Christ visible for 50 km and there are three large crosses on another mountain. It is also worthwhile going up the skyscraper Torre de Cali for a view of the city, but you have to buy an expensive meal as well.

Museums

Museo de Arte Moderno La Tertulia, Av Colombia, No 5-105 Oeste (10 mins from centre) has an exhibitions of S American including local art, open Tues-Sat 0900-1300, 1500-1900, Sun and holidays, 1500-1900. **Museo de Historia Natural**, Cra 2 Oeste, No 7-18, precolombian exhibits as well as biological specimens from the area, similar opening hours. **Museo Calima**, C 7, No 4-69, Banco de la República building, precolombian gold work and pottery, open Mon-Sat 0900-1700, entrance US$0.50.

Parks & zoos

Zoo on the S bank some distance from the centre, entrance US$0.50. Orchid garden, **Orchideorama**, Av 2N No 48-10, T 664-3256, free.

Local festivals

Fair from 25 Dec to 3 Jan at Plaza Canaveralejo; bullfights, horse parades, masquerade balls, sporting contests. National Art Festival in June (painting, sculpture, theatre, music, etc). Also in June Feria Artesanal at Parque Panamericano, C 5, handicrafts and excellent leather goods.

Local information
● **Accommodation**

L1 *Intercontinental*, Av Colombia, No 2-72, T 882-3225, F 882-2567, tennis and pool, pleasant garden, *Los Farallones* restaurant with shows, good barbecues and buffets (weekend discounts); **L3** *Aristi*, Cra 9, No 10-04, T 882-2521, F 883-9697, weekend discounts, rec, art-deco style, large and old by Cali standards, unmodernized rooms much cheaper, turkish baths, rooftop pool, restaurant; **L3** *Dann*, Av Colombia, No 1-40, opp *Intercontinental* (with weekend discounts), T 882-3230, F 883-0129, all suites, large units, good (also *Dann Carlton*, Cra 2 Oeste No 1-60, T 882-3230, F 883-0129); **L3** *Obelisco*, Av Colombia, No 4 Oeste-39, T 883-7420, F 883-0219, smart, riverside location, small but good.

A1 *Torre de Cali*, Av de las Américas, No 18N-26, T 667-4949, restaurant on top floor;

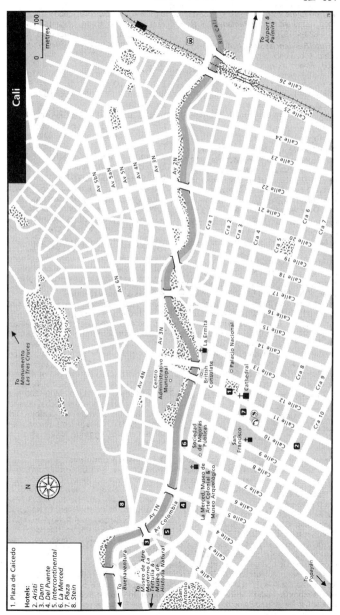

A3 *Don Jaime*, Av 6, No 15N-25, T 668-1171, good, restaurant rec; **A3** *Ramada*, C 5, No 5-25, T 883-4219, central.

B *Hotel Residencias Stein*, Av 4N, No 3-33, full board, **C** bed only, very good, quiet, excellent food, French, German and English spoken, Swiss-run, swimming pool; **B** *La Merced*, C 7, No 1-65, T 882-2520, swimming pool, pleasant young staff are very helpful, restaurant expensive, English spoken, rec.

C *Río Cali*, Av Colombia, No 9-80, T 880-3156, good, reasonably priced meals, old colonial building.

D *del Puente*, C 5, No 4-36, T 887-1490, will store luggage, rec; **D** *María Victoria*, C 10, No 3-38, 24-hr restaurant; **D** *Plaza*, Cra 6, No 10-29, T 882-2560, luggage stored, reasonably priced; **D** *La Familia*, C 14 N, No 6-42, T 661-2925, fan, small rooms, cold water, safe, good area; **D** *Los Angeles*, Cra 6, No 13-109, good.

E *Amoblador las Américas*, C 25, 2S-47, **F** without bath, cold water, safe; **E** *Sartor*, Av 8 N, No 20-50, T 668-6482, with bath, central, Italian spoken; *Las Palmas*, C 15, No 21-75, by the hour/night, comfortable.

F *Canaima*, Cra 6, No 12-61, T 776-1998, some rooms with bath, cold water; **F** *Paseo Bolívar II*, Av 3N, No 13N-43 (T 668-2863), cold water, safe (cheaper rates for long stay); **F** *Residencial 86*, Av 8N, No 14-01, hospitable, small rooms but good value, motorcycle parking; **F** *Calidad House*, C 17N, No 9AN-39, T/F 661-2338, taxi fare US$1 from bus terminal, kitchen, BBQ, laundry, will store luggage, run by Nick and Brenda, excellent travellers guest house, rec; **F** *La Margarita*, Cra 14, No 1-46, T 882-8259, use of kitchen, 5 mins from bus terminal, good.

G pp *del Río*, Cra 2 N, No 24-82; **G** *El Porvenir*, Cra 1, No 24-29, shared bath, cold water, no keys, no windows but quiet.

Out of town: **C** *Turístico La Luna*, Autopista Sur, No 13-01, T 558-7449, safe, large pool, restaurant, good parking.

Camping: on S outskirts *Balneario Campestre*, Brisas Tropicales, swimming pools, refreshments, car camping, armed guards and dogs.

● **Places to eat**
Las Dos Parrillas, Av 6N y C 35, good steaks but expensive; *Da Massimo*, Av 5N, No 46-10, good Italian; *Caballo Loco*, Av 6N y Cra 16N, European food; *Don Carlos*, Cra 1, No 7-53, excellent seafood, elegant and expensive; *Restaurante Suizo*, Cra 30 y Diagonal 29, Swiss, excellent fondue bourguignonne, pleasant atmosphere, reasonably priced; *El Quijote*, Cra 4, No 1-64, atmospheric, European dishes, expensive; *Simonetta*, Diagonal 27, No 27-117, pleasant, Italian dishes; *Balocco*, Av 6, No 14-

04, Italian and Colombian, good value; *La Terraza*, C 16, No 6N-14, elegant, music and dance, nice atmosphere; *Aragonesa*, Av 6 N, No 13N-68, good breakfasts; *Guacamole*, Av 6 N, No 14-73, Mexican, good quality, good portions; *Mac Club*, Centro Comercial Imbanaco (C 5 y Cra 39), hamburgers and hotdogs, excellent, cheap, good hamburgers also at *Primos*, nr C 5, Cra 34. At least 10 eating places in the bus station.

Vegetarian: *Raíces*, C 18N, No 16-25, open Mon-Sat lunch and dinner, good; *Punto Verde*, Cra 6, No 7-40, Mon-Sat, lunch only; *Govindas*, C 14, No 4-49, lunch at 1300, dinner 1900. *Centro Naturista Salud*, C 17N, No 6-39, set lunch US$2; *Casona Vegetariana*, Cra 6, No 6-56, good food, juices and bread.

You can find lots of European-style side-walk places along Av 6 at good prices. Also there many fast food places eg *Punto Sabroso*, C 12, No 8-06, central, open 24 hrs; *Oasis*, Av 6N y C 17; *La Flora* C 44, No 6-15. Cheaper are the *fuentes de soda*, mostly with Colombian-style cooking, a decent meal for US$3-4. Try *buñuelos* (cheesy fritters) and *pandebono* (cheesy buns). Cafés and ice-cream parlours abound nr the university, across the river from the main part of town.

● **Banks & money changers**
Banco Anglo Colombiano, C 11, No 4-48 (Plaza de Caicedo), and agencies in La Tertulia, Sur, and Av 6; **Banco de Bogotá** on the Plaza de Caicedo quickest in giving Visa cash advances. **Banco Industrial de Colombia**, C 11, No 6-24, cashes Amex TCs, good rates. **Credencial** in Unicentro, Cra 5, advances against Mastercard. Money can be changed at *Almacén Gerado*, C11, No 5-39, Almacén Stella, Cra 8, No 9-64, open 0800-1200, 1400-1800, very helpful, or at travel agents (eg at bus terminal, open Sat am). **Universal de Cambios**, Edif Lloreda, Plaza de Caicedo, rec. **Intercontinental de Cambios**, C6 Norte, No 2N-36, oficina 536, cash only.

● **Embassies & consulates**
Swiss, Cra 5, No 8-50; **US Consul** from Bogotá visits monthly at the centro Colombo-Americano, C 13N, No 8-45, T 667-3539; **British**, Ed Garcés, C 11, No 1-07, No 409, T 783-2752; **Norwegian**, Av de las Américas, No 23-33, T 668-6735; **Danish**, Av 4 N, No 4-46, T 661-4368; **Finnish**, C 4 Norte, No 1N-52, p 3, Barrio Centenario, T 661-1161; **French**, Av 3N, No 18N-24, Of 405.

● **Entertainment**
Nightclubs: locally known as "Grills". The ones along Av 6 N and C 5 are safest and best known. Try: *Tin Tin Deo*, C 5 y Cra 22, good atmosphere, salsa at weekends; *Nuestra Her-*

encia, C 5, Cra 34, popular, reggae and salsa; *Taberna Latina*, C 5, Cra 36, small and friendly; *Café Libro*, C 17 N, No 8N-49, very popular, more expensive; *Classicos*, C 22 N, No 2-58, good jazz concerts, drinks more expensive than C 5; *London Bar*, C 22N y Av 5N. There is a nightly tour on a *chiva* (open-sided bus) to various discos. There is a school, Profesional Académia de Baile, Cra 4B, No 44-24, T 446-2765, director Oscar Borrero, where you can perfect your Salsa.

Theatre: Teatro Experimental, C 7, No 8-63, T 778-1249; films Wed nights at Centro Colombo-Americano (see above). Also films on Fri nights at the Alianza Colombo-Francesa, Av 6 N, No 21-34. *Club Imbanaco*, C 5A, No 38A-14, old, popular movies. Good films also shown at the Museo La Tertulia (see above).

● **Hospitals & medical services**
Health: good clinic for women, *Grupo Mujeres*, C 6, No 3-64, T 880-0050; *Optica Cali*, Cra 5, No 13-105, good optician service; *Centro de Ortopedia y Fracturas*, Av 2N, No 21-65, for specialist treatments, doctors speak English and French.

● **Laundry**
Lavandería x kilo, C 23 Norte, No 7N-08, T 661-2184.

● **Post & telecommunications**
Post Office: Adpostal for national service, C 10, No 6-25; Avianca for international service, C 12N, No 2a-27.

Telecom: C 10, No 6-25. Faxes sent to Telecom 0057-2-883-0797 with name and local phone number will reach you. Small charge for receiving, about US$8/page to send fax to Europe.

● **Security**
Although still associated with drug and anti-drug operations, the atmosphere in Cali is quite relaxed. However, carry your passport (or photocopy) at all times and be prepared for police checks. Avoid C 15 S of the river and Cra 10, especially nr its junction with C 15, at night.

● **Shopping**
Platería Ramírez, Cra 11b, No 18-64, factory and shop good for gold, silver, brass, jewellery, table settings, etc: dubious area, best to take a taxi; *Artesanías de Colombia*, C 12, No 1-20 and for larger purchases Av 6 N, No 23-45. For boots and shoes *Chaparro (Botas Texanas)*, Av 6, No 14N-14, T 665-1007, good, owner Edgar speaks a little English. Best shopping districts are: Av 6N, from Río Cali to C 30 Norte and on Cra 5 in the S with new shopping malls: Unicentro and Holguines Trade Center, open also Sun 1000-1300.

Bookshop: *Librería Nacional*, on main plaza, has a café, as do branches elsewhere in the city. Bookstalls on the sidewalk on Cra 10 nr C 10.

● **Sports**
Within its Villa Olímpica in San Fernando, Cali has three stadia: the Pascual Guerrero Stadium, holding 50,000 people, the Olympic Stadium, holding 7,000 people and the Piscinas Olímpicas, 3,000. Another stadium holding 18,000, the Monumental de Cali, is 10 mins from the city on the road to Meléndez. Outside the city also is the new, first-class bullring.

● **Tour companies & travel agents**
Viajes Sinisterra, Edif Colseguros, p 2, T 889-3121, good service especially for airline advice. *Viajes Camino Real*, Av 4 N, No 22 N-32, T 661-6840, trips locally and to Popayán, Puracé, Leticia etc. *American Express* at Tierra Mar Aire SA, C 22N, No 5BN-53, PO Box 44-64, T 667-6767, clients' mail service, helpful. Thomas Cook office at Wagons-Lits, Cra 4, No 8-20.

● **Tourist offices**
Cortuvalle, Av 4N, No 4N-10, T (923) 675-614/13, F 680862. For national parks, **MA**, Av 4N, 37 AN-37, T 664-9334 (bus Blanco y Negro 2A from centre).

● **Useful addresses**
DAS office: Av 3N, No 50N-20 (T 664-3809).

● **Transport**
Local Taxi: ensure that meters are used. Prices, posted in the window, start at US$0.15. On holidays, Sun and at night, an extra charge is made.

Air Palmaseca, 20 km from city, has *casa de cambio*. International standard, with good *Hotel Aeropuerto Palmaseca*. Frequent services to Bogotá, Medellín, Cúcuta, Ipiales, Cartagena, Barranquilla, San Andrés, and other Colombian cities. Minibus from airport, from far end of pick-up road outside arrivals, to bus terminal (2nd floor), every 10 mins from 0500 up to 2100, approximately 30 mins, US$1.50. Colectivo to city about US$1.20; taxi, US$10, 30 mins. Avianca, Av 1N, No 7-59, T 889-4018/667-4141.

Buses Terminal (connected by tunnel to railway station) is at C 30N, No 2A-29, 25 mins walk from the centre (leave terminal by the taxi stands, take first right, go under railway and follow river to centre). Hotel information available, left luggage US$0.60/item, good food at terminal. Casa de cambio, cash only. Showers on second level (US$0.40). Buses between the bus station and the centre charge US$0.10. Taxi from centre to bus station, US$1.20. To **Popayán**, US$6, 2½-3 hrs, also colectivos, US$7.50. To **Pasto**, US$9.50, 9 hrs; to **Ipiales** (direct), US$14, 12 hrs or by Bolivariano Pullman, US$9.50, departures at 0400 and 0615 and

0800; Coomotor have a direct service to **San Agustín** via Popayán, Coconuco and Isnos, US$12.75, and a service at 0900 to San Agustín via La Plata (much slower than the new road via Isnos); Sotracauca also run Cali-Popayán-Coconuco-Isnos at 0500, 9 hrs, US$10. To **Cartago**, 3½ hrs, US$4.20; to **Armenia**, US$6; to **Ibagué**, US$7.50, 7 hrs; to **Buenaventura**, US$5, 4 hrs; to **Manizales**, US$11-US$13, 7 hrs; to **Medellín**, US$22, 10-12 hrs; to **Bogotá**, 10-15 hrs, by Magdalena (rec) and Palmira, US$18 (sit on left hand side of the bus). *Busetas* (Velotax and others) charge about 50% over bus prices but save time; taxi-colectivos about 2½ times bus prices and save even more.

BUENAVENTURA

145 km by road from Cali over a pass in the Western Cordillera is **Buenaventura** (*pop* 186,935), Colombia's only important port on the Pacific. It was founded in 1540, but not on its present site. It stands on the island of Cascajal, 16 km inside the Bay of Buenaventura. Beaches such as La Bocana, Juanchaco and Ladrilleros (many small hostels and restaurants) may be reached by motor launch, but they are not very safe. Trips to beaches cost between US$10-40 for 10-person launch (rate per launch, not pp).

Buenaventura is 560 km by sea from Panamá, 708 km by road from Bogotá. Mean temperature, 27°C. It rains nearly every day, particularly at night; the average annual rainfall is 7,400 mm (relative humidity 88%). There are still problems with malaria. The port handles 80% of Colombia's coffee exports, and 60% of the nation's total exports, including sugar and frozen shrimps.

The commercial centre is now entirely paved and has some impressive buildings, but the rest of the town is poor, with steep unpaved streets lined with wooden shacks. It is more expensive than Cali and it is difficult to eat cheaply or well. Festive atmosphere every night (see under **Music and dance** for festivals). South of the town a swampy coast stretches as far as Tumaco (see page 976); to the N lies the deeply jungled Chocó Department.

Local information
● Accommodation
A3 *Estación*, C 2, No 1A-08, T 243-4070, good restaurant.

D *Del Mar*, Cra 4 y C 3, T 242-3861, restaurant, TV, phone; **D** *Felipe II*, C 3 y Cra 3, T 22820, a/c, restaurant.

Several **F** and **G** hotels on Cra 5, eg **E** *Continental*, Cra 5, No 4-05, with bath; opp is **F** *Europa*, without bath; **F** *Las Gaviotas*, C 3, No 3-83, T 242-4652, OK; **F** *Niza*, C 6, No 5-38, with bath and fan.

● Places to eat
Los Balcones, C 2 y Cra 3, very good, but expensive; *Mediterráneo*, C 3, No 3-92, local and international food. Self-service restaurant on main plaza, clean, modern, open 24 hours. *La Sazón de Merceditas*, opp *Edif de Café*, good seafood, soups, reasonable prices. Good seafood at Pueblo Nuevo market, but not very cheap.

● Banks & money changers
Change money in Cali, not Buenaventura.

● Tourist offices
C 1, No 1-26, Mon-Fri, 0800-1200, 1400-1800. Cámara de Comercio nearby is also helpful; maps at CAM, 3rd floor of office block at the far end of the seafront.

● Useful addresses
Shipping agent: Navemar, C 1, No 2A-25, T 22571, for Sudamericana de Vapores, for shipping vehicles to/from Panama.

● Transport
Air Local airport only; flights to Cali.

Road There are plenty of buses to Cali, US$5, 4 hrs. Colectivos run at ½-hourly intervals to Cali, US$5.75 pp.

The **toll road** to Cali is fully paved; the toll is about US$1.30 for cars and US$0.30 for motorcycles. The ordinary road is not paved.

River From Buenaventura to Quibdó (see page 940) on the Río San Juan: boats are scarce out of Buenaventura (lumber boats from El Piñal only go about a day and a half upstream, and port authorities are strict about allowing passengers on cargo boats). One way is to take a bus from Pueblo Nuevo, Buenaventura, to San Isidro on the Río Calima (28 km, 6 hrs, terrible road), then a motorized dugout (*panga*) to Palestina on the Río San Juan. From there take a dugout going upstream; they rarely go as far as Istmina, which is connected by road and bus to Quibdó. Try to get as far as Dipurdú (no hotels, but friendly locals who offer sleeping space, shops with tinned goods), from where daily boats go to Istmina.

Sea Boats can also be found going S to Tumaco.

Whale watching

25 km NW of Buenaventura on the coast, near the mouth of the Río San Juan, is **Juanchaco**, a small fishing village, but the location of spectacular dolphin and humpback whale sightings between June and October. By launch from Buenaventura US$22, 1 hr, and by boat US$16.50, 3 hrs. Whale watching tours about US$12.50 for 2 hrs. Accommodation is basic.

FARALLONES NATIONAL PARK

Both the toll and ordinary roads out of Buenaventura give beautiful views of mountains and jungle, and from the old road you can reach the **Parque Nacional Farallones**. Take the dirt road S from the plaza in Queremal, at 1,460m, about 1 hr from Cali, 3½ hrs from Buenaventura. Alternatively, take the road SW out of Cali to Pance, on which there is an entrance to the park at El Topacio. Busy at weekends, camping possible at US$0.55 pp/day. Information from CVC, Cra 56, No 11-36, Cali, T 309755.

GORGONA ISLAND

The island of **Gorgona** is about 150 km down the coast from Buenaventura. Until a few years ago, it was Colombia's high security prison (a sort of Alcatraz), convicts were dissuaded from escaping by the poisonous snakes on the island and the sharks patrolling the 30 km to the mainland. It was made a nature reserve in 1985. Many parts are unspoilt with deserted sandy beaches. Some parts have been closed to visitors owing to excessive traffic. There is a good hike across the island through the jungle via a series of lakes, now dry due to earthquake activity. From the paths you can see monkeys, iguanas, and a wealth of flora and fauna. (Rubber boots are provided and recommended.) There is an abundance of birds (pelicans, cormorants, geese, herons) that use the island as a migration stop-over. Snorkelling is rewarding, equipment can be hired (but take your own if possible), exotic fish and turtles to be seen. July to Sept, killer whales visit the area.

● **Access** All visitors, research students and scientists must have a permit, obtainable from MA in Bogotá (other MA offices will give advice), US$15, US$10 embarcation – disembarcation fee. At holiday times application must be made 4 weeks in advance and you pay for 3 nights' accommodation at the time. Diving permit US$10. If you want to volunteer your services as a Park guard, contact MA, Bogotá. Facilities on the island are run by MA employees.

● **Accommodation** Cabins on the island: for 4 US$94 (80 low season), US$187 for 8 (156 low). Try to book bunk beds in advance; if you can't, prepare for a scramble. There is a restaurant with a mainly fish menu. You can take your own food but all non-biodegradable items must be taken off the island. Collect your own coconuts, but there is no other fruit on the island. Don't take alcohol, it will probably be confiscated. Do take drinking water, it is in short supply and expensive on the island.

● **Tours & transport** Organized tours: rec are *Ecotur*, Cra 56, No 5-31, Cali, T 551-7248, with a 4 day, 5 night tour from Cali for US$350 inc permission from MA, and an official guide. *Panturismo*, C 8, No 1-38, Cali, T 889-3135, offer a 4-day visit via Guapi, or 6 days via Buenaventura. To arrange on your own, find a boat at Buenaventura; they leave most days at 1600 from the El Piñal dock (Bodega Liscano) in Buenaventura. The trip, US$40 return, takes up to 10 hrs depending on conditions and can be an experience in itself.

You may be able to make arrangements in **Guapi** on the mainland for the 1½ hr boat trip to Gorgona Island, and Guapi can be visited from Gorgona with MA staff going to the market, but don't count on it. A launch costs US$300 to be shared by up to 10 passengers.

Local basket-weaving is on sale in Guapi, as are musical instruments such as the guaza (a hollow tube filled with seeds) and the marimba (about US$15). The only passable place to stay in Guapi is the *Hotel El Río* run by Pedro Arroyo, who speaks a little English, and his brother Camilo. The only way out of Guapi is by boat or by plane to Cali, US$36.

Popayán, Tierradentro and San Agustín

THE Pan-American Highway climbs out of the valley to Popayán, a richly historic city which gives access to the *páramo* of the Cordillera Central and the burial caves of Tierradentro – excellent walking country. This section also contains the upper reaches of the Río Magdalena and the remarkable archaeological site of San Agustín.

The paved Pan-American Highway (142 km) runs S from Cali to Popayán through splendid scenery in the Cauca Valley. Rich pastures are interspersed with sugar-cane plantations; to left and right are the mountain walls of the two Cordilleras. The valley narrows and the road begins to climb, with occasional glimpses E of the Nevado del Huila (5,750m).

Warning Both Valle del Cauca and Cauca departments have had guerrilla problems in the recent past. Enquire locally before travelling on minor roads in the area.

POPAYAN

Popayán (*pop* 201,000; *alt* 1,760m) is in the valley of the Pubenza, a peaceful land-scape of palm, bamboo, and the sharp-leaved agave. The early settlers after setting up their sugar estates in the hot, damp Cauca valley, retreated to Popayán to live, for the city is high enough to give it a delightful climate. To N, S, and E the broken green plain is bounded by mountains. To the SE rises the cone of the volcano Puracé (4,646m).

Popayán was founded by Sebastián de Belalcázar, Francisco Pizarro's lieutenant, in 1536. After the conquest of the Pijao Indians, Popayán became the regional seat of government, subject until 1717 to the Audiencia of Quito, and later to the Audiencia of Bogotá. It is now the capital of the Department of Cauca.

Popayán has given no fewer than eleven presidents to the Republic. The scientist Francisco José de Caldas was born here in 1771; it was he who discovered how to determine altitude by variation in the boiling point of water, and it was to him that Mutis (of the famous *Expedición Botánica*) entrusted the directorship of the newly founded Observatory at Bogotá. He was a passionate partisan of independence, and was executed in 1815 during Morillo's 'Reign of Terror'.

Places of interest

Popayán has been fully restored after the Mar 1983 earthquake. It has managed to retain its colonial character. The streets of 2-storey buildings are in rococo Andalusian style, with beautiful old monasteries and cloisters of pure Spanish classic architecture. **The Cathedral** (C 5, Cra 6), beautifully restored, has a fine marble madonna sculpture behind the altar by Buenaventura Malagón. Other churches are **San Agustín** (C 7, Cra 6), note the gilt altar piece and the unusual statue of Christ kneeling on the globe; **Santo Domingo** (C 4, Cra 5), used by the Universidad del Cauca, **La Ermita** (C 5, Cra 2), **La Encarnación** (C 5, Cra 5), also used for religious music festivals, **San Francisco** (C 4, Cra 9 – restoration continuing) and **El Carmen** (C 4, Cra 3). Walk to **Belén** chapel (C 4 y Cra 0), seeing the statues en route, and then continue to **El Cerro de las Tres Cruces** if you have the energy, and on to the equestrian statue of Belalcázar on the **Morro de Tulcán** which overlooks the city; this hill is the site of a precolumbian pyramid. There are plenty of guides offering their services: check for safety before making these walks alone. It is said that Bolívar marched over the **Puente Chiquito** (C 2 y Cra 6), built in 1713.

Museums

Not open Mon: **Museo Negret**, C 5, No 10-23, US$0.40, with works, photographs and furniture of Negret. **Museo Guillermo Valencia**, Cra 6 y C 3, birthplace of the poet; **Museo Casa Mosquera**, C 3, No 5-14; **Museo de Historia Natural**, Cra 2, No 1A-25, good displays of archaeological and geological items with sections on insects (particularly good on butterflies), reptiles, mammals and birds. Small collection in **Banco de la República**.

Local festivals

Easter processions, every night of Holy Week until Good Friday, are spectacular; the city is very crowded. The childrens' processions in the following week are easier to see. As at Pasto (but less violent), there are the Día de los Negros on 5 Jan and Día de los Blancos on 6 Jan; drenching with water is not very common.

Local information

● **Accommodation**

NB Hotel prices include taxes, but are subject to a 30% increase in some cases for Holy Week and festivals, eg 5-6 January. Continental breakfast is included in most category E and above hotels.

Central area: *Monasterio*, C 4, No 10-50, in what was the monastery of San Francisco, lovely grounds, swimming pool, very good, T (939) 232191/6, F 243491, reopened in 1996 after renovation; **A2** *Camino Real*, C 5, No 5-59, T 241254, PO Box 248, good service, excellent restaurant, rec; **A2** *El Herrero*, Cra 5 No 2-08, T 241637, converted large colonial house, family owned, good restaurant, highly rec; **A3** *Hostal Santo Domingo*, C 4, No 5-14, T 240676, good value, in restored colonial building; **A3** *Los Balcones*, C 3, No 6-80, T 242030, F 241814, hot water, Spanish-style restaurant for breakfast and lunch, good, will change TCs, rec.

B *La Casona del Virrey*, C 4, No 5-78, T 231836, hot water, big rooms, nice colonial house, warmly rec.

C *La Posada del Rancho*, 5 km on road to Cali,

T 234710, excellent restaurant; **C** *Los Olivares*, Cra 7, No 2-38, T 242186, quiet, good local and international restaurant.

D *Pakandé*, Cra 6, No 7-75, T 240846, good beds, hot shower, rec; **D** *Casa Grande*, Cra 6, No 7-11, T 240604, family run, attractive, hot water, convenient, stores luggage, highly rec.

E *Casa Familiar Turística*, Cra 8, No 3-25, T 242100, hot water, family-run, no sign, rec; **E** *Don Blas*, Cra 6 y C 8, No 240817, with bath, modern, rec; **E** *Ermita*, C 5, No 2-77, nr Capilla Ermita, T 241936, private bath, TV, good breakfast, accepts Visa, rec; **E** *La Posada*, Cra 6, No 2-35, with bath, use of kitchen, TV room, cheaper for longer stays, Spanish lessons arranged; **E** *Casa Familiar Haydée de Varela*, Cra 5 No 2-41, good breakfast, hot water, no sign, highly rec.

F *Casa Suiza*, C 4, No 7-79, T 240751, hot water, secure; **F** *Bolívar*, Cra 5, No 7-11, T 244844, hot water, pleasant, good restaurant, spacious flowery courtyard, safe motorcycle parking, car parking across street; nearby **G** *Residencia Panamá*, Cra 5, No 7-33, good, laundry service, good food, rec. Private accommodation at C 3, No 2-53, T 240602, Karin and Luis Cabrera, **G**, meals, Spanish lessons arranged.

Outside the central area, not safe walking alone at night: there are many hotels in the Mercado Bolívar area on Cra 6 to the N of the river, eg **F** *Plaza Bolívar*, Cra 6, No 2N-12, with bath, good cheap restaurant, safe, good value; **G** *Residencia Líder*, Cra 6, No 4N-70, good; **G** *Residencias San Agustín*, Cra 6, No 1N-15, family run, good beds, laundry facilities. Also, on and S of C 8: **D** *Berioska*, C 8, Nos 5-47, T 223145, well run; **F** *Residencias El Viajero*, C 8, No 4-45, T 243069, with bath, otherwise basic, popular, watch your belongings, modern; **F** *Residencias Cataluña*, C 8, Nos 8-27, popular; **F** *Amalia*, Cra 6, No 8-58, hot water, same owners as *Berioska*, cooking and laundry facilities, good base for young travellers, rec. For longer stays, finca accommodation nr Popayán suitable for families is available, enquire at the Tourist Office.

● **Places to eat**

The best restaurants are attached to hotels. For good food at reasonable prices, take a short taxi ride to the road to Cali to *Rancho Grande*, Autopista Norte 32N-50, T 235788, two thatched restaurants, delicious *chuzos* (barbecued beef), credit cards accepted, rec, or *Torremolino*, Autopista Norte 33N-100, T 234000, similar, also evening entertainment. In the centre, the best are: *La Viña*, C 4, No 7-85, open 24 hrs, good set lunch and dinner, also *panadería*; *Pizzería don Sebastián*, C 3, No 2-54, good food in a colonial mansion; *Cascada*, Cra 7, No 6-46, good for breakfast; *La Oficina*, C 4, No 8-01, huge servings, good value; *Los Quingos de Belén*, C4, No 0-13, very good Colombian food, try *empanadas* and *tamales pipianes*; *La Brasa Roja*, Cra 8 No 5-90, set lunch and evening meal, good food and value; *Jengibre*, Cra 8, No 7-19, T 242732, vegetarian; *Belalcázar*, Cra 6, No 7-55, T 241911, good value; *Caldas*, Cra 6 y C 8, filling 3-course set meals, their *sancocho* rec; *Mey Chow*, Cra 10A, No 10-81, good Chinese; *Chung Wah*, Cra 6, No 9-64, huge, good Chinese, also vegetarian; *Pizzeria Italiano*, C 4, No 8-83, Swiss owned, good pizzas and pastas etc, vegetarian dishes, fondues, lunch US$2.40, good meeting place, rec; *La Fontana*, C 6, No 7-72, excellent bakery with café serving meals, pizzas and sandwiches. For light refreshments: *Peña Blanca*, Cra 7, No 6-73, best bread and cakes; rec; *Comamos*, C4, No 8-41, in front of cinema, cheap, try the *arepas de queso*; *Delicias Naturales*, C 6, No 8-21, good, cheap, vegetarian; *Olafo*, C6, No 7-42, good pizzas and *patacones con guacamol* and great vanilla ice-cream.

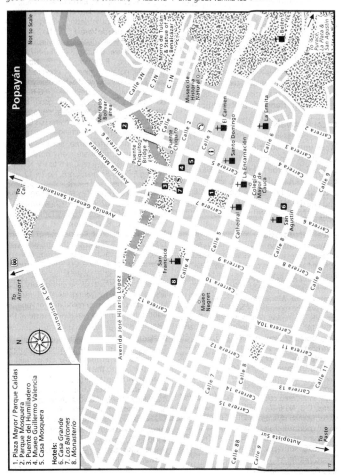

Popayán

Not to Scale

1. Plaza Mayor / Parque Caldas
2. Parque Mosquera
3. Puente del Humilladero
4. Museo Guillermo Valencia
5. Casa Mosquera

Hotels:
6. Casa Grande
7. Los Balcones
8. Monasterio

● **Bars**
Los Balcones, Cra 7, No 2-20; *Salón Azteca*, Cra 9, C 2 y 3; *Café Galería*, Cra 3 y C 4.

● **Banks & money changers**
Banco Cooperativo, Cra 6, Banco del Estado, and others will change TCs. Some, eg Banco Popular, will give cash advances against Visa cards or Banco del Occidente against Mastercard. Salvador Duque at Diana shop on the main plaza, nr the cathedral. Cash dollars can be changed at a *casa de cambio* on Cra 7 between C 6 and 7, also open on Sat. There are other *cambios*, but their rates are poor. Change dollars elsewhere; if coming from the S, Pasto is a good place.

● **Post & telecommunications**
Post Office: Cra 7, No 5-77.
Telephone Office: Telecom, Cra 4 y C 3; closes 2000.

● **Security**
Take care if you cross any of the bridges over the river going N, especially at night.

● **Shopping**
During the week, the open markets are interesting – Bolívar market, C 1N, Cra 5 is best in the early morning – local foods such as *pipián*, *tamales* and *empanadas*.

● **Sports**
At weekends people play 'sapo', see under **Sports** in **Information for travellers**. A good place is along the La Plata road nr Belén Church. At the Universidad del Cauca, Cra 3, there is a good, clean swimming pool, entry US$0.50.

● **Tourist offices**
Casa Caldas, C 3, No 4-70 (T 242251), has good maps of the city, prices of all lodgings, and bus schedules and prices. Ask for Sra Haydée de Varela about accommodation. All staff are very helpful, will tell you where horses may be hired for exploring, and will store luggage. In addition to normal hours, they are open Sun until 1200. Ask at the Tourist Office about which areas of the city are unsafe. (For information on travel beyond Popayán ask elsewhere and check with other travellers.) They also sell local crafts at good prices; telephone and mail service. The Tourist Office and the Colegio Mayor de Cauca have details on art exhibitions and concerts. Try also the **Casa de la Cultura**, C 5, No 4-33, for information on cultural events. **MA**: Cra 9, No 18N-143, T 239932.

● **Transport**
Local Taxi: no meters; normal price within city is US$0.75, or US$0.90 at night.

Air The airport is 20 mins' walk from the centre. Service to **Bogotá** with Avianca.

Buses Popayán's bus terminal is nr the airport, 15 mins walk from the centre (Ruta 2-Centro bus, terminal to centre, US$0.30, or taxi, US$0.75). Luggage can be stored safely (receipt given); there is a charge to use the toilets, and a US$0.07 departure tax. From the bus station, turn left to statue of Bolívar, then take second right to Parque Bolívar; here are the market and cheap hotels. **Care**: thefts of luggage in bus station reported in 1997.

To/from **Bogotá**, Expreso Bolivariano, US$23, 16 hrs. To **Cali**, US$6, 2½-3 hrs, or Velotax microbus, US$7.50, colectivos leave from the main plaza; to **Pasto**, with Coop de Nariño, Cra 6, No 2-16, 1130, Cootranar (cheapest US$9, 1030, but not too reliable), Flota Magdalena, Exp Bolivariano, 0930 and Supertaxis del Sur, US$11.25, 5-8 hrs, spectacular scenery (sit on right); to **Medellín**, US$30, 12 hrs; to **Ipiales**, something runs every hour but many buses arrive full from Cali, book in advance; Supertaxis at 1230, or bus, up to US$12 (Transportes Ipiales at 0700, Bolivariano at 0530 or 0900 the best), 7½-10 hrs. To **San Agustín** (confusing routes and schedules), La Gaitana, 11 hrs, at 0900 and 2000, Coomotor, 13 hrs, US$10.75 each once a day. Cootranshuila buses run over the new road via Isnos to San Agustín from bus terminal, twice a day (0600 and 1300), US$9.50, 6 hrs or more depending on the weather; also Sotracauca at 0900, 6 hrs, US$7.80. Sit on the left side for the best views. To **Tierradentro** (Cruce de Pisimbalá, also known as Cruce de San Andrés), with Sotracauca, 5 a day between 0500 and 1500, US$5.50, 4-6 hrs (see page 961) continues to La Plata. Flota Magdalena to **La Plata**, US$5.50, 5 hrs, also Unidos del Sur (not via Tierradentro) and Sotracauca at 0730. To **Puracé**, US$1.20, 2 hrs (Pullman is slightly more, Sotracauca at 0600, La Gaitana 0700, Coomotor later in am).

SILVIA

Silvia (*alt* 2,521m) lies in a high valley NE of Popayán. The local Guambiano Indians wear their typical blue and fuchsia costumes, and are very friendly and communicative. The Tues market seems to be full of Otavalo Indians from Ecuador and their goods – more expensive than in Otavalo, but sucres accepted. The market is at its best between 0600 and 0830. Not much to buy, but very colourful. A typical Indian settlement, La Campana, is 1 hr on the *lechero*; 2-3 hrs' walk downhill back to Silvia. It is not safe to park cars in the street at night in Silvia. Tourist information

1½ blocks up from plazuela on righthand side. Horse hire from Sr Marco A Mosquiro, US$1.50/hr.

Silvia is reached either through Totoró on the Popayán-Tierradentro road (partly paved), or through **Piendamó** (paved), two beautiful routes.

- **Accommodation In Silvia**: **C** *Comfandi*, Cra 2, No 1-18, T 251253, F 251076, opp church on main square, safe, restaurant; **D** *Casa Turística*, helpful, hot shower, good food, beautiful garden; **E** *Cali*, an old house, with good craft shop, inc food, a little primitive, but very pleasant; **E** *Ambeima* (3 beds/room), efficient, good simple meals, rec; **F** *La Parrilla*, water supply erratic, basic, restaurant has reasonable, cheap food; **G** *Residencias La Villa*, about 200m up main road, basic, negotiate your price; *Taberna El Buho*, with live music Sats pm. **Caja de Agraria** gives cash against Visa card. **In Piendamó**: **E** *Central*, behind old train station, quiet, dubious electrics; **E** *Motel*, next to Mobil, with cold shower, TV.

- **Buses** From Popayán, daily Coomotorista and Belalcázar, several *busetas* in the morning (US$2); additional buses on Tues; or take Expreso Palmira bus to **Piendamó**, every 30 mins, US$0.75; from there, colectivo to Silvia, US$0.85. On market day (Tues) you can take a bus to **Totoró**, 1200, US$1.50, 1 hr and then a bus to **Tierradentro**, 5 hrs, US$8.50. Direct bus to **Cali**, US$3.50, 3 hrs.

TIERRADENTRO

67 km beyond Totoró is **Inzá** (hotels *Inzá*, *Sayonara* and *Ambalá*). There are several stone statues in the new plaza.

9 km beyond Inzá is the **Cruce de Pisimbalá**, sometimes known as the Cruce de San Andrés, where a road turns off to **San Andrés de Pisimbalá** (4 km), the village at the far end of the Tierradentro Park. At Pisimbalá there is a unique and beautiful colonial church with a thatched roof; for the key ask behind the church. A few km before reaching Pisimbalá (20 mins down the hill, E, on foot) you pass the Tierradentro Museum of indigenous culture: 0700-1100, 1300-1700, very good local information. The second floor is dedicated to the work of the Páez Indians, not to be missed.

The Páez Indians in the Tierradentro region can be seen on market days at Inzá (Sat), and Belalcázar (Sat); both start at

0600. The surroundings have spectacular natural beauty, with small Indian villages in the mountains (get exact directions before setting out).

TIERRADENTRO ARCHAEOLOGICAL PARK

At the archway directly opposite the museum or at Pisimbalá village you can hire horses (US$2 an hr, make sure they are in good condition) – or you can walk – to the **Tierradentro** man-made burial caves painted with geometric patterns.

There are four cave sites – Segovia, El Duende, Alto de San Andrés and El Aguacate. The main caves are now lighted, but a torch (your own or one borrowed from the park administration) is advisable.

At Segovia (15 mins' walk up behind the museum across the river), the guard is very informative (Spanish only) and turns lights on in the main tombs. Segovia has over 20 tombs, 5 of which are lit (these 5 are not opened until 0800-0900). Nos 8, 9, 10, 12 and 28 are impressive. 15 mins up the hill beyond Segovia is El Duende (two of the four tombs are very good). From El Duende continue directly up to a rough road descending to Pisimbalá (40 mins). El Tablón, with 8 stone statues, is just off the road 20-30 mins walk down. El Alto de San Andrés is 20 mins from Pisimbalá (Nos 1 and 5 tombs the best – the guard is very helpful). From the back of El Alto it's 1½ hrs up and down hill, with a final long climb to El Aguacate. Only one tomb is maintained although there may be 30 more. The views from El Aguacate are superb. **NB** The whole area is good for birdwatching.

Steven Gilman from Georgia, USA, says: "Go to Tierradentro for a week, walk in the hills, people are very friendly. You can stop and ask at almost any house to buy *guarapo*, a local slightly fermented drink. Delicious to sit and talk and enjoy the hospitality." If you do not have that much time, 2 days is adequate.

Local information
- **Access**

Entry to Park and Museum US$7.50, valid for 4 days.

● **NB**

Walking between the sites, take a hat and plenty of water. It gets crowded at Easter-time. Single women are advised not to wander around this area at night unaccompanied.

● **Accommodation**

A short way up from the museum (see above), state-owned **C** *El Refugio*, good, restaurant and swimming pool (also available to non-residents); **E** *Residencias Pisimbalá*, "opposite the museum and up a bit", cheaper without bath, good, set meal and good other meals, garden, laundry facilities, mosquitos; **F** *Hospedaje Los Lagos de Tierra Adentro*, family run, good restaurant, hot water, pleasant, rec; **F** *Hospedaje Luzerna*, next to museum, cold showers, quiet, excellent fresh orange juice, free coffee in am, laundry facilities, highly rec, will let you camp for US$0.50.

Accommodation in the village: **F** *El Cauchito*, pleasant, family atmosphere, meals available, will arrange horse rentals, rec; camping; **F** *Residencia El Bosque*, cold showers, cheap meals, friendly dueña collects coins, rec; **F** *Residencias El Viajero* (Marta Veláquez), meals US$1, rec; **F** pp *Residencias Las Veraneras*, 2 houses, 300m from Archaeological Park, run by friendly young couple, restaurant, attractive garden and murals painted by locals. Ask about others who rent rooms.

● **Places to eat**

Pisimbalá, good food, cheap, rec; *El Diamanto*, opp museum, big portions, good value, order in advance; *Restaurante 56*, next to *Luzerna*, small but very good meals, also vegetarian dishes, also rents horses. Good fruit juices at the *Fuente de Soda y Artesanía* store and at *Los Alpes* (try their *mora con leche*), also good breakfasts. The house of Nelli Parra de Jovar, opp the museum with the long antenna, is rec for abundance; you must book meals in advance. She can also give up to date information on accommodation.

● **Transport**

The road from Popayán to **Tierradentro** is difficult and narrow, but this is compensated by the beautiful scenery. There are possibly 3 buses a week from Pisimbalá to **Popayán**, Mon, Wed, Fri, 0800, but on other days buses go from the Cruce (schedule from Popayán to Pisimbalá unknown). Sotracauca buses from Popayán, US$5.50, 4-6 hrs to **Cruce Pisimbalá**. Best to take the 0500 or 1000 bus, as the 1300 and 1500 will land you at the Cruce when it's dark, leaving you with a long unlit uphill walk. Walk (about 2 km) to the museum and on, 20 mins, to the village. Bus Cruce Pisimbalá-Popayán, 0600 (unreliable), 0800 and 1300, 4 hrs. If you want to go to **Silvia**, take this bus route and

change to a colectivo (US$1.50) at Totoró. For Inzá market (Sat) buses leave Tierradentro from 0200, US$0.55; best to go into Pisimbalá and out again to be sure of a seat. Buses from the Cruce to **La Plata** leave at 0900 and 1500 (unreliable), US$3, 4-5 hrs; if you cannot get a direct Cruce-La Plata bus, take one going to Belalcázar (US$1.20), alight at Guadualejo from where there is a more frequent service to La Plata; or one can hitch. On Fri only, a bus leaves from Pisimbalá village for La Plata at 0400.

NEVADO DE HUILA

17 km E of Inzá is Guadualejo, where one road heads SE to La Plata (see below), and another N to **Belalcázar** (12 km, a dusty drive). A further 23 km N along this road to Santander de Quilichao is **Tóez** on the Río Páez from where there is an access track, following the upper reaches of the river, to the **Nevado del Huila** National Park. At 5,750m, this is the second highest massif in Colombia and one of the least accessible. Near the source of the Páez is an MA hut with some facilities. Owing to heavy rain and snow in this area, especially April-June and Oct-Dec, and to thermal activity, there is a serious danger of landslides and flooding. Seek professional and MA advice before visiting or climbing in the area.

POPAYAN TO SAN AGUSTIN VIA LA PLATA AND GARZON

From Popayán a road crosses the Central Cordillera to Garzón on the paved highway S of Neiva. At Km 18 from Popayán, the road turning up to the right (S) leads to Coconuco and San Agustín (see below).

PURACE AND NATIONAL PARK

The valley road climbs to the small town of **Puracé**, at Km 12 (ie 30 km from Popayán), which has several old buildings. Behind the school a 500m path leads to Chorrera de las Monjas waterfalls on the Río Vinagre, notable for the milky white water due to concentrations of sulphur and other minerals.

● **Accommodation & places to eat** **F** *Residencias Cubina*, safe, cold showers, secure parking. *Restaurant Casa Grande* just above the church, meals around US$3.

● **Buses** There are several buses daily to Puracé from Popayán, the last returning around 1730.

At Km 22, look for the spectacular San Francisco waterfall on the opposite side of the valley. At Km 23 is the turning right to Puracé sulphur mines (6 km) which can be visited by applying to Industrias Puracé SA, C4, No 7-32 Popayán, best through the Popayán tourist office. 1 km along this road is a turning left leading in 1½ km to **Pilimbalá** in the **Puracé National Park** at 3,350m. Here there is a Park office, 7 sulphur baths at 28°C, entrance US$0.75, children ½ price, bring your own towels. The National Park contains Volcán Puracé (4,640m), Pan de Azúcar (4,670m) with its permanent snow summit, and the line of 9 craters known as the Volcanes los Coconucos (a strenuous 2-day hike can be made around the summits). The Park also encompasses the sources of four of Colombia's greatest rivers: the Magdalena, Cauca, Caquetá and Patía. Virtually all the park is over 3,000m. The Andean Condor is being reintroduced to the wild here from Californian zoos. There are many other birds to be seen. The Park's fauna include the spectacled bear and mountain tapir. Pilimbalá is a good base from which to explore the northern end of the park.

- **Climbing Volcán Puracé** On the hike to the summit, loose ash makes footholds difficult. Avoid getting down wind of the fumaroles, and do not climb down into the crater. Although the best weather is reported to be Dec-Mar and July-Aug, this massif makes its own climate, and high winds, rain and sub-zero temperatures can come in quickly at any time. A marked trail goes from behind the park office and eventually joins the road leading to a set of telecommunications antennae. These installations are guarded by the military and the area around them is mined, don't take shortcuts. Land mines are placed on the road itself at night, so climb only during daylight hours. The soldiers have been helpful to climbers in need of assistance. The summit is about 1 hr beyond the garrison, total time from Pilimbalá at least 4 hrs up and 2½ down. High altitude camping and mountaineering equipment required and a guide is strongly recommended.

Continuing on the main road to La Plata, at Km 31 there is a viewpoint for Laguna Rafael, at Km 35 the Cascada de Bedón (also chemically charged water) and at Km 37 the entrance to the most northerly part of the Puracé National Park. Here there is a visitor centre, a geology/ethnology museum (entrance US$0.75), and the very interesting Termales de San Juan, 700m from the road, entry US$0.40, where 112 hot sulphur springs combine with icy mountain creeks to produce spectacular arrays of multi-coloured mosses, algae and lichens – a must if you are in the area.

- **Park services** The Park is open all week, but reduced service on Mon. **At Pilimbalá:** saloon cars will struggle up the last stretch to the centre, but it is an easy 2½ km walk from Km 23. The centre has picnic shelters, a good restaurant (rainbow trout a speciality – also has cheap *hospedaje*, very cold) and 3 *cabañas* that hold 8, US$37.50 minimum for up to 6 and US$50 for 8 people. Firewood is provided. Camping costs US$3. Sleeping bags or warm clothing recommended to supplement bedding provided. **At Km 37:** the centre has a cafeteria (arrange meals beforehand through Popayán Tourist Office).

- **Transport** All these places beyond Puracé village can be reached by any bus from Popayán to La Plata or Garzón. The bus service can be erratic so check time of last daylight bus to Popayán and be prepared to spend a cold night at 3,000m. The rangers will allow you to stay in the centre.

At **Santa Leticia**, on the road to La Plata there is a cheap *hospedaje*, F, basic, to the right of the church.

La Argentina, 8 km off the Puracé-La Plata road beyond Santa Leticia, is an archaeological site in beautiful surroundings. The Museo Arqueológico de la Platavieja contains statues and ceramics. Ask for Sr Carlos Hernández, who runs the museum and is extremely knowledgeable. (He also keeps bees and sells honey.)

LA PLATA

La Plata (*municipal pop* 37,275), whose central plaza has an enormous tree, is 147 km from Popayán, 210 km from San Agustín.

- **Accommodation** E *Berlin*, by church on square, 3 blocks from the suite, F without bath, unappealing toilets and bugs in the beds; F *Brisas de la Plata*, nr bus station, door locked at 2300; F *Hospedaje Exclusivo*, nr bus station; next door to *Berlin* is G *Residencias Tunubalá*, OK; G *Viajero*, opp Sotracauca office, basic but convenient; G *Residencia Orense*, nr bus offices, meals available; G *El Terminal*, basic, nr bus station.

● **Places to eat** Most closed by 2000. *Noche y Luna*, just off main square, very good. Good set meals opp Banco Cafetero. Excellent bakery on main plaza.

● **Buses** Direct service with Coomotor from La Plata to **Bogotá**, via Neiva, 10 hrs, at 0900 and 2100, US$11; to **Garzón**, bus or jeep 1¹/₂ hrs, US$3; to **San Agustín** at 0600 and 0700, US$5; to **Popayán** (Sotracauca) 0500 and others, US$5.50, 5¹/₂ hrs. On Fri only, a bus goes at 1200 to **Pisimbalá**, otherwise for **Tierradentro** take a bus towards Popayán and alight at the Cruce. Private jeep hire La Plata-Tierradentro US$32, cheaper if you agree to pick up other passengers. Ask around for best options.

LA PLATA TO SAN AGUSTIN

Southeast of La Plata is Pital where the road forks, SE to Garzón, and S to near Altamira.

Garzón is a pleasant cathedral town set in mountains, 54 km SE of La Plata, 92 km S of Neiva (see page 930).

● **Accommodation** D *Damasco*, C 16, No 10-67, T 2091, colonial building, rec, good meals; **E** *Abeyma*, state hotel, rec, Cra 10 y C 12, T 2022, it is possible to camp in the grounds; **E** *Residencias Pigoanza*, on main square, with bath, rec.

At Altamira, 29 km further SW, a road heads SE to Florencia, capital of the Intendencia of Caquetá (see page 971). Southwest leads to **Timaná** (basic accommodation in G range) and continues paved past Pitalito to San Agustín.

Pitalito (*municipal pop* 62,890), has little to offer the tourist.

● **Accommodation** 2 hotels with swimming pools: **C** *Calamó*, Cra 5, No 5-41, T 360600, hot water, and **D** *Timanco*, 3-star, C 3 Sur, No 4-45, T 360666; **E** *Los Helechos*, C 7, No 6-48, T 360122, convenient for buses, family run; **F** *Residencia Pitalito*, without shower, reasonable, C 5 round corner from police station; **F** *Residencial El Globo*, main street, basic. *Crêperie*, 1 block S of main plaza, good value, excellent.

● **Transport** Plenty of buses and colectivos to **San Agustín**, US$1.50. Buses in Pitalito go from C 3a; Taxis Verdes from the main square (US$18 to Bogotá). Bus to **Mocoa** (in the Putumayo), US$8.50, 7 hrs, also jeeps from market square, 2 in am. Aires fly from Bogotá to Pitalito, via Neiva, on Sun at 1300, 1³/₄ hrs, returning to Bogotá Thur 1645, but the plane only goes if there are enough passengers (confirm tickets 24 hrs in advance).

South of Pitalito is the **Cueva de los Guácharos** National Park; take a bus to Palestina, US$1.20, 1 hr, and then walk for 6 hrs along an eroded, muddy path. Between Dec and June swarms of oilbirds (*guácharos*) may be seen; they are nocturnal, with a unique radar-location system. The reserve also contains many of the unusual and spectacular cocks-of-the-rock. The rangers are particularly friendly, providing tours and basic accommodation; permission to visit the park must be obtained from the MA offices in Pitalito, Neiva or Bogotá.

POPAYAN TO SAN AGUSTIN DIRECT

COCONUCO

Turn to the right off the Popayán-La Plata road at Km 18, then 7 km along is **Coconuco** (*alt* 2,734m). Coconuco's baths, Aguas Hirviendas, 1¹/₂ km beyond the *Hotel de Turismo* on a paved road (mostly), have one major and many individual pools with an initial temperature of at least 80°C. There is one pool where you can boil an egg in 5 mins. A track from town is quicker than the road. Entry US$0.60, crowded at weekends, but during the week it is a fine area for walking and relaxing in the waters. 6 km beyond Coconuco, near the road, are Aguas Tibias, warm rather than hot, with similar facilities for visitors.

● **Accommodation** B *Hotel de Turismo*, 500m out of town on the way to the baths, full service, colonial style hotel run by Cali Tourist authority, restful atmosphere; **E** *Coconuco*, in town, basic; **F** *Casa Familiar*, basic. Several other modest hotels and restaurants in town. **At Aguas Hirviendas**: 3 cabins at US$25/day that will hold up to 6.

24 km S of Coconuco is **Paletará** with high grassland on a grand scale with the Puracé/Pan de Azucar volcanoes in the background. Below the village (roadside restaurant and MA post) flows the infant Río Cauca. 10 km S of Paletará, the road enters the Puracé National Park and there is a track NE to Laguna del Buey. The road then enters a long stretch of virgin cloud forest. This section links Paletará with Isnos and San Agustín. Heavy rain

has weakened this stretch, 25 km of which is impassable to light vehicles and very tedious for buses and trucks. No efforts are being made currently to improve this road. 62 km from Paletará at the end of the cloud forest is Isnos (see page 966) followed by a steep drop to a dramatic bridge over the Río Magdalena and shortly to the main road between Pitalito and San Agustín.

● **NB** Avoid travelling by night between Popayán and San Agustín, the roads have been reported dangerous. Cyclists should avoid the new direct route. Also we have received many reports of theft on the buses between these towns; do not trust "helpfuls" and do not put bags on the luggage rack.

SAN AGUSTIN AND THE HEADWATERS OF THE MAGDALENA

Here, in the Valley of the Statues, are some hundreds of large rough-hewn stone figures of men, animals and gods, dating from roughly 3300 BC to just before the Spanish conquest. Nothing is known of the culture which produced them, though traces of small circular bamboo straw-thatched houses have been found. Various sculptures found here are exhibited in the National Museum at Bogotá, and there are some life-sized copies of San Agustín originals along the highway from Bogotá to the superseded Techo airport, near Fontibón. There are about 20 sites, described below. The area offers excellent opportunities for hiking, although some trails to remote sites are not well marked.

Rainy season April-June/July, but it rains somewhat during most of the year, hence the beautiful green landscape; the driest months are Nov-March. The days are warm but sweaters are needed in the evenings; average temperature 18°C.

SAN AGUSTIN

The town of **San Agustín** (*alt* 1,700m) is 27 km W of Pitalito.

Places of interest

The nearest archaeological sites are in the **Parque Arqueológico**, which includes the **Bosque de las Estatuas** (open 0800-1600

daily, entrance to both costs US$2.50, valid 2 days, also permits entry to the museum and the Alto de los Idolos – see below). The Park is about 2½ km from San Agustín, less than 1 km from the *Hotel Osoguaico*. The statues in the Parque are *in situ*, though some have been set up on end and fenced in; those in the Bosque (a little wood) have been moved and rearranged, and linked by gravel footpaths. Of particular interest are the carved rocks in and around the stream at the **Fuente de Lavapatas** in the Parque, where the water runs through carved channels. The **Cerro de Lavapatas**, above the Fuente, has an extensive view (closes at 1600; refreshment stands at 'Fuente' and on the way up to Lavapatas). There is a museum in the Parque which contains pottery and Indian artefacts (closes at 1700). Guides: Spanish US$12.50, other languages US$20. Guidebook in Spanish/English US$3.75. You can get a very good idea of the Parque, the Bosque and the museum in the course of 3 hrs' walking, or add in El Tablón and La Chaquira (see below) for a full day. The whole site leaves an unforgettable impression, from the strength and strangeness of the statues, and the great beauty of the rolling green landscape.

Museo Arqueológico, Cra 11, No 3-61, open Mon-Sat until 2300, with cultural events in the evenings, books and videos in Spanish and English, light refreshments. **El Tablón** is reached up Cra 14, over the brow of the hill and 250m to a marked track to the right. El Tablón (5 sculptures brought together under a bamboo roof) is shortly down to the left. Continue down the path, muddy in wet weather, ford a stream and follow signs to the Río Magdalena canyon. **La Chaquira** (figures carved on rocks) is dramatically set half way down to the river. Walking time round trip from San Agustín, 2 hrs. Plenty of houses offer refreshments as far as El Tablón.

At the site of **La Pelota**, two painted statues were found in 1984 (a 3 hr return trip, 6 hrs if you include El Tablón and La Chaquira, 15 km in all). The latest archaeological discovery (1986) in the

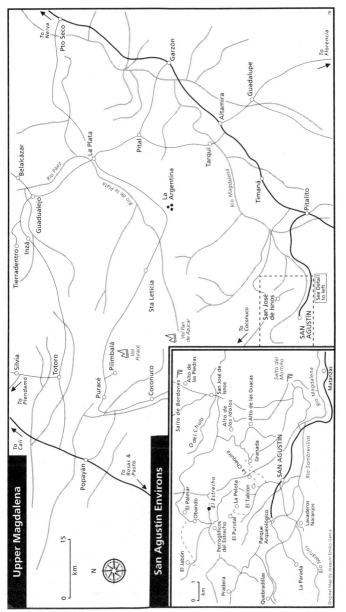

Upper Magdalena

San Agustín Environs

area is a series of at least 30 stones carved with animals and other designs in high relief; they are on the right bank of the Río Magdalena, near the **Estrecho** (narrows) to which jeeps run.

Alto de los Idolos is about 10 km by horse or on foot (small charge, less if you have a student card), a lovely (if strenuous) walk, steep in places, via **Puente de la Chaquira**. Here on a hill overlooking San Agustín are more and different statues known as *vigilantes*, each guarding a burial mound (one is an unusual rat totem). The few excavated have disclosed large stone sarcophagi, some covered by stone slabs bearing a sculpted likeness of the inmate (the site is open until 1600). 500m from the Alto is **D** *Parador de los Idolos* (3 rooms, bath, hot water).

Alto de los Idolos can also be reached from **San José de Isnos** (5 km NE) 27 km by road from San Agustín. The road passes the **Salto del Mortiño**, a 300m fall 7 km before Isnos, 500m off the road. Isnos' market day is Sat (bus 0500, US$1.20, return 1100, 1300, otherwise bus from Cruce on Pitalito road, or hitch); hotels in Isnos, **E** *Casa Grande*, central, cheaper without bath; **E** *El Balcón*.

6 km N of Isnos is **Alto de las Piedras**, which has a few interesting tombs and monoliths, including the famous 'Doble Yo'. Only less remarkable than the statues are the orchids growing nearby. 8 km further is Bordones; turn left at end of the village and there is (500m) parking for the **Salto de Bordones** falls; nearby **D** *Parador Salto de Bordones*, hot water, restaurant.

Local festivals

Santa María del Carmen in mid-July (not on a fixed date) in San Agustín. Two festivals in June are San Juan (24th) with horse races and dances, and San Pedro (29th) with horse races, dances, fancy dress, competitions and other events. In the first week of Oct, the Casa de Cultura celebrates La Semana Cultural Integrada, with many folklore events from all parts of the country. There are cockfights in San Agustín on Sun 100m behind the church at 1900, US$1.

Local information

● **Warning**

Beware of 'guides' and touts who approach you in the street. Have nothing to do with anyone offering drugs, precolumbian objects, gold, emeralds or other precious minerals for sale. Enquire about safety before walking to the more distant monuments.

● **Accommodation**

Between San Agustín and the Parque Arqueológico are **A2** *Yalconia*, 1 km from town, full board, some rooms with hot water, very pleasant, swimming pool, T (980) 373001; and **B** *Osoguaico*, T 373069, warm water, restaurant, laundry, swimming pool, camping site US$1 pp.

D *Cabañas Los Andes*, Cra 11, No 3-70, cabins, hot water and rooms with excellent views, cooking facilities, owner Sra María Muñoz de Hoyos.

E *Central*, C 3, No 10-32, T 373027, nr bus offices (cheaper without bath, or **G** for a room just to dump your luggage in during day's visit), good meals, laundry facilities, secure motorcycle parking, will hire horses, English and French spoken; **E** *Colonial*, C 3, No 10-54, T 373159, hot shower, pleasant, good restaurant, parrots in the garden, rec; **E** *Mi Terruño*, C 4, No 15-85, some rooms with bath, hot water, attractive garden, motorbike parking, owner Carlos Arturo Muñoz also has 3 cabins, *Los Andaqui*, for rent; **E** *Residencias El Imperio*, Cra 13, No 3-42, good; **E** *Residencial Familiar*, C 3, No 11-47, one block down from Coomotor-Autobuses Unidos del Sur office, hot water, laundry, book meals in advance or eat next door at the *Colonial*, horses for hire, but noisy disco nearby at weekends; **E** *Residencias Luis Tello*, C 4, No 15-33, run by a teacher, hot water, pleasant, laundry facilities, good value; **F** *Residencias Eduardo Motta*, C 4, No 15-71, T 373031, hot water, hard beds, but with morning coffee, quiet, rec; **F** *Residencias Menezu*, Cra 15, No 4-74, shared bath, hot water, family atmosphere, safe, central, rec; *Ullumbe*, Cra 13, No 3-36, T 373799, hot water, helpful, TV, family atmosphere; **F** *Residencias El Jardín*, Cra 11, No 4-10, T 373455, hot water, quiet, cooking and laundry facilities, free coffee.

There is accommodation in private houses for about US$2 pp. The farm of Constantino Ortiz is rec, 3½ km from town, first turn on left after the Parque Arqueológico, 4 rooms, best to take a sleeping bag, meals and horses available, peaceful, inexpensive, good cooking, plenty of morning coffee, also has camping, reservations at C 5, 11-13 in town. Another farmhouse rec is **G** *Posada Campesina*, Cra 14, Camino al Estrecho (on the route to El Tablón), owned by

Doña Silviana Patiño, who makes good pizza and cheese bread, meals with family, simple working farm, use of kitchen, camping possible, good walks nearby; **G** *Casa de Nelly*, Vía la Estrella, 1½ km W along 2 Av, T 373221, attractive peaceful finca run by Nelly Haymann (French), hot water, good food nearby, free coffee; **G** *Donde Clemencia*, Vía Antigua just beyond *Pizzería Cataluña*, rustic finca, good views, family atmosphere, riding available; **G** *Residencias Náñez*, C 5, No 15-78, T 373087, hot water, good value, rec; **G** *Magnola Pérez Urbano*, C 3, No 10-66, hot shower, cooking facilities.

Youth Hostel: *Albergue Juvenil Sindayo*, Cra 12, No 5-23, T 373208, F non-members, G members 1 YHA, dormitory, 50 beds, all inclusive 2 and 3 day programmes available.

Camping: next to *Yalconia* is *Camping San Agustín*, US$2 pp with your own tent, US$3 pp with theirs, clean, pleasant, toilets, lights, laundry service, horse hire (see below).

● **Places to eat**

La Brasa, opp *Yalconia Hotel*, good steaks, rec; *Brahama*, C 5, No 15-11, vegetarian meals and *comida* inc soup and drink (also meat dishes), good fruit salads, not expensive, rec; *Surabhi*, C 5, No 15-10, vegetarian dishes or meat, pizzas, *menú*, good juices, desserts etc, rec; *Superpollo*, Diagonal a la Iglesia, good; *Acuario*, C 3, very good, breakfasts and juices, sandwiches etc, good music; *Copacabana*, Cra 13 y C 5, good *comida* and breakfasts; *Arhuac*, C 3, Cra 13, filling meals, good quality steaks and meat dishes; *La Negra*, Cra 12, No 3-40, good tamales, weekends only; *Palacio de Jugos*, Cra 13, No 3-32, excellent fruit juices; also at *Heladería Tauro*, Cra 14, No 2-23, excellent salads and fruit juices; next to *Osoguaico* is *Mulales*, very good. *Santa Catalina*, up Cra 13, past brickworks and to right 1 km on Vía Antigua, closed Mon and all Dec, very good pizzas, crêpes, vegetarian, choose your own music, highly rec. Tap water in San Agustín is not safe to drink.

● **Banks & money changers**

Change TCs before arriving in San Agustín; the small shop opp police station will exchange cash only, at a poor rate. Caja Agraria will give cash advances against Visa card.

● **Shopping**

Film is available in several shops. Leather goods are beautiful and priced reasonably. Machetes are good value here. Many local shops make boots to your own design; *Calzado Líder* (José Pepicano) is highly rec, but if you want made-to-measure, he will need at least a couple of days, or *Artesanías El Viajero*, C 3 No 11-33. Rec handicraft shop is *Taller Orfebrería*, C 5, No 14-28, for masks using precolombian designs, copper and gold items. Market day is Mon.

● **Tourist offices**

As elsewhere in Colombia, the former national tourism office has been closed. However, Sr Joaquín Emilio García, who was well known as head of the office for many years, has now formed his own private company, **World Heritage Travel Office**, C 3, No 10-84, T 373940, which we strongly recommend you visit on arrival. Sr García is most helpful in all matters, he speaks English, French, Italian and a little German. Free maps to the area can only be obtained here. He has a list of all hotels, their prices and quality, cabins, and a price list for guides, taxi rides and horse hire. Tours can be arranged at the office. The Director of the Parque (Sr Alvaro León Monsalve) can arrange transport and guide to outlying sites.

Recommended reading: the best books on the subject are *Exploraciones Arqueológicas en San Agustín*, by Luis Duque Gómez (Bogotá, 1966, 500 pages) or *San Agustín, Reseña Arqueológica*, by the same author (1963, 112 pages). The Colombian Institute of Archaeology has published a booklet (English/ Spanish), at US$1.80, on San Agustín and Tierradentro, available at museums in San Agustín and San Andrés.

Horse hire: you are strongly advised to hire horses for trips around San Agustín through hotels or **World Heritage Travel**. The centre for horses is on the road to the Park (Asociación de Acompañantes y Alquiladores de Caballos) and charges about US$12/day and US$3/hr/rider. If you require a guide, you must add the hire cost of his horse. There are fixed tariffs for 20 or so standard trips.

Vehicle tours: jeeps may be hired for between 4-5 people. Prices vary according to the number of sites to be visited, but the daily rate is about US$70. For those who like a good walk however, most sites can be reached on foot, see above.

Guides: there are 27 guides available at any one time authorized by the authorities at US$15 for a half day, US$30 for a full day, up to 10 people for guide. You can make your own arrangements, and it may cost less, but we have received many reports of unsatisfactory experiences of unregistered guides. Always ask to see a guide's identity badge; if you have any problems, ask at **World Heritage Travel**.

● **Transport**

Buses San Agustín may be reached directly from **Bogotá** by colectivo (Taxis Verdes at 0300 and 0600, US$20, 8-9 hrs will pick you up at your hotel in Bogotá – ticket must be bought 1 day in advance; from San Agustín, C 3, No 11-57, 0500 direct, or 0400 and 0600, change at Neiva, just as quick, pickup at your hotel) or by bus (Coomotor, 4 a day, am buses US$15.50, pm buses US$12, 10-12 hrs; from San Agustín, C 3, No 10-71). Alternatively there are frequent services from Bogotá to **Neiva** as well as some to Pitalito (Taxi Verde costs US$14, leaving Bogotá at 0730 and 1030). From Neiva there are 6 buses a day to San Agustín, inc Coomotor and Cootranshuila, taking 6 hrs and costing US$6; to Neiva the 1000 Autobusco bus arrives in time for 1640 flight to Bogotá. The journey from Pitalito takes 1½ hrs, costs US$1.20 by jeep. To **Popayán** and **Cali**, Coomotor daily via Pitalito, Garzón and La Plata, US$10.75 to Popayán, US$12.75 to Cali. The bus stops at La Plata, 5-6 hrs, US$6. To **Tierradentro**, take early transport to Garzón (eg Taxis Verdes 0700, US$5.50), then a colectivo jeep to La Plata, US$2. With luck, you will get a *chiva* to Tierradentro the same day. Alternatively, take the daily bus to **La Plata** at 1700, stay half a night at a hotel, then, next morning, take the 0500 Sotracauca bus to Cruce de Pisimbalá (more details and alternatives given under La Plata). Buses to **Garzón** at 1230, 1430 and 1730, US$4, 3 hrs, from where more buses go to La Plata for Tierradentro. To appreciate the scenery, do not take a night bus to Tierradentro. There are daily buses from San Agustín to Popayán via Paletará and Coconuco with Cootranshuila at 0700 and 1300 (office on C 3, No 10-58), slow, 6 hrs, US$9.50; also Sotracauca (C 3, No 10-53) at 0600, continuing to Cali (US$12) and Coomotor on this route to Cali at 1700, 9 hrs. It may be advisable to book seats the day before. (For information ask at *World Heritage Travel*; the services are sometimes cut.) Rápido Tolima (C 3, No 10-53) goes to **Medellín** at 2100, 15 hrs, US$45.

Excursion to the source of the Río Magdalena

It is possible to walk from San Agustín to the Lago Magdalena, involving a bus ride or 6 hrs' walk the first day, 7 hrs' walk the second, and 8-10 hrs' walking on the third, either to the lake and back to the second *refugio*, or on to Valencia. From Valencia, there are buses to Popayán. It is also possible to ride from San Agustín via Lago Magdalena to Popayán, some 100 km, in 5 days or less. A recommended guide is Jorge Caitán, ask at *World Heritage Travel*, cost about US$70.

If walking in the opposite direction, take a bus from Popayán to Valencia, a dismal village with a very basic place to stay, but food available. A recommended guide for the way to San Agustín is Marnix Beching, Cra 7, No 2-56, Ap 7, Popayán, T 241850. He is a Dutchman working at the University of Popayán as a biologist. Seek advice on safety etc before committing yourself.

- **Accommodation** **Good bases** for this excursion from San Agustín are *Residencias El Paraíso*, at Puerto Quinchana, 30 km away on the road to the source of the Río Magdalena, 2 km from the Cementerio Indígena de Quinchana, owned by Sr Arsenio Guzmán, peaceful, restaurant; *Residencias El Páramo* at Juntas, beautiful countryside, owner Alvaro Palechor, safe, restaurant.

The Llanos and Leticia

THE extensive cattle lands from the Cordillera Central to the Orinoco are a good place to get away from it all – in the dry season. Leticia is Colombia's foothold on the Amazon.

META AND VICHADA

VILLAVICENCIO

A spectacular 110-km road runs SE from Bogotá to **Villavicencio** (*pop* 273,510; *alt* 498m), capital of Meta Department in the Llanos at the foot of the eastern slopes of the Eastern Cordillera. Rice is the main local crop.

Villavicencio is a good centre for visiting the Llanos stretching 800 km E as far as Puerto Carreño, on the Orinoco. Cattle raising is the great industry on the plains, sparsely inhabited by *mestizos*.

Local festivals See under **Music and dance.**

● **Accommodation A3** *Del Llano*, Cra 30, No 89-77, T 41119, F 41125, a/c, TV, bar, restaurant, pools; **B** *Villavicencio*, Cra 30, No 35A-22, T 26434, suites available, a/c, hot water, very comfortable, good restaurant; **D** *Centauros*, C 38, No 31-05, T 25106, small rooms, reasonably clean and quiet, central; **E** *Residencias Don Juan*, Cra 28, No 37-21 (Mercado de San Isidro), attractive family house, with bath and fan, sauna, safe, rec; **F** *Residencias Medina*, C 39D, 28-27, shared shower, fair, washing facilities.

● **Places to eat** Some on main plaza: others, some with swimming pools, on the road to Puerto López.

● **Transport Air** Aires to **Bogotá** daily. For flights into the Llanos, ask locally. Taxi to town, US$2; bus US$0.30. **Buses** Bus station outside town, taxi US$1. La Macarena and Bolivariano run from Bogotá about every 30 mins, US$3.30, 4 hrs; or colectivos Velotax, US$4.20, or Autollanos who run every hour, US$6.30. Be prepared to queue for tickets back to Bogotá. **Driving in the Llanos** Plenty of reserve gasoline should be carried as there are few service stations. Take food with you, unless you can live by gun and rod. Everybody lets you hang up your hammock or pitch your tent, but mosquito nets are a must. 'Roads' are only tracks left by previous vehicles but easy from late Dec till early April and the very devil during the rest of the year. More information on the Llanos can be obtained from the office of the Gobernación del Departamento de Meta, C 34 y Cra 14, Bogotá.

NORTHWEST FROM VILLAVICENCIO

A good asphalt road has been built E from Villavicencio to **Puerto López** on the Río Meta, a port of call for large river boats (hotels, *residencias* and restaurants). You can, with some patience, arrange to go downstream by boat to Puerto Carreño, 3-6 days. The road E (unpaved) continues through horse and cattle country for another 150 km to **Puerto Gaitán**, where there are hotels and restaurants (several buses a day from Puerto López to Puerto Gaitán, 3 hrs, US$3.20). Good views from the bridge across the Río Manacacías and great sunsets. The road goes on a further 60 km to San Pedro de Arimena, after which the road to Puerto Carreño degenerates to a rough track impassable in the wet season.

PUERTO CARREÑO

More than 500 km down the Río Meta, at its junction with the Orinoco, is **Puerto Carreño** (*pop* about 5,000).

Pico de la Bandera, a black rocky outcrop, can be climbed. It offers an excellent view over the Llanos and the confluence of the Ríos Meta and Orinoco. There are good beaches and bathing during the dry season at Tiestero, 15 mins from town by taxi, 1½ hrs' walk. Popular with locals at weekends.

● **Accommodation** E *Martha Helena*, 2 blocks from plaza nr navy headquarters, T 54086, family run, with bath and fan; E *La Vorágine*, off Av Orinoco nr plaza, T 54066, F without bath. Along Av Orinoco going from the plaza to the waterfront are the following: E *Apart Hotel Las Cabañas*, T 54018, with bath, fridge and TV; E *Safari*, T Bogotá 430-2926, with bath, fan or a/c, tame birds in courtyard, fridge facilities; E *Residencias Mami*, T 54046; E *Samanaré*, T 54181, rooms and 1 cabin for large group, disco-bar next door, a bit run down but clean, set menu is good value, other food and drinks expensive. Several restaurants along the same street, *Dona Margarita* is rec; also *Donde Mery*, which serves breakfast, *Kitty*, nr *Hotel Safari*, and *Oasis*, on main street, for refreshing juices.

● **Banks & money changers** Banks will not change cash or TCs. Shopkeepers will change cash, good rates for Venezuelan bolivares, extremely poor rates for US$. Try *Almacén Safari* or *Ferreteria Pastuzo* on Av Orinoco. If arriving from Venezuela, best to bring enough bolivares to be able to pay for your onward transport into Colombia.

● **Sports** For fishing excursions contact Victor Parra at *Taller Milton Guarín* nr *Panadería Pompey* or Sr Feliciano Morán, owner of *Almacén Safari*. Equipment can be bought in Puerto Carreño or Puerto Ayacucho.

● **Transport Air** From Bogotá Aero República fly Sat. **Buses** There are 2 weekly buses to Villavicencio during the dry season, but the route passes through guerrilla-held territory. **River** Launches upstream on Orinoco to Casuarito, 0800 and 1500, similar times return, US$6 one way. To Primavera on Río Meta, Mon and Fri, 8-10 hrs, US$45. It is possible to carry on up the Río Meta on another launch, then bus to Villavicencio.

FRONTIER WITH VENEZUELA

● **Colombian immigration**
DAS office is 2 blocks from the plaza, walking away from the river, near Casa de Cultura. Entry/exit stamps are given here.
The DAS agent meets all flights arriving from Bogotá. Foreigners must show passport and register with him.

To Venezuela There are two routes. Launches run throughout the day to El Burro (US$1.50) via Pto Páez. From El Burro, *por puestos* leave when full for Pto Ayacucho, US$3 (DIEX office for documentation), total time from Pto Carreño is 2-3 hrs. Alternatively, take an 0700 boat to

Casuarito (often full, buy ticket the day before at the foot of Av Orinoco) and then cross directly to Pto Ayacucho, reporting to the DIEX office there for your Venezuelan entry stamp (closes 1500). This takes 3-4 hrs, with an interesting ride along the river. There is no DAS in Casuarito, so that you must, in all cases, get your exit stamp in Pto Carreño.

● **Venezuelan consulate**
On Av Orinoco, one block from the plaza, walking towards the river. Official requirements are onward ticket, 2 photos, and US$30, visa issued the same day, but procedures are extremely arbitrary. Only single entry visas are given here, maximum 30 days. Try to obtain visa in Bogotá.

PARQUE NACIONAL TUPARRO

The Park is in Colombia, but has to be reached via Venezuela. Birds, orchids, bromeliads and dolphin can be seen; there are excursions to beaches, rapids and the burial site of the now extinct Maypure Indians.

● **Access** Follow the procedure as above for going to Pto Ayacucho, including having all documents stamped. From Pto Ayacucho take a taxi S along the road beside the Orinoco to Montaña Fría, US$10, where a launch can be hired for about US$80 to take you to the administrative centre of the Park near the confluence of the Río Tomo with the Orinoco. There may be a tour boat from Camturama Lodge, a short distance upstream from Montaña Fría. It is about 1½ hrs by launch to the visitor centre. Bring your own food, which can be supplemented with local fish. Admission US$10, cars US$4, camping US$26, hammock US$17. It is possible to reach the Park by road in the dry season from Villavicencio, about 700 km, but there are only isolated settlements for the last 500 km beyond Puerto Gaitán. There are two landing strips in the Park, one in El Tapón at the W extremity, and one near the MA admin centre on the Río Tomo.

SOUTH FROM VILLAVICENCIO

The road S from Villavicencio is paved through San Martín, a cattle town (bus 1½ hrs, US$1.50) to **Granada** and from there deteriorates rapidly. **Vistahermosa** (Macarena bus from Bogotá, 0845, US$6, 9 hrs), situated near the break-point between the Llanos and the jungle, lies further S along this road (G *Pampa Llanura*, opp the Flota La Macarena office).

SIERRA DE LA MACARENA

From Vistahermosa, a road (very muddy in the wet, Mar-Nov) goes to **Sierra de la Macarena**, a Tertiary outcrop 150 km long by 35 km broad. Its vegetation is so remarkable that the Sierra has been designated a National Park exclusively for scientific study, although the flora is under severe threat from colonization and drug cultivation. Trekking is not advisable because of guerrilla activity. If you wish to visit the Sierra, seek advice on conditions in advance, preferably from MA in Bogotá. There is also an office in the Park where you can hire guides (eg for hikes to waterfalls). Admission US$10, camping US$13.

MITU

To the SE of Villavicencio, along the Río Vaupés, and near the border with Brazil, is **Mitú**. Ask around for guides. In the wet season, traders will take you down river to Brazil (July-August). After several hundred kilometres, the Vaupés joins the Río Negro. Good local buys are baskets and bark paintings. There is a small hospital near the airport.

● **Accommodation** E *La Vorágine*, shower, fan, owned by Sr León who will help you to arrange trips; **F** *JM*, helpful, morning coffee, next to Satena office.

● **Places to eat** Plenty of restaurants around; rec: *de la Selva*, a meeting place of the pilots who fly into Mitú.

CAQUETA

Lying to the E of the Cordillera Oriental is the Intendencia of Caquetá, reached by air, or by road from Neiva or Garzón. The natural forest cover around Florencia, the capital of the Intendencia, has been cleared, creating undulating pasturelands for livestock raising, dotted with tall palms. To the SE, beyond the cleared lands, lie little-touched expanses of tropical forest inhabited by indigenous tribes and wide varieties of Amazonian flora and fauna.

The route Neiva-Florencia is 260 km: possible in 1 day, but it is recommended that the last 100 km over the mountains into Florencia be driven in daylight. The road branches SE at Altamira, 28 km SW of Garzón. Here the paving ends to become a single-track dirt road. The climb up over the mountains passes through a region of small farms and sugar-cane cultivation up into cloud. Soon after the summit, and on a clear day, there are extensive views out over Caquetá. The road winds down through substantial forests – ablaze with tropical flowers in the dry season (Jan-Mar) and into the lowlands. The lower section of the road into the lowlands is prone to frequent landslides.

In Caquetá the main lines of communication into the lowlands are along the Ríos Caquetá and Guayas and their tributaries.

FLORENCIA

Florencia (*pop* 101,275) was originally established in 1908. The plaza contains sculptures, fountains, a large forest tree (*saba*) and flower beds. Overnight, cars are best left in the care of the fire-station (US$0.20 a night).

Local festivals The local Saint's day is 16 July: candlelight procession in the evening.

● **Accommodation** Located around the central plaza are reputed to be the more salubrious. **C** *Kamani*, C 16, No 12, T 4101; **D** *Metropol*, Cra 11, No 16-52, T 6740; **D** *Royal Plaza*, Cra 11, No 14-64, T 7504; **F** *Residencias Don Quijote*, Cra 11, No 13-28, T 3190; and others in same price range.

● **Transport Air** Aires daily to **Neiva**; 5 a week to **Bogotá**. **Buses** There are regular services from Neiva (US$7.80, 7 hrs), Garzón and Altamira to **Florencia** (bus Altamira to Florencia, US$3.75) and frequent services as far as Puerto Rico and Belén. Bus to **Bogotá** costs US$23.50.

From Florencia the road runs NE as far as San Vicente del Caguán. It is paved for 67 km to El Doncello, passing through **El Paujil** (*pop* 2,750); *residencias* along the road into the town. **El Doncello** itself (*pop* 10,660; *residencias*) is a pleasant town, overlooked by the church which has a brightly painted steeple. Popular Sun market. Next comes the small settlement of Esmeralda with a hotel (ford for trucks and buses, wooden suspension bridge over the river for which there is a toll).

Puerto Rico (*pop* 8,325) is a river port on the Río Guayas, which is crossed by ferry (US$0.10). Houses built down by the river are raised on stilts above possible flood levels. River boats are made and repaired by the riverside. **Accommodation** and *residencias* are full on Sat nights – book a room early in the day. Buses then go as far as San Vicente.

● **NB** The area downstream of this road, along the Río Caguán and its tributaries is a cannabis growing region. Tourists are not welcome.

Anyone wanting to look at wildlife in Caquetá must travel beyond the settlement area. Toucans, monkeys, macaws etc are kept as pets, but there is little wild-life. Boats and canoes are easily hired.

LETICIA AND THE AMAZON

Leticia is on the southern tip of a spur of territory which gives Colombia access to the Amazon, 3,200 km upstream from the Atlantic. There is a land frontier with Brazil a short distance to the E beyond which are Marco and Tabatinga. Directly S across the river is another important Brazilian port, Benjamin Constant, which is close to the border with Peru. On the N side of the Amazon, Colombia has a frontage on the river of 80 km to the land border with Peru. For travellers interested in Amazonian wildlife the Putumayo is more accessible than Leticia; it is best reached from Pasto (see page 977).

LETICIA

The city (*pop* 23,200) is clean, modern, though run down near the river. It is rapidly merging into one town with neighbouring Marco in Brazil. There is a modern, well equipped hospital. The best time to visit the area is in July or Aug, the early months of the dry season. At weekends, accommodation may be difficult to find. Leticia is a good place to buy typical products of Amazon Indians, and tourist services are better than in Tabatinga or Benjamin Constant.

Museums

Set up by **Banco de la República**, local ethnography and archaeology, a beautiful building at Cra 11 y C 9 with a library and a terrace overlooking the Amazon.

Parks & zoos

Small Amazonian **zoo**, entry US$0.90 (huge anacondas) and **botanical garden** on road to airport, within walking distance of town (20 mins).

Local information
● **Accommodation**

A2 *Anaconda*, Cra 11, No 7-34, T 27119, F 7005, large a/c rooms, hot water, restaurant, good terrace and swimming pool.

B *Parador Ticuna*, Av Libertador (Cra 11), No 6-11, T 27241, spacious apartments, hot water, a/c, sleep up to 6, swimming pool, bar and restaurant. Under same ownership: *Jungle Lodge*, on Monkey Island (see below) and, in town, **B** *Colonial*, C 10, No 7-08, T 27164, with a/c or fans, swimming pool, cafeteria, noisy, not inc tax and insurance.

C *Residencias Fernando*, Cra 9, No 8-80, T 27362, well equipped, rec.

D *Residencias Marina*, Cra 9 No 9-29 (T 27201/9), TV, some a/c, cold water, good breakfast and meals at attached restaurant; **D** *Residencias La Manigua*, C 8, No 9-22, T 27121, with bath, fan.

E *Primavera*, C 8 between Cras 9 and 10, with bath and fan, noisy; **E** *Residencia Internacional*, Av Internacional, basic, bath, between centre and Brazilian border, fan, hard beds.

F *Residencias Colombia*, Cra 10 y C 8, good value, shared bath.

● **Places to eat**
Sancho Panza, Cra 10, No 8-72, good value, good meat dishes, big portions, Brazilian beer. Several small sidewalk restaurants downtown, good value *plato del día*. *Señora Mercedes*, C 8 nr Cra 11, serves good, cheap meals until 1930. Cheap food (fried banana and meat, also fish and pineapples) is sold at the market nr the harbour. Also cheap fruit for sale. Many café/bars overlook the market on the river bank. Take your own drinking water and anything stronger that you desire.

● **Banks & money changers**
There are street money changers, plenty of *cambios*, and banks for exchange. Shop around. TCs cannot be changed at weekends, and are hard to change at other times, but try Banco de Bogotá.

● **Post & telecommunications**
Post Office: Avianca office, Cra 11, No 7-58.
Telecom: Cra 11, nr Parque Santander.

● **Tourist offices**

Tourist office: at C 10, No 9-86.

MA: Cra 11, No 12-05, will arrange tours and find guides.

● **Transport**

Air Airport is 1½ km from town, taxi US$1.60; small terminal, few facilities. Expect to be searched before leaving Leticia airport, and on arrival in Bogotá from Leticia. SAM and Aero República each fly to **Leticia** (Tabatinga airport if Leticia's is closed) from Bogotá, 2-6 days a week. Varig has 4 flights a week from Manaus to Tabatinga.

River The cheapest way to get to Leticia is by bus to **Puerto Asís**, and then by boat (see page 978).

THE BRAZILIAN/COLOMBIAN/PERUVIAN FRONTIER

All information is given in the **Brazil** chapter, page 598, where Colombian, Brazilian and Peruvian procedures are detailed in one section.

JUNGLE EXCURSIONS

Monkey Island

Visits can be made to Yagua and Ticuna Indians. There are not many monkeys on the island now, those left are semi-tame. Agencies run overnight tours with full board.

Parque Nacional Amacayacu

60 km upstream, at the mouth of the Matamata Creek. There is a jungle walk to a lookout (guides will point out plants, including those to avoid); boats go to a nearby island to see Victoria Regia water lilies. The MA in Leticia arranges visits to its centre. Accommodation for 40-50 in three large, clean cabins with beds and hammocks, US$16 full board, mess-style meals, friendly, efficient; lights out 2130; small handicraft shop run for the local Indian communities. Park entry US$1. Boat from Leticia US$10, 2 hrs; two operators (if you buy a return check that your operator runs the day you wish to return).

Puerto Nariño

A small, attractive settlement up the Amazon, beyond the Parque Nacional Amacayacu. Hotel, **D** *Brisas del Amazonas*, charming location, simple rooms. Tours include fishing, visits to Indians and cayman watching, 4-5 days (eg with *Punto Amazónico*, Cra 24, No 53-18, p 2, Bogotá, T 249-3618). 3-hr trips from Leticia cost US$25.

● **Tour operators** Companies include *Turamazonas*, *Parador Ticuna*, Apdo Aéreo 074, T 7241; *Amaturs*, in lobby of *Hotel Anaconda*; *Amazonian Adventures*, ask for Chiri Chiri; *Kapax*. The following tours are available: to Monkey Island; to Benjamin Constant to see a rubber plantation, 8 hrs; 3 day trips to visit Indian communities with *Turamazonas*, price depends on number of people in group.

If you choose to go on an organized tour, do not accept the first price and check that the equipment and supplies are sufficient for the length of the tour.

● **Independent guides** Many guides can be found at the riverfront. They may be cheaper and better than organized groups, but you must seek advice about the guide's reputation and fix a firm price before setting out. Rec are Luis Daniel González, Cra 8, No 9-93 (Apdo Aéreo 256, Leticia), he can be found at the airport or through the *Hotel Anaconda*, knowledgeable, speaks Spanish, Portuguese, English, runs a variety of tours; Daniel Martínez, also knowledgeable, speaks good English. The cheaper the guide, usually the less experienced he will be. Check that adequate first aid is taken and whether rubber boots are provided (or buy your own in Leticia, US$5-6).

● **Hints** On night excursions to look for cayman, the boat should have powerful halogen lamps. You can swim in the Amazon and its tributaries, but do not dive; this disturbs the fish. Do not swim at sunrise or sunset when the fish are more active, nor when the water is shallow in dry season, nor if you have a wound which may open up and bleed. Take water purification tablets since almost all the water here is taken from the river.

Southern Colombia

FROM Popayán to Ecuador, including the mangrove swamps of the Pacific coast and the Amazonian-type lowlands of the Río Putumayo.

The Pan-American Highway continues S from Popayán to Pasto (248 km, 5 hrs driving). The entire road is paved. At 42 km S of Popayán is Rosas, a small friendly town with one small *hospedaje* and a good view to the valley of the Río Patía. **El Bordo** follows at 86 km (**E** *Hotel Patía*, fan, cold water, recommended; **G** *Residencias Central*, on Panamericana, basic, fan). 93 km S of Popayán is a tourist complex, *El Patio* (hotel and campsite, good), and at El Estrecho, Km 113, there are places to stay and eat. The road drops to 700m in the valley of the Río Patía before climbing to Pasto with big temperature changes. 28 km before Pasto is **Chachagüí: E** *Hotel Imperio de los Incas*, T 218054, with bath, swimming pool, restaurant, 2 km from Pasto airport; cheaper is **G** *Casa Champagnat*, with bath, cold water, swimming pool, helpful.

PASTO

The capital of the Department of Nariño, stands upon a high plateau in the SW, 88 km from Ecuador. **Pasto** (*pop* 282,310; *alt* 2,534m) is overlooked from the W by Galeras Volcano (when not in cloud) and to the E by green hills not yet suburbanized by the city, a very attractive setting. The city, which retains some of its colonial character, was founded in the early days of the conquest. During the wars of independence, it was a stronghold of the Royalists and the last town to fall into the hands of the patriots after a bitter struggle. Then the people of Nariño Department wanted to join Ecuador when that country split off from Gran Colombia in 1830, but were prevented by Colombian troops. Today Pasto is a centre for the agricultural and cattle industries of the region. Pasto varnish (*barniz*) is mixed locally, to embellish the strikingly colourful local wooden bowls.

Places of interest

The church of **Cristo Rey** (C 20, No 24-64, near the centre) has a striking yellow stone W front with octagonal turrets; **La Merced**, C 18 y Cra 22, has rich decoration and gold ornaments. From the church of **Santiago** (Cra 23 y C 13) there is a good view over the city to the mountains; **San Felipe** (C 12 y Cra 27) has green tiled domes. The interior courtyard of the **municipal building** on the main plaza (corner of C 19 and Cra 24) has 2 tiers of colonnaded balconies.

Museums

The **Museo de Oro del Banco de la República**, C 18, No 21-20, T 239100, 0830-1150, 1400-1830, US$0.30, has a small well-displayed collection of precolumbian pieces from the cultures of S Colombia, a library and auditorium. **Museo Zambrano**, C 20, No 29-78, houses indigenous and colonial period arts.

Local festivals

During the new year's *fiesta* there is a Día de los Negros on 5 Jan and a Día de los Blancos next day. On "black day" people dump their hands in black grease and smear each other's faces. On "white day" they throw talc or flour at each other. Local people wear their oldest clothes. On 28 Dec and 5 Feb, there is also a Fiesta de las Aguas when anything that moves gets drenched with water from balconies and even from fire engines' hoses. All towns in the region are involved in this legalized water war! In Pasto and Ipiales (see page 979), on 31 Dec, is the Concurso de Años Viejos, when huge dolls are burnt; they represent the old year and sometimes lampoon local people.

Local information
● Accommodation
A1 *Morasurco*, Av de los Estudiantes, y C 20, T 235017, F 235639, rec, reasonable restaurant; **A2** *Don Saul*, C 17 No 23-52, T 230618, F 230622, comfortable, good restaurant, rec; **A3** *Cuellar's*, Cra 23, No 15-50, roomy, T 232879, well-furnished, bowling centre underneath, rec; **A3** *Galerías*, Cra 26, No 18-71, T 237390, F 237069, above shopping mall, comfortable, good restaurant, rec.

B *Eldorado*, Pasaje Dorado No 23-42, T/F 233260, good; **B** *Sindagua*, C 20, No 21B-16, T 235404, rec.

C *San Diego*, C 16 A No 27-27, T 235050, good; **C** *El Paisa*, Cra 26, No 15-37, T 234592, F 239664, good restaurant, bar, laundry facilities.

D *Isa*, C 18, No 22-23, T 236663, helpful, safe; **D** *Río Mayo*, Cra 20, No 17-12, T 214905, small rooms, restaurant downstairs; **D** *Metropol*, C 15, No 21-41, T 212636, restaurant, laundry facilities.

E *Canchala*, C 17, No 20A-38, T 213337, big, safe, hot water, TV, central.

F *Embajador*, C 19, No 25-57, quiet, private bath, motorcycle parking, cold water; **F** *Koala Inn*, C 18, No 22-37, T 221101, cheaper without bath, laundry facilities, helpful, English speaking Oscar is the well-travelled owner, popular, hot water, book exchange, pleasant, good base for travellers, highly rec; **F** *Nueva York*, Cra 19 bis, 18-20, hot shower, motorcycle parking; **F** *Residencia Indi Chaya*, C 16, No 18-23 (corner of Cra 19 and C 16, up the steps), T 234962, good value, good beds, carpets, safe; **F** *María Belén*, C 13, No 19-15, safe, quiet, hot water.

G *Residencia Aica*, C 17, No 20-75, T 235311, safe, shared bath, but dirty; **G** *Viena*, clean, Cra 19B, No 18-36, cheap, restaurant downstairs, noisy.

● Places to eat
Central: *La Merced*, Cra 22, No 17-37, pizzas and local dishes, good; *Punto Rojo*, Cra 24, Parque Nariño, self service, 24 hrs, good choice of dishes; *El Mundo de los Pasteles*, Cra 22, No 18-34, cheap *comidas*; *Rancho Grande*, C 17, No 26-89, cheap and open late; *El Vencedor*, C 18, No 20A-40, good value, open 0600-1900; *Las Dos Pavrillas*, Pasaje Dorado, No 23-22, steaks, chicken, reasonable prices; *La Cabaña*, C 16, No 25-20, varied menu;

Govinda, Cra 24, No 13-91, vegetarian, set lunch US$2; *Riko Riko*, various locations, good fast food.

Away from centre: *Sausalito*, Cra 35A, No 20-63, seafood, good; *La Casa Vasca*, C 12A, No 29-10, Spanish, rec; *Cokorín*, bus terminal, T 212084, meat, chicken, local dishes.

Local speciality: try *arepas de choclo*, made with fresh ground sweet corn, at the kiosks beside the main road going N.

● Banks & money changers
For changing TCs, **Banco Industrial de Colombia**, C 19, No 27. **Banco Anglo Colombiano**, C 17, No 21-32 (best rates), Visa advances. **Banco de Bogotá** will change TCs 0930-1130. If going to Tumaco, this is the last place where TCs can be cashed. **Casas de cambio**, at Cra 25, No 18-97, T 232294, and C 19, No 24-86, T 235616, by the main plaza, changes sucres into pesos and vice versa, and will change US dollars into either.

● Embassies & consulates
Ecuadorean Consulate, C 17, No 26-55, p 2. Four photos needed if you require a visa.

● Entertainment
Bar/Discotheque: *Honey Bar*, C 16, No 25-40, T 234895, pleasant atmosphere.

● Post & telecommunications
Post Office: Cra 23, 18-42 and C 18, No 24-86.

Telecom: long distance calls, C 17 y Cra 23.

● Shopping
Casa del Barniz de Pasto, C 13, No 24-9, *Artesanías Nariño*, C 26, No 18-91; *Artesanía-Mercado Bomboná*, C 14 y Cra 27; *Artesanías Mopa-Mopa*, Cra 25, No 13-14, for *barniz*. Leather goods shops are on C 17 and C 18. Try the municipal market for handicrafts. *Mercado Campesino*, southern end of C 16, esq Cra 7. *Supermercado Confamiliar de Nariño*, C 16b, No 30-53, rec; *Ley* on C 18, next to Avianca postal office. On main plaza (C 19 y Cra 25) is a shopping centre with many shops and restaurants.

Maps: of Colombia and cities from Instituto Geográfico Agustín Codazzi, in Banco de la República building, C 18, No 21-20, limited selection.

● Sports
Every Sun a game of paddle ball is played on the edge of the town (bus marked San Lorenzo) similar to that played in Ibarra, Ecuador.

● Tourist offices
Just off the main plaza, C 18, No 25-25, T 234962, friendly and helpful, open 0800-1200 and 1400-1800 Mon-Fri, closed Sat-Sun.

● **Useful addresses**
DAS: C 16, No 28-11, T 235901, will give exit stamps if you are going on to Ecuador.

● **Transport**
Air Daily to Bogotá and Cali, Avianca. The airport is at Cano, 30 km from Pasto; by colectivo (beautiful drive), 45 mins, US$2.40 or US$13.50 by taxi. There are no currency exchange facilities, but the shop will change US$ bills at a poor rate. Avianca, C 18, No 25-86, T 232044.

Buses All interurban buses leave from the new terminal, Cra 6, C 16, 4 km from centre, taxi, US$1. To Bogotá, 23 hrs, US$30 (Bolivariano Pullman). To Ipiales, 2 hrs, US$2.40, sit on left hand side for the views. To Popayán, ordinary buses take 10-12 hrs, US$9; expresses take 5-8 hrs, cost US$11.25. To Cali, US$9.50, expresses, 8½-10 hrs. To Tumaco, 11 hrs by bus, 10 hrs by minibus, US$7.80. To Puerto Asís, 11 hrs, US$8 with Trans Ipiales or Bolivariano, 0500 and 1100. To Mocoa, 8 hrs, US$7.25.

VOLCAN GALERAS

The volcano, **Galeras** (4,276m), quiescent since 1934, began erupting again in 1989. Check at the tourist office on whether it is safe to climb on the mountain and whether you need a permit. A highway traversing all kinds of altitudes and climates has been built round it; the trip along it takes half a day. A rough road goes to the summit where there is an army post guarding a TV relay station. A taxi will take you to about 200m from the top; there is a fine view and the soldiers are glad to see people.

On the N side of the volcano lies the village of **Sandoná** where Panama hats are made; they can be seen lying in the streets in the process of being finished. Sandoná market day is Sat. 4 buses daily, US$1.50, the last back to Pasto is at 1700. There are good walks on the lower slopes through Catambuco and Jongovito (where bricks are made).

PASTO TO TUMACO

The 250-km road W from Pasto to Tumaco is paved, but is subject to landslides – check in Pasto. It leaves the Panamericana 40 km S of Pasto at El Pedregal, passing the brick factories of the high plains of the Cordillera Occidental. At **Túquerres** (*alt* 3,050m) the market is on Thur, good for ponchos (**F** *Residencias Santa Rita*, C 4, No 17-29; several restaurants including *Cafetería La 14*, Cra 14, C 20 near Trans Ipiales bus office. Bus to Pasto US$1.70, 2 hrs; jeep service to Ipiales from Cra 14, C 20, US$1.45, 1½ hrs). Ask in Túquerres about walking and climbing in the Laguna Verde/Volcán Azufral area.

The road continues to El Espino (no hotels) where it divides, left 36 km to Ipiales (see page 979), and right to Tumaco. About 90 km from Túquerres, at the village of **Chucunez**, a dirt road branches S to **Reserva Natural La Planada**, a private 3,200 ha nature reserve. This patch of dense cloud forest on a unique flat-topped mountain is home to a wide variety of flora and fauna. Day visitors are welcome but camping is prohibited. For further information contact Reserva Natural la Planada, Apdo Aéreo 1562, Pasto.

At **Ricaurte** is **F** *El Oasis*, central, last reasonable place to stay before Tumaco. The road passes through beautiful cloud forest, excellent for birdwatchers.

At **Junín** (36 km from Ricaurte; restaurants), a road N, 57 km goes to the interesting town of **Barbacoas** on the Río Telembí, a former Spanish gold-producing centre which still retains the remains of an extensive water-front, a promenade and steps coming down through the town to the river. Gold is still panned from the rivers by part-time prospector-farmers. The town has *residencias* and restaurants. Bus to Pasto, US$7.20, rough trip.

TUMACO

The region is very different from highland Colombia, with 2-storey Caribbean-style wooden houses and a predominantly black population. Small farms are mixed with cattle ranches, rice farms and oil-palm plantations. Cocoa is grown.

Tumaco (*pop* 71,370) has high unemployment, poor living conditions, and the roads, water and electricity supplies are not good. It is in one of the world's rainiest areas; the yearly average temperature is in the 25-35°C range. The northern part of the town is built on stilts out over the sea (safe to visit only in daylight). A natural arch on the main beach, N of the town and port, is reputed to be the hiding place of Henry Morgan's treasure. Swimming is not recommended from the town's beaches, which are polluted; stalls provide refreshment on the beach. Swimming is safe, however, at El Morro beach, N of the town, only on the incoming tide (the outgoing tide uncovers poisonous rays).

Excursions The area is noted for the archaeological finds associated with the Tumaco culture. Ask for Pacho Cantin at El Morro Beach who will guide you through the caves.

The coastal area around Tumaco is mangrove swamp, with many rivers and inlets on which lie hundreds of villages and settlements; negotiate with boatmen for a visit to the swamps or the beautiful island tourist resort of **Boca Grande**, the trip takes 30 mins, US$8 return; ask for Felipe Bustamante, C Comercial, Apto 224, T 465, who rents canoes and cabins, has a good seafood restaurant on the island, where water and electricity supplies are irregular. There are several places to stay in the **F** category.

There are water taxis N up the coast, across the bay to Salahonda and beyond.

● **Accommodation D** *Villa del Mar*, C Sucre, modern, with shower, toilet and fan, no hot water, good café below, also has well equipped cabins at El Morro Beach; *Residencias Don Pepe*, Calle de Comercio, near water-front and *canoa* dock, basic. Children meet arriving buses to offer accommodation; most cheap places are in C del Comercio, many houses and restaurants without signs take guests – nearly all have mosquito nets.

● **Places to eat** The main culinary attraction of the town is the fish, in the market and restaurants, fresh from the Pacific. A number of good restaurants on the main streets, Cs Mosquera and del Comercio, though the best is probably *Las Velas* on C Sucre. **NB** Be very careful of food and water because there are many parasites.

● **Banks & money changers** There are no money exchange facilities, except in some shops that will buy dollars and sucres at a poor rate; change money in Cali or Pasto.

● **Entertainment Discos**: many discos specializing in Afro/S American rhythms; try *Candelejas*.

● **Transport Air** There are daily flights to and from Cali with Avianca, 35 mins. **Buses** Tumaco to Pasto, 5 hrs, US$7.80, with Supertaxis del Sur or Trans Ipiales (better), 4 a day, interesting ride; minibus 4 hrs. From Ipiales go to El Espino

(US$0.75, colectivo, US$1.15) and there change buses for Tumaco (US$4.80).

PARQUE NACIONAL SANQUIANGA

The ranger headquarters is at La Vigía, N of Tumaco. The park extends for some 30 km along the coast and a similar distance inland consisting of mangrove covered sandbanks formed by rivers flowing down from the Andes. There are fresh and salt water fish in abundance and a rich variety of bird life. It can also be reached from Guapí and Górgona. Cost about US$20 from Tumaco.

FRONTIER WITH ECUADOR

It is possible to travel to Ecuador by boat. Part of the trip is by river, which is very beautiful, and part on the open sea, which can be very rough; a plastic sheet to cover your belongings is essential. Take suncream.

● **Colombian immigration**
DAS: Alcaldía Municipal, C 11 y Cra 9, Tumaco; obtain stamp for leaving Colombia here; office open weekdays only.

Entering Colombia: through Tumaco: you will have to go to Ipiales to obtain the entry stamp. Apparently the 24/48 hrs 'unofficial' entry is not a problem, but do not obtain any Colombian stamps in your passport before presentation to DAS in Ipiales. DAS in Pasto is not authorized to give entry stamps for overland or sea crossings, and the DAS office in Tumaco seems to be only semi-official.

● **Ecuadorean consulate**
Visas for Ecuador (if required) should be obtained in Cali or Pasto. Entry stamps for Ecuador must be obtained in the coastal towns.

● **Transport**
Daily service at 0800 to San Lorenzo, 7 hrs (but can take 14) tickets from C del Comercio (protective plastic sheeting provided). Señor Pepello, who lives in the centre of Tumaco, owns two canoes: he leaves on Sat at 0700 for San Lorenzo and Limones in Ecuador – book in advance. Also ask around the water-front at 0600, or try at the fishing centre, El Coral del Pacífico for a cheaper passage, but seek advice on safety before taking a boat (robberies en route reported). Fares: motorized canoe US$20; launch US$50.

THE PUTUMAYO

LAGUNA LA COCHA

1 hr E of Pasto, on the road to Mocoa is

Laguna La Cocha, the largest lake in S Colombia (sometimes called Lago Guámez). In the lake is the **Isla de La Corota** nature reserve with interesting trees (10 mins by boat from the *Hotel Sindanamoy*).

● **Accommodation** By the lake, 3 km from the main road, is the **C** *Chalet Guámez*, rec, particularly for the cuisine, cabins for 6 can be hired; free van-camping allowed. The chalet will arrange a US$22 jeep trip to Sibundoy, further along the road; boats may be hired for US$2.50/hr. **B** *Sindamanoy*, chalet style, government-run, good views, inviting restaurant with good but expensive food, free van, and tent camping allowed with manager's permission. There are also cheap and friendly places to stay in and nr El Encano where there are also many restaurants serving trout.

● **Transport** La Cocha may be reached by taxi from Pasto, US$9, or colectivo from C 20 y Cra 2. Also you can take a bus to El Encano and walk the remaining 5 km round to the chalets area, or 20 mins from the bus stop direct to the lake shore and then take a *lancha* to the chalets for US$3.

The road from Pasto to the Putumayo deteriorates rapidly after El Encano. It is steep but spectacular. It is also dangerous between Sibundoy and El Pepino (the junction for Mocoa) and care should be taken (especially by cyclists), but there is a magnificent view out over the Putumayo by a large statue of the Virgin, just before the final descent.

SIBUNDOY

There is a beautiful church on the main plaza, completed in 1968. About a quarter of the valley is now reserved for Sibundoy Indian occupation. Market Sun. Bus from Pasto (3 hrs, US$4), passing through Colón (*residencias*) and Santiago.

● **Accommodation & places to eat D** *Hotel Turista*, pleasant; better meals at **F** *Hotel Sibundoy*, but hotel dirty, unhelpful, not rec; **F** *Residencia Valle*, double rooms, hot water. *Restaurant Viajero*, just off main street. You can camp in the hills, where there are lovely walks and you can see all kinds of flora and fauna.

MOCOA

Mocoa (*pop* 18,960), the administrative capital of the Intendencia of Putumayo, has a very modern plaza, new offices and modern developments. Sugar-cane is grown in the area. The main DAS office

for the region is in Mocoa.

● **Accommodation D** *Central*, off main plaza, very good; opp is **D** *Continental*, C 8 y Cra 6, T 395428, fan, good, modern; **F** *Viajero*; **G** *Macaritama*, safe, TV, cold water; **G** *Residencia Colonial*, Cra 6, No 8-10, spartan but safe.

● **Buses** 8-12 hrs by bus and jeeps to **Pasto**, US$7.25; bus to Pitalito, 7 hrs, US$8.20. Bus to **Sibundoy**, US$4, 5 a day; to **Puerto Asís**, US$5, a few police checks.

PUERTO ASIS

The road continues from El Pepino, through cattle-ranching country, to **Puerto Asís**, the main town and port of the Putumayo. The water front is 3 km from the centre. River traffic is busy. For those interested in flora and fauna it is necessary to travel down river, beyond new areas of settlement or by canoe up the river for monkeys and many birds.

NB Puerto Asís is a marketing centre for cocaine and has been the scene of much guerrilla and counter-insurgency activity.

● **Accommodation F** *Residencias Gigante*, C 10, 24-25, clean; **F** *Residencias Nevado*, Cra 20, close to the airport, well kept and comfortable, a/c optional; **F** *Residencia Liz*, C 11, with bath, very friendly; **F** *Residencia Volga*, C 10, No 23-73, basic, safe. There are plenty of cheap hotels in the port, but it is hard to find a room late in the day.

● **Transport Air** Aires flies to Leguízamo, Neiva, Cali and Lago Agrio in Ecuador. **Boat** All boats that leave for Leticia (with connections to Manaus) are cargo boats, and only sail when they have cargo. They leave from the Hong Kong, Bavaria and Esmeraldas wharves (*muelles*): taxi from town US$4. Local information in town is poor, you must check with the boat personnel yourself. Those carrying gasoline (and most do) are not supposed to take passengers. Only one company, Navenal, normally takes passengers, and it can be weeks between their sailings. One can also try the army for a passage. Fares are about US$100; at least 10-15 days; it is best to see the Jefe de la Marina, or the Oficina de Transporte Fluvial, about a passage. By boat to Leguízamo takes 2-3 days, or by speedboat (canoa), 7 hrs, US$27 one way, twice a week. Boats will not go unless the rivers are high. Take supplementary food and water with you. **Buses** Bus to **Bogotá** US$24, 18 hrs; to Mocoa US$5. To **Pasto** (10 hrs, 3 a day, US$8, be prepared for military checks). Bus Sibundoy-Puerto Asís, US$4.

250 km downstream on the Río Putumayo is **Leguízamo** where there is a helpful MA

office. Several basic hotels, all **G**, eg *Caucaya* (comfortable, nice owners). *Caja Agraria* will give cash against Visa.

● **Transport Air** Aires from Neiva and Puerto Asís, 3 a week. **Boat** For river information go to Naval at the port, Transporte Fluvial Estrella del Sur (Cra 27, off C 10) or Transporte Fluvial Amazonas (Cra 20, 14-59 – English spoken).

Parque Nacional La Paya, downstream from Puerto Asís and just above Leguízamo, welcomes visitors. Many animals and birds to be seen. For further information on El Paya, ask at the *Joyería El Ruby* in Leguízamo where Ramiro will give details and may offer to show you the Park. River transport there costs about US$25, and takes about 1½ hrs. You should take water, food and a hammock.

It is possible to carry on down the Putumayo which forms the boundary between Colombia and Peru, then crosses into Brazil, becoming the Rio Iça to join the Amazon at Santo Antônio. The border town is **Tarapacá** (airport; basic *Residencial*).

TO ECUADOR FROM PUERTO ASIS

Five buses a day go from Puerto Asís to **San Miguel**, 4 hrs, near the Ecuadorean border (US$3.60) where the Sun market provides a meeting place, and where *canoas* may be hired to visit villages 2-4 hrs away on the river.

(Several very basic hotels, eg **F** *Mirador*, safe and *Residencias Olga*.) You can cross to Ecuador from here, get your exit stamp from the DAS office in Puerto Asís or Mocoa. The boat trip up the Río San Miguel via Puerto Colón to La Punta takes 1 hr and costs US$2.20. There is a bus to Lago Agrio (US$0.60).

SOUTH TO ECUADOR FROM PASTO

IPIALES

Passing through deep valleys and a spectacular gorge, buses on the paved Pan-American Highway cover the 84 km from Pasto to Ipiales in 1½-2 hrs. The road crosses the spectacular gorge of the Río Guáitara at 1,750m, near El Pedregal, where *choclo* (corn) is cooked in many forms by the roadside. **Ipiales** (*pop* 30,000; *alt* 2,740m), "the city of the three volcanoes", is famous for its colourful Fri morning Indian market. The Catedral Bodas de Plata is worth visiting and there is a small museum, set up by **Banco de la República**.

Excursions

7 km E of Ipiales on a paved road is the Sanctuary of the Virgin of **Las Lajas**. Seen from the approach road, looking down into the canyon, the Sanctuary is a magnificent architectural conception, set on a bridge over the Río Guáitara: close to, it is very heavily ornamented in the gothic style. The altar is set into the rock face of the canyon which forms one end of the sanctuary with the façade facing a wide plaza that completes the bridge over the canyon. There are walks to nearby shrines in dramatic scenery. It is a 10-15 mins' walk down to the sanctuary from the village. There are great pilgrimages to it from Colombia and Ecuador (very crowded at Easter) and the Sanctuary must be second only to Lourdes in the number of miracles claimed for it. The Church recognizes one only. Ipiales town buses going 'near the Sanctuary' leave you 2½ km short. Take a colectivo from Cra 6 y C 4, US$1 pp, taxi, US$6 return. Several basic hotels and a small number of restaurants at Las Lajas. You may also stay at the convent. Try local guinea pig and boiled potatoes for lunch (or guinea pig betting in the central plaza may be more to your taste).

15 km NW of Ipiales is **Cumbal** which sits beneath two 4,700m volcanoes, Cumbal, immediately above the town, and Chiles, further S and close to the Ecuador border. There is accommodation, F, at Cra 8, No 20-47 (no name), basic, and very good food at *Rincón de Colombia*, C 18, No 8-48, good value. Jeep from Ipiales (C 15, No 7-23) US$1, 1 hr.

Local information
● **Accommodation**
B *Mayasquer*, 3 km on road to frontier, modern, nice restaurant, very good, T 3984.

D *Angasmayo*, C 16, No 6-38, comfortable;
D *Dinar*, Cra 4A, No 12A-18, T 3659, cafeteria, private parking; **D** *Korpawasy*, Cra 6, No 10-47,

T 2634, good food, plenty of blankets.
E *Bachué*, Cra 6 y C 11-68, safe; **E** *Pasviveros*, Cra 6, No 16-90, T 2622, bath, hot water; **E** *Rumichaca Internacional*, C 14, No 7-114, T 2692, comfortable, good restaurant.

F *Belmonte*, Cra 4, No 12-111 (nr Transportes Ipiales), hot water, parking opp, good value but crowded, rec; **F** *Colombia*, C 13, No 7-50, hot water, clean except for toilets, helpful, parking for motorbikes; **F** *San Andrés*, Cra 5, No 14-75, hot water; **F** *ABC*, Cra 5, No 14-43, with bath, hot water, good value.

G *India Catalina*, Cra 5a, No 14-88, T 4392, hot shower, run down, 2 blocks from main plaza; **G** *Nueva York*, C 13, No 4-11, nr main plaza, run down, plenty of blankets; **G** *Oasis*, Cra 6, No 11-34, 1 block from main plaza, shower, ask for hot water, quiet after 2100, clean, helpful.

Camping: free behind last Esso station outside town on road N.

● **Places to eat**
Don Lucho (Los Tejados), Cra 5, No 14-13 (*antioqueño*); *Don José*, Cra 5, No 14-53. Plenty of cheap restaurants, better quality ones on Cra 7; *Panadería Galaxia*, C 15, No 7-89, for a good cheap breakfast. Outside town towards the frontier, *La Herradura*, good food, reasonable prices, try their excellent *trucha con salsa de camarones* (rainbow trout with shrimp sauce), rec.

● **Banks & money changers**
It is not possible to cash TCs, but cash is no problem eg **Banco Anglo Colombiano**, Cra 6, No 16-59, T 2331; **Banco de Colombia**, cash against Visa. **Casa de Cambio** at Cra 6, No 14-09, other *cambios* on the plaza. There are money changers in the street, in the plaza and on the border, but they may take advantage of you if the banks are closed. Coming from Ecuador, peso rates compare well in Ipiales with elsewhere in Colombia.

● **Post & telecommunications**
Telecommunications: International calls from Cra 6 y C 14.

● **Transport**
Air San Luis airport is 6½ km out of town. Aces flights to/from Cali daily.

Buses To **Popayán**, Expreso Bolivariano, US$12, 7½ hrs, hourly departures, 0430-2030; Transportes de Ipiales (neither on main plaza, best to take taxi from border), also transport from main plaza, Super Taxis and Cootranar *busetas*, sit on right side for views. Bus to **Cali**, US$14-15, 12 hrs, from main plaza. To **Pasto** from main plaza, colectivo US$3.50; Flota Bolivariano buses every hr, US$2.40, 3 hrs. Buses to **Bogotá** leave every other

hour between 0500 and 0830, 24 hrs, US$32.80 (note, if coming from Bogotá, there is an hour's stop in Cali; bus leaves from a different level from which it arrived). To **Medellín**, Expreso Bolivariano, 22 hrs, US$40. To **Túquerres** and **Ricaurte** on the Tumaco road, *camperos* (4WD taxis) leave from in front of San Felipe Neri church; for **Tumaco** change at El Espino.

FRONTIER WITH ECUADOR

Ipiales is 2 km from the Rumichaca bridge across the Río Carchi into Ecuador. The frontier post stands beside a natural bridge, on a concrete bridge, where customs and passport examinations take place from 0600 to 2100.

● **Colombian immigration & customs**
All Colombian offices are in one complex: DAS (immigration, exit stamp given here), customs, INTRA (Dept of Transportation, car papers stamped here; if leaving Colombia you must show your vehicle entry permit) and ICA (Dept of Agriculture for plant and animal quarantine). There is also a restaurant, Telecom for long-distance phone calls, clean bathrooms (ask for key, US$0.10) and ample parking. See page 1050 for the Ecuadorean side and see also **Documents** in **Ecuador**, **Information for travellers**.

● **Crossing by private vehicle**
If entering Colombia by car, the vehicle is supposed to be fumigated against diseases that affect coffee trees, at the ICA office; the certificate must be presented in El Pedregal, 40 km beyond Ipiales on the road to Pasto. (This fumigation process is not always carried out.) You can buy insurance for your car in Colombia at Caja Agraria, in the plaza.

● **Ecuadorean consulate**
In the DAS complex described above; open weekdays 0830-1200, 1430-1800.

● **Transport**
From Ipiales to **Tulcán**: colectivo from C14 y Cra 11 (waits till all seats are full), US$0.40 to the frontier (buses to Ipiales arrive at the main plaza – they may take you closer to the colectivo point if you ask). Colectivo from frontier to **Tulcán** US$0.45 (ask the fare at the tourist office at the border); to go to bus terminal, take blue bus from central plaza, US$0.05. Taxi to or from border, US$3.50. From Ipiales airport to the border by taxi, about US$6.50; to centre of Ipiales US$4.

Information for travellers

BEFORE YOU GO

ENTRY REQUIREMENTS

● **Documents**

A passport is always necessary; an onward ticket is officially necessary, but is not always asked for at land borders. Visitors are sometimes asked to prove that they have US$20 for each day of their stay (US$10 for students). You are normally given 90 days permission to stay on entry, though this is not automatic. If you intend to stay more than 30 days, make sure you ask for longer. If not granted at the frontier, extension (*salvoconducto*) for 15-day periods can be applied for at the DAS (security police) office in any major city up to a maximum of 6 months. There may be delays, so apply in good time. Better, apply at the DAS office, C 100, No 11B-27, Bogotá (see under Bogotá, **Useful addresses**) who are empowered to grant longer stays immediately. Alternatively, if you have good reason to stay longer (eg for medical treatment), apply at the embassy in your home country before leaving. Note also that if you are going to take a Spanish course, you must have a student visa. You may not study on a tourist visa. Leaving the country and re-entering to get a new permit is not always allowed. To visit Colombia as a tourist, nationals of Afghanistan, Algeria, China, Cuba, Czech Republic, Dominican Republic, Haiti, India, Iran, Iraq, Jordan, Lebanon, Libya, Morocco, Nicaragua, North Korea, Pakistan, Palestine, Slovakia, Sri Lanka, Sudan, Syria, Taiwan, Vietnam and Yemen need a visa (this information was correct according to the Colombian consulate in London, Mar 1997). You must check regulations before leaving your home country. Visas are issued only by Colombian consulates. When a visa is required you must be prepared to show 2 photographs, police clearance and medical certificates, an application form (£16 or equivalent), as well as a passport (allow 48 hrs). Various business and temporary visas are needed for foreigners who have to reside in Colombia for a length of time. Fees range from £54 (or equivalent) for a student visa, £112 for a business visa, to £131 for a working visa. If you do not receive an entry card when flying in, or lose the card while in Colombia, apply to any DAS office who should issue one and restamp your passport for free. Note that to leave Colombia you must get an exit stamp from the DAS. They often do not have offices at the small frontier towns, so try to get your stamp in a main city, and save time.

NB It is highly rec that you have your passport photocopied, and, for added insurance, witnessed by a notary. This is a valid substitute (although some travellers report difficulties with this variant), and your passport can then be put into safe-keeping. Also, photocopy your TCs, flight ticket and any other essential documents. For more information, check with your consulate.

● **Representation overseas**

Australia, 2nd floor, 101 Northbourne Ave, Canberra, PO Box 2892, ACT 2601, T 257-2027, F 257-1448; **Austria**, Stadiongasse 6-8A, 1010 Vienna, T 405-4249, F 408-8303; **Canada**, 360 Albert St, Suite 1130, Ottawa, Ontario, K1R 7X7, T 230-3760, F 230-4416; **Denmark**,

Kastelsvej 15, st tv 2100, Copenhagen; **France**, 22 rue de L'Elysée, 75008, Paris, T 42-65-46-08, F 42-66-18-60; **Germany**, Friedrich Wilhelm-Str 35, 5300 Bonn 1, T 234-565, F 236-845; **Holland**, Groot Hertoginelaan 14, 2517 EG The Hague, T 361-4545, F 361-4636; **Israel**, 52 Pinkas St, Apt 26, floor 6, 62261 Tel Aviv, T 546-1434, F 546-1404; **Japan**, 310-53 Kami-Osaki, Shinagawa-ku, Tokyo 141, T 3440-6451, F 3440-6724; **New Zealand**, Wool House, level 11, Wellington, T 472-1080, F 472-1087; **Spain**, Gen Martínez Campos 48, 28010 Madrid, T 310-3800, F 412-7828; **Sweden**, Ostermlamsgatan 46, Stockholm, T 218489, F 218490; **Switzerland**, Dufourstrasse 47, 3005 Bern, T 351-1700, F 352-7072; **UK**, 3 Hans Crescent, London SW1X 0LR, T 0171-581-9177, F 0171-581-1829; **USA**, 2118 Leroy Place, NW Washington, DC 20008, T (202) 387-8338, F (202) 332-8643.

● **Tourist information**

The Corporación Nacional de Turismo (CNT), with its headquarters at Bogotá, is in the course of reorganization. Other, mainly Departmental and City entities now have offices responsible for providing visitors with information, although the CNT remains in charge of national tourist assets. See text for local details. These offices should be visited as early as possible not only for information on accommodation and transport, but also for details on areas which are dangerous to visit. Enquire at embassies and consulates abroad for information on Colombia. For details on National Parks, go to the MA Office in Bogotá (address on page 873).

The Automobile Club in Bogotá has offices on Av Caracas, No 46-64 (T 245-1534 and 245-2684). Branches are at Manizales, Medellín, Cali, Barranquilla and Cartagena. It supplies Esso, Texaco and Mobil maps: good, but not quite up-to-date; a full set of Hojas de Ruta costs US$2.50. The Texaco map has plans of the major cities. Even the Shell series lacks detail. Maps of Colombia are obtainable at the Instituto Geográfico Militar, Agustín Codazzi, Cra 30 y C 45, open 0800-1530, Bogotá, or from their office in Pasto. Drivers' route maps are available from the CNT. See also under Bogotá, **Maps**.

WHEN TO GO

● **Best time to visit**

The best time for a visit is Dec, Jan and Feb: the driest months, but many local people are then on holiday. Easter is a busy holiday time, many hotels put up their rates, and transport can be overloaded. There is heavy rain in many places in April/May and Oct/Nov though intermittent heavy rain can fall at any time almost anywhere.

● **Climate**

Climate is entirely a matter of altitude: there are no seasons to speak of, though some periods are wetter than others.

HEALTH

Emergency medical treatment is given in hospitals: if injured in a bus accident, for example, you will be covered by insurance and treatment will be free. Bogotá has well-organized sanitary services, but bottled water is recommended for drinking. Outside the capital take sterilise with you, or boil the water, or use the excellent mineral waters. Choose your food and eating places with care everywhere. Hepatitis is common; get protection before your trip. Falmonox is rec locally for amoebas. Mosquito nets are useful in the coastal swampy regions. There is some risk of malaria and yellow fever in the coastal areas and the eastern *llanos*/jungle regions; prophylaxis is advised. For up to date information, ask at the bigger clinics and hospitals. See also **Health** in the Introductory pages. Tampons are not always available, but can easily be found in big city supermarkets.

MONEY

● **Currency**

The monetary unit is the peso, divided into 100 centavos. There are coins of 5, 10, 20, 50, 100, 200 and 500 pesos; there are notes of 100, 200, 500, 1,000, 2,000, 5,000, 10,000 and 20000 pesos (introduced in 1996 and already being forged). Large notes of over 1,000 pesos are often impossible to spend on small purchases as change is in short supply, especially in small towns, and in the morning.

There is a limit of US$25,000 on the import of foreign exchange, with export limited to the equivalent of the amount brought in.

Cash and TCs can in theory be exchanged in any bank, except the Banco de la República. Go early to banks in the smaller places to change cash or TCs: some close the service as early as 1000, though bank hours are generally getting longer. There are some legitimate *casas de cambio*, which are quicker to use than banks. Always check which rate of exchange is being offered. Hotels may give very poor rates of exchange, especially if you are paying in dollars, but practice varies. It is generally dangerous to change money on the streets, and you are likely to be given counterfeit pesos, sucres or bolívares. Also in circulation are counterfeit US dollar bills in denominations of US$50 and US$100; US$20 bills are therefore more readily accepted. If you do not present your passport when changing money (a photocopy is not always accepted), you may be liable for a 10% tax charged to residents on foreign exchange.

Travellers' cheques When changing TCs, a photocopy of your passport may be taken, best to take a supply of photocopies with you. Owing to the quantity of counterfeit American Express TCs in circulation, travellers may experience difficulty in cashing these cheques. For changing Amex TCs, use Banco Industrial de Colombia (BIC). You must always provide proof of purchase. The procedure is always slow, maybe involving finger printing and photographs. Obtaining reimbursement for lost American Express TCs can be straightforward if you have the numbers recorded (preferably proof of purchase), a police certificate (*diligencia de queja*) covering the circumstances of loss, and apply to their agents, *Tierra Mar Aire*, Bogotá (see Bogotá, **Exchange**). Take dollar TCs in small denominations, but, better still, take a credit card (see below). Thomas Cook/Mastercard refund assistance point in Bogotá is Aviatur, Av 19, No 4-62, T 282-7111, Bogotá. Sterling TCs are practically impossible to change in Colombia.

● **Credit cards**

As it is unwise to carry large quantities of cash, credit cards are widely used, especially Mastercard and Visa; Diner's Club is also accepted, while American Express is only accepted in highpriced establishments in Bogotá. Many banks will accept Visa: Banco de Colombia and Banco Popular advance pesos against Visa, through ATMs; Caja Agraria is a Visa agent; Cajero BIC (Banco Industrial de Colombia) gives cash advances against Cirrus/Mastercard through ATMs. American Express credit cards are rarely accepted for cash advances. At present cash advances against credit cards give the best rates of exchange. Cash advances against credit cards are not predictable as the voucher indicates only the amount in pesos (not dollars) and the rate of exchange is determined at the time the charge is posted to your account.

NB In addition to counterfeit US\$ notes, Colombia has been flooded with large quantities of legitimate US\$ cash which have come into the country through the drugs trade. Thus cash dollars are difficult to exchange and rates for cash are lower than for credit cards and TCs. The latter can be exchanged in the main branches of banks in Bogotá, Medellín, and Cali and some of the other major centres. Difficulties and very poor rates of exchange can be expected in smaller towns and tourist resorts. Many banks are reluctant to exchange money for anyone but account holders. Because of the great difference between the rates of exchange available (official, cash, TCs and credit cards), travellers may find variations of between 10 and 20% for prices of services and those quoted in the text.

GETTING THERE

AIR

From Europe British Airways and Avianca each have a twice weekly service from London to Bogotá, the former via Caracas, the latter direct. Avianca also flies from Frankfurt, Paris and Madrid. Airlines with services from continental Europe are Air France, Iberia, Alitalia and Lufthansa.

From N America Frequent services to and from the US by Avianca and American, the latter from Miami, daily to Bogotá, Cali and Barranquilla. Other flights from Miami: Avianca to Bogotá, Cartagena, Barranquilla, Medellín, Pereira (via Bogotá) and Cali; Aces to Bogotá, Cali and Medellín. From New York, Avianca flies to Bogotá (also Continental and Servivensa), Barranquilla, Cali, Cartagena and Medellín. Continental also flies from Houston. From Los Angeles, Avianca and Aerolíneas Argentinas to Bogotá.

Enquire when you book if there are special offers for internal flights.

● **From Neighbouring Republics**

Lacsa flies from San José to Barranquilla. From Mexico City with Avianca and Mexicana to Bogotá. SAM flies to Bogotá and San Andrés from San José (daily), and Guatemala City (3 a week). From Panama, Avianca daily to Bogotá (Aces 6 a week), SAM 3 days a week to Medellín and San Andrés; Copa daily to Bogotá, Barranquilla, Cartagena, Cali and Medellín.

If flying from Guatemala to Colombia with SAM, via San Andrés, you have to purchase a round-trip ticket, refundable only in Guatemala. To get around this (if you are not going back to Guatemala) you will have to try to arrange a ticket swap with a traveller going in the other direction on San Andrés. There is, however, no difficulty in exchanging a round-trip ticket for a San Andrés-Colombian ticket with the airline, but you have to pay extra. To obtain a refund on an unwanted onward ticket out of Colombia, you must first go to the DAS, Extranjería section, show your passport and ticket and obtain a permit for a refund. **Colombia-Panama** with Copa: one may not enter, or obtain a visa for, Panama without a return or onward ticket, so you must buy a return ticket and then sell half in Panama once you have purchased a flight ticket out of Panama, or purchase a Panama-San José ticket and get your money back, less the tax. Obtaining refunds is time consuming and you will not get your money in dollars outside Panama.

Avianca, Iberia, Lufthansa, Saeta, Ecuatoriana, LAB, AeroPerú, Servivensa, Aerolíneas Argentinas, Varig and LanChile go S from

Colombia. Avianca, Servivensa, Saeta and Ecuatoriana fly Bogotá-Caracas.

For a cheap means of flying from Venezuela to Colombia, see page 892.

See page 905 if you are travelling from Panama to Colombia by land or by short sea route.

BOAT

Shipping a vehicle from Panama to Colombia: The *Crucero Express* vehicle/passenger ferry service between Cristóbal, Panama, and Cartagena has been suspended, hopefully, temporally (see page 905 for details). For the present, the best advice is to shop around the agencies in Panama City or Colón to see what is available when you want to go. Both local and international lines take vehicles, and sometimes passengers, but schedules and prices are very variable. Agents include: Sudamericana de Vapores, T 229-3844, Cristóbal-Buenaventura; Boyd Steamship Corporation, T 263-6311, Balboa-Buenaventura. Panamá- Cartagena: Central American Lines sail once a week, agent in Panama, T Colón 441-2880, Panama City 236-1036. Geminís Shipping Co SA, Apdo Postal No 3016, Zona Libre de Colón, Rep de Panamá, T 441-6269/441-6959, F 441-6571. Mr Ricardo Gil was helpful and reliable. If sending luggage separately, make enquiries at Tocumen airport, eg Tampa, T 293-4439.

Bureaucratic delays at either end of the passage are considerable, but can be reduced if you have a *carnet de passages* for entering Colombia. Once you have a bill of lading, have it stamped by a Colombian consulate (the Colombian consul in Colón will only stamp a bill of lading if the carrier is going to Cartagena or Barranquilla). The consulate also provides tourist cards. They may require proof, in the form of a letter from your Embassy (or the Embassy representing your country in Panama) that you do not intend to sell the vehicle in Colombia. Then go to customs to have the vehicle cleared for export. After that the vehicle details must be removed from your passport at the customs office at the port of departure. Customs in Panama City, C 80 y 55; in Colón, behind the post office; in Cristóbal, at the entrance to the port on your left. The utmost patience is needed for this operation as regulations change frequently.

Some small freighters go only to intermediate ports such as San Andrés, and it is then necessary to wait for a connection to the mainland. Navieras Mitchell ship cars regularly to San Andrés and Barranquilla. Office at Coco Solo Wharf, Colón, T 441-6942. From Colón to San Andrés takes 2 days and from San Andrés to Cartagena takes 3 days. Shipping companies on San Andrés know that they have a monopoly, so take care when dealing with them and do not believe all they tell you.

Customs formalities at the Colombian end will take 1-3 days to clear (customs officials do not work at weekends). Clearance from the Colombian consul at the Panamanian port of embarkation may reduce the bureaucracy when you arrive in Colombia, but it will cost you US$10. In Colombia you have to pay US$15/cu m for handling, as well as other document charges. An agent can reduce the aggravation but neither the waiting time, nor the cost (they charge US$55-70/day).

CUSTOMS

● **Duty free allowance**

Duty-free admission is granted for portable typewriters, radios, binoculars, personal and cine cameras, but all must show use; 200 cigarettes or 50 cigars or up to 500 grams of manufactured tobacco in any form, 2 bottles of liquor or wine pp.

WHEN YOU ARRIVE

● **Clothing**

Tropical clothing is necessary in the hot and humid climate of the coastal fringe and the eastern *llanos*. In Bogotá medium-weight clothing is needed for the cool evening and night. Medellín requires light clothing; Cali lighter still; Manizales very similar to Bogotá. A dual-purpose raincoat and overcoat is useful in the uplands. Higher up in the mountains it can be very cold; woollen clothing is necessary.

● **Hours of business**

Mon to Fri, commercial firms work 0800 to 1200 and 1400 to 1730 or 1800. Certain firms in the warmer towns such as Cali start at 0700 and finish earlier. Government offices follow the same hours on the whole as the commercial firms, but generally prefer to do business with the public in the afternoon only. Embassy hours for the public are 0900 to 1200 and 1400 to 1700 (Mon to Fri). Bank hours in Bogotá are 0900 to 1500 Mon to Thur, 0900 to 1530 on Fri except the last Fri in the month when they close at 1200; banks in Medellín, Cali, Barranquilla, Bucaramanga, Cartagena, Pasto, Pereira and Manizales open from 0800 to 1130 and 1400 to 1600 on Mon to Thur; on Fri they are open until 1630 but shut at 1130 on the last Fri in the month; banks in Popayán, Cúcuta, Neiva, Tunja, Ibagué and Santa Marta open from 0800 to 1130 and 1400 to 1530 on Mon to Fri and 0800 to 1100 on Sat and the last day of the month. Shopping hours are 0900 to 1230 and 1430 to 1830, inc Sat.

● **Official time**

Colombia is 5 hrs behind GMT.

● **Safety**

Most travellers confirm that the vast majority of Colombians are honest and very hospitable.

In addition to the general advice given in the **Introduction and Hints** section, the following local conditions should be noted. Colombia is part of a major drug-smuggling route. Police and customs activities have greatly intensified and smugglers increasingly try to use innocent carriers. Do not carry packages for other people. Be very polite if approached by policemen. If your hotel room is raided by police looking for drugs, try, if possible, to get a witness to prevent drugs being planted on you. Colombians who offer you drugs may well be setting you up for the police, who are very active on the N coast and San Andrés island, and other tourist resorts.

There is sporadic guerrilla activity in Colombia. At present it appears to be confined to rural areas down the eastern part of the country from Guajira to Putumayo, and near the frontier with Panama. In some cases, it is related to oil production and pipeline areas and to the current destruction of drug crops by the authorities, causing local hardship and resentment. This has no anti-tourist implications except that, in Cocuy, 1996, US citizens have been targeted. Posing as a Canadian proved to be successful in one case reported to us! In 1997, tourists have been caught up in problems near the border with Panamá. Detailed local enquiry is essential before entering this, or indeed any, potentially hazardous area. *The Latin American Travel Advisor* (published by Latin American Travel Consultants, PO Box 17-17-908, Quito, Ecuador, F 593-2-562-566, E-mail, LATA@pi. pro.ec on Internet) is a quarterly publication which reviews the public safety situation in Colombia and South American as a whole.

● **Shopping**

Best buys Emeralds in Bogotá; handworked silver (excellent); Indian pottery and textiles. The state-run Artesanías de Colombia for craft work (see under Bogotá). In Antioquia buy the handbag – *carriel antioqueño* – traditionally made from otter skin, but nowadays from calf skin and plastic trimmed at that. At Cartagena crude rubber is moulded into little dyed figurines: odd but attractive. Clothing and shoes are cheap in Medellín. The Colombian *ruana* (poncho) is attractive and warm in any cool climate, and comes in a wide variety of colours. Leatherwork is generally good and not expensive especially in southern Colombia. Film is cheaper in Colombia than in neighbouring countries.

● **Tipping**

Upmarket restaurants 10%. Porters, cloakroom attendants, hairdressers and barbers, US$0.05-0.25. Taxi-drivers are not normally tipped.

● **Voltage**

120 volts AC, is general for Colombia. Transformer must be 110-150 volt AC, with flat-prong plugs (all of same size).

● **Weights and measures**

Weights and measures are metric, and weights should always be quoted in kilograms. Litres are used for liquid measures but US gallons are standard for the petroleum industry. Linear measures are usually metric, but the inch is quite commonly used by engineers and the yard on golf courses. For land measurement the hectare and cubic metre are officially employed but the traditional measures *vara* (80 cm) and *fanegada* (1,000 square *varas*) are still in common use. As in many other countries food etc is often sold in *libras* (pounds), which are equivalent to $^1/_2$ kilo.

ON DEPARTURE

● **Airport and other taxes**

There is an airport exit tax of US$24 (in cash, dollars or pesos), US$48 for stays of over 60 days. Travellers changing planes in Colombia and leaving the same day are exempt. When you arrive, ensure that all necessary documentation bears a stamp for your date of arrival; without it you will have to pay double the exit tax on leaving. You should also obtain the tax exemption certificate (that is, for the 50% exemption) which shows the expiry date, before leaving the customs zone. Do not buy tickets for domestic flights outside Colombia; they are much more expensive. When getting an onward ticket from Avianca for entry into Colombia, reserve a seat only and ask for confirmation in writing, otherwise you will pay twice as much as if purchasing the ticket inside Colombia. There is also a small tax on internal air tickets, not usually included in price quotations.

WHERE TO STAY

● **Accommodation**

The more expensive hotels and restaurants add on 16% VAT (IVA), but not on San Andrés. Some hotels add a small insurance charge. Between 15 Dec and 30 April, 15 June and 31 Aug, hotels in main holiday centres may increase prices by 20-30%. The Colombian tourist office has lists of authorized prices for all hotels which can be at least a year out of date. If you are overcharged the tourist office will arrange a refund. Most hotels in Colombia charge US$1 to US$6 for extra beds for children, up to a maximum (usually) of 4 beds/room. Although most hotels, except the very cheapest, offer private WC and shower as a matter of course, hot water often comes only in the more expensive hotels or in colder zones. Prices are normally displayed at reception, but in quiet periods it is always worth negotiating.

● **Camping**

Sites are given in the text. Colombian Tourist Office has a list of official sites, but they are seldom signposted on main roads, so can be hard to find. Permission to camp with tent, camper van or car is usually granted by landowners in less populated areas. Many *haciendas* have armed guards protecting their property: this can add to your safety. Do not camp on private land without permission. Those in camper vans may camp by the roadside, but it is neither particularly safe, nor easy to find a secluded spot. Vehicles may camp at truck drivers' restaurants or ask if you may overnight beside police or army posts.

'White gas' for camping stoves etc is readily available. Also available is Coleman fuel imported from the US sold at 19 Av C 123, Bogotá; C 3, No 42-135, Cali; and Av 30 de Agosto, No 37-23, Pereira.

FOOD AND DRINK

FOOD

Colombia's food is very regional; it is quite difficult to buy in Medellín, say, a dish you particularly liked in Bogotá. Restaurants in smaller towns often close on Sun, and early on weekday evenings: if stuck, you will probably find something to eat near the bus station. If you are economising, ask for the *plato del dia* or *plato corriente* (dish of the day).

Locro de choclos is a potato and maize soup so rich and nourishing that, with salad and coffee, it would make a meal in itself. Colombia has its own variant of the inevitable *arroz con pollo* (chicken and rice) which is excellent. For a change *pollo en salsa de mostaza* (chicken in mustard sauce) is rec. *Ajiaco de pollo* is a delicious chicken, maize, manioc, cabbage and potato stew served with cream and capers, and lumps of avocado; it is a Bogotá speciality; another Bogotá speciality is *sobrebarriga* (belly of beef). *Bandeja antioqueña* consists of meat grilled and served with rice, beans, potato, manioc and a green salad; the simpler *carne asada* is cheaper. *Mazamorra*, boiled maize in milk, is a typical *antioqueño* sweet, and so is *salpicón*, a tropical fruit salad. *Lechona* (sucking pig and herbs) is a speciality of Ibagué. Cartagena's rice with coconut can be compared with rice *a la valenciana*. In Nariño, guinea pig (*cuy, curi* or

conejillo de Indias) is typical. *Tamales* are meat pies made by folding a maize dough round chopped pork mixed with potato, peas, onions, eggs and olives seasoned with garlic, cloves and paprika, and steaming the whole in banana leaves (which you don't eat); the best are from Tolima. A baked dish of squash, beaten eggs and seafood covered with sauce is known as the *soufflé de calabash*. *Magras* is a typical Colombian dish of eggs and chicken baked together and served with a tomato sauce. *Sancocho* is a filling combination of all the tuberous vegetables, inc the tropical cassava and yam, with chopped fresh fish or any kind of meat, possibly chicken. From stalls in the capital and the countryside, try *mazorcas* (roast maize cobs) or *arepas* (fried maize cakes). On the Caribbean coast, eat an egg *empanada*, which consists of two layers of corn (maize) dough that open like an oystershell, fried with eggs in the middle, and try the *patacón*, a cake of mashed and baked plantain (green banana). *Huevos pericos*, eggs scrambled with onions and tomatoes, are a popular, cheap and nourishing snack – available almost anywhere. *Pandebono*, cheese-flavoured bread is delicious. A good local sweet is the *canastas de coco*: pastry containing coconut custard flavoured with wine and surmounted by meringue. *Arequipe* is very similar to fudge, and popular (it is called *manjarblanco* in other parts of South America). *Almojábanas*, a kind of sour-milk bread roll, are delicious if fresh. There is, indeed, quite an assortment of little fruit pasties and preserves. Then there are the usual fruits: bananas, oranges, mangoes, avocado pears, and (at least in the tropical zones) *chirimoyas, papayas*, and the delicious *pitahaya*, taken either as an appetizer or dessert. Other fruits such as the *guayaba* (guava), *guanábana* (soursop), *maracuyá* (passion fruit), *lulo* (*naranjilla*), *mora* (blackberry) and *curuba* (banana passion fruit) make delicious juices, sometimes with milk added to make a *sorbete* – though *sorbetes* are best left alone unless you are satisfied the milk is fresh. There is also *frejoya*, a green fruit with white flesh, high in vitamin C. Fruit yoghurts are nourishing and cheap (try Alpina brand; *crema* style is best). *Tinto*, the national small cup of black coffee, is taken at all hours. Colombian coffee is always mild. (Coffee with milk is called *café perico*; *café con leche* is a mug of milk with coffee added.) *Agua de panela* is a common beverage (hot water with unrefined sugar), also taken with limes, milk, or cheese.

DRINK

Many acceptable brands of beer are produced, almost all produced by the Bavaria group, but also popular is Leona. The local rum is good and cheap; ask for *ron*, not *aguardiente*, because in Colombia the latter word is used for a popular drink containing aniseed (*aguardiente anisado*). Try *canelazo* – cold or hot rum with water, sugar, lime and cinnamon. Local table wines include Santo Tomás; none is very good. Preferable are Chilean or Argentine wines; European wines are very expensive.

Warning It has been reported that bottles of imported spirits bearing well-known labels have often been 'recycled' and contain a cheap and poor imitation of the original contents. This can be dangerous to the health, and travellers are warned to stick to beer and rum.

GETTING AROUND

AIR TRANSPORT

Internal air services are flown principally by Avianca, SAM, Aces, Aires and Aero República. Avianca offers a round ticket (*Conozca a Colombia*) giving unlimited domestic travel for 21 days on Avianca, Aires or SAM; conditions are that it allows up to five stops, it must be bought outside Colombia in conjunction with an international air ticket, children aged 2-11 pay 67%, infants 10%, the Air Pass is non-refundable unless the whole has been unused, one may not pass through each city more than once (except for transfers), and a proposed itinerary (not firm) must be submitted when buying the ticket (Leticia and San Andrés may be included). Prices are determined during high season (15 June-15 Sept and 13 Dec-14 Jan), or low season (rest of year): Air Pass 1 is open to all nationalities inc Colombians legally resident abroad, passengers must fly Avianca transatlantic, US$290 (high), US$260 (low) for 5 stops, with the option to add 3 extra coupons at US$40 each. With Air Pass 2 (which is not available to Colombians), any transatlantic carrier may be used, US$539 (high), US$509 (low) for 5 stops, plus US$40 for extra coupons, max 3. The Airpasses are also available without Leticia and San Andrés: Air Pass 1 US$200 (high), US$160 (low); Air Pass 2 US$419 (high), US$399 (low). These prices and conditions change from time to time, enquire at any Avianca office. Ask about discount fares which may be available on certain days of the week. Stand-by tickets are available to Barranquilla, Cali, Medellín; known as PET, *pasajero en turno*. Domestic airports are good, though the tourist facilities tend to close early on weekdays, and all Sun. Most airports levy a US$4.25 tax, payable when you buy your ticket or before issue of a boarding pass. In-flight service and airline services on the ground tend to be poor. Security checks tend to be thorough, watch your luggage.

LAND TRANSPORT

The 107,377 km of roads have eastern and western systems, with inter-communicating laterals (see maps and text). Only about 12% of the road system is paved.

● Bus

Travel in Colombia is far from dull. The scenery is generally worth seeing so travel by day if possible: it is also safer and you can keep a better eye on your valuables. There have been increasing reports of robberies of night buses in the S of Colombia. On main routes you usually have choice of company and type of bus. The cheapest (*corriente*) are basically local buses, stopping frequently, uncomfortable and slow but offering plenty of local colour. Try to keep your luggage with you. *Pullman* (each company will have a different name for the service) are long distance buses usually with a/c, toilets, hostess service, videos (almost always violent films, Spanish/Mexican or dubbed English) and limited stop. Be prepared for lack of a/c and locked windows. Sit near the back with your walkman to avoid the video and the need to keep the blinds down. Luggage is normally carried in a locked compartment against receipt. *Colectivos*, also known as *vans* or *busetas*, run by Velotax, Taxis Verdes, etc are usually 12-20 seat vehicles, maybe with a/c, rather cramped but fast, saving several hours on long journeys. You can keep your eye on luggage in the back of the van. Fares shown in the text are middle of the range where there is a choice but are no more than a guide. Note that meal stops can be few and far between, and short; bring your own food. Be prepared for climatic changes on longer routes. If you entrust your luggage to the bus companies' luggage rooms, remember to load it on to the bus yourself; it will not be done automatically. There are few interdepartmental bus services on holidays. If you are joining a bus at popular or holiday times, not at the starting point, you may be left behind even though you have a ticket and reservation. Always take your passport (or photocopy) with you: identity checks on buses are frequent.

● Motoring

Roads are given in the text. Motor fuel: 'premium' 95 octane (only in large cities), about US$1.55/US gallon; 'corriente' 84 octane, US$1.05/US gallon. All gasoline is lead free. Diesel US$1. Roads are not always signposted. If driving yourself, avoid night journeys; vehicles may be unlighted and it can be dangerous. The roads are often in poor condition, lorry- and bus-drivers tend to be reckless, and stray animals are often encountered. Police checks are frequent in troubled areas, keep your documents handy. There are toll stations every 60-100 km on major roads: toll is about US$1.50. Motorcycles and bicycles don't have to pay. In town, try to leave your car in an attended car park (*parqueadero*), especially at night. If you are planning to sleep in your car, it is better to stop in a *parqueadero*; you will be charged a little extra. In many guarded carparks, only the driver is allowed in; passengers must get out at the entrance. Alternatively, find a police station and ask to sleep in your car nearby. You can also stay overnight in *balnearios campestres*, which normally have armed guards.

National driving licences may be used by foreigners in Colombia, but must be accompanied by an official translation if in a language other than Spanish. International drivers licences are also accepted. To bring a car into Colombia, you must also have documents proving ownership of the vehicle, and a tourist card/transit visa. These are normally valid for 90 days and must be applied for at the Colombian consulate in the country which you will be leaving for Colombia. Only third-party insurance issued by a Colombian company is valid, cost around US$70; there are agencies in all ports. In Cartagena, *Aseguradora Solidaria de Colombia*, near Plaza de la Aduana is rec. You will frequently be asked for this document while driving in the country. According to a law of 31 December 1992, if you do not have a *carnet de passages* (see **Motoring** in **Introduction and Hints**) you have to pay a bond worth 10% of the value of your vehicle when bringing a car into Colombia. This will be stamped into your passport. Entering the country with a *carnet* is a lot quicker than without. Carry driving documents with you at all times.

Spare parts are plentiful for Renault, Mazda and Chevrolet cars, which are assembled in Colombia. VW is also well represented.

● **Car hire**

Car hire is very expensive. In addition to passport and driver's licence, a credit card may be asked for as additional proof of identity (Visa, Mastercard, American Express), and to secure a returnable deposit to cover any liability not covered by the insurance. Check carefully. Main international car rental companies are represented at principal airports but may be closed Sat pm and Sun.

● **Cycling**

Cycling is a popular sport in Colombia. There are good shops for spares in all big cities, though the new standard 622/700 size touring wheel size is not very common. Take your own spare tyres. Recommended is *Bicicletas de Montaña*, C 23, No 43A-121, Medellín. There have been reports of muggings of cyclists in the Caribbean coastal area.

● **Hitchhiking**

Hitchhiking (*autostop*) seems to be quite easy in Colombia, especially if you can enlist the co-operation of the highway police checkpoints outside each town and toll booths. Truck-drivers are often very friendly, but be careful of private cars with more than one person inside, especially if you are travelling on your own.

● **Motorcycles**

Bringing a bike in by land only takes a few minutes. Bringing a bike by sea may require up to 3 days to clear customs, with costs of up to US$50; passport and shipping documents required. Shippers charge by cubic metre, so knock the bike down to use as little space as possible. You must drain the fuel, oil and battery acid. Remove anything breakable and tape cardboard over fragile bits. Insist on loading the machine yourself. Most people have to go to Customs at the port to get permission for the bike to be released. If you bring a bike in by air to Bogotá, try to stay as close as possible to it while it is cleared through freight forwarders (eg Cosimex) and the Customs, to save time and damage. You can airfreight from Panama, or from Guatemala by SAM via San Andrés. A *carnet de passage* is strongly advised (see above). At Bogotá airport, you can have it stamped and be through in 2 hrs. Otherwise you must go to the *Aduana Nacional* in C 68 to complete formalities. Parking at night can be a problem, but some hotels listed have patios or their own lock up garages nearby. Otherwise use *parqueadores* (see **Motoring** above). Local insurance costs around US$30 for a bike over 200 cc. You may find that wearing helmets is inadvisable in trouble spots, eg Medellín; take advice. Spare parts, tyres, etc readily available in Colombia for Yamaha XT and Honda XL models (although supplies are less good for models over 500 cc), so Colombia is a suitable country for rebuilding a bike on a long trip. Medellín is the best place for spare parts. BMW, Triumph spares sold by Germán Villegas Arango, C 1 B, No 11A-43, Bogotá, T 289-4399. Other rec motorcycle repairs: *Racing Lines Ltda*, Av 30 de Agosto, No 40-51, T (963)361970, Pereira; *Motoservicio Asturias*, Cra 5, No 24-35, T 893616, Cali.

● **Rail**

Originally there were over 3,000 km of railways, but most lines have been closed. At present there is only a tourist service N of Bogotá and an intermittant connection between Medellín and Barrancabermeja.

● **Taxis**

Whenever possible, take a taxi with a meter, and ensure that it is switched on, otherwise you will be overcharged. Recent reports suggest that meters are in disuse in some cities, in which case bargain and fix a price. All taxis are obliged to display the additional legal tariffs that may be charged after 2000, on Sun and fiestas. Don't take a taxi which is old; look for 'Servicio Público' on the side. There is a small surcharge for Radio Taxis, but they normally offer reliable service. The dispatcher will give you the cab's number which should be noted in case of irregularities. Women should not travel alone in taxis at night. If the taxi 'breaks down', take your luggage out if you are asked to push, or let the driver push; it may be a trick to separate you from your luggage.

COMMUNICATIONS

● **Newspapers**
Bogotá: *El Tiempo, El Espectador* (both Liberal); *La República* and *La Prensa* (Conservative), *El Siglo* (extreme Conservative). Medellín: *El Mundo, El Colombiano*; Cali: *El País, Occidente, El Pueblo,* all major cities have daily papers. Magazines are partisan, best is probably *Semana*. US and European papers can be bought at Drugstore Internacional, Cra 10, No 26-71, just N of *Tequendama Hotel* in Bogotá and at *Librería Oma*, Cra 15, No 82-58, or at the stand on the corner of Cra 7/C 19 in the centre of Bogotá. Worth bargaining for a better price. *Colombian Post*, once weekly in English, available in Bogotá.

● **Postal services**
There are two parallel postal systems, **Avianca**, operated by the national airline, and **Correos de Colombia**, the post office proper. Both have offices in all major cities, but only Correos can be found in small towns and rural areas. Both will accept mail for all destinations. Prices are identical for overseas airmail (which is carried by Avianca in any event), but Correos is much more economical, and can be more efficient, for internal service. Anything of importance should be registered. Avianca controls all airmail services and has offices in provincial cities. It costs US$0.80 to send a letter or postcard to the US, US$0.90 to Europe or elsewhere; a 1 kg package to the US costs US$16, to Europe, US$18 by air (Avianca). The Amex agent, Tierra Mar Aire, accepts mail to be held for Amex customers.

● **Telephone services**
Inter-city calls must be made from Telecom offices unless you have access to a private phone. Long-distance pay 'phones are located outside most Telecom offices, also at bus stations and airports. They take 50 peso coins. From the larger towns it is possible to telephone to Canada, the USA, the UK, and to several of the Latin American republics. International phone charges are high (about US$7 for 3 mins to USA, US$8 to Europe,

US$12 to Australia) but there is a 20% discount on Sun and sometimes less in the evening. A deposit is required before the call is made which can vary between US$18 and US$36, US$1 is charged if no reply, for person-to-person add an extra minute's charge to Canada, 2 mins' to UK; all extra minutes' conversation costs 1/3 more. The best value is to purchase a phone card and dial direct yourself. Canada Direct is 980-19-0057, AT&T for the US dial 980-110010 and for the UK, 980-44-0057; BT Chargecards can be used for calls within Colombia as well as country-to-country and to the UK. Other collect, or reversed-charge, telephone calls can be made from El Dorado airport (enquire) but otherwise are only possible from private telephones; make sure the operator understands what is involved or you may be billed in any case. Fax to Europe costs US$4/page, but is almost double this from hotels.

SPORT

Association football is the most popular game and is of high quality, especially in Cali and Medellín. American baseball is played at Cartagena and Barranquilla. The game of *tejo* is played in Cundinamarca, Boyacá, Tolima, Valle, Caldas and elsewhere. A stone is thrown from a set distance at a mudbank in which an explosive device is embedded. Hopefully, the winner survives! Another similar game is played in Pasto and Popayán under the name of *sapo* (toad). This is the Spanish *juego de la rana*, in which a small quoit has to be thrown from an improbable distance into a metal frog's mouth. There are bullrings at Bogotá, Cali, Manizales, Medellín, Sincelejo and Cerrito. Polo is played at Medellín and Bogotá. Cockfights, cycling, boxing and basketball are also popular.

Fishing is particularly good at Girardot, Santa Marta, and Barranquilla; marlin is fished off Barranquilla. There is good trout fishing, in season, in the lakes in the Bogotá area, particularly at Lago Tota, in the mountains.

Climbing For information ask at the Federación Colombiana de Montañismo, Cra 28, No 25-18, p 3, Bogotá, President: Mauricio Afanador, who can also be contacted at *Café y Crepes* (see Bogotá, **Places to eat**). Maps can be obtained at the Instituto Geográfico (see under Bogotá, **Maps**). If you have a guide or are invited on a mountain tour, make certain costs/charges are clear before you start. For specific area details, see under Sierra Nevada del Cocuy, Valledupar, Ibagué, Manizales and Pereira. If you intend to climb, bring all your own equipment. It may be impossible to find easily in Colombia, eg compass. Some equipment available at *Almacén Aventura*, Cra 13, No 67-26, Bogotá, T 248-1679, F 201-9543, rope, boots etc; *Deportivos* *del Campo*, C 64, No 18-15, Bogotá, T 248-1855, F 217-4756, tents, mattresses etc, mostly imported; *Sierra Nevada* shops: Cra 24, No 72-75, T 225-0827, Bogotá; Av 37, No 41-53, T 648029, Ibagué; Cra 39, No 8-03, T 268-4296, Medellín. Also at *Eco-Guías*, T 284-8991, Bogotá. Light equipment, rucksacks etc of reasonable quality, can be bought in markets.

HOLIDAYS AND FESTIVALS

Public Holidays are on the following days: 1 Jan: Circumcision of our Lord; 6 Jan: Epiphany*; 19 Mar: St Joseph*; Maundy Thursday; Good Friday; 1 May: Labour Day; Ascension Day*; Corpus Christi*; Sacred Heart*; 29 June: SS Peter and Paul*; 20 July: Independence Day; 7 Aug: Battle of Boyacá; 15 Aug: Assumption*; 12 Oct: Columbus' arrival in America*; 1 Nov: All Saints' day*; 11 Nov: Independence of Cartagena*; 8 Dec: Immaculate Conception; 25 Dec: Christmas Day. When those marked with an asterisk do not fall on a Mon, or when they fall on a Sun, they will be moved to the following Mon.

FURTHER READING

A brief, introductory selection: John Hemming, *The Search for Eldorado*; Alexandre von Humboldt, *Travels*. For an account of travelling in modern Colombia (specifically his adventures in the cocaine trade), Charles Nicholl's *The Fruit Palace* is highly recommended. For birdwatchers, *A Guide to the Birds of Colombia*, by Steven Hilty and William Brown, is recommended. Colombian literature: Jorge Isaacs, *María* (1867); José Eustacio Rivera, *La Vorágine* (*The Vortex*, 1924); and, of course, the novels and short stories of Gabriel García Márquez. *Colombian News Letter*, published monthly by the Colombian American Association Inc, 150 Nassau Street, New York, NY 10038.

ACKNOWLEDGEMENTS

This section has been updated with the welcome assistance of Peter Pollard, who visited Colombia in Feb 1997. In addition to the thanks given at the end of the book, we are most grateful to Lynda Cheetham (Medellín), Mark Duffy, Germán Esobar and Nadia Diamond (all of Bogotá) for their invaluable help.

Ecuador and the Galápagos Islands

HORIZONS

Ecuador, named after its position on the equator, is bounded by Colombia to the N, Peru to the E and S and the Pacific Ocean to the W. In area it is the second smallest republic in South America.

The Andes, running from N to S, form a mountainous backbone to the country. There are two main ranges, the Central Cordillera and the Western Cordillera, separated by a 400-km long Central Valley, whose rims are from 40 to 65 km apart. The rims are joined together, like the two sides of a ladder, by hilly rungs, and between each pair of rungs lies an intermont basin with a dense cluster of population. These basins are drained by rivers which cut through the rims to run either W to the Pacific or E to join the Amazon. The whole mountain area is known as the Sierra.

THE LAND

The Sierra There are altogether 10 intermont basins strung along the Sierra, at an elevation of between 1,800 and 3,000m. Quito, the capital, lies in one of the northern basins. Over half the area is now grassy land on which cattle and sheep are raised.

What crops are grown is determined by altitude, the hardiest of them being the potato. The intermont basins also produce poultry, wheat, barley, oats, maize, quinoa, fruit and vegetables.

Some 47% of the people of Ecuador live in the central trough of the Andes, and the majority are pure Indians. Most of the land is held in large private estates worked by the Indians, but some of it is held by Indian communities. With the limited application of an agrarian-reform programme, the *huasipungo* system whereby Indians were virtual slaves on the big highland *haciendas* has been all but replaced by co-operatives. Though many Indian communities live at subsistence level and remain isolated from national centres, others have developed good markets for products using traditional skills in embroidery, pottery, jewellery, knitting, weaving, and carving.

Both rims of the Central Valley are lined with the cones of more than 30 volcanoes. Several of them have long been extinct, for example, Chimborazo, the highest (6,310m), Cayambe (5,790m), standing directly on the equator, Illiniza (5,263m), Altar (5,319m) and Carihuairazo (5,146m). At least eight, however, are still active; Cotopaxi (5,897m), which had

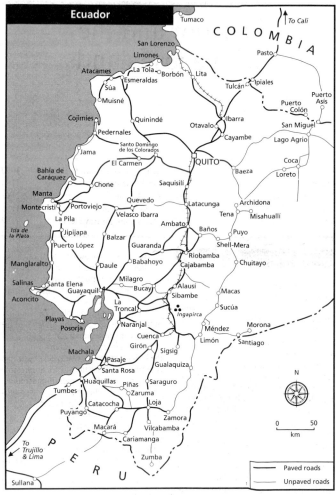

Ecuador

several violent eruptions in the nineteenth century; Tungurahua (5,016m), which had a major eruption early this century; Antisana (5,704m), which showed signs of activity in the 1960s; Pichincha (4,794m), which vents fumes and steam through its west-facing crater, and Sangay (5,230m) one of the world's most active volcanoes, continuously emitting fumes and ash. Nowadays all the main peaks except for Altar and Sangay, which are less accessible, are climbed fairly regularly.

The Costa Between the Western Cordillera and the Pacific lies the coastal alluvial plain, the Costa, 685 km from N to S and some 100 km wide. It is from this area that Ecuador draws the majority of its agricultural products for export. Guayaquil, the main city of this region, is 464 km from Quito.

Most of the Costa region is lowland at an altitude of less than 300m, apart from a belt of hilly land which runs NW from Guayaquil to the coast, where it turns N and runs parallel to the shore to Esmeraldas. In the extreme N there is a typical tropical rain forest. The forests thin out in the more S lowlands, and give way to tropical dry forest.

The main agricultural exports come from the lowlands to the SE and N of Guayaquil, between the coastal hills and the Andes. The heavy rains and high temperature and humidity suit the growth of tropical crops. One part of this Guayas lowland is subject to floods from the four rivers which traverse it. Bananas and mango are grown here while rice is farmed on the natural levees of this flood plain. The main crop comes from the alluvial fans at the foot of the mountains rising out of the plain. High on these same alluvial fans excellent coffee is also grown. A major employer and foreign exchange earner now is shrimp farming, which has greatly altered the coastal landscape in some areas and destroyed mangroves. Add to this that the Guayas lowland is a great cattle-fattening area in the dry season, and its importance in the national economy becomes obvious. Along the N coast, the main areas of population are at Esmeraldas, along the highways inland, in the irrigated lands of N Manabí, and near Manta, Montecristi, and Jipijapa.

Two areas of the coastlands have experienced spectacular rises in population and agricultural production: in El Oro Province in the extreme S, centred on the town of Machala; irrigation has produced a thriving zone of very intensive banana plantations. In the Quevedo-Santo Domingo area, along the Andean fringe to the N of Guayaquil, large areas of forest have been cleared. Bananas used to be the main crop, but have been replaced by African palm.

The Selva East of the Central Cordillera the forest-clad mountains fall sharply to a chain of foothills (the Eastern Cordillera) and then the jungle – the Oriente – through which meander the tributaries of the Amazon. This E lowland region makes up 36% of Ecuador's total territory, but is only sparsely populated by native Indians and agricultural colonists from the highlands. In total, the region has only 5% of the national population, but colonization is now proceeding rapidly owing to population pressure and in the wake of an oil boom. There are substantial oil reserves in the Oriente.

CLIMATE

In the Sierra, there is little variation by day or by season in the temperature in any particular basin: temperature depends on altitude. The range of shade temperature is from 6°C to 10°C in the morning to 19°C to 23°C in the afternoon. Temperatures can get considerably higher in the lower basins. There are two rainy seasons, from Feb to May and Oct to Nov, when the average fall in Quito is 1,270 mm; the skies are mostly cloudy or overcast at this time and there are frequent rainfalls during the afternoons and nights.

In the northern coastal lowlands there are two rainy seasons, which tend to merge into one, running from Dec to June. Further S, the later the rains begin, the sooner they end: at Guayaquil the rains normally fall between Jan and April. The Santa Elena Peninsula and the SW coast near Peru have little or no rainfall. During the dry season, May-Nov, the coast from Punta Blanca to Puerto López (provinces of Guayas and Manabí) is subject to mists (garúa) and cool grey days.

HISTORY

Conquest and Colonial Rule The Incas of Peru, with their capital at Cusco, began to conquer the Sierra of Ecuador, already densely populated, towards the middle of the 15th century. A road was built between Cusco and Quito, and the empire was ruled after the death of the Inca Huayna Capac by his two sons, Huáscar at Cusco and Atahualpa at Quito. Pizarro's main Peruvian expedition took place in 1532, when there was civil war between the two brothers. Atahualpa, who had won the war, was put to death by Pizarro in 1533, and the Inca Empire collapsed.

Pizarro claimed the N kingdom of Quito, and his lieutenants Sebastián de Benalcázar (also Belalcázar) and Diego de Almagro took the city in 1534. Pizarro founded Lima in 1535 as capital of the whole region, and 4 years later replaced Benalcázar at Quito for Gonzalo, his brother. Gonzalo later set out on the exploration of the Oriente. He moved down the Napo River, and sent Francisco de Orellana to prospect. Orellana did not return. He drifted down the river finally to reach the mouth of the Amazon: the first white man to cross the continent in this way.

Quito became an *audiencia* under the Viceroy of Peru. For the next 280 years Ecuador reluctantly accepted the new ways brought by the conqueror. Gonzalo had already introduced pigs and cattle; wheat was now added. The Indians were Christianized, colonial laws, customs and ideas introduced. The marriage of the arts of Spain to those of the Incas led to a remarkable efflorescence of painting, sculpting and building at Quito. In the 18th century black slave labour was brought in to work the plantations near the coast.

Independence and after There was an abortive attempt at independence in the strongly garrisoned capital in 1809, but it was not until 1822 that Sucre, moving N from Guayaquil, defeated the Spanish at Pichincha and occupied Quito. Soon afterwards Bolívar arrived, and Ecuador was induced to join the Venezuelan and Colombian confederation, the Gran Colombia of Bolívar's dream. On 26 and 27 July 1822, Bolívar met San Martín, fresh from liberating Lima, at Guayaquil. What happened at that mysterious encounter is not known, but San Martín left it silently for a self-imposed exile in France. Venezuela separated itself from Gran Colombia in 1829, and Ecuador decided on complete independence in August 1830, under the presidency of Juan Flores.

Ecuador's 19th century history was a continuous struggle between pro-Church conservatives and anti-Church (but nonetheless devotedly Catholic) liberals. There were also long periods of military rule from 1895, when the liberal Gen Eloy Alfaro took power. During the late 1940s and the 1950s there was a prolonged period of prosperity (through bananas, largely) and constitutional rule, but the more typical pattern of alternating civilian and military governments was resumed in the 1960s and 1970s. Apart from the liberal-conservative struggles, there has been long-lasting rivalry between Quito and the Sierra on one hand and Guayaquil and the Costa on the other.

Return to democracy Following 7 years of military rule, the first presidential elections under a new constitution were held in 1979. They were won by Jaime Roldós Aguilera, whose government began a policy of gradual reforms. President Roldós was killed in an air crash in 1981 and was succeeded by Vice-president Oswaldo Hurtado Larrea. In the next three presidential elections power oscillated between the centre-right and centre-left with conservative León Febres Cordero of the Partido Social Cristiano (PSC) being elected in 1984 followed by Rodrigo Borja Cevallos of the Izquierda Democrática(Democratic Left) in 1988 and Sixto Durán Ballén of the Partido de Unidad Republicana in coalition with Alberto Dahik of the Partido Conservador (who became vice-president) in 1992.

The popularity of President Durán Ballén's government declined steadily with the implementation of an economic modernization programme aimed at reducing inflation and replenishing foreign reserves by cutting public spending and public sector jobs and by privatizing state enterprises.

The country's political situation changed dramatically when Ecuadoreans responded to the Jan-Feb 1995 border conflict with Peru (see below) with a massive display of national unity, backing their government and armed forces to an extent not seen in recent years and sending the President's popularity ratings well above 90%. This backing was short-lived as a combination of the financial cost of the conflict and electricity rationing because of insufficient rain to fill hydroelectric reservoirs led to major economic problems. Confidence in both the economy and the political establishment was rocked by a huge corruption scandal which culminated with Vice-President Dahik fleeing the country in Oct 1995 in the face of charges of misuse of public funds. In all 23 ministers were impeached or resigned; at one stage the president himself was under threat of impeachment. The public's exasperation was amply demonstrated by the rejection in a referendum in Nov 1995 of all constitutional reforms, even those which, before the vote, were seen to have majority support.

In May 1996 general elections, Durán Ballén's party was rejected by the voters and the presidency was won by Abdalá Bucaram of the Roldosista party, who defeated Jaime Nebot Saadi, the Social Christian candidate. In early Feb 1997, the people and Congress lost patience with the president. A 48-hr strike and mass demonstrations against the huge price rises in his economic austerity programme were followed by a congressional vote to remove Bucaram from office on the grounds of 'mental incapacity'. Bucaram resisted his deposition for a few days, during which time Ecuador had three presidents: Bucaram, vice-president Rosalía Arteaga, who claimed the office, and Fabián Alarcón, chosen by Congress, of whom he was president. On 8 Feb the army withdrew its support for Bucaram and, 5 days later, Congress voted for Alarcón to become president until new elections in 1998. A referendum in May 1997 ratified both Bucaram's removal and Alarcón's appointment.

After the dissolution in the 1820s of Gran Colombia (largely present-day Venezuela, Colombia and Ecuador), repeated attempts to determine the extent of Ecuador's eastern jungle territory failed. This has caused periodic increases in tension between the two countries. The dispute reached an acute phase in 1941 when war broke out; it ended with military defeat for Ecuador and the signing of the Rio de Janeiro Protocol of 1942 which allotted most of the disputed territory to Peru. Since 1960 Ecuador has denounced the Protocol as unjust (because it was imposed by force of arms) and as technically flawed (because it refers to certain non-existent geographic features). According to Peru, the Protocol demarcated the entire boundary and all the features are provable to US aerial photographic maps. Ecuador's official policy remains the recovery of a sovereign access to the Amazon. In Peru's view, the Protocol gives Ecuador navigation rights, but does not and cannot return land that Ecuador never had in the first place. Sporadic border skirmishes culminated in Jan 1995s undeclared war over control of the headwaters of the Río Cenepa. Argentina, Brazil, Chile and the USA (guarantors of the Rio de Janeiro Protocol) intervened diplomatically and a ceasefire took effect after 6 weeks of combat. A multinational team of observers was dispatched to the region in Mar 1995 to oversee the disengagement of forces and subsequent demilitarization of the area of the conflict.

CULTURE

PEOPLE

Roughly 48% of Ecuador's people live in the coastal region W of the Andes, and 47% in the Andean Sierra. Migration is occurring from the rural zones of both the coast and the highlands to the towns and cities, particularly Guayaquil and Quito, and agricultural colonization by highlanders is occurring in parts of the coastal lowlands and the Oriente. National average population density is the highest in South America. Average income per head has risen fast in recent years like that of other oil-exporting countries, but the distribution has not improved and a few citizens are spectacularly wealthy.

According to 1989 figures, about 40% of the population was classed as Amerindian, 40% *mestizo*, 15% white and 5%

black. Different classifications state that there are 2-3 million Quichua-speaking Indians in the highlands and about 70,000 lowland Indians. The following indigenous groups maintain their distinct cultural identity: in the Oriente, Siona-Secoya, Cofán, Huaorani (also known as Aucas, which is a derogatory term), Záparo, Quichua, Achuar and Shuar (formerly known as Jívaro); in the Sierra, Otavalo, Salasaca (province of Tungurahua), Puruha (Chimborazo), Cañar and Saraguro (Loja province); on the coast, Chachi (also known as Cayapas, Esmeraldas province), Tsáchilas (also known as Colorados, lowlands of Pichincha) and Awas (also known as Cuaiquer, Esmeraldas and Carchi provinces). Many Amazonian Indian communities are fighting for land rights in the face of oil exploration and colonization. The main Indian organization is the National Confederation of Indigenous Nationalities of Ecuador, CONAIE, Casilla 17-17-1235, Quito, T 593-2-248-930, F 442-271.

Indigenous Groups

The Quichua, Shuar and Siona-Secoya Indians in Pastaza welcome tourists in a controlled way, in order to sell their beautiful products; some work as guides. Contact the Organización de Indígenas de Pastaza (OPIP) in Puyo, T 885-461, they can also give you a list of indigenous museums and artesan workshops. Also contact Federación de Centros Shuar-Achuar, Domingo Comín 17-38, Sucúa, Morona-Santiago, T/F 593-7-740-108 (or in Quito 2-504-264). CONFENIAE, the confederation of Amazon Indians is another good contact at Km 5 outside Puyo, T 885-343, or at their office in Quito, Av 6 de Diciembre y Pazmino, Edif Parlamento, p 4, of 408, T 593-2-543-973, F 220-325. Care is required when visiting the Oriente and taking tours to Huaorani villages without prior arrangement, the Huaorani are at great risk from the tourist invasion and do not appreciate being treated as a spectacle. ONHAE, the Huaorani Indigenous organization, has stated that it will only allow guides approved by them to enter their territories.

The term *cholo* refers to people in the Sierra who are an ethnic mixture of white and Indian. The same term is used in Peru. In Ecuador, however, it is also a name given to people of white/Indian/black descent who live in the Santa Elena peninsula, W of Guayaquil. Another, more common name is given to people of this three-way mixture in the area around Guayaquil and throughout the northern Pacific lowlands: *montuvio*. The *montuvios* (also spelt *montubios*) generally make their living from farming and fishing.

MUSIC AND DANCE

Culturally, ethnically and geographically, Ecuador is very much two countries – the Andean highlands with their centre at

Ecuador - National Parks & Reserves

COLOMBIA

Pacific Ocean

Cayapas-Mataje Ecological Reserve

Bilsa

Cotacachi-Cayapas Ecological Reserve

El Angel Ecological Reserve

Pululahua Geobotanical Reserve
Maquipucuna Biological Reserve

Cayambe-Coca Ecological Reserve

Cuyabeno Wildlife Reserve

Mindo Forest Reserve

Limoncocha Biological Reserve

Rio Guajalito Reserve
Pasochoa Forest Reserve

Antisana Ecological Reserve

Sumaco Forest Reserve

Cotopaxi National Park

Boliche National Recreation Area

Yasuni National Park

Llanganates Bilogical Reserve

Isla de la Plata

Machalilla National Park

Chimborazo Fauna Resrerve

El Salado National Park

Sangay National Park

Cerro Blanco

Manglares Churute Ecological Reserve

El Cajas National Park

N

Puyango Petrified Forest

Podocarpus National Park

0   50
km

PERU

Quito and the Pacific lowlands behind Guayaquil. In spite of this, the music is relatively homogeneous and it is the Andean music that would be regarded as 'typically Ecuadorean'. The principal highland rhythms are the Sanjuanito, Cachullapi, Albaza, Yumbo and Danzante, danced by Indian and mestizo alike. These may be played by brass bands, guitar trios or groups of wind instruments, but it is the *rondador*, a small panpipe, that provides the classic Ecuadorean sound, although of late the Peruvian *quena* has been making heavy inroads via pan-Andean groups and has become a threat to the local instrument. The coastal region has its own song form, the Amorfino, but the most genuinely 'national' song and dance genres, both of European origin, are the Pasillo (shared with Colombia) in waltz time and the Pasacalle, similar to the Spanish Pasodoble. Of Ecuador's three best loved songs, 'El Chulla Quiteño', 'Romántico Quito' and 'Vasija de Barro', the first two are both Pasacalles. Even the Ecuadorean mestizo music has a melancholy quality not found in Peruvian 'Música Criolla', perhaps due to Quito being in the mountains, while Lima is on the coast. Music of the highland Indian communities is, as elsewhere in the region, related to religious feasts and ceremonies and geared to wind instruments such as the *rondador*, the *pinqullo* and *pifano* flutes and the great long *guarumo* horn with its mournful note. The guitar is also usually present and brass bands with well worn instruments can be found in even the smallest villages. Among the most outstanding traditional fiestas are Inti Raymi in Cayambe and Ingapirca, the Pase del Niño in Cuenca and other cities, the Mama Negra of Latacunga, carnival in Guaranda, the Yamor in Otavalo, the Fiesta de las Frutas y las Flores in Ambato, plus Corpus Cristi and the Feast of Saint John all over the highlands. Among the best known musical groups who have recorded are Los Embajadores (whose 'Tormentos' is superb) and the Duo Benítez-Valencia for guitar- accompanied vocal harmony, Ñanda-Mañachi and the Conjunto Peguche (both from Otavalo) for highland Indian music and Jatari and Huayanay for pan-Andean music.

There is one totally different cultural area, that of the black inhabitants of the Province of Esmeraldas and the highland valley of the Río Chota. The former is a southern extension of the Colombian Pacific coast negro culture, centred round the marimba xylophone. The musical genres are also shared with black Colombians, including the Bunde, Bambuco, Caderona, Torbellino and Currulao dances and this music is some of the most African sounding in the whole of South America. The Chota Valley is an inverted oasis of desert in the Andes and here the black people dance the Bomba. It is also home to the unique Bandas Mochas, whose primitive instruments include leaves that are doubled over and blown through.

THE ECONOMY

Structure of production In the 1970s, Ecuador underwent a transformation from an essentially agricultural economy to a predominantly petroleum economy. Substantial oil output began in 1972, from when economic growth has largely followed the fortunes of the international oil market.

The contribution of agriculture and fishing to gdp has dwindled from over 22% in 1972 to about 17% in the mid-1990s, but about one third of jobs are in farming and agro-exports generate around 40% of foreign earnings. Ecuador is the world's largest exporter of bananas. Efforts have been made to expand markets following the introduction of EU import restrictions, to introduce a variety of banana resistant to black sigatoka disease and to reduce costs and increase efficiency. Coffee is the most extensive of Ecuador's cash crops, accounting for over 20% of total agricultural land, but it is very low yielding. Cocoa yields have also fallen and a programme for better maintenance and replacement of old trees is under way. Several non-traditional crops are expanding rapidly, including roses and other flowers in the Sierra within reach of Quito airport, mangoes, strawberries, palm hearts, asparagus and other fruits and vegetables, many of which are processed before export.

The fishing industry is a major export earner, partly from the catch offshore of tuna, sardines and white fish, but mostly from shrimp farming along the coast. Shrimp farms offer employment in underdeveloped areas where other jobs are scarce, but their development is controversial and a large portion of Ecuador's mangroves have been destroyed. Most of the forest around Bahía and Muisne has gone but the Government has declared a large area of mangrove in Esmeraldas province a reserve, so several shrimp projects have been shelved. In the Gulf of Guayaquil, where most of the farms are, the shrimp have suffered from high mortality, allegedly because of the pollution from agrochemicals used intensively by banana growers.

Mining is not yet an important sector, but the discovery of about 700 tonnes of gold reserves around Nambija (Zamora) in the SE created intense interest and over 12,000 independent miners rushed to prospect there. Over 9 tonnes of gold are produced a year by prospectors along the Andean slopes, polluting the waters with cyanide and mercury. New legislation in 1991 was designed to encourage investors in large projects with better technology which would be less harmful and could be more strictly controlled. Foreign companies are interested in deposits of gold, silver, lead, zinc and copper in the S.

Although Ecuador's share of total world oil production is small (0.6%), foreign exchange earnings from oil exports are crucial, producing about a third of exports and nearly half of government revenue. Ecuador left Opec in 1992 because of production quota disagreements and now produces 385,000 b/d, of which 250,000 b/d are exported. The main producing area is in the N Oriente, and a 495-km trans-Andean pipeline carries the oil to Esmeraldas on the coast, where it is refined and/or exported. A planned second trans-Andean pipeline was scrapped in 1997 in favour of extending the existing pipeline's capacity. Another

Ecuador: fact file	
Geographic	
Land area	272,045 sq km
forested	56.3%
pastures	18.4%
cultivated	11.0%
Demographic	
Population (1996)	11,698,000
annual growth rate (1991-96)	2.2%
urban	59.3%
rural	40.7%
density	43.0 per sq km
Education and Health	
Life expectancy at birth,	
male	67.5 years
female	72.6 years
Infant mortality rate	
per 1,000 live births (1994)	39.3
Calorie intake as %	
of FAO requirement	113%
Population age 25 and over	
with no formal schooling	12.7%
Literate males (over 15)	90.5%
Literate females (over 15)	86.2%
Economic and Employment	
GNP (1994 market prices)	US$14,703mn
GNP per capita	US$1,310
Public external debt (1994)	US$10,384mn
Tourism receipts (1994)	US$252mn
Inflation (annual av 1990-95)	39.1%
Population economically active (1990)	3,359,767
Unemployment rate	1.3%
Military forces	57,100
Source Encyclopaedia Britannica	

pipeline takes oil directly to Colombia, but neither has the capacity required for planned development of new wells. The Durán Ballén administration opened millions of hectares of Amazon forest to exploration (disregarding Indian reserves and national parks) in the mid-1990s, which could add 2 billion barrels of oil to existing reserves of 3.5 billion. The oil industry has had a considerable adverse affect on indigenous communities, who have seen their lands polluted and deforested. However, after a protracted campaign, Texaco, which ended two decades of operations in Ecuador in 1992, agreed in 1995 to pay for environmental and community development projects. Another oil company, Maxus, is also being asked for compensation.

Despite the abundance of oil, over two-thirds of electricity generation comes from hydropower. Hydroelectric projects on the Paute, Pastaza and Coca rivers could raise capacity from 2,300MW to 12,000MW. However, in the mid-1990s drought revealed the dangers of overdependence and power shortages were widespread. Several thermal plants came into operation in 1996 and the Government eased restrictions on diesel imports. A new Energy Law was strongly opposed by unions in the power sector who took strike action in 1996 against the privatization of the state power utility, Instituto Ecuatoriano de Electrificación (INE-CEL). Progress in this, and other privatizations, was held back by the political upheavals of early 1997.

Recent trends After a sharp rise in debt in the 1970s, Ecuador joined other debtor nations in the 1980s in refinancing its external obligations. Adherence to free market economic policies in IMF programmes brought international approval and by 1985 Ecuador was widely acclaimed as a model debtor with sufficient creditworthiness to return to the voluntary market for loans. However, in 1986 oil prices crashed, cutting oil receipts by half, followed in 1987 by an earthquake which destroyed part of the trans-Andean pipeline and damaged other oil installations, halting oil exports. Huge amounts of finance were necessary for reconstruction, which put strain on public finances while inflation and poverty increased. Subsequent loss of confidence in the Government's economic management resulted in a massive demand for dollars and a heavy devaluation of the sucre. Arrears on debt payments to all creditors built up and it was only in 1989 that the Government felt able to begin negotiations with both official and private creditors. However, agreements were not made until 1994 when the IMF granted a standby facility, the Paris Club of creditor governments rescheduled maturities and commercial bank creditors restructured US$4.5bn of principal and US$3bn of overdue interest.

The Government introduced reforms to streamline the public sector and liberalize trade and the financial markets. Debt remains a burden on the economy, representing 95% of gdp, but servicing costs have been halved to about 20% of exports of goods and services.

At the beginning of 1995 the border war with Peru caused direct costs to the budget of some US$300m, or 2% of gdp, but indirect costs were much higher. Despite approaching elections, the Government imposed austerity measures, allowed interest rates to rise and the sucre to devalue more rapidly. Confidence was restored and foreign reserves were soon back to the level before the war. In Dec 1996 President Bucaram announced an economic plan which focussed heavily on fiscal policy. The plan was badly received, especially austerity measures, and this, plus Bucaram's erratic style and a remarkable rise in corruption, contributed greatly to his deposition. His successor, President Alarcón, inherited a fiscal deficit of almost 7% of gdp and his first priority was to cut this to 2.7%. He intended to achieve the target without inflicting social costs on the poorest sectors of the community.

GOVERNMENT

There are 21 provinces, including the Galápagos Islands. Provinces are divided into *cantones* and *parroquias* for administration.

Under the 1978 constitution, the vote was extended to include all citizens over the age of 18. The president and vice-president are elected for a 4-year term. The president may not stand for re-election. The legislative branch consists of a single Chamber of Representatives of 77 members, of which 65 are provincial representatives elected for a 2-year term and 12 are national representatives elected for a 4-year term. Constitutional amendments under consideration since August 1994 include permitting presidential re-election, the introduction of a bicameral congress, reorganization of the judiciary, and recognizing dual citizenship.

Quito

FEW cities have a setting to match that of Quito, the second highest capital in Latin America (La Paz, the administrative capital of Bolivia, is the highest). The city is set in a hollow at the foot of the volcano Pichincha (4,794m). It was an Inca city, refounded by Sebastián de Benalcázar, Pizarro's lieutenant, in 1534. Today it is a city of two distinct parts, the colonial centre and, to the north, the modern city.

The city's charm lies in its colonial centre, where cobbled streets are steep and narrow, dipping to deep ravines. Through this section hurries the Machángara River, nowadays too polluted to wash clothes in. From the top of **Cerro Panecillo**, 183m above the city level, there is a fine view of the city below and the encircling cones of volcanoes and other mountains. There is a statue on the hill to the Virgen de Quito; Mass is held in the base on Sun. There is a good view from the observation platform up the statue (entry US$1; see page 1020).

Modern Quito extends N of the colonial city. It has broad avenues, fine private residences, parks, embassies and villas. The district known as La Mariscal (Mcal Sucre: Av Amazonas, from Av Patria to about Av Orellana and the adjoining streets) comprises Quito's modern tourist and business area. On Sun La Alameda, Carolina and El Ejido parks are filled with local families. The Parque Metropolitano, behind Estadio Atahualpa, is reputed to be the largest urban park in South America and is good for walking, running or biking through the forest. Take bus Batán-Colmena from the city. To reduce worsening air pollution, the municipal authorities began to control motor vehicle emissions in 1994. The situation was further helped by the introduction of a trolley bus service (see page 1030).

CLIMATE

Quito (*Pop* 1,100,847; *Alt* 2,850m; *Phone code* 02) is within 25 km of the equator, but it stands high enough to make its climate much like that of spring in England, the days warm or hot and the nights cool. Because of the height, visitors may initially feel some discomfort and should slow their pace for the first 24 hrs. Mean temperature, 13°C, rainfall, 1,473 mm. Rainy season, Oct to May with the heaviest rainfall in April, though heavy storms in July are not unknown. Rain usually falls in the afternoon. The day length (sunrise to sunset) is almost constant throughout the year.

PLACES OF INTEREST

The heart of the city is **Plaza de la Independencia**, dominated by a somewhat grim **Cathedral**, built 1550-1562 (open 0800-1000, 1400-1600) with grey stone porticos and green tile cupolas. On its outer walls are plaques listing the names of the founding fathers of Quito, and inside are the tomb of Sucre (tucked away in a corner) and a famous Descent from the Cross by the Indian painter Caspicara. There are many other 17th and 18th century paintings; the interior decoration, especially the roof, shows Moorish influence. Beside the Cathedral, round the corner, is the beautiful **El Sagrario**, originally built as the Cathedral chapel. Facing the Cathedral is the old **Palacio Arzobispal**, which now houses shops. On the NE side is the concrete **Municipal Alcaldía** which fits in quite well. The low colonial **Palacio de Gobierno**, silhouetted against the flank of Pichincha, is on the NW side of the Plaza (open 0900-1200, 1500-1800, free but you can only see the patio); on the first floor is a gigantic mosaic mural of Orellana navigating the Amazon. The balconies looking over the main square are from the Tuilleries in Paris; sold by the French government shortly after the French Revolution.

Calle Morales, main street of La Ronda district (traditionally called C La Ronda and now a notorious area for pickpockets and bag slashers, avoid the area after dark), is one of the oldest streets in the city. Go past Plaza Santo Domingo to C Guayaquil, the main shopping street, and on to **Parque Alameda**, which has the oldest astronomical observatory in South America (open Sat 0900-1200). There is also a splendid monument to Simón Bolívar, various lakes, and in the NW corner a spiral lookout tower with a good view. The traditional colonial area is being preserved, but elsewhere the city is being radically altered as a result of road improvements and new construction.

From Plaza de la Independencia two main streets, C Venezuela and García Moreno, lead straight towards the Panecillo to the wide Av 24 de Mayo, at the top of which is a concrete building where street vendors are supposed to do their trading. Street trading still takes place daily, however, from Sucre down to 24 de Mayo and from San Francisco church W up past Cuenca.

Plaza de San Francisco (or Bolívar) is W of Plaza de la Independencia; on the NW side of this plaza is the great church and monastery of the patron saint of Quito, **San Francisco**. The church (open 0600-1100, 1500-1800), is said to be the first religious building constructed in South America by the Spanish (1553) and is rich in art treasures. The two towers were felled by an earthquake in 1868 and rebuilt. A modest statue of the founder, Fray Jodoco Ricke, the Flemish Franciscan who sowed the first wheat in Ecuador, stands at the foot of the stairs to the church portal. See the fine wood-carvings in the choir, a magnificent high altar of gold and an exquisite carved ceiling. There are some paintings in the aisles by Miguel de Santiago, the colonial *mestizo* painter. His paintings of the life of Saint Francis decorate the monastery of San Francisco close by (see below). Adjoining San Francisco is the **Cantuña Chapel** with sculptures.

Plaza de Santo Domingo (or Sucre), to the SE of Plaza San Francisco, has to the SE the church and monastery of **Santo Domingo**, with its rich wood-carvings and a remarkable Chapel of the Rosary to the right of the main altar. In the centre of the plaza is a statue to Sucre, pointing to the slopes of Pichincha where he won his battle against the Royalists.

There are altogether 86 churches in Quito. The fine Jesuit church of **La Compañía**, in C García Moreno, one block from Plaza de la Independencia (open 0930-1100, 1600-1800) has the most ornate and richly sculptured façade and interior. See its coloured columns, its 10-sided altars and high altar plated with gold, and the gilded balconies. Several of its most precious treasures, including a painting of the Virgen Dolorosa framed in emeralds and gold, are kept in the vaults of the Banco Central del Ecuador and appear only at special festivals. Agree a price first if you use a guide (in Jan 1996, during restoration work, it was badly damaged by fire, compounding 1987 earthquake damage). Not far away to the N is the church of **La Merced** (open 1500). In the monastery of La Merced is Quito's oldest clock, built in 1817 in London. Fine cloisters are entered through a door to the left of the altar. La Merced contains many splendidly elaborate styles; note the statue of Neptune on the main patio fountain. The **Basílica**, on Plaza de la Basílica (C Venezuela), is very large, has many gargoyles, stained glass windows and fine, bas relief bronze doors (under construction since 1926).

Many of the heroes of Ecuador's struggle for independence are buried in the monastery of **San Agustín** (Flores y Mejía), which has beautiful cloisters on 3 sides where the first act of independence from Spain was signed on 10 August 1809. In the monastery of **San Diego** (by the cemetery of the same name, just W of Panecillo) are some unique paintings with figures dressed in fabrics sewn to the canvas – a curious instance of present-day collage. Ring the bell to the right of the church door to get in, entrance US$0.75, 0900-1200, 1500-1700, all visitors are shown around by a guide.

The **Basílica de Guápulo** (1693), perched on the edge of a ravine E of the city, is well worth seeing for its many paintings, gilded altars, stone carvings of indigenous animals and the marvellously carved pulpit. Take bus 21 (Guápulo-Dos Puentes) from Plaza de Santo Domingo, or walk down the steep stairway behind *Hotel Quito*.

MUSEUMS

Check museum opening times in advance. In the Parque El Ejido, at the junction of 12 de Octubre and Av Patria, there is a large cultural and museum complex housing the Casa de la Cultura and the museums of the Banco Central del Ecuador (entrance on Patria). Museums belonging to the Casa de la Cultura (T 565-808): **Museo de Arte Moderno**, paintings and sculpture since 1830; **Museo de Traje**

Indígena, traditional dress and adornments of indigenous groups; **Museo de Instrumentos Musicales**, an impressive collection of musical instruments. Open Tues-Fri 1000-1800, Sat 1000-1400; entry for the 3 museums, US$1.60, students with ISIC and national student card, US$0.70.

Museums belonging to the Banco Central del Ecuador (T 223-259): **Museo Arqueológico**, with beautiful precolumbian ceramics and gold and a video film on Ecuadorean culture and the different Indian tribes, guided tour every hour, open Tues-Fri 0900-1700, Sat-Sun 0900-1500, US$2, students with ISIC or national student card, US$1; **Museo Colonial y de Arte** (3 sections colonial, modern and contemporary art), guided tours in English, French and Spanish, same hours and entrance fee.

Museo de Ciencias Naturales, Rumipamba 341 y Los Shyris, at E end of Parque La Carolina, Mon-Fri 0830-1630, Sat 0900-1300, US$2, students, US$1. **Museo Nacional de Arte Colonial**, Cuenca y Mejía, T 212-297, a small collection of Ecuadorean sculpture and painting, housed in the 17th-century mansion of Marqués de Villacís, Tues-Fri 1000-1800, Sat 1000-1500, Sun 1000-1400, US$1. **Museo del Convento de San Francisco**, Plaza de San Francisco, T 211-124, has a fine collection of religious art (under restoration since 1991, completed sections are open to the public), Mon-Fri 0830-1130, 1500-1630, US$0.50. Similar collections in: **Museo de San Agustín**, Chile y Guayaquil, interesting exhibition of restoration work, Mon-Sat 0830-1200, Mon-Fri 1500-1800, US$0.25; and **Museo Dominicano Fray Pedro Bedón**, Plaza de Santo Domingo. The **Museo Jijón y Caamaño**, in the Catholic University library building, has a private collection of archaeological objects, historical documents, portraits, uniforms, etc, very well displayed, Mon-Fri 0900-1600, US$0.40. There is also a museum of jungle archaeology (0830-1200), at the university.

Municipal Museum of Art and History, Espejo 1147, near main plaza, free entry,

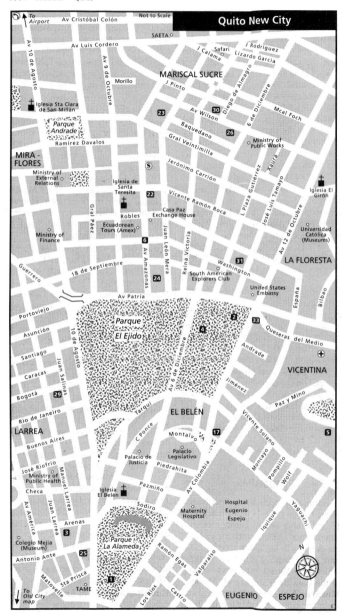

Quito New City

To Airport
Av Cristóbal Colón
Not to Scale
SAETA
Av Luis Cordero
J Calama J Rodríguez
Safari
Lizardo García
Av 10 de Agosto
Av 9 de Octubre
Morillo
MARISCAL SUCRE
J Pinto
Diego de Almargo
6 de Diciembre
Mcal Foch
Iglesia Sta Clara de San Millán
23
Av Wilson
30
Parque Andrade
Baquedano
26
Ramírez Davalos
Gral Veintimilla
Ministry of Public Works
MIRA-FLORES
Jerónimo Carrión
Ministry of External Relations
Iglesia de Santa Teresita
22
Vicente Ramón Roca
Iglesia El Girón
Gral Paez
Robles
Casa Paz Exchange House
José Luis Tamayo
Ministry of Finance
Ecuadorean Tours (Amex)
6
Juan León Mera
Reina Victoria
Washington
31
Av 12 de Octubre
Universidad Católica (Museums)
LA FLORESTA
Guerrero
18 de Septiembre
Av Amazonas
24
South American Explorers Club
United States Embassy
España
Bilbao
Portoviejo
Av Patria
Asunción
Parque El Ejido
2
33
Queseras del Medio
Santiago
Juan Salinas
4
Andrade
VICENTINA
Caracas
10 de Agosto
6 de Diciembre
Jiménez
Bogotá
29
Río de Janeiro
Tarqui
Paz y Mino
Larrea
Buenos Aires
EL BELÉN
Vicente Solano
5
José Riofrío
C Ponce
Montalvo
17
Moncayo
Pompilio
Wolf
Ministry of Public Health
Palacio de Justicia
Palacio Legislativo
Av Colombia
Checa
Manuel Larrea
Juan Larrea
Piedrahita
Pazmiño
Av América
Iglesia El Belén
Sodiro
Maternity Hospital
Hospital Eugenio Espejo
Iquique
Yaguachi
Arenas
3
Colegio Mejía (Museum)
Parque La Alameda
Ramón Egas
N
Antonio Ante
25
Valparaíso
Matovelle
Sta Prisca
1
TAME
Los Ríos
Castro
To Old City map
EUGENIO
ESPEJO

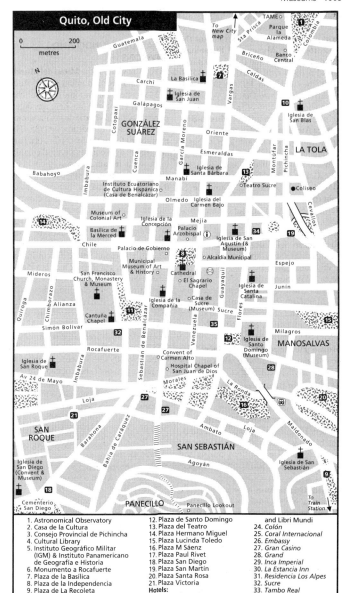

Quito, Old City

0 — 200 metres

1. Astronomical Observatory
2. Casa de la Cultura
3. Consejo Provincial de Pichincha
4. Cultural Library
5. Instituto Geográfico Militar (IGM) & Instituto Panamericano de Geografía e Historia
6. Monumento a Rocafuerte
7. Plaza de la Basílica
8. Plaza de la Independencia
9. Plaza de La Recoleta
10. Plaza de San Blas
11. Plaza de San Francisco
12. Plaza de Santo Domingo
13. Plaza del Teatro
14. Plaza Hermano Miguel
15. Plaza Lucinda Toledo
16. Plaza M Sáenz
17. Plaza Paul Rivet
18. Plaza San Diego
19. Plaza San Martín
20. Plaza Santa Rosa
21. Plaza Victoria

Hotels:
22. Alameda Real
23. Alston Inn, Super Papa

and Libri Mundi
24. Colón
25. Coral Internacional
26. Embassy
27. Gran Casino
28. Grand
29. Inca Imperial
30. La Estancia Inn
31. Residencia Los Alpes
32. Sucre
33. Tambo Real
34. Viena International
35. Yumbo Imperial

Labels on map:
TAME
To New City map
Parque la Alameda
Sta Prisca
Colombia
Banco Central
Guatemala
Briceño
Caldas
La Basílica
Iglesia de San Juan
Carchi
Vargas
Iglesia de San Blas
Galápagos
GONZÁLEZ SUÁREZ
Cotopaxi
García Moreno
Oriente
LA TOLA
Babahoyo
Imbabura
Cuenca
Manabí
Esmeraldas
Montúfar
Pichincha
Iglesia de Santa Bárbara
Teatro Sucre
Coliseo
Instituto Ecuatoriano de Cultura Hispánica (Casa de Benalcázar)
Olmedo
Iglesia del Carmen Bajo
Cevallos
Museum of Colonial Art
Iglesia de la Concepción
Mejía
Palacio Arzobispal
Iglesia de San Agustín (& Museum)
Basílica de la Merced
Chile
Palacio de Gobierno
Alcaldía Municipal
Espejo
Mideros
San Francisco Church, Monastery & Museum
Municipal Museum of Art & History
Cathedral
El Sagrario Chapel
Iglesia de Santa Catalina
Junín
Quiroga
Chimborazo
Alianza
Iglesia de la Compañía
Casa de Sucre (Museum)
Sucre
Cantuña Chapel
Simón Bolívar
Iglesia de Santo Domingo (Museum)
MANOSALVAS
Venezuela
Flores
Milagros
Rocafuerte
Convent of Carmen Alto
Sebastián de Benalcázar
Iglesia de San Roque
Hospital Chapel of San Juan de Dios
Morales
La Ronda
Av 24 de Mayo
Loja
Imbabura
SAN ROQUE
Barahona
Bahía de Caráquez
Ambato
Loja
Maldonado
SAN SEBASTIÁN
Agoyán
Iglesia de San Diego (Convent & Museum)
Cementerio San Diego
Iglesia de San Sebastián
PANECILLO
Panecillo Lookout
To Train Station

underneath is the cell where the revolutionaries of 1809 were executed (waxwork), well worth a visit, but not for the claustrophobic; **Museum of Ethnology**, Dpto de Letras, Ciudad Universitaria, Tues-Fri 0900-1230, Wed and Fri 1500-1700, Tues and Thur 1500-1830; **Museo de Artesanía**, 12 de Octubre y Madrid, has a good collection of Indian costume, helpful guides and a shop; **Museo-Biblioteca Aureliano Polit** at the former Jesuit seminary beyond the airport has a unique collection of antique maps of Ecuador, Mon-Fri 0900-1200, 1500-1800, take Condado minibus from Plaza San Martín in Av Pichincha. **Cima de la Libertad**, museum at the site of the 1822 Battle of Pichincha, splendid view, 0900-1200, 1500-1800, US$1.25, take a taxi there (US$12) as the suburbs are dangerous. **Museo del Colegio Mejía**, natural science and ethnographic exhibits, Ante y Venezuela, Mon-Fri 0700-1300, 1530-2000; **Vivarium** Fundación Herpetológica Gustavo Orces, Reina Victoria y Sta María, impressive number of South American and other snakes, reptiles and amphibians, entry US$2, open Tues-Sun, 0900-1300, 1500-1830.

Museo Histórico Casa de Sucre, the beautiful house of Sucre on the corner of Venezuela y Sucre, US$2, closed Mon.

The **house of Benalcázar** is at Olmedo y Benalcázar, a colonial house with a courtyard and some religious statues on view to the public. The **house of Camilo Egas**, a recent Ecuadorean artist, on Venezuela, has been restored by the Banco Central; it has different exhibitions during the year, entrance US$0.75, open Mon-Fri 1000-1300.

Museo Guayasamín, Bosmediano 543, Bellavista, NE of Quito, T 446-277, as well as the eponymous artist's works there is a precolumbian and colonial collection, highly rec; Mon-Fri 0900-1230 and 1500-1830, Sat 0900-1230, US$1.50. Works of art may be purchased and also modern jewellery made by the artist, ask to see the whole collection as only a small portion is displayed in the shop. Take Batán-Colmena bus No 3 marked Bellavista.

EXCURSIONS

MITAD DEL MUNDO AND ENVIRONS

23 km N of Quito is the **Mitad del Mundo** Equatorial Line Monument at an altitude of 2,483m near San Antonio de Pichincha. The exact equatorial line here was determined by Charles-Marie de la Condamine and his French expedition in 1735. The monument forms the focal point of a park and leisure area built as a typical colonial town, with restaurants, gift shops, Post Office with philatelic sales, tourist office 0900-1600, and has a museum inside (open Tues-Sun, 1000-1600), very crowded on Sun. Admission to the monument and the museum US$1.60. The museum is run by the Central Bank; a lift takes you to the top, then you walk down with the museum laid out all around with different Indian cultures every few steps. There is a Planetarium with hourly 30-min shows and an interesting model of old Quito, about 30-ft sq, with artificial day and night, which took 7 years to build, very pretty; entry US$0.65. 2 mins walk before the Monument is the restaurant *Equinoccio*, about US$10 a meal, live music, open from 1200 daily, T 394-091, F 545-663. Available at the restaurant or at stalls outside are 'certificates' recording the traveller's visit to the Equator (free if you have a meal).

● **Transport** From Quito: a paved road runs from Quito to the Monument, which you can reach by a 'Mitad del Mundo' bus (US$0.35, 1 hr) from Av América or the Parque Hermano Miguel (see Old City map, No 14), bus fills instantly; outside rush hour you can board at 10 de Agosto; beware of pickpockets on the bus. An excursion to Mitad del Mundo by taxi with 1 hr wait is about US$25 per taxi.

A few kilometres beyond the Monument, off the paved road to Calacalí, is the **Pululahua** crater. It is a geobotanical reserve, entry US$6.60. Try to go in the morning, there is often cloud later. Trucks will take you from the Mitad del Mundo bus stop, round trip US$5. *Calimatours*, Manzana de los Correos, Oficina 11, Mitad del Mundo, T 533-506 in Quito, PO Box 17-03-638, organizes tours to all the sites in the vicinity, US$5 pp, rec.

● **Access** Continue on the road past the Monument towards Calacalí. After a few kilometres (1 hr walk) the road bears left and begins to climb steeply; the paved road to the right leads to the rim of the volcano and a view of the farms on the crater floor. Buses to Calacalí (infrequent) will drop you at the fork, from where it is a 30-min walk. Plenty of traffic at weekends for hitching a lift. There is a rough track down from the rim to the crater, to experience the rich vegetation and warm micro-climate inside. Continuing past the village in the crater, turn left and follow an unimproved road up to the rim and back to the main road, a 15-20 km round trip.

Also in the vicinity of the Monument, 3 km from San Antonio beyond the Solar Museum, are the Inca ruins of **Rumicucho**. Restoration poor, but situation magnificent (entry US$1.25). Start early if you want to visit all these in 1 day.

8 km from Quito on the road to San Antonio de Pichincha, is the village of **Pomasqui**, near where was a tree in which Jesus Christ appeared to perform various miracles, El Señor del Arbol, now enshrined in its own building. In the church nearby is a series of paintings depicting the miracles (mostly involving horrendous road accidents). You may have to find the caretaker to unlock the church (we are grateful to Hilary Bradt for this information).

From San Antonio a dirt road heads N towards Perucho. S of Perucho another road turns sharply SE to Guayllabamba via **Puéllaro** (eat at the house on the plaza which is also a radio/TV workshop). A left turn (NE) off this road, just before Guayl-labamba, goes to Malchinguí, Tocachi and Cayambe (see next section).

The Equator line also crosses the Pan-American Highway 8 km S of Cayambe, where there are a concrete globe beside the road. Take Cayambe bus (2 hrs, US$0.80) and ask for Mitad del Mundo by Guachala.

SANGOLQUI

Another day-trip is to Sangolquí about 20 mins from Quito by bus. There is a busy Sun market (and a lesser one on Thur) and few tourists, and there are thermal baths, reported dirty, nearby (*Pop* 18,000).

● **Accommodation C** pp *Hostería Sommergarten*, Urb Santa Rosa, Chimborazo 248 y Río Frío, T/F Quito 332-761, 330-315, bungalow resort, inc breakfast, lots of activities available, sauna, pool, 30 mins by bus from Quito.

LOCAL FESTIVALS

New Year, *Años Viejos*: life-size puppets satirize politicians and others. At midnight on 31 Dec a will is read, the legacy of the outgoing year, and the puppets are burnt; good from Amazonas between Patria and Colón, very entertaining and good humoured. On New Year's day everything is shut. 6 Jan is *Día de los Inocentes*, a time for pranks, which closes the Christmas – New Year holiday season. **27 Feb**: is *Día del Civismo* celebrating the victory over Peru at Tarqui in 1829.

Carnival at Shrovetide is celebrated, as elsewhere in the Andes, by throwing water at passers-by: be prepared to participate. The solemn **Good Friday** processions are most impressive. **24 May**: is *Independence*, commemorating the Battle of Pichincha in 1822 with military and school parades, everything closes. **Aug**: *Mes de los Artes*, organized by the municipality, dance and music in different places throughout the city. Fancy-dress parades for Hallowe'en, celebrated **last Sat in Oct**, along Av Amazonas. The city's main festival, *Día de Quito*, celebrated throughout the week ending 6 Dec, commemorates the foundation of the city with elaborate parades, bullfights, performances and music in the streets; hotels are allowed to charge extra, everything except a few restaurants shuts on 6 December. Foremost amongst **Christmas** celebrations is the *Misa del Gallo*, midnight mass. Over Christmas Quito is crowded, hotels are full and the streets are packed with vendors and shoppers.

LOCAL INFORMATION

● **Accommodation**

Hotel prices

L1	over US$200	**L2**	US$151-200
L3	US$101-150	**A1**	US$81-100
A2	US$61-80	**A3**	US$46-60
B	US$31-45	**C**	US$21-30
D	US$12-20	**E**	US$7-11
F	US$4-6	**G**	up to US$3

Unless otherwise stated, all hotels in range **D** and above have private bath. Assume friendliness and cleanliness in all cases.

The *Ecuador Handbook* provides a full list with greater detail than there is space for here.

Major hotels quote their prices in dollars and foreigners are expected to pay in dollars. There is a different price structure for Ecuadoreans and sometimes for citizens of other Latin American countries.

The top-class hotels listed have all services, restaurants, etc, and are rec.

In the New City: **L1** *Oro Verde*, 12 de Octubre 1820 y Cordero, T 566-479, F 569-189; **L1** *Holiday Inn Crowne Plaza*, Shyris 1757 y Naciones Unidas, T 445-305, F 251-985, free transport to the airport; **L2** *Colón Internacional (Hilton)*, Amazonas y Patria, T 560-666, F 563-903, good disco, many useful services, food excellent (see **Places to eat** below), non-residents should dress neatly for best service; **L3** *Alameda Real*, Roca 653 y Amazonas, T 562-345, F 565-759, can be booked through KLM airline, good breakfast buffet US$6, 24-hr cafeteria, business centre;

L3 *Quito*, T 544-600, high up on González Suárez, often room on weekdays as business travellers prefer the more central *Colón*, good restaurant open to non-residents.

There are many good hotels in the US$46-100 bracket: **A1** *Akros Hotel*, 6 de Diciembre 3986, T 430-610, F 431-727, small, excellent restaurant; **A1** *Tambo Real*, 12 de Octubre y Patria opp US Embassy, T 563-822, F 554-964, rec, good rooms, TV, ideal for business visitors, restaurant very good; **A2** *Sierra Madre*, Veintimilla 464 y Luis Tamayo, T 505-687, F 505-715, old style villa fully renovated in 1993, comfortable, sun roof; **A2** *Hostal Los Alpes*, Tamayo 233 y Washington, T 561-110, behind US Embassy, 'alpine' interior, comfortable, excellent restaurant with reasonable prices, breakfast inc, many handicrafts and artworks, free papers, English paperbacks, warmly rec; **A2** *Sebastián*, Almagro 822, T 222-400, F 222-500, comfortable, rec; **A3** *Hostal Villantigua*, Jorge Washington 237 y Tamayo, T 545-663, beautiful, renovated colonial house, open fire, quiet, furnished with antiques; **A3-B** *Sierra Nevada*, Pinto 637 y Amazonas, T 553-658, F 554-936, in renovated house, very quick, fireplace, multilingual staff, gardens and terraces, price inc breakfast in *Café Colibrí*, hot showers, coffee shop, laundry service, climbing wall, travel information.

B *Café Cultura*, Robles 513 y Reina Victoria,

T/F 224-271, beautiful rooms, garden, luggage store, excellent breakfasts, shop with local crafts and foods, rec; **B** *Embassy*, Wilson 441 y 6 de Diciembre, T 561-990, inc tax, clean, well furnished, parking, restaurant, noisy disco next door at weekends; **B** *Floresta*, Isabel La Católica 1005 y Salazar, T 236-874, parking, restaurant, safe and very quiet, rec; **B** *Hostal de la Rábida*, La Rábida 227 y Santa María, T 222-169, F 221-720, Italian owner, bright, comfortable, good restaurant, rec; **B** *Hostal Plaza Internacional*, Plaza 150 y 18 de Septiembre, T 522-735/549-397, F 505-075, E-mail: hplaza@uio.satnet.net, comfortable, multilingual staff, very helpful, good location, free shuttle service from airport for Handbook readers; **B** *Res Cumbres*, Baquedano 148 y 6 de Diciembre, T 560-850, no credit cards, helpful, inc large breakfast; **B-C** *Hostal La Quinta*, Cordero 1951, T 230-723, an old renovated mansion, Italian owner speaks English, safe, parking, breakfast available, rec.

C *Alston Inn*, J L Mera 741 y Baquedano, T 229-955, laundry service, many restaurants nearby; **C** *Ambassador*, 9 de Octubre 1046 y Colón, T 561-777, rec; **C** *Hostal Charles Darwin*, La Colina 304 y Orellana, T 234-323, F 529-384, very quiet, safe, inc breakfast, rec; **C** *Hostal La Carolina*, Italia y Vancouver, T 542-472, suites **B**, helpful, safe deposit US$2.50, hot water, credit cards, ask for quiet rooms at the back; **C** *Hostal Residencial Los Andes*, Muros 146 y González Suárez behind the British Embassy, T 550-839, good area for walking, hot water, cable TV in lounge, English spoken, rec; **C** *Palm Garten*, 9 de Octubre 923, T 526-263/523-960, German run, good breakfasts, beautiful house, luggage store; **C** *Rincón de Bavaria*, Páez 232 y 18 de Septiembre, T 509-401, restaurant with good German food; **C** *Rincón Escandinavo*, Leonidas Plaza 1110 y Baquerizo, T 222-168, small, modern, well-furnished, convenient location, English spoken, rec; **C** *San Jorge*, Reina y Cordero 1361, T 525-606, modern, new 1996.

D *Casa Helbling*, Veintimilla 531 y 6 de Diciembre, T 226-013, good breakfast US$3.50, hot water even during power cuts, use of kitchen in afternoon, luggage store, use of washing machine US$3, helpful, will help arrange medical help, German spoken, family atmosphere, good information on tours, highly rec; **D** *Dan*, Av 10 de Agosto 2482 y Colón, T 553737, F 225083, a/c, good food and laundry, rec; **D** *Hostal Amazonas*, Pinto 471 y Amazonas, T 225-723, some sunny rooms; **D** *Hostal El Ciprés*, Lérida 381 y Pontevedra, T/F 549558/549561, inc breakfast, shared rooms, kitchen, very helpful owner; **D** *Hostal Jardín Quiteño*, Versalles 1449, T 526-011, F 564-924, carpeted rooms, restaurant, parking; **D** *Hostal Vizcaya*, Rumipamba 1726 y

Manuela Saenz, T 452-252, 450-288, owned by Sra Elsa de Racines, reservations essential, getting there involves a taxi ride, comfortable beds, good breakfast, evening meal on request, laundry service, English spoken, kind family, rec; **D** *La Estancia Inn*, Wilson 508 y D de Almagro, T 235-993, F 543-522, secure, helpful; **D** *Loro Verde*, Rodríguez 241 y Diego de Almagro, T 226-163, secure, good location; **D** *Majestic*, Mercadillo 366 y Versalles, T 543-182, F 504-207, well-furnished, bar, cafetería, restaurant, quiet; **D** *Nueve de Octubre*, 9 de Octubre 1047 y Colón, T 552-424, modern, very comfortable, secure, night watchman, rec; **D** *Pensión Lotys*, Marchena 592 y América, T 522-531, F 226-438, garden, all rooms are on the ground floor and are a bit gloomy and cold, good value laundry, secure, peaceful, rec; **D** *Posada del Maple*, Rodríguez 148 y 6 de Diciembre, T 237-375, warm atmosphere, inc breakfast, laundry, cooking facilities; the owners also run *Posada de Arupo*, **D**, at Berlin 147 y 9 de Octubre, English and French spoken; **D** *Res Carrión*, Carrión 1250 y 10 de Agosto, T 234-620, rooms without bath **E**, restaurant, bar, garden, luggage stored, good value, TV, accepts Visa, fills early, rec.

E *El Cafecito*, Luis Cordero 1124 y Reina Victoria, T 234-862, **F** pp in dormitory, Canadian-owned, relaxed atmosphere, café serves superb pancakes and pastries and an excellent vegetarian dish of the day, good information, 24 hr laundry; **E** pp *El Centro del Mundo*, Lizardo García 569 y Reina Victoria, T 229-050, **F** pp in dormitory, safe, modern, hot gas showers, laundry, kitchen, restaurant with good home-cooked food, bar, cable TV in lounge, language school, notice board, good meeting place, "a real gringo hang-out", highly rec; **E** pp *El Taxo*, Foch 909 y Cordero, T 225-593, hostal-type, large family house, helpful, open fire, constant hot water, kitchen facilities, good meeting place; **E** *Hostal Los Frailes*, Guanguiltagua 234 y F Páez, nr La Carolina, T 455-052, beautiful guest house, inc breakfast, use of kitchen, luggage stored, free airport pick-up, family-run, owners speak English, rec; **E** *La Casa de Eliza*, Isabel La Católica 1559, T 226-602, central, hot water, kitchen and laundry facilities, very popular and homely, Eliza organizes treks through the Cerro Golondrinas Cloudforest Reserve with research and volunteer opportunities, see page 1048, rec; **E** *La Casona de Mario*, Andalucía 213 y Galicia, nr La Católica University, T 230-129, Argentine-run, shared room, comfortable, kitchen, laundry and storage facilities, big garden, cable TV, book exchange, very comfortable, highly rec; **E** *Pickett*, Wilson 712 y JL Mera, T 551-205, shared bathrooms not always too clean, **D** with bath and TV, hot water, free coffee for breakfast, restaurant, laundry, popular, rec; **E** *Posada La Herradura*, Pinto 570 y Amazonas, T 226-340, kitchen and laundry facilities, convenient location, rec; **E** *Rincón de Castilla*, Versalles 1127 y Carrión, T 224-312, F 548-097, shared bath, safe, luggage stored, motorcycle parking, owner speaks German, French and English, laundry facilities, also travel agency and Spanish classes, highly rec.

F pp *Hostal Eva Luna*, Pasaje de Roca, C Roca entre Amazonas y JL Mera, T 234-799, women-only hostel, new, comfortable, kitchen facilities, secure, highly rec; **F** pp *Casa Paxee*, Romualdo Navarro 326 y La Gasca, T 500-441/525-331, price inc fruit for breakfast, use of kitchen area, laundry facilities, clean bathroom, 3 rooms only, discounts for longer stays, highly rec; **F** pp *Casapaxi*, Navarro 364 y La Gasca, PO Box 17-03-668, T 542-663, clean, hot water, friendly, will store luggage, TV, kitchen, owner Luigiana Fossati speaks perfect English and is very helpful, frequently rec as excellent value; **F** *Mi Casa*, Bartolome de las Casas 435 y Versalles, T 225-470, converted family house, shared bath, hot water, cooking facilities, dinner available for US$1-2 (inc vegetarian), camping possible in garden for US$2, laundry, highly rec.

Youth Hostel: *Albergue Juvenil Mitad del Mundo*, Pinto 325 y Reina Victoria, T 543-995, F 226-271, HQ of Asociación Ecuatoriana de Albergues, take IYHA card, new building, modern, dormitory or private room with bath, **F** pp without bath for members, **E** with bath, inc breakfast, cafetería, laundry, hot water, safe deposit, luggage store, fax service, self-service laundrette next door, rec; also at Madrid 868 y Pontevedra La Floresta, T 554-621, **D** pp, inc breakfast, hot showers, very nice and comfortable, friendly.

Near the airport: **B** *Aeropuerto*, opp the terminal, T 458-708, some rooms with kitchen; **D** *Res Maromi*, Pedro del Solar 479 e Isla Seymour, T 433-822, shared bath, hot water, TV, laundry service, meals available, family run, quiet, in residential area; *Terraza Suites*, Isla San Cristóbal 880 y Río Coca, T 249-567, large rooms, hot water, TV, safe, good, breakfast on room service.

If you prefer not to stay in a hotel: Cecilia Rivera, a doctor, offers full board, **D**, at Fco Salazar 327 y Coruña, T 548-006, 569-961, central, with a view across the valley, quiet, safe, hot water, laundry, luggage store; also Sra Anita Gomezjurado, Julio Zaldumbide 387 y Coruña, nr *Hotel Quito*, central, convenient (No 2 Colón-Camal bus), T 237-778, German and English spoken, hot water, safe, full board available, massage by appointment; Sra Rosa Jácome has an apartment in the new city, T 503-180 (eve-

nings), one double room with bath and 2 singles, **E** pp, use of kitchen and phone, she will arrange outings and is friendly and helpful, she meets most incoming flights at the airport in her taxi; Marcia de Sandoval, Galavis 130 y Toledo, T 543-254, rents small apartments, well equipped, US$180/month.

For longer stays with room, kitchen, TV, laundry service etc, the following have been rec: **A2** *Apart-Hotel Amaranta*, Leonidas Plaza 194 y Washington, PO Box 4967, T 560-585/586, comfortable, well-equipped suites, from US$900 a month, good restaurant. *Apartamentos Modernos*, Amazonas 2467 y Mariana de Jesús, T 553-136/543-509, from US$400/month (nr La Carolina park) English, French and German spoken; **B** *Apart-Hotel Antinea*, Rodríguez 175 y Diego de Almagro, T 506-839, suites and apartments, lovely rooms; *Apartotel Mariscal*, Robles 958 y Páez, US$17 pp/night, 20% less a month, T 528-833.

Apartments for rent are advertised in *El Comercio*, especially in 'Suites (Sector Norte)' section, US$125-300/month, usually unfurnished.

In between the new and old cities: **D** *Coral Internacional*, Manuel Larrea 164, T 572-337, spacious, popular with families, cafetería, open 0730-2200; **D-E** *Res Margarita*, Elizalde 410 y Colombia (nr Los Ríos), T 512-599/510-441, helpful, baggage stored, rec.

E *Baraka*, Asunción y América, T 509-260, noisy, good value; **E** *Hostal El Ejido*, Juan Larrea 535 y Riofrío, T 526-066, **D** with bath, hot water, good value; **E** *Res Marsella*, Los Ríos 2035 y Espinoza, T 515-884, hot water 0600-1200, 1800-2000, some rooms with bath, good rooftop terrace with views over Parque La Alameda, top floor rooms best, luggage stored for US$1/bag/15 days, not a safe area, often full by 1700, expensive laundry, safe deposit, notice board, good value, doors may be locked as early as 2100, otherwise rec; **E** *Res Portoviejo*, Portoviejo y América, T 235-399, Chilean owner, safe, use of kitchen for breakfast, cheap laundry service, luggage stored, rec; the owner has another rec hotel on América y Colombia 558, no sign, knock on the door, popular with Iraelis.

F *Casa Patty*, Tola Alta, Iquique 2-33 y Manosalvas, T 510-407, large rooms, hot shower in the morning, kitchen, terrace, laundry facilities, helpful, safe for left luggage, it is at the top of a steep hill, take bus no 8, 'Tola-Pintado' from the old town, take a taxi at night; **F** *Hostal Farget*, Pasaje Farget, T 570-066, helpful; **F** *L'Aubergine*, Av Colombia 1138 y Yaguachi, T 569-886, shared rooms, laundry and cooking facilities; **F** *Oriente*, Yaguachi 824 y Llona (nr Instituto Geográfico Militar), T 546-157, with bath and kitchen, safe, family-run, weekly or monthly rentals only, rec.

G *Atahualpa*, Manuel Larrea y Riofrío, convenient location, basic, no hot water, safe.

Accommodation in the Old City: note that there can be water shortages in Aug. **C** *Real Audiencia*, Bolívar 220 y Guayaquil, T 512-711, F 580-213, spacious, well furnished rooms, laundry service, baggage stored, restaurant/bar on top floor, great views, highly rec, convenient for the Trolley bus; **C** *Viena Internacional*, Flores y Chile, T 519-611, English spoken, large rooms, hot water, phone, laundry, good meals, safe.

D *Catedral Internacional*, Mejía 638 y Cuenca, T 683-119, hot shower, good rooms; **D** *Hostal La Casona*, Manabí 255 entre Flores y Montúfar, T 514-764, F 563-271, good beds, TV, phone, safe, use of kitchen, discount for longer stays, rec; **D** *Huasi Continental*, Flores 3-22 y Bolívar, T 517-327, cheaper without bath, TV, phone, hot water, safe, luggage stored, helpful, good restaurant; **D-E** *Plaza del Teatro Internacional*, Guayaquil, 1373 y Esmeraldas, T 514-293/512-980, F 519-462, Casilla 3443, restaurant, bar, café, conference room, parking, rec; **D-E** *Res San Marcos*, Junín 452 y Almedia, T 212-913, hot shower, cooking and washing facilities, safe, rec.

E-F *Flores*, Flores 355 y Sucre, T 580-148, with bath, hot water, ask for a room on the 1st floor, safe, laundry facilities, convenient for bus station; **E** *Gran Casino Internacional*, 24 de Mayo y Loja, T 514-905, with bath, cold water, luggage store, good restaurant, see under Travel Agencies for trips to the Galápagos and Oriente, good value; **E** *Hostal Belmonte*, Antepara 413 y V León, T 519-006, 1 block from La Marín underpass, good meeting place for backpackers, safe, family-run, hot showers, phone for incoming and outgoing calls, nice terrace, use of kitchen and laundry facilities, free tea and coffee, laundry service, book exchange, free luggage storage, son has opened Spanish school (see below), repeatedly rec; **E** *La Posada Colonial*, Paredes 188 y Rocafuerte, T 212-859, bar, restaurant, garage, rec; **E** *Rumiñahui*, Montúfar 449 y Junín, T 211-407/219-325, with bath, hot water, safe deposit box, laundry facilities; **E** *San Agustín*, Flores 626 y Chile, T 212-847, with bath, hot water, restaurant variable.

F *Gran Casino Colonial*, García Moreno 337 y Loja, T 211-914, converted colonial house, TV, restaurant, luggage stored, second-hand books, shared showers have hot water; **F** *Montúfar*, Sucre 160 y Flores, T 211-419, without bath, hot water, safe, good value; **F** pp *Yumbo Imperial*, Guayaquil 647 y Bolívar, nr Plaza Santo Domingo, T 518-651, cheaper without bath, safe luggage store, laundry facilities, top rooms overlook the old city; **F** *Venezia*,

Rocafuerte y Venezuela, cheaper without bath, water tepid, basic, often full.

G pp *Hostal Junín*, Junín y Flores, T 500184, hot water; **G** pp *Hostal Félix*, Guayaquil 451, nr Plaza Santo Domingo, hot shower in basement, reliable; **G** *Res Sucre*, on Plaza San Francisco, corner of Bolívar and Cuenca, cold showers, a bit noisy, has terrace with great views over the old city, laundry facilities, not for the hygenically-minded but very cheap.

In the vicinity of the Terminal Terrestre: **E** *Gran*, Rocafuerte 1001, T 519-411, with or without bath, run down, some rooms dingy, secure, free bag storage, same-day laundry attached, good breakfast in restaurant, Spanish school attached; **E** *Juana de Arco*, Rocafuerte 1311 y Maldonado, T 214-175, only back rooms with shower, front rooms cheaper but noisier, good restaurant next door.

On Calle Morales: **D** *Cumandá*, No 449, T 516-984/513-592, comfortable, hot showers, TV, phone, travel agency, laundry, restaurant, garage, safe, noisy from proximity to bus station but quieter at the back; **F** *Los Shyris*, No 691, T 515336, shared bath, hot water, spacious rooms, secure, laundry, restaurant downstairs.

On Maldonado: **E** *Colonial*, No 3035 (at the end of an alley), T 580-762, with bath, hot water most of the time, safe although not a safe area at night, quiet, laundry; **E** *Piedra Dorada*, No 3210, T 517-460, modern, with bath, hot shower, phone, TV, laundry service unreliable, restaurant; **F** *Guayaquil No 1*, No 3248, hot water, will store luggage for small fee, safe, basic.

NB Those travelling by car may have difficulty parking in the centre of Quito and are therefore advised to choose the less central hotels.

● **Places to eat**

There are few restaurants in the Old City, although these tend to be cheaper, with more local and fast food than in the New City, where more foreign styles can be found. Fast food is usually hamburgers or chicken, spit roasted. Note that hygiene in hamburger and *salchipapa bars* is sometimes poor. Many restaurants throughout the city close on Sun and, in the Old City, most close early evening. **NB** Prices listed are often inaccurate. Restaurants with credit card stickers do not necessarily take them. In more expensive restaurants 20% tax and service is added to the bill. The following list is by type and all are in the New City unless otherwise stated. In all cases, assume good food, service and value. All have been rec.

Ecuadorean: *Taberna Quiteña*, Amazonas y Calama, in cellar, rec; *Mamá Clorinda*, Reina Victoria y Calama, large portions, moderately priced; *Inti*, Mariana de Jesús y Hungría; *La*

Querencia, Eloy Alfaro 2530 y Catalina Aldaz, good views and atmosphere.

Latin American and US: *El Coyote de Eduardo*, El Universo 645 y Los Shyris, T 432-580, Mexican, very popular; *Churrascaría Tropeiro*, Veintimilla 564 y 6 de Diciembre, Brazilian-style, salad bar; *Tex Mex*, Reina Victoria y Pinto, US$3-4/dish, the Tex Mex Mixta especially rec US$5, lively, open daily; *Rincón Ecuatoriano Chileno*, 6 de Diciembre y Orellana, delicious, very good value; *La Bodeguita de Cuba*, Reina Victoria y Pinta, good food and music, reasonably priced; *The Magic Bean Restaurant and Coffee House*, Foch 681 y J L Mera, excellent atmosphere, specializes in coffees and natural foods, more than 20 varieties of pancakes, salads are relatively expensive, but "safe", slow service but rec; *Fried Green Bananas*, L Plaza y Washington, Tex-Mex; *Coconut Willy's*, Calama y J L Mera, salads, sandwiches and burgers; *Clancy's*, Toledo y Salazar, classy.

French: usually very smart: *Rincón de Francia*, Roca 779 y 9 de Octubre, excellent but very expensive, reservation essential, slow service; *Le Bistrot*, González Suárez 139, T 523-649, best gourmet food in town, expensive, live music at 2100, closed Sun; *Amadeus Restaurant and Pub*, Coruña 1398 y Orellana, T 230-831 and 566-404, very good French cuisine and concerts, usually at 2300 on Fri, rather formal; *Rincón de Borgoña*, Eloy Alfaro 2407, excellent; *Chantilly*, Roca 736 y Amazonas, restaurant and bakery, reasonably priced, second branch at Whimper 394; *Chalet Suisse*, Calama 312 y Reina Victoria, steaks and some Swiss dishes, expensive; *Grain de Café*, Baquedano 332 y Reina Victoria, T 234-340, excellent cheesecakes, pies, lunch, inc vegetarian, good coffee, book exchange, films in English on Tues pm, informative owner (Daniel – French Canadian), good meeting place for francophones.

German: *El Ciervo*, Dávalos 270 y Páez, slow service, southern German food, German newspapers available.

Italian: *Vía Margutta*, San Ignacio 1076 y González Suárez, expensive; *La Gritta*, Santa María 246 y Reina Victoria, smart, home made pasta, expensive; *La Scala*, Salazar y 12 de Octubre, good atmosphere, not cheap; *La Trattoria de Renato*, San Javier y Orellana, nice atmosphere, expensive; *Vecchia Roma*, Roca 618 y J L Mera, good atmosphere, excellent antipasti, US$10-12 pp inc drinks; *Romulo & Remo Spaghettería*, Pinto 419 y JL Mera, small, good, cheap, pasta dishes around US$1.50; *Portofino*, Calama 328 y Reina Victoria, good pasta selection; *Il Risotto*, Pinto 209 y Diego de Almagro, T 220-400, very popular, very good Italian specialities, no pizzas; *Spaghetti Café*, Portugal y Eloy Alfaro, nice atmosphere.

Spanish: *El Mesón de la Pradera*, Orellana y 6 de Diciembre, converted hacienda, also tapas bar; *La Paella Valenciana*, República y Almagro, huge portions, superb fish and paella, US$10-12/dish; *La Puerta de Alcalá*, Lizardo García 664 y J L Mera, delicious tapas.

International: the *Oro Verde* has a superb international restaurant, a very expensive but good Japanese restaurant, and *Café Quito*, with lunch and breakfast buffets. *Hotel Colón Internacional* has spectacular Sun buffet, all you can eat for US$12, also buffet breakfast in the restaurant, cheaper in snack bar. *La Casa de al Lado*, Valladolid 1018 y Cordero, with bar and cinema Mon-Sat 1100-0100, classy; *Palladino*, 10 de Agosto 850 y Patria, p 19, continental cuisine, expensive but good views; *Barlovento*, 12 de Octubre y Orellana, seafood and inexpensive steak; *El Arabe*, Reina Victoria y Carrión, good Arabic food.

Oriental: *Casa Asia*, Amazonas at bullring, excellent Korean and Japanese; *Chifa Mayflower*, Carrión 442 y 6 de Diciembre, good food, excellent service, 30-mins' home delivery service till 2200; *Gran Ciudad de China*, Carrión 1238, good service, great value; *Chifa China*, Carrión y 10 de Agosto, authentic; *Hong Kong*, Wilson 246 y G Córdova, good; *Palacio Real de China*, Calama 434 y Amazonas, cheap, large portions; *Hong Tai*, Niña 234 y Yanez Pinzon, reasonable prices; *Casa Guang Zhou*, 18 de Septiembre y Amazonas, good food for US$3-4.

General: *Terraza del Tártaro*, Veintimilla 1106 y Amazonas (no sign), top floor, steaks, pleasant atmosphere; *Taller del Sol*, Salazar 1063 y Camilo Destruge, always busy, great atmosphere, US$20 pp; *Rincón del Amazonas*, Ramírez Dávalos 152, parrilladas, moderately priced; *Café Stop*, Amazonas y Moreno Bellido, good atmosphere, moderate prices; *El Frutal*, Reina Victoria 328, fresh fruit juices and set lunches; *Super Papa*, J L Mera 761 y Baquedano, stuffed baked potatoes, some vegetarian, sandwiches and salads, cakes, takeaway service, great breakfasts, popular for notices, open daily, 0730-2100; *Café 3.30*, Whimper 330 y Coruña, first class.

Pizza: *Che Farina Pizzería*, Carrión, entre J L Mera y Amazonas and Naciones Unidas y Amazonas, fast service, popular, expensive, open Sun; *Eccos Pizzas*, Los Shyris nr Parque La Carolina, large-screen video; *Pizza Pizza*, Santa María y Diego de Almagro, relatively cheap; *Pizza Hut*, Av Naciones Unidas y Amazonas, 24 hrs, excellent, also JL Mera y Carríon, not 24 hrs.

Seafood: *Pedro El Marino*, Lizardo García 559 y Reina Victoria, rec for lunch; *Las Redes de Mariscos*, Amazonas 845 y Veintimilla, lovely atmosphere, closed Sun; more upmarket is

Mare Nostrum, Foch 172 y Tamayo; *El Cebiche*, J L Mera 1232 y Calama, and on Amazonas, delicious seafood, best ceviche in town; *El Viejo José*, Reina Victoria y Pinto, cheap, highly rec, same menu at *El Viejo Jorge*, Calama y Reina Victoria; *Ceviches y Banderas*, Av 12 de Octubre 1533 y Foch, reasonably priced; *Bar y Grill Buon Gustaio*, Isla San Cristóbal 881, seafood and local; *Ceviches de la Rumiñahui*, 3 branches: Nazareth 1777 y Dalias; Real Audiencia, Manzana 12, casa 38 entre Av del Maestro y Tufiño (the original branch and less clean), these two are N of the airport runway; Quicentro Shopping Centre, Naciones Unidas y Shyris (a bit more expensive than the others): all three are popular for *ceviche* (US$2-3), seafood and fish.

Steak: *Casa de mi Abuela*, J L Mera 1649, T 565-667, steak and salad US$7; *Columbia*, Colón 1262 y Amazonas, popular, open Sun; *Shorton Grill*, Calama 216 y Almagro, huge platter US$5-6; *Texas Ranch*, J L Mera y Calama, also good burgers and seafood, moderately priced.

Vegetarian: *El Márquez*, Calama 433, between J L Mera and Amazonas, cheap set lunch, Mon-Fri; *Girasol*, Oriente 581 y Vargas, cheap, closes 1700; *Windmill*, Versalles y Colón 2245, reasonable; *Maranatha*, Riofrío y Larrea, lunch Mon-Fri, clean and cheap; *El Maple*, Paez 485 y Roca, lunch US$1.25, open daily except Sun for dinner, good natural yoghurt at the shop next door, rec; *Casa Naturalista*, Lizardo García 630, also a health food store; *Chapati*, Calama y Diego de Almagro, vegetarian *almuerzos*; *El Holandés*, Reina Victoria 600 y Carrión, T 522-167, cheap, delicious, also Indian, Indonesian, Greek and Italian, dishes US$3.50, open Mon-Fri; *Manantial*, at 9 de Octubre 591 y Carrión and Luis Cordero 1838 y 9 de Octubre, good, cheap set lunch.

In the Old City: *El Criollo*, Flores 825, clean, Ecuadorean food, cheap, tasty, chicken specialities; *La Vieja Colonia*, García Moreno 8-34, clean, Ecuadorean food, nice atmosphere; *La Cueva del Oso*, elegant covered court of Edif Pérez Pallares on Chile y Venezuela, reasonable prices, great atmosphere; *Las Cuevas de Luis Candela*, Benálcazar y Chile and Orellana y Coruña, Spanish, reasonable prices, closed Sun; *Viena*, Chile y Flores, for breakfasts; *El Amigo*, Guayaquil, between Esmeraldas y Oriente, good food and coffee; *Cafetería Dimpy*, Venezuela y Mejía, cheap lunches, snacks, juices, breakfast and coffee; *Chifa El Chino*, Bolívar y Venezuela, Chinese, cheap, good lunch. You can find cheap meals in the market behind the shoe shops on Flores y Olmedo between 1130 and 1400.

Cafés/Pastry Shops/Bakeries: *Café Cultura*, Robles y Reina Victoria, nice atmosphere, converted colonial building, expensive but excellent cakes, homemade bread, open daily for breakfast (0800-1130) and afternoon tea (1500-1700); *Galería de Arte Libri Mundi*, JL Mera 804 y Wilson, good art exhibits in lovingly restored building, nice garden café; *La Cosecha*, main bakery on Los Shyris nr Villaroel across from Parque Carolina, several other outlets for homemade breads, doughnuts, oatmeal cookies; *El Cyrano*, Portugal y Los Shyris, wholemeal bread, pastries, French owner also runs excellent ice cream shop, *Corfu* next door; *Bangaló*, Carrión 185 y Tamayo, excellent cakes, quiches, coffees, Mon-Sat, open at lunchtime and 1600-2000, great atmosphere, good jazz at weekends; *Café Colibri*, Pinto 619 y Cordero, German-owned, breakfast, coffee and snacks, good atmosphere, nice garden, German and English newspapers, open 0700-2100; *Haripan*, Wilson y 6 de Diciembre, good breads and pastries; *San Fernando*, Asunción 136, excellent; *Baguette*, Amazonas 2525 y Mariana de Jesús, sells excellent bread, pasteurized cheeses, another branch in Colón 900 block, rec; *Delicatessen Español* next to Libri Mundi, J L Mera y Wilson, sandwiches, sausages, salmon, cheese, etc; *Top Cream*, Naciones Unidas, nr Amazonas, and on 6 de Diciembre, for high-quality ice cream, milkshakes. **In the Old City**: *Café del Teatro*, Flores y Manabí, nr Teatro Sucre, great atmosphere, coffee, desserts; *Café Modelo*, Sucre y García Moreno, cheap breakfast; *Su Café*, Flores 5-46, small coffee shop, rec for breakfast; *Las Cerezas*, García Moreno 1355 y Olmedo, nice patio, friendly, good juices and fruit salads; *Heladería Zanzibar*, on Guayaquil, nr Plaza Santo Domingo and on Benalcázar 860, excellent ice cream; *Jugos Naturales*, Oriente 449 y Guayaquil, safe juices and extracts.

● **Bars**

In the New City: *Rumors*, J L Mera at Veintimilla, relatively cheap, good atmosphere, open daily 1700-0200; *El Pub*, San Ignacio y González Suárez, English menu, nice fish and chips; *Reina Victoria*, Reina Victoria 530 y Roca, open Mon-Sat from 1700, darts, relaxed atmosphere, English beer in cans for US$2.50, happy hour 1700-1800, moderately priced bar meals, both places are meeting points for British and US expats; *Night Rider's*, J Martínez 489 y Portugal, nice atmosphere, US, popular; *Ghoz Bar*, La Niña 425 y Reina Victoria, T 239-826, Swiss owned, excellent Swiss food, pool, darts, videos, games, music, German book exchange; *El Pobre Diablo*, Santa María, nr *La Gritta* restaurant, popular, trendy, also serves good local food and plays great music, good atmosphere; *Papillon*, Almagro y Santa María, open every day, very popular for 'casual assignments', selective admission policy, passport needed at door; a few yards away is *Tequila Bar*, packed every night with young professionals, good atmosphere; *Bar People's*, Amazonas 585 y Carrión, rock and reggae, open 0800 for breakfast and 1600-0300; *Arribar*, JL Mera 1238 y Lizardo García, pool table, trendy, rap and other music, happy hour 1600-1800, Swiss-owned, more gringos than locals; *Cats*, Lizardo García y Almagro, quaint hideaway, good selection of music; *Ogui's World*, Baquedano 358 y JL Mera, bar and disco, loud, popular with local teenagers, happy hour 1800-2000; *Kizomba*, Almagro y L García, rec for atmosphere and creative drinks, good music; *L'petit Tango*, Almagro y Colón, live tango music, no beer served; *Patatus*, Pres Wilson y Amazonas, outdoor seating, fireplaces, nice; *The Lion of Judah Reggae Bar*, Amazonas y Orellana, p 2, good for a dance and drinks; *Blues*, La Granja 112 y Amazonas, good, passport needed at door; *No Bar*, Calama between Amazonas and JL Mera, always packed, latin and rock, rec. Try the *Cervecerías* around the Universidad Central for salsa and merengue. **In the Old City**: Teatro Bolívar has a good wine bar.

● **Airline offices**

Local: Aerogal, Italia 241 y Eloy Alfaro, T 563-646; **Ecuatoriana**, Reina Victoria y Colón, Torres de Almagro, T 563-923, F 563-931; **Saeta**, Colón y Amazonas, T 542-148 (British Airways agents, T 540-000); **SAN**, Santa María y Amazonas, T 564-969; **TAME**, Colón y Rábida, T 509-382, also 10 de Agosto 239.

Foreign airlines: AeroPerú, Jorge Washington 718, T 561-699/700; **Air France**, Amazonas y 18 de Septiembre, T 523-596; **Alltalia**, Ernesto Novoa 474 y Av 6 de Deciembre, T 509-061; **American Airlines**, América y Robles, T 561-144, 561-526; **Americana**, Eloy Alfaro 266, Edif Doral, p 10, internal Peru airline, T 549-478, rec; **AOM**, 12 de Octubre 394, T 541-627; **Avensa Servivensa**, Naciones Unidas y Amazonas, Edif Previsora, Torre B, of 410, T 466-461; **Avianca**, 6 de Diciembre 511 y 18 de Septiembre, T 508-842; **Iberia**, Amazonas y Washington; **KLM**, Edif Xerox, Amazonas 3617 y Juan Pablo Sanz, T 455-233; **Lacsa**, Av 12 de Octubre 394, T 504-691; **Lufthansa**, Av 6 de Diciembre 955 y 18 de Septiembre, T 508-682; **TAP Air Portugal**, Edif de los Andes, Amazonas 477 y Roca, on p 7, opp Lloyds Bank, T 550-308; **Varig**, Amazonas 1188 y Calama, T 543-257.

● **Banks & money changers**

Banking hours are 0900-1400. (Some banks open till 1530 for dollar services.) You can withdraw inward transfers in US dollars. US$ money orders of any kind are not accepted anywhere in Ecuador. It is possible to change German mark TCs without problems. **Lloyds Bank**, Av Amazonas 580 y Carrión, with Torres de Colón and

Jipijapa agencies, no commission, closes 1530; **Citibank**, Reina Victoria y Patria, only accepts its own cheques, money transfers from most European countries; **Bank of America**, Patria y Amazonas, cash only on its own Visa cards; **Filanbanco**, 10 de Agosto, opp Central Bank, and other branches, cash against all Visa cards, helpful if cards lost; **Banco Internacional**, opp Bank of America, cash only; **Banco de Pichincha**, Amazonas y Colón, good rates for cash, also on Venezuela in the old town, ½ block from Plaza de la Independencia; **Banco Guayaquil**, Colón y Reina Victoria, p 3, cash advances on Visa without limit (but depends on limit set by your own country), efficient, cash advances from Ban NET ATM at rear of bank in sucres only, with Visa, maximum withdrawal US$100, changes Visa TCs; **Banco Popular**, Amazonas 648, Mastercard, good service.

Banco del Pacífico, at Japón branch, W of Shyris, good rates for TCs (only until 1400), no commission changing into dollars, cash advance on Mastercard in dollars or sucres (min US$100); at the branch at Centro Comercial El Jardín, Amazonas y Av República can buy TCs with Mastercard, excellent service; there is also a branch in *Hotel Oro Verde*, no commission for cashing dollars, open until 1800 weekdays. The bank in the departure lounge at the airport is open Sat and Sun. The **American Express** representative is Ecuadorean Tours, Amazonas 339, T 560-488, no cash advances. Amex cheques available at Casa Paz, Amazonas 370. **Master Card** is at Amazonas y Veintimilla, in Banco Pacífico building.

Money changers: Casa Paz, Sucre y García Moreno, T 518-500, Amazonas 370 y Robles (open also Sat morning), T 563-900, Centro Comercial El Bosque, T 455-075, Centro Comercial Plaza Aeropuerto, T 241-865, airport lobby and *Hotel Colón*, will change TCs into US$ cash up to US$300, 1% commission, plus all major currencies, slightly better rates for holders of international student cards, open 0900-1300, 1500-1800, Mon-Fri, branches also in Multicentro, 6 de Diciembre y Orellana (T 525-153, Mon-Fri 0915-1800, Sat 0930-1330) and in Centro Comercial Iñaquito, open Sat to 2000 and Sun to 1200.

Casa Paz, Centro Comercial Iñaquito and the *Hotel Colón* are the only places you can change money on Sat afternoon and Sun (*Hotel Colón*, Sat 0800-1300 and 1500-1800, Sun 0900-1300, quick service, no commission). The airport *cambio* is also open at these times and late at night. **Multicambio**, Venezuela 689, T 511 364, Roca 720, T 567-347/351, and Colón 919 y Reina Victoria, T 561-747, open Mon-Fri, 0830-1330, 1430-1730 and Sat morning, also at the airport, no commission charged, good rates, no queues, better rate with ISIC card, change Citibank and Thomas Cook TCs. **Delgado Travel**, Av Amazonas 1225 y Foch.

Vazcambios, Amazonas y Roca, *Hotel Alameda Real*, T 548-010, good rate for TCs; **Ecuacambio**, República 192 y Almagro, T 540-129, change TCs to dollars cash for 1% commission, best rate for a *casa de cambio*. You are advised not to buy Peruvian soles until you get to the border; you will get a much better rate in Peru.

● **Cultural centres**

British Council: Amazonas 1646 y La Niña, T 232-421, F 565-720, Casilla 1197. There is a library, open Mon-Fri, 0800-1915, and back copies of British newspapers are stocked in the *La Galeria* café which serves a full English breakfast for US$3, also book exchange, vegetarian restaurant, tea and cakes, free films every Wed, E-mail service.

Alliance Française: at Eloy Alfaro 1900, French courses, films and cultural events. **Casa Humboldt**, Vancouver y Polonia, T 548-480, German centre, inc Goethe Institute, films, talks, exhibitions.

● **Embassies & consulates**

Argentina, Amazonas 477, Edif Banco Pacífico, T 562-292; **Bolivia**, Borja Lavayen y J P Sanz, T 458-863; **Brazil**, Edif España, Av Colón y Av Amazonas, T 563-086, 563-141; **Chile**, Juan Pablo Sanz 3617 y Amazonas, T 249-403, 453-327, open 0900-1300; **Colombia**, Colón 133 y Amazonas, T 553-263, insists on a ticket to leave Colombia before issuing a visa; **Costa Rica**, Francisco de Nates 165, T 568-615; **Cuba**, 6 de Diciembre 5113, T 458-282; **Guatemala**, República 192 y Almagro, T 545-714; **Mexico**, 6 de Diciembre 4843 y Naciones Unidas, T 457-820; **Panama**, Diego de Almagro 1550 y La Pradera, T 566-449; **Peru**, Edif España, Av Colón y Av Amazonas, T 520-134, 554-161; **Uruguay**, Lizardo García 1025, T 541-968; **Venezuela**, Coruña 1609 y Belo Horizonte, T 564-626, 562-038, visa US$30 plus 1 photo, it can take from a full morning up to 3 working days.

USA, Av 12 de Octubre y Patria, T 562-890. An official copy of a US passport, US$2. **Canadian Consulate**, Edif Josueth González, 6 de Diciembre 2816 y James Orton, p 4, T 543-214, F 503-108.

Austria, Veintimilla 878 y Amazonas, T 524-811, PO Box 17-01-167, T 503-456; **Belgium**, JL Mera 863 y Wilson, T 545-340, F 507-367, Apdo Postal 17-21-532; **Czech Republic/Slovakia**, Grecia 210, T 460-220; **Denmark**, Av República del Salvador 733 y Portugal, Edif Gabriela 3, T 458-585/786, 437-163, open 0900-1700; **Finland**, Av 18 de Septiembre 368, p 3, T 523-493; **France** Diego de Almagro y Pradera, Edif Kingmann, p 2,

T 569-883 for the consulate, the embassy is at Gen Plaza 107 y Patria, T 560-789, 562-270; **Germany**, Av Patria y 9 de Octubre, Edif Eteco, p 6, T 232-660, 567-231; **Honorary Irish Consul**, Montes 577 y Las Casas, T 503-674; **Italy**, La Isla 111 y H Albornoz, T 561-077/074; **Netherlands**, 12 de Octubre 1942 y Cordero, World Trade Center, p 1, T 229-229, F 567-917 (open 0900-1200, in pm by appointment only); **Norway**, Pasaje Alonso Jerves 134 y Orellana, T 566-354; **Poland**, Eloy Alfaro 2897, T 453-466; **Russia**, Reina Victoria 462 y Roca, T 505-089; **Spain**, La Pinta 455 y Amazonas, T 564-373/377; **Sweden**, Amazonas s/n y República, Edif Las Cámaras, p 20, T 452-010, open mornings only; **Switzerland**, Amazonas 3617 y Sanz, Edif Xerox, p 7, T 434-948/9 (open 0900-1200); **UK**, Av González Suárez 111 y 12 de Octubre (opp *Hotel Quito*), letters to Casilla 314, T 560-309/670. The Consulate is a few doors away, it has travel information on Peru, helpful, open Mon-Fri 0830-1230, 1400-1700.

Israel, Eloy Alfaro 969 y Amazonas, T 565-509/512; **Japan**, JL Mera 130 y Av Patria, Edif Corp. Financiero Nacional, p 7, T 561-899.

● **Entertainment**

Cinema: Multicines, CCI, Amazonas y Naciones Unidas, in basement, best selection of films; *Colón*, 18 de Agosto y Colón; *Universitario*, América y A Pérez Guerrero, Plaza Indoamérica, Universidad Central; *Benalcázar*, 6 de Diciembre y Portugal; *24 de Mayo*, Granaderos y 6 de Diciembre. *Colón* often has documentaries with Latin American themes. The Casa de la Cultura often has film festivals, as well as showing foreign films. Expect to pay around US$3 in these cinemas. There are many others, especially in the Old City, mostly showing violent films; usually there is a standard entry charge (US$0.75 or less) and you can stay as long as you like. Section D of *El Comercio* lists the films every day.

Music: local folk music is popular in *peñas*. Places inc *Dayumac*, J L Mera y Carrión, a meeting place for local musicians, dark, bohemian; *Cuerdas Andinas Disco Bar*, Carrión y J L Mera, entrance only for couples; *Ñucanchi*, Av Universitaria 496 y Armero, Thur-Sat 2230-0300. Most places do not come alive until 2230.

Nightclubs: *Licorne*, at *Hotel Colón Internacional*; discos inc *JK*, Amazonas 541; *Dreams*, Naciones Unidas y Los Shyris; *Río Club*, Av 12 de Octubre y Colón; *Carpenix*, Almagro y La Niña, cover charge, popular with young crowd; *Cali Salsoteca*, Almagro y Orellana, great atmosphere; *Seseribó*, Veintimilla y 12 de Octubre, salsa and rock, rec, Thur-Sun, US$2; *El Solar*, Amazonas 2563 y Mariana de Jesús, salsa, Wed-Sat, good music, popular; *Footloose*, Baquerano 188 y J L Mera, gay disco, cover charge US$4; *Ku*, Orellana y 6 de Diciembre, popular disco.

Theatre: *Teatro Sucre*, Flores with Guayaquil, the most elegant. Symphony concerts are free. Advance tickets from Metropolitan Touring; the theatre was closed for major renovation in mid 1996. *Teatro San Gabriel*, América y Mariana de Jesús, Ecuadorean folk ballet 'Jacchigua' presented Wed and Fri 1930, entertaining, colourful and loud. *Teatro Prometeo* adjoining the Casa de la Cultura Ecuatoriana, 6 de Diciembre y Tarqui, also closed for renovation in mid 1996. *Agora*, open-air theatre of Casa de la Cultura, 12 de Octubre y Patria, stages many concerts. There are also plays at the *Patio de Comedia*, 18 de Septiembre, between Amazonas and 9 de Octubre. Good music at *Teatro Equitorial Experimental*; check posters in Plaza Teatro for details. *Centro Cultural Afro-Ecuatoriano* (CCA), Tamayo 985 y Lizardo García, Casilla 352, Sucursal 12 de Octubre, T 522318, sometimes has cultural events and published material, a useful contact for those interested in the black community. There are always many cultural events in Quito; see the listings section of *El Comercio* for details.

● **Hospitals & medical services**
Most embassies have the telephone numbers of doctors who speak non-Spanish languages. **Hospital Voz Andes**, next to Voz Andes radio station, Villalengua 267, T 241-540, emergency room, quick, efficient, staffed by US, British and Ecuadorean doctors and nurses, fee based on ability to pay, run by Christian HCJB organization, has out-patient dept, they stock a rabies vaccine; reached by No 1 bus to Iñaquito. **Metropolitano**, Av Mariana de Jesús y Av Occidental, T 431-520, just E of the western city bypass, very professional, prices almost the same as in the USA, gamma globulin US$12; typhoid US$16 (buy vaccine from pharmacy on ground floor). Catch a Quito Sur-San Gabriel bus from El Tejar downtown, via Av Universitaria and Av América, or a bus on 10 de Agosto or Av América and walk up, or take a taxi, about US$0.60. A rec paediatrician is Dr Ernesto Quiñones, at ProSalud, Coruña 1761 y Novoa Camaño, T 223-591/223-593, F 223-590, e-mail: 04150,1472@compuserve.com.

Among the rec health centres are: **Centro Médico Alemania**, Eloy Alfaro y Alemania; **Clínica Pichincha**, Veintimilla 1259, T 561-643, amoebic dysentry tests, results within hours, US$15; **Clínica Americana Adventista** (some English spoken), 10 de Agosto 3366, 24 hrs, US$5; **Clínica San Francisco**, 6 de Diciembre y Colón, 24 hrs, x-rays.

For amoebic dysentery tests, **Análisis Médicos Automatizados**, Alpallana 477 y Whymper, Ramírez Dávalos 202, T 545-945. **Dra Johanna Grimm**, Salvador 112 y Los Shyris, T 240-332, Lab 462-182; **Lab León**, Edif Torrealba, Amazonas,

facing British Council, Dr León speaks English, does test and can prescribe, popular with foreign residents; **Centro Médico Martha Roldós**, Plaza Teatro, Hepatitis B injections for US$0.30, but buy your own syringe, needle and phial from *Fybeca* chemist (see below). **Dr Vargas Uvidia**, Colombia 248, T 513-152, speaks English and French; **Dr Rodrigo Sosa**, Cordero 410 y 6 de Diciembre, T 525-102, English-speaking; **Dr Wilson Pancho**, Av República de El Salvador 112, T 463-139/469-546, speaks German.

Dr John Rosenberg, internal and travel medicine, he has a wide range of vaccines, consultation US$20, Hepatitis A vaccine costs US$25, speaks English and German, very helpful general practitioner, office at Med Center Travel Clinic, Foch 476 y Almagro, T 521-104, paging service 506-856 beeper 135, home 441-757.

Chemist: *Farmacia Alaska*, Venezuela 407 y Rocafuerte, T 210-973; *Fybeca* on Guayaquil in the Old City (sells typhoid/paratyphoid pills – Vivatif, Swiss); *Fybeca* at Venezuela y Mejía sells tampons. Check the listing of *farmacias en turno* in *El Comercio* on Sat for 24-hr chemists in the following week. Chloroquine is available for malaria prevention but not Paludrine. For injections and prescriptions, Rumipampa 1744 y Vasco de Contreras, opp Coliseo de Colegio San Gabriel (old city), T 457-772.

Dentists: *Dr Aldo Grundland*, Rep de El Salvador 210 y Av de Los Shyris, Edif Onix p 7, speaks English, Hebrew, Italian, good value and efficient, great view of Pichincha from his chair; *Drs Sixto y Silvia Altamirano*, Av Amazonas 2689 y Av República, T 244-119, excellent; *Dra Rosa Oleas*, Amazonas 258 y Washington (T 524-859); *Dr Hesam Foroodi*, Inglaterra 113 y Eloy Alfaro, T 569-739, excellent, fluent English; *Dr Fausto Vallejo*, Madrid 744 (1 block from the end of the No 2 Camal/Colón bus line), T 554-781, rec, very reasonable; *Dr Roberto Mena*, Tamayo 1237 y Colón, T 525-329, speaks English and German; *Dr Víctor Peñaherrera*, Edif Banco Amazonas 4340 y Villalengua, T 255-934/5, speaks English, rec.

Gynaecologist: *Dr Steven Contag*, Cordero 410 y 6 de Diciembre, T 560-408, speaks English.

Opticians: *Optica Luz*, Amazonas y Colón, T 521-818, also 10 de Agosto y Riofrío, professional, helpful, good value; *Optica Gill*, Amazonas, opp the British Council, English spoken, glasses, contact lenses, helpful.

● **Language courses**
At the *Universidad Católica*, Octubre 1076 y Carrión, *Instituto de Lenguas y Lingüística*, T 529-240: 5-week Spanish courses, US$425, large classes; courses in Quichua. They will provide student cards, which are valid for reductions in Peru.

Language schools: *The South American Explorers Club* provides a free list of rec schools and these may give club members discounts. It is impossible to list all the schools offering Spanish courses in Quito. We list schools for which we have received positive recommendations each year. This does not necessarily imply that schools not mentioned are not rec. Although few schools are registered with the Ministry of Education, many of the others offer a high standard of teaching. Schools usually offer courses of 7 hrs or 4 hrs tuition/day, either in groups or on a one-to-one basis. Many correspondents have suggested that 4 hrs a day is normally sufficient. Charges range between US$1.50 and US$8/hr for one-to-one classes, but beware of extras which may not be mentioned in the initial quote.

Some of the most expensive schools spend a great deal on multi-media equipment and advertising abroad, check how much individual tuition is provided. It is possible to arrange some trial lessons. Do not arrange accommodation through intermediaries or 'fixers' and make sure you get a receipt for money paid. It is normally more expensive and not necessary to book from abroad. Most schools can arrange accommodation with families from US$10 to US$25 a day, full board (book for 1 week initially). Many also offer excursions.

Favourable reports in 1996 were received on the following schools. In the New City: *Mitad del Mundo*, Terán 1676 entre Versalles y 10 de Agosto, T/F 567-875, PO Box 17-15-389C, repeatedly rec; *Cumbre Andina*, Av América 1530 y Ramírez Dávalos, T/F 552-072; *Academia Latinoamericano*, José Queri 2 y Eloy Alfaro, PO Box 17-17-593, T 433-820, F 465-500; *Amazonas One to One Spanish School*, Washington 718 and Amazonas, Edif Rocafuerte, p 3, PO Box 17-21-1245, T/F 504-654; *Instituto Superior de Español*, Darquea Terán 1650 y 10 de Agosto, PO Box 17-03-00490, T 223-242, F 221-628, E-mail: Institut@superior.ecx.ec (they have also opened a school in Otavalo and can arrange voluntary work with La Cruz Roja Ecuatoriana, at Mindo, Fundación Jatun Sacha and others); *Galápagos Spanish School*, Amazonas 258 y Washington, PO Box 1703744, T/F 565-213/ 540-164/220-939; *Estudio de Español Pichincha*, Andrés Xaura 182, entre Lizardo García y Foch, PO Box 17-03-0936, T 528051/452-891, F 601-689; *Academia de Español Quito*, Marchena 130 y Av 10 de Agosto, T 553-647/554-811, F 506-474/504330; *Asociación Ecuatoriana de Enseñanza de Español*, Av Amazonas 629 y Carrión, T/F 547-275; *South*

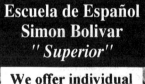

American Spanish Institute, Av Amazonas 1549 y Santa María, T 544715/226348, F 226348 (UK 0181 983 6724); *Rainbow Spanish Centre*, Armero 749 y Sta Rosa, PO Box 1721-01310, T 548-519, F 440-867; *New World Spanish School*, Orellana 290, PO Box 17-04-1052, F 502066; *World Wide Language School*, Versalles 1449, T 656-573/526-001, F 564-924; *Belmonte*, Ríofrio y J Larrea, T 520-177, PO Box 17-15-133B; *San Francisco*, Veintimilla 1106 y Amazonas, Edif Amazonas, p 7, T 553-476; *Atahualpa*, Veintimilla 910 y J L Mera, T 545-440, F 505-151, PO Box 17-07-9581; *La Lengua*, Colón 1001 and J L Mera, p 8, PO Box 17-07-9519, T/F 501-271; *Academia de Español Equinoccial*, Roca 533 y J L Mera, T 564-488, F 529-460; *Bipo & Toni's Academia de Español*, Carrión 300 y Plaza, T 540-632, F 547-090, e-mail bipo@pi.pro.ec, PO Box 17-12-587; *America Spanish School*, 768 Carrión and 9 de Octubre, T 229-166, F 568-664; *Simón Bolívar*, Calle Leonidas Plaza y Wilson, T/F 226-635, also salsa lessons on Fri; *Escuela de Español Ecuador*, Queseras del Medio 741 y Av 12 de Octubre, p 2, T 502-460, F 520-667; *Cristóbal Colón*, Foch 649 y Reina Victoria, T 560-872, PO Box 17-03-543, website http://www.qni.com/~mj/ccolon, also has *Hostal Bientur* (**E** pp) and *Bientur* travel agency.

In the Old City: *Beraca School*, Vargas 275 y Oriente, T 518-873, they also have a new school in Mindo; *Pacha Mama*, Guayaquil 1258 y Manabí, Plaza del Teatro, p 3, Of 305, PO Box 17-01-2535, T 218-416; *Los Andes*, 1245 García Moreno entre Mejía y Olmedo, p 2, T 583-086; *Nueva Vida*, Venezuela 1389 y Oriente, PO Box 17-01-2518, T 216-986; *Interandina*, García Moreno 858 y José Antonio Sucre, F 583-086; *Quito's Information Center*, Guayaquil 1242 y Olmedo, p 2, F 229-165, PO Box 17-03-0062, for information and worldwide phone and fax service.

● **Laundry**

Lavyseca, Cordero y Tamayo, laundry and dry cleaning, same day; *Lavandería*, 552 Olmedo, T 213-992, will collect clothes; *Lavahotel*, Almagro 818 y Colón, good value, inc soap powder; *Lavandería Opera de Jabón*, Pinto 325, T 543-995, open 7 days, 0700-2000. *La Química*, Mallorca 335 y Madrid; *Norte*, Amazonas 7339, and Pinzón y La Niña; *Almagro*, Wilson 470 y Almagro, T 225-208, laundry by weight. Ave US$1.65/kg.

Dry-cleaning: *Martinizing*, 1 hr service, 12 de Octubre 1486, Diego de Almagro y La Pradera, and in 6 shopping centres, plus other locations, expensive.

● **Places of worship**

Joint Anglican/Lutheran service is held (in English) at the Advent Lutheran Church, Isabel la Católica 1419, Sun, 0900. Synagogue at 18 de Septiembre y Versalles, services Fri 1900 and Sa 0900.

● **Post & telecommunications**

Post Office: the old sucursal mayor (main branch) is in the old city, on Espejo, entre Guayaquil y Venezuela. The new head office (philatelic service 7th floor) is located at Eloy Alfaro 354 y 9 de Octubre. For parcels and surface-air-lifted reduced priority (SAL/APR) Correo Marítimo Aduana, Ulloa 273 y Ramírez Dávalos, next to Santa Clara market.

Other offices at: Japón y Naciones Unidas (fax service); Colón y Almagro (fax service); Ulloa y Ramírez Dávalos (fax service); and at the airport (national departures). All sell stamps Mon-Fri 0730-1930, Sat 0800-1400; special services, eg parcels, collection of registered mail until 1530 only. *Poste Restante*, at the post offices at Espejo and at Eloy Alfaro (less efficient); all *poste restante* letters are sent to Espejo unless marked 'Correo Central, Eloy Alfaro', but you are advised to check both *postes restantes*, whichever address you use. Letters can be sent care of American Express, Apdo 2605, Quito. The *South American Explorers Club* holds mail for members. For more details and for parcels service and letters to Europe via Lufthansa, see page 1157

Telecommunications: international and inter provincial calls from Emetel at Av 10 de Agosto y Colón, in the Old City at Benalcázar y Mejía, the Terminal Terrestre, open 0800-2200; the airport open 0800-1900. *Hotel Oro Verde* will send faxes; *Hotel Colón* is cheaper but only for residents.

Fax service and 1-min international phone calls (Europe US$7/minute; Canada US$5.10) so tha you can be called back if necessary, are available through Intimexpo, Amazonas 877 y Wilson Edif Visecom, Oficina 306, T 568-617/632 F 568-664; Mon-Fri 0900-1800. It is also possi ble to make a collect call to some, but not all countries. Note that Emetel offices charge only US$0.70 for an unsuccessful transmission, un like some offices which advertise fax service and charge per minute whether successful or not.

● **Security**

Quito has become a tourist centre and unfortu nately theft is on the increase, especially in the old city, some areas of which are very dangerous at night. The police are reported helpful. Har assment of single women also appears to be on the increase. Do not walk through city parks in the evening or in daylight at quiet times (this inc Parque La Carolina). Joggers are recommended to stay on the periphery.

Panecillo: new neighbourhood brigades are patrolling the area, improving public safety. Tak ing a taxi up is safer than walking up the series of steps and paths to the Virgin which begin on García Moreno (where it meets Ambato). A taxi up and down with 30 mins wait costs US$3. Do not take valuables with you and seek local advice before going.

● **Shopping**

Most shops in the Old City are shut on Sat afternoon. Articles typical of Ecuador can be bought in the main shopping districts of Avenidas Amazonas and Guayaquil. There are carved figures, plates and other items of local woods, balsa wood boxes, silver of all types, Indian textiles, buttons, toys and other things fashioned from tagua nuts, hand-painted tiles, hand-woven rugs and a variety of antiques dating back to colonial days. Panama hats are a good buy. Indian garments (for Indians rather than tourists) can be seen and bought on the N end of the Plaza de Santo Domingo and along the nearest stretch of C Flores.

Bookshops: the *South American Explorers Club* in Quito and USA (see page 1029) has the best selection of guidebooks in English (new and second-hand at good prices) and maps covering Ecuador and the rest of South America. *Libri Mundi*, J L Mera 851 y Veintimilla, open Mon-Sat, 0800-1800, and at the *Hotel Colón Internacional*, open Mon-Fri, 0800-1800, Sat-Sun, 1700-2000, Spanish, English (some second-hand available), French, some Italian books, records, Ecuadorean maps when in stock, though these are cheaper at other bookshops, has a notice-board of what's on in Quito; very highly rec. *The Travel Company*, JL Mera 517 y Roca and JL Mera 1233 y Lizardo García, for books (secondhand at No 1233), postcards, T-shirts, videos, rec; *Imágenes*, 9 de Octubre y Roca, for books on Ecuador and art, postcards; *Libro Express*, Amazonas 816 y Veintimilla, has a good stock of maps, guides and international magazines; *Confederate Books*, Calama 410 y JL Mera, open 1000-1900, excellent selection of second-hand books, inc travel guides, mainly English but German and French are also available, the owner Tommy will exchange damaged dollar bills; *Ediciones Abya-Yala*, 12 de Octubre 14-36 (T 562-633), also has excellent library and museum; *Libros Para El Alma*, Diego de Almagro 129, entre Pinto y Pres Wilson, T 226-931, also café and library and will organize rainforest trips. *Biblioteca Luz*, Oriente 618 y Vargas, runs a book exchange (mainly Spanish) charge US$1. Bookshop at Centro Comercial Popular, Flores 739 y Olmedo, T 212-550, sells half price books and magazines, some French and English books, also book exchange. Foreign newspapers are for sale at the news stand in *Hotel Colón* (approx US$3). Lufthansa will supply German newspapers if they have spare copies.

Camera repairs and equipment: *Difoto*, Amazonas 893 y Wilson, professional processing, English and German spoken; *Kis Color*, Amazonas 1238 y Calama, will develop and print 36 exposure film for US$8, better quality for 24-hr printing than 1 hr service, passport photos in 3 mins. There are several places for cheap processing on Plaza Santo Domingo.

Suba Foto, Maldonado 1371 y Rocafuerte, sells second-hand cameras, and *Foto Estudio Grau*, Bolívar 140 y Plaza Santo Domingo for repairs and parts; *Cemaf*, Asunción 130 y 10 de Agosto, Edif Molina, p 1, T 230 855, helpful, also repairs video cameras; *Adolfo Alvarez*, Carvajal 749, T 236-034, for camera repairs, speaks perfect English. Film is cheap but only ASA100, 200, 400 and Kodak Gold 35 mm are available, no Kodachrome. Lots of shops on Amazonas sell film at good prices. *Ecuacolor/Kodak*, Amazonas 888 y Wilson, Orellana 476 y 6 de Diciembre, and 10 de Agosto 4150 y Atahualpa.

A rec processing lab is that of Ron Jones, Brieva 641 y Diguja (Granda Centeno), take a bus to Av América, get off at TV channel 4, then walk up the hill, he develops Fuji and Kodak, slides/prints, B/W or colour, helpful and informative. Also for black and white, *Fotomania*, 6 de Diciembre y Patria, and for new and second-hand cameras. The average price for processing US$6.50 for 24, US$8.50 for 36.

Foodstuffs: *Supermaxi* supermarkets offer 10% discount on purchases if you buy a Supermaxi card: at the Centro Comercial Iñaquito, Centro Comercial El Bosque (Av Occidental), Centro Comercial Plaza Aeropuerto (Av de la Prensa y Homero Salas), at the Multicentro shopping complex on 6 de Diciembre y La Niña, about 2 blocks N of Colón, and at Centro Comercial El Jardín at Amazonas y Mariana de Jesús; all open Mon-Sat 0930-2000, Sun 0930-1300; *Mi Comisariato*, Centro Comercial Quicentro, Naciones Unidas y 6 de Diciembre, supermarket and department store, also sells 10% discount cards; *La Feria* supermarket, Bolívar 334, entre Venezuela y García Moreno sells good wines and spirits, and Swiss, German and Dutch cheeses. Macrobiotic food is available at *Vitalcentro Microbiótico*, Carrión 376 y 6 de Diciembre. *Sangre de Drago*, the Indian cure all, is sold at the juice bar at Oriente y Guayaquil.

Handicrafts: *Hilana*, 6 de Diciembre 1921 y Baquerizo, beautiful unique 100% wool blankets in Ecuadorean motifs, excellent quality, purchase by metre possible, inexpensive. *Folklore*, Colón 260, the store of the late Olga Fisch, a most attractive array of handicrafts and rugs, but distinctly expensive, as accords with the designer's international reputation; also at *Hotel Colón*, where *El Bazaar* also has a good selection of crafts, and *Hotel Oro Verde*.

Fundación Sinchi Sacha, Reina Victoria 1780 y La Niña, T 230-609, F 567-311, PO Box 17-07-9466, cooperative selling ceramics and other crafts from the Oriente; *Marcel Creations*, Roca 766, entre Amazonas y 9 de Octubre, panama hats; *Artesanías Cuencanas*, Av Roca 626 entre Amazonas y J L Mera, knowledgeable, wide selection; *El Aborigen*, Washington 536 y J L Mera; *Ecuafolklore*, Robles 609 entre Amazonas y J L Mera (also stocks guide books). *Coosas*, J L Mera 838, the factory outlet for Peter Mussfeldt's attractive animal designs (bags, clothes etc); *The Ethnic Collection*, esq Amazonas 1029 y Pinto, PO Box 17-03-518, T 522-887, F 567-761, wide variety, clothing, leather, bags, jewellery, etc (in UK contact Richard Hartley, The Alpaca Collection, 16 Warstone Parade East, Hockley, Birmingham B18 6NR, T 0121 212 2550, F 0121 212 1948).

Nomada, Pinzón 199 y Colón, exellent quality T-shirts at factory prices; *Amor y Café*, Foch 721 y JL Mera, quality ethnic clothing; *Los Colores de la Tierra*, JL Mera 838 y Wilson, hand-painted wood items and unique handicrafts; *La Guaragua*, Washington 614, sells *artesanías* and antiques, excellent selection, reasonable prices.

Leather goods at *Chimborazo*, Amazonas (next to Espinal shopping centre) and *Aramis*, Amazonas 1234; *Su Kartera*, Sucre 351 y García Moreno, T 512-160, also Veintimilla 1185 entre 9 de Octubre y Amazonas, manufacturers of bags, briefcases, shoes, belts etc.

Jewellery: *Alquimia*, Juan Rodríguez 139, high quality silversmith; *Edda*, Tamayo 1256 y Cordero, custom-made jewellery, rec; *Argentum*, J L Mera 614, reasonably priced; *H Stern*, at the airport, Hotels *Colón* and *Quito*.

Markets: *Mercado Ipiales*, on Chile from Imbabura uphill, or *Mercado Plaza Arenas* on Vargas are where you are most likely to find your stolen camera for sale – or have it stolen, also try *Grau* camera shop, Plaza Santo Domingo, on your left as you face the church. The other market is on 24 de Mayo and Loja from Benalcázar onwards.

Miscellaneous: there is a chain of hardware stores called *Kywi* which have a good selection of items such as padlocks; one is on Av 10 de Agosto, just S of Colón.

There is an exhibition and sale of paintings in El Ejido park, opp *Hotel Colón*, on Sat mornings. On Amazonas, NE of *Hotel Colón*, are a number of street stalls run by Otavalo Indians, who are tough but friendly bargainers. Bargaining is customary in small shops and at street stalls.

● **Sports**
Basketball: is palyed in the Coliseo.
Bowling: centre, pool, at Amazonas y Alfaro.

Bullfighting: the first week of Dec is the main bullfighting season. Tickets are on sale at 1500 the day before the bullfight; an above-average ticket costs US$8 but you may have to buy from touts. The Unión de Toreros, Edif Casa Paz, Av Amazonas, has information on all bullfights around the country; these take place all year, except Christmas to March. They do not have details of the parochial *corridas del pueblo*.

Bungee jumping: every Sun at 1000 with Andes Bungee, T 226-071/524-796, US$40 for 2 jumps.

Camping: *Cotopaxi*, Av Colón 942 y Reina Victoria, Mon-Fri 0900-1300, 1500-1900, T 563-560, good value equipment and camping gas. *The Explorer*, Reina Victoria y Pinto, T 550-911, F 623-580, PO Box 17-07-9692, reasonable prices for renting or buying, very helpful, will buy US or European equipment. There are several new camping stores on Colón, E and W of Amazonas, which stock camping gas. Kerex or kerosene can be found on the corner of Bogotá y Uruguay, knock on the back gate.

Climbing: for climbing the volcanoes, proper equipment and good guidance are essential. The dangers of inadequate acclimatization, snow blindness, climbing without equipment or a guide must be taken very seriously, especially on Chimborazo and Cotopaxi, which are not technically difficult and tempting targets for the less experienced. The Quito climbing clubs (see below) welcome new members, but they do not provide free guiding service. It is not really worth joining if you are in Ecuador for only a few weeks. The clubs are a good source for locating professional guides. **Aseguim**, The Mountain Guide Association, Juan Larrea 657 y Rio de Janeiro, PO Box 17-03-357, F 568-664, open 0830-1230, provides courses for their members and checks standards and equipment. You can check the validity of any guide through any of the rec climbing stores. Aseguim also organizes mountain rescues. The Association is non-profit and its members appreciate donations. Mountain rescue facilities are inadequate, it can take many hours to start a rescue operation and lack of equipment severely hinders success.

Safari Tours (see **Tour companies**, below), chief guide Javier Herrera speaks English, uses only Aseguim guides, maximum 2 climbers/guide, several languages spoken, very knowledgable, well organized and planned, small groups. *Surtek*, Amazonas y Ventimilla, T 561-129, branch of original Ambato office, chief guide Camilo Andrade, 8 languages spoken, all guides Aseguim, large and small groups, experienced; *La Compañía de Guías*, Jorge Washington y 6 de Dicembre, T 533-779, 7

Aseguim guides, several languages spoken, expensive; *Sierra Nevada*, Pinto 637 y Cordero, T 553-658, F 554-936, Email: marlopez@pi.pro.ec, chief guide Freddy Ramírez (fluent English, French, German), uses mostly Aseguim guides, has own equipment for rent at good rates, professional, mostly large groups; *Pamir*, JL Mera, 741 y Ventimilla, T 322-331, F 569-741, chief guide Hugo Torres, very experienced, speaks English; *Agama*, Venezuela 1163 y Manabí, T 518-191, chief guide Eduardo Agama, large groups, few guides, inexpensive. Independent guides do not normally provide transport or full service, ie food, equipment, insurance, all Aseguim: Cosme León, T 603-140; Oswaldo Freire, T 265-597; Benno Schlauri, T 340-709; Gabriel Llano, T 450-628. The only woman guiding at this time is Damaris Carlisle, T 220-674. Oswaldo Freire and Gabriel Llano have opened a hostal/restaurant, *Campo Base*, at Veintimilla 858 y Baquedano 355, T 224-504, free information on all kinds of outdoor activities, excellent food, 4 rooms with bath, friendly, English spoken, rec.

Climbing clubs: Padre José Ribas at *Colegio San Gabriel Climbing Club* is helpful, their club meets Wed 1930. *Club de Andinismo* of the University Católica meets every Tues and Thur at 1930 and welcomes visitors, it is probably the most active club at this time. *Nuevos Horizontes Club* at Colón 2038 y 10 de Agosto, T 552-154, welcomes non-members their increasingly infrequent trips and will provide climbing information. *Sadday* is at Alonso de Angulo y Galo Molina.

Climbing & trekking equipment: useful climbing equipment stores (and sources of information) are: *Equipo Cotopaxi*, 6 de Diciembre y Patria, equipment rentals, expensive; *Campo Abierto*, Baquedano y Reina Victoria, Casilla 17-03-671, T 524-422, publishes a guide to climbing Ecuador's mountains, *Montañas del Sol* (1994); *Altamontaña*, Jorge Washington 425 y 6 de Diciembre, F 524-422, reasonable prices; *Altamontaña* and *Campo Abierto* both sell imported gear. Usual charge for hiring equipment is US$1-2/item/day, plus US$60 deposit in cash or cheques; stores may buy your used equipment.

Reading: mountaineering journals include *Campo Abierto* (not produced by the Travel Agency of the same name), an annual magazine on expeditions, access to mountains etc, US$1; *Montaña* is the annual magazine of the *Colegio San Gabriel* mountaineering club, US$1.50. **Recommended books are**: *Montañas del Sol*, by Marcos Serrano, Iván Rojar and Freddy Landazuri, Ediciones Campo Abierto, 1994; it covers 20 main mountains and is an excellent introduction, it costs US$5; *Cotopaxi: Mountain of Light*, by Freddy Landazuri, Ediciones Campo Abierto, 1994, in English and Spanish, is a thorough history of the mountain. *The High Andes, A Guide for climbers*, by John Biggar (Castle Douglas, Kirkcudbrightshire, Scotland: Andes, 1996), has a chapter on Ecuador. A rec guide to climbing is *Climbing and Hiking in Ecuador*, by Rob Rachowiecki, Mark Thurber and Betsy Wagenhauser (published by Bradt Publications, 4th edition due Dec 1997). Edward Whymper's, *Travels among the Great Andes of the Equator* (published by Gibbs M Smith, Salt Lake City) is available from Libri Mundi. Jorge Anhalzer publishes a series of five mountain guides, for each of Ecuador's most frequently climbed peaks, with updated information on routes to the summits. Available from book and camping shops, and by mail order from Latin American Travel Consultants (see above). *Die Schneeberge Ecuador* by Marco Cruz, a German translation from Spanish is excellent.

Cockfighting: takes place in the Pollodrome, C Pedro Calixto y Chile, Sat, 1400-1900, US$0.25 plus bet.

Dance classes: *Ritmo Tropical*, Av 10 de Agosto 1792 y San Gregorio, Edif Santa Rosa, of 108, T 227-051, teach Salsa, Merengue,

Cumbia, Vallenato and Folkloric dance in groups or one-to-one, US$6/hr, rec.

A local game, *pelota de guante* (glove ball), is played, Sat afternoon and Sun at Estadio Mejía. **Football** is played Sat afternoons (1200 or 1400) and Sun mornings (maybe as early as 0800) at Estadio Atahualpa, 6 de Diciembre y Naciones Unidas, any northbound bus on 6 de Diciembre marked 'Estadio' goes there.

Hiking gear: for hiking boots, *Calzado Beltrán*, Cuenca 562, and other shops on the same street. For a lockable rucksack cover *Equipos Cotopaxi*, Alianza 351 y Chimborazo, T 517626, made to measure, around US$25.

Jogging: the Hash House Harriers is a club for jogging, runners and walkers, enquire at *Reina Victoria Pub*, T 233-369.

Mountain biking: *Biking Dutchman Mountain Bike Tours*, Foch 714 y JL Mera, T 542-806, T/F 449-568, 1-day tours, great fun, good food, very well organized, English, German and Dutch (of course) spoken; *Páramo Mountain Bike Shop*, 6 de Diciembre 3925 y Checoslovaquia, T 255-403/404, F 465-507, stocks high quality bikes; *Bicisport*, Los Shyris 1300 y Portugal,

T 442-984, rec. Also *Biciteca y Renta Bike*, Av Brasil 1612 y Edmundo Carvajal, T/F 241-687, subida al Bosque, for sales, spares, repairs, tours, rentals and information, rents high quality bikes for US$20/day; *Safari* (see **Tour companies**, below) rents bikes and has free route planning; also does 1, 2 and 3 day full support trips. A rec mechanic is Alex Morillo, T 434-570.

Paragliding: *Escuela Pichincha*, Alemania 339 y Eloy Alfaro, T Jaime 540-347, Cicque 455-076, US$250 complete course, good .

Rugby: is played at Colegio Militar on Sun 1000; enquire at *El Pub*.

Snorkelling: *Globo* shops (eg on 10 de Agosto) stock cheap snorkelling gear, also *Importaciones Kao*, Colón y Almagro, and *Casa Maspons*, Orellana entre 6 de Diciembre y Pinzón. *Captain Peña*, on the corner of Plaza Santo Domingo and Flores, also sells snorkelling equipment and for your personal security they stock C S Gas spray.

Swimming: there is a cold spring-water swimming pool on Maldonado beyond the Ministry of Defence building (US$0.10), hot shower (US$0.10). A public heated, chlorinated pool is

in Miraflores, at the upper end of C Universitaria, corner of Nicaragua, a 10-min walk from Amazonas, you must take swimming cap, towel and soap to be admitted, open Tues-Sun, 0900-1600, US$1.50. There is another public pool at Batán Alto, on Cochapata, nr 6 de Diciembre and Villaroel, very good but expensive at US$3.

Whitewater rafting: *Explorandes* (see **Tour companies** below), the first rafting company in Ecuador, has very experienced guides, rec; *Sierra Nevada* (see **Climbing** above), excellent trips from 1 to 3 days, chief guide Edison Ramirez (fluent English/French) is certified by French Association; *Ríos Ecuador*, based in Tena, T 06-887-438 (see **Oriente** section), Gynner Coronel has equipment, lessons and information on kayaking, rafting trips in the jungle, highly rec, very experienced, T 553-727, or book through Quito agencies; *Row Expediciones*, Noriega 374 y Villaroel, T 458-339, contact Juan Rodríguez for 1-day trips on the Río Blanco and Toachi, depending on the water levels, very professional operation; also connected to *ROW* (River Odysseys West) of the USA, offering 6-day professionally-guided trips down the Río Upano in the southern Oriente (T 1-800-451-6034, or PO Box 579, Coeur d'Alene, ID 83816); *Eco-Aventur*, Alfredo Meneses runs day trips on the Ríos Blanco and Toachi, T 524-715, F 223-720, also

affiliated with *Small World Adventures* in the USA; *Amu Yacu*, Amazonas y Wilson. All these outfits charge US$50-70/day.

● **Tour companies & travel agents**
Note that many agencies offer 'nature tourism', which is not the same as 'ecotourism'. While nature tourism may offer trips to natural areas, there is no commitment to the environment, or economic benefits to indigenous groups. This is particularly true of the Oriente region.

Ecuadorean Tours (American Express agent), Av Amazonas 339, T 560-488, also sell local student cards, US$17, to those with proof of home student status, useful for discounts (Poste Restante can be sent to Aptdo 2605, Quito), office at *Hotel Colón* helpful; *Metropolitan Touring*, Av República de El Salvador 970, PO Box 17-12-310, T 464-780, F 464-702; also Amazonas 239 y 18 de Septiembre and at *Hotel Quito*; Thomas Cook representative; general agents for Galápagos Cruises and Transtur; runs tours to the Galápagos, also arranges climbing, trekking expeditions led by world-known climbers, as well as tours of Quito, Machalilla National Park, rail journeys to Cuenca and Guayaquil, jungle camps, generally rec, *Transturi*, part of Metropolitan Touring, operate a cruise ship, the *Flotel Francisco de Orellana*, in 4-5 day trips

along the jungle rivers; *Quasar Nautica*, Av Los Shyris 2447, T 446-996, F 436-625, tailor made tours to historic sites, haciendas, national parks and jungle lodges accompanied by highly qualified guides. Quasar Nautica also have a fleet of six luxurious sail and power yachts available for charter in the Galapagos Islands. (UK agent: Penelopie Kellie, T 01962 779317, F 01962 779458, E-mail: pkellie@yachtors.u-net.com. *Ecoventura*, Av Colón 535 y 6 de Diciembre, T 507-408, F 507-409, has tours throughout Ecuador and to the Galápagos; *Ecuaviajes*, Av

Eloy Alfaro 1500 y Juan Severino, T 233-386, F 504-830, highly rec for everything, Cristina Latorre de Suárez speaks excellent English, very helpful.

Angermeyers Enchanted Excursions, Foch 726 y Amazonas, T 569-960, F 569-956, for Galápagos cruises, and tours of jungle, sierra and costa (inc economy); *Safari*, Calama 380 y J L Mera (also in the cul-de-sac opp *Hotel Alameda Real* on Roca), T 552-505, F 220-426, E-mail: admin@safariec.com.ec, David Gayton and Jean Brown, excellent adventure travel,

Galápagos booking services, customized trips, mountain climbing, rafting, trekking, 4WD jeeps available (Fabian Espinosa is an excellent guide and runs birdwatching trips), open 7 days; *Explorandes*, Shyris 2657 y Gaspar de Villaroel, T 441-587, F 432-723, E-mail: explore@uio.sat-net.net, trekking, rafting (see **Whitewater rafting** above), climbing, jungle tours; *Sierra Nevada Expeditions* (see **Climbing** and **Whitewater rafting** above), specialized tours, also jungle expeditions, experienced multi-lingual guides; *Etnotur*, Luis Cordero 1313 y J L Mera, T 564-565, F 502-682, helpful, English and German spoken, jungle, mountain, rafting and Galápagos tour; *Canodros*, run Galápagos cruises and the Kapawi Ecological Reserve, see Guayaquil **Tour companies**, page 1040.

Latin Tour, office at airport and in Av Amazonas, T 508-811/528-522, various trips around the country in a jeep and by motorbike (eg to Cotopaxi), also have good crews and boats for Galápagos, English speaking, ask for Juan López, very friendly staff; *Free Biker Tours*, Guipuzcoa 339 y La Floresta, T 560-469, or in Switzerland, Grenzweg 48, 3645 Gwatt, T 033-365-128, run by Patrick Lombriser, Enduro-Motorcycles 600cc, good tours, spectacular roads; *Klein Tours*, Av Los Shyris 1000 y Holanda, T 430-345, F 442-389, Galápagos and mainland tours, tailor-made, specialist and adventure, English, French and German spoken; *Naturgal*, Foch 635 y Reina Victoria, T 522-681, T/F 224-913, good value for Galápagos; *Pablo Prado*, Rumipamba 730 y República, T 446-954, for tours in 4WD vehicle, nature adventures, ecological excursions, Galápagos, rainforest.

Tropic Ecological Adventures, Av 12 de Octubre 1805 y Cordero, Edif Pallares, T 508-575/222-389, F 222-390, E-mail Larry@lz-iegler.ecx.ec. Run by Welshman Andy Drumm, a naturalist guide and divemaster on the Galápagos. He is also director of the Amazon Project run by the *Asociación Ecuatoriana de Ecoturismo* and works closely with conservation groups; a sizeable percentage of each fee is given to indigenous communities and ecological projects. *Explorer Tours*, Reina Victoria 1235 y

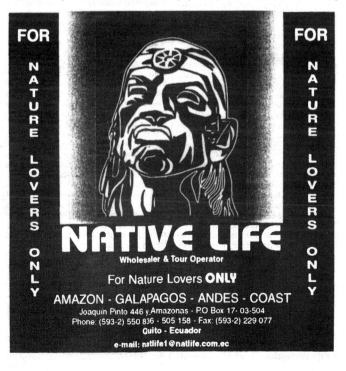

Lizardo García, T 522-220/508-871, F 508-871, owns *Sacha Lodge* and *La Casa del Suizo* on the Río Napo, first rate educational jungle tours; *Napo Tour*, J L Mera 1312 y Cordero, T 545-426/547-283, efficient, it is better value to book Napo's *Anaconda Hotel* (nr Misahuallí) in Quito than to book in Misahuallí (it is also cheaper to make your own way there than to go with Napo Tour); *Native Life*, J Pinto 446 y Amazonas, T 505-158/550-836, F 229-077, PO Box 17-03-504, e-mail: natlife1@natlife.com.ec, run tours to their Nativo Lodge in the Cuyabeno reserve.

Andes Discovery Tours, Av Amazonas 645 y Ramírez Dávalos, T 550-952, F 437-470, Galápagos tours, helpful, rec; *Elinatour*, Bejarano 150 y Suárez, T 525-352, 7 blocks from *Hotel Quito*, gives time and effort to finding what people want; *La Mondea Tours*, Av Naciones Unidas 825 y Av de Los Shyris, T 256-214, F 256-113, specializes in coastal and archaeological tours; *Palmer Voyages*, Alemania 575 y Mariana de Jesús, T 506-915, small specialist company, good rates, speak to Dominique Olivares; *Sudamericana de Turismo*, Av Amazonas 11-13 y Pinto, good, Ricardo speaks German; *Terracenter*, Reina Victoria 1343 y J Rodríguez, T/F 507-858, all variety of tours, inc to the Galápagos (special arrangement with Simón Bolívar language school).

Galasam Cía Ltda, Amazonas 1316 y Cordero, Pinto 523 y Av Amazonas (branch office), T 507-079/80/81/561-470, F 567-662, operates Economic Galápagos Tours as well as tours throughout the country, flight tickets, etc. 4-star hotel at Amazonas y Cordero offers discounts to *South American Handbook* owners (open 1997). Their tours can be purchased in Switzerland: Mondorama, T (41) 12-622-2306, and Alpin Travel (41) 81-735-2317; Germany: Gebeco, T (49) 43-197-8756, or Aquator (49) 89-314-9945; UK: Journey Latin America, T (44) 181-742-1312; USA: Andean Treks, T (617) 924-2158, LAST (410) 922-5538, Galapagos Inc (305) 661-1457, Forum Travel, (510) 671-2993, or Holbrook Travel (352) 377-1559. *The Galápagos Boat Company*, Pasaje Roca 630, T 220-426, is a broker for up to 80 boats in the islands, purchase in Quito for non-commissioned prices; *Neptunotour*, Enrique Gangotena 290, PO Box 17-04-10502, F 502-066, Galápagos cargo boat tour; *Nixe Cruises*, El Comercio 125 y Av de los Shyris, T 467-980, F 437-645, PO Box 6646 CCI, catamaran cruises of Galápagos, maximum 10 passengers, 4 crew, 1 guide, diving available, also tours of the coast, Machalilla National Park and the Oriente; *Taurus Viajes*, Amazonas 678 y Ramirez Davalos, p 2, T 223-639, rec for Galápagos tours, Luis Tipan speaks English; *Tierra del Sol*, Amazonas 338 y Jorge Washington, T/F 228-655, Galápagos

tours, rafting, climbing and adventure tours.

Galapagos Network, 7200 Corporate Center Drive, Suite 404, Miami, Florida, T (305) 592-2294, F (305) 592-6394, in Quito T 564-969, F 564-592, Guayaquil, T 201-516, F 201-153, modern yachts. For other agencies organizing tours to the Galápagos, see page 1145.

Galapagos Classic Cruises, 6 Keyes Road, London, NW2 3XA, T 0181 933 0613, offer group as well as tailor-made mainland tours in addition to those to the islands

NB When booking tours, note that National Park fees are rarely inc.

● **Tourist offices**

Corporación Ecuatoriana de Turismo (Cetur), Eloy Alfaro 1214 y Carlos Tobar (between República and Shyris), T 507-559/560, F 507-564, and at Venezuela 976 nr Mejía, p 1, open Mon to Fri, 0830-1700, T 514-044; and at airport, 0700-1900 (last two can make hotel bookings); provide maps and other information, very helpful. Some staff speak English.

Maps and guide books: Instituto Geográfico Militar on top of the hill to the E of El Ejido park. From Av 12 de Octubre, opp the Casa de la Cultura, take Jiménez (a small street) up the hill. After crossing Av Colombia continue uphill on Paz y Miño behind the Military Hospital and then turn right to the guarded main entrance; you have to deposit your passport or identification card. There is a beautiful view from the grounds. Map and air photo indexes are all laid out for inspection. The map sales room (helpful staff) is open 0800-1600, Mon-Fri. They sell the best topographic maps, covering most areas of Ecuador, scales 1:250,000, 1:100,000, 1:50,000, 1:25,000, US$2 each. Maps of border areas are 'reservado' (classified) and not available for sale without a military permit (requires approx 6 weeks). There are four sheets covering the Oriente, 1:250,000 Mapas Amazónicas, very accurate, US$2.75 each. Buy your maps here, they are rarely available outside Quito. If one is sold out you may order a photo-copy. Map and geographic reference libraries are located next to the sales room. A comprehensive road map (1989 edition) is also available as well as various other maps; e-mail igm2@igm.mil.ec. ITMB's 1:1,000,000 map of Ecuador, by Kevin Healey, 1994-96 edition, is available from ITMB Publishing Ltd, 345 West Broadway, Vancouver, BC, Canada, 5Y 1P8. A good series of pocket maps and city guides by Nélson Gómez, published by *Ediguias* in Quito, inc: *The Pocket Guide to Ecuador* (English), *Guía Turística del Ecuador* (Spanish), *Guía Vial del Ecuador* (road atlas), *Guía Informativa de Quito* (city guide), *Quito: Guía de Bolsillo* (pocket map), *Guía del Area Metropolitana de Quito* (road atlas of the areas surrounding Quito), *Guía Informativa de Guayaquil* (city guide), and *Guía Informativa de Cuenca* (city guide). These are available in book shops throughout the country and by mail order from *Latin American Travel Consultants* (for address, see above). Tourist maps and information are available from *Ecuatorial Publicaciones*, Av 10 de Agosto 4111 y Av Atahualpa, T 439-281, F 443-844, Casilla 17-16-1832 CEQ, Quito.

Many maps are now available at the **Centro de Difusión Geográfica** in the Casa de Sucre, Venezuela 573, helpful. All IGM maps are available by mail order from **Latin American Travel Consultants**, PO Box 17-17-908, Quito, Ecuador, F 562-566, e-mail: LATA@pi.pro.ec. Website: http://www.amerispan.com/latc. They produce a quarterly news bulletin with up-to-date detailed and reliable information on countries throughout South and Central America. The publication focuses on public safety, health, weather and natural phenomena, travel costs, the economy and politics in each country. Annual airmail subscriptions US$39, a single current issue US$15, information transmitted by fax or e-mail $10 per country. Payment by US$ cheque, MC or VISA (no money orders, credit card payments by mail or fax with card #, expiry date, card-holder's name and signature).

South American Explorers Club: Jorge Washington 311 y Leonidas Plaza, T/F 225-228, Mon-Fri 0930-1700, is a non-profit organization staffed by volunteers which provides a wide range of information on South America through its resource centre, library and quarterly journal as well as selling guidebooks, maps and equipment, both new and used. New, enlarged premises in a beautiful colonial house. Also has information on mountain biking in Ecuador. Highly rec. Annual membership US$40 single, US$60 for a couple. You can arrange incoming faxes through SAEC. Write to Apdo 17-21-431, Eloy Alfaro, Quito; e-mail: explorer@saec.org.ec (to send e-mail to a member, send to member@saec.org.ec and put member's full name in Subject field). In USA, 126 Indian Creek Rd, Ithaca, NY 14850, T (607) 277-0488, F 607-277-6122; e-mail: explorer@samexplo.org. US office offers books, maps, trip-planning service and can ship books and maps worldwide. For information and travel tips on-line: http://www.samexplo.org. Official representatives in UK: Bradt Publications, 41 Nortoft Rd, Chalfont St Peter, Bucks, SL9 0LA, T/F 01494-873478.

Telephone directories: in Ecuador have 'green

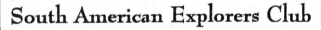

pages' giving useful tourist information, some-times in English.

● **Useful addresses**

Immigration Office: tourist visas will only be extended on the last valid day. **Policía Nacional de Migración**, Amazonas 2639, Mon-Fri 0800-1200 and 1500-1800; take bus 15 or a double-decker bus along Amazonas; go early and be prepared to wait. Those with visas other than tourist may obtain information from the **Cancillería** (Asuntos Migratorios, Sección Visas, Edif Zurita, Páez y Carrión, p 1, T 561-010, Mon-Fri 0930-1230), the **Extranjería** (Carrión y Páez, diagonally across from Asuntos Migratorios, T 563-353, Mon-Fri 0800-1300), and **Policía Nacional de Migración** (as above). Paperwork at any or all of these offices may be required to change, extend, or renew non-tourist visas.

Police: Criminal Investigations, Cuenca y Mideros, in the Old City. To report a robbery, make a *denuncia* within 48 hrs on official paper; if one officer is unhelpful, try another. If you wait more than 48 hrs, you will need a lawyer. Centralized number for all emergency services, T 101.

● **Transport**

Local Bus: Standard fare on local buses and *busetas* is US$0.10. Red and blue municipal buses on El Ejido-Quito Norte route (along Amazonas and by airport) US$0.25; *selectivos* and *ejecutivos* (sitting only), US$0.16-25. Buses are very slow in the Old City owing to traffic jams. **Trolley bus**: 'El Trole', running since May 1996, serves the southern and northern parts of the city, and two routes cross the city along 10 de Agosto. The northern station is at 'La Y', the junction of 10 de Agosto, Av América and Av de la Prensa, and the southern station is at El Recreo, on Av Maldonado. For the train station, use Chimbacalle if heading N, Machángara if heading S. For the main bus terminal use the Cumandá stop, at Maldonado y 24 de Mayo. In the N, some services run past the airport. The fare is US$0.25; US$0.15 for students. There is a special entrance for wheelchairs. **Car rentals**: all the main car rental companies are at the airport (Hertz, Avis, International, Ecuacar, Budget, Carros Diligentes and Arrancar). City offices: **Budget**, Colón y Amazonas, T 548-237 and *Hotel Colón* (closed Sat-Sun), T 525-328. **Avis**, Colón 1741 y 10 de Agosto, T 550-238. **Dollar**, Juan de Ascaray 281 y 10 de Agosto, T 430-777. **Ecuacar**, Colón 1280 y Amazonas, T 529-781. **Premium**, Orellana 1623 y 9 de Octubre, T 552-897. **Localiza**, 6 de Diciembre 1570 y Wilson, T 505-986. **Santitours**, Maldonado 2441, T 212-267/251-063 also rent minibuses, buses and 4WD, chauffeur driven rental only. Budget and Ecuacar have been par-

ticularly rec, helpful staff. **Car repairs**: **AMIPA**, *Auxilio Mecánico Inmediato para Automóviles*, T 238-032 or through paging service at 228-444 *receptor* No 958, is a reliable roadside mechanical assistance in the Quito metropolitan area, service for members and non-members, also run a good repair shop. Unleaded fuel is now widely available in the city. **Land rover**: specialists at Inglaterra 533, Talleres Atlas. Also Luis Alfredo Palacios, Iturralde y Av de la Prensa, T 234-341. **Motorcycle repairs**: Sr Lother Ranft, Euro Servicio, Av Los Shyris y Río Coca, T 454-261; main business is BMW, Mercedes and Porsche cars (very busy) but is a bike enthusiast and can get BMW motorcycle parts from Germany in 2 weeks. Paco Olmedo, Domingo Espinar 540 y La Gasca, T 550-589, has a well-equipped mechanical shop. Talleres Kosche, Eiffel 138 y Los Shyris, T 442-204, rec. Juan Molestina, Av 6 de Diciembre y Bélgica, T 564-335, fuel and travel equipment shop, helpful for motorbike spare parts. **Taxi**: standard taxi tariff in the city is US$0.50 to US$4 and not more than double by night; no increase for extra passengers; by the hour, from US$5. Although the taxis now have meters and are required by law to use them, drivers sometimes say they are out of order. Insist on the meter being used, it is always cheaper. If they have no meter, it is imperative to fix the fare beforehand. Taxis for local journeys in front of the big hotels nearly always ask more. Insist that the taxi drops you precisely where you want to go. A negotiated fare from the airport of US$4-5 to the new city and US$5-6 to the old city is reasonable but they will often try to charge up to US$10. If arriving on an international flight before 1830 walk back to domestic arrivals where they charge less, or walk out of the airport to Av de la Prensa and hail a taxi which will use a meter, or catch a bus. At night there are only taxis parked outside the airport (no cruising taxis), and they charge more. All legally registered taxis have the number of their co-operative and the individual operator's number prominently painted on the side of the vehicle. Note these and the license plate number if you wish to complain to the transit police or tourist office, but be reasonable as the amounts involved are usually small and the majority of taxi drivers are honest and helpful. For trips outside Quito taxi tariffs should be agreed beforehand: usually US$50-70 a day. Outside main hotels cooperative taxi drivers have a list of agreed excursion prices. For taxi tours with guide, Hugo R Herrera, T 267-891/236-492, speaks good English, rec. To order taxis by phone, T 220-800, 222-999, 492-492.

Air Mariscal Sucre Airport. From the airport catch bus 16 to go to the old and new cities.

The No 1 Iñaquito and Aeropuerto buses go to the airport, look for a sign '*Aeropuerto*' on the windscreen; also No 43, Marín-Carcelén. The connecting trolley bus service runs from outside the airport to the northern terminal at La Y. See also **Local buses** above for buses on Amazonas and taxis.

Beware of self-styled porters who grab your luggage in the hope of receiving a tip. There are no facilities for long-term left luggage at the airport, but there are at *Hotel Aeropuerto*, just outside the terminal, US$2/day. Watch bags at all times and watch out for theft by security officials when searching your bags; it has been reported that while you walk through the metal detector they remove money from your hand baggage. After checking in and before going through immigration, pay airport tax. The *Casa de cambio* opens at 0700. There are duty-free shops in the international departure lounge.

There is a monthly transport guide which gives details of international and national flights, and phone numbers of airlines in Quito and Guayaquil.

Internal flights: prices are payable in US$ or sucres and are increased every 6 months, all airlines charge the same. Cancellations are frequent. Services are given in the text.

Trains The railway station is 2 km S of the centre, along the continuation of C Maldonado, reached by buses along that street (eg Iñaquito-Villa Flora No 1 or Colón-Camal, No 2), and the trolley bus (see above). The ticket office at this beautiful but decrepit old station is frequently closed and employees are not well-informed.

There are no trains going straight through from Quito to Durán (Guayaquil), an overnight stay in Riobamba is necessary. The passenger service between Quito and Riobamba is limited to Sat 0800, US$10. This route provides spectacular views along the 'Avenue of the Volcanoes'. There is a service Riobamba-Durán (details under Riobamba **Transport**).

A tourist train, pulled by a steam locomotive runs from Quito to Parque Nacional Cotopaxi, Sun 0800, return 1430, US$20 return, for information T 513-422. Special arrangements can be made for group excursions from Quito to Riobamba and further S as far as Chunchi (118 km from Riobamba). A written request (*oficio*) must be presented at least 10 days prior to the date of the trip.

Metropolitan Touring (T 464-780) offers tours involving train travel to Riobamba, an extension by train from Riobamba to Guayaquil over the famous *Nariz del Diablo* (Devil's Nose) the following day, and to Cuenca.

Buses The Terminal Terrestre, at Maldonado and Cumandá (S of Plaza Santo Domingo), handles most long-distance bus services and is really the only place to get information on schedules. 24-hr luggage store, US$0.15 to use terminal. It is unsafe at night and in queues. Buses within the province of Pichincha leave from 'La Marín', which extends the length of Av Pichincha; a few others leave from San Blas (Trans Minas), Villaflora, or nr the Patria/10 de Agosto intersection.

From Terminal Terrestre to anywhere in the city, take a taxi, or the trolley bus along 10 de Agosto (if it does not go where you want, change at Marín or San Blas). There are company booking offices but staff shout destinations of buses leaving; you can pay them and get on board. For buses out of Quito it is often advisable to reserve the day before. See under destinations for fares and schedules.

Several companies run luxury coaches on the longer routes; those with stations in the new city are: Flota Imbabura, Manuel Larrea 1211 y Portoviejo, T 236940, for Cuenca and Guayaquil; Transportes Ecuador, JL Mera 330 y Jorge Washington, to Guayaquil; Panamericana Internacional, Colón 852 y Reina Victoria, T 501584-5, for Huaquillas, Machala, Cuenca, Loja, Guayaquil, Manta and Esmeraldas, they also run an 'international' bus to **Bogotá**, but it is quicker and cheaper to take a bus to the border and change. The route to Peru via Loja and Macará takes much longer than the Machala route. Tepsa has an office at Pinto 539 y Amazonas; do not buy Peruvian (or any other country's) bus tickets here, they are much cheaper outside Ecuador.

Drivers should note that there is a ring road around Quito, and a by-pass to the S via the Autopista del Valle de Los Chillos and the Carretera de Amaguaña.

CLIMBING NEAR QUITO

Cruz Loma is the low, southern one of the two antenna-topped peaks overlooking Quito from the W (to the N is a peak with loads of antennae, known as Las Antenas). On a clear day you can see about 50 km down the central valley and to the E.

Rucu Pichincha (4,627m) can be seen from some parts of Quito, and can be climbed either via Cruz Loma or via its neighbour. The path to its foot runs due W over and around hummocks on the rolling, grass-covered *páramo*. The climb up to the peak is not technical, but it is rocky and requires a bit of endurance. From Cruz Loma to Rucu Pichincha peak takes about 4 hrs up and 2 down. Take rainproof and cold-weather gear just in case. You can continue from Rucu to Guagua Pichincha, the higher of the two peaks, be careful at Paso de la Muerte, a narrow ledge, about half an hour beyond Rucu Pichincha.

● **Safety** Do not to walk in this area without checking safety first, ask at the South American Explorers Club. Widespread and frequent attacks reported – on no account go alone.

● **NB** No water is available so be sure to carry adequate supplies, especially if going to Rucu Pichincha. Please pick up your flotsam; the area is rubbish-strewn enough as it is.

● **Transport** To save time and energy take a taxi or bus, eg No 14, to Toctiuco, to the upper reaches of the city and start climbing to Cruz Loma from there (allow at least 5 hrs to reach the summit). There are poor roads up to both peaks, but traffic is sparse. Try hitching early in the morning, but remember that it is difficult to hitch back after about 1730 and you will have to walk in the dark. The road to the radio station on the northern hill is better for hitching.

Another recommended route for climbing **Guagua Pichincha** volcano (4,794m) is to take a bus to Mena 2 at Calle Angamarca, or to Chillogallo (US$1), from where the road goes to the small, friendly village of **Lloa**, then a 4 x 4 track goes to the rim of the crater. There are no regular buses to Lloa. It is possible to catch a lift on a truck or *camioneta*, but, if you're in a small group, take a taxi to Lloa, which costs around US$12. Set off early as you will need all day to walk up to the *refugio*, just below the summit.

The *refugio*, which is maintained by the Defensa Civil, is manned and will provide a bed and water for US$2 pp. Full details are given in *The Ecuador Handbook*.

HOT SPRINGS NEAR QUITO

In the valley of Los Chillos (to the SE, 1 hr by car) are the thermal pools of **La Merced** and **El Tingo**. Take a 'La Merced' bus from La Marín (lower end of Av Pichincha). If driving, take Autopista de Los Chillos to San Rafael, where the divided highway ends, turn left at the traffic lights, it is 4 km to El Tingo where there are thermal baths; excellent food and good

atmosphere at the German-owned *Mucki's Garden* restaurant, T 320-789. 7 km past El Tingo is La Merced, which also has thermal baths. 4 km from La Merced is Ilaló, privately owned pools, admission US$2, these are cleaner, with fewer mosquitoes and people. All three are best on weekdays.

At the Termas de **Papallacta**, 80 km E from Quito, 1 km from the road to Baeza, there are 8 thermal swimming pools and 2 cold pools fed by a river, open 0700-2300, entrance US$3. There are showers, toilets, steam room, changing rooms and a restaurant. The baths are usually quiet through the week. The view, on a clear day, of Antisana while enjoying the thermal waters is superb. In the village are municipal pools, simple, clean, US$1. The Fundación Ecológica Rumicocha has a small office on the main street (open 0800-1200, 1400-1600). There are leaflets on the Cayambe-Coca reserve.

● **Accommodation** Two cabins, 1 with private thermal bath, the other with kitchen facilities, US$50/cabin, 10 more rooms are available, for reservations T (Quito) 435-292 (Núñez de Vela 903, edif El Doral 2, p 1, of 15). **C** *Hostal La Posada Papallacta*, inc entry to the pools, fireplace, shared bunk rooms, restaurant at pools, food expensive. **In town: F** *Res El Viajero*, basic, shared bath, restaurant with reasonable meals, avoid the rooms in the old building. **G** *Hotel Quito*, clean and friendly, restaurant also with reasonable meals. **Camping**: US$5 per tent, clean, emphasis on recycling of rubbish.

● **Buses** From Quito, Terminal Terrestre, 2 hrs, US$1.75: ask to be let off at the road to the springs; it's a steep 1 km walk up to the baths. On Sat and Sun there is a bus from Plaza San Blas at 0800, returning 1430.

PROTECTED AREAS NEAR QUITO

Maquipucuna Biological Reserve

2 hrs NW of Quito; 14,000 acres: the cloud forest at 1,200-2,800m contains a tremendous diversity of flora and fauna, including over 325 species of birds. The reserve has five trails of varying length (15 mins to 5 hrs). Entry fee for foreigners, US$5 pp; one night's accommodation, US$45; guide, US$8.50.

● **Reservations** Fundación Maquipucuna,

Baquerizo 238 y Tamayo, Quito, Casilla 17-12-167, T 507-200, F 507-201, e-mail: root@maqui.ecx.ec. The British charity, **Rainforest Concern**, can also be contacted for information (and fund-raising), c/o Peter Bennett, 27 Lansdowne Crescent, London W11 2NS, T 0171-229-2093, F 0171-221-4094.

At Km 68 on the old road to Mindo via Tandayapa is Bellavista, with **C** pp *Finca Bellavista* (Cabins in the Clouds), with or without full board, hot showers, excellent birdwatching and botany, T Quito c/o Richard Parsons (593-2) 509-255, or T/F 223-381. Advance booking essential. For Maquipucuna and Bellavista take a bus to Nanegalito then hire a truck, or arrange everything with the lodges or in Quito.

Aldea Salamandra

140 km NW of Quito, a beautiful nature reserve in tropical rainforest: good for birdwatching (over 200 species including toucans and hummingbirds), swimming or kayaking, or trekking through the forest. US$15 pp/day including all meals and excursions; accommodation only is US$7 pp. For reservations T 551-188 (Quito).

● **Access** 3 hrs by bus from Quito. Take any Esmeraldas bus and ask the driver to stop 2 km before Puerto Quito. It is a 10-min walk from the main road; well signposted. From Esmeraldas with Trans Esmeraldas, 2 hrs; stop 2 km after Puerto Quito.

MINDO

Mindo is a small town (*Pop* approx 1,700) surrounded by dairy farms and lush cloud forest climbing the western slopes of Pichincha. 19,200 ha, ranging in altitude from 1,400 to 4,780m have been set aside as the **Bosque Protector Mindo-Nambillo**. The reserve features spectacular flora (many orchids and bromeliads), fauna (butterflies, birds including the cock of the rock) and spectacular cloud forest and waterfalls. Two ecological organizations are involved in the reserve: *Amigos de la Naturaleza de Mindo* and *Fundación Pacaso*, both with offices in Mindo. The former runs 2 refuges: Centro de Educación Ambiental (CEA), 4 km from town, within the 5 ha buffer zone, capacity for 25-30 people; and Refugio Enrique Grosse-Leumern, 12 km from Mindo,

with capacity for 15. Guide service, lodging and food are available at these shelters. Admission is US$2, lodging US$6 pp, full board US$18 pp. Take sleeping gear (none provided) and food if you wish to prepare your own (nice kitchen facilities available). Arrangements have to be made in advance, contact Amigos de la Naturaleza de Mindo, on the main road into Mindo, before reaching the plaza, on the left (signposted). If closed, enquire about Pedro Peñafiel or his family. In Quito: Sra María Guerrero, Casilla 17-03-1673, T 455-907. Visitors are recommended to stop at the office in Mindo before heading towards the reserve. During the rainy season, access to the reserve can be very difficult or impossible. Vinicio Pérez is an excellent resident birding guide, Spanish only, rec.

● **Accommodation B** pp *Hostería El Carmelo de Mindo*, in 32 ha, 700m from the town centre, T/F 408-355, cabins or room with or without bath, **E** pp dormitory, bring sleeping bag, **F** pp camping, US$ prices for foreigners, meals available, horse rental, excursions, 50% discount for IYHA card holders; **E** pp *Hacienda San Vicente*, 'Yellow House', 500m S of the plaza, inc all meals, family-run, very friendly, clean, nice rooms, TV, excellent food, good walking trails nearby, great value, rec; **E** *El Bijao*, on the left approaching the village, basic but nice, friendly; **E-F** *Familia Patiño*, 2 attractive cabins, new, cheap, clean, friendly, ask at *Restaurant Omarcito*; **F** *Noroccidental*, basic, clean, some rooms with private bath; **F** *El Guadual*, clean, hot shower, good food to order.

● **Transport** Buses at 1500 and at 0800 Fri-Sun, US$1.90, 2½ hrs (up to 7 hrs in the wet). From Santo Domingo de los Colorados, daily 1200 and Sat 0800, US$3, 4 hrs. The most direct access from Quito is along the road to San Miguel de los Bancos, Puerto Quito (accommodation available in both towns) and La Independencia where it joins the Santo Domingo-Esmeraldas road. It is now paved. If driving go to Mitad del Mundo, follow the signs for Calacalí and continue on to Nanegalito. It is a beautiful ride through native cloud forest. 24 km beyond Nanegalito, to the left is the turnoff for Mindo. It is about 7 km down a new road to the town.

BOSQUE PROTECTOR PASOCHOA

45 mins SE by car from Quito, is a natural park set in humid Andean forest, run by the Fundación Natura, América 5653 y Voz Andes, T 447-341/4 (entrance for for-

eigners US$7, Ecuadoreans US$1.70; very touristy at weekends). The reserve has more than 120 species of birds (three condors often seen) and 50 species of trees, situated between 2,700 and 4,200m. Its average temperature is 10°C and its dry season occurs between June and September. There are walks of 30 mins, 1 hr, 2, 4 and 8 hrs. Camping is permitted in the park (US$3 per tent); take food and water as there are no shops and take your rubbish away with you. There is also a refuge (US$5 pp/night, with shower, has cooking facilities), but you will need a sleeping bag.

• **Transport** From Quito buses run from Marín to Amaguaña (ask the driver to let you off at the 'Ejido de Amaguaña'); from there follow the signs. It's about a 8 km walk, with not much traffic for hitching, except at weekends. By car, take the highway to Los Chillos, at San Rafael (traffic light) continue straight towards Sangolquí and on to Amaguaña. 1.4 km past the sign 'Amaguaña Os Da La Bienvenida' turn left onto cobblestone road and follow the signs to Pasochoa, 5.4 km to the park. Tours with Safari Tours in Quito cost US$45 pp; a price negotiated with a taxi driver from a good hotel is about US$15 each way; a pick-up truck from Amaguaña is about US$6.

Northern Ecuador

AN AREA of outstanding ecological importance, the landscape is mountainous, with views of the Cotacachi, Imbabura, Chiles and glacier-covered Cayambe, interspersed with lakes. This is also a region renowned for its *artesanía* and for Otavalo's famous Saturday market.

ROUTES The Pan-American Highway and a railway line run NE from Quito to Otavalo (94 km) and Ibarra (114 km). Train services to Otavalo are indefinitely suspended and on the spectacular railway line from Ibarra. Northwest to the Pacific port of San Lorenzo, passenger services were all but terminated in 1996. North of Ibarra, the highway runs for another 108 km to Tulcán and on to Ipiales in Colombia. The Pan-American Highway is paved for the whole stretch Quito-Tulcán.

QUITO TO CAYAMBE

Calderón 32 km N of Quito, Calderón is the place where miniature figurines are made of bread. You can see them being made, though not on Sun, and prices are much lower than in Quito. Especially attractive is the Nativity collection. Prices range from about US$0.10 to US$4. On 1-2 Nov, the graves in the Indian cemetery are decorated with flowers, drinks and food for the dead. The Corpus Christi processions are very colourful. Many buses leave

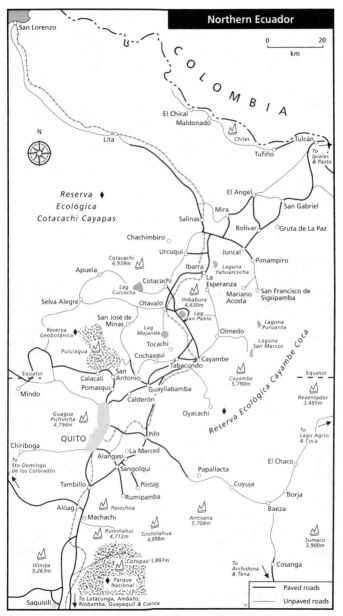

Northern Ecuador

0   20
km

COLOMBIA

San Lorenzo

El Chical
Maldonado
Chiles
Tulcán

Lita

Tufiño

To
Ipiales
& Pasto

*Reserva
Ecológica
Cotacachi Cayapas*

El Angel

Mira
San Gabriel

Salinas
Bolívar
Gruta de La Paz

Chachimbiro

Urcuquí
Juncal
Pimampiro

Apuela
*Cotacachi
4,939m*
Cotacachi

Ibarra
*Laguna
Yahuarcocha*

La
Esperanza

*Lag
Cuicocha*

Mariano
Acosta
San Francisco de
Sigsipamba

Selva Alegre

Otavalo
*Imbabura
4,630m*

*Lag
San Pablo*

San José de
Minas

*Lag
Mojanda*

Olmedo
*Laguna
Puruanta*

*Reserva
Geobotánica*

Tocachí

*Laguna
San Marcos*

Pululagua

Cochasqui

Tabacundo
Cayambe

Equator
*Cayambe
5,790m*
Equator

Calacalí
San
Antonio

Pomasqui

Guayllabamba

Mindo

Calderón
Oyacachi

Reserva Ecológica Cayambe Coca

*Reventador
3,485m*

*Guagua
Pichincha
4,794m*

QUITO

Pifo

To
Lago Agrio
& Coca

Chiriboga

La Merced
El Chaco

To
Sto Domingo
de los Colorados

Alangasí
Sangolquí

Papallacta

Tambillo

Píntag
Cuyuja

Borja

Alóag

Rumipamba
Baeza

Pasochoa
Machachi

*Antisana
5,704m*

*Rumiñahui
4,712m*

*Sincholahua
4,898m*

*Sumaco
3,900m*

*Illiniza
5,263m*

Cotopaxi 5,897m

*Parque
Nacional*

To
Archidona
& Tena

Cosanga

Saquisilí

To Latacunga, Ambato,
Riobamba, Guayaquil & Cuenca

14

Paved roads

Unpaved roads

from Plaza San Martín, Quito (often unwilling to take backpackers).

After Calderón the road N descends into the spectacular arid Guayllabamba gorge and climbs out again to the fertile oasis of **Guayllabamba** village, noted for its avocados and chirimoyas (**D** *Hostería Guayllabamba*, cabins on eastern outskirts of town). At Guayllabamba, the highway splits: to the right, the Pan-American Highway runs NE to Cayambe. The left branch goes to Tabacundo, from where you can rejoin the Pan-American travelling E to Cayambe.

Tolas de Cochasquí

10 km past Guayllabamba on the road to Tabacundo (8 km before Tabacundo), a gravel road to the left (signed Pirámides de Cochasqui) leads to Tocachi and further on to the national Tolas de Cochasqui archaeological site. The protected area contains 15 truncated clay pyramids, nine with long ramps, built between 900 and 1500 AD by Indians of the Cara or Cayambi-Caranqui tribe. Festivals with dancing at the equinoxes and solstices. There is a site museum.

● **Access** Only with a free 1½-hr guided tour; open 0900-1530. Be sure to take a bus that goes on the Tabacundo road and ask to be let off at the turnoff. From there it's a pleasant 8 km walk. If you arrive at the sign between 0900-0930, you should get a lift from the site workers. A taxi from Cayambe costs US$8 for the round trip.

CAYAMBE

Cayambe (*Pop* 16,849), NE of Guayllabamba, is dominated by the snow-capped volcano of the same name. Worth a visit are the pyramids of the Sun and Moon at Puntiachil; a descriptive route for the Pyramid of the Sun is displayed.

Nearby dairy farms produce a fine range of European-style cheeses; try the local *bizcochos con queso*. Cayambe is the Agrarian Reform Institute's showplace and its only major project. *Fiesta* in Mar for the equinox with plenty of local music; also IntiRaymi, last weekend in June.

Local information
● **Accommodation & places to eat**
Hotels may be full on Fri during June-September.

B *Hacienda Guachala*, S of Cayambe on the road to Cangahua, a beautifully restored hacienda (1580), spring-fed swimming pool, basic but comfortable rooms with fireplaces, delicious food, good walking, Anglo-Arabian horses for rent, excursions to nearby pre-Inca ruins, highly rec, reservations in Quito: Reina Victoria 1138 y Foch, T 563-748; **D** *Cabañas Nápoli*, Panamericana Norte Km 2, good restaurant; **E** *Hostal Cayambe*, Bolívar 23 y Ascázubi, T 361-007, Youth Hostel, clean, friendly, stores luggage; **E** *Hostal Mitad del Mundo*, on the Panamericana, clean, pool, sauna, restaurant.

Restaurant El Unicorno, nr the market, cheap, good. There are several cheap restaurants on Bolívar. *Casa de Fernando*, Panamericana Norte, good.

● **Transport**
Some Otavalo-Quito buses stop in Cayambe; dep every few minutes, 40 mins to Otavalo. Cayambe-Olmedo every 30 mins, till 1600 Mon-Fri, and 1800 Fri-Sun, 1 hr, US$0.35; bus to Ibarra 0700 only, 1½ hrs, US$0.50, returns 1230. Direct with Flor del Valle from M Larrea in Quito.

Cayambe (5,790m) is Ecuador's third highest peak and the highest point in the world which lies directly on the Equator. About 1 km S of Cayambe is an unmarked cobbled road heading E via Juan Montalvo, leading in 26 km to the Ruales-Oleas-Berge refuge at about 4,800m. The *refugio* costs US$10 pp/night, can sleep 37 in bunks, but bring a sleeping bag, it is very cold. There is a kitchen, fireplace, eating area, running water, electric light and a radio for rescue.

The standard route, up from the W, uses the refuge as a base. The climb is heavily crevassed, especially near the summit, and is more difficult and dangerous than either Chimborazo or Cotopaxi. Full details in *The Ecuador Handbook*.

● **Access** You can take a camioneta from Cayambe to *Hacienda Piemonte Alto* (at about 3,500m) or a taxi for US$15. From the *hacienda* to the *refugio* it is a 3-4-hr walk minimum, the wind can be very strong but it is a beautiful walk. It is difficult to get transport back to Cayambe. A milk truck runs from Cayambe hospital to the *hacienda* at 0600, returning between 1700-1900. 4WD jeeps go to the refugio (eg *Safari Tours*), 1½ to 2 hrs.

CAYAMBE TO OTAVALO

The road forks N of Cayambe. **To the right**: a cobbled road, the very scenic *carretera vieja*, runs in good condition to **Olmedo** (no hotels or restaurants; a couple of shops and lodging with the local nuns, ask; Emetel office, in the old Tenencia Política, on the plaza). A road runs E to the **Laguna de San Marcos**, 40 mins by car, 3 hrs on foot. After Olmedo the road is not so good (4WD rec). It is 9 km from Olmedo to **Zuleta**, where beautiful embroidery is done on napkins and tablecloths; *feria* on Sun. 15 km beyond is La Esperanza (see **Excursions** from Ibarra), and 8½ km further on is Ibarra.

To the left: the main paved road crosses a *páramo* and suddenly descends into the land of the Otaveño Indians, a thriving, prosperous group, famous for their prodigious production of woollens.

OTAVALO

Otavalo (*Pop* 21,548; *Alt* 2,530m; *Phone code* 06) is set in beautiful countryside which is worth exploring for 3 or 4 days. The town itself, consisting of rather functional buildings, is notable for its textiles and its enormous Sat market. In the Plaza Bolívar is a statue of Rumiñahui, Atahualpa's general, who was instrumental in the war between Atahualpa and Huáscar, and in the resistance to the Spaniards.

Otavalo men wear their hair long and plaited under a broad-brimmed hat; they wear white, calf-length trousers and blue ponchos. The women's colourful costumes consist of embroidered blouses, shoulder wraps and many coloured beads. All families speak Quichua (the Ecuadorean equivalent of Quechua) as their first tongue and Spanish as their second.

Places of interest

The Sat market comprises three different markets with the central streets filled with vendors. The *artesanías* market is held 0700-1800, and based around the Plaza de Ponchos. The livestock section begins at 0600 until 1000, and takes place outside town in the Viejo Colegio Agricultural: go W on C Colón from the town centre. The produce market lasts from 0700 till 1400, in Plaza 24 de Mayo and E across town to the Plaza Copacabana.

The *artesanías* industry is so big that the Plaza de Ponchos is now filled with vendors every day of the week not only Otavaleños, but people from all over Ecuador and South America. The selection is better on Sat but prices are a little higher than Wed or Sun when the atmosphere is more relaxed. Bargaining is appropriate in the market and shops. There is a good book market also at Plaza de Ponchos. Indigenous people in the market respond better to photography if you buy something first, then ask politely. Reciprocity and courtesy are important Andean norms.

Museums

Instituto Otavaleño de Antropología, exhibition, W of the Panamericana Norte. The **Museo Arqueológico César Vásquez Fuller** is at *Pensión Los Andes*, Roca y Montalvo, Mon-Sat 1400-1800, US$1, rec. **Centro Histórico**, is just outside town, in the direction of Cotacachi.

Excursions

Otavalo weavers come from dozens of communities. The easiest to visit are Ilumán (visit the Conterón-de la Torre family of *Artesanías Inti Chumbi*, on the NE corner of the plaza; there are also many felt hatmakers in town); Agato (the Andrango-Chiza family of *Tahuantinsuyo Weaving Workshop*, gives weaving demonstrations and sells textiles); Carabuela (many homes sell crafts including wool sweaters); Peguche (the Cotacachi-Pichamba family, off the main plaza behind the church, sells beautiful tapestries). These villages are only 15-30 mins away and all have a good bus service; buses leave from the Plaza Copacabana. You can also negotiate a price with a taxi driver.

To reach the **Cascadas de Peguche** follow the old railway track through the woods in the direction of Ibarra until the track drops away to the left and a dirt path continues up the hill towards the waterfall. Allow 1-1½ hrs each way. From the top of the falls you can continue the walk to Lago de San Pablo (see below). Attacks have been reported – don't go alone.

Local festivals

From 24 to 29 June, at the *Fiesta de San Juan*, there are bullfights in the plaza and regattas on the beautiful Lago de San Pablo, 4 km away, see below (bus to Espejo, US$0.20). *Fiesta del Yamor* **from 3 to 14 Sept**, local dishes are cooked, roulette played and bands in the plaza, as well as bullfights. If you wish to visit fiestas in the local villages, ask the musicians in the tourist restaurants, they may invite you.

Mojandas Arriba is an annual 2-day hike from Quito over Mojanda to reach Otavalo for the 31 Oct foundation celebrations.

Local information
● **Accommodation**

Hotels may be full on Fri nights, before market, when prices go up. Water is not always available in Otavalo.

B *Ali Shungu*, Quito y Miguel Egas, Casilla 34, T 920-750, run by friendly US couple, lovely garden, hot water, safe deposit boxes, good restaurant with vegetarian dishes on request, folk music at weekends, popular, apartments, **A2**, highly rec.

C *El Indio*, Bolívar 904, T 920-325, also suites, hot water, clean, attractive; also at C Sucre next to Plaza de Ponchos, T 929-960, and Colón 507 y Sucre, T 920-161.

D pp *El Coraza*, Calderón y Sucre, T 921-225,

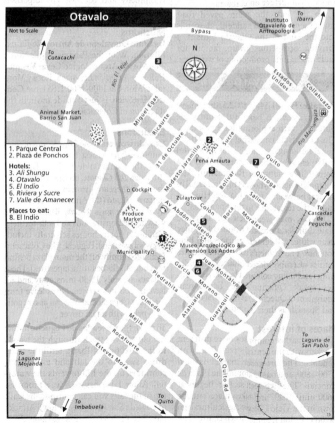

Otavalo

Not to Scale

To Cotacachi

To Ibarra

Instituto Otavaleño de Antropología

Bypass

Río El Tejar

Animal Market, Barrio San Juan

Miguel Egas

Ricaurte

Estados Unidos

Collahuazo

Río Machángara

1. Parque Central
2. Plaza de Ponchos

Hotels:
3. Ali Shungu
4. Otavalo
5. El Indio
6. Riviera y Sucre
7. Valle de Amanecer

Places to eat:
8. El Indio

31 de Octubre

Modesto Jaramillo

Sucre

Peña Amauta

Quito

Quiroga

Cockpit

Zulaytour

Av Abdón Calderón

Colón

Roca

Salinas

Morales

To Cascadas de Peguche

Produce Market

Bolívar

Museo Arqueológico & Pensión Los Andes

Municipality

García Moreno

Juan Montalvo

Atahualpa

Guayaquil

Piedrahíta

Olmedo

Mejía

Rocafuerte

Esteves Mora

To Lagunas Mojanda

To Imbabuela

To Quito

Old Quito Rd

To Laguna de San Pablo

F 920-459, hot water, very clean, nice rooms, quiet; **D** *Los Pendoneros*, Av Abdón Calderón 510 y Bolívar, T 921-258 clean, safe, hot showers, some rooms can be noisy, **E** without bath, rec; **D** *Otavalo*, Roca 504 y J Montalvo, T 920-416, **E** without bath or outside window, attractive patio, car and motorbike park, indigenous music on Fri nights, restaurant, homemade ice cream in the *Golden Eagle* coffee shop.

E *El Cacique* and *El Gran Cacique*, both on 31 de Octubre, entre Quito y Panamericana Norte, T 921-740, F 920-930, the latter is newer and better, bath, TV, parking clean, spacious, laundry, hot water, nice rooftop area; **E** *La Cascada*, Colón y Sucre, T 920-165, small rooms, hot water, clean, safe; **E** *Res San Luis*, Abdón Calderón 6-02 y 31 de Octubre, T 920-614, shared bath, family run, safe, café; **E** *Riviera Sucre*, García Moreno 380 y Roca, T 920-241, cheaper with shared bath, hot water, laundry facilities, cafetería, good breakfasts, book exchange, safe, nice garden, mostly rec; **E** *Rincón de Belén*, Roca 8-20 y J Montalvo, T 920-171/921-860, nice, modern, bath, TV, parking, restaurant.

F *Hostal Ingrid*, 31 de Octubre y Colón, T 920-191, quiet, clean; **F** *Inti Ñan*, J Montalvo 602 y Sucre, shared bath, nice clean rooms, small, noisy; **F** *Isabelita*, Roca 1107 y Quiroga, 2 shared gas showers, laundry facilities, clean, helpful, basic, parking space, noisy Sat night, good value; **F** *La Herradura*, Bolívar 10-05, T 920-304, shared bath, clean, hot water, rec; **F** *Res Irina*, Jaramillo 5-09 y Morales, T 920-684, clean, shared bath, tepid showers, laundry facilities, excellent breakfast, discount for longer stay, top rooms best, mountain bike hire, rec; **F** *Res Otavalo*, J Montalvo 4-44, shared bath, basic, small rooms; **F** *Samaj Huasy*, Jaramillo 6-11 y Salinas, ½ block from Plaza de Ponchos, T 921-126, shared bath, hot water, clean, safe, rec; **F** pp *Valle del Amanecer*, Roca y Quiroga, T 920-990, F 920-286, with bath, hot water, relaxed atmosphere, nice colonial building, very clean, popular,

good restaurant, *peña* on Fri evening, mountain bike hire, cheap laundry, rec.

Out of town: in Peguche (see **Excursions** above) is **E** *Aya Huma Hotel*, on the railway, 5 mins from the falls, T 922-663, F 922-664, excellent restaurant with vegetarian food and delicious pancakes, lovely place, hot water, clean, quiet, run by a Dutch lady, live folk music on Sat, highly rec. Closer to the centre of the village is *Tío Peguche*, T 922-619, same prices, new. Ask to leave the Otavalo-Ibarra bus at Peguche village.

North of town: **A3** *Hacienda Pinsaqui*, T/F (06) 920-387, beautiful original antiques, lovely dining room, lounge with fireplace, colonial ambience, gardens, horse riding. By Carabuela is **C** *Troje Cotama*, T/F (06) 922-980, inc breakfast, converted grain house, very attractive, fireplace in rooms, good food, horses available.

A3 *Casa de Mojanda*, Vía Mojanda Km 3, Casilla 160, Otavalo, e-mail: mojanda@uio.telconet.net, T 09-731-737, F (06) 922-969, beautiful setting on 25 acres of farmland and forested gorge, organic garden, inc all meals, healthy cooking, comfortable, library, horse riding, mountain bikes, highly rec. 5 mins on the road to Lagunas Mojanda, is *Hospedaje Camino Real*, T 920-421, in a eucalyptus wood, cabins, hot water, kitchen, laundry, good meals, library, rec.

● **Places to eat**

The restaurant of *Hotel Ali Shungu* (see above) serves all meals, open 0700-2100, wide variety, rec; *El Indio*, Sucre y Salinas, good fried chicken (weekends especially) and steaks; *Quino Pequeño*, Roca 740 y Juan Montalvo, good typical food, good value; *Fontana di Trevi*, Sucre entre Salinas y Morales, open 0600 to midnight, good pizzas and pasta, good juices, good views from top balcony, friendly service, helpful; *Pizza Siciliana*, Sucre 10-03 y Calderón, good large pizzas, vegetarian dishes, good juices; *Fuente del Mar*, Bolívar 815, ½ block from main plaza, seafood, also has some rooms with hot showers, rec; *Jack Daniels Rock Café*, next to Plaza de Ponchos, good music, good, cheap set meals, crêpes not so good; *Chifa China*, Morales y Sucre, excellent value; *Cafetería Shanandoa Pie Shop*, Salinas y Jaramillo, good pies, milk shakes and ice cream, expensive, good meeting place, rec for breakfast, book exchange, daily movies at 1700 and 1900; *L'Olivier*, on Roca, good cheap breakfasts, crepes, evening meals, French run, rec; *Plaza Café*, Plaza de Ponchos, good food and atmosphere, free coffee refill, safe storage for shopping, rec; *Café Galería*, Plaza de Ponchos, vegetarian, mainly snacks, open Mon, Wed, Fri, Sat only, good music and atmosphere. *Oraibi Bar*, Colón y Sucre, open Thur, Fri, Sat July and Aug, Swiss owner, pleasant courtyard, snacks, live music Fri and Sat evenings, good service, book exchange. Cheap food in the fruit and vegetable market (suitable for vegetarians).

● **Banks & money changers**
Imbacambios, Sucre 1205. There are several other Cambios on Sucre and Morales. **Banco Previsora**, on Sucre, Visa ATM, cash advance.

● **Entertainment**
Peña Amauta, Jaramillo y Salinas, and Jaramillo y Morales, the best, good local bands, friendly and welcoming, mainly foreigners, Italian food upstairs; *Peña Tucano*, Morales 5-10 y Sucre, nice place, good music, restaurant; *Peña Tuparina*, Morales y 31 de Octubre, rec. Peñas normally only on Fri and Sat from 2200, entrance US$1. *Habana Club*, Quito y 31 de Octubre, lively disco.

● **Language schools**
Instituto Superior de Español, Sucre 11-10 y Morales, p 2, T (06) 992-414, F 922-415 (see also **Quito language schools**). *Jatun Pacha*, Av 31 de Octubre 19 y Panamericana, cooperative, offers Spanish classes, also select handicrafts. Classes with Helena Paredes Dávila, at C Colón 6-12, T 920-178, rec.

● **Laundry**
Lavado en Seco, C Olmedo 32. Also laundry at Roca 942 y Calderón, US$1.20/kg.

● **Post & telecommunications**
Post Office: behind the Municipal building, approach from Piedrahita.

● **Security**
To prevent theft, ensure that your hotel room door is always locked, even if your absence is very brief. Never leave anything in your car or taxi, even if it is being watched for you. The streets of Otavalo are safe at night, but the surrounding areas are not. Lone walkers have been attacked on some of the trails around the town, so it's best to go in company. Take a stick to fend off dogs.

● **Sports**
The cockpit (*gallera*) is at 31 de Octubre y Montalvo, fights are on Sat and Sun 1500-1900, US$0.50. On the Panamericana, *Yanuyacu* has 3 swimming pools, volleyball courts: full on Sun.

Near the market, a ball game is played in the afternoons. It is similar to the game in Ibarra described below except that the ball is about the size of a table-tennis ball, made of leather, and hit with the hands, not a bat.

Mountain bikes: for hire at *Ecoturismo*, Jatun Pacha, 31 de Octubre y Panamericana, T 548-068, US$5 for 5 hrs or US$8/day. *Taller Ciclo Primaxi*, García Moreno y Atahualpa 2-49, has good bikes for rent, US$5/day, rec.

● **Tour companies & travel agencies**
Zulaytur, Sucre y Colón, T 921-176, run by Rodrigo Mora, English spoken, information, map of town, slide show, horse-riding, repeatedly rec; *Intiexpress*, Sucre 11-06, rec for 3/4-hr trek on horseback, US$15 pp, ask them to prepare the horses before you arrive, good for those with or without experience; *Zulay Diceny Viajes*, Sucre 1014 y Colón, T 921-217, run by an indigenous Otavaleña; *Lassotur*, Calderón 402 y Bolívar, T 902-446, also organizes horseriding; *Ecuapanorama*, Calderón y Roca, T 920-889/563, ecological tours of Intag, horseriding, hikes. All rec; all run tours with English-speaking guides to artisans' homes and villages, US$10 pp, which usually provide opportunities to buy handicrafts cheaper than in the market.

● **Transport**
Trains There is a regular ferrobus service to Ibarra, several daily, 1 hr.

Road New terminal at Atahualpa y Collahuazo (see map). To Quito 2 hrs, US$1.50-US$2. To Ibarra, every 15 mins, US$0.35, 30 mins. From Quito by taxi takes 1½ hrs, US$30-40; *Hotel Ali Shungu* (see above) runs a shuttle bus from any hotel in the new city, Quito, to Otavalo, US$12 pp, not restricted to *Ali Shungu* guests, dependable service. All buses from Quito dep from the Terminal Terrestre (Cooperativa Otavalo, Coop Las Lagos), every 15 mins on Sat, the last bus is about 1800. To **Tulcán**, via Ibarra, frequent departures. Buses and trucks to Apuela and points W leave from Colón y 31 de Octubre. The organized tour sold by the hotels is expensive. Travelling on Fri is rec.

LAGO DE SAN PABLO

There is a network of old roads and trails between Otavalo and Lago de San Pablo, none of which takes more than 2 hrs to explore. It is worth walking either to or back from the lake for the views. To explore the lake itself, canoes can be hired at the *Club de Tiro, Caza y Pesca*.

● **Accommodation at the lake: A1** *Hostería Cusín* in a converted 17th century *hacienda* on the E side of the lake, San Pablo del Lago, T 918-013, F 918-003, US$70 pp extra full board plus use of sports facilities (horses, mountain bikes, squash court, pool, games room), library, lovely grounds, book in advance, 2 nights minimum, run by an Englishman, Nick Millhouse, French and German spoken, credit cards not accepted; **A3** *Hostería Puerto Lago Country Inn*, Panamericana Sur, Km 6 y Lago San Pablo on the W side of the lake, T 920-920, F 920-900, beautiful setting, a good place to watch the sunset, very hospitable, restaurant, **A2** inc dinner; **B** *Cabañas del Lago*, on NE shore of the lake, T 918-001 (in Quito, Unicentro Amazonas, Amazonas y Japón, PO Box 17-11-6509, T 435-936/461-316), price includes breakfast, clean, mediocre restaurant, boats and pedalos for hire; **D** *Hotel Chicapán*, T 920-331, on the lakeshore, a bit run-down, good expensive restaurant with fine views.

From **San Pablo del Lago** it is possible to climb **Imbabura** volcano (4,630m, almost always under cloud), allow at least 6 hrs to reach the summit and 4 hrs for the descent. Easier, and no less impressive, is the nearby Cerro Huarmi Imbabura, 3,845m.

● **Transport** Buses from Otavalo-San Pablo del Lago every 30 mins, US$0.15, from esq Montalvo y Atahualpa; taxi US$1.70.

Lagunas de Mojanda

It is possible to hike S to **Caricocha** (or Laguna Grande de Mojanda; 1,200m higher than Otavalo, 18 km – 4-5 hrs). 25 mins walk above Caricocha is **Laguna Huarmicocha** and a further 25 mins is **Laguna Yanacocha**. Take a warm jacket, food and drinks. The views on the descent are excellent. From Caricocha the route continues S about 5 km before dividing: the left-hand path leads to Tocachi, the right-hand to Cochasqui (see page 1036). Both are about 20 km from Laguna Grande and offer beautiful views of Quito and Cotopaxi (cloud permitting). You can climb Fuya Fuya (4,263m; 2-3 hrs up, 1-1½ hrs down) and Yanaurco (4,259m). (See Otavalo **Accommodation** for *Casa de Mojanda*.)

● **Access** By car on a cobbled road. Take a tent, warm sleeping bag, and food; there is no accommodation. Or take a Quito bus as far as Tabacundo, hitch to Lagunas (difficult at week-ends), then walk back to Otavalo by the old Inca trail, on the right after 2 or 3 km. A taxi or camioneta from Otavalo US$18 return, arrange in advance but don't pay full fare.

COTACACHI

West of the road between Otavalo and Ibarra is **Cotacachi**, where leather goods are made and sold, although quality varies a lot. Credit cards are widely accepted but with a 10% surcharge.

● **Accommodation L2-3** *La Mirage*, ex-hacienda 500m W of town, T 915-237, F 915-065, beautiful garden, pool and gymnasium, very good suites with fireplace and antiques, lovely restaurant, arrive early for lunch as tour parties stop here, good excursions, price inc breakfast and dinner, rec; **L2** *Hostería La Banda*, W of town along 10 de Agosto, T 915-176, F 915-873, lavish bungalows and suites, restaurant, cafetería, tours, horse riding; **A2** *El Mesón de las Flores*, T 915-009, F 915-828, converted ex-hacienda off main plaza, meals in a beautiful patio, often live music at lunch, highly rec; **E** *Hostal Plaza Bolívar*, 10 de Agosto y Bolívar, Edif de la Sociedad de Artesanos, p 3, T 915-327, luggage store, secure, comfortable, use of kitchen, meeting place; **F** *Bachita*, Sucre y Peñaherrera, modern, bath, clean, rec.

● **Places to eat** *Don Ramiro*, Sucre y 9 de Octubre, nice, clean, trout is a speciality; *Asadero La Tola*, Rocafuerte, in an old courtyard; *Chifa Nueva*, González Suárez y 10 de Agosto, authentic Chinese.

● **Transport** From Otavalo, Calderón y 31 de Octubre, US$0.20, 15-20 mins.

LAGUNA CUICOCHA

The lake (*Alt* 3,070m) lies about 15 km beyond Cotacachi, past the town of Quiroga. The area is part of the **Parque Nacional Cotacachi-Cayapas**, which extends from Cotacachi volcano to the tropical lowlands on the Río Cayapas in Esmeraldas. The US$7 park fee need not be paid if only going to the lake. This is a crater lake with two islands, although these are closed to the public for biological studies.

There is a well-marked, 8 km path around the lake, which takes 4-5 hrs and provides spectacular views of the Cotacachi, Imbabura and, occasionally, Cayambe peaks. The best views are in the early morning, when condors can sometimes be seen. There is lookout at 3 km,

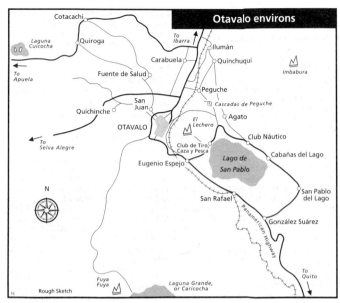

Otavalo environs

Rough Sketch

---

2 hrs from the start. It's best to go anti-clockwise; take water and a waterproof jacket. Don't go alone as robberies have been reported recently. Motor boats can be hired for groups, US$17.50 for minimum 6 persons. To climb the slopes of Cerro Cotacachi (4,944m), N from the lake, approach from the ridge, not from the side with the antennae which is usually shrouded in cloud.

● **Warning** The blue berries which grow near the lake are *not* edible: they are highly poisonous and render the eater helpless within 2 hrs. **NB also** On the road between Cotacachi and Cuicocha, children stretch string across the road to beg, especially at weekends.

● **Accommodation & places to eat F** pp *El Mirador*, with food, rooms with hot water and fireplace, camping possible, hikes arranged up Cotacachi for the fit, excellent view, return transport to Otavalo US$7, the restaurant, *Muelle*, has a dining room overlooking the lake, clean, moderate prices.

● **Transport** Bus Otavalo-Quiroga US$0.20 (from Calderón y 31 de Octubre), Cotacachi-Quiroga US$0.10; camioneta Quiroga-Cuicocha US$2.50, Cotacachi-Cuicocha US$3.50. Alternatively, hire a taxi (US$12.50) or camioneta (US$7) in Otavalo. Taxi from Cotacachi US$4 one way. The 3-hr walk back to Cotacachi is beautiful; after 1 km on the road from the park entrance, turn left (at the first bend) on to the old road.

On the SW boundary of the Cotacachi-Cayapas park is **Los Cedros Research Station**, 6,400 ha of cloudforest. Contact CIBT, Casilla 17-7-8726, Quito, T/F 221-324 for details.

● **Accommodation** At **Los Cedros**: US$25/day, inc food, negotiable for researchers. **C-D** *Reserva Río Guaycayacu*, exotic fruit farm, birdwatching, several hours' hike, maximum 8, booking essential, write to: Galápagos 565, Quito (includes 3 hearty vegetarian meals a day).

● **Transport** Bus from Quito; from San Blas with Transportes Minas, to Saguangal, 6 hrs, then it's a 6-hr walk; or through Safari Tours in Quito. A 4WD can reach the road-end.

Near **Apuela**, in the lush tropical valley of the Zona del Intag, are the thermal baths of Nangulví (**G** *Cabañas*, basic). Buses for Apuela leave from Otavalo on a dirt road; 3 hrs, 5 a day, book in advance, three of the buses pass Nangulví.

● **Accommodation & places to eat** Before Apuela is **B-C** pp *Intag Cloud Forest/Hacienda La Florida*, price inc all meals, wide range of nature walks and excursions, book in advance: Casilla 18, Otavalo, Imbabura, Ecuador; **D** *Gualiman*, T 953-048, new cabins up the road to Peñaherrera overlooking the Nangulví area, pre-Inca *tolas* and archaeological finds. In town is *Res Don Luis*, basic, cold showers, fairly clean, friendly.

IBARRA

(*Pop* 80,990; *Alt* 2,225m). This pleasant colonial town, founded in 1606, has an interesting ethnic mix, with blacks from the Chota valley and Esmeraldas alongside Otavaleños and other highland Indians.

Places of interest

The city has two plazas with flowering trees. On **Parque Pedro Moncayo**, stand the Cathedral and Casa Cultural, the Municipio and Gobernación. One block away is the smaller **Parque Dr Victor Manuel Peñaherrera**, at Flores y Olmedo, more commonly called Parque de la Merced after its church. Some interesting paintings are to be seen in the church of **Santo Domingo** and its museum of religious art, at the end of Cra Simón Bolívar, Mon-Sat 0900-1200, 1500-1800, US$0.15. **San Agustín** church, is on the small Parque Abdón Calderón. On Sucre, at the end of Av A Pérez Guerrero is the **Basílica de La Dolorosa**. A walk down Pérez Guerrero leads to the large covered **market** on Cifuentes, by the railway station, open daily. Take care in the downtown area, especially at night.

Excursions

La Esperanza is a pretty village, 10 km directly S on the road to Olmedo, in beautiful surroundings on the pre-Inca road which goes to Cayambe.

You can climb **Cubilche** volcano in 3 hrs from La Esperanza for beautiful views. From the top you can walk down to Lago de San Pablo, another 3 hrs. You can also climb Imbabura volcano more easily than from San Pablo del Lago. Allow 10-12 hrs for the round trip, take a good map, food and warm clothing.

● **Accommodation & transport G** pp *Casa Aída*, with bath, clean, hot water, laundry, Aída

speaks some English and cooks good vegetarian food, rec, Sr Orlando Guzmán is rec for Spanish classes, $2.40/hr; next door is **G** pp *Café María*, basic rooms, will heat water, helpful, use of kitchen, laundry facilities. Ask in town for makers of fine clothes and embroidery. The bus from Parque Germán Grijalva in Ibarra passes the hotels, US$0.17, 1 hr; taxi from Ibarra, US$5.

Urcuquí is a pretty little town with a basic hotel and a park. On Sun the locals play unusual ball games. To get there, a bus from Ibarra leaves from the open space opposite the old bus station (now a car showroom). Urcuquí is the starting point for walking to the Piñán lakes.

Off the main road between Otavalo and Ibarra is **San Antonio de Ibarra**, well known for its wood carvings. Bargaining is difficult, but it is worth seeing the range of styles and techniques and shopping around in the galleries and workshops.

● **Accommodation & transport F** *Hostal Los Nogales*, T 955-000, cheaper without bath, restaurant, good value. Buses leave from Ibarra, 13 km, 10 mins.

It is possible to walk the 4 km to **Lago Yahuarcocha** in about 1½ hrs. The beauty of the lake has been disfigured by the building of a motor-racing circuit round its shores. The lake is gradually drying up with *totora* reeds encroaching on its margins. They are woven into *esteras* (mats) and sold in huge rolls at the roadside. Reed boats can sometimes be seen.

● **Accommodation & places to eat D** *Parador El Conquistador*, 8 rooms, large restaurant, rec, run by Cetur; *Hotel del Lago*, no accommodation, only refreshments; *Rancho Totoral*, T/F 955-544, excellent local dishes, beautiful, tranquil setting, accommodation planned. Camping on the lakeside is possible.

● **Buses** There are frequent buses between Ibarra (market area) and the village, 30 mins, US$0.08.

Local festivals

Fiesta de los Lagos, last weekend of Sept, Thur-Sun. 16 July, *Virgen del Carmen*.

Local information

● **Accommodation**

The better class hotels tend to be fully booked during Holy Week, Fiesta de los Lagos and at weekends. Along the Pan-American Highway S towards Otavalo are several country inns, some in converted haciendas. **From South to North**

are: **C** *Hostería Natabuela*, Km 8, PO Box 683 (Ibarra), T 957-734, F 640-230, comfortable rooms, covered pool, sauna, restaurant; **B** *Hostería Chorlaví*, set in a converted hacienda, Km 4, PO Box 828, T 955-777, F 956-311, also cabins, excellent *parrillada* and folk music on Sun, disco at weekends, sauna, good restaurant, pool open to non-residents US$0.30; up the same drive is **B** *Rancho Carolina*, PO Box 78, T 953-215, F 955-215, nice cabins, restaurant; **D** pp *Hostería San Agustín*, Km 2½, T 955-888, clean, good service, hot water, good food; **C** *Hostería El Prado*, off the Pan-American at Km 1, barrio El Olivo, T/F 959-570, inc tax, luxurious, set in fruit orchards, restaurant, pool; **C** *Ajaví*, Av Mariano Acosta 16-38, T 955-555, F 952-485, along main

road into town from S, pool and restaurant.

In town: **C** *Montecarlo*, Av Jaime Rivadeneira 5-63 y Oviedo, T 958-266, F 958-182, inc tax, restaurant, heated pool, Turkish bath, jacuzzi.

D *El Dorado*, Oviedo 5-47 y Sucre, T 950-699, F 958-700, clean, good restaurant, parking; **D** *Imbaya Real*, Pedro Moncayo 7-44, T 959-729, nice, modern, good value, smaller rooms cheaper.

E *Hostal Madrid*, Moncayo y Sánchez, T 952-177, clean, comfortable, with bath, TV, parking, doors locked at 2300, rec; **E** *Nueva Colonial*, Carrera Olmedo 5-19, T 952-918/543, clean, restaurant, parking.

F *Hostal El Retorno*, Pasaje Pedro Moncayo 4-32; between Sucre and Rocafuerte; T 957-

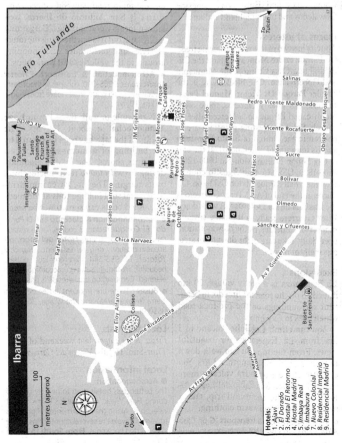

Ibarra

Hotels:
1. Ajaví
2. El Dorado
3. Hostal El Retorno
4. Hostal Madrid
5. Imbaya Real
6. Imbabura
7. Nuevo Colonial
8. Residencial Imperio
9. Residencial Madrid

722, without bath, hot water, clean, nice view from terrace, restaurant, rec; **F** *Imbabura*, Oviedo 9-33 y Narváez, T 950-155, shared bath, cheap, clean, will store luggage, splendid showers, big rooms, breakfast and snacks in the patio, basic, take your own padlock, the owner has considerable local knowledge, highly rec; **F pp** *Res Colón*, Narváez 5257 y Velasco, with bath, hot water, pleasant, clean, laundry facilities, stores luggage, rec; **F Res Imperio**, Olmedo 8-62 y Oviedo, T 952-929, with bath, hot water, reasonable value, disco at weekends till 0400; **F** pp *Res Madrid*, Olmedo 857 y Oviedo, T 951-760, with bath, hot water, TV, parking, good views from upper rooms. There are several others in the **F** and **G** categories along Bolívar, Moncayo and Olmedo.

● **Places to eat**

El Chagra, Olmedo 7-48, *platos típicos*, good trout, reasonable prices, rec; *Marisquería Los Redes*, Moreno 3-80, seafood; *Marisquería Rosita*, Olmedo 7-42, cheap fish and seafood. There are many restaurants on Olmedo: eg *Imperio*, No 8-62 y Oviedo, excellent, good value, rec; *Miravalle*, No 7-52, good value *almuerzo* and *merienda*; *El Cedrón*, No 7-37, vegetarian food, poor coffee and breakfast; breakfast with good bread at **Café Pushkin**, Olmedo 7-75, opens 0730; *Rith's*, Olmedo 7-61, good set meals and à la carte. There are also many Chinese restaurants on Olmedo, but choose carefully: *Chifa Muy Bueno*, No 7-23, does a good *Chaulafan*; *Chifa Gran Kam*, at No 7-62, exceptionally good food, not expensive. *Mr Peter's*, Oviedo 7-30 y Bolívar, good pizza, wide choice, good service, nice atmosphere, reasonable prices, open 1100-2200; *Casa Blanca*, Bolívar 7-83, excellent, family-run, seating around a colonial patio with fountain, open for breakfast and on Sun, delicious food, US$2/dish, warmly rec; *Mesón Colonial*, Rocafuerte 5-53, at Parque Abdón Calderón, also in a colonial house, good food and service, most main dishes around US$3-4, rec; *El Torreón*, Oviedo 7-62 y Olmedo, smart, expensive, good service and wine list.

Café Floralp, Bolívar y Gómez de la Torre, open 0700-2100, Swiss-owned, good breakfast, bread, own cheese factory, yoghurt, excellent coffee, Chilean wines, warmly rec; *Café Moliendo*, Velasco 7-12 y Bolívar, excellent coffee and cappucino, good breakfasts and pastries; *La Estancia*, García Moreno 7-66, very good grill but not cheap; *Pizzería*, at Av Gómez de la Torre s/n, nr the Bolívar intersection, smart, open late, also serves pastas; *George's Snack Bar*, Bolívar 10-84, cable TV with giant screen, open late.

There are several excellent *heladerias*, inc: *La Bermejita*, Olmedo 7-15; *Hielo y Dulce*, Olmedo 7-08; also *Heladería Rosalia Suárez*, Oviedo y Olmedo (100 years old in 1996), good home made *helados de paila*, also try *mora* or *guanábana*.

Local sweet specialities inc walnut nougat, guava jam and bottled blackberry syrup concentrate (*arrope de mora*). These are sold in the small shops along Olmedo 700 block and in the kiosks opp the Basílica de la Merced, in Parque Peñaherrera. *Helados de paila*, fruit sherbets made in large copper basins (*pailas*), are available in many *heladerías* throughout the town.

● **Banks & money changers**

Several national banks on Olmedo and **Banco del Austro**, Colón 7-51, have ATMs and are open Mon-Fri 0845-2000. Only *Casas de Cambio* change TCs: *Ecuafactor*, Pedro Moncayo 6-35, T 641061; *Imbacambios*, Oviedo 7-13 y Bolívar, p 2, T 955-129. Many shops change US$ notes: eg, *Las Redes* restaurant, *Res Colón*, *Farmacia Sudamericana*, Olmedo 8-64 y Moncayo, and *Delgado Travel* (see below); some also change Colombian pesos.

● **Entertainment**

Nightlife: piano bar, *El Encuentro*, Olmedo 9-59, interesting drinks, pleasant atmosphere, unusual décor; *Nexus*, Velasco y Bolívar; *Studio 54*, Autopista y Yahuarcocha. Ibarra is very quiet, even on Sat nights, as the locals go to Otavalo for the *peñas* and bars.

● **Hospitals & medical services**

Clínica Médica del Norte, Oviedo 8-24, open 24 hrs.

● **Language courses**

Centro de Español Imbabura, PO Box 10-01505, T 959-429.

● **Post & telecommunications**

Post Office: Salinas 6-64, entre Oviedo y Moncayo. **Emetel**: Sucre 4-56, open 0800.

● **Shopping**

Good supermarkets in the centre of town: *Supermercado El Rosado*, Olmedo 9-46; *Supermercado Universal*, Cifuentes y Velasco; *Mi Supermercado*, Bolívar 7-83.

● **Sports**

A unique form of paddle ball is played on Sat and Sun nr the railway station and other parts of town; ask around for details. The players have huge spiked paddles for striking the 1 kg ball. On weekdays they play a similar game with a lighter ball.

Balneario Primavera, Sánchez y Cifuentes 3-33, heated pool, turkish bath, also offers aerobics classes and remedial massage, for membership T 957-425; also *Baños Calientes*, at Sucre 10-68; *Ibarra Tennis Club*, at Ciudad Jardín, T 950-914.

● **Tour companies & travel agents**

Nevitur Cia Ltda, Bolívar 7-35 y Oviedo, T 958-

701, F 640-040, excellent travel guides, trips throughout the country and the Pasto region of Colombia; *Delgado Travel*, Moncayo y Bolívar, T/F 640-900, excellent service. A rec **taxi driver** for excursions is Luis Cabrera Medrano, Cooperativa de Taxis, Pascual Monge, 'El Obelisco'.

● **Tourist offices**

Cetur, J Rivadeneiro 6-48 y Mariano, p 2, T 958-547, F 955-711, very helpful, English spoken.

● **Useful addresses**

Immigration: Olmedo y LF Villamar (T 951-712), very quick for extensions.

● **Transport**

Trains Ferrobus service to **Otavalo** several times daily, 1 hr.

Buses There are four separate terminals, each for a different company: Flota Imbabura is at Flores y Cabezas Borja; Trans Andina, Av M Acosta y L C Borja; Trans Otavalo, Av F E Vacas cuadra 3 (beside the railway track). Other bus companies leave from alongside the railway tracks nr the obelisk, on the corner of Velasco, at the entrance to the city; beware of bagslashers here.

To/from Quito 2-3 hrs, US$1.95, about 50 departures a day; colectivo taxis (Supertaxis Los Lagos) for about US$2.65, taxis US$20. To Tulcán, US$2, 2 hrs. To **Otavalo**, 30 mins, US$0.35; most of the companies above go to Otavalo, and to Cotacachi (US$0.25, 1 hr) and Quiroga.

IBARRA TO THE COAST

5 hrs by train, 3 hrs by road from Ibarra is **Lita** (*Alt* 512m), 93 km before San Lorenzo on the Pacific coast. The tropical forests on the surrounding hill tops contain an immense variety of plants. Be careful taking photos in Lita, due to its proximity to the Colombian border.

● **Accommodation & places to eat In Lita**: 1 km uphill from the station is a *residencia*, **G** pp, adequate, clean, frequent water cuts. Several restaurants. Lights go out at 2200.

● **Transport Trains** The Ibarra-San Lorenzo train service has been mostly replaced by buses on the new road from Ibarra to the Pacific. It is doubtful if rail services will ever be fully restored. *Ecuagal* has bought a carriage with a view to running tourist trips. **Road** The road to San Lorenzo is paved as far as Guallupe, 20 km before Lita. From there it is in poor condition during and after the rainy season and often blocked by landslides. **Buses**: to San Lorenzo, 6 a day, between 0700 and 1400, 6-7 hrs, US$5.75; return from 0700; Coop Valle de Chota. Also Coop Espejo from Quito. To Lita, 0600, 0900 and 1300, 3 hrs, US$2.30; return to Ibarra 0600, 1000, 1300; the last San

Lorenzo-Ibarra bus passes Lita at 1800. Buses depart from behind the train station. **NB** Beware of thieves on the bus to San Lorenzo.

PIMAMPIRO

The quiet town of **Pimampiro** lies NE of Ibarra, 8 km off the Panamericana along a paved road; take the turnoff at Juncal. The surrounding countryside offers excellent walking. There is a Sun market.

● **Accommodation & places to eat G** *Residencial* run by the Hurtado family on C Flores, no sign, ask around, basic, friendly, poor water supply. *El Forastero*, on the corner of Flores and Olmedo, good food; also *El Vecino*, Espejo 3-028; and *Picantería Riobambeñita*, Espejo 3-054.

● **Buses** From Ibarra, Cooperativa Oriental, leaves every 20 mins, US$0.60, 45 mins; also Expreso Turismo from P Moncayo y Flores.

From Pimampiro a steep dirt road along the beautiful canyon of the Río Pisquer goes 20 km to the village of **Sigsigpamba**. Ask directions frequently if walking; 4WD is rec if driving. There are no hotels or restaurants in Sigsigpamba, only a few basic shops. Bus from Pimampiro at 1100, Thur to Sun, crowded.

Laguna de Puruanta, a 4-5-hr strenuous hike from Sigsigpamba is set amid the high *páramo*. From the lake you can walk to the village of Mariano Acosta, from which buses run back to Ibarra through Pimampiro. Allow 3 or more days for the excursion and take a tent, sleeping bag, warm waterproof clothing, food (trout fishing possible at Purnanta), stove and fuel.

NORTH TO COLOMBIA

ROUTES The Pan-American Highway goes past Laguna Yahuarcocha and then descends to the hot dry Chota valley. 24 km N of Ibarra is the turnoff W for Salinas and Lita along the new road to San Lorenzo. 8 km further N, at Mascarilla, is a police checkpoint (have your documents at hand), after which the highway divides. One branch follows an older route NE through Mira and El Angel to Tulcán on the Colombian border. This road is paved and in excellent condition as far as El Angel, but deteriorates rapidly thereafter (unpaved but the scenery is beautiful; no facilities along its 49 km). The second branch (the modern Pan-American Highway), in good repair but with many heavy lorries, runs E through the Chota valley to Juncal, before turning N to reach Tulcán via Bolívar and San Gabriel. An excellent paved road runs between Bolívar and El Angel, connecting the two branches. A second lateral road, between San Gabriel and El Angel, is in poor shape and is often impassable during the rainy season.

THE OLD ROUTE

Along the old route, which climbs steeply from Mascarilla, is the town of **Mira** (*Pop* 5,500), 15 km past the fork. Some of the finest quality woollens come from this part of the country. There are two festivals held each year, on 2 Feb, and 18 Aug, with fireworks and free flowing Tardón, the local *aguardiente*.

- **Accommodation & places to eat** G *Res Mira*, basic but clean, good beds. Few restaurants; the best is the *Bar Latino*.

- **Buses** From Ibarra, US$0.55, 1 hr; from Tulcán, 1600, 1½ hrs, US$1.

EL ANGEL

20 km NE along the old Panamericana is **El Angel** (*Pop* 5,700; *Alt* 3,000m), with a Mon market. The main plaza retains a few trees sculpted by José Franco (see Tulcán Cemetery, below).

- **Accommodation & places to eat** E pp *Hostería El Angel*, at the village entrance, T (06) 977-584, inc breakfast, hot showers, trips into the reserve (see below), US$20 pp (minimum 4 people), reservations in Quito T/F 332-761, 330-315; G *Res Viña del Mar*, José Grijalva 05-48 on main plaza, shared bath, basic, restaurant next door; G *Res Alvarez*, José Grijalva 02-59, no sign, basic, shared bath, cold water, no shower, but very friendly, rec. *Asadero Los Faroles*, José Grijalva 5-96, roast chicken and trout, expensive. Several other chicken places in town. *Pastelería Mi Pan*, José Grijalva esq Bolívar, very good bread and pastries.

- **Buses** Trans Espejo, hourly to Quito via Ibarra, US$2.50, 4 hrs; to Tulcán at 0530 and 0700 daily, US$0.95. Trans Mira, hourly to Mira and Tulcán.

3 km S of town, along the road to Mira, is the turnoff for the thermal baths of **La Calera** (6½ km) in a lovely valley. Admission US$0.50; the baths are deserted during the week, when only the smaller pool is filled. There is no public trans-

port, US$15 round trip to hire a jeep from El Angel; camioneta Fernando Calderón, T 977-274. The baths are crowded at weekends and holidays, when the same jeeps charge US$0.50 pp. There is basic accommodation; bring sleeping bag and food.

RESERVA ECOLOGICA EL ANGEL

Created in 1992 to protect 15,715 ha of *páramo* ranging in altitude from 3,400 to 4,150m, the reserve contains the southernmost large stands of the velvet-leaved *frailejón* plant, also found in the Andes of Colombia and Venezuela. Also of interest are the spiny *achupallas* with giant compound flowers, related to the *Puya Raymondii* of Peru and Bolivia. The fauna includes *curiquingue* hawks, deer, foxes, and a few condors. There are several small lakes scattered throughout the reserve. It can be very muddy during the rainy season and the best time to visit is May to August.

- **Park information** The reserve is administered by *Inefan*, El Angel office José Grijalva 04-26. The staff is helpful. The Reserve entry fee is US$7 for foreigners. The *Fundación El Angel*, offices in the municipal building, can also provide information. Gerardo Miguel Quelal knows the area well and can be hired as a guide. Contact him through either of the above offices.

- **Access** From El Angel follow the poor road N towards Tulcán for 16 km to **El Voladero** (parking area but no sign) where a trail climbs over a low ridge (30 mins' walk) to two crystal clear lakes. Camping is possible here, but you must be self-sufficient and take great care not to damage the fragile surroundings. Jeeps can be hired in the main plaza of El Angel for a day trip to El Voladero, US$40 return, but bargain.

A longer route follows an equally poor road to Cerro Socabones, beginning in the town of **La Libertad**, 3½ km N of El Angel. This route climbs gradually through haciendas, where fighting bulls are bred, to reach the high *páramo* at the centre of the reserve. After Socabones, in the village of **Morán**, the local guide Hugo Quintanchala can take you further through the valley. There are many paths criss-crossing the *páramo* and it is easy to get lost. Jeeps from El Angel to Cerro Socabones US$50 return, or Sr Calderón, as above.

A third access is from the N along the Tufiño-Maldonado road (see below) from which the Lagunas Verdes (green lakes) can be seen. According to local legend, they are enchanted.

There are sulphur gas vents here, so take care.

Beyond the Morán valley, in the forested hills towards the Mira valley, is the **Bosque Protector Cerro Golondrinas.** The Fundación Golondrinas' main sources of income are their *Hostal La Casa de Eliza* in Quito and the *Hostal El Tolondro*, in Guallupe (see page 1046). The foundation also organizes a 4-day trek from El Angel, through the **Golondrinas Reserve,** down to Guallupe in the subtropical lowlands, US$50/day; 2 simple cabins to stay in during the trek. Those interested in volunteer work, or merely visiting the reserve, contact: *La Casa de Eliza*, Quito, T (02) 226-602, F 502-640, e-mail: member@saec.org.ec; or Hugo in Morán.

THE NEW ROUTE TO THE BORDER

Following the new route of the Pan-American Highway E past Mascarilla for 2 km, is the turnoff for the town of **El Chota** with the **Honka Monka** museum of Afro-Ecuadorean culture.

● **Accommodation B** *Aruba Hostería*, T (06) 937-005, modern, small pool, very smart restaurant; **D** *Hostería Oasis*, Casilla 208, Ibarra, T (06) 937-001, F (06) 996-304, cabins for up to 6, or 2, 3 large pools, playground, several snack bars, disco, good restaurant with live music on weekends, good value, day use US$3 pp; **E** *Hostería El Jordán*, T (06) 937-002, similar but not as elaborate. Several others. Next to the *hosterías* is a Cetur kiosk with limited information.

Just beyond is **El Juncal**, the turnoff E to Pimampiro (see above), after which the highway turns N to cross the Río Chota into the province of Carchi and begins its steep climb out of the valley.

A further 17 km N is **Bolívar** (*Pop* 15,175), a neat little town with houses and the interior of its church painted in lively pastel colours, a well kept plaza and a Fri market.

● **Accommodation & places to eat G** *Hospedaje* run by Sra Lucila Torres, Carrera Julio Andrade s/n, 1 block N of the plaza, no sign, shared bath with electric shower, basic. *Restaurant Los Sauces*, by highway, good food, good value, rec. Good bakery on the main plaza, García Moreno esq Julio Andrade.

5 km N of Bolívar is the turnoff E for the town of **La Paz**, from which a steep but good cobbled road descends for 5 km to the **Gruta de La Paz**. Views along the road are breathtaking, including two spectacular waterfalls. The place is also called *Rumichaca* (Quichua for stone bridge) after the massive natural bridge which forms the *gruta* (grotto); not to be confused with the Rumichaca on the Colombian border.

The entire area is a religious shrine, receiving large numbers of pilgrims during Holy Week, Christmas, and especially around 8 July, feast day of the Virgin of La Paz.

There are clean thermal baths (showers and one pool) just below the grotto, open Wed to Sun (crowded at weekends), admission US$0.50, showers US$0.25; look for the caretaker if the gate to the pool is locked. Several scenic trails through the valley start from behind the hotel.

● **Access** Excursions to La Paz from Tulcán on Sat and Sun. Also jeeps from San Gabriel, US$0.60 pp (20 mins) on weekends; US$10 to hire a vehicle during the week. A second, signposted access road has been built from the Panamericana, 3 km S of San Gabriel.

10 km N of La Paz is **San Gabriel** (*Pop* 19,500), an important commercial centre. The spectacular 60m high **Paluz** waterfall is 4 km N of town; follow C Bolívar out of the main plaza and turn right after the bridge.

● **Accommodation & places to eat G** *Res Montúfar*, Colón 03-44, some rooms with private bath, hot water, clean, safe, motorcycle parking, basic, "has seen better days". *Su Casita*, Bolívar 12-07, good set meal; *Asadero Pío Riko*, Bolívar 10-15, chicken and others. *Heladería Zanzibar*, Colón 3-16, for ice-cream.

● **Transport Buses**: to Quito, every 45 mins, US$2.50, 4 hrs. **Jeeps**: for outlying villages leave from main plaza when full.

20 km E of San Gabriel is the tiny community of **Mariscal Sucre**, the gateway to the **Guandera Cloudforest Reserve**, where you can see bromeliads, orchids, toucans and other wildlife. The reserve is part of the **Fundación Jatun Sacha**. Reservations should be made at the office in Quito; Av Río Coca 1734, T 441-592.

● **Access** From San Gabriel, take a taxi to Mariscal Sucre, US$8, or one of the 'blue patrols' which leave from there, US$0.50. José Cando, in Mariscal Sucre, will act as a guide for hikes in the reserve.

TULCAN

The old and new branches of the Panamericana join at Las Juntas, 2 km S of **Tulcán** (*Pop* 37,069; *Alt* 2,960m), a commercial centre and capital of the province of Carchi. It is always chilly. Tulcán thrives as a shopping destination for Colombians who arrive by the busload. There is a frantic textile and dry goods fair on Thur and Sun. Prices are generally lower than Colombia, but higher than other parts of Ecuador.

Places of interest

In the cemetery, 2 blocks from Parque Ayora, the art of topiary is taken to beautiful extremes. Cypress bushes are trimmed into archways, fantastic figures and geometric shapes in *haut* and *bas* relief. To see the various stages of this art form, go to the back of the cemetery where young bushes are being pruned. The artistry, started in 1936, is that of the late Sr José Franco, born in El Angel (see above), now buried among the splendour he created. The tradition is carried on by his sons.

Local information
● Accommodation
On Fri nights and at weekends it can be difficult to find a room.

C *Parador Rumichaca*, on old road to the frontier, a short walk from the old bridge, T 980-276, swimming and thermal pools, popular, reservations required, rec; **C-D** *Frailejón*, Sucre y Rocafuerte, T 981-129/980-149, with bath, hot water, TV, good but expensive restaurant.

D *Sáenz Internacional*, Sucre y Rocafuerte, T 981-916, F 983-925, very nice, modern, good value.

E *Azteca*, Bolívar y Atahualpa, T 981-447, F 980-481, TV, restaurant, good, clean rooms, but noisy from the disco downstairs; **E** *Florida*, Sucre y 10 de Agosto, T 983-849, **F** without bath, modern section at back, good value; **E** *Hostal Alejandra*, Sucre y Quito, T 981-784, bath, clean, hot water, TV, safe indoor parking, restaurant, good value, rec; **E** *Los Alpes*, opp the bus station, with hot shower, TV, clean, rec; **E** pp *Torres de Oro*, Esq Sucre y Rocafuerte, T 980-226, with bath and TV.

F *Pensión Minerva*, Olmedo 40-50, hot water, a bit smelly but otherwise clean, beds not too comfortable, friendly, quiet; **F** *Res Colombia*, Colón 52-017 y Ayacucho, T 982-761, shared bath, simple.

G *Quito*, Ayacucho 450, T 980-541, OK.

● Places to eat
You can find Colombian specialities at *Los Arrieros*, Bolívar 51-053; and *El Patio*, on Bolívar, more expensive. Seafood at: *Cevichería el Viceño*, Bolívar 48-049; *Marisquería Anzuelo Manabita*, Sucre y Boyacá. There are various Chinese restaurants on Sucre; *Café México*, Bolívar 49-045, excellent vegetarian dishes, good value, friendly staff rec; *Parrilladas*, Sierra y Bolívar, good typical food, nr the cemetery. There are many other places to eat in town.

● Banks & money changers
There is an association of informal money changers in Tulcán, look for photo ID. A good place to change cash is in the main plaza, where the rates are better than at the border. To change TCs, try **Casa Paz cambio**, on Ayacucho in front of *Hotel Quito*, or **Carlos Burbano**, Bolívar y Junín. *Casas de cambio* in Tulcán give better rates than Ipiales. For those arriving in Ecuador, change only what you need to get to Quito or Ibarra, where the rate is better. **Filanbanco**, Sucre y Junín and **Banco de Préstamos**, on the parque, change foreign currencies. Few places accept credit cards.

● Security
It is prudent not to wander about late at night (ie after 2200).

● Transport
Air The airport is on the new road to Rumichaca. TAME flies to Cali and to Quito.

Buses The bus terminal is 1½ km uphill from centre; best to take a taxi, US$1.50, or a little blue bus from Parque Ayora; keep a sharp look out on the right for the terminal, or the bus will not stop. To Quito, 5 hrs, US$4.10, every 15 mins; to Ibarra, 2 hrs, US$1.95. Otavalo, US$1.95, 3 hrs (make sure the bus is going to Otavalo; if not get out on the Highway at the turnoff), or take a bus to Ibarra and then a colectivo. To Guayaquil, 20 a day, 11 hrs, US$7. There are also plenty of colectivos.

HOT SPRINGS NEAR TULCAN

The area surrounding **Tufiño** has various hot mineral springs arising from the nearby Chiles volcano and geothermal energy projects are planned here.

Crossing the border from Tufiño towards Chiles, in Colombia, turn left at the large green sign for the *Balneario* and continue uphill for 1½ km. There are no formalities at the border, but you must return the same day. The water here is warm, the public baths are free and dirty, the private *Baños Termales 'Juan Chiles'* cost US$0.65 and are somewhat cleaner. There are many other springs all along this hillside, follow the trail from behind the public pool.

● **Buses** Every 2 hrs from opp Colegio Nacional Tulcán, C R Sierra, US$0.50, 45 mins; it's a rough road, with a military checkpoint just before the village. Last bus back at 1700.

By far the best hot springs of the region are **Aguas Hediondas** (stinking waters), a stream of boiling sulphurous mineral waters in a wild, lonely valley. An ice-cold irrigation channel passes nearby; you need to direct it to make the hot water cold enough to enter. These waters are said to cure everything from spots to rheumatism; they are deserted on weekdays. Condors can sometimes be seen hovering above the high cliffs.

● **Warning** Several visitors have died after being overcome by fumes from the source of the sulphurous water. Bathe in the lower pools and do not follow the stream uphill. Do not go alone.

● **Access** Follow the winding road 3 km W of Tufiño, to where a rusting white sign marking the turnoff to the right. From here it is 8 km through strange scenery to the magnificent natural hot river. Only the midday Tulcán-Tufiño bus goes up the hill to the turning to Aguas Hediondas.

Past the turnoff for Aguas Hediondas the road climbs to the *páramo* on the southern slopes of **Volcán Chiles**, whose summit is the border with Colombia. The volcano can be climbed in about 6 hrs, but you must be self-sufficient. Enquire about the route in Tufiño, where guides can sometimes be hired.

To the S lies the Reserva Ecológica El Angel and the Lagunas Verdes (see above). The road then begins its long descent to **Maldonado** and Chical in the subtropical lowlands.

● **Buses** One bus leaves from opp Colegio Nacional Tulcán, C Sierra, daily at noon, US$2.20, 5 hrs, returning early next morning.

FRONTIER WITH COLOMBIA

● **Ecuadorean immigration**
Border hours are 0600 to 2100. The Ecuadorean side is older and more chaotic than the modern Colombian complex, but nonetheless adequate.

There is a modern Emetel office for phone calls. 90 days are given on entering Ecuador.

NB You are not allowed to cross to Ipiales for the day without having your passport stamped. Both Ecuadorean exit stamp and Colombian entry stamp are required. Although no one will stop you at the frontier, you risk serious consequences in Ipiales if you are caught with your documents 'out of order'.

● **Exchange**
The many money changers on both sides of the border will exchange cash; good rates have been reported at the Rumichaca bridge, but double-check all calculations.

● **Transport**
Colectivos Tulcán-border (blue and white minivans) leave when full from Parque Ayora (near the cemetery) US$0.45; from terminal to border, US$1. A city bus from the terminal to Parque Ayora, US$0.07, though this is often too crowded for luggage. Taxis to border US$0.85 pp from Parque Ayora; US$3.50 to hire a cab from anywhere in town (inc the bus terminal, though it's cheaper from the upper level).

The Central Sierra

SOUTH FROM QUITO is some of the loveliest mountain scenery in Ecuador. Colourful Indian markets and colonial towns nestle among volcanic cones over 5,000m high.

ROUTES The Pan-American Highway and the railway to the S climb gradually out of the Quito basin towards Cotopaxi. At Alóag, a road heads W to Santo Domingo de los Colorados and the Pacific lowlands.

MACHACHI

In a valley below the bleak *páramo* **Machachi** is famous for its mineral water springs and cold, crystal clear swimming pool (open 0700-1600 daily, US$0.25). The water, 'Agua Güitig', is bottled in a plant 4 km from the town and sold throughout the country (free tours 0800-1200, take identification). Machachi produces a very good cheese. Cockfights on Sun; annual highland 'rodeo', La Chagra in July.

- **Accommodation** **D** *La Estación de Machachi*, T 315-246, across the highway in the village of Aloasi, beautiful, family-run, fireplaces, access to Volcán Corazón; **E** *Tambo Chisinche*, Km 44, 200m from the Panamericana, T 315-041, take El Chaupi bus from Machachi, small sign, very good horse riding to nearby mountains US$40/day, clean, spartan, hot water, good meals extra, owner-guides Andrés and Carlos speak English, rec.

- **Places to eat** *Restaurante Pedregal*, good, cheap, basic food, log-cabin style, located off the park on the bus road into town; *El*

Chagra, good typical food, reasonably priced, take the road that passes in front of the church, on the right-hand side, about 5 km from church; *Cafe de la Vaca*, on the Highway, open Wed-Sun, fresh produce from a farm.

- **Buses**: To Quito (Villaflora), 1 hr, US$0.45. **Taxi**: to Cotopaxi, about US$30/car.

Machachi is a good starting point for climbing **Illiniza**. Illiniza Norte can be climbed without technical equipment in the dry season but a few exposed, rocky sections require utmost caution, allow 2-4 hrs for the ascent, take a compass, it's easy to mistake the descent. Illiniza Sur (5,305m) is a 4-hr ice climb: full climbing gear and experience are absolutely necessary. There is a *refugio* below the saddle between the two, at 4,750m, fully equipped with beds for 12 and cooking facilities, take a mat and sleeping bag, US$10/night.

- **Access** A pick-up truck along the deteriorating road to the 'Virgen' is about US$20, from there 4 hrs' walk to the refuge. Cheaper to get a bus from Machachi to El Chaupi, 10 km S and about 7 km from the Panamericana. From El Chaupi it is an 8-hr walk to the refuge, beautiful view of the peaks. The refuge can be reached in a day from Quito, but start very early. (With thanks to Dan Walker).

- **Accommodation** **E** *Hacienda Las Nieves*, T 330-872 (Mario), in village of El Chaupi, horse riding on Illiniza and Corazón; **E** *Hacienda San José del Chaupi*, nr El Chaupi, T (09) 737-985, or T 891-547 (Rodrigo), good base for climbing Illiniza, horse riding US$5/hr, US$20/day.

COTOPAXI NATIONAL PARK

Cotopaxi volcano (5,897m) is at the heart of a much-visited national park. The park authorities are breeding a fine llama herd on the pine clad lower slopes. Visitors to the Parque Nacional Cotopaxi must register at the main entrance; fee US$7 (open 0700-1500, although you are allowed to leave until 1800). The park administration and a small museum (open 0800-1200, 1400-1600) are located 10 km from the park gates, just before the plateau of Laguna Limpio Pungo, where wild horses may be seen. The museum has a 3D model of the park and stuffed animals.

Park information

● Access

There is an entrance to the Cotopaxi National Park 16 km S of Machachi, near a sign for the Clirsen satellite tracking station, which cannot be visited. This route goes past Clirsen, then via El Boliche National Recreation Area (shared entry fee, US$7 for foreigners), for over 30 km along a signposted dirt road, through the National Park gates, past Laguna Limpio Pungo to a fork, where the right branch climbs steeply to a parking lot (4,600m). From here it is 30 mins to 1 hr on foot to the José Ribas refuge, at 4,800m; beware of altitude sickness.

A second entrance, about 9 km further S, near the village of Mulaló, is marked by a small Parque Nacional Cotopaxi sign. It is about 36 km from here, through the main park gates, to the refuge. Nearly 1 km from the highway, turn left at a T junction and a few hundred metres later turn sharp right. Beyond this the road is either signed or you take the main fork. It is shorter and easier to follow than the first route which you join just at the Park gates. Walking from the highway to the refuge may exhaust you for the climb to the summit.

Cyclists should approach Cotopaxi from the N because the route from the S is too soft to climb on a bike. For more details and equipment, ask Jan But, 'The Biking Dutchman', or South American Explorers Club in Quito.

By public transport, take a **Quito-Latacunga** bus and get off at **Lasso** (see below). Do not take an express bus as you cannot get off before Latacunga. A truck from Lasso to the parking lot costs US$30 for 4 people, one-way, no bargaining. If you do not arrange a truck for the return you can sometimes get a cheaper ride down in a truck which has just dropped off another party. Alternatively, get off the bus at the southern entrance and hitchhike into the park from there. This is usually possible at weekends. Trucks and a jeep are available from Latacunga for about US$30 round trip – ask at the Hotel Estambul, leaves 0700 (see page 1022 for guides).

● Accommodation

There are two rustic cabañas (register at administration, US$0.65 pp) and many campsites (US$0.65 pp) in the Park. Take warm sleeping gear, water purifier and protect food from foxes. The José Ribas refuge has a kitchen, water, and 30 beds with mattresses; US$10 pp/night, bring sleeping bag and mat, also padlock for your excess luggage when you climb, or use the lockable luggage deposit, US$2.50.

Climbing Cotopaxi

The ascent from the refuge takes 5-8 hrs, start climbing at 0100 as the snow deteriorates in the sun. A full moon is both practical and a magical experience. Equipment and experience are required. Take a guide if you're inexperienced on ice and snow.

The best season is Dec-April. There are strong winds and clouds in Aug-Dec but the ascent is still possible for experienced mountaineers. More details are given in The Ecuador Handbook.

Just N of Cotopaxi are the peaks of Sincholahua (4,893m), Rumiñahui (4,712m) and Pasochoa (4,225m).

Rumiñahui can be climbed from the park road, starting at Laguna Limpio Pungo. The area around the base is excellent for birdwatching. You should also watch out for wild horses, mountain lions and, most of all, wild bulls. From Laguna Limpio Pungo to the mountain base takes about 1-1½ hrs.

LASSO

The railway and the Pan-American Highway cross one another at **Lasso** a small village, 33 km S of Alóag, with a milk bottling plant and two recommended cafés serving dairy products. Just N of Lasso, E of the highway, is the San Agustín hill, thought to be a prehistoric monument.

The area around San Agustín is owned by the Plaza family, which has two large *haciendas* and breeds bulls for the bullfights in Quito in December. One of the two *haciendas* is actually at the base of the San Agustín hill and includes some converted Inca buildings (limited accommodation in Inca rooms, **A1**, T 03-719-160).

● Accommodation & transport B Hostería La Ciénega, 2 km S of Lasso, an historic hacienda with nice gardens, an avenue of massive eucalyptus trees, nice rooms with heater, expensive restaurant, reserve in advance Thur and weekends, horse-riding US$1.50/hr, it belongs to the Lasso family, but is administered by others, T (03) 719-052, Camioneta to Cotopaxi parking area, US$22; C San Mateo, Km 16 S of Lasso, comfortable; D Parador Cotopaxi, Km 13 S of Lasso, T 719-046, simple cabins by the roadside.

LATACUNGA

Capital of Cotopaxi Province (*Pop* 39,882), a place where the abundance of light grey pumice has been artfully employed. Cotopaxi is much in evidence, though it is 29 km away. Provided they are not hidden in the clouds, which unfortunately is all too often, as many as nine volcanic cones can be seen from Latacunga; try early in the morning. The colonial character of the town has been well preserved.

Places of interest

The central plaza, **Parque Vicente León**, is a beautifully maintained garden (locked at night). There are several other gardens in the town including **Parque San Francisco** and **Lago Flores**.

Casa de los Marquéses de Miraflo-res, Sánchez de Orellana y Abel Echeverría, in a restored colonial mansion has a modest museum, with exhibits on Mama Negra (see below), colonial art, archaeology, numismatics and a library (free).

Casa de la Cultura, Antonio Vela 71-53 y Padre Manuel Salcedo, built around the remains of a Jesuit Monastery and the old Monserrat watermill, houses an excellent museum with precolumbian ceramics, weavings, costumes and models of festival masks; also art gallery, library and theatre (open Tues-Sat 0900-1200, 1400-1730, US$0.35). It presents a *fiesta de música indígena* on 5 May. **Escuela Isidro Ayora**, Sánchez de Orellana y Tarqui, and the **Cathedral** both have museums.

There is a Sat **market** on the Plaza de San Sebastián. Goods for sale include

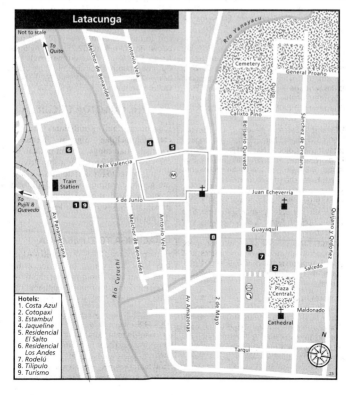

Latacunga

Hotels:
1. Costa Azul
2. Cotopaxi
3. Estambul
4. Jaqueline
5. Residencial El Salto
6. Residencial Los Andes
7. Rodelú
8. Tilipulo
9. Turismo

shigras (fine stitched, colourful straw bags) and homespun wool and cotton yarn. Market along C Guayaquil, between Quevedo y 2 de Mayo, Tues.

Local festivals

The *Fiesta de la Mama Negra* is held on 24 Sept, in homage to *Nuestra Señora de la Merced*. It celebrates the black slaves brought by the Spanish to work on the plantations. The civic festival of Mama Negra is on the first Sun in Nov.

Local information
● **Accommodation**

C *Rodelú*, Quito 7331, T 800-956, F 812-341, with bath, TV, clean, excellent restaurant, parking, rec; mountain guide Fernando Tovar is next door.

D *Cotopaxi*, Salcedo 42-32, Parque Vicente León, T 801-310, parking nearby, hot water after 0700, rooms with view over plaza are noisy at weekends; **D** *El Aventurero*, Echeverría y 2 de Mayo, T 801-043, helpful, rec. Along the Pan-American Highway, known as Av Eloy Alfaro are: **D** *Hostal Quilotoa*, No 78A-17, T 800-099, F 802-090, *Pollo a la Brasa* restaurant downstairs; **D** *Los Illinizas*, No 79-213, T/F 801-895, hot water, restaurant, parking; **D** *Res Santiago*, 2 de Mayo y Guayaquil, T 802-164, comfortable, good value; **D** *Tilipulo*, Guayaquil y 2 de Mayo, T 802-130, parking, varied rooms, good restaurant, helpful.

E *Estambul*, Belisario Quevedo 7340 y Salcedo, T 800-354, shared bath, clean, quiet, luggage store, trips to Cotopaxi National Park, highly rec; **E** *Los Nevados*, 5 de Junio 53-19 y Eloy Alfaro, T 800-407, nr the Panamericana, hot water, **F** with shared bath, restaurant.

F *Costa Azul*, Av 5 de Junio, very basic, good meals; **F** *Jackeline*, Antonio Vela 78-33, T 801-033, basic, hot water, clean; **F** *El Turismo*, 5 de Junio 53-09 esq Alfaro, T 800-362, basic, very cold shower.

G *Res El Salto*, Valencia 47 s/n, warm showers, clean, noisy, safe, restaurant, small rooms; next door is *Amazonas*, Valencia 47-36, T 801-156, better, best place to eat around the mercado central.

● **Places to eat**

Los Copihues, Quito 70-83, slow service, lunch US$4, popular with businessmen; *El Mashca*, Valencia 41-54, good value, open until 2200, rec; *Chifa Tokio*, Guayaquil 45-58, good value; *Chifa Casa China*, Av Amazonas 70 s/n, between Maldonado y Tarqui, smart, good food and service, open late; *El Portón*, Quito 73-107, cheap, open for break-

fast, popular with travellers, no sign, rec; *Pizzería Santa Bárbara*, Orellana 74-49, good; *La Borgoña*, Valencia 41-40, good value. *Pingüino*, Quito 73-106, good milk shakes and coffee; *Beer Center*, Orellana 74-20, good atmosphere, cheap beer. Two well-stocked supermarkets on C Quito. For breakfast before 0800-0900 try the *comedor* in the mercado central. A local dish is *chugchucaras*, fried pork with corn, bananas, potatoes, popcorn and porkskin (best at *Mama Rosa* on the main road).

● **Banks & money changers**

Banco Popular, Parque Vicente León, cash and TCs, only 0900-1300, good rate. Many shops on the Quito/Salcedo intersection buy dollars.

● **Post & telecommunications**

Post Office and Emetel: both at Belisario Quevedo y Maldonado.

● **Transport**

Road Buses: to Quito from *mercado central*, every 15 mins, 2 hrs, US$1.25; to Ambato, 3/4 hr, US$0.70; to Guayaquil, US$3.35, 6 hrs. To Saquisilí from C Melchor de Benavides 78-35 next to *mercado central*, every 20 mins (see below). To Quevedo (US$2.75), from Av 5 de Junio y Eloy Alfaro. Buses on the Zumbahua, Quilotoa, Chugchilán, Sigchos circuit are given below. **Taxi**: day-trip by taxi to **Zumbahua, Quilotoa**, return to Latacunga is US$40.

THE QUILOTOA CIRCUIT

Latacunga - Pujilí - Zumbahua - Quilotoa crater-Chugchilán - Sigchos - Toacazo - Saquisilí - Latacunga, 200 km in total. By car it would take 7 hrs of non-stop driving but it is better to break it up into 2-3 days (no gasoline stations beyond Pujilí and Saquisilí). All bus times quoted are approximate; buses are often late owing to the rough roads.

LATACUNGA TO ZUMBAHUA

A fine paved road leads W to **Pujilí** (15 km, bus US$0.30), which has a beautiful church but it is closed most of the time. Good market on Sun, and a smaller one on Wed. Beware of local illicit liquor and pickpockets.

ROUTES The road goes on over the Western Cordillera to Zumbahua and Quevedo. It carries very little traffic and is extremely twisty in parts but is one of the most beautiful routes connecting the highlands with Portoviejo, Manta and the coast. Beyond

Zumbahua are the pretty towns of **Pilaló** (2 restaurants and petrol pumps) and **El Tingo** (2 restaurants and lodging at *Carmita's*). The road is paved to 10 km past Pujilí and from just after Pilaló, through **La Maná** to Quevedo (2½ km beyond La Maná is **E** *Rancho Hostería Inmisahu*, T 688-003/281, with pool, clean, restaurant). Paving of the road continues, making it even more pleasant. This is a great downhill bike route.

Quevedo can also be reached by turning off this road through El Corazón. Transporte Cotopaxi (C 5 de Junio 53-44) runs daily buses to El Corazón via Angamarca; a spectacular ride.

Zumbahua lies 1 km from the main road, 65 km from Pujilí. It has an interesting Sat market (starts at 0600) for local produce, not tourist items. Fri nights involve dancing and drinking. Take a windcheater, as it can be windy and dusty. Many interesting crafts are practised by the Indians in the neighbouring valley of Tigua, skin paintings, hand-carved wooden masks and baskets.

The Sat trip to Zumbahua market and the Quilotoa crater is one of the best excursions in Ecuador, despite the poor accommodation in Zumbahua. The walk from Zumbahua to Pujilí, 6 hrs, is also recommended.

• **Accommodation F** *Pensión Quilotoa*, grey building at the bottom of the plaza, small sign, clean, with hot shower; **G** *Pensión Zumbahua*, green building at the top of the plaza, lots of rooms; **G** *Res Oro Verde*, first place on the left as you enter town, friendly, has small store and restaurant, sells purified water; unnamed *pensión*, in white house behind the church and up the hill a bit; look for someone to open it up for you. The only restaurant is on the main road outside the village, can find a cheap meal in the market. Just below the plaza is a shop selling dairy products and cold drinks.

• **Buses** Many daily on the Latacunga-Quevedo road and transport between Latacunga and Zumbahua is easy at almost any time. Buses leave every 2 hrs from 0600 (check evening before) from Av 5 de Junio, opp *Res Costa Azul* across the river; US$1.25. Four buses daily with Trans Vivero also leave from here, starting at 1100 and then every 30 mins, 2½ hrs. These buses continue up to Laguna Quilotoa, if there are passengers who wish to go,

which takes another hour, US$0.75. A pick-up truck can be hired from Zumbahua to Quilotoa for US$10-15; also to Chugchilán for around US$25-30. On Sat mornings there are many trucks leaving the Zumbahua market for Chugchilán which pass Quilotoa.

QUILOTOA

Zumbahua is the point to turn off for a visit to **Quilotoa**, a volcanic crater filled by a beautiful emerald lake, to which there is a steep path from the rim. From the rim of the crater several snowcapped volcanoes can be seen in the distance.

The crater is reached by a road which runs N from Zumbahua (about 14 km, 3-4 hrs walk). Go down from the village and cross the river. After a few kilometres along the road turn right and over the bridge at the fork in the road; there are no road signs. Keep climbing past Quilopungo and the Ponce turn-off to a colourfully-painted tombstone-shaped sign for Quilotoa, where there is a road to the right towards a small group of houses. The crater is just beyond; it can only be recognized when you are on top of it. Do not walk alone or after dark; also take a stick to fend off dogs on the road. Also be prepared for sudden changes in the weather. Everyone at the crater tries to sell the famous naïve Tigua pictures and carved wooden masks, so expect to be besieged.

• **Accommodation G** *Cabañas Quilotoa*, T (03) 812-044, owned by Humberto Latacunga (no relation to Jorge below), very friendly, warm fireplace, beds and wool blankets, cooks traditional food, vegetarian or *cuy* on request, Humberto will lead treks and provide mules, he is a good painter and has a small store, rec; *Refugio Quilotoa*, owned by Jorge Latacunga, take a sleeping bag as you sleep on the floor, he will cook food and take you on a day trek round the lake if you wish, he also paints masks; *Hostal Quilotoa*, owned by José Guamangate, friendly, with giant fireplace, offers bicycle rental, food, paintings and excursions. Camping is possible here.

• **Buses** Trans Vivero takes teachers to schools in Zumbahua and Quilapungo, leaving Latacunga daily at 0600 arriving 0815 in Quilapungo (0750 in Zumbahua), from where it is about 1 hr walk to the crater. Alternatively, hitch a truck on Sat morning from Zumbahua market bound for Chugchilán; you will be dropped close to the volcano. Hitching a return trip should not be left till late in the afternoon. Buses bound for Chugchilán/Sigchos drop the traveller 5 mins from the lake. Trans Vivero services Ponce a few times a week; from the Ponce turnoff it is about a 40-min walk N.

CHUGCHILAN TO TOACAZO

Chugchilán, a very poor village in one of the most scenic areas of Ecuador, is 22 km by road from the Quilotoa crater. It is a 6-hr walk; or walk around part of the crater rim, then down to Huayama, and across the canyon (Río Sihui) to Chugchilán, 11 km, about 5 hrs.

● **Accommodation** **F** pp *The Black Sheep Inn*, a few minutes below the village, run by Andy Hammerman and Michelle Kirby, hot showers, 2 bunk rooms and 2 private rooms at a slightly higher rate, excellent vegetarian restaurant, book exchange, organic garden, highly rec, a good base for hiking to Quilotoa, Toachi canyon and Inca ruins (Apdo 05-01-240, Correos Central Latacunga, Provincia Cotopaxi).

● **Buses** Daily (except Thur) from Latacunga at 1100 from C Melchor de Benavides, US$1.75, 4 hrs. On Thur the bus leaves from Saquisilí market at 1100, via Sigchos. On Sat two Illinizas buses leave Latacunga at 1030 and 1300. On Fri and Sat a 14 de Octubre bus leaves from opp *Res Costa Azul* in Latacunga at 1030, via Zumbahua and Quilotoa, 3-4 hrs, US$1.75. Buses return to Latacunga at 0300, via Sigchos. On Sat another bus leaves at 0300 for Latacunga, via Zumbahua. A bus leaves for Quito, via Zumbahua, on Sun at 1030; also on Sun to Sigchos at 1200 and to Latacunga, via Zumbahua, at 0600.

Continuing from Chugchilán the road runs through **Sigchos** (Sun market). The road E to Toacazo has been improved and from there to Saquisilí it is paved. Sigchos is the starting point for the Toachi Valley walk, via Asache to San Francisco de las Pampas (0900 bus daily to Latacunga).

● **Accommodation & places to eat** **E** *Res Sigchos*, basic but clean, large rooms, shared bath, hot water; **G** *Hostal Tungurahua*, shared bath, cold water. Few restaurants, but ask in advance for food to be prepared.

● **Buses** 3-5 daily to and from Latacunga (C Melchor de Benavides), US$1.25, 3 hrs. On Wed to Pucayaco, via Zumbahua, Quilotoa and Chugchilán, at 0400, 9 hrs (returns Thur at 0400); and to La Maná, via Zumbahua, Quilotoa

and Chugchilán, at 0500, 9 hrs (returns Thur at 0500 and Sat at 0400).

SAQUISILI

Some 16 km S of Lasso, and a couple of km W of the highway, is the small but very important market town of **Saquisilí**. Its Thur market (0700-1400) is famous throughout Ecuador for the way in which its plazas and most of its streets become jam-packed with people, the great majority of them local Indians with red ponchos and narrow-brimmed felt hats.

The best time to visit the market is between 0900 and 1200 (0700 for the animal market). Be sure to bargain, as there is a lot of competition. Saquisilí has colourful Corpus Christi processions. The bank near the main square exchanges dollars at poor rates.

● **Accommodation** **D** *Hostería Rancho Muller*, 5 de Junio y González Suárez, S end of town, T 721-380, F 721-103, cabins with bath, restaurant, German owner organizes tours and rents vehicles, rec; **F** *Pensión Chavela*, main plaza, very basic, no water in am, rock-hard beds, billiards hall downstairs, holes in walls; **F** *Salón Pichincha*, Bolívar y Pichincha, restaurant-bar below, good beds, cheap meals, basic, secure motor cycle parking.

● **Places to eat** Some basic restaurants at the entrance to the village, beware of overcharging. Try *colada morada*, a sweet, warm blueberry drink, with bread.

● **Buses** The Saquisilí and Cotopaxi bus companies have frequent services between **Latacunga** and Saquisilí, US$0.15, 30 mins; many buses daily from **Quito**, depart from the bus terminal, 0530 onwards, US$1.50, 2½ hrs. Buses and trucks to many outlying villages leave from 1000 onwards. Bus tours from Quito cost about US$26 pp, taxis can be found for US$45, with 2 hrs wait at market.

SALCEDO

11 km S of Latacunga is **Salcedo**, with good Thur and Sun markets. The town's Mama Negra festival is on 1 November.

● **Accommodation & places to eat** At Rumipamba, 1 km N, is **A3** *Hostería Rumipamba de las Rosas*, T (03) 726-128, F 727-103, hot showers, clean, guarded, nice garden with small zoo, swimming pool, good restaurant, highly rec; **F** *Res Las Vegas*, Bolívar y Paredes, hot water, private showers. *Restaurant Ritz*, Bolívar y Sucre, chicken.

AMBATO

The city (*Pop* 124,166) was almost completely destroyed in the great 1949 earthquake, so lacks the colonial charm of other Andean cities. Its nickname is "the city of fruits and flowers" and it is a major centre for the leather industry.

Places of interest

The modern cathedral faces the pleasant **Parque Montalvo**, where there is a statue of the writer Juan Montalvo (1832-1889) who is buried in a neighbouring street. His house (Bolívar y Montalvo) is open to the public; entrance free (T 821-024). In the **Colegio Nacional Bolívar**, at Sucre entre Lalama y Martínez, there is a Museo de Ciencias Naturales with stuffed birds and animals and items of local historical interest; US$1.65, open Mon-Fri 0800-1200, 1400-1800, closed for school holidays, rec. The **Quinta de Mera**, an old mansion in beautiful gardens in Atocha suburb, is open 0900-1200, 1400-1800, and can be reached by bus from Espejo y 12 de Noviembre.

Out along the Río Ambato, a pleasant walk from the centre, is the prosperous suburb of Miraflores, which has several hotels and restaurants. Buses leave from the centre to Av Miraflores.

The main market, one of the largest in Ecuador, is held on Mon, and smaller markets on Wed and Fri. They are interesting, but have few items for the tourist.

Excursions

To **Picaihua** by frequent bus to see the local work from *cabuya* fibre. At Pillaro outside the city there is a bull run and fight in early August.

Local festivals

Ambato has a famous festival in Feb, the *Fiesta de frutas y flores*, during carnival when there are 4 days of bullfights, parades and festivities. It is impossible to get a hotel room unless you book ahead. The town prohibits water-throwing at carnival (see **Holidays and festivals**, page 1158).

Local information

● **Accommodation**

NB A new street numbering system was being implemented in mid-1996, causing considerable confusion. Some numbers shown here correspond to the new system, while others to the old one.

A2 *Ambato*, Guayaquil y Rocafuerte, T 827-598, F 827-197, clean, good restaurant, casino, squash court, rec; **A2** *Miraflores*, Av Miraflores 2-27, T 843-224, F 844-395, clean, heating, good restaurant, parking; **A3** *Villa Hilda*, Av Miraflores 09-116 y Las Lilas, T 840-700, F 845-571, also apartments, German and Italian spoken, laundry, ask if you want hot water before 0700, restaurant good, big garden.

B *Florida*, Av Miraflores 1131, T 843-040, F 843-074, pleasant, clean, good food, sauna US$2.60, buses from the centre stop outside.

C *Colonial*, Sucre y Martínez, opp Parque Cevallos, T 827-134, with bath, TV, in restored colonial building, elegant, ask for a room away from the street; **C** *Gran*, Lalama y Rocafuerte, T 824-235, with bath, hot water, TV, friendly.

D *Bellavista*, Oriente y Napo Pastaza, T 847-535, rec; **D** *Cevallos*, Montalvo y Cevallos, T 847-457, F 824-877, good; **D** *Ejecutivo*, 12 de Noviembre 12-30 y Espejo, T 825-506, hot water, parking; **D** *Pirámide Inn*, Cevallos y Mariano Egüez, T 825-252, F 854-358, clean, comfortable, owner speaks English, very helpful, rec; **D** *San Ignacio*, Maldonado y 12 de Noviembre, cafetería, rec.

E *Portugal*, Juan Cajas 05, nr bus station, T 823-218, F 840163, with bath, hot water, TV, good value; **E** *San Francisco*, Egüez 8-37 y Bolívar, T 821-739, electric shower, cheaper with shared bath, central; **E-F** *Hostal La Liria*, Atahualpa y Caspicara, rec.

F *América*, Vela 06-46 y Mera, basic, shared hot shower; **F** *Nueve de Octubre*, Mera 07-56 y 12 de Noviembre, shared bath, hot water, good, basic. There are a lot of cheap *residenciales*, hotels and restaurants around Parque 12 de Noviembre.

● **Places to eat**

El Alamo Chalet, Cevallos 560 y Montalvo, Swiss-owned, good meals; also *El Alamo*, Sucre 660 y Mera, more economical, and *Gran Alamo*, Montalvo 535 y Sucre; *La Buena Mesa*, Quito 924 y Bolívar, French, rec; *Café Alemán*, Quito 778 y Bolívar, good food, ice cream; *La Casa Brasilera*, Rocafuerte 1513 y Castillo, Brazilian, good; *Vegetariano*, Lalama y Bolívar, vegetarian meals and health food products. *Miramar*, 12 de Noviembre y Juan Cajas, Redondel de Cumandá, nr the bus terminal, good; *Casa del Cangrejo*, Los Guaytambos y Los Manzanos, Barrio Los Huertos, crabhouse.

Mexican at *Tacolandia*, Martínez y Bolívar, good; *El Coyote Disco Club*, Bolívar y

Guayaquil, Mexican-American food, disco at weekends. Pizzas at *Cominos*, Guayaquil 9-34 y Bolívar, home-made desserts; *Carlinho's*, Mariano Egüez y Bolívar, pizza and good set meals; *El Gaucho*, Bolívar y Quito, rec. Oriental at *Chifa Nueva Hongkong*, Bolívar 768 y Martínez, good; *Chifa Jao Fua*, Cevallos 756, popular. There are many good cafeterías and snackbars: eg *Las Cañas*, 13 de Abril y Mera, open 24 hrs; *Mama Miche*, 13 de Abril y Mera, Centro Comercial, 24 hrs.

● **Banks & money changers**
Banco de Guayaquil, Sucre y Mera, cash and TCs, cash advance on Visa, charges commission; **Banco del Pacífico**, Cevallos y Lalama, and Cevallos y Unidad Nacional, cash and TCs, cash advance on Mastercard, 3% commission; **Banco del Pichincha**, Lalama y Cevallos, on Parque Cevallos and Av El Rey y Av de las Américas, nr the bus terminal, cash and TCs. **Cambiato**, Bolívar 17-15, changes Visa and Amex cheques, cash, European and Latin American currencies, no commission, Mon-Fri 0900-1300 and 1430-1800, Sat 0900-1230. Money exchange at *Café Español*, Montalvo 607, Mon-Sat, 0900-1800.

● **Entertainment**
Peña del Tungurahua, Fri and Sat, in block 2 of the Centro Comercial. **Discos**: *Imperio Club*, Paccha y Saraguro, international music; *Villa Blanca*, Vía a Baños Km 5, international music, restaurant, snackbar; and others.

● **Post & telecommunications**
Post Office: Castillo y Bolívar, at Parque Montalvo, 0730-1930; fax service at EMS express mail office. **Emetel**, Castillo 03-31 y Rocafuerte, 0800-2130.

● **Shopping**
Supermercado, Centro Comercial Ambato, Parque 12 de Noviembre, or *Supermaxi*, Centro Comercial Caracol, Av de los Capulíes y Miravalles, in Ficoa. Good leather hiking boots from *Calzado Piedrahita*, Bolívar 15-08 y Lalama. Leather jackets, bags, belts on Sucre between Lalama and Eloy Alfaro and Vela between Lalama and Montalvo. Many stores for leather shoes along Bolívar.

● **Tour companies & travel agents**
Ecuadorean Tours, Cevallos 428, Amex agent, but no help with TCs, go instead to Banco del Tungurahua, Montalvo 603 y Rocafuerte. *Surtrek*, Av Amazonas 897 y Wilson, Quito, T 561-129, F 561-132, E-mail: surtrekl.surtrek.com.ec, is a climbing agency, arranges guided climbs of most major peaks, rents and sells equipment, manufactures good quality backpacks to order, German, Spanish, English spoken, member of Mountain Guide and Ecuadorian Ecotourism Associations, manages the only lodge in the Cuyabeno Wildlife

Reserve, rec. For airline reservations *TAME*, Sucre 09-62 y Guayaquil, T 826-601; *SAN/Saeta*, Bolívar 17-52, T 825-028.

● **Tourist offices**
Cetur, Guayaquil y Rocafuerte, T 821-800, open 0800-1200, 1400-1800, Mon-Fri, helpful.

● **Useful addresses**
Immigration: Av Fermín Cevallos y Juan León Mera, T 820-000, Edif Asociación de Empleados, p 2, Mon-Fri 0830-1230, 1430-1800.

● **Buses**
The main bus station is on Av Colombia y Paraguay, 2 km N from the centre, nr the railway station. Town buses go there from Plaza Cevallos in the city centre. To **Quito**, 2¾ hrs, US$1.90. To **Cuenca**, US$4.60, 7 hrs. To **Guayaquil**, 6½ hrs, US$6; to **Baños**, 45 mins, US$0.60. To **Riobamba**, US$0.80, 1 hr. To **Guaranda**, US$1.50, 1 hr. To **Latacunga**, ¾ hr, US$0.70. To **Santo Domingo de los Colorados**, 4 hrs, US$2.65. To **Tena**, US$4, 6 hrs. To **Puyo**, US$2.60, 3 hrs (see below). To **Macas**, US$3.30, 7 hrs. To **Esmeraldas**, US$4.80, 8 hrs. To **Loja**, US$6.90, 12 hrs. To **Machala** US$5.30, 7 hrs.

ROUTES To the E of Ambato, an important road leads to Salasaca, Pelileo, and Baños and then on along the Pastaza valley to Mera, Shell Mera, Puyo and Tena in the Oriente (see page 1131). In 1996 work was in progress to rebuild the road from Baños to Puyo and construction is expected to continue until 1998. It was open to vehicular traffic only Sun 1800 to Tues 0600. Buses to the Oriente take an alternate, longer routes the rest of the week. **NB** Motorists driving through Ambato to other cities should avoid going into the centre as traffic is very slow.

Salasaca is a modernized village 14 km (30 mins) from Ambato. The Salasaca Indians wear distinctive black ponchos with white trousers and broad white hats. This is said to reflect perpetual mourning for the death of their Inca, Atahualpa. Most are farmers, but they are best known for weaving *tapices*, strips of cloth with remarkable bird and animal shapes in the centre. A co-operative has fixed the prices on the *tapices* it sells in its store near the church. Throughout the village the prices are the same, somewhat cheaper than in Quito, and the selection is much better. If you have the time (4-6 weeks) you can order one to be specially made. You can watch the Indians weaving in the main workshop opposite the church.

Pelileo, 5 km beyond Salasaca, is a lively little market town which has been almost completely rebuilt since the 1949 earthquake (the fourth such disaster in its 400-year history). The ruins of Pelileo Viejo can be seen about 2 km E of the present site, on the N side of the road to Baños. This is the blue jean manufacturing capital of Ecuador. Market day is Saturday. The town's *Fiesta* is held on 22 July. There are regular buses from Baños making the 25-mins' journey.

From Pelileo, the road gradually descends to Las Juntas, the meeting point of the Patate and Chambo rivers to form the Río Pastaza, and where the road from Riobamba comes in. The road then continues along the lower slopes of the volcano Tungurahua to Baños (25 km from Pelileo). The road gives good views of the Pastaza gorge and the volcano.

BAÑOS

(*Pop* 12,984; *Alt* 1,800m; *Phone code* 03) This major holiday resort is bursting at the seams with hotels, *residenciales* and restaurants. Tourists come here for the hot springs, to climb Tungurahua, or to escape the Andean chill in the sub-tropical climate.

The Río Pastaza rushes past Baños to the Agoyán falls 10 km further down the valley, nearly dry now because of the construction of a hydroelectric dam. The rainy season is usually from May to Oct, especially July and August.

Places of interest

The **Basílica** attracts many pilgrims. The paintings of miracles performed by Nuestra Señora del Agua Santa are worth seeing; also a museum with stuffed birds and Nuestra Señora's clothing; open 0800-1600.

Three sets of thermal baths are in the town. The **Baños de la Virgen** are by the waterfall opposite the *Hotel Sangay*. The water in the hot pools is changed three times a week, and the cold pool is chlorinated (best to visit early am). The **Piscinas Modernas** are next door and are open weekends and holidays only. The **El Salado** baths are 1½ km out of town off the Ambato road; entrance to each, US$0.75; open 0400-1700. All the baths can be crowded at weekends, but the water is usually clean (its brown colour is the result of mineral content) and is almost always hot. There are also the **Santa Clara baths**, which are thermal, but only tepid. They are popular with children and have a gym and sauna.

Excursions

There are many interesting **walks** in the Baños area. You can cross the Pastaza by the San Francisco suspension bridge across the main road from the bus station. It is possible to recross the river by another suspension bridge, a round trip of 2-3 hrs. It is a 45-min hike to the new statue of the Virgin (good views of the valley). Take the first path on the left after the hospital.

To the **Bella Vista cross**, it is a steep climb from C Maldonado, 45 mins-1 hr. **Illuchi** village is a steep 1¾ hr climb with marvellous views over the valley and Tungurahua. The **San Martín shrine** is a ¾ hr walk away and overlooks a deep rocky canyon with the Río Pastaza thundering below. Beyond the shrine is a path to the **Inés María waterfall**, a thundering, but smelly, cascade. The round trip takes 2 hrs. 50m from Inés María is the **zoo**, with a large variety of animals but small cages; entry US$1.25.

Along the old road from Ambato is **Lligua**, a flowery little village straddling the Río Lligua at its junction with the Pastaza. **Runtún** is a village of a dozen mud dwellings, from which there is a splendid view of Tungurahua. It is a 5-6 hrs round trip. Cold drinks are sold at the billiard hall. There are two paths from Baños: one from S end of Calle 9, the other from Calle 6.

20 km from Baños on the Puyo road are the spectacular **Río Verde** falls, better known as El Pailón del Diablo. A bus goes from the Baños terminal, 30 mins, US$0.25. For a thrill, ride on the roof. A worthwhile trip is to cycle to Río Verde and take a bus back to Baños (see above for road conditions). It is possible to cycle to Puyo (4-5 hrs) but very difficult with panniers trying to get around the road-works. In Río Verde, cross the river and

take the path to the right after the church, then follow the trail down to the suspension bridge with a view of the falls.

● **Accommodation** *El Otro Lado*, on the other side of the bridge, beautiful *cabañas* run by an Israeli couple, surrounded by waterfalls and mountains, will be closed until the reopening of the road to Puyo. Enquire at *Café Cultura* in Quito.

Local festivals

Oct: *Nuestra Señora del Agua Santa* in Oct with processions, bands, fireworks, sporting events and a lot of general partying. **15 Dec**: the town's anniversary, when each *barrio* hires a *salsa* band and there are many processions. The following day there is a grand parade.

Local information

● **Accommodation**

A2 *Hostería Luna Runtún*, Caserío Runtún Km 6, T 740-882/3, F 740-376, also suites **L3**, rustic design, beautiful setting, gardens, very comfortable rooms with balconies, wonderful views of the town and the surrounding mountains, delicious meals on request US$15-25, excellent service, English, French and German spoken, hiking, horse riding and biking tours, laundry, sports and nanny facilities, videos, internet service, highly rec; **A3** *Villa Gertrudis*, Montalvo 2975, T 740-441, with lovely garden, pool, demi-pension, reserve in advance, rec.

B *Cabañas Bascún*, on the edge of town, nr El Salado baths, T 740-334, **A3** for a cabin for 5, quite comfortable, pools (cold), sauna, health spa (US$5 to non-residents), tennis, good restaurant and service; **B** *Monte Selva*, Halflants y Montalvo, T 740-566, private cabins, sauna, bar, restaurant, pool, excellent service.

C *Casa Nahuazo*, Vía El Salado, T 740-315, reported re-opened in 1997 after being closed for over a year, bath, hot water, clean, quiet country house 15-min walk from town with beautiful setting and views of Tungurahua, hot baths 2 mins away; **C** *Sangay*, Plazoleta Isidro Ayora 101, T 740-490, F 740-056, beautifully situated close to the waterfall, good restaurant, sauna, whirlpool, steam bath and pool all open to non-residents (US$5), tennis and squash courts, also more luxurious chalets, **A3**, a few rooms in the basement are cheaper, information and some equipment for expeditions to the jungle and volcanoes may be provided.

D *Flor de Oriente*, Ambato y Maldonado, T 740-418, F 740-717, inc breakfast, accepts credit cards, very good, can be noisy at weekends, electric showers; **D** *Isla de Baños*,

Halflants 1-31 y Montalvo, T/F 740-609, owned by Christian and Gabby Albers Weltz (see **Horse riding** below), nice atmosphere, garden with parrots and monkeys, rec; **D** *La Casa Amarilla*, on mountainside on path to Runtún, T 740-017, 15-mins' walk uphill from Baños, lovely and quiet, bed and breakfast, 3 rooms, longer stays encouraged; **D** pp *Palace*, opp *Sangay* (even closer to waterfall), T 740-470, good for groups, old-fashioned, choose an airy room at the front with balcony, nice garden and pool, Turkish bath, sauna and jacuzzi, open to non-residents for US$5, friendly, restaurant; **D** *Petit Auberge*, 16 de Diciembre y Montalvo, T 740-936, inc breakfast, hot showers, homely, rooms with fireplace, quiet.

E *Achupallas*, 16 de Diciembre y Ambato, T 740-389, clean, hot showers, laundry; **E** *Alborada*, on the plaza nr the Basilica, T 740-614, with shower, modern, safe, luggage store; **E** pp *Café Cultura*, Montalvo y Santa Clara, T 740-419, beautiful, colonial-style house, garden, 4 rooms with shared bath, excellent breakfasts, closed Thur, highly rec; **E** *El Castillo*, Martínez y Santa Clara, with bath, nr the waterfall, quiet, hot water, good beds, parking, restaurant, rec; **E** *Hospedaje Santa Cruz*, 16 de Diciembre y Martínez, T 740-648, with bath, hot water, modern, nice, noisy, rec; **E** *Hostal Magdalena*, Oriente y Alfaro, T 740-233, with bath, warm water, rec, closes at 2200; **E** *Hostal Plantas y Blanco*, 12 de Noviembre y Luis Martínez, Casilla 1980, T/F 740-044, European owners, laundry, change cash and TCs at good rates, excellent breakfast on roof terrace, good restaurant (*El Artesano*), steam bath 0730-1100, US$2, jeep, motorbike and mountain bike hire, fax service, luggage store, warmly rec; **E** *Las Esteras*, Montalvo 20-13 y 12 de Noviembre, hot showers, good beds, good value, breakfast; **E** *Las Orquídeas*, Rocafuerte y Halflants, T 740-911, with bath, good beds; **E** *Mario's Place*, JL Mera y Rocafuerte, **G** pp in dormitory, inc breakfast, comfortable, Mario speaks good English, offers rec jungle tours; **E** *Posada El Marqués*, Montalvo, T 740-053, spacious, bright rooms, hot water, bath, laundry, use of kitchen, garden, good restaurant; **E** *Venus & Bacchus*, Montalvo, entre Reyes y Pastaza, quiet, excellent breakfast, terrace and tea-room serving imported teas and delicious homemade cakes and pies, Canadian owners, massages by appointment, rec; **E** *Víctor's House*, Martínez y 16 de Diciembre, T 740-913, with bath, hot water, inc good breakfast, comfortable, restaurant with vegetarian food, rec.

F *Anita*, Rocafuerte y 16 de Diciembre, behind the market, moderately clean, use of kitchen, parking for motorcycles; **F** *El Oro*, Ambato y

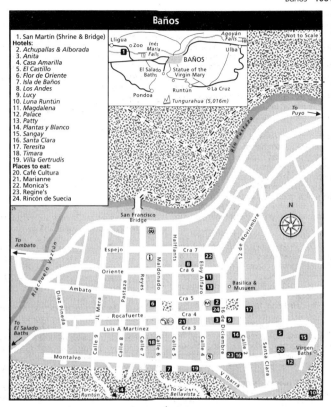

Baños

1. San Martín (Shrine & Bridge)
Hotels:
2. Achupallas & Alborada
3. Anita
4. Casa Amarilla
5. El Castillo
6. Flor de Oriente
7. Isla de Baños
8. Los Andes
9. Lucy
10. Luna Runtún
11. Magdalena
12. Palace
13. Patty
14. Plantas y Blanco
15. Sangay
16. Santa Clara
17. Teresita
18. Timara
19. Villa Gertrudis
Places to eat:
20. Café Cultura
21. Marianne
22. Monica's
23. Regine's
24. Rincón de Suecia

Mera, with bath, use of kitchen, laundry facilities, good value, rec; **F** *Lucy*, opp *Anita*, T 740-838, **G** without bath, comfortable beds, parking for motorcycles; **F** *Los Andes*, Oriente 1118 y Alfaro, without bath, 24-hr hot water, restaurant (*Le Gourmet*); **F** *Pensión Patty*, Alfaro 556, nr the market, T 740-202, basement rooms poor, otherwise good facilities, use of kitchen, laundry, comfortable and quiet, family-run, popular, safe, motorcycle parking; rec; **F** *Res Baños*, Ambato y Alfaro, T 740-284, good, washing facilities, luggage store, ask for a top room; **F** *Res El Rey*, Oriente y Reyes, nr the bus station, motorbike parking, rec; **F** *Res Kattyfer*, 16 de Diciembre entre Luis A Martínez y Montalvo, T 740-856, with bath, hot water, nice rooms, safe, helpful with local information, laundry facilities, rec; **F** *Res Timara*, Maldonado 381, T 740-709, hot water, use of kitchen, laundry facilities, nice garden, rec; **F** *Res Rosita*, opp

Bamboos Bar on 16 de Diciembre, T 740-396, hot water, big rooms with sitting room, kitchen for every 2 rooms, motorcycle parking, highly rec; **F** *Santa Clara*, 12 de Noviembre y Montalvo, T 740-349, without bath, rooms in new part with bath, **E**, or *cabañas*, hot water, use of kitchen, washing facilities, nice garden, motorcycle parking, good value, rec.

G *Familia Reyes y Alvarez*, J L Mera y Ambato, T 740-017, hot water, helpful; **G** pp *Res Dumary*, Halflants 656, T 740-314, hot water, only one shower, small rooms, Spanish lessons from English/German speaking daughter, rec; **G** *Res Teresita*, Parque de la Basílica, hot water, prices vary, shuts early.

● Places to eat

Many close by 2130. *Monica's*, Alfaro y Espejo, good, very slow service; *Closerie des Lilas*, Oriente 620 y Eloy Alfaro, excellent Fench cuisine at reasonable prices; *Donde Marcelo*, Ambato nr 16 de Diciembre, good breakfasts, friendly gringo bar upstairs; *Le Petit Restaurant*, 16 de Diciembre y Montalvo, Parisian owner, excellent food, US$7 for 2 courses, great atmosphere, also rents rooms; *Marianne*, on Martínez, opp Emetel, French and North African, excellent food, reasonable prices, closed Mon; *El Jardín*, 16 de Diciembre y Rocafuerte, good garden, vegetarian food, juices and bar; *Rincón de Suecia*, Carrera 5 y Parque Basílica and Rocafuerte y 16 de Diciembre, pizzas, good, Swedish and English spoken; *Regines Café Alemán*, 12 de Noviembre y Montalvo, good breakfasts, cakes, meeting place, very popular, expensive; *Mi Pan*, 16 Diciembre y Ambato, good meeting place, excellent fresh bread, pastries and coffee, 3 tables, not cheap; *Cafetería Chushi*, on Maldonado opp bus station, good and cheap breakfast and snacks, fast service, notice board; *Rico Pan*, Ambato y Maldonado, cheap breakfasts, hot bread, good fruit salads and pizzas.

La Abuela, nr Ambato 636, small, good pizzas, good breakfasts; next door is *Café Blah Blah*, good coffee, snacks, small, cosy, popular; *Café Cultura*, Montalvo y Santa Clara, book exchange; *Higuerón*, 12 de Noviembre 270 y Luis Martínez, open daily 0900-2230 except Wed, good European, local and vegetarian food, nice garden, friendly; *Café Hood*, 16 de Diciembre y Martínez, excellent vegetarian food, dishes around US$1.50, all water and milk boiled, English spoken, always busy, American/Ecuadorean run, owner Ray Hood also has bookstore, shows movies at cultural centre, closed Tues; next door is *Paolo's Pizzeria*, good pizzas, very friendly, nice ambience.

● **Banks & money changers**
Banco del Pacífico, Montalvo y Alfaro, changes TCs and cash, best rates for TCs, Mon-Sat from 0900-1800, very slow on Mon am. Banco del Pichincha, Ambato y Halflants; and Banco Tungurahua, Ambato y Maldonado, ground floor, both good for TCs.

● **Entertainment**
Peñas Ananitay, 16 de Diciembre y Espejo, good live music and dancing; *Ilusion Bar*, Montalvo y 16 de Diciembre, peña; *Hard Rock Café*, Eloy Alfaro nr the market, a favourite travellers' hangout, fantastic piña colada and juices; *Bamboos Bar*, Rocafuerte y 16 de Diciembre, good music, pool table, strong drinks. Films are shown at Centro Cultural, programme available at *Café Hood*.

● **Language classes**
Spanish is taught by José M Eras, Montalvo 5-26 y Santa Clara, T 740-453/740-232, English speaking retired teacher, US$4/hr; *Baños Spanish School*, run by Elizabeth Barrionuevo, at Calle 2 y Av Oriente, T 740-632, English and German speaking, US$4/hr, flexible and rec; Sandra Alvarez Solís, next to Familia Reyes Alvarez (see hotels) T 740-531, US$3.50/hr; Esther Romo, Maldonado opp bus terminal, T 740-703; Martha Vacas Flores, C 16 de Diciembre y Espejo, T 740-612, university trained, US$3/hr; *Instituto de Español Alternativo*, Montalvo y Alfaro, T/F 740-799.

● **Laundry**
Municipal washhouse next to the main baths, US$1.20 a bundle, or do it yourself for free. *El Marqués*, next to *Hotel Palace* has laundry service.

● **Security**
On all walks in the area (eg at the San Francisco bridge), beware robberies and unfriendly dogs. The police make late night passport checks in bars; without a passport you may spend a night in prison.

● **Shopping**
Street vendors sell canelazo, a sweet drink of aguardiente, naranjilla, water and cinnamon, and canario, aguardiente with egg, milk and sugar. Look out for jawsticking toffee (taffy, also known as melcocha de caña or alfeñique) made in ropes in shop doorways.

For painted balsa-wood birds see *El Chaguamango* shop by the Basílica, open 0800-1600. *Tucán*, Maldonado y Ambato, T 740-417/114, good for handicrafts. *Monilu T-shirts*, Rocafuerte 275 y Alfaro, large selection of good quality handicrafts and t-shirts, reasonable prices. Ask for the weaver José Masaquiza Caizabanda, Rocafuerte 2-56, who sells Salasacan weaving, gives demonstrations and explains the designs, materials, etc to visitors. *Galería de Arte Contemparáneo Huiliac Cuna*, next to *Café Cultura* on Montalvo, has modern art exhibits and a pizza restaurant, owner Marcelo Mazo organizes jungle trips.

Fruit and vegetable market on Sun am, and on Wed, in Plaza 5 de Junio on C Ambato.

Book exchange: *Café Cultura*, Artesanía *El Tucán*, Cafetería *Chushi*, Café *Hood*.

Camping equipment: Varoxi, Maldonado 651 y Oriente, T 740-051, also makes packs and jackets, and repairs luggage, rec.

Cycle hire: *Sierra Salva Adventures*, Maldonado y Oriente, T 740-298, for mountain bikes and motorcycles, owner Adrián Carrillo, reliable machines. Many other places rent bikes but quality is variable, US$4/day; check brakes and tyres, find out who has to pay for repairs, and insist on a puncture repair kit and pump.

● **Sports**
Horse riding: Christian and Gabby Albers Wetzl have excellent horses for rent, 6 hrs with a guide and jeep transport costs US$22 pp English, Spanish, German spoken, not rec for novices,

contact Christian at *Hostería & Cafetería Isla de Baños* (address in **Accommodation**). Also Caballos José, Maldonado y Martínez, T 740-746, good rates, flexible hours; and Angel Aldaz, Montalvo y JL Mera, US$3/hr (on road to the Virgin).

River rafting: is organized in Baños by Esther and Héctor Romo-Oester; trips down the Patate and Pastaza rivers, 1/2 day, US$30, full day, US$60. Check with Geotours, C Maldonado, Terminal Terrestre, or write to Casilla 18-02-1933, Baños, T 740-703.

● **Tour companies & travel agents**
Baños is a good meeting place to form a group to visit the Oriente. It is more interesting than Misahuallí, if you have to wait a few days, but can be more expensive. While the road to Puyo is closed, fewer tours are using this route. To avoid unscrupulous operators, only use qualified guides and seek advice, eg from the *South American Explorers Club*, or recommendations. In Baños, the Club says, mountain guides are not of the same standard regarding equipment or technique as in other climbing centres, even though they may be cheaper. For exceptions see below.

Guides in Baños: Carlos Saant Mashu, *Agencia de Viajes Kaniats Cia Ltda*, Residencial Santa Clara, T 740-349, knowledgeable, honest, rec, US$40/day inc transport. *Tsantsa Expeditions*, Oriente y Eloy Alfaro, T 740-957, have good jungle guides, Spanish-speaking only, and they can arrange fly-in trips, eg Sebastián Moya, a Shuar Indian, who will lead tours anywhere, US$45/day, not inc optional air travel. *Julio Verne*, Oriente 11-69 y Alfaro, T 740-249, climbing, trekking, equipment rental and sale, good laundry service US$3.25/load, Ecuadorean-Dutch run, rec.

Contactable through *Pensión Patty* (where equipment can be hired, helpful) are mountain guide Carlos Alvarez, who takes climbs in both the Sangay and Cotopaxi National Parks, and Fausto Mayorga, who is safe and good. *Geovanny Romo*, small, experienced agency on Maldonado, jungle tours and horseback tours from Baños. Juan Medinas and Daniel Vasco (based in Misahuallí), are at *Vasco Tours*, Eloy Alfaro y Martínez, T 740-017, PO Box 18-02-1970, 6-28 trips days available, also mountains and national parks, 6-8 people needed, excellent and plentiful food, up to 4 guides/tour.

NB There are four tour agencies in Baños who are recognized by Cetur and who use qualified guides; they are the above-mentioned Tsanta Expeditions, *Sangay Touring* (excellent trips down the Curaray, Amazonas y Cordero esquina, Quito, T 542-476, F 230-738), *Aventurandes* and *Explorsierra*, Rocafuerte y Eloy Alfaro, T 740-426/302. The above mentioned Juan Medinas of Vasco Tours is also recognized.

We have received some critical reports of tours out of Baños; in all cases, insist on a written contract and pay half after the tour. In late 1996 only 5 guides were authorized to enter Huaorani territory in the Oriente; Juan Medinas, Carlos Sevilla, Canadian Randy Smith, Juan Enomenga and Caento Padilla (both Huaoranis).

Guides and equipment for climbing: check all equipment carefully before hiring (see also page 1023). *Willie Navarrete*, at *Café Higuerón*, is highly recommended for climbing and is the only ASEGUIM member in Baños. Dosto Varela of *Expediciones Amazónicas*, in C Oriente, T 740-506. For a guide and pack animals enquire at Baños tourist office or Pondoa shop; guide and mule for 1 pack US$5, for 2 packs, US$7. Horses can be hired for US$0.90 an hour; contact Julio Albán, Segundo Sánchez or Víctor Barriga through the tourist office.

● **Tourist offices**
Tourist information office is nr the bus terminal, helpful, but not state-run. Good maps, town map US$1, hiking maps US$0.30, but distances and times reported incorrect; also high-pressure selling of jungle tours. Local artist, J Urquizo, sells an accurate Baños map, 12 de Noviembre y Ambato, T 740-589.

● **Buses**
The bus station is on the Ambato-Puyo road a short way from the centre, and is the scene of vigorous volleyball games most afternoons. To/from **Quito**, via Ambato, US$3, 3 1/2 hrs, Trans Baños 1/2 hourly; going to Quito sit on the right for views of Cotopaxi, buy tickets early for weekends and holidays. To **Ambato**, from the market place, 45 mins, US$0.60; to **Riobamba**, 1 hr, US$1; to **Latacunga**, 2-2 1/2 hrs, US$0.80; to **Puyo**, 2 hrs, US$1.50; pack your luggage in plastic as all goes on top of the bus. The road to Puyo is currently closed till 1998, except Sun 1900 to Tues 0600; this will affect services to **Tena**, 5 1/2 hrs, US$250, to **Misahuallí**, change at Tena, or at the Río Napo crossing, see page 1129 and **Macas**, 7 hrs, US$1.75 (sit on right).

CLIMBING TUNGURAHUA

From Baños it is possible to climb **Tungurahua**, 5,016m – part of Sangay National Park, entry US$7. A guide is highly recommended for this climb; see **Tour companies & travel agents** above. Depending on the season, you may need rubber boots to get to the refuge and crampons for the summit, check in Baños beforehand. The best season is Dec to Mar.

● **Access** Follow the road opposite the police control on the Ambato side of town, then take the first mule track to the right of the store and follow the path to **Pondoa**. If you are driving to Pondoa, take the main Ambato road and turn off to the left about 1 km from the town centre. The road runs parallel to the main road for several km before turning E into the mountains. Park at the shop in Pondoa. The walk from the shop to the beginning of the trail takes 30 mins. There is an occasional bus from Baños around 0900 to Pondoa; and a milk truck leaves at 0900 daily from *Pensión Patty* and *Explorsierra* to the Park office, 1 hr, US$1.75. Trucks return from Pondoa around 1300-1400. A pickup truck from Coop Agoyán on central plaza, C Maldonado, costs US$15 to the park entrance.

● **Accommodation** It is 3-4 hrs from the park entrance up to the Santos Ocaña *refugio* at 3,800m, US$3.50 pp, pay the warden at the refuge. Do not leave baggage unattended in the refuge. Take a sleeping bag and mat (a hammock can be slung), and food. There are cooking facilities at the *refugio*, but no eating utensils and rarely any lighting, so don't forget your torch. There is no heating and it can be cold.

ROUTES To the W of Ambato, a winding road leads up the valley of the Río Ambato, over a high area of desert called the Gran Arenal, past Carihuairazo and Chimborazo, and down through the Chimbo valley to Guaranda. This spectacular journey to the highest paved road in Ecuador takes about 3 hrs. It reaches a height of 4,380m and vicuñas can be seen.

GUARANDA

(*Pop* 15,730; capital of Bolívar Province) This beautiful, clean, quiet town, proudly calls itself 'the Rome of Ecuador' because it is built on seven hills. There are fine views of the mountains all around.

Places of interest

Locals traditionally take an evening stroll in the palm fringed main plaza, **Parque Libertador Simón Bolívar** around which are the Municipal buildings and a large **Cathedral**.

Towering over the city, atop one of the hills, is an impressive statue of '**El Indio Guaranga**', a local leader after whom the city may have been named; museum (entry free), art gallery and auditorium. To get there, take a taxi (US$0.80); or take a 'Guanujo' bus to the stadium, walk past the stadium to Av La Prensa and follow

it till you reach the first turning on the right (5-10 mins' walk).

The **Casa de la Cultura**, Manuela Cañizares 511, has a very small museum with pottery and a library.

Market days are Fri and Sat (larger), when many indigenous people trade at the Mercado Minorista (at the N end of Calle Azuay), by Plaza 15 de Mayo (9 de Abril y Maldonado) and at Plaza Roja (Av Gen Enríquez). Carnival in Guaranda is among the best known in the country.

Excursions

North of Guaranda, 1½ hrs by car along poor roads, is **Salinas de Guaranda** (*Pop* 5,000), noted for its geological formations, dairy cooperative (El Salinerito brand cheese) and sweaters. The nearby villages of Santiago and San Simón are picturesque.

● **Accommodation & transport E** *Hotel Refugio Salinas*, T 758-778 (Guaranda office: Gen Enríquez y Cándido Rada, Plaza Roja, T 980-703, F 982-140), run by the village cooperative, with bath, **F** with shared bath, **G** pp in dormitory, meals available. Transportes 10 de Noviembre buses from Verbo Divino School, Guaranda, daily about 0600 and 1400, return 0530 and 1300; taxi US$16.50 (US$23 wait inc).

There is an interesting church museum in **Huayco** (Santuario de Nuestra Señora de la Natividad), with interesting pre-Spanish artefacts, 30 mins' taxi ride (24 km) from Guaranda.

Local information
● **Accommodation**

B *La Colina*, high up on Av Guayaquil (No 117, T/F 980-666), bright and attractive, restful, covered swimming pool open to non-residents US$2, restaurant mediocre.

D *Res Bolívar*, Sucre 704 y Rocafuerte, T 980-547, intermittent hot showers, cheaper with shared bath, restaurant not open for breakfast, motorbike parking; **D** *Cochabamba*, García Moreno y 7 de Mayo, T 981-958, F 982-125, PO Box 01-02-0095, nice rooms, good service, cheaper with shared bath, good restaurant.

E *Matiaví*, Av Eliza Mariño 314, T 980-295, next to the bus station, clean, motorbike parking; **E** *Res Acapulco*, 10 de Agosto y Amazonas, basic, restaurant downstairs; next door is **E** *Santa Fé*, 10 de Agosto y 9 de Abril, T 981-526, cheaper with shared bath, very thin walls, clean, restaurant.

F *Pensión Rosa Elvira*, Sucre 606, shared bath,

basic; **F-G** *Res La Posada*, General Enríquez y 10 de Agosto, T 980-867, shared bath, cold water, not very clean, basic, motorbike parking.

● **Places to eat**
Marisquería El Conchal, Plaza Roja, not open in the evening, open Sun, good, cheap, family-run; *Chifa Hong Kong*, Parque Simón Bolívar, very good and cheap; *Amazonas*, 9 de Abril y García Moreno, family run, good set meals and à la carte, closed Sun, rec; *Rumipamba*, General Enríquez, Plaza Roja, fresh fruit juices, set meals and à la carte. A popular meeting place in the evenings is *Heladería El Pingüino*, next to *Chifa Hong Kong*.

● **Banks & money changers**
Filanbanco, on Av Kennedy, changes Amex and Visa TCs, 0900-1300 only.

● **Post & telecommunications**
Post Office: Azuay y Pichincha, Mon-Fri 0800-1200 and 1400-1800; fax service. Emetel, Rocafuerte 508 y Sucre, 0800-2200 daily; and at bus terminal.

● **Tour companies & travel agents**
Delgado Travel, on Parque Simón Bolívar at Moreno y Sucre, T 980-232, car hire, exchanges dollars cash, airmail service to the USA.

● **Transport**
Buses Terminal at Eliza Mariño Carvajal, on road to Riobamba and Babahoyo; if staying in town get off at Plaza Roja. Many daily buses to: **Ambato**, US$1.40, 2 hrs; **Riobamba**, US$1.40, 2 hrs; **Babahoyo**, US$1.65, 3 hrs, beautiful ride; **Guayaquil**, US$2.30, 4½ hrs; **Quito**, 3 companies run almost 30 daily services, US$3.85, 4-5 hrs. Taxi to **Riobamba** 1½ hrs, US$11.50.

AMBATO TO RIOBAMBA

After Ambato, the Pan-American Highway and railway pass apple orchards and onion fields. Between Ambato and Riobamba is **Mocha**, where guinea-pigs (*cuy*) are raised for the table and sold, roasted, by the road. On the houses a small crucifix crowns the roof, where figurines of domestic animals are also found. The Quito-Guayaquil railway's highest point, Urbina (3,609m) is between Cevallos and Riobamba. At the pass there are fine views in the dry season of Chimborazo and Carihuairazo.

● **Accommodation E** *Posada de la Estación (Youth Hostel)*, PO Box 523, Riobamba, T/F 942-215. The converted station at Urbina nr the Pan-American Highway at 3,609m, is a good place for acclimatization, clean, helpful, horses, trips and equipment arranged.

Riobamba (*Pop* 95,505; *Alt* 2,750m) is the capital of Chimborazo Province. It is built in the wide **Tapi Valley** and has broad streets and many ageing but impressive buildings. Because of its central location Riobamba is known as the heartland of Ecuador and it boasts the nickname 'La Sultana de Los Andes' in honour of its style and elegance.

Places of interest

The main plaza is **Parque Maldonado** around which are the **Santa Bárbara Cathedral**, the **Municipality** and several colonial buildings with arcades.

Four blocks NE of the railway station is the **Parque 21 de Abril**, named after the Batalla de Tapi, 21 April 1822, the city's independence from Spain. The park, better known as **La Loma de Quito**, affords an unobstructed view of Riobamba and Chimborazo, Altar and Tungurahua. It also has a colourful tile tableau of the history of Ecuador. **San Antonio de Padua** church, at the E corner of Parque 21 de Abril, tells bible stories in the windows.

There is a new market building, but at the Sat market buying and selling go on all over town. The 'tourist' market in the small plaza S of the Convento de la Concepción museum (see below) is a good place to buy local handicrafts. Since Indian-style clothing is also sold here, the plaza is full of colourful Indians from different parts of Chimborazo province, each group wearing its distinctive costume.

Two blocks E, there is a huge produce market in another plaza, also pottery, baskets, hats. All the streets in this area are filled with traders. There are also two markets on Wed, **Mercado La Condamine** and **Mercado San Alfonso**, which only sell local products. You should compare shop prices before buying from the markets.

Museums

The **Convento de la Concepción**, Orozco y España, entrance at Argentinos y J Larrea, restored by the Banco Central, now functions as a religious art museum; open

Tues-Sat 0900-1200 and 1500-1800, admission, US$1 for Ecuadoreans, US$1.65 for others. The guides are friendly and knowledgeable (tip expected). The priceless gold monstrance, Custodia de Riobamba Antigua, is the museum's greatest treasure, one of the richest of its kind in South America.

Museo Particular Familiar Córdoba-Román, Velasco 24-25 y Veloz, a private photo collection, paintings, sculptures, furniture and documents; open Mon-Fri, 1000-1300 and 1500-1700.

Excursions

Guano (*pop* 6,000) is a sisal-working and carpet-making town 10 km to the N, with prehistoric monoliths on a nearby hilltop. There are lovely views of El Altar from the plaza. A good handicraft shop is *Almacén Ciudad de las Fuentes*, in the plaza. You can have rugs made to your own design, Sun market very quiet other days.

● **Transport** There are frequent buses from NE Riobamba nr the road to Guano, US$0.15, or taxi, US$2.65.

After Guano you can take the bus on to Santa Teresita from where it is a 20-min walk downhill to **Balneario Los Helenes**, with 3 pools; 1 tepid, 2 cool. Camping is possible nearby.

Local festivals

2 Jan: *Fiesta de los Niños*, with street parades, music and dancing. **21 April**: independence celebrations lasting several days: hotel prices rise. **11 Nov**: *Foundation of Riobamba*.

Local information

● **Accommodation**

In Jan, schools from the coast bring children here on vacation and many hotels are full.

B *Hostería Abraspungo*, Km 3½ on the road to Guano, T 940-820, F 940-819, beautiful house in country setting, excellent restaurant, pool, horse riding; **B** *Chimborazo Internacional*, Los Cipreces y Argentinos, T 963-475, F 963-473, attentive service, spacious rooms, central heating, sauna, Turkish bath, jacuzzi, noisy discotheque, restaurant overpriced; nearby is **B** *El Galpón*, Argentinos y Zambrano, T 960-981, pleasant location on a hill overlooking the city, but a bit run-down; **B** *El Cisne*, Av Daniel L Borja y Duchicela, T 964-573, F 941-982, with bath, TV, restaurant, sauna and Turkish bath, modern; **B** *Hostería El Troje*, 4½ km

on the road to Chambo, T 960-826, nice rooms, good views, tourist centre, camping, good restaurant; **B** *Hostería La Andaluza*, Km 17, Panamericana Norte, T 904-223, views of Tungurahua and Altar, good walking, good restaurant.

C *Whymper*, Av Miguel Angel León 23-10 y Primera Constituyente, T 964-575, F 968-137, hot water, spacious rooms, safe parking, cafetería serves breakfast any time, but slow; **C** *Zeus*, Av Daniel L Borja 41-29, T 962-292, F 963-100, modern, comfortable, nice, 24-hr cafeteria, good restaurant, cash discounts.

D *Humboldt*, Borja 35-48 y Uruguay, T 961-788, clean, restaurant, parking; **D** *Manabí*, Colón 19-58 y Olmedo, T 967-967/305, clean, hot water, safe, restaurant, parking; **D** *Montecarlo*, Av 10 de Agosto 25-41 entre García Moreno y España, T/F 960-554, clean, comfortable, **E** without window, hot water, restaurant, English spoken; **D** *Riobamba Inn*, Carabobo 23-20 y Primera Constituyente, T 961-696, parking, restaurant, basic but clean, group discounts; **D** *Tren Dorado*, Carabobo 22-35 y 10 de Agosto, T 964-890, with bath, modern, reliable hot water, clean, nice, parking.

E *Hostal Ñuca Huasi*, 10 de Agosto 28-24 y Dávalos, T 966-669, **F** with shared bath, laundry facilities, noisy, poor beds, a bit dark and gloomy, hot water, safe parking, will arrange transport to the *refugio* on Chimborazo; **E** *Hostal Segovia*, Primera Constituyente 22-28 y Espejo, nr Parque Maldonado, T 961-259, cheaper with shared bath, clean, laundry service, good value, can arrange guides for Chimborazo; **E** *Imperial*, Rocafuerte 22-15 y 10 de Agosto, T 960-429, hot water 24 hrs, shared baths, expensive laundry, stores luggage, good beds, clean, comfortable, good views from the roof, loud music from bar on Fri and Sat nights, tours to Chimborazo arranged, US$20-25/car but don't pay in advance as they may be cancelled, also check their equipment.

E *Los Nevados*, Luis Costales 24-37 y Av Daniel L Borja, across from Parque Guayaquil, T 964-696, with bath, constant hot water, safe, clean, very good, laundry US$1.75/load, garage extra; **E** *Los Shyris*, 10 de Agosto y Rocafuerte 2160, T 960-323, F 967-934, nr the train station, cheaper rooms without bath on 4th floor, hot water 0500-1000 and 1500-2200, good rooms and service, rooms at the back are quieter, clean, nicely furnished, good value; **E** *Metropolitano*, Borja y Lavalle, T 961-714, nr the train station, with bath, central, traditional, large rooms, good beds, but noisy, insecure, water problems; **E** *Patricia*, Falconi y Brasil, T 961-525, quiet back street, family run, safe; **E** *Res Rocío*, Brazil 21-68, y Av Daniel L Borja, T 961-848, bath, warm water (but water problems

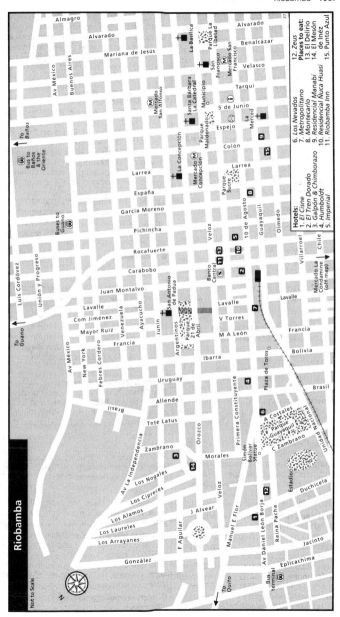

Riobamba

Not to Scale

To Baños

To Guano

To Quito

Hotels:
1. El Cisne
2. El Tren Dorado
3. Galpón Chimborazo
4. Humboldt
5. Imperial
6. Los Nevados
7. Metropolitano
8. Montecarlo
9. Residencial Manabí
10. Residencial Ñuca Huasi
11. Riobamba Inn

Places to eat:
12. Zeus
13. El Delirio
14. El Mesón
15. de Inéz
15. Punto Azul

1000 to 1800), towels and soap supplied, cheaper with shared bath, clean, quiet, parking.

F *Luzia Bártsch de Noboa*, Espejo 27-28 y Junín, T 961-205, Ecuadorian-Swiss run, no sign, clean, hot water intermittent, very comfortable, secure, car parking, helpful; **F** *Monterrey*, Rey Cacha 44-29 y Eplicachima, opp bus terminal, T 962-421, some with bath, hot water only in shared bath; **F** pp *Oasis*, Veloz 15-32 y Almargo, with bath, hot water, very clean, rec; **F** *Res Colonial*, Carabobo 21-62 y 10 de Agosto, opp train station, T 966-543, shared bath, very basic, run-down colonial house; **F** *Res Las Colinas*, Av Daniel L Borja y Pasaje El Espectador, nr the bus terminal, T 968-708, with bath, parking extra, basic.

G *Guayaquil*, Montalvo y Unidad Nacional, by the train station, T 964-512, shared bath, basic.

● **Places to eat**

None is open after 2200. *El Delirio*, Primera Constituyente 2816 y Rocafuerte (Bolívar's house in Riobamba), T 960-029, closed Mon and Sun, excellent steaks, highly rec; *El Mesón de Inéz*, Orozco y Morales, excellent; *Cabaña Montecarlo*, 10 de Agosto 25-45, T 962-844, Viennese atmosphere, excellent food and service, good breakfasts; *Tambo de Oro*, Zambrano y Junín, smart, expensive, excellent cuisine, good wine list; *La Biblia*, Primera Constituyente s/n, nr V Torres intersection, good regional cooking, moderate prices; *Parrillada de Fausto*, Uruguay y Av Daniel L Borja, good meat; *Che Carlitos*, Colón 22-44, between 10 de Agosto and Primera Constituyente, *parrilladas argentinas* and *empanadas*, expensive but authentic, *peña* at weekend; *Charlie's Pizzería*, García Moreno entre Guayaquil y 10 de Agosto, great pizza, vegetarian lasagne.

Chinese: *Chifa Joy Sing*, Guayaquil 29-27, behind the station, cheap, good; *Chifa China*, León Borja 43-49, good, cheap; *Chifa Internacional*, Veloz y Dávalos, good.

Seafood: *Punto Azul*, Colón y Olmedo, excellent, open 0800-1500, closed Sun; *La Fuente*, Primera Consituyente s/n y García Moreno, very good, reasonably priced, open 0900-1300, 1500-1900, rec; *El Portón Dorado*, Diego de Ibarra 22-50 y Av Daniel L Borja, set meals, à la carte, seafood, English and Italian spoken.

Snacks and coffee: *Café Montecarlo*, Av 10 de Agosto 25-40 y Moreno, popular, good breakfast, meals around US$2; *Gran Pan*, Moreno 22-46, nr Primera Constituyente, bakery and *cafetería*, good coffee and breakfast, opens at 0800; also at Borjas s/n, nr V Torres; *Caffe Johnny*, Espejo 22-45 y Primera Constituyente, breakfast from 0700, good, closed Sun; *Bambario*, 10 de Agosto y Rocafuerte, coffee bar, helpful, rents mountain bikes and runs tours

to Sangay National Park. Many snackbars along 10 de Agosto. Opp the railway station, on 10 de Agosto is *Sandy's Pastelería*, good for cakes and coffee, friendly owner. For early departures, there are several small cafés at the back of the bus terminal, open early till late, serving breakfast and other meals.

● **Banks & money changers**

Banco de Préstamos, Primera Constituyente y Espejo at Parque Maldonado, in a beautiful refurbished colonial building, cash and TCs, cash advances on Mastercard; **Banco del Pacífico**, García Moreno 11-40, cash advance on Mastercard, also at Miguel A León y Veloz; **Banco la Previsora**, Colón 22-35 y 10 de Agosto, cash advance on Visa; **Casa de Cambio Chimborazo**, 10 de Agosto 25-33, will change TCs, major European and American currencies, fair rates, Mon-Fri 0900-1330 and 1500-1800, Sat 0900-1300; **Delgado Travel** and **Coltur**, addresses below, cash only, good rates. Cash dollars are easy to change on the street and in shops showing *compra dolares* sign.

● **Entertainment**

Gens-Chop bar, León Borja 42-17 y Duchicela, good music, music and sport videos, open daily, popular, rec; *Peña* at *La Casa Vieja*, Orozco y Tarqui. The *Casa de la Cultura*, 10 de Agosto y Rocafuerte, has a good *peña* on Fri and Sat evenings. *Unicornio*, St Armand y Av Lizarzaburo, Vía Ambato Km 2, Piano Bar, Salsateca, cultural place, open Thur-Sat; *Pin Chop*, video bar at Borja 37-70; *Vieja Guardia* is a bar at Av Flor 40-43 y Av Zambrano; also *Juventus*, bar-disco at 10 de Agosto 26-57.

● **Post & telecommunications**

Post Office: 10 de Agosto y Espejo, closed Sat; also fax service. **Telephone**: **Emetel** at Tarqui entre Primera Constituyente y Veloz. National and international calls, 0800-2200; also at the bus terminal.

● **Shopping**

Porcelain masks and figurines at *Galerias Lys*, Argentinos y Juan Larrea, across from Convento de la Concepción Museum.

● **Sports**

Cockfights: at Coliseo San Pedro, Alvarado 33-36 y Chimborazo, 2 blocks from the Baños bus terminal, on Sat at 1800, US$0.50.

Mountain biking: *Pro Bici*, at Primera Constituyente 23-51 y Larrea, T 960-189/961-877, F 961-923, run by guide and mechanic, Galo J Brito, bike trips and rental, guided tours with support vehicle, full equipment, US$25-30 pp/day, excluding meals and overnight stays.

A variety of *pelota* games can be seen on Sun afternoons.

● **Tour companies & travel agents**
Metropolitan Touring, Av Daniel L Borja 37-64, T 969-600, F 969-601, tours, Western Union money transfers and airline tickets; *Coltur*, 10 de Agosto 24-55 y España, T/F 940-950, tickets and tours; *Alta Montaña*, Av Daniel L Borja 35-17 y Diego de Ibarra, T/F 942-215, PO Box 060123, trekking, climbing, cycling, running, bird watching, photography and horse riding tours in mountains and jungle, logistical support for expeditions, transport, equipment rental, souvenirs, English spoken; *Andes Trek*, Colón 22-25 y 10 de Agosto, T 940-964, F 940-963, climbing, trekking and mountain biking tours, transport, equipment rental, good rates, English spoken; *Expediciones Andinas*, Argentinos 38-60 y Zambrano, T 964-915, climbing expeditions; *Delgado Travel*, 10 de Agosto y Larrea, T 961-152, F 963-914, also handles airmail and giros to USA and Europe.

● **Tourist offices**
Cetur, 10 de Agosto 20-72 y 5 de Junio, T/F 941-213, open Mon-Fri 0830-1700, helpful, knowledgeable, English spoken.

● **Useful addresses**
Immigration: *Policia Nacional, Jefatura Provincial de Migración*, is at España 20-50, entre Guayaquil y Olmedo, open Mon-Fri 0800-1200 and 1400-1800.

Inefan: for information about Parque Nacional Sangay, Ministerio de Agricultura (MAG), Av 9 de Octubre y Quinta Macají, at the western edge of town, N of the roundabout at the end of Av Isabel de Godin, T 963-779; park people are only in the office in the early morning, be there before 0800. From town take city bus San Gerardo-El Batán.

● **Transport**
Trains To Durán (Guayaquil) daily except Tues and Thur at 0600, US$15 for foreigners; arrives Alausí 0930 (US$8), Bucay 1330 (US$12), get out at Bucay and change to bus to avoid arriving in Guayaquil in the dark. Interruptions to service occur. Tickets for Durán go on sale at 0530, but get there at 0500. The station is closed on Sun; for train information T 969-972/930-126. If time is limited, take the most spectacular section of the railway, take a bus before 0730 to Guayaquil and get out at Bucay (US$2.50), catch the train to Alausí, change to Riobamba by bus. **Train** to **Quito**, 0900 Fri (but not reliable), from Quito Sat 0800, US$10 for foreigners, 8 hrs; tickets sold on day of departure around 0800. You can ride on the roof on both services; sit as far back as possible to avoid oily exhaust. Be prepared for cold, wet and fruit-throwing farmers.

A privately-owned *autoferro* runs from Quito, details from Metropolitan Tours, rec, or other travel agencies. The railway administration office is on Espejo, next to the Post Office, during office hours, T 960-115.

Buses Terminal Terrestre on Eplicachima y Av D L Borja for buses to Quito, Guayaquil, Ambato, etc, but buses to Baños and the Oriente leave from the Terminal Oriental, Espejo y Córdovez. Taxi from one terminal to the other, US$0.75. **Quito**, US$2.95, 3½ hrs, about every 30 mins; to **Guaranda**, US$1.40, 2 hrs, road, paved to San Juan, crosses a 4,000m pass, sit on the right, beautiful views; to **Ambato**, US$0.85, 1 hr, sit on the right; to **Babahoyo** via Guaranda, US$3, 5 hrs; to **Alausí**, US$1.15, 2 hrs; to **Huigra**, US$2.15, 3 hrs. To **Cuenca**, 6 a day via Alausí, 5½ hrs, US$4. This road is paved but landslides are a constant hazard and the road is often under repair. For a day trip to **Ingapirca** (see page 1072), take the 0530 bus to Cuenca, getting off at El Tambo at about 1000. Bus back to Riobamba passes through El Tambo at about 1600; last one about 1930. Bus to **Santo Domingo**, hourly, US$3.30, 5 hrs; to **Baños**, US$1, 1 hr. To **Huaquillas** at 2100 with Patria, avoiding Guayaquil, daily except Tues and Sat, US$5.45, 9 hrs; also with Panamericana at 2200, 8 hrs, US$8. To **Guayaquil**, about 35 a day, first one leaves at 0600, US$4, 4½ hrs, the trip is really spectacular for the first 2 hrs.

CLIMBING AROUND RIOBAMBA

Chimborazo

At 6,310m, this is a difficult climb owing to the altitude. No one without mountaineering experience should attempt the climb, and rope, ice-axe and crampons must be used. It is essential to have at least 1 week's acclimatization above 3,000m. The best seasons are Dec and June-September.

● **Guides** There is a provincial association of mountain guides, Asociación de Andinismo de Chimborazo, which registers approved guides. **Enrique Veloz Coronado**, technical adviser of the Asociación de Andinismo de Chimborazo, Chile 33-21 y Francia, T 960-916, best reached after 1500, very helpful, his sons are also guides and work with him. **Marcelo Puruncajas** of Andes Trek (see **Tour companies** above), member of ASEGUIM, highly rec, speaks English, when not leading tours uses good guides, also offers trekking, 4WD transport and mountain biking. **Silvio Pesántez**, Argentinos 1140 y Darquea, PO Box 327, T 962-681, member of ASEGUIM, an experienced climber and adventure-tour leader, speaks French, rec; **Marco Cruz** of Expediciones Andinas (see above), T 962-845 (home), rec, he is a certified guide of the German Alpine Club and considered among the best and most expensive guides; **Rodrigo Donoso** of Alta Montaña (see above), for climbing and a variety of trekking and horse riding trips, speaks English. Trekking including guide, transport, equipment, shelter and food US$40-50 pp/day, min 2 persons; climbing with guides who belong to the Asociación de Andinismo about US$70 pp/day; overall cost for 2 between US$250-400. Sr Héctor Vásquez at Colegio Nacional Bolívar, Ambato, has helped many expeditions with travel arrangements and information; he is a top-grade mountaineer.

The **Fiesta de las Nieves** is celebrated at the 4,800m shelter on the second or third Sun in December. There is much music and dancing, although no folkloric roots, but at least buses from Riobamba go up to the mountain. There are two routes up the mountain:

The Southwest Face

● **Access** There are no direct buses so arrange with a travel agency, or a taxi from Riobamba; US$35 for 5-6 hrs, US$40 return next day or later, US$21 one way. There are usually several taxis and other vehicles at the car park in the early afternoon. Rec drivers are Segundo López, Taxi 89, at the taxi stand in Mercado Santa Rosa, Av Guayaquil y Rocafuerte, Riobamba, or Juan Fuenmayor, Veloz 25-31 y España, or arrange through Riobamba hotels, eg *Imperial*. You can also take a bus to San Juan village and hitch from there (better chance at the weekend). It is 56 km from Riobamba and takes about 1½ hrs.

● **Accommodation** The road ends at 4,800m, at the Hermanos Carrel refuge: guard, bunk beds with mattresses for 8, 1 private room for 2, dining area, cooking facilities, running water, toilet, electricity, bring food and warm gear, it gets very cold at night. In about 45 mins you can walk up to the Edward Whymper refuge at 5,000m at the foot of the Thielman glacier. The same facilities are available here, with capacity for 40, in 5 separate rooms. Both refuges are managed by Alta Montaña, US$0.50 fee for a day visit; overnight stays are US$10 but card carrying members of a club or Youth Hostel Association pay less. Take padlock for the small lockers under the bunks; the guards also have a locked room for valuables, and you can leave your gear with them.

   NB Beware of theft at the refuge or in your car at 4,800m. Also beware of robbery when driving up to the refuge. Check the situation with *Alta Montaña* in Riobamba, or *Safari Tours* in Quito (see page 1022).

The Northwest Face (Pogyos Route)

● **Access** Take the Guaranda bus from Ambato along the new paved road or a truck along the spectacular old road (50 km) to the valley of Pogyos. At Pogyos (4,000m) there is a house with a metal roof where you can hire mules for US$4 each to carry your luggage. Beware of pilfering from your bags on the ascent. Walk about 3 hrs to the Fabián Zurita refuge (4,900m) which is uninhabitable. From the refuge to the summit is about an 8-hr climb and 3-4 hrs descent. It's advisable to start at 2330-2400 at the latest. Take tents and water (obtainable at Pogyos, containers in Ambato). (We are grateful to Enrique Veloz Coronado, page 1069, for much of this information.)

   From Riobamba to the NW face, a trip can be made by jeep via San Juan and a road to Arenal, which is W of Pogyos. This road also permits a round-trip Riobamba-Chimborazo-Ambato.

El Altar and Sangay

Guides and horses to El Altar can be hired; the approximate cost per day in 1996 was US$60 for a guide, US$5 per mule, US$5 per porter. Because of mudslides, the track is hazardous and should not be done alone. Consult the National Park Office about conditions, they are in radio contact with the Guardería at Releche.

● **Access** Travel to Penipe by bus from Baños or Riobamba/Ambato, then to Candelaria by truck, or by bus which passes between 1200 and 1400. Walk out of the village, cross the bridge and go up about 2 km to the park station, a green building with a National Park sign, where you pay your entrance fee of US$7. In Penipe ask for Ernesto Haro, who will take you to the station in his jeep (US$8 one way) and pick you up from there at a pre-arranged time.

● **Accommodation** You can stay in the park station overnight, although it is not a *refugio*; US$0.50, beds, warm water, shower, cooking facilities and friendly keeper. It is not always open, so it's a good idea to ask in Riobamba beforehand at the Ministry of Tourism or the Inefan office. *Hacienda Releche* rents horses and is building rooms.

For **Sangay** (see page 1133), take a taxi to Alao and hire guides or carriers of food, tents, etc there; ask for Tom Gillespie. Remember you have to pay for and organize the food for your porters separately, otherwise you have to pay them a lot more. Make sure the fee covers the return journey as well. For information go to the Inefan offices (see **Useful addresses** above). **NB** Sangay is one of the most active volcanoes in the world and can be dangerous even on quiet days.

CAJABAMBA

A small, rather poor town. In 1534 the original Riobamba was founded on this site, but in 1797 a disastrous earthquake caused a large section of the hill on the N side of the town to collapse in a great landslide, which can still be seen. It killed several thousand of the original inhabitants of Riobamba and the town was moved almost 20 km NE to its present site. The new Riobamba has prospered, but Cajabamba has stagnated. A colourful, Colta Indian market on Sun is small but uncommercialized and interesting.

● **Transport & places to eat** The town is easily reached by bus from Riobamba, 25 mins, US$0.15. There are few restaurants out of town on the Panamericana towards Cuenca.

ROUTES A fairly good dirt road leaves the Pan-American Highway 6 km N of Cajabamba, to the W. It is one of the oldest of the coast-Sierra routes and links Cajabamba with Guaranda and Babahoyo. 5 km S of Cajabamba, a paved highway branches SW to Pallatanga, Bucay, Milagro and Guayaquil.

CAJABAMBA TO GUAMOTE

Road and rail skirt the shores of **Laguna de Colta**, just after the fertile Cajabamba valley. The lake and surroundings are very beautiful. At the edge of the village along the main road on the shore of Laguna de Colta is a small chapel, **La Balbanera**, dating from 1534, making it the oldest church in Ecuador, although it has been restored several times because of earthquakes.

28 km S of Cajabamba is **Guamote** (3,056m); interesting, colourful market on Thur with lots of animals and few tourists. Good half day walks in the area. A road to Macas is under construction (see page 1132). Sit at the front of the bus for a splendid view of the volcanoes.

● **Accommodation & places to eat F** *Hostal Turista*, at the railway station; **F** *Ramada Inn*, Vela y Riobamba, T 916-242, cold water, friendly, helpful, new. There are some places to eat nr the station.

● **Transport** Lots of buses from Riobamba, especially on Thur.

Palmira is a windswept village S of Guamote, close to the highest point on the Riobamba-Guayaquil railway. Between here and Guamote the newly-fixed dirt road to Osogoche, 32 km, is well-signed. A wild, cold, beautiful area of lakeland, it has good hiking and camping. Arrange pack animals and guides with the local community leader; take food and camping equipment.

Tixan has a beautifully restored church and many old houses. It is the home of many workers in the nearby sulphur mines. The *finados* on 2 Nov are very colourful.

The Southern Sierra

THE COLONIAL CITY of Cuenca, built on the site of an older, indigenous settlement, is the focal point of the region. A pleasant climate and magnificent mountain scenery make the Southern Sierra ideal walking country, while undisturbed *páramo* and cloud forest are home to many birds and other wildlife.

ALAUSI

84 km S of Riobamba (*Pop* 5,500), Alausí is the station where many passengers join the train for the amazing descent to Bucay. Sun market, in the plaza by the church, just up the hill from the station; *fiesta* late June.

- **Accommodation** **E** *Americano*, García Moreno 159, T 930-159, modern, private bath, hot water, rec; **E** *Gampala*, 5 de Junio 122, T 930-138, with bath, good; **E** *Res Alausí*, Orozco y 5 de Junio, T 930361, nr the station, with bath, **F** without, comfortable, restaurant; **E** *Res Tequendama*, inc breakfast, shared bath, hot water, quieter rooms upstairs, rec; **F** *Panamericano*, nr the bus stop, T 930-156, with and without bath, quieter at the rear, hot water, food cheap and good value; **G** *Res Guayaquil*, C Eloy Alfaro 149, behind station, very noisy, basic, not too clean.

- **Places to eat** *Momentos Bar*, 5 de Junio, at the end away from the station, good; *San Juan*, nr the station, on main street, owner speaks Eng-

lish, good; *Danielito*, opp Tequendama, good, cheap, will cook vegetarian meals; *El Flamingo*, behind the *Tequendama*, good set meals.

- **Transport Trains** Train at 0900-0930 daily except Tues and Thur (not Mon or Wed in other direction), 7-9 hrs to Durán, US$12; 4 hrs to Bucay, US$10; to Huigra, US$8. T 930-126 to check if the train is running; tickets go on sale from 0730. If the train to Durán is delayed and you may miss the last ferry to Guayaquil (2200), get out at Bucay and take a bus to Guayaquil bus station. From Riobamba to Alausí, US$8. **Buses** From Riobamba, 1½ hrs, US$1, 84 km, all paved, through a windswept plain, pine forest and, after Km 72, steep hills and valleys. To **Quito**, from 0600 onwards, about 20 a day, 5½ hrs, US$3.10; often have to change in Riobamba. To **Cuenca**, 4 hrs, US$3.20; to **Ambato** hourly, 3 hrs, US$1.35. Coop Patria has a small office where you can buy bus tickets to Guayaquil, Cuenca, or Riobamba. Other cooperatives have no office, but their buses pass through town, some at the highway and others outside the *Hotel Panamericano*.

INGAPIRCA

Ecuador's most important Inca ruin lies 5½ km E of Cañar, at 3,160m. The central structure is an *usnu* platform probably used as a solar observatory. It is faced with fine Inca masonry. Nearby is the a throne cut into the rock, the **Sillón de Inga** (Inca's Chair) and the **Ingachugana**, a large rock with carved channels. A 10-min walk away from the site is the **Cara del Inca**, or 'face of the Inca', an immense natural formation in the rock looking over the landscape.

Entry to the site is US$4, including museum. Open Mon-Sat 0900-1700; they sell a guide book, US$0.80, and will look after your belongings. An audio-visual guide in English is available, and there are guides at the site.

On Fri there is an interesting Indian market at Ingapirca. There is a good co-operative craft shop next to the church.

Local information
- **Accommodation & places to eat**
C *Posada Ingapirca*, 500m from the site, T (07) 838-508, F 832-340, 8 luxurious rooms with bath, inc breakfast, excellent restaurant, in a converted farm, good service, warmly rec; **F** *Inti Huasi*, in the village, nice rooms, quiet, hot water, good restaurant, rec. Ask at the museum and for permission to stay overnight; camping

at the site is possible, there is a small café opp the museum and in the village there's a *chifa*.

In El Tambo: the nearest town to Ingapirca (see **Transport** below): **F** *Pensión Ingapirca* on main street, nr the service station at the N end, hot water, not too clean but friendly, very noisy, can leave luggage for a small fee; *Restaurant El Turista*, good and cheap food but unfriendly; also good is *Restaurant Ingapirca* and *Restaurant Jesus del Gran Poder*, at the truck stop on the hill 400m N of town. There is a small Sat food market.

● **Transport**
A direct bus from the Terminal Terrestre in Cuenca leaves at 0900 and 1000, returning at 1300 and 1500, 2 hrs, US$1.60, with Transportes Cañar. Organized excursions and taxi tours from Cuenca US$45 from bus terminal. Any Guayaquil, Riobamba or Quito bus passes El Tambo, 2 hrs, US$1.30. Coop Cañar runs hourly buses Cañar-El Tambo from 0600, US$0.50. There is a daily 0600 bus from Cañar direct to Ingapirca (slower, rougher road than from El Tambo). From the plaza on the Panamericana in El Tambo, morning trucks and Transportes Juhuay buses pass the railway and continue to the ruins. Taxi El Tambo-Ingapirca US$5; camionetas US$1.30, beware of overcharging. Taxis can also be caught at the railway station. Last colectivos leave Ingapirca at 1800 for El Tambo. It is a beautiful 2½-hr walk from Ingapirca to Cañar. The start of the road is clearly signposted, along the main street.

INCA TRAIL TO INGAPIRCA

The 3-day hike to Ingapirca on an Inca trail starts at **Achupallas**, 25 km from Alausí. The IGM map (Juncal sheet, 1:50,000) is very useful; also a compass. The name Ingapirca does not appear on the Cañar 1:50,000 sheet and you may have to ask directions near the end. There are persistent beggars, especially children, the length of the hike. If you want to give them something, take pencils or something useful. Good camping equipment is essential. Take all food and drink with you as there is nothing along the way. A shop in Achupallas sells basic foodstuffs. The route is described in the *Ecuador Handbook* and Rob Rachowiecki, Mark Thurber and Betsy Wagenhauser's *Climbing and Hiking in Ecuador*.

● **Transport** A truck leaves Alausí almost every day, between 0900-1200 from outside *Residencia Tequendama*, US$0.40 to Achupallas. The trip takes a couple of hours and is spectacular in its own right.

SOUTH TO CUENCA

ROUTES The Pan-American Highway and railway S of Sibambe to Cuenca run through mountainous country and high above the valleys of the W-bound rivers. The railway was officially closed in Mar 1995 after flooding. The countryside is poor, dry, chilly and wind-swept, and the Indians withdrawn and wrapped-up. Near Zhud and Cañar, more Indians, dressed in black, are seen. At Zhud a paved road runs to Cochancay and La Troncal in the coastal lowlands, from where there are paved roads to Guayaquil and Machala. Towards Cuenca the road loses height and the land is more intensively farmed. There are excellent roads linking Quito-Guayaquil and Guayaquil-Cuenca, which meet at El Triunfo on the coastal plain.

CHUNCHI

At 2,300m, 37 km S of Alausí along the Pan-American Highway and one stop from Sibambe on the line to Cuenca, it is a friendly village with a Sun market.

● **Accommodation & places to eat** **F** *Res Patricia* just off the main plaza, shared bath, basic, clean, beware of overcharging; **G** *Res Carmita*, clean, basic, hot water, nr the station. Many restaurants along the highway.

● **Transport** Buses from the plaza, several daily, to Riobamba.

CAÑAR

(*Pop* approx 20,000; province 189,347) 67 km N of Cuenca, 36 km N of Azogues, Cañar is a pleasant colonial town, very much the indigenous capital of the province, set in a good area for walking. Its famous double-faced weaving is now difficult to find, although prisoners in the jail (Centro de Rehabilitación Social) sell backstrap weavings to pay for food. Several shops sell Cañar hats and the Sun market is very colourful.

● **Accommodation & places to eat** **F** *Res Mónica*, main plaza, T 235-486, often full, clean, shared bath, hot water, laundry facilities, owner's daughter offers tour service to Ingapirca, 2 hrs, US$2; **F** *Res Cañar*, T 235-682, small. *Los Maderos Restaurant*, nr the centre; *Chifa Florida*, on plaza, good, cheap.

● **Buses** Every 30 mins to the Terminal Terrestre in Cuenca, US$0.80, 2 hrs; also to Quito and El Tambo (7 km).

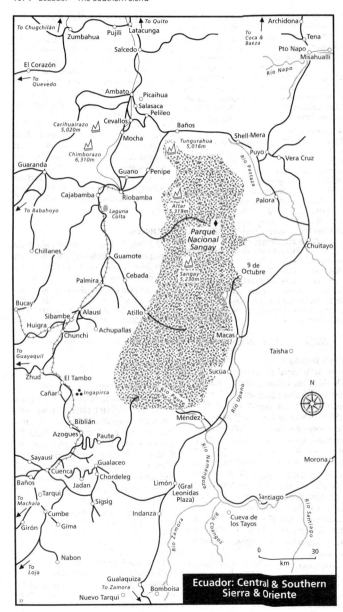

Ecuador: Central & Southern Sierra & Oriente

Between Cañar and Azogues is **Biblián** with a sanctuary, La Virgen del Rocío, built into the rocks above the village. Pleasant walk up with impressive views of the river valley and surrounding countryside.

AZOGUES

(*Pop* 21,060) The city is the administrative capital of the province, and a centre of the panama hat industry. The *sombrerías* are very happy to show visitors, but rarely sell, their hats; eg *La Sin Rival*, C Luis Cordero y 3 de Noviembre, or *Cahuzhun*, near the plaza, highly rec. The market is colourful and beautifully situated on the hill from the Panamericana to the city's huge church and convent San Francisco de la Virgen de las Nubes. Some of the older buildings around the plaza still have traditional painted ceilings over the pavements.

● **Accommodation & transport E** *Charles 1*, Solano y Rivera, nr plaza, T 241-364, clean, simple; *Charles 2*, Serrano y Abad, T 241-883, 1 block E of the plaza, **E** pp with bath; *Chicago*, 3 de Noviembre y 24 de Mayo, T 241-040, the best. 45 mins by bus to Cuenca (31 km).

CUENCA

Cuenca (*Pop* officially 194,981, more like 250,000; *Alt* 2,530m; *Phone code* 07), is capital of the province of Azuay and the third largest city in Ecuador. It was founded by the Spaniard Gil Ramírez Dávalos in 1557 on the site of the Inca settlement of Tomebamba. Much of its colonial air has been preserved, with many of its old buildings constructed of the marble quarried nearby and recently renovated. The climate is spring-like, but the nights are chilly.

Places of interest

On the main plaza, **Parque Abdón Calderón**, are the Old Cathedral, **El Sagrario**, begun in 1557, and the immense 'New' **Catedral de la Inmaculada**, started in 1885. It contains a famous crowned image of the Virgin, a beautiful altar and an exceptional play of light and shade through modern stained glass. Sun evening worship is recommended.

Other churches which deserve a visit are **San Blas**, **San Francisco**, **El Cenáculo**, and **Santo Domingo**. Many churches are open at irregular hours only and for services. The church of **El Carmen de la Asunción**, close to the SW corner of La Inmaculada, has a flower market in the **Plazoleta El Carmen** in front. **Turi church and mirador**, S of city on Av Fray Vicente Solano, beyond the football stadium, a 40-min walk or take a bus, has great views and a tiled panorama explains what you see. There are attractive walks along country lanes further S.

There is a colourful daily market in Plaza **Plaza Cívica** where pottery, clothes, guinea pigs and local produce, especially baskets, are sold. Thur is the busiest.

Museums

The **Banco Central 'Pumapungo'** museum, Larga y Huayna Capac, on the edge of town is at the Tomebamba site where excavations are continuing. Open Sat 0900-1200, Tues-Fri 0900-1800, US$1.50; entrance is on the far left of the building. It contains all the pottery, bones, statues etc found at the site. Padre Crespi used these artefacts to support his theory that the Phoenicians reached Cuenca via the Amazon. His statue stands in Plaza María Auxiliadora. It is believed that Tomebamba was the principal Inca administrative centre in Ecuador. There are book and music libraries, free cultural videos and music events. In the new Banco Central building (beside the old) there are museums of local and religious art and ethnography. About 300m from Pumapungo, at Larga 287, there are excavations at the Todos Los Santos site, which reveal traces of Inca and Cañari civilizations and show how the Spanish reused the stonework; open Mon-Fri, 0800-1600.

The **Instituto Azuayo de Folklore**, Escalinata 303 y Larga, extension of Hermano Miguel, open Mon-Fri 0800-1200, 1400-1800, has an exhibition of popular art and a library. It also supports research and promotes sales for artesan workers; rec craft shop, good information.

Museo de las Culturas Aborígenes, Av 10 de Agosto 4-70, entre F Moscoso y J M Sánchez, T 811-706, a good private collection of precolumbian archaeology, in the house of Dr J Cordero López; guided tours in English, Spanish and French, US$2, open Mon-Fri 0900-1230, 1530-1830, Sat 0900-1230, but phone in advance (taxi from centre US$1.50).

Museo del Monasterio de las Conceptas, Hermano Miguel 6-33 entre Pdte Córdova y Juan Jaramillo, T 830-625, well-displayed collection of religious and folk art housed in a cloistered convent founded in 1599. Open Tues-Fri 0900-1600, Sat 0900-1230, US$2.

Museo de Arte Moderno, Sucre y Talbot, on Plaza San Sebastián, often has shows of artists from around the world. There's a small museum, art gallery and bookshop in the **Casa de la Cultura**, Luis Cordero y Sucre (second floor). In the courtyard are niches each containing a statue of a saint. A lovely, restored colonial house is the **Casa Azul**, Gran Colombia y Pedro Aguirre, housing some small shops, restaurant and a little museum, cultural visits can also be arranged.

The **Casa de los Canónigos**, C Luis Cordero 888 opp Parque Calderón, houses the **Galería del Portal**, T 833-492, original Latin American works of art for exhibition and sale. **Museo Remigio Crespo Toral Municipo**, C Larga 7-27 y Pres Borrero, open Mon-Fri 0930-1300, 1500-1800, various collections housed in a beautifully-restored colonial mansion, free admission, nice café in basement.

Excursions

There are sulphur baths at **Baños**, with a domed, blue church in a delightful landscape, 5 km SW of Cuenca. These are the hottest commercial baths in Ecuador. Above *Hostería Durán* are two separate complexes of warm baths, *Marchan* and *Rodas*: the lower one is better, US$0.80 for private bathroom, US$0.40 for swimming pool; the upper one also costs US$0.40, neither is very clean. They are very crowded at weekends.

● **Accommodation** At the baths is **B** *Hostería Durán*, Km 8 Vía Baños, T 892-485, F 892-488, with a restaurant, its own well-maintained, very clean pools, US$1.60 for non-residents, also tennis courts, steam bath US$3, camping is allowed. There are also four residencias, all **F**.

● **Transport** Buses marked Baños go to and

from Cuenca every 5-10 mins, 0600-2330, US$0.15; buses turn around at the airport, pass the front of the Terminal Terrestre, cross the city on Vega Muñoz and Cueva, then down Todos los Santos to the river, along 12 de Abril and onto Av Loja to the end where it joins Av de Las Américas. Taxis cost US$2.40, or walk 1½ hrs.

Local festivals

On the Sat before Christmas day there is an outstanding parade: *Pase del Niño Viajero*, probably the largest and finest Christmas parade in all Ecuador. Children and adults from all the *barrios* and surrounding villages decorate donkeys, horses, cars and trucks with symbols of abundance. Little children in colourful Indian costumes or dressed up as Biblical figures ride through the streets accompanied by Indian musicians. The parade starts at about 0800 at San Sebastián, proceeds along C Simón Bolívar, past the Plaza Calderón at about 1030 and ends at San Blas.

At **New Year's Eve**, the festivities include the parading and burning at midnight of effigies called *Años Viejos* (some political, some fictional) which symbolize the old year. The festivities seem to go on until Lent and there are several smaller Pase del Niño parades between Christmas and Carnival.

On **6 Jan** is the *Festival de Los Inocentes*, and **10-13 April** is the *Foundation of Cuenca*. On **Good Friday** there is a fine procession through the town to the Mirador Turi. Cuenca hosts an internationally famous art competition every 2 years, which begins in **Nov** and ends April or May, coordinated by the Museo de Arte Moderno.

June: *Septenario*, the religious festival of Corpus Christi in June, lasts a week. On Plaza Calderón a decorated tower with fireworks attached, known as the 'vaca loca' or mad cow, is burnt every night after a mass and hundreds of hot air paper balloons are released. There are also dozens of dessert sellers and games in the streets.

3 Nov: is *Independence of Cuenca*, with street theatre, art exhibitions and nighttime dances all over the city.

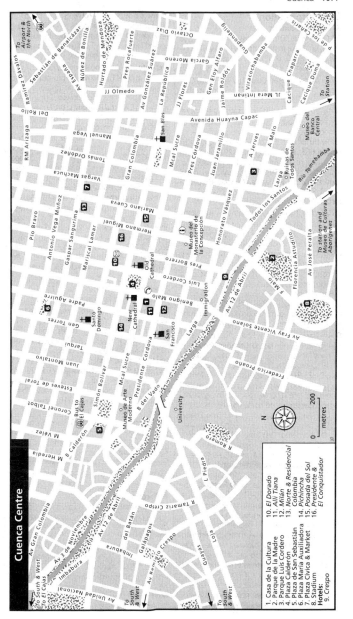

Cuenca Centre

To Airport & the North
To South & West
To El Cajas
To South & West

Av Gran Colombia
Ramírez Dávalos
Sebastián de Benalcázar
Av España
Av Núñez de Bonilla
Hurtado de Mendoza
Pres Rocafuerte
Av González Suárez
La República
García Moreno
Gen Eloy Alfaro
Octavio Díaz
Biguependilla
Guapondelig
Cacique Chaparra
Cacique Duma
P de los Cañaris

Del Rollo
RM Arizaga
Manuel Vega
JJ Olmedo
Tomás Ordóñez
Gran Colombia
Mcal Sucre
Pres Córdova
JJ Flores
Jaime Roldós
Gen Roldós
Viracochabamba
Museo del Banco Central

Pío Bravo
Antonio Vega Muñoz
Vargas Machuca
Mariscal Lamar
Gaspar Sangurima
Mariano Cueva
Hermano Miguel
Honorato Vásquez
Juan Jaramillo
A Malo
A Jerves
Avenida Huayna Capac
San Blas
Larga
O Ruinas de Todos Santos
Río Tomebamba
JL Mera Intiñan
To Station

Padre Aguirre
Gen Torres
Santo Domingo
New Cathedral
Old Cathedral
Pres Borrero
Luis Cordero
Benigno Malo
Immigration
Museo de Monasterio de la Concepción
Florencia Astudillo
Av José Peralta
To station and Museo de Culturas Aborígenes

Tarqui
Juan Montalvo
Esteves de Toral
Coronel Talbot
Simón Bolívar
Mcal Sucre
Presidente Córdova
San Francisco
Larga
Av 12 de Abril
Av Fray Vicente Solano
Federico Proaño

Museo de Arte Moderno
B del Vado
University
R Romero
L Piedra
L Loyola
Guayas

M Vélez
M Calderón
M Heredia
Av Gran Colombia
Imbabura
Av 3 de Noviembre
Av 12 de Abril
Galápagos
R Tamariz Crespo
del Batán
Av Remigio Crespo
To South & West
To South & West

Bus to El Cajas

N
0   200
metres

1. Casa de la Cultura
2. Parque de la Madre
3. Parque Luis Cordero
4. Plaza Calderón
5. Plaza de San Sebastián
6. Plaza María Auxiliadora
7. Plaza Cívica & Market
8. Stadium

Hotels:
9. Crespo
10. El Dorado
11. Alli Tiana
12. Milán
13. Norte & Residencial Colombia
14. Pichincha
15. Posada del Sol
16. Presidente & El Conquistador

Local information

● Accommodation

L3 *Oro Verde*, Ordóñez Lasso, on the road to Cajas, on a lake in the outskirts of town, T 831-200, F 832-849, completely refurbished, small pool, restaurant, cable TV.

A2 *El Dorado*, Gran Colombia 787 y Luis Cordero, T 831-390, F 831-663, nightclub, hot water in am only, good restaurant, good view.

B *Crespo*, C Larga 793, T 842-571, F 839-473, comfortable, some lovely rooms, others dark or windowless, restaurant overlooking river, a lovely building; **B** *El Conquistador*, Gran Colombia 665, T 831-788, F 831-291, inc breakfast, discounts for Youth Hostel members, disco, avoid back rooms Fri and Sat, very clean, good food and wine; **B** *Presidente*, Gran Colombia 659, T 831-979, F 824-704, good value, comfortable, convenient, good restaurant.

C *Catedral*, Padre Aguirre 8-17 y Sucre, T 823-204, clean, cheerful, spacious, modern, but not very warm, English-speaking manager, safe, laundry service, good food, coffee shop opens 0700; **C** *Internacional*, Benigno Malo 1015 y Gran Colombia, T 831-348, vaulted ceilings, a/c, TV, comfortable beds, hot water all day, pleasant but expensive restaurant, good bar, rec; **C** *Posada del Sol*, Bolívar 5-03 y Mariano Cueva, T 838-695, F 838-995, refurbished colonial building, owner Juan Diego also runs horse and bike treks into El Cajas, rec.

D *Allí-Tiana*, Córdova y Padre Aguirre, T 831-844, clean, inc breakfast; **D** *Cabañas Yanuncay*, 10-mins' drive from centre, C Cantón Gualaceo 21-49, between Av Loja y Las Américas (Yanuncay), T 883-716, rustic cabins with bath for 2-4 people, or room with bath, inc breakfast and dinner, fireplace in house, solarium, library, sauna, organic gardens, good home-cooked meals, run by Beto and Teresa Chico, Spanish and English spoken, helpful, transport to airport/bus terminal, rec; **D** *Chordeleg*, Gen Torres y Gran Colombia, T 824-611, charming, colonial style, clean; **D** *Gran*, Torres 9-70 y Bolívar, T 831-934, clean, hot water, phone, inc American breakfast, laundry service, good restaurant, beautiful patio, popular meeting place, good value, rec; **D** *Hostal Caribe Inn*, Gran Colombia 10-51 y Padre Aguirre, T/F 835-175, pleasant, comfortable, phone, restaurant; **D** *Hostal Macondo*, Tarqui 11-64 y Lamar, T 840-697, restored colonial house, Youth Hostel, apartment available, mostly shared bathrooms, hot water, laundry, kitchen facilities, excellent breakfast, US run, Spanish classes, "a real treat", highly rec; **D** *Hostería El Molino*, Km 7.5 on road Azogues-Cuenca, T 800-150, pleasant position between road and river, Spanish run, typical Ecuadorean dishes, pool, rustic style, rec, advisable to book; **D** *Las Américas*, Mariano Cueva 13-59, T 831-160/835-753, clean, TV, ask for room with windows, friendly, parking, restaurant; **D** *Tomebamba*, Bolívar, between Torres and Tarqui, T 823-797, quiet, clean, hot water, laundry service, good breakfast.

E *El Cafecito*, Hermano Vásquez 7-36 y Luis Cordero, T 827-341, colonial house, discount for longer stay, good breakfast in restaurant with charming patio, clean, hot showers, F pp in shared room, rec; **E** *Hostal Paredes*, Luis Cordero 11-29 y Lamar, T 835-674, F 834-910, beautifully-refurbished colonial mansion, with bath, international phone and fax, laundry, luggage stored, money exchange, garage, highly rec; **E** *Milán*, Pres Córdova 989 y Padre Aguirre, T 831-104, cheaper without bath, rooms with balconies, good view over market, rooms variable but clean, reliable for storing luggage, laundry facilities, often full, best to reserve; **E** *Norte*, Mariano Cueva 11-63 y Sangurima, T 827-881, renovated, large rooms, clean, safe, hot showers, comfortable, not a nice area after dark, motorcycle parking, good restaurant downstairs, rec; **E-F** *Pichincha*, Gral Torres y Bolívar, T 823-868, spacious, helpful, clean, laundry facilities, hot water, luggage stored; **E** *Res París*, Grl Torres 10-48, T 842-656, private bath, intermittent hot water, inc breakfast, clean, rec.

F *Res Colombia*, Mariano Cueva 11-61, T 827-851, clean, basic, large rooms, noisy, helpful.

Near the bus terminal are: **D** *Hurtado de Mendoza*, Sangurima y Huayna Cápac, T 843-611, good, restaurant, parking; **D** *Res España*, Sangurima 1-17, T 831-351, F 831-291, **E** without bath, clean, hot water, also communal showers and toilets, good restaurant, front upstairs rooms are best; **D** *Res Tito*, Sangurima 149, T 829-734, F 843-577, shared bath, safe, clean, hot water, restaurant very good value; **E** *Samay*, Tomás Ordóñez y Sangurima, T 831-119, cheaper without bath, clean, can be noisy, parking.

Furnished apartments: *El Jardín*, Av Pumapungo y Viracochabamba, cooking facilities and parking, T 804-103, or write to Casilla 298; **C** *Apartamentos Otorongo*, Av 12 de Abril y Guayas, T 811-184, 10-15-mins' walk from centre, with kitchenette, TV, phone, cleaning service inc, very friendly owners, discount for longer stay.

● Places to eat

International: *El Jardín*, Presidente Córdova 7-23, lovely, closed Sun-Mon, very expensive; *El Puente*, Remigio Crespo 1-20 y Av Solano, international food, nice atmosphere; *Villa Rosa*, Gran Colombia 12-22 y Tarqui, elegant, excellent, international and local dishes; *Molinos de Batan*, 12 de Abril y Puente El Vado, good setting by river, expensive; *El Che Pibe*, Av Remigio Crespo 2-59, *parrillada argentina* and other dishes, excellent service, open till late, expensive, 20% tax and service; also at Gran

Colombia, 8-33 y Cordero, excellent pizzas, pleasant courtyard; *Fuente del Sabor*, Cueva 11-71, next to *Hotel Norte, parrillada*, also seafood, chicken, etc, moderate prices, breakfast from 0730; *Atún*, Gran Colombia 8-80, pizzas and trout, popular; *La Napolitana*, C Solano nr Crespo, S of the river, nice atmosphere; *NY Pizza*, Borrero 838 y Sucre, good value; *Los Pibes*, Gran Colombia 776 y Cordero, opp *Hotel El Dorado*, pizzas and lasagne, moderately priced.

Los Capulíes, Córdova y Borrero, bar-restaurant, excellent Ecuadorean food, lovely setting, reasonable prices, Andean live music Thur-Sat 2030, reservations rec at the weekend, T 832-339; *Las Tres Caravelas*, part of hotel *El Conquistador*, good value Ecuadorean food, Andean live music at weekends; *Casa Grande*, San Joaquín-La Cruz Verde, local dishes, in picturesque San Joaquín district where flowers and vegetables are grown and baskets made; *Los Sauces*, Bolívar 6-17, original dishes, reasonable prices; *D'Bernardo*, Antonio Borrero 9-68 y Gran Colombia, opp the Post Office, breakfast, dinner, quiet music, coffee, excellent, open daily 0800-2300; *El Tequila*, Gran Colombia 20-59, local food and more, good value and service; *El Túnel*, Gral Torres 8-60, T 823-109, reasonably priced, quick service, romantic atmosphere, cheap lunch menu; *Salad Bar*, Sucre y M Cueva, popular for lunch.

The Zona Rosa, at the junction of Av Unidad Nacional and Gran Colombia has a variety of *pizzerías, heladerías*, burger and sandwich bars, steak houses, bars and discos.

Vegetarian: *El Paraíso*, Hermano Vásquez 6-46, open Mon-Sat 0800-1600, good breakfast; *Govinda*, Aguirre 8-15, behind the Cathedral, limited menu; *Mañjaris*, Hermano Vázquez 6-46, English spoken, cheap; *Vegetariano Madre Tierra*, Gran Colombia 14-35, entre Talbot y Esteves de Toral, open Mon-Sat 0800-2000, organic food, excellent.

Oriental: *Chifa Pack How*, Presidente Córdova 772 y Cordero, not cheap, rec; *Chifa Asia*, Cueva 11 s/n, entre 34 y 68, medium price, rec; *La Gran Muralla*, Juan Jaramillo 8-38 y Luis Cordero; *Sol Oriental*, Gran Colombia y Vega, cheap.

Snackbars and cafés: *Raymipampa*, Benigno Malo 8-59, on Plaza Calderón, open daily, very popular, local dishes, crepes, ice-cream, clean, excellent value; *Wunderbar*, Hermano Miguel y C Larga, behind the Instituto Azuayo de Folklore, German-run, good atmosphere, food and coffee, also vegetarian, expensive, book exchange, German magazines; *Café Chordeleg*, Gran Colombia 7-87, open 24 hrs, excellent breakfast; *Café Italia*, Pres Córdova 8-35, entre Luis Cordero y Benigno Malo, excellent cheap

snacks; *Helados Honey*, Mcal Lamar 4-21, clean, rec milkshakes; *Café Capuchino*, Bolívar y Aguirre, open 0930, hamburgers, real coffee and liqueur coffees; *Monte Bianco*, Bolívar 2-80 y Ordóñez, nr San Blas church, cakes, ice cream, open Sun; *Café Austria*, Benigno Malo 5-99, cakes, pies, sandwiches, coffee, fruit, ice cream, yoghurt, open Sun; *Heladería Holanda*, Benigno Malo 9-51, open 0930, yoghurt for breakfast, ice cream, fruit salads, great toilets; *MiPan*, Pres Córdova 824 between Cordero y Malo (also Bolívar y Aguirre), opens 0730, excellent bread, cakes, tarts, doughnuts, tea, coffee and chocolate.

● **Bars**

Picadilly Pub, Borrero 7-46 y Pres Córdova, upmarket, clean, relaxing; *La Morada del Cantor*, Av Ordóñez Lazo, 500m from *Hotel La Laguna*, T 837-197, restaurant and *peña*, excellent atmosphere; *Eclipse Bar*, Bolívar 952 y P Aguirre; *Chaos*, H Vásquez y H Miguel; *Ubu Bar*, Solano y Tres Puentes; all popular.

● **Airline offices**

TAME, Gran Colombia 6-61 y Hermano Miguel, in passage, T 827-609; **SAN**, Bolívar 5-33 y M Cueva, T 823-403; **Saeta**, Sucre 770 y Luis Cordero, T 831-548; **Aerogal**, L Cordero y Sangurima.

● **Banks & money changers**

Citibank, Gran Colombia 749, charges commission, no cheques; **Filanbanco**, several branches, no commission, quick service; **Banco del Pacífico**, Benigno Malo 9-75, advances money on Mastercard, good rates for TCs; **Banco del Austro**, Sucre y Borrero, T 842-492, changes cash and Citicorp TCs, cash on Visa on Sat; **Banco La Previsora** (main branch only) Gran Colombia y Benigno Malo, T 831-444, gives cash dollars on Visa; **Banco de Guayaquil**, Sucre entre Hermano Miguel y Borrero, cash on Visa and changes TCs of all brands; **Banco del Pichincha**, Bolívar 9-74 y B Malo T 831-544, changes cash and TCs of all brands; **Granturs**, M Cueva y Gran Colombia, good rates, quick, usually open Sat afternoon; **Cambidex**, Luis Cordero 9-77, T 835-755, helpful, good rates; **Cambistral**, Sucre 664 y Cordero, T 822-213, changes European currencies, TCs and cash; **Cambiosur**, Borrero 8-20 y Sucre, good rates for cheques and cash, no commission, fast, rec; **Cambiazuay**, Antonio Borrero 838 y Bolívar, T 823-536, cash and TCs; **Vaz Cambios**, Gran Colombia 7-98 y Cordero, T 833-434, open Sat morning, efficient. *Casas de Cambio* give the best rates but they are variable. No Peruvian currency is available.

● **Embassies & consulates**

Colombian Consulate, Cordero 9-55; **British Honorary Consul**, Sr Teodoro Jerves, Pasaje San

Alfonso (same block as Iglesia San Alfonso), T 831-996; **Alliance Française**, Tadeo Torres 1-92, open Mon-Fri, 0830-1230, 1430-1830.

● **Entertainment**

Cinemas: there are four cinemas, the one opp the Casa de la Cultura shows interesting films at 1430 and 2100. Films also at the Casa de la Cultura itself, evenings. *Teatro Cuenca*, P Aguirre 10-50, also shows films.

Discos: at Hotels *Conquistador* and *Alli-Tiana*, and *Las Galaxias*, Núñez de Bonilla 239. See also **Bars** above.

● **Hospitals & medical services**

Clinics: *Clínica Santa Inés*, Dr Jaime Moreno Aguilar speaks English, Toral, T 817-888; *Clínica Los Andes*, Mariano Cueva 14-68 y Pío Bravo, T 842-942/832-488, excellent care, clean, 24-hr service. *Farmacia Bótica Internacional*, Gran Colombia 7-20 y Borrero, experienced staff, wide selection.

● **Language courses**

Centro de Estudios Interamericanos, Gran Colombia 11-02 y Gral Torres, Edif Assoc de Empleados, Casilla 597, T 839-003, F 833-593, classes in Spanish and Quichua, rec, accommodation, *Hostal Macondo* attached; *Centro Abraham Lincoln*, Borrero y Vásquez, T 830-373, small Spanish language section; *Lenguas y Culturas*, Galápagos 2-37 y Guayas, T 817-552; *Nexus Lenguas y Culturas*, Av 12 de Abril 2-75 y Paucarbamba, T 884-016, F 814-575, also teach English and German, short-term basis family stays, well-run, rec.

● **Laundry**

La Química, Borrero 734 y Córdova, same day service, expensive; *Lavamás*, Av España y Benalcázar, nr the Terminal Terrestre.

● **Post & telecommunications**

Post Office: on corner of Calles Gran Colombia and Borrero, helpful. **Emetel**: on Benigno Malo between Córdova and Sucre, deposit required, twice the price of the call, buy long distance *fichas* before contacting the international operator, collect calls.

● **Security**

There is a man who asks female travellers to write letters for him to non-existent friends, and then invites them out. He claims also to be a businessman planning to travel abroad, who asks women to answer questions and then go with him to meet his 'sister', or a 'woman friend', by way of thanks. Furthermore, he claims to be a homosexual businessman with good links abroad and invites couples to share a glass of wine with him on his 'birthday'. He is a known rapist and dangerous, but seems to have close relations with the police. Avoid him.

NB Also take care around the market at night.

● **Shopping**

The Cuenca basin is noted for its *artesanía*. Good souvenirs are carvings, leather, basketwork, painted wood, onyx, woven stuffs (cheapest in Ecuador), embroidered shirts, etc. There are many craftware shops along Gran Colombia, in *El Dorado* hotel (good quality), and on Benigno Malo. *Arte Artesanías y Antigüedades* at Borrero y Córdova, textiles, jewellery and antiques; *El Tucan*, Borrero 7-35, Ecuadorean *artesanía*, rec. *Galería Claudio Maldonado*, Bolívar 7-75, unique precolumbian designs in silver and precious stones; *Centro Cultural Jorge Moscoso*, Pdte Córdova 6-14 y Hermano Miguel, T 822-114, weaving exhibitions, ethnographic museum, antiques and handicrafts; *Galería Pulla*, Jaramillo 6-90, famous painter, sculpture and jewellery. There are several good leather shops in the arcade off Bolívar between Benigno Malo and Luis Cordero, the quality and price are comparable with Cotacachi. *Artesa*, Presidente Córdova 6-96 y Borrero, several branches, modern Ecuadorean ceramics at good prices. *Joyería Turismo*, owned by Leonardo Crespo, at Gran Colombia 9-31, rec. *Unicornio*, L Cordero entre Gran Colombia y Lamar, good jewellery, ceramics and candelabra.

High quality Panama hats are made by *Homero Ortega Pe Hijos*, Av Gil Ramírez Dávalos 3-86, T 823-429, F 834-045, he will show you his factory opp bus station, open 0900-1200, 1500-1800 for visits. Also *Exportadora Cuenca*, Mcal Lamar 3-80, Jaime Ortega Ramírez and his wife, Tania, highly rec, will make to order and won't apply bleach if so asked.

There's an interesting market behind the new cathedral. There is a well-stocked supermarket behind *Res España*; *Supermaxi*, Colombia y Américas. Camping Gas is available at several locations; camping equipment at *Bermeo Hnos*, Borrero 8-35 y Sucre, T 831-522, and *Créditos y Negocios*, Benigno Malo y Pdte Córdova, T 829-583.

Photography: *Foto Ortiz*, Gran Colombia y Aguirre, wide range of film, good same day developing, not rec for slides; *Asefot*, Gran Colombia 7-18, T/F 839-342, rec for colour prints; *Ecuacolor*, Gran Colombia 7-44 y Cordero, good service.

● **Tour companies & travel agents**

Santa Ana Tours, Presidente Córdova y Borrero, T 832-340, run day tours, to Cajas US$35 pp, to Ingapirca, US$50; *Metropolitan Touring*, Gran Colombia y Cordero, T 831-185; *Viajes Enmotur*, Borrero 7-51 y Sucre, tours to Ingapirca US$45, will buy US dollars inc Sat am; *Ecotrek*, C Larga 7-108 y Luis Cordero, T 842-531, F 835-387, contact Juan Gabriel Carrasco, trips to Kapaw Ecological Reserve, excellent, experienced guides and great adventure travel, monthly departures, specialize in Shaman trips; *Río Arriba Eco-Turismo*, Hno Miguel 7-14 y Córdova, T 840-031, rec; *Apullacta*, Gran Colombia y G Torres, rent tents. **Rec guides:** *José Rivera Baquero*, Pedro Carbo 1-48 y Guapondelig, very knowledgeable; *Eduardo Quito*, T 823-018, F 834-202, has his own 4WD, special tours for up to 10 people, speaks good English, highly rec; *Luis Astudillo*, C Azuay 1-48 entre Guayas y Tungurahua, T 815-234, tours to Ingapirca, US$30, good. **Club Andinismo Sangay**, T 806-615/844-313, for Sun treks, main one 2nd Sun of month, US$3.

● **Tourist offices**
Cetur, Hno Miguel 686 y Córdova, open Mon-Fri only, 0800-1200, 1430-1600 (1800 in July-Sept). Has maps of Cuenca. A map of the city is also available from major hotels.

● **Useful addresses**
Immigration: Policía Nacional de Migración, Benigno Malo y Larga, T 831-020.

● **Transport**
Local Bus: city buses US$0.08. **Car rental:** *Budget Renta-Car*, Huayna Cápac 1018 y González Suárez, T 801-892/831-888, also at airport, T 804-063. *International*, Huayna Cápac y Suárez, T 801-892. **Taxis:** US$0.70-1 for short journey; US$1.80 to airport or bus station; US$3/hr; US$22/day.

Air The airport is 5-mins' walk from the Terminal Terrestre. No ticket reservations at airport. Local buses run along the road outside. To **Quito** and **Guayaquil;** with TAME. Reconfirm tickets, beware extra charges at check-in, try getting advanced boarding pass (precheques). Arrive at least 1 hr before departure.

Buses The Terminal Terrestre, well-organized and policed, is on Av España, a 20-min walk NW of the city centre, or take a minibus, US$0.10. The terminal for local or within-the-province buses is at the Feria Libre on Av Las Américas; many city buses pass here too. Take daytime buses to enjoy scenic routes. To **Riobamba**, 5½ -6 hrs, US$4, sit on the left. To **Baños**, US$7, 7½ hrs, the road goes from 2,600m to under 200m and up again). To **Baños**, from 12 de Noviembre, Turismo Baños. To/from **Quito**, 9½-10½ hrs, US$6, US$8 by minibus, 8 hrs; Panamericana Internacional, Huayna Cápac y España, T 840-060; luxury coach service with Sucre Express, 8½ hrs, US$10. To **Alausí**, US$3.90, 4 hrs, all Quito-bound buses pass through, about 20 a day, from 0600 onwards. To **Loja**, 4½ hrs with San Luis, US$5, sit on the left, passport checks are likely. To **Machala**, 3-4 hrs, every 20 mins, US$3, sit on the left. To

Guayaquil, 5 hrs, US$4, road paved – shop around for the most comfortable bus. Turismo Oriental (4 daily, better buses) and Coop Sucúa (3 nightly, one at 1000) go to **Sucúa** (11 hrs) and **Macas** (12 hrs, US$6, the left side is best overall although the right side is good for the last part with views of approach to lowlands. To **Huaquillas**, 4-6 hrs (frequent police checks), US$4.10, at 0530, 2000, 2300; to avoid a possible 2-hr wait in Machala get off at the large roundabout (well known to drivers) for the local bus to Huaquillas. To **Azogues**, US$0.35, every 30 mins. To **Saraguro**, US$2.65, 3½ hrs. To **Gualaquiza**, 10 hrs.

EAST OF CUENCA

Gualaceo and Paute
Gualaceo is a thriving, modern town set in beautiful landscape, with a charming plaza and fine new church with splendid modern glass. Its Sun market doesn't cater to tourists. Woollen goods are sold on the main street near the bus station, while embroidered goods are sold from a private home above the general store on the main plaza. Inexpensive good shoes are made locally.

● **Accommodation** C *Parador Turístico*, T 255-110, outside town, chalets, rooms, modern, nice, swimming pool, good restaurant; F *Res Carlos Andrés*, T 255-379, new, clean; F *Res Gualaceo*, T 255-006, Gran Colombia, clean, friendly, camping possible; G *Español*, T 255-158, very basic.

● **Buses** From the corner of the Terminal Terrestre in Cuenca to Gualaco, US$0.65, 2 hrs.

From Gualaceo take a taxi to **Bulzhun** (10 mins) where backstrap weavers make *Macanas* (Ikat dyed shawls); from there walk back down to Bulcay, another weaving community, and catch a bus back to Cuenca.

In 1993 heavy rains caused a huge landslide at La Josefina, destroying the paved route from El Descanso (between Azogues and Cuenca) to Paute and Gualaceo. The old riverside road was due to reopen after reconstruction in Oct 1996. To go to Paute you turn off to the E between Azogues and El Descanso, and to get to Gualaceo turn off S of El Descanso through the village of Jadan.

North of Gualaceo, on the Río Palma, is **Paute**, the site of Ecuador's largest hydroelectric plant. Deforestation is causing the dam to silt up, so it has to be continually dredged to function.

● **Accommodation B** *Hostería Huertas de Uzhpud*, set in the beautiful Paute valley, deluxe, rooms at the back have best views, swimming pool, sports fields, small zoo, gardens, lots of orchids, highly rec, Casilla 01-01-1268, Uzhupud, Paute, T 250-339, T Cuenca 806-521 (taxi from Cuenca US$7, bargain hard); also **G** *Res Cutilcay*, T 250-133; *San Luis*, T 250-165; and *Las Tejas*, T 250-176.

South of Gualaceo

Chordeleg is a touristy village famous for its crafts in wood, silver and gold filigree (though very little is available nowadays), pottery and panama hats. Watch out for fake jewellery. *Joyería Dorita* and *Joyería Puerto del Sol*, on Juan B Cobos y Eloy Alfaro, and *Joyería Campoverde* on the main plaza, have been recommended (the latter for gold filigree). The small Museo de Comunidad of local textiles, ceramics and straw work, sells some items at reasonable prices. The church is interesting with some lovely modern stained glass. It's a good uphill walk from Gualaceo to Chordeleg, and a pleasant hour downhill in the other direction.

● **Transport** Plenty of colectivos, or by local bus, US$0.15 from Gualaceo market, every 30 mins; direct bus from Cuenca, 1½ hrs, US$0.50.

South of Gualaceo, 83 km from Cuenca, **Sígsig**, with a Sun market and a few *sombrerías*, is worth a visit.

● **Buses** 1½ hrs, US$0.65, hourly bus also from Chordeleg.

A road is being built between Sígsig and Gualaquiza in the Southern Oriente, along a beautiful and unspoilt route. Until it is completed, the route can be done as follows: bus Sígsig-Chigüinda, then hike to **Aguacate** (see page 1135), thence to Río Negro for transport to Gualaquiza, or hike. Full details in the *Ecuador Handbook*.

Aguacate (see page 1135)

CAJAS NATIONAL PARK

Northwest of Cuenca, **Cajas** is a 28,000 ha national recreation area with over 230 lakes. Near the entrance is an altar and pilgrim area where a teenager saw 'Our Lady of the Faith' in 1988. Entrance to the park is US$6. There is a new visitors' centre and cafetería at Laguna Toreadora (3,810m), next to the old refuge.

The *páramo* vegetation, such as chuquiragua and lupin, is beautiful and contains interesting wildlife: Andean gull, black frogs, humming birds, even condors. On a clear morning the views are superb, even to Chimborazo, some 300 km away.

● **Walking conditions** The park offers ideal but strenuous walking, at 3,500-4,400m altitude, and the climate is rough. Deaths have occurred from exposure. The best time to visit is Aug-Jan, when you may expect clear days, strong winds, night-time temperatures to -8°C and occasional mist. From Feb-July temperatures are higher but there is much more fog, rain and snow. It is best to arrive in the early morning since it can get very cloudy, wet and cool after about 1300. Local maps are not always exact. It is better to get the IGM maps in Quito. It is easy to get lost as signs (if any) are of little help. Walks are described in the *Ecuador Handbook*.

● **Access** It's a 2½-hr bus trip to the park; one daily with Occidental, except Thur and Sun, between 0600 and 0630 from the San Sebastián church, esq Simón Bolívar y Col Talbot. The bus back is between 1400 and 1600, US$1.35, daily except Wed or Sat; arrive early as the bus can get very full. Hitchhiking is difficult as there is little traffic. A taxi costs anything up to US$40, bargain hard.

● **Accommodation G** pp *Refugio*, cold, with four bunks and cooking facilities. There are also two primitive shelters by the shore of the lake, a 20 and 40-mins' walk from the refuge. Take food, fuel, candles, sleeping bags, warm clothes and strong sun cream.

● **Tours** There are organized tours to the lakes from Cuenca, fishing possible, but these tend to be up to US$34. Alternatively, hire a private truck, US$16 with driver. Jorge Moscoso, see under Cuenca *Shopping*, is knowledgeable and helpful about Cajas. A group of ramblers welcomes visitors for Sun walks in Aug and Sept, look for posters in Cuenca.

ROUTES The new road from Cuenca to Guayaquil via Molleturo is open and paved for much of its length. The road passes through Cajas National Park and continues over the mountains to the towns of Miguir, Molleturo and on to Naranjal on the coast. The scenery is spectacular and there are still a few places where there is undisturbed forest. There is nowhere to stay after the *refugio* at Laguna Toreadora (see above) until you reach the lowlands between Naranjal and La Troncal. Some buses are running on this road (eg San Luis and Semeria to Guayaquil). It is still prone to landslides during the rainy season (Feb-May).

CUENCA TO MACHALA

From Cuenca, the Pan-American Highway runs S to La Y, about 20 km away. Here the road divides into two: one continuing the Pan-American to Loja and the other, which is faster, running through sugar cane fields to Pasaje and Machala. Most buses between Cuenca and the Peruvian border at Huaquillas (see page 1101), go NW to La Troncal, then S down the coast.

1 hr from Cuenca is **Girón** whose beauty is spoiled only by a modern concrete church. After the battle on 27 February 1829 between the troops of Gran Colombia, led by Sucre, and those of Peru under Lamar, at nearby Portete de Tarqui, a treaty was signed in Girón. The building, **Casa de los Tratados**, is shown to visitors, as is the site of the Peruvians' capitulation (entry fee). Ask directions to El Chorro waterfall with cloudforest above.

The route continues through the Yungilla valley and **Santa Isabel** (C *La Molienda*, by Cataviña, just before Santa Isabel; **D** *Sol y Agua*, below the village, a weekend place for Cuencanos; **G** *Hostería al Durán*, basic, no water; many other small weekend farms), then descends through desert to the stark, rocky canyon of the Río Jubones. The next town is **Casacay** (**E** *Hostería San Luis*, attractive, good, pool, pleasant climate), after which lush banana plantations are entered. Before Casacay, at a military checkpoint, a road climbs S to **Chilla**, where crowds throng in annual pilgrimages during September. In the lowlands is **Pasaje** (*Pop* 27,000; **D** *San Martín*, clean, a/c, safe; many basic *pensiones*, F, and *Santa Isabel*.)

SOUTH OF CUENCA

The Pan-American Highway climbs S from La Y through **Cumbe** (small, colourful Wed market), to the Tinajillas pass, 3,527m.

It descends sharply into the warm upper Jubones valley past cane fields and rises again after Río León (Km 95, 1,900m) to the small town of **Oña**, at Km 105, 2,300m (*Pop* 3,244; one hotel on the plaza and several places to eat). From Oña the road weaves and climbs through highland *páramo* pastures (3,040m) and then descends towards Saraguro (Km 144).

SARAGURO

(*Pop* 19,883) is a very cold town. Here the Indians, the most southerly Andean group in Ecuador, dress all in black. They wear very broad flat-brimmed hard felt hats. The men are notable for their black shorts, sometimes covered by a whitish kind of divided apron, and a particular kind of saddle bag, the *alforja*, and the women for their pleated black skirts, necklaces of coloured beads and silver *topos*, ornate pins fastening their shawls. The town has a picturesque Sun market and interesting Mass.

● **Accommodation & places to eat** F *Res Armijos*, C Antonio Castro, cold shower, clean, quiet, good; **F** *Res Saraguro*, C Loja No 03-2 y Antonio Castro, shared bath, nice courtyard, hot water, laundry facilities, rec. *Salón Cristal*, Azuay y Castro, lunch only, simple but good food, clean; *Gruta Azul*, on plaza, OK. Cheap food in the market.

● **Buses** To Cuenca with Coop Viajeros, 4 daily, US$2.65, 4½ hrs; to Loja, US$1.80, 1½ hrs.

ROUTES South from Saraguro there are two passes, at Km 150 and 156.5. Two further passes come after the village of San Lucas (Km 164), the highest of the two at Km 185, before a long descent towards Loja. The road between Cuenca and Loja is now paved and is one of the most beautiful and breathtaking in Ecuador.

LOJA

This friendly, pleasant city (*Pop* 94,305; *Alt* 2,063m), lies near the Oriente. It was founded on its present site in 1548, having been moved from La Toma, and was rebuilt twice after earthquakes, the last of which occurred in the 1880s. The city, encircled by hills, has been a traditional gateway between the highlands and southern Amazonia. Tropical forest products such as chinchona (the natural base for quinine) first entered European pharmacopia through Loja. The city has two universities, with a well-known law school. The Universidad Nacional has good murals on some of its buildings. There are also crude but original paintings on the patio walls of many of the old houses.

Places of interest

The **Cathedral** and **Santo Domingo** church, Bolívar y Rocafuerte, have painted interiors. **El Valle** church, on the S edge of the city is colonial, with a lovely interior. The **Banco Central museum** on the main plaza, 0900-1500, has exhibits of local folklore and history, and the **Casa de la Cultura**, Bolívar y Imbabura, sponsors cultural events. **Mercado Modelo**, 10 de Agosto y 18 de Noviembre, rebuilt in 1991, is worth a visit. It is clean and efficient, open 0800-1800 Mon to Sat, 0800-1500 Sun. There is a market on Sat, Sun and Mon, attended by many Saraguro Indians. There are souvenir and craft shops on 10 de Agosto between Iberoamérica and 18 de Noviembre.

Loja is famed for its musicians and has one of the few musical academies in the country. Musical evenings and concerts are often held around the town.

Excursions

Parque Educacional Ambiental y Recreacional de Argelia is superb, with trails through the forest to the *páramo*. It is 500m before the police checkpoint on road S to Vilcabamba. Take a city bus marked 'Argelia'; it is open 0830-1700 except Tues and Wed. Across the road and 100m S is the **Jardín Botánico Reynaldo Espinosa**, open Mon-Fri 0800-1700. It is nicely laid out and has several chinchona trees.

Local festivals

16-20 Aug: *Fiesta de la Virgen del Cisne*, the image of the Virgin remains in Loja until 1 Nov. The statue of the Virgin spends a month each year travelling around the province; the most important peregrination is the 3-day 70 km walk from El Cisne to Loja cathedral, beginning 17 Aug. The last 2 weeks of Aug and the first week of Sep are very crowded: rooms hard to find, all prices rise.

Local information

● **Accommodation**

C *Grand Hotel Loja*, Iberoamérica y Rocafuerte, T 575-200, F 575-202; **C** *Hostal Aguilera Internacional*, Sucre 01-08 y Emiliano Ortega, T 563-189, F 572-894, nice rooms, restaurant, sauna, parking; **C** *Libertador*, Colón 14-30 y Bolívar, T 570-344, F 572-119, Casilla 412, suites available, noisy, good restaurant *La Castellana*, parking.

D *Hostal La Riviera*, Universitaria y 10 de Agosto, T 572-863, good; **D** *Ramsés*, Colón 14-31 y Bolívar, phone, good restaurant.

E *Acapulco*, Sucre 749 y 10 de Agosto, T 570-651, clean, hot water, private bath, safe for leaving luggage, 1st floor rooms are quieter in the mornings, rec; **E** *Hostal Crystal*, Rocafuerte y 18 de Noviembre, clean, safe, large rooms; **E** *Los Ejecutivos*, Universitaria 1076, T 560-004, good, also 'video club'; **E** *Metropolitano*, 18 de Noviembre 6-41 y Colón, T 570-007, with bath and TV, hot water, clean; **E** *Saraguro Internacional*, Universitaria 724 y 10 de Agosto, T 570-552, hot water, TV, parking, restaurant open Mon-Fri.

F *Alborada*, Sucre 1279 y Lourdes, with shower, clean; **F** *Caribe*, Rocafuerte 1552 y 18 de Noviembre, T 572-902, shared bath, hot water, rec; **F** *Colonial*, Sucre 8-64, shared bath, basic; **F** *Hostal Carrión*, Colón 1630 y 18 de Noviembre, T 561-127, basic, hot water on request, safe; **F** *Hostal San Luis*, Sucre 4-56 e Imbabura, T 570-370, cheaper without bath, hot water, parking; **F** *Loja*, Rocafuerte 15-27, T 570-241, shared bath, intermittent hot water, nicely renovated; **F** *Londres*, Sucre 741 y 10 de Agosto, clean, nice big rooms, hot water.

G *Primavera*, Colón 1644, clean, cold shower; **G** pp *San Andrés*, Miguel Riofrío, more or less clean, very cheap. **Youth Hostel**, Av Miguel Riofrío 1661 y 18 de Noviembre, T 560-895. There are basic *residenciales* in our **G** range on Rocafuerte.

● **Places to eat**

José Antonio, Imbabura 15-30 entre Sucre y 18 de Noviembre, excellent *cebiche* and seafood, enthusiastic chef, highly rec; *La Cascada*, Sucre y Lourdes, very good; *Don Quijote Pizzería*, Eguiguren, ½ block W of El Río Malacatos, excellent food, wholewheat bread; *Trece*, Universitaria y Colón, also Eguiguren 1468, good; *México*, Eguiguren 1579 y Sucre, good set meals or à la carte, popular, rec; *El Rincón de Francia*, Bolívar y Riofrío, good; *La Tullpa*, 18 de Noviembre y Colón, cheap, good *churrasco*; *Parrillada Uruguaya*, Iberoamérica y Azuay, opens 1700, good grilled meat, owner helpful; *El Paraíso*, Sucre 0435 y Quito, good

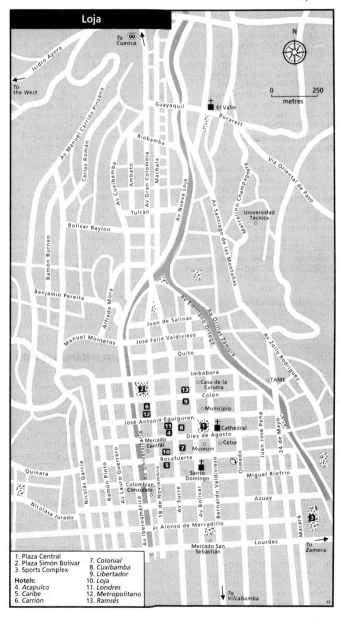

Loja

To Cuenca

To the West

N

0 — 250
metres

Guayaquil · El Valle · Bucarest

Isidro Ayora

Av Manuel Carrión Pinzano

Carlos Román

Riobamba

Av Cuxibamba

Ambato

Av Gran Colombia

Machala

Av Nueva Loja

Av Santiago de las Montañas

Via Oriental de Paso

Marcelino Champagnat

Universidad Técnica

Tulcán

Bolívar Baylon

Ramón Burneo

Benjamín Pereira

Alfredo Mora

Manuel Monteros

Juan de Salinas

José Félix Valdivieso

Av Emiliano Ortega

Av Olías Zamora

Av Zoilo Rodríguez

Quito

Imbabura · Casa de la Cultura

Colón

Municipio

José Antonio Eguiguren

Diez de Agosto

Cathedral

Cetur

Mercado Central

Museum

Rocafuerte

Santo Domingo

Olmedo

Juan José Peña

24 de Mayo

TAME

Quinara

Nicolás García

Ramón Pinto

Av Universitaria

Av Lauro Guerrero

Colombian Consulate

18 de Noviembre

Av Sucre

Av Bolívar

Bernardo Valdivieso

Miguel Riofrío

Azuay

Nicolasa Jurado

Av Iberoamérica

Av Alonso de Mercadillo

Mercado San Sebastián

Lourdes

Macará

To Zamora

To Vilcabamba

1. Plaza Central
2. Plaza Simón Bolívar
3. Sports Complex

Hotels:
4. *Acapulco*
5. *Caribe*
6. *Carrión*

7. *Colonial*
8. *Cuxibamba*
9. *Libertador*
10. *Loja*
11. *Londres*
12. *Metropolitano*
13. *Ramsés*

vegetarian; *Salud y Vida*, Azuay nr Olmedo, vegetarian; *Marisquería Las Castañuelas*, 10 de Agosto 1167, clean, set meal US$1. *Chifa El Arbol de Oro*, Eguiguren y 18 de Noviembre, good Chinese. Loja has many excellent bakeries. Good snacks, pastries and yoghurt at *Pastelería Persa* (2 locations – one at Rocafuerte 14-58). *Helados de Paila*, Av Iberoamérica, nr the market, good ice-cream and snacks; *Topoli*, Riofrío y Bolívar, best coffee and yoghurt, good for breakfast (not open for lunch); *Top Cream Ice Cream*, Iberoamérica y Colón, best ice cream.

● **Banks & money changers**

Filanbanco on the main plaza, changes Amex TCs, best rates; **Banco de Loja**, Rocafuerte y Bolívar, good rates for TCs; **Banco del Azuay**, on the main plaza, changes cash and TCs; **Banco Mutualista Pichincha**, on plaza, cash advance on Mastercard. No *casas de cambio*, good rates for US dollars in the gift shop in front of *Hotel Acapulco*; also *Loayza*, Riofrío 1450, helpful; *Librería Reina del Cisne*, Bolívar y Riofrío; *Frankhitur*, Centro Comercial Episcopal, Valdivieso y 10 de Agosto, T 573-378; *Joyería San Pablo*, Sucre 7-26 y 10 de Agosto, T 560-715, open Sat, good rates; *Vílcatur Travel Agency*, Colón 14-30 y Bolívar, good rates for cash; also *Delgado Travel*, opp the Post Office on Colón y Sucre.

● **Embassies & consulates**

Colombia 18 de Noviembre y Azuay, T 960-573; **Peru** Lazo y Rodríguez, T 961-668.

● **Post & telecommunications**

Post Office: Colón y Sucre; no good for sending parcels. **Emetel**: on Rocafuerte y Olmedo.

● **Shopping**

Cer-Art Ceramics, precolumbian designs on ceramics, produced at the Universidad Técnica. Above the Universidad Técnica is the 'Ceramics Plaza', where you can buy directly from the crafts studio. A little higher on the same road is Productos Lacteos, selling cheeses and fresh butter, all produced by the university.

● **Tourist offices**

Cetur, Valdivieso 08-22 y 10 de Agosto, T 572-964, F 570-485, open Mon-Fri, 0800-1300, 1500-1800. *Loja tradición, cultura y turismo*, is a useful guidebook. *El Siglo* and *Crónica* give news of events.

● **Useful addresses**

Immigration: Venezuela y Argentina, T 960-500.

● **Transport**

Air TAME office is at Zamora y 24 de Mayo, 0830-1600. Reserve your seat in Cuenca if you want to leave from Loja the next day; or get an open ticket at the airport and push and shout to get on the plane. There are flights from Quito direct or via Guayaquil to La Toma (Catamayo, 35 km away). At La Toma airport, shared taxis wait to take you to Loja; 45 mins, US$3. They fill up quickly so choose a driver, give him your luggage claim ticket and he will collect your checked luggage. Bus to Loja US$0.80, or stay in Catamayo (see below). Flights are often cancelled due to strong winds.

Buses Terminal at Av Gran Colombia e Isidro Ayora, buses every 2 mins to/from centre, 10-mins' journey; left luggage, information desk, shops, Emetel office, US$0.15 terminal tax. Taxi from centre, US$1. To **Cuenca**, 4½ hrs, 7 a day, US$4.50 with Trans Viajeros (18 de Noviembre y Quito); **Machala**, 10 a day, 7 hrs, US$3 (2 routes, one through Piñas, rather bumpy with hairpin bends but better views, the other paved and generally quicker). **Quito**, Cooperativa Loja (10 de Agosto y Guerrero), and Trans Santa, 4 a day, US$10-12, 13-14 hrs. **Guayaquil**, 5 a day, 8 hrs, US$5.85. Panamericana Internacional, office at *Grand Hotel Loja*, luxury service to Quito (US$15) and Guayaquil (US$10). To **Huaquillas** at 2030 and 2230, US$4.50, 6-8 hrs; get off at Machala crossroads, *La Avanzada*, and take a local bus from there. To **Macará**, 4 daily, 6-8 hrs, US$5; roadworks at El Limón, half way to Macará is paved, but the rest is terrible, numerous passport checkpoints. To **Saraguro**, 6 daily, 1½ hrs, US$1.80. To **Vilcabamba**, a spectacular 1½-hr bus ride, Sur Oriente hourly from Loja bus terminal, US$0.90; taxi about US$7.50, 1 hr. To **Zamora**, 1½ hrs, with Coop Nambija.

PODOCARPUS NATIONAL PARK

There are 3 entrances to this park. **1**: The entrance to the upper premontane section is about 15 km S of Loja on the Vilcabamba road at Cajanuma: spectacular walking country, lush tropical cloud forest and excellent bird-watching, but take waterproofs and warm clothing. Permits (US$7) and an adequate map from Inefan, C Azuay entre Valdivieso y Olmedo, Loja (T 571-534), office open 0800; or at the entrance. There is a comfortable refuge at the information centre in the park; make bookings at office in Loja before going. Camping is possible but it can be very wet. Park guardian Miguel Angel is very knowledgeable and helpful. Additional information from conservation groups: Arco Iris, Olmedo y Riofrío, T 572-926, PO Box 860, Loja, or contact member Rodrigo Tapiz, T 560-895; Fundación Ecológica Podocarpus, Sucre 8-47 y 10 de Agosto, PO Box 11-01-436, Loja.

● **Access** Take a Vilcabamba bus, the park entrance is 20 mins from Loja, US$0.80, then it's a 8 km hike uphill to the guard station. Direct transport by taxi only, US$10 round trip. You can arrange a pick up later from the guard station.

The lower subtropical section of Podocarpus Park can also be reached by 2 entrances from Zamora (see below).

2: The lower altitude of the Zamora side makes wet weather less threatening but waterproof hiking boots are essential. Permission to enter the Park from Inefan, US$14 entrance, is essential. Inefan office at the entrance to Zamora, open Mon-Fri, 0830-1800. At weekends pay at the Park headquarters at the Bombuscara refuge. Camping is possible near the refuge. Park guardians can suggest walks. Incredible bird life: mountain tanagers flock around the refuge.

3: The other entrance is 2 hrs S by bus. This area is unmatched for the virgin cloud forest and amazing quantity of flora and fauna. It contains one of the last major habitats for the spectacled bear and many birds, such as the mountain toucan, Andean cock-of-the-rock, umbrella bird, green jay, etc. A 3- to 5-day hike is possible into this part of the park, but permission is needed from the Inefan office in Zamora and from the mining company. Inefan will get the permission for you after filling out a few papers; T 900-141. Ing Luis Cuenca is in charge of the Podocarpus Park. Most food supplies can be obtained in Zamora, though all camping gear must be carried, as well as fuel for stoves.

● **Access 2**: Taxi US$2 to the entrance, 1 km walk to refuge. **3**: From the Zamora bus terminal, you can take a *ranchero*, or wooden, open-sided bus to Romerillos, which is a collection of a few houses and an Inefan office. Bus departs Zamora 0630 and 1415, return to Zamora at 0815 and 1600.

EAST FROM LOJA

The road to the Oriente (see page 1083) crosses a low pass and descends rapidly to **Zamora** (*Pop* 8,736), an old mission settlement about 65 km away at the confluence of the Ríos Zamora and Bombuscara. The road is beautiful as it wanders from *páramo* down to high jungle, crossing mountain ranges of spectacular cloud forest, weaving high above narrow gorges as it runs alongside the Río Zamora. The area has scarcely been affected by tourism yet. The town itself is a midway point for miners and gold prospectors heading further into the Oriente. The best month is Nov, but except for April-June, when it rains almost constantly, other months are comfortable.

● **Accommodation D** *Internacional Torres*, new, best in town; **D** *Maguna*, Diego de Vaca, T 605-113, fridge, TV, bath, parking; **E** *Orillas del Zamora*, Diego de Vaca nr car bridge, **F** without bath, family run; **F** *Seyma*, 24 de Mayo y Amazonas, T 605-583, clean, rec; **F** *Zamora*, Sevilla de Oro y Pío Jaramillo, T 605-253, shared bath, clean; **F** *Res Venecia*, Sevilla de Oro, shared bathroom, basic.

● **Places to eat** Restaurants in *Hotel Maguna* (best), *GranRitz*, good, and *Comedor Don Pepe*; *Esmeraldas* in market area opp bus terminal, rec.

● **Immigration Office**: C José Luis Tamayo S of the park, visitors may be asked for documents, always carry your passport.

● **Buses** All buses leave from Terminal Terrestre. To **Loja**, 4 a day, 2½ hrs; to **Cuenca**, 1 daily via Loja, 6-7 hrs; to **Yantzaza** and **La Paz**, 6 a day.

The road to the Southern Oriente passes near **Nambija**, a gold mining town with its own, limited law and order, and, further N, **Zumbi**, reached by 0800 bus from Zamora, last bus back 1500, a very scenic ride. The road continues through **Yantzaza**, with 4 hotels, including the new *Inca*, **F**, and several *comedores*, and **El Pangui** (**G** *Hotel Estrella del Oriente*) on its way N to Gualaquiza (see page 1135).

VILCABAMBA

(*Pop* 3,894; *Alt* 1,520m; *Phone code* 07) Once an isolated village, Vilcabamba has become increasingly popular with foreign backpackers, a 'must' along the gringo trail between Ecuador and Peru. There are many places to stay and several good restaurants. The whole area is beautiful and tranquil, with an agreeable climate (17°C min, 26°C max). The local economy has benefitted from the influx of tourists, but responsible tourism should not be neglected here.

There are many good walks in the Río Yambala valley (maps are available at

Cabañas Río Yambala), and on the Mandango mountain trail (exposed and slippery in parts, directions obtainable at *Madre Tierra*). The Vilcagua factory produces cartons of drinking water; visits to the plant can be arranged. There is a Tourist Office on the main plaza next to Emetel, which is helpful, with good information and maps. There are no banks or cambios, but hotels and shops will change at a poor rate.

Local information
● Accommodation

C *Hostería Vilcabamba*, T 580-271, F 580-273, excellent, comfortable, pool, may be used by non-residents for US$0.50, jacuzzi, bar, good Ecuadorean restaurant, massage, fitness instruction, language school, US$3/hr minimum 4 hrs daily, run by Cortez family.

D *Parador Turístico*, T 673-122, also run by Cortez family, good rooms, with restaurant and bar, free use of pool at *Hostería Vilcabamba*, rec; **D** *Posada Real*, C Agua del Hierro s/n, T 673-114, with bath, hot water, very clean, comfortable, excellent views, laundry facilities, relaxing atmosphere, rec.

E *Cabañas Paraíso*, 5 mins from town on the main road, cabins with bath, restaurant, good value; **E** *Madre Tierra*, T 580-269, a health farm set in idyllic surroundings about 2 km before village, coming from Loja, take dirt track on the right, just before the bridge, cabins of varying quality, but comfortable, shared bath, inc breakfast, dinner and free drinking water, reductions for long stay, excellent food, vegetarian to order, non-residents should reserve meals a day in advance, horses to rent (about US$15/day for 2 horses, food and gear), language school, small swimming pool, videos, massage, steam baths, English and French spoken, rec, often full, the Mendoza family are very welcoming, they have details of trails for walking, write to Jaime Mendoza, PO Box 354, Loja, Ecuador; **E** *Pole House*, 10-mins' walk from town by the Río Chamba, cabin built on stilts for 4 people, fully furnished kitchen, drinking water supplied, owned by Orlando and Alicia Falco, ask at their handicraft shop, *Prima Vera*, on the plaza, which will also double as the post office until 1997, Sr Falco also speaks English and runs excellent nature tours in and around the Podocarpus National Park, US$15 pp/day, inc boxed lunch; **E** *The Hidden Garden*, T/F (07) 580-281, shared bath, quiet, clean, use of kitchen, lovely gardens, rec.

F *Hostal Mandango*, behind bus terminal, family run, with bath, water shortages on upper floors if full, inexpensive restaurant, pretty quiet, good value; **F** *Hotel Valle Sagrado*, proprietor Abel Espinoza, on main plaza, shared baths not too clean, cold water, basic, noisy, good vegetarian restaurant (Luis will organize horse riding trips), excellent breakfast for US$1, luggage store, laundry facilities, use of kitchen; **F** *Sra Olivia Toledo*, Bolívar esq Clodoveo, 1 block from plaza, shared bath, hot water, family run. At the upper end of the Vilcabamba Valley, a beautiful 4 km walk from the village, are the highly rec **F** *Cabañas Río Yambala*, owned by Charlie and Sarah, different types of cabins for 3 to 6, or room, beautiful views, kitchen facilities, shopping done for you, vegetarian restaurant open all day, hot showers, laundry service, clean, helpful, do not leave belongings on balcony or porch, horses for rent with or without guide, trekking arranged in the Podocarpus National Park with tents, sleeping bags, food etc provided.

● Places to eat
There are four restaurants on the plaza, inc an unnamed, good vegetarian place. Also *Café Pizzería Pepito's*, 5 mins from the plaza on the road to Cabañas Yambala, excellent pizzas and pasta, cheap, rec (good book exchange nearby).

● Language schools
Academia de Castellano Vilcabamba, T 580-271, F 575-202, PO Box 107, Loja, rec.

● Tour companies & travel agents
New Zealander, Gavin Moore, runs *Caballos Gavilan*, offering 3-day horse treks to his farmhouse at 2,500m, overlooking Vilcabamba, or a trek in the cloud forest; US$75 pp, inc food (vegetarian specialities), sleeping bags (if necessary), and basic lodging, highly rec. He lives a couple of km outside the town; contact him through the tourist office or Casilla 1000, Loja, F (07) 673-186.

Horses can be hired from Roger Toledo who organizes 3-day trips into the mountains; also Wilson Carpio and Ernesto Avila, cost varies from US$4-8/1/2 day. There's a campsite at the nature reserve, *Las Palmas*, on the edge of the Park, take taxi or pick-up, US$4, try Miguel Carpio who lives 1/2 block from Tourist Office; for reservations call Comercial Karmita T 673-186, also fax service and tourist information.

LOJA TO THE PERUVIAN BORDER

An alternative to the Huaquillas border crossing is the more scenic route via Macará. Leaving Loja on the main paved highway going W, the airport at **La Toma** (1,200m) is reached after 35 km.

If flying to or from La Toma, it's best to stay at **Catamayo**, nearby.

● Accommodation & places to eat In
Catamayo: **D** *Hostería Bella Vista*, T 962-

450, tropical gardens, pool; **F** *Hotel San Marcos*, on the plaza; **G** pp *Hotel El Turista*, Av Isidro Ayora, shared bath, basic, friendly, poor beds. Opp is *Restaurant China*, good, cheap.

● **Transport** Taxi to airport US$1, or 20-mins' walk.

ROUTES At La Toma, where you can catch the Loja-Macará bus, the Pan-American Highway divides: one branch running W, the other S. The former, which is faster, runs via Velacruz and Catacocha, with 4 passport checks. The Loja to Catacocha section is paved, and Catacocha to Macará is paved halfway. **Catacocha** is a spectacularly placed town built on a rock; there are pre-Inca ruins around the town. From Catacocha, the road runs S to the border at Macará.

51 km from Catacocha, at Empalme, a road heads W to Celica, then 82 km SW to **Zapotillo** (*Pop* 5,000; *Alt* 325m), a charming riverside town on the Peruvian border, SW of Macará. It is said to be one of the best preserved towns in the S. Lots of locals cross to Peru here, but no tourists. Migración/police is in town.

● **Accommodation** **G** *Pensión Zapotillo* and **F** *Hotel Los Angeles*.

The S route from Catamayo to Macará is via Cariamanga. The road is paved to **Cariamanga**, via **Gonzanamá**, a pleasant, sleepy little town famed for the weaving of beautiful *alforjas* (multi-purpose saddlebags); **F** *Res Jiménez* (cold shower).

It's 27.5 km to Cariamanga (hotels, banks), then the road twists its way westwards to **Colaisaca**, before descending steeply 2,000m to **Utuana** (not rec for cyclists in the other direction). From there the road heads NW to **Sozoranga**, 75 km from Gonzanamá (hotel, **G**, shared cold shower) and on, S for 36 km, to Macará.

MACARA

(*Pop* 14,296; *Alt* 600m), a dusty town on the border, is in a rice-growing area. There are road connections to Sullana near the Peruvian coast.

● **Accommodation** **E** *Espiga de Oro*, opp the market, cheaper without bath, fan, TV, clean, rec; **E** *Paradero Turístico*, best, pool, restaurant, not far from centre; **F** *Amazonas*, Rengel 418, clean, basic; **G** *Res Paraíso*, Veintimilla 553, shared bath, clean, laundry facilities, noisy, unfriendly.

● **Places to eat** *Colonial Macará*, Rengel y Bolívar, helpful, but food not too good; *Dragón Dorado*, Calderón, seafood, popular; *Heladería Cream*, Veintimilla y Sucre, great ice cream; *Soda Bar Manolo* for breakfast.

FRONTIER WITH PERU

● **Ecuadorean immigration**
Open 0800-1800, closed 1200-1400, 7 days a week. Formalities last about 30 mins. It is reported as a much easier crossing than at Huaquillas.

A Peruvian tourist card can be obtained from the Peruvian Honorary Consul in Macará, if he is available, or at the border if not already obtained in Quito or Guayaquil.

● **Exchange**
The bank at Macará does not change money, so change sucres on the street to give you enough new soles to last you until you reach Sullana (Peru). You can change money at the market in the town centre, where the rates are better than at the border or in Loja. Better to change sucres in Ecuador, but beware of rip-offs changing sucres to soles.

● **Transport**
There is a 2½-km walk or taxi ride to the international bridge over the Río Macará; US$0.50 shared, up to US$2 in a pick-up from Macará market. A truck leaves the plaza in Macará at 0745. Beware of overcharging coming from Peru. Coop Loja and Cariamanga, 13 buses a day Macará to Loja, 6 to 8 hrs, US$3.50. The whole journey can be done in a day if you arrive at the border at noon. The Loja-border journey takes only 3½ hrs by car. On the Peruvian side, colectivos run to Sullana for US$3 pp, 2 hrs, 1 passport checkpoint. Colectivos take you to where camionetas leave for Piura, 30 mins, US$0.70.

Guayaquil and South to Peru

THRIVING and ever increasing banana plantations with shrimp farms among the mangroves are the economic mainstay of the coastal area bordering the east flank of the Gulf of Guayaquil; rice, sugar, coffee and cacao are also produced. The Guayas lowlands are subject to flooding, humidity is high and biting insects are fierce. Mangroves characterize the coast leading south to Huaquillas, the main border crossing to Peru.

GUAYAQUIL

Ecuador's largest city (*Pop* officially 1,508,000, more like 2,400,000; *Phone code* 4) and the country's chief seaport, industrial and commercial centre lies on the W bank of the Río Guayas, some 56 km from its outflow into the Gulf of Guayaquil. Founded in 1535 by Sebastián de Belalcázar, then again in 1537 by Francisco Orellana, the city has always been an intense political rival to Quito. Guayaquil is also hotter, faster and brasher than the capital, and Guayaquileños are certainly more lively, colourful and open than their Quito counterparts.

The Puerto Marítimo handles about 90% of the country's imports and 50% of its exports. The huge influx of people caused by rural migration and population explosion, has stretched the city's services beyond the limit. Water supply and rubbish collection have improved, but the installation of new water pipes and traffic schemes mean chaos for drivers (until 1997 at the earliest). It is often quicker to walk short distances in the centre, rather than take a bus or taxi (but don't walk after dark).

The climate from May to Dec is dry with often overcast days but pleasantly cool nights, whereas the hot rainy season from Jan to April can be oppressively humid.

Places of interest

A wide, tree-lined waterfront avenue, the Malecón, runs alongside the Río Guayas from the exclusive **Club de la Unión**, by the Moorish clock tower, past the imposing **Palacio Municipal** and **Government Palace** and the old Yacht Club to Las Peñas. Half way along, the Blvd 9 de Octubre, the city's main street, starts in front of La Rotonda, a statue to mark the famous yet mysterious meeting between Simón Bolívar and San Martín in 1822. There are 11 piers (*muelles*) running along the Malecón; from the most northerly, near Las Peñas, ferries across the river to Durán (see page 1098).

The old district of **Las Peñas** is a last picturesque, if ramshackle and small, vestige of colonial Guayaquil with its wooden houses and narrow cobbled street (Numa Pompilio Llona). Now occupied mostly by artists, there is a large open-air exhibition of paintings and sculpture every July. It makes a pleasant walk, but this is a poor area and you are strongly advised not to walk there at night, nor at any time on the adjacent streets of the Cerro Santa Ana that overlook Las Peñas.

The main plaza half way up 9 Octubre is the **Plaza Centenario** with a towering monument to the liberation of the city erected in 1920. In the pleasant, shady **Parque Bolívar** tame iguanas scuttle out of the trees for scraps. On it stands the **Cathedral**, in classical Gothic style, inaugurated in the 1950s.

There are several noteworthy churches.
Santo Domingo, the city's first church
founded in 1548, stands just by Las Peñas.
Also **San Francisco,** with its restored colonial interior, off 9 de Octubre and P

Carbo, and the beautiful **La Merced.**

At the N end of the centre, below Cerro
El Carmen, the huge, spreading **Cemetery** with its dazzling, high-rise tombs
and the ostentatious mausolea of the rich

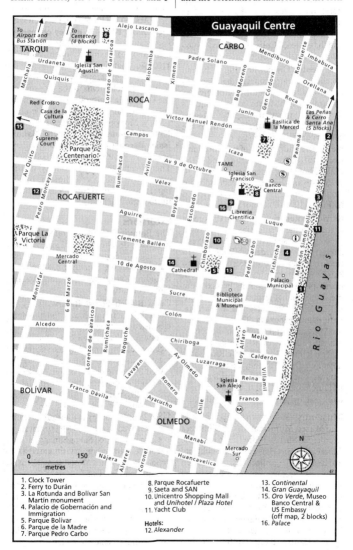

1. Clock Tower
2. Ferry to Durán
3. La Rotunda and Bolívar San Martín monument
4. Palacio de Gobernación and Immigration
5. Parque Bolívar
6. Parque de la Madre
7. Parque Pedro Carbo

8. Parque Rocafuerte
9. Saeta and SAN
10. Unicentro Shopping Mall and *Unihotel / Plaza Hotel*
11. Yacht Club

Hotels:
12. *Alexander*

13. *Continental*
14. *Gran Guayaquil*
15. *Oro Verde,* Museo Banco Central & US Embassy (off map, 2 blocks)
16. *Palace*

is worth a visit. A flower market over the road sells the best selection of blooms in the city. It's best to go on a Sun when there are plenty of people about.

There are numerous sports clubs and the horse race track of **El Buijo** is set in delightful surroundings some 5 km outside the city. There are two football stadia and the enclosed Coliseo Cerrado for boxing, basketball and other entertainments.

The **Centro Cívico**, heading S, has an excellent theatre/concert hall and is home to the Guayaquil Symphony Orchestra which gives free concerts throughout the year. The new **Teatro Centro de Arte** on the road out to the coast is another first class theatre complex with a wide variety of presentations. Colourful markets are at the S end of the Malecón or along 6 de Marzo between 10 de Agosto and Ballén. The Mercado Sur, next to Club de la Unión, prefabricated by Eiffel (1905-07), is not safe to enter.

Barrio Centenario to the S of the centre is the original residential sector, now a peaceful, tree-shaded haven. Newer residential areas are **Urdesa**, NW of the centre, in between two branches of the Estero Salado (about 15 mins from downtown, traffic permitting). 5 mins by taxi from the international airport and bus terminal, are the districts of **La Garzota**, **Sauces** and **Alborada**. They are cleaner, less congested and safer than the centre, but with all services, 10-15 mins by taxi.

Two long bridges span the Ríos Babahoyo and Daule, as they merge into the Guayas. The road across the bridges leads to Durán and the rail terminal on the E bank (see below).

Museums

The **Museo Municipal**, in the Biblioteca Municipal, Sucre y Pedro Carbo (near the *Hotel Continental*) has paintings, gold and archaeological collections, shrunken heads, a section on the history of Guayaquil and a good newspaper library. Open Wed-Fri 0900-1600, Sat 1000-1500, Sun 1000-1300; US$0.15 for Ecuadoreans and US$0.40 for foreigners (free on Sat, but passport must be left at desk).

The Central Bank's **anthropological museum**, Anteparra 900 y 9 de Octubre, has excellent displays of ceramics, gold objects and paintings; entry US$1.20, open Mon to Fri 1000-1800, Sat 1000-1600, Sun 1000-1400. The Pinacoteca Manuel Rendoy Seminario is on the first floor. **Museo del Banco del Pacífico** (address under **Banks & money changers**) is a beautiful small museum mainly of archaeological exhibits, open Tues-Fri 1100-1800, Sat-Sun 1100-1300.

There is an impressive collection of prehistoric gold items at the museum of the **Casa de la Cultura**, together with an archaeological museum, 9 de Octubre 1200 y Moncayo, open Tues-Fri 1000-1700. **Religious Art Museum Nahim Isaias Barquet** is at Pichincha y Ballén, open Tues-Fri 0900-1700, Sat 1000-1300. There is a pinacoteca (art gallery) on the ground and first floors of the same building. There is a **small zoo**, open on Sun, at the Colegio Nacional.

Excursions

The **Botanical Gardens** are NW on Av Francisco de Orellana to Las Orquídeas housing estate; good views and a pleasant walk. Entrance US$2. Over 3,000 plants, including 150 species of Ecuadorean and foreign orchids.

Cerro Blanco Forest Reserve is set in tropical dry forest with over 190 bird species listed so far, eg the Guayaquil green macaw, crane hawk, snail kite, etc, and with sightings of howler monkeys, ocelot, puma, jaguar, and peccaries among others. It is owned by La Cemento Nacional: reservations and prepayment from Multicomercio, Of 91, p 1, Eloy Alfaro y Cuenca, T 871-900, F 872-236; US$0.85 plus US$6.25 per group, up to 8, for guide. Trails are open Wed to Sun 0800-1600. Advance booking not needed Sat or Sun; pay at the site office. Early morning visits are best for seeing more wildlife. Mosquito repellent is a must. Camping US$2.50/night.

On the other side of the road is **Puerto Hondo**. Canoe trips through the mangroves can be arranged on the spot at weekends from the Fundación Pro-Bosque kiosk for US$7 pp with guides, or through the week with La Cemento Nacional.

● **Access** The reserve is at Km 14.5 on the coast road to Salinas; entrance beyond the Club Rocafuerte. Taxi from Guayaquil US$10-20. The yellow and green 'Chongonera' buses leave every 30 mins from Parque Victoria and pass the park entrance on the way to Puerto Hondo.

Heading E then S from Guayaquil, 22 km beyond the main crossroads at Km 26 on the road to Naranjal, lies the **Ecological Reserve of Manglares Churute**. Canoe trips into the mangroves with guides can see waterbirds, animals and dolphins; arrange through Inefan in Guayaquil, Dept Forestal, Av Quito 402 y P Solano, p 10, T 397-730, or through *Chasquitur*, Urdaneta 1418 y Av Del Ejército, T 281-085. To walk self-guided nature trail over the hills costs US$14; a boat trip costs an extra US$50.

● **Buses** Buses leave the terminal nr the airport every 30 mins going to Naranjal or Machala. Ask to be let off at Churute information centre.

Local festivals
In addition to national holidays, **25 July**, *Foundation of the City*. At *Carnival* before Lent, watch out for malicious throwing of water balloons, mud, ink and paint, women are prime targets. In contrast New Year's Eve is lots of fun. *Años Viejos* parade along the Malecón, children beg for alms for their life-size *viejos*, families take their *viejos* for car rides through the centre of town, and all these figures are piled onto a vast conflagration and explode at midnight.

Local information
● **Accommodation**

Hotel prices

L1	over US$200	**L2**	US$151-200
L3	US$101-150	**A1**	US$81-100
A2	US$61-80	**A3**	US$46-60
B	US$31-45	**C**	US$21-30
D	US$12-20	**E**	US$7-11
F	US$4-6	**G**	up to US$3

Unless otherwise stated, all hotels in range **D** and above have private bath. Assume friendliness and cleanliness in all cases.

Hotel prices are higher than in Quito and are set by the Tourist Board. Upmarket establishments often have one rate for nationals and a much higher one in dollars for foreigners. Always check the rate and whether the 20% service and taxes are included. In the better hotels booking is advised. Most hotels are downtown, so take

a taxi from the airport or bus station. The cheap hotels are pretty basic, many cater to short stay customers, and singles seem hard to find. The following list includes 20% service and tax in the prices.

NB All of the downtown area is unsafe; caution is especially important at night. It is rec to stay in the districts of La Garzota, Sauces and Alborada, nr the airport and bus terminal.

L1 *Hilton Colón*, Av Francisco Orellana, T 689-000, F 689-149, new Jan 97, superb rooms, price does not include breakfast, 4 restaurants, 2 pools; **L1** *Oro Verde*, 9 de Octubre y García Moreno, T 327-999, F 329-350, PO Box 09-01-9636, restaurants, bar, disco, pool, rec; **L3** *Continental*, Chile y 10 de Agosto, T 329-270, F 325-454 (a KLM Golden Tulip hotel), 5-star, cable TV, good coffee shop, rec; **L3** *Gran Hotel Guayaquil*, Boyacá 1600 y 10 de Agosto, T 329-690, F 327-251, good restaurants, swimming pool, sauna, etc, non residents can use pool, US$2/day; **L3** *Ramada*, Malecón y Orellana, T 565-555, pleasantly situated overlooking the river, with pool, mostly used by businessmen; **L3** *Unihotel*, Clemente Ballén 406 y Chile, T 327-100, F 328-352, good restaurant and breakfast.

A1 *Boulevard*, 9 de Octubre 432, T 566-700, F 560-076, very central, casino, shows, rec; **A2** *Palace*, Chile 214 y Luque, T 321-080, excellent, good value for business travellers, traffic noise on Av Chile side, restaurant, travel agency, fax service, highly rec; **A2** *Sol de Oriente*, Aguirre 603 y Escobedo, T 325-500, F 329-352, excellent value, rec; **A3** *Del Rey*, Aguirre y Marín, T 453-037, F 453-351, behind tennis club, inc breakfast, clean.

B *Doral*, Aguirre y Chile 402, T 328-490, F 327-088, good rooms and value, central, rec.

C *Majestic*, 9 de Octubre 709, T 324-134, central, fan or a/c; **C** *Plaza*, Chile 414 y Clemente Ballén, T 324-006, some cheaper rooms, international newspapers; **C** *Rizzo*, Clemente Ballén 319 y Chile, T 325-210, F 326-209, a/c, safe, central on Parque Bolivar, some windowless rooms, room service, *Café Jambeli* downstairs for seafood.

D *Acuario*, Luque 1204 y Quito, T 533-715, a/c, fridge, **E** with fan; **D** *Alexander*, Luque 1107 y Pedro Moncayo, T 532-000, F 514-161, a/c, comfortable, good value, some rooms without windows, noisy; **D** *Capri*, Luque y Machala, T 326-341, a/c, fridge, cafeteria, very clean and safe, busy at weekends; **D** *Paseo Real*, Luque 1011 y 6 de Mayo, T 532-710, a/c, **E** for inner rooms, cheaper with fan; **D** *Venezia*, Quisquis y Rumichaca, clean.

E *Centenario*, Vélez 726 y Santa Elena, T 524-467, with bath, TV, a/c, cheaper with fan;

Guayaquil Northern Suburbs

Not to scale

N

La Rotonda

ALBORADA

Av Benjamin Rosales

Av B Carrión

Av Jaime Roldos

Av Isidro Ayora

Av Egas

SAUCES

OBEV

Roldos Statue

Plaza Mayor

Av Orellana

Av Freire

Garzo Centro

GARZOTA

Terminal Terrestre

Av Juan Tanca Marengo

CC Plaza Quil

To Urdesa

Av Las Americas

To City Centre

Hotels:	Places to eat:
1. Youth Hostel	2. Cangrejo Criollo
	3. Manantial del Marisco

47A

with many in the larger hotels, around Urdesa, or La Alborada and La Garzota, which have many good eating houses. 20% service and tax is added on in the smarter places.

Chinese: a wide variety in the city, most do take-away, good value. *Gran Chifa*, P Carbo 1016, wide variety, good value; *Cantonés*, Av G Pareja y C 43, La Garzota, huge rather glaring emporium with authentic dishes and all-you-can-eat menu for US$9, karaoke. **Japanese**: *Tsuji*, Estrada 815, wonderful, authentic dishes, Teppan Yaki, expensive; *UniBar* in *Uni Hotel* complex, sushi.

Italian: *La Trattoria da Enrico*, Bálsamos 504, expensive but fun surroundings, good antipasto. Pizzas: *Pizza Hut* on 9 de Octubre in Urdesa, La Garzota and Barrio Centenario; *El Hornero*, Estrada y Higuerilla, part of Quito chain; *Pizzería Del Ñato*, Estrada 1219, good value, sold by the metre.

Mexican: *Noches Tapatías*, Primera y Dátiles, Urdesa, fun, good live music at weekends; *Mi Cielito Lindo*, Circunvalación 623 y Ficus, good.

Spanish: *Casa Basca*, Chile 406 y C Ballén, wonderful hole-in-the-wall place, expensive food, cash only, house wine good value, great atmosphere, gets very crowded; *Puerta de Alcalá*, Circulación y Ficus, upmarket.

International: *El Fortín* in *Hotel Continental*; *1822* in the *Gran Hotel*; *Le Gourmet* at the *Oro Verde*; *La Banca*, Icaza 115 y Pichincha, popular with business community; *Posada de las Garzas*, Urdesa Norte, Circunvalación Norte 536, also French style dishes; *El Parque*, top floor of Unicentro, popular buffet lunches at the weekends; *Caracol Azul*, 9 Octubre 1918 y Los Ríos, excellent seafood; *Juan Salvador Gaviota*, Kennedy Norte, Av Fco de Orellana, good seafood; *La Balandra*, Sa 504 entre Monjas y Dátiles, Urdesa, for good fish, upmarket ambience, also has a crab house at Circunvalación 506 y Ficus, Urdesa.

General: *Canoa Bar* in *Hotel Continental* for traditional dishes rarely found these days, with different specials during the week, open 24 hrs; *Salón Melba*, Córdova 720 y Junín, old fashioned eating house/coffee shop; *Muelle 5*, Malecón y Urdaneta, on a pier, good seafood; *Pique Y Pase*, Lascano 16-17 y Carchi, popular with students, lively; *El Patio* in the *Oro Verde*, for reasonably priced food, open 24 hrs; *El Caribe*, VE Estrada 1017 y Jiguas, Urdesa, good value and service, cheap set lunches, rec, wonderful *chupes de pescado*; *El Taller*, Quisquis y Esmeraldas, tiny place decked out with odd bits and pieces of old Guayaquil, live music in evenings. *Viejo Barrio*, over the bridge from the Policentro in Urdesa, lots of cafés offering a variety of dishes, all in fake old Guayaquil style.

E Danubio, P Icaza 604 y Escobedo, T 300-197, with bath, fan, some a/c; *E Jitur*, Colón 804 y Rumichaca, T 523-073, with bath, fan, clean; *E Res Pauker*, Baquerizo Moreno 902 y Junín, T 565-385, shared bath, run down, old-time haunt for travellers, safe; *E Vélez*, Vélez 1021 y Quito, T 530-356, with bath, a/c, cheaper without a/c and TV, clean, good value, rec.

F-G pp *Berlín*, Rumichaca 1503, T 524-648, with bath, fan, clean, front rooms noisy; *F* pp *Libertador*, Garaycoa 893, Parque Centenario, T 304-637, fan, bath.

G Hostal Miami, P Montúfar 534, T 519-667, fan, bath; *G Imperial*, Urdaneta 705, T 560-512, basic.

Youth Hostel: *E* pp *Ecuahogar*, Sauces I, Av Isidro Ayora, opp Banco Ecuatoriana de La Vivienda, T 248-357, F 248-341, member of IYHA and Ecuadorean Hostelling Association, 10% discount for members, non-members welcome, inc breakfast, bunk rooms and rooms with bath, cooking and laundry facilities, tourist information, safe, will pick up from bus station and airport, or take buses 2 or 66, discount for longer stay, English and German spoken, set meals in restaurant US$2, very helpful, highly rec.

● **Places to eat**
The main areas for restaurants are the centre

Seafood Crab Houses: these are almost an institution and great fun. *Manny's*, Av Miraflores y Segunda, not cheap but try the excellent *arroz con cangrejo*; *Casa del Cangrejo*, Av Plaza Dañin, Kennedy, for crab dishes of every kind; several others along the same street; *El Cangrejo Rojo*, Rumichaca 2901; *El Cangrejo Criollo*, Av Principal, Villa 9, La Garzota, excellent, varied seafood menu, etc. **Oyster Bars**: cultivated oysters are all the rage and many menus carry them. *Oystercatcher*, Higueras y Mirtos, Urdesa, varied menu; *Bodegas del Mar*, Centro Comercial Plaza Quil opp the Policentro, a fish shop selling 12 fresh, opened oysters for US$2.25.

Steak Houses: *Donde el Ché*, F Boloña S21A, holds competition to see who can eat the biggest steak, winner doesn't pay, music, tango and shows; *Parillada Del Ñato*, Estrada 1219, huge variety and portions, excellent value; *La Selvita*, Av Olmos y Las Brisas, Las Lomas de Urdesa, good atmosphere and fine panoramic views, also at Calle D y Rosa Borja, Centenario; *El Torro*, Luque y Garaycoa, huge steaks, pay in advance, fast food atmosphere.

Vegetarian: *Maranatá I*, Chile y Cuenca, and *II*, Quisquis y Rumichaca; *Super Nutrión I*, Chimborazo y 10 de Agosto, and *II* Chimborazo y Letamendi; *Girasol*, Chile y Colón; *Renacer*, G Avilés y Sucre; *Hare Krishna*, 1 de Mayo y 6 de Marzo; *Salud Solar*, Pedro Moncayo y Luque; *Bocado Natural*, Multicomercio, p 1; *Ollantay*, Tungurahua 508 y 9 de Octubre; *Paraíso*, Av Juan Tanca Marengo, Km 1.5; *Paxilandia*, Guayacanes 208 y C Primera in the Valmor Centre, Urdesa.

Fast Food: *Italian Deli*, in Albán Borja and Policentro, good self-service meals, great salads; *Pollos Gus*, Maracaibo 530 y Quito, Plaza Triángulo in Urdesa, Terminal Terrestre, good chicken and typical dishes.

Snacks: there are many places selling all sorts of snacks. Try *pan de yuca*, or *empanadas*, but beware of eating at street stalls. Excellent sandwiches at *Submarine*, 9 Octubre y Chile; *Miami Subs*, Chimborazo 425 y Ballén, and Estrada y Alborada, Urdesa, salads and sandwiches; *Uni Deli* in the Unicentro, good salami and cheese; *La Chiveria*, Circunvalación y Ficus for good yoghurt and *pan de yuca*; *La Selecta*, Estrada y Laureles, good sandwiches.

Ice-cream: *Top Cream*, the best, with many outlets throughout the city, try their local fruit sorbets.

● **Airline offices**

TAME, 9 de Octubre 424, edif Gran Pasaje, T 561-751; Saeta and SAN, main admin office at Av Arosemena Km 2.5, sales office at 9 de Octubre 2002 y Los Ríos, T 200-600 (bilingual information line), 200-614; Ecuatoriana, 9 de Octubre y Malecón, T 322-025, F 288-020; Cedta, T 301-165; AELA, T 288-580/228-110; AeroPerú, Icaza 451, T 563-600; British Airways, Velez 206 y Chile, T 325-080.

● **Banks & money changers**

Lloyds Bank, Pichincha 108-110, with Mercado Central and Urdesa agencies, high commission on TCs; Citibank, 9 de Octubre, Citicorp cheques only and before 1330; Banco del Pacífico, Icaza 200, p 4, no commission on TCs, advances money on Mastercard; Filanbanco, 9 de Octubre entre Pichincha y P Carbo, cash advance with Visa ATM, good rates, no commission; American Express, 9 de Octubre 1900 y Esmeraldas, for purchase of TCs. Queues are much longer in the afternoon. Banco de Guayaquil, ATMs advance cash with Visa (Sucres only). There is a Mastercard office on Rocafuerte, nr Parque Rocafuerte.

There are various Casas de Cambio on Av 9 de Octubre (eg Cambio Paz) and C Pichincha; also Cambiosa, in Albán Borja and Cambitur on Baquerizo Moreno 113 y Malecón, rec. Most open 0900-1900, closed Sat. Wander Cambios at airport (see below). It's difficult to change money at the bus station. When all the rest are closed (eg Sun) try Hotel Oro Verde and similar places, quite good exchange rate for cash, will change small TC amounts.

Street changers on 9 de Octubre y Pichincha, best rates for cash, very organized.

● **Embassies & consulates**

Argentina, Aguirre 104, T 323-574; Bolivia, P Ycaza 302 y Córdova, T 564-260; Brazil, Ciudadela Nueva Kennedy, C 9 Este A 208, T 393-979; Colombia, Gral Córdova 808 y VM Rendón, T 563-854; Peru, 9 de Octubre 411, p 6, T 322-738, 0900-1330; Venezuela, Chile 331, T 326-566.

Austria, 9 de Octubre 1312, T 282-303; Belgium, Lizardo García 310 y Vélez, T 364-429; Denmark, Gen Córdoba 604 y Mendiburu, T 308-020, open 0900-1200; Finland, Luis Urdaneta 212 y Córdova, T 304-381; France, Aguirre 503 y Chimborazo, p 6, T 328-159; Germany, 9 de Octubre 109, T 513-876; Netherlands, 9 de Octubre 2309, p 5, T 366-410; Norway, Blvd 9 de Octubre 109 y Malecón, T 329-661; Switzerland, 9 de Octubre 2105, T 453-607l; UK, Córdova 623 y P Solano, T 560-400.

Canada, Córdova 812 y Rendón, T 563-580; USA, 9 de Octubre 1571 y García Moreno, T 323-570.

● **Entertainment**

There are discos, bars and casinos in most of the major hotels. Other discos at *Infinity*, Estrada

505; *Latin Palace*, Av J Tanca Marengo y Roldós; *El Corsario*, Los Ríos y Piedrahita; *Disco Gente*, Estrada 913, for café-theatre style comedy show with dancing afterwards; *Reencuentros*, entrance to Urdesa Norte, C 6, music, bar, live show; *Cato's Pub*, Estrada 608 y Las Monjas; *Falls*, VE Estrada y Las Monjas, Urdesa, pool tables; *Aló*, VE Estrada y Dátiles, bar, disco, outdoor eating, cheap set lunches. For an unforgettable and alcoholic evening 'city tour' take *La Chiva* (open-sided bus) from *Infinity* on Fri at 2130, which provides en route as many rum punches as you can hold, stopping off occasionally for a ceviche, dancing, fireworks, crab sandwich before depositing you back at *Infinity* for US$14 pp. Usually for groups only, details available from *Viajes Horizontes*, T 281-260. Trips on the Río Guayas with the (fake) paddle boat *El Pedregal* to the Club Pedregal on E side; US$3.70, inc boat ride, use of pool etc, the complex has restaurant and bar. Boat departs Muelle Pedregal Sat and Sun 1130 and 1330 returning 1630 and 1730. See *El Universo* for cinemas and other entertainments. Cinemas cost US$2.25, one double bill.

● **Hospitals & medical services**
Doctors: *Dr Angel Serrano Sáenz*, Boyacá 821, T 301-373, English speaking. *Dr Alfonso E León Guim*, Centro de Especialidades, Boyacá 1320 y Luque, T 517-793, English speaking. *Clínica Santa Marianita*, Boyacá 1915 entre Colón y Av Olmedo, T 322-500, doctors speak English and Spanish, special rates for SAHB users.

Hospitals: the main hospital used by the foreign community is the *Clínica Kennedy*, Av del Periodista, T 286-963, which contains the consulting rooms of almost every kind of specialist doctor and diagnostic laboratory (Dr Roberto Morla speaks German); very competent emergency department.

● **Places of worship**
Anglican-Episcopalian Church, Calle D entre Bogotá y A Fuentes, T 443-050; Centro Cristiano de Guayaquil, Pastor John Jerry Smith, Av Juan Tanca Marengo, Km 3, T 271-423; many other sects represented.

● **Post and telecommunications**
Post Office and Emetel are in the same block at Pedro Carbo y Aguirre. Buy long-distance *fichas* for telephone calls before contacting the international operator. Good *poste restante* service. Parcels to be sent abroad have to be sealed in front of postal assistant, reliable service, p.1, ventanilla 12. Branch post offices in Urdesa, Estrada y Las Lomas; Policentro; airport and Terminal Terrestre. The major hotels also sell stamps. Many courier services for reliable delivery of papers and packages.

● **Security**
Guayaquil is becoming increasingly insecure, especially around hotel or bank entrances, attackers usually working in pairs. The Malecón in early morning and from dusk onwards is bad for snatch thieves. Also near the toilets in the Terminal Terrestre bus station where thieves work in pairs. Street robbery also occurs in Durán. Do not walk anywhere with valuables and take taxis at night. Cholera, dengue and rabies are present.

● **Shopping**
Books: *Librería Científica*, Luque 223 y Chile and Plaza Triángulo on the Estrada in Urdesa, has English books and is good for field guides to flora and fauna and travel in general; *Nuevos Horizontes*, 6 de Marzo 924 for book exchange. *Selecciones* in Albanborja has a choice of pricey novels and lots of magazines in English.

Shopping malls: *Unicentro*, Aguirre y Chile; *Policentro* and *Plaza Quil*, both on Av San Jorge, N Kennedy; *Albán Borja*, Av Arosemena Km 2.7; *Garzocentro 2000*, La Garzota, Av R Pareja; *La Rotonda*, entrance to La Garzota, US-style shopping; *Plaza Mayor*, La Alborada, Av R Pareja and, nearby, *Albocentro*. *Riocentro*, Av Samborondón, for good, expensive, US-style shopping. *Mall del Sol*, nr airport, to open end-1997.

For handicrafts: good quality but expensive products are found at Madeleine Hollander's shop in the *Oro Verde*; *Manos* in Urdesa (Cedros 305 y Primera); *Artesanías del Ecuador*, 9 Octubre 104 y Malecón are good and reliable as is *Ocepa*, Rendón 405 y Córdova, where prices compare favourably with the towns where the goods are made. Good variety of *artesanías* in Albán Borja Mall at *El Telar*; *Ramayana* for good ceramics; *Centro de Artesanías Montecristi*, Juan Tanca Marengo Km 0.5 for straw and wicker goods and furniture.

For bargains and variety try the *handicrafts market* between Loja y Montalvo and Córdova y Chimborazo, almost a whole block of permanent stalls; the Otavalan Indians sell their crafts along Chile between 9 Octubre y Vélez. Panama hats, good quality, authentic, from *Sombrero Barberán*, 12 de Mayo 112, N end of Parque Centenario; also in the handicraft market.

Photos: developed reliably at *Rapi-Color*, Boyacá 1418 y Luque, or *Photo Market*, VE Estrada 726 y Guayacanes, Urdesa, prints and slides. Camera repairs at *Cinefoto*, Luque 314 y Chimborazo, English spoken. Cheap film and instant ID photos from *Discount New York* in Albán Borja.

Camping equipment: (expensive) and camping gas are available from *Casa Maspons*, Ballén 517 y Boyacá, *Marathon*, 9 de Octubre y Escobedo, or in Policentro (also sells cheap T-shirts, choose your own motif). *Kao Policentro*, has fishing, camping and sports gear at good prices.

The **Bahía**, or black market, on either side of Olmedo from Villamil to Chile, is the most popular place for electrical appliances, clothing, shoes, food and drink. It was traditionally where contraband was sold from boats which put into the bay and is one of the city's oldest market places. Watch your valuables and be prepared to bargain.

● **Sports**
Swimming: pool at Malecón Simón Bolívar 116.

● **Tour companies & travel agents**
Wanderjahr, P Icaza 431, Edif Gran Pasaje, T 562-111, branches in Policentro, T 288-400, the *Hotel Oro Verde*, Albanborja, T 203-913; *Ecuadorean Tours*, 9 Octubre 1900 y Esmeraldas, T 287-111, is agent for Amex, branches Chile y 10 de Agosto and in Urdesa, Estrada 117, T 388-080; *Metropolitan Touring – Galapagos Cruises*, Antepara 915, T 320-300; *Ecoventura*, Av CJ Arosemena Km 2.5, T 206-748/9, F 202-990, see also under Quito **Tour companies** and under the Galápagos; *Galasam Cía Ltda*, Edif Gran Pasaje, 9 Octubre 424, ground floor, local 9A, and p 11 of 1108, T 304-488/311-485/ 306-289/311-042, F 313-351/562-033, see Galápagos section (page 1145) for their Economic Galapagos Tours programmes. *La Moneda Tours*, Av Las Américas 809, T 690900, F 690911, E-mail: travel@lamonedea.com.ec, has branches in Riocentro shopping center, T 831-201, F 831-214, Quito, Machala and in the USA (T (305) 379-8110), specializes in coastal and archaeological tours; *Canodros*, Luis Urdaneta, 1418 y Av del Ejército, T 285-711, F 287-651, PO Box 09-01-8442, E-mail: eco-tourism1@canodros.com.ec; run Galápagos cruises on MV *Renaissance*. They also operate the Kapawi Ecological Reserve, in conjunction with OINAE (Organization of Ecuadorean Achuar Nationalities), at the junction of the Pastaza and Kapahuari rivers, in Morona Santiago province; 4 nights in a double cabin with bath costs US$700, plus US$200 return flight from Quito; highly rec (see also page 1133).

Whale watching is gaining in popularity; a rec company is *Whale Tours*, Vélez 911 y 6 de Marzo, El Forum, p 5, T 524-608, a day trip costs US$16 pp. Trips can also be arranged out of Puerto López.

Most agencies arrange city tours, 2$\frac{1}{2}$ hrs, US$8-10 pp with English-speaking guide, eg *Royal Tours Service*, T 326-688. Also Fernando Icaza, bilingual tourist services, T/F 200-925, has his own minibus.

● **Tourist offices**
Cetur, Aguirre 104 y Malecón, p 1, T 328-312; friendly but poorly informed about anything outside their area or other than standard tourist attractions, Spanish only, open 0900-1730, Mon-Fri. They sell a map of Ecuador. Maps also from **Instituto Geográfico Militar**, 9 de Octubre y Rumichaca. A Policía de Turismo man can be hired for a guided tour of Guayaquil. Cost will be about US$4/hr for taxi (2 hrs is enough) and US$3 to the Policía de Turismo.

● **Useful addresses**
Immigration: Av Pichincha y Aguirre (Gobernación), T 514-925/516-789, for visa extensions.

● **Transport**
Local Buses City buses are clean, modern and comfortable, US$0.25; also minibuses (*furgonetas*), US$0.20, which post up their routes in the windscreen. Buses are not allowed in the centre; almost all go along the Malecón. Bus No 15 from the centre to Urdesa, 13 to Policentro, 14 to Albanborja, 74 to La Garzota and Sauces. **Car hire**: Budget T 288-510 (airport), 328-571 (by *Oro Verde*); **Ecucars** T 283-247 (airport); **Avis** T 287-906 (airport); **Arrancar** T 284-454 (airport); **Delgado** T 287-768 (airport), 398-687 (centre); **Internacional** T 284-136 (airport). Cheapest rates US$26-30/day, inc 10% tax and insurance, mileage extra. All offer 3-day weekend rates (US$147-154, not inc tax and insurance, 600 km free, Group C-D) and weekly rates with 1,200 km free. **Taxis**: have no meters, so prices are very negotiable and overcharging is notorious. It should be approx US$3 from centre to Urdesa or Policentro, short runs US$1 (if you are very persistent). To Durán, across the bridge, see under **Trains**. *Taxi rutas* run a set route, charging US$0.40; they are yellow with contrasting bonnets, or stripes over the roof, eg ones with red bonnets run from the Bahía, Centro, Urdesa to Mapasingue and back.

Air Simón Bolívar International Airport, 10 mins N by taxi (1 hr on foot) from the city centre (US$3-5). US$0.25 by bus; No 2 from Malecón, No 3 from Centro Cívico, No 69 from Plaza Victoria. If going straight on to another city, get the bus directly to bus station, which is close by; a taxi from the airport to the bus terminal is US$1.50. If you are arriving in Guayaquil and need a taxi from the airport, walk $\frac{1}{2}$ block from the terminal out to Av Las Américas, where taxis and camionetas wait for passengers and charge about half the fare of the airport taxi cooperative.

Facilities at the airport include an information desk; Cetur office (erratic hours); *Wander Cambio*, open 7 days a week, closed at night, rates lower than other *cambios* or banks, but better than hotels; several bank ATMs; car hire;

a modern cafetería (but none beyond customs) and a post office. To get to the baggage reclaim area you must leave the airport and re-enter further down the building. Show your boarding pass to enter and baggage ticket to leave.

Air services: many flights daily to **Quito**, (TAME, Saeta, SAN; ensure seats are confirmed, not standby, though seats are usually available outside peak hours of early morning and evening). Sit on the right side for the best views. To **Cuenca, Loja, Machala**. Daily to **Galápagos** (see page 1135). Commuter flights daily on 5-17 seater planes from the Terminal de Avionetas on the city side of the international airport, on Cedta to Machala, or AELA, to Bahía de Caráquez, Manta, Portoviejo and **Pedernales** (reported unreliable).

Road There is a 3¼-km bridge from Guayaquil across the river to Durán. A good paved road from there (summit at 4,120m) connects with the Andean Highway at Cajabamba, nr Riobamba (see page 1065). Also from Durán main roads go to Babahoyo, Quevedo and Santo Domingo, to Cuenca, and to the southern lowlands. **Buses**: the Terminal Terrestre is just N of the airport, just off the road to the Guayas bridge. The company offices are on the ground floor, departures on top floor. There is no left luggage depot and do not leave anything unattended. The terminal is chaotic and busy at weekends. There are some expensive restaurants, use of toilet US$0.10, bus tickets include terminal tax of US$0.05. A great many local buses go from the bus station to centre. Taxi to centre, US$3-5. Several companies to/from **Quito**, 8 hrs, from US$5 to US$13.35 for Rey Tours non-stop, a/c service (office in *Gran Hotel*). To **Cuenca**, 5½ hrs, US$6; **Riobamba**, 5 hrs, US$3.25; **Santo Domingo de los Colorados**, 4¾ hrs, US$4-5; **Manta**, 3 hrs, US$4; **Esmeraldas**, 7 hrs, US$5; **Portoviejo**, 3½ hrs, US$4, and to **Bahía de Caráquez**, 5½ hrs, US$4.45. To **Ambato**, 6½ hrs, US$6. To **Alausí**, 4 hrs, US$3.25. Regular and frequent buses to **Playas**, 2 hrs, US$1.35; and to **Salinas**, 2½ hrs, US$1.85. **Machala** (for Peru) 3½ hrs, US$2.65, frequent, or by minibus 2½ hrs, leave at 20-min intervals between 0600 and 1900, 10 kg baggage limit. For the **Peruvian border**, to **Huaquillas**, avoiding Machala, US$3.45, 4 hrs; via Machala, 6 hrs. Colectivos are not rec for journeys to the Sierra, they drive too fast and are dangerous. **Trucks**: carry freight and passengers, slower, bumpy, cheaper than buses, and you see better. Enquire at Sucre 1104.

Sea Shipping agent: Luis Arteaga, Aguirre 324 y Chile, T 533-592/670/F 533-445, rec, fast, US$120 for arranging car entry.

The spectacular 464-km railway line (1.067m gauge), which was opened in 1908, passes through 87 km of delta lands and then, in 80 km, climbs to 3,238m. At the summit, at Urbina, 3,609m is reached; it then rises and falls before reaching the Quito plateau at 2,857m. The line's greatest achievements are the Alausí loop and the Devil's Nose double zigzag, between Sibambe and Alausí.

DURAN

The train station is in **Durán**, reached by ferry from Guayaquil, Malecón Bolívar y Montúfar about 10 blocks N of the Palacio de Gobernación: the first is at 0530, the last at 2200, every 15 mins, US$0.10. Bus 17 goes to Durán, US$0.25, but drops you some blocks from station. Taxi to Durán from Guayaquil early is US$4.50 (beware 'special service' with prostitute as uninvited extra). Transport to Durán in the early morning is hard to find.

• **Accommodation & places to eat** Sparse and, in most cases, short-stay only. **E-F** *La Paz*, Esmeraldas 123 y Cuenca, main street, 2 blocks from and parallel to railway, T 803-465, with bath, fan, cheaper without, clean, light, early morning call for train passengers. Plenty of small restaurants on Esmeraldas and by the market.

• **Trains** Durán-Riobamba, daily except Mon and Wed at 0625, 12 hrs (*autoferro* sometimes 0620, 8-10 hrs), fare US$15; to Alausí, US$12, 9 hrs. Tickets for Riobamba go on sale from 0600, they cannot be bought in advance; check details before departure. It is rec to ride on the roof for the best views, but dress warmly and protect clothes from dirt. On the train, lock all luggage, even side pockets, as pilfering from luggage compartments is common. Popular, especially at weekends and public holidays; queue early or go midweek.

Leaving the river the train strikes out across the broad, fertile Guayas valley. It rolls through fields of sugar cane, or rice, past split cane houses built on high stilts. Everywhere there are waterways, with thousands of water-birds. The first station is **Yaguachi**. On 15 and 16 Aug thousands of visitors pour into this little town to attend the feast of San Jacinto, who is honoured for having put an end to many epidemics.

The first stop of importance is **Milagro** (*Pop* 93,637), centre of a pineapple growing region: sellers swarm about the train.

● **Accommodation & places to eat** E-F *Hotel Oasis*, nr. the railway station, safe, clean; *Restaurant Topo-Gigio*, nearby, good, cheap food.

● **Buses** To Guayaquil US$0.40.

About 87 km from Durán the train stops for an hour or less at **Bucay** (proper name General Elizalde), at the base of the Andes. There's a market on Sun.

● **Accommodation** F *California*, clean, cold water; F *El Rey*, opp rail station, clean, secure, fan, TV, rec.

● **Transport Trains** Train leaves Bucay at 1045. Tickets may only be bought on the day of travel; to Alausí, US$10, Riobamba US$10. If sitting on the roof for the stunning views, be ready for the cold after Palmira in the late afternoon. **Road Buses**: run parallel to the train between Bucay and Guayaquil. Bus to Guayaquil 2 hrs, with Santa Marta in the town centre. To Riobamba, US$1.50, and Ambato, 3 hrs, US$3, change at either for Quito. Bus to Cuenca: go to El Triunfo, 50 mins, US$0.65, then change, US$2.65, 3½ hrs.

The train follows the gorge of the Río Chanchán until it reaches **Huigra**, a very pleasant little town. This offers a better option than Bucay for those who don't have time to do the full trip and wish to return to Riobamba by bus.

● **Accommodation** C *Hostería La Eterna Primavera*, T (04) 885-015/886-749, F (04) 885-015, inc tax and service, bath, hot water, restaurant, bar, pool, horse riding, trips by train to Nariz del Diablo, lovely place to relax for a few days in a pleasant climate. In the town itself are G *Huigra*, and *Res Paraíso*, nr the station.

● **Buses** Daily to Riobamba at 0530, 0600 and 1300; direct to Alausí at around 1000.

After Huigra the most exciting part of the trip begins. The first mountain town reached is **Chanchán**, where the gorge is so narrow that the train has to pass through a series of tunnels and bridges in its zigzag course.

Next is **Sibambe** (no hotels, ask in the village for a room, or bring camping gear, but do not stay at the station). Shortly after leaving Sibambe the train starts climbing the famous Nariz del Diablo (Devil's Nose), a perpendicular ridge rising in the gorge of the Chanchán to a height of 305m. This almost insurmountable engineering obstacle was finally conquered when a series of switchbacks was built on a 5.5% grade.

Next comes **Alausí** (see page 1072), popular with Guayaquileños wishing to escape the tropical heat and humidity. After crossing the 120m long Shucos bridge, the train pulls into **Palmira**, on the crest of the first range of the Andes crossed by the railway. One by one the great snow-capped volcanoes begin to appear: Chimborazo, Carihuairazo, Altar, Tungurahua, and the burning head of Sangay, all seeming very close because of the clear air.

ROUTES The road from Durán or Milagro heads S to Naranjal and on to Machala, a main crossroads and useful stopover before heading onto Huaquillas, Arenillas and Loja (216 km), or via Pasaje and Girón to Cuenca (188 km).

MACHALA

This booming agricultural town (*Pop* 144,197; *Phone code* 04) is in a major banana producing and exporting region with an annual banana fair in September. It is also a large pond shrimp producing area.

Excursions

Puerto Bolívar, on the Estero Jambelí among mangroves, is a major export outlet for over 1 million tonnes of bananas annually. There is a pleasant waterfront and from the old pier a motorized canoe service crosses to the beaches of **Jambelí** on the far side of the mangrove islands which shelter Puerto Bolívar from the Pacific. Lots of birdlife can be seen in the mangroves; rent a canoe for an hour and explore the narrow channels. Canoes depart at 0700, 1000 and 1500, returning at 0800, 1200 and 1600, US$1.35. Take repellent against mosquitoes and other biting insects.

The beach at Puerto Bolívar is pleasant but waves and currents can be dangerous.

● **Accommodation In Puerto Bolívar**: F *Jambelí*, basic, fan, bath; better value is G pp *Pacífico*, Gral Páez 244. **At Jambelí**: *Cabañas del Pescador*, and *María Inez*, both E, clean, OK.

● **Places to eat Puerto Bolívar**: *El Acuario* one block back from pier for good seafood, *Restaurant Sarita* nearby; *Miramar* at the pierhead. There are lots of seafood kiosks between the old and new piers. Good, cheap cafés at **Jambelí**.

30 km S on the main road to Peru is **Santa Rosa**; by the air strip is a turnoff for **Puerto Jelí**, a tiny fishing village 4 km at the road's end. Good eating at *Picantería Jambelí* and *Riberas del Pacífico*. Canoe trips can be arranged through the mangroves with Segundo Oyola (ask for him opposite the dock) to the beach of Las Casitas, or fishing or clam collecting. Negotiate a fair price.

● **Accommodation & places to eat In Santa Rosa**: **D** *América*, El Oro y Colón T 943-130, a/c, TV, bath; **E** *Santa Rosa*, one block from plaza, good, a/c, bath. Cheap *residencias* on Av Colón. Several good *chifas*.

Local information
● **Accommodation**
In Machala: **L3** *Oro Verde*, Circunvalación Norte, Urb Unioro, T (07) 933-140, F 933-150, luxury, nice pool (US$9 for non-residents) and grounds, tennis courts, restaurant.

B *Rizzo*, Guayas y Bolívar, T 921-906, F 921-502, a/c, TV, suites available, recently refurbished, pool (US$2 for non-residents), casino, cafetería, restaurant, noisy late disco.

C *Oro*, Sucre y Juan Montalvo, T 930-783, F 937-569, a/c, good, helpful, expensive restaurant but good, cheaper café downstairs.

D *Araujo*, 9 de Mayo y Boyacá, T 935-257, hot water, a/c, parking, cheaper with fan, clean, some rooms are small, restaurant, parking, good value, rec; **D** *Edison*, Boyacá y Colón, T 938-120, a/c, cheaper with fan, modern, clean, nice large rooms, restaurant, rec; **D** *Gran Hotel Machala*, Juan Montalvo 835 y Rocafuerte, T 920-159, undergoing renovations, fan, some a/c, bath; **D** *Mosquera*, Olmedo entre Guayas y Ayacucho, T 931-752, F 930-390, cheaper with fan, TV, hot water, restaurant, rec.

E *Julio César*, 9 de Mayo 1319 y Boyacá, T 937-978, with bath, fan, TV.

F *Hostal La Bahía*, Olmedo y Junín, T 920-581, fan, cheaper with shared bath, by market, good value, basic; **F** *Res Pesantes*, 9 de Mayo y Pasaje, T 920-154, with bath, fan, basic. A mosquito net may be needed for sleeping.

● **Places to eat**
The best food is found in the better hotels. *Parrillada Sabor Latina*, Sucre y Guayas, good steaks and grills; *Don Angelo*, 9 de Mayo just off main plaza, open 24hrs, elaborate set meals and à la carte, good for breakfast; *Copa Cabana*, on main plaza, good clean snack bar; *Chifa Central*, Tarqui y 9 de Octubre, good Chinese; *Las Redes*, 9 de Mayo 18-23 y Bolívar, à la carte seafood and choice of cheap set meals; *Aquí es Correita*, Av Arízaga y 9 de Mayo, popular for seafood, closed Sun.

● **Banks & money changers**
Banco del Pacífico, Rocafuerte y Tarqui, changes TCs and cash; **Banco Machala**, advances cash against Visa, efficient; **Filanbanco**, Rocafuerte y Guayas, Visa cash advances; **Banco Continental**, 9 de Octubre y Juan Montalvo, cash and TCs, good rates.

● **Embassies & consulates**
Peruvian Consulate, at the NW corner of Colón y Bolívar, p 1, T 930-680.

● **Post & telecommunications**
Post Office: Bolívar y Montalvo. **Emetel**, 9 de Octubre nr the stadium.

● **Tour companies & travel agents**
Glendatur, Bolívar 613 y Guayas, T/F 921-855, helpful, sells Faucett air tickets for Peru; *La Moneda Tours*, Rocafuerte 518 entre Junín y Tarqui, T 562-230.

● **Tourist offices**
Cetur, 9 de Mayo y Pichincha, little information.

● **Transport**
Air Daily flights from Guayaquil with CEDTA (light aircraft), Mon-Fri, depart Guayaquil from the Terminal de Avionetas 4 a day, US$16 each way; also with TAME, Juan Montalvo y Bolívar, T 930-139.

Road Buses: to Quito, with Occidental (Buenavista entre Sucre y Olmedo), 12 hrs, US$6, 8 daily; with Panamericana (Colón y Bolívar), 9 daily, luxury service, 9 hrs US$10 a/c, US$8 without a/c. To **Guayaquil**, 4 hrs, US$3.80, hourly with Ecuatoriano Pullman (Colón y 9 de Octubre), CIFA and Rutas Orenses (9 de Octubre y Tarqui). To **Esmeraldas**, 11 hrs, US$7.40, with Occidental at 2200. To **Loja**, 7 hrs, US$4, several daily with Transportes Loja (Tarqui y Bolívar). To **Cuenca**, hourly with Trans Azuay (Sucre y Junín), 3½ hrs, US$3.80. To **Huaquillas**, with CIFA (Bolívar y Guayas) and Ecuatoriano Pullman, direct, 1 hr, US$1.40, every 30 mins; via Arenillas and Santa Rosa, 2 hrs, US$1.15, every 10 mins. There are passport checks on this route. **Warning** Do not take night buses into or out of Machala, they are not safe. **Taxis**: to **Guayaquil**, Orotaxis run a scheduled taxi service between the *Hotel Rizzo*, Machala and

Hotel Rizzo, Guayaquil, every 30 mins or so for US$7 pp.

ZARUMA

Southeast from Machala is the gold-mining town of **Zaruma** (118 km; *Alt* 1,170m). It is reached either by paved road via the military post at Saracay and **Piñas** (two orchid growers show their collections), or via Pasaje and Paccha on a scenic, dirt road. Founded in 1549 on orders of Felipe II to try to control the gold extraction, Zaruma is a delightful town perched on a hilltop, with steep streets and painted wooden buildings. Beside the plaza is a lovely little museum showing the history of gold mining in the area. South of Zaruma, **Portovelo** was once the HQ of the Vanderbilt mining company, down in the valley. There are hot thermal springs at **Aguas Calientes**, 6 km from Portovelo, but no facilities.

● **Accommodation D** *Rosales de Machay*, up the Busa valley between Zaruma and Piñas, access is difficult without a car or taxi, pool, restaurant, tennis, popular at weekends, clean, comfortable cabins; **F** *Colombia*, on the main plaza, very basic; and others.

● **Buses** Transportes Paccha departs Machala nr the market, or Trans TAC, Sucre y Colón departs every hour from 0500 to 1700 via Piñas, last bus back at 1800, US$1.70, 3 hrs to Zaruma.

A nice walk is 5 km on the Loja road to Río Pindo or Río Luis.

PUYANGO

The petrified forest of **Puyango**, due S of Machala, is supposedly the most extensive outside Arizona. Over 120 species of birds can be seen. No accommodation in the village but ask around for floor space or try at the on-site information centre. If not, basic accommodation is available in Alamor. Campsites are also provided. For further information, contact Comisión Administradora de Los Bosques Petrificados de Puyango, Ciudadela Las Brisas, Manzana B-6, Villa 2, Apto No 05, Machala, T 930-021, F 924-655.

● **Buses** For Alamor 0830 and 1400, 3 hrs, US$2.50, ask to be dropped off at Puyango. Several military checkpoints between Puyango and Machala.

HUAQUILLAS

The most commonly used route overland to Peru is via Machala. Many buses (see **Transport** above) go to **Huaquillas**, the Ecuadorean border town, which is something of a shopping arcade for Peruvians. It has grown into a small city with a reasonable selection of services.

● **Accommodation D** *Lima*, Portovelo y Machala, T 907-794, a/c, phone, **E** with fan, mosquito net; **D** *Vanessa*, 1 de Mayo 323, T/F 907-263, a/c, phone; **E** *Alameda*, Tnte Córdovez y José Mendoza, bath, fan, TV, mosquito net, basic; **E** *Internacional*, Machala y 9 de Octubre, T 907-963, fan, small rooms, basic, cheaper with shared bath; **E** *Rodey*, Tnte Córdovez y 10 de Agosto, T 907-736, bath, fan, fridge, clean, basic; **F** *Gaboeli*, Tnte Córdovez 311 y Portovelo, T 907-149, fan, mosquito net, cheaper without bath, parking; **F** *Res Fabiolita*, Tnte Córdovez y Santa Rosa, shared bath, mosquito net, basic; **F** *Res San Martín*, Av la República opp the church, 1 block from immigration, T 907-083, shared bath, fan, basic, noisy, mosquito nets, convenient. **NB** A number of the cheaper hotels in Huaquillas are primarily for short stay customers.

● **Places to eat** *Acuario*, Portovelo y José Mendoza, a/c, good set meal and à la carte, rec; *Guayaquil*, Remigio Gómez, behind immigration, basic; *Mini*, opp Transportes Loja, good set lunch. Excellent patisseries on main street sell delicious *pan de chocolate* and cheese empanadas. Expect bananas with everything here.

● **Banks & money changers** Verify rates of exchange with travellers leaving Peru. Fair rates are available for soles, sucres and dollars cash on both sides of the border but you will always be offered a low rate when you first enquire. Don't be rushed into any transaction. The money changers (recognized by their black briefcases) are very clever, particularly with calculators, and often dishonest. It is difficult to change TCs.

● **Post & telecommunications Post Office**: Av la República, in the same building as Immigration. **Emetel**: Av la República, opp Immigration.

● **Tourist offices** An information centre is just by the international bridge. It is staffed by tourism students and is friendly and helpful, but has limited information.

● **Buses** There are three checkpoints (Transit Police, Customs and military) along the road N from Huaquillas, keep your passport to hand. To **Machala**, with CIFA (Santa Rosa y Machala) and Ecuatoriano Pullman (Av la República y 9 de Octubre), direct, 1 hr, US$1.40, every hour between 0400 and 2000; via Arenillas and Santa Rosa, 2 hrs, US$1.15, every 10 mins. To **Quito**, with Occidental (Remigio Gómez 129), 3 daily, 12 hrs, US$7; with Panamericana (Remigio Gómez, behind Immigration), luxury service, 11½ hrs, 6 daily via Santo Domingo, US$10 a/c, US$8.30 without a/c; 2 daily via **Riobamba** and **Ambato**, 12 hrs, US$10. To **Guayaquil**, frequent service with CIFA and Ecuatoriano Pullman, about 5 hrs, US$3.70. To **Cuenca**, several daily, 6 hrs, US$4. To **Loja**, with Transportes Loja (Tnte Córdovez y Arenillas) daily at 1330 and 1800, 7 hrs, US$4.

FRONTIER WITH PERU

● Ecuadorean Immigration
Complete Ecuadorean formalities at customs (several hundred metres before the border) and immigration, Av de la República y Portovelo, in Huaquillas.

The border is officially open 0800-1800, but long lunches are common (Ecuadorean lunch 1200-1400). On Sun facilities may close at 1600. It is always best to cross before 1700. Allow up to 1-2 hrs to complete formalities, although it can sometimes be much quicker.

Then walk along the main street and across the bridge. Tricycle porters operate between customs and the border, US$1, never let go of your bags. Arrange the price in advance and the currency in which it is to be paid to avoid rip-offs. At the bridge, the police check passports. Immigration formalities are, generally, straightforward.

● Peruvian immigration
The main Peruvian immigration and customs complex is outside Zarumilla, about 3 km past the international bridge, however there is also a small immigration office in Aguas Verdes, just past the bridge on the right hand side, as you go into Peru. Enquire locally which office performs which functions.

● Exchange
Coming from Peru, you can buy sucres at the official rate with the money changers outside Peruvian immigration, but you also need to be careful here.

● Transport
There are three forms of transport between the frontier and Tumbes. Some colectivos leave from near the bridge; they charge higher prices, especially for foreigners. Other, cheaper ones leave 2 blocks down along the main street by a small plaza opp the church; US$1 pp, or US$6/car. Colectivos should stop and wait at the immigration complex on the Peruvian side. Buses and minivans leave from an esplanade 3 blocks E from the colectivo stop and go to the market in Tumbes, US$0.50 (they don't wait at immigration). There are also mototaxis from the bridge to the Zarumilla immigration complex, US$0.90 for up to 2 people. Taxi to Tumbes, inc the wait at immigration, US$6.

Coming from Peru into Ecuador, take a colectivo from Tumbes to the border. A ticket out of Ecuador is not usually asked for at this border.

Pacific Lowlands

THIS VAST tract of Ecuador covers everything west of the Andes and north of the Guayas delta. Though popular with Quiteños and Guayaquileños, who come here for weekends and holidays, the Pacific Lowlands receive relatively few foreign visitors, which is surprising given the natural beauty, diversity and rich cultural heritage of the coast. Here you can surf, watch whales, visit archaeological sites, or just relax and enjoy the best food that this country has to offer. The Machalilla National Park protects an important area of primary tropical dry forest, precolumbian ruins, coral reef and a wide variety of wildlife.

WESTERN LOWLANDS

The main route from Quito goes down the valley of the Ríos Naranjal/Pilatón/Blanco, turning off the Panamericana at Alóag and continuing past Tandapi. Sit on right for views, but on the left look for El Poder Brutal, a devil's face, carved in the rock face, 2.5 km W of Tandapi. This road is very busy, gets much heavy truck traffic and it can be dangerous owing to careless drivers passing on the many curves, especially when foggy and at night.

SANTO DOMINGO DE LOS COLORADOS

Santo Domingo de los Colorados, in the hills above the western lowlands (*Pop* 114,442; 129 km from Quito) became Ecuador's main transport hub in the mid 1960s when the road from Quito through Alóag was completed. Since then it has experienced very rapid growth. Sun is market day, shops are only open from Tues to Sun. There is a cinema.

Excursions

The name de los Colorados is a reference to the traditional red hair dye, made with achiote (annatto), worn by the native Tsáchila men. Today the Tsáchila only wear their native dress on special occasions and they can no longer be seen in traditional garb in the city. There were approximately 1900 Tsáchilas in 1996, living in eight communities off the roads leading from Santo Domingo to Quevedo, Chone and Quindé. Their lands make up a reserve of some 8,000 ha. Visitors interested in their culture are welcome at the Complejo Turístico Huapilú, in the Chihuilpe Commune, where there is a small but interesting museum (contributions expected) run by Augusto Calazacón.

● **Access** Via the turnoff E at Km 7 on the road to Quevedo, from where it is 4 km. Tours are available from travel agencies in town. A taxi is US$5-10, or take a city bus Centro-Vía Quevedo-Km 7 and walk.

Local information
● **Accommodation**
NB Many hotels are along Av 29 de Mayo, a noisy street, so request a room away from the road.

In town: C *Diana Real*, 29 de Mayo y Loja, T 751-380, F754-091, modern spacious rooms, hot water, fan; **D** *Aracelly*, Vía Quevedo y Galápagos, T 750-334, F 754-144, large rooms, electric shower, restaurant, parking; **D** *Caleta*, Ibarra 141, T 750-277, good restaurant, **E** without TV, friendly, good; **D** *Genova*, 29 de Mayo e Ibarra, T 759-694, clean, comfortable, electric shower, **E** without TV, parking, good value, rec;

E *Jennifer*, 29 de Mayo y Latacunga, T 750-577, with bath, some with hot water, rooms away from the street are quieter, parking, restaurant, good value; E *Las Brisas #2*, Cocaniguas y Río Pilatón, T 753-283, with bath, clean, modern, parking extra; E *San Fernando*, 2 blocks from the bus terminal, T 753-402, with bath, clean, modern, comfortable, cheaper with shared bath, parking.

On Av Abraham Calazacón, opp the bus terminal are: E *Sheraton*, T 751-988, modern, clean, with bath, hot water, parking, new in 1996, good value, rec; F *Res España*, entrance on the side street, with bath, clean, basic; F *Hostal Ejecutivo*, 29 de Mayo y Ambato, T 751-943, basic, cheaper with shared bath; F *Res El Viajero*, 29 de Mayo y Latacunga, cold water, basic, cheaper with shared bath.

Out of town: 20 km from Santo Domingo, on the road to Quito, is **A2** *Tinalandia*, pleasant and small, chalets with bathrooms, inc meals, own golf course overlooking the Toachi valley, and excellent food, many species of birds, flowers and butterflies in the woods behind (and many biting insects in the evening), lunch with right to use facilities US$10 for non-residents; also self-catering bunk rooms, E. It is poorly signposted, take small road between Km 16 and 17 from Santo Domingo on the right; T 09-494-727, in Quito T 449-028, F 442-638; **A3** *Zaracay*, Av Quito 1639, T 750-316, F 754-535, 1½ km from the centre on the road to Quito, restaurant, casino, noisy disco, gardens and a swimming pool, good rooms and service, breakfast inc, best available, advisable to book, especially at weekend; C *Hostería Los Colorados*, 12 km from Santo Domingo on the road to Quito, just W of the toll booth and police control, T/F 753-449, nice cabins with fridge, TV, pool, artificial lake with fish, restaurants, good cafetería; C *Hotel del Toachi*, Vía a Quito, Km 1, just W of Zaracay, T/F 754-688, spacious rooms, with bath, good showers, TV, swimming pool, parking.

● **Places to eat**
Mocambo, Tulcán y Machala, good; *La Fuente*, Ibarra y 3 de Julio, good. There are several chicken places in the Cinco Esquinas area where Avs Quito and 29 de Mayo meet; *Tacos Mexicanos*, Quito, a super deli, highly rec; two *chifas*, *Tay Happy* and *Central*, on Tulcán by the Parque Zaracay.

Seafood: *Juan El Marino*, 1.5 km from Monument Circle on road to Quevedo, reasonably priced, huge portions, good seafood, rec.

Ice-cream: *Heladería* at Edificio San Francisco, Av Quito entre Río Blanco y Río Toachi, good, made on the premises, also sell fresh cheese; opp is *Pingüino*.

● **Banks & money changers**
Banco Internacional, Av Quito y Río Blanco, US$ cash and TCs (4% commission); **Filanbanco**, Av Quito y Av de los Tsáchilas, by Parque Zaracay, cash and TCs, 0900-1400. Western Union money transfers at Hotel Diana Real.

● **Post & telecommunications**
Post Office: Av de los Tsáchilas y Río Baba, 0800-1830; fax service 0800-1630. **Emetel**, Edificio San Francisco, Av Quito entre Río Blanco y Río Toachi, p 2, and at bus terminal, 0800-2200 daily.

● **Security**
Santo Domingo is not safe late at night, caution is recommended at all times in the market areas, inc the pedestrian walkway along 3 de Julio and in peripheral neighbourhoods.

● **Tour companies & travel agents**
Turismo Zaracay, 29 de Mayo y Cocaniguas, T 750-546, F 750-873, runs tours to Tsáchila commune US$12 pp, minimum 5 persons; fishing trips US$24 pp, 8 hrs, bird/butterfly watching tours, exchanges cash. *Cayapatours*, 29 de Mayo y Tulcán, T/F 762-933, tickets and tours. *Delgado Travel*, Av Quito 148 y Cocaniguas, T 760-036, F 759-967, tickets, money transfers and exchange, courier service, car rentals,

● **Useful addresses**
Immigration: Subjefatura de Migración, Av de los Tsáchilas, across from the cemetery, just S of the bus terminal, T 750-225.

● **Transport**
Drivers do not need to enter the congested centre of the city, as there is a bypass around it. The bus terminal is on Av Abraham Calazacón, at the N end of town, along the city's bypass; long-distance buses do not enter the city. Taxi downtown, US$1, bus US$0.09.

As it is a very important transportation centre, you can get buses going everywhere in the country. To **Quito** via Alóag US$2, 3 hrs, via San Miguel de los Bancos US$3,50, 5 hrs; to **Guayaquil** US$3.25, 4 hrs; to **Machala**, US$4.55, 6 hrs; to **Huaquillas** US$5.20, 7½ hrs; to **Esmeraldas** US$1.95, 3 hrs; to **Ambato** US$2.60, 4 hrs; to **Loja** US$9.70, 12 hrs; to **Manta** US$4.40, 6 hrs; to **Bahía de Caráquez** US$3.60, 4 hrs; to **Pedernales** US$2.60, 3 hrs.

ROUTES TO THE COAST

A busy paved highway connects Santo Domingo de los Colorados with Esmeraldas, 185 km to the N (see page 1117). On this road is La Concordia (**D** *Hotel Atos*, new, very good), just before which is the private La Perla Forest Reserve, 40 km from Santo Domingo (you can hike in for free), La Independencia (junction with road from San Miguel de Los Bancos and the Sierra) and **Quinindé** (**Rosa Zárate**). The road deteriorates after Quinindé.

● **Accommodation & places to eat** D *Sanz*, on main street, clean, parking; E *Turista*, 8 blocks S of town, on main road, quiet, parking; *Restaurant Jean*, T 736-831, at bottom of hill 3 blocks S of town on the main road, excellent steaks and seafood, good salads, reasonable prices, possibly the best restaurant for miles.

A paved road runs W to **El Carmen**, with a cattle market on the outskirts. From El Carmen a paved road goes to **Pedernales** (see page 1115). Continuing SW of El Carmen is Chone where the road divides, either to Bahía de Caráquez (207 km from Santo Domingo, 340 km from Quito, see page 1113), or to Portoviejo and Manta (257 km from Santo Domingo, 390 km from Quito).

SOUTH FROM SANTO DOMINGO

Another highway goes S to **Quevedo** (*Pop* 86,910) 1½ hrs by bus. Set in fertile banana lands and often flooded in the rainy season, Quevedo has a fair-sized Chinese colony. It is a dusty, noisy and crowded.

● **Accommodation** At Km 47 from Santo Domingo on the Quevedo road is B *Río Palenque*, lodge with capacity for 20, cooking facilities, US$5 for day visit. Set in a biological field station, good bird watching, T 561-646 or 232-468 in Quito for information and reservations. In town, all are noisy: C *Quevedo*, Av 7 de Octubre y C 12, modern rooms with fridge, TV, good restaurant; D *Olímpico*, Bolívar y 19a, restaurant best in town, nr stadium; E *Ejecutivo Internacional*, 7 de Octubre y C Cuarta, modern, large rooms, a/c, private bath, good value, the least noisy.

● **Places to eat** On 7 de Octubre: *Rincón Caleño*, No 1103, Colombian; several *chifas*; *Tungurahua*, No 711, good breakfast.

● **Buses** Quevedo is an important route centre. To **Quito**, US$4, 7 hrs; to **Guayaquil**, 3 hrs, US$1.65; to **Portoviejo**, from 7 de Octubre y C 8, 5 hrs, US$1.85, uncomfortable, watch your possessions. Portoviejo, Tosagua and several coastal towns can be reached via Velasco Ibarra, Pichincha (*Residencial Z*), Rocafuerte and Calceta.

Quevedo is connected with Guayaquil by two paved highways, one through Balzar and Daule, one through **Babahoyo** (*Pop* 50,250).

● **Accommodation** *Hotel Emperador*, Gral Barona, T 730-535, bath, a/c, TV, restaurant; *Hotel Cachari*, Bolívar 120, T 731-205, acceptable, restaurant nearby.

THE GUAYAS COAST

The popular beach resorts of the Guayas coast can be reached along a paved toll highway from Guayaquil. The road divides after 63 km at El Progreso (Gómez Rendón).

PLAYAS

One branch leads to General Villamil, normally known as **Playas**, the nearest seaside resort to Guayaquil. Look out for the bottle-shaped ceibo (kapok) trees between Guayaquil and Playas as the landscape becomes drier, turning into tropical thorn scrub where 2-5m cacti prevail. Fishing is still important in Playas and a few single-sailed balsa rafts can still be seen among the motor launches returning laden with fish. These rafts are unique, highly ingenious and very simple. The same rafts without sails are used to spread nets close offshore, then two gangs of men take 2-3 hrs to haul them in. The beach shelves gently, and is 200-400m wide, lined with singular, square canvas tents hired out for the day.

As the closest resort to Guayaquil, Playas is popular with local city dwellers and the authorities are trying to keep the packed beaches cleaner and safer than in the past. Out of season, when it is cloudier, or midweek the beaches are almost empty especially N towards Punta Pelado (5 km). Change will come with the completion in 1997/98 of large new complexes. Playas is also a popular surfing resort with six good surf points.

NB Thieving is rampant during busy times – do not leave **anything** unattended on the beach.

Excursions

An interesting walk, or short drive, is to the village of **El Morro**, with a disproportionately large wooden church with impressive façade (under 'permanent' repair) and the nearby mysterious rock formation of the Virgen de la Roca, where there are a small shrine and marble stations of the cross (regular camioneta service from Av Guayaquil y Av Paquisha).

Some 3 km further down the road is **Puerto del Morro**, up a scenic mangrove estuary: traditional boats can be seen and canoes rented for 3-hr trips in the mangroves (about US$25). A few basic eating places.

Northwest up the coast is **Engabao**, a small settlement with deserted beaches, wooden fishing boats and surfing points. A camioneta goes here from the crossroads, a 30-min bumpy ride.

Local information
● Accommodation
C *Hostería Bellavista*, Km 2 Data Highway, T 760-600, rooms or suites in bungalows on beach, booking necessary, Swiss-run, clean, camping at the S end of beach.

D *Hostería La Gaviota*, 500m out on Data road, T 760-133, a/c, good clean restaurant; **D-E** *Playas*, T 760-121, on Malecón, accepts credit cards, beach hotel, plain rooms with fans, clean, safe, restaurant, parking, rec.

E *El Delfín*, Km 1.5, T 760-125, old fashioned, big rooms, on beach, hacienda type building, nice but sporadic water supply, electric showers, restaurant sometimes closed at night; **E** *El Galeón*, T 760-270, beside the church, clean, mosquito protection, cheap restaurant with seafood (closes 1800 Sun), good breakfast, cheaper for long stay; **E** *Hostería Costa Verde*, T 760-645, excellent meals, cheaper rates for longer stays; **E** *La Casa de Gabriel y Marie*, Av Roldós, 1 block in from Malecón, T 760-047, family atmosphere, basic suites with bath, cooking and laundry facilities, French, English spoken, long-term rates; **E** *Parasoles*, Principal y Alfonso Jurado, T 760-532, clean, helpful.

F *Miraglia*, T 760-154, popular with surfers, run-down but clean, sea view, showers, fresh drinking water, parking for motorcycles, cheaper rates for longer stays. Most hotels are 5 mins' walk from the Transportes Villamil bus station. Some are connected to Guayaquil's mains water supply, but many have wells which take water from the sea which is slightly brackish. Downmarket places have buckets for washing, if you're lucky.

● Places to eat
Excellent seafood and typical dishes from over 50 beach cafés (all numbered and named). Rec are *Cecilia's* at No 7 or *Barzola* at No 9. *Mario's*, central plaza opp Banco de Guayaquil, big hamburgers, good yoghurt. Giant oysters and 'mule foot' black conchs are opened and served from stalls in a side road down from *La Costa Verde*; worth a look if nothing else.

● Entertainment
Discos: *Motivos*, S end of Malecón; *Mr Frog*, diagonally opp *Miraglia*; *Peña de Arturo*, opp Transportes Villamil bus terminus.

● Post & telecommunications
Post Office: reliable.

Emetel: on Av Jaime Roldós Aguilera, service good, open Sun.

● Useful services
There are showers, toilets and changing rooms along the beach, with fresh water, for a fee.

● Transport
Buses To Guayaquil, 2 hrs by frequent bus, US$1.35; US$40 by taxi.

WEST TO SANTA ELENA
West of El Progreso (Gómez Rendón) a good quality road runs to **Santa Elena** where the road forks W for Salinas or N for the northern coastal towns. Near Santa Elena is the **Museo de los Amantes de Sumpa**, opened May 1996, which has a very interesting display on the Las Vegas culture. Beyond Zapotal, by the old race course (now stables), is the turnoff for **Chanduy**, a tiny, picturesque port, where 12 km along is the Real Alto Museum: well laid-out explanation of the peoples, archaeology and customs of the area; open daily 1000-1700, US$0.70.

7 km before Santa Elena, a well-signed turnoff leads 8 km to **Baños San Vicente**, Cetur-run hot thermal baths, which consist of swimming pools, a sauna and a big mud-hole which claim to cure assorted ailments. US$0.30 entrance, massages extra, open from 0600-1800.

● Accommodation
F *Hotel Florida*, basic, clean, next to baths.

West of Santa Elena the road passes a petroleum refinery and enters the busy port and regional market centre of **La Libertad**.

● Accommodation
The only reason for stopping here is for transport connections. It is not a safe town. **B** *Samarina*, Av 9 de Octubre, Cetur-run, some bungalows, swimming pool, restaurant, coffee shop, bar, with views of the oil refinery and tankers; **E** *Hostal Viña del Mar*, in town centre, T 785979, clean, fan, bath.

● Buses
To Guayaquil, with Coop Libertad

Peninsular, Av 9 de Octubre (opp *Hotel Turis Palm*) and CICA across the street, US$2.50, 2½ hrs, every 15 mins (the two companies alternate departures), rec; get off at Progreso for **Playas**, 1 hr, US$1.15. Buses every hour, until 1715 to **Manglaralto** (US$1.25), **Puerto López**, **Jipijapa** (US$3.65) and **Manta** (US$4.35) from the terminal nr the market. To **Quito** with Trans Esmeraldas (opp Coop Libertad Peninsular), 2 nightly, 9½ hrs, US$8.50.

SALINAS

A few kilometres further on, surrounded by miles of salt flats, is **Salinas** (*Pop* 19,298), Ecuador's answer to Miami Beach. There is safe swimming in the bay and high rise blocks of holiday flats and hotels line the sea front. The town is dominated by the Choclatera hill on the western point of the bay overlooking the well-equipped and very exclusive Salinas Yacht Club. During *temporada* (Jan to April/May) it is overcrowded and its services are stretched to the limit. During off season it is quieter, but still not for 'getting away from it all'.

● **Accommodation A3** *El Carruaje*, Malecón 517, T 774-282, a/c, hot water, good restaurant; **C** *Salinas*, Gral Henríquez Gallo y 27, T 774-267, modern, off Malecón, good restaurant; **C** *Yulee*, Diagonal Iglesia Central, T 772-028, **D** without bath, clean, excellent food, nr the beach; **E** *Florida*, Malecón y C 2, Chipipe, T 772-780, with bath, cheaper inside rooms.

● **Places to eat** *Mar y Tierra*, close to *Hotel Miramar* on Malecón, excellent seafood, especially lobster; also nr the *Miramar* is *Flipper*, cheap, simple, clean. Good freshly-cooked seafood in the market, 2 blocks in from the Malecón. *Oystercatcher*, Malecón y 32, rec, safe oysters, bird and whale watchers ask here for local expert, Ben Haase.

● **Banks & money changers** Banco del Pacífico changes cash and TCs, good rates on Mastercard; also **Filanbanco** opp the market.

● **Post & telecommunications Emetel**: at Radio Internacional, good service.

● **Tour companies & travel agents** Tours, hire of sailing boats, water skis, fishing trips arranged through *Pesca Tours*, on the Malecón, T (04) 772-391, or *Salitour*, T 772-800, F 772-789.

● **Buses** To Guayaquil, US$2.50, 2½ hrs; for the return journey, go to La Libertad by bus or colectivo (US$0.25, 15 mins, they pass by the market) and take a bus from there.

PUNTA CARNERO

On the S shore of the Santa Elena peninsula, 8 km S of La Libertad, a magnificent 15-km beach with wild surf and heavy undertow, virtually empty during the week. In July, Aug and Sept there is great whale watching.

● **Accommodation A2** *Punta Carnero*, T 775-450, all rooms with sea view, restaurant, swimming pool; **A3-C** *Hosteria del Mar*, T 775-370, with or without a/c, restaurant, pool, family suites to let on weekly basis.

A few kilometres to the E of Punta Carnero, along the coast, lies **Anconcito**, a fishing port at the foot of steep cliffs. Pelicans and frigate birds gather round the colourful boats when the catch is brought in.

The northern fork of the road at Santa Elena leads past **Ballenita** which has a pleasant beach.

● **Accommodation & places to eat B** *Hostería Farallón Dillon*, Lomas de Ballenita, T 786-643, F 785-611, restaurant, museum; **C** *Ballenita Inn*, T 785-008, at the fork, cottages to rent. Good food at *La Cabaña*, at the fork, where the filling station has good bathrooms.

Most of this coastal road is paved as far as Puerto Cayo and beyond, when it turns inland for Jipijapa and Manta, some sections are bad. The vegetation is tropical desert scrub as far as **La Entrada** with very little rainfall, giving onto a lusher landscape as far as Ayampe, with the hills of the Colonche range falling to the coast. Most of the numerous small fishing villages have good beaches, though beware of rip currents and undertow. Before **Punta Blanca** are several seafood stands on a wild beach. Look for the *semilleros* all along the coast trudging through waves to collect larvae to sell to the shrimp farms. There is basic accommodation in Punta Blanca at *La Cabaña*. The road then passes **Monteverde**, **Palmar**, and **Ayangue**, with popular beaches and beach cafés, in a horseshoe bay, just off the main highway (accommodation includes **E** *Hostal Un Millón De Amigos*, with fan and bath, T 916-975). It gets very crowded and dirty at peak weekends/holidays.

VALDIVIA

San Pedro and Valdivia are two unattractive villages which merge together. There are many fish stalls. This is the site of the 5,000 year-old Valdivia culture. Many houses offer 'genuine' artefacts and one resident at N end of the village will show you the skeletons and burial urns dug up in his back garden.

It is illegal to export precolumbian artefacts from Ecuador. The replicas are made in exactly the same manner as their predecessors, copied from genuine designs, and whilst sacrificing historic authenticity, their purchase prevents the trafficking of originals and provides income for the locals. Ask for Juan Orrala, who makes excellent copies, and lives up the hill from the museum. Most artefacts discovered at the site are in museums in Quito and Guayaquil.

MANGLARALTO

(*Pop* 18,510) The main centre of the region N of Santa Elena, with a hospital and Emetel office. A tagua nursery has been started; ask to see examples of worked 'ivory' nuts. It is a nice place, with a quiet, clean beach, good surf but little shade. *Pro-pueblo* is an organization promoting ecotourism, reforestation, organic gardening, recycling, health, and tagua-nut carving. Their office is beside *Las Tangas*, T (04) 901-195.

- **Accommodation D** *Sr Ramón's house*, S of main plaza, orange/beige building, with bath, hot water, clean, safe, fan, mosquito net; **F** *Posada del Emperador*, T 901-172, basic rooms and a cabin, long stays arranged, Doña Lupita will cook vegetarian meals; **F** rooms in house beside church, on Av 24 de Mayo, new, clean, good value.

- **Places to eat** *Restaurante Las Tangas*, on beach, seafood, slow service; *Comedor Familiar*, weekends only; *Comedor Florencia*, moderately cheap.

- **Buses** To La Libertad, US$1; Jipijapa, US$2, 3½ hrs, 100 km via Salango; Puerto López, 1 hr, US$1.50.

MANGLARALTO TO PUERTO LOPEZ

3 km N of Manglaralto, **Montañita** has a good beach but watch out for the strong undertow and stingrays close to the water's edge. If stung, the small hospital in Manglaralto will treat you quickly. Here is the best surfing in Ecuador; board rental US$1.50/hr. Various competitions are held during the year; at weekends the town is full of Guayaquileños and it's a good place to hang out. Major development has taken place at the surfing end of the beach.

- **Accommodation & places to eat A3-C** *Baja Montañita*, T 901-218, F 287-873, a/c, cabins and rooms, pool, jacuzzi etc, 2 restaurants, bars, loud beach parties during the high season; **E** *Rincón de Amigos*, T 02-225-907, cheaper without bath, cold water, cabins or rooms, relaxed, vegetarian food, expensive breakfast, beach bar, snorkelling trips offered; **F** *Vito's Cabañas*, T 241-975, next door, clean, camping facilities, mostly rec; in the same building is *Pelicano* restaurant, good pizzas, open till 2200; **F** *El Puente*, by bridge on main road, basic. *Camping Los Delfines* has tents for hire, restaurant; several other rooms for rent nr the surfing beach. It's cheaper to eat in the village S of the surf beach. Emetel phone, T 901-190. **At Olón**, a few km N with a spectacular long beach: **A3** *Hotel Al Risco*, at Las Nuñez beyond Olón, T 09-410-022 (cellular), rustic, cabins and restaurant, horse riding; **G** *Hostería Olón Beach*, clean, basic, with Emetel. Fanny Tomalá rents rooms in the village. *Veronica*, just off the beach, scruffy, good seafood, Emetel phone. Accommodation is impossible to find during holiday weekends.

- **Buses** Transportes Manglaralto from Montañita to La Libertad, 1 hr, US$1. CLP 3 direct buses a day to Guayaquil, 0500, 1300, 1430 (return 0600, 1300, 1430).

Further N, by **La Entrada**, the road winds up and inland through lush forest and continues to **Ayampe**.

- **Accommodation & places to eat** Just before Ayampe is the new **A3** *Hotel Atamari*, T 02-226-072, beautiful, expensive cabins in spectacular surroundings, wonderful food, no public transport.

- **Alandaluz Ecological Centre:** 5 km beyond Ayampe, just before Puerto Rico, T 604-103, an ecologically and socially sound hotel, bamboo cabins with thatched roofs and fresh flowers; very peaceful, clean beach and stunning organic vegetable and flower gardens in the middle of a desert, working demonstrations of recycling of rubbish and water and composting toilets. It is a good base for exploring the nearby area and Machalilla National Park. The hotel will arrange excursions to Isla de la Plata if there are enough people, though tours are expensive. Prices from **F** pp camping, to **D** pp in cabins; student and youth hostel discount, 10% discount if you pay in sucres cash; good home-made food, vegetarian or seafood, breakfast costs US$2.80, other meals US$5.15, bar. More information and reservations (necessary) T 604-173 in Puerto López, or in Quito, *Pacarina*, Baquedano 330 y Reina Victoria, T 543-042/505-084, or write to Casilla 17-15-006-C. Cheaper meals can be ordered in **Puerto Rico**, on the main road, ask for Don Julio Mero, at the first house by the road that branches off to left, also rents cabins for longer stays. **D** *Piqueros Patas Azules*, N on Río Chico beach, nice setting, has a museum; **D** *Hostería Río Chico*, by the road at Río Chico, new, clean, also **F** bunk rooms in Albergue, T (05) 604-181.

● **Buses** Trans Manglaralto from La Libertad, US$2, or from Jipijapa if coming from the N. Ask to get off at Puerto Rico, though the centre is easily seen from the road. The last bus from the S passes at 1930, from the N at 1730; hitching is difficult. It's 20 mins from Puerto López.

PUERTO LOPEZ

This pleasant little fishing town (*Pop* 10,212) is beautifully set in a horseshoe bay. The beach is cleaner at the northern end, away from the fleet of boats moored offshore; watch the fishermen arrive in the morning and evening. The town is becoming increasingly visited by foreign tourists since the Parque Nacional Machalilla and Isla de la Plata (see below) have become budget alternatives to the Galápagos. Scooter rental is US$3/hr, with daily and weekly rates available.

Excursions

The Presley Norton archaeological museum in the nearby village of **Salango** is worth visiting; entry US$1. Artefacts from the excavations in the local fish meal factory's yard are housed in a beautiful museum on the plaza.

● **Places to eat** *El Delfín Mágico* (order meal before visiting museum), try the *spondilus* (spiny oyster) in fresh coriander and peanut sauce with garlic coated *patacones*.

● **Buses** To and from Puerto López every 20 mins; US$0.40, 10 mins.

Local information
● **Accommodation**

In Puerto López: **C** *Hotel Pacífico*, nr the Malecón, T 604-133, hot showers, safe, com-

fortable, a/c, cheaper with fan, need mosquito net, **D** in cabañas with shared bath, good breakfast, rec; **D-E** *Hotel Buenos Aires*, at least a 15-min walk from the highway, away from the beach, with bath, clean, comfortable, fan; **D** *La Terraza*, on the hill behind the clinic, new, fresh breeze, great views; **F** *Res Isla de la Plata*, on the main street from the highway, T 604-114, one block from beach, basic but clean, shared bath, mosquito nets, good restaurant downstairs.

● **Places to eat**

Carmita on the Malecón, seafood, rec for freshness, try *pescado al vapor*, rents rooms for longer stays, **G** pp; next door is *Mayflower*, good but not cheap; *Spondylus*, on seafront, also videobar and disco, good cheap breakfast, good juices; *Acapulco*, nr the bus stop, on corner, good value; *Flipper*, next to bus stop, cheap, rec; *Diana's Pizzería*, originally in Playas, due open 1997. Try the local avocado *licuados* and *chuzos*, rec. Excellent banana bread from the *panadería* behind church.

● **Tour companies & travel agents**

Local companies run tours to Isla de la Plata, Agua Blanca, San Sebastián and Los Frailes, as well as diving trips. **Whale watching** trips can be arranged out of Puerto López with *Pacarina*, or with *Whale Tours* in Guayaquil (see page 1097). *Sercapez*, T 604-130, arranges tours in the area, as does *Machalilla Tours*, T 604-206. Cheaper trips are available in open fishing boats, which are smaller and faster and can get closer, but have no toilet. American Kevin Gulash runs cheaper, alternative trips and is found next door to Alándaluz.

● **Transport**

Buses every 30 mins to **Jipijapa**, 1½ hrs, US$1.30; **La Libertad**, 2 hrs; and **Manglaralto**, 1 hr, US$1.35. To **Portoviejo**, 1 hr, good road, 68 km. To **Manta** direct, every 2 hrs.

MACHALILLA NATIONAL PARK

The Park extends over 55,000 has, including Isla de la Plata, Isla Salango, and the magnificent beach of Los Frailes and preserves marine ecosystems as well as the dry tropical forest and archaeological sites on shore. The continental portion of the park is divided into three sections which are separated by private land, including the town of Machalilla. Entrance is US$14 (ask for 5-6 days), payable at the Park Office next to the market in Puerto López (open 0700-1800), or directly to the park rangers (insist on a receipt). Rec for bird watching, also several species of mammals and reptiles.

To **Los Frailes** Take a bus towards Jipijapa and alight at the turnoff just S of the town of **Machalilla**, then walk for 30 mins. Show your national park ticket on arrival. No transport back to Puerto López after 1630.

About 5 km N of Puerto López, at Buena Vista, a dirt road to the right leads to **Agua Blanca**. Here, 5 km from the main road, in the National Park, amid hot, arid scrub, is a small village and a fine, small archaeological museum containing some fascinating ceramics from the Manteño civilization. Entry US$1.15; open 0800-1800. It is cheaper to find a guide for Agua Blanca in the village itself for a visit to the pre-Inca ruins; US$1.50 pp for a 2-3-hr tour for 2 people. It's a 45-min walk to the ruins, or hire horses for US$7.50 pp/day.

San Sebastián, 9 km from Agua Blanca, is in tropical moist forest at 800m; orchids can be seen and possibly howler monkeys. Although part of the national park, this area is administered by the Comuna of Agua Blanca, which charges its own fees in addition to the park entrance. A tour to the forest costs US$15 per day for the guide (fixed rate), US$1.50 pp to stay overnight at guide's house, US$5 for meals, US$15 per horse. Transportation to Agua Blanca is an extra US$5 pp. 5 hrs on foot or by horse.

● **Accommodation & places to eat** In Machalilla is **D** *Hotel Internacional Machalilla*, T 345-905, conspicuous building, clean, fan, overpriced, enquire about cheaper rates for longer stays. Next door is *Comedor La Gaviota*. *Bar Restaurant Cabaña Tropical* at S end of town. A few shops with basic supplies. Camping and one very basic room for rent above the museum at Agua Blanca; US$1.50 pp, minimal facilities. Camping is possible at San Sebastián, US$1.50.

● **Transport** Public transport to Agua Blanca leaves Sat only from *Carmita's* in Puerto López at 0630 and 1200, returning 0700 and 1300.

Trips to the **Isla de la Plata**, about 24 km offshore, have become popular because of the similarities with the Galápagos. Wildlife includes nesting colonies of waved albatross, frigates and three different booby species. Whales can be seen in July, Aug and September, as well as dolphins. It is also a precolumbian site with substantial pottery finds, and there is good diving and snorkelling. There are two walks, of 3 and 5 hrs; take water.

● **Access** The island can be visited in a day trip. Reservations can be arranged at most nearby hotels in Puerto López, Puerto Cayo or Machalilla and there are touts only too willing to organize a trip. Cheapest trips are with *Machalilla Tours*, US$20 pp for a full day, including guide and snack, 6-8 people. The park wardens in Puerto López will arrange trips which don't use pirate operators. Take dry clothes, water, precautions against sun and seasickness and snorkelling equipment.

PUERTO LOPEZ TO MANTA

The road turns inland for Jipijapa at Puerto Cayo. The beach gets cleaner as you walk away from town. Ask the fishermen about whale-watching tours, June-Sept.

● **Accommodation B-D** *Puerto Cayo*, pleasant, S end of beach, good food, overpriced rooms; **D** *Hostal Jipijapa*, clean, fridge, restaurant; **E** *Mar del Plata*, basic, with bath, cabins nearby **C**; **E** *Res Zavala's*, Malecón, with bath, clean, ask for sea view, meals available.

● **Places to eat** *La Cabaña* just back from the beach for good seafood; *D'Comer*, next to *Zavala's*, good cheap seafood.

The paved road climbs over humid hills to descend to the dry scrub around **Jipijapa** (*Pop* 32,225), an important centre for cotton, cocoa, coffee and kapok.

● **Accommodation** **D** *Hostal Jipijapa*, T 600-522, 2 blocks S of the cemetery, clean, overpriced.

● **Buses** To Manglaralto, 2 hrs, US$2; to Puerto López, 1½ hrs, US$1.10; to Manta, 1 hr. Buses leave from the plaza. The last bus to the coast is 1800.

At **La Pila**, due N of Jipijapa, the road turns E for Portoviejo. The village's main industry is fake precolumbian pottery, with a thriving by-line in erotic ceramics.

A few kilometres further W is **Montecristi**, below an imposing hill, high enough to be watered by low cloud which gives the region its only source of drinking water. The town is renowned for Panama hats; also varied straw and basketware and wooden barrels which are strapped to donkeys for carrying water. Ask for José Chávez Franco, Rocafuerte 203, T/F 606-343, where you can see Panama hats being made; wholesale and retail. The statesman Eloy Alfaro was born here.

MANTA

(*Pop* 125,505; *Phone Code* 04) Ecuador's second port after Guayaquil, it is a busy town that sweeps round a bay filled with all sorts of boats. The western section comprises steep, narrow streets and the Malecón that fills in the evenings with impromptu parties and cars cruising, music blaring. The constant breeze makes it pleasant to walk along the front or stop for a drink at one of the many small bars. Playa Murciélago at the W end of the Malecón is very wide but unprotected. Further W towards the point, beaches are spotless and isolated. The town's fine wooden church was destroyed by a cargo plane crash in Oct 1996. Miraculously, the statue of the Virgin survived.

A bridge joins the main town with **Tarqui** on the E side of the Río Manta. The Tarqui beach is more popular, but dirtier. Do not leave **anything** unattended anywhere (in Tarqui or Manta).

Museums

The Banco Central museum, Av 6 y C4, has a small but excellent collection of ceramics of the Huancavilca-Manteño culture (AD 800-1550), open 0830-1630, the curator speaks English and French.

Local information

Water shortages are very common. All streets have numbers; those above 100 are in Tarqui (those above C110 are not safe). Most offices, shops and the bus station are in Manta. There is a wider selection of hotels in Tarqui.

● **Accommodation**

In Manta: A3 *Cabañas Balandra*, Av 8 y C20, Barrio Córdova, T 620-316, F 620-545, a/c cabins, breakfast inc, secure; **B** *Manta Imperial*, Malecón by Playa Murciélago, on beach, T 621-955, F 623-016, inc taxes, a/c, pool, parking, disco and dancing, plenty of insect life.

In Tarqui: B *Las Gaviotas*, Malecón 1109 y C 106, T 620-140, F 611-840, the best in Tarqui by some length, a/c, poor restaurant, tennis court; **B-C** *Las Rocas*, C 101 y Av 105, T 610-856, a/c, cheaper with fan, pool, private parking, restaurant poor.

C *El Inca*, C 105 y Malecón, T 610-986, phone, fan or a/c, good value restaurant, OK.

D *Pacífico Inn*, Av 106 y C 101, T 622-475, a/c, discount for longer stay; **D** *Panorama Inn*, C 103 y Av 105, T 611-552, a/c, pool, restaurant, parking, helpful, rec.

E *Boulevard*, Av 105 y C 103, T 625-333, with bath, TV, garage; **E** *Hostal Miami*, Av 102 y C 107, T 611-743, hot showers, fan, basic, clean; **E-F** *Res Viña del Mar*, Av 106 y C 104, T 610-854, with bath and fan; **F** *Res Monte Carlo*, C 105 y Av 105, with bath, no fan, dirty and basic; **F** *Playita Mía*, Malecón y C 103, restaurant, shared bath, very basic.

● **Places to eat**

Club Ejecutivo, Av 2 y C 12, top of Banco de Pichincha building, first class food and service, great view; *Paraná*, C 17 y Malecón, nr the port, local seafood and grill, cheap, highly rec; *Shamu*, C11 No 1-12, downtown, good set meals and à la carte; *Mima*, C 104 y Malecón, Tarqui, good fish and seafood. Many good, cheap *comedores* on Tarqui beach which are open at weekends.

● **Banks & money changers**

Banco de Pichincha and Banco del Pacífico

change TCs. **Filanbanco** accepts Visa. *Casa de Cambio Zanchi*, Av 2 No 11-28, T 613-857, *Cambicruz*, Av 2 No 11-22, T 622-235.

● **Post & telecommunications**
Post Office: above Banco de Pichincha. **Telephone**: Emetel, Malecón nr C 11.

● **Tour companies & travel agents**
Ecuadorean Tours, Av 2 y C 13; *Metropolitan Touring*, Av 3 No 11-49, T 623-090; *Delgado Travel*, C 12 y Av 2, T 624-614, F 621-497, also changes dollars.

● **Tourist offices**
Cetur, Pasaje José María Egas, Av 3 y C 11, T 622-944, helpful, Spanish only.

● **Useful addresses**
Immigration: Av 4 de Noviembre y J-1 (police station).

● **Transport**
Air Eloy Alfaro airport. TAME to Quito daily.
Buses All buses leave from the terminal behind the new central bank building. To **Quito**, 9 hrs, US$6.60, hourly 0400-2300; **Guayaquil**, 4 hrs, US$4, hourly; **Esmeraldas**, 0630, 0800 and 2000, 8 hrs, US$6.80; **Santo Domingo**, 4½ hrs, US$5.65; **Portoviejo**, 45 mins, US$0.70, every 10 mins; **Jipijapa**, 1 hr, US$1, every 20 mins; **Bahía de Caráquez**, 3 hrs, US$2.20, hourly.

PORTOVIEJO

40 km inland from Manta and 65 km NE from Jipijapa, Portoviejo is capital of Manabí province and a major commercial centre (*Pop* 132,937). The cathedral overlooks Parque Eloy Alfaro, where sloths may be seen in the trees. Kapok mattresses and pillows are made here from the fluffy fibre of the seed capsule of the ceibo and in C Alajuela items made by *montubios* (coastal farmers) are sold.

● **Accommodation** B *Hostería California*, Ciudadela California, T 634-415, a/c, very good; C *Cabrera Internacional*, García Moreno y Pedro Gual, T 633-201, a/c, clean, noisy; C *New York*, Fco de P Moreira y Olmedo, T 632-037/051, F 632-044, a/c and fridge, D with fan, clean, poor service, restaurant downstairs; E *Pacheco*, 9 de Octubre 1512 y Morales, T 631-788, with or without bath, fan; E *París*, Plaza Central, T 652-727, one of the oldest hotels, classic.

● **Places to eat** *Zavalito*, Primera Transversal entre Duarte y Alajuela, lunch only, popular; *Los Geranios*, Chile 508 nr Quito, good set lunch; *Mariano Internacional*, Córdova y García Moreno, good food. There's a good Chinese restaurant at the bus terminal. *El Palatino*, off main plaza, good coffee and cheap local specialities.

● **Banks & money changers** Banco del Pacífico changes TCs.

● **Tourist offices** Cetur, Morales 613 y Sucre.

● **Transport Air** Flights to Quito. **Buses** to **Quito**, 8 hrs; routes are either E via Quevedo (147 km), or, at Calderón, branch NE for Calceta, Chone and on to Santo Domingo de los Colorados. Services also to **Guayaquil**. Bus station is on the edge of town, taxi US$0.70.

CRUCITA

(*Pop* 8,300) A rapidly growing resort, 45 mins by road from Portoviejo, Crucita is popular with bathers on Sun. Other than during carnival, it is relaxed and friendly. Hang gliding and parasailing are practised from the dry cliffs S of town. The beach and ocean are lovely but do not go barefoot as there are many pigs roaming loose and *nigua* (a flea which likes to nest under toenails) are common. Beaches are cleaner on either side of town. There is an abundance of sea birds in the area.

● **Accommodation** From N to S along the beach: E *Hipocampo*, oldest in town, private bath, simple, good value; E *Res San José*, shared bath, intermittent water supply, basic; D *Hostería Zucasa*, T 634-908 (Portoviejo), 244-713/320-271 (Quito) fully equipped cabins for up to 6, best in town; D *Fernando's*, some rooms with bath; D *Hostería Las Cabañitas*, T 931-037, cabins for 4-5 people, basic.

● **Places to eat** Many simple restaurants and kiosks serving mainly fish and seafood.

● **Post & telecommunications** Emetel: for long distance phone calls (no international service), 2 blocks back from beach on main highway.

● **Transport** Buses and open sided trucks with slatted seats, called *chivas* or *rancheros*, leave from the beach and plaza for Portoviejo, US$ 0.45, 45 mins. Regular buses to **Manta**.

2 km N along a paved road running parallel to the beach is the fishing village of **Las Gilces**, which has been less influenced by tourism. *Hotel Centro Turístico Las Amazonas.*

NORTH TO BAHIA

About 60 km N of Portoviejo (30 km S of Bahía de Caráquez) are **San Clemente** and, 3 km S, **San Jacinto**. Both get crowded during the holiday season. The ocean is magnificent but be wary of the strong undertow. Also, do not go barefoot because of the *nigua*, especially in the towns.

● **Accommodation In San Clemente**:
C *Hostería San Clemente*, T 420-076, modern clean cabins for 6 to 10 persons, swimming pool, restaurant, book ahead in season, closed in low season; **E** *Las Acacias*, 150m from the beach, 800m N of San Clemente, clean, T 541-706 (Quito), bath, nice 3-storey wooden building with huge verandas, prices go up in high season, good seafood, rec; **E** *Hostal El Edén*, 1 block from beach along the main street, some rooms have bath, some have sea views, clean, basic; **E** *Cabañas Espumas del Mar*, on the beach, good restaurant, family run. **San Jacinto**: **D** *Hostal San Jacinto*, on the beach, with bath; **D** *Cabañas del Pacífico*, T 523-862 (Quito), private bath, fan, fridge; **E** *Cabañas Los Almendros*, T 533-493 (Quito), private bath, basic, cramped. **Between San Clemente and San Jacinto**: **E** *Cabañas Tío Gerard*, T 459-613, F 442-954 (Quito), with bath and kitchenette, small rooms, clean, fan.

● **Places to eat In San Clemente**: *Tiburón*, and *El Paraíso del Sabor*, both on beach, good, cheap.

● **Buses** Most Guayaquil-Portoviejo-Bahía de Caráquez buses pass San Clemente. To Jipijapa, 1 hr, US$1.50.

BAHIA DE CARAQUEZ

Set on the southern shore at the seaward end of the Chone estuary (*Pop* 15,308; *Phone code* 05), Bahía has an attractive river front laid out with parks on the Malecón Alberto Santos, which becomes Circunvalación Dr Virgilio Ratti and goes right around the point. The beach stretches around the point and is quite clean. While there are still some buildings with wooden windows and balconies, and some arcaded shops in the centre, the point is built up with smart houses and blocks of flats. The town has become popular as a beach resort (busiest July to Sept, Christmas and Easter). It is also a centre of the shrimp farming industry.

Museums
The archaeological museum of the Central Bank is in Casa de la Cultura next door. Admission free, open 1500-1700, it has a collection of precolumbian pottery.

Guacamayo Adventures (see below) has the concession for visiting the **Isla de Fragatas**, 15 mins by boat in the middle of the Bahía de Caráquez estuary, which has a stunning number of bird species, including a higher concentration of frigate birds than on the Galápagos (excellent for photographers). The frigate birds can be seen displaying their inflated red sacks as part of the mating ritual (best Aug-Jan). The 3-hr trip costs US$14 for 4 (less for larger groups). Dolphins can also be seen in the estuary.

The **Chirije** archaeological site can be visited with Bahía Dolphin Tours (see below). This site was a seaport of the Bahía Culture and is an important archaeological discovery; museum on site. The tour costs US$150 for 2, inc accommodation in basic huts; take mosquito repellent.

Local information
● **Accommodation**
Only hotels with their own supply do not suffer water shortages. **A3** *La Piedra*, Circunvalación y Bolívar, T 690-780, F 690-154, inc taxes, pool, good restaurant but expensive, laundry, modern, good service, access to beach, lovely views; **A3** *Herradura*, Bolívar y Circunvalación, T 690-446, F 690-265, inc taxes, a/c, cheaper with fan, comfortable, restaurant, very pretty.

C *Italia*, Bolívar y Checa, T 691-137, F 691-092, fan, hot water, restaurant.

D *Americano*, Ascázubi 222, 690-594, a/c, some rooms are nice, others not so good; **D** *Bahía*, on Malecón nr Banco Central, rooms at the back are nicer, fan, clean; **D** *Bahía Bed & Breakfast Inn*, Ascázubi 322 y Morales, T 690-146, clean, quite good value; **D** *Hostal Querencia*, Malecón 1800 by main road out of town, T 690-009, some rooms with bath, clean, popular, rec.

E *Palma*, Bolívar 914 y Arenas, T 690-467, with bath, clean, basic, restaurant below, good set meals, excellent value breakfast.

F *Pensión Miriam*, Montúfar, entre Ascázubi y Riofrío, shared bath, basic but clean, rooms at front have windows, own water supply.

G *Hostal San José*, Ascázubi y Juan de Velasco, clean, safe, big rooms; **G** *Res Vera*, Montúfar y Ante, T 691-581, rec.

● **Places to eat**
Brisas del Mar, Hidalgo y Circunvalación, good fish, cheap; nearby is *Albatros*, good; *Los Helechos*, Montúfar y Muñoz Dávila, by Circunvalación, good and clean; *Chifa China*, Bolívar

y Ascázubi, cheap, good; *La Chozita*, on the Malecón nr the San Vicente ferry station, barbecue style food, good; nearby is *Genesis*, popular, good seafood; *Donatella's*, 1 block from Reina del Camino bus terminal, good, cheap pizza.

● **Banks & money changers**
Banco Comercial de Manabí, Malecón y Ante; nearby, heading out of town is Banco Central, changes dollars cash; Filanbanco, Aguilera, nr Malecón, cash advance on Visa.

● **Post & telecommunications**
Post Office is at Morales y Ante; Emetel is on Intriago.

● **Tour companies & travel agents**
Marina Tours – Guacamayo Adventures, Av Bolívar y Arenas, T 691-412, F 691-280, excursions to Isla de Fragatas (see above), coastal caves N of Canoa (see below), to see the shrimp ponds, mangroves and the great migratory bird watching of the wetlands of the estuary and into the fascinating tropical dry forest at Punta Bellaca. Also offered are 3-day trips on horseback to an organic farm at Río Muchacho; accommodation is with a family in a bamboo house or tree house, traditional food, 'an eye opener to rural coastal culture', US$70-86 depending on numbers, highly rec, reservation necessary. *Bahía Dolphin Tours*, C Salinas, Edif Dos Hemisferios, PO Box 25, T 692-097/086, F 692-088, Email archtour@srv1.telconet.et, home page http//www.qni.com/~mj/bahia/bahia.html; owners of Chirije, for tours there and to other local and national destinations.

● **Tourist offices**
Cetur, Malecón y Arenas, T 691-124, Mon-Fri 0830-1800.

● **Transport**
Air Airport at San Vicente. Direct flights from Quito twice weekly.

Buses Coactur and Reina del Camino offices are on the Malecón 1600 block. To **Quito**, 8 hrs, US$6.60; **Santo Domingo de los Colorados**, 4-4½ hrs, US$4.10; **Esmeraldas**, at 1515, 8 hrs, US$6.90; **Portoviejo**, 2 hrs, US$1.55, hourly; **Puerto López** or **Manta**, go to Portoviejo or Jipijapa and change; to **Guayaquil**, 6 hrs, US$5.50, hourly; to **Manta**, 3 hrs, US$2.20, hourly. Open-sided *rancheros* leave from the park on Aguilera to Chone (US$1.05) and other nearby destinations.

ROUTES From Bahía de Caráquez to the highlands there are two main roads. The first one is via Chone and **El Carmen** to Santo Domingo. This road, which has many potholes, climbs quickly over the coastal range, with views of the estuary, the remaining mangroves and the shrimp ponds that destroyed them. In the following wetlands,

with more shrimp ponds, are cattle fincas and bamboo houses on stilts. **Chone** (*Pop* 41,437), is 1½ hrs E from Bahía. At the Santo Domingo exit is a strange sculpture of 4 people suspending a car on wires across a gorge. It represents the difficulty faced in the first ever trip to Quito by car (C *Atahualpa de Oro*, Av Atahualpa y Páez, T 696-627, with bath, TV, restaurant, garage, clean, very good). The second road is via San Clemente and Rocafuerte to Pichincha, Velasco Ibarra and on to Quevedo.

NORTH TO ESMERALDAS

SAN VICENTE

San Vicente, on the N side of the Río Chone, reached by ferry from Bahía, or by road W from Chone. The stretch of coast between San Vicente and Canoa (see below) is said to have the most tourist potential in the country and is therefore under development, including the upgrading of the airport. The Santa Rosa church, 100m to the left of the wharf, contains excellent mosaic and glass work by José María Peli Romeratigui (better known as Peli).

● **Accommodation** On the road to Canoa: **A3** *Cabañas Alcatraz*, T 674-179, nice, a/c, pool; **A3-B** *Monte Mar*, Malecón s/n, T 674-197, excellent food, pool, views; **B** *El Velero*, cabañas and suites, pool, restaurant, good; **C** *Las Hamacas*, T 674-134, rooms or cabañas, restaurant, bar, disco, pool, tours; **D** *El Montés*, T 674-201, bar, no restaurant, pleasant; **D** *Restaurant Las Gaviotas*, 3 rooms with bath, nice. **In town: C-D** *Vacaciones*, T 674-116/8, nr the old market, a/c, pool, tennis court, restaurant; **E** *San Vicente*, Av Primera y C 1, opp the old market, T 674-182, cheaper with shared bath, basic, clean, mosquito nets.

● **Transport Buses** Coactur, opp *panga* dock, to Portoviejo, Manta, Guayaquil. Reina del Camino (nr *Hotel Vacaciones*), to **Portoviejo**, 4 daily, US$1.55; **Chone**, 7 daily, US$1, 45 mins; **Guayaquil**, 4 daily, 6 hrs, US$5.70; Quito, at 0630 and 2215, 7½ hrs, US$6.60; **Esmeraldas**, US$5.65; **Santo Domingo**, US$3.70; **Quinindé**, US$4.50. Several companies to **Pedernales**, US$4, 3 hrs, and **Cojimíes**. The road is paved as far as Pedernales. **Boats** *Pangas* cross to Bahía continually until 2200, 10 mins, US$0.20; car ferry every 20 mins or so, free for foot passengers, very steep ramps very difficult for low clearance cars.

On the beautiful 17 km beach between San Vicente and **Canoa** (a good walk or bike ride), many people harvest shrimp larvae, especially at full and new moon. Just N along the beach are nine natural caves at the cliff base; walk there at low tide but allow time to return (guide rec). The clean beach is 800m wide, the widest in Ecuador, relatively isolated and great for surf.

● **Accommodation & places to eat E** *Bamboo*, on beach, good food, very popular, English, Dutch spoken; **E** *Posada de Daniel*, at back of village, attractive, with or without bath, Franklin Macay will guide to the caves; **E** *Bamboo*, on beach, good food, very popular, English and Dutch spoken; **F** *Hostería La Posada*, with bath, good service, laundry, restaurant, also cabins; several other rooms and *comedores*. *El Torbellino*, good for typical dishes, cheap, large servings; *Arena Bar* on the beach, snacks, beer, T-shirts, hammocks.

PEDERNALES

The road cuts across Cabo Pasado to Jama ($2^{1}/_{2}$ hrs; *Pensión Jamaica*), then runs parallel to the beach past coconut groves and shrimp hatcheries, inland across some low hills and across the Equator to **Pedernales**, an undeveloped small market town on the coast with nice beaches. The town is being touted as a major future beach resort. A mosaic mural on the church overlooking the plaza is one of the best pieces of work by Peli (see above); exquisite examples of his stained glass can be seen inside the church.

● **Accommodation C** *América*, García Moreno, on the road to the beach, T 681-174, fans, balcony, very comfortable, expensive restaurant; **D** *Playas*, Juan Pereira y Manabí, nr airport, T 681-125, fans, nets, clean, comfortable; **E** *Pedernales*, on Av Eloy Alfaro, 2 blocks from plaza, basic but clean, rooms at front have windows, fans, nets, good value.

● **Places to eat** *El Rocío*, on Eloy Alfaro, good cheap food; *La Fontana*, just off main plaza, good vegetarian food; *Habana Club*, next to *Hotel Playas*, good seafood, cheap.

● **Buses** To Santo Domingo, via El Carmen, 6 daily, $2^{1}/_{2}$ hrs, US$3, and on to Quito, 6 hrs, US$5.70; to Esmeraldas, at 0515 and 1630, US$5.30, and on to Muisne, US$7.15.

COJIMIES

A real one-horse town, with unpaved streets. It is continually being eroded by the sea and has been moved about three times in as many decades.

● **Accommodation & places to eat F** *Costa Azul*, shared bath, very basic; **F** *Mi Descanso*, with bath, slightly better looking; *Cabañas* for rent, **E**, ask at *Mi Descanso*. 14 km before Cojimíes on the beach is **C** *Cocosolo*, cabins with bath, set among palm trees, French, English and Italian spoken, clean, restaurant, breakfast US$2.25, lunch US$4.50, also rooms without bath, **E** pp, camping **E**/tent, horses for hire, US$7.50/hr; reservations through Guacamayo Tours in Bahía, T (05) 691-412 or Safari Tours in Quito, T (02) 552-505. *Restaurant Flavio Alfaro*, is by the beach where boats leave for Muisne, friendly, cheap.

● **Transport Buses** To Pedernales by a rough, unpaved road, $1^{1}/_{2}$ hrs, US$1.90, last one departs at 1500, minibuses depart more frequently; pick-ups also ply back and forth along the beach at low tide, an exhilarating 30-mins' ride, US$1.90, last one leaves around 1500. **Boat** Horacio Gostalle sails to Bahía twice a week. Daily canoes to Muisne, 2 hrs, US$5.70 pp, not for the faint-hearted, those prone to sea-sickness or weak swimmers; the entry into Cojimíes and Muisne is treacherous and many boats have been thrown into the shallows by the swell.

MUISNE

The town, on an island, is a bit run down but lively and friendly. 15 mins' walk from town (or a tricycle ride for US$0.35), is a long expanse of beach, a pleasant walk at low tide but practically disappears at high tide. Some 50,000 stems of bananas a month are exported through Muisne via Esmeraldas, though the main trade is now shrimps. On the Río Sucio, inland from Muisne and Cojimíes, is an isolated group of Cayapa Indians, some of whom visit the town on Sun. No banks; change TCs at a slightly lower rate at Marco Velasco's store, near the dock. Marcelo Cotera and Nisvaldo Ortiz arrange boat trips to see the mangrove forests which are being replanted by the Fundación Ecológica Muisne, donations welcome, contact them through the tourist office.

● **Accommodation** New hotel on the beach, price **C**. **E** *Galápagos*, 200m from beach, with bath, modern, clean, fans, mosquito nets, restaurant, rec; **E** *Oasis*, nearby, clean, fans, nets, secure, rec; **E** *Playa Paraíso*, clean, basic, nets; **F** *Cabañas Ipanema*, 100m from beach, with bath, water shortages, basic, nets; **F** *Cabañas*

San Cristóbal, wooden cabins on beach to the right coming from town, no sign, very basic, toilet, fetch water from well nearby, cheaper for long stay; **F** pp *Calade*, 150m away at the S end of the beach, clean, comfortable, negotiable for longer stays, excellent meals. **In town are**: **F** *Res Isla*, and **F** *Sarita*, both very basic. Insist on a mosquito net.

● **Places to eat**

Mi Delfín, on the beach, clean, rooms to let **G**, rec; *El Tiburón*, cheap, rec; *Las Palmeiras*, excellent seafood, try *camarones a la plancha*; nr beach is *Restaurante Suizo-Italiano*, good pizza and pasta, breakfast, good atmosphere; *Habana Club*, good rum and reggae. Several other excellent kiosks on the beach; try *encocada de cangrejo*, crab in coconut.

● **Transport**

Canoes ply the narrow stretch of water between the island and mainland (El Relleno); US$0.10. Buses to **Esmeraldas** US$1.50, 3 hrs; to **Quito** once a night, direct. Boats to **Cojimíes** at 0930 and 1300, US$5.70, 2 hrs, buy your ticket at the dock, take waterproofs and be prepared to wait until the boat is full.

Tonchigüe is a quiet fishing village, 2 hrs N from Muisne, with expensive *cabañas*, 2 cheap hotels and buses to Atacames, US$0.50, and Esmeraldas, US$1, 1 hr.

Playa Escondida 2 km S of Tonchigüe is the turn-off for **Playa Escondida**, at Km 14 via Tonchigüe-Punta Galera. This charming beach hideaway, run by Canadian Judith Barrett on an ecologically sound basis, is set in 100 ha stretching back to secondary tropical dry forest. Rustic cabins overlooking a lovely little bay; **E** pp, camping, **F** pp, 3 meals US$10-15; excellent food, safe swimming; completely isolated and wonderfully relaxing. For reservations, T (09) 733-368.

● **Access** To get there take a *ranchera* or bus from Esmeraldas for Punta Galera; El Pacífico departs at 1330 and La Costañita at 1630, 2 hrs. From Quito take a Trans Occidental bus at 2300, arriving in Tonchigüe at 0530-0600, then wait till 0730 for the *ranchera* to Punta Galera.

Beyond Tonchigüe is Playa de **Same**, with a long, grey sandy beach lined with palms and, mostly, high-rise apartment blocks. Safe swimming; good birdwatching in the lagoon behind the beach.

● **Accommodation A3** *Club Casablanca*, restaurant, tennis courts, swimming pool, luxurious (reservations through Metropolitan Tour-

ing in Quito); **D** *La Terraza*, on beach, T 544 507 (Quito), cabins, with bath, fan, hammocks Spanish and Italian owners, good restaurant **D** *Seaflower*, T/F 861-789, reasonable value restaurant. On the hill by the sea, S of Same i **C** *El Acantilado*, T 235-034 in Quito, cabins o rooms, excellent food. Booking is advisable a holiday times and weekends. In the low season good deals can be negotiated.

● **Buses** Every 30 mins to and from Atacames La Costeñita, 15 mins, 18 km, US$0.35, make sure it drops you at Same and not at *La Casab lanca*; to Muisne, US$0.60.

Súa is another resort, a 15-min bus ride S of Atacames. The beach is not very clear but it's a quiet and friendly place set in a beautiful bay.

● **Accommodation & places to eat D** *Pensión del Súa*, in the village, good, clean, restaurant; **D** *Súa*, on the beach, 6 rooms, hot water fans, clean, comfortable; **D-E** *Buganvillas*, on the beach, T 731-008, with bath, very nice; **F** *Le Weekend*, 150m from beach French/Ecuadorean owners, T 731-486, shared bath, clean, fan, mosquito nets, terrace, ar ranges boat trips; **G** pp *Malibu*, on the beach basic but good value. *La Plage*, on the beach French-run restaurant, excellent seafood, rec.

ATACAMES

25 km S of Esmeraldas (*Phone Code* 06) Atacames is one of the main resorts on the Ecuadorean coast. It's a real 24-hr party town during the high season (April-Oct), a weekends and local holiday times. The palm trees on the beach, washed away in 1983, are growing again. **NB** The sale of black cora jewellery has led to the destruction of much of the offshore reef. Consider the environmental implications before buying.

Local information
● **Accommodation**

Prices quoted are for the high season; discounts are available in the low season. Hotels are generally, expensive for Ecuador. Most accommodation has salt water in the bathrooms; fresh water is not always available and not very good. It's best to bring a mosquito net as few hotels supply them.

A3 *Complejo Turístico Piriapolis*, at the S end of the beach, T 731-238, T/F 713-500, a/c, TV, pool.

B *Lé Castell*, T 731-542, F 731-442, cabins, pool, garage, restaurant, comfortable; **B** *Villas Arco Iris*, at the N end of the beach, T 525-544

(Quito), or T 731-069, F 731-437, fridge, clean, charming, English, German and French spoken, rec.

C *Cabañas Caída del Sol*, 150m from the beach, T/F 731-479, fan, clean, spacious, quiet, good value, Swiss-run.

D *La Casa del Manglar*, 150m from the beach beside the footbridge, T 731-464, shared bath, clean, rec; **D** *Cabañas Los Bohíos*, T 731-094, bungalows with fresh water showers, clean, comfortable, quite good value; **D** *Galería Atacames*, T 731-149, on the beach, fresh water, clean, good restaurant, money exchange, cash and TCs, book exchange, safe deposit.

E *Bachita*, on main road leading to beach, large rooms with bath, good; **E** *Tahiti*, with bath, pool, fan, nets, breakfast, good restaurant, also cabins, **F** pp; **E** *Cabañas Rincón del Mar*, on the beach, T 731-064, new, with bath, clean, fresh water, secure, cosy, English, French and German spoken, highly rec; **E** *Rincón Sage*, 120m from beach,T 731-246, with bath, quiet, money exchange, clean, comfortable; **E** pp *Rodelú*, T 731-033, with bath, fridge, fan, clean, OK; **E-F** *Cabañas de Rogers*, at the S end of the beach, T 751-011, quiet, constant water supply, restaurant, bar, rec.

G pp *Res Rebecca*, round corner from *Galerías Atacames*, clean, noisy at night.

● **Places to eat**
The beach is packed with bars and restaurants, too numerous to list; most offer seafood at similar prices. The best and cheapest ceviche is found at the stands at the S end of the beach and at the market, but avoid concha. Many restaurants on the beach rent rooms. *La Terraza*, very good, nice views; *Cafetería*

The Capital of Rhythm

Esmeraldeños prefer the livelier sound of Caribbean *salsa* to the *cumbia* heard in the sierra, and have retained the African-influenced marimba, usually accompanied by a bomero, who plays a deep-pitched bass drum suspended from the ceiling, and a long conga drum. Where there is a marimba school you will also find dancers, and the women who are too old to dance play percussion and chant songs handed down the generations, many with Colombian references, but the best marimba can only be seen in the backwoods of the province on Sundays and holidays.

Pelícanos, good, menu includes vegetarian dishes and salads; *Comedor Popular*, good Italian and criollo cooking, order special requests in advance; *Paco Foco*, great seafood, very popular. Cocada, a sweet made from coconut, peanut and brown sugar, is sold in the main plaza.

● **Security**
Camping is unsafe. Walkers along the beach from Atacames to Súa regularly get assaulted at knife point where there is a small tunnel. Gangs seem to work daily. Note also that the sea can be very dangerous, there is a powerful undertow and many people have been drowned.

● **Transport**
Buses to/from Esmeraldas, every 15 mins, US$0.70, 40 mins; to/from Muisne, hourly; to Guayaquil, US$7.

ESMERALDAS

(*Pop* 98,558) The city has little to recommend it and it suffers from water shortages. There are gold mines nearby, tobacco and cacao grown inland, cattle ranching along the coast, timber exports, and an oil pipeline from the Oriente to an ocean terminal and refinery at nearby Balao. The development of shrimp farms has destroyed much mangrove forest. A road bridge over the river at San Mateo upstream from Esmeraldas gives a direct road link to the General Rivadeneira airport.

NB Mosquitoes and malaria are a serious problem throughout the province of Esmeraldas in the rainy season, including on the beaches at night. Most *residencias* provide mosquito nets (*toldos* or *mosquiteros*). It's best to visit in the June-Dec dry season. Use sun tan lotion or cover up, even when it's cloudy.

Excursions
Las Palmas, just N of Esmeraldas, is being developed as a resort, but, despite its broad sandy beach, it has yet to settle into a safe, clean environment for visitors. The best hotels are along Av Kennedy.

● **Transport** Buses to Las Palmas, US$0.18, taxi US$1.50; leave regularly from the main plaza in Esmeraldas.

Local information
● **Accommodation**
Generally, hotels in the centre of **Esmeraldas**

are not up to much and you are advised to stay in the outskirts.

D *Apart Hotel Casino*, Libertad 407 y Ramón Tello, T 728-700, F 728-704, excellent, good restaurant, casino.

E *Galeón*, Piedrahita 330 y Olmedo, T 713-116, bath, a/c; **E** *Miraflores*, on plaza, shared bath, clean, fans, basic, good; **E** *Diana*, Mañizares y Sucre, showers, safe.

F *Asia*, 9 de Octubre 116, T 711-852, nr the bus station, basic but clean.

G *Hostal Domínguez*, on Sucre nr the Plaza Central, noisy, hot water, open all night; **G** *Turismo*, Bolívar 843, basic, with bath and fan, clean and friendly; **G** *Valparaíso I*, Libertad y Pichincha, very basic but good value, cheap restaurant.

● **Places to eat**
Chifa Restaurante Asiático, Mañizares y Bolívar, Chinese, excellent; *La Marimba Internacional*, Libertad y Lavallén, rec; *Las Redes*, main plaza, good fish, cheap. *Budapest*, Cañizares 214 y Bolívar, Hungarian-run, clean, pleasant; *Balcón del Pacífico*, Bolívar y 10 de Agosto, nice atmosphere, good view overlooking city, cheap drinks; *Los Alamos*, 9 de Octubre, nr the plaza, good, popular. There are numerous typical restaurants and bars by the beach selling *ceviches*, fried fish and *patacones*.

● **Banks & money changers**
Banco Popular, Bolívar entre Cañizares y Piedrahita; Filanbanco, upstairs at both until 1200; *Botica Koch*, Sucre y 9 de Octubre, good rates.

● **Entertainment**
El Portón peña and discotheque, Colón y Piedrahita; *El Guadal de Ña Mencha*, 6 de Diciembre y Quito, peña school, marimba school at weekends; good *Bar Asia* on Bolívar by central Parque.

Cockfights: Eloy Alfaro y 9 de Octubre, at weekends.

Cinema: *Ciné Bolívar*, Bolívar y 9 de Octubre, with a/c and upholstered seating. *Cine Esmeraldas* shows newer movies.

● **Shopping**
There is a Cayapa basket market across from the Post Office, behind the vegetables. Also three doors down, Tolita artefacts and basketry. The market nr the bus station is good for buying mosquito nets. *Más por Menos* supermarket has a good selection of imported goods.

● **Useful addresses**
Immigration: Av Olmedo y Rocafuerte, T 720-256.

● **Transport**
Air Gen Rivadeneira Airport is on the road to La Tola; taxi to centre, 30 km, about US$5; buses to the Terminal Terrestre from the road outside the airport pass about every 30 mins; several buses to La Tola and Borbón, so it's not necessary to go into Esmeraldas if you want to go on to San Lorenzo or other places. Daily flights to Quito with TAME, 30 mins. Check in early, planes may leave 30 mins before scheduled time.

Buses To Quito, US$6, 5-6 hrs, 30 a day, good paved road (or 7 hrs via Mindo, San Miguel de los Bancos and La Independencia), with Trans-Esmeraldas (best buses, Av Piedrahita 200), Occidental and Trans Ibarra; also with Pan Americana (at *Hotel Casino*) twice daily, slow but luxurious, US$10; by Aerotaxi (small bus), 5 hrs, 12 passengers, reserved seats, their office is nr the main plaza. To **Santo Domingo**, US$2.25, 4 hrs; to **Ambato**, 5 times a day with Coop Sudamericana, 8 hrs, US$6.50; to **Guayaquil**, TAME, US$7, 7 hrs; to **Bahía de Caráquez**, via Santo Domingo de los Colorados, US$7; to **Portoviejo**, US$2.75; **Manta**, US$7; to **Quevedo**, 6 hrs. La Costeñita buses go to: La **Tola**, every 2 hrs, between 0600 and 1500, US$2.85, 3½ hrs; to **Muisne**, hourly, US$1.50, 3½ hrs; to **Súa**, **Same** and **Atacames**, every 15 mins from 0630 to 2030; to **Borbón**, every 2 hrs, US$3, 4 hrs.

Boat To Limones and San Lorenzo: the service is irregular; ask at the Port Captain's office at Las Palmas. A combined boat/bus service leaves for San Lorenzo at 1330.

NORTH OF ESMERALDAS

There are no good beaches for swimming N of Esmeraldas. **Río Verde**, where the paved road ends, has a dirty beach. It was the setting for Moritz Thompson's books on Peace Corps life, *Living Poor* and *Farm on the River of Emeralds*. Beyond Río Verde is **Rocafuerte**, recommended as having the best seafood in the province.

At **La Tola**, where you catch the boat for Limones and San Lorenzo, the shoreline changes from sandy beaches to mangrove swamp. The wildlife is varied and spectacular, especially the birds. Try to avoid staying overnight in La Tola; women especially are harassed.

● **Transport** The road to Esmeraldas is dusty and uncomfortable and buses often get stuck in the wet season. Boats between La Tola and San Lorenzo connect with buses to/from Esmeraldas; 2 hrs La Tola-San Lorenzo, US$4.25, via Limones and Tambillo. Boats can be rather overcrowded at times but the scenery makes it worthwhile.

LIMONES

The town is the focus of traffic down-river from much of northern Esmeraldas Province where bananas from the Río Santiago are sent to Esmeraldas for export. The Chachi Indians live up the Río Cayapas and can sometimes be seen in Limones, especially during the crowded weekend market, but they are more frequently seen at Borbón.

The people are mostly black and many are illegal immigrants from Colombia. Smuggling between Limones and Tumaco in Colombia is big business (hammocks, manufactured goods, drugs) and there are occasional drug searches along the N coastal road.

Limones has two good shops selling the very attractive Chachi basketry, including items from Colombia. The first is opposite *Restaurant El Bongó* and the second by the dock opposite Banco de Fomento. There are two hotels, both barely habitable. Limones and Borbón dispute the title 'the mosquito and rat capital of Ecuador'. It's a much better idea to stay at San Lorenzo.

● **Transport** A hired launch provides a fascinating trip through mangrove islands, passing hundreds of hunting pelicans; 6 people US$1.75 pp, 1½ hrs. Information on boat journeys from the Capitanía del Puerto, Las Palmas, reached by bus No 1 from the main plaza in Esmeraldas. From Limones you can also get a canoe or boat to Borbón.

BORBON

On the Río Chachi past mangrove swamps, Borbón is a dirty, unattractive, busy and dangerous, with the highest rate of malaria in the country. It is developing as a centre of the timber industry. Ask for Papá Roncón, the King of Marimba, who, for a beer or two, will put on a one-man show. Across from his house are the offices of *Subir*, the NGO working in the Cotacachi-Cayapas reserve, they have information on entering the reserve and guide services. Inefan can also provide information.

● **Accommodation & places to eat** E *Tolita Pampa de Oro*, T Quito 525-753, bath, clean, mosquito nets, helpful. *Comedor*, where the *ranchero* buses stop, excellent fish.

● **Transport** Buses to/from Esmeraldas, US$3 with El Pacifico, 4 hrs, 0600-1700, beware of theft or sit on the roof; by boat to Limones and San Lorenzo 3 hrs, US$5.20, at 0730 and 1100.

UPRIVER FROM BORBON

Upstream are Chachi Indian villages. From Borbón hire a motor launch or go as a passenger on launches running daily around 1100-1200 to the mouth of the Río Onzole; US$5 pp, 3½ hrs.

Santa María is just beyond the confluence of the Cayapas and Onzole rivers.

● **Accommodation** Board and lodging with Sra Pastora at the missionary station, F, basic, mosquito nets, meals US$2, unfriendly, her brother offers river trips; or at the **G** *Residencial*, basic, will prepare food but fix price beforehand, owner offers 5 hrs' jungle trips to visit Chachi villages (beware deadly red and black river snakes); or camp in front of school free. At the confluence of the Cayapas and Onzole rivers, there is a fine lodge built by a Hungarian (for advance bookings write to Stephan Tarjany, Casilla 187, Esmeraldas), **C** with full board, good value, clean, warm showers. Jungle walk with guide and small canoes at no extra charge. Water skiing available, US$12/hr. Steve organizes special tours to visit remote areas and a trip to the Ecological Reserve, US$250 for 3 days including transport and food.

Zapallo Grande, further upriver, is a friendly village with many gardens, where the American missionary Dr Meisenheimer has established a hospital, pharmacy, church and school; there is an expensive shop. You will see the Chachi Indians passing in their canoes and in their open long houses on the shore.

San Miguel has a church, a shop (but supplies are cheaper in Borbón) and a few houses beautifully situated on a hill at the confluence of two rivers.

Trips from San Miguel into the **Cotacachi-Cayapas National Park** (entry US$14) cost US$22.50 for a group with a guide, US$5 for boat rental, US$5/meal. Ask for an official guide, eg Don Cristóbal.

● **Accommodation** You can sleep in the rangers' hut, **F**, basic (no running water, no electricity, shared dormitory, cooking facilities), or camp alongside, but beware of chiggers in the grass; also **F** *residencial*.

● **Transport** Borbón to San Miguel, US$8 pp, 5 hrs, none too comfortable but interesting jungle trip.

SAN LORENZO

The hot, humid town of San Lorenzo stands on the Bahía del Pailón, which is characterized by a maze of canals. The area around San Lorenzo is rich in timber and other plants, but unrestricted logging is putting the forests under threat. The prehistoric La Tolita culture thrived in the region.

Owing to the large number of Colombian immigrants the culture has a distinct feel.

Excursions

To **Playa de Oro**, on the Río Santiago up in the Cotacachi-Cayapas Reserve. For information ask for Victor Grueso, who has a store in town and also works for the Insituto Permacultura Madre Selva, on the outskirts, near the football field (T 780-257; lodging **F** pp inc breakfast). Basic accommodation is available on the trip, but bring your own food and water; meals are cooked on request. Trips can also be made upriver from Playa de Oro into unspoiled rainforest where you can see howler and spider monkeys and jaguar prints; an unforgettable experience. Contact Mauro Caicedo in San Lorenzo. For information on how to contact Mauro, T 529-727 (Quito), or contact Jean Brown at Safari Tours in Quito (see page 1026).

At the seaward end of the bay is a sandy beach at San Pedro, with fishing huts but no facilities, canoes Sat and Sun 0700 and 1500, 1 hr; contact Arturo or Doris, who will cook meals.

Local information

When arriving in San Lorenzo, expect to be hassled by children wanting a tip to show you to a hotel or restaurant. Insect repellent is a 'must'.

● **Accommodation**

E *Carondelet*, on the plaza, with or without bath, some rooms are small, fans, mosquito nets, reliable; **E** *Continental*, C Imbabura, T 780-125, F 780-127, with bath, TV, mosquito nets, clean, family-run, breakfast on request; **E** *Pampa de Oro*, C 26 de Agosto, clean, cheaper without bath; **E** *San Carlos*, C Imbabura, nr the train station, T 780-240, F 780-284, with bath, clean, fans, nets, rec; **E** *Res Patricia*, cheaper without bath, good, clean, fans, noisy from nearby disco.

F pp *Res Imperial*, cheaper without bath, clean, nets, fans; **F** *Yeaniny*, 3 large rooms, fan, clean, mosquito nets, 1 private bath, 2 shared, rec.

● **Places to eat**

La Red, Imbabura y Ayora, good seafood; *La Conchita*, 10 de Agosto, excellent fish, rec; *La Estancia*, next to *Hotel San Carlos*, good food and service, rec.

● **Entertainment**

Marimba can be seen during the local fiesta on 30 September. Groups practice Thur-Sat; one on C Eloy Alfaro. Two discos nr *Hotels Ecuador* and *Patricia*.

● **Transport**

Buses To Ibarra, depart 0700 and 1500 (and others), 5-6 hrs, US$5.70; they leave from the train station or nr *Hotel San Carlos*.

Trains The train journey to Ibarra, has been almost completely superseded by buses (see under **Ibarra**).

Sea Launches to La Tola; 2 companies with sailings hourly between 0630 and 1430, 2$\frac{1}{2}$ hrs, US$4.25; to Borbón, at 0700 and 1300, 3 hrs, US$5.20, stops at Tambilla and Limones en route.

CROSSING TO COLOMBIA

From San Lorenzo there are boats to **Tumaco** in Colombia every other day at 0700 and 1400. It's 1$\frac{1}{2}$ hrs to the frontier at **Palmarreal**, US$3.20, from there take another canoe to **Monte Alto** and then a *ranchero* to **Puerto Palmas**, cross the Río Mira, then take a Land Rover taxi to Tumaco; 6-7 hrs in total.

Entry stamps in Colombia must be obtained by crossing the border at Ipiales and returning again. When arriving in San Lorenzo from Tumaco, the customs office run by navy personnel is in the harbour, but you have to get your passport stamped at the immigration office in Ibarra or Esmeraldas. Problems may arise if you delay more than a day or 2 before getting an entry stamp, as the immigration police in Ibarra are less easy-going.

NB If taking an unscheduled boat from Colombia, be prepared for anti-narcotics searches (at least). This can be a dangerous trip, try to seek advice before taking a boat. Gringos are not normally welcome as passengers because contraband is being carried.

The Oriente

EAST of the Andes the hills fall away to tropical lowlands, sparsely populated with indigenous settlements along the tributaries of the Amazon. Agricultural colonists have cleared parts of the forest for cattle rearing, while even more isolated areas are major oil producers, leading to the gradual encroachment of towns into the jungle.

The vast majority of this beautiful green wilderness, comprising the provinces of Sucumbíos and Napo in the N, Pastaza in the centre, Morona Santiago and Zamora Chinchipe in the S, remains unspoiled and unexplored. Yet, for the tourist, it is relatively accessible. Much of the Northern Oriente is taken up by the Yasuni National Park, the Cuyabeno Wildlife Reserve and most of the Cayambe-Coca Ecological Reserve.

NB Anti-malaria precautions (tablets, net and effective repellent) are recommended, especially below 600m. A yellow fever vaccination is also recommended.

Communications Ecuador's eastern tropical lowlands can be reached by four road routes, from Quito, Ambato, Cuenca or Loja. These roads are narrow and tortuous and subject to landslides in the rainy season, but all have regular, if poor bus services and all can be attempted in a jeep or in an ordinary car with good ground clearance. Several of the towns and villages on the roads can be reached by air services from Quito and places further into the immense Amazonian forests are generally accessible by river canoe or small aircraft from Shell or Macas.

The Oriente also has an unpredictable air service provided by army planes. Fares are low and the flights save a lot of time. There are frequent military checks, so always have your passport handy. You may be required to register at Shell-Mera, Coca, Misahuallí, Puerto Napo and Lago Agrio.

Types of tourism These fall into four basic types: lodges; guided tours; indigenous ecotourism; and independent travel without a guide. When staying at a **jungle lodge**, you will need to take a torch, insect repellent, protection against the sun and a rain poncho that will keep you dry when walking and when sitting in a canoe. Rubber boots can be hired. Getting to the lodge may involve a long canoe ride, with a longer return journey upstream to the airport, perhaps with a pre-dawn start.

Guided tours of varying length are offered by tour operators, river cruise companies and independent guides. These should be licenced by the Ecuadorean Tourism Corporation (CETUR). Tour companies and guides are mainly concentrated in Quito, Tena, Coca and Misahuallí.

A number of **indigenous communities and families** offer ecotourism programmes on their properties. These are either community-controlled and operated, or organized as joint ventures between the indigenous community or family and a non-indigenous partner. These programmes usually involve guides who are licensed by CETUR as *guías nativos* with the right to guide within their communities.

Though economically attractive, touring without a guide is not encouraged: from an ecotourist perspective, it does not contribute adequately to the local economy and to intercultural understanding and it may be environmentally damaging. Furthermore, it involves a greater risk of accident or injury.

ROUTES From Quito, through Pifo, to Baeza, the road is paved to a point 9 km beyond the top of the Papallacta pass (4,064m), 5 km before the turn to the Papallacta hotsprings. Thereafter it worsens. It crosses the Eastern Cordillera at the pass, just N of the extinct volcano **Antisana** (5,705m), and then descends via the small villages of Papallacta (see page 1032) and Cuyuja to the old mission settlements of Baeza and Borja. The trip between the pass and Baeza has beautiful views of Antisana (clouds permitting), high waterfalls, tropical mountain jungle, *páramo* and a lake contained by an old lava flow.

Antisana gets vast quantities of snow and has huge glaciers. It is very difficult to climb, experience is essential; information on the reserve (not climbing) from *Fundación Antisana*, Av Mariana de Jesús y La Isla, T 433-851, in Quito.

BAEZA

The mountainous landscape and high rainfall have created spectacular waterfalls and dense vegetation. Because of the climate, *ceja de montaña*, orchids (in flower June/July) and bromeliads abound. Baeza, in the beautiful setting of the Quijos pass, is about 1 km from main junction of the Lago Agrio and Tena roads. Get off the Lago Agrio bus at the gas station and walk up the hill; the Tena bus goes through the town. Baeza Colonial (Old Baeza) is being replaced by Andalucía (New Baeza), where the post office and Emetel are located.

There are many hiking trails in this region which generally can be done without a guide. A recommended source for maps and route descriptions is *The Ecotourist's Guide to the Ecuadorian Amazon*, by Rolf Wesche, which is available in Quito, or in the *Hostal San Rafael*. See also *The Ecuador Handbook*.

• **Accommodation** **F** *Samay*, in the new town, shared bath, basic, clean; **F** pp *Hostal San Rafael*, in the new town, shared bath, clean, spacious, cheaper cabins at rear, parking, restaurant, rec; **G** pp *El Nogal de Jumandí*, in old town, basic, holes in walls, hot water on request. 30 mins S of Baeza, in the Cosanga Valley, **A3** *Cabañas San Isidro*, comfortable cabins, excellent birding, good exploring in the surrounding primary cloudforest, reservations only, T (Quito) 547-403, F 228-902.

• **Places to eat** The best restaurants are in the old town: *El Fogón*, very good, cheap; *Gina*, the best, cheap; *Guaña*, breakfasts US$1, best. Everything closes by 2030.

• **Buses** Many buses to Tena (2 hrs) and Coca, best caught in centre of new town.

NORTHERN ORIENTE

At Baeza the road divides. One branch heads S to Tena, with a newly constructed branch road going directly via Loreto to Coca (7 hrs). The other goes NE to Lago Agrio, following the Río Quijos past the villages of **Borja**, a few kilometres from Baeza, and **El Chaco** to the slopes of the still active volcano **Reventador**, 3,485m.

• **Accommodation** At the village of Reventador there is *Pensión de los Andes*, basic, clean, and a restaurant.

The road winds along the N side of the river, past the impressive 145m **San Rafael Falls**, the highest in Ecuador. To get to the falls take a Quito-Baeza-Lago Agrio bus. About 2-3 hrs past Baeza, look for a covered bus stop and an INECEL sign on the right-hand side of the road. From here, walk about 5 mins to the guard's hut, just beyond a small bridge; US$3.75 entry. It's an easy 1½ hr round trip to the falls through cloudforest. Near the guard's hut is accommodation in some functional cabins, **D** pp, inc entry fee. Camping is possible, but take all equipment and food.

From San Rafael the road crosses the watershed between the Coca and Aguarico rivers and runs along the N bank of the river to the developing oil towns of Santa Cecilia and Lago Agrio.

LAGO AGRIO

Lago Agrio (*Pop* 13,165), capital of Sucumbíos (*Pop* 77,500), is primarily an oil town. It was once a rough frontier town, but infrastructure and sanitation are improving. The name comes from Sour Lake, the US headquarters of Texaco, the first oil company to exploit the Ecuadorean Amazon, but the town's official name is Nueva Loja. Cofan, Siona and Secoya Indians still come into town at the weekend, though you'll rarely see them in traditional dress.

Excursions

From Lago Agrio it is possible to take a bus to **Chiritza** and then a 2-hr boat ride to **San Pablo de Kantesiya**, a small village on stilts with one hut where visitors can stay.

Local information
● **Accommodation & places to eat**
Virtually everything can be found on the main street, Av Quito. **C** *El Cofán*, 12 de Febrero y Av Quito, T 830-009, inc taxes, a/c, best in town, but overpriced, no hot water, TV, fridge, clean, restaurant mediocre and expensive.

E *Cabaña*, next to *Hotel Willigram*, clean, rec; **E** *Machala 2*, with bath, TV, fan, clean, safe, restaurant, sometimes water shortages.

F *Guacamayo*, inexpensive, good meeting place, good restaurant; **F** *La Mexicana*, reason-able, mosquito nets; **F** *San Carlos*, clean, safe, a/c, cheaper with fan; **F** *Res Sayonara*, with bath, good, sometimes water shortages; **F** *Willigram*, with bath, doors unlockable, noisy, above bar. *Comercial Calvopeña* is the best place to buy groceries and supplies. *Mi Cuchita* beside *El Cofán*, cheap, good chicken.

● **Banks & money changers**
Several *casas de cambio* on Av Quito, good rates for notes. You can change TCs at *Banco de Préstamos*, next to *Res Sayonara*.

● **Tour companies & travel agents**
Harpia Eagle Tours, Cuyabeno, Robin Torres arranges tours, rec only if Robin is the guide.

● **Transport**
Air TAME flight to **Quito** (not Sun), book 1-2 days in advance.

Buses To **Quito**, US$7.50, 10-11 hrs, 2 luxury buses (one at 1300, one overnight); **Baeza**, 7 hrs; **Coca**, 3 hrs; also many *ranchero* buses which leave when full; to **Tena**, US$8.30, 9 hrs.

CUYABENO WILDLIFE RESERVE

Down the Aguarico from Lago Agrio is an extensive jungle river area on the Río Cuyabeno, which drains eventually into the Aguarico 150 km to the E. In the National Park there are many lagoons and abundant wildlife (entry US$14). Transport is mainly by canoe and motorboat, except for one road to Río Cuyabeno, 3 hrs by truck from Lago Agrio.

● **Tour companies & lodges** To visit Cuyabeno contact *Jungletur*, Amazonas 854 y Veintimilla, Quito, who have 6 day tours of the area. An experienced guide is Alejandro Quezada, T 571-098, Quito. *Neotropic Tours*, Rik Pennartz, PO Box 09-01-4690, Guayaquil, F (593-4) 374-078, takes trips to the Cuyabeno National Park, lodges, everything provided. *Pacarina*, in the same Quito office as *Hostería Alandaluz*, runs 5 day tours to a Secoya community down the Río Aguarico; *Native Life*, J Pinto 446 y Amazonas, T 505-158/550-836, F 229-077, PO Box 17-03-504, e-mail: natlife1@natlife.com.ec, run tours to their Nativo Lodge in the Cuyabeno reserve, rec. *Mariana Ortiz and Diego Holger Garces*, Av Río Amazonas y 12 de Febrero, T 830-515, PO Box 77, run highly rec tours with guide who speaks English and German. Also rec is *Edwin Ceballos* of Inefan.

Transturi of Quito (Orellana 1810 y 10 de Agosto, T 544-963) do trips into the jungle on a floating hotel, *Flotel Orellana*, US$567 (4 nights, 3 days) pp in double cabin with fan, inc all meals, guides, etc. Services and food are good. Flights extra: bus to Chiritza on the Río

Aguarico, then launch to the *Flotel*. Metropolitan Touring run excursions (3/4, 4/5, 5 night/6 day) to the **Imuya** and **Iripari** camps. Depending on length, tours involve stops at the Aguarico Base Camp and the *Flotel*; **Imuya** (220 km from Lago Agrio) involves a speedboat trip to get there, earplugs provided; it is very unspoilt, with good birdlife. **Iripari**, on Lake Zancudo, involves a 5 km walk, plus a paddle across the largest lake in Ecuador's Oriente; the camp itself is basic but adequate.

FRONTIER WITH COLOMBIA

Get an exit stamp from Migración in Lago Agrio (Quito 111 – police station, T 125) before taking a bus N to **La Punta** (US$0.50, 1¼ hrs), where you hand in your Tourist Card to the military and get a boat across the Río San Miguel to the village of **San Miguel** in Colombia (La Punta-San Miguel, 1 hr, US$2.65). From there you can catch a jeep or bus (5 hrs) to **Puerto Asís** and on to **Hormiga** (1 hr, hotels and restaurants), then a bus to Mocoa and on to Pasto. There are DAS office and border formalities at Mocoa. A Colombian entry stamp can be obtained at the Consulate in Lago Agrio.

ROUTES At Lago Agrio, a temporary ferry crosses the Río Aguarico (bridge washed away), then the road heads S to Coca.

COCA

Officially named Puerto Francisco de Orellana, Coca is a hot, dusty, noisy, sprawling oil town at the junction of the Ríos Coca and Napo (*Pop* 15,199).

All foreigners going beyond town into the jungle have to register with the police, and all guides who accompany foreigners have to be licensed. If going alone beyond the bridge at Coca into the jungle, you must get permission from the Ministerio de Defensa, Av Maldonado, Quito (full details from South American Explorers Club). Considering its relative isolation, food and supplies are not that much more expensive than more accessible parts of the country. There is usually no electricity after midnight.

Local information
● **Accommodation**
C *La Misión*, T 553-674, F 564-675 (Quito), in Coca 880-260/1, a/c, very smart, English spo-

ken, restaurant, arranges tours.

D *Auca*, cabins with bath, cold water, comfortable, big garden with monkeys roaming free, small rooms without bath **F** pp, manager speaks English, friendly, good meeting place to make up tour party, restaurant.

E *Oasis*, nr the bridge at the end of town, clean, comfortable, hot water and fans, rec; **E** *Florida*, on main road from airport, with fan, basic, dark rooms, clean.

F *Lojanita*, new rooms, clean, good; **G** pp *Res Tungurahua*, basic but OK, showers clean.

● **Places to eat**
Los Cedros, down by the river, 2 blocks from Capitanería, good fish, *patacones*, *yuca*, fairly expensive; *Doña Erma's* set meal is cheap and filling; *Escondito*, by river, good, cheap, filling, popular with locals; *Pappa Dan's*, Napo y Chimborazo, by river, hamburgers, chilli, tacos etc, good; *Mama Carmen*, good for early breakfast; *El Buho*, good food, jungle specialities, capibara etc, reasonably priced.

● **Banks & money changers**
Banks won't change TCs; reasonable rate for cash and TCs at Napo y Eloy Alfaro.

● **Post & Telecommunications**
Emetel on Eloy Alfaro; 0800-110 and 1300-1700.

● **Transport**
Air Flights to **Quito** with TAME, reserve 48 hrs in advance, planes are small and flights can be very bumpy, flights in and out of Coca are heavily booked; also military and oil workers have priority on standby; also flights to **Tena** and **Shell-Mera** from Coca on Mon, Wed and Fri. TAME office at Napo y Rocafuerte, T 881-078, always reconfirm.

Buses The bus terminal is a 20-min walk from *Hotel Auca*, away from river, ask to be let off in town. Buses leave from company offices on Napo. To **Quito**, 10 hrs, US$10.50, several daily 1030-2200, Trans Baños and Putumayo, depart from their offices on Napo y Cuenca; to **Lago Agrio**, 3 hrs, US$3.40; to **Tena**, 6 hrs, US$6; to **Misahuallí**, 7 hrs; to **Baeza**, 8 hrs.

River For passenger boats out of Coca, ask the Capitanía at the dock; to Misahuallí, US$20 pp; Nueva Rocafuerte, US$28; canoes go if there are 8 or more passengers, taking about 14 hrs, if it is not reached before nightfall, the party will camp beside the river.

JUNGLE TOURS FROM COCA

Most of the Coca region is taken up by the Yasuní National Park and Huaorani Reserve. This area is unsuited to tours of less than 3 days owing to the remoteness of its

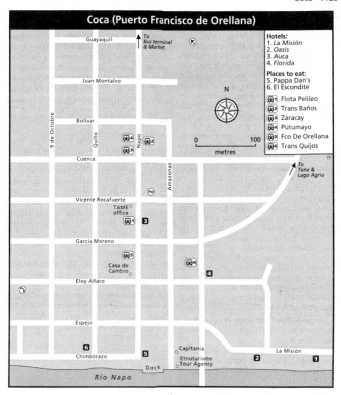

Coca (Puerto Francisco de Orellana)

To Bus terminal & Market

Guayaquil

Juan Montalvo

Bolívar

Cuenca

Vicente Rocafuerte

TAME office

Garcia Moreno

Casa de Cambio

Eloy Alfaro

Espejo

Chimborazo

Dock

Capitanía

Etnoturismo Tour Agency

La Misión

Río Napo

9 de Octubre
Quito
Napo
Amazonas

N

0   100
metres

Hotels:
1. La Misión
2. Oasis
3. Auca
4. Florida

Places to eat:
5. Pappa Dan's
6. El Escondite

1 Flota Pelileo
2 Trans Baños
3 Zaracay
4 Putumayo
5 Fco De Orellana
6 Trans Quijos

main attractions. Shorter visits of 3-4 days are worthwhile in the Coca-Yuturi segment of the Río Napo, where the lodges are concentrated. Tours to the Huaorani Reserve and Yasuní Park really need a minimum of 5 days. Wildlife in this area is under threat and visitors should insist that guides and members of their party take all litter back and ban all hunting and shooting; it really can make a difference.

All guides out of Coca charge about US$30-50 pp per day, but you may have to bargain down to this. Check what precisely is being offered and that the price includes items such as rubber boots, tents, mosquito nets, cooking equipment and food, and transport. Essential equipment for a trip of any length are suitable footwear (rubber boots, or two pairs of light shoes – keep one pair dry), light sleeping bag, rain jacket, trousers (not shorts), binoculars, insect repellent, sunscreen lotions, water-purifying tablets, sticking plasters. Wrap everything in several small plastic bags. The South American Explorers Club can provide updated information on how to arrange your trip.

NB Guides must have permission to take tourists into Huaorani territory. The only licensed guides are Samuel Padilla, Juan Enomenga, Moi Enomenga (with Tropic Tours) and Expediciones Jarrín. If any other guide offers a trip into their territory, do not accept, it would be in contravention of an authorization of Feb 1992.

● **Agencies**
Luis Alberto García, *Emerald Forest Expeditions*, Amazonas 1023 y Pinto, Quito, T 526-403, ext 13, speaks English, knowledgeable, rec; *Jumandy Explorers*, Wilson 718 y J L Mera, T 220-518/551-205, Quito, guide Isaias Cerda is an indigenous Quichua, very knowledgeable, speaks some English, does trips on the Río Arajuno. The Vasco brothers, Wilson, Daniel, Jonas and Walter, of *Vasco Tour Travel Agency*, can be contacted only in Baños, T (03) 740-017, rec, no litter, no killing of animals, no intrusion of Indians' privacy, their guide, Juan Medina, is frequently rec. Also in Baños, *Tsantsa Expeditions*, T 740-957.

● **Guides in Coca** *Ejarsytur*, opposite *Hotel Oasis*, T 887-142, Santa Prisca 260 y 10 de Agosto, Quito, T 583-120, run by the Jarrín family, German and English spoken, US$40 pp/day, rec. Canoes and guides for jungle trips can be hired from *Fernando Silva*, who lives at the end of the riverside lane next to the bridge, his nephew Ricardo Silva has been described as an enthusiastic guide and a good cook. *Etnoturismo Amasanga Supay*, run by indigenous co-operative to help local communities, opposite Capitanía, or contact César Andi at *Hotel Oasis*. Other rec guides are *Klever* and *Braulio Llori*, T 880-487/141; *Wimper Torres*, T 880-336, or through *Hotel Auca*.

● **Jungle lodges** *Hacienda Primavera* is 2 hrs downstream from Coca. There are clean, basic rooms (**F** pp), or you can camp (US$0.50). Meals cost US$2.50, breakfast US$1.50, bring bread. There is a generator but candles are used for after-generator hours. Excursions: US$13 to Monkey Island, US$30 to Monkey Island and Pompeya Catholic Mission, US$45 to the above and Limón Cocha, divide prices by the number of people (1-10) and add 10% service. There is not much wildlife to see apart from birds, but it is possible to hire canoes from the *hacienda* to visit other places along the Napo.

La Selva, a jungle centre 3 hrs down the Napo from Coca, has been frequently rec for the quality of its accommodation (built of natural materials) and food. It holds the highest award in ecotourism. It offers interesting excursions into the jungle, 140 ft observation tower, a butterfly farm for breeding and observation. Over 550 birds have been listed, inc some virtually unknown species, and the calibre of guiding is described as unequalled. *La Selva* runs the Neotropical Field Biology Institute, a field studies programme in conjunction with Harvard University and other institutions; genuine field biologists may apply to work at *La Selva* (subject to approval, discounts may be awarded). Guests often meet biologists in the field. 4-night packages from Quito inc all transport, lodging, and food, not cheap, but worth it. There is a slow laundry service. Also available 6-night, 7-day 'Amazon Light Brigade' adventure expedition, with 8 guests, 15 staff and a free bar, the height of luxury. Best to book directly at *La Selva*, 6 de Diciembre 2816 y James Orton, PO Box 635/Suc 12 de Octubre, Quito, T 550-995/554-686, Tx 2-2653 JOLEZ ED, F 567-297 (extra Fax 563-814), alternatively through most travel agencies in Quito.

Sacha Lodge, 2½ hrs by motor boat from Coca, owned by Swiss Benny, comfortable, hot water, excellent food, good jungle trips, prices lower than *La Selva*, rec. Has a good tree tower for canopy observations and uses biologist guides. Bookable through *Explorer Tours*, Lizardo García 613 y Reina Victoria, Quito, T 522-220.

Yuturi, 5 hrs downriver from Coca, on a tributary river, good value, prices lower than *Sacha*, uses local guides with a translator in English, very good birdwatching, sandflies may be a problem; *Yuturi Jungle Adventure*, Amazonas entre Pres Wilson y Pinto, Quito, T 233-685.

COCA TO NUEVO ROCAFUERTE

An irregular canoe service (best to hire your own) passes Coca carrying passengers and cargo down-river. En route is Laguna de **Limoncocha**, an excellent spot for birding now a Biological Reserve. Nearby is the Pompeya Capuchin mission, with a school and museum of Napo culture, about 2 hrs down-river from Coca. Upriver from Pompeya is Monkey Island. You can rent a canoe to visit the small island with free-roaming monkeys.

Halfway between Coca and Nuevo Rocafuerte is **Pañacocha**, near which is the magnificent lagoon of Pañacocha on the Río Panayacu. This was recently declared a protected forest region.

● **Accommodation** G *Pensión*, in Pañacocha, friendly, but beware chiggers in the mattresses.

The end of the line is **Nuevo Rocafuerte**, where the missionaries and Sra Jesús let rooms; there are no restaurants.

● **Transport** To take a boat from Coca to Nuevo Rocafuerte, you must get a military permit to enter the area. The officer has to write exactly the area you wish to visit and you have to leave your passport. The boat takes 8 hrs (hammocks provided). There is a cargo boat back on Mon, but it doesn't always run and you may have to wait until Fri. To Coca it is a 2½-day ferry ride (US$9) with an overnight stop at Sinchichieta and a meal stop at Pañacocha. It is not possible to cross from Nuevo Rocafuerte into Peru.

CENTRAL ORIENTE

ARCHIDONA AND TENA

Roads from both Baeza and Coca go S to **Archidona**, 65 km from Baeza. It has a striking, small painted church.

10 km further S, **Tena** is the capital of Napo Province (*Pop* 13,790). Like Archidona, it was founded in 1560 and both were important colonial missionary and trading posts. It is now a commercial centre with an attractive plaza overlooking the confluence of the Ríos Tena and Pano. A recommended walk is to Parque Amazónica, on the island. Cross by the wooden footbridge.

Tena has a large lowland Quichua Indian population living in the vicinity, many of whom are panning for gold in the rivers. These Indians are unlike the Indian groups further into the Oriente forests, they are Quijos, of Chibcha stock.

Excursions

The road leaving Archidona's plaza to the E goes 10 km to an old bridge over the Río Hollin and on to the access for the **Galeras Reserve**. To enter the Reserve you must have a guide and permission.

Tours can be arranged by special arrangement to the **Izu Mangallpa Urcu (IMU) Foundation**, 3 km E of Archidona off a side turning down the road to Galeras, set up by the Mamallacta family to protect territory on Galeras mountain. They charge US$35/day for accommodation and day trips, taking groups of 8-10; US$65/day, 5 days trekking, groups of 2 minimum; tough going but the forest is wonderful. Ask around or book through *Safari Tours* in Quito, T 552-505.

Just outside Archidona, to the S, a small turning leads to the river. About 200m along there is a large rock with many petroglyphs carved on its surface, the easiest to find of several within a 30 km radius.

The famous **Jumandí caves** are 5-6 km N of Archidona. Take a taxi, or bus from Archidona, 30 mins. It is advisable to go with a guide; take good boots and a strong torch. It is very muddy (sometimes full of water) so it can be useful to take spare clothes. The side ducts of the caves are extremely narrow and claustrophobic. There are several colonies of vampire bat (*Desmodus rotundus*) in the caves. A tourist complex has been built with swimming pool, waterslide and restaurant.

Local information
● **Accommodation**

Archidona: E *Res Regina*, Rocafuerte 446, T 889-144, modern, clean, rec, cheaper without bath, pleasant; *Hostal Archidona*, hidden down a back street, 5 blocks S of the plaza. There are few decent places to eat, though *Restaurant Los Pinos*, nr *Res Regina*, is good.

Tena: the water supply in most cheaper hotels is poor. **C** *Los Yutzos*, at the S end of town overlooking the Río Pano, superior, clean, comfortable, beautiful grounds, family-run; **D** *Mol*,

Sucre 432, T 886-215, clean, garage, rec; **D** *Hostal Turismo Amazónico*, Av Amazonas y Abdón Calderón, T 886-487, fan, fridge, parking. **E** *Auca*, on the river out of town, 1½ km on road to Archidona, T 886-461, modern resort-style hotel, Cetur-owned, restaurant and bar, nice grounds, discotheque, casino, swimming in river, electricity and water unreliable; **E** *Hostal Traveler's Lodging*, 15 de Noviembre by pedestrian bridge, T 886-372, F 886-015, modern, cheaper with cold shower, run by *Amarongachi Tours*; **E** *Hostal Villa Belén*, on Baeza road (Av Jumandy), T 886-228 N of town, new, clean, cold shower, quiet, rec; **E** *Media Noche*, 15 de Noviembre 1125, T 886-490, nr the bus station, cheaper without bath, good, clean, inexpensive restaurant; **E** *Res Alemana*, Díaz de Pineda 210 y Av 15 de Noviembre, T 886-409, good and fairly clean, **D** for cabin.

F *Res Nápoli*, Díaz de Pineda 147, T 886-194, fan, shared bath, parking; **F** *Jumandy*, clean, balcony, breakfast from 0600, the Fausto Cerda family arrange jungle tours, US$20 pp/day.

G *Hostal Baños*, nr the bus station, basic, clean, restaurant; **G** *Hostal Cambahuasi*, opp the bus terminal, basic but clean.

● **Places to eat**

Cositas Ricas, Av 15 de Noviembre 432, tasty meals, vegetarian available, good fruit juices, run by Patricia Corral of *Amarongachi Tours*; *Chuquitos*, Montalvo y Calderón, popular; *El Toro*, on the left arriving from Archidona, good almuerzo. There are also *chifas* in town. *Tatus* is a riverside bar, built of river mangrove and thatched, attractive and popular.

● **Tour companies & travel agents**

Ríos Ecuador, 12 de Noviembre, opp *Cositas Ricas*, run 1-day trips on remote rivers in the area and specialize in white water rafting and guided kayak excursions; also 5-day kayak school. Contact Gynner Coronel at the *Hostal Cambahuasi*, T 887-438, or T (Quito) 553-727.

● **Tourist offices**

Near the market at the N end of town.

● **Transport**

Air To Shell-Mera (see below). US$15-20 for 15-min flight over the canopy in superlight plane, one person at a time, contact Jorge through *Ríos Ecuador*.

Buses Quito, via Baeza, 11 daily 0200-2345, US$4.50, 5 hrs, book in advance; Baeza, 2 hrs; Ambato, via Baños, Mon only, US$5, 5 hrs; Baños, 4 hrs; Riobamba, via Puyo and Baños, 6 daily from 0200, 5 hrs, US$4.50; Archidona every 20 mins, US$0.20, 15 mins; Misahuallí, hourly, US$0.70, 45 mins, buses leave from the local bus station not the long distance terminal;

to **Coca**, 6 hrs, US$6, 8 daily 0600-2200; to **Lago Agrio**, with Jumandy at 1830, 9 hrs, US$8.30; **Puyo**, 3 hrs; to **Ahuano** 0600 and 1100, return 0800, 1400.

JUNGLE TOURS FROM TENA

Trips are organized to **Amarongachi** by Patricia Corral and Jesús Uribe; *Amarongachi Tours*, 15 de Noviembre 422, PO Box 278, T 886-372, F 886-015, highly recommended. They also own *Shangri-La* cabins S of Río Jatunyacu.

Comunidad Capirona is 1 hr by bus, then 3 on foot from Tena. It is run by FOIN, Federación de Organizaciones Indígenas de Napo. Information is available from Sr Tarquino Tapuy, C Augusto Rueda, Casilla Postal 217, Tena, T 886-288. Fees per day are from US$30-40 pp depending on the number in the party. (Ricancie in Quito, c/o Ayuda en Acción, T 529-934, also take reservations.) Alternatively contact the Cerda family, who act as guides for tour agencies, only US$20 pp/day. Nelli (daughter) lives at C 9 de Octubre 356, Barrio Bella Vista Baja, a 10-min walk from the bus station. You can also contact the family through *Hotel Jumandy*, who will have details on how to find Olmedo and Oswaldo Cerda (father and son, both rec guides), if Nelli is not home.

Sr Delfín Pauchi, T 886-434, Casilla 245, Tena, has built *Cabañas Pimpilala*, 45 mins by taxi from Tena, where for 2-5 days you can live with a Quichua family, US$30 pp/day, including lodging, meals, transport and guide. Trails for hiking have been made on his 30 ha of undeveloped land, but emphasis is on culture rather than animals. Delfín speaks only Quichua and Spanish. He knows about plants and their medicinal uses, legends and music. Also, *Hacienda Jatún Yacu*, a family farm in the rainforest, is excellent. Contact through *Ríos Ecuador* (see above) or *Safari* in Quito.

ROUTES From Tena the main highway (unpaved) runs S to Puyo. **Puerto Napo**, a few kilometres S of Tena, has a bridge across the Río Napo. (Pato García, a guide, has a nice room to rent, **G**, full board, but not recommended for single women. He will also take independent tours, but works mostly for Quito agencies.) On the N bank a road runs E to Misahuallí, about 17 km downstream. From the **Napo bridge** you can get a ride in a truck, US$0.50, or colectivos.

MISAHUALLI

This small port (*Pop* 3,579) at the junction of the Napo and Misahuallí rivers, is almost totally devoted to tourism. Being one of the easiest jungle places to reach, it attracts many visitors. Plants, butterflies and birds are plentiful and there is good hiking, but for wildlife you are advised to go to Coca or to take an excursion lasting several days. There is a fine, sandy beach on the Río Misahuallí, but don't camp on it as the river can rise unexpectedly.

Excursions

A nice walk is along the **Río Latas**, 7 km W of Misahuallí, where there are some small waterfalls. You walk through dense vegetation for about 1½ hrs, often through water to get to the largest fall and pass quite a few pools where you can swim. To get there catch the bus towards the Napo bridge and ask to be set down by the river at the third bridge out of Misahuallí.

A strenuous day trip can be made to **Palmeras**, a friendly village with no food or safe water, where many birds can be seen.

Local information

● **Accommodation**

C *Misahuallí Jungle Hotel*, across the river from town, cabins for up to 6, nice setting, restaurant operates sporadically, US$165 for 3 days/2 nights inc full board and excursions: in Quito, Ramírez Dávalos 251, T 520-043, F 454-146.

D *El Albergue Español*, PO Box 254, Tena, Quito T/F 584-912, owned by Dr José Ramón Edesa, best restaurant in town, some vegetarian meals, all rooms with bath, clean and screened with balconies overlooking Napo, family room sleep 6, highly rec, jungle tours to Coca; **D** *Txalaparta*, just before Misahuallí, T 584-964 for messages, peaceful cabins.

E *Dayuma Hotel*, T (Tena) 584-964, 2 and 3-bedded rooms with bath, fan, balcony, clean, often fully booked with tour groups, same owners as *Dayuma Camp* (see **Guides** below); **E** *El Paisano*, clean, cheaper without bath, intermittent water supply, laundry facilities, hammocks, nice garden, rec, good breakfast, information on guides; **E** *Milca Isca*, on the main plaza, clean, cheap, good restaurant, English spoken; **E** *Res Pepe*, on the main plaza, basic rooms with fan, safe to leave luggage, information on jungle tours; **E** *Sacha*, very basic, bamboo walls, noisy bar, at the point where the rivers meet, monkeys in the garden, good value souvenirs of the Oriente here.

F *Balcón del Napo*, basic, central, meals available, clean, noisy from disco at weekends, safe motorcycle parking, may change currency; **F** *Etsa*, with or without bath, very simple, owner is guide Carlos Cordero; **F** *Fifty*, on the main plaza, communal baths, safe, family run (familia Vasco), vegetarian restaurant.

● **Places to eat**

Douglas Clarke's *Restaurant Dayuma* is reasonably good and cheap; as is *El Paisano*, mostly good vegetarian food (but meat should be treated with caution), popular meeting place for gringos, hence its nickname *Restaurant Paleface*, closes 2100 sharp; *Jenifer*, cheap, good restaurant on plaza; *Cactus*, on the road to *El Paisano*, drinks, Mexican, breakfast. The bars down by the river have a frontier feel to them, as do the handful of general stores.

● **Transport**

Buses From **Quito** via Baños and Tena, about 8 hrs, Mon only until Baños-Puyo road is completed; or via Baeza and Tena, about 5 hrs, the route most used by buses; the road has been improved.

River There are still twice weekly canoes scheduled to Coca, leaving Wed and Sun, returning Thurs and Mon, or if you are in a group you can charter a canoe; 6 hrs to Coca, 9-14 back. Tickets are available across the street from the port captain's office, which has a list of approved prices to various destinations.

During and after heavy rainfall there are obviously no services, nor are there any services during a long dry period. You can rent a boat to Coca, US$115 for up to 20 people, it leaves only in the morning. Take a cushion and waterproofs.

On river journeys or jungle trips If going downstream, you must register with the port captain's office. The office will want to keep your passport after stamping it. If you are returning the same way, it's a safe place to leave it. However, if you want to keep it, or are not returning to Misahuallí, tell them you are returning via Coca or Ahuano, if they ask where you are leaving from. Every canoe pilot is supposed to have his passenger list checked before going downstream but this is not always done. For your own safety ensure that the authorities have a record.

JUNGLE TOURS FROM MISAHUALLI

There are many guides available to take parties into the jungle for trips of 1 to 10 days, all involving canoeing and varying amounts of hiking. Travellers should ask to see a guide's licence (we have frequent reports of unlicensed guides cheating tourists). It is advisable to insist on paying part of the cost on completion of the trip (for tour agencies based in Quito, see page 1025). Prices are the same as in Coca (see above) and depend on the season, size of group and length of trip. Overnight tours are recommended only for the hardy. The same advice applies as in Coca on checking equipment and supplies, and a guide's written permission to visit Indian villages. Some guides visit zoos of hotels where animals are kept in unsatisfactory conditions; make sure beforehand that zoos are not on the itinerary. Also see under Coca for what personal effects to take.

● **Guides**

We list only those guides who have been recommended to us: *Héctor Fiallos*, of Fluvial River Tours (information in Quito T 239-044, or write PO Box 225, Tena-Misahuallí, or Baños T 740-002); arranges outings from 1-15 days. A 6-day tour takes in the Cuyabeno National Park (special permit needed, US$14, passport must be left at the naval office) and the Río Aguarico. A 10-day tour goes down the Napo to Nuevo Rocafuerte and up the Aguarico to the Cuyabeno National Park. There are also other tour operators using Hector's name.

Douglas, Wilfred Clarke and *Albin Caicedo* (speak English), from the *Hotel Dayuma*, Casilla 291, Tena, T 584-964, or Av 10 de Agosto 3815 y Mariana de Jesús, edif Villacis Pazos, of 301, T/F 564-924, Quito, arrange trips with other guides. Their 1-and 2-day walks are rec. Also trips to Coca, to smaller rivers and lagoons, Limoncocha, and longer ones into the jungle of up to 10 days, similar to those organized by Héctor Fiallos. They also have *Dayuma Camp* at the junction of the Arajuno and Puni rivers (15 mins by canoe plus a 4-hr walk from Misahuallí).

Viajes y Aventuras Amazónicas, on the plaza, friendly, good food, ask for Celso, US$25/day. *Julio Angeles*, at *Crucero Fluvial Cononaco*, will arrange anything you wish to do; a 4-day tour on Río Tiputini is the minimum time to see animals.

At *Hotel Balcón del Napo* contact *Carlos Sevilla*, whose tours up to 18 days are well rec (also contactable via his sister in Quito, T 241-981). *Marcos Estrada* of *Crucero Fluvial Yasuni* is knowledgeable, honest and offers tours of different lengths. *Jaime Recalde* is interesting on fauna and flora, good meals; contact him at *Balcón del Napo*.

Sócrates Nevárez, PO Box 239, Tena, runs 1-10 day tours inc trips further down the Río Napo, well-organized. *Carlos Herbert Licuy Licuy*, locally born, is good on history, legends and culture of the area. *John Cordero*, at *Etsa. Alfredo Andrade*, T 584-965, or PO Box 268, Tena, English spoken, money exchanged. *Pepe Tapia González* of *El Oriente*, PO Box 252, Tena, speaks English, knowledgeable, 1 to 10 day tours, good cook (Gary), can pay by TCs. *Luis García* at *Emerald Forest Expeditions* in Quito is rec.

● **Jungle lodges**

B *Anaconda*, on Anaconda Island in the Río Napo, about 1 hr by canoe, US$1.20 downstream from Puerto Misahuallí, reservations required: 10 bungalows of bamboo and thatch, no electric lights, but flush toilets and cold showers, water available most of the time. There is a zoo with animals in small, unsatisfactory cages. Watch out for thieving monkeys. The meals are good. Canoe and hiking trips arranged, US$50 for 4 days, meals and guides included, guides only speak Spanish.

Opposite, on the river bank at **Ahuano**, is **A3** *Casa del Suizo*, Swiss, Ecuadorean-owned, price pp full board, but little scope for vegetarians, cheaper with shared bath, highly rec for hospitality and location, electricity till 2200, pool, animal sanctuary, trips arranged. For further information contact Giulliano Bonello, Koescherruetistr 143, 8052 Zurich, Switzerland, T 01-302-37-27, or *Explorer Tours*, Reina Victoria y Lizardo García, Quito, T 522-220, F 508-872.

There are no public canoes from Misahuallí on Sun afternoon, only private hire, US$30, but there are buses Tena-Ahuano, 2 hrs, US$1.50, ask to be dropped at the ferry point.

C *Hotel Jaguar*, 1½ hrs downstream from Misahuallí, congenial atmosphere, price pp with full board, vegetarians catered for, good value, a full tour (3 days) inc meals and good excursions into the jungle costs US$70 from Misahuallí with an extra charge of US$32 for each additional day. Avoid paying in US$ as they give you a very bad rate (independent canoe journey there costs US$30, except by public canoe at 1100); in Quito reservations at Luis Cordero 1313, T 230-552.

2 hrs downstream is *Yachana Lodge*, part of the Funedesin Project, based in the indigenous village of Mondaña; US$50/day inc 3 meals, hiking, bird watching, river trips, etc. Reservations at Funedesin, Francisco Andrade Marín 188 y Diego de Almagro, Quito, PO Box 17-17-92, T 543-851, F 220-362.

8 km downriver is **Jatun Sacha** Biological Station (quichua meaning 'big forest'). The station and the adjacent Aliñahui project together conserve 1,300 ha of tropical wet forest. So far, 507 birds, 2,500 plants and 765 butterfly species have been identified at Jatun Sacha. Activities include environmental education, field research, ecotourism and excursions with good views and a well-developed trail system.

● **Access** 25-mins by boat, US$2.50; or by road on the S bank of the Río Napo, 25 km from the bridge in Puerto Napo, bus to La Punta or Campacocha from Tena passes, but it has to ford the river, can be difficult if the level is high.

● **Accommodation** At *Cabañas Aliñahui*, 8 cabins with 2 bedrooms and bathroom, lush tropical garden; US$44/day, inc three delicious meals in dining hall, or US$6 for entrance only; profits contribute to rainforest conservation. Reservations are necessary: Fundación Jatun Sacha, Av Río Coca 1734, Casilla 17-12-867, Quito, T 253-267/441-592, F 253-266.

PUYO

This is the most important centre in the whole Oriente (*Pop* 15,563); the junction for road travel into the Southern Oriente and for traffic heading to or from **Ambato** via Baños (see page 1059). The Policía Nacional in Puyo handles visa extensions. Sangay and Altar can be seen.

Excursions

A 20-min walk along the footpath by the Río Puyo, across two footbridges, there is a good place for swimming.

22 km from Puyo is the 40 ha **Reserva de Bosque Tropical**, a private nature reserve administered by *Fundación Hola Vida*, US$1 per day, shelter for 10 people. Access is 16 km S on the road to Macas then turnoff W 6 km to the reserve.

Local information
● **Accommodation**

D *El Araucano*, Celso Marín 576, T 885-227, **F** without bath, Chilean owned, rooms on the road side best, family atmosphere, clean, hot water, video club, restaurant, stores luggage; **D** *Hostería Turingia*, Orellana y Villamil, T 885-180, small huts with bath, tropical garden, comfortable but noisy, good restaurant.

E *Europa Internacional*, 9 de Octubre y Orellana, T 885-407, with bath, shower, bright, pleasant, good restaurant; **E** *Hostería Safari*, Km 5.5 on the road to Puerto Napo outside town, T 885-465, peaceful.

F *California*, 9 de Octubre 1354, T 885-189, noisy.

● **Places to eat**
Mesón Europeo, Mons Alberto Zambrano, nr the bus station, the fanciest in town; *Europa*, next to *Hotel Europa*, 9 de Octubre y Marín, good; *Rincón Ambateño*, on the river front, follow 29 de Julio, restaurant and pool complex; *Viña del Mar* and *El Delfín* (both seafood), on Marín; *Chifa China*, 9 de Octubre y 24 de Mayo, clean; *Mistral*, Atahualpa y 9 de Octubre, good for breakfast; *Pan Selecto*, Marín y 9 de Octubre, good, fresh bread; *Vitapán*, also Marín y 9 de Octubre, good breakfast with eggs and fresh bread, US$0.75; *El Chileno*, fuente de soda run by owner of *El Araucano*, rec.

● **Banks & money changers**
Cambios Puyo, 9 de Octubre y Atahualpa, T/F 883-064, good rates.

● **Tour companies & travel agents**
Entsa Tours, PO Box 16-01-856, T 885-500, rec

for tours into the jungle, Mentor Marino helpful and knowledgeable; *Amazonia Touring*, 9 de Octubre y Atahualpa, T 883-219, F 883-064, land based and fly-in trips for 1-10 people.

● **Transport**
Air Military flights to Tena; Macas via Taisha, good views; Shell-Mera (see below) can be reached from Quito, 30 mins; also flights from Shell-Mera to Montalvo and Tiputini. Military passenger flights only go if there are 16 people.

Buses To Baños, US$1.50, Mon only, many delays, 4 hrs at least (roadworks); **Ambato**, US$2.60, 3 hrs; **Quito**, US$2.75, 7 hrs (9 hrs via Baeza, US$3.50); **Tena**, US$1.25, 3½ hrs, fight for a seat, rough road; **Riobamba**, US$1.60, 3½ hrs. Most buses leave from the new Terminal Terrestre on the outskirts of town, 10-15 mins' walk or bus from centre. Those for **Macas** leave from the old terminal, before going to the new terminal nr the market at far end of Atahualpa, past Amazonas (sign says Transportes Amazónicas); they leave daily 0600, 0900, 1100 and 1500, US$3.70, 3 hrs.

PUYO TO BAÑOS

The road from Puyo to Baños is a dramatic journey with superb views of the Pastaza valley and a plethora of waterfalls. **NB** Road is closed until 1998 at least, except Sun 1800 to Tues 0600.

Shell-Mera is 8 km W of Puyo, 50 km from Baños, 1½ hrs. It has an airfield and an army checkpoint where foreigners must register (passport required) if coming from Baños or Ambato. The Brigada in Shell will give permission for visiting the jungle.

● **Accommodation D** *Hostal Germania*, new, quiet; **F** *Hostal Cordillera*, with bath, restaurant; **G** *Hotel Esmeraldita*, basic, restaurant.

SOUTHERN ORIENTE

ROUTES The first leg of the Puyo-Macas bus journey goes as far as **Chuiguaza**, a small settlement at the junction of the Chiguaza and Pastaza rivers. There is a bridge suitable only for cars and small *busetas*. On the opposite shore, a bus carries passengers the rest of the way to the Macas bridge (this bus is rather smaller than the first). It stops often at small settlements, mostly inhabited by Shuar descendants. The ride is slow and rough, the road hard packed dirt, full of potholes. The jungle which borders this road is rapidly being removed.

MACAS

(*Pop* 9,720; *Alt* 1,000m approx) capital of Morona-Santiago province, situated high above the broad Río Upano valley, is developing rapidly thanks to nearby oil deposits and beef production. Sangay volcano can be seen on clear mornings from the plaza, creating an amazing backdrop to the tropical jungle surrounding the town. The modern cathedral, with beautiful stained-glass windows houses the much venerated image of La Purísima de Macas. Several blocks N of the cathedral, in the park which also affords great views of the Upano Valley, is an excellent orchid collection. The climate is not too hot and the nights are even cool.

● **NB** In 1997, the wooden suspension bridge giving access to the town was washed away (the concrete bridge it replaced was destroyed in 1996). Until a new bridge is built (due in 1997), long queues form to cross by a cage on pulleys.

Excursions

To the Salesian Sevilla-Don Bosco mission, E of town (slow journey until the bridge is replaced). The modern archaeological museum, Don Bosco y Montalba, is a good place to rest and see views of the river, and there is a recreation area nearby. 3 km N is La Cascada, beside the Río Copueno, picnic area, swimming, slide, football, volleyball. **Complejo Hombre Jaguar** archaeological site, with many *tolas* is N, near Santa Rosa and Guapula on the way to Sangay National Park. Allow 2 days to see everything; ask for directions if using public transport; day tours with *Sunka* US$25 pp.

Local information
● **Accommodation**
C pp *Cabañas Ecológicas Yuquipa*, T 700-071, 3 km walk from Km 12 on road to Puyo, minimum 3 days, inc accommodation, guiding, meals, transport, cheaper for groups of 6 or more, contact *Pancesa* bakery, Soasti y Tarqui.

D *Cabañas del Valle*, Vía Sur Km 1½, T 700-226, renovated, quiet, helpful; **D-F** *Peñón del Oriente*, Domingo Comín 837 y Amazonas, T 700-124, F 700-450, modern, clean, secure, hot water, good views from roof, rec; **D-F** *Splendit*, Soasti 1518, clean, modern, hot water, helpful, parking.

E *Amazonas*, Guamote y 29 de Mayo, T 700-198, nr university, **F** without bath, parking; **E** *Esmeralda*, Cuenca 612 y Soasti, T 700-160, modern, clean, hot water, cheaper with cold; **E** *La Orquídea*, 9 de Octubre 1305 y Sucre, T 700-970, with bath, hot water, cheaper with cold, clean and bright, quiet.

F *Emperatriz*, Amazonas y Tarqui, T 700-748, more basic rooms without bath **G**; **F** *Res Macas*, 24 de Mayo y Bolívar, T 700-254, above *Restaurante Carmitas* (good, simple cooking), quiet, clean, cheaper without bath.

G *Casa de la Suerte*, Tarqui 626 y Soasti, T 700-139, basic, helpful; **G** *Sangay*, Tarqui 605, T 700-457, basic, friendly.

● **Places to eat**

Chifa Pagoda, opp Peñón del Oriente, delicious, generous portions, good value, rec; *La Randimpa*, 24 de Mayo, on Parque Central, good, Cuban inc cigars, bar; *Los Helechos*, Soasti entre Cuenca y Sucre, good, popular with guides; *Café El Jardín*, Amazonas y D Comín, good breakfast not before 0800; *Donde Iván*, next door, bar.

● **Banks & money changers**

Banco del Austro, 24 de Mayo y 10 de Agosto, cash or TCs; *Delgado Travel*, cash only.

● **Post & telecommunications**

Post Office: 9 de Octubre y Domingo Comín, next to the park. **Emetel**: 24 de Mayo y Sucre, F 700-110, use this number to contact any establishment (be patient).

● **Tour companies & travel agents**

It is possible to visit the jungle from Macas and there are agencies specializing in tours to villages. However, contact the Shuar Federation (see below, Sucúa) before taking a tour and verify what is involved before signing any contract. Malaria precautions are recommended.

ETSA, 24 de Mayo y 10 de Agosto, T 700-550; *Ikiaam*, 10 de Agosto, 2nd floor in house opp bus terminal, T 700-457, tours to jungle and Sangay National Park; *Tuntiak Tours*, in bus terminal, T 700-082, Carlos Arcos is half Shuar and speaks the language, very experienced; *Sunka*, Sucre y 24 de Mayo, T 700-088, Pablo Velín guide, rec, typical Shuar restaurant next door; *J&B*, 10 de Agosto y Soasti, mail service to USA; *Delgado*, D Comín y Amazonas.

ROW, Amazonas y Quito, a US company from Idaho is offering whitewater rafting on the Upano (River Odysseys West, PO Box 579, Coeur d'Alene, Idaho, 83816-0579, T (208) 765-0841). Ecuador contact: Juan, Quito, T 458-339. Seasons are limited owing to the extreme unpredictability of the Upano river.

Kapawi Ecological Reserve: run by *Canodros*, Luis Urdaneta 1418 y Av del Ejército, Guayaquil, T (04) 285-711/280-173, F 287-651, e-mail eco-tourism1@canodros.com.ec, PO Box 09-01-8442: developed in Achuar Territory with the full participation of the local people. Built according to the Achuar concept of architecture, it is in a zone rich in biodiversity, with a lodge and many opportunities for seeing the forest and its inhabitants. From Quito you go either to Shell-Mera or Macas, then a plane takes you to Sharamentza; from here canoes go 1½ hrs down the Río Pastaza to the confluence with the Kapawari; 4 nights in a double cabin costs US$700, plus US$200 for transport to and from Quito. Location, service, accommodation and food all highly rec.

● **Transport**

Air Flight to **Quito**, TAME, Mon, Wed, Fri, sit on left for best views of Sangay. The air force flies Shell, Taisha, Macas, Morona and vice versa Tues, Thur and Fri.

The paved runway at Macas is the main access for the southern jungle, but local airlines are only licensed to transport missionaries, volunteers, Indians and people needing medical attention. The only way round this is to charter a plane from a licensed company in Shell or Quito, which is obviously much more expensive. It may sometimes be possible to get a flight from Sucúa's grass strip, a 40-min taxi ride to the S (see below).

Buses To **Cuenca**, 12 hrs, US$7, 4 a day with Turismo Oriental; Transportes Sucúa, 1700, spectacular views, 0530 bus to see it in daylight; hourly to **Sucúa**, 1 hr, no regular service on Thur. Two bus companies Macas-**Puyo**: Coop San Francisco 5 a day, US$4.50, 6 hrs; Coop Macas almost hourly from 0600-1500.

ROUTES A new road from Macas to Guamote in the mountains (see page 1071) may be finished in 1997. (see page 1071)

SANGAY NATIONAL PARK

The surrounding hills give excellent views of the volcano **Sangay**, 5,230m, within the Sangay National Park, entrance US$20, information from Inefan in Macas, Juan de la Cruz y 29 de Mayo. Sangay is an active volcano; the South American Explorers Club has information on organizing a trip, equipment, helmet, etc, and guide essential. The trek takes 7 days and is only for those who can endure long, hard days of walking and severe weather. Protection against falling stones is vital. Mecánica Acosta, Plaza Arenas, Quito (near the prominent basilica), will make shields, arm loops welded to an oil drum top, for US$2-3. Dec/Jan is a good time to climb Sangay.

● **Access** The park may be reached by bus 1½ hrs to village of 9 de Octubre, Wed, Fri and Sun 0730 and 1600, then walk.

SUCUA

23 km from Macas, is of particular interest as the centre of a branch of the ex-head-hunting Shuar (Jívaro) Indians. Their crafts can be seen and bought but it is tactless to ask them about head-hunting and shrinking (a practice designed to punish those who bewitched others or to deter anyone wishing to cause sickness or disaster in future). Outside the schools, scenes from Shuar mythology are displayed in painted tableaux. You can contact the **Shuar Federation** at Domingo Comín 17-38 (C Tarqui 809), T/F 704-108, about visiting traditional villages. This is possible with an Indian guide, but takes time as the application must be considered by a council of seven and then you will be interviewed. Allow at least 1½ days. There is a small craft shop across the street from the Shuar Federation. There is an interesting bookshop and, 10 mins' walk from the town centre, a small museum and zoo (very few animals) run by Shuar Indians, in the Centro de Formación Kimi.

Nearby is the Río Upano, a 1½-hr walk, with plenty of Morpho butterflies. A cablecar crosses the river. Also close by is the Río Tutanangoza, a 15-min walk, with rapids and good swimming, but be careful after rain.

● **Accommodation** E *Karina*, SW corner of plaza, above *farmacia*, light, clean; F *Hostería Orellana*, at the S end of town, T 704-193, one room with bath, others without; F *Hostal Alborada*, cheap, restaurant; F *Rincón Oriental*, shared bath, clean, parking, rec; G *Sangay*, very basic; G *Cuenca*, small rooms, basic, toilets filthy.

● **Places to eat** *Restaurant La Fuente*, Domingo Comín nr the plaza, good; bar/restaurant *Sangay*, opp *Rincón Oriental*; *Paolita*, Domingo Comín S of centre. *Jefralisavi*, N of the plaza, snacks and drinks, open till midnight, changes US$ cash and TCs.

SOUTH OF SUCUA

From Sucúa, the road heads S for 1 hr to Logroño and then, another 1 hr S (Santiago de) **Méndez**, a nice town with a modern church. Market day Sun.

● **Accommodation & places to eat** All on Calle Cuenca, none has hot water. E *Hostal Los Ceibos*, T 760-133, with bath; F *Res Vanessa*, and 3 basic *pensiones*, all G: *Miranda*, *Amazonas*, *Anita*. The restaurant under *Anita* is popular; several others.

● **Buses** To Gualaquiza 1600, 1900; **Cuenca** 4 a day; Macas 0600, 1100. To **Morona**, E of Méndez in the jungle (see *The Ecuador Handbook*), 1200 and 2000. More buses pass through Bella Unión, 4 km E of the town.

ROUTES   A road is being built to connect Méndez and Paute, NE of Cuenca. It will go via Libertad (driveable to this point, Mar '97), Guarumales, and Amaluza. It follows an ancient trade route, which is walkable.

Heading S of Méndez, passports are checked at the checkpoint at Patuca, the first village after the bridge over the Río Upano; photocopies not accepted. If permission to proceed is denied, don't argue. The road is subject to landslides in the wet season.

LIMON

2 hrs, 50 km S of Méndez is **Limón**, official name Gen Leónidas Plaza, a mission town founded in 1935, now a busy, friendly place, surrounded by high jungle.

● **Accommodation & places to eat** 3 *residenciales* on C Quito, all F: *Limón*, T 770-114, modern, basic, clean, front rooms noisy; *Domínguez*, friendly; *Santo Domingo*, basic. *Chifa Rincón de Taiwán*, C Quito.

● **Buses** All from C Quito, go to Cuenca, Macas and Gualaquiza.

ROUTES   From Limón, the road to Cuenca (132 km) passes through Gualaceo, via Jadán. It is a longer route (Macas-Cuenca) than from Quito, but just as spectacular. From Limón the road rises steeply with many breathtaking turns and the vegetation changes frequently, partly through cloud forest and then, at 4,000m, through the *páramo*, before dropping very fast down to the valley of Gualaceo. There is a police checkpoint at Plan de Milagro, where foreigners have to register. There is nowhere to stay along the Limón-Gualaceo road.

GUALAQUIZA

Continuing S from Limón the road passes **Indanza** (very basic *residencial* and *comedor*), before reaching **Gualaquiza**, a pioneer town off the tourist track. It is surrounded by densely forested mountains, in which are interesting side trips.

Among the excursions are the caves near Nuevo Tarqui, the Salesian mission at Bomboisa and Tutusa Gorge. It's a 3-hr walk, 2 hrs by boat, take a guide, eg Sr José Castillo.

Also **Aguacate**, a 6-hr walk, near which are precolumbian ruins; food and bed at Sr Jorge Guillermo Vázquez. Yumaza is a 40-min walk, for more precolumbian ruins (2 sites).

- **Accommodation** F *Amazonas*, Domingo Comín 08-65, basic; **E** *Turismo*, Gonzalo Pesantes 08-16, **F** without bath, good value, restaurant; **F** *Guaquiz*, Orellana 08-52, shared bath. *Cabaña los Helechos*, opp the bus station, rec.

- **Post & telecommunications Emetel**: García Moreno y Ciudad de Cuenca, Mon-Sat 0800-1100, 1400-1700, 1900-2100.

- **Transport** Buses to **Cuenca**, 1900, 2000 and 2100, 6 hrs; **Loja**, 0300 and 2200; **Macas**, 1800, 10 hrs. *Rancheros* leave for Yantzaza in the morning, from where a bus reaches Zamora before dark (see **Southern Sierra**).

Galápagos Islands

Lying on the Equator, 970 km W of the Ecuadorean coast, the Galápagos consist of 6 main islands (San Cristóbal, Santa Cruz, Isabela, Floreana, Santiago and Fernandina – the last two uninhabited); 12 smaller islands (Baltra and the uninhabited islands of Santa Fe, Pinzón, Española, Rábida, Daphne, Seymour, Genovesa, Marchena, Pinta, Darwin and Wolf) and over 40 islets. The islands have a total population of nearly 10,000 and because of immigration the annual growth rate is about 12%. The largest island, Isabela (formerly Albemarle), is 120 km long and forms half the total land area of the archipelago. Its notorious convict colony was closed in 1958; some 1,000 people live there now, mostly in and around Puerto Villamil, on the S coast. San Cristóbal (Chatham) has a population of 3,000 with the capital of the archipelago, Puerto Baquerizo Moreno. Santa Cruz (Indefatigable) has 7,000, with Puerto Ayora, the main tourist centre; and Floreana (Charles) fewer than 50. The group is quite widely scattered; by boat, Puerto Baquerizo Moreno and Puerto Ayora are 6 hrs apart.

GEOLOGY

The islands are the peaks of gigantic volcanoes, composed almost exclusively of basalt. Most of them rise from 2,000 to 3,000m above the seabed. Eruptions have taken place in historical times on Fernandina, Isabela, Pinta, Marchena, Santiago and Floreana. The most active today are Fernandina, Isabela, Pinta and Marchena, and fumarolic activity may be seen intermittently on each of these islands.

FLORA AND FAUNA

The Galápagos have never been connected with the continent. Gradually, over many hundreds of thousands of years, animals and plants from over the sea arrived there and as time went by they adapted themselves to Galápagos conditions and came to differ more and more from their continental ancestors. Thus many of them are unique: a quarter of the species of shore fish, half of the plants and almost all the reptiles are found nowhere else. In many cases different forms have evolved on the different islands. Charles Darwin recognized this speciation within the archipelago when he visited the Galápagos on the *Beagle* in 1835 and his observations played a substantial part in his formulation of the theory of evolution. Since no large land

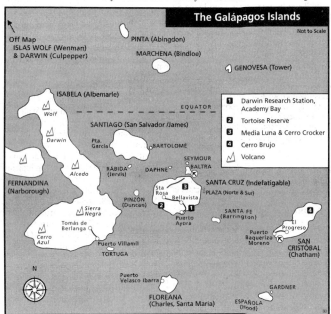

The Galápagos Islands

Not to Scale

Off Map
ISLAS WOLF (Wenman)
& DARWIN (Culpepper)

PINTA (Abingdon)

MARCHENA (Bindloe)

GENOVESA (Tower)

ISABELA (Albemarle)

EQUATOR

Wolf

SANTIAGO (San Salvador / James)

Darwin

Pta.
Garcia

BARTOLOMÉ

SEYMOUR

Alcedo

RÁBIDA
(Jervis)

DAPHNE

BALTRA

FERNANDINA
(Narborough)

Sta
Rosa

SANTA CRUZ (Indefatigable)

PLAZA (Norte & Sur)

Sierra
Negra

PINZÓN
(Duncan)

Bellavista

Tomás de
Berlanga

Cerro
Azul

SANTA FE
(Barrington)

Puerto
Ayora

El
Progreso

Puerto Villamil

TORTUGA

Puerto
Baquerizo
Moreno

SAN
CRISTÓBAL
(Chatham)

N

Puerto
Velasco Ibarra

GARDNER

FLOREANA
(Charles, Santa Maria)

ESPAÑOLA
(Hood)

1 Darwin Research Station, Academy Bay
2 Tortoise Reserve
3 Media Luna & Cerro Crocker
4 Cerro Brujo
Volcano

mammals reached the islands, reptiles were dominant just as they had been all over the world in the very distant past. Another of the extraordinary features of the islands is the tameness of the animals. The islands were uninhabited when they were discovered in 1535 and the animals still have little instinctive fear of man.

The most spectacular species to be seen by the visitor are the giant tortoise (species still survive in 6 or 7 of the islands, but mostly on Isabela); marine iguana (the only seagoing lizard in the world and found throughout most of the archipelago; it eats seaweed); land iguana (on Fernandina, Santa Cruz, Santa Fe, Isabela, Seymour and Plaza); Galápagos albatross (which nests only on the island of Española – apart from 2 pairs on Isla de la Plata; it leaves in December and returns in late March-early April); Galápagos hawk, red-footed, blue-footed and masked boobies, red-billed tropic-bird, frigate birds, swallow-tailed gulls, dusky lava gulls, flightless cormorants (on Isabela and Fernandina), mockingbirds, 13 species of Darwin's finches (all endemic and the classic examples of speciation quoted by Darwin); Galápagos sea-lion (common in many areas) and the Galápagos fur-seal (on the more remote and rocky coasts).

The most-visited islands from Puerto Ayora are Plaza Sur (an estimated 1,000 sea-lions living on 1 ha, land and sea iguana, many birds flying close to the cliff top), Santa Fe (land and sea iguanas, cactus forest, swimming with sea-lions), Seymour Norte (sea-lions, marine iguanas, swallow-tailed gulls, magnificent frigate birds, blue-footed boobies – the latter not close to the tourist trail), Rábida (sea-lions, flamingoes, pelican rookery), and Santiago (James Bay for fur seals, snorkelling with sea-lions, migratory coastal birds; Sullivan Bay and Bartolomé Island for fantastic lava fields on the climb to the summit, fine views, snorkelling around Pinnacle Rock and maybe a few penguins). On a tour of these islands it may be possible to go also to Punto García on Isabela to see flightless cormorants (it takes at least a full day to climb up Sierra Negra volcano to see the tortoises – it can be climbed on foot, horseback or by pickup). Daphne Island with very rich birdlife may be visited by each boat only once a month (a permit is required).

More distant islands from Puerto Ayora, but visited from there or from Puerto Baquerizo Moreno are Española (blue-footed boobies, masked boobies, waved albatross, many other birds, brightly-coloured marine iguanas, sea-lions, snorkelling at Tortuga Islet), Genovesa (red-footed boobies – brown and white phase, masked boobies, swallow-tailed and lava gulls, frigate birds and many others, marine iguanas, snorkelling) and Floreana (flamingoes, sea-lions, endemic plants, snorkelling at Corona del Diablo). There is a custom for visitors to Post Office Bay on the N side of Floreana since 1793 to place unstamped letters and cards in a barrel, and deliver, free of charge, any addressed to their own destinations. Fernandina is best visited on longer cruises which include Isabela. For more details on Santa Cruz, San Cristóbal and Isabela, see below. Never miss the opportunity to go snorkelling, there is plenty of underwater life to see, including rays, sharks (not all dangerous) and many fish. All the other islands are closed to tourists.

Do not touch any of the animals, birds or plants. Do not transfer sand or soil from one island to another. Do not leave litter anywhere; it is highly undesirable in a National Park and is a safety and health hazard for wildlife. Do not take raw food on to the islands.

The number of tourists to the islands is controlled by the authorities to protect the environment but critics claim that the ecology is seriously threatened by current levels. Limits were increased from 12,000 in 1974 to 60,000 in 1990, but tourism infrastructure remains fairly basic. In April 1997, President Alarcón signed an emergency decree covering migration to, and development in the islands and a new Tourism Law will prevent any new permits for tourist operations being issued until 31 December 2005. There are reports that galapagueños often charge foreigners

more than locals. Understand that they feel overrun by people who must be rich; be courteous but firm. Avoid visiting in July and especially August (high season).

CLIMATE

The Galápagos Climate can be divided into a hot season (Dec to May), when there is a possibility of heavy showers, and the cool or *garúa* season (June to Nov), when the days generally are more cloudy and there is often rain or drizzle. July and Aug can be windy, force 4 or 5. Daytime clothing should be lightweight. (Clothing generally, even on 'luxury cruises' should be casual and comfortable.) At night, however, particularly at sea and at higher altitudes, temperatures fall below 15°C and warm clothing is required. Boots and shoes soon wear out on the lava terrain. The sea is cold July-Oct; underwater visibility is best Jan-March. Sept is the low point in the meteorological year.

TRAVEL TO THE ISLANDS

● By Air
There are 2 **airports**, one at Baltra (South Seymour), across a narrow strait from Santa Cruz, the other at Puerto Baquerizo Moreno, on San Cristóbal. The two islands are 96 km apart; regular boat services between them with Ingala (see page 1141). When booking make sure your flight goes to the island of your choice. Cruises leave from both islands so itineraries depend on which port of departure is used, the capability of the boat and the length of the cruise. From either port prearranged tours can be paid for in advance. In Puerto Ayora, Santa Cruz, cruises can be arranged on the spot and can be arranged to finish at Baltra for the airport. It is more difficult in very high or low season to arrange tours. There are few opportunities to do this in Puerto Baquerizo Moreno.

All flights originate in Quito and make a long stopover in Guayaquil. Normal return fare in 1997, US$378 from Quito, US$333 from Guayaquil; 21-day excursion low season fare is US$323 from Quito and US$290 from Guayaquil with TAME to Baltra (16 Jan-14 June; 1 Sept-30 Nov), valid for 21 days from date of purchase. Independent travellers must reconfirm outward and return flights 2 days before departure and see their name written on the Manifest, not the 'Lista de Espera'. This is especially critical during high season.

TAME flies daily (not Sun out of the high season) **to Baltra**, and offers 15% reductions on normal fare flights to holders of International Student Identity Cards with evidence of home student status (details from office at Edif Pichincha, p 6, Amazonas y Colón, Quito, two photocopies of ID required, allow at least 4 hrs for documents to be endorsed); reductions available in Quito or Guayaquil but paperwork must be done in the relevant city. TAME office in Puerto Ayora opens 0800 and closes Sat pm and all day Sun.

Boat owners make block bookings with the airlines in the hope of filling their boat. Visitors may buy tickets where they like, but in the busy season will have to take the ticket to the tour operator for the reservation. Tickets are the same price everywhere, except for student discounts on TAME.

SAN flies to **Puerto Baquerizo Moreno** (daily, except Sun). One-way tickets are available and it is possible to buy an open-ended ticket (valid one year). SAN will change dates for return to mainland. SAN offers 20% discount to holders of International Student Identity Cards; your home college ID card, 3 copies of each and the originals plus a passport and US$ cash (not credit cards) required. Go to the office in Av Cristóbal Colón y 6 de Diciembre. Saeta has excellent 30-day excursion packages Miami-Quito/Guayaquil-Galápagos (SAN to San Cristóbal)-Guayaquil/Quito-Miami (US$584), usually the cheapest deal.

The **Air Force flights**, known as *logísticos*, may be booked at the military airport, Colegio Técnico y Escuela 1, Av de la Prensa 3212, T 445-043, just past the civil airport; single fare US$140, payable only in dollars. Reservations can only be made in advance for the Wed or Sat flight; the office is open 0800-1200. For those who succeed, a Lockheed C-130 Hercules departs Quito for Guayaquil, San Cristóbal and Baltra at 0700, be there at 0500. This can be very time consuming and there is no guarantee. The flights are not reliable and flying for 2 hrs in a cargo aircraft with no windows and no facilities is not much fun. To return, make reservation at the Marine Station by the harbour (if they say 'no' foreigners, show the used ticket from Quito), pay the exact fare in dollars at the airport, no change given. *Café Booby* in Puerto Ayora sells tickets at 0715 before 0800 bus to the airport.

● Airport transfer
From the airport on Baltra, one takes a combination of bus (US$1), ferry (US$0.50) and bus (US$2.50) to Puerto Ayora, Santa Cruz. The whole process takes 2½ hrs. Airport buses leave Puerto Ayora (supermarket at the pier) at 0730, 0745 and 0800 for Baltra (best buy a ticket the night before – not possible for Sat bus though). Hotels may make prior arrangements. The airport in Puerto

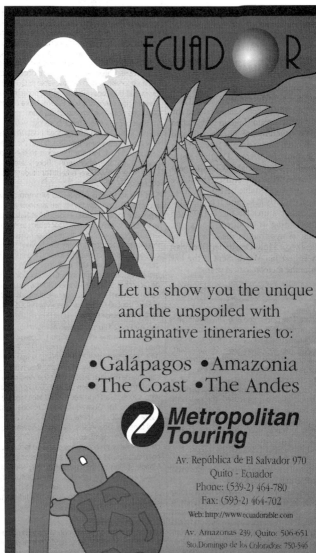

Baquerizo Moreno is within walking distance of town, but those on prearranged tours will be met at the airport.

● **By Sea**

The supply vessel (tramp steamer) *Piquero* takes 10 passengers between Guayaquil and the Galápagos, US$200 pp in a double cabin, $3^1/_2$ days inc food (US$150 without food). The ship leaves Guayaquil on the 25th (usually) of each month. You can return after 5-7 days or next month. To stay on board during its sailing round the islands costs US$40 plus US$7/day for food. Information from Johnny Franco, Tulcán 1824 y Ayacucho, F 04-450-441 (04-360-779 in evening), or go on board and speak to the purser or captain, it docks on the Malecón in Guayaquil. Take care of the cranes, etc, and be very alert to theft at all times (report of very basic facilities, inadequate food, accommodation and guides): "an experience, but not a way to see the Galápagos". The park entry tax must be paid on arrival.

● **Entry tax**

Every visitor has to pay a National Park Tax of US$80, payable only in sucres or US$ cash. It is paid on arrival, or at Quito or Guayaquil airports on request. On San Cristóbal there is a municipal tax of US$30; on Santa Cruz or on Baltra the tax is US$12. In each case it is paid by arriving plane passengers. Do not lose your park tax receipt; boat captains need to record it. A 50% reduction on the national park fee is available to children under 12 and students with a student identity card from their home university who are under 26.

● **Travel between the islands**

Internal flights can be made from *Grand Hotel* in San Cristóbal, T (05) 520-179, charter only, max 6 passengers, US$300/flight.

Ingala sails from Puerto Ayora to Puerto Baquerizo Moreno Tues 1000, returning Wed 1000, and Sat 0800, returning Mon 1000, US$9 for locals, US$18 for Ecuadoreans, US$42 for foreigners; at 0800 on Thur it sails Puerto Ayora-Isabela (US$36), returning Fri via Floreana. Buy all tickets the day before sailing. The Ingala office in Puerto Ayora is on Padre Herrera, near the petrol station on the outskirts; in Puerto Baquerizo Moreno it is up the hill on the road leading inland, on the edge of town.

ISLAND CRUISES

There are two ways to travel around the islands: a 'tour navegable', where you sleep on the boat, or less expensive tours where you sleep ashore at night and travel during the day. On the former you travel at night, arriving at a new landing site each day, with more time ashore. On the latter you spend less time ashore and the boats are smaller with a tendency to overcrowding in high season. In the low season and with last minute bookings (Feb-May, Sept-Nov), luxury boats rarely offer discounts, but if they do it could be as much as 40%, tourist boats offer about 20% discount and budget boats 5-10%.

Itineraries are controlled by the National Park to distribute tourism evenly throughout the islands. Boats are expected to be on certain islands on certain days. They can cut landings, but have to get special permission to add to a planned itinerary. An itinerary change may be made if time would be better spent elsewhere. A good guide will explain this and you can trust their advice. Altering an itinerary to spend more time in Puerto Ayora or San Cristóbal is unacceptable (except in extreme bad weather). This sometimes occurs because not all passengers are on the same length of tours and boats come into port to change passengers.

Legitimate complaints should be made to Edgar Vargas, the Jefe de Turismo at the park in Puerto Ayora, or to Jimena Larrea, the head of Cetur, who is helpful. Any 'tour navegable' will include the days of arrival and departure as full days. Insist on a written itinerary or contract prior to departure as any effort not to provide this probably indicates problems later. The South American Explorers Club (in Quito, Lima or Ithaca, NY) has produced a useful, brief guide to the Galápagos which includes a specimen contract for itinerary and living conditions.

Choosing a tour

The less expensive boats are normally smaller and less powerful so you see less and spend more time travelling, also the guiding is likely to be in Spanish only (there are some exceptions to this). The more expensive boats will probably have 110 volts, a/c and private baths, all of which can be nice, but not critically important. All boats have to conform to certain minimum safety standards (check that there are enough liferafts) and have VHF radio, but the rules tend to be quite

arbitrary (eg windows and portholes may have domestic, rather than safety glass). A watermaker can make quite a difference as the town water from Puerto Ayora or Puerto Baquerizo Moreno should not be drunk. Note that boats with over 18 passengers take quite a time to disembark and re-embark people, while the smaller boats have a more lively motion, which is important if you are prone to seasickness.

The least expensive tours, about US$300-450 tend to travel during the day, with nights spent ashore in a hotel. For US$450-800 for 8 days you will be on a smaller boat but travelling at night, with more time ashore in daylight. US$800-1,400 is the price of the majority of the best boats, most with English guiding. Over US$1,400 is entering the luxury bracket, with English guiding the norm, more comfortable cabins and better cuisine. No boat may sail without a park-trained guide: Naturalists II have little or no English and only basic knowledge; Naturalists III are English-speaking naturalist guides.

Booking a cruise

If wishing to plan everything ahead of time, there are many good tour operators. In Britain, David Horwell, naturalist and author of *Galápagos, the Enchanted Isles*, London, Dryad Press, 1988 (£9.95 through his agency), arranges tailor-made tours to Ecuador and the Galápagos islands. For further details write to him at Galapagos Adventure Tours, 37-39 Great Guildford St, London SE1 0ES, T/F 0171 261 9890, E-mail: pinzon@compuserve.com. Also rec is Penelope Kellie, T 01962-779317 who is the UK agent for Quasar Nautica (see under **Agencies and boats**). *Galapagos Classic Cruises*, 6 Keyes Road, London NW2 3XA, T 0181 933 0613, F 0181 452 5248, E-mail: galapagoscruises@compuserve.com, specialise in tailor-made cruises and diving holidays to the islands with additional land tours to Ecuador and Peru available on request. In the USA, *Wilderness Travel* (801 Allston Way, Berkeley, CA 94710, T 1-800-368-2704) and *Inca Floats* (Bill Robertson, 1311 63rd St, Emeryville, CA 94608) have been rec.

Shopping around the agencies in Quito is a good way of securing a value-for-money cruise, but only if you can deal with the boat owner, or his/her representative, rather than someone operating on commission. It is worth asking if the owner has 1-3 spaces to fill on a cruise; you can often get them at a discount. A much simpler way is to fax from home to an agency which acts as a broker for the cruise ships. The broker can recommend a vessel which suits your requirements. Allow about 2 months for arrangements to be made. Rec are *Safari Tours*, F (593-2) 220-426, e-mail admin@safariec.ecx.ec, and *Angermeyer's Enchanted Excursions*, F (593-2) 569-956, full addresses under Quito **Tourist Agencies**.

Arranging a tour from the islands

If you wish to wait until you reach the islands, Puerto Ayora, Santa Cruz, is the only practical place for arranging a cruise. Here you can hire boats (lists available from National Park Service) and a 2-week sojourn will allow you to see most of the Islands. Reservations are strongly recommended for June-Aug, Dec-Jan and Easter Week. Out of season boats do not run unless they are full, so either book in advance or be prepared to wait until a group forms.

For cheaper tours it is generally recommended that you form a group once you reach the Islands, talk to people about the boats they may have used and then visit the office of the small boat owners (*armadores*). Negotiate the route (don't include the Darwin Research Station or Tortuga Bay as these are easy from Puerto Ayora) and the price, and get a firm commitment from the owner on dates and itinerary, leave a deposit 'to buy food' and get a receipt.

Prices are fixed by the *armadores*; if you believe you have been misled see the Port Captain who is usually honest, but changes annually. A small boat taking 8 or 12 people costs US$55 pp/day (low season) – US$80 (high season) for a full load, often excluding food, drinks and US$2 harbour exit tax. Prices are set according to the 8, 12 or 16 capacity of the boats; parties of other sizes may upset calculations. Check that the small boats can carry enough food and supplies for the length of journey so you do not waste a day restocking. Many boats require you to provide your own drinking water: check this when you make arrangements.

NB If not booking a cruise in advance, it can take several days to arrange a tour, so allow yourself plenty of time (a week, maybe more). If you do get stuck, the Tourist Office in Puerto Ayora offers 1-day tours (US$36 pp with lunch; departure 0600-0800) to Seymour Norte, Plaza Sur or Santa Fe. These smaller islands have a good sample of animal species (although fewer in numbers) and, together with sightseeing on Santa Cruz, can be a worthwhile experience for the tourist with only limited time.

Agencies and boats

With over 100 boats operating in the islands, we cannot give them all. We list those for which we have received positive recommendations. Exclusion does not imply poor service.

Quasar Nautica-Galápagos Expeditions, Av Los Shyris 2447, Edif Autocom, Quito, T 441-550, F 436-625 (USA T 305-599-9008, F 305-592-7060, UK representative, Penelope Kellie, T 01962-779-317, F 01962-779-458), 7-10 day inter-island cruises on 8-18 berth luxury sail and power yachts with multi-lingual guides and high class cabin service. Both naturalist and diving cruises are available. Also arrange mainland tours accompanied by highly qualified guides.

In Guayaquil, *Galasam* (Economic Galapagos Tours), Av 9 de Octubre 424, Edif Gran Pasaje, ground floor, local 9A, and p 11 (T 306-289/313-724, F 313-351/562-033, website http://www.galasam.com.ec, e-mail galapago@ galasam.com.ec) sell flights and country-wide tours as well as their own Galápagos cruises. Special rates are offered on TAME and SAN flights, depending on season. Cargo voyage from Guayaquil to the islands and back can be booked here. They have 8 boats for cruises, *Dorado*, *Cruz del Sur*, *Estrella del Mar*, *Islas Plazas*, *Moby Dick*, *Darwin* (all 16 passengers), *Yolita* (12) and *Antártida* (10). Departures are daily except Tues and Fri for 4, 5 and 8-day cruises, costing from US$540 to 1,350 (ask about last minute discounts). Also available are 2-day/1-night tour to Isabela, US$150 and a diving package at special prices. An office is to open in Puerto Ayora in 1998. See also under Quito **Tour companies**. If purchasing via the Internet a discount is available. *South American Handbook* owners are also entitled to discounts; make full enquiries.

Metropolitan Touring, Av República de El Salvador 970, PO Box 17-12-310, Quito, T (593-2) 464-780, F 464-702, website http://www.ecuadorable.com (represented in the USA by Adventure Associates, 13150 Coit Rd, Suite 110, Dallas, Texas 75240, T 214-907-0414, F 783-1286) offers 7-night cruises on the MV *Santa Cruz* (90 passengers), said to be the best boat, very professional service, with multilingual guides, also the *Isabella II*. They also use *Yate Encantada* and *Delfín II*, and have yachts for private charters (eg Ecuacruceros' *Rachel III* and *Diamante*) and can arrange tours on a number of boats of all types, from 8 to 34 passengers. Metropolitan can also arrange scuba diving trips. Bookings can also be made for the *Reina Silvia*, owned by Rolf Siebers, who also owns the *Delfín Hotel* in Puerto Ayora. This vessel makes daily sailings, returning to the hotel each night, but its speed means that the day trips are worthwhile and comfortable, rec.

Ecoventura, Av CJ Arosemena, Km 2.5, Guayaquil, T 593-4-203-080/206-749, F 202-990 (in Quito Av Colón 535 y 6 de Diciembre, T 593-2-507-408, F 507-409) is another agency with Galápagos cruises, operating in conjunction with *Galapagos Network*, 7200 Corporate Center Drive, Suite 309, Miami, FL 33126, T (305) 592-2294, F 592-6394, e-mail gpsnet@aol.com: 3 motor yachts, *Eric*, *Flamingo* and *Letty* (good guides, atmosphere and food, highly rec); 1 motor vessel, *Corinthian*; and *M/S Sea Cloud*; 3, 4 and 7-night cruises available out of Puerto Baquerizo Moreno. 7-night fares start at US$1,375 on *Corinthian* to US$1,600 on *Eric*.

Angermeyer's Enchanted Expeditions, Foch 726 y Amazonas, Quito, T 593-2-569-960, F 569-956, have been rec for their professional, well-organized cruise on the *Beluga*, good English-speaking guide, lots of good food, worth the expense. They also operate the *Cachalote*, which is also rec.

Canodros SA, Luis Urdaneta 14-18, Guayaquil, T 280-164, F 287-651. *Galatravel*, Amazonas 623 y Carrión, T 222-885, F 505-772, Quito. *Eurogalapagos*, Amazonas 333 y Washington, T 553-750, F 500-075, Quito. Other rec agencies with tours to/in the Galápagos are given under Quito and Guayaquil **Tourist Agencies**.

Two boats with consistently high recommendations are the sailing brigantine *Andando* and the motor trawler *Samba*, both owned by Jane and Fiddi Angermeyer; book through *Andando Tours*, T/F (593-5) 526-308, Puerto Ayora, or PO Box 17-21-0088, T (593-2) 465-113, F 443-188, Quito; personal service always given.

Other recommendations: Pepe Salcedo's *Sulidae*, an old Norwegian fishing boat; Pepe is very experienced (Sulidae Charters, PO Box 09-01-0260, Guayaquil, T 593-4-201-376, F 323-478). Georgina and Agustín Cruz' *Beagle III*, friendly, good cooking (bookable through Metropolitan Touring). The motor yacht *Orca* (Etnotours, J L Mera y Cordero, Quito, T 593-2-230-552) and *Angelique* (owner Franklin Angermeyer), the latter has lots of character, good food.

Rolf Wittmer, son of Margaret Wittmer of the famous 1930s Galápagos Affair, owns and runs *Tiptop III*, no snorkelling equipment. His son has the sailing yacht *Symbol*, a converted ship's lifeboat, very basic, but a good way to drift between the islands (Wittmer Turismo, Amazonas 621 y Carrión, Quito, PO Box 17-07-8989, T 593-2-449-337, F 448-173). *Seaman*, run by Galápagos Travel, has good tours but cramped lower cabins (Amazonas 519 y Roca, Quito, T 593-2-500-064, F 505-772). Jenny Devine, *Moonrise* travel agency, opp Banco de Pacífico, Puerto Ayora, T 05-526-348, F 05-526-403, 5-day trips on *Stella Maris*. The sailing catamaran *Pulsar* is rec, US$580/8 days, but best when the owner Patric is on board; some cabins are very small indeed (Ecuagal, Amazonas 1113 y Pinto, p 2, T 593-2-229-579, F 550-988).

Good service on the *Golondrina*, *Frigata*, Golondrina Turismo, J L Mera 639 y Carrión, Quito, T 593-2-528-570, F 528-570. *Isla Galápagos* is rec; the guide is Peter Freire, good, but fair English. *Elizabeth II*, good crew and food; *Angelito* of Hugo Andrade, with a new *Angelito* in service; *Española* (8 passengers, good food); *Lobo del Mar* (12 passengers); *Daphne* (8 – good cook); and *San Antonio* (12 – good food, nice crew).

Day tours can be arranged on *North Star*, small but fast, contact David Asencio at *Hotel Darwin*; *Santa Fe II*, owned by Byron Rueda, T (05) 526-593; *Esmeraldas*, owned by Ninfa Tours.

It must be stressed that a boat is only as good as its crew and when the staff change, so will these recommendations. The South American Explorers Club in Quito has an extensive file of trip reports for members to consult and David, at *Safari Tours*, Quito, tries to keep abreast of all new developments.

PUERTO AYORA

Places of interest

In 1959, the centenary of the publication of Darwin's *Origin of Species*, the Government of Ecuador and the International Charles Darwin Foundation established, with the support of Unesco, the Charles Darwin Research Station at Academy Bay 1½ km from Puerto Ayora, Santa Cruz, the most central of the Galápagos islands, open Mon-Fri 0700-1300, 1400-1600, Sat 0700-1300. A visit to the station is a good introduction to the islands as it provides a lot of information. Collections of several of the rare sub-species of giant tortoise are maintained on the station as breeding nuclei, together with a tortoise-rearing house incorporating incubators and pens for the young. The Darwin Foundation staff will help bona fide students of the fauna to plan an itinerary, if they stay some time and hire a boat. See their website for more information, page 1151.

Excursions on Santa Cruz

Ask at *Neptuno Tours* in Puerto Ayora for tours of the interior. Walk to **Tortuga Bay** on a marked path for excellent sunsets and nice beach (very strong undertow), 5 km. Take drinking water and do not go alone (armed robbery reported). Overnight camping is possible with permission from the Park offices in Puerto Ayora. There are several beaches by the Darwin Station, very crowded at weekends.

Hike to the higher parts of the island called Media Luna, Puntudo and Mt Crocker. The trail starts at Bellavista, 7 km from Puerto Ayora. A round trip from Bellavista is 4 to 8 hrs, depending on the distance hiked, 10-18 km (permit and guide not required, but a guide is advisable). Take water, sun block and long-sleeved shirt and long trousers to protect against razor grass.

To see giant tortoises in the wild, go to Steve Devine's Butterfly ranch beyond Bellavista on the road to Santa Rosa (the bus passes the turn-off), only in the dry season; in the wet season the tortoises are breeding in the arid zone. Vermillion fly-catchers can be seen here also. Entry US$2, inc free cup of *hierba luisa* tea, or juice. Steve Devine is a guide on the island, highly rec (ask for him or Jack Nelson at *Hotel Galápagos*).

There are several natural tunnels (lava tubes): one 3 km from Puerto Ayora on the road to Bellavista, unsigned on the left, look for the black-and-white posts (tread carefully); barn owls may be seen here. Two more are 1 km from Bellavista; on private land, US$1.50 to enter, bring torch or pay for one – it takes about 30 mins to walk through the tunnels. Ask for Bolívar at *Pensión Gloria*, his ex-wife's family have lands with lava caves, a *mirador* and other attractions.

Hike to the **Chato Tortoise Reserve**, 7 km; the trail starts at Santa Rosa, 22 km from Puerto Ayora. Horses can be hired at Santa Rosa, US$6 each, guide compulsory, US$6.50 (again ask Bolívar at *Pensión Gloria*). A round trip takes 1 day. The Puerto Ayora-Bellavista bus stops at the turnoff for the track for the reserve (US$0.95). It's a hot walk; take food and drink. From Santa Rosa, distance to different sites within the reserve is 6-8 km (permit and guide not required). To walk to the Reserve from Santa Rosa, turn left past the school, follow the track at the edge of fields for 40 mins, turn right at the memorial to the Israeli, 20 mins later turn left down a track to Chato Trucha.

Two sinkholes, **Los Gemelos**, straddle the road to Baltra, beyond Santa Rosa; if you are lucky, take a *camioneta* all the way, otherwise to Santa Rosa, then walk. A good place to see the Galápagos hawk and barn owl.

The highlands and settlement area of Santa Cruz are worth seeing for the contrast of the vegetation with the arid coastal zones. Ask for Tim Grey and Anita Salcedo at *Garapata* in Puerto Ayora, they have a *finca* for arranging barbecues.

- **Transport To Santa Rosa and Bellavista**
From San Francisco school in Puerto Ayora buses leave for Santa Rosa and Bellavista at 0630, 1230 and 1630, 30-min trip, return immediately; fare for all destinations US$1. There are also trucks (cheaper). On roads to the main sites hitching is easy but expect to pay a small fee.

Local information – Puerto Ayora
Electricity is off between midnight and 0600 and INECEL cuts power to a different section of town from 1900-2200 every night. Most hotels have a portable generator. Carry a passport at all times.

- **Accommodation**
Hotel space is limited and reservations are strongly rec in high season.

L3 *Delfín*, on the far side of Academy Bay, with lovely beach (local class 1), expensive, accessible only by boat, write to Mrs Sievers.

A1 *Angermeyer*, Av Darwin y Piqueros, T (2) 222-198, F (2) 230-981, a/c extra, meals available, bath, laundry, pool, tours, bicycle hire, diving; **A3** *Galápagos*, bungalows with private bathroom, hot water, ocean-view, laundry service, generator, restaurant with fixed menu, fruit and meat from hotel farm, nr Darwin Research centre, reservations can be made through Ecuadorean travel agencies, day excursions can be made from hotel in Pedro and Sally García's own dinghy for 10, the *Fernandina*, also *Scuba Iguana*; **A3** *Red Mangrove Inn* (in Guayaquil T 880-618, F 880-617), 4 rooms oceanfront, hot showers, jacuzzi, deck bar, restaurant, warmly rec, owner Polo Navaro offers tours inc sea kayaking, highland farm, cruises in *Azul* and diving (*Nauti Diving*).

B *Las Ninfas*, very close to harbour, basic, cold showers, good restaurant, has its own boat at reasonable price for day trips and Fernando Jiménez is helpful with arrangements.

C *Castro*, with private bath, owned by Sr Miguel Castro, he arranges 7-day inclusive tours, includes Fri TAME flight, rec. He is an authority on wildlife and his tour includes 1 or 2 nights away visiting the islands of Plazas and Santiago, and a day-trip to Santa Fe, with visits to the tortoise reserve and the Darwin Institute.

D *Salinas*, opp *Lirio del Mar*, with bath and fan, clean, good value; **D** *Sol y Mar*, next to bank, cabins, meals available, 10% discount for stays of 2 weeks or more; reservations can be made by writing to the owner (Sr Jimmy Pérez), or Transgalapagos Inc, PO Box 11227, T 562-151, F (593) 4-382-444, Guayaquil; **D** *Las Palmeras*, good.

E *Elizabeth*, with bath, reasonable, owner very helpful; **E** pp *Lirio del Mar*, private bath, cafetería, laundry facilities, pleasant, clean; **E** pp *Lobo de Mar* with bath, modern, clean, can do laundry on roof.

F *Darwin*, with bath, restaurant (order meals in advance), rec but don't leave valuables in your room; **F** *España*, clean, good beds, hot water, excellent value, rec; **F** *Flamingo*, opp, with private bath, fan, decent, clean; **F** *Pensión Gloria*, 12 beds, simple, you can cook your own food over a wood fire, mosquito repellent needed, new rooms with unusual decor, laundry facilities; **F** *Los Amigos*, Av Darwin in front of TAME office, without bath, run by Sra Rosa Rosera, cool, reasonable, airy rooms (upstairs best), laundry facilities, clean, rec; **F** pp *Peregrino*, on main street behind *Restaurante Pippo*, inc good breakfast, highly rec.

- **Places to eat**
Expect slow service and shortages of items such as flour which will reduce menu availability. *Rincón del Alma*, nr the plaza, best, good food, reasonable prices; *Sir Francis Drake*, Av Darwin, excellent food, slow service; *Don Guillo*, next to tortoise roundabout on Av Darwin, good, slow service; *La Garrapata*, open air, on road to research station, popular meeting place for travellers, morning and evening but not Sun, drinks expensive; *Viña del Mar*, on main street, good value, popular with locals, OK; *Sol y Mar*, good but expensive breakfast on terrace full of marine iguanas; *4 Linternas*, pizza and Italian; *Trattoria de Pippo*, Italian; *Salvavida*, on the docks, good breakfast, *almuerzo*, seafood; *Media Luna Pizza*, also sandwiches, good; *Moon Rise Café*, good breakfast, highly rec. Restaurants serving cheap fish and seafood on the side streets.

- **Banks & money changers**
Banco del Pacífico, Av Charles Darwin, 0800-1700, good rates for TCs, but no cash advance. In emergency offers international telephone service, via Guayaquil, by Telex, Fax and satellite. Most boats accept US$ cash and TCs. The *Hotel Sol y Mar* will change notes and cheques, but at a poor rate. Several shops change US$ notes.

- **Embassies & consulates**
British Consul, David Balfour, c/o Etica, Barrio Estrada, Puerto Ayora.

● **Entertainment**

Cinema: each evening at 2015.

Music: *Disco La Panga*; *5 Fingers* disco and bar, popular; *Bar Frank*, Av Darwin next to Galápagos Sub-Aqua, travellers' hang-out.

● **Shopping**

For boat charters and camping trips most basic foodstuffs generally can be purchased on the islands, eg *Proinsular* supermarket opp the pier. The *mercado municipal* is on Padre Herrera, beyond the telephone office, on the way out of town to Santa Rosa. Fresh milk available in Puerto Ayora from Christine Aldaze, 0930, on main road (24 hrs notice appreciated). Medicines, sun lotions, mosquito coils, film, and other useful items are either not available or cost a lot more than on the mainland. *Galapaguito* can meet most tourists' needs, the owners are both naturalists, very helpful. There is a wide variety of T-shirt and souvenir shops, eg *Galápagos Souvenirs*; *Artesanías Bambú*, nr *Hotel Galápagos*. Do not buy items made of black coral; it is an endangered species.

● **Hospitals & medical services**

Hospitals: there is a hospital in Puerto Ayora; consultations US$10, medicines reasonably-priced, but they can not perform operations.

● **Laundry**

Ask at the *farmacia* nr *Hotel Santa Cruz*, good service. *Lavagal*, by football stadium, machine wash and dry US$0.80/lb, good, reliable, US$1 taxi ride from town.

● **Post & telecommunications**

Post Office: the Post Office sometimes runs out of stamps (never leave money and letters), ask in the 'red boat' (*Galería Jahanna*) or *Artesanías Bambú*. **Telephone office**: on Padre Herrera.

● **Sports**

Diving: *Galápagos Sub-Aqua*, Av Charles Darwin, the owner Fernando Zambrano provides courses for beginners and trips for the experienced, all equipment for hire, inc for snorkellers, T/F 526-350 (Dátiles 506 entre Quinta y Sexta, Guayaquil, T 304-132, F (593-4) 314-510), safe, rec. Day tours US$75 to US$100, inc boat, gear, instructor, 2 dives (mainly drift diving). Multi day tours inc meals, accommodation from US$130 pp/day. Introductory courses US$75/day. *Scuba Iguana*, Jack Nelson and Mathias Espinosa at *Hotel Galápagos*, experienced on the islands, knowledgeable about different sites; *Nauti Diving*, Polo Navaro at *Red Mangrove Inn*. Also Alvaro Solorzano, Rosa Borja de Icazay, El Oro, Barrio Centenario, US$80 for certification course.

For snorkelling, masks and snorkels can be rented from dive shops, US$4-5 a day, US$60 deposit. 1-day snorkelling tours US$15-20, 3 locations, rec, ask for Marcello through Marcos Martínez at *Bar/Restaurant Five Fingers*. **NB** Please help to maintain standards by not disturbing or touching underwater wildlife.

● **Tourist offices**

Cetur, on main road, open Mon-Fri 0800-1200, 1500-1600, T 328-312, 324-471. Information also available at the boat owners' cooperative office nearby.

● **Useful services**

Immigration: the immigration police will extend visas with a little persuasion for those who overstay their visa or tourist card.

Lost property: information and retrieval of lost property from Radio Santa Cruz, next to Catholic Church.

PUERTO BAQUERIZO MORENO

(*Pop* 3,023) on San Cristóbal island to the E, is the capital of the archipelago. The island is being developed as a second tourist centre.

Places of interest

In town, the cathedral, 2 blocks up from the post office, has interesting, mixed-media relief pictures on the walls and altar. Next door is the municipal museum of natural history; 0830-1200, 1530-1730, US$1, stuffed exhibits, old photos, a tortoise called Pepe.

Excursions on San Cristóbal

Bus (shuttle) to **El Progreso**, then 2½-hr walk to El Junco lake, tortoises may be seen on the way (but nothing to see if it's cloudy). The road continues to a school, above which is a shrine, a deserted restaurant and a *mirador* overlooking the different types of vegetation stretching to the coast. From El Progreso (tree house *El Tarzan* for rent; eating places), a trail crosses the high lands to **Cerro Brujo** and **Hobbs Bay**; also to **Stephens Bay**, past lakes.

A 3-hr hike to **Galapaguera** in the NE allows you to see tortoises in the wild. **At La Lobería**, beyond the airport, is a bay with shore birds, sea-lions and huge marine iguanas. You can continue along the cliff, but do not leave the trail, to see tortoises and rays.

Boats go to **Punta Pitt** in the far N

where you can see all three boobies. Off the NW coast is **Kicker Rock** (León Dormido), the basalt remains of a crater; many seabirds, including a masked and blue-footed boobies, can be seen around its cliffs (5-hr trip, inc snorkelling, rec). Up the coast is **Cerro Brujo** beach with sea-lions, birds, crabs (none in any abundance). Raul Sánchez offers short trips on his boat *Ana Mercedes*, ending in Puerto Ayora, much time spent travelling, T 529-163. Española (Hood) is within day trip reach.

Local information
● Accommodation
C *Orca*, OK, good food, has its own boat for cruises.

D *Hostal Galápagos*, E end of town, a/c cabins, fridge; **D** *Chatham*, on road to airport, with bath; **D** *Mar Azul*, on road to airport, with bath, hot showers, clean, nice gardens, rec, restaurant.

E *Res San Francisco*, with bath, good, clean; **E** *Res Northia*, with bath.

F pp *Cabañas Don Jorge*, close to beach, clean, 'not luxurious', member of Ecuadorean and International Youth Hostal Associations; **F** *Res Miramar*, good value, clean restaurant, good; **F** *Res Flamingo*, basic, clean.

● Places to eat
Rosita, best in town; *Nathaly*, good food, open late; *Chatham*; *Laurita*, fair; *La Terraza*, disco, on beach; *Fragata*, on road to airport. *Cafetería Tagu*, cheap.

● Banks & money changers
Banco del Pacífico, 0800-1700, 0800-1300 Sat, changes cash, cheques and gives cash against Mastercard. SAN office on Darwin, Mon, Tues, Wed, Fri 0800-1600, Thur and Sat 0800-1200.

● Hospitals & medical services
There is a hospital but if you need an operation you have to go yourself to the pharmacy to buy everything they need.

● Language school
Iguana Spanish School, Playa de Oro, T/F 520-233, Email: pat@etnet.ecx.ec, dive base, kayaking and mountain biking as well as Spanish courses.

● Post & telecommunications
Post Office: next to Banco Central on Av Charles Darwin (main street). **Telephone office**: on Av Quito.

● **Shopping**
There are a few souvenir shops (poorer quality than Puerto Ayora); best is *Edliz* for T-shirts, in Moorish-style house opp the jetty with the whale. Do not buy black coral.

● **Transport**
See **Travel Between the Islands**, above. Be warned that it can take several days to find room on a boat to Puerto Ayora.

ISABELA ISLAND

Isabela is not highly developed for tourism but if you have a few days to spare it is worthwhile spending time there.

Excursions

Good walks in the highlands (eg to Cerro Negro volcano) and beautiful beaches; also to the 'walking wall' left from the penal colony. Tours to the volcanoes can be made with two guides, compare prices. Horses can be hired. A 3-5 day trip can be arranged in Puerto Ayora at Darwin 606, 10 people required. Also ask Chino at Galápagos Sub-Aqua in Puerto Ayora about 3-day tours, inc riding, snorkelling, accommodation and food, US$150 pp. Marcos Martínez in Puerto Ayora offers 4 day/3 night tours, min 6 people, US$275 pp, inc food and lodging. The climb up the volcanoes takes 3 days, 1 for the ascent, 1 at the top and 1 to come down.

● **Accommodation** E *Alexandra*, nice site on the beach; E *Loja*, on the road to the highland, clean, sometimes water shortages, patio, cheap and very good restaurant; *El Rincón del Bucanero*, on the beach, more expensive; F *Isabela del Mar*, good food, water supplied, rec; F *El Capitán*, pleasant; E-F pp *Ballena Azul*, T (593-5) 529-125 or through *Safari Tours*, Quito, safe, clean, family atmosphere, rooms or cabins, meals available, rec, run by Dora Gruber, Swiss; G *Antonio Gil*, rents 2 rooms with shower, friendly, helpful, tours arranged with horses. There are a few *comedores* but food is seldom available unless you order in advance.

● **Transport**
An airport is being built at Villamil and a light aircraft shuttle is operating from San Cristóbal. Besides Ingala on Thur (see above), *Estrella del Mar* sails from Puerto Ayora on Wed, or contact fishermen, US$20-30; ask for Don Vicente at Proinsular office.

GENERAL ADVICE

● **Tipping**
On a cruise, it will be suggested to you that you tip US$50-100/passenger for the crew and the same for the guide. As elsewhere, tips should always reflect service, and should be given according to the service in relation to what you requested. On first and secondhand evidence, it appears that US$25-30/cabin is the top limit, and that for outstanding service.

● **If you have problems**
See above for complaints regarding itineraries. If a crew member comes on strong with a woman passenger, the matter should first be raised with the guide or captain. If this does not yield results, a formal complaint, in Spanish, giving the crew member's full name, the boat's name and the date of the cruise, should be sent to Sr Capitán del Puerto, Base Militar de Armada Ecuatoriana, Puerto Ayora, Santa Cruz, Galápagos. Failure to report such behaviour will mean it will continue. To avoid pilfering, never leave belongings unattended in Puerto Ayora, or on a beach when another boat is in the bay.

● **What to take**
A remedy for seasickness is rec; the waters S of Santa Cruz are particularly choppy. A good supply of sun block and skin cream to prevent windburn and chapped lips is essential. A hat and sunglasses are also rec. You should be prepared for dry and wet landings, the latter involving wading ashore.

Take plenty of film with you; the birds are so tame that you will use far more than you expected; a telephoto lens is not essential, but if you have one, bring it. Also take filters suitable for strong sunlight. Snorkelling equipment is particularly useful as much of the sea-life is only visible under water. Most of the cheaper boats do not provide equipment and those that do may not have good snorkelling gear. If in doubt, bring your own, rent in Puerto Ayora, or buy it in Quito. It is possible to sell it afterwards either on the islands or try the *Gran Casino* travel agency in Quito.

● **The cost of living**
The cost of living in the Galápagos is high, particularly in the peak season (Dec, July and Aug). Most food has to be imported although certain meats, fish, vegetables and fruit are available locally in the Puerto Ayora market. Bottled drinks are expensive, beer US$1.50.

● **Recommended reading**
The *Galápagos Guide* by Alan White and Bruce White Epler, with photographs by Charles Gilbert, is published in several languages; it can be bought in Guayaquil in Librería Científica and

the airport, Libri Mundi (US$5) in Quito, or at the Charles Darwin station. The South American Explorers Club in Quito sells a useful brief guide, *Galapagos Package*, US$4.

Galápagos: the Enchanted Isles by David Horwell (London: Dryad Press, 1988, available through his agency).

The Enchanted Isles. The Galápagos Discovered, John Hickman (Anthony Nelson, 1985).

The Galápagos Affair, John Treherne (Jonathan Cape, 1983).

Journal of the Voyage of HMS Beagle, by Charles Darwin, first published in 1845. Penguin Books of the UK have published Darwin's account of the Galápagos in their Penguin 60s Classics series.

The Galápagos Islands, 1:500,000 map by Kevin Healey and Hilary Bradt (Bradt Publications, 1985).

Galápagos: A Natural History Guide, Michael H Jackson (University of Calgary Press, 1985).

Reef Fish Identification, Paul Humann (Libri Mundi, 1993).

A Field Guide to the Fishes of Galápagos, Godfrey Merlen (Libri Mundi, 1988).

Plants of the Galápagos Islands, Eileen Schofield (New York: Universe Books, 1984).

A Guide to the Birds of the Galápagos Islands, Isabel Castro and Antonia Phillips (Christopher Helm, 1996).

The Galápagos Conservation Trust (18 Curzon Street, London W1Y 7AD, T 0171 626 5049, F 0171 629 4149, publishes a quarterly Newsletter for its members.

Noticias de Galápagos is a twice-yearly publication about science and conservation in the Islands. It is the official publication of the Charles Darwin Foundation. 'Friends of the Galápagos' (US$25/year membership) receive the journal as a part of their membership.

The Charles Darwin Research Station can be reached via the Internet: http://fcdarwin.org.ec/welcome.html.

The Galápagos Coalition web pages are also worth visiting: http://www.law.emory.edu/PI/ GALAPAGOS.

Information for travellers

BEFORE TRAVELLING

ENTRY REQUIREMENTS

● **Documents**

A passport (valid for at least 6 months required on arrival at Quito airport), and a tourist card valid for 90 days obtainable on arrival. Tourists are now allowed only 90 days on entry in any 365-day period; you can leave the country and return within that 90 days, but if your 90 days end on 31 Dec, you cannot return in Jan, you have to wait 12 months for another 90-day entitlement. You are required to say how many days you intend to stay and the card and your passport will be stamped accordingly; most travellers are given 15 or 30-day stamps irrespective of their requests (at Huaquillas, Macará and Tulcán), and travellers arriving by air may be given a stamp valid for only 10 days (transit pass) unless they request otherwise. It is therefore better to overestimate as you can be fined on leaving the country for staying too long.

Extensions can be routinely obtained at the Policía Nacional de Migración in Quito, or at the Jefatura Provincial de Migración in any provincial capital (except Portoviejo, go to Manta instead); 30 days are given for each extension, which cost approximately US$2.50 (payable in sucres), up to a maximum of 90 additional days (180 days total). If you are late in applying there is a US$3 fine. Evidence of sufficient funds (see below) is sometimes required.

French citizens need a **visa**; US$30, 4 photos, a return ticket and at least 6 months validity on passport required. A visa is also required for those from China, N and S Korea, Vietnam, Cuba, Guatemala, Costa Rica, Honduras, India, Sri Lanka, Pakistan and Bangladesh. Business people and students who stay longer than 90 days must apply for a visa in their home country and they must get an exit permit (*permiso de salida*, once obtained this is valid for multiple trips out of Ecuador during one year) with both tax and police clearance. It costs US$17 for renewing a visa after its expiry date; extending a 90-day consular visa is not easy. If travelling on anything other than a 90-day tourist card, check if you need to register upon arrival with the Extranjería and Policía Nacional de Migración as well as obtaining an exit permit.

Tourists attending a course at a language school do **not** need a student visa (unless staying more than 90 days). A **student visa** for a longer course is given for 6 months and involves a lot of paperwork in your home country and in Ecuador. Verify all details at the Consulate before departure.

NB Students visiting the Galápagos, and in other cases, are entitled to discounts. Because of local, counterfeit international student cards, they do not accept Ecuadorean-issued student cards. ISICs are sometimes honoured, but proof of home student status is essential. See page 1025 on purchasing student ID in Quito.

Tourists crossing from Colombia or Peru may be asked for evidence that they possess US$20 pp for each day they propose to spend in Ecuador. Theoretically you must have an onward ticket out of Ecuador, but this is almost never enforced if you are travelling overland. However, travellers arriving from Miami by plane have been refused entry without a ticket and an MCO may not be sufficient.

Warning Always carry your passport with you, or a photocopy with the immigration visa date, except when travelling in the Oriente on flights or border areas when the real thing is required. Failure to produce this as identification could result in imprisonment. Tourists are not permitted to work under any circumstances.

● **Representation overseas**

Australia, 388 George St, Suite 1702 A, American Express Tower NSW 2000, Sydney, 223-3266, 223-0041; **Belgium**, Chaussée de Charleroi No 70, 1060 Brussels, T 0 537-9193, F 0 537-9066; **Canada**, 50 O'Connor Str #,1311, Ottawa, ON K1P 6L2, T 613 563-8206, F 613 235-5776, 151 Bloor St West, Suite 470 Toronto, Ontario M5S 1S4, T 416 968-2077, F 416 968-3348, 1010 Sainte Catherine W #,440, Montreal, QC H3B 3R3, T 514 874-4071, F 514 874-9078; **France**, 34 Ave de Messine, 75008 Paris, T 1 456 11021, F 1 425 60664; **Germany**, Koblenzer Strasse 37, 5300 Bonn 2, T 0 288 352544, F 0 228 361765; **New Zealand**, Ferry Bldg, 2 Floor, Quai St, Auckland, T 09 309-0229, F 09 303-2931; **Sweden**, Engelbrektsgatan 13, Box 260 95, S-100 41 Stockholm, T 0 679-6043, F 0 611-5593; **Switzerland**, Helvetiastrasse 19-A, 3005 Berne, T 031 351-1755, F 031 351-2771; **UK**, Flat 3B, 3 Hans Crescent, Knightsbridge, London, SW1X 0LS, T 0171 584-1367.

● **Tourist information**

Corporación Ecuatoriana de Turismo (Cetur), Eloy Alfaro 1214 y Carlos Tobar, Quito, T 507-559/560, F 507-564. The addresses of tourist offices are given in the **Local information** sections. Cetur has constructed an internet site http//mia.lac.net/mintur/ingles. Limited at the moment, Cetur are promising great things in the future.

● **Tour Operator**

Amerindia, based in Quito, is a new regional ground operator, who cover Ecuador, Bolivia, and Peru (as well as Belize, Costa Rica and Guatemala). It has been created to rediscover the wonders of Latin America. Tours are of the highest quality with experienced guides. Accommodation is in superb lodges. Among tours being offered will be luxury safari-style tents, land rover circuits and yacht charters along the coasts. Further information from Amerindia's head office T (593) 2 439736/469455, F (593) 2 439735, Email amerindi@pi.pro.ec, in UK from Penelope Kellie T (44) 1962 779317, F (44) 1962 779458, Email pkellie@yachtors.u-net.com, in USA T (1) 305 599 9008, F (1) 305 592 7060.

MONEY

● **Currency**

The sucre is the unit of currency. Bank notes of the Banco Central de Ecuador are for 100, 500 (both being phased out), 1,000, 5,000, 10,000, 20,000 and 50,000 sucres; there are nickel coins of 50, 100 and 500 sucres. (A 100,000 sucre note and a 1,000 sucre coin were expected by end-1996.)

There is no restriction on the amount of foreign money or sucres you can take into or out of Ecuador. It is very easy to change US$ cheques into US$ notes at the *cambios*; the commission varies so it is worth shopping around and *cambios* sometimes run out of US$ notes; you can try to bargain for a better rate than shown on the blackboard. Most banks charge no commission on US$ cheques into sucres. Note that although many hotels and restaurants have signs indicating acceptance of credit cards, this is often not the case; always check first. ATMs in the Mastercard/Cirrus network can be found in branches of Banco del Pacífico, Banco General de Crédito, Banco de Préstamos and Banco Holandés Unido. Visa ATMs are at Banco de Guayaquil and Filanbanco branches. Note that difficulties have been reported with Amex cards, an alternative credit card may be more useful. It is quite difficult to change TCs outside the main towns, especially in the Oriente. US$ money orders cannot be exchanged anywhere in Ecuador. For Western Union money transfers, T (2) 565-059 in Quito.

GETTING THERE

AIR

● **From Europe**

Air France three times from Paris to Quito. Iberia flies from Madrid to Quito via Santo Domingo, Dominican Republic, twice weekly. KLM flies 4 times weekly from Amsterdam to Guayaquil and Quito via Aruba and/or Curaçao. Lufthansa flies from Frankfurt to Quito three times weekly via Bogotá.

● **From North America**

There are flights from New York to Quito and Guayaquil with Saeta, which also flies from Miami. Ecuatoriana flies from New York to Quito and from Miami to Quito and Guayaquil. American Airlines fly daily from Miami to Quito and Guayaquil. Continental flies from Houston to Quito and Guayaquil and from Newark via Panama. LanChile flies Miami-Guayaquil. Servivensa flies from Los Angeles via Central America. From other US cities make connections in Miami.

● **From Latin American cities**

Bogotá (Lufthansa, Air France, Continental, Saeta, Avianca, Servivensa and AeroPerú to Quito; Saeta to Guayaquil); Cali to Esmeraldas with TAME; Lima (LAB, Saeta, Servivensa, Avianca and Aeroperú to Quito, Copa, Saeta and AeroPerú to Guayaquil); Caracas (Saeta to Quito and Guayaquil, Avianca, Servivensa to Quito only, LanChile to Guayaquil only); Panama (to Quito and Guayaquil Saeta, Tame, Continental and Copa); Santiago de Chile (LanChile to Guayaquil, Ecuatoriana and Tame to Quito and Guayaquil – Ecuatoriana's flights start in Buenos Aires, Saeta to Quito). From Brazil Lacsa and Ecuatoriana to Guayaquil and Quito from São Paulo and Rio de Janeiro, Ecuatoriana also from Manaus; Lacsa also flies to San José. Connections with other Central American capitals in San José or Panama City; Copa's Lima-Guayaquil-Panama routes continues to Santo Domingo and San Juan, 4 times a week.

CUSTOMS

Personal effects, a litre of spirits and a reasonable amount of perfume are admitted free of duty.

ON ARRIVAL

● **Clothing**

Spring clothing for Quito (mornings and evenings are cold). In Guayaquil tropical or lightweight clothes. An unkempt look is said to attract a 'gringo tax' and reduce friendliness. Laundering is excellent.

● **Official time**

Local time is 5 hrs behind GMT (Galápagos, 6 hrs behind.)

● **Safety**

Although Ecuador has been generally one of the safer countries in the region, there have been reports of increased crime and violence: police searches are now more frequent. If your luggage is searched, make sure that you are present during the search: women travelling alone, especially in Otavalo, should beware of police officers who ask to look at their passport and then insist on taking them to a police station. Theft and mugging are on the increase throughout Quito, particularly in the old city, climbing Panecillo and Pichincha direct from the city side; also Tungurahua and on the beaches at Manta and near Atacames. Guayaquil has long been plagued with gang violence, which is also present in the city of Esmeraldas, caution is also advised at nearby beaches. Robberies on city buses, even in the morning, and intercity bus holdups are now more common. There have been guerrilla incursions from Colombia and drug related violence in the northern jungle province of Sucumbios, but many of the public safety problems are worst in the big cities while the countryside has remained generally safer and more tranquil. See *Latin American Travel Advisor* above for safety information.

● **Tipping**

In restaurants, 10% usually in the bill (in cheaper restaurants, tipping is uncommon – but obviously welcome!). Taxi, nil. Airport and railway porters, US$0.10-0.20, according to number of suitcases; cloakroom attendants, US$0.05, hairdressers, 20%.

● **Voltage**

110 volts, 60 cycles, AC throughout Ecuador. Very low wattage bulbs in many hotel rooms, keen readers are advised to carry a bright bulb.

● **Weights and measures**

The metric system is generally used in foreign trade and must be used in legal documents. English measures are understood in the hardware and textile trades. Spanish measures are often used in the retail trade.

ON DEPARTURE

● **Airport tax**

There is a 10% tax on international air tickets for flights originating in Ecuador, regardless of where bought, and 12% on domestic tickets, and a tax of US$25 on all passengers departing on international flights (except those who stay under 24 hrs in the country).

WHERE TO STAY

● **Hotels**

Outside the main towns; almost standard prices are charged of US$2.50-4 pp (without bath) in a *pensión*, *residencial*, or hotel (where this is the minimum charge). One can bargain at cheaper *pensiones* and *residenciales*. Outside the provincial capitals and the resorts of Salinas and Playas, there are few higher-class hotels. Service of 10% and tax of 10% are added to 1st and 2nd class hotel and restaurant bills. The cheaper hotels charge at most 5%, if anything. Hotel owners tend to try and let their less attractive rooms first, but they are not insulted if you ask for a bigger room, better beds or a quieter area. The difference is often marked.

● **Camping**

Bluet Camping Gas is easily obtainable, but white gas, like US Coleman fuel, is not available. Stoves should either burn Camping Gas, a compressed gas which comes in a non-refillable cylinder, kerosene, or unleaded car gas/petrol (generally an acceptable substitute for white gas). For stoves, kerosene is known as 'kerex' and is available at many rural petrol stations and in outdoor markets in towns and cities outside Quito; it is, however, very impure. Unleaded gasoline is better (Eco 85 or Super SP). Pure alcohol fuel is sold in hardware stores, *ferreterías*, take your own bottle or ask for it 'en bolsa' (in a plastic bag).

FOOD AND DRINK

FOOD

The cuisine varies extensively with region. The following are some typical dishes worth trying. **In the highlands**: *locro de papas* (potato and cheese soup), *mote* (corn burst with alkali, a staple in the region around Cuenca, but used in a variety of dishes in the Sierra), *caldo de patas* (cowheel soup with *mote*), *llapingachos* (fried potato and cheese patties), *empanadas de morocho* (fried snacks: a ground corn shell filled with meat), *morocho* is a drink made from *mote*, milk, sugar and cinnamon, *sancocho de yuca* (vegetable soup with manioc root), roast *cuy* (guinea pig), *fritada* (fried pork), *hornado* (roast pork), *humitas* (tender ground corn steamed in corn leaves), and *quimbolitos* (similar to *humitas* but prepared with corn flour and steamed in banana leaves). *Humitas* and *quimbolitos* come in both sweet and savoury varieties.
On the coast: *empanadas de verde* (fried snacks: a ground plantain shell filled with cheese, meat or shrimp), *sopa de bola de verde* (plantain dumpling soup), *ceviche* (marinaded fish or seafood, popular everywhere, see below), *encocadas* (dishes prepared with coconut milk, may be shrimp, fish, etc, very popular in the province of Esmeraldas), *cocadas* (sweets made with coconut), *viche* (fish or seafood soup made with ground peanuts), and *patacones* (thick fried plantain chips served as a side dish).
In Oriente: dishes prepared with yuca (manioc or cassava root) and a wide variety of river fish.
Throughout the country, if economizing ask for the set meal in restaurants, *almuerzo* at lunch time, *merienda* in the evening – very cheap and wholesome; it costs US$1-2. *Fanesca*, a fish soup with beans, many grains, ground peanuts and more, sold in Easter Week, is very filling. *Ceviche*, marinated fish or seafood which is usually served with popcorn and roasted maize, is very popular throughout Ecuador. Only *ceviche de pescado* (fish) and *ceviche de concha* (clams) which are marinated raw, potentially pose a cholera hazard. The other varieties of *ceviche* such as *camarón* (shrimp/prawn) and *langostino* (jumbo shrimp/king prawn) all of which are cooked before being marinated, are

generally safe (check the cleanliness of the establishment). *Langosta* (lobster) is an increasingly endangered species but continues to be illegally fished. It is out of season until the year 2000, please be conscientious. Ecuadorean food is not particularly spicy. However, in most homes and restaurants, the meal is accompanied by a small bowl of *ají* (hot pepper sauce) which may vary greatly in potency. *Colada* is a generic name which can refer to cream soups or sweet beverages. In addition to the prepared foods mentioned above, Ecuador offers large variety of delicious temperate and tropical fruits, some of which are unique to South America. Chocolate lovers can try the Superior and Rico bars, good quality, excellent value.
VAT/IVA of 12% is charged in food shops.

DRINK

Argentine and Chilean wines are available in the larger cities and cheaper than European or US ones. The best fruit drinks are *naranjilla*, *maracuyá*, *taxo* and *mora* (blackberries), but note that fruit juices are often made with unboiled water. Main beers available are Pilsener and Club. Good *aguardiente* (unmatured rum, Cristal is rec), *paico* and *trago de caña*. The usual soft drinks, known as *colas*, are available. Instant coffee or liquid concentrate is common, so ask for *café puro* if you want real coffee.

GETTING AROUND

AIR TRANSPORT

The local airlines Saeta, SAN, TAME and Aerogal operate internal flights between the main cities. TAME and SAN fly to the Galápagos; both have received favourable reports on reliability and baggage control. Also local airline Cedta operating Santa Rosa, near Machala-Guayaquil. Ecuavia and Icaro operate charter flights. There are air taxis (Cessnas or Bonanzas) to anywhere you want to go, also helicopters. On internal flights passengers may have to disembark at intermediate stops and check in, even though they have booked all the way to the final destination of the plane. Seats are not assigned on internal flights, except to the Galápagos. *Prechequeo* procedures speed up boarding as passes are issued up to 8 days in advance. If you miss the plane you need half a day and US$5 to revalidate your ticket for another flight. Your space on the plane is held until loading.

LAND TRANSPORT
● Trains
The future of all trains is under debate (a combination of severely decaying infrastructure, a

lack of money and possible privatization). A 2-tier price system operates for Ecuadoreans and foreigners. Rail services are often unreliable, depending on weather.

● **Bus**

Bus travel is generally more convenient, and cheaper, than in other Andean countries. Since most buses are small they fill up and leave at frequent intervals. Several companies use luxury a/c units on their longer routes. All are called Volvo, even if they are other makes. Fares for these are higher and some companies have their own stations, away from the main bus terminals, exclusively for the new buses. The length of paved highway is developing rapidly, inc Quito-Guayaquil, Quito-Riobamba, Quito-Tulcán, Quito-Cuenca, Guayaquil-Cuenca, Guayaquil-Riobamba, Riobamba-Baños and the lowland (Costa) road Huaquillas-Machala-Guayaquil-Babahoyo-Santo Domingo-Esmeraldas. New tolls are due to be introduced on main highways.

● **Motoring**

Driving in Ecuador has been described as 'an experience', partly because of unexpected pot-holes and other obstructions and the lack of road signs, partly because of local drivers' tendency to use the middle of the road. Some surfaces at high altitude are slippery and some, that appear paved, are crude oil sprayed onto compacted gravel. Beware the bus drivers, who often drive very fast and rather recklessly (passengers also please note). Driving at night is not rec, especially in rural areas where speed humps to reduce speed in villages have become places for robbers to lurk.

'Extra' gasoline, 82 octane, costs US$1.20/US gallon, Eco 85 (85 octane unleaded, also known as *gasolina verde*, although it is coloured red rather than green), US$1.25, Super SP (92 octane unleaded), US$1.40, diesel US$1.20. Unleaded gasoline is becoming increasingly common throughout the country although it may still be unavailable in the more remote rural areas and in parts of Oriente. Super is only available in the main cities.

Documents A *carnet de passage* (or *libreta de pasaje*, known locally as a *triptico*) is no longer required to enter Ecuador with a car or motorcycle, but many have found their passage eased by being able to present one.

If intending to buy a car or motorcycle, you must have an international drivers licence (bring one from home, costs US$70 in Ecuador). Use a lawyer to help sort out ownership documentation. **NB** Vehicles imported from Peru cannot be sold in Ecuador.

Shipping Shipping in a vehicle through Guayaquil is also hazardous; you will be charged by customs for every day the car is left there and will need assistance from an agent. Spare cash may be needed. Manta is a smaller, more relaxed and efficient alternative port. If bringing in a motorcycle by air it can take over a week to get it out of customs. You need a customs agent, who can be found around the main customs building near the airport, fix the price in advance. Best to accompany the agent all the time and a letter from the Ecuadorean Automobile Club (ANETA) can be helpful. If you need boxes/cartons to send bicycles home, *Global Transportes*, Veintimilla 878 y Av Amazonas, p 3, might be able to help you (German-run).

● **Car hire**

In 1996, a small car at Budget cost, including 10% tax, US$10/day, plus US$0.10/km or US$168 for a week with unlimited kms. A 4WD Trooper (rec for trips to the Oriente and the higher peaks) cost US$19/day inc tax, plus US$0.19/km or US$328 for a week with unlimited kms. A 10% tax is always added to the posted prices, insurance is in the range of US$5.50-7/day, drop off charge (for returning the vehicle in a city other than where it was rented) US$70. Be sure to check the car's condition and make sure it has good ground clearance. Always make sure the car is securely garaged at night.

In order to rent a car you must be 25 and have an international credit card. You may pay cash, which is cheaper and may allow you to bargain, but they want a credit card for security. You may be asked to sign two blank credit card vouchers, one for the rental fee itself and the other as a security deposit, and authorization for a charge of as much as US$1,000 may be requested against your credit card account. These arrangements are all above board and the uncashed vouchers will be returned to you when you return the vehicle, but the credit authorization may persist on your account (reducing your credit limit) for up to 30 days. Be careful when dealing with some of the smaller agencies. Some car hire firms do not have adequate insurance policies and you will have to pay heavily in the event of an accident.

● **Hitchhiking**

Hitchhiking on the main roads is reported to be easy in the N, but nearly impossible S of Riobamba, and it can be very cold in the mountains in the back of a truck (when hitching, it is common to pay a small sum). In the arid S the unpaved roads are dusty; use a wet cotton handkerchief to filter the air you breathe. Whether hitching or driving always take plenty of drinking water. Be judicious when accepting a ride or picking up hitchhikers, armed car robberies by the latter are increasingly common.

COMMUNICATIONS

● Language

The official language is Spanish. English and other European languages are spoken in many establishments catering for tourists in Quito and popular tourist destinations. Away from these places, knowledge of Spanish is essential.

● Newspapers

The main newspapers are *El Comercio*, *Hoy*, *Tiempo*, and *Ultimas Noticias*, in Quito; *Expreso*, *El Telégrafo*, *El Universo* (with good international news), *La Prensa*, *La Razón* and *Extra* (an afternoon paper), in Guayaquil; *El Mercurio*, in Cuenca; *La Opinión del Sur*, in Loja; and *El Espectador*, in Riobamba. *City* is a free weekly magazine in Quito, with tourist information and details of what's on; a similar magazine is *The Explorer*.

● Postal services

Many post offices away from Quito may not know the foreign rates (20g airmail to the Americas US$0.65, Europe and rest of world US$0.84) and give incorrect ones. For US$1.15 you can certify your letters and parcels; ask for 'con certificado' when you buy stamps, so that they are stamped separately. The only post office (probably in all Ecuador) which deals in International Reply Coupons is in Quito, at Eloy Alfaro 354 y 9 de Octubre (new city). **For sending parcels**: up to 20 kg maximum dimensions permitted is 70 x 30 x 30 cms. Take contents and packaging (unsealed) to the Correo Marítimo Aduana, Ulloa 273 y Ramírez Dávalos (next to the Santa Clara Market – not a safe area), for customs inspection. Ask for SAL/APR (surface-air-lifted, reduced priority) rates for the cheapest tariffs. Parcels under 20 kg can also be sent from the post office at Reina Victoria y Colón. The Post Office at the airport is more helpful and the smaller quantity of packages being handled should mean less chance of them going astray. Rates vary according to weight and destination. Packages under 2 kg can be sent 'certificado' (US$5.50 for 1 kg to the Americas, US$16 to rest of world; 2 kg US$9.15 within the Americas, US$30 other continents; for 3-5 kg US$33 within Americas, US$76 other continents) from the post offices at Espejo, entre Guayaquil y Venezuela, and at Eloy Alfaro. Rates quoted are for airmail: SAL/APR, surface-air-lifted rates are US$23 (3-5 kg) and US$32 (5-10 kg) to USA, US$28 and 43 elsewhere. Transpak (also called STAIR), Amazonas y Veintimilla, will ship out packages for about US$4/kg to USA, minimum charge about US$50. Letters for Europe bearing the correct Ecuadorean postage can be dropped off at the Lufthansa office, 6 de Diciembre 955 y 18 de Setiembre, to be sent in the next international bag; by 1200 on the day before the flight. Packages coming in to Ecuador should be less than 2 kg and of no stated value to avoid hefty import duty.

NB Some correspondents report that parcels and letters sent 'certificado' are more vulnerable to theft and that packages should be marked as 'used clothing' and 'no commercial value'. Even if not certifying your mail, watch to see that the stamps are franked (then they cannot be stolen). For cardboard boxes and large, strong, plastic-lined envelopes, try Japon Color Film Lab on Amazonas, Quito.

● Telephone services

All the principal towns have long-distance telephone facilities. Interprovincial phone calls must be prefixed by the following codes: Pichincha 02; Bolívar, Cotopaxi, Chimborazo, Pastaza, Tungurahua 03; Guayas 04; Galápagos, Los Ríos, Manabí 05; Carchi, Esmeraldas, Imbabura, Napo, Sucumbios 06; Azuay, Cañar, El Oro, Loja, Morona, Zamora 07. For cellular phones 09. Discount period 1900-0700 and all day Sat-Sun: 3 mins to USA US$11 person to person (regular), US$9 (discount); to Europe US$13.60 person to person (regular), US$11 (discount). For international operator dial 116, normally only 5-20 mins wait for call to UK. There is an acute shortage of lines, expect long waits from outlying areas. Direct lines to foreign countries for collect or credit cards are available: dial 999 then for Brazil 177, Canada 175, Chile 179, Italy 174, Spain 176, Switzerland 160, UK 178, USA 119, 170, 171, 172. Collect calls can be made from Ecuador to some countries (not Australia, Denmark, Germany or Belgium). A charge is made for person-to-person calls even when the person is not there. Fax to Europe from US$7.10/page; to USA US$5.80/page; US$8.40 Asia and Oceania; US$3.70 Andean countries. Telegrams, ordinary US$4.30 first 7 words and US$0.57/word thereafter, nightletter US$0.20/word. There are public telex booths in the best hotels in Quito and Guayaquil (US$13.50 for 3 mins), and at Cuenca.

SPORT

The Sierra country is excellent for riding, and good horses can be hired. Quito, Guayaquil and Riobamba have polo clubs. There are golf clubs at Guayaquil and Quito and on the Santa Elena Peninsula. There is excellent big-game fishing for bonito and marlin off Playas, Salinas and Manta. Bull fighting is rarely seen at Guayaquil, but there is a well-known bullfight festival during the week preceding 6 Dec at Quito. A favourite sport is cock fighting; every town has its pits, but association football is fast taking over as the national sport. Volleyball and basketball are also popular. There is Sun horse-racing at Guayaquil.

HOLIDAYS AND FESTIVALS

1 Jan: New Year's Day; **6 Jan**: Reyes Magos y Día de los Inocentes; **27 Feb**: Día del Civismo; **Lent**: Mon and Tues before Lent (Carnival); **Easter**: Holy Thursday, Good Friday, Holy Saturday; **1 May**: Labour Day; **24 May**: Battle of Pichincha; **early June**: Corpus Christi; **24 July**: Birthday of Bolívar; **10 Aug**: first attempt to gain the Independence of Quito, Opening of Congress; **9 Oct**: Independence of Guayaquil; **12 Oct**: Columbus' arrival in America; **1 Nov**: All Saints' Day; **2 Nov**: All Souls' Day; **3 Nov**: Independence of Cuenca and Manta; **4 Nov**: Independence of Azóguez and Bahía; **6 Dec**: Foundation of Quito; **25 Dec**: Christmas Day.

ACKNOWLEDGEMENTS

We are most grateful to Alan Murphy for updating this chapter. For their assistance in the preparation of the text, thanks are due to Gavin Clark (London), and Jean Brown (Quito), and to the South American Explorers Club in Quito and Robert and Daisy Kunstaetter (Quito) for additional information.

Paraguay

HORIZONS

THE LAND

Paraguay is entirely landlocked, surrounded by Argentina, Bolivia and Brazil. It is divided into two by the Río Paraguay.

The only practicable water route is by the Paraná to the Plata estuary, and Buenos Aires, 1,450 km from Asunción. So difficult is the river that communication with Buenos Aires was mainly by road before the railway to Asunción was opened in 1913. Although river barges still ply along the Paraná, and plans for new waterways from the Paraná to the Atlantic are being drawn up, most freight is moved to Buenos Aires, or to Santos or Paranaguá in Brazil, by good paved roads.

Eastern Paraguay East of the river is Paraguay proper (159,800 sq km), a rich land in which most of the population live. This part of the country consists of two contrasting areas separated by an escarpment which runs almost due N from the Río Alto Paraná, W of Encarnación, to the Brazilian border. East of the escarpment is the Paraná Plateau which extends across neighbouring parts of Argentina and Brazil. The Plateau, which is crossed by the Río Paraná, ranges from 300 to 600m in height, was originally forest and enjoys relatively high levels of rainfall. West of the escarpment and stretching to the Río Paraguay lies a fertile plain with rolling, wooded hills, drained by several tributaries of the Río Paraná. Most of the population of Paraguay lives in these hilly lands, stretching SE from the capital, Asunción, to Encarnación. Much of the plain is flooded once a year; it is wet savanna, treeless, but covered with coarse grasses.

Western Paraguay The Chaco, 246,950 sq km, nearly 61% of the country's area, is a flat, infertile plain stretching N along the W bank of the Río Paraná. The marshy, unnavigable Río Pilcomayo, which flows SE across the Chaco to join the Río Paraguay near Asunción, forms the frontier with Argentina. The landscape and people are described in full on page 1191. The *quebracho* (axe-breaker) tree, the world's principal source (with mimosa) of tannin, comes from the scrub forests of the Chaco and of the Río Paraná.

CLIMATE

The climate is sub-tropical, with a marked difference between summer and winter and often between one day and the next throughout the year. Summer (Jan-Mar) is hot (and humid in Asunción). Temperatures range from 25° to 43°C. The autumn (April-June) is mild, but nights are cold. During winter (July-Sept) the temperature can be as low as 5°C, though it can also be much higher. Temperatures below freezing are rare, and it never snows. The

Paraguay

1. Asunción
2. East from Asunción
3. South from Asunción
4. North from Asunción
5. The Paraguayan Chaco

This map has been tilted in order to fit the whole country on a single page. See angle of North symbol for true north.

heaviest rains are from Oct to April, but some rain falls each month.

HISTORY

Spanish colonization The original inhabitants of present day Paraguay were the semi-nomadic Guaraní Indians; by the 16th century they had spread to the foothills of the Andes, along the coast of Brazil, and even into the basin of the Amazon. In 1524, the first Spaniards reached the Río Paraguay, under the navigator Diego de Solís. A member of Solís's expedition, Alejo García, was the first European to cross Paraguay, leading an expedition NW through the Chaco in search of El Dorado in 1525; he was also the first European to fight against the Incas, as his career included an attack on them with a Guaraní army of 2,000. Spanish settlement in the area came later: an expedition led by Juan de Ayolas came from Buenos Aires, where the earliest Spanish settlement was planted unsuccessfully in 1536. Finding no gold along the Río de la Plata, and harassed by the hostile Indians of the Pampa, they pushed N along the river, seeking a short route to the gold and silver of Peru. They reached the Guaraní Indians in 1537 and a member of the party, Juan de Salazar de Espinosa, is generally credited with founding Asunción on 15 August.

Asunción became the nucleus of Spanish settlement in southeastern South America. Spaniards pushed NW across the Chaco to found Santa Cruz, in Bolivia, eastwards to occupy the rest of Paraguay, and southwards down the river to re-found Buenos Aires in 1580, 43 years after they had abandoned it.

The Jesuit Missionaries During the colonial era one of the world's most interesting experiments in dealing with a native population was carried out, not by the Spanish conquerors, but by their missionaries, over whom the civil power had at first little control. In 1609 the Society of Jesus sent missionaries to Paraguay to convert and 'civilize' the Indians. During the 158 years until they were expelled in 1767, the Jesuits established 30 *reducciones*, or settlements, run along theocratic-socialist lines. They induced the Indians to leave the forests and settle in the *reducciones* where they helped build magnificent churches, employing unsuspected native skills in masonry, sculpture, and painting. Selected natives were even given a sound classical education. The first *reducciones* were further N, but they were forced to abandon these because of attacks by the *bandeirantes* of São Paulo, Brazil. They settled finally in Misiones; parts of the area of settlement are now in Argentina and southern Brazil. After the expulsion of the Jesuits, the *reducciones* fell to pieces: the Indians left, and were reduced to peonage under other masters. Most of the great churches have fallen into ruin, or been destroyed; the few that remain are dealt with in the text (see also under San Ignacio Miní, Argentina, page 178 and page 474 in Southern Brazil).

Independence and dictatorship The disturbances in Buenos Aires in 1810-1816 which led to independence from Spain enabled creole leaders in Asunción to throw off the rule of Buenos Aires as well as Madrid. The new republic was, however, subject to pressure from both Argentina, which blocked Paraguayan trade on the Río de la Plata, and Brazil. Following independence Paraguay was ruled by a series of dictators, the first of whom, Dr Gaspar Rodríguez de Francia (1814-1840) known as 'El Supremo', imposed a policy of isolation and self-sufficiency. The opening of the Río de la Plata after the fall of the Argentine dictator Rosas enabled de Francia's successor, Carlos Antonio López (1840-62) to import modern technology: in 1856 a railway line between Asunción and Villarrica was begun; an iron foundry and telegraph system were also developed. Carlos López was succeeded by his son, Francisco Solano López (López II), who saw himself as the Napoleon of South America. Believing Paraguay to be threatened by Brazil and Argentina, Solano López declared war on Brazil in 1864. When Argentina refused permission to send troops through Misiones to attack Brazil, López declared war on Argentina. With Uruguay supporting Brazil and Argentina, the ensuing **War of the Triple Alliance** was disastrous for the Paraguayan forces who held on against overwhelming odds until the death of López at the Battle of Cerro Corá in Mar 1870. Of a pre-war population of 400,000, only 220,000 survived the war, 28,000 of them males, mostly either very young or very old. In the peace settlement Paraguay lost territory to Brazil and Argentina, although the rivalry between these neighbours prevented a worse fate.

After the war Paraguay experienced political instability as civilian factions competed for power, often appealing to army officers for support. Although there were few policy differences between the two political parties (the National Republican Association, known as Colorados from its red banner, and the Liberal party who adopted the colour blue), rivalry was intense. Elections were held regularly, but whichever party was in government invariably intervened to fix the result and the opposition rarely participated.

The Chaco War While Paraguayan leaders were absorbed with domestic disputes, Bolivian governments began occupying disputed parts of the Chaco in an attempt to gain access to the sea via the Río Paraguay. Although Bolivian moves started in the late 19th century, the dispute was given new intensity by the discovery of oil in the 1920s. In the three years of the Chaco War (1932-1935) 56,000 Bolivians and 36,000 Paraguayans were killed. Despite general expectations Paraguayan troops pushed the Bolivian army out of most of the Chaco.

Victory in war only increased dissatisfaction in the army with the policies of governments before the war. In Feb 1936 nationalist officers seized power and appointed the war hero, Col Rafael Franco as President. Although Franco was overthrown in a counter-coup in 1937, the so-called 'February Revolution' began major changes in Paraguay including the first serious attempt at land reform and legal recognition of the small labour movement. Between 1939 and 1954 Paraguayan politics were even more turbulent, as rival ci-

vilian factions and army officers vied for power. In 1946 civil war shook the country as army units based in Concepción fought to overthrow President Morínigo.

The Stroessner Years A military coup in May 1954 led to Gen Alfredo Stroessner becoming President. Stroessner retained power for 34 years, the most durable dictator in Paraguayan history. His rule was based on control over the army and the Colorado party, both of which were purged of opponents. While a network of spies informed on dissidents, party membership was made compulsory for most official posts including teachers and doctors. In fraudulent elections Stroessner was re-elected eight times. Paraguay became a centre for smuggling, gambling and drug-running, much of it controlled by Stroessner's supporters. Meanwhile the government spent large amounts of money on transportation and infrastructure projects, including the giant hydroelectric dam at Itaipú. Although these projects brought employment, the completion of Itaipú in 1982 coincided with recession in Brazil and Argentina on whose economies Paraguay was heavily dependent. Meanwhile rivalry intensified within the regime over the succession, with Stroessner favouring his son, Gustavo. Opposition focussed around Gen Andrés Rodríguez, who was married to Stroessner's daughter. When Stroessner tried to force Rodríguez to retire, troops loyal to Rodríguez overthrew the 75 year old Stroessner, who left to live in Brazil.

Liberalization Rodríguez, who became provisional president, easily won multi-party elections in May 1989. The commitment to greater democracy permitted opponents, who had previously boycotted, or been banned from elections, to gain an unprecedented number of seats in the legislative elections of the same date. Despite considerable scepticism over Gen Rodríguez's intentions, political liberalization became a reality. The presidential and congressional elections that he promised were held on 9 May 1993. The presidency was won by Juan Carlos Wasmosy of the Colorado Party,

Domingo Laíno of the Authentic Radical Liberal Party came second and Guillermo Caballero Vargas of the coalition Encuentro Nacional third. In congress the Colorados won the most seats, but insufficient to have a majority in either house.

The government's commitment to market reforms, privatization and to economic integration with Argentina and Brazil within Mercosur inspired protests from all quarters, even from within its own ranks. 1994 saw the first general strike for 35 years. There were also demands for land reform. To these problems was added in 1995 a worsening of relations between the military and the legislature. Various measures, such as reshuffling the Army High Command and breaking the link between the armed forces and the Colorados, led to a critical few days in April 1996. Army commander Gen Lino Oviedo was dismissed for threatening a coup; Wasmosy offered him the defence ministry but then withdrew the offer after massive public protest. Oviedo was later arrested on charges of insurrection, but from jail he made many accusations about corruption at the highest level. He also conducted his campaign for the presidency in 1998, adding to the split in the Colorado Party, which elected as its leader Luis María Argaña, a staunch supporter of Stroessner and opponent of Wasmosy. In municipal elections in Nov 1996, the Colorados won most of the rural votes, but lost in Asunción to a coalition of the Partido Liberal Radical Auténtico and the Partido Encuentro Nacional. Whether PLRA-PEN would use this for a successful campaign for the 1998 presidential election remains to be seen.

CULTURE

PEOPLE

Because Spanish influence was less than in many other parts of South America, most people are bilingual, speaking both Spanish and Guaraní. Outside Asunción, most people speak Guaraní by preference. There is a Guaraní theatre, it is taught in private schools, and books and periodicals are published in that tongue, which has official status as the second national language. According to official figures, the indigenous population is about 39,000; non-government sources put it as high as 99,000 (see *Return of the Indian* by Phillip Wearne, London 1996, page 212). Two-thirds of them are in the Chaco, and one-third in the rest of the country. There are 17 distinct ethnic groups with five different languages, among which Guaraní predominates. The 1981 Law of Native Communities in theory guarantees Indian rights to ownership of their traditional lands and the maintenance of their culture. Contact Tierra Viva, Casilla de Correo 789, Asunción, T/F (595) 21-85209.

MUSIC AND DANCE

The music of Paraguay is a curiosity. Although this is the only South American country the majority of whose population still speak the original native tongue, the music is totally European in origin. The 17th and 18th century Jesuits found the Guaraní people to be highly musical and when their missions were established, the natives were immediately and totally indoctrinated into European music, of which they became fine performers, albeit not composers or innovators. A good example is Cristóbal Pirioby (1764-94), who changed his name to José Antonio Ortiz and moved to Buenos Aires to perform. At his death he left a large collection of musical instruments and sheet music of works by Haydn, Boccherini, etc. After the disastrous War of the Triple Alliance there was an abandonment of things national and even the national anthem was composed by a Uruguayan. Although black slaves were introduced to the country, they became quickly absorbed and there is no trace of black influence in the music. Neither is there any Guaraní element, nor infusion from Brazil or Argentina. Virtually the only popular instruments are the guitar and harp and it is the latter in particular that has come to be the hallmark of all that is musically Paraguayan, with the assistance of such brilliant performers as Félix Pérez Cardoso and Digno

García. Paraguayan songs are notably languid and extremely sentimental and the present repertoire is not 'traditional', but of 20th century origin and by known composers. Of the three principal musical genres, two are slow and for singing, while one is lively and purely for dancing. The two singing genres are the Canción Paraguaya (or Purajhéi) and the Guarania, the former being a slow polka, of which the earliest and most famous example is 'Campamento Cerro León' about the War of the Triple Alliance. The Guarania was developed by José Asunción Flores as recently as the 1920s and includes most of the country's best loved and oft-repeated songs, such as 'India', 'Mi Dicha Lejana' and 'Recuerdos de Ypacaraí'. Equally celebrated and far more vigorous is that favourite of harp virtuosos, the wordless but onomatopeic 'Pájaro Campana'.

For dancing there are the lively Polca Paraguaya and Polca Galopada, first mentioned in print in 1858. They have similarities with the Argentine 'Gato' for instance and are not a true polka nor a gallop, the names of these popular European dances having been attached to an existing Paraguayan dance of unknown name. The Polca is a dance for couples, whilst the even livelier Galopa is usually danced by groups of women, the so-called 'Galoperas', who swing round barefoot, balancing a bottle or jar on their heads. This in turn has developed into the 'Danza de la Botella' or bottle dance, a more recent variant for virtuoso individual performance. Other less well known dances are the Valseadas (a local variant of the waltz), the Chopi or Santa Fé (for three couples), the Taguato, Golondrina, Palomita and Solito, the last named a kind of 'musical chairs'.

Paraguayan music first came to the attention of the outside world soon after the second world war and a number of artists such as Luis Alberto del Paraná and Los Paraguayos have achieved world fame. At the other end of the spectrum the four barefoot old men of the Banda Peteke Peteke from Guajayvity near Yaguarón play their own traditional music on two *mimby* flutes and two little drums, a small idiosyncratic island in an ocean of harp music.

THE ECONOMY

Structure of production Paraguay is essentially an agricultural country; farming accounts for 27% of gdp and manufacturing is mostly processing of agricultural products. The country's major export items are cotton and soya, which make up 55-60% of total exports. Other agricultural exports include leather, beef, timber, oilseeds and wood manufactures. The 1994/95 soya crop was the biggest ever, at 2.3 million tonnes, of which 1.5 million was exported as beans and the balance used by local processing plants, the number of which grew rapidly in the 1990s. The trend towards adding value locally is also seen with cotton, as more spinning plants open and less raw cotton is sold abroad. Paraguay is self-sufficient in wheat and maize. Tobacco, sugar cane, essential oils (mainly petit grain) and *quebracho* are also grown. Land reform is a political issue and has led to riots by landless peasants and strikes in their support. Only 341 landowners hold 40% of cultivable land.

Manufacturing contributes 15% of gdp and apart from soyabean processing and cotton ginning agricultural based industries include sugar milling, distilling alcohol for fuel, textiles, meat packing, timber processing and extraction of *quebracho*, industrial and essential oils. Cement and steel industries, now being privatized, were developed because of cheap and abundant hydroelectricity.

Two massive hydroelectricity generating plants have been built on the river Paraná. The largest, Itaipú, was built with Brazil at a cost of over US$15bn. Its capacity of 12,600MW is shared equally, but Paraguay exports much of its share to Brazil, earning valuable foreign exchange. The second project, Yacyretá, is a joint operation with Argentina and has a potential capacity of 2,800MW. A third dam, Corpus, is planned to be built between the two by Paraguay and Argentina, with a capacity of 4,000MW. Paraguay has a smaller hydroelectric facility at Acaray. No hydrocarbons are produced in Paraguay and all needs are imported. None of the 50 exploratory wells dug in as many years has discovered oil in substantial quantities. Bolivia is to route a gas pipeline to Asunción on its way to the southern states of Brazil.

Recent trends Until 1983, Paraguay managed to offset its current account and trade deficits with capital inflows for Itaipú. After the completion of civil works, the overall balance of payments fell into deficit, with a consequent drain on international reserves. In 1986 the situation was exacerbated by the World Bank and the Inter-American Development Bank refusing to disburse loans until a more realistic exchange rate was adopted. The new administration which replaced the Stroessner regime in 1989 moved quickly to introduce economic reforms, including freeing the exchange rate and lifting many controls. In the short term, this had the effect of dramatically improving registered imports and exports; previously about half of all trade was contraband. In 1991, Paraguay joined Mercosur, the customs union formed with Argentina, Brazil and Uruguay, and a tariff reduction programme was begun. Lower tariffs and an appreciation of the guaraní led to a huge increase in imports, mostly non-durable consumer goods, electrical appliances, machinery and motors, and by 1993-95 the trade deficit was running at over US$1bn a year, while the current account deficit had risen to 10% of gdp.

The Wasmosy Government made slow progress with its privatization schedule, largely as a result of congressional opposition. The state airline, Lapsa, was sold in 1994 to Saeta, of Ecuador, and local investors in a consortium known as Cielos de América. It was later sold to Brazil's TAM group (1996). In 1995 Cañas Paraguayas (brandy) was sold to its employees, who constitutionally have first refusal, but the sale of the state steel company, the merchant fleet and the railway were delayed.

Reform of the financial sector is underway to create a more conducive climate for investments and eliminate Paraguay's reputation for money laundering and contraband transactions esti-

mated at some US$70bn a year. In 1995 a ban was put on the formation of any new banks or finance companies, which had mushroomed since the end of the 1980s. However, a series of bank frauds during the year involving unregistered deposits which could not be indemnified, led to a run on domestic banks and a sharp contraction of liquidity and credit. Four banks were liquidated, several finance companies and other financial players collapsed and the Government spent US$337mn in propping up the system. The crisis had a knock-on effect throughout the economy: the collapse of bank credit hit growth as retail sales dropped and tax revenues fell. In spite of this, gdp

Paraguay: fact file

Geographic

Land area	406,752 sq km
forested	32.4%
pastures	54.6%
cultivated	5.7%

Demographic

Population (1996)	4,964,000
annual growth rate (1991-96)	2.8%
urban	50.5%
rural	49.5%
density	12.2 per sq km

Education and Health

Life expectancy at birth,	
male	64.8 years
female	69.1 years
Infant mortality rate	
per 1,000 live births (1992)	47.1
Calorie intake as %	
of FAO requirement	116%
Population age 25 and over	
with no formal schooling	13.6%
Literate males (over 15)	93%
Literate females (over 15)	90.6%

Economic and Employment

GNP (1994 market prices)	US$7,606mn
GNP per capita	US$1,570
Public external debt (1994)	US$1,370mn
Tourism receipts (1994)	US$197mn
Inflation (annual av 1990-95)	18.2%
Population economically active (1992)	
	1,390,580
Unemployment rate (1989)	9.2%
Military forces	20,200
Source Encyclopaedia Britannica	

growth of 4.7% was recorded in 1995, thanks to a good year for the agricultural sector. In 1996, agricultural results were less good, with the result that growth overall was modest.

GOVERNMENT

A new Constitution was adopted in 1992. The country is divided into 19 departments. Executive power rests with the President, elected for 5 years. There is a two-chamber Congress (Senate 45 seats, Chamber of Deputies 80). Voting is secret and obligatory for all citizens over 18.

Asunción

Asunción, the capital and largest city in Paraguay, has over a quarter of the national population (*pop* over 1.2 million; *phone code* 021). The city has expanded S and E far beyond its original site on the shore of a bay on the eastern bank of the Río Paraguay, almost opposite its confluence with the Río Pilcomayo. Most of the public buildings are near the river, but none is older than the last half of the 19th century, most of them dating from the Presidencies of Carlos Antonio López and his son, Francisco Solano López. The central plazas of the city are drenched in colour during July-Aug with the prolific pink bloom of the *lapacho* trees, which grow everywhere. Dwelling houses are in a variety of styles; new villas in every kind of taste have replaced the traditional one-storey Spanish-Moorish type of house, except in the poorer quarters.

PLACES OF INTEREST

Most of the public buildings can be seen by following El Paraguayo Independiente SE from the **Aduana** (Customs House). The first is the **Palacio de Gobierno**, built 1860-1892 in the style of Versailles (open Sun). In **Plaza Independencia** or **Constitución** stands the **Congreso Nacional** (debates can be attended during the session from April to Dec, on Thur and sometimes Fri). On the NW side of the Plaza is the **Antiguo Colegio Militar**, built in 1588 as a Jesuit College and now housing the Casa de la Cultura and the military history museum (see below). On the SE side of the Plaza is the **Cathedral**. Two blocks SW, along C Chile, is **Plaza de los Héroes**, with the **Pantéon Nacional de los Héroes**

based on Les Invalides in Paris, begun during the Triple Alliance War and finished in 1937. It contains the tombs of Carlos Antonio López, Mariscal Francisco Solano López, Mariscal Estigarribia, the victor of the Chaco War, an unknown child-soldier, and other national heroes. Under the Plaza de los Héroes (in reality four squares) are parking areas. Four blocks SE is the **Plaza Uruguaya** with, nearby, the railway station, built 1856, and a steam engine, the *Sapucai*, dating from 1861. The national cemetery (**Cementerio Recoleta**), resembling a miniature city with tombs in various architectural styles, is on Av Mariscal López, 3 km SE of the centre. It contains the tomb of Eliza Lynch, the Irish mistress of Solano López (ask guide to show you the location), and, separately, the tomb of their baby daughter. Eliza Lynch's home at the corner of Yegros and Mcal Estigarribia is now the Facultad de Derecho.

The best of several parks is **Parque Carlos Antonio López**, set high to the W along Colón and, if you can find a gap in the trees, with a grand view. Good views are also offered from *Restaurant Zodiac*, on top floor at 14 de Mayo y Benjamín Constant (opens 1500) and from Cerro de Lambaré, 7 km S (buses 9 and 29 from Gral Díaz). The **Jardín Botánico** (250 ha) is 6 km E, on Av Artigas y Primer Presidente, reached by bus (Nos 2, 6, 23, and 40, US$0.15, about 35 mins from Luis A Herrera, or Nos 24, 35 or 44B from Oliva or Cerro Corá). The gardens lie along the Río Paraguay, on the former estate of the López family, and contain only trees (no labels, but nice and shady), an 18-hole golf course, and a little zoo, which has

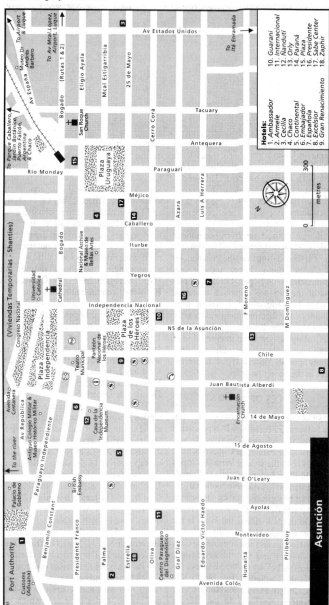

Asunción

Hotels:
1. Ambassador
2. Armele
3. Cecilia
4. Chaco
5. Continental
6. Embajador
7. Española
8. Excelsior
9. Gran Renacimiento
10. Guaraní
11. Internacional
12. Nanduti
13. Orly
14. Paraná
15. Plaza
16. Presidente
17. Sabe Center
18. Zaphir

inspired some unfavourable comments and protests. Entrance fee US$0.50. In the gardens are the former residences of Carlos Antonio López, a one-storey typical Paraguayan country house with verandahs, which now houses a natural history museum and library and of Solano López, a two-storey European-inspired mansion which is now the Museo Indigenista. The beautiful church of **Santísima Trinidad** (on Santísimo Sacramento, parallel to Av Artigas), where Carlos Antonio López was originally buried, dating from 1854 with frescoes on the inside walls, is well worth a visit. It is 10 mins' walk from the zoo entrance. The **Maca Indian reservation** (since 1985) is N of the Gardens (take bus 42 or 44, entrance US$0.15, guide US$0.80); the Indians, who live in very poor conditions, expect you to photograph them (US$0.25).

MUSEUMS

Museo Nacional de Bellas Artes, Iturbe y Mcal Estigarribia, a good collection of Spanish paintings (formerly privately owned) including works by Tintoretto and Murrillo; also an interesting selection of 20th century Paraguayan art, open Tues-Fri, 0700-1900, Sat-Sun 0800-1200. In the Jardín Botánico are the **Museo de Historia Natural** and the **Museo Indigenista**, both open Mon-Sat 0730-1130, 1300-1730, Sun 0900-1300, both free, neither in good condition. In the **Casa de la Independencia** (14 de Mayo y Presidente Franco) is an interesting historical collection; this was where the 1811 anti-colonial revolution was plotted; open Tues-Fri 0700-1200 and 1430-1830, Sat and Sun 0800-1200, entry free. **Panteón Nacional de los Héroes**, Palma y Chile, open every day. **Museo Histórico Militar** in the Antiguo Colegio Militar, on Plaza de la Independencia, open Mon-Fri 0730-1200, 1330-1800, Sat-Sun 0800-1200, containing collections focussing on the War of the Triple Alliance and the Chaco War. There is also a room each dedicated to artefacts from the lives of Solano López and Estigarribia, including 2 portraits of Eliza Lynch. **Museo Dr Andrés Barbero**, España y Mompox, open Mon-Fri 0700-1100, and

Mon, Wed, Fri 1500-1700, anthropological, free, with a good collection of tools and weapons, etc, of the various Guaraní cultures, rec. **Museo Gral de Div Bernardino Caballero**, Parque Caballero, memorabilia and furniture, Mon-Fri 0800-1300, Sat 0800-1200. **Centro de Artes Visuales**, at Isla de Francia, access via Av Gral Genes, bus 30 or 44A from the centre, open daily, except Sun and holidays, 1600-2030; contains **Museo Paraguayo de Arte Contemporáneo**, with some striking murals, **Museo de Arte Indígeno** and **Museo de Barro**, containing ceramics, highly rec. **Museo del Ferrocarril**, Mcal López y Antequera, Mon-Fri 0700-1300.

EXCURSIONS

From the former FME (Flota Mercantil del Estado) dock a ferry leaves daily across to the Rowing Club, frequency depends on demand; many facilities, welcoming people. Boat trips to Isla Chaco'y from Calle Montevideo, on left of Palacio de Gobierno, US$0.50, pleasant.

The town of **Luque** (*pop* 24,917), near the airport, founded 1636 with some interesting colonial buildings, is famous for the making of Paraguayan harps (*Guitarras Sanabria* is one of the best-known firms, Km 13, T 021-2291), and for fine filigree work in silver and gold (ask around for Alberto Núñez). There are also many fine musical instrument shops on the road to Luque; get off the bus – No 30 – from Asunción just before the major roundabout. Mariscal López' house may be visited. 8 km from Luque is Balneario Yukyry, with an artesian well, springs, swimming pools, football pitches and a snackbar; for details and reservations, T 23731 (closed in winter, but pleasant trip anyway).

Many towns close to Asunción can be visited on a day trip, eg Itauguá, San Bernardino and Aregua on Lago Ypacaraí (see page 1176) and Sapucay (see page 1183). For a longer look at the countryside, take a tour for US$45 from any travel agent (pick-up at your hotel – about US$100 with private taxi drivers) to drive the 'Circuito Central' also called 'Circuito de Oro': Asunción - San Lorenzo - Itá - Yaguarón - Paraguarí - Piribebuy - Caacupé - San Bernardino - Itauguá - Asunción. Some 200 km on paved roads, 7 hrs. An alternative circuit, through Guarambaré is given under **South from Asunción**. In all cases, the towns themselves are described in the text below.

LOCAL INFORMATION

NB Plaza de la Independencia is often referred to as Plaza Constitución, it should also be noted that Plaza de los Héroes is called Plaza Independencia on some sources, Plaza de la Democracia on others. On Sat am, till 1200, Av Palma becomes a pedestrian area, with scores of stores selling anything that can be carried, or learnt. Av España originally extended as far out as Av San Martín, but the section between Av Kubitschek and Av Santísimo Sacramento was renamed Av Generalísimo Franco (not to be confused with Presidente Franco) and the remaining section between Av SS Sacramento and Av San Martín was renamed Av General Genes. Many people still use the name Av España for the whole of its original length.

● **Accommodation**

Hotel prices

L1	over US$200	**L2**	US$151-200
L3	US$101-150	**A1**	US$81-100
A2	US$61-80	**A3**	US$46-60
B	US$31-45	**C**	US$21-30
D	US$12-20	**E**	US$7-11
F	US$4-6	**G**	up to US$3

Unless otherwise stated, all hotels in range **D** and above have private bath. Assume friendliness and cleanliness in all cases.

The hotel bill does not usually include a service charge. Check out time is usually 1000.

Outside Asunción: 12 km from town, at Lambaré, on its own beach on the Río Paraguay is **L1** *Hotel del Yacht y Golf Club Paraguay*, PO Box 1795, T 36117/36121, F 36120, 3 restaurants, super luxury, with pool, gym, golf, tennis, airport transfers, etc; many extras free and special deals.

In Asunción: **L3** *Chaco*, Caballero 285 y Estigarribia, T 492066, F 444223, with breakfast, parking nearby, rooftop swimming pool, good restaurant (US$15-20); **L3** *Guaraní*, Oliva e Independencia Nacional, T 491131/139, F 443647, efficient, courteous, central, good value, reasonable restaurant with good buffet; **L3** *Sabe Center*, 25 de Mayo y México, T 450093, F 450101, has luxury suites, central, on busy corner; **L3-A2** *Excelsior*,

Chile 980, PO Box 2863, T 495632, best, new 175-rooms tower, another under construction, conference facilities, etc; **A1** *Cecilia*, Estados Unidos 341, T 210365, F 497111, very smart, comfortable, rec, good restaurant; **A1** *Gran del Paraguay*, De La Residenta y Padre Pucheu, T 200051/2, F 214098, in a wooded garden, with swimming pool, a nightclub on Fri, traditional dance show on Sat (rec, food not as good), a former gentleman's club, full of character, English spoken, helpful; **A2** *Continental*, 15 de Agosto 420 y Estrella, T 493760, 1st class, all rooms a/c, TV, swimming pool, restaurant, rec cafetería, bars, laundry service; **A3** *Gran Armele*, Palma y Colón, T 444455, F 445903, with breakfast, good restaurant, a/c, used by tour groups, rec; **A3** *Gran Renacimiento*, Chile 388 y Estrella, T 445165, central, a/c, good service; **A3** *Paraná*, Caballero y 25 de Mayo, T 444236, F 494793, with breakfast, central, secure, helpful, discounts negotiable, restaurant rec, also short-stay.

B *Asunción Palace*, Colón 415, T/F 492151, with breakfast; **B** *Orly*, Humaitá 209, T 491497, F 442307, good value (**D** for stays over 2 months); *City* cafetería in lobby is good; **B** *Premier*, 25 de Mayo y Curipaty, T 23881, 15 rooms, 16 suites, not central but rec; **B** *Presidente*, Azara y Independencia Nacional, T 494931, F 496500, with breakfast and a/c; **B-C** *Embajador*, Pdte Franco 514, T/F 493393, with breakfast, a/c, **C** with fan, central, parking.

Specially for German-speaking travellers: **L3-A3** *Westfalenhaus*, M Benítez 777 y Stma Trinidad, T 292374/293323, F 291241, e-mail westfalenhaus@pla.net.py, TV, comfortable, German run, swimming pool, a/c; **A-B** *Castillo*, Cruz del Chaco 959, T 605356, German-owned, a/c, laundry; **B** *Zaphir*, Estrella 955, T 490025, small, comfortable, good value; **C** *Omega*, Independencia Nacional y Luis Herrera, **D** without bath.

C *Española*, Herrera y Yegros, T 447312, parking, highly rec; **C** *Ñandutí*, Pdte Franco 551, T 446780, with breakfast, comfortable, luggage stored, rec; **C** *Sahara*, Oliva 920 y Montevideo, T 494935, F 493247, with breakfast, a/c, parking, small pool, large garden; **C-D** *Miami*, México 449 (off Cerro Corá), T 444950, with breakfast, a/c, attractive, highly rec; **C** *Plaza*, Eligio Ayala y Paraguarí, T/F 444772, **D** without bath, spacious rooms, a/c, luggage stored, highly rec.

D *Amigo*, Cerro Corá y Caballero, without bath, with breakfast, cooking and laundry facilities, cheap, rec but noisy; **D** *Azara*, Azara 860, T 449754, attractive mansion but run down, with breakfast and a/c, parking, most rooms face a shady patio and pool; **D** *Hispania*, Cerro Corá 265, T 444018, noisy front rooms, poor breakfast, central, some rooms have no windows; **D** *India*, General Díaz 934, nr Av Montevideo, T 493327, with breakfast and fan, pleasant, small beds, cheaper in old part; **D** *Residencial Itapúa*, Fulgencio R Moreno 943, T 445121, Mennonite run, breakfast and a/c, quiet, comfortable, lunch available; **D** *Stella di Italia*, Cerro Corá 933, T 448731, a/c, with breakfast; **D** *Viajero*, Antequera entre 25 de Mayo y Cerro Corá, hot water, fan, Korean family, will store luggage; **D-E** *Oasis*, Azara 736, T 495398, with bath, small rooms,no windows Korean owned, safe.

E *Ambassador*, Montevideo 111, T 445901, on riverbank, with bath, dirty showers, fan, kitchen and laundry facilities, run down, basic, noisy; **E** pp *Ayuda Social Alemana*, España 202, with breakfast, double rooms only, a/c, fan, quiet, German and English spoken; **E** *Residencial Familiar*, Eligio Ayala 843, T 446381; **E** *Residencial Ideal*, Azara 1549, T 445901, quiet; **E** *Residencial Rufi*, Cerro Corá 660, T 447751, hot water, fans, dark rooms, rec.

Near Bus Terminal on Av F de la Mora: **C** *Adelia*, on corner with Lapacho, T 553083, with breakfast, modern; **C-D** *Yasy*, No 2390, T 551623,with fan. Many more behind these in C Dolores eg **C-D** *Anahi*, T 554943, with breakfast and fan; **E** *El Paraíso*, Lapacho 236, T 555948, shower, quiet, safe, no breakfast.

Camping: the pleasant site at the Jardín Botánico charges US$1.50 pp plus tent, cars also permitted, cold showers and 220v electricity, busy at weekends. If camping, take plenty of insect repellent. You can camp at rear of *Restaurant Westfalia*, T 331772, owner speaks English, French, German, very knowledgeable, US$1 per night for car, hot showers, clothes washing facilities, noisy, animals. Take Av Moreno, towards Ciudad del Este, turn right after going under two bridges into General Santos. *Rest Westfalia* is 3 km on, 5 km from Asunción (bus 19, 23 or 40). Buy camping supplies and gas canisters from *Safari Sport*, Montevideo 258.

● **Places to eat**

Some closed Sat and at holiday times. Most are closed Sun daytime, though some open evenings. Average price of a good meal in quality restaurants, US$20-35. *La Preferida*, Estados Unidos y 25 de Mayo 1005, T 210641, US$25, rec (part of *Hotel Cecilia*); *Oliver's* in *Hotel Presidente*, very good, pricey, live music; *Bistro*, 15 de Agosto y Estrella, excellent, US$25; *Talleyrand*, Estigarribia 932, T 441163, French; *Bolsi*, Estrella 399, wide choice of wines, good for breakfast, excellent food (open Sun 1200-1430), snack bar next door also good; under same ownership *El Jardín del Bolsi*, Perú 363, excellent; *Brasilera*, Mcal López y Tte Zolti, for barbecued meat, rec; *Amstel*, Rep Argentina 1384, good traditional food, expensive; *La Molleja*, Av Brasília 604, very good traditional grill; *Amandau*, Rep Argentina y Boggiani, not cheap but good. *Munich*, Eligio Ayala 163, good German food, excellent value; *Hostería del Caballito Blanco*, Alberdi 631, good food and service; *San Marcos*, Alberdi y Oliva, friendly, part a/c, good food, reasonably priced, good for snacks in café; *Le Gran Café*, Oliva 476, good value, friendly, occasional live music; *Di Trevi*, Palma 573, excellent; *San Roque*, Eligio Ayala y Tacuary, traditional, turn of the century atmosphere, inexpensive, rec; *Baby Grill*, Villa Mora shopping plaza, open 1800-2400 (poorly signposted in building), good food, pricey; *Boule Bar*, Caballero y 25 de Mayo, opp Paraná, tasteful setting, friendly; *Colonial*, Plaza 25 de Mayo, French cuisine; *Arche Noah*, Tacuary y 25 de Mayo, German run, quite expensive but good; *Westfalia*, Bavarian style, see above under **Camping**; *Zodiac*, 14 de Mayo y Benjamín Constant (see above, **Places of interest**).

La Piccola Góndola, Av Mcal López y Juan de Motta, good Italian (and other) food; also *Buon Appetito*, 25 de Mayo nr Av Mcal López y Juan Motta; *Italia*, Cerro Corá 150, Italian and Spanish management, good food, good value; *Da Vinci*, Estrella 695, nice terrace, rec; *Navajo*,

Av San Martín y del Maestro, good pizzas.

American Bar, Estrella y 14 de Mayo, self service restaurant open Sun, clean; *Lucho*, Estados Unidos 564, good local food, cheap, try *churrasco* with *choclo* (maize); *Rincón Chilena*, Estados Unidos 314, friendly, excellent *empanadas*; also at Av 5, No 937, nr Presidente Franco, open Sun; *Café San Francisco*, Brasil y Estigarribia, good coffee, closed weekends; *Copetín Micael*, Herrera y Yegros, good coffee and *empanadas*; *Chiquilín*, mostly pizza, Av Perú y Estigarribia; *El Molino*, España 382 nr Brasil, good value, downstairs for sandwiches and home-made pastries, upstairs for full meals in a nice setting, good service and food (particularly steaks) but pricey, rec; also 2 outlets in Super Centro shopping, Palma 488. *Estrella*, Estrella y 15 de Agosto, pizzas and *empanadas*; *Biggest*, 14 de Agosto y Estrella, pizzas and café. On Palma there are *Pizza Hut* and *Space Burger*, both a/c, reasonable prices. For good roast chicken try *Nick's Restaurant*, Azara 348 nr Iturbe (open Sun). Also open on Sun is *Lido*, Plaza de los Héroes, good for breakfast and *empanadas*. Cheap lunches at *La Flor de la Canela*, México casi Moreno and *Amílcar*, Estados Unidos y 5a Proyectada. Most cheap lunch places close around 1600. *Bar Victoria*, Chile y Oliva, popular for cheap meals.

There are many good oriental restaurants inc: *Sinorama*, Av Próceres de Mayo 262; *Corea*, Perú y Francia, excellent; *Hoy*, Alberdi 642; *Hiroshima*, authentic Japanese, Chóferes del Chaco y Av Moreno. Plenty of Korean places around Perú y Francia.

Wagner, Presidente Franco 828, excellent bread and sweet shop. For ice cream try *Sugar's*, several branches inc *Shopping Excelsior* on Chile; also *Heladería París*, Brasilia y Siria, very popular; *Heladería Amanday*, Estrella 330, plus coffee and cakes.

Paraguayan harp music, bottle dancing, reasonable food and service, but commercialized, at *Jardín de la Cerveza*, Av República Argentina y Campos Cervera, US$20 meal and show, and *Yguazú*, Chóferes del Chaco 1334 (San Lorenzo), good meat, both some distance from centre. Also in *El Gran Hotel Del Paraguay*, Sat only. Good Paraguayan harp/guitar group at *Churrasquería Sajón*, Av Carlos A López, bus 26 from centre. More central is *La Curva*, Av Próceres de Mayo 212, reasonable food, several 'typical' groups play 2100 to 0300, check bill carefully. *Cafecitos*, Colón 320, pub and art gallery, good atmosphere, music, highly rec; *Casa del Sur*, Cerro Corá 150, live music, good atmosphere; *El Circo Bizarro*, Antequera esq E Ayala, bohemian pub, rec; *Summer Pub*, Cruz del Chaco 847, good value, excellent meat; *Britannia Pub*, Cerro Corá 851, evenings only, closed Tues, good variety of drinks, English spoken, popular, book exchange;

Austria Pub, Austria just off Av San Martín, German run, brews own beer, popular, rec; *Pub Viejo Bavaria*, Estados Unidos 410, good beer, chicken, sandwiches and burgers.

● **Airline offices**

LAB, 14 de Mayo 563, Oficina B, T 441586, F 448218; **Arpa**, Perú 456 y España, T 491039; **Lapsa/TAM**, Perú y España, T 495261; **Ladesa**, Mcal López 4531, T 443346; **Varig**, 14 de Mayo y Gen Díaz; **Iberia**, 25 de Mayo y Independencia; **Nacional**, T 493351.

● **Banks & money changers**

See **Currency** section in **Information for travellers**. Lloyds Bank, Palma y O'Leary (and 4 agencies in Greater Asunción, accepts Visa); **Citibank**, Estrella y Chile, will change Citibank TCs into US$ cash, and gives US$ cash on Mastercard; **Banco Alemán Paraguayo**, Estrella y 14 de Mayo (fast service for money sent from Germany, paid by cheque which can be cashed into dollars at Cambio Guaraní); **Banco de Desarrollo**, VE Haedo y NS de la Asunción, no commission on cash advances on Mastercard, guaraníes only, US$200 limit. Also Argentine, Brazilian and local banks. **Banco Unión**, Estrella y Alberdi, gives cash advances in US$ and guaraníes on Visa or Mastercard, no commission in about 15 mins, also has ATMs, English spoken, friendly, only between 0845-1130. Similarly, **Creditcard**, 15 de Agosto y Humaitá, and **Unicard**, 15 de Agosto between Haedo and Humaitá, Mastercard only. **Amex**, Yegros 690 y Herrera, poor rates.

Many *casas de cambio* on Palma, Estrella and nearby streets (open Mon-Fri 0730-1200, 1500-1830, Sat 0730-1200). Deutsche Marks can be changed at good rates, and all rates are better than at frontiers. Some will accept sterling notes. Some *casas de cambio* change one type of dollar TC. Shop around as there are wide variations in commission. **Cambio Guaraní**, Palma 449, T 90032/6, is good, changes US$ TCs into US$ cash, Argentine pesos or reais, but commission charged per cheque. German spoken at **Cambios Menno Tour**, Azara 532. **Cambios Yguazú**, 15 de Agosto 451, T 490135, Thomas Cook, but can't replace lost or stolen TCs. Be careful to count money received from street money changers (Palma and surrounding area – their rates are poor when banks and *cambios* are closed).

● **Cultural centres**

Centro Cultural de la Ciudad, Haedo 347, organizes concerts, exhibitions and shows films; **Casa de la Cultura**, Plaza Independencia, organizes exhibitions and other activities, Mon-Fri 0830-1330, 1600-2000, Sat 0900-1930, Sun 1000-1900.

The **US-Paraguay Cultural Centre** has a good library at España 352 (open Mon-Fri 0900-

2000, Sat 0900-1200, also has snack bar). **Instituto Anglo-Paraguayo**, Artigas 356 y Toledo, T 25525, F 203871, snack bar, library with British newspapers, book exchange; also US TV. **Alianza Francesa**, Mcal Estigarribia 1039, T 210382, snack bar. **Goethe Institut**, J de Salazán 310, library with a few newspapers, open 1600-2000. **German-Paraguayan Culture Institute**, Av Artigas 303 y Juan de Salazar, T 26242, rec. All these institutes have special events, film shows, etc. If you have the time, these institutes may be able to use volunteers to give classes/lectures in their subjects.

Spanish and Guarani classes at **IPEE**, Carlos Antonio López 1057, T 80132, friendly and efficient.

● **Embassies & consulates**
Brazilian Consulate, 25 de Mayo esq Gen Aquina, open 0800-1200, Mon-Fri, US$22 for visa, T 448084/069; **Argentine Consulate**, España y Perú, T 212320, visas issued at Edif Banco Nacional de Argentina, Palma 319, p 1, open 0800-1300, 2 hr service, photo needed; **Chilean**, Guido Spano y Juan B Molta, T 660344; **Bolivian Consulate**, Eligio Ayala 2002 y Gral Bruguez, T 22662; **Peruvian Consulate**, Av Mcal López 648, T 200949; **Uruguayan**, Gen Aquina 432 y 25 de Mayo, T 25022 (visas processed immediately if exit ticket from Uruguay, overland travel to Uruguay and onward country visas can be shown, US$42 for Australians); **Mexican**, O'Leary y Estrella, T 444421; **Ecuadorean**, Herrera y Yegros, T 446150; **Venezuelan**, Mcal Estigarribia y Estados Unidos, T 444243.

US Embassy and Consulate, Av Mcal López 1776, T 210489; **South African**, Banco Sudameris, Cerro Corá e Independencia Nacional, p 4, T 496031.

British, Pdte Franco 706, p 4 (Casilla 404), T 449146, Mon-Fri 0800-1300, holds mail; **Swiss**, O'Leary 409, Edif Parapiti, p 14, esq Estrella, T 448022; **Spanish**, 25 de Mayo 175, T 490686/7; **Danish Consulate**, Nuestra Señora de la Asunción 766, T 493160; **Swedish Consulate**, Bogado 1039-47, T 205561/9; **Finnish Consulate**, Elias Ayola y Yasú, T 291175; **Dutch Consulate**, Chile 680, T 492137; **Austrian Consulate**, Gen Díaz 525, Edif Internacional Faro, T 443910; **German**, Av Venezuela 241, T 24006/7; **French**, España 893, T 213840; **Israeli**, Yegros 437 y 25 de Mayo, Edif San Rafael, p 6, T 495097.

● **Entertainment**
Cinema: Centro Cultural de la Ciudad, E V Haedo 347, for quality foreign films, US$1.50. Cinema programmes are given in the press; some offer 3 films at one price (US$2.50).

Theatre: *Teatro Municipal*, Pdte Franco, nr Alberdi, has an extensive winter programme of concerts and ballets (entry US$4). *Teatro Ar-*

lequin, de Gaulle y Quesado, *Teatro Latino*, 16 de Julio y 16 de Agosto, and *Teatro El Lector*, San Martín y Austria have productions most of the year. Concerts are given at the *Teatro de las Américas*, J Bergés 297.

Nightclubs and discotheques: *Musak*, Bertoni y José Ocampos; *Caracol Club*, Gen Santos y Porvenir; *Playboys*, 14 de Mayo y Oliva; *Tabasco Club*, 1 de Marzo y Felicidad; *La Salsa*, Papa Juan XXIII y Oddone (Latin American Disco); *Karim*, 25 de Mayo nr Estados Unidos. There are floor shows in several hotels, eg *Hotel del Yacht* (Scruples).

● **Hospitals & medical services**
Health: *Doctor Carlos M Ramírez Boettner*, Díaz 975, T 493021, general practitioner.

● **Laundry**
Lavamático, Yegros 808 y Fulgencio Moreno, good, fairly cheap. *Lavarap*, Galería Friuli, 25 de Mayo y Tacuari, and Hernandarias 636, 1 block from Colón and Díaz, open all day, T 447478. *Lavandería Centro*, Pdte Franco y O'Leary, T 440286; *Lave Speed*, Eligio Ayala 619; *Blue Bubbles*, Paraguarí 484 y Cerro Corá. Average price US$4/load.

● **Places of worship**
Anglican: St Andrew, España y Uruguay.
Synagogue: Díaz 657.

● **Post & telecommunications**
General Post Office: Alberdi, between Benjamín Constant y El Paraguayo Independiente, T 493784. A fine set of buildings around a colonnaded patio with plants and fountains. Open Mon-Fri 0700-2000, Sat 0700-1200. *Poste Restante* (ask at the Casillas section) charges about US$0.25 per item, but you may have to insist they double-check if you are expecting letters (poste restante closes 1100). Postcards for sale, but better ones in nearby bookshops. Also philatelic museum, open 0700-1800, Mon-Fri; 0700-1200, Sat. Post boxes throughout the city carry address of the nearest place to buy stamps. Register all important mail; you must go to main PO for this. There are sub-offices at the railway station and at the docks.

Telephone: Antelco, Azara y Alberdi, Gral Bruguez y M Domínguez and at Terminal de Omnibus, all for international calls and fax, 24 hrs.

● **Shopping**
Colón, starting at the port, is lined with good tourist shops, and so are Pettirossi, Palma and Estrella. *Galería Colón 185* is rec. For leather goods several places on Colón and on Montevideo inc *Boutique Irene*, No 463, *La Casa Del Portafolio*, No 302 and *Boutique del Cuero*, No 329. *Casa Vera* at Estigarribia 470 for Paraguayan leatherwork, cheap and very good. For wooden articles and carvings go to *Artes de Madera* at Ayolas 222; *Viva*, José Borges 993,

Chaco and Oriental crafts, rec. Other recommended shops, **Casa Overall**, Mcal Estigarribia 397, nr Plaza Uruguaya, good selection; **Victoria**, **Arte Artesanía**, Iturbe y Ayala, interesting selection of wood carvings, ceramics etc, rec. Many leading tourist shops offer up to 15% discount for cash. Check the quality of all handicrafts carefully, lower prices usually mean lower quality. The markets are worth a visit, especially the Pettirossi (food and ordinary clothes). There is a daily market on Av Dr Francia, best visited during the week, and a Sat one on Plaza de la Independencia, where the nuns from Villeta sell their hand-made clothing for children. There is a handicraft market on Plaza de los Héroes selling lace and items from Peru and Bolivia. Supermarkets are usually well stocked, especially with imported liquor; rec is the one at El Paraguayo Independiente y 14 de Mayo (bakes its own bread, open daily 0800-2100). Also opp **Excelsior Hotel** at Chile 959. **Unicentro**, Palma y 15 de Agosto is a modern shopping centre. Outside Asunción, visit Luque (musical instruments and jewellery – see page 1169) and Itauguá (lace) – see page 1176. Prices of electronic goods in the Korean-run shops are very low.

Bookshops: **Librería Internacional**, Oliva 386, Estrella 723 at Palma 595, good for maps; also 'Books' at Mcal López 3971, at Villa Morra shopping centre, second-hand English language books, also magazines and newspapers; **El Lector** at Plaza Uruguaya y 25 de Mayo has a selection of foreign material; **Librería Alemana**, Av Luis A de Herrera 292, warmly rec for German books and publications.

Photographic: repairs: **Panatronic**, Benjamín Constant 516; **Rodolfo Loewen**, **Camera Service**, Blas Garay y Morelo, T 23807. Slide film costs US$4, print film US$3.50 (35 mm). Good place for buying cameras, **Casa Fanny**, Mcal Estigarribia 144. Kodak-Ektachrome slide film is difficult to find; try **Kodak Express** on Palma. **Time 45**, Yegros 550, rec for good quick developing service; also **Rochester**, Nuestra Señora de la Asunción 632 y Gen Díaz.

● **Tour companies & travel agents**
All very helpful.

Inter-Express (Amex), Yegros 690, T 490111; **American Tours**, Alberdi y Oliva, T 490672, German and English spoken; **Menno Tour**, Azara 551, German spoken; **Inter Tours**, Brasil y Estigarribia 1097, T 211747, tours to Chaco and Jesuit missions rec; **Abysa**, Azara 229, T 441569, sells bus tickets in the centre of town; **Maya Viajes**, Yegros 748 p 6, T 444666, T 448961; **Time Tours**, 15 de Agosto y Díaz, T 493527, fluent English, rec; **Lions Tours**, Alberdi 454, T 490591. Most agencies offer tours of the Circuito de Oro and the 'Triangle' (Encarnación, Jesuit Missions, Ciudad del Este, Itaipú and Iguazú), 3 days, 2 nights, US$185

double. For more information contact **Itra Travel**, T 491667/494302, or Dirección General de Turismo.

● **Tourist offices**
Dirección General de Turismo, Palma esq Alberdi, open Mon-Fri 0800-2000, T 441530, F 491230. Free map, information on all parts of Paraguay, but you may need to be persistent. Another map is sold in bookshops.

● **Useful addresses**
Immigration: O'Leary 625, p 8. Ministerio de Relaciones Exteriores, O'Leary y Pdte Franco.
Mennonite Centre: Colombia 1090, T 200697.
Police: T 446105.

● **Transport**
Local Car rental: Only Rent-a-Car, 15 de Agosto 441, T 492731, also airport; **Localiza**, E Ayala 695, T 446233, and airport, T 206193, rec, rates from US$55/day; **Hertz** at airport, T 22012, km 4½, and C Recalde y Av E Ayala, T 605708, US$67-93/day depending on vehicle (inc tax, insurance and 100 km free); **National**, Yegros 501, T 492157, F 445890; **Fast**, 15 de Agosto 588, T 447069, F 447112, good, helpful. See **Motor repairs** page 1198.

City buses: the system is extensive, running from 0600-2400; buses stop at signs before every street corner. Journeys within city, US$0.30. For buses to the new bus terminal, see below. Buses only rec outside rush hours, with light luggage. Keep your ticket for inspection until you leave bus.

Taxi: minimum fare in Asunción is US$0.70 plus US$0.05 for every 100m. About 30% more at night. The average journey costs about US$2, there is an extra charge for luggage. Hire by the hour; minimum US$10, up US$20 outside the city. Radiotaxi rec, T 550116, or 311080.

Trams: service temporarily suspended in 1997.

Air Silvio Pettirossi Airport, 15 km NE of centre. Several agencies have desks where you can book a taxi to your hotel, US$15. Bus 30A goes every 15 mins between the red bus stop outside the airport and Plaza de los Héroes, US$0.30, difficult with luggage, allow 30-45 mins. Minibus service from your hotel to airport run by Tropical, T 84486, book in advance, US$8.

The new terminal building contains a tourist office (free city map and hotel information), bank (turn right as you leave customs), handicraft shop, restaurant and several travel agencies which can arrange hotel bookings and change money (very poor rates). Left luggage US$0.50/piece.

Trains San Roque Station at Eligio Ayala y México, T 447316. Pdte Carlos Antonio López Railway to Encarnación: no trains in 1997 as part of the track was flooded. Only one passenger service, Mon-Fri 1315, Sun 0900, to Aregua and Ypacaraí, return service 0430, US$0.50, 2½ hrs.

See page 1183 for a trip to see the locomotive workshops at Sapucay.

River boats Sailings to Concepción every 15-20 days, 27-30 hrs, US$27 1st class, US$17 2nd, US$11 deck space. Not very comfortable (eg *Cacique II*, Wed 0700, basic restaurant, essential to arrive early, watch luggage). *Guaraní* sails to Concepción Sat 1100, returns Thur, 30 hrs, US$8 pp + US$7 for cabin.

River services to **Corumbá** (Brazil) were not operating in 1996/97. Enquire at the dock at the end of C Montevideo, or at *Hotel Ambassador*, where Blanca is very helpful and knowledgeable. On all sailings take your own food, water, toilet paper, warm clothes for the night (or mattress and blanket, or sleeping bag), mosquito repellent.

Corumbá can be reached by bus, through Pedro Juan Caballero, Ponta Porã and Campo Grande (approx US$50). See also page 1189.

Ferry to **Puerto Pilcomayo** (Argentina) about every 30 mins (US$0.50, 5 mins) from Itá Enramada (Paraguayan immigration), take bus 9 from Asunción (Argentine immigration closed at weekends for tourists). Boats S to **Pilar** and Argentina are few and irregular.

Buses Terminal, S of the centre at República Argentina y Fernando de la Mora, reached by taking local bus No 8 (the only direct one), on Oliva, Haedo, or Cerro Corá in the centre and get off outside the terminal, US$0.20. In the centre get off at Chile y Díaz. Allow 30-40 mins (other buses Nos 10, 25, 31, 38 and 80, follow very circuitous routes). Taxi to/from centre, rec if you have luggage, US$4, journey time depends on the amount of traffic, minimum 20 mins. The terminal has a bus information desk, free city/country map, restaurant (quite good), café, *casa de cambio* (poor rates) and shops. Bus company offices on the top floor are in three sections: short-distance, medium and long. Local departures, inc for Yaguarón and Paraguarí from the basement. Hotels nearby: turn left from front of terminal, 2 mins' walk. Bus times and fares within Paraguay are given under destinations.

To Uruguay COIT (Eligio Ayala 693, T 496197) runs to **Montevideo**, 0800, Sat and Wed, 20 hrs; Brújula/Cynsa (Pte Franco 985, T 441720) Tues and Fri, with a third service in summer, US$70 (the route is Encarnación, Posadas, Paso de los Libres, Uruguaiana, Bella Unión, Salto, Paysandú – the only customs formalities are at Bella Unión; passport checks here and at Encarnación).

To Argentina There is a road N from Asunción (passing the Jardín Botánico on Primer Presidente) to a concrete arch span bridge (Puente Remanso – US$1 toll, pedestrian walkway on upstream side, 20 mins to cross) which leads to the border at Puerto Falcón (about 40 km) and then to **Clorinda** in Argentina. The border is open 24 hrs a day; local services are run by Empresa Falcón to Puerto Falcón (US$1, every hour, last bus from Puerto Falcón to the centre of Asunción 1830; from Falcón to Clorinda costs US$0.25), but it is cheaper to book direct from Asunción to Argentina.

Buses to Buenos Aires (18 hrs) daily, many companies, via Rosario and Santa Fe (average fare US$68 luxury, US$50 *diferencial*, US$48 *común*). To **Resistencia** (5 hrs, US$21) and **Formosa**, 4 a day, Brújula/La Internacional (US$6, plus US$1 luggage) many drug searches on this road; to **Córdoba** (US$55), Brújula 4 a week and Cacorba (3 times). To **Posadas**, Singer 3 a week at midnight, or go to **Encarnación** (frequent service and cheaper) and cross the river. To **Salta**, Stel, T 510757, Fri, 1300, 18 hrs, US$66.

To Chile Several buses weekly to **Santiago**, 28 hrs, US$75 (plus extra charge for luggage) with Sirena Del Paraná (excellent service) and Brújula.

To Brazil Many Paraguayan buses advertise that they go to destinations in Brazil, when, in fact you have to change buses and book again at the frontier. Note also that through services to Campo Grande and Corumbá via Pedro Juan Caballero do not stop for immigration formalities. Check all details carefully. Nuestra Señora and Rysa, and the Brazilian companies Pluma and Unesul, have services to Ciudad del Este, continuing to **Foz do Iguaçu**, US$9.75, 5-7 hrs, 6 direct buses a day in all. Seat reservations recommended. (It is possible to visit the Brazilian side of the Iguaçu Falls in one day, either by leaving Asunción soon after midnight, or at 0730. Either way you have less than half a day at the Falls – remember to buy *reais* in Asunción beforehand.) To **Curitiba**, with Pluma, buses daily, 15$\frac{1}{2}$ hrs; to **São Paulo**, Rápido Yguazú, Pluma and Brújula, 20 hrs, US$41 (*leito*, US$82). Pluma to **Rio de Janeiro**, US$53; to **Porto Alegre**, Unesul, 4 a week; Nacional Expresso to **Brasília** 3 a week. Services also to **Blumenau** (Catarinense) and **Florianópolis**, US$32 (Pluma and Catarinense).

To Bolivia Via the Chaco, to Santa Cruz, Yacyretá, T 551725, Tues, Fri, 0900, US$65, some food provided, best to bring plenty of your own plus water, theoretically 32 hrs, in reality 40-45, good service but be prepared to help dig the bus out; Bolipar dep Mon and Thur, US$65, good; Santaniana, Thur 1300, T 551607, 36-40 hrs, US$60; Stel, Wed 1530, US$60. Foreigners must get an exit stamp in Asunción if leaving the country on this route; take bus ticket to Migraciones. Don't wait until the border. Alternative route to Bolivia via Salta, Argentina (see above).

East from Asunción

S MALL towns with interesting local crafts, leading to jungle on the Brazilian border, Ciudad del Este and the attractions of the Itaipú dam and the nearby Iguazú Falls.

ROUTE TWO TO CORONEL OVIEDO

The Mariscal Estigarribia Highway leaves Asunción past typical markets, reached by bus from Asunción (Nos 20, 26 and 27 from Herrera, US$1.50). At Km 12 is **San Lorenzo** (*pop* 74,400), an industrial town with the National School of Agriculture (Universidad de Agronomía – it has an extensive insect collection) and Museo de Historia Natural, open Mon-Fri 0730 to 1530 with some emphasis on ecology. Also in town are the small but interesting Museo Aqueológico, near cathedral, free, though not always open, good Indian section, and the Museo Guido Boggiani, Bogado 888, Tues-Sat 1000-1200, 1500-1800, a collection built up by the Italian anthropologist who researched the tribes of the northern Chaco at the turn of the 19th/20th century. It has become a social and artistic centre for the Indians with music, dancing and crafts. Basketry and wood carvings on sale, no explanations but worth a visit. Here is the Balneario El Tigre, with swimming pool and shady trees. (**C-D** *Hotel San Lorenzo*, Gral Caballero 148 y 14 de Mayo,

T 2261, with breakfast, excellent, can commute into city, laundry).

Capiatá, at Km 20, founded in 1640, has a fine colonial church, with simple interior and beautifully carved beams and uprights supporting the tiled roof (buses every few minutes from San Lorenzo).

ITAUGUA

(*Pop* 5,400) At Km 30, founded in 1728, Itauguá is where the famous ñandutí, or spiderweb lace, is made. There are over 100 different designs. Prices are lower than in Asunción and the quality is better; try the *Taller Artesanal* (Km 29) or the *Mutual Tejedoras* (Km 28). To watch the lace being made, ask around. The old town lies 2 blocks from the main highway: the blocks of uniform dwellings around the plaza, with their red tile roofs projecting over the sidewalk and their lines of pillars, are very close to the descriptions we have of Guaraní Jesuit settlements. Worth seeing are the church, the Museo Parroquial San Rafael, with a display of indigenous art and Franciscan artefacts (open daily 0800-1130, 1500-1800) and the market (closed Sun). No accommodation, but Itauguá is only 1 hr by frequent bus service from Asunción, US$1; cheap lunches at the market.

Local festival There is a 4-day festival in early-July, including processions and the crowning of Señorita Nandutí.

LAGO YPACARAI

The lake is 24 km by 5. There are facilities for swimming and watersports, with a sandy beach. The water was reported to be a health risk in 1996 – ask locally. There are frequent cruises from the pier during the tourist season, Dec-Feb, when it is crowded.

At Capiatá (see above), a left turn (signposted) goes via a toll road (US$0.75) 7 km to **Aregua**, a pretty resort on the slopes above Lago Ypacaraí. It has an interesting ceramics cooperative, a church and convent. An increasing number of houses are being built around the lake. From here boat trips run across the lake at weekends to San

Asunción surroundings

Bernadino, on the opposite side.

● **Accommodation and places to eat**
E *Hospedaje Ozli*, reasonable, restaurant mediocre. *La Rotunda*, restaurant on the waterfront; *Mozart Pub*, open Thur-Sun, rec; *Las Palmeras*.

● **Transport** For details of the daily steam train from Asunción see under **Asunción, Train**. Buses from Asunción, Transportes Ypacaraínse, every 30 mins, but do not leave from the terminal; alternatively take local bus to Capiatá and change.

At Km 40 on Route 2 a branch road, 8 km long, leads off to **San Bernardino**, on the E bank of Lago Ypacaraí (buses from Asunción, 56 km, 1 hr, US$1.70). Boats can be hired and there is good walking in the neighbourhood, for example from San Bernardino to Altos, lake views, wooded hills and valleys, round trip about 3 hrs. Shortly after the turn off from the main road towards San Bernardino is a sign to La Grota; turn right here, and the road leads to a secluded national park.

There are grottoes with still water and overhanging cliffs.

● **Accommodation** A2 *San Bernardino Pueblo*, Paseo del Pueblo y Mbocayá, T 2195, swimming pool, a/c, by the lake; **B** *Acuario*, lakeside, 2 km from town centre, T 2375; **B-C** *Del Lago*, lakeside in town, T 2201, with breakfast, attractive 19th century building, a/c, pool, gardens. It is possible to find rooms in private houses. **Camping** At Km 43 is *Casa Grande Camping Club* with all facilities. For information, Corfín Paraguaya, Ayolas 437 y Estrella, T 492360/1, Asunción, or direct, T (0511) 649. It is possible to camp right on the lake but there are many mosquitoes, inadequate sanitary facilities and not much safety for your personal belongings.

● **Places to eat** *Como-Rap*, good food, pleasant atmosphere, reasonable prices, proprietor, Tito, owns next door laundry. Several places near lake, eg *Ypanamena*.

CAACUPE

(*Pop* 9,105; *phone code* 0511) At Km 54 on

Route 2, this is a popular resort and religious centre on the Azcurra escarpment. Although the old church has been demolished, a small replica has been built about 5 blocks away. The centre is dominated by the modern Basilica of Our Lady of the Miracles, with copper roof, stained glass and polychrome stone esplanade,which was consecrated by the Pope in 1988. There is a market next to it. Parque Anka, outside town on the Asunción road, has a swimming pool, tennis courts, ponies, a Disneyland, camp site and good restaurants. Bus from Asunción US$0.50, get off at Basilica rather than Caacupé station.

Local festival Thousands of people from Paraguay, Brazil and Argentina flock to the shrine, especially for the Feast of the Immaculate Conception on 8 December. Prices are somewhat higher than normal in Paraguay. Go midweek if you can. Besides fireworks and candlelit processions, pilgrims watch the agile gyrations of Paraguayan bottle-dancers; they weave in intricate measures whilst balancing bottles pyramided on their heads. The top bottle carries a spray of flowers and the more expert dancers never let drop a single petal.

● **Accommodation** B *Virgen Serrana*, on plaza, T 2366, with a/c, **D** with fan; **D** *El Mirador*, on plaza, with bath; **D** *El Uruguayo*, large rooms, a/c, hot water, parking, delightful restaurant but poor food, OK breakfast; and others. Chicken restaurant 1 block N of *El Uruguayo*, then 1 block E, on Highway, rec. **Camping** Club de Camping Melli, 1 km E of town, all facilities, T 313.

Excursions Poor, busy roads lead to several interesting churches. One is at **Tobati**, a tobacco centre, with local pottery and woodwork, 16 km to the N. It is also a brick-making centre; wood-burning kilns for bricks and tiles can be seen in many yards. It is a good walk from Caacupé, with excellent views of the country below and the outcrops of the escarpment above (rec).

At Km 64 beyond Caacupé a paved road runs 13 km SE to **Piribebuy** (*pop* 5,902; **F** *Pensión Santa Rosa*, basic; **E** *Rincón Viejo*, reasonable), founded in 1640 and noted for its strong local drink, *caña*. In the central plaza is the church (1640), with fine sculptures, high altar and pul-pit. The town was the site of a major battle in the War of the Triple Alliance (1869), commemorated by the Museo Histórico Pedro Juan Caballero, which also contains artefacts from the Chaco War (entry free). Buses from Asunción by Transportes Piribebuy. Near the town are the attractive small falls of Piraretá. The road goes on via Chololó, 13 km S, and reaches Route 1 at Paraguarí, 28 km from Piribebuy (see below, page 1183).

VAPOR CUE NATIONAL PARK

24 km N of Route 2 from Eusebio Ayala (Km 72) is **Vapor Cué** with peaceful swimming and fishing in the river in the middle of fertile cattle country. It contains the remains of seven steamships sunk during the War of the Triple Alliance. Several boilers and one ship have been reconstructed. Camping is permitted, public transport runs to within 4 km of the site. Transport can be hired in the village.

Continuing along Route 2 at Km 87 is **Itacurubí** (**D** *Hotel Aguila*, a/c, and nearby *Restaurant Estrella Suiza*, Swiss owned, though for sale in late 1996, good food, helpful, camping at the back, showers, rec).

CORONEL OVIEDO

(*Pop* 21,782; *phone code* 0521) An important route centre (but not worth a stopover), situated 3 km S of the junction of Route 2 and the major N-S Route 8; buses drop passengers at the junction (El Cruce). Excursions can be made to the village of Yataíty (reached by a turning 22 km S of Coronel Oviedo) where a local cooperative sells ponchos, fine weaving and embroidery. At the end of Nov there is a *feria artesanal* with folk music and dancing, exhibitions etc. There are German agricultural communities nearby.

● **Accommodation** **D** *El Rey*, Estigarribia 213, T 2117, clean, modern, with breakfast, rec; **E** *San Pedro*, 100m from *El Rey*, rec; **F** *Hospedaje Juancito*, Juan E O'Leary y Carmelo Peralta, with bath, mosquito net, nice garden, rec; **F** *Casa Kolping*, Iturbe y 1 de Marzo, T (521) 3065, with breakfast, German spoken; at El Cruce, *Hotel Alemán*, rec.

NORTH FROM CORONEL OVIEDO

Route 8 (paved) runs N to Yby Yaú, where it meets Route 5 (Concepción to Pedro Juan Caballero). At **Mbutuy** (Km 56, good *parador*, restaurant, petrol station) Route 10 (paved as far as Cruce Carambey) branches off NE to the Brazilian frontier at Saltos del Guaira.

Saltos del Guaira is named after the waterfalls now under the Itaipú lake. Here there is a 900 ha wildlife reserve. Saltos del Guaira can also be reached by a paved road which runs N from Hernandarias, via Itaquyry to meet Route 10 at Cruce Carambey. Nowhere to change TCs.

- **Accommodation** **C** *Colonial*, T 530; *Imperio*, T 208; **C-D** *Peralta*, T 235, pleasant, with breakfast and bath, **E** without; **E** *El Lago*, basic.

- **Buses** To Asunción, US$18; to Ciudad del Este, US$13. **To Brazil** Regular launches cross the lake to Guaíra, 20 mins, US$1. There is also an hourly bus/launch service, 30 mins, US$1. Buses also run N of the lake to Mondo Novo, where they connect with Brazilian services.

36 km N of Mbutuy is **San Estanislao**, museum, hotel (E). At Santa Rosa, 107 km N of San Estanislao, there is petrol, *pensión* and restaurants. Here a dirt road runs SW to the Mennonite colony of **Nueva Germania**, 27 km. This road goes on to San Pedro and Puerto Antequera on the Río Paraguay (88 km). A further 23 km N of Santa Rosa, a dirt road runs NE through jungle to the interesting and tourist-free **Capitán Badó** (120 km) in the Cordillera Amambay which forms the frontier with Brazil. From here another road follows the frontier N to PJ Caballero (100 km). 50 km N of the turn off to Capitán Badó is Yby Yaú, see page 1190.

VILLARRICA

(*Pop* 21,203; *phone code* 0541) Situated 42 km S of Coronel Oviedo, 173 km SE of Asunción and 219 km N of Encarnación, Villarrica is delightfully set on a hill rich with orange trees. A very pleasant, friendly place, it has a fine cathedral, built in traditional style with verandah. The Plaza de los Héroes contains many statues and memorials, and a battle-by-battle description of the Chaco War around the perimeter (walk clockwise). There are other tree-filled plazas with botanic name plates, not all of which are accurate. The museum (closed weekends) behind the church has a foreign coin collection; please contribute. Products of the region are tobacco, cotton, sugar, *yerba mate*, hides, meat and wine produced by German settlers. Horse-drawn taxis.

- **Accommodation** **C** *Ybytyruzú*, C A López y Dr Bottell, T 2390, with breakfast, more with a/c, fairly clean; **D** *Asunción*, Thompson y Aquideban, T 0541-2542, a/c, fan; **D** *Guaíra*, N Talavera y Mcal Estigarribia, T 2369, nr bus terminal, shower, fan, noisy; **D** *Plaza*, Mcal López, clean, friendly, beautiful patio; **E** *Hospedaje El Porvenir*, Thompson 144, basic, hospitable; **E** *Hospedaje La Guairana*, with restaurant, and next door, **E** *Pensión el Toro*, Mcal López 521, single beds only.

- **Places to eat** Many on CA López and Gral Díaz. *Mesón Universitario*, González 623, in part of a colonial pavilion, open all day; *París*, CA López 100, good food; *Refugio*, Gral Díaz 578, reasonable prices; *El Tirol*, CA López 205, German owned, set lunch; *El Palacio de las Empanadas*, Gral Díaz 533; *Los Amigos*, Melgarejo 828, good food, poor service, sidewalk eating at night; *Capri*, San Roque y Gral Díaz, local food, inexpensive; *Miami Bar*, La Plaza de Municipalidad, good food, rec; *Angelo's* on main plaza, decent.

- **Buses** To Coronel Oviedo, US$1.50; to Asunción, frequent, US$5, 3 hrs (Empresa Guaireña); also direct service to Ciudad del Este, 4 daily, US$6, 4 hrs.

German colonies near Villarrica

7 km N is a turn off to the E, then 20 km to **Colonia Independencia**, **D** *Hotel Tilinski*, out of town, peaceful, German spoken, swimming pool (filled with river water), meals for residents; *Che Valle Mi*, Sr Jacob Esslinger, Correo Melgarejo, T 05418-241, rec; next door is *Ulli y Klaus* restaurant, also rec; also a good restaurant, with German chalet style accommodation, *Hotel Restaurant Panorama*, set on top of a hill on the road 12 km from Colonia Independencia. It makes a good stop, especially for German-speaking travellers, who can also visit the German cooperative farms. There is camping nearby at Melgarejo with full facilities. Direct bus to Asunción, three daily (US$2.75, 4 hrs), as well as to Villarrica.

From Villarrica Route 8 continues S 222 km (unpaved) through Caazapá to Coronel Bogado, where it joins Route 1.

EAST FROM CORONEL OVIEDO

The paved Route 7 runs 195 km through cultivated areas and woods and across the Caaguazú hills to the spectacular 500-metre single span 'Friendship Bridge' across the Paraná (to Brazil) at Ciudad del Este.

CIUDAD DEL ESTE

(*Pop* 83,000; *phone code* 061) Originally founded as Ciudad Presidente Stroessner in 1957, this was the fastest growing city in the country until the completion of the Itaipú hydroelectric project, for which it is the centre of operations. Ciudad del Este has been described as the biggest shopping centre in Latin America, attracting Brazilian and Argentine visitors who find bargain prices for electrical goods, watches, perfumes etc. (Don't buy perfume at tempting prices on the street, it's only coloured water. Make sure that shops which package your goods pack what you actually bought.) Prices are decidedly high for N American and European visitors. Also watch the exchange rates if you're a short-term visitor from Argentina or Brazil. It's dirty, unfriendly and hotels and restaurants are more expensive than elsewhere in Paraguay. The leather market is well worth a visit, be sure to bargain.

Local information
● Accommodation
A3 *Convair*, Adrián Jara y García, T 500342, a/c, comfortable, cheaper rooms without bath; **A3** *Executive*, Adrián Jara y Curupayty, T 500942/3, inc a/c, breakfast – restaurant only; **A3** *Residence de la Tour* at Paraná Country Club, 5 km from centre, T 60316, superb, Swiss-owned, excellent restaurant (US$12-16 pp), swimming pool, gardens, beautiful view.

B *Catedral*, C A López 838, T 500378, inc breakfast, TV, a/c, several blocks from commercial area, large, modern with swimming pool, restaurant; **B** *Gran Hotel Acaray*, 11 de Septiembre y Río Paraná, T/F 511471/5, also has new extension, swimming pool, casino, nightclub, restaurant; **B** *San Rafael*, Abay y Adrián Jara, T 68134, large rooms, with breakfast, German and English spoken.

C *Itaipú*, Rodríguez y Nanawa, T 500371, breakfast, a/c; **C** *Mi Abuela*, Adrián Jara 128, T 500348, with breakfast, fan, poor beds; **C** *Munich*, Fernández y Miranda, T 500347, with breakfast, a/c, garage, rec; **C** *Puerta del Sol*, Rodríguez y Boquerón, T 500798, a/c, just off main street; **C-D** *El Cid*, Recalde 425, T 512221, breakfast, a/c, cheaper with fan.

D *Austria* (also known as *Viena*), Fernández 165, T 500883, above restaurant, with good breakfast and a/c, Austrian family, good views from upper floors, warmly rec; **D** *Tripolis*, San Blas 331, T 512450, a/c, poor restaurant, unhelpful, unsafe.

● Places to eat
Coreio, San Blas 125, T 0448, good Korean food; *Osaka*, Adrián Jara and, 100m away, *New Tokyo*, Adrián Jara 202, both good, authentic Japanese; *Seoul*, Curupayty y Adrián Jara, good parrillada; *Hotel Austria/Viena*, good Austrian food, clean, good value. Cheaper ones along García and in market. Many restaurants close on Sun.

● Banks & money changers
Banco Holandés Unido, cash on Mastercard, 5% commission; local banks (open Mon-Fri 0730-1100). Dollars can be changed into *reais* in town, but exchange may be better and easier in Foz do Iguaçu. Several *Casas de Cambio*: *Cambio Guaraní*, Av Monseñor Rodríguez, changes TCs for US$0.50, branch on Friendship Bridge has good rates for many currencies inc dollars and *reais*; *Tupi Cambios*, Adrián Jara 351; *Cambios Chaco*, Adrián Jara y Curupayty. *Casa de cambio* rates are better than street rates. Money changers (not rec) operate at the bus terminal but not at the Brazilian end of the Friendship Bridge.

● Post & telecommunications
International Phone: Antelco, Alejo García y Pai Pérez, near centre on road to bus terminal.

● Transport
Air Full jet airport. To **Asunción**, Arpa 3 flights Mon-Sat, 1 on Sun; also Lapsa/TAM daily en route to São Paulo. TAM, Edificio SABA, Monseñor Rodríguez.

Buses Terminal is on the southern outskirts (No 4 bus from centre, US$0.50, taxi US$3.50, rec as it's not a safe area). Many buses (US$17.25 *rápido*, 4½ hrs, at night only; US$9.50 *común*, 6 hrs) to and from **Asunción**. Nuestra Señora and Rysa reported to run the best; to **Villarrica**, 3 a day, last 0015, 4 hrs, US$6 (San Juan Nepomuceno); to **Pedro Juan Caballero**, 7 hrs, US$19; to **Concepción**, García, 11 hrs, comfortable; to **Encarnación** (for Posadas and Argentina), along fully paved road, frequent, 4 hrs, US$9 (this is probably cheaper than via Foz do

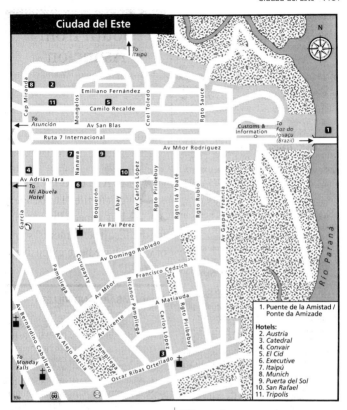

Ciudad del Este

To Itaipú

To Asunción

Emiliano Fernández

Camilo Recalde

Av San Blas

Ruta 7 Internacional

Av Mñor Rodríguez

Customs & Information

To Foz do Iguaçu (Brazil)

Av Adrián Jara

To Mi Abuela Hotel

Av Pai Pérez

Av Domingo Robledo

Francisco Cedzich

A Matiauda

To Monday Falls

Oscar Ribas Ortellado

Río Paraná

1. Puente de la Amistad / Ponte da Amizade

Hotels:
2. Austria
3. Catedral
4. Convair
5. El Cid
6. Executive
7. Itaipú
8. Munich
9. Puerta del Sol
10. San Rafael
11. Tripolis

Iguaçu).

FRONTIER WITH BRAZIL

● Immigration

Paraguay and Brazilian immigration formalities are dealt with on opposite sides of the bridge. **The border crossing over the Friendship Bridge** to Foz do Iguaçu is very informal but keep an eye on your luggage and make sure that you get necessary stamps – so great is the volume of traffic that it can be difficult to stop, especially with the traffic police moving you on. It is particularly busy on Wed and Sat, with long queues of vehicles. Pedestrians from Brazil cross on the N side of the bridge allowing easier passage on the other side for those returning with bulky packages. There is a US$3 tourist charge to enter Paraguay. **NB** Remember to adjust your watch to local time.

● Transport

The international bus goes from outside the Ciudad del Este terminal to the new bus terminal (*Rodoviária*) in Foz. There are also local buses from the terminal and along Av Adrián Jara, every 15 mins, 0600-2000, US$1, which go to the city terminal (*terminal urbana*) just outside Foz. Most buses will not wait at immigration, so disembark to get your exit stamp, walk across the bridge (10 mins) and obtain your entry stamp; keep your ticket and continue to Foz on the next bus free. Paraguayan taxis cross freely to Brazil (US$18) but it is cheaper to walk across the bridge and then take a taxi, bargain hard. You can pay in either currency. **To Iguaçu Falls** On the Brazilian side a 32-km road leads to the Iguaçu Falls and Tancredo Neves Bridge to Argentina. From the *terminal urbana* in Foz buses run to both the Brazilian and Argentinian sides of the Falls; if only visiting the Falls, immigration procedure on the Paraguayan and Brazilian sides of the Friendship Bridge is minimal, even for those normally requiring a visa to visit Brazil. If in doubt, though, obtain all necessary exit and entrance stamps. **To Argentina** Direct buses to Puerto Iguazú, frequent service by several companies from outside the terminal, US$3.50, you need to get Argentine and Paraguayan stamps (not Brazilian), bus does not wait so keep ticket for next bus.

ITAIPU

The huge **Itaipú** hydroelectric project, which covers an area of 1,350 sq km, is close to Ciudad del Este, and well worth a visit. Take a bus from Rodríguez y García, outside the terminal to the Visitors' Centre, open 0730-1200, 1330-1700, Sun and holidays 0800-1200, 1330-1630. Free conducted tours of the project include a film show (versions in several languages – ask) 45 mins before bus tours which start at 0830, 0930, 1030, 1400, 1500, 1600, Mon-Sat (Sun and holidays closed), check times in advance. Take passport.

Hernandarias, N of Ciudad del Este (*pop* 32,000, **D** *Hotel El León*, cleanish, poor breakfast, quiet; frequent buses from Ciudad del Este, US$0.60) grew rapidly with the building of Itaipú. From Hernandarias a paved road runs N to Cruce Carambey, where it meets Route 10 (see above, page 1179).

From Hernandarias, boat trips on Lago Itaipú go to Puerto Guaraní where there is a museum.

Puerto Presidente Franco (*pop* 24,000), S of Ciudad del Este, also benefitted from Itaipú investment. It is reached by the Tres Fronteras bus which leaves you 2 km from its small port on the Paraná, opposite Puerto Iguazú, Argentina (**E** *Hotel Rosa*, B Caballero y Piribebuy, T 061-512425, with bath). Regular launches cross here, but immigration formalities must be carried out in Ciudad del Este.

The **Monday** Falls, where the Río Monday drops into the Paraná gorge, 10 km S of Ciudad del Este, are worth visiting by taxi (return fare US$20). They are known locally as Cascada de Monday, or Lunes Cascada. There is good fishing below the falls.

South from Asunción

A N ATTRACTIVE area of fertile landscapes, but especially notable for the Jesuit settlements, some of which have been extensively restored.

GUARAMBARE AND VILLETA

At Km 28 on Route 1 (LP Petrol station) a road goes W to **Guarambaré**, a sleepy town in the sugar area with many Peace Corps trainees. From May to Nov bullock carts and trucks take the cane to the factory, 1 km past the electricity sub-station. Bus Asunción-Guarambaré, 45 mins, US$0.25, every 10 mins from terminal. From Guarambaré you can go to **Villeta** (27 km S of Asunción, *pop* 5,232), on the E bank of the Río Paraguay, which has undergone a rapid economic expansion. It is known for the fine children's clothing hand-made by nuns at a local convent. A little N is a park at Ytororó where trenches used in the war of the Triple Alliance can still be seen. From either place, the route back to Asunción, through typical farmlands and citrus orchards is via Ypané and Nemby.

Route One runs through some of the old mission towns to Encarnación, 370 km SE, on the Alto Paraná. **Itá** (*pop* 9,310), Km 37 from Asunción, founded 1539, is famous for rustic pottery (by Rosa Britez as you enter village).

YAGUARON

Km 48, founded in 1539, Yaguarón was the centre of the Franciscan missions in colonial times. It is set on a river at the foot of a hill in an orange-growing district. Most of Paraguay's petit-grain comes from the area. The town's famous church, in Hispano-Guarani Baroque style, was begun by the Franciscans in 1640 and finished in 1720, reconstructed in 1885 and recently renovated. (Open 0700-1100, 1330-1630, daily except Sun when am only; Sr Palacios has the key.) The tints, made by the Indians from local plants, are still bright on the woodcarvings. The pulpit is particularly fine. Stations of the Cross behind the village lead to a good view of the surroundings.

"The corridor, or outside walk under a projecting roof supported by pillars, is a typical feature of Paraguayan churches. Generally it runs all the way round the church, forming an entrance portico in front. An excellent example is the church at Yaguarón. It is the prototype of the mission sanctuaries of the early 18th century, when the structure was built with a sturdy wooden skeleton and the walls – simple screens of adobe or brick – had no function of support. The belfry is a modest little wooden tower somewhat apart from the church; in the missions it also served as a *mangrullo*, or watch tower." Paul Dony.

Museum Museo Del Doctor Francia, 500m down the road opposite the church, with artefacts from the life of Paraguay's first dictator, 'El Supremo', plus paintings and artefacts from the 18th century. The 18th century single-storey adobe building with bamboo ceilings and tiled roof belonged to Francia's father. Open Tues to Sun 0730-1130, free guided tour in Spanish.

Local festivals *Fiesta patronal*, mid-July.

● **Accommodation & places to eat** E *Hotel Silva*; E *Bar Elsi. Restaurant Ani Rejhaserei*, opp the church, basic accommodation, good meal.

● **Buses** Every 15 mins from Asunción.

PARAGUARI

(Km 63; *pop* 5,725), founded 1775, the N entrance to the mission area, at the foot of a range of hills with many streams. Its church, much restored, has two bell towers, both separate from the main structure. Buses between Asunción and Encarnación stop here.

● **Accommodation & places to eat** D *Hospedaje Alemán*, vegetarian meals; E *Hospedaje Bonanza*, friendly owners, basic. Excellent steaks at *Parador La Estación*.

DETOURS FROM PARAGUARI

Sapucay, 25 km E of Paraguarí, is the location of the workshops for the wood-burning steam locomotives (open Mon-Fri only). Bus from Asunción, 88 km – 0700, 1200, 3 hrs; road closed from Paraguarí after heavy rain. There are cheap *hospedajes*.

15 km NE from Paraguarí is **Chololó** (B *Parador Chololó*, T 0531-242, rec), with a small but attractive series of waterfalls and rapids with bathing facilities and walkways, mainly visited in the summer. It is a picturesque bus ride from Paraguarí, with good views of the surrounding countryside.

PARQUE NACIONAL YBICUY

At **Carapeguá**, Km 84 (*hospedaje* on main street, basic, friendly; blankets and hammocks to rent along Route 1, or buy your own, made locally and cheaper than elsewhere), a road turns off to Acahay, Ybicuy and the **Parque Nacional Ybicuy**, 67 km SE, one of the most accessible National Parks.

Founded in 1973, the 5,000 ha park includes one of the few remaining areas of rainforest in eastern Paraguay. Good walks, a beautiful camp site (hardly used in the week, no lighting, some facilities may not be available) and lots of waterfalls. At the entrance is a well set out park and museum as well as the reconstructed remains of the country's first iron foundry (La Rosada). Crowded on Sun but deserted the rest of the week. The only shops (apart from a small one at the entrance selling drinks, eggs, etc, and a good

T-shirt stall which helps support the park) are at **Ybicuy**, 30 km NW (**D** *Hotel Pytu'u Renda*, Av Gen Caballero 509, good food, cooking facilities; *Pensión Santa Rosa* and *San Juan*, both **E**, latter has no sign but is nice).

● **Buses** Bus from Ybicuy at 0430 and 1120, returning 0700 and 1345, goes as far as camp site, 2 km beyond the museum. From Asunción take a bus to Acahay, Transportes Emilio Cabrera, 8 daily and change, or bus to Ybicuy, 0630 which connects with a minibus.

Just before Km 141 is **Caapucú** (**E** *Hotel Misiones*; *Hotel Parados*; bus from Asunción, US$3.75). At Km 161 Route 1 crosses the Río Tebicuary which in colonial times formed the border between the missionary areas of the Franciscans (to the N) and the Jesuits (to the S). At the crossing is **Villa Florida**, an ideal holiday resort (but often overpriced) for sailing, fishing and relaxing, with several hotels: **B** *Nacional de Turismo*, Km 162, Mcal F Solano López, T 083-207, good and 2 *paradores*, camping nr the river (good fishing); also **A3** *Estancia Las Mercedes*, 7 km NE, T 083-220, full board, idyllic, river bathing, beaches, camping, highly rec. At **Centú Cué**, 5 km S of Villa Florida, there are hotels (**D** *Parador Centú Cué*, full board, pleasant, peaceful; **D** *Dorado*) and camping facilities; for reservations at either, T Asunción 206570 or directly to Centú Cué 083-219. At San Miguel (Km 178), all types of woollen articles are on sale (blankets, shawls, ponchos, hammocks, etc). At Km 196 is the small, peaceful town of **San Juan Bautista** (*pop* 6,872; **E** *Hotel Waldorf*, pleasant, rooms off a domestic courtyard). Its neatly cobbled streets, paved footpaths and substantial houses suggest a prosperity, unusual for rural Paraguay. The relatively recent cathedral on the main square has more than a touch of Jesuit severity.

SAN IGNACIO GUAZU

Km 226, a delightful town on the site of a Jesuit *reducción* (*guazú* is big in Guaraní). Several typical Hispano-Guaraní buildings survive, with pavilions and colonnades.

Museums The **Museo Jesuítico**, housed in the former Jesuit art workshop, reputedly the oldest surviving civil building in Paraguay, contains an important collection of Guaraní art and sculpture from the missionary period, open daily 0800-1130, 1400-1730, US$0.50. Videos in Spanish and English on the Jesuit missions can be seen. Nearby is the **Museo Histórico Semblanza de Héroes**, featuring displays on the Chaco War, open Mon-Sat 0745-1145, 1400-1700, Sun 0800-1100.

● **Accommodation** **E** pp *Unión*, T 082-544, with bath, a/c and breakfast; **B** *Parador Piringó*, T 082-262, modern, on outskirts, with a/c, **E** pp without, rec, restaurant open 24 hrs, most of the other places in town are *parrilladas*; **E** *Hospedaje San Antonio*, T 082-404, fan, basic; **E** *Hospedaje Miriam*, with fan, without bath, basic; **E** *Hospedaje Santa Rita*, without bath, fan, old-fashioned, basic. Camping is possible outside the town.

● **Buses** Regular bus services to/from Asunción, US$6 *común*, US$9 *rápido*; to Encarnación, frequent, US$7.50 *común*, US$10.50 *rápido*.

Santa María is 12 km to the NE along a cobbled road. (**F** pp *Pensión San José*, basic.) Here there is another fine museum in restored mission buildings containing some 60 Guaraní sculptures among the exhibits (open 0800-1130, 1330-1700, free). The modern church has a lovely altar-piece of the Virgin and Child (the key is kept at a house on the opposite side of the plaza). Good local *artesanía* shop. Transport from San Ignacio by bus from the Esso station, 6 a day from 0500, 45 mins.

From San Ignacio Guazú Route 4 runs 156 km W to **Pilar** (*pop* 13,135) opposite the confluence of the Ríos Paraguay and Bermejo. The road continues SW to the extreme SW tip of Paraguay, near Humaitá, the site of a heroic siege during the War of the Triple Alliance. There are occasional boats to Argentina and Asunción.

At **Santa Rosa** (Km 248), founded 1698, only a chapel of the original church survived a fire. The chapel houses a museum; on the walls are frescoes in poor condition; exhibits include a sculpture of the Annunciation considered to be one of the great works of the Hispanic American Baroque (ask at the *parroquia* next door for entry). The former bell tower can also be visited. The plaza is laid out in typical Jesuit mission style, surrounded by one-storey dwellings. One local hotel: **E** *Avenida*, on the outskirts. Buses from San Ignacio Guazú.

A road at Km 262 leads 52 km SW to **Ayolas**, associated with the Yacyretá hydroelectric scheme (**B** *Hotel Nacional de Turismo*, Av Costanera, T 072-2273, with shower, poor breakfast, otherwise OK; **E** *El Dorado*, with good restaurant). At Km 18 is **Santiago**, another important Jesuit centre founded in 1669 with a modern church containing a fine wooden carving of Santiago slaying the Saracens. Next door is a small museum containing a collection of wooden statuary from the old church including reredos depicting San Francisco Javier and San Felipe. Ask around the village for the key-holder. In the plaza one mission house (at far end from the church) is maintained in its original state. **Coronel Bogado** (*pop* 5,180), Km 319, is the southern limit of the mission area. Museum next door to the church, collection of wooden images from old church including reredos of San Francisco and San Felipe. The Fiesta de la Tradición Misionera is held here in the second half of January.

SAN COSME Y DAMIAN

At Km 306 a road turns off Route 1 to **San Cosmé y Damián**, 25 km S. Although founded as a Jesuit mission in 1632, it was moved to the present site in 1760. When the Jesuits were expelled from the Spanish colonies, 7 years later, the great church and ancillary buildings were unfinished. A huge completion project has recently been carried out following the original plans. Open 0700-1100, 1300-1700, entry US$0.25. (**E** *hospedaje* opp Antel building, dirty. Camping is possible in the school grounds but ask first.) Buses from Encarnación, La Cosmeña, US$4.25, 2 hrs, 0830, also services by Perla del Sur. Nearby is a neat new town where some of the Yacyretá dam workforce live.

Route 1 reaches the Alto Paraná at Carmen del Paraná, Km 331, 40 km W of Encarnación.

ENCARNACION

(*Pop* 60,000; *phone code* 071) A bridge connects this busy port on the Alto Paraná (founded 1614) with the Argentine town of Posadas. The old town has been badly neglected as it is due to be flooded when the Yacyretá-Apipé dam is completed. A modern town has been built higher up. This is less interesting than the lower part which forms the main commercial area selling a wide range of cheap goods to visitors from Argentina and Brazil. The town exports the products of a rich area: timber, soya, *mate*, tobacco, cotton, and hides; it is fast losing its traditional, rural appearance. The town is a good centre for visiting the nearby Jesuit missions of San Cosmé y Damián, Trinidad and Jesús. The cost of living is higher than in most other parts of Paraguay, but at present tourist goods, electrical equipment and accommodation are much cheaper than in Posadas.

Local information
● **Accommodation**

A2 *Novohotel Encarnación*, first class, on outskirts Route 1, Km 2, T 4131, comfortable, very well run, highly rec; **A3** *Cristal*, Estigarribia 1157, T 2371, restaurant.

B *Paraná*, Estigarribia 1414, T 4440, good breakfast, helpful, rec.

C *Acuario*, Mallorquín 1550, T 2676, with breakfast, central, pleasant, parking; **C** *Viera*, 25 de Mayo 413, T 2038, with breakfast and a/c, **D** with fan.

D *Central*, Mcal López 542, T 3454, with breakfast, nice patio, German spoken; **D** *Germano*, Cabañas y C A López, opposite bus terminal, T 3346, **E** without bath, German and Japanese spoken, small, very accommodating, highly rec; **D** *Itapúa*, C A López y Cabanas, T/F 5045, opp bus station, dark rooms, modern; **D** *Hotel Liz*, Av Independencia 1746, T 2609, comfortable, restaurant, parking, rec; **D** *Viena*, PJ Caballero 568, T 3486, beside Antelco, with breakfast, German-run, good food, garage.

E *La Rueda*, C A López y Memmel nr bus station, a bit run down but OK.

● **Places to eat**

Rubi, Chinese, Mcal Estigarribia 519, good; *Buez Brasil*, Av Irrazábal, good and popular buffet; *Parrillada las Delicias*, Estigarribia 1694, good steaks, comfortable, Chilean wines; *Rancho Grande*, Estigarribia y Cerro Corá, large

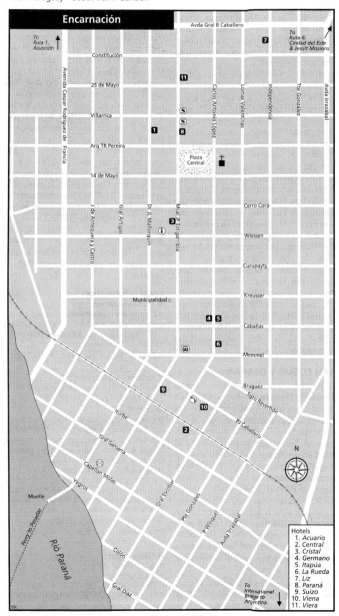

Encarnación

Avda Gral B Caballero

To Ruta 1, Asunción

To Ruta 6: Ciudad del Este & Jesuit Missions

Constitución

25 de Mayo

Villarrica

Arq TR Pereira

Plaza Central

14 de Mayo

Avenida Caspar Rodríguez de Francia

Carlos Antonio López

Lomas Valentinas

Independencia

Tte González

Avda Irrazábal

Cerro Corá

Wiessen

Curupayty

Kreusser

Cabañas

Memmel

Bruguez

Sato Reverflón

Pj Caballero

J de Antequera y Castro

Gral Artigas

Dr JL Mallorquin

Mcal JF Estigarribia

Municipalidad

Iturbe

Gral Ganarra

Capellán Molas

Yegros

Muelle

Gral Escobar

Pre González

P Wriquel

Avda Irrazábal

Colón

Gral Díaz

Río Paraná

ferry to Posadas

N

To International Bridge to Argentina

Hotels
1. *Acuario*
2. *Central*
3. *Cristal*
4. *Germano*
5. *Itapúa*
6. *La Rueda*
7. *Liz*
8. *Paraná*
9. *Suizo*
10. *Viena*
11. *Viera*

parrillada, live music; *Cuarajhy*, Estigarribia y Pereira, terrace seating, good food, open 24 hrs; *Ñasaindy*, Estigarribia 900, for snacks; *Karanday*, Gral Caballero, good grill; *Tokio*, Mcal Estigarribia 472, good Japanese, real coffee.

● **Banks & money changers**
Most banks now in the upper town, eg **Banco Continental**, Mcal Estigarribia 1418, Visa accepted; **Lloyds Bank**, Villarrica y Mcal Estigarribia, open Mon-Fri 0845-1215; **Banco Unión**, Mcal Estigarribia 1404, will change TCs (with purchase receipt), cash advance on Visa. Money changers at the Paraguayan side of the bridge but it is best to change money in town. *Casas de cambio* for cash on Mcal Estagarribia (eg *Cambios Guaraní* at No 307, *Cambio Iguazú* at No 211).

● **Embassies & consulates**
Argentina, Mallorquín y Cabañas; **Brazil**, Memmel 452; **Germany**, Memmel 627; **Japan**, C A López 1290.

● **Laundry**
Laverap, 25 de Mayo 552.

● **Post & telecommunications**
International Phone: Antelco, Capitán PJ Caballero y Mcal López, 0700-2200, very unfriendly.

● **Tourist offices**
Wiessen 345, 3 blocks from bus station, helpful, open 0800-1200; street map of city. In the afternoon map of city can be obtained from the Municipalidad, Estigarribia y Kreusser, oficina de planificación.

● **Transport**
Trains Passenger trains were suspended in 1997.

Buses The bus terminal is at Estigarribia y Memmel; good cheap snacks. To/from **Asunción**, Alborada, Flecha de Oro, Rysa, Nuestra Señora de la Asunción, all except last named at least 4 a day, 6 hrs, US$15. Stopping (*común*) buses US$9, but much slower (6-7 hrs). To **Ciudad del Este**, US$9, several daily, 4 hrs.

Taxi A few horsedrawn (about US$0.50), but prices tend to be high if drivers suspect you don't know the distance you want to travel. Some motor driven ones for those in a hurry.

FRONTIER WITH ARGENTINA

The new San Roque road bridge connects Encarnación with **Posadas**.

● **Immigration**
Formalities are conducted at respective ends of the bridge. Argentine side has different offices for locals and foreigners; Paraguay has one for both. **NB** Paraguay is 1 hr behind Argentina, except during Paraguayan summer time.

● **Transport**
Take any 'Posadas/Argentina' bus from opp bus terminal over the bridge, US$1.50, 30 mins, *común* and US$3, *rápido* (faster treatment at the frontier). Bus passengers should keep all luggage with them and should retain bus ticket; buses do not wait. After formalities (queues common), use ticket on next bus. Taxi costs US$5. Cycles are not allowed to use the bridge, but officials may give cyclists a lift. A ferry still operates, but only for locals as there are no immigration officials on the Argentine side.

ENCARNACION TO CIUDAD DEL ESTE

JESUIT MISSIONS

From Encarnación a paved road (Route 6) goes NE to Ciudad del Este. At Km 21, just beyond Capitán Miranda, is **A2** *Hotel Tirol*, T 075-555, with 40 double rooms, chalets, 2 swimming pools, terraces, used as a stopover for Argentine coach tours. A further 7 km towards Ciudad del Este is **Trinidad**, the hilltop site of a Jesuit *reducción*, built 1706-1760, now a Unesco World Cultural Heritage site. The Jesuit church, once completely ruined, has been partially restored. Note the restored carved stone pulpit, the font and other masonry and relief sculpture. Also partially rebuilt is the bell-tower which is near the original church (excellent views from the top). You can also see another church, a college, workshops and the Indians' living quarters. It was founded in 1706 by Padre Juan de Anaya; the architect was Juan Bautista Prímoli. For information, or tours, contact Sr Augusto Servián Goana, the curator who lives close by. Many buses go from Encarnación to and through Trinidad, take any bus from the terminal marked Ciudad del Este, US$1 (beware overcharging). A taxi tour from Encarnación costs about US$30. You can stay at the Centro Social, food and shower available, take sleeping gear; camping permitted behind the souvenir stall. Hotel under construction.

10 km NW of Trinidad, along a rough road (which turns off 300m N from Trinidad entrance) is **Jesús**, now a small town where another group of Jesuits finally settled in 1763. In the five years before

they were expelled they commenced a massive construction programme including church, sacristy, *residencia* and a baptistry, on one side of which is a square tower. There is a fine front façade with three great arched portals in a Moorish style (opening hours as for Trinidad, entry US$1). Beautiful views in all directions. Camping permitted at entrance to ruins. Unreliable bus service from Trinidad, 30 mins, US$1, last return bus 1700, also collective taxis, US$4.25. Enquire locally as taxis try to overcharge.

From Trinidad the road goes through or near a number of German colonies including Hohenau (Km 36), Obligado, Santa Rita (**B** *Hotel Staufenberg*, Km 41, T 600-756, good, restaurant), Bella Vista (Km 42, **C** *Hotel Bella Vista Plaza*, Samaniego 1415, T 0757-236; **C** *Papillón*, Km 44, T 0757-235, clean) and, at Km 67, a cobbled side road leads to Pirapó, a Japanese settlement (**E** *Hotel Pirapó*). This is a prosperous agricultural area, attractive countryside with facilities for travellers en route. Significant areas of forest which used to cover this region were cleared between 1945 and 1985 to plant soybeans and other crops. Eventually Route 6 meets Route 2 close to Ciudad del Este.

North from Asunción

THE Paraguay river, still a main trade route between Brazil and Argentina, dominates this section.

ASUNCION TO CONCEPCION

A boat trip up the Paraguay to Concepción, about 312 km N of Asunción, is one of the easiest ways of seeing the country. The winding river is 400m wide, with a lot of traffic, for in the absence of a direct road between Concepción and Asunción, this is the main trade route for the products of northern Paraguay: cattle, hides, *yerba mate*, tobacco, timber and *quebracho*. For passenger sailings, see under Asunción, **River boats**.

North from Asunción by river, you pass Villa Hayes where the bridge marks the beginning of the Trans-Chaco Highway. About 120 km upstream is Puerto Rosario where an unpaved road goes SE to San Estanislao. A further 50 km upstream is Puerto Antequera and 100 km beyond is Concepción.

By road there are two alternative routes: via the Trans-Chaco Highway and Pozo Colorado. The Pozo Colorado-Concepción road, 146 km, is now paved apart from a 30 km section which is very bad in the wet. This route offers spectacular views of bird life.

Via Route 3 to Coronel Oviedo, Route 8 to Yby Yaú (paved) and thence E along Route 5 (paving in progress but very bad in wet weather).

CONCEPCION

(*Pop* 35,000; *phone code* 031) A free port for Brazil, Concepción stands on the E bank. This pleasant, friendly, quiet and picturesque town is the trade centre of the N, doing a considerable business with Brazil. The market is E of the main street, Agustín Pinedo; from here Av Pdte Franco runs W to the port. The Museo Municipal is at Mcal Lopéz y Cerro Corá (Mon-Fri 0700-1230); it contains a collection of guns, religious art and other objects. About 9 km S is a new bridge across the Río Paraguay, offering an interesting walk across the shallows and islands to the W bank, about 1 hr return trip, taxi US$9.

Local information
● **Accommodation**

B *Francés*, Franco y C A López, T 2283, with a/c, **C-D** with fan, with breakfast, good value, restaurant, rec.

C-D *Victoria*, Franco y Caballero, T 2826 with a/c, **D** with fan, with breakfast, attractive old building with patio, restaurant, rec.

E *Boquerón*, Iturbe y Brasil, basic, nice staff, dirty toilets, quiet area; **E** *Center*, Franco 240, with bath, hot water when the weather is hot, a/c on second floor; **E** pp *Concepción*, Don Bosco y Colombia, T 2506, with bath, breakfast and a/c, cheaper with fan, basic, poor beds; **E** *Imperial*, Garay y Villarica, fan, without bath, basic.

● **Places to eat**

The restaurants of *Hotels Victoria* and particularly *Francés* are good. Also, *Tedacar*, on Franco, good food, pleasant with seating in the garden behind. *Bar El Trébol*, in the centre, has chamamé and polka paraguaya music on Thur pm. *Heladería Amistad*, Franco y 31 de Mayo, good sandwiches and ice cream.

● **Consulate**

Brazilian Vice Consulate, Franco 972, Mon-Fri 0800-1200.

● **Transport**

Air Asunción-Concepción flights are operated by LATN, Aeronorte, Arpa and TAM (which tends to be cheapest). TAM to Asunción daily at 0800, 40 mins, book as early as possible (only 25 seats), free colectivo from TAM office on main street to airport. Arpa daily at 1530. On Mon, Wed and Fri at 0700 TAM flies from Asunción and Concepción to Vallemí, Fuerte Olimpo and Bahía Negra, all three villages to N of Concepción on the Río Paraguay. Air services to these places are irregular because runways are sometimes flooded or muddy. There is no direct air connection between Concepción and Pedro Juan Caballero.

Buses The terminal is on the outskirts, 8 blocks N along Gen Garay, but buses also stop in the centre. A shuttle bus (Línea 1) runs between terminal and the port. Several companies to **Asunción**, most services overnight; most go via Pozo Colorado, 5½ hrs, US$18 *directo*, 6½ hrs, US$15 *semi-directo*, though a few go via Yby Yaú and Coronel Oviedo, 8 hrs (rough to Yby Yaú). Until paving work on the roads to Pozo Colorado and Yby Yaú is completed, expect long delays in wet weather. To **Pedro Juan Caballero**, *semi-directo* 6 hrs, US$6, *directo* 4 hrs, US$7. To **Horqueta**, 1 hr, US$1.50. To **Filadelfia**, *rápido*, 6 hrs.

Shipping To **Asunción**, 15 hrs, several companies (fares under Asunción **River boats**). For details of sailings ask at the Agencia Marítima, Nanawa 547, near dock.

NORTH OF CONCEPCION

Normally it is possible to find a passage on boats going upstream from Concepción to the small 'ports' serving local communities, though there are few places to stay. North of the confluence with the Río Apá, the Río Paraguay becomes the border with Brazil. You can enter Brazil, by taking a boat to Isla Margarita, where you can get a ferry to Porto Murtinho, Brazil, but the Paraguayan officials cannot give you an exit stamp so this route cannot be used for travel further into Brazil (see page 625 Brazil, **The Centre-West**).

The limit of river traffic if the river is in flood is **Bahía Negra**, the northernmost river port on the border. It has flights to Asunción, but neither hotel nor bank. To cross to Porto Coimbra and thence to Porto Esperança in Brazil requires a yellow fever certificate and much red tape because it is not a regular border crossing. Local river traffic is sparse. From Porto Esperança a road runs to Corumbá. Above Bahía Negra, the river leaves Paraguay and for a few kms is the border between Bolivia and Brazil. Thereafter it enters the **Pantanal** – see Brazil, **The Centre-West**, page 629.

EAST OF CONCEPCION

There is a 215 km road (Route 5 – paving in progress on first 112 km to Yby Yaú) from Concepción, eastwards to the Brazilian border. This road goes through Horqueta, Km 50, a cattle and lumber town of 10,000 people, then passes near Arroyito where an experimental land resettlement programme began after the political changes of 1989. Further on the road is very scenic. From **Yby Yaú** (junction with Route 8 S to Coronel Oviedo, fuel, restaurants) the road is paved to Pedro Juan Caballero.

PARQUE NACIONAL CERRO CORA

6 km E of Yby Yaú a road branches off to the very pleasant, uncrowded **National Park of Cerro Corá** (22,000 ha), which is the site of Mariscal Francisco Solano López' death and the final defeat of Paraguay in the War of the Triple Alliance. There is a monument to him and other national heroes; the site is constantly guarded. It has hills and cliffs (some with precolumbian caves and petroglyphs), camping facilities, swimming and hiking trails. The rocky outcrops are spectacular and the warden, Carmelo Rodríguez, is helpful and will provide free guides. When you have walked up the road and seen the line of leaders' heads, turn right and go up the track passing a dirty-looking shack (straight on leads to a military base). Administration office is at Km 180 on Ruta 5, 5 km E of the main entrance.

THE BRAZILIAN BORDER

The border town of **Pedro Juan Caballero** (*pop* 37,331; *phone code* 036), is separated from the Brazilian town of Ponta Porã, by a road (Av Internacional): locals cross as they please (see below for immigration formalities). The contrast between the two sides of the border is stark: most of the shops are on the Paraguayan side, which is good for cheap liquor and electronics. Ponta Porã has a road to São Paulo and the Atlantic coast and a railway to Campo Grande. Near the bus terminal at Teniente Herrero 998 y Estigarribia, is a natural history museum run by the Fundación Kayamo, entry free, open Mon-Sat 0800-1200, 1300-1700.

Local information
● **Accommodation**
B *Casino Amambay*, Dr Francia 1, T 2718, luxury, good restaurant, close to border; **B** *Eiruzú*, Estigarribia 4-8, T 2259, with breakfast, modern, rec, swimming pool, good restaurant.

D *Corina*, 14 de Mayo, T 2960, with breakfast, T 2960, rec; **D** *La Negra*, Mcal López 1342, T 2262. Several others which are less good.

● **Places to eat**
In hotels, or the Brazilian side. *Parrillada El Galpón*, Mcal López 892, is rec; *Nasaindy*, Av Internacional 778, not cheap; *Pepe*, Av Internacional 748, expensive, live music.

● **Banks & money changers**
Bancopar changes TCs. At least 6 *casas de cambio* for TCs (also deal in European currencies) inc *Cambios Chaco*, Mcal López 1462. At weekends try *Game Centre Guaraní* or *Casa China*. TCs not changed for US$ cash anywhere in town.

● **Transport**
Air Daily flights to Asunción, twice on Tues and Fri (though they may be suspended after heavy rain).

Buses To **Concepción**, 4 hrs, US$7, *preferencial*, 5 hrs, US$6 *común*. To **Asunción**, direct, 7-7½ hrs, US$13 (US$24 deluxe sleeper) and slower buses, 9-10 hrs, eg Cometa del Amambay at 0900 and 1900, US$11. Most buses for **Campo Grande** leave from Ponta Porã.

THE FRONTIER WITH BRAZIL
● **Paraguayan immigration**
To cross into Brazil officially, first obtain a Paraguayan exit stamp at Tte Herrero 2068, T 2047, Mon-Fri 0700-1200, 1400-1700, Sat 0700-1200. Then report to Brazilian federal police in Ponta Porã. It is essential to observe immigration formalities or you will run into problems later.

● **Brazilian Consulate**
Francia y Iturbe: go there first if you need a Brazilian visa.

There is another crossing to Brazil at Bella Vista on the Río Apá, NW of PJ Caballero; buses run from the Brazilian border town of Bela Vista to Jardim and thence to Campo Grande.

The Paraguayan Chaco

A REMARKABLE area of marshes and farm-lands developed by German-speaking Mennonites, with a substantial population of Indian peoples. Birds are spectacular and common, while other wildlife is equally interesting but less frequently seen.

The Paraguayan Chaco covers 24 million ha, but has fewer than 100,000 inhabitants, most of those living just across the Río Paraguay from Asunción (the average density is less than one person to the square kilometre). A single major highway, the Ruta Trans-Chaco, runs in a straight line N-W to the Bolivian border 20 km beyond Nueva Asunción, at Gen E A Garay. As far as Mariscal Estigarribia, its paved surface is excellent, but beyond that point its dirt surface, after rain, is negotiable only by 4WD vehicles. The elevation rises very gradually from 50m opposite Asunción to 450m on the Bolivian border.

The Chaco is divisible into 3 sections. The Low Chaco, just W of Asunción across the Río Paraguay, is a picturesque palm savanna, much of which is permanently inundated because of the impenetrable clay beneath the surface, although there are 'islands' of high ground. Cattle ranching on gigantic *estancias* is the pre-

vailing economic activity; some units lie several hundred km down tracks off the highway. Cattle breeds are very mixed – English Herefords, Indian Brahmins, and Brazilian. Most *estancias* are chronically overstocked and overgrazed; the stock are in poor condition and calving rates are very low. Remote *estancias* have their own airfields, and all are equipped with 2-way radios. Motorists should beware of cattle on the Trans-Chaco, especially at night.

The Middle Chaco, near Filadelfia, has been settled by Mennonites, Anabaptist refugees of German extraction who began arriving in the late 1920s. There are three administratively distinct but adjacent colonies: Menno (from Russia via Canada and Mexico); Fernheim (directly from Russia) and Neuland (the last group to arrive, also from Russia, after WW2). Among themselves, the Mennonites speak 'plattdeutsch' ('Low German'), but they readily speak and understand 'hochdeutsch' ('High German'), which is the language of instruction in their schools. Increasingly, younger Mennonites speak Spanish and Guaraní, while English is not unknown. Altogether there are 118 villages with a population of about 10,000 Mennonites, 10,000 Indians and much smaller numbers of 'Paraguayans' and other immigrants. The natural vegetation is scrub forest, with a mixture of hardwoods, and cactus in the N. The *palo borracho* (bottle-tree) with its pear-shaped, water-conserving, trunk, and the tannin-rich *quebracho* (axe-breaker) are the most important native species.

Parque Nacional Defensores del Chaco From Filadelfia an alternative route goes N to this 780,000 ha park, where most of the country's remaining jaguars are found. Puma, tapir and peccary also inhabit the area, but none is commonly seen except, with great patience, around water holes at nightfall. This road is very rough and negotiable only by 4WD vehicles; park rangers and very limited facilities can be found at Fortín Madrejón and Aguas Dulces. Most settlements beyond the orbit of Filadelfia are under military

The People of the Chaco

🐌 The **Mennonites**, who run their own banks, schools, hospitals and agricultural cooperatives, have created a prosperous community in an area that has attracted few other settlers. They are mainly crop-farmers raising citrus, groundnuts, sorghum and cotton, but their dairy products are excellent and widely distributed throughout the country. About half the country's milk production comes from the Chaco.

Very few of the remaining **Chaco Indians**, most notably the Ayoreo, still rely on hunting and gathering for their livelihood to any great degree. Many have settled among or near Mennonite colonies, where they cultivate cotton and subsistence crops, and work as day labourers for the Mennonites or on Paraguayan cattle *estancias*. They speak a variety of indigenous languages, including Guaraní, but are often more likely to know German than Spanish. Controversial fundamentalist Christian missionaries proselytize actively among them.

jurisdiction and a letter of authorization or military introduction may be useful.

The High Chaco consists of low dense thorn forest, an impenetrable barricade of hard spikes and spiny branches resistant to fire, heat and drought, and very tough on tyres. Occasional tracks lead off the Trans-Chaco for a short distance. Towards Bolivia cactus becomes more prevalent as rainfall decreases. There are a few *estancias* towards the S, where the brush is bulldozed into hedges and the trees left for shade. Summer temperatures often exceed 45°C.

No expedition should leave the Trans-Chaco without plentiful supplies of water, food and fuel. In the Middle and Low Chaco, there are service stations at regular intervals along the highway, but none beyond Mariscal Estigarribia. Since this is a major smuggling route from Bolivia, it is unwise to stop for anyone in the night. There is almost no traffic in the

High Chaco, and ill-equipped expeditions have had to be rescued by the army or have come to grief. Clear the area around your camp to deter poisonous snakes. Winter temperatures are warm by day, cooler by night, but summer heat and mosquitoes can make it very unpleasant (pyrethrum coils – *espirales* – are available throughout the region). The rapid improvement of the highway has opened the area to agricultural colonization, especially by foreigners, but oil exploration is as yet unsuccessful.

To reach the Ruta Trans-Chaco, you leave Asunción by the route across the Río Paraguay to Villa Hayes. Bird life is especially abundant and visible in the palm savanna, but other wild animals occur mostly as road kills. At Km 270 is **Pozo Colorado**, the turning for Concepción (see page 1189). There are two restaurants, a service station and a military post; for hitching, try truck drivers at the truck stop. Toll point US$0.75. At this point, the tidy Mennonite homesteads, surrounded by flower gardens and citrus orchards, begin to appear. A good place to stay or eat on the Trans-Chaco is **Cruce de los Pioneros** (ex-Cruce Loma Plata), at Km 415, a popular weekend excursion from Asunción where accommodation (**C** *Los Pioneros*, hot shower, a/c, clean, friendly, good breakfast), a bank and fuel are available.

FILADELFIA

The service centres of the Mennonite area are Filadelfia (Fernheim Colony), Loma Plata (Menno Colony), and Neu-Halbstadt (Neuland Colony). **Filadelfia**, 472 km from Asunción, is the largest of the three. A knowledge of German is very helpful in this area. The bank does not change bolivianos; good rates for US$ cash. Sieghart Friesen, Av Trébol, Filadelfia, rec as guide, knowledgeable on the area, speaks Spanish and German.

Museum

The **Unger Museum** (US$1 admission inc video) provides a glimpse of pioneer life in the Chaco, as well as exhibiting artefacts of the aboriginal peoples of the region. The Manager of the *Hotel Florida* will open the museum upon request, when things are not too busy.

Local information
● Accommodation
Note that accommodation in Filadelfia and elsewhere in the Chaco is heavily booked in Sept when there is a national motor rally centred in the town.

C *Florida*, T 091-258, modern motel-style wing with a/c, very comfortable, good restaurant, slow service, **E** pp in annex, good German pastries available, expensive breakfast; **C** *Safari*, a/c, pool, comfortable.

E *Edelweiss*, basic, fan. 5 km E of town, Parque Trébol has basic camping facilities at no charge, but lacks running water.

● Places to eat
La Estrella rec for good ice cream and *asados*; another good restaurant *El Girasol*, opp; *Remi*, on same street, pizzas and ice cream. Plenty of good, but basic homemade ice cream, more than welcome in the heat.

● Shopping
A craft shop, *Libería El Mensajero*, next to *Hotel Florida*, is run by Sra Penner, very helpful and informative. Next to the Unger Museum is a useful supermarket.

● Transport
Buses from Asunción, Stel Turismo, Mon, Tues, Thur, Sun 2100, Sat 1230, 6 hrs, US$17; Nasa, Colombia 1050, T 200697, 2200, Mon-Fri, Sat 1430, Sun 2000 7 hrs, US$14 (also calls at main terminal) less comfortable.

Loma Plata, the centre of Menno Colony, is 25 km E of Filadelfia (**E** *Hotel Loma Plata*, a/c, friendly, clean, with restaurant). Good museum open on request; ask at nearby Secretariat building. Bus from Filadelfia, Stel Turismo, 1845, US$2.50. 33 km S of Filadelfia is **Neu-Halbstadt**, centre of Neuland Colony (**C** *Hotel Boquerón*, with excellent restaurant and tasty ice cream). Neu-Halbstadt is a good place to purchase local Indian crafts. Bus, Stel Turismo, 0100. 40 km W of Filadelfia, across the Trans-Chaco, is **Fortín Toledo**, where the San Diego Zoo supports a small reserve for Wagner's peccary, a Pleistocene relic thought extinct until 1975 (visitors not generally welcomed); nearby are abandoned fortifications and a military cemetery from the 1930s Chaco War.

TO BOLIVIA
From Filadelfia to the Bolivian border, 20 km beyond Gen Eugenio A Garay, is 304 km. Best to fill up with fuel and supplies at Filadelfia in the Mennonite Co-op supermarket. There are sparse facilities (food, fuel) until **Mariscal Estigarribia**, Km 540 (**D** *Hotel Alemán*, with breakfast, also cheaper rooms without bath; accommodation also available from Ecmetur Agency next to service station, US$8; the military post may provide a meal and bed; at Km 516, turn left and go 25 km to Rosaleda, to **C** *Hotel-Restaurante Suizo*, with breakfast, shower, fan, clean, Swiss run). You can change money at the supermarket *Chaparral*, and local German priests may offer you a bed. (Daily bus from Filadelfia 1500, 2 hrs; daily colectivo 1900; daily bus to Asunción 0700. From Asunción Ecmetur, Mon-Fri 2115, Sat 1330, Sun 2030, 9½ hrs, US$14). Thereafter military outposts or *estancias* are the only alternatives.

At **Estancia La Patria**, Km 662, a Centro Urbano Rural includes a motel (**E**, pleasant, good value), supermarket and fuel. Bus from Filadelfia, Fri 0500, US$9.25, leaves La Patria Fri 0700, also truck transport US$12. From here safaris can be made into the 40,000 ha Parque Nacional Teniente Enciso (entrance 18 km along the Trans-Chaco; little wildlife to be seen except at night; trenches from the Chaco War are visible). At Nueva Asunción, 95 km beyond La Patria, there is an airbase where you can get water, but you may have to show your papers and be registered.

Identity checks at the numerous military checkpoints are common, and photographs should be a good likeness of the bearer. Backpackers need expect no special difficulties, but motorists should carry plenty of food and water since even small amounts of rain turn the highway into mud and cause major delays. Motorcycling beyond Mariscal Estigarribia can be difficult because of the deep sand and can be dangerous in wet weather. Passport control is at Fortín Mister Long, 13 km short of Gen Garay (state whether you are entering or leaving). Camping is possible and water is available here, but do not surrender your passport to the *guardia* if staying overnight, since you may have to wait until the following day to have it returned. The commandant of Fortín Gral Garay is friendly and has allowed travellers to stay the night and use the showers (1995). There is no official charge but a contribution is appropriate. Exit stamps should be obtained in Asunción: take your bus ticket to Migración, do not wait until the border. For the continuation of this route, see under **Boyuibe** in **Bolivia**, page 323. Take small denomination dollar notes as it is impossible to buy bolivianos before reaching Bolivia (if entering from Bolivia street changers in Santa Cruz sell Guaraníes at good rates).

● **Transport**
Hitching is possible but traffic is sparse (fee US$10-15). Trucks travel into Bolivia and may take passengers in Filadelfia; the Esso Station on Hindenburgstrasse and the police checkpoint are the most convenient places to ask, but Mariscal Estigarribia and other checkpoints on the Trans-Chaco are also possible: ask the police for help, but be prepared to wait up to a week.

● **Tours from Asunción**
Many agencies offer tours, staying for up to 6 days in Cruce de los Pioneros. If you wish to explore the remoter parts of the Chaco, guides can be found in Asunción, often German speaking, at around US$100 per day. Some travellers report that it is difficult to visit Indian areas because most tours are operated by Mennonites who only visit Mennonite communities.

Information for travellers

BEFORE TRAVELLING

ENTRY REQUIREMENTS
● **Documents**

A passport is required for a stay of up to 90 days. Visitors are registered on arrival by the immigration authorities and get their documents back immediately. This procedure applies to those who do not require visas. Citizens of the following countries do NOT need a visa (June 1997): USA, UK, Germany, Austria, Belgium, Spain, Italy, Holland, Luxembourg, Norway, Sweden, Finland, Switzerland, Israel, Japan, South Africa, Argentina (some crossings accept identity cards instead of passports), Uruguay, Brazil, Chile, Ecuador, Colombia, Costa Rica, Bolivia, Peru. All others must apply for a visa, which is free, presenting a valid passport, photograph (for a business visa a supporting letter from one's employer should suffice). If you do not get an entrance stamp in your passport you can be turned back at the border, or have trouble when leaving Paraguay.

● **Representation overseas**

Germany, Mainzer Landstrasse 46 D, 6000 Frankfurt Main 1, T (69) 720170; **UK**, Braemar Lodge, Cornwall Gardens, London SW7 4AQ, T 0171 937-6629, F 0171 937-5687; **USA**, 2400 Massachusetts Avenue NW, Washington, DC 2008, T 202 363-8207.

● **Tourist information**

The Dirección General de Turismo has an office at Palma y Alberdi in Asunción. Information about weather and roads from Touring y

Automóvil Club Paraguayo (TACP) at Brasil y 25 de May (who also produce a road map), and the office of the traffic police in Asunción. The best maps, inc ones of the Chaco, are available from Instituto Geográfico Militar, Av Perú y Jardín Botánico, take passport (an IGM map of the country can be bought at bookshops in Asunción). Small national maps, made by the Army, can be bought from the TACP, at bookshops and bus terminals.

For information on national parks: Dirección de Parques Nacionales y Vida Silvestre, Presidente Franco 736 y Ayolas, Edif Ayfra p 1, bloque B, Asunción, T 445214, Mon-Fri 0715-1300 (a permit is required to visit the 10 National Parks open to the public; there are 8 protected areas closed to the public); on conservation: Fundación Moisés Bertoni para la Conservación de la Naturaleza, Prócer Argüello 208 y Mcal López y Boggiani, T 608740/1, open Mon-Fri 0800-1700, permits must be obtained here for the Moisés Bertoni Park and Museum in Alto Paraná.

Business visitors Foreign business is transacted in Asunción, Ciudad del Este and Pedro Juan Caballero (with retail outlets particularly in the last two).

WHEN TO GO
● **Best time to visit**

May to Oct is the best time for a visit.

HEALTH

Tuberculosis, typhoid, dysentery, and hepatitis are endemic. Hookworm is the most common disease in the country, and there is much venereal disease, goitre and leprosy. Visitors should be inoculated against tetanus, typhoid, and paratyphoid. Be very careful over salad and tap water (bottled water is available). Local mosquito repellent, *Repel*, and pyrethrum coils are effective. Dengue fever (see **Health Information**) has recently been reported. Medical fees and medicine costs are high. The Centro Paraguayo del Diagnóstico, Gral Díaz 975 y Colón, Asunción, is rec as inexpensive, foreign languages spoken. Clínica Integral de Mujer, Mcal Estigarribia 1085 y Brasil, Asunción, T 94722, has been rec as a good gynaecological clinic. Dentists can be found either at the centre, or at Odontología 3, Mcal Estigarribia 1414 y Pai Pérez, T 200175, Asunción.

MONEY

● **Currency**

The Guaraní (plural Guaraníes) is the unit of currency, symbolized by the letter G (crossed). There are bank notes for 100, 500, 1,000, 5,000, 10,000 and 50,000 guaraníes and coins for 100, 50 and 100 guaraníes. Get rid of all your guaraníes before leaving Paraguay; there is no market for them elsewhere (except in some *cambios* in Buenos Aires or Montevideo). Asunción is a good place for obtaining US$ cash for TCs or on Access or Visa especially if heading for Brazil. Many banks in Asunción (see page 1172) give US$ cash, but charge up to 5½% commission. Rates for all foreign currencies, except bolivianos, are reasonable. *Casas de cambio* sometimes want to see customers' records of purchase before accepting TCs. Visitors are advised to check on the situation on changing TCs in advance. Visa and Mastercard cash advances are possible in Asunción, Caacupé and Encarnación. Mastercard/Cirrus ATMs are located in branches of Banco Unión. Street dealers operate from early in the morning until late at night, even at weekends or public holidays. **NB** Dirty and/or torn US$ bills are very difficult to change or spend, especially in the Chaco. Check notes carefully before accepting them in *casas de cambio*. A bank, such as Lloyds, will replace all legitimate bills with acceptable ones.

● **Cost of living**

Paraguay is cheaper than Argentina and Brazil. There are a few hotels in our F range and many good ones in our C-E ranges, with breakfast, private shower and toilet. Most hotels have 2 rates – one for a room with a/c, the other without.

● **Credit cards**

Visa and Mastercard credit cards are widely accepted even for small purchases. Foreign-issued Visa cards may not always be accepted though a phone call will often resolve the problem; Visa is displayed as Unioncard. Credit card transactions are sometimes subject to a surcharge. For Western Union T (21) 496683.

GETTING THERE

BY AIR

● **From Europe**

Iberia has 6 flights a week to Asunción from Madrid, with a change of plane in Buenos Aires. From other points in Europe, slow connections can be made via Rio or São Paulo. Routes from Europe via Brazil offer greater ticketing flexibility than other options.

● **From North America**

American operates daily from Miami via São Paulo, also from Dallas; flights from other US cities connect in Miami. From California, connections via Lima or Miami.

● **Within South America**

From Montevideo Lapsa/TAM and Pluna 3 times a week; from Buenos Aires by Aerolíneas Agentinas daily, direct from Ezeiza, also daily with Lapsa/TAM; from Santiago 5 a week with National of Chile or LanChile, 4 with Lapsa/TAM; from Lima 2 a week with Lapsa/TAM, once with AeroPerú; from Santa Cruz, Bolivia, twice a week with LAB and Lapsa/TAM; from Río and São Paulo, daily with Varig; from São Paulo direct, daily with American, and daily with Lapsa/TAM via Ciudad del Este. See **Getting there: Air**, in Brazil, **Information for travellers**, on the Mercosur airpass.

BY ROAD

● **From Argentina**

From Buenos Aires the two main road routes to Asunción are 1) via Santa Fe to Clorinda and then on a paved road via the border at Puerto Falcón and the Remanso Castillo suspension bridge to Asunción: 1,370 km, about 23 hrs. 2) via Posadas to Encarnación across the new San Roque bridge. Good bus services on these routes.

● **From Brazil**

The main road connections are between Foz do Iguaçu and Ciudad del Este, and between Pedro Juan Caballero and Ponta Porã.

BY RIVER

There are no scheduled boat services to either Buenos Aires on the Río Paraná, or northward along the Río Paraguay to Porto Esperança or Corumbá in Brazil.

Under Mercosur (Southern Cone Common Market) regulations, borders between Paraguay,

Brazil and Argentina should be open 24 hrs a day, 7 days a week.

CUSTOMS

'Reasonable quantities' of tobacco products, alcoholic drinks and perfume are admitted free of duty.

ON ARRIVAL

● Clothing

In summer, Jan to Mar, tropical clothing, sunglasses and an umbrella are needed. From May to Sept the heat is not too oppressive.

● Hours of business

Many shops, offices and businesses open between 0630 and 0700. *Siesta* (generally observed all year round) is from 1200 to 1500. Commercial office hours are from 0730 to 1100 or 1130, and 1430 or 1500 to 1730 or 1900. Banks: from 0830 to 1200, closed on Sat and Sun. Government offices are open 0630 to 1130 in summer, 0730 to noon, in winter, open on Sat.

● Official time

3-4 hrs behind GMT (clocks go on 1 hour in local summer time, Oct-Feb/Mar, dates change annually).

● Safety

Generally, travellers find Paraguay safer than the neighbouring countries, but check prices and change.

● Shopping

The famous *ñandutí* lace, made exclusively by the women of Itauguá (see page 1176). The local jewellery is also attractive. Handmade *aó po'í* (fine cloth) is suitable for shirts and blouses, and there are cotton thread belts in all colours. Bags, hammocks and blankets are also good. The best place to buy these items is Villarrica. Also leather articles, the pottery and *pau de santo* (small articles made from Paraguayan woods). See also 'Shopping', under Asunción (page 1173). Imported goods, especially cameras, film and tampons, are cheaper in Paraguay than in most other Latin American countries (although prices in the UK, for instance, are cheaper). The selection of all types of consumer goods is better in Ciudad del Este than Asunción, and there are good prices in Pedro Juan Caballero.

● Tipping

Restaurants, 10%. Porters US$0.15 a suitcase. Taxis, 10%. Porters at docks US$0.40 a suitcase.

● Voltage

Nominally 220 volts AC and 50 cycles, but power surges and voltage drops are frequent. European round pin plugs are used.

● Weights and measures

The metric system is used except by carpenters, who use inches.

ON DEPARTURE

● Airport tax

Airport tax is US$16, payable in US$ or guaraníes (tends to be cheaper).

FOOD AND DRINK

FOOD

Typical local foods include *chipas* (yuca bread flavoured with egg and cheese), *chipa soo* (maize bread with meat filling) and *sopa paraguaya* (a kind of dumpling of ground maize and cheese). *Soyo* is a soup of different meats and vegetables, delicious; *albóndiga* a soup of meat balls; *bori bori* another type of soup with diced meat, vegetables, and small balls of maize mixed with cheese. *Palmitos* (palm hearts) should not be missed; the beef is excellent in better class restaurants (best cuts are *lomo* and *lomito*). Paraguayan *chorizos* (sausages) are good. *Parrillada completa* is rec. *Surubí*, a Paraná river fish, is prepared in many different ways, and is delicious. Sugar-cane juice, greatly beloved, is known as *mosto*. Fruit is magnificent.

DRINK

The national wine is not rec (better is imported from Chile), but Baviera, a local lager beer is very good (beer is usually sold in litre bottles). *Cerveza de invierno* is Brazilian black beer. The cane-sugar spirit, *caña* is good (the best is 'Aristocrat'; ask for 'Ari'). *Guaraná* is a good local soft drink (originally from Brazil). Very typical of Paraguay is *tereré* (cold *mate* with digestive herbs) for warm days and hot *mate* to warm you up on cold days.

GETTING AROUND

AIR TRANSPORT

There are scheduled services to most parts of the country by Aerolíneas Paraguayas (Arpa, in joint operation with Lapsa), Líneas Aéreas de Transporte Nacional (LATN) and Ladesa, and to Concepción, Vallemí, Bahía Negra and Fuerte Olimpo by Transportes Aéreos Militares (TAM). Planes can be chartered. Domestic fares are subject to 2.5% tax.

RAILWAYS

There are 441 km of railways: most passenger services have been withdrawn (see page 1174).

ROAD TRANSPORT

The major roads are: Route 1 from Asunción SE to Encarnación, 372 km, paved; Route 2 from Asunción E to Coronel Oviedo, continuing E as Route 7 to Ciudad del Este and the Iguazú falls, 362 km, paved; Route 5 from Concepción E to the Brazilian frontier at Pedro Juan Caballero, 215 km, partly paved; Route 8 which runs N from Coronel Bogado (junction with Route 1) via Coronel Oviedo (Route 2) to meet Route 5 at Yby Yaú, paved; Route 9 from Asunción NW across the Río Paraguay at Remanso, continuing via Villa Hayes through the Chaco to Filadelfia and Bolivia, paved to Mariscal Estigarribia, 805 km.

Buses ply on the main roads. For motorists, there are sufficient service stations, except in the Chaco area. Motorists should beware stray cattle on the road at night. Gasoline/petrol prices: 95 octane US$0.64/litre; 97 octane US$0.68/litre; unleaded US$0.55/litre; diesel US$0.32/litre. It is highly rec that drivers use diesel-powered vehicles as almost all the locals do: not only is diesel usually cheaper than gasoline, but a diesel engine will not stop in water, has no ignition/carburettor problems, and will not encounter the corrosive effects of alcohol in the fuel. Motor fuel and oil are sold by the litre. The documents needed for private cars are international car registration and driver's licence. For entry into Brazil the only document necessary is the title to the car (or other proof of ownership).

Motor repairs A rec mechanic is Lauro C Noldin, Dr Moleón Andreu 493 y 4ta Proyectada, Barrio Santa Librada, Asunción, T 333933; he repairs Land Rover, Range Rover, Jaguar and all makes of British, European, American and Japanese cars, diesel and petrol engines, motorcycles, power generators for motor homes. For diesel service, MBT service garage at Av Eusebio Ayala y Lapacho Km 4, T Asunción 553318. A rec Land Rover parts source is Repuestos Agromotor at Herrera 604, Asunción. Mechanics at **Santo Domingo**, Núñez y Farin, very good for VWs and Japanese cars. Spares are available in Paraguay for all makes of car (European, North American, Asian); also available are most makes of tyre.

CAR HIRE

Weekly and free-kilometre rates available. See under Asunción, **Car Rental**.

COMMUNICATIONS

● **Newspapers**

Hoy, Ultima Hora, Noticias and *ABC Color* are published daily in Asunción. English-language papers from Argentina and Brazil are sometimes available the following day at corner of Estrella and Chile. German language paper *Aktuelle Rundschau*. CNN, in English, is available on Channel 8.

● **Postal services**

Postal services are expensive and not reliable. A normal airmail letter to USA costs US$0.60 and to Europe US$0.67. To register a letter costs US$0.70. Register important mail if you want it delivered. Parcels may be sent from the main post office on El Paraguayo Independiente, Asunción. Rates to Europe by APR/SAL US$10 up to 1 kg, US$25 up to 5 kg; to USA US$7.60 and US$19 respectively. Airmail parcels cost US$14.30 to Europe and US$10 to USA for first kg. Packages under 2 kg should be handed in at the small packages window, over 2 kg at the 'Encomiendas' office in the same building, but on corner of Alberdi and El Paraguayo Independiente. Customs inspection of open parcel required.

● **Telephone services**

The telephone service (few telephone boxes) links the main towns, and there is a telephone service with most countries, operated by Antelco. Tokens for 'phone boxes are sold in shops next to the box. Rates: to Europe US$2.90/minute; USA, Canada, US$2.70/minute, 20% cheaper 1900-2400, 40% cheaper 2400-0800. To make a collect call anywhere in the world, dial 0012. Antelco phone cards for calling other South American countries cost US$3, and for 4 mins to USA or 3 mins to Europe US$9.25; can be used in any phone box in Greater Asunción.

SPORT

Football is very popular. Fishing, basketball, tennis, horse-racing and rugby football are popular. There are two rowing and swimming clubs of some 2,000 members, and a motor-boat club with 150 members, in Asunción. Swimming in the Río Paraguay is not rec: beware stinging starfish where there is mud on the islands and beaches. Golf is played in the Jardín Botánico, and there is a Paraguayan Aviation Club. There are two boxing rings.

HOLIDAYS AND FESTIVALS

1 Jan; 3 Feb; 1 Mar; Maundy Thursday, Good Friday; 1, 14, 15 May; Corpus Christi, 12, 23 June; 15, 25 Aug; 29 Sept; 12 Oct; 1 Nov; 8, 25 Dec.

FURTHER READING

Así es el Paraguay (with maps and very useful information) and *Paraguay, Land of Lace and Legend* (first published 1960, reprinted 1983, available from bookshops and Anglo-Paraguayan and US-Paraguay cultural institutes in

Asunción); also *Green Hill, Far Away*, by Peter Upton. Books on the history of Paraguay include: *The Origins of the Paraguayan War* (2 vol) by Pelham Horton Box; *Tragedy of Paraguay* by Gilbert Phelps; *Portrait of a Dictator* by RB Cunninghame- Grahame, on López II; *Eliza Lynch, Regent of Paraguay*, by Henry Lyon-Young; *Seven Eventful Years in Paraguay* by George F Masterman, and *The Lost Paradise* by Philip Caraman, an account of the Jesuits in Paraguay 1607-1768, published in London in 1975. *Land Without Evil*, by Richard Gott (Verso 1993) is also on Jesuit history. For further reading on the origin and aftermath of the War of the Triple Alliance, see *Paraguay: un destino geopolítico*, by Dra Julia Velilla Laconich de Aréllaga; *Genocídio Americano: a Guerra do Paraguai*, by Júlio José Chiavenalto; *Woman on Horseback*, by William E Barrett. Michael Gonin highly recommends, in addition, *The British in Paraguay* by Josefina Plá, for a complete study of this subject, and *Forgotten Fatherland* by Ben MacIntyre, about New Germany (Nueva Germania) in Paraguay. Paraguay's most renowned contemporary novelist is Augusto Roa Bastos: *Yo, el Supremo, Hijo de hombre*.

ACKNOWLEDGEMENTS

We are most grateful to Rachel Rogers for doing the updating and, for their help in the preparation of this chapter, Mick Day (Colchester, UK) and Marcelo Martinessi (Asunción).

Peru

HORIZONS

Peru, the third largest South American country (over twice the size of France), presents formidable difficulties to human habitation. The whole of its W seaboard with the Pacific is desert on which rain seldom falls. From this coastal shelf the Andes rise steeply to a high Sierra which is studded with massive groups of soaring mountains and gouged with deep canyons. The highland slopes more gradually E; the mountains in its E zone are deeply forested and ravined. Eastward from these mountains lie the vast jungle lands of the Amazon basin.

THE LAND

THE COAST

The coastal region, a narrow ribbon of desert 2,250 km long, takes up 11% of the country and holds 44% of the population. It is the economic heart of Peru, consuming most of the imports and supplying half of the exports. When irrigated, the river valleys are extremely fertile, creating oases which grow cotton throughout the country, sugar-cane and rice in the N, and grapes, fruit and olives in the S. At the same time, the coastal current teems with

fish, and Peru has on occasion had the largest catch in the world.

THE SIERRA

In the Sierra, at an average altitude of 3,000m, which covers 26% of the country, live about 50% of the people, an excessive density on such poor land. The population is mostly Indian in this region. Here, high-level land of gentle slopes is surrounded by towering ranges of high peaks. Ten are over 6,000m; the highest, Huascarán, is 6,768m. There are many volcanoes in the S. The continental divide is the western rim of mountains looking down on the Pacific. Rivers which rise in these mountains and flow towards the Amazon cut through the cold surface of the plateau in canyons, sometimes 1,500m deep, in which the climate is tropical. The N and E highlands are heavily forested up to a limit of 3,350m: the grasslands are between the forest line and the snowline, which rises from 5,000m in the latitude of Lima to 5,800m in the S. Most of the Sierra is covered with grasses and shrubs, with Puna vegetation (bunch grass mixed with low, hairy-leaved plants) from N of Huaraz to the south.

Pastoral farming is possible on about 13 million ha of the plateau; the deep valley basins contain the best land for

arable farming. The wide areas of high and wind-swept Altiplano in southern Peru are near the limit of agriculture – though some potatoes and cereals (*quinua*, *kiwicha* and *kañiwa*) are grown – but the Indians use it for grazing llamas, alpacas and sheep; it cannot support cattle. Some sheep-farming areas are at altitudes ranging up to 4,250m. The pastoral Indians of the area live off their flocks; they weave their clothes from the wools, eat the meat, use the dried dung for fuel and the llamas for transport. They are, in short, almost entirely self-supporting.

A mostly Indian labour force of over 80,000 was for many years engaged in mining (minerals are extracted as far up as 5,200m). In the early 1990s, many mines were forced to close and the Indians have either returned to agriculture or left the highlands to seek work in Lima.

THE SELVA

The forested eastern half of the Andes and the land beyond covered with tropical forest and jungle is 62% of the country's area but holds only about 5% of the population. Its inhabitants are crowded on the river banks in the cultivable land – a tiny part of the area. The few roads have to cope with dense forest, deep valleys, and sharp eastern slopes ranging from 2,150m in the N to 5,800m E of Lake Titicaca. Rivers are the main highways, though navigation is hazardous and the draught of the vessels shallow. The economic potential of the area includes reserves of timber, excellent land for rubber, jute, rice, tropical fruits and coffee and the breeding of cattle. The vast majority of Peru's oil and gas reserves are also E of the Andes.

CLIMATE

Each of Peru's geographical zones has its own climate. The coast: from Dec to April, summertime, temperature from 25° to 35°C; hot and dry. Wintertime, May-Nov; the temperature drops a bit and it is cloudy.

On the coast, climate is determined by cold sea-water adjoining deserts: prevailing inshore winds pick up so little moisture over the cold Peruvian current that

only from May to Nov does it condense. The resultant blanket of cloud and sea-mist extends from the S to about 200 km N of Lima. This *garúa* dampens isolated coastal zones of vegetation (called *lomas*) and they are grazed by livestock driven down from the mountains.

At intervals during Dec-April a current of warm water, known as 'El Niño', is blown S from the equator over the cold offshore waters, the surface temperature rises and evaporation is so great that the desert is deluged with rain which creates havoc (most recently in 1992). It is not possible to predict the exact timing or strength of 'El Niño', although it seems to have a frequency of every 5-6 years; scientific study can tell each year if there will be one or not.

The sierra: from April to Oct is the dry season, hot and dry during the day, around 20°-25°C, cold and dry at night, often below freezing. From Nov to April is the wet season, dry and clear most mornings, some rainfall in the afternoon, with a small temperature drop (18°C) and not much difference at night (15°C).

The jungle: April-Oct, dry season, temperatures up to 35°C. In the jungle areas of the S, a cold front can pass through at night. Nov-April, wet season, heavy rainfall at any time, humid and hot.

HISTORY

Three major obstacles restrict our knowledge of ancient Peru. First, the very terrain of the country is a challenge to present, let alone past inhabitants. The Andes are the most seismically active mountain range on Earth; devastating earthquakes and landslides have damaged or destroyed whole cities. The tropical lowlands have defied exploration; remains of the past may still be hidden in the undergrowth. Flashfloods unleashed by the El Niño current sweep down the N coast at intervals, driving away the fish and washing away the adobe houses and irrigation canals. Fortunately the coastal desert from Chan Chán S to Paracas has revealed an 'American Egypt' for archaeologists, although this has meant a bias towards the coastal region and a reliance on the contents of tombs for information.

Secondly, the lack of the written word has deprived us of any firsthand record of the everyday lives of the earliest settlers. The Spanish chroniclers based their accounts on the Incas' own version of the past, but this was inevitably coloured with propaganda, myth and folklore. The third problem is looting, incited by demand from the international antiquities market. Gangs of *huaqueros* plunder sites too numerous to be policed or protected by archaeologists. In spite of these handicaps, Peru has revealed a precolumbian history of highly advanced societies that prevailed against awesome odds.

PRECOLUMBIAN HISTORY

The Incas told the Spaniards that before they established their Tawantinsuyo Empire, the land was overrun by primitives constantly at war with one another.

There were, in fact, many other civilized cultures dating back as far as 2000 BC. The most accomplished of these were the Chavín-Sechín (c 900-200 BC), the Paracas-Nasca (c200 BC-500 AD), the Huari-Tiwanaku (c750 BC-1000 AD), and the Moche-Chimú (200 BC-1400 AD).

Early settlement

It is generally accepted that the earliest settlers in Peru were related to people who had crossed the Bering Straits from Asia and drifted through the Americas from about 20,000 BC. Theories of early migrations from across the Pacific and Atlantic have been rife since Thor Heyerdahl's raft expeditions in 1947 and 1969-70.

Human remains found in a cave in Lauricocha, near Huánuco, have a radiocarbon date of c7500 BC, but the earliest signs of a village settlement in Peru, were found on the central coast at Pampa, dating from 2500 BC. Between these two dates it is thought that people lived nomadically in small groups, mainly hunting and gathering but also cultivating some plants seasonally. Domestication of llamas, alpacas and guinea pigs also began at this time, particularly important for the highland people around the Titicaca basin.

The abundant wealth of marine life produced by the Humboldt Current, especially along the N coast, boosted population growth and settlement in this area. Around 2000 BC climatic change dried up the *lomas* ('fog meadows'), and drove sea shoals into deeper water. People turned more to farming and began to spread inland along river valleys.

As sophisticated irrigation and canal systems were developed, farming productivity increased and communities had more time to devote to building and producing ceramics and textiles. The development of pottery also led to trade and cultural links with other communities. Distribution of land and water to the farmers was probably organized by a corporate authority, and this may have led to the later 'Mit'at' labour system developed by the Incas.

The earliest buildings constructed by organized group labour were *huacas*, adobe platform mounds, centres of some cult or sacred power dating from the second millennium BC onwards. Huaca Florida was the largest example of this period, near the Río Rimac, later replaced by Huaca Garagay as a major centre for the area. Many similar centres spread along the N coast, most notably Aspero and Piedra Parada.

During this period, however, much more advanced architecture was being built at Kotosh, in the central Andes near Huánuco. Japanese archaeological excavations there in the 1960s revealed a temple with ornamental niches and friezes. Some of the earliest pottery was also found here, showing signs of influence from southern Ecuador and the tropical lowlands, adding weight to theories of Andean culture originating in the Amazon. Radiocarbon dates of some Kotosh remains are as early as 1850 BC.

Chavín-Sechín

For the next 1,000 years or so up to c 900 BC, communities grew and spread inland from the N coast and S along the N highlands. Farmers still lived in simple adobe or rough stone houses but built increasingly large and complex ceremonial centres, such as at Las Haldas in the Casma Valley. As farming became more productive and pottery more advanced, commerce grew and states began to develop throughout central and North-central Peru, with the associated signs of social structure and hierarchies.

Around 900 BC a new era was marked by the rise of two important centres; Chavín de Huántar in the central Andes and Sechín Alto, inland from Casma on the N coast.

The chief importance of Chavín de Huántar was not so much in its highly advanced architecture as in the influence of its cult coupled with the artistic style of its ceramics and other artefacts. The founders of Chavín may have originated in the tropical lowlands as some of its carved monoliths show representations of monkeys and felines.

Objects with Chavín traits have been found all along the coast from Piura to the Lurín valley S of Lima, and its cult ideology spread to temples around the same area. Richard L Burger of Yale University has argued that the extent of Chavín influence has been exaggerated. Many sites on the coast already had their own cult practices and the Chavín idols may have been simply added alongside. There is evidence of an El Niño flood that devastated the N coast around 500 BC. Local cults fell from grace as social order was disrupted and the Chavín cult was snatched up as a timely new alternative.

The Chavín cult was paralleled by the great advances made in this period in textile production and in some of the earliest examples of metallurgy. The origins of metallurgy have been attributed to some gold, silver and copper ornaments found in graves in Chongoyape, near Chiclayo, which show Chavín-style features. But earlier evidence has been discovered in the Andahuaylas region, dating from 1800-900 BC. The religious symbolism of gold and other precious metals and stones is thought to have been an inspiration behind some of the beautiful artefacts found in the central Andean area. The emergence of social hi-erarchies also created a demand for lux-ury goods as status symbols.

The cultural brilliance of Chavín de Huántar was complemented by its contemporary, Sechín. This huge granite-faced complex near Casma, 370 kms N of Lima, was described by JC Tello as the biggest structure of its kind in the Andes. According to Michael Moseley of Harvard University, Chavín and Sechín may have combined forces, with Sechín as the military power that spread the cultural word of Chavín, but their influence did not reach far to the S where the Paracas and Tiwanaku cultures held sway.

The Chavín hegemony broke up around 500 BC, soon after which the Nasca culture began to bloom in southern Peru. This period, up to about 500 AD, was a time of great social and cultural development. Sizable towns of 5-10,000 inhabitants grew on the S coast, populated by artisans, merchants, government administrators and religious officials.

Paracas-Nasca

Nasca origins are traced back to about the 2nd century BC, to the Paracas Cavernas and Necropolis, on the coast in the national park near Pisco. The extreme dryness of the desert here has preserved remarkably the textiles and ceramics in the mummies' tombs excavated. The technical quality and stylistic variety in weaving and pottery rank them amongst the world's best, and many of the finest examples can be seen in the museums of Lima.

The famous Nasca Lines are a feature of the region. Straight lines, abstract designs and outlines of animals are scratched in the the dark desert surface forming a lighter contrast that can be seen clearly from the air. There are many theories of how and why the lines were made but no definitive explanation has yet been able to establish their place in Peruvian history. There are similarities between the style of some of the line patterns and that of the pottery and textiles of the same period. It is clear from the sheer scale of the lines and the quality of the work that, whatever their purpose, they were very important to the Nasca culture.

In contrast to the quantity and quality of the Nasca artefacts found, relatively few major buildings belonging to this period have been uncovered in the southern desert. Dos Palmas is a complex of rooms and courtyards in the Pisco Valley and Cahuachi in the Nasca Valley is a large area including adobe platforms, a pyramid and a 'wooden Stonehenge' cluster of preserved tree trunks. As most of the archaeological evidence of the Nasca culture came from their desert cemeteries, little is known about the lives and social organization of the people. Alpaca hair found in Nasca textiles, however, indicates that there must have been strong trade links with highland people.

Moche-Chimú

Nasca's contemporaries on the N coast were the militaristic Moche who, from about 100-800 AD built up an empire whose traces stretch from Piura in the N to Casma, beyond Chimbote, in the S. The Moche built their capital in the middle of the desert, outside present day Trujillo. The huge pyramid temples of the Huaca del Sol and Huaca de la Luna, overlook the biggest adobe city in the world. Moche roads and system of way stations are thought to have been an early inspiration for the Inca network. The Moche increased the coastal population with intensive irrigation projects. Skilful engineering works were carried out, such as the La Cumbre canal, still in use today, and the Ascope aqueduct, both on the Chicama river.

The Moche's greatest achievement, however, was its artistic genius. Exquisite ornaments in gold, silver and precious stones were made by its craftsmen. Moche pottery progressed through five stylistic periods, most notable for the stunningly lifelike portrait vases. A wide variety of everyday scenes were created in naturalistic ceramics, telling us more about Moche life than is known about other earlier cultures, and perhaps used by them as 'visual aids' to compensate for the lack of a written language.

A spectacular discovery of a Moche royal tomb at Sipán was made in Feb 1987 by Walter Alva, director of the Bruning Archaeological Museum, Lambayeque. Reports of the excavation in the National Geographic magazine (Oct 1988 and June 1990), talked of the richest unlooted tomb in the New World. The find included semi-precious stones brought from Chile and Argentina, and seashells from Ecuador. The Moche were great navigators.

The cause of the collapse of the Moche Empire around 600-700 AD is unknown, but it may have been started by a 30-year drought at the end of the 6th century, followed by one of the periodic El Niño flash floods (identified by meteorologists from ice thickness in the Andes) and finished by the encroaching forces of the Huari Empire. The decline of the Moche signalled a general tipping of the balance of power in Peru from the N coast to the S sierra.

Huari-Tiwanaku

The ascendant Huari-Tiwanaku movement, from c 600-1000 AD, combined the religious cult of the Tiwanaku site in the Titicaca basin, with the military dynamism of the Huari, based in the central highlands. The two cultures developed independently but, as had occurred with the Chavin-Sechín association, they are generally thought to have merged compatibly.

Up until their own demise around 1440 AD, the Huari-Tiwanaku had spread their empire and influence across much of S Peru, N Bolivia and Argentina. They made considerable gains in art and technology, building roads, terraces and irrigation canals across the country. The Huari-Tiwanaku ran their empire with efficient labour and administrative systems that were later adopted and refined by the Incas. Labour tribute for state projects had been practised by the Moche and was further developed now. But the empire could not contain regional kingdoms who began to fight for land and power. As control broke down, rivalry and coalitions emerged, and the system collapsed. With the country once again fragmented, the scene was set for the rise of the Incas.

THE INCA DYNASTY

The origins of the Inca Dynasty are

shrouded in mythology and shaky evidence. The best known story reported by the Spanish chroniclers talks about Manco Capac and his sister rising out of Lake Titicaca, created by the Sun as divine founders of a chosen race. This was in approximately AD 1200. Over the next 300 years the small tribe grew to supremacy as leaders of the largest empire ever known in the Americas, the four territories of Tawantinsuyo, united by Cusco as the umbilicus of the Universe (the four quarters of Tawantinsuyo, all radiating out from Cusco, were 1 – Chinchaysuyo, N and NW, 2 – Cuntisuyo, S and W, 3 – Collasuyo, S and E, 4 – Antisuyo, E.

At its peak, just before the Spanish Conquest, the Inca Empire stretched from the Río Maule in central Chile, N to the present Ecuador-Colombia border, containing most of Ecuador, Peru, W Bolivia, N Chile and NW Argentina. The area was roughly equivalent to France, Belgium, Holland, Luxembourg, Italy and Switzerland combined, 980,000 sq km. For a brief description of **Inca Society,** see under Cusco.

The first Inca ruler, Manco Capac, moved to the fertile Cusco region, and established Cusco as his capital. Successive generations of rulers were fully occupied with local conquests of rivals, such as the Colla and Lupaca to the S, and the Chanca to the NW. At the end of Inca Viracocha's reign the hated Chanca were finally defeated, largely thanks to the heroism of one of his sons, Pachacuti Inca Yupanqui, who was subsequently crowned as the new ruler.

From the start of Pachacuti's own reign in 1438, imperial expansion grew in earnest. With the help of his son and heir, Topa Inca, territory was conquered from the Titicaca basin S into Chile, and all the N and central coast down to the Lurin Valley. The Incas also subjugated the Chimú, a highly sophisticated rival empire who had re-occupied the abandoned Moche capital at Chan Chán. Typical of the Inca method of government, some of the Chimú skills were assimilated into their own political and administrative system, and some Chimú nobles were even given positions in Cusco.

Perhaps the pivotal event in Inca history

came in 1532 with the death of the ruler, Huayna Capac. Civil war broke out in the confusion over his rightful successor. One of his legitimate sons, Huascar, ruled the southern part of the empire from Cusco. Atahuallpa, Huascar's half-brother, governed Quito, the capital of Chinchaysuyo. In the midst of the ensuing battle Francisco Pizarro arrived in Tumbes with 179 men. When Atahuallpa got wind of their presence there was some belief that Pizarro and his *conquistadores* on horseback were Viracocha and his demi-gods predicted in Inca legend. In need of allies against Huascar, Atahuallpa agreed to meet the Spaniards at Cajamarca.

Francisco Pizarro's only chance against the formidable imperial army he encountered at Cajamarca was a bold stroke. He drew Atahuallpa into an ambush, slaughtered his guards, promised him liberty if a certain room were filled with treasure, and finally killed him after receiving news that another Inca army was on its way to free him. Pushing on to Cusco, he was at first hailed as the executioner of a traitor: Atahuallpa had ordered the death of Huascar in 1533 when Atahuallpa himself was a captive of Pizarro and his victorious generals (at the Battle of Huancavelica) were bringing the defeated Huascar to see his half-brother. Panic followed when the *conquistadores* set about sacking the city, and they fought off with difficulty an attempt by Manco Inca to recapture Cusco in 1538. (For the whole period of the Conquest John Hemming's *The Conquest of the Incas* is invaluable; he himself refers us to Ann Kendall's *Everyday Life of the Incas*, Batsford, London, 1978. Also *Oro y tragedia* by Manuel Portal Cabellos, excellent on division of the empire, civil war, the conquest and *huaqueros*.)

CONQUEST AND AFTER

Peruvian history after the arrival of the Spaniards was not just a matter of *conquistadores* versus Incas. The vast majority of the huge empire remained unaware of the conquest for many years. The Chimú and the Chachapoyas cultures were powerful enemies of the Incas. The Chimú developed a highly sophisticated culture and a powerful empire stretching for 560 km along the coast from Paramonga S to Casma. Their history was well-recorded by the Spanish chroniclers and continued through the Conquest possibly up to about 1600. The Kuelap/Chachapoyas people were not so much an empire as a loose-knit 'confederation of ethnic groups with no recognized capital' (Morgan Davis 'Chachapoyas: The Cloud People', Ontario, 1988). But the culture did develop into an advanced society with great skill in roads and monument building. Their fortress at Kuelap was known as the most impregnable in Tawantinsuyo. It remained intact against Inca attack and Manco Inca even tried, unsuccessfully, to gain refuge here against the Spaniards.

In 1535, wishing to secure his communications with Spain, Pizarro founded Lima, near the ocean, as his capital. The same year Diego de Almagro set out to conquer Chile. Unsuccessful, he returned to Peru, quarrelled with Pizarro, and in 1538 fought a pitched battle with Pizarro's men at the Salt Pits, near Cusco. He was defeated and put to death. Pizarro, who had not been at the battle, was assassinated in his palace in Lima by Almagro's son 3 years later. For the next 27 years each succeeding representative of the Kingdom of Spain sought to subdue the Inca successor state of Vilcabamba, N of Cusco, and to unify the fierce Spanish factions. Francisco de Toledo (appointed 1568) solved both problems during his 14 years in office: Vilcabamba was crushed in 1572 and the last reigning Inca, Túpac Amaru, put to death. For the next 200 years the Viceroys closely followed Toledo's system, if not his methods. The Major Government – the Viceroy, the *Audiencia* (High Court), and *corregidores* (administrators) – ruled through the Minor Government – Indian chiefs put in charge of large groups of natives: a rough approximation to the original Inca system.

Towards independence

The Indians rose in 1780, under the leadership of an Inca noble who called himself Túpac Amaru II. He and many of his lieu-tenants were captured and put to death under torture at Cusco. Another Indian leader in revolt suffered the same fate in 1814, but this last flare-up had the sympathy of many of the locally-born Spanish, who resented their status, inferior to the Spaniards born in Spain, the refusal to give them any but the lowest offices, the high taxation imposed by the home government, and the severe restrictions upon trade with any country but Spain.

Help came to them from the outside world: José de San Martín's Argentine troops, convoyed from Chile under the protection of Lord Cochrane's squadron, landed in southern Peru on 7 September 1820. San Martín proclaimed Peruvian independence at Lima on 28 July 1821, though most of the country was still in the hands of the Viceroy, José de La Serna. Bolívar, who had already freed Venezuela and Colombia, sent Antonio José de Sucre to Ecuador where, on 24 May 1822, he gained a victory over La Serna at Pichincha. San Martín, after a meeting with Bolívar at Guayaquil, left for Argentina and a self-imposed exile in France, while Bolívar and Sucre completed the conquest of Peru by defeating La Serna at the battle of Junín (6 August 1824) and the decisive battle of Ayacucho (9 December 1824). For over a year there was a last stand in the Real Felipe fortress at Callao by the Spanish troops under General Rodil before they capitulated on 22 January 1826. Bolívar was invited to stay in Peru, but left for Colombia in 1826.

Important subsequent events were a temporary confederation between Peru and Bolivia in the 1830s; the Peruvian-Spanish War (1866); and the War of the Pacific (1879-1883), in which Peru and Bolivia were defeated by Chile and Peru lost its southern territory. A long-standing legacy of this was the Tacna-Arica dispute, which was not settled until 1929 (see under Tacna).

MODERN PERU

A reformist military Junta took over control of the country in Oct 1968. Under its first leader, Gen Juan Velasco Alvarado, the Junta instituted a series of measures to raise the personal status and standard of living of the workers and the rural Indians, by land reform, worker participation in industrial management and ownership, and nationalization of basic industries, exhibiting an ideology perhaps best described as 'military socialism'. In view of his failing health Gen Velasco was replaced in 1975 by Gen Francisco Morales Bermúdez and policy (because of a mounting economic crisis and the consequent need to seek financial aid from abroad) swung to the Right. Presidential and congressional elections were held on 18 May 1980, and Fernando Belaúnde Terry was elected President for the second time. His term was marked by growing economic problems and the appearance of the Maoist guerrilla movement Sendero Luminoso (Shining Path).

Initially conceived in the University of Ayacucho, the movement gained most support for its goal of overthrowing the whole system of Lima-based government from highland Indians and migrants to urban shanty towns. The activities of Sendero Luminoso and another guerrilla group, Túpac Amaru (MRTA), frequently disrupted transport and electricity supplies, although their strategies had to be reconsidered after the arrest of both their leaders in 1992. Víctor Polay of MRTA was arrested in June and Abimael Guzmán of Sendero Luminoso was captured in Sept; he was sentenced to life imprisonment. Although Sendero did not capitulate, many of its members in 1994-5 took advantage of the Law of Repentance, which guaranteed lighter sentences in return for surrender, and freedom in exchange for valuable information. Meanwhile, Túpac Amaru was thought to have ceased operations (see below).

The April 1985 elections were won by the APRA party leader Alán García Pérez. During his populist, left-wing presidency disastrous economic policies caused increasing poverty and civil instability. In presidential elections held over two rounds in 1990, Alberto Fujimori of the Cambio 90 movement defeated the novelist Mario Vargas Llosa, who belonged to the Fredemo (Democratic Front) coalition. Fujimori, without an established political network behind him, failed to win a majority in either the senate or the lower house. Lack of congressional support was one of the reasons behind the dissolution of congress and the suspension of the constitution on 5 April 1992. With massive popular support, President Fujimori declared that he needed a freer hand to introduce free-market reforms, combat terrorism and drug trafficking, and root out corruption.

In elections to a new, 80-member Democratic Constituent Congress (CCD) in Nov 1992, Fujimori's Cambio 90/Nueva Mayoría coalition won a majority of seats. Three major political parties, APRA, Acción Popular and the Movimiento de Libertad, boycotted the elections to CCD. In municipal elections held in Feb 1993 the trend against mainstream political groups continued as independent candidates won the lion's share of council seats.

A new constitution drawn up by the CCD was approved by a narrow majority of the electorate in Oct 1993. Among the new articles were the immediate re-election of the president (previously prohibited for one presidential term), the death penalty for terrorist leaders, the establishment of a single-chamber congress, the reduction of the role of the state, the designation of Peru as a market economy and the favouring of foreign investment. As expected, Fujimori stood for re-election on 9 April 1995 and beat his independent opponent, former UN General Secretary, Javier Pérez de Cuéllar, by a resounding margin. The coalition that supported him also won a majority in Congress.

The government's success in most economic areas did not accelerate the distribution of foreign funds for social projects. Furthermore, rising unemployment and the austerity imposed by economic policy continued to cause hardship for many. During 1996, Fujimori's popularity declined rapidly as his authoritarianism, his relationship with the armed forces, and his apparent lack of concern for dubiously convicted political prisoners caused disquiet. Economic progress also began to falter, casting further doubt on the government's ability to alleviate poverty. Dramatic events on 17 December 1996 thrust several of these issues into sharper focus: 14 Túpac Amaru guerrillas infiltrated a reception at the Japanese Embassy in Lima, taking 490 hostages. Among the rebel's demands were the release of their imprisoned colleagues, better treatment for prisoners and new measures to raise living standards. Most of the hostages were released and negotiations were pursued during a stalemate that lasted until 22 April 1997. The president took sole responsibility for the successful, but risky assault which freed all the hostages (one died of heart failure) and killed all the terrorists. By not yielding to Túpac Amaru, Fujimori regained much popularity. But this masked the fact that no concrete steps had been taken to ease social problems. It also deflected attention from Fujimori's plans to stand for a third term following his unpopular manipulation of the law to persuade Congress that the new constitution did not apply to his first period in office.

CULTURE

PEOPLE

The indigenous population of Peru is put at about 3 million Quechua and Aymara Indians in the Andean region and 200,000-250,000 Amazonian Indians from 40-50 ethnic groups. In the Andes, there are 5,000 Indian communities but few densely populated settlements. Their literacy rate is the lowest of any comparable group in South America and their diet is 50% below acceptable levels. About two million Indians speak no Spanish, their main tongue being Quechua, the language of the Incas; they are largely outside the money economy. The conflict between Sendero Luminoso guerrillas and the security forces caused the death of thousands of highland Indians. Many Indian groups are under threat from colonization, development and road-building projects. Some have been dispossessed and exploited for their labour.

EDUCATION

Education is free and compulsory for both sexes between 6 and 14. There are public and private secondary schools and private elementary schools. There are 32 State and private universities, and five Catholic universities. A new educational system is being implemented as too many children cannot complete secondary school.

MUSIC AND DANCE

Peru is the Andean heartland. Its musicians, together with those of Bolivia, have appeared on the streets of cities all over Europe and North America. However, the costumes they wear, the instruments they play, notably the *quena* and *charango*, are not typical of Peru as a whole, only of the Cusco region. Peruvian music divides at a very basic level into that of the highlands ('Andina') and that of the coast ('Criolla').

The highlands are immensely rich in terms of music and dance, with over 200 dances recorded. Every village has its fiestas and every fiesta has its communal and religious dances. Those of Paucartambo and Coylloriti (Q'olloriti) in the Cusco region moreover attract innumerable groups of dancers from far and wide. The highlands themselves can be very roughly subdivided into some half dozen major musical regions, of which perhaps the most characteristic are Ancash and the N, the Mantaro Valley, Cusco, Puno and the Altiplano, Ayacucho and Parinacochas.

There is one recreational dance and musical genre, the Huayno, that is found throughout the whole of the Sierra, and has become ever more popular and commercialized to the point where it is in danger of swamping and indeed replacing the other more regional dances. Nevertheless, still very popular among Indians and/or Mestizos are the Marinera, Carnaval, Pasacalle, Chuscada (from Ancash), Huaylas, Santiago and Chonguinada (all from the Mantaro) and Huayllacha (from Parinacochas). For singing only are the mestizo Muliza, popular in the Central Region, and the soulful lament of the Yaravi, originally

Indian, but taken up and developed early in the 19th century by the poet and hero of independence Mariano Melgar, from Arequipa.

The Peruvian Altiplano shares a common musical culture with that of Bolivia and dances such as the Auqui-Auqui and Sicuris, or Diabladas, can be found on either side of the border. The highland instrumentation varies from region to region, although the harp and violin are ubiquitous. In the Mantaro area the harp is backed by brass and wind instruments, notably the clarinet, in Cusco it is the *charango* and *quena* and on the Altiplano the *sicu* panpipes.

Two of the most spectacular dances to be seen are the Baile de las Tijeras ('scissor dance') from the Ayacucho/Huancavelica area, for men only and the pounding, stamping Huaylas for both sexes. Huaylas competitions are held annually in Lima and should not be missed. Indeed, owing to the overwhelming migration of peasants into the barrios of Lima, most types of Andean music and dance can be seen in the capital, notably on Sun at the so-called 'Coliseos', which exist for that purpose.

Were a Hall of Fame to be established, it would have to include the Ancashino singers La Pastorcita Huaracina and El Jilguero del Huascarán, the *charango* player Jaime Guardia, the guitar virtuoso Raul García from Ayacucho and the Lira Paucina trio from Parinacochas. However, what the young urban immigrant from the Sierra is now listening to and, above all, dancing to is 'Chicha', a hybrid of Huayno music and the Colombian Cumbia rhythm, played by such groups as Los Shapis.

The 'Música Criolla' from the coast could not be more different from that of the Sierra. Here the roots are Spanish and African. The immensely popular Valsesito is a syncopated waltz that would certainly be looked at askance in Vienna and the Polca has also suffered an attractive sea change, but reigning over all is the Marinera, Peru's national dance, a splendidly rhythmic and graceful courting encounter

and a close cousin of Chile's and Bolivia's Cueca and the Argentine Zamba, all of them descended from the Zamacueca. The Marinera has its 'Limeña' and 'Norteña' versions and a more syncopated relative, the Tondero, found in the N coastal regions, is said to have been influenced by slaves brought from Madagascar. All these dances are accompanied by guitars and frequently the *cajón*, a resonant wooden box on which the player sits, pounding it with his hands. Some of the great names of 'Música Criolla' are the singer/composers Chabuca Granda and Alicia Maguiña, the female singer Jesús Vásquez and the groups Los Morochucos and Hermanos Zañartu.

Also on the coast is to be found the music of the small black community, the 'Música Negroide' or 'Afro-Peruano', which had virtually died out when it was resuscitated in the 50s, but has since gone from strength to strength. It has all the qualities to be found in black music from the Caribbean – a powerful, charismatic beat, rhythmic and lively dancing, and strong percussion provided by the *cajón* and the *quijada de burro*, a donkey's jaw with the teeth loosened. Some of the classic dances in the black repertoire are the Festejo, Son del Diablo, Toro Mata, Landó and Alcatraz. In the last named one of the partners dances behind the other with a candle, trying to set light to a piece of paper tucked into the rear of the other partner's waist. Nicomedes and Victoria Santa Cruz have been largely responsible for popularizing this black music and Peru Negro is another excellent professional group.

Finally, in the Peruvian Amazon region around Iquitos, local variants of the Huayno and Marinera are danced together with the Changanacui, to the accompaniment of flute and drum.

THE ECONOMY

Structure of production Agriculture, forestry and fishing account for 14% of gdp and employ about a third of the labour force. In 1995 a new agriculture law abolished the land reform law imposed by the military régime and eliminated limits on land holding, aiming to encourage large scale investment in agroindustry and export crops. The Costa is the most productive area of the country and has traditionally been the dominant economic region. Occupying 11% of the total land area, most of the export crops are grown here, with excellent crops of cotton, rice, sugar and fruit where the coastal desert is irrigated. Irrigation is, however, costly and the Government is hoping to substitute luxury fruit and vegetables for export instead of the thirsty sugar cane and rice. Most food production is in the Sierra, where revitalization of agriculture is a government priority, with the aim of returning to the self-sufficiency of Inca times. Pacification in the highlands and good weather have helped food supply, and there have been improvements in living standards, although two thirds of the inhabitants of the Sierra still live in poverty. Fishing suffered a dramatic decline in 1983 as the Niño current forced out of Peruvian waters the main catch, anchovy, whose stocks were already seriously depleted by overfishing in the 1970s. Peru lost its position as the world's leading fishmeal exporter to Chile, but by the 1990s was exporting high quality fishmeal again, helped by rising fish catches and the abolition of the state monopoly, which encouraged private investment in new technology. Pescaperú began selling its assets in 1994 and seven fishmeal plants were sold in a year.

Manufacturing contributes 23% of gdp. After high growth rates in the early 1970s, manufacturing slumped to operating at 40% of its total capacity as purchasing power was reduced and the cost of energy, raw materials and trade credit rose faster than inflation. A consumer-led recovery in 1986 led to most of manufacturing and the construction industry working at full capacity, but the boom was followed by a severe slump in 1988-90. Growth returned in the 1990s and the areas of greatest expansion were food processing, fishmeal and transport equipment, while those sectors still adjusting to increased competition from imports, such as electrical appliances, remained stagnant or declined.

Although mining has traditionally been important in Peru since pre-Conquest times, the sector contracted sharply in the 1980s because of poor world prices, strikes, guerrilla activity in mining areas, rising costs and an uncompetitive exchange rate. The Fujimori Government passed a new Mining Law in 1992 to attract private investment, both domestic and foreign, and growth in mining has boomed in the 1990s with over 80 mining companies operating in the country. Copper and iron deposits are found on the S coast, but the Sierra is the principal mining area for all minerals, including silver, gold, lead and zinc. Centromín and Mineroperú, the state mining companies, are having their assets sold off to private mining companies. Mines sold to US companies include Tintaya, a high-grade copper deposit between Cusco and Arequipa, and Cerro Verde, an open pit copper mine in the S. Many under-capitalized Peruvian mining companies have joined forces with foreign companies to develop concessions. The largest locally-controlled company is Compañía de Minas Buenaventura, which in a joint venture owns the largest gold mine in Latin America, Yanacocha, in Cajamarca, which produced 811,400 oz in 1996. The US-owned Southern Peru Copper Corporation (SPCC) was the only major mining company not to be nationalized by the military in the 1970s, and it now produces some two thirds of all Peru's copper at its Cuajone and Toquepala mines. Official estimates for exploration, development and expansion of existing projects start at investment of US$8.7bn in 1993-2003; new projects will push up investment still further and call for spending on energy generation, roads and other infrastructure, together with housing, health and education facilities for employees. In the same period the value of metals production is forecast to rise from US$2bn to US$5bn a year with exports doubling to US$4bn. Copper output will increase from 400,000 to 900,000 tonnes a year and gold will double to 2 million troy oz.

Peru: fact file

Geographic

Land area	1,285,216 sq km
forested	66.3%
pastures	21.2%
cultivated	3.2%

Demographic

Population (1996)	23,947,000
annual growth rate (1985-94)	2.0%
urban	71.2%
rural	28.8%
density	18.6 per sq km

Education and Health

Life expectancy at birth,	
male	64.4 years
female	69.2 years
Infant mortality rate	
per 1,000 live births (1993)	58.3
Calorie intake as %	
of FAO requirement	80%
Population age 25 and over	
with no formal schooling	12.3%
Literate males (over 15)	92.9%
Literate females (over 15)	81.7%

Economic and Employment

GNP (1994)	US$44,110mn
GNP per capita	US$1,890
Public external debt (1994)	US$17,890mn
Tourism receipts (1994)	US$402mn
Inflation (annual av 1991-95)	78.4%
Population economically active (1993)	
	7,109.527
Unemployment rate (1993)	7.1%
Military forces (1996)	125,000

Source *Encyclopaedia Britannica*

Oil production comes from the NE jungle, although some is produced on and off the NW coast. No major new reserves have been found since 1976 and proven oil reserves have declined to 380 million barrels. Oil output fell from a peak of 195,000 b/d in 1982 to about 130,000 b/d in the mid-1990s. However, the Camisea gas and condensates field in the SE jungle is huge, with reserves in two deposits estimated at 12 trillion cu ft of natural gas and 700 million barrels of condensates, equivalent to 2.4 billion barrels of oil, more than six times current reserves. The field was discovered by Royal Dutch Shell in the 1980s and development of the field by the company was eventually agreed in 1996. Since the passing of new legislation in 1993, several contracts have been signed with private oil companies for exploration and development. The privatization of the state oil company, Petroperú, began piecemeal in 1996.

Recent trends Growing fiscal deficits in the 1980s led to increasing delays in payments to creditors and as arrears accumulated to both official agencies and commercial banks, the IMF declared Peru ineligible for further loans in 1986. President García limited public debt service payments to 10% of foreign exchange revenues but reserves continued to fall. By 1987 the free-spending policies had pushed the country into bankruptcy and inflation soared as the Government resorted to printing money.

President Fujimori inherited an economy devastated by financial mismanagement and isolationist policies, with Peruvians suffering critical poverty, high infant mortality, malnutrition and appalling housing conditions. His Government had to deal with hyperinflation, terrorism and drug trafficking, compounded in 1991 by a cholera epidemic which affected hundreds of thousands of people, cut food exports and sharply curtailed tourism revenues. An economic austerity package introduced in 1990 raised food and fuel prices and was the first stage of sweeping reforms. Monetary and fiscal control was accompanied by liberalization of the financial system, foreign investment rules, capital controls and foreign trade; the tax code, ports and customs and labour laws were reformed, monopolies eliminated and state companies privatized. Successful negotiations with creditors reinstated Peru in the international community and investors returned, but the *auto golpe* in 1992 rocked confidence and international aid was suspended until after the elections at the end of the year.

Arrears to the IMF and World Bank were repaid in 1993 and the Paris Club of creditor governments rescheduled debts due in 1993-94. The reform programme remained on course with emphasis put on control of inflation and tight control of the money supply. Exports and imports grew strongly and the new economic and political stability also encouraged foreign tourists to return. In 1994 Peru registered the highest economic growth rate in the world, as gdp expanded by 13%. An agreement with commercial bank creditors was signed in 1995 when Peru became the last major Latin American debtor nation to convert loans at a discount into bonds, known as Brady bonds. Servicing of the new debt was deemed possible because of a steep rise in tax receipts from 4% of gdp in 1990 to 14% in 1995 and forecast to grow further to 20% of gdp by 2000. The pace of privatization was slowed because of fears of overheating and inflation, and the Government's limited capacity to spend all the proceeds on poverty reduction as required by law, but it was planned that no state companies would remain by the end of the decade. Monetary policy was tightened in 1996 to keep control of inflation, but at the expense of slower growth. Prospects were brighter in 1997 with debt restructuring allowing a return to international capital markets, a competitive exchange rate promoting exports, privatization showing renewed progress and a manageable budget deficit allowing a real increase in spending on social welfare and education.

GOVERNMENT

Under a new constitution (approved by plebiscite in Oct 1993), a single chamber, 80-seat congress replaced the previous, two-house legislature. Men and women over 18 are eligible to vote; registration and voting is compulsory until the age of 60. Those who do not vote are fined. The President, to whom is entrusted the Executive Power, is elected for 5 years and may, under the constitution which came into force on 1 January 1994, be re-elected for a second term.

Tourists invade as terrorists retreat

Tourism is booming in Peru after several years of decline. Numbers of foreigners entering Peru fell from 359,300 in 1988 to 216,534 in 1992, but with the elimination of the terrorist threat and greater security visitors began to return. The Fujimori Government privatized the many state-owned hotels and introduced new tax benefits for investors. Services have subsequently improved and the number of airlines and flights to Peru have increased. In 1995 485,000 tourists generated income of US$520mn, making tourism the third largest foreign exchange earner in Peru. 1996 arrivals were forecast at 600,000, with income of US$700mn, and were projected to increase by about 20% a year until 2005. Market surveys show that tourists' average length of stay has risen to 21 days and they are less likely to be including Peru as part of a whistle-stop tour of South America. Although niche tourism, such as ecotourism or adventure tourism, is flourishing, large international hotel chains are also moving in. Management contracts have been signed with big players such as Marriott, Hilton and Sheraton for new hotels in the Cusco area, where there is a shortage of rooms in the four and five star category. Nationwide the basic infrastructure is lacking to cope with greater numbers of visitors and the extra demand is putting strain on the supply of transport, guides, restaurants and entertainment for both the small, special interest groups and traditional tours.

Lima

UNDER the fog which lasts 8 months of the year, Lima's shady colonial suburbs are fringed by the *pueblos jóvenes* which sprawl over the dusty hills overlooking the flat city. It has a great many historic monuments and its food, drink and nightlife are the best in the country. Although not the most relaxing of South America's capitals, it is a good place to start before exploring the rest of the country.

Lima (*Phone code* 01), capital of Peru, is built on both sides of the Río Rímac, at the foot of Cerro San Cristóbal. It was originally named *La Ciudad de Los Reyes*, in honour of the Magi, at its founding by Francisco Pizarro in 1535. From then until the independence of the South American republics in the early 19th century, it was the chief city of Spanish South America. The name Lima, a corruption of the Quechua name *Rimac* (speaker), was not adopted until the end of the 16th century.

History
The Universidad de San Marcos was founded in 1551, and a printing press in 1595: among the earliest of their kind in South America. Lima's first theatre opened in 1563. The Inquisition was introduced in 1569 and was not abolished until 1820. For some time the Viceroyalty of Peru embraced Colombia, Ecuador, Bolivia, Chile and Argentina. The city's wealth attracted many freebooters and in 1670 a protecting wall 11 km long, which was demolished in 1869, was built round it. Lima's power was at its height during the 17th century and the early 18th, until the earthquake of 1746 destroyed all but 20 houses and killed 4,000 inhabitants.

There were few cities in the Old World that could rival its wealth and luxury. It was only comparatively recently, with the coming of industry, that Lima began to change into what it is today.

Modern Lima is very dirty and seriously affected by smog for much of the year, and is surrounded by 'Pueblos Jóvenes', or shanty settlements of squatters who have migrated from the Sierra. Villa El Salvador, a few miles SE of Lima, may be the world's biggest 'squatters' camp' with 350,000 people building up an award-winning self-governing community since 1971.

Over the years the city has changed out of recognition. Many of the hotels and larger business houses have moved to the fashionable seaside suburbs of Miraflores and San Isidro, thus moving the commercial heart of the city away from the Plaza de Armas. Among the traditional buildings which still survive soar many skyscrapers which have changed the old skyline.

Half of the town-dwellers of Peru now live in Lima. The metropolitan area contains eight million people, nearly one third of the country's total population, and two-thirds of its industries.

Climate

Only 12° S of the equator, one would expect a tropical climate, but Lima has two distinct seasons. The winter is from May to Nov, when a damp *garúa* (Scotch mist) hangs over the city, making everything look greyer than it is already. It is damp and cold, 8° to 15°C. The sun breaks through around Nov and temperatures rise as high as 30°C. Note that the temperature in the coastal suburbs is lower than the centre because of the sea's influence. Also protect against the sun's rays when visiting the beaches around Lima, or elsewhere in Peru.

PLACES OF INTEREST

Street names: several blocks, with their own names, make up a long street, a *jirón* (often abbreviated to Jr). Street corner signs bear both names, of the *jirón* and of the block. The new and old names of streets are used interchangeably: Colmena is also Nicolás de Piérola, Wilson is Inca Garcilaso de la Vega, and Carabaya is also Augusto N Wiese. The city's urban motorway is often called 'El Zanjón' (the ditch) or Via Expresa.

The traditional heart of the city, at least in plan, is still what it was in colonial days. Even though many of the buildings are run down, there being no money to restore them, it is still worth visiting the colonial centre to see the fine architecture and works of art. Most of what the tourist wants to see is in this area.

Plaza de Armas

One block S of the Río Rímac lies the Plaza de Armas, which has been declared a World Heritage by Unesco. Around it stand the Palacio de Gobierno, the Cathedral, the Archbishop's Palace, the Municipalidad and the Club Unión. The Correo Central (Post Office) is opposite the visitors' entrance to the Government Palace. Running along two sides are arcades with shops: Portal de Escribanos and Portal de Botoneros. In the centre of the Plaza is a bronze fountain dating from 1650.

The Palacio de Gobierno (Government Palace), on the N side of the Plaza, stands on the site of the original palace built by Pizarro. In 1937, the palace was totally rebuilt. The visitors' entrance is on Jr de la Unión. Visits are organized only by *Lima Tours* (see below).

The Cathedral reduced to rubble in the earthquake of 1746, is a reconstruction on the lines of the original, completed 1755. Note the splendidly carved stalls (mid-17th century), the silver-covered altars surrounded by fine woodwork, mosaic-covered walls bearing the coats of arms of Lima and Pizarro and an allegory of Pizarro's commanders, the 'Thirteen Men of Isla del Gallo'. The old remains of Franscisco Pizarro lie in a small chapel, the first on the right of the entrance, in a glass coffin, though later research indicates that they reside in the crypt. Museo de Arte Religioso in the cathedral, free guided tours (English available, give tip), ask to see the picture restoration room. Open to visitors Tues-Sun 1000-1800; all-inclusive entrance ticket, US$2, students US$1. Next to the cathedral is the **Archbishop's Palace**, rebuilt in 1924, with a superb wooden balcony.

For **The Municipalidad de Lima's** collection of paintings and interior, see **Pinacoteca Municipal** under **Museums**, below.

From the Plaza, passing the Government Palace on the left, straight ahead is the **Desamparados** Station of the Central Railway. **The Puente de Piedra**, behind the Palacio de Gobierno is a Roman-style stone bridge built in 1610. Across the Río Rímac is the district of the same name, in which are the **Alameda de los Descalzos** (see Convento de los Descalzos under **Churches** below) and the **Paseo de Aguas**, two fashionable places for a stroll in days gone by (no longer so). On Jr Hualgayoc is the bullring in the **Plaza de Acho**, inaugurated on 20 January 1766 (see **Museo Taurino** below).

Between Av Abancay and Jr Ayacucho is **Plaza Bolívar**, where General José de San Martín proclaimed Peru's independence. The plaza is dominated by the equestrian statue of the Liberator. Behind lies the

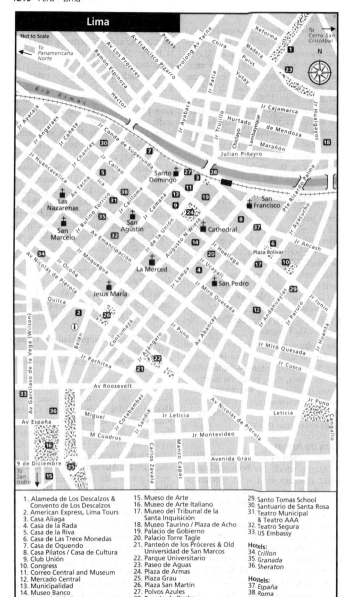

Lima

Not to Scale

To Panamericana Norte

1. Alameda de Los Descalzos & Convento de Los Descalzos
2. American Express, Lima Tours
3. Casa Aliaga
4. Casa de la Rada
5. Casa de la Riva
6. Casa de Las Trece Monedas
7. Casa de Oquendo
8. Casa Pilatos / Casa de Cultura
9. Club Unión
10. Congress
11. Correo Central and Museum
12. Mercado Central
13. Municipalidad
14. Museo Banco Central de la Reserva

15. Mueso de Arte
16. Museo de Arte Italiano
17. Museo del Tribunal de la Santa Inquisición
18. Museo Taurino / Plaza de Acho
19. Palacio de Gobierno
20. Palacio Torre Tagle
21. Panteón de los Próceres & Old Universidad de San Marcos
22. Parque Universitario
23. Paseo de Aguas
24. Plaza de Armas
25. Plaza Grau
26. Plaza San Martín
27. Polvos Azules
28. Puente de Piedra

29. Santo Tomas School
30. Santuario de Santa Rosa
31. Teatro Municipal & Teatro AAA
32. Teatro Segura
33. US Embassy

Hotels:
34. Crillon
35. Granada
36. Sheraton

Hostels:
37. España
38. Roma

Congress building which occupies the former site of the Universidad de San Marcos.

The Jr de La Unión, the main shopping street, runs to the Plaza de Armas. It has been converted into a pedestrian precinct which teems with life in the evening. In the two blocks S of Jr Unión, known as C Belén, several shops sell souvenirs and curios. The newer parts of the city are based on **Plaza San Martín**, S of Jr de la Unión, with a statue of San Martín in the centre. One and a quarter km W is the **Plaza Dos de Mayo**. About 1 km due S of this again is the circular **Plaza Bolognesi**, from which many major avenues radiate.

Colonial Mansions

At Jr Ucayali 363, is the **Palacio Torre Tagle**, the city's best surviving specimen of secular colonial architecture. It was built in 1735. Today, it is used by the Foreign Ministry, but visitors are allowed to enter courtyards to inspect the fine, Moorish-influenced wood-carving in balconies, wrought iron work, and a 16th-century coach complete with commode. The Palace is closed to the public Mon-Fri.

The late 16th century **Casa de Jarava** or **Pilatos** is opposite San Francisco church, Jr Ancash 390, open 0830-1645, Mon-Fri. **Casa La Riva**, Jr Ica 426, T 428-2643, open 1000-1300, 1400-1600, has an 18th century porch and balconies, a small gallery with 20th century paintings. **Casa de Oquendo** or **Osambela**, Conde de Superunda 298, stages art exhibitions; open 0900-1300. **Casa Negreiros**, Jr Azángaro 532, is now a restaurant. **Casa de las Trece Monedas**, Jr Ancash 536, still has the original doors and window grills.

The **Casa Aliaga**, Unión 224, is still occupied by the Aliaga family but has been opened to the public. *Lima Tours* has exclusive rights to include the house in its tours; T 424-5110/7560/9386. The house contains what is said to be the oldest ceiling in Lima and is furnished entirely in the colonial style. **Casa Barbieri**, Jr Callao, near Jr Rufino Torrico, is a fine old 18th-century town house in the Sevillian style. Ring the bell in the entrance hall for permission to look at the patios. **Casa Museo Prado**, Jr Cusco 448, visitable when Sr Prado is in residence, is a beautifully maintained house with early 19th-century front and, apparently, a 17th-century patio. **Casa de Riva Agüero**, Jr Camaná 457, has the library and archives of the Universidad Católica on the 1st floor; the 2nd floor has a small folk art museum. A special appointment is needed to visit the rest of the house. **AAA Theatre** (Amateur Artists' Association), Jr Ica 323, is in a lovely 18th-century house. **Casa de la Rada**, or **Goyoneche**, Jr Ucayali 358, opposite Palacio Torre Tagle, is an extremely fine mid-18th-century town house in the French manner which now belongs to a bank. The patio and first reception room are open occasionally to the public.

Churches

La Merced is in Plazuela de la Merced, Unión y Huancavelica. The first mass in Lima was said here on the site of the first church to be built. The restored façade is a fine example of colonial Baroque. Inside are some magnificent altars and the choir stalls and the vestry's panelled ceiling are worth seeing. A door from the right of the nave leads into the Monastery. The cloister dates from 1546. The church is open 0700-1230, 1600-2000, and its monastery 0800-1200, 1500-1730 daily.

Santo Domingo Church and Monastery is on the 1st block of Jr Camaná, built in 1549. The Cloister, one of the most attractive in the city, dates from 1603. The second Cloister is less elaborate. Beneath the sacristy are the tombs of San Martín de Porres, one of Peru's most revered saints, and Santa Rosa de Lima (see below). In 1669, Pope Clement presented the alabaster statue of Santa Rosa in front of the altar. Entrance, US$2.75, students US$1.25; monastery and tombs open 0900-1300, 1500-1800 Mon-Sat; Sun and holidays am only.

San Francisco, first block of Jr Lampa, corner of Ancash: the baroque church, finished in 1674, withstood the 1746 earthquake. The nave and aisles are lavishly decorated in Mudejar style. The monastery is famous for the Sevillian tile-work and panelled ceiling in the cloisters (1620). The Catacombs under the church and part of the monastery are well worth seeing. The church and monastery are open 0930-1745, entry US$1.60, US$0.50 children, only with guide, Spanish and English (recommended), last groups start at 1245 and 1745 daily.

San Pedro (0700-1300, 1740-2030 every day), 3rd block of Jirón Ucayali, finished by Jesuits in 1638, has marvellous altars with Moorish-style balconies, rich gilded wood carvings in choir and vestry, and tiled throughout. Several Viceroys buried here; the bell called La Abuelita, first rung in 1590, sounded the Declaration of Independence in 1821.

Santuario de Santa Rosa (Av Tacna, 1st block), small but graceful church. A pilgrimage centre; here are preserved the hermitage built by Santa Rosa herself, the house in which she was born, a section of the house in which she attended to the sick, her well, and other relics. Open 0930-1300, 1500-1800 daily; entrance to grounds free.

Las Nazarenas Church (Av Tacna, 4th block, open 0700-1130 and 1630-2000 daily), built around an image of Christ Crucified painted by a liberated slave in 1655. This, the most venerated image in Lima, and an oil copy of El Señor de los Milagros (Lord of Miracles), encased in a gold frame, are carried on a silver litter – the whole weighing nearly a ton – through the streets on 18, 19, and 28 Oct and again on 1 Nov (All Saints' Day).

San Agustín (Jr Ica 251), W of the Plaza de Armas: its façade (1720) is a splendid example of churrigueresque architecture. There are carved choir stalls and effigies, and a sculpture of Death, said to have frightened its maker into an early grave. Open 0830-1200, 1530-1730 daily, ring for entry. The church has been sensitively restored after the last earthquake, but the sculpture of Death is in storage.

The 18th century **Jesús María** (Jr Moquegua, 1st block), contains fine paintings and gilded Baroque altars in all of Lima. **Magdalena Vieja**, built in 1557,

but reconstructed in 1931, has altar pieces of gilded and carved wood. It can be seen during a visit to the Museum of Archaeology on Plaza Bolívar in Pueblo Libre (see **Museums** below). Another church worth seeing for its two beautiful colonial doors is **San Marcelo**, at Av de la Emancipación, 4th block. The interior is also remarkable.

The **Convento de Los Descalzos** on the Alameda de Los Descalzos in Rímac was founded in 1592 and contains over 300 paintings of the Cusco, Quito and Lima schools which line the four main cloisters and two ornate chapels. The chapel of El Carmen was constructed in 1730 and is notable for its baroque gold leaf altar. The museum shows the life of the Franciscan friars during colonial and early republican periods. The cellar, infirmary, pharmacy and a typical cell have been restored. The convent is open daily 0930-1300, 1500-1745, except Tues, entrance US$1. Guided tour only, 45 mins in Spanish, but worth it.

NB Churches are open between 1830 and 2100 unless otherwise stated. Many are closed to visitors on Sun.

MUSEUMS

The older of two museums of anthropology and archaeology is **Museo Nacional de Antropología y Arqueología**, Plaza Bolívar in Pueblo Libre, not to be confused with Plaza Bolívar in the centre. On display are ceramics of the Chimú, Nasca, Mochica and Pachacámac cultures, various Inca curiosities and works of art, and interesting textiles. The museum houses the Raimondi Stela and the Tello obelisk from Chavín, and a reconstruction of one of the galleries at Chavín. It also has a model of Machu Picchu.

Open Tues-Sat 0900-1800, admission US$1.50; T 463-5070. Guides are available. Take bus 12 or colectivo along Av Tacna or Av Venezuela, get off at Av Vivanco and walk two blocks; or any bus or colectivo going along Av Brasil, get off at block 22, Av Vivanco, and walk seven blocks. Taxi US$2.

Museo de la Nación, on Javier Prado Este

2466, San Borja, T 476-9875/476-6577, in the huge Banco de la Nación building, is the new anthropological and archaeological museum for the exhibition and study of the art and history of the aboriginal races of Peru. There are good explanations in Spanish on Peruvian history, with ceramics, textiles and displays of almost every ruin in Peru. There is an excellent copy of the tomb of the Señor de Sipán and a display of the discoveries. Another exhibition shows artefacts from Batán Grande near Chiclayo (Sicán culture). The museum holds a concert every Sun and most evenings there is a lecture, or an event in the theatre (see the monthly programme, or newspaper).

Open Tues-Fri 0900-1700, Sat/Sun 1000-1700, entry US$1.50. Take a colectivo from Miraflores or the centre to the Universidad de Lima and get out at block 24 on Javier Prado; taxi US$2-3.

Museo Peruano de Ciencias de la Salud, now part of the Museo de la Nación, has a collection of ceramics and mummies, plus an explanation of precolumbian lifestyle, divided into five sections: *micuy* (Quechua for food), *hampi* (medicine), *onccoy* (disease), *hampini* (healing) and *causay* (life).

Museo de Oro (Gold Museum) is the private collection of Miguel Mujica Gallo, in the 18th block of Prolongación Av Primavera (Av de Molina 1110), Monterrico (T 435-2917). This excellent collection includes precolumbian gold, silver and bronze, ceramics, weavings, mummies, etc. Allow plenty of time to appreciate it fully. The catalogues cost US$20 or US$40 and the complete book US$70. Upstairs is a remarkable arms collection with an impressive exhibition from Spanish colonial times. In the garden are high quality, expensive craft shops.

Open every day 1200-1900. Admission US$5, children half price. No photography allowed. Take a colectivo from Tacna or Av Arequipa to the corner of Av Arequipa y Av Angamos (you can walk to Av Angamos from Miraflores) and take bus 11, 72, 112 or 985, or a colectivo, to the 18th block of Av Primavera, then walk 250m. Taxi US$3-4.

Museo Arqueológico Rafael Larco Herrera, Av Bolívar 1515, Pueblo Libre, T 461-1312, is the Chiclín pottery museum brought from Trujillo. The greatest number of exhibits stem from the Mochica period (AD 400-800). The Cupisnique period, dating back to 1000 BC, and the Nasca, Chimú, and Inca periods are also well represented. There is an erotica section in a separate building. This museum gives an excellent overview on the development of Peruvian cultures through their pottery. It is very much like a warehouse with few explanations, but also has an excellent collection of precolumbian weaving, including a sample of 2-ply yarns with 398 threads to the inch. There are also several mummified weavers buried with their looms and a small display of gold pieces.

Admission US$5 (half price for student-card holders), open Mon-Sat 0900-1800, Sun 0900-1300; texts in Spanish, English and French. Photography not permitted. Take Bus 23 or colectivo from Av Abancay, any bus or colectivo to the 15th block of Av Brasil, and another one on Av Bolívar. Taxi US$2-3.

Museo Arqueológico Amano, C Retiro 160, 11th block of Av Angamos, Miraflores: private collection of artefacts from the Chancay, Chimú and Nasca periods, owned by the late Mr Yoshitaro Amano. It has one of the most complete exhibits of Chancay weaving, and is particularly interesting for pottery and precolumbian textiles, all superbly displayed and lit.

Visits are by appointment Mon-Fri in afternoons only, T 441-2909. Admission free (photography prohibited). Take bus or colectivo to the corner of Av Arequipa y Av Angamos and another one to the 11th block of Av Angamos, or bus 1, 73, or colectivo from Av Tacna y Av La Vega to corner Av Comandante Espinar y Av Angamos and walk to the 11th block.

Museo Banco Central de Reserva, Av Ucayali 291 and Lampa, one block from San Pedro Church, on same side as Torre Tagle Palace, T 427-6250, ext 2657. This is a large collection of pottery from the Vicus or Piura culture (AD 500-600) and gold objects from Lambayeque, as well as

19th and 20th century paintings: both sections highly recommended. Open Tues-Fri 1000-1600, Sat-Sun 1000-1300. Photography prohibited.

Museo Nacional de la Cultura Peruana, Av Alfonso Ugarte 650, Lima, T 423-5892. The mock Tiahuanaco façade houses a rather disjointed collection of precolumbian and modern artefacts, including *mate burilado* (carved gourds), *retablos*, textiles, *keros* and *huacos*. There are examples of ceramics and cloth from some Amazonian tribes and a set of watercolours by Pancho Fierro, the 19th century *costumbrista* artist. Open Tues-Fri 1000-1630, Sat 1000-1400. Admission US$1, free guide in Spanish.

Poli Museum, Lord Cochrane 466, T 422-2437, Miraflores, is one of the best private collections of precolumbian and colonial artefacts in Peru, including material from Sipán. Guided tours (not in English) by Sr Poli cost US$50 irrespective of the size of the group; allow 2 hrs.

Museo de Arte, 9 de Diciembre 125, T 423-4732, in the Palacio de la Exposición, built in 1868 in Parque de la Exposición. There are more than 7,000 exhibits, giving a chronological history of Peruvian cultures and art from the Paracas civilization up to today. It includes excellent examples of 17th and 18th century Cusco paintings, a beautiful display of carved furniture, heavy silver and jewelled stirrups and also precolumbian pottery.

Between April and Oct, and with special programmes in the holiday season, the cinema shows films and plays almost every night (cheap); see the local paper for details, or look in the museum itself. Free guide, signs in English. Open Tues-Sun 1000-1700, entry US$1.50.

Museo de Arte Italiano, Paseo de la República, 2nd block, T 423-9932, is in a wonderful neo-classical building, given by the Italian colony to Peru on the centenary of its independence. Note the remarkable mosaic murals on the outside. It consists of a large collection of Italian and other European works of art and houses the Instituto de Arte Contemporáneo, which has many exhibitions. Open Mon-Fri 0900-1630, US$1.

Contemporary Folk Art Museum, on Saco Olivero 163, between Arenales and 3rd block of Arequipa, is recommended. There is a shop in the museum grounds. Open Tues-Fri, 1430-1900; Sat 0830-1200.

Pinacoteca Municipal, housed in the Municipal Building on the Plaza de Armas, contains a large collection of paintings by Peruvian artists. The best of the painters is Ignacio Merino (1817-1876). The rooms and furnishings are very ornate. Open Mon-Fri, 0900-1300.

Colección Pedro de Osma is on Av Pedro de Osma 421, Barranco, a private collection of colonial art of the Cusco, Ayacucho and Arequipa schools; T 467-0915/0019 for an appointment. Take bus 2, 54 or colectivo from Av Tacna. The number of visitors is limited to ten at any one time. Admission US$3.

Museo Nacional de Historia, Plaza Bolívar, Pueblo Libre, T 463-2009, is in a mansion occupied by San Martín (1821-1822) and Bolívar (1823-1826); next to the old Museo de Antropolígía y Arqueología. It exhibits colonial and early republican paintings, manuscripts, portraits, uniforms, etc. Open daily 0900-1700. Admission US$1.50.

Museo del Tribunal de la Santa Inquisición, Plaza Bolívar, C Junín 548, near the corner of Av Abancay. The main hall, with a splendidly carved mahogany ceiling, remains untouched. The Court of Inquisition was held here from 1584; 1829-1938 it was used by the Senate. In the basement there is a recreation *in situ* of the gruesome tortures. A description in English is available at the desk. Admission free. Students offer to show you round for a tip; good explanations in English. Mon-Fri 0900-1300, 1430-1700.

Museo Histórico Militar, Parque Independencia, in Real Felipe Fortress, Callao, T 429-0532. There are many interesting military relics and the remains of the small Bleriot plane in which the Peruvian pilot, Jorge Chávez, made the first crossing of the Alps from Switzerland to Italy. Open 0930-1400, US$2 including guide, no cameras allowed. Take bus 25, 74, 94 or colectivo from Av La Vega.

Museo Naval, Av Jorge Chávez 121, off Plaza Grau, Callao, T 429-4793, contains a collection of paintings, model ships, uniforms, etc. Open Mon-Fri 0900-1400. Admission free.

Museo de los Combatientes del Morro de Arica, Cailloma 125, Lima, T 427-0958, gives the Peruvian view of the famous battle against the Chileans during the War of the Pacific. Open Tues-Sat 1000-1500, admission US$0.50.

Museo Miguel Grau, Jr Huancavelica 170, Lima, T 428-5012, is the house of Admiral Grau and has mementoes of the War of the Pacific. Open daily 0900-1400, admission free.

Museo de Historia Natural Javier Prado, Av Arenales 1256, Jesús María, T 471-0117, belongs to Universidad de San Marcos. Exhibits: Peruvian flora, birds, mammals, butterflies, insects, minerals and shells. Open Mon-Sat 0900-1800; admission US$1 (students US$0.50). Take a colectivo from Av Tacna.

La Casa O'Higgins, Unión 550, is an interesting colonial house which holds temporary exhibitions from the Universidad de Lima (entry US$1). Bernardo O'Higgins, president of Chile from 1817-23, died here on 24 October 1842.

Museo Taurino, Hualgayoc 332, Plaza de Acho Bull Ring, Rímac, T 482-3360. Apart from matadors' relics, the museum contains good collections of paintings and engravings – some of the latter by Goya. Mon-Sat 0800-1600. Admission US$1; students US$0.50, photography US$2.

Philatelic Museum, at the Central Post Office, off Plaza de Armas, T 427-5060, ext 553. Incomplete collection of Peruvian stamps and information on the Inca postal system; stamp exchange in front of the museum every Sat and Sun, 0900-1300. Stamps particularly commemorative issues can be bought here; shop hours, Mon-Fri 0800-1200, 1400-1500; museum open 0915-1245, Mon-Fri.

Museo Numismático, Banco Wiese, 2nd floor, Cusco 245, T 427-5060 ext 2009. Displays Peruvian coins from the colonial era to the present.

Museo Teatral, Teatro Segura, Jr Huancavelica 251, Lima, T 427-7437, open during performances; a collection of mementoes and photographs of people who have appeared on the Lima stage.

NB Some museums are only open between 0900 and 1300 from Jan to Mar, and some close altogether in January. Some close early if there are few visitors.

SUBURBS OF LIMA

The Av Arequipa connects the centre of Lima with Miraflores. Parallel to this is the Vía Expresa, a highway carrying fast traffic to the suburbs (six lanes for cars, two for buses). San Isidro, Pueblo Libre, Miraflores and parts of Lince have some good examples of Art Deco and Estilo Barca residential architecture.

San Isidro

To the E of Av La República, down C Pancho Fierro, is **El Olivar**, an old olive grove planted by the first Spaniards which has been turned into a delightful park (best visited in daylight). Beyond this is the Lima Golf Club and the Country Club, primarily a hotel, which incorporates the Club Real (open to members only). This is an 8 km taxi ride from the centre of Lima. There are many good hotels and restaurants in San Isidro; see main Lima lists, hotels page 1227 and restaurants page 1229.

Between San Isidro and Miraflores, at C Nicolás de Rivera 201, is **the Pan de Azúcar**, or **Huallamarca**, a restored adobe pyramid of the Maranga culture, dating from about AD 100-500. There is a small site museum, open daily, 0900-1700. Take bus 1 from Av Tacna, or minibus 13 or 73 to Choquechaca, then walk.

West of San Isidro is the rundown seaside resort of **Magdalena del Mar**, inland from which is **Pueblo Libre** (formerly Magdalena Vieja), where many important museums are located (see under **Museums**, above).

Parque las Leyendas, is on the 24th block of Av de La Marina, Pueblo Libre, between Lima and Callao, T 452-6913. It is arranged to represent the three regions of Peru: the coast, the mountainous Sierra,

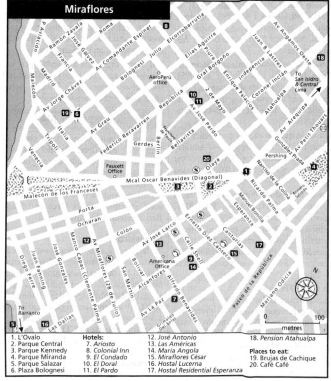

Miraflores

1. L'Ovalo
2. Parque Central
3. Parque Kennedy
4. Parque Miranda
5. Parque Salazar
6. Plaza Bolognesi

Hotels:
7. Ariosto
8. Colonial Inn
9. El Condado
10. El Doral
11. El Pardo

12. José Antonio
13. Las Américas
14. Maria Angola
15. Miraflores César
16. Hostal Lucerna
17. Hostal Residencial Esperanza

18. Pensión Atahualpa

Places to eat:
19. Brujas de Cachiche
20. Café Café

and the tropical jungles of the Selva, with appropriate houses, animals and plants, children's playground. Elephants and lions have been introduced so the zoo is no longer purely Peruvian. It gets very crowded at weekends. The Park is open daily 0900-1700, entrance US$2. There is a handicrafts fair (Feria Artesanal) at the entrance to the park; particularly good insect specimens can be bought here. Take bus 23 or colectivo on Av Abancay, or bus 135A or colectivo from Av La Vega.

Miraflores

Av Arequipa continues to the coast at **Miraflores**, the largest, most important suburb of Lima (see main Lima lists for hotels, page 1226, Youth Hostel, page 1229 and restaurants, page 1229). Together with San Isidro this is now the social centre of Lima.

There is a handsome park in the middle of the shopping centre and at the end of Av Mcal Benavides, which is commonly called Av Diagonal, you can get the best view of the whole Lima coastline from Chorrillos to La Punta. The Mcal Necochea clifftop park, or Parque de los Amantes, overlooks the Waikiki Club, a favourite with Lima surfers.

Concerts are held in the summer in **Parque Salazar**, overlooking the bay, and on Thur-Sun in **Parque Kennedy**. In this park is an artists' and craftsmen's market most evenings of the week. Calle San Ramón, opposite Parque Kennedy off Av Diagonal, is closed to traffic and lined

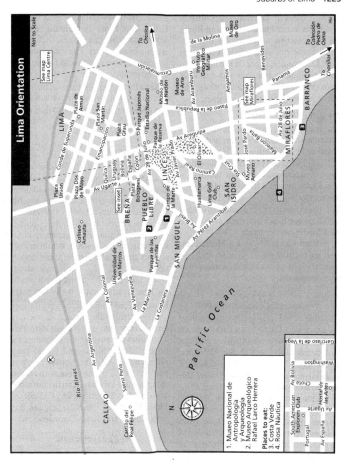

Lima Orientation

Not to Scale

See map
Lima Centre

To
Chosica

To
Colección
Pedro de
Osma

To
Chorrillos

Museo
de Oro

de la Molina

Benavides

Panama

BARRANCO

Instituto
Geográfico
Militar

Museo
de Arte

Circunvalación

Av Arambúru

Angamos

See map
Miraflores

MIRAFLORES

Av 28 de Julio

Malecón Balta

José Pardo

Av Amano

Sta Cruz

Museo
de la Nación

Av Aramburu

Paseo de la República

LIMA

Conde de Superunda

Plaza San
Martín

Plaza de
Armas

Plaza
Grau

Parque
Japonés

Estadio Nacional

Av 28 de Julio

Parque de
la Reserva

Av Arequipa

El Olivar

Av Javier Prado

Camino Real

LINCE

SAN
ISIDRO

Lima Golf
Club

Huallamarc

Emancipación

Quilca

Uruguay

Bolivia

España

Colón

Plaza
Bolognesi

Campo de
la Marte

Av Pérez Aranibar

Plaza
Unión

Plaza Dos
de Mayo

Av Ugarte

See inset

BREÑA

PUEBLO
LIBRE

Av Brasil

SAN MIGUEL

Av Colonial

Universidad de
San Marcos

Parque de las
Leyendas

Av Venezuela

La Marina

Av La Costanera

Coliseo
Amauta

Río Rímac

CALLAO

Saenz Peña

Av Argentina

Castillo del
Real Felipe

Pacific Ocean

N

1. Museo Nacional de
   Antropología
   y Arqueología
2. Museo Arqueológico
   Rafael Larco Herrera

Places to eat:
3. Costa Verde
4. Rosa Náutica

Garcilaso de la Vega

Washington

Av Bolivia

Chota

Hostal de
las Artes

South American
Explorers Club

Av Ugarte

Av España

Portugal

with many pizzerias, hence its nickname of Pizza Street. The house of the author **Ricardo Palma**, Gral Suárez 189, is now a museum, open Mon-Fri 0930-1230, 1330-1800, small entrance fee, T 445-5836. The Miraflores branch of **Banco Wiese** has an exhibition of finds from El Brujo archaeological site N of Trujillo. Open Mon-Fri, 0900-1230, free admission.

At Borgoña, 8th block s/n, turn off Av Arequipa at 45th block, is **Huaca Pucllana**, a pre-Inca site which is under excavation: guided tours only (give tip);

small site museum; admission free.

Barranco

Further S is **Barranco**, which was already a seaside resort by the end of the 17th century. Nowadays, a number of artists have their workshops here. The attractive public library, formerly the town hall, stands on the plaza. Nearby is the interesting *bajada*, a steep path leading down to the beach. **The Puente de los Suspiros** (bridge of sighs), leads towards the Malecón, with fine views of the bay. Barranco is quiet by day but comes alive at night (see Lima **Places to eat** and **Bars**). Take a colectivo to Miraflores then another. Some run all the way to Barranco from Lima centre; check on the front window or ask, same fare. It is a 45-min walk from Miraflores to Barranco along the Malecón; lovely sunsets in summer.

Chorrillos

The next development on the coast is at **Chorrillos**, a fashionable resort with a cliff promenade, and boating. At Hacienda La Villa, an old Spanish *hacienda* worth visiting, there is occasionally open air dancing to *salsa*. Down the beach from Chorrillos is the fish market, with several seafood stalls (the fish is fresh, but is caught in polluted water), the clean beach of Playa Agua Dulce, and the Club Regatas de Lima.

Beyond Chorrillos is **La Herradura**, another bathing resort with several restaurants. The private Club Unicornio is open to tourists.

CALLAO

Founded in 1537, Callao quickly became the main port for Spanish commerce in the Pacific. The merchants were plagued by English raids from Drake, Hawkins, and others. The 1746 earthquake caused a massive wave which completely destroyed the port.

Callao (*Pop* 588,600) is now contiguous with Lima. The road between the two is lined by factories. Shipyards, far from sea, load the fishing vessels they build on huge lorries and launch them into the ocean at Callao. The port handles 75% of the nation's imports and some 25% of its exports. San Lorenzo island, a naval station, protects the roadstead from the S. **The Club**, the oldest English club on the W coast, is at Pasaje Ronald, C Constitución, Callao. There is also an English cemetery. The **Castillo del Real Felipe** is still a military post, and tourists are allowed to visit it. The **Museo Histórico Militar** is in the old barracks. There is also the **Museo Naval** (see page 1220 for both). The Naval College is at **La Punta**, just beyond Callao, served by municipal buses and colectivos through Callao from Lima. La Punta is on a spit of land stretching out to sea, once a fashionable beach resort. The walk along the seafront between Callao and La Punta has its charms.

● **Security** Callao has a serious theft problem, avoid being there in the evening.

● **Transport** Lima is at least 20 mins by car, colectivos US$0.30, bus US$0.25, taxi US$3-4 to the centre or Miraflores.

LIMA BEACHES

In summer (Dec-April) the city's beaches get very crowded at weekends and lots of activities are organized. Even though the water of the whole bay has been declared unsuitable for swimming, Limeños see the beach more as part of their culture than as a health risk. Do not camp on the beaches as robbery is a serious threat and for the same reason, take care on the walkways down. Don't take any belongings with you to the beach, only what is really necessary.

Beaches S of Lima can be very dangerous because of the strong Pacific current. Every year people are drowned. The following beaches are considered to be safe: Santa María and Naplo (near Pucusana). All the other famous beaches have a strong current and swimming should be treated with caution or avoided: Las Señoritas, Los Caballeros, Punta Hermosa, Punta Negra, San Bartolo, Chilca and León Dormido.

EXCURSIONS

CIENEGUILLA

Cieneguilla, about 20 km E of Lima, on the Río Lurín, is a small village in the country, an easy escape from the city and cloud cover of Lima. It is a popular place on Sun, with good restaurants, gardens and swimming pools. The valley of Lurín is good for bird-watching in the early morning.

PACHACAMAC

Pachacámac is in the Lurín valley, 31 km from Lima. When the Spaniards arrived, Pachacámac was the largest city and ceremonial centre on the coast. A wooden statue of the creator-god, after whom the site is named, is in the site museum. Hernando Pizarro was sent here by his brother in 1533 in search of gold for Atahualpa's ransom. In their fruitless quest, the Spaniards destroyed images and killed the priests. The ruins encircle the top of a low hill, whose crest was crowned with a **Temple of the Sun**, now partially restored. Hidden from view is the reconstructed **House of the Mamaconas**, where the 'chosen women' spun fine cloth for the Inca and his court. Open 0900-1700; closed 1 May; US$1.25, includes the small site museum which sells soft drinks.

● **Transport Bus or colectivo from Lima**: from Av Montevideo y Ayacucho. The buses (US$0.40, 1 hr) and colectivos (US$0.60) go via Chorrillos; tell the driver you are going to the *ruinas*, not Pachacámac town further on. A yellow Enatru bus marked Lurín-Pachacámac No P1 leaves from Parque Campo de Marte along Av Grau to Pachacámac. Taxi, round trip with a few hours at the site, US$25. Several travel agencies offer 3 hrs excursions inc English-speaking guide for US$35; *Lima Tours* run daily trips, about 3½ hrs, for about US$15 pp.

PURUCHUCO

On the way to Chosica, up the Rímac valley, turn off at Km 4½ to Puruchuco, the reconstructed palace of a pre-Inca Huacho noble; small museum with ceramics and textiles from the lower Rímac valley and a selection of indigenous plants and animals. Open 0900-1700, Tues-Sun (closed 1 May and 28 July); US$1; transport as for Chosica.

    Cajamarquilla, a large adobe pre-Inca city, can also be visited. The turnoff (left, at Huachipa) is about 6 km on from the Puruchuco turn. The site cannot be seen from the road; look for a sign 'Zona Arqueológica' in the middle of a brick yard. Cajamarquilla is at the end of an ill-kept dirt road. Open daily 0900-1700.

PUCUSANA

Pucusana, 60 km S of Lima, is a pleasant, relaxed fishing village with some good restaurants serving seafood, not cheap, and some basic hotels (in our E range). All are very popular from Dec to Mar, school holidays, and at weekends. There are plenty of buses from the bus station area in Lima. Take the same security precautions as on all Lima's beaches.

ANCON

In the 19th and early 20th centuries, this was the smart seaside resort in Peru, but has now been deserted by the wealthy and in summer is crowded with daytrippers. It has a mix of elegant 19th century houses with wooden balconies and modern apartment blocks. Also bathing, tennis, and a yacht club. The beaches are very small and crowded during Jan-Mar holidays. On the way to Ancón is the pleasant Santa Rosa beach (entrance fee). Beyond Ancón is a cemetery, from which has come much Chancay weaving and pottery (as seen in the Museo Amano). In the valley of Chillón, N of Callao, are several interesting pre-Inca and Inca ruins; the Templo de la Media Luna y El Paraíso and **Chuquitanta**. For more information contact Dr Richard Holmberg at the Instituto Nacional de Cultura, Callao.

● **Accommodation & places to eat** **D** *Hostal del Pirata*, antique furniture, good views, excellent seafood; *Restaurant Cinco Luches*, has rooms to rent, **E**; *Los 5 Tenedores*, is a rec restaurant on the Corniche.

● **Transport** 30 km NW of Lima, reached by a double-lane asphalted highway. Colectivo from Plaza 2 de Mayo in Lima, US$0.60, returns 1 block from Ancón Cathedral.

LOCAL FESTIVALS

18 Jan: Founding of Lima. The whole of **Feb** is Carnival during which time there is water-throwing on Sun. Some 'jokers' mix paint, oil, etc, with the water, so watch out. **Semana Santa**, or Holy Week, is a colourful spectacle with processions. **28-29 July**: is Independence, with music and fireworks in the Plaza de Armas on the evening before. **July-Aug**: Feria del Hogar, which gives a good insight into current Peruvian attitudes and interests. **Oct**: is the month of Our Lord of the Miracles with impressive processions (see *El Comercio* for dates and routes). The Pacific International Fair is held every other year in **November**.

LOCAL INFORMATION

● **Accommodation**

Hotel prices

L1	over US$200	**L2**	US$151-200
L3	US$101-150	**A1**	US$81-100
A2	US$61-80	**A3**	US$46-60
B	US$31-45	**C**	US$21-30
D	US$12-20	**E**	US$7-11
F	US$4-6	**G**	up to US$3

Unless otherwise stated, all hotels in range **D** and above have private bath. Assume friendliness and cleanliness in all cases.

All hotels and restaurants in the upper price brackets charge 18% VAT and 10% service on top of prices (neither is included in prices below). In cheaper hotels water may be scarce in the middle of the day. The more expensive hotels charge in dollars according to the parallel rate of exchange at midnight. More visitors stay in the Miraflores area than in the centre, as it is more organized, cleaner and safer, but more expensive. Backpackers prefer the cheaper *hostales* in the centre, which has more theft problems, is more chaotic, but which, with care and attention to your belongings, is OK. Don't carry any valuables with you, inc TCs. Consult the general **Security** section in the **Information for travellers** and see also the **Warning** under **Buses** below. Note that many parks are used as meeting places for drug pushers and thieves.

Miraflores: L1-L2 *Miraflores César*, La Paz y Diez Canseco, T 444-1212, F 444-4440, luxury, pool, gym, sauna, facilities for the handicapped; **L2** *Las Américas*, Av Benavides 415, T 445-9494, F 444-1137, 5-star, commercial centre, pool, gym, restaurant; **L2** *María Angola*, Av La Paz 610, T 444-1280, F 446-2860, rec; **L2-L3** *El Pardo*, Independencia 141, T 444-2283, F 444-2171, a/c, satellite TV, fax and telex service, pool, gym, good restaurant, rec.

A2 *Ariosto*, Av La Paz 769, T 444-1414, F 444-3955, rec; **A2** *La Hacienda Resort*, 28 de Julio 511, T 444-4346, F 444-1942, English spoken, excellent 5-star service, inc breakfast; **A2** *Grand Hotel Miraflores*, Av 28 de Julio 151, T 447-9641, casino, disco, very pleasant; **A2** *José Antonio*, 28 de Julio 398, T/F 445-6870, good restaurant, rec.

A3 *El Doral*, Av José Pardo 486, T 447-6305, F 446-8344, nice rooms with lounge and kitchenette, safe, pool, rec; **A3** *Hostal Miramar Ischia*, Malecón Cisneros 1244, overlooking Pacific, inc breakfast, good value restaurant, rec; **A3** *Hostal San Antonio Abad*, Ramón Ribeyro 301, T 447-6766, T/F 446-4208, quiet, secure,

very helpful, free airport transfer, highly rec; **A3-B** *Hostal Huaychulo*, Av Dos de Mayo 494, T 445-1195, German owner-manager, English spoken, rec.

B *Hostal El Ejecutivo*, Av 28 de Julio 245, T 447-6310, F 444-2222, inc breakfast, overpriced, tariff negotiable for long stay, safe, luggage can be left; **B** *Hostal La Castellana*, Grimaldo del Solar 222 (nr US consulate), T 444-3530/4662, F 446-8030, pleasant, good value, nice garden, safe, restaurant, laundry, English spoken, 15% discount for South American Explorers Club (SAEC) members, rec; **B** *Hostal Lucerna*, Las Dalias 276 (parallel with 12th block of Larco), T 445-7321, F 446-6050, safe, quiet, cosy, excellent value, rec; **B** *Hostal El Patio*, Diez Canseco 341a, T 444-2107, inc breakfast, reductions for long stays, comfortable, English and French spoken; **B** *Hostal Res Esperanza*, Esperanza 350, T 444-2411/4909, F 444-0834, café, bar, TV, phone, pleasant, secure; **B** *Hostal Palace*, Av 28 de Julio 1088, T 445-6040, F 440-0450, inc breakfast, comfortable, keeps luggage, English spoken; **B** *Hostal Qosqo*, Malecón Cisneros 1070, T/F 992-6596, hot water, TV, inc breakfast, simple rooms, nice location, bar with ocean views; **B** *Hostal Res Torreblanca*, Av José Pardo 1453, T/F 447-9998/3363, inc breakfast, quiet, safe, laundry, restaurant and bar, cosy rooms, will help with travel arrangements, rec; **B** *Hostal Señorial*, José González 567, T 445-7306, inc breakfast, comfortable, nice garden, rec; **B** *Las Palmas*, Bellavista 320, T 444-6033, F 444-6036, helpful, rec; **B** *Res Alemán*, Arequipa 4704, T 445-6999 (no sign), comfortable, quiet, excellent breakfast, laundry service extra; **B** *Suites Eucaliptas*, San Martín 511, T 445-8594, F 444-3071, European-style, kitchenette, sauna, jacuzzi, pool, safety deposit, laundry, credit cards accepted.

C *Armendariz*, Av Armendariz 375 (between Miraflores and Barranco), on No 2 bus line, T 445-4565, inc breakfast, rec; **C** *Hospedaje Atahualpa*, Atahualpa 646c, T 447-6601, **D** without bath, inc breakfast, parking, hot water, cooking and laundry facilities, luggage stored, taxi service, rec; **C-D** *Pensión Yolanda*, Domingo Elias 230, T 445-7565, use of kitchen, owner speaks English, family house, quiet, safe, reservation required, highly rec.

D *Pensión José Luis*, Fr de Paula Ugarriza 727, San Antonio district, T 444-1015, F 446-7177, well-equipped apartments, small kitchen, reservation required, laundry facilities, English-speaking owner, highly rec; **D** pp Sra Jordan, Porta 724, T 445-9840, inc breakfast, 5 rooms, family home, comfortable, quiet; **D** *Pensión San Antonio*, Paseo de la República 5809, T 447-5830, shared bath, comfortable, helpful, hot water on first floor, rec.

E *Hostal Andalucia*, Jr Tacna 472, T 445-8717, with bath, good value, helpful, quiet, rec.

San Isidro: L3 *El Olivar de San Isidro*, Pancho Fierro 194, T 441-1454, F 441-1382, luxury, modern, restaurant, coffee shop, garden, swimming pool, quiet, popular with business visitors. **A2** *Country Club*, Los Eucaliptos, T 440-4060, F 440-8912, all services, restaurant and coffee

shop, quiet, helpful, reasonable rates (except for overseas faxes), gaming room; **A2** *Garden*, Rivera Navarrete 450, T 442-1771, good, large beds, shower, restaurants, rec.

A3 *Hostal Beech*, Los Libertadores 145, T 442-8713, F 442-8716, inc breakfast, noisy, but rec. **B** *Hostal Limatambo*, Av Aramburú 1025, T 441-9615, 24-hr snack bar, good service and quality; **B** *Residencial Francia*, Samuel Velarde 185, 11th block of Ave Ejército, T 461-7054, price inc taxes and breakfast, hot water, laundry

facilities, swimming pool, gardens, very helpful;
B *Sans Souci*, Av Arequipa 2670, T 422-6035,
F 441-7824, safe, good services, garden, garage.

In **Santa Beatriz**, between San Isidro and Centre:
C-D *Hostal Mont Blanc*, Jr Emilio Fernández 640,
T 433-8055, inc breakfast, quiet area, safe (video
monitoring), 15 mins walk or 5 mins by minibus
to centre, owner arranges excursions; **D** *Res Los
Petirrojos*, Petirrojos 230, Corpac (Sra Miri),
T 441-6044, spacious, inc breakfast.

In **Lince** is **D** *Hostal Ambassador*, Julio C Tello
650, T 470-0020, safe, hot water, changes
money for guests, highly rec.

In **Central Lima**, rec in the upper price brackets:
L2 *Lima Sheraton*, Paseo de la República 170,
T 433-3320, F 433-6344, *Las Palmeras* coffee
shop good, daily buffet breakfast, all you can
eat for US$15 pp, casino; **L3** *Crillón*, Av Nicolás
de Piérola, or Colmena 589, T 428-3290, F 432-
5920, good food and service in *Skyroom* (open
1200-2400 Mon-Sat, Peruvian/international
cuisine, buffets and live music at weekends,
great view over Lima).

A1 *Grand Bolívar*, Unión 958, Plaza San
Martín, T 427-2305, F 433-8626 (may be negotiable to C out of season), palatial old building,
good ambience, helpful, excellent restaurant,
have a pisco on the terrace overlooking plaza,
highly rec.

B *El Plaza*, Nicolás de Piérola 850, T 428-6270,
quiet at the back (except Sat), convenient, good,
safe for luggage (cheaper in low season), inc
breakfast; **B** *Grand Castle*, Av Carlos Zavala
Loayza 218, T 428-3181, opp Ormeño bus station, inc breakfast (poor), hot water, comfortable, good service, Japanese restaurant, rec;
B *Kamana*, Jr Camaná 547, T 426-7204, F 426-
0790, modern, TV, phone, comfortable, safe,
restaurants, French and some English spoken,
rec; **B-C** *Hostal Renacimiento*, Parque Hernán
Velarde 52, T 433-2806, nice rooms, quiet,
parking, colonial building, very close to national
stadium, not all rooms with bath, helpful; **B-
C** *Hostal San Martín*, Av Nicolás de Piérola 882,
p 2, Plaza San Martín, T 428-5337, a/c, inc
breakfast served in room, helpful, safe, money
changing facilities, Japanese run, good restaurant, good service, rec.

C *Hostal Los Virreyes*, Jr Cañete 826, T 431-
2733, comfortable, hot water, central, rec; **C-
D** *Res Roma*, Jr Ica 326, T 427-7576, 426-0533,
F 427-7572, hot water all day unless full, safe
to leave luggage, basic, often full, motorcycle
parking, highly rec (*Roma Tours*, helpful for trips,
reservations, flight confirmations, Dante Reyes
speaks English).

D *Granada*, Huancavelica 323, T 427-9033, inc
breakfast, hot water, English spoken, safe, safety

deposit, laundry facilities; **D** *Hostal Belén*,
Belén 1049, just off San Martín, T 428-8995,
discount for groups of 3 or more but give prior
notice, Italian spoken, hot water, sometimes
water shortage pm, basic; **D** *Res Kori Wasi*, Av
Washington 1137, T 433-8127, pleasant, safe.

E *Gran*, Av Abancay 546, T 428-5160, enormous hotel, old house, popular with locals;
E *Hostal de las Artes*, Jr Chota 1454, T433-
0031, Dutch owned, English spoken, safe luggage store, nice colonial building, usually hot
water, good restaurant, close to SAEC, rec;
E *Hostal Iquique*, Jr Iquique 758, Breña, round
corner from SAEC (discount for members),
T433-4724, use of kitchen, hot water, storage
facilities; **E** pp *Hostal Wilson*, Jr Chancay,
T 424-8924, a bit run down but safe for luggage
deposit; **E** *Pensión Ibarra*, Av Tacna 359, Apt
162, p 15 and 16, T 427-1035/428-8656, no
sign, breakfast extra, discount for longer stay,
use of kitchen, laundry facilities, balcony with
views of the city, very helpful owner, hot water,
full board available, highly rec; **E** *Hostal
España*, Jr Azángaro 105, no sign (**G** pp in
dormitory), fine old building being restored,
T 428-5546, shared bath, hot water if you're
quick, run by a French-speaking Peruvian painter
and his Spanish wife, English spoken, travel
agency, motorcycle parking, luggage store
(free), laundry service reported as unreliable,
roof garden with some animals in tiny cages,
mixed reports on security, always busy, good
café, rec; **E-F** *Familia Rodríguez*, Av N de
Piérola 730, 2nd floor, T 423-6465, with breakfast, popular, some rooms noisy, will store luggage, dormitory accommodation with only one
bathroom, transport to airport US$9.50, rec.

F pp *Hostal Samaniego*, Av Emancipación 184,
Apto 801, reservation required, 15 spaces available (4 rooms), noisy, use of kitchen, will store
luggage for foreigners; **F** *Universo*, Azángaro
754, front rooms better, rec.

Outside Lima is the 5-star, **A2** *El Pueblo*, Santa
Clara, Km 11.2, Vitarte (along the Central Highway), huge luxurious complex in the country,
with restaurants, bars, discos, swimming pool,
tennis, shows, shops; you can visit for the day
and use the facilities for a small fee, reservations
T 494-1616/170. Next door is *La Granja Azul*,
Carretera Central (turn off between Km 13 and
14 of Carretera Central, buses from Parque
Universitario every 15 mins; last bus back leaves
2000 but a minibus leaves the hotel for Lima at
2200), restaurant specializing in exotic cocktails
and chicken dishes, dancing every night, rec.

If arriving by air, especially at night, you can try
the tourist office at the airport (beyond passport
control) if you want to arrange a hotel room, but
they are not always helpful. **Hotel reservations**

for Lima and elsewhere in Peru can be made through Reservaciones Central, a travel agency, Av Panamericana 6251, San Antonio/Miraflores, T 446-6895; it charges a small commission, also offers all usual services.

Youth hostel: *Albergue Turístico Juvenil Internacional*, Av Casimiro Ulloa 328, San Antonio between San Isidro and Miraflores, T 446-5488, F 444-8187, basic cafeteria, travel information, cooking (minimal) and laundry facilities, US$9 members, US$10 non-members, dormitory, more for double room, swimming pool often empty, extra charge for kitchen facilities, clean and safe, situated in a nice villa, rec. 20 mins walk from the beach. Bus No 2 or colectivos pass Av Benavides to the centre; taxi to centre, US$2.50. *Qorpawasi*, Av J Pardo de Zela 877, Lince, T 471-2480/445-5548, F 440-9021, US$9 pp inc breakfast in dormitories, US$12 pp in double room, highly rec. Hotel run by Henry Kleinberg, Los Lirios 165, San Isidro, T 442-0162.

Camping: under no circumstances camp on or nr the beach at Miraflores, theft and worse is rife in these areas. Camping gas (in small blue bottles) available from any large hardware store or bigger supermarket, about US$3. Backpack makers and repairers, *Ursus* (Alberto Abalero), Av El Ejército 1982, Miraflores, T 422-6678. *Alpamayo*, Larco 345, sells camping equipment.

● **Places to eat**
Menu prices fail to show that 18% government tax and 10% service will be added to your bill in middle and upper class restaurants. A cheap *menú* (set lunch) costs US$1.30-3, while a meal in a moderate café/bistro will cost US$15-20; in middle-range restaurants a meal costs US$25-30, rising to US$60-80 at the upper end of the range. Chinese is often the cheapest at around US$5 inc a drink. Unless stated otherwise, prices of places listed below are in the moderate range.
In **Miraflores** we recommend the following: *Rosa Náutica*, T 447-0057, built on old British-style pier (Espigón No 4), in Lima Bay, nr Miraflores, not to be missed, delightful opulence, finest fish cuisine, experience the atmosphere by buying an expensive beer in the bar, sunset rec, open 1230-0200 daily; *La Costa Verde*, on Barranquito beach, T 441-4084, excellent fish and wine, pecan pie highly rec, very expensive, Amex accepted, open 1200-2400 daily, Sun buffet; *Las Brujas de Cachique*, Plaza Bolognesi, an old mansion converted into bars and dining rooms, beautifully decorated, traditional food, live criollo music, expensive but affordable, highly rec.
    The Vila Nova precinct, Av Ricardo Palma 251, has 9 smart restaurants offering different cuisines. *Don Beta*, José Gálvez 667, expensive, rec for seafood; *Carlín*, La Paz 646, cosy, international, expensive; *Pizzería Restaurant Erik*,

Av Benavides 1057, cheap local and international food, highly rec, try the *salsas*; *Don Rosalino*, Juan Figari 135, pizzas; *Stefanos*, Av José Pardo 779, closed Mon, pastas and pizzas; *Las Tejas*, Diez Canseco 340, good, typical Peruvian food; *El Señorío de Sulco*, Malecón Cisneros 1470, at the end of Av Pardo, authentic Peruvian dishes; *Rincón Chami*, Esperanza 1st block, *comida criolla*, very good value; *C'est Si Bon*, Cdte Espinar 663, French style; *Alfresco*, Malecón Balta 790 (also Santa Luisa 295, San Isidro, and Carabaya 445), middle price range, very good service and food.
    El Alamo, La Paz y Diez Canseco, cosy spot for wines, raclettes and fondues, expensive; *Cheese and Wine*, Av La Paz 522, good fondues, raclette, salads and wines, warm, cosy atmosphere, excellent service; *Oriental*, José de San Martín 561, 1130-1500 only Sun, great Chinese food; *Asia Garden*, Diez Canseco 493, Chinese; *Palachinke*, Shell 120, excellent, large pancakes; *The Steak House*, La Paz 642, steaks and salads, another branch in San Isidro (Las Camelias 870); *La Tranquera*, Av Pardo 285, steaks; *El Rodizio*, Ovalo Gutiérrez y Santa Cruz, good meats and salad bar; *Martín Fierro*, Malecón Cisneros 1420, Argentine, good Sun buffet; *El Rincón Gaucho*, Parque Salazar, closed Mon, grills and steaks, and *El Otro Gaucho*, Rep Panamá 6488.
    Manolo, Av Larco 608, good food, popular, expensive; *New York Pizza Company*, Av Larco 1145, tasty, English spoken; *Whatta Burger*, Grau 120, American-style hamburgers; *Mediterráneo Chicken*, Av Benavides block 420, chicken and salads (branch in San Isidro); next door is *Silvestre*, good fresh juices and vegetarian sandwiches, fairly expensive; *Tomás*, 2nd floor of Santa Isabel Supermarket, Benavides 486, open 24 hrs, good, cheap, fast food; *Varsovia 2000*, Esperanza 135, good set lunch; *La Tasca*, Espinar 300, good value *menú*; *Rebecca*, Jr Atahualpa 192, good, cheap *menú*. Best ice cream, *Quattro D*, Angamos Oeste 408; second best at *Fragola*, Av Benavides 468. Best yoghurt *Mi Abuela*, Angamos 393; *Media Naranja*, Shell 130, good for breakfast, Brazilian owner; *Pastelería Sueca*, Av Larco 759, good hamburgers, pastries, salads; *Brenchley Arms*, Atahualpa 174, British pub, British owner, typical food, informal and relaxed, tourist information, expensive (US$10 for bar snacks), darts.

Vegetarian: *Bircher Berner*, Av Shell 598, closed Sun, with store, slow service, good cheap *menú*; *Govinda*, Shell 630, good; *La Huerta del Sol*, El Alamo precinct, La Paz y Diez Canseco, lunch menu US$3, main dishes US$5, good food, pleasant setting; *Rincón Vegeteriano*, Los Pinos 173, entre 2 y 3 de Benavides, cheap lunch US$1.75.

Cafés: *Vivaldi*, Ricardo Palma 258, also snacks and drinks, good cappucinos; *Haiti*, Diagonal 160, drinks, café snacks, expensive, popular meeting place; *Café Suisse*, Av Larco 111, on main plaza, for very good cakes, coffee, European-style food and delicatessen, expensive; *Café Café*, Mártir Olaya 250, nr Ovalo, very popular, good atmosphere.

In **San Isidro**: *La Réserve*, Las Flores 326, expensive, French cuisine; *Aquarium* (at the Country Club Hotel), expensive, rec. **Seafood**: *Punta Sal*, Conquistadores 948, expensive; also *La Caleta*, D Deteano 126, expensive; *Puerto Azul*, Conquistadores 1018; similar is *El Pirata*, Av Dos de Mayo 674, closes 1800 Sun-Wed; also *Cebiches El Rey*, Av Aramburu 975, closes 1800 Sun, with branches in Miraflores, Callao and Barranco.

Valentino's, M Bañón 215 (nr Camino Real and Av Javier Prado), great Italian food; *Fredos*, Conquistadores 512, excellent homemade pastas; *José Antonio*, B Monteagudo 200, closed Sun, creole and Peruvian dishes, expensive; *Mi Casa*, Augusto Tamayo 150, closed Sun; *Lung Fung*, Av Rep de Panamá 3165, Chinese; *El Dorado*, Av Arequipa 2450, Chinese, good views of Lima, expensive; *La Casa de España*, Conquistadores 331, closes 1600 Sun, Spanish; *La Carreta*, Rivera Navarrete 740, Peruvian and international, good steaks; *Don Alfredo*, M Bañón 295, closes 1500 Sun, expensive, excellent, helpful, friendly; *La Ronda*, Las Begoñas y Andrés Reyes, excellent value, US$10-15. La Plaza de Miguel Dazzo is a place for nightlife, restaurants, bars and discos, popular with Limeños.

In **Barranco**: *El Otro Sitio*, Sucre 317, closed Sun, in a fine 18th century house, excellent creole buffet, expensive with live music; *Manos Morenas*, Av Pedro de Osma 409, creole cuisine with shows some evenings (cover charge for shows); *El Buen Gusto*, Av Grau 323, good for atmosphere, service, selection of meat dishes and desserts; *El Cortijo*, Rep de Panamá 675, Peruvian; *El Florentino*, Av Grau 680, bar/restaurant/peña; *Abdala*, Av Grau 340, German owner, good; *La Ermita*, Bajada de Baños 340, Puente de Suspiros, international cuisine, romantic, expensive. **Seafood**: *Canta Rana*, Génova 101, good, also for *ceviche*; *El Catamarán*, Av Rep de Panamá 258, lunch only. Around the main plaza are several good bars, pizza restaurants and *peñas*.

In **Pueblo Libre**: *Taberna Quierolo*, Av San Martín 1090, 2 blocks from Museo Nacional de Antropología y Arqueología, old bar, good seafood and atmosphere, not open for dinner; *Puerto Coral*, La Marina 1004, friendly, huge dishes (try *parihuela*).

In **Monterrico**, nr the Gold Museum: *Pabellón de la Caza*, Alonso de Molina 1196, open weekdays, Sun brunch 1030-1600, expensive, very good food and service, delightful surroundings; *Puerto Fiel*, Av Primavera 1666, 3 blocks from Gold Museum, seafood, rec.

Chorrillos: *El Salto del Fraile*, Herradura Beach, beautifully-located, Peruvian and seafood; *El Encuentro Otani*, San Pedro 182, La Campina, excellent seafood, creole and oriental, very good value. **San Borja**: *El Piqueo Trujillano*, Av San Luis 1956-58, open till 1830 Mon-Thur, 1200-2100 Fri-Sun, creole cooking; *Shanghai*, Av San Luis 1988, Chinese. **Surco**: *El Mono Verde*, Av Vicus F-56, Urb La Capullana, T 448-7288, evening by reservation only, good creole and Peruvian cuisine; *Punta Pez*, Camino del Inca 398, seafood.

Jesús María: *El Centro Cultural Peruano Japonés*, Gregorio Escobedo 803, good, cheap Japanese food.

In **central Lima**: *L'Eau Vive*, Ucayali 370, across from the Torre Tagle Palace, run by nuns, open Mon-Sat, 1245-1430, 1930-2130, set lunch US$7.50, Peruvian-style in interior dining room, or à la carte in either of dining rooms that open on to patio, French spoken, excellent, profits go to the poor; *El Mesón del Frayle*, in the cloisters of San Francisco, very good, pleasant ambience, 1200-1800 (later by arrangement); *Maury*, Ucayali 201, Peruvian/international, good pisco sours; *Chifa Cai*, Carabaya y Ucayali, clean, cheap, good fish dishes, ask about vegetarian if they're not too busy; *Daruma*, Nicolás de Piérola 712, closed Sun, Japanese; *Gigi's*, Uruguay 411, good chifa, open for lunch; *Raimondi*, Quesada 110 (no sign), Peruvian, good (especially *ceviche*); *Buena Muerte*, Junín y Abancay, Plaza Bolívar, lunch only, good *cevicheria*; *Hedi*, Puno 367, good, cheap seafood, lunch only, popular; *Rolando's*, Washington 988, good seafood/*ceviche*; *Lucky Star*, N de Piérola 733 (3 blocks from Plaza San Martín), good, Peruvian; *El Damero de Pizarro*, Jr de la Unión 543, huge helpings, popular with locals, loud music; *El Pan Nuestro*, Ica 129, 2 blocks from Res Roma, closed Sun, good value, good food; *Machu Picchu*, nr Hostal España on Jr Azángaro, excellent set menus for breakfast (US$1.50, but ask as it's not on the menu) and lunch, huge portions; *Casa del Cappelletti*, Av Tacna, block 7, cheap, good Italian; *Nuevo Siglo*, Jr Moquegua 585, good menú US$1.30. The restaurant/bar opp the railway station serves good food, old-world atmosphere, good pisco sours. Very close to SAEC on Jr Breña is *La Choza Náutica*, excellent ceviche and friendly service. Also nr SAEC is *Nakasone*, good chicken, fries and salad for US$2.75, good service.

Vegetarian restaurants: *Natur*, Moquegua 132, rec, some English spoken; *Govinda*, Av Callao 480 y Tacna, good value lunch and at Av Arenales 674, Jesus María; *Centro Aplicación Naturista Sebastián Kneipp*, Jr Loreto 379, Rímac, highly rec; *Centro de la Salud 'La Naturaleza'*, Jr de la Unión, 819, No 107, or Jr Lampa 440, T 427-3832, 1000-1900, Mon-Fri; *San Juan*, Camaná 949; *Comedor Vegetariano Nuevo Mundo*, Camillo Carrillo 159, Jesus María, cheap, acceptable.

A good coffee bar for snacks and sandwiches is *Googies* in Plaza San Martín; also *Sandwich Tacna*, Tacna 327, popular and crowded at lunchtime. Good coffee at *Café de Paso*, Carabobo y Cusco (stand-up coffee shop); *Café Azzurra*, Jr Unión 574, for coffee and ice cream, also serves food during the day and breakfasts; *Bar Edén*, Huancavelica 285, good strong expresso served from a 1950s Italian machine, male clientèle meet to discuss the day's events; *Pastelería Lobatón*, Jr Unión 672, good *churros*. There are plenty of other cafés and snackbars in the centre of Lima.

● **Bars**

In **Barranco**: *Johann Sebastian Bach*, Av Grau 687, classical music, has concerts nightly; *Pizzelli Latina*, Pedro de Osma, great local bar; *Barman's House*, Piérola 109, cheap takeaway cocktails; *Juanito's Bodega Bar*, on the plaza, rec for local colour; *La Noche*, popular, video bar. There are many others by the plaza in Barranco, also on the pedestrian street (Sánchez Carrión) leading from Barranco plaza to Av Bolognesi and others nr Puente de los Suspiros, eg *El Age Acantilado*, great view, nice atmosphere.

In **Miraflores**: *Medi Rock*, Benavides 420, good live rock music, US$2.50 cover charge, US$2 for a small beer; *Phantom Video y Café*, Diagonal 344, open weekends 2000-0400, music videos, good record shop downstairs; *Nautilus*, Ricardo Palma 130, open late till dawn for food and drink.

In **central Lima** there are many good discos and video bars on and around Jr de la Unión.

● **Airline offices**

Peruvian airlines with international and national flights: **Faucett**, Garcilaso de La Vega 865, Lima, T 433-6364; Av Diagonal 592, Miraflores, T 446-3444; reservations, T 464-3322. **AeroPerú**, head office at Av Pardo 601, Miraflores, T 241-1797; reservations, T 241-0606; Av Garcilaso de la Vega 870, T 447-8255. Peruvian airlines with national flights only: **Expreso Aéreo**, Av Larco 101, edif Caracol, of 303, Miraflores, T 444-9984. **Aero Cóndor**, Jr Juan de Arona 781, San Isidro, T 442-5215/441-8484. **Aero Continente**, Francisco

Masias 528, p 8, San Isidro, T 442-8770/7829. **Aero Ica**, Tudela y Varela 150, San Isidro, T 421-6653, F 440-1030. **Grupo Ocho**, military airline, T 452-9560, at airport (desk not always staffed).

International airlines: Aeroflot 444-8716; **Air France** 470-4702; **Alitalia** 442-8506; **American Airlines** 442-8555/475-6161; **Avianca** 470-4232; **Iberia** 428-3833; **KLM** 447-1394; **Lan Chile** 446-6958/6995; **LAB** 447-3292; **Varig** 442-4031/4148; **Servivensa** 447-2694; **Saeta**, Andalucía 174, Miraflores, block 42 of Av Arequipa, T 422-4526/27/28; **Lacsa** 446-0758 (often have cheaper flights from USA).

● **Banks & money changers**

Most banks at their main branch change TCs without commission into soles, but will charge 2-3% for changing cheques into dollars cash. Banco de Crédito and Interbanc give the best rates. There are especially large queues on Mon. Banks are the best place to change TCs and *casas de cambio* for cash. Open Mon-Fri 0900-1300, 1500-1700, unless stated otherwise; many also open Sat am. **Citibank**, Las Begoñas 580, San Isidro, charges no commission on its own TCs, open 0830-1245 in summer. **Bank of America**, Augusto Tamayo 120, San Isidro, will change Bank of America TCs into local currency, 1.5% commission. **Interbanc**, Jr de la Unión 600, esq Huancavelica changes cash and Amex TCs, no commission into soles, open 0900-1500, and Sat 0900-1200; Av Larco 5th block, Miraflores, US$5 commission on TCs up to US$1,000; R Navarrete 857, San Isidro, open Sat am, no commission into soles; cash against Visa card. **Banco de Crédito**, Av Lampa 499; Larco y Shell, Miraflores; Amex and Citicorp TCs, no commission; cash against Visa card, US$300/day max; **Banco Wiese**, Diagonal 176, Miraflores, 1% commission on Amex and Citicorp TCs, cash against Mastercard. **Banco Continental**, at Lampa y Emancipación; República de Panamá 3055, San Isidro; Larco 467, Miraflores; 1% commission to soles or dollars, min US$5. **Banco Mercantil**, Ucayali y Carabaya, changes Amex and Citicorps TCs (soles only, no commission) and gives cash on Visa and Mastercard; also branches in Miraflores and San Isidro. **LAC Dolar**, Jr Camaná 779, 1 block from Plaza San Martín, p 2, T 428-8127, T/F 427-3906, open Mon-Sat 0900-1900, Sun and holidays 0900-1400, good rates, very helpful, safe, fast, reliable, 2% commission on cash and TCs (Amex, Citicorp, Thomas Cook, Visa), will come to your hotel if you're in a group, repeatedly rec. **P & P Cambios**, N de Piérola 805, Mon-Fri 0900-1700, Sat 0900-1200; Av Benavides 735, Miraflores, Mon-Fri 0900-1300, 1500-1700; 2% commission on TCs in soles or dollars; **Cambios MFB**, Jr Camaná 825, T 428-7102/0004, 1 block from Plaza San Martín, friendly and reliable, will change Thomas Cook TCs. Lima

Sheraton Casino changes TCs into dollars, no commission. Always check your money in the presence of the cashier, particularly bundles of pre-counted notes. See also **Airport**, below. The banks which deal with credit cards are very efficient in replacing stolen cards; similarly the American Express office (see **Travel agents** below) in replacing stolen cheques (police report needed). **Diners Club**, Canaval y Moreyra 535, San Isidro, T 441-4272, Mon-Fri 0900-1330, 1430-1800.

The **gold dealers** on Pasaje Los Pinos, Miraflores, give good street rates. Many money changers at corner of Plaza San Martín and Jr de la Unión, in the streets behind *Hotel Bolívar*, and nr L'Ovalo in Miraflores, identified by their calculators and hiss of 'dollars', change money at the parallel rate; some change other South American currencies (see **Warning** under **Currency** in **Information for travellers**). Double-check amounts shown on calculators. Damaged dollar bills can be changed on Calle Ocoña, at a poor rate.

● **Cultural centres**

Peruvian-British Cultural Association, Av Arequipa 3495, San Isidro, T 470-5577, with reading room and British newspapers (bus 1, 2, 54A). For other offices, library and film shows, Jr Camaná 787, T 427-7927, classes only; theatre, Av Benavides 620, Miraflores, T 445-4326. British Council, Alberto Lynch 110, San Isidro 27, T 704-350. The theatre of the British Cultural Association is the Teatro Británico (amateur productions of plays in English), C Bella Vista, Miraflores, T 445-4326. Cámara de Comercio Peruano-Británico, Av Rep de Panamá 3563, of 202, San Isidro, T 441-3268, F 442-2135. Instituto Cultural Peruano y Norteamericano, Cusco 446, T 428-3530, in centre, with library; branch at Av Arequipa 4798, Miraflores, T 446-0381. Language tuition, US$80 for 4 weeks, Mon-Fri, 2 hrs a day. The American Society of Peru, Av Angamos 1155, Miraflores, T 441-4545. Goethe-Institut, Jr Nasca 722, Jesus María, Lima 11, T 433-3180, Mon-Fri, 1100-1200, 1500-2000, library, theatre, German papers, tea and cakes, you will need your passport. Alliance Française, Av Garcilaso de la Vega 1550, T 423-0139, also in Miraflores, Av Arequipa 4598, T 446-8511. Euroidiomas, Juan Fanning 520, Miraflores, T 445-7116, English papers, tea room, Ciné Club.

● **Embassies & consulates**

Argentine Consulate, Pablo Bermúdez 143, p 2, Jesús María, T 433-5709, open 0800-1300. Bolivian Consulate, Los Castaños 235, San Isidro, T 422-8231 (0900-1330), 24 hrs for visas. Brazilian Consulate, José Pardo 850, Miraflores, T 446-2635, Mon-Fri 0930-1300. Chilean Consulate, Javier Prado Oeste 790, San Isidro, T 440-7965, open 0900-1300, need appointment. Ecuadorean Consulate, Las Palmeras 356, San Isidro (6th block of Av Javier Prado Oeste), T 442-4184. Colombian Consulate, Natalio Sánchez 125, p 4, T 433-8922/3, Mon-Fri 0900-1300. Paraguayan Consulate, Los Rosarios 415, San Isidro, T 441-8154, open 0900-1300. Uruguayan Consulate, Av Larco 1013, p 2, Miraflores, T 447-9948, open 0930-1330. Venezuelan Consulate, Av Salaverry 3005, San Isidro, T 441-5948.

US Embassy, Av Encalada block 17, Monterrico, T 434-3000, F 434-3065, for emergencies after hours T 434-3032, the Consulate is in the same building. Canadian Embassy, Libertad 130, Casilla 18-1126, Lima, T 444-4015. New Zealand Embassy, contact British Embassy. South African Consulate, contact Swiss Embassy.

British Embassy and Consulate, Edif Pacífico-Washington, Plaza Washington, corner of Av Arequipa (5th block) and Natalio Sánchez 125, p 11 (Casilla de Correo 854), T 433-5032/4839/4932/5137, open Mon-Thur 0830-1700, Fri 0830-1315, good for security information and newspapers (yellow bus No 2 passes the Embassy). Irish Consulate, Santiago Acuña 135, Urb Aurora, Miraflores, T 445-6813. Austrian Embassy, Av Central 643, p 5, San Isidro, T 442-8851. German Embassy, Av Arequipa 4202, Miraflores, Casilla 18-0504, T 445-7033. French Consulate, Arequipa 3415, San Isidro, T 470-4968. Belgian Consulate, Angamos 380, Miraflores, T 446-3335. Spanish Embassy, Jorge Basadre 498, San Isidro, T 470-5600/78, open 0900-1300. Swiss Embassy, Av Salaverry 3240, Magdalena, Lima 17 (Casilla 378, Lima 100), T 264-0305/0719. Swedish Embassy, Camino Real 348, p 9, Torre del Pilar, San Isidro, T 440-6700. Norwegian Consulate, Canaval Moreyra 595, T 440-4048. Danish Consulate General, at Bernardo y Monteguido, San Isidro, T 462-1090. Netherlands Consulate, Av Principal 190, Santa Catalina, La Victoria, T 476-1069, open Mon-Fri 0900-1200. Italian Embassy, Av G Escobedo 298, Jesús María, T 463-2727. Israeli Embassy, Natalio Sánchez 125, p 6, same building as British Embassy, Santa Beatriz in Lima, Aptdo 738, T 433-4431. Japanese Embassy, Av San Felipe 356, Jesus María (postal address: Apdo 3708, Lima), T 463-0000.

NB During the summer, most embassies only open in the morning.

● **Entertainment**

Cinemas: some *Ciné Clubs* are: *El Cinematógrafo*, Pérez Roca 196, Barranco; *Filmoteca de Lima*, Museo de Arte, closed Mon; *La Otra Vía*, Valdelomar 665, Pueblo Libre; *Raimondi*, Alejandro Tirado 274, Lima. Free films also at Banco Central, Lampa y Ucayali, Wed at 1630, arrive early. Also the cultural institutions (see above) usually show a film once a week (often Thur). Entry about US$1. The section 'C' (Cultural) in *El Comercio* is good for checking film and theatre programmes. Many good cinemas throughout the city. Most films are in English with Spanish subtitles; US$2 in the centre, US$4.50 in Miraflores. Cinemas in centre tend to have poor sound quality.

Discotheques: good nightlife in Miraflores nr Parque Diagonal and Av Larco, with discos, video-pubs and pizzerías. All discos have a cover charge of between US$8 and US$20 pp or couple, inc one drink. In most discos only couples are allowed in; most are expensive for drinks, and open from 2100 till 0400. *Keops*, Camino Real 149, San Isidro, is very popular with young Limeños. *Casablanca*, P Fierro 117, San Isidro, cheaper, casual; *Amadeus*, close to the Gold Museum, Lima's most expensive and luxurious disco, US$20 cover; *La Rosa Naútica*, above restaurant of same name, young crowd, US$10 cover; *Casa Vieja*, San Martín y La Paz, Miraflores, casual, US$10 cover; *Psicosis*, Bella Vista, 1st block, Miraflores, expensive, young clientele, US$15/couple; *Nirvana*, Shell y Paseo de la República, Miraflores, modern, casual, US$8/couple; *Bizzaro*, Lima y Diez Canseco facing Parque Kennedy, Miraflores, 2nd Floor Edif D'Anafrio, US$5 cover, New York-style, dancing and billiards. In Surquillo, *Africa*, Av Tomás Marsano 826, and *El Zalonazo*, C Uno 157, both rec. There are several discos along the beach in Miraflores, most of them are *salsatecas*, where only salsa is played, cover charge about US$10 pp.

Folklore: every Sun at the *Coliseo Cerrado*, Av Alfonso Ugarte. Also at the *Teatro Municipal*, Jr Ica (tickets US$0.60-3.60), Tues 2000. *Cooperativa Santa Elisa*, Cailloma 824, p 3, has a folk group every Wed, 2000. The *Museo de Arte* has seasons of Peruvian folklore on Wed, at 2000, US$1.20 entrance. Peñas are generally cheap, tavern-like places with Peruvian music, much dancing and audience participation: *Hatuchay Peña*, Trujillo 228 (across the bridge past the Post Office), Fri, Sat, 2100, entrance US$3, inexpensive, crowded, good, but take a taxi there and back; *Las Brisas de Lago Titicaca*, just off Plaza Bolognesi, US$4.50 entry, rec; *Peña El Ayllu*, Jr Moquegua 247, open every night, entrance free, rec; *Taberna 1900*, Av Grau 268, Barranco, folklore and creole; *El Buho Pub*, Sucre 315, Barranco, creole music; *La Casona de Barranco*, Grau 329, modern music, creole and jazz. Many others in Barranco around Plaza Grau and Puente de los Suspiros; *La Estación de Barranco*, at Pedro de Osma

112, good, family atmosphere, varied shows, live music at weekends, US$8-US$15 cover charge, and *Latinoamericano* on same street.

Theatre: most professional plays are put on at the **Teatro Segura**, C Huancavelica, block 2, Lima, T 427-7437; **Teatro Municipal**, Jr Ica, block 3, Lima, T 428-2303 (also orchestral and ballet performances). Open air theatre in Parque Salazar, Miraflores (end of Av Larco) between Nov and April; check press for programme. Others are produced by amateur and university groups. **Teatro Cabaña** in the Parque de la Exposición puts on a strong programme of progressive theatre, take student card. **AAA Theatre Workshop**, Jr Ica 323. English speaking theatre occasionally by the Good Companions at **Teatro Británico**, details in *Lima Times*. The Sun edition of *El Comercio* publishes all cinema and theatre details.

● **Health, hospitals & medical services**

Dentists: *Dr Zuelei Cornejo*, Octavio Espinoza 443, San Isidro, T 422-9638. *Ribamar Camacho Rodríguez*, Clínica Los Pinos, Miraflores, T 446-4103/2056, speaks a little English, highly rec. *Víctor Melly*, Av Conquistadores 965, San Isidro, T 422-5757. *Dr Víctor Aste*, Antero Aspillaga 415, San Isidro, T 441-7502. *Dra Ada Lucía Arroyo Torres*, Jr Laredo 196, Centro Comercial Monterrico, T 436-0942.

Doctors: *Dr Augusto Saldarriaga Guerra*, Clínica Internacional, T 433-4306. *Dr Alejandro Bussalleu Rivera*, Instituto Médico Lince, León Velarde 221, Lince, T 471-2238, speaks English, good for stomach problems. Also good for stomach or intestinal problems, *Dr Raul Morales*, Clínica Padre Luis Tezza, Av del Polo 570, Monterrico, T 435-6990/6991 (no English spoken). *Dr Jorge Mejía*, Analisisclinicos, Av J Pardo Oeste 910, T 440-0643, stool analysis.

Hospitals: *Anglo-American Hospital*, Av Salazar, 3rd block, San Isidro, T 221-3656, rec for injections, but not typhoid, stocks gamma globulin and anti-rabies vaccine, US$45/consultation. *Instituto de Medicina Tropical*, Universidad Particular Cayetano Heredia, Av Honorio Delgado, Urb Ingeniería, San Martín de Porres, T 482-3903/3910, for tropical diseases, or any medical help or advice, very good, cheap, for check-ups after a long jungle trip. *Hospital del Niño*, Av Brasil, vaccination centre for yellow fever, tetanus and typhoid at the side. *Clínica Internacional*, Jr Washington 1475, Lima, T 428-8060, US$30 per consultation; *Clínica San Borja*, Av del Aire 333, San Borja, T 475-3141/4997; *Clínica de Fracturas San Francisco*, Av San Felipe 142, Jesus María, T 463-9855/6202. *Policlínico Japonés*, Av Gregorio Escobedo 783, Jesús María, T 461-9291, x-rays, check-ups and analysis, reasonable prices. All clinics have 24-hr emergency service and most of them have English-speaking doctors. A consultation costs between US$25 and US$45, not inc any medicines. *Centro Especializado de Diagnóstico*, Av Arequipa 1840, Lince, T 471-8506, for x-rays, analyses, etc, no English. *Centro Anti-Rabia*, Jr Austria, Chacra Rios, Lima, T 425-6313.

Pharmacy: *Botica Inglés*, Jr Cailloma 336, sells Dr Scholl foot supplies for those contemplating or recovering from the Inca Trail, among others in the centre. Tampons are available everywhere.

● **Language schools**
Most institutes have standard packages for 1 month, 2 hrs a day from Mon to Fri, about US$80; you can arrange for 2, or 3 weeks, or private tuition (about US$10/hr). **Instituto de Idiomas Pontífica Universidad Católica del Perú**, Jr Camaná 956, Lima, T 431-0052; **La Católica Universidad Instituto de Idiomas**, Camino Real 1037, San Isidro, T 441-5962; **Centro de Idiomas de Lima**, Av Manuel Olguín 215, Monterrico, T 435-0601, F 435 5970 (PO Box 772, Lima 100), US$12/hr, classes suited to students' travelling schedules, full board accommodation can be arranged with families US$120/week. See also Instituto Cultural Peruano y Norteamericano above. **Quechua Classes** Señora Lourdes Gálvez, Los Insurgentes 154, Urb Santa Constanza de Monterrico, opp Javier Prado Oeste 41 in Surco, T 435-3910, gives 3-month courses for US$6/hr; at the same address is Señora Llorgelina Savastizagal, T 438-2676. **Universidad San Marcos**, T 452-4641, dept of Idiomas, Sats only, 4½ hrs, US$15.

● **Laundry**
Laundries charge per item (eg US$3-4 for a pair of trousers). There are some in Miraflores and San Isidro which charge per kilo, about US$1.50-2. Mostly next day service. *Continental*, Callao 422, same-day and next-day laundry and drycleaning, good, charge per item. *Burbujitas*, Porta 293, Miraflores, 4 kg wash and dry for US$4.50. *Lavaquik*, Av Benevides 604, Miraflores; *Lava Center*, Víctor Maurtúa 140, San Isidro, T 440-3600; *Tokai*, Cantuarias 380, Miraflores, Mon-Sat 0900-1900, rec; coin laundromat at Berlin 315, US$4.35 per load, same day service, reliable, rec; *Centro de Autoservicios Lavaphilp*, Av Arica 448, Breña, rec as cheapest.

● **Places of worship**
Non-catholic: the *Union Church of Lima* (Interdenominational), Av Angamos 1155, Miraflores, Worship Sun 1030, T 441-1472. *Church of the Good Shepherd*, Av Santa Cruz 491, Miraflores (Anglican) T 445-7908, Sun 0800 Holy Communion, 1000 morning service. *International Baptist Church of Lima*, Col Inclán 799, Miraflores, T 475-7179, Worship Sun 1000. *English Bene-*

dictine Monastery, Jr Olivares de la Paz, Las Flores (57M minibus from Plaza de Acho); Sunday Mass 0900, weekdays 1900. *Synagogue*, Av 2 de Mayo 1815, San Isidro, T 440-0290. **Catholic Mass in English**, La Iglesia de Santa María Reina, Ovalo Gutiérrez, Av Santa Cruz, Miraflores, T 424-7269, Sun 0930.

● **Post & telecommunications**
Air freight: most companies are in Callao (see Yellow Pages under 'Agencias de Carga'). They all charge about the same and only handle large amounts: by air about US$15/kg, surface US$3-5/kg. You can deal direct with the airlines, all have a cargo office at the airport. KLM is best. UPS, Paseo de la República 6299, Miraflores, T 446-0444, documents or freight to USA US$37/kg, to Europe US$96.

Post Offices: central office is on Pasaje Piura, 1 block from the Plaza de Armas, T 427-5592, hours: Mon-Sat 0800-2000, Sun 0800-1400. *Poste restante* is in the same building, but on the other side (unreliable). In Miraflores, Av Petit Thouars 5201, Mon-Sat 0800-2000. There are many sub-post offices in all districts of Lima, but sending a letter from the suburbs takes longer. Express letters can be sent from the Central Post Office or the airport (mail posted at the airport reaches Europe in 5 days). There are private companies for express letters, eg: EMS, T 432-3950/278531; DHL, T 451-8587/452-1278; Letter Express, T 444-4509; Peru Express, T 431-1769; VEC, T 442-0830/0866; Skyway, T 422-9225/440-2353. When receiving a package of over 1 kg, it must be collected from the Aduana post office, Av Tomás Valle, nr the airport, open Mon-Fri 0830-1400, or from Teodoro Cárdenas 267, Lince, T 471-6877. For parcels see page 1411, **Mail**.

Telecommunications: Telefónica del Perú, Jr Carabaya 933, Plaza San Martín, T 433-1616, open daily 0800-2200; also at Diez Canseco y La Paz, Miraflores, opp *Hotel César*, open daily 0730-2100; Tarata 280, off Larco, Miraflores, open Mon-Sat 0830-2130, Sun 0800-1300. Payphones on the street, and at airport, can be used for national and international calls with coins or phonecards. Telefónica offices can be found all over Lima; phone and fax. For full details on phone operation, see **Telephones** in **Information for travellers**, page 1412.

● **Shopping**
Since so many artesans have come from the Sierra to Lima, it is possible to find any kind of handicraft in the capital. The prices are the same as in the highlands, and the quality is high. Silver and gold handicrafts of all kinds; Indian handspun and hand-woven textiles; manufactured textiles in Indian designs; llama and alpaca wool products such as ponchos, rugs, hats, blankets,

slippers, coats, sweaters, etc; *arpilleras*, appliqué pictures of Peruvian life (originated in Chile with political designs), made with great skill and originality by women in the shanty towns; fine leather products mostly hand made. The *mate burilado*, or engraved gourd found in every tourist shop, is cheap and a genuine expression of folk art (cheaper in villages nr Huancayo). For handicrafts produced by cooperatives, with benefits going directly to the producers, contact the non-profit organization *Minka*, Av Grau 266, Edif El Portal, p 2, Barranco, open Tues-Sat 1100-1900, good selection of handicrafts; for further information contact Norma Velásquez. *Silvania Prints*, Conquistadores 915, San Isidro, also at Diéz Canseco 337A, Miraflores; sell modern silk-screen prints on Pima cotton with precolumbian designs. On Av Nicolás de Piérola vendors sell oil paintings of Andean scenes, bargains abound. *Centro Artesanal 'El Arte Peruano'*, Av Alfonso Ugarte 901-925, T 424-1978, open 0900-2000, ask for Carlos Ramos for especially fine retablos, or Guillermo Arce for fine Cajamarca mirrors in colonial style; they also sell rugs from Ayacucho and San Pedro de Cajas, ceramics from Ayacucho and Cusco and other items (there is a nationwide handicraft association of this name). *Artesanías Perú SA* government store for Peruvian handicrafts in San Isidro (Av Jorge Basadre 610, T 440-1925/228847). *La Casa de la Mujer Artesana*, Av Perú 1550 (Av Brasil cuadra 15), Pueblo Libre, T 423-8840, F 423-4031, cooperative run by Movimiento Manuela Ramos, excellent quality work mostly from *pueblos jóvenes*. *Textiles Peruanos*, at Jr Ancash 350, is rec for ceramics.

Miraflores is the best place for high quality, pricey handicrafts; there are many shops on and around **Av La Paz**, and particularly on **Petit Thouars**, blocks 53/54. Rec is *Kuntur Wasi*, Ocharan 182, T 444-0557, high quality, English-speaking owner very knowledgeable about Peruvian textiles, frequently has exhibitions of fine folk art and crafts; *Antisuyo*, Jr Tacna 460, Miraflores, Mon-Fri 0900-1930, Sat 1030-1830, an indigenous cooperative run by an English-woman, sells high-quality handicrafts from all regions, reasonable prices, T 447-2557 (another outlet in Cusco). *Agua y Tierra*, Diez Canseco 337b, excellent fine crafts and indigenous art. *Centro Comercial El Alamo*, La Paz (close to *César Hotel*), 0900-2000, *artesanía* shops with good choice. *Las Pallas*, Cajamarca 212, 5th block of Av Grau, Barranco, T 477-4629, Mon-Sat 0900-1900, good quality handicrafts. Antiques available in Miraflores on Av La Paz. See *H Stern's* jewellery stores at *Hotels Miraflores César, Bolivar* and *Sheraton*, and at the International Airport.

NB It is better to buy pullovers in the Sierra. However, although Lima is more expensive, it is often impossible to find the same quality of goods elsewhere; geniune alpaca is odourless wet or dry, wet llama 'stinks'. Alpaca cloth for suits, coats, etc (mixed with 40% sheep's wool) can be bought cheaply from factories: *Cinsa*, Av Argentina 2400, microbus 93, 70 or 84 from Plaza Castilla; *Lanificio*, Nicolás Arriola 3090, San Luis, T 432-0859, better quality in their Arequipa factory (see page 1321) (gives 10% discount to foreigners attached to their embassies). Alpaca wool for knitting or weaving from *Alpaca III*, Av Larco 859, Miraflores. Made-to-measure cotton shirts in 24 hrs from Sr Hurtado, 'Sir', Jr Carabaya 1108, and in 48 hrs from Luz Manrique, Cailloma 328, T 427-9472. A good tailor is *Navarro Hermanos*, in Belén, below the Tourist Office. Another is *Creaciones Vargas*, Jr Ica 380, T 427-8680, good value. For mohair, *Grupo Prestige*, Centro Comercial San Isidro, shops 204-207, T 422-7476. Export quality jeans are made by *Sombrería Palacio*, Unión 214. There are bargains in clothing made from high quality Pima cotton.

Bookshops: fair selection of foreign-language books at *Librería Delta*, N de Piérola 689, Lima, and Av Larco 970, Miraflores; and at *ABC Bookstores*, Av Paseo de la República 3440, No 32B, San Isidro, also by *Cine El Pacífico*, Miraflores. *Librería Studium*, Plaza Francia 1164 (with several branches), sells history/travel books in English. *Studium* and *Librería de la Universidad de San Marcos* give student discounts. Books in English, French and German also available from *Librería Ayza*, Jr Unión 560, rec, will supply works in Quechua. *Librería Internacional*, Jr Unión (corner of Plaza San Martín) has a wide selection of books on South America in all languages, good for regional maps. Good English selection at *Epoca*, on Belén in the centre, on José Pardo in Miraflores and other branches, T 445-7430/0282. *Portal* on the plaza in Barranco has good selection, with a gallery, excellent handicrafts for sale and coffee shop. Rare books, many shops on Av Azángaro. **NB** Foreign language books are subject to a high tax (US$12) and there are no guidebooks for sale. International newspapers, from newstands, Block 6, Av N de Piérola, or in the Parque Central, Miraflores (taken from aircraft).

Secondhand books are found in the 5th to 6th block of Av Grau in the centre, some English books are sold, but poor selection. Also around Plaza Francia on the pedestrian street that runs to block 10 of Garcilaso de la Vega.

Film: Agfa distributor at E Diez Canseco 176; for cheap film try at the black market at Feria Polvos Azules, at Puente de Piedra. Many developers using Kodak equipment offer same-day service; all at similar prices. Many on Jr Unión and Plaza San Martín; also Av Larco, Miraflores. Good but expensive place for developing photos and slides at Grimaldo del Solar 275, between Shell and Benavides, Miraflores, T 444-2304, open Mon-Fri 0945-1300, 1400-1830, Sat 0945-1300. *Profesa*, Av Petit Thouars 3231, San Isidro, T 442-3542, specialist shop for photographic equipment. **Camera repairs**: *Camera House*, Larco 1150, Office 39, p 2, Miraflores, Mon-Fri 1530-1900, ask for Clemente Higa, who is often there later in pm; *Frankitec*, Jr Lampa 1115, oficina 104, Lima 1, T 428-4331, Swiss technician, better for mechanical cameras; *Foto Magnum*, Ocoña 190, also very good for spares and repairs.

Maps: a good map of the Lima area is available from street sellers in the centre of Lima, or in better bookshops (published by Lima 2000, US$10, or US$14 in booklet form). A cheaper, less accurate, and less discreet map is published by Cartográfica Nacional for US$3-4. The **Instituto Geográfico Nacional** (Av Aramburu 1198, Surquillo, Lima 34, T 475-9960, F 473-3075), sells a standard map of Peru (1:2,200,000), US$10, department maps, US$7, a Peru road map, US$10 and a beautiful 4-sheet map of Peru, 1:1,000,000, US$30; at the same size and for the same price is a geological map; topographical maps, 1:100,000, which only cover Peru from the coast to the highest mountains and most of the Department of Loreto, cost US$7. Satellite map of most of the jungle area, 1:100,000, is US$8; black-and-white aerial photos available at US$8. Passport is needed to enter; they are open 0900-1700, Mon-Fri. Maps of N and S border areas are not sold. If you submit a letter to the IGN, giving your credentials and adequate reasons, plus a photocopy of your passport, you may be able to obtain maps of the border regions. Aerial photographs are available at **Servicio Autofotográfico Nacional**, Las Palmas airforce base, Chorrillos, T 467-1341, open Mon-Fri 0800-1300, 1330-1545. **Ingement**, Pablo Bermúdez 211, Jesus María, T 433-6234, open 0730-1400, has information on geology and sells some maps. **Senamhi**, República de Chile 295, Jesus María, T 433-7624, open 0830-1345, has good information on Peruvian meteorology. Petroperú maps for town centres rec.

Markets: Parque Diagonal/Kennedy, Miraflores (by *Restaurant Haiti*): secondhand books, jewellery, sandals made to measure, paintings and other handicrafts, Dec-June, Wed to Mon, in winter Sat and Sun only; **Feria Artesanal**, Av de la Marina 790 and Av Sucre Oeste, in Pueblo Libre, the biggest crafts market in Lima, but expensive, bargaining is expected; take any colectivo that says Brasil/La Marina from Plaza Bolognesi or Ugarte; taxi US$2-3; watch your possessions, as thieves are numerous. Extensive market selling woollen goods, leatherwork, bric-a-brac and Peruvian goods and souvenirs on sidestreets off **Lampa**; for hardware, sidestreets off **Av Colmena**; for books, **Parque Universitario**; also good markets on Av Abancay, Jr Huallaga and Jr Cusco. **Polvos Azules**, behind Central Post Office, 1 block from Plaza de Armas, sells just about anything (inc stolen cameras), small handicraft section (ask directions) which sells the best and cheapest earrings, inc the parts for making them; the market is generally cheap and very interesting, it doesn't get going until around 1000; beware pickpockets. The handicrafts markets in Miraflores on Av Petit Thouars, blocks 52-54, have a good selection.

In every suburb you can find one or more food market. Some of the bigger supermarkets are **Wong** (at Banavides y Panama, nr Youth Hostel) and **Santa Isabel** (24-hr supermarket at Benavides y La Paz – excellent stock).

● **Sports**

Association football matches and various athletic events take place at the National Stadium, in the centre of the city on ground given by the British community on the 100th anniversary of Peru's Declaration of Independence. The local soccer derby is Universitario against Alianza Lima (tickets US$2.50-25).

Baths: Baños Pizarro, Unión 284, steam rooms, US$3, cold showers only, café and swimming pool. Windsor Turkish Baths, on Miguel Dasso, San Isidro, separate facilities for men and women, steam, sauna, cold pool and whirlpool, US$4. See Yellow Pages for other addresses.

Bull fighting: there are two bullfight seasons: Oct to first week in Dec and during July. They are held in the afternoons on Sun and holidays. Tickets can be bought at Plaza Acho from 0930-1300 (T 481-1467), or Farmacia Dezza, Av Conquistadores 1144, San Isidro, T 440-8911/3798. Prices range from US$14 to US$90 (see page 1215).

Cockfights: are frequently organized and advertised: the Plaza de Gallos is at C Sandía 150, nr Parque Universitario.

Cycling: popular, without yet becoming a serious sport: *Bike Touring Club* meets every Sun at 0730 outside *Cine Orrantia*, Javier Prado y Av Arequipa, T 463-1747 (planning meetings at Cabo Gutarra 613, Pueblo Libre), contact Tito López and Mónica Miranda (Tito repairs bikes, but does not have spares). *Mountain Bike Club*, at *Cicling* shop, Av Benavides 2997, Miraflores, president Gustavo Prado. *Centro Comercial de Bicicletas*, Av San Juan de Miraflores 1281, Miraflores, T 446-0228. Hard to find

28" tyres, try *Casa Okuyama*, Jr Montevideo, Lima. Good shop is *Biclas*, Av Los Conquistadores, San Isidro.

Diving: for information and equipment contact; *Mundo Submarino*, Av Conquistadores 791, San Isidro, T 441-7602, Sr Alejandro Pez Z is a professional diver and arranges trips; *Kailua Dive Shop*, Av Conquistadores 969, San Isidro, T/F 441-4057, owner Paolo is Italian, also runs PADI diving course.

Golf: the Lima (T 426006), Inca, Granja Azul and La Planicie golf clubs and the Country Club de Villa all have 18-hole courses. The Santa Rosa, Cruz de Hueso and Huampani golf clubs have 9-hole courses.

Horse racing: Hipódromo Monterrico, on Tues and Thur evenings (1900) and Sat and Sun (1400) in summer, and in winter on Tues evening and Sat and Sun afternoons. Foreigners must bring their passport. Preferred seating US$2, first class US$0.75, second class US$0.20; T 436-5677 or 435-1035 ext 2316/2317. For Caballos de Paso, which move in four-step amble, extravagantly paddling their forelegs, **National Paso Association**, Miraflores, T 447-6331. Races are held at the Peruvian de Paso breeding farm in Lurín, S of Lima, T 435-6574.

Lima Cricket and Football Club: Justo Vigil 200, Magdalena del Mar, T 461-0080/4030. The club has extensive sports facilities, as well as football, rugby (training at 1700 on Thur, May-Oct) and cricket, squash, swimming, snooker, etc. Also restaurant, pub and friendly place to meet people. If you play cricket get in touch, Dec-February.

Mountaineering: the information provided by the informal mountaineering clubs is questionable. *Club Andino*, Av Paseo de la República 932, Santa Beatriz, contact Lucho Sherpela, T 463-7319, meetings Thur 1900-2200; *Asociación de Andinismo de la Universidad de Lima*, Pabellón F (Bienestar Universitario), Universidad de Lima, Javier Prado Este s/n, T 437-6767 ext 2107/2134, F 437-8066, meetings Wed 1800-2000; *Club de Montañeros Américo Tordoya*, Jr Tarapacá 384, Magdalena, T 460-6101, meetings Thur 1930, contact Gonzalo Menacho. *Asociación Andes Perú*, Av Larco 853, of, D, Miraflores, T 445-6055, contact Pedro Marchetti.

Parapenting, Hangliding, Ballooning: contact Sr José Bustamante, *High Flight Peru*, Parque San Carlos 217, Lima 21, just off 14th block of Av Bolívar, T 463-4199 (Sr Bustamante is opening a new Youth Hostel, E, at Los Sauces 418, Chaclacayo, Km 24, T 497-2343, F 462-7998).

Surfing: *Federación Peruana de Tabla* is located at Club Waikiki, Costa Verde s/n, Bajada Baños, Miraflores, PO Box 180007, T/F 442-3830; several surf shops, best is *O'Neills*, Av Santa Cruz 851, Miraflores, T 445-0406, contact Gino, very knowledgeable, speaks English; the surfing magazine '*Tablista*' is published in Dec and July, available at kiosks in Lima.

Trekking and backpacking: for information contact Percy Tapiá, *Trek Andes*, Av Benavides 212, of 1203, Miraflores, PO box 01-3074, Lima 100, T/F 447-8078, good information. *Instituto Nacional de Recreación*, Educación Física y Deportes (Inred), has an Andean specialist, César Morales Arnao, at the Estadio Nacional, Tribuna Sur, door 4, p 3, T 433-4192, ext 42, rec. *Trekking and Backpacking Club*, Jr Huáscar 1152, Jesus María, Lima 11 (T 423-2515), run by Miguel Chiri Valle, free information on Peru and South America, storage and gas cylinders available. *Meiggs Trekking Club*, Casilla 41-0091, Lima 41, T/F 446-3493, runs trips once a month, contact Fernando Pinto. Good advice from Richard Hidalgo, T 448-2691. Good climbing and hiking equipment shop, *Alpamayo*, at Av Larco 345, Miraflores, T 445-1671, F 445-0370; owner Sr Enrique Ramírez speaks fluent English.

● **Tour companies & travel agents**

Most of those in Lima specialize in selling air tickets, or in setting up a connection in the place where you want to start a tour. Shop around and compare prices; also check all information carefully. It is best to use a travel agent in the town closest to the place you wish visit; it is cheaper and they are more reliable.

Those listed below are divided into the following groups: a) standard tours, well-organized but expensive; b) standard tours, less expensive; c) adventure tours; d) specialized tours.

a) *Lima Tours*, Jr Belén (or extension of Unión) 1040 (PO Box 4340), Lima, T 424-5110/7560/9386, F 426-3383, highly rec; in the same building is the American Express agent, which will not change TCs into dollars cash but is the only place to give TCs against an Amex card; also at Los Rosales 440, San Isidro, T 442-0750, F 441-1405; Av Pardo 392, Miraflores, T 241-7551, F 446-8716. *Cóndor Travel*, Mayor Armando Blondet 249, San Isidro, T 442-7305, F 442-3634; *Kinjyo Travel*, Las Camelias 290, San Isidro, T 442-4000, F 442-1000; *Solmartur*, Av La Paz 744, Miraflores, T 444-1313, F 444-3060; *Perú Chasqui*, Mariana de los Santos 198-201, San Isidro, T 441-1455, F 441-1459; *Panorama*, Bella Vista 210, of A, Miraflores, T 446-9578, F 445-0910; *Hada Tours*, 2 de Mayo 529, Miraflores, T/F 446-2714.

b) *Nuevo Mundo*, Jr Camaná 702, Lima, T/F 427-0635; *Turismo Pacífico*, Alcanfores 373, Miraflores, T 444-3363; *Setours*, Cdte Espinar 229, Miraflores, T 446-7090, F 446-7129; *Tecnitur*, Manuel Freyre y Santander 282, Miraflores, T/F 447-1289; *Julia Tours*, Francia 597, Miraflores, T 447-9798, F 447-3021; *Peruvian's Life*, Diez Canseco 332, Miraflores, T/F 444-8825.

c) *Explorandes*, Bellavista 518, Miraflores, T 445-0532, F 445-4486; *Andean Tours*, Jr Shell 319, of 304, Miraflores, T 447-8430; *Hirca*, Bellavista 518, Miraflores, T/F 447-3807; *Alpamayo Tours*, Emilio Cavanecia 160, of 201, San Isidro, T/F 442-3886, Duilio Vallutino and 'Pepe' López are two of the most experienced rafters and kayakers in Peru, rec for river rafting; *Panamericana*, Jr Tarata 294, Miraflores, T 444-9364, F 444-1377, specialized tours to all parts of Peru, trekking, rafting, paragliding and mountaineering; *Irré Tours*, Av Boulevard 1012, T 475-8808, Julio speaks good English, arranges trips and guides for small groups.

d) *CanoAndes*, Av San Martín 455, Barranco, T 477-0188, F 474-1288, rafting and kayaking trips; *Viento Sur Expediciones*, Av La Molina 400, Ate-Vitarte, T 435-6226, sailing tours to Paracas and day tours from Lima.

Useful addresses: *Apavit*, Asociación Peruana de Agencias de Viajes y Turismo, Antonio Roca 121, Santa Beatriz, T 433-7610; *Apta*, Asociación Peruana de Operadores de Turismo de Aventura, Benavides 212, of 1203, Miraflores, T 447-8078; *Agotur*, Asociación de Guías Oficiales de Turismo, Jr Belén 1030, Lima, T 424-5113.

Private guides: Rolando Peceros, contact Lima Tours, T 427-6720 or 448-5562 (home), specialist in Peruvian archaeology from Chiclayo to Nasca, charges US$25/day. Tino Guzmán Khang, T/F (home) 429-5779, 24-hr cellphone

997-7060, or South American Explorers Club, cultural tours, especially Pachacámac, museums, special interest tours, English and French speaking, US$10/hr up to 3 people, highly rec. Jaime Torres, Los Algarrobos 1634, Urb Las Brisas, T 462-9400, very knowledgeable, fluent in English, good contacts throughout Peru, will make all transport arrangements.

NB We have received complaints about agencies, or their representatives at bus offices or the airport arranging tours and collecting money for companies that either do not exist or which fall far short of what is paid for. Do not conduct business anywhere other than in the agency's office and insist on a written contract.

● **Tourist offices**
Tourist offices throughout Peru are operated by the Ministerio de Industria, Comercio, Turismo e Integración, C 1 Oeste, Corpac, p 14, T 442-9280. In Lima, the tourist office is Infotur, Jr Unión (Belén) 1066, Oficina E-2, T 431-0117, Mon-Fri 0930-1730, Sat 1000-1300; they give out tourist information, make reservations and are very helpful. Copetur (Corporación Peruana de Turismo), Schell 120 of 25, Miraflores, T 445-3083, F 446-1593. There is a tourist booth at the airport, just past passport control, which will make local reservations, or you can call the hotel direct, very helpful. Ask for the helpful, free, *Peru Guide* published in English by Lima Editora, T 444-0815, available at travel agencies or other tourist organizations. 24-hr hotline for travellers' complaints, T 224-7888 (dial 01 first from outside Lima), or toll free on 0-800-4-2579 (not from pay phones); this is run by the Tourist Bureau of Complaints for matters regarding customs, airlines, travel agencies, accommodation, restaurants, public authorities or if you have lost, or had stolen, documents.

South American Explorers' Club: Av Rep de Portugal 146 (Breña ~ on the 13th block of

Alfonso Ugarte), T/F 0051 (01151 from USA)-1-425-0142, e-mail montague@amauta.rcp.net, is a non-profit, educational organization which functions primarily as an information network for Peru and South America. Membership is US$40 a year (US$60/couple), plus US$7 for postage of its quarterly journal, *The South American Explorer* (outside the US) and numerous member services such as access to files of travel information, equipment storage, personal mail service, trip planning, etc. Open 0930-1700 Mon to Fri; non-members are welcome, but asked to limit their visits, staff very helpful. The clubhouse is attractive and friendly; it is not necessary to 'explore' to feel at home here. They will sell used equipment on consignment (donations of used equipment, unused medicines etc, are welcome). Their map of the Inca Trail is good (US$4), and they sell an excellent map of the Cordillera Huayhuash. Other useful dyeline trekking maps inc the Llanganuco-Santa Cruz trek in the Cordillera Blanca, and the Cordillera Vilcanota (Auzangate). There is a good library and they sell travel books (inc this one) and guides (at a discount to members), book swap facilities are available, and some excellent handicrafts. For further information, and the most recent views on where and

how to travel safely, write to: Casilla 3714, Lima 100, Peru; 126 Indian Creek Rd, Ithaca, NY 14850, USA (T 607-277-0488, F 607-277-6122, e-mail explorer@samexplo.org); or Apdo 21-431, Eloy Alfaro, Quito, Ecuador (T/F 225-228, e-mail explorer@saec.org.ec). The US office can supply books, maps and trip-planning services; book and maps can be shipped worldwide. Online information http://www.samexplo.org.

Tourist and archaeological information: Federico Kaufmann-Doig is a great source of information on Peruvian archaeology, for serious students and archaeologists. He has worked on various sites in Peru and is currently engaged on a 3-year project in the Kuelap area. He is the director of the Instituto de Arqueología Amazónica, T 449-0243, or (home) 449-9103. His book, *Historia del Perú: un nuevo perspectivo*, in 2 volumes (*Pre-Inca*, and *El Incario*) is available at better bookshops. The Instituto Nacional de Cultura, in the Museo de la Nación, should be contacted by archaeologists for permits and information. The Museo Nacional de Antropología y Arqueología in Pueblo Libre (address above) is the main centre for archaeological investigation and the Museo de la Nación holds exhibitions.

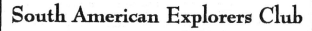

A useful book is *The City of Kings: A guide to Lima*, by Carolyn Walton.

The Peruvian Touring and Automobile Club: Av César Vallejo 699 (Casilla 2219), Lince, Lima (T 403270), offers help to tourists and particularly to members of the leading motoring associations. Good maps available of whole country; regional routes and the South American sections of the Pan-American Highway available (US$2.10).

● **Useful addresses**

Tourist Police, Museo de la Nación, J Prado 2465, p 5, San Borja, T 476-9896, F 476-7708, friendly, helpful, English and some German spoken, open 0800-2000; rec to visit when you have had property stolen. **Dirección General de Migraciones**, España 700, Breña, open 0900-1300; if passport stolen can provide new entry stamps, also for visa extensions, given same day. **Intej**, Av San Martín 240, Barranco, can extend student cards, T 477-4105. **YMCA**, Av Bolívar 635, Pueblo Libre, membership required. **Biblioteca Nacional**, Av Abancay (cuadra 4) y Miró Quesada, T 428-7690, open 0830-2000.

● **Transport**

Local Bus: the bus routes are shared by buses and colectivos (small vans); the latter run from 0600-0100, and less frequently through the night, they are quicker and stop wherever requested. Bus fares US$0.30, colectivos US$0.35-0.45, depending on length of journey. The principal routes are from the centre of Lima to Miraflores, San Isidro, Pueblo Libre, central market and airport. The centre, between Tacna, Abancay and Nicolás de Piérola is now free of buses. Look for route names on bus windscreen, but check that the bus is going in the direction you want.

Buses to Miraflores: plenty of colectivos run the route between the centre and Miraflores, along Tacna, Garcilaso de la Vega, Arequipa and Larco, 24 hrs, US$0.30 by day, US$0.35 on Sun, US$0.45 after midnight. Routes are displayed on the windscreen. Some buses also run this route for US$0.30; check the route before you get in. On Vía Expresa, buses can be caught at Avs Tacna, Garcilaso de la Vega and Ugarte (faster than Av Arequipa, but watch for pickpockets). The main stop for Miraflores is Ricardo Palma, 4 blocks from Parque Kennedy. Taxi US$2.30.

Car rental: all rental companies have an office at the airport, where you can arrange everything and pick up and leave the car. Cars can be hired from **Hertz**, Rivera Navarrete 550, San Isidro, T 442-4475; **Budget**, Francisco de Paula Camino 231-A, Miraflores, T 445-1266; **Avis**, Av Camino Real 1278, San Isidro, T 441-9760;

Dollar, Av La Paz 438, Miraflores, T 444-4920; **National**, Av España 449, Lima, T 433-3750; **Thrifty**, Aristides Aljovin 472, Miraflores, T 444-4441; **VIP**, Conquistadores 697, San Isidro, T 441-3705. Prices range from US$40 to US$60 depending on type of car. The condition of vehicles is usually very poor. Beware of deep street potholes. Make sure that your car is in a locked garage at night. Russian-made 4WD Niva vehicles are often rented; they are up to the conditions of Andean driving, but Lada saloon cars are not. Note that it can be much cheaper to rent a car in a town in the Sierra for a few days than to drive all the way from Lima. Also, if there are any problems with the rental car, companies do not have a collection service.

Cycling: into or out of Lima is not rec, difficult and dangerous.

Taxis: no taxis use meters and anyone can operate as a taxi driver. You must bargain the price beforehand and insist on being taken to the destination of your choice, not the driver's. Fares: within city centre US$1.50-2; to Miraflores and most suburbs US$2-3.50; from outside airport to centre US$4-5, San Isidro/Miraflores US$6-7, Breña US$3.50; from inside airport gates to centre US$8-9, Miraflores US$12-13. After dark and on holidays, 35%-50% surcharge. Always have exact fare ready. Licensed taxis are blue and yellow, but there are many other types. VWs are cheapest, the bigger black taxis charge US$15-20 from centre to suburbs. Licensed and phone taxis are safest. There are several reliable phone taxi companies, which can be called for immediate service, or booked in advance; prices are 2-3 times more than ordinary taxis; eg to the airport US$12, to suburbs US$7-8. Some are *Taxi Real*, T 470-6263; *Taxi Metro*, T 437-3689; *Lady's*, T 470-8528; *Taxi Phono*, T 422-6565; *Taxi Seguro*, T 448-7226. Paco, T 461-6394, is dependable for phone hiring, similarly Willy, T 452-7456, speaks perfect English, highly rec, works with SAEC. Drivers don't expect tips; give them small change from the fare. If hiring a taxi for over 1 hr agree on price/hour beforehand. To Callao, La Punta, San Miguel, Magdalena, Miraflores (US$4), Barranco, Chorrillos, by agreement, basis US$5/hr. Rec, knowledgeable driver, Hugo Casanova Morella, T 485-7708 (he lives in La Victoria), for city tours, travel to airport, etc. 'Trici-Taxis', 3-wheel cycle carts, can be hired for moving about with heavy baggage.

Air Jorge Chávez Airport, 16 km from the centre of Lima. There is control of people entering and leaving the airport; tourists have to show passports. Luggage may be checked several times, so arrive 2-3 hrs before your departure (1½ hrs for domestic flights).

Strict controls at the airport may mean that an official will demand to search your luggage. Legally they cannot ask for money and this also applies on arrival. This is not true if you are importing goods or bringing a large quantity of new merchandise, when taxes are charged. Taxes cannot be charged on new personal possessions. At the customs area, insist that you are a tourist and that your personal effects will not be sold in Peru; if necessary ask them to stamp in your passport that you are bringing a bicycle, stereo, whatever, and that you will leave with it.

Only official Corpac porters are allowed in the customs area. Do not give your bags to unofficial porters who are desperate to carry your luggage (they will expect a tip if you even so much as look at them). 24-hr left luggage costs US$3/item/day (make sure luggage is locked, or use the US$1 plastic loop to seal bags).

Banco Mercantil and **Banco del Comercio** in Departures change TCs (Amex and Citicorp), no commission and give cash advance on Visa or Mastercard, open 24 hrs; the latter handles airport tax along with Banco Continental; also Visa ATM in Departures. **Casa de Cambio** in Arrivals changes cash and TCs, open 24 hrs. Avoid getting left with soles at the airport when leaving; changing them back into dollars can take a lot of time, and you need to show the official exchange slips. **Post Office** upstairs in Departures, open 24 hrs. **Telefónica del Perú** has a 24-hr office; lots of payphones. **Information** on arrivals and departures: international T 452-3135; national T 452-9570. The **Prohotel** agent at the airport is very helpful with hotel bookings of all classes; there is a second hotel booking agency. Taxi drivers also tout for hotel business, offering discounts – don't let yourself be bullied.

There are several cafes, restaurants and shops and a duty-free shop in the Departure lounge which will accept Amex cards. Prices on some items higher than at supermarkets. Safe to stay all night in 24-hr expresso-snack bar upstairs but expensive; also in VIP lounge, US$10. There is an airport workers' canteen 'comedor de los trabajadores' also open to the public, just beyond the perimeter fence to the right of the main terminal. For those in transit, refreshment options are expensive, although temporary access to shops in the main lobby of the terminal building is possible.

Taxi from desk outside Arrivals, US$8-9 to centre, US$12-13 to Miraflores. See above for other taxi fares. The gate for cars leaving the airport is in the middle of the parking area; for pedestrians it is at the lefthand corner of the parking area, from where you can catch a cheaper taxi to the city – do not do this after dark (US$4 to

centre, US$7 to Miraflores). There is a service called Airport Express, every 20 mins to Miraflores from the national exit, comfortable micro buses, US$4.50 pp, only during the day. Local buses and colectivos run between the airport perimeter and the city centre and suburbs, their routes are given on the front window (eg 'Miraflores' for Miraflores, 'Brasil' for South American Explorers Club). Outside the pedestrian exit are the bus, colectivo and taxi stops, but there is more choice for buses at the roundabout by the car entrance. Luggage is not allowed on buses. Colectivo service from Av Tacna y Colmena (N de Piérola) 733, from 0600 to 2000, colectivos wait until they have 5 passengers, US$0.75 pp, and US$0.25 for luggage. By bus: go from Av Tacna to Av Brasil then change to a 'Faucett' bus, allow 1¼ hrs. The big hotels have their own buses at the airport, and charge US$6.

Internal air services: to most destinations there are daily flights by several airlines (most options are given in the text) but flights may be cancelled in the rainy season. Grupo Ocho's flights to selected destinations are fixed schedule, but must be booked well in advance, at least 10 days (Cusco, Pucallpa, Andahuaylas, Chachapoyas).

Trains There has been no passenger service to La Oroya or Huancayo since 1991, although trains are running from Huancayo to Huancavelica. Check South American Explorers Club for information. For these destinations there are bus and colectivo services. On Sun in the dry season there is a train to San Bartolomé at 0830, returning at 1600: Desamparados station, behind Palacio de Gobierno. (For description of line see page 1365.)

Bus companies: there are many different bus companies, but the larger ones are better organized, leave on time and do not wait until the bus is full. For approximate prices, frequency and duration of trip, see destinations. Bus companies which serve all Peru (in Lima unless stated otherwise): *Ormeño*, Carlos Zavala 177, T 427-5679, also at J Prado Este 1059, more expensive luxury service to Trujillo and Chiclayo, well-organized and rec; *Cruz del Sur*, Quilca 531, T 427-1311/423-5594, expanding network, good buses, rec; *Expreso Sudamericano*, Montevideo 618, T 427-6548/6549, fewer buses, cheaper, older buses.

Companies with routes to the N: *Perú Express*, Guillermo Dansey 235, T 424-8990, luxury buses to Chimbote, Trujillo, Chiclayo; *Chiclayo Express*, Av Grau 653, T 428-5072, to Chiclayo direct; *Expreso Panamericano*, Av Alfonso Ugarte 951, T 424-9045, to Chimbote, Trujillo, Chiclayo. *Transporte Cinco*, Jr Sandia 205, T 428-1915, to Barranca, Paramonga; *Olano/*

Oltursa, Jr Apurímac 567 y Av Grau 617, T 428-2370, to Chiclayo, Piura, Jaén, Bagua, Tumbes; *Atahualpa*, Jr Sandia 266, T 427-5838, to Chimbote, Cajamarca, Celendín; *Rodríguez*, Av Roosevelt 354, T 428-0506, to Huaraz and Caraz, rec; *Movil Tours* and *Paradise Tours*, both at Abancay 947, to Huaraz, both rec (as is Ormeño); *Cóndor de Chavín*, Montevideo 1039, T 428-8122, to Chavín. *Cruz de Chalpón*, Montevideo 809, T 427-0981, to Chimbote, Trujillo, Piura; *Espadín*, Carlos Zavala 140, T 428-5857, to Churín; *Turismo Chimbote*, Huarochiri 785 (2 blocks off 2 de Mayo), T 424-0501, Chimbote direct and Caraz; *Chinchaysuyo*, Av Grau 525, T 427-5038, to Casma, Caraz, Chimbote, Trujillo, Pacasmayo and Piura; *Antisuyo*, Av Abancay 947, T 428-1414, to Trujillo; *Las Dunas*, Paseo de la República 821, La Victoria, T 431-0235, to Chimbote, Trujillo, Chiclayo, luxury. *Transporte Piura*, Montevideo 801, to Trujillo, Chiclayo, Piura, Tumbes.

Companies with routes to the S: *Cañete*, Av Grau 427, T 428-2729, to Cañete direct; *General de San Martín*, Montevideo 552, T 428-1423, to Pisco and Ica; *Paracas Express*, Jr Montevideo 553, to Pisco. *Señor Luren*, Av Abancay 1165, T 428-0630, to Ica and Nasca; *Cóndor Aymaraes*, Jr Condesuyos 477, T 428-6618, to Ica, Nasca and Abancay; *Morales Moralitos*, Av Grau 141, T 427-6310, to Abancay and Cusco; *Señor de Animas Apurímac*, Av Luna Pizarro 453, La Victoria, T 431-0904, to Apurímac, Abancay, Cusco; *Expreso Jacantaya*, Av Grau 486, T 432-8987.

Companies to the Central Highlands and Eastern Lowlands: *Mariscal Cáceres*, Av 28 de Julio 2195, La Victoria, T 474-7850, good 'Imperial' service to Huancayo (similarly Cruz del Sur, address above). *León de Huánuco*, Av 28 de Julio 1520, T 432-9088, to Huánuco, Tingo María, Pucallpa; *Chanchamayo*, Av Luna Pizarro 453, La Victoria, T 432-4517, to Tarma, San Ramón, La Merced, etc; *Satipo Expreso*, Av Luna Pizarro 488, La Victoria, T 423-9272, to La Merced; *Transmar*, Av 28 de Julio 1511, La Victoria, T 433-7440, to Tingo María and Pucallpa, also *Etposa*, Av José Gálvez 1121, Lince, T 472-1402; *Trans Rey*, Av 28 de Julio 1192, La Victoria (terminal), Av Luna Pizarro 398, La Victoria (ticket office), T 431-9808, luxury bus to Pucallpa.

Comités are small vans which run on some routes throughout Peru; they are quicker, more comfortable, but double the price of buses. They only leave when full. In Lima unless otherwise stated: *Comité No 14*, Leticia 604, T 428-6621, to Huaraz; *No 25*, Jr Azángaro 839, T 428-7524, to Chimbote; *No 12*, Montevideo 736, T 427-3327, to Huancayo and Huánuco; *No 30*, Av

Bolívar 1335, La Victoria, T 432-9459, and *No 22*, Ayacucho 997, T 428-9082, to Huancayo; *No 1*, Luna Pizarro 377, T 431-0652, to Tarma; *No 18*, Av N de Piérola 1470, T 428-8143, to Huacho and Barranca. Colectivos to Huacho and Huaral leave from Plaza de Acho.

International buses: to enter Peru, a ticket out of the country may be required. If you have to buy a bus ticket, be warned: they are not transferable or refundable.

Ormeño international buses leave from Javier Prado 1059, T 472-1710, no change of bus at border: to Guayaquil (US$60) and Quito (US$70) twice a week; Cali (US$130) and Bogotá (US$145) once a week; Cúcuta (US$185) and Caracas (US$195) once a week; Santiago (US$70) on Tues and Sat, 2$\frac{1}{2}$ days, 3 meals inc; Mendoza (US$130) and Buenos Aires (US$160) twice a week, 3$\frac{1}{2}$ days, inc 3 meals and hotel in Santiago, good buses. *El Rápido*, Av Carlos Zavala Loayza 177, T 420-2958, weekly to **Mendoza** and **Buenos Aires**, fare inc meals and one night in a hotel, takes 4 days. Connecting twice weekly services to **Guayaquil** and **Quito** (although there are no through buses; you can buy through tickets but they are very expensive and give no priority), leaving Lima on Wed and Sun at 0845. The trip takes 2$\frac{1}{2}$ days; often long frontier delays. Bear in mind that international buses are more expensive than travelling from one border to another on national buses.

Warning The area around the bus terminals is very unsafe; thefts and assaults are more common in this neighbourhood than elsewhere in the city. You are strongly advised to consider taking a taxi to and from your bus. Make sure your luggage is well guarded and put on the right bus. It is also important not to assume that buses leave from the place where you bought the tickets.

In the weeks either side of 28/29 July (Independence), and of the Christmas/New Year holiday, it is practically impossible to get bus tickets out of Lima, unless you book in advance. Prices for bus tickets double at these times.

Lima to Callejón de Huaylas

A REGION of geographic and cultural contrasts. From the relentless grey coastal desert to the jewelled lakes and mountains of the Callejón de Huaylas. From smelly fishing ports like Chimbote, to the delicate artistry of pre-Inca ruins at Chavín de Huantar and others still being explored deep in the Andes.

LIMA TO CHIMBOTE

Between Lima and Pativilca there is a narrow belt of coastal land deposited at the mouths of the rivers and, from Pativilca to the mouth of the Río Santa, N of Chimbote, the Andes come down to the sea. Between Lima and Pativilca cotton and sugar-cane are grown, though the yield of sugar is less than it is further N where the sunshine is not interrupted by cloud. Much irrigated land grows vegetables and crops to supply Lima and Callao. Between June and Oct, cattle are driven down from the Highlands to graze the *lomas* on the mountain sides when the mists come.

The Pan-American Highway parallels the coast all the way to the far N, and feeder roads branch from it up the various valleys. Just N of Ancón (see page 1225), the Pasamayo sand dune, stretching for 20 km, comes right down to the seashore. The old road which snakes along the base beside the sea is spectacular, but is now closed except to commercial traffic. The new toll road (US$0.85), which goes right over the top, is much safer and you get spectacular views over the nearby coast and valleys.

CHANCAY VALLEY

At **Chancay** on the coast, the sea can be dangerous and heavily polluted.

- **Accommodation & places to eat** C *Hostal Villa de Arnedo*, pool open in summer, restaurant, rec; **E** *Hostal Chancay*, safe, good beds, can wash clothes. *Pizzería Donatello* on Plaza, expensive and *Costa Azul*, with gardens, overlooking sea; both good.

Just inland from Chancay is **Huaral**, which gives access to the Chancay Valley, up which are the extraordinary, little-visited ruins of **Chiprac**, **Rupac** and **Añay**.

Chiprac is a $2\frac{1}{2}$ hrs climb from Huascoy (Fiesta de San Cristóbal in the week before 28 July – see below). The Salvador family have accommodation and Carlos is a recommended guide. It is a good day's walk there and back with time to take photographs and eat. Rupac is best reached from La Florida. Its ruins are the best preserved of the group, though less extensive than Chiprac. All the ruins have complete roofs, which is unique in Peru. For Añay, go to Huaral as for the other ruins, then get transport to Huayopampa (basic accommodation) or La Perla from where the ruins can easily be reached. Get a guide to show you up from either village.

- **Transport** Take a bus from Lima to Huaral; from Plaza de Acho, by the bullring – beware of thieves. Then take the Juan Batista bus, Tues and Fri, to Huascoy US$2, 2 km beyond San Juan, which is up beyond Acos: "A hair-raising, breath-taking and bone-shaking ride, up to 3,500m above sea-level."

Turn right 1 km N of turn off to Sayán (see below) where, a further 3 km, the **Loma de Lachay** reserve has thousands of snail shells, locust-trees and much bird life. In Sept-Oct the plants are in bloom and very beautiful. Visitors' centre, trails, camping and picnic areas; very popular at weekends.

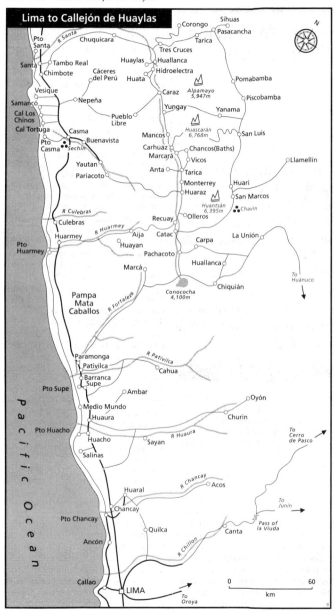

Lima to Callejón de Huaylas

HUAURA VALLEY

The Pan-American Highway is 4-lane (several tolls, US$1) to Km 101, at **Huacho** with, 19 km W **Puerto Huacho** (*Pop* 35,900). The beaches S of the town are clean and deserted. Just across the river from Huacho, is **Huaura** where the balcony is still preserved from which San Martín declared the country's independence from Spain. Try *guinda*, the local cherry brandy. Bus from Lima 2½ hrs, US$2, or Comité 18, daily colectivos, US$2.50.

- **Accommodation In Puerto Huacho**: **C** *Hostal Villa Sol*, pleasant, restaurant, pool, playground; **E** *Hostal Maury*, basic but hospitable; **E** *Italia*, communal bathrooms; and others. Camping is possible at El Paraíso beach.

The journey inland from Huacho, up the Huaura valley, is splendid. Beyond Sayán are terrific rock formations, then the road passes through subtropical vegetation around the spa of **Churín**, with hot, sulphurous springs which are used to cure a number of ailments. The climate is dry, temperatures ranging from 10° to 32° C; the area is heavily forested. It is famous for its cheeses. There are also hot springs nearby at **Chiuchín** (**C** *Albergue San Camilo*, excellent).

- **Accommodation** *Hostal San Juan de Churín*, Av Victor Larco Herrera 315, Local T 12, with bath, hot water, restaurant, bar, TV; *Hostal La Meseta* (member of Peruvian Youth Hostel Association), contact in Lima at Paul Harris 367, San Isidro, T 422-7619; *Internacional*, Av Victor Larco Herrera 410, T 15, with bath, hot water, moderately priced.

- **Transport** Buses from Lima go to Churín and beyond to Oyón (between Churín and Raura, a coal mine in the Cordillera of the same name); Espadín y Hnos (see Lima, **Bus Companies**), 2 daily, 6½ hrs, US$3.50. Only travel to this area in daylight, and check with locals on safety in villages beyond Churín.

Midway between Huaura and Supe, on the coast road, is **Medio Mundo**, with a lake between the village and the sea. The turnoff is outside the village on the Pan-American Highway, to the left, look for the sign, 'Albufera de Medio Mundo'. It is hot and busy in summer (good camping, tents for rent, guarded at weekends; no running water; bring food).

There is more desert and then the cotton-fields of San Nicolás lead to **Supe** at Km 187, a small busy port shipping fishmeal, cotton, sugar and minerals (*hostales*; restaurants). At **Aspero**, near Supe, is one of the earliest prehistoric sites in Peru (see History section, page 1206).

BARRANCA, PATIVILCA, PARAMONGA

At **Barranca** (Km 195; *Phone code* 034) the beach is long, not too dirty, though windy. The straggling town of **Pativilca** (Km 203), has a small museum.

- **Accommodation & places to eat In Barranca**: **D** *Hotel Chavín*, warm water, good value, rec, also restaurant on 1st floor for lunch and dinner (try *arroz con conchas*), breakfast bar and café; **F** *Jefferson*, Lima 946, pleasant; **F** *Pacífico*, with bath, good value; **G** *Colón*, Jr Gálvez 407, basic. There are many other hotels on the main street, and plenty of bars and restaurants; good for fish is *Cevichería Fujino*, at Arica 210. Here and in Supe try the *tamales*.

- **Banks & money changers** Banco de la Nación, Barranca, accepts TCs, good rates.

- **Transport** Buses stop opp the service station (*el grifo*) at the end of town. From **Lima** to **Barranca**, 3½ hrs, US$3; to **Pativilca**, 3½ hrs, US$3.50. As bus companies have their offices in Barranca, buses will stop there rather than at Pativilca or Paramonga. Bus from Barranca to **Casma** 155 km, several daily, 3 hrs, US$3. From Barranca to **Huaraz**, 4 hrs, US$6, daily buses or trucks. The good, paved road to Huaraz turns off the Panamericana just past Pativilca.

4 km beyond the turn-off to Huaraz, beside the Highway, are the well preserved ruins of the Chimú temple of **Paramonga**. Set on high ground with a view of the ocean, the fortress-like mound is reinforced by eight quadrangular walls rising in tiers to the top of the hill. Admission US$1.20; caretaker may act as guide.

- **Transport** Buses run only to Paramonga port (3 km off the Highway, 4 km from the ruins, about 15 mins from Barranca). Taxi from Paramonga to the ruins and return after waiting, US$4.50, otherwise take a Barranca-Paramonga port bus, then a 3 km walk.

Between Pativilca and Chimbote the mountains come down to the sea. The road passes by a few very small protected harbours in tiny rock-encircled bays – Puerto Huarmey, Puerto Casma, and Vesique.

- **Accommodation** At **Huarmey** town, on the Pan-American Highway is **C-D** *Hotel de Turistas*, small, good service, restaurant, noisy from traffic on highway; and **D** *Hostal Santa Rosa*, on plaza.

CASMA

The town, largely destroyed by the 1970 earthquake, has since been rebuilt. It has a pleasant Plaza de Armas, several parks and two markets including a good food market.

About 15 km SE of Casma are the ruins of **Chanquillo** with a cemetery and a Chimú fortress of four concentric rings, with three towers in the middle. Visible from Chanquillo is a large wall with 13 towers atop a ridge.

- **Access** Take a truck going to San Rafael and ask for Castillo de Chanquillo (irregular departures from the E end of town, before bridge over Río Sechín; ask when last truck returns to Casma). After alighting, walk 2 km uphill.

- **Accommodation D** *Hostal El Farol*, Tupac Amaru 450, T/F 711064, best in town, inc continental breakfast, hot water in most rooms, good restaurant, pleasant garden, parking, rec; **D** *Hostal Ernesto's*, Garcilaso de la Vega y Gamarra, T 711475, modern, hot water, bakery downstairs; **D** *Indoamericano*, Av Huarmey 130, T 711395, cheaper without bath, hot water, dirty bathroom, owner speaks English and changes cash dollars; **E** *Gregori*, Luis Ormeño 579, T 711073, cheaper without bath, noisy, restaurant downstairs; **F** *Hostal Central*, Plaza de Armas 140, dirty, cold water, very basic, helpful.

- **Places to eat** *Sechín*, Nepeña esq Mejía, nr plaza, good; *Tío Sam*, Huarmey 138, Chinese and *criollo*, cheap, rec. Several *cevicherías* on Av Ormeño 600 block and cheap restaurants on Huarmey. *Heladería El Pibe*, Gamarra 466, good ice-cream.

- **Useful services Bank**: good rates for cash and TCs, no commission, at **Banco de Crédito**, Bolívar 181. **Post Office**: at Fernando Loparte, 1 block from Plaza de Armas. National and International **phone** and **fax** at *Sonia's*, Huarmey 302; and *Luz*, Av Ormeño 118.

- **Buses** From **Lima**, 370 km, several buses daily, 5 hrs, US$5; to **Lima**, Turismo Chimbote, Ormeño 515, T 711370, at 1000 and 2400; Vista Alegre, Ormeño 529, T 711073; Chinchaysuyo, Ormeño 526, at 0100. To **Chimbote**, 55 km, several buses and colectivos daily, 1 hr, US$1. To **Trujillo**, 175 km, daily buses, 3 hrs, US$2.50. Most buses N pass Casma 0400-0600; buses S 0900-1200; wait by gas station at E end

of Av Ormeño. At other times, take a bus to Chimbote. To **Huaraz**: from Casma a road runs inland over the **Callán pass** (4,224m) 150 km to Huaraz. A difficult but beautiful trip, worth taking in daylight. Not all buses take this route, so check before leaving. From Casma the first 30 km are paved, a good dirt road follows for 30 km to **Pariacoto** (basic lodging). From here to the pass the road is rough (landslides in rainy season), but once the Cordillera Negra has been crossed, the wide, gravel road is better with spectacular views of the Cordillera Blanca. Bus to **Huaraz**, via Pariacoto, 6-7 hrs, US$6, Transportes Moreno, Ormeño 555, 0800 and 2100 daily, or trucks; via Pativilca, US$6.60, Turismo Chimbote at 2200, Chinchaysuyo at 2330.

SECHIN

This is one of the most important ruins on the Peruvian coast. It consists of a large square temple completely faced with carved stone monoliths – probably over 500 of them – narrating, it is thought, a gruesome battle, with the fates of the conquerors and the conquered graphically depicted. The style is unique in Peru for its naturalistic vigour. The complex as a whole is associated with the pre-Chavín Sechín culture, dating from about 1500 BC. Three sides of the large stone temple have been excavated and restored, but you cannot see the earlier adobe buildings inside the stone walls because they were covered up and used as a base for a second storey which has been completely destroyed.

The site is open 0830-1830 daily, photography best around midday (US$2.25, children and students half price); ticket also valid for the Max Uhle Museum by the ruins and Pañamarca (see page 1247).

- **Access** To walk to the ruins from Casma, follow Av Ormeño E, at the circle turn right and follow the Pan-American Highway, walk about 3 km S to a well posted sign showing a left turn for Huaraz (this is at Km 370), then simply follow the road for 2 km to the ruins. Frequent colectivos leave from in front of the market in Casma, US$0.30 pp, or motorcycle taxi.

CHIMBOTE

In one of Peru's few natural harbours, a port has been built to serve the national steel industry. Chimbote (*Pop* 296,600; *Phone code* 044) is also Peru's largest fishing port; fishmeal is exported and the smell of the fishmeal plants is very strong. The city's importance will grow with the paving of the road through the Cañon del Pato to the Cordillera Blanca. The modern Municipal building has a small art gallery downstairs (open 0900-2000). Flocks of brown pelicans and masked boobies may be seen from the beach. **NB** The main street, Av Victor Raul Haya de la Torre, is also known by its old name, José Pardo.

Excursions

About 25 km S of Chimbote, at Km 405 on the Pan-American Highway, a paved road leads E to the Nepeña valley, where several precolumbian ruins can be found: just beyond Capellanía (11 km from junction) is **Pañamarca**. The site includes a 2-storey stone structure, built on a hill, dating from the formative period (2000 BC-100 AD) and many adobe structures from the Mochica period. 20 km from Pañamarca is **Paredones**, a large stone structure, with 4m high granite walls and a very impressive gateway known as 'Portada de Paredones' or 'Puerta del Sol'.

In the same valley is another site with similar characteristics known as **Siete Huacas**. A large carved monolith (Monolito de Siete Huacas), reminiscent of the Sechín carvings was found at the site.

Local information
● Accommodation
Water shortages can be a problem, make sure your hotel has a tank before taking a room.

A1 *Gran Hotel Chimú*, ex-State Tourist Hotel, José Gálvez 109, T/F 321741, inc breakfast, safe parking.

B *Hostal Antonio's*, Bolognesi 745, T/F 325783, hot water, minibar; **B** *Ivansino Inn*, Haya de la Torre 738, T 331395, F 321927, inc breakfast, comfortable, modern; **B** *Presidente*, L Prado 536, T 322411, F 321988, hot showers, safe parking (extra), poor snack bar, rec.

C *Hostal Karol Inn*, Manuel Ruiz 277, T/F 321216, hot water, good, family run, laundry service, cafeteria; **C-D** *Residencial El Parque*, E Palacios 309, on plaza, T 323963, converted old home, hot water, nice.

D *Felic*, Haya de la Torre 552, T 325901, **E** without bath, quiet, rec; **D** *San Felipe*, Haya de la Torre 514, T 323401, hot water, comfortable, restaurant; **D** *Venus*, Haya de la Torre 675, T 321339, dirty but friendly, nr bus stations,

useful if you arrive at night.

E *Hostal Playa*, Malecón Miguel Grau 185, OK, safe; **E** *Hostal Paraíso*, Haya de la Torre 1015, T 323718, cheaper without bath, basic, nr Ormeño bus station.

F *Hostal El Santa*, Espinar 671, basic.

● Places to eat
Pollo Gordo, Prado y Aguirre, good chicken and cold beer; *Buenos Aires*, Aguirre nr the beach, popular lunch place; *Marisquito*, Bolognesi nr Palacios, good local food, disco at night; *Chifa Cantón*, Bolognesi, Chinese, good; *La Fogata Inn*, Villavicencio, good grilled food; *Aquarius*, Haya de la Torre 360, vegetarian. An excellent bakery is *Delca*, at Haya de la Torre 568.

● Banks & money changers
Banco de Crédito and Interbanc, both on Bolognesi and M Ruiz, for TCs and cash; Casa Arroyo, M Ruiz 292, cash only. There are other *casas* and street changers along M Ruiz between Bolognesi and VR Haya de la Torre.

● Post & telecommunications
Post: Serpost, Jr Tumbes behind market.

Telecommunications: Telefónica main office, Tumbes 356, national and international fax and phone; also at Haya de la Torre 420 and M Ruiz 253.

● Security
Chimbote suffers from a high level of street crime. Avoid the shanty towns around the city and be especially careful nr the market and bus stations, day or night.

● Tour companies & travel agents
Chimbote Tours, Bolognesi 801, T 325341, F 324792, helpful and friendly, English spoken.

● Transport
Local Taxis: radio taxis from T 334433, T 327777 and T 322005.

Air Airport is at the S end of town. To **Lima**, 1 hr, 5 a week, Expreso Aéreo; also to **Cajamarca**.

Buses From **Lima**, to Chimbote, 420 km, 6 hrs, US$7-9, several buses daily inc: Turismo Chimbote, VR Haya de la Torre 670, T 321400, 9 daily, rec; Cruz del Sur, Haya de la Torre 626; Continental (Ormeño), J Balta 289, esq Haya de la Torre; Vista Alegre, Gálvez 225, T 331048. To **Trujillo**, 130 km, 2 hrs, US$2.50, several buses and colectivos daily. To **Tumbes**, 889 km, 13 hrs, US$11, Continental at 1630, Cruz del Sur at 2200. It is 8-10 hrs to **Huaraz** via the Santa Valley (for a description of this route, see page 1256), US$6; daily buses (Transportes Moreno, J Gálvez 1178, T 321235, 0800, rec), book the previous day. To Huaraz via Casma and Pariacoto, with Moreno, 0645 and 2000, US$6; via Pativilca, Cruz del Sur at 2145 and Turismo Chimbote at 2100, US$7.

THE CORDILLERA BLANCA AND THE CALLEJÓN DE HUAYLAS

Apart from the range of Andes running along the Chile-Argentina border, the highest mountains in South America are along the Callejón de Huaylas and are perfectly visible from many spots. From the city of Huaraz alone, one can see over 23 snow-crested peaks of over 5,000m, of which the most notable is Huascarán (6,768m), the highest mountain in Peru.

Although the snowline is receding, the Cordillera Blanca still contains the largest concentration of glaciers found in the world's tropical zone. From the retreating glaciers come the beauty and the plague of the Callejón. The turquoise-coloured lakes which form in the terminal moraines are the jewels of the Andes, but at the same time these *cochas* (glacial lakes) have caused much death and destruction when dykes have broken, sending tons of water hurtling down the canyons wiping out everything in their path. The levels of some high mountain lakes have been artificially lowered for flood control and to feed the huge Cañon del Pato dam.

Probably the easiest way to see the Santa Valley and the Callejón de Huaylas, is to take the paved road which branches E off the Pan-American Highway N of Pativilca (see page 1245), 203 km from Lima.

The road climbs increasingly steeply to the chilly pass at 4,080m (Km 120). Shortly after, Laguna **Conococha** comes into view, where the Río Santa rises. A dirt road branches off from Conococha to **Chiquián** (see page 1261) and the **Cordilleras Huayhuash** and **Raura** to the SE. After crossing a high plateau the main road descends gradually for 47 km until **Catac**, where another road branches E to Chavín and on to the **Callejón de Conchucos**. Huaraz is 36 km further on and the road then continues N between and towering Cordillera Negra, snowless and rising to 4,600m, and the snow-covered Cordillera Blanca. This valley, the Callejón de Huaylas, has many picturesque villages and small towns, with narrow cobblestone streets and odd-angled house roofs.

The alternative routes to the Callejón de Huaylas are via the Callán pass from Casma to Huaraz (see page 1246), and from Chimbote to Caraz via the Cañón del Pato (page 1257).

HUARAZ

The valley's focus is **Huaraz** (*Pop* 80,000; *Alt* 3,091m; *Phone code* 044), capital of the Department of Ancash, 420 km by road from Lima. The city was almost completely destroyed in the earthquake of May 1970. The Plaza de Armas has been rebuilt, except for the Cathedral, which is being resited elsewhere. The setting, at the foot of the Cordillera Blanca, is spectacular. For good views of the surrounding peaks go to the *Mirador Rataquenua* at the cross (visible from Huaraz) 1 hr walk from the town (turn left past the cemetery and head uphill through a small forest). For an amazing view of the whole valley, continue past the *Mirador* to *Pukaventana*. **NB** Reports of armed hold-ups at the *Mirador*.

Huaraz is a tourist centre, especially busy on market day (Thur).It is a prime destination for hikers and a mecca for international climbers.

Museums

Museo Regional de Ancash, Instituto Nacional de Cultura, Plaza de Armas, containing stone monoliths and *huacos* from the Recuay culture, well labelled; Tues-Sat 0800-1900, Sun-Mon 0800-1500; entry US$1.80, includes entry to Willkawain ruins on same day. **Museo de Miniaturas del Perú**, Jr Lúcar y Torre 460, models of Huaraz and Yungay before the earthquake, plus a collection of Barbie dolls in Peruvian dress, strange but interesting; Mon-Sat, 0800-1300, 1500-2200, US$0.85.

Excursions

Willkawain About 8 km to the NE is the Willkawain archaeological site. The ruins (AD 700 to 1000, Huari Empire) consist of 3 large 2-storey structures with intact stone slab roofs and several small structures.

• **Access** Take a colectivo N along Luzuriaga (or walk) past the *Hotel Huascarán*. After crossing a small bridge take a second right marked

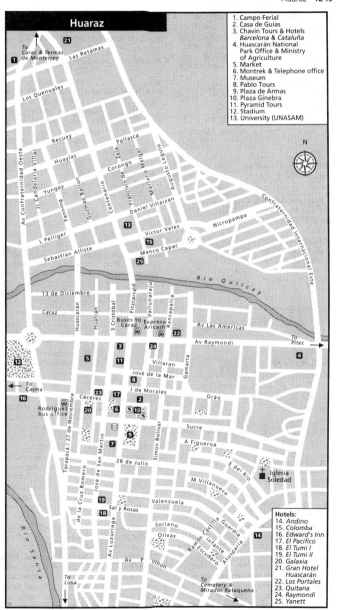

Huaraz

1. Campo Ferial
2. Casa de Guías
3. Chavin Tours & Hotels *Barcelona* & *Cataluña*
4. Huascarán National Park Office & Ministry of Agriculture
5. Market
6. Montrek & Telephone office
7. Museum
8. Pablo Tours
9. Plaza de Armas
10. Plaza Ginebra
11. Pyramid Tours
12. Stadium
13. University (UNASAM)

Hotels:
14. Andino
15. Colomba
16. Edward's Inn
17. El Pacifico
18. El Tumi I
19. El Tumi II
20. Galaxia
21. Gran Hotel Huascarán
22. Los Portales
23. Quitana
24. Raymondi
25. Yanett

by a blue sign, it is about 2 hrs uphill walk; ask frequently as there are many criss-crossing paths. About 500m past Willkawain is Ichiwillkawain with several similar but smaller structures. Beware of dogs en route (and begging children). Take a torch. The ruins are along the road to Laguna Llaca, colectivos leave from Jr Caraz above Fitzcarrald (US$0.45 to Willkawain); there is also an alternative road from the ruins to Monterrey.

North of Huaraz, 6 km along the road to Caraz, are the thermal baths at **Monterrey** (*Alt* 2,780m): the lower pool is US$0.90; the upper pool, which is nicer (closed Mon for cleaning), US$1.35; also individual and family tubs US$1.35 pp for 20 mins; crowded at weekends and holidays.

● **Accommodation & places to eat** B *Baños Termales Monterrey*, Av Monterrey, at top of hill, T/F 721717, classic old spa, price inc breakfast and use of pools, restaurant, bar; B *El Patio*, Av Monterrey, 250m down hill from baths, T/F 01-437-6567 (Lima), inc breakfast, meals on request, bar, colonial-style, rec; C *El Nogal*, on side street off Av Monterrey across from El Patio, modern. There are several country style restaurants which are busy at weekends, serving regional specialities. Others along the Huaraz-Caraz road.

● **Transport** City buses along Av Luzuriaga go as far as Monterrey (US$0.22), until 1900; taxi US$2-3.

Local festivals

Patron saints' day, *El Señor de la Soledad*, week starting **3 May**. Independence celebrations, **28 July**. *Semana del Andinismo*, in **June**, international climbing and skiing week. *San Juan* and *San Pedro* throughout the region during the last week of **June**. *Semana Santa* is widely celebrated.

Local information

● **Accommodation**

Hotels fill up rapidly during high season (May-Sept), especially during public holidays and special events when prices rise (beware overcharging).

In town: **A2-3** *Hostal Andino*, Pedro Cochachín 357, some way SE from centre, T 721662, T/F 722830, inc breakfast, best in town, restaurant (fondue expensive), safe parking, Swiss run, beautiful view of Huascarán, climbing and hiking gear for hire, rec; **A3** *Gran Hotel Huascarán*, Av Centenario block 10, at the N end of town, T 721640, F 722821, uninspiring ex-state hotel, large rooms, poor restaurant, **C** for camping in courtyard with

use of facilities.

B *Hostal Saxofón*, Cascapampa 250, 1 block from *Gran Hotel Huascarán*, T/F 721722, pleasant with garden, parking.

C *Hostal Montañero*, Plaza Ginebra 30-B (ask at Casa de Guías), T/F 722306, hot water, modern, comfortable, good value, climbing equipment rental and sales, rec; **C** *El Tumi I*, San Martín 1121, T 721784, good restaurant, fairly good (*No II*, cheaper, San Martín 1089, T 721784); **C** *Hostal Colomba*, Francisco de Zela 210, on Centenario across river, T 721241, lovely old hacienda, bungalow, family-run (German), garden, safe car parking; **C** *Hostal Los Portales*, Raymondi 903, T 721402, F 721247, hot water, parking, pleasant.

D *Casablanca*, 27 de Noviembre/Tarapacá 138, T 722602, F 721578, pleasant, modern, nr market; **D** *Edward's Inn*, Bolognesi 121, T/F 722692, cheaper without bath, not always hot water, laundry, food available, insist on proper rates in low season, popular, Edward speaks English and knows a lot about trekking and rents gear (not all guides share Edward's experience); **D pp** *Familia de Alcides Ames*, 27 de Noviembre 773, T 723375, with breakfast, Sr Ames is an expert on glaciers, his son is a climbing and rafting guide; **D** *Hostal Oscar*, La Mar 624, T 721145, hot water, cheap breakfast, good beds, **E** out of season, rec; **D** *Hostal Raymondi*, Raymondi 820, T 721082, central, hot water (am only in ground floor shower), comfortable, charges for left luggage, café serves good breakfast; **D** *Hostal Yanett*, Av Centenario 164, at N end of town across river, T 721466, hot water, large rooms, restaurant for breakfast, rec.

E *Alojamiento Norma*, Pasaje Valenzuela 837, nr Plaza Belén, T 721831, inc breakfast, cheaper without bath, hot water, rec; **E** *Hostal Chong Roca*, J de Morales 687, T 721154, with bath, hot water 24 hrs, huge rooms, rec; **E** *Hostal Copa*, Jr Bolívar 615, cheaper without bath, limited hot water, laundry facilities, owner's son, Walter Melgarejo is a well-known guide, popular with trekkers, restaurant; **E** *Hostal Estoico*, San Martín 635, T 722371, cheaper without bath, safe, hot water, laundry facilities, rec; **E** *Hostal Galaxia*, Jr de la Cruz Romero 688, T 722230, cheaper without bath, hot water, laundry facilities, basic, rec; **E** *Hostal Los Andes*, Tarapacá 316, T 721346, cheaper without bath, hot water, laundry facilities, attractive but noisy, hard beds; **E** *Hostal Quintana*, Mcal Cáceres 411, T 726060, cheaper without bath, hot shower, laundry facilities, basic, stores luggage, popular with trekkers; **E** *Hostal Tany*, Lúcar y Torre 468, T 722534, with bath, hot water at night, spotless; **E** *Hostal Virgen del*

Carmen, Jr de la Cruz Romero 664, T 721729, or 481-5311 (Lima), cheaper without bath, hot water, run by a lovely, helpful old couple from Lima, homely atmosphere, nice rooms, cheap laundry service, highly rec; **E** *Residencial Cataluña*, Av Raymondi 822, T 721117, with bath, basic, restaurant open only in season, safe, noisy, tepid water; **E-F** pp *Alojamiento Alpes Andes*, at Casa de Guías (see below), Plaza Ginebra 28-g, T 721811, member of Peruvian Youth Hostel Association, nice dorms for up to 6 people, rec restaurant, muesli, yoghurt in am, pastas and pizzas in evening; **E-F** *Casa Jansy's*, Jr Sucre 948, hot water, meals, laundry, owner Jesús Rivera Lúcar is a mountain guide, rec.

F *Albergue El Tambo*, Confraternidad Internacional Interior 122-B, laundry and cooking facilities, 3 rooms with 12 beds; **F** *Alojamiento San Martín de Porres*, Pasaje San Martín de las Porres off Las Américas 300 block, T 721061, rec; **F** pp *Hostal López*, behind *Edward's Inn*, ask nr Estadio just off Av Bolognesi at Santa river end, lukewarm showers, laundry facilities, beautiful garden and restaurant, good views, luggage stored; **F-G** *Alojamiento Nemys*, Jr Figueroa 1135, T 722949, safe, hot shower, breakfast US$2.40, good for climbers, luggage store of fee.

G pp *Alojamiento El Rey*, Pasaje Olivera 919 nr Plaza Belén, T 721917, dormitory style, shared bath, hot water 24 hrs, cooking and laundry facilities, family run, charming people, meals available, rec; **G** pp *Casa de Jaimes*, C Alberto Gridilla 267, T 722281, two blocks from main plaza, hot showers (but insufficient when full), washing facilities, maps and books of region, use of kitchen, popular, very noisy, rec; **G** *Familia Sánchez*, Jr Caraz 849, basic, warm water, helpful, cheap breakfast; **G** pp *Hostal Maguiña*, Av Tarapacá 643, T 722320, opp Rodríguez bus terminal, noisy in am, hot water, laundry facilities, breakfast available, luggage stored, English and French spoken, helpful in arranging trekking and equipment hire, rec. There are usually people waiting at the bus terminals offering cheap accommodation in their own homes.

Youth Hostels: see *Alojamiento Alpes Andes* above; *Hostal la Montañesa*, Av Leguía 290, Centenario, T 721287.

● **Places to eat**

Restaurant and bar at *Ebony 86*, Plaza de Armas; *Monttrek Pizza Pub*, Luzuriaga 646, T 721124, good pizzas and pastas, indoor climbing wall, shows videos; *Chez Pepe*, Luzuriaga 570, good pizza, chicken, meat, run by Pepe from *Residencial Cataluña*; *La Familia* at Luzuriaga 431, popular, vegetarian dishes, good food but slow service; *Créperie Patrick*,

Luzuriaga 424 y Raymondi, excellent crêpes, fish, quiche, spaghetti and good wine, rec; *Chifa Jim Hua*, Luzuriaga 643, large, tasty portions for US$2-3; *Monte Rosa*, Av Luzuriaga 496, good pizzería, reasonable prices, open 1830-2300, Swiss owner is Victorinox representative, offering knives for sale and repair service, climbing and trekking books to read; *Café Central*, Luzuriaga 808, good for breakfast; *Miski Huasi*, Jr Sucre 476, small, cheap, some vegetarian; *Las Cuyas*, Morales 535, good cheap meals and breakfasts, popular; *Pío Pío*, Av Centenario 329, rec; *Pizza Bruno*, Luzuriaga 834, T 725689, French-owned, good, open from 1830, pricey, owner Bruno Reviron organizes treks; *Querubín*, Jr J de Morales 767, traditional dishes, also vegetarian, cheap, rec; *Huaraz Querido*, Jr Huascarán 184, excellent *cevichería*, rec. Also good for *ceviche* is *Warmi Juicio*, Pasaje Octavio Hinostroza 522, 2 blocks from Plaza de Armas. *La Fontana*, Av Tarapacá 561, excellent pancakes and juices, cheap; *La Estación*, Luzuriaga 928, video pub with good lunch for US$1, also good steaks for US$2, rec. *Recreos* are restaurants that specialize in typical local dishes, open only at weekends.

Note that middle and high-class restaurants charge a 31% tax on top of the bill.

● **Banks & money changers**

Banco de Crédito, on Plaza de Armas, closed 1300-1630, changes cash, no commission on TCs into soles, good rates, into cash dollars 5% commission, cash advance on Visa; Interbanc, on Plaza de Armas, 5% commission on TCs, cash advance on Visa. Casa de Cambio *Oh Na Nay*, across from Interbanc, cash only, good rates. Street changers on Luzuriaga (be careful). Travel agents also change dollars and TCs, but generally offer poor rates.

● **Entertainment**

Imantata, Luzuriaga 424, disco and folk music; *La Cueva del Oso*, Luzuriaga 674, taverna-style, good peña; *Taberna Tambo*, José de la Mar, folk music daily, disco, open 1000-1600, 2000-0200, rec, knock on door to get in; *Amadeus*, Parque Ginebra, bar-disco; *Bad Boy Pub Disco*, Jr J de la Mar 661, live rock groups.

● **Laundry**

Fitzcarrald, Fitzcarrald, close to bridge; *Lavandería Liz*, Bolívar 711, US$2/kg; another at San Martín 732. Also at the Casa de Guías (see below).

● **Post & telecommunications**

Post: Serpost, Luzuriaga opp Plaza de Armas, open 0800-2000 daily.

Telecommunications: Telefónica del Perú, Luzuriaga esq Sucre, national and international phone and fax, open 0700-2300 daily.

● **Shopping**

Daily market (1600-2000) in covered sidewalks of Luzuriaga for local sweaters, hats, gloves, etc, wall hangings, good value. *Andean Expressions*, Jr J Arguedas 1246, nr La Soledad church, T 722951, run by Lucho, Mauro and Beto Olaza, rec for hand-printed clothing and gifts.

Camping gear: several shops of the trekking agencies sell camping gaz cartridges. White gas is available from *ferreterías* on Raymondi below Luzuriaga and by Parque Ginebra. The following agencies are rec for hiring gear: *Andean Sport Tours* (see address below); *Casa de Guías* rents equipment and sells dried food; *Monttrek* (see address below); *Chavín Tours* (Willy Gordillo at *Hostal Casablanca*, address above, T 722602); *Lobo*, Luzuriaga 557, T 725994; *Pablo Tours* (see below). Check all camping and climbing equipment before taking it. Gear is usually of poor quality, mostly second hand, left behind by others. Best to bring your own. All prices standard, but not cheap, throughout town. All require payment in advance, passport or air ticket as deposit and will only give 50% of your money back if you return gear early.

● **Sports**

Climbing and trekking: the Cordillera Blanca is the main climbing and hiking centre of Peru. The season is from May to Sept, although conditions vary from year to year. See also under **Tourist Information** below and in the same paragraph for *Casa de Guías*. Recommended mountain guides are: Hugo Cifuentes Maguiña and his brother César (speaks English and French), Av Centenario 537; also in *Casa de Guías*; Augusto Ortega, Jr San Martín 1004, T 724888, the only Peruvian to climb Everest; Juan José Tome, Av Gamarra 782, dpto 1; Walter Baumann, T 721195, aptdo 17. Several of the agencies and *Casa de Guías* run rock climbing courses at Monterrey (behind *Hotel Baños Termales Monterrey*) and Huanchac (30 mins' walk from Huaraz); US$7.50-10 pp/day, inc guide and transport.

Mountain biking: contact Julio Olaza at *Mountain Bike Adventures*, Lúcar y Torre 538, T 721203, Julio speaks excellent English, US$15 for 5 hrs, various routes; also rents rooms, **F** pp.

River rafting and canoeing: contact Carlos Ames *River Runners*, Calle 27 de Noviembre 773 y La Mar 661, T 723375, F 724888.

● **Tour companies & travel agents**

All agencies run conventional tours to Llanganuco, Pastoruri (both US$9 pp) and Chavín (US$11 pp). Many hire equipment (see above) and also offer rafting on Río Santa (US$15/half day), climbing and trekking tours and ski instruction. Most agencies provide transport, food, mules and guides.

The following are rec: *Pablo Tours*, Luzuriaga 501, T 721145; *Chavín Tours*, Luzuriaga 502, T 721578; *Hiroshanka Sport*, Julián de Morales 611, T 722562, climbing, trekking, horse riding, 4WD hire (also rents rooms, **E** pp, with bath, hot water, breakfast). *Monttrek*, Luzuriaga 640, T 721124, good trekking and climbing information, advice and maps, also run ice and rock climbing courses (at Monterrey); tours to Lago Churup and 'spectacular' *Luna Llena* tour; also mountain bike hire, ski instruction and trips, river rafting. Upstairs in Pizzería is a climbing wall, good maps, videos and slide shows. For new routes and maps contact Porfirio Cacha Macedo, 'Pocho', at *Monttrek* or at Jr Corongo 307, T 723930. *Andean Sport Tours*, Luzuriaga 571, T 721612, basic practice wall behind office, also organizes mountain bike tours, ski instruction and river rafting. *Nueva Aventura*, Av Centenario 713, T 722977, F 721582, for climbing and trekking, good quality equipment, French spoken. On the 2nd floor of the *Hotel Residencial Cataluña*, Av Raymondi, T 72117, José Valle Espinosa, 'Pepe', hires out equipment (pricey), organizes treks and pack animals, sells dried food, and is generally helpful and informative.

● **Tourist offices**

Basic tourist information from OPTUR (Oficina de Promoción Turística) on Luzuriaga by Plaza de Armas, Mon-Fri 0900-1300, 1600-1900, Sat 0900-1300. **Casa de Guías**: Plaza Ginebra, T 721811, climbers and hikers' meeting place, useful with information, arrangements for guides, *arrieros*, mules, etc. The Dirección de Turismo issues qualified guides and *arrieros* a photo ID, check for this when making arrangements. Prices for specific services are set so enquire before hiring someone. You are required to provide or pay for food for all porters and guides.

● **Transport**

Air No regular service; private charter from AeroCóndor from Lima. Taxi to airport (at Anta) about 23 km from town, 20 mins, US$3. All transport N to Carhuaz goes past the airport; minivan, 40 mins, US$0.50.

Buses to Lima: Huaraz-Lima, 420 km, 7 hrs, US$5-9. There is a large selection of buses to Lima, both ordinary service and luxury coaches; departures throughout the day. Many of the companies have their offices along Fitzcarrald and on Av Raymondi. Some rec companies are: *Cruz del Sur*, Lúcar y Torre 573, T 723532; *Transportes Rodríguez*, Tarapacá 622, T 721353; *Expreso Ancash* (Ormeño), Raymondi 845, T 721102; *Movil Tours*, Raymondi 616, T 722555.

Other buses: to Casma and Chimbote via the
Callán pass (150 km) 6-7 hrs, US$6, sit on left
for best views: Transportes Moreno, Raymondi
892, T 721344, daily 0830 and 2000; Transportes Huandoy, Fitzcarrald 261, T 722502,
daily 0800. To **Chimbote**, 185 km: Transportes
Moreno, daily 0700, US$6, 8-9 hrs via Caraz and
Cañón del Pato, see under Chimbote, sit on the
right for the most exciting views (see page
1256). Other companies go to Chimbote via
Pativilca; Turismo Chimbote, Tarapacá 182,
T 721024, US$7, 6 hrs. To **Pativilca**, 160 km, 4
hrs, US$3.50. To **Trujillo**: Cruz del Sur, Chichay-
suyo (Fitzcarrald 369), Rodríguez, Turismo
Chimbote, Empresa de Transportes 14 (Fitzcarrald 216, T 721282); all buses go at night, 8-9
hrs, US$7. Several buses and minivans run daily,
0500-2000, between Huaraz and **Caraz**, 2 hrs,
US$1.10. They stop at all the places in between;
depart from Fitzcarrald esq Jr Caraz. To **Chavín**,
110 km, 4 hrs, US$3, and on to Huari, 150 km,
6 hrs, US$4.50 from Huaraz: Chavín Express,
Mcal Cáceres 338, T 724652, daily 0900, 1100
and 1300; Cisper Tours, Tarapacá 621,
T 722025, daily 0900 and 1300; Lanzón de
Chavín, Tarapacá 602, daily 1000 to Huari, to
Llamellín, Tues and Sat 1000, US$8. To **Chacas**
(US$7) and **San Luis** (US$7.60), Transportes
Huandoy, 7 hrs (also to Llamellín). To **Huallanca**,
via Pachacoto (see below), US$3.50; some
trucks and buses run this route, continuing to
La Unión and Huánuco. Colectivos to Recuay,
Ticapampa and Catac daily 0500-2000,
US$0.65, from Mcal Cáceres y Tarapacá.

Taxi: standard fare in town is about US$0.90;
radio taxis T 721482 or 722512.

HUASCARAN NATIONAL PARK

Established in July 1975, the park includes the entire Cordillera Blanca above
4,000m, with a total area of 3,400 sq km. It
is a UNESCO World Biosphere Reserve
and part of the World Heritage Trust. The
park's objectives are to protect the unique
flora, fauna, geology, archaeological sites
and extraordinary scenic beauty of the
Cordillera. Please help by taking all your
rubbish away with you when camping.
The park administration officially
charges visitors US$1/day to enter the
park but this was not always enforced in
1995. The park office is in the Ministry of
Agriculture, at the E end of Av Raymondi
in Huaraz, open am only, T 722086; limited general information but useful for
those planning specific research activities.

HUARAZ TO CHAVIN

South of Huaraz, on the main road, is
Recuay, one of the few provincial capitals
which survived the 1970 earthquake and
conserves its colonial features (27 km, 30
mins). The road passes **Olleros** at 3,450m.
Some basic meals and food supplies available, but no accommodation. The famous,
easy 3-day hike to Chavín, along a precolumbian trail, with spectacular views of
snow-covered peaks, starts from Olleros.

● **Transport** You can get off at the main road
and walk the 2 km to Olleros, or catch a truck
or minibus from Tarapacá y Jr Cáceres, nr Edward's Inn, to the village, 29 km, US$0.30.

The main road continues from Recuay to
Catac, 11 km, where a good dirt road
branches E for Chavín.

● **Accommodation & places to eat** *Hostal
Central* and one other, both basic. *Restaurant
La Familia*, good.

7 km S of Catac on the main road is **Pachacoto** from where a road goes to **Huallanca**
on the other side of the Cordillera Blanca
(133 km, 6-7 hrs). In this southern part of
the Cordillera there are few high, snow-
covered peaks, but the glacier of **Pastoruri**
is used as the only skiing area in Peru. It is
nothing compared to other skiing areas in
South America, but it is a place to get in a
little practice. Tours and private transport
can be arranged in Huaraz; US$80 for a van
up to 10 people.

A good place to see the impressive
Puya Raimondi plants is the Pumapampa
valley. Hike up the trail from Pachacoto
to the park entrance, 2½ hrs, where there
is a park office. You can spend the night
here. Walking up the road from this point,
you will see the gigantic plants.

From Catac to Chavín is a magnificent,
scenic journey, if frightening at times.
The road passes Lago Querococha, has
good views of the Yanamarey peaks and,
at the top of the route, is cut through a
huge rock face, entering the Cauish tunnel at 4,550m. On the other side it descends the Tambillo valley, then the Río
Mosna gorge before Chavín.

CHAVIN DE HUANTAR

Chavín de Huantar, a fortress temple, was built about 600 BC. It is the only large structure remaining of the Chavín culture which, in its heyday, is thought to have held influence in a region between Cajamarca and Chiclayo in the N to Ayacucho and Ica in the S. In Dec 1985, UNESCO designated Chavín a World Heritage Trust site. The site is in good condition despite the effects of time and nature. The main attractions are the marvellous carved stone heads and designs in relief of symbolic figures and the many tunnels and culverts which form an extensive labyrinth throughout the interior of the structures. The carvings are in excellent condition, though many of the best sculptures are in Huaraz and Lima. The famous Lanzón dagger-shaped stone monolith of 800 BC is found inside one of the temple tunnels. In order to protect the site some areas are closed to visitors. Although some of the halls have electric lights, take a torch. The guard is also a guide and gives excellent explanations of the ruins; Marino González is another knowledgeable guide. There is a small museum at the entrance, with carvings and some Chavín pottery. Entry US$2.25, students US$1.35; open 0800-1600 Mon-Sat, 1000-1600 Sun and holidays. Camping is possible with permission from the guard.

The town of Chavín (*Alt* 3,140m), just N of the ruins has a pleasant plaza with palm and pine trees. There is nowhere to change money in town. Local *fiesta* July 13-20.

There are not hot sulphur baths (Baños Termales de Chavín) about 2 km S of Chavín at Km 68 in the village of Quercos. Camping is possible here. Buy detergent in the shop above baths and scrub your tub before bathing; entry US$0.45.

- **Accommodation** E *Inca*, Wiracocha 160, **F** without bath, good beds, hot water on request, nice garden; **F** pp *La Casona de JB*, on plaza next to town hall, hot showers; **F** pp *Casa del Sr Benigno Peña*, N end of town, past police checkpoint, unsigned, cold showers, laundry service; **F** *Gantu*, Huayna Capac 135, basic, shared bath, cold water; **F** *Montecarlo*, 17 de Enero S, shared bath, cold water, cold at night.

- **Places to eat** Several along the main street, 17 de Enero: *La Ramada*, regional dishes, also trout and set lunch; *Chavín Turístico*, 439S, best in town, good *menú* and à la carte, nice courtyard; *El Lanzón de Chavín*, 216N, regional dishes, set lunch.

- **Post & telecommunications** Post office and telephone, 17 de Enero 365N; open 0630-2200.

- **Transport** Buses to Huaraz, 110 km, 4 hrs, US$3, see under Huaraz. Buses to Huaraz from Huari pass through Chavín between 0400-0600 daily but are often full; trucks go in the afternoon from the police checkpoint. There is plenty of transport to Catac, 2½ hrs, US$2; many buses or trucks from there to Huaraz, 1 hr, US$0.50. Huaraz travel agencies organize daily tours to the ruins; sometimes you can hitch a ride back with them. Taxi, 4 hrs, US$20. To Lima, 438 km, 14 hrs, US$9 with Cóndor de Chavín twice a week. Most buses from Lima go on to Huari and Pomabamba. From Chavín to **Huari**, 38 km, 2 hrs, in pm, **San Luis**, a further 61 km, 3 hrs, and **Piscobamba**, 62 km, 3 hrs: several buses and trucks serve this route as far as Huari on quite a good dirt road. The scenery is very different from the other side of the Cordillera Blanca, very dry and hot. Gasoline is available at N end of Chavín.

CHAVIN TO POMABAMBA

From Chavín one circuit by road back to Huaraz is via Huari, San Luis, Yanama and Yungay (see page 1258) but the bus service is infrequent.

The road N from Chavín descends into the dry Mosna river canyon. After 8 km it reaches **San Marcos**, a small, friendly town with a nice plaza and a few basic restaurants and *hostales*. 32 km further on is **Huari**, perched on a hillside at 3,150m. *Fiesta of Nuestra Señora del Rosario* first 2 weeks of Oct.

- **Accommodation & places to eat** F *El Dorado*, Bolívar 341, basic, comfortable, sunny patio, shared bath, hot water; **F** *Añaños*, Alvarez 437, next to market, very basic but clean. There are a few others which are very basic, all **F**. Several places to eat, inc *Centro Virgen del Rosario*, San Martín by Parque Vigil, coffee, sweets and snacks, very clean and friendly, open evenings and Sun, run by an Italian nun and her students.

- **Post & telecommunications** The post office is at Luzuriaga 324 by Parque Vigil. Telephone at Libertad 940, open 0700-2200 daily.

- **Transport** Bus companies have their offices around Parque Vigil. To **Huaraz**, 5-6 hrs, US$4.50, all companies depart daily 0200-

0400, also on Fri at 1500. Services also to San Luis and Lima.

There is a spectacular 2-3 days walk from Huari to Chacas via Laguna Purhuay. Alberto Cafferata of Caraz writes: "The Purhuay area is beautiful. It has splendid campsites, trout, exotic birds and, at its N end, a 'quenoal' forest. This is a microclimate at 3,500m, where the animals, insects and flowers are more like a tropical jungle, fantastic for ecologists and photographers." A day walk to Laguna Purhuay is recommended for those who don't want the longer walk to Chacas.

In **Chacas**, 10 km S of San Luis, off the main road, is a fine church. The local *fiesta patronal* is in mid-Aug, with bullfights, a famous *carrera de cintas* and fireworks. Seek out the Taller Don Bosco, a woodcarving workshop run by an Italian priest.

● **Accommodation & places to eat** There are a few basic shops, restaurants, a small market and 2 or 3 basic hostels, inc *Hostal de Pilar*.

It is a 2-day hike from Chacas to Marcará (see page 1259) via the Quebradas Juytush and Honda (lots of condors to be seen). The Quebrada Honda is known as the Paraíso de las Cascadas because it contains at least seven waterfalls. From Huari the road climbs to the Huachacocha pass at 4,350m and descends to **San Luis** at 3,130m (**G** *Hostal Rotta*, also a few basic restaurants, shops and a market).

28 km N of San Luis, a road branches left to **Yanama**, 50 km from San Luis, at 3,400m. It has one marked hotel outside and one unmarked hotel, **G**, on the plaza; ask at the pharmacy. Food is available, but no electricity in the village, which is beautifully surrounded by snow-capped peaks. A day's hike to the ruins above the town affords superb views.

● **Transport** Daily bus between Yungay and Yanama, US$4.50, 5 hrs, continuing to Pomabamba Tues, Sat (returning twice a week, US$11). Trucks also go along this route.

A longer circuit to Huaraz can be made by continuing from San Luis 62 km to **Piscobamba**. There is a basic, but clean and friendly hotel, and one other, both **F**; also a few shops and small restaurants.

POMABAMBA

22 km beyond Piscobamba, this town is worth a visit for some very hot natural springs (the furthest are the hottest). There is a small museum opposite the restaurant on the corner of the main plaza, which the people in the courtyard offices will open free on request.

● **Accommodation & places to eat** **F** *Estrada*, C Lima, good; **F** *Hostal Pomabamba*, on main plaza, basic, safe for luggage; *San Martín de Porres*, off the smaller plaza, basic; **G** *No nos Ganan*, ½ block from plaza, basic but OK. Family lodging, **F**, at the house of Sr Alejandro Via, Jr Primavera s/n, behind the school. The restaurant on the corner of the main plaza is friendly and good.

● **Tour companies & travel agents** One Pyramid Travel, Huaraz 209, T 721283, run by Victor Escudero, who speaks English, specializes in archaeological tours, inc some little known, unspoilt places, rec.

● **Transport** Occasional buses run from San Luis. Bus to Lima twice a week via San Luis and Chavín. To Chimbote twice a week via Sihuas.

Treks from Pomabamba Several good walks into the Cordillera Blanca start from near Pomabamba: via Palo Seco or Laurel to the Lagunas Safuna, from which one can go on, if hardy, to Nevado Alpamayo, dubbed 'the most beautiful mountain in the world'. The glacier of Alpamayo is an incredible sight. From there, continue down to Santa Cruz and Caraz for several days' hard walking in total.

For the less energetic, it is a good 4½-5 hrs walk up to the quite large and extensive, though sadly dilapidated, ruins of **Yaino**, on top of a very steep mountain and visible from the main plaza of Pomabamba. Take food and lots of water; you can get very dehydrated climbing and perspiring in the thin dry air. It's also very cold high up if the sun goes in, so go with warm, waterproof clothes.

From Pomabamba to the Cañon del Pato, the road goes N through cold, wild mountains and valleys, passing in 23 km Palo Seco and Andeymayo. The mining town of **Pasacancha** (hotel and restaurant), 56 km beyond Palo Seco, is the junction for a road N to Sihuas (expensive, basic hostales). Buses twice a week from Pomabamba via Sihuas to Chimbote, 16 hrs. Daytime trucks run from Pasacancha, through Tarica and Yanac, past pre-Inca *chullpas* to Tres Cruces (basic friendly restaurant, no accommodation). Transportes Moreno buses from Tres Cruces go to Yuramarca, before the Cañon del Pato, and on to Caraz (and from there to Yungay and Huaraz).

Places like San Luis, Piscobamba, Pomabamba and Sihuas were on the royal Inca Road, that ran from Cusco to Quito.

CAÑON DEL PATO TO HUARAZ

The route from Chimbote via the Santa Valley: just N of Chimbote, a road branches NE off the Pan-American Highway and goes up the Santa valley following the route, including tunnels, of the old Santa Corporation Railway which used to run as far as **Huallanca** (not to be confused with the town SW of Huaraz), 140 km up the valley. *Hotel Huascarán*, good, friendly; everything closes early. At the top of the valley the road goes through the very narrow and spectacular **Cañon del Pato** before reaching the Callejón de Huaylas and going on S to Caraz and Huaraz.

An alternative road for cyclists is the private road known as the 'Brasileños', used by a Brazilian company which is building a water channel from the Río Santa to the coast. The turn-off is 15 km S of the bridge in Chao, on the Pan-American Highway.

CARAZ

Now almost totally restored after the 1970 earthquake, this pleasant town (*Alt* 2,250m) is a good centre for walking, parasailing and the access point for many excellent treks and climbs. Tourist facilities are expanding as a more tranquil alternative to Huaraz: splendid views of Huandoy and Huascarán as well as the northern Cordilleras in July and August. In other months, the mountains are often shrouded in cloud. Caraz has a milder climate than Huaraz and is more suited to day trips.

Museums

Museo Arqueológico de Caraz is at 1 de Mayo y Mcal Cáceres, open 0800-1400, free; small but interesting collection of ceramics and artefacts from the region; also a good place to ask about the ruins of **Tunshukaiko**, which are in the suburb of Cruz Viva, to the N before the turn-off for Parón. This is a poor area so be discrete with cameras etc.

Local festivals
20 Jan: Virgen de Chiquinquirá. **July**: Semana Turística, last week in July.

Local information
● **Accommodation**

D *Hotel Restaurant Chamanna*, Av Nueva Victoria 185, T 791223, 25 mins walk from centre of town, run by Germans Ute Baitinger and Reiner Urban, clean cabañas set in beautiful gardens, hot water, secure, excellent French/international cuisine, will lend free tents for Llanganuco-Santa Cruz trek, highly rec; D *Regina*, Los Olivos s/n y Gálvez, at S end of town 1 block W of road to Yungay, T 791520, modern, hot water, good value; D *Chavín*, San Martín 1135 just off Plaza, T 791171, sometimes hot water, owner can arrange trips to Lago Parón.

E *El Cafetal*, San Martín 307, T 791137, 7 blocks from the plaza, very basic, 2 rooms with bath, hot water; E *Hostal La Casona*, Raymondi 319, 1 block from plaza, T 791334, F without bath, cold water, lovely little patio; E *Morovi*, Luzuriaga 3a cuadra, at S end of town, T 791409, F without bath, helpful, hot water.

F *Ramírez*, D Villar 407 above Moreno terminal, T 791368, basic, shared bath, cold water, helpful.

In private homes: F pp *Caballero Lodging*, D Villar 485, T 791637, enquire at Pony's Travel on plaza, shared bath, basic; F *Familia Aguilar*, San Martín 1143, T 791161, basic, shared bath, hot water, rec, Prof Bernardino Aguilar Prieto has good information on the Cordillera Negra.

● **Places to eat**

Jeny, on plaza, good food and prices; also on plaza, *El Mirador*, Sucre 1202, nice view from terrace, good for afternoon coffee, and *Café Heladería El Portal*, on San Martín, good snacks and sweets; *Café d'Rat*, above *Pony's Expeditions* (see below), balcony overlooking plaza, vegetarian and international cuisine; *La Punta Grande*, D Villar, inexpensive local meals; *Esmeralda*, Av Alfonso Ugarte 404, good meat and local food, friendly, good value, rec; *La Olla de Barro*, Sucre 1004, good, English spoken; *Palmira*, 500m S of town, E of main road, serves excellent trout, reasonably priced (open 1200-1800), pleasant outdoor setting; *Añañu Caraz*, Sucre 1107, *menú*, popular with locals.

● **Banks & money changers**
Banco de Crédito, D Villar 217, cash and TCs

at good rates, no commission. *Comercial Fournier*, Sucre 907, cash only, daily 0800-1330, 1600-2000; *Pony's Travel* (see below) cash only; *Importaciones América*, Sucre 721, T 791479 (Esteban), good rates and service, open weekends and evenings.

● **Entertainment**

Taberna Discoteca Gato Negro, 28 de Julio s/n, on the way to Parón, good atmosphere, reasonable prices; *Taberna Discoteca Alpamayo Inn*, Bolognesi, moderate prices, a bit impersonal; *Taberna Disco Huandy*, Mcal Cáceres 119.

● **Post & telecommunications**

Post Office: at San Martín.

Telecommunications: national and international phone and fax at Raymondi y Sucre.

● **Shopping**

The best shop for camping supplies is *Kike*, at Sucre 918. Some dehydrated food is available from *Pony's Travel* (see below).

● **Sports**

Swimming: there is a cold water pool at the S entrance to town; adults US$0.45, children US$0.20.

● **Tour companies & travel agents**

Pony's Expeditions, Sucre 1266, Plaza de Armas, T/F 791642 (24 hrs), or Lima 447-4696, open daily 0900-2100, English, French and Quechua spoken, excellent and reliable information about the area, owners Alberto and Haydée Cafferata are very knowledgeable about treks and climbs; local tours and trekking arranged, equipment for hire; also mountain biking to Lago Parón (5 hrs, moderate difficulty) and Portachuelo de Llanganuco (10 hrs, difficult), bike hire US$10/day, US$1/hr, maps and guides inc, helmets and gloves available, rec. Another trekking guide is Mariano Araya, who is also keen on photography and archaeology.

● **Tourist offices**

At Plaza de Armas, in the municipality, T 791029, limited information.

● **Transport**

Buses From Caraz to **Lima**, 470 km; buses go via Huaraz. Most buses on the Lima-Huaraz route continue to Caraz. 6 companies daily, fares ranging from US$6 (eg Chinchaysuyo) to US$10 (Expreso Ancash), 14 hrs. From Caraz to **Huaraz**, several buses and many colectivos daily, 0500-2000, 2 hrs, US$2.25, road in good condition; taxi US$15. To **Yungay**, 12 km, 30 mins, US$0.45. To **Chimbote**, Transportes Moreno, US$5.80, via Huaraz and Casma at 0600 and 1730 daily; via Huallanca 0830 daily (see under Chimbote); Turismo Chimbote, San Martín 1121, T 792146. To village of **Parón** (for trekking in Laguna Parón area) pickups from

corner Santa Cruz and Grau by market, 0500 and 1300, 1 hr, return from Parón 0600 and 1400; to **Cashapampa** (Quebrada Santa Cruz) buses from Santa Cruz between Grau and Sucre by market, 1000, 1100, 1200 and 1500, 2 hrs, US$1.50.

TREKS FROM CARAZ

A good day hike with good views of the Cordillera Blanca is to **Pueblo Libre** (about 4 hrs round trip, or you can take a colectivo back to Caraz). A longer day walk – about 7 hrs in total – with excellent views of Huandoy and Huascarán follows the foothills of the Cordillera Blanca, from Caraz S (head for Punyan, from where transport goes back to Caraz).

Lago Parón From Caraz a narrow, rough road goes E 32 km to Lago Parón, in a cirque surrounded by several, massive snow-capped peaks, including Huandoy, Pirámide Garcilazo and Huaraz. The water level has been lowered to protect Caraz, and the water from the lake is used for the Cañon del Pato hydroelectric scheme. The gorge leading to it is spectacular. It is about a 2-day trek (25 km) up to the lake at 4,150m, or a 3-4 hr walk from the village of Parón (you need to be acclimatized). If there is room, you can stay at the refuge run by Edelnor (kitchen, bathroom); there is usually a charge for use of the facilities.

● **Transport** From Caraz, colectivos go to the lake if there are enough passengers and only in the dry season, US$3-4 pp. Taxi from Caraz US$30. *Pony's Expeditions* in Caraz organize day-trips to the lake, June-Oct, for US$7 pp (min 6 people).

Santa Cruz Valley The famous Llanganuco-Santa Cruz hike is done most easily starting in the Santa Cruz valley (see transport above). It takes about 4 days, up the Santa Cruz Valley, over the pass of Punta Unión, to Colcabamba or Vaquería (see Llanganuco to Santa Cruz below). In this direction the climb is gentler, giving more time to acclimatize, and the pass is easier to find. You can hire an *arriero* and mule for about US$8/day. 3 km N of Cashapampa, 1-2 hrs hike, are the hot-baths of Huancarhuas. It is almost impossible to hitch from the end of the trail back to

Yungay. There are 2 daily buses from Yanama to Yungay; you have to be on the road at Vaquería by 0800-0900, US$4, 3 hrs. Travellers describe this journey down to Yungay as exhilerating and terrifying.

The Alpamayo valley This offers a beautiful, but difficult, 6-8 day trek from Cashapampa to Pomabamba; for the experienced only.

For hikes in the **Cordillera Negra**, a truck leaves from Caraz market at 1000 to Huata at 2,700m (dirty hotel, **F**). From here you can climb to the Quebrada de Cochacocha (3,500m) at the top of which is the Inca ruin of Cantu (excellent views), and on to the Inca lookout, **Torreón Andino** (5,006m). Take water, food and tent with you. Allow 3 days for the hike; there are lagoons near the peak.

Seek advice from Prof Bernardino Aguilar Prieto in Caraz, San Martín 1143, T 791161; refer to his Torreón Andino Information book before climbing it.

YUNGAY

The main road goes on to **Yungay**, 12 km S of Caraz, which was completely buried during the 1970 earthquake by a massive mudslide; a hideous tragedy in which 20,000 people lost their lives. The earthquake and its aftermath are remembered by many residents of the Callejón de Huaylas. The original site of Yungay, known as Yungay Viejo, desolate and haunting, has been consecrated as a *camposanto* (cemetery). The new settlement is on a hillside just N of the old town, and is growing gradually. It has a pleasant plaza and a concrete market, good on Thur and Sun.

Local fiestas Oct 17: Virgen del Rosario; **Oct 28**: anniversary of the founding of the town.

● **Accommodation E** pp *COMTURY*, Complejo Turístico Yungay, Prolongación 2 de Mayo 1019, 2.5 km S of the new town, 700m E of main road in Aura, the only neighbourhood of old Yungay that survived, T 722578, nice bungalows, pleasant country setting, hot water, fireplace, restaurant with regional specialities, camping possible; **E** *Hostal Gledel*, Av Arias Graziani, N past plaza, T 793048, a few cheaper rooms available, owned by Sra Gamboa, who is

hospitable and a good cook, shared bath, hot water, excellent meals prepared on request, nice courtyard, highly rec; **E** *Hostal Yungay*, Jr Santo Domingo on plaza, T 793053, basic, shared bath; **F** *Hostal Blanco*, follow the hospital street at N end of plaza and continue up hill, there are signs, T 793115, shared bath, basic, nice views.

● **Places to eat** *Alpamayo*, Av Arias Graziani s/n, at N entrance to town, good; *El Portal*, by the market, fair. There are several small *comedores* in and around market and by the plaza.

● **Transport** Buses, colectivos and trucks run the whole day to Caraz, 12 km, US$0.45, and Huaraz, 54 km, 1½ hrs, US$1.10. To Yanama, via the Portachuelo de Llanganuco pass at 4,767m, 58 km: buses and trucks leave Yungay daily from in front of the Policía Nacional, 1 block S of plaza, at around 0800 but you may have to wait until they are full, 4-5 hrs, US$4.50. Some buses and trucks continue to San Luis, a further 61 km, 3 hrs, US$2.50, Huari (61 km) and Chavín (38 km, 6 hrs, US$3.50); on Tues and Sat the bus continues N to Piscobamba and Pomabamba (US$11 Yungay-Pomabamba). Buses or colectivos will do the route to the Llanganuco lakes when there are enough people, and only in the dry season, 1½ hrs; colectivo US$4.50, bus US$2.50. Huaraz travel agencies organize trips to Llanganuco for about US$8.

EXCURSIONS FROM YUNGAY

A day walk from Yungay to **Mirador de Atma** gives beautiful views of Huascarán, Huandoy and the Santa valley. It is about a 3-hr round trip.

Matacoto, 6 km from Yungay, is in the Cordillera Negra at 3,000m, with excellent views of Huascarán, Huandoy and other major peaks. The turn-off is at Huarazcucho (Km 251), 3 km S of new Yungay; it is another 3 km W from here, across the bridge over the Río Santa. Camping possible, kitchen and hot baths, US$6, ask for Susana Scheurich (German, she also speaks English, French and Italian). Horse hire in Matacoto US$3/half day, ask for Pachamanca, recommended. Daily minibuses from Yungay; also trucks on Wed and Sun 0700-1300, US$0.50. Matacoto can also be reached from Mancos (3 hrs trekking; see below).

LLANGANUCO TO SANTA CRUZ TREK

For trekkers, one of the finest walks (trees, flowers, birds, midges) is over the path by Huascarán and the lakes at **Llanganuco** (Orcon Cocha and Chinan Cocha) from Yungay to Piscobamba. The Park office is situated below the lakes at 3,200m, 17 km from Yungay. Accommodation is provided for trekkers who want to start from here, US$2 pp. The entrance fee to the park is US$1/day, but is based purely on trust.

Although you can start hiking up the Llanganuco valley from the park office, most hikers continue by bus or truck to Vaquería or Colcabamba where the Llanganuco-Santa Cruz trail starts. From the park office to the lakes takes about 5 hrs (a steep climb). There is a *refugio* at the lakes. From the lakes to the pass will take a further 2-3 hrs, with perfect views of the surrounding peaks.

From the Portachuelo de Llanganuco down to **Vaquería** at 3,700m, about 9 km, takes $2\frac{1}{2}$ hrs. The trail makes a short cut to **Colcabamba**, 4 km, 3 hrs. There is basic lodging and food in Colcabamba, should you decide to stay there. Familia Calonge is recommended, friendly, good meals. You can arrange an *arriero* and mule for about US$9/day.

From Colcabamba, the Santa Cruz trek goes to Huaripampa, Punta Pucaraju, then up the steep climb to the highest point, Punta Unión, 4,750m. From here it is downhill through the Santa Cruz valley to Cashapampa (trucks to Caraz, US$1.35, 2 hrs, and buses) and the village of Santa Cruz, 5 hrs' walk from Caraz.

CARHUAZ

After Yungay, the main road goes to Mancos (8 km S, 30 mins) at the foot of Huascarán. There is one hostal, some basic shops and restaurants.

From Mancos it is 14 km to Carhuaz, a friendly, quiet mountain town with a pleasant plaza. There is very good walking in the neighbourhood (eg to thermal baths; up the Ulta valley). Market days are Wed and Sun (the latter is much larger). The local fiesta of *Virgen de las Mercedes*, Sept 14 to 24, is rated as the best in the region.

● **Accommodation D** pp *Casa de Pocha*, 1 km out of town towards Hualcán, at foot of Nevado Hualcán, ask directions in town, T cellular 613-058 (Lima 462-1970), inc all meals, country setting, entirely solar and wind energy powered, hot water, sauna, home-produced food (vegetarian available), horses for hire, camping possible; **E** *Hostal Residencial Carhuaz*, Av Progreso 586, T 794139, just off plaza, cheaper without bath, varying standards of rooms (check first), basic but pleasant, hot water, nice courtyard and garden; **F** *Hostal La Merced*, Ucayali 600, T 794327, excellent, hot water, rec. Due to open in 1997 is *Casa Blanca*, in Acopampa, 3 km S of town, T 794149, ask at *Heladería El Abuelo* on the plaza.

● **Places to eat** *Los Pinos*, Av Amazonas 645, good typical food and set meals, rec; *El Palmero*, Av Progreso 490, good value. Several other restaurants on the plaza. *Café Heladería El Abuelo*, Plaza de Armas, D'Onofrio and local ice-cream, sweets, also sells regional maps and guides.

● **Transport** There are trucks (only 1 or 2 a day) and one minivan (0800) going up the Ulta valley to Chacas (see page 1255), 87 km, 4-5 hrs, US$4.50. The road works its way up the Ulta valley to the pass at Punta Olímpica from where there are excellent views. The dirt road is not in a very good condition owing to landslides every year (in the wet season it can be closed). The trucks continue to San Luis (see page 1255), a further 10 km, $1\frac{1}{2}$ hrs. Each Thur, a bus (Transportes Huandoy) does the trip from Carhuaz to Chacas and returns, US$6 one way, 5 hrs. To Huaraz, colectivos and buses, 0500-2000, US$0.65, 1 hr; to Caraz, 0500-2000, US$0.90, 1 hr.

Carhuaz to Huaraz The main road goes on from Carhuaz 6 km to **Marcará**; **E** *Alojamiento Restaurant Suárez*, Leguia 144, basic, shared bath, and other basic restaurants and shops. Pick-ups and colectivos go from here **E** along a branch road 3 km to **Chancos**, a little settlement with hot baths (two very basic *alojamientos* and several basic restaurants and food stalls).

From Marcará the road and transport continue to **Vicos**, 3 km further up the Huandoy valley (7 km, from Marcará, $1\frac{1}{2}$ hrs, US$1.50). Vicos is in superb surroundings with views of Nevados Tocllaraju and Ranrapalca. It is a 2-hr hike Chancos to Vicos. From Vicos, one can walk through the Quebrada Honda, over the Portachuelo de Honda at 4,750m, to Chacas; about 4 days, an excellent, not difficult hike.

The main Carhuaz-Huaraz road goes on to **Taricá**, where there is a home pottery industry (good value purchases from Francisco Zargosa Cordero) and thence to Huaraz, 26 km from Marcará, 1 hr, US$0.50.

● **Accommodation F** *Hostal Sterling*, no hot water, food, friendly.

TREKKING IN THE CORDILLERA BLANCA

Hilary Bradt writes: The Cordillera Blanca offers the most popular backpacking and trekking in Peru, with a network of trails used by the local people and some less well defined mountaineers' routes. Most circuits can be hiked in 5 days. Although the trails are easily followed, they are rugged and the passes very high – between 4,000 and nearly 5,000m – so backpackers wishing to go it alone should be fit and properly acclimatized to the altitude, and carry all necessary equipment. Essential items are a tent, warm sleeping bag, stove, and protection against wind and rain (climatic conditions are quite unreliable here and you cannot rule out rain and hail storms even in the dry season). Trekking demands less stamina since equipment can be carried by donkeys.

● **Sources of information The South American Explorers' Club** publishes a good map with additional notes on the popular Llanganuco to Santa Cruz loop, and the Instituto Geográfico Nacional has mapped the area with its 1:100,000 topographical series. These are more useful to the mountaineer than hiker, however, since the trails marked are confusing and inaccurate. Apart from the book by Hilary Bradt (see Information for travellers), a useful guide to the area currently in print is *Peruvian Andes* by Philipe Beaud, costs US$24, available through Cordee in the UK, some shops in Huaraz and the South American Explorers' Club. See also *Callejón de Huaylas y Cordillera Blanca*, a good guide to the area, by Felipe Díaz, in Spanish, English and German; *The High Andes*, John Biggar (Castle Douglas: Andes, 1996); *Climbing in The Cordillera Blanca*, by David Sharman. The hikes mentioned in this chapter, and others, are described in more detail in the *Peru Handbook*.

● **Maps** An excellent map of the Callejón de Huaylas and Cordillera Huayhuash, by Felipe Díaz, is available in many shops in Huaraz and at Casa de Guías. Maps of the area are available from the IGN in Lima. Hidrandina, the state hydroelectric company, at 27 de Noviembre 773, has dye-line maps of the Cordillera Blanca, open in morning only. Several guides and agencies have their own sketch maps of the most popular routes. Maps are also available by mail-order from Latin American Travel Consultants, PO Box 17-17-908, Quito, Ecuador, F (593-2) 562566, Internet: LATC@pi.pro.ec.

Advice to climbers

The height of the Cordillera Blanca and the Callejón de Huaylas ranges and their location in the tropics create conditions different from the Alps or even the Himalayas. Fierce sun makes the mountain snow porous and the glaciers move more rapidly. The British Embassy advises climbers to take at least 6 days for acclimatization, to move in groups of four or more, reporting to the Casa de Guías or the office of the guide before departing, giving the date at which a search should begin, and leaving the telephone number of your Embassy with money. Rescue operations are very limited; insurance is essential (cannot be purchased locally), since a guide costs US$40-50 a day and a search US$2,000-2,500 (by helicopter, US$10,000).

Be well prepared before setting out on a climb. Wait or cancel your trip when weather conditions are bad. Every year climbers are killed through failing to take weather conditions seriously. Climb only when and where you have sufficient experience.

NB Check locally on political conditions. A few robberies of hikers have taken place; do not camp near a town or village, never leave a campsite unattended and always hike with others when heading into the remote mountain districts.

On all treks in this area, respect the locals' property, leave no rubbish behind, do not give sweets or money to children who beg and remember your cooking utensils, tent, etc, would be very expensive for a campesino, so be sensitive and responsible.

CORDILLERA HUAYHUASH AND RAURA

The **Cordillera Huayhuash** lying S of the Cordillera Blanca, is perhaps the most spectacular in Peru for its massive ice faces which seem to rise sheer out of the contrasting green of the Puna. Azure trout-filled lakes are interwoven with deep quebradas and high pastures around the hem of the range. You may see tropical parrokeets in the bottom of the gorges and condors circling the peaks. The circuit is very tough; allow 12 days. There are up to eight passes over 4,600m, depending on the route. Both ranges are approached from Chiquián in the N, Oyun in the S or Cajatambo to the SW.

A 5-day minimum hike to Laguna Jahuarcocha from Chiquián is recommended for those not wishing to do the full circuit: fantastic landscapes and insights into rural life.

Chiquián is usually the starting point for the Huayhuash circuit. It is a town of narrow streets and overhanging eaves. An interesting feature is a public television mounted in a box on a pedestal which sits proudly in the Plaza de Armas.

● **Accommodation & places to eat** F *Hostal San Miguel*, Jr Comercio 233, nice courtyard and garden, many rooms, popular, rec; F *Hostal Inca*, 1 block from plaza. A good, basic restaurant is *Yerupajá*, Jr Tarapacá 351. Buy all your food and supplies in Huaraz as there is little in Chiquián.

● **Transport** Three daily buses run from Huaraz to Chiquián (El Rápido, between Raymondi and Tarapacá, Huaraz, Virgen del Carmen and one other), 120 km, 3-4 hrs, US$2, dep Huaraz about 1400, Chiquián 0500. There are also trucks on the route, leaving from the market, not daily. A minibus can be hired for up to 10 people, US$40. It is not well-travelled. Direct buses go from Chiquián to Lima, 353 km, 8 hrs, US$5.25, with Tubsa, Firesa and Cavassa overnight. There is also a connection from Chiquián to Huallanca, some trucks and buses doing this route, not daily. Trucks and buses go on to La Unión and Huánuco. **Mule hire** It may take a day to bring the mules to Chiquián from Llamac or Pocpa where they are kept. (Very basic supplies only can be bought in either village.) Ask for mules (US$5/day) or horses (US$7/day) at the hotels or restaurants in Chiquián. A guide for the Huayhuash is Sr Delao, ask for him in Chiquián.

Cajatambo is the southern approach to the Cordillera Huayhuash, a small, friendly market town. Electricity supply 1800-2200.

● **Accommodation & places to eat** G *Hostal Miranda*, Jr Huascarán 120, just behind the church, homely, laundry, small rooms, rec; G *Hostal Cajatambo*, Plaza de Armas 173, basic, cheap, restaurant; G *Hostal Trinidad*, Jr Raimondi 141, behind town hall, basic, bring your own door lock. Good restaurants are *Andreita*, *Carmencita* and *Vicky*, all around the plaza.

● **Transport** Two buses to Lima at 0600, US$7, daily with Empresa Andina (office on plaza next to *Hostal Cajatambo*), and daily except Thur with Tours Bello Perú; stop at Pativilca for lunch, fantastic views, sit on right side.

Northern Peru

A N AREA of great and diverse interest: elegant Spanish cities, some restored (Trujillo), some in ruins (Saña), former Indian settlements transformed into quaint towns (Cajamarca, Chiclayo, Piura), monumental ruins of highly-skilled pre-Inca cultures (Chan-Chan, Kuelap, Tucumé) and a region poised for major tourist development (Sipán, Batán Grande, Huaca El Brujo and Moro). There are mountain villages with local customs and on the coast, deep-sea fishing, surfing, and the "caballitos de totora" reed rafts at Huanchaco and Pimentel. Between the oases, all the way to Ecuador, the desert, with sweeping grey dunes and dusty cliffs contains rare flora and fauna, including the iguana and the *huerequeque*, the long-legged bird portrayed on prehispanic pottery to symbolize hospitality.

North of the mouth of the Río Santa the Andes recede, leaving a coastal desert belt 8 to 16 km wide containing the three great oases of Northern Peru – the areas of Trujillo, Chiclayo and Piura.

North of Chimbote the Highway crosses the valleys of Chao and Virú, and after 137 km reaches Trujillo. In the valley there is an abrupt line between desert and greenery. Cultivation requires irrigation ditches which take their water from far up in the mountains.

TRUJILLO

Trujillo (*Pop* 750,000; *Phone code* 044), capital of the Department of La Libertad, disputes the title of second city of Peru with Arequipa. The greenness surrounding the city is a delight against the backcloth of brown Andean foothills and peaks. Founded by Diego de Almagro in 1534 as an express assignment ordered by Francisco Pizarro, the city was named after the latter's native town in Spain.

Places of interest

The focal point is the pleasant and spacious **Plaza de Armas**. The prominant sculpture represents agriculture, commerce, education, art, slavery, action and liberation, crowned by a young man holding a torch depicting liberty. Fronting it is the **Cathedral**, dating from 1666, with its museum of religious paintings and sculptures next door (Mon-Sat 0800-1400, US$2). Also on the Plaza are the *Hotel Libertador*, the colonial style Sociedad de Beneficencia Pública de Trujillo and the Municipalidad.

The **Universidad de La Libertad**, second only to that of San Marcos at Lima, was founded in 1824. Near the Plaza de Armas, at Jr Pizarro 688, is the spacious 18th century **Palacio Iturregui**, now occupied by the **Club Central**, an exclusive and social centre of Trujillo, open 1100-1300 and 1600-2000. Exhibitions of local ceramics are often held.

Also on the Plaza is the Republican-style **Casa Urquiaga (or Calonge – Banco Central de Reserva)**, Pizarro 446, free entry, open 0900-1600 Mon-Sat, which contains valuable precolumbian ceramics; the other is **Casa Bracamonte (or Lizarzaburo)**, Independencia 441, now closed; and the **Lynch House**, next to the Cathedral, boasting the oldest façade in the city.

Other mansions, still in private hands, include **Casa del Mayorazgo de Facalá**, Pizarro 314, now Banco Wiese, free entry when bank is open; **Casa de la Emancipación**, Jr Pizarro 610 (Banco Continen-tal), is where independence from Spain was sworn, open daily 0900-1300 and 1700-2000; the **Casa del Mariscal de Orbegoso**, Orbegoso 553, is a museum owned by Banco Internacional, open daily 0900-1300 and 1600-1900, free entry; **Casa Ganoza Chopitea**, Independencia 630, architecturally the most representative house in the city.

One of the best, the 17th century **La Merced** at Pizarro 550, with picturesque

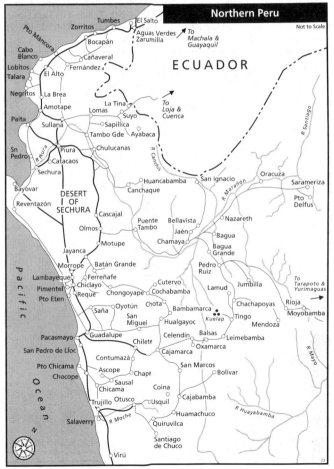

Northern Peru

Not to Scale

moulded figures below the dome, is being restored, but part of the dome has collapsed because of building work next door. **El Carmen** church and monastery at Colón y Bolívar, has been described as the 'most valuable jewel of colonial art in Trujillo'. Next door is the Pinacoteca Carmelita. **La Compañía**, near Plaza de Armas, is now an auditorium for cultural events. **San Francisco** on the 6th block of Almagro; **Santa Clara** on the 4th block of Junín; **San Agustín** on the 6th block of Mcal Orbegoso; **Santa Ana** on the 2nd block of the same street; and **Santo Domingo** on the 4th block of Bolognesi.

Museums

Museo de Arqueología, Casa Risco, Junín y Ayacucho, open 0800-1300 (entrance, US$1), houses a large and interesting collection of pottery.

The basement of the **Cassinelli** garage on the fork of the Pan-American and Huanchaco roads contains a superb private collection of Mochica and Chimú pottery, recommended. Demonstrations of the whistling *huacos* are given; entry, US$2.50, open 0830-1130, 1530-1730.

Museo de Zoología de Juan Ormea, Jr San Martín 349 (0800-1400); interesting displays of Peruvian animals, en-

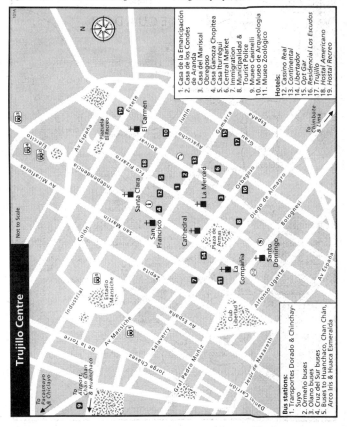

Trujillo Centre

Not to Scale

1. Casa de la Emancipación
2. Casa de los Condes de Aranda
3. Casa del Mariscal Obregoso
4. Casa Gamoza Chopitea
5. Casa Iturregui
6. Central Market
7. Immigration
8. Municipalidad & Tourist Police
9. Museo Casinelli
10. Museo de Arqueología
11. Museo Zoológico

Hotels:
12. Cassino Real
13. Continental
14. Libertador
15. Pizarro
16. Residencial Los Escudos
17. Trujillo
18. Hostal Americano
19. Hostal Recreo

Bus stations:
1. Transportes Dorado & Chinchay-Suyo
2. Ormeño buses
3. Chiari buses
4. Cruz del Sur buses
5. Buses to Huanchaco, Chan Chán, Arco Iris & Huaca Esmeralda

trance free (but donations welcome, and needed).

Local festivals

The two most important festivals are the *National Marinera Contest* (last week of Jan) and the *Festival Internacional de La Primavera* (last week of Sept), featuring beauty pageants and Trujillo's famous *Caballos de Paso*. First week of May is the Festival del Mar, a celebration of the disembarkation of Taycanamo, the leader of the Chimú period. A procession is made in Totora boats.

Local information

NB Trujillo has confusing double street names: the smaller printed name is that generally shown on maps, in guide books and in general use.

● Accommodation

A1 *Libertador*, Independencia 485 on Plaza de Armas, T 232741, F 235641, inc tax, pool, full of character, cafeteria and restaurant, continental breakfast US$5, excellent buffet lunch on Sun, rec; **A2** *El Gran Marqués*, Díaz de Cienfuegos 145-147, Urb La Merced, T/F 249582, inc tax and breakfast, modern, pool, restaurant, rec; **A3** *Los Conquistadores*, Diego de Almagro 586, T 244505, F 235917, inc tax and American breakfast, bar, restaurant, very comfortable.

C *Continental*, Gamarra 663, T 241607, F 249881, opp market, inc tax, good, safe, restaurant rec; **C** *Hostal Residencial Las Terrazas*, Av Manuel Vera Enríquez 874, Urb Primavera, behind Hotel Primavera, T 232437, hot water, phone, garage, cafeteria, garden, pool, good value; **C** *Opt Gar*, Grau 595, T 242192, good, excellent restaurant (lunch only for non-guests) and snack bar, rec; **C** *Res Los Escudos*, Orbegoso 676, T 255961, make sure you ask for the hot water to be switched on, small garden, expensive laundry service, secure, rec; **C** *San Martín*, San Martín 743-749, T 234011, **D** without bath, good value, small restaurant, good for breakfast, noisy, rec; **C** *Vogi*, Ayacucho 663, T 243574, inc tax, safe, quiet, rec.

D *Hostal Recreo*, Estete 647, T 246991, safe, restaurant, rec; **D-E** *Hostal Residencial Las Flores*, Atahualpa 282-284, T 242527, big rooms, good value; **D-E** *Primavera*, Av N de Piérola 872, Urb Primavera, nr Empresa Díaz bus terminal, T 231915, F 257399, hot water, restaurant, bar, good value; **D-E** *Roma*, Nicaragua 238, next to El Aguila bus station, T 259064, secure, helpful, luggage stored, rec; **D-E** *Trujillo*, Grau 581, T 243921, good value, rec.

E *Grau*, Grau 631, T 242332, with bath, good value; **E** *Hostal Americano*, Pizarro 792,

T 241361, a vast, rambling old building, next to cinema, rooms without bath are noisy and very basic, most rooms without window (Nos 134 and 137, and those either side of 303, have windows, balconies and good views), safe, good meeting place.

There are several cheap hotels on Ayacucho, all of which are decaying and very basic, eg **F** *Hostal Lima*, 718, T 244751, popular with gringos, dirty, baths terrible. Familia Moreno, Húascar 247, **E**, nr centre, quiet, safe, or Catrina Castillo, Pedro Muñiz 792 (10 blocks from the Plaza de Armas) **F**.

Youth hostel: **E** *Hostal Rossel*, Av España 252, T 253583, F 256282.

● Places to eat

Typical restaurant with good reputation and higher prices is *El Mochica*, Bolívar 462. *Chifa Oriental*, Gamarra 735, rec; *El Pesquero*, Junín 118, good fish; *Pollería El Bolívar*, Pizarro 501 y Plaza de Armas, good chicken and salad for US$2.50; *24 Horas*, Jr Gamarra 700 block, reasonably priced meals, always open; *ABC*, Orbegoso y San Martín, good for chicken; *De Marco*, Pizarro 725, good, especially the ice creams and coffee, set menu US$2.50, desserts and cakes, good source of information for passing cyclists (Lucho D'Angelo who works there, has accommodation for cyclists); *El Sol*, Pizarro 660, good, cheap set meals, vegetarian dishes; *Juguería San Agustín*, Pizarro 691, good juices, good *menú*, popular, excellent value; *La Nonna*, Pizarro 722, good, cheap local food; *Pizzería Valentino*, Orbegoso block 2, very good; *Reyno del Sol*, Bolívar 438, good breakfasts and vegetarian meals, friendly, open 0800; *La Selecta*, Pizarro 870, set lunch for US$1.75, good value; *El Paraíso*, Pizarro 871, rec vegetarian; *La Pizza Nostra*, Pizarro 568, Italian dishes, cheap chicken and fries. Good, cheap seafood restaurants at Plazuela El Recreo, at the end of Pizarro, outdoor seating, pleasant atmosphere. Wholewheat bread at *Panadería Chalet Suizo*, Av España e Independencia. Cheap meals in the market at Grau y Gamarra. It's difficult to find a meal before 0800. A Mon speciality is *shambar*, a thick minestrone made with ham.

● Airline offices

Faucett, Pizarro 532, T 232771, F 232689; AeroPerú, Pizarro 470, T 234241/242727; Aero Continente, Av España 307, T 248174, T/F 244592.

● Banks & money changers

Banco de Crédito, Gamarra 562, no commission on cash or TCs (Amex) into soles only, good rates, Visa cash advance; Interbanc, Pizarro y Gamarra, good rates for cash, no commission on TCs, reasonable rate, Visa cash advance; Banco Wiese, Pizarro 314, *Casa de Mayorazgo* de Facalá, good rates for TCs, no commission into soles, cash on Mastercard. Banks close 1300-1615, they give same rate for cash dollars as street changers, casas de cambio and travel agencies.

● **Embassies & consulates**
British, Honorary Consul, Mr Winston Barber, Jesús de Nazareth 312, T 235548; **Finnish**, Bolívar 200, T 276122; **German**, Honorary Consul, Dr Guillermo Guerra Cruz, C Estados Unidos 105-107, Urb El Recreo, T 245903, F 261922.

● **Entertainment**
Las Tinajas, Pizarro y Almagro, on Plaza de Armas, pub-disco, live rock music and peña on Sat; Luna Rota, América Sur 2119, at end of Huayna Capac, popular; La Taberna, Av Húsares de Junín 350, Urb La Merced, good for Andean folk music; Camana Video Pub, San Martín 791, good at weekends.

● **Hospitals & medical services**
Hospital: Clínica Peruana Americana, Av Mansiche 702, T 231261, English spoken, good.

● **Post & telecommunications**
Post Office: Independencia y Bolognesi.
Telecommunications: Telefónica del Perú, Bolívar 658, national and international phone calls and faxes.

● **Security**
The city is generally safe but be especially careful at bus stations when arriving or leaving; guard your luggage very carefully. Also take care beyond the inner ring road, Av Mansiche, towards the hill and in the Sánchez Carrión district at night.

● **Shopping**
Camera repairs: Laboratorios de Investigación Científica, San Martín 745, over Fuji shop opp Hotel San Martín, good. Hugo Guevara, **G&M Color**, Ayacucho 825, T 255387, and España 2787, T/F 259483, 1 hr developing service and electrical repairs.

Markets: Mercado Central on Gamarra; Mercado Mayorista on Roca.

NB Tourists may be approached by vendors selling huacos and necklaces from the Chimú period; the export of these items is strictly illegal if they are genuine, but they almost certainly aren't.

● **Sports**
Outdoor swimming pool next to Mansiche stadium, where buses leave for Chan Chán and Huanchaco; open 0900-1300 and 1600-1800, US\$0.50.

● **Tour companies & travel agents**
Trujillo Tours, San Martín y Almagro 301,

T 233091, F 257518, work with Lima Tours; Sigma Tours, Pizarro 570, T 201335, F 201337, rec; many others. Prices vary and competition is fierce so shop around for best deal. Few agencies run tours on Sun and often only at fixed times on other days. To Chan Chán, el Dragón and Huanchaco, US\$15 pp; to Huacas del Sol and de la Luna, US\$13 pp; to El Brujo, US\$20-25 pp; city tour US\$6.50 pp (minimum of 2 people; discounts for 4 or more).

Guides: Clara Bravo, Huayna Capac 542, T 260003/243347, is an experienced official tourist guide with her own transport; she speaks Spanish, English, German and understands Italian. She takes tourists on extended circuits of the region and is good for information (archaeological tour US\$16 for 6 hrs, city tour US\$7 pp). She also offers accommodation in Trujillo and Huanchaco, US\$5 pp. Another rec official guide is José Soto Ríos, who can be contacted at the Tourist Police office on Independencia (see below) or at Atahualpa 514, T 251489, he speaks English. Pedro Puertas, English speaking, not an official guide but very knowledgeable, often unavailable, at Km 560 on the Panamericana Norte, 2½ km from the Plaza de Armas, he can also be contacted through Hostal Americano. Other experienced guides are Oscar and Gustavo Prada Marga, Miguel Grau 169, Villa del Mar. The tourist office has a list of official guides; average cost US\$7/hr.

● **Tourist offices**
Caretur, Independencia 628, T/F 258216, private organization, helpful, free information. Maps available from Touring and Automobile Club, Argentina 278, Urb El Recreo, T 242101; also from Librería Ayacucho, Ayacucho 570. **Tourist Police** have an office at Pizarro 402, on the corner of Plaza de Armas, open daily 0800-2000; also at Independencia 630, Casa Ganoza Chopitea. They are very helpful, provide useful information, and most of the staff speak English. They will negotiate a good price for taxis to visit sites; expect to pay around US\$24 per car for 3-4 hrs. Any complaints about tourist services should be addressed to the Ministerio de Industria y Turismo, Av España 1801, T 245345/245794.

● **Useful addresses**
Immigration: Av Larco 1220, Urb Los Pinos. Gives 30-day visa extensions, US\$20 (proof of funds and onward ticket required), plus US\$1 for formulario in Banco de la Nación (fixers on the street will charge more).

● **Transport**
Local Bus and colectivos: on all routes, US\$0.20-0.35; colectivos are safer as there are fewer people and fewer pick-pockets. **Taxi**: town trip, US\$1. Chan Chán, airport US\$5;

Huanchaco, US$6.50. Beware of overcharging, check fares with locals. Taxi from *Hotel Libertador*, US$7/hr, or contact Tourist Police (see above). Taxi driver Jorge Enrique Guevara Castillo, Av del Ejército 1259, Altos 1, rec. Another taxi driver, Félix Espino, T 232428, reliable, good value. English chartered accountant Michael White (speaks fluent Spanish and a useful amount of German) provides transport, plus translation and business services, very knowledgeable about tourist sites, he also produces and sells t-shirts with local motifs; see under **Guides** above, Clara Bravo, for address.

Air To Lima, 1 hr, daily flights with Faucett, AeroPerú and Aero Continente; to Chiclayo 30 mins, Faucett; to Piura, 45 mins, AeroPerú; to Tarapoto, Aero Continente; to Iquitos, AeroPerú. Check flight times as they change frequently. Taxi to airport, US$5; or take bus or colectivo to Huanchaco and get out at airport turn-off (US$0.25); or take colectivo from Huanchaco and pay extra US$0.40 to be dropped off at entrance.

Buses To Lima, 548 km, 8-9 hrs on good road. There are many bus companies doing this route, among those rec are: Ormeño, Av Ejército 233, T 259782, normal service 4 daily, US$7.50, super especial (meal, drinks inc), US$19.50; Cruz del Sur, Av Ejército 285 and Av Mansiche 331, T 261801, US$8.70; Empresa Díaz, Nicolás de Piérola 1079 on Panamericana Norte, T 234476, US$6.50, at 2130. Trans Olana (Oltursa), Av Ejército 342, T 2603055, offer a *bus cama* service to Lima, with full reclining seats, a/c, heating, meals and drinks, US$22.50, dep 2300; connection at Lima for Arequipa. Cheaper buses tend to arrive at night and do not have terminals, dropping passengers in the street. To **Pacasmayo**, 120 km, 2 hrs, US$1.50, several buses and colectivos a day; similarly to **Chiclayo**, 209 km, 3 hrs, US$3-3.50, Trans Chiclayo, Mansiche 301, T 243341; and on to **Piura**, 278 km, 6 hrs, US$6.50 (Transportes Dorado, Daniel Carrión y Av Mansiche, T 242880, at 1830, 1930; Chinchay-Suyo, González Prada 337, also at Carrión, T 246818, US$5.30, at 1215, 2220); and **Tumbes**, 282 km, 1530, 9-10, 12 hrs (Cruz del Sur at 2000); to **Huaraz**, 319 km, via Chimbote and Casma (169 km), direct, 9-11 hrs (Cruz del Sur, US$6.50, Chinchay-Suyo, US$7.85, both at 1930) several buses and colectivos to **Chimbote**, El Sol/LitPerú/América Express from Tupac Yupanqui 300, 135 km, 2 hrs, US$2.50. To **Cajamarca**, 300 km, 7-8 hrs, US$6.50; Trans Vulcano, Carrión 140, T 235847, at 1030, 2130 (also to Chiclayo); Trans Mercurio, Av Mansiche 403, at 2230; Empresa Díaz at 1300, 2200. Transportes Guadalupe, Av Mansiche 331, has buses to **Tarapoto**, via Jaén, Chachapoyas and Moyobamba, departing at 1000 daily, 24 hrs, US$20.

ARCHAEOLOGICAL SITES NEAR TRUJILLO

The crumbling ruins of **Chan Chán**, the imperial city of the Chimú domains and largest adobe city in the world, are about 5 km from the city. The ruins consist of nine great compounds built by Chimú kings. The 9m high perimeter walls surrounded sacred enclosures with usually only one narrow entrance. Inside, rows of storerooms contained the agricultural wealth of the kingdom, which stretched 1,000 km along the coast from near Guayaquil to Paramonga.

Most of the compounds contain a huge walk-in well which tapped the ground water, raised to a high level by irrigation higher up the valley. Each compound also included a platform mound which was the burial place of the king, with his women and his treasure, presumably maintained as a memorial. The Incas almost certainly copied this system and transported it to Cusco where the last Incas continued building huge enclosures. The Chimú surrendered to the Incas around 1471 after 11 years of siege and threats to cut the irrigation canals.

The dilapidated city walls enclose an area of 28 sq km containing the remains of palaces, temples, workshops, streets, houses, gardens and a canal. What is left of the adobe walls bears well-preserved moulded decorations and painted designs have been found on pottery unearthed from the debris of a city ravaged by floods, earthquakes, and *huaqeros*. Heavy rain and flooding in 1983 damaged much of the ruins and although they are still standing, many of the interesting mouldings are closed to visitors. The **Ciudadela of Tschudi** has been reconstructed (15 mins walk from the road), open 0900 to 1700 (but it may be covered up if rain is expected). Museum on the main road, US$1, at least 500m before the turn-off to the site.

● **Access to Chan Chán** A ticket which covers the entrance fees for Chan Chán, Huaca El Dragón and Huaca La Esmeralda (for 2 days) costs US$2.50. A guide costs US$6-7; map and leaflet in English US$0.75. Buses and combis

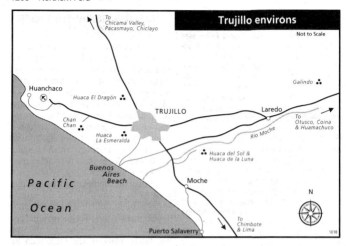

Trujillo environs

Not to Scale

To Chicama Valley, Pacasmayo, Chiclayo

Huanchaco

Huaca El Dragón

TRUJILLO

Galindo

Laredo

To Otusco, Coina & Huamachuco

Chan Chán

Río Moche

Huaca La Esmeralda

Pacific Ocean

Buenos Aires Beach

Huaca del Sol & Huaca de la Luna

Moche

N

To Chimbote & Lima

Puerto Salaverry

leave from José Gálvez 394, corner of Los Incas, nr Mercado Mayorista, or corner of España and Industrial; nos 114A or B and 6B, US$0.35, 20 mins to the turn-off (see also Huanchaco **Transport** below); taxi, US$5. Tourist police are on duty at the turn-off on the Trujillo-Huanchaco road and at Chan Chán. It is relatively safe to walk on the dirt track from turn-off to site, but go in a group and don't stray from the road as robberies have occurred; a mototaxi can be taken from the turn-off, US$1. If alone, contact the Tourist Police in Trujillo to arrange for a policeman to accompany you. On no account walk the 4 km to, or on Buenos Aires beach nr Chan Chán as there is serious danger of robbery, and of being attacked by dogs.

The restored temple, **Huaca El Dragón**, dating from Huari to Chimú times (1000-1470 AD), is also known as **Huaca Arco Iris** (rainbow), after the shape of friezes which decorate it. It is on the W side of the Pan-American Highway in the district of La Esperanza; taxi costs US$2; open 0800-1700.

The poorly restored **Huaca La Esmeralda** is at Mansiche, between Trujillo and Chan Chán, behind the church (not a safe area). Buses to Chan Chán and Huanchaco pass the church at Mansiche. The tour to Chan Chán includes a visit to these ruins.

A few kilometres S of Trujillo are the huge Moche pyramids, the **Huaca del Sol** and the **Huaca de la Luna** (open 0800-1600, entry US$2). The interior passageways of the Huaca de la Luna are not open to visitors, though a guided tour from on-site archaeologists may be possible; the site is under the control of the tourist police; interesting friezes are being excavated by students from the University (five discovered since 1992). The Trujillo Pilsen brewery is currently sponsoring excavations.

● **Access** Taxi about US$8 return; bus or colectivo marked Mayorista or Huacas, 20 mins, US$0.30 from corner of Zela near Mercado Mayorista, or colectivos about hourly from C Suárez y Los Incas. If you want a walk, get out at Bodega El Sol on the right hand side of the road; opposite is a huge Pilsen sign. Here starts a path to Moche, about an hour's interesting walk through farmland; it is inadvisable to walk unless in a large group.

North of Trujillo is the sugar estate of **Hacienda Cartavio**, in the Chicama valley (43 km). One of the biggest sugar estates in the world, also in the Chicama valley, is the Casa Grande cooperative. It covers over 6,000 ha and employs 4,000 members. Visits (guided) are only possible before 1200; many buses and combis, US$0.75.

60 km N of Trujillo, is considered one of the most important archaeological sites

on the N coast. The complex, covering 2 square km, consists of Huacas Prieta, Cortada and Cao Viejo. This complex is collectively known as **El Brujo** and was an important Moche ceremonial centre.

Huaca Cortada (or El Brujo) has a wall decorated with high relief stylized figures. Huaca Prieta is, in effect, a giant rubbish tip dating back 5,000 years, which once housed the very first settlers to this area. In front of Cao Viejo are the remains of one of the oldest Spanish churches in the region. It was common practice for the Spaniards to build their churches near these ancient sites in order to counteract their religious importance.

● **Access To El Brujo**: you can reach the complex from Cartavio (possibly combining with a visit to the rum factory). Taxis and mototaxis are available from Cartavio market; better to pay them to wait at the site and take you back. Alternatively take a bus to Chocope on the Pan-American Highway N; from there take a combi to Magdalena de Cao and walk 8 km to the site, or ask a combi to take you to El Brujo and wait or drop you off and return later (don't pay full fare in advance, US$5 each way from Chocope). It is better to go in the morning as there are more people around. There is a better chance of finding transport in Cartavio. Buses to Cartavio and Chocope leave Trujillo from González Prada y Los Incas and pass along Av Mansiche. It may be easier to hire a car if you're in a group, or take a guided tour. Clara Bravo (see **Guides** above) charges US$53/car (4 people) to El Brujo for the 4-5 hrs round trip (extension to Sipán, Tucumé, Brüning museum possible). For more information, ask the Tourist Police (see above).

HUANCHACO

Narrow pointed fishing rafts, known as *caballitos* (little horses) *de totora*, made of totora reeds and depicted on Mochica and Chimú pottery are still a familiar sight in many places along the northern Peruvian coast. Unlike those used on Lake Titicaca, they are flat, not hollow, and ride the breakers rather like surfboards (you can rent one on the beach, beware of rocks in the surf). You can see fishermen set off in their reed rafts at around 0500, returning to shore about 0800 when they stack the boats upright to dry in the fierce sun.

The village, now developed with the beach houses of the wealthy of Trujillo, is overlooked by a huge church from the belfry of which are extensive views. Children sell imitation precolumbian *objets d'art* and beads. It's cheaper to stay in Huanchaco than Trujillo but the choice of restaurants is more limited. Entry to pier, US$0.10.

NB The strength of the sun is deceptive; a cool breeze off the sea reduces the temperature, but you can still be badly sunburned. The beaches S of the pier are quite dirty, but are much cleaner northwards around the bay.

Local festivals Several times a year, especially at Easter, Festival del Mar (the biggest *fiesta* in Huanchaco), the annual Olímpidas Playeral and El Festival Internacional de la Primavera (see also under Trujillo). Surf competitions are held.

● **Accommodation** C *Caballito de Totora*, Av La Rivera 217, T 232201, inc taxes, **D** in low season, pool, nice garden, restaurant, parking, good value, rec; **C** *Hostal Bracamonte*, Los Olivos 503, T 230808, comfortable, good, chalets with private bath, or converted caravans, you can camp on the grass, pool, own water supply, emergency generator, rents bicycles, secure, good restaurant, English spoken, highly rec; **D** *Hostal Sol y Mar*, Los Ficus 570, T 245524, pool, restaurant, garden, rec; **D** *Hostal Huanchaco*, Larco 287 on Plaza, T 230813, shared bath, cold water, pool, expensive cafeteria with home-made cakes and other good meals, video, pool table, rec; **D** *Hostal Los Esteros*, Av Larco 618, T 230810, hot water, restaurant, safe motorcycle parking; **E** *Casa de los Amigos*, Las Gardineras 373, nr *Hotel Bracamonte*, German-owned, basic, intermittent cold water supply, kitchen facilities, sun terrace, **F** to camp in garden; **F-G** *Hostal Solange*, Ficus 484, 1 block from beach, with bath, hot water, good food, highly rec; **F** pp *Golden Club*, Av La Rivera 217, T 241189, 8 rooms, gym, pool, restaurant, use of kitchen, popular with surfers, laid back, excellent value, rooms on first floor cheaper, rec; **F** pp *La Casa Suiza*, run by Heidi and Oscar Stacher, Los Pinos 451, 3 blocks from beach, shared bath, 3 rooms with private bath, cold water, nice roof balcony, excellent breakfast US$1, highly rec, good juices at shop next door. Basic accommodation at the house of the very friendly Señora Lola, Manco Capac 136, **G** pp, basic, laundry, noisy at weekends. Opposite is Sr Carlos Sánchez Leyton, **G**, good, safe, cold water. Señora Nelly Neyra de Facundo offers accommodation at Las Palmeras 425, **G**, rec.

Accommodation, inc food, with families is easy to find, US$2-3 a day, such as friendly English-speaking Sra Mabel Díaz de Aguilar, nr the football ground.

● **Places to eat** Good fish restaurants on the sea front, eg Malecón Larco 602; *Violetta*, a private house – 4 blocks directly inland from the pier (good meals provided for US$1) and Familia Flores, popular; *El Tramboyo*, nr the pier, good, helpful, friendly; *Lucho del Mar*, excellent seafood, check the bill; next door is *Estrella Marina*, good fish, great value; *Piccolo*, 5 blocks from plaza, cheap, friendly, live folk music weekend evenings, excellent; *Club Colonial*, on plaza, run by Belgians, fish, chicken or meat, excellent but expensive, US$20 for 2, rec. Good fish also at *Pisagua*, just past the pier, and *La Esquina*, C Unión 299, opp the pier. *Arroyitos Chickens*, C Atahualpa 135, excellent roast chicken, fries and salad for US$2. Try *picarones*, people come from Trujillo at weekends especially to eat them. Do not eat fish in the hut-like restaurants on the way into town from Trujillo as they aren't hygienic.

● **Post & telecommunications** Post Office at Manco Kapac 306, open 0900-1445.

● **Transport** Combis between Trujillo and Huanchaco are 114A or B; they both do a clockwise circuit of Huanchaco and run to the Cassinelli museum, then A goes round the W side of Trujillo onto Av 28 de Julio and Av Vallejo/Los Incas as far as Zela, while B goes round the E side on Av Industrial, España and Vallejo/Los Incas also to Zela. At night B goes only to España y Grau; both run till 2300 (later at weekends). Fare US$0.35, 20 mins. 'Micros' follow similar routes to Los Incas, but in daylight only; colectivos and some radio taxis run at night. Taxi US$6.50.

Puerto Chicama, 70 km N of Trujillo is known by surfers as the best surf beach in Peru, claiming that it has the longest left-hand point-break in the world. There are a few basic places to stay and eat. It's a real surfers' hang-out with friendly locals.

FROM THE COAST TO CAJAMARCA

---

1. FROM TRUJILLO

To the NE of Trujillo is Cajamarca, which can be reached either from Trujillo or from Pacasmayo (paved throughout). The old road NE to Cajamarca is terrible and (for cyclists especially) lonely, taking 12-15 hrs (as opposed to 8 hrs via Pacasmayo – see below), but it is more interesting, passing over the bare puna before dropping to the Huamachuco valley. Off it lies **Otusco**, an attractive Andean town with narrow cobbled streets. In **Agallpampa** there is one, unsigned *hostal*. Further on, at the mining town of Shorey, a road branches off to **Santiago de Chuco**, birthplace of the poet César Vallejo, where there is the annual festival of Santiago El Mayor in the second half of July. The main procession is on 25 July, when the image is carried through the streets. Close to Yancabamba is *Hostería El Viajero* and in Quiruvilca there is one hotel.

HUAMACHUCO

The road runs on to this colonial town, 181 km from Trujillo, formerly on the royal Inca Road. It has a huge main plaza and a controversial modern cathedral. There is a colourful Sun market. A 2-hr walk (take the track which goes off to the right just after crossing the bridge on the road to Trujillo) takes you to the extensive ruins of hilltop pre-Inca fortifications, **Marca-huamachuco** (taxi US$25 for 3-4 hrs, US$5 pp if 5 people). Nearby, beyond the local radio station, 1 hr's walk, are the pre-Inca ruins of **Viracochabamba**.

Worth seeing in the Huamachuco area are **Laguna Sausacocha** (with Inca ruins nearby) and *haciendas* Yanasara and Cochabamba, deep down in the valley of the Río Chusgón, about 2-3 hrs by truck E of the town. At **Yanasara**, there are hot springs, good, US$1, basic accommodation, run by priests. There is a guesthouse at Cochabamba, which used to be the Andean retreat of the owners of the Laredo sugar plantation, near Trujillo. The climate, at about 2,300m, is mild.

● **Accommodation** F *Hostal Okay*, C Atahualpa 147, no sign, new; F *Hostal Noche Buena*, on plaza, new; F *Hostal San Francisco*, Sánchez Carrión 380, hot shower; G *Fernando*, Bolívar 361, good value; G *La Libertad*, not rec, rooms and bathrooms filthy.

● **Places to eat** *Café Venezia*, San Martín 315, superb snacks and cakes; *El Caribe* on plaza serves local dishes; *El Cairo*, Sánchez Carrión 754, good food and service, rec.

● **Buses** From Trujillo, Trans Sánchez López,

Vallejo 1390, T 251270, and Trans Palacios, España 1005, T 233902, spectacular journey through mining settlements, views of snow-capped peaks, over 4,100m pass, US$6, 8 hrs, most buses at night (take warm clothing), try to go by day. There are also colectivos from Trujillo. Direct bus to Lima, 24 hrs. Regular combis to **Cajabamba**, almost hourly, 2 hrs, US$4.

CAJABAMBA

From Huamachuco the road runs on 48 km through impressive eucalyptus groves to **Cajabamba**, which lies in the high part of the sugar-producing Condebamba valley. It has an attractive Plaza de Armas.

● **Accommodation** F *Flores*, toilet, on the Plaza de Armas. Other hotels and restaurants.

● **Buses**   Regular combis daily to Huamachuco; US$4, 2 hrs. Two direct buses a day from Trujillo, 12 hrs. To Cajamarca, via San Marcos (below) with Trans Palacios and Empresa Atahualpa, 6 hrs, US$6, 0700, 1400, 1900.

Cajabamba can also be reached in a strenuous but marvellous 3-4 days hike from **Coina**, 132 km E of Trujillo at 1,500m in the Sierra Alto Chicama. The first day's walk brings you to Hacienda Santa Rosa where you stay overnight. Then you cross the mountains at about 4,000m, coming through Arequeda to Cajabamba. The ruins at Huacamochal may be seen en route; the scenery is spectacular. It is advisable to hire a guide, and a donkey to carry the luggage. A map of the route is available from the Post Office in Coina.

● **Accommodation** D *Hostería El Sol*, full board or bed only, built by the late Dr Kaufmann, who opened a hospital for local people here; details from *Hostería El Sol*, Los Brillantes 224, Santa Inés, Trujillo, T 231933, Apdo 775.

The road continues from Cajabamba through **San Marcos** to Cajamarca. San Marcos is important for its Sun cattle market; both it and Cajabamba are on the Inca Road.

● **Accommodation & transport** There are 3 hotels inc **G** pp *Nuevo*, with bath, water shortages, but clean and quiet. Bus to Cajamarca (124 km), Atahualpa and Empresa Díaz leaving early in the morning, takes 6 hrs US$3.60.

2. PACASMAYO TO CAJAMARCA

Pacasmayo (*Pop* 12,300), port for the next oasis N, is 142 km N of Trujillo, and is the main road connection from the coast to Cajamarca. The paved 180 km road to Cajamarca branches off the Pan-American Highway soon after it crosses the Río Jequetepeque. The river valley has terraced rice fields and mimosas may often be seen in bloom, brightening the otherwise dusty landscape.

A few kilometres N on the other side of Río Jequetepeque are the ruins of **Pacatnamú** comparable in size to Chan Chán – pyramids, cemetery and living quarters of nobles and fishermen, possibly built in the Chavín period. Evidence also of Moche tribes. Micro bus to Guadelupe, 10 km from ruins, and taxi possible from there (Ortiz family, Unión 6, T 3166), US$20. Where the Pan-American Highway crosses the Jequetepeque are the well-signed ruins of **Farfan** (separate from those of Pacatnamú, but probably of the same period).

● **Accommodation**   E *Ferrocarril*, 1½ blocks from Pacasmayo seafront on small plaza, quiet, no hot water (ask for water anyway); F *Duke Kalanamoku*, C Ayacucho 44, safe, quiet, rec; F *Panamericano*, Leoncio Prado 18, with private cold shower, good value, safe, reasonable restaurant downstairs; F *San Francisco*, opp *Panamericano*, basic, OK. Several cheap restaurants on the main street.

103 km E of Pacasmayo is the mining town of **Chilete**. 21 km from Chilete, on the road N to San Pablo, are the stone monoliths of **Kuntur Wasi**. The site is undergoing new development under a Japanese archaeological team.

● **Accommodation** Hotels *Amazonas* and *San Pedro*, **G**, filthy bathrooms. Rooms are hard to find on Tues because of Wed market.

40 km S of Chilete is the attractive town of **Contumazá** on an alternative route from Trujillo to Cajamarca. This passes through the cane fields and rice plantations of the Chicama valley before branching off to climb over the watershed of the Jequetepeque. Further along the road to Cajamarca is **Yonán**, where there are petroglyphs.

CAJAMARCA

Cajamarca (*Pop* 70,000; *Alt* 2,750m; *Phone code* 044), is a beautiful colonial town and the most important in the northern mountain area. Here Pizarro ambushed and captured Atahualpa, the Inca emperor.

Places of interest

The **Cuarto de Rescate** is not the actual ransom chamber but in fact the room where Atahualpa was held prisoner. It is open 0900-1300, 1500-1745, 0900-1245 Sat and Sun, closed Tues, US$1.35, entrance on Amalia Puga beside San Francisco church (ticket also valid for Belén church and nearby museums). The room was closed to the public for centuries and used by the nuns of Belén hospital. The Plaza where Atahualpa was ambushed and the stone altar set high on **Santa Apolonia hill** where he is said to have reviewed his subjects can also be visited (small entrance fee). There is a road to the top, or the physically fit can walk up from C 2 de Mayo, using the steep stairway.

The **Plaza de Armas**, where Atahualpa was executed, has a 350-year-old fountain, topiary and gardens. The **Cathedral**, opened in 1776, is still missing its belfry. On the opposite side of the Plaza is the 17th century **San Francisco Church**, older and more ornate than the Cathedral, with the **Museo de Arte Colonial**. A guided tour of the museum includes entry to the church's catacombs.

The **Complejo Belén** comprises the Institute of Culture, a museum, art gallery and a beautifully ornate church, considered the city's finest. Connected to the church is the **Pinacoteca**, a gallery of local artists' work, which was once the kitchen of an 18th century hospital for men. Across the street is a maternity hospital from the same era, now the **Archaeological Museum** (see below).

Other churches well worth seeing are **San Pedro** (Gálvez y Junín), **San José** (C M Iglesias y Angamos), **La Recoleta** (Maestro y Casanova) and **Capilla de La Dolorosa**, close to San Francisco.

The city has many old colonial houses with garden patios, and 104 elaborate carved doorways. See the **Bishop's Palace**, next to the Cathedral; the **Palace of the Condes de Uceda**, now occupied by the Banco de Crédito on Jr Apurímac 719; the house of **Toribio Casanova**, Jr José Gálvez 938; the house of the **Silva Santiesteban family**, Jr Junín 1123; and the houses of the **Guerrero** and **Castañeda** families.

Museums

The **Education Faculty of the University** has a museum at Del Batán 283 with objects of the pre-Inca Cajamarca culture, not seen in Lima. Open 0800-1200, 1500-1700 in winter, and 0800-1200 in summer, US$0.20 (guided tour). The University maintains an experimental **arboretum** and agricultural station. The **Archaeological Museum**, opposite the Belén church at Junín y Belén, has a wide range of ceramics from all regions and civilizations of Peru, samples of local handicrafts and costumes used during the annual carnival celebrations. All museums are closed on Tues but open at weekends.

Excursions

The surrounding countryside is splendid.

Aylambo is a village which specializes in ceramics. You can visit the *Escuela/Taller* where children learn pottery, open Mon-Fri 0730-1200, 1300-1700, Sat 0730-1230.

6 km away are the warm sulphurous thermal springs known as **Los Baños del Inca**, where there are baths whose temperature you can control. The baths are cleaned after each user; open 0500-2000 daily, public bath US$0.65, private bath US$0.90, swimming pool US$0.45 (take your own towel). Atahualpa tried the effect of these waters on a festering war wound. Buses and combis marked Baños del Inca every few minutes from Amazonas, US$0.25, 15 mins.

Other excursions include **Llacanora**, a typical Andean village in beautiful scenery. **La Colpa**, a *hacienda* which is now a cooperative farm of the Ministry of Agriculture, breeds bulls and has a lake and gardens. **Ventanillas de Otusco**, part of an old pre-Inca cemetery, has a gallery

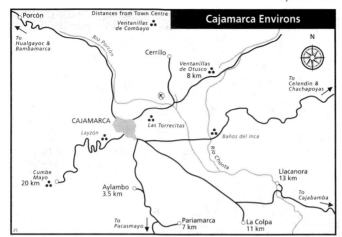

Cajamarca Environs

Distances from Town Centre

Porcón

To Hualgayoc & Bambamarca

Río Porcón

Ventanillas de Combayo

Cerrillo

Ventanillas de Otusco 8 km

To Celendín & Chachapoyas

N

CAJAMARCA

Layzón

Las Torrecitas

Baños del Inca

Río Chonta

Cumbe Mayo 20 km

Aylambo 3.5 km

Llacanora 13 km

To Cajabamba

To Pacasmayo

Pariamarca 7 km

La Colpa 11 km

of secondary burial niches (US$0.75 entry). A 1-day round trip can be made, taking a bus from Del Batán to Ventanillas de Otusco (30 mins) or colectivos leaving hourly from Revilla 170, US$0.15, walk to Baños del Inca (1½ hrs, 6 km); walk to Llacanora (1 hr, 7 km); then a further hour to La Colpa.

A road goes to **Ventanillas de Combayo**, some 20 km past the burial niches of Otusco. These are more numerous and more spectacular, being located in a rather isolated, mountainous area, and are distributed over the face of a steep 200m high hillside.

Cumbe Mayo, a *pampa* on a mountain range, is 20 km SW of Cajamarca. It is famous for its extraordinary, well-engineered pre-Inca channels, running for several kilometres across the mountain tops. It is said to be the oldest man-made construction in South America. The sheer scale of the scene is impressive and the huge rock formations are strange indeed, but do take with a pinch of salt your guide's explanations. On the way to Cumbe Mayo is the Layzón ceremonial centre.

● **Access to Cumbe Mayo** There is no bus service; guided tour prices are about US$7 pp (rec in order to see all the pre-Inca sites); taxi US$15. The *hostal* at the site is **F** pp. A milk truck

goes daily to Cumbe Mayo leaving at 0400 from C Revilla 170. Ask Sr Segundo Malca, Jr Pisagua 482; small charge, dress warmly. To walk up takes 4 hrs. The trail starts from the hill of Santa Apolonia (Silla del Inca), and goes to Cumbe Mayo straight through the village and up the hill; at the top of the mountain, leave the trail and take the road to the right to the canal. The walk is not difficult and you do not need hiking boots. Take a strong torch. The locals use the trail to bring their goods to market.

Local festivals

The *pre-Lent Carnival* is very spectacular and regarded as one of the best in the country; it is also one of the most raucous. In Porcón, 16 km to the NW, **Palm Sunday** processions are worth seeing. On **24 June**: is *San Juan* in Cajamarca, Chota, Llacanora, San Juan and Cutervo. An agricultural fair is held in July at Baños del Inca; on the first Sun in Oct is the *Festival Folklórico* in Cajamarca.

Local information

● **Accommodation**

During Oct there are numerous school trips to this area, so most of the budget hotels are full at this time. Similarly at Carnival.

A2 *Laguna Seca*, at Baños del Inca, T 923149, in pleasant surroundings, private hot thermal baths in rooms, swimming pool with thermal water, restaurant, bar, disco, horses for hire, rec.

B *Continental*, Jr Amazonas 760, T 922758, hot water, good restaurant, noisy, rec; **B-C** *Hostal*

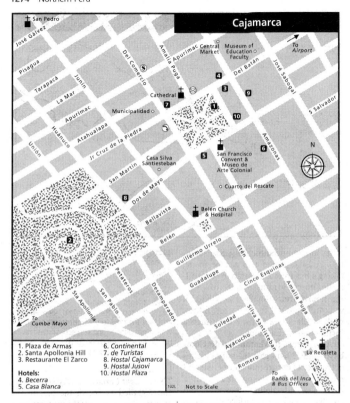

Cajamarca

1. Plaza de Armas
2. Santa Apollonia Hill
3. Restaurante El Zarco

Hotels:
4. Becerra
5. Casa Blanca
6. *Continental*
7. *de Turistas*
8. *Hostal Cajamarca*
9. *Hostal Jusovi*
10. *Hostal Plaza*

Not to Scale

Cajamarca, in colonial house at Dos de Mayo 311, T 922532, F 928813, hot water, phone, food excellent, travel agency next door, rec; owners also run **A3-B** *Albergue San Vicente*, outside the town at Santa Apollonia, T 922644, in an old hacienda, totally remodelled in the style of Gaudi; **B-C** *Hostal Los Pinos*, Jr La Mar 521, T/F 925992, inc breakfast, a lovely colonial-style house.

C *Turistas* (60 rooms) on Plaza de Armas, T 922470/71, T 922472, laundry service, 2 restaurants, bar, parking extra; **C** *Casa Blanca*, Dos de Mayo 446 on Plaza de Armas, T/F 922141, safe, nice building and garden, good.

D *Hostal Atahualpa*, Pasaje Atahualpa 686, T 922157, hot water in mornings only, good value; **D** *Hostal Becerra*, Del Batán 195 (unsigned), T 923496, intermittent tepid water, modern; **D** *Hostal Jusovi*, Amazonas 637, T 922920, comfortable, hot water only in am, safe; **D** *Hostal José Gálvez*, Av Manco Capac 552, at Baños del Inca, T 920203, with private thermal bath, good value; **D** *Hostal San Lorenzo*, Amazonas 1070, T 922909, T/F 926433, hot water, helpful; **D** *Hostal Turismo*, Dos de Mayo 817, T 923427, can be noisy at weekends, rec.

E *Hostal Delfort*, Apurímac 851, nr market, with bath, spacious, good value; **E** *Hostal Dos de Mayo*, Dos de Mayo 585, T 922527, shared bath, hot water am and evening, good value *menú* in restaurant, rec; **E** *Hostal Plaza*, Plaza de Armas 669, T 922058, old building with handmade wood furnishings, mainly large rooms with many beds, private bath and balcony (F without bath), hot water but poor water supply, quiet, rec (especially rooms 4 and 12), with new annex (dirty but is open at 0200); **E** *Hostal Sucre*, Amalia Puga 815, T 922596, with toilet and wash basin in each room, water am only, good value, sometimes noisy, not very safe, poor restaurant upstairs.

F *Hostal San José*, Angamos 358, T 922002, shared bath, basic, cheap, hot water. Rooms to rent at *Restaurant Encuentro Tupanakuy*, Huánuco 1279, **G** pp; also at *Restaurant Carimbó*, Dos de Mayo 712, **E** pp inc meals.

● **Places to eat**

Los Faroles, Jr Dos de Mayo 311, in *Hostal Cajamarca*, local specialities, friendly, informal, rec, *peña* in the evening; *Salas*, on Plaza, fast service, good, cheap local food, best *tamales* in town; *El Zarco*, Jr Del Batán 170, very highly rec, much frequented by local residents, inexpensive, also has short *chifa* menu, good vegetarian dishes, excellent fish; *El Real Plaza*, Jr Dos de Mayo 569, good food; *Las Rocas*, Dos de Mayo 797, excellent sandwiches, cheap; *La Namorina*, on edge of town on road to Baños del Inca, opp Ché service station, renowned for its speciality, *cuy frito*; *El Cajamarqués*, Amazonas 770, excellent, tables in garden of colonial building; *Rocco's Pizza Bar*, Jr Cruz de Piedra 653, 1500-0030, good pizza, popular with local kids; *Om-Gri*, San Martín 360, nr Plaza de Armas, Italian dishes, rec; *El Batán Gran Bufet*, Del Batán 369, arty bar/restaurant, live music, craft shop, great food and atmosphere; *Michelangelo*, on the corner of Del Batán y Amazonas, fast food, pizza, chifa. *Los Maderos*, Amazonas 807, local specialities and *peña*, open 2100-0300 Mon-Sun; *Bananas*, Dos de Mayo on Plaza, good juices, fruit salads, yoghurt, sandwiches, pizza, good music. For early breakfasts go to the market.

Food specialities: *Queso mantecoso* (full-cream cheese); *manjar blanco* (sweet); *humitas* (ground maize with cheese); *cuy frito* (fried guinea pig); eucalyptus honey (sold in the market on C Amazonas; said to be a cure for rheumatism). Try the flaky pastries filled with apple or *manjar blanco* from the street sellers. The area is renowned for its dairy produce; many shops sell cheese, *manjar blanco*, butter, honey, etc: try *La Pauca* at Amazonas 713, or *Manos Cajamarquiñas* at Tarapacá 628.

● **Banks & money changers**

Banco de Crédito, Jr del Comercio y Apurímac, changes TCs without commission, cash advance on Visa; Banco Continental, Tarapacá 721, changes TCs US$5 commission minimum. Dollars can be changed in most banks, travel agencies and the bigger hotels; better rates from street changers on Jr Del Batán and Plaza de Armas.

● **Language schools**

Instituto de Idiomas de Cajamarca, Jr Dos de Mayo 360, T/F 926054, full range of courses in Spanish.

● **Laundry**

Jr Amalia Puga 545, expensive.

● **Post & telecommunications**

Post Office: Serpost at Del Batán 133 on Plaza de Armas, 0800-2045.

Telecommunications: Telefónica del Perú main office on Plaza de Armas, Jr Del Comercio s/n; also at Amalia Puga 1022, and Amazonas 518; for national and international calls.

● **Shopping**

Handicrafts are cheap, but bargain hard. Specialities inc cotton and wool saddlebags (*alforjas*). Items can be made to order. The market on Amazonas is good for *artesanía*.

● **Tour companies & travel agents**

A group of local guides has formed *Cumbemayo Tours*, Amalia Puga 635 on Plaza, T/F 922938, highly rec, with tours to Ventanillas de Otusco (US$5 pp), Cumbe Mayo (US$6.50 pp), Kuelap and Gran Vilaya (US$30 pp a day, 7 day tour). *Aventuras Cajamarca*, office next to *Hotel Casa Blanca*, T/F 923610, run by Jorge Caballero, rec. *Inca Baths Tours*, Amalia Puga 807, rec for Cumbe Mayo (US$7 pp). Several travel agenices around the Plaza de Armas offer trips to local sites and further afield (eg Kuelap, normally a 5-day trip, US$200 pp). A rec tour guide is Edwin Vásquez, ask for him in the *Cuarto de Rescate* or *Hostal Dos de Mayo*.

● **Tourist offices**

In the cultural centre next to the Belén church, open 0900-1800, T 922834, helpful. Also tourist information at the Museum at Del Batán 283.

● **Transport**

Air Expreso Aéreo flies Lima-Cajamarca daily, direct or via Chimbote, 1½ hrs; also Cajamarca-Chachapoyas, 3 a week; office at Jr Del Comercio 700, T/F 923419. Airport 3 km from town; taxi US$3.

Buses To Lima, 856 km, 17-19 hrs, US$9-11; the road is paved, several buses daily. To Pacasmayo, 189 km, 5-6 hrs, US$8, several buses and colectivos daily. To Trujillo, 296 km, 7½ hrs, US$5-7, 10-12 buses daily, 1200-2230; most continue to Lima. To Chiclayo, 260 km, 7 hrs, US$6, several buses daily, most continuing to Piura (US$11.15) and Tumbes. To Celendín, 112 km, 4 hrs, US$4.35, at 0630 and 1300; the route follows a fairly good dirt road through beautiful countryside. Also to Cajabamba, 75 km, US$6, 6 hrs, several daily. Most bus companies are on Atahualpa, eg: Expreso Sudamericano, No 300, T 923270; Palacios Transporte, No 322, T 925855; Trans Vulcano, No 318, T 921090; Nor Perú, No 302, T 924550; Atahualpa, No 299, T 923060; Empresa Díaz, Ayacucho 753, T 923449; Empresa Trans Mercurio, Juan XXIII s/n, T 925630; Expreso Cajamarca, Independencia 319, T 923337; El Cumbe, Independencia 242, T 923088; Tepsa, Sucre y Reina Farje, T 923306. The bus offices on

Atahualpa and Independencia are 15-20 mins' walk S of the centre.

THE CHACHAPOYAS REGION

Cajamarca is a convenient starting point for the trip E to the province of Amazonas, which contains the archaeological riches of the Chachapoyans, also known as Sachupoyans. Here lie the great pre-Inca cities of Gran Vilaya, Cerro Olán and the immense fortress of Kuelap, among many others.

● **Recommended reading** The whole area is full of largely unexplored remains; some of them have been studied by the Swiss archaeologists Henri and Paula Reichlen (who surveyed 39 sites in 1948 – see *Récherches archaeologiques dans les Andes du haut Utcubamba*, in *Journal des Américanistes*, which includes an accurate map), and the American archaeologist Gene Savoy (who went further than the Reichlens; see his book *Antisuyo*). Kaufmann Doig refers to them as the "12 Cities of the Condors"; his map showing their location is in his *Arqueología Peruana*. In 1992 he started a new project in the area. Ask if he is in Chachapoyas as he is worth contacting. See also Morgan Davis' book, *The Cloud People, an Anthropological Survey*. Also the booklet on Kuelap, available in Chachapoyas, very informative (ask Carlos Torres Mas, see below). *The Peru Handbook* gives more details.

CELENDIN

East from Cajamarca, the first town of note is **Celendín**, where there is a cinema and cock fighting Sun night in the local arena. Festival 16 July (Virgen del Carmen). There is also an interesting local market on Sun where you can buy cheap sandals and saddlebags. The town has electricity from 1800 to 0100.

3 hrs SE from Celendín by bus (US$2.25) is the village of **Oxamarca**. From here it is 10 km, or a 2½ hrs walk, to the ruins of **La Chocta**. Ask Gregorio Sánchez Junio in Celendín at Jr San Martín 423 for maps and information about local ruins.

● **Accommodation** A few basic *hostales*, all on Jr 2 de Mayo: **E** *Hostal Celendín*, with bath, on the plaza, good restaurant; **E** *Amazonas*, J Gálvez, 4 blocks from plaza, OK, clean, helpful.

● **Places to eat** *Santa Isabel*, Jr José Gálvez 512, clean, OK; *Bella Aurora*, good but not open in evenings; the market is OK as well.

● **Transport** To Cajamarca, 107 km, 4½ hrs, see under Cajamarca **Buses**. Atahualpa dep at 0500, continue to Chiclayo, 3 hrs stop in Cajamarca, US$11.40, arrive early to get a seat. Bus to Balsas, 55 km, 5 hrs, US$3. Trucks daily. On to Leimebamba, 89 km, 7 hrs, US$5.20. It is almost impossible to get transport from Balsas to Leimebamba, except the one pick-up a week from Celendín; probable waiting time 2-3 days. On to Tingo, 45 km, 2 hrs, US$6; several combis daily. On to Chachapoyas, 38 km, 1½ hrs, US$1.75; several combis daily. To Chachapoyas, 227 km, Trans Virgen del Carmen and Jaura twice a week each (usually in convoy), 20-25 hrs (35 or more in the rainy season, US$12). **NB** It is common for buses to leave later than the set time, to break down and to suffer long delays (up to several days) in the wet season. Always bring warm clothing and food on these journeys.

ROUTES The road, in bad condition to Chachapoyas (but due for improvement as far as Leimebamba in 1997), follows a winding course through the N Andes, crossing the wide and deep canyon of the Río Marañón at Balsas. The road climbs steeply with superb views of the mountains and the valleys below. The fauna and flora are spectacular as the journey alternates between high mountains and low rainforest. After rain, landslides can be quite a problem.

LEIMEBAMBA

There are plenty of ruins around this pleasant town, many of them covered in vegetation. Among them are: La Congona, La Joya, Torre Puco and Tim Bamba. Find a local to explain the area and show the way to the ruins as it is easy to get lost.

Of the ruins in the area **La Congona**, a Chachapoyan site, is easily reached without a guide. It is a brisk 2½ hrs walk along a clearly-marked trail which starts at the end of the street with the hotels. La Congona is a system of three hills: on the easterly, conical hill, the ruins are clustered in a small area, impossible to see until you are right above them. The views are stupendous and the ruins worth the effort. This is the best preserved of three sites, with 30 decorated round stone houses (some with evidence of 3 storeys) and a watch tower. The other hills have been levelled. There are two other sites, El Molinete and Pumahuanyuna, nearby. All three can be visited in a day but a guide (US$5) is essential.

- **Accommodation** Two hotels, the better of which is **G** *Escobedo*, very basic, water in mornings and evenings, electricity in evenings only.
- **Places to eat** Several restaurants, inc *El Sabor Tropical*, good chicken and chips; breakfast at restaurant a few doors down. *Oasis*, just off Plaza de Armas, and *El Caribe* on the Plaza, basic meals.
- **Transport** Two buses leave Chachapoyas for Celendín on Tues and arrive in Leimebamba around 1400-1500; US$5.20; no guarantee of a seat. There are also combis, minibuses and trucks.

NORTH FROM LEIMEBAMBA

The road to Chachapoyas crosses the Utcubamba river, passes through **Palmira** and heads North. Before Puente Santo Tomás there is a turn-off which heads E beyond **Duraznopampa** to the small town of **Montevideo**. An hour's walk SE of Montevideo is the ruined complex of **Rumichaco/Monja**, spread along a ridge above the town. Local guides can be hired; ask for Tito Rojas Calla in Montevideo. There are no hotels in the town but ask the owner of the only restaurant if you can sleep there.

Another Chachapoyan site is **Cerro Olán**, reached by colectivo to San Pedro de Utac, a small village beyond Montevideo, then a 30-min walk. From the Plaza a trail rises directly into the hills E of town to the ruins, which can be seen from the village. Here are the remains of towers which some archaeologists claim had roofs like mediaeval European castles.

Further N are the towns of Yerbabuena and **Puente Santo Tomás**, which is at the turn-off for the burial *Chullpas* of **Revash**, belonging to the Revash culture (AD 1350-1538). In Yerbabuena there is one unnamed basic *hospedaje*, **G**, running water but no electricity. There is also *Restaurant Karina*, which is cheap.

The attractive town of **Jalca Grande** (or La Jalka as it is known locally), at 2,600m, lies between Montevideo and Tingo, up on the E side of the main valley. In the town itself, one block W of the Plaza de Armas, is the interesting and well-preserved Chachapoyan habitation of **Choza Redonda**, which was inhabited

until 1964. Half an hour W of the town are the ruins of **Ollape**, a series of platforms with intricate fretwork designs and wide balconies.

- **Accommodation** There are no hotels but ask the alcalde. Take a torch.
- **Transport** One combi daily from Ubilon, on the main road N to Tingo, or a strenuous 3 hr walk uphill.

TINGO

Tingo (*Alt* 1,800m) is about 25 km from Leimebamba, 37 km S of Chachapoyas, up the Utcubamba valley. Much of the village was washed away in the floods of 1993. High up on mountains above Tingo is Tingo Nuevo. There is no running water or electricity in Tingo. Police register all foreigners going up the hill to Kuelap.

- **Accommodation & places to eat** **F** pp *Albergue León*, basic, behind *Restaurant Kuelap*, run by Lucho León, who is very knowledgeable. *Miss Tony*, by the police station, good food; *Kuelap*, almost opp, clean, okay. Also reasonable is *El Edén*, at Jr Kuelap 120.
- **Transport** There are combis (from 0500) and pick-ups daily to Chachapoyas, 1½ hrs, US$1.50, last back around 1400-1500. For Celendín, see **Transport** under that town. Several camionetas daily to Kuelap, US$2.20. There are occasional combis to Puente Santo Tomás, US$1.35; or walk part of the way and board a passing combi.

KUELAP

Kuelap (3,000m) – or Cuelap as it is locally known – is a spectacular pre-Inca walled city which was re-discovered in 1843. It was built over a period of 200 years, from AD 1100 to 1300 and contained 3 times more stone than the Great Pyramid at Giza in Egypt. The site lies along the summit of a mountain crest, more than a kilometre in length. The massive stone walls, 700m long by 175m wide at their widest, are as formidable as those of any precolumbian city. Some reconstruction has taken place, mostly of small houses and walls, but the majority of the main walls on both levels are original, as is the cone-shaped dungeon.

Entrance fee is US$4.50 (including US$1 for use of camera), opening hours 0800-1700. The ruins are locked; the guardians, Vargas Silva family, have the keys. They offer basic accommodation, meals and camping space.

- **Access** From Chiclayo to Chachapoyas (see below). Best to leave Chachapoyas early am to get to Kuelap, then spend the night near the ruins before returning to Chachapoyas the following morning. You need at least 5 days to visit Kuelap from Chiclayo. The new road from Tingo to Kuelap is very circuitous (1½ hrs by car from Tingo; very few vehicles make it up to the ruins). Horses, donkeys and guides can be hired in Tingo for US$5-7/day. It's a steep 4 hrs' walk uphill from Tingo; take waterproof, food and drink, and start early as it gets very hot. Only the fit should try to ascend and descend in one day on foot. In the rainy season it is advisable to wear boots; at other times it is hot and dry (take all your water with you as there is nothing on the way up). Camionetas or combis go very early, usually Sat/Sun from Tingo market, to Pueblo María (US$3.50, 1 a day), from where it's a 2 hr walk to the ruins; sleep at the ruins, then walk back down to Tingo.

- **Accommodation** The last house to the right of the track (El Bebedero) offers accommodation (bed, breakfast and evening meal US$6, good meals, friendly, helpful); see also above. There is also a camping area.

- **Further accommodation & services** Oscar Arce Cáceres based at 'El Chillo' nr the Río Utcubamba, 4½ km outside Tingo, who owns a farm and knows the area very well, will help the traveller. He has accommodation with bath (US$10pp), good meals at US$5, stores luggage. The trek into this area, like the walk up to Kuelap, starts from Tingo; the way is all mule track. The walk from El Chillo to Kuelap is shorter than from Tingo; the return to El Chillo can be made via the village of Nogalcucho (ask for directions). In Magdalena (a 30-min walk from Tingo), Abram Torres will be happy to provide one with his services as guide, and his mule, for the first leg of the journey as far as Choctamal, about 4 hrs away. A lodge is being built at Choctamal by Los Tambos Chachapoyanos; the first floor and six bathrooms are complete. Choctamal is the midpoint on the 36-km tortuous road from Tingo to Kuelap. It is also three quarters of the way up the Abra Yumal pass, which crosses the cordillera to Gran Vilaya (see below). Staying at Choctamal thus makes it much easier to hike to Gran Vilaya; the lodge fee of US$10 includes food and guide for expeditions.

GRAN VILAYA REGION

US explorer Gene Savoy discovered this extensive set of ruined complexes in 1985. There are about 30 sites spread over this vast area, among which are Pueblo Alto, Pueblo Nuevo, Paxamarca and Machu Llacta. It is recommended to take a letter of introduction from Dr Carlos Torres Mas in Chachapoyas. Ask the alcalde for accommodation, meals and assistance in finding a guide, which is essential.

- **Access** The whole area stretches W from the Río Utcubamba to the Río Marañon. Head N from Tingo or S from Chachapoyas as far as the Huinchuco bridge across the Río Utcubamba. On the W bank of the river a road leads to the left, if heading N, to the town of Colcamar, which is the starting point for exploring this area.

CHACHAPOYAS

Chachapoyas (Pop 15,000; Alt 2,234m), is the capital of the Department of Amazonas. PNP (Amazonas-police) are based on block 11 of C Amazonas. Archaeological and anthropological information can be sought from the local anthropologist, Carlos Torres Mas, who is the head of the Instituto Nacional de Cultura, Jr Junín 817; he also advises about walks in the area. The Instituto has a map of local ruins. César Torres Rojas, who also works here, is very helpful. Another local authority on the region is German ethnographer, Dr Peter Lerche, who has lived here for almost 10 years. His excellent guide to the region (in Spanish) is available for US$10.

Excursions

Huancas, which produces unique pottery, can be reached by a 2-hr walk on the airport road. There are also Inca and pre-Inca ruins.

Local information
- **Accommodation**

A3 Gran Vilaya, Jr Ayacucho 700 block, T/F 757208, part of Los Tambos Chachapoyanos, a plan to build lodges to facilitate visits to this region (for information contact Charles Motley, 1805 Swann Ave, Orlando, Florida, USA 32809). Besides the above hotel and the INC lodge at Kuelap, projects are under way at Choctamal (see above) and Levanto (see below).

E El Dorado, Ayacucho 1062, T 757047, with bath, hot water, helpful; **E** Hostal Kuelap, Amazonas 1057, T 757136, shared bath, hot water extra, rec; **E** Johumaji, Jr Ayacucho 711, T 757138, with bath, cold water.

F Continental, Jr Ortiz Arrieta 441, T 751705,

hot water, not great; **F** *Hostal Amazonas*, Plaza de Armas, T 757199, hot water extra, large rooms, nice patio, rec.

● **Places to eat**
Chacha, on Plaza de Armas, clean, good, huge portions, friendly, rec; *Burguer Mass*, Plaza de Armas, excellent juices, cakes, fruit salads; *Patisserie*, Jr 2 de Mayo 558, good pastries; *Kuelap*, on Ayacucho, good, large portions, friendly, rec; *Chifa El Turista*, Amazonas 575 nr post office, is reasonable, friendly and helpful; *Las Chozas de Marlissa*, Ayacucho 1133, friendly, good for typical food, pub-type place at night, serves the strangest *pisco sour* you'll ever taste; *La Estancia*, Amazonas 861, just off Plaza, video pub, cheapish and good place for a night out. Good bakery at Ayacucho 816.

● **Banks & money changers**
Banco de Crédito, on plaza, gives cash on Visa card, changes TCs. Street changers for cash nr market.

● **Post & telecommunications**
Post Office: Dos de Mayo 438.

● **Tour companies & travel agents**
Guide: Martín Chumbe, Jr Piura 909, or via Comercial Zegarra on Plaza de Armas, or via *Gran Vilaya Hotel*, T/F (074) 757208. He is an official guide to most of the sites described above, charges US$25/day, and speaks some English at a push. He can store luggage. He has a copy of Gene Savoy's video on the Gran Vilaya expedition. On Plaza de Armas are *Kuelap Tours* and *Revash* (Rosario Muñoz and Carlos Burga), both run tours to Kuelap, Wed and Sat, depart 0700, 12 hrs, US$15 pp (min 5), inc meals and entry to ruins. Tourist information at Chincha Alta 445.

● **Transport**
Air A new airport has been built; Expreso Aéreo flies Lima-Cajamarca-Chachapoyas Tues, Thur and Sun, US$94. Grupo Ocho (army) flies every Sat, US$53: also every other Tues, Lima-Saposa-Mendoza-Chachapoyas-Chiclayo; on Wed, Chiclayo-Chachapoyas-Mendoza-Saposa-Lima.

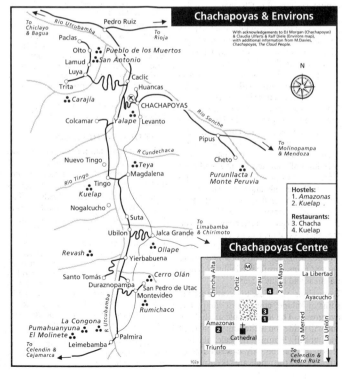

Chachapoyas & Environs

With acknowledgements to DJ Morgan (Chachapoyas) & Claudia Ulferts & Ralf Diele (Environs map), with additional information from M.Davies, *Chachapoyas, The Cloud People*.

Hostels:
1. *Amazonas*
2. *Kuelap*

Restaurants:
3. *Chacha*
4. *Kuelap*

Chachapoyas Centre

Truck from Plaza de Armas to airport up to 2 hrs before flights leave, US$1; taxi US$3. Flights are not reliable and are often cancelled.

Buses To **Chiclayo** 230 km, 10-12 hrs (longer in the rainy season, Nov-April), US$12; if blocked, take a colectivo to Pedro Ruiz and try to book for 1600 departure from there; also trucks daily. The route is via Bagua (see below) and Jaén (40 km from Bagua). The road is in bad condition and can be very difficult in the wet; but it is still an easier route than via Celendín. To **Pedro Ruiz**, 54 km, 2½-3 hrs, US$2.15, several combis daily; to **Bagua Grande** (141 km) 4-5 hrs, US$5.20, combis daily; easy to find a bus or truck on to Chiclayo. To **Celendín**, 227 km, for details see under Celendín. It is advised to travel by day on buses in the Chachapoyas area.

LEVANTO

The Spaniards built this, their first capital of the area, directly on top of the previous Chachapoyan structures. Although the capital was moved to Chachapoyas a few years later, Levanto still retained its importance, at least for a while, as it had been one of the seven great cities of the Chachapoyans as described by Cieza de León and Garcilaso de la Vega.

The Kuelap East-West Highway starts at Levanto and links with the Inca military highway at Jalca Grande (see above). Levanto was about mid-way on the N/S route from Colombia to the Huari, then Inca hub, at Huánuco. This stone road crosses the modern vehicle road at La Molina, about 5 km from Chachapoyas. A 16 km walk downhill on this road from Levanto is worthwhile. Nowadays Levanto is a small, unspoilt, and very beautiful colonial village set on flat ground overlooking the massive canyon of the Utcubamba river. Kuelap can, on a clear day, be seen on the other side of the rift. Levanto is a good centre for exploring the many ruins around, being the centre of a network of ancient ruins, fortified redoubts, residential areas and many others.

Excursions Very close to Levanto are the ruins of **Yalape**, now almost completely overgrown. The local people are helpful and will guide you to the ruins, a pleasant walk uphill (30 mins). Its scale, like that of Kuelap, can be only described as titanic. In fact the whole area is covered in

ruins, almost every prominent hilltop in the immediate vicinity has at least a watchtower of some sort.

Morgan Davis has reconstructed an Inca military garrison at Colla Cruz; on a classic Inca stone terrace, a regional-style round building has been constructed, with a 3-storey high thatched roof. This garrison guarded the road which ran past Colcamar, over the Cordillera Oriental on a 1.5 km staircase, through Gran Vilaya, to Cajamarca's central N/S road and on to the coastal highway.

● **Accommodation & services** As yet there is no official accommodation in Levanto, although the village council and *Los Tambos Chachapoyanos* are planning to restore a colonial house on the square as a lodge. However, small groups of travellers are very welcome and beds and bedding are provided in the mayor's office and village meeting hall. There is one small shop and bar in the village (selling coffee and Pepsi, but little food).

● **Transport** Levanto is 2 hrs by truck or 6 hrs walk from Chachapoyas by new road. Trucks leave from the market in Chachapoyas most days at 0600, US$0.90, also from outside *Bodega El Amigo* on Jr Hermosura at 1400, 1½-2 hrs depending on the number of stops; or 3½ hrs by mule track, ask in Chachapoyas market if anyone returning to Levanto will guide you for a small fee. Taxi from Cachapoyas to Levanto and back, inc driver waiting while you look around, US$25.

EAST OF CHACHAPOYAS

40 km E from Chachapoyas, on the road to Mendoza, are the pre-Inca ruins of **Monte Peruvia** (known locally as Purunllacta), hundreds of white stone houses with staircases, temples and palaces. The ruins have been cleared by local farmers and some houses have been destroyed. A guide is not necessary.

● **Access & accommodation** There is no direct transport from Chachapoyas. Take a combi at 0930 and 1500 from Jr Salamanca, 4th block down from market, to Pipus, at the turn-off to Cheto; 1½ hrs, US$1.35. A camioneta leaves Pipus for Cheto early am, US$0.90; or a 2-hr walk on a rough road. If stuck in Pipus, ask to sleep at restaurant *Huaracina* or police station next door. There are no hotels in Cheto but a house high up on the hill above the town with a balcony has cheap bed and board. The same family also has a house on the Plaza. The ruins are 2-hr walk from Cheto.

The road E from Chachapoyas continues through Pipus to **Molinopampa**, 2 hrs drive from Chachapoyas, the starting point of a difficult 5-day hike to Rioja (see below). The road carries on to **Mendoza**, the starting point for an ethnologically interesting area in the Guayabamba Valley where there is a high incidence of very fair people. See *The Peru Handbook* for more information.

● **Transport** 4 hrs, 86 km, from Chachapoyas to Mendoza by truck, daily at 1000, US$4.35 (return 0200, sometimes 0700).

NORTHWEST OF CHACHAPOYAS

37 km NW of Chachapoyas, on a turn-off on the road N to Pedro Ruiz, is **Lamud**, which is a convenient base for several interesting sites. At **San Antonio**, 30 mins from Lamud, is a sandstone cliff face with several groups of burial tombs high on a ledge. 3 hrs from Lamud (10 km on a very poor mule track), are the ruins of **Pueblo de los Muertos**, circular stone houses overlooking the valley. The view is spectacular but it is easy to lose your way and the ruins are very difficult to find as they are overgrown.

● **Accommodation & places to eat** F *Hostal Kuelap*, Jr Garcilaso de la Vega, on Plaza, basic, cold water only between 0700-0900. A few doors down is Restaurant *María*, which is cheap and obliging, excellent value, popular, the owner's son is a good local guide and charges around US$10/day.

● **Transport** Buses and combis to Lamud, and Luya, leave between 1000 and 1230 when full from nr market by Plaza, US$1.50, 1 hr 20 mins. The road is unpaved but in reasonable condition.

A 20 mins' drive S of Lamud, on the same road, is the village of **Luya**.

3 km or 1 ½ hrs walk from Luya is **Chipuric**, a residential complex belonging to the Chachapoyas culture. The site consists of burial tombs (all looted) set in a cliff face on a high ledge with circular stone buildings on the hill above. **Carajía**, also known as Solmol, is 2½ hrs walk from Luya but more accessible from Trita. A short walk from Trita, in the valley behind the village, are the stone burial figures set into an impressive cliff face. Ask for directions in Luya (2 hotels, both G). Best to take a local guide (US$3.50-5 a day).

CHACHAPOYAS TO THE AMAZON

From Chachapoyas the road heads N through the beautiful river canyon for 2-3 hrs to a small crossroads, **Pedro Ruiz**, where you return to the coast or continue to Yurimaguas, making the spectacular descent from high Andes to high jungle.

● **Accommodation & transport** There is basic accommodation in **G** *Hostal Marginal* with good, cheap restaurant, and one other, **F**. A pick-up truck leaves Chachapoyas about 0830, or when full. Plenty of trucks in Pedro Ruiz go to the Selva and regular combis go to Bagua Grande from where trucks go to Chiclayo. It is advisable to stay the night if you arrive late as most trucks to Rioja leave at 0500-0700. Pedro Ruiz to Rioja is 198 km, about 14 hrs, US$8.70, on an appalling piece of road. In the rainy season, this and the continuation to Moyobamba and Tarapoto can be very bad.

Half an hour before Rioja on this road is the new town of **Nueva Cajamarca**, with a few thousand inhabitants. There is a large market for local produce.

● **Accommodation & transport** F *Puerto Rico*, on main road, and F *Perú*, off to the right towards Rioja. Hourly colectivo to Rioja, US$1.30, 45 mins; colectivo to Chachapoyas US$12, 11-12 hrs. All trucks to Rioja stop here.

RIOJA

From **Rioja** there is a road to Naranjillo and Aguas Verdes, with a 5-hr walk to Venceremos, a pleasant way to see the jungle in good weather, but don't attempt otherwise.

An easy excursion can made to the Cueva de los Huácharos, unexplored caves, take a torch. Take a truck to La Unión (45 mins), walk 40 mins to Palestina then 50 mins more to the caves, ask locals for directions.

● **Accommodation & places to eat** Hostal *San Martín*, Gran 540, *San Ramón*, Jr Faustino Maldonado 840 and *Carranza*, Jr Huallanga, all basic. *Restaurante Los Olivos* is rec.

● **Transport Air** To Lima from Rioja, 2 hrs, US$75 one way, 3 times a week on Aero Continente. **Road** There is a mini-bus to Tarapoto at 1400, US$5.

MOYOBAMBA

A road with plenty of transport (about 30 mins, US$1.30) runs 21 km to **Moyo-**

bamba (*Pop* 14,000; *Alt* 915m; *Phone code* 094), capital of San Martín district. Tourists must register with the PNP. Moyobamba is a pleasant town, in an attractive valley. Mosquito nets can be bought cheaply. This area has to cope with lots of rain in the wet season; in some years the whole area is flooded. **NB** There have been guerrilla and drug activities in this region so take good care.

Excursions Puerto Tahuiso is the town's harbour, where locals sell their produce at weekends. From **Morro de Calzada**, there is a good view of the area; take a truck to Calzada, 30 mins, then walk up, 20 mins. There are Baños Termales, 4 km from Moyobamba on the Rioja road, which are worth a visit.

The more adventurous can hike to the **Jera waterfalls**, 21 km from Moyobamba in the jungle. Also on the road to Tarapoto are the waterfalls at **Lahuarpía**, which are easier to get to. Children in the village will guide you.

● **Accommodation A3** *Turistas*, Puerto Mirador, Jr Sucre, T 562594/848, F 562050, with breakfast, 1 km from centre, fine situation, pool, good restaurant (in Lima T 442-3090, F 442-4180, Av R Rivera Navarrete 889, of 208, San Isidro); **E** *Hostal Inca*, with bath, good but noisy; **E-F** *Royal*, nice, will change money, good restaurant; **F** *Hostal Country Club*, comfortable, nice garden, rec; **F** *Hostal Cobos*, with bath, good; **F** *Hostal Los Andes*, clean.

● **Banks & money changers** Viajes Turismo Río Mayo, Jr San Martin 401.

● **Tourist information & guides** Information on excursions and hikes is available from the Instituto Nacional de Cultura, Jr Benavides, 3rd block. Guides: Emigdio Soto, an expert on trips to native communities in the Alto Mayo area, contact him at the Proyecto Especial Alto Mayo; Orlando Peigot Daza, for jungle trips (no English), at Yurayacu village.

● **Transport Air** To Lima, US$71 one way: 3 weekly; with Expreso Aéreo; also to Huánuco, Juanjui, Tarapoto and Tingo María. **Buses** To Yurimaguas, Guadalupe (Jr Callao block 5), US$8.75.

TARAPOTO

The road is paved for a short way out of Moyobamba, then deteriorates to **Tarapoto** (*Phone code* 094), a busy town with several hotels. Good local market 1½ blocks from Plaza de Armas on Av Raimondi. Rioja, Moyobamba and Tarapoto are growing centres of population, with much small-scale forest clearance beside the road after Balsapata. The road is heavily used by trucks, with fuel and meals available, but until the road is improved, food and accommodation will remain expensive.

Excursions

La Mina de Sal is a salt mine outside the city. **Laguna Venecia** is a weekend resort with restaurant, 5 km from Tarapoto. **Laguna Azul** (or **Laguna Sauce** as it is sometimes known), is a big lake with *cabañas* for rent on the shore, US$80/night (4 beds and shower), very simple, no fresh water or food available, overpriced. Fishermen will offer trips on the lake. Trucks from bus station in Tarapoto, 52 km, 2½ hrs, US$3-5.

Between Tarapoto and Moyobamba a road leads off to **Lamas** where there is a small museum, with exhibits on local Indian community (Lamistas), ask at the café opposite if museum shut. Market in the early morning. Colectivo from Tarapoto, 30 mins, US$0.70, 35 km.

About 14 km from Tarapoto on the spectacular road to Yurimaguas are the 50m falls of **Ahuashiyacu**, which can be visited by tour from Tarapoto (US$18 including lunch) or by hiring a motorcycle from *Grand Prix*, Shapajo y Raimondi, US$3.50 an hour.

Local information
● **Accommodation**
A3 *Río Shilcayo*, Pasaje Las Flores 224, T 522225, F 524236 (in Lima T 447-9359), excellent meals, 1 km out of town, non-residents can use the swimming pool for a fee.

D *Edinson*, Av Raimondi, 1 block from Plaza de Armas, T 522723, less without bath, cold water, comfortable; **D** *Hostal San Antonio*, Jr Jiménez Pimentel 126, T 522226, courtyard, noisy, rec.

E *Tarapoto*, T 522150, with fan.

F *Hostal Americano*, fan and private bath; **F** *Juan Alfonso*, with shower, noisy, Jr Pedro de Urzúa.

G *Los Angeles*, nr plaza, good value, laundry facilities, restaurant.

● **Places to eat**
Best are *Real* and *El Camarón*. *Las Terrazas*,

typical food, rec. Many others.

● **Banks & money changers**
Banco de Crédito, Maynas 134, efficient, no commission on TCs. Many street changers around Plaza de Armas.

● **Tour companies**
Los Chancas Expeditions, Jr Rioja 357, T 522616, F 525279, e-mail:postmaster@unsm.edu.pe, white-water rafting on the Río Mayo, 30 km from Tarapoto on paved road, trips of up to 5 days; 1¹⁄₂ hr trip on grade III rapids US$15.

● **Transport**
Air US$1.75/taxi airport to town (no bus service, but no problem to walk). To **Lima**, 1 hr, US$76, Faucett, Expresso Aéreo, Aero Continente. **Yurimaguas**, 20 mins, US$23, 1 a week with Faucett. To **Pucallpa**, Expresso Aéreo, 3 a week. Expreso Aéreo has flights to/from Chiclayo, Huánuco, Juanjui, Yoyobamba, and Tingo María. Book in advance, particularly in rainy season. Many smaller airlines operate flights to Yurimaguas, eg Aerotaxi Ibérico (US$40): enquire at airport.

Buses The journey from Rioja to Tarapoto costs about US$7 and it is best to carry food and water because of road problems. To/from **Moyobamba**, 116 km, 3¹⁄₂ hrs, US$7 by colectivo, US$3.50 by colectivo, 5 hrs, several daily. There is a direct connection by bus (Chinchaysuyo) or truck from Tarapoto to **Chiclayo** via Moyobamba, Rioja, Bagua and Olmos, 690 km, 35-40 hrs, US$20. The same bus company also runs to Trujillo, at least 36 hrs. To **Yurimaguas**, US$5-10, trucks and pick-ups daily (see below for road conditions). Truck/pick-up leaves for Yurimaguas (usually 0800-0900, and in pm) from Jorge Chávez 175, down Av Raimondi 2 blocks, then left 5 blocks along Av Pedro de Uruaz (pick-ups from this street to other destinations).

TARAPOTO TO YURIMAGUAS

The journey from Tarapoto to Tingo María (see page 1384) is not advisable. In the rainy season the roads are impossible and it is a drugs-growing area. From Tarapoto to Yurimaguas on the Río Huallaga (136 km – see page 1386), the spectacular road can be very bad in the wet season, taking 6-8 hrs for trucks (schedules above). Once the plains are reached, the road improves and there is more habitation. **Shapaja** is the port for Tarapoto, 14 km from town, served by colectivos. At Shapaja cargo boats can be caught to Yurimaguas; plenty of birdlife and river traffic to be seen. From Yurimaguas on the Río Huallaga, launches ply to Iquitos.

The road from Pedro Ruiz (see page 1281) goes W to Bagua Grande (see page 1280) and then follows the Río Chamaya. It climbs to the Abra de Porculla (2,150m) before descending to join the old Pan-American Highway at Olmos (see page 1290). The section Jaén-Olmos is paved. From Olmos you can go SW to Chiclayo, or NW to Piura.

Bagua Grande is the first town of note heading W and a busy, dusty place with many hotels on the main street. *Restaurant Central* at Av Chachapoyas 1553 is good. Cars and camionetas depart from Av Chachapoyas when full to Pedro Ruiz, 1¹⁄₂ hrs, around US$2.70.

47 km W of Bagua Grande, a road branches NW at Chamaya to **Jaén**, a convenient stopover en route to the jungle, which has recently been revived as a rice-growing centre and is being modernized. Festival, Nuestro Señor de Huamantanga, 14 September.

● **Accommodation & places to eat** **D** *Prim*, Palamino 1353, modern, most upmarket in town; **E** *Monaco*, Ureta 1353, T (074) 731583, garden, café, secure, helpful, bath, rec; similar price and standard is *Guerrero*, Pardo Miguel 424; **F** *Hostal Requejo*, R Castilla 345, attractive, economical, often full. Very good food at *Chifa El Azuelo*, nr main plaza; several other *chifas*, and more, on Palamino.

● **Transport** Bus to Chiclayo, Civa US$4.35, 7 hrs.

When Spanish conquistadores first encountered the broad, northern Peruvian coastal valley oases, they marvelled at the creativity and sophistication of these desert farmers and fishermen. Early 16th century accounts describe enormous precolumbian settlements and sacred places. Recent archaeological discoveries near Chiclayo, the centre for today's rural population and capital of Lambayeque department, now attract scientists and tourists to the area.

Today's rural peasantry are inheritors

of many of the customs and technologies of their Moche forebears, who were master craftsmen in many fields. Artisan markets, primitive ocean going vessels, folk curing sessions and colourful religious 'fiestas' enliven any visitor's stay. In addition, the N, with a rain free climate all year, sports Peru's finest beaches for bathing and surfing.

Sandwiched between the Pacific Ocean and the Andes, Lambayeque is one of Peru's principal agricultural regions, and its chief producer of rice and sugar cane. Even so, archaeological studies indicate that prehispanic people have cultivated some 25% more land than farmers today. The extensive irrigation canals and reservoirs of northern Peru constitute one of the major technological achievements of ancient America.

CHICLAYO

Chiclayo (*Pop* 280,000; *Phone code* 074), founded in the 1560s as a rural Indian village by Spanish priests, has become a major commercial hub, with distinctive cuisine and musical tradition (*Marinera, Tondero* and afro-indian rhythms), and an unparalleled archaeological and ethnographic heritage (see **Excursions**). A walking tour in the centre reveals the mixture of creole, Spanish and Indian architecture along curving, narrow streets, once precolumbian canals now filled and paved with cobble stones.

Places of interest

On the Plaza de Armas is the 19th century neoclassical **Cathedral**, designed by the English architect Andrew Townsend. The **Palacio Municipal** and private **Club de la Unión** are on C Balta, the major avenue. Continue five blocks N on Balta to the **Mercado Modelo**, one of northern Peru's liveliest and largest daily markets. Don't miss the colourful fruits, handicrafts stalls (see *Monsefú*) and the well-organized section (off C Arica on the S side) of ritual paraphernalia used by traditional curers and diviners (*curanderos*). James Vreeland, a North American anthropologist, considers the Chiclayo *mercado de brujos* (witch

doctors' market) to be one of the most comprehensive in South America, filled with herbal medicines, folk charms, curing potions, and exotic objects used by *curanderos* and *brujos* to cure all manner of real and imagined illnesses. **NB** As in all markets, take good care of your belongings.

Excursions

Lambayeque 12 km NW from Chiclayo (*Pop* 20,700), its narrow streets are lined by colonial and republican houses, many retaining their distinctive wooden balconies and wrought iron grill-work over the windows. For example, on 8 de Octubre are **Casona Iturregui Aguilarte,** No 410, and, at No 328, **Casona Cúneo** with the only decorated façade in the town; opposite is **Casona Descalzi,** perhaps the best preserved. On Calle 2 de Mayo see especially **Casa de la Logia o Montjoy/Munyeo** (in need of repair), whose 64m long balcony is said to be the longest in the colonial Americas. Also of interest is the 16th century **Complejo Religioso Monumental de San Pedro** and the baroque church of the same name which stands on the **Plaza de Armas 27 de Diciembre.**

The reason most people visit is the highly recommended **Brüning Archaeological Museum,** in an impressive modern building. It specializes in Mochica, Lambayeque, Sicán and Chimú cultures, and has a fine collection of Sipán and Lambayeque gold. The magnificent treasure from the tomb of a Moche warrior priest, found at Sipán in 1987, has also been displayed here (see below), open 0830-1830 daily; entry US$1, guided tour in Spanish extra US$2.

• **Places to eat & transport** There are no hotels in the town but several good restaurants. Colectivos from Chiclayo US$0.50, 20 mins, leave from Elías Aguirre nr Plazuela Aguirre; also Brüning Express from Vicente de la Vega y San Martín, every 15 mins, US$0.20.

Colonial and traditional towns

The colonial town of **Ferreñafe**, NE of Chiclayo, is worth a visit, as is the traditional town of **Monsefú**, SW, also known for handicrafts; good market, 4 blocks from Plaza, open 0930-1700 (see also **Local festivals** below). **Mórrope**, on the Pan-American

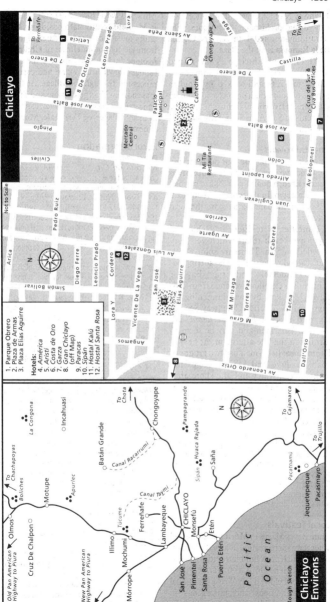

Chiclayo

Not to Scale

1. Parque Obrero
2. Plaza de Armas
3. Plaza Elías Aguirre

Hotels:
4. América
5. Aristi
6. Costa de Oro
7. Garza
8. Gran Chiclayo
   (off Map)
9. Paracas
10. Sipán
11. Hostal Kalú
12. Hostal Santa Rosa

Chiclayo Environs

Rough Sketch

Pacific Ocean

Highway N of Chiclayo still produces pottery using prehispanic techniques. The beautifully-restored 16th century **Capilla de la Ramada** is on the Plaza.

51 km S of Chiclayo is the ruined Spanish town of **Saña**, destroyed by floods in 1726, and sacked by English pirates on more than one occasion. There are ruins of five colonial churches and the convents of San Agustín, La Merced and San Francisco.

Coastal towns

North from Trujillo are four ports serving the Chiclayo area. The more southerly is **Puerto Etén**, a quaint port 24 km by road from Chiclayo. In the adjacent roadstead, Villa de Etén, panama hats are the local industry.

Pimentel, N of Etén, is a chic and expensive beach resort which gets very crowded on Sun. There are some excellent seafood restaurants. The surfing between Pimentel and the Bayovar Peninsula is excellent, reached from Chiclayo (14½ km) by road branching off from the Pan-American Highway. Sea-going reed boats (*caballitos de totora*) are used by fishermen and may be seen returning in the late afternoon. At nearby **Santa Rosa**, fishermen use two groups of boats *caballitos* and *bolicheros* – pastel-painted craft which line the shore after the day's fishing, 1-hr walk from Pimentel. The most northerly port is **San José**, from where you can walk along deserted beaches to Pimentel.

● **Transport** All four ports may be visited on a pleasant half day trip. Aspcarpi combis from Vicente de la Vega 400, 20 mins, US$0.25 to Pimentel. Colectivos run frequently from Pimentel to Santa Rosa, and on to Etén and back to Chiclayo (10 mins from Santa Rosa, 15 mins from Pimentel), from Av Ugarte, near junction with Pedro Ruiz, US$0.30.

Local festivals

6 Jan: Reyes Magos in **Mórrope**, **Illimo** and other towns, a recreation of a medieval pageant in which precolumbian deities become the Wise Men. On **4 Feb**: *Túcume* devil dances (see below). Holy Week, traditional Easter celebrations and processions in many villages. **2-7 June**: Divine Child of the Miracle, *Villa de Etén*. **27-31 July**: Fexticum in **Monsefú**, traditional foods, drink, handicrafts, music and dance. **5 Aug**: pilgrimage from the mountain shrine of **Chalpón** to **Motupe**, 90 km N of Chiclayo; the cross is brought down from a cave and carried in procession through the village. At Christmas and New Year, processions and children dancers (*pastorcitos* and *seranitas*) can be seen in many villages, eg **Ferreñafe**, **Mochumi**, **Mórrope**.

Local information

● **Accommodation**

A1 *Costa de Oro*, Balta 399, T/F 233280, inc continental breakfast, parking nearby, good services but a bit pricey, good restaurant, casino; **A1-2** *Gran Hotel Chiclayo*, Villareal 115, T 234911/224031, ex-Turistas, refurbished 1995/96 to high standard, inc taxes and breakfast, pool, safe car park, changes dollars, still undergoing improvements but rec; **A3** *Garza*, Bolognesi 756, nr Balta, T 228172, F 228171, excellent bar and restaurant, pool, car park, tourist office in lobby provides maps, information in English, Land Rovers, jeeps and minibuses for hire, highly rec; **A3** *Sipán*, Virgilio Dall'Orso 150, T 242564, F 242408, **B** without a/c, restaurant, parking, rec.

B-C *América*, L González 943, T 229305, F 241627, inc continental breakfast, comfortable, restaurant, good value, Travel Agency in reception, rec; **B-C** *El Sol*, Elías Aguirre 119, T/F 231070, inc taxes, hot water, restaurant, pool, TV lounge, comfortable, free parking, good value; **B-C** *Inca*, Av L González 622, T 235931, with fan, restaurant, garage, comfortable.

C *Hostal Santa Victoria*, La Florida 586, Urb Santa Victoria, T/F 241944, hot water, restaurant, free parking, cash dollars exchanged, quiet, 15-20 mins' walk from the centre.

D-E *Europa*, Elías Aguirre 466, T 237919, cheaper without bath, hot water, restaurant, good value; **D** *Hostal Kalú*, Pedro Ruiz 1038, T 228767, F 229293, taxi service, will reserve bus and air tickets, laundry, helpful, excellent value, rec; **D-C** *Hostal Santa Rosa*, L González 925, T 224411, F 236242, laundry service, international phone service, good breakfast downstairs in snack bar, rec; **D** *Paraíso*, Pedro Ruiz 1064, T 228161, T/F 240190, nr market, hot water, cafeteria, good value; **D** *Paracas*, Pedro Ruiz 1046, T 221611, T/F 236433, good value, rec.

E-F *Aries II*, Av Pedro Ruiz 937, T 235235, shared bath, cheap, cold water; **E** *Hostal Colonial*, Lora y Lora 344, T 237871, with bath, hot water, basic, noisy, convenient for buses; **E** *Hostal San Ramón*, Héroes Civiles 169, T 233931, with bath, hot water, noisy, cheap restaurant, laundry service, good value; **E** *Sol Radiante*, Izaga 392, T 237858, hot water, comfortable, owner will provide breakfast; **E** *Tumi de Oro*, L Prado 1145, T 227108, shared bath, **D** with bath, hot water, simple, good value. On Juan Cuglievan are: **E** *Hostal Kuelap*, No 1041, with bath; and **F** *Hostal San José*, 1 block from Mercado Modelo, basic, acceptable, cold water. There are several cheap hotels on Av Balta, nr bus offices, which range from basic to unhygienic. Most have only cold water. It is difficult to find decent cheap accommodation in Chiclayo.

● **Places to eat**
Fiesta, Av Salaverry 1820 in Ocho de Octubre suburb, T 228441, local specialities, first class, very expensive; *Le París*, MM Izaga 716, T 235485, excellent but expensive, international and creole food. First-class and very reasonably priced food (usually good breakfast) at *Romana*, Balta 512, T 238601, popular with locals. Many cheap *pollerías* on Balta and Pedro Ruiz nr market; *Mi Tía*, Aguirre 650, just off Plaza, cheap, huge portions, great value *menú*, very popular at lunchtime, rec; *Govinda*, Balta 1029, good vegetarian, cheap, open daily 0800-2000, rec; *Blue Garden*, Fco Cabrera 638, vegetarian, meat and fish dishes, rec; *Men Wha*, Pedro Ruiz 1059, expensive Chinese but delicious, huge portions; *Las Tinajas*, Elías Aguirre 957, excellent seafood at reasonable prices; *Kafé D'Kaly*, San José 728, good *menú*, friendly; *24 Horas*, E Aguirre 884, good food, cheap, open 24 hrs; *Las Américas*, Aguirre 824, open 0700-0200, good food and service, US$3-4 per dish; *El Algorrobo*, Av Saenz Peña 1220, good set lunch for US$1.10; *Flippy*, San José 710, good fried chicken and salad for US$1.50, also juices, sandwiches etc.
Lo Más Natural, Arica 755, nr market, sells good natural/organic yoghurt, also dried fruits and granola; *La Panadería*, Aguirre 610, for good bread, *pan integral*, rec.

Local food and drink: *Ceviche* and *chingurito* (a *ceviche* of strips of dried guitar fish, chewy but good); *cabrito*, spiced stew of kid goat; *arroz con pato*, paella-like duck casserole; *humitas*, *tamale*-like fritters of green corn; *King Kong*, baked pastry layered with candied fruit and milk caramel; *chicha*, fermented maize drink with delicious fruit variations.

● **Airline offices**
Faucett, MM Izaga 711, T 237932; *AeroPerú*, Elías Aguirre 712, T 242865; *Aero Continente*, A Ugarte 687, T 241202; *Expresso Aéreo*, San José 490, T 224802.

● **Banks & money changers**
Banco de Crédito, Balta 630, no commission on TCs for US$100 or more (US$11 commission

if less), cash on Visa; **Interbanc**, on Plaza de Armas, no commission on TCs, OK rate, good rates for cash, Visa cash advance; **Banco Wiese**, on Plaza, cash on Mastercard. Be prepared to wait. Beware of counterfeit bills, especially among street changers on 6th block of Balta, on Plaza de Armas and 7th block of MM Izaga.

● **Cultural centres**
Instituto Peruano Británico, Av 7 de Enero 296; Instituto Nacional de la Cultura, Av L González 375, occasional poetry readings, information on local archaeological sites, lectures, etc; Instituto de Cultura Peruano-Norteamericana, Av Izaga 807.

● **Entertainment**
Folklore: *Los Hermanos Balcázar*, Lora y Cordero 1150, T 227922; *El Embrujo*, Vicente de la Vega, T 233984; *Recreo Parrillada El Gaucho*, Fco Cabrera 1291, T 234441.

● **Hospitals & medical services**
Doctors: *Juan Aita*, Clínica Chiclayo, Av Santa Victoria, T 239024, rec as good general medical practitioner; *José Gálvez Jaime*, eye specialist, English spoken, Elías Aguirre 011, T 238234.

● **Post & telecommunications**
Post Office: on 1 block of Aguirre, 6 blocks from Plaza.

Telecommunications: Telefónica del Perú on 7 de Enero 724, open 0700-2300, international phone and fax; also on 8th block of Aguirre.

● **Shopping**
Paseo de Artesanías, at 18 de Abril nr Balta, stalls sell woodwork, basketwork and other handicrafts in a quiet, peaceful, custom-built open-air arcade.

● **Tour companies & travel agents**
Indiana Tours, Colón 556, T 242287, F 240833, daily tours to Sipán (US$15), Thor Heyerdahl's Kon Tiki museum, archaeological excavations in Túcume, Brüning Museum in Lambayeque, Batán Grande and a variety of other daily and extended excursions with 4WD vehicles; English and Italian spoken, Handbook users welcome. *Sipán Tours*, Av Luis González 741, T/F 237413; *Lambayeque Tours*, Av Santa Victoria 300, T 244327, F 274452; *Kaly Tours*, San José 728, T 238830, friendly, helpful, English spoken. The Brüning Museum, Sipán and Tucumé can easily be done by public transport. Expect to pay US$18-25 pp for a 3 hr tour to Sipán; US$25-35 pp for Túcume and Brüning Museum (5 hrs); Batán Grande is US$45-55 pp for a full-day tour inc Ferreñafe and Pomac; to Saña and coastal towns, US$35-55 pp. These prices are based on 2 people; discount for larger groups.

● **Tourist offices**
The tourist police, San José 733 y Plaza de Armas, T 233132, are very helpful and may store luggage and take you to the sites themselves. The regional tourist board plans to open an office in the same building; their current office is at Sáenz Peña 838.

● **Transport**
Local Mototaxis are a cheap way to get around; US$0.50 anywhere in city.

Air José Abelardo Quiñones González airport 1 km from town; taxi from centre US$1. Daily flights to/from Lima daily, with all major airlines; to Piura and Tumbes (Aero Continente), daily; to Tarapoto, with Expresso Aéreo, who also fly to Tingo María, Juanjui and Huánuco. AeroPerú to Iquitos 4 times a week.

Buses No *terminal terrestre*; most buses stop outside their offices on Bolognesi. To **Lima**, 770 km, US$8-9; Chiclayo Express, Mcal Nieto 119, T 237356; Cruz del Sur, Bolognesi 751, T 242164 (also Roggero, T 223216); Ormeño, Bolognesi 954A; Turismo Las Dunas, L González 291, T 229328, luxury service with a/c, toilet, meals, US$17.50, at 2000; Ortursa, Balta 598, *cama* service; most companies leave from 1600 onwards. To **Trujillo**, 209 km, with Emtrafesa, Av Balta 110, T 234291; and Vulcano, Av Bolognesi 638, T 234291; hourly 0530-2000, US$3.50, 3-4 hrs. Bus to **Piura**, US$3.50, hourly 0630-1930; **Sullana**, US$4.35; and **Tumbes**, US$6.50, 9-10 hrs, with Transportes Chiclayo, Av L Ortiz 010, T 233632l; Oltursa has night service 2015, arriving 0530 (a good bus to take for crossing to Ecuador next day, seats can be reserved, unlike other companies which tend to arrive full from Lima late at night).

Many buses go on to the Ecuadorean border at **Aguas Verdes**. Go to *Salida* on Elías Aguirre, mototaxi drivers know where it is, be there by 1900. All buses stop here after leaving their terminals to try and fill empty seats, so it's possible to get a substantial discount on the fare to the border. **NB** Bear in mind that the cheapest buses may not be the most secure.

Direct bus to **Cajamarca**, 260 km; with Vulcano, El Cumbe (Av Quiñones 425), Sud Americano (Colón 272, T 238566) and Turismo Arberia (Av Bolognesi 638, T 236981), US$6, 7 hrs, 3 a day at 1300, 2130 and 2200. To **Jaén** and **Bagua Grande**, regular buses, 0600-0700, from Nor-Oriente petrol station beside Panamericana on N side of city. To **Chachapoyas**, 230 km, US$8, 12 hrs. To **Tarapoto**, Chinchay-Suyo, Av Balta 179, T 231731, via Moyobamba, at 1030 and 1400, 24 hrs, US$17.50. Bus to **Huancabamba**, with Etipthsa, Mon, Wed and Fri from Tepsa terminal at Av Bolognesi 536, T 229217, at 1700, 12 hrs, US$9. Trucks going in all directions leave from C Pedro Ruiz 948 and from the market.

ARCHAEOLOGICAL SITES NEAR CHICLAYO

SIPAN

At this imposing twin pyramid complex a short distance E of Chiclayo, excavations since 1987 have brought to light a cache of funerary objects considered to rank among the finest examples of precolumbian art. Peruvian archaeologist Walter Alva, leader of the dig, continues to probe the immense mound that has revealed no less than five royal tombs filled with 1,800-year-old offerings worked in precious metals, stone, pottery and textiles of the Moche culture (ca AD 1-750). In the most extravagant Moche tomb discovered, El Señor de Sipán, a priest was found clad in gold (ear ornaments, breast plate, etc), with turquoise and other valuables. A fine site museum features photos and maps of excavations, technical displays and replicas of some finds.

Following the 4-year restoration of the principal treasures in Germany, the Lord of Sipán's physical remains and extraordinary funerary paraphernalia were recently returned to the Brüning Museum in Lambayeque. In another tomb were found the remnants of what is thought to have been a priest, sacrificed llama and a dog, together with copper decorations. In 1989 another richly-appointed, unlooted tomb contained even older metal and ceramic artefacts associated with what was probably a high-ranking shaman or spiritual leader, called 'The Old Lord of Sipán'.

Tomb contents are being restored in the Brüning Museum. At the time of writing, yet another unlooted tomb is currently being excavated, which will take several years. You can wander around the previously excavated areas to get an idea of the construction of the burial mound and adjacent pyramids. For a good view, climb the large pyramid across from the Sipán excavation.

● **Accommodation** At nearby **Huaca Rajada** is **F** *Parador Turística*, 2 rooms, meals possible, camping and use of facilities for US$1 pp.

● **Entry & access** The site museum is open 0800-1800. Entrance for tombs and museum is

US$1. To Sipán, colectivos leave from 7 de Enero y Juan Fanning (take a taxi there, US$1; it can be a dangerous area), US$0.40, 40 mins; guide at site US$2. To visit the site takes about 3-4 hrs in total.

25 km from Sipán is **Pampagrande**, a Mochica settlement interpreted by Canadian archaeologists in the 1970s as the first true N coast city, ca AD 550. At that time, it was the largest Moche complex, with as many as 10,000 inhabitants. The precise reason for the downfall of this once-powerful city remains a mystery.

A minor road runs to **Chongoyape**, a quaint old town 60 km to the E (3 km W are the Chavín petroglyphs of Cerro Mulato). Nearby are the vast Taymi precolumbian and modern irrigation systems. Also near Chongoyape are the aqueduct of Racarrumi, the hill fort of Mal Paso and the ruins of Maguín.

● **Transport** Bus from Chiclayo, US$1, 1½ hrs, leaves from Leoncio Prado block and Saenz Peña.

Batán Grande, 50 km from Chiclayo, has revealed several sumptuous tombs dating to the middle Sicán period, AD 900-1100. The ruins comprise some fifty adobe pyramids, where some of the best examples of precolumbian gold artefacts, notably the 915-gram Tumi, were found. The site, in 300 ha of desert-thorn forest of mezquite (*Prosopis pallida*), is now a national sanctuary and is protected by police.

● **Access** Colectivos, US$1.20, leave from 7 de Enero block 15 and J Fanning to the main square of the sugar cane cooperative (in which the ruins are set). You must get permission to visit the site from the cooperative (need to speak Spanish and to pay), and go with site archaeologist; Mon-Fri only; private car (taxi) from cooperative to site, US$8.50. Need full day to visit; impossible in wet season, Jan-March. Seek sound advice before you go.

TUCUME

About 35 km N of Chiclayo, beside the old Panamericana to Piura, lie the ruins of this vast city built over a thousand years ago. A short climb to the *mirador* atop **Cerro La Raya** (or **El Purgatorio**) offers the visitor an unparalleled panoramic vista of 26 major pyramids, platform mounds, walled citadels and residential compounds flanking a ceremonial centre and ancient cemeteries. One of the pyramids, Huaca Larga, where excavations are currently going on, is the largest adobe structure in the world, measuring 700m long, 280m wide and over 30m high. There is no evidence of occupation of Túcume previous to the Lambayeque people who developed the site between AD 1000 and 1400 until the Chimú conquered the region, establishing a short reign until the arrival of the Incas around 1470. The Incas built on top of the existing structure of **Huaca Larga** using stone from Cerro La Raya. Among the other pyramids which make up this huge complex are: **Huaca El Mirador** (90m by 65m, 30m high), **Huaca Las Estacas**, **Huaca Pintada** and **Huaca de las Balsas** which is thought to have housed people of elevated status such as priests. (Do not climb on the fragile adobe structures.)

Excavations at the site, which were once led by Norwegian explorer-archaeologist, Thor Heyerdahl of *Kon-Tiki* fame, are quickly challenging many conventional views of ancient Peruvian culture. Some suspect that it will prove to be a civilization centre greater than Chan Chán. There is also evidence, including art and remains of navigation gear, that the people of Túcume were intrepid seafarers.

A site museum, entrance US$1, contains architectural reconstructions, photographs and drawings, a ceremonial oar and a fabulous bas relief and mural depicting maritime scenes suggesting former sea trade and interregional contact. A café is attached, but take water. Fatima Huaman Vera is a good English-speaking guide US$2.50.

The town of Túcume is a 10-15 min walk from the site. On the Plaza is the interesting **San Pedro Church**. The surrounding countryside is pleasant for walks and swimming in the river. **Fiesta de la Purísima Concepción**, the town's Patron Saint, 8 days prior to Carnival in Feb, and also in September.

● **Transport** Combi buses go from Chiclayo, Manuel Pardo block 6, US$1.50 pp, 1 hr; a combi from the village to Come passes the ruins, hourly. Combi Túcume-Brüning Museum, US$0.50, 30 mins.

CHICLAYO TO CAJAMARCA

The Chiclayo – Chota bus passes through Chongoyape to Cochabamba (no hotels, not a friendly place, police searches for drugs), 34 km before Chota, from where you can hitch in a truck to **Cuervo** (*Pop* 6,000; *Alt* 2,800m), a very friendly town which tourists rarely visit. There is a local market on Thur and Sun.

● **Accommodation & places to eat** G pp *Hospedaje Marlen Central*, Jr 22 de Octubre, just off Plaza, cold water in mornings; *San Juan* on plaza, cheap but has bugs; nicer one by Cine San Juan, several more. *Restaurant Salón Azul*, very good; *La Casita*, Jr Lima 717, nr the Plaza, good, helpful with local information.

● **Transport** Many trucks to Cuervo, Tues-Sat, return Mon-Fri, bus from Chiclayo Sat, returns Sun 2000.

Chota is an attractive town with a fine Sun market where weavings are cheaper than in Cajamarca. Cheap, friendly shops at 27 de Noviembre 144 and 246.

● **Accommodation & places to eat** Several hotels: **F** *Plaza*, is the best; also *Continental*, which is poor. *Restaurant San Juan* is good.

● **Transport** Daily bus to Chiclayo am, 12-14 hrs; bus to Cajamarca daily 1500 and 2000.

Occasionally buses, and many trucks, run on to **Bambamarca**, which has an attractive Sun morning market.

● **Accommodation & places to eat** *Hotel Bolívar*, is the best; and others. *Restaurant Pollos a la Brasa* is very good.

● **Transport** Truck from Chota US$1. Empresa Díaz bus to Cajamarca daily at 0600, 9 hrs, frequent stops, US$4; there is a 2-hr stop in Bambamarca for the market; some days also with Peregrino.

ROUTES The road continues to **Hualgayoc**, a beautifully situated, quaint old mining town, and Cajamarca. It is a very interesting and beautiful journey, but few buses. The stretch from Bambamarca, about 90 km, to Cajamarca is exhilarating. The road climbs to about 4,000m through the Andean highlands with beautiful scenery of a *puna* landscape, nearly uninhabited, no fuel supply; it takes about 6 hrs in a 4WD car. The whole trip between Chongoyape and Cajamarca takes about 2 days in a car, the road is particularly bad between Chongoyape and Chota.

ROUTES On the old Pan-American Highway 885 km from Lima, **Olmos** is a tranquil place (Festival de Limón last week in June). A paved road runs E from Olmos over the Porculla Pass for Jaén, continuing to Bagua Grande. The old Pan-American Highway continues from Olmos to Cruz de Caña and Piura. At Lambayeque the new Pan-American Highway, which is in good condition, branches off the old road and drives 190 km straight across the Sechura Desert to Piura. There is also a coast road, narrow and scenic, between Lambayeque and Sechura via Bayovar.

● **Accommodation** At Olmos: G *Hospedaje San Martín*, very dirty, bargain hard; *Hotel Remanso*, is in a restored farmstead, good food, friendly, but not cheap.

The Sechura Desert is a large area of shifting sands separating the oases of Chiclayo and Piura. Water for irrigation comes from the Chira and Piura rivers, and from the Olmos and Tinajones irrigation projects which bring water from the Amazon watershed by means of tunnels (one over 16 km long) through the Andes to the Pacific coast. The northern river – the Chira – has usually a superabundance of water: along its irrigated banks large crops of Tangüis cotton are grown. A dam has been built at Poechos on the Chira to divert water to the Piura valley. In its upper course the Piura – whose flow is far less dependable – is mostly used to grow subsistence food crops, but around Piura, when there is enough water, the hardy long-staple Pima cotton is planted. In 1983 the Niño current brought heavy rains and turned the Sechura desert into an inland sea.

NB Solo cyclists should not cross the Sechura Desert as muggings have been known to occur. Take the safer, inland route. In the desert, there are restaurants between Km 845 and 848 and one at the junction for Bayovar where you can sleep, but no hotels. Do not camp out if possible. Heading S, strong headwinds may make camping unavoidable. Do not attempt this alone.

PIURA

A proud and historic city, 264 km from Chiclayo (*Pop* 324,500; *Phone code* 074) was founded in 1532, 3 years before Lima, by the *conquistadores* left behind by Pizarro. There are two well kept parks, Cortés and Pizarro (with a statue of the *conquistador*), and public gardens. Old buildings are kept in repair and new buildings blend with the Spanish style of the old city. Four bridges cross the Río Piura to Castilla, the oldest from C Huancavelica, for pedestrians, others from C Sánchez Cerro, from C Bolognesi, and the newest from Av Panamericana Norte, at N end of town.

The winter climate, May-Sept, is very pleasant although nights can be cold and the wind piercing; Dec to Mar is very hot.

Places of interest

Standing on the **Plaza de Armas** is the **cathedral**, with gold covered altar and paintings by Ignacio Merino. A few blocks away is **San Francisco**, where the city's independence from Spain was declared on 4 January 1821, nearly 8 months before Lima. The colonial church of **Las Mercedes** has ornately carved balconies, 3-tiered archway, hand-hewn supports and massive furnishings. **San Sebastián**, on Tacna y Moquegua, is also worth seeing. The birthplace of Admiral Miguel Grau, hero of the War of the Pacific with Chile, is **Casa Museo Grau**, on Jr Tacna 662, opposite the Centro Cívico. It is a museum and contains a model of the *Huáscar*, the largest Peruvian warship in the War of the Pacific, which was built in Britain. Interesting local craftwork is sold at the **Mercado Modelo**. **Museo Complejo Cultural**, with archaeological and art sections, is open on Sullana, near Huánuco, and though small it is very interesting.

Excursions

12 km to the SW of Piura, **Catacaos** is famous for its *chicha* (be careful, quality not always reliable), *picanterías* (local restaurants, some with music, *La Casa de Tales*, recommended), tooled leather, gold and silver filigree jewellery, wooden articles, straw hats (expensive) and splendid celebrations in Holy Week. 2 km S of Catacaos is the **Narihualá** archaeological site.

● **Transport** Colectivos leave from Plaza Pizarro, US$0.50, bus US$0.35.

Also from Piura, one can visit the coastal town of **Sechura**. The fine 17th-century cathedral has a splendid W front which has been under renovation for a long time and is normally closed to the public.

San Pedro has a huge lagoon with edible crabs, flamingoes and a superb beach and a fierce sun. Best visited in the week. There are no hotels or facilities whatsoever. **Yacila** is a picturesque fishing village with a few fish restaurants and a church on the beach. Nearby are La Tortuga, Parachique, Matacaballo (which is the best beach of these four places), Chullachay (the nearest beach to Sechura), Los Puertos and Angostura. Balsa boats are common on the coast.

Local information

● **Accommodation**

A1 *Los Portales*, Libertad 875, Plaza de Armas, T 322952, F 325920, ex-government hotel being refurbished, a/c, some rooms with hot water, pleasant terrace and patio, nice pool, the city's social centre; **A3** *El Angolo*, Fortunato Chirichigno 661, Urb San Eduardo, T/F 326461, suites and bungalows, hot water, a/c, pool, cable TV, restaurant, airport pickup service.

B *Perú*, Arequipa 476, T 333421, F 331530, a/c, **C** with fan, safe, laundry service, cold water, restaurant.

C *El Sol*, Sánchez Cerro 411, T 324461, F 326307, hot water, small pool, snack bar, parking, accepts dollars cash or TCs but won't change them; **C** *Esmeralda*, Loreto 235, T/F 327109, hot water, fan, comfortable, good, restaurant; **C** *Miraflores*, Cayetano Heredia 503 y Av Guardia Civil, Castilla, T 327236, a/c, hot water, **E** with fan, comfortable, family run; **C** *Vicus*, Av Guardia Civil B-3, in Castilla across river on Sánchez Cerro bridge, T 322541, F 325687, hot water, fan, quiet, parking; **C-D** *San Jorge*, Jr Loreto 960, T 327514, F 322928, with bath and fan, hot water, clean.

D *Cocos Inn*, José Olaya 197, Castilla, T 329004, inc breakfast, cheaper with cold water, converted colonial home in quiet residential area, terrace; **D** *El Almirante*, Ica 860, T/F 335239, fan, modern; **D** *Turismo*, Huánuco 526, T 325950, fan, pleasant, front rooms noisy.

E *Hostal Aruba*, on Junín esq Huancavelica, opp *Hotel Lalo*, small rooms but comfortable, fan on request, rec; **E** *California*, Jr Junín 835, T 328789, shared bath, own water-tank, mosquito netting on windows, roof terrace, pleasant, rec; **E** *Continental*, Jr Junín 924, T 334531, some rooms with bath, comfortable; **E** *Lalo*, Junín 838, T 325798, shared bath, cold water, very basic, **F** with double bed, laundry facilities; **E** *Oriental*, Callao 446, T 328891, cheaper without bath and fan, good value but very noisy, TV in reception.

It is extremely difficult to find a room in the last week of July because of Independence festivities. The city suffers from water shortages.

● **Places to eat**

Carburmer, Apurimac 343 in Centro Comercial, very good but not cheap; *El Puente Viejo*, Huancavélica 167, very good seafood, rec; *Gran Prix*, Loreto 395, good food, reasonable prices; *Casab-*

lanca, Jr Arequipa 902 esq Ayacucho, good local and international food, music at weekends, open 0900-0100, rec. Several good restaurants on Ayacucho between Cuzco and Arequipa, some are discos at night: *Las Tradiciones*, No 579, regional specialities, nice atmosphere, also an art gallery; *Bar Román*, No 580, excellent set meal for US$1.75, highly rec; *La Cabaña*, No 598, esq Cuzco, serves pizzas and other good Italian food, not cheap; *Ferny's*, next to *Hotel San Jorge*, good food, clean. *Café Concierto*, Cuzco 933, pleasant, popular, not cheap; *Chifa Canton*, Libertad 377, excellent, US$2.50 per dish, always busy; *Chifa Oriental*, on Huancavelica, 1 block W of Plaza, cheap and good; *Snack Bar*, Callao 536, good fruit juices; *Chispita*, Sánchez Cerro 210, nr bridge, good set meal, à la carte, fruit juices. Good little cheap restaurants on Jr Junín: *Chalán del*

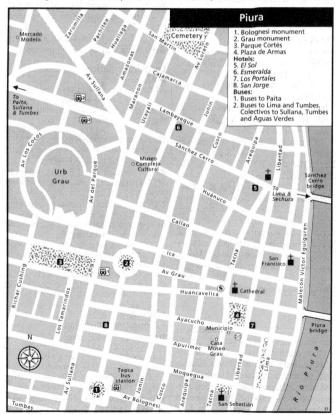

Piura

1. Bolognesi monument
2. Grau monument
3. Parque Cortés
4. Plaza de Armas
Hotels:
5. El Sol
6. Esmeralda
7. Los Portales
8. San Jorge
Buses:
1. Buses to Paita
2. Buses to Lima and Tumbes. Colectivos to Sullana, Tumbes and Aguas Verdes

Norte at 722, *Bianca* at 732, *El Capri* at 715. *Ganímedes*, Sánchez Cerro y Lima, vegetarian, very popular set lunch, à la carte. Two good places for sweets and ice-cream are: *El Chalán*, Tacna 520 on Plaza de Armas; and *D'Pauli*, Lima 541.

Local specialities: Piura's special dishes include *Majado de Yuca*, manioc root with pork; *Seco de Chavelo*, beef and plantain stew; and *Carne Seca*, sun-dried meat. Its best- known sweet is the delicious *natilla*, made mostly of goats milk and molasses. Its local drink is *pipa fría*, chilled coconut juice drunk from the nut with a straw.

● **Airline offices**
Faucett, Huancavélica 268, T 332165; **Aero Continente**, Grau 140, T 328223; **Aeroperú**, Libertad 951, T 328297.

● **Banks & money changers**
Banco de Crédito, Grau y Tacna, cash and TCs (no commission), TCs changed am only; **Banco Continental**, Plaza de Armas, changes TCs with commission, helpful, open Sun. **Banco Latino**, cash only. *Casa de cambio* at Edif Plaza Fuerte, Arequipa cuadra 6; street changers on Grau and Arequipa.

● **Embassies & consulates**
Honorary British Consul, Casilla 193, T 325693, Mr Henry Stewart. **Honorary German Consul**, Jutta Moritz de Irazola, Las Amapolas K6, Urb Miraflores, Casilla 76, T 332920, F 320310.

● **Post & telecommunications**
Post Office: on the corner of Libertad and Ayacucho on Plaza de Armas.

Telecommunications: Loreto 259, national and international phone and fax; also at Ovalo Grau 483.

● **Shopping**
Fuji film at Grau 202; Kodak at Huancavelica 199 and 258. The *natilla* factory on Sánchez Cerro, Miraflores, 4 blocks from bridge, sells *natilla* and *algarrobina* syrup. Market on Sánchez Cerro, good for fruit.

● **Laundry**
Lavandería Liz-to, Tacna 785, charges by weight.

● **Tour companies & travel agents**
There are several travel agents around the Plaza. Particularly helpful is *Piura Tours*, C Ayacucho 585, T 328873, the manager Mario speaks very good English. Also helpful is *Amauta Tours*, Apurimac 580, T 322976, F 322277.

● **Tourist offices**
Information at the Ministerio de Industria y Turismo, Gobierno Regional, Urb San Eduardo, at N end of town, helpful when there are problems. Touring y Automóvil Club del Perú, Sánchez Cerro 1237.

● **Transport**
Local Car rental: daily rates range between US$40 for a small car and US$75 for a 4WD; book ahead as availability is limited. **Piura Rent-a-car**, Sánchez Cerro 425, T 325510, F 324658; **Sun Rent-a-car**, Arequipa 504, T/F 325456; **S y S Rent-a-car**, Libertad 777, T/F 326773. **Taxis**: Radio Taxis, T 324509/324630.

Air To Lima daily with Faucett, AeroPerú, Aero Continente, 1½ hrs. To Chiclayo with AeroPerú, Faucett and Aero Continente, 30 mins. To Trujillo with AeroPerú, 40 mins. To Guayaquil, Mon and Thur, with AeroPerú. Taxi to airport, US$1.50.

Buses Unless stated otherwise, companies are on Av Sánchez Cerro, blocks 11 and 12. To Lima, 1,038 km, 14-16 hrs, US$13, on the Panamericana Norte; most buses stop at the major cities on route. To Chiclayo, 190 km, 3 hrs, US$3.50, several buses daily. To Trujillo, 7 hrs, 487 km, US$6, only at night. To Tumbes, 282 km, 5 hrs, US$5.25, several buses daily, eg Cruz del Sur (on Bolognesi) and El Dorado; colectivos, US$8, 3½ hrs (very cramped). Bus to **Aguas Verdes** US$5.50 leaving 2300 arriving 0500. To **Sullana**, 38 km, 30 mins, frequent buses, US$0.50, and colectivos, US$1, from Roma y Sánchez Cerro and Loreto y Sánchez Cerro; to **La Tina** for Ecuadorean frontier, a further 122 km, 2-3 hrs, US$3; best to take an early bus to Sullana (start at 0630, every 20 mins), then a colectivo. To **Talara**, US$1.75, 2 hrs, with Talara Express and EPPO. To **Máncora**, US$3.50, 3 hrs, with EPPO and El Dorado.

EAST FROM PIURA

Chulucanas, 50 km NE of Piura and 10 km off the old Pan-American Highway (minibus US$1.50), is the centre of the lemon and orange growing area and of local pottery production. Excellent ceramics can be bought at a shop on the Plaza and three others within one block (**F** *Hotel Ica*, Ica 636; *Restaurant Cajamarquino*, Ayacucho 530, good).

The paved road continues from Chulucanas SE to Morropán from where a dirt road goes to **Canchaque**, a delightfully-situated small centre for coffee, sugar-cane and fruit production (**F** *Hostal Don Félix*, central plaza, just tolerable; otherwise simple clean accommodation for about US$2 on right hand side of church).

The difficult and tiring road, impossible for ordinary vehicles in the wet season, continues over a pass in the Andes of more than 3,000m for 69 km to **Huancabamba**.

This very pretty, friendly town in a wonderful setting has three claims to fame. First, the predominance of European features, due to the fact that it was an important Spanish settlement in colonial times. Second, it is called 'the walking town, *la ciudad que camina*', as it is built on irregularly slipping strata which cause much subsidence. Third, and by far the most remarkable it is the base for reaching **Las Guaringas**, a series of lakes at about 4,000m. Around here live the most famous witchdoctors of Peru, to whom sick people flock from all over the country and abroad.

Buses to the lakes leave at 0400 from the main Plaza. Horses to the lakes can be hired, US$5. Also trips to the village of San Antonio below Lago Carmen, and the village of Salalá below Lago Shumbe (**G** *Hotel San José*, very basic, take own food). Ignacio León, who owns a *bodega* opposite *El Dorado* runs an early pick-up service to outlying villages and takes trips at negotiable prices.

Local specialities include *rompope*, a rich and strong drink made of egg, spices and *cañazo* (sugar-cane spirit), roast *cuy* (guinea-pig) and local cheeses.

- **Accommodation F** *Hotel El Dorado*, good, clean, informative owner, with restaurant, on the main Plaza. There are also a couple of others on the Plaza.

- **Transport** Buses from C Sánchez Cerro in Piura to Canchaque and Huancabamba leave daily 0700-0800, 0930, 1900 and 2000, 8-10 hrs (and return from Huancabamba 0700 and 1000), US$6. If driving, take the Pan-American Highway S of Piura for 66 km where there is a signpost to Huancabamba.

PAITA

The port for the area, 50 km from Piura, **Paita** (*Pop* 51,500) exports cotton, cotton seed, wool and flax. Built on a small beach, flanked on three sides by a towering, sandy bluff, it is connected with Piura and Sullana by paved highways. It is a very old fishing port. Several colonial buildings survive, but they are in poor condition. Bolívar's mistress, Manuela Sáenz, lived the last 24 years of her life in Paita, after being exiled from Quito. She supported herself until her death in 1856 by weaving and embroidering and making candy after refusing the fortune left her by her husband. The house may be visited if you ask the people living in it, but there's not much to see. Fishing, fishmeal and whaling (at Tierra Colorada, 6½ km S of Paita) are prosperous industries.

On a bluff looming over Paita is a small colonial fortress built to repel pirates. Paita was a port of call for Spanish shipping en route from Lima to Panama and Mexico. It was a frequent target for attack, from Drake (1579) to Anson (1741).

- **Places to eat** *El Mundo*, Jr Junín, quite good; much better is the restaurant on 2nd floor of Club Liberal building, Jorge Chávez 161, good fish, seafood and crêpes, good value; others on Plaza de Armas.

- **Transport** From Piura, colectivos and buses; TUPPSA, Sullana 527, Parque Cortez, every hour, 45 mins, US$0.90.

SULLANA

Sullana (*Pop* 154,800), 39 km N of Piura, is built on a bluff over the fertile Chira valley and is a busy, modern place. San Martín is the main commercial street. Parks and monuments were added in 1994/5, which have greatly improved the city's appearance. The local fiesta and agricultural fair is *Reyes*, held on 5-29 January.

NB Although the city is safer than it once was, caution should still be exercised by the market and where colectivos leave for the Ecuadorean border.

- **Accommodation A3** *Hostal La Siesta*, Av Panamericana 400, T/F 502264, at entrance to town, hot water, fan, **B** with cold water, pool, restaurant, laundry; **D** *Hostal Aypate*, Av José de Lama 112, T 502013, hot water, fan, comfortable; **D** *Hostal Turicarami*, San Martín 814, T 502899, some rooms have hot water, **E** without bath or fan; **E** *Hostal Fernando*, Grau 703, T 500727, with bath, fan; **E** *Hostal Lion's Palace*, Grau 1030, T 502587, with bath, fan, patio, pleasant, quiet; **E** *Hostal San Miguel*, C J Farfán 204, T 500679, cheaper without bath, basic, helpful, good showers, staff will spray rooms against mosquitoes, cafeteria; **E** *Hostal Príncipe*, Espinal 588.

- **Places to eat** *El Parque*, E Palacios 173, corner San Martín, good value set meal, expensive à la carte, good quality and service, rec; *Chifa Canton*, Farfán 248, good cheap food, open evenings only; ***Due Torri***, E Palacios 122, Italian and regional, popular with locals; ***Pollería Ibañez***, J de Lama 350, grilled meats and chicken.

- **Banks & money changers** Banco de **Crédito**, San Martín 685, will change cash and TCs. *Casas de cambio* and street changers on San Martín by Tarapacá.

- **Post & telecommunications Post Office**: at Farfán 326. **Telecommunications**: telephone and fax at Miró Quesada 213.

- **Useful addresses Immigration**: Grau 939.

- **Tour companies & travel agents** *Pesa Tours*, Espinar 301 y Tarapacá, T/F 502237, for airline tickets (flights from Piura) and information, helpful and friendly.

- **Transport Local Taxis**: Radio Taxis, T 502210/504354. **Buses** Most bus companies are on Av José de Lama. To **Tumbes**, 244 km, 4-5 hrs US$5, several buses daily. **Piura**, 38 km, 30 mins, US$0.50, frequent buses, colectivos, US$1, taxi US$2 (if you have time, it is worth continuing to Piura); **Chiclayo** and **Trujillo** see under Piura. To **Lima**, 1,076 km, 14-16 hrs, US$9-18, several buses daily, most coming from Tumbes or Talara, luxury overnight US$18; Cruz del Sur, Ugarte 1019; Continental (Ormeño), Tarapacá 1007. Colectivos to Paita leave from the main road parallel to the market; buses to Máncora and Talara (Empresa EPPO) from market area.

NORTH TO ECUADOR

At Sullana the Pan-American Highway forks. To the E it crosses the Peru-Ecuador frontier at La Tina and continues via Macará to Loja and Cuenca. The excellent paved road is very scenic. The more frequently used route to the border is the coastal road which goes from Sullana NW towards the Talara oilfields and then follows the coastline to Máncora and Tumbes.

FRONTIER AT LA TINA-MACARA

● Peruvian immigration

The border crossing is described as problem-free and officials are helpful. The Peruvian immigration officer can be found at the nearby *cevichería* if not at his desk. The border is reported open 0800-1800 but it may close for lunch, so it is better to cross in the morning.

● Accommodation

There is one basic hotel in Suyo and two in Las Lomas (75 km from Sullana).

● Transport to border

Minivans leave from Sullana to the international bridge from Mercadillo Bellavista, Av Buenos Aires y Calle 4, which is a crowded market area. They leave between 0400 and 1300 when full, US$3 pp, 2 hrs. The Buenos Aires area is not safe, so it's best to take a taxi or moto-taxi to and from here. To get to Macará, walk over the bridge and take one of the pick-ups which run from the border. Buses leave the Ecuadorean side for Loja every few hours, so you can go from Sullana to Loja in 1 day.

TALARA

135 km from Piura and 1,177 km from Lima, is Talara (*Pop* 44,500), the main centre of the coastal oil area, with a State-owned 60,000 barrel-a-day oil refinery and a fertilizer plant. Set in a desert oasis, the city is a triumph over formidable natural difficulties, but was badly damaged in the 1983 floods and has many shanty districts. Water is piped 40 km from the Río Chira. Talara is reached via a 5 km side road E off the Pan-American Highway. La Peña beach, 2 km away, is still unspoilt.

Of historical interest are the old tarpits at La Brea, 21 km inland from Punta Pariñas, S of Talara, and near the foot of the Amotape mountains. Here the Spaniards boiled the tar to get pitch for caulking their ships. Punta Pariñas itself is the westernmost point of South America.

- **Accommodation NB** All hotels in Talara have problems with water supply. **A3** ***Pacífico***, Av Aviación y Arica, T/F (074) 381719, most luxurious, suites, hot water, pool, restaurant, bar, parking, pay in dollars; **D** ***Hostal César***, Av Salaverry 9, T 382364, T/F 381591, fan, safe, snack bar; **D** ***Residencial Grau***, Av Grau 77, T 382841, nr main plaza, possible to park one motor bike, owner changes dollars; **E** ***Hostal Talara***, Av del Ejército 217, T 382186, comfortable.

- **Places to eat** There are many cheap restaurants on the main plaza. The better restaurants can be found in the main hotels.

- **Transport Air** Airport with daily flights by Faucett to Lima, 1½ hrs. **Buses** To **Tumbes**, 171 km, 3 hrs, US$3.50, most coming from Piura and most stop at major towns going N; several daily. To **El Alto** (Cabo Blanco), 32 km, 30 mins, US$0.75, continuing to Máncora, 28 km, 30 mins, US$0.75 to **Piura**, 111 km, 2 hrs, US$1.75. To **Lima**, US$15.

BEACHES NORTH OF TALARA

32 km N of Talara, is the small port of **Cabo Blanco**, famous for its excellent sea-fish-

ing and surfing. The scenery has, unfortunately, been spoilt by numerous oil installations. The film of Hemingway's *The Old Man and the Sea* was shot here.

● **Accommodation** **B** *Fishing Club Lodge* (former Fishing Club), clean, attractive, rec, restaurant, pool, watersports, likely to be full in New Year period, secure camping; cheaper is **D** pp *El Merlín*, good value, huge rooms, situated right on the beach, good restaurant.

28 km further N is **Máncora**, a small, attractive resort with good beaches, water warm enough for bathing. This stretch of coast is famous for surfing (best Nov-Mar) and for its excellent *mero* (grouper). South of Máncora along the coastal road (old Pan-American Highway) are some excellent beaches which are being developed.

● **Accommodation** Prices can increase by up to 100% in high season (Dec-Mar). From S to N: **D** *Punta Ballenas*, S of Cabo Blanco bridge at the S entrance to town, T 447-0437 (Lima), **B** in high season, lovely setting on beach, garden with small pool, expensive restaurant, rec; **D** *La Posada*, by Cabo Blanco bridge, follow the dry river bed away from the beach, **C** in high season, nice garden, hammocks, rooms for larger groups, meals on request, parking, camping possible, good local knowledge, owner sometimes does tours in the hinterland; **E** *Sol y Mar*, Piura cuadra 2, on beach, with bath, basic, restaurant, popular with surfers, rec; **E** pp *El Angolo*, Piura 262, on the beach, with bath, basic, nice terrace, restaurant, camping permitted in garden, rec; **E-F** *Bambú*, Piura 636, basic, shared bath; **E-F** *Hospedaje Crillon/Tía Yola*, Paita 168, 1 block E of Piura, behind Tepsa office, shared bath, plenty of water, rec; **F** *Máncora*, Piura 641, shared bath, very basic, cheapest in town.

● **Places to eat** You can find excellent seafood, inc lobster and grouper, on Av Piura by the centre of town. *César*, rec, also hires out bicycles for $2.50 per day; *El Arpón*, good value, rec; *Kiosko Betty*, close to *Sol y Mar*, friendly, good value meals; *Regina's*, for fruit salad.

● **Post & telecommunications** **Telephone**: at Piura 509, opp the church, national and international calls, also collect. This is the only telephone in town. For hotel reservations leave message at (074) 320212.

● **Sports** **Horse riding**: German Heidi Ritter hires horses at her ranch, US$4.50 pp for 2-hr guided tour through beautiful countryside, rec. Take moto-taxi or bicycle to El Angolo, then take main road N and turn right after the bridge. After about 1 km, just before the corrals on the right, turn right and you'll see a doorway

which leads to Heidi's corrals.

● **Transport** To Piura with EPPO, US$3.50, 3 hrs; to Tumbes (and points in between), minivans leave when full, US$1.55, 2 hrs.

5 km E of Máncora are hot mud baths (*baños del barro*), reported to be medicinal. The access is N of town, at Km 1168, from where it is about 2 km to the baths. Continuing along this road to Quebrada Fernández you can reach the **El Angolo game reserve**, which extends as far S as the Río Chira. Ask at *Hostal La Posada* for tours to this area.

16 km N of Máncora is the *Carpitas* customs checkpoint, where southbound vehicles are checked. 6 km further N, at Km 1187, is the turn-off for **Punta Sal Grande**, a resort town at the S end of beautiful Playa Punta Sal, a 3 km long sandy beach. A few restaurants operate in high season only and the town is very quiet in the low season.

● **Accommodation** For reservations in any of the hotels in the area, leave a message at Cancas public telephone, T/F 320251. High and low season prices given where known; full board usually available. In town, from N to S are: **A3-C** *Los Delfines*, nr beach, shared bath, nice rooms, restaurant in high season, meals on request in low season, vegetarian available, Canadian-run; **B-C** *Hua*, on beach, T 448-5667 (Lima), with bath, pleasant terrace overlooking ocean, discount for IYHF card holders, meals available; **B-D** *Estancia*, Calle Carrosable, back from beach, 4 rooms, 1 with bath, ask José Devescovi at first house at entrance to town; **D** *Las Terrazas*, at S end of bay, T/F 433-7711 (Lima), on a terraced hill overlooking the ocean, cheaper rooms without bath, comfortable, meals available, British-run; **D** *Caballito de Mar*, at S end of bay, T 442-6229 (Lima), some rooms with bath, overlooking the ocean, comfortable. The beach is known as Punta Sal Chica: **A3** *Puerto Azul Beach Resort*, access from Panamericana Km 1190, T/F 444-4131 (Lima), spacious bungalows, pool, tours to mangroves and Tumbes, Tumbes airport pick-up US$20; **L3** *Punta Sal Club Hotel*, access road at Km 1192, T (074) 521386 (radiophone via Tumbes), T/F 442-5961 (Lima), 18 bungalows, 12 rooms, solar heated water, attractive, comfortable, relaxing, good beach, watersports, pool, horse riding, deep-sea fishing, transport to Tumbes airport US$10 pp, rec. **Camping**: is reported to be safe along the beach between Talara and Punta Sal (Punta Negra rec).

The fishing village of **Cancas** is just N of Punta Sal Chica (Km 1,193). It has a few shops, restaurants, a gas station and a police checkpoint where vehicles must stop and southbound foreigners may be required to register. From Punta Mero (Km 1,204) N, the beach is used by *larveros*, extracting shrimp larvae from the ocean for use in the shrimp industry.

● **Accommodation** Several new resorts are being built between Punta Mero and Tumbes. Between Bocapán and Los Pinos, 30 km from Tumbes, is **E** pp *Casa Grillo Centro Ecoturistico Naturista*, Los Pinos 563, Youth Hostel, take colectivo from Tumbes market to Los Pinos, or get off bus on Pan-American Highway at Km 1236.5, T/F (074) 525207, T/F 446-2233 (Lima), excellent restaurant inc vegetarian, great place to relax, variety of rooms, shared bath, hot water, laundry, also surfing, scuba diving, fishing, cycling, trekking, camping available, rec.

Zorritos, 27 km S of Tumbes, is an important fishing centre with a good beach (the water is not oily). The first South American oil well was sunk here in 1863. This is the only part of the Peruvian coast where the sea is warm all year. There is a good beach at **Caleta La Cruz**, 16 km SW of Tumbes, where Pizarro landed in 1532. Regular colectivos run back and forth, US$0.80 each way.

Puerto Pizarro is a small fishing beach 13 km NE of Tumbes; colectivo No 6 from Plazuela Bolognesi in Tumbes, US$0.80. Take a motor or sailing boat to visit the mangroves from Puerto Pizarro pier (US$8), or across the lagoon to reach a good clean sandy beach (about 10 mins' journey, bargain hard). The Festival of San Pedro y San Pablo takes place 29-30 June.

TUMBES

Tumbes (*Pop* 34,000; *Phone code* 074), about 141 km N of Talara, and 265 km N of Piura is the most N of Peruvian towns. It is a garrison town: do not photograph the military or their installations – they will destroy your film and probably detain you. There is a long promenade, the Malecón Benavides, decorated with arches, beside the high banks of the Río Tumbes.

Places of interest

There are some old houses in **Calle Grau**, and a colonial public library in the **Plaza de Armas** with a small museum. The **cathedral** is 17th century but restored in 1985. There are two pedestrian malls, Paseo de Los Libertadores on Bolívar and Paseo de la Concordia on San Martín, both leading N from the Plaza de Armas. There is a sports stadium and cockfights in the Coliseo de Gallos, Av Mcal Castilla, 9th block, Sun at 1500, special fights 28 July and 8 Dec. The water supply is poor.

Local information
● **Accommodation**

NB Av Tumbes is still sometimes referred to by its old name of Teniente Vásquez.

A3 *Sol de la Costa*, San Martín 275, Plazuela Bolognesi, T 523293, F 523298, ex-state run hotel, hot water, minibar, fan, restaurant, good food and service, parking extra, nice garden with swimming pool, racketball court.

D *Asturias*, Mcal Castilla, T 522569, fan, cafeteria, comfortable, rec; **D** *Chicho*, Tumbes 327, T/F 523696, fan, mosquito net; **D** *Florián*, Piura 400 nr El Dorado bus company, T 522464, F 524725, fan, rec; **D** *Lourdes*, Mayor Bodero 118, one block from main plaza, T/F 522758, fan, roof restaurant, slow service, rec.

E *Amazonas*, Av Tumbes 317, T 520629, with bath, fan, water in mornings unreliable; **E** *Córdova*, J R Abad Puell 777, with bath, no hot water, safe, safe for motorcycle parking; **E** *Elica*, Tacna 319, T 523870, with bath, fan, quiet, good; **E** *Estoril*, Huáscar 317, 2 blocks from main plaza, T 524906, with bath, good, discount for long stay; **E** *Hostal Tumbes*, Grau 614, T 522203, with bath, cold water, fan, good value, rec; **E** *Italia*, Grau 733, T 520677, cold showers, noisy, good; **E** *Toloa 1*, Av Tumbes 430, T 523771, with bath, fan, safe, helpful; **E** *Toloa 2*, Bolívar 458, T 524135, with bath, fan, OK.

F *Cristina*, Mcal Castilla 758, nr market, T 521617, with bath, basic, cheap; **F** *Hostal Bolívar*, Bolívar 115, on Plaza de Armas, T 523007, shared bath, mosquito net; **F** *Sudamericano*, San Martín 130, Paseo de la Concordia, shared bath, basic but good value. Many other cheap hotels by the market. At holiday times it can be very difficult to find a vacant room. Camping is possible nr Rica Playa, by the waterfall on Río Tumbes; ask at the tourist office.

● **Places to eat**

Curich, Bolívar, on the Plaza de Armas, good for fish, friendly, rec; *Europa*, off Plaza de Armas, rec, particularly for omelettes, expensive; *Lat-*

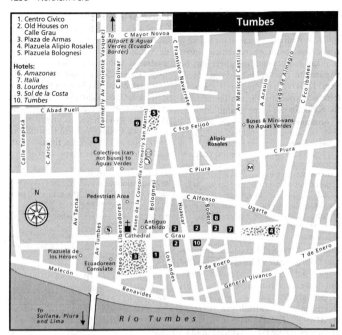

1. Centro Cívico
2. Old Houses on Calle Grau
3. Plaza de Armas
4. Plazuela Alipio Rosales
5. Plazuela Bolognesi

Hotels:
6. Amazonas
7. Italia
8. Lourdes
9. Sol de la Costa
10. Tumbes

Tumbes

ino, Bolívar 163, on Plaza de Armas, good set meals, à la carte expensive, also *peña* most evenings; *Chifa Wakay*, Huáscar 417, smart, good, US$5-8, rec; *Río Tumbes*, Malecón Benavides s/n, at E end of seafront, excellent views of river, pleasant atmosphere, seafood specialities, not cheap; *Hawaii*, Av Bolívar 235, nr Plaza de Armas, good, big portions; *Juliban*, Grau 704, good, generous set meal; *El Algarrobo*, Huáscar across from Club Social, good. There are other inexpensive restaurants on the Plaza de Armas and nr the markets. *Heladería La Suprema*, Paseo Libertadores 298, good ice cream, sweets and cold drinks; next door at 296 is *Bam Bam*, for breakfast and snacks. Try *bolas de plátano*, soup with banana balls, meat, olives and raisins, and *sudado*, a local stew.

● **Banks & money changers**
Interbanc, Bolívar 129, Plaza de Armas, cash and TCs at same fair rate, cash advance on Visa; Banco Continental, Bolívar 121, cash and Amex TCs only, US$5 commission. All banks close for lunch. Bad rates at the airport. Cambios Ocoña, Galería San Carlos, Piura nr Paseo de la Concordia, US$ cash at good rates; Cambios Internacionales, Av Tumbes 245, cash

only, good rates. Money changers on the street (on Bolívar, left of the Cathedral), some of whom are unscrupulous, give a much better rate than banks or *cambios*, but don't accept the first offer you are given. None changes TCs. If you are travelling on to Ecuador, it is better to change your Soles at the border as the rate is higher.

● **Embassies & consulates**
Ecuadorean Consulate, Bolívar 155, Plaza de Armas, T 523022, 0900-1300 and 1400-1630, Mon-Fri.

● **Post & telecommunications**
Post Office: San Martín 208; Entel Telephone office, San Martín 210; both on Paseo de la Concordia.

● **Tour companies & travel agents**
Rosillo Tours, Tumbes 293, T/F 523892, information, tickets, Western Union agents; *Tumbes Tours*, Tumbes 351-A, tickets and information.

● **Tourist offices**
Centro Cívico, Bolognesi 194, p 2, helpful, provides map and leaflets. Federación Peruana para la Conservación de la Naturaleza (FPCN), Av Tarapacá 4-16, Urb Fonavi, T 523412.

● Transport

Air To Lima, 6 a week with Faucett via Talara, daily with Aero Continente via Chiclayo and Piura buy tickets outside Peru to avoid paying sales tax. It is essential to reconfirm flights 24 hrs before departure. It is better to buy tickets in Tumbes rather than at the airport. Taxi to airport, US$4, 20 mins; minivans charge US$1.50; taxis meet flights to take passengers to border, US$7-9; no minivans from airport to border, beware of overcharging.

Buses Daily to and from **Lima**, 1,320 km, 12-20 hrs, depending on stopovers, US$15 (normal service), US$22 (luxury service), long trip on an excellent Panamericana Norte. Several buses daily. All on Av Tumbes: Expreso Continental (Ormeño group), 314; Cruz del Sur, 319; Oltursa, 324 and 359, daily 1330, rec; Tepsa, 199, old buses, unsafe, often full, not rec. For other companies, ask around; cheaper ones usually leave 1600-2100, more expensive ones 1200-1400. Except for luxury service, most buses to Lima stop at major cities en route, although you may be told otherwise. You can get tickets to anywhere between Tumbes and Lima quite easily, although buses are often booked well in advance, so if arriving from Ecuador you may have to stay overnight. Piura is a good place for connections. To **Talara**, 171 km, US$3.50, 3 hrs. To **Sullana**, 244 km, 3-4 hrs, US$4.50, several buses daily. To **Piura**, 4-5 hrs, 282 km, US$5.25 with Empresa Chiclayo, Cruz del Sur, El Dorado (Piura 459) 6 a day, Dorado Express (Tumbes 297); Colectivo (Tumbes 302), US$7 pp, 3½ hrs. To **Chiclayo**, 552 km, 6 hrs, US$7, several each day with Cruz del Sur, El Dorado, Dorado Express, Oltursa. To **Trujillo**, 769 km, 10-11 hrs, US$9, Continental, Cruz del Sur, El Dorado, Dorado Express. To **Chimbote**, 889 km, 13-14 hrs, US$10. Transport to the border, see **Frontier with Ecuador**, below.

EXCURSIONS FROM TUMBES

The Río Tumbes is navigable by small boat to the mouth of the river, an interesting 2 hr trip with fantastic birdlife and mangrove swamps.

The **Santuario Nacional los Manglares de Tumbes** protects the mangrove ecosystem in the northernmost part of the Peruvian coast. The mangrove swamps are full of pelicans; best to visit them at high tide. Three islands, Isla Hueso de Ballena, Isla del Amor and Isla de los Pájaros may be visited by boat; bargain hard, good for swimming and picnics, take food and water. The remains of the Cabeza de Vaca cult centre of the Tumpis Indians can be found at Corrales, 5 km S of Tumbes. They were heavily damaged by 1983 rains; Museo de Sitio nearby.

The **Parque Nacional Cerros de Amotape** protects an area of the equatorial forest. It extends SE from the S bank of the Tumbes river, towards the El Angolo game preserve NE of Máncora. Some of the endemic species are the Tumbes crocodile, the river otter and white-winged turkeys. Access is via the road which goes SE from the Pan-American Highway at Bocapán (Km 1,233) to Casitas and Huásimo, it takes about 2 hrs by car from Tumbes, best in the dry season (July-Nov); also access via Quebrada Fernández from Máncora and via Querecotilo and Los Encuentros from Sullana.

The **Zona Reservada de Tumbes** (75,000 ha), lies to the NE of Tumbes, between the Ecuadorean border and Cerros de Amotape National Park. It protects dry equatorial forest and tropical rainforest. The wildlife includes monkeys, otters, wild boars, small cats and crocodiles. Access from Tumbes is via Cabuyal, Pampas de Hospital and El Caucho to the Quebrada Faical research station or via Zarumilla and Matapalo.

● Mosquito repellent is a must for Tumbes area.

FRONTIER WITH ECUADOR

● Peruvian Immigration

Immigration for those leaving Peru is at an office 3 km before the border; for those entering Peru, immigration is at the end of the international bridge, W side, at Aguas Verdes. PNP is on the E side. All offices are open Mon-Sat 0800-1300 and 1400-1800, Sun 0800-1300 and 1400-1600. Best to arrive well in advance of closing times on either side.

NB Peruvian immigration formalities are reported as relatively trouble-free, but if you are asked for a bribe by police officers on the Peruvian side of the international bridge, be courteous but firm. Porters on either side of the border charge exorbitant prices; don't be bullied. Also note that relations between Peru and Ecuador are not good; Ecuadorean customs may confiscate guidebooks and maps of Peru which show areas claimed by Ecuador as belonging to Peru.

● Entering Ecuador

Having obtained your exit stamp, proceed across the bridge into Huaquillas; 100m up is

Ecuadorean immigration on the left. You may have to buy two photocopied embarkation cards, which touts will try to sell for US$0.50, but which can be bought at the photocopy shop behind immigration for US$0.01.

● **Peruvian Customs**
There are virtually no customs formalities at the border for passengers crossing on foot, but spot-checks sometimes take place. There is a well-organized customs checkpoint S on the Pan-American Highway between Cancas and Máncora.

● **Crossing by Private Vehicle**
When driving into Peru vehicle fumigation is not required, but there is one outfit who will attempt to fumigate your vehicle with water and charge US$10. Beware of officials claiming that you need a carnet to obtain your 90-day transit permit; this is not so, cite Decreto Supremo 015-87-ICTI/TUR (but check that rules have not changed). Frequent road tolls between Tumbes and Lima, approx US$1.

● **Accommodation**
If stuck overnight in the border area there is a hotel in **Aguas Verdes**: **E** *Hostal El Bosque*, at S end of town on Av República de Perú 402, shared bath, basic, mosquito nets. Aguas Verdes also has phone booths and airline ticket offices.

There are 4 hotels in **Zarumilla**, at Km 1290 on the Pan-American Highway, 5 km S of Aguas Verdes. There is a signpost on the highway and the main plaza is only a few blocks away from the turn-off: **E** *Imperial*, on the plaza, small, modern, very basic, cold water turned off at night, mosquito nets, rec; **D** *Caribe*, newest and nicest.

● **Exchange**
The money changers on the Ecuadorean side sometimes give a better rate. Beware sharp practices by money changers using fixed calculators. If you are going to change TCs into Ecuadorean sucres in Huaquillas, make sure you cross the border in morning because the bank is closed after lunch. Do not change money on the minibus to Aguas Verdes, very poor rates.

● **Transport**
From Tumbes to border: colectivos leave from Calle Piura nr corner of Bolívar, US$1 pp or US$6 to hire car, and wait at the immigration office before continuing to the border, 30-40 mins. **Make sure the driver takes you all the way to the border and not just as far as the complex 3 km S of the bridge**. Minivans leave from the market area along Mcal Castilla across from Calle Alipio Rosales, US$0.50, luggage on roof. They leave passengers at the immigration office. Run down city buses ply the same route

as minivans, US$0.40, slower. Ortursa bus from Chiclayo also leaves passengers at the immigration complex. From the border complex to the bridge take colectivo, minibus (US$0.25) or moto-taxi (US$0.50). All vehicles only leave when full. They pass the turn-off for the airport from which it is a 500m walk to the terminal; colectivos to the airport charge US$1.50 pp, but often ask for much more. From the border to Zarumilla by moto-taxi costs US$0.50 pp.

Entering Peru, it is easier to take a colectivo to Tumbes and then a bus S, rather than trying to get on a bus from the border to a southern destination.

The South Coast

T HE mysterious Nazca lines, the precious Paracas bird reserve and Peru's wine and pisco-producing oases in and around Ica punctuate the desert south of the capital. The Pan-American Highway carries on down to Chile, with a dramatic branch inland, climbing to Arequipa.

SOUTH FROM LIMA

The first 60 km from Lima are dotted with a series of seaside resort towns and clubs: first is **El Silencio** (30 km, good), then **Punta Hermosa** (35 km), **Punta Negra** (40 km) and **San Bartolo** (43 km; *Posada del Mirador*, Malecón San Martín 105, T 290388, **C** in bungalows or **A3** full board, *Handbook* users are welcome). **Santa María**, 45 km from Lima, has the beautiful **A3** *Santa María Hotel*, meals included.

Pucusana is a charming fishing village, 60 km from Lima. There are excellent panoramas from the cliffs above the village. You can hire a boat for an hour, but fix the price beforehand and stick to it. Don't sail in the direction of the smelly factory, but to the rocks where you can see seabirds close at hand. There is a compulsory police checkpoint before the turning to Pucusana. *Hotel Bahía* has good seafood.

Chilca is a small beach resort 14 km S of Pucusana, 30 mins by colectivo from the

market place. You can walk along the beach from Chilca to Salinas (5 km), which has mineral baths. There are a few restaurants and *pensiones*. In summer (Dec-Feb), these places fill up with holidaymakers from Lima.

NB Most beaches have very strong currents and can be dangerous for swimming; if unsure, ask locals.

SAN VICENTE DE CAÑETE

About 150 km S of Lima, on the Río Cañete, this prosperous market centre is set amid desert scenery. It is commonly called Cañete (festival last week in Aug). At Cerro Azul, 13 km N of Cañete, is a unique Inca sea fort known as **Huarco**, which is now badly damaged.

- **Accommodation & places to eat** **D** *Hostal San Francisco*, Santa Rosa 317, 2 blocks N of plaza, T 912409, with bath, **E** without, new, quiet, rec. A rec restaurant is *Cevichería Muelle 56*, Bolognesi 156.

- **Buses** The main bus stop is on the highway; wait for the service you want going N or S and hope there are free seats. To **Pisco**, US$1.30. To Lunahuaná: unless you are on a Lima-Cañete-Imperial bus, take a combi from the highway to Imperial, then a bus to Lunahuaná.

LUNAHUANA

A paved road runs inland, mostly beside the Río Cañete, through **Imperial** (market Sat, Sun and Mon for every type of household item), and **Nuevo Imperial** to the Quebrada de Lunahuaná. After the town of **Lunahuaná** (40 km from Cañete), the road continues unpaved to Huancayo up in the sierra; bus US$9 (see page 1367).

Lunahuaná is 8 km beyond the Inca ruins of **Incawasi**, which dominated the valley. The town of Lunahuaná has several *anexos* – Paullo (with the ruin of the valley's first church), San Gerónimo, Langla, Jita, Condoray, Uchupampa and Catapalla (near which is the pre-Inca site of Cantagallo). It is interesting to visit the *bodegas* (wine cellars) in the valley and try the wine (the best-known is *Los Reyes*, in the *anexo* of **Condoray**).

Several places offer rafting and kayaking; eg *Camping San Jerónimo*, *Aldea Aventura Perú* in San Jerónimo and

Paullo. From Nov-April rafting is at levels 4-5. May-Oct is low water season with only boat trips possible (levels 1-2). Excellent kayaking is 2½ hrs upriver. Rafting costs US$15 pp for 1½ hrs. Annual championships are held every February.

Local festivals Fiesta de la Vendimia, grape harvest, first weekend in March. At the end of Sept/beginning Oct is the Fiesta del Níspero (medlar festival).

● **Accommodation A3-B** *Embassy* and *Embassy Río*, in Uchupampa, 3 km, T 472-3525, all facilities, restaurants, disco, gardens, rafting, large property, good, popular with families; **B** *Río Alto*, T 463-5490, in Condoray, just outside Lunahuaná, rooms, bungalows for 7, pool, hot water, restaurant, disco, rafting, very nice. **In Lunahuaná: D** *Los Casuarinos*, Grau 295, T Cañete 034-912627; **D-E** *Grau*, Grau 205, shared bath, all meals available.

● **Places to eat In Lunahuaná are:** *Lester*, on block 3 of Grau, good; *Sol y Río*, Malecón Araoz, arranges rafting. There are several other restaurants in town and in the surrounding *anexos*.

CHINCHA ALTA

35 km N of Pisco, near Chincha Baja, is **Tambo de Mora**, with nearby archaeological sites at Huaca de Tambo de Mora, La Centinela, Chinchaycama and Huaca Alvarado. **Chincha** itself is a fast-growing town where the negro/criollo culture is still alive. The famous festival, *Verano Negro*, is at the end of February.

● **Accommodation B** *Hacienda San José*, is a 17th century ranch-house, just outside town, full board, great lunch stop, buffet rec, pool, garden, small church, colonial crafts, the tunnels believed to link up with other ranches and the catacombs, where many slaves are interred, can be visited, US$15 pp. In the town of Chincha is **F** *Hostal La Rueda*, nr the plaza, breakfast extra, hot showers, pool, lounge; several other hotels.

PISCO

(*Pop* 82,250; *Phone code* 034) The largest port between Callao and Matarani, 237 km S of Lima, serves a large agricultural hinterland. It is a short distance to the W of the Panamerican Highway. The two parts of town, Pisco Pueblo with its colonial-style homes, and Pisco Puerto, which, apart from fisheries, has been replaced as a port by the deep-water Puerto Gen San Martín, have expanded into one.

Places of interest

In Pisco Pueblo, half a block W of the quiet Plaza de Armas, with its equestrian statue of San Martín, is the **Club Social Pisco**, Av San Martín 132, the HQ of San Martín after he had landed at Paracas Bay. There is an old Jesuit church on San Francisco, 1 block from the plaza, separated from the Municipalidad by a narrow park. The newer **Cathedral** is on the main plaza. Avenida San Martín runs from the Plaza de Armas to the sea.

Local information
● **Accommodation**

The town is full at weekends with visitors from Lima.

A3 *El Candelabro*, Av San Martín, 1 block from plaza, F 534620, midweek rates available, TV, fridge, fax service, hot water, café, bar on roof, laundry, safe.

C *Hostal Candelabro*, Av San Martín 1148, T 534616, TV, fridge, restaurant.

D *Embassy Boulevard*, Jr Comercio just off Plaza de Armas, noisy, nice bar on roof, has disco, trips to Ballestas Islands; **D** *Hostal Belén*, Plaza Belén, comfortable, electric showers, rec (on same plaza, *Hostal Perú*); **D** *Pisco*, on Plaza de Armas, T 532018, **F** without bath, hot water, rooms without windows, good tour company adjoining hotel, parking for motorcycles; **D** *Posada Hispana Hostal*, Bolognesi 236, T 536363, F 461-4907 (Lima), 5 rooms each with loft, bath, hot water, can accommodate groups, comfortable, information service, English, French, Italian and Catalonian spoken, highly rec.

E *Hostal San Jorge*, Juan Osores 267, sometimes hot water, rec; **E-F** *Colonial*, Comercio, pedestrianized part, shared bath, large rooms with balcony overlooking plaza.

F *Hostal Progreso*, Progreso 254, communal bathrooms, water shortages, rec. Mosquitoes are a problem at night in the summer; **F** pp *Hostal Pisco Playa* (Youth Hostel), Jr José Balta 639, Pisco Playa, T 532492, kitchen and washing facilities, quite nice, breakfast US$1.50.

● **Places to eat**

As de Oro, San Martín 472, good, reasonable prices, closed Mon; *Don Manuel*, Comercio 187, US$2-4 for main dish; *Ch'Reyes*, Jr Comercio (same block), good, set meal US$1; also on pedestrianized block of Comercio, *El Boulevard*, *Snack Pizza Catamarán*; *Chifa Progreso*, Callao at Plaza de Armas, good lunches.

There are seafood restaurants along the shore between Pisco and San Andrés, and in San Andrés (buses from Plaza Belén, nr *Hostal Perú*) there are: *La Fontana*, Lima 355, good food and pisco sours; *La Estrellita*; *Olimpia*, Grecia 200; and *Mendoza*, for fish and local dishes; all are rec.

● **Banks & money changers**
Banco de Crédito on Plaza de Armas gives good rates, for Amex and cash; also on Plaza, Interbanc.

● **Post & telecommunications**
Telephone: telephone and fax office on Plaza de Armas between Av San Martín y Callao.

● **Transport**
Local Taxis on Plaza de Armas. Combis from Cruce (see below), stop at Comercio by Plaza Belén.

Buses If arriving by bus, make sure it is going into town and will not leave you at the Cruce which is a 10-min combi ride, US$0.30, from the centre. To **Lima**, 242 km, 3-4 hrs, US$3.50, buses and colectivos every hour. Company offices in Pisco are: Ormeño, San Francisco, 1 block from plaza, and San Martín at San Martín 199. To **Ayacucho**, 13 hrs, US$6, several buses daily, leave from San Clemente 5 km N on Panamericana Sur, take a colectivo; make sure to take warm clothing as it gets cold at night. To **Huancavelica**, 269 km, 12-14 hrs, US$8, at 0800 and 1900 with Ormeño, old buses; also a few trucks. To **Ica** US$2 by colectivo, US$1 by bus, 1 hr, 70 km, 11 daily; with Ormeño; also Saavedra (Callao 181). To **Nasca**, 210 km, by bus, US$3.20, 3 hrs, via Ica, at 0830 with Oropesa, and 1600 with Ormeño. To **Arequipa**, US$11, 10-12 hrs, 3 daily.

PARACAS NATIONAL RESERVE

15 km down the coast from Pisco Puerto is the bay of **Paracas**, sheltered by the Paracas peninsula. (The name means "sandstorm" – they can last for 3 days, especially in Aug; the wind gets up every afternoon, peaking at around 1500). Paracas can be reached by the coast road from San Andrés, passing the fishing port and a large proportion of Peru's fishmeal industry. Alternatively, go down the Pan-American Highway to 14.5 km past the Pisco turning and take the road to Paracas across the desert. After 11 km turn left along the coast road and 1 km further on fork right to Paracas village. The peninsula, a large area of coast to the S and the Ballestas Islands are a National Reserve (entrance US$1

pp); it is one of the best marine reserves, with the highest concentration of marine birds, in the world.

Return to the main road for the entrance to the Reserve (ask for a map here). There are an archaeological museum (US$0.65, open daily 0900-1700) and a shop (guide books, film, drinks) and a natural history museum. You can walk down to the shore from the museum to see flamingoes feeding in Paracas bay (boat trips do not go to see flamingoes; in Jan-Mar the flamingoes go to the Sierra). The tiny fishing village of Lagunillas is 5 km from the museum across the neck of the peninsula; it has clean, safe beaches free from sting rays and good eating places, eg *Rancho de la Tía Fela*. A network of firm dirt roads, reasonably well signed, crosses the peninsula; for walking, details available from Park Office or ask for 'Hoja 28-K' map at Instituto Geográfico Militar in Lima for US$5 (it is not safe to walk if alone). Also note that it is easy to get lost in the hot, wide desert area. Other sites on the peninsula include Mirador de los Lobos at Punta El Arquillo, 6 km from Lagunilla, with view of sealions; and a rock formation in the cliffs called La Catedral, 6 km from Lagunilla in the opposite direction.

About 14 km from the museum is the precolumbian Candelabra (Candelabro in Spanish) traced in the hillside, at least 50m long, best seen from the sea, but still impressive from the land. Hitch along the paved road which leads to Punta Pejerrey, get off at left fork and you will see a trail (1½ hrs walk to Candelabra under a blazing sun, take water and sunscreen). Condors may be seen (Feb/Mar) from the (bad) road between Paracas and Laguna Grande.

Local information
● **Accommodation**
A3 *Paracas*, good hotel, bungalows on beach (T Pisco 532220 or Lima 472-3850, F 447-5073) good food, not cheap, good buffet lunch on Sun, fine grounds facing the bay, it is a good centre for excursions to the Peninsula and flights over Nasca; it has tennis courts and an open-air swimming pool (US$2 for non-residents); it also houses the Masson ceramics collection which is worth seeing.

C *Hostal Santa Elena*, a few kilometres from

the Paracas National Park, reservations in Lima T 718222; with restaurant 'the cook is legendary', the beach is safe for swimming as there are no manta rays – dangerous fish with a sharp dorsal fin which hide in sand, local trips can be organized, the hotel is now sandwiched between two fishmeal factories; **C El Mirador**, at the turn-off to El Chaco, hot water, no phone, good service, boat trips arranged, meals available, sometimes full board only, reservations in Lima, T 445-8496, ask for Sra Rosa. Camping is possible on the beach nr the *Hotel Paracas* at a spot called La Muelle, no facilities, sea polluted. Ask for permission to camp in the reserve, but note that there is no water. Do not camp alone as robberies occur.

● **Places to eat**
Excellent fried fish at open-sided restaurants at El Chaco (see below), eg *Jhonny y Jennifer*, friendly; *El Chorito*, close to *Hotel Paracas*.

● **Transport**
Local Taxi from Pisco to Paracas about US$3-4; combis to/from El Chaco beach (marked 'Chaco-Paracas-Museo') when full, US$0.50, 25 mins; several buses, US$0.30, leave from the market in Pisco. Make sure you catch the last bus back at about 1600. By private transport it takes about 50 mins to Lagunilla, 45 mins to La Mina and 1 hr to Mirador de los Lobos. Make sure your car is in good condition, never leave it unattended, and travel in a group as robbery has been a problem in the past. There is no public transport on the peninsula.

BALLESTAS ISLANDS

Trips to the **Islas Ballestas** leave from the jetty at El Chaco, the beach and fishing port by Paracas village. The islands are spectacular, eroded into numerous arches and caves (*ballesta* means bow, as in archery), which provide shelter for thousands of seabirds, some of which are very rare, and sea lions. The book *Las Aves del Departamento de Lima* by Maria Koepcke is useful.

● **Tours** For trips to Islas Ballestas: *Blue Sea Tours*, C Chosica 320, San Andrés, Pisco, T 034-533469, anexo 35, also at El Chaco, guides Jorge Espejo and Hubert Van Lomoen (speaks Dutch) are frequently rec; there is no time limit on tours. On C San Francisco, Pisco: *Paseo Turístico Islas Ballestas*, No 109, multi-lingual guide, rec; *Ballestas Travel Service*, No 249, T 533095, rec; *Paracas Tours*, No 257. *The Zarcillo Connection*, Arequipa 164, T 262795, also good for Paracas National Reserve. The main hotels in Pisco and Paracas will also arrange tours (eg *Hotel Paracas*, US$30 in their own speed

boat, 0900-1700). Short trips last 3 hrs; it's better to go in the morning when the sea is not so rough. The full trip includes Isla San Gallán, where there are thousands of sea lions, and is rec. All boats are speedboats with life jackets, some are very crowded; wear warm clothing. You will see, close up, thousands of inquisitive sea lions, guano birds, pelicans, penguins and, if you're lucky, dolphins swimming in the bay. The boats pass Puerto San Martín and the Candelabra en route to the islands. Tours to the islands cost US$11 pp; to the peninsula US$20 pp; out of season tours are a lot cheaper.

INLAND FROM PISCO

A 317 km road goes to Ayacucho in the sierra, with a branch to Huancavelica. It is paved as far as Huaytará and is being paved thereafter. At Castrovirreyna it reaches 4,600m. The scenery on this journey is superb.

Tambo Colorado, one of the best-preserved Inca ruins in coastal Peru, is 48 km from Pisco, up the Pisco valley. It includes buildings where the Inca and his retinue would have stayed. Many of the walls retain their original colours. On the other side of the road is the public plaza and the garrison and messengers' quarters. The caretaker will act as a guide, he has a small collection of items found on the site. Entrance US$1.50. From Humay, go to Hacienda Montesarpe, and 500m above the hacienda is the line of holes known as 'La avenida misteriosa de las picaduras de viruelas' (the mysterious avenue of smallpox spots) which stretches along the Andes for many kilometres. Its purpose is still unknown.

● **Transport** Buses from Pisco, 0800, Oropesa US$1.60, 3 hrs; also colectivos, US$1.20 pp. Alight 20 mins after the stop at Humay; the road passes right through the site. Return by bus to Pisco in the afternoon. For the bus or truck back to Pisco wait at Sr Mendoza, the caretaker's house. Taxi from Pisco US$30.

Huaytará is 4 hrs by bus from Pisco. The whole side of the church is a perfectly preserved Inca wall with niches and trapezoidal doorways. 20 mins from town are the ruins of **Incahuasi** with thermal baths. On 24 June is the Fiesta of San Juan Bautista, which involves a week of processions, fireworks, bullfights and dancing day and night.

• **Accommodation & transport D** *Hotel de Turistas*, lodging, food and tours; **E** *Municipal*, no restaurant, warm water. Bus from Pisco US$2.25 (US$5.50 for festival); also Molina from Lima, 6 hrs.

ICA

From Pisco the Pan-American Highway runs 60 km S to **Guadalupe** (*Restaurant Sol de Mayo*, 1 block N of main plaza, good *menú* for US$1.50), then continues a further 10 km to **Ica** (*Pop* 152,300; *Phone code* 034), on the Río Ica. The San Jerónimo church at Cajamarca 262 has a fine mural behind the altar. Ica is famous for its *tejas*, a local sweet of *manjarblanco*, which is sold behind the Luren church. The waters of the Choclacocha and Orococha lakes from the eastern side of the Andes are tunnelled into the Ica valley and irrigate 30,000 ha of land. The lakes are at 4,570m. The tunnel is over 9 km long.

Wine and Pisco
Ica is Peru's chief wine centre. Bodegas that one can visit are: **El Carmen**, on the right-hand side when arriving from Lima (has an ancient grape press made from a huge tree trunk). **Vista Alegre** (Spanish is essential), its shop is recommended; official tours on Fri and Sat 0830-1130. A local bus drops you at the entrance, or it's a 10-15 mins' walk on the other side of the river. **El Catador**, José Carrasco González, 10 km outside Ica, in the district of Subtanjalla, a shop selling home-made wines and pisco, and traditional handicrafts associated with winemaking. In the evening it is a restaurant-bar with dancing and music, best visited during harvest, late Feb to early April, wine and pisco tasting usually possible. Open daily 0800-1800; bus from the 2nd block of Moquegua, every 30 mins, US$0.10. Near El Catador is **Bodega Alvarez**, whose owner, Umberto Alvarez, is very hospitable and won the gold medal for the best pisco in Peru in 1995. Ask about *pisco de mosto verde* and the rarer, more expensive, *pisco de limón*. A very good, strong *moscatel* is made by Sr Luis Chipana who lives on the main plaza beside his bodega; ask for him in the bar on the plaza (take your own bottle).

Museums
Museo Regional houses mummies, ceramics, textiles and trepanned skulls from the Paracas, Nasca and Inca cultures; a good, well-displayed collection of Inca counting strings (*quipus*) and clothes made of feathers. Behind the building is a scale model of the Nasca lines with an observation tower; a useful orientation before visiting the lines. The attendant paints copies of motifs from the ceramics and textiles in the original pigments (US$1), and sells his own good maps of Nasca for US$1.65. Take bus 17 from the Plaza de Armas (US$0.50); open 0745-1900, Mon-Sat: Sun 0900-1300 (US$1.15, students US$0.65).

Excursions
5 km from Ica, round a palm-fringed lake and amid impressive sand dunes, is the attractive oasis and summer resort of **Huacachina**. Its green sulphur waters are said to be curative and thousands of visitors come to swim and relax here. Sleeping in the open is pleasant and swimming in the lake is beautiful, but watch out for soft sand (and, as elsewhere, watch your belongings). Sandboarding on the dunes is a major pastime here; board hire US$1.20/hr, from Manuel's restaurant, where you can also pitch a tent.

• **Accommodation C** *Hotel Mossone* (4 hrs' drive from Lima), or **A3**, full board, is at the eastern end of the lake, T 231651, F 236137. Another good hotel is the **F** *Salvatierra*, with private bath. Both are great places to relax.

• **Transport** Bus from plaza in Ica to Huacachina, US$0.50, 10-15 mins; taxi US$1.50.

Local festivals
Wine harvest festival in early March. The image of El Señor de Luren, in a fine church in Parque Luren, draws pilgrims from all Peru to the twice-yearly festivals in Mar and Oct (15-21), when there are all-night processions.

Local information
● **Accommodation**
Hotels are fully booked during the harvest festival and prices rise greatly.

A2 *Las Dunas*, Av La Angostura 400, T 231031, F 231007, plus 18% tax and service, about 20% cheaper on weekdays, highly rec, in a complete resort with restaurant, swimming pool, horse riding and other activities, it has its own airstrip for flights over Nasca, 50 mins. Lima offices: Ricardo Rivera Navarrete 889, Oficina 208, San Isidro, Casilla 4410, Lima 100, T/F 442-4180.

C-D *Hostal Siesta I*, Independencia 160, T 233249, hot water, hospitable owner; *Siesta II*, T 234633, similar.

E *Colón*, Plaza de Armas, **F** without bath, basic, dirty, old, noisy, restaurant; **E** *Confort*, La Mar 251, 4 blocks from plaza, possible to park motorcycle; **E** *Hostal El Aleph*, Independencia 152, good.

F *El Colibri*, C Grau 387, T 225364, small, very helpful; **F** *Lima*, Lima 262, basic but quiet; **F** *Europa*, Independencia 258, cold water, good.

● **Places to eat**
Macondo, Jr Bolívar 300, fish good, rec; *El Otro Peñoncito*, Bolívar 255, friendly, clean, good toilets; *El Fogón*, Municipalidad 276, good and cheap. Good one at Ormeño bus terminal. *El Edén*, *Casa Naturista*, vegetarian at Andahuaylas 204. *Pastelería La Spiga*, Lima 243, rec; *Pastelería Velazco*, on Plaza de Armas, clean, good service, rec.

● **Banks & money changers**
Avoid changing TCs if possible as commission is high. If necessary, use **Banco de Crédito**.

● **Post & telecommunications**
Post office at Lima y Moquegua; **telephone** at Av San Martín y Huánuco.

● **Tourist offices**
On Cajamarca, 1/2 block from Plaza de Armas. **Touring y Automóvil Club del Perú**, Manzanilla 523.

● **Transport**
Buses To Pisco, 70 km, 1 hr, US$1 by bus, several daily; colectivos from opp Ormeño. To Lima, 302 km, 4 hrs, US$5, several daily inc Soyuz and Flores (see also Lima, **Bus Compa-**

nies); in Ica Ormeño is at Lambayeque 180. All bus offices are on Lambayeque blocks 1 and 2 and Salaverry block 3. To **Nasca**, 140 km, 2 hrs, US$2, several buses and colectivos daily, inc Ormeño, last bus 2100. To **Arequipa** the route goes via Nasca, see under Nasca.

Warning Beware of thieves in the market, at the bus station and around the Plaza de Armas, even in daylight.

SOUTH TO NASCA

The southern oases, S of Ica to the Chilean frontier, produce enough to support themselves, but little more. The highlands grow increasingly arid and the coast more rugged. There are only thin ribbons of cultivable lands along valley bottoms, and most of these can be irrigated only in their upper reaches. However, the cotton plantations between Ica and Nasca and the orange-growing centre at Palpa are exceptions. In several places the Highway is not protected against drifting sand and calls for cautious driving.

NASCA

(*Pop* 30,000; *Alt* 619m; *Phone code* 034); 141 km S of Ica by the Pan-American Highway, set in a green valley amid a perimeter of mountains, 444 km from Lima. Its altitude puts it just above any fog which may drift in from the sea. The sun blazes the year round by day and the nights are crisp. Overlooking the town is Cerro Blanco (2,078m), the highest sand dune in the world, which is popular for sandboarding and parapenting.

Dr Cabrera's stones

The museum on the Plaza de Armas, run by Dr Javier Cabrera, has a collection of several thousand engraved stones. Open Mon-Sat 0930-1230 and 1730-2000 and sometimes open Sun. If visiting in a group T 234363. We are informed that some of these stones are fakes: people have talked to the craftsmen concerned. If authentic, the stones suggest the existence of a technologically-advanced people contemporary with the dinosaurs, but the archaeological establishment seems very reluctant to study them. If interested, contact Ms Sophia Afford, Le Petit Canadeau, Le Plan du Castellet, Le Beausset, 83330, France, T 94 987241, a geologist who has written several articles on the subject. (There are so many stones that its is impossible to believe they are all fakes. Most are in a recognisably pre-Inca style, but, for instance, kangaroo and a giraffe in the style of a modern children's story book, strain the visitor's credulity.)

The Nascas had a highly developed civilization which reached its peak about AD 800. Their polychrome ceramics, wood carvings and adornments of gold are on display in many of Lima's museums (see after **Local information** for the Nasca Lines).

Museums

The Nasca municipality's museum, on the main plaza, has a small but fine collection. Entry, US$1, open Mon-Sat 0900-1200, 1600-1700.

Excursions

The Nasca area is dotted with over 100 cemeteries and the dry, humidity-free climate has preserved perfectly invaluable tapestries, cloth and mummies. At **Chauchilla** (30 km S of Nasca), grave robbing *huaqueros* ransacked the tombs and left bones, skulls, mummies and pottery shards littering the desert, but latest reports suggest that practically nothing is left. A tour takes about 2 hrs and should cost about US$7 pp with a minimum of 3 people. 20 km from Nasca, **Poroma** cemetery is on the right, signed (poorly). Cemetery tours usually include a visit to a gold shop. Gold mining is one of the main local industries and a tour usually includes a visit to a small family processing shop where the techniques used are still very old-fashioned. Some tours also include a visit to a local potter's studio. That of Sr Andrés Calle Benavides, who makes Nasca reproductions, is particularly recommended.

To the Paredones ruins and aqueduct: the ruins, also called Cacsamarca, are Inca on a pre-Inca base. They are not well-preserved. The underground aqueducts, built 300 BC-700 AD, are still in working order and worth seeing. 33 aqueducts irrigate 20 ha each; they are cleaned end Oct/early Nov. By taxi it is about US$10 round trip, or go with a tour.

Cantalloc is a 30 mins-1 hr walk through Buena Fe, to see markings in the valley floor. These consist of a triangle pointing to a hill and a *tela* (cloth) with a spiral depicting the threads. Climb the mountain to see better examples.

Cahuachi, to the W of the Nasca Lines, comprises several pyramids and a site called **El Estaquería**. The latter is thought to have been a series of astronomical sighting posts, but more recent research suggests the wooden pillars were used to dry dead bodies and therefore it may have been a place of mummification. Tours cost about US$5 pp with a minimum of 3 people.

Sacaco, 30 km S of Nasca, has a museum built over the fossilized remains of a whale excavated in the desert. The keeper lives in a house nearby and is helpful. Take a bus from Nasca, C Bolognesi, in the morning (check times in advance) towards Puerto de Lomas, ask the driver where to get off and be ready for a 30-min (2 km) walk in the sun. Return to the Pan-American Highway no later than 1800 for a bus back. Do not go 2-3 days after a new moon as a vicious wind blows at this time.

Puerto de Lomas is a fishing village to the S of Nasca, with safe beaches which are popular in Feb-Mar. It is 1½ hrs by bus, US$1.75 (1 hr by car).

● **Accommodation & places to eat** **C** *Hostal Capricho de Verano*, T 210282, beautifully-situated on the cliffs, bungalows with bath, clean, same owner as *Hostal Don Agucho* in Nasca, run by very friendly elderly couple, special rates for young travellers, rec. 100m beyond is *Restaurant Alojamiento Melchorita*; also several fish restaurants.

Tours

Alegría Tours, run by Efraín Alegría, Jr Lima 168, T/F 522244, cellular 667177/667718, offer inclusive tours to the different archaeological sites of the area (see *Hotel Alegría* below) which have been repeatedly recommended (they also run tours to Lima, Arequipa, Cusco and Puno). Guides with radio contact and maps can be provided for hikes to nearby sites. Juan Valdivia is very knowledgeable on the Nasca and Paracas cultures and speaks English. The Fernández family, who run the *Hotel Nasca*, also run local tours. Ask for the hotel owners and speak to them direct. Also rec is Juan Tohalino Vera of *Nasca Trails*, at Ignacio Morsesky 122, T 522858, he speaks English, French, German and Italian. Ask Efraín Alegría or the Fernández family to arrange a taxi for you to one of the sites outside Nasca (eg US$50 to Sacaco, 30 mins at site) as it is recommended only to visit the sites with a trustworthy person. Taxi drivers usually act as guides, but most speak only Spanish. All guides must be approved by the Ministry of Tourism: ask to see an identity card. Tour and hotel touts try to overcharge or mislead those who arrive by bus: do not conduct any business at the bus station. We have received reports of some hotels putting pressure on guests to take their tours, or offering a two-tier service for those who buy their tours and those who do not.

Local festivals

29 Aug-10 Sept: Virgen de la Guadelupe.

Local information

● **Accommodation**

A3 *Nasca Lines*, Jr Bolognesi, T 522293, F 522293, a/c, comfortable, rooms with private patio, hot water, peaceful, restaurant, good but expensive meals, safe car park, pool (US$5 for non-guests, or free if having lunch), they can arrange package tours which include 2-3 nights at the hotel plus flight over the lines and a desert trip for around US$250, rec; **A3** *De La Borda*, T 522576, old hacienda at Majoro, about 5 km from town past airstrip, lovely gardens, 2 pools, excellent restaurant, quiet, helpful, English-speaking manageress, rec.

B *Maison Suisse*, opp the airport, T/F 522434, nice, comfortable, safe car park, restaurant, pool, new rooms with jacuzzi, accepts Amex, good giftshop, shows video of Nasca lines.

C *Hostal Don Agucho*, Paredones y San Carlos, T 522048, very nice, good, garage; **C** *Albergue Villa Verde*, Pasaje Angela s/n, T 523373, small, country-style lodge in quiet gardens, pursues environmental improvements, pool, bar, parking; **C-D** *Hostal Las Líneas*, Jr Arica 299, T 522488, spacious, restaurant, rec; **C-E** *Hotel Alegría*, Jr Lima 166, T 522702, T/F 522444, cellular 667177/667718, nr bus station, 4 new bungalows and 20 rooms with bath and continental breakfast, inc tax, or rooms with communal bath, basic, hot water, cafeteria, swimming pool, garden with coffee shop, manager (Efraín Alegría) speaks English and Hebrew, rec, tours (see above), laundry service and facilities, safe luggage deposit (inc for bus passengers not needing a hotel), book exchange, very popular, flights and bus tickets arranged, those arriving by bus should beware being told that *Alegría* is closed, or full, and no longer runs tours, if you call the hotel they will pick you up at the bus station free of charge day or night.

D *El Huarango*, Av Los Incas 117, opp Ormeño bus terminal, T 522497, **E** without bath, hot water, good facilities, TV; **D** *Internacional*, Av Maria Reiche, T 522166, quiet, hot water, garage, café, new bungalows; **D** *Montecarlo*, Jr Callao, T 522577, hot water (ask for it), quite old, small

pool, offers flights over the Lines plus 1 night's lodging in bungalow but not all year round, mixed reports; **D** *Via Morburg*, JM Mejía 108, T 522566, fan, hot water, quiet, pleasant, the hotel is associated with *Restaurant El Huarango*, good food and prices, bar, live entertainment.

E *Hostal El Sol*, Jr Tacna, on Plaza de Armas, T 522064, with hot shower, basic, small.

F *Nasca*, C Lima 438, T/F 522085, hot water, noisy, laundry facilities, luggage store, hard sell on tours and flights, bargain hard for better price, mixed

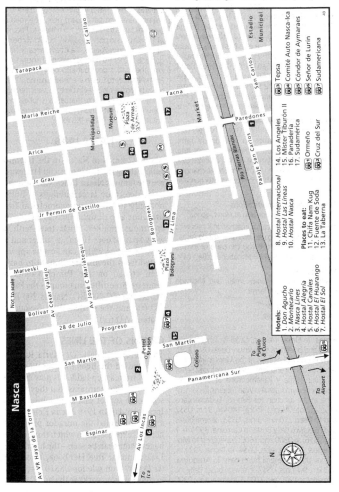

Hotels:
1. Don Agucho
2. Montecarlo
3. Nasca Lines
4. Hostal Alegría
5. Hostal Canales
6. Hostal El Huarango
7. Hostal El Sol
8. Hostal Internacional
9. Hostal Las Líneas
10. Hostal Nasca

Places to eat:
11. Chifa Nam Kug
12. Fuente de Soda
13. La Taberna
14. Los Angeles
15. Mister Tiburón II
16. Panadería
17. Sudamerica

🚌1 Ormeño
🚌2 Cruz del Sur
🚌3 Tepsa
🚌4 Comité Auto Nasca-Ica
🚌5 Cóndor de Aymaraes
🚌6 Señor de Lurin
🚌7 Sudamericana

Not to scale

Nasca

reports, safe motorcycle parking; dirty bathrooms; **F** *San Martín*, Arica 116, basic, hot showers.

Camping: in the grounds of *Restaurant Nido del Cóndor* opp the airport.

● **Places to eat**

Nido del Cóndor, opp airport, also has shop, videos, swimming pool; *Aviance*, Arica 213, rec for *menú*; *Cañada*, Lima 160, cheap, good *menú*, excellent pisco sours, rec; *Los Angeles*, ½-block from Plaza de Armas, good, cheap, try *sopa criolla*, and chocolate cake; similar is *Concordia*, Lima 594, which rents bikes at US$1/hr; *Chifa Nam Kug*, on Bolognesi nr Plaza, rec; *La Púa*, Jr Lima, next to *Hotel Alegría*, good; *La Taberna*, Jr Lima 326, excellent food, live music, friendly, popular with travellers, worth a look just for the graffiti; *Mister Tiburón II*, C San Martín, clean, good food; *Sudamérica*, Lima 668, good local food, especially meat; *Fuente de Soda Jumbory*, nr cinema, good *almuerzo*; *Panadería Pin-Pan*, Lima y F de Castillo. The pisco sours are rec as the best in Peru.

● **Banks & money changers**

Banco de Crédito, Lima y Grau, changes cash and TCs, cash advance on visa, decent rates. Banco de la Nación exchanges at poor rate. Interbanc, on the Plaza de Armas, changes cash and will advance on Visa. Some street changers will change TCs for 3% commission after bargaining.

● **Post & telecommunications**

At Lima 816, post office also at *Hotel Alegría*.

Telephone: Telefónica for international calls with coins on Plaza Bolognesi; also on Plaza de Armas and at Lima 359 where you can send or receive fax messages and make international collect calls.

● **Shopping**

Markets at Lima y Grau, small, and Mercado Central entre Arica y Tacna.

● **Useful addresses**

Police: at Av Los Incas.

● **Transport**

Buses To Lima, 446 km, US$5-8, 7 hrs, several buses and colectivos daily, luxury buses US$12.50, Ormeño, on Av Los Incas nr the *Montecarlo* hotel, rec; Cruz del Sur and Tepsa also on Los Incas; Señor de Luren, Lima y Panamericana at the Ovalo; Cóndor de Aymaraes and Wari Tours on Panamericana at the junction for Puquio; Sudamericana office in *Hotel Alegría*. To Ica, 140 km, 3 hrs, US$2 and to Pisco 210 km, 3 hrs, US$3, several buses and colectivos daily. Buses to Camaná, 390 km, 7 hrs, US$6, at 0300 and 1600; continuing to Moquegua, 244 km, 4 hrs, US$4. To Tacna, 793 km, 12 hrs, US$12, several buses daily. To Arequipa, 623 km, 9-11 hrs, US$7-9; several buses daily, inc Ormeño, at 1900 and 2100, Sudamericano, 0300

and 2030; and Cruz del Sur at 2000 and 2230, delays possible out of Nasca because of drifting sand across the road or because of mudslides in the rainy season. Travel in daylight if possible – buses that leave around 0300, 0330 do most of the journey in daylight. Book ticket on previous day. Watch out for bus companies charging the full fare from Lima to Arequipa and for overbooking.

Cóndor de Aymaraes and Wari run buses to Cusco, 659 km, 25 hrs, US$18, at night only; the route goes through **Reserva Nacional Pampas Galeras**, which has a vicuña reserve. There is a military base and park guard here. The road is paved as far as the Reserve; from there to Puquío, at 155 km, it is in poor condition, but slowly being upgraded. From Puquío, via Chalhuanca (where gasoline is sold from the drum) to Abancay (309 km), the road is poor but also being upgraded. From Abancay to Cusco the road is paved. These buses begin their journey in Lima, so seats may not always be available. Note that safety is not assured (terrorists or bandits) and most major bus lines have not resumed services on this route.

NASCA LINES

About 22 km N of Nasca, in the Ingenio valley, along the Pan-American Highway, are the famous Nasca Lines. Cut into the stony desert are large numbers of lines, not only parallels and geometrical figures, but also designs such as a dog, an enormous monkey, birds (one with a wing span of over 100m), a spider and a tree. The lines, which can best be appreciated from the air, are thought to have been etched on the Pampa Colorada sands by three different groups – the Paracas people 900-200 BC, Nascas 200 BC-AD 600 and the settlers from Ayacucho at about AD 630.

ORIGINS OF THE LINES

The German expert, Dr Maria Reiche, who studied the lines for over 40 years, mostly from a step ladder, is now over 90 years old. She maintains that they represent some sort of vast astronomical pre-Inca calendar. In 1976 Maria Reiche had a platform called the mirador put up at her own expense, from which three of the huge designs can be seen – the hands, the Lizard and the Tree. Her book, *Mystery on the Desert*, is on sale for US$10 (proceeds to conservation work) at the hotel. In Jan

1994 Maria Reiche opened a small museum (entry US$0.50), 5 km from town at the Km 416 marker. Another good book is *Pathways to the Gods: the mystery of the Nasca Lines*, by Tony Morrison (Michael Russell, 1978), obtainable in Lima.

Another theory is that the ancient Nazcas flew in hot-air balloons; this is based on the fact that the lines are best seen from the air, and that there are pieces of ancient local pottery and tapestry showing balloonists, and local legends of flying men (which would be supported by the engraved designs on stones in Ica – see page 1306) if these are proved authentic. See *Nasca, the flight of Condor 1*, by Jim Woodman, Murray, 1980 (Pocket Books, NY 1977).

Georg A von Breunig (1980) discounts both the above theories, claiming that the lines are the tracks of running contests. He bases his argument on the asymmetrical surface level at curves in the designs and on the triangular fields which accord with human running characteristics, and with a number of runners starting from a straight line, then becoming an extended string of contestants. A similar theory was proposed by the English astronomer Alan Sawyer.

Other theories are that the Nasca designs represent weaving patterns and yarns (Henri Stirlin) and that the plain is a map demonstrating the Tiahuanaco Empire (Zsoltan Zelko). *The Nazca Lines – a new perspective on their origin and meaning* (Editorial Los Pinos, Lima 18), by Dr Johan Reinhard, brings together ethnographic, historical and archaeological data, including current use of straight lines in Chile and Bolivia, to suggest that the Lines conform to fertility practices throughout the Andes.

● **Tours on land**
Taxi-guides to the mirador, 0800-1200, cost US$7 pp, or you can hitch, but there is not always much traffic. Travellers suggest the view from the hill 500m back to Nasca is better. Ormeño bus leaves for the lines at 0900 (US$1.75); hitch back, but have patience. Go by an early bus as the site gets very hot. Better still, take a taxi and arrive at 0745 before the buses.

● **Tours by air**
Small planes take 3-5 passengers to see the Nasca Lines. Reservations can be made at the airport for flights with Aerocóndor; their office is opposite *Hotel Nasca Lines*. Flights can also be booked at Alas Peruanas (*Hotel Alegría*, experienced pilots fluent in English), *Hotel Nasca*, Aero Montecarlo (from hotel of that name), or Aerolca in Jr Lima and at the airport. These companies are recommended; there are others. The price for a flight is US$40-50 pp, plus US$1.50 airport tax. It is best to organize a flight with the airlines themselves, or with Familia Fernández at *Hotel Nasca*. Flights should last from 30 to 45 mins, but are sometimes cut to 20, and are bumpy with many tight turns – many people are airsick. Best times to fly are 0800-1000 and 1500-1630 when there is less turbulence and better light. Aerocóndor in Lima (T 442-5663, or at the *Sheraton Hotel*, T 433-3320) and Aerolca (T 441-8614/8608) both offer flights over the lines from Lima in a 1-day tour (lunch in Nasca) for US$260 pp; or flights from Ica for US$130 pp. Aerolca also offers a night in *Maison Suisse* plus flight for US$65, but book 48 hrs in advance. Taxi to airport, US$1.35, bus, US$0.10. Make sure you clarify everything before getting on the plane and ask for a receipt. Also let them know in advance if you have any special requests.

SOUTH OF NASCA

After Nasca the Pan-American Highway returns through impressive desert scenery to the coast at Puerto de Lomas and passes by Chala, **Atico** and Ocoña, to Camaná (392 km from Nasca). The road from Atico to Camaná is cut into steep cliffs and offers great views. Basic accommodation in Atico at **E** *Hostal Unión*, Av Arequipa 700. Cyclists warn that the headwinds between Nasca and Atico can be very severe.

Chala, 173 km from Nasca, is a friendly fishing village with beaches where condors may be seen. Good fresh fish is available in the morning and possibilities of fishing with the local fishermen. There is no electricity after midnight. Many of the locals work in gold-panning.

● **Accommodation** C *Turistas*, in renovated building, **D** without bath, large rooms, good beds, hot water, restaurant, great sea view, rec; **F** *Hostal Grau*, has rooms facing the ocean; next door is *Hostal Evelyn*, similar, both good. There are dozens of restaurants, mostly catering for passing buses.

PUERTO INCA

10 km N of Chala are the large precolumbian ruins of **Puerto Inca** on the coast. This was the port for Cusco. The site is in excellent condition: the drying and store houses can be seen as holes in the ground (be careful where you walk). On the right side of the bay is a cemetery, on the hill a temple of reincarnation, and the Inca road from the coast to Cusco is clearly visible. The road was 240 km long, with a staging post every 7 km so that, with a change of runner at every post, messages could be sent in 24 hrs.

● **Accommodation & access** C *Beach Resort Puerto Inka*, Km 603 Panamericana Sur (for reservations; Central Telefónica Chala (054) 210260, or Arequipa T 254827, T/F 237122), **D** without bath, the water is brackish, excellent food, by the beautiful beach, great place to relax, boat hire, diving equipment rental, safe camping for US$2, discount for longer stay, highly rec. Taxi from Chala US$6.75; 1-day tour from Nasca, US$10 pp. From Chala, at Km 603 on the Panamericana, follow an unpaved road on the left for a few kilometres to the hotel and ruins.

Southern Peru: Arequipa, Lake Titicaca

AREQUIPA and Lake Titicaca share great local pride and major tourist popularity: colonial architecture in Arequipa; the tranquility of Lake Titicaca and the bustling folklore of Puno. All are set in the southern cordilleras of the Peruvian Andes, with smoking volcanoes, deep canyons, bleak altiplano and terraced valleys.

THE COAST TO AREQUIPA

CAMANA

This nice, lively coastal town is 222 km S from Chala. 5 km away is **La Punta**, the most popular of Camaná's beaches, especially during summer weekends when young Arequipeños come to party in the many bars and discos. The beach is pleasant but has little shade and is dangerous for swimming owing to the strong undertow. Colectivos leave frequently day and night from Camaná, US$0.25.

32 km S of Camaná is the pleasant village of **Quilca**, perched on a cliff overlooking the Río Siguas, on the Río Quilca. In colonial times the nearby port, now seedy, was the unloading point for goods im-

ported via Arequipa to Potosí. A bus leaves daily at 0900 and returns from Quilca at 1330; US$1.40, 2 hrs. The coastal village of **Chira**, 12 km N of Camaná is worth a visit for its impressive sea cliffs, sea birds and quiet beaches. Catch a colectivo to **Atico** and ask to get off at Chira; US$0.70, 30 mins.

- **Accommodation C-D** *Turistas*, Av Lima 138, T 571113, old colonial building, with breakfast, big rooms, helpful, safe, restaurant downstairs, rec; **D** *Lider 2*, Av Mcal Castilla 678 (new Pan-American Highway), T 571365, hot water, comfortable; **D** *Residencial Selva*, Prolongación 2 de Mayo 225, Urb Granada, T 572063, cold water, modern, spacious, laundry facilities, cafeteria, patios and gardens, not very central but the owner will collect you if you call him on arrival in Camaná, discount for longer stays, highly rec; **E** *Lider 1*, Av Lima 268 (old Pan-American Highway), with bath, clean, good restaurant, safe motorcycle parking for US$3. **NB** Hotels tend to be full in Jan, Feb and Mar.

- **Places to eat** *Chifa Hong Kong*, Plaza de Armas, excellent food at reasonable prices, popular; *Turístico*, Av Pizarro 304, T 210280, seafood and *peña*. The best place for breakfast is the food market. The freshwater shrimps are delicious.

- **Buses** To Lima, many buses daily, US$12, 12 hrs. To Arequipa, many daily, US$4, 3½ hrs. To Pisco Flores Hnos, Sudamericano, US$7, 8 hrs. Many companies have their offices on Av Lima.

ROUTES The Pan-American Highway swings inland from Camaná and runs along the top of a plateau with strange crescent-shaped dunes (see page 1326). The sudden descents into the canyons of the Siguas and Vitor rivers are interesting, as is the pink stone valley at Km 945. West of Arequipa, 74 km before Repartición, a dirt road branches left off the Pan-American Highway leading to Corire, Aplao and the valley of the Río Majes.

TORO MUERTO

The world's largest field of petroglyphs at **Toro Muerto** is near **Corire**. Turn-off on the right heading back out of Corire; 1 hr walk; ask directions. The higher you go, the more interesting the petroglyphs, though many have been ruined by graffiti. The sheer scale of the site is awe-inspiring and the view is wonderful. Take plenty of water and protection against the sun, including sunglasses.

- **Accommodation F** *Hostal Willys*, Plaza de Armas, helpful; *Hostal Manuelito*, 3 blocks from the plaza, good. Another *Hostal*, 1 block from plaza, is OK, hot water. Several restaurants around the plaza; **Banco de Crédito**.

- **Buses** To Corire leave from Arequipa main terminal hourly from 0500, 3 hrs.

COTAHUASI CANYON

Simon Harvey and Mark Duffy write: "Beyond Aplao the road heads N through **Chuquibamba** (festivals 20 Jan; 2-3 Feb; 15 May) traversing the western slopes of Nevado Coropuna (6,425m), before winding down into **Cotahuasi** (*pop* 4,000; *alt* 2,600m). The peaceful colonial town nestles in a sheltered hanging valley beneath Cerro Huinao. Its streets are narrow, the houses whitewashed. Several kilometres away a canyon has been cut by the Río Cotahuasi, which flows into the Pacific as the Río Ocuña. At its deepest, at Ninochaca (just below the village of Quechualla), the canyon is 3,354m deep, 163m deeper than the Colca Canyon and the deepest in the world. From this point the only way down the canyon is by kayak and it is through kayakers' reports since 1994 that the area has come to the notice of tourists (it was declared a Zona de Reserva Turística in 1988). There is little agriculture apart from some citrus groves, but in Inca times the road linking Puerto Inca and Cusco ran along much of the canyon's course.

One of the main treks in the region follows the Inca trade road from Cotahuasi to Quechualla. From the football pitch the path goes through Piro, the gateway to the canyon, and Sipia (3 hrs), near which are the powerful, 150m high Cataratas de Sipia (take care near the falls if it is windy). The next 3-hr stretch to Chaupo is not for vertigo sufferers as the path is barely etched into the canyon wall, 400m above the river in places. At Chaupo ask permission to camp in the citrus groves; do not pick the fruit (it's a cash crop); water is available. Next is Velinga, then the dilapidated but extensive ruin of Huña, then **Quechualla**, a charming village and administrative capital of the district. Ask Sr Carmelo Velásquez Gálvez for permission to sleep

Southern Peru

in the schoolhouse. On the opposite side of the river are the ruined terraces of Maucullachta. A 16 km hike continues to the ruins of Marpa (no water en route, allow 4 more days). If it rains, Quechualla can be cut off for days as sections where the river has to be waded become too deep and treacherous (eg just past Velinga).

Other treks To Pampamarca, 3 hrs walk N of Cotahuasi: ruins, waterfall, village known for rugmaking. To the thermal baths of Luicho: take bus to Tomepampa (first at 0600, several more); Luicho is between Tomepampa and Alca. A days' walk beyond Tomepampa is the rock forest of Santo Santo; start trek from Huaynacotas, near Luicho.

Rafting It is possible to raft or kayak from a point on the Upper Cotahuasi, just past the town, almost to the Pacific (boats are usually taken out of the water at the village of Iquipi), a descent of 2,300m. Season May-Aug; rapids class 3 to 5; some portaging unavoidable."

Local festival 4 May.

● **Accommodation & places to eat** F *Hostal Villa*, just off plaza; G *Alojamiento Chávez*, Jr Cabildo 125, T 210222, rooms around pleasant courtyard, friendly, rec, Sr José Chávez is helpful on places to visit, if a little vague on timings. *Restaurant El Pionero*, Jr Centenario, clean, good *menú*. Three small restaurants/bars on Jr Arequipa offer basic fare. There are many well-stocked *tiendas*, particularly with fruit and vegetables.

● **Useful services** No money exchange. **PNP**, on plaza; advisable to register with them on arrival and before leaving. **Maps**: some survey maps in Municipalidad and PNP; they may let you make photocopies (shop on the corner of the plaza and Arequipa). Sr Chávez has photocopies of the sheets covering Cotahuasi and surroundings.

● **Buses** Two companies daily from Arequipa bus terminal, 13-14 hrs, US$9: Emp Mendoza, 1400, returning from Cotahuasi plaza 1600; Emp Virgen del Carmen 1430, returning 1500 from plaza. On arrival in Cotahuasi you may sleep on the bus till dawn. Both companies stop for refreshments in Chuquibamba.

TOWARDS THE VALLEY OF THE VOLCANOES

A road goes to the E from the Cotahuasi road to **Andagua**, a village lying at the head of the valley of the volcanoes (bus from Arequipa, Sun, Wed, Fri, 1530, Empresa Delgado; there are also trucks on this route). Basic accommodation at the mayor's house in Andagua. The Arequipa-Andagua bus goes on to **Orcopampa**, from which the thermal springs of Huancarama can be visited. A mining lorry leaves Orcopampa for Cailloma on the 12th and the last day of each month; this enables one to make a round trip from Arequipa.

From Andagua there is a road to **Chachas** (3,100m), a picturesque village on the edge of a lake (*hostal* on the plaza; no restaurants). Trucks sometimes run between the two villages. The area is heavily cultivated and there are perfect views of the valley of the volcanoes from the top of the hill above Chachas. It is possible to hike from Chachas to Choco and on to Cabanaconde via the Río Colca in 4 days (see page 1325).

AREQUIPA

The city of **Arequipa**, 1,011 km from Lima by road, stands in a beautiful valley at the foot of El Misti volcano, a snow-capped, perfect cone, 5,822m high, guarded on either side by the mountains Chachani (6,057m), and Pichu-Pichu (5,669m). The city has fine Spanish buildings and many old and interesting churches built of *sillar*, a pearly white volcanic material almost exclusively used in the construction of Arequipa. The city was re-founded on 15 August 1540 by an emissary of Pizarro, but it had previously been occupied by Aymara Indians and the Incas. It is the main commercial centre for the S, and its people resent the general tendency to believe that everything is run from Lima.

BASICS *Pop* 1 million; *Alt* 2,380m; *Phone code* 054. The *climate* is delightful, with a mean temperature before sundown of 23°C, and after sundown of 14½°C. The sun shines on 360 days of the year. Annual rainfall is less than 150 mm.

Places of interest

The elegant **Plaza de Armas** is faced on three sides by colonial arcaded buildings with many restaurants, and on the fourth by the Cathedral. Behind the cathedral there is a very attractive alley with handicraft shops. The central **San Camilo market**, between Perú, San Camilo, Piérola and Alto de la Luna, is worth visiting, as is the Siglo XX market, to the E of the rail station. At **Selva Alegre** there is a shady park in front of the *Hotel Libertador* (ex-*de Turistas*), which is within easy walking distance of all the famous churches and main plaza. Arequipa is said to have the best-preserved colonial architecture in Peru, apart from Cusco. The oldest district is **San Lázaro**, a collection of tiny climbing

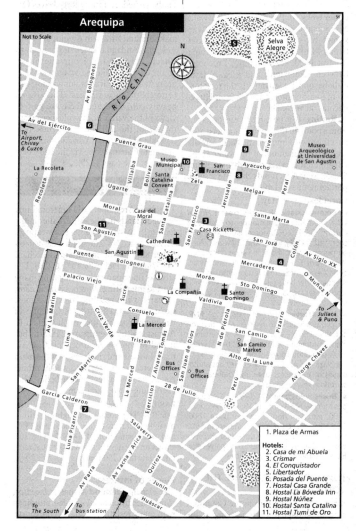

Arequipa

Not to Scale

Selva Alegre

To Airport, Chivay & Cuzco

Av del Ejército

Av Bolognesi

Rio Chili

Puente Grau

La Recoleta

Recoleta

Villalba

Bolívar

Museo Municipal **10**

Santa Catalina Convent

Ugarte

Zela

San Francisco

Ayacucho

Rivera

Museo Arqueológico at Universidad de San Agustín

Peral

2

9

8

Melgar

Moral

Casa del Moral

Santa Catalina

San Francisco

Jerusalén

Santa Marta

11

San Agustín

Casa Ricketts

3

San José

San Agustín

Cathedral

Puente Bolognesi

Palacio Viejo

Sucre

1

Morán

Mercaderes

Colón

Av Siglo XX

4

O Muñoz N

To Juliaca & Puno

Av La Marina

Cruz Verde

Consuelo

La Compañía

Valdivia

Sto Domingo

Santo Domingo

N de Piérola

Pizarro

Lima

La Merced

Tristán

Álvarez Tomás

San Juan de Dios

San Camilo

San Camilo Market

Alto de la Luna

Perú

Av Jorge Chávez

San Martín

García Calderón

7

Bus Offices

Bus Offices

28 de Julio

Ejercicios

Salavery

Luna Pizarro

Pizarro

Av Tacna y Arica

Quiroz

Junín

Huáscar

To The South

To bus station

1. Plaza de Armas

Hotels:
2. *Casa de mi Abuela*
3. *Crismar*
4. *El Conquistador*
5. *Libertador*
6. *Posada del Puente*
7. *Hostal Casa Grande*
8. *Hostal La Bóveda Inn*
9. *Hostal Núñez*
10. *Hostal Santa Catalina*
11. *Hostal Tumi de Oro*

streets and houses quite close to the *Hotel Libertador*, where you can find the ancient **Capilla de San Lázaro**. **A cheap tour** of the city can be made in a Vallecito bus, 1½ hrs for US$0.30. It is a circular tour which goes down Calles Jerusalén and San Juan de Dios.

Churches

Because of the danger of earthquakes churches in the city were built low. They are usually open 0700-0900 and 1800-2000. The twin-towered **Cathedral**, founded in 1612 and largely rebuilt in the 19th century, is remarkable for having its façade along the whole length of the church (entrance on Santa Catalina and San Francisco). Inside is the fine Belgian organ and elaborately-carved wooden pulpit.

At **La Compañía**, General Morán and Ejercicios, the main façade (1698) and side portal (1654) are striking examples of the florid Andean *mestizo* style. To the left of the sanctuary is the **Capilla Real** (Royal Chapel); its San Ignacio chapel has a beautiful polychrome cupola; admission, US$0.50, 0900-1200, 1500-1800 daily.

Also well worth seeing are the churches of **San Francisco** (Zela 103), **San Agustín** (corner of San Agustín y Sucre), the early 17th century **La Merced** (La Merced 303), and **Santo Domingo** (Santo Domingo y Piérola). Opposite San Francisco is a handicraft centre, housed in a beautiful former prison.

La Recoleta, a Franciscan monastery built in 1647, stands on the other side of the river, on Recoleta. It contains several cloisters, a religious art museum, a precolumbian museum, an Amazon museum and a library with many rarities. Open Mon-Fri 0900-1200, 1500-1700, Sat 0900-1200; entry US$1.90. The church itself is open only 0900-1200, 1500-1800.

The **Santa Rosa Convent** is at San Pedro y Santa Rosa. It was founded on 12 July 1747, by nuns from the much larger Santa Catalina Convent.

Santa Catalina Convent By far the most remarkable sight is Santa Catalina Convent, opened in 1970 after four centuries of mystery. The convent has been beautifully refurbished, with period furniture, pictures of the Arequipa and Cusco schools and fully-equiped kitchens. It is a complete miniature walled colonial town of over 2 ha in the middle of the city, where about 450 nuns lived in total seclusion, except for their women servants. The few remaining nuns have retreated to one section of the convent, allowing visitors to see a maze of cobbled streets, flower-decked cloisters and buttressed houses. These have been painted in traditional white, browns and blues. The Convent is at Santa Catalina 301, T 229798; open 0900-1600 daily, admission US$3.60. The tour they offer you at the entrance is worthwhile; 1½ hrs, no set price, many of the guides speak English. There is a small café, which sells cakes made by the nuns and a special blend of tea.

Colonial houses

Arequipa has several fine seignorial houses with large carved tympanums over the entrances. Built as single-storey structures, they have mostly withstood earthquakes. They have small patios with no galleries, flat roofs and small windows, disguised by superimposed lintels or heavy grilles. Good examples are the 18th century **Casa Tristan del Pozo**, or **Gibbs-Ricketts house**, with its fine portal and puma-head waterspouts (now Banco Continental, San Francisco 108 y San José; open to the public 1700-2000).

Casa del Moral, or Williams house (with museum, Banco Industrial, Moral 318 y Bolívar); **Casa Goyeneche**, La Merced 201 y Palacio Viejo (now an office of the Banco Central de la Reserva, ask the guards to let you view the courtyard and fine period rooms).

Museums

Opposite the San Francisco church is the interesting **Museo Histórico Municipal** with much war memorabilia, open Mon-Fri 0800-1800; entry, US$0.50. The **archaeological museum** at the Universidad de San Agustín, Av Independencia entre La Salle y Santa Rosa, has a good collection of ceramics and mummies. Open Mon-Fri 0800-1400, entry US$1. Apply to Dr E Linares, the Director, T 229719.

Excursions

In the hillside suburb of **Cayma** is the delightful 18th century church (open only until 1600), and many old buildings associated with Bolívar and Garcilaso de la Vega. Many local buses go to Cayma.

Another suburb is **Yanahuara**, where there is a 1750 *mestizo*-style church (opens 1500), with a magnificent churrigueresque façade, all in *sillar*. The thermal baths of Jesús are 30 mins by car, on the slopes of Pichu-Pichu; open 0500-1230. To get there cross the Gran Puente bridge and turn right up Lima.

Yura, is a pleasant town, 29 km from Arequipa in a small, interesting valley on the W slopes of Chachani. It is popular for its warm thermal baths and riverside picnic spots; open Tues-Sat, until 1500; entry US$1.50. Bus to Yura every 3 hrs from San Juan de Dios, US$0.40.

Tingo, which has a very small lake and three swimming pools, should be visited on Sun for local food; *anticuchos* and *buñuelos*; bus 7, US$0.20. 3 km past Tingo, beside the Sabandía river on the Huasacanche road, is **La Mansión del Fundador**. Originally owned by the founder of Arequipa, Don Garcí Manuel de Carbajal, it has been restored as a museum with original furnishings and paintings. Entrance US$2.50, with cafeteria and bar. 8 km N of Arequipa is the **Molino de Sabandía**, the first stone mill in the area, built in 1621. There is a swimming bath and the surrounding countryside is pleasant. Entrance US$1.50; round trip by taxi US$4. Adjoining Sabandía is **Yumina**, with many Inca terraces which are still in use.

Local festivals

10 Jan: *Sor Ana de Los Angeles y Monteagudo*, festival for the patron saint of Santa Catalina monastery. **Mar-April**: Semana Santa celebrations involve huge processions every night, culminating in the burning of an effigy of Judas on Easter Sunday in the main plazas of Cayma and Yanahuara, and the reading of his 'will', containing criticisms of the city authorities. Afterwards, people eat *Adobo a la Antaño* with some *pan de tres puntas*. **27 April**: the celebration of the apostle Santiago.

May is known as the *Mes de Las Cruces*, with ceremonies on hilltops throughout the city. **3 Aug**: a procession through the city bearing the images of Santo Domingo and San Francisco. **6-31 Aug**: *Fiesta Artesanal del fundo El Fierro* is a sale and exhibition of artesanía from all parts of Peru, taking place beside Plaza San Francisco. **6-17 Aug**: celebration of the city's anniversary (the 15th, many events including a mass ascent of El Misti). **2 Nov**: Day of the Dead celebrations in cemeteries. A full list of the department's many festivals is available locally and in *The Peru Handbook*.

Local information

● **Accommodation**

A2 *Portal*, Portal de Flores 116, T 215530, F 234374, excellent, wonderful views, expensive, rooftop swimming pool, *El Gaucho* restaurant; **A2** *Posada del Puente*, Av Bolognesi 101, T 253132, F 253576, beside Puente Grau, alongside Río Chili, attractive, small, good, restaurant, rec; **A2-3** *Libertador*, Plaza Simón Bolívar, Selva Alegre, T 215110, F 241933, safe, swimming pool (cold), gardens, good meals, pub-style bar, cocktail lounge, tennis court; **A3** *El Conquistador*, Mercaderes 409, T 212916, F 218987, safe, lovely colonial atmosphere, owner speaks English, thin walls; **A3** *Hostal Casa Grande*, Luna Pizarro 202, Vallecito, T 214000, F 214021, inc taxes, small, cosy, well-furnished, quiet, good services, rec; **A3** *Hostal La Gruta*, La Gruta 304, Selva Alegre, 5 mins form centre, T 224631, e-mail: studio@amauta.rcp.net.pe, inc breakfast, cable TV, garden, laundry, 24-hr café, fax service, parking; **A3** *Maison Plaza*, Portal San Agustín 143, T 218929, F 212114, with breakfast, good value.

B *Crismar*, Moral 107, T 215290, F 239431, opp the main Post Office, with shower, modern, safe, noisy, central, food good; **B-C** *Jerusalén*, C Jerusalén 601, T 244441/81, F 243472, hot water, comfortable, modern, good restaurant, safe, parking.

C *Casa de Melgar*, Melgar 108-A, T 222459, 2 rooms, hot water all day (solarpanel), safe; **C** *Hostal Las Mercedes*, Av La Marina 1001, end of C Consuelo, T/F 213601, inc breakfast, will provide sandwiches and a soft drink instead for early morning tour, safe (but its surroundings are not too secure), snacks available, highly rec; **C** *Hostal Latino*, Carlos Llosa 135, T 244770, cafeteria, garden, parking, rec; **C** *Maison d'Elise*, Av Bolognesi 104, T/F 253343, Sra Elsa Podigo is very helpful; **C** *Miamaka*, San Juan de Dios 402, T 241496, F 227906, excellent service, helpful, English spoken, highly rec; **C** *Villa*

Baden Baden (Sra Bluemel de Castro), Manuel Ugarteche 401, Selva Alegre, T 222416, 6 rooms, breakfast inc, German, French, English spoken, very informative about city's environs and climbing, safe, rec; **C-D** *Casa de Mi Abuela*, Jerusalén 606, T 241206, F 242761, safe, hot water, laundry, self-catering if desired, English spoken, tours and transport organized in own agency, which has good information (T 226414), small library of European books, breakfast or evening snacks on patio or in beautiful garden, apartment for 5 US$40, highly rec.

D *El Gobernador*, Rivero 303, T 244433, **E** without bath, hot water, safe motorcycle parking, good beds, luggage store, rec; **D** *Hostal Le Foyer*, Ugarte 114 y San Francisco, T 286473, beautiful colonial house, hot water 24 hrs, laundry, luggage store, safe, helpful, breakfast inc, rec; **D** *Hostal Tumi de Oro*, San Agustín 311A, 2½ blocks from Plaza de Armas, T 281319, F 231633, cheaper without bath, French and English spoken, hot water, roof terrace, cooking facilities, safe, rec; **D-E** *Posada de Sancho*, Santa Catalina 213 A, nr convent, T 287797, hot showers 24 hrs, safe, nice patio and terrace with a view of El Misti, good breakfast, English and German spoken, good travel information, offer cheap tours, very good value.

E *Embajador*, Jerusalén 619, T 281048, with bath, cheaper without, hot water, helpful, English-speaking staff, **E** *Hostal El Cóndor*, San Juan de Dios 525, T 213323, good; **E** *Hostal Fernández*, Quesada 106, Yanahuara, T 254152, 10 mins from centre, good for a longer stay, beautiful garden with parrot, views of El Misti, family affair, safe, breakfasts, hot water, rec; **E** *Hostal La Portada del Mirador*, Portal de Flores 102, Plaza de Armas, T 211539, basic, safe, will store luggage, great views from the roof; **E** *Hostal Núñez*, Jerusalén 528, T 233268, cheaper without bath, hot water, laundry, safe, comfortable, small rooms, breakfast on roof terrace overlooking the city, rec; **E** *Hostal Regis*, Ugarte 202, T 226111, colonial house, French-style interior, hot water all day, cooking and laundry facilities, sun terrace with good views, safe, luggage store, rec; **E** *Hostal Santa Catalina*, Santa Catalina 500, T 233705, hot water, noisy, safe, luggage stored, Jimmy organizes tours to Colca, rec; **E** *La Bóveda Inn*, Jerusalén 402, above *Lashmivan* restaurant, T 281685, safe, good showers, rec; **E** *Lluvia de Oro*, Jerusalén 308, F 235730, English-speaking, basic, **F** pp without bath, breakfast US$1.40, restaurant, pisco sours rec; **E** *Residencial Rivero*, Rivero 420, T 229266, with bath, helpful, washing facilities, rec but not a very safe area.

F pp *Albergue Internacional El Misti*, Salaverry 302, 3 blocks from rail station, T/F 245760, family rooms with bath, singles and shared rooms in elegant old mansion, arranges cultural tours, also Spanish classes; **F** *Colonial House Inn*, Puente Grau 114, T/F 223533, hot water, big rooms, quieter at the back, good breakfast; **F** pp *Rooms for tourists (Hostal La Reina)*, Zela 209, T 286578, shared bath, 24 hrs hot water, the daughter speaks a little English, great breakfast, also other meals available, rooftop seating, will store luggage, arrange trips to Colca canyon, excellent value, very highly rec; **F** pp *Tambo Viejo*, Av Mcal Cáceres 107, IV Centenario, unsigned, 6 blocks S of Plaza nr rail station, family home, quiet, nice garden, hot water early am, laundry, cable TV, breakfast available (inc vegetarian), excellent, very highly rec; **F** pp *Tito*, C Perú 105-B, T 234424, shared bath, good value.

G *Hostal Moderno*, Alto de la Luna 106, large rooms, laundry, hot water, safe, rec.

● **Places to eat**
Central Garden, San Francisco 127, good food but expensive; *Anushka*, Santa Catalina 204, open 1800-2300, live music, Fri and Sat, only place to get a hot meal after 2200, German specialities, friendly, handicrafts for sale; *Bacuch*, Melgar 413, good Swiss food; *Balcón Arequipa*, Merced y Bolognesi, good view over Plaza, popular with locals, good breakfasts and fruit juice, slow service; *El Dólar*, San Juan de Dios 106, cheap, all meals available, rec; *La Casa del Pino*, Jerusalén 308, pleasant courtyard, good set lunch; *Bonanza*, Jerusalén 114-116, for meat and pasta dishes, very good, US$5; *Pizzería Los Leños*, Jerusalén 407, nr San Francisco, excellent, good atmosphere, evenings only; *Snack Don Guido*, San José 206, excellent home-cooked Italian food; *La Rueda*, Mercaderes 106, excellent *parrilladas*; *Las Quenas*, San Francisco 215, opp Santa Catalina convent, excellent *menú* for US$1.50, but expensive for dinner, also a *peña* in the evening. There are many good, cheap restaurants on Av Estados Unidos. *André de París*, better known as *El Emperador*, Santa Catalina 207, excellent cheap set lunches, breakfast also rec; *Tradición Arequipa*, Av Dolores 111, Paucarpata, T 242385, high quality restaurant serving excellent, moderately priced food, popular with tourists and locals alike.

Vegetarian: *Govinda*, Jerusalén 505, excellent set meal US$1.25, good yoghurt and muesli (also called *Madre Natura*, which has a branch at Grau 310), rec; *Lashmivan*, Jerusalén 402, good set lunch US$1.25, pleasant courtyard; *Come y Vive Mejor*, C Nueva 410A, cheap and good; *Mathesis*, Jerusalén 224, a bit more expensive than others; *La Avellana*, Santa Marta 317-B, good, cheap lunch *menú*.

Cafés: *Café Manolo*, Mercaderes 113, great

cakes and coffee; *Pastelería Salón de Té*, Mercaderes 325, very clean, open early, good breakfasts; *Café Suri*, on the Plaza, for sandwiches and pastries; *Harumi* snack bar, San José 216, Chinese, good value; *El Café*, San Francisco 125, popular meeting place.

There are several good cheap places down San Juan de Dios, eg *El Chuquibambino*, No 625, or *La Empanadita*, No 205, excellent *empanadas* and snacks. *La Canasta*, Jerusalén 115, bakes authentic-tasting baguettes twice daily, excellent. At Jerusalén 603, Jutta Grau and Carlos Gutierrez bake wonderful German breads, speak English, French and German, non-profit making, money goes to help the disadvantaged.

A score of *picanterías* specialize in piquant foods: *rocoto relleno* (hot stuffed peppers), *cuy chactado* (seared guinea-pig), *papas con ocopa* (boiled potatoes with a hot yellow sauce) and *adobo* (pork stew). Try them at lunchtime in Yanahuara suburb and *Sol de Mayo*, Jerusalén 207, T 254148. Arequipeño food is also available at the San Camilo market. A good local speciality is Mejía cheese. *Queso helado* is frozen fresh milk mixed with sugar and a sprinkling of cinnamon. The local chocolate is excellent (*La Ibérica* – the factory on Jerusalén, NE of Plaza de Armas, gives tours on weekdays only), as is the toffee. The fruit drinks called *papayada* and *tumbada*, are local specialities in the market and restaurants.

● **Airline offices**

All airline offices are on the Plaza de Armas: **AeroPerú**, Portal San Agustín 145, T 211616; **Faucett**, Portal San Agustín 143-A, T 212352; **Aero Continente**, Portal San Agustín 113, T 219914/219788. Most tour agencies sell air tickets; prices are quoted in dollars but payment is in soles so check exchange rate carefully.

● **Banks & money changers**

Banco Internacional, Mercaderes 217, exchanges Citicorp dollar cheques. **Banco de Crédito**, Santo Domingo y Jerusalén, accepts Visa Card and gives good rates, no commission, rec. **Banco Continental**, La Uruguaya Department Store, Mercaderes 133, Mon-Fri 0900-1200, 1600-1830. **Banco del Sur del Perú**, C Jerusalén, close to Post Office, will change TCs, low rates, accepts Mastercard, has ATM for withdrawals with Visa; **Arequipa Inversiones**, Jerusalén 190-C, T 238033; **Sergio A del Carpio D**, Jerusalén 126, T 242987, good rates for dollars; **Ideal Travel**, Zela 212; **Lima Tours**, Santa Catalina 120; **Via Tours**, Santo Domingo 114, good rates; **Diners Club**, San Francisco 112. It is almost impossible to change TCs on Sat pm or Sun; try to find a sympathetic street changer. Better rates for cash dollars in banks and *casas de cambio*.

● **Cultural centres**

Instituto Cultural Peruano-Norte Americano, in the Casa de los Mendiburo, Melgar 109, T 243201, has an **English Library**. **Instituto Cultural Peruano Alemán**, Ugarte 207, T 218567. **Instituto Regional de Cultura**, Gen Morán 118 (altos), T 213171; **Instituto Nacional de Cultura**, Alameda San Lázaro 120, T 213171; **Alianza Francesa**, Santa Catalina 208, T 218406/215579.

● **Embassies & consulates**

British Consulate, Mr Roberts, Tacna y Arica 145, T 241340, Mon-Fri 0830-1230, 1430-1800, reported as very friendly and helpful; **French Consulate**, Estadio Oeste 201-A, IV Centenario, T 232119 (Sun T 224915), Mon-Fri 1530-1900; **German Consulate**, in Colegio Max Uhle, Av Fernandini s/n, Sachaca, Mon-Fri 0900-1300, Casilla 743; **Dutch Consulate**, Mercaderes 410 (Banco Wiese), Sr Herbert Ricketts, T 219567, F 215437, Casilla 1, open Mon-Fri 0900-1300, 1630-1830; **Swedish Consulate**, Av Villa Hermosa 803, Cerro Colorado, T 259847/270616, open Mon-Fri 0830-1300, 1500-1730; **Swiss Consulate**, Av Miguel Forga 348, Parque Industrial, T 232723; **Italian Consulate**, La Salle D-5, T 221444, open 1130-1300, in the afternoon T 254686 (home); **Spanish Consulate**, Ugarte 218, p 2, T 214977 (home T 224915), open Mon-Fri 1100-1300, Sat 0900-1300; **Chilean Consulate**, Mercaderes 212, p 4, Of 401-402, Galerías Gameza, T/F 233556, entrance to lift 30m down passageway down Mercaderes on left, open Mon-Fri 0900-1300, present passport 0900-1100 if you need a visa; **Bolivian Consulate**, Piérola 209, p 3, Of 321, T 213391, open Mon-Fri 0900-1400, 24 hrs for visa, go early.

● **Entertainment**

Romie, Zela 202, T 234465, bar with *peña*, Tues-Sat; *El Sillar*, Santa Catalina 215, T 215468, 'salón concierto', typical folk music, rec, Mon-Sat from 2000; *Blues Bar*, San Francisco 319-A, T 283387, 5 bars, large but intimate disco, pool tables, good pizzas, live blues and rock Thur-Sat, US$5 cover if live band is playing, includes a drink, drinks US$1.50, very popular; *Peña Waykopac*, Jerusalén 204, good atmosphere, Fri and Sat; *Peña Chunenea*, Pasaje la Catedral 4; *Discoteca Casablanca*, Av Sucre, Puente Bolognesi, garage entrance, clean, well-run and safe; downstairs pool room; *Disco Fragavoss*, Santa Catalina 109-A, T 232651, young crowd, rec. There are many good discos on Av Ejército in Yanahuara. Watch out for the local folk-music group Chachani, said to be one of Peru's best.

● **Hospitals & medical services**

Hospitals: *Regional Honorio Delgado*, Av A Carrión s/n, T 238465/231818. *General Base Goyeneche*, Av Goyeneche s/n, T 211313. *Nacional del Sur*, Filtro y Peral s/n, T 214430 in emergency.

Dentist: *Dr José Corrales*, San Juan de Dios 216.

Doctors: *Dr Julio Postigo*, Independencia 225; *Dr Jorge A del Carpio Alvarez*, Santo Domingo 123, of 303, T 215483, rec, only Spanish spoken.

Clinics: *Clínica Arequipa SA*, esq Puente Grau y Av Bolognesi, T 253424, fast and efficient with English- speaking doctors and all hospital facilities, consultation costs US$18, plus US$4 for sample analysis and around US$7 for a course of antibiotics. *San Juan de Dios*, Av Ejército 1020, Cayma, T 252256/255544. *Monte Carmelo*, Gómez de la Torre 119, T 231444, T/F 287048. *Clínica de Urgencias Meza*, Urb Aurora J-11, cercado, T 234883.

Pharmacy: *Farmacia Libertad*, Piérola 108, owner speaks English.

● **Language courses**

Silvana Cornejo, 7 de Junio 118, Cerrito Los Alvarez, Cerro Colorado, T 254985, US$6/hr, negotiable for group, rec, she speaks German fluently; her sister Roxanna charges US$3/hr. Fidelia and Charo Sánchez, T 224238, highly rec, Fidelia speaks French, Charo English. Also at Instituto Peruano-Norte Americano and Instituto Cultural Peruano Alemán.

● **Post & telecommunications**

The central Post Office is at Moral 118, opp *Hotel Crismar*. Letters can only be posted at the Post Office during opening hours, Mon-Sat, 0800-2000, Sun 0800-1400. Telephone and fax at Alvarez Thomas y Palacio Viejo.

● **Security**

Though theft can be a problem in the market area, especially after dark, and at the bus offices in San Juan de Dios, the police are friendly, courteous and efficient.

● **Shopping**

Casa Secchi, Av Víctor Andrés Belaunde 124, in Umacollo (nr the aeroplane statue), sells good arts, crafts and clothing; also *Artesanías Peruanas*, Puente Bolognesi 147. *Empresa Peruana de Promoción Artesanal (EPPA)*, Gen Morán 120. *Alpaca 111*, Jerusalén 115, Of 208, T 212347, rec for high-quality alpaca and wool products. The covered market opp the Teatro Municipal in C Mercaderes is rec for knitted goods, bags, etc. Also the market around Valdivia and N de Piérola. The main street of saddlers and leather workers is Pte Bolognesi. At *Fundo del Fierro* shop 14, on Plaza San Francisco,

alpaca-wool handicrafts from Callalli in the Colca canyon are sold. *Lanificio*, La Pampilla s/n, T 225305, the factory for high-quality alpaca cloth at better prices than Lima outlets. *Sombrería El Triunfino*, N de Piérola 329-331, good selection of hats, but expensive. *El Zaguán*, Santa Catalina 105, good for handicrafts. There are three antique shops in C Santa Catalina.

Bookshops: there are good bookshops nr the Post Office. For international magazines, look along C San Francisco, between Mercaderes and San José.

Laundry: *Magic laundry*, Av Cayma 617, coin-operated, open daily; *Lavendería del Pueblo*, Ejercicios 558; *Don Marcelo*, T 421411 (am), T 229245 (pm), delivery service.

Photography: Sr Fernando Delange, N-10 Urbanización Adepa, T 233120, repairs all kinds of electrical equipment as well as cameras. *Foto Esparza*, Mercaderes 132-2, English spoken, cameras mended; *Foto Mundo Color*, San Francisco 218-A, will develop good quality prints in 1 hr, US$3.50 for 24.

● **Tour companies & travel agents**

Ideal Travels, Zela 212, on plaza San Francisco, T 244439, F 242088, Mon-Fri 0800-1900, Sat 0830-1300, tours to Colca Canyon (2 days, 1 night, US$60, all meals, rafting US$33), Cotahuasi Canyon, Andagua Volcanic valley, Majes River, Cotahuasi River, Toro Muerto, Callalli alpaca and vicuña ranch; jeep and microbus rentals, excellent bilingual guides, international ticket reservations, accepts credit cards. Also rec are: *Conresa Tours*, Jerusalén 409, Casilla 563, T 211847/ 223073/215820, specializes in trips to the Colca Canyon, and to the Toro Muerto petroglyphs, Las Salinas and Mejía lakes, and city tours; *Santa Catalina Tours*, Santa Catalina 204, T 216994, F 217352, good value Colca tours; *Colonial Tours*, Santa Catalina 205, of 1, T 285980, daily tours to Colca; *Wasi Tours*, Jerusalén 613 and Santa Catalina 207, friendly, helpful advice; *Illary Tours*, Jerusalén 204-B, T 220844, friendly, English-speaking guides; *Expeandes*, La Merced 408, of 1, T 212888, F 228814, PO Box 1403, owner Ricardo Córdoba Mercado, adventure trips, well-organized, reliable, rents equipment. A rec guide for climbing, trekking, mountain biking and river rafting in the Colca Canyon is Vlado Soto, he can be contacted at La Merced 125, CC Unicentro, of 139, PO Box 1988, T 234818/225494, F 226610; he is knowledgeable and helpful and also rents equipment.

Many agencies on Jerusalén, Santa Catalina and around Plaza de Armas sell air, train and bus tickets and offer tours of Colca, Cotahuasi, Toro Muerto, Campiña and city; prices vary so shop around. **NB** Don't pay for a tour in advance;

always settle the details before starting the tour and check that there are suitable numbers (neither too many, nor too few people) for the tour. Quite often travel agents work together to fill buses and use lots of touts. If a travel agency puts you in touch with a guide, make sure he/she is official.

Climbing: Sr Carlos Zárate of the Mountaineering Club of Peru, has good information and advice, acts as a guide and rents some equipment, highly rec; contact him through Alianza Francesca, T 215579.

● **Tourist offices**
Office on Plaza de Armas, opp the Cathedral, T 211021, ext 113, open 0800-1900, helpful, friendly, free street plans. **Oficina de Protección al Turista**, T 0800-42579, 24 hrs, toll-free, or T 212054, during office hours. Tourist Police, Jerusalén 317, T 251270/239888, very helpful with complaints or giving directions. **Ministry of Tourism**, La Merced 117, T 213116, will handle complaints. **Touring y Automóvil Club del Perú**, Av Goyeneche 313, T 215631, mechanical assistance T 215640.

● **Transport**
Local Car hire: National, Bolívar 25, US$70/day inc tax, insurance and 200 km; **Avis**, Puente Bolognesi nr plaza. **Car repairs**: Automec, Av Tahuaycani cuadra 2, Tahuaycani. **Bicycle repairs and equipment**: Hoz Trek Bicicletas, Villalba 428, T 223221. **Taxi**: US$4-5 airport to city (can be shared). US$1.75 bus terminal to Plaza de Armas; US$1.75 railway station to centre. Nova Taxi, T 252511; Fono Car, T 212121; Telemóvil, T 221515; Taxitur, T 422323.

Air Rodríguez Ballón airport is 7 km from town, T 443464. To and from **Lima**, 1 hr 10 mins, several daily with Faucett, AeroPerú, Aero Continente, Aerosanta. To **Tacna**, 30 mins, daily flights with all major airlines. To **Cusco**, 40 mins, daily flights. To **Juliaca** 30 mins, daily flights. National flies 3 times a week to Arica, Iquique and Antofagasta.

A reliable means of transport to and from the airport is the hotel of your choice is with **King Tours**, T 243357/283037, US$1.30 pp; give 24 hrs notice for return pick-up from your hotel; journey takes 30-40 mins depending on traffic. Transport to the airport may be arranged when buying a ticket at a travel agency, US$1 pp, but not always reliable. Local buses go to about ½ km from the airport.

Trains The railway system goes from Arequipa to Juliaca, where it divides, one line going N to Cusco, the other S to Puno.

To Juliaca-Puno: the train leaves Tues, Wed, Fri and Sun at 2100. It arrives in Juliaca at 0645, and in Puno at 0830. The train returns from Puno

at 1945; arrives in Juliaca at 2045; and arrives in Arequipa at 0600. To Cusco: the train leaves Puno at 0735, arrives 1800. Trains are subject to delays and cancellation in the rainy season, always check.

There are four different classes: 2nd class, no seat reservations, not rec; 1st class, reserved seats, but anyone is allowed into the carriage (inc thieves), it's a good local experience if you do not mind watching your belongings all the time; pullman (turismo ejecutivo) class, with closed doors, only ticket holders are allowed in the carriage, safe, heating, rec for the night journey which can be extremely cold; and Inca class, with reclining seats and video, only ticket holders are allowed in the carriage. You can travel all the way through if you stay in the same class; you only need change trains in Juliaca when changing classes. Fares: Arequipa-Puno, 2nd class US$9, 1st class US$11, pullman US$19, Inca US$23. Arequipa-Cusco, 2nd class US$16, 1st class US$20, pullman US$30, Inca US$46.

Tickets are sold the day before departure. To reserve a seat in advance, you must pay a deposit (if the ticket seller doesn't mention a deposit, remind him of it). It is wise to reserve tickets at least 48 hrs before the day of departure, especially if you're travelling on weekends or public holidays. The ticket office is at Av Tacna y Arica 201; for reservations T 223600, information T 233928/229012; open 0630-1030, 1400-1800 Mon-Fri; 0800-1200, 1500-1800 Sat/Sun. You can buy tickets through travel agencies (check date and seat number). Try to board the train as early as possible as there isn't much room for luggage.

Warning Theft is a major problem on 1st and 2nd class. Thieves are very well-organized and work in groups, using all the tricks to distract you while someone else steals your bags. The best way is to lock your luggage on the rack and watch it (it is easier if you have only one bag). Pay attention at all times and do not leave the train. Sit with a group if possible to help each other. Always have a torch/flashlight to hand. Take a taxi to and from the train station and do not hang around the station area.

If you feel bad on the train ask for the oxygen mask at once.

Buses The bus terminal is at Av Andrés A Cáceres s/n, Parque Industrial, opp Inca Tops factory, S of the train station; 15 mins from the centre by colectivo US$0.20, or taxi US$1.75 (10 mins). A terminal tax of US$0.35 must be paid on entry. All the bus companies have their offices in the terminal. **Warning** Theft is a serious problem in the bus station area and the surrounding restaurants. Take a taxi to and from the bus station and do not wander around with your belongings.

To **Lima**, 1,011 km, 16-18 hrs, 'normal' service US$9, 'Imperial' US$22 (video, toilet, meals, comfortable seats, blankets) several daily, Ormeño (T 219126, or San Juan de Dios 657, T 218885) and Cruz del Sur (T 232014, or Av Salaverry 121, T 213905) rec. The road is paved and in good condition but drifting sand and breakdowns may prolong the trip.

To **Nasca**, 566 km, 9 hrs, US$9, several buses daily, mostly at night and most buses continue to Lima. Beware, some bus companies to Nasca charge the Lima fare. To **Moquegua**, 213 km, 3 hrs, US$4, several buses and colectivos daily. To **Tacna**, 320 km, 4 hrs, US$5, several buses daily; colectivo, Expreso Tacna, San Juan de Dios 537, T 213281, will collect you from your hotel, US$7.

To **Cusco**, 521 km, 13-17 hrs (longer in the rainy season), US$10-13; several daily, Cruz del Sur at 1600. The road is in good shape and the views are superb. In the rainy season the journey is not rec because of mudslides. To **Juliaca**, 279 km, 8-9 hrs, US$5-8; colectivos charge US$12 and take 8 hrs in the dry season, leaving from C Salaverry, only when full. Most buses and colectivos, of which a few go daily, continue to Puno. Mudslides are a problem in the rainy season and the road is in poor condition, it also gets bitterly cold at night, but the scenery is superb. To **Puno**, 297 km, 8$\frac{1}{2}$-10 hrs, US$7.50, a few buses and trucks daily, 1600 and 1700; colectivo US$12, 9 hrs. Although the route does not go via Juliaca, the road conditions are identical. **NB** Check on the security situation before travelling Arequipa-Cusco by overnight bus.

CLIMBING EL MISTI

At 5,822m, **El Misti** volcano offers a relatively straightforward opportunity to scale a high peak. Start from the hydroelectric plant, after first registering with the police there, then you need 1 day to the Monte Blanco shelter, at 4,800m. Start early for the 4-6 hrs to the top, to get there by 1100 before the mists obscure the view. If you start back at 1200 you will reach the hydroelectric plant by 1800. Alternatively, buses leave Arequipa for Baños Jesús, then on to Chiguata, where one can walk to the base of El Misti. Be sure to take plenty of food and water; it takes 2 days to reach the crater. Guides may be available at Cachamarca. Further information is available from Carlos Zárate (address above, **Climbing**). Also some travel agencies have information.

COLCA CANYON

The Colca Canyon is twice as deep as the Grand Canyon. The Río Colca descends from 3,500m above sea level at Chivay to 2,200m at Cabanaconde. The roads on either side of the canyon are at around 4,000m.

In the background looms the grey, smoking mass of Sabancaya, one of the most active volcanoes in the Americas, and its more docile neighbour, Ampato (6,288m). Unspoiled Andean villages lie on both sides of the canyon, inhabited by the Cabana and Collagua peoples, and some of the extensive precolumbian terraced fields are still in use.

Tours

Travel agencies in Arequipa arrange a '1-day' tour to the Mirador for US$18-20: depart Arequipa at 0400, arrive at the Mirador at 0800-0900, expensive lunch stop at Chivay and back to Arequipa by 2100; not recommended, especially for those with altitude problems, as it is too much to fit into 1 day. 2 day tours cost US$20-26 pp with an overnight stop in Chivay. Allow at least 2-3 days when visiting the Colca Canyon.

Local festivals

Many in the Colca region: **2-3 Feb**: *Virgen de la Candelaria*, Chivay, Cabanaconde, Maca, Tapay. *Semana Santa*. **3 May**: *Cruz de la Piedra*, Tuti. **13 June**: **San Antonio**, Yanque, Maca. **14 June**: *San Juan*, Sibayo, Ichupampa. **21 June**: anniversary of Chivay. **29 June**: *San Pedro y San Pablo*, Sibayo. **14-17 July**: *La Virgen del Carmen*, Cabanaconde. **25 July**: *Santiago Apóstol*, Coporaque. **26 July-2 Aug**: *Virgen Santa Ana*, Maca. **15 Aug**: *Virgen de la Asunta*, Chivay. **8 Dec**: *Immaculada Concepción*, Yanque, Chivay. **25 Dec**: *Sagrada Familia*, Yanque. Many of these festivals last several days and involve traditional dances and customs.

CHIVAY TO CABANACONDE

A poor dirt road runs N from Arequipa, over the altiplano, to **Chivay** (3,600m), the first village on the edge of the Canyon. About an hour out of Arequipa is the **National Vicuña Reserve**. If you're lucky,

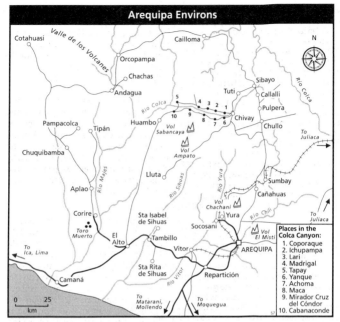

Arequipa Environs

Places in the Colca Canyon:
1. Coporaque
2. Ichupampa
3. Lari
4. Madrigal
5. Tapay
6. Yanque
7. Achoma
8. Maca
9. Mirador Cruz del Cóndor
10. Cabanaconde

you can see herds of these rare near the road. This route affords fine views of the volcanoes Misti, Chachani, Ampato and Sabancaya. There is a US$0.80 entrance fee to the canyon.

Chivay is the linking point between the two sides of the canyon, as it has the only bridge over the river. The road continues NE to **Tuti**, where there is a small handicrafts shop, and **Sibayo**, with a *pensión* and grocery store. A long circuit back to Arequipa heads S from Sibayo, passing through **Callalli**, **Chullo** and **Sumbay**. This is a little-travelled road, but the views of fine landscapes with vicuña, llamas, alpacas and Andean duck are superb.

Another road from Sibayo goes W, following the northern side of the Colca mountain range to **Cailloma**, **Orcopampa** and **Andagua** (see page 1315).

Crossing the river at Chivay going W to follow the canyon on the far side, you pass the villages of **Coporaque**, **Ichupampa** (where a foot bridge crosses the river), **Lari**, **Madrigal** (which is connected to Maca) and **Tapay** (connected to Cabanaconde).

Chivay is the gateway to the canyon. The hot springs of **La Calera** are 4-5 km away, regular colectivos (US$0.25) or a 45-mins' walk from town, entrance US$1.20; highly recommended after a hard day's trekking.

From Chivay, the main road goes W along the Colca Canyon. The first village encountered is **Yanque** (8 km, 4 hrs' walk, excellent views), with an interesting church and a footbridge to the villages on the other side of the canyon. Two nuns, Sisters Antonia and Sara will allow you to climb the old bell tower of the church. They also run a food help programme for poor families in the area; donations much appreciated. *Refugio* across river near thermal baths, G pp, food extra (ask directions). Next is **Achoma**, with a luxury bungalow complex outside the village. There is also an old settlement for road workers where you can camp.

The road continues to **Maca**, which barely survived an earthquake in Nov 1991 (people are still living in tents that were provided at the time), and to the Mirador, or **Cruz del Cóndor** at the deepest point of the canyon. The view is wonderful and condors can be seen rising on the morning thermals (0900) and sometimes in the late afternoon (1800). There is good hidden camping here. The bus will stop here for about 10 mins (if not, ask). Take the return bus from Cabanaconde (0330) and ask to be dropped off at the Mirador to wait for sunrise and condors.

From the Mirador it is a 20 mins' ride to **Cabanaconde** (3,287m), a friendly, typical village, very basic (take a torch/flashlight). It is the last village in the Colca Canyon; the views are fine and condors can be seen from the hill just W of the village, a 10 mins' walk from the plaza. A path winds down into the canyon and up to the village of Tapay. A dirt road goes back from Cabanaconde to Arequipa via Huambo and El Alto. This is not a well-used route and there are no services between Cabanaconde and the Panamericana.

Trekking

There are many hiking possibilities in the area. Make sure to take enough water as it gets very hot and there is not a lot of water available. Moreover, sun protection is a must. Some treks are impossible if it rains heavily in the wet season, but most of the time the rainy season is dry. Check beforehand. Ask locals for directions as there are hundreds of confusing paths going into the canyon. Buy food for longer hikes in Arequipa. Topographical maps are available at the Instituto Geográfico Militar in Lima, and good information at the South American Explorers Club. From Chivay you can hike to Coporaque and Ichupampa, cross the river by the footbridge and climb up to Achoma, a 1-day hike. It is a 2 hrs' walk from the Mirador to Cabanaconde (or the other way round – horses can be hired) by a short cut, following the canyon instead of the road, which takes 3 hrs. It takes 2 days to walk from Chivay to Cabanaconde, you can camp along the route.

2 hrs below Cabanaconde is an 'oasis' of palm trees and swimming areas (4½ hrs back up, ask for the best route), rec. The hike from Cabanaconde to Tapay takes 4 hrs; possible to stay overnight in Tapay, or camp. You can continue to Madrigal on foot, through a red-walled valley, about 4 days. A longer hike from Cabanaconde goes to Chachas (4-5 days – see page 1315): heading W, you descend into the canyon, cross the Inca Bridge (Puente Colgado, 1,800m) then climb to Choco (2,473m) and the pass at 5,000m, then down to Chachas. This is a superb walk through untouched areas and villages. You need all camping equipment, food and plenty of water.

- **Accommodation & places to eat Chivay**: **D** *El Posada del Inca*, with bath and breakfast, hot water, modern, safe, restaurant next door; **D-E** *Hostal Colca*, Salaverry 307, 2 blocks from plaza, dormitory rooms and some with private bath, good restaurant, water infrequent; **E** *Inca*, on Salaverry, spacious rooms, good restaurant; **F** *El Parador del Inca*, no hot water, roof garden, laundry; **F** *Hostal Municipal*, on W side of plaza, with bath, cold water, rec; **F** *Los Leños*, hot water, pizzería, rec; **F-G** *Hostal Inti*, several blocks from plaza, rec; **F-G** *Hostal Plaza*, on the plaza, basic. *El Volante*, on W side of plaza, excellent cheap set meals, popular; *Casa Blanca*, on main plaza, good, cheap, lunch buffet US$4.25. There are other basic restaurants and a small market. **Yanque**: **A3** *Colca Lodge*, reservations at Zela 212, Arequipa, T 245199, F 242088, with bath, hot water, swimming pool, restaurant, hiking, riding, cycling tours. **Achoma**: **E** *Aldea Turística de Colca*, luxury bungalows for 6 **C**, all meals, it has the only electricity, heating and hot water in the valley; book through Receptur in Lima or Arequipa, or Ricketts Turismo, Mercaderes 407, Arequipa, T 225382, open April-Nov only. **Cabanaconde**: electricity from 1900-2200. Several basic hotels: **G** pp *Cruz del Cóndor*, on the plaza, nice; **G** *Solarex*, C Tingo 105, 1 block from plaza, these two may not have either water or enough blankets (take sleeping bag); **G** *Hostal San Pedro*, bright rooms, no shower; **G** *Hostal Valle del Fuego*, 1 block from the plaza, good meals available for around US$3 at restaurant *Rancho del Sol*, the owner, Pablo Junco, is a wealth of information. There are several basic restaurants around the plaza, inc *Rancho del Colca*, which is mainly vegetarian.

- **Tour companies & travel agents** Tours to *Cruz del Condor* (US$4 pp), river rafting

(US$20/3 hrs) and mountain bike rental at the pizza restaurant on a side street just off the main plaza.

● **Transport** From Arequipa there are two routes to Chivay: the old route, via Cayma, called 'Cabreritas'; the new route, through Yura, following the railway, longer but quicker. Several buses daily, some very old (Cristo Rey etc), from Arequipa to Chivay, 4 hrs (longer if it rains), US$3.85; they leave from the bus offices in C San Juan de Dios at 0300-0400 and from the terminal at 1230-1330. Get your ticket the previous day and be there early to claim your seat. It is a rough route and cold in the morning, reaching 4,825m in the Pata Pampa pass, but the views are worth it. Buses continue to Cabanaconde, 2 hrs, US$1.40. Buses return to Arequipa at 1300 from the market. Arequipa-Cabanaconde 6 hrs, US$4.35; buses return to Arequipa 0900-0930. From Chivay to Sibayo, 35 km, 1 hr, US$0.75, several pick-ups daily. From Sibayo to Arequipa, via Callalli, 147 km. From Sibayo to Andagua, via Cailloma and Orcopampa, 194 km, and a further 290 km back to Arequipa; about 12 hrs, US$7. It is possible to go to Cusco from Chivay: take colectivo to Callalli and the friendly local police will flag down a passing Cusco-bound bus for you.

SOUTH TO CHILE

ROUTES At **Repartición**, 42 km SW of Arequipa, 134 km from Camaná, a branch of the Panamericana Sur leads S to the Chilean border. From this latter road a branch leads off from La Joya W to Mollendo and Matarani.

MOLLENDO

130 km S of Arequipa, **Mollendo** (*Pop* 14,650; *Phone code* 054) has now been replaced as a port by Matarani 14½ km to the NW. Three beautiful sandy beaches stretch down the coast. The small beach nearest town is the safest for swimming; the swimming pool on the beach is open Jan-March. Mollendo now depends partly upon the summer attraction of the beaches, during which time hotels can be full, and partly upon the 15,000 ha of irrigated land in the nearby Tambo valley. On the coast, a few kilometres SE by road, is the summer resort of Mejía. The small national reserve at the lagoons has 72 resident species of birds and 62 visiting species.

Local festivals 6 Jan: anniversary of the district and start of the summer season.

● **Accommodation & places to eat C** *Hostal Cabaña*, Comercio 240, good; **D** *Hostal Willy*, Deán Valdivia 437-443, hot water, modern, spacious, rec. There are several other cheap options in the **E-F** range on Arica: **F** *Hostal California*, Blondel 541, T 535160, best rooms at top, restaurant, rec. Several restaurants inc *La Cabaña*, Comercio 208, excellent, cheap set meals; *La Pizzería*, Comercio 301, good.

● **Buses** To Arequipa, 129 km, buses and colectivos daily, 3 hrs, US$3, many companies on Comercio opp the church. To Moquegua, 156 km, 2 hrs, US$2-3, several buses and colectivos daily. To Tacna, 315 km, direct transport Thur only; otherwise take colectivo from C Comercio early am to 'fiscal', where you can connect with Arequipa-Tacna buses.

ROUTES The Pan-American Highway runs S from La Joya through Moquegua to Tacna and Arica (Chile). Cyclists warn that the road to Moquegua is very hilly. The ash-grey sand dunes near La Joya, on the Pan-American Highway and almost half way to the coast to Arequipa, are unique in appearance and formation. All are crescent shaped and of varying sizes, from 6 to 30m across and from 2 to 5m high, with the points of the crescent on the leeward side. The sand is slowly blown up the convex side, drifts down into the concave side, and the dunes move about 15m a year.

MOQUEGUA

Moquegua (213 km from Arequipa; *Pop* 110,000; *Alt* 1,412m), is a peaceful town in the narrow valley of the Moquegua river and enjoys a sub-tropical climate. The old centre, a few blocks above the Pan-American Highway, has winding, cobbled streets and 19th century buildings. The Plaza de Armas, with its mix of ruined and well-maintained churches, colonial and republican façades and llama-shaped hedges, is one of the most interesting small-town plazas in the country.

Museo Contisuyo on the Plaza de Armas, is within the ruins of the Iglesia Matriz. It covers the Pucara, Huari, Tiahuanaco, Colla, Lupaca and Inca cultures and displays artefacts from around the area. Open Tues 1700-2000, Wed-Sun 1000-1300, 1500-1700.

A highly recommended excursion is to **Cerro Baúl**, 2,590m, a tabletop mountain with marvellous views and many legends, which can be combined with the Huari ruins at Torata, 24 km NE.

The main **festival** is *Día de Santa Catalina* on 25 Nov, the anniversary of the founding of the colonial city.

● **Accommodation** Several hotels inc **C** *Limoneros*, Jr Lima 441, T 761649, hot water, **D** without bath, helpful, car park, old house with basic rooms, nice garden; **D** *Los Angeles*, Jr Torata 100-A, T 762629, hot water, rec; **D** *Hostal Adrianella*, Miguel Grau 239, T 763469, modern, hot water; **F** *Hostal Carrera*, Jr Lima 320, T 762113, rec.

● **Buses** From Lima, US$16. Moquegua-Ilo, 95 km, 1½ hrs, US$1, a few buses daily. To Tacna, 159 km, 2 hrs, US$2, several buses and colectivos daily; to Puno, 262 km, 10 hrs, San Martín and others daily, US$7. To Arequipa, 3½ hrs, US$4, several buses daily.

ILO

There are three Ilos: Ilo Viejo; Ilo Nuevo; and the present town, a fast developing industrial city and important port (*Pop* 95,000; *Phone code* 054). Ilo Viejo was founded by the French as a port. In precolumbian times, between 900 and 1300 AD, it was the centre of the Chiribaya culture. The present town is pretty ugly, with a fishmeal factory, oil tanks, and dusty cobbled streets and 'half-door' saloons. Uglier still is Ilo Nuevo, a breezeblock town built by the Southern Peru Copper Corporation for its engineers and their families. In 1992, Bolivia was given part of the beach S of Ilo, now called Bolivia Mar, got half of the tax free zone, for the import and export of goods.

● **Accommodation** **C** *Karina*, esq Abtao 780 y Mcal Nieto, T 781531, breakfast inc, hot water, modern and very clean, very friendly, telephone, TV US$2 extra, car parking US$2 extra per day; many other hotels in town.

TACNA

Backed by the snow-capped peak of Tacora, **Tacna** (*Pop* 150,200; *Alt* 550m; *Phone code* 054) is 156 km S of Moquegua by the Pan-American Highway, 42 km from the Chilean frontier, and 64 km from the international port of Arica, to which there is a railway. It is 1,292 km from Lima by road.

Tacna was in Chilean hands from 1880 to 1929, when its people voted by plebiscite to return to Peru. There are good schools, housing estates, a stadium to seat 10,000 people, an airport, many military posts and one of the best hospitals in Peru.

Around the city the desert is gradually being irrigated. The local economy includes olive groves, vineyards and fishing.

Places of interest

Above the city, on the heights, is the **Campo de la Alianza**, scene of a battle between Peru and Chile in 1880. The cathedral, designed by Eiffel, faces the main square, Plaza de Armas, which contains huge bronze statues of Admiral Grau and Colonel Bolognesi. The interior is austere but the round stained glass windows, each with a different motif, accentuate the fine, clean lines. The bronze fountain is said to be the duplicate of the one in the Place de la Concorde (Paris) and was also designed by Eiffel. The **Parque de la Locomotora**, near the city centre, has a British-built locomotive, which was used in the War of the Pacific. There is a very good railway museum at the station (0800-1300, US$0.45). The museum in the **Casa de la Cultura** has precolumbian pottery and war relics, it is very good and entry is free.

Local information

NB Everything closes 1300-1600.

● **Accommodation**

Accommodation is hard to find in the centre, especially at Christmas-time, because of Chileans on shopping sprees.

A2 *Gran Hotel Tacna*, Av Bolognesi 300, T 724193, F 722015 (ex Hotel Turistas), gardens, 2 swimming pools, safe car park, good breakfast for US$4, English spoken, disco, casino, gym.

B *Gran Hotel Central*; San Martín 561, T 712281, F 726031, central, secure, English spoken, rec; **B-C** *El Mesón*, Unánue 175, T 725841, F 721832, modern, nice.

D *Lima*, San Martín 442, T 711912, on Plaza de Armas, sporadic hot water, bar, good restaurant, stores luggage, smelly; **D** *San Diego*, Ayacucho 86-A, T 712398, shared bath, basic.

E *Hostal HC*, Zela 734, T 712391, hot water, discounts available, cafeteria next door, laundry service, videos, rec; **E** *Lido*, C San Martín 876, nr Plaza de Armas, with hot showers, good value restaurant, rec.

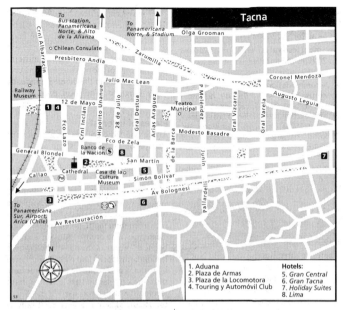

Tacna

1. Aduana
2. Plaza de Armas
3. Plaza de la Locomotora
4. Touring y Automóvil Club

Hotels:
5. *Gran Central*
6. *Gran Tacna*
7. *Holiday Suites*
8. *Lima*

F *Hostal Buen Amigo*, 2 de Mayo 445, secure, no water at night; **F** *Hostal Arica*, Pasaje Bacigalupo, Av Leguía, T 715818, good value, hot water.

● **Places to eat**
Sur Perú, Ayacucho 80, rec; *Los Tenedores*, San Martín 888, good, clean, expensive; *El Sameño*, Arias Aráguez, entre Zarumilla y Olga Grooman, good value fish restaurant; *Delfín Azul*, Zela 747, good; *Helados Piamonte*, 1 block from *Hotel Tacna*, good ice cream. Hot food from supermarket *Caneda y Cía*, San Martín 770.

● **Airline offices**
Aero Continente, Apurímac 265; Faucett, Apurímac 205; AeroPerú, Ayacucho 96.

● **Banks & money changers**
Banco de Crédito, San Martín 574, no commission for TCs (Amex, Citicorp, City Bank) into soles; similarly at Banco Wiese, San Martín 476; Banco de Perú, C Gral Blondel, between Gral Deustua y Arias Aráguez, changes TCs into soles at reasonable rate, open Sat 0930-1200. Best rates are at the *cambio* on Junín, between *Hotel Junín* and Av Bolognesi.

● **Post & telecommunications**
Telefónica del Perú: Zela 727.

● **Tourist offices**
Secretaría de Estado de Turismo, Av Bolognesi 2088, T 3778. **Touring y Automóvil Club del Perú**, Av 2 de Mayo 55.

● **Transport**
Air To **Lima**, 2 hrs; daily flights with AeroPerú, Aero Continente and Faucett. To **Arequipa**, 35 mins, all airlines; with connecting flight to **Juliaca**. Taxi to town and bus terminal US$5. There is no transport direct to the border; cheapest way is to take a taxi to town first, then take a colectivo.

Buses Bus station on Hipólito Unánue, 1 km from plaza (colectivo US$0.25); well-organized, local tax US$0.40, baggage store, easy to make connections to the border, Arequipa or Lima. To **Moquegua**, 159 km, 2 hrs, US$2, several buses and colectivos daily. There are no direct buses to **Mollendo**, so catch one of the frequent buses to El Fiscal (US$4, 4 hrs), then a colectivo to Mollendo for US$1.50. To **Arequipa**, 4 hrs, US$5, several buses daily, 0800-1000, 1900-2200 (eg Ormeño, Aráguez 698 y Grooman). To **Nasca**, 793 km, 12 hrs, US$9, several buses daily, most en route for Lima. Several buses daily to **Lima**, 1,239 km, 21-26 hrs, US$27 with Cruz del Sur and Ormeño, rec.

Tickets can be purchased several days before

departure and buses fill up quickly. At the Tacna/Moquegua departmental border there are checkpoints at which all buses stop for inspection of imported goods from Chile (there are loads!). This can take time as negotiation with the officials is required and they can be impossible. Do not carry anything for a Peruvian, only your own belongings.

Buses leave from the Zona Franca nr the airport and market area, **not** the bus terminal, to **Ilave** on the Puno-La Paz highway, 320 km, 16 hrs (can be longer in the rainy season), US$6; Gironda, Río Blanco and Ponce companies. The road, via Tarata (where Inca terraces are still in use) and Challapalca, is in fair condition, but it is a bumpy and cold journey and can be hard in the wet, though the views are spectacular. Luggage packed on the roof racks has been known to disappear. It might be better to fly to Juliaca and then take a bus. Plenty of local buses and colectivos leave all day from Ilave to **Puno**, a further 55 km, 1 hr, US$1. To **La Paz**, either go from Puno to Yunguyo, or take the direct Litoral bus, T 724761, Wed 0700, US$20, 13-16 hrs (but it can be much longer in the rainy season).

NB Soon after buses leave Tacna, passengers' passports and luggage are checked, whether you have been out of the country or not.

FRONTIER WITH CHILE

● Peruvian immigration

There is a checkpoint before the border, which is open 0900-2200. Peruvian immigration is closed on public holidays. You need to obtain a Peruvian exit stamp (quick) and then a Chilean entrance stamp, which can take a while, but formalities are straightforward. Drivers will help, or do it all for you. If you need a Chilean visa, you have to get it in Tacna (open only during office hours, closed weekends and holidays). Note that no fruit or vegetables are allowed into Chile.

● Crossing by private vehicle

For those leaving Peru by car buy *relaciones de pasajeros* (official forms, US$0.45) from the kiosk at the border or from a bookshop; you will need 4 copies. Next, return your tourist card, visit the PNP office, return the vehicle permit and finally depart through the checkpoints.

● Exchange

Coming into Peru from Chile, you can only change pesos into soles with street money changers in Tacna at a poor rate. Money changers line Av Bolognesi, they are also at one end of the new bus terminal where the rates are described as 'not too bad' (see also **Banks & money changers** above).

● Transport

Road 46 km, 1-2 hrs, depending on waiting time at the frontier. Buses to Arica charge about US$2 and colectivo taxis about US$4 pp. All leave from the bus terminal in Tacna throughout the day. If you're in a hurry, make sure that the colectivo you choose is full (most of the time 6 passengers) because it will not leave before. You can change your remaining soles at the bus terminal. A Chilean driver is perhaps more likely to take you to any address in Arica. 'Agents' operate on behalf of taxi drivers at the bus terminal; you may not see the colectivo until you have negotiated the price and filled in the paperwork.

Trains Mon, Wed and Fri at 0530 and 0700 (check times) from Tacna to Arica, US$1.60, 2 hrs. The station opens 1 hr before departure to prevent smugglers from entering as the trains are normally used by smugglers. There are customs, but no immigration facilities for those arriving by train from Chile.

NB Between Oct and Mar Peruvian time is 1 hr earlier than Chilean time, 2 hrs earlier Oct to Feb or Mar, varies annually.

AREQUIPA TO JULIACA

The railway from Arequipa winds its way up the valley towards Juliaca. Skirting El Misti and Chachani the train climbs steadily past Yura, Socosani and Pampa de Arrieros. After another 80 km it reaches Crucero Alto, the highest point on the line, at 4,500m. On the descent, streams become more plentiful. The scenery changes over the next few hours from desolate mountain peaks to a fertile pampa with a fairly populous agricultural community. **NB** Since there is no day train, much of this stunning scenery is, unfortunately, not visible en route. The train, however, is more comfortable than travelling by bus.

The rough road from Arequipa to Juliaca climbs steeply for the first 50 km, before reaching a plateau. Its highest point is at Alto de Toroya, 4,693m. The scenery is beautiful as the road passes lakes, salt flats and small villages. If driving, a 4WD is strongly recommended. Even in the dry season, there are rivers to cross and sand stretches. After heavy rain it is impassable.

This takes 3 days by bicycle. If heading for Puno it is better to go via Juliaca than taking the direct branch to Puno. Restaurants along the way sell mostly basic foodstuffs and drinks: at **Chiguata**, Km 30; **Salinas**, Km 82; at Km 113, S from **Pati**; **Alto de Toroya**, Km 176; **Tincopalca**, Km 176, where it is also possible to sleep; **Santa Lucía**, Km 218, also *alojamiento*; and at **Deustua**, Km 252. The route covers 282 km in total. The road is paved to Chiguata, then poor as far as Santa Lucía, and paved from there to Juliaca. Gasoline is sold from the drum at the villages along the road.

JULIACA

289 km NE of Arequipa, **Juliaca** (*Pop* 134,700; *Alt* 3,825m; *Phone code* 054), is freezing cold at night and not particularly attractive. On the huge Plaza Melgar, several blocks from the main part of the town, is an interesting colonial church. At the large market in the plaza on Mon, you can buy wool and alpaca goods. There is another daily market in the plaza outside the railway station, which is more tourist oriented. Túpac Amarú market, on Moquegua 7 blocks E of railway line, is a cheap black market. A first class hospital is run by the Seventh Day Adventists.

Excursions

23 km NW of Juliaca is the unspoiled little colonial town of **Lampa**, known as the 'Pink City', with a splendid church, La Inmaculada, containing a copy of Michelangelo's 'Pietà'. Also of interest is the Kampac Museo, Ugarte 462, a museum with sculptures and ceramics from the Lampa and Juli areas; the owner lives next door. It also has a good Sun market. There is a basic *hostal*, G pp. Buses and trucks daily, 1 hr, US$0.65, from Plaza de Armas in Juliaca.

The town of **Pucara** lies 63 km to the N, with pre-Inca ruins and fine pottery. 71 km NE is the old town of **Azángaro** with a famous church, La Asunción, filled with *retablos* and paintings of the Cusco school. There are good thermal springs at **Putina**, 84 km NE, 5½ hrs by bus or truck, US$2.50.

Local information
● **Accommodation**

B *Turistas*, Av Arequipa 1381, T 71524, on the outskirts of town, good, but the water is turned off at 2300, meals US$3-5.

C *Hostal Samari*, Noriega, T 321870, F 321852, modern, with restaurant.

D *Karlo's Hostal*, Unión 317, T 322568, comfortable, hot water; **D** *Royal Inn*, San Román 158, T 321561, F 321572, decent accommodation, rec, restaurant good.

E *Hostal Perú*, Bracesco 409, railway plaza, T 321510, cheaper without bath, comfortable, hot water sometimes, rec, has a basic restaurant; **E** *Yasur*, Jr M Núñez 414, **F** without bath, safe, a small bar and restaurant are open in the evening.

G *Hostal Ferrocarril*, San Martín 249, water until 1900. There are water problems in town, especially in the dry season.

● **Places to eat**

Trujillo, on San Martín, basic, typical food, good value, US$3-4 for a meal.

● **Security**

Beware of pickpockets and thieves, especially at the station, where they get on the train to join those already on board. Also beware of overcharging by taxi drivers at the railway station.

● **Transport**

Air Airport is small but well-organized. To Lima, 1 hr, 45 mins, daily with AeroPerú, Faucett and Aero Continente (special promotional deals are often available). To Arequipa, 30 mins, daily with all main airlines. To Cusco, 35 mins, Faucett 3 a week, and Aero Continente daily. Taxi to airport 15 mins, US$2.10. Alternatively, walk 200m to airport entrance and catch a city bus, US$0.15. A colectivo runs direct from the airport to Puno, US$2 pp, 1 hr.

Trains See information under Arequipa (inc **Warning**), Puno or Cusco. The station at Juliaca is the junction for services between Arequipa, Puno and Cusco. Carriages are put onto the right rails for their next destination, a process which can take several hours and can prove too much for tired passengers. It is advisable to get off the train and continue to Puno by bus or colectivo (US$0.45, 1 hr), which is much quicker, safer and more comfortable. You do not have to change trains in Juliaca if you buy a through ticket from one terminus to the other using the same class all the way. Stay in your carriage at Juliaca and watch your possessions closely.

You have the opportunity to buy alpaca goods through the carriage window, but bargain hard. The ticket office opens when the train comes in. Trains for Puno arrive about 0645; for

Arequipa at about 2045. Prices to Cusco and Arequipa are the same as from Puno.

Buses To **Cusco**, 344 km, 12 hrs (longer in the rainy season), US$8; buses and trucks daily. The road is in very poor condition as the train is used more frequently. When the train does not run in the rainy season, the bus has to be taken, unless conditions are so bad that buses are not running either. It is not advisable to take a night bus to or from Cusco, as robberies, or worse, can occur; at least take the more expensive tourist bus. To **Puno**, 44 km, 1 hr, US$0.50, leaving from Calle Nicolás de Piérola, past the rail station; combis to Puno leave from Plaza Bolognesi, also US$0.50. Taxi to Puno is about US$15. To **Huancané** (on the N side of Lake Titicaca), 51 km, 3½ hrs, US$1.75, several buses and trucks daily; it is a bumpy ride on a poor road, but the views are wonderful. It is a further 50 km, US$1.75, to the Bolivian border; there are several checkpoints and the trip can take a few hours. Buses and trucks leave daily, but not very frequently, on this route.

PUNO

On the NW shore of Lake Titicaca, **Puno** is Capital of its Department and Peru's folklore centre with a vast array of handicrafts, festivals and costumes and a rich tradition of music and dance.

Cathedral, completed in 1657, has an impressive baroque exterior, but an austere interior. Beside the Cathedral is the **Balcony of the Conde de Lemos**, Deustua esquina Conde de Lemos, where Peru's Viceroy stayed when he first arrived in the city. A short walk up Independencia leads to the **Arco Deustua**, a monument honouring those killed in the battles of Junín and Ayacucho. Nearby, is a mirador giving fine views over the town, the port and the lake beyond. The walk from Jr Cornejo following the Stations of the Cross up a nearby hill, with fine views of Lake Titicaca, has been recommended, but be careful and don't go alone.

BASICS *Pop* 80,000, with 8,000 students; *Alt* 3,855m. *Climate* Puno gets bitterly cold at night: in June-Aug the temperature at night can fall to -25°C, but generally not below -5°C.

Museums

The **Museo Municipal** has been combined with the private collection of Sr Carlos Dreyer; Conde de Lemos 289; open Mon to Fri 0730-1330, US$1.

The *Yavari*, the oldest ship on Lake Titicaca, is berthed in the port and is now open as a Museum and Bar. She is moored alongside the jetty from which the launches to Los Uros leave. The ship was built in England in 1862 and was shipped in kit form to Arica, thence by rail to Tacna and by mule to Lake Titicaca. The journey took 6 years. The *Yavari* was eventually launched on Christmas Day 1870. The ship is being restored by an Anglo-Peruvian Association. Visitors are very welcome on board; entrance US$2 to help with maintenance costs.

● **Project addresses** England: 61 Mexfield Road, London, SW15 2RG, T/F (44) 181 874 0583; Peru/Lima: c/o *Invertur*, Av Las Magnolias 889, Of 208, San Isidro, Lima 27, T 442-3090, F 442-4180; Puno: c/o *Solmartours*, Jr Arequipa 140, Puno, T 352901, F 351654.

Excursions

Anybody interested in religious architecture should visit the villages along the western shore of Lake Titicaca. An Inca sundial can be seen near the village of **Chucuíto**, which has an interesting church, La Asunción, and houses with carved stone doorways. Beside the Plaza Menor is the site of ancient fertility rituals; a rectangular room filled with stone penises. (**D** *Las Cabañas*, 4-bedded bungalow, quiet location, T 352108, leave message for Alfredo Sánchez.) At Chichiflope, nearby, are cave paintings.

The best examples of religious architecture are at **Juli**. **San Pedro**, designated as the Cathedral, has been extensively restored. It contains a series of superb screens, some fine paintings, and a collection of coloured objects in the sacristy. **San Juan Bautista** has two sets of 17th century paintings of the lives of St John the Baptist and of St Teresa, contained in sumptuous gilded frames. San Juan is a museum, open in the morning only (US$1.15); it also has intricate *mestizo* carving in pink stone. **Santa Cruz** is partly roofless, so that it is easy to photograph the carvings of monkeys, papayas and grapes. The keys to Santa Cruz and San Juan Bautista are kept by the couple who look after San Juan Bautista. The fourth church, **La Asunción**,

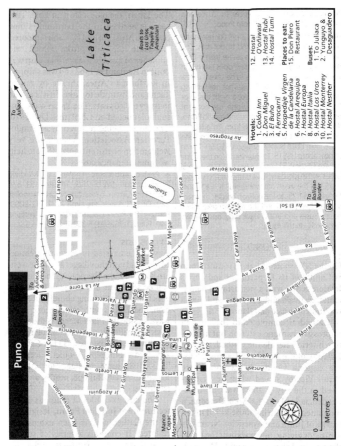

Hotels:
1. Colon Inn
2. Don Miguel
3. El Buho
4. Ferrocaril
5. Hospedaje Virgen de la Candelaria
6. Hostal Arequipa
7. Hostal Europa
8. Hostal Italia
9. Hostal Los Uros
10. Hostal Monterrey
11. Hostal Nesther
12. Hostal Q'oñiwasi
13. Hostal Rubi
14. Hostal Tumi

Places to eat:
15. Don Piero Restaurant

Buses:
1. To Juliaca
2. Yunguyo & Desaguadero

now abandoned and its fine bell tower damaged by earthquake or lightning, has an archway and atrium which date from the early 17th century. A school of picture restoration is working on its mass of paintings. Beautiful needlework can be bought at the plaza in Juli. There is a nice walk from Juli to the red rock formations known as Caballo Cansado. Near Juli is a small colony of flamingos. Many other birds can be seen from the road. Colectivo Puno-Juli US$0.80.

● **Accommodation F** *Hostal Municipal*, opp market, clean, big rooms; **G** *Alojamiento El*

Rosal, Puno 128, just off the Plaza, basic but OK.

The church at **Pomata**, under restoration, has beautiful carvings in Andean *mestizo* baroque of vases full of tropical plants, flowers and animals in the window frames, lintels and cornices. The frieze of dancing figures inside the dome is unusual in Peru (John Hemming). The church at **Zepita** is also worth visiting.

Near Puno, are the *chullpas* (precolumbian funeral towers) of **Sillustani** in a beautiful setting on a peninsula in Lake Ayumara, 32 km from Puno on an excellent road. "Most of the towers date from the period of Inca occupation in the 15th century, but they are burial towers of the Aymara-speaking Colla tribe. The engineering involved in their construction is more complex than anything the Incas built – it is defeating archaeologists' attempts to rebuild the tallest 'lizard' *chullpa*. Two are unfinished: one with a ramp still in place to raise blocks; the other with cut stones ready to go onto a very ambitious corbelled false dome" (John Hemming). There are local people at the site, in traditional costume. Photography is best in the afternoon light, though this is when the wind is strongest. The scenery is desert, but impressive. The site has a restaurant, but no electricity; admission, US$2.25.

● **Transport** Take an organized tour; about 3-4 hrs, leave 1430. Some include transport and entrance fee, about US$7-8; some offer only transport US$3. Bus, inc site entrance, from C Tacna, 1430, US$5. Taxi from Puno US$25.

Local festivals

Feb: at the *Fiesta de la Virgen de la Candelaria*, first 2 weeks in Feb, bands and dancers from all the local towns compete in a *Diablada*, or Devil Dance. The festivities are better at night on the streets than the official functions in the stadium. Check the dates in advance as Candelaria may be moved if pre-Lentern carnival coincides with it.

A candlelight procession through darkened streets takes place on **Good Friday**. **3 May**: *Invención de la Cruz*, an exhibition of local art. **29 June**: colourful festival of *San Pedro*, with a procession at Zepita (see page 1332); also 20 July. **4-5 Nov**: pageant dedicated to the founding of Puno and the emergence of Manco Capac from the waters of Lake Titicaca.

Local information
● **Accommodation**

Hotel rooms are difficult to find after the trains arrive but hotel touts besiege arriving train passengers. Check on the early morning water supply, as some only have water after 0730, too late if you are going out by train or on an island tour. There are clean public showers nr the football stadium. Note that Puno suffers from power and water shortages.

L3 *Isla Esteves* (ex Tourist Hotel), T 353870, spacious, good views, on an island linked by a causeway 5 km NE of Puno (taxi US$1.75), built on a Tiahuanaco-period site, phone, bar, good restaurant, disco, good service, electricity and hot water all day.

A3 *Hostal Hacienda*, Jr Deustua 297, T/F 356109, refurbished colonial house, hot water, inc breakfast, carpeted rooms, café, comfortable, rec.

B-C *El Buho*, Lambayeque 142, T 351409, hot water, nice rooms, ask for a room with a radiator, rec; **B-C** *Ferrocarril*, Av La Torre 185, T 351752, opp station, hot water, **E** without bath and with cold water in the old part of building, modern, good rooms, but noisy, poor service, central heating adequate, accepts many credit cards and changes Bolivian currency; **B** *Hostal Colón Inn*, Tacna 290, T 351432, recently renovated, colonial style, good rooms with hot shower, good service, restaurant and pizzería, the Belgian manager Christian Nonis is well known, especially for his work on behalf of the people on Taquile island; **B** *Sillustani*, Jr Lambayeque 195, T 351431, inc breakfast, good service, ask for an electric heater, hot water; **B-C** *Hostal Italia*, Teodoro Valcarcel 122, T 352521, 2 blocks from the station, good, safe, hot water, good food, helpful, rec.

C *Don Miguel*, Av La Torre 545, T 351371, with shower, with restaurant, clean; **C** *Internacional*, Libertad 161, T 352109, with shower, hot water morning and evening, restaurant, secure, central.

D *Hostal Arequipa*, Arequipa 153, T 352071, cold water, will change TCs, stores luggage, secure, arranges tours to the islands, adequate; **D** *Hostal Imperial*, Teodoro Valcarcel 145, T 352386, hot water, helpful, stores luggage, comfortable, safe; **D** *Hostal Rubi*, Jr Cajamarca 152-154, T 356058, T/F 353384, safe, breakfast US$2, good; **D** *Hostal Tumi*, Cajamarca 237, T 353270, safe, plenty of hot water, breakfast available, helpful, highly rec; **D-E** *Hostal Monterrey*, Lima 447A, T 351691, popular, reasonable, some rooms with bath, better than those without, communal bathrooms are reported dirty, hot water 0630-0900 but unreliable, restaurant poor, secure for luggage, motorcycle parking US$0.50, has colectivo service to La Paz, US$12; **D-E** *Hostal Nesther*, Deustua 268, T 351631, also 3-bedded rooms, with bath, hot water, 0730-0900, rec.

E *Europa*, Alfonso Ugarte 112, nr the station, T 353023, very popular, luggage may be stored, but don't leave your valuables in the room, shared bathrooms, hot water sometimes, garage space for motorcycles; **E** *Los Uros*, Teodoro Valcarcel 135, T 352141, cheaper without bath, hot water 1900-2200, plenty of blankets, breakfast available downstairs, quiet, good value, small charge to leave luggage, laundry service, often full, changes TCs at a reasonable rate, rec. **F** *Hostal Extra*, Moquegua 124, hot water 24 hrs, safe, popular, luggage stored; **F** pp *Hostal Q'oñiwasi*, Av La Torre 135, T 353912, opp rail station, warm rooms, luggage store, breakfast available, safe, rec; **F** *Hostal Santa Rosa*, Jr Los Incas 208, T 356733/356746, cheaper without bath, hot water, good beds, helpful; **F-G** pp *Hospedaje Virgen de la Candelaria*, Jr Tarapacá 139, T 353828, no sign, shared rooms, hot water, breakfast US$1.50, laundry service, luggage store, helpful, family atmosphere, secure, cooking facilities, can arrange local tours, rec.

Youth hostel: F-G pp *Albergue Juvenil Virgen de Copacabana*, llave 236, T 354129, no sign, huge rooms, well-furnished, hot water, "awesome bathroom", good location, quiet, helpful owners, laundry service at reasonable fee, breakfast US$1.30, a real bargain, highly rec.

● **Places to eat**
Don Piero, Lima 360, huge meals, live music, slow service, popular, tax extra; the restaurant next door is also called *Don Piero*, decent chicken, salad, fries and a soft drink for US$1.50; *Café Internacional*, Libertad 161, 2 blocks from Plaza, popular with travellers, excellent trout, not cheap and service variable; *Pizzería del Buho*, Jr Libertad 386, good pizza, cosy atmosphere, open 1800 onwards; *Al Paso Antojitos*, Lima 373, rec snack bar for cake, pies and coffee; *Peña Hostería*, Lima 501, good music, rec; *Pascana*, Lima 339, specializes in *parrilladas*, vegetarian dishes available, folk shows; *Hilda's House*, Moquegua 189, excellent food, reasonable prices; *Samaná*, Puno 334, inconsistent service, sometimes has live folk music from 2100, open fire and snacks and drinks; *Chez Maggy*, Grau 138, delicious pizza and pasta, great atmosphere, friendly staff, evening meal US$2.50, great value; *Ricardos*, Jr Lambayeque 117, clean, good breakfasts, sandwiches, friendly, rec; *Monterrey*, behind hotel of same name, good fish, good value lunches, otherwise expensive. *Café Ayllu*, Arequipa y Puno, very good pastries. Excellent patisserie at Lima 430, for croissants, fresh bread and cakes. *Café Delissa*, Libertad 215, open 0600, espresso coffee, good vegetarian food, excellent set lunch US$1.50; *Rico Pan*, Arequipa 459, café and bakery, great cakes, excellent capuccino, espresso and Irish coffee, good juices and pastries, good breakfasts and other dishes, reasonable prices, great place to relax, open 0600-2300, closed Sun; *Mi Perú*, on the corner of Arequipa and Jr Deza, popular with locals, cheap, huge portions, friendly; *Adventista*, Jr Deza 349, good. Above the city is a quinta called *Kantuta*, Arequipa 1086, good local dishes, open until 1700, rec.

● **Banks & money changers**
Banco de Crédito, Lima y Grau, before 1300 for TCs, US$1 commission, cash advance on Visa. For cash go to the *cambios*, the travel agencies or the better hotels. Best rates with money changers at the market but check your Peruvian soles carefully. The rates for soles to Bolivianos is poor; it's better to wait till Yunguyo at the border.

● **Embassies & consulates**
Bolivian Consulate, Jr Arequipa between Parque Pino y Jr Deza, visa on the spot, US$10, open 0830-1330 Mon to Fri.

● **Laundry**
Lavandería América, Jr Moquegua 169; *Lavandería Lava Clin*, Deustua 252, El Sol 431 and Teodoro Valcarcel 132, all expensive. It's better to wait until Cusco, where laundries are better value.

● **Post & telecommunications**
Post Office: Jr Moquegua 267.

Telephone: Telefónica at Arequipa y Moquegua. International phone and fax office next to the church on Parque Pino.

● **Shopping**
In the covered part of the market mostly fruit and vegetables are sold, but there are also model reed boats, attractive carved stone amulets and Ekekos (household goods). The *Market* on the railway between Av Los Incas and Lampa is one of the best places in Peru (or Bolivia) for llama and alpaca wool articles, but bargain hard, especially in the afternoon. You will be hassled on the street, and outside restaurants to buy woollen goods, so take care! Food and clothing market next to the stadium. **NB** Reports of robbery in the market.

● **Tour companies & travel agents**
Agencies organize trips to the Uros floating islands and the islands of Taquile and Amantaní (which is usually included in the Taquile trip), as well as to Sillustani, and other places. Make sure that you settle all details before embarking on the tour. Alternatively, you can easily go down to the lake and make your own arrangements with the boatmen.

We have received good reports about the following: *Servitur*, Jr Melgar 173; *Kinjyo Travel Service*, C Arequipa 401; *Kontiki Tours*, Melgar 188 for 'mystical tours'; *Cusi Tours*, Valcarcel 103, T 352591; *Kolla Tour*, Jr Moquegua 679, T 352961, F 354762, airline tickets, own boat for tours on the lake; *Feiser Tours*, Teodoro Valcarcel 155, T 353112; *Ecoturismo Aventura*, Jr Lima 458, T 355785, very helpful; *Always Travel*, Jr Puno 318, T 352823, very helpful, speak German, French, English and Italian, ask for Eliana if you have any problems in general; *Imperio Tours*, Valcarcel 191, T 367690, good for travel to La Paz; *León Tours*, Jr Libertad 176, T 852771.

● **Tourist offices**

InfoTur, C Lima y C Deustua on Plaza de Armas, helpful with general information, friendly, city guide and map US$1.20; **Ministry of Tourism**, Jr Ayacucho 682, T 351261, helpful with complaints; **Touring Automóvil Club del Perú**, C Arequipa 457.

● **Useful addresses**

Immigration: Libertad 403, T 352801, for renewing entry stamps, etc. The process is very slow and you must fill in 2 application forms at a bank, but there's nothing else to pay.

● **Transport**

Trains The railway runs from Puno to Juliaca (44 km), where it divides, to Cusco (281 km) and Arequipa (279 km). To **Cusco** Mon, Wed, Thur, Sat at 1925, arriving about 0600 (try to sit on the right hand side) and to **Arequipa** Mon, Wed, Fri, Sun at 1945, arriving about 0600. In the wet season the services may be cut to 2-3 times a week, or even be cancelled for short periods. Always check.

Fares: Puno-Cusco, 2nd class, US$11; 1st class, US$19; pullman US$24; Inca class, US$26. Puno-Arequipa, 2nd class, US$9; 1st class, US$11; pullman (*turismo ejecutivo*), US$19; Inca US$23. The ticket office is open from 0630-1030, 1600-1900 Mon-Sat, Sun pm only and tickets can be bought 1 day in advance, or 1 hr before departure if there are any left. Travel agencies are sometimes the only option, but they can be unreliable and charge 25% commission; do not pay in full before receiving the tickets and always check the date and seat number. Hotels can help with getting tickets as well. See under Arequipa **Trains** for the standards and safety of the classes. See also under Arequipa and Juliaca on safety. There is a *menú* available in the pullman and Inca carriages (US$6.50 for lunch or dinner).

A good idea in Puno, Juliaca and other Andean towns, when moving about with heavy baggage, is to hire a 3-wheel cycle cart, 'Trici-Taxi', which costs about US$0.20/km.

Buses Most companies have offices on Av Sol, eg Cruz del Sur. To Arequipa, 297 km, 8-10 hrs (longer in the rainy season), US$7-8 (US$5.50 with Emes Tours, depart 0700, 1700). A few buses and trucks go daily, the route does not go through Juliaca. Colectivos charge US$12, 9 hrs, minimum. The road is in poor condition and mudslides cause problems in the rain. All buses seem to go at night; a very cold journey. Continuing to Lima, 1,011 km, US$18, all buses go through Arequipa, sometimes with a change of

bus. See under Arequipa. To **Juliaca**, 44 km, 45 mins, US$0.50, minibuses run all day from Jr Tacna, nr corner with Libertad. Taxi to Juliaca about US$15. To **Cusco**, 388 km, 12 hrs, US$8, buses (only at night) and trucks daily, but the train is more commonly used. **NB** There is a serious danger of robbery on this route; not advised. To **Moquegua**, 262 km, 10 hrs, US$7, a few buses daily, poor road, bumpy and cold.

To **Tacna**, via **Ilave** (a typical, gaunt *altiplano* town; good Sun market with woven goods): US$1.40 by frequent bus or colectivo Puno-Ilave. Ilave-Tacna 375 km unpaved, 17 hrs (in dry season), US$7, Transportes Ponce (better) and Gironda. The road is not too bad but it is rough and cold and can be difficult in the rainy season. The views are spectacular.

Boats on Lake Titicaca Boats to the islands leave from the rebuilt terminal in the harbour (see map); *trici-taxi*, US$1.20.

LAKE TITICACA

UROS

Although the Uros of the 'floating islands' have intermarried with the Aymara and no pure Uros exist, the present Puno Bay people still practise some Uro traditions. They fish, hunt birds and live off the lake plants, most important of which are the reeds they use for their boats, houses and the very foundations of their islands. Tourism has opened their simple lives to the scrutiny of cameras and camcorders, contributing to the erosion of their culture. Some visitors find the 'peep show' nature of this type of tourism unsettling. There is no drinking water on the islands.

● **Transport** Motorboats charge upwards of US$3.50 pp; prices should not be over US$5-6 (which is what agencies charge in season). Pay half before you leave and half on your return. Boats go about every 30 mins from about 0630 till 1000, or whenever there are 10 or more people to fill the boat, and take 3-5 hrs. The earlier you go the better, to beat the crowds of tourists. Out of season there are no regular boats, so either get a group together and pay US$10 for the boat, rent a boat at US$1-2 pp, or pay an agency US$15-20.

TAQUILE

A much more interesting island to visit is **Taquile**, some 45 km from Puno, on which there are numerous pre-Inca and Inca ruins, and Inca terracing. The island is narrow, only about 1 km wide, but 6-7 km long. Ask for the (unmarked) museum of traditional costumes and also where you can see and photograph local weaving. There is a cooperative shop on the plaza that sells exceptional woollen goods which are not cheap but of very fine quality.

Easter, from the 2 to 7 June, the *Fiesta de Santiago* over 2 weeks in mid-July, and 1 and 2 Aug are the principal festival days with many dances in between.

● **Accommodation** Plentiful accommodation can be found in private houses but it is best to take warm clothes and a sleeping bag. No previous arrangements can be made; on arrival you walk up a steep path for 30 mins (remember you are at 3,800m), are greeted by the locals, pay a US$0.10 fee, sign the guest book and, if wishing to stay, are 'assigned' a family to stay with **G** pp, or **F** pp inc all meals.

● **Places to eat** There are several small restaurants on the island; eg *El Inca* on the main plaza. Fish is plentiful and the island has a trout farm, but meat is rarely available and drinks often run out. Meals are a little more expensive than on the mainland. You are advised to take with you some food, particularly fruit, bread and vegetables, water, plenty of small-value notes, candles and a torch. Take precautions against sunburn.

● **Transport** Boats leave Puno daily at 0800-0900; 4 hrs, return 1400/1430, arriving 1830, US$4.50 one way. This doesn't leave enough time to appreciate the island fully in 1 day. Organized tours can be arranged for about US$16 pp, but only give you about 2 hrs on the island. Boats sometimes call at Uros on the outward or return journey.

AMANTANI

Another island well worth visiting, is **Amantaní**. It is very beautiful and peaceful, and many say less spoiled than Taquile. There are six villages and ruins on both of the island's peaks, Pacha Tata and Pacha Mama, from which there are excellent views. There are also temples and on the shore there is a throne carved out of stone. On both hills, a fiesta is celebrated on 15 Jan (or thereabouts). The festivities are very colourful, musical and hard-drinking. There is also a festival the first Sun in Mar with brass bands and colourful dancers. The residents make beautiful textiles and sell them quite cheaply at the Artesanía Cooperativa. The people are Quechua speakers, but understand Spanish.

● **Accommodation & places to eat** There are no hotels but you are assigned to stay with local families on a rota basis; or ask your boat owner where you can stay. Accommodation, inc 3 meals, is in our **F** range. There is one restaurant, *Samariy*.

● **Transport** Boats from the harbour in Puno at 0800 daily, return 1430, US$9 round trip. The journey takes 4-5 hrs, take water. A 1-day trip is not possible as the boats do not always return on the same day. Several tour operators in Puno offer 2-3 day excursions to Amantaní, Taquile and a visit to the floating islands, US$16-30 pp (depending on the season and size of group); inc meals, 1 night on Amantaní and 3-4 hrs on Taquile. It may be better to visit the islands independently and go at your own pace. If you wish to visit both Taquile and Amantaní, it is better to go to Amantaní first; from there a boat goes to Taquile around 0800, US$2.50 pp. There is no regular service; the boat leaves if there are enough passengers.

● **Responsible tourism** The influx of tourists to all the above islands unfortunately prompts persistent requests for sweets and money which irritates many travellers. Above all, stay good-humoured. Gifts of fruit, torches (there is no electricity), moisturizer or sun block (the children suffer sore cheeks), pens, pencils or notebooks are appreciated. Buy their handicrafts instead of handing out sweets indiscriminately.

FRONTIER WITH BOLIVIA

There are four different routes across the border. The first three described are the least travelled.

● **Along the east side of Lake Titicaca**
This is the most remote route, via **Huancané**, **Moho** and **Puerto Acosta** (Bolivia). There is accommodation in Moho, **G**; one bus leaves on weekdays to Juliaca, 7 hrs, but it is often cancelled. This route is recommended only on weekends when there is more traffic. After Puerto Acosta, the road is very bad. Make sure you get an exit stamp in Puno.

● **Puno-Desaguadero**
This is the most direct route road (150 km paved), passing through **Chucuíto**, **Ilave**, **Juli** and **Pomata**. Desaguadero is a cold, miserable place, with dubious accommodation at **F** *Alojamiento Internacional*. Colectivos and buses run Puno-Desaguadero (see Puno map), 3 hrs, US$2 by bus, last one around 1600. Get your exit stamp on the Peruvian side, cross the border

and get an entrance stamp on the Bolivian side. Border offices are open 0800-1200 and 1400-1930. There are buses to La Paz (105 km from Desaguadero), 3-4 hrs, US$1.40; last one around 1700. Frequent buses run to Puno until 1930. It is easy to change money on the Peruvian side. This particular border crossing allows you to stop at Tiahuanaco en route.

● **To La Paz by hydrofoil or catamaran**
There are luxury services from Puno/Juli to La Paz by *Crillon Tours'* hydrofoil, with connections to tours, from La Paz, to Cusco and Machu Picchu. All Puno travel agents have details, or contact head office in La Paz, see page 280 for details. The itinerary is: Puno-Copacabana by bus; Co-pacabana-Isla del Sol-Huatajata (Bolivia) by hy-drofoil; Huatajata-La Paz by bus; 13 hrs. Similar services, by catamaran, are run by *Transturin*, whose dock is at Chúa, Bolivia; bookings through Transturin: offices in Puno at Libertad 176, ask for Esther de Quiñones, T 352771; Cusco, Portal de Panes 109, of 1, Plaza de Armas, T 222332; or in La Paz.

PUNO-LA PAZ VIA YUNGUYO AND COPACABANA

● **Peruvian immigration**
Is located 5 mins' drive from **Yunguyo** (shared taxi from plaza US$0.25 pp); open 0700-1800. When leaving you must get an exit stamp before crossing the border and a tourist visa on the other side. 90 days is normally given when entering Peru. Be aware of corruption at cus-toms and look out for official or unofficial people trying to charge you a departure fee (say that you know it is illegal and ask why only gringos are expected to pay the 'embarkation tax').
NB Peruvian time is 1 hr behind Bolivian time.

● **Bolivian Consulate**
Near the main plaza in Yunguyo, open Mon-Fri 0830-1500, for those who need a visa; some nationalities have to pay.

● **Accommodation**
Is available in **Yunguyo**: **F-G** pp *Hostal Isabel*, San Francisco 110, nr Plaza de Armas, T 856019/856084, shared bath, hot water, modern, good value, will change money and arrange transport; **G** *Hostal Amazonas*, basic, restaurant, and *Hostal Yunguyo*.

● **Exchange**
Good rates are available in the main plaza, Yunguyo, better than at the border, and good for changing Bolivianos, cash only. TCs can be exchanged in the *cambio* here, poor rates.

● **Transport**
The road is paved from Puno to Yunguyo and the scenery is interesting. Several travel agencies

in Puno (all on Jr Tacna) sell bus tickets for the direct route from Puno to La Paz, taking 6-8 hrs, US$13-US$15.50; check in advance that your ticket includes the Tiquina ferry crossing and other charges. They leave Puno at 0800 and stop at the borders and for lunch in Copacabana, arriving in La Paz at 1700. You only need to change money into Bolivianos for lunch on this route. Bus fare Puno-Copacabana, US$4. There are local buses and colectivos all day between Puno and Yunguyo, 3 hrs, US$2; they leave from Av El Sol in Puno. From Yunguyo to the border (Kasani), combis charge US$0.20. From the bor-der it is a 20-min drive to Copacabana; colectivos and minibuses leave from just outside Bolivian immigration, US$0.50. Taxi from Yunguyo to Copacabana costs about US$1.50 pp.

PUNO TO CUSCO

On the way from Puno to Cusco there is much to see from the train, which runs at an average altitude of 3,500m. At the sta-tions on the way, people sell food and local specialities, eg pottery bulls at Pucara (rooms available at the station); for Sicuani, see below; knitted alpaca ponchos and pullovers and miniature llamas at Santa Rosa (rooms available). There are three hotels in **Ayaviri**.

The railway crosses the altiplano, climbing to **La Raya**, the highest pass on the line; 210 km from Puno, at 4,321m. Up on the heights breathing may be a little difficult, but the descent along the Río Vilcanota is rapid. To the right of **Aguas Calientes**, the next station, 4 km from La Raya, are steaming pools of hot water in the middle of the green grass; a startling sight. The temperature of the springs is 40°C, and they show beautiful deposits of red ferro-oxide. The springs are not developed, but bathing is possible to the left, where the hot spring water joins the cold creek. At **Marangani**, the river is wider and the fields greener, with groves of eucalyptus trees.

By **road Puno-Cusco**: the paved road ends at Juliaca, from where it is very rough gravel over La Raya pass up to **Tinta**, 69 km S of **Urcos**; it is paved from Tinta all the way to Cusco. The road may be impassable in the rainy season as there are many rivers to cross. There are reports that it is to be paved. Most people take the train but, as said above, in the wet season, trains may be cancelled.

SICUANI

38 km beyond La Raya pass **Sicuani** (*Alt* 3,960m) is an important agricultural centre. Excellent items of llama and alpaca wool and skins are sold on the railway station and at the Sun morning market. Around Plaza Libertad there are several hat shops. There are mineral baths at Uyurmiri. (For more information about places between Sicuani and Cusco, see page 1352.)

- **Accommodation & places to eat D** *Centro Vacacional*, best in town, some way from centre, rec; **F** *Manzanaral*, Av 28 de Julio, cold shower, basic, noisy, parking in *taller*, about 2 blocks away; **G** *Obada*, communal shower, basic; **G** *Quispe*, basic, no shower. *Viracocha* restaurant on main plaza, OK.

ROUTES A road S of Sicuani leads to the alternative route Cusco-Arequipa. It is a spectacular journey, rough in parts (landslides in the wet). From Sicuani, the road passes the pretty lake, Laguna Langui Layo, then climbs to a radio-transmission antenna. At El Descanso is a checkpoint. The road forks SW to **Yauri**, isolated on a plateau by a canyon (**G** *Hostal El Tigre*, nice rooms, water shortages), then leads on to Sibayo, Chivay and Arequipa. Alternatively, to the SE, the road skirts **Laguna Condorama**, one of the highest lakes in South America (4,700m), past mining operations, the Majes irrigation scheme and on to the Arequipa-Juliaca road. Sicuani to Arequipa is about 400 km. If driving this route, check directions with the police.

The Vilcanota plunges into a gorge, but the train winds above it and round the side of the mountain. At **Huambutío** the railway turns left to follow the Río Huatanay on the final stretch to Cusco. The Vilcanota here widens into the great Urubamba canyon, flanked on both sides by high cliffs, on its way to join the Ucayali, a tributary of the Amazon.

Cusco and the Sacred Valley

CUSCO

The ancient Inca capital is said to have been founded around 1100 AD, and since then has developed into a major, commercial centre of 275,000 inhabitants, most of whom are Quechua. The city council has designated the Quechua, Qosqo, as the official spelling.

Today, the city is a fascinating mix of Inca and colonial Spanish architecture: colonial churches, monasteries and convents and extensive precolumbian ruins are interspersed with countless hotels, bars and restaurants that cater for the hundreds of thousands of visitors. Almost every central street has remains of Inca walls, arches and doorways; the perfect Inca stonework now serves as the foundations for more modern dwellings. This stonework is tapered upwards (battered); every wall has a perfect line of inclination towards the centre, from bottom to top. The stones have each edge and corner rounded. The curved stonework of the Temple of the Sun, for example, is probably unequalled in the world.

Information and advice (*Phone code* 084) Cusco stands at 3,310m, a little lower than Puno, so respect the altitude: 2 or 3 hrs' rest after arriving makes a great difference; avoid meat and smoking, eat lots of carbohydrates and drink plenty of clear, non-alcoholic liquid; remember to walk slowly. To see Cusco and the surrounding area properly – including Pisac, Ollantaytambo, Chinchero and Machu Picchu – you need 5 days to a week, allowing for slowing down because of altitude.

Visitors' tickets A combined entry ticket allows entry to the Cathedral, San Blas, Santa Catalina, Museo de Arte Religioso, Museo de Historia Regional, the Piquillacta ruins, Pisac, Chincheros, Ollantaytambo, Sacsayhuamán, Qenqo, Puku Pukara and Tambo Machay. The ticket (Boleto Turístico Unico, or "BTU") costs US$10 and is valid for 5 or 10 days. It can be bought from: a) the OFEC office, Av Sol 103, on the ground floor of Galerías Turísticas, just before the Banco de Crédito; or b) any of the sites included on the ticket. There is a 50% discount with

Inca society

🦶 Cusco was the capital of the Inca empire – one of the greatest planned societies the world has known – from its rise during the 11th century to its death in the early 16th century. (See John Hemming's *Conquest of the Incas* and B C Brundage's *Lords of Cuzco* and *Empire of the Inca*.) It was solidly based on other Peruvian civilizations which had attained great skill in textiles, building, ceramics and working in metal. Immemorially, the political structure of the Andean Indian had been the *ayllu*, the village community; it had its divine ancestor, worshipped household gods, was closely knit by ties of blood to the family and by economic necessity to the land, which was held in common. Submission to the *ayllu* was absolute, because it was only by such discipline that food could be obtained in an unsympathetic environment. All the domestic animals, the llama and alpaca and the dog, had long been tamed, and the great staple crops, maize and potatoes, established. What the Incas did – and it was a magnificent feat – was to conquer enormous territories and impose upon the variety of *ayllus*, through an unchallengeable central government, a willing spiritual and economic submission to the State. The common religion, already developed by the classical Tiwanaku culture, was worship of the Sun, whose vice-regent on earth was the absolute Sapa Inca. Around him, in the capital, was a religious and secular elite which never froze into a caste because it was open to talent. The elite was often recruited from chieftains defeated by the Incas; an effective way of reconciling local opposition. The mass of the people were subjected to rigorous planning. They were allotted land to work, for their group and for the State; set various tasks (the making of textiles, pottery, weapons, ropes, etc) from primary materials supplied by the functionaries, or used in enlarging the area of cultivation by building terraces on the hill-sides. Their political organization was simple but effective. The family, and not the individual, was the unit. Families were grouped in units of 10, 100, 500, 1,000, 10,000 and 40,000, each group with a leader responsible to the next largest group. The Sapa Inca crowned the political edifice; his four immediate counsellors to whom he allotted responsibility for the northern, southern, eastern and western regions (*suyos*) of the empire.

Equilibrium between production and consumption, in the absence of a free price mechanism and good transport facilities, must depend heavily upon statistical information. This the Incas raised to a high degree of efficiency by means of their *quipus*: a decimal system of recording numbers by knots in cords. Seasonal variations were guarded against by creating a system of state barns in which provender could be stored during years of plenty, to be used in years of scarcity. Statistical efficiency alone required that no one should be permitted to leave his home or his work. The loss of personal liberty was the price paid by the masses for economic security. In order to obtain information and to transmit orders quickly, the Incas built fine paved pathways along which couriers sped on foot. The whole system of rigorous control was completed by the greatest of all their monarchs, Pachacuti, who also imposed a common language, Quechua, as a further cementing force.

a green ISIC card, which is only available at the OFEC office on Av Sol.

Note that all sites are very crowded on Sun. No photographs are allowed in any museums. Many churches are closed to visitors on Sun, and the 'official' opening times are unreliable.

Machu Picchu, the Museo Arqueológico, Santo Domingo-Qoricancha and the church of La Merced are not included on the ticket. Tickets for Machu Picchu and the Inca Trail can be bought at the INC office, on Garcilaso y Heladeros.

Places of interest

The heart of the city, as in Inca days, is the Plaza de Armas. Around it are colonial arcades and four churches. To the NE is the early 17th century baroque **Cathedral**, built on the site of the Palace of Viracocha. The high altar is solid silver and the original altar *retablo* behind it is a masterpiece of Andean wood carving. In the sacristy are paintings of all the bishops of Cusco and a painting of Christ attributed to Van Dyck. The choir stalls, by a 17th-century Spanish priest, are a magnificent example of colonial baroque art. The elaborate pulpit and the sacristy are also notable. Much venerated is the crucifix of El Señor de los Temblores, the object of many pilgrimages and viewed all over Peru as a guardian against earthquakes. The Cathedral is open until 1000 for genuine worshippers – Quechua mass is held 0500-0600; otherwise Mon-Sat 1400-1730. The doors from the Cathedral open into the church of **Jesús María** (1733), which stands to its left as you face it.

The tourist entrance to the Cathedral is through **El Triunfo** (1536), on its right, the first Christian church in Cusco. It has a statue of the Virgin of the Descent, reputed to have helped the Spaniards repel Manco Inca when he besieged the city in 1536. It also has a painting of Cusco during the 1650 earthquake – the earliest surviving painting of the city – in a side chapel. In the far right hand end of the church is an interesting local painting of the Last Supper replete with *cuy*, *chicha*, etc.

On the SE side of the plaza is the beautiful **La Compañía de Jesús**, built on the site of the Palace of the Serpents (*Amarucancha*) in the late 17th century. Its twin-towered exterior is extremely graceful, and the interior rich in fine murals, paintings and carved altars.

Much **Inca stonework** can be seen in the streets and most particularly in the Callejón Loreto, running SE past La Compañía de Jesús from the main plaza. The walls of the *Acllahuasi* (House of the Chosen Women) are on one side, and of the *Amarucancha* on the other. There are also Inca remains in Calle San Agustín, to the E of the plaza. The famous stone of 12 angles is in Calle Hatun Rumiyoc halfway along its 2nd block, on the right-hand side going away from the Plaza.

Churches La Merced, on Calle Márquez, was first built 1534, and rebuilt in the late 17th century. Attached is a very fine monastery with an exquisite cloister. Inside the church are buried Gonzalo Pizarro, half-brother of Francisco, and the two Almagros, father and son. The church is most famous for its jewelled monstrance, on view in the monastery's museum during visiting hours.

The church and monastery are open 0830-1200, 1430-1730; admission US$1.75, students US$1.25. The church was closed for restoration, late 1996.

San Francisco, on Plaza San Francisco, 3 blocks SW of the Plaza de Armas, is an austere church reflecting many indigenous influences. Its monastery is being rebuilt and was still closed in 1996. The church is open 0600-0800, 1800-2000. **Santa Catalina** church, convent and museum are on Arequipa, opposite C Santa Catalina; open Mon-Thur and Sat 0800-1800, Fri 0800-1900. There are guided tours by English-speaking students; tip expected. Delicious marzipan is sold next to the museum by the nuns through a revolving wooden door, US$1 for 200 grams. **San Pedro**, in front of the Santa Ana market, was built in 1688. Its two towers were made from stones brought from an Inca ruin (open Mon-Sat 1000-1200, 1400-1700).

The smaller and less well-known church of **San Blas**, on Carmen Bajo, has a beautiful carved *mestizo* cedar pulpit, which is well worth seeing; open Mon-Sat 1400-1730. Above Cusco, on the road up to Sacsayhuamán, is **San Cristóbal**, built to his patron saint by Cristóbal Paullu Inca. North of it, you can see the 11 doorway-sized niches of the great Inca wall of the Palacio de Colcampata.

Belén de los Reyes, in the southern outskirts of the city, was built by an *indígena* in the 17th century. It has a striking main altar, with silver embellishments at the centre and goldwashed *retablos* at the sides. The church is open 1000-1200, 1500-1700 except Thur and Sun.

Santo Domingo, SE of the main Plaza, was built in the 17th century on the walls of the Qoricancha Temple of the Sun and from its stones. Current excavation is revealing more of the five chambers of the Temple of the Sun, which shows the best Inca stonework to be seen in Cusco. The Temple of the Sun was awarded to Juan Pizarro, the younger brother of Francisco, who willed it to the Dominicans after he had been fatally wounded in the Sacsayhuamán siege.

The baroque cloister has been gutted to reveal four of the original chambers of the great Inca temple – two on the W have been partly reconstructed in a good imitation of Inca masonry. The finest stonework is in the celebrated curved wall beneath the W end of Santo Domingo. This was rebuilt after the 1950 earthquake, at which time a niche that once contained a shrine was found at the inner top of the wall. Below the curved wall was a garden of gold and silver replicas of animals, maize and other plants. Excavations have revealed Inca baths below here, and more Inca retaining walls. The other superb stretch of late Inca stonework is in C Ahuacpinta outside the temple, to the E or left as you enter (John Hemming). Santo Domingo is open 0900-1700; entry US$0.85; English-speaking guides, tip expected.

Colonial buildings The **Palacio del Almirante**, just N of the Plaza de Armas on Ataud, is impressive. It houses the Museo de Arqueología (see below). Note the pillar on the balcony over the door, showing a bearded man and a naked woman. Nearby, in a small square on Cuesta del Almirante, is the colonial house of **San Borja**, where Bolívar stayed after the Battle of Ayacucho.

The **Palacio Arzobispal** stands on Hatun Rumiyoc y Herrajes, 2 blocks NE of Plaza de Armas. It was built on the site of the palace occupied in 1400 by the Inca Roca and was formerly the home of the Marqueses de Buena Vista. It contains the Museo de Arte Religioso (see below).

Above San Cristóbal church, to the left, is a private colonial mansion, once the home of the infamous explorer and murderer, Lope de Aguirre. Also worth a visit is the palace called **Casa de los Cuatro Bustos** at San Agustín 400, which is now the *Libertador-Marriott Hotel*. The **Convento de las Nazarenas**, on Plaza de las Nazarenas, now houses the offices of Copesco. You can see the Inca-colonial doorway with a mermaid motif, but ask permission to view the lovely 18th century frescos inside. Also on Plaza Nazarenas is **Casa Cabrera**, which is now a gallery and used by Banco Continental.

Other sites On the way to the airport on Av del Sol, 20 mins' walk from the Plaza de Armas, there is a statue of the Inca Pachacútec placed on top of a lookout tower, from which there are excellent views of Cusco. Open 1000-2000; entrance free; small galleries and restaurant.

The **Astronomical Observatory** is at Km 3 on the road W to Cachimayo and affords fine views of Cusco and the Sacred Valley. It has a pleasant restaurant where you can enjoy the views while you are dining. Observations are 1830-2300.

Museums

Museo Arqueológico in the Palacio del Almirante (see above) contains a first-rate precolumbian collection, Spanish paintings of imitation Inca royalty dating from the 18th century, as well as an excellent collection of textiles. Visitors should ask to see the forty miniature pre-Inca turquoise figures found at Piquillacta and the golden treasures, all kept under lock and key but on display. Open Mon-Fri 0800-

1730, Sat/Sun 0800-1400, but check in advance as the museum is frequently closed; US$2 entry; the staff will give a guided tour but please give a tip.

Museo de Arte Religioso, in the Palacio Arzobispal (see above), has a fine collection of colonial paintings and furniture. The collection includes the paintings by the Indigenous master, Diego Quispe Tito, of a 17th century Corpus Christi procession that used to hang in the church of Santa Ana, insist on seeing them. Open Mon-Sat, 0830-1200, 1500-1730.

Museo de Historia Regional, in the Casa Garcilaso, Jr Garcilaso y Heladeros, tries to show the evolution of the Cuzqueño school of painting. It also contains Inca agricultural implements, colonial furniture and paintings, a small photographic exhibition and mementos of more recent times; open 0800-1800.

Museo de Arte Contemporáneo is in the Casa de Gobierno, on Plaza Recojijo.

Excursions

Sacsayhuamán There are some magnificent Inca walls in this ruined ceremonial centre, on a hill in the northern outskirts. The Incaic stones are hugely impressive. The massive rocks weighing up to 130 tons are fitted together with absolute perfection. Three walls run parallel for over 360m and there are 21 bastions. Sacsayhuamán was thought for centuries to be a fortress, but the layout and architecture suggest a great sanctuary and temple to the Sun, which rises exactly opposite the place previously believed to be the Inca's throne – which was probably an altar, carved out of the solid rock. Broad steps lead to the altar from either side. The hieratic, rather than the military, hypothesis was supported by the discovery in 1982 of the graves of priests, who would have been unlikely to be buried in a fortress. The precise functions of the site, however, will probably continue to be a matter of dispute as very few clues remain, owing to its steady destruction.

The site is about a 30-min walk up Pumacurco from Plaza de las Nazarenas. Open daily 0700-1730; free student guides, give them a tip.

Along the road from Sacsayhuamán to Pisac, past a radio station, is the temple and amphitheatre of **Qenqo** with some of the finest examples of Inca stone carving *in situ*, especially inside the large hollowed-out stone that houses an altar. On the same road are **Cusillyuioc** (K'usilluyuq), caves and Inca tunnels in a hillside (take a torch/flashlight); **Puka Pukara** (Red Fort, but more likely to have been a *tambo*, or post-house), wonderful views; and the spring shrine of **Tambo Machay**, which is in excellent condition. Water still flows by a hidden channel out of the masonry wall, straight into a little rock pool traditionally known as the Inca's bath. Take a guide to the sites and visit in the morning for the best photographs. Carry your multi-site ticket, there are roving ticket inspectors. You can visit the sites on foot, a pleasant walk of at least half a day through the countryside; take water, sun protection, and watch out for dogs. Alternatively, take the Pisac bus up to Tambo Machay (US$0.35) and walk back, or arrange a horseback tour with an agency (US$16 pp for 5 hrs).

NB It is safest to visit the ruins in a group, especially if you wish to see them under a full moon. Take as few belongings as possible, and hide your camera in a bag.

Local festivals

20 Jan: procession of saints in the San Sebastián district. *Carnival* in Cusco is a messy affair with flour, water, cacti, bad fruit and animal manure thrown about in the streets. (The length of the Sacred Valley, Carnival is lively.) **Easter Monday** sees the procession of *El Señor de los Temblores* (Lord of the Earthquakes), starting at 1600 outside the Cathedral. A large crucifix is paraded through the streets, returning to the Plaza de Armas around 2000 to bless the tens of thousands of people who have assembled there. **2-3 May**: *Vigil of the Cross* takes place at all mountaintops with crosses on them, a boisterous affair.

June: On *Corpus Christi* day, the Thur after Trinity Sunday, statues and silver are paraded through the streets. The Plaza de Armas is surrounded by tables with women selling *cuy* and a mixed grill called *chiriuchu* (*cuy*, chicken, *tortillas*, fish eggs, water-weeds, maize, cheese and sausage). **Mid June**: *Q'Olloriti*, the ice festival, is held at a 4,700m glacier beyond Ocongate. Several agencies offer tours.

24 June: the pageant of *Inti Raymi*, the Inca festival of the winter solstice, is enacted at 1300 at Sacsayhuamán, 2½ hrs, in Quechua. Tickets for the stands can be bought a week in advance from the Municipalidad, and cost US$25. Standing places

on the ruins are free but get there at about 1030 to defend your space. Travel agents who try to persuade you to buy a ticket for the right to film or take photos are being dishonest. On the night before Inti Raymi, the Plaza de Armas is crowded with processions and food stalls. Try to arrive in Cusco 15 days before Inti Raymi for the Cusqueña beer festival (US$6 entry) and other festivals, parades etc.

16-22 June: the *Huiracocha* dance festival takes place in the village of Raqchi (see

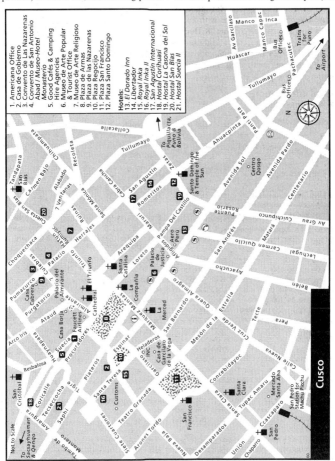

1. Americana Office
2. Casa de Gobierno
3. Convento de Las Nazarenas
4. Convento de San Antonio Abad / Museo-Hotel Monasterio
5. Good Cafés & Camping Hire Agencies
6. Museo de Arte Popular & Tourist Office
7. Museo de Arte Religioso
8. Plaza de Armas
9. Plaza de las Nazarenas
10. Plaza Regocijo
11. Plaza San Francisco
12. Plaza Santo Domingo

Hotels:
13. El Dorado Inn
14. Libertador
15. Royal Inka
16. Royal Inka II
17. San Agustín Internacional
18. Hostal Corihuasi
19. Hostal La Casona del Sol
20. Hostal San Blas
21. Hostal Suecia II

Cusco

also page 1354). **28 July**: Peruvian Independence Day. Prices shoot up during these celebrations. **Aug**: on the last Sun is the *Huarachicoy* festival at Sacsayhuamán, a spectacular reenactment of the Inca manhood rite, performed in dazzling costumes by boys of a local school. **8 Sept**: *Day of the Virgin* is a colourful procession of masked dancers from the church of Almudena, at the SW edge of Cusco, near Belén, to the Plaza de San Francisco. There is also a splendid fair at Almudena, and a free bull fight on the following day. **1 Nov**: *All Saints Day*, celebrated everywhere with bread dolls and traditional cooking. **8 Dec**: is Cusco day, when churches and museums close at 1200. **24 Dec**: *Santuranticuy*, 'the buying of saints', with a big crafts market in the plaza.

Local information
● **Accommodation**

Hotel prices

L1	over US$200	**L2**	US$151-200
L3	US$101-150	**A1**	US$81-100
A2	US$61-80	**A3**	US$46-60
B	US$31-45	**C**	US$21-30
D	US$12-20	**E**	US$7-11
F	US$4-6	**G**	up to US$3

Unless otherwise stated, all hotels in range **D** and above have private bath. Assume friendliness and cleanliness in all cases.

Book more expensive hotels well in advance through a good travel agency, particularly for the week or so around Inti Raymi, when prices are greatly increased. Prices given are for the high season in June-Aug. When there are fewer tourists hotels may drop their prices by as much as half. Always check for discounts. On the Puno-Cusco train there are many hotel agents for medium-priced hotels. Prices can often be negotiated down but it is best to pay the agent for 1 day only and then negotiate with the hotel. Rooms offered at Cusco station are usually cheaper than those offered on the train. Taxis and tourist minibuses meet the train and take you to the hotel of your choice for US$0.50, but be insistent. It is cold in Cusco, and many hotels do not have heating. It is worth asking for an 'estufa', a space heater which some places will provide for an extra charge. The whole city suffers from water shortages, and hotels usually only have supplies in the mornings, so plan your day accordingly.

The best are **L1** *Monasterio del Cusco*, Palacio 140, T 226871, F 237111 (in Lima T 440-8043, F 440-6197), price includes tax, 5-star, beautifully restored Convent of San Antonio Abad, inc the chapel, wonderful rooms, courtyards and cloisters (the president has his own suite), good restaurant; **L3** *Libertador* (5-star), in the Casa de los Cuatro Bustos at C San Agustín 400, T 232601/231961, 28% tax, good, especially the service, but in July and Aug rooms in the older part of the hotel are cold and dark.

A1 *Cusco*, Heladeros 150, T 224821, administered by Sociedad de Beneficencia Pública del Cusco, hot water, largest and best known, central location; **A2** *Holiday Inn Court*, Av Sol 602, T 224457, F 233315, all rooms with safe, fridge, heating, TV, rooms with handicapped facilities, stylish; **A2** *Royal Inka I*, Plaza Regocijo 299, T 231067, inc taxes and breakfast, bar, dining room, good service, rec; **A2** *Royal Inka II* on the same street, larger, good sauna, US$7, highly rec; **A2** *San Agustín Plaza*, Av Sol 594, T 238121, inc taxes and breakfast, phone, modern, very good, safe, English spoken; **A2** *San Agustín Internacional*, San Agustín y Maruri 390, T 231001, F 221174, inc taxes and breakfast, more expensive than *Plaza* but higher standard.

On Plazoleta Las Nazarenas, the colonial Casa de la Torre (No 211) is being converted into *Posada Las Nazarenas*, 13 rooms, 3-4 star, due open mid-late 1997, T 232829, Tierras Altas SA, or Los Pinos 584, San Isidro, Lima 27, T 440-5476.

B *Conquistador*, Santa Catalina Angosta 149, T 224461, inc breakfast, safe, phone, restaurant, parking, good; **B** *Hostal Carlos V*, Tecseccocha 490, T 223091, inc tax and breakfast, has charm and character, restaurant, refurbished, pleasant; **B** *Wiracocha*, Plaza de Armas, corner of Mantas, T 222351, PO Box 502, hot water, restaurant opens at 0600, good breakfast; **B-C** *Raymi*, Av Pardo 950, T 225141, heater, inc breakfast, rec.

C category *Hostal Corihuasi*, C Suecia 561 (not a safe street at night), T/F 232233, inc breakfast, colonial house, laundry arranged, hot water, quiet, electric heaters, good views, rec; *Hostal Garcilaso*, Garcilaso de la Vega 233, T 233031, safe for luggage, refurbished, historic charm, rec; *Hostal Garcilosa III*, Garcilosa de la Vega 237, quiet, helpful; *Hostal Qosqo*, Portal Mantas 115, nr Plaza de Armas, hot water, helpful, inc breakfast, rec; *Los Portales*, Matará 322, T 223500, inc airport pickup, tastefully renovated, modern facilities, plenty of character, helpful, English spoken, safe deposit, luggage store, highly rec; *Loreto*, Pasaje Loreto 115, Plaza de Armas, rooms with Inca walls and electric heaters, a bit dark, cheap laundry service, great atmosphere, taxis and other travel can be arranged, Lucio here is a good guide, safe luggage deposit, rec; *Los Marqueses*, Garcilaso 256, T 232512, heaters extra, early colonial house, beautiful patio, comfortable, convenient.

D category *California*, Nueva Alta 444, T 235770, hot water, cheaper without breakfast, quiet, safe; *El Inca*, Quera 251, heating, hot water variable, luggage store, restaurant, inc breakfast, Wilbur speaks English, and is helpful, rec, noisy disco in basement till 0100; *Hostal Amaru*, Cuesta San Blas 541, T 225933, cheaper without bath, hot water 24 hrs, laundry, safe, nice views, rec; *Hostal Amparito*, Av Regional 898, nr train station, 15 mins' walk from Plaza de Armas, T 224898, hot water, quiet, owner is a policeman who will help organize tours to Machu Picchu; *Hostal Apu Wasi*, Pumacurco y Concepción, T 237249, **E** downstairs, inc breakfast, colonial house, helpful, hot showers, big rooms, good views, laundry facility; *Hostal Cahuide*, Saphi 845, T 222771, discount for long stay, hot water, good rooms, quiet, good laundry service, storage facilities, helpful, café serving good value breakfasts; *Hostal Corregidor*, Portal de Panes, Plaza de Armas, T 232632, good; *Hostal El Arqueólogo* (room or dormitory), Ladrillos 425 not far from Sacsayhuamán (T 232569, not a safe street at night), inc breakfast, hot water, helpful, French and English spoken, will store luggage, garden, cafeteria and kitchen, rec; *Hostal El Solar*, San Francisco 162, T 232451, rec; *Hostal Imperial Palace*, Tecseccocha 492, T 223324, with breakfast, prices negotiable for longer stays, café, bar, restaurant, a bit cold, but well furnished, English spoken, good, safe deposit open only 0700-1100; *Hostal Incawasi*, Portal de Panes 147, Plaza de Armas, T 238245, hot water 0800-0900, 2000-2200, good beds, bargain for long stays, secure, helpful, good value, quieter rooms on 3rd floor; *Hostal San Blas*, Cuesta San Blas 526, T 225781, basic, secure for luggage, inc breakfast; *Huaynapata*, Huaynapata 369, T 228034, small rooms, quieter rooms at the back, family-run, hot water, stores luggage; *Inca World*, Tecseccocha 474 (opp *Suecia II*), hot water, small restaurant, rooms 1-4 are good, others without windows, safe, stores luggage; *Suecia II*, Tecseccocha 465, T 239757, rooms with or without bath, good beds and blankets, good security procedures, breakfast at 0500, US$1.50, beautiful building, good meeting place for trekkers doing the Inca Trail, best to book if arriving on same day as Puno train; *Tambo*, Ayacucho 233, T 236788, heating in rooms, laundry facilities, safe for luggage, central, hot water intermittent, restaurant fair, rec.

E category *Hostal Bellavista*, Av Santiago 100, **F** without bath, hot water, safe, 10 mins' walk from centre, not a safe area at night, breakfast available, will store luggage, rec; *Hostal Bosanova*, on Afligados entre Sol y Loreto, no sign, enter through *Café Canela* 2nd floor, hot showers, laundry service, small; *Hostal Cáceres*, Plateros 368, 1 block from Plaza de Armas, sometimes hot water, big rooms, luggage store, laundry service, can put motorcycle in patio; *Hostal El Puerto*, Fierro 571-577, nice, family-run, use of kitchen, garden; *Hostal Familiar*, Saphi 661, cheaper without bath, hot water 0700-0900, luggage store US$2/item, owner Cecilia speaks excellent English; *Hostal Pakcha Real*, Tandapata 300, San Blas, T 237484, no sign, brown house, family run, hot water, cooking and laundry facilities, TV and video lounge, use of kitchen, rec; *Hostal Quipu*, Fierro 495, T 236179, F 260721, hot water 24 hrs, good value, colonial-style house, attractive courtyard, laundry service, luggage store, safe deposit, not a safe part of town; *Hostal Resbalosa*, Resbalosa 494, T 224839, charming, good value; *Suecia*, C Suecia 332, shared rooms, uncomfortable beds, will store luggage, can use their bulletin board to arrange groups for the Inca trail.

F category *El Arcano*, Carmen Alto 288, San Blas district, T 232703, hot water 24 hrs, safe to leave luggage, laundry, 7 rooms for 1-4 people, good beds, toilet paper provided, highly rec; *Hostal Choquechaca*, Choquechaca 436B, T 237265, hot water am, rec; *Hostal Familiar Carmen Alto*, Carmen Alto 197, 1 block from Choquechaca, hot water, use of kitchen, laundry facilities, quiet, safe, rec; *Hostal Familiar Casa*, Pasaje España 844, T 224152, off Pardo, shared bath, basic rooms, quiet, safe, hot water in mornings only, baggage stored for a small fee, laundry, rec; **F** pp *Hostal Pumacurco*, Pumacurco 336, Interior 329, T 227739, 3 mins from Plaza de Armas, newly restored part of colonial house, hot water, owner Betty is very helpful, some large rooms, safe, laundry facilities; **F** pp *Hospedaje Sol Naciente*, Av Pardo 510, T 228602, hot water, comfortable, laundry facilities, luggage stored for a small fee, family-run; *Hostal Unión*, Unión 189, T 231580, 5 blocks from Plaza de Armas, 1/2 block from Santa Ana market, shared bath, hot water, safe, laundry facilities, kitchen/café, luggage store, knowledgeable, helpful, very noisy but rec; **F** pp *Hospedaje Virgen de los Remedios*, 156 Santa Catalina Angosto, 1 block from Plaza de Armas, no sign, follow the passage to the back to find the entrance, quiet, very nice owners, comfortable beds, water intermittent; *Imperio*, C Chaparro, run by Elena and family, nr San Pedro station, T 228981, be careful at night in this part of town, hot water, noisy, motorcycle parking, safe to leave luggage, rec; **F** pp *Qorichaska*, Nueva Alta 458, T 228974, close to centre, hot water, will store luggage, cafeteria open till 2100, safe, great value, rec; next door is **F** *Hostal Naty*, warm water, luggage store, quiet, rec.

G pp *Hostal Chaski*, Portal Confituría 257, Plaza de Armas, T 236093, hot water, laundry service, cafetería, safe deposit; **G** *Hostal Colonial*, Meson de la Estrella y Ayacucho, hot water 0600-0900, laundry, luggage store, rec; **G** pp *Hostal San Cristóbal*, Quiscapata 242, nr San Cristóbal, in dormitory, cooking and clothes-washing facilities, baggage deposit, reliable, if full, Sra Ema de Paredes will let you spread a sleeping bag on the floor, rec.

Youth hostel: *Albergue Municipal*, Quiscapata 240, San Cristóbal, T 252506, US$7 pp in dormitories, reliable hot water supply, helpful staff, luggage store, great views, bar, cafetería, laundry, safe deposit, discount for members; *El Procurador*, Qoricalle 425, T/F 241447, US$7 pp with bath, US$5 without, includes breakfast, hot water, laundry, kitchen facilities, book exchange, motorcycle parking, friendly, rec.

Camping: is not safe anywhere in the Cusco area. For renting equipment, there are several places around the Plaza area. Check the equipment carefully as it is common for parts to be missing. An example of prices per day: tent US$3, sleeping bag US$2, stove US$3. A deposit of US$100 is asked, plus credit card, passport or plane ticket. *Soqllaq'asa Camping Service*, owned by English-speaking Louis Aedo, at Plateros 354, T/F 222224, is rec for equipment hire. White gas (*bencina*), US$1.50/litre, can be bought at hardware stores, but check the purity; stove spirit (*alcoól para quemar*) is available at pharmacies; blue gas canisters, costing US$5, can be found at some hardware stores and at shops which rent gear. You can also rent equipment through travel agencies. A shop with useful, imported (so expensive) camping gear: *Camping Deportes*, Centro Comercial Ollanta, Av del Sol 346, shop no 118; it also sells insect repellent, Deet, US$10 for a small bottle.

● **Places to eat**

International and local cuisine, expensive: for a good meal and décor try *Inti Raymi* in the *Libertador*; *Mesón de los Espaderos*, Espaderos y Plaza de Armas, *parrilladas*, good; *Paititi*, Plaza de Armas, live music, good atmosphere, Inca masonry; next door is *Taberna del Truco*, live music at dinner time.

Medium class, local cuisine: *Trattoria Adriano*, C Mantas y Av Sol, just off SE corner of Plaza de Armas, open for breakfast at 0700, Italian, great desserts, not cheap; *Peña Los Incas*, Plaza de Armas, good *menú* at lunchtime for US$3, expensive at night; *Pucará*, Plateros 309, highly rec, good meals throughout the day, pleasant atmosphere, pottery, silver jewellery and designer alpaca sweaters for sale; *Los Tomines*, Triunfo 384, excellent, 4-course set meal for US$5.50, rec.

Pizzerías: *Chez Maggy*, Plateros 339, open 1800, good atmosphere, popular, live music nightly, pasta, soups, pizzas freshly baked in wood-burning oven; *Pizzería América*, at 316 and *Americana*, at 369, both on Plateros, highly rec; *Pizzería Cyrano*, Procuradores 347, good pizzas, also meat dishes; *Los Balcones*, upstairs at Espaderos 125, also has vegetarian menu; at Espaderos 136 is *Pizzería Espaderos*, good pizzas, smokey atmosphere; *Tizziano Trattoria*, Tecseccocha 418, good Italian food, homemade pasta, excellent value *menú* Mon-Sat 1200-1500 and 1800-2300, also vegetarian, rec.

Cheaper restaurants, local cuisine: *El Nevado*, Plateros 345, 3-course set meals, good soups and fish, rec; *Urpi*, Procuradores 332, good, popular; *Punto Viejo*, at the end of Procuradores, good, pizza and pasta; *La Yunta*, Portal de Carnes, Plaza de Armas, vegetarian, good salads, pancakes and juices, popular with gringos, same owners as *Instinct Travel Agency*, rec; next door upstairs is *Café Bagdad*, nice balcony with good views, cheap set lunch, good atmosphere, happy hour 1930-2130, German owner Florian Thurman speaks good English; *El Solar*, San Francisco, good lunch menu, rec; *Conde*, Plaza San Francisco 364, 24 hrs, rec; *Víctor Victoria*, Tigre 130, Israeli and local dishes, highly rec for breakfast, good value; *Chifa El Paso*, Garcilaso 220, large selection, good; *El Cuate*, Procuradores 386, Mexican food, rec; *Ama Lur*, Plaza de las Nazarenas 159, clean, varied menu, excellent food, vegetarian dishes available, foreign newspapers and magazines; *Chez Víctor*, Ayacucho 217, good, popular; *El Mariño*, Espinar y Mantas, good seafood; *Tronquito*, Plateros 327, huge portions; *La Tranquera*, Plaza Túpac Amaru 137, local and international food; *El Trujillo*, Matará, northern Peruvian specialities. To try other local specialities, in the suburbs: *Quintas Eulalia*, Choquechaca 384, closed on Mon. Cheap local food at the market on the corner of Huáscar and Av Garcilaso.

Vegetarian: *Govinda*, Espaderos 128, just off W corner of Plaza de Armas, always busy, slow service; *El Tordo*, Tordo 238, good value, tiny place, very cheap 1-course lunch, also has rooms to let; *John Bore*, Tecseccocha 418, open daily 0600-2400, rec; *Acuarium*, Cuesta del Almirante 211, good *menú*.

Cafés and snackbars: *Café Hualliy*, Plateros 363, set lunch US$1.20, good for comments on guides, popular meeting place, especially for breakfast, also good vegetarian *menú*; *Ayllu*, Portal de Carnes 208, open at 0600, Italian, classical/folk music, good atmosphere, superb range of milk products and wonderful apple pastries, good breakfast, rec; *Café Literario Varayoc*, Espaderos 142, good meeting place, excellent coffee, pizzas and chocolate cake; *Oasis*, Av Sol 453, good set lunch; *Misky Wasi*, Tigre 110, for breakfasts, snacks; *Tumi's Video Bar*, Saphi 478, good café, local and European dishes, open late, good value lunch, 4 movies daily, US$1.30, pool table, book exchange, owner Maurice Drews has good local information (see also **Language classes** below); *Café Plus*, Portal de Panes 151, p 2, same owners as *Hostal Apu Wasi*, delicious cakes, excellent coffee, good service; *La Tertulia*, Procuradores 50, p 2, nice setting above courtyard, run by Johanna Berendse and her Peruvian husband, who also run the *Amauta* Language School (see below), excellent breakfast buffet is served 0700-1300, eat as much as you like for around US$3, also book exchange, newspapers, classical music, vegetarian buffet served daily 1800-2200.

● **Bars**
Cross Keys Pub, Plaza de Armas, Portal Confiturías 233, p 1, open 1800-0130, run by Barry Walker, a bird expert, darts, great atmosphere, happy hour once or twice a night (1800 and 2000/2100), not for beer; *Kamikaze*, Plaza Regocijo, *peña* at 2200, folk and rock music, candle-lit cavern atmosphere, many gringos, entry US$2.50, T-shirts for sale, rec; *Mama Africa*, Espaderos 135, p 2, live music at weekends, very popular with gringos; *Taberna Cusicusi*, S side of Plaza de Armas, nice atmosphere, reasonable prices, good music, sometimes live; *Puputi Pub*, on the corner of Procuradores and Plaza de Armas, café until 1800, good, cheap breakfast, cakes, juices, good view of plaza, bar afterwards with live music every night, happy hour 1900-2130 Sun-Thurs, great atmosphere; *Ukuku's*, Plateros 316, US$1.35 entry, good, friendly atmosphere, happy hour 0730-0930. Also, *Manu Pub*, Procuradores 351, p 2; *El Manguare Jungle Bar*, Triunfo 393; *Las Quenas* in the basement of the *Hotel Savoy*, rec; *Uptown Club*, Suecia 302 y Procuradores, good music and atmosphere.

● **Airline offices**
AeroPerú, Av Sol 317; **Aero Continente**, Portal Comercio 179, Plaza de Armas, T 252635; **Faucett**, Portal Comercio 195, and Portal de Carnes, T 233151.

● **Banks & money changers**
The best places are the banks along Av del Sol, although it can be time-consuming and, in some cases, only at certain hours (not at weekends): **Interbanc**, Av del Sol y Puluchapata, no commission on TCs, Visa; and next door **Banco Continental**, US$5 commission. For cash on Mastercard, **Banco del Sur**, Av Sol 459, also Amex and Thomas Cook TCs, Mastercard, reasonable rates. You can withdraw dollars or soles from the several ATMs at the banks along Av Sol. Many travel agencies and *casas de cambio* change dollars; some of them change TCs as well, but charge 4-5% commission. The street changers hang around Av del Sol, blocks 2-3, every day; they will also change TCs. In banks and on the street check the notes. Dollars are accepted at many restaurants and at the airport.

● **Embassies & consulates**
US Agent, Olga Villa García, Apdo 949, Cusco, T 222183 or 233541. **German**, Sra Maria-Sophia Júrgens de Hermoza, San Agustín 307, T 235459, Casilla Postal 1128, Correo Central, open Mon-Fri, 1000-1200, appointments may be made by phone, also book exchange. **French**, C Espinar (M Jean Pierre Sallat, *Farmacia Vallenas* – may let French people leave luggage if going to Machu Picchu). **British**, Dr Raul Delgado de la Flor, *Hotel San Agustín Internacional*, T 222322 or 231001, address above, the Austrian Consul is also there. **Finnish**, Emmel 109, Yanahuara, T 223708.

● **Entertainment**
Folklore shows: regular nightly folklore show at *Centro Qosqo*, Av del Sol 604 next to *Holiday Inn*, at 1900, entrance fee US$6; and at *Teatro Inti Raymi*, Saphi 605, nightly 1845, US$4.50 and well worth it. Local *peña* at *Inka's Restaurant Peña*, Portal de Panes 105, Plaza de Armas; at Portal de Panes 109, **Clave del Sol**, good fun. *Teatro Municipal*, C Mesón de la Estrella 149, T 227321 for information 0900-1300 and 1500-1900, a venue for plays, dancing, shows, mostly Thur-Sun; ask for their programmes.

● **Hospitals & medical services**
Dentists: *Tomás Flores*, T 222844; *Gilbert Espejo*, T 228074.

Health: *Hospital Regional*, Av de la Cultura, rec. If lab tests are needed, Lab Pasteur, Tullumayo 768 is rec. Dr *Oscar Tejada* (PO Box 425, Cusco, T 233836 or 240449 day or night) is a member of the International Association for Medical Assistance to Travellers and is prepared to help any visitor in an emergency, 24-hr attention; he charges according to that organization's scales, which are not expensive. Dr *Gustavo Garrido Juárez*, Matará 410, T 239761, English and French spoken. *Dr Ramon Figueros*, Matara 410, of 201, T 223190/239636 (home), speaks English and French.

● **Language classes**
Exel, Cruz Verde 336, T 235298, Señorita Sori is highly rec, US$3-4/hr; the school can arrange accommodation with local families. *Tumi's* have a school at Awaqpinta 732, Spanish US$3/hr

one-to-one; they also employ English teachers. *Amauta*, Procuradores 50, p 2, T/F 241422, PO Box 1164, classes in Spanish and Quechua, workshops in Peruvian cuisine, dance and music, also apartments to rent for US$50/week, arrange excursions; can help find voluntary work, owners also have *La Tertulia* café (see above). Spanish classes are run by the *Acupari*, the German-Peruvian Cultural Association, San Agustín 307.

● **Laundry**
Laundry service at *Lavamatic*, Procuradores 341, US$1.20/kg, laundry brought early in the morning will be returned the same afternoon, rec; *Lavanderías Superchick*, Saphi 635, US$1.25 for 2 kg. Cheap laundry service at Siete Cuartones 317, US$1/kilo. There are several cheap laundries on Procuradores, and also on Suecia and Tecseccocha. **NB** In damp or overcast weather, allow plenty of time for clothes to be dried properly.

● **Post & telecommunications**
Post Office: Av del Sol, block 5, Mon-Sat 0730-2000; 0800-1400 Sun and holidays. Stamps and postcards available. Sending packages from Cusco is not cheap, reliable or quick; it's much better to wait until Lima or La Paz. *Poste restante* is free and helpful.

Telecommunications: Telefónica del Perú, Av del Sol 386, for telephone and fax, open Mon-Sat 0700-2300, 0700-1800 Sun and holidays. International calls by pay phone or go through the operator (long wait possible), deposit required, national calls US$3, international US$12. Fax to Europe costs US$3.50/page; to receive a fax costs US$2/page, the number is (084) 241111.

Radio messages: Radio Tawantinsuyo, Av del Sol 806, open Mon-Sat 0600-1900, Sun 0600-1600, messages are sent out between 0500 and 2100 (you can choose the time), in Spanish or Quechua, price/message US$1; this is sometimes helpful if things are stolen and you want them back. Radio Comercial, Av del Sol 457, of 406, T 231381, open daily 0900-1200, 1600-1900, for making contact with other radio-users in Cusco and the jungle area. Helpful if you wish to contact people in Manu; price US$1.50 for 5 mins.

● **Security**
More police patrol the streets, trains and stations than in the past, which has led to an improvement in security, but one should still be vigilant. Look after your belongings, leaving valuables in safe keeping with hotel management, not in hotel rooms. Places in which to take care are: when changing money on the streets; in the railway and bus stations; the bus from the airport; the Santa Ana market (otherwise rec); the San Cristóbal area and at out-of-the-way ruins.

Also take special care during Inti Raymi. Avoid walking around alone at night on narrow streets, between the stations and the centre, or in the market areas.

● **Shopping**
Santa Ana Market, opp Estación San Pedro, is the best market for a variety of goods; best value is at closing time or in the rain. There's another market on the corner of San Andrés and Quera, which is good for local handicrafts. *Mercado Artesanal*, Av del Sol, block 4, is good for cheap crafts. *Coordinadora Sur Andina de Artesanía*, C del Medio 130, off Plaza de Armas, has a good assortment of crafts and is a non-profit organization. *La Pérez*, Urb Mateo Pumacahua 598, Huanchac, T 232186/222137, is a big co-operative with a good selection; they will arrange a free pick-up from your hotel.

Cusco is the weaving centre of Peru, and excellent textiles can be found at good value: *Alpaca Llampu*, C Ruinas, genuine, 100% alpaca goods, but not cheap. *Artesanía La Paloma*, Cuesta San Blas 552 and Plazuela Santa Catalina 211, good but expensive. *Sr Aller*, Plaza Santo Domingo 261, sells interesting antiques. *Josefina Olivera*, Santa Clara 501, sells old ponchos and antique mantas, without the usual haggling. *Kaliran*, Cuesta San Blas 522, sells musical instruments and Andean music. Be very careful of buying gold and silver objects and jewellery in and around Cusco; we have received many reports of sharp practices. Cusco market is said to be the cheapest for slide and print film, eg Fuji US$4.50.

A good supermarket for buying supplies for the Inca trail is *Carrillo*, at C Plateros 348, nr Plaza de Armas.

Bookshops: *Librería Estudio*, San Agustín 293. *Los Andes*, Portal Comercio 125, Plaza de Armas, has a good range of books and large boxes of postcards.

Local crafts: in the Plaza San Blas and the surrounding area, authentic Cusco crafts still survive. Wood workers may be seen in almost any street. Leading artisans who welcome visitors include Hilario Mendivil, Plazoleta San Blas 634, who makes biblical figures from plaster, wheatflour and potatoes and Edilberta Mérida, Carmen Alto 133, who makes earthenware figures showing the physical and mental anguish of the Indian peasant. Víctor Vivero Holgado, at Tandapata 172, is a painter of pious subjects, while Antonio Olave Palomino, Siete Angelitos 752, makes reproductions of precolumbian ceramics and colonial sculptures. Maximiliano Palomino de la Sierra, Triunfo 393, produces festive dolls and wood carvings, and Santiago Rojas, nr San Blas, statuettes. Luis Aguayo Revollar, *Galería de Arte Aguayo*, Cuesta del Almirante 211-256, y Av Sol 616, T 237992, makes fine wood carvings. Museo Inca Art Gallery of Amílcar Salomón Zorrilla, Huancaro M-B – L8, T 231232 (PO Box 690), telephone between 0900 and 2100, is good for contemporary art. Visit Nemesio Villasante, Av 24 de Junio 415, T 222915, for Paucartambo masks, and Miguel Chacón Ventura, Portal Confituría 265, Plaza de Armas, for watercolour paintings.

● **Tour companies & travel agents**

There are many travel agencies in Cusco. We divide them into two categories: a) the expensive, long-established, reliable, well-organized agencies, with English-speaking staff, and b) the cheaper, less reliable agencies which are always changing. Most tours have set prices, but the second category agencies will offer cheaper packages. Always check details before making arrangements, shop around and be aware that overcharging and failing to keep to arrangements are common, especially in the high season. Also beware agencies quoting prices in dollars then converting to soles at an unfavourable rate when paying. Do not deal with guides who claim to be employed by agencies listed below without verifying their credentials; do not prepay for a tour other than at an agency's office. Seek advice from visitors returning from trips for the latest information. Beware also of tours which stop for long lunches at expensive hotels. In Cusco, its environs and Machu Picchu, check the standard of your guide's English (or whichever language is required) as some have no more than a memorized spiel.

A day tour Pisac-Ollantaytambo-Chinchero costs US$10-15 pp; ½-day tour visiting the four ruins around Cusco, US$6 pp, not inc entrance fees; ½-day city tours cost US$3-3.50.

Category a) *Lima Tours*, Portal de Harinos 177, Plaza de Armas, T 228431/223791, F 221266, Amex representative, gives TCs against Amex card, but no exchange; also DHL office, to receive a parcel you pay 35% of the marked value of customs tax; *Explorandes*, Av del Sol, block 5, T 238380, F 233784, good equipment for rent; *Southern Cross Adventures*, Portal de Panes 123, of 301, on Plaza de Armas, T 237649, F 239447, manager Hugo Paullo, friendly, helpful, good for information, specializes in horseback trips; *APU Expediciones*, Portal Comercio 157, Plaza de Armas, PO Box 24, T 235408/235061, F 241111, adventure tours and river trips, mountaineering expeditions with good equipment, nature tours and packages to Manu National Park, Tambopata and other jungle areas, transport facilities, guide Mariella Bernasconi Cilloniz is highly rec; *Tambo Treks*, Atocsaycuchi 589, Plaza San Blas, T 237718, adventure trips; *Peruvian Andean Treks*, Av Pardo 705, T 225701, manager Tom

Hendrikson, adventure tours; *Kinjyo Travel Service*, Portal de Panes 101, Plaza de Armas, T 231101, F 239044; *El Aventurero*, Portal Confiturías 265, T/F 263278, run by Julio Vargas. For Cusco agencies operating in Manu, see page 1397 below.

Category b) *Kantu Tours*, Portal Belén 258, T 221381, F 232012, rec for local tours, competitive, offers good horse treks around Cusco (US$10 for 6 hrs), experience not necessary, but sun protection is, manager Gloria Hermosa Tapiá speaks good English; *Río Bravo*, Almagro 120 (off Av Sol), T 232301, white water rafting specialists; *Instinct*, Procuradores 107, T 233451, Benjamín speaks good English and is rec, also Juan Muñil, white water rafting trips, mountain bike hire, rec; *Mach Tour*, Arequipa 275, T 234033, will arrange personalized tours, rec; *Ecotours*, Heladeros 150, T 231288, reliable and competitively priced; *Eco Amazonia Lodge*, Plateros 351, T 236159, Julio Vargas Vega, friendly, rec. The following are rec, all on Plaza de Armas: *Naty's Travel*, Portal de Confiteria 273, T/F 239437, US$60 op for Inca Trail; *United Mice*, Plateros 348, T 221139, F 238050, repeatedly rec for the Inca Trail, especially Vicente Gómez, US$65 pp, discount with student card; *Compania de Servicios Turísticos (CST)*, Portal Comercio 141, T 231515, Humberto, Silverio and Octavio are reliable guides, rec for Sacred Valley and Machu Picchu; *Luzma Tours*, Portal de Panes Los Ruiseñores, of 308, T 235370, F 236229, good for information, helpful, friendly, manager Luz-Marina, rec. River rafting trips cost on average US$20 pp. *Ecomontaña*, Procuradores 351, T/F 252670, mountain bike hire and tours, US$12/day, Sacred Valley tour US$35/day inc accommodation.

Recommended private guides, divided into two groups: c) classic, standard tours, and d) adventure trips. All of those listed speak English. Set prices: city tour US$15/day; trekking, Machu Picchu and other ruins US$30/day. Private guides can be contacted through the tour companies.

Category c) *Amalia Escobar*, T 222258, also does trekking; *Juana Pancorbo*, Av Los Pinos D-2, T 227482; *Haydee Mogrovejo*, T 221907; *Marco Arragón*, T 233733; *Boris Carnas*, T 221482; *Wilbert Yáñez*, T 232511; *Elisha García*, T 237916; *Satoshi Shinoda*, T 227861 and *Michiko Nakazahua*, T 226185, both Japanese-speaking guides; *Victoria Morales Condori*, San Juan de Dios 229, T 235204; *David Quintana*, T 225757, or through *SAS Travel*, Plaza de Armas 109, Portal Belén, T 224247, he speaks English; *Rubén Huallapuma*, works out of *Hostal Garcilaso*, he is very knowledgeable about Inca civilization, and flexible; **Fredy Palacios Paiva**, T 240281/239716, English-speaking; **Luís Guillén Pinelo**, T 224385; **Dimas Mirando Arroyo**, at *Aventuras Peruanas*, C Espaderos, T 224372, speaks English; **Antonio Aguilar Argandona**, T 262603, speaks English.

Category d) **Aurelio Aguirre**, T 232797; **Darwin Camacho**, T 233884; **Manuel Luna**, T 226083; **Pieter Bohn**, T 234234, German; **Gunther Haue**, T 236916; **Marco Pérez**, T 227414; **Roger Valencia Espinoza**, T 251278; **Tino Aucca**, Urb Titio Q-1-13 Wanchaq, T 235850, a biologist studying the birds of the Polylepis forest. **Victor Estrada**, Parque España E-3, Urb Ucchullo Grande, T 224049, is a shaman and spiritual guide who is also very knowledgeable about local history, architecture, etc; US$75/day.

● **Tourist offices**
Av del Sol 103, same entrance as Museo de Arte Popular. INC tourist office is at Garcilaso y Heladeros for buying tickets for Machu Picchu and the Inca Trail. Official tourist information and Servicio de Protección al Turista is at Mantas 188, opp La Merced, T 263176, open 0800-2000; 24-hr hotline 252974. **Ministry of Tourism**, Av Manco Capac 1020, p 4, Huanchac, T 233701/232347, Mon-Fri 0800-1300. The University is also a good source of information, especially on archaeological sites. They sell good videos of Cusco and surroundings.

Automóvil Club del Perú, Av del Sol 457, next to Banco del Sur, p 3, of 305, has some maps. Motorists beware; many streets end in flights of steps not marked as such. There are very few good maps of Cusco available.

Maps and guidebooks: maps of the city, the Inca Trail and the Urubamba Valley are available at tour companies. There are lots of information booklets on Machu Picchu and the other ruins at the bookshops. The best book on Cusco, the Sacred Valley, Inca Trail, Machu Picchu and other ruins is *Exploring Cusco*, by Peter Frost, which is available in Cusco bookshops. Also rec for general information on Cusco is *Cusco Peru Tourist Guide*, published by Lima 2000. *The Sacred Center*, by Johan Reinhard, explains Machu Picchu in archaeological terms. Another rec book on Machu Picchu, with colour photographs, is *The Machu Picchu Historical Sanctuary*, by Peter Frost (Nuevas Imagenes SA). *Apus and Incas*, by Charles Brod, describes cultural walks in and around Cusco, and treks in the Cordilleras Vilcabamba, Vilcanota and Urubamba, plus the Manu National Park (2nd edition, Inca Expeditions, 2323 SE 46th Ave, Portland, OR 97215, USA, US$10.95 plus US$1.50 postage, or from bookshops in N America, Europe and Peru).

● **Useful addresses**
Police: Tourist police, in Av Sol, on the W side of the grounds of Santo Domingo-Qoricancha, T 221961, they are very helpful. If you need a *denuncia* (a report for insurance purposes), which is available from the Banco de la Nación, they will type it out. Always go to the police when robbed, even though it will cost you a bit of time. Stolen cameras often turn up in the local market and can be bought back cheaply; remember the person selling them is not the thief. If you can prove that the camera is yours, contact the police; National Police, C Saphi, block 4.

● **Transport**
Local Motorcycle mechanics: Eric and Oscar Antonio Aranzábal, Ejercicios 202, Tahuantinsuyo, T 223397, highly rec for repairs; also Autocusa, Av de la Cultura 730 (Sr Marco Tomaycouza), T 240378/239054. **Motorcycle hire**: *Kantu*, Urb Santa Monica, Jr Ricardo Palma L-8, T 233155/223896, owner Enrique Polack has about 15 on/off road 250/350 cc bikes, US$70-80/day, inc guide. **Taxis**: in Cusco are inexpensive and rec when arriving by air, train or bus. They have fixed prices: in the centre US$1.10; to the suburbs US$1.25. Trips to Sacsayhuamán US$10; to the ruins of Tambo Machay US$15-20 (3-4 people); for a whole day trip US$40.

Recommended taxi drivers: Angel Salazar, Saguán del Cielo B-11, T 224597 to leave messages, English speaking, highly rec, helpful, arranges good tours. José G Valdivia Díaz, T 222210, he is not an official guide but has been rec as knowledgeable and helpful. Ferdinand Pinares Cuadros, Yuracpunço 155, Tahuantinsuyo, T 225914, English, French and German spoken, reasonable prices, rec. Taxis on call are reliable but expensive, in the centre US$1.25: Radio Car T 222222; El Dorado, T 221414.

Tourist transport: to rent a minibus for the day costs US$80 (US$40 for ½-day), inc guide (less without guide), maximum 10 people: *Gardenias Tours*, José Castillo, T 222828, tours around Cusco; *Orellana*, Edilberto Orellana, T 239167/225996, tours around Cusco; *Explorers Transporte*, C Plateros 345, T 233498, to all places in Peru.

Air. The airport is at Quispiquilla. To **Lima**, 1 hr, daily flights with Faucett, AeroPerú, Aero Continente and Expresso Aéreo; there are often promotional offers. Grupo Ocho (military) flies every Wed. Flights are heavily booked on this route in the school holidays (Jan-Feb) and national holidays. To **Arequipa**, 35 mins, with Faucett, AeroPerú, Aero Continente and Expresso Aéreo. To **Juliaca**, Faucett, Aero Continente. To **Puerto Maldonado**, 45 mins, daily with Aero Continente. Grupo Ocho has 2 flights a month via Iberia from which there is a dry season route to Brazil (see under Iñapari, page 1402). To La Paz, AeroPerú flies daily.

Airport information T 222611/222601. Taxi to and from the airport costs US$2.50 (US$3.50 by radio taxi), extra US$0.50 if you enter the car park. Colectivos cost US$0.20 from Plaza San Francisco or outside the airport car park. You can book a hotel at the airport through a travel agency, but this is not really necessary. Many representatives of hotels and travel agencies operate at the airport, with transport to the hotel with which they are associated. Take your time to choose your hotel, at the price you can afford.

Warning Cusco-Lima, high possibility of cancelled flights during the wet season; tourists sometimes stranded for several days. Planes may leave early if the weather is bad. Sit on right side of the aircraft for the best view of the mountains when flying Cusco-Lima; it is worth checking in early to get these seats. Reconfirm 24 hrs before your flight departure.

Trains There are two stations in Cusco. To Juliaca, for the Arequipa and Puno services, trains leave from the Av Sol station. When arriving in Cusco, a tourist bus meets the train to take visitors to hotels whose touts offer rooms on the train. Machu Picchu trains leave from Estación San Pedro, opp the Santa Ana market.

The train to **Juliaca** leaves at 0800, Mon, Wed, Fri and Sat, arriving at about 2100; sit on the left for the best views. If going to Puno, it is quicker to get off at Juliaca and take a bus or colectivo from there. See under Juliaca for details on the splitting of the train and services to **Arequipa** and **Puno**; also for a description of the three classes of travel. A popular choice is 1st class to Juliaca and then pullman to Arequipa; this will involve changing carriages in Juliaca. Always check on whether the train is running, especially in the rainy season, when services can be reduced or completely cancelled.

Fares are given under Arequipa and Puno. Tickets are sold 1 day in advance, open Mon-Sat 0700-1230, 1430-2100, Sun 0900-1200. Tickets sell out quickly and there are queues from 0400 before holidays in the dry season. In the low season tickets to Puno can be bought on the day of departure. You can buy tickets through a travel agent, but check the date and seat number. Meals are served on the train.

Warning See under Arequipa, but note that 1st class Cusco-Puno is much emptier than Puno-Cusco and therefore more liable to theft.

To Anta, Ollantaytambo, Machu Picchu and Quillabamba, see page 1355, 1361 and page 1363.

Buses Most bus offices are in C Pachacútec. To Juliaca, 344 km, 12 hrs, US$8, a few buses and trucks do this route daily. The same cautions about road conditions, bad weather and safety apply Cusco-Juliaca-Puno as in the other direction (see pages 1331 and 1331). See under Puno for more details and routes to La Paz. A tourist bus to Puno in the daytime is worth paying the extra for the views.

To **Arequipa**, 521 km, 13-17 hrs, US$10-13, the new road leaves the Puno-Cusco road at Sicuani and runs close to the Colca Canyon, via Chivay; it is very rough in parts. Buses travel mostly at night and it's a very cold journey, so take a blanket. See under Arequipa and the relevant sections for continuation to Nasca and Lima. Most buses to **Lima** go via Arequipa, 36-40 hrs (Cruz del Sur at 1600), US$18-22; but there are some direct buses from Cusco to Lima.

To **Abancay**, 195 km, 7-9 hrs (longer in the rainy season), US$7, several buses and trucks leave daily from Av Arcopata, eg Transcusal 0600, 1000, 1300. The road continues to **Andahuaylas**, 135 km, 5½ hrs minimum, US$5, and on to **Ayacucho**, 252 km, 12 hrs (again longer in the wet), US$8-9. Note that the only direct bus to Andahuaylas leaves at 0300. Most companies will claim that they go direct, but you will have to change in Abancay and wait several hours for another. From Limatambo to Abancay the road is mostly paved and in fairly good condition, otherewise road conditions are poor, but the spectacular scenery compensates.

Continuing from Abancay to **Nasca** via Puquío, the road is mostly paved from Puquío to Nasca (155 km, 6 hrs) but otherwise in very bad condition; Expresso Cusco, Av Grau 820, 3 times a week, US$20, 24 hrs but can be up to 2½ days. The scenery is stunning. There are many military checkpoints and the route has been described as peaceful, but seek advice before taking this route to the coast.

Buses to the Sacred Valley: to Pisac, 32 km, 1 hr, US$0.60 (beware pickpockets); to Calca, 18 km, 30 mins, US$0.10; to Urubamba a further 22 km, 45 mins, US$0.40. Colectivos, minibuses and buses leave from bus station at Tullumayo 125 (½ block S of the plaza on C Zetas) whenever they are full, between 0600 and 1600; also trucks and pick-ups. Buses returning from Pisac are often full; last one back leaves around 2000. An organized tour can be fixed up anytime with a travel agent for US$5 pp. Taxis charge about US$25 for the round trip. To Chinchero, 23 km, 45 mins, US$0.45; to Urubamba a further 25 km, 45 mins, US$0.45 (or US$0.85 Cusco-Urubamba direct). To get to Ollantaytambo, catch a bus to Urubamba; no direct buses from Cusco. Colectivos, minibuses and buses leave from C Arcopata when full, or from Inticahuarina 305 (between Tullumayo and

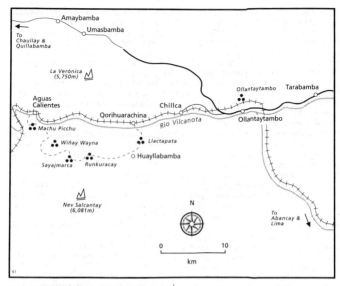

Ahuacpinta), every 20 mins; also from the same place as buses from Cusco via Pisac. Again tours can be arranged to Chinchero, Urubamba and Ollantaytambo with a Cusco travel agency. To Chinchero, US$6 pp; taxi US$25 round trip. Usually only day tours are organized for visits to the valley; see under **Travel Agencies**. Using public transport and staying overnight in Urubamba, Ollantaytambo or Pisac will allow much more time to see the ruins and markets.

For US$50 a taxi can be hired for a whole day (ideally Sun) to take you to Cachimayo, Chinchero, Maras, Urubamba, Ollantaytambo, Calca, Lamay, Coya, Pisac, Tambo Machay, Qenqo and Sacsayhuamán. If you wish to explore this area on your own, Road Map (*Hoja de ruta*) No 10 from the Automóvil Club del Perú is an excellent guide.

THE SACRED VALLEY

Cusco is at the W end of the gently sloping Cusco valley, which stretches 32 km E as far as Huambutío. This valley, and the partly isolated basin of Anta, NW of Cusco, are densely populated. Also densely populated is the Urubamba valley, stretching from Sicuani (on the railway to Puno) to the gorge of Torontoi, 600m lower, to the NW of Cusco. The best time to visit

is April-May or Oct-Nov. The high season is June-Sept, but the rainy season, from Dec to March, is cheaper and pleasant enough.

SOUTHEAST FROM CUSCO

There are many interesting villages and ruins on this road. **Tipón** ruins, between the villages of Saylla and Oropesa, include baths, terraces, irrigation systems and a temple complex, accessible from a path leading from just above the last terrace. **Oropesa** church contains a fine ornately carved pulpit. **Huacarpay**, the well-preserved ruins of the Inca town of Kañaracy, are nearby, reached from a path behind the *Albergue Urpicancha* which is on the shore, of Lago Muina. At **Lucre**, 3 km from Huacarpay, there is an interesting textile mill, and many unexplored ruins. About 3 km from Huacarpay is *C El Dorado Inn*, in a converted monastery, some of the rooms are done in a remarkable style and the service is very good.

At **Huambutío**, N of Huacarpay, the road divides; NW to Pisac and N to **Paucartambo**, on the eastern slope of Andes. This remote town has become a popular

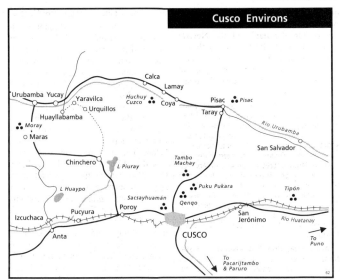

Cusco Environs

map showing: Urubamba, Yucay, Calca, Lamay, Yaravilca, Huchuy Cuzco, Coya, Pisac, Taray, Urquillos, Huayllabamba, Moray, Maras, Chinchero, L Piuray, Tambo Machay, San Salvador, Río Urubamba, L Huaypo, Sacsayhuamán, Puku Pukara, Tipón, Izcuchaca, Pucyura, Poroy, Qenqo, San Jerónimo, Río Huatanay, Anta, CUSCO, To Puno, To Pacarijtambo & Paruro

tourist destination. The *Fiesta del Carmen* is a major attraction, with masked dancers: 16 July, but check dates in Cusco. (**G** *Albergue Municipal Carmen de la Virgen*, basic.) From Paucartambo, in the dry season, you can go 44 km to **Tres Cruces**, along the Pilcopata road, turning left after 25 km. Tres Cruces gives a wonderful view of the sunrise in June and July and private cars leave Paucartambo between 0100 and 0200 to see it; they may give you a lift. You can walk from Paucartambo to the *chullpas* of **Machu Cruz** in about an hour, or to the *chullpas* of **Pijchu** (take a guide).

● **Transport** Private car hire for a round trip Cusco-Paucartambo on 16 July, US$30; travel agencies in Cusco arrange this. A minibus leaves for Paucartambo from Av Huáscar in Cusco, every other day, US$4.50, 3-4 hrs; alternate days Paucartambo-Cusco. Trucks and a private bus leave from the Coliseo, behind Hospital Segura in Cusco, 5 hrs, US$2.50.

Further on from Huacarpay are the Huari (pre-Inca) adobe wall ruins of **Piquillacta**, the monkey temple and the wall of Rumicolca. Piquillacta is quite large, with some reconstruction in progress. Buses to Urcos from Av Huáscar in Cusco will drop you at the entrance on the N side of the complex, though this is not the official entry. Walk through to the official entry and continue to Rumicolca on the other side of the highway; open daily, 0700-1730.

Andahuaylillas is a village 32 km SE from Cusco, with a fine early 17th century church, with beautiful frescoes, a splendid doorway and a gilded main altar. Taxis go there, as does the Oropesa bus (from Av Huáscar in Cusco) via Tipón, Piquillacta and Rumicolca.

Beyond Andahuaylillas is **Urcos**. There is accommodation in municipal rooms on the plaza, or better ones in the 'hotel'; ask for directions. A spectacular road from Urcos crosses the Eastern Cordillera to Puerto Maldonado in the jungle (see page 1399). 47 km after passing the snow-line Hualla-Hualla pass, at 4,820m, the super-hot thermal baths of Marcapata, 173 km from Urcos, provide a relaxing break (entry US$0.10).

82 km from Urcos, at the base of **Nevado Ausangate** (6,384m), is the town of **Ocongate**, which has two hotels on the Plaza de Armas. Beyond Ocongate is **Tin-**

qui, the starting point for hikes around Ausangate and in the Cordillera Vilcanota. On the flanks of the Nevado Ausangate is Q'Olloriti, where a church has been built close to the snout of a glacier. This place has become a place of pilgrimage (see Cusco **Local festivals**, page 1343).

● **Hiking around Ausangate** *Arrieros* and mules can be hired in Tinqui for US$4/day. Make sure you sign a contract with full details. The hike around the mountain of Ausangate takes about 5 days: spectacular, but quite hard, with 3 passes over 5,000m, so you need to be acclimatized. Temperatures in high season (Apr-Oct) can drop well below zero at night. It is rec to take a guide or *arriero*. Buy all food supplies in Cusco. Maps are available at the IGM in Lima or the South American Explorers Club. Some tour companies in Cusco have details about the hike, or check with the Mountain Guide Club, T 226844.

● **Accommodation & transport G** *Hostal Tinqui Guide*, on the right-hand side as you enter the village, friendly, meals available, the owner can arrange guides and horses; also **G** *Ausangate*, very basic, friendly. From Cusco, take a truck to Tinqui, via Urcos and Ocongate; 172 km, 8 hrs, US$8.

Southeast from Urcos, **Huaro** has a church whose interior is covered entirely with a colourful mural painting. **Cusipata**, with an Inca gate and wall, is where the ornate bands for the decoration of ponchos are woven. Close by is the Huari hilltop ruin of Llallanmarca.

Between Cusipata and Checacupe a road branches W to **Acomayo**, a pretty village which has a chapel with mural paintings of the 14 Incas. Accommodation is available in *Pensión Aguirre*.

● **Transport** To Acomayo, take a Cusco-Sicuani bus or truck, US$1, 1½ hrs, then a truck or bus to Acomayo, 3 hrs, same price. Alternatively, alight at Checacupe and take a truck on to Acomayo.

The church at **Checacupe** is, according to John Hemming, very fine, with good paintings and a handsome carved altar rail.

Tinta, 23 km from Sicuani, has a church with brilliant gilded interior and an interesting choir vault (**F** *Casa Comunal*, dormitory accommodation, clean with good food). There are frequent buses and trucks

to Cusco, or take the train from Cusco. Continuing to Sicuani, **Raqchi** is the scene of the region's great folklore festival in mid-June, when dancers come to Raqchi from all over Peru. Through music and dance they illustrate everything from the ploughing of fields to bull fights.

John Hemming adds: "The Viracocha temple is just visible from the train, looking from the distance like a Roman aqueduct. What remains is the central wall, which is adobe above and Inca masonry below. This was probably the largest roofed building ever built by the Incas. On either side of the high wall, great sloping roofs were supported by rows of unusual round pillars, also of masonry topped by adobe. Entrance to the site is US$2. Nearby is a complex of barracks-like buildings and round storehouses. This was the most holy shrine to the creator god Viracocha, being the site of a miracle in which he set fire to the land – hence the lava flow nearby. There are also small Inca baths in the corner of a field beyond the temple and a straight row of ruined houses by a square. The landscape is extraordinary, blighted by huge piles of black volcanic rocks."

● **Transport** To reach Raqchi, take a bus or truck from Cusco towards Sicuani, US$1.50.

NORTHWEST FROM CUSCO

Chinchero (3,762m), is on a direct road to Urubamba. It has an attractive church built on an Inca temple. The church is only open Sun for mass. Recent excavations there have revealed many Inca walls and terraces. The site is open daily, 0700-1730, on the combined entrance ticket (see page 1339). The food market and the handicraft market are separate. The former is held every day, on your left as you come into town. The latter, on Sun only, is up by the church, small, but attractive. On any day but Sun there are few tourists. *Fiesta*, day of the Virgin, on 8 Sept (**F** *Hotel Inca*, with restaurant).

Hikes from Chinchero: there is a scenic path from Chinchero to Huayllabamba, a village on the Río Urubamba, between Yucay and Calca (see below). It offers fine views of the peaks of the Urubamba range and takes about 3-4 hrs. Another hike follows the Maras-Moray-Pichingoto salt mines route, reaching the main Urubamba valley road about 10-12 km beyond Urubamba town.

At **Moray**, there are three 'colosseums', used by the Incas as a sort of open-air crop laboratory, known locally as the greenhouses of the Incas. Peter Frost (*Exploring Cusco*) writes: "There are no great ruined structures here to impress visitors. Moray is more for the contemplative traveller with an affinity for such phenomena as the Nasca Lines, the stone rings of Avebury and the menhirs of Brittany."

● **Access** The easiest and most interesting way to get to Moray is from Urubamba via the Pichingoto bridge over the Río Urubamba. The climb up from the bridge is fairly steep but easy. The path passes by the spectacular salt pans, still in production after thousands of years. Moray is about 1½ hrs further on. The *Hotel Valle Sagrado de los Inkas* in Urubamba can arrange horses and guide and a pick-up truck for the return; US$30-40 pp (see page 1357). Alternatively, wait for a pickup on the bridge on the Chinchero road. This will take you near to Maras. Walk to Maras (30 mins) and on through it, bearing left a little, and ask directions to Moray; 1½ hrs walk in total. Hitching back to Urubamba is quite easy, but there are no hotels at all in the area, so take care not to be stranded.

At **Tiobamba**, near Maras, a fascinating indigenous market-festival is held on 15 Aug, where Sacred Valley yellow maize is exchanged for pottery from Lake Titicaca.

WEST FROM CUSCO

The Cusco-Machu Picchu train reaches the heights N of the city by a series of switchbacks and then descends to the floor of the Anta basin, with its herds of cattle. In **Anta** itself, felt trilby hats are on sale. *Restaurant Dos de Mayo* is good. Bus to Anta, US$0.30. The railway goes through the Anta canyon for 10 km, and then, at a sharp angle, the Urubamba canyon, and descends along the river valley, flanked by high cliffs and peaks.

76 km from Cusco, beyond Anta, on the Abancay road, 2 km before Limatambo at the ruins of **Tarahuasi**, a few hundred metres from the road, is a very well-preserved **Inca temple platform**, with 28 tall niches, and a long stretch of fine polygonal masonry. The ruins are impressive, enhanced by the orange lichen which give the walls a beautiful honey colour.

100 km from Cusco along the Abancay road is the exciting descent into the Apurímac canyon, near the former Inca suspension bridge that inspired Thornton Wilder's *The Bridge of San Luis Rey*. Also, 153 km along the road to Abancay from Cusco, near Curahuasi, famous for its anise herb, is the stone of **Sahuite**, carved with animals, houses, etc, which appears to be a relief map of an Indian village. Unfortunately, 'treasure hunters' have defaced the stone. There are other interesting carvings in the area around the Sahuite stone.

THE URUBAMBA VALLEY

From Cusco a paved road climbs to the pass, continues over the pampa before descending into the Urubamba valley. It crosses the river by bridge at Pisac and follows the N bank of river to the end of the paved road at Ollantaytambo. It passes through Calca, Yucay and Urubamba (also reached from Cusco via Chinchero, see above). There is always transport, and it is always full. Since the valley (*alt* 2,800m) is 600m lower than Cusco, it is a good area to acclimatize, physically and culturally, before going up to the former Inca capital.

PISAC

30 km N of Cusco, high above the town, on the mountainside, is a superb Inca fortress. Pisac has a Sun morning market, which comes to life after the arrival of tourist buses around 1000; it is usually over by 1500. Pisac has other, somewhat less crowded, less expensive markets on Tues and Thurs morning. It's best to get there before 0900. On the plaza are the church and a small interesting Museo Folklórico. The town is worth strolling around; look for the fine façade at Grau 485. There are many souvenir shops on Bolognesi. Local fiesta: 15 July.

The walk up to the ruins begins from the plaza (but see **Access** below), past the

Centro de Salud and a new control post. The path goes through working terraces, giving the ruins a context. The first group of buildings is Pisaqa, with a fine curving wall. Climb then to the central part of the ruins, the Intihuatana group of temples and rock outcrops in the most magnificent Inca masonry. Here are the Reloj Solar ('Hitching Post of the Sun') – now closed because thieves stole a piece from it, palaces of the moon and stars, solstice markers, baths and water channels. From Intihuatana, a path leads around the hillside through a tunnel to Q'Allaqasa, the 'military area'. Across the valley at this point, a large area of Inca tombs in holes in the hillside can be seen. The end of the site is Kanchiracay, where the agricultural workers were housed. Road transport approaches from this end. For full details, see Peter Frost's *Exploring Cusco*. The descent takes 30 mins. At dusk you will hear, if not see, the *pisaca* (partridges), after which the place is named. If lucky you will also see deer.

● **Access** To appreciate the site fully, allow 5 hrs if going on foot. If you do not show your multi-site ticket on the way up, you will be asked to do so by the warden. The site is open 0700-1730; guides charge US$5. There is transport up to the archaeological site on market days only so, at other times, you must walk, at least 1 hr uphill all the way. Horses are available for US$3 pp, but travellers with a couple of dollars to spare should get a taxi from near the bridge up to the ruins and walk back down. A van from the plaza to the ruins costs US$2.50 each way.

● **Accommodation D** pp *Pisaq*, Pardo y Arequipa, on the plaza in front of the church and marketplace, T (084) 203062, run by Roman Vizcarra and his wife Fielding Wood from New Mexico, 15 rooms, 3 with bath, price with shared bath is **E** pp, constant hot water, pleasant decor, sauna, knowledgeable, meals available at the hotel's café on the plaza, good homemade pizza, highly rec; **F** *Residencial Beho*, Intihuatana 642, ask for room in main building, good breakfast for US$1, owner's son will act as guide to ruins at weekend. A new 5-star hotel, *Royal Inca III*, opened mid-1996, 1 km out of town, a converted hacienda with 75 rooms, pool, sauna, jacuzzi, phone the *Royal Inca I* or *II* in Cusco for further details.

● **Places to eat** *Samana Wasi*, on the plaza, reasonable. Good, cheap trout is available in many restaurants. The bakery at Mcal Castilla 372 sells excellent cheese and onion *empanadas* for US$0.25, suitable for vegetarians, and good wholemeal bread.

● **Tours** You can continue the Sun morning tour to Pisac along the Urubamba to Ollantaytambo, with lunch at Yucay or at the *Hotel Valle Sagrado de Los Inkas* (or elsewhere) in Urubamba. Tours from Cusco usually allow only 1½ hrs at Pisac. This is not enough time to take in the ruins and splendid scenery. Apart from Sun when Pisac is crowded, there are very few tourists. If you're not interested in the market, it would be a good idea to ask the driver to do the tour clockwise, Chinchero, Ollantaytambo, then Pisac, thereby missing the crowds.

PISAC TO URUBAMBA

Calca, 2,900m, is 18 km beyond Pisac. The plaza is divided in two: Urubamba buses stop on one side; and Cusco and Pisac buses on the other side of the dividing strip. *Fiesta de la Virgen Asunta* 15-16 Aug. There are a couple of very basic hotels and **E** *Hostal Pitusiray*, on the edge of town. There are some basic restaurants around the plaza.

It is a 2-day hike from Cusco to Calca, via Sacsayhuamán, Qenqo, Puka Pukará, Tambo Machay and **Huchuy Cusco** (a small, ruined Inca town) with excellent views of the Eastern Cordilleras, past small villages and along beautifully built Inca paths. There are many places to camp, but take water (Calca to Huchuy Cusco is a stiff 3-4 hr climb). At **Coya**, between Calca and Pisac, there's a fiesta during 14-18 Aug.

There are mineral baths (cold) at **Minas Maco**, 30 mins' walk along the Urubamba, and at **Machacancha**, 8 km E of Calca. 3 km beyond Machacancha are the Inca ruins of **Arquasmarca**.

● **Guides** Walter Góngora Arizábal, T 202124, is a combi driver who does private trips; US$31 to Cusco, US$18 to Pisac, including wait.

● **Accommodation Between Calca and Yucay**: a bridge crosses the river to the village of **Huayllabamba**. East along the bank of the river, near the community of Urquillos, on a working maize farm is **A1** *Posada-Hacienda Yarivilca*, due open in mid-late 1997. Due open earlier in 1997 is *Albergue Hacienda Urpi Wata*, on the headwaters of the Río Urquillos just below Chinchero; this is also a working farm, with maize and milk/cheese production. *Urpi Wata* will accommodate both backpackers and other guests; visitors to the farm are welcome at any time. Both hotels are run by Tierras Atlas SA (managing director Scotsman Ken Duncan); further information in Cusco, at Las Nazarenas 211, T 232829; or Lima: Los Pinos 584, San Isidro, Lima 27, T/F 440-5476.

3 km E of Urubamba, **Yucay** has two grassy plazas divided by the restored colonial church of Santiago Apóstol, with its oil paintings and fine altars. On the opposite side from Plaza Manco II is the adobe palace built for Sayri Túpac (Manco's son) when he emerged from Vilcabamba in 1558. In Yucay monks sell fresh milk, ham, eggs and other dairy produce from their farm on the hillside.

● **Accommodation** On the same plaza as the adobe palace is the **A2** *Posada del Inca*, a converted 300-year-old monastery, T 201107, inc tax, it is like a little village with plazas, chapel, different types of room (all well-appointed), restaurant, conference centre and a museum with the owner's private collection of pre-Inca ceramics, gold and silver pieces and weavings. Also **B-C** *Hostal Y'Llary*, on Plaza Manco II, T 201112, inc breakfast.

URUBAMBA

Like many places along the valley, Urubamba (*Alt* 2,863m) is in a fine setting with snow-capped peaks in view. The main plaza, with a fountain capped by a maize cob, is surrounded by buildings painted blue. Calle Berriozabal, on the W edge of town, is lined with pisonay trees. The large market square is 1 block W of the main plaza. The main road skirts the town and the bridge for the road to Chinchero is just to the E of town. Visit the ceramics workshop of Pablo Seminario, who uses precolumbian techniques and designs, highly recommended, M Castilla cuadra 9 y Zavala, T 201002.

6 km W of Urubamba is **Tarabamba**, where a bridge crosses the Río Urubamba. Turn right after the bridge to **Pichingoto**, a tumbled-down village built under an overhanging cliff. Also, just over the bridge and before the town to the left of a small, walled cemetery is a salt stream. Follow the footpath beside the stream to Salinas, a small village below which are a mass of terraced Inca salt pans which are still in operation

there are over 5,000. The walk to the salt pans takes about 30 mins. Take water as this side of the valley can be very hot and dry.

Local festivals May and June are the harvest months, with many processions following ancient schedules. Urubamba's main festival, *El Señor de Torrechayoc*, occupies the first week of June.

● **Accommodation A2** *Valle Sagrado de los Inkas* (ex-*Turistas*, being upgraded), 5 mins walk from the centre, special rates available, 67 comfortable bungalows with gardens, 15 suites and 50 rooms, English-owned, restaurant, bar, disco, 2 pools, T 201126/27, F 201071, horse riding (eg to Moray), mountain biking, kayaking, rafting; **A2-3** *Turquesa*, 20 mins' walk from town, towards Yucay, small pool, restaurant, buffet on Tues/Thur/Sun US$3.50, room service, comfortable, part of San Agustín chain, reservations at *San Agustín Internacional* in Cusco; **D** pp *Hostal Urpihuasi*, without private bath, **C** pp with full board, pleasant modern rooms, small outdoor pool, sauna, quiet and relaxing, rec (manager Rae Pieraccini runs a project for street children, financed by the hotel's income); **E** pp *Hostal Rumichaca*, 3 km W of Urubamba, back from the Rumichaca bus stop, full board, beautiful location, vegetarian food available, run by Martín and Ada, Martín is also a mountain guide, Ada is a great cook, great place to relax. **In the town of Urubamba: F** *Hostal Urubamba*, Bolognesi, basic, pleasant, cold water.

● **Places to eat** Several restaurants on M Castilla: *Hirano's*, good food. *Luna Nueva*, Grau y Mainique, homemade pasta, good food and atmosphere, live music, rec. On the main road, before the bridge is *Quinta los Geranios*, excellent lunch for US$3.

● **Useful services** Banco de la Nación, with **Correos** behind it, is on the main road, opp the petrol station at M Castilla.

● **Transport** From Urubamba to Calca, Pisac (US$0.80, 1 hr) and Cusco, about 2 hrs, US$1, with Caminos del Inca, M Castilla y Mainique, from 0530; buses to Cusco via Chinchero leave from the W side of the plaza. El Señor de Huanca combis run to Calca from the petrol station on M Castilla when full between 0700 and 1900; from the opp side of the street combis run to Ollantaytambo, 45 mins, US$0.30. Buses to Quillabamba from M Castilla outside *Hirano's*.

OLLANTAYTAMBO

The Inca town, or Llacta, on which the present-day town is based (*Alt* 2,800m) is clearly seen in the fine example of Inca *canchas* (blocks), which are almost entirely intact and still occupied behind the main plaza.

Entering Ollantaytambo from Pisac, the road is built along the long wall of 100 niches. Note the inclination of the wall: it leans towards the road. Since it was the Incas' practice to build with the walls leaning towards the interiors of the buildings, it has been deduced that the road, much narrower then, was built inside a succession of buildings. The road out of the plaza leads across a bridge, down to the colonial church with its enclosed *recinto*. Beyond is a plaza (and car park) with entrances to the archaeological site, which is open 0700-1730.

The so-called **Baño de la Ñusta** (bath of the princess) is of grey granite, and is in a small area between the town and the temple fortress. Some 200m behind the Baño de la Ñusta along the face of the mountain are some small ruins known as Inca Misanca, believed to have been a small temple or observatory. A series of steps, seats and niches have been carved out of the cliff. There is a complete irrigation system, including a canal at shoulder level, some 6 inches deep, cut out of the sheer rock face (under renovation). The flights of terraces leading up above the town are superb, and so are the curving terraces following the contours of the rocks overlooking the Urubamba. These terraces were successfully defended by Manco Inca's warriors against Hernando Pizarro in 1536. Manco Inca built the defensive wall above the site and another wall closing the Yucay valley against attack from Cusco. These are still visible on either side of the valley.

The temple itself was started by Pachacuti, using Colla Indians from Lake Titicaca – hence the similarities of the monoliths facing the central platform with the Tiahuanaco remains. The Colla are said to have deserted half-way through the work, which explains the many unfinished blocks lying about the site.

● **Access and information** Admission is by combined entrance ticket, which can be bought at the site. If possible arrive very early, 0700, before the tourists. The guide book *Ollan-taytambo* by Víctor Angles Vargas is available in Cusco bookshops, and Peter Frost's *Exploring Cusco* is also useful. Ask for Dr Hernán Amat Olazábal, a leading Inca-ologist, at the Parador for further explanation.

Recently a "pyramid" has been identified on the W side of the main ruins of Ollan-taytambo. Its discoverers, Fernando and Edgar Elorietta, claim it is the real Pacaritambo, from where the 4 original Inca brothers emerged to found their empire. Whether this is the case or not, it is still a first-class piece of engineering with great terraced fields and a fine 750m wall aligned with the rays of the winter solstice, on 21 June. The mysterious "pyramid", which covers 50-60 ha, can be seen properly from the other side of the river. This is a pleasant, easy 1-hr walk, W from the Puente Inca, just outside the town. There are great views of the Sacred Valley, the river and the snowy peaks of the Verónica massif as a backdrop.

A major excavation project has been carried out since 1977 under the direction of Ann Kendall in the **Cusichaca** valley, 26 km from Ollantaytambo, at the intersection of the Inca routes. Only 9 km of this road is passable by ordinary car. The Inca fort, Huillca Raccay, was excavated in 1978-80, and work is now concentrated on Llactapata, a site of domestic buildings. Ann Kendall is now working in the Patacancha valley NE of Ollantaytambo. Excavations are being carried out in parallel with the restoration of Inca canals to bring fresh clean water to the settlements in the valley.

Local festivals The Sun following Inti Raymi, there is a colourful festival, the *Ollanta-Raymi*. On **6 Jan** there is the festival of Reyes (the Three Wise Men), with music, dancing, processions. Around **26 Oct** there is a 2-day, weekend festival with lots of dancing in traditional costume and many local delicacies for sale.

● **Accommodation D** pp *El Albergue*, next to, and access via, the railway station, T/F (084) 204014, or in Cusco at Expediciones Manu, T 226671, manager Wendy Weeks (American), 6 rooms, charming, homely, with sauna, meals available on request, convenient for Machu Piccu train, good place for information, highly rec. Next door is **D** *Albergue Kapuly*. **E** *Hostal*

Chuza, 3 mins below the main plaza, rec; **E-F** *Hostal Miranda*, between the main plaza and the ruins, with shower, basic; **G** pp *Alojamiento Yavar*, 1½ blocks from the main plaza, if they're full, they'll let you sleep on the floor for free, basic, no water in the evening, they have information on horse riding in the area.

● **Places to eat** There are several restaurants on the Plaza: *Bahía*, on the S side of Plaza, very friendly, vegetarian dishes on request; also rec is **Ollantay**.

● **Sports Horse riding**: horses can be hired for US$5/day; a gentle day's ride or hike is to La Marca, along the beautiful river valley; ask Wendy Weeks for details. You can also visit the Inca quarry on the other side of the river.

● **Transport** For those travelling by car and intending to go to Machu Picchu, it is rec to leave the car at Ollantaytambo railway station, which costs US$1/day; ask Wendy Weeks at *El Albergue* for details. Also safe car parking in Sra Carmen's backyard at the train station. Check in advance the time trains pass through here. It's best to have your ticket in advance. The Ollantaytambo ticket office has to check if there's room on the train. Both the tourist and local trains stop on the way to and from Machu Picchu. The station is 10-15 mins walk from the plaza. There are colectivos at the plaza for the station when trains are due.

THE INCA TRAIL TO MACHU PICCHU

The spectacular 3 to 5 day hike runs from Km 88, Qorihuayrachina (2,299m), a point immediately after the first tunnel 22 km beyond Ollantaytambo station. A sturdy suspension bridge has now been built over the Río Urubamba. An entrance ticket for the trail must be bought at Km 88: US$17; 50% discount for students with an ISIC card. It also gives entry to Machu Picchu if you get it stamped there. Guided tours often start at Km 83; check whether the price includes site entrance.

● **Equipment**
The trail is rugged and steep (beware of landslides), but the magnificent views compensate for any weariness which may be felt. It is cold at night, however, and weather conditions change rapidly, so it is important to take not only strong footwear, rain gear and warm clothing but also food, water, insect repellent, a supply of plastic bags, coverings, a good sleeping bag, a torch/flashlight and a stove for preparing hot food and drink to ward off the cold at night. A stove using paraffin (kerosene) is preferable, as fuel can be bought in small quantities in markets. Camping gas (white gas) is available in hardware stores in Cusco, US$1.50/litre. A tent is essential, but if you're hiring one in Cusco, check carefully for leaks. Walkers who have not taken adequate equipment have died of exposure. Caves marked on some maps are little better than overhangs, and are not sufficient shelter to sleep in.

All the necessary equipment can be rented; see page 1349 under **Travel agencies**. Good maps of the Trail and area can be bought from the South American Explorers Club in Lima. If you have any doubts about carrying your own pack, reasonably-priced porters/guides are available, most reliably through Cusco agencies. You can also hire porters in Ollantaytambo; speak to the men in the plaza wearing red ponchos. Expect to pay US$7/day plus basic foodstuffs. Carry a day-pack nonetheless in case you walk faster than the porters and you have to wait for them to catch you up. Horses can also be hired on the trail for around US$5 per pack.

● **Tours**
You can do the Inca Trail independently or with a Travel Agency in Cusco who will arrange transport to the start, equipment, food, etc, for an all-in price, generally around US$60-70 pp. Agency treks range from the more expensive, with smaller groups, better equipment and transport arrangements, to cheaper, cost-cutting outfits with large groups and basic gear. Almost everyone reports that things do not go to plan. Most complaints are minor, but do check equipment carefully. Ask around for people who have done the trip and take extra food and water. Do not accept under-age porters or inexperienced guides.

● **Transport**
Only the local train stops at Km 88; about 3 hrs after leaving Cusco. The tourist train does not stop here. Be ready to get out at Km 88, at the village called Chamana, as it's easy to pass it; from Ollantaytambo US$0.80. If you do not wish to travel on the local train, the simplest method is to go to Ollantaytambo, or Chillca and start walking from there.

From Ollantaytambo it takes about 8 hrs to the start of the Inca Trail: follow the railway in the direction of Machu Picchu until you come to Chillca village where you can cross the river. Sometimes there is a truck going to Chillca. From Chillca to the start of the Trail takes 5 hrs: climb up to a path that runs parallel to the river. This is an original Inca trail (still in use) that leads to Llaqtapata on the Inca Trail. **Warning** It's best not to spend a night on this trail. Theft is possible because you have to sleep near the villages.

● **The Trail**

The walk to Huayllabamba, following the Cusichaca river, needs about 3 hrs and isn't too arduous. Beyond Huayllabamba, a popular camping spot for tour groups, there is a camping place about an hour ahead, at **Llulluchayoc** (3,200m). A punishing 1½-hr climb further is Llulluchapampa, an ideal meadow for camping. If you have the energy to reach this point, it will make the second day easier because the next stage, the ascent to the first pass, **Warmiwañuska** (4,200m), is exhausting, 2½ hrs.

Afterwards take the steep path downhill to the Pacamayo valley. You could camp by a stream at the bottom (1½ hrs from the first pass). It is no longer permitted to camp at **Runkuracay**, on the way up to the second pass (a much easier climb, 3,850m). Magnificent views nr the summit in clear weather. A good overnight place is past the Inca ruins at **Sayacmarca** (3,500m), about an hour on after the top of the second pass.

A gentle 2-hr climb on a fine stone highway leads through an Inca tunnel to the third pass. Near the top there's a spectacular view of the entire Vilcabamba range. You descend to Inca ruins at **Phuyopatamarca** (3,650m), well worth a long visit. There is a 'tourist bathroom' here where water can be collected (but purify it before drinking).

From there steps go downhill to the impressive ruins of **Wiñay-Wayna**, with views of the recently cleared terraces of Intipata. Access is possible, but the trail is not easily visible. There is a basic hostel with bunk beds, F pp, showers and a small restaurant, but the facilities are badly run-down. There is a small campsite in front of the hostel. After Wiñay-Wayna there is no water and no camping till Machu Picchu.

The path from this point goes more or less level through jungle until the steep staircase up to the **Intipunku** (2 hrs), where there's a magnificent view of Machu Picchu, especially at dawn, with the sun alternately in and out, clouds sometimes obscuring the ruins, sometimes leaving them clear.

Get to Machu Picchu as early as possible, preferably before 0830 for best views but in any case before the tourist train arrives at 1030. **NB** Camping is not allowed at Intipunku; guards may confiscate your tent. You can, however, go down through Machu Picchu (your ticket will be stamped but you can use it the next day) to a patch of grass 300m-500m past the hotel, where you can camp. There is water at a tap 100m further down and meals are available at the small house nearby.

4 days would make a comfortable trip (though much depends on the weather) and you would not find yourself too tired to enjoy what you see. **NB** You are not allowed to walk back along the trail, though you can pay US$4.50 at Intipunku to be allowed to walk back as far as Wiñay-Wayna. You cannot take backpacks into Machu Picchu; leave them at ticket office, US$0.50.

NB The first 2 days of the Trail involve the stiffest climbing, so do not attempt it if you're feeling unwell. Try to camp in groups at night, leave all your valuables in Cusco and keep everything inside your tent, even your shoes. Security has, however, improved in recent years. Avoid the July-Aug high season and the rainy season from Nov to April (note that this can change, check in advance). In the wet it is cloudy and the paths are very muddy and difficult. Also watch out for coral snakes in this area (black, red, yellow bands).

Please remove all your rubbish, including toilet paper, or use the pits provided. Do not light open fires as they can get out of control. The Earth Preservation Fund sponsors an annual clean-up July-Aug: volunteers should write to EPF, Inca Trail Project, Box 7545, Ann Arbor, Michigan 48107, USA. Preserving the Inca Trail: in Lima contact APTA, Percy Tapiá, T 478078, or Antonio Bouroncle, T 450532. In Cusco, different agencies organize the clean-up each year.

A short Inca trail starts at Km 104, where a footbridge gives access to the ruins of Chachabamba and the trail which ascends through the ruins of Choquesuysuy to connect with the main trail at Wiñay-Wayna. This first part is a brutal ascent (take water) and the trail is narrow and exposed in parts. It takes about 2½-3½ hrs to reach Wiñay-Wayna. The regular train arrives around 0930-1030; arrange with conductor to make sure it stops. Entry to the trail is US$12. There is a good hike from Aguas Calientes (see page 1362) to Km 104.

MACHU PICCHU

42 km from Ollantaytambo by rail (2,380m), **Machu Picchu** is a complete city. For centuries it was buried in jungle, until Hiram Bingham stumbled upon it in 1911. It was then explored by an archaeological expedition sent by Yale.

The ruins – staircases, terraces, temples, palaces, towers, fountains and the famous Intihuatana (the so-called 'Hitching Post of the Sun') – require at least a day. Take time to appreciate not only the masonry, but also the selection of large rocks for foundations, the use of water in the channels below the Temple of the Sun and the surrounding mountains.

Huayna Picchu, the mountain overlooking the site (on which there are also ruins), has steps to the top for a superlative view of the whole site, but it is not for those who are afraid of heights and you shouldn't leave the path. The climb takes up to 90 mins but the steps are dangerous after bad weather. The path is open 0700-1300, with the latest return time being 1500; and you must register at a hut at the beginning of the trail. The other trail to Huayna Picchu, down near the Urubamba, is via the Temple of the Moon, in two caves, one above the other, with superb Inca niches inside, which have sadly been blemished by graffiti. For the trail to the Temple of the Moon: from the path to Huayna Picchu, take the second trail to the left – both are marked 'Danger, do not enter'. The danger is in the first 10 mins, after which it is reasonable, although it descends further than you think it should. After the Temple you may proceed to Huayna Picchu. The round trip takes about 4 hrs. Before doing any trekking around Machu Picchu, check with an official which paths may be used, or which are one way.

The famous Inca bridge is about 45 mins along a well-marked trail S of the Royal Sector. The bridge – which is actually a couple of logs – is spectacularly sited, carved into a vertiginous cliff-face. East of the Royal Sector is the path leading up to **Intipunku** on the Inca Trail (45 mins, fine views).

Local information
● **Access**

The site is open from 0700 to 1700. You can deposit your luggage at the entrance for US$0.50, though theft has been reported; check for missing items and demand their return. Entrance fee is US$10, half price with ISIC card; second day ticket half price. If paying in dollars, only clean, undamaged notes will be accepted. Guides are available at the site, they are often very knowledgeable and worthwhile, US$15 for 2½ hrs. Permission to enter the ruins before 0630 to watch the sunrise over the Andes, which is a spectacular experience, can be ob-

tained from the Instituto Nacional de Cultura in Cusco, but it is often possible if you talk to the guards at the gate. After 1530 the ruins are quieter, but note that the last bus down from the ruins leaves at 1700.

Mon and Fri are bad days because there is usually a crowd of people on guided tours who are going or have been to Pisac market on Sun, and too many people all want lunch at the same time. The expensive hotel is located next to the entrance, with a self-service restaurant. Lunch costs US$15 pp, so it's best to take your own food and drink, and take plenty of drinking water. Note that food is not officially allowed into the site.

● **Recommended reading**

Lost City of the Incas by Hiram Bingham (available in Lima and Cusco); *A Walking Tour of Machu Picchu* by Pedro Sueldo Nava – in several languages, available in Cusco. See also *The Sacred Center*, by Johan Reinhard, and *The Machu Picchu Historical Sanctuary*, by Peter Frost. *Exploring Cusco*, also by Peter Frost has good information about the site. The Tourist Hotel sells guides, although at a rather inflated price. The South American Explorers Club in Lima has detailed information on walks here, and so have Hilary Bradt's and Charles Brod's books.

● **Accommodation**

L2 *Machu Picchu Ruinas*, electricity and water 24 hrs a day, will accept American Express TCs at the official rate, restaurant for residents only; the hotel is usually fully booked well in advance, try Sun night as other tourists find Pisac market a greater attraction; for reservations T (511) 221-0826/440-8043, F 221-0824/440-6197, San Isidro, Lima. The South American Explorers Club in Lima advise against trying to make your own reservation as this can be very frustrating; they will do it for you; call them several months in advance with details, inc credit card number; T 51-1-425-0142.

● **Transport**

Trains The railway runs from Cusco (San Pedro station), up the zig-zag route to the pass before descending all the way to Quillabamba, 130 km. It passes through Ollantaytambo, Km 88, Aguas Calientes (the official name of this station is 'Machu Picchu') and Machu Picchu (officially called 'Puente Ruinas'). There is a paved road between 'Machu Picchu' and 'Puente Ruinas'. There are two local trains, two *autovagones* and one tourist train a day.

The local train has 2nd and 1st class; US$4.50 and US$6 one way respectively. The train is really crowded and you should watch your possessions carefully as bag-slashing is common. Take as little as possible, and no valuables, on the train. When on your way to hike the Inca Trail, equipped with a big backpack, try to be in a group, watching each other's gear. The first train leaves Cusco Mon-Sat at 0645, stopping in Ollantaytambo at about 0900 and Puente Ruinas at 1025; it continues to Quillabamba, arriving about 1130; leaves Quillabamba at 1430, stopping at Puente Ruinas at 1600, Ollantaytambo 1730 and arrives in Cusco at 2100. Be at Puente Ruinas station by 1400 for a ticket; very few are available so jump on and pay on board. The train is always crowded, so in order to avoid standing all the way back to Cusco, it's a good idea to get off at Ollantaytambo (2 hrs), spend the night there and return by bus the next day. Alternatively, spend the night in Aguas Calientes and catch the early morning train from there. The second train leaves Cusco daily at 1310, stops in Ollantaytambo at 1545, Puente Ruinas 1730, arriving in Quillabamba at 1830. It leaves Quillabamba the next day at 0530, arriving at Puente Ruinas at 0700, Ollantaytambo 0815 and Cusco 1100.

The tourist train has one class, pullman, with closed doors (only ticket holders allowed on); US$27 return. It leaves Cusco daily at 0625, stopping at Ollantaytambo at 0830 and Puente Ruinas at 1000; it returns from Puente Ruinas at 1600, arrives in Ollantaytambo at 1740 and arrives in Cusco at 2000.

There are two *autovagones*; US$47 return, with toilets, video, snacks and drinks for sale. The first one leaves Cusco at 0600, stops in Ollantaytambo at 0745 and Puente Ruinas at 0930 (it also stops at Km 88 to let the local train pass). It returns at 1500, reaches Ollantaytambo at 1630 and Cusco at 1830. The second one leaves Cusco at 0900; arrives in Ollantaytambo 1100; Puente Ruinas 1220. It returns at 1800; arrives in Ollantaytambo at 1950, and Cusco at 2150.

The *autovagón* and tourist train do not stop at Aguas Calientes. Travellers on inclusive tours often return by bus from Ollantaytambo, leaving the trains emptier for the slower uphill journey to Cusco.

Train schedules are unreliable and delays of hours are common, especially on the local train. In the rainy season mudslides cause cancellations. Tickets can be bought in advance or on the day at the railway station or at a travel agency (always check date and seat number, and don't pay the agency in advance). Theoretically, the ticket office is open daily 0600-0830, 1000-1100 and 1500-1700. Expect long queues at Cusco for the morning local train in the high season and on holidays.

Tourist tickets: there are two types, 1) round trip in the *autovagón*, round trip in the bus up to the ruins, entrance fee and guide, for US$110. 2) Round trip on the local train, buffet class, round trip in the bus to the ruins, entrance fee and guide, US$60. These tickets can be booked through any travel agency, who will pick you up at your hotel and take you to the train station. On the *autovagón* and tourist train try to get tickets with seat numbers. Independent travellers should try to buy their return leg to Cusco as soon as they arrive at Puente Ruinas.

Buses leave Puente Ruinas station for Machu Picchu at 0630 and 0730, and every 30 mins until after the last morning train has arrived; 25 mins, US$3.30 one way. From Aguas Calientes to the ruins, there is a bus service from 0730-1130, US$7 return. There is a bus from the ruins to Puente Ruinas and Aguas Calientes from 1230-1700. The walk up takes 2 hrs, and 1 hr down, following the zig-zag road.

AGUAS CALIENTES

1½ km back along the railway from Puente Ruinas. Most activity is centred around the railway station, on the plaza, or on Av Pachacútec, which leads from the plaza to the thermal baths (a communal pool), 10 mins' walk from the town. They are open 0500-2200, US$2.50. You can rent towels and bathing costumes (US$0.65) at several places on the road to the baths; basic toilets and changing facilities and showers for washing *before* entering the baths; take soap and shampoo.

• **Accommodation** **A1-2** *Machu Picchu Pueblo Hotel*, Km 110, Aguas Calientes (Cusco 232161/223769, Procuradores 48; Lima 461915, F 455598, Andalucía 174, Lima 18), individual bungalows, hot water, heating, meals extra in nice, expensive restaurant, pool, lovely gardens, rec, 5 mins walk along the railway from the town, the tourist train from Puente Ruinas stops here; **B** *Hostal Inka*, at station, T 211034, includes breakfast, rec; **B** *Hostal Machu Picchu Inn*, Av Pachacútec, **C** without bath, good; **C** *Hostal Ima Sumac*, Av Pachacútec, 5 mins before the baths, T 211021, will exchange money; **D** *Gringo Bill's* (*Hostal Q'oñi Unu*), Qoya Raymi, third house to left of church, T 211046, shared bath, relaxed, hot water, laundry, money exchange, good but expensive meals served (usually slowly), they offer a US$2 packed lunch to take up to the ruins, luggage stored, good beds, don't stay in the rooms nearest the entrance as they flood during heavy rain; **D-E** *Hostal Machu Picchu*, at the station, basic, quiet, Wilber helps, the owner's son, with travel information, hot water, nice balcony over the Urubamba, grocery store, rec; **E** *Hostal Inti Sumi*, at the top of the hill nr the baths, hot water; **E** pp *Hostal Los Caminantes*, by the railway just beyond the station, **F** pp without bath, basic; **E** *Hostal Pachacuctec*, up the hill beyond *Hostal La Cabaña*, T 211061, with bath, hot water 24 hrs, good breakfast, quiet, family-run, rec. **Camping**: the only official campsite is in a field by the river, just below Puente Ruinas station. Do not leave your tent and belongings unattended.

● **Places to eat** At the station: *El Refugio*, good food, slow service; *Aiko*, immaculately clean, rec; *El Chosa Pizzería*, pleasant atmosphere, good value; *Wiñay-Wayna*; and many others. *Clave de Sol*, Av Pachacútec 156, same owner as *Chez Maggy* in Cusco, good cheap Italian food US$3.70, changes money, has vegetarian menu, great atmosphere. Also on this street: *Govinda*, just off the plaza, vegetarian, cheap set lunch, rec; *Machu Picchu*, good, friendly; *Chifa Hong Kong*; *Waisicha Pub*, good music and atmosphere; and others. *Inka's Pizza Pub*, on the plaza, good pizzas, changes money, accepts TCs, rec.

● **Tour companies & travel agents** Travel agency, *Información Turística Rikuni*, is at the station, Nydia is very helpful; also *Qosqo Service*, by the railway.

● **Useful information** There are lots of places for exchange. The **Post Office** at the station sells maps of Machu Picchu. The telephone office is on the plaza. The town has electricity 24 hrs a day.

QUILLABAMBA

The railway goes on 79 km through Chaullay to **Quillabamba** (*Pop* 24,000; *Alt* 1,054m) in the Urubamba Valley, where there is a Dominican mission.

The train follows the Río Urubamba much of the way from Machu Picchu, and the improvised station at Quillabamba is right on the river. Cross a footbridge and then climb up a 100-odd flight of stairs to reach the town. Not many attractions for the tourist, but this is a good place to bask in the sun or take a swim in the river, though ask the locals where the safe stretches are, as the current is quite rapid in places. The high season is June and July.

● **Accommodation D** *Quillabamba*, Prolongación y M Grau 590, unmarked entrance next to Autoservicio behind market, roof terrace restaurant, laundry service, rec; *Hostal Don Carlos*, private shower, generally hot water; **F** *Hostal Cusco*, with patio and roof terrace, rec;

F *Hostal Alto Urubamba*, on Dos de Mayo, good, with or without bath, hot water, restaurant. There is other accommodation, **G** and upwards, nr the market.

● **Places to eat** *Pub Don Sebas*, Jr Espinar 235 on Plaza de Armas, good place to eat, great sandwiches, run by Karen Molero who is very friendly and always ready for a chat; *El Gordito*, on Espinar, good place for chicken, US$3. There are many *heladerías*, which are much needed in the heat; the best is on the NW corner of the Plaza.

● **Banks & money changers** Banco de Crédito, good for TCs.

● **Transport Trains** See above for train information. **Road** A minibus leaves Cusco in the morning when full, from C Gen Buendía nr Machu Picchu station; also trucks go in the daytime; 233 km, 6-11 hrs, US$4.50.

ROUTES The road between Ollantaytambo and Quillabamba passes through Peña, a place of great beauty with snowy peaks on either side of the valley. Once out of Peña, the climb to the pass begins in earnest – on the right is a huge glacier. Soon on the left, Verónica begins to appear in all its huge and snowy majesty. After endless zig-zags and breathtaking views, you reach the Abra Málaga pass. The descent to the valley shows hillsides covered in lichen and Spanish moss. At Chaullay, the road meets the railway to Quillabamba, Machu Picchu and Cusco. The road crosses the river at the historic Choquechaca bridge. You can drive from Chaullay to Santa Teresa, where there are hot springs, but ask the locals for directions. From here, the railway goes to Machu Picchu. Note that driving in this area is very demanding owing to the number of hairpin bends.

VITCOS

From Chaullay you can drive to the village of **Huancacalle**, the best base for exploring the nearby Inca ruins of **Vitcos**, with the palace of the last four Inca rulers from 1536 to 1572, and Yurac Rumi, the impressive sacred white stone of the Incas. Huancacalle can be reached from Quillabamba daily by truck and bus, 4-7 hrs. There is a small hotel at Huancacalle, or villagers will accept travellers in their very basic homes (take sleeping bag). Vicente Macias has a 3 room *hostal* (no light or water, gets very busy on market days), and is also a guide for Vitcos, Ñustahispanan (a temple with holy waters), the sacred stone and the grave of Túpac Amaru. The Cobo family permits travellers to put up their tents on their property; Juvenal Cobo is a good guide and can supply mules for the trek to Vilcabamba Vieja (see below). Allow plenty of time for hiking to, and visiting Vitcos. It takes 1 hr to walk from Huacacalle to Vitcos, 45 mins Vitcos-Yurac Rumi, 45 mins Yurac Rumi-Huacacalle. Horses can be hired if you wish.

The road from Chaullay continues to **Vilcabamba La Nueva**. You can also hike from Huancacalle; a 3-hr walk through beautiful countryside with Inca ruins dotted around. There is a missionary building run by Italians, with electricity and running water, where you may be able to spend the night.

VILCABAMBA VIEJA

Travellers with ample time can hike from Huancacalle to **Espíritu Pampa**, the site of the **Vilcabamba Vieja** ruins, a vast pre-Inca ruin with a neo-Inca overlay set in deep jungle at 1,000m.

The site is reached on foot or horseback from Pampaconas. From Chaullay, take a truck to Yupanca, Lucma or Pucyura: there rent horses or mules and travel through breathtaking countryside to Espíritu Pampa.

To visit this area you must register with the police in Pucyura. You are advised to seek full information before travelling. Distances are considerable – it is at least 100 km from Chaullay to Espíritu Pampa – the going is difficult and maps appear to be very poor. Essential reading, *Sixpac Manco*, by Vincent R Lee, available in Cusco with accurate maps of all the archaeological sites in this area, and describes 2 expeditions into the region by the author and his party in 1982 and 1984, following in the footsteps of Gene Savoy, who first identified the site in the 1960s. His book, *Antisuyo*, which describes his expeditions here and elsewhere in Peru, is also recommended reading.

Allow 5-8 days if going on foot. The best time of year is May-Oct. During the wet season it really does rain, so be prepared to get very wet and very muddy. Insect repellent is essential. Also take pain-killers and other basic medicines.

Guides for Vilcabamba Vieja: Vidal Albertes, contact in Huancacalle; Paulo Quispe Cusi in Yupanca; and Oswaldo Saca in Espíritu Pampa. Another local guide in Pucyura is Gilberto Quintanilla. Adriel Garay at *White River Tours*, Plateros, Cusco, or C Bayoneta 739, Cusco, T 234575.

The Central Highlands

T HE CENTRAL AN-DES are remote mountain areas with small, typical villages. The vegetation is low, but most valleys are cultivated. Roads, all dirt, are in poor condition, sometimes impassable in the rainy season; the countryside is beautiful with spectacular views and the people are friendly. The road into the central Andes has been improved and is paved throughout, offering fine views. Huancayo lies in a valley which produces many crafts; the festivals are very popular and not to be missed.

Because of heavy terrorist disruption in the 1980s and early 1990s, large parts of the central highlands are only just opening up to tourism once more. People in these parts are relieved to see tourists return to their towns and cities and treat them with great friendship and hospitality. Knowledge of Spanish is essential, as is informing yourself regularly of the current political situation.

LIMA TO HUANCAYO

On the Central Railway passenger trains have not run since 1991. All passenger traffic now goes by road until there is sufficient demand for the service to be restored. See under La Oroya, **Roads and Buses**, for transport details. The Central Highway between Lima and Huancayo more or less parallels the course of the railway.

CHOSICA

Chosica (*Pop* 31,200; *Alt* 860m) is the real starting place for the mountains, 40 km from Lima. It is a popular winter resort because it is above the cloudbank covering Lima in winter. Beyond the town looms a precipitous range of hills almost overhanging the streets.

● **Accommodation** There are four basic *hostales*, two are off the main road nr the market, and the other two up the hill on the left. All have water problems and are in **E** range. The best is *Residencial Chosica*, a big old building on the pedestrian street perpendicular to 28 de Julio, rec.

● **Transport** Colectivos for Chosica leave from the first block of Montevideo (around the corner from Ormeño), when full, between 0600 and 2100, US$0.60.

MARCAHUASI

40 km beyond Chosica, up the picturesque Santa Eulalia valley, is **Marcahuasi**, a table mountain about 3 km by 3 km at 4,200m, near the village of **San Pedro de Casta**. The *meseta* was investigated by the late Daniel Ruzo. There are 3 lakes, a 40m high 'monumento a la humanidad', and other mysterious lines, gigantic figures, sculptures, astrological signs and megaliths which display non-American symbolism. Ruzo describes this pre-Incaic culture in his book, *La Culture Masma*, Extrait de l'Ethnographie, Paris, 1956. Others say that the formations are not man-made, but the result of wind erosion. The trail starts behind the village of San Pedro, and bends to the left. It's about 2 hrs to the *meseta*; guides cost about US$3 a day, and are advisable in misty weather.

● **Accommodation & transport** The bus to San Pedro de Casta leaves Chosica from Parque

Echerique, opp the market, daily except Sun, at about 0800 (when full), 3 hrs, US$2. The road is in a reasonable condition until the Callahuanca hydroelectric station. The only accommodation in San Pedro is in a cold shelter, for less than US$1. Take all necessary camping equipment and buy food in Chosica as there is nothing beyond that point. Tours can be arranged with travel agencies in Lima.

CHOSICA TO LA OROYA

For a while, beyond Chosica, each successive valley looks greener and lusher, with a greater variety of trees and flowers.

San Bartolomé, Km 57, at 1,513m, is the terminus of the only passenger train service currently running from Lima on Sun, in the dry season only.

Matucana, Km 84, at 2,390m, is set in wild scenery, where there are beautiful walks. The road continues to climb, passing **San Mateo** (Km 107, 3,215m), where the San Mateo mineral water originates. Beyond San Mateo is **Infiernillo** (Little Hell) Canyon, at Km 100. Car excursions can be made from Lima. (**Accommodation**: **F** *Ritz*, fair; and *Grau*, cheap.)

Between Río Blanco and **Chicla** (Km 127, 3,733m), Inca contour-terraces can be seen quite clearly. After climbing up from **Casapalca** (Km 139, 4,154m), there are glorious views of the highest peaks, and more mines, at the foot of a deep gorge. The road ascends to the Ticlio Pass, before the descent to **Morococha** and **La Oroya**. A large metal flag of Peru can be seen at the top of Mt Meiggs, not by any means the highest in the area, but through it runs Galera Tunnel, 1,175m long, in which the Central Railway reaches its greatest altitude, 4,782m. **Ticlio**, at Km 157, is the highest passenger station in the world, at 4,758m. It lies at the mouth of the tunnel, on one side of a crater in which lies a dark, still lake. There are still higher points on the railway on the branch of the line that goes through Morococha – 4,818m at La Cima, and 4,829m on a siding. At Morococha is the Centromín golf course, which welcomes playing visitors. It stands at 4,400m and disputes the title of the world's highest with Mallasilla, near La Paz, in Bolivia.

LA OROYA

The main smelting centre for the region's mining industry is full of vitality. It stands at the fork of the Yauli and Mantaro rivers, 187 km from Lima by a road (*Pop* 36,000; *Alt* 3,755m). (For places to the E and N of La Oroya, see page 1378 and 1380 respectively.)

● **Accommodation F** *Hostal Regional*, Lima 112, T 391017, with bath, basic, hot water in the morning; **F** *Hostal Inti*, Arequipa 117, T 391098, shared bath, hot water; **F** *Hostal Chavín*, Tarma 281, shared bath, good, cheap restaurant.

● **Places to eat** *La Caracocha*, Lima 168, cheap, good menú; *Punta Arenas*, Zeballos 323, good seafood, chifa; *El Tambo*, 2 km outside town on the road to Lima, good trout and frogs, rec as the best restaurant. There are lots of *pollerías* in front of the train station in C Lima.

● **Transport** To Lima, 4½ hrs, US$5.20; comité 3 hrs, US$7.85. To Jauja, 80 km, 1½ hrs, US$1; and on to Huancayo, a further 44 km, 1 hr, US$1. To Tarma, 1½ hrs, US$1.35. To Cerro de Pasco, 131 km, 3 hrs, US$2.20. To Huánuco, 236 km, 6 hrs, US$4.35; on to Tingo María, 118 km, 3-4 hrs, US$1.75, and on to Pucallpa, 284 km, 7-9 hrs, US$7.85. Buses leave from Zeballos, adjacent to the train station. Colectivos also run on all routes (see under Lima).

ROUTES   At La Oroya, the central highway divides: S, following the valley of the polluted Río Mantaro, to Huancayo, and on to Huancavelica or Ayacucho; N to Cerro de Pasco and on to Huánuco, Tingo María and Pucallpa. 25 km N along this road is the fork E for Tarma and La Merced. The road is paved from Lima to Huancayo, but all the other roads are in poor condition, especially when wet.

JAUJA

80 km SE of La Oroya is the old town of **Jauja** (*Alt* 3,330m), Pizarro's provisional capital until the founding of Lima. It has a very colourful Wed and Sun market. Jauja is a friendly, unspoilt town, in the middle of a good area for walking. There is an **archaeological museum**, which is recommended for the Huari culture. A modernized church retains 3 fine 17th-century altars. The **Cristo Pobre** church is claimed to have been modelled after Notre Dame and is something of a curiosity. On a hill above Jauja there is a fine line of Inca storehouses, and on hills nearby the ruins of hundreds of circular stone

buildings from the Huanca culture (John Hemming). There are also ruins near the **Paca lake** 3½ km away (mototaxi US$0.90 for 2, combi from Jr Tarma US$0.45).

18 km to the S, on the road to Huancayo, is **Concepción** (*Alt* 3,251m), with a market on Sun as well as a colourful bullfight later in the day during the season. From Concepción a branch road (6 km) leads to the **Convent of Santa Rosa de Ocopa**, a Franciscan monastery set in beautiful surroundings. It was established in 1725 for training missionaries for the jungle. It contains a fine library with over 20,000 volumes and a biological museum with animals and insects from the jungle. Open 0900-1200 and 1500-1800, and closed Tues.

- **Accommodation** *E Cabezon's Hostal*, Ayacucho 1027, T 362206, with bath, hot water, best; *E* **Ganso de Oro**, R Palma 249, T 362165, shared bath, hot water, good restaurant; *E Hostal Los Algarrobes*, Huancayo 264, T 362633, shared bath, hot water in morning; *E Hostal Francisco Pizarro*, Bolognesi 334, opp the market, T 362082, shared bath, hot water.

- **Places to eat** *Marychris*, Jr Bolívar 1166, T 362386, lunch only, excellent; *Hatun Xauxa*, Jr Ricardo Palma 165, good, cheap food and hot rums; *Centro Naturista*, Huarancayo 138, fruit salad, yoghurt, granola, etc; *Fuente de Soda "Rossy's"*, Jr Bolognesi 561, great cakes, OK pizza and snacks.

- **Banks & money changers** Dollar Exchange **Huancayo**, on Jr Huarancayo, gives a much better rate than Banco de Crédito (no TCs).

- **Post & telecommunications** Correo Cen-tral: Jr Bolívar. **Telefónica**: at Bolognesi 546, T (064) 362020, T/F 361111; also at Ricardo Palma, opp *Hotel Ganso de Oro*, T/F 362395, better service and prices.

- **Transport Buses** To Lima, direct with Mcal Cáceres, from Plaza de Armas, daily 1100 and 2230, US$5.35-6.65, service from Huancayo, highly rec; also with Sudamericano, Plaza de Armas, and Costa Sierra, R Palma 145, rec. To Cerro de Pasco, with Oriental (28 de Julio 156) and Turismo Central (28 de Julio 150), 5 hrs, US$3.55. Oriental and Turismo Central also go to Huánuco, 7 hrs, US$5.35; Tingo María, 12 hrs, US$6.65; and Pucallpa, 24 hrs, US$12. To Tarma, US$2.25, hourly with ET San Juan from Jr Tarma; continues to Chanchamayo, US$4.50. To Satipo, with Turismo Central, 12 hrs, US$6.25.

ROUTES The road to Satipo branches off near the Convento de Santa Rosa de Ocopa. The scenery is spectacular, with snow-capped mountains in the Paso de la Tortuga, followed by a rapid drop to the Caja de Silva in Satipo (see page 1379).

HUANCAYO

The city (*Pop* 359,000; *Alt* 3,271m; *Phone code* 064) is in the beautiful Mantaro Valley. It is the capital of Junín Department and the main commercial centre for inland Peru. All the villages in the valley produce their own original crafts and celebrate festivals the year round. At the important festivals in Huancayo, people flock in from far and wide with an incredible range of food, crafts, dancing and music. The Sun market gives a little taste of this every week (it gets going after 0900), but it is better to go to the villages for local handicrafts. Jr Huancavelica, 3 km long and 4 stalls wide, still sells typical clothes, fruit, vegetables, hardware, handi-crafts and, especially, traditional medicines and goods for witchcraft. There is also an impressive daily market behind the railway station.

Museums

The museum at the Salesian school has over 5,000 pieces, including a large collec-tion of jungle birds, animals and butter-flies, insects, reptiles and fossils. *Wali Wasi* ('sacred house' in Quechua), Hualahoyo 2174, run by mystic, Pedro Marticorena Oroña Laya, has paintings of Andean vi-sions, masks made of cow dung and roots turned into gods and animals; also Quechua lessons and cheap accommoda-tion. Take a *micro* marked 'Umuto' and get off 1 block before the cemetery.

Excursions

The whole Mantaro valley is rich in culture. On the outskirts of town is **Torre-Torre**, impressive, eroded sandstone towers on the hillside. Take a bus to Cerrito de la Libertad and walk up. Not far from here is a large park with a depressing zoo, but with a good swimming pool; entry US$0.25.

West of the Mantaro river, 8 km from Huancayo, at **Sapallanga**, the *fiesta* of the Virgen de Cocharcas on 8 Sept is famous. **Viques** (19 km) is known for the production of belts and blankets. **Huayucachi** (7 km) organizes festivals with dancing and impressive costumes in Jan and Feb and also makes embroidery. The ruins of **Warivilca** (15 km) are near **Huari**, with the remains of a pre-Inca temple of the Huanca tribe. Museum in the plaza, with deformed skulls, and modelled and painted pottery of successive Huanca and Inca occupations of the shrine. Ruins open 1000-1200, 1500-1700 (museum am only), US$0.15 admission. Take a *micro* for Chilca from Calle Real. Between Pilcomayo and Huayo (15 km) is the **Geophysical Institute of Huayo**, on the 'Magnetic Equator' – $12\frac{1}{2}°$ S of the geographical equator (best to visit in the morning, or when the sun is shining).

Details of other villages and their festivals, archaeological and natural sites will be found in *The Peru Handbook*, or from local sources.

East of the Mantaro river The villages of **Cochas Chico** and **Cochas Grande**, 11 km away, are where the famous *mate burilado*, or gourd carving, is done. You can buy them cheaply direct from the manufacturers, but ask around. Beautiful views of the Valle de Mantaro and Huancayo. *Micros* leave from esq Amazonas y Giráldez, US$0.25.

Hualahoyo (11 km) has a little chapel with 21 colonial canvases. **San Agustín de Cajas** (8 km) makes fine hats, and **San Pedro** (10 km) makes wooden chairs; **Hualhuas** (12 km) fine alpaca weavings.

The village of **San Jerónimo** is renowned for the making of silver filigree jeweller; Wed market. Fiesta in August. There are ruins 2-3 hrs' walk above San Jerónimo, but seek advice before hiking to them.

Local festivals

There are so many festivals in the Mantaro Valley that it is impossible to list them all. Practically every day of the year there is a celebration of some sort in one of the villages. We offer a selection. **Jan**: 1-6, New Year celebrations; 20, *San Sebastián y San Fabián*. **Feb**: there are carnival celebrations for the whole month, with highlights on 2, *Virgen de la Candelaria*, and 17-19 *Concurso de Car-*

naval. **Mar-April**: *Semana Santa*, with impressive Good Friday processions. **May**: *Fiesta de las Cruces* throughout the whole month. **June**: 15 *Virgen de las Mercedes*; 24, *San Juan Bautista*; 29, *Fiesta Patronal*. **July**: 16, *Virgen del Carmen*; 24-25, *Santiago*. **Aug**: 4, *San Juan de Dios*; 16, *San Roque*; 30, *Santa Rosa de Lima*. **Sept**: 8, *Virgen de Cocharcas*; 15, *Virgen de la Natividad*; 23-24, *Virgen de las Mercedes*; 29, *San Miguel Arcángel*. **Oct**: 4, *San Francisco de Asís*; 18, *San Lucas*. **Nov**: 1, *Día de Todos los Santos*. **Dec**: 3-13, *Virgen de Guadalupe*; 8, *Inmaculada Concepción*; 25, *Navidad* (Christmas).

Local information

● **Accommodation**

NB Prices may be raised in Holy Week. Note that the Plaza de Armas is called Plaza Constitución.

B *Huancayo Plaza*, Ancash 729, T 231072, F 235211, ex Turistas, old building, some rooms small, quiet, good meals for US$3.50; **B** *Presidente*, C Real 1138, T 231736, F 231275, helpful, safe, breakfast only, rec.

C *Hostal Alpaca*, Giráldez 494, T 223136, hot water, carpets, snack bar downstairs; **C** *Santa Felicita*, Plaza Constitución, T 235476, F 235285, hot water, good.

D *El Dorado*, Piura 428, T 223947, hot water, some rooms with TV in **C** category; **D** *Hostal La Breña*, Arequipa 510, T 223490, hot water all day, new, carpets; **D** *Hostal Plaza*, Ancash 171, T 210509, hot water, ask for rooms at front; **D** *Percy's*, Real 1399, T 231208, shared bath, hot water in morning, basic; **D** *Roger*, Ancash 460, T 233488, hot water, basic.

E pp *Casa Alojamiento de Aldo y Soledad Bonilla*, Huánuco 332, ½ block from Mcal Cáceres bus station, T 232103 (Lima 463-1141), inc breakfast, **D** pp full board, beautiful colonial house, hot water all day, heaters, owners speak English, laundry, secure, relaxing, nice courtyard, can arrange tours, book ahead to gaurantee a reservation, highly rec; **E** *Confort*, Ancash 231, 1 block from the main Plaza, T 233601, all rooms with bath, those with hot water are nicer, but more expensive, car parking US$1; **E** *Hogar Metodista*, Abancay 200, T 232524, hot water, safe, parking; **E** *Hostal Palace*, Ancash 1127, T 238501, with bath, hot water, restaurant; **E** *Pussy*, Giráldez 359, T 231565, **F** without bath, hot water all day, safe, luggage stored, comfortable beds.

F pp *Hostal Baldeón*, Amazonas 543, T 231634, kitchen and laundry facilities, hot shower; **F** pp *La Casa de Mi Abuela*, Av Giráldez, hot shower, inc breakfast, good value, laundry facilities, meals available, run by Lucho Hurtado's mother (see page 1370); **F pp** *Peru Andino Lodging & Excursions*, Pasaje San Antonio 113-115, 3 blocks from Av Centenario, 10-15 mins' walk from the centre, T 223956, inc breakfast, hot showers, several rooms with private bath, safe area, cosy atmosphere, run by Sra Juana, daughter speaks some English, owner runs trekking and mountain bike tours, cooking and laundry facilities, rec.

The following *hostales* are all **F** with shared bath and cold water, unless stated otherwise: *Central*, Loreto 452, T 211948, large place, basic, hot water in the morning; *Hostal San Martín*, Ferrocarril 362, charming place, nr the rail station; *Los Angeles*, Real 245, T 231753, hot water, basic, restaurant; *Prince*, Calixto 578, T 232331, large and basic, hot water in the morning; *Torre-Torre*, Real 873, T 231118, shared bath, hot water. Luis Hurtado has 2 rooms, **G** inc breakfast, with hot water, washing and cooking facilities at La Cabaña restaurant (see below).

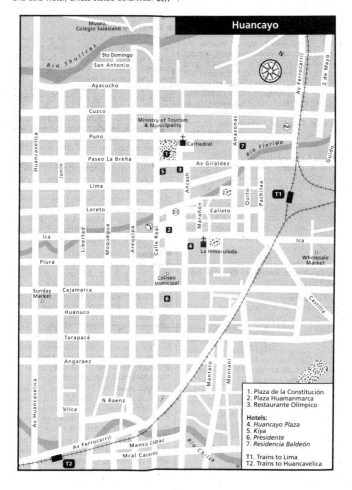

Huancayo

Museo, Colegio Salesiano

Río Shullcas

Sto Domingo
San Antonio

Ayacucho

Cuzco

Ministry of Tourism & Municipality

Puno

Cathedral

Paseo La Breña

Av Giráldez

Amazonas

Río Florido

Lima

Ancash

Pachitea

Quito

Loreto

Marañón

Calixto

Ica

Libertad

Moquegua

Arequipa

Calle Real

Piura

La Inmaculada

Ica

Wholesale Market

Sunday Market

Cajamarca

Coliseo Municipal

Huánuco

Tarapacá

Castilla

Angaraez

Mantaro

Montani

Av Huancavelica

N Raenz

Vilca

Av Ferrocarril

Manco Capac

Mcal Cáceres

Río Chilca

T2

Av Ferrocarril

2 de Mayo

Guido

Pol

T1

Huancavelica
Junín

1. Plaza de la Constitución
2. Plaza Huamanmarca
3. Restaurante Olímpico

Hotels:
4. *Huancayo Plaza*
5. *Kiya*
6. *Presidente*
7. *Residencia Baldeón*

T1. Trains to Lima
T2. Trains to Huancavelica

● **Places to eat**

Better class, more expensive restaurants, serving typical dishes for about US$4-5, plus 18% tax, drinks can be expensive: *El Inca*, Puno 530, good salads; *Inti Palacio*, Lima 354; *Olímpico*, Av Giráldez 199, rec as the best in town, but not cheap.

Recommended cheaper places for typical food, about US$2-3 a dish, or with a fixed price *menú*, inc: *Lalo's*, Giráldez 365; *El Pino*, Real 539; *Pinkys*, Giráldez 147; *Los Tres Sillares*, Lima 170, serves typical Arequipeña food; *Chifa El Centro*, Giráldez 238, Chinese, good service; *La Cabaña*, Av Giraldez 652, outstanding pizzas, ice-cream, *calentitos*, and other dishes, great atmosphere, repeatedly rec (owned by Beverly Stuart and Lucho Hurtado – see below); *Marco Antonio*, Av Giráldez 255, cheap, excellent set lunch, friendly; *Los Maduros*, Puno 599, nr main plaza, good pizzas; *Nuevo Horizonte*, Jr Ica 578, excellent set meal for only US$1. There is an excellent vegetarian restaurant on Arequipa 700 block, between Loreto and Ica. Lots of cheap restaurants along Av Giráldez serving set *menú*. *Chez Viena*, Puno 125, good cakes. *Café Billar*, Paseo de Breña 133, open 0900-2400, serves beer and snacks, pool tables. Breakfast is served in Mercado Modelo from 0700.

● **Banks & money changers**

Banco de Crédito, Real 1039, changes TCs with no commission, cash advance on Visa. **Western Union Money Transfer**, Ancash 540, Of 302, T 224816/235655, open Fri-Fri 0900-1300 and 1600-2000; Sat 0900-1300. There are several *casas de cambio* on the 4th and 5th blocks of Real; street changers hang out there as well. Also travel agencies and banks will change dollars.

● **Cultural centres**

Peruvian-North American Cultural Institute: Jr Guido 740.

● **Entertainment**

Discotheques: *A1A*, Bolognesi 299. Most discos open around 2000 and close at 0200. Some charge an entrance fee of US$3-4.

Peñas: all the *peñas* have folklore shows with dancing, open normally Fri, Sat and Sun from 1300 to 2200. Entrance fee is about US$2 pp. *Taki Wasi*, Huancavelica y 13 de Noviembre; *Ollantaytambo*, Puno, block 2. *Restaurante La Cabaña*, see above, has folk music at weekends.

● **Security**

Be careful in the market and at the train and bus stations. You should travel only by day, especially in the coca growing areas in the central jungle beyond Huancayo.

● **Shopping**

Crafts: all crafts are made outside Huancayo in the many villages of the Mantaro Valley, or in Huancavelica. The villages are worth a visit to learn how the items are made. *Casa de Artesano*, on the corner of Real and Paseo La Breña, at Plaza Constitución, has a wide selection of good quality crafts. There is a large cooperative, *Kamaq Maki*, Santa Isabel 1856, which exports alpaca goods, open Mon-Fri 0900-1400. It is very helpful and will be happy to take you to meet the manufacturers of the goods. The workshop has a small shop. Contact Arturo Durán, T 231206/233183. *Artesanía Sumaq Ruray*, Jr Brasilia 132, San Carlos 5th block, T 237018, produces fine weaving, not cheap.

● **Tourist offices**

Ministry of Tourism, in the *Casa de Artesano* (see above), has information about the area, helpful, open 0730-1330 Mon-Fri. **Lucho (Luis) Hurtado**, who is from Huancayo and speaks good English, and his wife, Beverly Stuart, from New Zealand, own *Pizzería La Cabaña* (see above); you are always welcome for a slice of pizza and a side order of information. They organize Spanish courses for beginners for US$150/week, inc accommodation with local families, rec, weaving, playing the pan flute, Peruvian cooking and lots of other things. They also have maps and a book exchange. Lucho is an excellent private guide who arranges adventurous, cultural trips in the mountains or jungle, giving a personal touch, and hires bikes for tours of rural communities. He has been highly and repeatedly rec as a guide. Contact him in Huancayo, or through the South American Explorers Club in Lima. **Turismo Huancayo**, C Real 517 Of 6, T 233351, organizes local tours, rec.

● **Transport**

Trains There are two unconnected railway stations. The Central station serves Lima, via La Oroya, 298 km; no passenger service.

From the small station in Chilca suburb (15 mins by taxi, US$1), trains run to **Huancavelica**, 142 km, narrow gauge 3 ft. There are 2 trains: the *autovagón (expreso)* at 0630 Mon-Sat, at 1400 on Sun; US$2.20 normal, US$3.50 buffet class. 4½ hrs, spectacular with fine views, passing through typical mountain villages. Meals, drinks and snacks are served on the train, and at the village stations vendors sell food and crafts. The local train leaves at 1230 Mon-Sat, and takes 6½ hrs; US$1.75 2nd class, US$2 1st class and US$3.50 buffet class. You can buy tickets 1 day in advance, or 1 hr before departure. Services can be suspended in the rainy season.

Road To Lima, 6-7 hrs on a good paved road, US$9-10. Travelling by day is rec for the fantastic views and, of course, for safety. If you must travel by night, take warm clothing. Recommended companies: Mcal Cáceres, Jr Huánuco 350, T 231232; Cruz del Sur, Ayacucho 287; Etucsa, Puno 220, several a day (*bus cama*, US$11). Many other companies ply this route, many are cheaper but also less comfortable and less safe. Small buses for Lima congregate 15 blocks N of Plaza Constitución on C Real; there is much competition for passengers. Comités 12 and 22, both on C Loreto, and Comité 30, C Giráldez, run to Lima in 6 hrs, when the car is full, which can mean waiting all day; US$12 pp.

To **Ayacucho**, 319 km, 11 hrs, US$8. Empresa Molina, C Angaraes 287, several daily from 0700-2100, and TransFano at 1830, both rec; also Antezana, Arequipa 1301, at 2100. The road has improved but is still very difficult in the wet. Take warm clothing. The military seem to have established control over this route after years of terrorist disruption. Check the situation in advance, though, and travel by day. After Izcuchaca, on the railway to Huancavelica, there is a good road to the Kichuas hydroelectric scheme, but thereafter it is narrow with hair-raising bends and spectacular bridges. The scenery is staggering, but sit on the right or you'll have 11 hrs of staring at a solid rock wall. From Huanta the road descends into Ayacucho.

To **Huancavelica**, 147 km, 5 hrs, US$3, several buses a day; Empresa Hidalgo, Loreto 350, San Pablo, Ancash 1248, at 1400. The road is in poor condition but being improved, and takes much longer in the wet. The scenery is spectacular. Most travellers use the train.

To **Cerro de Pasco**, 255 km, 5-6 hrs, US$3-4. There is quite a good paved road to La Oroya, but a dirt road from there to Cerro de Pasco. Transporte Salazar, Giráldez 245, Sun and Mon at 2100. Oriental, Ferrocarril 146, 3 a week; on to Huánuco, 105 km, US$2; Tingo María, 118 km, 5 hrs; and Pucallpa, 11 hrs. Comité 12 does this route for US$15 pp when full.

To **Satipo**, 229 km, 12 hrs, on a very difficult road, which is impossible in the wet; San Juan, Quito 136, rec. The bus goes via Jauja, Tarma and La Merced; 5 hrs, US$4.50. San Juan and Los Canarios (Puno 725) go to Oxapampa, 12 hrs. To **Cañete**, 289 km, 10 hrs, US$4, some trucks and a few buses travel this route. It is a poor road, with beautiful mountain landscapes before dropping to the valley of Cañete. To **Jauja**, 44 km, 1 hr; colectivos leave from Huamaumarca y Amazonas; ones via San Jerónimo and Concepción have 'Izquierda' on the front. Most buses to the Mantaro Valley leave from several places around the market area. Buses to Hualhuas, Cajas and Huamancaca leave from block 3 of Pachitea. Buses to Cochas leave from Amazonas y Giráldez.

Between Huancayo and Huancavelica, **Izcuchaca** is the site of a bridge over the Río Mantaro. The name in Quechua means 'stone bridge'. The bridge was partly rebuilt in the 18th century. On the edge of town is a fascinating pottery workshop whose machinery is driven by a water turbine (small shop).

A nice hike is to the chapel on a hill overlooking the valley; 1-1½ hrs each way.

● **Accommodation & places to eat** There are 2 hotels: one is on the plaza, **G**, with no bathroom, you have to use the public bath by the river; the other is just off the plaza, a yellow 3-storey house, **G**, no shower, toilet suitable for men only, chamber pot supplied, only blankets on bed, cold. *Restaurant El Parque* on plaza, opens 0700, delicious food.

● **Transport** The 0630 train from Huancavelica arrives at 0800, then continues to Huancayo; US$1.15. The train tends to be very crowded. Sit on the left for the best views. The train from Huancayo passes at around 1700. Daily colectivo to Ayacucho at 1000-1100, 8 hrs.

ROUTES There is an alternative route to Ayacucho, little used by buses, but which involves not so much climbing for cyclists. Cross the pass into the Mantaro valley on a road to **Quichuas**, which has no hotel, but there is a basic place, 3 km away by a dam. Then on to **Anco**, rebuilding after a flood in 1977, where there is a small, basic lodging with running water, and to **Mayocc** (lodging). At Mayocc a bridge is being repaired. From Mayocc go to **Huanta**, crossing a bridge after 10 km, 20 km from Huanta, then it's a paved road to Ayacucho.

HUANCAVELICA

Capital of its Department, a friendly and attractive town (*Pop* 37,500; *Alt* 3,680m), surrounded by huge, rocky mountains. It was founded in the 16th century by the Spanish to exploit rich deposits of mercury and silver. It is predominantly an Indigenous town, and people still wear traditional costume. There are beautiful mountain walks in the neighbourhood.

Places of interest

The cathedral, located on the Plaza de Armas, has an altar considered to be one of the finest examples of colonial art in Peru. Also very impressive are the five other churches in town. The church of San Francisco, for example, has no less than

11 altars. Sadly, though, most of the churches are closed to visitors.

Bisecting the town is the Río Huancavelica. S of the river is the main commercial centre. North of the river, on the hillside, are the thermal baths; US$0.15 for private rooms, water not very hot, US$0.10 for the hot public pool, also hot showers, take a lock for the doors, open 0600-1500. There is a colourful daily market. Most handicrafts are transported directly to Lima, but you can still visit craftsmen in neighbouring villages. There is a daily food market at Muñoz or Barranca. The Potaqchiz hill, just outside the town, gives a fine view, about 1 hr walk up from San Cristóbal.

Local festivals

The whole area is rich in culture. In Sept there is a tourist week with a huge crafts market, music and dancing. Typical festivals: **6 Jan**: Niño Occe. **12 Jan**: Fiesta de Negritos; carnival in **Feb**; Palm Sunday procession; Semana Santa. **June**: Fiesta de Torre-Torre. **Nov**: Todos los Santos. **25 Dec**: Los Galos.

Local information

NB Always carry your documentation, travel by day and find out about latest conditions in the Department of Huancavelica before travelling.

● **Accommodation**

C *Presidente*, Plaza de Armas, T 952760, ex Tourist Hotel, cheaper without bath, lovely colonial building, overpriced.

E *Mercurio*, Jr Torre Tagle 455, T 952773, unfriendly, basic, cold water.

F *Camacho*, Jr Carabaya 481, best of the cheap hotels, hot shower in the morning only, well maintained, excellent value; **F** *Hostal Tahuantinsuyo*, Carabaya 399, T 952968, with bath, hot water in mornings, dirty and dingy; **F** *Santo Domingo*, Av Barranca 366, T 953086; and **F** *Savoy*, Av Muñoz 294, both very basic, shared bath, cold water; **F** *Virrey*, Av Barranca 317, basic, cold water.

● **Places to eat**

There are lots of cheap, basic restaurants on C Muñoz and Jr Virrey Toledo. All serve typical food, mostly with set *menú*, US$1.50. Better are: *Paquirri*, Jr Arequipa 137, good, expensive; *Mochica Sachún*, Av Virrey Toledo 303, great *menú* US$1.50, otherwise very expensive, popular; *Pollería Joy*, Toledo y Arequipa, good for chicken; *La Casona*, Jr Virrey Toledo 230, cheap

and good *menú*, also a *peña*; *Las Magnolias*, Manuel Muñoz 1 block from the Plaza, OK.

● **Banks & money changers**

Banco de Crédito, Virrey Toledo 300 block.

● **Post & telecommunications**

Post Office: on Toledo, 1 block from the Plaza de Armas.

Telephones: Carabaya y Virrey Toledo.

● **Tourist offices**

Ministerio de Industria y Comercio, Turismo y Artesanías, Jr Nicolás de Piérola 180, open Mon-Fri 0730-1400, very helpful. **Instituto Nacional de la Cultura**, Plaza San Juan de Dios, open Mon-Sat 1000-1300, 1500-1900, director Alfonso Zuasnabar, a good source of information on festivals, archaeological sites, history, etc. Gives courses on music and dancing, and lectures some evenings. There is also an interesting but small archaeology and anthropology museum.

● **Transport**

Trains See under Huancayo; the *autovagón/expreso* leaves for Huancayo daily at 0630, the local train at 1230, Mon-Sat.

Road All bus companies have their offices on and leave from C Muñoz. To **Huancayo**, 147 km, 5 hrs, US$3.50, it's a rough road but is being improved, several buses a day, eg Expreso Huancavelica and Empresa Hidalgo. To **Lima** there are two routes: one is via Huancayo, 445 km, 13 hrs minimum, US$8. Most buses to Huancayo go on to Lima, there are several a day. The other route is via **Pisco**, 269 km, 12 hrs, US$9. Only one bus a day at 0600, with Oropesa, buy your ticket 1 day in advance. Some trucks also travel this route. The road is in very poor condition, but the views are spectacular and worth the effort. Be prepared for sub-zero temperatures in the early morning as the bus passes snowfields, then for temperatures of 25-30°C as the bus descends to the coast in the afternoon.

Getting to **Ayacucho** (247 km) is a problem, as there are no buses. Either take the train to Izcuchaca, stay the night and take the colectivo (see above), or take the morning train to La Mejorada where you can catch the 1000 Expreso Molino bus from Huancayo to Ayacucho. Alternatively take a bus to Santa Inés, then a truck to Rumichaca, the junction where buses and trucks on the Lima-Ayacucho route pass. Buses go through Rumichaca at 0300-0400 only, but there are many trucks and police at the checkpoint who may help with lifts. Take an Oropesa bus from Huancavelica to Santa Inés at 0600, which allows plenty of time for a truck to Rumichaca and then another to Ayacucho. Rumichaca-Ayacucho is 7 hrs by truck and 4 hrs by bus. The road is in an appalling condition. The journey is a cold one but spectacular as it is the highest continuous road in the world, rarely dropping below 4,000m for 150 km.

HUANCAVELICA-AYACUCHO VIA SANTA INES

Out of Huancavelica the road climbs steeply with switchbacks between herds of llamas and alpacas grazing on rocky perches. Around Pucapampa (Km 43) is one of the highest habitable *altiplanos* (4,500m), where the rare and highly prized ash-grey alpaca can be seen. **Santa Inés**, 78 km, has one very friendly restaurant where you can sleep and several others. Nearby are two lakes (Laguna Choclacocha) which can be visited in 2½ hrs. 50 km beyond Santa Inés at the Abra de Apacheta (4,750m), 98 km from Ayacucho, the rocks are all colours of the rainbow, and running through this fabulous scenery is a violet river. These incredible colours are all caused by oxides. 11 km later is the Paso Chonta and the turnoff to Huachocolpa. By taking the turnoff and continuing for 3 km you'll reach the highest drivable pass in the world, at 5,059m.

AYACUCHO

Ayacucho (*Pop* 101,600; *Alt* 2,740m; *Phone code* 064), capital of its Department, was founded on 9 January 1539. On the Pampa de Quinua, on 9 December 1824, the decisive Battle of Ayacucho was fought, bringing Spanish rule in Peru to an end. In the middle of the festivities, the Liberator Simón Bolívar decreed that the city be named Ayacucho, 'City of Blood', instead of its original name, Huamanga.

Following the violence of Shining Path's most active period in the 1980s and early 1990s, peace has returned to this beautiful city, which is now eager to promote tourism.

The city is built round Parque Sucre, the main plaza, with the Cathedral, Municipalidad and Palacio de Gobierno facing on to it. It is famous for its Semana Santa celebrations, its splendid market and its 33 churches. The climate is lovely, with warm, sunny days and pleasant balmy evenings.

Places of interest

For a fascinating insight into Quechua art and culture, a visit to **Barrio Santa Ana** is a must. The district is full of *artesanía* shops, galleries and workshops (eg *Galería Latina*, Plazuela de Santa Ana 605, and *Wari Art Gallery*, Jr Mcal Cáceres 302).

The **Mirador Turístico**, on Cerro Acuchimay, offers fine views over the city. Take a *micro* from the corner of 28 de Julio and Plaza de Armas to Carmen Alto, then walk 2 blocks.

Churches

The **Cathedral**, built in 1612 has superb gold leaf altars; open daily 1730-1845. See also **San Cristóbal**, the first church to be founded in the city; **La Merced**, whose high choir is a good example of the simplicity of the churches of the early period of the Viceroyalty; **La Compañía de Jesús** (1605), with a baroque façade guarded by two 18th century towers (open Sun 1200-1230 and 1730-1800); **San Francisco de Asís** (open daily 1000-1200 and 1500-1700) and **Santa Teresa** (1683, open daily 0600-0700), both with magnificent gold-leafed altars heavily brocaded and carved in the churrigueresque style. **Santa Clara** is renowned for its beautifully delicate coffered ceiling; open Wed-Sun 0630-1600. One of the city's most notable churches is **Santo Domingo** (1548). Its fine façade has triple Roman arches and Byzantine towers. Open daily 0700-0800.

Colonial houses and museums

To the N of Parque Sucre, on the corner of Portal de la Unión and Asamblea, are the **Casonas de los Marqueses de Mozobamba y del Pozo**, also called Velarde-Alvárez. **Casa Jaúregui** is situated opposite the church of La Merced, and **Casa Olano** is in C De la Compañía. On the 5th block of Jr Grau, before San Blas, is the house where Simón Bolívar and José Antonio de Sucre stayed. On the 5th block of 28 de Julio is **Casona Vivanco**, which now houses the **Museo Andrés A Cáceres**, open 0900-1230, 1400-1700, Mon-Sat, US$0.45, displaying prehispanic, colonial, republican and contemporary art.

Museo Histórico Natural, Jr Arequipa 175, in the University (closed 1996). **Museo Arqueológico Hipólito Unanua** is opposite the University Residences, on Av Independencia, at the N end of town, open 0800-1300, 1500-1700, Mon-Fri, 0900-1300 Sat, US$1.30. It has many Huari artefacts.

Excursions

The Inca ruins of **Vilcashuamán** are to the S, beyond Cangallo. John Hemming writes: "There is a 5-tiered, stepped *usnu* platform faced in fine Inca masonry and topped by a monolithic 2-seat throne. The parish church is built in part of the Inca sun temple and rests on stretches of Inca terracing. Vilcashuamán was an impor-

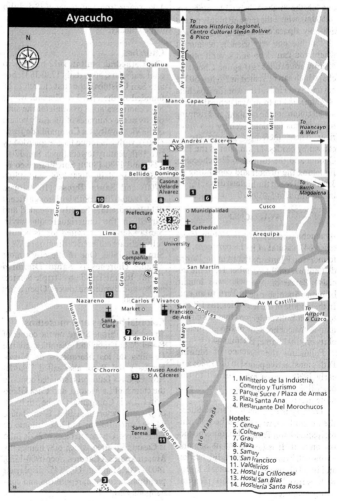

Ayacucho

To Museo Histórico Regional, Centro Cultural Simón Bolívar & Pisco

To Huancayo & Wari

To Barrio Magdalena

To Airport & Cuzco

Quinua
Manco Capac
Av Andrés A Cáceres
Santo Domingo
Casona Velarde Alvarez
Prefectura
Municipalidad
Cathedral
University
La Compañía de Jesús
San Martín
Carlos F Vivanco
Market
San Francisco de Asís
Av M Castilla
Santa Clara
S J de Dios
C Chorro
Museo Andrés A Cáceres
Santa Teresa
Bolognesi
Río Alameda

Libertad · Garcilaso de la Vega · 9 de Diciembre · Asamblea · Tres Mascaras · Los Andes · Miller · Sol · Cusco · Arequipa · Sucre · Callao · Lima · Bellido · Grau · 28 de Julio · Nazareno · Huancasolar · Libertad · 2 de Mayo · Londres

1. Ministerio de la Industria, Comercio y Turismo
2. Parque Sucre / Plaza de Armas
3. Plaza Santa Ana
4. Restaurante Del Morochucos

Hotels:
5. Central
6. Colmena
7. Grau
8. Plaza
9. Samary
10. San Francisco
11. Valdelirios
12. Hostal La Crillonesa
13. Hostal San Blas
14. Hostelería Santa Rosa

tant provincial capital, the crossroads where the road from Cusco to the Pacific met the empire's north-south highway." Tours can be arranged with Travel Agencies in Ayacucho, US$55 pp for 2 people, full day tour, including **Intihuatana** (Inca baths about 1 hr uphill from the village of Vischongo, 1 hr from Vilcashuamán, 5 from Ayacucho); alternatively stay overnight (3 **F** hotels, basic but clean). Market day is Wed.

• **Transport** Buses and colectivos run from Av M Castilla, Tues, Thurs and Sat at 0600, returning Wed, Fri and Sun at 0600, 5-6 hrs, US$4.50.

La Quinua village, 37 km NE of Ayacucho, has a charming cobbled main plaza and many of the buildings have been restored. There is a small market on Sun. Nearby, on the Pampa de Quinua, a 44m-high obelisk commemorates the battle of Ayacucho. There is also a small, poorly displayed museum; US$1.40. The village's handicrafts are recommended, especially ceramics. Most of the houses have miniature ceramic churches on the roof. San Pedro Ceramics, at the foot of the hill leading to the monument, and Mamerto Sánchez, Jr Sucre, should be visited. *Fiesta de la Virgen de Cocharcas*, 7-8 Sept.

It is a beautiful 18 km walk downhill from La Quinua to Huari, where trucks leave for Ayacucho until about 1700.

A good road going N from Ayacucho leads to **Huari** (see page 1368), dating from the 'Middle Horizon', when the Huari culture spread across most of Peru. This was the first urban walled centre in the Andes. The huge irregular stone walls are up to 12m high and rectangular houses and streets can be made out. The most important activity here was artistic: ceramics, gold, silver, metal and alloys such as bronze, which was used for weapons and for decorative objects.

• **Transport** Buses leave from Ovalo in Barrio Magdalena. There are no specific times, they leave when full from 0700 onwards. Buses go on to La Quinua, US$1, and Huanta, US$1.35 (see below). Trips can be arranged to Huari, La Quinua village and the battlefield; US$16-17 pp for 2 people (see **Travel agents** below).

The Huanta valley is a picturesque region, 48 km NE of Ayacucho. The town of Huanta is 1 hr from Ayacucho, on the road to Huancayo. From Huanta, several lakes can be visited, also the valley of Luricocha, 5 km away, with its warm climate. Huanta celebrates the *Fiesta de las Cruces* during the first week of May. Its Sun market is large and interesting.

24 km from Ayacucho, on the road to Huanta, is the site of perhaps the oldest known culture in South America, 20,000 years old, evidence of which was found in the cave of **Pikimachay**. The remains are now in Lima's museums.

Local festivals

The area is well-known for its festivals throughout the year. Almost every day there is a celebration in one of the surrounding villages. Check with the Ministry of Tourism. *Semana Santa* begins on the Fri before Holy Week. There follows one of the world's finest Holy Week celebrations, with candle-lit nightly processions, floral 'paintings' on the streets, daily fairs (the biggest on Easter Saturday), horse races and contests among peoples from all central Peru. All accommodation is fully booked for months in advance. Many people offer beds in their homes during the week. Look out for notices on the doors, especially on Jr Libertad. *Carnival* in **Feb** is reported as a wild affair. **25 April**: anniversary of the founding of Huamanga province. **4-10 Dec**: *Semana de la Libertad Americana*, to honour the Battle of Ayacucho.

Local information

NB As in all areas previously affected by terrorism, travel only by day and get the latest information before you go.

● **Accommodation**

Ayacucho suffers from water shortages. There is usually no water between 0900 and 1500. Many hotels have their own water tanks.

A3 *Plaza*, 9 de Diciembre 184, T 912202, F 912314, beautiful colonial building but the rooms don't match up to the palatial splendour of the reception, comfortable, TV, some rooms overlook plaza.

B *Valdelirios*, Bolognesi 520, T 913908, F 914014, lovely colonial-style mansion, beautifully-furnished, pickup from airport US$1.30, restaurant, bar, disco at weekends, reserve at least 24 hrs in advance, rec; **B-C** *Yañez*, Mcal Cáceres 1210, T 912464, well furnished rooms, it's a former hospital so the decor is slightly clinical, a bit pricey.

C *Hostelería Santa Rosa*, Jr Lima 166, T/F 912083, lovely colonial courtyard, hot water am and pm, car park, restaurant, rec; **C** *San Francisco*, Jr Callao 290, T 912959, F 914501, inc breakfast, comfortable, nice patio, rec.

D *Colmena*, Jr Cusco 140, T 912146, hot water 0700-0900, small rooms, secure, pleasant courtyard; **D** *Hostal El Mirador*, Jr Bellido 112, T 912338, large rooms, laundry facilities, great view; **D** *Hostal Las Orquídeas*, Jr Arequipa 287, T 914435, intermittent hot water, basic, noisy from disco next door at weekends; **D** *Hostal Plateros*, Jr Lima 206, hot water, comfortable; **D** *Residencial La Crillonesa*, Nazareno 165, T 912350, hot water, laundry facilities, discount for longer stay, great views; **D** *Samary*, Jr Callao 335, T/F 912442, discount for foreigners, safe, hot water in am, rec; **D** *Hostal San Blas*, Jr Chorro 167, T 910552, hot water all day, laundry facilities, nice rooms, cheap meals available, discount for longer stay, Carlos will act as a local tour guide and knows everyone, rec.

E *Central*, Jr Arequipa 188, T 912144, shared bath, large rooms, good value, **F** in low season; **E** *Grau*, Jr San Juan de Dios 192, T 912695, with bath, hot water, laundry facilities, good value; **E** pp *Hostal El Sol*, Av Mcal Castilla 132, T 913069, hot water all day, well-furnished large rooms, rec; **E** *Hostal Luz Imperial*, Jr Libertad 591 (altos), cheaper without bath, hot water in am, basic; **E** *Hostal Wari*, Mcal Cáceres 836, T 913065, shared bath, hot water in am, basic, large rooms; **E** *Magdalena*, Mcal Cáceres 810, T 912910, cheaper without bath, basic but good.

F *Hostal Ayacucho*, Jr Lima 165, T 912759, shared bath, cold water, basic; **F** *Santiago*, Nazareno 177, T 912132, shared bath, hot water in am, OK.

● **Places to eat**

Tradición, San Martín 406, popular, good cheap *menú*; *San Agustín Café Turístico*, Jr Cusco 101, good food and lemon meringue pie, rec for snacks; *La Casona*, Jr Bellido 463, regional specialities, rec; *Del Morochucos*, Jr 9 de Diciembre 205, opp Santo Domingo church, large selection, *parrillada* etc, very popular, live music, colonial-style building; *Portales*, on Plaza, Portal Unión, popular; *Urpicha*, Jr Londres 272, typical food, rec; *La Buena Salud*, Jr Asamblea 206, vegetarian, cheap *menú*; *Pollería Nino*, Jr Garcilaso de la Vega 240, rec for chicken, US$2.25; same owner as *Restaurant Nino*, Jr Salvador Cavero 124, which is rec for local dishes. Also good for chicken is *Tivole*, Jr Bellido 492. *Fuente de Soda La Compañía*, 28 de Julio 151, good for juices, cakes and snacks. Try *mondongo*, a soup made from meat, maize and mint, at the market nr Santa Clara on Jr

Carlos Vivanco; Sra Gallardo has been rec. Those wishing to try *cuy* should do so in Ayacucho as it's a lot cheaper than Cusco.

● **Airline offices**

Aero Continente, Jr 9 de Diciembre 160, T 912816; Faucett, Grau y Lima.

● **Banks & money changers**

Banco de Crédito, 28 de Julio y San Martín, no commission on TCs, cash advance on Visa. Many street changers at Portal Constitución on Plaza, good rate for cash. **Casa de Cambio DMJ**, at Portal Constitución 4, good rates for cash, TCs at 1% commission, open Mon-Sat 0800-1900. To change cash or TCs on a Sun, contact Andrés Harhuay Macoto or Carito Acevedo Vallejo at Portal Constitución, or T 913547.

● **Entertainments**

Bars: *Taberna Liverpool*, Mcal Cáceres 620, good for blues and rock music, owner Edwin is a great Beatles fan, he also plays Quechua rock music, also videos and pizzas; *Punto Caliente Video Pub*, Asamblea 131, open Tues-Sun, very popular, good atmosphere; *Crema Rica*, restaurant and video pub, very popular; *Peña Machi*, on Jr Grau, *peña* on Fri and Sat, the rest of the week it's a disco.

● **Post & telecommunications**

Post Office and **Telefónica**: Asamblea 293.

● **Shopping**

Handicrafts: Ayacucho is a good place to buy local crafts inc filigree silver, which often uses *mudéjar* patterns. Also look out for little painted altars which show the manger scene, carvings in local alabaster, harps, or the pre-Inca tradition of carving dried gourds. The most famous goods are carpets and *retablos*. In both weaving and *retablos*, scenes of recent political strife have been added to more traditional motifs.

For carpets, go to Barrio Santa Ana, *Familia Sulca*, Jr Mcal Cáceres 302 (see under **Places of interest** above); or *Familia Fernández*. In Barrio Belén, *Familia Pizarro*, Jr San Cristóbal 215, works in textiles and *piedra huamanga* (local alabaster), good quality.

● **Tour companies & travel agents**

Morochucos Travel Service, Portal Constitución 14, T/F 912261, city tours, tours to Huari, Quinua, Huanta and Inca ruins at Vilcashuamán, also agent for AeroPerú. Also local tours with *Wari Tours*, Portal Independencia 70, T 913115; and *Quinua Tours*, Jr Asamblea 195, T 912191, manager Zumilda Canales de Pérez is very helpful.

● **Tourist offices**

Ministerio de Turismo (MICTI), Asamblea block 4, T 912548/913162, open Mon-Fri 0800-1300, helpful.

● **Useful addresses**
Tourist Police: at Dos de Mayo y Arequipa.

● **Transport**
Air To Lima, 40 mins, Faucett 4 a week and Aero Continente daily flights. A taxi to the airport costs US$1; buses or colectivos leave from the Plaza de Armas. At the airport walk 1/2 block down the street for a bus to the centre.

Buses To Pisco, 332 km, 10-12 hrs in the dry season, US$7-10, between 1500 and 1700. It is a poor road but with good views. Most buses go on to Lima, 14-15 hrs, US$9-11. Companies inc: Fano, Pasaje Cáceres 150, T 912813; Trans-Mar, Av Mcal Cáceres 896; Trans Molina, Tres Máscaras 551. To Pisco you are dropped off at San Clemente, 5 km from town on the Panamericana. This area is dangerous at night, so take a taxi. To Huancayo, 319 km, 8-10 hrs, US$6-7; Trans Molina, Fano, Yazala (Av Mcal Cáceres 879, T 914422) and Antezana (Av Manco Cápac 467) daily at 1800-1900, Trans Molina also at 0630. The road is paved as far as Huanta, thereafter it is rough, especially in the wet season, but the views are breathtaking. For Huancavelica, take a Pisco bus to Pámpano, via the Abra de Apacheta (Apacheta-Pámpano, 5 hrs). In Pámpano wait in a restaurant till next day; there are no hotels. A bus runs to Santa Inés at 1100 or 1200, arriving at 1900. From Santa Inés take a truck to Huancavelica, or there is a bus between 1600-1700. It is 3 hrs Santa Inés-Huancavelica.

To Andahuaylas, 252 km, 12 hrs (more in the rainy season), US$8-9. Trans Fano, Mon, Wed, Fri, Sat at 0600; Ayacucho Tours, Av Mcal Cáceres 880, daily at 0630, continuing to Abancay, 135 km, 5 1/2 hrs, US$5, and on to Cusco, a further 195 km, 7 hrs in the dry season, US$7. It takes 2 days to Cusco, with an overnight stop in Andahuaylas. There are no direct buses. Trucks to Abancay and Cusco leave from opp Hostal El Sol, 0500-0600. Road conditions are terrible, and landslides a common occurrence in the wet season. The scenery, though, is stunning and makes up for it. Terrorist activity has declined in recent years, but robberies are a problem and there are numerous military checkpoints. Buses sometimes even travel in convoy with a police escort. The route is reasonably safe.

AYACUCHO TO CUSCO

The road towards Cusco goes through **Chincheros**, 158 km from Ayacucho and 3 hrs from Andahuaylas. It's a picturesque town and a nice place to break the Andahuaylas-Ayacucho trip. Ask for the bakery with its outdoor oven. 15 mins from Chincheros, on the road from Andahuaylas,

is Uripa with a good Sun market. *Micros* regularly run between the two towns.

● **Accommodation G** pp *Hostal Don José*, clean, friendly, pleasant courtyard, warm; **G** pp *Hostal Municipal*, on the plaza, clean, very quiet.

● **Transport** A bus leaves for Ayacucho at 0400 and 1300. You may be able to hitch a lift with one of the trucks, if you're up before daybreak.

ANDAHUAYLAS

80 km further on, in a fertile, temperate valley of lush meadows, cornfields and groves of eucalyptus, alder and willow. The town offers few exotic crafts, no lighting except in the plaza, poor transport, but beautiful scenery. There is a good market on Sun.

Excursions The scenery is pleasant on the old road by the river to **Talavera**. **San Jerónimo** is another picturesque town nearby.

Most worth seeing is **Pacucha** (*pop* 2,000), the largest of six villages on the shores of a large lake, with a view of the mountains to the NW. In the plaza, where the trucks stop, women sell bread, coffee and hot lunches, the only food for 16 km. There are dirt roads around the lake. Allow at least 3 hrs to walk round its circumference, but be back in Pacucha before dark to ensure transport back to Andahuaylas. The wildlife includes many types of wild duck and other birds. Opposite Pacucha, some 2 km past the lake, are the ruins of a Chanka fortress called **Sóndor**. Except for Andahuaylas itself, this is a mainly Quechua-speaking region. It is also one of the poorest parts of Peru. Mini-vans leave daily when full from the centre of Andahuaylas, about every 30 mins; 40-min ride, US$0.65. Sun is market day.

● **Accommodation & places to eat C-D** *Turístico Andahuaylas*, Av Lazaro Carrillo 620, T (084) 721224; **E** *Las Américas*, nr *Delicias*, hot water am and pm, rec; **F** *Cusco*, Casafranca 520, hot shower; **F** *Delicias*, Ramos 525, hot showers, basic but rec, 7 rooms, ask for extra blankets, cold at night; **F** *Wari*, Ramos 427, hot shower; **G** pp *Hostal Waliman*, Av Andahuaylas 266, nr where buses leave for Cusco, basic. Good, cheap food can be found at *Corazón Ayacuchano*, Av Andahuaylas 145; *Las Floridas*, good set meal US$0.80; *Chifa*, Jr Juan A Trellas 279, rec Chinese.

● **Transport Air** Daily flights to Lima with Imperial Air; Grupo Ocho every Wed. **Buses** To **Ayacucho**, a minimum of 12 hrs, US$8-9, daily buses with Ayacucho Tours, also Fano, leave between 1300 and 1500. There are no direct buses early in the morning, so you will miss most of the stunning scenery. To **Abancay** with Señor de Huanca at 0600 and 1300 daily, 5½ hrs, US$5; also buses at 1200 and 1800. To **Cusco**, Señor de Huanca at 0600, and Emp Andahuaylas at 1300, 12 hrs, US$9.

ABANCAY

Nestled between mountains in the upper reaches of a glacial valley, this friendly town is first glimpsed when you are 62 km away. There is a petrol station.

● **Accommodation & places to eat B** *Hotel de Turismo Abancay*, Av Díaz Barcenas 500, T (084) 321017 (Cusco, 223339), good food, US$3, comfortable, old-fashioned house, safe car park, camping permitted US$3; **F** *Hostal Sawite*, on Nuñez, hot water 24 hrs, ask them to turn off the TV in the main passage if you want to sleep; and other cheap places. *Elena*, on the same street as the bus companies, is a good place to eat.

● **Transport** Several bus companies leave for Cusco on Av Arenas nr the market, daily at 0600 and 1300, US$7, 6-7 hrs (in the dry season), also colectivos. The scenery is dramatic, especially as it descends into the Apurímac valley and climbs out again. There is a checkpoint at the Apurímac border. Coming from Cusco, after the pass it takes an hour to zig-zag down to Abancay. The 2000 bus from Cusco arrives around 0300, there is no guarantee of a seat to Andahuaylas, even with a through ticket. See page 1355 for sites of interest between Abancay and Cusco. Services to Andahuaylas US$4, 6 hrs, 5 daily; change there for Ayacucho. Landslides are common on this route, as well as lots of checkpoints, which involve getting off the bus. To **Nasca** on the Panamericana Sur, 464 km, via Chalhuanca and Puquío, 20 hrs, US$14, bus or truck daily. **NB** The route from Cusco to Nasca is still considered unsafe and many bus companies are not yet travelling this road.

EAST OF LA OROYA

ROUTES The 60-km surfaced road to Tarma follows the Cerro de Pasco road for 25 km, then branches off to rejoin the old road quite near Tarma, which is 600m lower than La Oroya.

TARMA

This nice little flat-roofed town, founded in 1545, with plenty of trees, is now growing, with garish modern buildings (*Pop* 105,200; *Alt* 3,050m). It still has a lot of charm. The Semana Santa celebrations are spectacular, with a very colourful Easter Sunday morning procession in the main plaza. Accommodation is hard to find at this time but you can apply to the Municipalidad for rooms with local families. The town is also notable for its locally-made fine flower-carpets. The cathedral is dedicated to Santa Ana. The surrounding countryside is beautiful.

Excursions 8 km from Tarma, the small hillside town of **Acobamba** has the futuristic **Santuario de Muruhuay**, with a venerated picture painted on the rock behind the altar. It also has fine *tapices* made in San Pedro de Cajas which depict the Crucifixion. There are festivities during May. Two *alojamientos*, both **G**, eg Doña Norma's, nr the plaza.

● **Transport** Daily buses leave Acobamba to Tarma (US$0.20, or a pleasant 2 hrs' walk), La Oroya (US$0.60) and Huancayo. 3 buses a week go direct to Lima (Coop San Pedro).

The **Grutas de Guagapo**, also known as *La gruta que llora* (the cave that weeps), is 4 km from the town of **Palcamayo**. The caves can be entered for about 300m. Even without a guide you can penetrate the cave for some way with a torch. A bus leaves twice daily from Tarma; US$1, 2 hrs.

Beyond Palcamayo, the road continues to **San Pedro de Cajas**, a large village which used to produce most of the coloured sheep-wool weavings for sale in Lima. Most of the weaving families have now moved to Lima. There are no buses, but you can walk in 3 hrs. **G** *Hotel Comercio*, in Calle Chanchamayo; also 2 restaurants, but no shops.

NB In this area it's best to travel by day for safety and scenery.

● **Accommodation B-C** *La Florida*, 6 km from Tarma (for reservations T Lima 424-6969, F 432-4361), 18th century hacienda, 6 rooms, hot water, inc breakfast, owned by German-Peruvian couple Inge and Pepe, excursions, highly rec, also camping US$3; **D** *Hostal Galaxia*, on Plaza de Armas, T 321449, hot water, car park US$1; **D** *Hostal Internacional*, Dos de Mayo 307, T 321830, hot water 1800-0800; **E** *Hostal Bolívar*, Huaraz 389, T 321060, with bath, hot water, reasonable; **E** *Hostal Central*, Huánuco 614, shared bath, hot water, has an observatory, open Fri 2000; **E** *Hostal El Dorado*, Huánuco 488, T 321598, hot water, reasonable.

● **Places to eat** *Señorial*, Huánuco 138, good *menú*, 'best in town'; *Chavín Café*, beneath *Hostal Galaxia*, on Plaza de Armas, trout is rec; *Don Lucho*, Lima 175, good; *El Rosal*, on Callao nr Transportes Chanchamayo, reasonable and clean. There are also several places on Lima, inc a vegetarian. The *manjarblanco* of Tarma is famous, as well as *pachamanca*, *mondongo* and *picante de cuyes*.

● **Banks & money changers** Banco de Crédito, Lima 407, changes Amex TCs.

● **Post & telecommunications** *Telefónica del Perú*: is on the Plaza de Armas.

● **Tourist offices** *Club de Turismo de Tarma*, Moquegua 653, offer tours of the local area, US$4.50-9, depending on the length of the tour: they go on weekends and need a minimum of 15 people, which may be difficult during the rainy season. *Comité de Exploradores Tarmeños Perú Profundo*, is a group of university students who will organize local tours, US$10 pp; you can find them in the bookshop at Jr Lima 440. Alfonso Tapía E at *Hostal Central* will show people around. He is very friendly and likes to practise his English and German.

● **Transport**
Buses to **Lima**, 231 km, 6 hrs, US$5.25, direct buses daily; Transportes Chanchamayo, Callao 1002, T 321882, is rec; also Expreso Satipo, Ucuyali 384. There is a good lunch stop at El Tambo before La Oroya, with superb fried trout. The road is paved throughout. To **Jauja**, US$1.80; and **Huancayo**, 3 hrs, US$2.50. Daily colectivos from Jr Huánuco 439 run almost hourly to Huancayo, US$4, 2½ hrs. Bus to **La Oroya**, US$2.40, colectivo, US$3. Bus to **La Merced**, US$2.65. Colectivos often leave for La Merced and San Ramón (Chanchamayo – see below), from Dos de Mayo blocks 2 and 3, US$3.45.

ROUTES Beyond Tarma the road is steep and crooked but there are few places where cars cannot pass one another. In the 80 km between Tarma and La Merced the road, passing by great overhanging cliffs, drops 2,450m and the vegetation changes dramatically from temperate to tropical. This is a really beautiful run.

CHANCHAMAYO

The towns of San Ramón and La Merced are collectively known as Chanchamayo. **San Ramón** (*pop* 7,000) is 11 km before La Merced.

● **Accommodation & places to eat B** *El Refugio*, outside town, beautiful botanical garden which can be visited for US$1; **E** *Conquistador*, on the main street, shower, parking. *La Estancia*, Tarma 592, serves local specialities. There are other places on the main street.

● **Transport Air** Flights leave from San Ramón. There is an 'air-colectivo' service to **Puerto Bermúdez**, 10 kg baggage allowance, US$5/kg of excess luggage. The service continues to Atalaya, Satipo, Puerto Inca (see page 1312) and Pucallpa. Air-colectivos go to Lima and to most places in the jungle region where there is an airstrip. Flights are cheap but irregular, and depend on technical factors, weather and demand.

La Merced (*pop* 10,000), lies in the fertile Chanchamayo valley. Sometimes Campa Indians come to town selling bows and arrows. There is a festival in the last week of September.

● **Accommodation & places to eat E** *Cosmos*, opp the police station, with bath, best value; **F** *Romero*, Plaza de Armas, T 2106, good but noisy and water pm only. Opp Transportes Chanchamayo is a Japanese-owned hotel, **E**, which is quiet and friendly. The best restaurant is *Shambari-Campa*, on the Plaza de Armas.

● **Transport** Many buses go here from **Lima**: Transportes Chanchamayo is the best; also Expreso Satipo; 9 hrs, US$6.40. Also many buses from **Tarma**, US$2.65, 3 hrs. Bus to **Puerto Bermúdez**, 8 hrs, US$6.40, at 1000 with Túpac Amaru. To get to **Pucallpa**, take a launch from Puerto Bermúdez to Laurencia (which takes 8 hrs or more, be prepared for wet luggage), then a truck to Constitución (20 mins), and from there a colectivo to Zungaro, 1½ hrs. From Zungaro, colectivos take 4½ hrs to Pucallpa. Alternatively, you can take a truck from La Merced to Pucallpa. The journey takes 3 days, and between 0830 and 1400 each day expect to be drenched by rain.

EAST OF LA MERCED

About 22 km N from La Merced is **San Luis de Shuaro**, 3 km before which a road runs E up the valley of the Perené river. There are large coffee plantations at an altitude of only 700m. Sat and Sun are market days. The jungle town of **Satipo** is the main centre of this region.

● **Accommodation D** *Hostal Majestic*, no

clothes-washing facilities, electricity 1900-2300 only; **F** *La Residencial*, 4 rooms, garden, swimming pool, rec. There are many smaller hotels, all very basic. For good food try *Dany's Restaurant*.

● **Buses** To get to Satipo take a Lobato or Los Andes bus from La Merced, US$7.20, 0800. Daily buses run direct from Satipo to Huancayo and Lima at night, a very cold journey, US$9.50, 12 hrs, with Los Andes and Lobato. Check whether the tunnels are open before travelling.

● **Warning** Latest reports suggest that Oxapampa, the Perené region and Satipo are still dangerous due to narco-terrorist activity. Check on the situation before travelling into these areas.

NORTH OF LA MERCED

The road has been extended from San Luis de Shuaro over an intervening mountain range. A turn-off E leads to **Puerto Bermúdez** on the Río Neguachi (**F** *Hostal Tania*, opposite the dock where motorized canoes tie up, clean; eating house opp the airstrip). Boat passages possible from passing traders.

56 km from La Merced is **Oxapampa** (*Pop* 5,140; *Alt* 1,794m), 390 km from Lima, in a fertile plain on the Río Huancabamba, a tributary of the Ucayali. A third of the inhabitants are descendants of a German-Austrian community of 70 families which settled in 1859 at **Pozuzo**, 80 km downstream, and spread later to Oxapampa. There is much livestock farming and coffee is planted on land cleared by the timber trade. 25 km from Oxapampa is **Huancabamba**, from where it is 55 km to Pozuzo. The whole road between La Merced and Pozuzo is very rough, depending on the season. There are no less than 30 rivers to be crossed.

● **Accommodation & places to eat In** Oxapampa: **E** *Rey*, with bath, cold water, small beds; **F** *Arias*, cheaper without bath, new, best value; **F** *José*, without bath, hot water, pleasant; **F** *Hostal Jiménez*, Grau 421, refurbished, cold water, shared bath; **F** *Hostal Liz*, Av Oxapampa 104, small rooms, cold water. The following are in old buildings: **F** *Santo Domingo*, no hot water; **G** *Hostal Santa Isolina*, Jr M Castilla 177, with bath, cold water. *Oasis*, is a highly rec restaurant. **In** Pozuzo: **E** *Hostal Tirol*, full board, rec; **F** *Hostal Prusia*; **F-G** *Hostal Maldonado*, rec.

● **Transport** Colectivo La Merced-Oxapampa; taxis at 0600, US$2, 4 hrs. Buses from Lima to Pozuzo with La Victoria, from 28 de Julio 2405, Mon, Thur, Sat, 0800, US$12, about 16 hrs.

NORTH OF LA OROYA

A paved road runs 130 km N from La Oroya to Cerro de Pasco. It runs up the Mantaro valley through narrow canyons to the wet and mournful Junín pampa at over 4,250m, one of the world's largest high-altitude plains. An obelisk marks the battlefield where the Peruvians under Bolívar defeated the Spaniards in 1824. Blue peaks line the pampa in a distant wall. This windswept sheet of yellow grass is bitterly cold and the only signs of life are the youthful herders with their sheep and llamas. The railway line follows the E shores of the Lago de Junín. The town of **Junín**, with its picturesque red-tiled roofs, stands beside the lake.

NB Before going to this region, check that there has been no resurgence of terrorist activity, only travel by day, and stay in contact with the locals.

LIMA TO CERRO DE PASCO

An alternative to the La Oroya route from Lima to Cerro de Pasco is the road via **Canta**. From Canta you can visit the pre-Inca ruins of **Cantamarca** – many of the buildings still have roofs, supported by pillars. It is a 2-3 hrs' walk up to the ruins, from where there are extensive views.

● **Accommodation & transport** Accommodation is limited, but *Hostal Kalapacho* is good value. There is one good restaurant in town. 3 buses daily to and from Lima, US$3.60 – El Canteño company, San Román 151-153, Lima.

Continuing through the beautiful high pass of La Viuda (4,748m), the road goes to the mines of **Alpamarca**, from where there are 2-3 buses per week to **Huayllay** (see below).

CERRO DE PASCO

The main line goes to this long-established mining centre (*Pop* 29,810; *Alt* 4,330m; *Phone code* 064), 130 km from La Oroya by road. The town is not attractive but is nevertheless very friendly. Copper, zinc, lead, gold and silver are mined here, and coal comes from the deep canyon of Goyllarisquisga, the 'place where a star fell', the highest coal mine in the world, 42 km N of Cerro de Pasco. The town seems to defy gravity as its buildings and streets cling precariously to the edge of a huge abyss; nights are bitterly cold. A new town – San Juan de Pampa – has been built 1½ km away.

Excursions 40 km SW of Cerro de Pasco is **Huayllay**, near which is the **Santuario Bosque de Piedras**, unique weathered limestone formations in the shape of a tortoise, elephant, alpaca, etc. Also near Huayllay are the Inca ruins of **Bon Bón Marca** and the thermal baths of **Calera**.

● **Access** Take a bus from Cerro de Pasco and get off at the crossroads near Villa de Pasco. It is about 15 mins out of town, on the road to Lima. Camionetas pass by bound for Huayllay, which is about 1 hr away.

80 km SE of Cerro de Pasco is the **Valle de Huachón**. There are excellent hiking opportunities in the valley and around several *nevados*, including Huaguruncho (5,730m), which is the snowy peak visible from the road on the way to Huánuco. To reach the valley, take a bus to **Tambo del Sol**, on the road to Lima.

Another recommended excursion is to the precolumbian funeral towers at **Cantamasia**, reached on muleback.

● **Accommodation & places to eat** E *Hostal Arenales*, Jr Arenales 162, nr the bus station, new, hot water; **F** *El Viajero*, on the plaza, no hot water; **F** *Santa Rosa*, also on the plaza, basic, very cold. UMI *Restaurant Los Angeles*, Jr Libertad, nr the market, rec; *El Espignol I*, Jr Libertad 195; *El Espignol II*, Jr Arenales 164, for fish, chicken, *menú* and other dishes. Local specialities are trout and fried frog.

● **Banks & money changers** Banco de Crédito is on Jr Bolognesi.

● **Buses** To Lima, at 0830 and 2000, 9 hrs, US$7, with Empresa de Transportes Carhuamayo, nr the Av Montivideo entrance to the market (in Lima: Av Grau 525, T 433-0785, F 427-8605). To La Oroya, bus from Plaza Arenales, 0900 and later, 3 hrs, US$2.20; cars also travel this route, leaving when there are enough passengers, US$9.50. To Huancayo, 5-6 hrs, US$3-4. Colectivos to Huánuco, US$6.20, from Plaza de Armas. There are also buses between 0800 and 0900; 5 hrs, US$2. Cerro de Pasco has a central bus station.

Some 65 km NW of Cerro de Pasco is **Yanahuanca**, in the beautiful valley of the same name. From the village one can reach one of the longest surviving stretches of Inca road. 2 km up the Yanahuanca Valley a lesser valley cuts northwards between the towering crags. The road, its paving uneven and disturbed by countless horse and donkey convoys, leads up the smaller valley, its course sometimes shared by a stream, to the village of **Huarautambo**, about 4 km distant. This village is surrounded by many pre-Inca remains. For more than 150 km the *Camino Incaico* is not only in almost continuous existence from the Yanahuanca Valley but is actually shown on the map issued by the Instituto Geográfico Militar. The clearest stretch ends at Huari in Ancash, having passed by such places as La Unión (see page 1382) and San Marcos. After Huari its route may be followed, less distinctly, through Llamellín and in the hills behind San Luis, Piscobamba and Pomabamba.

The Central Highway from Cerro de Pasco continues NE another 528 km to Pucallpa, the limit of navigation for large Amazon river boats. The western part of this road (Cerro de Pasco-Huánuco) has been rebuilt into an all-weather highway (see map, page 1385, for its contour).

The sharp descent along the nascent **Río Huallaga** is a tonic to travellers suffering from *soroche*. The road drops 2,436m in the 100 km from Cerro de Pasco to Huánuco, and most of it is in the first 32 km. From the bleak vistas of the high ranges the road plunges below the tree line revealing views of great beauty. The only town of any size before Huánuco is **Ambo**.

NB The Huallaga valley is the country's main coca-growing area, with both drug-trafficking and guerrilla activity. The main centre of activity is between Tingo María and Tarapoto, so it is best to avoid the region at present. It does appear to be safe to visit Huánuco, Tingo María and Pucallpa, but as the area is under military control there are many checkpoints. Travelling during the day is advised and seek full information before going.

HUANUCO

An attractive Andean town (*Pop* 82,240; *Alt* 1,894m; *Phone code* 064) on the Upper Huallaga with an interesting market.

Places of interest

The two churches of **San Cristóbal** and **San Francisco** have both been much restored. The latter has some 16th century paintings. The small but interesting natural history museum is at Gen Prado 495, **Museo de Ciencias**, US$0.50.

5 km away on road W to La Unión is **Kotosh** (*alt* 1,812m), the Temple of Crossed Hands, the earliest evidence of a complex society and of pottery in Peru, dating from 2000 BC. A new bridge leads to partly-restored ruins; entry US$1.

Local festivals

20-25 Jan: is *Carnaval Huanuqueño*. **3 May**: *La Cruz de Mayo*. **16 July**: *Fiesta de la Virgen del Carmen*. **12-18 Aug**: Tourist Week in Huánuco. **28-29 Oct**: *Fiesta del Rey y del Señor de Burgos*, the patron of Huánuco. **25 Dec**: *Fiesta de los Negritos*.

Local information

● **Accommodation**

B *Gran Hotel Huánuco*, Jr D Beraun 775, T 514222, F 512410, restaurant, pool, sauna, gym, parking, rec.

D *Cusco*, Huánuco 616, 2 blocks from Plaza de Armas, cafeteria, OK.

E *Hostal Residencial Huánuco*, Jr Huánuco, nr Plaza de Armas, with bath, hot water, garden, use of kitchen, laundry facilities, excellent value, highly rec.

F *Imperial*, Huánuco 581, with cold shower (intermittent water), reasonable value, quiet; *Las Vegas*, on Plaza de Armas, rec; **F** *Lima*, Plaza de Armas, 28 de Julio 9222, with bath. Hotels are often fully booked, so you should arrive early.

Camping: it's possible to camp by the river, nr the stadium.

● **Places to eat**

La Casona de Gladys, Gen Prado 908, good, cheap local food; *Vegeteriano*, Dos de Mayo 751; *Chifa Confort*, 28 de Julio 811, good. Also try the *chifas* on Damaso Beraun, 1 block W of the Plaza de Armas.

● **Banks & money changers**

Banco de Crédito, at Dos de Mayo 1005, ATM for visa withdrawal, look for 'Telebanco' sign.

● **Telecommunications**

Telefónica del Perú: at 28 de Julio 1157.

● **Tourist offices**

Gen Prado 716, on the Plaza de Armas. A good contact for adventure tours is *César Antezana*, Jr Pedro Puelles 261, T 513622.

● **Transport**

Buses To Lima, US$9, 9 hrs, with León de Huánuco, Malecón Alomía Robles 821 (28 de Julio 1520, La Victoria, Lima); 3 a day in the early evening. A colectivo to Lima, US$20, leaves at 0400, arrives 1400; book the night before at Gen Prado 607, 1 block from the Plaza, rec. Transportes del Rey, 28 de Julio 1201 (28 de Julio 1192, La Victoria, Lima), also have buses to Lima. Daily buses to **Cerro de Pasco**, 5 hrs, US$2. 'Mixto' Huánuco-Cerro de Pasco, half bus, half truck, departs at 0400, 3 hrs, US$3.60; also colectivo 1 or 12, US$6.20 at 0500. To **Huancayo**, 8-9 hrs, US$5-6. Buses to **Tingo María**, 3-4 hrs, US$1.75; colectivo, US$4.35, 2 hrs, many start from nr the river bridge, 2 blocks from the main plaza. Bus to **Pucallpa**, US$11, with La Perla del Oriente (Etposa), 0800 and 1600, 10-12 hrs, rec. Buses make stops for meals but some of them are few and far between, so take your own food, especially given the frequency of breakdowns. This route has many checkpoints and robberies can occur.

The road NW to Tantamayo and La Unión passes the 'Crown of the Inca', also known as Lacsahuarina, meaning 'Two Princesses' in Quechua. This distinctive rock formation is at the pass before the descent into the upper canyon of the Río Marañon. **Tantamayo** (3,600m) is a farming village surrounded by precolumbian ruins from the Yarowillca culture: **Japallan**, **Selinin**, **Piruru** and **Susupillu**. All are visible from Tantamayo and can be reached on foot in about 3-4 hrs; guides are available. The walks to the ruins are arduous; take warm clothing, a hat and suntan lotion. The scenery is stunning. Pictures and information from Huánaco Post Office. In Tantamayo there are 4 basic hotels and one restaurant, *Ortega*, on the corner of the Plaza.

● **Buses** From Huánuco: Transportes Balla, San Martín 575, US$6.50, 10 hrs, depart 0730 and 0800, return 1800 and 0100.

From Huánuco, a road leads to **La Unión**, capital of Dos de Mayo district. It's a friendly town, but electricity can be a problem and it gets very cold at night. On the pampa above La Unión are the Inca ruins of **Huánuco Viejo**, a 2½ hr walk from the town, a great temple-fortress with residential quarters.

● **Accommodation & Places to eat E** *Hostal Turista*, on main street, not very clean, parking; and **G** *Hostal Dos de Mayo*; neither are safe for left luggage. *Restaurant El Danubio*, nr the market, good home cooking.

● **Transport** From Huánuco, 2 buses daily at 0745, leave from Tarapacá, return 0600 and 0700, US$4.35, 7-8 hrs. A truck leaves in the late morning, 10½ hrs. La Unión-Tingo Chico, US$2.70. There is a daily bus to Lima which gets crowded.

ROUTES It is possible to get to the Callejón de Huaylas from here. La Unión-Huaraz direct is very difficult because most transport does the route La Unión-Chiquián-Lima: change buses in Chiquián (see page 1248) or at the Conococha crossroads, but check times if you can to avoid being stranded in the dark. Alternatively ask for trucks going to Huallanca and from there to Pachacoto, 1 hr S of Huáraz. Check local political conditions before taking this route.

Amazon Basin

COOLED by winds sweeping down from the Andes but warmed by its jungle blanket, this region contains some of the most important tropical flora and fauna in the world. The frontier town, Puerto Maldonado, only a 30-minute flight from Cusco, is the starting point for expeditions to one of the national parks at Manu, Tambopata or Heath. Besides its natural attractions, the area also harbours gold-diggers, loggers, hunters, drug smugglers and oilmen.

It is a very varied landscape, with grasslands and tablelands of scrub-like vegetation, inaccessible swamps, and forests up to 2,000m above sea level. The principal means of communication in the jungle is by its many rivers, the most important being the Amazon, which rises high up in the Andes as the Marañon, then joins the Ucayali to become the longest river in the world.

THE NORTHEASTERN JUNGLE

ROUTES The journey to Tingo María from Huánuco, 135 km, is very dusty but gives a good view of the jungle. Some 25 km beyond Huánuco the road begins a sharp climb to the heights of Carpish (3,023m). A descent of 58 km brings it to the Huallaga river again; it then continues along the river to Tingo María. The road is paved from Huánuco to Tingo María, including a tunnel through the Carpish hills. Landslides along this section are frequent and construction work causes delays. Although this route is reported to be relatively free from terrorism, robberies do occur and it is advisable to travel only by day. There are three police/army checkpoints where soldiers may demand money to pass through; it is not necessary to pay.

TINGO MARIA

Tingo María (*Pop* 20,560; *Alt* 655m; *Phone code* 064; *Climate* tropical, annual rainfall 2,642 mm) is on the middle Huallaga, in the Ceja de Montaña, or edge of the mountains, isolated for days in rainy season. The altitude prevents the climate from being oppressive. The Cordillera Azul, the front range of the Andes, covered with jungle-like vegetation to its top, separates it from the jungle lowlands to the E. The mountain which can be seen from all over the town is called La Bella Durmiente, the Sleeping Beauty. The meeting here of Sierra and Selva makes the landscape extremely striking. Bananas, sugar cane, cocoa, rubber, tea and coffee are grown. The main crop of the area, though, is coca, grown on the *chacras* (smallholdings) in the countryside, and sold legitimately and otherwise in Tingo María.

Places of interest

A small university outside the town, beyond the *Hotel Madera Verde*, has a little museum-cum-zoo, with animals native to the area, and botanical gardens in the town. Entrance is free but a small tip would help to keep things in order. 6½ km from Tingo, on a rough road, is a fascinating cave, the **Cueva de las Lechuzas**. There are many oilbirds in the cave and many small parakeets near the entrance. Take a motorcycle-taxi from town, US$1.75; US$0.45 for the ferry to cross the Río Monzón just before the cave; entry to cave, US$0.90. Take a torch, and do not

wear open shoes. The Cave can be reached by boat when the river is high.

13 km from Tingo is the small gorge known as **Cueva de las Pavas**, good swimming. 10 km away, on the Huánuco road, are the **Cuevas de Tambillo**, with beautiful waterfalls and refreshing pools for swimming.

Local information
● **Accommodation**

A3 *Madera Verde*, on road to Huánuco nr University, some way out of town, T/F 561608/562047, several chalets set in beautiful tropical surroundings, with and without bath, restaurant, swimming pool.

E *Hostal Marco Antonio*, Jr Monzón 364, T 562201, quiet, restaurant next door.

F *Hostal Aro*, Av Ucayali 553, safe; **F** *Hostal Mieses*, Av Alameda Perú 365, nr the plaza; **F** *La Cabaña*, Raimondi 6th block, fairly clean, good restaurant; **F** *Viena*, Jr Lamas, with bath, good value. Hotels are often fully-booked.

● **Places to eat**

Gordon's Café, Jr José Pratto 229, good food and service, cheap pisco sours; *El Antojito 2*, Jr Chiclayo 458, good local food.

● **Security**

Watch out for gangs of thieves around the buses and do not leave luggage on the bus if you get off. Note that this is a main narco-trafficking centre and although the town itself is generally safe, it is not safe to leave it at night. Also do not stray from the main routes, as some of the local population are suspicious of foreign visitors.

● **Tour companies & travel agents**

Tingo María Travel Tours, Av Raimondi 460, T 562501, for local excursions.

● **Transport**

Air Expreso Aéreo fly daily to Lima, Huánuco, Juanjui and Tarapoto; check the times. Their office is at Av Raimondi 218. Services are unreliable; there are cancellations in the rainy season or if the planes are not full.

Buses To Huánuco, 118 km, 3-4 hrs, US$1.75, several micros; colectivos US$4.35, 2 hrs. Direct buses continue to Lima. To Pucallpa, 284 km, 12 hrs, US$5.50. Many of the big bus companies (eg: León de Huánuco, Transmar and Transportes del Rey) pass through Tingo María on their way to Pucallpa, from Lima, in the middle of the night. Ucayali Express colectivos leave from the corner of Raimondi and Callao; also other colectivos and taxis, which all leave in the early morning in convoy. To Juanjui, 340 km, 15-20 hrs, US$9, daily transport, not a rec journey because of narco-terror-

La Oroya to Pucallpa

Elevation of Road LIMA - PUCALLPA

Lima		156m
Chosica		860m
Matucana		2,390m
Anticona		4,843m
Oroya		3,826m
Carhuamayo		4,104m
Junín		4,128m
Cerro de Pasco		4,330m
Salcachupán		2,819m
Ambo		2,072m
Huánuco		1,812m
Rancho		1,750m
Acomayo		2,114m
Carpish		3,023m
Pto Durand		791m
Cayumba		1,050m
Tingo María		655m
Punahuasi		660m
El Boche		1,613m
Boquerón Abad		470m
Pucallpa		200m

Pampas del Sacramento

Km 100 200 300 400 500 600 700 800 841

0 ——— 40 km

115

ist activity; continuing to **Tarapoto**, a further 145 km, 4 hrs, US$2.

NORTH TO YURIMAGUAS

The Río Huallaga winds northwards for 930 km. The Upper Huallaga is a torrent, dropping 15. 8m/km between its source and Tingo María. The Lower Huallaga moves through an enervation of flatness, with its main port, Yurimaguas, below the last rapids and only 150m above the Atlantic ocean, yet distant from that ocean by over a month's voyage. Between the Upper and Lower lies the Middle Huallaga: that third of the river which is downstream from Tingo María and upstream from Yurimaguas. Down-river of Tingo María, beyond Bellavista, the orientation is towards **Yurimaguas**, which is connected by road with the Pacific coast, via Tarapoto and Moyobamba (see page 1282).

At **Tulumayo**, soon after leaving Tingo María, a road runs N down the Huallaga past **La Morada**, successfully colonized by people from Lima's slums, to **Aucayacu** and **Tocache**, which has an airport. The road is paved to 20 km past Aucayacu, thereafter it is gravel.

● **Accommodation** In **Aucayacu**: E *Hotel Monte Carlo*, with bath, and one other hotel; both are poor. In **Tocache**: F *Hostal San Martín*; and F *Hostal Sucre*.

● **Transport Air** A small plane flies between Tocache and Juanjui; 25 mins. **Road** Colectivos run Tingo-Tocache US$13, 4½ hrs; or bus US$9.50, 6 hrs. The road has been pushed N to join another built S from Tarapoto and has now been joined at Tarapoto to the Olmos-Bagua-Yurimaguas transandine highway to the coast at Chiclayo. Tarapoto-Tocache, US$7.50 by colectivo. Colectivos and taxis run from Tocache to Yurimaguas on a serviceable unpaved road; daily camioneta Tarapoto-Yurimaguas, US$7-9, 6-8 hrs. The Juanjui-Tocache road has five bridges, but the last one across the Huallaga, just before Juanjui, was washed away in 1983 to be replaced by an efficient ferry; US$9.20/vehicle. Juanjui-Tarapoto by colectivo US$12.50. **River** For the river journey, start early in the morning if you do not wish to spend a night at the river village of Sión. There are no facilities, but the nights are not cold. The river runs through marvellous jungle with high cliffs. Boats sometimes run aground in the river near Sión.

Take food and water purifier. Balsa wood rafts also ply this stretch of river.

YURIMAGUAS

The town (*Pop* 25,700) has a fine church of the Passionist Fathers, based on the Cathedral of Burgos, in Spain. A colourful market is held from 0600-0800, full of fruit and animals. Tourist information is available from the Consejo Regional building on the main plaza. Interesting excursions in the area include the gorge of Shanusi and the lakes of Mushuyacu and Sanango. Mopeds can be hired for US$2.35 per hour, including fuel.

● **Accommodation** E *Leo's Palace*, Plaza de Armas 104-6, good, reasonably-priced, restaurant; F *Camus*, Manco Capac 201, no sign, cheap.

● **Banks & money changers** Interbanc or travel agents; poor rates.

● **Security** There has been guerrilla activity in the Yurimaguas region; visitors can expect attention from the police. It is also a centre for anti-narcotics operations. A good contact is Lluis Dalman; The South American Explorer's Club in Lima has his address and telephone number.

● **Transport Air** To Lima, 2 hrs, Aero Continente (3 a week), and Faucett (1 a week). To **Tarapoto**, 20 mins, same airlines, same frequency. To **Iquitos**, 45 mins, Aero Continente (3 a week). Flights are cancelled in the wet season or if they're not full. **Buses** To Moyobamba, with Guadalupe (Raymondi y Levean, T 3990), 0630, US$8.75. **River** By ferry to Iquitos takes 2 days and 2 nights (upstream takes longer), take a hammock, mosquito net, waterpurification, fruit and drinks; there are police inspections at each end of the trip. Fares usually include meals, US$18, cabins cost more. To buy a hammock costs US$20-30 in Yurimaguas, mosquito nets are poor quality.

YURIMAGUAS TO IQUITOS

The river journey to Iquitos can be broken at **Lagunas**, 12 hrs from Yurimaguas. You can ask the local people to take you on a canoe trip into the jungle where you will see at very close range alligators, monkeys and a variety of birds, but only on trips of 4 days or so.

● **Accommodation** G *Hostal La Sombra*, Jr Vásquez 1121, shared bath, basic, good food; *Montalbán*, Plaza de Armas, no sign, owner Sr Inga, 2 rooms, 20-min walk from the jetty, also accommodation at the Farmacia.

● **Transport River** The *Constante* plies Yurimaguas to Lagunas 2-3 times a week (US$4.50); from there connections are difficult to Iquitos; you should confirm departures the day before by radio. The boats pass by the villages of Castilla and Nauta, where the Huallaga joins the Ucayali and becomes the Amazon.

There are good jungle trips from Lagunas to the **Pacaya-Samiria Reserve**. When arranging a guide and boat from Lagunas, make sure you take enough fuel for the boat. Before entering the Reserve you pass through a village where you must pay US$4.50. Officially, you need a permit from INRENA in Lima.

Edinson and Klever Saldaña Gutiérrez, Sgto Flores 718, are good guides; also Job and Genaro (ask at *Hostal La Sombra*), who include basic food, with fishing and hunting; Juan Huaycama, at Jáuregui 689, is highly rec, mostly on the river, sleeping in hammocks, and fishing. The typical cost for a party of 5 for 12 days is US$200, with 2 guides and 2 boats. One person for 5 days with one guide is charged US$45. Take water purifier and mosquito repellent on excursions that involve living off the land.

TINGO MARIA TO PUCALLPA

From Tingo María to the end of the road at Pucallpa is 288 km, with a climb over the watershed – the Cordillera Azul – between the Huallaga and Ucayali rivers. The road is paved and good for 60-70 km after Tingo María and 70 km before Pucallpa. In between it is affected by mud and landslides in the rainy season. There are eight army checkpoints. When the road was being surveyed it was thought that the lowest pass over the Cordillera Azul was over 3,650m high, but an old document stating that a Father Abad had found a pass through these mountains in 1757 was rediscovered, and the road now goes through the pass of Father Abad, a gigantic gap 4 km long and 2,000m deep. At the top of the pass is a Peruvian Customs house; the jungle land to the E is a free zone. Coming down from the pass the road bed is along the floor of a magnificent canyon, the Boquerón Abad. It is a beautiful trip through luxuriant jungle and ferns and sheer walls of bare rock punctuated by occasional waterfalls plunging into the roaring torrent below. East of the foot of the pass the all-weather road goes over the flat pampa, with few bends, to the village of **Aguaytía** (narcotics police checkpoint, gasoline, accommodation in the **F** *Hostal San Antonio*, clean, and 2 restaurants). From Aguaytía the road continues for 160 km to Pucallpa – 5 hrs by bus, US$4.35. There are no service stations on the last half of the journey.

PUCALLPA

The capital of the Department of Ucayali is a rapidly expanding jungle town (*Pop* 400,000; *Phone code* 064) on the Río Ucayali, navigable by vessels of 3,000 tons from Iquitos, 533 nautical miles away. The town's newer sections have paved streets, sewers and lights, but much of the frontier atmosphere still exists. The floating ports of La Hoyada and Puerto Italia are about 5 km away and worth a visit to see the canoe traffic and open-air markets. The economy of the area includes sawmills, plywood factories, a paper mill, oil refinery, fishing and boat building. Large discoveries of oil and gas are being explored, and gold mining is underway nearby.

The climate is tropical: dry during July and Aug; rainy Oct-Nov and Feb-Mar. The town is hot and dusty between June and Nov and muddy from Dec to May. **NB** There is much military control because of narcotics activity. The city itself is safe enough to visit, but don't travel at night.

Places of interest

Museo Regional, at Jr Inmaculada 999, has some good examples of Shibipo ceramics, as well as some delightful pickled snakes and other reptiles; open 0800-1200 and 1600-1800, US$0.90. **Parque Natural Pucallpa** is a zoo on the left on the road to the airport; many jungle animals (most of the cages are OK). Entry US$0.90.

Excursions

The Hospital Amazónico Albert Schweitzer, which serves the local Indians, is on picturesque Lake **Yarinacocha**, the main tourist attraction of the area. River dolphins can be seen in the lake. The Indian market of Moroti-Shobo ('The House of Selling and Buying') is a cooperative, organized by Shipibo-Conibo craftsmen. Fine handicrafts are sold in their shop; visit them in Yarinacocha; T 571551.

A good place to swim is at **San José**. Take the road out behind the power station round the lake beyond the Summer School of Linguistics (also on the lake).

San Francisco and **Santa Clara** can be visited at the far end of the lake on its western arm. Both are Shibipo villages still practising traditional ceramic and textile crafts.

● **Accommodation** In San Francisco a nice place to spend the night is in the house of Alberto Sánchez Ríos, *Casa Artesanal Shibipo*, which is very friendly and warmly rec.

● **Transport** To reach these villages take one of the motorized canoes, *peke-pekes*, which leave from Puerto Callao when full, US$0.90.

The beautifully-located reserve, **Jardín Botánico Chullachaqui**, can be reached by boat from Puerto Callao to Pueblo Nueva Luz de Fátima, 45 mins, then 1 hr's walk to the garden, entry free. For information about traditional medicine contact Mateo Arevalomayna, San Francisco de Yarinacocha (president of the group Ametra; T 573152, or ask at Moroti-Shobo).

● **Accommodation** In Yarinacocha: **C** pp *La Cabaña*, by appointment only, price rises in high season, inc all meals and transport to and from Yarinacocha harbour, same Swiss owner as *Mercedes* in Pucallpa, good service and food, excellent guide, Isabel, for short expeditions, will organize plane excursions to Indian villages, or elsewhere; next door is **B-C** pp *La Perla*, inc all meals, German-Peruvian owned, English and German spoken, no electricity after 2100, good, jungle tours organized; **D-E** *Los Delfines*, T 571129, new rooms with bath, fan, fridge, some with TV; **F** *El Pescador*, in Puerto Callao, cheapest in town, restaurant, extension planned for 1997. Some small houses for rent on weekly basis.

● **Places to eat** There are many restaurants and bars on the waterfront and nr the Plaza. *El Cucharón*, good food; *Grande Paraíso*, good view, also has a *peña* at night, popular with young people; *Orlando's*, Jr Aguaytía, good local food.

● **Transport** Yarinacocha is 20 mins by colectivo or bus from the market in Pucallpa, US$0.30, or 15 mins by taxi, US$2.

6-7 hrs by boat S are **Laguna Imitia** and **Laguna Chauya**. There are many indigenous villages on the shores and boats sometimes glide through the dense, overhanging vegetation around the lakes. Take a colectivo (US$9 pp), *peke-peke* or a hired boat from the port in Pucallpa.

Local festivals

Feb: Carnival. **24 June**: San Juan. **5-20 Oct**: Pucallpa's *Aniversario Political* and the Ucayali regional fair.

Local information

● **Accommodation**

A3 *Sol del Oriente*, Av San Martín 552, T 575154, T/F 575510, pool, good restaurant.

B *Hostal Antonio*, Jr Progreso 547, T 573122, F 573128, has gym.

D *Arequipa*, Jr Progreso 573, good; **D** *Mercedes*, good, but noisy with good bar and restaurant attached, swimming pool.

E *Barbtur*, Raymondi 670, T 572532, **F** without bath, central, opp the bus stop, good beds; **E** *Komby*, Ucayali 300 block, comfortable, swimming pool, excellent value; **E** *Sun*, Ucayali 380, cheaper without bath, good value, next to *Komby*.

F *Marinhor*, Raymondi 699, grubby but economical, helpful; **F** *Hostal Mori*, Jr Independencia 1114, basic.

● **Places to eat**

El Alamo, Carretera Yarinacocha 2650, good typical food; *El Sanguchón*, Jr Tarapacá 829, nr Banco de Crédito, clean, good sandwiches and coffee; *El Golf*, Jr Huáscar 545, cevichería; *Jugos Don José*, Jr Ucayali y Raimondi, one of the oldest in town; *Cafetería Antonio*, Cnel Portillo 307, 2 blocks from the Museo Regional, good coffee.

Typical dishes: *patarashca* is barbecued fish wrapped in *bijao* leaves; *zarapatera*, a spicy soup made with turtle meat served in its shell, but consider the ecological implications of this dish; *chonta salad*, made with palm shoots; *juanes*, rice with chicken or fish served during the San Juan festival; *tacutacu* is banana and sauces. The local beer 'San Juan' has been rec.

● **Banks & money changers**

It is easy to change dollars cash at the banks, travel agencies, the better hotels and bigger stores. There are also lots of street changers (watch them carefully). Banco de Crédito is the only place to change TCs. Cash on Visa at Banco de Crédito and Interbanc.

● **Cultural centres**

Art school: *Usko Ayar Amazonian School of Painting*, in the house of artist Pablo Amaringo, a former *vegetalista* (healer), Jr LM Sánchez, Cerro 465-467. The school provides art classes for local people, and is financially dependent upon selling their art. The internationally-renowned school welcomes overseas visitors for short or long stays to study painting and learn Spanish and/or teach English with Peruvian students.

● **Shopping**

Artesanías La Selva, Jr Tarapacá 868, has a reasonable selection of indigenous craftwork. For local wood carvings visit the workshop of sculptor, Agustín Rivas, at Jr Tarapacá 861. Many Shibipo women carry and sell their products around Pucallpa and Yarinacocha.

● **Tour companies & travel agents**

Laser Viajes y Turismo, Jr 7 de Junio 1043, T 571120, T/F 573776, helpful, rec for planning a jungle trip. If organizing a group tour with the

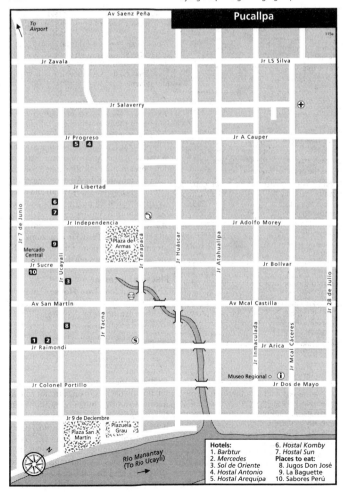

Pucallpa

Hotels:
1. Barbtur
2. Mercedes
3. Sol de Oriente
4. Hostal Antonio
5. Hostal Arequipa
6. Hostal Komby
7. Hostal Sun

Places to eat:
8. Jugos Don José
9. La Baguette
10. Sabores Perú

boatmen on the waterfront; expect to pay around US$30/day pp. Only use accredited guides.

● **Tourist offices**
Ministerio de Industria y Turismo (MICTI), Jr Dos de Mayo 999, T 571303, T/F 575110, helpful.

● **Transport**
Local Small **motorcycles** for hire from Karen Motorbikes, Av San Martín 634, US$3.50/hr, plus deposit.

Air To **Lima**, 1 hr, daily flights with Faucett, Americana and Aero Continente, less frequently with Expresso Aéreo; Grupo Ocho every Fri. To **Iquitos**, 40 mins, with AeroPerú and Aero Continente, daily. To **Huánuco** and **Tingo María**, with Expresso Aéreo. Airport to town, bus US$0.25; *motos* US$1; taxi US$2-3.

Buses There are regular bus services to **Lima**, 812 km, 18-20 hrs (longer in the rainy season, Nov-Mar), US$11. To **Tingo María**, 284 km, 7-9 hrs, US$7.80, combis leave at 0600, 0700 and 0800 with Ucayali Express, 7 de Junio y San Martín. All buses have police guard and go in convoy. Take blankets as the crossing of the Cordillera at night is bitterly cold. It's rec to cross the mountains by day as the views are wonderful.

River Buses and colectivos go to the port, La Hoyada. In the dry season boats dock 3 km from the bus stop, it's a dusty walk, or taxi US$3. To **Iquitos**, some are better than others; only 3 boats with cabins, don't count on getting one (hammocks are cooler): *Florico, Carolina* and *Manuel*, trip takes 3-4 days, US$22 pp, US$27 inc food.

NB Travellers to Iquitos may need confirmation from the PNP that their documents are in order, this must then be signed by the Capitanía otherwise no passenger can be accepted on a trip leaving Pucallpa. No such clearance is necessary when returning to Pucallpa. Passenger services are in decline owing to competition by air and priority for cargo traffic; it may be better to make journeys in short stages rather than Pucallpa-Iquitos direct. There's a risk of illness as the river water is used for cooking and drinking. Tinned food, mosquito netting, hammock and fresh water are necessary purchases, and fishing line and hooks are advisable. Vegetarians must take their own supplies. Bottled drinking water is reportedly impossible to find in Pucallpa. 2 litre bottles of carbonated water are readily available but expensive at US$4-6 a bottle. Also take lots of insect repellent, water purifier and tummy pills.

The smaller boats call often at jungle villages if you want to see them, but otherwise the shores can only be seen at a distance. Boats leave very irregularly. When conditions are bad they leave in convoy and none may leave afterwards for 4 to 6 weeks. Avoid boats that will be loading en route, this can take up to 6 days. Further down the Río Ucayali are **Contamaná**, with a frontier-town atmosphere, and **Requena**, from which launches sail to Iquitos, taking 12 hrs. Unlike most other villages, which are *mestizo*, **Roroboya**, about 12 hrs downstream from Pucallpa, is Shipibo Indian.

You can go to Puerto La Hoyada and Puerto Italia to find a smaller boat going to Iquitos; the Capitanía on the waterfront may give you information about sailings, but this is seldom reliable. Do not pay for your trip before you board the vessel, and only pay the captain. Some boat captains may allow you to leave on board a couple of days before sailing. Boats going upstream on the Amazon and its tributaries stay closer to the bank than boats going down, which stay in mid-stream.

IQUITOS

Capital of the Department of Loreto and chief town of Peru's jungle region, **Iquitos** (*Pop* 350,000; *Phone code* 094) stands on the W bank of the Amazon. Some 800 km downstream from Pucallpa and 3,646 km from the mouth of the Amazon, the city is completely isolated except by air and river. Its first wealth came from the Rubber Boom (late 19th century to second decade of 20th century). It is now the centre for oil exploration in Peruvian Amazonia and the main starting point for tourists wishing to explore Peru's northern jungle.

Places of interest

The incongruous **Iron House** stands on the Plaza de Armas, designed by Eiffel for the Paris exhibition of 1889. It is said that the house was transported from Paris by a local rubber baron and is constructed entirely of iron trusses and sheets, bolted together and painted silver. It now houses a snack bar.

Belén, the picturesque, friendly waterfront district, is lively, but not safe at night. Most of its huts are built on rafts to cope with the river's 10m change of level during floods, which are most likely Nov to April. *Pasaje Paquito* and *La China* are bars with typical local drinks. The main plaza has a bandstand made by Eiffel. Canoes can be hired on the waterfront to visit Belén, US$3/hr, but don't try paddling yourself as the current is very strong. The market at the end of the Malecón is well worth visiting, though you should get there before 0900 to see it in full swing.

See the old Hotel Palace, now the army barracks, on the corner of Malecón Tarapacá and Putumayo. Of special interest are the older buildings, faced with *azulejos* (glazed tiles). They date from the rubber boom of 1890 to 1912, when the rubber barons imported the tiles from Portugal and Italy and ironwork from England to embellish their homes. Werner Herzog's film *Fitzcarraldo* is a *cause célèbre* in the town and Fitzcarrald's house still stands on the Plaza de Armas.

Museums

Museo Municipal, Tăvara 3rd block s/n, has a large, old collection of stuffed Amazonian fauna. The guide will explains the exhibits; open Mon-Sat 0800-1800, US$1.30.

Excursions

There is a beautiful white, sandy beach at **Bellavista**, which is safe for swimming and very popular at weekends in summer. Boats can be hired from here to see the meeting of the Nanay and Amazon rivers, and to visit villages en route. There are lots of food stalls selling typical local dishes. Take a bus from Jr Próspero to Bellavista, 15 mins, US$0.40.

Launches leave Iquitos for the village of **Indiana**. Get off at the 'Varadero de Mazán' and walk through the banana plantations to the Río Mazán. A trail leads from the village of Mazán through the jungle to Indiana, where there is hotel; it's about a 2-hr walk. Catch the launch back to Iquitos at 1300.

13½ km S of the city is beautiful **Lake Quistococha** in lush jungle, with a fish hatchery at the lakeside. The Parque Zoológico de Quistococha on the lake gives an example of the local wildlife, though conditions are pretty squalid. At the entrance are pictures and texts of local legends. The ticket office will supply a map of the lake and environs. There's a good 2-hr walk through the surrounding jungle on a clearly marked trail. See particularly the *paiche*, a huge Amazonian fish whose steaks (*paiche a la loretana*) you can eat in Iquitos' restaurants. There are also bars and restaurants on the lakeside and a small beach. Boats are for hire on the lake and swimming is safe but the sandflies are vicious, so take insect repellent. Entry is US$1.30, open daily 0900-1700.

● **Transport** Combis leave every hour until 1500 from Plaza 28 de Julio; the last one back leaves at 1700. Alternatively take a *motocarro* there and back with a 1-hr wait, which costs US$13. Perhaps the best option is to hire a motorbike and spend the day there. The road can be difficult after rain.

On the road to Quistococha, is the turn-off to the village of **Santo Tomás** (*fiesta* 22-25 Sept), about 20 km away, and a favourite weekend retreat of inhabitants of Iquitos. The village has a good restaurant and canoes may be hired. Trucks go there, taking passengers.

Local festivals

5 Jan: founding of Iquitos. **Feb-Mar**: Carnival. **Third week in June**: tourist week. **24 June**: San Juan. **28-30 Aug**: Santa Rosa de Lima. **8 Dec**: Immaculate Conception, celebrated in Punchana, near the docks.

Local information

If possible, avoid visiting Iquitos around Peruvian Independence Day (27 and 28 July) and Easter as it is very expensive and crowded and excursion facilities are overloaded. Hotels are generally more expensive than the rest of the country, but discounts of 20% or more can be negotiated in the low season (Jan-April).

● **Accommodation**
A1 *Real Hotel Iquitos*, Malecón Tarapacá, 1 block from Plaza de Armas, T 231011, F 236222, ex Tourist Hotel, recently upgraded, inc tax and breakfast, good a/c rooms; **A2** *El Dorado*, Napo 362, T 237326, F 232203, pool (open to restaurant users), cable TV, bar and restaurant, highly rec; **A2-3** *Victoria Regia*, Ricardo Palma 252, T 231983, F 232499, a/c, fridge, free map of city, safe deposit boxes in rooms, good restaurant and pool, rec; **A3** *Hostal Acosta*, Calvo de Araujo y Huallaga, T 235974, similar to *Victoria Regia* minus the swimming pool; **A3** *Jhuliana*, Putumayo 521, T/F 233154, inc tax and breakfast, nice pool, restaurant, rec.

B *Amazonas*, Plaza de Armas, Arica 108, T 232015, modern, a/c, phone, frigo bar, TV; **B** *Hostal Ambassador*, Pevas 260, T 233110, inc tax, a/c, transport to and from airport, member of Peruvian Youth Hostel Association, cafeteria, owns Sinchicuy Lodge (see below), rec; **B** *Europa*, Brasil 222, T 231123, F 235483, a/c, cable TV, phone and fridge in every room, pleasant café/bar, good views from 5th floor.

C *Internacional*, Próspero 835, T/F 234684, a/c, cable TV, fridge, phone, secure, medium-priced restaurant, good value, rec.

D *El Sitio*, Ricardo Palma 541, T 239878, fan, cafeteria, highly rec; **D** *Hostal Bon Bini*, Pevas 386, T 238422, fridge, good value, rec; **D** *Hostal La Pascana*, Pevas 133, T 231418, with cold shower, basic, fan, breakfast available, luggage store, TV lounge, luxuriant garden, relaxed, popular, book exchange, highly rec, ask for Coby, a Dutch lady who will take tours on

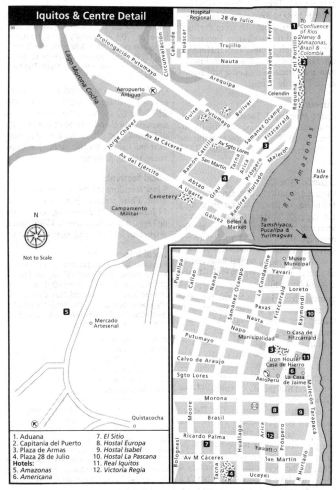

Iquitos & Centre Detail

1. Aduana
2. Capitanía del Puerto
3. Plaza de Armas
4. Plaza 28 de Julio
Hotels:
5. *Amazonas*
6. *Americana*
7. *El Sitio*
8. *Hostal Europa*
9. *Hostal Isabel*
10. *Hostal La Pascana*
11. *Real Iquitos*
12. *Victoria Regia*

her houseboat, the 'Miron Lenta'.

E *Hostal Don José Inn*, Fitzcarrald 456, T 234257, with bath, fan, TV, good, breakfast and evening meal on request; **E** *Hostal Rolando's Amazon River*, Esq Fitzcarrald y Nauta 307, T 233979, with bath and fan, restaurant, also own *Albergue Supay* (see **Jungle tours** below); **E** *Hostal Vargas*, Av Quiñones, outside town on the road to the airport, good value, rec; **E** *Isabel*, Brasil 164, T 234901, with bath, very good, but plug the holes in the walls, secure, often full; **E** *Pensión Económico*, Moore 1164, T 265616, large rooms, water all day, quiet, not central, no sign outside, breakfast on request, rec.

F pp *Hostal Aeropuerto*, Av Corpac block 100 y Malvinas, nr airport, OK, fan in room, other 'services' available; **F** *Hostal Anita*, Ramírez Hurtado 742, T 235354, with bath, no fan, basic; **F** *Hostal Tacna*, Tacna 516, T 230714, fans, basic, good value, rooms at front with balcony noisy.

● **Places to eat**

El Dorado Inn, C Huallaga 630, good value and good menu; *El Mesón*, Jr Napo 116, local specialities, rec; *La Terraza*, Malecón Tarapacá y Napo, commanding views of river, good; *La Casa de Jaime*, Malecón Tarapacá 137, excellent steaks, also vegetarian meals, owner Jaime Acevedo is charming, speaks perfect English, and will give excellent advice about jungle trips, the wonderful, locally-produced mozzarella cheese comes from water buffaloes brought from Africa by Cubans, also book exchange, frequented by tour operators, consuls and ex-pats, interesting ambience, very highly rec; *La Pascana*, Ramírez Hurtado 735, good fish and *ceviche*, popular, try the *vientequatro raices*, 20% discount for Handbook users; *Wai Ming*, San Martín at Plaza 28 de Julio, good, expensive; *Hueng Teng*, esq Pucallpa y Nauta, Chinese, cheap, rec. The cheapest restaurants are on and around Plaza 28 de Julio. *Heladería La Favorita*, Próspero 415, good ice-cream; *Juguería Paladar*, Próspero 245, excellent juices; *Casa de Hierro*, Plaza de Armas, Próspero y Putumayo, friendly snack bar inside Eiffel's iron house, good chocolate cake, try malta beer with egg and fresh milk, a useful pick-me-up; *Ari's Burger*, Plaza de Armas, Próspero 127, medium-priced fast food, popular with gringos; *Olla de Oro*, Calvo de Araujo 579, close to the main indoor market, excellent food, good service, rec.

Bars: the liveliest are along the riverside in the first couple of blocks of Malecón Tarapacá: *Pipi Vela*, live music Fri; *La Ribereña*, Raymondi 453, terraced seats on a newly-built plaza with jukebox; *El Encanto del Amazonas*, Malecón Tarapacá block 4, palm-roofed bar with river view, sells *siete raices* (see below); *Snack Bar Arandu*, beers, drinks, good views of the Amazon river; *El Mirador*, Requena next to steps leading down to the wharf, cheap drink, fantastic view; *Teatro Café Amauta*, Nauta 248, live music, open 2200-2400, good atmosphere, popular, small exhibition hall.

Pineapples are good and cheap. Try the local drink *chuchuhuasi*, made from the bark of a tree, which is supposed to have aphrodisiac properties but tastes like fortified cough tincture (for sale at Arica 1046), and *jugo de cocona*, and the alcoholic *cola de mono* and *siete raices* (aguardiente mixed with the bark of 7 trees and wild honey), sold at *Exquisita Amazónica*, Abtao 590. You can eat cheaply, especially fish and *ceviche*, at the three markets. Palm heart salad (*chonta*), or a *la Loretana* dish on menus is excellent; also try *inchicapi* (chicken, corn and peanut soup), *cecina* (fried dried pork), *tacacho* (fried green banana and pork, mashed into balls and eaten for breakfast or tea), *juanes* (chicken, rice, olive and egg, seasoned and wrapped in bijao leaves and sold in restaurants) and the *camu-camu* is an interesting but acquired taste, said to have one of the highest vitamin C concentrations in the world.

● **Airline offices**

Aero Continente, Próspero 331, T 233162, F 233990; **Faucett**, Próspero 632-40, T 239766, F 243198; **AeroPerú**, Próspero 248, T 232513; **SAA** (Servicios Aéreos Amazónicos), Arica 273, T 230776, F 243776.

● **Banks & money changers**

Banco de Crédito, Plaza de Armas, Visa, cash and TCs, good rates, ATM. **Banco Continental**, Sgto Lores 171, Visa, Mastercard, 1% commission on TCs. **Banco de la Nación**, Condamine 478, good rates, 0915-1530, changes Deutschmarks. **Banco Wiese**, Próspero 282, Visa, Mastercard, changes TCs into Soles with no commission, 1% into dollars, rates for cash not great. *Casas de Cambio* stay open late: Tacna 380 and Fitzcarrald 120. There are many money changers on Próspero in the 3 blocks S of Plaza de Armas. Their rates are good on weekdays but not at the weekend.

● **Embassies & consulates**

Consulates: Brazil, Sgto Lores 363, T 232081, Mon-Fri 0800-1200, 1500-1800, need photo and yellow fever certificate for visa; Britain, Mr Lewis Power, Arica 253, T 234110 or 234383; Colombia, Putumayo 247, T 231461; Spain, Av La Marina, T 232483; France, Napo 346, T 232353; Germany, Max Drusche, Yavari 660, T 232641, F 236364.

● **Entertainment**

Cinemas: *Bolognesi*, San Martín 390, on Plaza 28 de Julio.

Discotheques: *Bamboleo*, Malecón Tarapacá 328, very popular, open 2300 till late; *La Pantera Rosa*, Moore 454, free entrance, Mon-Sat until 0300; *La Estancia*, Napo 1 block, restaurant by day, dancing at night, popular; *Yutopia Karaoke*, Napo 168; *Dreams*, Samanez Ocampo 120; *Calipso*, Putumayo 15 block.

● **Hospitals & medical services**
Medical services: *Clínica Loreto*, Morona 471, T 233752, 24-hr attention, rec, but only Spanish spoken; *Hospital Iquitos*, Av Grau, emergency T 231721; *Hospital Regional de Loreto*, 28 de Julio, emergency T 235821.

● **Post & telecommunications**
Post Office: on the corner of C Arica with Morona, nr Plaza de Armas, open daily 0700-2000. **Telefónica del Perú**, at Arica 276.

● **Shopping**
Artesanías del Perú, Putumayo 128; *Mercado Artesanal de Productores*, 4 km from the centre in the San Juan district, on the road to the airport, take a colectivo; *Artesanías de la Selva*, R Palma 190. Camera accessories at *Aspinwall*, Raimondi 138. There are pharmacies at Tacna 156 and at Próspero 361-3. Records and tapes at *Discotiendas Hikari*, San Martín 324.

NB Locals sell necklaces made with red and black rosary peas (Abrus pecatorius), which are extremely poisonous. Do not give them to children. They are illegal in Canada, but not in the USA.

● **Tour companies & travel agents**
Cumacebo Expediciones, Putumayo 263, T/F 232229, tours of 2-8 days to their jungle lodge, cheaper and more basic than the other lodges, 3 days/2 nights US$120 pp; *Amazonia Expeditions*, Napo 156, T 222049, owned by Carlos Grández Pérez, camping, wildlife, jungle survival and trekking; tours from 2-15 days, US$50 pp/day; *Amazon Experience*, Echenique 473, T 236224. Also see **Jungle tours** below. A rec, accredited guide is Hernán Silva Peixoto, Requena 142. For good advice ask Jaime Acevedo at *Casa de Jaime*, see above, **Places to eat**.

● **Tourist offices**
At Napo 176, 0730-1330, for maps and general tourist literature; try the Gobierno Regional de Loreto, Ricardo Palma 113, T 233321. Useful town maps, maps of the Quistacocha zoo and literature are available from the main jungle tour operators. You can also get a town map from *Librería Mosquera*, Jr Próspero.

PARD, Preservation of the Amazon River Dolphin, Pevas 253, T/F (51-94) 238585, Roxanne Kremer or Frank Aliaga for information.

● **Useful addresses**
Immigration: Malecón Tarapacá 382, quick service.

● **Transport**
Local Motorcycle hire: *Rider*, Pevas 219; *Park Motors*, Tacna 579, T/F 231688.

Air Francisco Secada Vigneta airport handles national and international flights (to/from Miami), T 231501/233094. Taxi to the airport costs US$2.50 pp; *motocarro* (motorcycle with 2 seats), US$2.20. A bus from the airport, US$0.20, goes as far as the market area, about 12 blocks from the Plaza de Armas, a taxi from there is US$1.30.

To **Lima**, daily; Faucett, Aero Continente and AeroPerú (via Trujillo or Chiclayo). Aero Continente flies via **Pucallpa**; also Faucett 5 a week. To **Cajamarca** and **Yurimaguas** Aero Continente, and **Tarapoto** Aero Continente and Faucett. To **Miami**, with Faucett Sat. When entering Peru on this flight, a 90-day tourist visa is given on arrival. Iquitos flights are frequently delayed; be sure to reconfirm your flight in Iquitos, as they are often overbooked, especially over the Christmas period; check times in advance as itineraries frequently change. SAA fly to Caballococha (45 mins) and Leticia, Colombia (55 mins) 3 times a week, returning the same day; they also charter 34-seater jets for US$1500/hr to any destination.

Shipping Upstream: river boats to **Pucallpa**, leave every second day, usually at 1700, 6/7 days when river is high, 3/4 days when low; price depends on demand, eg US$22 pp in hammock, US$26 pp with bed and cabin. To **Yurimaguas**, 4/5 days, longer if cargo is being carried, which is usually the case, US$13-18 pp, more or less daily. Information on boats and tickets at Bellavista, Malecón Tarapacá 596; or Puerto Masusa district of Puchana, Av La Marina with Masusa, bus from centre, 10 mins. Cabins are 4 berth and you have to buy both a first class ticket, which entitles you to food (whether you want it or not) and deck space to sling your hammock, and a cabin ticket if you want the 'luxury' of a berth. Adequate washing and toilet facilities, but the food is rice, meat and beans (and whatever can be picked up en route) cooked in river water. There is a good cheap bar on board.

Downstream: a weekly luxury 54-passenger boat, *Río Amazonas*, plies between Iquitos and Tabatinga (Brazil), leaving Sun, operated by Amazon Tours and Cruises (see **Jungle tours** below), US$525 pp (US$445 for groups of 10 plus), return journey to Iquitos Wed; also M/V *Arca*, US$495 pp (US$420 groups of 10 plus), return journey Wed-Sat.

There are no boats direct to Manaus. Take a boat to **Islandia**, opp Tabatinga (Brazil); US$26 pp cabin plus food, US$22 pp hammock plus food. It takes 3 days to Islandia; 4/5 boats leave each week on Thurs and Sat, usually at 1700-1800. From Islandia take a small boat to Benjamín Constant and from there boats leave for Manaus. It is roughly 8 days from Islandia to Manaus. Boats for Manaus also leave from a little way down-river from Marco, the port for Tabatinga. Speedboats run between Iquitos and Islandia with Amazon Tours and Cruises, US$75, Tues, Fri and Sun, book ahead (2 days upstream, 11 hrs downstream). The *Ruiz* is highly rec for river journeys to the frontier; 3 days, US$20 with your own hammock, no food, or Pucallpa. *Ecograss* is also rec, US$25-30 pp inc food.

NB From May to July the river rises and the port in Iquitos moves. Boats leave from Puerto Nanay at Bellavista or from Puerto de Moronacocha.

General hints for river travel A hammock is essential, but they are expensive in Iquitos. A double, of material (not string), provides one person with a blanket. Board the boat many hours in advance to guarantee hammock space. If going on the top deck, try to be first down the front; take rope for hanging your hammock, plus string and sarongs for privacy. On all boats, hang your hammock away from lightbulbs (they aren't switched off at night and attract all sorts of strange insects) and away from the engines, which usually emit noxious fumes. Guard your belongings from the moment you board. There is very little privacy; women travellers can expect a lot of attention. Stock up on drinking water, fruit and tinned food in Iquitos. Take plenty of prophylactic enteritis tablets; many contract dysentery on the trip. Also take insect repellent.

● **Crossing the Frontier**
Details on exit and entry formalities seem to change frequently, so when leaving Peru, check in Iquitos first at Immigration (see above) or with the Capitanía at the port. All details are given in the **Brazil** chapter, page 598.

JUNGLE TOURS FROM IQUITOS

All agencies are under the control of the local office of the Ministry of Tourism. They arrange 1 day or longer trips to places of interest with guides speaking some English. Package tours booked in Lima are much more expensive than those booked in Iquitos. Some agencies are reported as too easy going about their responsibilities on an organized trip. Take your time before making a decision, shop around, and don't be bullied by the hustlers at the airport. Find out all the details of the trip and food arrangements before paying; expect to pay about US$40-

50/day. Launches for river trips can be hired by the hour or day; prices are negotiable, but usually about US$20-30/hr.

● **Tour operators**
Explorama Tours, rec as the most efficient and the longest established: Av La Marina 340, PO Box 446, T 51-94-252526/252530, F 51-94-252533; in USA, Selective Hotel Reservations, Toll Free, T 800-223-6764; MA (617) 581-0844, F 581-3714. They have three sites: *Explorama Inn*, 40 km ($1\frac{1}{2}$ hrs) from Iquitos, hot water, comfortable bungalows in a jungle setting, good food, attractive walks, a rec jungle experience for those who want their creature comforts, US$175 pp for 1 night/2 days, US$75 for each additional night (1-2 people); *Explorama Lodge* at Yanamono, 80 km from Iquitos, $2\frac{1}{2}$ hrs from Iquitos, palm-thatched accommodation with separate bath and shower facilities connected by covered walkways, US$250 for 3 days/2 nights and US$75 for each additional day (1-2 people); *Explornapo Camp* at Llachapa, 160 km (4 hrs) from Iquitos, primitive, but better for seeing fauna, with an impressive new canopy walkway some 35m above the forest floor and 500m long, set in 105,000 ha of primary rainforest, "a magnificent experience and not to be missed". It is also possible to stay in the ACEER laboratory, a scientific research station, only 10 mins from the canopy walkway; the basic programme costs US$1,000 for 5 days/4 nights (2 people), the first and last nights spent at Explorama Lodge. A US$25 donation to the Foundation for Conservation of Peruvian Amazon Biosphere (Conapac) is included if visiting the walkway; to spend a night at the ACEER lab is US$55; each extra night to the basic programme costs US$90. Prices include transfers, advance reservations, etc; local rates are much lower. Flight inclusive packages are available from Miami with Faucett.

Paseos Amazónicos Ambassador, Pevas 246, T/F 233110, operates the *Amazonas Sinchicuy Lodge*, US$70 pp/night; the lodge is 1 hr 15 mins from Iquitos on the Sinchicuy river, 10 mins by boat from the Amazon river.

Lima Tours offers 3 days/2 night tours to Iquitos and the Amazon from Lima for US$510 pp, flight included (US$900 for 2 passengers).

Amazon Tourist Services, Requena 336, T (51-94) 233931, F 231265; in USA, 8700 W Flagler St, suite 190, Miami, FL 33174, T 305-227-2266, toll free 800-423-2791, F 305-227-1880, American owned company: Lodge itineraries to 42-room *Amazon Camp*, 1 night/2 days US$105, extra night US$55. Various cruises available: on M/V *Arca* Iquitos-Leticía-Iquitos, US$500 pp; nature cruises on M/V *Delfin*. They also organize rugged expeditions to various jungle *tambos* (thatched shelters), rec as conscientious and efficient.

Anaconda Lara Lodge, Pevas 210, T 239147, F 232978, 40 km from Iquitos, full day tours US$50, also offers adventure expeditions to Río Yarapa, 180 km away.

Las Colinas de Zungarococha Amazon Resort, operated by Paucar Tours, Próspero 648-Altos, T 235188/232131, or through *Hostal Acosta*, or Ricardo Rivera Navarrete 645E, San Isidro, Lima, T/F 442-4515, comfortable lakeside bungalows, swimming pool, watersports, mini-zoo, full day US$40, 1 night/2 days US$70.

Amazon Lodge, Raymondi 382, T 237142; Av Alvarez Calderón 155, Of 302, San Isidro, Lima, T (51-1) 221-3341, F 221-0974, 48 km downriver from Iquitos, rec as friendly and comfortable; 3 days/2 nights, US$200 pp, 2-4 people, US$50 pp for each additional night.

Albergue Supay is a floating hotel on Supay lake close to the Río Nanay, 2 hrs by boat from Iquitos, or taxi and canoe, 1 to 5 day tours from US$60 to US$290 pp, run by Austrian Roland Röggl and Peruvian Luz Elena Montoya; contact Apdo 532, Correo Central, Iquitos, or Jr Próspero 635, T 234785; they also have *hostal* at Fitzcarrald y Nauta 307 (see above).

Yacumama Lodge, Jr Arica 513-A, T/F 241022; Av Benavides 212, Of 1203, Miraflores, Lima; 4 days/3 nights, US$389, 6 days/5 nights, US$559 (minimum 2 people); part of the fee is invested in local conservation.

● **General information & advice**
It is advisable to take a waterproof coat and shoes or light boots on such trips, and a good torch, as well as *espirales* to ward off the mosquitoes at night – they can be bought from drugstores in Iquitos. *Premier* is the most effective local insect repellent. The dry season is from July to Sept; Sept is the best month to see flowers and butterflies.

THE SOUTHEASTERN JUNGLE

The southern selva is in Madre de Dios department, which contains the Manu National Park (1,881,000 ha), the Tambopata-Candamo Reserved Zone (1,170,000 ha), the Bahauja-Sonene National Park (330,000 ha) and the Heath National Sanctuary.

The forest of this lowland region (*Alt* 260m) is technically called Sub-tropical Moist Forest, which means that it receives less rainfall than tropical forest and is dominated by the floodplains of its meandering rivers. The most striking features are the former river channels that have become isolated as ox-bow lakes. These are home to black caiman and giant otter. Other rare species living in the for-

est are jaguar, puma, ocelot and tapir. There are also howler monkeys, macaws, guans, currasows and the giant harpy eagle. As well as containing some of the most important flora and fauna on Earth, the region also harbours gold-diggers, loggers, hunters, drug smugglers and oilmen, whose activities have endangered the unique rainforest. Fortunately, various conservation groups working to protect it.

The climate is warm and humid, with a rainy season from Nov to Mar and a dry season from April to October. Cold fronts from the South Atlantic, called *friajes*, are characteristic of the dry season, when temperatures drop to 15-16°C during the day, and 13° at night. Always bring a sweater at this time. The best time to visit is during the dry season when there are fewer mosquitoes and the rivers are low, exposing the beaches. This is also a good time to see nesting and to view the animals at close range, as they stay close to the rivers and are easily seen. Note that this is also the hottest time. A pair of binoculars is essential and insect repellent is a must.

● **Recommended reading** *Birds of Venezuela* (Princeton University) and *South American Birds*, by John Dunning, give the best coverage of birds of Peru; also *Neotropical Rainforest Mammals, A field guide*, by Louise H Emmons. *Tropical Nature*, by Adrian Forsyth and Ken Miyata, gives an explanation of the rainforest. *Manu National Park*, by Kim MacQuarrie and André and Cornelia Bartschi, is a large, expensive and excellent book, with beautiful photographs. *Birds of Tambopata – a checklist, Mammals, Amphibians and Reptiles of Tambopata*, both by TReeS (address on page 1401). *Madre de Dios Packet*, by the South American Explorers Club, gives practical travel advice for the area.

MANU BIOSPHERE RESERVE

The Manu Biosphere Reserve covers an area of 2,233,693 ha and is one of the largest conservation units on Earth, encompassing the complete drainage of the Manu river. No other reserve can compare with Manu for the diversity of life forms. The reserve holds over 850 species of birds and covers an altitudinal range from 200 to 4,100m above sea-level. Giant otters, jaguars, ocelots and 13 species of primates abound in this pristine tropical wilderness, and uncontacted indigenous tribes are present in the more remote areas, as are indigenous groups with limited access. **The reserve is divided into** the **Manu National Park** (1,532,000 ha), where only government sponsored biologist and anthropologists may visit with permits from the Ministry of Agriculture in Lima, the **Reserve Zone** of the Manu Biosphere reserve (257,000 ha), which is set aside for applied scientific research and ecotourism, and the **Cultural Zone** (92,000 ha), set aside for these two Nomadic Native groups, where the locals still employ their traditional way of life.

The cultural zone is accessible to anyone and several lodges exist in the area (see **Accommodation** below). The reserved zone of the Manu Biosphere Reserve is accessable by permit only. Entry is strictly controlled and visitors must visit the area under the auspices of an authorized operator with an authorized guide. Permits are limited and reservations should be made well in advance. In the reserved zone of the Manu Biosphere Reserve the only accommodation is in the comfortable Manu Lodge or in Safari-style camps.

Park information

In Lima: Asociación Peruana para la Conservación de la Naturaleza (Apeco), Parque José Acosta 187, p 2, Magdalena del Mar, T 616316. Fundación Peruana para la Conservación de la Naturaleza (FPCN), Av de los Rosales 255, San Isidro, T 426706/426616.

In Cusco: Asociación para la Conservación de la Selva Sur (ACSS), is a local NGO that can help with information, at Of 305, Centro Comercial Ruiseñores, Plaza de Armas, T 226392, open 1000-1300, 1500-1900. Further information can be obtained from the Manu National Park Office, Of 1, Av El Sol, Edif San Jorge, Pasaje Grace, Cusco, T 224683, F 221020. Their office is next door to *Manu Nature Tours*, open 0800-1400. They issue a permit for the Reserve Zone which costs US$10. The two tour companies given below will answer any question on the park. *Manu Nature Tours* has a good video on the area.

● **Tour companies**

The following companies organize trips into the Culture and Reserve Zones. Contact them for more details. *Manu Nature Tours EIRL*, Av Pardo 1046, Cusco, T 252721, F 234793, e-mail: mnt@amauta.rcp.net.pe, owned by Boris Gómez, they run lodge-based trips and are owners of Manu Lodge, and part owners of Manu Cloudforest Lodge, highly rec; or Centro Plaza Conquistadores, 396-S-101, San Isidro, Lima, T/F 428990. They own the only lodge in the Reserve Zone (*Manu Lodge*) open all year, situated on an ox-bow lake, providing access to the forest, US$75 a night inc meals. Guides are available. Activities include river-rafting and canopy-climbing. It is highly rec for experiencing the jungle in comfort. An 8-day trip with flights both ways costs US$1,493, with road/boat transport there, plane back, US$1,695; 4-day trip US$998, plane both ways. At the same address is Eco-tour Manu, a non-profit making organization made up of tour operators which assures quality of service and actively supports conservation projects in the area. When you travel with an Eco-tour member you are assuring your support for tropical rainforest conservation projects. Eco-tour Manu comprises Expediciones Manu, Manu Nature Tours, Pantiacolla Lodge, *Aventuras Ecológicas Manu* (Plateros 361, Cusco) and *Inka Natura Travel* (Portal de Panes 123, Of 305, Cusco, T 240911, Daniel Blanco Zamalloa); contact Boris Gómez Luna.

Expediciones Manu, Av Sol 582, Cusco, T 226671, F 236706, owned by ornithologist, Barry Walker. They operate 4-9 day trips in Safari camps and lodges and specialize in birdwatching trips; US$889/6 days.

Beware of pirate operators on the streets of Cusco who offer trips to the Reserved Zone of Manu and end up halfway through the trip changing the route "due to emergencies", which, in reality means they have no permits to operate in the area.

● **Accommodation**

In the Cultural Zone, where no permit is needed, are four lodges. *Amazonia Lodge*, on the Río Alto Madre de Dios just across the river from the small town of Atalaya, on the road to Shintuya, US$40 a night, is a pleasant family run converted Hacienda, a great place to relax; contact Sr Santiago Yavar in Cusco, T/F 231370. *Erika Lodge*, on the Río Alto Madre de Dios, 25 mins from Atalaya, is a biological station used by the FPCN, which now accepts small numbers of visitors. It offers basic accommodation and is cheaper than the other, more luxurious lodges, inc food but not transport. Contact: *Aventuras Ecológicas Manu*, Plateros 361, Cusco; or Ernesto Yallico, Casilla 560, Cusco, T 227765.

Pantiacolla Lodge, located in Itahuania, 30 mins downriver from the road's end at Shintuya. owned by Marianne (Dutch) and Gustavo Moscoso. Book through *Pantiacolla Tours*, Calle Plateros 360, Cusco, T 238323, F 233727/252696. US$25pp/night (US$40 pp inc meals). They organize trips into the Reserve at US$110 pp for 5 or more for boat and boatman and US$55/day for guide, 8-day camping trip into the Reserve, US$450. Also 9-day trips en route from Shintuya-port, guide, food, boat, gear for US$950 (minimum 6, maximum 19 people).

Manu Wildlife Centre, run by *Expeciones Manu*, on the Río Madre de Dios 1 hr downstream from Boca Manu, small cabins for up to 30 people, macaw salt licks nearby and also a tapir lick, if you make your own way there by boat going downriver en route from Shintuya to Colorado (8 hrs) it costs US$75 pp/night.

A rec guide is Percy Núñez, biologist, Umanch'ata 136, Cusco. *Manu Cloud Forest Lodge* is situated at 1,800m above sea level in the cloud forest, only basic camping facilities are available at present but plans to construct bungalows are under way.

Routes

Cusco-Puerto Maldonado via Mazuko
From Cusco take a bus to Urcos; 1 hr, US$2.25. Trucks leave from here for **Mazuko** around 1500-1600, arriving around 2400 the next day, US$6.65. Catch a truck early in the morning from here for Puerto Maldonado, US$4.50, 13-14 hrs. It's a painfully slow journey on an appalling road; trucks frequently get stuck or break down. **Quincemil**, 240 km from Urcos on the road to Mazuko, is a centre for alluvial gold-mining with many banks. Accommodation is available in **F** *Hotel Toni*, friendly, clean, cold shower, good meals. Quincemil marks the half-way point and the start of the all-weather road. Gasoline is scarce in Quincemil because most road vehicles continue on 70 km to Mazuko, which is another mining centre, where they fill up with the cheaper gasoline of the jungle region.

The changing scenery is magnificent and worth the hardship and discomfort. The trucks only stop 4 times each day, for meals and a short sleeping period for the driver. You should take a mosquito net, repellent, sunglasses, sunscreen, a plastic sheet, a blanket, food and water.

To Puerto Maldonado via Pilcopata and Shintuya The arduous 255 km trip over the Andes from Cusco to Pilcopata takes about 12-15 hrs by local truck (20-40 hrs in the wet season). On this route, too, the scenery is magnificent. From Cusco you climb up to the pass before Paucartambo (very cold at night), before dropping down to this mountain village at the border between the departments of Cusco and Madre de Dios. The road then ascends to the second pass (also cold at night), after which it goes down to the cloud forest and then the rainforest, reaching **Pilcopata** at 650m. At Pilcopata you can stay at a little hostal (the only one) of Sra Robella for US$2.50 pp, very basic.

● **Transport** Trucks leave from Cusco from behind the Coliseo Cerrado at about 1000, on Mon, Wed and Fri; US$10. Be there by 0800 and make sure your driver is not inebriated! They return the following day, but there is no service on Sun. Rec are: Príncipe, Armando Cana, Carrasco and Tigre. There is also a local bus owned by Angel Valencia; T 224458 for reservation.

Private transport can be arranged through *Explorers Transportes*, T 237518, or ask at the tour companies. Only basic supplies are available after leaving Cusco, so take all your camping and food essentials, including insect repellent. You may be able to rent a seat on a more comfortable tour bus by asking at the agencies.

Pilcopata to Shintuya After Pilcopata, the route is hair-raising and breath-taking, passing through **Atalaya**, the first village on the Alto Madre de Dios river (meals available at the family of Rosa and Juan, where you can camp). The route continues to Salvador, where the Park Office and the Park Entrance are situated. If you did not get a permit in Cusco, this is your last chance. There are basic hostals and restaurants. From Pilcopata, truck traffic is infrequent to Atalaya (1 hr, US$5) and Shintuya (4-6 hrs, US$8). Trucks leave in the morning between 0600 and 0900. Make sure you go with a recommended truck driver. Basic restaurants can be found in Pilcopata and Atalaya.

The end of the road is **Shintuya**, at 485m, the starting point for river transport. The inhabitants are Masheos Indians. It is a commercial and social centre, as wood from the jungle is transported from here to Cusco. There are a few basic restaurants and you can camp (beware of thieves). The priest will let you stay in the dormitory rooms at the mission. Supplies are expensive.

Shintuya to Puerto Maldonado Cargo boats leave for the gold mining centre of Boca Colorado on the Río Madre de Dios, via Boca Manu, but only when the boat is fully laden; about 6 to 8 a week, 9 hrs, US$15. Very basic accommodation can be found here, but it is not recommended for lone women travellers. To Boca Manu is 3-4 hrs, US$12. From Colorado you can catch a truck to Laberinto, 6-7 hrs, US$20, from where regular colectivos run to Puerto Maldonado, 1½ hrs.

NB It is not possible to arrange trips to the Reserved Zone of the Biosphere Reserve from Shintuya, owing to park regulations. All arrangements must be made in Cusco.

Boca Manu is the connecting point between the rivers Alto Madre de Dios, Manu and Madre de Dios. It has a few houses, an air strip and some food supplies. It is also the entrance to the Manu Reserve. The Park Office is located in Limonal. You need to show your permit here. There are huts available for accommodation and it is possible to camp. At Boca Manu there is an airstrip and semi-regular flights are available 3 times a week during the dry season (check with the tour operators in Cusco). Aero Sur flies to Boca Manu from Cusco when there are sufficient passengers, T (084) 224638.

To the Reserve Zone Upstream on the Río Manu you pass the *Manu Lodge* (see Manu Nature Tours), on the Cocha Juárez, 2 hrs by boat; visitors are charged an entrance fee of US$5 (taken care of by tour companies). You can continue to Cocha Otorongo, 2½ hrs and Cocha Salvador, 30 mins, the biggest lake with plenty of wildlife. From here it is 2-3 hrs to Pakitza, the entrance to the Park Zone. This is only for biologists with a special permit.

PUERTO MALDONADO

Puerto Maldonado (*Pop* 17,000; *Alt* 250m; *Phone code* 084) is the capital of the Department of Madre de Dios. Overlooking the confluence of the rivers Tambopata and Madre de Dios, it is an important starting point for visiting the rainforest, or for departing to Bolivia. Its isolation makes it an expensive town and because of the gold mining and timber industries, the surrounding jungle (including most of the mahogany trees) has been destroyed and cultivated.

Excursions

The beautiful and tranquil **Lago Sandoval** is a 1-hr boat ride along the Río Madre de Dios, and then a muddy 5-km walk into the jungle (take boots). There is a newly built **G** *Sandoval Lodge* (contact *Inka Natura Travel*, Av Benavides 634-D, Of 301, Lima 33, T/F 271-8156 or at Portal de Panes 123, Of 305, Cusco, T/F 243408, e-mail inkanatura@ aol.com.pe). Boats may be hired at the Madre de Dios port for about US$30 a day to go to Lago Sandoval, bargain hard, and don't pay the full cost in advance. (See **Tour companies** below).

For those interested in seeing a gold rush, a trip to the town of **Laberinto** is suggested. There is one hotel, several poor restaurants. Combis and trucks leave from Puerto Maldonado, 1½ hrs, US$2.50, and returns in the afternoon daily. Boats leave from here to Manu.

Local information
● Accommodation

C *Turistas*, Av León Velarde s/n, T 571029, T/F 571323, nice view over Río Tambopata, a/c, restaurant, TV, phone, good.

D *Cabañaquinta*, Cusco 535, T 571863, F 571890, fan, good restaurant, lovely garden, very comfortable, airport transfer, rec; **D** *Bahuaja Research Lodge*, price inc meals and transport to lodge, for research students or work volunteers, write to Tina Smith at *poste restante* or ask for her at Tambopata port; **D** *Hostal Libertador*, just out of town on León Velarde, comfortable, pool, good restaurant, rec.

E *Hostal El Astro*, Velarde 617, T 572128, with bath, basic, cheap; **E** *Hostal El Solar*, González Prada 445, T 571571, basic, fan; **E** *Hostal Gamboa*, Jaime Troncoso 293, T 571388, with bath, a bit run down, large rooms; fan; **E** *Huasai*, Billinghurst, cabins with thatched roofs overlooking the Madre de Dios, comfortable, good restaurant, contact Willy Wither here; **E** pp *Hostal Iñapari*, 4 km from centre, 5 mins from the airport, run by a Spanish couple Isabel and Javier, inc breakfast and dinner, excellent food, very relaxing, rec; **E** *Hostal Kross*, Velarde 721, with bath, basic, fairly clean, cheap, fans but no nets; **E-D** *Rey Port*, Av León Velarde 457, T 571177, with bath, fan, insecure; **E** *Wilson*, Jr González Prada 355, T 571086, with bath, basic, good value, popular, the best of the lower range hotels, rec.

F *Tambo de Oro*, Av Dos de Mayo 277, T 572057, cheap, basic, water 24 hrs.

● Places to eat

La Cusqueñita 2, Av Ernesto Rivero 607, good, cheap; *Kalifa*, Piura, some regional specialities, closed in evening, rec; *El Hornito*, on Plaza, good pizzas; *Chifa Wa Seng*, Dos de Mayo 353. Cheap set lunch at *Club Madre de Dios*, Carrión esq Plaza.

● Airline offices

Aero Pua, González Prada 360, T 571656.

● Banks & money changers

Banco de Crédito, cash advances with Visa, no commission on TCs. Banco de la Nación, cash on Mastercard, quite good rates for TCs. The best rates for cash are at the *casas de cambio* on Puno 6th block, eg *Cárdenas Hnos*, Puno 605.

● Embassies & consulates

Peruvian immigration: is on Billinghurst, get your exit stamp here.

● Post & telecommunications

Serpost: at Velarde 6th block. **Telefónica**: on Puno.

● Tour companies & travel agents

Turismo de los Angeles, Jr Puno 657, T 571070, run trips to Lago Sandoval (US$25pp/day) and Lago Valencia. *Luly Tours*, Av Velarde 620, T 572133, informative. Reputable guides are: Hernán Llave Cortez, who can be contacted through *Hotel Wilson*; Willy Wither, Av León Velarde 391, T/F 571183; Edwin Latorre, T 571340, or through *Hotel Cabañaquinta*. Insist on a detailed explanation of the tour offered, if necessary sign a contract and make sure that, once you have paid, the programme is not scaled down.

● Transport

Local Motorcycle hire: scooters and mopeds can be hired from *Oconita*, on the corner of Puno and G Prado for US$1.35. This is the standard rate in town.

Air To **Lima** via **Cusco**, daily with Aero Continente (office on Velarde 500 block). Grupo Ocho (military flight) have flights to Iberia and then Iñapari once a week. Their office is at the airport. To **Rio Branco** (Brazil), with Aero Pua, once a week. A moto-taxi from town to the airport is US$1.35.

Road and River routes from Cusco are given above. Trucks for Cusco leave Puerto Maldonado usually between 1600 and 1900 from the market at León Velarde y Jr Troncoso.

A daily cargo boat leaves Puerto Maldonado for Colorado, 8 hrs, US$12; from there you continue to Boca Manu and Shintuya, 9-10 hrs.

To **Puerto Heath** (Bolivian border), it can take several days to find a boat going all the way to the Bolivian border. Motorized dugout canoes go to Puerto Pardo on Peruvian side, 5 hrs, US$4.50 pp (no hotels or shops); wait here for a canoe to Puerto Heath. It is fairly hard to get a boat from the border to Riberalta (a wait of up to 3 days is not uncommon), 3 days, US$15-20; alternatively, travel to the naval base at América, then fly.

JUNGLE TOURS FROM PUERTO MALDONADO

Trips can be made to **Lago Valencia**, 60 km away near the Bolivian border, 4 hrs there, 8 hrs back. It is an ox-bow lake with lots of wildlife. Many excellent beaches and islands are located within an hour's boat ride. Mosquitoes are voracious. If camping, take food and water.

It is quite easy to arrange a boat and guide from Puerto Maldonado (see **Tour companies** below) to the **Tambopata-Candamo Reserved Zone**, between the rivers Madre de Dios, Tambopata and Heath. Some superb ox-bow lakes can be visited and the birdwatching is wonderful.

Some of the lodges along the Tambopata river offer guiding and research placements to biology and environmental science graduates. For more details send an SAE to TReeS: UK – J Forrest, 64 Belsize Park, London, NW3 4EH. USA – W Widdowson, 5455 Agostino Court, Concord, CA 94521.

The **Bahauja-Sonene National Park** was declared in 1996 and stretches from the Heath river across the Tambopata, incorporating the Río Heath National Sanctuary. It is closed to visitors.

● **Jungle Lodges**

Cusco Amazónico Lodge (Albergue Cusco Amazónico), 45 mins by boat down the Río Madre de Dios, jungle tours and accommodation, US$80 pp/day (inc meals and guides), a naturalists programme is also provided, negotiable out of season, about 30 bungalows with private bathrooms, friendly staff but mixed reports; avoid in Feb when everyone goes on holiday inc the mechanic. Book at Andalucía 174, Lima 18, T 462775, F 455598, or Procuradores 48, Cusco, T 232161/223769.

Explorers Inn, book through Peruvian Safaris, Garcilaso de la Vega 1334, Casilla 10088, T 313047 Lima, or Plateros 365, T 235342 Cusco. The lodge is located in the Tambopata-Candamo Reserved Zone, in the part where most research work has been done, 58 km from Puerto Maldonado. It's a 3-hr ride on the Río Tambopata (2 hrs return, in the early morning, so take warm clothes and rain gear), one of the best places in Peru for seeing jungle birds (587 species have been recorded here), butterflies (1,200-plus species), dragonflies (over 150 species) as well as tree species and mammals (inc giant otters), but you probably need more than a 2-day tour to benefit fully from the location. The guides are biologists and naturalists from around the world who study in the reserve in return for acting as guides. They provide interesting wildlife-trips, inc to the Collpa macaw lick and speak English. US$160 for 3 days, 2 nights,

at the lodge; 5 days/4 nights at the Collpa lick US$450 pp; discounts are available in the low season Jan-Mar, and for larger groups; mixed reports on the food and service.

Tambopata Jungle Lodge, on the Río Tambopata, make reservations at Peruvian Andean Treks, Av Pardo 705, Cusco, T 225701, F 238911; from US$65 pp/night (children half price), all inclusive, naturalists programme provided, rec; US$160 for 3 nights 4 days.

EcoAmazonia Lodge, 1 hr by boat down the Madre de Dios, nr Lago Sandoval, a bit cheaper than other lodges in the area, book through offices in Cusco (C Plateros 351, T 236159), or Lima (Pasaje Los Pinos 114, Of 306, Miraflores, T 446-2286).

Colpa Lodge, run by *Rainforest Expeditions*, Galeón 120, Lima 41, T 438-9325, the most remote lodge in the area and therefore more expensive; 10-12 hrs trip up the Río Tambopata from Puerto Maldonado, opp one of the largest macaw licks in Amazonia.

TO IBERIA AND IÑAPARI

A very worthwhile 1 or 2-day excursion by motorcycle (see hire rates above) is by boat across the Río Madre de Dios and follow the road towards **Iberia** and **Iñapari** on the border with Brazil. This can only be done in the dry season. Along the road are picturesque *caseríos* (settlements) that serve as collecting and processing centres for the Brazil nut. Many trucks, of varying vintage, take this road and will offer lifts for US$10-20, 10 hrs to Iberia.

At **Planchón**, 40 km up the road, there is a hotel, **G**, which is clean, but has no mosquito nets, and 2 bar/restaurants. **Alegría** at Km 60 has a hotel/restaurant and Mavilla, at Km 80, a bar.

At **Alerta**, Km 115, there are several cheap, basic hotels and plenty of places to eat. If coming from Brazil, dollar bills can be changed. There are no immigartion facilities; continue to Puerto Maldonado, regular *combis*, 3 hrs, US$10. The river is safe to swim in. If there is a boat here, it is the quickest route to Brasiléia in Brazil (see page 610) apart from the plane. Take a cargo boat or motor canoe (*peque-peque*) to Porvenir (*Hotel La Marimba*, **F** pp, good, clean); times are approximate, allow for breakdowns. From Porvenir buses run to Cobija, in Bolivia (1 hr, US$1.50), across the border from Brasiléia.

At **San Lorenzo**, Km 145, is the *Bolpebra* bar, which serves cheap food and drink and is generally merry.

Iberia, Km 168, has two hotels, the best is **F** *Hostal Aquino*, basic, cold shower, rooms serviced daily.

Iñapari, at the end of the road, Km 235, has one hotel and a restaurant, but **Assis Brasil** across the border is much more attractive. Just wade across the river to get there.

There is a road from Assis Brasil into Brazil and connections to Bolivia. It can be cold travelling this road, so take a blanket or sleeping bag. There are no exchange facilities en route and poor exchange rates for Brazilian currency at Iñapari. From time to time it is possible to get a boat from Puerto Maldonado all the way to Iñapari. Note that taking shorter trips may mean getting stuck for days, or even weeks.

CROSSING TO BOLIVIA AND BRAZIL

Ensure that you get an exit stamp in Puerto Maldonado at the Peruvian immigration office or at the PNP. You cannot get an exit stamp in Iberia or Iñapari at the border. Consular visas for Brazil or Bolivia are not issued at the border.

To Bolivia: take the boat to Puerto Heath (see above) and get a tourist visa at the Bolivian immigration office (though it was closed at the time of writing).

To Brazil: by truck to Iñapari or flight to Iberia and truck from there. Get a tourist visa at the Brazilian immigration in Iñapari.

Information for travellers

BEFORE TRAVELLING

ENTRY REQUIREMENTS

● **Documents**

Tourist cards No visa is necessary for citizens of Western European and Scandinavian countries, Canada, the USA, Japan, Australia, New Zealand, Israel, Hong Kong, all Latin American and Caribbean countries (except Cuba), South Africa, Indonesia, Malaysia, Thailand, Taiwan, the Philippines and South Korea. A Tourist Card (*Cédula C*, obligatory) is obtained free from the immigration authorities on arrival in Peru for visits up to 90 days (insist on getting the full 90 days, at some borders cards valid for 60, or even only 30 days have been given). It is in duplicate, the original given up on arrival and the copy on departure, and may be renewed (see below). A new tourist card must be obtained for each re-entry or when an extension is given. If your tourist card is stolen or lost, apply for a new one at Migraciones, Paseo de la República 585, Lima, 0900-1300; very helpful. If you try to leave Peru without your tourist card, the fine is US$40.

Tourist visas, for citizens of countries not listed above, cost £8.40 or equivalent, for which you require a valid passport, a departure ticket from Peru (or a letter of guarantee from a travel agency), two colour passport photos, one application form and proof of economic solvency. All foreigners should be able to produce on demand some recognizable means of identification, preferably a passport. You must present your passport when reserving tickets for internal, as well as, international travel. An alternative is to photocopy the important pages of your passport – including the immigration stamp, and legalize it by a 'Notario público' (US$1.50). This way you can avoid showing your passport. We have received no reports of travellers being asked for an onward ticket at Tacna, Aguas Verdes, Macará, Yunguyo or Desaguadero. If you do not have one on arrival at the border, you may be forced to pay US$15 minimum for an out-going bus ticket. The best bet is to buy a bus ticket, Tacna-Arica if travelling to Chile, and Puno-La Paz if going to Bolivia, at the Ecuadorean border, eg Machala. Alternatively, a Tumbes-Guayaquil ticket will do. Travellers arriving by air report no onward flight checks at Lima airport.

Renewals and extensions Tourist visas and entry permits may be renewed for 60 days at Migraciones in Lima, address above (also in major towns like Cusco, Iquitos or Arequipa). You must present your passport, a valid return ticket to a destination outside Peru, a *solicitud* (written request for an extension) and payment of US$40 or the equivalent in soles. If you wish to extend your entry permit after 90 days have already elapsed since your entry into Peru this is possible at the discretion of the authorities, but on payment of a fine of US$20. The maximum stay in such a case would be 150 days from the first entry. If you are in the Puno area when your visa expires, it is sometimes quicker and easier to cross the border to Bolivia for a day and return with a new visa, often for 90 days, which you would not get in Lima or Cusco.

Business visas If a visitor is going to receive money from Peruvian sources, he/she must have a business visa: requirements are a valid passport, two colour passport photos, return ticket and a letter from an employer or Chamber of Commerce stating the nature of business, length of stay and guarantee that any Peruvian taxes will be paid. The visa costs £18.90 (or equivalent) and allows the holder to stay 90 days in the country. Visas are generally granted in 24 hrs. If wishing to extend, an application must be lodged with the Dirección General de Migraciones. On arrival business visitors must register with the Dirección General de Contribuciones for tax purposes.

Student visas To obtain a 1 year student visa you must have: proof of adequate funds, affiliation to a Peruvian body, a letter of recommendation from your own and a Peruvian Consul, a letter of moral and economic guarantee from a Peruvian citizen and 4 photographs (frontal and profile). You must also have a health check certificate which takes 4 weeks to get and costs US$10. Also, to obtain a student visa, if applying within Peru, you have to leave the country and collect it in La Paz, Arica or Guayaquil from Peruvian immigration (it costs US$20).

● **Tourist information**

The Fondo de Promoción Turística (Foptur) closed its national and international offices in 1992. Tourism was placed under the Ministerio de Industria, Comercio, Turismo e Integración, which has an office in each major town. Staff are helpful with advice. Some former Foptur offices in large cities have been taken over by former employees within a private organization called Infotur.

Outside Peru, information may be obtained from Peruvian Embassies and Consulates.

● **Tour Operator**

Amerindia, based in Quito, is a new regional ground operator, who cover Peru, Bolivia and Ecuador (as well as Belize, Costa Rica and Guatemala). It has been created to rediscover the wonders of Latin America. Tours are of the highest quality with experienced guides. Accommodation is in superb lodges. Among tours being offered will be luxury safari-style tents, land rover circuits and yacht charters along the coasts. Further information from Amerindia's head office T (593) 2 439736/469455, F (593) 2 439735, Email amerindi@pi.pro.ec, in UK from Penelope Kellie T (44) 1962 779317, F (44) 1962 779458, Email pkellie@yachtors.u-net.com, in USA T (1) 305 599 9008, F (1) 305 592 7060.

HEALTH

In addition to the advice given in **Health information**, visitors to Peru should be aware that eating from street vendors is considered safe only if the food is boiled or can be peeled. Most middle-class restaurants are safe. Do not eat ceviche unless you are sure that it has been thermally cooked; usually it is *cocinado en limón* (marinated in lemon). Tap water should not be drunk anywhere in Peru unless it has been boiled or treated with iodine, as that will kill all pathogens, including giardia. Boiled water is available throughout Peru. Note that at high altitudes boiling may be insufficient to purify water (since the boiling point is less than 100°C); additional forms of purification may be necessary. Of the water purification tablets sold in local chemists, Certimil do not dissolve; Micropur are much better.

Typhoid and hepatitis are common; get inoculated, either before you go, or in Lima. Be careful about buying gamma globulin in Peru as most pharmacists do not keep it under refrigeration, rendering it valueless. Buy a disposable syringe for US$0.25 to obviate the risk of hepatitis from the clinic or doctor's needle.

In Lima, there is a Centro de Antirrabia if you are unfortunate enough to be bitten by a rabid dog. In other cities, hospitals give anti-rabies injections (always have a check-up if bitten by a dog; rabies is not uncommon). Because of a TB epidemic, avoid non-pasteurized dairy products.

Further to the general advice about altitude sickness, note that, when walking at high altitude, the body needs sugar, which can be carried conveniently in the form of a block of crystallized pure cane sugar, called *chancaca*, and easily found in markets. Tonopan has been recommended for altitude sickness and headaches: take first pill 15 mins before landing, then 3 times a day.

Tampons are easy to obtain in the better pharmacies in large cities, but they are expensive. Hotels and chemists/pharmacies often let visitors use their toilets.

MONEY

● **Currency**

The new sol (S/) is divided into 100 céntimos. Notes in circulation are: S/100, S/50, S/20 and S/10. Coins: S/5, S/2, S/1, S/0.50, S/0.20 and S/0.10. The last remaining inti note in circulation, 5,000,000, is being replaced by the S/5 sol coin. Some prices are quoted in dollars in more expensive establishments, to avoid changes in the value of the sol. You can pay in soles, however. Try to break down large notes whenever you can.

Warning A large number of forged notes (especially US$20 and larger bills) are in circulation; check the numbers if possible, and hold notes up to the light to inspect the line which can be seen on the lefthand side of the bill spelling out the bill's amount. There should also be tiny pieces of thread in the paper (not glued on). Always check every bill when changing money. There is a shortage of change in museums, post offices, railway stations and even shops, while taxi drivers are notorious in this regard – one is simply told "no change". Do not accept this excuse.

● **Credit cards**
Visa (most common), Diners Club, and Mastercard (Access/Eurocard) are accepted. An 8% commission is charged on their use. Visa is accepted at Banco de Crédito, at better rates than for TCs and cash can be withdrawn – local currency only – at no commission, in most cities. Mastercard is not as widely accepted as shop signs indicate. Cash against Mastercard can be obtained, with commission, at Banco del Sur and Banco Wiese. ATMs of the Mastercard/Cirrus network can be found at all branches of Banco Regional del Norte. Credit cards cannot be used in smaller towns, only in the main cities. Credit card loss can be reported in Lima, T 444-1891/1896; card number required.

● **Exchange**
There are no restrictions on foreign exchange. Banks are the best place to change TCs into new soles; most charge no commission. They will also change cheques into dollars cash at 2-3% commission. The services of the Banco de Crédito have been repeatedly rec. *Casas de cambio* are good for changing dollars cash into soles. There is no difference in the exchange rate given by banks and *casas de cambio*. Always count your money in the presence of the cashier. It is possible to have US\$ or DM sent from your home country. Take the cheque to the banks and ask for a *liquidación por canje de moneda extranjera*. You will be charged 1% commission in US\$ or soles. US dollars are the most useful currency (take some small bills), but Deutsche marks can be negotiated in all large towns; other currencies carry high commission fees. For changing into or out of small amounts of dollars cash, the street changers give the best rates avoiding paperwork and queuing, but they also employ many ruses to give you a bad deal (check your soles before handing over your dollars, check their calculators, etc, and don't change money in crowded areas). If using their services think about taking a taxi after changing, to avoid being followed. Street changers usually congregate near an office where the exchange 'wholesaler' operates; he will probably be offering better rates than on the street.

Soles can be exchanged into dollars at the banks at Lima airport, and one can change soles for dollars at any border. Dollars can also be bought at the various frontiers.

NB No one, not even banks, will accept dollar bills that look 'old', or are in any way damaged or torn.

American Express state that they will sell TCs and give out emergency money, but only in Lima. Travel agents are allowed to accept foreign currencies in payment for their services, and to exchange small amounts. Try to avoid changing TCs outside the main cities: commission is high and it is often a difficult process. Travellers have reported great difficulty in cashing TCs in the jungle area, even Iquitos, and other remote areas. Always sign TCs in blue or black ink or ballpen. Thomas Cook/Mastercard refund assistance point: Viajes Laser, C Espinar, 331, Lima, T 449-0134/137. For Western Union, T Lima 440-7934.

● **Cost of living**
Living costs in the provinces are from 20 to 50% below those of Lima. Peru is expensive for the tourist, especially for those on a tight budget. For low and middle-income Peruvians, prices of many items are beyond their reach. In 1997 the South American Explorers Club estimated a budget of US\$25-30 pp a day for living comfortably, inc transport, or US\$12-15 a day for low budget travel. Accommodation rates range from US\$3-4 pp for the most basic *alojamiento* to over US\$100 for luxurious hotels in Lima and Cusco. For meal prices, see **Food** below.

Students can obtain very few reductions in Peru with an international student's card, except in and around Cusco. To be any use in Peru, it must bear the owner's photograph. An ISIC card can be obtained in Lima from San Martín 240, Barranco, T 774105, for US\$20.

GETTING THERE

BY AIR
● **From Europe**
Direct flights Amsterdam (KLM), Frankfurt (Lufthansa), Rome (Alitalia) and Madrid (Iberia). Cheap flights from London: one way is to go via Madrid with Iberia, or standby to Miami, then fly the airlines shown below. Aeroflot fly to Peru from Moscow via Stockholm and Cape Verde. To avoid paying Peru's 18% tax on international air tickets, take your used outward ticket with you when buying return passage.

● **From Latin America**
Regular flights to all South American countries and most Central American; in most cases, daily. Lloyd Aéreo Boliviano (LAB) is usually the cheapest airline for flights out of Lima but tickets bought in Peru are more expensive. Lacsa and AeroPerú fly from Mexico (in latter case Mexico City and Cancún).

● **From USA and Canada**

Miami is the main gateway to Peru with flights every day with American, United, also AeroPerú, daily, and Faucett, 6 a week (Faucett also flies Miami-Iquitos-Lima once a week). Other direct flights from New York (Lan Chile; Continental; United and AeroPerú/Mexicana via Miami, Servivensa via Caracas; Lacsa with change in San José; Avianca in Bogotá), Dallas (American), Houston (Continental), Boston (American via Miami), and Los Angeles (Lacsa, Continental, AeroPerú, Aerolíneas Argentinas, Varig, Lan Chile). Regular connections can be made from many other North American cities. AeroPerú and Faucett offer discounts on internal flights when you buy a Miami-Lima return ticket, eg US$250 for unlimited flights (check in advance for restrictions). See **Introduction and Hints**, page 17, on AeroPerú's Sudameripass round Latin America flight ticket and on the Mexi-AmeriPass of AeroPerú, AeroMéxico and Mexicana.

CUSTOMS

● **Duty free allowance**

400 cigarettes or 50 cigars or 500 grams of tobacco, 2 litres of alcoholic drinks, new articles for personal use or gifts up to value US$200.

● **Export ban**

No object of archaeological interest may be taken out of Peru.

ON ARRIVAL

● **Hours of business**

Shops: 0900 or 1000-1230 and 1500 or 1600-2000. In the main cities, supermarkets do not close for lunch and Lima has some that are open 24 hrs. Some are closed on Sat; most are closed on Sun. *Banks*: most are open 0900-1230, 1500-1800 the year round. Closed Sat. Some banks in Lima open from 0900-1600 and do not close for lunch. **NB** All banks close on 30 June and 31 Dec for balancing; if it falls on Sat or Sun, banks may close 1 day before or after. This does not apply to the banks at Jorge Chávez international airport which are open 24 hrs every day. *Offices*: 0830-1230, 1500-1800 the year round; some have continuous hours 0900-1700; most close on Sat. *Government Offices*: Jan to Mar, Mon-Fri 0830-1130. Rest of year: Mon-Fri 0900-1230, 1500-1800, but this changes frequently.

● **Official time**

5 hrs behind GMT.

● **Safety**

The following notes on personal safety should not hide the fact that most Peruvians, particularly outside those areas affected by crime or terrorism, are hospitable and helpful.

Thieves are active in markets, streets, buses and trains, choosing especially tourists as their targets. We have received reports of robbery from hotel rooms and safes from places as diverse as Huaraz, Paracas and Cusco. Snatch thieves in Lima are very fast, they often use beggars to distract you. The most common method of attack is bag-slashing. Take care everywhere, but especially when arriving in or leaving a town at night by bus or train; in fact, it is better to travel by day whenever possible. Take taxis to stations, when carrying luggage, before 0800 and after dark (look on it as an insurance policy). It is worth taking extra care during festivals when streets are crowded. For general hints on avoiding crime, please see the **Security** section at the beginning of the book. All the suggestions given there are valid for Peru. Avoid staying in hotels too near to bus companies, as drivers who stay overnight are sometimes in league with thieves; avoid restaurants near bus terminals if you have all your luggage with you, it is hard to keep an eye on all your gear when eating. On trains, one large bag is easier to watch, and lock to a rack (more than once), than lots of small ones. In poor areas of cities be on your guard as this is where most theft takes place. Try to find a travel companion if alone, as this will reduce the strain of watching your belongings all the time. If checking valuables into a hotel safe, ask for an itemized receipt, which should prevent any discrepanices later. The police presence in Lima, Arequipa, Puno and Cusco has been greatly stepped up. It is a good idea to inform your Embassy in Lima of your passport data (or leave a photocopy), so that if the passport is stolen delays for replacement are minimized. In general, common sense is the best policy. Outside the July-Aug peak holiday period, there is less tension, less risk of crime, and more friendliness. A friendly attitude on your part, smiling even when you've thwarted a thief's attempt, can help you out of trouble. In addition, do not be discourteous to officials.

Although certain illegal drugs are readily available anyone carrying any is almost automatically assumed to be a drug trafficker. If arrested on any charge the wait for trial in prison can take a year and is particularly unpleasant. Unfortunately, we have received reports of drug-planting, or mere accusation of drug-trafficking by the PNP on foreigners in Lima, with US$1,000 demanded for release. If you are asked by the narcotics police to the toilets to have your bags searched, insist on taking a witness. **Drugs use or purchase is punishable by up to 15 years' imprisonment**.

Tricks employed to get foreigners into trouble over drugs include slipping a packet of cocaine into the money you are exchanging, being invited to a party or somewhere involving a taxi ride, or simply being asked on the street if you want to buy cocaine. In all cases, a plain clothes 'policeman' will discover the planted cocaine, in your money, at your feet in the taxi, and will ask to see your passport and money. He will then return them, minus a large part of your cash. Do not get into a taxi, do not show your money, and try not to be intimidated. Being in pairs is no guarantee of security, and single women may be particularly vulnerable. Beware also thieves dressed as policemen asking for your passport and wanting to search for drugs; searching is only permitted if prior paperwork is done.

Insurgency It remains hard to tell how many followers and sympathizers Sendero Luminoso has, but the military now seems to have taken control of most departments. With the reestablishment of military control in the Central Highlands, there has been much improvement in safety there. It is still essential to inform yourself of the latest situation before going. There are many checkpoints, which present no problem. Travel only by day. Avoid the Huallaga Valley because of drug trafficking and terrorism.

For up-to-date information contact the Tourist Police, T Lima 437-8171/435-1342/437-8262, your embassy or consulate, fellow travellers, the South American Explorers Club, who issue the pamphlet 'How Not to Get Robbed in Peru' (T Lima 425-0142, or in Quito) and, also in Quito, *The Latin American Travel Advisor* (published by Latin American Travel Consultants, PO Box 17-17-908, Quito, F 593-2-562-566, e-mail LATA@pi.pro.ec).

● **Tipping**
Restaurants: service is included in the bill (see below), but if someone goes out of his way to serve tips can be given. Taxi drivers, none (in fact, bargain the price down, then pay extra for good service if you get it). Cloakroom attendants and hairdressers (very high class only), US$0.50-$1. Railway or airport porters, US$0.50. **NB** Anyone who as much as touches your bag will expect a tip. Usherettes, none. Car wash boys, US$0.30, car 'watch' boys, US$0.20.

● **Voltage**
220 volts AC, 60 cycles throughout the country, except Arequipa (50 cycles).

● **Weights and measures**
The metric system of weights and measures is compulsory.

ON DEPARTURE

● **Airport departure taxes**
There is a US$25 airport tax on international flight departures, payable in dollars or soles. For non-Peruvians, there is a security tax of US$4-5 and an airport tax of US$3.50-4 (depending on the airport) on domestic flights (if you are working in Peru, carry a letter stating this and insist you are 'residente' and pay local tax of US$2). 18% VAT is charged on air tickets.

WHERE TO STAY

● **Hotels**
All de luxe and 1st class hotels charge 28% in taxes, which includes VAT and service charges; lower category hotels charge 20-23% (similarly restaurants). Most hotels have this surcharge included in their prices, but best check first. By law all places that offer accommodation now have a plaque outside bearing the letters H (Hotel), Hs (Hostal), HR (Hotel Residencial) or P (Pensión) according to type. A hotel has 51 rooms or more, a hostal 50 or fewer; the categories do not describe quality or facilities. Many hotels have safe parking for motor cycles. All hotels seem to be crowded at the end of July, Independence celebrations. Reception areas may be misleading; it is a good idea to see the room before booking. Hotels tend to be more expensive in the N than in the S. When booking a hotel from an airport, or station by phone, always talk to the hotel yourself; do not let anyone do it for you (except an accredited hotel booking service). You will be told the hotel of your choice is full and be directed to a more expensive one. Information on youth hostels and student accommodation can be obtained from INTEJ, Av San Martín 240, Barranco, Lima, T 477-4105. Also Asociación Peruana de Albergues Turísticos Juveniles, Av Casimiro Ulloa 328, Miraflores, Lima, T 446-5488, F 444-8187. Always take a torch and candles, especially in remoter regions.

NB Hotels are checked by the police for drugs, especially the rooms of foreigners. Make sure they do not remove any of your belongings. You do not need to show them money. Cooperate, but be firm about your rights.

● **Camping**
Easy in Peru, especially along the coast. There can be problems with robbery when camping close to a small village. Avoid such a location, or ask permission to camp in a backyard or *chacra* (farmland). Most Peruvians are used to campers, but in some remote places, people have never seen a tent. Be casual about it, do not unpack all your gear, leave it inside your tent (especially at night) and never leave a tent unattended. Camping gas in little blue bottles is available in the main cities. Those with stoves designed for lead-free gasoline should use *ron de quemar*, available from hardware shops (*ferreterías*). White gas is called *bencina*, also available from hardware stores.

FOOD AND DRINK

FOOD

The high-class hotels and restaurants serve international food and, on demand, some native dishes, but the taverns (*chicherías*) and the local restaurants (*picanterías*) supply the highly seasoned native food at its best. Soups tend to be very good, and a meal in themselves. In the Lima area the most popular fish dishes are the *ceviche* – raw fish, seasoned with lemons, onions and red peppers (see **Health** above); the *escabeche* – fish with onions, hot green pepper, red peppers, prawns (*langostinos*), cumin, hard eggs, olives, and sprinkled with cheese; and *chupe de camarones*, a shrimp stew made with varying and somewhat surprising ingredients. *Parihuela* is a popular bouillabaisse which includes *yuyo de mar*, a tangy seaweed. *Yacu-chupe*, or green soup, has a basis of potato, with cheese, garlic, coriander leaves, parsley, peppers, eggs, onions, and mint. *Causa* and *carapulca* are two good potato dishes; *papa a la huancaína* is another potato dish, topped with a spicy sauce made with milk and cheese; *causa* is made with yellow potatoes, lemons, pepper, hard-boiled eggs, olives, lettuce, sweet cooked corn, sweet cooked potato, fresh cheese, and served with onion sauce. Favourite meat dishes are *ollucos con charqui* (a kind of potato with dried meat), *caucau*, made with tripe, potatoes, peppers, and parsley and served with rice; *anticuchos*, hearts of beef with garlic, peppers, cumin seeds and vinegar; *estofado de carne*, a stew which often contains wine; *carne en adobo*, a cut and seasoned steak; *fritos*, fried pork, usually eaten in the morning; *sancochado*, meat and all kinds of vegetables stewed together and seasoned with ground garlic; *lomo a la huancaína*, beef with egg and cheese sauce; *lomo saltado* is a beef stew with onions, vinegar, ginger, chilli, tomatoes and fried potatoes, served with rice; and *sopa a la criolla* containing thin noodles, beef heart, bits of egg and vegetables and pleasantly spiced. *Cuy* is guinea pig; *chicharrones*, deep fried chunks of pork ribs and chicken; *lechón*, suckling pig. Any dish described as *arequipeño* can be expected to be hot and spicy. *Mondonguito* is a boiled small intestine. The best beef is imported from Argentina and is expensive. Duck is excellent. *Rocoto relleno* is spicy bell pepper stuffed with beef and vegetables. Corn dishes: *choclo con queso*, corn on the cob with cheese; *tamales*, boiled corn dumplings filled with meat and wrapped in banana leaf; *cancha*, toasted corn. For snacks, Peruvian *empanadas* are good. *Palta rellena* is avocado filled with chicken salad.

Among the desserts and confections are *cocada al horno* – coconut, with yolk of egg, sesame seed, wine and butter; *picarones* – frittered cassava flour and eggs fried in fat and served with honey; *mazamorra morada* – purple maize, sweet potato starch, lemons, various dried fruits, sticks of ground cinnamon and cloves and perfumed pepper; *manjar blanco* – milk, sugar and eggs; *maná* – an almond paste with eggs, vanilla and milk; *alfajores* – shortbread biscuit with *manjar blanco*, pineapple, peanuts, etc; *pastelillos* – yucas with sweet potato, sugar and anise fried in fat and powdered with sugar and served hot; and *zango de pasas*, made with maize, syrup, raisins and sugar. *Turrón*, the Lima nougat, is worth trying. *Tejas* are sugar candies wrapped in wax paper; the pecan-flavoured ones are tastiest. The various Peruvian fruits are of good quality: they include bananas, the citrus fruits, pineapples, dates, avocados (*paltas*), eggfruit (*lúcuma*), the custard apple (*chirimoya*) which can be as big as your head, quince, *papaya*, mango, guava, the passion-fruit (*maracuyá*) and the soursop (*guanábana*).

The tea hour starts about 1800 at the good hotels. If asked to a party ask the hostess what time you are *really* expected unless the time is specified on the invitation card as *hora inglesa* – English time; Peruvians tend to ask guests for dinner at 2000.

A normal lunch or dinner costs US$5-8, but can go up to about US$80 in a first-class restaurant, with drinks and wine included. Middle and high-class restaurants add 11% tax and 17% service to the bill (sometimes 18% and 13% respectively); this is not shown on the price list or menu, check in advance. Lower class restaurants charge only 5% tax, while cheap, local restaurants charge no taxes. Lunch is the main meal: dinner in restaurants is normally about 1900 onwards, but choice may be more limited than lunchtime. There are plenty of cheap and good restaurants around the centre of Lima and most offer a 'business lunch' called *menú* for US$1.30-3 for a 3-course meal. There are many Chinese restaurants (*chifas*) in Peru which serve good food at reasonable prices. For really economically-minded people the *Comedores populares* in most cities of Peru offer a standard 3-course meal US$1. Meals at this price, or little more, can be found under name of *menú económico* at many restaurants throughout Peru.

DRINK

The usual international drinks with several very good local ones: *pisco*, a brandy made in the Ica valley, from which pisco *sour* is made; *chilcano*, a longer refreshing drink made with *guinda*, a local cherry brandy; and *algarrobina*, a sweet cocktail made with the syrup from the bark of the carob tree, egg whites, milk, pisco and cinnamon. Wine is acidic and not very good, the best of a poor lot are the Ica wines Tacama and

Ocucaje; both come in red, white and rosé, sweet and dry varieties. Tacama blancs de blancs and brut champagne have been rec, also Gran Tinto Reserva Especial. Viña Santo Tomás, from Chincha, is reasonable and cheap. Casapalca is not rec. Beer is best in lager and porter types, especially the Cusco and Arequipa brands (lager) and Trujillo Malta (porter). In Lima only Cristal and Pilsener (not related to true Pilsen) are readily available, others have to be sought out. Look out for the sweetish 'maltina' brown ale, which makes a change from the ubiquitous pilsner – type beers. *Chicha de jora* is a maize beer, usually homemade and not easy to come by, refreshing but strong, and *chicha morada* is a soft drink made with purple maize. Coffee is often brought to the table in a small jug accompanied by a mug of hot water to which you add the coffee essence. If you want coffee with milk, a mug of milk is brought. There are many different kinds of herb tea: the commonest are *manzanilla* (camomile) and *hierbaluisa* (lemon grass).

GETTING AROUND

AIR TRANSPORT

Air services link towns which are often far apart and can only be reached otherwise with difficulty. The two main companies are Faucett and AeroPerú. Aero Continente flies mostly the same routes as these for about the same fares, but with better service. Expreso Aéreo fly to towns in the mountains and the jungle using smaller aircraft (not very reliable). The airforce runs some commercial flights to jungle areas, only a few times a month, not reliable, but half the price of other airlines. Tickets are not interchangeable between the companies, but may be permitted in the case of cancelled flights. See under Lima (page 1241) for airline addresses, and above for taxes. Note that flight schedules and departure times change often, and that delays are common. In the rainy season cancellations occur, sometimes for 2 days. There are also unannounced route changes and poor time-keeping. Always allow an extra day between national and international flights, especially in the rainy season. Internal flight prices are fixed in US dollars (but can be paid in soles) and have 18% tax added. Prices given in the text were valid in Sept 1995. It is possible to buy AeroPerú domestic tickets more cheaply outside Peru, but the offer changes frequently. You cannot alter the destinations in Peru, only the date. (If you fly Cusco-Juliaca you go via Arequipa and can stop over, completing the Juliaca leg later.) If you fly to Peru with AeroPerú from Miami, you are given one free internal flight and any other routes for US$50 each. AeroPerú and Faucett offer 2, 3, 4 or 5-stop tickets for US$99, US$149, US$179 or US$209 if bought outside Peru; also an unlimited ticket for US$269, valid for 30 days. If you have a choice, remember time-keeping tends to be better early am than later. When buying an internal flight, check with travel agencies for occasional special deals, but scrutinize the ticket carefully. Also check with the different airlines; even though they maintain the same set price, they sometimes do promotions on flights.

NB If possible travel with hand luggage only (48 cm x 24 cm x 37 cm) so there is more chance of you and your baggage arriving at the same destination. Unpredictable weather contributes to poor time-keeping, but companies are also criticized for their passenger service, especially as regards information and overbooking. Note that flights into the mountains may well be put forward 1 hr if there are reports of bad weather. Neither AeroPerú or Faucett has enough aircraft and both are in financial difficulties. Flights to jungle regions are also unreliable. See also warning on page 1351.

Flights must be reconfirmed in the town you will be leaving from 24 hrs in advance, but 72 hrs is advised. 20 mins before departure, the clerk is allowed by law to let standby passengers board, taking the reserved seats of those who haven't turned up. AeroPerú offers senior citizen discounts (40%) but some offices may not grant them. Tickets can be bought through travel agencies (but check them carefully), or direct through the airline; the price is the same.

Air Freight Luggage, packets, etc, are not handled with care; make sure there are no loose parts, or put your rucksack in a separate bag. Always lock your luggage when possible. Check that the correct destination label has been attached. Never put valuables into luggage to be checked in.

LAND TRANSPORT
● **Trains**
Two railways run up the slopes of the Andes to reach the Sierra. These railways runs from Lima in the centre to La Oroya, at which point it splits, one section going to Cerro de Pasco and the other to Huancavelica, via Huancayo. One of the ports of Matarani and Mollendo in the S through Arequipa to Juliaca; here again the line splits, to Cusco and to Puno. A separate part links Cusco with Quillabamba via Machu Picchu. There are in all 2,121 km of railway (1993). There are passenger services on the following lines, which are often quicker and more comfortable than buses: Huancayo-Huancavelica, Arequipa-Juliaca-Puno, Puno-Juliaca-Cusco, and Cusco-

Machu Picchu-Quillabamba. Details of services in the text. Good cheap meals are usually served on trains. **NB** Train schedules are cut in the rainy season, sometimes to 2-3 times a week, occasionally are cancelled for weeks or months.

● **Road**

There are three main paved roads: the Pan-American Highway runs N-S through the coastal desert; it is much improved. Paved spurs run from Pacasmayo to Cajamarca and Olmos to Jaén. Holes are a constant problem. South of Lima another spur runs NE into the Sierra to Arequipa, with a partially paved continuation to Puno on Lake Titicaca which then skirts the lake to Desaguadero, on the Bolivian frontier, a total of 3,418 km. The road to Arequipa is much improved (1995); that to Puno is not good. Improvement is under way on the routes Arequipa-Cusco, Nasca-Abancay-Cusco and Pisco-Ayacucho. The Central Highway from Lima to Huancayo is mostly well-paved; it continues (mostly paved) to Pucallpa in the Amazon basin. Also paved and well-maintained is the direct road from Lima N to Huaraz.

All other roads in the mountains are of dirt, some good, some very bad. Each year they are affected by heavy rain and mud slides, especially those on the E slopes of the mountains. Repairs are limited to a minimum because of a shortage of funds. Note that some of these roads can be dangerous or impassable in the rainy season. Check beforehand with locals (not with bus companies, who only want to sell tickets) as accidents are common at these times. Total road length in 1995 was 71,400 km.

Toll roads in Peru include Aguas Verdes-Tumbes, many on the Pan-American Highway between Tumbes and Lima, Pativilca-Huaraz, Lima-Pucusana, Ica-Nasca, Lima (highway around city), Variante-Pacasmayo, which vary from US$1.50 to US$0.50. Ecuador to Chile/Bolivia on main roads comes to about US$17. (Motorcycles are exempt from road tolls: use the extreme righthand lane at toll gates.)

If you have to drive at night, do not go fast; many local vehicles have poor lights and street lighting is bad. Be sure to check with the Peruvian Touring and Automobile Club regarding road conditions before driving in the Sierra.

● **Motoring**

The Touring y Automóvil Club del Perú, Av César Vallejo 699, Lince, Lima (T 403270, F 419652), with offices in most provincial cities, gives news about the roads and hotels along the way (although for the most up-to-date information try the bus and colectivo offices). It sells a very good road map at US$6.25 (Mapa Vial del Perú, 1:3,000,000, Ed 1980, reliable information about road conditions) and route maps covering most of Peru (Hoja de Ruta, detail maps 1:1,000,000, very good but no information on road conditions). Good maps are available from the South American Explorers Club, who will give good advice on road conditions. Buy maps separately or in packages of 8. Cuadernos de Viaje are travel notebooks covering all Peru with valuable information and maps, in Spanish. Other maps can be bought from street vendors in Colmena and Plaza San Martín, Lima. 'Westermanns Monatshefte; folio Ecuador, Peru, Bolivien' has excellent maps of Peru, especially the archaeological sites.

Gasoline is sold as: 'extra' (84 octane), US$2.10 a gallon, and 'importada' (95 octane), US$2.60-2.75 a gallon, found in Lima, the coastal towns and Arequipa; unleaded fuel (90 and 97 octane SP) is sold on the coast, US$2.25-US$3. Fuel in remote jungle areas can be double the price of urban areas. Diesel costs US$1.40 a gallon. Filling stations are called *grifos*.

In Lima never trust the green light; Peruvian drivers tend to regard traffic lights as recommendations, at most. When parking remove detachable accessories and screen wipers. No-parking signs are painted at the roadside: illegally parked cars are towed away. Do not leave your vehicle on the street in Lima, always put it in a car park (called *playa*, usual charge US$0.50/hr). If you want to sleep in your car, check with the local tourist police first. They may allow you to park near their office.

Roads go to very high altitudes in Peru – make sure that the spark is properly adjusted and consider use of smaller carburettor jets if driving much at altitude. Avoid mountain travel between Nov and April. Take 2 planks of wood in case car gets stuck in soft soil when allowing other vehicles to pass. Never travel off the main roads without being self-sufficient. Always make sure your fuel tank is full when branching off a major highway, fill up whenever possible and make sure you do not receive diesel or kerosene. If you need mechanical assistance in the mountains ask for the nearest mining or road construction camp. If you take your own car you are immediately a symbol of wealth and will be liable to have it broken into. Disadvantages of travelling in your own vehicle include the difficulties of getting insurance, theft, finding guarded parking lots, maintenance on appalling roads and nervous exhaustion, which may outweigh the advantages of mobility and independence.

Imported car spares available and cheaper than in neighbouring countries. Makes with well-established dealerships are easiest to obtain (eg Volvo, Peugeot, VW). VW Beetles, Toyota Coronas and Datsun Stanzas are assembled in Peru and are therefore easier to get spares and service for. There is also a booming black market in motor parts involving both contraband and stolen parts.

You must have an international driving licence – especially with a number. If you don't have a number on your licence, improvise. (It has been reported that a UK driving licence is acceptable.) A 90-day transit permit for vehicles is available at land borders without a *carnet de passages*, contrary to what officials may tell you (see **Motoring** in **Introduction and Hints**). The minimum age for renting a car is 25.

● **Bus**

Services along the coast and to Arequipa are usually quite good, but try to avoid travel at night, assaults on buses have occurred; buses in the mountain areas generally are small, old, crowded and offer little comfort. The larger companies are usually the best as they tend not to cancel services; the smaller companies will cancel if they do not have enough passengers. The main companies (and some others) have luxury services on the coastal routes, with toilet, video and reclining seats. Tickets cost 30% more than normal. For bus lines, see Lima, **Bus Companies**. For long journeys take a water bottle. Blankets and emergency food are a *must* in the mountains. Always possible to buy food on the roadside, as buses stop frequently. Luggage can be checked in on a bus, but it is your own responsibility to look after it when the bus stops. Backpacks can be protected by a rice sack, for further security use chicken wire as well. Always carry your valuables with you, even when leaving the bus at a stop. If your bus breaks down and you are transferred to another line and have to pay extra, keep your original ticket for refund from the first company. If possible, on country buses avoid the back seats because of the bumpiness, and the left side because of exhaust fumes. Prices given in the text are the minimum for the route. Colectivos usually charge twice the bus fare. They leave only when full. They go almost anywhere in Peru; most firms have offices. Book 1 day in advance. They pick you up at your hotel or in the main plaza. Trucks are not always much cheaper than buses; they charge 3/4 bus fare, but wholly unpredictable, not for long hops, and comfort depends on the load. Always try to arrive at your destination in daylight: much safer.

NB Prices of bus tickets are raised by 50-75%, 2-3 days before 28 July (Independence Day) and Christmas. Tickets are sold out 2-3 days in advance at this time and transport is hard to come by.

● **Hitchhiking**

Hitchhiking is difficult. Freight traffic has to stop at the police *garitas* outside each town and these are the best places to try (also toll points, but these are further from towns). Drivers usually ask for money but don't always expect to get it. In mountain and jungle areas you usually have to pay drivers of lorries, vans and even private cars; ask the driver first how much he is going to charge, and then recheck with the locals. Private cars are very few and far between. Readers report that mining trucks are especially dirty to travel in, avoid if possible.

● **Taxi**

Taxi prices are fixed in the mountain towns, about US$0.80 in the urban area. Fares are not fixed in Lima even though there are standard fares (see under Lima). Most taxi drivers will try to charge more for foreigners, so ask locals. The main cities have taxis which can be hired by phone, which charge a little more, but are reliable and safe.

Many taxi drivers work for commission from hotels. Choose your own hotel and get a taxi driver who is willing to take you there.

Taxis at airports are always more expensive; seek advice about the price in advance and do not use the taxis in front of the airport.

COMMUNICATIONS

● **Language**

Spanish. Quechua, the language of the Inca empire, has been given some official status and there is much pride in its use; it is spoken by millions of Sierra Indians who have little or no knowledge of Spanish. Another important Indian language is Aymara, used in the area around Lake Titicaca.

● **Newspapers**

Lima has several morning papers: *La Nación*, *El Comercio* (good international news), *La República* (liberal-left), *Expreso*, *Ojo*, *El Mundo*; *El Peruano* (with parliamentary gazette); *Síntesis* and *Gestión* are business dailies. Weekly magazines are *Caretas* and *Sí*; monthlies include *Business*, *Proceso Económico*, *Debate* and *Idede*. There is a monthly magazine in English, the *Lima Times*, with useful information and articles, and a weekly economic and political report, the *Andean Report*. The main provincial cities have at least one newspaper each.

● **Postal services**

Sending parcels abroad must be done at Centro de Clasificación de Correos, Tomás Valle, block 600, Lima (take bus 128, direction San Germán); open Mon-Fri 0900-1330, Sat 0800-1300. Staff in the post office help with all checking and then sew parcels into sacks for US$1. It can cost about US$20/kg to send a parcel abroad. To avoid paying a tax of US$0.20/kg on parcels sent abroad, take your passport and onward ticket, plus a photocopy of each to the post office. Better still, take your parcels to another country for mailing home; it will almost certainly be cheaper. Try not to have articles sent by post to Peru; taxes can be 200% of the value. To send a letter up to 20 grams anywhere in the Americas costs US$1, to the rest of the world US$1.20. For US$0.50 extra letters can be sent 'con certificado', which is rec. A Dutch company called EMS are reliable for sending smaller packages, eg film, home. Expensive US$34/kilo (to Europe). More expensive still is UPS; see under Lima, **Air Freight**.

● **Telephone services**

The state company, Entel, has been privatized and is now called Telefónica del Perú. There are offices in all large and medium-sized towns. Overseas calls made through the operator cost on average US$12 for 3 mins (minimum). Collect calls can now be made (most of the time) to North America and some European countries at the CPT office on Plaza San Martín, Lima, or elsewhere from Telefónica offices. The best place to try is Lima. Local, national and international calls can be made from public phone boxes with coins or phone cards which can be bought at Telefónica offices (though cards don't work everywhere). Telephone directories found in most hotel rooms have a useful map of Lima and show itineraries of the buses. Fax and telex abroad can be sent from major Telefónica offices, US$4-5/page/minute. (See also Lima, **Telecommunication**.)

SPORT

Association football is the most popular. Basketball and other sports are also played on the coast, particularly around Lima and Callao. Golf clubs and racecourses are mentioned in the text. Riding is a favourite recreation in the Sierra, where horses can be hired at reasonable rates. Cricket is played at the Lima Cricket Club. Bullfights and cockfights are held throughout the country. There is excellent deep-sea fishing off Ancón, N of Lima, and at the small port of Cabo Blanco, N of Talara (see text). In that part of the Andes easily reached from La Oroya, the lakes and streams have been stocked with trout, and fly fishing is quite good.

For details about the best rainbow trout fishing in Peru (near Juliaca and in Lakes Arapa and Titicaca) write to Sr José Bernal Paredes, Casilla 874, Arequipa.

Swimming   Between Dec and April the entire coast of Peru offers good bathing, but during the rest of the year only the northern beaches near Tumbes provide pleasantly warm water. There are many bathing resorts near Lima (do not swim at, or even visit, these beaches alone). The current off the coast can be very strong, making it too dangerous to swim in places. A Foptur brochure lists the many surfing beaches.

Walking   The South American Explorers Club has good information and advice on trekking and sells books. Serious walkers are advised to get *Back-packing and Trekking in Peru and Bolivia* (Bradt Publications, T/F (UK) 01494-873478) which describes 3-5 day treks in the Cordilleras Blanca, Vilcabamba and Vilcanota (Cusco region), and in the Cajamarca area (6th edition, 1995). John Richter's *Yurak Yunka* can be obtained from the South American Explorers' Club or from *Lima 2000* bookshop, J Bernal 271, Lima. For an account of the Andean Inca road, see Christopher Portway, *Journey Along the Andes* (Impact Books, London, 1993). See also page 13507.

The popular trekking routes in Peru are becoming damaged because of over use. Little is done by the government to maintain the trails and less is done by locals. Trekkers are given no information and no guards control the routes. A few conservation groups are trying to combat this problem, but with very little success. Please give everyone a good example by not dropping litter and by picking up that left by others. Point out the importance of this to guides and porters.

HOLIDAYS AND FESTIVALS

1 Jan: New Year. Mar or April: Maundy Thursday (pm). Good Friday. 1 May: Labour Day. 29 June: Saints Peter and Paul. 28, 29 July: Independence (when all prices go up). 30 Aug: Santa Rosa de Lima. 7 Oct: Battle of Angamos. 1 Nov: All Saints. 8 Dec: Immaculate Conception. 25 Dec: Christmas.

NB Everything closes on New Year's Eve, Christmas Eve, and other holidays designated 'family holidays', especially July-Aug. At these times, expect prices to rise.

Between mid-July and the beginning of Sept is the Peruvian tourist season: prices rise, transport can be difficult and hotels are heavily booked. The big national holidays are Dec, Jan and Feb.

FURTHER READING

The Peru Reader, edited by Orin Starn, Carlos Iván Degregori and Robin Kirk (Duke University Press; Durham and London, 1995) contains history, culture and politics and is an excellent introduction to these topics; the anthology ranges from the precolonial to the present.

ACKNOWLEDGEMENTS

We are deeply grateful to Alan Murphy and Gavin Clark for updating this chapter. For their invaluable help in the preparation of this chapter, thanks go to the South American Explorers' Club, Lima; Peter Frost, Cusco; Alberto Cafferata, Caraz; James Vreeland and Cecilia Kamiche, Arequipa; John Hemming; and John Forrest of TReeS, London.

Uruguay

HORIZONS

Uruguay is the smallest Hispanic country in South America; its official name is República Oriental del Uruguay.

LANDSCAPE AND CLIMATE

Apart from a narrow plain which fringes most of the coast (but not near Montevideo), and an alluvial flood plain stretching N from Colonia to Fray Bentos, the general character of the land is undulating, with little forest except on the banks of its rivers and streams. The long grass slopes rise gently to far-off hills, but none of these is higher than 600m. Five rivers flow westwards across the country to drain into the Río Uruguay, including the Río Negro, which rises in Brazil and on which a number of dams have been built, creating a series of large, artificial lakes across the centre of the country.

Climate Temperate, if somewhat damp and windy, and summer heat is tempered by Atlantic breezes, but there are occasional large variations. In winter (June-Sept), when the average temperature is 10° to 16°C, the temperature can fall now and then to well below freezing. It is generally humid and hardly ever snows. Summer (Dec-Mar), with an average temperature of 21° to 27°C, has irregular dry periods. There is always some wind and for the most part the nights are relatively cool. The rainfall, with prolonged wet periods in July and Aug, averages about 1,200 mm at Montevideo and some 250 more in the N, but the amount varies yearly.

HISTORY

Colonization The Spanish explorer, Juan Díaz de Solís, sailed up the Río de la Plata in 1516 and landed E of the site of Montevideo, near what is now Maldonado. His second landing was in the present Department of Colonia, where he was killed by the Charrúa Indians. There was no gold or silver in Uruguay, and it was only after about 1580 that the Spaniards showed any interest in it. Military expeditions against the Indians were unsuccessful, but Jesuit and Franciscan missionaries, landing in 1624, founded a settlement on Vizcaíno Island. It is said that cattle were first introduced during an unsuccessful expedition by Hernando Arias in 1607; they were successfully established between 1611 and 1620.

By 1680, the Portuguese in Brazil had pushed S to the Plata and founded Colonia de Sacramento as a rival to Buenos Aires, on the opposite shore. It was the Portuguese who planned, but the Spaniards who actually founded, Montevideo in 1726 as a fortress against the Portuguese at Colonia. It changed hands several times and was also taken by the British in 1807, but after their failure to hold Buenos Aires, they withdrew altogether.

Uruguay

1. Montevideo
2. East from Montevideo
3. Montevideo North - East to Brazil
4. Montevideo North to Brazil
5. West from Montevideo
6. Up the River Uruguay

The struggle for independence In 1808 Montevideo declared its independence from Buenos Aires. In 1811, the Brazilians attacked from the N, but the local patriot, José Gervasio Artigas, rose in arms against them. In the early stages he had some of the Argentine provinces for allies, but soon declared the independence of Uruguay from both Brazil and Argentina. Buenos Aires invaded again in 1812 and was able to enter Montevideo in June 1814. In Jan the following year the Orientales (Uruguayans) defeated the Argentines at Guayabos and regained Montevideo. The Portuguese then occupied all territory S of the Río Negro except Montevideo and Colonia. The struggle continued from 1814 to 1820, but Artigas had to flee to Paraguay when Brazil took Montevideo in 1820. In 1825 General Juan Lavalleja, at the head of 33 patriots (the Treinta y Tres Orientales), crossed from Argentina and returned to Uruguay, with Argentine aid, to harass the invaders. After the defeat of the Brazilians at Ituzaingó on 20 February 1827,

Britain intervened, both Argentina and Brazil relinquished their claims on the country, and independence was finally achieved in 1828.

19th century upheavals The early history of the republic was marked by a civil war (known as the Guerra Grande) which began as a conflict between two rival leaders, José Fructuoso Rivera with his Colorados and Manuel Oribe with his Blancos; these are still the two main parties today. Oribe was helped by the Argentine dictator, Juan Manuel de Rosas, but was overthrown in 1838. Blanco forces, backed by Rosas, beseiged Montevideo between 1843 and 1851. Although Rosas fell from power in 1852, the contest between Colorados and Blancos continued. A Colorado, Gen Venancio Flores, helped by Argentina, became president, and, in 1865, Uruguay was dragged into the war of the Triple Alliance against the Paraguayan dictator, López. Flores was assassinated in 1868 3 days after his term as President ended.

Batlle y Ordoñez The country, wracked by civil war, dictatorship and intrigue, only emerged from its long political turmoil in 1903, when another Colorado, a great but controversial man, José Batlle y Ordóñez was elected president. During Batlle y Ordóñez' two terms as president, 1903-07 and 1911-15, Uruguay became within a short space of time the only "welfare state" in Latin America. Its workers' charter provides free medical service, old age and service pensions and unemployment pay. Education is free and compulsory, capital punishment abolished, and the church disestablished.

Guerrillas and Military rule As the country's former prosperity has ebbed away since the 1960s, the welfare state has become increasingly fictitious. The military promised to reduce bureaucracy and spend more on the poor and development after the turmoil of 1968-1973, the period in which the Tupamaros urban guerrilla movement was most active. In practice the military, which effectively wiped out the Tupamaros by 1972, expanded state spending by raising military and security

programmes. Real wages fell to less than half their 1968 level and only the very wealthy benefited from the military regime's attempted neo-liberal economic policies. Less than 10% of the unemployed received social security payments. Montevideo began to sprout shanty towns, once unheard of in this corner of the hemisphere. Nevertheless, the country's middle class remains very large, if impoverished, and the return to democracy in 1985 raised hopes that the deterioration in the social structure would be halted. Almost 10% of the population emigrated for economic or political reasons during the 1960s and 1970s: the unemployed continue to leave, but the political and artistic exiles have returned *en masse*.

Allying himself with the Armed Forces in 1973, the elected President, Juan M Bordaberry, dissolved Congress and stayed on to rule as the military's figurehead until 1976. Scheduled elections were cancelled in that year, and a further wave of political and trade union repression instituted. Unable to convince the population to vote for a new authoritarian constitution in 1980, the military became increasingly anxious to hand back power to conservative politicians. However, moderate politicians refused to accept the harsh conditions the military continued to propose.

Return to democracy In Aug 1984 agreement was reached finally on the legalization of most of the banned leftist parties and elections were held in November. Under the moderate government of Julio María Sanguinetti (of the Colorado party) the process of national reconstruction and political reconciliation began with a widespread political amnesty (endorsed by referendum in April 1989). The moderate conservative Partido Nacional (Blancos) won Nov 1989 presidential and congressional elections and Luis Alberto Lacalle took office as president on 1 March 1990. There was considerable opposition to plans for wage restraint, spending cuts, social reforms and privatization. Owing to the unpopularity of

Lacalle's market-oriented policies, his Blanco Party lost the Nov 1994 elections: Colorado ex-president Sanguinetti won 32.2% compared with 31.1% for the Blancos and 30.7% for the Frente Amplio, a broad left front. Each party won about a third of the seats in Congress. Soon after taking office in Mar 1995, President Sanguinetti managed to forge an alliance with the Blancos to introduce economic restructuring and steps towards implementing social security reforms which, although much needed, no previous administration had managed to draw up. While the coalition worked together to reduce the influence of the public sector, the Frente Amplio gained support for its aim of maintaining the welfare state.

In Dec 1996 a referendum was held on constitutional reforms, including changes to the presidential selection process which would restrict political parties to a single candidate for each election, the introduction of a second ballot for the presidency, further modernization of the election process and some increases in presidential power. The Blancos and Colorados were in favour of the changes, but the Frente, fearing that the two main parties would maintain their cooperation to keep it from power, was opposed. The electorate voted in favour of the changes.

CULTURE

PEOPLE

Settlement There was little Spanish settlement in the early years and, for a long time, the area was inhabited mainly by groups of nomadic *gauchos* who trailed after the herds of cattle killing them for food and selling their hides only. Organized commerce began with the arrival of cattle buyers from Buenos Aires who found it profitable to hire herdsmen to look after cattle in defined areas around their headquarters. By about 1800 most of the land had been parcelled out into large *estancias*. The only commercial farming was around Montevideo, where small *chacras* grew vegetables, wheat and maize for the near-by town.

It was only after independence in 1828 that immigration began on any scale. Montevideo was then a small town of 20,000 inhabitants. Between 1836 and 1926 about 648,000 immigrants arrived in Uruguay, mostly from Italy and Spain, some into the towns, some to grow crops and vegetables round Montevideo. The native Uruguayans remained pastoralists, leaving commercial farming to the immigrants. More recent immigrants, however, Jewish, Armenian, Lebanese and others have chosen to enter the retail trades, textiles and leather production rather than farming.

Population Just under half of the population lives in Greater Montevideo. Only some 14% are rural, and the drift to the towns is 1.6% per year. Uruguayans are virtually all European, mostly of Spanish and Italian stock. A small percentage in parts of Montevideo and near the Brazilian border are of mixed African and European descent. Less than 10% are *mestizos*.

MUSIC

Most musical influences came with the European immigrants who arrived after the disappearance of the Amerindian population. The folk songs and dances are very closely related to those of the Argentine pampas, except in the N, where they are shared with the neighbouring Brazilian state of Rio Grande do Sul. The major song genres are the Estilo, Cifra, Milonga and Vidalita, whilst the "national" dance is the stately Pericón for six or more couples. The Milonga is also danced, as are the Tango, Cielito, Media Caña and Ranchera. The guitar is the instrument that accompanies most country music and as in Argentina, the gauchos like to engage in Payadas de Contrapunto, where two singers vie with each other, alternating improvised verses. Nineteenth-century Europe introduced other popular dances into Uruguay, such as the polca, waltz, chotis and mazurca, all of which were given a local touch.

"Although the tango originated in Argentina, many composers, musicians and singers of Uruguay created first rate tango music since the beginning of the 20th century. One of the best known of all tangos, 'La Cumparsita', was composed by the Uruguayan Gerardo Matos Rodríguez in Montevideo in 1917." (John M Raspey)

In the northern departments a number of dances are shared with Brazil, such as the Chimarrita, Carangueijo and Tirana, which are also sung, either in Spanish or Portuguese or a mixture of both.

There were many black slaves in the Río de la Plata during colonial times and the African ritual of the Candombe was practised in Montevideo until late in the 19th century. Less than 3% of the population is black and the only musical remains of African origin are to be found in the presence during carnival of the Morenada groups of up to 50 Candomberos, who take part in the procession, playing their *tamboril* drums, while smaller groups take part in these so-called "Llamadas" from Dec through to Holy Week. There are four sizes of drums – *chico*, *repique*, *piano* and *bajo* – and the complex polyrhythms produced by the mass of drummers advancing down the street is both unexpected and impressive. (See also under Montevideo for more details on music. A useful booklet is *El Candombe* by Tomás Olivera Chirimini and Juan Antonio Varese, Ediciones El Galeón, 1992.)

THE ECONOMY

Structure of production Agriculture accounts for only 19% of gdp yet raw and processed agricultural products make up the great majority of exports. The soil is black and rich in potash, producing grasses superior even to those in Argentina, so that over three quarters of the land is given over to livestock rearing. Uruguay has historically been a major meat and meat product exporter, whose fortunes have fluctuated in line with world prices and, more recently, Brazilian demand. The cattle herd is almost 11 million head and rising. Sales of meat abroad have benefitted from the fact that the herd is free of foot and mouth disease and BSE ('mad cow disease'). The number of sheep

also rose in the 1980s and 1990s because of demand for live and slaughtered animals as well as wool, of which Uruguay is a major world producer. Sales of wool and meat account for about 15% and 21% respectively of total exports. The only grain exported is rice, but others grown for the domestic market include maize, sorghum and wheat. Also important are vegetable products, oilseeds (sunflower and linseed), and citrus fruits which are exported. Only a small portion of the country is forested but investment in forests is growing, with the aim of raising the area planted from 120,000 ha in the mid-1990s to 450,000 ha by 2015. The industry is expected to produce about 2.6 million tonnes of timber worth US$200mn by 2000.

Manufacturing, contributing 18% of gdp, is concerned largely with agroindustrial activities. The most important of these are meat packing, drinks, tobacco, textiles, clothing and footwear. The top ten exporting companies in Uruguay are involved in rice, dairy products, leather, wool, meat and vehicles. Medium-technology industries include oil refining, plastics, rubber products, electrical appliances and motor vehicle assembly.

Uruguay is heavily dependent on the economic fortunes of its neighbours, Argentina and Brazil, over and above its membership of the Mercosur customs union. An Argentine economic contraction hits Uruguay's tourism industry in Punta del Este and hotel construction falls, at the same time as lower demand cuts electricity output from the jointly owned power station. Changes in Brazilian demand and the fluctuations of the Brazilian exchange rate greatly affect Uruguayan exports of foodstuffs such as dairy produce and beef. Brazil accounts for about a quarter of exports and Argentina for about 20%. The financial sector's fortunes also fluctuate according to the economic health of Argentina and Brazil. Uruguay has been called the Switzerland of Latin America and is the repository of much of the region's exported capital.

Uruguay has no major mining industry, apart from the extraction of marble, gypsum and other construction materials. It has no known reserves of oil or natural gas. Its coal deposits are of poor quality and are not suitable for commercial mining. Most electricity generation comes from hydroelectric plants whose output, as in 1996-97, can be limited by drought.

Recent trends Like many Latin American debtors, Uruguay became unable to service its debts normally in the 1980s and had to reschedule its loans to commercial bank and government creditors in the context of an IMF stabilization programme. By the late 1980s Uruguay's external position had strengthened and net new borrowing from multilateral and commercial creditors took place on a voluntary basis. However, gdp growth slowed, the fiscal deficit grew and inflation soared to three figures. Debt servicing absorbed over half of all exports of goods and services. In 1990 the Government secured a debt reduction agreement covering US$1.6bn owed to commercial banks, supported by another IMF programme and structural adjustment loans from other multilateral and bilateral lenders. Gdp growth was restored and maintained, inflation was cut and the deficit of the non-financial public sector was cut from 3.5% of gdp in 1989 to record a surplus of 0.4% the following year.

The improvement in public finances came to a halt by the end of 1993, principally because of higher spending by both the central government and public enterprises. In 1994 inflation, which had been held down by slow depreciation of the exchange rate, came under pressure again as the public sector deficit widened. Privatization of state enterprises began slowly, but the airline, Pluna, a state bank and an airport were sold in 1995, the telecommunications company began to contract out services to a private company and the gas company was leased out to an international consortium. The Sanguinetti Government made its priorities restoring export competitiveness, lowering the fiscal deficit, public sector reform and social security system reform. On taking office it moved quickly to introduce an austerity budget with tax rises

Uruguay: fact file

Geographic

Land area	176,215 sq km
forested	5.3%
pastures	77.3%
cultivated	7.5%

Demographic

Population (1996)	3,140,000
annual growth rate (1990-95)	0.3%
urban	88.7%
rural	11.3%
density	17.8 per sq km

Education and Health

Life expectancy at birth,	
male	70.9 years
female	77.5 years
Infant mortality rate	
per 1,000 live births (1992)	18.7
Calorie intake as %	
of FAO requirement	103%
Population age 25 and over	
with no formal schooling	7.5%
Literate males (over 15)	94.5%
Literate females (over 15)	95.4%

Economic and Employment

GNP (1994 market prices)	US$14,725mn
GNP per capita	US$4,650
Public external debt (1994)	US$3,774mn
Tourism receipts (1994)	US$632mn
Inflation (annual av 1990-95)	60.9%
Population economically active (1993)	
	1,261,000
Unemployment rate (1993)	2.4%
Military forces	25,600

Source *Encyclopaedia Britannica*

and spending cuts. By dampening domestic demand and granting tax incentives to exporters, it was hoped that companies would turn to export markets and thereby reduce the trade deficit. Social security reform was essential, as the bankrupt system was the main reason for the fiscal deficit. In 1995, 15% of gdp was spent on pensions (10% in 1990); Uruguay's workforce of 1.3 million supported 0.7 million pensioners. Legislation was passed to end the state monopoly on insurance and a new pension law allowed private pension funds to be set up to compete with those of the state banks.

The fiscal and trade deficits were cut

in 1995 as a result of the austerity measures, but 1996 did not record the same success. Higher oil prices and increased oil imports to cover electricity generating shortfalls because of drought adversely affected both the budget and the import bill. The costs of restructuring the public sector, high public sector wages and the shift away from state to private pension schemes also added to the fiscal deficit. Nevertheless, the government anticipated gdp and exports to continue to grow and did not plan new austerity measures for 1997.

GOVERNMENT

Uruguay is a republic with a bicameral legislature: a Senate with 31 seats and a Chamber of Representatives with 99 seats. The president, who is head of state and of the government, holds office for 5 years. The country is divided into 19 provinces.

Montevideo

Montevideo, the capital (*pop* 1,311,976, in and near, 1994; *phone code* 02), was founded in 1726 (see **History** above). The original site is on a promontory between the Río de la Plata and an inner bay, though the fortifications have been destroyed. In addition to some colonial Spanish and Italian, French and Art Deco styles can be seen. The city not only dominates the country's commerce and culture: it accounts for 70% of industrial production and handles almost 90% of imports and exports. It is also a summer resort and the point of departure for a string of seaside resorts to the E (see **East from Montevideo**).

PLACES OF INTEREST

In the **Ciudad Vieja** (the old city – in poor shape) is the oldest square in Montevideo: the **Plaza de la Constitución**, also known as the Plaza Matriz. Here on one side is the **Catedral** (1790-1804), with the historic **Cabildo** (1808) opposite. Still further W along Calle Rincón is the small **Plaza Zabala**, with a monument to Zabala, founder of the city. N of this Plaza are the **Banco de la República** (Cerrito y Zabala), the **Aduana** (Rambla 25 de Agosto), and the **houses of Generals Rivera** (Rincón 437) and **Lavalleja** (Zabala 1469). Together, the last two form part of the Museo Histórico Nacional (see **Museums** below). Three blocks N of Plaza Zabala are the docks, while 3 blocks S is the Río de la Plata. The seafront road, the Rambla, has been opened round the point to the port. In the port (which one can visit on Sat from 1300 till sunset and on Sun from 0800 till sunset), opposite the Port Administration Building, the ship's bell of

HMS *Ajax* has been set up to commemorate the scuttling of the *Graf Spee*. The anchor of the *Graf Spee* was erected inside the port area in 1964 to commemorate the 25th anniversary of the battle. The old railway station (by the port, at end of Río Negro) is a romantic old building with an old train on display.

Between the Ciudad Vieja and the new city is the grandest of Montevideo's squares, **Plaza Independencia**, a short distance E of Plaza de la Constitución along the pedestrianized Calle Sarandí. In the middle is the impressive black marble mausoleum of Artigas. On three sides it is surrounded by colonnades, with pavement cafés at the eastern end. Also at the eastern end is the **Palacio Salvo**, a major landmark. On the southern side is the **Casa de Gobierno Histórico** (Palacio Estévez). The unfinished modern block to the W of the Casa de Gobierno will be the Palacio de Justicia (still unfinished in mid-1997). The Casa de Gobierno itself is now used for ceremonial purposes only as the executive offices have been moved to the Edificio Libertad, far from the centre. Just off the plaza to the W is the splendid **Teatro Solís**, in a wing of which is the **Museo de Historia Natural**, Buenos Aires 652, T 9060908, open Tues-Sun 1400-1800 (library 1230-1730).

The Avenida 18 de Julio, whose pavements are always thronged, runs E from Plaza Independencia. Along this avenue, between Julio Herrera and Río Negro, is the **Plaza Fabini**, or **del Entrevero**, with a statue of a group of *gauchos* engaged in battle, the last big piece of work by sculptor José Belloni; and the **Plaza Cagancha** (or Plaza Libertad), with a statue of Liberty.

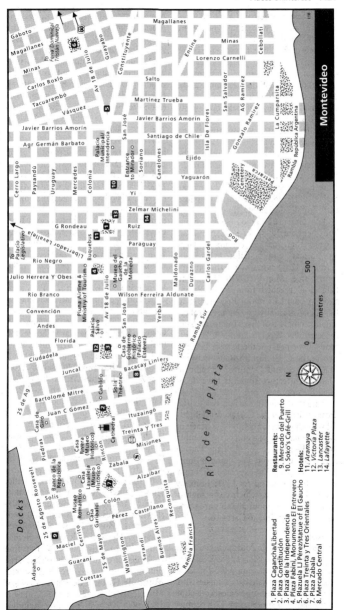

Montevideo

1. Plaza Cagancha/Libertad
2. Plaza Constitución
3. Plaza de la Independencia
4. Plaza Fabini, Monumento El Entrevero
5. Plazuela LJ Pérez/statue of El Gaucho
6. Plaza Treinta y Tres Orientales
7. Plaza Zabala
8. Mercado Central

Restaurants:
9. Mercado del Puerto
10. Soko's Café-Grill

Hotels:
11. Aramaya
12. Victoria Plaza
13. Lancaster
14. Lafayette

The **Palacio Municipal** (La Intendencia) is on the S side of Av 18 de Julio, just before it bends N, at the statue of **El Gaucho**. The best view of the city is from the top of the Palacio Municipal; external glass elevators take you up to a *mirador* (glass-fronted terrace) on the 22nd floor. Entrance at the back of the building on Soriano, between Ejido and Santiago de Chile; open 1230-2230, US$0.45. The road which forks S from the Gaucho is Constituyente, and leads to the beach at Pocitos.

Further E along Av 18 de Julio is the University; the avenue ends at an intersection with Bulevar General Artigas. Here is an obelisk commemorating the makers of the 1830 Constitution, by José Luis Zorrilla de San Martín (born 1891).

The immense **Palacio Legislativo** was built between 1908 and 1925 from local marble: there are 55 colours of Uruguayan marble in the Salón de los Pasos Perdidos, 12 types of wood in the Library (tours, free, Mon-Fri 0930-1200). The Palacio is reached from Plaza Fabini along Av del Libertador Brig Gen Juan Lavalleja (normally known as Av Libertador), 5 blocks E of Plaza Independencia (buses 150, 173, 175 from Calle Mercedes). Northeast of the Palacio Legislativo is the Calle Emilio Reus, between Blandengues and Domingo Aramburú, where architecture students have decorated the houses.

Among the main seaside residential areas are **Pocitos** and **Carrasco**, a delightful semi-rural place behind the beach of the same name at the end of the Rambla Sur, backed by the forest of the Parque Nacional Roosevelt. The international airport is nearby. The express bus DI runs every 30 mins along Av 18 de Julio; by using this service, which costs slightly more (US$1.20) about 30 mins are saved on the journey time to Carrasco.

Museums

Museo Nacional de Antropología, Av de las Instrucciones 948, T 956060, open Tues-Fri 1300-1900, Sun 1400-1800, ex-Quinta de Mendilaharsu, a modest but well-presented anthropological collection in the hall of a superb, late 19th century mansion (see, among other things, the Music Room with its huge, Chinese silk tapestry), bus 149 from Ejido. **Museo Zoológico**, Rambla República de Chile 4215, Buceo, Tues-Sun 1500-1900, free, well-displayed and arranged, rec, great for children too (bus 104 from 18 de Julio); **Cabildo** (History), Gómez y Sarandí (Mon-Fri 1400-2000); **Museo Casa Lavalleja**, Zabala 1469, Ciudad Vieja, Tues-Fri 1300-1900, Sun and holidays 1400-1800, free, historical mementos, furniture, etc, vast panoramic painting of the Battle of Sarandí by Juan Manuel Blanes; **Museo Casa Rivera**, Rincón 437, Tues-Fri 1300-1900, Sun 1400-1800. **Casa de Giró**, Cerrito 584-6, eleven rooms exhibiting the work of Uruguayan writers, historians, painters, etc, also has a library, open Tues-Fri 1300-1900, Sun and holidays 1400-1800. On 25 de Mayo are the **Casa del Gral José Garibaldi** (at No 314), Uruguayan history from 1843-48 (open daily 1300-1900), and **Casa de Montero**, **Museo Romántico**, No 428, with late 19th, early 20th century exhibits (both open as Casa de Giró, but Garibaldi 1 hr earlier on weekdays). The **Panteón Nacional**, Av Gonzalo Ramírez y Yaguarón, houses the burial monuments of local families, many with sculptured façades and inscriptions.

Museo Municipal de Bellas Artes Juan Manuel Blanes, Millán 4015 y Castro, Tues-Sun 1400-1800, free, ex-Quinta Raffo (late 19th century mansion) dedicated to the work of the artist Blanes (1830-1901), plus a room of the works of Pedro Figari (1861-1938), a lawyer who painted strange, naïve pictures of peasant life and negro ceremonies, also work by other Uruguayan artists; has a room with paintings by Courbet, Vlaminck, Utrillo, Dufy, etchings by Orozco and engravings by Goya; temporary exhibitions, admission free (buses 146, 148, 149, 150 from Mercedes). **Museo Nacional de Artes Visuales**, Herrera y Reissig y Tomás Garibaldi, Tues-Sun 1500-1900, free, fine collection of contemporary plastic arts, plus a room devoted to Blanes, rec. **Museo de Historia de Arte**, at Palacio Municipal (Ejido 1326), open Mon-Fri 1430-2000; **Centro de Exposiciones**,

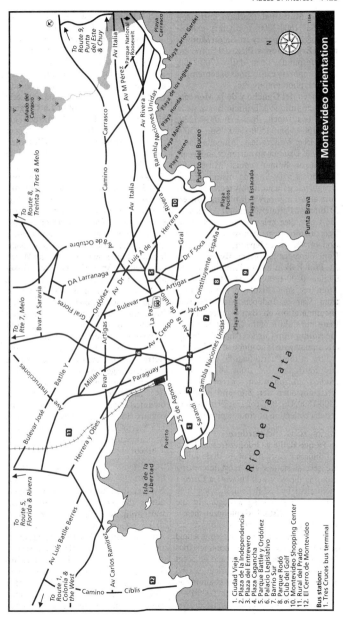

Montevideo orientation

1. Ciudad Vieja
2. Plaza de la Independencia
3. Plaza del Entrevero
4. Plaza Cagancha
5. Parque Battle y Ordóñez
6. Palacio Legislativo
7. Barrio Sur
8. Parque Rodó
9. Club del Golf
10. Montevideo Shopping Center
11. Rural del Prado
12. El Cerro de Montevideo

Bus station:
1. Tres Cruces bus terminal

Palacio Municipal (Soriano entrance), Mon-Sat 1600-2000, temporary exhibitions of contemporary art. **Salón Municipal de Exposiciones**, Plaza del Entrevero (underground), open daily 1700-2100, free, temporary exhibitions of contemporary art, photography, etc.

Museo del Gaucho y de la Moneda, Av 18 de Julio 998, Edificio Banco de la República, open Tues-Fri 0930-1230, 1300-1900, Sat 1530-1900, Sun 1500-1900, free: Museo de la Moneda has a survey of Uruguayan currency and a collection of Roman coins; Museo del Gaucho is a fascinating history of the Uruguayan gaucho, highly rec, but closed Sun; also temporary exhibitions. **Museo Militar**, at Fortaleza General Artigas, at the Cerro (see below), daily 1400-1900, free, historical mementos, documentation of War of Independence (bus 125 from Mercedes goes near). **Museo Naval**, Av Prof E Peluffo esq Rambla Rep de Chile, 0800-1200, 1400-1800, closed Thur, free, small display of naval history from War of Independence onwards, documentation on Battle of the River Plate and sinking of the *Graf Spee*, and on the sailing ship *Capitán Miranda*, which circumnavigated the globe in 1937-8 and is now in the Puerto (can be visited Sat and Sun), bus 104 from 18 de Julio. **Museo Aeronáutico**, Plaza de la Aviación, open Sat, Sun and holidays, 1400-1800, US$0.15 (bus 71, 79 from Mercedes), collection of vintage planes.

Parks, zoos and gardens

In **Parque Batlle y Ordóñez** (reached by a continuation eastwards of Av 18 de Julio), are several statues: the most interesting group is the very well-known **La Carreta** monument, by José Belloni, showing three yoke of oxen drawing a wagon. In the grounds is the **Estadio Centenario**, the national football stadium with a seating capacity of 70,000 and a football museum, a field for athletics and a bicycle race-track (bus 107). The **Jardín Zoológico** and adjacent **Planetarium** are SE of this park at Av Gral Rivera 3254 (buses 141, 142 or 144 from San José). The zoo is open Wed-Sun 0900-1900, entry US$0.15; the planetarium (free) gives good, 40-minute shows on Thur at 1730, Sat and Sun at 1630 and 1730.

From the Palacio Legislativo, Av Agraciada runs NW to **Parque Prado**, the oldest of the city's many parks, situated about 5 km from Av 18 de Julio (bus 125 and others). Among fine lawns, trees and lakes is a rose garden planted with 850 varieties, the monument of **La Diligencia** (the stage coach), the Círculo de Tenís and the Sociedad Rural premises. Part of the park is the adjacent **Jardín Botánico** (in fine condition, visits with a guide Mon-Fri, without a guide Sat-Sun, T 394420). It is reached via Av 19 de Abril (bus 522 from Ejido next to Palacio Municipal), or via Av Dr LA de Herrera (bus 147 from Paysandú). The largest and most popular park is **Parque Rodó**, on Rambla Presidente Wilson. Here are an open-air theatre, an amusement park, and a boating lake studded with islands. The Museo Nacional de Artes Visuales (see **Museums**) is at the eastern end.

At the eastern limits of the city is **Parque Nacional Roosevelt**, a green belt stretching N to the marshes of Carrasco (which are being drained). The city itself is expanding beyond Roosevelt.

At the western end of the bay is the **Cerro**, or hill, 139m high (from which Montevideo gets its name), with an old fort on the top, now the Museo Militar (see **Museums**). The Cerro is surmounted by the oldest lighthouse in the country (1804). Bus from centre to Cerro: 125 "Cerro" from Mercedes, and others, or boat Sat and Sun 1500-1900, US$5, T 618601/2.

THE BEACHES

Nine sandy bathing beaches stretch along almost the whole of the metropolitan water front, from Playa Ramírez in the W to Playa Carrasco in the E. Along the whole waterfront runs the Rambla Naciones Unidas, named along its several stretches in honour of various nations. Bus 104 from Aduana, which goes along Av 18 de Julio, gives a pleasant ride (further inland in winter) past Pocitos, Punta Gorda and all the beaches to Playa Miramar, beyond Carrasco. Much of the Rambla between the centre and Pocitos underwent major reconstruction while a new sewage system was installed, but all the beaches seem to be clean now.

LOCAL FESTIVALS

Easter week is also *Fiesta Criolla* (Tourist Week), with rodeo-type competitions held in the Parque Prado (US$1.50 entry – bus 185 from Pocitos, or 522 from Ejido) horse-breaking and handicrafts, music (mostly folk). Large barbecues are held in the open air. Also in the Parque Prado is the *Exposición Rural*, an agricultural show held every Aug; horse-riding competitions among other events. **Christmas Eve** and **New Year's Eve** are celebrated with drummers and firecrackers in the streets. During **carnival** week and a few days after there are many live shows; especially recommended is the traditional *candombe* singing and dancing in the Barrio Sur. There is an annual *Tango Festival* in Oct and the first half of Nov (information from Joventango, Soriano 956, T 915561, a non-profit organization which offers tango lessons and other events, open weekdays 1800-2000).

LOCAL INFORMATION

NB Some streets have changed name in recent years but this fact may not be marked on all maps: Michelini was Cuareim; Hector Gutiérrez Ruiz was Ibicuy; Convención was Latorre; Wilson Ferreira Aldunate was Río Branco.

● **Accommodation**

Hotel prices

L1	over US$200	**L2**	US$151-200
L3	US$101-150	**A1**	US$81-100
A2	US$61-80	**A3**	US$46-60
B	US$31-45	**C**	US$21-30
D	US$12-20	**E**	US$7-11
F	US$4-6	**G**	up to US$3

Unless otherwise stated, all hotels in range **D** and above have private bath. Assume friendliness and cleanliness in all cases.

During the tourist season, 15 Dec-15 Mar hotels should be booked in advance. At the beaches many hotels offer full board only during the season. After 1 April prices are greatly reduced and some hotel dining rooms shut down. For Carnival week, on the other hand, prices are raised by 20%.

The city is visited by many Argentines at weekends: many hotels increase prices; ask in advance. When not included, breakfast (*café completo*) costs US$4 or more in a hotel.

The tourist office has information only on more expensive hotels. For more information and reservations contact Asociación de Hoteles y Restaurantes del Uruguay, Gutiérrez Ruiz 1213, T 900346, F 980141. Hotels add a 14% charge to bills, on top of which there is 23% value-added tax.

In the Ciudad Vieja: L1 *Plaza Fuerte*, Bartolomé Mitre 1361, esq Sarandí, T 959563, F 959569, each room with different design, a/c, many other facilities, restaurant, bar, all in a historic building; **A2** *Columbia Palace*, Reconquista 470, T 960001, F 960192, first class, breakfast, IDD phone in every room, minibar, TV, restaurant, sauna, mixed music show; **B** *Palacio*, Bartolomé Mitre 1364, T 963612, safe, balconies, TV, highly rec; **D** *City*, Buenos Aires 462 (opp Correos), good value; **D** *Solís*, Bartolomé Mitre 1314, T 962887, basic; *Hospedaje Pensión Roy*, Sarandí 437, T 955328, good value budget hotel, access to kitchen, laundry facilities; **E** *Hostal Universal*, Piedras 272, small and basic rooms.

Centre, E of Ciudad Vieja: L1-L2 *Holiday Inn*, Colonia 823, T 920001, F 921242, rec for business visits, all services, convenient, pool and health club, has fax and telex; **L2** *Gran Hotel América*, Río Negro 1330, T 920392, F 920485, modern, a/c, central; **L3** *Claridge*, Mercedes 924, T 915746, F 916907, rec; **L3** *Lafayette*, Soriano 1170, T 922351, F 921301, with breakfast, good suites, spacious, but rooms are small, not suitable for business visitors, restaurant good, free parking.

A1 *Victoria Plaza*, Plaza Independencia, T 920111, F 921628, a/c, excellent restaurant (rooftop, fine views), casino in basement, friendly, faded old world charm (some cheaper rooms, see below), new 5-star wing; **A2** *Klee*, San José 1303, T 920606, F 987365, restaurant, business services; **A2** *Oxford*, Paraguay 1286, T 920046, F 923792, good breakfast, rec; **A2** *Alvear*, Yí 1372, T 920244, F 923728, good service, rec for business travellers; **A3** *Balfer*, Z Michelini 1328, T 921418, good, safe deposit, excellent breakfast; **A3** *Lancaster*, Plaza Cagancha 1334, T 921054, F 921117, a/c, with breakfast and fridge/bar; **A3** *London Palace*, Río Negro 1278, T 920024, F 921633, with breakfast (15% discount for Argentine ACA members), garage, parking; **A3** *Mediterráneo*, Paraguay 1486, T 905090, comfortable; **A3** *Ermitage*, Juan B Blanco 779-83, Playa Pocitos, business services.

B *King's*, Andes 1491, N of Plaza Independencia, T 920927, with breakfast, rec; **B** *Río* *de la Plata*, Av 18 de Julio 937, T 985174, F 921624; **B** *Montevideo*, Yaguarón 1309, T 904634, rec, small garage; **B** *Aramaya*, Av 18 de Julio 1103, T 921058, F 929039, old, comfortable.

C *Arapey*, Uruguay 925, T 907032, good value, heating, TV; **C** *Casablanca*, San José 1039, T 910918, good value; **C** *Itá*, San José 1160, T 913363, quiet, 10% discount if you stay more than a week; **C** *Royal*, Soriano 1120, T 983115, dark rooms, rec; **C** *Victoria Plaza*, Plaza Independencia 759, new annex of more expensive hotel (see above), nice rooms, helpful.

D *Ateneo*, Colonia 1147; **D** *Cifre* (10% discount on stays of over 2 weeks) Mercedes 1166, **E** with shared showers/toilets, use of kitchen; **D** *Hospedaje Diagonal 2*, Convención 1326 entre Av 18 de Julio y San José (not to be confused with *Diagonal 1*, Colonia 1168, which is red light); **D** *Ideal*, Colonia 914, T 916389, hot water, higher rates on Sat; **D** *Libertad*, Gutiérrez Ruiz 1223, quiet, laundry facilities and food available; **D** *Litoral*, Mercedes 887, T 905812, good value; **D** *Hospedaje del Centro*, Soriano, T 901419, cooking facilities, rec; **D** *Nueva Pensión Ideal*, Soriano 1073, excellent washing facilities, no breakfast; **D-E** *Windsor*, Michelini 1260, T 915080, simple, good location, helpful staff, hot water, pleasant, with bath.

D *El Aguila*, Colonia y Yí, clean, basic; **D** *Solanas*, Yí 1423, T 981070, good but check rates carefully; **D** *Torremolinos*, San José 774, T 900305.

Suburbs E of centre: L1 *Belmont House*, Av Rivera 6512 y Sanlúcar, Carrasco, T 600430, F 608609, 5-star, small, beautifully furnished, top quality, excellent restaurant and service, Pub/bar *Memories*, pool, 4 blocks from beach, highly rec; **L3** *Hostería del Lago*, Arizona 9637, T 612210, F 612880, E of Carrasco, Depto de Canelones, excellent; **A2** *Oceania*, Mar Artico 1227, Playa Los Ingleses, T 600444, F 602273, pleasant view, good restaurant and night club, highly rec; **A2** *Villa Biarriz*, Francisco Vidal 613, T 712543/716491, rec; **A3** *Cottage*, Miraflores 1360, Carrasco, T 600867, F 607114, no restaurant; **B** *Carrasco*, Rambla República de México, with breakfast, good, "ancient splendour, reasonable service", highly rec; **D** *Riviera*, Rambla Rep de México 6095, Carrasco, built in 1926 in Louis XV style, must be seen, pleasant, good service; **D** *Maracana*, Rambla Rep de Chile 4667, Malvín Beach, T 630418, good value, rec, take bus 60 from Plaza Cagancha (if coming from Brazil, buses stop outside the hotel).

Youth Hostel: the headquarters of the Association are at Pablo de María 1583, apartment 008, T 404245/400581, open 1130-1900 Mon-Fri. Hostel (members only) is at Canelones 935,

T 981324, open all year. US$8 pp (with seasonal variations, breakfast included, sheets US$1 extra), doors locked at 2400 (but security lax), friendly, clean, dormitory style, cooking facilities, cold, but plenty of hot water, shortage of bathrooms, closed Sat and Sun 1000-1700, events in pm can make it unwelcoming.

Camping: information on camping from Camping Club del Uruguay, Agraciada 3096. Parque Roosevelt, nr Carrasco, US$5 pp, free, hot showers, safe, no electricity, 15 km from centre, open all year. For vans and caravans only at Punta Ramírez on Rambla República Argentina, free for stays under 48 hrs, central, basic facilities, 24 hr security.

● **Places to eat**
There is a 23% value added tax on restaurant bills, plus 14% service. Dinner in "top class" establishments is taken between 2000-0100. Less formal restaurants serve from 1930 onwards. A meal costs from US$12 pp up to US$25 with wine. First-class restaurants at the centre are *Morini*, Ciudadela 1229, serves excellent steaks, simple, good value for US$18 pp inc wine, very popular for functions; *La Casa del Gobernador*, Plaza Zabala, new, good. Don't miss eating at the *Mercado del Puerto*, opp the Aduana, on Calle Piedras, between Maciel and Pérez Castellano (take "Aduana" bus), closed Sun, delicious grills cooked on huge charcoal grates (menus are limited to meat); colourful atmosphere and friendly, but not cheap; *La Pradera*, *La Estancia del Puerto*, *La Proa* and *Cabana Verónica* have been particularly rec; *Roldós*, specializes in sandwiches and *medio medio*; several are open at night, eg *El Palenque* (Pérez Castellano 1579, excellent), *La Posada del Puerto* (seafood), *La Tasca del Puerto* (plus dance show) and *La Marina Café-Bar*, nearby ones on Calle Pérez Castellano stay open later, eg *El Patriota*. Other good grill rooms (*parrilladas*) inc *Forte di Makale*, Requena García y Wilson; *Del Ferrocarril*, Río Negro 1746, in railway station, excellent, expensive; *Anticuario*, Maldonado 1602, expensive *parrillada*, atmospheric; *del Aguila*, Buenos Aires 694, good, traditional, piano music, good US$27 pp; *El Puertito de Pescadores*, Arenal Grande 2690, T 294272, excellent fish, N of centre, taxi US$4.

In the central Plaza Cagancha district: *La Genovesa* (Spanish), San José 1242, excellent, *marisquería* and *parrillada*; *Las Brasas*, San José 909, good typical food, US$20-25; *Otto*, Río Negro y San José, good value, restaurant and tea room; *Viejo Sancho*, San José 1229, excellent, US$25-30, popular, complimentary sherry or vermouth to early arrivals, tearoom by day; *Gran César*, Gutiérrez Ruiz 1285, similar, rec; *Danubio Azul*, Colonia 835, very good value, US$15-20. A reasonable place for lunch is restaurant on 6th floor of YMCA building, Colonia 1870, good views, ask for the Asociación Cristiana de Jóvenes; cheap lunches also at *Comedor Universitario*, Michelini 1175 y Canelones, and at Yaguarón 1234.

Vegetarian: *Vegetariana*, Av Brasil 3086, Pocitos, and other locations, excellent, self-service buffet; *Sabor Integral*, F Crespo 1531; *Vida Natural*, San José 1184; *Natura*, Rincón 414 and Scosería 2754 (Pocitos).

A good place for lunch is the *Golf Club*, Artigas 379, good food, international cuisine, smart, expensive, excellent surroundings and grand view.

Many good restaurants on seafront in Pocitos (names and ownership change frequently): *Spaghetería 23*, Scosería 2584, Tues-Sun, very good Italian; *Doña Flor*, Artigas 1034, classy French restaurant, limited menu but superb, moves to Punta del Este in summer; *Bungalow Suizo*, Sol 150, very good; *La Bizon*, Luis B Cavia 2719, cheap. In Carrasco, *Las Tablitas*, P Murillo 6666, *parrillada*; *Picapiedras*; and *La Casa Violeta*, opp each other on Av Arocena (discounts for non-smokers); *Dackel*, Dr Gabriel Otero 6438, T 606211, German/Swiss/Austrian food, average prices.

Confiterías: a *confitería* is an informal eating/drinking place which serves meals at any time, as opposed to a *restaurante*, which serves meals at set times. A *confitería* may describe itself as a *cafetería, bar, repostería, cervecería, coctelería, sandwichería, grill, pizzería, salón de té* or *whiskería*. Many serve *preparación*, a collection of hors d'oeuvres. There are a great many; the following is a selection: on Av 18 de Julio, *Lusitano*, esq Paraguay; *Lion d'Or*, No 1981; *Soko's*, No 1250, popular, good if expensive food, good coffee, open till 0100, 0400 on Sat. *Suizo*, Andes 1421; *Oro del Rhin*, Convención 1403, open 0830-2100, good cakes; *Beer Garden*, San José, good *empanadas*; *Café Sorocabana*, Yí 1377, good coffee and ice cream, another branch at 25 de Mayo 485, Ciudad Vieja. *Universal Bar*, Piedras y Gómez, last of the real dock bars, worth a visit. *Cake's*, Marco Bruto 1004 and Dr A Schroeder 6536, Carrasco, expensive, rec; *Canaprole*, Rambla M Gandhi 697 y S Antuña; *Jelly*, Av Arocena 1556, tearoom/restaurant behind *Casino/Hotel Carrasco*, has children's menu.

Heladerías: ice-cream parlours produce very good, unusual ice creams in the summer. Try *La Cigale*, R Graseras 845 (Pocitos), Ejido 1368 and several other locations; *Las Delicias*, Schroeder 6454, Carrasco; *Batuk*, 26 de Marzo y Pérez, Pocitos, and at 18 de Julio y Yí, both open daily 1000-0200; *Papitos*, 18 de Julio 1060, excellent but pricey.

● **Airline offices**

Pluna, Colonia y Julio Herrera y Obes, T 921414; **Aviasur**, T 08768, at airport, T 614618; **Aero Regionales**, Yí 1435, T 925632, Airport, T 614852 int 1254; **Aerolíneas Argentinas**, Colonia 851, T 919466; **Varig**, Río Negro 1362, T 924676; **American**, Sarandí 699 bis y Plaza Independencia, T 963979; **KLM**, T 611020, airport. *ASATEJ Uruguay*, Student Flight Centre, Río Negro 1354.

● **Banks & money changers**

Casas de cambio on Plaza Cagancha open daily until 2200, inc Sun, but most banks open only from 1300 to 1700. Many banks give cash advances against Visa and Mastercard. Airport bank open every day 0700-2200. **Lloyds Bank**, Calle Zabala 1500, and 11 city agencies; **Citibank**, Cerrito 455 (corner Misiones), no commission on own cheques; **Banco Holandés Unido**, 25 de Mayo; **Banco Comercial**, Cerrito 400 and Av Libertador (up to US$1,000 available on Mastercard or Visa, best rates for deutschemark cheques); **American Express Bank**, Rincón 473, T 960092/961162, does not change cash or TCs (see Turisport under **Travel Agents**). Thomas Cook/Mastercard refund assistance point: Viajes Continental, 25 de Mayo 732, T 920930. There are exchange houses, especially along 18 de Julio, eg **Almar** at 1077, **La Favorita** (Amex agents) at 1459, **Suizo** at 1190, **Zito** at 1841, but do shop around for best rates (rates for cash better than for TCs, but both are often better than in banks, and quicker service too). **Exprinter** on Plaza Independencia (also travel agency), **Delta**, Río Negro 1341, and **Cambio Indumex**, Rincón 464, 18 de Julio 1128 and at Buquebus terminal, have been rec.

● **Cultural centres**

American Chamber of Commerce, Bartolomé Mitre 1337, esq 108, T 959048. **Alianza Cultural Uruguay-Estados Unidos**, Paraguay 1217, T 915234, library open Mon-Fri, 1400-2000, US publications and books (excellent selection), theatre, art gallery. **British Chamber of Commerce**, Av Libertador 1641, piso 2, of 201, T 900936. **Instituto Cultural Anglo-Uruguayo** (known as the "Anglo"), San José 1426, T 908468 (theatre, rec, library open Mon-Fri 0930-1200, 1430-1930). **The British Hospital**, Av Italia 2420, T 409011. **The English Club**, Treinta y Tres 1309, T 951212. **Alliance Française**, Soriano 1180, T 911979 (theatre, concerts, exhibitions in French and Spanish, library, excellent bookshop). **Goethe Institut**, Canelones 1524, T 405813/493499, F 404432 (open Mon, Tues, Thur, Fri 1000-1300, 1600-1930). **Casa Cultural Uruguay-Suecia**, Ejido 1444, T 900067. **Instituto Italiano de Cultura**, Paraguay 1177, T 903354. **Instituto de Cultura Uruguayo-Brasileño**, Av 18 de Julio 994, T 986531.

● **Embassies & consulates**

Argentine Consulate, Wilson Ferreira Aldunate 1281, T 900897, open 1400-1900, visa US$15, one day work, English spoken. **Brazilian Consulate**, Convención 1343, Edif La Torre, piso 6, T 912024/1460, open 0930-1230, 1430-1730 (service for visas takes 24 hrs and is more complicated than Buenos Aires – need photo, onward ticket, entry ticket, proof of finances), Embassy is at Andes 1365, Torre Independencia, 6 piso, T 905043. **Paraguayan Consulate**, Blvd Artigas 1191, T 485810, open 0900-1200 summer, 1400-1730 winter. **Chilean Embassy**, Andes 1365, T 982223, open 0900-1400, visa US$5, same day.

US Embassy and Consulate, Lauro Muller 1776 esq Abadie Santos, T 236276/236061. **Canadian Consulate**, Gómez 1348, T 958583.

British Embassy, Marco Bruto 1073, T 623597/623581. **Spanish Consulate**, Libertad 2750, T 780048. **Swedish Embassy**, Av Brasil 3079, piso 6, Pocitos, T 780088. **Swiss Embassy**, Ing Federico Abadie 2934-40, T 704315. **German Embassy**, La Cumparsita 1417-35, T 904958 (open 0930-1230). **Belgian Embassy**, Leyenda Patria 2880, Apt 202, T 701265. **French Embassy**, Uruguay 853, T 904377. **Israeli Embassy**, Blvd Gral Artigas 1585, T 404164. **Italian Embassy**, JB Lamas 2857, T 780542. **Austrian Consulate- General**, Misiones 1372, T 960152/960718, F 951283. **Netherlands Embassy**, Leyenda Patria 2880, Apt 202, T 701631. **Portuguese Embassy**, Av Dr F Soca 1128, T 96456.

● **Entertainment**

Boliches: (Café-Concerts/Peñas/Folk-Pubs, offering the most typical local night-life) *Clave de Fu*, 26 de Marzo 1125, Pocitos, Wed-Sat from 2200, best local folk-rock groups live at weekends; *TK*, Bulevar Artigas 1031, from 2200 nightly, the place to hear *candombe*; *Vieja Viola*, Pampas 1995 esq Venezuela, 2400 onwards, folk songs, *candombe*, tango; *Amarcord*, Julio Herrera y Obes 1321, Wed-Sun 2200 onwards, traditional pop music. *Clyde's*, Costa Rica y Rivera, lively, live music. *Subterráneo Magallanes*, Gonzalo Ramírez 1701, T 494415, live shows, Fri and Sat only, book in advance; *Lobizón*, Michelini 1329, good food, good price; *Taj Mahal*, Andes 1255, sangria, good food; *Fun-Fun*, Ciudadela 1229, amateur and local music. *Pizza Sing*, Schroeder 6411, Carrasco, good.

Casinos: *Parque Hotel*, Luis Piera 1992, 1400-0200, 0300 Sat and Sun; *Hotel Carrasco*, Rambla República de México, daily 1800-0300; *Victoria Plaza Hotel*.

Cinema: is very popular. Price is almost the same in all cinemas, at US$7 (US$4 on Tues and Wed). During the week no cinemas open before 1730. Classic and serious films at Cinemateca film club (3 separate cinemas – at L Carnelli 1311, Soriano 1227 and A Chucarro 1036), monthly membership US$6, and Ciné Universitario (2 halls, Lumière and Chaplin, Canelones 1280). Films are released quite soon after the UK and USA, and often before they get to Buenos Aires. Details in *Guía del Ocio* and monthly *Cinemateca Uruguaya* (free). At least half Montevideo's cinemas show blue films – marked *sexo explícito*.

Discos: (*Boites* are the more expensive discos which provide live music for dancing; prices, US$15-30.) *Zum Zum*, Rambla Armenia 1647, from 2200 nightly, rock, live music weekends; *New York*, Mar Artico 1227, Punta Gorda; *La Base*, Ruta 101, No 3258, nr Airport (for people over 25): these three are expensive and you need to book ahead. *Rock Café*, Bulevar España 2721, Pocitos, Fri, Sat 2400 onwards, rock 'n' roll, open air terrace is a nice retreat from the heat, noise and lasers; *Flannagans Pub*, Luis B Cavia 3082, Pocitos, young, lively, pop, rock and salsa; cheaper discos include *San Telmo*, Maldonado 1194, live music, always full and *Chantclaire*, Soriano 1338.

Music: every Sat, from midnight to Sun morning, thousands of dancers crowd into the Palacio Sud América, Yatay 1429, nr Palacio Legislativo, 3 dance salons, Caribbean music on 1st floor, Tango on 2nd, tickets half price if bought before 2400. Pop concerts are held in Centenario stadium and Parque Rodó. During the two weeks around Carnival there is a music and dance competition, in the Parque Rodó amphitheatre, in "Murga", a form of satirical revue, at 5 hrs every night, US$0.50 entry, starting at 2100. See also under **Tanguerías**, etc and **Theatres**, below.

Nightclubs: (*Clubes Nocturnos*) These all-night clubs, of which there are many, provide striptease, music and willing sexual partners; all expensive. The red light district, around Piedras y Juan Carlos Gómez in Ciudad Vieja, is a very friendly environment, safe, active only in the late afternoon on weekdays.

Tanguerías: *La Vieja Cumparsita*, C Gardel 1811, nightly 2330-0500, no singles admitted, also has *candombe* shows, book ahead; *Sorocabana*, Yí 1377, tango shows Fri, Sat, 2100-2400.

Besides tango and candombe, other popular music forms in Montevideo are Música Campestre-Folklórica (of guacho origin), Música del Caribe by Uruguayan orchestras dedicated to dance music from Puerto Rico, and "the best New Orleans Dixieland Jazz Bands" in Latin America (John Raspey).

Theatres: *Solís*, Buenos Aires 678, two auditoria, home of the Comedia Nacional. About 10 others present professional productions. *Teatro Millington-Drake* at the Anglo (see **Cultural Institutions**) puts on occasional productions, as do the theatres of the Alianza Uruguay-Estados

Unidos and the Alianza Francesa (addresses above). Opera and ballet at *Auditorio del Sodre*, Sala Brunet, Av 18 de Julio 930 (a new Sodre Cultural Complex is under construction at Mercedes y Andes. Many theatres close during Jan and February.

● **Laundry**
Automatic laundrettes can be found in all parts of the city.

● **Places of worship**
The Roman Catholic Cathedral is known locally as the Iglesia San Juan. Anglican Church (Holy Trinity), Reconquista 522 (a national monument) T 954037 (English Service 1015 Sun). Methodist services at Christ Church, Carrasco. Holy Trinity Episcopal (British), and the Emanuel Methodist Church (American), hold regular services in English. The German Evangelical Church holds services in German at Calle JM Blanco 2. There is a synagogue.

● **Post & telecommunications**
Post Office: Misiones 1328 y Buenos Aires; 0800-1800 Mon-Fri, 0800-1300 Sat and holidays; philatelic bureau on top floor sells back issues. *Poste restante* at main post office will keep mail for 1 month, 2 if authorized in advance by administrator. Next to Pluna office on Av Libertador, next to Montevideo Shopping Center, 0800-1300, and under Intendencia at corner of Av 18 de Julio and Ejido.

Telecommunications: Antel, Fernández Crespo 1534 (headquarters) and at San José 1108 (Plaza), Arocena 1666 (Carrasco), Ariel 4914 (Sayago), Cádiz 3280 (Mercado Modelo), Garzón 1806 (Colón), José Belloni 4445 (Piedras Blancas); for international phone calls (inc USA Direct Express), telex, fax, cables, etc, open 0800-2000 daily. Long distance operator 120; for Latin America 0007, other countries 0008; telegrams 125; special service 124.

   NB All phone numbers in Montevideo will become 7-digit on 26 October 1997; the new system of numbering was not known at the time of going to press.

● **Shopping**
The main shopping area is Av 18 de Julio. Suede and leather are good buys; styling is more traditional than in Buenos Aires; try *Casa Mario*, Piedras 641 (expensive); several shops and workshops around Plaza Independencia (*Montevideo Leather Factory*, No 832, rec); for leather and woollen goods, *Artesanal*, Av 18 de Julio 1197, Río Negro 1320 L 2, good prices. Amethysts, topazes, agate and quartz are mined and polished in Uruguay and are also good buys: rec is *Benito Sityá*, Sarandí 650 (Ciudad Vieja) and *Cuarzos del Uruguay*, Sarandí 604. For woollen wall hangings see *Manos del Uruguay*, which also sells floor

cushions, crafts, high quality woollen goods, etc at Reconquista 587, in an old colonial-style house, in Montevideo Shopping Center (144-45), and at San José 1111. Other good craftwork (cheaper) in daily covered craft market on Plaza Cagancha (and indoors at No 1365, nr the cinema). Ciudad Vieja is an excellent district in which to buy antiques, especially antique jewellery; go to Bartolomé Mitre: at No 1368 is *Portobello Road*; next door, No 1366, is *Mariano*, a wig-maker; at No 1388 is *Naftalina*, good. Many galleries here, and in Maldonado and Punta del Este, selling contemporary paintings. For stamps, Carlos Camusso, Galería Central, 18 de Julio 976. On Sun, 0800-1400, there is a large, crowded street market on Tristán Narvaja (good for silver and copper, and all sorts of collectibles) opp Facultad de Derecho on 18 de Julio. A small Sat am market and a Sun antique fair are held in Plaza Constitución; there is also a big market, Villa Biarritz, on Vásquez Ledesma nr Parque Rodó, Pocitos, selling fruit, vegetables, clothes and shoes (Tues and Sat 0900-1500, and on Sun in Parque Rodó, 0800-1400).

   The Montevideo Shopping Center on the E edge of Pocitos (Herrera 1290 y Galanza, 1 block S of Rivera): it is open daily 1000-2100 and has a self-service restaurant, a cinema and *confiterías*. It also has wide range of shops inc *Manos del Uruguay* as well as others selling leather goods, *Foto Martín*, *Bookshop*, supermarkets and more (bus 141 or 142 from San José). Outside is a *McDonalds*, serving economical breakfasts. A new Shopping Centre has opened at Punta Carretas in the old prison, Ellauri 306, very popular; other shopping centres are Portones in Carrasco, the Tres Cruces bus station and Plaza Arozena Shopping Mall.

Bookshops: the following have English and American books: *Librería Barreiro y Ramos*, 25 de Mayo y JC Gómez, 18 de Julio 937, 21 de Septiembre (Pocitos) and Av Arocena 1599 (Carrasco); *Ibana*, International Book and News Agency, Convención 1479, specializes in foreign publications. *Librería Británica*, Sarandí 580, specializes in language and children's books. Others include *Librería Mosca Hermanos*, Av 18 de Julio 1578 and Av Arocena 1576 (Carrasco); *Feria del Libro*, Av 18 de Julio y Río Negro; *Paseo del Lector*, Av 18 de Julio y Michelini; *Librería Papacito*, Av 18 de Julio 1415. *Ruben*, Tristán Narvaja 1736. *Librería Oriente Occidente*, Cerrito 477 and *Librería El Aleph*, Bartolomé Mitre 1358, both sell used and rare books (former has English books, also exchange of books in perfect condition). The only shop with exclusively English stock is *Bookshop SRL*, JE Rodó 1671 (at Minas y Constituyente), T 409954, Cristina Mosca, very friendly staff, also at Montevideo

Shopping Center; specializes in travel. The Sun market on Paysandú is good for second-hand books.

Cameras and film: for developing films: Foto Martín, Av Libertador and Uruguay; Fuji Plaza, Andes 1369 y 18 de Julio, 1 hr service, good quality; Delucchi, on Herrera y Obés, good for slides; Foto Tecnifilm, Av 18 de Julio 1202, helpful, English spoken; camera repairs by Fotocámara, on Michelini between Mercedes and Colonia. Film developing and equipment is quite expensive in Uruguay; better to bring film from abroad.

● **Sports**
There are two good 18-hole golf links, Cerro and Punta Carretas. There are several lawn tennis clubs, and two for polo. Horse racing at Las Piedras (see page 1443).

● **Tour companies & travel agents**
JP Santos, Colonia 951, and Jetmar, Plaza Independencia 725-7, both helpful. Exprinter, Sarandí 700; Turisport Ltda, Mercedes 942, T 900474, F 920852 (American Express for travel and mail services, good; sells Amex dollar TCs on Amex card and personal cheque at 1% commission); Golden Tours, Colonia 1221, T 90 7500, English spoken. Turinter, Río Negro 1388, very helpful. Orientur, Río Negro 1356bis, Plaza Fabini, T 983369; also on Plaza Fabini, Buquebus, address below, is a travel agent. Jorge Martínez, Río Branco y Colonia 949; Freeway, Colonia 994, T 908931/33. 1-day tours of Punta del Este are organized by many travel agents and run from several hotels, US$40-100 inc meals. Bilingual guide: Marian Whitaker, T 706842, F 715411, for tours of Montevideo and Uruguay, riding, hiking, camping, fishing, also visits to Santa Sofia estancia in Río Negro. The Palacio Municipal organizes city tours, Sat-Sun, US$5, T 930648/9 Mon-Fri 1000-1800.

● **Tourist offices**
Tourist information is at the new Tres Cruces bus terminal, and booth in entrance to Ministerio de Turismo, Av Libertador 1409 (Pluna building, just off Plaza Fabini), both helpful. Also at Carrasco international airport, T 602261.

Information: Dial "16" for exact time. The Guía del Ocio, a weekly guide with Fri edition of El País, gives information on museums, cultural events, nightlife and entertainment, inc addresses, rec.

Maps: best street maps of Montevideo are at the beginning of the Guía Telefónica (both white and yellow page volumes). Eureka Guía De Montevideo is rec for streets, sector by sector, with index and bus routes (US$4.75 from bookshops).

● **Transport**
Local Bus: US$0.60 (pay the conductor on board); express buses D2 US$0.65, D3, 5, 8, 10,

11 US$0.90, D1 (see above) US$1.20. There are many buses to all parts from 18 de Julio; from other parts to the centre or old city, look for those marked "Aduana". For Pocitos from city centre take bus No 121 from San José behind the former Onda station. **Car hire**: without chauffeur, from US$30 to US$60 per 24 hrs (insurance included), plus extra per kilometre if only hiring for the day; guarantee of US$500 required. Hire for 3-day weekend is US$130 (rates are much lower out of season and vary according to size of vehicle). Cheaper weekly rates available. Best to make reservations before arrival. Collision damage waiver (amounting to US$1,000), US$15/day. Hertz, Maderal SA, Uruguay 839, T 939338, F 921596, rec; National, Av de las Américas 5026, T 615267; Snappy, Andes 1363, T 907728; Punta Car, Cerro Largo 1383, T 902772, also at Aeropuerto Carrasco. Budget, Mercedes 935, T 916363; Sudancar, Piedras 533, T 958150; and Avis at airport, T 611929, and Yaguarón 1527, T 930303; many others. **Remises**: US$8 per hour; Remises Montevideo, Joaquín Requena 1303, F 411149; Uruguay, Plaza Cagancha 1120; Guillermo Muñoz, Bartolito Mitre 2636, T 773928, rec. **Taxis**: US$0.90 for first 600m, and US$0.21 for each 140m afterwards; on holidays and Sun, 20% more; charge per hour US$15. There is a small charge for each piece of luggage, but tipping is not expected. Beware of taxi drivers telling you that long-distance buses are full and offering to take you instead; this is unlikely to be true.

Air The main airport, T 602261, is at Carrasco, 21 km outside the city; with coffee shop and children's play area in departure lounge; left luggage about US$1/day/item; if exchange facilities closed, buses will accept dollars for fares to town. To Montevideo 30 mins by taxi or remise (US$15-22, depending on destination in the city – may be able to charge it to hotel bill if without cash); if driver offers to take the coastal route, it may have fewer hold-ups, but it will be more expensive; about 50 mins by bus. Many buses from Aduana pass the airport US$1; dark brown "Copsa" bus terminates at the airport. Pluna has a bus service from Colonia 1321 to airport, US$5. Concorde Travel (Robert Mountford), Germán Barbato 1358, apto 1302, T 926346/8, has a service from hotel to plane (almost) US$10-25.

Trains The station is at the N end of Calle Río Negro (with Cerro Largo). Fine building with information office, post office, restaurants and historical display. Commuter trains run N to 25 de Agosto (Florida), Mon-Fri dep 25 de Agosto 4 times between 0440 and 0655, returning from Montevideo 4 times 1728-1930, 1 hr 50 mins,

US$1.90. On Sat, dep 25 de Agosto 0440, 0530, return 1320, 1420. You can take the train to Santa Lucía, the stop before 25 de Agosto, and return by bus (2 hrs); the train goes via Canelones also. Ferrotransporte (T 941387) arrange return trips to Florida, with lunch and tours, US$15.80 for the train ride.

Road Buses within Uruguay: excellent new terminal, Tres Cruces, Bulevar Artigas y Av Italia (10-15 mins by bus from the centre); it has a shopping mall, tourist office, restaurants, left luggage (free for 12 hrs at a time), post and phone offices, toilets, good medical centre, Banco de Montevideo and Indumex cambio (accepts Mastercard). Close by is the 3-star *Hotel Tres Cruces*, Miguelete 2356 esq Acevedo Díaz, T 423474, F 424400. All buses leave from here and bus company offices are here, too. During the summer holiday season buses are booked heavily; it is rec to book in advance (also for Fri and weekend travel all year round). Fares and journey times from the capital are given under destinations.

To Paraguay, Brazil, Chile To Asunción, Paraguay, US$70, 18 hrs: twice a week (Wed and Sat, plus Mon in summer) by COIT, Río Branco 1389, T 986469, or Tres Cruces, T 415628, and 3 a week by Brújula, T 915143, both services rec, meals served. Alternatively take bus to **Santa Fe**, Argentina (US$30), via Paysandú bridge, for easy access to Asunción. The through bus route is via Paysandú, Salto, Bella Unión, Uruguaiana, Paso de los Libros, Posadas, Encarnación, to Asunción (there are no passport or customs formalities except passport checks at Bella Unión and at Encarnación). There are very comfortable buses to **Porto Alegre** (US$40, 10 hrs) and **São Paulo** (US$79 daily, 32 hrs) at 2200 and 2230 daily, with TTL (Tres Cruces or Plaza Cagancha 1385, T 917142/411410), *coche cama* daily except Sat 2100 US$63 to Porto Alegre; the route is Pelotas, Porto Alegre, Florianópolis (US$55), Camboriu (US$58, arr 2000, a good place to stop over), Curitiba (US$66), São Paulo (arr 0500 on second morning); often booked very early. Also EGA, Tres Cruces, T 425164, or Rio Branco 1409, T 925335, and Planalto to Santa Maria and Rio Grande do Sul (Rondeau 1475). A cheaper alternative route (which also avoids the risk of being stranded at the border by through-bus drivers) is to Chuy (US$11-12, 4½ hrs), then catch an onward bus to Porto Alegre (7½ hrs, US$13.25), either direct or via Pelotas. To **Santiago** via Mendoza, US$90, 28 hrs, by El Rápido (T 414764), Thur 1200, COIT and Tas Choapa, Río Negro 1356 bis, T 483539, or Tres Cruces, T 498598. Round trips to Argentina, Chile or Brazil by bus or plane, booked at travel agents

are reported to be good value.

NB One needs a passport when buying international tickets. On through buses to Brazil and Argentina, one can expect full luggage checks both by day and night.

To Argentina: Ferries and buses Direct to Buenos Aires: **Buquebus**, Río Negro 1400, T 920670, and Terminal Las Cruces, Local B29, T 488146, 'Avión de Buquebus', Mon-Sat at 0730 (0800 Sat), 1130, 1530 and 1900, plus Fri 2330, Sun 1200, 1530, 2000, 2200, 3 hrs, US$47 tourist class, US$59 1st class (bus service from *Hotel Carasco* 1¼ hrs before sailings). At Montevideo dock, go to Preembarque 30 mins before departure, present ticket and pay exit tax; then go to Migración for Uruguayan exit and Argentine entry formalities. The terminal has been redesigned like an airport. On board there is duty free shopping, video and expensive food and drinks. **Services via Colonia**: bus/ferry services by Buquebus; hydrofoils (*aliscafos*) daily at 0730, 1130, 1530 and 1915, buses leave Tres Cruces bus terminal 3 hrs earlier, US$20 (28 inc bus), alternative service at 0400 and 1900 (Sun 1900 only), bus from Tres Cruces 3½ hrs earlier, US$17 (23 inc bus). Buquebus on either route carries cars, US$93.50-US$103.50 Montevideo, US$33-US$41 Colonia. **Ferryturismo**, Río Branco 1368, T 900045, Sea Cat 4 hrs Montevideo-Buenos Aires via Colonia: bus leaves 0645, 1215 and 1730 daily, catamaran leaves Colonia 3 hrs after bus departure, US$18, plus US$7 bus Colonia-Montevideo, cars carried US$40, also has bus/ferry service, 2 a day (once Sat and Sun), US$8 + US$7 for bus (break of journey in Colonia on all services is allowed; cheaper, if you do this, to buy bus ticket only in Montevideo, and then ferry ticket in Colonia). Services **via Carmelo and Tigre** (interesting trip): bus/motor launch service by Cacciola, 0040, 0800, 1500, Tres Cruces T 419350, Plaza Cagancha 1326, T 910755, US$18.50. Bus service **via Fray Bentos** (Bus de la Carrera): joint service by El Condor (old buses, not rec), Cita and COT (Tres Cruces, T 421313) at 1000, 2200, 2220 and 2300 daily, US$20, and *dormibus* at 2230, US$27, 9 hrs, slow journey. Bus service to Santa Fé and Córdoba (US$57, 15 hrs), via Paysandú and Paraná, Cora (Tres Cruces, T 498598), daily 1800, snacks served. Advanced booking is advisable on all services at busy periods.

For air services to Argentina via Colonia see page 1449.

NB If intending to travel through Uruguay to Brazil, do not forget to have Uruguayan entry stamped in your passport when crossing from Argentina. Without it you will not be able to cross the Brazilian border.

East from Montevideo

A BEAUTIFUL coast, 320 km long, consisting of an endless succession of small bays, beaches and promontories, set among hills and woods. Punta del Este, 139 km from Montevideo is a major international resort. From Punta del Este to the Brazilian frontier is much less developed; good bird watching in the coastal lagoons. The beach season is from Dec to the end of February.

MONTEVIDEO TO PUNTA DEL ESTE

Two paved roads go to Punta del Este. The northern branch via Pando and Soca, is Route 8 (toll just before Route 9 branch); at Km 75 Route 8 continues NE towards Minas (see page 1441), while Route 9 branches off to San Carlos (14½ km N of Maldonado and 19 km N of Punta del Este) through beautiful rolling country with views of the Laguna del Sauce. The other road, the "Interbalnearia", runs largely along the coast, with short branches to some of the resorts, and is the one described in the text. It is being made into a dual carriageway. There are toll posts (US$4) at Arroyo Pando and at Arroyo Solís Grande (you are charged only on the way out from Montevideo). For the first 15 km or so out of Montevideo an alternative road to the Interbalnearia runs parallel between it and the coast (recommended during heavy traffic to avoid dangerous junctions).

Route 9 runs from San Carlos through the towns of Rocha and Castillos to Chuy. A spur of the road turns S to La Paloma and there are secondary roads to some of the resorts further along the coast.

ATLANTIDA

This resort (*phone code* 0372), 45 km from Montevideo, is ringed by fir forest and has a good country club. About 2 km before the resort is an old, derelict house, shaped like an eagle's head and overlooking the beach; interesting to explore. A short distance beyond, in groves of eucalyptus and pine, is the small and intimate beach of Las Toscas (*Camping Costa de Oro*), followed by Parque del Plata, on the Solís Chico river (Km 50, *Camping Les Amis*, expensive; many sports and services).

● **Accommodation & places to eat Atlántida**: **C** *Rex*, is main hotel; **C** *Munday*, is clean and friendly; many good *residenciales* charging **E** off season; campsite *El Ensueño* at Km 46, T 2371; some good restaurants. *Francisco Fischer*, ask for Pancho, an Austrian coordinator for interuniversity projects who speaks German and English, offers accommodation, **E** pp, tours by minibus US$30-50 pp/day, help in emergencies, and much else besides, between Nov and May, highly rec; Calle 3 entre 22 y 24, T/F 0372-4437. 5 km before Atlántida, in an old fortress set in pine woods, is **A2-B** *El Fortín de Santa Rosa* hotel and restaurant, rooms face onto a beautiful patio, excellent food and service, rec; 2 mins from a lovely sandy beach, Ruta Interbalnearia Km 42, T 7376. Small zoo not far off. Also nr Atlántida is *El Renacimiento*, a dairy farm which is open to the public, with produce on sale.

La Floresta: 8 km further E across a (toll) bridge, surrounded by woods (*Oriental*, highly rec). The chalets are pretty, reminiscent of the villages of the Landes, nr Biarritz. *Pueblo Chico*, Km 55.5, T (037) 39565, F 39775, is a dairy farm open to the public, with cabins, pool, live music Sat pm, riding, excellent food, Greek owner, highly rec. At Km 64.5 is Sr Garabedian's **campsite**, for bookings, telephone Sr Garabedian at Montevideo 561230.

Solís, over a toll bridge at the mouth of the Río Solís, is at Km 85. It has a very long beach, good fishing, delightful river and hill scenery. About 8 km beyond Solís lies the small village of Las Flores, with a better beach than that at Solís.

● **Accommodation & places to eat Bellavista**: (Km 87, Ruta 10) **A2** *Hostería Bellavista*, with breakfast, T (0432) 3192, F 4059, horseriding and other sports. **Las Flores**: **B** pp *Hostería del Mar*, T (043) 800 99 or Montevideo 786657, bed and breakfast (**C** low season), clean, well-run, open all year, and *Edén Camping*, T 3504, with room at US$3 pp or *El Quijote Camping* at Km 90, T Montevideo 907648. *Restaurant Charma*, rec.

PIRIAPOLIS

The next resort, **Piriápolis** (*pop* 6,000; *phone code* 0432), is 16 km from Solís, 101 from Montevideo. Set among hills, it is laid out with an abundance of shady trees, and the district is rich in pine, eucalyptus and acacia woods. It has a a good beach, a yacht harbour, a country club, a motor-racing track and is particularly popular with Argentines. 6 km N on the R37 is Cerro Pan de Azúcar (Sugar Loaf Hill), crowned by a tall cross with a circular stairway inside, fine coastal views; there is only a steep path, marked by red arrows, up to the cross.

Museum and zoo

Just N of Piriápolis R 37 passes the La Cascada Municipal park (open all year) which contains the Museo Castillo de Piriá, open daily in summer 1200-2000, T 3268. By the entrance to the municipal park is a good zoo ('Reserva de la Fauna'), containing among other things live specimens of all snakes and most animals native to Uruguay including endangered pampas deer.

Local information
● **Accommodation**
Many, situated along the sea front. Most close end-Feb until mid-December. Reservation advisable in high season.

A1 *Argentino*, Rambla de los Argentinos, T 2791, a fine hotel with casino and medicinal springs, ice rink and pool open to public for US$3.50, also sauna; **B** *Danae*, Rambla 1270 y Freire, T 2594, **E** out of season, breakfast, heating; **B** *Rivadavia*, Rambla 1208, T 2532, open all year (**C** in summer), hot water. Many others in our price ranges C and up. The Centro de Hoteles y Anexos

de Piriápolis runs a reservation office at Edificio Piria on Rambla de los Argentinos.

Youth Hostel: *Albergue de Piriápolis*, behind *Hotel Argentino*, Simón del Pino 1136, T 0432-2157, US$6 pp (open all year), mostly double bedrooms, hot showers, cooking facilities (but no utensils!). Student cards accepted. Reserve in high season.

Camping: international YMCA camp on the slope of Cerro del Toro, double rooms in bungalows, and tents, T 3454. Site at Misiones y Niza, T 3275, poor showers, smelly toilets, US$6.

● **Places to eat**
Many small restaurants nr the harbour, eg *Don Anselmo*, between Puntas Fría and Colorada (shellfish, excellent, overlooking sea) and *Náutico*, both rec. Also *Posada de los Reyes*, Gorlero 629.

● **Tourist offices**
Asociación de Fomento y Turismo, Rambla de los Argentinos 1348, T 2560.

● **Transport**
Road Piriápolis may be reached either by following the very beautiful R10 from the end of the Interbalnearia, or by taking the original access road (R37) from the town of Pan de Azúcar, which crosses the R93. The shortest route from Piriápolis to Punta del Este is by the Camino de las Bases which runs parallel to the R37 and joins the R93 some 4 km E of the R37 junction. **Bus**: to/from **Montevideo**, US$4, 1½ hrs. To **Punta del Este**, US$2.50. For **Rocha**, **La Paloma** and **Chuy**, take bus to Pan de Azúcar and change.

PORTEZUELO AND PUNTA BALLENA

R93 runs between the coast and the Laguna del Sauce to **Portezuelo**, which has good beaches. The Arboreto Lussich (open 1030-1630) on the W slope of the Sierra de la Ballena (north of R93) contains a unique set of native and exotic trees. There are footpaths, or you can drive through; two *miradores*; worth a visit. From Portezuelo it is possible to drive N towards the R9 by way of the R12 which then continues, unpaved, to Minas. Just off R12 is *El Sosiego*, T (042) 20000, F 20303, a dairy farm open to the public, selling goats' cheese, *dulce de leche* and other products.

At **Punta Ballena** there is a wide crescent beach, calm water and very clean sand. The place is a residential resort but is still quiet. At the top of Punta Ballena there is a panoramic road 2½ km long with remarkable views of the coast. **Casa Pueblo**, the house and gallery of Uruguayan artist Carlos Páez Villaro, is built in a Spanish-Moroccan style on a cliff over the sea; the gallery can be visited (US$3.50), there are paintings, collages and ceramics on display, and for sale; season: 1 Nov to 1 April. Walk downhill towards the sea for a good view of the house.

● **Accommodation** There is a hotel at **L'** *Casa Pueblo*, T 042-78101, F 78818, highly rec; also time-share apartments, restaurant and, lower down the hill, a *parrillada*. **L2** *Solana del Mar*, Km 126.5, T 75868, modern, restaurant on the beach, full board. *Cumbres de Ballena*, Ruta 12 Km 3.5, T 78689, F 79241, new hotel 1997, with restaurant. Campsite nr Arboreto Lussich, turn off at Km 128 on Interbalnearia, T 42-78902/24181, or Montevideo 801662, US$5.60 for 2 with tent, many facilities, very clean.

MALDONADO

Maldonado (*pop* 33,000; *phone code* 042), capital of Maldonado Department, is 140 km E of Montevideo. This peaceful town, sacked by the British in 1806, is now a dormitory suburb of Punta del Este, but it has many colonial remains.

Places of interest

El Vigia watch tower, Gorriti y Pérez del Puerto; the Cathedral (started 1801, completed 1895), on Plaza San Fernando; the windmill; the Cuartel de Dragones exhibition centre and the Cachimba del Rey (an old well – local legend claims that those who drink from the well will never leave Maldonado).

Museums

Museo Mazzoni (Ituzaingó 787, T 21107, Tues-Fri 1800-2200), regional items, indigenous, Spanish, Portugues and English; **Museo San Fernando** (Sarandí y Rafael Pérez del Puerto, T 25929, Tues-Sat 1300-2000), in the colonial customs house; **Museo de Arte Americano** (José Dodera 648 y Treinta y Tres, T 22276, open summer only 1800-2200), private museum of national and international art, interesting.

Local information
● **Accommodation**

Hotel accommodation is scarce in summer.

A3 *Colonial*, 18 de Julio s/n, T 23346; **A3** *Esteño*, Sarandí 881, T 25222; **A3** *Sancar*, Dr Edye 597, T 23563.

C *Hospedaje Isla de Gorriti*, Michelini between Ituzaingó and Florida, rec; **C** *Maldonado*, Florida 830, T 24664, quiet; **C** *Celta*, Ituzaingó 839, T 30139, helpful, Irish owner, No 7 bus stop outside.

Camping: in Parque El Placer, T 70034, free.

● **Places to eat**

Matias Módena, 3 de Febrero 642, good fish and meat, US$14 pp; *Cantina del Italiano*, Sarandí 642, pizzería, old building, good value; *Lo de Tere*, Calle 20 y 21, terrace overlooking sea, good food; *Piano-Bar JR Pizzetas*, Rincón y Gutiérrez Ruiz, pizzas and pastas. Best ice-cream at *Popy's*, 2 branches.

● **Banks & money changers**

Banco Pan de Azúcar, accepts Mastercard; Cambio Bacacay, Florida 803, good rates, TCs.

● **Tourist offices**

Edif Comunal, p 2, Av Acuña de Figueroa.

Information: concerts and exhibitions in summer T 22276. Tourist information at bus station, T 25701.

● **Transport**

Buses to/from **Montevideo**, US$7.50; to **Minas**, 2 hrs, 5 a day, US$3.75.

SAN CARLOS

A charming old town (*pop* 20,000) on Route 9, 14½ km N of Maldonado; of interest are the church, dating from 1722, heavily reconstructed, an excellent zoo in Parque Municipal Medina, and the historical museum.

● **Accommodation D** *Hospedaje*, on main plaza (limited hot water, good but cold and damp in winter) and *El Amanecer*, Treinta y Tres 634. Free camping, with poor facilities, in municipal park.

● **Banks & money changers** Two *cambios* which exchange TCs.

● **Shopping** *Benítez*, Treinta y Tres y Maldonado, for good leather items.

● **Buses** San Carlos is a good point for connections to La Paloma (2 buses a day), and Chuy on the Brazilian border. Buses from Plaza Artigas run to Maldonado every 15 mins.

At Km 130 on Route 9, before San Carlos, the Camino de los Ceibos heads SE to join Route 39 at Km 13.5 S of San Carlos. Off this road (2 km from Km 130) is a turning to *Las Vertientes*, a delightful place to have afternoon tea (mostly home-made produce). Best to book in advance, T 69997.

PUNTA DEL ESTE

7 km from Maldonado and 139 km from Montevideo, facing the bay on one side and the open waters of the Atlantic on the other, lies the largest and best known of the resorts, **Punta del Este** (*phone code* 042), which is particularly popular among Argentines. The narrow peninsula of Punta del Este has been entirely built over. On the land side, the city is flanked by large planted forests of eucalyptus, pine and mimosa.

Places of interest

Two blocks from the sea, at the tip of the peninsula, is the historic monument of El Faro (lighthouse); in this part of the city no building may exceed its height. On the ocean side of the peninsula, at the end of Calle 25 (Arrecifes), is a shrine to the first mass said by the Conquistadores on this coast, 2 February 1515. 3 blocks from the shrine is Plaza General Artigas, which has a *feria artesanal* (handicraft market); along its side runs Av Gorlero, the main street. There are a golf course, two casinos and many beautiful holiday houses.

Museum

Museo Rally of Contemporary Latin American Art, Barrio Beverly Hills, T 83478, open Dec to end of Holy Week, Tues, Thurs, Sat and Sun, 1700-2100, entrance free. Worth a visit but car needed to get there.

Beaches and watersports

Punta del Este has excellent bathing beaches, the calm *playa mansa* on the bay side, the rough *playa brava* on the ocean side. There are some small beaches, hemmed in by rocks, on this side of the peninsula, but most people go to where the extensive *playa brava* starts, opposite the *Hotel Playa*. Papa Charlie beach on the Atlantic (Parada 13) is preferred by families with small children as it is safe.

There are an excellent yacht marina, yacht and fishing clubs. There is good fishing both at sea and in three nearby lakes and the Río Maldonado. The *Muriel*, a late 19th century yacht, makes 3 sailings daily, lasting 3 hrs, US$35.

Islands

Isla de Gorriti, visited by explorers including Solís, Magellan and Drake, was heavily fortified by the Spanish in the 1760's to keep the Portuguese out. The island, densely wooded and with superb beaches, is an ideal spot for campers (boats from 0800-1700, return 0915-1915, US$7). On **Isla de Lobos**, which is a government reserve within sight of the town, there is a huge sea-lion colony; excursions to it every morning at 0900 if demand is sufficient, US$30; ticket should be bought at the harbour the day before (T 44352/21445).

Local information

NB Streets on the peninsula have names and numbers; lowest numbers at the tip.

Seasons High season is 15 Dec-28 Feb; mid season 1 Oct-15 Dec; low season 1 Mar-30 September. From 10 Mar to Easter and from Easter onwards the place is deserted and on sunny days it is still warm enough to swim.

● Accommodation

Very many, but expensive: we list only those with positive confirmations. Rates in those few hotels that are open after the end of Mar are as much as halved. In the high season, for which prices below apply, it is better to find a hotel in Maldonado and commute, or look for a hotel that is rebuilding, so that you can negotiate on prices. Visitors without a car are forced to take a hotel on the peninsula, unless they want to spend a fortune on taxis.

On the peninsula: **L3** *Amsterdam*, El Foque (Calle 14) 759, T 44170, ocean view, good service, rec; **L3** *Iberia*, Calle 24, No 685, T 40405/6, 43348, about centre-peninsula, pleasant, breakfast included, open all year, good covered garage opp; **L3** *Palace*, Gorlero y 11, T 41919 (A1 in Mar, closed in winter), breakfast only (expensive restaurant, *La Stampa*, in the hotel), lovely courtyard, colonial style, well kept; **L3** *Embajador*, Risso, by new bus terminal, T 81008, good.

Just off the peninsula, but within walking distance: **L3** *Arena's*, Costanera y Parada 3, T 84556; **L3** *Ajax*, Parada 2, Malvarosa, T 84550; **A2** *Jamaica*, Amazonas y Santa Teresa, parada 2, T 82225, F 86637, inc breakfast, a/c, bigger rooms on 3rd floor, **A3** low season, good; **A2** *Gorlero*, Av Artigas y Villa Serrana

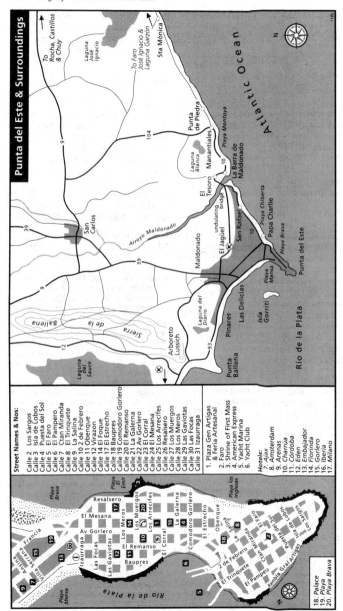

Punta del Este & Surroundings

Street Names & Nos:

Calle 2   Los Sargos
Calle 3   Isla de Lobos
Calle 4   Puesta del Sol
Calle 5   El Faro
Calle 6   El Pampero
Calle 7   Ctan Miranda
Calle 8   El Trinquete
Calle 9   La Salina
Calle 10 Obenque
Calle 11 2 de Febrero
Calle 12 Virazon
Calle 14 El Foque
Calle 17 El Estrecho
Calle 18 Baupres
Calle 19 Comodoro Gorlero
Calle 20 El Remanso
Calle 21 La Galerna
Calle 22 Av Gorlero
Calle 23 El Corral
Calle 24 El Mesana
Calle 25 Los Arrecifes
Calle 26 Resalsero
Calle 27 Los Muergos
Calle 28 Los Meros
Calle 29 Las Gaviotas
Calle 30 Las Focas
Calle 31 Izaurraga

1. Plaza Gen Artigas & Feria Artesanal
2. Faro of First Mass
3. Antinea
4. American Express
5. Yacht Marina
6. Yacht Club

Hotels:
7. Ajax
8. Amsterdam
9. Arenas
10. Charrúa
11. Córdoba
12. Edén
13. Embajador
14. Florinda
15. Gorlero
16. Iberia
17. Milano
18. Palace
19. Playa
20. Playa Brava

(Parada 2), T 82648.

Bus services pass close to hotels on Pedragosa Sierra (**L2** *Clarion Hotel*, Av Pedragosa Sierra y Las Delicias, T 91515, F 91530), Av Roosevelt and **L3** *Salto Grande*, Salto Grande 3½, T 82137. **L3** *Barradas*, Río Branco y Francia, T 81527, F 84895, pool, gardens, tennis, a/c. **L1** *L'Auberge*, nr golf course, T 82601, F 83408, own transport essential, a/c, "lo más refinado", open all year, special weekend offers, good restaurant. Newest resort is **L1** *Conrad*, Biarritz y Br Artigas, T 91111, F 89999, with casino, Las Vegas-style. *Cantegril* country club lets cottages and hotel apartments at a high price, or one may hire from an "Inmobiliaria".

● **Places to eat**

La Lutèce, Los Sauces casi Pedragosa Sierra, French cuisine, superb, very expensive; *L'Etoile*, Rambla Claudio Williman, C 32, top floor, revolving, top quality, very expensive, opens 2130, summer only; *La Bourgogne*, Av del Mar y Pedragosa Sierra, also French and excellent restaurant and afternoon tea in stylish surroundings, expensive; *Pierre* (in hotel of same name), Artigas y Lourdes, good but very expensive; *Floreal*, Pedragosa Sierra, posta 5, elegant, French, rec, *casa de té* 1600-2030, restaurant after 2130; *Mariskonea*, Calle 26, No 650, one of the oldest restaurants, very good quality and service, but very expensive; *Bungalow Suizo*, Av Roosevelt y Parada 8, excellent, US$40 pp, must book; at the port: *El Pobre Marino* (rec) and *Sea Port*, both seafood; *El Mastil*, Av de las Palmeras esq 8 (behind port), charming atmosphere, open all year; *El Ciclista*, Calle 20 y 27, one of the oldest restaurants, Italian food; *Los Caracoles*, Calle 20 y 28, excellent food at good prices; *Viejo Marino*, Calle 11 entre 14 y 15, Las Palmeras, fish restaurant, very busy so go early; *Forte di Makalle*, Calle 8-828 y 11, rec; *Andrés* on a terrace at the Edificio Vanguardia, Rambla Costanera; *Harpers*, Rambla Costanera y 21, good but expensive; *Portofino*, Rambla Artigas entre 10 y 12, good Italian; *da Carmela*, Gorlero 635 y Rambla Gen Artigas, pizza and pasta, pleasant; *Blue Cheese*, Calle 20 No 717, Rambla de Circunvalación y 23, for steaks and unlimited salads, good value; *Yacht Club Uruguayo*, Gral Artigas y 8, very good, US$20-US$30 pp, friendly, views over the port (not to be confused with the exclusive Yacht Club, which is members only, but excellent); *El Metejón*, Gorlero 578 y 19, good food, good value; *La Fragata*, Gorlero 800, open 24 hrs all year, a good meeting place; *El Monarca II*, Calle 27 y 24 on Playa El Emir, expensive, seafood specialities; *Monaco*, 12 y 11, good value fixed price meals or expensive à la carte; *Lo de Tere*, 20 y 21, good food, reasonable prices, open all

year; *parrillas*: *Rahuel*, 24 y 25, expensive, and *Nitos*, 19 y 24; *Avenida Rotisería*, Calle 21 (La Galerna), good, cheap; *Gure-etxe* (also in La Coronilla), Calle 9 y 12, good food and price; *La hamburguesa*, Calle 27 entre Gorlero y 24, for burgers and other dishes. Many enticing ice-cream parlours on Gorlero. *Rosario*, Av Francia esq Ansina, excellent but expensive coffee shop, pastries, sandwiches.

● **Banks & money changers**

Best rates of exchange from **Banco de la República Oriental de Uruguay**, which opens earlier and closes later than the other banks and accepts Mastercard, but no TCs. **Amex Bank**, Gorlero y 21, will give cash against card. Also *casas de cambio*, eg **Indumex**, Av Gorlero y 28, **Brimar**, C 31 No 610.

● **Entertainment**

Discotheques: often don't begin till 0200. Entry US$25-50 a couple, inc 2 drinks. *New Faces*, Calle 20; *Caras y Caretas*, nr yacht club; *Space*, nr Playa Chiberta; many others.

● **Post & telecommunications**

Post Office and telephone, telex and fax on Calle 24 at Calle 25, by the square. Telefónica phones at Ancap station, Gorlero y C 30, T/F 46018.

● **Shopping**

Crafts: *Manos del Uruguay* on Gorlero, in front of the Casino Nogaró.

● **Sports**

Riding: Nueva Escuela de Equitación at *Cantegril Country Club*, Av Saravia, T 25013, classes, guided rides, all levels and ages catered for.

● **Tour companies & travel agents**

Madrid, T 41654, excursions from US$12, car hire, fishing trips and to islands; *Tuttie*, Local 1 de Servicio de Tráfico de Lanchas, T 44352, for trips to islands and fishing.

● **Tourist offices**

Tourist information at **Liga de Fomento**, Parada 1, T 45979/438, open 0800-2000, or at airports.

● **Transport**

Local Traffic is directed by a one-way system; town bus services start from Calle 5 (El Faro), nr the lighthouse. **Car hire**: Punta-Car, Cont Gorlero, *Hotel Playa*, T 82112/82761, telex Punt-Car UY 28105; **Hertz** (Maderal SA), 31 y Gorlero, T 89775, F 89778; Serracar, T 88855. See Madrid Viajes above. **Scooter hire**: US$10/hr, US$25/day, with drivers licence (US$50 fine if caught without it) and ID documents; one place opp bus terminal, others on same street as *Taller Los Angeles*, Parada 2 casi Blvr Artigas, T 86732. *Los Angeles* rents scooters and bicycles (US$1.50-US$2.20/hr, US$5.15-US$6/day depending on number of gears,

padlock and chain included, leave ID as deposit).
Air Direct daily Boeing 737 flights from Buenos Aires to Punta del Este airport during the high season. Laguna del Sauce, Capitán Curbelo (T 73056), which handles flights to Buenos Aires (AR, Pluna and Lapa, US$90). Airport tax US$6. Exchange facilities, tax-free shopping. Regular bus service to airport from Punta del Este bus station, US$4, 90 mins before departure, also connects with arriving flights. Taxi US$25; *remise* US$18-US$38 depending on destination (T 41269 or Punta del Este 433221). El Jagüel airport is used by private planes. Pluna, Gorlero 940, T 41840, or 78386 Laguna del Sauce, 84378 El Jagüel; Aerolíneas Argentinas, T 78782 Laguna del Sauce, or Edif Santos Dumont, T 44343.

Buses New terminal at Av Gorlero, Blvd Artigas and C32, T 89467 (served by local bus No 7); has toilets, left luggage at COT, newsagent, café. To/from **Montevideo**, COT (T 86810) or Copsa (T 89467, ext 13), US$6.70, just over 2 hrs, frequent in the summer; to Piriápolis, US$2.50. To San Carlos (US$2.25) for connections to Porto Alegre, La Paloma, Chuy. Direct to Chuy, 4 hrs, US$7.50. To Gen José Artigas bridge (Argentina) US$25. Local bus fare about US$0.60. For transport Montevideo-Buenos Aires, *Buquebus* T 84995, Gorlero 732, and *Ferryturismo* T 45312/42820, Galería Sagasti, Av Gorlero.

BEACHES EAST OF PUNTA DEL ESTE

Between the Peninsula and the mouth of the Río Maldonado, a road runs along the coast, passing luxurious houses, dunes and pines. At **Playa San Rafael**, there is an 18-hole golf course. The river is crossed by a unique, undulating bridge, like a shallow M, to **La Barra**, a fashionable place with beaches and restaurants. The coast road climbs a headland here before descending to the beaches further N, Montoya and **Manantiales** (reached by Condesa bus). 30 km from Punta del Este is the fishing village of **Faro José Ignacio**, with a lighthouse (open Fri-Sun, 1700-1900), a beach club and other new developments now the road is paved. Coastal R10 runs some way E of José Ignacio, but there is no through connection to La Paloma as a new bridge across the mouth of the Lago Garzón is not operational. A car ferry sometimes runs, but rowing boats will take pedestrians and cyclists across.

- **Accommodation & places to eat At San Rafael**: **L1** *Casino San Rafael*, A2 low season, closed after Easter, no credit cards, no balconies, much used for conferences, Tx 28035, T/F 82161; **L1** *Hotel Porto Bari*, T 84304, F 84021, Parada 13, French restaurant, swimming pool, tennis. **L3** *San Marcos*, T 82251, very pleasant; **L3** *La Capilla*, San Rafael, 100m from casino, T 81843, cheaper out of season, gardens, good. *Camping San Rafael*, T 86715, good facilities, US$7, bus 5 from Maldonado. Restaurant *La Plage*, Rambla L Battle parada 12, very pleasant; same address is *Gitana*, good beach restaurant (open Christmas to end-Feb). **At La Barra**: **L1** *Hostal de la Barra*, Ruta 10 Montoya, T 71521, F 71524, with breakfast. 2 campsites after the bridge, the second is cheaper, US$9.75, good showers and toilets. **Restaurants**: *Lo de Miguel*, Ruta 10 y C 7, excellent, small, booking essential (US$30 pp); *Pizza Bruja*, Ruta 10, just across the bridge, crêpes, pizzas and pasta; *Yenny's*, Ruta 10, good seafood; other *pizzerías* and restaurants up the hill. **At Manantiales**: **L1-L3** *Las Dunas*, T 71211, F 71210, good rooms, but no breakfast, meals US$25-US$30, opulent; *Nueva Puebla Youth Hostel*, US$5, kitchen and washing facilities, small. **At Faro José Ignacio**: **A2** *Parador Renner*, with breakfast, good dining room. The well-known restaurant *Parador Santa Teresita* (T 0486-2004), serves seaweed omelette as a speciality, very popular, US$25 pp. Many other small restaurants, eg *Los Negros Franceses*.

PUNTA DEL ESTE TO THE BRAZILIAN BORDER

ROCHA

Rocha *(pop 52,000)*, capital of Rocha Department, is 211 km from Montevideo. Groves of palms dotted about the fields give the area an unusual beauty. The city has an interesting central plaza and cathedral. There is a cinema on the plaza and the Club Social has dancing. The zoo is free to enter.

- **Accommodation & places to eat B** *Trocadero*, 18 de Julio y 25 de Agosto; **D** *Municipal*, on 19 de Abril, very good. Good *confitería* on the plaza; try also *Titar Grill* opp old Onda bus terminal; *Las Brasas*, 25 de Agosto 113; *Sirocco*, Ramírez y Rodó.

- **Buses** To Montevideo, 3 hrs, US$8.50 (COT); to Chuy, US$6.25. No direct services to Punta del Este, but easy connections at San Carlos.

LA PALOMA

28 km from Rocha, **La Paloma** *(pop 5,000;*

phone code 0473), protected by an island and a sandspit, is a good port for yachts. The surrounding scenery is attractive, with extensive wetlands nearby. You can walk for miles along the beach. The freshwater and sea fishing are good and the pace is more relaxed than Punta del Este.

● **Accommodation A2** *Portobello*, Las Tres Marías s/n, T 6159, rec; **A2** *Cabo Santa María*, with casino, Av Solari, T 6004; **A3** *Tirrenia*, Av del Navío, T/F 6230; **B** *La Tuna* (T 6083), Neptuno y Juno, rec; **B** *Perla del Este*, Aldo y Jupiter, T 6078; **B** *Bahía*, rec, T 6029, good restaurant; and others in **B** range. In nearby La Aguada, **B** *Bungalows de Piemonte*, Costanera, T 6096. **Youth Hostel**: at Parque Andresito, T 6396, 50 beds, US$5 pp, clean, friendly, good meals available, kitchen facilities, open 1 Nov to 30 Mar, essential to book at Montevideo office. **Camping**: in Parque Andresito, T 6107, US$11.75, overpriced, thatched *cabañas* for rent, US$22-38/day with maid and kitchen facilities, sleep 4-6; *Grill del Camping* for *parrillas*, La Aguada, T 6239, 2 km E of town, US$5, good, friendly, each site with own barbecue, tap, sink, water and electricity.

● **Places to eat** *La Marea*, nr tourist office, very popular, has outstanding seafood. *Arrecife*, on main street, excellent. Excellent bread at *Confitería La Farola*.

● **Useful services** Bike rental opp the casino, US$3.50 a day; horses can be hired. One bank which changes TCs; also a supermarket and post office. Tourist office on Av Solari at entrance to town, very helpful, T 6088.

● **Buses** Frequent buses run to and from Rocha, and to and from **the capital** (5 hrs, US$18). 4 buses daily to Chuy, US$4.35, 3¾ hrs, 2 a day to San Carlos, Pan de Azúcar and Aguas Dulces, all with Rutas del Sol company.

NORTHEAST OF LA PALOMA

Coastal R10 runs to Aguas Dulces (regular bus services along this route). 10 km from La Paloma is **La Pedrera**, a beautiful village with sandy beaches. Beyond La Pedrera the road runs near pleasant fishing villages which are rapidly being developed with holiday homes, eg **Barra de Valizas**, 50 mins N. At **Cabo Polonio**, visits to the islands of Castillos and Wolf can be arranged to see sea lions and penguins. It has a great beach (some topless bathing and 'old hippy' atmosphere). It can be reached from Valizas by walking 8 km over the dunes (very interesting, but hot, unless

you go early). From **Aguas Dulces** the road runs inland to the town of **Castillos** (easy bus connections to Chuy; several hotels including **D** *Hotel A Mi Gente*, Acosta 1235; several restaurants including *La Strada* on 19 de Abril), where it rejoins R9. At Km 298 there is a turn off for **Punta del Diablo**, a fishing village in dramatic surroundings, again with fine beaches.

● **Accommodation & places to eat At La Pedrera**: **A3** *Hotel La Pedrera*, T 6028, swimming pool, tennis, comfortable rooms, rec; *Restaurant Costa Brava*, overlooking the sea. Campsite *La Palomita*, 8 blocks from the sea, wooded, electricity, US$5, open summer only. **At Barra de Valizas**: **A3** *Posada Eirete*, small, tasteful, good breakfasts, owned by painter María Beloso, rec; ask around for cottage rental at US$25/day, sleep 4, fully equipped; Youth Hostel, US$5 pp, open 1 Nov-30 Mar, reserve in Montevideo first; free campsite, no facilities; fresh fish available if you ask. No electricity. **At Cabo Polonio**: a few restaurants, simple hotels, and houses or rooms to rent; informal camping at your own risk; bring your own food as prices are high. No electricity, cooking gas, or phone. **At Aguas Dulces**: *Hotel Gainford*, with restaurant; *Restaurant La Terraza*; *Chivito Veloz*, good, large portions for US$5; camping fairly organized. 2 km from Aguas Dulces is the private *Reserva Ecológica La Laguna*, T (099) 602410, on a 25 ha lake, with cabins for 4-6 (**B**), youth hostel (**D-E**), meals extra, IYHA affiliated, open all year, English, German, French, Italian, Spanish spoken, pick-up from bus stop in jeep or horse-drawn carriage, tours arranged, riding, boating on lake, sandboarding, birdwatching, credit cards accepted. At Km 280.5, 17 km N of Castillos is *Camping Esmeralda*. **At Punta del Diablo**: **A3** *Hostería del Pescador*, T (0472) 1611 LD17; private houses for rent US$50/day for 4; several restaurants, eg *La Posada*, excellent food, highly rec. Food and fish shops and handmade jewellery for sale.

PARQUE NACIONAL SANTA TERESA

About 100 km from Rocha, 308 km from Montevideo, is **Parque Nacional Santa Teresa**, with curving, palm-lined avenues and plantations of many exotic trees. It also contains a modest zoo, an aviary, botanical gardens, fresh-water pools for bathing and beaches which stretch for many kilometres (the surf is too rough for swimming). It is the site of the impressive colonial fortress of Santa Teresa, begun by the Portuguese in 1762 and seized by the Spanish in 1793. The fortress houses a museum of artefacts from the wars of independence, open 1000-1700 except Mon (winter hours shorter). Entry US$0.30, tickets from restaurant *La Posada del Viajero*, opposite, recommended. On the inland side of Route 9, the strange and gloomy Laguna Negra and the marshes of the Bañado de Santa Teresa support large numbers of wild birds.

● **Park services** Park entry is US$1.20 (check opening times, maybe 1300 on weekdays). There are countless campsites (open all year), and a few cottages to let in the summer (which are usually snapped up quickly). At the *capatacia*, or administrative headquarters, campers are expected to register (although the staff can be gloriously indifferent to your desire to do so and to pay). Here there are also a small supermarket, greengrocer, butcher, bakery, medical clinic, petrol station, auto mechanic, post and telephone offices, and the *Club Santa Teresa*, where drinks and meals are available, but food and drinks are expensive. Practically every amenity is closed off-season. Tour by taxi (US$12, daily) from La Coronilla (see below) to Santa Teresa fortress, Laguna Negra, and the collection of native and exotic plants.

LA CORONILLA

10 km beyond Santa Teresa, 20 km S of Chuy, is the bathing resort of **La Coronilla**; excellent ocean shark fishing, plus skate and corvina from the rocks; there is an annual competition in January. The sea water is reported to be highly polluted by a drainage canal.

● **Accommodation** Most close in winter, but try **B** *Gure-Etxe*, on beach, T 2783, small and very pleasant, with rec restaurant; **B** *Mesón Las Cholgas*, T 2860, restaurant, rec, but hot water is scarce in bathrooms of rooms facing beach; **B** *Parador La Coronilla*, on Route 9 at Km 312.5, T 2883; **B** *Costa del Mar*, on beach, rec, swimming pool, casino, restaurant; **C** *Rivamare*, T 2782. Cheapest is **D** *Las Maravillas*, on Leopoldo Fernández, T 2786. **Campsite:** *La Coronilla*, with restaurant, open Dec to Holy Week, 300m from the ocean, T 0474-1611-77. It also rents tent-cabañas, US$15 for up to four persons.

● **Places to eat** Besides hotel restaurants, there are also *La Ruta*, open all year, rec; *Niko's*, nr beach, good and cheap, and *El Mejillón*.

● **Buses** Between Chuy and Montevideo

stop at La Coronilla (US$13.25, COT, 5 hrs to the capital). To Santa Teresa fortress, take Rutas del Sol bus to junction, then walk 1 km.

CHUY

At **Chuy**, 340 km from Montevideo (*pop* 9,000; *phone code* 0474), the Brazilian frontier runs along the main street, Avenida Brasil. There are duty free shops in Chuy and tourists from Uruguay may buy limited amounts of manufactured goods on the Brazilian side without formalities (but see below). Quality underwear shops abound, excellent prices. There is also a casino. For details on the Brazilian town of **Chuí**, see Brazil chapter, page 475.

Excursions

On the Uruguayan side, on a promontory overlooking Laguna Merín and the gaúcho landscape of southern Brazil, stands the restored fortress of **San Miguel**, dating from 1752 and surrounded by a moat. It is set in a park in which many plants and animals are kept. (Bus from Chuy US$0.45, entry US$0.20, closed Mon.) The hotel nearby, **A2** *Parador San Miguel*, is excellent, beautiful rooms, fine food and service, highly recommended. Tours (US$9 from Chuy) end for the season after 31 March.

Local information
● **Accommodation**

All are open the year round. **C** *Alerces*, Laguna de Castillos s/n, T 2260, heater, breakfast, nice.
D *International*, Río San Luis 121, T 2055;
D *Madrugada*, Calle S Priliac.
F *Hospedaje Vitoria*, Numancia 143, T 2280, clean, friendly. Cheaper hotels available.

Camping: from Chuy buses run every 2 hrs to the Barra del Chuy campsite, Ruta 9 Km 331, turn right 13 km, T 2425; good bathing, many birds. *Cabañas* for up to 4 persons cost US$20 daily or less, depending on amenities.

● **Places to eat**

Most restaurants are on Av Brasil: eg *Restaurant Jesús*, good, cheap, friendly; *Parrillada Maldonado*, Brasil at Cebollati, good, quite cheap. Casino open till 0400.

● **Banks & money changers**

Exchange at *Hotel Chuy* (open until 0300); several *cambios* on Av Brasil (open until 1830), give slightly better rates. No exchange facilities on Sun. Brazilian currency can be bought here.

Banco de la República Oriental Uruguay changes TCs.

● **Post & telecommunications**
Post Office: Av Brasil, 4 blocks from Gen Artigas. Antel, 1 block behind plaza, between Calles L Olivera and Gen Artigas.

● **Tourist offices**
In middle of Av Brasil, at Av Argentina/Gen Artigas junction.

● **Transport**
Buses to **Montevideo** (COT or Cita) US$11-12, 4½ hrs; to **Maldonado** US$7.50; to **La Paloma**, 4 a day, US$4.25, 3¾ hrs. To **Treinta y Tres**, Transportes Puentes.

FRONTIER WITH BRAZIL

● **Uruguayan immigration**
Uruguayan passport control is 2½ km before the border on the road into Chuy, US$2 by taxi, officials said to be friendly and cooperative; Ministry of Tourism kiosk here is very helpful, especially for motorists. If travelling by bus, make sure the driver knows you want to stop at Uruguayan immigration, it will not do so automatically.

Tourists may freely cross the border in either direction.

Entering Uruguay To enter Uruguay, you must have a Brazilian exit stamp and a Uruguayan entry stamp, otherwise you will not be permitted to proceed (eg at the customs post between Chuy and San Miguel fortress, on Route 19 toward Treinta y Tres). Those requiring a visa must have a medical examination before a visa can be issued in Chuí, cost about US$20 and US$10 respectively.

● **Leaving Uruguay by private vehicle**
Taking a car into Brazil is no problem, especially if the car is not registered in Brazil or Uruguay.

● **Brazilian consulate**
Fernández 147, Chuy.

● **Transport**
Uruguayan taxis are allowed 25 km into Brazil. Bus from Chuy to **Rio Grande** at 0700 and 1530, 4 hrs, with stop at immigration; to **Porto Alegre**, 7½ hrs, US$18.50, 1200 and 2300.

Montevideo northeast to Brazil

TWO ROADS run towards Melo, heart of cattle-ranching country: Route 8 and Route 7, the latter running for most of its length through the Cuchilla Grande, a range of hills with fine views.

ROUTES Route 8 is the more important of these two roads to the border and it is completely paved.

MINAS

This picturesque small town (*pop* 34,000; *phone code* 0442) 120 km N of Montevideo, is set in wooded hills, which supply granite, marble and other minerals. Juan Lavalleja, the leader of the Thirty-Three who brought independence to the country, was born here (equestrian statue), and there is an equestrian statue to Artigas, said to be the largest such in the world, on the Cerro Artigas just out of town. The church's portico and towers, some caves in the neighbourhood, and the countryside around are worth seeing. In Mar and April you can buy *butea* palm fruit, which is grape size, orange and tastes bitter-sweet. Good confectionery is made in Minas; the largest firm, opposite *Hotel Verdun*, shows tourists round its premises. Museum in the Casa de la Cultura.

Excursions

The Parque Salus, on the slopes of Sierras de las Animas, is 8 km to the S and very attractive; take the town bus marked "Cervecería Salus" from plaza to the Salus brewery, then walk 2 km to the mineral spring and bottling plant (**C** pp *Parador Salus*, full board, acceptable; reasonable set lunch.) It is a beautiful 3-hr walk back to Minas from the springs. The Cascada de Agua del Penitente waterfall, about 11 km E off Route 8, is interesting and you may see wild rheas (protected) nearby. It is difficult to get to the falls in the off-season.

Between Minas and Punta del Este is the *estancia Peña Blanca*, owned by a member of the Batlle family; the library covers 200 years of the family's, and Uruguay's, history. Meals are provided at any time of day. It is a beautiful place, worth a visit.

Local information

● **Accommodation**
A2 *Verdun*, 25 de Mayo 444, T (0442) 2110; **D** *Residencia Minas*, 25 de Mayo 502 on main plaza; **D** *Ramos*, 18 de Julio nr bus station, basic (discount for IYHA members); **D-E** *Las Sierras*, 18 de Julio 486, T 3631, inc breakfast, very good value.

Youth Hostel: Route 8, Km 145, in small village of Villa Serrana, US$5 pp a night (open all year), 28 km beyond Minas on road to Treinta y Tres; basic, poor facilities, take plenty of food and drink as there is no shop. Direct bus from Montevideo or Minas, ask driver to set you down and walk 3 km to Villa Serrana; essential to book through Montevideo office.

Camping: *Arequita*, T 1611-70, beautiful surroundings, US$6.

● **Places to eat**
San Francisco, 25 de Mayo 586, is rec as is *El Portal*, Aníbal del Campo 743, for *parrillada*. The best pastry shop is *Irisarri*, Calle Treinta y Tres 618, known for *yemas* (egg candy) and *damasquitos* (apricot sweets).

● **Banks & money changers**
Lloyds Bank and national banks, open 1300-1700 Mon-Fri.

● **Tourist offices**
Tourist office at the bus station.

● **Transport**
Buses to Montevideo, US$5.75 (Núñez), US$5 (Minuano), 2½ hrs. To **Maldonado**, US$3.75, 5 a day, 2 hrs.

TREINTA Y TRES

286 km from Montevideo, this is the next centre of any importance (*pop* 28,000; *phone code* 0452), picturesquely placed a little way from the Río Olimar.

Excursions

Some 20 km from Treinta y Tres on Route 8, a dirt road, left, runs 19 km among and over hills to a rocky region with small streams, the **Quebrada de los Cuervos**, now a beautiful and quite unspoilt national park.

● **Accommodation & places to eat B** *Treinta y Tres*, JA Lavalleja 698, T (0452) 2325; *Central*, and pensions *Jorgito* or *Mota*. Free camping and swimming at Municipal Park on the Río Olimar. The main plaza has all the major restaurants and grills.

● **Buses** Núñez and Minuano from Montevideo, US$12.

TO THE BRAZILIAN BORDER

There are two routes from Treinta y Tres: Route 8 through Melo (113 km) to near Aceguá (59 km), or Route 18 through Vergara to Río Branco. Route 26 links Melo and Río Branco (88 km).

12 km SE of **Melo** (*pop* 42,000; *phone code* 0462) is the Posta del Chuy (2 km off Route 26). This house, bridge and toll gate (built 1851 by 2 Frenchmen) was the only safe crossing place on the main road between Uruguay and Brazil. Nowadays it houses a display of gaucho paintings and artefacts relating to its history.

● **Accommodation** At Melo **L3** *Gran Hotel Virrey*, J Muñiz 727, T 2411, better rooms in new part, TV, mini bar, good café.

● **Buses NB** Melo is also reached by Route 7 direct from the capital. Bus from Montevideo US$16.30 (Núñez). Several buses daily to Río Branco.

Río Branco was founded in 1914, on the Río Yaguarón. The 1½ km-long Mauá bridge across the river leads to the Brazilian town of Jaguarão.

● **Accommodation** **D** *Italiano*, with bath.
Youth Hostel: Av Artigas 279, cooking, laundry facilities, open all year (reservations in Montevideo).

● **Places to eat** *Oasis*, good, *pollo a la brasa*. *Pluna*, Ituzaingó 720, T 2272.

FRONTIER WITH BRAZIL

For road traffic, the frontier at Chuy is better than Río Branco or Aceguá.

Entering Uruguay Before crossing into Uruguay, you must visit Brazilian Policia Federal to get an exit stamp; if not, the Uruguayan authorities will send you back.

● **Brazilian consulates**

Melo: Av Aparicio Saravia 711, T 2084. **Río Branco**: Lavalleja y Palomeque, T 3.

● **Exchange**

Rates are usually better at Melo than at the frontier.

Montevideo north to Brazil

D AMS ON the Río Negro have created an extensive network of lakes near Paso de los Toros, with camping and sports facilities. South of the Río Negro is gently rolling cattle country, vineyards, orchards, orange, lemon and olive groves. North is hilly countryside with steep river valleys and cattle ranching.

ROUTES Route 5, the 509 km road from Montevideo to the border town of Rivera runs almost due N, bypassing Canelones before passing through Florida, Durazno and Tacuarembó. The road is dual carriageway as far as Canelones; there is a toll 67.8 km N of Montevideo. If driving this route, note that on the narrow bridges on the single carriageway traffic coming from the N has preference.

DEPARTMENT OF CANELONES

Las Piedras (*pop* 58,000), 24 km from Montevideo, in vineyard country, has a Gothic Chapel of the Salesians. Race meetings (pari-mutuel betting) Tues, Thur, Sat and Sun, entry US$0.50, take bus 102 from Av Paysandú in Montevideo.

Canelones, 45 km from the capital, is a typical small town (*pop* 17,000) in a grain growing area (it has a municipal campsite). It was the seat of Artigas' first government in 1813 (in what is now the Police station). Bus from Montevideo, Cita, US$2.20.

FLORIDA

52 km further N is the pleasant country town of **Florida** (*pop* 28,000), where the Act of Uruguayan Independence was signed in 1825. This is celebrated by a folklore festival on Independence Day (25 Aug) each year.

- **Accommodation C** *Español*, José Rodó 360, T 2262, **E** without bath, no food. **Camping**: Parque Robaina, on southern entrance to town and at Municipal Campsite in centre. **Tourism Farm**: *Estancia Tornero*, 51 km E of Florida (go 30 km E on Route 56, 10 km on Route 6 to Km 121, then right), T (02) 386623, Matilde y Francisco Gorlero, accommodation, meals, riding, walking on the farm.

- **Places to eat** *Restaurant Negro el 8*, Independencia y Gral Flores, Italian food.

- **Buses** From Montevideo US$4.75 (Núñez), US$4.10 (Cita). See also **Trains** in Montevideo section.

DURAZNO

Durazno (*pop* 28,000; *phone code* 0362), 182 km from Montevideo on the Río Yí, is a friendly provincial town with tree-lined avenues and an airport. There is a good view of the river from the western bridge.

- **Accommodation C** *Durazno*, Herrera 947, T 2371; **D** *Hotel Central*, Manuel Oribe 699 y Mons Arrospiede, T 2324. **Camping**: *33 Orientales*, in park of same name by river, T 2806, nice beach, hot showers, toilets, laundry sinks. **Youth Hostel**: Campus Municipal, T 2835, between 1300 and 1900, Mon-Fri, open all year. **Tourism Farm**: *Estancia Albergue El Silencio*, 12 km W of Durazno, T 2014 (or 1611 and ask for 'dos rural'), 15 mins walk E of bridge over Río Yí where bus will stop: basic, clean rooms, simple tasty food, very friendly, riding, swimming, fishing, bird watching, can help the gauchos, rec.

- **Buses** From Montevideo US$7.80, Núñez, Nossar.

Trinidad is 42 km W of Durazno; it is capital of Flores Department and is on Route 3 (Montevideo-Paysandú).

- **Accommodation B-C** *Gran Hotel*, on plaza, with bath, clean, comfortable. **Campsite** on road to Durazno.

- **Buses** Montevideo-Trinidad US$8.25 (Núñez, Nossar, Copay).

LAGO RINCON DEL BONETE

Paso de los Toros (*pop* 13,000) is close to the huge lake created by the Rincón del Bonete dam on the Río Negro, tourist information at Parador Municipal, Durazno s/n, T 2074. East of Paso de los Toros, along R43 (1½ hrs by bus) is **San Gregorio de Polanco** (*pop* 3,000), a small, picturesque village, with sandy beaches on the lake shore. A number of public and private buildings are decorated with wall paintings. Tourist information at *Pinolanda* handicraft shop, Artigas 201. There is a ferry across the lake several times a day.

- **Accommodation At Paso de los Toros**: **C** *Sayonara*, Rivera 484, T 0366-2535, basic; beautiful camping, *La Correntada*, *El Sauce* by the river. **At San Gregorio**: campsite, restaurant and hotel (**C**).

- **Buses** Montevideo-Paso de los Toros, US$10.20, Núñez, Nossar, Turil.

TACUAREMBO

390 km N of Montevideo, an agro-industrial town and major route centre (*pop* 40,000; *phone code* 0632). Museo del Indio y del Gaucho at Flores y Artigas.

- **Accommodation L3** *Central*, Gral Flores 300, T 2341; **A3** *Tacuarembó*, 18 de Julio 133, T 2104, breakfast, central; *Hospedaje 25*, 25 de Mayo 358, basic, garden; campsite 1 km out of town in the Parque Laguna de las Lavanderas, T 4761, and 7 km N on R26 at Balneario Iporá; *Restaurante Parrilla La Rueda*, W Beltrán 251, good.

- **Buses** From Montevideo, US$15.50 (Turil, Núñez). Train service to Rivera at 0600 (see below).

Minas de Corrales (*pop* 3,000) is in an area of abandoned goldmines, including long tunnels under the town. It is 23 km E of a turning off Route 5, 38 km N of Tacuarembó, 73 km S of Rivera (daily bus 2 hrs).

THE BRAZILIAN BORDER

Rivera (*pop* 55,400; *phone code* 0622) is divided by a street from the Brazilian town of Santa Ana do Livramento. Points of interest are the park, the Plaza Internacional, and the dam of Cañapirú. There are a casino and many duty-free shops.

- **Accommodation A3** *Casablanca*, Sarandí

484, T 3221, shower, breakfast, a/c, comfortable, pleasant; **B-C** *Comercio*, Artigas 115, comfortable, **C** without bath; **B-C** *Sarandí*, Sarandí 777, T 3521, fan, good, **C** without bath; **C** *Uruguay-Brasil*, Sarandí 440, T 3068, a/c, breakfast; **D** *Ferrocarril*, Lavalleja y Uruguay, T 3389, without bath, basic, quiet. **Youth Hostel**: Uruguay y Brasil. **Camping**: in Municipal site nr AFE station, T 3803, and in the Parque Gran Bretaña 7 km S along Route 27.

● **Banks & money changers** Plenty of exchange offices.

● **Transport Air** Aviasur from Montevideo; Pluna, Paysandú 1079, T 3404. **Trains** Passenger service to Tacuarembó leaves Rivera 1700, Mon-Sat, 3½ hrs; dep Tacuarembó 0600, US$3. The train goes through beautiful countryside abundant with animal life. **Buses** Terminal at Uruguay y Viera (1½ km from the terminal in Santa Ana). To/from **Montevideo**, US$21 (Turil, Núñez); to **Fray Bentos** and **Durazno**; to **Paysandú**, Copay at 0330, 1600, US$15; to **Tacuarembó**, US$4.50 (Núñez or Turil), no connections for Paysandú. To **Salto**, Mon and Fri 1630, 6 hrs, US$16. For **Artigas**, take bus in Livramento to Quaraí, then cross bridge.

FRONTIER WITH BRAZIL

● **Uruguayan immigration**
In the new Complejo Turístico at Sarandí y Viera, 14 blocks, 2 km, from the border (take bus along Agraciada). There is also a tourist office here.

NB This is not a straightforward border crossing by public transport. Remember that you must have a Brazilian exit stamp to enter Uruguay.

● **Uruguayan customs**
Luggage is inspected when boarding buses out of Rivera; there are also 3 checkpoints on the road out of town.

● **Brazilian consulate**
Ceballos 1159, T 3278/4470; **Argentine consul**, Ituzaingó 524, T 3257.

West from Montevideo

THIS IS the route from the capital to Colonia del Sacramento, with its colonial quarter and connections for Argentina.

ROUTES Route 1, part of the Pan-American Highway, runs W from Montevideo (toll at the Santa Lucía bridge, Km 22.5) for 177 km to Colonia del Sacramento. At Km 67, Route 3 turns N to San José de Mayo (**Hotels** *El Centro* and **A1** *El Parque*), Trinidad, Paysandú and Salto. 10 km W of San José, at Juan Soler, is *Parador El Cien*, painted violet, with *cabañas* (**B**) and a nice restaurant selling local produce (cheese, jams, etc). From Juan Soler, Route 23 goes to Cardona on Route 2 (82 km) and Route 11 goes to Route 1 at Scavino.

Route 1 is lined with ribbon development for much of the way to Libertad (Km 51). Roads lead off to several beaches, notably Playa Pascual at Km 34, Kiyú (campsite) at Km 76 and Boca del Cufre (campsite) at Km 101.

● **Tourism Farm** *Estancia Los Macachines*, Km 93.5, Route 1, T (0349) 2062 (or T Montevideo 619182, Calle Luis Andreoni 7246, CP11500), day trips only, for typical meals, horse riding, carriage trips, football, volleyball and tours of the working *estancia*, attended by the owners, US$30/day, highly rec.

COLONIAS VALDENSE AND SUIZA

At Km 121 from Montevideo the road passes **Colonia Valdense**, a colony of Waldensians who still cling to some of the old customs of the Piedmontese Alps.

(**Hotel** *Parador Los Ceibos*.) A road branches off N here to **Colonia Suiza**, a town of Swiss settlement also known as **Nueva Helvecia** (*pop* 9,000; *phone code* 0552). The Swiss national day is celebrated with great enthusiasm.

- **Accommodation** **L3** *Nirvana*, Av Batlle y Ordóñez, T 4052/4081, F 4175, Best Western, Montevideo office Rincón 728, T 924122, F 920365, restaurant (Swiss and traditional cuisine), sports facilities, gardens, rec; **A3** *Granja Hotel Suizo*, T 4002, fine restaurant, rec; **C** *Del Prado* – Youth Hostel – open all year, T 4169. Campsite in a park at the turnoff for Col Suiza, on main road, free, toilets (locked after 2100), no showers. Snack Bar/Restaurant *Don Juan*, main plaza, excellent food, pastries and bread. The area is famous for its cheeses and other dairy produce. **Tourism Farm** *El Terruño*, Ruta 1, Km 140, 35 km before Colonia, T 0556-2700, F 3078, full day tours US$20, inc rural safari, lunch.

- **Buses** Montevideo-Colonia Suiza, frequent, with COT, 2½ hrs, US$5.30; Turil, goes to Colonia Suiza and Valdense; to **Colonia del Sacramento**, frequent, 1 hr, US$1.85; local services between Colonia Valdense and Nueva Helvecia connect with Montevideo/Colonia del Sacramento buses.

ROUTES Route 2, for Mercedes and Fray Bentos, leads off at Km 128. At Km 5 **Rosario** is a typical agricultural town. It has 2 fishing clubs and the Club Cyssa, a social, cultural and sports club.

COLONIA

Colonia del Sacramento was founded by Portuguese settlers from Brazil in 1680. Throughout the seventeenth century it was an important centre for smuggling British goods across the Río de la Plata into the Spanish colonies. The small historic section juts into the Río de la Plata, while the modern town (*pop* 22,000; *phone code* 0522; from Buenos Aires 0222) extends around a bay. It is a charming, lively place with streets lined with plane trees, a pleasant Plaza 25 de Agosto and a grand Intendencia Municipal (Méndez y Av Gen Flores – the main street). The whole town is kept very trim. The best beach is Playa Ferrando, 2 km to the E (buses from Gen Flores every 2 hrs). There are regular sea and air connections with Buenos Aires and a free port.

The Barrio Histórico

The Barrio Histórico, with its narrow streets (see the **Calle de los Suspiros**), colonial buildings and reconstructed city walls, is interesting because there are few such examples in this part of the continent. It has been declared Patrimonio Cultural de la Humanidad by Unesco. The **Plaza Mayor** is especially picturesque. Grouped around it are the **Museo Municipal** in the former house of Almirante Brown (with indigenous archaeology, historical items, paleontology, natural history), the **Casa Nacarello** next door, the **Casa del Virrey**, the **Museo Portugués** and the ruins of the Convento de San Francisco, to which is attached the **Faro** (lighthouse, entry free – tip or donation appreciated). At the eastern end is the **Puerta del Campo**, the restored city gate and drawbridge. Just N of the Plaza Mayor is the **Archivo Regional**. The **Iglesia Matriz**, on Calle Vasconcellos (beside the Plaza de Armas/Manuel Lobo), is the oldest church in Uruguay. At the end of Calle Misiones de los Tapes, the Casa Portuguesa is now the tiny **Museo del Azulejo**. The house of Gen Mitre, Calles de San José y España, now houses the **Museo Español**. At the N edge, the fortifications of the **Bastión del Carmen** can be seen; nearby is the Teatro Bastión del Carmen, Rivadavia 223. (All museums open 1130-1830, entry by combined ticket bought from Museo Municipal; not all may be open on the same day.)

Real de San Carlos

Around the bay (5 km, take blue bus from Av Gen Flores y A Méndez, 30 mins, US$0.40), is Real de San Carlos, an unusual, once grand but now sad tourist complex, built by Nicolás Mihanovic between 1903-1912. The elegant bull-ring, in use for a mere 2 years, is falling apart (it is closed to visitors but a local guide will take you through a gap in the fence). The casino, the nearest to Buenos Aires (where gambling was prohibited), failed when a special tax was imposed on Mihanovic's excursions; it and its hotel are decaying. A huge Frontón court can still be used, but the building is rotting. Only the racecourse (Hipódromo) is still operational

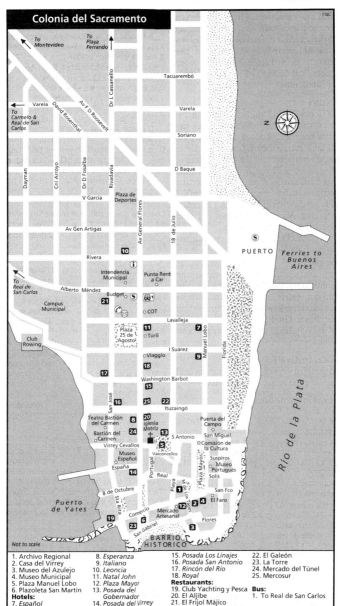

Colonia del Sacramento

Not to scale

1. Archivo Regional
2. Casa del Virrey
3. Museo del Azulejo
4. Museo Municipal
5. Plaza Manuel Lobo
6. Plazoleta San Martín
Hotels:
7. Español

8. Esperanza
9. Italiano
10. Leoncia
11. Natal John
12. Plaza Mayor
13. Posada del Gobernador
14. Posada del Virrey

15. *Posada Los Linajes*
16. *Posada San Antonio*
17. *Rincón del Río*
18. *Royal*
Restaurants:
19. Club Yachting y Pesca
20. El Aljibe
21. El Frijol Májico

22. El Galeón
23. La Torre
24. Mercado del Túnel
25. Mercosur
Bus:
1. To Real de San Carlos

(US$1 for men, women free) and you can see the horses exercising and swimming in the sea. Also in Real de San Carlos is a Museo Municipal; by the beach are two restaurants. At Parada 20, about 7 stops before Real de San Carlos, is the Capilla de San Benito.

Excursions

To **Conchillas**, 45 km N, pop 700, an unusual village of attractive one-storey terraced houses, abandoned quarry and mill, all built in 1890s by HJ Walker & Co to extract stone to build the port facilities of Buenos Aires. From Colonia take Tauriño bus for Carmelo, changing to connecting service at Radial Conchillas, 6 km from the village, bus waits in Conchillas 1 hr before returning. About 6 km further is Puerto Conchillas, with similar stone houses, disused port facilities and camping site. Intertur bus from Montevideo, US$9.

Parque Anchorena, N of Colonia, is the president's summer residence, at the mouth of the Río San Juan. It has native and non-native trees and animals in its beautiful park and several interesting buildings. Guided tours at weekends 1430-1700, US$2 pp, rec; fewer tours on weekdays.

Local festivals

In the third week of Jan, festivities are held marking the founding of Colonia.

Local information
● **Accommodation**
L3 *El Mirador*, Av Roosevelt, Km 176½, T 2004, a/c, casino, sports facilities.

In **Barrio Histórico**: **L3-A2** *Plaza Mayor*, Del Comercio 111, T/F 3193, lovely, English spoken; **L3-A2** *Posada del Virrey*, España 217, T/F 2223, suites and rooms; **A1** *Posada del Gobernador*, 18 de Julio 205, T 3018, with breakfast, charming, rec.

In the **centre**: **A2** *Esperanza*, Gral Flores 237, T/F 2922, charming; **A2** *Posada Los Linajes*, Washington Barbot 191, T 24181, central, a/c, TV, cafeteria, warmly rec; **A2** *Royal*, General Flores 340, T 2169, with breakfast, comfortable, good restaurant, pool, noisy a/c but rec; **A3** *Italiano*, Lobo 341, T 2103, **B** without bath, good restaurant, hot water but no heating, rec; **A3** *Leoncia*, Rivera 214, T 2369, F 2049, a/c, modern, good; **A3** *Natal John*, Gral Flores 382 on plaza, T 2081; **A3** *Posada San Antonio*,

Ituzaingó 240, T 5344, with breakfast, **B** during week.

B *Posada de la Ciudadela*, Washington Barbot 164, T 2683, pleasant, a/c, simple; **B** *Posada del Río*, Washington Barbot 258, T 3002, shower, with breakfast; **B** *Los Angeles*, Roosevelt 213, T 2335, small rooms, no restaurant, English spoken; **B** *Beltrán*, Gral Flores 311, T 2955, shared bath, comfortable.

C-D *Hospedaje Colonial*, Flores 436, T 2906, rec but noisy, restaurant below.

D *Hospedaje Las Tejas* Rosenthal y Fray Bentos, T 4096, with breakfast, shower; **D** pp *Español*, Lobo 377, without bath, large dark rooms, lots of character; **D** *Señora Raquel Suárez*, T 2916, has spacious rooms to rent, good value. The municipal sports complex has 2 dormitories with 80 beds, which are sometimes available – ask at the tourist office.

Camping: Municipal site at Real de San Carlos, T 4444, US$3.50 pp, **C** in mini-cabañas, electric hook-ups, 100m from beach, hot showers, open all year, safe, excellent, rec.

● **Places to eat**
La Torre, Av Gral Flores y Santa Rita, in old town, bar and restaurant, loud disco music, but fine panoramic views especially at sunset; *Pulpería Los Faroles*, just off Plaza Mayor, old town, rec, friendly. *Yacht Club* (at Puerto de Yates) and *Esperanza* (at hotel) are good; *Mercado del Túnel*, Flores 227, good meat dishes, but encourages eating of fresh vegetables; *Mercosur*, Flores e Ituzaingó, rec; *El Aljibe*, Flores 248 e Ituzaingó, good fish dishes. Good unnamed *parrillada* and pasta at Ituzaingó 168, nice atmosphere, value for money; *El Galeón*, Ituzaingó y 18 de Julio. *Club Colonial*, Gen Flores 382, good value. *El Frijol Mágico*, Galería Americana at Rivadavia y Méndez, good vegetarian food, 1130-1400.

● **Banks & money changers**
Banks open in pm only; **Banco Comerical**, on plaza, gives cash against Visa. *Cambio Viaggio*, Flores 350 y Suárez, T 2070, Mon-Sat 0900-1200, 1300-1800, Sun 1000-1800 (also outside the ferry dock, with car hire). *Cambio Colonia* and Banco de la República Oriental del Uruguay at the ferry port (dollars and South American currencies).

● **Embassies & consulates**
Argentine Consulate, Flores 215, T 2091, open weekdays 1200-1700.

● **Post & telecommunications**
Post Office: on main plaza.
Telephones: Antel, Rivadavia 420, open till 2300, does not accept foreign money.

● **Shopping**

El Patio, Flores 184, wool, leather, ceramics, Uruguayan stones. *Mercado Artesanal*, del Comercio y de la Plaza, old city; also *Rincón del Turista*, Santa Rita, old city.

● **Tourist offices**

Flores y Rivera, T 2182, open Mon-Fri 0800-1830, Sat and Sun 0900-2200, good maps of the Barrio Histórico; also at passenger terminal at the dock.

● **Transport**

Air Lapa (Rivadavia 383, T 2006/2461) flies to Aeroparque, Buenos Aires, most days, US$30 inc connecting bus services to/from Montevideo. This is generally quicker than hydrofoil. The airport is 17 km out of town along Route 1; for taxi to Colonia, buy ticket in building next to arrivals, US$2. **NB** Book in advance for all sailings and flights in summer, especially at weekends.

Buses To Montevideo, 2½ hrs, COT (Flores 432) and Turil (Flores y Suárez), half-hourly service between the two, US$7.50; Chadre at 0555, 1350; Turil to Col Valdense, US$2.35; to **Carmelo**, 1½ hrs, Tauriño (Flores 436), 4 a day (not Sun), US$2.50; Chadre/Agencia Central to Carmelo, **Salto**, 8 hrs, US$18.75 and on to **Bella Unión** en route from the capital. Turil to **Tacuarembó**, US$14.85, **Rivera**, US$19.10, and **Artigas**, US$23.40. **Car hire**: Budget, Flores 472; Punta, Paseo de la Estación L3, on Méndez nr Flores; also car hire at airport. Motorcycle and bicycle hire at Flores y Rivera and outside ferry dock, US$5/hr, US$15/day, rec as a good way of seeing the town, traffic is slow.

Sea To Buenos Aires: By ferry, 2½ hrs crossing, by hydrofoil (*aliscafo*), 1 hr, with Buquebus (T 0522-2975/3364), cars carried, and Ferryturismo (T 2919/3145), fares and schedules given under Montevideo.

Up the Río Uruguay

THE RIO URUGUAY marks the frontier with Argentina (international crossings at Fray Bentos, Paysandú and Salto). On the Uruguayan side are rolling hills crossed by a network of rivers. At all the major towns on the Uruguay are beaches and campsites and there are thermal springs at Guaviyú, Daymán and Arapey.

CARMELO

From Colonia, Route 21 heads N then NW to reach **Carmelo** (74 km; *pop* 18,000), on the banks of Arroyo Las Vacas. A fine avenue of trees leads to the river, crossed by the first swing bridge built in Uruguay. Across the bridge is the Rambla de los Constituyentes, with terraces and the Fuente de las Tentaciones. The town is pleasant, with the church, museum and archive of El Carmen on Plaza Artigas (named after the founder of the city). In the Casa de Cultura, 19 de Abril 246, is a tourist office and museum.

Before crossing the bridge into town, a road left goes to the Rowing Club, the Reserva de Fauna (with birds and mammals), the casino, the Yacht Club and continues to Playa Seré, Carmelo's beach at the river mouth. In summer, several hundred yachts visit Carmelo.

- **Accommodation A3** *Casino Carmelo*, Rodó s/n, T 2314; **B** *Bertoletti*, Uruguay 171, T 2030, modern; **C** *Rambla*, Uruguay y 12 de Febrero, T 2390; **D** *Palace*, Sarandí 308, T 2622; **D** *San Fernando*, 19 de Abril 161, T 2503, full of character, temperamental showers, rec. **D** *Oriental*, 19 de Abril 284. **Camping**: at Playa Seré, hot showers.

- **Banks & money changers** The banks will only exchange bills and not TCs.

- **Embassies & consulates** Argentine Consulate, FD Roosevelt 318, T 266.

- **Buses** To Montevideo, 1210, 2240, US$8.40, Intertur; to **Fray Bentos**, **Salto**, from main plaza 0710, 1540; to **Colonia**, Tauriño, 4 a day, 1½ hrs, US$2.50. **To Argentina**: via Tigre, across the Paraná delta, a most interesting bus/boat ride past innumerable islands: Cacciola 3 a day; office in Carmelo, Constituyente 263, T (0542) 8062, see under Montevideo for more details, page 1431.

NUEVA PALMIRA

Some 30 km N by road, passing Balneario Zagarzazu and *El Faro*, a private Argentine summer club, is **Nueva Palmira** (*pop* 7,000), a popular yachting resort with a free zone and campsite. Worth visiting in the vicinity are the Pirámide de Solís dating from 1888 (8 km out of town), the Estancia de las Vacas (also known as the Calera de las Huérfanas), an 18th century Jesuit estate, and the Estancia de Narbona, built in 1732, with a chapel and 3 storey bell tower (both in poor condition, 12 km from town, and 3 km off the road).

La Agraciada, some 20 km further N is the historic beach famous for the landing of the Thirty-Three patriots on 19 April 1825, which led to Uruguayan independence. On the beach is a statue of General Juan Lavalleja, leader of the Treinta y Tres. A festival is held on each anniversary.

MERCEDES

The road continues N through the small port of **Dolores** (*pop* 13,000), 32 km upriver from the confluence of the Río San Salvador with the Río Uruguay. On the plaza is a large brick church. Campsite 8 blocks W of the centre in a riverside park, free, cold showers; Intertur bus from Montevideo US$11, also Chadre.

Mercedes, a livestock centre and resort on the Río Negro best reached by Route 2 from the main Colonia-Montevideo highway. Founded in 1788, this pleasant town (*pop* 37,000; *phone code* 0532) is a yachting and fishing centre during the season. Its charm (it is known as "the city of flowers") derives from its Spanish-colonial appearance, though it is not as old as the older parts of Colonia. There is a pleasant *costanera* (riverside drive). 4 km W of town is the Parque Mauá, dating from 1757, with a castle and Museum of Palaeontology and Natural Sciences. There is also a small, well-maintained zoo (1300-1930), picnic tables, barbecues, camping possible in season. It takes 45 mins to walk to the park, a pleasant route passing interesting ruins (Calera Real) dating back to 1722, on the river bank.

Excursions To the islands in the Río Negro – the largest has an inn. To the small town of **Villa Soriano** (formerly **Santo Domingo de Soriano**), first town to be founded in Uruguay, see a fine colonial church and the old Casa de los Marfetan. It also has a river port, fishing, beaches and many orange trees. Difficult to do this trip easily in one day.

- **Accommodation A2** *Brisas del Hum*, Artigas 201, T 2740; **A3** *Marín*, Rodó 668, T 2987, a/c; **D** *El Dragón*, Giménez 659, T 3204, dark; **D** *San Martín*, Artigas 305, T 3212; **D** *Mercedes*, on Giménez, basic; **D** *Club de Remeros*, Youth Hostel, on riverside, T 0532-2534, kitchen and laundry facilities. Good food at *La Brasa*, Artigas 426, and at *Círculo Policial*, Calle 25 de Mayo. *El Emporio de los Panchos*, Roosevelt 711, good range of dishes. **Camping**: site at Mercedes, on an island in mid-river, reached by a small road, toilets, showers, US$2.20. **Tourism Farm**: A 200-year-old Colonial Estancia, a peaceful and novel alternative for visitors to Uruguay who want to experience traditional country living. Estancia "La Sirena" offers excellent accommodation, four daily meals as well as riding, fishing, hunting, tennis, sailing, swimming, etc; highly rec (also has timeshare). Attended by Rodney, Lucia and Patricia Bruce its friendly owners. 26 km E of town on Route 14. T/F Montevideo 607029, address: E Pittaluga 6396, Montevideo 11500, Uruguay; estancia T (598) 530-2046, F 532-4193.

- **Banks & money changers** Cambio Fagalde, Giménez 709; **Banco Comercial** on Colón (just off plaza) and **Banco de la República**, on plaza.

- **Tourist offices** **Colón**, on the plaza, maps and hotel lists available.

- **Buses** To **Paysandú**, with Sabelín, Sánchez 782, T 3937, 2½ hrs, US$6.25; also Chadre on the Montevideo-Bella Unión route. Bus to **Argentina** and **Montevideo**, CUT, Artigas (on plaza).

70 km inland from Mercedes is **La Palmar**, a pleasant small town with a hydroelectric power station and tourist complex with motels, campsite by the lake (free), fishing and sports facilities.

FRAY BENTOS

Route 2 continues westwards (34 km) to **Fray Bentos** (*pop* 22,000), the main port on the E bank of Río Uruguay, 193 km above Buenos Aires. Here in 1865 the Liebig company built its first factory producing meat extract. The original plant, much extended and known as **El Anglo**, has been restored as the Museo de La Revolución Industrial, and business park (there is a restaurant, *Wolves*, and a disco, *Fuel Oil*), open daily except Mon, entry by guided tour only, US$1.50, 1000, 1430 (more frequently in summer), tour 1½ hrs in Spanish, may provide leaflet in English. Nearby in the Barrio El Anglo, the workers' and manager's housing can be seen.

Excursions
There are beaches to the NE and SW and also at Las Cañas, 8 km S (where there is a tourist complex including motels, T 2597, C, campsite, sports facilities and services).

Local information
- **Accommodation**
A2 *Gran Hotel Fray Bentos*, Paraguay y Zorilla, T 2358, overlooking river, casino; **B** *Plaza*, 18 de Julio y 25, T 2363, comfortable; **D** *Colonial*, 25 de Mayo 3293, T 2260, attractive old building with patio; **E** pp *25 de Mayo*, 25 de Mayo y Lavalleja, T 2586, basic.

Camping: at the *Club Remeros*, nr the river and at Colegio Laureles, 1 km from centre, T 2236.

- **Places to eat**
Enramada, España y 25 de Agosto, the best; several cafés and pizzerias on 18 de Julio nr Plaza Constitución.

- **Banks & money changers**
Cambio Fagalde, Plaza Constitución, open Mon-Fri 0800-1900, Sat 0800-1230.

- **Tourist offices**
In Museo Solari, Plaza Constitución, T 2233, very friendly.

- **Transport**
Terminal at 18 de Julio y Blanes, buses call here, but do not alight as buses also call at company offices around Plaza Constitución. To/from **Montevideo**, ETA, 4½ hrs, US$9, also Chadre; to **Mercedes**, ETA, US$1, frequent, ½ hr; to **Paysandú**, US$4.75.

- **Crossing to Argentina**
9 km upriver from Fray Bentos is the San Martín International Bridge, the most popular overland route with Argentina, toll US$4 per car (tourist office). Bicycles are not allowed to cross, but officials will give you a lift if there is no other traffic.

Customs Formalities are separate, at opp ends of the bridge.

Argentine Consulate Sarandí 3195, Fray Bentos.

Buses To **Gualeguaychú** (Argentina), ETA, 2 a day, 1 hr, US$5, passports inspected on bus. To **Buenos Aires**, *bus de la carrera*, 3½ hrs, US$18.

PAYSANDU

The city (*pop* 100,000; *phone code* 0722) is on the E bank of the Río Uruguay, 122 km N of Fray Bentos along Route 24 and 480 along Route 3 from Montevideo via Trinidad. Temperatures in summer can rise as high as 42°C. There is a golf club, and a rowing club which holds regattas. The cathedral is 19th century. The cemetery on the outskirts is worth a look.

Museums
Museo de la Tradición, N of town at the Balneario Municipal, Tues-Fri 1230-1700, Sat 0900-1200, Sun 1330-1700, reached by bus to Zona Industrial, gaucho articles, worth a visit; **Museo Histórico**, Zorilla y Sarandí; **Museo Salesiano**, Florida 1278, attached to Cathedral, interesting, open Mon-Fri 0830-1130.

Excursions

To the **Río Quequay waterfalls**, 25 km to the N; the **Termas del Guaviyú** thermal springs 50 km N ($1\frac{1}{2}$ hrs by bus, US$2.50, 4 a day) with four pools, restaurant, motel accommodation and excellent cheap camping facilities, entrance to springs US$0.50, and to the **Meseta de Artigas**, 90 km N of Paysandú, 13 km off the highway to Salto. The Meseta, 45m above the Uruguay river, which here narrows and forms whirlpools at the rapids of El Hervidero, was used as a base by Gen Artigas during the struggle for independence. A terrace commands a fine view, but the rapids are not visible from the Meseta. The statue, with Artigas' head topping a tall shaft, is very original. There are pleasant, somewhat primitive, chalets available from Erwin Frey, 90 Estación Chapieny, Depto Paysandú. Early booking recommended. Bus to Km 462 on Paysandú-Salto road.

Local festivals

During Holy Week (book hotels in advance).

Local information

● **Accommodation**

L3 *Gran Hotel Paysandú*, 18 de Julio y 19 de Abril, T 3400, a/c, with breakfast, comfortable; **A2** *Mykonos*, 18 de Julio 768, T 9052, F 7990, with breakfast, TV, a/c; **A3** *Lobato*, Gómez 1415, T 2241, with breakfast, a/c, modern, good; **A2** *Nuevo Hotel Paysandú*, Herrera y Gómez, T 3062, a/c, TV.

B-C *Rafaela*, 18 de Julio 1181, T 5053, with breakfast, large rooms, modern; **C** *Concordia*, 18 de Julio 984, T 2417, **D** without bath, old-fashioned, pleasant patio; **C** *Plaza*, Gómez 1211, T 2022, with breakfast, fan.

D *Sarandí*, Sarandí 931, T 3465, good, comfortable; **E** pp *Victoria*, 18 de Julio 979, T 4320, highly rec, cheaper without bath, very helpful; **D** *LAF*, Sarandí 1190, T 8188, fan, with bath.

Youth Hostel: Liga Deportiva de Fútbol, Baltasar Brum 872, T 4247, US$1 pp, neither clean nor well-maintained. Cabins for 5 or more people.

Camping: Balneario Municipal, 2 km N of centre, by the river, no facilities. Also at the Parque Municipal, S of centre, some facilities.

● **Places to eat**

Artemio, 18 de Julio 1248, "best food in town"; *Asturias*, Pereda 917, very popular, good food, rec; *Don Diego*, 19 de Abril 917,

parrillada. *Los Tres Pinos*, Av España 1474, *parrillada*, very good.

● **Banks & money changers**

Several *casas de cambio* on 18 de Julio, inc **Cambio Fagalde**, No 1004; **Cambio Bacacay**, No 1008; both change TCs, open Sat 0830-1230. Also **Banco de la República**, 18 de Julio y 19 de Abril, and others on 18 de Julio.

● **Embassies & consulates**

Argentina, Gómez 1084, T 2253, Mon-Fri 0800-1300; **Brazil**, Herrera 932, T 2723.

● **Post & telecommunications**

Post Office: 18 de Julio y Montevideo. **Antel**: Montevideo 875.

● **Tour companies & travel agents**

Viñar Turismo, Artigas 1163, helpful.

● **Tourist offices**

Plaza de Constitución, 18 de Julio 1226, Mon-Fri 0800-1900, Sat-Sun 0800-1800.

● **Transport**

Air Aviasur flights to Montevideo (US$80 return; Pluna, Florida 1249, T 3071).

Buses Terminal at San Martín y Artigas. To/from **Montevideo**, US$14.70 (Núñez), 15.50 (Copay), 5-6 hrs, also Chadre/Agencia Central, many buses. To **Salto** US$5, 6 a day. To **Rivera**, US$15. To **Fray Bentos**, 4 a day, $1\frac{1}{2}$ hrs direct, 4 hrs via Young, US$5. To **Paso de los Toros** 1430 (return 0430), US$6.25, or by Alonso bus to **Guichón** at 0600, 1100, 1430 and change. To **Colonia** by Chadre, 1700, 6 hrs, US$7.50. It can be difficult to get a seat on long-distance buses going N.

● **Crossing into Argentina**

The José Artigas international bridge connects with Colón, Argentina (toll US$4 per car), about 8 km away.

Buses To **Colón** and **Concepción del Uruguay**, 5 a day, 2 on Sun, US$3 to Colón, US$4 to Concepción.

● **Tourism Farm**

L3 *La Calera*, nr Guichón (T Montevideo 904873, F 923177, Mara Morán, Colonia 881, piso 10), cheaper Mon-Thur, 20 luxurious suites with fireplace, full board, dining room with home made food, swimming pool, riding, rodeo, conference facilities, highly rec, transport from Paso de los Toros.

SALTO

A centre for cultivating and processing oranges and other citrus fruit, **Salto** (*pop* 80,000; *phone code* 073) is 120 km by paved road N of Paysandú. The town's commercial area is on Calle Uruguay, between

Plazas Artigas and Treinta y Tres. Next to the Club Uruguay, Calle Uruguay, is the *Farmacia Fénix*, "la más antigua de Salto", over 100 years old. See the beautiful but run down **Parque Solari** (on Ruta Gral Artigas, NE of the centre) and the **Parque Harriague** (S of the centre) with an open air theatre and a zoo (free, closed Mon, 7 blocks from centre, feeding time 1400-1500).

Museums
The **Fine-arts museum** in the French style mansion of a rich *estanciero*, Uruguay 1067, opens at 1400, well worth a visit. **Museo de Historia Natural**, Zorrilla de San Martín y Brasil, **Museo de Tecnología** in the old Mercado Central (same street intersection).

Excursions
The most popular tourist site in the area is the large **Salto Grande** dam and hydroelectric plant 20 km from Salto, built jointly by Argentina and Uruguay; a tour can be arranged with the tourist office, US$5, minimum 5 people, every 30 mins, 0700-1400. A road runs along the top of the dam to Argentina. By launch to the **Salto Chico** beach, fishing, camping. Nearby is the resort **A1** *Hotel Horacio Quiroga*, T 34411, sports facilities, staffed by nearby catering school.

Local festivals
Shrove Tuesday carnival.

Local information
● **Accommodation**
A3 *Gran Hotel Uruguay*, Brasil 891, T 35197, a/c, parking, cafetería; **A3** *Gran Hotel Salto*, 25 de Agosto 5, T 34333, with breakfast, best, a/c, rec, good restaurant, reasonably priced; **A3** *Los Cedros*, Uruguay 657, T 33984, with breakfast, a/c, comfortable.

B *Argentina*, Uruguay 892, T29931, with breakfast, a/c, cafetería, comfortable; **B** *Biasetti*, San Martín 94, T 32141, old-fashioned, large rooms; **B** *Libertador*, Lavalleja 55, T 28992, breakfast, fan, modern.

C *Concordia*, Uruguay 749, T 32735, breakfast, fan; **C** *Artigas Plaza*, Artigas 1146, T 34824, run down, log fire in winter, some rooms without windows; **C** *Plaza*, Plaza Treinta y Tres, T 33744, simple, old-fashioned.

D *Pensión 33*, Treinta y Tres 269, basic, central;

Pensión Pocholo, 18 de Julio y Varela, basic.

Youth Hostels: Club Remeros de Salto, Rambla Gutiérrez y Belén (by the river) T 33418, open all year, friendly, no cooking facilities, pool (US$5/day), US$5, US$6.50 without IYHA card; Club de Leones, Uruguay 1626, need a student to sign you in.

● **Places to eat**
Pizzería Las Mil y Una, Uruguay 906, popular, good atmosphere; *Pizzería La Farola*, Uruguay y Julio Delgado; *Don Diego*, Chiazzaro 20, pasta; *Club de Uruguay*, Uruguay 754, good breakfast and good value meals.

● **Banks & money changers**
Banco Pan de Azúcar does cash advances on Visa and Mastercard; Banco de Crédito, Mastercard only; both on Uruguay. Several exchange houses on Uruguay.

● **Places of worship**
Anglican Church: Calle República de Argentina, close to Calle Uruguay.

● **Post & telecommunications**
Post Office: Treinta y Tres y Artigas.

● **Tourist offices**
Uruguay 1052, T 4096, open 0800-2000, Sun 0800-1200, free map.

● **Transport**
Air Aviasur flights to/from the capital, US$80 return. Pluna, Uruguay 657, T 2724. Bus to airport, US$2.

Buses Terminal 6 blocks S of centre at Latorre y Larrañaga. To/from **Montevideo**, 7½ hrs, 4 a day, US$20, TTN on Ascencio, between Artigas and Uruguay, good service (also El Norteño, Núñez and Chadre); to **Termas del Arapey**, 2 hrs, daily, US$5.25. Paysandú US$5, 2 hrs, 6 a day. To **Rivera**, US$16. To **Bella Unión**, 2 hrs, US$6, 6 a day. To **Colonia** by Chadre, 0555, 1555, 8 hrs, US$18.75; to **Fray Bentos**, same times, US$10.

● **Crossing to Argentina**
North of the town, at the Salto Grande dam, there is an international bridge to Concordia, Argentina. **Immigration** is carried out on the bus.

Argentine consul Artigas 1162, T 32931, open Mon-Fri 1300-1700.

Transport Buses To Concordia, Chadre and Flecha Bus, 2 a day each, not Sun, US$3, 1½ hrs. To **Buenos Aires**, US$29, Flecha Bus. To **Posadas** night buses only, to **Puerto Iguazú**, 12 hrs, US$44. **Ferry** To Concordia, Sanchristobal/Río Lago joint service, 5 a day, Mon-Fri, 4 Sat, 2 Sun, US$3, dep from port on Calle Brasil, 20 mins.

Hot springs

Medicinal springs at Fuente Salto, 6 km N of the city. 10 km S of Salto, reached by bus No 4 every 30 mins from Calle Artigas (US$0.15) is **Termas del Daymán**, beautifully laid out with 8 swimming pools (entrance US$0.35, towel US$0.50, locker US$0.10; it is cheaper to buy combined bus/entrance ticket in Salto). 3 hotels, including **B** *La Posta del Daymán*, T 29701, F 28618, a/c, half-board, pool, massage, free medical assistance, good restaurant, discounts for long stay, recommended. **Youth Hostel** On Route 3, Km 490, T 0732-4361 (open all year, book well in advance during holiday season), restaurant, souvenir shop, campsite (no electricity or services).

The road to **Termas del Arapey** branches off the partially paved Route 3 to Bella Unión, at 61 km N of Salto, and then runs 35 km first E and then S. Pampa birds, rheas and metre-long lizards much in evidence. Termas del Arapey is on the Arapey river S of Isla Cabellos (Baltazar Brum). The waters at these famous thermal baths (five pools) contain bicarbonated salts, calcium and magnesium. There is a hotel with pool, **L3-B** *Hotel Termas del Arapey*, price depends on cabin size and facilities, a nice swimming pool, a very simple *parador* (meals only) and a good restaurant. Book ahead at tourist offices in Salto or Montevideo. Camping US$2 pp, good facilities (beware of theft at campsite and take food as local markets very expensive).

TO THE BRAZILIAN BORDER

Route 3 runs N to the little town of **Bella Unión** (*pop* 12,000), near the confluence of the Ríos Uruguay and Cuaraim, 144 km N of Salto. The Brazilian frontier, nearby, is crossed by the Barra del Cuaraim bridge. Bella Unión has 3 hotels and a campsite in the Parque Fructuoso Rivera (T 0642-2261), insect repellent needed.

- **Brazilian consul** Lirio Moraes 62, T 54.

- **Transport** Bus from **Salto**, US$6, 2 hrs. From **Montevideo**, US$26.15, El Norteño, Chadre. Launches go from Bella Unión to Monte Caseros. Buses to Barra del Cuareim (the 'town') leave every 30 mins, US$0.60, from Plaza 25 de Agosto. If entering from Brazil by car take plenty of fuel as there are few service stations on the roads S.

ARTIGAS

From near Bella Unión Route 30 runs E to **Artigas** (*pop* 40,000; *phone code* 0642), a frontier town in a cattle raising and agricultural area (excellent swimming upstream from the bridge). The town is known for its good quality amethysts.

- **Accommodation** **L3** *Hotel Municipal*, Dr LA de Herrera y Lecueder, T 3832; Ramón Carrea's hotel, **D**, Lavalleja 466, T 4666/2736, TV and fridge. *Pensión Hawaii*, basic. **Youth Hostel**: Club Deportivo Artigas, Pte Berreta and LA de Herrera, 4 km from city, T 3015, open all year, communal room, camping, restaurant, closes early. **Camping**: at Paseo 7 de Septiembre (by river), T 2261, and at Club Zorrilla, T 4341.

- **Places to eat** *Municipal*, Lecueder y Berreta; *Donatello*, Lecueder, good bar, pizza; *Deportivo*, Herrera, good value. Disco *Mykonos*, A Saravia.

- **Transport** **Air** Airport at Bella Unión (Tamu to Montevideo US$30); Pluna, Garzón y Baldomir, T 2545. **Buses** To **Salto**, 225 km, Oribe 279, US$6.85. Turil and others from **Montevideo** via Durazno, Paso de los Toros and Tacuarembó, US$30.

CROSSING TO BRAZIL

There is a bridge across the Río Cuaraim to the Brazilian town of Quaraí opposite.

- **Brazilian Consul** Lecueder 432, T 2504.

Information for travellers

BEFORE YOU GO

ENTRY REQUIREMENTS

● **Documents**

A passport is necessary for entry except for nationals of other American countries, who can get in with national identity documents. Visas are not required for a stay of less than 3 months by nationals of Argentina, Austria, Belgium, Belize, Bolivia, Brazil, Colombia, Costa Rica, Chile, Denmark, Dominican Republic, Ecuador, Finland, France, Greece, Guatemala, Germany, Honduras, Hungary, Italy, Israel, Iceland, Republic of Ireland, Japan, Luxembourg, Liechtenstein, Malaysia, Malta, Mexico, Netherlands, Nicaragua, Norway, Panama, Paraguay, Peru, Poland, Portugal, Slovenia, Spain, Sweden, Switzerland, Seychelles, UK, USA. Visas are required for Australians and New Zealanders, for example, £27 (June 1997, details from consulate in London), and you need a passport photograph and to show a ticket out of Uruguay. Tourist cards (obligatory for all tourists, obtainable on entry) are valid for 3 months, extendable for a similar period. For extensions (small fee) go to Migraciones office, Calle Misiones 1513, T 960471/961094.

● **Tourist information**

The Comisión Nacional de Turismo information office, see under Montevideo **Tourist offices**, issues tourist literature. On the Internet, visit http://www.turismo.gub.uy. The local papers publish 'what's on' columns on Fri evenings and on Sat.

● **Maps**

Automóvil Club del Uruguay, Av Libertador General Lavalleja 1532, Montevideo, T 984710, publishes road maps of the city and the country, and so do Esso and Ancap at about US$2 each. Official maps are issued by Instituto Geográfico Militar, Abreu y 8 de Octubre, open 0800-1230, T 816868.

WHEN TO GO

● **Best time to visit**

Most tourists visit during the summer (Dec-mid March). Business visits can be paid throughout the year, but it is best to avoid the tourist months.

HEALTH

Milk and tap water can be drunk and fresh salads eaten fairly freely throughout the country. Medical services are reported to be expensive. Emergency ambulance and care is provided by UCM and SUAT, US$14/month. The British Hospital in Montevideo is rec.

MONEY

● **Currency**

The currency is the peso uruguayo. Bank notes issued are for 50, 100, 200 (do not confuse with old peso 2,000 notes – pre-1993, which are now worth 2 pesos), 500 (don't confuse with 50), 1,000, 5,000 and 10,000 pesos uruguayos. Coins: 10, 20 and 50 centavos; 1, 2 pesos. Any amount of currency can be taken in or out.

● **Cost of living**

Uruguay is expensive, not as expensive as

Argentina. Prices vary considerably between summer and winter, Punta del Este being the most expensive summer resort in Latin America. Some Argentines find that generally prices and quality of clothing, for instance, are better in Montevideo than Buenos Aires. Someone staying in a cheap hotel, eating the *menú del día* and travelling by bus, should allow US$28-34/day.

● **Banks & money changers**

Rates change frequently because of the floating exchange rate and inflation differentials against the US dollar; see the 'Exchange Rates' table near end of book. No restriction on foreign exchange transactions (ie an excellent place to stock up with US$ bills, though American Express and some banks refuse to do this for credit cards; most places charge 3% commission for such transactions). Those banks which give US$ cash against a credit card are given in the text. Dollars cash can be purchased when leaving the country. Changing Argentine pesos into Uruguayan pesos is usually a marginally worse rate than for dollars. Brazilian *reais* get a much worse rate. US$ notes are widely accepted.

● **Credit cards**

Argencard is a member of the Mastercard organization, so one may use Mastercard at outlets displaying their sign. Many shopkeepers are unaware of this but a phone call will confirm it. Also American Express, Diners Club and Visa. Most hotels outside Montevideo do not accept credit cards. There is a 10% charge on the use of credit cards.

GETTING THERE

BY AIR

● **From Europe**

Direct flights by Pluna (Madrid), Iberia (Barcelona and Madrid) and Air France (Paris). Flying by other carriers, a change must be made at Rio or Buenos Aires.

● **From North America**

United Airlines from New York via Buenos Aires daily, and American daily from Miami via São Paulo.

TO URUGUAY FROM SOUTH AMERICA

● **From Argentina**

Ferry and hydrofoil services (Montevideo and Colonia to Buenos Aires) and launch services (Carmelo to Tigre) are given in the text. Aerolíneas Argentinas and Pluna have several flights a day between Aeroparque in Buenos Aires and Carrasco Airport, flights can be very full, especially in high season. Service intensified during holiday period. Also flights to Punta del Este from Buenos Aires. Lapa has a bus/plane service via Colonia to Buenos Aires. Buses run across the Paysandú and Fray Bentos bridges. Direct bus between Buenos Aires and Montevideo via Fray Bentos takes about 10 hrs. Ferries cross the Río Uruguay between Salto and Concordia.

● **From Bolivia**

LAB four times a week from Santa Cruz.

● **From Brazil**

Direct connection between Brazil and Uruguay by all the international airlines landing at Montevideo. Pluna flies from Rio de Janeiro to Montevideo direct and via São Paulo. Varig has a daily flight from Rio via Porto Alegre and a daily flight from Rio via São Paulo. Pluna also flies daily from São Paulo direct. Pluna flies Florianópolis-Montevideo once a week. By road: the Pan-American Highway runs 2,880 km from Rio de Janeiro to Montevideo and on to Colonia. It is poorly surfaced in parts. There are several bus services.

See under Brazil, **How to get to Brazil: By Air**, for the Mercosur airpass.

● **From Chile**

Pluna (3 a week) and LanChile (5) from Santiago.

● **From Paraguay**

Three a week by Lapsa and by Pluna. Five buses a week between Asunción and Montevideo.

CUSTOMS

● **Duty free allowance**

Duties are not usually charged on a reasonable quantity of goods brought in obviously for the traveller's own use: 400 cigarettes or 50 cigars or 250 grammes of tobacco are admitted duty-free; so are 2 litres of alcoholic drink, 3 little bottles of perfume and gifts up to the value of US$5.

WHEN YOU ARRIVE

● **Hours of business**

Most department stores generally are open 0900 to 1200 (or 1230), 1400 (or 1430) to 1900, but 0900 to 1230 on Sat. Business houses vary but most work from 0830 to 1200, 1430 to 1830 or 1900, according to whether they open on Sat. Banking hours are 1300 to 1700 in Montevideo; there are special summer hours (1 Dec-15 Mar) in Montevideo (1330-1730), in the interior (0800-1200) and in Punta del Este, Maldonado and other resorts (1600-2000); banks are closed on Sat. Government offices, mid-Mar to mid-Nov, 1300 to 1830 from Mon to Fri; rest of the year, 0700 to 1230 (not Sat).

● **Safety**
Personal security offers few problems in Uruguay to travellers who are reasonably prudent.

● **Tipping**
Normally all hotel and restaurant bills include a percentage service charge plus 23% value-added tax, but an additional small tip is expected. In other cases give 10% of the total bill. Porters at the airport expect about US$1 per piece of luggage; although there is an official rate of tips for porters at seaports, the actual charges are mostly higher. Taxi drivers are tipped 10% of the fare. Tips at cafés are about 10%. Cinema ushers get a small tip, as do cloakroom attendants and hairdressers (10%-15%).

● **Voltage**
220 volts 50 cycles AC.

● **Weights and measures**
Metric units alone are legal.

ON DEPARTURE

● **Airport tax**
Airport tax of US$6 on all air travellers leaving Uruguay (but US$12 to Ezeiza); US$12 for all other countries, US$0.50 on internal flights, and a tax of 3% on all tickets issued and paid for in Uruguay.

WHERE TO STAY

● **Accommodation**
Hotel accommodation can be very scarce in summer: reserve in advance. High, mid and low season dates are given under Punta del Este. For accommodation on farms (*Estancias de Turismo*) contact the Tourist Office in Montevideo, in addition to those mentioned in the text. Travel agents who specialize in *estancias* are: **Estancias Gauchas**, Cecilia Regules Viajes, Bacacay 1313, Montevideo, T 963011, F 963012; **Estancias de Turismo**, Rosa O'Brien, Wilson Ferreira Aldunate 1407, apto 306, T 910698.

● **Camping**
Lots of sites. Most towns have municipal sites (quality varies). Many sites along the Ruta Inter-balnearia, but most of these close off season. The Tourist Office in Montevideo issues a good guide to campsites and youth hostels; see references in main text. *El País* newspaper publishes a *Guía de turismo juvenil y tiempro libre* to complement the Instituto Nacional de la Juventud's Programa de Turismo Juvenil: aimed at backpackers, it gives useful information on camping and travelling cheaply in Uruguay. Methylated spirits, called *alcohol de quemar*, is sold in *Dispensas*.

● **Youth hostels**
Asociación de Alberguistas del Uruguay, Calle Pablo de María 1583 (open 1300-1900), Montevideo (T 404245) operates hostels (IYHA members only) at Montevideo (Canelones 935), Artigas, Paysandú, Piriápolis, Salto, La Paloma, Colonia Suiza, Villa Serrana (near Minas), Barra de Valizas (between La Pedrera and Aguas Dulces), Durazno and Río Branco. Many of the hostels are poorly equipped. A 10% rebate is available on Lapa plane tickets between Colonia and Buenos Aires, and rebates have also been reported (10-20%) for bus fares and hotel prices.

FOOD AND DRINK

FOOD
Beef is eaten at almost all meals. The majority of restaurants are *parrilladas* (grills) where the staple is beef. *Asado* (barbecued beef) is popular; the main cuts are *asado de tira* (ribs); *pulpa* (no bones), *lomo* (fillet steak) and entrecote. To get a lean piece of *asado*, ask for *asado flaco*. *Costilla* (chop) and *milanesa* (veal cutlet) are also popular; usually eaten with mixed salad or chips. *Chivitos* are Uruguayan steak burgers; *chivitos canadienses* are sandwiches filled with slices of meat, lettuce, tomato, egg, etc (normally over US$2 – very filling). Two other good local dishes are *puchero* (beef with vegetables, bacon, beans and sausages) and the local varieties of pizza. Other specialities are barbecued pork, grilled chicken in wine, *cazuela* (or stew) usually with *mondongo* (tripe) or sea foods (eg squid, shark – *cazón*, mussels – *mejillones*). The sausages are very good and spicy (*chorizos, morcillas, salchichas*). *Morcilla dulce*, a sweet black sausage, made from blood, orange peel and walnuts, has been highly praised; so has the *morcilla salada*, which is savoury. For snacks, *media lunas mixtas* are a type of croissant filled with ham and cheese, either hot or cold; toasted sandwiches are readily available; *panchos* are hot dogs, *húngaros* are spicy sausage hot dogs. *Preparación* is a selection of crisps, nuts, vol-au-vent, etc. An excellent dessert is *chajá*, from Paysandú, a type of sponge-cake ball with cream and jam inside, also with peaches – very sweet; others there are *massini* (a cream sponge), *Martín Fierro* (*dulce de membrillo* with cheese) and the common lemon pie. Pastries are very good indeed, and crystallized egg-yolks, known as *yemas*, are popular sweets. Ice cream is excellent everywhere.

The dinner hour is usually from 2000 to 0100. Note that restaurants generally charge *cubierto* (bread), which ranges from US$0.30 to US$1 in Punta del Este.

DRINK

The local wines are very varied, not only from bodega to bodega, but also from vintage to vintage. **NB** 'Del museo' indicates the bodega's vintage reserve. The beers are good. Imported drinks are freely available in Montevideo, eg whisky, and Chilean wines. *Mate* is a favourite drink between meal hours. The local spirits are *caña* and *grappa*; some find the locally-made whisky and gin acceptable. In the Mercado del Puerto, Montevideo, a *medio medio* is half still white wine, half sparkling white (a must! Elsewhere a *medio medio* is half *caña* and half whisky). *Espillinar* is a cross between whisky and rum. Try the *clérico*, a tasty mixture of wine, fruit juices and fruits. Coffee is good: a *cortado* is a strong, white coffee, *café con leche* is milk with a little coffee. Milk is available, in plastic sacs.

GETTING AROUND

AIR TRANSPORT

Internal flights are very cheap with Pluna and Aviasur (addresses under Montevideo). Provincial airports are given in the text.

LAND TRANSPORT

● **Train**

The only passenger services in operation in 1995 were Tacuarembó-Rivera and commuter services Montevideo – 25 de Agosto (in Florida department). There are plans to resume services to Minas and Río Branco (on the Brazilian border).

● **Road**

There are 52,000 km of roads, 23% of them paved and a further 60% (approximately) all-weather. The Comisión Nacional de Turismo will help to plan itineraries by car.

● **Bus**

Bus services are given in the text.

● **Motoring**

Vehicles do not stop, nor is there a right of way, at uncontrolled intersections. Driving in Montevideo has become very dangerous; take care. Outside Montevideo there is little traffic and few filling stations (many close at weekends). Care is needed at night since vehicle lights do not always work. There are many ancient cars (1920s and 1930s models are called *cachilas* and skilled mechanics keep them on the road). Insurance is not required by law. Uruguay is said to be much better than Argentina or Brazil to ship a car to, but vehicles are admitted for 6 months only, with the possibility of a further 3 months extension. Gasoline prices are

US$1.03/litre *eco supra*, US$0.97/litre *super*, US$0.84/litre *común*; diesel is US$0.45/litre. Automóvil Club del Uruguay has a fuel and service station for its members only at Yí y Colonia, Montevideo, T 921691 (head office is Av Libertador General Lavalleja 1532, T 924792). Reciprocity with foreign automobile clubs is available all year round, members no longer have to pay for affiliation.

Car spares are expensive. The area around Galicia and Yí in Montevideo is rec for new parts. Warnes, Minas y Cerro Largo, have been rec for second-hand parts. Land-Rover garage in Montevideo at Cuareim 2082, nr old railway station.

● **Hitchhiking**

Hitchhiking is not easy following attacks on drivers who have given lifts.

COMMUNICATIONS

● **Postal services**

Postal services are very unreliable; all items should be registered and sent by air mail to avoid delay (probably better to go direct to airport, avoiding chaos of the sorting office). Rates to USA and Europe, up to 20g US$1, up to 100g US$3; to South Africa and Asia up to 20g US$1, up to 100g US$3.20. Courier services are used increasingly: to Europe US$30-40, USA US$25, South Africa US$35, Middle East US$45, Buenos Aires US$12.

● **Telephone services**

Provided by Antel (see under Montevideo). Direct dialling to any country abroad is straightforward – public phones cannot receive incoming calls. Collect calls available to most countries (collect calls are the cheapest way of phoning USA and Canada). With competition from fax, and new equipment, phone prices have fallen: US$2/min to Argentina and Brazil; US$3 to most of the Americas and Europe; US$4 to USA; US$5 to rest of world. Phone calls are cheaper by 25% between 2200 and 0700 and Sat 1300 to Mon 0700. Fax from Antel, first sheet costs US$1 more than a minute's phone call to USA, Europe and Australia (US$0.50 more to Argentina and Brazil).

ENTERTAINMENT

● **Newspapers**

There are 3 Montevideo morning newspapers: *El País, La República* and *La Mañana*, and *El Diario* and *Ultimas Noticias* which come out in the evening. *Búsqueda* and *Ambito Financiero* are published weekly. The town of Paysandú has the *Telégrafo*. At about 1000 the main Buenos Aires papers, including the *Buenos Aires Herald*, can be had in Montevideo.

● **Radio**

There are 35 radio stations (8 private FM) in Montevideo and 65 in the rest of the country.

● **Television**

Of the 20 colour-TV stations, 4 transmit from Montevideo (channel 12 is the most popular). Also satellite and cable TV.

SPORT

The beach is more popular than the water. Uruguay has three important yacht clubs, the Uruguayo, the Nautilus and the Punta del Este. Fishing. Association football is played intensively. Rugby football is also played, and there is an annual championship.

HOLIDAYS AND FESTIVALS

● **Holidays**

1 Jan, 6 Jan; Carnival (see below); Easter week; 19 April; 1, 18 May; 19 June; 18 July; 25 Aug; 12 Oct; 2 Nov; 25 December. (8 Dec is a religious holiday which also marks the official start of the summer holiday.)

Business comes to a standstill also during Holy Week, which coincides with La Semana Criolla (horse-breaking, stunt riding by cowboys, dances and song, many Argentine visitors). Department stores close only from Good Friday. Banks and offices close Thur-Sun. Easter Monday is not a holiday.

● **Festivals**

Carnival week is officially the Mon and Tues immediately preceding Ash Wednesday, but a great many firms close for the whole of the week.

FURTHER READING

Satius Guiatur publishes a *Guía de Montevideo* in Spanish and English, with factual and cultural information, and a guide to Uruguay. Pirelli of Argentina is publishing a guide to Uruguay. Uruguay has a strong tradition of critical writing, eg José Enrique Rodó (*Ariel*, 1900), Angel Rama and Eduardo Galeano (*Venas abiertas de América Latina, Memoria del fuego, Días y noches de amor y de guerra*, etc). Two novelists who have gained international fame are Juan Carlos Onetti and Mario Benedetti (also a poet and critic).

ACKNOWLEDGEMENTS

Our thanks go to Rachel Rogers, who updated the chapter, and to Sonya Ayling, resident in Montevideo, for her help in the preparation of this chapter.

Venezuela

HORIZONS

When the Spaniards landed in Venezuela in 1498, in the course of Columbus' third voyage, they found a poor country sparsely populated by Indians who had created no distinctive culture. 400 years later it was still poor, almost exclusively agrarian, exporting little, importing less. The miracle year which changed all that was 1914, when oil was discovered near Maracaibo. Today, Venezuela is one of the largest producers and exporters of oil in the world.

THE LAND

Venezuela has 2,800 km of coastline on the Caribbean Sea, and 72 islands. To the E is Guyana, to the S Brazil, and to the W Colombia. It was given its name – 'Little Venice' – by the Spanish navigators, who saw in the Indian pile dwellings on the Lago de Maracaibo a dim reminder of the buildings along Venetian waterways.

The country falls into four very different regions: the Venezuelan Highlands to the W and along the coast; the Maracaibo Lowlands around the fresh water lake of Maracaibo; the vast central plain of the Llanos of the Orinoco; and the Guayana Highlands, which take up over half the country.

The Venezuelan Highlands are an offshoot of the Andes. From the Colombian border they trend, at first, towards the NE to enfold the Maracaibo Lowlands. This section is known as the Sierra Nevada de Mérida. Beyond they broaden out into the Segovia Highlands N of Barquisimeto, and then turn E in parallel ridges along the coast to form the Central Highlands, dipping into the Caribbean Sea only to rise again into the Northeastern Highlands of the peninsulas of Paria and Araya.

The natural obstacles to farming, cattle breeding, and communications explain why the country was poverty-stricken for so long.

NATIONAL PARKS

Venezuela has 35 national parks and 15 smaller national monuments, some of which are mentioned in the text. A full list is published by the Instituto Nacional de Parques (Inparques), Museo de Transporte, Edif Sur, Av Rómulo Gallegos, Parque del Este (exit Parque del Este metro opposite park, turn left, office is a few hundred metres further on up a slight incline), T 284-1956, Caracas. Each park has a regional director and its own guards (guardaparques). Permits (free) are required to stay in the parks (up to 5), although this is not usually necessary for those parks visited frequently. For further information on the National Parks system,

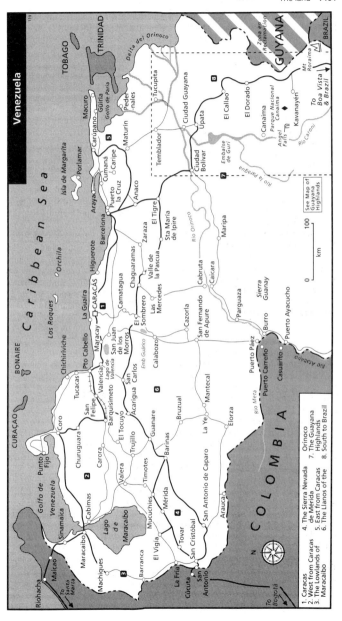

Venezuela

1. Caracas
2. West from Caracas
3. The Lowlands of Maracaibo
4. The Sierra Nevada de Mérida
5. East from Caracas
6. The Llanos of the Orinoco
7. The Guayana Highlands
8. South to Brazil

visit the Ministerio del Ambiente y de los Recursos Naturales Renovables (MARNR), Centro Simón Bolívar, Torre Sul, p 19, Caracas 1010, T 483-3164/1071. The book *Guía de los Parques Nacionales y Monumentos Naturales de Venezuela*, is obtainable in Audubon headquarters, 0900-1230 and 1430-1800, Las Mercedes shopping centre, Las Mercedes, Caracas in the La Cuadra sector next to the car parking area (it is difficult to find), T 913813 (and also at Librería Noctúa, Villa Mediterránea, in the Centro Plaza shopping centre). The society will plan itineraries and make reservations.

CLIMATE

Climate is tropical, with little change between seasons. Temperature is a matter of altitude. Mean annual temperatures are given in the text. At Caracas it is 20°C, but during the dry season (Dec to April), there is a great difference between day and night temperatures, and during the whole year there is a burst of heat around midday. Rainfall in mm: Caracas, 762; Maracaibo, 573; Barcelona, 660; Mérida, 1,295; Amazonas and parts of Barinas state 2,540.

HISTORY

At the beginning of the 16th century, Venezuela was inhabited by various tribes of Caribs and Arawaks, who could make no effective resistance against the Spaniards. The first permanent Spanish settlement was at Cumaná, in 1520. Soon afterwards settlers reached Coro, at the foot of the Paraguaná Peninsula. Indian slaves were used to mine and pan for gold, but the results were disappointing and the settlers turned to agriculture, forming settlements at Barquisimeto in 1552, at Valencia in 1555, and at Caracas in 1567. It was not until after a century of consolidation in these areas that they began to occupy the rest of the country, intermarrying freely with the Indians and later introducing black slaves to work the sugar plantations.

THE STRUGGLE FOR INDEPENDENCE

Centralized colonial control from Spain was as irksome here as in the rest of Latin America: three risings reflecting these discontents took place in 1749, 1775 and 1797, and there were two abortive attempts by Francisco Miranda to achieve independence in 1806 and 1811. After Miranda had been captured, the movement was led by Simón Bolívar, a *criollo* with a touch of Indian ancestry, born in Caracas in 1783. He met with mixed success until his capture of Angostura, now Ciudad Bolívar, in 1817. There he was joined by a contingent of experienced Peninsular veterans recruited in London. At their head, together with the horsemen of the *llanos* commanded by Gen José Antonio Páez, he undertook a dramatic march over the Andes in 1819 to win the battle of Boyacá and capture Bogotá. Three months later, the revolutionary congress at Angostura – with most of Venezuela still in Spanish hands – declared the independence of Gran Colombia, a union of what is now Ecuador, Colombia, Venezuela, and Panamá. Bolívar returned from Bogotá, and on 24 June 1821, the revolutionaries routed the Spanish forces at Carabobo. There was some desultory fighting for 2 more years, but the last of the Spanish forces surrendered at Puerto Cabello in 1823. Before Bolívar's death in 1830 Páez declared Venezuela an independent republic.

THE 20TH CENTURY

In the first half of the century presidents of note were Juan Vicente Gómez (1909-35), a brutal but efficient dictator, and Isaías Medina Angarita, who introduced the oil laws. There was much material progress under the 6-year dictatorship of Gen Marcos Pérez Jiménez (1952-58), but his Gómez-like methods led to his overthrow in Jan 1958. A stable democracy has been created since, with regular presidential elections every 5 years. Sr Carlos Andrés Pérez of the centre-left Democratic Action party (AD) took office in 1974, presiding over a period of rapid development following the first great oil-price rise, and was succeeded in 1979 by Sr Luis Herrera Campins of the Christian Democratic party, Copei. Dr Jaime Lusinchi of Democratic Action was elected president in 1983, to be followed by Carlos Andrés Pérez, who began his second term in 1989.

THE 1990s: INSTABILITY AND ECONOMIC CRISIS

Pérez' second term was marked by protests, some violent, against the economic adjustment programme and growing levels of poverty. In 1992 there were two unsuccessful coup attempts by military officers. Among reforms designed to root out corruption, the Supreme Court and Central Bank were given greater independence. Both bodies were instrumental in the decision that Pérez himself be tried on corruption charges in 1993. The president was suspended from office, arrested and, after 2 years of house arrest, was found guilty in May 1996. An interim president, Senator Ramón José Velázquez, took office until the presidential elections of Dec 1993, in which Rafael Caldera, now standing as an independent, was re-elected to office. The coalition which supported him did not win a majority in Congress, so Caldera had to forge alliances with all parties to see his policies through. Many of his aims, such as improvement in social conditions, tax reform and the control of inflation, had to be postponed in favour of solving an economic and financial crisis which began in 1994 (see below, **The Economy**). The stubbornness of the economic difficulties forced Caldera in June 1996 to reverse his policies, which helped him to conclude an agreement with the IMF. Public protest at declining salaries and deteriorating public services included a strike by the medical service in late 1996, early 1997. The government eventually granted doctors a 100% pay rise, followed by 40% for public sector workers. While this threatened efforts to reduce inflation, it also led to agreement with trades unions on issues such as reform of employment regulations and pensions. The very public demolition of the notorious Catia prison in Caracas in Mar 1997 was a start towards improving conditions in the penal system, generally regarded as violating human rights.

CULTURE

PEOPLE

A large number are of mixed Spanish and Indian origin. There are some pure Africans and a strong element of African descent along the coast, particularly at the ports. The arrival of 800,000 European immigrants, mostly in the 1950s, has greatly modified the racial make-up in Venezuela. One in six of all Venezuelans is foreign born.

About 1% of the population (150,000) is Indian. Among the best-known are the Yanomami, who live in Amazonas, and the Bari in the Sierra de Perijá (on the NW border with Colombia). An Indian Reserve gives the Bari effective control of their own land, but this has not prevented infringement from mining, plantation or settlers. Other groups do not have title to their territory. These groups include the Wayuu (in the Guajira), the Panare and the Piaroa.

Venezuela, despite its wealth, still faces serious social problems. Many rural dwellers have drifted to the cities; one result of this exodus is that Venezuelan farmers do not provide all the food the nation needs and imports of foodstuffs are necessary, even for items such as beans and rice.

Elementary schools are free, and education is compulsory from the age of 7 to the completion of the primary grade.

MUSIC AND DANCE

Venezuelan music is more homogenous than that of some of the other republics. Its highly distinctive sound is based on an instrumental combination of harp, *cuatro* (a small, four stringed guitar) and *maracas*. Many of the rhythms have a very fast, almost headlong pace to them, stimulating both to the senses and to the feet, music here being almost inseparable from dance. The recipe for Venezuelan music is a classic European/African/Amerindian mix. The country's national dance is the Joropo, a name deriving from the Arab 'Xarop', meaning syrup and which originally meant a country dance. This is a dance for couples with several sequences, such as the Valseao, Zapatiao, Escobillao and Toriao. Closely related to the Joropo are the Corrido, with a ballad content, Galerón (slow for singing or fast for dancing), Pasaje (lyrical, very popular in the Llanos) and Golpe, from the State of Lara, to all of which styles the Joropo may be danced in different parts of the country. Note that the little *cuatro* is normally referred to as 'guitarra', while the Spanish guitar is called the 'guitarra grande'. Some of the dance rhythms have been imported from abroad or are shared with neighbouring countries, such as the urban Merengue (introduced into Caracas in the 1920s), the Jota and Malagueña of Anzoátegui State, the Pasillo (shared with Colombia and Ecuador), the Polo of the Oriente and Isla Margarita and the Bambuco, found in Lara and Táchira states near the border with Colombia.

There is a wealth of dances and musical forms found in particular towns or states at religious festivities. Outstanding among these is the Tamunangue of Lara State, danced in the second fortnight of June to the accompaniment of drums and small guitars and made up of seven individual dances, varying from the 'Batalla', where men battle with sticks, to the 'Bella', a flirtatious dance for couples. Corpus Cristi is the time to visit San Francisco de Yare in Miranda State and see the 80 or so male 'Diablos' of all ages, dressed entirely in red and wearing large horned masks, who dance in the streets to the sound of their own drums and rattles. The Bailes de Tambor take place among the largely black people of the Barlovento coast during the feasts of San Juan and San Pedro and at Christmas. This is brilliant polyrhythm on huge drums (*cumacos*, *minas* and *curvetas*) held between the legs. Also in Barlovento, but in May, can be heard the Fulias, chant-and-response songs addressed to a venerated saint or cross, to the accompaniment of *cuatro*, *tambora* drum and *maracas*. Christmas is a great period for music from the Gaitas of Zulia to the ubiquitous Aguinaldos, both in Merengue rhythm, with solo verses responded to by a chorus and varied instrumental accompaniment. Notable in the eastern states are the folk thea-

tre dances of the Pájaro Guarandol (a hunter shoots a large bird that is brought back to life), Carite (from Margarita, using a large model fish), Chiriguare (a monster that is duly despatched) and Burriquita (a hobby horse). More surprising is to find the Calipso, played on steel bands by the black inhabitants of El Callao in the Orinoco region, whose ancestors came from Trinidad and who also perform the Limbo.

Venezuelans enjoy Salsa as much as other Hispanic peoples around the Caribbean, but they are also very keen on their own music, whether rustic 'folk' or urban 'popular'. The virtuoso harpist Juan Vicente Torrealba has performed with his group Los Torrealberos for more than three decades, usually with Mario Suárez as vocal soloist. Another famous singer is Simón Díaz. Outstanding among the folk groups who strive for authenticity are Un Solo Pueblo, Grupo Vera and Grupo Convenezuela. Choral and contrapuntal singing of native music in a more sophisticated style has also been perfected by Quinteto Contrapunto and Serenata Guayanesa.

THE ECONOMY

Structure of production

Venezuela has vast natural resources and is especially rich in energy, possessing 65 billion barrels of proved oil reserves, the largest in the Western Hemisphere. Oil production is concentrated in three major sedimentary basins: the Maracaibo, the eastern and the Apure-Barinas basins. Apart from proved and exploitable reserves there are another 1.2 trillion barrels in potential reserves of very heavy oil in the Orinoco belt. There are 3.6 trillion cu m of natural gas reserves (plus 5 trillion probable) and 500 million tonnes of coal (9 billion estimated) in the provinces of Zulia and Táchira. There is believed to be a hydroelectricity generating potential of 80,000MW; so far the largest project is the 10,300MW Guri dam near Ciudad Guayana.

Venezuela is a founding member of Opec, but consistently exceeds its output quota of 2.35 million b/d in a bid to maximize foreign exchange earnings. It is the largest supplier of oil to the USA. Petróleos de Venezuela (PDVSA), the state oil company, was created out of the nationalization of oil companies in 1976. It was only in 1996 that foreign participation in exploration and production was invited back as the Government realized that it had not the means to increase reserves fast enough to meet demand. Bids for ten exploration areas under profit sharing participation contracts were invited, both offshore and onshore. The Government hopes to have attracted US$65bn in foreign investment by the year 2005, raising proven reserves by about 40 billion barrels and increasing production to more than 5 million b/d.

The mining sector is buoyant, with important ventures in bauxite, iron ore, ferronickel, coal and gold. As a result of cheap energy, the country has been able to build up heavy industry using local raw materials and now has a huge iron and steel industry and is one of the world's largest producers of aluminium. The state steel and aluminium companies were part of a package of 24 state companies to be privatized by 1997, raising up to US$3.5bn.

Agriculture is relatively unimportant, contributing only 4.6% of gdp, but it employs many more people than the oil industry. The main grain staples are maize and sorghum, while sugar and rice are also important. The main export crop is coffee, with other cash crops being cocoa and cotton. Over 20% of land is used as pasture, mainly for the cattle herd, which numbers over 14 million head. Less than 5% is cultivated for crops and Venezuela is not self-sufficient in foodstuffs, although imports are much less than in the days of the oil price boom.

Recent trends

Venezuela accumulated huge foreign reserves of over US$20bn by the mid-1980s from oil wealth, yet the country became unable to service its external debt normally from 1982 because of a bunching of maturities. A US$21bn debt rescheduling agreement was signed with commercial banks in 1986 but was almost immediately renegotiated because of a collapse in oil prices; oil

Venezuela: fact file	
Geographic	
Land area	912,050 sq km
forested	34.0%
pastures	20.2%
cultivated	4.4%
Demographic	
Population (1996)	22,311,000
annual growth rate (1991-96)	2.2%
urban	84.6%
rural	15.4%
density	24.5 per sq km
Education and Health	
Life expectancy at birth,	
male	70.1 years
female	76.0 years
Infant mortality rate	
per 1,000 live births (1994)	27.7
Calorie intake as %	
of FAO requirement	106%
Population age 25 and over	
with no formal schooling	23.5%
Literate males (over 15)	93.5%
Literate females (over 15)	91.1%
Economic and Employment	
GNP (1994 market prices)	US$59,025mn
GNP per capita	US$2,760
Public external debt (1994)	US$28,039mn
Tourism receipts (1994)	US$486mn
Inflation (annual av 1990-95)	44.3%
Population economically active (1993)	
	7,546,200
Unemployment rate	6.3%
Military forces	79,000
Source Encyclopaedia Britannica	

revenues fell by 44% in 1986. The Government avoided taking adjustment measures and chose instead to spend reserves, until by end-1988 liquid foreign exchange reserves were exhausted. In 1989 the new administration turned to the IMF and World Bank for support for a comprehensive macroeconomic adjustment programme to rebuild reserves, encourage domestic savings and cut the public sector deficit. Previous policies were reversed with the freeing of interest rates and the exchange rate. A debt restructuring package was implemented in 1990 which allowed banks to choose from a menu of options including debt reduction, debt service reduction or new loans.

The initial impact of the reforms was a severe recession and gdp fell by 8.1% in 1989, accompanied by a burst of inflation and higher unemployment. Between 1990 and 1992 the economy rebounded, strengthened by the reforms, a higher level of investment and buoyant oil revenues. The political instability of 1993-94, compounded by lower oil prices, brought renewed recession and inflation. In 1994 the Caldera administration tried to lower the fiscal deficit, but a banking crisis which spread to the rest of the financial system in fact increased the consolidated public sector deficit from 2.7% of gdp in 1993 to 14.4% in 1994 as the state spent heavily on propping up illiquid and undercapitalized banks, which eventually were nationalized. This increased spending and a loose monetary policy caused heavy capital outflows, a precipitous fall in the exchange rate and higher inflation.

In mid-1994 exchange controls were imposed to prevent further loss of reserves and a fixed rate of Bs170=US$1 was introduced. These controls and a contraction in the economy led to a 30% drop in imports and consequent surpluses in trade of US$8bn and the current account of US$4bn, but capital flows remained sharply negative and net international reserves declined by US$1bn in 1994. Delays in servicing external debt and economic uncertainties adversely affected Venezuela's position in international financial markets, leading to credit limitations. The Government was forced to turn to domestic sources of finance and domestic debt rose from 5% of gdp in 1993 to 14% in 1994.

In 1995 arrears in payments to some foreign creditors and domestic bond holders continued to mount and there was constant speculation that despite its political unpopularity, an IMF programme was inevitable. Gasoline prices were raised by 140% from a very low base to US$0.06-0.08 a litre to raise budget revenues, but diesel prices were lowered to avert a rise in public transport costs and avoid riots. No structural economic reforms were implemented, inflation remained higher than interest rates, the bolívar became increasingly overvalued and capital flight persisted. The public sector deficit was about 13% of gdp, financed by debt arrears, debt issues and printing money. Eventually, in December 1995, when the parallel exchange rate (determined by the local market for debt reduction bonds known as Brady bonds) had reached Bs390=US$1, the Government devalued the official rate to Bs290.

1996 was dominated by negotiations with the IMF for a 12-month, US$1.4bn standby arrangement, which was eventually signed in June, enabling the disbursement of over US$3bn in related multilateral lending. The economic reform programme included the lifting of exchange controls and the floating of the bolívar in April, tax increases, lifting price controls and raising gasoline prices by up to 500% to reduce the fiscal deficit to 2.2% of gdp in 1996. Opposition was muted, giving the Government confidence to proceed with structural reform, particularly in the public sector.

As a result of the IMF-inspired austerity of 1996, real incomes declined by about 60% and gdp again failed to show positive growth (-1.8% in 1996). On the other hand, the international investment climate improved, renewing confidence in the privatization programme, despite congressional opposition, and giving a massive boost to the bidding for rights to operate in the oil sector. The investment in oil helped stabilize the bolívar in 1996-97 and inspired prospects for gdp growth of at least 4% a year until 2001. The government hoped to cut inflation from 103% in 1996 to 25% in 1997, but public sector pay increases and other factors made such a target unrealistic. It also intended to focus on streamlining the public sector, tackling corruption and eliminating inefficiency while asking the IMF to extend its stand-by facility until Dec 1998.

GOVERNMENT

Venezuela is a federal republic of 22 states and a Federal District. There are two legislative houses, a Senate with 49 seats and a Chamber of Deputies with 201 seats. The current Constitution is dated 23 January 1961. Voting is compulsory for all over 18.

Caracas and environs

THE CAPITAL and nearby excursions to mountain towns, the Monte Avila National Park, beaches and Los Roques, a beautiful Caribbean atoll.

The capital, together with the cities of Valencia and Maracay, is in the Central Highlands, the most important upland area in Venezuela. The mountains here rise abruptly from a lush green coast to heights of from 2,000-3,000m. **Caracas**, founded in 1567, lies in a small basin, a rift in the thickly forested mountains which runs some 24 km E and W.

Caracas' growth since WW2 has been greater than that of any other Latin American capital. Colonial buildings have given way to modern multi-storeyed edifices and many visitors find the metropolis lacking in character, as there is no single centre. A broad strip some 10 km from W to E, fragmented by traffic-laden arteries contains several centres, eg Plaza Bolívar, Plaza Venezuela, Sabana Grande, Chacaíto, Altamira, La Floresta, Boleíta.

BASICS Caracas has a *population* of around 4 million (the city proper 1.3 million). *Altitude* 960m, but the southern parts of the city are 160m higher. *Temperatures* are moderate (a maximum of 32°C in July and Aug, and an occasional minimum of 9°C in Jan and Feb) and it is always cool at night. *Phone code* 02.

Orientation
A comparatively low pass (1,040m) in the mountains gives Caracas access by a magnificently engineered road from its port, La Guaira, and its international and domestic airports nearby at Maiquetía (toll is charged only when going up, US$0.05).

The modern *autopista* and the winding old road from La Guaira converge at Catia, an industrial area in the W. From here, Av Sucre runs E to the city centre. Three main routes branch E from Av Sucre or its viaduct continuation: Av Urdaneta begins between Palacio Miraflores and the Palacio Blanco, housing presidential offices. It passes the Post Office and Santa Capilla Church, looking like a wedding cake by a Parisian master pastrycook. Turn right here for Plaza Bolívar and the Capitolio Nacional, or carry straight on down the Av Urdaneta to San Bernardino. Av Urdaneta becomes Av Andrés Bello, with a link road to Av Libertador which goes to the Country Club and the E. Just below Av Libertador is Parque Los Caobos, with the fine mahoganies which give it its popular name.

From the Av Sucre viaduct, Av Universidad passes the Biblioteca Nacional (former University), Capitol and San Francisco church. Two corners later, on the left, is Bolívar's birthplace, before continuing to the Museo de Bellas Artes and on round Parque Los Caobos.

From the Plaza Venezuela intersection at the eastern end of the park, the Av Abraham Lincoln leads E through Sabana Grande and continues as the Av Francisco Miranda to Altamira, with its fine plaza and obelisk and Parque del Este. Sabana Grande, a modern shopping, hotel and business centre, is closed to vehicular traffic and a popular place to take a stroll or sit at one of its many open-air cafés.

The third route E from Av Sucre and crossing the viaduct is via El Silencio, and from there through the Centro Simón Bolívar, with its twin skyscrapers, underground parking and shopping centre (with an interesting mosaic at the lowest level), and finally along the Av Bolívar past Nuevo Circo bullring to Los Caobos. Here it joins the Autopista del Este which passes Ciudad Universitaria and the Sports Stadium. The *autopista* splits at Las Mercedes, Del Este going E past La Carlota airfield, Parque del Este and La Casona, residence of the President to Petare, Autopista Caracas Baruta going S past the *Hotel Tamanaco*.

An alternative W-E route is along the Av Boyacá from Av Baralt in the W, skirting the Cordillera de la Costa, including Monte Avila, and giving fine views along the length of the city. It passes a monument commemorating the battle of Boyacá, and a viaduct over the park in Los Chorros suburb before joining the Autopista del Este to become Route 9 to Barcelona.

PLACES OF INTEREST

The shady **Plaza Bolívar**, with its fine equestrian statue of the Liberator and pleasant colonial cathedral, is still the official centre of the city, though no longer geographically so. There are squirrels (quite tame) and sloths (harder to see) in the trees.

Capitolio Nacional Open to visitors Tues-Sun, 0900-1200, 1500-1700. The Elliptical Salon has some impressive paintings by the Venezuelan artist Martín Tovar y Tovar and a bronze urn containing the 1811 Declaration of Independence. One of the paintings on the ceiling shows a British regiment fighting in the Battle of Carabobo, and the names of the officers appear on the wall.

The present **Cathedral** building, dating from 1674 has a beautiful façade, gilded altar, the Bolívar family chapel and pictures by Michelena, Murillo and an alleged Rubens 'Resurrection'. **San Francisco**, Av Universidad y San Francisco (1 block SW of Plaza Bolívar), should be seen for its colonial altars and Murillo's 'San Agustín' (oldest church in Caracas, rebuilt 1641). **Santa Teresa**, between La Palma and Santa Teresa, just SE of the Centro Simón Bolívar, has good interior chapels and a supposedly miraculous portrait of Nazareno de San Pablo (popular and solemn devotions on Good Friday).

Panteón Nacional Open Tues-Sun, 0900-1200 and 1430-1700 (Plaza Panteón, Av Norte y Av Panteón). The remains of Simón Bolívar, the Liberator, lie here, but the tomb of Francisco Miranda (the Precursor of Independence), who died in a Spanish prison, has been left open to await the return of his body, likewise the tomb of Antonio José de Sucre, who was assassinated in Colombia. Every 25 years the President opens Bolívar's casket to verify that the remains are still there. Daniel O'Leary, Bolívar's Irish aide-de camp, is buried alongside. There is a small military ceremony at 1515 daily.

Modern Caracas The **Ciudad Universitaria** is an enormous and coherent complex in which paintings, sculpture and stained glass are completely integrated with the architecture (which is now showing signs of wear). South of the university, reached by Autopista El Valle, is **Paseo de los Próceres** with its twin monoliths and other monuments to the heroes of independence (it also has flowers and gardens). Beside the Av de los Próceres is the magnificent **Círculo Militar**.

MUSEUMS

Museo de Bellas Artes, Plaza Morelos in Parque Los Caobos, the oldest museum in Caracas, designed by Carlos Raúl Villanueva: open Tues-Fri, 0900-1200, 1500-1730, weekend 1000-1700. Pictures include an El Greco among works by mainly Venezuelan artists. Adjacent is the Galería de Arte Nacional, T 571-0176, same opening hours, which also houses the Cinemateca Nacional (Tues-Sun 1830 and 2130, Sun 1100 for children's films).

Museo de Ciencias Naturales, also in Plaza Morelos in Parque Los Caobos; open Tues-Fri, 0900-1200, 1500-1730, weekend 1000-1700: archaeological, particularly precolumbian, zoological and botanical exhibits.

Museo de Arte Colonial, Quinta Anauco, Av Panteón, San Bernardino, take *por puesto* from Bellas Artes metro (at the same stop as the metro bus), those bound for San Bernardino go past Quinta Anauco: open Tues-Sat, 0900-1200, 1400-1700, Sun, 1000-1730. Guided tour in Spanish available. A delightful house built in 1720, the residence of the Marqués del Toro. Chamber concerts most Sat at 1800. The beautiful suburb of San Bernardino is full of tropical flowers and whole avenues of forest trees, smothered in blossom in season, highly recommended.

Casa Natal del Libertador Open Tues-Fri, 0900-1200 and 1430-1700, Sun and holidays, 1000-1700: a reconstruction of the house where Bolívar was born (on 24 July 1783). It contains interesting pictures and furniture. The first house, of adobe, was destroyed by an earthquake. The second became a stable, and was later pulled down. **The Museo Bolivariano** is alongside the Casa Natal and contains the Liberator's war relics.

Cuadra Bolívar, Bárcenas y Las Piedras, 8 blocks S of Plaza Bolívar; 'El Palmar', the Bolívar family's summer home, a beautifully preserved colonial country estate: walled gardens, stables, Bolívar memorabilia. Tues-Sat, 0900-1300, 1430-1700; Sun and holidays 0900-1700.

House of Arturo Michelena, La Pastora y Puente Miraflores, four blocks N of Miraflores palace, in the La Pastora section, is a typical 19th century home. Open 0900-1200 and 1500-1700 (closed Mon and Fri).

Museo de Transporte, Parque Nacional del Este (to which it is connected by a pedestrian overpass), includes a large collection of locomotives and old cars, as well as a fascinating series of scale models of Caracas a century ago, although much has been neglected. Open Sat, Sun, 0900-

1600; admission US$0.10.

In the **Parque Central**, between Av Lecuna (E end) and the elevated section of Av Bolívar there are four museums in a complex which includes two octagonal towers (56 floors each) and four large apartment buildings with shopping below: **Museo de Arte Contemporáneo**, Parque Central, Cuadra Bolívar, entrance beside *Anauco Hilton*, very good, European and Venezuelan painters, a room devoted to Picasso ink and pen drawings, and interesting modern sculptures. Tues-Sun 1000-1800; entry free.

Museo de los Niños, Parque Central, next to E Tower, open Wed-Sun and holidays, 0900-1200, 1400-1700, otherwise is for school visits; a highly sophisticated modern science museum, extremely popular, US$0.75 (adults). Allow 2-3 hrs for a visit. Book a day or so in advance in school holidays or August. Also in the Parque Central complex, **Museo Audiovisual**, Tues-Fri, 0900-1700, US$1, includes a library of Venezuelan television programmes, a practice TV studio, and **Museo del Teclado** (keyboard instruments).

Casa Amarilla (The Ministry of Foreign Relations), NW corner of Plaza Bolívar, pictures mostly of national heroes and historical events.

Museo Histórico Fundación John Boulton, Torre El Chorro, 11th floor, Av Universidad y Sur 3, entre El Chorro y Dr Díaz, previously in La Guaira (see page 1484), contains many unique historical items and a library of 19th-century research material and commercial records of the Casa Boulton (easy access, free). Open Mon-Fri 0800-1200, 1300-1700, 2 tours a day by knowledgeable guides; underground parking on presentation of ID.

The Concejo Municipal (City Hall) on Plaza Bolívar contains three museums: a collection of the paintings of Emilio Boggio, a Venezuelan painter; the Raúl Santana Museum of the Creole Way of Life, a collection of miniature figures in costumes and poses characteristic of Venezuelan life, all handmade by Raúl Santana; and the Sala de Arqueología Gaspar Marcano, exhibiting ceramics,

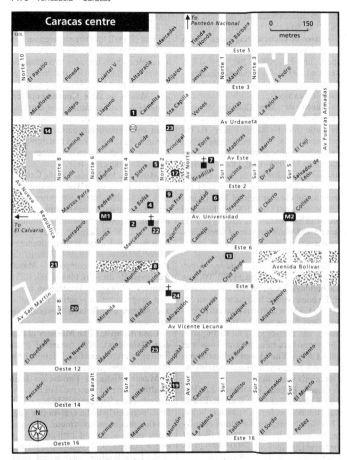

Caracas centre

To Panteón Nacional

0   150
metres

In the centre of Caracas, each street corner has a name, and addresses are generally given as, for example, 'Santa Capilla a Mijares', rather than the official 'Calle Norte 2, No 26'. On some maps Av Luis Rocha is still shown as Av España (Altamira). For maps see **Tourist Information**, below, and **Maps** in Information for travellers.

mostly discovered on the coast. All three open Tues-Fri, 0930-1200, 1500-1800; Sat and Sun, 0930-1800. Informative guides are available.

Those with a deeper interest in archaeology might like to contact the Junta Nacional Protectora y Conservadora del Patrimonio Histórico y Artístico de la Nación, Palacio de Miraflores, Av Urdaneta.

NB Museums and art galleries throughout Venezuela are closed on Mon. Check museum schedules in *El Universal*, *El Nacional* or the *Daily Journal* (which also have

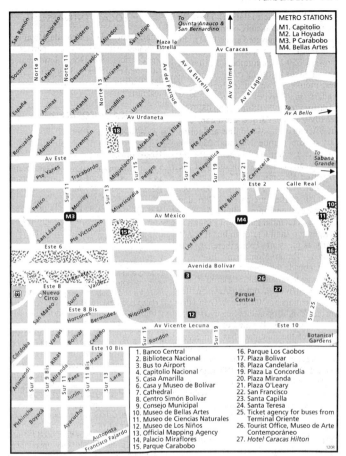

MAP LABELS:
To Quinta Anauco & San Bernardino

METRO STATIONS
M1. Capitolio
M2. La Hoyada
M3. P Carabobo
M4. Bellas Artes

Plaza la Estrella
Av Caracas

San Ramón, Chimborazo, Tenidero, Mirador, San Felipe

Socorro, Calero, Norte 11, Desamparados, Avilanes

Norte 9

España, Animas, Platanal, Norte 13, Candilito, Urapal

Av del Parque, Av la Estrella, Av Vollmer, Av el Lago

Av Urdaneta

To Av A Bello

Romualda, Manduca, Terrenquin

Av Este

Pte Yanes, Tracabordo

Perico, Montoy, Pte Victoriano

San Lázaro

Este 6

Miguelacho, Peligro, Misericordia

Sur 11, Sur 13, Sur 15, Sur 17, Sur 19, Sur 21

Alcabala, Campo Elías, Pte Anauco, Pte Republica, Pte Brion

T Caracas, Cerveceria

Este 2, Calle Real

Av México

Los Naranjos

Avenida Bolívar

Este 8, Urdaneta, Valdez, Sucre, Este 8 Bis, Horcones, Bermúdez, Niquitao

Nuevo Circo

San Mateo

Parque Central

Av Vicente Lecuna

Sur 25, Este 10

Córdoba, Este 10 Bis, Rondón, Sur 15, Sur 19

Botanical Gardens

Armendi, Pidincha, Boyaca, Sur 9, Sur 9 Bis, Ribas, Miranda, Sur 11, Sur 11 Bis, Páez, Plaza, Sur 13, Lara

Vargas, Bolívar, Cerbeño

Junín, Ayacucho

Autopista Francisco Fajardo

1. Banco Central
2. Biblioteca Nacional
3. Bus to Airport
4. Capitolio Nacional
5. Casa Amarilla
6. Casa y Museo de Bolívar
7. Cathedral
8. Centro Simón Bolívar
9. Consejo Municipal
10. Museo de Bellas Artes
11. Museo de Ciencias Naturales
12. Museo de Los Niños
13. Official Mapping Agency
14. Palacio Miraflores
15. Parque Carabobo
16. Parque Los Caobos
17. Plaza Bolívar
18. Plaza Candelaria
19. Plaza La Concordia
20. Plaza Miranda
21. Plaza O'Leary
22. San Francisco
23. Santa Capilla
24. Santa Teresa
25. Ticket agency for buses from Terminal Oriente
26. Tourist Office, Museo de Arte Contemporáneo
27. Hotel Caracas Hilton

details of events for children). Many museums and most religious buildings will refuse entry to anybody wearing shorts.

PARKS AND ZOOS

Jardín Botánico, near Plaza Venezuela, entrance by Ciudad Universitaria (US$0.30, guide US$1 in English), is worth a visit. There are extensive plant collections and a small area of 'natural forest'. Here you can see the world's largest palm tree (*Corypha Sp*) and the Elephant Apple with its huge edible fruit. **Parque Los Caobos** is peaceful and has a cafeteria in the middle. By the entrance in Av México is the cultural centre, Ateneo de Caracas, with a theatre, art gallery, concert room, bookshop and the imposing Teresa Carreño theatre complex. **Parque Nacional del Este** (renamed the Parque Rómulo Betancourt in 1989) is a popular place to relax, especially at weekends, entrance US$0.15, closed Mon, otherwise opens 0530 for joggers, 0800 for mere mortals, till 1730 (reached from

Parque del Este metro station). There is a boating lake, a replica of Columbus' *Santa María* (being renovated since 1991), the Humboldt Planetarium (weekend shows, US$0.25), a number of different sunken lakes featuring caiman and turtles, monkeys, two frustratingly caged jaguars, many types of water birds, a terrarium (open Sat-Sun, US$0.05). The heavily-wooded **Parque Caricuao** is at the SW end of the Metro line, and forms part of the Parque Nacional Macuro. There is a small, well kept zoo (better than Parque el Este) with many of the birds free. Recommended for a pleasant day out. Open Tues-Sun 0900-1700, US$0.20. Take metro to Caricuao Zoológico, then 5 min walk up Av Principal La Hacienda. **Parque El Pinar** has a larger zoo than Caricuao but it is not nearly as pleasant. To get there take bus marked 'Paraíso-Montalban' from Av Baralt, outside the Capitolio metro station (exit La Pedrera), and ask to be let off at park entrance on Av Páez, corner of Av Guadalajara, the entrance is 500 m up Av Guadalajara on the right; open Tues-Sun 0900-1745, entry US$0.65. The **Parque Los Chorros** at the foot of the mountain has impressive waterfalls, entrance US$0.05 (take bus marked Petare and La Urbina), also recommended. **El Calvario**, W of El Silencio, with the Arch of Confederation at the entrance, has a good view of Centro Simón Bolívar, but muggings have been reported. It has a small Museo Ornitológico, botanical gardens and a picturesque chapel. A new park, **Parque Vargas**, is planned, similar in concept to the Champs Elysées, some is already in place. A model of the area is on display in the Galería de Arte Nacional.

EXCURSIONS

El Hatillo, 30 mins from the city centre by car, or take bus from Av Humboldt, 2 blocks from Plaza Chacaíto. It has well-preserved colonial style housing, with many art galleries, souvenir shops, restaurants and a famous Christmas market. On the plaza is a tearoom serving good cakes. Nearby is the wealthy residential district, La Lagunita.

LOCAL FESTIVALS

3 May, Velorio de la Cruz de Mayo still celebrated with dances and parties in some districts. 18-25 Dec, Yuletide masses at different churches leading up to Christmas. Traditional creole dishes served at breakfasts.

LOCAL INFORMATION

● Accommodation

Hotel prices			
L1	over US$200	L2	US$151-200
L3	US$101-150	A1	US$81-100
A2	US$61-80	A3	US$46-60
B	US$31-45	C	US$21-30
D	US$12-20	E	US$7-11
F	US$4-6	G	up to US$3

Unless otherwise stated, all hotels in range **D** and above have private bath. Assume friendliness and cleanliness in all cases.

Cheap *pensiones* are usually full of long-stay residents and have very few rooms available for travellers. Hotels tend to be particularly full at weekends and in July and August. In the centre all cheap hotels take only short stay customers on Fri pm. Better hotels often try to give you a suite instead of a double room. Hotel prices below do not inc 12.5% tax. Hotels marked with an asterisk (*) are bookable through Fairmont International (see below).

Hotels in Chuao/Las Mercedes Business/commercial district SE of centre, not on metro: The **L1** *Tamanaco**, Av Principal Las Mercedes, PO Box 467, Caracas 1060A, T 924522, F 208-7116, is the best hotel in Caracas, superb pool, luxury business hotel, difficult to get room as it is normally fully booked (inc service, tax 15%, rooms are priced in dollars), courteous staff, good facilities, changes TCs for guests only (poor rate); **L1** *Eurobuilding*, Centro Ciudad Comercial Tamanaco, T 959-1133, F 993-9285, PO Box 64487, 5-star, modern, has all-suite wing, well-furnished, a/c, inc breakfast, efficient service, large pool, gym, restaurants, many services, weekend rates available; also in CCCT **L3-A1** *CCCT Venantur**, T 959-0611, F 959-6409, smart business hotel with a pool terrace, approached through shopping mall, not that easy to find; **A2** *Hotel Paseo de las Mercedes*, Las Mercedes, T 910444, F 993-0341, almost next door to the *Tamanaco*, good sized rooms, restaurant, bar, small pool on pleasant rear terrace.

Parque Central (metro Bellas Artes), an area of tower blocks, concrete walkways and underpasses: **L1** *Hilton**, Av Libertador and Sur 25,

T 503-5000, F 503-5003, ageing luxury hotel, impressive conference facilities, excellent business centre, spectacular city views, especially at night, noisy (traffic and a/c), useful long-term luggage deposit and good breakfast, nice pool, fax service open to non-residents, very helpful, good sushi bar, rec.

Near Altamira metro station, a respectable comercial and residential area, E of centre: **A3** Continental, Av San Juan Bosco, T 261-9091, F 261-0131, smart, gardens front and rear and a good, private swimming pool; **B/C** El Cid, Av San Felipe, between 1a and 2a, T 263-2611, F 263-5578, Spanish style interior, large suites with living area, breakfast rooms, kitchenette ensuite, a/c, good value for money.

Sabana Grande/Chacaíto, varied area with many restaurants and shops, convenient for metro and safest area for cheap hotels: **A2** Lincoln Suites, Av Francisco Solano, entre San Jerónimo y Los Jabillos, T 761-2727, F 762-5503, top of the range in this area, high quality accommodation and service, no pool; **A2** Cumberland, 2da Av de las Delicias, T 762-9961, F 762-5549, very good, nice restaurant, taxi service to airport; **A3** Las Américas, C Los Cerritos, T 951-7387, F 951-1717, a modern tower, with new block attached, tiny roof pool and restaurant, taxi service to airport, good value; **A3** Tampa*, Av Francisco Solano López, T 762-3771, F 762-0112, comfy but noisy a/c, plain interior, interesting bodega-style restaurant; **B** Atlántida, Av La Salle, Los Caobos, 2 blocks up from Av Libertador, T 793-3211, F 781-3696, safe, noisy, a/c, restaurant; **B** Coliseo, T 762-77916, F 761-7333, Coromoto y Bellomonte, a/c, good breakfast, 100m from Sabana Grande metro station, rec; **B** Crillon*, Av Libertador, esq Av Las Acacias, T 761-4411, F 761-6911, highrise block with good bar and Le Chalet restaurant; **B** Plaza Palace, Av Los Mangos, Las Delicias, T 762-4821, good; **C/D** El Condor, Av Las Delicias, T 762-9911, comfortable but plain, outstanding restaurant in Spanish bodega style; **C** Kursaal, Av Casanova y El Colegio, T 762-2922, safe, a/c, cheap taxi service to airport; **C** Luna*, Av Casanova y El Colegio, T 762-5851, rec; **C/B** Savoy*, Av Francisco Solano y Av Las Delicias, T 762-1971, F 762-2792, good food, efficient, secure vehicle park, taxi service to airport; **D** Broadway, Av Casanova between C Guaicaipuro and C Chacaíto, T 951-1922, nr Chacaíto metro, Italian specialities in restaurant, rec; **D** Cristal, Pasaje Asunción, just off Av Abraham Lincoln, nr Sabana Grande metro, T 761-9131, a/c, comfortable, safe, good value, disco at weekends, restaurant; **D/E** Escorial, C Colegio, nr Plaza Venezuela, T 762-8820, F 762-7505, central, a/c, secure,

mediocre restaurant and bar, fax service, cheap taxi service to airport, good value; **D** Ritz, Av Las Palmas y Av Libertador, nr Plaza Venezuela, T 793-7811, a/c, safe provided, good beds, luggage store, restaurant, secure free parking, ask for cheapest rooms; **E** La Mirage, Prolongación de Las Acacias, T 793-2733, F 793-0629, with bath, a/c, restaurant, reasonable value; **E** Odeon, Las Acacias y Av Casanova, T 793-1322, F 781-9380, modern, stores luggage, restaurant serves Colombian food, reported as the best place to stay on Las Acacias. There are many hotels around this area, but the majority are short-stay.

In San Bernardino, residential area 2 km N of Bellas Artes metro: **A3** Avila*, Av Jorge Washington (T 515128/515173, F 523021, Tx 21637 Avila), set in park-like gardens ('magical nighttime atmosphere from tropical birdsong'), very pleasant, good service, most of staff speak English and German, fans, mosquito screens, pool, Metrobus nearby, very good restaurant and poolside bar, rec, phones which accept Visa/Mastercard; **B** Aventura*, Av Sorocaima y Av Francisco Fajardo, T 514011, F 519186, big rooms, suites for long lets, small pool in rear courtyard; **D** Waldorf, Av Industria, T 571-4733, hot water erratic, restaurant, English sometimes spoken, good value, will store luggage; Banco Consolidado next door for exchange, good value Chinese restaurant next door (the airport tourist office often rec this hotel).

In the downtown area (the cheapest hotels are around the Nuevo Circo bus terminal, which is not a safe area): **C** Plaza Catedral*, Blvd Plaza Bolívar, next to Cathedral, T 564-2111, F 564-1797, beautiful location in the colonial part of town, Amex accepted, a/c, some English spoken, good restaurant; **D** Avenida, C Sur 4 (nr Capitolio), T 426440, hot water sporadic, a/c, safe, rec; **D** Hospedaje Fidelina, Sur 4 No 120, safe, fan, **F** with shared bath/toilet; **D/E** Inter*, Animas a Calero, on corner of Av Urdaneta, nr Nuevo Circo, T 564-0251, helpful, English spoken, very popular, poor restaurant, accepts credit cards; **D** La Neve, Sur 4, Pilita a Glorieta No 126 – Sur 4, nr Metro Capitolio, a/c or fan, good, safe, quiet, good restaurant, rec; **D** Limón, C Este 10, No 228, nr metro Bellas Artes, safe, parking, often rec; **D** Palais, Sur 4, Pilita a Glorieta, modern, a/c, helpful, luggage stored, the restaurant is highly rec; **E** Caroní, Av Baralt, between Muñoz and Piñango, popular, safe but a bit noisy, not very clean, bar; **E** Guarapiche, Este 8, Zamuro a Pájaro (diagonal to Palacio de Justicia), T 545-3073, safe, a/c, hot water; **E** Hospedaje Torreiro, Sur 11, Bolívar a Sucre, next to Lagoven, T 577-2148, nice, helpful, bath, fan, safe, rec; **E** Pensión San Gregorio,

San Agustín Este 12 Arismendi, 2½ blocks from Nuevo Circo, many single rooms, more or less clean, shared or private bath; **F Nueva Lucía**, Sur 9, Arismendi a Pichincha, fan, helpful owner. For other cheap hotels look on C Sur 2, but better to go several blocks WSW to a quieter area, eg **E Pensión San Marcos**, Hoya a Santa Rosalía, T 545-3723, basic.

Santa Teresa is a dormitory town SE of Caracas; 1½hrs by bus from Nuevo Circo. It is an alternative to the capital, with cheaper, safe accommodation and scenic mountain setting. **E Hotel Tahay**, a/c, private bath, small, safe; **F Hotel Lamas**, opp, with fan and private bath, small, secure, luggage store, rec.

Hotel reservations: *Fairmont International*, Torre Capriles, Planta Baja, Plaza Venezuela, Caracas, T 782-8433, Tx 21232 SNRHO, F 782-4407, will book hotel rooms in Caracas and also in 102 hotels in the rest of the country and in other countries, eg Colombia, with no booking fee, rec as helpful. The airport tourist office is very helpful and will book hotel rooms. If you book from abroad, make sure you receive confirmation before beginning your journey. If you arrive by air in the evening without a reservation it is often easier to get a taxi to Macuto, rather than Caracas, where there are several hotels only 15 mins drive away. For apartment rental, consult *El Universal* daily paper, small ads columns. *Residencias Taormina*, Av María Teresa Toro, una cuadra Plaza Tiuna delante CANTV, Las Acacias, good apartments US$25/night, best value for 2 weeks or more.

● **Places to eat**
There is such a profusion of eating places in Caracas that we give the following general advice, with a mention of just a few places currently reported reliable, rather than attempt the impossible task of keeping up to date with all the changes. Guides to eating inc *Guía gastronómica de Venezuela*, available in most bookshops, US$5.60. Don't be shy about asking the price before you order in a bar as beer in one will cost three times as much as in another, and a modest portion of manchego cheese will cost more than a good steak. Food on display in a bar is free with your drink if they offer it as a *pasapalo*, but will be charged for if offered as a *ración*. You can save on the service charge by eating at the bar and not at a table. Restaurants must put up a list of prices on or nr the front door, and are prohibited from charging for place settings (*cubiertos*) or bread, butter, condiments etc (*guarnición*). A meal costs between US$4-5 minimum, not inc beer (an extra US$1 or so), 1997 prices. Midday is the most economical time to eat the main meal of the day and about the only opportunity to find fresh vegetables. Particularly

good value is the 'menú ejecutivo' or 'cubierto', which is a 3-course meal for US$2-3. Breakfast in your hotel is likely to be poor (poor bread or none, insipid coffee and orange juice which is half artificial). It is better and cheaper in a *fuente de soda* – once you have purchased your ticket you will find there is little sense of queuing, shout your order to the staff like the locals, and cheaper still in a *pastelería* or *arepería*.

There is a wide selection of good restaurants around Av Urdaneta and in the districts of La Castellana (eg: *La Estancia*, Av Principal La Castellana, esq C Urdaneta, nr Altamira metro, very good beef in traditional style and popular with young Caracas business set; next door is *Primi*, Italian/Creole cuisine, quite chic and friendly, plenty of vegetarian dishes), Altamira, Las Mercedes and in Sabana Grande (see below).

In the downtown area: there are plenty of eating places around Plaza Bolívar: *Plaza Mayor*, Torre a Veroes, NE corner of Plaza Bolívar, very good, rec; *El Paso*, Hospital a Glorieta, Ed Atlántico, Plaza La Concordia, Chinese, cheap, good. Seafood at *Las Vegas* nr *Hotel Plaza Catedral*. *Casa de Italia*, in the Italia building, next to *Waldorf Hotel*, best Italian food for the price, excellent service, view and bar.

Sabana Grande: the area is full of cafés, bars and restaurants to suit all tastes and budgets. Tables in the open air on the main boulevard (Av Abraham Lincoln), however, are expensive; the waiters overcharge, so check prices on the displayed list.

Among the **rec restaurants**: *Tívoli*, El Colegio between Lincoln and Casanova, good pasta dishes from US$1.70-2.50; *Casiero*, on Fco Solano, and *Urrita*, Fco Solano y Los Mangos, both very good for national dishes; *Bohío Habanero*, in La Previsora, Cuban food, rec; *La Buca* in *Hotel Kursaal*, international food; *Victor's Pollo*, Av F Solano y El Bosque (Chacaíto end), has 20 different chicken dishes; *Shorthorn*, Av Libertador y El Bosque, very good.

Vegetarian: *Buffet Vegetariano*, Av Los Jardines; *El Acuarino*, Truco a Caja de Agua; neither open for dinner. *Almuerzo*, Hoyo a Sta Rosalía, good, cheap; *Comida Arabe*, Colegio, nr *Hotel Kursaal*, excellent. Also *Delicatesen Indú*, specializes in southern Indian dishes, good quality, small portions, on C Villa Flor, in Sabana Grande just off Av Abraham Lincoln between metro stations Sabana Grande and Plaza Venezuela. There is a good selection of Arabic, Chinese and Hindu restaurants on C Villa Flor and all Arabic restaurants have vegetarian options.

Fast foods: there are many burger and pizza places, also hot dog stalls of doubtful hygiene (when the police don't close them down). *Arturo's*, is a chain of clean, modern, chicken-

and-chips style restaurants in various locations. *El Arepazo*, 1 block S of Chacaíto metro station, has every kind of arepa filling you could wish for. *El Coco*, in the Centro Comercial Chacaíto, has very good Venezuelan food at much lower prices than the sidewalk cafés on nearby Sabana Grande.

● **Airline offices**
Avensa, Edif Atlántida, Av Universidad, T 561-3366 (airport 551-555), Metro La Hoyada; Aerotuy, Av Lincoln y Blvd Sabana Grande, Edif Gran Sabana p 5 (T 761-6247/9782/8043); Aerolíneas Argentinas, Av Sur 25, Plaza Morelos, Torre Viasa, p 8, Los Caobos (T 576-7969, F 576-9645); Air Aruba, Av Libertador, Torre Maracaibo (T 719781); Air France, Parque Cristal, Torre Este, p 2, Los Palos Grandes (T 283-5855); Alitalia, Edif Atlantic p 5, Av Andrés Bello, Los Palos Grandes (T 800-66666); ALM, Edif Exa p 8, Av Libertador (T 953-7086/6424); American, Centro Plaza, Torre B (T 209-8111); Avianca, Av F de Miranda, Edif Roraima (T 953-7254); British Airways, Torre Británica p 11, Altamira (T 261-8006); BWIA, Oficentro Rovica p 1, Blvd Sabana Grande (T 711307); Iberia, T 562-6444; KLM, Torre KLM, Av R Gallegos (T 285-3333); LIAT, Torre Británica, Mezz 2, Av JF Sosa, Altamira Sur (T 265-7542); Lufthansa, Av Tamanaco, Edif Bayer (T 951-0044); United, Av F de Miranda, Edif Parque Canaima, p 8, Los Palos Grandes (T 285-5753); Varig, Av Principal de Los Ruices, Centro Emp Los Ruices p 3 (T 238-2111).

● **Banks & money changers**
(See **Currency** page 1572.)
Citibank will exchange Citicorp cheques; Banco Unión for **Visa** transactions. For cash advances on **Mastercard**, go to Credimático for a voucher then to Banco Mercantil for the cash from a side office, up to US$250 a day. Many banks accept Visa cards in their ATMs. For **Thomas Cook** cheques try Banco Internacional or Banco Mercantil. **American Express** cheques, Banco Consolidado, Av San Francisco, Edif Torre California, p 9, Urb Colinas de La California, am and pm, or any other branch; **Amex rep** is Turisol, Centro Comercial Tamanaco, level C-2, Local 53F-07, Chuao suburb, PO Box 62006, T 959-3050, F 959-2867, rec as helpful and efficient. Stolen or lost travellers' cheques can be replaced, and US$ cash exchanged, at the Amex office in Torre Consolidada, Plaza La Castellana, Av Principal La Castellana, nearest metro Altamira.

For **exchange** go to *Italcambio*, they require proof of TC purchase, commission 1.70%, open Mon-Fri till 1630, Sat till 1200. Offices at: esq Veroes and Urdaneta (or *Visesta CA* opp, highly rec, accepts Eurocheques, also for travel arrangements, Walter Kleebinder speaks several languages and is very helpful, T 562-4698/562-

5333); Av Casanova (Sabana Grande); Av L Roche (Altamira Sur), Simón Bolívar Airport (may limit transaction to US$100, open public holidays); *La Moneda*, Centro Financiero Latino, Urdaneta, p 8, and Av Fco Solano, 1 block from Plaza Venezuela metro, opp El Molino Rosso restaurant and next to Banco Profesional, open Mon-Fri only; *Infesa*, Av Libertador, between Negrín and Jabillos; *Confinanzas*, Centro Comercial Paseo Las Mercedes, Local PA-CI, open 0800-1200, 1400-1700, commission 1% usually charged on TCs; *MVS Cambios*, Av Francisco Solano, between Calles El Cristo and Los Manguitos, Edif Torre Oasis, Sabana Grande, less waiting, good rates.

● **Cultural centres**
British Council, Edif Torre la Noria, 6th floor, Las Mercedes; English classes and modest library. Centro Venezolano-Americano, Av Las Mercedes, good free library of books in English, and free concerts; also Spanish courses, eight different levels, each lasts 17 days and costs US$50, highly rec. Asociación Cultural Humboldt (Goethe Institut), Av Juan Germán Roscio, San Bernardino, T 527634, library, lectures, films, concerts, Spanish courses.

● **Embassies & consulates**
Argentina, Centro Capriles, 2a, Mezz Entrada Este, Plaza Venezuela, T 781-1487, PO Box 569, Caracas 1010-A; Colombian Consulate, Guaicaipuro, Sector Chacaíto, Urb El Rosal, T 951-3631; open Mon-Fri 0800-1400 for visas, photo and US$10 (maybe free), can take anything from 10 mins to 1 day; Ecuadorean Consulate, Centro Empresarial Andrés Bello 13th Floor, Av Andrés Bello, Torre Este, Parque del Este metro, T 781-6090; Mexican Embassy (visa section), Edif Parque Cristal, Torre Este, p 14, T 286622 (Mon-Fri 0900-1300), next to Parque del Este metro, tourist cards issued on the spot, free; Brazilian Embassy, Plaza La Castellana, Av Principal La Castellana, T 261345, nearest metro Altamira (visa US$13, 1 photo, valid 3 months maximum, 24 hrs); Brazilian Consulate, Edif 'Centro Gerencial Mohedano', p 6, entre C Los Chaguaramas y Av Mohedano, La Castellano, open Mon-Fri 0830-1230; Cuban Consulate, Av 3/2, Campo Alegre, behind Clínica Sanatriz, 0900-1300; Guyanese Embassy, Edif Los Frailes, C La Guanita, Chuao (same for Jamaican Embassy), T 978-1779, visa Mon, Wed, Fri, 0830-1200, same day if early, passport, airline ticket, yellow fever certificate, 2 photos required; Peruvian Consulate, Centro Empresarial Andrés Bello 7th floor, Av Andrés Bello, Torre Este, T 781-6168, next to Parque del Este metro; Suriname Embassy, 4a Av, between 7a and 8a Transversal, Urb Altamira, T 262-1616; Trinidadian Embassy, beside the Suriname

Embassy, Quinta Serrana, 4a Av, between 7a and 8a Transversal, Altamira, T 261-3748/4772 (visa US$17, 2 photos, up to 1 week).

USA Embassy and Consulate, Calle S con Calle Suapure, Colinas de Valle Arriba, take metro to Chacaíto then taxi US$3, T 977-2011, F 977-0843, PO Box 62291; **Canadian Embassy**, Edif Torre Europa, p 7, Av Francisco de Miranda, corner of Av Escuela, 2 blocks E of Chacaíto metro (T 951-6166); **Australian Embassy**, 'Yolanda', Av Luis Roche, between transversal 6 and 7, Altamira, T 283-3090; **Japanese Embassy**, Av San Juan Bosco, between 8th and 9th Transversal, Altamira, T 261-8333.

Austrian Embassy, Torre Las Mercedes, Chuao, T 913863; **British Embassy and Consulate**, Torre Las Mercedes, 3rd floor, Av La Estancia, Chuao (T 751-1022/1166/1454/1966), Apdo 1246 for letters; **Danish Embassy**, Av Venezuela, esq C Mohedano, Edif Centuria, p 7, El Rosal, nr Chacaíto metro station, T 951-5606; **Finnish Embassy**, Torre C, p 14, Centro Plaza, Av Francisco de Miranda, T 284-5013; **French Embassy**, Ed Las Frailes, p 6, La Guairita, T 910333/324; **German Embassy**, Edif Panavén, p 2, Av San Juan Bosco, Altamira, T 267-0181/1205, open Mon-Fri 0900-1300; **Greek Embassy**, Av San Gabriel 60, Alta Florida, T 2617696/2621590; **Israeli Embassy**, Av Francisco de Miranda, Centro Empresario Miranda, p 4, T 239-4511, F 239-4320; **Netherlands Consulate**, Edif San Juan, p 9, San Juan Bosco y Av Transversal 2, Altamira, T 266-6522, F 263-0462, send post to Apdo 62286, Caracas 1060a; **Spanish Embassy**, Ed Banco Unión, Sabana Grande, p 1, T 326526; **Swedish Embassy**, Edif Panavén, p 5, Av San Juan Bosco con Tercera Transversal, Altamira, T 323911; **Swiss Embassy**, Torre Europa, p 6, Av Francisco de Miranda, corner of Av Escuela, 2 blocks E of Chacaíto metro (T 951-4064).

● **Entertainment**
There are frequent Sun morning concerts in the Teatro Municipal, 1100. Concerts, ballet, theatre and film festivals at the Ateneo de Caracas, Paseo Colón, Plaza Morelos; and similar events, inc foreign artists, at the Complejo Cultural Teresa Carreño, see above. There are numerous **cinemas**, normally four showings a day, usual price US$3, except the *Lido* in Chacao, US$4.20 (half price Mon). For details of these and other events, see the newspapers, *El Universal*, *El Nacional* and *Daily Journal*, and the Sun issue of *El Diario de Caracas*.

Discotheques: a great many; recent recommendations: *Pida Pizza*, Sabana Grande; *Weekend*, Las Mercedes; *Palladium*, in CCCT shopping centre, popular, big, you do not have to be in a couple as in many other places.

Nightclubs: Caracas is a lively city by night.

Caraqueños dine at home around 2000, and in restaurants from 2100 to 2300, so nightclubs don't usually come to life until after 2300, and then go on to all hours of the morning. *Un Solo Pueblo*, typical Venezuelan music, 3rd Transversal, Altamira (there are many small clubs, restaurants and bars on Plaza Altamira Sur); opp is *Café Rajatabla*, in the Ateneo cultural complex, young crowd and often has live music; *El Maní es Así*, C El Cristo, 1 block up from Av Fco Solano, good for live salsa and dancing, US$6 after 2200. 1 block E of Nuevo Circo, opp the filling station, *Rica Arepa*, an *areparia*, has traditional Venezuelan folk music, free, on Fri, Sat, Sun nights. *La Padrona*, C Humboldt, Chaguaramas, Brazilian music.

● **Hospitals & medical services**
Hospital de Clínicas, Av Panteón y Av Alameda, San Bernardino, T 574-2011.

● **Laundry**
Lavandería Austria, Lecuna y Sur 3, self-service or service wash, helpful, reasonably priced; *Lavandería Automática Jescal*, San Agustín, Sur 11, Sucre 106, self-service, cheap, open 0700-2000. *Lavandería Automática*, Sur 17, Este 2, 1 block from *Hotel Waldorf*, self-service or service wash, open 0800-1600, sometimes later.

● **Places of worship**
(With times of services in English): **San Ignacio College**, C Santa Teresa, La Castellana, Sunday mass 0915. **Protestant**: The United Christian Church, Av Arboleda, El Bosque, Sun 1000; St Mary's Anglican and Episcopal, C Chivacoa, San Román, Sun 1030. **Shalom Temple**, Av Jorge Washington, San Bernardino, Sat 0900 and 1600.

● **Post & telecommunications**
Post Office: Central at Urdaneta y Norte 4, close to Plaza Bolívar. Mail packages abroad from here; fast and efficient but not much help with packing boxes (no tape etc). *Lista de correos* costs US$0.30, Mon-Fri 0700-1945, Sat 0800-1700, Sun 0800-1200. Ipostal office in Centro Comercial Cediáz, on Av Casanova between C Villaflor and San Jerónimo, open Mon-Fri office hours, Sat till 1200; also at airport.

Telecommunications: are operated by CANTV, on 1st floor of Centro Plaza on Francisco Miranda in the E (corner of Andrés Bello between metros Parque del Este and Altamira), open Mon-Sat 0800-1945, T 284-7932, phone cards sold here. Public telex at Centro Simón Bolívar and *nivel* C-I, Centro Ciudad Comercial Tamanaco. Few public phones, use those in metro stations.

● **Security**

It is advisable not to arrive in Caracas at night and not to walk down narrow streets or in parks after dark. Avoid certain areas such as all suburbs from the El Silencio monument to Propatria, other than main roads, the area around the *teleférico*, Chapellín near the Country Club, and Petare. Street crime is on the increase, even armed robbery in daylight. Never carry valuables. Car theft is common. Police searches are frequent and thorough, especially around Av Las Acacias after dark and in airports; always carry ID. If you have entered overland from Colombia, you can expect thorough investigation (once you've left the border, better to say you flew in).

● **Shopping**

For gems and fine jewellery, visit the *H Stern* shops at the Hotels *Hilton* and *Tamanaco* and at the International Airport; try also *Labady*, Sabana Grande 98, beautifully-made gold jewellery, English spoken. *Pro-Venezuela Exposición y Venta de Arte Popular*, Gran Av at C Olimpo, between Plaza Venezuela and beginning of Av Casanova (opp Torre La Previsora), sells Venezuelan crafts, very crowded, no prices, bargain hard. Good quality Sun craft market between Museo de Bellas Artes and Museo de Historia Natural (metro Bellas Artes). Indian market on SW corner of Plaza Chacaíto has selection of Venezuelan, Peruvian and Ecuadorean crafts. The **CCCT shopping centre** is worth a visit, as is the Centro Comercial Plaza Las Americanas, mostly for fashion stores and beach wear. Large-size shoes (up to 47) at Catedral Sur 4 y Mercaderes. **Centro Plaza Altamira**, between metro stations Altamira and Parque del Este, has shops, cafés, *tascas* and the **Centro Mediterráneo**, with boutiques and cafés and a good quality cinema.

Color Express in the Centro Comercial Chacaíto does good, cheap and quick slide developing.

Bookshops: English language ones: *English Bookshop*, Concresa, Prados del Este, will exchange nearly new books and stocks the *Caribbean Islands Handbook*; *Lectura*, Centro Comercial Chacaíto; *American Bookshop*, Av San Juan Bosco, Edif Belveder, T 263-5455/267-4134, nr Altamira metro, Mon-Fri 0900-1730, Sat 0900-1400, good selection of second-hand English books; also available in bookstalls in the street; *Librería del Este*, Av Francisco de Miranda 52, Edif Galipán, and *Librería Unica*, Centro Capriles, ground floor local 13N, Plaza Venezuela, have foreign language books; *Librería Washington*, La Torre a Veroes No 25, good service. *Novedades* has branches all over the city; *Librería Ecológica*, Plaza Caracas, between Torres Norte and Sur, Centro Simón Bolívar, nr CANTV office, for environmental books, also has some maps. A French bookshop is *Librería La France*, Centro Comercial Chacaíto; Italian bookshop, *El Libro Italiano*, Pasaje La Concordia (between Sabana Grande pedestrian street and Av Fco Solano López), and for German books, *Librería Alemana* (Oscar Todtmann), Centro El Bosque, Av Libertador, T 710881, open Tues-Sat, 0900-1230, 1500-1800. *Alcaldía de Caracas*, Puente Brion, Av Méjico, used foreign language books.

● **Sports**

Horse-racing every Sat and Sun at La Rinconada (magnificent grandstand; betting is by a tote system). Races start at 1300, admission to grandstand US$1.10. Several buses go to La Rinconada. Bull fights at Nuevo Circo, 2nd Sun in Jan, also in Feb. Golf, tennis, riding, fishing. Baseball (Oct-Jan), football, swimming, etc. To hire fishing boats contact Ani Villanueva, T 740862.

Clubs: there are three country clubs in Caracas, all of which have excellent restaurants. The Country Club in the eastern part has an 18-hole golf course. The Social Centre of the British Commonwealth Association, Quinta Alborada, Av 7 with Transversal 9, Altamira, T 261-3060, bar and swimming pool, British and Commonwealth visitors only, entry fee according to length of stay. The sports club run by the *Tamanaco Hotel* is open to non-guests and suitable for people staying a short time. Radio Club Venezolano is a very welcoming organization of amateur radio operators which is eager to meet amateurs from around the world (address: PO Box 2285, Caracas 1010-A, T 781-4878, 781-8303 – Av Lima, Los Caobos; branches around the country).

● **Tour companies & travel agents**

Maso Internacional, Plaza Altamira Sur, Av San Juan Bosco, T 313577, reps for Thomas Cook, generally good reports of tours. *Lost World Adventures*, Edif 3-H, p 6, Oficina 62, Av Abraham Lincoln, Caracas 1050, T 761-7538, tours to Roraima and Canaima. *Candes Turismo*, office in lobby of *Hilton* and Edif Celeste, Av Abraham Lincoln, T 934-4710, F 953-6755, E-mail: candes@telcel.net.ve, Web: http://www.candesturismo.com.ve, helpful, English, Italian, German spoken; *Orinoco Tours*, Edif Galerías Bolívar, p 7, Av Abraham Lincoln, Caracas 1050-A, PO Box 51505, T 761-7712, F 761-6801, flights and tours, very helpful; *Selma Viajes*, Av Universidad, Monroy a Misericordia, Edif Dorado Locales A y B, T 572-0225, run recexcursions to Canaima.

In the USA *Lost World Adventures* specialize in tours of Venezuela, ranging from the Caribbean, to the Andes, plus tours of Panama and Ecuador, 1189 Autumn Ridge Drive, Marietta, GA 30066, T (404) 971-8586, (800) 999-0558 outside GA, F (404) 977-3095. UK based *Last Frontiers*, Swan House, High Street, Long Crendon, Bucks, HP18 9AF, T 01844-208405, F 01844 201400 (Internet http://www.lastfrontiers.co.uk), run by Edward Paine (who used to live in Venezuela), organizes tailor-made itineraries to any part of the country, also photographic and painting tours. Also *Geodyssey* run adventure and general tours of Venezuela, inc Angel Falls, Mt Roraima, upper Orinoco, Andes treks and specialist tours for birdwatchers, 29 Harberton Rd, London N19 3JS, England, T (0171) 281-7788, F (0171) 281-7878. *Forum Travel International*, 91 Gregory Lane, Suite 21, Pleasant Hill, CA 94523, T (510) 671-2900, F (510) 671-2993, runs tours to *Las Nieves Eco-Adventure Jungle Lodge*, in the transition zone of savannahs and jungles of the Orinoco; lots of wildlife, nature tours, canoing, etc.

Tours to Cuba: *Ideal Tours*, Centro Capriles, Plaza Venezuela, T 267-3812, 4 days, 3 nights, US$649, inc flight, hotel, half board and city tour. *The Tour Hunters*, T 91-2511, 5 days, 4 nights US$286, 6 days, 5 nights US$340, inc everything except flights.

● **Tourist offices**
Corpoturismo, administrative office on floor 35, Torre Oeste, Parque Central (metro Bellas Artes is closest), T 507-8607/8600; open Mon-Fri 0830-1200, 1400-1630, helpful but not much information or maps. There is a smaller office at the airport (see below). See page 1572 for **Maps** and further rec reading.

● **Useful addresses**
Diex: for visa renewal, Av Baralt, El Silencio (**NB** Don't believe anyone who tells you visa extensions are not available).

Touring y Automóvil Club de Venezuela, Torre Phelps, p 15, of A y C, Plaza Venezuela,

T 794-1032/781-7491, ask for Sr Oscar Giménez Landínez (treasurer, speaks some English), or Zonaida R Mendoza (Secretary to the Club President).

YMCA: Edif YMCA, Av Guaicaipuro, San Bernardino, T 520291.

● **Transport**
Local Buses: many buses start from Nuevo Circo bus station in the city centre, overcrowded in the rush hours, additional fare after 2100 (the correct fare helps to speed things up). On the longer runs these buses are probably more comfortable for those with luggage than a *por puesto*. Midibuses are known as *carmelitas*. *Por puesto* minibuses run on regular routes, fares depend on the distance travelled within the city; fares rise for journeys outside. Many *por puesto* services start in Silencio.

Driving: Self-drive cars (Hertz, Avis, Volkswagen, Budget, Dollar, ACO) are available at the airport and in town. They are cheaper than guided excursions for less than full loads. Driver's licence from home country accepted. Major credit card or cash deposit over US$200 required. Rates are given in **Information for travellers**, **Motoring**. Budget is the only company giving unlimited mileage, if you book and pre-pay outside the country. Auto and personal insurance (US$10-17.50/day) strongly rec as you will be lucky to survive 2 or 3 days as a newcomer to Caracas traffic without a dent or a scrape. All cars should be checked carefully as most have some defect or other, and insist on a short test drive.

Garage: *Yota-Box*, 3a Transversal Mis Encantos, Quinta Morava, No 1 15, Chacao, T 313772/331035, owner Gerardo Ayala, rec, especially for Toyota; *Bel-Cro*, Av Intercomunal de Antímano, very good for VWs, also sells new and used parts, very cheap and highly rec.

Motorcycles: may not be ridden in Caracas between 2300 and 0500. Also see **Motoring**.

Taxis: are required by law to instal and use

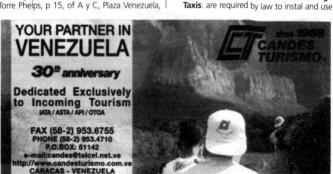

taxi-meters, but they never use them, if they have not already been removed. Fares must be negotiated in advance. Most city trips are US$1 absolute minimum during the day (most fares US$2). Taxi drivers are authorized to charge an extra 20% on night trips after 1800, on Sun and all holidays, and US$0.45 for answering telephone calls. After 1800 drivers are selective about where they want to go. Beware of taxi drivers trying to renegotiate fixed rates because your destination is in 'a difficult area'. The sign on the roof of a taxi reads 'Libre'. There are pirates, however, with possibly a taxi sign, but without yellow licence plates/registration-number plate, which are to be avoided. Never tell a taxi driver it is your first visit to Caracas. See yellow pages for radio taxis.

The Metro: operates 0530-2300; a/c, clean, well-patrolled, safe and more comfortable and quicker than any other form of city transport; no smoking, best to take rucksacks only during off-peak hours. There are 3 lines: Line 1 (W-E) from Propatria to Palo Verde; Line 2 (N-S), from Capitolio to Las Adjuntas, with connection to Caricuao Zoológico; Line 3, S from Plaza Venezuela to El Valle, plus metrobus El Valle-Los Teques. Tickets cost US$0.20-0.25 per journey; 10-journey tickets (Multi Abono), US$2 (US$3.60 inc Metrobus). Student discounts are available with ISIC card. Metrobuses connect with the Metro system (US$0.20): get transfer tickets (*boleto integrado*, US$0.20) for services to southern districts, route maps displayed at stations – retain ticket after exit turnstile. Good selection of maps at shop in La California station.

Air 28 km from Caracas, nr the port of La Guaira: Maiquetía, for national flights, Simón Bolívar for international flights, adjacent to each other (5 mins' walk – taxis take a circular route, fare US$2.25; airport authorities run a shuttle bus between the two every 10 mins from 0700). The Tourist Office at the international airport has good maps, helpful; some English spoken, open 0700-2400, T 551060; tourist office at national terminal open 0700-2100, T 551191. When manned, both offices are useful, will book hotels, reconfirm flights, English spoken, better service than Corpoturismo head office. Flight enquiries T (031) 522222; passenger assistance T 552424; police T 552498. Many facilities close 1 Jan, inc duty free and money exchanges. Duty free shops close 2230. At Simón Bolívar: several *casas de cambio* open 24 hrs (good rates at Italcambio, outside duty-free area); also Banco Industrial branch in International terminal and another, less crowded, in baggage reclaim area. If changing TCs you may be asked for your receipt of purchase; commission 2.5%. There are cash machines for Visa, Amex and Mastercard. Pharmacy, bookshops, basement café

(good value meals and snacks, open 0600-2400, hard to find); cafes and bars on 1st floor viewing terrace also good value. No official left luggage; ask for Paulo at the mini bar on the 1st floor. Look after your belongings in both terminals. Direct dial phone calls to USA only, from AT&T booth in international departure lounge. CANTV at Gates 15 and 24, open 0700-2100, long-distance, international and fax services, inc receipt of faxes.

Always allow plenty of time when going to the airport, whatever means of transport you are using: the route can be very congested (2 hrs in daytime, but only 30 mins at 0430). Allow at least 2 hrs checking-in time before your flight. When several flights arrive close together there are long queues for immigration. Taxi fares from airport to Caracas cost on average US$14 minimum, depending on the quality of the taxi, the part of city, or on the number of stars of your hotel (give the name of a cheaper hotel nearby); overcharging is rife. Fares are supposedly controlled, but it is essential to negotiate with the driver. Check the official fares outside airport terminal. After 2200 and at weekends a surcharge of 20% may be added; you may get charged up to US$40. Drivers may only surcharge you for luggage (US$0.50/large bag). From the city centre to the airport is US$10. If you think the taxi driver is overcharging you, make a complaint to Corporturismo or tell him you will report him to the Departamento de Protección del Consumidor.

The airport shuttle bus (blue and white with 'Aeropuerto Internacional' on the side) leaves from E end of terminal, left out of exit. To airport catch it under the flyover at Bolívar and Av Sur 17, 250m from Bellas Artes metro (poorly lit at night, not rec to wait here in the dark); regular service from 0400 to 0030, bus leaves when there are enough passengers, US$1.80. If heading for a hotel in Sabana Grande on arrival, ask to be dropped off at Gato Negro metro station and take metro from there to Plaza Venezuela or Sabana Grande. The shuttle bus or *por puesto* to airport can also be caught at Gato Negro metro station. To catch bus to Macuto, leave terminal from upper level, cross the parking lot, pass the exit, climb steps and cross the 4-lane highway. **NB** Don't attempt this at night.

Long distance buses The chaotic, dirty, Nuevo Circo bus station is in the city centre (nearest metro La Hoyada). It serves all **western** destinations. Give yourself plenty of time to find the bus you need although there are bus agents who will assist in finding a ticket for your destination. Tickets are sold, at most, 24 hrs before departure, sometimes only on the morning of departure. This adds to the chaos at busy periods. Nevertheless, do not

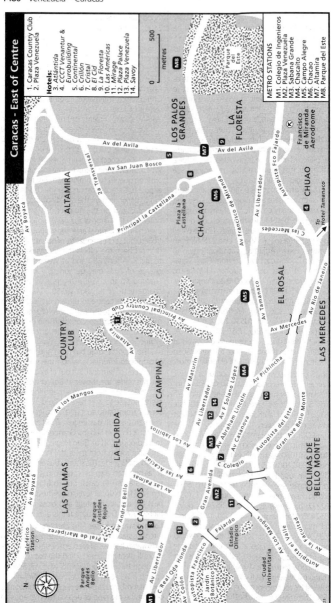

Caracas - East of Centre

1. Caracas Country Club
2. Plaza Venezuela

Hotels:
3. Atlántida
4. CCCT Venantur & Eurobuilding
5. Continental
6. Crillon
7. Cristal
8. El Cid
9. La Floresta
10. Las Américas
11. Mirage
12. Plaza Palace
13. Plaza Venezuela
14. Savoy

METRO STATIONS
M1. Colegio de Ingenieros
M2. Plaza Venezuela
M3. Sabana Grande
M4. Chacaíto
M5. Campo Alegre
M6. Chacao
M7. Altamira
M8. Parque del Este

0   500
metres

be tempted to buy tickets from the touts who wait by buses. Those first on get the best seats so it is advisable to arrive 1 hr before departure. Buses may also leave early. Watch your baggage carefully up until the baggage door is closed (see also **Road Transport**, page 1576).

Buses for **eastern** destinations leave from Terminal Oriente at Guarenas, clean, modern, safe. City buses leave Nuevo Circo bullring every 30 mins, US$0.30, 45 mins, 1 hr in rush hour; or take *por puesto* from Petare metro station; an easier option but take care at night. Taxi to terminal US$4. Bus from terminal to centre: turn left outside main entrance towards main parking area where buses wait; get off at Bellas Artes or El Silencio, US$0.50. Tickets for eastern destinations can be bought from agency on Av Lecuna, opp INGEVE, between Miracielos y Hospital.

Buses for places close to Caracas leave from the other side of the road from Nuevo Circo bus station, via the underpass (eg Los Teques, Higuerote, Catia La Mar, La Guaira). From La Hoyada metro, do not go under the bridge, but walk straight down the road for 300m.

On public holidays buses are usually fully booked leaving Caracas and drivers often make long journeys without stopping. Sat and Sun morning are also bad for travel into/out of Caracas, no problem on journeys of 4 hrs or less. Always take identification when booking a long-distance journey. Times and fares of buses are given under destinations. Buses going W on the Panamericana route are not recommended because the old road suffers from many accidents. The best lines are: to Maracaibo, Expresos los Llanos; to Guayana, Rápidos de Guayana. Aetoexpresos Ejecutivos, Av Principal de Bello Campo, Quinta Marluz (between Chacao and Altamira metro stops), T 266-3601/9011, rec for Valencia, Barquisimeto and Puerto La Cruz, reserve 2 days in advance, except for buses leaving on Fri (no left luggage). Fares are 3-4 times higher than other companies, but worth it. Ormeño has buses to Bogotá (US$75), Cali (US$90), Quito (US$130), Guayaquil (US$140), Lima (US$190), Santiago (US$270), Mendoza (US$330) and Buenos Aires (US$340); safe, comfortable, a/c, video, toilet; terminal at Final Av San Martín, Sector Oeste, C Sucre con C Nueva, nr Metro La Paz.

MONTE AVILA

The cable railway (*teleférico*) up Monte Avila from Av Perimetral de Maripérez, giving a stupendous view of the city and the coast, seems to be out of action permanently (still closed, early 1997). The future of the *Humboldt Hotel* on the summit

(2,159m) has not been decided. It has been refurbished, but not even the ground floor bar/restaurant/disco is open. Camping is possible with permission. A dirt road runs from La Puerta section of San Bernardino to the summit, 45 mins in 4WD vehicle. A recommended trip is to ride up in a vehicle and hike back down (note that it is cold at the summit, average temperature 13°C). The *Tamanaco* offers jeep with driver US$50 pp.

There are three good places to start a hike in the Monte Avila National Park: to Pico Naiguatá, 2,765m; to Pico Oriental, 2,600m; to the *Hotel Humboldt*, 2,150m. Hikers should go in groups of at least three, from the point of view of both mountain and personal safety (Monte Avila is not a dangerous place, but the occasional thief lurks there). Always take water and something for the cold at altitude. The unfit should not attempt any of the hikes.

Pico Naiguatá is a very strenuous hike. Take the metro to La California, then a bus going up Av Sanz, ask for the Centro Comercial El Marqués. From there walk up Av Sanz towards Cota Mil (Av Boyacá), about 4 blocks. At the end of Av Sanz, underneath the bridge, is the entrance to the Naiguatá trail. In about 40 mins you reach La Julia *guardaparques* station, where you have to state your destination and pay US$0.25 entrance.

Pico Oriental: from the Altamira metro station take a bus to 'La entrada de Sabas Nieves', where the *Tarzilandia* restaurant is. From here a dirt road leads up to the Sabas Nieves *guardaparques* station (about 40 mins). The path to Pico Oriental starts at the back of Sabas Nieves and is extremely easy to follow.

Hotel Humboldt is a relatively easy route, 3 hrs. Take the metro bus from Bellas Artes station to El Avila stop, US$0.25; opposite is a grocery. Turn the corner and walk 2 blocks up towards the mountain. At the top of the street turn left; almost immediately on your right is the park entrance. **NB** This area is not safe before 0800 or after dark. Plenty of people take this route, starting 0830-

0900, giving plenty of time to get up and down safely and in comfort.

On the La Guaira side (and best reached from La Guaira) is a Museo Ecológico known as 'El jardín de las piedras'. It is owned by Zoez, a self-styled prophet, and reflects his beliefs. Open weekends, remove shoes before entering, very interesting; take a picnic, enjoy the designs and views. It can also be reached from Macuto, 20 mins by jeep, or 1½-2 hrs walk, but ask directions as there are two paths, the first of which goes through a *barrio* which must be avoided.

Full descriptions of the hiking routes are given in the *Venezuela Handbook*.

● **Agencies**
Camel Tours: La California Sur, Av Trieste, Qta Reycara, T Caracas 223261, or 014-255356 (cellular), ask for Roberto Andara (speaks English), runs day trips to Galipán, a *bodega* on the Hotel Humboldt hike, for US$25 pp (inc horseriding and barbecues).

The hiking club, Centro Excursionista de Caracas, C Chivacoa, San Román, T 235-3155 (Sr Contreras) or 573-8515 (Sr Barcón), meet Sat 1430, arranges day and weekend hikes, very welcoming, speak some English and German.

DISTRITO FEDERAL

WEST OF CARACAS

Ruta 4 leaves the capital at Antímano and climbs gently W for l9 km to the market town of **El Junquito**, popular with Caraqueños at weekends (several short-stay hotels, parking, magnificent views); roadside stalls sell souvenirs, fruit and barbequed *chorizos* (pork sausages). The road then winds another 19 km to a paved turnoff, where several roads lead down to the coast (see below). To the S of the road is the **Parque Nacional Macarao**, small but attractive; from one point on this road Caracas can be seen to the E and the Caribbean to the N. At the coast turnoff (Km 44) is an arch over the road marking the Aragua state border; 3½ km beyond is the *Charcutería Tovar*, a good place to stock up on picnic supplies, closed all Mon and Tues am. Nearby is a grass ski slope, skis rented by the hour.

COLONIA TOVAR

The mountain town of **Colonia Tovar** (*pop* 4,330; *alt* 1,890m), was founded in 1843 by German immigrants from Kaiserstuhl in the Black Forest, recruited by the geographer Agustín Codazzi with the promise of free land and little interference. They retained their customs and isolation until a paved road reached the settlement in 1963. It is now very touristy, but the blond hair, blue eyes and Schwartzwald-accented German of the inhabitants are still much in evidence. *Tovarenses* make unsurpassed bread, blackberry jam and bratwurst, and grow strawberries, coffee, garlic, rhubarb and flowers for the Caracas market. Colonia Tovar offers delightful landscapes, mild climate, old architecture (see the Scandinavian-style ceramics) and dignified hospitality. There is a small museum which tells the history of the 241 pioneers who founded Tovar (117 died on the outward voyage) and the nearby offshoot of El Jarillo (museum open 1000-1800, Sat and Sun, and holidays). The church of San Martín de Tours is L-shaped, a copy of the one in Emmendingen, Germany. Carnival preserves European traditions and is unique in Venezuela.

Local information
● **Accommodation & places to eat**
Credit cards widely accepted. *Alta-Baviera*, T 51483, 0.8 km above village on La Victoria road (Prolongación C Codazzi), heated, good view from restaurant terrace; *Bergland*, T 51229, on same road, some cabins, beautiful views, good cheap breakfasts; *Drei-Tannen*, T 51246, private road on right just before entering village from E, 7 rooms, 2 heated apartments, parking, owner Señora Klemperer; *Edelweiss*, T 51139, just past the *Alta Baviera*, highest hotel in town! – superb vistas, 8 rooms, 3 cabins, parking; *Freiburg*, T 51313, cross river at 'El Molino' sign in village and continue along hillside until signs to hotel, rooms and cabins, heated, restaurant; *Kaiserstuhl*, T 51132, C Bolívar in centre, parking, good views, 2 restaurants (A2 with breakfast and dinner); *Selva Negra**, T 51072, in centre nr church, some cabins, heated, children's park, popular restaurant, parking. All are at least **B** and are normally full at weekends; room rates inc good, German-style food; **D-E** *Guest House Alicia*, beside *Selva Negra*, nice.

Other rec restaurants: *El Codazzi*, in centre on C Codazzi, traditional German and Hungarian dishes, strudel and biscuits, open 1100-1600, closed Mon and Tues; *El Molino*, on Molino next to the historic old mill (worth a visit), has *cabañas* (C), use of kitchen, good restaurant, great *jugo de fresas*, wide selection of German dishes, open 0900-1000, 1200-1600, 1800-1900, Mon 0900-1400, highly rec; *Perolón*, C Codazzi, only open weekends and holidays 1100-1900, homemade vegetable soup a speciality; *Café Munstall*, opp the church, interesting location in oldest house in Colonia Tovar, pastry and coffee at weekends; *La Ballesta*, turn left at sign before entering Tovar, restaurant on 3 tiers with prices to match, snacks and meals weekends and holidays, adjoining rifle and archery ranges, equipment for hire. Local fruit, vegetables and flowers sold at *Frutería Bergman*, next to Lagoven station at E entrance to town; across the street is *Panadería Tovar* for delicious bread; many food stalls on weekends along Av Codazzi.

● **Transport**
Road The 1½-hrs' drive up from Caracas is easy during the week, but murder on weekends – long traffic jams, difficult to find picnic spots or accommodation, definitely not recommended. Keep your passport with you in case of military checks. It is generally easy to get a lift if there are no buses. Taxi fare for the round trip from Caracas to Colonia Tovar (driver will wait) is about US$20. **Buses**: from Av Sur 9 y El Rosario, next to Nuevo Circo, to El Junquito (1 hr, US$0.40), then change for Colonia Tovar (1 hr, US$0.55). *Por puesto* from Plaza Catia or O'Leary (more frequently), Caracas, 1 hr, US$1. Alternatively, take a *por puesto* from Plaza Capuchino to El Junquito, then one from there to Colonia Tovar, US$1. If changing *por puesto*, make sure the driver stops at the right place. Last bus to Caracas 1800.

COLONIA TOVAR TO THE COAST

The road which leaves Ruta 4, 8 km before Tovar divides soon after into three paved roads which wind down the mountains through beautiful scenery to Puerto Cruz, Chichiriviche and Carayaca respectively. It is 43 km to **Puerto Cruz**, a tiny harbour with a good beach. Boats can be hired here for a 14 km trip W to the even smaller settlement of **Puerto Maya** (*pop* 200), on a beautiful bay and accessible only by boat; the villagers are mostly descended from African slaves. The second road leads down the valley to Chichiriviche (40 km

from Tovar, not to be confused with the resort W of Puerto Cabello), a neat little town with no accommodation; potholes in the last section of the road make a high-clearance vehicle useful. (A new coastal jeep track now links Chichiriviche with Puerto Cruz, not yet suitable for conventional cars.) The paved coast road begins at Chichiriviche and runs E to Catia La Mar and Maiquetía. First resort is **Oricao** with a lovely palm-rimmed but private beach, then comes **Puerto Carayaca**, where the third paved road down from Tovar reaches the coast. At Pto Carayaca is **D** *Casa Francisco*, hotel and restaurant, attractive setting. A few kilometres inland are the small towns of Tarma and **Carayaca** (only other gas station in the area apart from Colonia Tovar), where yet another paved road runs from the Tovar-El Junquito road to the coast (at Arrecifes). Many of the coves along this coast are good for swimming and renowned for sport fishing; the vegetation covering the mountainsides is lush and attractive: ferns, orchids, bromeliads, etc.

From Colonia Tovar, Ruta 4 continues (well-paved but hair-raising) S down the slopes for 34 km to La Victoria on the Caracas – Valencia Highway (see below); 4 buses a day, US$1.50; glorious scenery.

EAST OF CARACAS

YARE

In **San Francisco de Yare** (*pop* 18,000), a celebration is held at Corpus Christi (early June); the dance before the church of the enormously masked red devils, and of most of the villagers lasts the whole day (see **Music and Dance** section). Yare is about 90 km from Caracas; the road to it is through Petare and down the Río Guaira as far as Santa Teresa, and then up the Río Tuy.

PARQUE NACIONAL GUATOPO

From Santa Teresa make a detour to this beautiful and little frequented **National Park** on the road to Altagracia de Orituco (bus from Nuevo Circo marked 'El Popular', US$1.50). You must return to Santa Teresa to continue your journey to Yare.

At the Parque Guatopo are various convenient places to picnic on the route through the forest. Take insect repellent. Free camping at Hacienda La Elvira; take jeep from Altagracia de Orituco (US$0.50) and ask to be let off at turn-off to Hacienda. A permit must be obtained at Inparques. There are a number of good nature trails in the park.

THE COAST

LA GUAIRA

Venezuela's main port (*pop* 26,420; *mean temperature* 29°C), only 45 mins by road from Caracas (traffic permitting). Dating back to 1567, La Guaira achieved its greatest importance in the 18th century when the Basque Guipuzcoana Company held the royal trading monopoly; many British export-import companies flourished here in the 1800s.

Places of interest The old town, 1 km E of the port, remains intact (much restoration work in progress), with delightful colonial houses along steep narrow streets, several of which climb up to the forts of **El Vigía** (the lookout), **La Pólvora** (the Powder Magazine) and the restored **Castillo de San Carlos** (1610), built on the classic star pattern and commanding a fine view of the port and its surroundings (if going to the Castillo, aim for C León, or take a *por puesto* up and walk down). See the imposing **Casa Guipuzcoana** (1734), on coast road (Av Soublette), original HQ of the company, now used as government offices, a busy cultural centre (free events advertised in Caracas newspapers), the art gallery of the **Ateneo de La Guaira** and the **Litoral branch of the Universidad Simón Bolívar**; interesting collections scattered throughout the three floors, including regional hammocks, Indian fishing implements, documents, open Tues-Sun 0800-1800. Many other mansions and churches, including the **Catedral**, the lovely **Ermita Carmen** (open only weekends pm, key at the cathedral) and the **Casa José María España**, home of the first 'martyr' in the War of Independence.

The old **Camino Real** continues upwards from the Castillo de San Carlos and can be hiked to Caracas; a second colonial road rises from Maiquetía, 2 km E.

MAIQUETIA

Founded 1670, **Maiquetía** (*pop* 103,000) was the terminus of the old supply road to Caracas. A pilgrimage is made on foot in Feb from La Pastora church in Caracas to the Maiquetía parochial church along the old supply route.

● **Accommodation E** *Crillon*, esq Navarvete, with shower and toilet, basic but adequate; **E** *Granada* (alias Coromoto), up the hill from Plaza Los Maestros, tiled entrance, reasonable. Others cater for short-stay couples.

● **Places to eat** *Avila*, good, nr Plaza Los Maestros; also rec is *Mesón Canarios* and *Cervecería Primera*; opp *Avila* is a good and cheap fish restaurant.

● **Buses** To La Guaira and Maiquetía from Gato Negro metro. Caracas-La Guaira US$0.40; many to Maiquetía, marked also Catia; taxi from Caracas US$9. If driving, note that streets in central Maiquetía and La Guaira are extremely narrow, best to park along Av Soublette rather than try to tour the towns by car. The coastal road E from La Guaira is slow and quite rough, but scenic and interesting, making a worthwhile round trip if you return to Caracas/La Guaira by the paved interior roads.

EAST FROM MAIQUETIA

The coast E of Maiquetía-La Guaira has a string of popular seaside resorts and residential districts with a total population of about 75,000. The divided Av Soublette sweeps eastwards past the Punta Mulatos market (which serves most of the Litoral) to Macuto, El Caribe, Naiguatá and so on to **Los Caracas**. All these places can be reached quite cheaply by most 'Litoral' buses from the W end of Nuevo Circo in Caracas.

MACUTO

5 km E of La Guaira, founded in 1740 (*pop* 19,370; *phone code* 031). The coastal promenade (Paseo la Playa) is lined with seagrape trees; there is a splendid yacht marina behind the *Sheraton*. It's a pleasant alternative to Caracas when arriving or before flying out. The beaches tend to be

overcrowded at weekends, go midweek if possible. They are now badly polluted, although less so the further E you go. **NB** Robberies reported on seafront between Macuto and Caraballeda.

Places of interest

From the Plaza de las Palomas (lots of pigeons) can be seen **La Guzmanía**, the coastal residence of the President, built by Guzmán Blanco, complete with guards in colonial uniforms. Opposite is the **presidential residence** built in 1888 for Joaquín Crespo; the initials J and C can be seen over the entrance (for Joaquín and Jacinta Crespo). The building is now a college but can be visited by arrangement. The **Castillete de las Quince Letras** is the only building on the beach facing the sea, built by Armando Julio Reveron, whose paintings are on display in the Galería Nacional del Arte in the capital; the museum preserves his daily life, paintings and the life-sized rag dolls he used as models. Open Tues-Sat 0800-1200, 1400-1700, Sun and holidays 1000-1500.

Local information
● Accommodation
In Macuto itself: B *Las Quince Letras**, Av La Playa, on eastern side of town, T 461551, F 461432, fully renovated, good restaurant, pool, a/c; **B** *Macuto**, Av La Playa y C 3, Urb Alamo, T 461310, F 461854, a/c, hot water, empty midweek, full weekends, 5 mins walk to beach, comfortable but poorly maintained, swimming pool, safe parking, good breakfasts, accepts credit cards; **C** *Santiago*, Av La Playa, T 44214, F 44118, a/c, small, bare rooms, large terrace, beautiful view over sea, tiny rooftop pool, noisy bar at night, good restaurant (*La Choza*), English spoken, accepts credit cards; **D** *Alamo*, Av La Playa, T 461263, with fan or a/c, good value, bargaining possible, English spoken, accepts credit cards, good restaurant on seafront; **D** *Colonial*, Paseo Macuto 48, T 461462, nr beach, good value, a/c, smart, good restaurant and service, accept credit cards; **D** *Diana*, Boulevard Caraballeda, T 461553, 50m from the beach, basic, hot water in some rooms, a/c, helpful, noisy on ground floor especially, safe for motorcycles; **D** *Isabel*, Isabel la Católica y C 3, 2 mins from sea, small, quiet, good; **D** *Pensión Guanchez*, Av Alamo Transversal, behind church, T 461253, with ceiling fan, breakfast US$1, excellent set lunch US$3-4, no sign

outside, noisy, nice balcony, manager speaks English and Swedish; **D-C** *Posada del Hidalgo*, Paseo del Mar, T 44107, F 45280, good value, helpful, accepts credit cards, safe, noisy, good restaurant/bar on ground floor (separate entrance), taxi service to airport; **D** *Riviera*, Blvd Caraballeda y C San Bartolomé, T 461332, 100m from beach, triples available, helpful, a/c, good French food; **E** *Alemania*, Paseo Macuto, T 461553, **F** without bath, fans, old building, sparse but clean, veranda overlooking sea, very noisy from disco next door; **E** *Canta Claro*, Boulevard Macuto con C Centenario, T 461035, basic, very small, 2 rooms with balcony overlooking Paseo, one with private bath; **E** *Plazamar*, Plaza Las Palomas, T 3, nr La Guzmanía, T 44291/44271, run by Italians, rooms with up to 6 beds, helpful, pleasant balcony, taxi service to airport; next door is **E** *Darimar*, T 44798, with bath, safe, rec.

The wealthier area of Caraballeda is 5 km E of Macuto: **L2** *Macuto Sheraton**, on public beach, Apdo 65 La Guaira, T 944300, F 944317, 3 restaurants (good food and value) and all 5-star facilities, sells phone cards for international calls, will store luggage (tip the porter), post office; **L3** *Meliá Caribe**, on beach just E of Sheraton, T 945555, 3 restaurants (good), pool, disco, noisy, try to get a room on the landside, free tennis, expensive gym; **C** *Fioremar*, nr *Meliá Caribe* and beach, T 941743, solarium, restaurant, pool; **F** pp *Tamacuro*, Av de la Playa, T 941325, a/c, large rooms. Quite a few aparthotels in the area, up to US$100 a day without meals.

● Places to eat
In Caraballeda, along Av Principal are *Neptuno*, good seafood, rec; *El Bodegón del Lino*, Spanish-style, rec; *El Portón del Timotes*, seafood, good service. *La Esquina*, nr *Hotel Alamo*, good; also on Paseo La Playa: *El Coral*, next to *Hotel Santiago*, good seafood; *Chifa*, good, huge portions; *Los Criollos*, cheap, good food.

● Transport
Por puesto from Caracas US$2, about 1 hr (taxi US$20); *por puesto* to airport, domestic terminal, US$1, 15 mins, or take Catia La Mar bus, 25 mins, starts at 0600, stops in front of airport. The taxi fare from the airport is officially US$12, 30 mins (plus US$0.50 for a large suitcase or rucksack – beware of overcharging); more to the *Macuto Sheraton*. To get a *por puesto* to Caracas at rush hour (weekend afternoons, etc), walk back to one of the early stops such as the *Macuto Sheraton*. Most *por puestos* go to El Silencio. Tourist transport with Andrés and Isabelino, T (031) 519146, in 8-seater van, Spanish only, rec.

To the W of the airport is **Catia La Mar** (*pop* 131,400), industrial, very littered and with polluted sea, but it is very convenient for Maiquetía airport, taxi, officially US$12 (but US$4-9 with bargaining). *Balneario Camuri Chico*, 3 good beaches, restaurant, showers, water fairly clean, recommended.

● **Accommodation B** *Aeropuerto*, shower, a/c, OK, stores luggage; **C** *Bahía del Mar*, clean, swimming pool, good restaurant; **D** *Catia del Mar*, modern, clean.

EAST TO HIGUEROTE

East of Caraballeda is a series of small resorts, most with their own walled-in public beaches (strong undertows), until the cliff-hugging road arrives at **Naiguatá** (*pop* 24,100), an old village in the shadow of the Avila National Park's highest peak (Fiesta of San Juan, 24 June, and Corpus Christi, costumed devil dancers, etc). There are lovely views of rocky coast and surf from the corniche road to **Los Caracas** (50 km from La Guaira), a holiday resort subsidized by the government for low-income workers. For information on accommodation, T 541-6487, Incret (Worker's Training and Recreation Institute).

It is possible to continue on along the Barlovento coast to Higuerote and return to Caracas on paved roads via Caucagua and Guatire, a round trip of about 300 km. Beyond Los Caracas (last gas until Carenero), the road is dirt and 4WD is recommended because of the rivers to be forded. It does not hug the coast as before but links many tiny fishing settlements. Near Osma (10 km) is the Granja Osmán, which has some cottages for rent (**A** inc meals and watersports equipment); in **Todasana** (22 km) is the German-run *Egua*, hotel and restaurant, **D**, fans, modest. The road continues on through La Sabana (very popular 2 km sandy beach, waterfall on right of road) and Chuspa (coconut palm-fringed sandy beach) to **Chirimena** (67 km from Caracas), where the highway paving begins again, and thence 14 km to Higuerote (see page 1520).

ISLAS LOS ROQUES

Islas Los Roques lie 150 km due N of Caracas; the atoll, of about 340 islets and reefs, constitutes one of Venezuela's loveliest National Parks (225, 153 ha). There are long stretches of white beaches and over 12 miles of coral reef with crystal-clear water ideal for snorkelling (best at Francisqui – Cayo Francés – and Cayo Agua). There are many bird nesting sites (eg the huge gull colonies on Francisqui and the pelicans, boobies and frigates on Selenqui); May is nesting time at the gull colonies. For more information write to La Fundación Científica Los Roques, Apdo No 1, Av Carmelitas, Caracas 1010, T 326771. This is one of the least visited diving spots in the Caribbean; best visited midweek as Venezuelans swarm here on long weekends and at school holidays. Prices are slightly higher than the mainland and infrastructure is limited but the islands are beautiful and unspoiled. Campers need a permit from Inparques, T (02) 234-7331, F 234-4238. Average temp 27°C with coolish nights. You will need strong sunblock as there is no shade. Park entry US$2.

Gran Roque is the main and only inhabited island. The airport is here, as is the national guard, food stores, public phones, medical facilities and accommodation. There is nowhere to change TCs. Park Headquarters are in the scattered fishing village (*pop* 900). You can negotiate with local fishermen for transport to other islands: you will need to take your own tent, food and (especially) water. **Nordisqui** is very isolated while **Madrisqui** has many summer houses. **Cayo Francés** is two islands joined by a sandspit, with calm lagoon waters on the S and rolling surf on the N (there is an abandoned house and enough vegetation to provide shaded hammock sites, and accommodation at US$30 pp, full board inc drinks, good food, friendly staff, nice beach, snorkelling gear, water and light 24 hrs, fan, bargaining possible if you stay for several days). The *Pelicano Club* has accommodation and organizes excursions, boat trips and dives, recommended. **Warning to would-be campers**: leave nothing out on the ground, the crabs eat everything! Tiny but irritating biting insects in the calmer months can make camping miserable.

Local information

● Accommodation

On Gran Roque: **A2** *Canto de la Ballena*, on seafront, T 302420, full board, excellent food, relaxed, fans, can pay with TCs; **A2** *Posada Bora La Mar*, T (02) 238-5408, run by Marta Agustí who can put you in touch with local fisherman to take you to other islands at reasonable prices, eg Nordisqui or Isla Larga; **C** *Posada Margot*, inc breakfast and dinner, often has water and electricity problems; **D** *Doña Magaly*, C Principal, Plaza Bolívar, T (014) 372113, basic, shared bath, fans; **D** pp *Posada La Lagunita*, basic, inc large breakfast and dinner. There are many other posadas, ranging from **D** pp to **L1**; most inc breakfast and dinner. 'Eola' is a yacht out of Gran Roque, fully equipped, with cabins, chartered for US$100/day, all inclusive, highly rec as a worthwhile way of getting some shade on the treeless beaches. Run by Italians Gianni and Jaqueline, book direct by phone, T (99) 216735.

● Sports

Diving: *Sesto Continente*, on the edge of the village, T/F (014) 241853, ask for Jakob, Saul or Hugo, very helpful, run PADI courses and night dives, rec.

● Getting there

Flights from Maiquetía or Porlamar. Chapi Air from Maiquetía at 0800, returning at 1600, US$110. Aereotuy (T 02-761-6231, F 762-5254) fly from Maiquetía 3 times a day: 2-day package (return flight, accommodation, meals, drinks, catamaran excursion with snorkelling and diving equipment), from US$300 pp. Aerotuy have several *posadas* of varying comfort; reported as very efficient but the catamaran trip is not rec.

West from Caracas

A VARIED region, through which run the Central Highlands; north of the highlands is the Caribbean, with secluded coves and popular resorts. Two coastal national parks are Morrocoy, offshore, and the dunes around the old city of Coro. Straddling the mountains is the birders' paradise of Henri Pittier National Park. South of the Highlands are Lake Valencia and the agricultural and industrial centres of Maracay and Valencia.

100 km W of Caracas is the great basin in which lies the Lago de Valencia and the towns of Maracay and Valencia. The basin, which is only 450m above sea-level, receives plenty of rain and is one of the most important agricultural areas in the country; sugar, cotton, maize, beans and rice are the main crops. In the other valleys and depressions in the Central Highlands are also grown manioc, bananas, cocoa and the superb local coffee.

ROUTES The Pan-American Highway, which links Caracas by road with the other capitals of South America, follows closely the route of Gómez' Great Andean Highway as far as the Lago de Maracaibo, though many sections have been widened and straightened. At the start, there is the choice of a direct toll motorway to Valencia (with exit to Maracay), toll US$0.60, or the old road called, familiarly, 'La Pan-Americana' and known for its dangerous bends. It leaves La Rinconada race course to its left and passes (Km 11) the Venezuelan Institute of Advanced Scientific Research (IVIC) which has an excellent Museo de Antropología and the most advanced scientific library in South America. The Panamerica continues its steady climb into the Teques mountains; past the turn off to Carrizal is the park of **Las Colinas de Carrizal**, with collections of local fish and birds.

LOS TEQUES

25 km from Caracas the highway reaches **Los Teques**, capital of Miranda state (*pop* 164,440; *alt* 1,180m; founded 1703). The city is a mixture of skyscrapers and colonial buildings around Plaza Guaicaipuro (statue of the Carib chief who fought the Spaniards here) and Plaza Bolívar (Cathedral etc), with several attractive parks. Parque Gustavo Knoop, named after the director of the German-built Caracas-Valencia railway which ran through the town in 1894-1951, opens 0800-1800 except Mon. Parque El Encanto in the mountains nearby, is reached by a 20-min ride aboard an 1891 German locomotive and antique carriages from the old Los Teques station, 1 km S of the town beside the highway (it is also the terminus for buses from Caracas); 3 trips weekdays, 9 weekends, starts 0900, last return 1800, adults US$1.50, children US$0.75 return.

● **Accommodation C** *Gran Casino*, Carabobo y Boyacá; central, noisy, disco, good restaurant 1100-2300, parking; many motels on the old highway from Caracas; **D** *Alemán*, Plaza Miranda, good food.

● **Places to eat** *Hípico*, in wooded suburb of Club Hípico, varied menu inc Spanish dishes, open 1100-2300, popular; *Don Blas*, in shopping centre at highway interchange for San Antonio, good steaks and fish, 1130-0100; *Hotel Los Alpes*, Km 28 on Panamericana S of city, dining room open 0800-1130, 1200-2200, closed Mon, bakery next door with hot chocolate, *empanadas* etc, good snack stop if avoiding Los Teques.

LA VICTORIA

24 km beyond Los Teques on the way down into the fertile valleys of Aragua, you can either join the Caracas-Valencia tollway or take the older road through several attractive towns such as **La Victoria** (*pop* 105,000). Venezuela's oldest bullring is here. Despite the surrounding industrial zones the city retains much of its 18th century charm; visit the beautiful Nuestra Señora de la Victoria church.

● **Accommodation A2** *Onix*, in Omni shopping complex, Urbanización Industrial Soco, in older E part of city, modern, all facilities, comfortable; **C** *El Recreo*, converted 1724 sugar hacienda on highway W of town, restaurant, pool, very pleasant.

The Quinta de Bolívar is at **San Mateo**, between La Victoria and Maracay. The Liberator spent much of his youth here and the museum is a must for anyone interested in Simón Bolívar, open 0800-1200, 1400-1700 except Mon. The rich San Mateo Church is also worth a visit. Soon after San Mateo, Highway 11 leads off S (45 km) to **San Juan de Los Morros** (page 1545).

ROUTES The new highway avoids city centres, so all that is seen of Maracay, Valencia and Barquisimeto are factories plus the huge concrete Barquisimeto Fourth Centenary Monument. Beyond Barquisimeto the mountains are dull grey until the green of the Andes.

MARACAY

Maracay (*pop* 538,620; *alt* 445m; *phone code* 043), capital of Aragua State, is a hot, humid, thriving industrial city. It is the centre of an important agricultural area, and the school and experimental stations of the Ministry of Agriculture are worth visiting.

Places of interest

In its heyday it was the favourite city of Gen Gómez and some of his most fantastic whims are still there. **Jardín Las Delicias** (on Av Las Delicias, en route to Choroní; take an Ocumare bus from terminal) with its beautiful zoo (closed Mon), park and fountain, built for his revels. The bull ring (1 block W of the Casa de la Cultura), is an exact replica of the one at Seville. The **Gómez mausoleum** (C Mariño), built in his honour, has a huge triumphal arch. The heart of the city is **Plaza Girardot**. Its colonial character has been lost to modern apartments, while the streets around the plaza are a bazaar of jewellery, clothing, electrical and shoe shops. On the plaza is the attractive, white **Cathedral**, dating back almost to the city's foundation in 1701. There is an interesting collection of prehispanic artefacts in the museum of the **Instituto de Antropología e Historia** on the S side of the plaza, revealing how densely-populated the shores of Lago de Valencia once were. Open Tues-Fri 0800-1200, Sat and Sun 0900-1300, admission free. At the opposite end of the same building is a poor history museum, with rooms dedicated to Gómez and Bolívar, open Tues-Fri 0800-1200, Sat and Sun 0900-1300, admission free. At the rear end of the building is the **Biblioteca de Historia** whose walls are lined with portraits of Bolívar. 500m E is **Plaza Bolívar**, said to be the largest such-named plaza Latin America. On one side is the **Palacio del Gobierno**, originally the *Hotel Jardín*, built by Gómez in 1924. Also here are the **Palacio Legislativo** and the modern **opera house** (1973). The park with its statues, colonnades and squirrels is a pleasant place to stroll.

Museums
The **FAV (Fuerza Aérea Venezolana) Museum** on Av Principal, Las Delicias suburb has been closed for renovation since 1992.

Local festivals
San José, 16-25 March.

Local information
● **Accommodation**
A3 *Byblos**, Av Las Delicias, a/c, good restaurant, some English spoken, good value, disco at weekend, rec; *Italo*, Av Las Delicias, T 322166, closer to town, on bus route, 4-star, a/c, lovely rooftop pool, safety deposit box; **A3** *Pipo**, Av Principal, El Castaño, pool, disco, rec restaurant (*parrillas* a speciality), in hills above the city, no public transport.

C *Princesa Plaza*, Av Miranda Este entre Fuerzas Aéreas y Av Bermúdez, T 336953, F 337972, new commercial hotel, 1 block E of Plaza Bolívar, convenient, inexpensive restaurant; **C** *Wladivar*, Av Bolívar Este 27, spacious, lots of insects.

D *Caroní*, Ayacucho Norte 197, Bolívar, a/c, hot showers, comfortable, rec; **D** *La Barraca*, Av

Bolívar Este 186, a/c, safe parking, noisy at weekends, good value.

E *Oma*, C Libertad 32, entre Av Páez y Av Miranda, with bath, run down. Budget hotels are located in the streets around Plaza Girardot. (* Bookable through Fairmont International.)

● **Places to eat**
Many excellent restaurants in the Av Las Delicias area, inc *Vroster*, grills, large portions, popular with locals, good service, rec; most are American style drive-up, fast-food outlets. *Carne Tropical*, Av Bolívar y 5 de Julio, OK; *Biergarten Park*, on E side of Plaza Bolívar, a pleasant, covered terrace with bar and restaurant, some German and Italian specialities, cheap and good. Many reliable Chinese restaurants and *loncherias*, *tascas* and inexpensive restaurants in the streets around Plaza Girardot.

● **Banks & money changers**
Banco Consolidado (American Express), Av Bolívar y Fuerzas Aéreas, in the basement of Parque Aragua shopping mall. *Cambio* in *Air Mar* travel agency, ground floor of CADA Centro Comercial, Av 19 de Abril, Local 20, 2 blocks N of Plaza Girardot, 2.5% commission.

● **Cultural centres**
Casa de Cultura, art and cultural exhibitions, 2 blocks NW of Plaza Bolívar, Mon-Fri 0800-1500.

● **Tour companies & travel agents**
Travel agency in Edif Elizoph, Av 19 de Abril Este, Rose-Marie speaks excellent English, helpful.

● **Transport**
Airport 5 km from the centre.

Buses Bus station is 2 km SE of centre; *por puesto* marked 'Terminal' for the bus station and 'Centro' for the town centre (Plaza Girardot). To Maracaibo Expresos los Llanos, US\$8; **Valencia**, US\$0.50, 1 hr; **Caracas**, US\$1.50, 2 hrs, *por puesto* US\$3; **Barinas** US\$5, 7 hrs; **Choroní** and **Ocumare/Cata** (see below); **Ciudad Bolívar**, US\$9.50, 10 hrs. To **Coro**, US\$4.55, 7¾ hrs. Oriente destinations inc **Margarita** served by Expresos Ayacucho, T 349765, daily departure to Margarita, 1400, US\$15 (inc first class ferry crossing). Many buses to every part of the country, most leave 0600-0900 and 1800-2300.

HENRI PITTIER NATIONAL PARK

The 107,800 ha **Henri Pittier National Park** (established 1937) is the oldest in the country. It extends from the N of Maracay to the Caribbean, excluding the coastal towns of Ocumare, Cata and Choroní, and S to the valleys of Aragua and the villages of Vigírima, Mariara and Turmero. A land of steep rugged hills and tumbling mountain streams, the park rises from sea level in the N to 2,430m at Pico Cenizo, descending to 450m towards the Lago Valencia. The dry season runs from Dec-Mar and the rainy season (although still agreeable) is from April-November. The variation in altitude gives great variety of vegetation, including lower and upper cloud forests. 578 species of birds have been recorded, representing 43% of all those found in Venezuela and some 5.4 different species for every square km, one of the highest densities recorded in the world. Included are no less than seven different eagles and eight kites. For further information refer to *Parque Nacional de Henri Pittier – Lista de Aves*, by Miguel Lentino and Mary Lou Goodwin, 1993. Park entrance fee US$0.65 pp.

Two paved roads cut through the Park. The Ocumare road climbs to the 1,128m high Portachuelo pass, guarded by twin peaks (38 km from Maracay). The road was built by Gómez as an escape route if things grew too hot for him. At the pass is Rancho Grande, the uncompleted palace/hotel Gómez was building when he died. It is in the shape of a question mark and is worth visiting, though now dilapidated. It is close to the migratory routes, Sept and Oct are the best months. There are many trails in the vicinity. Rancho Grande is the favoured base in the park for ornithologists and naturalists; on the 4th floor is a biological research station run by the Institute of Agronomy, Vía El Limón, Maracay, T (043) 450153, situated on the road towards El Limón and Ocumare. When visiting look for Edif 11 and ask for Iris. No permit required in advance.

Local information

● **Accommodation**

There are plenty beds available for those wishing to stay at the station, US$5 pp/night, use of kitchen facilities, bring warm sleeping bag, candles and food; nearest supplies at El Limón, 20 km before Rancho Grande.

● **Transport**

A taxi can be hired at Maracay for a day's outing in the park for about US$30 (bargain hard). Buses dep from Maracay Terminal; pay full fare to Ocumare or hitch from El Limón Alcabala.

THE ARAGUA COAST

VIA OCUMARE

The road to the coast from Rancho Grande goes through **Ocumare de la Costa** (*pop* 6,140; 48 km from Maracay), to La Boca de Ocumare and **El Playón**.

● **Accommodation & places to eat In Ocumare**: B *Montemar*, D *Casona*, next door, family-run, restaurant, D *Playa Azul*, modest. **In El Playón**: hotel-restaurants *Posada María Luisa*, T (043) 931184; E *La Abuela*, stuffy, nice restaurant and *El Playón*. Many other restaurants.

● **Buses** From Maracay, 2-2½ hrs, US$1.10.

A few kilometres E is **Bahía de Cata**, once a beautiful beach, now overdeveloped particularly at W end, basic cabins for rent on beach (D), good fish restaurant, run by Pepe (in low season, May-June, restaurants close 1530).

The smaller beach at **Catita** is reached by fishing boat ferries (10 mins, US$0.70). In **Cata** town (5 km inland, *pop* of town and beach 3,120) is the small colonial church of San Francisco; devil dancers here fulfill an ancient vow by dancing non-stop through the morning of 27 July each year. **Cuyagua** beach, unspoilt, is 23 km further on at the end of the road. Good surfing, dangerous rips for swimmers. Devil dancers here too, on movable date in July or August.

● **Buses** *Por puesto* to Cata from Ocumare US$0.70; from El Playón US$0.25 from plaza.

VIA CHORONI

The second road through the Henri Pittier National Park is spectacular and goes over a more easterly pass (1,830m), to Santa Clara de **Choroní**, a beautiful colonial town. The Fiesta de San Juan on 31 May is worth seeing.

Choroní is a good base for walking in the park. There are numerous opportunities for exploring the unmarked trails, many of them originate in picturesque spots such as the river pools, 'pozos', of El Lajao (beware of the dangerous whirlpool), and Los Colores, 6 km above Choroní. Agua Fuerte (9 km above Choroní), has an interesting cultural centre, converted from an old hydroelectric power station. From behind the entrance gate rises a trail which soon divides, one branch extends to the heights above the valley. Watch out for snakes when walking in the park. Other recommended 'pozos' are La Virgen, 10 km from Choroní and La Nevera, 11 km away. 8 km N of Choroní are two waterfalls at a dam, El Dique, where one can bathe; in Uraca village (drinks on sale), ask for directions, they are easy to find. For more challenging hikes consult Edilberto at the *Robin Hood Restaurant* (see below).

- **Accommodation** B *Hacienda La Aljorra*, breakfast and dinner inc, 9 colonial rooms in 62 ha of wooded hillside, reservations T Caracas (02) 237-7462, F 238-2436; **B** *Posada Pittier*, on road to Puerto Colombia, 8 small but immaculate rooms, a/c, good meals, Sat night sale US$10, helpful, garden, rec, T (043) 911028, or Caracas (02) 573-7848, F 577-4410; **B** *La Gran Posada*, 5 km N of Choroní on steep hillside above Maracay road, neat, pleasant bar and restaurant, short walks in the park, T Maracay (043) 549307, F 545776; **D** *Choroní*, colonial building on plaza, bed and breakfast, dinners available, basic, attractive, small, shared bath, T Caracas (02) 951-7607, F 951-0661.

- **Transport** Maracay-Choroní, beautiful journey, every 2 hrs from around 0630-1700, more at the weekend, US$1.25, 2½ hrs. Romerito, 16 km from Choroní in the heart of the park, is reached by 'Metro-Mar' bus from Puerto Colombia, 6 times a day.

PUERTO COLOMBIA

Just beyond Choroní is the fishing village of **Puerto Colombia**, where tourists flock to enjoy the dazzling white beach of Playa Grande, 5 mins' walk across the river. Bus journeys start and end here. At weekends the beach is crowded and littered; if swimming, beware the strong undertow. The usually deserted three beaches of Diario are a 50-min walk.

Excursions Many fishing boats for hire in the harbour, US$55 for a day trip to one of the several nearby beaches (although not accessible by road they can be popular, especially at weekends). Launches to Cepe, 30 mins E, US$8.50-12.50 pp depending on numbers, boats usually take 6-10 people. Beautiful unspoiled beach,

accommodation at *Posada Puerto Escondido* (T 043-413614), 4 rooms, clean, homely, owner Freddy Fisher organises fishing and diving trips.

From Puerto Colombia launches go to the colonial village of **Chuao** (30 mins, prices as above), famous in the past for its cocoa. The most reliable boatman is Amado (return trip by vehicle, US$4). The bay is very pleasant with a couple of bars. It has a festival 28-29 May, with dancing devils. The best store is out of town on the Choroní road (sells cuatros, hammocks, besides groceries); next door is an excellent Romanian/Venezuelan *panadería* with chairs outside, cheap for breakfast or snacks.

- **Accommodation In Puerto Colombia**: L3 *La Posada de Humboldt*, nr checkpoint at entrance to village, beautifully reconstructed colonial house, inc all meals (and drinks from 1800-2300!), T Caracas (02) 976-2222, cellular (016) 310608; **D** *Costa Brava*, nr Malecón, T 911057 (cheaper without bath), basic, ceiling fans, laundry facilities, good food, English spoken, family-run, Nora (who also works in *Robin Hood* restaurant) arranges trips to her home village of Chuao, rec; **D** *Don Miguel*, nr *Posada de Humboldt*, T 911081, 15 rooms, a/c, safe; nearby is **D** *Posada Alfonso*, T 911037, German owner, quiet, hammocks, laundry facilities, rec; **D** *La Montañita*, nr Malecón, T (043) 911132, nice courtyard, charming owners, packages available (B inc all meals), rec; **E** *La Abuela*, nr bridge to Playa Grande, basic, fan; **E** *Posada Los Guanches*, off C colón nr plaza, T 911209, costs more at weekends, 9 rooms, with bath, rec. Camping possible on the beach; beware of theft.

- **Places to eat** *Araguaney*, nr bridge to Playa Grande, large portions, good breakfast for US$1, main gringo hangout, changes cash and TCs at poor rates; on same street is *Tasca Bahía*, cheap, poor service, beware of salads (rooms to rent upstairs, **D**, safe, fan or a/c); *Robin Hood*, excellent food, pizza, salads etc, also vegetarian, US$3-5, rec, owner organizes 1-day treks, US$10 pp; *El Abuelo*, just before bridge to Playa Grande, very good food, prices OK.

- **Transport** Buses for Maracay dep from opp licorería beside bridge every hr or so from 0500, last one at 1700.

ROUTES 50 km to the W of Maracay the road reaches Valencia, through low hills thickly planted with citrus, coffee and sugar.

VALENCIA

Valencia (*pop* 955,000; *alt* 480m; *phone code* 041), the capital of Carabobo State, was founded in 1555. It stands on the W bank of the Río Cabriales, which empties into the Lago de Valencia (352 sq km, the second largest in the country, with no outlet, consequently it is polluted; it has also been shrinking for centuries and is 40% smaller than when Humboldt took measurements in 1800). Valencia is Venezuela's third largest city, the centre of its most developed agricultural region, and the most industrialized. Annual mean temperature 24°C; the valley is hot and humid; annual rainfall, 914 mm.

Places of interest

The **Cathedral** (open 0630-1130, 1500-1830 daily, 0630-1200, 1500-1900 Sun), built in 1580 yet remodelled to retain its original style, is on the E side of **Plaza Bolívar**, where there are sloths and iguanas in the trees. The statue of the Virgen del Socorro (1550) in the left transept is the most valued treasure; on the second Sun in Nov (during the Valencia Fair) it is paraded with a richly jewelled crown. See also **El Capitolio** (Páez, between Díaz Moreno y Montes de Oca), the **Teatro Municipal** (Colombia y Av Carabobo), the old **Carabobo University** building and the handsome **Plaza de Toros** (S end of Av Constitución beyond the ring road) which is the second largest in South America after Mexico City; it seats 27,000 spectators and features renowned international matadors during the Nov Valencia Fair. At Páez y Boyacá is the magnificent former **residence of General Páez** (hero of the Carabobo battle), now a museum where annual painting competitions take place in the Michelena Salon, open Mon-Fri, free admittance. Equally attractive is the **Casa de Célis** (1766), which houses the Museo de Arte e Historia with precolumbian exhibits; C 98 and Av 104 (open Tues-Sat 0800-1400). The **Girardot Monument** commemorates Atanacio Girardot, one of Bolívar's warriors. There are also several pleasant parks: Parques Cristóbal Mendoza, Andrés Eloy Blanco and Metropolitano have fountains, nicely-tended flower gardens and leisure activities. The landscaped **Parque Humboldt**, 6 blocks E of the Cathedral, was the terminus of the old railway to Caracas, the station now houses an art gallery and the old passenger cars have become boutiques and restaurants. There is an **Aquarium**, at the W end of C 107, which displays a selection of Latin American aquatic life and features a dolphin show at 1600 (open Tues-Sun, 0930-1800, admission US$1). There is a small, unremarkable zoo at the snackbar/restaurant behind the aquarium (open Tues-Sun 0900-2400, closed Mon). From the centre Av Bolívar extends several kilometres N towards the smart residential area of La Viña. Like its Spanish namesake, Valencia is famous for its oranges. There is a nice country club and a celebrated race track. Construction of a Metro began in late 1994. (**NB** Most of the interesting sights are closed on Mon.)

Excursions

One of the largest groups of petroglyphs in Venezuela is to be found in the **Parque Nacional Piedras Pintadas**, 22 km NE, reached by turning off the tollway at Guacara (14 km E of Valencia) and driving 6 km N on the road to Vigírima; turn left at a small blue 'Cadafe Tronconero' sign then a further 3 km. Lines of prehispanic stone slabs, many bearing swirling glyphs, march up the ridges of Cerro Pintado. Navy-blue buses run to Vigírima from Valencia at regular intervals (US$1), ask to get off at the 'Cerro Pintado' turnoff.

Near the S shore of Lake Valencia, about 34 km E of Valencia, is the regional centre of Güigüe (*pop* 44,320). At the nearby village of **La Taimata** other extensive ancient petroglyphs have been discovered. There are more sites along the W shore, and on the rocks by the Río Chirgua, reached by 10 km paved road from Highway 11 (turn N at La Mona Maraven gas station), 50 km W of Valencia. Park by the cemetery in Chirgua and walk along the E side to the river. A further 5 km past Chirgua, at the Hacienda Cariprima, is the country's only geoglyph, a remarkable 35m-tall humanoid figure carved into a steep mountain slope at the head of the valley; it is above and to the left of the ranch house.

30 km SW of Valencia on the highway to San Carlos is the site of the **Carabobo** battlefield, an impressive historical monument surrounded by splendid gardens. Two battles were fought here: although Bolívar won the first in 1814, his forces were subsequently routed by the *llaneros* of Tomás Boves ('The Butcher') and Bolívar had to flee the country. 7 years later came the famous battle which established Venezuelan independence. The view over the field from the *mirador* where the Liberator directed the battle is impressive. Historical explanations Wed, weekends and holidays. Buses to Carabobo leave from bottom of Av Bolívar Sur y C 75, or from Plaza 5 de Julio, US$0.25, ask for Parque Carabobo (1¼ hrs). Take drinks, none available at the park. Those dressed too casually will be denied entrance to the monument.

Local festivals

Late Mar, Valencia Week; 15 Nov, Patrocinales de NS de Perpetuo Socorro (1 week Valencia Fair), with bull fights.

Local information

● **Accommodation**

L2 *Intercontinental Valencia**, 5 km N of centre at C Juan Uslar, La Viña, T 211533, F 211033, luxury style resort with pool, garden and all comforts.

A1 pp *Hacienda Guataparo*, 20 mins from centre, owned by Vestey family, 9,000 ha peaceful farm, all meals, riding and mountain bikes, good birding, must be booked in advance through *Last Frontiers*, UK, T 01844-208405, F 201400; **A2** *Ucaima*, Av Boyacá 141, T 227011, F 220461, nr *Intercontinental*, suites, pool, tennis.

C *Canaima*, Av Lara con Branger, rec; **C** *Continental*, Av Boyacá 101-70, T 83014, restaurant, good value. There are many hotels across the price range on Av Bolívar, but it is a long avenue, so don't attempt to walk it; **C** *Marconi*, Av Bolívar 141-65, T 213445, a/c, helpful, safe, laundry, rec (next to a petrol station, good pharmacy and health food store), take bus or colectivo from bus station to stop after 'El Elevado' bridge.

D *Carabobo*, C Libertad 100-37, esq Plaza Bolívar, OK, with large a/c lobby; **D** *Caribe*,

T 571157/571209), a/c, safe, central, popular.

F *Palermo*, Av 97 Farriar, Italian owned, restaurant, quite good.

● **Places to eat**

Fego, Av Bolívar 102-75, rec; *El Bosque*, opp *Hotel Marconi*, cheap. *La Rinconada*, Plaza Bolívar, rec, open Sun; *Caballo Blanco*, Av 97 Farriar, cheap and good food, clean, well-lit, Italian run.

● **Banks & money changers**

Banco Consolidado (American Express), Av Bolívar Norte, Edif Exterior; *Italcambio*, Av Bolívar Norte, Edif Talia, Loc 2, bring original purchase receipt of TCs, a long way from centre in Urbanización Los Sauces, get off bus at junction with C 132.

● **Embassies & consulates**

British Vice-Consul, (Hon): Corporación Mercantil Venezolana, C Silva No 100-70, Edif Comersa, T 50411/7.

● **Laundry**

La Fuente, C Martín Tovar y Colombia, T 86657, rec.

● **Shopping**

Artesanía Típica Edy, Av Bolívar Norte, Urbanización La Alegría, opp Banco República, rec.

Bookshop: selling and trading English books between pharmacy and health food store by *Hotel Marconi* on Av Bolívar.

● **Transport**

Air 6 km SE of centre. Avensa/Servivensa flights daily to Caracas, Aruba, Barcelona, Maracaibo, Porlamar, Puerto Ordaz, San Antonio. Aserca flies to Maracaibo, Caracas, Puerto Ordaz, Porlamar and Aruba. Servivensa daily to Bogotá and Miami.

Buses Terminus 3 km E of centre, part of shopping mall Big-Low (24-hr restaurants). Entry to platforms by *ficha* (token), US$0.05. Left luggage store. Minibus to centre, frequent and cheap, but slow and confusing route at peak times; taxi US$3 to centre. To Caracas, US$1.75, *por puesto* US$3.50, Autoexpresos Ejecutivos (T cellular 014-405010), US$6, 8-9 a day; **Mérida**, 10-12 hrs, US$8; to San Cristóbal, 10 hrs, US$10; Barquisimeto, US$3.25, 3 hrs; Maracay, 1 hr, US$0.50. Puerto Cabello, US$0.70, frequent, 1 hr or so; Tucacas, US$1.40, or US$3 by frequent *por puesto* service. To Coro US$4.20, 4½ hrs. To Puerto Ordaz/Ciudad Guayana, US$12, 13 hrs. To Ciudad Bolívar, 10 hrs.

VALENCIA TO PUERTO CABELLO

The Caracas-Valencia motorway (Ruta 1 to Puerto Cabello) continues down the mountains, reaching the sea near El Palito (refinery and pier). Turn right here to Puerto Cabello. 18 km from Valencia, the road passes **Las Trincheras** (*pop* 1,350), a decaying spa with the second hottest sulphur springs in the world (98°C); there are three baths (hot, hotter, very hot), a mud bath and a Turkish bath; delightful setting. Entrance US$1.50, facilities open 0800-1800 daily. **B** *Hotel Termales Las Trincheras*★, rooms only for guests on cures, min 21 days, good restaurant open to public 1200-1600, 1800-2100, *fuente de soda* 0700-2100. Opp is **D** *Hotel Turístico*, good. Frequent buses from Valencia.

PUERTO CABELLO

55 km from Valencia, this is an industrial city and Venezuela's second most important port (*pop* 137,250; *mean temperature* 28°C; *phone code* 042).

Places of interest

The **Museo de Historia** (Mon-Fri 0800-1200, 1500-1800, Sat-Sun 0800-1200) is in one of the few remaining colonial houses (1790) on C Los Lanceros (No 43), in the tangle of small streets between the Plaza Bolívar and the seafront. The **forts of San Felipe** (1732, also called the Castillo del Libertador) and **Solano** (1765) recall Spain's strength in the Caribbean. Solano is in a military zone (access unrestricted, take a taxi, it's a long walk); the Navy runs free launches across the channel to San Felipe, which was a prison until Gómez' death in 1935. **El Aguila monument** in the colonial section (El Casco) marks the site where North American mercenaries in the pay of Francisco de Miranda were executed by the Royalists in 1806 during the War of Independence.

Excursions

A recommended hike is on the old, cobbled Camino Real from Valencia to the village of San Esteban, 8 km inland from Puerto Cabello.

A paved road runs 18 km E past the picturesque village of Borburata (pilgrimages during Holy Week) to Patanemo, both within the **Parque Nacional San Esteban** (or Miguel J Sanz),

44,000 ha abutting the Henri Pittier Park on the E and stretching almost to Puerto Cabello.

About 30 mins E on this road is La Bahía, a beautiful horseshoe-shaped beach shaded by palms (refreshment stand, changing rooms, toilets and lifeguards, but take lunch).

There are two other attractive sandy beaches, **Quizandal** (restaurant, showers, drive-in theatre, parking fee), with a coral reef, near the naval base (difficult to find, take a taxi, US$4, but you may find it hard to get one on the way back), and **Bahía de Patanemo**. The latter is a little resort tucked away in the trees (**C** *La Churuata*, family-run hotel, without bath, English, French, Spanish, Italian spoken, pool, horses, excellent food and drink, local excursions, highly recommended but very small rooms). Offshore is Isla Larga, where sunken ships make for ideal snorkelling; *lanchas* from Quizandal, US$2, 15 mins, 0700-0800, take shade, buy tickets at weekends at wharf, on weekdays seek out individual boatmen. All these beaches are very crowded and noisy at weekends. **NB** The beach to the W of Puerto Cabello is not so attractive; be careful of going beyond the bathing area as the beach is notorious for armed robbery.

Local festivals

Shrove Tuesday, carnival festivities.

Local information
● **Accommodation**

B *Balneario Caribe*, Urbina Palma Sol, on beach front, T (052) 71395, cold showers.

C *Cumboto*, on beach in old Hacienda Cumboto, a/c, pool, open-air restaurant, being renovated.

D *Miramar*, at El Palito, T 3853, with its own beach.

● **Places to eat**

Marisquería Romar, Edif Sabatino (below Ondas del Mar radio station), Av Bolívar, Rancho Grande, seafood, rec; *Briceñoven*, Paseo Malecón, 1½ blocks from Plaza El Aguila, good criollo cuisine; *Mar y Sol*, C El Mercado 6-110, facing sea, local favourite for seafood.

● **Tourist offices**

On main plaza, helpful, friendly, no English spoken, few maps or brochures.

● **Transport**
Air Airport W on highway, to Maiquetía 30 mins, Coro 40 mins, one daily non-stop; Maracaibo 80 mins, 2 daily (LAV). Taxis to the old town, US$4. Hertz agency at the airport.

Trains To and from Barquisimeto twice daily (see under Transport, page 1501 for details).

WEST OF PUERTO CABELLO

24 km W of Puerto Cabello, at the junction of the Pan-American Highway and the road to Tucacas, is **Morón** (*pop* 56,450), from where a road goes to Coro via Tucacas, 1 hr from Puerto Cabello.

Quite near Morón is the lovely beach of **Palma Sola**, 16 km long and deserted save at Easter time when Venezuelans camp out there in crowds. The water can be dangerous but the sands and palms are superb. There are hotels, many closed in the off season.

SAN FELIPE

From Morón the Pan-American Highway strikes up into the hills, a well-paved and scenic road, reaching 550m at **San Felipe** (*pop* 30,750), capital of Yaracuy State.
Local festivals 2 April, *día patronal*; 3 May, *Velorio de la Cruz de Mayo*; 23 June, San Juan.
● **Accommodation** *Turístico Río Yorubi*, pleasant, safe, good but expensive restaurant, at the end of Av Los Baños at city's edge; **D** *Hostería Colonial**, Av La Paz, pool; and others in **D** and **E** range, eg on 6A Av.

PARQUE NACIONAL MORROCOY

The **National Park of Morrocoy** comprises hundreds of coral reefs, palm-studded islets, secluded beaches and calm water for water-skiing, snorkelling, and skin-diving. The Park is reached from Tucacas in the S and Chichiriviche in the N. With appropriate footwear it is possible to walk between some of the islands. The largest, cleanest and most popular of the islands is **Cayo Sombrero**. It's very busy at weekends but has some deserted beaches, with trees to sling a hammock. **Playuela** is beautiful and better for snorkelling (beware of mosquitoes in the mangrove swamps), while **Playa del Sol** has no good beach and no palm trees. **Bocaseca** is more exposed to the open sea than other islands and thus has fewer mosquitoes. Cayo Borracho is one of the nicest islands. **NB** Much of the coral in the park was destroyed in 1996 and the potential for scuba diving has fallen greatly. Beginners will still get good value for money but there isn't much to interest advanced divers.

Adjoining the park to the N is a vast nesting area for scarlet ibis, flamingoes and herons, the **Cuare Wildlife Sanctuary**. Most of the flamingoes are in and around the estuary next to Chichiriviche, which is too shallow for boats but you can walk there or take a taxi. Birds are best watched early morning or late afternoon.

● **Access From Tucacas**: prices per boat range from US$17 return to Paiclas to US$36 return to Cayo Sombrero (max 7 per boat). Ticket office is to the left of the car entrance to the Park. Recommended boatmen are Orlando and Pepe. **From Chichiriviche**: prices per boat vary according to distance; eg, US$7.50 to Cayo Muerto, US$28 to Cayo Sombrero. There are 2 ports; one close to the centre and Playa Sur. The latter has a ticket system which is supposed to guarantee that you will be picked up on time for return trip. **NB** Playa Sur is not safe after dark; muggings reported. 3-4 hr trip US$42 per boat; 5-6 hr trip US$63; bargaining possible.

● **Camping** You may camp on the islands but must first make a reservation with Inparques (National Parks), T 800-8487, 0800-2000 Mon-Sun; reserve at least 8 working days in advance giving all details; US$2.10 pp/night, 7 nights max, pay in full in advance (very complicated procedure). Very few facilities and no fresh water; Cayo Sombrero and Paiclas have restaurants, Boca Seca has a small café (closed Mon); Sombrero, Playa Azul and Paiclas have ecological toilets. At weekends and holidays it is very crowded and litter-strewn (beware rats).

TUCACAS

Tucacas (*pop* 15,100, *phone code* 042) is a hot, busy, dirty and expensive town, 30 mins from Morón, with lots of new building in progress, where bananas and other fruit are loaded for Curaçao and Aruba.

● **Accommodation** The only accommodation within the park is **A1** pp *Villa Mangrovia* on the Lizardo Spit between Tucacas and Chichiriviche, 3 rooms, excellent food and service, charming owner, book through Last Frontiers, UK (T 01844-208405) or Journey Latin America, UK (0181 747 8315): **B** *Manaure*, Av Silva, T 830286, a/c, hot water, good restaurant;

D *La Suerte* on main street, a/c, **E** with fan, small shop; next door is **E** *Las Palmas*, with shower, basic, fan, kitchen and laundry facilities, helpful, cheap boat trips to islands, rec; opp is **E** *La Esperanza*, fan, with bath, fridge, German owner arranges trips to islands. Cheap accommodation is difficult to find, especially in high season and at weekends, hotels are generally more expensive than elsewhere in Venezuela. **Camping**: gas available in Tucacas or Puerto Cabello.

- **Places to eat** *La Entrada*, rec. Good, cheap meals for US$2 at *Marisquería Bodegón del Mar* and *Lotería Cayo Sombrero*, open weekday lunchtime only.

- **Banks & money changers** Banco Unión, cash advance on credit cards only. Hotels and Travel Agents will change money but at very low rates.

- **Sports Diving**: equipment can be hired from nr the harbour. *Submatur*, C Ayacucho 6, T 830082, F 831051, owner Mike Osborn, 4 day PADI course US$330, 1 day trip 2 dives US$65 (US$45 with own equipment); also rents rooms, **E**, fan and cooking facilities. **Bicycles**: can be hired in town.

- **Tour companies & travel agents** *Guilica*, 2 blocks up from *Hotel La Esperanza* on Av Principal, T 830939, tours to islands, also bird watching; *Valadero Tours*, round corner from *Hotel La Esperanza*, tours to islands, also Canaima, Mérida etc, fax service, will reconfirm flights.

- **Transport** Frequent *por puesto* from Valencia, US$3, bus US$1.40; Coro, US$3.

CHICHIRIVICHE

A few kilometres beyond Tucacas, towards Coro, is the popular and expensive beach resort of **Chichiriviche** (*pop* 4,700; *phone code* 042); the town is filthy and crowded at holidays and long weekends.

- **Accommodation B** *La Garza*, Av Principal, attractive, pool, restaurant, full board, cheaper without, comfortable, popular, post box in lobby, daily collection, changes cash, rec; **B** *Náutico*, T 99-35866, inc breakfast, dinner and trip to islands, good meals, fans, popular; **B** *Parador Manaure*, on C Marina, T 86121, F 86569, apartments for 5, small pool, fully-equipped kitchen; **B** *Villa Marina*, T 86503, aparthotel, good, safe, pool, rec; **C** *La Puerta*, out of town, next to the port, nice bar and restaurant, helpful owners, rec; **D** *Capri*, nr docks, shower, fan or a/c, pleasant, Italian owned, good restaurant and supermarket; **D** *Gregoria*, C Mariño, 1 block N of bus stop, fan, laundry facilities, hammocks, Spanish run, highly rec; **E** *Posada La Perrera*, C Riera, nr centre, 150 m from bus stop, quiet, fan, laundry facilities, patio,

hammocks, luggage stored, Italian owner, tours arranged, very good; **D** *Res Linda*, 1 block from docks, with or without bath, modern, Italian owners, helpful, use of kitchen, rec; **E** *Centro*, opp *Capri*, tiny rooms, fan, shared bath; **E** *Res Delia*, C Mariño 30, 1 block from *Gregoria*, T 86089, inc breakfast, 4 double rooms, shared bath, organizes tours.

- **Places to eat** *Veracruz*, at top of main street overlooking beach, good fish; *Taverna de Pablo*, opp Banco Industrial, good pizzas, seafood etc.

- **Banks & money changers** Banco Industrial, opp bus terminal on main street, the only bank in the state of Falcón which changes dollars cash, open 0930-1530. *Valadero Tours* (see below) may change cash and TCs at very poor rates.

- **Sports Diving**: *Centro de Buceo Caribe*, Playa Sur, runs PADI courses for US$360, 1 day diving trip US$65, rents equipment, rooms for rent, **D**, with cooking facilities; *Aqua-Fun Diving*, Casa El Monte, C El Sol, Virgen del Valle, T 86265, run by Pierre and Monika who speak German, English, French and Spanish, high quality dive equipment, PADI courses from beginner to pro level, excursions for divers with certification card (US$40-65 pp, US$30-55 with own equipment), 2 double rooms to rent, **D**, inc breakfast, with fan.

- **Tour companies & travel agents** *Valadero Tours*, 2 blocks from Banco Industrial on opp side, tours to islands US$16-19 pp, and to other parts of the country. Cheaper tours available with *Morrocoy Tours*, behind gas station nr *Hotel La Garza*, or from *Ulrich's Lodge* restaurant on main street towards port.

- **Transport Buses** To Puerto Cabello, frequent *por puestos*, 2 hrs, US$2; to Barquisimeto, 3 hrs; to Valera, 9 hrs. Direct buses from Valencia or take bus from Morón to Coro and get out at turnoff, 1½ hrs, US$1.

CORO

From Tucacas it is 177 km to **Coro** (*pop* 131,420; *mean temperature* 28°C; *phone code* 068), capital of the State of Falcón. Founded in 1527, Coro is clean and well kept and the colonial part is lovely with many beautiful buildings and shaded plazas. It's a good place to relax for a few days.

Places of interest

The **Cathedral**, a national monument, was begun in 1583. **San Clemente** church is built in the shape of a cross with arms pointing to the cardinal points. The wooden cross in the square in front of the church is said to mark the site of the first mass said in Venezuela and is believed to be the country's oldest such monument. It is undergoing reconstruction. There are several interesting colonial houses: **Los Arcaya**, Zamora y Federación, one of the best examples of 18th century architecture (see Museo de Cerámica below); **Los Senior**, Talavera y Hernández, where Bolívar stayed in 1827; **Las Ventanas de Hierro**, Zamora y Colón, built in 1764/65, now a museum of period furniture, open Tues-Sat 0900-1200 and 1500-1800, Sun 0900-1300, US$0.20; opp is the **Casa del Tesoro**, art gallery shows local artists' work, free entry. The **Jewish cemetery**, on C 23 de Enero esq C Zamora, is the oldest on the continent.

Museums

The **Museo de Coro 'Lucas Guillermo Castillo'**, C Zamora opp plaza San Clemente, in old monastery, good collection of church relics, recommended, open Tues-Sat 0900-1200 and 1500-1800, Sun 0900-1400, entry US$0.20; **Museo de Cerámica**, housed in Los Arcaya (see above), small but interesting, beautiful garden, open Tues-Sat 0900-1200 and 1500-1800, Sun 0900-1300, entry US$0.10; **Museo de Arte**, C 16A Talvera, between Plaza Bolívar and Cathedral, open Tues-Sat 0900-1230, 1500-1630, Sun 0900-1600, free, daily collection from post box in entrance.

Excursions

Coro is surrounded by sand dunes, **Los Médanos de Coro**, which form a **National Park**. The place is guarded by police and generally safe to visit but stay close to the entrance and on no account wander off across the dunes. Kiosk at entrance sells drinks and snacks; open till 2400. To get there take bus marked 'Carabobo' from Av Falcón, it goes past the road leading to the Médanos on Av Independencia (look out for sign saying Santa Ana de Coro); from here walk 500m to entrance, or take a taxi.

Near the village of La Vela along the Morón road rocking chairs of all sizes are made from cactus wood. On the road to La Vela, near the turnoff is the **Jardín Botánico Xerofito Dr León Croisart**, which has plants from Africa, Australia, etc, very interesting, guided tours in Spanish Mon-Fri 1430-1730, Sat 1000-1500, Sun 0830-1200, free. Take Vela bus from corner of C Falcón, opp Banco Coro, and ask to be let off at Pasarela del Jardín Botánico – the bridge over the road.

Local festivals

26 July, Coro Week; 9-12 Oct, state fair; 24-25 Dec, *Tambor Coriano* and *Parranda de San Benito* (Coro, La Vela and Puerto Cumarebo). August Regatta, Curaçao to La Vela, competitors from USA, Holland, Caribbean take part, ask at Capitanía (Port Captain's office) for information.

Local information

● Accommodation

A3 *Miranda Cumberland**, Av Josefa Camejo, opp old airport, T 523011, beautiful hotel, restaurant, swimming pool.

D *Arenas*, opp bus terminal, cold water, a/c, pool, restaurant; **D** *Falcón*, Av Los Médanos, a/c, fridge, good restaurant, 15 mins walk to centre; **D** *Intercaribe*, T 068-511811, Av Manaure entre Zamora y Urdaneta, expensive food, good, pool, a/c, rec.

E *Coro*, Av Independencia, 1/2 block from Av Los Médanos, helpful, a/c, accepts credit cards; **E** *Posada Alemania*, Av Cementos, German owner, inc good breakfast, use of kitchen, rents snorkelling gear; **E** *Roma*, on C Zamora, small rooms, fan, very basic; next door is **E** *Martín*, basic, owner organizes trips to Los Médanos and Sierra de San Luis; **E pp** *Zamora*, nearby on C Zamora, T 516005, with bath, cold water but no shortages, huge rooms with table and chairs, a/c, rec.

F *Capri*, nr Plaza Bolívar, very basic, large selection of rooms, with fans, poor maintenance and water supply.

Camping: about 30 km W of Coro at *La Cumara*, nice, good beach and dunes, US$1.20 pp.

● Places to eat

Mersi, off C Zamora, 1 block down from *Hotel Venezia*, good pizzas; *Cervecería Alhambra*, C Zamora, good, cheap; next door is *Casa Vieja*, good food, lovely atmosphere, rec; *Chupulún*, Av Manaure esq C Monzón, rec for lunch, homemade *chicha*; *El Bogovante*, Av Los Médanos, cheap and reasonable, *Rica Pizza*, in the same building, also rec; *Makokas Café*, on the boulevard between Plaza Falcón and Cathedral, rec for breakfast; *Dulzura y algo más*, corner of Alameda boulevard, rec for ice cream.

● **Banks & money changers**
Banco Unión, Av Manaure esq Av Romulo Gallegos, gives cash on Visa or Mastercard. Banco Venezuela, Plaza Talavera, Visa; otherwise try hotels and travel agents.

● **Post & telecommunications**
Telephone: CANTV is in the very fine 100 windows house; international calls from the Centro de Monedas on Plaza Sucre, opp the jail.

● **Tour companies & travel agents**
Kuriana Travel, C Zamora, opp Cathedral, Edif Avila, p 2, oficina 2B, T 522058, F 513035, ask for Mercedes Medina, who has an excellent campsite nearby (*Llano Largo*), highly rec, specializing in eco-tourism, English-speaking guide.

● **Tourist offices**
On Paseo Alameda, English spoken, helpful. Office at airport will help to find a hotel.

● **Transport**
Air Airport 10 mins' walk from centre; good restaurant on 1st floor, no money changing facilities. Flights to Caracas and Barquisimeto. Ask at airport for details of private flights to Curaçao, eg, *Aero Caribe*, US$70 one way (see also Las Piedras, below).

Buses To/from **Caracas** US$7.25, 10 hrs; **Maracaibo**, US$4, 4½ hrs, *por puesto* US$8; **Tucacas**, US$3, 3 hrs. Buses to terminal go up C Falcón (US$0.10), taxi US$1.20. Expreso Occidente has its own terminal on Av Manaure between C Libertad and C Monzón, T 512356, daily bus to San Cristóbal, 1900, 12 hrs, US$10.25, also to Caracas, Maracaibo, Valencia, Punto Fijo.

Sea The port of La Vela de Coro is called Muaco, 3 km E of town. Several small launches make trips to Curaçao weekly. Contact Oscar Guerrero at Oficina de Migración, La Vela, T 068-78922; Nelson García (T 522553), owner of *Carmen Reynely* and Douglas Zavala (T 78268), of *Trinidad II*, neither speaks English. A newly-restored ferry runs to Curaçao and Aruba (room for cars). The coaster *Don Andrés* makes a weekly run to Bonaire. Captains can be contacted through the maritime agency, 2 blocks from Plaza Bolívar.

ROUTES From Coro, there is a good but uninteresting road to Maracaibo and another paved road along the isthmus leading to the Paraguaná Peninsula.

PARAGUANA PENINSULA

AROUND PUNTO FIJO

The western side of the peninsula is industrialized, with oil refineries at Cardón and Amuay connected by pipeline to the Lago de Maracaibo oilfields. The main town is **Punto Fijo** (*pop* 89,500; *phone code* 069), a busy, unappealing place. 5 km from Punto Fijo is the residential area of **Judibana**, a much nicer place to stay, with shopping centre, cinema and restaurants. Beaches around Los Taques are at least 30 mins N of Punto Fijo, many are accessible by car, few visitors, good camping but no shade or facilities.

Zoo A very interesting zoo with exclusively Venezuelan species, many of which you will never see in the wild, is at **Comunidad Cardón Maraven**, Av 6, T (069) 403485/54222, open Tues-Fri 1400-1800, Sat-Sun 1000-1800; US$0.20; *por puestos* from Av Brasil entre C Arismendi y Falcón in Punto Fijo. Opp the zoo the **Museo de Historia Natural de Paraguaná** is due to open.

● **Accommodation & places to eat In Punto Fijo**: C *Concord Suites*, Av Jacinto Lara next to Franco Italiano supermarket, a/c, large rooms, restaurant, lounge, accepts credit cards, changes US$ cash; D *Satri*, Av Colombia 78-15, T 468419, F 464175, central, changes US$ cash; E *Comercio*, Av Bolívar con C Carnevali, nr terminal, T 465430, with bath, a/c, highly rec, good *panadería* opp. A rec and cheap restaurant is *Colonial*, C Libertad entre Colombia y Ecuador. **At Judibana**: C *Jardín*, on Av Mariscal y C Falcón, nr airport, T 461727, a/c, adequate rooms, pool, restaurant, accpets credit cards, changes US$ cash; C *Luigi*, C 10 next to Banco Venezuela, T 460970, a/c, pleasant, good restaurant, changes US$ cash, accepts credit cards.

● **Banks & money changers** Banco Provincial, Av Bolívar y C Zamora, only place to get cash on Visa or Mastercard; Banco Consolidado, C Falcón y Av Bolívar, changes Amex TCs; Casa Fukayama, Av Bolívar entre C Altagracia y Girardot, changes US$ cash.

● **Embassies & consulates** Dutch Consul in Judibana at Urb La Laguna, C Mucubaji 38, Roque Hernández, T 407211, open weekdays 1600-1700.

● **Transport Air** Airport is at **Las Piedras**: *por puestos* from C Garcés y Av Bolívar; taxi from Punto Fijo US$3.50; from Coro US$29. Avensa (T 461893), Avensa and Acerca (T 475596) fly to Aruba (US$76 return), Avensa to Curaçao (US$149 return). **Buses** Terminal on C Peninsular entre Colombia y Ecuador; *por puestos* to Pueblo Nuevo, Adícora, Coro, Valencia and Maracaibo. Long distance buses: Expresos Occidente, on C Comercio entre Ecuador y Bolivia;

Expresos San Cristóbal, C Carnevali just behind *Hotel Comercio*.

ADÍCORA

Adícora (*pop* 4,500, *phone code* 069) is a quiet little resort on the E side. The beaches are very windswept and not great but Adícora is a good base for exploring the peninsula and a must for windsurfers (there are 3 windsurfing schools in town).

Excursions Cerro Santa Ana (830m) is the only hill on the peninsula and commands spectacular views. Entrance is at El Moruy; take bus to Pueblo Nuevo (0730-0800), then take one to Punto Fijo and ask to be dropped off at the entrance to Santa Ana. From the plaza walk back to signpost for Pueblo Nuevo and take the dirt road going past a white building; 20m to the left is *Restaurant La Hija*. Walk 1 km through scrubby vegetation (watch out for dogs) to the Inparques office (closed Mon-Fri but busy at weekends). Register here before attempting the steep 3-hr climb. It's safer to go at weekends. **Laguna Boca de Caño** (also known as Laguna Tiraya) is a nature reserve N of Adícora, inland from Supi, along a dirt track normally fit for all vehicles. Bird life here is abundant, particularly flamingoes. It is the only mangrove zone on the E side of the peninsula. There are five other protected nature reserves on the peninsula, organized by a project called Bioma (information from their office at: Av Arévalo Gonzales y C Páez 10, Pueblo Nuevo, T/F 069-81048). **NB** The N part of the peninsula is a deserted place and there have been reports of armed robbery of vehicles.

● **Accommodation D** *Posada Kitzburger*, on Malecón, fan, German owners, good restaurant, rec; **E** *Hotel Montecano*, 88174, Italian-owned, meals, rec.

● **Buses** To Coro, several daily from 0630-1830, US$0.70, 50 mins; to Pueblo Nuevo and Punto Fijo, several daily from 0600-1730.

SOUTH FROM CORO

South of Coro, on the road to Barquisimeto, is the **Sierra de San Luis** which includes the **Parque Nacional Juan C Falcón**. This area is a paradise for nature lovers and recommended for hiking, with tropical forest, caves and waterfalls.

The picturesque village of **Curimagua** is best for visiting the park; jeeps leave from Coro terminal, US$1.50. The lovely colonial town of **Cabure** is the capital of the Sierra. Jeeps leave from Coro terminal, US$2.15. A few kilometres up the road is a huge series of waterfalls, Cataratas de Hueque.

The Spanish Road is a fantastic 3-hr walk through orange groves and tropical forest from Curimagua to Cabure. Take water as there is none en route. Ask at any of the hotels listed below. Also recommended is the beautiful village of **San Luis** with its interesting church, reached by taxi from Coro. Ask for the Cueva de Pereguey to the S and the falls nearby.

● **Accommodation Curimagua:** 10 km from the village is **D** *Finca El Monte*, run by Swiss couple on an ecological basis, hot water, meals, highly rec, Ernesto takes tours round the park; also *Falconese* and *Apolo* (both **C-D**, restaurant, run tours in park) and *El Trapichito* (**D**, 5 km outside Curimagua). **Cabure:** 20 mins uphill is **E** *Hotel El Duende*, T 611079/483626, a beautiful old posada, restaurant, highly rec. In town are **D** *Camino Viejo*, and **E** *La Montaña*; also restaurants, bars, bakery, supermarket, pharmacy. **San Luis:** accommodation is not easy to find; try renting a room with Señora Jovita, nr the liquor store (there is a sign outside 'se vende comida').

BARQUISIMETO

Barquisimeto, capital of Lara State, is Venezuela's fourth largest city (*pop* 723,000; *alt* 565m; *phone code* 051; *mean temperature* 25°C), with the University of Lara. The town was moved three times before its present location, founded in 1563. The city was largely destroyed by an earthquake in 1812, but is a nice enough place to spend a few days visiting the area.

Places of interest

Many fascinating corners have been preserved and a law prohibiting demolition of older buildings means that more are being restored. The **Museo de Barquisimeto**, at Av 15 between C 25 and 26, displays the town's history, also contemporary art (open Tues-Fri 0900-1700, Sat-

Sun 1000-1700, free). More old buildings are a block away around **Plaza Jacinto Lara**. The **San Francisco church** faces the plaza. On the opp side is the small **Anteneo gallery** which has temporary exhibitions in an 18th century house; Carrera 17 y C 23 (Mon-Fri 0830-1200, 1500-1830, Sat 0900-1200); also restaurant, occasional evening concerts, admission free. The **Cathedral**, C 30 y Carrera 26 (Venezuela), is a modern structure of reinforced concrete and glass. At the heart of the old city is **Plaza Bolívar**, with towering palms, a heroic statue of the Liberator and an assortment of ancient and modern buildings. Most attractive is the white-painted **Iglesia Concepción**, on the S side. Also on the plaza, the **Palacio Municipal**, Carrera 17 y C 25, is an attractive modern building. On Carrera 15 (Av Francisco de Miranda) between C 41-43 there is **Parque Ayacucho**, with lush vegetation, paths, fountains and a bronze statue of Mcal Sucre. There is a **zoo** on Av 21, reputed to be one of the best in the country; open Tues-Sun 0900-1730, US$0.55. Bus No 6 from the centre goes past the entrance. The **Concha Acústica** park is a block E of Plaza Lara.

Excursions

About 24 km SW of Barquisimeto is the busy agricultural centre of **Quíbor** (*pop* 53,525; *phone code* 053). Accommodation in *Hostería El Valle de Quíbor*, **D**, and *Hotel El Gran Duque*, **F**. Festivals on 18 Jan (NS de Altagracia) and 12 June (San Antonio de Padua). The Centro Antropológico de Quíbor exhibits work of the Indians who used to live in the region. Stop in the plaza for a *chicha de maíz* or *arroz*, a refreshing local drink. Turn right a few km before Quíbor to get to a tiny *rancho* in the village of Tintorero where 'blankets' are made from local wool. These are in bright coloured stripes or plaids and serve well as colourful rugs. They are very good value. Ask for Quíbor's renowned ceramics factory. About 18 km from Quíbor is the attractive, friendly mountain village of **Cubiro** (*pop* 4,780; *alt* 1,600m), ideal for walking. Festival in Oct (Festival de Los Sueños) writers and poets gather for spiritual peace; ask Lucy or Juan Torres at *Las Rosas Delicias* for information. There are several hotels, **D-E**. Direct buses from Barquisimeto or from Plaza Bolívar in Quíbor; better to get a jeep from Av Florencio Jiménez, 1 block from *Hotel El Duque*.

South of Quíbor and 40 mins from Barquisimeto is **Sanare** (1,360m), on the edge of the **Yacambu National Park**, where you can hike through tropical forest up the Fumerola, a sleeping volcano. **E-D** *Posada Turística El Cerrito*, Sanare, T (053) 49016, manager speaks English, small restaurant and bar, tours to local sights and Yacambu, highly recommended.

Further SW, about 30 mins drive from Barquisimeto, is **El Tocuyo** (*pop* 44,000) with a good hotel in a delightful colonial setting, **C** *La Posada Colonial*, with moderately priced restaurant.

About 60 km E of Barquisimeto is **Chivacoa** (*pop* 40,400). Passing sugar-cane fields you reach the mountain of Sorte which is the holy region for the María-Lionza cult (similar to Voodoo) practised throughout Venezuela. Celebrations are held there mostly at weekends with 12 Oct (Día de la Raza) being the most important day. There is a Catholic festival, La Inmaculada Concepción, from 8-14 December.

Another pleasant excursion from Barquisimeto by bus or car is to **Río Claro**, about 28 km S, 'where the Andes begin'. You follow a lush river valley through the mountains. There are banana plantations in the area and many dirt trails you can follow on horseback or in a 4WD vehicle. From Río Claro a gravel road (dry season only) goes to Buena Vista and on to Quíbor; good views and pleasant villages.

Local festivals

On 28 Dec (am) is the fiesta of La Zaragoza, when colourfully clad participants and children pass through the streets accompanied by music and dancing. Huge crowds are attracted to the procession of La Divina Pastora in early Jan, when an image of the Virgin Mary is carried from the shrine at Santa Rosa village into the city.

Local information
● Accommodation

L3 *Hilton**, Urb Nueva Segovia, Carrera 5 entre 5 y 6, T 536022, F 544365, excellent restaurant, pool, good value.

B *Hostería Obelisco**, Av Panamericana, T 410311, F 422133, motel-style, pool, a/c, restaurant, always full.

C *Bonifran*, Carrera 19 y C 31, T 321314, F 317509, a few blocks from centre; **C-D** *Gran Hotel Barquisimeto**, on C 59 1 block from Av Pedro León Torres (not a nice area), T 420511, F 420354, pool, restaurant, a/c; **C** *Príncipe*, Av 18 entre C 22 y C 23, T 312111, F 311731, pool, restaurant, rec.

D *Hevelin*, Av Vargas entre 20 y 21, T 523986, hot water, a/c, good value, rec; **D** *Motel El Parador*, excellent, Av Intercommunal nr El Obelisco, a great roundabout in the northern suburbs; **D** *Yacambú*, Av Vargas, between C 19 and 20, T 513022, F 522474, pool, a/c.

E-F *Avenida*, Av Vargas, No 21-124, p 2, fan or a/c; **E** *Centro*, Av 20, between C 26-27, T 314524, good value; **E** *La Casona*, Av 17 con C 27 nr Plaza Bolívar, T 315311, a/c, hot water, parking, restaurant, rec; **E** *Lido*, Av 16 between C 26 and 27, a/c, bath; **E** *Savoy*, Av 18 entre C 21 y 22, T 315134, a/c, OK. Many small cheap hotels nr the bus terminal, but not a nice area: **E** *Yaguara*, basic.

● Places to eat
Barquipan, C 26 entre Carreras 17 y 18, good breakfasts, snacks; vegetarian retsaurant opp; *Majestic*, Av 19 con C 31, good breakfast and vegetarian.

● Banks & money changers
Banco Provincial, Av 20 entre C 31 y 32 and C 23 entre Avs 18 y 19, for Visa and Mastercard; also **Banco de Lara**, Av 20 entre C 27 y 28, and **Banco Unión**, Av Vargas entre C 21 y 22. **Capital Express**, Av Los Leones, Centro Comercial Paseo, next to *Caffe 90*, changes US$ cash at low rates; also **Turisol**, Av Vargas entre C 20 y 21, next to *Hotel Hevelin*, for Amex.

● Hospitals & medical services
Health clinic: Clínica Rozetti, efficient and not expensive.

● Post & telecommunications
Post Office: Av 17 con C 25.
Telephone: C 30 entre Avs 24 y 25.

● Tourist offices
Corpoturismo Edo Fundalara, on Av Libertador.

● Tour companies & travel agents
Turisol (address above), for local day trips; *Danesa Tours*, Av 20 entre C 28 y 29, T/F 327227, will arrange guide.

● Transport
Air Jacinto Lara, international, 8 km SW of the centre, 10 mins, US$3 by taxi. Local buses stop outside, US$0.12. Avensa flies daily to Miami via Maracaibo; flights also to Caracas (also Servivensa, Aeropostal and Aserca), Maracaibo, San Antonio, Coro, Porlamar and Valencia.

Trains To Puerto Cabello (175 km, 2¾ hrs) twice a day in each direction, tickets sold 2 hrs before departure, timetable unreliable, many extra trains at carnival time, but always full, bad track but a worthwhile experience; daily trains run from Yaritagua en route to/from Acarigua for Puerto Cabello.

Buses Terminal is on the edge of the city at Carrera 25 and C 44: to **Mérida**, 3 to 4 a day, at 1020 and several between 2000 and 0200, 8 hrs via Agua Viva and El Vigía, US$7; to **Acarigua** (see page 1544), 1 hr, US$1.75. To **Valera** *por puesto*, 3½ hrs, US$5. To **Tucacas** every 2 hrs; to **Coro** every 2 hrs, 7 hrs, US$5. To **Caracas**, US$5, 6 hrs. For **renting cars** (Volkswagen best), Av Pedro León Torres y C 56, also at airport.

75 km past Barquisimeto the Lara-Zulia motorway to Maracaibo forks off to the right (Caracas-Maracaibo 660 km), through the cattle farming centre of **Carora** (*pop* 82,500). The town has a nice colonial centre with a very pleasant Plaza Bolívar. It is possible to visit the Bodega Pomar Winery on the Lara-Zulia road, 1 km out of town. Call beforehand to organize your trip, T (052) 212191, F 341014. *Madre Vieja* and *Katuka* are the best hotels, each with a good restaurant and good value (in *Madre Vieja* you can sit outside, under a very old vine).

The small village of **Altagracia** where the grapes are grown, is nearby. Cross the bridge next to Plaza Bolívar and it is about 20 km away. In the village there are some typical restaurants serving mixed grill, highly recommended (iguana is on the menu).

The Lowlands of Maracaibo

V ENEZUELA'S main oil producing zone has the city of Maracaibo as its centre, on the western shore of the entrance to the Lago de Maracaibo. To the north is the border crossing to Colombia on the Guajira Peninsula.

The Lowlands of Maracaibo, lying in the encircling arms of the mountains, are more or less windless and extremely humid. Average annual temperature is higher than anywhere else in Latin America. Rainfall decreases steadily from the foothills of the Sierra Nevada to the coast. In these lowlands is the semi-salt Lago de Maracaibo, of about 12,800 sq km, 155 km long and in places over 120 km wide. It is joined to the sea by a waterway, 3 to 11 km wide and 55 km long, at the mouth of which is the bar of Maracaibo.

Once dependent on fishing and the transport of coffee across the lake from the Sierra, the discovery of one of the world's greatest oilfields in 1914, has brought a great transformation, both in appearance (a forest of oil derricks covers the shore swamps and some of the lake), and in prosperity. The Lara-Zulia motorway reaches Maracaibo by the beautiful 8 km long Gen Rafael Urdaneta bridge, which has the longest pre-stressed concrete span in the world.

MARACAIBO

Venezuela's second largest city (*pop* 1,218,800; *phone code* 061), on the north-western shore of Lago de Maracaibo, capital of the State of Zulia, is Venezuela's oil capital: 70% of the nation's output comes from the Lake area. It's a modern commercial city with wide, clean streets and, apart from the intense heat, is pleasant to walk around, especially around Plaza Bolívar.

CLIMATE The hottest months are July, Aug and Sept, but there is usually a sea breeze from 1500 until morning. The mean temperature of 28°C and average humidity of 78% are most felt at sea level.

Places of interest

The traditional city centre is **Plaza Bolívar**, on which stand the **Cathedral** (at E end), the **Casa de Gobierno**, the **Asamblea Legislativa** and the **Casa de la Capitulación** (or Casa Morales, a colonial building and national monument, tour free, copies of Tovar y Tovar paintings of Bolívar's life and times). The Casa has an extensive library dedicated to the Liberator, open Mon-Fri, 0800-1600. Next door is the 19th century **Teatro Baralt**. Running W of Plaza Bolívar is the **Paseo de las Ciencias**, a 1970s development which levelled all the old buildings in the area. Only the **Iglesia de Santa Bárbara** stands in the Paseo. **Calle Carabobo** (1 block N of the Paseo de las Ciencias) is a very good example of a colonial Maracaibo street. One block S of the Paseo is **Plaza Baralt** on Av 6, stretching to C100 and the old waterfront market (**Mercado de Pulgas**). The **Centro de Arte de Maracaibo Lía Bermúdez** is housed in the 19th century Mercado de Pulgas building, where the work of national artists is displayed (it is a/c, a good place to escape the midday heat). The museum also has a good historical display of photographs of Maracaibo and makes a good starting place for a walking tour of the city centre. The new part of the city round **Bella Vista** and towards the University is in vivid contrast with the **old town** near the docks. The latter, with narrow streets and brightly-painted, colonial style adobe houses, is hardly changed from the last century, although many buildings are in an advanced state of decay. The buildings facing **Parque Urdaneta** (3 blocks N of Paseo de las Ciencias) have been well-restored. Also well-preserved are the church of **Santa Lucía** and the streets around. This old residential area is a short ride (or long walk) N from the old centre. **Parque La Marina**, on the shores of the lake, contains sculptures by the Venezuelan artist, Jesús Soto depicting scenes from the Battle of the lake in 1823 which consolidated the country's independence. More of his work can be seen in the **Galería de Arte Brindhaven** (free), nr Santa Lucía, where he is often in residence.

Excursions

Paseo de Maracaibo, or del Lago, is a lakeside park built in the late 1970s, near the *Hotel del Lago*. It offers walks along the shores of the Lake at its narrowest point, spectacular views of the Rafael Urdaneta bridge and of oil tankers sailing to the Caribbean. There are also places to sit and watch life go by. The park attracts a wide variety of birds. To get there, take a Milagro bus northbound from the Mercado de los Guajiros, and ask the driver to let you off at the entrance, which is well-marked.

From the port, you can take a ferry to Altagracia for US$0.40, the first at 0645, 25 mins. Return the same way or take a minibus (US$0.55), travelling through exotic scenery for almost an hour and crossing the Gen Urdaneta bridge.

Local festivals

Festivals at Cabimas on the E shore of the lake, *gaitas* (see **Music and Dance**) 1-6 Jan; Virgen del Rosario, 5 Oct; 18 Nov, NS de Chiquimquira (La Chinita), processions, bullfights – the main regional religious festival. At Lagunillas, San Isidro processions and games, 15 May.

Local information

● **Accommodation**

It is difficult to obtain rooms without making reservations well in advance.

L3-A2 *Hotel del Lago Intercontinental**, El Milagro, Av 2, T (061) 924022, F 914551, T 924180 for reservations, PO Box 90, plastic atmosphere, pool open to non-residents; **A1** *Maruma Internacional**, Circunvalación No 2, T 972911, F 981258, old and new sections, hot water, a/c, reasonable restaurant; **A2** *Kristoff**, Av 8 entre C 68 y 69, T 972911, F 980796, a/c, nice pool open to non-residents US$6, disco, laundry service, restaurant, changes US$ cash at terrible rates.

B *Gran Hotel Delicias**, Av 15 esq C 70, T 976111, F 973035, a/c, rec restaurant, good value, pool, disco, accepts credit cards, changes dollars.

D *Doral*, C 75 y Av 14A, T 981792, a/c, helpful, rec.

E *Almería*, Av 3H No 74-78, T 914424, a/c, with bath, hot water; **E** *Astor*, S side of Plaza de la República, Bella Vista, T 914510, a/c, popular; **E** *Europa*, C 93 y Av 4, a/c, run down but OK; **E** *Falcón*, Av 4, No 84-158, T 220967, a/c, laundry facilities; **E** *Novedades*, C 78 (also known as Dr Portillo) No 9-43, Bella Vista, T 75766, a/c, shower, safe, small rooms, safe parking, basic. Also in Bella Vista: **E** *Roma I*, C 86, 3F-76, T 220868, a/c, restaurant, laundry service; **E** *San Martín*, Av 3Y (San Martín) con C 80, T 915097, a/c, restaurant next door, accepts credit cards.

● **Places to eat**

Most are closed on Sun. *Pizzería Napoletana*, C 77 nr Av 4, excellent, closed Tues; *Mi Vaquita*, Av 3H con C 76, Texan steak house, best meat in town, popular with locals, good atmosphere, rec; *El Carite*, C 78, No 8-35, T 71878, excellent selection of fish and seafood, delicious and moderately-priced; *La Habana*, Av Bella Vista (Av 4) nr C 76, good salads and milkshakes, open 24 hrs; *La Friulana*, C 95 con Av 3, good cheap meal, repeatedly rec, closes 1900; *San José*, Av 3Y (San Martín), 82-29, good; *El Gaucho*, Plaza Banderas, Argentine-style, good. Many restaurants on *palafitos* (stilts) in Santa Rosa de Agua district, good for fish (*por puesto* US$0.20 to get there). There are good restaurants around the Plaza de la República (C77/5 de Julio and Av 31, Bella Vista), such as *Chips*, Av 31 opp Centro Comercial Salto Angel, regional fast food, *tequeños* and *patacones*, rec. *Larga Vida*, Av 13A between C 75 and C 76, health food store; *Bambi*, Av 4, 78-70, Italian run with good capuccino, pastries, rec, cheap; 1 block away, nr C 76, is *Panadería Bella Vista*, rec for *quesillo* and *tiramisu*. Many good clubs and restaurants on C 72, eg *Malanga Café*, with outdoor patio and live music most nights; *Pizza Pizza*, for good pizza and other Italian foods. On C Carabobo (see above) *Zaguán* serves traditional regional cooking at reasonable prices.

● **Banks & money changers**

Banco Mercantil, on corner of Plaza de la República, cash advance on Visa and Mastercard; also at Banco Unión; Av 4 y C 78. Best for dollars and TCs is *Casa de Cambio de Maracaibo*, C 78 con Av 9B; *Turisol*, Av 4 (Bella Vista) con C 67 (C Acosta), Amex rep; *Citibank*, Av 15 (Las Delicias) con C 77 (5 de Julio) for Citicorp TCs. All banks shut at 1630, exchange am only. All Thomas Cook transactions have to be verified in Caracas. *Cambio* at bus terminal will change Colombian pesos into bolívares at a poor rate.

● **Embassies & consulates**
Colombia, Av 3Y (San Martín) 70-16 nr Av 4/Bella Vista (T 921483, F 921729), 10 km from centre, take bus or *por puesto* (Bellavista) out of town on Av 4 to C 70; open Mon-Fri, 0700-1300 prompt, 60-day visa in 5 hrs, no questions, no tickets required (better than Caracas). **Spain**, Av Sabaneta y C El Prado No 9B-55, T 213445. **Denmark**, Av 15, No 88-78, Las Delicias, Apdo 301, T (61) 591579, F 595763, open 0800-1200, 1400-1800. **France**, Av 3F y C70, T 912921, F 77671; **Germany**, C77 No 3C-24, Edif Los Cerros p 9, T 912406, F 912506; **UK**, Av 9B No 66-146, T 73745, F 82794; **Netherlands**, Av 3C y C67, La Lago, Unicentro Virginia, office 6, p 2, T/F 922885; **Italy**, Av 3H No 69-79, T 72182, F 919903; **Norway**, Km 1 Carretera a Perijá, Sector Plaza Las Banderas-Los Haticos, T 616044, F 616555; **Sweden**, Av 15 Las Delicias No 88-78, T 595843, F 595763; **Switzerland**, Av 9B No 75-95, T 77710, F 71167.

● **Hospitals & medical services**
Doctors: *Dr García, Hospital Coromoto*, Av 3C and C 72, T 912222, speaks English, as does *Dr Carlos Febres*, a dentist, Av 8, No 84-129, Mon-Fri 0900-1200, 1500-1800, T 221504.

● **Laundry**
Lavandería Laza, C 72 nr Av 3H, Bella Vista, rec.

● **Places of worship**
Anglican Church: Christ Church, Av 8 (Santa Rita) a C 74.

● **Post & telecommunications**
Post Office: Av Libertador y Av 3.
Telecommunications: Servicio de Telecomunicaciones de Venezuela, C 99, esq Av 3, payphones for local calls only, CANTV, C 76 nr Av 3E, Bella Vista, open 0700-2330, Mon-Fri. If offices are closed, phone cards are available at the desk of the nearby *Hotel Astor*, S side of Plaza de la República.

● **Security**
The old part of the city is not safe after 1700 and even requires care in daylight.

● **Shopping**
Fin de Siglo department stores sell records, tapes, posters of local sights. *Foto Bella Vista*, Av Bella Vista, C 78, rec service. The outdoor market, *Las Pulgas*, is enormous, mostly clothes, shoes, and general household goods, S side of C 100 entre Av 10 y 14. *Centro Comercial Costa Verde*, Av 4 (antes Bella Vista), good new shopping complex. *El Mercado de las Indias Guajiras*, open market at C 96 y Av 2 (El Milagro), a few crafts, some pottery, hammocks, etc. Most of the shops on C Carabobo sell regional crafts, eg *La Salita*.

Bookshops: *Librería Universal*, Av 5 de Julio y Av 4, maps, stationery, Caracas newspapers but poor selection of books; *Librería Cultural*, Av 5 de Julio, best Spanish language bookstore in town; *Librería Italiana*, Av 5 de Julio, Ed Centro América, postcards and foreign publications (inc US). Good bookshop in Arrivals lounge of airport. Staff at the public library, Av 2, are helpful to tourists.

● **Transport**
Local *Por puestos* go up and down Av 4 from the old centre to Bella Vista. Ruta 6 goes up and down C 67 (Cecilia Acosta). The San Jacinto bus goes along Av 15 (Las Delicias). Buses from Las Delicias also go to the centre and terminal. From C 76 to the centre *por puestos* marked 'Las Veritas' and buses marked 'Ziruma'. Look for the name of the route on the roof, or on the front window, passenger's side. A ride from downtown to Av 5 de Julio in a 'Bella Vista' *por puesto* costs US$0.20. **Taxis**: US$1.50-2. *Luquis Taxis* will do city tours for US$6.50/hr; on Av 14A entre C 76 y 77, nr *Hotel Doral*, T 971556.

Air Airport, La Chinita, is 25 km SW of city centre: terminal has international and national lounges. Shops, inc bookshop selling city map; *casa de cambio* open 0600-1800 daily, no commission; Banco Venezolano; car hire offices outside. Taxis charge between US$5-6, there are no *por puestos*. There are frequent flights with Aserca, Avensa, Servivensa and Aeropostal to Maiquetía, Valencia, Barquisimeto, Las Piedras, Mérida, San Antonio (be early to guarantee seat), Barcelona, Porlamar and Puerto Ordaz. International flights to Maracaibo with Curaçao and Aruba (Servivensa) and Miami (Servivensa).

Buses Bus station is 15 mins walk from centre, 1 km S of the old town. Ask for buses into town, local services are confusing. There are several fast and comfortable buses daily to **Valencia** (US$7.75 by Expresos del Lago), **San Cristóbal** (US$6.50, 6-8 hrs, *por puesto*, US$19), **Barquisimeto**, 5½ hrs inc police checks (US$5), **Coro** US$4, 4 hrs, and **Caracas** (US$12, 10-13 hrs, *por puesto* US$24). To **Mérida**, 2300, US$7, 5-7 hrs, or *por puesto*, US$10, 6½ hrs.

NORTH OF MARACAIBO

About 1 hr N is the Río Limón. Take a bus (US$0.40, from terminal or Av 15 between

C 76 and 77) to **El Moján**, riding with the Guajira Indians as they return to their homes on the peninsula. Near the bus terminal is a jetty from where launches go to the Isla San Carlos (US$1.20 each way). The restored Castillo San Carlos, built in the late 17th century, protected the entrance to Lake Maracaibo with mixed success. There are guided tours of the fort (US$0.40). You can swim on the beach nearby. The last launch back to El Moján leaves between 1600 and 1700; be ready to leave the island by 1530.

SINAMAICA LAGOON

From El Moján, *por puestos* go to **Sinamaica** (US$0.80; taxi US$3). From there another can be taken to the lagoon (US$0.50) at the small port of Puerto Cuervito. Hire a boat (US$17/boat for 1 ½ hrs on the lake), and go up the river for an hour to La Boquita (*pop* 2,500) where Indians live in houses made of woven reed mats built on stilts (concrete). There are also excursions by boat from Maracaibo to the Sinamaica lagoon, ask for *el libro de reclamaciones* which should give the maximum official price. Sinamaica has an agricultural show on 15-21 August.

Beyond Sinamaica, a paved road leads to the border with Colombia. Along the way you see Guajira Indians, the men with bare legs, on horseback; the women with long, black, tent-shaped dresses and painted faces, wearing the sandals with big wool pom-poms which they make and sell for US$2, as against the US$7-10 in the tourist shops. The men do nothing: women do all the work, tending sheep and goats, selling slippers and raising very little on the dry, hot, scrubby Guajira Peninsula. There is an interesting Guajira market at Los Filudos, 2 km beyond Paraguaipoa, where you can buy the local tent-dress (manta) for about US$5-10, depending on the quality, but much cheaper than in Maracaibo. Because of the proximity of the border, it is best not to stay in this area after 1600.

FRONTIER WITH COLOMBIA

The frontier opens at 0800; formalities said to slow on Venezuelan side. Ask for 90 days on entering Colombia. Venezuela is 1 hr ahead of Colombia.

● **NB**
Bus passengers from Maracaibo to Maicao have to pay US$5 at a booth in Maracaibo bus terminal. Receipt must be shown at the border.

● **Entering Venezuela**
To enter Venezuela by land a visa is essential despite what may be said by Venezuelan Consulates. Only 72-hr transit visas are issued at this border; *tarjetas de turismo* must be obtained from DIEX in Maracaibo – not an easy task. Get a visa in advance. You can expect vigorous searches at the border and en route to Maracaibo.

● **Colombian consulate**
See under Maracaibo, above.

● **Buses**
Maracaibo-Maicao, with Expreso Maicao or Expreso Gran Colombia, US$3.50, 3 hrs, from 0500-1600, leaves when full, risk of ambush by bandits/guerrillas. *Colectivos* US$5 pp, 6 in car.

SOUTH TO THE ANDES

MACHIQUES

Machiques (*pop* 43,200) is on the fast Ruta 6 from Maracaibo via La Fría to San Cristóbal, and has the good **D** *Motel Tukuko*; **E** *Hotel Italo Zuliano*. Machiques celebrates the Fiesta de San José on 19 Mar, and the Feria de Virgen del Carmen, with agricultural shows, on 14-18 July.

On the W side of the lake, between the rivers Santa Ana and Catatumbo, a large area of swampland is crossed by the road to La Fría. The swamp is inhabited by the Motilones, who, until 1960, refused to have dealings either with white men or other Indians. The southern border of the Motilones' territory, the Río Catatumbo, is famed for its almost nightly display of lightning for which there is, as yet, no accepted explanation and which caused it to be known in the old days as 'The Lighthouse of Maracaibo'. The easiest mission to reach is Los Angeles del Tocuco, 51 km from Machiques (*por puesto* US$0.80, 1¼ hrs), where they welcome visitors; it helps to take a present, such as dried milk. Shop-cum-restaurant, family-run, simple, filling food, accommodation F.

To the Sierra Nevada de Mérida or the State of Trujillo from Maracaibo, return over the lake and turn sharp right through Cabimas (**A2** *Cabimas Internacional**, T 45692, luxury, pool, discotheque), Lagunillas (**D** *Hotel Lagunillas**, T 21423, pool), Bachaquero and Mene Grande, all oil towns, to rejoin the Pan-American Highway at **Agua Viva**.

The Pan-American Highway from Agua Viva is asphalted and runs along the foot of the Andes through rolling country planted with sugar or bananas, or park-like cattle land. At **Sabana de Mendoza**, 24 km S of Agua Viva (*Hotel Panamérica*, good, a/c), a road branches to Valera for the Sierra Nevada.

The Pan-American goes straight on, with plenty of restaurants, hotels and filling-stations, especially at Caja Seca and **El Vigía** (*pop* 70,290; hotels include **E** *La Suiza*, Av 15, opp bus terminal, recommended). Here the road from Mérida to Santa Bárbara (Zulia) crosses the Río Chama by a fine bridge over 1 km long. Flights diverted from Mérida often land at El Vigía. **Santa Bárbara** (56 km NW) is a milk, meat and plantain producing centre, with an important annual cattle show.

From El Vigía, the road continues fairly flat until **La Fría** (*pop* 26,000), to join Ruta 6 from Maracaibo. In La Fría the family-run **E** *Hotel Turística*, on main plaza, basic but clean, is recommended, as is **E** *Hotel Miramar*, C 6-50, near Plaza Bolívar, T (077) 41790. From La Fría the Highway climbs through **San Juan de Colón** to San Cristóbal (see page 1518).

The Sierra Nevada de Mérida

VENEZUELA'S high Andes offer hiking and mountaineering, and fishing in lakes and rivers. The main tourist centre is Mérida, but there are many interesting villages, often with colonial churches. The Pan-American Highway runs through the Sierra entering Colombia at the notorious town of Cúcuta.

The **Sierra Nevada de Mérida**, running from S of Maracaibo to the Colombian frontier, is the only range in Venezuela where snow lies permanently on the higher peaks. Several basins lying between the mountains are actively cultivated; the inhabitants are concentrated mainly in valleys and basins at between 800 and 1,300m above sea level. The three towns of Mérida, Valera and San Cristóbal are in this zone. There are two distinct rainy and dry seasons in the year. Two crops of the staple food, maize, can be harvested annually up to an elevation of about 2,000m.

VALERA

Roads from Agua Viva and Sabana de Mendoza go to **Valera**, the most important town in the State of Trujillo (*pop* 119,400;

phone code 071). In Valera you can choose between two roads over the Sierra, either via Timotes and Mucuchíes to Mérida, or via Boconó and down to the Llanos at Guanare. Agricultural and industrial fair in August.

Local information
● **Accommodation**
B *Camino Real*, Av Independencia, nr terminal, T 53795, F 51704, a/c, restaurant, bar, parking.

C-B *Valera**, Av Maya, 4 blocks from terminal, T 57511, F 57937, inc taxes, a/c, restaurant, parking.

D *Albergue Turístico*, Av Independencia, nr terminal, T 56997.

E pp *Miramar*, C 9 No 5-38, T 316293, with bath, restaurant. *Hidrotermal San Rafael*, 4 km off road between Valera and Motatán, notable for its hot water springs and the thermal bath.

● **Places to eat**
There are lots of Italian restaurants, eg *Aurora*, Av Bolívar between C 9 and 10, good, cheap; *Italio* opp *Hotel Valera*, rec; *Fuente de Soda Bulevar*, Av Bolívar between C 11 and 12, good breakfast and juices.

● **Banks & money changers**
Banco Consolidado, Av Bolívar con C 5, changes Amex TCs, no commission; ATM at Banco Unión nearby. Banco de Venezuela, C 7 con Av 10, cash on Visa and Mastercard, very efficient and helpful.

● **Transport**
Air To Caracas, via Barquisimeto, daily with LAI, book well in advance (eg at *Teresita Viajes*, C 8 entre Avs 9 y 10, T 55997).

Buses Terminal on the edge of town. To Boconó, US$2.25, 3 hrs; to Trujillo, regular *por puestos*, ½ hr, US$0.45; to Caracas, 9 hrs, US$7.50 (direct at 2230 with Expresos Merida); to Mérida, 4 daily with Empresa Barinas (0800, 1000, 1300, 1500), US$2.60, 4½ hrs; *por puestos* to Mérida, 3 hrs US$5.20, leave when full; to Maracaibo, *micros* every ½ hr until 1730, 4 hrs, US$3.85.

TRUJILLO

From Valera a road runs via the restored colonial village of **La Plazuela** to the state capital, **Trujillo** (*pop* 44,460; *alt* 805m; *phone code* 072). This beautiful historic town consists basically of two streets running uphill from the Plaza Bolívar. It's a friendly place with a warm, sub-tropical climate.

Places of interest
The **Centro de Historia de Trujillo**, on Av Independencia, is a restored colonial house, now a museum. Bolívar lived there and signed the 'proclamation of war to the death' in the house. A monument to the **Virgen de la Paz** (47m high) was built in 1983; it stands at 1,608m, 2½ hrs walk from town. Jeeps leave when full from opp *Hotel Trujillo*, 20 mins, US$0.55 pp; open 0900-1700, US$0.75 entry, good views to Lake Maracaibo but go early.

Local information
● **Accommodation & places to eat**
C *Trujillo*, 1 km uphill from Plaza Bolívar on Av Independencia, T 33952, a/c, pool, restaurant, international phone calls; **E** *Los Gallegos*, Av Independencia 5-65, T/F 33193, with bath, hot water, highly rec; **E** *Palace*, Av Independencia nr plaza, crumbling old building, basic, cold water. *Tasca Restaurant La Gran City*, Av Independencia, good, US$4-5 main dish; *Café D'Adria*, next to *Hotel los Gallegos*, good lunches and breakfast.

● **Banks & money changers**
Banco Provincial, on main plaza, cash on Visa and Mastercard; Banco de Venezuela, 1 block down from cathedral, has ATM.

● **Transport**
To Caracas, 9 hrs, US$7.50, at 2000, 2100 and 2130; to Barinas and Mérida, at 0700; to Boconó, regular *por puestos*, US$1.50.

TRUJILLO TO BOCONO

From Trujillo there is a high, winding, spectacular paved road to **Boconó** (*pop* 39,220), a town built on steep mountain sides and famed for its crafts. The Centro de Acopio Artesanal Tiscachic is highly recommended for *artesanía* (turn left just before bridge at entrance to town and walk 300-400m). 27 km before Boconó, just off the road, is the village of **San Miguel de Boconó**; colonial church built 1597; festival of Romería de los Pastores de San Miguel 4-7 Jan (**E** *Hostería San Miguel*, inc breakfast, homely; **E** *Los Valles*, 2 km on road to Boconó, cabañas, nice views). *Por Puestos* dep frequently to Trujillo and Valera from C Páez.

● **Accommodation F-E** pp *Colonial*, on plaza, with bath, hot water, restaurant, basic; **E** *Venezia*, ½ block uphill from plaza, with bath, hot water, restaurant; **E** *Italia*, 1 block downhill from plaza, with bath, cold water, basic, cheap meals. *Estancia de Mosquey*, at Mosquey, 10 km from Boconó towards Biscucuy, family run, great views, good beds, good restaurant, pool, rec.

From Boconó you can continue down to **Guanare** (bus US$2, 3½ hrs) in the Llanos via **Biscucuy** (*pop* 27,000).

● **Accommodation & places to eat In Guanare**: D *Colina*, nr the river at bottom of town, motel-style, comfortable, restaurant; E *Colonial*, Av Miranda; E *Vega del Río**, restaurant; E *Venezia*, with shower, rec. *Turística La Casa Vieja*, good food, good value, lots of old photos of the area; *El Paisano*, popular restaurant.

NIQUITAO

The small town of **Niquitao**, founded 1625 (*pop* 4,400) is 1 hr by public transport SW of Boconó. It is still relatively unspoilt, colonial-style, celebrating many festivals, particularly Holy Week, when paper is rolled out in the streets for children to create a giant painted mural. Excursions can be made to the Teta de Niquitao (4,007m) 2 hrs by jeep, the waterfalls and pools known as Las Pailas, and a nearby lake. Southwest of Niquitao, by partly-paved road is **Las Mesitas**; continue up a steep hill towards **Tuñame**, turn left on a good gravel road (no signs), cross pass and descend to Pueblo Llano. From the bottom, at 1,600m, you can climb to the National Park of Sierra Nevada at 3,600m, passing Santo Domingo. There is good hiking in the area. Johnny Olivio at the video shop on Plaza Bolívar is a knowledgeable guide.

● **Accommodation** D *Posada Turística de Niquitao*, T (072) 53111/31448 and D *Na Delia*, T (072) 52113/52522, on a hill ½ km out of town, both have restaurants. *La Estancia*, T 52499/52888, Plaza Bolívar, owner Golfredo Pérez, helpful, kind, knows area well, excellent pizzas; F pp *Posada Don Jérez*, corner of Plaza Bolívar, a few rooms, simple local food; *Posada Mama Chepi*, family atmosphere, good cooking; also F pp *Posada Guirigay*. **Pueblo Llano**: E *La Gruta*, good, cheap restaurant, rec. *El Campesino*, for good pizza. There is a good campsite with shelters and cooking-fire places in **Parque Las Piedras**, ask Mérida-Barinas bus driver to stop, about 2 km walk from road, US$1 to Mérida (3½ hrs) or Barinas (1½ hrs).

VALERA TO MERIDA

40 km beyond Valera on a good paved road is **Timotes** (*pop* 10,550), surrounded by lush, forested hills. Bus from Valera, US$1.50.

● **Accommodation** C *Las Truchas*, very nice, good food; D *Carabay*, family run, good rooms, excellent restaurant; E *Posada Caribe*, good value, restaurant.

PICO EL AGUILA

The road climbs through increasingly wild, barren and rugged country and through the windy pass of **Pico El Aguila** (4,007m, best seen early in the morning, frequently in the clouds). This is the way Bolívar went when crossing the Andes to liberate Colombia, and on the peak is the statue of a condor. At the pass is the tourist restaurant *Páramo Aguila*, reasonably priced with open fire; also food stalls, souvenir sellers and horses for hire. Across from the monument is a small chapel with fine views. A paved road leads from here 2 km up through *frailejones* to a CANTV microwave tower (4,118m, grand view). It continues N as a lonely track to the Piñango lakes (45 km), noted for their large trout, and the traditional village of Piñango (2,480m). Splendid views of high altitude lakes and even to Lake Maracaibo. The Aranjo family provides food and lodging and hires horses. Cyclists should note that the road from Pico El Aguila is downhill all the way until Km 718, before Mérida, with lots of posadas, hostels and campsites en route.

SANTO DOMINGO

On the spectacular road up from Barinas to Mérida, before the Sierra Nevada National Park, is the town of **Santo Domingo**, (*pop* 3,200). There are good handicraft shops and fishing.

● **Accommodation** B *Las Cabañas* for small groups, or *Cabañas Halcón de Oro* (cheap rooms for rent next door, opp *Panadería Santo Domingo*). The beautiful C *Hotel Moruco**, T (073) 88155, F 88225, is a little further out in a lovely setting, good value, alt 2,300m, food very good, bar expensive, reservations can be made through *Hotel Río Prado* in Mérida; D *Hotel La Trucha Azul*, open fireplace, rec;

D *Santo Domingo*, 20 mins from town centre, log cabins for up to 4 people, log fireplace, games room with pool, table tennis, hot water, excellent restaurant with good selection of wines. *Restaurant Brisas de la Sierra*, rec. Sr Izarra's grilled chicken, simple but highly rec, also sells trout, US$2.

● **Tourist offices** On the right, leaving town; a 10-min hike from centre.

● **Buses** Buses or busetas pass through in either direction at approximately 2-hr intervals through the day. Mérida 2 hrs, US$2.35 *por puesto*; Barinas 1½ hrs, US$2.50.

Between Santo Domingo and Laguna Mucubají is the former monastery, **A3** *Hotel Los Frailes*★, at 3,700m, international menus, expensive wines, poor service. Book ahead through Hoturvensa, T (02) 9078054/9078153, but don't pay in advance as money will not be reimbursed you in case of transport problems. On the other side of the river is **C** *Hotel Paso Real*, which is almost as good. *Mucubají* restaurant, at the highest point of the road that passes Laguna Mucubají, is very good for trout.

SIERRA NEVADA NATIONAL PARK I

A few km before the road from Barinas meets the road from Valera is the entrance to the **Parque Nacional Sierra Nevada** (Trans Barinas bus, 2 hrs, or *por puesto* from Mérida US$2, 2 hrs, 60 km). At the turn-off to the park is a motel, **E**, restaurant (good coffee and *arepas*) and shop. The park is clean and very well kept. Near the entrance is **Laguna Mucubají**, at 3,600m (free campsite and visitors' centre, good coffee, bookshop, good maps, interesting museum. A 1½-hr walk takes you to Laguna Negra. A permit is required from Inparques office at the entrance. Be prepared for near-freezing temperatures if camping out. A further 1½-hr walk from Laguna Negra is the Laguna Los Patos (very beautiful in fine weather). Horses can be hired (US$5 pp including guide). Guides (not absolutely necessary) can be found at Laguna Mucubají or at the hotels in Santo Domingo. (See Sierra Nevada National Park II, page 1515.) Throughout park you will see a plant with curious felt-like leaves of pale grey-green, the *frailejón* (or great friar), which blooms with yellow flowers from Sept to December.

APARTADEROS

The road then dips rapidly through **Apartaderos** (12½ km; *pop* 2,000; *alt* 3,473m), a scattered town at the junction of Route 7 and the road over the Sierra Nevada to Barinas, with a handful of shops and hotels serving the tourist traffic between Mérida, Laguna Mucubají and Santo Domingo/Pueblo Llano. Over the centuries the Indians have piled up stones from the rocky mountainside into walls and enclosures, hence the name. On Sun they all stand and watch the tourists, their potential income (there is some high pressure selling); the children sell flowers and fat puppies called *mucuchíes* (a variant of the Grand Pyrené) after a nearby town.

● **Accommodation B** *Parque Turístico*, attractive modern chalet-style building, heating, very hot showers, helpful owner, expensive but rec restaurant; **B** *Hotel y Restaurant Mifafi*, good food, beautiful, no heating; **E** *Posada Viejo Apartaderos*, with bath, good value, good restaurant with reasonable prices. Several places to eat; eg, *Posada Molineras*.

● **Buses** to Mérida US$1.20; bus to Barinas on the road over the Sierra Nevada is unreliable, best to catch it in Mérida.

3 km above Apartaderos, a narrow paved road (signposted) turns W off the highway at the 1-room 'Escuela Estatal 121' and winds its way to **Llano del Hato** (at 3,510m, the highest place in Venezuela served by road) and on to the 3-domed CIDA *Astrophysical Institute* at 3,600m. At least two viewing points on the way in give great views of the Lake Mucubají plateau. CIDA's four telescopes and modern facilities are open to visitors daily 1000-2230 during school holidays, Easter Week, and in Aug and Dec; otherwise open Sat 1000-2230, Sun 1000-1630; US$1.75 entry. To confirm T (074) 712780. The old access road, now paved, descends 7 km from Llano del Hato to the Mérida highway at La Toma, just above Mucuchíes. Many prehispanic terraces and irrigation systems, adobe houses and ox-ploughed fields (*poyos*) are visible from this road, which is safe and in good condition.

APARTADEROS TO MERIDA

From Apartaderos the road to Mérida (2 hrs), follows the Río Chama valley and drops 1,850m. This is the heart of the cultivated highlands and the fields extend up to the edge of the *páramo*, clinging to the steepest slopes.

SAN RAFAEL DE MUCUCHIES

The road leads up to **San Rafael de Mucuchíes** (*alt* 3,140m), said to be the highest village in Venezuela. You should visit the remarkable church by Juan Félix Sánchez and his wife Epifania Gil. They live beside the church and are happy to receive visitors. From San Rafael you can go to remote **Páramo El Tisure** where Juan Félix and his wife also built a stone house and church (free accommodation; take your own food and bedding).

An old colonial trail, **El Camino Real**, can be taken from Apartaderos to Mucuchíes (3-4 hrs), sometimes joining the main road, sometimes passing through small villages; below San Rafael is an old flour mill still in operation.

● **Accommodation E** *El Rosal*, hot water, good. Sra Crys, a French artist, will provide meals if you book in advance.

MUCUCHIES

A few km beyond San Rafael is **Mucuchíes** (*pop* 9,175; *alt* 2,980m), where there is a trout farm. Beside the Liberator on the statue in Plaza Bolívar is a representation of the Indian boy, Tinajaca, and the Mucuchíes dog, Snowy, given to Bolívar in 1813 and, according to legend, devoted to him until their deaths on the same day at the Battle of Boyacá. The patron saint of Mucuchíes is San Benito; his festival on 29 Dec is celebrated by participants wearing flower-decorated hats and firing blunderbusses continuously.

● **Accommodation E** *Los Andes*, old house above plaza, 4 rooms, hot water, shared bathrooms, excellent restaurant (closes 2030), highly rec. Between Mucuchíes and Mucurubá is *Posada San Remón*, T 526877, great kitchen, good meals, nice relaxing courtyard.

35 mins before Mérida is **Los Aleros**, a reconstruction of a 1930s town; entry US$5. Staff wear appropriate rustic costume (the drunks are not acting; they're paid by the government). Restaurant *El Caney*, colonial style, in front of bus stop, cheap, good steak, trout, *arepas andinas*, highly recommended, busy at weekends.

TABAY

10 km before Mérida is **Tabay**. From Plaza Bolívar a jeep can be taken to the cloud forest at **La Mucuy** and to Aguas Calientes (or Termales), two pools in a stream, warm and luke warm.

● **Accommodation** 1.5 km from the plaza on the Mérida road is **D-E** *La Casona de Tabay*, T 074-830089, beautiful colonial-style hotel, surrounded by mountains, comfortable, home cooking, family-run, highly rec, take *por puesto*, 2 signposts; **G** pp *Posada de la Mano Poderosa*, dormitory rooms, lovely, quiet, hot showers, good food, great value, get off at La Plazuela then walk 15 mins towards Vivero Tutti Flor.

● **Places to eat** *El Morichal*, 50m from plaza, good, cheap. A few km before Tabay look out for *Catalina Delicattesses*, fantastic jams and chutneys, hundreds of flavours to taste, open 0800.

● **Transport** Regular *por puesto* service, buses from Mérida C 19 entre Avs 3 y 4. Gasoline in Tabay.

MERIDA

The road continues to descend through increasingly lush, tropical vegetation until the city of Mérida becomes visible. It stands on an alluvial terrace 15 km long, 2½ km wide, surrounded by cliffs and plantations and within sight of Pico Bolívar, the highest in Venezuela, crowned with a bust of Bolívar. Mérida (founded 1558), the capital of Mérida State, retains some colonial buildings which contrast with the fine modern buildings, such as those of the Universidad de los Andes (founded 1785). The main plaza with rebuilt Cathedral is pleasant, but is no longer colonial.

BASICS *Pop* 222,700 including students (about 37,000 from South America and the Caribbean); *alt* 1,640m; *phone code* 074. *Mean temperature* 19°C; in Jan-Feb, the coldest months, and Aug-Sept, it rains almost every late afternoon (in the latter also throughout the night, too). 173 km from Valera; 674 km from Caracas.

Places of interest

Mérida is known for its many parks (33, some very small, little more than roundabouts) and statues. **Parque de las Cinco Repúblicas** (C 13, between Avs 4 and 5), beside the barracks, had the first monument in the world to Bolívar (1842, replaced in 1988) and contains soil from each of the five countries he liberated (photography strictly prohibited). Three of the peaks known as the Five White Eagles (Bolívar, 5,007m, Toro, 4,755m, and León 4,740m) can be clearly seen from here (Humboldt, 4,942m and Bompland, 4,882m are out of view). The **Parque La Isla** contains orchids, basketball and tennis courts, an amphitheatre and fountains. In the **Plaza Beethoven**, a different melody from Beethoven's works is chimed every hour (when working); *por puestos/busetas*, run along Av 5, marked 'Santa María' or 'Chorro de Milla', US$0.15. The **Parque Los Chorros de Milla** has a zoo (some cages disgracefully small) in a hilly setting with a waterfall, closed Mon, (*buseta*, US$0.35); plenty of handicraft shops near the zoo. On the way, there is a new chapel, built on the site where the Pope said mass in 1985. **Jardín Acuario**, beside the aquarium, is an exhibition centre, mainly devoted to the way of life and the crafts of the Andean *campesinos*, US$0.10, Tues-Sun 0800-1200, 1400-2000 (*busetas* leave from Av 4 y C 25, US$0.10, passing airport).

Museums

Museo de Arte Colonial, Av 4, between C 17 and C 18, 3 blocks from Plaza Bolívar (Tues-Fri, 0900-1200, 1500-1800, Sat 1500-1800, and Sun, 1000-1200, 1500-1800). More interesting is the small **Museo Arqueológico**, Av 3, Edif del Rectorado de la Universidad de los Andes, just off Plaza Bolívar, precolombian exhibits from the Andean region; open Tues-Fri 0800-1200 and 1400-1800, Sat-Sun 1500-1900. **Museo de Arte Moderno**, Centro Cultural Don Tulio Febres Cordero, between Avs 2 and 3, diagonally opp Plaza Bolívar (check here for cultural events). Roger Manrique has an impressive butterfly collection (more than 10,000), also knowledgeable about Andean wildlife, T 660962 for directions.

Local festivals

For 2 weeks leading up to Christmas there are daily song contests between local students on Plaza Bolívar, 1700-2200. Feria del Sol, held on the week preceding Ash Wednesday. This is also the peak bullfighting season. 1-2 Jan, Paradura del Niño; 15 May, San Isidro.

Local information

● **Accommodation**

It is difficult to get rooms during school holidays and the Feria del Sol. The week of 4 Dec hotels will only let for the whole week. Recommended to book in advance.

B *Chama*, Av 4 con C 29, T 521011/521224, F 521157, pleasant, restaurant, *Candilejas* disco, guarded car parking, rec; **B** *Park Hotel**, Parque Glorias Patrias, T (074) 637014, F 634582, car hire, noisy, good service, good restaurant, rec; **B** *Pedregosa**, Av Panamericana, T 663181, F 664295, on the edge of town, laid out like an Andean village with guests' cottages, pool, restaurant, *Tops* disco open later than others, rec, particularly for families with children, safe, armed guards, National car hire office, horse riding, rowing boats and bicycle rental nearby.

C *Caribay**, Av 2 Lora Prolongación, T 636451, F 637141, excellent restaurant; **C** *Gran Balcón*, Paseo de las Ferias, T 524056, a few mins walk to cable car, safe; **C** *Mintoy*, Av C 25 (Ayacucho), No 8-130, T 520340, F 526005, 10% discount for cash, comfortably furnished, poor breakfast, good value, parking, suites with separate sitting area (sleeps 5), rec; **C** *Prado Río**, Cruz Verde 1, T 520633, F 525192, views from garden, pool, in main building or individual cabins, rec.

D *Hispano Turístico*, Av 3 Independencia No 27-51, T 528019, comfortable; **D** *La Casona de Margot*, Av 4 entre C 15 y C 16, T/F 523312, hot water, owners both speak English and organize trips, barbecues in back garden, parking, rec; **D** *Oviedo*, Av 3 No 34-37, T 636944, excellent restaurant.

E *Alemania*, Av 2 y C 18, T 524067, **F** without bath, quiet, family atmosphere, nice patio, busy, German owner runs excursions; **E** *De Paz*, Av 2, C 24/C 25, T 523666, with bath, good value, rec; **E** *Glorias Patrias*, Plaza Glorias Patrias, Av 2, No 35-64, T 638113, with bath, stores luggage, laundry facilities, rec; **E** *Las Nieves*, Av 2 y C 19, hot water, cooking facilities, TV, good, rec; **E** *Luxemburgo*, C 24, between Avs 6-7, T 526865, with bath, cold water, new annex

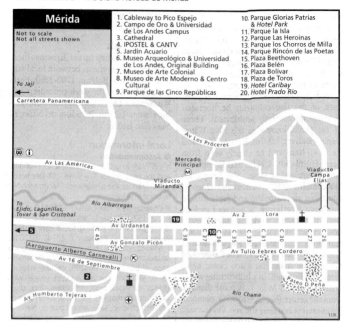

Mérida

Not to scale
Not all streets shown

To Jají

Carretera Panamericana

1. Cableway to Pico Espejo
2. Campo de Oro & Universidad de Los Andes Campus
3. Cathedral
4. IPOSTEL & CANTV
5. Jardín Acuario
6. Museo Arqueológico & Universidad de Los Andes, Original Building
7. Museo de Arte Colonial
8. Museo de Arte Moderno & Centro Cultural
9. Parque de las Cinco Repúblicas
10. Parque Glorias Patrias & Hotel Park
11. Parque la Isla
12. Parque Las Heroinas
13. Parque los Chorros de Milla
14. Parque Rincón de las Poetas
15. Plaza Beethoven
16. Plaza Belén
17. Plaza Bolívar
18. Plaza de Toros
19. Hotel Caribay
20. Hotel Prado Río

Av Los Próceres

Av Las Américas

Mercado Principal

Viaducto Campa Elías

Viaducto Miranda

To Ejido, Lagunillas, Tovar & San Cristobal

Río Albarregas

Av 2   Lora

Av Urdaneta   19

Aeropuerto Alberto Carnevalli

Av Gonzalo Picón

Av Tulio Febres Cordero

Av 16 de Septiembre

Paseo D Peña

2

Av Humberto Tejeras

Río Chama

guesthouse when hotel is full, safe, rec; **E** *Montecarlo*, Av 7 with C 24 and C 25, T 526688, safe, parking, hot water, restaurant, ask for a back room with mountain view, rec; **E** *Posada Doña Pumpa*, Avs 5 y C 14, good showers, spacious rooms, cable TV, quiet, very comfortable, English-speaking owner; **E** *Posada Encanto Andino*, C 24 No 6-53, entre Avs 6 y 7, T/F 526929, cheaper without bath, fully-equipped kitchen, highly rec; **E** *Posada La Merideña*, Av 3 No 16-39 entre C 16 y 17, T 525738, F 520647, with bath, hot water, inner rooms noisy, charming, with washing machine; **E** *Posada Luz Caraballo*, Av 2 No 13-80, opp La Plaza de Milla, T 525441, excellent cheap restaurant, good bar, 40 rooms with bath, hot water, colonial style old building; rec; **E** *Posada Turística Marianela*, C 16 entre Av 4 y 5, T 526907, hot showers, breakfast available, terrace, laundry and kitchen, owner Marianela speaks English and is helpful, often full, rec.

F *Italia*, C 19 between Avs 2 and 3, with bath, hot water (cheaper, smaller rooms available), laundry facilities, rec, post box, has own travel agency, speak English and French, changes dollars, rec; **F** pp *Panamá*, Av 3 entre 18 y 19, hot water, with bath, popular with students and backpackers, changes dollars and TCs, rec; **F** pp

Posada Calle 18, C 18 entre Avs 3 y 4, rooms for 3 or 4, shared bath, hot water 24 hrs, cooking facilities, laundry, salsa lessons, rec; **F** pp *Posada Mucumbari*, Av 3 entre C 14 y 15, T 526015, German spoken, shared bath, hot water 24 hrs, laundry, breakfast and snack bar, travel agency, rec; **F** *Res de Rafael Cuevas*, Av 8 entre C 20 y 21, No 20-49, helpful, rec; **F** pp *Residencias San Pedro*, C 19, No 6-36, entre Avs 6 y 7, T 522735, family run, fully equipped, cheaper without bath, hot water, laundry facilities, kitchen, luggage store, highly rec.

G pp *Posada Las Heroínas*, C 24, No 8-95, Plaza Las Heroínas, T 522665, owners Raquel and Tom Evenou, shared bath, hot water, helpful, popular, safe, stores luggage, use of kitchen, laundry, good atmosphere, parking facilities, highly rec (see also Bum Bum Tours below). Also on Plaza las Heroínas: **E-F** *Posada Mara*, with bath, pleasant; **F** *Posada La Joya*, shared bath, hot water, Italian owner, very helpful, secure, stores luggage, kitchen facilities, rec.

Camping: *Gasolina blanca* sold in *Mérida Gas*, Av 4 No 29-47, beside *Hotel Chama*.

● **Places to eat**

Chipen, Av 5, C 24/C 23, good meat; *Tatuy*, C 24, No 8-197, Plaza Las Heroínas, good food,

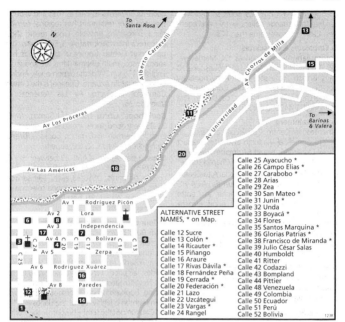

ALTERNATIVE STREET NAMES, * on Map.

Calle 12 Sucre
Calle 13 Colón *
Calle 14 Ricauter *
Calle 15 Piñango
Calle 16 Araure
Calle 17 Rivas Dávila *
Calle 18 Fernández Peña
Calle 19 Cerrada *
Calle 20 Federación *
Calle 21 Lazo
Calle 22 Uzcátegui
Calle 23 Vargas *
Calle 24 Rangel

Calle 25 Ayacucho *
Calle 26 Campo Elias *
Calle 27 Carabobo *
Calle 28 Arias
Calle 29 Zea
Calle 30 San Mateo *
Calle 31 Junín *
Calle 32 Unda
Calle 33 Boyacá *
Calle 34 Flores
Calle 35 Santos Marquina *
Calle 36 Glorias Patrias *
Calle 38 Francisco de Miranda *
Calle 39 Julio César Salas
Calle 40 Humboldt
Calle 41 Ritter
Calle 42 Codazzi
Calle 43 Bompland
Calle 44 Pittier
Calle 48 Venezuela
Calle 49 Colombia
Calle 50 Ecuador
Calle 51 Perú
Calle 52 Bolivia

try filled trout with seafood; *Zaguán de Milla*, Av 2, C 13/C 14, pizzas cooked over wood-fired stove, very good service; *Chino*, Av Los Chorros de Milla, a few hundred metres before zoo, 15 mins by bus, excellent Chinese; *Fortune*, C 21 entre Av 2 y 3, good Chinese food, English and German spoken; *La Taberna de Eugenio*, off Av 5 below the viaduct, cheap, rec; *La Mamma*, Av 3 and C 19, good pizza, pasta and set lunches, excellent salad bar, popular in the evening, live music at weekends, very cheap local wine; *El Sabor de los Quesos*, C 13, Av 1-2, very good and cheap pizzería; *Sancho Panzas*, Plaza Las Heroínas, excellent, cheap variety with good service, rec; *Mesón La Cibeles*, C 25 y Av 3, good food, well-priced, open until late; *D'Angelos Pizzería*, Edif El Col, Paseo Las Ferias, excellent; *Café Atico*, C 25 nr Plaza Las Heroínas, excellent lunch for US$1.70, rec. Many places offer student set lunches for US$1-1.50.

El Puntal, C 19, entre Avs 3 y 4, part of Centro Comercial La Glorieta, good cakes and coffee, Arabian food, falafel rec; *Sarkis*, C 26 y Av 5, Arabic, vegetarian, falafel etc, rec; *El Palacio*, C 23 entre Av 4 y 5, good batidos, cheap set meal, friendly Lebanese owner speaks French; *Café París Tropical*, on Boulevard de los Pintores, nr Plaza Bolívar, good service, highly

rec for sandwiches and fruit drinks, very popular; *Café Gala*, in Centro Comercial at Av 2 y C 26, good coffee, cakes, breakfasts, dinner, excellent salads, reasonable prices, German and US magazines, Finnish owner; *Tía Nicota*, Av 3 entre C 25 y 26, Galería 1890, rec for coffee, pancakes, pies; *Panadería Roma*, Av 8 y C 24, rec for breakfast. The *Heladería La Coromoto*, Av 3 y C 29, T 523525, open 1400-2200, closed Mon, offers 529 flavours, 150 choices each day, eg, trout, avocado, garlic, spaghetti and even Handbook flavour!

Vegetarian restaurants: *Almuerzos Vegetarianos*, Av 4 y C 18, cheap set lunch, good food and tranquil atmosphere, rec; *Fonda Vegetariana*, C 29/Av 4, rec; *Anfora de Acuario*, Av 2, C 24 and C 23, good set lunches; *El Vegeteriano*, Av 4 y C 18, set lunch US$1.40, good service, rec.

● **Banks & money changers**
Banco Unión, Av 4, C 23/24, cash advance on Visa and Mastercard; **Banco Consolidado**, Av Las Américas y C 1, opp Centro Comercial Mamayeya and next to Mercado Principal, only bank for Amex TCs (no commission), may change cash dollars if you insist; **Banco Mercantil**, Av 5 y C 15, ATM takes Cirrus (commission lower than Visa),

changes Thomas Cook TCs. Some shops advertise that they change dollars, or try travel agencies. Cash is less welcome than TCs.

● **Embassies & consulates**
Colombian, Av Las Américas, CC Mamayeya, p 5, T 448607, open 0800-1400, visas take 10 mins. **British**, Professor Robert Kirby, honorary vice-Consul, Pedregosa Media, Conjunto Residencial Las Ardillas 2a, Transv C Las Dantas, Qta Lothlorlen, T 448050 ext 2011.

● **Entertainment**
Cinemas: in Centro Comercial Las Tapias, in Centro Comercial Viaducto at the first viaduct on Av Las Américas and **Multicine Tibisay** on Av La Universidad after Charlie Chaplin statue.

Nightclubs: *La Basura*, Comercial Alto Chama on the road to Parroquía; *La Jungla*, Av 4 y C 36, very popular; *La Cucaracha*, in Centro Comercial Las Tapias, taxi US$2, good; *Birosca Carioca*, Av 2 y C 24, popular, with live music. *Alfredo's*, C 19 y Av 4, bar, very popular with locals and travellers, good atmosphere. There is no overall charge for nightclubs but always take your passport or a copy.

● **Hospitals & medical services**
Doctor: *Dra María Yuraima C de Kirby* at *Clínica Médica*, C 22 (opp Cultural Centre), T 521859, speaks English, rec.

● **Language schools**
Iowa Institute, Av 4 y C 18, T 526404, run by Cathy Jensen de Sánchez, US$85 for 20 hrs, rec; Website: http://www.ing.ula.ve/~iowainst/; E-mail: iowainst@ing.ula.ve.; *Latinoamericano de Idiomas*, CC Mamayeya, p 4, of C-5-38, T/F 447808, contact Marinés Asprino, Conjunto Residencial Andrés Bello, Torre C, p 5, Apt 6-1, T 711209 for private lessons and cheap accommodation, highly rec; *María Eugenia Olívar*, Renjifo and Nora, Av 2 con C 19, Edif Chiquinquirá No 19-11 Apt 3, T 520845, US$4/hr, rec. Many tutors place ads in posadas and bars.

● **Laundry**
Lavandería Estudiante, Av 2, nr Plaza de Milla, quick service.

● **Post & telecommunications**
Post Office and telephones: Ipostel, C 21 entre Avs 4 y 5, 0800-1900 daily; CANTV, C 21 y Av 4, Mon-Sat 0800-1930. Post office also in bus terminal, 0800-1200, 1400-1700, weekdays only.

● **Shopping**
Handicraft market on La Plaza de Las Heroínas, by *teleférico*, good café. Market on C 26 nr Av T Febres Cordero has expensive but beautiful and unusual jewellery. **Mercado Principal** on Av las Americas (buses for bus station pass by), huge building containing many small shops,

good for souvenirs as well as fruit and vegetables, top floor restaurant has regional *comida típica*, bargaining possible. Good record shop *Discoteca Internacional*, Av 3, Edif Trujillo. The up-market Centro Comercial **Las Tapias** has shops, disco, multi cinema (films are shown in English), 1½ km SW of the airport on Av Andrés Bello, opp Jardín Acuario. Cheaper is the Centro Comercial *Viaducto*, Av Las Américas at Viaducto 26.

Bookshops: *Libros Usados*, J Santos, Av 6, 21-45, very good prices, inc some second-hand English, German and French books. *Librería Universidad*, Av 3 C 29/30, superb.

Films: 1-day service, *CA*, C 23 between 5 y 6, T 527981. *Kodak*, on Plaza Bolívar, rec, good colours on prints, US$0.33 each, 1-hr service, slides developed in 2-3 days, good selection of films; *Profot*, Av 3, C 25, best for Fuji film, good colour quality for prints.

● **Tour companies & travel agents**
Bum Bum Tours, final C 24, No 8-301, beside Teleférico, T/F 525879, e-mail: raquele@bolivar.funmrd.gov.ve; owned by Tom and Raquel from *Posada Las Heroínas*, tours with great guides, fair prices, very hospitable, highly rec for Los Nevados and the Llanos, horse riding, river rafting, book exchange, English-speaking guide Alan Highton is highly rec for the Llanos and the Río Catatumbo (also sell the best jam in the world). *NAtour A*, Av 4, No 18-19 and C 24 nr Teleférico, T/F 524075/524216, e-mail: miriamb@ing.ula.ve; open Mon-Sun 0830-1900, rec for tours on foot or by car, climbing, trekking, hang-gliding, horse riding, mountain biking, fishing, birdwatching, 4WD hire with guide and driver, and trips in Barinas state, small, friendly company run by José Luis Troconis and Renate Reiners, English, French, German and Italian spoken; *Montaña Adventure*, Edif Las Américas PB, Av Las Américas, Mérida, T/F 661448, Apdo Postal 645, also at airport; ask for Gustavo García-Quinttana, excellent guide, especially in Andes, offers climbing holidays, horseriding, birdwatching, hang gliding, mountain biking, trout fishing, trips elsewhere in Venezuela, English-speaking guides; *Guamanchi Tours* (owned by John Peña), C 24, No 8-39, T/F 522080, e-mail: geca@bolivar.funmrd.gov.ve; Internet: http://www.ftech.net/~geca, rec for hiking, paragliding, horse riding, biking, equipment hire, exchange, information, mountain climbing, tours to Llanos, Amazonia and Angel Falls. Ponciano Dugarte Sánchez, T 665096/528416, rec for jeep hire, Spanish only spoken; also Lucio (T 528416) and Nicolas Savedra (T 712618).

Several agencies offer paragliding courses. Beginners must recognise that this is a dangerous sport and conditions in Mérida (lots of wind and thermals) are much better suited to those with experience. Accidents are not uncommon. A rec instructor is Raul Penso (contact through *Bum Bum Tours*).

● **Tourist offices**
Centro de Información Turística Norte, between Avs Próceres and Universidad, T 441076, low season 0800-1200, 1400-1800, high season 0800-1800, closed Sun. At airport, in waiting lounge, T 639330 (very informative), same low season hours, 0730-1330 in high season. In bus terminal, T 633952, same hours as Centro Norte, has free map of city. At Terminal Sur, helpful, map, hotel list, useful addresses and guide to events, English spoken. **Centro de Información Acuario**, Av Andrés Bello, T 633117, low season 0800-1200, 1400-1800, high season 0830-1830. The Tourist Offices are probably a better bet than the police if you need to register a theft report for insurance purposes. **Inparques** (National Parks) office at C 19 entre Av 5 y 6, map of Sierra Nevada national park (mediocre) US$1; also at Teleférico for permits.

● **Useful addresses**
Immigration Office: DIEX, Av 4 y C 16.

● **Transport**
Local Car hire: several companies at the airport, inc *Mérida Rent a Car*, T 630722, ask for José Félix Rangel, or *Dávila Tours*, Av Los Próceres opp Urb la Trinidad, T 660711, or airport T 634510. **Taxis**: in town about US$1; from bus terminal to centre US$1.50. **Línea Tibisay**, outside Park Hotel, T 637930, rec.

Air Airport is on the main highway, *por puesto* into town US$0.10, taxi US$1.50. No exchange facilities. Watch out for unofficial tour guides touting for business. Daily flights to Caracas (1 hr direct) at least 5 a day with Avensa, Servivensa, Air Venezuela and LAI; San Antonio (1, 25 mins), Maracaibo (4 daily with Air Venezuela, Bárbara and Oriental de Aviación); Air Venezuela to Cumaná (daily except Sat), Maturín (daily except Sat and Sun) and Porlamar (daily). In the rainy season, especially on afternoon flights, planes may be diverted to San Antonio (3-5 hrs by road), or El Vigia (2½ hrs away). Avensa office at C 25, Av 3-4, T 522244, open Mon-Fri 0800-1200, 1500-1800.

Buses The bus terminal is about 3 km from the centre on the W side of the valley, connected by frequent minibus service from C 25 entre Avs 2 y 3. Good tourist information office, will book hotels, free maps. To call a taxi ring bell on left just outside entrance as you leave. A small exit tax of US$0.10 is charged at the information desk, make sure you pay, officials check buses before departure. On interstate buses, it is essential to book in advance; for buses within the state you pay on board. Those hitchhiking E from Mérida should take a minibus to Tabay (US$0.45) and try from there.

Bus companies: **Expresos Occidente**, daily direct to Caracas at 0830, US$12.50, 12 hrs; via Valencia and Maracay at 0800, US$11; to Coro/Pto Fijo at 0700, US$11, 12-14 hrs. **Expresos San Cristóbal** (T 631881), daily direct to Caracas at 1930, 12 hrs, via Valencia and Maracay at 1700, 2030; to Maracaibo, at 1930, 8 hrs, US$5-7. **Expresos Mérida** (T 633430/639918), to Caracas hourly from 1800, some direct others via Valencia and Maracay (US$9, 10-11 hrs); also to Barquisimeto (US$7, 8 hrs), Maracaibo and Pto Fijo. **Transportes Barinas** (T 634651), 4 daily to Barinas via Santo Domingo, US$2.50, 5 hrs; 3 to Valera, US$2.60, 5 hrs. **Expresos Unidos** (T 631592), to San Cristóbal (US$5, 6 hrs), direct to San Antonio at 0300. **Expresos Los Llanos** (T 655927), to Caracas at 1900; to San Fernando, via Valencia and San Juan, at 2045, 18 hrs, US$17.70.

Also *por puestos* leave from upper level of terminal to: Jaji, Chiguará, Apartaderos (US$2.50), Barinas (US$4, 4 hrs), Maracaibo (US$10), Barquisimeto, Caracas, El Vigía, San Cristóbal (US$7), Valera (US$5.45).

SIERRA NEVADA NATIONAL PARK II

The world's alleged highest and longest aerial cableway runs to **Pico Espejo** (4,765m) in four stages; it was built by the French in 1958. In Nov 1991 a cable snapped on the final section and now (mid-1997) it runs as far as Loma Redonda; US$15.65, closed Mon & Tues in low season.

An alternative to the cableway is to take a jeep as far as the little hamlet of **Los Nevados** (2,711m).

● **Accommodation In Los Nevados**: 9 *posadas*; rec are *Posada Bella Vista*, Sánchez family, **E** pp inc breakfast and dinner, behind church; *El Buen Jesús* and *Florencia*, both **F** pp; *Posada Guamanchi*, owned by travel agency of same name in Mérida, solar power, great views. All *posadas* will arrange food and mules for climbing to El Alto de la Cruz or to Loma Redonda.

● **Transport** Jeep Los Nevados-Mérida, late pm (dep 0700 from Plaza Las Heroínas in Mérida), 4-6 hrs, US$20-25 pp, very rough but spectacular.

Hikes from Los Nevados

It is a very testing 2-day trek to Pico Espejo;

strong possibility of altitude sickness as the ascent is more than 2,000m. It is best done early in the morning (before 0830 ideally), before the clouds spoil the view, and from Nov to June. In summer the summit, with its statue to Nuestra Señora de las Nieves (Our Lady of the Snows, patron saint of mountaineers), is clouded and covered with snow and there is no view. It is a 1-day return to Mérida. **It is not recommended to attempt Pico Espejo alone; better to go with a guide as it is easy to get lost**. Reputable trekking companies can provide suitable clothing, temperatures can be as low as 0°C. Aug is the coldest month on the peaks. The glacier on Pico Bolívar can be seen clearly; so can Picos Humboldt and Bompland, forming the Corona, and to the E, on a clear day, the blue haze of the llanos.

From Los Nevados to Loma Redonda (4,045m), the penultimate station on the *teleférico*, takes 5-7 hrs (14 km). The hike is not too difficult; breathtaking views; be prepared for cold rain in the afternoon, start very early. Mules do the journey daily, 4 hrs; US$4/mule, US$4/guide.

You can walk down from Loma Redonda to La Aguada station (3,452m) on a rough path, wear boots, walk slowly, about 2 hrs, not for children or the elderly, take water. *Posadas* at La Aguada charge US$4 for dinner, bed and breakfast. At La Aguada station you can see the *frailejón* plant and throughout the area there is a great variety and quantity of flora. From La Aguada you can walk to the main road to Mérida (3-5 hrs) and catch a *por puesto* to town. It is a 30-min walk from La Aguada to Los Calderones' farm, accommodation and horses for hire. From La Aguada to the next station down, La Montaña (2,442m), it's a tough 2½ hrs walk (wet and overgrown). From La Montaña, the penultimate station on the way down, it's a 2½-3½ hr walk to Mérida.

The walk from Los Nevados to the village of **El Morro** (24 km) takes 7-9 hrs (very steep in parts). Sr Oviller Ruiz provides information on the history of the church and Indian cemetery. From here it is 47 km to Mérida, do not walk unless sure of facilities en route. Jeeps make the trip.

● **Accommodation In El Morro**: *Posada Abel Gámez*, run by Adriana Dugerte, meals, rec; *Posada* run by Doña Chepa, as you enter from Los Nevados, warm, highly rec; **F** pp *Posada El Oregano*, inc meals, basic, good food, rec; **G** *Hospedaje Nerios*, meals, rec.

A recommended hike from Pico Espejo, is to the cloud forest at La Mucuy (see page 1510), 2-3 days walking at over 4,000m altitude, passing spectacular snow peaks and several lakes. A tent and a warm sleeping bag are essential, as is a good map (local guides may lend theirs to photocopy). Water supply en route is plentiful. The refuge at the foot of **Pico Humboldt** is in disrepair but camping area at Laguna Verde.

● **Access** Because this is a national park, you need a permit to hike this mountain range and camp overnight. It must be obtained from the Inparques (National Parks) office in Mérida (see above). Permits are not given to single hikers (except to Los Nevados): a minimum of 2 people is required. It costs US$0.20 per person. Have your passport available. Return permit after your hike. If camping, remember that the area is between 3,500 and 4,200m so acclimatization is necessary as is warm clothing for night-time. (See **Altitude** in **Health Information** at the beginning of the book.) Some treks are very difficult so be sure to check with the tourist office before leaving. Water purification is also recommended.

● **Mountain Guides** The *Casa del Montañista*, run by Carlos Reyes in Mérida, organizes trips to the top with guides and all equipment (PO Box 66); enquire at the *teleférico* station at the end of C 24, beyond Av 8. *Carlos Torres*, Av 2, No 9-81, or through *Hotel Italia*, rec, US$30/day for 2. Guides can often be found at *Café París* in the centre. See also Mérida **Tour companies and travel agents**.

SOUTHWEST OF MERIDA

El Valle-La Culata is an easy trip by buseta from C 19, Av 1/2 (US$0.30, 30 mins, ask for La Culata; some *busetas* stop short). The road up the superb valley ends at La Culata. Thereafter a stony track leads up to the head of the valley and beyond, crossing the watersheds. You can go around the locked gate marked 'propiedad privada' after about 1 km.

● **Food & lodging** Many snack stops and marmalade/preserves shops along the way to La

Culata; **B** *La Culata*, El Valle, Carretera via Páramo La Culata, T (074) 523915/526128, Cellular (014) 740340, F 638802, 24 km from Mérida, rather gaudy, up-market retreat in magnificent setting; **D** *Valle Grande*, T 443011, scenic setting, expensive restaurant.

JAJI

43 km from Mérida, this town (*pop* 1,500) is famous for its colonial architecture, including a nice main plaza. The main plaza and adjoining streets are mainly given over to *artesanías* from all over the continent. Out of season, there are few visitors. There is good walking in the hills.

● **Accommodation & places to eat E** *Aldea Vieja*, nr plaza, with bath, hot water, nice rooms, free coffee am, restaurant, rec; **F** *Hospedaje Familiar*, good, nice roof terrace. *El Bosque*, good local food, US$7 for 2 inc drinks, excellent parrilladas, bar, open 1600-2230; *La Montaña*, rec.

● **Transport** *Buesetas* leaves Terminal Sur hourly, 50 mins, US$0.60; journey passes forested mountains, cliffs and waterfalls, sit on left.

Continuing for 62 km – narrow, but mostly paved – beyond Jají, the Panamericana is reached at Santa Elena de Arenales (several gas stations on the way).

On the way is **La Mesa de Ejido** village (**D** *Posada Turística Papá Miguel*, recommended, good food). **Mesa de Los Indios** is a small village beyond Ejido, near which there are fantastic hot springs where cold rain water from the mountains meets hot spring water. Watch out for fierce dogs on property next door. Off the road to Jají, 20 mins from Mérida, is *Venezuela de Anteayer*, where regional culture is recreated in a series of displays, including typical music and food, US$8. *Por puesto* from C 26, Mérida.

AROUND LAGUNILLAS

Transandean Route 7 leaves Mérida and passes through the Chama valley, heading for Lagunillas and Bailadores. At La González, one rough road turns S to **San José**, a pleasant village, 2½ hrs from Mérida, a dusty but beautiful trip into the mountains, green and cultivated higher up.

● **Accommodation E** pp *Posada Mochabá*, at the end of town, owner Martín Sosa, choice of cabaña or house, excellent cuisine, trips to

lakes organized; *El Porvenir*, simple, with restaurant; Haydee Ruiz rents a cottage, T 074-792-2222.

● **Road** Take bus from Av 2 in Mérida to El Ejido, 30 mins, then *por puesto* from main plaza, 2 hrs, US$1.50. From San José a track runs up the S slope of the Andes to El Morro (see above).

Another road from La González goes NW to **San Juan de Lagunillas**, believed to be the first site of Mérida (*pop* 15,900). It has a striking church and is noted for its craftwork especially weaving. Fiestas from Christmas to Candlemas (2 Feb), 3 weeks in May (14 and 15 the highpoint) and in July.

From San Juan, or from further along Route 7, Lagunillas can be reached. On the edge of Lagunillas is **Jamu**, a reconstructed Indian village, named after an Indian tribe, where demonstrations of weaving and other skills are given; entry US$1.20.

PUEBLO NUEVO

Soon after the second turn-off for Lagunillas, a turning on the left leads to **Pueblo Nuevo**, a pretty colonial village (*alt* 2,050m). The well-paved road climbs up steeply, giving impressive views all around. The whole village has very lively celebrations starting 10 days before Christmas when everyone runs around the cobblestone streets, setting off fire-crackers, firing blunderbusses into the air, playing violins and getting extremely drunk, but is otherwise quiet. There are also pleasant walks in the hills.

30 mins beyond Lagunillas lies the little church of **Estanques** (seldom open except on Christmas Day) with a stupendous gold colonial altar. Near Estanques is the colonial village of **Chiguará** with mineral springs, quiet, beautiful, nice walking. At El Pedregal there are botanical gardens and a good view over the town. Giant cacti in the area are said to be 300-years-old.

In the Valle de Mocotíes, by the Alcabala La Victoria, is the Museo del Inmigrante in a reconstructed coffee *finca*, open daily 0800-1800 (also has *cafetería*). Puente Victoria is a few kilometres beyond Estanques; a road branches off N to El Vigía on the Panamericana.

● **Accommodation Pueblo Nuevo**:
F *Posada Doña Eva*, on the SE corner of the main plaza, is basic but with a family atmosphere, delicious and cheap vegetarian meals served to order, highly rec (the building is 300-years-old and has been restored). Also **Comedor Doña Rosa**, cheap and good. **Chiguará**: **E** *Posada Colonial Cantarranos*, pool fed by mineral springs, owner Fanny speaks some English and is very helpful; **E** *Posada Los Rurales*, at entrance to village.

TOVAR

96 km beyond Mérida is **Tovar** (*pop* 30,000), a nice little town with pleasant excursions, from where you can rejoin the Panamericana via Zea, itself a pleasant village, or tackle the wild and beautiful old mountain road over the Páramo de La Negra to San Cristóbal.

● **Accommodation & places to eat D** *Hostería Sabaneta*, private bath; **E** *Valle del Mocoties*, opp bus terminal; **F** *Pensión Ideal*, basic, laundry facilities; **F** *Hospedaje Tovar*; *Restaurant Kek Duna*, Hungarian owner speaks 6 languages and serves interesting food.

BAILADORES

15 km from Tovar is **Bailadores** (*pop* 10,330), which also celebrates its fiesta from Christmas to Candlemas; beautiful walk to the waterfall with strawberries and cream half-way at La Capellería.

From Bailadores the road climbs up into the mountains. **La Grita** is a pleasant town, good Sunday market, festival 6 August. **San Pedro del Río** is a well preserved colonial village.

● **Accommodation Bailadores**: **C** *La Cascada*, modern – Wilfredo plays electric organ in the bar on Sat night, and at Mass on Sun in the beautiful church, entertaining on both occasions; **E** *Hospedaje Villa*; **C** *Hotel de Montaña*, private bath, T 077-82401/2, is rec, 7 km before La Grita. **La Grita**: **E** *La Casona*, Carrera 2A, No 6-69; **E** *Capri*, Carrera 3, good value; good pizza restaurant next door. **San Pedro del Río**: **D** *Posada Valparaíso*, T 077-911032, beautiful garden, rec.

● **Transport** From **Mérida** to: Pueblo Nuevo, taxi-jeeps from Av 2 nr new cultural centre, US$1.50; Chiguará, *buseta* US$0.90; Tovar, bus US$1.50. From **Tovar** to: Bailadores, US$0.75; La Grita 0900 and 1530 on old road. From **Bailadores** to: La Grita, US$1.80; San Cristóbal, US$3.60, *por puesto*, US$1.50; bus.

SAN CRISTOBAL

San Cristóbal, the hot, humid capital of Táchira State, is on a plateau 55 km from the Colombian border (*pop* 290,900; *alt* 830m; *average temperature* 22°C). The city was founded in 1561, and the Spanish colonial appearance – the appearance only – is preserved. The Cathedral, finished in 1908, had its towers and façade rebuilt in colonial style for the 400th anniversary of the foundation. There is a good road over the mountains, with beautiful Andean views, to San Antonio.

Local festivals

Fiesta de San Sebastián, 7-30 January.

Local information

● **Accommodation**

B *Círculo Militar De Ferias El Tamá**, Av 19 de Abril, overlooking the town, safe, spacious, good pool and gymnasium, rec.

C *Korinu*, Carrera 6 bis, shower, restaurant, rec.

D *Del Rey*, Av Ferrero Tamayo, T 432703/430561, good showers, fridge, quiet, rec; **D** *Machirí*, C 7 No 4-30, hot water, central.

E *Ejecutivo*, C 6, No 3-45, old and basic but clean and central; **E** *Tropicana*, next to bus terminal, with bath, basic; **E** *Río*, outside bus station, big rooms, hot shower; **E** *Unisa*, also nr bus terminal, OK. There are several cheap hotels on Av 6A, just off the central plaza, and around Avs 5-7, C 4-8; **E-F** category.

Camping: *El Petroleo*, 15 km from city on old road to Rubio (first oilfield in South America), ask for Hacienda Santa Teresa, owner Carlos Eduardo Cruz, very good site on coffee and sugarcane farm, good atmosphere, helpful, English spoken US$2/day.

● **Places to eat**

Café in Casa Francesa, good *merengadas*, pleasant, reasonable prices, nr Cathedral. *Fuente de Soda La Bohème*, Av García de Hevia y 7 Av, Centro Cívico, expensive, breakfasts all day; *El Rancho de Esteban*, 500m from *Hotel Del Rey*, open air with fine view over city, special barbecue dishes, highly rec; *Pietro*, C 14 y Carrera 20, pizzería.

● **Banks & money changers**

Banco Consolidado (American Express), 5a Av, Edif Torre E.

● **Embassies & consulate**

German, Edif Torovega, Carrera 8, La Concordia, T 448866.

● **Laundry**
Launderette: in Cada shopping centre next to *Hotel El Tamá*, open 0800-1200, 1400-1800.

● **Post & telecommunications**
Post Office: Palacio Municipal, next to Cathedral. **CANTV**, on Carrera 23, C 10 y Pasaje Acueducto.

● **Tourist offices**
Cotatur, Pabellones de Exposición, Av España, Pueblo Nuevo, very helpful, good city map and hotel list. **Touring y Automóvil Club**, Av Libertador C y Av Principal Las Lomas, Edif Olga, T 442542/664/675, ask for Sr Hernán Sojo González.

● **Transport**
Air For San Cristóbal: at Santo Domingo (flights on the Caracas-Bogotá-Guayaquil route, Servivensa), taxi to San Cristóbal US$11, or walk 30 mins to highway and catch bus, 1 hr, US$0.30; at San Antonio (1 hr) and La Fría (90 mins).

Buses The bus station is well-equipped; the information booth has maps of town and some hotel information. To **Maracaibo**, 6-8 hrs, US$6.50, *por puesto*, US$19. To **Mérida**, US$5, 6 hrs, US$7 by *por puesto*. To/from **Bailadores** US$1.50, lovely trip via La Grita. To **Caracas**, US$12.50, 15 hrs (Expresos Occidente), executive service US$13.50; **Valencia**, US$10. To **San Antonio**, 2½ hrs by bus, US$2, or *por puesto*, which continues to **Cúcuta**, stopping at Immigration in both countries, runs every 20 mins. By taxi to Cúcuta: US$11 to San Antonio, US$5 to wait at border, then US$6 to Cúcuta.

SAN ANTONIO

The frontier town (*pop* 42,630), is connected by international bridge with Cúcuta on the Colombian side (about 16 km); continue by road or air to Bogotá. San Antonio has an attractive colonial cathedral and some pleasant parks, but is not tourist-oriented. 13 km N on the Venezuelan side lies the spa of Ureña, with natural hot springs (**B** *Hotel Aguas Calientes**, private thermal bath, swimming pool); crossing the border at Ureña is not permitted.

Local festivals
San Antonio, 13-20 May; Ureña, 3-12 December.

Local information
● **Accommodation**
D *Neveri*, C 3, No 3-11, esq Carrera 3, a/c, TV, safe, parking nearby, by border.

E *Colonial*, Carrera 11, No 2-51, T 78018, with bath, basic, restaurant; **E** *Lorena*, Carrera 6, No 6-57, fan; **E** *Terepaima*, Carrera 8, No 1-37, safe, rec, good meals.

F *Frontera*, C 2 y Carrera 9, No 8-70, T 77366, pleasant, good value. Many hotels nr town centre.

● **Places to eat**
Refugio de Julio, Carrera 10, good value pizzas; *La Giralda de Sevilla*, next door to *Hotel Neveri* (above), very good, open on Sun evenings, unlike everywhere else.

● **Banks & money changers**
Visa at **Banco Unión**; Amex at **Banco Consolidado**, all on main plaza. TCs are difficult to change. *Casas de cambio* nr the international bridge will not all change cheques and some will only change Colombian pesos, not even US dollars cash. The exchange rate for changing bolívares to pesos is the same in San Antonio as in Cúcuta.

● **Transport**
Air The airport has exchange facilities (mainly for Colombian pesos). Taxis run to DIEX (emigration) in town, and on to Cúcuta airport, US$8.50. *Por puesto* to airport, US$0.20. Internal flights, Aeropostal, Aserca, Avensa and Servivensa to Maiquetía, Puerto Ordaz, Barquisimeto, Maracaibo and Valencia. Servivensa also to Bogotá and Medellín daily.

Buses Caracas-San Antonio US$13.50, a/c, to Caracas at 1600 and 1800, 12 hrs.

FRONTIER WITH COLOMBIA
● **Venezuelan immigration**
DIEX, Carrera 9 y Av 1 de Mayo, San Antonio.
To get a Venezuelan exit stamp here, buy stamp from opp DIEX (US$2), then take it back to DIEX for exit stamp.

Entering Venezuela There is no point in buying a bus ticket to San Cristóbal before going through formalities. Go to DIEX first. Resist any demands to pay extra 'because your visa is incorrect'. **NB** Venezuelan time is 1 hr ahead of Colombian.

Air travellers It is cheaper, if slower, to fly Caracas-San Antonio, take a taxi to Cúcuta, then take an internal Colombian flight, than to fly direct Caracas-Colombia. The airport transfer at San Antonio is well-organized and taxi drivers make the 25-min trip with all necessary stops. Air tickets out of Cúcuta can be reserved in advance in a Venezuelan travel agency.

● **Venezuelan customs**
Customs is often closed at weekends; at such times it is not possible to cross from Cúcuta. There is a customs post 5 km after San Antonio;

be prepared for strip searches and for further searches between San Cristóbal and Mérida.

● **Crossing by private vehicle**

Car documents are checked at DIEX. You must have a visa and a *carnet de passages* (but see **Additional Notes on Motoring** in Introduction, and page 1576). See Cúcuta, **Colombia**, page 892, for details on exit formalities. Once in Venezuela, you may find that police are ignorant of requirements for foreign cars.

● **Colombian consulate**

10 Centro Cívico San Antonio, p 2, open 0800-1400; better to go to Mérida for visas.

● **Transport**

Buses San Antonio to border bridge US$0.80, in bolívares or pesos. Bus to **Cúcuta**, US$7.20. On any form of transport that crosses the border, make sure that the driver knows that you need to stop to obtain stamps. *Por puesto* drivers may refuse to wait. Taxi drivers will stop at all the right offices.

Just to visit Cúcuta, no documents are needed.

East from Caracas

SOME of Venezuela's most interesting coast lies east of the capital. Beautiful beaches, islands, forested slopes and a strong colonial influence all help to make this one of the most visited parts of the country. In the far east you can cross to Trinidad by boat (if you're lucky), or the less persistent can make the short crossing to Isla Margarita.

The eastern part of the North-Eastern Highlands, with summits rising to 2,000m, has abundant rainfall in its tropical forest. The western part, which is comparatively dry, has most of the inhabitants and the two main cities, Cumaná and Barcelona.

HIGUEROTE

It is 5 hrs from Caracas to Barcelona by road through Caucagua, from which there is a 58 km road NE to **Higuerote** (*pop* 13,700). Surrounded by sandy beaches and currently the focus of large-scale tourist projects, Higuerote remains quite tranquil but is expensive, especially during the festival of the Tambores de San Juan (23-26 June, see **Music and Dance**). The partly-paved coastal road from Los Caracas (see page 1486) also goes to Higuerote; beautiful views, many beaches.

The Riches of the Highlands

Eastern Venezuela, with the Highlands in the NE, the great *llanos* of the Orinoco to the S, and S of the Orinoco again the range of Guayana Highlands, was until quite recently not of much account in the Venezuelan economy. Some coffee and cacao are grown on the eastern slopes of the northeastern highlands in the tropical forest, but the western slopes are subject to drought. Cattle roam the *llanos*, and the Guayana Highlands produce gold and diamonds. The picture has now been changed, as about 30% of Venezuelan oil now comes from this area. South of the Orinoco vast iron ore deposits are mined.

Excursions To the nearby village of **Caruao**, rebuilt in old style (population almost entirely black), friendly, good beach, one hotel. Ask for Josefa, who cooks delicious seafood; the sports club has a wild beach party each Sat pm. Near Caruao is the Pozo del Cura, a waterfall and pool, good swimming.

● **Accommodation** **C** *Mar-Sol*, modest rooms, Plaza Bolívar on beachfront esplanade, open-air restaurant 0730-2300; **D** *Barlovento*, on littered beachfront NE of Jardín Higuerote condos, colonial style, bare rooms, fan, safe, small pool, restaurant; **D** *Posada El Mar*, motel-style rooms, no hot water, open-air restaurant, 2 blocks N of the Mar-Sol; **E** *Cabañas Brisas Marinas*, Av Serrano at Plaza Bertorelli, huts for 3-4 people, simple restaurant 0800-2200 serving Barlovento specialities, good.

LAGUNA DE TACARIGUA NATIONAL PARK

14 km before Higuerote on the road from Caucagua is Tacarigua de Mamporal, where you can turn off to the **Laguna de Tacarigua National Park**. The road passes a Tunnel of Vegetation (almost 3 km long), cocoa plantations, the towns of San José de Río Chico and **Río Chico** (*pop* 14,900), with a number of colonial homes and the derelict remains of the old railway station, on the 54 km French-built 1889 railway from El Guapo to Carenero. 4 km N the road reaches the coast, where many of the canals snaking from the olive-green Laguna de Tacarigua have been incorporated into private subdivisions, with modest hotels and bridges to the sandy beaches. Off this road is the *Caballerizas Dos Estrellas*, a paso fino stud farm; the owner, Sr Pérez Mata, is happy to show

visitors around. The road runs a further 8 km E along the coast to the fishing village of Tacarigua de la Laguna. The 18,400 ha national park enclosing the lagoon is an important ecological preserve, with mangroves, good fishing and many water birds, including flamingos (usually involving a day-long boat trip to see them, best time to see them 1700-1930); an unmotorized ferry crosses the lagoon (ask at Restaurant Poleo Lebranche Asado). All boats leave from National Park office; fixed price of US$9 for 2. Boats can be hired to anywhere in the Park (beware of overcharging) and to *Club Miami* beach resort, **B** including two meals, on the Caribbean side of the eastern sandspit. The beaches beyond here are unspoilt and relaxing, but mosquitoes are a problem after sunset.

● **Accommodation** Río Chico: **E** *Hotel Italia*, C Miranda, T (034) 74248, a/c or fan, bath, excellent; **E** *Hotel Iberia*, similar standard, also on C Miranda. *Pizzería Río Chico*, takeaways, open to midnight on weekends; excellent natural fruit icecream at several kiosks on C Miranda. **Tacarigua de la Laguna**: Rooms to rent, hostel from where boat tours leave, **E** *Ciudad Tablita*, **F** without bath, quiet, cooking facilities, some German spoken, rec, *por puesto* from Río Chico, US$0.30. You can eat delicious lebranche fish at the *Bar-Restaurant Poleo Lebranche Asado*.

ROUTES Highway 9 (Caracas-Barcelona) can be joined 25 km S of Río Chico at **El Guapo** (**E** *Hotel Casa Vieja*, a/c, cheaper without, very basic with dirty bathrooms); it then runs E near the coast, looping inland at **Boca de Uchire** (*pop* 4,500; many vacation homes and **E** *Hotel Uchire*, on main road, a/c, private bath, good restaurant behind) over a ridge of the famous Morro de Unare to Clarines (a paved road runs straight on from Boca de Uchire along the sandbar sealing off the Laguna Unare to Clarines).

Clarines (*pop* 9,000) is a quiet, beautiful little town with one of the best-restored colonial churches in Venezuela (1760). Religious festivities and street processions mark San Antonio de Padua's day (13 June) and the Virgin is honoured with dance and music each 16 July. There are comfortable cabañas, restaurant, snack bar, pool and sports facilities at the *Parador Turístico Clarines* at the W entrance to the town.

PIRITU

16 km on are the twin towns of **Píritu** and Puerto Píritu (3 km apart, combined *pop* of 18,000): worth seeing in Píritu is the imposing 18th century Franciscan church of Nuestra Señora de la Concepción; Puerto Píritu has long stretches of lovely beaches, a new *balneario* (only open weekends) and a modern resort, with safe swimming.

● **Accommodation C** *Balneario Casacoima Puerto Píritu*, T 411511, a/c, restaurant, pool open to public; **C** *Hotel Bella Mar*, C Bolívar, a/c, pool, restaurant, parking, sports; **E** *La Posada*, on top of small hill overlooking main road in Píritu, with bath and fan, safe and quiet, excellent, easy 30 mins walk from Puerto Píritu which now has many expensive hotels, restaurants and snack bars.

BARCELONA

Barcelona (*pop* 266,750; mean temperature 27°C), founded 1671, capital of Anzoátegui State, straddles the Río Neveri, 5 km from the sea. With its colonial streets and old buildings, it makes a more agreeable base for budget travellers than neighbouring Puerto La Cruz. The state is named after Gen Anzoátegui, a hero of the Battle of Boyacá. His statue stands in the main **Plaza Boyacá** with the Palacio de Gobierno and San Cristóbal Cathedral.

Places of interest

The **Cathedral** (started 1748, rebuilt 1773 after an earthquake in 1766) contains the embalmed remains of the Italian martyr, San Celestino (open 0600-1200, 1500-1930). Several blocks N on Av 5 de Julio are the twin **plazas of Bolívar** (with statue)

and **Miranda**. Facing Plaza Bolívar are the ruins of the **Casa Fuerte**, a national monument, where 1600 of Bolívar's followers were massacred in 1817. Details of this and other historic epics can be found next door in the **public library**, weekdays only. **Teatro Cajigal**, facing the small Plaza at Carrera 15 with C 3a, is a replica of the Teatro Municipal in Caracas. **Museo de la Tradición**, C Juncal, in a 1671 building once the centre of the slave trade, houses a wide collection of indigenous and Spanish religious art, open Mon-Fri 0800-1200, 1400-1700, weekends 0900-1500. An overgrown park follows both banks of the Río Neveri right through the city and provides a pleasant stroll. Next to the bus and *por puesto* station on Av San Carlos, over 1 km S of Plaza Boyacá, is the **Mercado Libre**, for food and just about anything else.

Local information
● **Accommodation**

C *Barcelona**, Av 5 de Julio, 1 block from Cathedral, T 771065, TV, parking, 6th floor restaurant (good fish); *Neveri*, Av Fuerzas Armadas, T 772376, similar, good restaurant *Castillo del Oriente*.

E *Venus*, Av Intercomunal y Lecherías, T 774202, a/c.

F *Plaza*, C Juncal opp Cathedral, in a colonial building, rec; **F** *Madrid*, just behind Cathedral, with restaurant, unfriendly owner; **F** *Toledo*, Juncal y Av 5 de Julio, basic, good value.

● **Places to eat**
There is a wide variety of restaurants in town, inc *Lucky*, Av Miranda No 4-26, N of Plaza Bolívar, Chinese, rec.

● **Tourist offices**
Carrera 13, No 3-7, just off Plaza Boyacá; open weekdays only.

● **Transport**
Air The airport also serves Puerto La Cruz, 3 km S. Avensa, Servivensa, Aserca and Laser: many daily flights to Maiquetía, daily flight to Porlamar, Puerto Ordaz, San Tomé, Valencia, San Antonio, and Maracaibo. Oficambio exchange facilities (no TCs), artesanía shops, small museum, car rental agencies, Corpoturismo booth (stays open late for some incoming flights, few handouts, friendly, cannot book hotels, a city map can be scrounged from National Car Rental). Taxi to airport from bus station US$2.25; taxi to Puerto La Cruz US$5-6.

Buses The Terminal de Pasajeros next to the

Mercado Libre is used mostly by *por puesto*, with regular departures to Valle la Pascua, Puerto Anaco, El Tigre, Maturín, Cumaná, Boca de Uchire, Valle Guanape and other nearby destinations. Buses go to **Caracas** (5 hrs, 11 daily, US$5); **San Félix** (Ciudad Guayana); **Ciudad Bolívar** (6 daily); **Maturín** (2 daily). Buses for **Puerto La Cruz** (40 mins) run every few minutes from the Terminal Pasajeros, along Av 5 de Julio, past Plaza Bolívar (take care around here).

Sea The port for Barcelona and Puerto La Cruz is **Guanta**. Vessels from La Guaira call here.

BARCELONA TO PUERTO LA CRUZ

Barcelona has been surpassed touristically and commercially by Puerto La Cruz, 12 km away by 4-lane highway (Av Intercomunal) skirting the pleasant residential resort of Lechería (minibus US$0.15, then walk or *por puesto* to the beach; several good restaurants).

Off the highway is the Polideportivo sports stadium seating 10,000 people: covered gymnasium, velodrome, basketball courts, 2 pools, etc. Most of the facilities are available to the public without charge (open daylight hours daily). Soon after Barcelona is El Morro Tourist Complex, with hotels, cultural centres, condos with access from the street or from a new system of canals, and the Marina Amérigo Vespucio (Horisub, the company which manages the docks, arranges diving and boat tours, friendly, English spoken). An inland road, very circuitous, goes around the tourist complex to Puerto La Cruz. Alternatively, a passenger ferry crosses the main channel to the Amérigo Vespucio Marina, US$0.05.

PUERTO LA CRUZ

Puerto La Cruz (*pop* 220,000; phone code 081), originally a fishing village, has fine avenues and modern hotels, holiday apartments and restaurants. Principally, though, it is a petroleum town, refining and exporting oil from the interior. The older part of town is a traffic-choked grid with a seafront avenue, the Paseo Colón, extending to the eastern extremity of a broad bay. To the W the bay ends at the prominent El Morro headland beneath which lies Lechería (see above). All types of watersport are well catered for and tourist facilities are above average, if expensive. Most (craft shops, *cambios*, discos, etc) can be found on Av 5 de Julio and Paseo Colón. The latter has excellent views of the Bahía de Pozuelas and the islands of the Mochima National Park (see below). The evening *paseo* along Colón is a relaxing, cheerful end to the day. The sea in the bay looks inviting, but you cannot swim in it because of sewage pollution.

Excursions

To the Chimana, La Plata and Borracha islands in Mochima National Park for good swimming and snorkelling: see **Ferries**, below. Take hat and sunscreen. The islands are very popular and consequently are badly littered. All have restaurants, snack bars and thatched shelters for hire. Iguanas can be seen on Chimana.

Local festivals

3 May, Santa Cruz. 8 Sept, Virgen del Valle (boats cruise the harbour clad in palms, balloons; afternoon party at El Faro, Chimana, lots of salsa and beer).

Local information
● **Accommodation**

The newer, up-market hotels are at Lechería and El Morro; middle grade and budget hotels and nightlife are concentrated in central Puerto La Cruz, though it's not easy to find a cheap hotel.

L2 *Meliá**, on Paseo Colón, at the eastern edge of the centre, T 691311, F 691241, best in this part of town, luxury hotel with all services and facilities, American Airlines office.

A1 *Maremares*, Av Amérigo Vespucio, El Morro, T 811011, F 814494, 5-star, fully-serviced resort of the Golden Rainbow group with a vast lake-style pool, 9-hole golf course and marina.

B *Gaeta*, Paseo Colón 9, T 691816, on boulevard, very modern, set back slightly from sea front, a/c, good location, restaurant, scooter rentals; **B** *Rasil*, Paseo Colón 6, T 672535, F 673121, rooms, suites and bungalows, 3 restaurants, bar, pool, gym, money exchange, car rental and other facilities, convenient for ferries and buses, highly rec.

C *Riviera*, Paseo Colón 33, T/F 691337, seafront hotel, noisy a/c, some rooms have balcony, phone, bar, watersports, very good location, poor breakfast; **C** *Caribbean Inn*, C Freites, T 674292, F 672857, big rooms, very well kept

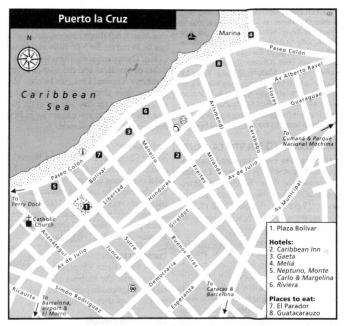

Puerto la Cruz

Caribbean
Sea

Marina

Paseo Colón

Av Alberto Ravel

Guaraguao

To
Cumaná & Parque
Nacional Mochima

Arismendi

Maneiro

Freites

Miranda

Carabobo

Av de Julio

Av Municipal

Paseo Colón

Bolívar

Libertad

Honduras

To
Ferry Dock

Catholic
Church

Anzoátegui

Av de Julio

Juncal

Sucre

Giraldot

Buenos Aires

Democracia

Esperanza

To
Caracas &
Barcelona

Ricaurte

Simón Rodríguez

To
Barcelona,
airport &
El Morro

1. Plaza Bolívar

Hotels:
2. Caribbean Inn
3. Gaeta
4. Meliá
5. Neptuno, Monte
   Carlo & Margelina
6. Riviera

Places to eat:
7. El Parador
8. Guatacarauzo

with quiet a/c, small pool, rec, very good service; **C** *La Marina*, Andrés Eloy Blanco, at the new ferry terminal, a/c, good views, expensive waterside restaurant, rec, parking for those using the Margarita ferry; **C** *Neptuno*, Paseo Colón at Juncal, T 653221, a/c, excellent restaurant *Terraza* on top floor, rec; **C** *Sorrento*, Av 5 de Julio, T 686745, F 688550, a/c, TV with US channels; **C-D** *Aparthotel Cristián del Valle*, Maneiro 15, T 650925, rec, Trinidadian owner speaks English, a/c, fans, dining room, kitchen, TV, nice staff.

D *Comercio*, Maneiro, 1 block from Paseo Colón, T 23465, phones, cold water only, a/c, rec; **D** *Europa*, Sucre, esq Plaza Bolívar, good, a/c; **D** *Monte Carlo*, Juncal at Paseo Colón, shower and a/c unreliable, central; **D** *Puerto La Cruz*, Av 5 de Julio, T 21698, phone, rec; **D** *Senador*, Miranda y Bolívar, T 22035, a/c, back rooms quieter, phone, restaurant with good view, parking, rec; **D** *Luna y Sol*, Ricaurte 5, close to beach, fan, a/c, safe, quiet, laundry around corner.

E *Pippo*, Freites 66, modern, good value, very noisy; **E** *Nacional Inn*, Miranda 44A, esq Av 5 de Julio, T 685252, basic, water problems.

● **Places to eat**

On Paseo Colón: *El Parador*, 2nd floor, excellent food and service; *Los Zulianos*, food average but Fri, Sat, Sun nights live folk music, good atmosphere, no cover charge, rec; *Da Luigi*, Italian, good; *El Espignon*, very good dinner in the open air, romantic; *Big Garden*, delicious sea food; *Casa Nápoli*, cheap, rec; *Reale*, No 69, pizzería, good for breakfast; *Ristorante O Sole Mio*, cheap, excellent, wide variety; *Pastelería Fornos* for breakfast; *Las Cabañas*, very good value and service. Try the *chwarmas* (roast meat in pitta bread) at the street stands, eg *Buen Gusto* opp Burger King. *La Taberna del Guácharo*, C Carabobo, eastern end of Paseo Colón, tacky interior with plastic guácharo statues but excellent cheap Venezuelan cuisine, good service, highly rec, not as tourist-orientated as the restaurants along the sea front; *El Guatacarauzo*, Paseo Colón, nr Pizza Hut, waiters wear silly hats and play practical jokes, live music, good atmosphere and good value; *El Teide*, Av 5 de Julio No 153, nr Plaza Bolívar, good and cheap local food, closes at 2000; *Nature*, vegetarian, Constitución 70, lunch and dinner, self-service buffet, tasteless, mostly corn-based dishes; *El Farao*, eastern corner of main bus station, gaudy interior, fair service, excellent, authentic, spicy Arab food. *Gamblers* nightclub, Paseo Colón, nr Burger King, excellent music, free entry. *Christophers*, a Canadian owned bar, C La Marina, 1 block from Paseo Colón, an informal cellar-type watering hole open from 1600 till late.

● **Airline offices**

Avensa, Av Municipal y Pepsi, and at Barcelona airport; **Alitalia** and **American Airlines** at Meliá; **Dominicana**, Independencia 124, Chapurín Central. For air services see Barcelona.

● **Banks & money changers**

Banco Consolidado (American Express), Av 5 de Julio, Local No 43; **Turisol**, Amex rep, T 662161/669910. No banks will change money. *Oficambio*, C Maneiro y Libertad, no commission on TCs, best rates, open 0800-1200, 1400-1730 Mon-Fri, or on the sea front between Calles Buenos Aires and Sucre, Mon-Fri 0800-2100.

● **Post & telecommunications**

Post Office/telecommunications: Freites y Bolívar, 1 block from Paseo Colón. Telephone office will hold faxes, F 651266.

● **Shopping**

Vendors of paintings, jewellery, leather, hammocks, etc on Paseo Colón in evenings, cheaper than in the souvenir shops.

● **Sports**

Diving: *Explosub, Hotel Meliá*, T 653611/ 650574, T/F 673256, PO Box 4784, efficient, helpful, will dive with 1 person, US$75/2 dives; *Lolo's Dive Centre*, Guanta Marina, Bahía de Guanta, T 683052, F 682885 (or contact Eddy Revelant T 014-801543 cellnet), very experienced, English spoken, collect you from hotel and provide lunch, US$60/2 dives, 2-3 person minimum, 4-day PADI course US$300. Hotels and travel agents also organize trips. The nearest recompression chamber is on Isla Margarita.

● **Tour companies & travel agents**

The travel agency in *Hotel Meliá* is rec for arranging and confirming flights.

● **Tourist offices**

On Paseo Colón opp *El Parador* restaurant, T 688170, French, English, Italian and Dutch spoken, very helpful and friendly, open Mon-Fri 0800-1200, 1400-1730.

● **Transport**

Buses The bus and *por puesto* terminal is at Av Juncal and C Democracia. A new bus terminal has been built to the E of town. To **Caracas**, 5 hrs, US$5-8, at least 15 through the night, Expresos Los Llanos (T 671373, rec, a/c, movies), Sol de Margarita (rec), *por puesto*, dep 1550, 4

hrs, US$17.50; Autoexpresos Ejecutivos to/from Caracas 4 a day, US$12.65 (T 678855, next to ferry terminal), highly rec (also to Maracay, Valencia, Barquisimeto and Maturín). To **Mérida**, US$22.35, 16 hrs; to **Ciudad Bolívar** US$5, US$2.50 student discount, but often full since service starts at Cumaná; if stuck, take *por puesto* to El Tigre, US$4.25 and *por puesto* to Ciudad Bolívar US$3.50. To **Cumaná**, US$3, Expresos Guyanesa, rec, *por puesto* US$6, 1½ hrs, fight to get on any bus which arrives. To **Barcelona**, US$1, 40 mins. To **Carúpano**, US$3, 5 hrs. *Por puesto* to Playa Colorada US$1.20 and to Santa Fe about US$1.10. There are also services to San Félix, Ciudad Bolívar, Río Caribe, Maracay, Valencia, Acarigua, Barinas, San Cristóbal, Güiria. *Por puestos* cover the nearest destinations and charge a little over double. Along Av 5 de Julio runs a bus marked 'Intercomunal'. It links Puerto La Cruz with Barcelona and intervening points, inc the entry to Lechería (connecting *por puesto* stop is 1 block further, along the Av Principal of Lechería, left side). Bus also passes within a few km of Barcelona airport. Another Barcelona bus is marked 'Ruta Alternativa' and uses the inland highway via the Puerto La Cruz Golf and Country Club and Universidad de Oriente (both 5 km SW of city), US$0.12.

Ferries Local islands can be visited through Embarcadero de Peñeros, Paseo Colón (behind *Tejas Restaurant*); departures throughout the morning to a dozen points along the coast (about US$15); return 1630. Ferries are cheaper from here than smaller beaches. Several small jetties reached from the central part of Paseo Colón offer island trips. For details of **Ferries** to **Isla Margarita**, see page 1537.

THE COASTAL ZONE

Starting E from Puerto La Cruz is the Costa Azul, with a seemingly endless series of beaches backed by some of Venezuela's most beautiful scenery, and offshore the islands of the **Mochima National Park**. Highway 9 follows the shore for much of the 85 km to Cumaná. The road is treacherous in parts, especially between Playa Colorada and Cumaná, and only recommended for experienced drivers in 4WD vehicles, but the scenery is beautiful. It passes the small Playa Blanca, excellent snorkelling, take own equipment. The locals cook and sell fish. Other recommended spots are El Faro, El Saco, Conoma, which has palm trees and

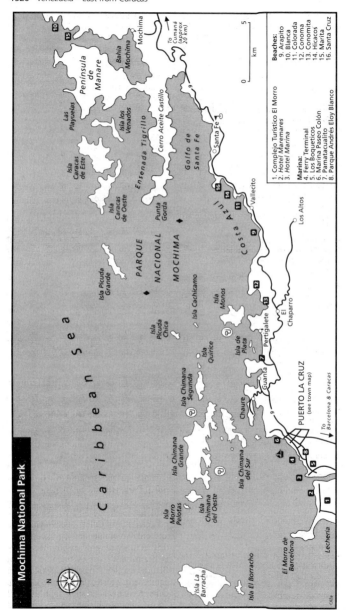

Mochima National Park

Caribbean Sea

Isla La Barracha

Isla El Borracho

El Morro de Barcelona

Isla Morro Pelotas

Isla Chimana del Oeste

Isla Chimana Grande

Isla Chimana del Sur

Isla Chimana Segunda

Chaure

Lecheria

PUERTO LA CRUZ
(see town map)

To Barcelona & Caracas

9

Guanta

Pertigalete

El Chaparro

Los Altos

Vallecito

Costa Azul

Isla de Plata

Isla Quirice

Isla Monos

Isla Cachicamo

Isla Picuda Chica

Isla Picuda Grande

PARQUE NACIONAL MOCHIMA

Punta Gorda

Golfo de Santa Fe

Santa Fe

Cerro Aceite Castillo

Ensenada Tigrillo

Isla Caracas de Oeste

Isla Caracas de Este

Isla los Venados

Las Playuelas

Península de Manare

Bahía Mochima

Mochima

To Cumaná (approx 20 km)

N

1. Complejo Turístico El Morro
2. Hotel Maremares
3. Hotel Marina

Marina:
4. Ferry Terminal
5. Los Boqueticos
6. Marina Paseo Colón
7. Pamatacualito
8. Parque Andrés Eloy Blanco

Beaches:
9. Arapito
10. Blanca
11. Colorada
12. Conoma
13. Conomita
14. Hicacos
15. Marita
16. Santa Cruz

km

0   5

is 'paradise-like', departure behind the Puerto La Cruz tourist office, on the beach (US$3.50, departure 0900-1000, return 1600). Further along is Playa Arapito (restaurant, parking US$0.35; see **NB** below). Here boats can be hired to La Piscina, a beautiful coral reef nr some small islands, for good snorkelling (lots of dolphins); US$8-10 per boat. The boatman will pick you up later and take you to a restaurant. The tourist office in Puerto La Cruz provides tour operators for day trips to various islands for swimming or snorkelling; 6 hr trip to 4 islands US$15 pp, inc drinks; bring your own food as the island restaurants are expensive.

PLAYA COLORADA

A popular beach (Km 32) with beautiful red sands and palm trees (*por puesto* from corner of terminal in Puerto La Cruz, US$0.80, or hitch).

● **Accommodation C** *Villas Turísticas Playa Colorada*, Av Principal, T 016-816365, clean pool, comfortable rooms, also trailers for 4, good restaurant, Apdo 61355, Caracas 1060-A, T (02) 952-1393; **D** *Bed and Breakfast Jali*, Quinta Jali, C Marchant, Playa Colorada, T (016) 818113, run by Lynn and Jack Allard, they have another house 4 blocks away, a/c, shared bathroom, hot water, very quiet, smaller rooms **E**, free transport to surrounding beaches, family atmosphere, English and French spoken, washing facilities, German books, rec, price inc a good American breakfast, dinner is also served on request. Sra Mónica lets rooms, **D**, and Doña Rosa lets out a house or apartment, **D**, while Seniorca, who runs a beach bar, hires tents, US$8/night. Camping is permitted for a small fee (but there is no fresh water) and there is a restaurant.

Nearby are Playas Vallecito (camping US$1.50/tent, security guard, car US$0.80, bar with good food and bottled water on sale, plenty of palm trees for hammock-slinging) and Santa Cruz (buy fresh seafood from the fishermen's huts). At Playa Los Hicacos is a beach club for the Universidad del Oriente, Cumaná; it has a lovely coral reef.

SANTA FE

40 km from Puerto La Cruz, in Sucre state is **Santa Fe**, a good place to relax, though plenty of loud music. It has a golf course

on the dark red, sandy but littered beach; market Sat.

● **Accommodation & places to eat D** *Hotel Cochaima*, difficult to find, take road parallel to main road, on the left hand side, and follow it to the end of the beach, run by Margot, noisy, popular, close to beach, fan, meals available, rec; **D-E** *Siete Delfines*, on beach, nr market, safe, fan, café and terrace where you can cook, excellent food available, bar, great atmosphere, warmly rec, ask here for tours or information about the area, tours organized for US$4-10, Ricardo runs PADI courses; **D** *Posada El Jardin*, on Cochaima beach, T/F (093) 210073, with continental breakfast, cheaper without bath, kitchen, garden, run by Diego Rubio and Cristina who speaks English, French and German, airport transfer and tours, snorkelling trips; **D-E** *Café El Mar*, Playa Cochaima, owner Matthias (German), rooms OK but toilets smelly, restaurant, bar, very good food, a/c. Private houses let rooms; accommodation at Señor Julio's home, a bit further down the beach from *Restaurant Cochaima*, sign 'Rooms for Rent', US$3 pp, cooking facilities, safe, very helpful, rec. *Salón de Juegos Chomena* has 1 basic, cheap room for real budget travellers, owner changes TCs. The pizzeria on the beach has good food and rooms to let, owner, José, will let you stay in his house if hotel is full, no locks on doors.

● **Transport** Gasoline is available; *por puesto* at 0600 and bus to Cumaná (US$1), and Puerto La Cruz (US$0.80). It is sometimes difficult to get the bus from Puerto La Cruz to stop at Santa Fe, *por puesto* may be a better bet, US$1.10, 1 hr, or taxi, US$13.30 inc wait. Jeep, boat or diving tours available. Francisco is rec for boat trips, he can be found a few houses to the W of the *Cochaima*. Fishermen offer similar trips but their prices are much higher. Boat trips to Playas Colorada or Blanca cost US$10 pp; better to hire your own boat for half the price, or hitch down the road to Colorada. Ask for Thomas, he has a boat and will take you wherever.

MOCHIMA

The small, colourful weekend resort of **Mochima** beyond Santa Fe, is 4 km off the main road, hitching difficult. The sea is dirty near the town. Boats take tourists to nearby beaches, such as Playa Marita and Playa Blanca (recommended), and around the islands; fares negotiable, about US$10 to one island, US$12 for a 2-hr trip round the islands (up to 6 people). Several huts on Playa Blanca serve fresh fish.

● **Accommodation** *Hotel Mochima*, good

restaurant, cheap, they will allow you to stay on the terrace if there are no more rooms; Sras Cellita Día, Gaby, Mama Inés and Doña María let out rooms, **E**; Señor Padriño, private rooms, **F**, basic but safe, they will store luggage when you go to the nearby beaches by boat, the house has no sign but it is just a few houses before Gaby's *pensión*. Houses to rent with kitchens and fans from US$12/day depending on length of stay.

- **Places to eat** *Los Mochimeros*, good (try the *empanadas* with ice cold coconut milk); *Don Quijote*, Av Bermúdez, very good. The only restaurant open during the week is *El Guyacán*.

- **Transport** From Puerto La Cruz, the trip can be organized by taxi, US$30 inc the journey home. Buses do not travel between Santa Fe and Mochima, *por puestos* can be taken, bargain hard on the price, US$10-12 is reasonable. Once in Mochima it is very difficult to find a taxi, you should arrange to be picked up again by the same driver if just staying for 1 day. Bus to Cumaná, 1400, US$0.80.

NB At holiday times this coast is very busy and has become littered and polluted, especially at Santa Fe and on the islands. Repeated warnings about broken glass on the beaches. Beware of fishermen robbing campers on the islands; it is only advisable to go to islands with guards (during the day) and where people live. Camping is not safe, either; robbery and rape have occurred.

CUMANA

Cumaná (*pop* 250,300; *phone code* 093; *average temperature* 27°C) capital of Sucre state, straddles both banks of the Río Manzanares, its economy based on coffee, sugar and cacao, supplemented by fishing, tourism and salt from the mines on the Araya Peninsula. It is possibly the oldest Hispanic city on the South American mainland, founded 1521 to exploit the nearby pearl fisheries. From here the strategies for conquest and colonization of the new continent were planned. Because of a succession of devastating earthquakes (the last in 1929), only a few historic sites remain. Cumaná is a charming place with its mixture of old and new, but the port area (1½ km) is not safe at night.

The older sections flow around the base of the hill dominated by the Castillo de San Antonio. The streets around the Gobernación and Plaza Bolívar are narrow and partly pedestrianized. More relaxing than the busy streets surrounding, they have several budget hotels and eating places; the tourist office is here also.

Places of interest

There are walks along the treelined river (beware mosquitoes), which has the **Parque Ayacucho, Parque Guaiqueri** on the W bank (clean toilets) and markets on both sides (food and craftwork). The **Castillo de San Antonio de la Eminencia** affords a wide view of the town, Araya Peninsula and coast. It was built in 1686 as a defence against pirates, with 16 mounted cannon, drawbridge and dungeons (Páez was held captive here 1849-50) from which there are said to be underground tunnels leading to the Santa Inés church. Restored in 1975, it is flood-lit at night. The **Castillo de Santa María de la Cabeza** (1669) is a rectangular fortress with a panoramic view of San Antonio and the elegant homes below. **Convento de San Francisco**, the original Capuchin mission of 1514, was the first school on the continent; its remains are on the Plaza Badaracco Bermúdez facing the beach. The **Church of Santa Inés** (1637) was the base of the Franciscan missionaries; earthquakes have caused it to be rebuilt five times. A tiny 400-year-old statue of the Vírgen de Candelaria is in the garden. The **home of Andrés Eloy Blanco** (1896-1955), one of Venezuela's greatest poets and politicians, on Plaza Bolívar, has been nicely restored to its turn-of-the-century elegance (photographs, poetry recordings, political notes and personal effects of the owner; open Tues-Sun 0900-1100, 1600-1900, free). On the opp side of the plaza is **La Gobernación** around a courtyard lined by cannon from Santa María de la Cabeza, note the gargoyles and other colonial features.

In the suburb of Chaima a bronze monument marks the 450th anniversary of the city's founding. It depicts in bas-relief the more martial encounters between Spaniards and natives. A Capuchin friar and a Cumanagoto Indian top the 16m column (take Brasil/Terminal bus near Plaza Ayacucho, US$0.30).

Museums

The **Museo Gran Mcal de Ayacucho** in the old Consejo Municipal in Parque Ayacucho commemorates the 150th anniversary of the battle of Ayacucho: mainly portraits, relics and letters of Bolívar and José Antonio Sucre (born 1795, Bolívar's first lieutenant, President of Peru in 1826, assassinated in Colombia in 1828). The maritime museum, **Museo del Mar**, has good exhibits of tropical marine life, at the old airport, Av Universidad with Av Industrial, open Tues-Sun 0830-1130, 1500-1800, US$0.60: take San Luis minibus from outside the cathedral.

Beaches

Los Uveros on the Ensenada de Manzanillo is the largest public beach in Venezuela, there are two restaurants and camping allowed on the 3 km long clean, sandy stretch just W of the airport. San Luis is a short local bus ride away, recommended but the water is dirtier than Los Uveros.

Excursions

A paved road runs S down the Manzanares to **Cumanacoa** (56 km; *pop* 18,750), a traditional creole town in a rich agricultural area (1 hotel, **E**; rooms for rent, **F**). At the Casa de Cultura, C Motedano 20, authentic folk music is performed by 'Los Carrizas Precolombinos', a band of local musicians and members of the Turimiquire tribe. Near the town is the Cuchivano grotto from which flares a jet of natural gas.

Local festivals

22 Jan, Santa Inés; pre-Lenten carnival throughout the state of Sucre; 2 Nov, Santos y Fideles Difuntos at El Tacal.

Local information
● **Accommodation**

B *Los Bordones*, Final Av Universidad, T 510352, F 515377, 8 km from the bus station, rec, beautifully situated on a good beach with excellent food and a swimming pool.

C *Gran Hotel**, Av Universidad, T 510671, beach, mid-way between Cumanagoto and town centre, good; **C** *Mariño*, T 320751, nr centre, C Mariño y Junín, a/c, not very clean; **C** *Minerva**, T 314-4171, F 662701, 5 km N of centre on seafront, Av Cristóbal Colón, little to do in area, modern; **C** *Turismo Guaiqueri*, Av Bermúdez 26, T 310821, comfortable, a/c.

D *Don Bosco Suite*, Av Perimetral and 19 de Abril, T 310969, a/c, no hot water, rec; **D** *Caribe*, Av Universidad, on San Luis beach, T 514548, with a/c, basic cabins, English spoken, highly rec; **D** *Regina*, Av Arismendi, T 321168, hot water, a/c, restaurant, good views from upper rooms, very helpful, good value, highly rec; **D** *Savoia*, Av Perimetral, T 314379, a/c.

Cheaper hotels can be found across the river, around Plaza Ayacucho, especially on C Sucre: **E** *Astoria*, C Sucre, T 662708, with cold shower, fan; **E** *Italia*, central, dirty, with fan, or a/c with bath, very safe.

F *Hospedaje La Gloria*, Sucre 31, opp Sta Inés church, with fan and bath, basic, helpful.

● **Places to eat**

El Colmao on Plaza Pichincha, C Sucre, T 663251, very good fish, charming service, not expensive; *Sand Hills* and *Los Montones*, nr Caribe Hotel, San Luis beach, rec. On Sucre: *Italia*, cheap and good; *Pucheff*, good pizza; *Ali Baba*, Av Bermúdez nr corner with C Castellón, excellent, cheap, middle eastern food, rec; *Jardín de Sport*, Plaza Bolívar, only outdoor café, good food, good atmosphere, rec. All central restaurants close Sun lunchtime. Many good restaurants on Av Perimetral in the area nr the *Savoia Hotel*.

● **Banks & money changers**

Banco Consolidado, Av Bermúdez y Perimetral, Edif Ajounián, Amex cheques only, no commission. Exchange at Oficambio, C Mariño, Edif Funcal, accepts all TCs, same rate as cash, open 0800-1200 and 1400-1800.

● **Tour companies & travel agents**

Araya Tours, Sucre 65, T 313134, organizes launches to Araya Peninsula and nearby beaches and scuba diving.

● **Tourist offices**

Tourist Office nr church of Santa Inés, ask to see their photos of surrounding area, very helpful, English spoken, information not always accurate.

● **Transport**

Air New airport 10 km E of centre (taxi fare US$2.50). To Caracas and Porlamar with Servivensa (T 312484).

Buses Terminal 3 km NW of the centre on Av Las Palomas, just before the junction with the peripheral road, T 662218. Local bus into centre US$0.10, taxi US$3. *Por puesto* to Puerto La Cruz, US$6, bus US$3, 1½ hrs. To Güiria, US$3.60, 1230, *por puesto* US$7.20 (5 hrs), beware of overcharging, often stop in Carúpano. To Caripe, 0730 and 1230, 4 hrs, get there early and buy ticket on the bus, US$4. To

Caracas, US$7 upwards depending on company (7-8 hrs), frequent service but not all advertised buses run, many cancellations; many daily to **Ciudad Guayana** and **Ciudad Bolívar,** US$6 with Expresos Guayanesa, T 66218, 6 hrs. Other destinations inc Maracay, Valencia, Carúpano (US$3), Cumanacoa, Maturín, Barcelona and San Félix.

Sea   For Ferries to **Isla Margarita,** see page 1537.

ARAYA PENINSULA

Desert landscapes and pink salt lakes characterize the peninsula, whose main settlement is **Araya** (*pop*, with Manicuare, 21,000). It has an airport and a ferry dock. The major sight is the Castillo de Santiago (or Fuerte Araya), built by Spain in 1625 to protect the salt mines. So important was salt in the preservation of food that the authorities spent 3 years constructing the fortress, bringing all materials, food and water in by sea. It was Spain's most expensive project to that time in the Americas. Very little remains of the fortress apart from the ruins of its walls, passageways and cistern. Entry is free, but the only facilities are a refreshment stand and a picnic area. Today the mines are exploited by a Government-owned corporation; annual production has almost reached 500,000 tonnes. Ask permission for a visit from Ensal (Empresa Nacional de Salinas); office near the pier at Puerto Sucre.

- **Accommodation & places to eat**
G *Hospedaje San José,* very basic. There's another hostel, even more basic, and the *Hotel Araya,* a long way from the dock, mainly used by the Salt Company for its visitors. Private houses also have rooms available. Bars on the beach nr the dock serve meals and a *panadería* at the end of the main street going uphill from the dock serves good breakfasts. Ensal has an a/c guesthouse and dining room open to the public and runs 2-hr tours of its saltworks up to 1400.

- **Transport**   A boat Cumaná-Araya, departs every hour, US$0.60; return boats (haphazard and difficult to get on at weekends as more cars than spaces) leave from main wharf at end of Av Bermúdez; several passenger launches a day, some with upper seating decks. By road from Cariaco, 78 km E on the Cumaná-Carúpano highway, no public transport. The peninsula road out to Araya is now paved (95 km).

CARÚPANO

The highway from Cumaná goes on to the port of Carúpano, on the Pariá Peninsula (135 km). The coastal route as far as Villa Frontado is beautiful, running along the Golfo de Cariaco past a succession of attractive beaches and small villages. Even the larger places along this stretch – Marigüitar and San Antonio del Golfo – are very quiet and have little accommodation (*Balneario Cachamaure,* 44 km from Cumaná, beautiful beach, cabins US$18, barbecue equipment, US$2). After Cereza, famed for its basket-making, and Cariaco (*pop* 25,350, gas/petrol) the road winds inland over the Pariá Ridge to **Carúpano** (*pop* 87,600), a colonial town dating back to 1647, from which 70% of Venezuela's cocoa is shipped. Here in 1816 Bolívar freed the black slaves who worked on the wealthy cocoa plantations, thus acquiring new allies. The town sits between the Ríos Revilla and Candoroso; its beach is wide and desolate but the waterfront boulevard is landscaped.

Beaches

An alternative road between Cariaco and Carúpano reaches the coast after 17 km, and runs E by the Caribbean for 38 km. The beaches on this coast are covered with shells which make swimming less attractive, but good sand can be found at Saucedo and the Balneario Costa Azul (2 km E of Guaca where clams packed with peppers are sold, restaurant). Escondido is a deep calm bay surrounded by sand dunes. Playa Copey is 7 km before Carúpano (ask buses from W to stop, or take taxi from town); no shops.

Local festivals

Carúpano is famous throughout Venezuela as the last place still celebrating a traditional pre-Lenten Carnival: days of dancing, rum drinking, completely masked women in black (*negritas*), etc. Book accommodation ahead at this time (Feb). 3 May, Velorios de la Cruz (street dances); 15 Aug, Asunción de la Virgen.

Local information

● Accommodation

A3 *Victoria**, Av Perimetral, seen better days but good, pool, restaurant.

C *Lilma*, Av Independencia 161, good restaurant.

D *San Francisco*, Av Juncal 87A, good restaurant; **D** *Bologna*, Av Independencia, excellent, cheap restaurant, a/c, cheaper rooms with fan only, intermittent water, owner speaks German, rec; **D** *Posada Nena*, Playa Copey, T 317624, F 317297, good meals extra, comfortable, one block from beach, garden, games room, German/Venezuelan owners, highly rec, tours arranged.

E *El Yunque*, Av Perimetral (about 2 km from centre), dirty, beach, good seafood restaurant; **E** *María Victoria*, Av Perimetral (100m from *Hotel Victoria*), safe, fan, basic, no hot water; **E** *Playa Copey*, on beach at nearby Santa Catalina, airy rooms, pool.

F *Carúpano*, Av Independencia, nr seafront, noisy, friendly and very basic.

● Places to eat

La Brasa Dorada, Av 5 Libertad, rec. *El Kiosko*, Paseo Boulevard, by the seafront, OK; *Pizza Haiti*, Av Independencia nr *Hotel Carúpano*, wide choice, good.

● Tour companies & travel agents

Travel agent next to *Hotel Lilma* on Av Independencia, sells tickets for *Windward* to Trinidad (see below).

● Transport

Buses To Caracas, Responsable de Venezuela, US$8, 8 hrs; to Cumaná, US$3, 2 hrs, *por puesto* US$6; Güiria US$1.75, 3 hrs, *por puesto* US$4, 3 hrs (from Plaza Colón). Bus to Puerto La Cruz, US$4.70, 5 hrs. No buses leave direct from Carúpano to **Caripe**: go first to Maturín or Cumaná; taxi Carúpano-Caripe US$35.

PARIA PENINSULA

Highway 9 continues a further 160 km E along the Peninsula to Güiria. The coast is left behind until Irapa, as the main highway climbs over the central spine through luxuriant forests of bamboo and Spanish moss to the village of **El Pilar** (33 km, *pop* 17,000), where there are a number of hot springs (El Hervidero and Cueva del Pato) and the river bathing resort of Sabacual. E of El Pilar is **Guaraúnos** (40 mins from Carúpano), the base of Claus Müller (C Bolívar 8, T 094-69052) who has worked with Indian communities and

in conservation for 25 years. His trips in the peninsula, to the cloud forest, and the delta are highly recommended, US$60/day for 4WD, food and lodging, money ploughed back into the local community.

RIO CARIBE

A second road which joins the highway beyond El Pilar follows the coast E of Carúpano to the fishing village of El Morro de Puerto Santo (15 km), on a sandspit between the coast and a rocky offshore island, then to the lovely town of **Río Caribe** (*pop* 25,100, about 20 km E of Carúpano), whose old pastel-hued houses testify to the former prosperity of the place when it was the chief cacao-exporting port. There are several sandy beaches on either side of the village and the best beach is another 25 km to the E. Turn off the main road at a sign for 'Medina', becoming a dirt track, to the Playa Medina in a beautiful setting. Pick-up truck from Río Caribe to La Entrada, 2 km from Playa Medina, 1 hr, US$0.50 followed by a very long walk. Try to find a truck that will take you directly to Playa Medina, bargain hard, get there early since the last form of transport back to Río Caribe is 1530.

● Accommodation Río Caribe: **C** *Mar Caribe*, inc breakfast, pool, restaurant, good coffee and cocktails; or rooms rented by Señora Ana at Av Las Bermudas 21, **G** pp. There are also private, unsigned pensions; ask for them. **A3** *Hotel Playa Medina*, T 094-315241/312283, reserve in advance, inc full board and drinks, cottages on the beach with small snackbar restaurant and toilets open to the public, changing facilities, carparking (US$1), well worth a visit.

IRAPA

At Bohordal, the paved road from Río Caribe across the mountains meets Route 9 55 km from Carúpano. Route 9 continues to **Irapa** (117 km, *pop* 11,500), a fishing town surrounded by a grove of coconut palms; it is said to be here that Papillon came ashore after his last escape from Devil's Island in 1945 (*fiesta* 19 Mar). Across the Gulf of Paría are the swamps of the Orinoco Delta. The climate is dry and very hot but the coast E of Irapa is a string of coves, palms and rich vegetation – Columbus was so impressed he named the region 'Los Jardines'.

- **Services** Bus terminal is 5 blocks from the sea; on the third street from terminal toward sea is the more expensive of the 2 hotels (**E** with a/c); the cheaper (**F**) is signed *Licorería Bacco*, ½ block from sea, clean, quiet. Food market near sea front in am, enough shops for supplies, no restaurants. Bus to Güiria at 0700-0800, check exact time, or take taxi, US$1 from same block.

GÜIRIA

The well-surfaced highway continues 42 km to **Güiria** (*pop* 20,200), a fishing town with a littered beach. It has been described as a delightfully friendly place which seems to come alive every 2 weeks when the *Windward* sails (see below). *Feria de la Pesca*, 14 July. Roads end here, but there are fuel supplies for the return journey. Bus to Balneario beach (US$0.10); good restaurant with cheap, cold beer, easy to hitch-hike back to town.

- **Accommodation C** *Playa Paraíso*, on the beach nr town, pool, restaurant, music; **E** *Hotel Oriente*, corner of main plaza, rec; **F** *Fortuna*, with bath; *Plaza*, basic but fine, good patio restaurant, fish is rec, most popular place in town; *Manzur*, cheapest, not rec.

- **Places to eat** There are a couple of basic places on the main plaza inc an Arab-run restaurant, with *falafel* and *humus*, highly rec; not much else. Good, cheap *empanadas* cooked outside Catholic Church on main plaza. Water restrictions at night in some places.

- **Banks & money changers** Banco Orinoco changes TCs, good rates, no commission.

- **Entertainment** Cinema: men should wear long trousers in the cinema.

- **Transport Air** Flights to Caracas, Margarita, Tucupita, Anaco. **Buses** To Maturín, US$3.50, 6 hrs, Expresos Maturín. Several buses daily to Cumaná, 6 hrs, and to Caracas, all leaving between 1600 and 1800. Travel agent offers **cruises** to Caribbean islands for US$150 pp (see also below).

MACURO

A good trip from Güiria is to **Macuro** (*pop* 1,500), a quiet town on the tip of the Peninsula. Being surrounded on its landward sides by jungle, it is accessible only by boat, passing dense jungle which laps against deserted, palm-fringed beaches. It

was in one of these coves – perhaps Yacúa, there is no record – that Spaniards of Columbus' crew made the first recorded European landing on the continent on 5 August 1498, before taking formal possession in the estuary at Güiria the next day (locals like to believe the landing took place at Macuro, and the town's official new name is Puerto Colón). A big party is held here every year on 12 Oct to mark the official 'discovery' of America.

Macuro is friendly, with a beach (narrow, has biting ants, nice sand but pollution in the sea and lots of vegetation in the sea – boatmen will take you to a better beach, at a price).

Eduardo manages the little history museum. He is knowledgeable about the immediate area and can advise on hiking on the Peninsula, the National Park which covers the N side of Paría, and boats to the Orinoco Delta, and through the Bocas del Dragón to the miniscule settlement of **Patao** (3 hrs), where one can hire a guide for a trek across the Peninsula or an ascent of Cerro Patas, climbing up from cacao and banana plantations into cool montane forest. Fishing boats can often be hired to take you to many small villages, making for a hot but relaxed trip in one of Venezuela's less-visited corners.

- **Services In Macuro**: a few understocked shops, one restaurant, 3 hotels (one of which is **F**, basic, good, big meals, free coffee) and rooms to let (easy to camp or sling your hammock somewhere).

- **Boats** Leave Güiria for Macuro Mon-Sat, possibly Sun, at 1000 (US$2.50, take protection against sun, and plastic sheeting in case of rough seas – ask for Don Pedro), returning 0530, taking 3 hrs.

- **Travel to Trinidad** Helpful for boats to Trinidad, accommodation in Trinidad, or for excursions, is Adrian Winter-Roach, a Trinidadian (also known by the name of his boat *El Cuchillo*): C Carabobo, Casa s/n, Macuro, or the Distribuidora Beirut, C Valdez 37, Güiria, T/F 81677, or Vereda Paramacuni 37, Banco Obrero, Güiria. He travels to Port of Spain about once a week (not weekends), clearing all necessary formalities, US$60 one way, US$100 return, 4-day trips with food and lodging US$170, reductions for large groups. Ask in the port for other sailings.

Windward Lines Ltd (Global Steamship Agencies Ltd, Mariner's Club, Wrightson Road, PO

Box 966, Port of Spain, Trinidad, T 624-2279, F 809-627-5091, or in Güiria, Acosta Shipping Agents, Bolívar 31, T 094-81679/81233, F 81112, English spoken) sails to Güiria every other week, arriving Tues 2130, departing Wed at 2300, on its route St Lucia, Barbados, St Vincent, Trinidad, Venezuela and back (on alternate weeks the ship goes to Margarita). Fares: US$40 one way, US$60 return.

Immigration etc: if leaving Venezuela, remember to get an exit stamp, probably in Macuro, but check. Officially, to enter Trinidad and Tobago you need a ticket to your home country, but often a return to Venezuela will suffice. Extending permission to stay in Trinidad is possible. Returning to Venezuela this way poses no problems.

PEDERNALES

You can visit the Orinoco delta from Güiria; there are motor boats trading between Güiria and **Pedernales** (*pop* 3,100), a small village in the delta. Only Indians live in the northern part of the village.

● **Accommodation** Hotel, **F**, rats, comfortable beds, meals available, owner meets boats; the store on the riverbank also has rooms with cooking facilities, **F**; also at the blue house opp, **G** pp. For a shower, ask Jesús, who runs a fish-freezing business.

● **Boats** Pedernales is only accessible by boat. From Güiria the trip takes about 5 hrs, US$13, check for boats at the harbour (the *Guadeloupe*, *Verónica* and *Mil del Valle*), the *Hotel Fortuna*, the *Hotel Plaza*, or ask for Andrecito, who lives on N side of small plaza nearest harbour entrance. Cargo boats operated by men from Pedernales, known in Güiria as 'Los Indios', charge US$7.50-10 negotiable according to number of passengers, no seats, deck space in open only, can be rough, 'the sun is very strong and you and your luggage will get wet!'. From **Tucupita** (see page 1560) boats are easier to find. To Tucupita, locals pay US$5, but you may get asked for US$40 (ask for Juan but be prepared to bargain hard), leave at daybreak, 6-7 hrs, rec as the boat stops in some of the Indian villages, where you can buy hammocks (*chinchorros*), fish, cheese, and some beautiful carved animal figures made of balsa wood (see also page 1560). Many birds and Orinoco dolphins may be seen en route.

ISLA DE MARGARITA

Margarita is the country's main Caribbean holiday destination. Some parts are crowded but there are undeveloped beaches, villages with pretty churches, colonial La Asunción and several national parks including the fascinating Restinga lagoon.

Isla de Margarita and two close neighbours, Coche and Cubagua, form the state of Nueva Esparta.

Isla de Margarita is in fact one island whose two sections are tenuously linked by the 18 km sandspit which separates the sea from the Restinga lagoon. At its largest, Margarita is about 32 km from N to S and 67 km from E to W. Most of its people live in the developed eastern part, which has some wooded areas and fertile valleys. The western part, the Peninsula de Macanao, is hotter and more barren, with scrub, sand dunes and marshes. Wild deer, goats and hares roam the interior, but 4WD vehicles are needed to penetrate it. The entrance to the Peninsula de Macanao is a pair of hills known as **Las Tetas de María Guevara**, a national monument covering 1,670 ha.

The climate is exceptionally good; very little rain. Water is piped from the mainland. The roads are good, and a bridge connects the two parts. Nueva Esparta's population is over 200,000, of whom 68,000 live in the main city, Porlamar (which is not the capital, that is La Asunción).

The island has enjoyed a boom since 1983, largely as a result of the fall in the value of the bolívar and the consequent tendency of Venezuelans to spend their holidays at home. Margarita's status as a duty-free zone also helps. Venezuelan shoppers go in droves for clothing, electronic goods and other consumer items. Gold and gems are good value, but many things are not. There has been extensive building in Porlamar, with new shopping areas and Miami-style hotels going up. A number of beaches are also being developed. Its popularity means that various packages are on offer, sometimes at good value, especially off-season.

Local industries are fishing and fibre work, such as hammocks and straw hats. Weaving, pottery and sweets are being pushed as handicraft items for the tourists. An exhibition centre has been opened at El Cercado, near Santa Ana, on

C Principal, near the church.

Despite the property boom and frenetic building on much of the coast and in Porlamar, much of the island has been given over to natural parks. Of these the most striking is the **Laguna La Restinga**. Launches provide lengthy runs around the mangrove swamps, but they create a lot of wash and noise. The mangroves are fascinating, with shellfish clinging to the

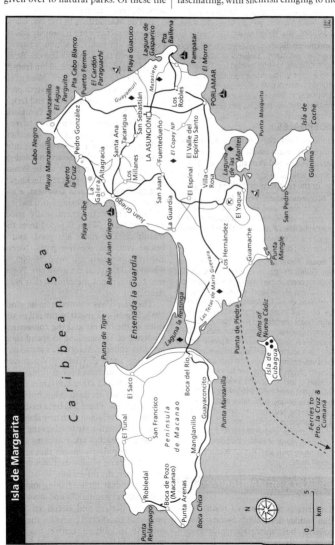

Isla de Margarita

roots. The launch will leave you on a shingle and shell beach (don't forget to arrange with your boatman to collect you), and you can rummage for shellfish in the shallows (protection against the sun essential – see below for prices, etc). Flamingoes live in the lagoon.

There are mangroves also in the **Laguna de las Marites** natural monument, W of Porlamar. Other parks are Las Tetas de María Guevara (see above), **Cerro el Copey**, 7,130 ha, and **Cerro Matasiete y Guayamurí**, 1,672 ha (both reached from La Asunción).

By boat from Porlamar you can go to the Isla de los Pájaros, or Morro Blanco, for both bird-spotting and underwater fishing. In Boca del Río there is a Museum of the Sea.

Festivals on Margarita

6-13 Jan at Altagracia; 20-27 Jan at Tacarigua; 16-26 Mar at Paraguachí (*Feria de San José*); 3-10 May at Los Robles; 24-30 May at La Guardia; 6 June at Tacarigua; 25-26 July at Santa Ana; 27 July at Punta de Piedra; 31 July (Batalla de Matasiete) and 14-15 Aug (Asunción de la Virgen) at La Asunción; 30 Aug-8 Sept at Villa Rosa; 8-15 Sept at El Valle; 11-12 and 28 Oct at Los Robles; 4-11 Nov at Boca del Río, 4-30 Nov at Boca del Pozo; 5-6 Dec at Porlamar; 15 Dec at San Francisco de Macanao; 27 Dec-3 Jan at Juan Griego. See map for locations.

PORLAMAR

Most of the hotels are at **Porlamar** (*phone code* 095), 20 km from the airport and about 28 km from Punta de Piedra, where most of the ferries dock. At Igualdad y Díaz is the Museo de Arte Francisco Narváez. The main, and most expensive, shopping area is Av Santiago Mariño; better bargains and a wider range of shops are to be found on Gómez and Guevara. The centre of the city is crowded with cars and shoppers. To the E there is continuing, apparently chaotic development of big holiday hotels and condominiums, separated by vast areas of waste ground and construction sites. At night everything closes by 2300; women alone should avoid the centre after dark. Porlamar has many casinos, all of which lack legal status.

Excursions

Ferries go to the **Isla de Coche** (11 km by 6), which has 4,500 inhabitants and one of the richest salt mines in the country. They also go, on hire only, to **Isla de Cubagua**, which is totally deserted, but you can visit the ruins of Nueva Cádiz (which have been excavated). Large catamarans take tourists on day sails to Coche, while the luxury motor yacht, *Viola*, goes to Cubagua, including drinks, lunch and snorkelling.

NB Aug and Sept are the vacation months when flights and hotels are fully booked.

NB Also, there is both a C Mariño and Av Santiago Mariño in the centre.

Local information
● **Accommodation**

L3 Hilton, C Los Uveros, Playa Moreno, Costa Azul, T 624111, F 620810, sailing dinghies for hire; other top class establishments.

A1 *Bella Vista**, Av Santiago Mariño, T 617222, F 612557, swimming pool, beach; **A2** *Dynasty*, T 621252, F 625101, opp Hilton, nice restaurant, pool; **A3** *Stauffer*, Av Santiago Mariño, T 612911, F 618708, large rooms, excellent service and restaurant, bar on roof, casino being added; **A3-B** *Marbella Mar*, Av Principal y C Chipichipi, T 624022, F 624488, clean rooms, friendly, especially with children, free bus service to the beach, highly rec.

B *Aguila Inn*, Narváez, ½ km N of centre, T 612311, F 616909, swimming pool, restaurant, rec; **B** *Colibrí*, Av Santiago Mariño, T 616346, new rooms, **D** in older rooms, a/c, rec; **B** *Imperial*, Av Raúl Leoni, Vía El Morro, T 616420, F 615056, best rooms in front have balcony, comfortable, safe, a/c, good showers, triple rooms available, English spoken, rec; **B** *Venus*, Milano y San Rafael, T 23722, a/c, safe; **B** *La Perla*, C Los Pinos, swimming pool, bar, restaurant, laundry service, shops in lobby inc travel agency Latsa, rec.

C *Contemporáneo*, C Mariño entre Igualdad y Velásquez, modern, a/c, bar, restaurant; **C** *Italia*, San Nicolás, cold water, a/c, safe, rec, but district is a bit rough.

D *Porlamar*, Igualdad y Fajardo, good restaurant and video bar La Punta, a/c or fan, hot water.

E *Brasilia*, San Nicolás, quiet, nice new rooms at back; **E** *Domino*, La Libertad 7-40, with fan or a/c, basic; **E** *España*, Mariño 6-35, T 095-612479, cold shower, good breakfast, fan, highly rec; **E** *La Viña*, La Marina, No 14-24,

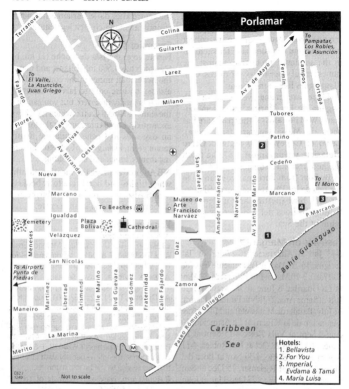

Porlamar

Hotels:
1. Bellavista
2. For You
3. Imperial, Evdama & Tamá
4. María Luisa

T 635723, bath, a/c, bar, restaurant, laundry; **E Malecón**, Marina y Arismendi, T 635723, seaview from front rooms, the Mexican owner, Luis and his wife are very helpful and generous, rec; **E Palermo**, C Igualdad, opp cathedral, best rooms on top floor with views of plaza; **E Robaldar**, Igualdad, nr Libertad, shower, a/c, rec. Many others around Plaza Bolívar (eg **F San Miguel**, good value); **E Tamá**, next to Imperial, gringo place with basic rooms, OK, excellent restaurant and atmosphere, bar is German-run, lots of languages spoken; **E Torino**, Mariño entre Zamora y Maneiro, T 610734, with bath, a/c.

● **Places to eat**

La Gran Pirámide, C Malave y JM Patiño, superb food, very good service, cocktails worth trying, very good value, highly rec; *Doña Martha*, Velázquez nr Hernández, Colombian food, good, inexpensive; *El Punto Criollo*, Igualdad nr *Hotel Porlamar*, excellent value, good; *Rancho Grande*, C Guevara, nr Playa El Agua bus stop, Colombian, good value, rec; *El Pollo de Carlitos*, Marcano y Martínez, nice location, live music most nights, good food and value; *Bahía* bar-restaurant, Av Raúl Leoni y Vía El Morro, excellent value, live music; excellent pizzas at *París Croissant* on Blvd Santiago Mariño; *Los 3 Delfines*, Cedeño 26-9, seafood, rec. *La Isla*, Mariño y Cedeño, 8 fast food counters ranging from hamburgers to sausages from around the world. *Dino's Grill*, Igualdad y Martínez, T 642366, open 0700-1400, buffet lunch, indoor/outdoor seating, grill, home-made sausages, wood-fired pizza oven, cheap, good service, rec.

● **Banks & money changers**

Banco Consolidado, Guevara y San Nicolás; banks generally slow with poor rates. *Casa de cambio* at Igualdad y Av Santiago Mariño; also *Cambio La Precisa*, Maneiro entre Mariño y Blvd Guevara, good rates. Amex office is opp *Hotel Bella Vista*, best rate for Amex TCs, open

0900-1200, 1400-1630, closed Mon. Banks are open 0830-1130, 1400-1630. Most shops accept credit cards.

● **Entertainment**
Mosquito Coast Club, behind *Bella Vista Hotel*, disco with genuine Venezuelan feel, good merengue and rock music, bar outside, also does excellent Mexican meals (beware of overcharging on simple items like water); discotheque for singles, *Village Club*, Av Santiago Mariño, rec for good music with variety of styles but expensive drinks, cover charge. *Doce 34*, Av 4 de Mayo, two dance floors, highly rec. Night life is generally good, but at European prices.

● **Post & telecommunications**
Post Office: C Arismendi.
Telephones: CANTV, Bolívar, entre Fajardo y Fraternidad.

● **Shopping**
Besides all the duty-free shops, *Del Bellorín*, Cedeño, nr Santiago Mariño, is good for handicrafts. Good selection of jewellery at *Sonia Gems*, on Cedeño; *Ivan Joyería* and *Inter Gold*, both on 4 de Mayo (latter is between *Ivan* and *Hotel Flamingo*); many other places on the main street are overpriced. When purchasing jewellery, bargain hard, don't pay by credit card (surcharges are imposed), get a detailed guarantee of the item. Designer clothes are cheap in many places, especially on Blvd Guevara, Blvd Gómez, and Calles Igualdad and Velázquez; cosmetics and perfumes also good value.

● **Tour companies & travel agents**
Supertours, C Larez, Quinta Thaid, T 618781, F 617061, tours of the island and elsewhere; *Zuluoga Tours*, San Nicolás entre Arismendi y Mariño No 16-40, helpful. Ask travel agents about excursions on the sailing catamaran, *Catatumbo*, rec.

● **Tourist offices**
A tourist information booth on 4 de Mayo has map, coupon booklet, *La Vista* tourist magazine. Travel agencies can also provide a tourist guide to Margarita. An outspoken and well-informed English-language newspaper, *Mira*, is published on the island; the editor/publisher acts also as an inexpensive tour guide; Av Santiago Mariño, Ed Carcaleo Suites, Apartamento 2-A, Porlamar (T 613351). The best map is available from Corpoven.

● **Transport**
Local Car hire: an economic proposition for any number above one and a good way of getting around the island, several offices at the airport. **Ramcar**, at airport and *Hotel Bella Vista*, rec as cheap and reliable, non-deductible insurance (as do Avis and Hertz; others on Av Santiago Mariño). **Lizmar** is the cheapest, watch

insurance excess, cars are in poor condition. In all cases, check the brakes. Scooters can also be hired from, among others, **Maruba Motor Rentals**, La Mariña (English spoken, good maps, highly rec, US$16 bikes for 2, US$13 bikes for one). Motor cycles may not be ridden between 2000 and 0500. **NB** Remember to keep an eye on the fuel gauge; there are service stations in towns, but a/c is heavy on fuel. Always check the gauge on the fuel pump carefully: overcharging is common.

Driving on Isla Margarita: the roads are generally good and most are paved. Signposts are often poorly-positioned (behind bushes, round corners), which adds to the night-time hazard of vehicles with badly-adjusted lights. It is best not to drive outside Porlamar after dark. Also beware of robbery of hired vehicles. Check conditions and terms of hire carefully.

Public: *Por Puestos* serve most of the island, leaving mainly from the corners of Plaza Bolívar in Porlamar. Fares: to Punta de Piedra (from 4 blocks from Plaza Bolívar, towards sea-front), US$0.50, to the ferry terminal US$0.65; to La Asunción, US$0.25, from C Fajardo, half a block from Igualdad; to Pampatar, US$0.15; to La Restinga (from La Marina y Mariño), US$0.70, El Agua (from corner of Guevara and Marcano), US$0.40; Juan Griego, US$0.40. **Taxi** fares are published by *Mira* but are not uniformly applied by drivers. If you want to hire a taxi for a day you will be charged US$7-10/hr. Always establish the fare before you get in the car. There is a 30% surcharge after 2100.

Air Gen Santiago Mariño Airport, between Porlamar and Punta de Piedra; comfortable and modern, has the international and national terminals at either end. Bus from Plaza Bolívar, US$0.70, taxi US$7. There are up to 12 flights a day from **Caracas**, with Servivensa, Aeropostal, Laser and Aserca, 50 mins flight; tickets are much cheaper if purchased in Venezuela in local currency. Reservations made from outside Venezuela are not always honoured. Daily Aeropostal flight to **Puerto Ordaz**, except Sun. Daily flights from Barcelona, Valencia, Canaima and weekdays from San Antonio, Maracaibo and Barquisimeto. Aeropostal flies twice a week from Barbados and Port of Spain. Avensa on C Fajardo, Porlamar, T 617111, airport 691021.

Ferries Very busy at weekends and Mon. From **Puerto La Cruz**, Margarita (**Punta de Piedra**): Conferries, Los Cocos terminal, T 677221, and *Meliá Hotel*, Pta La Cruz, T 653001, to Margarita, 4 a day between 0700 and 2400 each way (extras at 0400 and 1600 at busy times), 4 hrs, passengers US$7.70 one-way 1st class, US$5.10 2nd (in enclosed middle deck with limited views), children and pensioners half price, cars,

US$16-17. A new fast ferry, *Margarita Express*, takes 2 hrs, US$24. Ferries not always punctual. Don't believe taxi drivers at bus terminal who may tell you there's a ferry about to leave. From **Cumaná**, Conferry Terminal, Cumaná Puerto Sucre, T 311462, ferries at 0700 and 1600 to Margarita, returning 1000 and 2000, US$5.75 one way for passengers. A ferry from Punta de Piedra to Coche sails Mon-Fri, 1600, returns 1730, Sat and Sun, 0800 and 1730, returns 0530 and 1730.

Windward Lines (Global Steamship Agencies Ltd, Mariner's Club, Wrightson Road, PO Box 966, Port of Spain, Trinidad, T 809-624-2279) sails to Isla Margarita every other week (Tues) from Trinidad, St Vincent, Barbados and St Lucia. It sails from Pampatar to Trinidad on Wed at 1800, and on alternate weeks from Güiria at 2300, arriving in Port of Spain at 0700 on Thur. Contact David Hart, Windward Lines agent, C José María Vargas, frente Monederos, Pampatar, T 623527, friendly, efficient, speaks English, ensures immigration/customs goes smoothly. Return fares: from Trinidad US$70 (see Travel to Trinidad, page 1532), St Lucia, St Vincent or Barbados US$155. Travellers' cheques can be changed on board at good rates.

Road Several bus companies in Caracas sell through tickets from Caracas to Porlamar, arriving about midday. Buses return from Porlamar from terminal at Centro Comercial Bella Vista, at bottom end of C San Rafael. By car from Caracas, it takes about 4 hrs.

LA ASUNCION

The capital, La Asunción (*pop* 16,660), is a few kilometres inland from Porlamar. It has several colonial buildings, a cathedral, and the fort of Santa Rosa, with a famous bottle dungeon (open Mon 0800-1500, other days 0800-1800). There is a museum in the Casa Capitular, and a local market, good for handicrafts. On Plaza Bolívar, as well as the statue of Simón Bolívar, there is a statue of Luisa Cáceres de Arismendi, heroine of the Liberation and second wife of Gen Arismendi. Nearby are the Cerro Matasiete historical site, where the defeat of the Spanish on 31 July 1817 led to their evacuation of the island, and the Félix Gómez look-out in the Sierra Copuy.

- **Accommodation B-C** *Ciudad Colonial*, C La Margarita, upmarket, nice; **E** pp *de la Hotel Asunción*, C Unión, 2 blocks from Plaza Bolívar, with bath, a/c, fridge (rooms with balcony cost more but face noisy road, rooms without window cost less). Frequent *por puesto* service stops in front of hotel.

EL VALLE DEL ESPIRITU SANTO

Between La Asunción and Porlamar are the Parque Francisco Fajardo, beside the Universidad de Oriente, and **El Valle del Espíritu Santo**. Here is the church of the Virgen del Valle, a picturesque building with twin towers, painted white and pink. The Madonna is richly dressed (one dress has pearls, the other diamonds); the adjoining museum opens at 1400, it displays costumes and presents for the Virgin, including the 'milagro de la pierna de perla', a leg-shaped pearl. A pilgrimage is held in early September. Appropriate dress is required to enter the church.

Throughout the island, the churches are attractive: fairly small, with baroque towers and adornments and, in many cases, painted pink.

BEACHES ON MARGARITA

Apart from the shopping, what attracts the holidaymakers from Venezuela and abroad are the beaches: long white stretches of sand bordered by palms, but rather hot, with little shade (sunscreen essential).

In Porlamar, the main beach suffers from its popularity: calm shallow water, pedalos for hire, windsurf classes. The *Bella Vista* beach, although crowded, is kept clean; lots of restaurants. Playa Morena is a long, barren strip of sand serving Costa Azul, the expanding hotel zone to the E of the city. La Caracola is a very popular beach for the younger crowd.

PAMPATAR

For a more Venezuelan atmosphere go NE to **Pampatar** (*pop* 10,590), which is set around a bay favoured by yachtsmen as a summer anchorage. Pampatar has the island's largest fort, San Carlos de Borromeo, built in 1662 after the Dutch destroyed the original, and the smaller La Caranta. Visit the church of Cristo del Buen Viaje, the Library/Museum and the customs house.

There is an amusement park to the SW of Pampatar, called Isla Aventura, with ferris wheel, roller coaster, water slide, dodgems etc, open Fri and Sat, 1800-

2400, Sun, 1700-2400, and more frequently in peak holiday season. Entrance in peak season is US$5 adults, US$3.35 children, all rides included; in low season entrance is US$0.50 and each ride US$0.30-0.60.

Jet skis for hire on the clean and pretty beach. A scale model of Columbus' *Santa María* is used for taking tourists on trips. A fishing boat can be hired for US$12 for 2½ hrs, 4-6 passengers; shop around for best price, good fun and fishing.

● **Accommodation & places to eat**
A2 pp *Flamingo Beach*, T (095) 624822, F 620271, 5-star, all-inclusive, food, drinks, entertainment, service, taxes, casino, good value; *Hippocampus Beach*, next door, T 623090, F 623510, 4-star, package holidays, gaudy; **D** *Res Don Juan*, with bath and fan; apartments sleeping 6 are available. Beach restaurant *Antonio's*, rec; also *Trimar*, good value; *El Farallon*, beside the Castillo, excellent seafood. **F** pp guesthouse of David Hart (Windward Lines agent), Av Principal 12, T 623527, next to supermarket, with bath, fan, welcoming, dark rooms, mosquitoes.

The beaches on the eastern side are divided into ocean and calm beaches, according to their location in relation to the open sea. The former tend to be rougher (good surfing and windsurfing) and colder. Water is uniformly clear and unpolluted. It is still possible, even in high season, to find practically deserted beaches. Restaurants, *churuatas* (bars built like Indian huts), sunshades and deckchairs are widespread. (Hire charges are about US$1.50/item.)

PLAYA GUACUCO

On the eastern coast is **Playa Guacuco**, reached from La Asunción by a road through the Guayamurí reserve. It's a popular local beach with a lot of surf, fairly shallow, palm trees, restaurant and parking lot; excellent horseriding here or up into the hills, US$30 for 2 hrs, contact Harry Padrón at the ranch in Agua de Vaca, or phone travel agent on 611311. *Hotel Guacuco Resort*, 1 km from beach, T/F (02) 242-9497, apartments for 4, pool, bar, German-owned, recommended. Paraguito beach is best for surfing (strong waves; full public services).

PLAYA EL AGUA

45 mins by bus from Porlamar (US$0.45), 4 km of stone-free white sand with many *kioskos*, which have palm-leaf shade areas. 2 sun chairs under one of these cost US$2-3, umbrella US$1 extra. The sea is very rough for children, but fairly shallow (beware the cross current when you are about waist deep, it gets very strong and can quickly carry you out to sea). This is the most popular beach on the island and at Venezuelan holiday times it is overcrowded. At other times it is ideal for sunbathing and walking; the fashionable part is at the southern end; the northern end is popular with younger people, is less touristy, has fewer facilities, and less shade. It's possible to see the island by Ultralight from here at weekends. Contact Omar Contreras, T 095-617632 or José-Antonio Fernández 095-623519, English spoken, US$35/flight. (Also possible from the old airport at Porlamar.)

● **Accommodation L2** *Playa El Agua Beach Resort*; **A1** *Lagunamar*, a few kilometres N of Pampatar, T 620711, F 621445, occupies a vast spread of flat coastland, beach, 9 pools and 6 restaurants; **A3** *Miragua Club Resort*. **C** *Residencias Miramar*, Av 31 de Julio-Carretera Manzanillo, esq calle Miragua, 3 mins from beach, 1 min from supermarket, family-run, self-catering apartments, comfortable, barbecue, rec; **B** *Casa Trudel*, T/F 589-548735, 4 rooms, bed and breakfast, homely atmosphere (Dutch/Canadian owners), no young children, evening food service, barbecue once a week, 5 mins walk from beach; **B** *Trudel's Garden Vacation Homes*, C Miragua, T/F 095-48735, 6 large 2-bedroom houses set in a beautiful garden, 200m from beach, fresh towels daily (fully equipped kitchens), for reservations by post write to Dan and Trudy O'Brien, Apdo 106, Isla Margarita, 6301, Porlamar, Venezuela; **E** *Hostería El Agua*, Av 31 de Julio vía Manzanillo, T 48935, contact Sarah Studer, English, French German and Italian spoken, clean bathroom, good beds, fan, fridge, laundry facilities, 4 mins walk from beach; **B** *Pelican Village*, northern end, small group of bungalows, satellite TV, pool, restaurant, bar, German run, quiet. An unnamed chalet park next to the *Miragua Club Resort*, self-catering, all facilities, very welcoming, highly rec.

● **Places to eat** *El Paradiso*, southern end, rents out cabins, US$12, small but comfortable; *Kiosko El Agua*, helpful, English spoken; *Posada Shangri-Lá*, rec, *Casa Vieja*, seafood,

La Dorada, French owned by Gérard and Hilda, with good beach view, rec as good value. Many beach restaurants stay open till 2200. Recommended are *Moisés* (Venezuelan-owned), *Sueño Tropical* (Italian-owned), also own *Jardín Tropical*, further down beach, spacious, pasta, traditional seafood dishes, rec, *Tinajón del Agua* (on main road nr beach entrance), small, popular, good.

Manzanillo (*pop* 2,000) is a picturesque bay between the mountains on the NE point of the island. The water gets deep rather suddenly, fishing huts, fish sold on beach, apartments, expensive restaurant, Playa Escondida is at the far end. **Puerto Fermín**/El Tirano is where Lope de Aguirre, the infamous conquistador, landed in 1561 on his flight from Peru; El Caserío handicrafts museum is nearby. **El Cardón** is an attractive limestone outcrop.

The coast road is interesting, with glimpses of the sea and beaches to one side. There are a number of clifftop lookout points. The road improves radically beyond Manzanillo, winding from one beach to the next. Playa Puerto la Cruz (wide and windy) adjoins **Pedro González** (*pop* 3,700), with a broad sweeping beach, running from a promontory (easy to climb) to scrub and brush that reach down almost to the water's edge. Ask for Antonietta Luciani at *Restaurant Pedrogonzález*, she has an apartment to rent, US$40/day, sleeps 6, well-equiped, recommended as is her restaurant. The next bay is accessible by scrambling over rocks (major building here).

● **Accommodation In Manzanillo**: **B** *Hotel Karibek*, overlooks the sea, wonderful view, quiet, balcony, fan, swimming pool, bar and restaurant adjacent, breakfast provided, evening meals not great but there are a couple of good restaurants down on the beach, easy taxi ride to other beaches, rec; **C** *Pahayda Vilas*, nice apartments, large rooms, 2 baths for 4 people, sign at main road; 100m further on towards Playa Azul, beach house with rooms to let and German-owned restaurant, good food. **Between Manzanillo and Pedro González**: **A1** *Isla Bonita*, T (095) 657111, F 657211, Playa Puerto Cruz, a monstrous edifice of reflective glass, 18-hole golf course, business centre, posh restaurants; **A3** *Dunes*, Playa Puerto Cruz, T 631333, F 632910, a more modest option, all-inclusive resort of low rise, tiled buildings in pinks and creams, activities, sports, fun and games.

JUAN GRIEGO

Further W is **Juan Griego** bay and town (*pop* 8,300), a small, sleepy town whose picturesque bay is full of fishing boats. The little fort of La Galera is on a promontory at the northern side, beyond which is a bay of the same name with a narrow strip of beach, more fishing boats and many seafront restaurants.

● **Accommodation & places to eat B** *El Yare*, T 55835, 1 block from beach, some suites with kitchen, owner speaks English, highly rec; *Hotel Nuevo Juan Griego*, Dutch owners, fan, right on beach; *Hotel La Galera*, rec; **D** *Gran Sol*, La Marina, entrance in shopping arcade, T 55736, a/c, TV; **D-E** *Aparthotel y Res El Apurano*, C La Marina y El Fuerte, T 530901, English-speaking manager, 2-bedroom apartments with bath, hot water, a/c, but no utensils or towels (because of theft); **E** *Res Carmencita*, C Guevara 20, T 55561, a/c, private bath, rec; **E** *Fortín*, a/c, cold water, opp beach, most rooms have good views, good restaurant and tables on the beach; **E** *La Posada de Clary*, C Los Mártires, T 530037, restaurant, rec, also apartments for 4, **D**, a/c, kitchen, parking. *Restaurant Mi Isla* is rec, also the Lebanese restaurant on the beach; *Viña del Mar*, opp *Hotel Fortín*, a/c, attractive, excellent food; *Juan Griego Steak House*, same building as *Hotel El Yare*, good value, rec; also rec, *El Buho*; *Viejo Muelle*, next door, good restaurant, live music, outside beach bar.

La Galera is to the E and a good place to relax and enjoy the famous Juan Griego sunset (**D** *Posada del Sol*, bedroom, kitchen, sitting area, fan, fridge). To the N is **Caribe**, which has many beach restaurants.

South of Juan Griego, the road goes inland to San Juan Bautista (a pleasant colonial town ringed by hills; Rosa Hernández has apartments, **E**, C La Vega, on left leaving town, past cemetery, spacious, fan, a/c, cold water; *por puesto* from Juan Griego). Thence to Punta de Piedra, the ferry dock, see above (a pleasant stretch through cultivated land and farms at regular intervals; *por puesto* Juan Griego to ferry).

Due S of San Juan is **El Yaque**, near the airport and the mouth of the Laguna de las Marites (the hinterland is very bleak). This is said to be the best place for windsurfing. Surf boards can be hired at the *Club El Mistral*, good service, very helpful, ½-day costs US$30. It is being rapidly developed with small hotels, but it suffers from aircraft noise and lacks public transport (taxi from Porlamar, US$5). **C** *California*, T (014) 951907, F 950908, 46 rooms, small pool; *Casarita*, T (016) 950290 (cellular number), resort, pleasant building in neo-colonial style, bed and breakfast, 400m from beach.

The **Peninsula de Macanao** is connected to the other section of Margarita by La Restinga, a dyke of broken seashells which is part of Fuentedueño National Park. On the right is a spotlessly clean beach, on the left the lagoon. At the far end are many little restaurants and a cluster of fishermen's huts with landing stages from which the launches make trips into the mangroves (US$14/boat taking 5 passengers; bus from Porlamar harbour front US$1, ask driver to drop you off). The peninsula is quite underdeveloped, although it is hardly an untouched paradise. Some of the beaches, however, are highly regarded: Manzanilla, Guayaconcito, Boca de Pozo, Macanao, Punta Arenas and Manglanillo. There is a harbour at Chacachacare.

STATE OF MONAGAS

MATURIN

Maturín (*pop* 268,650; *phone code* 091), capital of Monagas State, is relaxed and pleasant place.

Excursions

Laguna Grande is a beautiful lake in the jungle about 32 km away, *por puesto* No 2 from the old market, US$0.50. By the lake is the *Club Naútico*, open 1100-1830, closed Mon. Return transport can be difficult as passing *por puestos* are usually full.

Local information
● **Accommodation**

C *Chaima Inn*, pool, satellite TV, good restaurant with buffet lunch, rec; *Perla Princess*, Av Juncal y Monagas, hot water, good, but restaurant overpriced; **C** *Friuli*, Carrera 9 with C 30, quiet, a/c.

D *París*, Av Bolívar 183, T 414028, a/c, hot water, safe, central, rec; **D** *Berlín*, Av Bolívar, lively bar, shows at weekends.

E *El Terminal*, at bus terminal, just out of town on road to Barcelona, very convenient, a/c, private bath, drinking water supplied, helpful owner, rec; **E** *Manolo*, Av Bolívar, pleasant, good restaurant with reasonable prices, bar; **E** *Trinidad*, Av Bolívar, English speaking, *Trinidad* is two hotels, one is rec, the other not rec.

● **Places to eat**

Yarúa (behind the Cathedral) most expensive, seafood and grilled meat; *Parador Turístico Arauguay*, via La Cruz, Argentine barbecue speciality; *Mister Pasta*, Av Juncal, 3 blocks from *Perla Princess*, good value, wide variety.

● **Banks & money changers**

Banco Consolidado (American Express), Av Raúl Leoni, Edif D'Amico, take bus 1 or 5 along Av Bolívar, heading away from bus terminal; **Banco Mercantil**, C Monagas and opp central market, most likely to accept TCs.

● **Transport**

Air Air services to Caracas (Aeropostal, Aserca and Servivensa), Ciudad Bolívar (Servivensa) and Puerto Ordaz (Avensa), good restaurant upstairs in airport.

Buses Bus station is at end of Av Bolívar, take bus No 1 or 5 to get there. Buses leave 3 times a day for **Caracas** from the central bus terminal, 2030, 2200 and 2245 hrs (US$6.50, 8 hrs, *por puesto* US$13); buses for **Ciudad Guayana**-San Félix (0815, 3 hrs, US$4, inc ferry) and **El Dorado** leave from the terminus nr the airport. To **Puerto La Cruz** or **Barcelona**, take a *por puesto* to Cumaná and change, 2 hrs, US$4.20. Bus only to **Ciudad Bolívar**, US$4.50, change in Ciudad Guyana-San Félix (no *por puesto*). Bus to **Carúpano**, at 1000, US$3, 3 hrs, beautiful landscape. To **Caripe**, 2½ hrs, US$1.10, *por puesto*, 2 hrs, US$4.50. Bus to **Río Caribe**, US$3, 4 hrs, at 1100 with Expresos Maturín, be quick to queue for the bus, ticket does not guarantee a seat or even transport. Bus to **Tucupita** at 1100, US$3 with Expresos Guayanesa (poor standard), 3-4 hrs. Bus to **Güiria**, US$3.50, 6 hrs, Expresos Maturín; to **Irapa** 1230, 4½ hrs, US$4. Travelling between the airport and town: *por puesto* Nos 1,5,6 (US$0.25), or bus from main road outside airport (US$0.10). Taxis from the Reponsable de Venezuela office will try to charge much more.

16 km W of Maturín is the oil camp at Jusepín, beyond which is **Santa Bárbara** (airport) where they sell native *chinchorros*, hammocks of woven *moriche* palm leaves, decorated with coloured yarn. They can also be found in Tucupita (see page 1560). They 'give' when you lie on them and do not absorb moisture when used on the beach. Very good for camping.

CARIPE

Just beyond Jusepín an unpaved 32 km road, left, joins the Maturín-Cumaná road (212 km, all paved but twisty; beautiful tropical mountain scenery). At San Francisco on this road is a branch road running 22½ km NE to **Caripe** (*pop* 23,880; *phone code* 092), set in a mountain valley. To the W of the town is a Mirador, from which there are great views over the whole valley. There is also a paved road between Carúpano and Caripe via Santa Cruz and Santa María, 2 hrs.

Local festivals
2-12 Aug, Feria de las Flores; 10-12 Oct, NS del Pilar.

Local information
● **Accommodation**
C *Samán**, Enrique Chaumer 29, T 51183, good atmosphere, moderate restaurant.

D *San Francisco*, Av Enrique Chaumer 55, T 51018, hot water, good restaurant.

E *Hacienda Campo Claro*, Teresén, T 51994, managed by Francisco Belancourt, rents cabins, can provide meals, horseriding; **E-F** *Berlin Caripe*, German-owned, bath, restaurant closes at 2000, rec; **E-F** *Venezia*, spacious, restaurant, owner speaks English.

F *La Fogata*, opp *San Francisco*, shared bath, large rooms, good value.

● **Places to eat**
Lonchería Arabe, rec; *Tasca Restaurant Río Colorado*, cheap, good local food, rec; *El Cafetín*, snack bar on main road, delicious food, rec; *La Solana*, local atmosphere, souvenir shop and very good food.

● **Transport**
Bus from Caripe to **Caracas** at 1800 stops in Cumaná, pick up at San Remo Sur office, next to *Hotel San Francisco*. Caracas direct leaves at 2000. Bus to **Maturín** direct, 0600, 2 hrs, US$1.

CUEVA DEL GUÁCHARO

12 km from Caripe is the remarkable **Cueva del Guácharo** National Monument. The cave was discovered by Humboldt, and has since been penetrated 10½ km along a small, crystal-clear stream. First come the caves in which live about 18,000 *guácharos* (oil birds) with an in-built radar system for sightless flight. Their presence supports a variety of wild-life in the cave: blind mice, fish and crabs in the stream, yellow-green plants, crickets, ants, etc. For 2 hrs at dusk (about 1900) the birds pour out of the cave's mouth, continuously making the clicking sounds of their echo-location system, coming back at dawn with their crops full of the oily fruit of certain local palms. Through a very narrow entrance is the *Cueva del Silencio* (Cave of Silence), where you can hear a pin drop. About 2 km in is the *Pozo del Viento* (Well of the Wind). The streams are bridged and the path is paved, but there is still quite a lot of water around; wear old clothes, stout shoes and be prepared to take off your shoes and socks. In the wet season it can be a bit slippery; tours into the cave may be shortened or even closed in Aug-Sept because of rising water level. There is a caving museum with a good range of publications, including a leaflet about the cave in English, US$0.80; good cafetería. Opposite the road is a paved path to Salto Paila, a 25m waterfall, about 30 mins' walk, guides available; orange and other fruit trees along the way. Other routes are suggested at the cave. A beautiful path, built by Inparqes, starts at the caving museum, with some nice shelters for picnics.

● **Access** The cave is open 0830-1700, US$4 entry with compulsory guide (Jesus speaks English, rec, Alexander speaks a little German, also rec); guided tour 2 hrs. Leave backpacks at the ticket office. Tape recorders and cameras are allowed, the guides inform you when you can use a flash. To go further than 1½ km into the caves, permits from Inparques in Caracas and special equipment are needed.

● **Accommodation** For a small tip you can stay the night at the museum, guarded, good birdwatching.

● **Transport** There are frequent buses from Caripe to the caves. If staying in Caripe, take a *por puesto* (a jeep marked Santa María – Muelle), at 0800, US$3, see the caves and waterfall and catch the Cumaná bus which goes past the caves between 1200 and 1230. Taxis from Caripe (US$5), hitching difficult. Bus from Cumaná direct to the Cueva del Guácharo leaves at 0715, US$2.50 and stops right in front of the caves. *Por puesto* from Cumaná US$7.50, 2 hrs. Private tours can be organized from Cumaná for about US$10 pp, with guide.

ANACO

From Puerto La Cruz a toll road goes inland, skirting Barcelona. At Km 52 a road forks left to Santa Bárbara and Maturín. Continuing straight on from Km 52, the road passes W of **Anaco** (*pop* 60,000). It has an airport and is a base for oil-well service contracting companies. Beyond Anaco a branch road leads to the oilfields of San Joaquín.

● **Accommodation D** *Motel Canaima*, Av Aeropuerto, good; **E** *Dragón Oriental* on same street nearby, central; **E** *Mand's Club*, Av Venezuela, restaurant, bar, a bit noisy; **E** *Muñiz*, Sucre, basic; **E** *Viento Fresco*, some fans, dark rooms, poor security.

EL TIGRE

The main road passes near Cantaura, a market town, and goes on to **El Tigre** (*pop* 105,000), a busy city on the edge of the Guanipa Plateau. It too is a centre for petroleum, but also for large peanut plantations. El Tigre and its neighbour, El Tigrito (also called San José de Guanipa, *pop* 48,220, 10 km E), are well-served by highways to all parts of the country. The local airport is at San Tomé, 5 km from El Tigrito (regular bus to El Tigre US$3.50). In San Tomé, the eastern headquarters of Menevén, the former Mene Grande oil company, the public relations office (C Guico) is happy to arrange tours to nearby wells.

● **Accommodation C** *Internacional Gran Hotel*, Av Intercomunal, pool, nightclub, best but not central; **D** *Tamanaco*, Av España, opp bus terminal, a/c, good, with highly rec restaurant; **D** *Orinoco*, Guayana, best of cheaper places, cafetería. On Av España, **E** *Caribe*, and **E** *La Fuente*, nr main plaza, **E** *Arichuna* and **E** *Santa Cruz*, clean and basic. Chilean restaurant serves excellent Chilean food and salads, on Av España. In El Tigrito is **D** *Hotel Rancho Grande*, acceptable; services better in El Tigre. **Warning** Pickpockets work the city buses, usually in pairs.

ROUTES From El Tigre, Highway 15 leads off to Caracas (via Valle de Pascua, Camatagua and Cúa – 550 km, see page 1545). The road S leads, straight and flat, 130 km over the *llanos* to the Angostura bridge across the Orinoco to Ciudad Bolívar (298 km from Puerto La Cruz).

The Llanos of the Orinoco

A SPECTACULAR route descends from the Sierra Nevada to the flat *llanos*, perhaps one of the best places in the world to see birds. South of these cattle lands stretch the forests through which flow the Orinoco and its tributaries. Out of the lowlands rise strange, flat-topped *tepuyes*.

This area of flat grasslands, 1,000 km by 320 km, lies between the Andes and the Río Orinoco. It is veined by numerous slow running rivers, forested along their banks. The vast flatland is only varied here and there by *mesas*, or slight upthrusts of the land. About 5 million of the country's 6.4 million cattle, many of the Zebu type from Brazil and India, are in the *llanos*, 30% of the country's area, but holding no more than 13% of the population. When the whole plain is periodically under water, the *llaneros* drive their cattle into the hills or through the flood from one *mesa* to another. When the plain is parched by the sun and the savanna grasses become uneatable they herd the cattle down to the damper region of the Apure and Orinoco. Finally they drive them into the valley of Valencia to be fattened.

Around Oct/Nov, when the vast plains

The Virgin Mary and Coromoto

After the first appearance of the Virgin to the Cospes Indians near Guanare, Chief Coromoto failed to be baptized, though he did hedge by getting other members of the tribe baptized. When the Virgin reappeared he made a grab at her and told her gruffly to be gone, but she vanished leaving in his hand a likeness of herself on the inner surface of a split stone now on display in the church (on a parchment in another version). For years little attention was paid to the image, and it was only in 1942 that this Virgin was declared the Patron of Venezuela.

are still partially flooded, wildlife abounds. Among the animals that can be seen are capibara, caiman, monkeys, anacondas, river dolphins, pumas and countless varieties of birds. Tours are best arranged in Mérida (see above).

VALENCIA TO BARINAS

There is a splendid road to the western *llanos* of Barinas, from Valencia. It goes through **San Carlos** (*pop* 71,650), capital of Cojedes State (festivals 18 Jan and 2-5 Nov – San Carlos Borromeo), **Acarigua**, a thriving agricultural centre in Portuguesa State, and **Guanare** (*pop* 32,500), a national place of pilgrimage with an old parish church containing the much venerated relic of the Virgin of Coromoto, Patron of Venezuela.

Festivals in Portuguesa State

Pilgrimages to Coromoto, 2 Jan and 8 Sept; Candlemas in Guanare, 1 Feb; Virgen de la Corteza in Acarigua, 11 Feb (bull-baiting, dancing).

● **Accommodation & places to eat** San Carlos: C *Central*, safe, a/c, good bar and restaurant, secure parking; F *San Carlos*, Av Carabobo, a/c, bath. Acarigua: C *Motel Payara**, on road to Guanare, pool, a/c; C *Hotel Parigua*, C 31, a/c, secure parking; E *Motel Rancho Grande*, safe, very mediocre restaurant attached; *Campeste*, nr bus terminal. Guanare: C *Italia*, Carrera 5, No 19-60, a/c, bar and restaurant, offstreet parking; others, inc *Motel Sultana*, on the main road to Acarigua, a/c, safe, reasonable bar and restaurant adjacent; C *Motel Portuguesa*, on northern outskirts – beware of dangerous intersection, a/c, cold water, good restaurant, pool, small zoo with tiny cages for animals; *Restaurant Don Quixote*, nr *Hotel Italia*, good atmosphere but expensive.

BARINAS

The road continues to Barinas (*pop* 179,660; *phone code* 073), the hot, sticky capital of the cattle-raising and oil-rich State of Barinas. The shady Parque Universitario has a botanical garden and a zoo open Mon to Fri. There are two museums. Barinas is a good base for fishing and wildlife-watching excursions into the *llanos*.

Local information
● **Accommodation**
On Av 23 de Enero, nr the airport: C *Bristol**, a/c, safe, good, rec, nondescript restaurant; C *Varyná*, a/c, rec; E *Motel La Media Avenida*, T 22278, cold showers, bar, restaurant, parking, rec; D *Internacional*, C Arzobispo Méndez on Plaza Zamora, T 22343, a/c, safe, good restaurant. Opp bus terminal are: E *Palacio*, a/c, good value; F pp *Lisboa*, basic, fan; F-E pp *Motel San Marino*, with bath, a/c, small rooms, not too clean.

● **Places to eat**
Adán y Eva, Av Sucre, criollo restaurant, good; *Don Enrique*, opp *Hotel Palacio*, good, cheap. Good patisserie opp the bus terminal. *Yoanna*, Av 7, 16-47, corner of Márques del Pumar, Arab owner, excellent; *Franko Café*, on Plaza Sucre, bar/restaurant, good, music; *El Estribo*, C Apure entre Av Garguera y Andrés Varela, roast and barbecued local meat, good, open 1100-2400.

● **Banks & money changers**
Banco Italo or Banco Unión, for Mastercard or Visa cash withdrawals. Banco de Barinas accepts Thomas Cook TCs.

● **Tourist offices**
On Plaza Bolívar, helpful, local maps available, no English spoken.

● **Transport**
Air Airport with local services and to Caracas (2 a day). The tourist office here is friendly and has a free town map and hotel list.

Buses To **Mérida**, 5 a day with Transportes Barinas, US$2.50, spectacular ride through the mountains, 5-7 hrs (sit on right for best views); *por puesto*, US$4; also to **Valera** at 0730, US$3.15, 7 hrs. To **Caracas**, US$6.70, 8 hrs, several companies go direct or via **Maracay** and **Valencia**, regularly 0730-2300. To **San Cristóbal**, several daily, US$3.75, 5 hrs; to **San Fernando de Apure**, US$8.15, 9 hrs with Expresos Los Llanos at 0900, 2300; the same company also goes to **Maracaibo** (at 2000 and 2200, US$7.80, 8 hrs), **San Antonio** (at 2330) and **Puerto La Cruz** (0730, 1445, US$14.25, 16 hrs). The bus terminal is on the edge of the town.

ROUTES From Barinas there is a beautifully scenic road to Apartaderos, in the Sierra Nevada de Mérida (see page 1509). Also from Barinas, Route 5 runs along the eastern edge of the Andes to San Cristóbal, via Santo Domingo (airport). Another road heads E, across the *llanos* to San Fernando de Apure (see below).

Motorists travelling E from Mérida to Ciudad Bolívar can either go across the *llanos* or via San Carlos, Tinaco, El Sombrero, Valle de la Pascua (see below) and El Tigre. The latter route requires no ferry crossings and has more places with accommodation.

● **Accommodation** In the *llanos*, nr El Baúl (turn off Tinaco-El Sombrero road at El Cantón), is a safari-type lodge at the working ranch of *Hato Piñero*, US$140 pp/day, fully inclusive, US$240 pp, inc return overland transport from Caracas, US$560 by chartered plane, free drinks, good room, and bi-lingual nature guide for excellent bird- and animal-watching trips, highly rec; address: Hato Piñero, Edif Gen de Seguros, p 6, Ofic 6B, Av La Estancia, Chuao, Caracas 1060, T (2) 916965/916854/916576, F 916776. No public transport to ranch but ask police in El Baúl for ride with Hato Piñero workers. Last part of the road very bad. From Caracas the direct route is 6 hrs; the expensive alternative is to use the airstrip. On the road to El Baúl at Km 93 (next to Hato Piñero turn off) is the *Reserva Privada de Flora y Fauna Mataclara*: lodging with full board, horse riding, fishing and animal watching trips costs US$50 pp a day; address Prof Antonio González-Fernández, Universidad de Los Llanos 'Unellez', Mesa de Caracas, Guanare 3323, Estado de Portuguesa, F 57-68130.

CARACAS SOUTH TO THE LLANOS

From the Panamerican Highway near Cagua (*pop* 92,000), 16 km E of Maracay, a good road leads S to **San Juan de los Morros** (*pop* 78,500). A cock-fighting tournament is held here each year. It has natural hot springs. Nearby are mountains with vertical cliffs, on which several climbing routes have been opened.

● **Accommodation D** *Gran Hotel Los Morros*, on Carrera Nacional towards Villa de Cura; **D** *Excelsior*, C Marino.

South of San Juan, just past Ortiz, is a crossroads: W to San Carlos, S to the *llanos* and San Fernando de Apure, and E to **El Sombrero** (large Indian population in the area), **Chaguaramas** and **Valle de la Pascua** (*pop* 75,200). East of Valle de Pascua is El Socorro, beyond which the road to El Tigre (see page 1543) is in poor shape, especially for cyclists. 53 km beyond El Socorro is **Santa María de Ipire**, a pretty, old village with narrow streets, but no hotel. 4 km E is a restaurant and petrol station which may provide accommodation. In **Pariaguán**, 83 km on, there is *Hotel Modín*, **E**, opp bus terminal, bath, a/c, small and filthy.

● **Accommodation El Sombrero**: **E-F** *Brasilia*, nr plaza, with bath, good fans, safe parking, rec. Very good food at *Restaurante Mary*, C Descanso 2, US$2-3 pp. **Chaguaramas**: **E** motel at W end, bath, a/c, check for scorpions in shoes and snakes in bedside tables; good restaurant across highway. **Valle de la Pascua**: **E** *Hotel Venezuela*, Plaza Bolívar; **E** *San Marcos*, Carretera Nacional towards El Socorro; **E** *Gran Hotel Monte Carlo*, opp bus station, suites available, a/c, shower, locked car park.

An alternative from Caracas to San Juan de los Morros and El Sombrero is Route 15 through **Cúa** (40 km S, **E** *Hotel Cúa*, with bath, a/c, unfriendly). From here to El Sombrero is via **Camatagua** (2 km off highway; *pop* 8,050; 2 hotels; 7 km from town is a very good campsite by a hydro-electric dam and lake, turnoff 1 km before town, US$0.30 pp, safe, drinking water, pit latrines, 'cabañas').

CALABOZO

South of Ortiz, on the road to San Fernando, is the Guárico dam and lake. From **Calabozo** (*pop* 91,000), S of Guárico, the main road goes to Puerto Miranda on the

Río Apure. A detour from Calabozo (**D** *Motel Tiuna*, Av via San Fernando, a/c, good restaurant, safe car park, good value, recommended; *El Castañuelo*, restaurant on main road junction, elegant, good food, popular) turns SE to Paso del Caballo (81 km).

A little trail goes on to **Cazorla** (85 km). On the swamps one can see egrets, parrots, alligators, monkeys (and hear howlers). Turn W in Cazorla to Guayabal, 21 km from San Fernando.

SAN FERNANDO DE APURE

This hot, sticky and unappealing town is the capital of the western *llanos* (*pop* 87,000).

Local information
● **Accommodation**
C *Hotel Plaza*, 2 blocks from the bus terminal, good.

D pp *Trinacria*, Av Miranda, nr bus station, T 23578, huge rooms, a/c, no breakfast.

E pp *La Torraca*, Av Boulevard y Paseo Libertador by Plaza Bolívar, excellent rooms, a/c, plush bathroom, balcony overlooking centre of town, rec.

F pp *Boulevard*, Paseo Libertador, with bath, a/c; **F** *Maracay*, Sucre 88, fan, a little run down, lots of bugs.

G pp *Hospedaje Central*, C. Bolívar 98, T 24120, with bath, colonial-style, basic. Most hotels are within 1 block of the intersection of Paseo Libertador and Av Miranda.

● **Places to eat**
Mister Pollo, Av Carabobo, good value chicken; *Punto Criollo*, Av Miranda, good value; *Europa*, opp *La Torraca*, cheap, excellent, creole Italian and other international food, good service, occasional evening cabaret, rec; *Gran Imperio Romano*, small, popular, along Av Boulevard from *Europa*, good and cheap; *Comedor* in building beside CANTV has good *menú*, Mon-Fri, 1100-1200.

● **Banks & money changers**
Banco Consolidado for American Express, Av Miranda, Res 19 de Abril; **Banco Unión**, Av Libertador and Carretera 5, cash advance on Mastercard and Visa.

● **Transport**
Air Daily Avensa flight to Caracas, and to **Puerto Ayacucho**; go early to airport, 30 mins journey, good views of *llanos*.

Buses Terminal is modern and clean, not far from centre; US$1.20 taxi ride. To **Caracas**, US$6.50, 7 hrs; to **Barinas**, Expresos Zamora, 5 daily, 9 hrs (take food and drink); rough ride, day and night bus, US$8.15; to **Maracay**, US$4.20; to **Puerto Ayacucho**, US$9, 8 hrs.

SAN FERNANDO TO BARINAS

From San Fernando you can drive W towards Barinas, the road is beautiful, but in terrible condition, between Mantecal and Bruzual. In the early morning, many animals and birds can be seen, and in the wet season caiman (alligators) cross the road; a highly recommended journey.

MANTECAL

Mantecal is a friendly cattle-ranching town. There are no tours on offer here but take a taxi to **Modelo Mantecal**, an eco-tourism area where caiman and capibaras can be seen. To view the waterbirds from the road be there before sunrise. *Fiesta*, 23-26 February.

● **Accommodation E** *Hotel El Pescador*, a/c, restaurant, OK; **F** *Hospedaje Centro Llano*, fan, shared shower, basic but good value. Two other hotels and many places to eat; *Gardenia*, excellent, cheap, very charming owner.

● **Ranches** About 30 mins by bus is *Hato Turístico Cedral*, where hunting is banned, visits arranged only through Turismo Aventura, Caracas, T 02-951-1143. Also in this area: *Doña Bárbara*, ranch, book through *Doña Bárbara* travel agency, Paseo Libertador, Edif Hotel La Torraca, PB y Mezzanina, Apdo 55, San Fernando de Apure, T (047) 25003, F 27902. Also *Hato El Frío*. All three charge about US$150 pp/night inc 3 meals, 2 tours/day, bath, a/c or fan, clean, comfortable, or US$45 for a daytime visit.

● **Buses** San Fernando de Apure-Mantecal 4-5 hrs (bad road), US$2.70; Mantecal-Barinas, 4 hrs, US$3.60. A road heads W after Mantecal at La Ye junction and goes over Guasdualito to San Cristóbal (take spare gasoline).

Bruzual (*pop* 4,800) is just S of Puente Nutrias over the Río Apure.

● **Accommodation** There are a few primitive hotels: **E** *Los Llaneros*, restaurant, dirty bathroom; **E-F** *Golpe Criollo*, on the plaza, with bath, a/c, good beds, safe parking, cheap and OK restaurant, basic rooms.

● **Road** To Mantecal, US$1.50; not many buses on Sun (one at 1000).

SAN FERNANDO TO CIUDAD BOLIVAR

From San Fernando you can travel E to Ciudad Bolívar by taking a boat (expensive and unreliable and not possible in the dry season) from opposite the airport to Caicara (see below). Alternatively, take a bus to Calabozo (1½ hrs, US$1.80) and *por puesto* from there to El Sombrero (US$1.10), where you can catch the Ciudad Bolívar bus at 1700.

There is a route across the *llanos* to Ciudad Bolívar: from Chaguaramas (see above) turn S through Las Mercedes (**E** *Gran Hotel Las Mercedes*, noisy a/c, mosquitoes, poor restaurant, safe parking) and flat cattle land to **Cabruta** (*pop* 4,300), 179 km, road badly potholed, daily bus to Caracas, US$6.75. There is a small hotel, infested with rats and cockroaches.

CAICARA

The town (*pop* 28,600) is across the Orinoco from Cabruta, 372 km W of Ciudad Bolívar by paved highway. Its recent growth is due to the continuation of the road to Puerto Ayacucho and the exploitation of bauxite at Los Pijiguaos. Manatees have been seen around the ferry at Cabruta.

- **Accommodation C** *Redoma*, nr airport, a/c, best; **E** *Bella Guayana*, C Merecey 3, bath, hot water, fan, dirty, dark, depressing; **D** *Venezuela*, Av Búlevard, a/c but regular power cuts leave rooms like furnaces; **E** *Miami*, Antigua C Carabobo, with bath, no hot water; **E** *Tres Ríos*, a/c, parking; **E** *La Fortuna*, run by blind family; **E** *El Diamante*, a/c (cheaper without), good value, English spoken, tours into Gran Sabana, Amazonas. Good open air restaurant by Río Orinoco for lunch.

- **Transport Air** 2 LAV flights a week (Wed and Sat) to **Ciudad Bolívar**, 55 mins, **Barinas**, 4 hrs, **San Fernando de Apure**, weekdays 30 mins, and **Puerto Páez**, 1 hr 25 mins. **Buses** From Caicara to **Ciudad Bolívar**, Transporte Orituco and Línea Bolívar, 0700 daily, 6 hrs, US$6.25; to **Puerto Ayacucho** 6 a day, 6 hrs (allow extra time for national guard searches) US$8. **River** Ferry from Cabruta, about 1 hr, 0500-2100, US$2 for car and passengers, or *lanchas* (*chalanas*) which leave when full every 30 mins or so, costing US$0.50 for the 25 mins journey.

Between Caicara and Ciudad Bolívar is the small town of **Maripa**, on the E bank of the Río Caura (*Hotel Maripa*, basic; bus to/from Ciudad Bolívar, 3½ hrs, US$3.50, several a day). Ask at Maripa gas station for taxi to **Las Trincheras**, 1½ hrs S, US$10-15. Carlos and Jonas have boat trips from here, US$60 a day. Take your own hammock, food and drink (inc enough for the guide), and cooking gear.

SAN FERNANDO TO PUERTO AYACUCHO

Due S of San Fernando is **Puerto Páez** (*pop* 2,600) at the confluence of the Meta and Orinoco rivers; here there are crossings to Puerto Carreño in Colombia, see below, and to El Burro W of the Caicara-Puerto Ayacucho road. A road is being built from San Fernando to Puerto Páez; for 134 km it is paved, then from the Río Capanaparo it is dirt, deeply rutted, passable only in the dry season by 4WD vehicles or buses (2 a day San Fernando-Pto Páez, dry season, 4 ferry crossings). Between the Capanaparo and Cinaruco rivers is the **Parque Nacional Santos Luzardo**, reached only from this road. If this road is closed, to get to Puerto Ayacucho from San Fernando involves a 15-hr (minimum) detour via the Caicara ferry.

From Caicara a new paved road runs 370 km SW to Puerto Ayacucho, passing scruffy settlements and bauxite-mining towns like Los Pijiguaos and Parguaza. The turn off to **El Burro**, where the boat crosses the Orinoco to Puerto Páez (ferry US$1, also to Puerto Carreño, Colombia), is 88 km N of Puerto Ayacucho (*por puesto* Burro-Pto Ayacucho, 1 hr).

On arrival in the Amazonas territory, it is necessary to register at a Guardia Nacional checkpoint about 20 km before Puerto Ayacucho. Around this area the national guard can be very strict and travellers are likely to be searched.

PUERTO AYACUCHO

Puerto Ayacucho (*phone code* 048) is the capital of the State of Amazonas, which has an area of 175,000 sq km and a population of 80,000, 73,660 of whom live in Puerto Ayacucho. At the end of the dry season (April), it is very hot and sticky. It is 800 km up the Orinoco from Ciudad Bolívar, deep in the wild, but no direct boats do the 5 day journey up river.

Museo Etnológico del Territorio Federal Amazonas, Monseñor Enzo Ceccarelli, opp church, open Tues-Sat, Sun am, US$0.80, has a library and collection of regional exhibits, recommended. In front of the museum is a market, open every day, where Indians sell handicrafts, eg wooden sculptures, musical instruments. One block away is the cathedral, which has colourful paintings, especially on the ceiling. The Salesian Mission House and boys' school on Plaza Bolívar may also be visited. Prices in Puerto Ayacucho are generally higher than N of the Orinoco. **NB** Malaria is prevalent in this area; take precautions.

Excursions

Locals recommend Oct to Dec as the best time for trips, when the rivers are high but the worst of the rains have passed. In the low season, May-June, it may be difficult to organize tours for only a few days.

You can walk up **Cerro Perico** for good views of the town, or go to the Mirador, about 1 km from centre, which offers good views of the Ature rapids. A recommended trip is to the small village of Pintado (12 km S), where petroglyphs described by Humboldt can be seen on the huge rock called **Cerro Pintado**. This most easily accessible petroglyph site of the hundreds scattered throughout Amazonas.

35 km S on the road to Samariapo is the **Parque Tobogán de la Selva**, a pleasant picnic area with tables and refreshments centred around a steeply inclined, smooth rock over which the Río Maripures cascades. This water-slide is great fun in the wet season; crowded on Sun, take swimsuit, bathing shoes and food and drink (stick to the right to avoid crashing into barrier, there are some painful rocks to the left near the bottom; few locals slide right from the top; also beware of broken glass). A small trail leads up from the slide to a natural jacuzzi after

about 20 mins. Taxi to Cerro Pintado and Parque Tobogán, US$15-20 return (be sure to organize your return with the driver, otherwise you may face a lengthy hike). Agencies in town arrange tours; easier but more expensive.

Nearby, also by paved road, is **Coromoto colony**, founded by the Salesian Fathers to protect and evangelize the 'howling Guaharibos' (as early explorers called this nomadic tribe).

The well-paved road from Puerto Ayacucho to Samariapo (63 km) was built to bypass the rapids which here interrupt the Orinoco, dividing it into 'Upper' and 'Lower'; the powerful Maripures Rapids are very impressive. The road (gravel, but being paved) continues for 17 km to Morganito, from where smaller launches continue on up river. Boats run from Samariapo to Isla de Ratón and Santa Rosa.

Local information
● **Accommodation**

D *Apure*, Av Orinoco 28, less than 1 km from centre, a/c, restaurant, rec; **D** *Guacharo's Amazonas Resort Hotel**, at end of Av Evelio Roa, 2 blocks from Av Río Negro, T 210328, a/c, restaurant.

E *Res Internacional*, Av Aguerrevere 18, T 21242, a/c (cheaper without), comfortable, shower, safe, laundry, warmly rec, good place to find tour information and meet other travellers, if no room available you can sling up your hammock, bus drivers stay here and will drive you to the terminal for early morning journeys; **E** *Res La Cueva*, Av 23 de Enero, 1 block from the Redoma (traffic roundabout, Corpoven station), a/c, luggage stored, rec; **E** *Res Siapa*, Av Orinoco, behind Banco de Venezuela, T 210138, a/c, modern, mixed reports, very crowded at weekends, some rooms without locks; **E** *Tobogán*, Av Orinoco con Av Evelio Roa, T 210320, popular, a/c, reasonable value.

F-G *Res Ayacucho*, Urb Pedro Camejo, 2 blocks off C Amazonas behind *Guacharo's amazonas Hotel*, bath, fan, cheapest in town.

● **Places to eat**

Las Palmeras, Av 23 de Enero, 2 blocks from the Redoma, pizzas and fast food; *El Padrino*, in Urb Andrés Eloy Blanco on Av Belisio Pérez off Av 23 de Enero, good Italian; *Cherazad*, C Aguerrevere y Av Orinoco, Arabic food; *El Encuentro*, cheap, good, ideal place for meeting travellers. Good food in restaurant at *Hotel Apure*. *Capi Fuente de Soda*, on Av Evelio Roa behind *gobernación*, vegetarian and other dishes.

● **Banks & money changers**
Banco Unión and Banco de Venezuela, both on Av Evelio Roa nr roundabout in town centre, cash on Visa and Mastercard. Changing dollars is difficult; try Hotel Tobogán or Hotel Orinoco.

● **Laundry**
Lavandería Automático Unión, Centro Unión on Av 23 de Enero.

● **Post & telecommunications**
Post office: Ipostal on Av Aguerrevere 3 blocks up from Av Orinoco.
Telephone: international calls from CANTV, on Av Orinoco next to *Hotel Apure*; also from *Las Chruwatas* on Av Aguerrevere with C Amazonas, 1 block from Plaza del Indio.

● **Shopping**
Good *artesanía* in the Plaza del Indio; also in **Artes Amazonas** on Av Evelio Roa, next to **Wayumi**, and in **Topocho** just up from Plaza del Indio. Many tourist souvenirs are on offer and Vicente Barletta, of *Típico El Casique*, Av Principal 583, Urb Andrés Eloy Blanco, has a good collection of masks (free); he also works as a guide (T 21389), rec, take own food and equipment.

● **Transport**
Air Airport 7 km SE along Av Orinoco. Scheduled LAV (Av 23 de Enero 27, T 21422) flights to Caracas, 2 a day, one non-stop, 1 hr, one via San Fernando de Apure and Calabozo, 3-4 hrs. Also Avensa once daily to Caracas via San Fernando. Daily flights to San Fernando de Atabapo and San Juan de Manapiare with Wayumi (Av Evelio Roa, 1 block from Av Río Negro) and Aguaysa (Av Río Negro, 1 block from the Redoma); no permit needed, charters also available. Charters also with Avisur (Av Río Negro 13).

Road Vehicle hire: *Servicio Amazonas de Alquiler*, Av Aguerrevere, T 210762. **Buses**: Expresos del Valle to Cuidad Bolívar (US$11, 10 hrs; take something to eat, bus stops once for early lunch), Caicara, Pto Ordaz and San Felix (T 210840); Cooperativa Cacique to San Fernando de Apure, US$9, 8 hrs (T 210091); both companies in bus terminal. Expresos La Prosperidad to Caracas and Maracay (T 210682) from Urb Alto Parima. Bus from Caracas, 2030, 2230 daily, US$12.50, 12 hrs (but much longer in wet season). *Por puesto* to Ciudad Bolívar, 3 daily, US$12, 10-12 hrs (Caicara Amazonas).

River Ferry across the Orinoco, US$0.50. Boat to Caicara, 1½ days, US$15 inc food, but bargain; repellent and hammock required.

FRONTIER WITH COLOMBIA

88 km N of Puerto Ayacucho a paved branch road leads W to El Burro, from where a ferry-barge crosses to Puerto Páez. On the S bank of the Meta opposite (ferry, US$1) is Puerto Carreño in Colombia.

Bongos and ferries run regularly across the river from Puerto Ayacucho to Casuarino (Colombia), which has quite good shopping, locals make these excursions without formalities, and many gringo travellers have experienced no problems or formalities crossing for a few hours (ferries leave from the Guardia Nacional post on the northern edge of town). On the other hand, some difficulty with the local authorities is not uncommon, both here and at Puerto Carreño. You may be asked how much money you have and where you are going; some travellers have had to obtain Colombian visas when only a passport and ticket out of the country were strictly necessary. From Ayacucho there is a cargo boat to Puerto Páez, 4 hrs. Check with Guardia Nacional and insist on exit stamp if crossing to Colombia.

TOURS IN AMAZONAS STATE

Much of Amazonas State is stunningly beautiful and untouched, but access is only by river. For starting out, the best base is Puerto Ayacucho. Do not travel alone. By ascending the Autana or Sipapo rivers, for example, one can see **Autana-tepuy**, a 1,200m-high soaring mass of rock resembling a petrified tree trunk, riddled with massive caves; it was first explored in 1971 by Charles Brewer Carias, who descended by helicopter (an Anglo-American expedition parachuted onto the summit in 1986 – no-one has yet climbed from the base). There are other *tepuis* in the region, including the great mass of the Sierra de la Neblina on the Brazilian border.

On the Río Negro, towards Brazil, is **San Carlos de Río Negro** (*pop* 1,500). Hotel at customs post. Flights from Puerto Ayacucho on Fri with Wayumi (see above). Permit required to visit.

San Juan de Manapiare (*pop* 3,700) is the regional centre for the middle Ventuari.

A beautiful track winds around the Cerro Guanay to get there. The road starts at Caicara and goes through Guaniamo and Sabana de Cardona.

● **Access** Travel in the southern part of Amazonas is heavily restricted to protect the Yanomami and the Alto Orinoco – Casiquiare Biosphere Reserve, which covers most of the SE portion of Amazonas state from the Neblina Range to the Orinoco headwaters. Permits are required from: the Bureau of Indian Affairs (Orai), in Caracas or Puerto Ayacucho (several copies of photograph and description page in passport required); from Inparques in Puerto Ayacucho (go through the Mercadito and 2 blocks further down); the Catholic Vicariato if you intend to visit missions along the rivers; and Servicio Autónomo para el Desarrollo Ambiental de Amazonas (Sada), in same building as Inparques in Caracas, T (02) 408-1822/1026, Dr W Frank. Travellers without a guide may be turned back by the Guardia Nacional in San Carlos de Río Negro.

● **Accommodation** There are a number of private river camps on the upper Orinoco but they do not welcome casual guests; the most welcoming is *Yutajé Camp*, located on a tributary of the Río Manapiare due E of Puerto Ayacucho. This can theoretically be reached from the track running S from Guaniamo to San Juan de Manapiare, but the passability of the track depends on how recently it was used and the season. The camp accommodates 30, with restaurant and bar, full board, fishing, canoes, horses, airboats, excursions to Indian villages, spectacular falls in the vicinity, much wildlife, expensive but professional. Also in the area is the *Campamento Camani*, T (02) 284-9006, F (02) 285-7352 (Centro Plaza, Torre C, p 19, Caracas), in a forest clearing on the banks of the Río Alto Ventuari, 2 hrs by launch from San Juan de Manapiare. A private aircraft leaves Caracas each Thur and Sun, 2 hrs 20 mins. From Puerto Ayacucho the daily aerotaxi takes 50 mins. Maximum 26 guests at any one time, mosquito nets provided, bathroom, restaurant, bar, TV, handicraft shop, football and petanque courts, excursions available, US$290 pp lodging and meals, excluding air fare, 3 day/2 night package. Near Puerto Ayacucho, in mixed jungle and dry forest setting, is *Jungle Camp Calypso*, run by *Calypso Tours*, T 210572 (or Caracas, T (02) 545-0024, F 541-3036), US$150 pp for 2 days inc food, basic cabin accommodation, highly rec, excursions in canoes. **B** *Canturama Amazonas Resort*, Puerto Ayacucho, ribera del río Orinoco, T 210266 (or Caracas, T (02) 941-8813, F 9435160), 20 mins by vehicle S of town, on the banks of the Orinoco amidst dry, open

Savannah, 40 km from nearest jungle, highly rec accommodation and food but very few animals and beware biting insects by the river; buffet meals US$4-7, full day tours US$10. *Dantos Adventure*, very basic jungle refuge, accommodation and canoe tours around US$45 pp/day, probably cheapest option available, also space for camping; run by Reni and Danitza Barrio (Reni is also a rec guide, speaks English), ask at *Aguas Bravas* (see below) or contact Juan Carlos Garcia, T 210478/211771.

● **Tour companies & guides** Tourists are strongly rec to go on tours organized by tour agents or guides registered in the *Asocación de Guías*, in the Cámara de Turismo, Casa de la Piedra, on the Arteria Vial de la Av Orinoco with Av Principal (the house on top of the large rock). Permission is required to visit Amazonas and some independent guides may not have access to this. Tours generally cost US$50-120 pp/day depending on agency and trip. Those listed below will arrange permits and insurance but shop around: *Tobogán Tours*, Av 23 de Enero nr *Instituto del Menor*, T 214553, F 214865; *Autana Aventura*, Av Aguerrevere, 1 block from Av Orinoco, T 212821, F 210605, owned by Julián Jaramillo; *Guaharibo CA*, C Evelio Roa 39, in same building as *Wayumi*, T 210635, or Caracas T 952-6996, F 953-0092, manager Levis Olivo; *Yutajé Tours*, in Urb Monte Bello, 1 block from Av Orinoco, past the Mercadito going out of town, T 210664, they give rides to doctors and nurses to remote parts; *Expediciones Aguas Bravas Venezuela*, Av Río Negro, No 32-2, in front of Plaza Rómulo Betancourt, T 210541, F 211529, whitewater rafting, 2 daily from 0900-1200 and 1500-1800, 3-13 people per boat, reservations required at peak times, take insect repellent, sun protector, light shoes and swimsuit (raincoat in rainy season), US$35 pp.

The Guayana Highlands

THE historic Ciudad Bolívar on the Río Orinoco is a good starting place for the superb landscapes further south, notably the table-top mountains and waterfalls around Canaima. The most spectacular of all is Angel Falls. From the industrial centre of Ciudad Guyana trips can be made to the huge hydroelectric scheme at Guri. Further east the Orinoco Delta is opening up to tourism.

These uplands, lying S of the Orinoco River, constitute half of Venezuela. They rise, in rounded forested hills and narrow valleys, to flat topped tablelands on the borders of Brazil. These lands with savannas interspersed with semi-deciduous forest are very sparsely populated. So far, communications have been the main difficulty, but a road has now been opened to Santa Elena de Uairén on the Brazilian frontier (see page 1566). This road can be followed to Manaus. The area is Venezuela's largest gold and diamond source, but its immense reserves of iron ore, manganese and bauxite are of far greater economic importance.

CIUDAD BOLÍVAR

Ciudad Bolívar (*pop* 261,000; *phone code* 085), on the S bank of the Orinoco, is 400 km from its delta and 640 by road from Caracas. Average temperature 29°C, but a cool and refreshing breeze usually springs up in the evening. It stands by the narrows of the Orinoco, not more than 300m wide, which gave the town its old name of Angostura. It was here that Bolívar came after defeat to reorganize his forces, and the British Legionnaires joined him. At Angostura he was declared President of that Gran Colombia which he had yet to build, and which was to fragment before his death. Though the city still has many beautiful colonial buildings around the Plaza Bolívar, it has spread outwards from the old centre to the airport.

Places of interest

At the Congress of Angostura, 15 February 1819, the representatives of the present day Venezuela, Colombia and Ecuador met to proclaim Gran Colombia. The building, on **Plaza Bolívar**, houses a museum (**Casa del Congreso de Angostura** built 1766-76 by Manuel Centurión, the provincial governor, guides in Spanish only). Also on this historic plaza is the **Cathedral** (started 1764, completed 1840), the **Casa de Los Gobernadores de la Colonia** (also built by Centurión in 1766), the **Real Intendencia**, and the **Casa de la Cultura**. Also on the N side of the plaza, at Bolívar 33, is the house where Gen Manuel Piar, the Liberator of Guayana from the Spanish, was held prisoner before being executed by Bolívar on 16 October 1817. Piar refused to put himself under Bolívar's command. The restored **Parque Miranda**, up C Carabobo, is a shady place to relax; on one side is the old theatre, recently converted into an art centre. At one time the theatre was the Antigua Prefectura (1900-20) and then a military prison. The present legislative assembly and **Consejo Municipal** are between Plaza Bolívar and Parque Miranda. When the town was still known as Angostura a physician invented the famous bitters there in 1824; the factory moved to

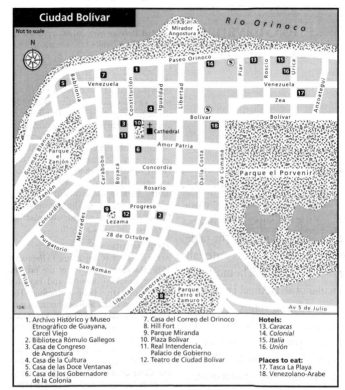

Ciudad Bolívar

Not to scale

1. Archivo Histórico y Museo Etnográfico de Guayana, Carcel Viejo
2. Biblioteca Rómulo Gallegos
3. Casa de Congreso de Angostura
4. Casa de la Cultura
5. Casa de las Doce Ventanas
6. Casa de los Gobernadore de la Colonia
7. Casa del Correo del Orinoco
8. Hill Fort
9. Parque Miranda
10. Plaza Bolívar
11. Real Intendencia, Palacio de Gobierno
12. Teatro de Ciudad Bolívar

Hotels:
13. *Caracas*
14. *Colonial*
15. *Italia*
16. *Unión*

Places to eat:
17. Tasca La Playa
18. Venezolano-Arabe

Port of Spain in 1875.

A walk along the river bank is recommended at dusk when the sun is setting. Launches take passengers across the river (US$0.25), but there are no other passenger boat services. The Paseo Orinoco leading W out of town goes to the **Angostura Bridge**, which can be seen from town. This is the only bridge across the Orinoco, 1,668m long (over a mile), opened in 1967 (toll US$0.80; cyclists and walkers are not allowed to cross, but military will flag down a car for you). The **Zamuro hill fort** (1902), on another hill in the centre, dominates the city (entrance on Paseo Heres, closed 1200-1400).

Just W of the centre is **El Zanjón**, an area of vegetation typical of the region.

To the E is **Parque El Porvenir**, with botanical gardens. Outside the airport is the *Río Caroní* aeroplane, which Jimmie Angel landed on top of Auyán-Tepuy (see page 1557).

Museums

The **Museo Soto**, Av Germania, some distance from the centre in pleasant gardens, has works by Venezuela's Jesús Rafael Soto and other modern artists, open Tues-Sun 1000-1700, guide in Spanish only, free, recommended. Museum at **Casa del Correo del Orinoco**, Paseo Orinoco y Carabobo, modern art and some exhibits of history of the city, inc the printing press of the newspaper which spread the cause of independence; has free town map (poor) and booklet on Ciudad Bolívar. **Museo**

Geológico y Minero at the School of Mines in the University of the East (UDO), Av Principal, La Sabanita. **Archivo Histórico y Museo Etnográfico de la Guayana**, housed in the former prison and governor's mansion, 2 blocks from Cathedral on Paseo Orinoco, has a very interesting and original display of Indian tools and artefacts. Many other museums in the city: **Casa de los Doce Ventanas**, Venezuela entre Babilonia y Las Delicias, the residence of President Soublette; **Museo Casa San Isidro**, Av Táchira (Tues-Sat 0900-1200, 1430-1700, Sun 0900-1200) a mansion where Simón Bolívar stayed.

Local festivals

Aug: *Fiesta del Orinoco*; 5-8 Sept, fair and exhibition.

Local information

● **Accommodation**

Near airport: **C** *Laja Real**, Av Andres Bello y Jesús Soto, opp airport, T 27911, T/F 28778, pool open to non-residents for US$2/day, a/c, excellent restaurant, highly rec; **D** *Laja City Hotel*, Av Táchira y Av Bolívar, T 29910/ 29920/ 29919, quiet, a/c, hot water, restaurant; **D** *Da Gino*, Av Jesús Soto, opp airport, T 20313, F 25454, good service and restaurant, rec; **D** *Valentina*, Av Maracay 55, quiet, a/c, comfortable, very good restaurant, rec; **E** *Táchira*, Av Táchira 40, T 27489, with bath, a/c, parking, OK.

On or nr Paseo Orinoco: **D** *Colonial*, T 24402, F 23080, has seen better days but good value, a/c, good travel agency, nice restaurant on balcony overlooking river, changes Amex TCs and cash, rec.

E *Caracas*, with bath, safe but very rundown, balcony overlooking river, noisy a/c; **E** *Italia*, **F** without bath, noisy a/c, very basic rooms, veranda overlooking the Río Orinoco, mixed reports on security, store luggage, cheap restaurant, small portions, very popular with travellers, changes cash, travel agency in lobby, all the guides hang around here, hard sell on tours; **E** *Unión*, C Urica 11, T 23374, with bath, a/c, **F** with fan, good value, rec; **F** *Pensión Yocaima*, C Zaraza, at E end, with bath and fan, laundry facilities, basic.

On Av Moreno de Mendoza, nr bus terminal: **D** *Universo*, rec and **F** *Brasilia*, shower and fan, basic, double beds only.

● **Places to eat**

Savoy, Venezuela y Dalla Costa, good value breakfast and lunch; *Mi Casa*, Venezuela, open air, good value; *América*, Paseo Orinoco esq Roscio, good food, dishes US$3-5, open late; *Arabe-Venezolano*, on Cumaná nr Bolívar, clean, a/c, good Arabic food, not cheap. Cheap food at the market at the E end of Paseo Orinoco. Good breakfast at *Lonchería Ché*, next to *Hotel Colonial*. *La Playa*, on C Urica entre Venezuela y Zea, good for fish, reasonable prices; *Lonchería Urica*, next to *Hotel Unión*, good lunch for US$1.25, get there early.

● **Banks & money changers**

Banco Consolidado, Edif Pinemar, Av Andrés Bello, Centro Comercial Canaima, nr airport, Amex TCs; **Banco de Venezuela**, nr *Hotel Colonial*, cash on Visa, ATM; **Banco Mercantil**, E end of Paseo Orinoco, changes TCs, has ATM.

● **Embassies & consulates**

Danish Consulate, Av Táchira, Quinta Maninata 50, of 319, T (85) 23490, 0800-1200, 1500-1700.

● **Post & telecommunications**

Post Office: Av Táchira, 15 mins' walk from centre.

Telephones: CANTV, Av 5 de Julio, 100m from Av Táchira; closed Sun.

● **Shopping**

You can buy baskets and items made by the Indians, and good hammocks. The gold orchid pin or earrings, or a gold nugget (known as *cochano*), are the best souvenirs of Venezuela (worth seeking out, but now rare, is the handmade orchid of red, yellow and white gold). There are many jewellers on Pasaje Guayana, which runs off Paseo Orinoco and nr *Hotel Colonial*. Gold items of comparable price and quality can also be found on the Plaza Bolívar in Caracas and in Santa Elena de Uairén. Supermarket close to the Museo Soto on Germania, large and well-stocked. Jewellery shop, *Van Buren*, Av Venezuela 27, behind Paseo Orinoco, fluent English spoken, highly rec. *La Carioca*, new shopping centre at the end of Paseo Orinoco, restaurants, shops, nice to walk around.

Camping equipment: white gas (stove fuel) is available at Av República 16, nr the bus terminal.

● **Tour companies & travel agents**

Soana Travel, Dalla Costa y Bolívar, T 014-851056 (cellular), 22536 (office), F 22030, run by Angelica and Martin Haars, tours to Canaima and Gran Sabana, 5 day tour to Río Caura highly rec, accommodation at their house out of town, **E** room for 4/5; *Cunaguaro Tours*, T 22041, F 27810, cellular 014-850344, at *Hotel Italia* entrance, Gran Sabana, Salto Angel, driver Lenin Linares is very good, friendly, rec; *Marina Río Orinoco*, at *Hotel Unión*, F 49868, run by Sean Starr, tours to Roraima, Canaima and Orinoco

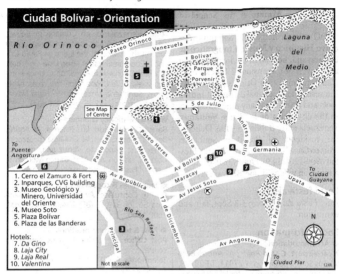

Ciudad Bolívar - Orientation

Río Orinoco

Paseo Orinoco

Laguna del Medio

1. Cerro el Zamuro & Fort
2. Inparques, CVG building
3. Museo Geológico y Minero, Universidad del Oriente
4. Museo Soto
5. Plaza Bolívar
6. Plaza de las Banderas

Hotels:
7. Da Gino
8. Laja City
9. Laja Real
10. Valentina

To Puente Angostura

To Ciudad Guayana

To Ciudad Piar

Not to scale

1248

Delta, good English spoken; *Turi Express* at airport, run by Guillermo Rodríguez, arranges tours to Canaima and the Guri dam, good English, rec; *Expediciones Dearuna*, at *Hotel Caracas*, T 014-851360 (Cellular), T/F 26089, run by Javier Cubillos, rec for Canaima, English, Dutch, German and French spoken. Miguel Gasca is rec for tours to Roraima, Gran Sabana and Canaima, T 014-235210/016-294600 (Cellular) or look for him at *Hotel Italia*; *Agencia de Viajes Auyantepuy*, C Bolívar, Ed Roque, Centro No 8, T 20748, very helpful for tickets to Canaima, English and French spoken. For 3 days/2 nights tours to Canaima expect to pay around US$220-260 pp; 4 days/3 nights to Gran Sabana US$200-250.

Unofficial touts swamp the bars and restaurants around Paseo Orinoco. It may be better to go to your destination and find a tour there, eg tours to Roraima and Gran Sabana are best in Santa Elena or San Francisco de Yuruaní. One option is to hire a jeep (about US$120/day) and do your own tour. Motorized canoe trips to the Angel Falls are best organized in Ciudad Bolívar. Before deciding to purchase a tour with anyone in Ciudad Bolívar ensure that the guide who sells the package is the guide who leads the tour, that all equipment is good and waterproof, that initial prices are not grossly inflated and that you agree on what is being offered. **NB** We have received several reports of tours being subcontracted to unskilled guides by unreliable operators. In addition, tourists

have been deceived, or worse, by unscrupulous guides. We suggest that you choose a company or guide from the list above, all of whom have received positive recommendations.

● **Tourist offices**
Av Táchira entre Avs M Briceño y Maracay, quite helpful, street map and info on Gran Sabana.

● **Transport**
Local Taxis: US$1-1.25 to virtually anywhere in town. US$1.50-2 from bus station to town centre.

Air Minibuses and buses (Ruta 2) marked Terminal to town centre. Taxi to Paseo Orinoco US$1.50. A yellow bus marked 'Aeropuerto' runs E along Paseo Orinoco; catch it 1 block W of *Hotel Colonial*. To Caracas daily with Servivensa, 1½ hrs, via Maturín, US$65. Rutaca fly to Canaima and Santa Elena, daily at 0700, US$65. For information on all flights and for trips to Canaima you should ask for Jorge at the Ciaca office at airport. Airport tax US$0.45. There are international phones at the airport and a good restaurant. Car hire at the airport. Check where tours start from as some fly from Ciudad Guayana (Turi Tours), and charge passengers for taxi transfers.

Buses Terminal at junction of Av República and Av Sucre. To get there take a bus marked Terminal going W along the Paseo Orinoco (US$0.15). Several daily to Caracas 9 hrs, US$12, student discount available (day and night buses, *por puesto* US$24). To Puerto La Cruz, US$5,

US$2.50 with student discount, *por puesto*, US$10, 5 hrs; to **Cumaná**, US$6, 6 hrs with Expresos Guayanesa (8 daily); to **Maracay**, US$8-9, 10 hrs; **Valencia**, via Maracay, US$10. **Tumeremo** US$5.25; Tumeremo bus through to El Dorado US$5.75, 3 daily. To **Santa Elena de Uairén** direct with Línea Orinoco, Transportes Mundial (5 daily) or Expreso Rápidos de Güiria at 0500, 0800 and 1900, spectacular views of the Gran Sabana at sunset (book in advance), US$9-10, 12 hrs. To **Boa Vista** with Transportes Mundial, Mon and Thur at 2000 (sometimes once a week) US$25, 20 hrs. To **Ciudad Guayana** hourly from 0700 by Expresos Guayanesa, US$1.35, 1½ hrs, *por puesto*, US$3.60, 1½ hrs. Bus to **Caicara**, 7½ hrs, inc 2 ferry crossings. Bus to **Ciudad Piar**, US$1.40, 3 hrs. Bus to **Luepa** (Canaima National Park), US$9, 10-12 hrs. *Por puesto* to **Puerto Ayacucho**, 3 daily, US$12, 10-12 hrs; direct with Caicara Amazonas, US$11, 10 hrs, take food.

LA ENCRUCIJADA

73 km E of Ciudad Bolívar is **La Encrucijada**, a road junction/truck stop/small community. One hotel, **F** *La Gran Parada*, bath, fan, good value, owner Tadeo Venarusso, speaks English and Italian and is very knowledgeable about the area. His family lives in Playa Blanca (see below). To the left of La Encrucijada is the freeway to Ciudad Guayana (37 km); straight on is the road to Upata via the Paso Carnachi (no ferry but private boats can be hired for the 2 min crossing); to the right is the road to Ciudad Piar and La Paragua. On the right hand road from La Encrucijada turn left after 8 km, past enormous black rocks, on to an almost hidden trail. After a further 2 km is the **Cueva del Elefante**, where precolumbian relics were found and rock paintings can be seen. Following the track (10 km) you reach **Playa Blanca** on the Río Caroní, where miners dive for gold and diamonds. Since the discovery of gold in 1991, the population of Playa Blanca has exploded. A visit is worthwhile, particularly to see the gold dredgers. Transport can be arranged with Tadeo Venarusso in La Encrucijada; his brother Gyani does boat trips. Tadeo also goes to rock paintings in the area; contact him at Apdo 186, Puerto Ordaz, Estado Bolívar, Código Postal 8015, or at *La Gran Parada*.

CIUDAD PIAR

Ciudad Piar (97 km, *pop* 21,100) is near the iron ore mountain (Cerro Bolívar – cheaper to visit from Ciudad Bolívar than from Ciudad Guayana). In this area is **A** *Hato El Burro*, run by the Ackerman family, English, German and Spanish spoken. Trips are arranged around their own extensive ranch, Guri dam, Angel Falls etc, first class service. Contact at Vía La Paragua, Km 434, Ciudad Piar, T 938148, or Caracas T/F 793-6515/6150, PO Box 60636, Este Caracas, 1060.

PARQUE NACIONAL CANAIMA

Angel Falls, the highest fall in the world (979m – its longest single drop is 807m) and **Canaima**, 70 km down-river, are best reached from Caracas or from Ciudad Bolívar. At Canaima is a beautiful tannin-stained lagoon with soft beige beaches (chiggers, *niguas*, in the sand). The Río Carrao tumbles spectacularly over seven waterfalls into the lagoon below. The surrounding countryside is very beautiful. There are several tourist lodges at Canaima and many package tours now visit on day trips, so it can be very busy and quite expensive. There is an expensive snack bar at the airport. Park entry US$4.50 pp.

Warning There are dangerous undercurrents in the lagoon; people have drowned while swimming near the falls. Tourists are not told of the possible dangers beforehand.

Tours

There are various excursions from Canaima, which are all worthwhile (and usually crowded). You can make walking expeditions into the jungle to Indian villages with a guide but bargain hard on the price. Other excursions are to the Mayupa Falls, including a canoe ride on the Río Carrao (US$45, half day), to Yuri Falls by jeep and boat (US$25, half day); to Isla Orquídea (US$65, full day, good boat ride, beach barbecue); to Saltos de Sapo and Sapito, 3 hrs, US$20.

Recommended guides in Canaima: Tomás Bernal, who has his own camp on an island in the lagoon, beds and hammocks, popular with travellers, very knowledgeable about flora and fauna, contact in Canaima or through *Soana Tours* in Ciudad Bolívar (see above). There is fierce competition at airport but agencies pretty much offer the same thing at the same price. *Kamaracoto Tours*, *Tiuna Tours* and *Hnos Jiménez* are recommended for trips to Salto Sapo, Kavac, Salto Angel; they will also help with finding accommodation.

Many agencies in Caracas, Ciudad Bolívar, etc, offer tours to Canaima, offering various accommodation, excursion and Angel Falls flight arrangements. Some are listed under Caracas and Ciudad Bolívar **Travel Agents**. When booking a package beware of agents telling you that all the guides speak English: some do, but many don't.

Local information
● Accommodation
Lodging in Hoturvensa's *Campamento Canaima*, T (Caracas 02) 562-3022, F 564-7936, PO Box 943, Caracas 1010, Tx 26282, is in quite comfortable cabins; each is complete with shower and toilet; there are no hardships whatsoever. Meals are basic, self-service, no choice; drinks are expensive (more than double the prices in Ciudad Bolívar) for those travelling independently, see below.

Hoturvensa's rates are: for 1 night, US$330, for 2, US$640, inc transfers, meals, boat trip and flight over the Angel Falls, weather permitting. The airfare with Servivensa is not inc, although a reduced price round-trip ticket is available for US$96 for those booked into the Canaima Camp.

Although the quickest and most convenient way to visit Canaima is on a Hoturvensa excursion, it is also possible to travel independently.

A2 *Campamento Ucaima*, run by the daughter of the late 'Jungle' Rudy Truffino, US$80 with 3 meals, 2 hrs walk from Canaima above Hacha Falls.

C *Camp Churún Vena*, in the village, clean rooms with bath and breakfast, hammock space with breakfast is also available at US$5, evening meals can be organized; also in the village is **C** pp *Camp Wey tupu*, T (086) 625955, fan, shower, bar.

D pp *Parakaupa Lodge*, 5 mins from airport, with bath, comfortable, hammocks outside rooms, restaurant; opp is **D** pp *Kaikusé Lodge*, basic but clean, with bath, **F** pp in hammocks. Some families in the village rent hammocks for US$5-10 pp. Travel agencies also rent hammocks for US$3-5 pp a night; ask at the airport.

Camping: camp for free; fires are permitted and plenty of wood is available. Obtain a *permiso de excursionistas* from Inparques, Caracas, see page 1460, in Ciudad Bolívar, Av Germania, Casa de Gobernador, or at the CVG building in Canaima, US$1.50. No tents available for hire.

● Services
It is advisable to take food, though the village near Canaima has a small store selling mainly canned foods; also souvenir shop in airport, and the *fuente de soda* overlooking the lagoon. Do not forget swimming costumes, insect repellent and sun cream; waterproof clothing may be advisable.

Food is expensive at the Hoturvensa restaurant. A cheaper option is Simon's restaurant in the village which is used by many of the agencies, US$3-4.

Warning Necklaces of poisonous red and black seeds (rosary peas) are on sale here.

● Transport
The full air fare from Caracas is US$157. Servivensa flies from Caracas, Porlamar, Puerto Ordaz, US$65 one way. Servivensa also has flights from Santa Elena de Uairén. Do not rely on being able to change the return date on your flight and be even more wary of getting an open return. The airline is quite happy to change your ticket, but the next available seat could be in 5 days time and Canaima is a very expensive place to kill time. All arrangements are made through Avensa/Servivensa, direct (best in Caracas – address as for *Los Frailes*, page 1509; Ciudad Bolívar Avensa office is closed for most of the weekend) or through travel agencies. Aereotuy runs 1 day excursions by 19-seat Dornier aircraft out of Ciudad Bolívar one landing at Canaima, the other at Kavac, giving good views of Falls. There is a connecting Aereotuy flight from Isla Margarita (0900, returning 1600) and direct excursions from Barcelona and Margarita (0730 departure returning 1800). They have a new camp nr the foot of Nonon-tepuy, bookable only through Aerotuy, rec (T 02-761-6231, F 762-5254). Various companies offer 5-seater Cessnas to Canaima from Ciudad Bolívar, day excursions, book early, 0630-0700 at airport, US$150-165 pp, inc flight over Angel Falls, boat across lagoon, lunch and trip to Salto Sapo; flight only US$65 one way with Rutaca and Ciaca; same price to Santa Elena. Arrange with Jorge at airport; you'll find him in the Ciaca office opp Avensa desk. Reductions are available for parties. Note that you may not even see the falls from the air in the rainy season – the additional cost of a trip to the Angel Falls may well bring the cost of your journey up to that of a package.

ANGEL FALLS

The Falls are named after Jimmie Angel, the US airman who first reported their existence in 1933; he landed his plane, the *Río Caroní*, on top of the mesa 9 October 1937 (see *South American Explorer*, No 40, May 1995, pp 22-30). The site is now marked with a plaque. The sheer rock face of was climbed in 1971 by three Americans and an Englishman, David Nott, who recounted the 10-day adventure in his book *Angels Four* (Prentice-Hall). **NB** The falls face E so only receive sun in the morning.

TRIPS TO THE FALLS

Trips by boat upriver to the **Angel Falls** only go June-Nov, leaving usually in the afternoon, staying the first night at Isla Orquídea, continuing to the Falls next day. 12 hr day trips cost around US$100; more relaxing, but showing nothing different, are 44 hr, '3 day' trips, US$200. If you have a *permiso de excursionistas* (see above), you may be able to go on one tour and come back with another, giving yourself more time at the Falls (take all food and gear). Trips can be arranged with agencies in Cuidad Bolívar (see above) or at Canaima airport. All *curiaras* (dugouts) must have 2 motors, by law, and carry first aid, life jackets, etc. Take wet weather gear, swimwear, mosquito net for hammock and insect repellent.

- **Flights** The cheapest way to fly over the falls is on scheduled flights from Ciudad Bolívar with Rutaca or Ciaca (see above). From Canaima a 45 min flight costs US$45 pp and does some circuits over and alongside the falls. There are also 20 min flights at 0930 for US$55-60 which return in time for the midday Servinesa flight out of Canaima. Better than organized flights is to go to the airstrip and ask around the pilots waiting there on business if they will fly over the Falls for the same price as a tour.

EXCURSIONS FROM CANAIMA

Although not the highest or largest of the tepuyes, **Auyán-Tepuy** (600 km2) is one of the more accessible. **Kamarata** is a friendly Indian settlement with a Capuchin mission on the plain at the E foot of the tepuy. It has a well-stocked shop but no real hotels; basic rooms can be found for about US$2.50 pp, camping also possible at the mission (mosquito nets necessary and anti-malarial pills advised). Take food, although there is one restaurant and locals may sell you dinner. Aerotuy fly from Ciudad Bolívar (2 hrs) on Thur and from Santa Elena de Uairén on Mon. A co-operative of Pemón guides called *Macunaima Tours*, headed by Tito Abati, is based in Kamarata and can arrange *curiaras*, tents and porters for various excursions, take your own food (guide Jorge Calcaño is very helpful). The whole area is within the Canaima National Park. The local Indians have closed Auyán-Tepuy to climbers (since 1995). For details on the latest situation, contact *Alechiven*, run by Edith Rogge, which has a base and radio at Kamarata. T (041) 211828, F 217018. They and *Macunaima Tours* run 6-day river trips from Kamarata to Angel Falls (May-Dec), descending the **Río Akanán** to the Carrao by motorized dugout then turning S up the 'Devil's Canyon' to the Falls; the tours continue downriver to Canaima. About US$200 pp, supply your own food. River trips in this region are easier in the rainy season.

KAVAC

Kavac, about a 2-hr walk NW of Kamarata, is a new Indian-run resort consisting of a dozen thatched huts (*churuatas*) for guests, a small shop, and an excitingly short airstrip serviced by Aerotuy propjets from Ciudad Bolívar and Isla Margarita daily except Mon; flights provide excellent views of Angel Falls and Auyán-Tepuy. There is a *carro* connection with Kamarata but it is expensive because all fuel has to be flown in. The prime local excursion is to **Kavac Canyon** and its waterfall known as La Cueva, which can be reached by joining a group or by setting out early W up the Río Kavac, following the waterpipe installed by the fathers at Kamarata to provide the settlement with water from the falls. A natural jacuzzi is encountered after a 30 min wade/scramble along the sparkling stream, after which the gorge narrows dramatically until the falls are reached. Go in the morning to avoid groups of day trippers from Porlamar. The sun's rays illuminate the vertical walls of the canyon only for a short time around 1100. Be prepared to get wet; bathing suits and shoes with good grip, plus a dry change of clothing are recommended; also insect repellent, since there is a mosquito invasion around dusk. Late afternoon winds off the savannah can make conditions chilly. Guide ropes have been installed where they are most needed along the river; there are pools and a further fall higher up the canyon but an Indian guide should be hired for this extension. A day excursion by light plane to Kavac from Canaima (45 mins flight) can be made with any of the tour operators at the airport; costs around US$120 pp depending on number of passengers. Trips from Ciudad Bolívar can be arranged with tour agencies in town or at airport; around US$230 pp inc flight via Angel Falls, meals, 1 night's accommodation. A Pemón guide in Kavac is Marino Sandoval (*Excursiones Pemón*).

CIUDAD GUAYANA

In an area rich in natural resources 105 km down-river from Ciudad Bolívar an entirely new metropolis, known as **Ciudad Guayana** (*phone code* 086), is still being built. It is forging into one the four separate centres of San Félix, Palúa, Puerto Ordaz and Matanzas. Its population has already exceeded half of the planned million, on the S bank of the Orinoco and both sides of the Caroní River before it spills into the Orinoco. The mixing of the rivers' waters is like 'pouring cream into coffee'. East of the Caroní are the commercial port of **San Félix** (work in progress to make a riverside walk and park) and the Palúa iron-ore terminal of the railway from El Pao. Across the Caroní by the 470m concrete bridge is **Puerto Ordaz** (airport), the iron-ore loading port connected by rail with the famous Cerro Bolívar open-cast iron mine (see below). The iron-tinted waterfall in the pretty Parque Cachamay is worth a visit. The Casa Machupicchu, C Guasipati, sells a city map.

Excursions

Just up the Caroní is the Macagua hydro-electric plant (with a second phase under construction); there are some truly beautiful cataracts called Salto Llovizna as you enter the grounds (known as Parque La Llovizna, reached by bus from San Félix most of the way, then hitch). Higher up the river is the massive Guri dam and hydroelectric undertaking, see page 1464. The trip to Guri takes 90 mins by taxi; the plant is open daily 0900-1030, 1415-1515, for a conducted tour (4 daily, 1 hr) phone Edelca, Puerto Ordaz 20-80-66 (Relaciones Institucionales del Guri); the area gets very full during holidays, Easter or carnival. You can also visit the rest of the complex including the hotel, C, a/c, comfortable; camping possible outside the entrance with permission. *Por puesto* from Ciudad Bolívar, Route 70, US$12.50 one way; for return, ask at Alcabala Río Claro (gatehouse) if they can get you a free lift. Excursion buses go from the main offices in the park at 1300 and 1500, take your passport. If no public transport, take a Ciudad Bolívar-Ciudad Guayana bus to Km 70 and take a taxi from there to Río Claro.

To Cerro Bolívar mine, take a *por puesto* (US$5.60) or hitchhike to Ciudad Piar, or go with guided tour organized by Ferrominera Orinoco at their headquarters building in Ciudad Guayana. Tours are free, and leave Ciudad Piar at 0900 and 1400. To visit industries in the area, ask at the Corporación Venezolana de Guayana, Departamento de Relaciones Públicas, or Sidor, T 907534. Do not expect immediate permission and check if you need your own vehicle. Boat trips from *Intercontinental*, US$32 for boat (say 12 passengers), or US$8.50 pp.

From San Félix or Puerto Ordaz go down the Orinoco to **Los Castillos** (either by *por puesto*, 1 hr, US$1.50, or by bus to Aceiles, US$0.35, ask to be let off where pick-up goes to Los Castillos 0700, 1130, 1530, returns 0830, 1300 and 1700, US$1; difficult to get there by boat). It is possible to camp on the beach. Candes Tours run an excursion from Puerto Ordaz but only if there are 4 people. There are two old forts here: one on a huge rock near the water, the other on top of a hill and both in good condition. A tiny village (*pop* 500) lies at their feet. It is said to have been here that Sir Walter Raleigh's son was killed in battle while searching for El Dorado. From Los Barrancos, on the N bank of the Orinoco, opp San Félix, *curiaras* and other boats can be taken to the delta; settle prices before setting out, take hammock, mosquito net and repellent, and canned food (in the rainy season, take a waterproof). A free ferry for foot passengers crosses to Los Barrancos; taxi from Puerto Ordaz to ferry, US$3, or take micro from bus terminal (not very safe); return trip about 1 hr.

Local information
● Accommodation
In Puerto Ordaz: **L2** *Intercontinental Guayana**, Parque Punta Vista, PO Box 293, T 222244, F 222253, next to Parque Cachamay, all facilities, little character, swimming pool; **B** *El Rasil*, Centro Cívico, with all comforts, swimming pool, intermittent hot water, car hire rep is helpful; **B** *Dos Ríos*, México esq Ecuador, T 220679, shower, a/c, has seen better days, helpful; **D** *Tepuy**, a/c, Carrera Upata, Edif Arichuna, T 220102, central; **E** *Habana Cuba*, Av Las Américas, a/c, organize trips to Orinoco delta, rec; **E** *Guayana**, Av Las Américas, a/c, no hot water, unfriendly, OK value; **E** *Turista*, Av Caracas, basic; **E** *Motel Los Faroles*, 1 km S on 4 lane highway to Upata, immaculate a/c rooms and grounds. Rolf and Rosa Kampen offer bed and breakfast at C Surinam 03-07, Villa Antillana, 3 km from central Pto Ordaz, T 220593, no buses, so take a taxi, **E**, breakfast US$1.30, restaurant serves Bavarian food, Rolf speaks English, German and Dutch, rec; **F** *Res Santa Cruz*, Av Principal de Castillito, opp Gen Electric, fan, also short-stay.

In San Félix: only **D** *Aguila* and *Yoli* (no hot water, otherwise OK) have decent restaurants; also, **D-E** *Mucuchíes*, Av Moreno de Mendoza, by Cine Cavoní, some rooms have TV and a/c, noisy, OK.

● Places to eat
There is a very good churrascaría restaurant 15 mins walk from *Hotel Guyana* towards the airport, in an old hacienda building on the left, next to a *cervecería*, very good food, rec.

● Banks & money changers
Banco Consolidado (American Express), C Urbana, Edif Don Andrés. Banco Unión for Visa. Banks will not exchange Brazilian currency.

● Embassies & consulates
Brazilian Consulate, Av Las Américas, nr CANTV, T 227246, 0900-1700, friendly, helpful, visa issued in 1 hr, no onward ticket requested (some nationalities have to pay, eg Australians US$45). Information on roads in Boa Vista area.

● Shopping
Bookshop: *Librería Orinoco*, Centro Cívico Puerto Ordaz, international magazines and English paperbacks.

● Tour companies & travel agents
Lobo Tours, C Zambia No 2, Villa Africana Manzana 39, Puerto Ordaz, T 616286, F 617708, Wolfgang Loffler organizes trips to Río Paragua, well-organized, excellent cooking, rec for excursions S of the Orinoco; *Keyla Tours*, Av Monseñor Zabalete y Los Llanos, T 229195, F 226123, camping trips to the Gran Sabana, excellent guides, inc Steve from the USA, strongly rec (US$280 pp, 3 nights, 4 days, all inc). Also rec, *Selva Tours*, T 225537/225044, for trips to the Gran Sabana; guides Carlos Quintero (T/F 622480) and Eleazer (T 612867) also act freelance. *Piranha Tours*, at *Hotel Intercontinental*, runs good river trips, US$10 pp, to nearby falls, meeting of Caroní and Orinoco, etc. Recommended guide, *Richard Brandt*, T/F 224370 (or in Santa Elena de Uairén, T 220078/226813), who has his own car, speaks English and tailors trips to your requirements. Will lead climb of Roraima, fees from US$50-80 pp a day.

● Transport
Local Car hire: Many different operators at the airport, Puma cars rec; Hertz, Puerto Ordaz, rents 4WD vehicles. A car is very useful in this area, especially for visiting the Cerro Bolívar mine and Guri dam.

Air Daily flights to Caracas, Maracaibo and Barcelona; also to Porlamar, Valencia, Maturín, San Antonio, Santa Elena and Canaima. Walk 600m to gas station on main road for buses to San Félix or Puerto Ordaz.

Buses Terminal at San Félix, frequent minibuses to centre. Bus 0500, 0800, 1900 from Ciudad Guayana to **Santa Elena de Uairén**, US$9 with Líneas Orinoco, 0730, at least 12 hrs (or overnight bus, which misses the fine scenery, 9 hrs), via El Callao, also with Transmundial, daily, US$9, 10 hrs, few stops. **Tumeremo** (US$2.50), El Dorado (US$3.60) and Km 88; book a day in advance. *Por puesto* to **Ciudad Bolívar** US$3.60 (bus US$1.50); bus to **Maturín** US$4, 2½ hrs; to **Caracas**, US$10, 10½ hrs. To **Barcelona** and **Puerto La Cruz**, 8 a day; to **Cumaná**, 4 a day. To **Tucupita**, US$5 with Expresos Guayanesa at 0730 and 1400, 3 hrs, booking office opens 1 hr before departure, be there early, passport check just before Tucupita, inc 30 min ferry crossing to Los Barrancos. Minibuses in town are fast, frequent and cheap; San Félix-Puerto Ordaz, US$0.50; buses run until about 2100. Taxis San Félix-Puerto Ordaz US$1.50, Puerto Ordaz-airport US$2, airport-bus terminal US$7.50, San Félix bus terminal-Puerto Ordaz bus terminal US$3.50, bus terminal-town centre US$1.80, town centre-San Félix bus terminal US$2.50.

TUCUPITA

A worthwhile side trip along asphalted roads can be made to **Tucupita** (*pop* 81,820), on the Orinoco delta. Though capital of Monaguas state and the main commercial centre of the delta, there's a one-horse feel about it. It has an interesting cathedral; climate is very humid. TCs only accepted in Banco Unión or Banco de Venezuela at the riverside.

Local information
● **Accommodation**
E *Gran Hotel Amacuro*, C Bolívar 23, a/c, very good; **E** *Delta*, C Pativilca 28, a/c, basic; **E-F** *Pequeño*, C La Paz, fan, good value, safe, stores luggage, closes at 2200.

● **Places to eat**
Mi Tasca, C Dalla Costa, popular, varied menu, highly rec; *El Río*, rec; on Paseo Manamo *Refresquería La Cascada*, English spoken; and *Capri*, very good.

● **Tourist offices**
At C Dalla Costa beside Sonido Color 2000. Tourists should go here first for information on tours.

● **Transport**
Buses *Por puesto* from **Maturín** about US$6, 2-3 hrs; bus to Maturín, US$3 with Expresos Guayanesa, 1100, 3-4 hrs. To San Félix at 0730 with Expreso La Guayanesa, 3 hrs, US$5. To **Caracas**, 10 hrs, 2000, US$10; **Puerto La Cruz** at 0730 and 1400, US$6, 6 hrs.

DELTA TRIPS

For a 3-4 day trip to see the delta, its fauna and the Indians, either arrange boats through the tourist office, or contact Juan Carrión (all the taxi drivers know him, but he is very expensive). Vessels are not easy to come by and are expensive except for large groups. Bargain hard and prices may drop considerably. Recent favourable reports received: Romero Ildemaro (ask at

Bar Warauno, or C Tucupita 19), US$40 pp/day, basic but watertight accommodation, good food, hammocks and mosquito nets, recommended; Raúl at the *Gran Hotel Amacuro* runs a 1-day trip for up to 4, including food and drink, visit to 'Indian village'; Abelardo of *Delta Tours*, C Bolívar, also recommended for trips deeper into the region, US$60 pp, owner, Toni, from the USA, has his own lodge in the delta, US$85 pp/day (reductions for backpackers); *Aventura Turística Delta SA*, C Centurión, No 62, T (087) 211391, 1-5 day trips to the Delta Orinoco, Nicolás and Vidalig are very helpful, they speak French and English, they charge US$85/day; *Wakeriana Tours and Paradise Camp* (C Pativilca 21, Tucupita, T/F 087-210224), 4 hrs by boat from Tucupita, private and shared rooms, shared bath, typical meals, tours to Indian settlements (general manager Danielle Homsiova); also recommended is *Viaje a la Naturaleza*, C Mariño 23, run by Trinidadian Yance, US$40 pp/day, very good value. Some boat owners visit hotels in the evenings looking for clients and may negotiate a price.

The quality of some guides is poor and trips are expensive. Some guides are reported to pester visitors as soon as they get off the bus; bargain hard and never pay up front. There are other guides from Ciudad Guayana whose boats are unsuitable and whose services untrustworthy. For shorter excursions by boat, ask at gas station (*bomba*) by the river, but you won't see much in 1 day. Excursions often only travel on the main river, not in the caños where wildlife can be seen. Alternatively, take a *por puesto* from Plaza Bolívar to the peaceful village of La Horqueta on the banks of the Orinoco (US$0.35, 45 mins), where it is easier to get a boat and where there are many Indians. There are no hotels, but there are shops selling drinks and dry foodstuffs. Be warned, if the river level rises after a downpour, arrangements may be cancelled. On all trips agree in advance exactly what is included, especially food and hammocks. Make sure there is enough food for yourselves, the guide and the Indians, and plenty of water. Hammocks and mosquito repellents are essential. You can buy hammocks and local handicrafts. Passports must be shown leaving La Horqueta. Ask permission before you take photos of the Indians.

BARRANCAS

An interesting and friendly village is **Barrancas** (*pop* 13,000). Founded in 1530, it is one of the oldest villages in the Americas. Situated on the Orinoco, it can be reached by road from Tucupita, 63 km, US$1 (buses return at 0945 and 1700) or from Maturín. **F-G** *Hospedaje San Judas*, nr church, basic, good value, cheap restaurant next door, run by a helpful Guyanese woman. The village has a large community of Guyanese people who speak English. It is possible to take a boat to Curiapo (Indian village) and Amacuro (near the Guyana border), check at harbour; Señora Yúñez, lives next door to the bank, recommended.

Warning Avoid boats that are carrying suspicious goods, those that do not have adequate shelter from the rain and those that do not stop in Curiapo, as this is the only place to get an exit stamp out of Venezuela.

It is possible to go to Georgetown from here, ask for boats to Amacuro (the trip to Bellavista, Cangrejito or San José de Amacuro, all at the mouth of the Orinoco, takes 12 hrs) and then onto Mabaruma (only for the adventurous), or check with the lady at the *librería* on the river at the bottom of the village. She is from Georgetown and travels there occasionally. The trip from Barrancas to Georgetown is likely to take 3-4 days.

South to Brazil

THE land route to Boa Vista, Brazil, passes over the beautiful Gran Sabana plateau, an ancient land of flat-topped mountains and waterfalls. The road is not difficult until you get to Brazil, or make excursions off it. The trek to Roraima, perhaps Conan Doyle's 'Lost World', begins at a point on the highway south.

SOUTH FROM CIUDAD GUAYANA

Travelling S from Ciudad Guayana to the Brazilian border is becoming an increasingly popular excursion for Venezuelan tourists, as well as for overland travellers heading for Manaus and the Amazon. The road to the border at Santa Elena de Uairén is completely paved, with all bridges in place.

Tours

5-day/4-night tours of the Gran Sabana can be arranged in Caracas (US$297, including hotel, food, excursions, eg *Passarini-Suárez*, Centro Comercial Los Altos, San Antonio de Los Altos, T 032-711327), or in Ciudad Bolívar (cheaper and easier).

Local information
● **Camping**
Camping is possible but a tent with good waterproofing is essential (see also above, under Canaima National Park). Insect repellent and

long-sleeved/trousered clothes are needed against *puri-puri* (small, black, vicious biting insects) and mosquitoes (especially in El Dorado, at Km 88 and at Icabarú); or use baby oil mixed with vitamin B12.

● **Driving to the Brazilian Border**
4WD is only necessary if you wander off the main road, particularly in the rainy season. It is highly recommended to take spare tanks of gasoline (spare tanks are available at Km 88, but better and cheaper to get one earlier). All petrol pumps have fuel, but not all octane levels. It is also advisable to carry extra water and plenty of food. There are police checks at the Río Cuyuni and at Km 126, and at a military check at San Ignacio de Yuruaní all driving permits, car registration papers, and identification must be shown. If hitchhiking note that if you're dropped away from a 'base' there will be no shade.

UPATA

South from Ciudad Guayana Highway 10 is a 4-lane *autopista* as far as **Upata** (*pop* 51,500).

● **Accommodation** **D** *Andrea**, Plaza Miranda, credit cards accepted, restaurant, safe parking, good; **E** *Adriático*, good; **E** *Comercio*, C Ayacucho, excellent, as is its restaurant. Water is rationed in Upata and hot water in hotels is rare S of Ciudad Guayana.

● **Shopping** There is a good place to buy provisions opp the petrol station in Upata.

ROUTES From Upata to Km 88 the road is resurfaced and widened with broad hard shoulders. 18 km beyond **Guasipati** (*pop* 8,600; **C** *Hotel La Reina*, a/c, good; also **E** *Hotel Venezuela*) is **El Callao** on the S bank of the Río Yuruari, off the highway.

EL CALLAO

A small, clean, bright town (*pop* 7,400) whose Trinidadian inhabitants add a touch of calypso to its pre-Lenten carnival. A plant reprocesses the old gold mine tailings from El Perú, 8 km away, but the centre of gold mining has moved to Km 88 and Las Claritas (see below). The gold mine can be visited, the director will show you around. The town has many jewellery shops.

● **Accommodation** **D** *Isidora*, a/c, on the road to El Perú but in town; **E** *Italia*, 10 rooms, central, no phone; **F** *Callao*, C Bolívar, 2 blocks from the plaza, shared bath, laundry facilities, very welcoming owners, rec; **E** *Ritz*, on same street as post office, basic, serves cold beer;

several restaurants. There is a chronic water shortage, check when it is available in your hotel.

● **Banks & money changers** You may be able to change US$ cash in Banco de Venezuela on main plaza, but not TCs.

TUMEREMO

On another 41 km is **Tumeremo** (*pop* 9,100), recommended as the best place to buy provisions. There is Banco de la Unión (Visa), Banco de Orinoco (Amex, after 1500 US$5 commission/transaction), and gasoline (all grades) at a normal price (better than El Dorado). 5 km from Tumeremo towards the Fuerte Tarabay is the beautiful artificial lake of San Pedro with an attractive campsite (free camping ruined by rubbish).

● **Accommodation & places to eat** **D** *Cacique*, very good, noisy, excellent shower, rec; **D** *Miranda*, OK, better than some of the others; **E** *Leocar*, next to the bus-stop, fair, with shower and toilet, fan and a/c, some rooms with fridges, restaurant rec; **E** *Central*, nr plaza, fan, good, bakery and snackbar; **F** *Hospedaje Tumeremo*, on C El Dorado, fan, clean bathroom, good. *El Esturión*, C El Dorado, Edif Bolívar, good, friendly restaurant; *Restaurante Turístico* expensive but OK, does not serve yucca with everything; *Restaurante Las Cuevas*, nr plaza, medium priced, very popular, food is average, service slow, check your bill.

● **Buses** To Santa Elena, US$8.75 (8-10 hrs), Líneas Orinoco, 1100, 2 blocks from plaza nr Leocar); El Dorado, US$1.10, 1½ hrs; bus to Ciudad Bolívar, US$5.25, 6 a day, 6½ hrs or *por puesto* (via San Félix and Puerto Ordaz); bus to San Félix (Ciudad Guayana), US$2.50, *por puesto* US$5; bus Tumeremo-**Caracas**, US$35. Direct bus to Caracas departs 1600, 14 hrs.

FRONTIER WITH GUYANA

From Tumeremo you can go to the **Isla Anacoco**, on the Río Venamo which forms the border with Guyana. A paved road runs through the jungle to San Martín (one military and one police post en route), where you can arrange a visit to the island. Much English spoken in San Martín. The area around San Martín is a mining area and there are few tourists.

● **Immigration**
Get a Venezuelan exit stamp before reaching the border and a Guyanese entry stamp at the earliest opportunity.

● River transport to Guyana

From San Martín boats go to Nuevo Maico on the Río Cuyuní, US\$0.12 fast boat, 1½ hrs, US\$0.07 slow boat, 3 hrs. Dugouts (*piragua*) go from Nuevo Maico to Puerto Dedos, or Soledad at 0400, 0900, 1300 and 1800, 1 hr, US\$0.20, from where you can travel to Bartika, 4 hrs, US\$7 (boats leave at 0700 and 1200). In Bartika transport can be arranged to Georgetown (eg on horseback to Parika, US\$4, then by road).

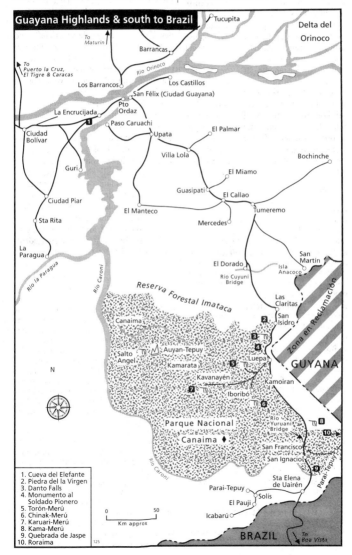

Guayana Highlands & south to Brazil

Tucupita

Delta del Orinoco

To Maturín

Barrancas

To Puerto la Cruz, El Tigre & Caracas

Río Orinoco

Los Castillos

Los Barrancos

San Félix (Ciudad Guayana)

La Encrucijada

Pto Ordaz

Paso Caruachi

Ciudad Bolívar

Upata

El Palmar

Guri

Villa Lola

Bochinche

Ciudad Piar

Guasipati

El Miamo

El Callao

Sta Rita

El Manteco

Mercedes

Tumeremo

La Paragua

Río la Paragua

El Dorado

Río Cuyuni Bridge

San Martín

Isla Anacoco

Zona en Reclamación

Reserva Forestal Imataca

Las Claritas

San Isidro

Canaima

Auyán-Tepuy

Salto Angel

Kamarata

Luepa

GUYANA

Kavanayén

Kamoirán

N

Iboribó

Parque Nacional

Río Yuruaní Bridge

Canaima

Río Caroní

San Francisco

San Ignacio

Paraí-Tepuy

1. Cueva del Elefante
2. Piedra de la Virgen
3. Danto Falls
4. Monumento al Soldado Pionero
5. Torón-Merú
6. Chinak-Merú
7. Karuari-Merú
8. Kama-Merú
9. Quebrada de Jaspe
10. Roraima

Parai-Tepuy

Sta Elena de Uairén

El Pauji

Solís

0   50

Km approx

Icabarú

BRAZIL

To Boa Vista

EL DORADO

278 km from Ciudad Guayana and 76 km from Tumeremo is **El Dorado** (*pop* 4,000), 7 km off the road on the Río Cuyuni, a hot, dirty and very noisy miners' supply centre in dense forest. On an island in the river stands the regional prison made famous by Papillon's stay there in 1945, in use again after renovation. It is possible to get police permission to cross the river and land on the island. The accompanying officer is full of interesting information. No charge for boat crossing. The local gold seams have been largely exhausted but mining still continues. El Dorado now relies for its existence mainly on its gas station (open 0800-1900, daily).

- **Accommodation NB** All hotels in El Dorado have problems with running water. **D** *San Antonio*, Edif Ceferino, next to bus stop, electricity intermittent, prefers to let by the hour, fan; **E** *Hospedaje Portugal*, 6 rooms, the Portuguese owner also runs the store next door; **F** *Mirador*, basic, noisy at weekends but good; *Alfonso*, quite good, will make excursions to the mines; **F** *El Dorado*, with bath, very large rooms, fan; **F** *El Valle*, basic, safe, rec.

- **Places to eat** *La Brasa*, on left when entering village, excellent food but small portions; *Archiven*, Plaza Bolívar, good, helpful owner; restaurant beside church serves delicious 'criolla vegetarian' food.

- **Banks & money changers** There is no bank, exchange at El Dorado is possible with the gold buyer on the main street; cash only, poor rates.

- **Buses** From Caracas to El Dorado, Expresos del Oriente, at 1830 daily, US$12, 14½ hrs, return at 1400 (925 km). The Orinoco bus line connects with Ciudad Bolívar (6 hrs) and Santa Elena, as does Transmundial (better buses, leaving 1100, US$5.40 to Santa Elena, US$3.60 to San Felix, 4 hrs). From El Dorado a bus runs to San Martín on the Guyanese border (see above). All buses stop on main plaza.

- **Tours** Contact Carlos at *Hotel San Antonio* for boat trips on the Río Cuyuni, US$25 pp/day, max 5 people, Indian guide. Boat trips can be taken 12 km up the Chicanán River to a gold camp, US$15, or other road excursions to miners' camps, US$7.

SOUTH FROM EL DORADO

The turn-off to El Dorado is marked Km 0; distances are measured from here by green signs 1 km apart. 6 km S of the turnoff to El Dorado, is the Río Cuyuni crossed by a bridge. From here it is possible to take boat trips to the gold mines, eg Payapal 1 hr 40 mins each way, US$25 for boat, beautiful trip; can also be visited by car, leaving from central plaza every hour or so, 30-mins journey, US$8 return, people are friendly and will let you look into the 30m deep mines. The roadside is dotted with tiny Indian villages – San Miguel de Betania, Araimatepui – and subsistence level farms. At Km 70 is *Manzanita* cabañas (E) and campsite (US$6), clean, good bathrooms, cold water, bar, restaurant, good.

At Km 85 is another gold-digging village, **Las Claritas**. This, and other settlements like it, is built out of oil cans and other rubbish, but complete with hotels, restaurants, small shops, hairdressers, brothels, etc. The miners guard their claims and diggings jealously; best to go with a guide or friendly local. If visiting independent miners at work, ask permission to take photos, and take a small gift.

At **Km 88** (also called **San Isidro**), there is gasoline (rarely 92 octane – the last before Santa Elena), a garage, the last telephone before Santa Elena and Banco Guayana. Everything is expensive, better food shops at Km 85.

- **Accommodation & places to eat** Las Claritas: **C** *Campamento Turístico Anaconda*, cabins with shower, WC, fan, well-furnished, with bar, table football and snooker; inc breakfast and dinner, run by Larri Master, who speaks English; another *campamento*, both reserved for tour groups. Restaurant; big market for food and gold; safe parking at Las Hermanitas de las Pobres (Convent), which can be better reached by the track from Km 88. **Km 88**: **D** *El Parador del Viajero*, restaurant, OK; **F** *La Pilonera*, opp Vargas store, with fan, safe parking, some rooms with bath, overpriced, restaurant with good fruit drinks, very friendly; good food and wide choice next door at the *Fuente de Soda*; *Restaurant Internacional*, despite the grotty exterior, excellent, cheap and friendly. Rooms for rent, **F**, with bath, fan, clean, ask at *farmacia*. Also at Km 88 is *Barquilla de Fresa*, owner Henry Cleeve speaks English and German, accommodation in bunk beds, no camping, good food, US$40/day, trails for hiking, early morning bird-watching, car parking, safe.

- **Transport** Bus Km 88-Caracas, US$10.50;

to Ciudad Bolívar wait at gas station for buses from Las Claritas (dep 0900, 1100, 1500, 1800). Frequent *por puestos* from El Dorado to Km 88, 1 hr, US$2. The only reliable public transport out of Km 88 is the bus from Ciudad Bolívar, which stops at 1400 daily, 6 hrs to Santa Elena, US$4.50; the alternative is to get a ride with passing jeeps and trucks (very little passes after 1030).

The wall of the Gran Sabana looms above Km 88 and the highway climbs steeply in sharp curves for 40 km before reaching the top; the road is, however, in very good condition and presents no problem for conventional cars. 4WD may be better in the wet season (May-Oct). At Km 100 the huge **Piedra de la Virgen** (sandy coloured with black streaks) is passed before the steepest climb (La Escalera) enters the beautiful **Canaima National Park** (30,000 sq km) one of the six largest parks in the world. To camp in the park, a permit must be bought at Inparques in Ciudad Bolívar, US$1.30 pp/night. Good views 100m W of the road at Km 102. The trail can be slippery, beautiful at sunrise.

Characteristic of this area are the large abrupt *tepuis* (flat-topped mountains or *mesas*), hundreds of waterfalls, and the silence of one of the oldest plateaus on earth. The landscape is essentially savanna, with clusters of trees, moriche palms and bromeliads; there is plenty of firewood should you wish to spend a night under the stars, but nights are very cool. At Km 119 (sign can only be seen going N) a short trail leads to the 40m **Danto** ('Tapir') **Falls**, a powerful fall wreathed in mosses and mist. If you are paying for your ride, try to persuade the driver to make a short stop; the falls are close to the road (about 5 mins slippery walk down on the left hand side), but not visible from it. (Buses cannot be flagged down here because of dangerous bends.) Further fine views at Km 135. The **Monumento al Soldado Pionero** (Km 137) commemorates the army engineers who built the road up from the lowlands, finally opened in 1973; barbecues, toilets, shelters. 4 km beyond is **Luepa**; all travellers must stop at the *ciudadela* (military checkpoint) a little way S. There is a popular camping place at Luepa, on the right going S which

belongs to a tour company. An informative guide on duty will rent you a tent or you can hang a hammock in an open-sided shelter (very cold at night, no water or facilities, possible to buy meal from tour group but expensive). There is a breakfast place, US$4.

8 km beyond Luepa, a graded gravel road leads 70 km W to **Kavanayén** (little traffic, best to have your own vehicle with high clearance, especially during the wet season, take plenty of snacks). The settlement is surrounded by *tepuis*.

Off this road after 25 km turn right to the falls of **Torón Merú** (17 km – road almost impassable for normal car, hell for cyclists, at the end is river impassable for 4WD, continue on foot, falls hard to find). Further on is a left turn at Km 30 to the falls of **Chinak-Merú**, 110m high and very impressive. Take the trail to the Río Aponguao and the very friendly Pemón Indian village of **Iboribó**, pay US$4 to cross the river and walk 45 mins to the falls, there is a trail descending to the bottom of the falls. This trip is reported not to be possible by normal car, take great care near the falls.

Beyond Kavanayén a beautiful but risky trail (18 km, 5 hrs walk) leads along flat-topped mountains to the **Karuari-Merú** falls (good swimming in the pool below).

Bargain with pilots to fly you over the Gran Sabana: a tour of Auyán-Tepuy, Angel Falls, Canaima and back to Kavanayén, costs US$200 for 5 passengers.

- **Accommodation & services** 18 km before Kavanayén is a rough road to the **E** *Hotel Chivaton*, good beds but icy water, no food, very isolated, rec. Kavanayén is the site of a Franciscan mission, founded in 1943; accommodation **G**, very friendly, cash TCs at better rate than in Santa Elena. One of the 2 grocery stores will prepare food, or restaurant opp serves cheap breakfasts and dinners, order in advance. Medical post near the airstrip.

TO SANTA ELENA DE UAIREN

For the remaining 180 km to Santa Elena de Uairén few people and only a handful of Pemón Indian villages are to be seen. Kampirán, **Kamoirán** (Km 176, restaurant, good breakfast, reasonable lunch, rapids in the back garden, rooms to let, **D**, gasoline) and Oriwarai are passed. The impressive falls at the **Kama** River should not be missed (Km 205, 82m high, but the viewpoint is used as a public toilet); there is also a small lake, Indian handicrafts for sale, canoe trips US$1.50/hr pp. Buses can be flagged down going S or N 3 times a day; check times in advance.

At Km 249 is the Río Yuruaní; in the **Quebrada Pacheco** is a small Inparques office; waterfalls and pools nearby where you can swim. Tour groups often stop here. A 15-min hike to the Yuruaní waterfall leaves the main road 250m after the crossing, turn left. Then comes the Pemón village of San Francisco de Yuruaní (see page 1569), followed, 9 km of bends later, by the larger village of **San Ignacio de Yuruaní** (military checkpoint; excellent regional food). As the highway crosses a wide plain, Kukenam and Roraima (the more southerly of the two) may be seen to the E on a clear day.

A trail at Km 275 leads to the **Quebrada de Jaspe** where a river cuts through striated cliffs and pieces of jasper glitter on the banks (don't take them home to glitter on your shelf, don't walk on the jasper and don't add to the graffiti on the rocks). Visit at midday when the sun shines best on the jasper, or at 1500 when the colour changes from red to orange, very beautiful.

● **Accommodation Km 205**: there is a native hut to rent, **E**, or you can sling a hammock in a *cabaña*, **F**, or pitch your tent in the camping area, **G**. No facilities, take water purification tablets. There is an overpriced restaurant and a small shop. **Km 245**: Río Sarapan falls, hotel, campsite, immaculately kept, with toilets, canned drinks sold but no restaurant, no charge for tents, small huts for rent, US$5-7.50/night. **Km 249**: cabins with hammocks for up to 12, **D**, cooking facilities. **Quebrada de Jaspe**: campsite beside the river, no facilities, bad drainage and exposed, not rec.

About 20 km from San Ignacio the highway begins to descend until, at the Río Cuquenán, it leaves Canaima National Park and runs the last few kilometres to Santa Elena, 642 km from Ciudad Guayana.

SANTA ELENA DE UAIREN

This growing, pleasant frontier town (*pop* 7,330; *phone code* 088) was established by Capuchin monks in 1931. Gold is a better buy here than in Ciudad Bolívar.

Local festivals
9-19 Aug, featuring music, dance and handicrafts.

Local information
● **Accommodation**

Accommodation is often difficult to find because of visiting mine workers and Brazilian shoppers (particularly at weekends).

B *Cabañas Familiares Friedenau*, S of town, off Av Perimetral, T 951353, self-contained chalets, pleasant, also run trips to Roraima (see below), English and German spoken.

C *Villa Fairmont*, Urb Akurimá, T (02) 782-8433, at N edge of town, a few mins' drive from bus station, has aviary; nearby is **C-D** *Cabañas Roraima*, fan, hot water, fridge, very comfortable, nr supermarket.

D *La Abuela*, C Urdaneta, T951422, hot water, fan, good, washing facilities; **D** *La Posada del Mesón*, Vía Penetración Sampai, T 951443, beautiful wooden bungalows, sanitary installations, modern and functioning, run by Margarita and José E Isurrualde, who are extremely helpful.

E *Fronteras**, C Icabarú y Zea, T951095, single or double, with bath, hot water, quiet, comfortable, fan, safe, good restaurant, rec; **E** *Gabriela*, on Mcal Sucre, 150m from bus terminal on opp side, with bath, water, fan, modern, comfortable, free coffee, rec, very good restaurant next door, US$4-5 per dish; **E** *Lucrecia*, Av Perimetral, nr terminal, with bath, fan, restaurant, nice rooms, arranges tours; **E** *Luz*, C Peña, 2 mins' walk from Plaza Bolívar, with bath, cold water, fan, comfortable beds, good meeting point, *Tayukasen Tours* have their office here (see below), rec, if hotel's full, owner will help to find a room in a private home; **E** *Panzarelli*, C Bolívar, nr plaza, T951196, with bath, hot water, fans, nice rooms, good value.

F *Casa de Gladys*, C Urdaneta 187, T 951171, with bath, fan, cooking and washing facilities, tourist information, day trips, rec; **F** *Las 5 Jotas*, nr *Cabañas Roraima*, comfortable, good value; **F-E** *José Gregorio*, next to bus terminal, with bath and fan, cold water, basic, OK; **F-E** *Tres Naciones*, on Zea, next to *Hotel Fronteras*, T 951190, with bath, fan, hot water, parking.

● **Places to eat**

Roraima, C Icabarú, opp hospital and CANTV, at W end of C Icabarú, not too expensive despite being tourist oriented, excellent steaks, highly rec creole and international cooking; *Agua Miel*, same location, very good vegetarian dishes and takeaway snacks, owner speaks good English; *Pizzería Texas*, on Av Perimetral, at bottom of C Urdaneta, excellent; almost opp is *Chivileayen*, expensive but tasty, great burgers; *La Carola*, around the corner from *Hotel Luz*, good lunches, popular, US$2-3 per dish, rec; *Panadería Trigopán*, next to *Anaconda Tours* on C Bolívar, good breakfasts and coffee. There are several restaurants on Mcal Sucre.

● **Banks & money changers**
Banco Orinoco, at C Bolívar and Mcal Sucre, changes Amex TCs at 5% commission, am only. Try the shops in the centre for dollars cash or TCs, eg *Casa de Los Cóchamos*, the gold shop S of main plaza, which changes TCs at lower rate than bank; *Inversiones Fortaleza*, C Urdaneta on plaza, cash, TCS or Brazilian currency; *La Boutique Zapatería* also changes TCs and cash at reasonable rates; also grocery store *El Gordito*, next to *La Abuela* on Urdaneta, for Brazilian currency (English and French spoken). Try at border with Brazilians entering Venezuela. Generally the rates are poor; check with travellers going in opp direction what rates should be). For better rates you must wait until Ciudad Guayana, or Boa Vista if going to Brazil (change some money into Brazilian currency before the bus leaves).

● **Post & telecommunications**
Telephone: CANTV office, on Av Perimetral, next to hospital at W end of C Icabarú, for international calls, but not all day.

● **Useful addresses**
Mechanic: Antonio Mejías, good, cheap, a miracle-worker. *Parks Auto Parts*, next to *Hotel Fronteras*, run by Floyd Park from Texas, USA, helpful.

● **Tour companies & travel agents**
Tayukasen Tours, at *Hotel Luz*, run by Roberto Fuenmayor Quintero, guides Pablo Vallenilla, Richard Mata, Andrés Emilio Pérez, Orlando Alder (El Gato) and Richard Prada, 1-5 day tours of Gran Sabana, US$20 pp/day guide and transport, US$45 pp/day all inc, 6 days to Roraima US$230 pp all inc, also trips to El Pauji and mines, Canaima, Angel Falls and Kavac, English spoken, highly rec; *Adventure Tours*, Av Perimetral at the end of C Urdaneta, T 951371, run by Frank Khasen and wife Arelis, tours of Gran Sabana or El Pauji, US$25 pp/day guide and transport only, or US$50 pp/day all inc, group discounts, 6 days to Roraima US$450 pp all inc; *Anaconda Tours*, Centro Comercial Augusto, C Bolívar, T 951016, tours of Gran Sabana/El Pauji, US$30-45 pp/day, not inc accommodation and meals; *Rodiske Tours*, C Mcal Sucre, T 951467,

tours to Gran Sabana and Roraima.

● **Transport**
Air Servivensa daily flights to Canaima (US$75) and Puerto Ordaz (US$80). Aereotuy has daily flights to Ciudad Bolívar, standby basis only on Sun; sometimes stops at Indian villages. To fly to Icabarú and the Indian villages of Uriman, Wonkin, and Kamarata you will have to charter an Airtaxi, quite expensive (eg Aerotécnica 6-seater, US$600/day). Book a week in advance. Airport, 10 km from town.

Road Corpovén gas station open 0800-1900.
Buses Terminal on C Mcal Sucre. From **Caracas** it is best to go to Ciudad Bolívar and take a bus direct to Boa Vista, or Santa Elena. From Santa Elena to **Ciudad Bolívar** (10-12 hrs), at 0700, 0930, 1330 and 1930 with Turgal (a/c, TV), US$9.50; at 1700 and 1900 with Línea Orinoco, US$9.30; at 0800 and 2000 with Travircan (some with a/c); with Ecuatur at 1130, US$11.60, 9 hrs (a/c, more comfortable). Alternatively take a daily bus to Tumeremo or El Dorado; Transmundial runs from **Tumeremo** to Santa Elena (US$8.75) and from **El Dorado** (US$5.40, 6 hrs), returning from Santa Elena at 0830. Santa Elena-**Ciudad Guayana**, 0600, 1900, 2000 (US$10, 10-11 hrs), or Expreso Maturín goes to Ciudad Guayana and Maturín daily. Transmundial go direct to San Félix daily, 1800, US$9, 10 hrs, very few stops. Take warm clothing for overnight buses with a/c (the driver may even insist that the shades be closed throughout the journey, so as not to affect the a/c).

Hitchhiking North from Santa Elena is said to be easy. Stand at the roadside at the garage just opp the terminal. Expect a small charge, up to US$5.

FRONTIER WITH BRAZIL

The 16 km road to the border is paved. The entire road links Caracas with Manaus in 4 days with hard driving; see Brazil, **Northern Brazil**, page 602, for a description of the road from the border.

● **Venezuelan immigration**
DIEX immigration office is uphill behind the bus terminal; opens at 0730-1130 and 1400-1700. All passports and car documents must be stamped here (not the border) on entry or exit.
   Staff at the Ministry of Justice next to DIEX, and the Guardia Nacional headquarters have been recommended as helpful with entry/exit difficulties.

Entering Venezuela Everyone who crosses the border from Boa Vista, Brazil, must have a visa, regardless of nationality (passport must be valid for 1 year). Venezuelan consulates are given in the Brazil chapter. Ask well in advance what health requirements are in force (yellow fever vaccination certificate, malaria test certificate and medical check-up may be required). Border officials may insist upon US$20/day for your stay; regulations state that a visa is sufficient. Fresh fruit and vegetables may not be brought into Venezuela. There are frequent road checks.

● **Crossing by private vehicle**
Allow 2 hrs to undertake all formalities.

● **Brazilian consulate**
Near bus terminal opp Corpoven gas station; open 0800-1200 and 1400-1800. You can get a visa here.

● **Transport**
Buses To Boa Vista with Unión Cascavel at 0830, 1200, 1500 and 1600, 4 hrs, US$13.70. There is no direct transport to Manaus.

EL PAUJI AND ICABARU

A road leaves the highway 8 km S of Santa Elena and after passing through a tunnel of jungle vegetation emerging onto rolling savannas dotted with *tepuis*. The road is in terrible condition. At Km 58 is a Guardia Nacional checkpoint at Paraitepuí, with a waterfall nearby. At Km 68 is *Shailili-ko* camp, English, Italian and French spoken, recommended.

17 km further is **El Pauji**, an agricultural settlement with a growing number of foreign residents. Ask for Luigi, an Italian at El Cajón mine (he speaks English). It is in a lovely area, with good walking. Excellent sights: Chirica Tepuy, huge, beautiful, jet black, surrounded by rolling savannah; Río Surucun, where the largest diamond in Venezuela was found; Salto Catedral, beautiful small hollow, lovely falls, bright red water below due to the tree roots, excellent for swimming; Salto La Gruta, very impressive falls, but very slippery; and Pozo Esmeralda, just outside El Pauji, fine rapids and pools for swimming. It is 20 mins to Los Saltos de Pauji, good for a bath. A good walk is to the small hill, 2 km from El Pauji beyond the airfield; views from the crest one side into El Abismo, a small tepuy, where the Brazilian jungle begins, 2-3 hrs from village, and on the other side down to the Venezuelan savanna (a beautiful area and walk, highly recommended). A German-speaking guide is Marco, recommended.

120 km W of Santa Elena is **Icabarú**, a diamond-producing centre with few facilities, where prices are high.

● **Accommodation & services In El Pauji**: **D** *Hospedaje Maripak Tepuy*, in the village, nr the airstrip and bus terminal, T (02) 234-3661 (Caracas), (088) 951459, run by Mariella Gill, cabins for 2/3 with bath, English spoken, US$5 per meal, good food, organizes tours, camping US$3 per tent; **E** *Chimanta*, with bath, solar powered, restaurant, run by Louise Scott; **F** pp *El Caminante* tourist camp, just after the bridge, coming from Santa Elena, run by Danielle, helpful, camping, trips arranged, good restaurant; **F** *Alojamiento Weimore*, on the other side of the bridge from Danielle's camp, has owner-designed space-age accommodation, peaceful, good food, natural pool; **F** *Hospedaje Karaware*, run by Nelson and Elizabeth, helpful. Just before the bridge is *El Merendero* restaurant. At *La Bodega* general store, Victoriano has information on guides for tourists. 15 km from El Pauji, at Solís, Arquimedes and Philippe have a tourist camp and organize tours. 25 km from the town is the *Canta Rana* tourist camp with basic accommodation (owners, Alfonso and Barbara Borrero, speak German, English and Spanish), waterfall and lovely surroundings, they have a private plane that collects people from Puerto Ordaz (T 086-226851 or 220709, Sr Haissan Al Atrache).

● **Transport Air** El Pauji to Ciudad Bolívar, US$60. **Road** Conventional cars and pick-ups can go no further than 30 km from Santa Elena on this road. 4WD can get to El Pauji. US$10 by jeep – if full, if not, cost increased – from Santa Elena, 0600, 3 hrs; ask in Santa Elena for possibility of a lift with families returning after buying supplies – you may have to pay. Jeep hire in El Pauji, US$50/day.

MOUNT RORAIMA

An exciting trip is to walk to Mt Roraima (2,810m), which it has been suggested was the 'Lost World' made famous by Arthur Conan Doyle's novel (although conflicting evidence points to the Brazilian Serra Ricardo Franco near the Bolivian border W of Cuiabá as the site). Roraima is a word in the Pemón indian language meaning 'The great, ever fruitful mother of streams'. Owing to the tough terrain and extreme weather conditions, this hike is only suitable for the fit. Supplies for a week or more should be bought in Santa Elena. If your food is being supplied by a tour company, check what food you will be eating; often vegetarians go hungry.

San Francisco de Yuruaní

The starting point is the Indian village of **San Francisco de Yuruaní**, 60 km N of Santa Elena and 9 km N of the San Ignacio military checkpoint (at which you are required to register). **G** *Hospedaje Mínima*, shower, very basic; also **G** *hostal* run by *Roraima Tours* (see below), usually full. There are 3 small shops selling basic goods but not enough for Roraima hike. Meals are available and tents can be hired, US$3 each/day, quality of tents and stoves is poor, try to get hold of good equipment. *Roraima Tours*, T (088) 951283, F 951339, recommended, Ana Fernández is very helpful, Roraima tour US$550 pp inc food, or US$100 for guide only (group rates can be arranged), also hire tents (US$10/6 days) and stoves. Guides in San Francisco charge about US$20-25 a day, more if they carry your supplies: Basílio is highly recommended, as is Donald Mitchel, speaks English; Carmelo is also good; Mario has not been recommended. Buses from Santa Elena will let you off here and pick up passengers en route to Ciudad Bolívar at 1700 and 1900. A jeep to Paraitepui is around US$40, cheapest is Oscar Mejías Hernández, US$25 one way, ask for him in village.

Paraitepuí

The badly eroded track to Paraitepuí (signposted), the nearest village to the mountain, leaves the highway a kilometre S of San Francisco. Very little traffic; difficult to hitch. In the rain many vehicles get stuck on the last stretch and the authorities are tired of pulling them out; the full 25 km can be walked in 7 hrs. Guides available here from US$12 a day and carriers for US$15, Spanish speaking guides available (see **Note also** below). Ask for El Capitán, he is in charge of guides. You can sleep free in the village if hiring a guide; camping is permitted. Few supplies available; one small shop sells soft drinks and biscuits. The Ayuso brothers are the best-known guides. The villagers speak Tauripen, the local dialect, but now most of them also speak Spanish.

CLIMBING RORAIMA

The foot trail winds back and forth on a more direct line than the little-used jeep track; it is comparatively straightforward and adequately marked descending from the heights just past Paraitepuí across rolling hills and numerous clear streams. The goal, Roraima, is the mountain on the right, the other massive outcrop on the left is Mata Hui (known as Kukenam after the river which rises within it). If leaving the village early enough in the day, you may reach the Río Cuquenán crossing early afternoon; this river floods quickly after rain, the bottom is slippery and the current swift; take a 50m rope if not going with a party and be prepared to get wet (good camping here, you can swim in the many pools, lots of mosquitoes and *puripuris* on river bank). 3 hrs' walk brings you to a lovely bird-filled meadow below the foothills of the massif, another perfect camping spot known as *campamento base* (10 hrs to base camp from Paraitepuí). The footpath now climbs steadily upwards through the cloud forest at the mountain's base and becomes an arduous scramble over tree trunks and damp rocks until the cliff is reached. From here it is possible to ascend to the plateau along the 'easy' rock ledge which is the only route to the top. It is quite broad and supports much vegetation; it manoeuvres around three spurs, drops sharply in places, and passes under an icy waterfall before heading steeply and directly to the summit. Walkers in good health should take about 4 hrs from the meadow to the top. The vistas across the Gran Sabana are magnificent, and the summit is an eerie world of stone and water, difficult to move around easily. There are not many good spots to camp; best is *El Hotel* – a sandy patch under an overhanging ledge – to which red painted arrows lead the way to the right after reaching the summit. From *El Hotel* a marked track leads to the survey pillar near the E cliff where Guyana, Brazil and Venezuela meet; allow a day as the track is very rough. Full camping equipment including stove is essential (an igloo-type tent is best for the summit), wear thick socks and boots to protect legs from snakes, also essential are warm clothes for the summit (much mist, rain squalls and lightning at night: beware) and effective insect repellent – biting *plaga* infest the grasslands. The whole trip can take anywhere between 5 days and 2 weeks; if you don't wish to camp on the summit, a trip to the top and return can be done in a day, but keep an eye on weather conditions. A cloud belt usually wells up around the massif after dawn and often remains all day to blot out Roraima, even though the summit may remain clear. The water on the summit and around the foot of Roraima is very pure, but bring bottled water or a purifier for the Savannah. There is very little firewood on top, better to bring gas or liquid fuel stoves. Litter is beginning to appear along the trail; please take care of the environment.

NB The dry season for trekking is Nov-May (with annual variations); June-Aug Roraima is usually enveloped in cloud. **Note also** that the National Guard requires first-time visitors to have a guide beyond Paratepuí, otherwise you will be fined. It is not recommended to go alone; best to go with a guide from Santa Elena or San Francisco (those hired in Paraitepuí have no accident insurance cover). A guide can be of great assistance for the hike's final stages (it is very easy to get lost) and for knowing best places to camp. Thorough searches are now made on your return. Do not remove crystals from the mountain; on the spot fines up to US$100 may be charged.

even take your photo. Visa and Mastercard transactions at banks offer good rates. Banco Consolidado is affiliated with American Express, no commission, some branches cash personal cheques from abroad on an Amex card; Banco Unión, Banco de Venezuela and Banco Mercantil (not all branches) handle Visa and ATM transactions, inc cash advances and Banco Mercantil handles Mastercard. Thomas Cook Mastercard refund assistance point, Edif Cavendes, p 7, of 706, Av Fco de Mirando, Los Palos Grandes, 1060 Caracas, T 284-3866/3255.

In 1997, it was becoming very difficult to change dollars cash or TCs in Venezuela. Visitors are strongly advised to use Visa or Mastercard. It was virtually impossible to change cash in banks; best to try *casas de cambio*. If changing money in hotels, do not take sterling or any other European currencies. There are cash machines for Visa, Mastercard and Amex at Simón Bolívar airport. Have money sent to you by telex and not by post, which can take weeks. Rates of exchange in hotels are generally poor.

NB It is quite common for tour companies not to accept credit cards, other than for flights, so you will need cash or TCs for buying tours.

Popular names for coins: Fuerte, Bs 5; Real, Bs 0.50; Medio, 0.25; Puya or Centavo, 0.05. The brown Bs 100 note is sometimes referred to as a marrón, or a *papel*, the Bs 500 note as an *orquidea*, because of its picture.

● **Cost of living**
Travelling on the cheapest possible budget will cost around US$15/day, depending on which part of the country you visit. A less basic budget would be about US$25/day, rising to US$95 for first class travel.

GETTING THERE

BY AIR

● **From Europe**
British Airways fly from London to Simón Bolívar twice a week direct. There are also services from Europe by Air France, KLM, Iberia, Alitalia and TAP.

● **From North America**
Direct flights with American Airlines (New York, Orlando, Miami, Chicago), United Airlines (New York, Miami, Los Angeles, Chicago), Servivensa (Miami, New York), LanChile (Miami).

● **Latin America and the Caribbean**
From Colombia (Bogotá-Caracas), there are direct flights by Avianca, Servivensa, Saeta and Ecuatoriana. Also Lacsa from Barranquilla. Lacsa flies from San José (Costa Rica) and Panama to Caracas. From Argentina, Brazil and Bolivia there

are direct services by Aerolíneas Argentinas, Varig and LAB. There is direct air service from Chile (LanChile twice weekly), Peru (Saeta, Ecuatoriana, AeroPerú, Servivensa, Avianca), Ecuador (Saeta, Servivensa, Avianca and Ecuatoriana – from Quito; from Guayaquil, Saeta, Ecuatoriana), Santo Domingo (Aeropostal), Puerto Rico (Lacsa), Curaçao (ALM, Servivensa), Aruba (Air Aruba, Servivensa, ALM, Aserca), Bonaire (Servivensa). BWIA have services to Port of Spain (5 days a week from Caracas). LIAT flies twice a week to St Lucia; Air France flies to Guadeloupe once a week; Cubana 3 days a week to Havana.

Avensa/Servivensa operate an airpass, which must be bought outside Latin America or the Caribbean. It is valid for 45 days and passengers must buy a minimum of 4 coupons. No route may be flown twice in the same direction. Economy class only; children pay 66% and infants 10% of the adult fare. Prices are by Zone: Caracas to Aruba, Bonaire or Curaçao US$50; Caracas-Miami (but not Barquisimeto or Maracaibo-Miami), Caracas-Bogotá, Bogotá-Quito, or Quito-Lima US$70; Caracas-Lima US$180; Caracas-Mexico City US$200; any internal Venezuelan flight US$40.

BY BOAT

Shipping routes are given in the Introduction and Hints, apart from those with Curaçao and Aruba, which can be found in the text under Coro.

● **Shipping a car from Europe**
Harms Hamburg of Bremerhaven ship a car in a container for US$4,100 plus port handling to Venezuela.

On arrival in Venezuela (La Guaira), you must get a letter from the shipping agent stating that the boat has arrived and go to the Tourism Department at Simón Bolívar airport where you must obtain a document identifying your car (take photocopies of driving licence, passport, tourist card, car documents and bill of lading). With this you can get your car out of the port: a shipping agent is not necessary, though knowledge of Spanish is useful. A freight forwarder can be useful; they charge US$40-45, agree price in advance. Go then to Aduanas Marítimas at the port with your bill of lading, ownership documents and passport, and 5 hrs to spare. They stop for lunch 1200-1300 and close at weekends. You will have to pay US$100 to the docks company to get your car out. If you will be taking your car out of Venezuela overland, make sure that the freight forwarder gives you a sealed letter for Venezuelan customs at your point of exit.

● **Shipping a car from the USA**

Shipping a car from Miami to Maracaibo or La Guaira: Venezuelan Line (agent Oceanic Steamship Co – rec, contact Gene Taylor) and Delta Line, fare is less Maracaibo-Miami; no passengers. From New Orleans: Delta Line, passengers carried, but very expensive. Alternatively, agent Hansen and Tiedemann charges same price as Delta for vehicle, but you can accompany it at much lower cost (5 days, inc meals). Also rec: Coordinadora del Caribe Transmodal CA (CCT), C Veracruz, Ed Torreón, p 7, Las Mercedes, Caracas, T 927133. Vencaribe (shipping) agent is Taurel y cía, Edif Taurel, C Cuji a Romualdo No 69, Apdo 1592, Caracas; representative is Sonigar on 3rd floor, but Paul Paulheim on 1st floor is helpful. In port of La Guaira Taurel is on main street, just ask; Johnny Hilahl is the representative, but Wendy the receptionist and Bobby Momighan are also helpful, all speak English. Taurel's shipping department is called 'vapores'. A rec agent for importing a vehicle is Sr Freddy Diz, T (031) 22028; for unpacking a containerized vehicle, Sr Gustavo Contreras V, Transporte Gusconval, T (Radio) 02-661-9222, or (031) 943901. At the shipping agent Transportadoras Marítimas Venezolanas, Centro Comercial Litoral, on the main street in Maiquetía, Carlos Hernández is very helpful.

● **Yacht**

Do not try and clear Customs and Immigration without an agent in a commercial port, well worth the fee. Get your tourist card at a Venezuelan embassy before arriving, although if you arrive during a major storm officials may make an exception. The time a yacht may stay in Venezuelan waters is to be increased from 6 to 18 months. During the busy hurricane season, **security** problems increase; thieves arrive by night in boats with bolt cutters and fast engines and steal dinghies, motors and other items left on deck. Best security is in marinas. Porlamar even has trouble with swimmers during the day. Fewer problems in the outer islands of La Blanquilla, La Tortuga, Los Roques, Los Aves and Los Testigos, but trouble reported in coastal anchorages, eg Cumaná, Mochima, Morrocoy, Puerto La Cruz. Take all precautions possible. Chris Doyle's *Guide to Trinidad and Tobago and Venezuela*, 1994 edition, has information on yachting. A new edition is expected for Venezuela and Bonaire.

CUSTOMS

● **Duty free allowance**

You may bring into Venezuela, free of duty, 25 cigars and 200 cigarettes, 2 litres of alcoholic drinks, 4 small bottles of perfume, and gifts at the inspector's discretion. New items to the value of US$1,000 may be brought in.

● **Clothing**

Tropical weight in normal city colours is best for business in Caracas, otherwise clothing is less formal, but smart jackets and ties are required in the most exclusive restaurants and clubs. In Maracaibo and the hot, humid coastal and low-lying areas, regular washable tropical clothing is used. For women: blouse and trousers (shorts quite acceptable on the coast); cotton dresses, with a wrap for cool evenings, and for air-conditioned restaurants and cinemas. Shoes are very good value. Cinemas may not admit men in shorts or anyone in flip-flops.

● **Hours of business**

Banks are open from 0830 to 1130 and 1400 to 1630. Mon to Fri only. Government office hours vary, but 0800-1200 are usual morning hours. Government officials have fixed hours, usually 0900-1000 or 1500-1600, for receiving visitors. Business firms generally start work about 0800 and some continue until about 1800 with a midday break. Shops, 0900-1300, 1500-1900, Mon-Sat. Generally speaking, Venezuelans start work early, and by 0700 in the morning everything is in full swing. Most firms and offices close on Sat.

● **Official time**

4 hrs behind GMT, 1 hr ahead of EST.

● **Safety**

In the cities, take the usual precautions to protect your valuables and belongings, but in addition, carry handbags, cameras etc on the side away from the street as motor-cycle purse-snatchers are notorious, especially in Caracas. Hotel thefts are becoming more frequent.

● **Tipping**

Taxi drivers are tipped if the taxi has a meter (hardly anywhere), but not if you have agreed the fare in advance. Usherettes are not tipped. Hotel porters, US$0.50; airport porters US$0.50/piece of baggage. Restaurants, between 5 and 10% of bill.

● **Voltage**

110 volts, 60 cycles, throughout the country.

● **Weights and measures**

Weights and measures are metric.

● **Airport information**

To avoid overbooking the Government obliges airlines to post a passenger list, but it is important to obtain clear instructions from the travel agent regarding confirmation of your flight and checking-in time. **NB** Passengers leaving Caracas on international flights must reconfirm their reservations not less than 72 hrs in advance; it is safer to do so in person than by telephone; not less than 24 hrs for national flights: if you fail to do this, you lose all rights to free accommodation, food, transport, etc if your flight is cancelled and may lose your seat if the plane is fully booked. Beware of counterfeit tickets; buy only from agencies. If told by an agent that a flight is fully booked, try at the airport anyway. International passengers must check in 2 hrs before departure or they may lose their seat to someone on a waiting list. Handling charge for your luggage US$0.50. When leaving Maiquetía airport, beware Gate 5. This is subdivided into gates A-D; hundreds of passengers with different destinations are crammed into a lounge where flights are not called and the monitor does not work. Keep asking the staff with the walkie-talkie if your flight is boarding. All flights are subject to delays or cancellation.

● **Airport and land departure taxes**
All tourists and diplomats leaving the country, except transit passengers, must pay US$18 (approximately) at the airport, land border or port of embarkation (payable in bolívares or dollars). Minors under 12 years of age do not pay the exit tax. Venezuelans, resident foreigners or those with a visa *transeunte* have to pay Bs 1,200 on departure. There is also an airport tax of US$0.45 for those passengers on internal flights, payable at every change of plane. Exit stamps for overland travellers, US$2 (except US$5 Maracaibo-Maicao, Colombia).

WHERE TO STAY

● **Accommodation**
Fairmont International (see page 1474) will book hotel rooms both in Caracas and in other towns, where they have 102 hotels on their books, not all of which are mentioned in these pages. Hotels marked with an asterisk (*) are bookable through Fairmont. Officially controlled prices exist for 1-star and 2-star hotels. Hotels of our B price category upwards are often heavily booked up, especially in Caracas; advance reservations are advisable. 3-star hotels start at about US$15-20 a night. Prices for singles are often not much less than doubles.

● **Camping**
Equipment, perhaps not of the highest standard, is available at sports-goods shops in Caracas. It is impossible, in fact illegal, to refill portable gas cylinders. Cylinders are sold at Deportes el Llanero, Caracas, T 545-1634. Those using gasoline stoves should note that even the higher octane fuels will cause blockages of fuel jets. Camping in Venezuela is a

popular recreation, for spending a weekend at the beach, on the islands, in the *llanos* and in the mountains. (People pitch their tents on Monte Avila overlooking Caracas.) Camping, with or without a vehicle, is not possible at the roadside. If camping on the beach, for the sake of security, pitch your tent close to others, even though they play their radios loud. For information on hiking, climbing and relevant equipment, telephone Alexander on (02) 573-0056 (Spanish only). See page 1565 on camping in the Canaima National Park.

FOOD AND DRINK

FOOD

There is excellent local fish (eg *pargo* or red snapper), crayfish, small oysters and prawns. Sometimes there is turtle, though it is a protected species. Turtle may appear on menus in the Peninsula of Paraguaná as *ropa especial*. Of true Venezuelan food there is *sancocho* (a stew of vegetables, especially yuca, with meat, chicken or fish); *arepas*, a kind of white maize bread, very bland in flavour; toasted *arepas* served with a wide selection of relishes, fillings or the local somewhat salty white cheese are cheap, filling and nutritious; cachapas, a maize pancake (soft, not hard like Mexican *tortillas*) wrapped around white cheese; *pabellón*, made of shredded meat, beans, rice and fried plantains (vegetarian versions available); and empanadas, maize-flour pies containing cheese, meat or fish. At Christmas only there are *hallacas*, maize pancakes stuffed with chicken, pork, olives, etc boiled in a plantain leaf (but don't eat the leaf). A *muchacho* (boy) on the menu is a cut of beef. *Ganso* is also not goose but beef. *Solomo* and *lomito* are other cuts of beef. *Hervido* is chicken or beef with vegetables. *Contorno* with a meat or fish dish is a choice of fried chips, boiled potatoes, rice or yuca. *Caraotas* are beans; *cachitos* are filled croissants. *Pasticho* is what the Venezuelans call Italian *lasagne*. The main fruits are bananas, oranges, grapefruit, mangoes, pineapple and pawpaws. **NB** Some Venezuelan variants of names for fruit: *lechosa* is papaya, *patilla* water melon, *parchita* passion fruit, and *cambur* a small banana. Excellent strawberries are grown at Colonia Tovar, 90 mins from Caracas. A delicious sweet is *huevos chimbos* – egg yolk boiled and bottled in sugar syrup. The Caracas *Daily Journal* (in English) lists many reliable restaurants in Caracas and Maracaibo. Venezuelans dine late.

DRINK

Venezuelan rum is very good; rec brands are Cacique, Pampero and Santa Teresa. There are four good local beers: Polar (the most popular),

Regional (with a strong flavour of hops), Cardenal and Nacional (a *lisa* is a glass of keg beer; for a bottle of beer ask for a *tercio*); Brahma beer (lighter than Polar), is imported from Brazil. There are also mineral waters and gin. Now there is a good, local wine in Venezuela. The Polar brewery has joined with Martell (France) and built a winery in Carora. Wines produced are 'Viña Altagracia' and 'Bodegas Pomar'. 'Bodegas Pomar' also produces a sparkling wine in the traditional champagne style. Liqueurs are cheap, try the local *ponche crema*. The coffee is excellent and very cheap (*café con leche* has a lot of milk, *café marrón* much less, *café negro* for black coffee, which, though obvious, is not common in the rest of Latin America); visitors should also try a *merengada*, a delicious drink made from fruit pulp, ice, milk and sugar; a *batido* is the same but with water and a little milk; *jugo* is the same but with water. A *plus-café* is an after-dinner liqueur. Water is free in all restaurants even if no food is bought. Bottled water in *cervecerías* is often from the tap; no deception is intended, bottles are simply used as convenient jugs. Insist on seeing the bottle opened if you want mineral water. *Chicha de arroz* is a sweet drink made of milk, rice starch, sugar and vanilla; fruit juices are very good.

GETTING AROUND

AIR TRANSPORT

Most places of importance are served by Avensa, Servivensa and Aeropostal. Aereotuy and Aserca (rec for good service) fly to a variety of destinations. For the Avensa/Servivensa airpass, see above. Internal airlines offer special family discounts and student discount but practice is variable, photocopies of ISIC card are useful as it allows officials to staple one to the ticket. Sometimes there is little difference between 1st class and tourist class fares. Beware of overbooking during holiday time, especially at Caracas airport; it is rec that you check in 2 hrs before departure, particularly at Easter.

LAND TRANSPORT

● **Trains**

The only passenger traffic of any importance is on the Barquisimeto to Puerto Cabello line. The 110 km Yaritagua-Acarigua-Turén electric railway line was opened at the beginning of 1983, intended mostly to transport agricultural products. Passengers are carried on the Acarigua-Yaritagua stretch.

● **Road**

Buses are relatively cheap, but the quality of long-distance travel varies a lot. There are numerous services between the major cities. Buses stop frequently, but there may not always be a toilet at the stop. For night journeys in a/c buses take a sleeping bag or similar because the setting is set to freezing. Also take earplugs against the loud stereo systems. The colectivo taxis and minibuses, known as *por puesto*, seem to monopolize transport to and from smaller towns and villages. For longer journeys they are normally twice as expensive as buses, but faster. They may be reluctant to take luggage and the ill-kempt. If first on board, wait for other passengers to arrive, do not take a *por puesto* on your own unless you want to pay for the whole vehicle. Outside Caracas, town taxis are relatively expensive. At peak periods *revendedores* (touts) will try to sell tickets at 2-3 times face value.

● **Motoring**

A tourist can bring in his/her car without paying duty. See above for **Shipping a car from the USA** or **Europe** and under **Additional notes on motoring** in **Introduction and Hints**. A visa is required for overland entry (this is necessary despite what Consulates may tell you). An entry permit for a car costs US$10 and requires one photograph (takes 24 hrs); ask for a permit for 6 months, or unspecified time. See also page 1520.

The Touring y Automóvil Club de Venezuela (addresses under Caracas, **Useful addresses**, and San Cristóbal, **Tourist offices** – the Maracaibo office only deals through Caracas) issues the *Libreta de Pasos por Aduana* for taking foreign-registered cars into other South American countries. Takes 24 hrs and your vehicle must be presented to the Club. Before shipping your vehicle to Venezuela, go to a Venezuelan consul to obtain all necessary documentation, inc visa, to allow you to enter the country prior to getting the *libreta*. You must also go to a Venezuelan consul in the country in which you land your car if other than Venezuela.

For vehicles with Venezuelan registration leaving Venezuela the following documents are required: an Automóvil passport book from the Touring y Automóvil Club de Venezuela; the original car papers; the registration document; a police *revisión* obtained from the Policía Técnica Judicial; and a temporary import/export licence for a vehicle obtainable from the Ministerio de Hacienda, Caracas, or from a customs agent in San Antonio de Táchira (border town) for about US$100. The export/import licence and the passport book must be signed and stamped by the Customs Administrator. In the border area with Colombia, police checks are frequent; make sure you have all your papers. If possible, check all details on bringing in/taking out a car in advance. For third party insurance contact Sra Joaqui l de Castaneda (Corredor de

Seguros, Av Andrés Bello y Av El Parque, Edif Oficentro, p 6, San Bernardino, Caracas, T (02) 575-2522/574-6111. Short term insurance policies are available with Seguros La Seguridad, offices all over the country.

All visitors to Venezuela can drive if they are over 18 and have a valid driving licence from their own country; an international driving licence is preferred. It is a good idea to hire a car (see page 1478); many of the best places are off the beaten track. Some companies such as National have a wide network of offices in towns and airports allowing a fly-drive approach to travel, using a number of different vehicles. You have to have a credit card to rent a vehicle. Car hire with insurance varies from company to company: basic rates for a car are from US$16-50/day depending on make; government tax of 12.5% is also added. Rates tend to be the same in all cities, except on Margarita, which is more expensive. If planning to hire a car for any length of time it is worth the trouble to obtain a *licencia temporal para conducir*; for this you require a medical certificate (eye examination, blood pressure, US$2, issued by an authorized medical centre, try Touring y Automóvil Club, Caracas), photocopy of your home driver's licence and two black-and-white passport photos which must be presented at the Ministerio de Transporte y Comunicaciones, Torre Este, Parque Central, Dep Licencias. If you have an accident and someone is injured, you will be detained as a matter of routine, even if you are not at fault. Do not drive at night if you can help it (if you do have to, don't drive fast). Carry insect spray if you do; if you stop and get out, the car will fill with biting insects.

The roads in Venezuela are generally poor, except for the 4-lane autopistas. Motoring restrictions in Caracas include a ban on parking in front of a bank; motorcycles may not be driven at night; pillion passengers may not be carried on motorcycles if of the same sex as the driver. You are more likely to be penalized for infringing these rules than for driving through a red light; they are designed to improve security for banks and pedestrians. In addition, motorcyclists are obliged to wear a crash helmet but it must not be of a type which obscures the face. Use private car-parks whenever possible as break-ins on streets are common in Caracas and all large cities.

There are five grades of gasoline: 'normal', 83 octane; 87, 89, 91 and 'alta', 95 octane (average cost US$0.10-0.12 a litre). Diesel (US$0.10 a litre) is used by most goods vehicles, available from many filling stations in Caracas. Fuel prices are due to rise, by an unknown amount (June 1997). Oil costs US$0.60 a litre. Service stations are open 0500-2100, Mon-Sat, except those on highways which are open longer hours. Only those designated to handle emergencies are open on Sun. In the event of breakdown, Venezuelans are usually very helpful. There are many garages, even in rural areas; service charges are not high, nor are tyres, oil or accessories expensive, but being able to speak Spanish will greatly assist in sorting out problems. Carry spare battery water, fan belts, the obligatory breakdown triangle, a jack and spanners. **Warning** There is an automatic US$20 fine for running out of fuel. See **Tourist Information** under Caracas, and Maps, above.

● **Hitchhiking**

Hitchhiking (*Cola*) is not very easy and not very safe in coastal regions, but elsewhere the Venezuelans are usually friendly and helpful if you know some Spanish. The best places to try are Guardia Nacional posts outside cities (may get free bus rides from them). It is illegal on toll roads and, theoretically, for non-family members in the back of pick up trucks. Some drivers may ask for money for the lift, especially if on a bus route, common in the Gran Sabana.

● **Boat**

In Amazonia wait at the police posts where boats are obliged to report.

COMMUNICATIONS

● **Newspapers**

Caracas: *El Universal*, *El Nacional* and *El Diario de Caracas*, *La Religión*, *Ultimas Noticias*. The *Daily Journal* (English), *El Mundo* and *2001* (evening), *Número* (weekly), *Resumen* (weekly), *Elite* (weekly), *Momento* (weekly), *Venezuela Gráfica* (weekly), *Páginas* (weekly), *Semana* (weekly), *Ve Venezuela*, tourist bi-monthly. Maracaibo: *Panorama*, *La Crítica*. Puerto La Cruz: *El Tiempo*. For economic news, *El Globo* (daily), *Economía Hoy* (daily) and *Reporte* (3 times a week). The Sun edition of *Hoy* contains the *Guardian Weekly* from the UK.

● **Postal services**

The postal service can be extremely slow and unreliable. For a letter up to 20 grams to the Americas the cost is US$0.30; to the rest of the world US$0.36. A 10 kg package is US$25 to Europe, airmail only. All boxes must be wrapped up and sewn up with cloth. Airmail letters to the USA or Europe can take from 1 to 4 weeks and registered mail is no quicker. Internal mail also travels slowly, especially if there is no PO Box number. As in other Latin countries removing stamps from letters occurs (Trish and Tony Wheeler suggest that you insist on seeing your letters franked because you are a collector). Avoid the mail boxes in pharmacies as some no longer have collections. A private parcel delivery company, such as DHL, will charge around US$60 for parcels of up to 500g to Europe.

● **Telephone services**

All international and long distance calls are operated by CANTV. Most major cities are now linked by direct dialling (*Discado Directo*), with a 3-figure prefix for each town in Venezuela. Otherwise CANTV offices deal with most long-distance and international calls in the cities outside Caracas. Collect calls are possible to some countries, at least from Caracas, though staff in offices may not be aware of this. Calls out of Venezuela are more expensive than calls into it and are subject to long delays. Local calls are troublesome and the connection is often cut in the middle of your conversation; calls are best made from hotels or CANTV offices, rather than from booths. Most public phones operate on prepaid CANTV cards in denominations of 1,000 and 2,000 bolívares. Buy them from CANTV or numerous small shops bearing the CANTV logo, or a scrap of card reading '¡Sí! ¡hay tarjetas!' They are also sold by street vendors. Make sure they are still in their clear plastic wrapper with an unbroken red seal. Many small shops impose a 25% handling charge and tarjetas may be out of stock particularly outside Caracas or larger towns. International calls can be made with a tarjeta, minimum needed Bs 2,000, but you get little more than 1 min to Europe. To make an international call, dial 00 plus country code etc. Canada direct: 800-11100. For UK, BT Direct, 800-11440 (BT chargecard works from any phone). International calls are charged by a series of bands, ranging from about US$1/min to USA and Canada, to US$2 to UK, to US$2.15. There are various reduced and economy rates according to band. Fax rates are as for phones.

NB Telephone, fax or telex are far preferable to cables. Ask your hotel for use of its telex or fax machine.

HOLIDAYS AND FESTIVALS

There are two sorts of holidays, those enjoyed by everybody and those taken by employees of banks and insurance companies. Holidays applying to all businesses inc: 1 Jan, Carnival on the Mon and Tues before Ash Wed (everything shuts down Sat-Tues; make sure accommodation is booked in advance), Thur-Sat of Holy Week, 19 April, 1 May, 24 June (24 June is the feast day of San Juan Bautista, a particularly popular festival celebrated along the central coast where there were once large concentra-

tions of plantation slaves who considered San Juan their special Saint; some of the best-known events are in villages between Puerto Cabello and Chuspa, to the E, such as Chuao, Cata and Ocumane de la Costa), 5, 24 July, 24 Sept, 12 Oct, 25 December. Holidays for banks and insurance companies only inc all the above and also: 19 Mar and the nearest Mon to 6 Jan, Ascension Day, 29 June, 15 Aug, 1 Nov and 8 December. There are also holidays applying to certain occupations such as Doctor's Day or Traffic Policeman's Day. From 24 Dec-1 Jan, most restaurants are closed and there is no long-distance public transport. On New Year's Eve, everything closes and does not open for a least a day. Queues for tickets, and traffic jams, are long. Business travellers should not visit during Holy week or Carnival.

Local: La Guaira: 10 March. Maracaibo: 24 Oct, 18 November.

FURTHER READING

● **Business visitors**

The *Guide to Venezuela* (925 pages, updated and expanded in 1989), by Janice Bauman, Leni Young and others, in English (available in Caracas) is a mine of useful information and maps (US$11). There are many fine coffee-table books on the various regions of Venezuela, for example Charles Brewer-Carias' books on Roraima and Venezuela as a whole. *Venezuala in Focus* (Latin America Bureau, £5.99), a guide to the history, politics, economy and culture of the country.

ACKNOWLEDGEMENTS

We should like to thank Alan Murphy for updating this chapter. Our warmest thanks are due to Frances Osborn (resident in Caracas), Tom and Raquel Evenou and all at Bum Bum Tours in Mérida, José Troconis of Mérida (NatourA), Martin and Angelika Haars of Soana Tours in Ciudad Bolívar, Miguel Gasca of Ciudad Bolívar, the guides at Tayukasen Tours in Santa Elena, María Eugenia Olívar of Mérida and her family in Trujillo, Edward Paine and Steven Chew (Last Frontiers), Kathy Irwin of Texas and Steve Collins (Journey Latin America) for much valuable assistance.

The Guianas

HORIZONS

LIKE the West Indians, the people of the three Guianas, Guyana (formerly British Guiana), Suriname (formerly Dutch Guiana) and French Guyane, are not regarded as belonging to Latin America. The explanation of these three non-Iberian countries on the South American continent goes back to the early days of the Spanish conquest of the New World. There was no gold or any other apparent source of wealth to attract the attention of the Spanish discoverers. This part of the coast, which Columbus had first sighted in 1498, seemed to them not only barren but scantily populated and seemingly uninhabitable. The English, the French and the Dutch, anxious to establish a foothold in this part of the world, were not so fastidious. All three countries are geographically very similar: along the coast runs a belt of narrow, flat marshy land, at its widest in Suriname. This coastland carries almost all the crops and most of the population. Behind lies a belt of crystalline upland, heavily gouged and weathered. The bauxite, gold and diamonds are in this area. Behind this again is the massif of the Guiana Highlands. They reach a height of 3,000 feet (915m) in the Tumuc-Humac range, the divide between French Guyane, Suriname and Brazil, and 9,219 feet (2,810m) at flat-topped Mount Roraima, where Guyana, Venezuela and Brazil all meet.

NB Flights through the Guianas are solidly booked; be certain to confirm and reconfirm your flights (in person for BWIA).

Guyana

THE LAND

GUYANA has an area of 83,044 square miles, nearly the size of Britain, but only about 2.5% (or 1,328,000 acres) is cultivated. About 90% of the population lives on the narrow coastal plain, either in Georgetown, the capital, or in villages along the main road running from Charity in the W to the Suriname border. Most of the plain is below sea level. Large wooden houses stand on stilts above ground level. A sea wall keeps out the Atlantic and the fertile clay soil is drained by a system of dykes; sluice gates, *kokers* are opened to let out water at low tide. Separate irrigation channels are used to bring water back to the fields in dry weather. In several places fresh water is supplied by reservoirs, known as conservancies. Most of the western third of the coastal plain is undrained and uninhabited. The strange cultural mix: Dutch place names and drainage techniques, Hindu temples, mosques, coconut palms and calypso music, reflect the chequered history of the country.

Four major rivers cross the coastal plain, (from W to E) the Essequibo, the Demerara, the Berbice, and the Corentyne (which forms the frontier with Suriname). Only the Demerara is crossed by bridges. Elsewhere ferries must be used. At the mouth of the Essequibo River, 21 miles wide, are islands the size of Barbados. The lower reaches of these rivers are navigable (75 miles up the Demerara to Linden and 45 miles up the Essequibo to the mouth of the Cuyuni River); but waterfalls and rapids prevent them being used by large boats to reach the interior.

Inland from the coastal plain most of the country is covered by thick rain forest, although in the E there is a large area of grassland. Some timber has been extracted, but the main economic activity is mining: principally bauxite, but gold and diamonds are sifted from the river beds by miners using mercury (at considerable environmental cost). The largest goldmine in the western hemisphere has been opened by Omai Gold Mines of Canada on the W bank of the Essequibo River. It is located in a fairly remote area and is planned to produce 250,000 ozs of gold for 10 years. In 1994 the government issued 12 new mineral prospecting licences, covering some 240 square miles. Large areas of rain forest are still undisturbed and even the more accessible areas have varied and spectacular wildlife, including brightly-plumaged birds. The timber industry has been based primarily on Greenhart, a wood renowned for its resistance to sea water. It is used in piers and piles around the world and, until the introduction of carbon fibre fishing rods, was a favourite with fishermen and women. When the Duke of Edinburgh visited Guyana in 1992 he was presented with two Greenhart rods. Also in 1992, however, a tract of land totalling between 7 and 8% of Guyana's land area was granted to a Korean/ Malaysian consortium, Barama, for logging (in 1994 Barama was meeting international standards for felling). At any event, general timber exports are increasing, although Guyana's loggers practise selective, as opposed to clear felling in an effort to foster

a sustainable timber industry. Towards the Venezuelan border the rain forest rises in a series of steep escarpments, with spectacular waterfalls, the highest and best-known of which are the Kaieteur Falls on the Potaro River. In the southwest of the country is the Rupununi Savanna, an area of open grassland more easily reached from Brazil than from Georgetown.

The area W of the Essequibo River, about 70% of the national territory, is claimed by Venezuela. In the SE, the border with Suriname is in dispute, the contentious issue being whether high or low water is the boundary (in the area of the Koeroeni and New rivers).

Until the 1920s there was little natural increase in population, but the eradication of malaria and other diseases has since led to a rapid growth in population, particularly among the East Indians (Asian), who, according to most estimates comprise about 50% of the population. The 1980 census showed the following ethnic distribution (1992-93 estimates in brackets): East Indian 51.4% (49.4%); black 30.5% (35.6%); mixed 11% (7.1%); Amerindian 5.3% (Carib 3.7%, Arawak 1.4%) (6.8%); Chinese 0.2% (0.4%); white (mostly Portuguese) 0.1% (0.7%); other 1.5%. Descendants of the original Amerindian inhabitants are divided into nine ethnic groups, including the Akawaio, Makuxi and Pemon. Some have lost their isolation and moved to the urban areas, others keenly maintain aspects of their traditional culture and identity.

HISTORY

The country was first partially settled between 1616 and 1621 by the Dutch West India Company, who erected a fort and depot at Fort Kyk-over-al (County of Essequibo). The first English attempt at settlement was made by Captain Leigh on the Oiapoque River (now French Guyane) in 1604, but he failed to establish a permanent settlement. Lord Willoughby, famous in the early history of Barbados, founded a settlement in 1663 at Suriname, which was captured by the Dutch in 1667 and ceded to them at the Peace of Breda in exchange for New York. The Dutch held the three colonies till 1796 when they were captured by a British fleet. The territory was restored to the Dutch in 1802, but in the following year was retaken by Great Britain, which finally gained it in 1814, when the three counties of Essequibo, Berbice and Demerara were merged to form British Guiana.

During the 17th century the Dutch and English settlers established posts upriver, in the hills, mostly as trading points with the Amerindian natives. Plantations were laid out and worked by slaves from Africa. Poor soil defeated this venture, and the settlers retreated with their slaves to the coastal area in mid-18th century: the old plantation sites can still be detected from the air. Coffee and cotton were the main crops up to the end of the 18th century, but sugar had become the dominant crop by 1820. In 1834 slavery was abolished. Many of the slaves scattered as small landholders, and the plantation owners had to look for another source of labour. It was found in indentured workers from India, a few Chinese, and some Portuguese labourers from the Azores and Madeira. At the end of their indentures many settled in Guyana.

The end of the colonial period was politically turbulent, with rioting between the mainly Indo-Guyanese People's Progressive Party (PPP), led by Dr Cheddi Jagan, and the mainly Afro-Guyanese People's National Congress (PNC), under Mr Forbes Burnham. The PNC, favoured over the PPP by the colonial authorities, formed a government in 1964 and retained office until 1992. Guyana is one of the few countries in the Caribbean where political parties have used race as an election issue. As a result, tension between the main ethnic groups has manifested itself mainly at election time.

On 26 May 1966 Guyana gained independence, and on 23 February 1970 it became a cooperative republic within the Commonwealth, adopting a new constitution. Another new constitution was adopted in 1980; this declared Guyana to be in transition from capitalism to socialism. Many industries, including bauxite and sugar, were nationalized in the 1970s and close relations with the USSR and Eastern Europe were developed. Following the death of President Forbes Burnham in Aug 1985, Mr Desmond Hoyte became President. Since then, overseas investors have been invited back and relations with the United States have improved.

Elections to the National Assembly and to the Presidency have been held regularly since independence, but have been widely criticized as fraudulent. The main opposition parties were the PPP, still led by Dr Jagan, and the Working People's Alliance, which attracts support from both East Indian and African communities. Having been delayed since May 1991, national assembly and presidential elections were finally held on 5 October 1992. The polling was monitored by both the Carter Center and a team from the Commonwealth, who declared the elections free and fair even though the campaign was not free of incidents. The PPP/Civic party, led by Dr Jagan, won power after 28 years in opposition, and the installation of a government by democratic means was greeted with optimism. The result also prompted foreign investors to study potential opportunities in Guyana. Recovery has to some extent begun, with several years of positive gdp growth recorded. Nevertheless, the economic recovery programme, part of an IMF Enhanced Structural Adjustment Facility, which aided economic improvement, has also seriously eroded workers' real income and hit the middle classes very hard.

In March 1997, President Jagan died after a heart attack. Samuel Hinds, the prime minister, was sworn in as his successor until elections which were due before Oct 1997.

THE ECONOMY

Structure of production The agriculture, fishing and forestry sector of the economy makes up almost 50% of gdp and is a major exporter. Most agriculture is concentrated on the coastal plain, where sugar is the main crop. Many sugar plantations are below sea level, necessitating an extensive system of dams, dykes, canals and pumps to prevent inundation. Production of sugar has risen steadily since the British company, Booker Tate, was awarded a management contract for the industry in 1991. From a low of 129,920 tonnes in 1990 output rose to 275,705 tonnes in 1996, with a target of 287,500 tonnes for 1997. Most of Guyana's sugar exports go to Europe under the EU quota system. The state-owned Guyana Sugar Corporation was put on the list for privatization in 1993, but no sale has yet been made. Output of rice has also grown in the 1990s, following a decade of decline. A harvest of 352,442 tonnes of rice was forecast for 1997 (it was 332,542 tonnes in 1996), up from 93,443 tonnes in 1990, because of greater investment in machinery and different varieties of rice with higher yields. Other farm products are coffee, cocoa, cotton, coconut, copra, fruit, vegetables and tobacco. Dairy herds are kept mostly on the coast and beef herds on the savannah inland. Fishing is mostly small scale, but both fish and shrimp are exported. Forestry is a booming area of growth with significant foreign investment, much of it from Malaysia, South Korea and Singapore. In 1991 the Government began leasing millions of acres of forest in the NW and Mazaruni districts for 'sustainable logging'. The largest company, Barama, leases 4,125,000 acres and is investing US$154mn in 1992-2001 in its forestry complex, which produces plywood for export. Most industrial production is processing of agricultural products (sugar, rice, timber, coconuts).

The area of greatest growth in the mining sector is gold, which is now the leading export earner. A new pricing system was introduced in 1990, which resulted in more of the gold produced being officially declared, but it was the development of the Omai gold mine, one of the largest open pit mines in South America, which pushed growth and it now produces 70% of total output. Expansion plans were announced in 1995, but were dashed by a tailings pond dam collapse and cyanide spill into the Omai River, which forced the closure of the mine for several months. A commission of inquiry called on the Government to prepare environment protection legislation and establish a regulatory agency to monitor compliance with environmental regulations. The mine was reopened in 1996 following concern about the loss of earnings of the 900-strong workforce. Reserves at the mine are 3.6 million ozs after the discovery in 1995 of a further 9 million tonnes of gold bearing ore representing 446,000 ozs of gold. Total gold production in 1996 was 372,000 ozs.

Guyana was the world's largest producer of calcined bauxite, the highest grade of the mineral, but has lost its dominance to China. Nationalized in 1971, bauxite and alumina were traditionally the biggest foreign exchange earners but the industry collapsed in the 1980s. In 1992 the heavily indebted state company, Guymine, was dissolved and replaced by two new entities, Linden Mining Enterprises (Linmine) on the Demerara River, offered for privatization in 1996, and Berbice Mining Enterprises (Bermine) at Kwakwani. A bauxite rehabilitation project was started, with the help of a World Bank loan. Production in 1995 and 1996 was just over 2 million tonnes a year, up from a low of 1.3 million in 1988. No alumina has been exported since 1982 when the Linden refinery closed.

Other mineral deposits include copper, molybdenum, tungsten, iron, nickel and quartz. Diamonds are mined, granite is being quarried to reconstruct sea defences and the coastal road system and oil is being sought offshore and onshore.

Recent trends Guyana's economy was in almost permanent recession between 1970 and 1990, apart from temporary prosperity brought about by a brief non-oil commodities boom in the mid-1970s. Venezuela's long standing claim to the Essequibo region discouraged exploitation of the natural resources in that area but the overall investment climate was damaged by inefficient management in the dominant state sector which undermined both domestic and foreign savings. During the 1980s the Government struggled to come to terms with the IMF, which declared Guyana ineligible for further lending in 1985 because of the accumulation of arrears. It was only in 1990 that the Bank for International Settlements and a group of other donors provided funds to clear the arrears to the IMF and other creditors. This opened the way for new loans from a variety of sources as well as debt rescheduling or cancellation agreements and the resumption of foreign aid.

The 1990s have seen a dramatic turnaround with gdp growth averaging 10.8%

Guyana: fact file

Geographic

Land area	215,083 sq km
forested	83.8%
pastures	6.3%
cultivated	2.5%

Demographic

Population (1996)	712,000
annual growth rate (1991-96)	-0.8%
urban	36.2%
rural	63.8%
density	3.3 per sq km

Education and Health

Life expectancy at birth,	
male	58.2 years
female	63.9 years
Infant mortality rate	
per 1,000 live births (1995)	51.4
Calorie intake as %	
of FAO requirement	105%
Population age 25 and over	
with no formal schooling	8.1%
Literate males (over 15)	98.6%
Literate females (over 15)	97.5%

Economic and Employment

GNP (1994 market prices)	US$434mn
GNP per capita	US$530
Public external debt (1994)	US$1,788mn
Tourism receipts (1994)	US$24mn
Inflation (annual av 1990-95)	23.0%
Population economically active (1987)	
	270,074
Unemployment rate (1992)	12.9%
Military forces	1,600

Source *Encyclopaedia Britannica*

in 1990-94. The economy slowed to 5.1% in 1995 as a result of the closure of the Omai gold mine, but grew by 7.9% in 1996 (with 7% expected for 1997), as gains continued in production of sugar, rice, gold and bauxite. Under an IMF-approved Economic Recovery Programme (1990-93), a number of state companies were privatized. Others are earmarked for divestment but progress has slowed. A second, 3-year Enhanced Structural Adjustment Facility was agreed with the IMF in 1994 and the Government has succeeded in meeting its targets. Tax reform and improved collection methods have greatly increased fiscal revenue. Following the passage of the

Financial Institutions Act and other legislation the InterAmerican Development Bank granted loans for strengthening and reform of the financial system, including privatization of state banks. The World Bank provided finance for several sectoral adjustment projects together with a Social Impact Amelioration Programme aimed at easing the hardship inflicted on lower income groups by economic restructuring. The Government is committed to poverty eradication and makes annual budget allocations. The drain imposed upon the economy by a foreign debt of US$1.8bn has been eased as the economy grows and deficits in the trade and current accounts are reduced. Further relief has come from the writing off of US$500mn of debt by the Paris Club of creditor nations in 1996 and of US$395mn by bilateral creditors in 1997.

● Guyana has suffered from serious economic problems for over 15 years. Wages are very low and many people depend on overseas remittances or 'parallel market' activities to survive. The country is basically self-sufficient for its food supply. Many foreign goods are readily available. The country's infrastructure is seriously run down. Electricity blackouts occur and last anywhere from 10 mins to days on end. New equipment, aimed to improve supply, is scheduled for early 1997. Outside Georgetown, facilities are much more basic.

GOVERNMENT

A Prime Minister and cabinet are responsible to the National Assembly, which has 65 members elected for a maximum term of 5 years. The President is Head of State. The country is divided into 10 administrative regions.

Georgetown

Georgetown, the capital, and the chief town and port, is on the right bank of the river Demerara, at its mouth. Its population is roughly 200,000. The climate is tropical, with a mean temperature of 27°C, but the trade winds provide welcome relief. The city is built on a grid plan, with wide tree-lined streets and drainage canals following the layout of the old sugar estates. Despite being located on the Atlantic coast, Georgetown is known as the 'Garden City of the Caribbean'. Parts of the city are very attractive, with white-painted wooden 19th century houses raised on stilts and a profusion of flowering trees. In the evening the sea wall is crowded with strollers and at Easter it is a mass of colourful paper kites. Although part of the old city centre was destroyed by fire in 1945, there are some fine 19th century buildings, particularly on or near the Avenue of the Republic (eg on Brickdam). The Gothic-style **City Hall** dates from 1887; its interior has been recently restored and may be viewed. **St George's Anglican Cathedral**, which dates from 1889 (consecrated 1894), is 44m (143 feet) high and is reputed to be the tallest wooden building in the world (it was designed by Sir Arthur Blomfield). Above the altar is a chandelier given by Queen Victoria. The **Public Buildings**, on Brickdam, which house Parliament, are an impressive neo-classical structure built in 1839. Opposite, is **St Andrew's Kirk** (18th century). **State House** on Main Street is the residence of the president. Much of the city centre is dominated by the imposing tower above **Stabroek market** (1880). At the head of Brickdam, one of the main streets, is an aluminium arch commemorating independence. Nearby is a monument to the 1763 slave rebellion, surmounted by an impressive statue of Cuffy, its best-known leader. Near the *Guyana Pegasus Hotel* on Seawall Road is the **Umana Yana**, a conical thatched structure built by a group of Wai Wai Amerindians using traditional techniques for the 1972 conference of the Non-Aligned Movement.

The **National Museum**, opposite the post office, houses an idiosyncratic collection of exhibits from Guyana and elsewhere, including a model of Georgetown before the 1945 fire and a good natural history section on the top floor (free, 0900-1700 Mon-Fri, 0900-1200 Sat). The **Walter Roth Museum of Anthropology**, opposite *Park Hotel* on Main Street, has a collection of Amerindian artefacts (closed until early 1998).

The **Botanical Gardens** (20 mins' walk from Anglican Cathedral, entry free), covering 50 hectares, have Victorian bridges and pavilions, palms and lily-ponds (undergoing continual improvements). Be alert in the Gardens at all times. Near the SW corner is the former residence of the President, Castellani House, which now houses the **National Art Collection** (Tues-Sun 1000-1700), and there is also a large mausoleum containing the remains of the former president, Forbes Burnham, which is decorated with reliefs depicting scenes from his political career. Look out for the rare cannonball tree (Couroupita Guianensis), named after the appearance of its poisonous fruit. The **zoo** (being upgraded) has a collection of local animals and the manatees in the ponds will eat grass from your hand. The zoo also boasts a breeding centre for endangered birds which are released into the wild. The zoo is open 0800-1800, US$0.30 for adults, half-price for children; to use personal video US$14.50. There are also beautiful tropical plants in the **Promenade Gardens** (frequently locked) on Middle Street and in the **National Park** on Carifesta Avenue. The National Park has a good public running track.

The **Georgetown Cricket Club** at

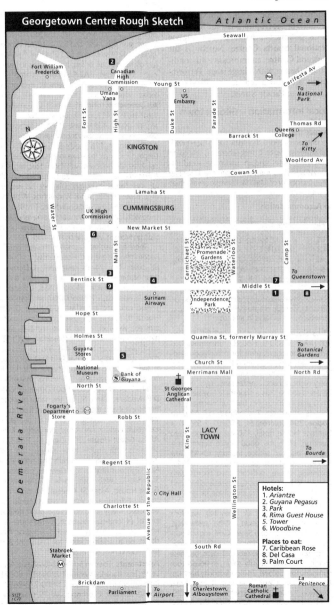

Georgetown Centre Rough Sketch

Atlantic Ocean

Seawall

Fort William Frederick

2 Canadian High Commission

Young St

Umana Yana

US Embassy

Fort St

High St

Duke St

Parade St

Carifesta Av

Pol

To National Park

Thomas Rd

Queens College

Barrack St

To Kitty

N

KINGSTON

Woolford Av

Cowan St

Lamaha St

CUMMINGSBURG

UK High Commission

New Market St

Water St

6

Main St

Carmichael St

Promenade Gardens

Waterloo St

Camp St

To Queenstown

Bentinck St

3

9

Middle St

7

1

8

Surinam Airways

Independence Park

Hope St

Holmes St

Quamina St, formerly Murray St

To Botanical Gardens

Guyana Stores

5

Church St

North Rd

Demerara River

National Museum

Bank of Guyana

Merrimans Mall

St Georges Anglican Cathedral

North St

Fogarty's Department Store

Robb St

LACY TOWN

To Bourda

Regent St

King St

Avenue of the Republic

City Hall

Wellington St

Charlotte St

Stabroek Market

South Rd

La Penitence

Brickdam

Parliament

To Airport

To Charlestown, Albouystown

Roman Catholic Cathedral

Hotels:
1. *Ariantze*
2. *Guyana Pegasus*
3. *Park*
4. *Rima Guest House*
5. *Tower*
6. *Woodbine*

Places to eat:
7. *Caribbean Rose*
8. *Del Casa*
9. *Palm Court*

Bourda has one of the finest cricket grounds in the tropics. Near the SE corner of the Botanic Gardens is a well-equipped **National Sports Centre**. Nearby is the **Cultural Centre**, an impressive air-conditioned theatre with a large stage. Performances are also given at the **Playhouse Theatre** in Parade Street.

Local Information – Georgetown
● NB

Despite the delights of this beautiful city, normal security precautions should be taken. Don't walk the streets at night. Check where it is safe to go with your hotel and in particular avoid Albouystown (S of the centre) and the Tiger Bay area, 1 block W of Main St. Leave your valuables in your hotel.

● Accommodation

Hotel prices			
L1	over US$200	**L2**	US$151-200
L3	US$101-150	**A1**	US$81-100
A2	US$61-80	**A3**	US$46-60
B	US$31-45	**C**	US$21-30
D	US$12-20	**E**	US$7-11
F	US$4-6	**G**	up to US$3

Unless otherwise stated, all hotels in range **D** and above have private bath. Assume friendliness and cleanliness in all cases.

L2-L3 *Guyana Pegasus*, Seawall Rd, PO Box 101147, T 52853-9, F 60532, undergoing extensive renovations (due for completion end-1997), very safe, a/c, comfortable, fridge, cable TV, lovely swimming pool, poolside barbecue every night, 2 bars, 2 restaurants, gym, tennis, business centre, has a shoeshine boy between 0700 and 1000, 24-hrs back up electricity, organizes tours to *Timberhead*; **L3-A1** *Cara Lodge*, 294 Quamina St, T 55301, F 55310, a Heritage House hotel, 150-year-old converted mansion, 14 rooms, good service, superb, restaurant, bar, taxi service, laundry; **L3-A1** *Cara Suites*, 176 Middle St, T 61612/5, F 61451, luxurious, secure, self-contained rooms with kitchen, Irish Bar serving Guinness and Irish and Scotch whiskies, grocery, shoeshine, laundry, no restaurant; **L3-A1** *Tower*, 74-75 Main St, T 72011-5, F 56021, a/c, lively bar, excellent restaurant, *The Cazabon*, 24-hrs restaurant, good breakfasts, *Main Street Café*, nightly buffets, swimming pool (membership for non-residents takes 4-5 days to process), gym, business centre, boutique, beauty salon, in-house tour company (see below), 24-hrs electricity back up; **L3-A2** *Ocean View*, Liliendaal, Rupert Craig Highway, 2 miles E of Georgetown, T 022-5429, pool, bar, dining room; **A2-B** *Park*, 37-38 Main

St, T 54914-16/70312-3, F 60351, a/c, secure, beautiful Victorian ballroom (worth a visit), beautiful restaurant too (vegetarian), but food could be better (average meal US$5.50); **L3-A3** *Woodbine*, 41-42 New Market St, T 59430-4, F 58406, just off Main St, a/c or fan, bar, restaurant, health club, overpriced; **A2** *Campala*, Camp St, T 52951, 61920/51620, modern, a/c, near prison (other meals: lunch US$4, dinner US$6); **A3** *Queenstown Inn*, 65 Anira St, Queenstown, T 61416, F 61411, 6 self-contained rooms with a/c, inc gourmet breakfast, US-style, family-run, safe, afternoon tea, laundry, non-alcoholic drinks; **A3-B** *Ariantze*, 176 Middle St, T 65363/70115, simple, fans, or a/c in deluxe rooms and suites, inc breakfast, dining room with TV and a/c, rec; **A3-C** *Friends*, 82 Robb St, T 72383, renovated with a/c, safe, fan, shower, mosquito net, bar, restaurant, travel agency; **A3-B** *Waterchris*, Waterloo St, between Murray and Church Sts, T 71980, a/c (E pp with fan), good restaurant, being renovated in 1997. A new hotel, *Main Street Plaza*, being built on Main St, was due open in mid-1997.

There are also many smaller, cheaper hotels. Recommended are: **B-C** *Hotel Glow*, 23 Queen St, clean, fan, 24-hrs restaurant; **C** *Demico*, near Stabroek Market, T 56372, with a/c, E without, no breakfast, lunch US$5; **C** *Randy's Inn*, 78 Robb St, T 76966/74297, a/c, free local phone calls, inc breakfast; **C-D** *Rima Guest House*, 92 Middle St, T 57401, good area, modernized, well-run, good value, central, safe, mosquito nets, restaurant (breakfast US$3.55, lunch and dinner US$5); **C-E** *Trio La Chalet*, corner of Camp St and Hadfield St, T 56628 (D in self-contained a/c unit), popular with locals but not very hospitable, 24-hrs bar (breakfast US$1.30, other meals US$1.60). Others include: **D** *Belvedere*, Camp St, on the same block as the hospital and thereby benefitting from constant electricity, unhelpful, breakfast available, ice cream parlour next door; opposite is **E** pp *Alpha Guest House*, 203 Camp St, T 54324, all rooms with double beds, shower, fan and mosquito nets, bar downstairs and noisy *Blue Note* nightclub next door; **E** *German's*, 81 Robb St, T 53972, with bath, no fan; **G** *Dal-Jean's Guest House*, Albert St, Queentown, noisy but friendly; **F** *Tropicana*, Waterloo and Middle Sts, very basic. Many small hotels and guest houses are full of long-stay residents, while some are rented by the hour. Try to book in advance. If in doubt, go to a larger hotel for first night and look around next day in daylight.

Apartments: *Toucan Suites*, 246 Anaida Ave, Eccles, East Bank Demerara, T 77094/5, F 60921 (reservations in USA/Canada 1-800-728-8657), US$50-55 a day, 1 bedroom, a/c, TV, maid service, washer, dryer, guard service, generator, free airport shuttle; *Blue Wave*, 3 locations, office at 8-9 North Rd, Bourda, T 64295, fully-furnished, kitchenette, TV, a/c, hot water, 24-hrs electricity and security, US$45-75. Mrs Lee has 3 flats on Middle St, 2 bedrooms, bathroom, kitchen, US$400/month, contact her at *Polly's Hairdressers*, Middle St, next to *Caribbean Rose*.

● **Places to eat**

Eating out is very cheap at present because of the favourable exchange rate. 10% service may be added to bill. Many restaurants are closed on public holidays. Prices given below are for an average main course. At Hotels: *Pegasus*, *El Dorado*, good atmosphere, Caribbean, Continental and Guyanese, flambé menu US$9; *Browne's Old Cafe*, lunch special US$4.70, main course from menu US$6, good breakfasts US$4; *Tower*, *Cazabon*, very good food, US$11-15, also *Main Street Café*, very good breakfast US$6, open 24 hrs; *Bottle Bar and Restaurant* at *Cara Lodge*, good, pleasant surroundings, must book, from US$10-17; very good breakfast from US$4 at *Waterchris*, lunch/dinner from US$6. Best in town are *Del Casa* (good food and atmosphere – no shorts, from US$12), *Tahli*, in same building, good Indian food, expensive; *Caribbean Rose*, opp *Ariantze* (US$8-16, slow service, mixed reports, up 4 flights of stairs and on the roof, the open sides will cool you down, credit cards not accepted but will take US$ or Guyanese dollars); *Return to Eden*, opp hospital, rec, cheap and vegetarian, all on Middle St (US$7.50-9.20); also rec at *Palm Court*, Main St (mixed menu inc Chinese, US$8, good food, fair service), and *Arawak Steak House*, in roof garden above Demico Hotel (casual atmosphere, busy in pm, good value, average price US$5, closes 2200). *Ranch*, Vlissengen Rd, T 66311, poor food and service, western decor, breeze at night. Good lunches for around US$4-5 at the *Rice Bowl* in Robb St, the *Coalpot* in New Town (no shorts allowed, cheaper cafeteria) and *Hack's Hallal*. Fresh daily baking at *Jerries*, 228 Camp St, and wild meats and seafood at *Anchor*, 136 Waterloo St. For good, cheap food, a/c, *Kwality Foods*, in *Kwality Supermarket*, Camp and Regent Sts. Good Chinese: *Yue Yuan*, Robb St, *Hing Loon*, Main St; *New Thriving*, Regent St, also in Alexander St, all good. Many Chinese restaurants (all pretty rough), inc *Double Dragon*, Av of the Republic; and *Diamond Food House*, 9 Camp St. For late night eating there are several Chinese restaurants on Sheriff St inc *Double Happiness*. For fast food, try *Creole Hot Pot*, 37C Cummings St, exclusively Guyanese dishes; *Arapaima*, Main St; *Idaho*, Brickdam; *Forest Hills*, Camp St; *Calypso*, Regent St; *Demico House*, Stabroek Market, convenient, but poor service. *KFC* at Stabroek

Market and on Vlissengen Rd. Cheap counter lunches at *Guyana Stores*, Main St. Haagan-Daz ice cream sold at *Shaynors*, Ave of the Republic, US$2.50. Ice cream at *Igloo*, Camp and Middle Sts; *Brown Betty's*, nr Stabroek. Excellent fruit juices at *Organic Juices*, Croal St, Bourda. *Juice Power*, Middle St, past the hospital, also sells drinking water. Beacon Foundation, 3 branches in Georgetown (ask a local for directions) is a charitable organization to feed the homeless and care for the terminally ill; it has good food at reasonable prices.

● **Entertainment**

Nightlife: Georgetown is surprisingly lively at night, mainly with gold miners, traders and overseas Guyanese throwing US$ around. Take care walking home at night. *The Library*, Camp St, very popular Wed night (ladies free), barbecue, beer garden, dance floor, bar (entrance US$2.50); *Blue Note*, Camp St, disco and beer garden, entry US$3.50, lively; also on Camp St *Rumour Bar* and *The Spectrum*. *Palm Court*, Main St, popular bar/café (French style), very lively Fri pm (entry US$3.50) and holidays, no entrance fee on other days; *Jazz Club* and *Sidewalk Cafe* in *Ariantze Hotel*, Middle St, US$2 on Thur, major international artists US$3.50-7; *Trump Card*, Church St, near St George's, sometimes has a live band. Near the Kitty Market are *Jazzy Jacks*, Alexander St (open till 0400 at weekends), and *Wee Place*, Lamaha St, but this area is unsafe unless you go with locals. Sheriff St is some way from the centre but is 'the street that never sleeps' full of late night Chinese restaurants and has some good bars inc *Tennessee Lounge*, *Burns Beat* and *Sheriff* (live band). Most nightclubs sell imported, as well as local Banks beer; many sell drinks by the bottle rather than shot, this works out cheaper. You can visit the steel pan yards and watch practice sessions. There are 2 theatres in Georgetown. **Cinemas**: *Astor*, Waterloo and Church Sts; *Strand*, Charlotte St; one on Main St; all worth a visit, US$0.75 for a double bill (protect against mosquitoes).

● **Shopping**

Normal shopping hours are 0830-1600, Mon-Thur, 0830-1700 Fri, 0830-1200 Sat. Market hours 0800-1600, Mon-Sat, except Wed 0900-1200, Sun 0800-1000. The main shopping area is Regent St. The two main department stores are *Guyana Stores* in Church St, and *Fogarty's*, but neither has a wide range of goods. Most Guyanese do their regular shopping at the four big markets: Stabroek (don't take valuables), Bourda, La Penitence and Kitty. Craft items are a good buy; Amerindian basketwork, hammocks, wood carvings, pottery, and small figures made out of Balata, a rubbery substance tapped from trees in the interior. *Houseproud*, 6 Avenue of the Republic, has a good selection of expensive craftwork, but there are many other craft shops including *Creations Craft*, Water St and *Amerindian Hostel*, Princess St. Also *Hibiscus Craft Plaza*, outside General Post Office; others are advertised in the papers. Good T-shirts are sold at *Guyana Stores* and in the markets. Gold is also sold widely, often at good prices but make sure you know what you are buying. Do not buy it on the street. Films over ASA400 are normally not available; bring your own stock. 24-hr developing is available at *Risans* on Main St (top end) and Ave of the Republic recommended as efficient, sells slide film (photocopying, too), also *Guyana Stores* and a 1-hr photo print service in Quamina St, near Main St.

Bookshops: some interesting books in *Houseproud*. Try also *GNTC* on Water St, *Argosy* and *Kharg* both on Regent St, *Dimension* on Cummings St, as well as *Guyana Stores* and *Fogarty's*, *Universal Bookstore* on Water St, nr *Fogarty's*, has a good selection of books and greetings cards. Hughes and Thorne Publishing House, 61 Hadfield and Cross Sts, copies of *Guyana Tourist Guide* and *El Dorado*, inflight magazine of Guyana Airways. *Newsweek* sold at *Hotel Tower*.

● **Vehicle rental**

Car hire is available through numerous companies (page 18 of Guyana Telephone Book gives details). Prices range from US$35/day to US$65/day for a new Nissan Sentra. **Budget** at *Ocean View Hotel*, US$28/day for a small car, US$57 for luxury; **N and R Rentals**, 301 Church and Thomas Sts, T 58079/66404, also at airport (book ahead as not always open), Toyota Camry and Corolla, Nissan Station Wagon. Scooters can be hired from Addis Scooter Enterprise Ltd, 38 Sussex St, Charlestown, T 66789, from US$14/day. A permit is needed from local police; rental agencies can advise. Bicycle hire: Roshan Ali at *Full Work Cycles*, Robb St and Light St, US$3.50/day plus deposit.

● **Local Transport**

Minibuses run regularly to most parts of the city, mostly from Stabroek market or Avenue of the Republic, standard fare US$0.20, very crowded. It is difficult to get a seat during rush hours. **Taxis** charge US$1.20 for short journeys, US$2.20 for longer runs, with higher rates at night (a safe option) and outside the city limits. Normal collective taxis ply set routes at a fixed fare; they stop at any point on request. Certain hand signals are used on some routes to indicate the final destination (ask). Special taxis at hotels and airports, marked 'special' on the windscreen, charge US$1.25 around town, stops and waiting time extra, or you can negotiate a 'by the hour' deal, usually US$6.

● **Exchange**

National Bank of Industry and Commerce; Guyana Bank of Trade and Industry; Bank of Baroda; Bank of Nova Scotia will give cash advance on Visa card. Bank hours are 0800-1230 Mon-Fri, plus 1500-1700 on Fri. **Exchange houses** (*cambios*) in shops may be open longer hours. Good, safe *cambios* are *Joe Chin Travel* on Main St and *Kayman Sankar*, Lamaha St. There is a *cambio* next to *Rima Guest House*, Middle St. Roving *cambios* at entrance to Stabroek Market, take care.

● **Laundry**

Car Wash Laundromat, Camp St, past the prison, going S; ask taxi drivers to take you to a laundry.

● **Post & telecommunications**

Post Office: main one on North St.

● **Places of worship**

Anglican: St George's Cathedral, Christ Church, Waterloo Street; St Andrew's (Presbyterian), nr Avenue of the Republic; Roman Catholic Cathedral, Brickdam; Pentecostal, Full Gospel Fellowship, South Rd corner of Albert Rd, welcoming.

● **Sports**

The national indoor sport is dominoes. There are sports clubs for cricket, tennis, football, rugby, hockey, riding, swimming, cycling, athletics, badminton, volley ball, netball, snooker, pool, golf, boxing, ballroom dancing and rifle shooting. At Easter there are kite flying competitions.

● **Bus Services**

There are regular services by minibuses and collective taxis to most coastal towns from the Stabroek Market. To **Rosignol** (for New Amsterdam, Springlands and Suriname), 2 hrs, US$3; to **Parika** US$1.50; to **Linden** US$3. Ask other passengers what the fare should be.

● **Travel agents**

Try Mr Mendoza or Nigel Buckley at *Frandec Travel Service*, Main St, repeatedly rec (no tours to the interior); *Wieting and Richter*, Middle and Camp Sts, very helpful, ask for Onassis Stanley; *H and R Ramdehol*, 215 South Rd, Lacytown, T 70639/73183/73486; *Joe Chin Travel*, rec (see **Exchange**, above). For **Tour Operators**, see below.

● **Tour Operators**

The tourism sector is promoting ecotourism in the form of environmentally friendly resorts and camps on Guyana's rivers and in the rainforest. There is much tropical wildlife to be seen.

Wilderness Explorers, 61 Hadfield and Cross Sts, 1st floor, Hadfield Foundation Bldg, Georgetown, T/F 62085, T 77698, after hours T 54929, also have an office at *Frandec Travel*, e-mail: wilderness-explorers@solutions2000.

net, offer ready-made itineraries and specialize in custom-designed, personal itineraries for any group size. Tours available to all of Guyana's interior resorts, day and overland tours to Kaieteur Falls, horse trekking, hiking and general tours in the Rupununi (agents for *Ranches of the Rupununi*) and rainforest (trips to Iwokrama Rain Forest Programme, see page 1597). Specialists in nature, adventure and bird-watching tours. Free tourism information, booklet and advice available. *Wonderland Tours*, 65 Main St, Georgetown, T 53122 (64956 after hours), T/F 59795, day trips to Kaieteur and Orinduik Falls, Santa Mission, Essequibo and Mazaruni Rivers (developing own camp on the Mazaruni River), city tours; special arrangements for overnight stays available. *Torong Guyana*, 56 Coralita Ave, Bel Air Park, Georgetown, T 50876/65298, F 50749, trips to Kaieteur and Orinduik Falls and 3-day Rupununi Safaris, inc Kaieteur (US$450). *Discover Tours*, Hotel Tower, 74-75 Main St, Georgetown, T 72011-5/58001, F 65691/56021, custom-designed itineraries to inland resorts, day and overland trips to Kaieteur Falls and other locations, rates fully inclusive, 4-14 day tours US$450-2,000 pp, group sizes 8-15. *Cattleya Rainforest Tours*, 228 South Rd, Georgetown, T 76590, F 70944, overland trips to Kaieteur. *Shell Beach Adventures* (Mary de Souza), T 52853/9, trips to Almond Beach in NW Guyana to see 4 species of nesting turtles in season and scalet ibis roosting, 2-day trip US$250 pp using light aircraft and camping on beach. *Rainbow River Marshall Falls (Guyana) Ltd*, c/o Allison, Guyenterprise Agency, 234 Almond St, F 2-56959 or phone Allison 2-69874, can provide tours into the interior, to its campsite on the Mazaruni River (see below), arranges overland tours to Kaieteur and Yvette Falls, director Mrs Louraine Sabat, resident at the campsite (London office, Gordon Duncan, T 0181-923 4496), US$60-90/day. *Greenheart Tours*, 36 Craig St, Campbellville, Georgetown, T/F 58219, itineraries for any group size, tours

of Georgetown City (US$25), to Santa Mission (US$50 pp), Essequibo/Mazaruni Rivers (US$100 pp), Kaieteur/Orinduik Falls (US$180 pp), Ituni Savannahs (US$150 pp). *Cortour*, 1651 Crabwood Creek, Corentyne, Berbice, T/F 020-4793/039-2430, tours to the Corentyne, river and land. *Evergreen Adventures*, 185 Shribasant St, Prashad Nagar, Georgetown, T 51048, tours on the Essequibo River to Baganara Island. *White Water Adventure Tours*, T/F 65225, daytrips to Barakara Island on the Mazaruni River from US$58; trips to Marshall Falls (rapids) available, uses 2 jetboats for tours. *Roraima Airways*, 101 Cummings St, Bourda, T 59648, F 59646.

● **Resorts**

Timberhead, operated by *Pegasus Hotel* in the Santa Amerindian Reserve, situated on a sandy hill overlooking Savannah and the Pokerero Creek, 3 beautifully appointed native lodges with bath and kitchen facilities, well-run, good food, lovely trip up the Kamuni River to get there, much wildlife to be seen, 212 species of bird have been recorded, activities include swimming, fishing, jungle treks, visit to Santa Mission Amerindian village, volley ball, US$90 pp for a day trip, US$145 pp for 1 night and 2 days, plus US$110 per night from second night on (includes all transport, meals, bar, guide, accommodation), highly rec. *Shanklands*, contact Patricia Affonso, PO Box 10448, Georgetown, T/F 78660 (or through *Wilderness Explorers*), on a cliff overlooking the Essequibo, 5 colonial style cottages with verandah and kitchen, activities include swimming, walking, bird watching, croquet, fishing, watersports, first class, overnight rate US$135-165. *Double 'B' Exotic Gardens*, 58 Lamaha Gardens, Georgetown, T 52023, F 60997, contact Boyo Ramsaroop, near Timehri Airport, good birdwatching, gardens specializing in heliconias, day tours US$35. *Emerald Tower Rainforest Lodge*, Madewini on the Demerara River, rain forest lodges, T 72011,

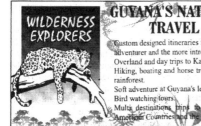

F 56021, reached by minibus from Georgetown, 8 private tree-level cabins, activities include swimming, bicycle and nature trails, croquet, putting green, sauna, birdwatching, archery, closed for ronovations until late-1997; organizes custom itineraries, including other interior resorts, Kaieteur and Orinduik Falls. *Barakara Resort*, beautifully designed resort on an island in the Mazaruni River, 10 mins by boat from Bartika, T/F 65225, from US$120 overnight. For *Rock View Ecotourism Resort*, *Karanambu Ranch* and *Dadanawa Ranch*, see under Rupununi, below.

● **Camps**

Maparri Wilderness Camp is on the Maparri River, whose source is high in the East Kanuku Mountains. The river is a tributary of the Rupununi River. The Kanuku Mountains have been recognized by Conservation International as one of the few remaining pristine Amazonian areas, rich in flora and fauna, with easy sightings of macaws, herons, toucans, kingfisher and maybe harpy eagles. Lucky wildlife watchers may be rewarded with sightings of tayra, labba, ocelot, agouti, monkeys, tapir, even jaguar. It can only be reached by a combination of air and river. *Maparri Camp* is built of wood, with open sides, and hammocks, with mosquito nets, are slung in the camp. The site overlooks a waterfall; the river water is crystal clear (unlike most rivers in Guyana) and the fall and surrounding pools are safe for swimming. Simple, nutritional meals, supplemented by fish from the river, are prepared over an open fire. Treks include along the river bank past a succession of waterfalls, up the mountain slopes into unexplored areas, and nighttime spotlighting trips to see caiman, electric eels and mammals coming to the water's edge to drink.

Rainbow River Marshall Falls, a 17,000 acre conservation site on the Mazaruni River, dormitory style accommodation in 3 large tented camps (chalets planned), pit latrines, washing in river, cooking over wood fire, US$60-90 pp all inclusive, day trips with 3 different jungle trails US$3.75, swimming, whitewater rafting, wildlife walking, birdwatching, hill climbing, gold panning, no music unless requested, no caged animals; 12 further camps are planned. Day trippers pay a landing fee of G$500. See above for contact addresses, which should be approached for all latest details. Agent in Bartica, Bell Boats, Monty Bell, T 05-2405, or Stephen Bell, T 05-2414, or Attack, T 05-2484.

● **NB**

For visiting many parts of the interior, particularly Amerindian districts, permits are required in advance from the Ministry of Home Affairs and the Minister of Amerindian Affairs in the office of the President, New Garden St in Georgetown. If venturing out of Georgetown on your own, you must check beforehand whether you need a permit for where you intend to visit.

SOUTHEAST TO SURINAME

Linden (*pop* 60,000), the second-largest town in Guyana, is a bauxite mining town 70 miles/112 km S of Georgetown on the Demerara River. A good road connects the two towns; the police checks are to stop drug and gun running. On the W bank of the river Linden is a company mining town. The opencast mine is 200-300 ft deep and is said to have the world's longest boom walking dragline. Across the river (bridge or ferry, G$5) are the poorer suburbs of Wismar and Christianburg. The town is dominated by a disused alumina plant and scarred by old bauxite pits. **Accommodation** is scarce: in town, in the lovely colonial guesthouse on the Demerara River, run by the mining company; *Crescent* and *Chez Docs*, cheap basic; *Hotel Star Bonnett*, three-quarters of a mile out of town on Georgetown road, clean, good lunches; nearby **E** *Summit Hotel*.

From Linden rough roads suitable for four-wheel drive vehicles run S to the bauxite mining towns of Ituni and Kwakwani. The road S to the logging centre at Mabura Hill is in excellent condition; it continues to Kurupukari (this stretch is being upgraded). A good road goes W from Linden to Rockstone ferry on the Essequibo River. From Rockstone very bad roads run N to Bartica and SW to Issano.

New Amsterdam (*pop* 25,000) is 65 miles S-E of Georgetown on the E bank of the Berbice River, near its mouth. From Georgetown, take a minibus (44, or express No 50) or collective taxi to Rosignol (**G** *Hotel Hollywood*, 'dubious') on the W bank of the Berbice, then cross the river by the ferry, 15 mins (US$0.30; also takes vehicles) or by launch to Blairmont, 1 mile past Rosignol. The town is picturesque.

● **Hotels C-D** *Church View Guest House*, 3 Main and King Sts, T (03) 2880, F 3927, inc breakfast, clean, rec; **C-D** *Parkway*, 4 Main St, T (03) 3928, clean, friendly, safe, with bath, rec but food poor; *Hotel Embassy*, at Rose Hall. **C-D** *Astor*, 7 Strand, T (03)3578, verandah with lounge chairs, breakfast from US$3, rec.

● **Places to eat** *Circle C*, Main and Charlotte Sts, Créole; *Brown Derby*, Main and Church Sts, Créole; both US$3-6 per meal, various Chinese on Main St; *Oik Banks Est*, Main St, nice, slow.

From New Amsterdam, it is sometimes possible to get a lift on a bauxite barge up the Berbice River to the small mining town of Kwakwani (there is a guesthouse, reasonable, check for vacancies at Guymine in Georgetown).

The road continues E from New Amsterdam (minibus, US$1), to **Springlands** and Skeldon at the mouth of the Corentyne River. The two towns are officially known as **Corriverton** (Corentyne River Town, *pop* about 31,000). Springlands is 2 km long, so you need to know where you want to get off the bus.

● **Hotels in Springlands** *Ambassador*, near point for ferry for Nieuw Nickerie; **D-F** *Swiss Guest House*, T (039) 2329, Pakistani run, rough but helpful. In Skeldon: **E** *Parapak*, no fan, no mosquito net, poor value; **F** *Mahogany*, fan, clean, friendly, rec; **G** *Arawak*, rough, avoid. Several good Chinese restaurants within a few blocks of Springlands town centre. Good Indian food at *Mansoor*, Skeldon.

● **Exchange** National Bank of Industry and Commerce; Guyana National Commercial Bank. *Cambio* (National Bank of Industry and Commerce) at Skeldon for arriving ferry passengers. Suriname guilders can officially be changed into Guyanese dollars.

CROSSING TO SURINAME

Before you leave Georgetown, check with the Suriname embassy whether you need a visa (without one, if required, you may be imprisoned before being sent back to Georgetown). See **Documents**, Suriname, **Information for travellers**. From Springlands there is a daily ferry (not Sun or national holidays of either country) to Nieuw Nickerie (foot passengers only). Queue at the booking office near the jetty from 0700, office opens 0800, booking fee US$0.25, all passports must be presented when booking, tickets are sold later on the ferry, Sf65 one way, payable in Suriname guilders only. Immigration and customs

formalities (very slow and thorough) take place from 0900, ferry sails in the afternoon depending on tides and weather, crossing time normally 2 hrs.

WEST FROM GEORGETOWN: ROUTES TO VENEZUELA

Travelling W from Georgetown, the road crosses the 1¼-mile long floating Demerara bridge (opens often for shipping, US$0.20 toll, pedestrians free) and continues to **Parika**, a small town on the E bank of the Essequibo River (minibus US$1). Speedboats cross the river from Stabroek market, US$0.30. If you need accommodation, there are two small guesthouses where you can stay fairly safely. From here ferries cross the river to **Adventure** on the W bank at 1700 daily and 0830 Wed and Fri, returning at 0300 daily and 1330 Wed and Fri; alternatively take a speedboat US$2.40. (See *Three Singles to Adventure* by Gerald Durrell.) There are also three ferries a day to Leguan Island (30 mins, US$0.25); accommodation available at the *Hotel President*.

The NW coastal area is mainly accessible by boat only. Speedboats cross from Parika to Supenaam, US$2.80, a very wet crossing. From Supenaam minibuses or taxis (US$3.50 pp) go to Charity. From Adventure a road runs N through Anna Regina. Nearby is Lake Mainstay, a small resort, reached by taxi; it is also known as the hot and cold lake because it varies in temperature from one place to another. The road goes on to **Charity**, a pleasant little town with two small hotels (**E** *Purple Heart*, cheaper than *Xenon*) and a lively market on Mon (quiet at other times).

Near the border with Venezuela are the small ports of **Morawhanna** (Morajuana to the Venezuelans) and **Mabaruma**. Mabaruma has replaced Morawhanna as capital of the region since it is less at risk from flooding. **D** *Kumaka Tourist Resort*, Maburama, contact *Somwaru Travel Agency*, Georgetown, T (02) 59276, meals (excellent, huge helpings), pool (filled if requested in advance), bath, balcony, hammocks, rec, owner Lincoln Broomes; offers trips to Hosororo Falls,

Babarima Amerindian settlement, rainforest, early examples of Amerindian art.

● **Transport** GAC flies from Georgetown Mon and Fri, US$72.50 return. An unreliable ferry from Georgetown (US$6.50) goes to Mabaruma. The journey is surprisingly rough and 'you will have to fight for hammock space and watch your possessions like a hawk'. From Mabaruma boats sail up the river to Port Kaituma, 40 miles/ 64 km inland, from where a small passenger railway connects with the isolated settlement of Matthews Ridge (more easily reached by chartered aircraft from Georgetown). The site of the Jonestown mass-suicide is nearby.

The Venezuelan border can be crossed at the river Cuyuni (at least from Venezuela into Guyana). On the Venezuelan side is San Martín, from which a narrow road goes to El Dorado on the road S to Brazil. It is possible to reach this border by boat from Georgetown (very infrequent), or by military plane, about 4 or 5 times a week, no schedule, US$60.

SOUTHWEST FROM GEORGETOWN: TO BRAZIL

From Parika there is a ferry up the Essequibo River to Bartica on Mon, Thur and Sat, returning next day, US$1.50 one way. The 36 mile/58 km journey takes 6 hrs, stopping at Fort Island; small boats come out from riverside settlements to load up with fruit. On Fort Island is a Dutch fort (built 1743, restored by Raleigh International in 1991) and the Dutch Court of Policy, built at the same time. There is also a small village; the rest of the island is dairy farms. Local people generally prefer to take a speedboat, US$4.35 pp, 1-2 hrs, depending on horsepower.

Bartica, at the junction of the Essequibo and Mazaruni rivers, is the 'take-off' town for the gold and diamond fields, Kaieteur Falls, and the interior generally. Here an Amazon-like mass of waters meets, but with an effect vastly more beautiful, for they are coloured the 'glossy copper' of all Guyanese rivers and not the dull mud-brown of most of the Amazon. Swimming very good. The *stelling* (wharf) and market are very colourful. Bars flank the main street; *Crystal Crest* has a huge sound system and will play requests. Easter regatta.

● **Accommodation D-E** *Main Hotel*, 19 Second Ave, T (05) 2243, meals available (breakfast US$3.20, lunch and dinner US$6.40); **E** *Harbour Cove*, very nice, eat elsewhere; **E** *The Nest* on Fifth Ave, unsafe, very noisy, meals to be had from disco after 1730, or 'Robbie's'. **F** *Modern*, nr ferry, 2 luxury rooms, others basic, with bath and fan, rec, good food; **F** *Pink House* (Mrs Phil's), Second Ave, cheaper, clean, without bath, basic, secure, family-run, quiet. Book ahead if possible. Mrs Payne, near Hospital, basic, clean. *Sea View*, condominium-style resort, under construction. *Riverview Beach Bar*, nr Bartica, popular hotel and bar, disco, videos, nice beach, safe swimming.

The Essequibo is navigable to large boats for some miles above Bartica. The Cuyuni flows into the Mazaruni 3 miles above Bartica, and above this confluence the Mazaruni is impeded for 120 miles by thousands of islands, rapids and waterfalls. To avoid this stretch of treacherous river a road has been built from Bartica to Issano, where boats can be taken up the more tranquil upper Mazaruni.

At the confluence of the Mazaruni and Cuyuni Rivers are the ruins of the Dutch stronghold Kyk-over-al, once the seat of government for the Dutch county of Essequibo. Nearby are the Marshall Falls (35 mins by boat from Bartica, US$38 per boat, return) where you can swim in the falls themselves ('a natural jacuzzi'), or the nearby bay, part of the Rainbow River Marshall Falls property, GS$500 landing fee.

The **Kaieteur Falls**, on the Potaro River, rank with the Niagara, Victoria, and Iguazú Falls in majesty and beauty, but have the added attraction of being surrounded by unspoilt forest. The Falls, nearly five times the height of Niagara, with a sheer drop of 228m (741 ft), are nearly 100m wide. They are unspoilt because of their isolation.

The Kaieteur Falls lie within the **Kaieteur National Park**, where there is a variety of wildlife: tapirs, ocelots, monkeys, armadillos, anteaters, and jungle and river birds. At the Falls themselves, one can see the magnificent silver fox, often near the rest house, the cock-of-the-rock and the Kaieteur swift, which lives behind the falls. At dusk the swifts swoop in and out of the gorge before passing through the deluge to roost behind the water. Permission to enter the national park must be obtained from the National Parks Commission in Georgetown, T 59142. In the dry months, April and Oct, the flow of the falls is reduced; in Jan and June/July the flow is fullest, but in June, the height of the wet season, the overland route is impassable.

A trip to the Kaieteur Falls costs US$145 (eg with GAC, T 52002, from Timehri airport, no regular schedule, inc 1½ hrs at Falls, lunch, drinks and guide, also goes to Orinduik Falls; see below, sit on left for best views, take swimming gear). Most agencies include the Orinduik Falls as well, US$160, including ground and air transport, 2 hrs at each fall, meal, drinks, US$5 national park entrance fee and guide. Trips depend on the charter plane being filled; there is normally at least one flight per week. Cancellations only occur in bad weather or if there are insufficent passengers. Operators offering this service are *Wilderness Explorers* (T 62085), trips to both falls by light aircraft, *Discover Tours* at Hotel Tower (T 72011-5), US$175, *Wonderland Tours* (T 65991, Richard Ousman), and *Torang Guyana*, Mrs Chan-A-Sue in Georgetown, T 65298. To charter a plane privately costs US$1,000 to Kaieteur and Orinduik. *Wilderness Explorers, Discover Tours and Cattleya Rainforest Tours*, all in Georgetown offer overland trips, as does *Rainbow River Marshall Falls (Guyana) Ltd* (7-10 days, not including rest days).

To go independently overland to Kaieteur involves much boating and some tough walking. The route starts at Kangaruma village (reached by truck from Bartica to Kangaruma junction, if the road is passable), then to Tukeit via Amatok falls and Waratok falls. From Tukeit you walk to Kaieteur in about 2 hrs in the dry season; not rec in the rainy season. In the dry season it is possible to walk from Kangaruma to Kaieteur. The whole route is very hard going and it would seem that there is much more chance of being near people if you go by boat.

Once at Kaieteur, you can walk to the top of the falls, at least 2 hrs, but worth it to watch the blue, white and brown water tumbling into the stupendous gorge.

● **Precautions** If going on your own, detailed planning and a guide are essential. Take adequate supplies of food and drink, a sleeping bag, a sheet and blanket, a mosquito net, and kerosene for Tilley lamps.

● **Accommodation** The rest house at the top of the Falls was not open in mid-1997, enquire first at the National Parks Commission, Georgetown, T 59142 (if planning to stay overnight, you must be self-sufficient, enquire whether the guesthouse is open or not; take your own food and a hammock, it can be cold and damp at night). It is nearly impossible to get down the gorge below the falls; the path is completely overgrown, a guide is essential and it takes a full day.

The Pakaraima Mountains stretch from Kaieteur westwards to include the highest peak in Guyana, Mount Roraima, the possible inspiration for Conan Doyle's *Lost World*. Roraima is very difficult to climb from the Guyanese side.

There are several other spectacular waterfalls in the interior, including Imbaimadai and Orinduik, but none is very easy to reach. **Orinduik Falls** are on the Ireng River, which forms the border with Brazil; the river pours over steps and terraces of jasper, with a backdrop of the grass-covered Pakaraima Mountains. There is good swimming at the falls. Vincent and Rose Cheong run a tourist shelter and are full of information about the area and about routes to Brazil from Orinduik (take hammock, food and fuel for outboard motors). It is a 3-hr walk from Orinduik to Urimutang, on the Brazilian side of the Ireng River (essential to get detailed description or a guide for the correct place to cross the river – no bridge); public transport runs from Urimutang to Boa Vista, 5 hrs. *Wilderness Explorers*, T 62085, offer 4 trips per year from Orinduik N on Ireng River in dugout canoes with Amerindian guides.

The **Rupununi Savanna** in the SW is an extensive area of dry grassland with scattered trees, termite mounds and wooded hills. The freshwater creeks, lined with Ite palms, are good for swimming. The region is scattered with occasional Amerindian villages and a few large cattle ranches which date from the late 19th century: the descendants of some of the Scots settlers still live here. Links with Brazil are much closer than with the Guyanese coast; many people speak Portuguese and most trade, both legal and illegal, is with Brazil.

Avoid visiting the Rupununi in the wet season (mid-May to Aug) as much of the Savanna is flooded and malaria mosquitoes widespread. The best time is Oct to April. River bathing is good, but watch out for the dangerous stingrays. Wild animals are shy, largely nocturnal and seldom seen. Among a wide variety of birds, look out for macaws, toucan, parrots, parakeets, hawks and jabiru storks. Note that a permit from the Ministry of Home Affairs is usually required to visit Rupununi, unless you are going with a tour operator. Check in advance if your passport is sufficient. A separate permit to visit Amerindian villages is needed from the Minister of Amerindian Affairs, office of the President in Georgetown.

Lethem, a small but scattered town on the Brazilian frontier, is the service centre for the Rupununi and for trade with Brazil. There are a few stores, a small hospital, a police station and government offices which have radio telephone links with Georgetown. A big event at Easter is the rodeo, visited by cowboys from all over the Rupununi. Prices are about twice as high as in Georgetown. About 1½ miles/ 2½ km S of town at St Ignatius there is a Jesuit mission dating from 1911. In the nearby mountains there is good birdwatching and there are waterfalls to visit.

• **Accommodation** A number of places take guests, full board, organize tours and transport. Accommodation in Lethem: **C** *Savannah Inn*, attached to General Store, T Georgetown 69716, or book through *Wilderness Explorers*, inc breakfast, good, clean, helpful, tours arranged; **F** pp *Takutu Guest House*, clean, basic, poor water supply, Claire cooks food on request (has information on trucks to Georgetown); *Casique Guest House*, OK, and *Regional Guest House*. The *Manari Ranch Hotel*, 7 miles N of Lethem, US$60/day, also *Pirara Ranch*, 15 miles further N, US$50/day, both on creeks for swimming. Duane and Sandy de Freitas at the *Dadanawa Ranch*, 60 miles S of Lethem, one of the world's largest

ranches, US$95 pp/day. They can organize trekking and horse riding trips (contact *Wilderness Explorers*, T 62085). Dianne McTurk at *Karanambo Ranch*, 60 miles NE of Lethem, on the Rupununi River, US$120/day (unique old home with cottages for visitors, fishing, excellent birdwatching and boat rides). The owner rears and rehabilitates orphaned giant river otters. Can be booked through *Wilderness Explorers*, T 62085. At the village of Annai on the road to Georgetown, some 70 miles from Lethem *The Rock View Ecotourism Resort* has 4 rooms and cheaper rooms in the main ranch house, several bars, zoo; it is located in the Pakaraima foothills, where the savannah meets the Iwokrama rainforest project (see below); T 64210, F 57211, can also be booked through *Wilderness Explorers*, T 62805; pony treks to nearby foothills, nature tours with opportunities for painting, photography and fishing, regional Amerindian and other local cooking, US$95/day full board, rec. All can be contacted at the Airport Shop in Lethem, where Don and Shirley Melville provide the most comprehensive information and assistance service in the Rupununi (accommodation due to open in late 1997). In Georgetown contact Wendella Jackson, T 53750 (for *Karanambo*), or Tony Thorne at *Wilderness Explorers*, T 62085.

• **Places to eat** *Foo Foods*; *Savannah Inn* (accommodation under construction; the Airport Shop.

• **Transport** At *Foo Foods* bicycles can be hired for US$8/day; also available at the Airport Shop, as are horses for US$8/hr. The Airport Shop can arrange landrovers and trucks at US$3 per mile. For birdwatching trips and transport contact Loris Franklin through the Airport Shop. The best time to ask for hiring a vehicle (always with driver), bicycle or horse is when the plane arrives, the only time when lots of people are around. Car hire is expensive and there are fuel shortages.

Transport around the Rupununi is difficult; there are a few four-wheel drive vehicles, but ox-carts and bicycles are more common on the rough roads. From Lethem transport can be hired for day-trips to the Moco-Moco Falls and the Kamu Falls and to the Kanuku Mountains (four-wheel drive and driver to Moco-Moco US$72.50, long, rough ride and walk, but worth it). Trucks may also be hired to visit Aishalton, 70 miles/110 km S along a very bad road, 6-hr journey, US$300; and to Annai, 60 miles/96 km NE along a better road, 3-hrs' journey, US$200. All trucks leaving town must check with the police so the police know all trucks that are departing.

A road link between Georgetown and Lethem via Mabura Hill and Kurupakari was opened in early 1991. Once completed it will provide a through route from Georgetown to Boa Vista

(Brazil), which will have a major impact on Guyana. The funding for the final section has not been found, and although much improved in 1997, it is not yet complete. The present route is: good road to Linden, and good for 50 miles beyond, then rapid deterioration for 100 miles to the Essequibo River. Creeks are often bridged by just 2 logs. It is either very dusty or very muddy, challenging, uncomfortable, and a great experience. The road is better in the dry season, but in the rains the worst sections are bypassed with boats.

Truck Georgetown-Lethem: contact Ministry of Regional Development, Georgetown; Eddie Singh, 137 Herstelling, nr Providence police station, 5 miles S of Georgetown, T (065) 2672; Ng-a-fook, on Church St, between Camp St and Waterloo St. Trip takes 2-3 days, can take 7, US$28 pp one-way, no seat but share truck with load, take food, lots of water and hammock. (Care is needed on this route, but it is exciting, through savannah and rainforest.) Guyana Airways Corporation flies from Georgetown to Lethem and back daily 0515, US$53 one-way (diversions available to Annai and Karanambu Ranch for extra US$90 per flight); book well in advance at the GAC office on Main St, Georgetown. Regular charter planes link the town with Georgetown, about US$200 return.

Iwokrama Rain Forest Programme is a 388,000 ha project, set up by Guyana and the Commonwealth to conserve about 2% of Guyana's tropical forest. In addition to conservation, the Programme will involve studies on the sustainable use of the rainforest and ecotourism. It is hoped that the results will provide a database for application worldwide. Tourists are being allowed to visit. Simple cabins are available at the Field Station at Kurukupari, on the northern boundary of the reserve. You can meet research teams, take boat trips and stay at satellite camps deep in the forest. The wildlife is exceptionally good, including macaws, toucans, black curacow, jaguar, peccary, howler monkeys and more. Fishing is also good, especially for peacock bass. Local guides escort visitors through the forest on many trails. One goes to the top of Mount Iwokrama, a difficult 20 km round trip; for the less fit there is a 10 km trail to the foot of the mountain to a pleasant stream and Amerindian petroglyphs.

Annai is a remote Amerindian village in the southern plains. It is possible to trek over the plains to the Rupununi River, or through dense jungle to the mountains. 1 hr on foot is Kwatamang village where Raleigh International built a Health Centre in 1995.

FRONTIER WITH BRAZIL

The Takutu River separates Lethem from Bonfim in Brazil. The crossing is about 1 mile N of Lethem (taxis, or pickups, US$2.15) and 2½ km/1½ miles from Bonfim. Small boats ferry foot passengers (US$0.35); vehicles cross by pontoon, or can drive across in the dry season. Formalities are generally lax on both sides of the border, but it is important to observe them as people not having the correct papers may have problems further into either country.

● **Guyanese immigration & customs**
All procedures for exit and entry are carried out at the police station, on the left as you approach the crossing. There is also immigration at Lethem airport.

For accommodation, exchange, transport, etc, see above under Lethem. **Buses** from Bonfim to Boa Vista (Brazil) about 6 a day, 2 hrs, US$5; colectivos charge US$18.

Information for travellers

BEFORE TRAVELLING

● **Documents**
Visa requirements have been relaxed; as of 15 February 1993, the following countries do not need a visa to visit Guyana: USA, Canada, Belgium, Denmark, France, Germany, Greece, Ireland, Italy, Luxembourg, the Netherlands, Portugal, Spain, UK, Norway, Finland, Sweden, Australia, New Zealand, Japan, Korea, and the Commonwealth countries. Visitors are advised to check with the nearest Embassy, Consulate or travel agent for further changes. All visitors require passports and all nationalities, apart from those above, require visas. To obtain a visa, two photos, an onward ticket and yellow fever certificate are required. Visas are charged strictly on a reciprocal basis, equivalent to the cost charged to a Guyanese visitor to the country concerned. Visitors from those countries where they are required arriving without visas are refused entry, unless a tour operator has obtained permission for the visitor to get a visa on arrival. To fly in to Guyana, an exit ticket is required, at land borders an onward ticket is usually not asked for. For **Tourist Information** see page 1618 below.

● **Customs**
Baggage examination can be very thorough. Duties are high on goods imported in commercial quantities.

● **Climate**
Athough hot, is not unhealthy. Mean shade temperature throughout the year is 27°C; the mean maximum is about 31°C and the mean minimum 24°C. The heat is greatly tempered by cooling breezes from the sea and is most felt from Aug to October. There are two wet seasons, from May to June, and from Dec to the end of Jan, although they may extend into the months either side. Rainfall averages 2,300mm a year in Georgetown.

● **Health**
There is a high risk of both types of malaria in the interior, especially in the wet season. Recommended prophylaxis is chloroquine 500 mg weekly plus paludrine 200 mg daily. Reports of chloroquine-resistant malaria in the interior (seek advice before going). If travelling to the interior for long periods carry drugs for treatment as these may not be available. Sleep under a mosquito net. Although there are plenty of mosquitoes on the coast, they are not malarial.

There is some risk of typhoid and water-borne diseases (eg cholera) owing to low water pressure. Purification is a good idea. Tapwater is usually brown and contains sediment. It is not for drinking; bottled water (Tropical Mist) should be bought for drinking. In the interior, use purification. The Georgetown Hospital is run down, understaffed and lacking equipment (a new outpatient block has just opened, however), but there are a number of well-equipped private hospitals, including St Joseph's on Parade St, Kingston; Prashad's on Thomas St, doctor on call at weekends, 24-hr malaria clinic, T 67214/9; and the Davis Memorial Hospital on Lodge Backlands. Charges are US$2 to US$8 per day and medical consultations cost US$2 to US$4. If admitted to hospital you are expected to provide your own sheets and food (St Joseph's and Davis provides all these). Rec doctor, Dr Clarence Charles, 254 Thomas St, surgery hours 1200-1400.

In the interior, travellers should examine shower pipes, bedding, shoes and clothing for snakes and spiders. Also, in most towns there is neither a hospital nor police. If travelling independently, you are on your own. Besides protecting against mosquitoes, take iodine to treat wounds and prevent infection (can also be used for water purification), a hammock with rope for securing it, and a machete, especially if in the jungle. Remember to drink plenty of water.

MONEY

● **Currency**
The unit is the Guyanese dollar. There are notes for 20, 100, 500 and 1,000 dollars. Coins are for 1, 5 and 10 dollars.

● **Exchange**
The devaluation of the Guyanese dollar in Feb 1991 aligned the official exchange rate with that offered by licensed exchange houses (known as *cambios*). Since that date the exchange rate was to be adjusted weekly in line with the market rate. On 15 April 1997, this stood at G$140 = US$1. At present *cambios* only buy US or Canadian dollars and pounds sterling. Most *cambios* accept drafts (subject to verification), travellers' cheques and telegraphic transfers, but not credit cards. Rates vary slightly between *cambios* and

from day to day and some *cambios* offer better rates for changing over US$100. Rates for changing travellers' cheques are good in *cambios* or on the black market. A few banks accept Thomas Cook travellers' cheques. Note that to sell Guyana dollars on leaving the country, you will need to produce your *cambio* receipt. The illegal black market on America St ('Wall Street') in Georgetown still operates, but the rates offered are not significantly better than the *cambio* rate and there is a strong risk of being robbed or cheated. The black market also operates in Springlands, the entry point from Suriname. If you arrive when *cambios* are closed and you need to change on the black market, go by taxi and ask someone to negotiate for you.

● **Cost of living**

The devaluation to the *cambio* rate means that, for foreigners, prices for food and drink are low at present. Even imported goods may be cheaper than elsewhere and locally produced goods such as fruit are very cheap. Hotels, tours and services in the interior are subject to electricity and fuel surcharges, which make them less cheap.

AIR

There are no direct flights to Guyana from Europe, but BWIA's flights from London, Frankfurt and Zurich to Antigua or Port of Spain connect; from North America BWIA flies daily from Miami, 5 a week from New York, and 3 times a week from Toronto; most BWIA flights involve a change of planes in Port of Spain. Guyana Airways fly 5 days a week from New York, once from Miami and twice from Toronto, most direct. BWIA flies to Guyana from Trinidad 9 times a week (Surinam Airways 2 a week). LIAT and BWIA fly daily from Barbados (the former with onward connections); BWIA flies 5 times a week from Antigua. LIAT have connecting flights with British Airways in Barbados to/from London and Air Canada from Toronto. Surinam Airways flies twice a week from Paramaribo, but these flights may leave early, so reconfirm. Guyana Airways twice a week from Curaçao. There are no direct flights to Caracas, Venezuela, which can be reached via Port of Spain with an overnight stop.

Flights are often booked weeks in advance, especially at Christmas and in Aug when overseas Guyanese return to visit relatives. Flights are frequently overbooked, so it is essential to reconfirm your outward flight, which can take some time, and difficult to change your travel plans at the last minute. A number of travel agents are now computerized, making reservations and reconfirmations easier. Foreigners must pay for airline tickets in US$ (most airlines do not accept US$100 bills), or other specified currencies. Luggage should be securely locked as theft from checked-in baggage is common.

ON ARRIVAL

● **Airports**

The international airport is at Timehri, 25 miles/40 km S of Georgetown. Check in 3 hrs before most flights, listen to the local radio the day before your flight to hear if it has been delayed, or even brought forward. Minibus No 42 to Georgetown US$1 (from Georgetown leaves from next to Parliament building); for a small charge they will take you to your hotel (similarly for groups going to the airport). Taxi US$14-18 (drivers charge double at night; if arriving on internal flights at night, ask a local to book minibus seats for you). There are three duty-free shops, one selling local and imported spirits (more expensive than downtown), one perfumes, etc, the third local handicrafts and jewellery. There is also an exchange house, open usual banking hours; if closed, plenty of parallel traders outside (signboard in the exchange house says what the rate is). It is difficult to pay for flight tickets at the airport with credit cards or TCs. The exchange desk will change TCs for flight ticket purchases. Internal flights go from Ogle airport; minibus from Market to Ogle US$0.20.

● **Embassies and consulates**

There is a large number of embassies in Georgetown, including: **British High Commission** (44 Main St, PO Box 10849, T 592-2-65881/4); **Canadian High Commission** (Young St) and the embassies of the **United States** (Young St, Kingston, near *Guyana Pegasus Hotel*), Honorary **French** Consul (7 Sherriff St, T 65238), **Venezuela** (Thomas St), **Brazil** (308 Church St, Queenstown, T 57970, visa issued next day, 90 days, 1 photo, US$12.75), **Cuba** (Main St) and **Suriname** (304 Church St, T 56995; 2 passport photos, passport, US$20 and 5 days minimum needed).

● **Official time**

4 hrs behind GMT; 1 hr ahead of EST.

● **Public holidays**

1 Jan, New Years' Day; 23 Feb, Republic Day and Mashramani festival; Good Friday, Easter Monday; Labour Day, 1 May; Independence Day, 26 May (instigated in 1996); Caricom Day, first Mon in July; Freedom Day, first Mon in Aug; Christmas Day, 25 Dec, and Boxing Day, 26 December.

The following public holidays are for Hindu and Muslim festivals; they follow a lunar calender, and dates should be checked as required: Phagwah, usually Mar; Eid el Fitr, end of Ramadan; Eid el Azah; Youm un Nabi; Deepavali, usually November.

Note that the Republic Day celebrations last about a week: during this time hotels in Georgetown are very full.

● **Things to take**

A good torch/flashlight and batteries (for the electricity cuts) is essential. Small gift items (eg imported cigarettes, batteries, good quality toiletries) may be appreciated in the interior (they are readily available in Georgetown).

● **Voltage**

100 v in Georgetown; 220 v in most other places, including some Georgetown suburbs.

● **Weights and measures**

Although Guyana went metric in 1982, imperial measures are still widely used.

ON DEPARTURE

● **Departure tax**

There is an exit tax of G$1,500, payable in Guyanese dollars, or US dollars at US$12. It can be paid when reconfirming your ticket at least 3 days before expected departure, in Georgetown, or at the airport after check-in. There is also a 15% tax on international airline tickets for all flights leaving Guyana even if bought abroad.

ACCOMMODATION

The largest hotels in Georgetown have their own emergency electricity generators and water pumps to deal with the frequent interruptions in supply. Other hotels usually provide a bucket of water in your room, fill this up when water is available. When booking an air-conditioned room, make sure it also has natural ventilation. A 10% room tax applies to hotels with more than 16 rooms.

FOOD AND DRINK

● **Food**

The blend of different national influences – Indian, African, Chinese, Creole, English, Portuguese, Amerindian, North American – gives a distinctive flavour to Guyanese cuisine. One well-known dish, traditional at Christmas, is pepper-pot, meat cooked in bitter cassava (casareep) juice with peppers and herbs. Seafood is plentiful and varied, as is the wide variety of tropical fruits and vegetables. The staple food is rice. The food shortages and import ban of the early 1980s had the positive effect of encouraging experimentation with local ingredients, sometimes with interesting results. In the interior wild meat is often available – try wild cow, or else labba (a small rodent).

● **Drink**

Rum is the most popular drink. There is a wide variety of brands, all cheap, including the best which are very good and cost less than US$2 a bottle. Demerara Distillers' 12-year-old *King of Diamonds* premium rum won the *Caribbean Week* (Barbados) Caribbean rum tasting for 2 years running (1992, 1993); its 15-year old *El Dorado* won in 1994. High wine is a strong local rum. There is also local brandy and whisky (Diamond Club), which are worth trying. The local beer, Banks, made partly from rice is good and cheap. There is a wide variety of fruit juices. A new drink, D'Aguiar's Cream Liqueur, produced and bottled by Banks DIH Ltd, is excellent (and strong).

GETTING AROUND

AIR TRANSPORT

Guyana Airways has scheduled flights between Georgetown and Lethem (see text above). There are several charter companies, including Mazaharally, Trans Guyana Airways (158-9 Charlotte St, T 73010), Roraima Airways (T 59648) and Kayman Sankar; US$320/hr. Ask the charter companies at Ogle airport for seats on cargo flights to any destination, they will help you to get in touch with the charterer. Prices vary, up to US$0.80 per pound. Returning to Ogle can be cheaper, even, if you are lucky, free.

LAND TRANSPORT

Most coastal towns are linked by a good 185 mile road from Springlands in the E to Charity in the W; the Berbice and Essequibo rivers are crossed by ferries, the Demerara by a toll bridge, which, besides closing at high tide for ships to pass through (2-3 hrs) is subject to frequent closures (when an alternative ferry service runs). Apart from a good road connecting Timehri and Linden, continuing as good dirt to Mabura Hill, most other roads in the interior are very poor, although the government has budgeted for the improvement of roads. Car hire is available from several firms, see under Georgetown. There are shortages of car spares. Gasoline costs about US$1.90 a gallon. Traffic drives on the left. Minibuses and collective taxis, an H on their number plate, run between Georgetown and the entire coast from Charity to Corriverton; also to Linden. All taxis also have an H on the number plate.

RIVER TRANSPORT

There are over 600 miles of navigable river, which provide an important means of communication. Ferries and river boats are referred to in the text, but for further details contact the Transport and Harbours Department, Water St,

Georgetown. 6-seater river boats are called *bal-lahoos*, 3-4 seaters *corials*; they provide the transport in the forest. Note that there is no vehicle ferry across the Courantyne to Suriname.

COMMUNICATIONS

● **Postal services**
Overseas postal and telephone charges are very low. Letters to N and S America US$0.21, to Europe US$0.25, to rest of world US$0.42; post cards US$0.15; aerogrammes US$0.18. Parcels sent abroad have to be weighed and checked by customs before scaling. Take all materials and passport; choose between ordinary and registered service.

● **Telecommunications**
Telecommunications are rapidly improving. It is possible to dial direct to any country in the world. Blue public telephones in Georgetown only allow collect calls overseas; phone booths have overseas, 3-digit codes printed inside. Yellow phones are for free calls to local areas. Some businesses and hotels may allow you to use their phone for local calls if you are buying something – usual charge about US$0.05. Overseas calls can be made from the Guyana Telephone and Telegraph Company office behind the Bank of Guyana building; open daily till 2000 (arrive early and be prepared for a long wait), or from the *Tower Hotel* (more expensive but more comfortable). Calls are subject to 10% tax. Travel agencies may allow you to make overseas collect calls when buying tickets. Hotels add high extra charges to phone bills. Canada Direct, dial 0161; UK direct 169. Fax rates to Europe are economical, under US$1 per page. Most hotels have fax service.

MEDIA

● **Newspapers**
The Chronicle, daily; *The Mirror*, weekly PPP-run; *The Stabroek News*, daily, independent; *The Catholic Standard*, weekly, well-respected and widely read. Street vendors charge more than the cover price, this is normal and helps them make a living.

● **Radio**
GBC Radio is government-run and is often difficult to receive.

● **Television**
There are eight TV channels, mainly broadcasting programmes from US satellite television. Local content is increasing.

TOURIST INFORMATION

● **Local tourist office**
The combination of incentives, the stabilization of the economy and government recognition of the foreign exchange earning potential of tourism has led to many new ventures since 1990. The Ministry of Trade, Tourism and Industry has a Tourism Department which can provide information through its office on South Rd near Camp St, Georgetown, T 62505/63182, F 02-544310. The Ministry has a booth (often closed) at Timehri Airport. Substantial private sector growth has led to the formation of the Tourism Association of Guyana (TAG – office and information desk at 157 Waterloo St, T 50807, F 50817, 24-hr emergency hotline, T 56699), which covers all areas of tourism (hotels, airlines, restaurants, tour operators, etc). The TAG produces a 40-page, full-colour booklet on Guyana; the *Tourist Guide* may be obtained by writing to the Association at PO Box 101147, Georgetown, or by phoning the above number.

● **Maps**
Maps of country and Georgetown (US$6) from Department of Lands and Surveys, Homestreet Ave, Durban Backland (take a taxi). T 60524-9 in advance, poor stock. A tour map and business guide of Georgetown has been produced by *Kojac Marketing*, US$3. Rivers and islands change frequently according to water levels, so maps can only give you a general direction. A local guide can be more reliable. City and country maps are sold at *Pegasus* and *Tower* hotels. City maps also from *Guyana Store*, Water St, next to the ice house (take a taxi). Maps of Georgetown and Guyana in 1996 *Guyana Tourist Guide*.

ACKNOWLEDGEMENTS

We are very grateful to Tony Thorne and Karen Waldren (Georgetown) for an update of the Guyana chapter.

Suriname

THE LAND

SURINAME has a coastline on the Atlantic to the N; it is bounded on the W by Guyana and on the E by French Guyane; Brazil is to the S. The principal rivers in the country are the Marowijne in the E, the Corantijn in the W, and the Suriname, Commewijne (with its tributary, the Cottica), Coppename, Saramacca and Nickerie. The country is divided into topographically quite diverse natural regions: the northern part of the country consists of lowland, with a width in the E of 25 km, and in the W of about 80 km. The soil (clay) is covered with swamps with a layer of humus under them. Marks of the old seashores can be seen in the shell and sand ridges, overgrown with tall trees. There follows a region, 5-6 km wide, of a loamy and very white sandy soil, then a slightly undulating region, about 30 km wide. It is mainly savannah, mostly covered with quartz sand, and overgrown with grass and shrubs. South of this lies the interior highland, almost entirely overgrown with dense tropical forest and intersected by streams. At the southern boundary with Brazil there are again savannahs. These, however, differ in soil and vegetation from the northern ones. A large area in the SW is in dispute between Guyana and Suriname. There is a less serious border dispute with Guyane in the SE.

The 1980 census showed that the population had declined to 352,041, because of heavy emigration to the Netherlands. By 1996 it was estimated to have grown to 436,000 (official statistics say 402,000 – 1995). The 1991 population consisted of Indo-Pakistanis (known locally as Hindustanis), 33%; Creoles (European-African and other descent), 35%; Javanese, 16%; Bush Negroes, called locally 'maroons' (retribalized descendants of slaves who escaped in the 17th century, living on the upper Saramacca, Suriname and Marowijne rivers), 10%; Europeans, Chinese and others, 3%; Amerindians, 3% (some sources say only 1%). About 90% of the existing population live in or around Paramaribo or in the coastal towns; the remainder, mostly Carib and Arawak Indians and bosnegers, are widely scattered.

The Asian people originally entered the country as contracted estate labourers, and settled in agriculture or commerce after completion of their term. They dominate the countryside, whereas Paramaribo is racially very mixed. Although some degree of racial tension exists between all the different groups, Creole-Hindustani rivalry is not as fundamental an issue as in Guyana, for example. Many Surinamese, of all backgrounds, pride themselves on their ability to get along with one another in such a heterogeneous country.

The official language is Dutch. The native language, called Sranan Tongo, originally the speech of the Creoles, is now a *lingua franca* understood by all groups, and standard English is widely spoken and understood. The Asians still speak their own languages among themselves.

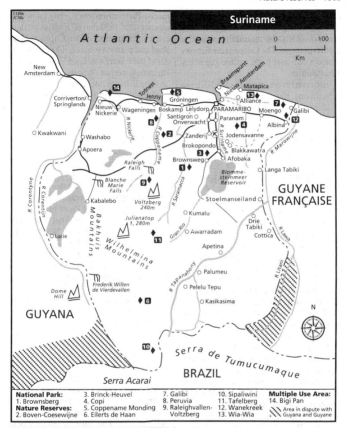

Suriname

National Park:	3. Brink-Heuvel	7. Galibi	10. Sipaliwini	Multiple Use Area:
1. Brownsberg	4. Copi	8. Peruvia	11. Tafelberg	14. Bigi Pan
Nature Reserves:	5. Coppename Monding	9. Raleighvallen-	12. Wanekreek	
2. Boven-Coesewijne	6. Eilerts de Haan	Voltzberg	13. Wia-Wia	Area in dispute with Guyana and Guyane

NATURE RESERVES

Stinasu, the Foundation for Nature Preservation in Suriname, Jongbawstraat 14, T 475845/476597, PO Box 436, Paramaribo, offers reasonably priced accommodation and provides tour guides on the extensive nature reserves throughout the country. One can see 'true wilderness and wildlife' with them, recommended. See also under **Tourist Agencies**, below.

Many reserves were badly damaged during the civil war. At present only **Brownsberg** has any organized infrastructure. Located atop hills overlooking the van Blommesteinmeer reservoir, it features good walking and three impressive waterfalls. There are all-inclusive tours from Paramaribo with Stinasu (1- and 3-day tours, price includes transport, accommodations, food, and guide). One can also make an independent visit. Buses for Brownsweg leave Paramaribo daily at approx 0830 from Saramacastraat by BEM shop, trucks at the same time. Go to Stinasu at least 24 hrs in advance of your visit to reserve and pay for accommodation in their guest houses and to arrange for a vehicle to pick you up in Brownsweg. Take your own food.

Raleighvallen/Voltzberg Nature Re-

serve (57,000 ha) is rainforest park, including Foengoe Island and Voltzberg peak; climbing the mountain at sunrise is unforgettable. The Coppename Estuary is also a national park, protecting many bird colonies.

Two reserves are located on the NE coast of Suriname. Known primarily as a major nesting site for sea turtles (five species including the huge leatherback turtle come ashore to lay their eggs), Wia-Wia Nature Reserve (36,000 ha) also has nesting grounds for some magnificent birds. The nesting activity of sea turtles is best observed April-July (July is a good month to visit as you can see adults coming ashore to lay eggs and hatchlings rushing to the sea at high tide). Since the beaches and consequently the turtles have shifted westwards out of the reserve, accommodation is now at Matapica beach, not in the reserve itself. (After a visit to the reserves please send any comments to Stinasu. Your support is needed to keep the reserve functioning.) There may also be mosquitoes and sandflies, depending on the season. The SMS riverboat from Paramaribo stops at Alliance on its journey up the Commewijne River. You then transfer to a Stinasu motorboat for a one-hour ride to Matapica. The motorboat costs US$50 for 4 people, round trip. Suitable waterproof clothing should be worn. Fishermen make the crossing for US$3-4. The beach hut accommodates 18 people in 4 rooms, and costs US$4 pp. Take your own bedding/food. Cooking facilities provided. Book the hut and boat through Stinasu and keep your receipts or you will be refused entry. Early booking is essential as the closure of the other reserves has made Matapica very popular.

The Galibi Nature Reserve, where there are more turtle-nesting places, is near the mouth of the Marowijne River. There are Carib Indian villages. From Albina it is a 3-hour (including ½ hour on the open sea) boat trip to Galibi.

HISTORY

Although Amsterdam merchants had been trading with the 'wild coast' of Guiana as early as 1613 (the name Parmurbo-Paramaribo was already known) it was not until 1630 that 60 English settlers came to Suriname under Captain Marshall and planted tobacco. The real founder of the colony was Lord Willoughby of Parham, governor of Barbados, who sent an expedition to Suriname in 1651 under Anthony Rowse to find a suitable place for settlement. Willoughbyland became an agricultural colony with 500 little sugar plantations, 1,000 white inhabitants and 2,000 African slaves. Jews from Holland and Italy joined them, as well as Dutch Jews ejected from Brazil after 1654. On 27 February 1667, Admiral Crynssen conquered the colony for the states of Zeeland and Willoughbyfort became the present Fort Zeelandia. By the Peace of Breda, 31 July 1667, it was agreed that Suriname should remain with the Netherlands, while Nieuw Amsterdam (New York) should be given to England. The colony was conquered by the British in 1799, and not until the Treaty of Paris in 1814 was it finally restored to the Netherlands. Slavery was forbidden in 1818 and formally abolished in 1863. Indentured labour from China and the East Indies took its place.

On 25 November 1975, the country became an independent republic, which signed a treaty with the Netherlands for an economic aid programme worth US$1.5bn until 1985. A military coup on 25 February 1980 overthrew the elected government. A state of emergency was declared, with censorship of the press, radio and TV. The military leader, Colonel Desi Bouterse, and his associates came under pressure from the Dutch and the USA as a result of dictatorial tendencies. After the execution of 15 opposition leaders on 8 December 1982, the Netherlands broke off relations and suspended its aid programme, although bridging finance was restored in 1988.

The ban on political parties was lifted in late 1985 and a new constitution was drafted. In 1986 guerrilla rebels (the Jungle Commando), led by a former bodyguard of Col Bouterse, Ronny Brunswijk, mounted a campaign to overthrow the government, disrupting both plans for political change and the economy. Nevertheless, elections for the National Assembly were held in Nov 1987. A three-party coalition (the Front for Democracy and Development) gained a landslide victory over the military, winning 40 of the 51 seats but conflicts between Assembly President Ramsewak Shankar and Col Bouterse led to the deposition of the government in a bloodless coup on 24 December 1990 (the 'telephone coup'). A military-backed government under the presidency of Johan Kraag was installed and elections for a new national assembly were held on 25 May 1991. The New Front of four traditional parties won 30 National Assembly seats. Twelve went to the army-backed National Democratic Party (NDP, led by Col Bouterse) and nine to the Democratic Alternative, which favours closer links with The Netherlands. Ronald Venetiaan of the New Front was elected president on 6 September 1991. Meetings between Suriname and the Netherlands ministers after the 1991 elections led to the renewal of aid in the second half of 1992. In Aug 1992, a peace treaty was eventually signed between the government and the Jungle Commando.

By 1993, the New Front's popularity had slumped as its handling of the economy failed to reap any benefit from the 1992 Structural Adjustment Programme and corruption scandals undermined its claim to introduce 'clean politics'. Because of wide ideological differences, the opposition parties presented no concerted campaign against the New Front until the 23 May 1996 general election. Until then, much greater impetus was given to popular discontent by the economic decline, which reached catastrophic proportions by 1995. Although the New Front won a small majority in the National Assembly, Venetiaan did not hold enough seats to become president. Several parties defected to the NDP with the result that, in Sept 1996, the United Peoples Assembly elected by secret ballot Jules Wijdenbosch as president. Wijdenbosch, who had been a vice-president during Bouterse's regime, formed a coalition government of his own NDP and five other parties.

THE ECONOMY

Structure of production Suriname has rich and varied natural resources, yet political upheavals and inconsistent economic management have damaged the country's prosperity. From 1980 gdp per capita declined every year by an average of 3% to only US$703 in 1994.

Agriculture is restricted to some districts of the alluvial coastal zone, covering about 0.8 million ha. At least two thirds of permanent crop and arable land is under irrigation. Farming (including fishing and forestry) accounts for 14% of gdp. The main crops are rice (the staple) and bananas which are exported to Europe, along with small quantities of sugar, citrus fruits, vegetables and coffee. The fishing subsector is predominantly of shrimp for export and processing facilities have expanded. Suriname has vast forestry potential but development has been hampered by civil war. In 1994 the Indonesian group, Musa, was granted a 150,000 ha concession to extract tropical hardwood for export. It also has plans to expand into wood processing.

The manufacturing sector is small, at only 10% of gdp, and includes beverages, edible oils, tobacco and some construction materials. Production is severely constrained by shortages of foreign exchange.

Mining accounts for 13% of gdp, its contribution having grown substantially since 1990, one of the few sectors of the economy to register any growth at all. Suriname has traditionally been a major producer of bauxite, with reserves estimated at nearly 2% of the world's total. However, fluctuations in world prices and the closure of the Moengo mines in the mid-1980s because of the civil war badly disrupted output of alumina, the country's major export. Two companies are involved in the bauxite/aluminium industry, the Suriname Aluminium Company (Suralco), a subsidiary of Alcoa and Western Mining (of Australia), and Billiton Maatschappij, part of Gencor of South Africa.

A joint operation between the state mining company, Grasalco, and the Canadian companies, Golden Star Resources and Cambior, is preparing a

Suriname: fact file

Geographic

Land area	163,820 sq km
forested	96.2%
pastures	0.1%
cultivated	0.4%

Demographic

Population (1996)	436,000
annual growth rate (1991-96)	1.5%
urban	49.6%
rural	50.4%
density	2.7 per sq km

Education and Health

Life expectancy at birth,	
male	67.8 years
female	72.8 years
Infant mortality rate	
per 1,000 live births (1994)	27.9
Calorie intake as %	
of FAO requirement	113%
Literate males (over 15)	95.1%
Literate females (over 15)	91.0%

Economic and Employment

GNP (1994)	US$364mn
GDP per capita	US$870
Public external debt (1990)	US$138mn
Tourism receipts (1994)	US$11mn
Inflation (annual av 1990-95)	163.5%
Population economically active (1992)	
	138,000
Unemployment rate	13.4%
Military forces	1,800

Source *Encyclopaedia Britannica*

feasibility study for development of a gold mine in the Gross Rosebel area. About 2,000 local gold miners were evicted from the area in 1995 and given the right to dig further S in another gold-bearing region.

Staatsolie, the state oil company, has about 129 wells producing some 4,620b/d, much of which comes from the Tambaredjo heavy oil deposit. Its refinery produces heavy fuel oil, asphalt, liquefied petroleum gas and diesel.

Recent trends After 5 years of decline and a fall in gdp of 8.1% in 1987 alone, the economy began to recover, helped by resumption of activity in the bauxite industry, the attenuation of the domestic insurgency and the resumption of aid from the Dutch Government. Consistent improvement was not maintained and international creditors urged Suriname to unify the exchange rates, reduce state involvement in the economy and cut the huge budget deficit to attract overseas investment. It was only after the 1990 coup and a 25% fall in the price of alumina in 1991 that these issues began to be addressed. In 1992 a Structural Adjustment Programme (SAP) was drawn up as a forerunner to a 1994-98 Multi-Year Development Programme. A complex system of exchange rates was replaced with a unified floating rate in 1994, but apart from that the Government made little progress in complying with the SAP. Monetization of Central Bank losses and purchases of gold led to a rapid increase in the money supply, which in turn caused soaring inflation (to an average of 370% in 1994) and a rapid depreciation of the parallel exchange rate, thereby cutting real incomes. Despite substantial inflows of remittances from Surinamese living in the Netherlands, consumption fell in real terms.

In 1995 inflation dropped sharply to 50%, partly because of a massive appreciation of the parallel exchange rate for the US dollar from 750 to 400 guilders because of Central Bank intervention in the market. The exchange rate remained stable well into 1997 (sf401 = US$1 in May) and during 1996 inflation also stayed low. The fiscal position improved as the Venetiaan Government campaigned against tax evasion and raised income tax for high earners to 60%. The proportion of taxpayers making returns grew from 10% to 70%. Subsidies on basic consumer goods were eliminated, interest rates were raised and the salaries of 40,000 public employees were increased. Of concern in 1997, in the light of events in Albania, were two pyramid investment schemes which had attracted more capital than all the country's commercial banks combined. In May, one, Roep, applied for a banking licence, but the outcome was not known at the time of going to press.

GOVERNMENT

There is one legislative house, the National Assembly, which has 51 members. The President is both head of state and government. Suriname is divided into ten districts, of which the capital is one.

Paramaribo

Paramaribo, the capital and chief port, lies on the Suriname River, 12 km from the sea. It has a population of about 257,000. There are many attractive colonial buildings.

The **Governor's Mansion** (now the Presidential Palace) is on Onafhanke-lijkheidsplein (also called Eenheidsplein and, originally, Oranjeplein). Many beautiful 18th and 19th century buildings in Dutch (neo-Normanic) style are in the same area. A few have been restored but much of the old city is sadly decaying. **Fort Zeelandia** houses the Suriname Museum, restored to this purpose after being repossessed by the military. The whole complex has been opened to the public again and its historic buildings can be visited. The fort itself now belongs to the Stichting (foundation) Surinaams Museum, but it needs to be restored. Very few exhibits remain in the old museum in the residential suburb of Zorg-en-Hoop, Commewijnestraat, 0700-1300. Look for Mr FHB Lim-A-Po-straat if you wish to see what Paramaribo looked like only a comparatively short time ago. The 19th century **Roman Catholic Sint Peter and Paul Cathedral** (1885), built entirely of wood, is said to be the largest wooden building in the Americas, and is well worth a visit (closed indefinitely for repairs since 1993). Much of the old town, dating from the nineteenth century, and the churches have been restored. Other things to see are the colourful **market** and the waterfront, **Hindu temples** in Koningstraat and Gravenstraat 31, one of the Caribbean's largest **mosques** at Keizerstraat (magnificent photos of it can be taken at sunset). There are two synagogues: one next to the mosque at Keizerstraat 88, the other (1854) on the corner of Klipstenstraat and Heerenstraat (services on Sat morning, alternating monthly between the two – to visit when closed T 498944 and ask for Dennis Kopinsky). A new harbour has been constructed about 1½ km upstream. Two pleasant parks are the **Palmentuin**, with a stage for concerts, and the **Cultuurtuin** (with well-kept zoo, US$1.20, busy on Sunday), the latter is a 20-mins walk from the centre. National

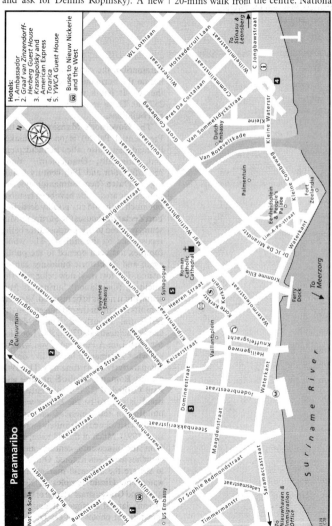

Paramaribo

Not to Scale

Hotels:
1. Ambassador
2. Graaf van Zinzendorff-Herberg Guest House
3. Krasnapolsky and American Express
4. Torarica
5. YWCA Guest House

🚌 Buses to Nieuw Nickerie and the West

dress is normally only worn by the Asians on national holidays and at wedding parties, but some Javanese women still go about in sarong and klambi. A university was opened in 1968. There is one public swimming pool at Weidestraat, US$0.60 pp. There is an exotic Asian flavour to the market and nearby streets. Cinemas show US, Indian and Chinese movies, with subtitles.

An interesting custom practised throughout Suriname is the birdsong competitions. These are held in parks and public plazas on Sundays and holidays. People carrying their songbird (usually a small black tua-tua) in a cage are a frequent sight on the streets of Paramaribo at any time; on their way to and from work, off to a "training session", or simply taking their pet for a stroll!

Local information – Paramaribo
● **Accommodation**

Hotel prices

L1	over US$200	**L2**	US$151-200
L3	US$101-150	**A1**	US$81-100
A2	US$61-80	**A3**	US$46-60
B	US$31-45	**C**	US$21-30
D	US$12-20	**E**	US$7-11
F	US$4-6	**G**	up to US$3

Unless otherwise stated, all hotels in range **D** and above have private bath. Assume friendliness and cleanliness in all cases.

Service charge at hotels is 10-15%. **L3-A2** *Torarica*, T 471500, F 411682, PO Box 1514, best in town, very pleasant, book ahead, swimming pool, and other sports facilities, sauna, casino, nightclub, tropical gardens, a/c, central, 3 restaurants (bar, poolside buffet), superb breakfast (opp is *Zeelandia Suites*, in traditional colonial style, art exhibition centre); **A3** *Krasnapolsky* Domineestraat 39, T 475050, F 420139, a/c, central, good breakfast and buffet, shops, launderette, takes Amex, bank (see **Exchange** below), swimming pool; **A3-B** *Ambassador*, Dr Sophie Redmondstraat 66-68, T 477555, F 477688, a/c, inc breakfast, good 24-hr restaurant, rec; **A3** *Era Fit*, Cornelis Prinsstraat 87, T 493284, 5 km from centre, exercise floor, swimming pool, good report; **A1-A3** *Stardust*, at Leonsberg (8 km from city), T 451544/453065/450854, F 452992, a/c, nightclub, small restaurant, swimming pool, golf course, tennis courts, sauna, fitness room; **A2-B** *ABC-plus*, Mahonylaan 55, central, new, a/c, TV; **A3-B** *Mets Residence Inn*, 10A Rode Kruislaan, T 431990/490739, F 432630, a/c, TV, minibar,

laundry, incl breakfast, credit cards accepted, new, 3-star, in a residential area.

C *Guesthouse Flair*, Kleine Waterstraat 7, T 422455/474794, opp *Torarica*, a/c, safe, helpful; **D** *Lambada*, Keizerstraat 162, T 411073, F 420603. For budget travellers, best is **E** *YWCA Guesthouse* at Heerenstraat 14-16, T 476981, cheaper weekly rates, full of permanent residents, essential to book in advance (office open 0800-1400); if it's full try the **E** *Graaf Van Zinzendorff-Herberg* at Gravenstraat 100, T 471607, large rooms, TV lounge, advance booking advisable; **C** *Doble R*, Kleine Waterstraat opp *Torarica*, T 473592, a/c, good value, but noisy bar downstairs, restaurant, often full, the Suriname Museum in Zorg-en-Hoop now has a good guest house; book in advance. Otherwise, try **E-G** *Fanna*, Princessestraat 31, T 476789, from a/c with bath to basic, breakfast extra, safe, family run, English spoken, rec, can book in advance; *La Vida* on the way in from the airport is 'cheap but nice'; **E** *Mivimost*, Anamoestraat 23, 3 km from centre, T 451002, a/c, cheaper with fan, toilet, safe, rec; *Mrs Robles' Guesthouse*, Roseveltkade 20, T 474770, family run, organizes tours; *Balden*, Kwattaweg 183, 2 km from centre on the road to Nickerie is probably the cheapest available accommodation; its Chinese restaurant serves cheap meals. Beware: many cheap hotels not listed above are 'hot pillow' establishments. A religious organization, Stadszending, Burenstraat 17-19, T 47307, **G**, good location, best to reserve. The *Salvation Army*, Saramaccastraat, will give the hard up a bed for a minimal price. Mrs Rudia Shair-Ali, Toenalaan 29, 20 mins walk from centre, not a hotel but a large private house: Mrs Shair-Ali charges US$1-2 a night if she has a free room, free use of fridge and kitchen equipment.

● **Places to eat**

There are some good restaurants, mainly Indonesian and Chinese dishes. Try a *rijsttafel* in an Indonesian restaurant, eg *Sarinah* (open-air dining), Verlengde Gemenelandsweg 187; *Bali*, Ma Retraiteweg 3, T 422325, very good food, service and atmosphere; *Jawa*, Kasabaholoweg 7, famous Indonesian restaurant; *De Smaak*, Sommelsdijckstraat 38; *La Bastille*, Kleine Waterstraat, opp *Torarica*, good, T 473991; also opp *Torarica*, **Restaurant 'T VAT'**; *Golden Dragon*, Anamoestraat 22, *Golden Crown*, David Simmonstraat; *Roja's*, corner of Mahonylaan and Grote Combeweg; *Fa Tai*, Maagdenstraat 64, a/c. *Oriental Foods*, Gravenstraat 118, for well-prepared Chinese food, rec. Many other Chinese restaurants. *Hofje*, Wagenwegstraat, and *Chalet Swiss*, Heerenstraat (more Chinese than Swiss). *Tori Oso* (literally 'Chat House'), Rust en Vredestraat 76, popular venue for good conversation. *Natura*, Rust-en-Vredestraat between Keizerstraat and Weidestraat, whole-grain bread and natural foods. Meat and noodles from stalls in the market are very cheap. Javanese foodstalls on Waterkant are excellent and varied, lit at night by candles. Try *bami* (spicy noodles) and *petjil* (vegetables). Especially recommended on Sun when the area is busiest. In restaurants a dish to try is *gadogado*, an Indonesian vegetable and peanut concoction. Good places for lunch include *Cartousj Terras*, Domineestraat. For breakfast, try *Klein Maar Fijn*, Watermolenstraat. The local beer is called Parbo; imported Heineken is more expensive.

● **Nightclubs**
Discothèques: *Touche*, Waaldijk/Dr Sophie Redmonstraat 60, Fri and Sat only 2300, small restaurant and the best disco; *Cartousj*, nr *Krasnapolsky*, on 1st floor. *Small Talk*, the only recognized gay disco in Suriname, but popular with gays and non-gays alike. There are many Brazilian girls seeking European husbands and several nightclubs cater for this trade. A good one where it is not blatant is *El Condor*, Zwartenhovenbrugstraat 158, not far from *Ambassador Hotel*, a/c, clean, restaurant, soft music, often full. Many other clubs.

● **Shopping**
Crafts of Amerindian and Maroon origin. *Arts & Crafts*, Neumanpad 13a. Amerindian goods, batik prints, carvings, basket work, drums are attractive. *Cultuurwinkel*, Anton de Kom Straat, bosneger carvings, also available at *Hotel Torarica*. Carvings are better value at the workshops on Nieuwe Dominee Straat and the Neumanpad. *Peet* woodworks have been rec for hardwood pieces. Local ceramics are sold on the road between the airport and Paranam, but they are rather brittle. The following sell international and local music on CD (the latter is heavily influenced by Caribbean styles); *Disco Amigo*, Wagenwegstraat, opp Theater Star; *Boom Box*, Domineestraat, opp *Krasnapolsky Hotel* and *Beat Box* in the *Krasnapolsky*. Old Dutch bottles are sold. **Bookshops** The two main bookshops are *Vaco* (opp *Krasnapolsky*) and *Kersten*, both on Domineestraat, and both sell English-language books. Also *Hoeksteen* (Gravenstraat 17) and the kiosk in *Krasnapolsky Hotel*. *Boekhandel Univers NV*, Gravenstraat 61, is rec for nature, linguistic and scholarly books on Suriname. Second hand books, English and Dutch, are bought and sold in the market. Maps are hard to find, but try *Vaco*.

● **Local Transport**
There are very few regular buses; the few services that are left leave from Waterkant or Dr Sophie Redmondstraat. There are privately run 'wild buses', also known as 'numbered buses' which run on fixed routes around the city; they are minivans and are severely overcrowded. **Taxis**: generally have no meters. The price should be agreed on beforehand to avoid trouble. If hiring a taxi for touring, beware of overcharging.

● **Long Distance Transport**
To **Nickerie** from Dr Sophie Redmondstraat, nr *Hotel Ambassador*, minibuses leave when full between 0500 and 1000; there are also buses after 1200, but the price then depends on the driver, 4-5 hrs (depending on ferry crossing), extra for large bag. Taxis from the same area are slightly faster. To **Albina** from near ferry dock or from Meerzorg, 2-3 hrs, Sf1,500, large bag extra (take an APB or PBA bus, which has a plain-clothes policeman on board). Taxis are available, but dishonest (usually). There are irregular bus services to other towns. For full details ask drivers or enquire at the tourist office. Verify all fares in advance and beware of overcharging. There is much jostling in the queues and pure mayhem when boarding vehicles. They are all minivans and have no luggage space. Try to accommodate baggage under your seat or you will have to hold it in your lap.

● **Exchange**
Algemene Bank Nederland (Kerkplein 1), **AMRO Bank**, **Surinaamsche Bank** (near the cathedral); **VCB** (Volks Crediet Bank – Waterkant 104), **Surinaamse Postspaar Bank** (Knuffelsgracht 10-14), **Lanbouw Bank** (Mr Lim a Postraat 28-30) and **Hakrin Bank**, 0700-1400 (closed Sat). Surinaamsche branch in *Hotel Krasnapolsky* open 0700-1430; 0800-1200 Sat, charges commission on each TC exchanged. Amex agent is C Kersten and Co, NV, in *Hotel Krasnapolsky*, T 477148. *Cambios* for exchange: *De Vries*, Waterkant 92-94; *Dallex*, Keizerstraat 8; *Surichange*, Dr Sophie Redmondstraat 71, and *Finbank*, No 61 (cambios are open on Sat). Black market changers congregate outside the *Hotel Krasnapolsky* and they are the best bet when banks are closed. Be very wary of money changers in the market and on the street, who approach you calling 'wissel' (exchange). Many visitors have been robbed or cheated and, as the black market is illegal, you have no recourse. Many shop keepers will change cash at parallel rates and this is a much safer option. Ask around for best rates.

● **Places of worship**
The Anglican Church is St Bridget's, Hoogestraat 44 (Sunday 0900 service in English). Roman Catholic Cathedral, Sint Peter and Paul, on Gravenstraat. Dutch Reformed Church and many other denominations.

● **Tourist Agencies**

NV Mets (Movement for Eco-Tourism in Suriname), PO Box 9080, 5 Rudielaan, Paramaribo, T 492892/497180, F 497062, the national tour operator (sales office Dr J F Nassylaan 2, T/F 477088, e-mail mets@sr.net; also in Cayenne, 15 rue Louis Blanc, T 317298, F 305786, and Georgetown, Surinam Airways, 91 Middle St, T 254894, F 252679), organizes trips to the interior at reasonable rates. Tours offered are City Tour, Rivercruise, Santigron (all day trips); Matapica Beach (2 days); 4/5 day trips to Tukunari Island; 4/5-day trips to Palumeu (see below) or to Gran Rio (Maroon area) staying in lodges; 8-day trip to Mount Kasikasima in remote southern Suriname (all transport, food and guides included). *Wild Coast Expeditions*, Poseidonstraat 62, T 454900, boat tours to Jodensavanne, Galibi, New Amsterdam, Matapica and Braamspunt; *Ara Cari Tours*, subsidiary of Gum Air, Kwattaweg 242, T 498888, nature tours, eg Tafelberg and Frederik Willem de Vierdevallen in W Suriname; *Mayedu*, Mateolistraat 22, T 410348, tours to Marowijne with emphasis on Maroon culture and nature, eg Stoelmanseiland, Langa Tabiki, Drie Tabiki; *Arinze Tours*, Gravenstraat, tours to Maroon villages of Santigron; *Cardy Adventures*, Heerenstraat 19 boven, T 422518, bicycle tours to Commewijne district, and tours to Amerindian village of Apetina in S, Braamspunt, Brownsberg; *Amar's Tours*, Estabrielstraat 16, T 400372, history and cultural tours to Jodensavanne, Brownsberg, Braamspunt, Raleighvallen, Blanche Marie Falls. Mrs W J Robles-Cornelissen, *Independent Tours*, Rosenveltkade 20, T 474770, and *Suriname Safari Tours*, Waterkant 54, T 471624, organize excursions to the interior. *CHM Travel*, Sophie Redmondstraat, opp Hakrin Bank building, 0730-1600, helpful for tours to the interior or abroad. *Ram's Tours*, Neumanpad 30 Ben, T 476011/ 476223. *Does Travel Service*, Domineestraat. *Amadine's Tours and Travel*, Alice Kasan, *Hotel Torarica* Arcade, T/F 477268, helpful. *Saramaccan Jungle Safaris* (John Ligeon), PO Box 676, Zwartenhovenbrugstraat 19, Paramaribo, for visits by canoe to Saramaccan Maroon villages and wildlife tours.

NB If intending to take a tour to the jungle and either Amerindian or Maroon villages, check how much time is spent in the jungle itself and on the conditions in the villages. One such trip is to Palumeu, an Amerindian village (Trio, Wajana and Akurio peoples) due S of Paramaribo, not far from the Brazilian border. 4-day, 3-night packages include flights, food, accommodation, jungle hikes and boat trips.

EXCURSIONS

Accaribo resort, about 1 hr by car from the capital on the Suriname River, near the villages of La Vigilantia and Accaribo: 7 rooms with bath, visit Amerindian settlement, pottery making, swimming in the river, Creole and Javanese cultures. **Powaka**, about 90 mins outside the capital, is a primitive village of thatched huts but with electric light and a small church. In the surrounding forest one can pick mangoues and other exotic fruit. An interesting half, or full day excursion is to take minibus 4, or taxi, to **Leonsberg** on the Suriname River (restaurant *Rusty Pelikan* on waterfront; at *Leonsberg* restaurant try *saoto* soup and other Javanese specialities, overlooking the river), then ferry to **Nieuw Amsterdam**, the capital of the predominantly Javanese district of Commewijne. There is an open-air museum inside the old fortress which guarded the confluence of the Suriname and Commewijne rivers (badly rundown, open only in mornings except Friday, 1700-1900, Sf20). There are some old plantation mansions left in the Commewijne district which are of interest; **Mariënburg** is the last sugar estate in operation in Suriname. The return trip can be made by bus to Meerzorg on the river, taking the vehicle ferry back to Paramaribo.

Braamspunt is a peninsula at the mouth of the Suriname River, about 10 km from Paramaribo. Nice beaches. Hire a boat at the Leonsberg scaffold for a trip up the river.

By private car to **Jodensavanne** (Jews' Savanna, established 1639), S of Paramaribo on the opposite bank of the Suriname River, where a cemetery and the foundations of one of the oldest synagogues in the Western Hemisphere has been restored. There is no public transport and taxis won't go because of the bad road. It is still only 1½ hrs with a suitable vehicle (see above for tours). There is a bridge across the Suriname River to Jodensavanne. **Blakawatra** is said to be one of the most beautiful spots in all Suriname (shame about the amount of rubbish strewn around). This was the scene of much fighting in the civil war. A full day trip to

Jodensavanne and Blakawatra, returning to Paramaribo via Moengo, has been recommended if one can arrange the transport. Some 5 km from the International Airport there is a resort called **Colakreek**, so named for the colour of the water, but good swimming (busy at weekends), lifeguards, water bicycles, children's village, restaurant, bar, tents or huts for overnight stay, entre Sf500 (children under 12 half price).

Approximately 30 km SW of Paramaribo, via **Lelydorp** (*Hotel De Lely*, Sastrodisomoweg 41), is the Bush Negro village of **Santigron**, on the E bank of the Saramaca River. Mini-buses leave from Saramacastraat in front of BEM store at approx 0700 and 1030, Mon-Sat, one afternoon bus on Sat, 1 hr, crowded. They return as soon as they drop off passengers in the village, so make sure you will have a bus to return on, no accommodation in Santigron. Nearby is the Amerindian village of **Pikin Poika**. The two make a good independent day trip. Tour agencies also visit the area about twice month, including canoe rides on the Saramaca River and a Bush Negro dance performance.

By bus or car to **Afobakka**, where there is a large hydro-electric dam on the Suriname River. There is a government guesthouse (price includes 3 meals a day) in nearby **Brokopondo**. Victoria is an oil-palm plantation in the same area. The Brownsberg National Park is one hour by car from here.

Tukunari Island, in Professor Van Blommesteinmeer lake, is about 3 hrs drive from Paramaribo to Brokopondo then a 2-hr canoe ride. The island is near the village of Lebi Doti, where Aucaners Maroons live. Tours with NV Mets include fishing, visits to villages to see Maroon culture, jungle treks and visits to rapids.

Stoelmanseiland, on the Lawa River in the interior, and the maroon villages and rapids in the area can be visited on excursions organized by tour operators. Price US$170 pp for 3 days (5 persons, minimum). They are, however, more easily reached by river from St-Laurent du Maroni and Maripasoula in Guyane.

WEST OF PARAMARIBO

Leaving Paramaribo, a narrow but well paved road leads through the citrus and vegetable growing districts of **Wanica** and **Saramaca**, connected by a bridge over the Saramaca River. At **Boskamp** (90 km from Paramaribo) the Coppename River is reached. Daytime only ferry to **Jenny** on the W bank takes about 20 mins.

A further 50 km is **Totness**, where there was once a Scottish settlement. It is the largest village in the Coronie district, along the coast between Paramaribo and Nieuw Nickerie on the Guyanese border. There is a good government guesthouse. The road (bad, liable to flooding) leads through an extensive forest of coconut palms. Bus to Paramaribo at 0600. 40 km further W, 5 km S of the main road is **Wageningen**, a modern little town, the centre of the Suriname rice-growing area. The road from Nickerie has recently been renewed. One of the largest fully mechanized rice farms in the world is found here (*Hotel de Wereld*, T 02-51544). The **Bigi-Pan** area of mangroves is a bird-watchers' paradise; boats may be hired from local fishermen.

Nieuw Nickerie, on the S bank of the Nickerie River 5 km from its mouth, opposite Guyana is the main town and port of the Nickerie district and is distinguished for its ricefields and for the number and voraciousness of its mosquitoes. The town has a population of more than 8,000, the district of 35,000, mostly East Indian. Paramaribo is 237 km away by road. For bus services, see under Paramaribo. Sit on the left-hand side of the bus to get the best views of the birdlife in the swamps. The coastal ferry service has been discontinued, but once a week the SMS company makes an interesting water trip, using inland waterways, to Nieuw Nickerie taking 36 hrs; it leaves Paramaribo on Mondays at 0800, departs Nieuw Nickerie 1200 Wednesday (times subject to 2 hrs variation due to tides), no cabins, only slatted seats, but there is hammock space; take food and drink; lots of mosquitoes.

- **Accommodation** E *Moksie Patoe*, Gouverneurstraat 115, T 02-32219, restaurant, owner rents a 2-bedroom house (3 beds) next door; **E** *De-Vesting*, similar quality, Balatastraat 6, T 02-31265; **E** *Ameerali*, Maynardstraat 32-36, T 02-31642, F 02-31066, a/c, good, clean, friendly; **F** *De President*, Gouverneurstraat, with bath, cheaper without, a/c, good value, friendly; **F** *Luxor*, St Jozefstraat 22, T 02-31365, private bath, friendly; **G** *Diamond*, Balatastraat 29, T 02-32210, some rooms with bath, close to ferry, basic; **G** *Tropical*, Gouverneurstraat 114, T 231796, noisy bar downstairs; *Het Park*, Slagenhoutstraat 11, T 02-31367. **NB** If phoning within town, omit 0 from prefix.

- **Places to eat** *Jean Amar*, Gouverneurstraat 115, run by Dr Jacques Durauchelle, provides European and Indian dishes with items rarely found elsewhere in friendly atmosphere, slow service; *Incognito*, Gouverneurstraat 44, Indonesian; *Pak-Hap*, Gouverneurstraat 101, Chinese (mice in the dining room). Many others on same street.

- **Exchange** The bank at the immigration office is reported to close at 1500 Mon-Fri, whether or not the ferry has arrived.

- **Transport Air** Surinam Airways to/from Paramaribo, twice weekly (booked up weeks in advance), office on main square on river, helpful, can book international flights, no credit cards, open till 1600.

Ferry to Springlands, Guyana Normally operates Mon to Sat (except public holidays of either country), foot passengers only, Sf65 one way, heavy luggage extra. Booking office at Landenstraat 26, open Mon-Sat, 0630-0645, 0900-1200, 1600-1700, essential to book the day before travelling, booking fee Sf2.50, must show passport.

All immigration and customs formalities take place at the ferry dock. Queue up at gate at 0600, expect about 3 hrs of waiting before sailing. The trip takes at least 2 hrs, Guyanese immigration and customs forms handed out on board, cold drinks are sometimes sold. There may be up to another 3 hrs of queuing for Guyanese formalities. Visa requirements have been relaxed (see Guyana, **Documents**) and a return ticket is not always asked for. Ferry returns to Nickerie the same afternoon (bookings in the am).

The entire journey from Paramaribo to Georgetown takes 2 days including overnight in Nickerie (Nickerie-Georgetown takes 10-12 hrs).

Apoera on the Corantijn can be reached by sea-going vessels. **Blanche Marie Falls**, 320 km from Paramaribo on the Apoera road, is a popular destination. There is a guesthouse, **B** *Dubois*, contact Eldoradolaan 22, Paramaribo T 476904/2. There is

a good guesthouse at Apoera (**C** with 3 meals, advance booking from Paramaribo advisable). **Washabo** near Apoera, which has an airstrip, is an Amerindian village. There is no public transport from Paramaribo to the Apoera-Bakhuis area, but there are frequent charter flights to the Washabo airstrip. Irregular small boats go from Apoera to Nieuw Nickerie and to Springlands (Guyana). Try to rent a canoe to visit the Amerindian settlement of Orealla in Guyana or Kaboeri creek, 12 km downstream, where giant river otters may possibly be seen in October or March.

EAST OF PARAMARIBO TO GUYANE

Eastern Suriname was the area most severely damaged during the civil war, and its effects are still evident. A paved road connects Meerzorg (vehicle ferry from Paramaribo, every 30 min, passengers Sf1) with Albina, passing through the districts of Commewijne and Marowijne. There is little population or agriculture left here. **Moengo**, 160 km up the Cottica River from Paramaribo, is a bauxite mining and loading centre for Suralco (*Government Guesthouse*). Bauxite is transported to be refined into alumina/aluminium at the refinery at Paranam, on the left bank of the Suriname River. It can be reached by medium draught ships and by cars.

East of Moengo, the scars of war are most obvious. Temporary wooden bridges replace those that were blown up, shell craters dot the road, and many abandoned or destroyed houses are seen. **Albina** is on the Marowijne River, the frontier with Guyane. Once a thriving, pleasant town and then a bombed-out wreck, it is now showing signs of recovery with new buildings, shops, a market and two restaurants. *The Creek Hotel* (8 rooms) is on the northern outskirts of town; the owner speaks English.

FRONTIER WITH GUYANE

Customs and immigration on both sides close at 1900, but in Albina staff usually leave by 1700. Be wary of local information on exchange rates and transport (both the ferry and buses to Paramaribo).

● **Exchange**

Changing money on the Suriname side of the border is illegal; see **Currency**, below. Money can be changed on the Guyane side.

● **Transport**

A passenger and vehicle ferry leaves Albina for St Laurent du Maroni Mon, Thur, 0800, 1000, 1500, 1700, Tues, Wed, Sat, 0800, 1000, Sun 1630, 1700, 30 mins voyage; the fare is US$4 pp, which is the same charged by *pirogues*, US$20 for cars.

Information for travellers

BEFORE TRAVELLING

● **Documents**

Visitors must have a valid passport (one issued by the Hong Kong government, and a few others, will not be accepted), a visa, or tourist card. Visas must be obtained in advance by citizens of all countries except Great Britain, Japan, Israel, The Gambia, South Korea, Denmark, Finland, Sweden, Switzerland, Netherlands Antilles, Brazil, Ecuador, Canada, Chile and Guyana (these require a tourist card, obtainable at the airport, US$14). To obtain a visa in advance, write to the Ministry of External Affairs, Department for Consular Matters, Paramaribo, sending 1 passport photo; cost is US$50. Visas issued at the consulate in Cayenne normally take 15 days and cost F150 (US$28), but may be obtained the same day (an extra charge for this is sometimes made). Take photocopy of exit ticket out of South America. In Georgetown a visa takes 5 days minimum and costs US$20. On entry to Suriname (by land or air) your passport will be stamped by the military police indicating a brief period (usually 7-10 days) for which you can remain in the country, regardless of the length of stay authorized by your visa. If you are considering a longer visit, you should go as soon as possible to the Immigration Office in Paramaribo to get a second stamp in your passport and to apply for a 'blue card' (foreigner registration card): Immigration Office, van't Hogerhuystraat, Nieuwe Haven, Paramaribo. To get this you need a receipt for Sf10 from the Commissariat Combé, Van Sommelsdijkstraat, opposite *Torarica Hotel*, take passport and two passport photos, allow a week to get it. Mon-Fri, 0700-1430. The procedure is relatively quick and painless and you will generally be authorized a 3 month stay (once again the length of your entry visa seems irrelevant). If you stay more than 2 weeks, you should return to Immigration at that time, to collect your blue card which you can carry instead of your passport (it is prudent to carry both). You must also return here for any further extensions and for an exit authorization stamp (called 'stamp out') 2 days before you leave the country. The final exit stamp is again given by the military police at the airport or land border.

Despite suggestions that these procedures be simplified, they remain law and failure to comply can result in very serious consequences. They are not usually explained to visitors on arrival.

● **Representation overseas**
USA: Embassy, Van Ness Center, 4301 Connecticut, NW Suite 108, Washington DC, 20008, T 202-244-7488, F 202-244-5878; Consulate, 7235 NW 19th St, Suite A, Miami, FLA 33126, T 305-593-2163. **Belgium**, Avenue Louise 379, 1050 Brussels, T 640-11-72; **Netherlands**: Embassy, Alexander Gogelweg 2, 2517 JH Den Haag, T 65-08-44; Consulate, De Cuserstraat 11, 1081 CK Amsterdam, T 642-61-37; **Brazil**, SCS Quadra 2 Lotes 20/21, Edif, OK, 2e Andar, 70457 Brasilia, T 244-1824; **Venezuela**, 4a Av de Altamira 41, entre 7 y 8a Transversal, Altamira, Caracas 1060A, PO Box 61140, Chacao, T 261-2095; **Guyana**, 304 Church St, Georgetown, PO Box 338, T 56995; **Guyane**, 38 TER, Rue Christoph Colomb, Cayenne, T 30-04-61.

For **Tourist information**, see page 1618, below.

● **Customs**
Duty-free imports include 400 cigarettes or 100 cigars or $1/2$ kg of tobacco, 2 litres of spirits and 4 litres of wine, 50 grams of perfume and 1 litre of toilet water, 8 rolls of still film and 60m of cinefilm, 100m of recording tape, and other goods up to a value of Sf40. Personal baggage is free of duty. Customs examination of baggage can be very thorough.

● **Climate**
Tropical and moist, but not very hot, since the NE trade wind makes itself felt during the whole year. In the coastal area the temperature varies on an average from 23° to 31°C, during the day; the annual mean is 27°C, and the monthly mean ranges from 26° to 28°C. The mean annual rainfall is about 2,340mm for Paramaribo and 1,930mm for the western division. The seasons are: minor rainy season, Nov-Feb; minor dry season, Feb-April; main rainy season, April-Aug; main dry season, Aug-November. None of these seasons is, however, usually either very dry or very wet. The degree of cloudiness is fairly high and the average humidity is 82%. The climate of the interior is similar but with higher rainfall.

● **Health**
No information has been made available about the incidence of cholera in Suriname. Since the disease is almost certainly present, take the approrprate precautions. Boil or purify water, even in the capital. Otherwise, no special precautions necessary except for a trip to the malarial interior; for free malaria prophylaxis contact the Public Health Department (BOG, 15 Rode Kruislaan), but better to take your own. METS and Suriname Safari Tours provide malaria prophylaxis on their package tours. Chloroquine-resistant malaria in the interior. Mosquito nets should be used at night over beds in rooms not air-conditioned or screened. In some coastal districts there is a risk of bilharzia (schistosomiasis). Ask before bathing in lakes and rivers. Vaccinations: yellow fever and tetanus advisable, typhoid only for trips into the interior. Swim only in running water because of poisonous fish. There is good swimming on the Marowijne River and at Matapica beach and on the Coppename River. There are five hospitals in Paramaribo, best is St Vincentius.

MONEY

● **Currency**
The unit of currency is the Suriname guilder (Sf) divided into 100 cents. There are notes for 5, 10, 25, 100, 500, 1,000 and 2,000 guilders. Coins are for 1 and 2.50 guilders and 1, 5, 10 and 25 cents (the 25-cent coin is usually known as a *kwartje*, 10-cent *dubbeltje*, 5-cent *stuiver* and Sf2.50 *doller*).

● **Exchange**
In July 1994 all exchange rates were unified and a floating rate was established at Sf183 = US$1. In May 1997 the rate was Sf401 = US$1. Dutch guilders and French francs are readily exchanged in banks and on the black market, cash only in the latter case. It is, however, illegal to change money on the black market; police pretend to be black marketeers.

On arrival, change a little money at the airport (where rates are poorer than in the city), then go to the main banks for further exchange. Officially visitors must declare their foreign currency on arrival. When arriving by land, visitors' funds are rarely checked, but you should be prepared for it.

GETTING THERE

AIR

Surinam Airways flies 3 times a week from Amsterdam (joint operation wtih KLM), Miami (3 times a week, 2 of which are joint operation with ALM), Belém (3 times a week), Macapá (twice), Port of Spain (twice), Porlamar (twice), Aruba (once), Curaçao (twice), Cayenne (4 times a week), and Georgetown (twice a week). ALM flies from Curaçao once a week. There is a weekly connecting flight from Miami via Curaçao with ALM. Many people go to Cayenne to take advantage of cheap Air France tickets to Europe as well as increased seat availability. Internal services are maintained by SLM and two small air charter firms.

SEA

Fyffes banana boats sail from Portsmouth, UK, and Flushing, Holland, to Paramaribo on 13-14 day schedule. Occasionally they call at Georgetown. The 35-38 day roundtrip costs £1,980 pp.

ON ARRIVAL

● Airports
The Johan Pengel International Airport (formerly Zanderij), is 47 km S of Paramaribo. Minibus to town costs Sf2,000 (eg De Paarl, T 479610); taxi costs Sf10,000/US$20 (Ashruf, T 450102), but negotiate. Surinam Airways, Dr Sophie Redmondstraat 219, T 432700, F 434925. (At Pengel Airport T 0325-181, F 0325-292.) Money exchange facilities, Central Bank of Suriname between Customs and Immigration (closed Sun). There is a guest house near the airport. Internal flights leave from Zorg-en-Hoop airfield in a suburb of Paramaribo (take minibus 8 or 9 from Steenbakkerijstraat).

● Clothing
Except for official meetings, informal tropical clothing is worn, but not shorts. An umbrella or plastic raincoat is very useful.

● Embassies
USA (Dr Sophie Redmondstraat 129, PO Box 1821, T 472900), Netherlands, Belgium, Brazil, France, Venezuela, India, Indonesia, Guyana, India, Japan, China (People's Republic).

● Consulates
There are consuls-general, vice-consuls or consular agents for Canada, Denmark, Dominican Republic, Ecuador, Finland, Germany, Haiti, UK, Mexico, Norway, Spain, and Sweden – all in Paramaribo. British Honorary Consul, Mr James Healy, T 472870 office/474764 house, is very helpful.

● Hours of business
Shops and businesses: Mon-Fri 0900-1630, Sat 0900-1300. Government departments: Mon-Thur 0700-1500, Fri 0700-1430. Banks are open Mon-Fri 0900-1400. The airport bank is open at flight arrival and departure times.

● Official time
3 hrs behind GMT.

● Public holidays
1 Jan, New Year; Holi Phagwa (Hindu festival, date varies each year, generally in Mar, very interesting but watch out for throwing of water, paint, talc and coloured powder); Good Friday; Easter (2 days); 1 May (Labour Day); 1 July (National Unity); 25 Nov (Independence Day); Christmas (2 days). For Moslem holidays see note under Guyana.

● Festivals
Avond Vierdaagse starts on the first Wed after Easter, a carnival parade of the young and old dressed in traditional costume or simple clothes; it is organized by Bedrijven Vereniging Sport en Spel (BVVS), Johannes Mungrastraat 48, Paramaribo, T 461020. **Suriname Tourist Fair**, first week of July, held in the Theater Unique, Rust en Vredestraat 23-25, T 71006, exhibition of tour operators' services and cultural activities. **Suri Flora**, in May, exhibition of the flower industry, run by KKF (the Chamber of Commerce and Industry), Mr Dr de Mirandastraat 10, T 473527/6. **Nationale Kunstbeurs**, annual art exhibition at *Ons Erf*, Prins Hendrikstraat 17a, Paramaribo, T 472319. **Year-end** festival on 31 Dec, everything closes, lots of music, celebration at 'T Vat opp *Hotel Torarica* until 2300, fireworks at 2400, some discos and other venues stay open after midnight.

● Security
Photography is now generally permitted. Only military installations remain off limits. When in doubt, ask first. Those travelling to the interior should inquire in the capital about the public safety situation in the areas they plan to visit. The presence of rival armed factions in some places remains a hazard and the government is not fully in control of the entire country. Street crime in Paramaribo is rising: take the usual precautions with cameras, watches, etc. Downtown and near the market should be avoided at night unless accompanied by a local.

● Voltage
110/127 volts AC, 60 cycles. Plug fittings are usually 2-pin round (European continental type). Lamp fittings are screw type.

● Weights and measures
The metric system is in general use.

ON DEPARTURE

● Departure tax
There is an exit tax of US$10, plus a terminal fee from the Departure Hall of US$5 (ie US$15 in total).

WHERE TO STAY

Hotels and restaurants are rare outside the capital, and you usually have to supply your own hammock and mosquito net, and food. A tent is less useful in this climate. Travelling is cheap if you change cash dollars on the black market; taking your own hammock and food will reduce costs.

FOOD AND DRINK

Surinamese cuisine is as rich and varied as the country's ethnic makeup. Rice is the main staple and of very high quality. Cassava, sweet potatoes, plantain, and hot red peppers are widely used. *Pom* is a puree of the tayer root (a relative of cassava) tastily spiced and served with *kip* (chicken). *Moksie Alesie* is rice mixed with meat, chicken, white beans, tomatoes, peppers and spices. *Pinda soep* (peanut soup with plantain dumplings) and *oker soep met tayerblad* (gumbo and cassava soup) are both worth a try. Well known Indonesian dishes include *bami* (fried noodles) and *nassie goreng* (fried rice), both spicy with a slightly sweet taste. Among the Hindustani dishes are *roti* (a crêpe wrapped around curried potatoes, vegetables and chicken), *somosa* (fried pastry filled with spicy potatoes and vegetables), and *phulawri* (fried chick-pea balls). Among the many tropical fruits of Suriname, palm nuts such as the orange coloured awarra and the cone shaped brown maripa are most popular.

GETTING AROUND

AIR TRANSPORT
E-W, Paramaribo-Nieuw Nickerie twice a week. N-S: the interior is currently open. Bush flights are operated by Surinam Airways, Gum-Air (T 498760) and ITA to several Amerindian and Maroon villages. Most settlements have an airstrip, but internal air services are limited. These flights are on demand.

LAND TRANSPORT
● **Motoring**
There are 2,500 km of main roads, of which 850 km are paved. East-west roads: From Albina to Paramaribo to Nieuw Nickerie is open; buses and taxis are available (details in the text above). North-south: the road Paramaribo - Paranam - Afobaka is open. **Self-Drive Cars** City Taxi, Purperhart, Kariem, Intercar, U-Drive Car rental, T 490803, and other agencies. All driving licences accepted, but you need a stamp from the local police and a deposit. Gasoline/petrol is sold as 'regular', or 'extra' (more expensive). **Bicycles** Can be bought from A Seymonson, Rijwielhersteller, Rust en Vredestraat. Rec rides from Paramaribo include to Nieuw Amsterdam, Marienburg, Alkmaar and back via Tamanredjo in the Javanese Commewijne district or from Rust en Werk to Spiering-

shoek to Reijnsdorp (3½ hrs) and return to Leonsberg via ferry, whence it is a 30 mins ride to Paramaribo. Driving is on the left, but many vehicles have left-hand drive.

FERRIES
The three ferries across the main rivers operate only in daytime (the Paramaribo-Meerzorg ferry until 2200). The Suriname Navigation Co (SMS) has a daily service, leaving 0700, on the Commewijne River (a nice four-hour trip; one can get off at *De Nieuwe Grond*, a plantation owned by an English couple, and stay overnight). SMS also has infrequent services on other rivers (Wayombo and Cottica), and makes an interesting water trip, using inland waterways, to Nieuw Nickerie (see text above).

● **Note**
It is advisable to check the weather conditions and probabilities of returning on schedule before you set out on a trip to the interior. Heavy rains can make it impossible for planes to land in some jungle areas; little or no provision is made for such delays and it can be a long and hungry wait for better conditions.

COMMUNICATIONS

● **Postal services**
The postal service is remarkably quick and reliable. Letters must be franked at the post office and posted the same day (no stamps sold). Both postal and telecommunications charges are very low at the black market exchange rate. **NB** Postcard rate for postcards means only 5 words. DHL, Van het Hogerhuystraat 55, Paramaribo, T 474007, F 473990; **Federal Express**, Keizerstraat 43, Paramaribo, T 474436, F 474696.

● **Telecommunications**
International telephone cards can be bought at the local phone company, TeleSur, Heiligenweg 01, Paramaribo (near the fountain, downtown), T 420222 for information, open 0700-1500, Mon-Fri. AT&T's USA Direct is available for collect calls from any phone; dial 156, 24-hr service. For Dutch PTT Holland Direct, dial 157, 24 hrs. Faxes can be sent or received through TeleSur, T 151 for information, 0700-2400 daily.

Useful telephone numbers:
Police emergency: T 115; other police numbers T 471111/7777/3101.
First Aid centre: T 499933.
Fire Brigade: T 473333/491111/451111.

MEDIA

● **Newspapers**
Newspapers are in Dutch, *De Ware Tijd* (morning) and *DeWest* (evening).

● **Radio**

Radio Zon (107.5 FM) has news bulletins in English at 1800. Radio Paramaribo (98.7 FM) broadcasts Voice of America after 0100 daily.

● **Television**

There are three stations, ATV, STVS and Apintie. All broadcast in Dutch, but there are programmes in Sarnami (the local Hindi language), Javanese and Sranan Tongo. All are in colour. STVS runs from 1500-2400, ATV 0800-2400, Apintie 0600-2400. ATV and STVS have good coverage of international sports, especially football; ATV carries CNN in English. Many cable TV stations are available.

TOURIST INFORMATION

Information about Suriname can be had from: Suriname representatives abroad (see above), the Suriname Tourism Foundation at Nassylaan 2, T 477694, F 420425, Telex 118 ALBUZA SN, Paramaribo, or Stinasu or NV Mets, address of both above.

The *Surinam Planatlas* is out of print, but can be consulted at the National Planning office on Dr Sophie Redmondstraat; maps with natural environment and economic development topics, each with commentary in Dutch and English.

Points of interest are: some colonial architecture, especially in and around Paramaribo; and the tropical flora and fauna in this very sparsely populated country. There are no beaches to speak of; the sea and the rivers in the coastal area are muddy, and mosquitoes can be a worry in places. Hitchhiking is not common, but it is possible. The **high seasons,** when everything is more expensive, are 15 Mar-15 May, July-Sept and 15 Dec-15 Jan.

ACKNOWLEDGEMENTS

We are very grateful to Jerry R A-Kum (Paramaribo) for a thorough review of this chapter.

Guyane

THE LAND

Guyane, an Overseas Department of France, has its eastern frontier with Brazil formed partly by the river Oiapoque (Oyapock in French) and its southern, also with Brazil, formed by the Tumuc-Humac mountains (the only range of importance). The western frontier with Suriname is along the river Maroni-Litani. To the N is the Atlantic coastline of 320 km. The area is estimated at between 83,900 and 86,504 square km, or one-sixth that of France. The land rises gradually from a coastal strip some 15-40 km wide to the higher slopes and plains or savannahs, about 80 km inland. Forests cover some 8 million hectares of the hills and valleys of the interior, and timber production is increasing rapidly. The territory is well watered, for over twenty rivers run to the Atlantic. There are widely divergent estimates for the ethnic composition of the population. Calculations vary according to the number included of illegal immigrants, attracted by social benefits and the high living standards. (The prefect stated in 1994 that Guyane had 30,000 illegal residents.) By some measures, over 40% of the population are Créoles, with correspondingly low figures for Europeans, Asians and Brazilians (around 17% in total). Other estimates put the Créole proportion at 36%, with Haitians 26%, Europeans 10% (of whom about 95% are from France), Brazilians 8%, Asians 4.7% (3.2% from Hong Kong, 1.5% from Laos), about 4% from Suriname and 2.5% from

Guyana. The Amerindian population is put at 3.6% (over 4% by some estimates). The main groups are Galibis (1,700), Arawak (400), Wayanas (600), Palikours (500), Wayampis-Oyampis (600) and Emerillons (300). There are also bush negroes (Bonis, Saramacas, Djukas), who live mostly in the Maroni area, and others (Dominicans, St Lucians, etc) at 0.7%. The language is French, with officials not usually speaking anything else. Créole is also widely spoken. The religion is predominantly Roman Catholic.

● **Note** The Amerindian villages in the Haut-Maroni and Haut-Oyapock areas may only be visited with permission from the Préfecture in Cayenne *before* arrival in Guyane.

HISTORY

Several French and Dutch expeditions attempted to settle along the coast in the early 17th century, but were driven off by the native population. The French finally established a settlement at Sinnamary in the early 1660s but this was destroyed by the Dutch in 1665 and seized by the British two years later. Under the Treaty of Breda, 1667, Guyane was returned to France. Apart from a brief occupation by the Dutch in 1676, it remained in French hands until 1809 when a combined Anglo-Portuguese naval force captured the colony and handed it over to the Portuguese (Brazilians). Though the land was restored to France by the Treaty of Paris in 1814, the Portuguese remained until 1817. Gold was discovered in 1853, and disputes arose about the frontiers of the colony with Suriname and Brazil. These were settled by arbitration in 1891, 1899, and 1915. By the law of 19 March, 1946, the Colony of

Guyane Française

Cayenne, or Guyane Française, became the Department of Guyane, with the same laws, regulations, and administration as a department in metropolitan France. The seat of the Prefect and of the principal courts is at Cayenne. The colony was used as a prison for French convicts with camps scattered throughout the country; Saint-Laurent was the port of entry. After serving prison terms convicts spent an equal number of years in exile and were usually unable to earn their return passage to France. Those interested should read *Papillon* by Henri Charrière. Majority opinion seems to be in favour of greater autonomy: about 5% of the population are thought to favour independence. Many prominent people were indicted on charges of corruption and diversion of funds in 1995 and 1996. The end of the latter year also saw riots which started when students demanded better facilities. Renewed rioting in April 1977 followed the arrest of members of the independence movement.

- *Rhum*, by the French Guyanese writer Blaise Cendras, is worth reading for its descriptions of the country's unique customs and traditions.

THE ECONOMY

Structure of production Most of the population lives in the coastal strip and it is here that farming is concentrated. The main crops are sugar cane, rice, maize and bananas; sugar is processed into rum, much of which is exported. Some market gardening is undertaken by Laotian Hmong immigrants, near Cacao, who produce fresh vegetables. The cattle farms on the coast are not large enough to meet domestic demand. Fishing is mainly for shrimp, with most of the 2,000-3,000 tonne annual catch exported to the USA or Japan. Guyane has renewable natural riches in its forests (about 75,000 sq km) and development of the timber industry is underway. Apart from the export of hardwood, trees are also used for the extraction of essence of rosewood and gum products.

There are deposits of gold, several of which have attracted Brazilian *garimpeiros* and consequent ecological damage through the silting of rivers and indiscriminate use of mercury. Officially gold production has risen from 330 kg in 1986 to 2.5 tonnes in 1995, largely as a result of increased declaration. An estimated 42 million tonnes of extractable bauxite have been located in the Kaw mountains to the SE of Cayenne, but development has not yet been started. Other minerals include sulphide of mercury, iron and clay; some 40 million tonnes of kaolin have been located at St-Laurent du Maroni.

Electricity is generated by three thermal power stations at Cayenne, Kourou and St-Laurent, but these may be replaced by the construction of a 120-MW hydroelectric scheme at Petit Sant on the Sinnamarie River. An estimated 1 million animals and 1.5 million birds lost their habitat when the area was flooded, but a French government-funded project rescued some of them and relocated them in Guyane's first nature reserve. More nature reserves are being created as a result of investment by the French government.

Recent trends Guyane is overwhelmingly dependent upon France for finance of about US$1.2bn a year, which is principally directed to providing social services and

French Guyane: fact file

Geographic
Land area	86,504 sq km

Demographic
Population (1996)	149,000
annual growth rate (1991-96)	3.2%
urban	79.4%
rural	20.6%
density	1.7 per sq km

Education and Health
Life expectancy at birth (1991),	
male	63.4 years
female	69.7 years
Infant mortality rate	15.4
per 1,000 live births (1993)	
Calorie intake as %	
of FAO requirement	124%
Literate males (over 15)	83.6%
Literate females (over 15)	82.3%

Economic and Employment
GNP (1994 market prices)	US$800mn
GNP per capita	US$6,000
Public external debt (1992)	US$36mn
Population economically active (1990)	
	48,800

Source *Encyclopaedia Britannica*

improving infrastructure. Most food-stuffs, consumer goods and manufactured products are imported from France or the French Caribbean and prices are consequently very high. Much of the country remains sparsely populated and underdeveloped despite French aid but the department is known internationally for its space station at Kourou, home to the European Ariane space programme, where economic activity and investment is concentrated. The site has been used to launch over half the world's commercial satellites and over 20,000 foreigners are employed there. Tourism is slowly being developed, but the lack of good beaches and the proximity of the Amazon which muddies the water has deterred many. About 10,000 tourists visit annually, mainly for adventure trips into the forests, but their numbers are dwarfed by the 60,000 other visitors, businessmen and those who work in the space programme.

GOVERNMENT

The head of state is the President of France; the local heads of government are a Commissioner of the Republic, for France, and the Presidents of the local General and Regional Councils. The General Council (19 seats) and the Regional Council (31 seats) are the two legislative houses. In regional council elections in March 1992, the Parti Socialiste Guyanais won 16 seats, while the other major party, the Front Democratique Guyanais, won 10. Guyane is divided into two *arrondissements*, Cayenne and St-Laurent du Maroni.

Cayenne

Cayenne, the capital and the chief port, is on the island of Cayenne at the mouth of the Cayenne River. It is 645 km from Georgetown (Guyana) and 420 km from Paramaribo (Suriname) by sea. Population estimated between 52,000 and 60,000. There is an interesting museum, the **Musée Departemental**, in rue de Remire, near the Place de Palmistes (Mon and Wed 0900-1330, Tues and Fri 0900-1330, 1630-1830, Sat 0900-1200; US$2, students US$1). It contains quite a mixture of exhibits, from pickled snakes to the trunk of the 'late beloved twin-trunked palm' of the Place de Palmistes; there is a good entomological collection and excellent paintings of convict life. Next door is the municipal library. The **Musée de L'Or**, Impasse Buzaré (Mon-Fri 0800-1200) has been restored. **L'Orstom** (scientific research institute), Route de Montabo, Mon and Fri 0700-1330, 1500-1800, Tues-Thur 0700-1300, has a research library and permanent exhibits on ecosystems and archaeological finds in Guyane. Also worth a visit are **La Crique**, the colourful but dangerous area around the Canal Laussat (built by Malouet in 1777); the Jesuit-built residence (circa 1890) of the Prefect (**L'Hôtel-de-Ville**) in the Place de Grenoble; the **Place des Amandiers** (also known as the Place Auguste-Horth) by the sea; the **Place des Palmistes**, with assorted palms; a swimming pool and five cinemas. The **fruit and vegetable market** on Monday, Wednesday, Friday and Saturday mornings has a Caribbean flavour, but it is expensive. There are bathing beaches (water rather muddy) around the island, the best is **Montjoly**, but watch out for sharks. Minibuses run from the terminal to Rémire-Montjoly for beaches. They leave when full – check when the last one returns. There is a walking trail called '**Rorota**' which follows the coastline and can be reached from Montjoly or the Gosselin beaches. Another trail, '**Habitation Vidal**' in Remire, passes through former sugar cane plantations and ends at the remains of 19th century sugar mills.

Excursions

43 km SW of Cayenne is **Montsinéry**, with a zoo featuring Amazonian flora and fauna (open daily 1000-1900), an orchid and a walking trail, '**Bagne des Annamites**', through remains of a camp where prisoners from Indochina were interned in the 1930s.

Local information – Cayenne
● Accommodation

Hotel prices			
L1	over US$200	**L2**	US$151-200
L3	US$101-150	**A1**	US$81-100
A2	US$61-80	**A3**	US$46-60
B	US$31-45	**C**	US$21-30
D	US$12-20	**E**	US$7-11
F	US$4-6	**G**	up to US$3

Unless otherwise stated, all hotels in range **D** and above have private bath. Assume friendliness and cleanliness in all cases.

L3 *Novotel Cayenne*, Chemin Hilaire-route de Montabo, T 30-38-88, F 31-78-98, not central, on beach, restaurant, a/c, very good; **A2** *Hotel des Amandiers*, Place Auguste Horth, T 30-26-00, F 30-74-84, a/c, excellent restaurant; **A2** *Phigarita Studios*, 47 bis, rue F Arago, T 30-66-00, F 30-77-49, spacious apartments with kitchenette, a/c, rec, helpful, breakfast; **A2** *Amazonia*, 26 Av Gen de Gaulle, good, a/c, luggage stored, central location, T 31-00-00, F 31-94-41; **A3** *Central Hotel*, corner rue Molé and rue Becker, T 31-30-00, F 31-12-96, downtown, a/c, very good; **A3** *Le Grillardin*, PK6 Route Matoury, 4 km from airport, T 35-63-90, a/c, restaurant; **A3** *Ket-Tai*, Ave de la Libertie corner Blvd Jubelin, T 30-11-00, new, modern; **A2** *Guyane Studios*, 16 rue Molé, T 30-25-11, a/c, kitchenette; **B** *Le Baduel*, Route de Baduel, T 30-51-58, F 30-77-76, a/c, TV, cooking facilities; **B** *Ajoupa*, T 30-33-08, F 30-12-82, Route Camp de Tigre, 2 km from town, helpful; **B-C** *Chez Mathilde/Hotel du Palais*, 42 Av Gen de Gaulle, T 30-25-13, cheaper with fan and without bath, hammock space, noisy, not safe

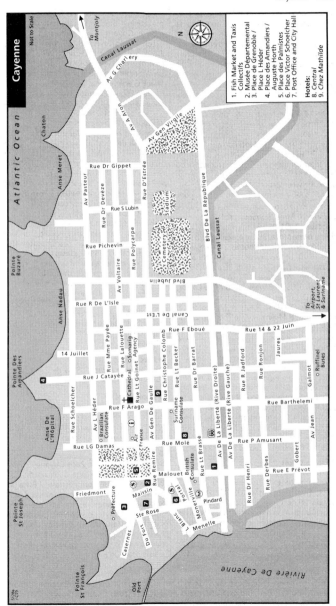

Cayenne

Not to Scale

Atlantic Ocean

To Montjoly

Canal Laussat

Av G Charlery

Av Aron

Chaton

Anse Meret

Rue Dr Gippet

Av Pasteur

Rue Dr Deveze

Rue D'Estrée

Av Gen Virgile

N

Pointe Buzaré

Rue S Lubin

Rue Pichevin

Rue Polycarpe

Av Voltaire

Stadium

Blvd Jubelin

Cemetery

Blvd De La République

Canal Laussat

Anse Nadau

Rue R De L'Isle

Canal De L'Est

To Airport, St Laurent & Suriname

Pointe Des Amandiers

Rue Mme Payée

Rue Lalouette

Rue F Eboué

Rue 14 & 22 Juin

4

14 Juillet

Rue J Catayée

Rue Lt Goinet

Somarig Agency

Rue Christophe Colomb

Rue Lt Becker

Rue Dr Barrat

Rue 14 & 22 Juin

Jaures

Rue Ronjon

Rue R Jadford

Ruffinel Buses

Anse De L'Hôpital

Rue Schoelcher

Av L Héder

Brazilian Consulate

Cathedral

Rue F Arago

Air France

Av Gen De Gaulle

Suriname Consulate

Rue De La Liberté (Rive Droite)

Av De La Liberté (Rive Gauche)

Rue Barthelemi

Galmot

1

Rue LG Damas

Rue Molé

Rue Lt Brassé

Rue P Amusant

Av Jean

Gobert

Rue E Prévot

5

Rue Remire

Malouet

British Consulate

7

Rue Dr Henri

Rue Derbes

Friedmont

Préfecture

3

Maissin

2

Portal

Monerville

Pindard

M

Ste Rose

6

L Blanc

Menelle

Casernes

Du Fort

Pointe St Joseph

Old Port

Pointe St François

Rivière De Cayenne

1. Fish Market and Taxis Collectifs
2. Musée Departemental
3. Place de Grenoble / Place L Héder
4. Place des Amandiers / Auguste Horth
5. Place des Palmistes
6. Place Victor Schoelcher
7. Post Office and City Hall

Hotels:
8. Central
9. Chez Mathilde

for left luggage, always full; **B** *Madeleine*, T 30-17-36, a/c, basic, breakfast, will book Raffinel bus to St-Laurent, 1 km out of town (good Surinamese snackbar nearby); **B** *Neptima*, rue F Eboué 21, T 30-11-15, F 37-98-60 (15 rooms), best value, a/c.

About 10 km from Cayenne is the **A2** *Beauregard*, route de Rémire, T 35-41-00, F 35-44-05, rec for business visitors, pool, tennis, squash, sauna, restaurant *Cric-Crac*; also *Hotel M*, a motel with a/c rooms and a small swimming pool; the owner hires out small cars, rec for business visitors, breakfast, T 35-41-00, Telex 010 310, and **A1** *Motel du Lac*, T 38-08-00, F 38-10-34, Chemin Poupon, Montjoly, 10 km from centre, pool, bar, restaurant, good business hotel. *Hotel-restaurant Le Polygone*, between airport and Cayenne, T 35-14-00, F 35-21-64, rooms, suites, bungalows, pool. The best value is to rent an apartment for a week or more: **C** *Mme Romieu*, PK 5.5 Route de Montabo, T 31-06-55, minimum stay of 3 nights; *Mme Mirta*, 35 Lot Alexandre, T 31-48-78, US$576/month; **M** *Roques*, 2 Lot Amarillys, T 38-18-20, US$230/week, a/c; **C** *Mme Stanistlas*, Villa Sonia PK 0.4 Rte de Rémire, T 38-22-13; *Mme Anastase*, 59 Av de Gaulle, T 35-17-70, US$203/week, a/c; **B** *Mme Castor*, 4 rue du Dr Gippet, T 31-27-38, F 31-66-13, a/c; **B** *Mme de Chadirac*, Route de Montjoly PK 6, T 38-23-01; **B** *M Firmin*, Cité Thémire, 28 rue René Maran, T 80-46-56; **B** *Mme Girard*, Route de Montabo PK3.5, T 30-61-28; **B** *M Benoît*, 117 rue Ch Colomb, T 31-42-81. Most hotels do not add tax and service to their bill, but stick to prices posted outside or at the desk. Hotel rooms are expensive—it is hard to find a room under 200F a night double. Bed and breakfast accommodation (gîte) is available for about 150F a night (breakfast is usually at extra cost)—contact the tourist office for details. Ask the Catholic Fathers at Cité Messaih, nr *Hotel Madeleine*, about sleeping possibilities. Amex cards are often not accepted but Visa is OK.

● **Places to eat**
Main hotels. *Hostellerie 'Les Amandiers'*, Place Auguste-Horth, excellent, the most famous, French, expensive (US$38); *Au Vieux Genois*, 89 rue Christophe Colomb, very good, French with local products, fish specialities, good business lunches; *La Caravelle*, 21 rue Christophe Colomb; *Le Vesuvio*, route Montabo, very good; *Armand Ti A Hing*, Place des Palmistes, French, excellent, 180F pp; *Cap St Jacques*, rue Docteur E Gippet, excellent Vietnamese food, reasonable; also *Thang-Long Vietnamese*, 1 rue Mentel; *Maxim'um*, Av Estrée; *La Croix du Sud*, 80, Av de Gaulle; *Tournesol*, rue Lt Goinet, real French food, fine wines, expensive, highly rec; *Porto Verde*, 58 rue Lt Goinet, Brazilian menu, mostly under 50F, rec; *Le Grillardin* (see **Hotels**), very good Créole; *Paris-Cayenne*, 59 rue Lalouette, French, very good, nice décor; *La Belle Epoque*, French, expensive; *Cric-Crac* at Hotel Beauregard, Créole cooking, lovely atmosphere; *Le Snack Créole*, 17 rue Eboué; *Mille Pâtes*, 16 rue Felix Eboué; *Palmiste*, Place des Palmistes, good daily menu, US$17, breakfast US$4, central and spacious; *Frégate*, Av de Gaulle; *Le Traiteur de la Forêt*, Blvd Jubelin, friendly, good; *Marveen Snack Bar*, rue Ch Colombe, near Canal de L'Est, food and staff pleasant, the patrons are very helpful regarding air travel and excursions (the elder of the two is a pilot for the Guyane Flying Club); *Ko Fei*, 18 rue Lalouette, T 312888, good Chinese; *Apsara*, 95 rue Colombe, Chinese, good value; *La Rose d'Asie*, 20 rue Samuel Lubin, very good Vietnamese; *Hindu-Creol*, rue J Catayée, Indian, good. Along the Canal Laussant there are Javanese snack bars; try *bami* (spicy noodles) or *saté* (barbequed meat in a spicy peanut sauce). Also along the canal are small, cheap Créole restaurants, not very clean. Vans around Place des Palmistes in evenings sell cheap, filling sandwiches. *Delifrance*, Av de Gaulle at rue Catayée, hot chocolate and croissants; *Epi D'or*, Av Jubelin, good sweets and cakes, rec. Food is about 38% more expensive than Metropolitan France: it is hard to find a meal for under 50F (small Chinese restaurants charge 50-80F for a full meal).

● **Bars**
Bar Cayenne Palace, 45 Av de Gaulle, disco 80F with first drink.

● **Bookshops**
Librairie AJC, 31 Boulevard Jubelin, has some stock in English. Also old maps and prints. Current map sold at *Librairie Alain Pion*, Av de Gaulle and in most bookshops.

● **Exchange**
Banque Nacional de Paris-Guyane, 2 Place Schoelcher; no exchange facilities on Sat. **Banque Française Commerciale**, 2 Place des Palmistes (best bank exchange rates); **Crédit Populaire Guyanais**, 93 rue Lalouette. Most banks have ATMs for cash withdrawals on Visa, sometimes Mastercard, never Amex. *Cambio Caraïbe*, Av Gen de Gaulle near Catayée (best rates for US$); *Guyane Change*, Av Gen de Gaulle near rue F Eboué. The Post Office exchanges cash and TCs at good rates, but complicated and time-consuming. There are no exchange facilities at the airport; if in extreme need on Sat you may be able to change money at Air France office in Place des Palmistes. Cen-

tral drugstore may help when banks closed. Almost impossible to change dollars outside Cayenne or Kourou. Buy francs before arrival if possible.

● **Laundromat**
Corner of rue Lalouette and rue Eboué, US$5 load; *Ros'in*, 87 Av Liberté, T 31-73-13.

● **Main Post Office**
Route de Baduel, 2 km out from town (15F by taxi or 20 mins on foot). Poste Restante letters are only kept for 2 weeks maximum. Also Poste Cayenne Cépéron, place L Heder.

● **Tourist offices**
Agence Régionale de Développement du Tourisme et des Loisirs de la Guyane (ARDTLG), 12 rue Lalouette (T 30-09-00), 0800-1200, 1500-1800. Free map and tourist guide (Guyane Poche). At the airport, **Chambre de Commerce et d'industrie de Guyane**, has plenty of hotel and tour information and map.

● **Travel Agents**
Takari Tour, Colline du Montabo, T 31-19-60 (BP 513) and at *Novotel*, rec for inland tours. *Guyane Excursions*, Centre Commercial Sima-rouba, Kourou, T 32-05-41, specializes in inland tours, particularly to the Maroni River, highly rec, US$700 for 5-6 days, but a wide variety of options. Also *JAL Voyages*, 1 ave des Plages, Montjoly, T 31-68-20, for a wide range of tours. *Somarig*, 32 rue Lalouette, T 30-29-80, is good for South American and European airline tickets. It also sells boat tickets to Ile Royale as well as meal tickets for the Auberge which are rec. *Agence Sainte-Claire*, 8 rue de Remire, T 30-00-38, for travel outside Guyane (inc charters to Caracas and Cuba); *Havas*, 2 place du Marché, T 31-26-22/31-27-26 (also 26 ave de l'Opéra, 75001 Paris, T 40-41-80-00).

● **Transport**
Bus terminal at corner of rue Molé and Av de la Liberté. Regular urban services. The only west-bound bus is run by Raffinel & Cie, 8 Av Galmot, T 31-26-66 (Kourou US$12, St Laurent US$25) leaves 0530 (not Sun). Minibuses to St-Laurent du Maroni leave when full from the terminal, 0400-1200, 3 hrs, US$25. Service to **Mana** Mon and Thur only. To Kaw, Wed. Otherwise transport is by shared taxis (collectifs), which leave from Av de la Liberté, near the fish market early in the morning (Kourou US$12, St Laurent US$30-38).

WEST TO SURINAME

Kourou, 56 km W of Cayenne, where the main French space centre (Centre Spatial Guyanais), used for the European Space Agency's Ariane programme, is located, is referred to by the Guyanais as 'white city' because of the number of metropolitan French families living there; its population is about 20,000. Tourist attractions include bathing, fishing, sporting and aero club, and a variety of organized excursions. The space centre occupies an area of about 4 km deep along some 30 km of coast, bisected by the Kourou River. Public guided tours are given Mon-Fri 0745-1130 and 1300-1630 (Fri am only). Write to Centre Spatial Guyanais, Jupiter 2, Acceuil Visite, 97310, Kourou, or T 33-44-82. The tour includes the new museum, which can be visited without reservation, open Mon-Thur 1000-1800, Fri and Sat 1400-1800, US$7.70. No public transport, take a taxi or hitch. Visits are free. To watch a launch you must write to M Le directeur du Centre Spatial Guyanais, BP726, 97387 Kourou Cedex, or F 33-50-55, saying you want to attend; fax, or T 33-44-82 to find out when launches take place. Supply full names and ID; ask for your invitation from Centre d'acceuil du CSG, or Syndicat d'Initiative de Cayenne, 7 ave G Monnerville, 97300 Cayenne (312919). Invitations must be collected 2-3 days before the launch; if you hear nothing, it's probably full, but you can try wait-listing (arrive early). There are five viewing sites: Toucan (for VIPs, but wait-listing, or enquiries, possible), Kikiwi, Colibri (both good), Agami (OK) and Ibis (not rec). Alternatively, you can watch the launch for free, from 10 km, at Montagne Carapa at Pariacabo.

Local Information – Kourou
● **Accommodation**
All hotels are overbooked and raise their prices when there is an Ariane rocket launch (about once a month).

L3 *Relais de Guyane* (*Hotel des Roches*), Avenues des Roches, T 32-00-66, F 32-03-28, not too good, a/c, inc breakfast, pool, beach, good restaurants; **A1** *Atlantis*, T 32-13-00, F 32-40-12, nr Lac Bois Diable, a/c, modern, pool, good restaurant, best value for business visitors; also at Lac Bois Diable, **L2** *Mercure*, T 32-07-00; **L3** *La Corissante*, 23 rue des Alizés, T 33-11-00, F 33-11-60, studios with 2-5 rooms, cooking facilities; **A2** *Studios Le Gros Bec*, T 32-91-91, 52 rue Dr Floch, cooking facilities; **A2** *Les Jardins D'Hermes*, 56 rue Duchense, T 32-01-

83, F 32-09-17, in heart of old Kourou, a/c, modern, good; *A3 Ballahou*, 1 rue Armet Martial, T 32-42-06, F 32-52-08, a/c, TV, nice, modern, good restaurant; **A** *Mme Moutton*, rue Séraphin 56, T 31-21-45, studios with or without kitchen. **E** *Centre d'Acceuil*, Av de Gaulle, T 32-25-40/32-26-33, various sizes of room, fans, good value. Cheap hotels and rooms for 100F on Av de Gaulle.

20 km S of Kourou on the road to Saramaca is *Les Maripas*, tourist camp, T 32-05-41, F 32-28-47, river and overland excursions available, D for tent, book at Guyane Excursion, 7 quartier Simarouba, nr *Restaurant Saramaca*.

● **Places to eat**
Many, especially on de Gaulle, offer 60F menu (Creole or Chinese) inc *Le Catouri*, *Cachiri Combo* (No 3, T 32-44-64, 100-150F, also has basic rooms, C), *Vieux Montmartre*. *La Grillade*, Av Berlioz; *L'Enfer Vert*, Av G Monnerville; *Le Paradisier* in Hotel des Roches (see above); *L'Hydromel*, rue Raymond Cresson, good pancakes; *Le Provence*, 11 passage G Monnerville, best French, expensive; *Ballahou* (see **Hotels**), best for fish and seafood (try *Guyabaisse*); pizza at *Le Valentino*, 4 place Galilé, pizzas, seafood Fri; *Le Saramaca*, place du Marché. *La Pirogue*, Quartier de l'Europe, 20m from post office, at 60F good value; in same area, *Le Citron Vert*, *Le Moaï*, *Le Roc*, *Le Gourbi*, *Viet Nam*, *Le Colibri* (good chicken) and **Bar des Sports** (beside Post Office, 50F). Many cheap Chinese (also take-away): *Le Chinatown*, rue Duchesne, rec; *Kong Loong*, rue du Levant; many vans sell sandwiches filled with Créole food, good. *Le Glacier des 2 Lacs*, 68 ave des 2 Lacs, ice cream, cakes, tea, very good.

● **Bars**
La Nouvelle Dimension (Créole and European style); *American Bar* in Hotel des Roches (see **Hotels**); *Le Forban*, rue Dreyfus, district 205, worth seeing the murals (also for the lonely, many young Brazilian women).

● **Entertainment**
Nightclubs: *3ème Dimension* (Créole style), *Le Vieux Montmartre*, both on de Gaulle; *Clibertown*, quartier de l'Anse, very good.

● **Exchange**
Banque National de Paris Guyane, near the Mairie; Banque Française Commerciale, Place Jeanne d'Arc; Crédit Populaire Guyanais, Simarouba; Crédit Martiniqueis, ave G Monnerville.

● **Post Office**
Avenue des Frères Kennedy.

● **Travel Agencies**
Guyane Excursions, T 32-05-41 (see under Cayenne); *Agence Sainte Claire*, T 32-36-98, F 32-50-40; *Air France*, place Newton, T 32-10-50; *Amazonie Détente*, 18 rue A Renoir, T 32-82-52.

● **Tourist offices**
Quartier de l'Europe, T 32-48-840.

● **Transport**
Taxi in town US$10, Lopez T 320560, Gilles T 320307, Kourou T 321444. To **Cayenne**, bus leaves from Shell service station, corner Av de France, Av Vermont Polycarpe; bus to **St-Laurent du Maroni** from same place, 2 between 0600 and 0700, US$30; *taxis collectifs*, 0600, 0630, 0700, 1330, US$12 to Cayenne. Taxi to Cayenne or airport, US$60 (US$85 at night); to St-Laurent du Maroni US$25 by *taxi collectif* (irregular) or by minibus from Shell Station.

The **Iles du Salut** (many visitors at weekends), opposite Kourou, include the Ile Royale, the Ile Saint-Joseph, and the Ile du Diable. They were the scene of the notorious convict settlement built in 1852; the last prisoners left in 1953. The Ile du Diable ("Devil's Island"), a rocky palm-covered islet almost inaccessible from the sea, was where political prisoners, including Alfred Dreyfus, were held. There is a 60-bed hotel on Ile Royale, **A3** *Auberge Iles du Salut* (address Sothis, 97310 Kourou, T 32-11-00, F 32-42-23), also hammock space US$20 pp; former guard's bungalow, main meals (incl with minimum US$36, breakfast US$8 (exmess hall for warders, with good food; bottled water sold); gift shop with high prices (especially when a cruise ship is in), good English guide book for sale. Camping is possible, but suitable sites are limited (try the NE end of Ile Royale), the stronghearted may try the old prison barracks; take food and water (you can also sling a hammock in the open, take a plastic sheet to protect yourself from morning mist); bread and water (check bottle is sealed) can be bought from the hotel stall. You can see monkeys, agoutis, turtles, humming birds and macaws, and there are many un-owned coconut palms. Beware the many open wells. Take a torch for visiting the ruins. Paintings of prison life are on show in the tiny church. Points of interest include the children's graveyard, hospital, mental asylum and death cells. These, and the church, are not always open. Little is being done to prevent the deterioration of the buildings. Boat from Kourou's port at the end of Av General de Gaulle, 4 km from old centre US$37 return (children under 12 half price), leaves 0810 and 1030 daily, returns from island at 1600 and 1800 (check, T 32-09-95), additional sailing Sat 1600, 1 hour each way. Tickets may be obtained from Somarig Voyages, address under Cayenne **Travel Agents**; Air Guyane Voyages, 2 rue Lalouette, T 31-72-00; in Kourou from au Carbet des Roches, cash only. There are no regular boats from Ile Royale to Ile Saint-Joseph, which is wilder and more beautiful, with a small beach (this island had solitary-confinement cells and the warders' graveyard). It may be possible to hire a private boat at the ferry dock, or ask for James on the Kourou-Ile Royale ferry. Surfing and swimming are possible, though not advised, between Ile Royale and Ile du Diable; strong currents at high tide, as well as sharks. Boat owners are very reluctant to visit Ile du Diable except around July-August when the sea is calmer.

Between Kourou and Iracoubo, on the road W to St-Laurent, is **Sinnamary** (116 km from Cayenne), a pleasant town where Galibi Indians at a mission make artifical flowers from feathers, for sale to tourists. Scarlet ibis can be seen in numbers on the Sinnamary estuary at Iracoubo. Also at Iracoubo is a pretty church with paintings by a convict. **C** *Hotel au Fil de l'Eau*, friendly but noisy.

St-Laurent du Maroni (*pop* 20,000), formerly a penal transportation camp, is now a quiet colonial town 250 km from Cayenne on the river Maroni, bordering Suriname. It can be visited as a day tour from Cayenne if you hire a car. There are no gîtes in St-Laurent; those on a tight budget wanting a room or hammock space can try to make advance arrangements in Cayenne with: Fédération d'Oeuvres Laïques, Centre d'Hebergement de Saint-Louis, T 34-11-40; CAS EDF, centre d'Hebergement, T 34-12-96/34-23-03; or Le Carbet du Balat, Mme Emilie Lamtoukai, T 34-04-04.

The old Camp de Transportation (the original penal centre) can be wandered round at will (an absolute must if visiting the country); closed Mon. Next door on Blvd Malouet is the tourist office. Guided tours of Les Bagnes (prison camps) daily 0815-1115, 1515-1715, chilling, buy tickets from tourist office, US$2.50. The Charbonière refugee camp, next to the ferry pier housed Surinamese Bush Negro refugees during that country's civil war. A few have remained and more have returned. (Nearby is St-Jean du Maroni, an Indian village.)

Local Information
● **Accommodation**
Sinnamary: **A3** *Sinnarive Motel*, T 34-55-55; **A3** *Hotel du Fleuve*, T 34-54-00, F 34-53-03, expensive. *Restaurant Madras*, good Creole; ask for *Gaya Baru*, Indonesian restaurant in an Indonesian village. Wood carvings and jewellery are on sale here and the workshops can be visited. There are 3 to 5 day excursions up the Sinnamarie River.

St-Laurent: **A1-A3** *Hotel La Tentiaire*, 12 Av Franklin Roosevelt, T 34-26-00, F 34-15-09, a/c, the best, breakfast extra; **B** *Hotel Toucan*, Boulevard Republique, T 34-12-59, F 34-17-06, a/c, dirty, TV, poor value; **B** *Star Hotel*, rue Thiers, T 34-10-84, a/c, pool, cheap restaurant, rec; **A3** *Chez Julienne*, Route des Malgaches, T 34-11-53, a/c, TV, shower, good.

In the countryside not far from St-Laurent are 2 *Auberge de brousse*, which are good places to stay for walking, or for trips to see turtles at Les Hattes (see below): **C** *Auberge Bois Diable*, PK8 Acarouany, T 34-19-35, 1 bedroom, hammock space, US$6, meals, US$16, breakfast US$4, good food, hospitable, tours arranged; **C** *Relais d'Acarouany*, T 34-17-20, 6 rooms, meals US$18, breakfast US$4. Cabins in forest available, sleeps several, US$100 total (inc transport by boat).

● **Places to eat**
St-Laurent: *Restaurant La Saramaca*, Av Felix Eboué, the best (also has rooms to rent at the back); *Restaurants Vietnam* and *La Goelette*, T 342897, rec (French/Brazilian, closed Sun pm, Mon) also has kayak and canoe tours, also *Loe*, nr hospital, Créole, excellent; many cheap Chinese.

● **Bars**
Jean Solis, opp Catholic church, rec.

● **Exchange**
BNP opp *Restaurant Le Saramaca* will change

US$ TCs. **Cambio COP**, 19 rue Montravel, nr BNP, T 34-38-23, changes Dutch and Suriname guilders, dollars

● **Transport**

Minibuses to Cayenne meet the ferry from Suriname, leaving when full, 3 hrs, US$25. Bus to Cayenne, US$30, same price to Kourou, 0500 daily, tickets and info at *Hotel Star*; *taxis collectifs* to and from Cayenne, 8 people, US$25 a head, 3½-hour trip. Freight *pirogues* sometimes take passengers inland along the Maroni River; alternatively a group can hire a *pirogue* at about US$200 a day. Avis has a car rental office in St-Laurent.

FRONTIER WITH SURINAME

Make sure you obtain proper entry stamps from immigration, not the police, to avoid problems when leaving. Customs and immigration close at 1900.

● **Exchange**

Many aggressive touts on the St-Laurent and Albina piers. It is best to change money in the Village Chinois in St-Laurent; although rates are lower than in Paramaribo, it is illegal to change money in Albina. Beware theft at St-Laurent's black market.

● **Transport**

Ferry for vehicles and passengers to Albina Mon, Thur, 0700, 0900, 1400, 1600, Tues, Wed, Sat 0700, 0900, Sun, 1530, 1600, ½ hr. Passengers US$4 one way, car US$20 one way. It can be quicker, more fun and the same price to hire a *pirogue*. Minibuses and taxis for Paramaribo meet the Albina ferry.

EXCURSIONS

About 3 km from St-Laurent, along the Paul Isnard Road, is Saint-Maurice, where the rum distillery of the same name can be visited, Mon-Fri 0730-1130. At Km 70 on the same dirt road is access to **Voltaire Falls**, 1½ hrs walk from the road (**A3** *Auberge des Chutes Voltaires*, T 34-27-16). 7 km S of St-Laurent on the road to St-Jean is the Amerindian village of **Terre Rouge**; canoes can be hired for day trips up the Maroni River (see Maripasoula below). These can be arranged with *Youkaliba (Maroni) Expeditions*, 3 rue Simon, T 34-16-45/31-23-98 and *Guyane Adventure*, T 34-21-28/34-13-78: eg 1-night trip to Apatou, US$140; to Saut Anana on Mana River, 10 days, US$655.

40 km N of St-Laurent du Maroni is

Mana, a delightful town with rustic architecture near the coast (**E** pp *Gîte d'Etape*, rooms OK, filthy kitchen, mosquitoes, disco next door; nuns next to the church rent beds and hammocks, US$8, clean and simple, T 34-17-29, Communauté des Soeurs de St-Joseph de Cluny, 1 rue Bourguignon; Mme Hidair, T 34-80-62, has rooms, **C**; **C** *Le Bougainvillier*, a/c, **D** with shared bath; restaurants *Le Bufalo* and *Le Manoa del Dorado*). 20 km W of Mana following the river along a single track access road is **Les Hattes**, or Yalimapo, an Amerindian village (**B** *Gîte Rureau*, clean; restaurant *Au Paradis des Acajous*; Indian restaurant near beach; ask M Daniel for permission to stay in the church). 4 km further on is Les Hattes beach where leatherback-turtles lay their eggs at night; season April-Aug with its peak in May-June. No public transport to Les Hattes and its beach, but hitching possible at weekends; take food and water and mosquito repellent. In spite of the dryish climate Mana is a malaria region. The fresh water of the Maroni and Mana rivers makes sea bathing very pleasant. Very quiet during the week.

Aouara, or Aiwala, an Amerindian village with hammock places, is about 16 km W of Les Hattes. It also has a beach where the leatherback turtles lay their eggs; they take about three hours over it. Take mosquito nets, hammock and insect repellent.

CENTRAL MASSIF

There are daily flights from Cayenne to **Maripasoula**; details in **Air transport**, page 1632 (**C** *Auberge Chez Dedè*, Av Leonard, T 37-20-05, US$4 per extra person; **A1** *Campement Touristique de Sant Sonnelle*, T 31-49-45, full board). It is up the Maroni from St-Laurent (2-4 day journey up river in *pirogue*). There may be freight canoes which take passengers (US$40) or private boats (US$150) which leave from St-Laurent; 5-6 day tours and other options with Guyane-Excursions or with Takari Tour (see under Cayenne **Travel Agents**). Maripasoula has 5,000 inhabitants in town and its surroundings. Many bush negros live here. 20 mins by canoe from Maripasoula is **A2** *Campement Touristique Lassort*, T 31-49-45.

Saül, a remote gold-mining settlement in the 'massif central' is the geographical centre of Guyane. The main attractions are for the nature-loving tourist. Beautiful undisturbed tropical forests are accessible by a very well-maintained system of 90 km of marked trails, including several circular routes. The place has running water, a radiotelephone, and electricity. Ten-day expeditions are run by Christian Ball, 'Vie Sauvage', 97314 Saül, US$86 (30% in advance) per day with meals, maps of local trails provided, own hammock and bedding useful but not essential. It can be cold at night. Another fascinating overland route goes from Roura (see below) up the Comte River to Belizon, followed by a 14 to 16-day trek through the jungle to Saül, visiting many villages en route, guide recommended. 7 km N of Saül is *Eden des Eaux Claires*, tourist camp, T 30-91-11, **A2** full board, **C** in hammock including breakfast and dinner (drinks extra).

● **Transport** Air service with Air Guyane from Cayenne or via Maripasoula (see **Air transport**, below); try at airport even if flight said to be full. By *pirogue* from Mana up Mana River, 9-12 days, then one day's walk to Saül, or from St-Laurent via Maripasoula along Moroni and Inini Rivers, 15 days and one day's walk to Saül, both routes expensive.

SOUTHEAST TO BRAZIL

30 km S of Cayenne at Carrefour de Gallion, the intersection of RN2 and CD5, is **B** *Emerald Jungle Village*, a tropical nature centre with a small botanical and zoological collection. Eco-tours can be taken into the forests by boat or canoe with expedition gear. Meals and drinks extra, airport transportation US$18, mountain bike hire US$10/day, canoes for hire. Owned by Joep Moonen and his wife, who both speak English, German and Dutch F 30-06-82; or write to CDS-PK0.5, 97356 Montsinéry.

28 km SE of Cayenne is the small town of **Roura** (**B** *Hotel-restaurant Amazone River*, T 31-91-13, a/c, good restaurant,

good views of the river; **B** *Auberge des Orpailleurs*, PK62 route de l'Est, T 37-62-97, hammock space US$5, breakfast and dinner available; rooms to rent from Mme Luap, **C**, T 31-54-84), with an interesting church; an excursion may be made to the Fourgassier Falls several km away (*L'Auberge des Cascades*, excellent restaurant). From Cayenne the road now crosses a new bridge over the Comte River. Excursions can be arranged along the Comte River. For information about the area contact the Syndicat D'Initiative de Roura, T 31-11-04. Nearby is Dacca, a Laotian village. 27 km from Roura is **C** *Auberge du Camp Caiman* (tourist camp, F to hang hammock), T 37-60-34, tours arranged to watch caiman in the swamps.

From Roura an unpaved road runs SE towards the village of Kaw. At Km 36 from Cayenne is the **C** *Hotel Relais de Patawa* (T 28-03-95), or sling your hammock for US$4, cheaper rates for longer stays, highly recommended. The owners, M and Mme Baloup, who are entomologists, will show you their collection, take you on guided tours of local sights and introduce you to their pet anaconda and boa constrictors. At Km 53 on the road to Régina is the turn-off to **Cacao** (a further 13 km), a small, quiet village, where Hmong refugees from Laos are settled; they are farmers and produce fine traditional handicrafts. The main attraction is the Sun am market with local produce, Laotian food, embroidery. (Accommodation: **C** *Restaurant La Lan*, one room, good value, good food; **E** *Quimbe-Kio*, hammock camp, breakfast US$3; M Levessier, T 30-51-22, has hammocks, **E**; best restaurant is *Chez By et David*, Laotian food; also good is *Degrad Cacao*). Minibus from Cayenne, Monday 1200; Friday 1800, return Mon 0730, Fri 1400. Halfway along the side road is the *Belle Vue* restaurant, which lives up to its name, because of the superb view over the tropical forest; the restaurant is open at weekends. SW of Cacao is the tourist camp **A2** *Carbet La Source*, with full board, T 31-96-64.

Kaw, at Km 83, is on an island amid swamps which are home to much rare wildlife including caymans. The village is reached by dugout either from the Cayenne road or from Régina, or by road from Roura (50 km dirt road through the mountains with the last 2 km by dugout). Basic accommodation available (Mme Musron, T 31-88-15; *Jacana Tour*, T 38-07-95, excursions by day or night on the river), take insect repellent. Southwest of Kaw on the river Approuague is **Régina**, linked with Cayenne by a mostly paved road. A good trip is on the river to Athanase with G Frétique, T 30-45-51.

A trail has been cut by the French army from the road-head at Régina to St-Georges de l'Oyapock, along which a road is currently under construction (planned for completion 1998). It is 4 to 5 days of hard trekking with many rivers to be forded, impassable during the rainy season.

FRONTIER WITH BRAZIL

St-Georges de l'Oyapock is 15 mins down river from Oiapoque (Brazil) US$4 pp by motorized canoe, bargain for a return fare. The **Saut Maripa** rapids (not very impressive with high water) are located about 30 mins upstream along the Oiapock River, past the Brazilian towns of Oiapoue and Clevelândia do Norte. Hire a motorized *pirogue* (canoe) to take you to a landing downstream from the rapids. Then walk along the remains of a narrow gauge railway line (one of only two in Guyane, formerly used for gold mining) for 20 mins through the jungle, to reach a small tourist complex with restaurant, bar, and guest houses by the rapids. A pleasant day trip. There are more rapids further upstream.

● Immigration
Immigration (*gendarmerie*) for entry/exit stamps at E end of town, follow signs, open daily 0700-1200, 1500-1800 (sometimes not open after early morning on Sun, in which case try the police at the airport); French and Portuguese spoken.

● Accommodation & services
B *Hotel Modestine*, T 37-00-13, restaurant, rooms to rent from M Carème; **D** unnamed hotel to left of supermarket opposite town hall, a dump, no fan, no window; also *Theofila*, lunch US$3, other restaurants and a night club. Two supermarkets with French specialities. Post Office; public telephone which takes phone card.

● Exchange
One of the Livre Service supermarkets and *Hotel Modestine* will sometimes change dollars cash into francs at very poor rates; if entering the country here, change money before arriving in St-Georges. Note that nowhere in town accepts Visa cards.

● Transport
For Air Guyane flights to Cayenne see below, **Air transport**. Air Guyane office at airport open 0700-0730, 1400-1430 for check in, open 0800-1100 for reservations. Flights are fully-booked several days in advance; you must check in at stated times. Extra flights are sometimes added. The police check that those boarding flights who have arrived from Brazil have obtained their entry stamp; also thorough baggage search.

Shipping A small vessel, the *Sao Pedro*, normally runs a shipping service to Cayenne, deck passengers US$30, but check it is not under repair. A cargo ship, the *Normelia*, calls at St-Georges about twice a month and will sometimes take passengers to Cayenne, 12-14 hrs, US$30 inc meals. Speak directly to the captain. The Elf petrol station has details on ship arrivals.

Information for travellers

cayou, Matoury, T 35-64-99; J-P Brugerie, Impasse France Equinociale, Kourou, T 32-12-58.

MONEY

● **Currency**

The currency is the French franc (5.71F = US$1 May 1997). Try to take francs with you as the exchange rate for dollars is low, many banks do not offer exchange facilities and most places demand cash. A better rate can be obtained by using Visa cards to withdraw cash from all the banks in Cayenne, Kourou and St-Laurent du Maroni.

GETTING THERE

AIR

Air France flies daily direct to Guyane from Paris, 10 times a week from Pointe-à-Pitre (Guadeloupe), Fort-de-France (Martinique), and once a week from Santo Domingo, once a week from Miami and once a week from Port-au-Prince. AOM French Airlines fly twice a week direct from Paris and are reported to be the cheapest from Europe (Paris T 40-74-00-04). Air Guadeloupe flies from Pointe-à-Pitre and Fort de France 4 times a week, Port-au-Prince and San Juan (Puerto Rico) twice and Santo Domingo once. Surinam Airways flies to Belém, Macapá and Paramaribo 3, 2 and 4 times a week; Surinam Airways sells tickets for Cayenne-Paramaribo-Georgetown-Port of Spain.

SEA

The Compagnie Général Maritime runs a passenger service to France once a month via Martinique and a freight service every 3 months. To Brazil from St-Georges to Oiapoque, see text above.

BEFORE TRAVELLING

● **Documents**

Passports are not required by nationals of France and most French-speaking African countries carrying identity cards. For EC visitors, documents are the same as for Metropolitan France (ie no visa, no exit ticket required – check with a consulate in advance). No visa (45F) required for most nationalities (except for those of Guyana, Australia, some Eastern European countries, and Asian – not Japan – and other African countries) for a stay of up to 3 months, but an exit ticket out of the country is essential (a ticket out of one of the other Guianas is not sufficient); a deposit is required otherwise. If one stays more than 3 months, income tax clearance is required before leaving the country. Inoculation against yellow-fever is officially required only for those staying in Guyane longer than 2 weeks, but advisable for all. Travel to certain Amerindian villages is restricted. For **Tourist information see page 1633** below.

● **Climate**

Tropical with a very heavy rainfall. Average temperature at sea-level is 27°C, and fairly constant at that. Night and day temperatures vary more in the highlands. The rainy season is from November to July, with (sometimes) a short dry interruption in February and (sometimes) March. The great rains begin in May.

● **When to go**

The best months to visit are between Aug and Nov, which are the usual months for trips to the jungle.

● **Health**

Tropical diseases, dysentery, malaria, etc, occur, but the country is fairly healthy. Malaria prophylaxis recommended.

Recommended specialist in tropical diseases, Dr P Chesneau, Place Europe, T 32-11-05, Kourou. Dentists: R Fournier, 115 Lot Mou-

ON ARRIVAL

● **Airports**

Cayenne-Rochambeau (T 29-97-00) is 16 km from Cayenne, 20 mins by taxi, and 67 km from Kourou (US$60-80). No exchange facilities. No public transport; only taxis (US$25 daytime, US$30 night, but you can probably bargain or share). The cheapest route to town is taxi to Matoury US$10, then bus to centre US$2. Cheapest method of return to airport is by collective taxi from corner of Av de la Liberté and rue Malouet to Matoury (10 km) for US$2.40, then hitch or walk.

● **Airline offices**

Air France, 13, rue L G Damas, Place des Palmistes, T 37-98-99; Air Guyane, 2 rue Lalouette,

T 31-72-00/35-65-55; Surinam Airways, 2 place Schoelcher, T 31-72-98.

● **Embassies & consulates**
British (Honorary), 16 Av Monnerville (BP 664, Cayenne 97300, T 31-10-34/30-42-42, F 30-40-94); **Brazilian**, 12 rue L Héder, at corner of Place des Palmistes, nr Air France offices (closed Sats T 30-04-67); **Dutch** (Honorary), Batiment Sogudem, Port de Dégrad des Cannes, BP139, Cayenne 97323, T 35-49-31, F 35-46-71; **Suriname**, 38 rue Christophe Colomb (T 30-04-61), Mon-Fri 0900-1200, visa 150F, two photos needed, takes 15 days (may be obtained same day, at extra cost).

● **Hours of business**
Hours vary widely between different offices, shops and even between different branches of the same bank or supermarket. There seem to be different business hours for every day of the week, but they are usually posted. Most shops and offices close for a couple of hours around midday.

● **Official time**
3 hrs behind GMT.

● **Public holidays**
Public holidays are the same as in Metropolitan France, with the addition of Slavery Day, 10 June.

Carnaval (Feb or Mar). Although not as famous as those of its neighbours in Brazil or the Caribbean, Guyane's Carnaval is joyous and interesting. It is principally a Créole event, but there is some participation by all the different cultural groups in the department (best known are the contributions of the Brazilian and Haitian communities). Celebrations begin in Jan, with festivities every weekend, and culminate in colourful parades, music, and dance during the 4 days preceding Ash Wednesday. Each day has its own motif and the costumes are very elaborate. On Sat night, a dance called 'Chez Nana – Au Soleil Levant' is held, for which the women disguise themselves beyond recognition as 'Touloulous', and ask the men to dance. They are not allowed to refuse. On Sun there are parades in downtown Cayenne. Lundi Gras (Fat Monday) is the day to ridicule the institution of marriage, with mock wedding parties featuring men dressed as brides and women as grooms. 'Vaval', the devil and soul of Carnaval, appears on Mardi Gras (Fat Tuesday) with dancers sporting red costumes, horns, tails, pitch-forks, etc. He is burnt that night (in the form of a straw doll) on a large bonfire in the Place des Palmistes. Ash Wednesday is a time of sorrow, with participants in the final parades dressed in black and white.

● **Shopping**
The best buys are handicrafts in wood in the Saramaca village (Kourou) and along the road in the W of the country, and in St-Laurent du Maroni; also white rum. Hmong embroidery is sold at Sunday markets in Cacao and Jahourey.

● **Weights and measures**
The metric system is in use.

WHERE TO STAY

Details of hotels are given in the text. For information on *Gîtes* and *Chambres chez l'habitant* write to Agence Régionale de Dévéloppement du Tourisme et des Loisirs de la Guyane (ARDTLG), 12 rue Lalouette, 97338, Cayenne Cedex, T 30-09-00, Telex 910364 FG; also, for *Gîtes*, Association pour le Tourisme Vert en Guyane, 27 rue Justin Cataye, 97300 Cayenne, T 31-10-11.

FOOD AND DRINK

Most food is imported, except seafood; it is of very high quality but expensive.

GETTING AROUND

AIR TRANSPORT

Internal air services are by Air Guyane. These flights are always heavily booked, so be prepared to wait or write or telephone Air Guyane, address above. There are regular connections with Maripasoula, daily at 0930; Saül on Mon, Wed and Fri, at 0930; St-Georges, daily at 0745 and usually one early pm, 30 mins; Régina, Mon, Wed and Fri at 0745. Baggage allowance 10 kg. No services on Sun. Locals are given preference on internal flights; reservations cannot be made other than at the office in Cayenne, with cash.

LAND TRANSPORT

● **Motoring**
There are no railways, and about 1,000 km of road. The main road, narrow but now paved, runs for 130 km from Pointe Macouris, on the roadstead of Cayenne, to Iracoubo. Another 117 km takes it to Mana and St-Laurent. It also runs to Régina and Cacao, although the last stretch has some rough patches.

● **Car hire**
Car hire can be a great convenience (there are 15 agencies in Cayenne; those at the airport open only for flight arrivals). All types of car available, from economy to luxury to pick-ups and jeeps. Cheapest rates are US$57 a day, US$385/week. Check insurance details carefully; the excess is very high. Gasoline/petrol costs 5.32F a litre; diesel 3.64F a litre.

● **Bus**

There is a lack of public transport.

● **Hitchhiking**

Hitching is reported to be easy and widespread.

FERRIES

One- to three-ton boats which can be hauled over the rapids are used by the gold-seekers, the forest workers, and the rosewood establishments. There is a twice-a-month shipping service which calls at nearly all the coastal towns of Guyane. Ferries are free. Trips by motor-canoe (*pirogue*) up-river from Cayenne into the jungle can be arranged.

COMMUNICATIONS

● **Language**

French, with officials not usually speaking anything else. Créole is more commonly spoken.

● **Telecommunications**

International calls can be made direct to any country from any phone: dial 00 + country code. Public telephones are widely installed and used. They take phonecards of 50 or 120 units (35F or 80F), which can be bought at tobacconists, bookshops or supermarkets. How to use the phone is displayed in each phone booth in French, English, Italian and Spanish. To call the USA, 1 unit buys 3.6 secs, to EC 2.5 secs; discounts at weekends and between 1700 and 0700. The system is totally interconnected with the French system. International code for Guyane is 594.

MEDIA

● **Newspapers**

La Presse de la Guyane is the daily paper (circ 1,500). *France-Guyane-Antilles* is a weekly newspaper with a good information page for the tourist.

TOURIST INFORMATION

The French Government tourist offices generally have leaflets on Guyane; good sources of information are **La Maison de La France**, 8 ave de l'Opéra, 75001 Paris, T 42-96-10-23, and **Ministere des Départements et Territoires D'Outre-Mer**, 27 rue Oudinot, 75007 Paris, T 47-83-01-23. The latter publishes a comprehensive directory, *CAP'97*, in six European languages. Two specialist travel agents in Paris are **Havas Voyages** (also in Cayenne, see above), 26 ave de l'Opéra, 75001 Paris, T 40-41-80-00, and **Fleuves de Monde**, 122 rue d'Assac, 75006 Paris, T 42-04-25-92. The Cayenne tourism offices are at 12 rue Lalouette, Cayenne (Tx 910356, T 300900); Délégation Régionale, 10, rue L-Heder, 97307 Cayenne, T 31-84-91; Syndicat d'initiative de Cayenne, Jardin Botanique, PO Box 702, 97338 Cayenne, T 31-29-19; Syndicat d'Initiative Rémire-Montjoly, Mairie de Rémire, 97305 Rémire, T 35-41-10.

ACKNOWLEDGEMENTS

We are most grateful to Rachel Rogers for updating the Guianas section, and to the travellers listed at the end of the book.

Falkland Islands/ Islas Malvinas

In accordance with the practice suggested by the UN, we are calling the Islands by both their English and Spanish names.

The Falkland Islands/Islas Malvinas comprise about 420 islands in two groups: East Falkland (Isla Soledad) with its adjacent islands, about 2,600 square miles; and West Falkland (Gran Malvina), with its islands, about 2,100 square miles. Approximately 480 miles NE of Cape Horn, the Islands lie between latitudes 51° and 53° S and between longitudes 57° and 62° W. Nearly all land combat during the 1982 war was confined to the northern half of East Falkland; its southern peninsula of Lafonia, and West Falkland were little affected. The population in April 1996 was 2,221. According to the 1991 census, slightly less than two-thirds of the residents were Falklands-born; another quarter were born in the United Kingdom. Slightly more than a quarter live and work on sheep farms. During the past decade, land reform through sale and subdivision of traditional large stations has resulted in more broadly based local ownership of pastoral land.

Climate

Although the *Sunday Express* once referred to a mutton freezer in the Falklands as a 'Colonial Development project near the South Pole' (8 March 1953), the Islands are in the same latitude S as London is N. The climate is cool and oceanic, dominated by persistent westerly winds which average 16 knots. Long periods of calm are rare except in winter. Though not always inclement, weather is very changeable but temperatures vary relatively little. At Stanley the mean month temperature in summer (Jan/Feb) is 10°C and in winter (June/July) 3°C. Stanley's annual rainfall of about 600mm is slightly higher than London's. In the drier camp, outside Stanley, summer drought sometimes threatens local water supplies. Snowfall is rare although a dusting may occur at any time of the year. Spring, autumn and winter clothing, as used in the United Kingdom, is suitable.

Flora and fauna

The main islands are covered by acidic peaty soil of low fertility, though at higher elevations (over 500m) the peat gives way to stony and clay soils. Large areas of the major islands are covered by oceanic heathlands, consisting of White Grass, dwarf shrubs, Mountain Berry and Christmas Bush. These heathlands support little fauna, but where they are crossed by small streams the valleys are covered by rich grasslands which attract several species, among them Upland and Ruddy Headed Geese.

Tussac grass, which was common on the larger islands until the introduction of livestock farming, covers about 270 of the smaller islands. Tussac grass, which grows to 3m in height and has leaves up to 2m long, thrives in marine environments subject to sea spray and moisture laden atmospheres with a high salt content. It provides ideal nesting for birds: 46 of the 62 species which regularly breed on the islands use tussac grass as a nesting or feeding habitat.

There are few trees on the islands and only where these have been introduced and carefully cultivated at settlements such as Hill Cove.

Early history

Records of early voyages are ambiguous, but Dutchman Sebald de Weert made the first universally acknowledged sighting in 1598. The Englishman John Strong landed in 1690 and named the Falkland Sound for a British peer; this name was later applied to the entire group. The Islands acquired their French appellation, Iles Malouines, from 17th century seafarers from the channel port of St Malo. This in turn became the Spanish Islas Malvinas.

In 1764 France established a small colony of Acadians at Port Louis under Bougainville. 2 years later France sold the settlement to Spain, under which it became a military garrison and penal colony. At about the same time as France, Britain had built an outpost at Saunders Island, West Falkland, whose occupants Spain discovered and expelled in 1770. Restored in the following year after threat of war, the post was abandoned in 1774.

Deserted by Spain in 1811, during the South American wars of independence, the Islands lacked formal authority until 1820, when the United Provinces of the River Plate (later part of Argentina) raised their flag at Port Louis (Soledad). In 1831, a United States warship destroyed a promising colonization project under the auspices of a German-born merchant from Buenos Aires, who had arrested and imprisoned United States sealers operating in the area. After British warships expelled a token Buenos Aires force in 1833, the Islands experienced nearly 150 years of stability until April 1982, when Argentina invaded and occupied. Britain's counter-invasion recaptured the Islands by June of that year.

Economy

Since the declaration of a 150 nautical mile fisheries protection zone in 1986, the economy has been transformed. License fees from Asian, South American and European fleets exploiting the Islands'

squid, hake, and whiting have quadrupled Government revenue, to £15-20 million a year. Revenues began to fall in 1993 following Argentina issuing cut-price fishing licences in neighbouring waters and the Falkland Islands Government lowering the price of its own licences. Much of the revenue is being used to fund overdue improvement in education and infrastructure, as well as social expenditures for increased pensions. A new telephone system has been installed and a community school has been built. The housing stock has doubled since the 1982 war, roads have been improved and there are many more vehicles in use.

In 1995 Argentina and Britain signed an agreement to allow oil development in the disputed waters around the islands. Should oil be found in commercially viable quantities, further substantial transformation of the way of life could be expected.

Most of the camp, as the countryside is known locally, is devoted to sheep grazing. There are some 600,000 sheep, all of whose wool is exported to the United Kingdom.

Administration

The Islands' Constitution provides for a Governor, appointed from London, an Executive Council composed of appointed and elected members, and an elected Legislative Council.

Education

A Junior and Senior Community School in Stanley cater to the needs of town children and rural children who board in the School Hostel. Instruction to GCSE Level is available locally (compulsory to the age of 16), but higher education requires overseas travel, usually to Britain. Rural children receive attention from settlement instructors or travelling teachers. Radio is used to keep in contact with the more isolated farms.

STANLEY

The capital, Stanley, on East Falkland, is the major population centre. Its 1,700 residents live mostly in brightly-painted houses, many of which have corrugated iron roofs. Port Stanley, surrounded by rolling moorland, resembles parts of the Hebrides. The outer harbour of Port William is larger but less protected. East Cove, 30 miles SE of the capital, is the principal port for the new military installations at Mount Pleasant.

Places of interest and events The Museum at Britannia House, Ross Road West, merits a visit (Tues-Fri, 1030-1200, 1400-1600, also Wed, 1800-2000, Sun, 1000-1200). Mr John Smith, the curator, is knowledgeable on the Islands' maritime history. Government House, the Anglican Cathedral (most southerly in the world, built in 1890), and monuments commemorating the naval battle of 1914 and the 1982 liberation are also worth seeing. The public library has a good selection of books on travel and on flora and fauna; in the same building is a public swimming pool and some good gym machines, for public use after 1600. During the December holidays, the annual sports meeting at the race course attracts visitors from all over the Islands. The equally popular West and East Falkland sports, at the end of the shearing season in February or March, rotate among various settlements.

● **Accommodation & places to eat** *Upland Goose Hotel*, Ross Road, T 21455, F 21520, between £40-70 bed and breakfast depending on the room, evening meal £14.95; *Malvina House Hotel*, 3 Ross Road, T 21355, F 21357, similar prices; *Emma's Guest House*, Ross Road, T 21056, F 21573, from £30.50 bed and breakfast. Prices are pp and subject to change. Full meals at all three, with reservations rec at *Upland Goose* and *Malvina* (restaurant is smart with good food, book 36 hrs in advance). *Warrah Guest House*, John Street, T 21252, from £25 bed and breakfast; *Cay's*, bed and breakfast, £15 pp. Fish and chips and pizza at *Woodbine Cafe*, 29 Fitzroy Road, T 21102, closed Sun and Mon. *Monty's/Deano's* bistro, bar snacks on John Street, inc vegetarian menu; *Boathouse Café*, Ross Road, Mon-Fri 0930-1600; *Clayton's Bakery*, T 21273, Mon-Sat, 0730-1530; *Stanley Bakery*, T 22692, Mon-Fri, 0830-1530, Sat 0900-1230; *Waverley House Café*, open all day.

On Sea Lion Island: *Sea Lion Lodge*, T 32004, £50 full board. **At Port Howard:** *Port Howard Lodge*, T 42150, £49 full board. **On Pebble**
Island: *Pebble Island Hotel*, T 41097, £47.50 full board. Each lodge has a long wheelbase Land Rover for transport to the airstrip and points of interest nearby. The comfortable tourist lodges at Sea Lion Island, the most southerly inhabited island of the group (35 mins flight fom Port Stanley), and Pebble Island (40 mins flight) are good bases to view wildlife. Also on Pebble Island *Marble Mountain Shanty*, at NW of the island, T 41098, Mr R Evans, self-catering, £15/night and room for up to 4. It is 12 miles from the rest of the population so is peaceful with plenty of wildlife (3 types of penguin within 1/2 hr walk). Bring food and bedding, all else provided. Scenic Port Howard's lodge on West Falkland, offers excellent trout fishing, a small but interesting war museum, and an opportunity to see the operations of a traditional large sheep station. *Blue Beach Lodge*, San Carlos, East Falkland, £49 full board. *Carcass Island Cottages*, Mr and Mrs McGill, Ross Road East, T 41106, £25/night/cottage, both on West Falkland. Further self-catering at Fox Bay Village and Fox Bay West, prices from £7.50 pp/night to £25/group/night. Also *Salvador* (Gibraltar Station, East Falkland, T 31199/31193, F 31194), £10/night (adult), £5/night (child).

Camping is not encouraged on the islands; there is a very real risk of fire and of disturbance to wildlife.

● **Services**
Stanley has an excellent new civilian-military hospital. Dental services are also available. Post Office, Philatelic Bureau, library and some other Government services are in Town Hall, Ross Road. Other Government offices are in the nearby Secretariat. Cable and Wireless, Ross Road, operate overseas telephone, fax, telegraph and telex services. The islands' telephone system has direct dialling worldwide. There are some well-stocked stores, open Mon to Sat. The few pubs, the *Globe* near the public jetty, the *Rose*, on Dury St, the *Victory* on Philomel Hill, *Deano's* on Dean St, the *Stanley Arms* at W end of Stanley, John Biscoe Rd, and the *Ship* behind the *Upland Goose Hotel* are popular meeting places (open all day, except Sun only from 1200 to 1400, and 1900-2200).

● **National Tourism Bureau**
Falkland Islands Tourist Board (FITB), representative, John Tourist Board, Ross Road, Stanley, T (010500) 22215/22281, F 22619, will provide all information on holidays on the islands. Bookings for lodgings and for fishing, riding, Range Rover hire, tours, inter-island travel are handled by Stanley Services Ltd, Airport Road, Stanley, T 22622, F 22623, Tx 2438. See below under communications for the Falklands Islands Tourist Board's London Office.

● **Transport**

Rentals: The Falkland Islands Company, Stanley, rents Fiat Strada 4 x 4 cars for about £125/week, for road use only. Carol and Dave Eynon, *South Atlantic Marine Services*, PO Box 140, Stanley, T 21145, F 22674, offer adventure tourism, overland tours, boat trips, safaris and have a dive centre with deck recompression chamber (PADI courses to be introduced in 1997/98); Falkland Images (SAMS) produce videos and stills photographs for sale, plus the book *Beneath Falkland Waters* (due late 1997). Ian Bury on Davis Street rents Land Rovers for £30-50 a day. Insurance is extra from the Falkland Islands Company. The *Malvina House Hotel*, T 21355, Mel Lloyd, Swan Inlet (rec as good value, experienced driver, 8-seater vehicle) and Tony Smith, T 21027 (or try at Ian Bury's House), offer overland Land Rover excursions from Stanley. Boats may be hired from Sullivan Shipping, T 22626, or the FIC, T 27630.

OUTSIDE STANLEY

For wildlife enthusiasts, especially birders, the Islands are an exceptional destination. On arrival, visitors are given a guide to respecting the Falklands wildlife and its habitat, with a checklist of breeding birds and mammals. Best months to visit are October to March. Make allowance for unpredictable weather. Always wear or carry waterproof clothing; wear good boots and a peaked hat to protect the eyes from rain or hail. Outside Stanley, there is a major road to the airport at Mount Pleasant, but great care should nevertheless be taken on it. Roads connect Stanley with San Carlos (70 miles) and Goose Green (64 miles). On West Falkland a new road connects most of the settlements. Elsewhere, tracks require Land Rovers or motorbikes. Remember to phone farms in the camp for permission to drive across private land. Off-road driving in the boggy terrain is a skill not easily learned by short-term visitors. Near Stanley and a few farm settlements there are still unexploded mines, but hazardous areas are clearly marked and fenced. Visitors should *never* enter these areas, and should report suspicious objects to the police or military authorities in Stanley. Free minefield maps are available from the Bomb Disposal Office, Ross Road, Stanley. Ordnance Survey maps of the Islands are available from the Secretariat, £2.50 each for the 1:50,000 sheets; there is also a two-sheet, 1:250,000 map suitable for most purposes.

Travel outside the vicinity of Stanley and the road to Goose Green is mainly by air. The Falkland Islands Government Air Service (FIGAS) operates three Islander aircraft to farm settlements and settled outer islands according to bookings, seat availability, and weather. To book a seat, visitors should telephone FIGAS no later than the morning of the day before travelling; flight schedules are announced that evening on local radio (airfares are about £1 per minute for non-islanders, luggage limit 14 kg/30 lbs, high excess charge). FIGAS tickets are also available from Stanley Services Ltd, Airport Road, Stanley, T 22622. Regular service operates 7 days a week. Flights leave from Stanley Airport, three miles E of town on the Cape Pembroke peninsula.

Places of interest

Sparrow Cove, Kidney Cove, and adjacent areas, only a short distance across Stanley Harbour by boat and out into Port William, are good areas to see penguins and other wildlife; dolphins often follow in the wake of your boat near The Narrows. Gypsy Cove, walking distance from Stanley, features a colony of burrowing Magellanic penguins and other shorebirds. Leopard seals, elephant seals and the occasional killer whale visit the area. Observe minefield fences which prevent close inspection of the penguins (they are not unduly inhibiting, though). At Cape Pembroke, around the town airport and the renovated lighthouse one can see Gentoo penguins and ground-nesting birds such as dotterels, snipe, and Upland geese.

Of particular interest are the hulks of old sailing ships at Stanley and Darwin. Examples at Stanley are the *Jhelum* (built in 1839 for the East India Company) near Government House, the *Charles Cooper* (the last US sailing packet to sail out of New York Harbour; in the Islands since 1866), and the iron-built *Lady Elizabeth* at the far end of the harbour (228 ft long, with three masts still standing). A Maritime History Trail has been set up around

Port Stanley (self-guided with interpretive panels at key points, and guide book available at FITB; a book describing the Stanley wrecks is sold by the museum). At Darwin are the *Vicar of Bray* (last survivor of the California Gold Rush fleet), and another old iron ship, the *Garland*. Some of these hulks are still used for storage. There are interesting old French buildings and ruins at Port Louis (the road between Stanley and Port Louis is a boulder-strewn clay track, very tricky when wet).

Neil Rogers of New Brighton, Merseyside, has suggested the following walk: From the 'Beaver' hanger opposite 'Strathcarron', Ross Road W, walk past the various ships and monuments, along the harbour, up to the Falkland Islands Company offices. Here it is possible to walk onto the jetty and visit the after section of a 19th century sailing vessel that is still being used as a warehouse. Also below the jetty you will see a couple of 19th century Welsh colliers. From here go E until you reach B slip, used by the British Forces during the 1982 conflict. Carry on E, past the floating harbour and around the head of the bay to the iron barque *Lady Elizabeth*. At low tide it is possible to walk out to her. Follow the bay round and eventually you will come to various penguin rookeries and Gypsy Cove.

Volunteer Point, N of Stanley, is a wildlife sanctuary. It contains the only substantial nesting colony of King penguins in the Falklands. Gentoo penguins, Magellanic penguins, geese, ducks, and elephant seals are very tame and easily photographed. The sanctuary was closed to visitors in 1996 and 1997; after Oct 1997 enquiries should be made to Mr George Smith, at Johnson's Harbour, T 31398, or at the Tourist Board, or Stanley Services. An exceptional wildlife hike is along the N coast of East Falkland, from Seal Bay to Volunteer Point. Ask permission of the manager of Port Louis as well, and allow three to four days.

Battlefield visits, to some of the sites associated with the 1982 conflict, can be arranged.

Carcass Island and New Island

On Carcass Island the farm at Settlement Harbour is home to the McGills. The farm is surrounded by an arbour, alive with Black-crowned Night Herons. A group of Dusky Dolphins often play in the harbour. Patagonian Crested Ducks, with their deep wine-red eyes, can be seen spinning in courtship displays in the shallows while brilliant white male Kelp Geese and their less conspicuous female partners pick their way along the shore. Like the other islands, Carcass is an idyllic place to explore on foot; the long white beaches and colonies of penguins and albatrosses, Upland Geese grazing in the fields and Military Starlings, with their crimson breasts, marching among the tussock. Anyone who pauses will soon be befriended by the small brown tussock bird, indigenous to the Falklands. There are lovely views to West Falkland.

The tussock grass in the southern sector of New Island is home to one of the largest colonies of Prions; it is magical at nightfall when the prions return in huge, cackling, flocks to feed their young. There is also a colony of Black-browed Albatrosses. These birds once seen are never forgotten, overwhelmingly graceful in flight, endearingly serene on the nest or in courtship, and amazingly comical when landing. Adjacent to the albatrosses there is a colony of Rockhopper Penguins. These aptly named birds are often considered the punks of the penguin world with erect yellow crests. Both of these species are at present declining: Rockhoppers are being considered for the globally threatened list; and Black-browed Albatross populations are being closely monitored. It is a privilege and incredibly rewarding to sit quietly near the edge of one of these colonies.

Kim Crosbie, Scott Polar Research Institute, Cambridge.

Sea Lion Island in the SE is a delightful place to explore and relax. Throughout the austral summer the lodge, run by David and Pat Gray, accommodates a maximum of 15 visitors. Many Southern Sea Lions breed on the beaches; Southern Elephant Seals also breed here. A pod of Orca whales is seen almost daily cruising the kelpbeds in search of an unsuspecting meal. The island also has magnificent birdlife: Gentoo, Magellanic and Rockhopper Penguins. Giant Petrels (known locally as 'stinkers'), King Cormorants, the incredible flightless Steamer Duck, Black-crowned Night Herons, the friendly Tussock Bird, Oystercatcher (Magellanic and Black) and the rare Striated Caracara.

The smaller islands off West Falkland, such as Carcass and New Island, are the most spectacular and attractive for wildlife and scenery. The southern half of New Island, on the extreme W of the archipelago, is run as a nature reserve by Ian and Maria Strange. The northern half, owned by Tony and Annie Chater, has a small sheep farm. The island has a grass airstrip and is served by FIGAS on flights limited to three passengers (owing to the length of the strip). There are basic self-catering facilities on the island and enquiries should be addressed to Ian and Maria Strange, Snake Hill, Stanley, T 21185, F 21186; on New Island 42017. Carcass can be visited more easily and has two self-catering cottages (see above). Saunders Island, besides a representative sample of wildlife, contains the ruins of the 18th century British outpost at Port Egmont and an accessible albatross colony.

Fishing Sea-trout fishing is excellent on the islands. The season runs from 1 September to 30 April. For information in the UK on fishing in the Falklands/Malvinas, contact Go Fishing Falklands (Maggi Smit), 6 Barons Gate, 33/35 Rothschilds Road, Chiswick, London W4 5HT, T 0181-742 3700, F 0181-994 7388; or Sport Elite Tours (J A Valdes Scott), Woodwalls House, Corscombe, Dorchester, DT2 0NT, England, T (0935) 891477, F (0935) 891797.

INFORMATION FOR TRAVELLERS

BEFORE TRAVELLING

● **Entry requirements**

All travellers must have full passports to visit the Falkland Islands/Islas Malvinas. Generally, visa requirements are the same as for the UK, but at present Argentine citizens are not permitted to visit unless they have relatives on the islands. If going to the islands from Argentina via Chile, check entry procedures. All visitors require a 4-month visitor permit, normally provided on arrival upon presentation of a return ticket. Visitors are also asked to have pre-booked accommodation and sufficient funds to cover their stay. Work permits are not available. Do not stay beyond the valid period of your visa without applying to the Immigration Office for an extension.

● **Currency**

The local £ is on a par with sterling. Local notes and coins. UK notes and coins are (except the new small 10p and 5p, Falkland Island coins are the old larger ones) also legal tender. Currency from Ascension Island, where the RAF Tri-Star stops for refueling, or Santa Helena, is not accepted, nor are Falklands notes or coins legal in the United Kingdom. Foreign currency may be changed at Standard Chartered Bank, Ross Road, Stanley.

● **Cost of living**

About the same as in Britain. Freight adds to the price of imported groceries. Since the construction of a hydroponic market garden near Stanley, fresh produce such as lettuce, tomatoes and aubergines are available year-round. Potatoes and other vegetables are grown in gardens and conservatories for household use, but are not readily purchased.

There is no value-added tax; only tobacco, wine, spirits and beer pay import duty. Small luxury goods on which freight is correspondingly low are sometimes cheaper than in the UK. Colour slide film, which can be scarce, should be brought from outside the islands.

● **Postal services**

Since the opening of Mount Pleasant, there is direct and dependable air mail service from the United Kingdom. Heavy parcels come by sea from the UK 4 or 5 times a year. Inter-island mail service is carried out by FIGAS and by the vessels *Tamar* (see below) and *Forrest*.

GETTING THERE

The RAF usually operates two Tri-Star flights a week from Brize Norton, Oxfordshire, to Mount Pleasant airport (every Mon and most Thur, returning to UK every Wed and most Sat). The fare is £2,180 return, but there are also cheaper APEX (£1,340) and group rates. Falkland Islands residents receive a discount (£940). Confirm your seat 12 hrs before departure to avoid disappointment from overbooking or lost reservations. Flight time is 18 hrs, but diversions to Montevideo owing to bad weather are not uncommon. Enquiries about passages can be addressed to Miss Jenny Smith, Falkland Islands Government London Office, Falkland House, 14 Broadway, Westminster, London SW1H 0BH, T 0171-222 2542, F 222 2375. The Falkland Islands Tourist Board (same address and phone number) answers enquiries about the islands themselves and gives information on organized tours.

Aerovias DAP of Chile operate a weekly schedule Santiago-Punta Arenas-Stanley, departing Wed, arriving in Stanley at 1815, returning from Stanley about 1530 on Thur. These flights connect with British Airways' London-Santiago service (overnight stop on Stanley-Santiago-London route). The plane is a Boeing 707; return fares are Santiago-Stanley US$1,580 business, US$980 economy, US$830 economy excursion; Punta Arenas-Stanley US$944, US$600, US$560 respectively, all one way. Booking offices: Aerovías DAP, O'Higgins 899, Punta Arenas, T (56-61) 243958/223340, F 221693; Falkland Islands Co, Crozier Place, Stanley, T (500) 27633, F 27603, or 94a Whitechapel High St, London E1 7RH, T (0171) 377 0566, F 377 6194 (all 3 offices accept credit cards: Visa, Mastercard, Eurocard).

MV *Tamar FI*, of Byron Marine Ltd, Stanley, T 22245 makes unscheduled sailings to Punta Arenas, £125 single, 2 cabins, 2 passengers per cabin, cramped though the ship is, 'relatively modern and a good sea-goer'. *Tamar* will take passengers around the islands.

ON ARRIVAL

● **Airport information**
Mount Pleasant, 35 miles from Stanley, is built to international specifications. C and M Travel, James Street, Stanley, T 21468, transports passengers and luggage to and from the capital for £12 single. Departing passengers should make reservations. Also, Lowes Taxi, T 21381, for transport between Stanley and the airport, and within Stanley (Mon-Fri, 0800-2000), and Ben's Taxi, Ross Road East, T 21437.

SOUTH GEORGIA

South Georgia, in latitude 54½° S and longitude 36° to 38° W, has an area of about 3,755 square km, and a small transient population of soldiers and British Antarctic Survey scientists. During the summer months, tourists may sometimes book a passage on a Royal Fleet Auxiliary vessel at Stanley for £520 return, but weather conditions sometimes prevent landings. Intending visitors must submit a request through the Commissioner in Stanley. The Island was briefly occupied by Argentina in April 1982 (21 days).

South Georgia is a mass of high, snow-covered mountains and glaciers. Between 1951 and 1980 at King Edward Point, at sea level, snow fell an average of nearly 200 days per annum, but the coastal area is free from snow and partially covered by vegetation in summer. Wildlife consists of most of the same species found in the Falklands, but in much larger numbers. Reindeer, introduced by Norwegian whalers in 1909, have flourished. Other points of interest are seven abandoned whaling stations, the little white church, and many wrecks. A South Georgia Whaling Museum has been established at Grytviken. If it is unmanned access may be obtained from the Magistrate (Garrison Commander) at King Edward Point, 1 km away. The museum has a display of artefacts, photographs and other items about the old Antarctic whaling and sealing industry. (Information is available from South Georgia Whaling Museum, Mr Bob Burton, 80 Caxton End, Eltisley, Huntingdon, UK, PE19 4TJ, T +44-1480- 880- 259, F 880-539.) Local administration of South Georgia is by the Magistrate, who also runs the island's post office with its distinctive stamps.

ANTARCTICA

Antarctica, the 5th largest continent, is 99.6% covered with perpetual ice. Although very inaccessible, approximately 8,000 tourists visit annually and it is well known for extraordinary scenery, wildlife, scientific stations, and historic sites. The weather may also be spectacularly severe, thus visits are confined to the brief summer. Presently 18 countries operate 42 scientific stations with wintering personnel there, and about a dozen summer stations also function. A wintering population of about 1,200 lives in a continent larger than Europe. These governmental stations are expensive to maintain thus, with only minor exceptions, they make no provision for visitors not connected with their work.

Governance of Antarctica is principally through the Antarctic Treaty (1959) signed by all countries operating there (43 countries were parties to the Treaty in 1997, these represent about 75% of the Earth's population). Most visitors will be affected by several provisions of the Treaty, in particular those of the Environmental Protocol made in Madrid in 1992. Seven countries have territorial claims over parts of Antarctica and three of these overlap (Antártida Argentina, British Antarctic Territory, and Territorio Chileno Antártico); the Treaty has neutralized these with provision of free access to citizens of contracting states. Some display of sovereignty is legitimate; many stations operate a Post Office where philatelic items and various souvenirs are sold.

The region S of South America is the most accessible part of the Antarctic, therefore over half the scientific stations are there and on adjacent islands. Fortuitously it is one of the most spectacular areas with many mountains, glaciers and fjords closely approachable by sea. One ice-breaker, other large ships, several private yachts, and an air company carry passengers there every austral summer. Three ports are used: Stanley (Falkland Islands/Malvinas), Punta Arenas (Chile), and Ushuaia (Argentina). Vessels sailing from one may return to another or go farther to South Africa, New Zealand, or Australia. Most are fully booked well in advance by luxury class passengers but sometimes late opportunistic vacancies can be secured by local agencies (on the basis that any vacant cabin is a loss). During the 1996-97 austral summer 18 passenger vessels made several voyages each to Antarctica carrying an average of about 100 tourists.

Voyages from South America and the Falkland Islands involve at least 2 days each way, crossing the Drake Passage where sea conditions may be very uncomfortable. No guarantee of landings, views or wildlife is possible and delays due to storms are not exceptional. Conversely, on a brilliant day, some of the most spectacular sights and wildlife anywhere can be seen. All visitors should be well prepared for adverse conditions with warm clothing, windproofs and waterproofs, and good boots for wet landings. Weather and state of the sea can change quickly without warning.

In 1991 the International Association of Antarctica Tour Operators was formed (contact Mr Darrel Schoeling, International Association of Antarctica Tour Operators, 111 East 14th St, Suite 110, New York, United States, 10003; T +1 212 460-8715, F +1 212 529-8684) which represents the majority of companies and can provide details of most Antarctic voyages planned during an austral summer (annual variation of these is great). Many vessels have a principal contractor and a number of other companies bring smaller groups, thus it is advantageous to contact the principal. Clipper Voyages, Albany House, Suite 404, 324/326 Regent St, London, W1R 5AA, T 0171 436 2931, has a 122-passenger expedition cruise ship which sails to Antarctica. Cruises often also visit South Georgia and the Falkland Islands. Adventure Network International (Canon House, 27 London End, Beaconsfield, Buckinghamshire, United Kingdom, HP9 2HN; T +44 1494 671808, F 671725), provides commercial flights landing in Antarctica which depart from Punta Arenas where there is a local office (935 Arauco, Punta Arenas,

Chile; T +56 61 247735, F 226167). Wheeled aircraft fly as far as a camp at Patriot Hills (80° 19'S, 81° 20'W) whence ski-aircraft proceed to the South Pole, vicinity of Vinson Massif (4,897m, Antarctica's highest peak), and elsewhere. Tickets start at about US$8,000. 1 day overflights are operated only by *Qantas* from Australia. More such flights are expected to operate in the future.

More opportunistic travel is possible with certain private yachts which have carried passengers for several summers. These are not coordinated but inquiries on the waterside of the ports listed may secure transport. Similarly opportunities to travel with the Argentine or Chilean navy occur but are virtually impossible to arrange other than in Ushuaia or Punta Arenas. Neither navy encourages passengers so your only chance is by approaching the captain of the vessel. No advance booking, fares about US$100 pp per day. Levels of comfort and prices are usually much lower than for the cruise ships. Many tourist ships and some yachts also visit South Georgia; there are other possibilities for reaching this Antarctic island from the Falkland Islands/Islas Malvinas.

RK Headland, Scott Polar Research Institute, Cambridge.

Section 4

Rounding up

ACKNOWLEDGEMENTS

We are very grateful to all travellers who have written to us over the last year. M Addis, Gooambat, Australia (Per, Bol, Chi); Peter Aeschlimann, Neukirch, Switzerland (Per, Bol, Par, Bra); Jose Nereu Afonso da Siva, São Paulo, Brazil (Bra, Bol, Per, Chi); Lucy Airey and Stephen Jefferson, Keswick, UK (Chi, Bol); Lisbeth Allemann, Balsthal, Switzerland (Ecu); Kurt Allenspach, Kleinvongen, Switzerland (Ven); Brigid Ammerschlaeger, Schorndorf, Germany (Per); Lillemor Andersson, Gothenburg, Sweden (Chi); Katja Andreas and Graf Hartl , Graz, Austria (Bra, Per, Ecu.Chi, Bol, Arg); Jo Andrere, (Arg); Belinda Andrews, Bradford on Avon, UK (Arg); Rhud Arazi, Hshiva, Israel (Ecu); Heidrun Arnold, Berlin, Germany (Bra); Barbara Augenstein and Ronald Krause, Dennach, Germany (Bol, Per); Gilad Avni, Israel, (Bol, Chi); Yamir Avraham and Helga Noorman, Israel and The Netherlands (Col).

Vivienne and Peter Baker, Melbourne, Australia (Per); Ute Balmacedo, Unna, Germany (Per); Bernhard Balmer, Bern, Switzerland (Per, Chi, Bol, Arg); Katie Barefoot, Lebanon, USA (Ecu); Jody Barnes and Patrick Teahan, Wellington, New Zealand (Ecu); Dom Barry, Grantham, UK (Bol, Ecu, Par, Per, Uru); Corrado Barrera, Asti, Italy (Bol); Didier Bauer, Jona, Switzerland (Per); J P Beaufils, Sommières, France (Per); Gesine Belser, Nurnberg, Germany (Arg); Keith Bennett, Cambridge, UK (Arg, Chi, Uru); Lucas Bergmans, London, England (Chi, Bol, Per); Lucas Bergmans, Chile (Chi); Robin Berman, Yosemite, California, USA (Bol, Per); Antje Bernhardt and Dr Steffen Heublein, Berlin, Germany (Bol, Ecu, Per); Arne Bertelsen, Vejie, Denmark (Ecu); Mrs

Consuelo Beumer, Maarssen, The Netherlands (Ven); Brady Binstadt, Santiago, Chile (Chi); Siri Birgen and Dag Hakon Hellevik, Rykkinn, Norway (Per, Col); Annette Bjornsen and Niels Ellerrog, Morvd, Denmark (Ven, Ecu); David Block, Ithaca, USA (Bol); Danny Bohni, Buthken, Switzerland (Bra); Jef and Bigouzi Boisson, Paris, France (Arg, Bol, Per); Kristian Bollerup, Copenhagen, Denmark (Ecu, Per, Bol, Chi, Arg); Wolfgang Bonaventura, Heidelberg, Germany (Col, Per, Ecu); Marcela Bonilla, Bogota, Colombia (Bol, Arg, Chi); Anne Bonwit and Susie Barnes, Brighton, England (Arg); Alistair Bool, Surrey, UK (Arg, Chi, Bra, Per, Ecu, Col); Willem Boom and Annette Valk, Rotterdam, Holland (Arg, Chi); Bibi van den Bos, Amsterdam. The Netherlands (Bol); Patrixia Bossi, Merida, Venezuela (Ven); Barnabas Bosshart, Alcantara, Brazil (Bra); Paul Bouwman, Engadine, Australia (Ecu, Per, Chi); Miriam & Albert Bouwmans, Feiderdorp, Netherlands (Per); Athel Cornish-Bowden, france (Chi); David and Susan Brady, Leeds, UK (Arg, Chi, Uru, Bra, Ven, Col, Ecu, Bol); Katja Breitenbucher, Schwetzingen, Germany (Chi); Kathrin Breuer and Martin Hoedt, Odenthal, Germany (Bra); John Brewer, USA (Ecu); Nick Britton and Michael Shanahan, St Helier, Jersey (Bol, Ecu, Per); Barbara Broeckelmann and Andreas Togge, Hannover, Germany (Ecu, Per); Jeanette Brooks, Glasgow, Scotland (Arg, Bol, Chi, Per); Jurg Buhler and Christine Blauer, Winterthur, Switzerland (Bol, Col, Per); Lane Buie, Buenos Aires, Argentina (Chi); Werner Bull, Salzburg, Austria (Per); Thomas Burg, Wiesbaden, Germany (Ecu); Werner Burkner, Wurzburg, Germany (Ven); Carol Burman, Sorsele, Sweden (Bol); Ralf Buschendorf, Goslar, Germany (Chi, Bra); Dirk Büttner, Berlin, Germany (Ecu); Yvonne Byman and Bas Geerts, Giekeek, The Netherlands (Arg, Bra, Bol, Chi, Col, Ecu, Per, Uru).

Lucy Cadbury, Cambridge, UK (Ecu); Ann Carroll, Freedom, USA (Per); Ronald Carter, Lima, Peru (Per); Karen Chapman, Tunbridge Wells, England (Bol, Bra, Chi, Per); Louis Chavance, Las Vegas, USA (Bol, Bra, Chi); Ian Coker, Cochabamba, Bolivia (Bol); Richard Collyer-Hamlin, London, UK (Chi); Marriame Considine, Edimauloree, France (Chi); Paul Cowling (Ven); Paul Cowling and Philippa Peel, Plymouth and Sheffield, UK (Ven); Alyson Cox and Michael Lutz, Washington, UK (Per); Niels Crama, Rotterdam, The Netherlands (Ecu, Per); Michael Crill and Monette Stephens, Santa Barbara, USA (Arg, Bol, Chi, Per); Glynis Crown and Charles Jeannin, N Ireland and Switzerland (Bol, Ecu, Per).

Thibaut d'Argoeuves and Jane Pares, Norfolk, UK (Arg, Chi); Jorg Danzenbacher, Putzbrunn, Germany (Arg, Bol, Chi, Ecu, Per, Uru); Patricia Davico, Oregon, USA (Ecu, Per); Tom Davies, Wha Katane, New Zealand (Bol, Chi, Per); Mck Day, Wivenhoe, UK (Bra, Par); David Dearhorn, Livermorr, USA (Bol); Alex Decker, Vienna, Austria (Bol); Tricia Deering and Tim Gorman, Prague, Czech Republic (Chi); Alexandrine Délèze, Nyon, Switzerland (Bra); Gaston Delgadillo, Sucre, Bolivia (Bol); Neil Dempsey, Perth, Australia (Ecu, Per, Ven); Albert Dempster, Seoul, South Korea (Bra); Denise and Dennis , Surrey, Canada (Bol); Carmen Diamantis, Muehlheim, Germany (Chi); Carmen Diamantis, Muehlheim, Germany (Chi); Tchau Dina (Bra); J W Dixon, London, UK (Bra, Chi, Uru); Alexandra Dobbs, Boulogne, France (Bol, Chi); Pierine Dodi, Chambery, France (Bol, Chi, Ecu, Per); Neil Donovan, Ballyporeen, Ireland (Arg, Bol, Bra, Chi, Par, Per, Uru); Gerdine wan den Dool and Jo Derkz, Leiden, The Netherlands (Ecu); Shlomi Doron, Ramat-Hasharon, Israel (Chi); Jon Dreyer, California, USA (Arg, Bra, Chi, Uru, Ven); Jon Dreyer, Mill Valley, USA (Bol, Bra, Per, Ven); Audrey and Jack Duchesne, Quebec, Canada (Guy); Daniel Duenser, Nueziders, Austria (Ecu); Marianne Dume, Rodgan, Germany (Bra, Chi, Par).

Matt Ebiner and Susan Almanza, Covina, USA (Arg, Bol, Bra); Eva Ekelund and Sinikka Aahtila, Stockholm and Jarfalla, Sweden (Ecu, Ven); James Evans and Eleanor Durie, Richmond, Surrey, UK (Ecu, Per); Raquel and Tom Evenou, Merida, Venezuela (Ven); Jan-Willem Evers, Rotterdam, Netherlands (Ecu, Col).

Elad Faltin, Israel (Col); Jack Farnsworth, London, UK (Ven); Paul Fässler, Pohlheim-Giessen, Germany (Bol, Col, Chi, Ecu, Per, Ven); Matthias Fehrenbach, Immedstaad, Germany (Bra, Col, Ecu, Par, Per); Matthias Fehrenbach, Spiegelberg, Germany (Bol, Chi, Col, Ecu, Per); Alain Fenart, Schwellbrunn, Switzerland (Ecu, Per); Jim Fenton, Los Angeles, USA (Bol); Christine Ferrario, Arbon, Switzerland (Ecu); Chris Fetto, St Albans, UK (Chi); Wiltrud Fischer and Philipp Jaesche, Goldronach, Germany (Ven); J Flannigan, USA (Chi); Edith Fohlinger, Karlsruhe, Germany (Per); Edith Fohlinger, Karlsruhe, Germany (Per); Barbara Forster, Erlach, Switzerland (Bol, Chi, Ecu, Per); Will Fox, Narberth, USA (Bol); Mr and Mrs Frank Systilo, Colorado Springs, USA (Ecu); Patrick Franke and Stefanie Ehling, Berlin, Germany (Arg); Emil and Renate Frehner, Herisau, Switzerland (Bol, Ecu, Per); Emil and Renate Frehner, Trogen, Switzerland (Arg, Chi); Bente Fremmerlid, Skodje, Norway (Per); Daniel Frens, Nyon, Switzerland (Bra); Filip Frimout, Gent, Belgium (Col, Ecu, Per); Oliver Fuchs and Sebastian Ladendorf, Ditzingen, Germany (Arg); Oliver Fuchs, Kempen, Germany (Chi); Ian Fuller, UK (Arg ,Chi, Per).

Marion Gaa, Vienna, Austria (Bol, Ecu); Eileen Gallagher, Chicago, USA (Bol, Par, Per); Suzanne Gasster, Grand Rapids, USA (Chi); Tim Gaunt (Chi); Erin Gemar, Gilroy, USA (Col, Chi); Luisa Georgov, Newark, USA (Ecu); John Gerstenberg, San Diego, USA (Arg); Theodor Gevert, Santana de Parnaiba, Brazil (Arg, Bol, Bra); Matiecke van der Gias, Utrecht, The Netherlands (Arg, Bra, Par); Dr Klaus Gierhake, Giessen, Germany (Arg, Bol, Chi, Par); Mark Gillard, Wokingham, UK (Bra); Alex van Ginkel, Amsterdam, The Netherlands (Ecu); Laurie Goering, Rio de Janeiro, Brazil (Bra); Dori Goldfard and Jeffrey Maggard, Sarasota, USA (Arg, Bra, Per); Shiry Goldberg, Ramat-Efal, Israel (Ecu); Kevin Golden, Spokane, WA, USA (Per); Michael Gonin, Canberra, Australia (Chi, Par); Jorge C Gordillo, Chile (Chi); Daniel Gordon, Santiago, Chile (Col, Ecu); Elliot Gotkine, London (Arg, Bol, Chi, Per, Uru, Ven); Kerstin Gotthardt, Freiburg, Germany (Per, Ecu); Pam Graff, Antwerp, Belgium (Ven); James Green, West Palm Beach, USA (Arg, Chi); Ralph Griese, Esslingen, Germany (Bra, Col, Per, Ven); Wolfgang Grubar, Babenshum, Germany (Ecu); Christian Guenat, Quito, Ecuador (Chi); William Guerrant, Albuquerque, USA (Arg, Bol, Chi, Ecu, Per, Uru); Jaime Guezado, Quebec, Canada (Ecu); David Guilfoyte, Gossau, Switzerland (Chi).

Klaus Haas, Bruckobel, Germany (Ecu); Siegfried Haberl, Los Angeles, Chile (Arg, Chi); Sarah Haggard, Montreal, Canada (Ecu); Marko Halla, Helsinki, Finland (Chi); Stuart Hamilton, Montevideo (Arg, Uru); Rhonda Hankins, Longview, USA (Arg, Chi, Fal); Kirsten Hannam and Nicole Brand, Victoria, Canada (Bol, Ecu, Per); Thomas & Christina Hansen, Denmark (Bol, Ecu); Douglas Hardy, Amherst, USA (Arg); David Hardcastle, Osford, UK (Per); Bernd Harle and Bernd Riegger, Salem, Germany (Arg, Bol, Bra); Steve Harris and Claire Bonnet, London, UK (Per); Sharon Harvey, Grasby, UK (Arg, Bra, Chi, Per); Ingrid Hauptmann, Tutzing, Germany (Arg, Chi); Marc Heim, Nyon, Switzerland (Bol, Chi, Col, Ecu, Per); Inge Heiurichsmeyer and Oliver Graj, Saarbeucken, Germany (Bol, Ecu, Chi); Freek Hemmings and Mrieke Assandelft, Bennebroek, The Netherlands (Ecu, Per); Clive Henman, Crawley, UK (Arg, Bol, Bra, Chi, Per); Sioibhan Hennessey, Urlingford, Ireland (Ecu, Chi); Lothar Herb, Singen, Germany (Ecu, Col); Sabine Herrmann, Berlin, Germany (Ecu); Steffen Heublien and Anlje Bernhorott, Berlin, Germany (Bol, Chi); W R Heyer, Woodside, USA (Per); Ms E S Higgins, Cambridge, UK (Ecu, Per, Ven); Jesper Hjorth, Copenhagen, Denmark (Ven); Anna Hogdahl and Lars Jonsson, Bjorkliden, Sweden (Ecu); Markus Holjchneider, Frankfurt, Germany (Col , Ecu, Ven); Ferdinand Höng, Quito, Ecuador (Ecu); Susanne Hong, Germany (Bra, Per); Dr Bernhard Hosius, Reckerhausen, Germany (Bol, Bra); Paul Howles, Hawthorndene, Australia (Arg, Bra, Par); Thomas Hugi, Oberwil, Switzerland (Arg, Bol, Ecu, Per); Wolfgang Huhn, Tübingen, Germany (Chi, Per); René Huser, Winterthur, Switzerland (Col); Martin Hutchings, California, USA (Guy); Regina Hutteri, Weinfelden, Switzerland (Col); Inon and Daphna, Ramut Gan, Israel (Chi, Per); Anders Jacobson and Lasse Hansen, Stourins, Denmark (Ecu,Per).

Daniel James and Partners, Huanchaco, Peru (Per); Jannette and Marcel , The Hague, Netherlands (Chi); Gonnie Janssens and Peter Peeters, Vught, The Netherlands (Bol, Per); Cathy Jensen de Sánchez, Mérida, Venezuela (Ven); Guillaume Johan, Sion, Switzerland (Bra, Col, Ven); Henk and Nita de Jong, The Netherlands (Ecu); Depoortere Joris, De Panne, Belgium (Ven); Elena Jurado, Ecuador (Ecu); Hans-Jurgen Walter, Berlin, Germany (Chi); Alan Juszyuski, Rehovot, Israel (Chi, Col, Ecu, Per).

Sebastian Kanzpw, Munich, Germany (Per); Wendy Kerselaers (Chi); Wendy Kerselaas, Betehorn, Belgium (Chi); Susanne Kienbaum, Berlin, Germany (Chi, Arg); John Killick, Steyning, UK (Per, Bol, Par, Arg); Dr J Kleinwachter, Am Wetzelsberg, Germany (Ecu); Dr J Koch and Brigit Glockle, Stuttgart, Germany (Chi, Arg); Eric Koehler, Paris, France (Chi); Mette Kold, Felding, Denmark (Ecu); Thomas Kolodzie, Hamburg, Germany (Bra); Martin Kolp, Dübendorf, Switzerland (Ecu); Peter Korner, Osterholz-Scharmbeck, Germany (Chi, Arg); Thomas Koodzn, Hamburg, Germany (Bra); Mart Kopp, Stuttgart, Germany (Col); Margaret Kostaszuk, Boston, USA (Ven); Jonas Krat, (Ven); Stefan Kraus, Feldleirchen-Westerham, Germany (Chi); Viola Krebs, Geneva, Switzerland (Bra); Tania Krupitza, Wellington, New Zealand (Ecu); Thomas Krusekamp, Hamburg, Germany (Arg); Claus Krygell, Copenhagen, Denmark (Arg, Bol, Bra, Chi, Ecu, Par, Per, Uru); Philipp Kuhn, Cordoba, Argentina (Arg); Kerstin Kuye, Wilnsohrf, Germany (Bra); Ales Kyzecka, Prague, Czech Republic (Bra).

Bernd Lamatsch, Marly, Switzerland (Bra); Peter Lambert, Perth, Australia (Chi); Sophie Lambin, London, UK (Col); Gert van Lancker and Sandra van Heyste, Mechelen and Vilvoorde, Belgium (Ecu, Chi, Arg, Per); Andreas Lasschuit bei Blume, Berlin, Germany (Bol, Par, Bra); Eileen and Andy Lattimore, Richmond, UK (Bra, Arg); Conny Leib, Mettmann, Germany (Arg); Rochus Leinert, Germany (Chi); Daniel Leiser and Nicole Zimmerli, Langnau, Switzerland (Ven, Bol, Bra, Ecu, Per); Antony Lempert, Leeds, UK (Ven, Ecu, Bol, Per, Chi); Gerard Lentiez, Paris, France (Chi); June Lewis, Birchington, UK (Per); Michael Lewis, Swanley, UK (Bol, Arg); Ayelet Libi Zabicky, Kfar Adumim, Israel (Col); Barry Lloyd, Newcastle upon Tyne. UK (Bra); Vivien Lo and Philipp Nimmerman, Frankfurt, Germany (Arg, Bra); Chuck Locherand Nancy Blackstock, Richmond, USA (Ven, Gui); Wilfred Lohmar, Los Angeles, Chile (Chi); Agnes and Antoine Lorgnier, Le Pecq, France (Chi); Markus Low, New York, USA (Ecu); V Lucy (Arg); Christine Luehrs, Bensee, Germany (Bra, Ven); Maya-Lusa Outinen, Helsinki, Finland (Chi, Arg); Daniel Lutz, Gossau, Switzerland (Chi, Col, Ecu, Per, Ven).

Sara Machlin, (Chi, Arg); Peter MacMurdie, London, UK (Ecu, Per); Ted Madden, St Paul, USA (Ecu); Franz Magerl, Santiago, Chile (Chi); Cedric Magnin, Geneva, Switzerland (Per, Col); Gur Mainzer, Haifa, Israel (Chi, Per); Robert Manley, Cincinnati, USA (Bra, Guy, Col); Mark Mann, London, UK (Ecu); Olly Del Mar, Basingstoke, UK (Per, Chi, Ecu, Bol, Par); Serge Marti and Clare Toms, Huenibach, Switzerland & Penzance, UK (Per); Jane Martin, La Paz, Bolivia (Bol); Bob Masters, London, UK (Ven); Brent Matsuda,

Vancouver, Canada (Per, Bol, Ecu, Col); Bernard Matz, Karlsruhe, Germany (Bol, Arg); Sue Maule, Poulsbo, WA USA (Chi, Bol); Agathe Mauron, Fribourg, Switzerland (Chi, Arg, Bra); Burkard May, Bergeheinfeld, Germany (Uru, Bra, Arg, Bol); Charles Mays, Ft Worth, USA (Per); Scott McCartney, Hamish Moline, Ollie Alcock and Nick Roberts, Sydney, Australia (Arg, Bol, Bra, Chi); Sara McFall, Oxford, UK (Chi); Ross McKean, Sevenoaks, UK (Bol, Per); Alasdair McLoed, Stirling, UKi (Ven, Col, Ecu, Per, Chi); Elizabeth Mcneil, Lisa Savage & Heide Getrost, Ozford, New Zealand (Ecu); Anne Meadows and Daniel Buck, New York, USA (Per, Bol, Arg); Thomas Meffert, Aachen, Germany (Ecu); Thomas Meier, Esmeraldas, Ecuador (Ecu); Ortrun Meinhard, Stuttgart, Germany (Chi, Bol, Per); Rolf Meier, Zug, Switzerland (Ecu); Oliver Meiser, Pfullingen, Germany (Chi, Bra); Chris Meyer, Hayden Lake, Idaho USA (Bol); Lee Min Min, Hong Kong (Bol); Tom Mindt, Winterthur, Switzerland (Chi, Arg, Uru, Par); Mattias Mohlin and Marianne Korkko, Vinslov, Sweden (Chi, Per, Bol); Gabriella Molnar and Csaba Korsos, Grand Cayman (Bol, Chi, Per); Alain Moretti, Geneva, Switzerland (Ecu); Harry Morgan, Dusseldorf, Germany (Arg); Harry Morgan, Dusseldorf, Germany (Arg); Thomas Moser, Schaffhausen, Switzerland (Per); Thomas Moser, Schaffhausen, Switzerland (Per); Yossi Mossel and Rami Rosenbaum, Ratanana, Israel (Bol, Per, Ecu, Col); Jean-Marc Motchane, Geneva, Switzerland (Uru); Caroline Muchlerlonie, Stuttgart, Germany (Chi, Bol, Per); Murcus Müller, Tübingen, Germany (Per, Bol, Arg, Par, Uru, Bra); J Muller-Seebeck, Berlin, Germany (Bol, Chi, Arg); Franziska Müller, Ittigen, Switzerland (Ecu); James Musters and Simon Cleary, UK (Bra, Per); Heiner Muth, Freiburg, Germany (Chi, Arg, Bol).

Klaus Nahr, Geretsried, Germany (Ven); Thomas Nauer, Sebwyz, Switzerland (Ecu, Col); Matthias Neubauer, Wurzburg, Germany (Chi, Bol); Ruth Neumaier, Schonach, Germany (Ecu); Catherine Newman, Exeter, UK (Ven); Catherine Newman, Exeter, UK (Ven); Alexander van Nierop, Leiden, The Netherlands (Chi); Bettina Nielsen and Dina Vejling, Denmark (Ven, Per, Ecu); Michael and Nir Nin-Nin, Haifa, Israael (Ecu, Per, Bol, Chi, Arg, Bra); Cordelia Nisbet, Cambridge, UK (Ecu, Per, Bol); Alexander Nord, Korntal, Germany (Arg, Chi, Bol).

Franziska Oberli, Langenthal, Switzerland (Arg, Chi); Ljubo Oblikov, Castle Hill, Australia (Chi); Kirsten Odellermann, Hamburg, Germany (Ecu); Siesta Oppi, Neunegg, Switzerland (Arg,

Chi); Yariv Oren, Even-Yemuda, Israel (Chi); Frank Oswald and Tania Krupitza, Rastalt, Germany (Chi, Per); Winifrid Ottmers, Moers, Germany (Ecu); David Owen, Virginia, USA (Ven, Col, Ecu, Per).

Gustavo Pacheco, Rio de Janeiro, Brazil (Bra); Patricia Pache, Lussy, Switzerland (Ecu); Christian Pagel and Ute Behrens, Cologne, Germany (Chi); Albert Palaus, Oxon, UK (Arg, Bol); Joe Palmer, Canterbury, UK (Chi, Bol, Per); Patrick Paluden, Copenhagen, Denmark (Bra, Arg); Gonzalo Panizo, (Per); Karin Pankow-Simrose and Phil Simrose, Parkbeg, Canada (Ven, Bra, Bol, Per, Ecu); Elba Paredes, Merida, Venezuela (Ven); Roland Paul, Bamberg, Germany (Col, Ecu, Per); Michael Paumgarten, Bologna, Italy (Ecu); Stefan Peerboom, The Netherlands (Ecu); Shay Perry, Haifa, Israel (Bol, Per, Ecu, Col); Gerald Petersen, Sparks, USA (Per, Chi); Barbara Petersen, Nuremberg, Germany (Bra, Par); Volken Peters, Munich, Germany (Bra, Bol, Arg, Chi, Per); J Robert peterson, Landrum, USA (Ecu); Luke Peters, Venezuela (Ven); John-Francis Phipps, Brighton, England (Bra); Lisa Pirinen, Cambridge, UK (Col); Namcy Pistole and Matt Oliphant, La Crescenta, USA (Col, Ecu, Per, Bol, Pan, Chi); Norman Plaster, Ahlhorn, Germany (Chi, Per); Marion van den Plas &A van Elzakkel, Nleuwefein, The Netherlands (Bra); Richard Plevin, Berkeley, USA (Arg, Per); Robin Pogalele, Dunstable, UK (Arg, Bol, Bra, Chi, Col, Ecu, Par, Per, Uru); Jorn Pohl, Nurtigen, Germany (Bol, Arg); Maike Potthast, Berlin, Germany (Ecu); Greg Powell and Yvonne Dings, Vancouver, Canada (Arg, Chi, Bra); Marcelo Pozzo, La Plata, Argentina (Arg); Alexander Prager and Meg Verhees, Innsbruck Austria (Bol); Fernando Prati, Buenos Aires, Argentina (Per); David Pugh, Winchester, UK (Chi).

Raffaela Ramos, Brazil (Arg); Scott Rasmussen, San Juan, Puerto Rico (Ven); Ralph Rebeyrol, Decize, France (Ecu); Paul Rebholz, Zurich, Switzerland (Per); Torben Redder, Arhus, Denmark (Per, Bra, Ecu); Monique Reeves, Victoria, Canada (Ecu, Per); Hans and Renate Reist, Kyburg-Buchegg, Switzerland (Ven); Ulli Rellenbenz, Süsseu, Germany (Ecu); Ulli Rellenbenz, Sussen, Germany (Ecu); Angelika Rempp, Ludwigshafen, Germany (Ecu); Dierk and Karin Reuter , Martinez, Argentina (Ecu, Per, Bra); Ori Reuveny, Kfar Saba, Israel (Bra, Ven, Ecu, Arg, Chi); Eduardo Rey, Quito, Ecuador (Ecu); Monica Ridolfi, Buenos Aires, Argentina (Arg); Franz Rigg, Hialeah, USA (Per); P Robinson, Leeds, UK (Par, Bra, Arg); Sergio G Rodríguez, Santiago, Chile (Arg); Ariel Rogers, Buenos Aires, Argentina (Arg); Stefan Rohloff, Heidelberg, Germany (Ecu); Daniel Rosazza, (Per); E Rosenmann, Jerusalem, Israel (Bra, Uru, Per, Arg); Arri Rotem, Petah-Tikva, Israel (Bol); Ellen Rotterink, Schuttorf, Germany (Chi); Siamak Rouhani, Bern. Switzerland (Bra); Louise Roy, Montreal, Canada (Bol, Chi); Yoav Rubenstein and Tal Benoudiz, Jerusalem, Israel (Col); Audrey Rudofski, Michigan, USA (Per); Wiliam Runely, London, UK (Arg, Chi).

Gil Salomon, Haifa, Israel (Ecu, Per, Bol); Víctor Sánchez, Trujillo, Venenuela (Ven); J Sandhuhl and R Robinson, Calgary, Canada (Per); Martin Saurle and Ursula Wermter, Gmund, Germany (Bol, Chi); Dr Michael Saxby, Dorking, UK (Chi); Britta Scheunemann and Stefan Bock, Bonn, Germany (Per); Hannes Scheiner, Argentina (Arg, Chi, Uru, Par, Bol); Bruno Schmid, Zurich, Switzerland (Ven, Bra, Per); Oda Schmellel, Bonn, Germany (Ecu); Rainer Schneuwly, Bern, Switzerland (Arg, Bol, Uru); Achin Schnegule, Berlin, Germany (Col); Pascal Schneider, La Chaux-de-Fonds, Switzerland (Chi); Rainer Schneuwly, Bern, Switzerland (Arg, Bol, Uru); Lucy Schottler, Erlangen, Germany (Arg, Bol); Angela Schottenhamel, Miunchen, Germany (Arg, Bol, Chi); Thorsten Schuller, Neustadt, Germany (Per); Thilo Schultze, Filderstadt, Germany (Bra); John Sebastian Stray Jorgensen, Copenhagen, Denmark (Arg); Matthew Seddon, Chicago, USA (Bol); Ilan Selig, Israel (Chi, Bol); Drrin Sellick, Oshawa, Canada (Ecu); Yiftah Shalev and Eran Shayshon, Jerusalem, Israel (Ven, Bra); Saar Shmueli, Tivon, Israel (Chi); D Shuttleworth, Kingsbridge, England (Chi); Volker Simon, Augsburg, Germany (Chi, Bol); Jeff Singer, Wheathampstead, UK (Col, Ecu); Dr Udo Skladny, Berlin, Germany (Arg); Joris Smets and Vanessa Vandenberghe, Brechem, Belgium (Ecu, Per); Robert Smith, Glasgow, UK (Ecu); Brian Smith (Arg); Gabriel and Joan Soares, Grand Rapids, USA (Bra); Michael Sonnenberg, Lonstanz, Germany (Chi, Ecu, Bol); Marcel Spaas, Eindhoven, The Netherlands (Guy); Alexander Spahn, Frankfurt, Germany (Per, Bol); Philip Spahr, Boblingen, Germany (Chi, Arg); Jorg Spieler, Malsch, Germany (Bra); Adolf Sprenger, Wertheim, Germany (Arg, Chi); Wolfram Spreer (Chi); Adolf Sprenger, Wertheim, Germany (Arg, Chi); N Stalker, Cambridge, UK (Chi); Derek Stansfield, Sutrminster Newton, Dorset (Ecu); Damien Steheli and Veronika Klein, Berlin, Germany (Bra); Cornelia Steinlechner (Ven); Anda Stampe, Herlufmagie, Denmark (Col, Ecu); Patrick Sterckx, Grez-Doiceau, Belgium (Arg); Geoffrey Stevenson, Mukilteo, USA

(Chi, Per); Marc Stockli, Muttenz, Switzerland (Ecu, Per, Bol); Tommie Stopp, Nuremberg, Germany (Chi); Adam and Samantha Stork, London, UK (Ecu); Terry Stord and Jack Cargil, Albuquerque, New Mexico USA (Chi, Bol); Nicholas Stott, Aberdeen, UK (Uru, Chi, Par, Col, Bra, Guy, Arg); Paul Stritter, Austria (Chi, Arg); Fred Stromsdorfer, Ettlingen, Germany (Bra); Soren Strom and Ane Jensen, Denmark (Arg); Jim and Miki Strong, Bishops, California USA (Per, Chi); Thomas and Majorie Stuehrenberg, St Catherine, Jamaica (Ecu); Luisa Summa, Cuneo, Italy (Ecu); Martin de Swart, Amsterdam, Netherlands (Per); Amy Swinnerton and Roland Webster, London, England (Chi, Arg, Par, Bra); Patrick Symmes, New York, USA (Arg, Chi, Per, Bol).

Christopher Tanfield, London, UK (Bol, Per); Horst Thomas, Aachen, Germany (Ecu); Paul Thomas, Pico Rivera, California , USA (Bol); Christian Thordal, Kastrup, Denmark (Bra, Ven, Bol); Mark Thurber and Jane Letham, Quito, Ecuador (Ecu); Marcia Tideman, New York, USA (Ecu); Truls Toggenburger, Winterthur, Switzerland (Bra); James Toplis, Paihia, New Zealand (Arg); Maurizio Trabacchi, Geneva, Switzerland (Col); Yossi Tunaami, Netanya, Israel (Per); Orit Turrel, Kiryat Bialik, Israel (Bol).

Simon Urwin , London, England (Ven); Maria & Anna Vantsos (Sydney, Australia), Johnny Jakobsen (Bodo, Norway), Richard Newman, Pamela Alice Holland and Tessa Hibbert (UK), Astrid & Graham Challice (Melbourne, Australia), (Chi); Muriel Vermeersch, Zeuven, Belgium (Ecu); Richard and Helen vine, Oldham, UK (Chi, Arg).

Hayley Walker, Harare, Zimbabwe (Bra, Par, Bol, Per, Ecu, Arg); Christopher Walker, Reston, USA (Bol); Clive Walker, San Jose, Costa Rica (Per, Chi, Bol, Arg); Alison Ware, Kidlington, UK (Ecu); Javier Wasserzug and Gabi Folchieri, Rio Negro, Argentina (Arg, Bra, Ven, Col); Mary Watson, Edinburgh, UK (Chi); Simon Watson-Taylor, (Ecu); Joanna Watts, Spalding, UK (Bol, Arg, Chi); Roland Webber and Amy Swinnerton, London, England (Bol); Thomas Weber, Los Andes, Chile (Chi); Roland Webster and Amy Swinnerton, London, UK (Ecu, Per, Chi); Volker Weinmann, Blumenau, Brazil (Chi, Arg, Bra, Uru); Markus Weinbacher, Basel, Switzerland (Arg); Martina Weinrich, Hausen, Germany (Bol); Peter and Marina Weisshaupt, Sargans, Switzerland (Arg, Chi, Per, Bol); Dick Welch, Genova, Spain (Arg, Par); Florian Werner, Bonn, Germany (Col, Ecu); Jennifer Wessely and Anne-Grit Albrecht, Lohfelden, Germany (Ven, Per,

Bol); Mark West, Santiago, Chile (Chi, Bol); Ronald Wilhelm, Laubach, Germany (Bra); Martyn Williams, Gwent, UK (Chi); Joy Wintersteen, Arkansas, USA (Arg); Jim Wishshaw, Skibby, Denmark (Bol, Chi, Ecu, Per); MOnika Wohlmann, Goettingen, Germany (Arg); Fritz Woldt, Munchen, Germany (Ecu); Elvina & Joseph Wolfisberg, Zurich, Switzerland (Per, Bra); Peter & Norma Wright, London, England (Bol, Arg, Bra, Chi); Ragnhild Wulfsberg, Oslo, Norway (Per).

Dennis Vah-Gruihleh, The Netherlands (Per);

Peter Vanquaille and Hilde Sleurs, Dikelvenne, Belgium (Ecu).

Richard Young, Auckland, New Zealand (Bol, Arg, Par); Oliver Zehnder, Baden, Switzerland (Per).

Helmut Zettl, Ebergassing, Austira (Per, Ecu, Bra, Arg, Bol); Jan Zielinski, Berlin, Germany (Bra); Jan Zomer, Rijnsburg, The Netherlands (Arg, Bol, Chi, Ecu, Par, Per); Roman Zubowksy, Karlsruhe, Germany (Chi, Arg, Bra); Cees Zuithoff, Capelle aan den lissel, The Netherlands (Arg).

Writing to us

Many people write to us - with corrections, new information, or simply comments. If you want to let us know something, we would be delighted to hear from you. Please give us as precise information as possible, quoting the edition and page number of the Handbook you are using and send as early in the year as you can. Your help will be greatly appreciated, especially by other travellers. In return we will send you details about our special guidebook offer.

For hotels and restaurants, please let us know:

- each establishment's name, address, phone and fax number
- number of rooms, whether a/c or air-cooled, attached (clean?) bathroom
- location - how far from the station or bus stand, or distance (walking time) from a prominent landmark
- if it's not already on one of our maps, can you place it?
- your comments - either good or bad - as to why it is distinctive
- tariff cards
- local transport used

For places of interest:

- location
- entry, camera charge
- access - by whatever means of transport is most approiate, eg time of main buses or trains to and from the site, journey time, fare
- facilities - nearby drinks stalls, restaurants, for the disabled
- any problems, eg steep climb, wildlife, unofficial guides
- opening hours
- site guides

TEMPERATURE CONVERSION TABLE

°C	°F	°C	°F
1	34	26	79
2	36	27	81
3	38	28	82
4	39	29	84
5	41	30	86
6	43	31	88
7	45	32	90
8	46	33	92
9	48	34	93
10	50	35	95
11	52	36	97
12	54	37	99
13	56	38	100
14	57	39	102
15	59	40	104
16	61	41	106
17	63	42	108
18	64	43	109
19	66	44	111
20	68	45	113
21	70	46	115
22	72	47	117
23	74	48	118
24	75	49	120
25	77	50	122

The formula for converting °C to °F is:
$$°C \times 9 \div 5 + 32 = °F$$

WEIGHTS AND MEASURES

Metric

Weight
1 Kilogram (Kg) = 2.205 pounds
1 metric ton = 1.102 short tons

Length
1 millimetre (mm)= 0.03937 inch
1 metre = 3.281 feet
1 kilometre (km) = 0.621 mile

Area
1 heactare = 2.471 acres
1 square km = 0.386 sq mile

Capacity
1 litre = 0.220 imperial gallon
 = 0.264 US gallon

Volume
1 cubic metre (m^3) = 35.31 cubic feet
 = 1.31 cubic yards

British and US

Weight
1 pound (lb) = 454 grams
1 short ton (2,000lbs) = 0.907 m ton
1 long ton (2,240lbs) = 1.016 m tons

Length
1 inch = 25.417 millimetres
1 foot (ft) = 0.305 metre
1 mile = 1.609 kilometres

Area
1 acre = 0.405 hectare
1 sq mile = 2.590 sq kilometre

Capacity
1 imperial gallon = 4.546 litres
1 US gallon = 3.785 litres

Volume
1 cubic foot (cu ft) = 0.028 m^3
1 cubic yard (cu yd) = 0.765 m^3

NB 5 imperial gallons are approximately equal to 6 US gallons

The manzana, used in Central America, is about 0.7 hectare (1.73 acres).

Climatic tables

The following tables have been very kindly furnished by Mr R K Headland. Each weather station is given with its altitude in metres (m). Temperatures (Centigrade) are given as averages for each month; the first line is the maximum and the second the minimum. The third line is the average number of wet days encountered in each month.

	Jan	Feb	Mar	Apr	May	Jun	Jul	Aug	Sep	Oct	Nov	Dec
Arica, Chile	26	26	25	23	21	19	19	18	19	21	22	24
29m	18	18	17	16	14	14	12	13	13	14	16	17
	0	0	0	0	0	0	0	0	0	0	0	0
Asunción, Par	34	34	33	28	25	22	24	25	27	29	31	33
64m	22	22	21	18	14	13	14	14	16	17	19	21
	7	6	9	7	5	4	4	4	6	5	6	7
Bariloche, Arg	21	21	18	14	10	7	6	8	10	11	16	18
825m	8	8	6	4	2	1	0	0	1	3	5	6
	2	3	5	7	11	13	11	11	8	6	4	4
Barranquilla, Col	31	31	32	33	34	33	33	33	33	32	32	30
12m	22	22	23	24	25	25	25	25	25	24	24	23
	0	0	0	1	4	8	5	6	8	11	6	4
Belém, Braz	31	30	30	31	31	32	32	32	32	32	32	32
24m	23	23	23	23	23	23	22	22	22	22	22	22
	24	26	25	22	24	15	14	15	13	10	11	14
Belo Horizonte	27	27	27	27	25	24	24	25	27	27	27	26
857m	18	18	17	16	12	10	10	12	14	16	17	18
	15	13	9	4	4	2	2	1	2	10	12	14
Bogotá	21	21	21	20	20	19	19	19	20	20	20	21
2560m	7	7	9	10	10	9	8	8	8	9	8	7
	9	7	10	18	16	10	16	10	13	18	16	13
Brasília	27	28	28	28	27	26	26	28	30	29	27	27
912m	18	18	18	17	15	13	13	14	16	18	18	18
	19	16	15	9	3	1	0	2	4	11	15	20
Buenos Aires	30	29	26	22	18	15	15	16	18	21	25	29
25m	18	17	15	12	9	6	6	6	8	11	13	16
	5	5	6	6	4	4	5	6	5	7	7	7
Caracas	26	26	28	28	28	27	26	27	28	27	27	26
1035m	15	15	16	17	18	18	17	17	17	17	17	16
	4	3	2	4	8	13	13	11	11	11	8	6
Córdoba, Arg	32	31	28	25	21	19	19	20	23	26	28	31
425m	17	16	14	11	7	4	4	5	8	11	13	16
	8	9	9	6	4	2	2	1	3	7	9	10

	Jan	Feb	Mar	Apr	May	Jun	Jul	Aug	Sep	Oct	Nov	Dec
Cuzco	20	21	21	22	21	21	21	21	22	22	23	22
3310m	7	7	7	4	2	1	-1	1	4	6	6	7
	18	13	11	8	3	2	2	2	7	8	12	16
Guayaquil	31	31	32	31	31	29	28	29	30	29	30	31
6m	22	22	23	23	22	21	20	20	20	21	21	22
	12	13	15	10	4	1	0	0	0	1	0	2
La Paz, Bol	18	18	18	19	17	17	17	17	18	19	19	19
3632m	6	6	6	5	3	2	1	2	3	5	6	6
	21	18	16	9	5	2	2	4	9	9	11	18
Lima	25	26	26	24	21	19	17	17	17	19	20	23
137m	19	20	19	18	16	15	14	13	13	14	16	17
	1	0	0	0	1	1	1	2	1	0	0	0
Manaus	30	30	30	30	31	31	32	33	33	33	32	31
48m	23	23	23	23	24	23	23	24	24	24	24	24
	20	18	21	20	18	12	12	5	7	4	12	16
Montevideo	28	28	26	22	18	15	14	15	17	20	23	26
22m	17	16	15	12	9	6	6	6	8	9	12	15
	6	5	5	6	6	5	6	7	6	6	6	7
Porto Alegre, Braz	31	30	29	25	22	20	20	21	22	24	27	29
10m	20	20	19	16	13	11	10	11	13	15	17	18
	9	10	10	6	6	8	8	8	11	10	8	8
Punta Arenas, Chile	15	14	13	9	6	4	3	4	7	10	12	14
	7	7	6	4	2	1	1	1	2	3	4	6
28m	6	5	7	9	6	8	6	5	5	5	5	8
Quito	21	21	20	21	21	21	21	22	22	21	21	21
2818m	8	8	8	8	8	7	7	7	7	8	8	8
	9	11	11	15	10	9	3	3	8	13	13	7
Recife, Braz	30	30	30	30	29	28	27	27	28	29	30	30
56m	24	25	24	23	23	22	21	21	22	23	24	24
	7	8	10	11	17	16	17	14	7	3	4	4
Rio de Janeiro	30	30	29	27	26	25	25	25	25	26	28	28
30m	23	23	23	21	20	18	18	18	19	20	20	22
	13	11	9	9	6	5	5	4	5	11	10	12
Salvador (Bahia)	29	29	29	28	27	26	26	26	27	28	28	29
8m	23	23	24	23	22	21	21	21	21	22	23	23
	6	9	17	19	22	23	18	15	10	8	9	11
Santa Cruz, Bol	30	31	30	28	25	23	24	28	29	30	31	31
437m	21	21	20	19	16	15	15	16	19	20	20	21
	14	10	12	9	11	8	5	4	5	7	8	11
Santiago de Chile	29	29	27	23	18	14	15	17	19	22	26	28
520m	12	11	9	7	5	3	3	4	6	7	9	11
	0	0	1	1	5	6	6	5	3	3	1	0
São Paulo	28	28	27	25	23	22	21	23	25	25	25	26
792m	18	18	17	15	13	11	10	11	13	14	15	16
	15	13	12	6	3	4	4	3	5	12	11	14

Sources: H.M.S.O. Meteorological Reports, K.L.M. Climatic Data Publication

Standard time zones

Argentina	3	Ecuador		5
Falkland Islands	4	Galápagos		6
	(3 Sept-Apr)	Paraguay		4
Bolivia	4		(3 Oct-Feb)	
Brazil		Peru		5
East	3	Uruguay		3
	(2 Oct-Feb: not all states)	Venezuela		4
West	4	Guyana		4
	(3 Oct-Feb: not all states)	Suriname		3
Acre	5	Guyane		3
Fernando de Noronha	2			
Chile	4			
	(3 Oct-Mar)			
Easter Island	6			
	(5 Oct-Mar)			
Colombia	5			

NB Times shown are hours *behind* GMT; figures in brackets are for summer time saving. Check exact dates locally.

Advertisers

Useful words and phrases

N O AMOUNT of dictionaries, phrase books or word lists will provide the same enjoyment as being able to communicate directly with the people of the country you are visiting. Learning Spanish is an important part of the preparation for any trip to South America (apart from Portuguese-speaking Brazil of course) and you are encouraged to make an effort to grasp the basics before you go. As you travel you will pick up more of the language and the more you know, the more you will benefit from your stay. The following section is designed to be a simple point of departure.

General pronunciation

The stress in a Spanish word conforms to one of three rules: 1) if the word ends in a vowel, or in **n** or **s**, the accent falls on the penultimate syllable (*venta*na, *venta*nas); 2) if the word ends in a consonant other than **n** or **s**, the accent falls on the last syllable (*habl*ar); 3) if the word is to be stressed on a syllable contrary to either of the above rules, the acute accent on the relevant vowel indicates where the stress is to be placed (*pantal*ón, *met*áfora). Note that adverbs such as *cuando*, 'when', take an accent when used interrogatively: *¿cuándo?*, 'when?'

Vowels

a not quite as short as in English 'cat'
e as in English 'pay', but shorter in a syllable ending in a consonant
i as in English 'seek'
o as in English 'shop', but more like 'pope' when the vowel ends a syllable
u as in English 'food'; after 'q' and in 'gue', 'gui', **u** is unpronounced; in 'güe' and 'güi' it is pronounced
y when a vowel, pronounced like 'i'; when a semiconsonant or consonant, it is pronounced like English 'yes'
ai, ay as in English 'ride'
ei, ey as in English 'they'
oi, oy as in English 'toy'

Unless listed below **consonants** can be pronounced in Spanish as they are in English.

b, v their sound is interchangeable and is a cross between the English 'b' and 'v', except at the beginning of a word or after 'm' or 'n' when it is like English 'b'
c like English 'k', except before 'e' or 'i' when it is as the 's' in English 'sip'
g before 'e' and 'i' it is the same as **j**
h when on its own, never pronounced
j as the 'ch' in the Scottish 'loch'
ll as the 'g' in English 'beige'; sometimes as the 'lli' in 'million'
ñ as the 'ni' in English 'onion'
rr trilled much more strongly than in English
x depending on its location, pronounced as in English 'fox', or 'sip', or like 'gs'
z as the 's' in English 'sip'

GREETINGS, COURTESIES

hello hola
good morning buenos días
good afternoon/evening/night buenas tardes/noches
goodbye adiós/chao
see you later hasta luego
how are you? ¿cómo está?/¿cómo estás?
pleased to meet you mucho gusto/encantado/encantada
please por favor
thank you (very much) (muchas) gracias
yes sí
no no
excuse me/I beg your pardon permiso
I do not understand no entiendo
please speak slowly hable despacio por favor
what is your name ¿cómo se llama?
Go away! ¡Váyase!

BASIC QUESTIONS

where is_? ¿dónde está_?
how much does it cost? ¿cuánto cuesta?
how much is it? ¿cuánto es?
when? ¿cuándo?
when does the bus leave? ¿a qué hora sale el autobus?
- arrive? - llega -
why? ¿por qué?
what for? ¿para qué?
what time is it? ¿qué hora es?
how do I get to_? ¿cómo llegar a_?
is this the way to the church? ¿la iglesia está por aquí?

BASICS

bathroom/toilet el baño
police (policeman) la policía (el policía)
hotel el hotel (la pensión, el residencial, el alojamiento)
restaurant el restaurante
post office el correo
telephone office el centro de llamadas
supermarket el supermercado
bank el banco
exchange house la casa de cambio
exchange rate la tasa de cambio
notes/coins los billetes/las monedas
travellers' cheques los travelers/los cheques de viajero
cash el efectivo
breakfast el desayuno
lunch el almuerzo
dinner/supper la cena
meal la comida
drink la bebida
mineral water el agua mineral
soft fizzy drink la gaseosa/cola
beer la cerveza
without sugar sin azúcar
without meat sin carne

GETTING AROUND

on the left/right a la izquierda/derecha
straight on derecho
second street on the left la segunda calle a la izquierda
to walk caminar
bus station la terminal (terrestre)
train station la estación (de tren/ferrocarril)
bus el bus/el autobus/ la flota/el colectivo/ el micro etc
train el tren
airport el aeropuerto
aeroplane/airplane el avión
first/second class primera/segunda clase
ticket el boleto
ticket office la taquilla
bus stop la parada

ACCOMMODATION

room el cuarto/la habitación
single/double sencillo/doble
with two beds con dos camas
with private bathroom con baño
hot/cold water agua caliente/fría
noisy ruidoso
to make up/clean limpiar
sheets las sábanas
blankets las mantas
pillows las almohadas
clean/dirty towels toallas limpias/sucias
toilet paper el papel higiénico
Chemist farmacia
(for) pain (para) dolor
stomach el estómago
head la cabeza
fever/sweat la fiebre/el sudor
diarrhoea la diarrea
blood la sangre
altitude sickness el soroche
doctor el médico
condoms los preservativos
contraceptive (pill) anticonceptivo (la píldora anticonceptiva)
period/towels la regla/las toallas
contact lenses las lentes de contacto
aspirin la aspirina

TIME

at one o'clock a la una
at half past two/ two thirty a las dos y media
at a quarter to three a cuarto para las tres or a las tres menos quince
it's one o'clock es la una
it's seven o'clock son las siete
it's twenty past six/six twenty son las seis y veinte
it's five to nine son cinco para las nueve/ son las nueve menos cinco
in ten minutes en diez minutos

five hours cinco horas
does it take long? ¿tarda mucho?
Monday lunes
Tuesday martes
Wednesday miercoles
Thursday jueves
Friday viernes
Saturday sábado
Sunday domingo
January enero
February febrero
March marzo
April abril
May mayo
June junio
July julio
August agosto
September septiembre
October octubre
November noviembre
December diciembre

NUMBERS

one uno/una
two dos
three tres
four cuatro
five cinco
six seis
seven siete
eight ocho
nine nueve
ten diez
eleven once
twelve doce
thirteen trece
fourteen catorce
fifteen quince
sixteen dieciseis
seventeen diecisiete
eighteen dieciocho
nineteen diecinueve
twenty veinte
twenty one, two veintiuno, veintidos etc

thirty treinta
forty cuarenta
fifty cincuenta
sixty sesenta
seventy setenta
eighty ochenta
ninety noventa
hundred cien or ciento
thousand mil

KEY VERBS

To Go
ir
I go voy; you go (familiar singular) vas; he, she, it goes, you (unfamiliar singular) go va; we go vamos; they, you (plural) go van.
To Have (possess)
tener
tengo; tienes; tiene; tenemos; tienen (also used as To Be, as in 'I am hungry' tengo hambre)
(**NB** haber also means to have, but is used with other verbs, as in 'he has gone' ha ido.
he; has; ha; hemos; han.
Hay means 'there is'; perhaps more common is No hay meaning 'there isn't any')

To Be (in a permanent state)
ser
soy (profesor - I am a teacher); eres; es; somos; son
To Be (positional or temporary state)
estar
estoy (en Londres - I am in London); estás; está (contenta - she is happy); estamos; están.
This section has been compiled on the basis of glossaries compiled by André de Mendonça and David Gilmour of South American Experience, London, and the Latin American Travel Advisor, No 9, March 1996.

Index

Maps

Map Symbols

Administration

International Border	
State / Province Border	
Cease Fire Line	
Neighbouring country	
Neighbouring state	
State Capitals	□
Other Towns	○

Roads and travel

Main Roads (National Highways)	
Other Roads	
Jeepable Roads, Tracks	
Railways with station	

Water features

River	*Amazon*
Lakes, Reservoirs, Tanks	
Seasonal Marshlands	
Sand Banks, Beaches	
Ocean	
Waterfall	
Ferry	

Topographical features

Contours (approx), Rock Outcrops	
Mountains	
Mountain Pass	
Gorge	
Escarpment	
Palm trees	

Cities and towns

Built Up Areas	
One Way Street	→
National Parks, Gardens, Stadiums	
Fortified Walls	▲ ▲ ▲
Airport	⊗
Banks	Ⓢ
Bus Stations (named in key)	
Hospitals	⊕
Market	Ⓜ
Police station	Pol
Post Office	⊗
Telegraphic Office	
Tourist Office	ⓘ
Key Numbers	❶ ❷ ❸ ❹ ❺
Bridges	
Cathedral, church	† ■
Guided routes	

National parks, trekking areas

National Parks and Bird Sanctuaries	◆
Hide	
Camp site	Å
Refuge	
Motorable track	
Walking track	

Other symbols

Archaeological Sites	
Places of Interest	○
Viewing point	

Footprint Handbooks

All of us at Footprint Handbooks hope you have enjoyed reading and travelling with this Handbook. As our story starts back in the early 1920s we thought it would be interesting to chronicle our development.

It all started 75 years ago in 1921, with the publication of the *Anglo-South American Handbook*. In 1924 the *South American Handbook* was created. This has been published each year for the last 74 years and is the longest running guidebook in the English language, immortalised by Graham Greene as the best travel guide in existence. Celebrations, presumably, next year as we hit the 75th annual edition!

One of the key strengths of the *South American Handbook* over the years, has been the extraordinary contact we have had with our readers through their hundreds of letters to us in Bath. From these letters we learnt that you wanted more Handbooks of the same quality to other parts of the world.

In 1989 my brother Patrick and I set about developing a series modelled on the *South American Handbook*. Our aim was to create the ultimate practical guidebook series for all travellers, providing expert knowledge of far flung places, explaining culture, places and people in a balanced, lively and clear way. The whole idea hinged, of course, on finding writers who were in tune with our thinking. Serendipity stepped in at exactly the right moment: we were able to bring together a talented group of people who know the countries we cover inside out and whose enthusiasm for travelling in them needed to be communicated.

The series started to steadily grow as we brought out new guides to the Indian subcontinent, Southeast Asia and Africa. At this stage we were known as Trade & Travel Publications, or the people who publish the Handbooks! In 1995 we felt that the time was right to look again at the identity that had brought us all this way. So, we commissioned London designers Newell & Sorrell to look at all the issues.

The result was the launch of our new identity, Footprint Handbooks in September 1996 which has, without doubt, lifted our profile across the globe in the travel guide scene.

For us here in Bath, it has been an exciting exercise working through this dramatic change. We have many new guidebooks in the pipeline and many ideas for the future but central to all of this is to maintain contact with all our readers. Do continue to write to us with all your news, comments and suggestions and in return we will keep you up-to-date with developments here in the West Country.

The Footprint list

Andalucía Handbook
Cambodia Handbook
Caribbean Islands Handbook
Chile Handbook
East Africa Handbook
Ecuador Handbook
  with the Galápagos
Egypt Handbook
India Handbook
Indonesia Handbook
Laos Handbook
Malaysia & Singapore Handbook
Mexico & Central America
  Handbook
Morocco Handbook
  with Mauritania
Myanmar (Burma) Handbook
Namibia Handbook
Pakistan Handbook
Peru Handbook
South Africa Handbook
South American Handbook
Thailand Handbook
Tibet Handbook
Tunisia Handbook with Libya
Vietnam Handbook

New in Autumn 1997
Bolivia Handbook
Goa Handbook
Israel Handbook
Nepal Handbook
Zimbabwe & Moçambique
  Handbook with Malawi

New in Spring 1998
Argentina Handbook
Brazil Handbook
Colombia Handbook
Cuba Handbook
Jordan, Syria & Lebanon Handbook
Sri Lanka Handbook (new edition)
Venezuela Handbook

Web site
Our website is up and running. Take a look
at http://www.footprint-handbooks.co.uk
for the latest news, to order a book or to
join our mailing list.

Mail Order
Footprint Handbooks are available worldwide in
good bookstores. They can also be ordered
directly from us in Bath either via the website or
via the address below.

Footprint Handbooks
6 Riverside Court
Lower Bristol Road
Bath BA2 3DZ, England
T +44(0)1225 469141
F +44(0)1225 469461
E Mail handbooks@footprint.cix.co.uk

Discover the amazing New World with us

Amerindia offers a style of travel in Latin America where comfort, beauty and style go hand in hand with a discovery - or rediscovery - of the many varied and often unique charms, attractions and elements of the New World.

We can organise high quality tours and circuits for groups and individuals which are tailored according to particular interest in soft adventure, history, culture, art and artifacts, natural history, and sheer beauty. We will be covering the whole of Latin America, but right away have offices in the following countries:

• Ecuador • Perú • Bolivia • Central America •

Amerindia
The Undiscovered World

Contact the following offices for more information

Amerindia UK • Steeple Cottage / Easton, Winchester / Hampshire SO21 1EH England • Tel: 01962-779317 • Fax: 01962-779458 • e-mail: pkellie@yachtors.u-net.com

Amerindia USA • 7855 N.W. 12th Street / Suite 115 / Miami,FL 33126 USA Tel: (305) 599-9008 • 1-800-247-2925 • Fax: (305) 592-7060 • e-mail: tumbaco@gate.net